IUS COMMUNE CASEBOOKS
FOR THE COMMON LAW OF EUROPE

CASES, MATERIALS AND TEXT
ON CONTRACT LAW

Cases, Materials and Text on Contract Law

Third Edition

Hugh Beale, Bénédicte Fauvarque-Cosson,
Jacobien Rutgers and Stefan Vogenauer

·HART·
OXFORD · LONDON · NEW YORK · NEW DELHI · SYDNEY

HART PUBLISHING

Bloomsbury Publishing Plc

Kemp House, Chawley Park, Cumnor Hill, Oxford, OX2 9PH, UK

HART PUBLISHING, the Hart/Stag logo, BLOOMSBURY and the Diana logo are
trademarks of Bloomsbury Publishing Plc

First published in Great Britain 2019

Copyright © The authors severally 2019

A catalogue record for this book is available from the British Library.

Library of Congress Cataloging-in-Publication data

Names: Beale, H. G., author. | Fauvarque-Cosson, Bénédicte, author. |
Rutgers, Jacobien W., author. | Vogenauer, Stefan, 1968- author.

Title: Cases, materials and text on contract law / Hugh Beale, Bénédicte
Fauvarque-Cosson, Jacobien Rutgers and Stefan Vogenauer

Description: Third edition. | Oxford, UK ; Portland, Oregon : Hart Publishing, 2019. |
Series: Ius commune casebooks for the common law of Europe

Identifiers: LCCN 2018040271 (print) | LCCN 2018041415 (ebook) |
ISBN 9781509912582 (Epub) | ISBN 9781509912575 (paperback)

Subjects: LCSH: Contracts—Europe. | BISAC: LAW / Comparative. | LCGFT: Casebooks (Law)

Classification: LCC KJC1720 (ebook) | LCC KJC1720 .B43 2018 (print) | DDC 346.402/2—dc23

LC record available at https://lccn.loc.gov/2018040271

ISBN: PB: 978-1-50991-257-5
ePDF: 978-1-50991-259-9
ePub: 978-1-50991-258-2

Typeset by Compuscript Ltd, Shannon
Printed and bound in Great Britain by TJ International Ltd, Padstow, Cornwall

To find out more about our authors and books visit www.hartpublishing.co.uk.
Here you will find extracts, author information, details of forthcoming events
and the option to sign up for our newsletters.

PREFACE

In the Preface to the second edition of this book, we wrote that the new edition came 'at an exciting moment for "European" contract law'. At that time the European Commission was consulting on whether the fragmentary European contract law contained in the various directives should be replaced or supplemented by European rules on contract law in general, possibly in the form of an 'Optional Instrument'.

The third edition comes at a more difficult and less hopeful moment. In 2011 the European Commission proposed a 'Common European Sales Law' for sales where one party is a consumer or a small or medium-sized enterprise. It would have dealt with most issues that are likely to arise in the life of such sales contracts. The proposal received strong support from the European Parliament but it foundered in the European Council and in 2014 the Commission withdrew it. The contract law measures now proposed by the Commission are important but much narrower, dealing only with certain aspects of the supply of digital content and the sale of goods to consumers. In the current climate, with debates raging over such matters as what to do about asylum seekers and refugees, the Eurozone, right- and left-wing populism and Brexit, there seems no prospect of more general contract law developments in the foreseeable future.

Even if European legislation on contract law remains sectoral and fragmented, the case law of the Court of Justice of the European Union (CJEU) interpreting it continues to develop at a fast pace. Many of the recent decisions are quoted or referred to in this new edition. National decisions are also relevant to European legislation, not only because they show how European law is interpreted (or possibly misinterpreted) in Member States but also because European solutions are heavily influenced by the case law and legislation of the Member States. The President of the CJEU, Koen Lenaerts, has stressed the importance of comparative law to the work of the Court,[1] even if the contribution is not always acknowledged or even identifiable;[2] and its contribution seems to be as important in contractual matters as in the fields of comparative constitutional law and tort law to which the President referred.

In addition, 'European' contract law and comparative contract law have had major impacts on national laws. Among the systems that are covered in this book – English, French and German law, and to a lesser extent Dutch Law – the reform of the BGB in 2002 was in part based on the provisions of the 1980 Vienna Convention on Contracts for the International Sale of Goods (CISG) and the Consumer Sales Directive of 1999; also

---

[1] In his address to the Annual Conference of the European Law Institute in 2016, cited below, p 6 n 9; see also K Lenaerts, 'La Cour de justice de l'Union européenne et la méthode comparative' in B Fauvarque-Cosson (ed), *Le droit comparé au XXIème siècle: Enjeux et défis* (Paris: Société de législation comparée, 2015) 35.

[2] See K Lenaerts, 'Interlocking Legal Orders or the European Union Variant of "*E pluribus unum*"' (2003) 52 ICLQ 873, 874, 876.

'soft' European principles profoundly influenced the reforms of the French Code civil in 2016. The 2016 reforms (and the 'reform of the reforms' that took place in 2018 when the original Ordonnance was confirmed) are considered in detail in this new edition.

Indeed it can be argued that the failure to adopt a general contract law measure for Europe makes it all the more important to compare and contrast the national laws that, for the most part, will continue to apply to both domestic and cross-border contracts in Europe. And that is the main purpose of this collection of cases, materials and texts on contract law. The book covers the nature and extent of European measures, and the detailed provisions of European soft law (referring mainly to the Principles of European Contract Law, but where relevant drawing contrasts with the provisions of the Draft Common Frame of Reference, the proposed Common European Sales Law, the CISG and the UNIDROIT Principles of International Commercial Contracts). However, the bulk of the material continues to focus on the four national systems, with the aim of exploring their similarities and differences, and the extent to which the 'soft law principles' are (as is often claimed) a restatement of a common core of shared solutions.

This approach means that though the book necessarily concentrates on European laws, it will be of world-wide interest, particularly to lawyers in systems that are to some extent inspired by one of the systems covered in detail. We have been delighted to discover that previous editions of the book have been used in, for example, both Latin America and Asia; we hope that the new edition will be of even wider interest, particularly because of the coverage of the new French law.

The book continues to concentrate on cases, legislation and 'black-letter' rules of law. We remain very aware that such an approach has serious limitations; there may be deeper differences of philosophy, of *mentalité*, which may be masked by a superficially similar result. A good comparatist should explore these, which requires a much more rounded study of the traditions and institutions of each legal system than can be offered here. However, we continue to think that a comparison of black-letter rules is the best place to start.

Users of the previous edition will notice that the third edition contains more chapters, as we have added new material to the introductory chapters and have re-organised them to make them easier to follow. To accommodate the new material we have had to sacrifice some older cases, or the book would have become too long and too expensive, but we have kept everything that we think is really important. We hope readers will agree. We have also tried to make the book more reader-friendly by working with a bigger variety of font sizes and by introducing grey-scale boxes to identify the Notes in which we comment specifically on the preceding extract. We hope that readers will find it easier to navigate the text.

As always, we owe many debts of gratitude. First, we wish to thank those copyright holders who granted us permission to quote extracts from their work in the first edition of this book and whose permission to do so in this edition is once again gratefully acknowledged. Secondly, Professors Andrew Burrows and Edwin Peel granted us permission to use (in chapter 18) extracts from Professor Vogenauer's essay 'Interpretation of Contracts: Concluding Comparative Observations' which first appeared in the volume *Contract Terms* (OUP, 2007). We also wish to express our deepest gratitude to the research assistants who have helped us at various stages of the process: at the Max-Planck

Institute in Frankfurt, Thorben Klünder, Christoph Resch, Grigorij Tschernjawskyj, Luca von Bogdandy, Simon Willaschek and Sarah Zimmermann; in Paris, Maxime Cormier, Léah Faust-Taïeb and Louis-Marie Morin and, previously, Adrien Tehrani; in Warwick, Marie Pillon and Simon Thorpe; and, previously, at the Oxford Institute of European and Comparative Law, Klaus Wiedemann and Susanne Zwirlein. Lastly, many thanks are due to Sinead Moloney and her staff at Hart Publishing for their patience with us and their skill and understanding in dealing with a long typescript and a difficult process of re-ordering and updating.

Sadly, since the last edition was published we have lost two wonderful colleagues and friends: Denis Tallon, who contributed to the first and second editions of the book; and Walter van Gerven, who founded the *Ius Commune Casebook* series. We would like to dedicate this edition to their memory.

Hugh Beale
Bénédicte Fauvarque-Cosson
Jacobien Rutgers
Stefan Vogenauer
December 2018

CONTENTS

PART 4
CONTENT OF CONTRACTS

PART 5
REMEDIES FOR NON-PERFORMANCE

PART 6
SUPERVENING EVENTS

PART 7
THIRD PARTY CONSEQUENCES

ABBREVIATIONS

AA	Ars aequi
AALR	Anglo American Law Review
ABGB	Allgemeines Bürgerliches Gesetzbuch (Austrian Civil Code)
AC	Law Reports, Appeal Cases, House of Lords and Privy Council (since 1890)
AcP	Archiv für die civilistische Praxis
Ad & E	Adolphus and Ellis' Reports, King's Bench and Queen's Bench (ER 110 ff)
AG	Amtsgericht (German first instance court); Aktiengesellschaft (German public limited company)
AGB	Allgemeine Geschäftsbedingung(en) (general term(s) and conditions)
AGBG	Gesetz zur Regelung des Rechts der Allgemeinen Geschäftsbedingungen (German Standard Terms Act of 1976)
Ala App	Alabama Appellate Court Reports
Aleyn	Aleyn's Reports, King's Bench (ER 82)
All ER	All England Law Reports
All ER Rep	All England Law Reports, Reprint
Am J Comp L	American Journal of Comparative Law
Anon	Anonymous (names of parties unknown)
App Cas	Law Reports, Appeal Cases, House of Lords and Privy Council (1875–1890)
Arr Cass	Arresten van het Hof van cassatie / Arrêts de Cassation
Art	article
Arts	articles
Ass plén	Cour de cassation, Assemblée plénière
BAG	Bundesarbeitsgericht (German Federal Supreme Court for Labour Law)
B & Ald	Barnewall and Alderson's Reports, King's Bench (ER 109–10)
BauR	Zeitschrift für das gesamte öffentliche und zivile Baurecht
BB	Der Betriebsberater
B & C	Barbewall and Cresswell's Reports, King's Bench (ER 107 ff)
BCLC	Butterworths Company Law Cases

Beav	Beavan's Reports, Rolls Court (ER 48 ff)
BG	Bundesgericht (Swiss Supreme Court)
BGB	Bürgerliches Gesetzbuch (German Civil Code)
BGE	Entscheidungen des schweizerischen Bundesgerichts (Decisions of the Swiss Supreme Court)
BGH	Bundesgerichtshof (German Federal Supreme Court)
BGHZ	Entscheidungen des Bundesgerichtshofs in Zivilsachen
Bing	Bingham's Reports, Common Pleas (ER 130–31)
BLR	Business Law Review
BRH	Jurisprudence Commerciale de Bruxelles / Belgische Rechtspraak in Handelszaken
B & S	Best & Smith's Reports, Queens's Bench (ER 121–22)
Building LR	Building Law Reports
Bull civ	Bulletin des arrêts de la Cour de cassation, Chambres civiles
Bull crim	Bulletin des arrêts de la Cour de cassation, Chambre criminelle
Bull Joly	Bulletin Joly Sociétés
BW	Burgerlijk Wetboek (Dutch Civil Code)
c	contre
CA	Court of Appeal (England and Wales); cour d'appel (French appellate court)
Cal 2d	California Reports, 2nd Series
Camp	Campbell's Nisi Prius Reports (ER 170–71)
Cass belg	Cour de cassation (belgique) (Belgian Supreme Court)
Cass civ	Cour de cassation, Chambre civile (with number of chamber)
Cass com	Cour de cassation, Chambre commerciale
Cass crim	Cour de cassation, Chambre criminelle
Cass it	Corte di cassazione (Italian Supreme Court)
Cass mixte	Cour de cassation, Chambre mixte
Cass req	Cour de cassation, Chambre des requêtes
Cass soc	Cour de cassation, Chambre sociale
CB	Chief Baron; Common Bench Reports (ER 135 ff)
CB (NS)	Common Bench Reports, New Series (ER 140 ff)
Cciv	Code civil (French Civil Code)
Ccom	Code commercial (French Commercial Code)

Cconsomm	Code de la consommation (French Consumer Code)
CE	Conseil d'État (French Supreme Administrative Court)
cf	confer
CFR	Common Frame of Reference
ch	chapter
Ch	High Court of Chancery; Law Reports, Chancery Division (since 1890)
Ch App	Law Reports, Chancery Appeals
Ch D	Law Reports, Chancery Division (1875–1890)
ChD	Chancery Division of the High Court of Justice
CJ	Chief Justice
chron	Chroniques
CISG	United Nations Convention on Contracts for the International Sale of Goods
CLC	Commercial Law Cases
CLJ	Cambridge Law Journal
CLR	Commonwealth Law Reports
Clark … Ex	Clark's House of Lords Appeal Cases
Clark & Fin	Clark and Finelly's Reports, House of Lords (ER 6 ff)
CMLR	Common Market Law Review
Cmnd	Command Papers
Co	Company
Col LR	Columbia Law Review
Com Cas	Commercial Cases
Com LR	Commercial Law Reports
Cons const	Conseil constitutionnel
Cowp	Cowper's Reports, King's Bench (ER 98)
Cox	SC Cox's Equity Cases (ER 29–30)
Cox's Crim Cas	EW Cox's Criminal Law Cases
C & P	Carrington and Payne's Reports, Nisi Prius (ER 171 ff)
CPD	Common Pleas Division of the High Court of Justice; Law Reports, Common Pleas Division (1875–1880)
D	Recueil Dalloz de doctrine, de jurisprudence et de législation (1945–1964); Recueil Dalloz

Davies's Rep	Davies' Irish Kings Bench Reports (ER 80)
DB	Der Betrieb
DC	Divisional Court
DCFR	Draft Common Frame of Reference
De GF & J	De Gex, Fisher & Jones' Chancery Reports (ER 45)
De GM & G	De Gex, Macnaghten and Gordon's Reports, Chancery (ER 42 ff)
DH	Dalloz, Recueil hebdomadaire de jurisprudence (1924–1940)
Defr	Defrénois, la revue du notariat
DLR	Dominion Law Reports
Doug KB	Douglas' Reports, King's Bench (ER 99)
DP	Dalloz, Recueil périodique et critique de jurisprudence, de législation et de doctrine (1825–1940)
Drew	Drewry and Smale's Chancery Reports (ER 62)
DS	Recueil Dalloz-Sirey
East	East's Term Reports, King's Bench (ER 102 ff)
E & B	Ellis & Blackburn's Queen's Bench Reports (ER 118 ff)
EAT	Employment Appeal Tribunal
EC	European Community
ECHR	European Convention of Human Rights
ECJ	European Court of Justice
ECR	European Court Reports
ECtHR	European Court of Human Rights
ed	editor
edn	edition
eds	editors
EEC	European Economic Community
eg	for example (Latin: *exempli gratia*)
ELJ	European Law Journal
ER	English Reports
ERCL	European Review of Contract Law
ERPL	European Review of Private Law
Esp	Espinasse's Nisi Prius Reports (ER 170)
esp	especially
et al	and others (Latin: *et alii*)

et seq	and the following (Latin: *et sequens*)
etc	et cetera
EU	European Union
EWCA	Court of Appeal, England and Wales
Ex D	Exchequer Division of the High Court of Justice; Law Reports, Exchequer Division and Court of Appeal (1875–1880)
Exch	Exchequer Reports (1847–1856)
f, ff	following page(s)
F 2d	Federal Reporter, 2nd Series
FF	French Francs
F & F	Foster and Finlason's Nisi Prius Reports (ER 175–76)
FLR	Family Law Reports
Foro it	Foro italiano
F Supp	Federal Supplement
Gaz Pal	Gazette du Palais
gen ed	general editor
GG	Grundgesetz (German Constitution)
GI	Giurisprudenza italiana
Gif	Giffard's Chancery Cases
Giff	Giffard's Chancery Reports (ER 65–66)
Giust civ	Giusticia civile
GmbHG	Gesetz betreffend die Gesellschaft mit beschränkter Haftung (German Limited Company Act)
H & C	Hurlstone and Coltman's Reports, Exchequer (ER 158–59)
H & N	Hurlstone and Norman's Reports, Exchequer (ER 156ff)
HL	House of Lords
Hobart	Hobart's Reports, Common Pleas (ER 80)
HR	Hoge Raad (Dutch Supreme Court)
Harv LR	Harvard Law Review
HGB	Handelsgesetzbuch (German Commercial Code)
ibid	in the same place (Latin: *ibidem*)
ICC	International Chamber of Commerce
ICLQ	International and Comparative Law Quarterly
ICR	Industrial Cases Reports

ie	that is (Latin: *id est*)
IR	Jurisprudence Informations rapides
IRLR	Industrial Relations Law Reports
J, JJ	Justice(s)
JCP	Juris-classeur périodique, La semaine juridique
JDI	Journal du droit international ('Clunet')
J Law & Society	Journal of Law and Society
JLS	Journal of Legal Studies
JW	Juristische Wochenschrift
JZ	Juristenzeitung
K & J	Kay and Johnson's Vice Chancellors' Reports (ER 69–70)
KB	Law Reports, King's Bench Division (1901–1952)
KBD	King's Bench Division
Knight's LGR	Knight's Local Government Reports
Law Com	Law Commission of England and Wales
LC	Lord Chancellor
Ld Raym	Lord Raymond's King's Bench Reports
LG	Landgericht (German Regional Court)
LJ, LJJ	Lord Justice(s)
Ll L Rep	Lloyd's Reports
Lloyd's Rep	Lloyd's Law Reports
LM	Lindenmaier-Möhring, Nachschlagewerk des Bundesgerichtshofs
LQR	Law Quarterly Review
LR … App Cas	Law Reports, Appeal Cases
LR … CA	Law Reports, Court of Appeal
LR … Ch App	Law Reports, Chancery Appeal Cases
LR … CP	Law Reports, Common Pleas (1865–1875)
LR … Ex; LR … Exch	Law Reports, Exchequer (1865–1875)
LR … HL	Law Reports, English and Irish Appeal Cases and Claims of Peerage before the House of Lords (1865–1875)
LR … QB	Law Reports, Court of Queen's Bench (1865–1875)
LT	Law Times Reports
Ltd	Limited Company

M & W	Meeson and Welsby's Reports, Exchequer (ER 150 ff)
Mass	Massimario
Mass Foro it	Massimario de Foro italiano
MDR	Monatsschrift für deutsches Recht
Mich LR	Michigan Law Review
Minn	Minnesota Supreme Court Reports
MJ	Maastricht Journal of European and Comparative Law
MLR	Modern Law Review
MR	Master of the Rolls
Münchener Kommentar	Münchener Kommentar zum Bürgerlichen Gesetzbuch, 7th edn (Munich: CH Beck, 2015 ff)
NJ	Nederlandse Jurisprudentie
NJW	Neue Juristische Wochenschrift
NJW-RR	Neue Juristische Wochenschrift, Rechtsprechungs-Report Zivilrecht
NLJ	New Law Journal
no., nos.	number(s)
NSWLR	New South Wales Law Reports
NW 2d	North Western Reporter, 2nd Series
OJ	Official Journal (of the EEC, EC or EU)
OJLS	Oxford Journal of Legal Studies
OLG	Oberlandesgericht (Higher Regional Appeal Court, Germany)
OLGZ	Entscheidungen der Oberlandesgerichte in Zivilsachen
OR	Obligationenrecht (Swiss Law of Obligations)
P	Law Reports, Probate, Divorcce, and Admiralty Division of the High Court of Justice (1890–1971)
p, pp	page(s)
P 2d	Pacific Reporter, 2nd Series
Palandt	Bürgerliches Gesetzbuch, 77th edn (Munich: CH Beck, 2018)
para, paras	paragraph(s)
Pas	Pasicrisie belge (Belgium)
PC	Judicial Committee of the Privy Council
P & CR	Planning (Property) and Compensation Reports
PECL	Principles of European Contract Law
Plc	Public limited company

QB	Queen's Bench Reports (1841–1852) (ER 113 ff); Law Reports, Queen's Bench Division (1891–1901, since 1952)
QBD	Law Reports, Queen's Bench Division (1875–1890)
QC	Queen's Counsel
Qd R	Queensland Reports
RabelsZ	Rabels Zeitschrift für ausländisches und internationales Privatrecht
RDC	Revue des contrats
Rec	Recueil des décisions du Conseil d'État statuant au Contentieux, du Tribunal des conflits, des arrêts des cours administratives d'appel et des jugements des tribunaux administratifs
regs	Regulations
Rep	Coke's King's Bench Reports (ER 76–77)
resp	respectively
Rev dr int dr comp	Revue de droit international et de droit comparé
RG	Reichsgericht
RGDC/TBBR	Revue générale de droit civil belge / Tijdschrift voor Belgisch Burgerlijk Recht
RGLJ	Revista General de Legislación y Jurisprudencia
RGZ	Entscheidungen des Reichsgerichts in Zivilsachen
RIDC	Revue internationale de droit comparé
RIW	Recht der internationalen Wirtschaft
Roll Abr	Rolle's Abridgement
RPC	Reports of Patent, Design and Trade Mark Cases
RT	Revue Thémis
RTD civ	Revue trimestrielle de droit civil
RTD com	Revue trimestrielle de droit commercial
RvdW	Rechtspraak van de Week
RW	Rechtskundig Weekblad
S	Recueil Sirey
s, ss	section(s)
SA	Société anonyme
SC (HL)	Session cases – Cases decided in the House of Lords
Seuff A	Seufferts Archiv für Entscheidungen der obersten Gerichte in den deutschen Staaten

Sez un	Sezione Unite (United Section of the Corte di cassazione)
SGA	Sale of Goods Act 1979 (UK)
SI	Statutory Instrument
SLR	Singapore Law Reports
SLT	Scots Law Times
Sm LC	Smith's Leading Cases in Various Branches of the Law
So	Southern Reporter
StGB	Strafgesetzbuch (German Penal Code)
Str	Strange's King's Bench Reports (ER 93)
TEC	Treaty Establishing the European Community
TFEU	Treaty on the Functioning of the European Union
TGI	Tribunal de grande instance (French first or second instance court)
The Times	The Times
TLR	Times Law Reports
TR	Durnford and East's Term Reports (ER 99 ff)
Trib civ	Tribunal civil (French first instance court)
Tul LR	Tulane Law Review
Tyr	Tyrwhitt's Exchequer Reports
UCC	Uniform Commercial Code (USA)
UCTA	Unfair Contract Terms Act 1977 (England)
UKHL	United Kingdom House of Lords
UKPC	United Kingdom Privy Council
UKSC	United Kingdom Supreme Court
UNIDROIT PICC	Unidroit Principles of International Commercial Contracts (4 edn, Rome: UNIDROIT, 2016)
UTCCR	Unfair Terms in Consumer Contracts Regulations 1999 (England)
UWG	Gesetz gegen den unlauteren Wettbewerb (German Unfair Competition Act)
v	versus
VersR	Versicherungsrecht
Ves Sen	Vesey Senior's Law Reports, Chancery (ER 27 ff)
viz	namely (Latin: *videlicet*)
VOB/A & VOB/B	Verdingungsordnung für Bauleistungen Teil A und B (German contracting rules for the award of public work contracts, parts A and B)

vol, vols	volume(s)
VOL/A & VOL/B	Verdingungsordnung für Leistungen, Teil A und B
Wash 2d	Washington Reports, 2nd Series
Wis 2d	Wisconsin Reports, 2nd Series
WLR	Weekly Law Reports
WM	Wertpapier-Mitteilungen
WN	Weekly Notes
Yale LJ	Yale Law Journal
YB … Edw	Year book … Edward
ZEuP	Zeitschrift für Europäisches Privatrecht
ZGB	Zivilgesetzbuch (Swiss Civil Code)
ZIP	Zeitschrift für Wirtschaftsrecht
ZPO	Zivilprozessordnung (German Code of Civil Procedure)

TABLE OF CASES

(Alphabetical order except where otherwise specified)

EUROPEAN CONVENTION OF HUMAN RIGHTS

EUROPEAN UNION

NATIONAL

AUSTRALIA

BELGIUM

CANADA

FRANCE (chronological order)

GERMANY (chronological order)

HONG KONG

ITALY (chronological order)

NETHERLANDS (chronological order)

NEW ZEALAND

SWITZERLAND (chronological order)

UNITED KINGDOM

UNITED STATES

(Alphabetical order except where otherwise stated)

INTERNATIONAL

NATIONAL

AUSTRIA

BELGIUM

CANADA

FRANCE

GERMANY

GREECE

ITALY

NETHERLANDS

PORTUGAL

SPAIN

SWEDEN

SWITZERLAND

UNITED KINGDOM

UNITED STATES

PART 1

INTRODUCTION

CHAPTER 1
GENERAL TRENDS IN MODERN CONTRACT LAW

In the absence a unified European or international contract law, the study of the various laws of contract is one of the core subjects of comparative law. Its practical importance is great. 'Of all areas of law, perhaps none has been subjected to comparative study as consistently, frequently, and intensely as contract law'.[1] According to Allan Farnsworth, there are three main reasons for this: 'First, the origins of modern comparative law lie in the civil law world (ie in Western Europe) of the late nineteenth and early twentieth centuries, and in that world, contracts have been widely considered the pre-eminent area of law. … Second, modern comparative law soon began to focus particularly on the study of the similarities and differences between the civil law and the common law, and contract law turned out to be an enormously fertile field for such studies. … Third, contract law is a favourite topic for comparative study because it is among the practically most salient areas of law, both in terms of economic importance and in terms of the realities of international negotiation and litigation'.[2]

National legislators, when reforming the law of contract, are more and more inspired by what has been done abroad as well as by transnational norms. Gradual convergences occurred, which enabled scholars from around the world to elaborate soft law instruments on a worldwide and European scale. These instruments, in turn, have provided guidance for converging developments of national contract laws. Competition between legal systems has dramatically developed. As measuring how friendly each system is towards foreign investment has become a constant trend worldwide, demonstrating the potential political explosiveness of comparative studies (the 'Doing Business' approach which ranks economies according to various sets of indicators based on the ease of doing business is typical of such an approach),[3] legislators are eager to modernise their own national

---

[1] A Farnsworth, 'Comparative contract law' in M Reimann and R Zimmermann (eds), *Oxford Handbook of Comparative Law* (Oxford University Press, 2006) 899, 900.

[2] ibid, 900-02.

[3] See the website of the Doing Business organisation to access the various reports: www.doingbusiness.org.

laws of contract and this may lead them to make a determined effort to forge an alliance between their legal tradition and the construction of a European and international legal order. As we shall see in the subsequent chapters of this book, the recent French contract law reform (2016, with slight modifications in 2018) is a prime example of this trend.

Over the decades, contracts have become more numerous, more sophisticated and also more international. As surprising as this may seem, most cross-border transactions are still governed by national laws of contract. However, the constant development of party autonomy, characterised by the parties' freedom to choose the applicable law in an international setting, increases the need for contracting parties (in particular business operators) to be well informed of the content of national contract laws. Whereas only large companies used to be active in international markets, an increasing proportion of parties to a contract (suppliers, customers, employees, students, retired persons, migrants, tourists) are now engaged in international transactions.

The first part of this chapter will present the main trends that affect national contract laws within the European Union, the second part will deal with contract law in a digital environment and the third part with contract law in an international environment.

1.1 NATIONAL CONTRACT LAWS WITHIN THE EUROPEAN UNION

1.1.A GRADUAL CONVERGENCES OF NATIONAL LEGAL SYSTEMS

Establishing a European contract law in the twenty-first century would not be an easy task. The biggest problem in this respect is not just, as we shall see further, the divide between the civil law tradition prevailing in continental Europe and the common law tradition prevailing in England and Ireland,[4] but rather the political implications of such a project, in terms of European integration, as the idea of a unified European contract code goes along with the idea of a unified Europe and the creation of the European Union.[5] In spite of the major European and international developments that our legal systems have experienced, there is no general common European contract law and so far the arguments in favour of a European unification of contract law have not been considered sufficiently strong. There is, however, an ever-increasing doctrinal framework and gradual convergence towards shared principles.

1.1.A.1 ARGUMENTS IN FAVOUR OF A EUROPEAN UNIFICATION OF CONTRACT LAW

There are various arguments in favour of a European unification of contract law.

First, the subject of contracts lends itself to unification because contracting parties develop their activities in an international context and this unification would lead to more legal certainty.

---

[4] See below, ch 4.
[5] See below, 1.1.A. 1; see also chs 2 and 3.

Secondly, some areas, or 'sectors' of contract law have been harmonised by the European legislator, while others have been left as a matter of national law. This so-called 'sectorial approach' has many disadvantages. They include, for example, the difficulty of transposing directives into national laws and the resulting fragmentation of the national laws. A more coherent and more complete set of European rules to govern contracts would be welcome (see Chapter 2).

Thirdly, consumer protection has led, within Europe, to the enactment of many specific uniform rules which are mandatory in the sense that the parties cannot contract out of them. Fundamental rights, particularly those linked to privacy and data protection, reinforce this trend.

Fourthly, establishing a European law of contract has a symbolic dimension for Europe.

However, the idea of a European *codification*, which would be complete, coherent and structured, gave rise to strong criticism, not only because it tended to embody the civil law tradition to the detriment of the common law, but also because it exceeded the scope of the powers held by the EU. The European system of conferred powers implies that both the principles of subsidiarity and proportionality are respected, and the arguments regularly put forward by the Commission, which focused on the fragmented legal framework in the area of contract law and its obstacles for cross-border trade,[6] were not judged sufficient to confer the necessary powers on the Commission. It also needed to be demonstrated that the diversity of laws does indeed create barriers, and the Court of Justice was of the view that a Community act must genuinely have as its objective the improvement of the conditions for the establishment and functioning of the internal market.[7] It is therefore not sufficient to find disparities between national rules, or to point out the abstract risk of obstacles to the exercise of fundamental freedoms or of distortions of competition likely to result therefrom to justify the process of European unification of law. Furthermore, and perhaps more importantly, such a task is charged with strong symbolism: codifying contract law is a significant step towards a European Civil Code, a project that can only be achieved if there is a strong desire for it within Europe.[8] This is not the case.

1.1.A.2 SHARED PRINCIPLES

There is a common legal basis across Europe, inherited from history and rediscovered in the second half of the twentieth century, with the effect that, in the last decades, a substantial doctrinal European framework has emerged. Even systems which share little by way of common origin, such as the common law and the French Civil Code, have influenced each other and often produce results that are not too dissimilar. Beyond the wide

---

[6] See the Explanatory Memorandum in the Proposal for a Regulation of the European Parliament and the Council on a Common European Sales Law, COM/2011/0635 final—2011/0284 (COD).

[7] C-376/98, *Federal Republic of Germany v European Parliament and Council of the European Union*, 5 October 2000, ECLI:EU:C:2000:544, at [83]–[84]; C-434/02, *Arnold André GmbH & Co. KG v Landrat des Kreises Herford*, 14 December 2004, ECLI:EU:C:2004:800; C-210/03, *Swedish Match AB and Swedish Match UK Ltd v Secretary of State for Health*, 14 December 2004, ECLI:EU:C:2004:802.

[8] W van Gerven, 'Codifying European private law? Yes, if …!' [2002] ELRev 156; O Lando, 'Culture and Contract Laws' (2007) 1 ERCL 1.

variety of national contract laws, there are indeed striking convergences, and a strong doctrinal framework forms part of what is currently called 'European private law'. The comparative law method, used in this book, has become 'a valuable interpretative tool that serves to strike the dynamic balance' between unity and diversity upon which the future of Europe and its law should be built.[9]

Principles which are found in the laws of the Member States have been elevated to the European level by the Court of Justice, which recognises general principles of EU law on the basis of the constitutional traditions of the Member States. Cross-fertilisations and reciprocal exchanges are thus facilitated. Principles which have been first affirmed in one State and then recognised at the level of the European Union subsequently spread across other countries; and they may also often be found in the law of the European Convention on Human Rights. As explained by French *conseiller d'État*[10] Bernard Stirn, these shared principles 'structure the European legal system'. Bernard Stirn identifies four of these, which 'make up the keystone of the construct of European law—these are the principles of equality, proportionality, subsidiarity, and legal certainty'.[11]

This comparative approach is rapidly spreading within the EU. And the decisions of national judges are contributing to the convergence of national legal systems.[12] Along-side the principles of equality, proportionality, subsidiarity and legal certainty, national contract laws share other guiding principles, notably contractual freedom, the binding force of contracts and, to a certain extent, good faith and legitimate expectations. These principles also belong to a common corpus of general principles in transnational instru-ments. As Stefan Vogenauer shows, while in the past general principles of contract law were neither codified in civil codes, nor so well-established that they could be regarded as self-evident, transnational instruments have greatly contributed to a major shift in this respect.

*General principles of contract law in transnational
instruments*[13]   **1.1 (INT)**

Stefan Vogenauer

General principles of contract law at the outset of these texts help us better understand the general nature of the instruments. Their presence or absence, their exact formulation and their position within the overall context of a given instrument provide us with an idea as to how their black letter rules will attempt to strike the balance between freedom

---

[9] K Lenaerts, 'The Court of Justice and the Comparative Law Method', the keynote address given by the President of the Court of Justice to more than 350 legal experts from all over Europe at the European Law Institute (ELI) 2016 Annual Conference on 9 September 2016, accessible at https://typo3.univie.ac.at/fileadmin/user_upload/p_eli/General_Assembly/2016/Conference_Materials_for_participants/Keynote_speeches/K._Lenaerts_ELI_AC_2016.pdf.

[10] Judge at the Conseil d'État.

[11] B Stirn, *Towards a European Public Law*, translated by E Bjorge (Oxford University Press, 2017) 106.

[12] G Canivet, 'La convergence des systèmes juridiques par l'action du juge' in *De tous horizons: Mélanges Xavier Blanc-Jouvan* (Paris: Société de législation comparée, 2005) 11.

[13] S Vogenauer, 'General principles of contract law in transnational instruments' in L Gullifer and S Vogenauer (eds), *English and European Perspectives on Contract and Commercial Law: Essays in Honour of Hugh Beale* (Oxford: Hart Publishing, 2014) 291, 316.

and social justice. Such guideposts are particularly useful in a transnational context where there is no shared background legal culture, as it exists in national jurisdictions … [Transnational instruments] will be applied by lawyers with very different understandings of the role and function of contracts in law, society and the economy. In these circumstances, there are no self-evident or obvious solutions, and laying down a number of fundamental provisions will help them in gradually finding common ground.

Notes

(1) As explained by Stefan Vogenauer, there is a sharp contrast between earlier approaches towards the codification of these principles in the civil codes of the eighteenth and early nineteenth century—typically the French Civil Code of 1804—which did not attempt to give a systematic overview of the fundamental principles, and the modern trend which is to formulate, in the shape of black-letter rules, the 'general principles' that underlie national contract laws and new transnational instruments, such as the Principles of European Contract Law[14] (PECL) and the UNIDROIT Principles of International Commercial Contracts[15] (UNIDROIT PICC).

(2) The codification of international and European shared guiding principles is desirable. However, it is not an easy task when there is no shared background legal culture. In his article, Stefan Vogenauer provides eight guidelines for the codification of these general principles, which should identify themselves as 'fundamental provisions' rather than 'general principles', so as not to create a confusion due to the 'inconsistent use of the enigmatic term "principle" across different jurisdictions'.[16]

(3) Transnational instruments which have codified general principles of contract law now serve as 'model codes' for national legislators. They thus play an important part in the evolution of national contract laws within Europe and facilitate cross-fertilisations.[17] A striking example of this phenomenon is the 2016 French contract law reform (the origin of which is presented in Chapter 4 of this book). The process leading to this reform led all those involved in it (the government, but also judges, scholars, practitioners and to some extent the French Parliament) to consider primarily international and European models (notably the PECL and the UNIDROIT PICC).[18] The first governmental draft of the French reform (July 2008) even placed contractual freedom, binding force and good faith in a chapter entitled 'Guiding Principles'. Due to strong criticism from some academics and business representatives, who feared that this would open the way to judicial discretion and a broad interpretation of these principles, the new French Civil Code (2016) does not contain a specific

[14] O Lando and H Beale (eds), *Principles of European Contract Law, Parts I and II* (The Hague: Kluwer, 2000); O Lando, E Clive, A Prüm and R Zimmerman (eds), *Principles of European Contract Law, Part III* (The Hague: Kluwer 2003).

[15] Now in a 2016 edition.

[16] Vogenauer (n 13 above) 317.

[17] ibid.

[18] This is obvious from the Report to the President of the Republic accompanying the 2016 Ordonnance (see ch 4.2.A below).

chapter titled 'Guiding Principles'. However, such principles are to be found in a preliminary chapter.[19]

(4) The Draft Common Frame of Reference[20] (DCFR) also contains such principles.[21] The introduction to the DCFR attempts to differentiate these 'underlying principles' from the ones mentioned in an earlier draft of the DCFR, the 'Interim Outline edition',[22] which are 'generally of a rather high political nature' and 'could be said overriding rather than underlying'.[23] The introduction cites, in this category, the protection of human rights, the promotion of solidarity and social responsibility, the preservation of cultural and linguistic diversity, the protection and promotion of welfare and the promotion of the internal market.[24]

(5) Within the context of the elaboration of a European contract law (see Chapter 2), a group of French scholars purported to draft 'guiding principles of European contract law' which were meant to be a useful guide to the interpretation and application of the PECL.[25] These scholars identified three main 'guiding principles': freedom of contract, contractual fairness and contractual certainty.

The general trends which affect all national contract laws can be identified throughout the main themes studied while analysing the general theory of contract law. The quest for legal certainty in contract law, the protection of weaker parties and the influence of constitutional laws, as well as of fundamental rights, on contract laws, successively examined below, all belong to these core themes.

1.1.B LEGAL CERTAINTY

Legal certainty is not only given different meanings but also a different scope in the various national legal systems studied in this book.

---

[19] *Dispositions liminaires*, Arts 1101 to 1111-1.

[20] Study Group on a European Civil Code and Research Group on EC Private Law (Acquis Group), *Principles, Definitions and Model Rules of European Private Law: Draft Common Frame of Reference* (Munich: Sellier, 2009), available in both six volumes and an Outline Edition.

[21] On the DCFR, see ch 3.2.C; for an account of the codification of contract law principles in the DCFR as well as in the other contract law transnational instruments, see Vogenauer (n 13 above) 299–310.

[22] Study Group on a European Civil Code and Research Group on EC Private Law (Acquis Group), *Principles, Definitions and Model Rules of European Private Law: Draft Common Frame of Reference* (Interim Outline Edition) (Munich: Sellier, 2008).

[23] DCFR (2009) (n 20 above) Introduction, no. 13.

[24] ibid, no. 16.

[25] Association H Capitant and Société de législation comparée (eds), *Projet de cadre commun de référence: Terminologie contractuelle commune* (Paris: Société de législation comparée, 2008); Association H Capitant and Société de législation comparée (eds), *Projet de cadre commun de référence: Principes contractuels communs* (Paris: Société de législation comparée, 2008). For an English translation: B Fauvarque-Cosson and D Mazeaud (eds), *European Contract Law: Materials for a Common Frame of Reference. Terminology, Guiding Principles, Model Rules* (Munich: Sellier, 2008). See also B Fauvarque-Cosson, 'The Need for codified Guiding Principles and Model Rules in European Contract Law' in R Brownsword, H-W Micklitz, L Niglia and S Weatherill (eds), *The Foundations of European Private Law* (Oxford: Hart Publishing, 2011) 73.

In continental law countries, legal certainty primarily derives from the fact that the law is codified. Provisions which reflect a movement towards a fairer general contract law (such as those on the exploitation of a state of dependence,[26] or on the controls on unfair terms, notably in standard-form contracts)[27] are therefore not viewed as a direct threat to legal certainty. The approach is different in English law, where legal certainty is the basis for the principles of 'legitimate expectations' and reliance.

Contracts, Contract Law and Contractual Principle[28]   **1.2 (EN)**

Simon Whittaker

Those who characterise English contract law as 'liberal' (or perhaps more liberal) than French law, mean by this that the law generally recognises the full force of the double principles of freedom of contract and the binding force of contract and so provides a framework for contracting parties which is facilitative of their own decision-making rather than normative or moralising. In my view, there are four key features of the English law which lend support to this view.

— First, the common law itself rarely provides the legal incidents of particular types of contract and, where it does so—whether directly as common law rules or indirectly as 'implied terms'—the norms so provided are overwhelmingly non-mandatory and thereby open to modification or exclusion by the agreement of the parties.[29]

— Secondly, apart from consumer contracts, there is no general control on the validity of the terms of the contract even in standard term contracts by reference to their 'reasonableness' or 'fairness' whether at common law or by statute, the exceptions here being all but limited to exemption clauses.[30]

— Thirdly, the common law provides the general framework of contract law and in its interpretation English courts remain very much concerned with the maintenance of the certainty of the law so as to ensure transactional (often termed commercial) certainty. In this respect, 'legal certainty' is used in a somewhat different sense from the typical use of French lawyers in relation to *la sécurité juridique*. For an English lawyer, legal certainty requires that the substance of the law should be sufficiently clear (and often therefore sufficiently detailed) to allow contracting parties

---

[26] Art 1143 Cciv.

[27] Art 1171 Cciv.

[28] S Whittaker, 'Contracts, Contract Law and Contractual Principle' in J Cartwright and S Whittaker (eds), *The Code Napoléon Rewritten: French Contract Law after the 2016 Reforms* (Oxford: Hart Publishing, 2017) 29, 31–33.

[29] The technique of the implication of terms at common law is *necessarily* subject to contrary agreement: *Marks & Spencer plc v BNP Paribas Securities Services Trust Co (Jersey) Ltd* [2015] UKSC 72, [2016] AC 742 [28], per Lord Neuberger PSC: 'it is a cardinal rule that no term can be implied into a contract if it contradicts an express term'. An example of the common law regulating the consequences of a contract may be found in the case of the contract of suretyship, where the contract of suretyship is discharged if the principal debt is varied unless the contract allows for variation or giving time: *Chitty on Contracts*, 33rd edn by H Beale (gen ed) (London: Sweet & Maxwell/Thomson Reuters, 2018) para 45–112.

[30] Unfair Contract Terms Act 1977 and the rule that one cannot exclude one's liability for personal fraud in *S Pearson & Son Ltd v Dublin Corp* [1907] AC 351. The other principal exceptions concern 'covenants in restraint of trade' (ie anti-competition clauses, which must be reasonable) and 'penalty clauses' (where the traditional common law restrictions have recently been *reduced* by the Supreme Court in the interests of freedom of contract): *Cavendish Square Holding BV v El Makdessi, ParkingEye Ltd v Beavis* [2015] UKSC 67, [2016] AC 1172.

to predict how it would apply to differing sets of facts. In the context of contracts, this is important in advance of parties entering a contract (so as to allow them to plan their contract in the light of their needs) and after doing so (so as to establish the parties' duties and proper performance and to provide a clear basis for the out-of-court settlement of any contractual dispute). For many French lawyers, and particularly, I think, for those enacting the new Code civil provisions, *la sécurité juridique* focuses on the need for *legislation* to express the rules which are in fact applied by the courts, the contrast being with the pre-reform position when the law as applied by the courts (*la jurisprudence*) sometimes bore only a distant relationship with the law set out by the Code civil.[31] While clearly the two understandings of legal certainty overlap, there are significant differences. A first difference is found in the accompanying attitude to the *content* of the law. For the French lawyer, the principal concern is that legislation should set out a series of legal propositions which are, in principle, relatively stable and also comprehensible to citizens as well as to lawyers—this is not a purely formal concern, as it concerns the accessibility of the substance of the law, and it has an important constitutional significance.[32] However, the law need not, and indeed, in principle should not be formulated in a very detailed way: accessibility to citizens requires a certain level of generality, as detail typically leads to complexity and technicality. This explains why the French tradition that the codification of civil law should be expressed in broad legal propositions remains so strong. By contrast, for an English lawyer, an area of the law which is formed of a complex pattern of court decisions (cases) is not on that ground 'uncertain' even if it is entirely opaque to the ordinary citizen: it is the nature of the common law to be contextual and fact-sensitive. Indeed, complexity may be seen as *enhancing* legal certainty by regulating in detail many of the factual or contextual permutations in which the law may be applied, as long as these permutations can be seen as justified. On the other hand, for an English lawyer, very broad legal propositions (legislative or judicial) which leave courts unguided as to their application in practice and which therefore give the courts wide powers of assessment or evaluation are seen as threatening to legal and, in the context of contract law, transactional certainty. So, a legislative proposition which to a French lawyer looks clear and accessible and therefore supportive of *la sécurité juridique* may well look to an English lawyer uncertain in its application and therefore disruptive of legal certainty.

— This leads to my fourth feature of English law: there is no general legal principle to counter or to qualify the principles of freedom of contract and the binding force of contract, such as good faith or fairness.[33] This does not mean, of course, that

---

[31] See further B Fauvarque-Cosson, 'Libres propos sur la sécurité juridique et l'entreprise' in B Fauvarque-Cosson and JL Dewost (eds), *L'entreprise et la sécurité juridique* (Paris: Société de législation comparée, 2015) 25. There are exceptions. P Stoffel-Munck defines *la sécurité juridique* as 'the foreseeability in the application of the law … This legal certainty allows a person to anticipate the legal consequences of his or her initiatives' and, as a result, he criticises a number of provisions in the draft *Ordonnance* on the basis that they use open and subjective legal concepts (P Stoffel-Munck, 'Les enjeux majeurs de la réforme "Attractivité, Sécurité, Justice"' in P Stoffel-Munck (ed), *Réforme du droit des contrats et pratique des affaires* (Paris: Dalloz, 2015) 17, 22–23).

[32] See C Bazy-Malaurie, 'La sécurité juridique et les droits fondamentaux' in Fauvarque-Cosson and Dewost (n 31 above) 58.

[33] For the details see *Chitty* (n 29 above) paras 1-044 ff. Some have argued that good faith should have a role to play in the general law of contract: eg Collins has argued that the law of implied terms rests on the idea of good faith in performance: H Collins, 'Implied Terms: The Foundation in Good Faith and Fair Dealing' (2015) 67 CLP 297.

English law itself makes no reference to the concept of good faith or fairness. Apart from its inclusion in legislation stemming from EU directives,[34] good faith is used on occasion in relation to particular types of contract (for example, the duties of agents to their principals).[35] And an implied term itself requiring good faith may sometimes be found by a court in a particular individual contract in its context or a particular type of contract, though the courts have made clear that implied terms should not be used as a vehicle to undermine the general *absence* of a legal principle of good faith.[36] For, rather than possessing a broad legal principle of good faith, the particular rules (legislative or common law) are seen as promoting the purpose of contract law, that is, to give effect to the reasonable expectations of honest people.[37]

Notes

(1) Throughout this book, we will see that 'legal certainty' is used in a different sense by the different legal systems. A topical issue which relates to legal certainty is the judge's power to interfere with contract terms, so as to restore some equilibrium or give effect to one party's reasonable expectations. As we will find out, issues of inequality and the techniques used to combat it are closely related to this issue of legal certainty.[38]

(2) While the primary purpose of contract law is to ensure legal certainty by giving effect to the contract as well as to the reasonable expectations of honest parties, the protection of the weaker party has become a major concern in general contract law. This goes far beyond consumer contracts—over the last decades, at least in some jurisdictions, there has been concern for any party who is not in a position to negotiate the contract. In some jurisdictions, therefore, the focus has moved from consumer law to the protection of the weaker party in general.

1.1.C THE PROTECTION OF THE WEAKER PARTY

The dissemination of standard form contracts and other fundamental changes to contract practices have turned the protection of the weaker party into a particularly stringent concern. Indeed, since the growth of standard form contracts has enabled one party to impose its contractual terms on other parties, the development of small business organisations and start-ups has increased the need to place limits upon the unfettered (rather

---

[34] Notably, the Consumer Rights Act 2015, s 62 implementing the test of unfairness of terms in Art 3 of the Council Directive 93/13/EEC on unfair terms in consumer contracts, OJ L 95/93, p 29.

[35] *Chitty* (n 29 above) para 31–120.

[36] I have argued that the legislative controls on trader behaviour to consumers and on consumer contracts themselves can be seen as reflecting a general *statutory* principle of good faith, but that the various legislative provisions give expression to this in a way which is particular, both in terms of their scope and in terms of the restrictions and qualifications on the rights or remedies which they create: S Whittaker, 'Distinctive Features of the New Consumer Contract Law' (2017) 133 LQR 47, 71.

[37] J Steyn, 'Contract Law: Fulfilling the reasonable expectations of honest men' (1997) 113 LQR 433.

[38] See in particular chs 11, 15, 16, 17, 18, 21.

than dishonest) exercise of contractual freedom. The many ways of protecting the weaker party will be examined further in this book (particularly in Chapters 15–21).

Many of the qualifications on party autonomy or freedom of contract, especially in the laws of the continental countries, can be explained by the idea that the weaker party (be it a consumer or even a business person) should be protected. This is particularly true in the development of precontractual duties and provisions on unfair contract terms. Not allowing a contracting party to gain an advantage from its dishonest or unfair conduct also testifies to the importance of contractual justice in contemporary laws of contracts. Party autonomy is protected (it may even be given constitutional status)[39] but it is tempered in many ways: good faith, duress, undue influence, specific rules on the interpretation of certain contracts, and, perhaps most importantly, the regulation of unfair standard terms are various techniques which all limit the parties' autonomy in favour of the weaker party.

European Contract Law[40]   **1.3 (DE)**

Hein Kötz

Standard terms are a product of the industrial revolution of the nineteenth century: as the production of goods and services was standardised, so were the terms of business on which such goods and services were supplied. Standard terms contribute to the rationalisation and development of mass transactions, for they save companies and their customers the cost and trouble of negotiating the terms of each contract individually, or of going to court to have the contract construed and amplified. Standard terms therefore make it easier to forecast the cost of doing business, simplify its procedures, and thus contribute to keeping costs and prices low.

But there is another side to the picture. Rationalising contracts is not the company's only aim in drafting terms of business; they are also used to shift as many risks as possible on to the other party. Of course, one can only speak of shifting risks in this sense if one knows what the distribution of risks would otherwise be. This can often be inferred from the default rules laid down by statute or judicial decision, and implied into contracts in the absence of any contrary term. Such rules are designed to produce a reasonable accommodation of the interests of both parties, whereas the company will be concerned only with its own. Accordingly, if the default rules are substituted by terms that protect the drafting party, these will be felt by the other party to be 'unfair'.

There is now general agreement that the law and courts must set limits to the validity of these clauses, but it is not so clear how to justify such control. It is not enough that the customer accept a disadvantageous clause without objection. The critical question is *why* the customer habitually accepts such prejudicial clauses without demur. The reason generally given is 'unequal bargaining power' between the parties: faced with the economic superiority of the company, the customer has no alternative but to submit to the standard terms. Sometimes the company has a monopoly position, and thus sees no need to negotiate over the content of its contracts. Even in a competitive environment, competitors often use very similar standard terms of business. Commentators often point to the psychological and intellectual superiority of the entrepreneur who knows so much more about law and business than his customers that they will think it futile to protest

[39] See below, ch 1.1.D.3.
[40] H Kötz, *European Contract Law* (2nd edn, Oxford University Press, 2017) 132–33.

against disadvantageous terms. In an influential and much-cited article in 1943, Friedrich Kessler wrote 'standard contracts in particular could ... become effective instruments in the hands of powerful industrial and commercial overlords enabling them to impose a new feudal order of their own making upon a vast horde of vassals'.[41] This idea that general terms of business must be controlled in order to protect the weak and inexperienced against the powerful and knowledgeable has really come to dominate discussions of legal policy. After this argument became the battle-cry of the consumer protection movement, most countries in Europe have passed laws since the 1970s based more or less on the view that as consumers are the 'weaker' of the contracting parties, they must be protected against contract terms forced upon them by companies abusing their economic superiority. The Council Directive of 5 April 1993 on unfair terms in consumer contracts is based on the concept that the justification for control of standard terms is to correct the 'abuse of power' between companies and 'consumers'.[42]

Yet it is far from clear that this is the nub of the matter. Certainly a customer will occasionally refrain from objecting to an unfavourable term because he thinks it futile to negotiate over it in view of the other party's superiority in economic or other respects, but this is not the normal case. Even in areas of commerce where competition is so lively that there can be no question of economic superiority, quite experienced contractors accept such terms without demur. Businesses do not haggle over the standard terms proffered by carriers, warehousemen, credit institutions, security firms or credit information agencies. In such cases, the customer 'submits' to the proffered terms of business because it is not worth investing the time and money involved in getting the terms modified or seeking out other firms whose terms are less unfavourable in some respect or other. A private person or even a businessman who parks his car in a garage or buys a computer or arranges for his goods to be carried accepts the terms on offer without discussion—not because they are forced on him by a 'powerful industrial or commercial overlord' but because the cost of negotiating, obtaining the necessary information or tracking down a more favourable offer would be out of all proportion to the advantage to be gained. The company exploits this fact by saddling the customer with the risks of the deal on the assumption that, for the reasons given, the customer will neither object nor go elsewhere. But the fact that the customer agrees to the conditions does not make it incompatible with the principle of freedom of contract for the law to control such terms, since it is only when both parties had a fair chance of influencing the content of contracts that the principle requires them to be respected. In the situations under consideration, the customer has no such opportunity—not because of the superiority of the company in economic or other respects, but because of the prohibitively high transaction costs of utilising any such opportunity.[43]

Notes

(1) There is now a general consensus that courts must set limits to the validity of unfair clauses. However, the extent and justifications for such a control vary. More detail is given in Chapter 21.

---

[41] F Kessler, 'Contracts of Adhesion—Some Thoughts About Freedom of Contract' (1943) 43 Col LR 629, 640.

[42] See Recital 9 to Directive 93/13/EEC (see n 34 above).

[43] See MJ Trebilcock and DN Dewees, 'Judicial Control of Standard Form Contracts' in P Burrows and C Veljanovski (eds), *The Economic Approach to Law* (London: Butterworths, 1981) 93; [further citations omitted] M Eisenberg, 'The Limits of Cognition and the Limits of Contract' (1955) 47 Stanford Law Review 211, 243.

(2) Hein Kötz's contribution is particularly relevant in this debate because his approach, inspired by Law and Economics is opposite to the French and European starting point whereby unfair terms primarily serve to correct the 'abuse of power' between companies and 'consumers': control of standard terms, for Kötz, is not a device to protect the 'weaker party' but to remedy market failure—no one reads the terms, and suppliers have no incentive to use fair terms.

1.1.D CONTRACT, CONSTITUTIONAL LAW AND HUMAN RIGHTS

Development of constitutional issues in private law is a common feature of modern national legal systems. The concept of 'constitutionalisation of contract law' refers to the impact of fundamental rights on contract law.[44] This justifies examining these two issues together. The extensive set of fundamental rights affects all parts of the law, including contract law even though it is not the most obvious candidate for such interactions.

1.1.D.1 THE INCREASED CONSTITUTIONAL DIMENSION OF CONTRACT LAW

1.1.D.1 (i) Human Rights: General Background

Fundamental rights are laid down in national constitutions or statutes and/or in international treaties. One of the most important of these is the European Convention for the Protection of Human Rights and Fundamental Freedoms (ECHR). Whether fundamental rights included in international treaties can be directly enforced depends on domestic constitutional law. This is possible, for instance, in the Netherlands and France. In Germany and the UK, in contrast, treaties have to be transposed into national legislation in order to be brought into force.

In Germany, the main source of fundamental rights is the national constitution, the Grundgesetz (Basic Law). In addition, the ECHR is transposed into a statute, the Act on the Convention for the Protection of Human Rights and Fundamental Freedoms.[45] It must be noted that the Basic Law is further up in the hierarchy of legal sources than the statute transposing the ECHR, but the fundamental rights included in the Basic Law are broadly similar to those included in the ECHR. In France also, the main sources of fundamental rights are the constitution (*Constitution*), more precisely the *bloc de constitutionnalité*, and the ECHR, which applies directly in the French legal order due to the doctrine of monism. Under Dutch law, the situation is rather similar: fundamental

---

[44] See further: OO Cherednychenko, *Fundamental Rights, Contract Law and the Protection of the Weaker Party: a Comparative Analysis of the Constitutionalisation of Contract Law, with Emphasis on Risky Financial Transactions* (Munich: Sellier, 2007); A Colombi Ciacchi, 'The Constitutionalization of European Contract Law' (2006) 2 ERCL 167; C Mak, *Fundamental Rights in European Contract Law: a Comparison of the Impact of Fundamental Rights on Contractual Relationships in Germany, the Netherlands, Italy and England* (Alphen an den Rijn: Wolters Kluwer, 2008); C Mak 'The Constitution of a Common Frame of Reference for European Contract Law' (2008) 4 ERCL 553.

[45] Gesetz über die Konvention zum Schutze der Menschenrechte und Grundfreiheiten of 7 August 1952, BGBl. II 685.

rights are included in the constitution (Grondwet) and the ECHR, which applies directly. In the UK there is no written constitution. The main source of fundamental rights is the Human Rights Act 1998 which (broadly speaking) incorporates the ECHR into domestic law.

The 1957 Treaty establishing the European Economic Community (EEC) was silent on the protection of fundamental rights within the legal order of the Community. This did not mean, however, that there was no legal protection. As early as 1969, and to answer the concerns expressed by some national courts, the Court of Justice held that fundamental rights form an integral part of the general principles of law whose observance the Court ensures.[46] However, the European Community (EC) still lacked a codified declaration of rights of its own.

EU fundamental rights were finally consecrated in the Charter of Fundamental Rights of the EU (the Charter), which was 'proclaimed' on 7 December 2000.[47] With the entry into force of the Lisbon Treaty in December 2009, the Charter became a legally binding and core element of the Union's legal order.[48] Moreover, under Article 6 of the Treaty on European Union (TEU), the EU also gained the constitutional power to seek accession to the ECHR. Article 6(3) TEU amended the previous treaty to provide that 'Fundamental rights, as guaranteed by the [ECHR] and as they result from the constitutional traditions common to the Member States, shall constitute general principles of the Union's law'.

The Court of Justice draws 'inspiration' from the constitutional traditions of the Member States, from international human rights treaties and from the case law of the ECHR. While the Court of Justice has no jurisdiction to apply the ECHR (as it does not constitute a formal source of EU law), the Court has referred extensively to the provisions of the ECHR and its case law, to assist its own interpretation of EU human rights standards.

The Charter's 50 'rights, freedoms and principles' do not simply codify existing fundamental rights contained in other sources (national or international). Some of the Charter's rights are modern and innovative (eg the right to the protection of personal data, the right to a high level of environmental protection, etc), as previously they had not been characterised as fundamental rights in the EU context.

1.1.D.1 (ii) The Constitutionalisation of Contract Law

We have just seen that the concept of 'constitutionalisation of contract law' refers to the impact of fundamental rights on contract law.

Historically, fundamental rights were addressed to States and did not permeate private law relationships between citizens. Thus they concerned the relationship between a State and a citizen: when a citizen's fundamental right was infringed by a State, he could enforce this right vis-à-vis the State. However, in Germany the question was raised in the 1950s whether fundamental rights should not also apply in private law relationships.

---

[46] C-29/69, *Erich Stauder v City of Ulm—Sozialamt*, 12 November 1969, ECLI:EU:C:1969:57.
[47] OJ C 364/2000, p 1.
[48] See below, ch 2.2.B.

This is referred to as the 'horizontal effect of fundamental rights'. Another way to put it is to ask whether individual rights have indirect effect or are indirectly enforceable as between individuals. This is now accepted in many European countries and it is the reason why the expansion of fundamental rights may affect a private law relationship created by contract. In other words, contracting parties may be bound by fundamental rights.

Contracting parties now invoke the ECHR. Among the various provisions of the ECHR which may play an important role in contract law are Article 14 (non-discrimination principle) and Article 1 of the First Protocol (peaceful enjoyment of one's possessions), since both discrimination and expropriation occur frequently. The right to an effective remedy before an independent and impartial tribunal is also one which may easily surface in contract litigation. Attempts to deny claimants the right to have their disputes resolved by a court of law may under certain circumstances (for instance an illegal arbitration clause in a consumer contract) involve a violation of Article 6(1) of the ECHR. This provision is applied vigorously by national courts. The French Cour de cassation regularly provides examples of this phenomenon, and this encourages litigants to take their chance and invoke the ECHR in situations which the other party may reasonably not have anticipated. Lease contracts offer good illustrations of this; both Article 8 (right to respect for one's 'private and family life') and Article 9 (a right to freedom of thought, conscience and religion) may impact contractual terms which attempt to restrict the lessee's rights.[49] In addition, the recent development of a broad control of proportionality by the Cour de cassation, which is based on human rights, is likely to increase this 'fundamentalisation' of contract law.

It has been argued that human rights may have such effects in English law also, as a result of the Human Rights Act 1998. However, the cases which are most often referred to do not deal with contract, but with privacy, for instance *Douglas v Hello*[50] or *Campbell v MGN Ltd*.[51] Moreover, while domestic laws develop within the framework of the EU requirements and standards of human rights, Brexit may have some impact.

The values that are protected by fundamental rights also play a role through general contract law doctrines, such as good faith and public policy. One of the best-known decisions in Germany is the *Bürgschaft* case, in which a daughter stood as a surety for her father's business debts to a bank. The bank had not pointed out the financial risk to her. The Bundesgerichtshof (BGH, the Supreme Court), initially upheld the contract of suretyship.[52] The Bundesverfassungsgericht (BVerfG, the Constitutional Court), however, held that the BGH had omitted to consider whether the bank had imposed the surety unilaterally on the daughter and had informed the daughter properly of the risks. Consequently, the daughter's right to self-determination, which is protected under Article 2(1)

---

[49] Some French writers denounce a 'fundamentalisation' of French law and of French contract law: F Terré, Y Lequette and F Chénédé, *Grands arrêts de jurisprudence civil*, vol 2, *Obligations, Contrats spéciaux, Sûretés* (13th edn, Paris: Dalloz, 2015) nos. 273–74.

[50] *Douglas v Hello! No 2* [2003] EWHC 786 (Ch), [2003] 3 All ER 996; sub nom *OBG Ltd v Allen* [2007] UKHL 21, [2008] 1 AC 1.

[51] [2004] UKHL 22, [2004] 2 AC 457. For an explanation of the impact of the Human Rights Act 1998 on the English law of contract, see *Chitty* (n 29 above) paras 1-064 ff.

[52] BGH 16 March 1989, NJW 1989, 1605.

of the Basic Law, had been violated and the case was referred back to the BGH.[53] In the end the BGH came to the conclusion that the contract was invalid, because it offended good morals (§ 138 BGB).[54] Dutch law seems similar to German law, because the courts use fundamental rights in their reasoning when they apply general doctrines such as good faith and public policy.

This is also the case in French law. The French Civil Code does not allow derogation from rules which are an expression of public policy, and though the Code does not expressly say so, rules protecting fundamental rights are so considered.[55] Interestingly, the Draft Ordonnance which preceded the French contract law reform (2008),[56] made an express reference to fundamental rights in its Article 1102. Due to the objections of many stakeholders, particularly of economic actors and business and professional organisations, this reference was deleted, but this does not mean that fundamental rights may not be applied, in particular via the general doctrine of public policy.[57]

The EU Charter of Fundamental Rights may also have a great potential impact on contractual practices. An example of this may be found in the fast emerging field of data protection (Article 8 of the EU Charter). Indeed, the legal definition of personal data is very broad (any information relating to an identified or identifiable person is considered personal data; examples of personal data are telephone numbers, addresses, financial information, photographs, satellite images, car registrations, ID numbers, e-mail addresses, health records, etc).

1.1.D.2 THE IMPACT OF BREXIT

We have seen above that the EU's area of competence was extended with the adoption of the Charter of Fundamental Rights. Not only must institutions and bodies of the EU comply with the Charter, but so must national measures that transpose directives or set out the rules for applying regulations. In its judgment of the Grand Chamber (*Akerberg Fransson*) of 26 February 2013, the Court of Justice stated: 'The applicability of European Union law entails applicability of the fundamental rights guaranteed by the Charter.'[58] Due to the principle of primacy and the direct effect of

---

[53] BVerfG 19 October 1993, BVerfGE 89, 214.

[54] BGH 24 February 1994, NJW 1994, 1341.

[55] The reference to 'bonne mœurs' has not been kept by the legislator: cf Art 6 Cciv. For further details, see ch 17 on immoral and illegal contracts.

[56] On the history of the 2016 reform of French contract law, see ch 4.2.A.

[57] It is interesting to compare, as regards the French contract law reform, the 2008 Draft Ordonnance and the solution finally retained (new Art 1102 of the French Code civil). Draft Ordonnance, Art 1102: 'Everyone is free to contract or not to contract, to choose the person with whom to contract, and to determine the content and form of the contract, within the limits imposed by legislation. However, this contractual freedom does not allow the parties to derogate from rules which are an expression of public policy, nor to infringe fundamental rights and freedoms recognised by a provision which applies to relationships between private parties except where such infringement is indispensable to the protection of legitimate interests and proportionate to the intended purpose.' New Art 1102 of the Code civil: 'Everyone is free to contract or not to contract, to choose the person with whom to contract, and to determine the content and form of the contract, within the limits imposed by legislation.'

[58] C-617/10, *Åkerberg Fransson*, 26 February 2013, ECLI:EU:C:2013:280, para 21.

EU law[59] this has consequences for the duties of the Member States with regard to their national contract laws.

Some rights are inherent and fundamental to democratic civilised society. Brexit currently seems unlikely to lead to the UK renouncing the ECHR but the EU Charter will no longer bind it, so Brexit may increase the role of UK constitutional principles. The common law does not offer a prescriptive list of rights but it still is a rich source of fundamental rights and values. While its development had been somehow stopped after the ECHR had been incorporated into domestic law, there is a strong desire to revitalise it. Even before the referendum which triggered Brexit Lord Toulson suggested, in *Kennedy v The Charity Commission*: 'it was not the purpose of the Human Rights Act 1998 that the common law should become an ossuary'.[60]

UK Constitutionalism on the March?[61]   **1.4 (EN)**

Lady Hale

[A]fter more than a decade of concentrating on European instruments as the source of rights, remedies and obligations, there is emerging a renewed emphasis on the common law and distinctively UK constitutional principles as a source of legal inspiration. Sometimes this expands the range of what is available, sometimes it may constrict it. ... One aspect of this resurgence has been the emphasis by the courts on the power and continuing primacy of common law rights. There has been a tendency to assume that after the enactment of the Human Rights Act 1998 the European Convention on Human Rights should be the first port of call. But, it is said, this is to misunderstand the relationship between the Convention and the common law in our domestic law, and to overlook the continued and developing protection offered by the latter.

Notes

(1) In a similar vein, see the judgment of Lord Mance in *Kennedy v The Charity Commission*.[62]

(2) The continued and developing protection offered by constitutional principles is also visible, although less explicitly, within other Member States of the EU. Not only do national courts expressly rely on their own national traditions, but they sometimes use them to go beyond the EU frame of reference.

(3) As judges and academics put strong emphasis on constitutional rights and on the relationship between EU law and national constitutional orders, there is a growing awareness of the extent to which fundamental rights as an expression of constitutional principles should be placed at the centre of the courts' analysis.

---

[59] The direct effect of EU provisions includes European regulations as well as the clear, specific and unconditional provisions of European directives that have not been regularly transposed into domestic law within the relevant timeframe.

[60] *Kennedy v The Charity Commission* [2014] UKSC 20, [2015] 1 AC 455 [133].

[61] Lady Hale, 'UK Constitutionalism on the March?', Keynote Address to the Constitutional and Administrative Law Bar Association Conference 2014, https://www.supremecourt.uk/docs/speech-140712.pdf, pp 1–2.

[62] *Kennedy* (n 60 above).

1.1.D.3 THE CONSTITUTIONAL DIMENSION OF FREEDOM OF CONTRACT

In continental law countries, there is a general move towards recognition of the constitutional dimension of freedom of contract.

In France, the Constitutional Council gradually acknowledged the constitutional dimension of freedom of contract. It first declared that freedom of contract was not a constitutional value, but that its infringement could endanger constitutionally guaranteed rights and liberties.[63] It then affirmed that severe intrusions into legally concluded contracts could be considered as an infringement of the liberty rights enshrined in Article 4 of the 1789 Human Rights Declaration.[64] In 2000, it acknowledged the constitutional value of freedom of contract,[65] a finding that was subsequently confirmed.[66]

In Germany, the constitutionalisation of private law has gone quite far and this has been criticised. The German doctrine also develops a reflection of the economic theory of law which justifies the control of general conditions of contract (*Allgemeine Geschäftsbedingungen*) in consumer contracts as well as in contracts concluded between professionals. Article 2 of the German Fundamental Law protects the right to self-determination (*Selbstbestimmung*). The Federal Constitutional Court used this constitutional principle to encourage courts to strike down unfair clauses. In the 1993 *Bürgschaft* decision mentioned above[67] the Federal Constitutional Court stated that the law on unfair terms as applicable at the time—and which has changed little in terms of abusive clauses since—was in accordance with the Constitution. The Court also enjoined civil judges to apply the general provision (now § 307 of the BGB) and to interpret it in such a way that contracts do not serve as a means of heteronomy: judges must therefore put aside the principle of the binding force of the contract where the content of the contract is clearly inappropriate to the interests of one of the parties and that party has been unable to exercise its autonomy of will and thus its constitutional right to self-determination upon concluding the contract.

1.2 CONTRACT LAW IN A DIGITAL ENVIRONMENT

EU institutions view the digitalisation of our economies as a challenge and an opportunity for the development of the internal market. New legal issues arise from the development of new technologies. National laws alone cannot respond to all the challenges resulting from the digital environment.

---

[63] Cons const 20 March 1997, no. 97-388 DC, RTD civ 1998, 99, annotated by N Molfessis.
[64] Cons const 10 June 1998, no. 98-401 DC, RTD civ 1998, 796, annotated by N Molfessis.
[65] Cons const 19 December 2000, no. 2000-437 DC, RTD civ 2001, 229, annotated by N Molfessis.
[66] Cons const 13 June 2013, no. 2013-672 DC, RDC 2013, 1285, annotated by C Pérès.
[67] BVerfG 19 October 1993, BVerfGE 89, 214.

1.2.A CONTRACT LAW AND INNOVATION

1.2.A.1 NEW TYPES OF CONTRACT

The way many services and assets are provided and consumed is rapidly changing.

New matters of trade lead to new types of contract. The traditional sales contract is no longer the archetype of contracts in today's world, challenged as it is by other types of contract. A collaborative economy is developing and a complex ecosystem of on-demand services and temporary use of assets, often based on exchanges via online platforms, is prospering.

The supply of digital content is an expanding new category of contract which includes the supply of videos, music clips, software or live sport events sold online. So far there are no EU-wide rules for faulty digital content and few Member States have already started designing their own legislation. A directive is likely to be adopted, based on the Proposal for a Directive of the European Parliament and of the Council on certain aspects concerning contracts for the supply of digital content.[68]

New forms of economic behaviour and activities, such as crowdfunding, couchsurfing and car-sharing, are induced by what is commonly termed a 'share economy'. Often, service providers are not professional traders but private persons (so that EU consumer contract law does not apply) and contracts are concluded through a platform which prescribes standard terms and conditions and thus determines most of the issues that traditionally were freely negotiated between contracting parties (price, quality, repartition of liabilities, remedies etc). The platform organises and controls the contract that the parties conclude. It is not a typical 'third party' because it does have some interest in or connection to the contract, and so the question of its own liability, particularly as regards the information duties which have become more and more predominant, is posed. Besides, the 'platform' sometimes provides more than just an intermediation service. The Court of Justice held that Uber is not a platform but a transporter:

> [A]n intermediation service such as that at issue in the main proceedings, the purpose of which is to connect, by means of a smartphone application and for remuneration, non-professional drivers using their own vehicle with persons who wish to make urban journeys, must be regarded as being inherently linked to a transport service and, accordingly, must be classified as "a service in the field of transport" within the meaning of Article 58(1) TFEU. Consequently, such a service must be excluded from the scope of Article 56 TFEU, Directive 2006/123 and Directive 2000/31.[69]

In the case, the main issue was therefore whether possible rules on how Uber operates are subject to the requirements of EU law, primarily those relating to the freedom

---

[68] COM/2015/0634 final—2015/0287 (COD). The proposed Directive notably includes rules on conformity of the digital content, remedies available to consumers in cases of lack of conformity of digital content with the contract, as well as certain aspects concerning the right to terminate a long term contract and the modification of the digital content. It is only applicable to business-to-consumer transactions. It covers the supply of all types of digital content, not only for a monetary payment but also in exchange for (personal and other) data provided by consumers. It does not cover services performed with a significant element of human intervention or contracts governing specific sectorial services such as healthcare, gambling or financial services.

[69] C-434/15, *Asociación Profesional Elite Taxi v Uber Systems Spain, SL*, 20 December 2017, ECLI:EU:C:2017:981, para 50.

to provide services, or whether they fall within the scope of the shared competence of the EU and the Member States in the field of local transport, a competence which has not yet been exercised at EU level. If the service of connecting potential passengers and drivers with one another had been regarded as independent of the supply of transport and, therefore, as an information society service, Article 3(2) of Directive 2000/31 could have precluded any requirement to have authorisation in order to provide such a service (the aim of Directive 2000/31 is to ensure the effectiveness of the freedom to provide information society services).

1.2.A.2 TOWARDS A DIGITAL SINGLE MARKET

Digital technologies are transforming many industrial sectors, leading to more efficient production and innovative business models. They are challenging established categories, such as business to business (B2B) or business to consumer (B2C) contracts.

In May 2015, in order to meet the challenges of the digital economy and improve access for consumers and businesses to online goods and services, the Commission adopted the Digital Single Market Strategy.[70] Two years later, in May 2017, in the Mid-Term Review on the implementation of the Digital Single Market Strategy, it reaffirmed that 'the completion of the EU Single Digital Market also needs a clear and stable legal environment to stimulate innovation, tackle market fragmentation and allow all players to tap into the new market dynamics under fair and balanced conditions'.[71] The Digital Single Market provides the basis for new developments that will affect European contract laws and bring further harmonisation, if not unification. A series of proposals is now being examined by the European institutions, with a set of targeted actions built on three pillars:

(1) better access for consumers and businesses to digital goods and services across Europe, notably through harmonised EU rules on contracts and consumer protection when you buy online. The idea is that EU regulation will boost confidence as consumers should benefit from a wider range of rights and offers while businesses will more easily sell to other EU countries.

(2) creating the right conditions and a level playing field for digital networks and innovative services to flourish and ensuring both e-Privacy and cybersecurity.

(3) maximising the growth potential of the digital economy and promoting the free movement of data in the European Union as well as a European Cloud initiative.

For more than 20 years now, the EU has been adopting directives in order to bring a legal response to practical changes, such as the directives on distance contracts, on electronic signatures, on electronic commerce, on distance marketing of consumer financial services etc. Major public consultations have also been launched, which relate to the new regulatory issues raised by a digital society: platforms, online intermediaries,

---

[70] European Commission, 'A Digital Single Market Strategy for Europe', COM(2015) 192 final.
[71] Mid-Term Review on the implementation of the Digital Single Market Strategy, A Connected Digital Single Market for All, COM(2017) 228 final.

cloud computing and others. Legal issues such as data protection and the use of data as a currency are also crucial in today's data driven economy.[72]

1.2.B NEW LEGAL ISSUES FOR CONTRACT LAW

The digital revolution has increased inequalities and brought changes to contractual practices that ought to be controlled by the law.

1.2.B.1 INFORMATION AND TRANSPARENCY

In his book *Economie du bien commun*, Jean Tirole, the economist and Nobel Prize Laureate in 2014, shows how pressing the need for information is as the question of information is everywhere.[73] Tirole stresses the hiatus between the quasi-infinite information that is offered and the limited time we have to deal with it. Transaction costs linked to reading the offers and selecting the partners (with the help of platforms) are more and more becoming the main ones, as other costs, such as transportation, customs, listing etc tend to decrease.[74]

Lack of transparency on platform tariffs (intermediation rates vary from 5% to 30% of the final price, including currently 20% for Uber and Airbnb) or on use of data (such as the unclear and non-transparent exploitation of personal user data for commercial purposes, as when personal data is sold to third parties) are important issues often raised by consumers' organisations.[75] In 2015, the European Commission launched a public consultation on platforms, online intermediaries, data, cloud computing and the collaborative economy so as to better capture market trends, the dynamics of platform-development and the various business models underpinning platforms. The responses acknowledged the benefits of online platforms which make information more accessible and communication easier, create new business opportunities and increase choice of products and services. However, both business and citizen respondents stated that platforms should be more transparent (notably about search results, clarity about the actual supplier and review mechanisms) and should provide more information on personal and non-personal data collected as well as on their terms and conditions.

---

[72] When the European Commission put forward its EU Data Protection Reform in January 2012 to make Europe fit for the digital age, many Europeans said they wanted the same data protection rights across the EU and regardless of where their data is processed. Regulation (EU) 2016/679 of the European Parliament and of the Council of 27 April 2016 on the protection of natural persons with regard to the processing of personal data and on the free movement of such data, and repealing Directive 95/46/EC (General Data Protection Regulation, GDPR) (OJ L 119/2016, p 1) is an essential step to strengthen citizens' fundamental rights in the digital age. The reform provides tools for gaining control of one's personal data. It will foster new contractual practices. For instance, the new right to data portability will allow individuals to move their personal data from one service provider to another.

[73] J Tirole, *Économie du bien commun* (Paris: PUF, 2016) 26.

[74] ibid, 501.

[75] Businesses and associations of businesses thus expressed recommendations such as the following: indication of copyright compliance eg, images on site, rights holders origins [B2B]; better information about how consumer data is used and sold, and highlighting how and when user data is being tracked [B2C]; improve traceability, through clearer contact information, including registration and business licenses [B2B & C].

Information should also be easy to understand and not presented in sets of Terms and Conditions that are too long. Too much information kills transparency and does not restore equality between contracting parties.[76]

1.2.B.2 THE RISE OF STANDARD FORM CONTRACTS

E-contracts have increased even further the use of standard form contracts. As we saw earlier, standardised 'one-size-fits-all' agreements allow sellers or service providers to mass-market their goods and services. They reduce transaction costs substantially by precluding the contracting parties to negotiate the many details of a contract each time the product is sold. Lengthy boilerplate terms are often in fine print and written in complicated legal language which seems all the more irrelevant as the contract is presented on a 'take it or leave it' basis. The time needed to read the terms is substantial, while the expected payoff from reading the contract is very low since the consumer is not in a position to bargain. In practice, standard terms are hardly ever read by consumers.

The software industry is a good example for this. Software represents a continuously growing and evolving product market. For instance, software license agreements establishing the purchaser's right to use the software are an important type of online standard form contract and have provoked various regulatory debates. Not only are license agreements often very long and complex; it is not always easy for the customer to review the license agreement before purchasing the software. In online contracts, the software license agreement is presented to the user on-screen during installation (the license is sometimes referred to as a click-wrap license).

In contrast to German law, English and French laws have traditionally treated standard form contracts like any other contract. This is now changing, and special rules are being developed with respect to them.[77] Because inequality of bargaining power is so salient, control over unfair contract terms has become one of the most challenging issues of modern contract law. While EU directives and regulations in contract law are targeting B2C contracts, more and more national legal systems have introduced rules which enable the courts to strike down unfair clauses even for B2B contracts. Control over unfair terms will be examined at length later in this book. This control may also take other routes, such as judicial interpretation of the contract. This too will be examined.

1.2.B.3 INCREASED INTERDEPENDENCE OF CONTRACTS

Multiplicity of actors and of contracts is an increasing phenomenon in our digitalised society. Complexity is everywhere. In the law of contracts, it is echoed by a new (or at

---

[76] Companies must also disclose high quality and relevant financial and also non-financial (environmental, social and governance related) information in a way that provides transparency to stakeholders. See the Guidelines on non-financial reporting published by the European Commission in June 2017 (OJ C 215/2017, p 1): 'The information may also be made more understandable by using plain language and consistent terminology, avoiding boilerplate, and, where necessary, providing definitions for technical terms' and '[t]he non-financial statement is also expected to be concise, and avoid immaterial information. Disclosing immaterial information may make the non-financial statement less easy to understand since it would obscure material information. Generic or boilerplate information that is not material should be avoided' (p 13).

[77] See ch 21.

least much more widespread) phenomenon, that of contractual interdependence between many actors, some with a strong position, others in a much more vulnerable one. Many contracts are concluded for the purpose of performing others (*ensembles indivisibles*). Interconnected contracts may appear in a wide range of cases: large construction projects but also simple situations where, for instance, a consumer takes a loan to buy specific goods but finds the goods are no longer on sale. They may also come into play in the case of contracts involving smart devices (smartphones, smartwatches, tablets etc) which depend for their operation on services to be provided under a contract with another party. If one of the contracts is avoided, the question is: what about the others? Should they still be performed when one of the parties no longer has an interest in performance, due to the termination of the other contract? Another questions is: if the service needed to make a device work is provided by a third party, who ceases to provide the service or does not perform it well, who is responsible?

If a consumer is involved, EU law applies (insofar as there are EU rules), while if the contract is one which does not involve a consumer, each national legal system may have its own solution—or may not yet have developed one.

1.2.B.4 SHARED LIABILITIES IN THE AGE OF THE INTERNET OF THINGS

The Internet of things (IoT) is a wide encompassing reality which includes self-driving cars, robots in smart factories and household appliances in smart houses. New legal issues, particularly those of contractual and extra-contractual liability, arise in respect to IoT (should liability be based on risk (strict liability) or on fault?). Who should be liable when there is a wide number of participants (each individual versus joint liability?). Is there any liability of algorithms?[78] These are all questions that sooner or later contract law and the law on extra-contractual liability will have to face.

1.2.B.5 SMART CONTRACTS

The automated conclusion of contracts defies the traditional models of conclusion of contracts via offer and acceptance, and so do 'smart contracts'. The expression 'smart contracts' was coined by computer scientists. Smart contracts are not 'contracts' but computer protocols intended to facilitate, verify or enforce the performance of a contract. A smart contract thus is a computerised transaction protocol that executes the terms of a contract. Smart contracts have been used primarily in association with blockchains and cryptocurrencies. The most prominent smart contract implementation is the Ethereum blockchain platform. Smart contracts—which may operate according to rigid and completely unforgiving algorithms—present yet another challenge for the law.

Writing the future contract law of the digital economy is a formidable task. This book does not purport to do so. Besides, much of the new or proposed legislation is aimed at consumers, and this book does not aim to give detailed coverage of consumer contracts. However, the same problems will arise in many B2B contracts, and then general contract

---

[78] Any set of rules about turning digital inputs into digital outputs is an 'algorithm'. An algorithm is decision-making software.

law will have to find a solution. Legislation will be needed, possibly at the national level, but preferably at the EU or international level.

1.3 CONTRACT LAW IN AN INTERNATIONAL ENVIRONMENT

In today's interconnected world, a vast proportion of contracts have an international dimension, and this gives the parties the freedom to choose the law that governs that contract (party autonomy). When parties enter into a contract that has connections with more than one State, the question of which set of legal rules governs the transaction arises. In planning the transaction the parties should determine in the contract which set of rules governs their obligations; and if they fail to do so, the law should provide default rules to determine the issue. At a European level the conflict rules are unified in the Regulation on the Law Applicable to Contractual Obligations (Rome I Regulation) which came into force on 1 August 2008.[79]

Another key question is: where will disputes arising under the contract be heard? Answers to these questions are to be found in the Brussels Regulation (EC) No 44/2001 of 22 December 2000 on Jurisdiction and the Recognition and Enforcement of Judgments in Civil and Commercial Matters (Brussels I Regulation).[80] A revised version of the Brussels Regulation (often called 'Brussels I bis') entered into force on 10 January 2015.[81]

The Rome I and Brussels I Regulations include terms and notions which are relevant in the area of contract law. Some of these have been given an interpretation by the Court of Justice and this is helping the development of a European contract law.

Within the EU, parties are allowed to select both the governing law for their contracts and the forum. If parties fail to select an applicable law, a court that accepts jurisdiction over the dispute will have to apply the relevant conflict rules of private international law in order to determine which law is applicable to the contract, including any international instruments that might apply by default. In this chapter, we shall focus on the promotion of party autonomy throughout the twentieth century and therefore on cases where parties have included in the contract a choice-of-law clause, which is usually accompanied by a choice-of-forum clause.

1.3.A THE PROMOTION OF PARTY AUTONOMY WITH REGARD TO CHOICE OF THE APPLICABLE LAW

Party autonomy is promoted by many legal systems as well as by the EU because it enhances certainty and predictability for the parties who usually are in the best position

---

[79] OJ L177/2008, pp 6–16.

[80] Brussels Council Regulation (EC) No 44/2001 of 22 December 2000 on Jurisdiction and Enforcement of Judgments in Civil and Commercial Matters (Brussels I Regulation), OJ L 12/2001, p 1.

[81] Regulation (EU) No 1215/2012 of the European Parliament and of the Council of 12 December 2012 on jurisdiction and the recognition and enforcement of judgments in civil and commercial matters, OJ L 351/2012, p 1.

to determine which set of rules is most suitable for their contract. The Rome I Regulation promotes freedom of choice.

Rome I Regulation[82]

1.5 (EU)

Article 3: Freedom of choice

1. A contract shall be governed by the law chosen by the parties. The choice shall be made expressly or clearly demonstrated by the terms of the contract or the circumstances of the case. By their choice the parties can select the law applicable to the whole or to part only of the contract.

2. The parties may at any time agree to subject the contract to a law other than that which previously governed it, whether as a result of an earlier choice made under this Article or of other provisions of this Regulation. Any change in the law to be applied that is made after the conclusion of the contract shall not prejudice its formal validity under Article 11 or adversely affect the rights of third parties.

3. Where all other elements relevant to the situation at the time of the choice are located in a country other than the country whose law has been chosen, the choice of the parties shall not prejudice the application of provisions of the law of that other country which cannot be derogated from by agreement.

4. Where all other elements relevant to the situation at the time of the choice are located in one or more Member States, the parties' choice of applicable law other than that of a Member State shall not prejudice the application of provisions of Community law, where appropriate as implemented in the Member State of the forum, which cannot be derogated from by agreement.

...

Notes

(1) Article 4 of the Rome I Regulation gives rules on how to determine the applicable law when the parties have not chosen a law. Article 6 of the Regulation, which sets specific and more protective choice of law rules for consumer contracts, has been one of the drivers behind many of the Commission's proposals in recent years.

(2) Recital 11 of the Regulation states that 'The parties' freedom to choose the applicable law should be one of the cornerstones of the system of conflict-of-law rules in matters of contractual obligations'. In private international law, party autonomy, which serves many purposes, expands beyond contract law to family law and the law of persons.

(3) Regulation (EC) No 864/2007 of 11 July 2007 on the law applicable to non-contractual obligations (Rome II) also promotes, in certain exceptional circumstances, party autonomy. Recital 31 of this Regulation explains: 'To respect the principle of party autonomy and to enhance legal certainty, the parties should be allowed to make a choice as to the law applicable to a non-contractual obligation'. See in particular Article 14, 'freedom of choice', which allows the parties to agree to

---

[82] Regulation on the Law Applicable to Contractual Obligations (EC) No 593/2008 of the European Parliament and of the Council of 17 June 2008, OJ L 177/2008, pp 6–16.

submit non-contractual obligations to the law of their choice in two types of situation: (i) by an agreement entered into after the event giving rise to the damage occurred, or (ii) in situations where parties are pursuing a commercial activity, before the event occurred. Tort/delict, unjust enrichment, *negotiorum gestio* and *culpa in contrahendo* are non-contractual obligations to which this Regulation applies.

(4) Drawing on the model set forth by the UNIDROIT PICC as well as by the Rome I Regulation, the Hague Conference on Private International Law ('the Hague Conference') has adopted the Hague Principles on Choice of Law in International Commercial Contracts (12 articles and a commentary) which affirm party autonomy.[83]

1.3.B NOTION OF INTERNATIONAL CONTRACT

As noted by the official Comment 1 to the Preamble of UNIDROIT PICC, 'The international character of a contract may be defined in a great variety of ways'. Flexible definitions are possible, such as contracts with '"significant connections with more than one State", "involving a choice between the laws of different States," or "affecting the interests of international trade"'. International instruments have identified contracts as 'international' when the parties concluding the agreement have their respective places of business in two or more different States (see United Nations Convention on Contracts for the International Sale of Goods (Vienna, 1980) (the 'CISG'), Article 1(1); Principles on Choice of Law in International Commercial Contracts (2015) (the 'Hague Principles'), Article 1(2)). The Rome I Regulation gives no definition of international contracts. However, Article 3(3) and (4) ensures that the parties do not seek to escape the applicable national or European mandatory rules. Article 3(3) provides that:

> Where all other elements relevant to the situation at the time of the choice are located in a country other than the country whose law has been chosen, the choice of the parties shall not prejudice the application of provisions of the law of that other country which cannot be derogated from by agreement.

Article 3(4) preserves, along the same line, the application of provisions of 'Community law' (EU Law).

1.3.C ARBITRATION AGREEMENTS AND AGREEMENTS ON CHOICE OF COURT

It is highly strategic for the parties to agree in advance on how disputes arising out of a contract concluded between them will be resolved. In some cases, the parties will

---

[83] www://hcch.net. It is the first time that the Hague Conference on Private International Law, the oldest of the Hague international legal institutions, adopts 'Principles' rather than an international treaty. While party autonomy is part of the law in many legal systems, some countries, notably in South America, do not accept party autonomy or limit it to a considerable and excessive extent. The Hague Convention of 30 June 2005 on Choice of Court Agreements, another significant achievement of the Hague Conference, also promotes party autonomy in international contracts on an international scale.

litigate before a designated State court, in others, they will prefer to refer the dispute to arbitration. Both State courts and arbitral tribunals closely scrutinise the validity of the choice of court and the arbitration agreement, the true intention of the parties and the coverage of the clauses.

At the stage of recognition and enforcement, important differences still exist. While arbitration agreements in international cases are almost universally recognised under the rules established by the 1958 New York Convention on the Recognition and Enforcement of Foreign Arbitral Awards, choice of court agreements are not always respected under national rules, particularly when cases are brought before a court other than the one designated by the parties. In order to remedy this, and create a climate more favourable to international trade and investment, the Hague Convention of 30 June 2005 on Choice of Court Agreements seeks to promote greater legal certainty for cross-border business. The Convention applies to choice of court agreements 'concluded in civil or commercial matters' (Article 1). The Convention excludes consumer and employment contracts and certain specified subject matters (Article 2).[84]

At the EU level, the ambit of the Brussels I bis Regulation[85] is much wider than contracts, so this Regulation will not be covered in this book.

1.3.D CHOICE OF LAW CLAUSES

Parties may and, for the sake of legal certainty, should also choose national laws to apply to their international commercial contracts. The party with greater bargaining power may insist on its national law, or parties may instead choose the law of a third State, usually one considered to have a well-developed law with regard to commercial transactions. For instance, Swiss law may be selected because of the perception that Switzerland's political neutrality makes it a neutral law. English law is frequently chosen in reinsurance, charterparties and the sea trade, among other areas. The ICC International Court of Arbitration 2013 Statistical Report also indicates the frequent choice of German and French law.[86]

The designated law will include, when applicable, the United Nations Convention on Contracts for the International Sale of Goods ('CISG'). The CISG is a treaty that provides for a uniform international sales law. Very broadly, if an international sales contract is made subject to the law of a State that has adopted the Convention, then (unless the parties agree otherwise, or 'opt out') the contract will be governed by the rules of the Convention rather than by the rules of the relevant State's law that would apply to

---

[84] For more information on the Choice of Court Convention, see the Hague Conference website www.hcch.net. In 2016, 28 States (all the EU Member States with the exception of Denmark, as well as Mexico, which was the first State to accede to the Convention on 26 September 2007) were bound by the Convention. In 2009, the US was the first country to sign the Choice of Court Convention. In 2016, it had not yet ratified the Convention. An Expert Group mandated by the Hague Conference is assisting in the preparation of a Convention on the Recognition and Enforcement of Foreign Judgments in Civil and Commercial Matters.

[85] See n 81 above.

[86] *2013 Statistical Report*, (2014) 25 ICC International Court of Arbitration Bulletin no. 1, 5, 13.

a domestic contract (at least, so far as the relevant issue is covered by the Convention). Although the Convention forms part of the law of each adhering State, and is to be applied by national courts as part of the law of the relevant State, its provisions should be interpreted uniformly, and so (on the issues covered) the law governing the international sale should (theoretically) be the same in each State that adheres to the Convention. This should reduce the transaction costs involved in international sales.

It has been a considerable source of inspiration for further international or European instruments in the law of contracts. To some extent, it has also inspired reforms in national contract laws. As of May 2018, the CISG had been ratified by 89 States that account for a significant proportion of world trade (including France, Germany and the Netherlands, but not the UK), making it one of the most successful international uniform laws. Its scope is limited to commercial contracts for the cross-border sale of goods (see CISG, Part I, Articles 1–5). Under its Article 6, contractual parties may opt out of the CISG or any of its provisions.

CISG 1.6 (INT)

Article 6: The parties may exclude the application of this Convention or, subject to article 12, derogate from or vary the effect of any of its provisions.

Notes

(1) Article 6 guarantees party autonomy over both the conflict rules and the substantive law. The Convention can be excluded by choice of law if the parties choose to apply a different domestic law. It is also possible simply to reject the CISG without choosing an applicable law. Substantively, any rule of the Convention can be altered or rejected by the parties, even by standard contract terms, as long as the requirements for their validity in domestic law are fulfilled.

(2) A much-debated issue was whether the parties must affirmatively choose the CISG in order for it to apply (the 'opting-in' solution) or whether the Convention would automatically apply, unless the parties agreed to apply a different law (the 'opting-out' solution). In the end, the 'opting-in' proposal, which would have turned the Convention into a set of standard contract terms, was rejected.

(3) The Convention does not mention the possibility of an 'implied' exclusion, but this does not mean that a tacit exclusion is impossible, though national courts should not be too quick to impute exclusion of the Convention. The fact that the parties have agreed on an arbitral tribunal or chosen a domestic law does not necessarily mean that country's local sales law applies. In case of doubt, it is for national judges to decide whether the parties' choice of a national law excludes the Convention (provided that State has adopted the Convention).

(4) Article 7 of the CISG creates an obligation for States, via their courts, to interpret the Convention with regard 'to its international character and the need to promote uniformity in its application'. National courts and arbitral tribunals make real efforts to interpret the CISG in a uniform manner so as not to create divergent precedents and

thus neutralise the benefits of a harmonised regime. The same concern also applies when courts interpret EU law and this approach is followed by soft law instruments, notably by Article 1:106, titled 'Interpretation and Supplementation' of the PECL.[87]

(5) The rules of the CISG do not cover all aspects of contract law. In particular, issues of validity and the question of the control of terms in general conditions of contract are left to be governed by the applicable domestic law.

1.3.E THE LIMITS TO PARTY AUTONOMY

In an international transaction, a dominant party may easily impose a particular contract law as a governing law if this best serves its interests. What are the limits on party autonomy? The answer is not straightforward, as various branches of the law are concerned: private international law, which is unified within the EU; international arbitration, insofar as parties may escape certain limits by choosing arbitration; and national contract law, since eventually it is for each national court to assess the limits established by its own national legal order.

1.3.E.1 OVERRIDING MANDATORY RULES AND PUBLIC ORDER

The traditional limits to party autonomy reside in the concepts of 'overriding mandatory rules' and public order. They are well expressed in the Rome I Regulation.

Rome I Regulation   **1.7 (EU)**

Article 9: Overriding mandatory provisions

(1) Overriding mandatory provisions are provisions the respect for which is regarded as crucial by a country for safeguarding its public interests, such as its political, social or economic organisation, to such an extent that they are applicable to any situation falling within their scope, irrespective of the law otherwise applicable to the contract under this Regulation.

(2) Nothing in this Regulation shall restrict the application of the overriding mandatory provisions of the law of the forum.

(3) Effect may be given to the overriding mandatory provisions of the law of the country where the obligations arising out of the contract have to be or have been performed, in so far as those overriding mandatory provisions render the performance of the contract unlawful. In considering whether to give effect to those provisions, regard shall be had to their nature and purpose and to the consequences of their application or non-application.

Article 21: Public policy of the forum

The application of a provision of the law of any country specified by this Regulation may be refused only if such application is manifestly incompatible with the public policy (ordre public) of the forum.

---

[87] PECL Art 1:106 (see below, p 33).

Notes

(1) The mandatory rules of the law of the forum are not all 'overriding mandatory provisions', so they do not all necessarily apply to an international situation. Usually, national contract rules are drafted in contemplation of domestic contracts. Depending on the facts of the case, the State may or may not have a legitimate interest in seeing them apply in an international context. For instance, the applicable rules on defects of consent, which are usually mandatory in a national context, are not necessarily so in an international one because the State then has a more remote interest in the application of its own law. This means that a court that applies the foreign law applicable to the contract will apply the provisions of the chosen law (foreign law) on defects of consent (mistake, fraud, violence, gross disparity). However, if the court finds the provisions of the foreign law really incompatible with its own law (for instance, a provision that would systematically bar a party who has been the victim of fraud by the other party from seeking avoidance of the contact), the court may use the public order exception to put aside the foreign provisions and substitute its own national law on this specific question.

(2) Overriding mandatory provisions may also derive from EU legislation.[88]

(3) The Rome I Regulation specifies that 'The concept of "overriding mandatory provisions" should be distinguished from the expression "provisions which cannot be derogated from by agreement" and should be construed more restrictively' (Recital 37). National mandatory rules exist when there are interests to protect such as the protection of weak parties (consumers, commercial agents etc). Some are considered overriding mandatory rules, but this is not systematic and mainly depends on judicial appreciation. Overriding mandatory rules may also serve to ensure undistorted competition, the transparency of certain markets, public security, tax collection.

(4) As regards consumer contracts, insurance contracts and individual employment contracts, the Rome I Regulation sets specific conflict-of-law rules which protect consumers, insured persons, employees (see Articles 6, 7 and 8).

(5) Considerations of public interest may also justify giving the courts of the Member States the possibility, in exceptional circumstances, of applying exceptions based on public policy of the forum, but within the EU, this should remain rather exceptional, as showed by the use of the phrase 'manifestly incompatible with the public policy'.

The value of arbitration as a method of settling disputes arising in international commercial relations is widely recognised, but it may give rise to some abuses, especially when one party imposes it upon the other, hence the limits set forth by EU law and national Member States for consumer contracts.

---

[88] A leading ECJ decision is C-381/98, *Ingmar GB Ltd v Eaton Leonard Technologies Inc.*, 9 November 2000, ECLI:EU:C:2000:605: 'Articles 17 and 18 of Council Directive 86/65 3/EEC of 18 December 1986 on the coordination of the laws of the Member States relating to self-employed commercial agents, which guarantee certain rights to commercial agents after termination of agency contracts, must be applied where the commercial agent carried on his activity in a Member State although the principal is established in a non-member country and a clause of the contract stipulates that the contract is to be governed by the law of that country'.

1.3.E.2 BEYOND STATE LAW: MAY PARTIES CHOOSE 'RULES OF LAW'
INSTEAD OF A DOMESTIC LAW TO GOVERN THEIR CONTRACTS?

Sometimes parties to international commercial contracts do not agree on a domestic law and provide that their contract shall be governed by the 'general principles of law'. They may even choose soft law instruments (ie non-State law) as the 'rules of law' governing their contract. The development of soft law instruments both in contract law and private international law is indicative of the development of private law 'beyond the State'.[89] Soft law instruments need not be signed and ratified by the States. Consequently, they can have a wide scope of application: for instance, the UNIDROIT PICC set forth general rules for international commercial contracts. This wide scope of application contrasts with the limited scope of international treaties in contract law, the most famous and probably also most wide-encompassing being the CISG. Soft law instruments may also adopt innovative solutions, in the hope that sooner or later, those solutions will inspire national legislators.

While domestic courts are bound by the private international law rules of the forum (within the EU, the provisions of the Rome I Regulation must be applied by the Member States), which usually limit the parties' freedom of choice to the choice of State laws, arbitrators may apply non-State rules such as the PECL or the UNIDROIT PICC. The promotion of party autonomy in the area of international contracts on a worldwide scale responds to a genuine need in international trade. In 2006, the Special Commission on General Affairs and Policy of the Hague Conference on Private International Law (the Hague Conference) invited the Permanent Bureau to prepare a feasibility study for an instrument relating to the choice of law in international contracts. Since its creation in 1893, the Hague Conference on Private International Law has developed international conventions in various areas but it had never adopted soft law instruments. The 'Hague Principles on the Choice of Law in International Commercial Contracts' ('the Hague Principles'), which consist of 12 articles and a commentary are the first instrument of this kind. They also are the first to address the choice of law in international commercial contracts at a global level.[90] They are intended to be used in both judicial and arbitral proceedings. They affirm party autonomy and promote contractual freedom to choose non-State rules.

Hague Principles on the Choice of Law
in International Contracts   **1.8 (INT)**

Article 3: Rules of Law
   Under these Principles, the law chosen by the parties may be rules of law that are generally accepted on an international, supranational or regional level as a neutral and balanced set of rules, unless the law of the forum provides otherwise.

---

[89] N Jansen and R Michaels, 'Private law beyond the State? Europeanization, Globalization, Privatization' (2006) 54 Am J Comp L 843. This phenomenon raises all sorts of new questions and challenges described in ch 3.

[90] For the text, the draft commentary, preparatory materials (notably those called Prel. Doc.), and a bibliography, see www.hcch.net.

Notes

(1) This provision is the result of a compromise between the members of the Expert Group and the EU Commission, which was concerned by the fact that, while drafting the Rome I Regulation, European institutions finally decided not to allow the choice of non-State rules. Where a dispute is subject to litigation before a national court, private international law regimes require that the parties' choice of law agreement designate a national system of law. Although parties may incorporate by reference in their contract 'rules of law' or trade usages, such a choice of norms or 'rules of law' is generally authorised only in an arbitral context. This provision reflects a novel approach.

(2) The criteria established by Article 3 relate both to the sources and characteristic features of 'rules of law'. They are restrictive.[91] In fact the provision allows for a small number of soft law instruments of international trade law to be chosen by the parties as *lex contractus*. The Commentary cites the UNIDROIT PICC, the CISG and the PECL. Another restriction comes from the fact that the Principles defer to the law of the forum which may confine the parties' freedom to a choice of a national law. Within the EU, Article 3 of the Rome I Regulation is interpreted as preventing the parties' choice of non-State law. Some jurisdictions have however adopted a more flexible approach and several courts have relied upon the parties' choice of law to make the CISG applicable. In spite of their success (the PECL still constitute the point of reference for further developments in European contract law and the UNIDROIT PICC have been several times revised, completed and modernised), these soft law instruments are rarely chosen as the applicable law governing the contract. To encourage such choices, UNIDROIT published model clauses for the use of the UNIDROIT PICC which reflect the different ways in which the UNIDROIT PICC may be chosen by parties or applied by judges and arbitrators. Where parties designate rules of law and these do not cover the specific issue upon which they litigate, adjudicators are faced with a gap and the Hague Principles do not address this situation. The parties should provide for a solution, for instance by referring, subsidiarily, to a national legal order. When no solution can be found in the soft law instruments they themselves provide guidelines as to how to proceed. Article 1:106 PECL, for example, has the title 'Interpretation and Supplementation' and states:

(1) These Principles should be interpreted and developed in accordance with their purposes. In particular, regard should be had to the need to promote good faith and fair dealing, certainty in contractual relationships and uniformity of application.

(2) Issues within the scope of these Principles but not expressly settled by them are so far as possible to be settled in accordance with the ideas underlying the Principles. Failing this, the legal system applicable by virtue of the rules of private international law is to be applied.

---

[91] B Fauvarque-Cosson, 'New Principles in the Legal World: The Hague Principles on the choice of law in international contracts' in L Gullifer and S Vogenauer (eds), *English and European Perspectives on Contract and Commercial Law: Essays in Honour of Hugh Beale* (Oxford: Hart Publishing, 2014) 455; S Symeonides, 'The Hague Principles on Choice of Law for International Contracts' (2013) 61 Am J Comp L 873, 894 ff.

To conclude this section, it is important to recall that, unlike international treaties in commercial matters (such as the CISG) which are applicable whenever the contract falls within their scope and the parties have not excluded their application, the 'Principles' may only be applied as if they were the governing law if the parties have validly designated them and, within the EU, where the contract provides for arbitration according to the relevant set of Principles. However, even in the law of EU Member States, the Principles may be incorporated as terms of the particular contract (save so far as they are compatible with the mandatory provisions of the national law and with the other terms of the contract.) This is the reason why parties who want these Principles to apply would be well advised to incorporate the provisions of Principles into the contract (especially when there is no arbitration clause).

As we shall see in Chapter 3 of this Book, the PECL, the UNIDROIT PICC and the Hague Principles on the Choice of Law in International Commercial Contracts add to a growing number of international instruments of other organisations (model laws, guides, international treaties) that have had some success in developing and harmonising the law of contracts. They contribute to the Europeanisation and globalisation of legal thinking in contract law. While contracting parties remain rather ignorant of them, national judges and legislators are more and more influenced by these instruments; and the instruments have created new convergences among national contract laws. For instance, in order to interpret the new French contract law provisions of the Code civil, a French judge will first pay attention to the new provisions of the Code civil, but also all the surrounding elements, including those European and international models which have indeed exerted an influence on the drafters of the 2016 Ordonnance. It is most likely that, drawing inspiration from the history of this reform, judges, practitioners and academics will interpret the texts in a way that will foster the construction of a European common contract law.

FURTHER READING

Farnsworth, EA, 'Comparative contract law' in M Reimann and R Zimmermann (eds), *Oxford Handbook of Comparative Law* (Oxford University Press, 2006) 899–935.

Fauvarque-Cosson, B, 'New Principles in the Legal World: The Hague Principles on the choice of law in international contracts' in L Gullifer and S Vogenauer (eds), *English and European Perspectives on Contract and Commercial Law: Essays in Honour of Hugh Beale* (Oxford: Hart Publishing, 2014) 455–65.

Jansen, N and Zimmermann, R (eds), *Commentaries on European Contract Laws* (Oxford University Press, 2018).

Kötz, H, *European Contract Law* (2nd edn, Oxford University Press, 2017).

Stirn, B, *Towards a European Public Law*, translated and edited by E Bjorge (Oxford University Press, 2017).

Vogenauer, S, 'General principles of contract law in transnational instruments', in L Gullifer and S Vogenauer (eds), *English and European Perspectives on Contract and Commercial Law: Essays in Honour of Hugh Beale* (Oxford: Hart Publishing, 2014) 291–318.

CHAPTER 2
EUROPEAN UNION LAW ON CONTRACTS

2.1 EUROPEAN CONTRACT LAW

2.1.A INTRODUCTION

In this chapter we will discuss the current situation concerning European contract law. In this respect a distinction must be made between binding rules of contract law and non-binding rules, also known as 'soft law'. In what follows, the binding rules of European contract will be discussed first. The non-binding rules will be dealt with in Chapter 3.

2.1.B BINDING RULES OF EUROPEAN CONTRACT LAW

Binding rules of contract law are no longer created merely on a national level. They may also follow from international conventions and European Union measures. An example of an international convention is the UN Vienna Convention on Contracts for the International Sale of Goods of 1980 (CISG). The manner in which these rules are applicable in a legal system depends on whether the country involved has adopted the doctrine of monism or dualism with respect to international conventions. Monism implies that international conventions are directly applicable in the legal system, whereas dualism means that in order for the convention to be applied in the legal system it must be transposed into national legislation. In France and the Netherlands, for instance, the CISG is directly applicable, whereas in Germany the CISG is incorporated by national legislation.[1] In the UK the same would have applied, had it ratified the CISG.[2]

In addition there are also EU measures, for instance regulations and directives, which include rules of contract law. In the area of substantive contract law a number of directives

---

[1] Gesetz zu dem Übereinkommen der Vereinten Nationen vom 11. April 1980 über Verträge über den internationalen Warenkauf sowie zur Änderung des Gesetzes zu dem Übereinkommen vom 19. Mai 1956 über den Beförderungsvertrag im internationalen Straßengüterverkehr (CMR) of 5 July 1989, BGBl 1989 II 586.

[2] Compare the Contracts (Applicable Law) Act 1990, which implemented the Rome Convention on the Law Applicable to Contractual Obligations (on which see below, p 50).

have been adopted.[3] Most of these directives are sector specific, in the sense that they are confined to a specific type of contract or a particular problem. Some of the directives concern minimum harmonisation, whereas others concern maximum harmonisation. Minimum harmonisation implies that Member States may provide more protection if they wish to do so.[4] In the case of maximum harmonisation, Member States neither have the possibility to include more stringent nor more lenient rules in their national legal systems than is provided for by a directive.

The effect on contract law of some of these European directives will be discussed in the specific chapters of this book.

Apart from these directives, there are also other rules of European law that may affect rules of national private law, for instance, the rules on competition law which are, inter alia, included in Article 101 of the Treaty of the Functioning of the European Union (TFEU). The effect of primary European law will be examined in Section 2.2 below.

The fact that there are rules of contract law on many different levels, ie the international, the European and the national levels, is sometimes referred to as the 'multi-level character' of European contract law.

2.2 EU PRIMARY LAW AND ISSUES OF CONTRACT LAW

2.2.A INTRODUCTION

In this section we will discuss a number of issues of EU primary law that may affect contract law.[5] Sometimes this is also referred to as constitutionalisation of contract law.[6]

---

[3] Council Directive 86/653/EEC of 18 December 1986 on the co-ordination of the laws of the Member States relating to self-employed commercial agents, [1986] OJ L382/17; Council Directive 93/13/EEC of 5 April 1993 on unfair terms in consumer contracts, [1993] OJ L95/29; Directive 94/47/EC of the European Parliament and the Council of 26 October 1994 on the protection of purchasers in respect of certain aspects of contracts relating to the purchase of the right to use immovable properties on a timeshare basis, [1994] OJ L280/83; Directive 97/5/EC of the European Parliament and the Council of 27 January1997 on cross-border credit transfers, [1997] OJ L43/25; Directive 1999/44/EC of the European Parliament and of the Council of 25 May 1999 on certain aspects of the sale of consumer goods and associated guarantees, [1999] OJ L171/12; Directive 2000/31/EC of the European Parliament and of the Council of 8 June 2000 on certain legal aspects of information society services, in particular electronic commerce, in the Internal Market, [2000] OJ L171/1; Directive 2000/35/EC of the European Parliament and of the Council of 29 June 2000 on combating late payment in commercial transactions, [2000] OJ L200/35; Directive 2005/29/EC of the European Parliament and of the Council of 11 May 2005 concerning unfair business-to-consumer commercial practices in the internal market and amending Council Directive 84/450/EEC, Directives 97/7/EC, 98/27/EC and 2002/65/EC of the European Parliament and of the Council and Regulation (EC) No 2006/2004 of the European Parliament and of the Council ('Unfair Commercial Practices Directive') [2005] OJ L149/22; Directive 2011/83/EU of the European Parliament and of the Council of 25 October 2011 on consumer rights, amending Council Directive 93/13/EEC and Directive 1999/44/EC and repealing Council Directive 85/577/EEC and Directive 97/7/EC, [2011] OJ L304/64; Directive (EU) 2015/2302 of the European Parliament and of the Council of 25 November 2015 on package travel and linked travel arrangements, amending Regulation (EC) No 2006/2004 and Directive 2011/83/EU of the European Parliament and of the Council and repealing Council Directive 90/314/EEC [2015] OJ L326/1.

[4] D Chalmers, G Davies and G Monti, *European Union Law* (3rd edn, Cambridge University Press, 2014) 693.

[5] See for an extensive discussion of these issues: AS Hartkamp, CH Sieburgh and W Devroe (eds), *Ius Commune Casebooks on the Common Law of Europe: European Law and Private Law* (Oxford: Hart Publishing, 2017).

[6] See also above, pp 15–17.

Rules of primary European law that may affect rules of contract law and the rights and obligations resulting from a contract are inter alia the free movement of goods, services, capital and persons, the Charter of Fundamental Rights of the European Union (CFREU)[7] and general principles of EU law.[8] Hereafter, we will look at the interaction between contract law and the CFREU, the general principles of EU law and the free movements.

2.2.B CHARTER OF FUNDAMENTAL RIGHTS OF THE EUROPEAN UNION

When the Lisbon Treaty came into force in 2009, the Charter of Fundamental Rights of the European Union became binding in the European Union.[9] The CFREU may also affect contractual relationships. Below, it will be discussed to what extent and how.

Charter of Fundamental Rights of the European Union **2.1 (EU)**

Preamble: The peoples of Europe, in creating an ever closer union among them, are resolved to share a peaceful future based on common values.

Conscious of its spiritual and moral heritage, the Union is founded on the indivisible, universal values of human dignity, freedom, equality and solidarity; it is based on the principles of democracy and the rule of law. It places the individual at the heart of its activities, by establishing the citizenship of the Union and by creating an area of freedom, security and justice.

The Union contributes to the preservation and to the development of these common values while respecting the diversity of the cultures and traditions of the peoples of Europe as well as the national identities of the Member States and the organisation of their public authorities at national, regional and local levels; it seeks to promote balanced and sustainable development and ensures free movement of persons, services, goods and capital, and the freedom of establishment.

To this end, it is necessary to strengthen the protection of fundamental rights in the light of changes in society, social progress and scientific and technological developments by making those rights more visible in a Charter.

...

Article 51: Field of Application.

1. The provisions of this Charter are addressed to the institutions, bodies, offices and agencies of the Union with due regard for the principle of subsidiarity and to the Member States only when they are implementing Union law. They shall therefore respect the rights, observe the principles and promote the application thereof in accordance with their respective powers and respecting the limits of the powers of the Union as conferred on it in the Treaties.

---

[7] Charter of Fundamental Rights of the European Union, OJ EU 2012, C 326/02.
[8] See below, ch 17, on immoral and illegal contacts.
[9] Chalmers et al (n 4 above) 247 ff. See above, pp 14–15.

Article 52: Scope and interpretation of rights and principles.

1. Any limitation on the exercise of the rights and freedoms recognised by this Charter must be provided for by law and respect the essence of those rights and freedoms. Subject to the principle of proportionality, limitations may be made only if they are necessary and genuinely meet objectives of general interest recognised by the Union or the need to protect the rights and freedoms of others.

2. Rights recognised by this Charter for which provision is made in the Treaties shall be exercised under the conditions and within the limits defined by those Treaties.

3. In so far as this Charter contains rights which correspond to rights guaranteed by the Convention for the Protection of Human Rights and Fundamental Freedoms, the meaning and scope of those rights shall be the same as those laid down by the said Convention. This provision shall not prevent Union law providing more extensive protection.

4. In so far as this Charter recognises fundamental rights as they result from the constitutional traditions common to the Member States, those rights shall be interpreted in harmony with those traditions.

5. The provisions of this Charter which contain principles may be implemented by legislative and executive acts taken by institutions, bodies, offices and agencies of the Union, and by acts of Member States when they are implementing Union law, in the exercise of their respective powers. They shall be judicially cognisable only in the interpretation of such acts and in the ruling on their legality.

6. Full account shall be taken of national laws and practices as specified in this Charter.

7. The explanations drawn up as a way of providing guidance in the interpretation of this Charter shall be given due regard by the courts of the Union and of the Member States.

Notes

(1) The addressees of the CFREU are the institutions of the EU. The Member States only have to observe the CFREU insofar as the implementation of EU law is concerned.

(2) It is generally accepted that fundamental rights have vertical effect, which implies that they apply in relationships between a state or a state authority and a citizen. Within the literature, there is a debate about the effects of human rights on private law relationships, which could occur by either direct or indirect horizontal effects. The Court of Justice tends to avoid this discussion by instructing national courts to interpret EU legislation in conformity with the CFREU, as it for instance did in *Kušionová,* a decision concerning the interpretation of Directive 93/13 on unfair terms in consumer contracts.[10] Since this directive applies in the private sphere, such an instruction is associated with the horizontal application of fundamental rights. It could be defended as an example of horizontal application of the CFREU turned into vertical application.[11]

---

[10] C-34/13, *Monika Kušionová v SMART Capital, a.s.*, 10 September 2014, ECLI:EU:C:2014:2189. See below, 2.5 (EU), p 40.

[11] For the horizontal application of the Charter, see D Leczykiewicz, 'Horizontal Application of the Charter of Fundamental Rights' (2013) 38 ELRev 479.

Charter of Fundamental Rights of the European Union   **2.2 (EU)**

Article 16: Freedom to conduct a business.
The freedom to conduct a business in accordance with Union law and national laws and practices is recognised.[12]

Court of Justice (Grand Chamber), 22 January 2013[13]   **2.3 (EU)**

Sky Österreich

Facts: Sky was authorised by KommAustria to broadcast via satellite the coded digital television programme 'Sky Sport Austria'. By a contract of 21 August 2009, Sky acquired exclusive rights to broadcast Europa League matches in the 2009/2010 to 2011/2012 seasons in Austrian territory. Sky stated that it had spent several million euros each year on the licence and production costs. Sky Österreich concluded a contract with ORF which granted the right to ORF to produce short news reports. In return ORF had to pay Sky Österreich €700,00 per minute for such reports. At the request of ORF, made in November 2010, KommAustria decided that Sky was required, as the holder of exclusive broadcasting rights, to grant ORF the right to produce short news reports, but was not entitled to demand remuneration greater than the additional costs directly incurred in providing access to the satellite signal, which were non-existent in this case. This ruling was based on Austrian implementation of the Audiovisual Media Services Directive.[14] Both parties appealed against that decision before the *Bundeskommunikationssenat*. The *Bundeskommunikationssenat* referred to the Court of Justice for a preliminary ruling and asked inter alia whether Article 15(6) of the Audiovisual Media Services Directive resulted in an infringement of fundamental rights included in the CFREU.

Held: By prohibiting to set a certain price for the services concerned Article 15(6) of Directive 2010/13/EU of the European Parliament and of the Council of 10 March 2010 on the coordination of certain provisions laid down by law, regulation or administrative action in Member States concerning the provision of audiovisual media services (Audiovisual Media Services Directive) does not result in an infringement of Article 16 CFREU.

Judgment: 42 The protection afforded by Article 16 of the Charter covers the freedom to exercise an economic or commercial activity, the freedom of contract and free competition, as is apparent from the explanations relating to that article, which, in accordance with the third subparagraph of Article 6(1) TEU and Article 52(7) of the Charter, have to be taken into consideration for the interpretation of the Charter (Case C-279/09 DEB [2010] ECR I-13849, paragraph 32).

43 In addition, the freedom of contract includes, in particular, the freedom to choose with whom to do business (see, to that effect, Joined Cases C-90/90 and C-91/90 Neu [1991] ECR I-3617, paragraph 13), and the freedom to determine the price of a service (see, to that effect, Case C-437/04 Commission v Belgium [2007] ECR I-2513, paragraph 51, and Case C-213/10 F-TEX [2012] ECR, paragraph 45).

...

---

[12] Explanations relating to the Charter of Fundamental Rights (2007/C 303/02) [2007] OJ, C303/23.

[13] C-283/11, *Sky Österreich GmbH v Österreichischer Rundfunk*, 22 January 2013, ECLI:EU:C:2013:28; cf C-544/10, *Deutsches Weintor eG v Land Rheinland-Pfalz*, 6 September 2012, ECLI:EU:C:2012:526.

[14] Directive 2010/13/EU of the European Parliament and of the Council of 10 March 2010 on the coordination of certain provisions laid down by law, regulation or administrative action in Member States concerning the provision of audiovisual media services (Audiovisual Media Services Directive), OJ L 95/2010, p 1, and corrigendum OJ L 263/2010, p 15.

45 However, in accordance with the Court's case-law, the freedom to conduct a business is not absolute, but must be viewed in relation to its social function (see, to that effect, Joined Cases C-184/02 and C-223/02 Spain and Finland v Parliament and Council [2004] ECR I-7789, paragraphs 51 and 52, and Case C-544/10 Deutsches Weintor [2012] ECR, paragraph 54 and the case-law cited).

46 On the basis of that case-law and in the light of the wording of Article 16 of the Charter, which differs from the wording of the other fundamental freedoms laid down in Title II thereof, yet is similar to that of certain provisions of Title IV of the Charter, the freedom to conduct a business may be subject to a broad range of interventions on the part of public authorities which may limit the exercise of economic activity in the public interest.

47 That circumstance is reflected, inter alia, in the way in which Article 52(1) of the Charter requires the principle of proportionality to be implemented.

Notes

(1) From Article 16 CFREU freedom of contract as a fundamental right is also inferred. This freedom, however, is not absolute. It can be curtailed by national and European secondary law, provided the principle of proportionality is observed.

(2) The *Alema-Herron* decision of the Court of Justice is a ruling in which the Court of Justice held that the fundamental right to freedom of contract was infringed.[15] This decision was met with criticism.[16]

The Court of Justice does not only answer preliminary questions as to whether secondary law is in conformity with the CFREU, but it also refers to the CFREU if it answers preliminary questions with respect to the interpretation of directives. Article 7 CFREU, for instance, plays a role in the interpretation of the Directive on unfair terms on consumer contracts[17] in contracts which concern housing.

Charter of Fundamental Rights of the European Union   **2.4 (EU)**

Article 7: Respect for private and family life. Everyone has the right to respect for his or her private and family life, home and communications.

Court of Justice, 10 September 2014[18]   **2.5 (EU)**

Monika Kušionová v SMART Capital

Facts: Monica Kušionová, who lived in Slovakia, was threatened with eviction from her home, because she had stopped paying a consumer credit of € 10,000, which was secured by a mortgage on her family home in

---

[15] C-426/11, *M. Alemo-Herron and Others v Parkwood Leisure Ltd*, 18 July 2013, ECLI:EU:C:2013:521.

[16] See eg, M Bartl and C Leone, 'Minimum harmonization and Art 16 CFREU, Difficult Times Ahead for Social Legislation' in H Collins (ed), *European Contract Law and the Charter of Fundamental Rights* (Cambridge: Intersentia, 2017) 113.

[17] [1993] OJ L95/29. See below, ch 21.

[18] C-34/13, *Monika Kušionová v SMART Capital, a.s.*, 10 September 2014, ECLI:EU:C:2014:2189.

which she lived. The mortgage agreement included a clause according to which the lender, SMART Capital, could sell the family home extra-judicially without any review by a court. Kušionová started proceedings against SMART Capital and asked for the terms of the credit agreement and the mortgage agreement to be annulled under the Directive 93/13 on unfair terms in consumer contracts. At first instance, the court held that some of the terms in the credit were unfair as well the mortgage agreement as such and annulled them. On appeal, the Court referred the case to the Court of Justice for a preliminary ruling.

The operative part of the decision is not reproduced, since it is not relevant in this respect.

Judgment: 'Under EU law, the right to accommodation is a fundamental right guaranteed under Article 7 of the Charter that the referring court must take into consideration when implementing Directive 93/13.'

Notes

(1) In this case the Court of Justice refers explicitly to Article 7 CFREU. In earlier cases the Court had referred implicitly to this fundamental right by using the language the European Court of Human Rights had used to interpret the equivalent provision in the European Convention on Human Rights.[19]

(2) The Court of Justice also refers to other rights in the CFREU in its case law on the Directive on Unfair Terms in Consumer Contracts, for instance to Article 47 (Right to an effective remedy and to a fair trial).[20]

2.2.C GENERAL PRINCIPLES OF EU LAW

From general EU law, the Court of Justice has inferred general principles which must be taken into account when applying and interpreting EU law. The Court of Justice has held that these principles may also play a role in horizontal relationships which are governed by private law.[21]

In his book *The General Principles of EU Law*, Tridimas distinguishes the following principles: the principles of equality, proportionality, legal certainty and protection of legitimate expectations, in addition to fundamental rights, the right to judicial protection, the rights of defence, transparency and access to documents, abuse of right, the principle of effective remedies in national courts and principles governing liability in damages.[22]

---

[19] C-415/11, *M. Aziz v Catalunyacaixa*, 14 March 2013, ECLI:EU:C:2013:164; C-488/11, *D.F. Asbeek Brusse, K. de Man Garabito v Jahani BV*, 30 May 2013, ECLI:EU:C:2013:341. See below, ch 21.

[20] C-472/11, *Banif Plus Bank Zrt v Csaba Csipai, Viktória Csipai*, 21 February 2013, ECLI:EU:C:2013:88; C-470/12, *Pohotovst's.r.o. v M. Vašuta*, 27 February 2014, ECLI:EU:C:2014:101; *Kušionová* (n 18 above); N Reich, *General Principles of EU Civil Law* (Cambridge: Intersentia, 2014) 90 ff.

[21] See for an elaborate discussion: Hartkamp et al (eds) (n 5 above) ch 5 General Principles of EU Law, 279 ff; J Basedow, 'General Principles of European Private Law and Interest Analysis' [2016] ERPL 331.

[22] T Tridimas, *The General Principles of EU Law* (2nd edn, Oxford University Press, 2007).

Within private law these principles also play a role. This was questioned in the *Audiolux* case, which concerned the interpretation of company law, but the Court of Justice held:

Court of Justice, 15 October 2009[23]   **2.6 (EU)**

Audiolux

EU law does not recognise a general principle of equal treatment of shareholders.

Facts: A minority shareholder in a company established under Luxembourg law wanted to rely on the general principle of equal treatment in EU law to secure its position.

Judgment: 63 The general principles of Community law have constitutional status while the principle proposed by Audiolux is characterised by a degree of detail requiring legislation to be drafted and enacted at Community level by a measure of secondary Community law. Therefore, the principle proposed by Audiolux cannot be regarded as an independent general principle of Community law.

64 Having regard to all the foregoing, the answer to the first and second questions must be that Community law does not include any general principle of law under which minority shareholders are protected by an obligation on the dominant shareholder, when acquiring or exercising control of a company, to offer to buy their shares under the same conditions as those agreed when a shareholding conferring or strengthening the control of the dominant shareholder was acquired.

[In her opinion Advocate General Trstenjak elaborated that these principles are not concerned with certain areas of law, but apply in all:]

Opinion Advocate General Trstenjak[24]

87. As has already been explained, general principles are distinguished primarily by their constitutional status within the Community legal order. As a rule, general principles embody fundamental legal concepts and values inherent in a legal order. Furthermore, they differ from specific rules of law in that they claim a certain degree of general validity and are not restricted to a certain area of law.

Notes

(1) In this case minority shareholders argued that a general principle of equal treatment of shareholders was infringed. The Court of Justice held that such a general principle does not exist, since it only applies in specific instances.

(2) In *Mangold* and other cases, the Court of Justice accepted a general principle of equal treatment.[25] *Mangold* involved a labour contract. With respect to labour

---

[23] C-101/08, *Audiolux SA and Others v Groupe Bruxelles Lambert SA (GBL) and Others, Bertelsmann AG and Others*, 15 October 2009, ECLI:EU:C:2009:626.

[24] Opinion of Advocate General Trstenjak of 30 June 2009 in C-101/08, *Audiolux SA and Others v Groupe Bruxelles Lambert SA (GBL) and Others, Bertelsmann AG and Others*, ECLI:EU:C:2009:410.

[25] C-144/04, *W Mangold v R Helm*, 22 November 2005, ECLI:EU:C:2005:709. See for an elaborate discussion: Chalmers et al (n 4 above) 574 ff; Hartkamp et al (eds) (n 5 above) ch 5 II.

contracts, the principle of non-discrimination on the grounds of sex, age and sexual orientation is especially relevant.[26]

(3) However, the principle of non-discrimination is not restricted to labour contracts, it is also applicable, for instance, with respect to services of general economic interest.[27]

(4) Some authors, for instance, Reich and Hartkamp, also infer tentatively a general principle of good faith from EU law.[28]

2.2.D THE FREE MOVEMENTS AND CONTRACT LAW; EX POST ASSESSMENT

The free movements of goods, services, capital and persons may affect contract law and contracts in various ways.[29] In this respect, three instances can be distinguished. First, it may be that national rules of contract law are contrary to the free movements; this will be discussed in this section. Secondly, the contract which the parties have entered into may be contrary to a rule of national public law, which, in its turn, is a barrier to trade and consequently must be set aside. This will influence the rights and obligations arising from the contract. These two instances are often referred to as the vertical effect of the free movements, since they may result in a national rule of either public or private law that results in an obstacle to trade being set aside.[30] The third issue is whether the free movements have horizontal effect or, in other words, whether contracts which are entered into by the parties may constitute an obstacle to free movement. Each issue involves an *ex post* assessment of a potential barrier to trade. However, before these instances are discussed, a few general remarks must be made with respect to the application of these free movements.

The free movements of goods, services, persons and capital is enshrined in the TFEU in Articles 34, 56, 45, 49 and 63. Their wording is rather hard to understand without taking into account the interpretation put on them by the Court of Justice. For instance, Article 34 TFEU relating to the free movement of goods provides:

All measures having equivalent effect are forbidden.

In this respect, it should be noted that within the literature there is an ongoing discussion about whether the case law with respect to the freedoms is converging or whether each free movement and its case law must be dealt with separately, since there are differences between them.

---

[26] C-144/04, *W Mangold v R Helm*, 22 November 2005, ECLI:EU:C:2005:709. See for an elaborate discussion: Hartkamp et al (eds) (n 5 above) ch 5 II; Reich (n 20 above) 59 ff.

[27] Reich (n 20 above) 81 ff.

[28] AS Hartkamp, *European Law and National Private Law* (Cambridge: Intersentia, 2016) 123 ff; Reich (n 20 above) 189.

[29] See also H-W Micklitz, J Stuyck and E Terryn (eds), *Ius Commune Casebooks on the Common Law of Europe: Consumer Law* (Oxford: Hart Publishing, 2010) 12–18.

[30] See also Hartkamp et al (eds) (n 5 above) ch 1. The authors use a different terminology.

A common characteristic of all the free movements is that the effect of a national rule on trade between Member States is decisive, regardless of whether it concerns a rule of public or private law. When national rules obstruct trade between the Member States, they must be set aside unless they are justified on one of the grounds mentioned in the Treaty (for instance ex-Article 30 EC). The first landmark case in which the Court of Justice held this was the *Dassonville* decision, which held that all national rules 'which are capable of hindering directly or indirectly, potentially or actually intra-Community trade' are liable to be set aside.[31] As a result, national rules that either openly or covertly discriminate between national and imported products are considered to be an obstacle to trade between the Member States.

In *Cassis de Dijon*, the category of rules that obstruct trade was enlarged to measures that do not discriminate.[32] In the absence of harmonisation, disparity of national legislation results in an infringement of the free movement of goods, unless the national legislation is justified. In order to counteract the enlargement of the number of rules that could be set aside, the Court of Justice also created a new non-exhaustive category of justification grounds, which is referred to as the rule of reason. However, as a consequence of *Cassis de Dijon*, the Court of Justice was flooded with cases in which rules that did not concern cross-border trade were challenged, since they allegedly were an obstacle to inter-Community trade.

In order to reverse this development, the Court of Justice rendered its decision in *Mithouard and Keck*, in which the Court distinguished between selling arrangements and product requirements.[33] The former are rules concerning the time and place of a sale, the latter involve rules on issues such as the quality of products and quantity of ingredients in products. This distinction was aimed at clarifying the existing case law at the time. It is, however, questionable whether the Court of Justice succeeded. The *Keck* test has met considerable criticism from academic writing[34] as well as from the Court of Justice's Advocates General.[35] One of the criticisms is that often a national rule does not fit easily into either category. Roth refers to rules of private law in this respect and argues that they do not fall in either category.[36] Moreover, the *Keck* test has not been applied with respect to the free movements of persons, capital and services. In those instances an 'access-to-market' test is applied, according to which national rule constitutes an obstacle to

---

[31] C-8/74, *Procureur de Roi v Benoît and Gustave Dassonville*, 11 June 1974, ECLI:EU:C:1974:82. Chalmers et al (n 4 above) 754–57.

[32] C-120/78, *Cassis de Dijon* (*Rewe-Zentral AG v Bundesmonopolverwaltung für Branntwein*), 20 February 1979, ECLI:EU:C:1979:42. Chalmers et al (n 4 above) 773 ff.

[33] Joined Cases C-267/91 and C-268/91, *Keck and Mithouard*, 24 November 1993, ECLI:EU:C:1993:905.

[34] S Weatherill, 'Some Thoughts on How to Clarify the Clarification' (1996) 33 CMLR 885; cf D Chalmers, G Davies and G Monti, *European Union Law* (Cambridge University Press, 2006) 686.

[35] See para 41 of the opinion of Advocate General Jacobs of 24 November 1994 in C-412/93, *Société d'Importation Edouard Leclerc-Sipouard v TF 1 Publicité SA and M6 Publicité SA*, ECLI:EU:C:1994:393; Opinion of Advocate General Geelhoed of 11 December 2003 in C-239/02, *Douwe Egberts NV v Westrom Pharma NV and others*, ECLI:EU:C:2003:668.

[36] P Oliver and WH Roth, 'The Internal Market and the Four Freedoms' (2004) 14 CMLR 414.

trade when it prevents access to the market. However, with respect to the free movement of goods, the Court of Justice seems to uphold the *Keck* test, despite the criticism, although there are authors that argue that *Keck* is outdated law on the basis of recent case law.[37]

The Court of Justice has not dealt in many instances with the issue as to whether rules of substantive contract law are contrary to the free movements. The most well-known decisions are *Alsthom Atlantique*[38] and *CMC Motorradcenter*.[39]

Court of Justice, 24 January 1991[40]   **2.7 (EU)**

Alsthom Atlantique v Compagnie de Construction mécanique Sulzer SA

Article 34 [now Article 35 TFEU] must be interpreted as meaning that it does not prohibit the application of a Member State's case law which, by not allowing persons selling goods by way of trade to prove that on the date on which the goods were delivered they were unaware of a defect in the goods.

The facts are not reproduced, since they are not relevant in this respect.

Held: … the answer to the question submitted for a preliminary ruling must be that the provisions of Articles 2 and 3(f) of the EEC Treaty, read together with … Article 34 [now Article 35 TFEU] … thereof, must be interpreted as meaning that they do not prohibit the application of a Member State's case law which, by not allowing persons selling goods by way of trade to prove that on the date on which the goods were delivered they were unaware of a defect in the goods, has the effect of preventing them from relying on provisions of national legislation which allow them to limit their liability when unaware of the defect, in the same way as their competitors in the other Member States may do.

Judgment: …

13. According to Article 34 of the Treaty [now Article 35 TFEU], quantitative restrictions on exports and all measures having equivalent effect are prohibited between Member States.

14. As the court has consistently held …, Article 34 [now Article 35 TFEU] of the Treaty concerns only those measures which have as their specific object the trade of other Member States.

15. It must be held that the case-law of the French Court of Cassation, to which reference is made in this case, applies without distinction to all commercial relations governed by French law and does not have as its specific object or effect the restriction of patterns of exports thereby favouring domestic production or the domestic market. Furthermore, the parties to an international contract of sale are generally free to determine the law applicable to their contractual relations and can thus avoid being subject to French law.

---

[37] C Barnard, 'Restricting Restrictions: Lessons for the EU from the US?' (2009) 68 CLJ 575; E Spaventa, 'Leaving *Keck* Behind? The Free Movement of Goods after the Rulings in *Commission v Italy* and *Mickelsson and Roos*' (2009) 34 European Law Review 914, 915 ff.

[38] C-339/89, *Alsthom Atlantique v Compagnie de Construction mécanique Sulzer*, 24 January 1991, ECLI:EU:C:1991:28.

[39] C-93/92, *CMC Motorradcenter GmbH v Pelin Baskiciogullar*, 13 October 1993, ECLI:EU:C:1993:838.

[40] C-339/89, ECLI:EU:C:1991:28.

Court of Justice, 13 October 1993[41] **2.8 (EU)**

CMC Motorradcenter GmbH v P Baskiciogullari

Article 30 of the EEC Treaty [now Article 34 TFEU] is to be interpreted as not precluding a rule established in the courts of a Member State from imposing an obligation to provide information prior to contract.

Facts: Ms Baskiciogullari, who lived in Germany, entered into a contract of sale concerning a Yamaha moped with CMC Motorradcenter GmbH, a non-authorised dealer for any individual brand of motorcycles. The general conditions of the contract specified that the purchaser could assert her rights under the guarantee as against either the vendor or undertakings approved by the manufacturer or the importer. Although Motorradcenter was aware that, despite those conditions, authorised German dealers generally refused to repair motorcycles which had been the subject of parallel imports under the guarantee, Motor-radcenter had not informed Ms Baskiciogullari thereof. When she became aware thereof, she refused to accept the moped at the moment of delivery. Motorradcenter initiated proceedings against Ms Baskiciogullari before a German court and claimed damages. In those proceedings the question arose whether this obligation to provide information prior to concluding a contract under German law obstructs trade between Member States.

Held: Article 30 of the EEC Treaty [now Article 34 TFEU] is to be interpreted as not precluding a rule established in the courts of a Member State from imposing an obligation to provide information prior to contract.

Judgment: ...

8. By the question referred to the Court, the Landgericht is in substance enquiring whether such an obligation to provide information constitutes a measure having an effect equivalent to a quantitative restriction within the meaning of Article 30 of the EEC [which is now Article 34 TFEU].

9. As the Court has consistently held ... any rule capable of hindering directly or indirectly, actually or potentially, intra-Community trade constitutes a measure having equivalent effect to a quantitative restriction.

10. In this case, the first point to note is that the obligation to provide information prior to a contract, imposed by the German law of contract, applies without distinction, at least as regards products coming from the Community, to all contractual relationships covered by that law and that its purpose is not to regulate trade.

11. As regards the question whether there is a risk of obstructing the free movements of goods, it is in any event not the obligation to provide information which would cause such a risk, but the fact that certain authorized dealers of the brand in question refuse to perform services under the guarantee on motorcycles which have been the subject of parallel imports.

12. It follows that the restrictive effects which the said obligations to provide information might have on the free movement of goods are too uncertain and too indirect to warrant the conclusion that it is liable to hinder trade between Member States (see the judgment in Case C-69/88 *Krantz* [1990] ECR I-583).

---

[41] C-93/92, ECLI:EU:C:1993:838.

Notes

(1) In *CMC Motorradcenter* the Court held that the effect of the German rule of *culpa in contrahendo*[42] was too uncertain and too indirect to constitute an infringement of the free movement of goods. In *Alsthom Atlantique*, in which the French rule on hidden defects[43] was at stake, the Court of Justice held that the French rules of substantive contract law were not contrary to the free movement of goods.

(2) In both cases, the facts were confined to one Member State, Germany and France respectively. On the basis of, inter alia, these cases, it can be argued that national rules of substantive law cannot constitute an infringement of one of the freedoms when the facts of a case are restricted to one Member State.

2.2.E EX ANTE ASSESSMENT OF THE FREE MOVEMENT OF GOODS

In accordance with Directive 98/34 on the notifications of technical regulations,[44] Member States must notify draft technical regulations to the European Commission. The Directive's aim is to prevent Member States from introducing new legislation that constitutes an obstacle to trade. After the notification, the Directive creates a standstill period, in which the European Commission examines the compatibility of the proposed national legislation with European law. At first sight, the link with rights and obligations arising from contract is not that clear, since this Directive imposes duties on the Member States rather than on private parties.[45] However, in *Unilever v Central Food*[46] the Court of Justice dealt with the issue of whether non-observance of the requirements which are included in this Directive also affect the rights and obligations of private parties.

Court of Justice, 26 September 2000[47]   **2.9 (EU)**

Unilever SpA v Central Food

A national court is required, in civil proceedings between individuals concerning contractual rights and obligations, to refuse to apply a national technical regulation which was adopted during a period of postponement of adoption prescribed in Article 9 of Directive 83/189.

Facts: Italy notified the European Commission of a draft act on the labelling concerning the indication of the geographical origin of the various types of olive oil. However, Italy did not observe the stand-still period which

---

[42] See below, pp 423 ff.

[43] See below, pp 485, 1154.

[44] Council Directive 83/189/EEC of 28 March 1983 laying down a procedure for the provision of information in the field of technical standards and regulations, OJ L 109/1983 p. 8, as amended by Directive 94/10/EC of the European Parliament and the Council of 23 March 1994, OJ L 100/1994 p 30.

[45] See also Hartkamp et al (eds) (n 5 above) ch 1 II B iii, ch 6 V.

[46] C-443/98, *Unilever Italia SpA v Central Food*, 26 September 2000, ECLI:EU:C:2000:496. See also C-159/00, *Sapod Audic v Eco-Emballages SA*, 6 June 2002, ECLI:EU:C:2002:343.

[47] C-443/98, ECLI:EU:C:2000:496.

it should have observed after the notification of the proposed legislation. In other words, the Italian legislation had come into force during the stand-still period. During that period, Unilever SA, an Italian company delivered a batch of olive oil to Central Food, which refused to pay the price. Central Food argued that there was non-performance on the side of Unilever, since it had not labelled the olive oil in accordance with the Italian rules that had been notified to the European Commission. Unilever argued that these rules were not applicable and consequently it had labelled the olive oil properly. Subsequently, Unilever started proceedings for payment of the price before the *pretore* of Milan, who asked the COURT OF JUSTICE a preliminary question whether the Italian legislation which had been notified to the European Commission could be applied during the stand-still period.

Held: A national court is required, in civil proceedings between individuals concerning contractual rights and obligations, to refuse to apply a national technical regulation which was adopted during a period of postponement of adoption prescribed in Article 9 of Directive 83/189.[48]

Judgment: ...

7. In paragraphs 54 and 55 of its judgment in Case C-194/94 *CIA Security v Signalson and Securitel* [1996] ECR I-2201 (hereinafter 'CIA Security') the Court held that Directive 83/189 was to be interpreted as meaning that breach of the obligation to notify rendered the technical regulations concerned inapplicable, so that they were unenforceable against individuals and that individuals might therefore rely on Articles 8 and 9 of Directive 83/189 before the national court, which must decline to apply a national technical regulation which has not been notified in accordance with that directive.

...

31. The question from the national court seeks, in essence, to ascertain whether a national court is required, in civil proceedings between individuals concerning contractual rights and obligations, to refuse to apply a national technical regulation which was adopted during a period of postponement of adoption prescribed by Article 9 of Directive 83/189.

...

44. Although, in paragraph 48 of CIA Security, after reiterating that the aim of Directive 83/189 was to protect freedom of movement for goods by means of preventive control and that the obligation to notify was essential for achieving such Community control, the Court found that the effectiveness of such control would be that much greater if the directive were interpreted as meaning that breach of the obligation to notify constituted a substantial procedural defect such as to render the technical regulations in question inapplicable to individuals, it follows from the considerations set out in paragraphs 40 to 43 of this judgment that breach of the obligations of postponement of adoption set out in Article 9 of Directive 83/189 also constitutes a substantial procedural defect such as to render technical regulations inapplicable.

45. It is therefore necessary to consider, secondly, whether the inapplicability of technical regulations adopted in breach of Article 9 of Directive 83/189 can be invoked in civil proceedings between private individuals concerning contractual rights and obligations.

46. First, in civil proceedings of that nature, application of technical regulations adopted in breach of Article 9 of Directive 83/189 may have the effect of hindering the use or marketing of a product which does not conform to those regulations.

47. That is the case in the main proceedings, since application of the Italian rules is liable to hinder Unilever in marketing the extra virgin olive oil which it offers for sale.

---

[48] See para 52 of the judgment.

48. Next, it must be borne in mind that, in CIA Security, the finding of inapplicability as a legal consequence of breach of the obligation of notification was made in response to a request for a preliminary ruling arising from proceedings between competing undertakings based on national provisions prohibiting unfair trading.

49. Thus, it follows from the case-law of the Court that the inapplicability of a technical regulation which has not been notified in accordance with Article 8 of Directive 83/189 can be invoked in proceedings between individuals for the reasons set out in paragraphs 40 to 43 of this judgment. The same applies to non-compliance with the obligations laid down by Article 9 of the same directive, and there is no reason, in that connection, to treat disputes between individuals relating to unfair competition, as in the CIA Security case, differently from disputes between individuals concerning contractual rights and obligations, as in the main proceedings.

50. Whilst it is true, as observed by the Italian and Danish Governments, that a directive cannot of itself impose obligations on an individual and cannot therefore be relied on as such against an individual (see Case C-91/92 *Faccini Dori* [1994] ECR I-3325, paragraph 20), that case-law does not apply where non-compliance with Article 8 or Article 9 of Directive 83/189, which constitutes a substantial procedural defect, renders a technical regulation adopted in breach of either of those articles inapplicable.

51. In such circumstances, and unlike the case of non-transposition of directives with which the case-law cited by those two Governments is concerned, Directive 83/189 does not in any way define the substantive scope of the legal rule on the basis of which the national court must decide the case before it. It creates neither rights nor obligations for individuals.

2.2.F HORIZONTAL EFFECT OF THE FREE MOVEMENTS

The rules concerning the free movements address the Member States. The question has arisen whether the free movements also apply to private parties. In this respect, a distinction must be made between the free movements of services and persons, on the one hand, and the free movement of goods, on the other.[49] With respect to the former, the Court of Justice held that they also apply to private parties, provided a private party acts collectively.[50] With respect to the free movement of goods, in *Fra.bo* the Court of Justice held that it applies to private parties insofar as they can 'restrict the free movement of goods in the same manner as a Member State can'.[51] Commentators agree that the Court of Justice did not intend to give the free movement of goods such an extensive interpretation.[52] The Court of Justice has not held yet that the free movement of capital has horizontal effect.[53]

---

[49] For an elaborate discussion see, Hartkamp et al (eds) (n 5 above) 10.

[50] See with respect to the free movement of services and persons: C-415/93, *Union royale belge des sociétés de football association and Others v Bosman and Others*, 15 December 1995, ECLI:EU:C:1995:463; C-309/99, *Wouters and Others*, 19 February 2002, ECLI:EU:C:2002:98; C-281/98, *Angonese*, 6 June 2000, ECLI:EU:C:2000:296. Hartkamp et al (eds) (n 5 above) ch 3 III A I, ch 3 IV A 1.

[51] C-171/11, *Fra.bo SpA v DVGW*, 12 July 2012, ECLI:EU:C:2012:453. See for a case note: H Schepel (2013) 9 ERCL 186. See also Hartkamp et al (eds) (n 5 above) ch 3 II A i.

[52] C-171/11, *Fra.bo SpA v DVGW*, 12 July 2012, ECLI:EU:C:2012:453. See for a case note: H Schepel (2013) 9 ERCL 189. Chalmers et al (n 4 above) 768 ff; Hartkamp et al (eds) (n 5 above) ch 3 II A i.

[53] Hartkamp et al (eds) (n 5 above) ch 3 V A i.

2.3 PRIVATE INTERNATIONAL LAW ISSUES[54]

Since there is no European Civil Code, each Member State has its own legal system, which includes inter alia the law of contract. In the case of cross-border contracts it is not obvious which legal system is applicable, since the contract is connected to more than one legal system. In those situations the choice of law rules or conflict rules provides a solution. Conflict rules refer a contract to a legal system and, in principle, that is the only role that conflict rules play.

On a European level the conflict rules on contract are unified in the Regulation on the Law Applicable to Contractual Obligations (Rome I Regulation), which came into force on 1 August 2008.[55] Prior to August 2008, the intergovernmental Convention on the Law Applicable to Contractual Obligations (1980 Rome Convention) prevailed.[56] From 1 August 2004, preliminary questions could be referred to the European Court of Justice by national courts concerning the interpretation of the 1980 Rome Convention. Also with respect to the Rome I Regulation, preliminary questions can be asked by the courts of each Member State.

Another instrument of private international law which must be mentioned at this stage is the Regulation (EU) No 1215/2012 of 12 December 2012 on jurisdiction and the recognition and enforcement of judgments in civil and commercial matters (Brussels I recast).[57] The Rome I and Brussels I recast Regulations are mentioned here because they both include terms and notions which are relevant in the area of contract law. Some of these have been given an interpretation by the European Court of Justice. This all may be helpful in dilineating a European contract law.

FURTHER READING

Brownsword, R, Micklitz, H-W, Niglia, L and Weatherill, S (eds), *The Foundations of European Private Law* (Oxford: Hart Publishing, 2011).
Collins, H, *The European Civil Code* (Cambridge University Press, 2008).
Collins, H (ed), *European Contract Law and the Charter of Fundamental Rights* (Cambridge: Intersentia, 2017).
Dougan, M, 'The Disguised Vertical Direct Effect of Directives?' (2000) 59 Cambridge Law Journal 586–611.
Hartkamp, AS et al, *Towards a European Civil Code* (4th edn, Dordrecht: Kluwer International, 2011).
Hartkamp, AS, *European Law and National Private Law: Effect of EU Law and European Human Rights Law on Legal Relationships between Individuals* (2nd edn, Cambridge: Intersentia, 2016).
Joerges, C, 'On the Legitimacy of Europeanizing of Private Law: Considerations on a Justice-making Law for the EU Multi-level System' (2003) 7 Electronic Journal of Comparative Law, www.ejcl.org/73/art73-3.html.

---

[54] See above, ch 1.3.
[55] [2008] OJ L177/6.
[56] [2005] OJ C334/1.
[57] Regulation (EU) No 1215/2012 of 12 December 2012 on jurisdiction and the recognition and enforcement of judgments in civil and commercial matters (recast) [2012] OJ L351/1.

Leczykiewicz D, Weatherill S (eds), *The Involvement of EU Law in Private Law Relationships* (Oxford: Hart Publishing, 2013).

Oliver, P, Roth, WH, 'The Internal Market and the Four Freedoms' (2004) 41 Common Market Law Review 407–41.

Reich, N, *General Principles of EU Civil Law* (Cambridge: Intersentia, 2014).

Roth, WH, 'Secured Credit and the Internal Market: The Fundamental Freedoms and the EU's Mandate for Legislation' (2008) Special Issue of the European Company and Financial Law Review 36–67.

Rutgers, JW, Sirena P (eds), *Rules and Principles in European Contract Law* (Cambridge: Intersentia, 2015).

Smits, J (ed), *The need for a European Contract Law: Empirical and Legal Perspectives* (Groningen: Europa Law Publishers, 2005).

Teubner, G, 'Legal Irritants: Good Faith in British Law or How Unifying Law Ends up in new Divergences' (1998) 61 Modern Law Review 11–32.

Twigg-Flesner, C (ed), *Research Handbook on EU Consumer and Contract Law* (Cheltenham: Edward Elgar, 2016).

Weatherill, S, 'Breach of directives and breach of contract' (2001) 26 European Law Review 177–86.

CHAPTER 3
PRINCIPLES, SOFT LAW AND LEGISLATIVE
PROPOSALS IN EUROPEAN CONTRACT LAW

3.1 INTRODUCTION

In the previous chapter we discussed the binding rules of EU law that may affect contract law. In this chapter we will focus on non-binding rules, also known as 'soft law', and also some legislative proposals made by the European Commission—one that subsequently was withdrawn and some that are on-going.

In respect of 'soft law' a distinction must be made between soft law originating from institutions of the European Union and other private initiatives. There is no EU soft law at present but it was contemplated, principally in the Communications issued by the European Commission with respect to contract law; these will be dealt with in Section 2 below.[1] Within this context, model rules were drafted, for instance those included in the Draft Common Frame of Reference. They could also be regarded as soft law.

Within Europe, the best known rules of soft law that resulted from a private initiative are the *Principles of European Contract Law* (PECL).[2] They were drafted by the 'Commission on European Contract Law'. In an article entitled 'My Life as a Lawyer' Ole Lando, the chairman, writes about its start:[3]

> I set out to try and unify the substantive contract law in the EU. My efforts started in 1976. I attempted to find scholars from the EC countries, who would be member of the *Commission*

---

[1] Communication from the Commission to the Council and the European Parliament on European Contract Law, COM(2001) 398 final; Communication from the Commission to the European Parliament and the Council, A more Coherent European Contract Law, An Action Plan, OJ C 63/2003 p 1; Communication to the European Parliament and the Council. European Contract Law and the Revision of the acquis: The Way Forward, COM(2004) 651 final; Report from the Commission, First Annual Progress Report on European Contract Law and the Acquis Review, COM(2005) 456 final; Report from the Commission, Second Progress Report on the Common Frame of Reference, Brussels 25 July 2007, COM(2007) 447 final.

[2] O Lando and H Beale (eds), *Principles of European Contract Law, parts I and II* (The Hague: Kluwer, 2000); O Lando, E Clive, A Prüm and R Zimmerman (eds), *Principles of European Contract Law, part III* (The Hague: Kluwer, 2003).

[3] O Lando, 'My Life as a Lawyer' (2002) 10 ZEuP 508, 519.

on European Contract Law (CECL). Many declined my invitation. Gradually, however, I succeeded in gathering a group of highly qualified lawyers … I also tried to persuade the European Commission to provide us with some means to hold our meetings. It took time, but *Claus Ehlermann,* who was now Director General of the Legal Service of the European Commission, saw to it that we got the funds. So in 1982 the CECL started to prepare the *Principles of European Contract Law (PECL).*

The goals of the PECL are set out in its first provision:

Article 1:101 PECL **3.1 (INT)**

1. These Principles are intended to be applied as general rules of contract law in the European Union.

2. These Principles will apply when the parties have agreed to incorporate them into their contract or that their contract is to be governed by them.

3. These Principles may be applied when the parties:

    a. have agreed that their contract is to be governed by 'general principles of law', the 'lex mercatoria' or the like; or

    b. have not chosen any system or rules of law to govern their contract.

4. These Principles may provide a solution to the issue raised where the system of law or rules of law applicable do not do so.

The European Commission on Contract Law as such no longer exists; its work was taken over by the Study Group on a European Civil Code (SGECC), which also no longer exists. This Group drafted principles in the area of contract law and beyond. Its chairman, Christian von Bar, described its aim in his foreword to the volumes that include Principles of European Law:[4]

Study Group on a European Civil Code, Foreword **3.2 (INT)**

The Study Group on a European Civil Code has taken upon itself the task of drafting common European Principles for the most important aspects of the law of obligations and for certain parts of the law of property in moveables which are especially relevant for the functioning of the common market. It was founded in 1999 as a successor body to the Commission on European Contract Law, on whose work the Study Group is building. …

… the results of the research conducted by the Study Group on a European Civil Code seek to advance the process of Europeanisation of private law. We have undertaken this endeavour on our own personal initiative and merely present the results of a pan-European research project.

---

[4] C von Bar, 'Foreword' in *Principles of European Law, Study Group on a European Civil Code, Commercial Agency, Franchise and Distribution Contracts (PEL CAFDC)* prepared by MW Hesselink, JW Rutgers, O Bueno Díaz, M Scotton, M Veldman (Munich: Sellier, 2006) vii.

Another group which was involved in writing principles was, for instance, the Research Group on the existing EC Private Law (the Acquis Group), which also no longer exists. Their aim is formulated in the Introduction to the Acquis Principles:[5]

Introduction to the Acquis Principles **3.3 (INT)**

The European Research Group on Existing EC Private Law was founded in 2002, as a successor to smaller networks founded in the 1990s, with the primary aim of formulating principles of existing European Community contract law. The short name, Acquis Group, confirms that these principles are formulated on the basis of the *acquis communautaire*, in particular Treaties, Regulations, and Directives, as applied and interpreted by the courts.

The UNIDROIT Principles of International Commercial Contracts (UNIDROIT PICC)[6] should also be mentioned. Their focus is beyond just the EU. Their aims are included in the Preamble:

UNIDROIT Principles, Preamble **3.4 (INT)**

These Principles set forth general rules for international commercial contracts.
  They shall be applied when the parties have agreed that their contract be governed by them.
  They may be applied when the parties have agreed that their contract be governed by general principles of law, the *lex mercatoria* or the like.
  They may be applied when the parties have not chosen any law to govern their contract.
  They may be used to interpret or supplement international uniform law instruments.
  They may be used to interpret or supplement domestic law.
  They may serve as a model for national and international legislators.

It will be seen that these purposes resemble those of the PECL, and indeed the two sets of principles are very similar in many ways, perhaps in part because a number of members of each group were also members of the other group. However, there are some significant differences of substance between the two sets of principles; we will note these where appropriate.

Upon the instruction of the European Commission, the Draft Common Frame of Reference was drafted primarily by academics. This set of rules also can be considered soft law and it will be discussed in Section 3.2.C.

---

[5] Research Group on the Existing EC Private Law (Acquis Group), *Principles of the Existing EC Contract Law (Acquis Principles) Contract I, Pre-contractual Obligations, Conclusion of Contract, Unfair Terms* (Munich: Sellier, 2007) XXIII.
[6] 4th edn, 2016.

3.2 THE INITIATIVES OF THE EUROPEAN UNION CONCERNING EUROPEAN CONTRACT LAW

3.2.A INTRODUCTION

Arguably the European Parliament started the discussion about a European Civil Code, by adopting a resolution in 1989 and another one in 1994. In both, the European Parliament called on the European Commission, the Council and the Member States to start working on a Code of European Private Law. It is not clear whether this was to be the same as a European Civil Code. In its 1989 Resolution, the European Parliament stated:[7]

European Parliament   **3.5 (EU)**

The European Parliament ...
    A. whereas the Community has to date harmonized many individual aspects of private law but [not] whole branches of it,
    B. whereas the legal coverage of individual subjects does not meet the needs and objectives of the single market without frontiers, particularly as formulated since the entry into force of the Single Act,
    C. whereas the most effective way of carrying out harmonization with a view to meeting the Community´s legal requirements in the area of private law is to unify major branches of that law,
    E. whereas unification can be carried out in branches of private law which are highly important for the development of the single market, such as contract law, without this, of course, exhausting the possibilities for unification,
    ...
    1. Requests a start to be made on the necessary preparatory work on drawing up a common European Code of Private Law, the Member States being invited, having deliberated the matter, to state whether they wish to be involved in the planned unification; ...

In 1994, the European Parliament repeated its call in another Resolution.[8] These resolutions did not have an immediate effect, but 'did help to keep the idea alive.'[9]

Despite these calls of the European Parliament, the European Commission did not start to work on a European Civil Code, but it started a discussion on the future of European contract law by the publication of the *Communication from the Commission to the Council and the European Parliament on European Contract Law* in July 2001.[10]

---

    [7] Resolution A2 157/89 of the European Parliament on action to bring into line the private law of the Member States, OJ C 158/1989, p 400.
    [8] Resolution A3 00329/94 on the harmonization of certain sectors of the private law of the Member States, OJ C 205/1994, p 518.
    [9] C Joerges, 'Europeanization as Process: Thoughts on the Europeanization of Private Law' (2005) 11 European Public Law 63, 66.
    [10] Communication on European contract law (n 1 above). Also see H-W Micklitz, J Stuyck and E Terryn (eds), *Ius Commune Casebooks on the Common Law of Europe: Consumer Law* (Oxford: Hart Publishing, 2010) 157, 165 ff.

Apparently the reason for this Communication was a conclusion reached during the European Council in Tampere in 1999.[11]

In its Communication of 2001, the European Commission asked interested parties whether differences between the national laws hindered the operation of the internal market, and sought views on what to do with contract law in Europe. It went on to offer four options:[12]

European Commission   **3.6 (EU)**

4.1. Option I: No EC Action; ...

4.2. Option II: Promote the development of common contract law principles leading to more convergence of national laws ...

4.3. Option III: Improve the quality of legislation already in place ...

4.4. Option IV: Adopt new comprehensive legislation at EC level ...

or, as it was phrased in the executive summary of the 2001 Communication,[13]

— To leave the solution of any identified problem to the market.

— To promote the development of non-binding common contract law principles, useful for contracting parties in drafting their contracts, national courts and arbitrators in their decisions and national legislators when drawing up legislative initiatives.

— To review and improve existing EC legislation in the area of contract law to make it more coherent or to adapt it to cover situations not foreseen at the time of adoption.

— To adopt a new instrument at EC level. Different elements could be combined: the nature of the act to be adopted (regulation, directive or recommendation), the relationship with national law (which could be replaced or co-exist), the question of mandatory rules within the set of applicable provisions and whether the contracting parties would choose to apply the EC instrument or whether the European rules apply automatically as a safety net of fallback provisions if the contracting parties have not agreed a specific solution.

It should be noted that the notion of contract which the European Commission used was broader than commonly employed in the legal systems of the EU Member States. It defined contract law as follows:[14]

European Commission   **3.7 (EU)**

12. Contract Law encompasses several areas of law. ... Contract law constitutes the principal body of law regulating cross-border transactions and some Community legislation regulating contract law already exists, although this legislation has taken a sector-by-sector approach.

---

[11] Presidency Conclusions, Tampere European Council, 15, 16 October 1999, SI(1999) 800, heading above nos. 28 ff; COM(2001) 398 final no. 4.

[12] Communication on European contract law (n 1 above) p 2.

[13] ibid.

[14] ibid, nos. 12, 13. See for a reaction of the European Parliament to the Communication of 2001: A5 0384/2001, European Parliament Resolution on the approximation of the civil and commercial law of the Member States (COM(2001)398 C5 0471/2001 2001/2187(COS)), [2002] OJ C140 E/538.

On the basis of its consultation, in its subsequent (second) *Communication, A More Coherent European Contract Law, An Action Plan* ('the Action Plan'), the European Commission referred to three different measures, which were (1) a 'Common Frame of Reference' (CFR), (2) 'Euro-wide general conditions' and (3) 'an optional instrument' or 'non-sector-specific instrument'.[15] The second measure, the Euro-wide general conditions, was subsequently abandoned by the European Commission in its First Annual Progress Report[16] and consequently will not be discussed.

Initially, the European Commission focused on the Common Frame of Reference (CFR). However, in the course of the CFR-process, the European Commission moved its focus from the CFR to a review of the Consumer Acquis[17] and subsequently to an optional instrument, which resulted in a proposal for a Regulation on a Common European Sales Law.[18]

The plans with regard to a review of the Consumer Acquis started off with a review of eight directives in 2007[19], which was subsequently reduced to a review of four directives in the European Commission's Proposal for a Directive of the European Parliament and the Council on consumer rights.[20] This would have required the full harmonisation of the rules on unfair contract terms and sales of goods to consumers, and partly because that would have resulted in the reduction of consumer's rights in some Member States, it ran into political opposition. The final directive, Directive 2011/83 on Consumer Rights, is restricted to a review of two directives: Directive 85/577/EEC on contracts negotiated away from business premises and Directive 97/7/EC on distance contracts on doorstep selling.[21] Since this chapter concerns principles and soft law in European contract law, the Consumer Rights Directive will not be discussed more elaborately.[22]

---

[15] Action Plan (n 1 above) p 1.

[16] First Annual Progress Report (n 1 above) p 10. However, the Council conclusions continued to refer to general conditions, and the statement by the then newly appointed Commissioner, Viviane Reding, to the Parliament also referred to providing 'standard terms and conditions' (7 January 2010, CM\800797EN. doc), as did the Commission's Communication Europe 2020, A strategy for smart, sustainable and inclusive growth, Brussels 3 March 2010, COM(2010), 2020 final, 21. It is not clear, though, what is meant by these references.

[17] Green Paper on the Review of the Consumer *Acquis* (presented by the European Commission), Brussels, 8 February 2007, COM(2006) 744 final; Commission Staff Working Paper, Report on the Outcome of the public consultation on the Green Paper on the Review of the Consumer *Acquis*; Preparatory Work for the Impact Assessment on the Review of the Consumer *Acquis*, DG Health and Consumer Protection, Analytical Report on the Green Paper on the Review of the Consumer *Acquis* submitted by the Consumer Policy Evaluation Consortium, 6 November 2007. See for a reaction of the Council: 2694th Council Meeting Competitiveness (Internal Market, Industry and Research), Brussels, 28–29 November 2005, 14155/05 (Presse 287). See H Beale, 'The European Commission's Common Frame of Reference Project' (2006) 2 ERCL 303; Micklitz et al (eds) (n 10 above) 20 ff, 165 ff.

[18] Proposal for a Regulation of the European Parliament and of the Council on a Common European Sales Law, COM(2011) 635 final, Brussels, 11.10.2011.

[19] Green Paper on the Review of the Consumer *Acquis* (n 17 above); Commission Staff Working Paper, Report on the Outcome of the public consultation on the Green Paper on the Review of the Consumer *Acquis* (n 17 above).

[20] Proposal for a Directive of the European Parliament of the Council on consumer rights, Brussels, 8 October 2008, COM(2008) 614 final.

[21] Directive 2011/83/EU of the European Parliament and of the Council of 25 October 2011 on consumer rights, amending Council Directive 93/13/EEC and Directive 1999/44/EC of the European Parliament and of the Council and repealing Council Directive 85/577/EEC and Directive 97/7/EC of the European Parliament and of the Council, [2011] OJ L304/64.

[22] See about the process of adopting Directive 2011/83: H-W Micklitz and N Reich, 'Crónica de una muerte anunciada: The Commission Proposal for a "Directive on Consumer Rights"' [2009] 46 CMLRev 471.

Hereafter, we will first focus on the CFR, which must be distinguished from the DCFR. The DCFR is discussed in Section 3.2.C and the optional instrument in Section 3.2.D.

3.2.B COMMON FRAME OF REFERENCE (CFR)

In its Action Plan the European Commission described the Common Frame of Reference as follows:[23]

European Commission   3.8 (EU)

59. A common frame of reference, establishing common principles and terminology in the area of European contract law is seen by the Commission as an important step towards the improvement of the contract law *acquis*. This common frame of reference will be a publicly accessible document which should help the Community institutions in ensuring greater coherence of existing and future *acquis* in the area of European contract law. This frame of reference should meet the needs and expectations of the economic operators in an internal market which envisages becoming the world's most dynamic economy.

...

.62 ... the Commission may use this common frame of reference in the area of contract law when the existing *acquis* is reviewed and new measures proposed. It should provide for best solutions in terms of common terminology and rules, ie the definition of fundamental concepts and abstract terms such as 'contract' or 'damage' and of the rules which apply, for example, in the case of the non-performance of contracts. In this context contractual freedom should be the guiding principle; restrictions should only be foreseen where this could be justified with good reasons.

It was often said that the aim was to provide a 'toolbox' for legislators.[24] In a subsequent Communication, *European Contract Law and the revision of the acquis: the way forward*,[25] (*'The Way Forward'*) the European Commission presented a possible structure and content of the CFR:

European Commission   3.9 (EU)

The structure envisaged for the CFR ... is that it would first set out common fundamental principles of contract law, including guidance on when exceptions to such fundamental principles could be required. Secondly, those fundamental principles would be supported by definitions of key concepts. Thirdly, these principles and definitions would be completed by model rules, forming the bulk of the CFR. A distinction between model rules applicable to contracts concluded between businesses or private persons and model

---

[23] Action Plan (n 1 above) p 11.

[24] See eg, Green Paper from the Commission on policy options for progress towards a European Contract Law for consumers and businesses, Brussels, July 2010, COM(2010) 348 final, p 7. On this Green Paper, see further below. On how the CFR might be used as a toolbox see H Beale, 'The Future of the Common Frame of Reference' (2007) 3 ERCL 257, 261–65.

[25] The Way Forward (n 1 above).

rules applicable to contracts concluded between a business and a consumer could be envisaged.[26]

In its Action Plan, the European Commission also explained how the CFR was going to be created and financed:[27]

European Commission   **3.10 (EU)**

66. As far as the organisational aspects are concerned, it should be emphasised that it is not the Commission's intention to 'reinvent the wheel' in terms of research activities. On the contrary, it is remarkable that never before in the area of European contract law has there been such a concentration of ongoing research activities. It is essential that these research activities are continued and exploited to the full. Therefore, the main goal is to combine and coordinate the ongoing research in order to place it within a common framework following several broad approaches.

67. Only where ongoing research does not cover all the areas concerned, would it be desirable that new research activities fill these gaps. Furthermore, the above-mentioned areas to be covered do not preclude ongoing research projects from going beyond these areas as they might have necessary links with other areas, like property law or tort law.

In *The Way Forward* it was stated:[28]

European Commission   **3.11 (EU)**

In order to ensure that the CFR is of high quality the Commission will finance three years of research under the Sixth Framework Programme for research and technological development. ...

By 2007, the researchers are expected to deliver a final report which will provide all the elements needed for the elaboration of a CFR by the Commission. It shall therefore include a draft CFR which the researchers believe to be fit for the purposes set out in the Action Plan.

...

Stakeholder participation to the process is essential... [F]our key criteria for successful participation were proposed and supported:

Diversity of legal traditions: account needs to be taken of the range of different legal traditions in the EU;

Balance of economic interests: account needs to be taken of the interests of a wide range of businesses in diverse economic sectors from SMEs to multi-nationals, as well as consumers as legal practitioners;

Commitment: stakeholders need to devote real resources to provide ongoing, substantive input;

Technical expertise: to provide detailed feedback and challenge to the academic researchers.'

...

Thus the European Commission identified, amongst others, two principal groups involved in the drafting of the CFR: the researchers and the representatives of parties which may

---

[26] The Way Forward (n 1 above) p 11; see also Annex I 'Possible Structure of the CFR', p 14.
[27] Action Plan (n 1 above) no. 59, p 12.
[28] The Way Forward (n 1 above) pp 9 ff. See also the Action Plan (n 1 above) nos. 63, 68.

be interested, also referred to as 'stakeholders'. The researchers who were to draft the CFR formed a 'Joint Network on European Private Law (CoPECL-Network)'.

The two main groups of researchers that worked on the actual drafting of the CFR were the Study Group on a European Civil Code and the Acquis Group.[29] An interim outline of the Draft Common Frame of Reference (DCFR) was presented to the European Commission by the CoPECL-Network in December 2007[30] and a final version was published in 2009.[31]

In a resolution of 2006 the European Parliament stressed the importance of the CFR, while the European Commission's main focus was on the revision of the consumer acquis:[32]

European Parliament   **3.12 (EU)**

3. Strongly supports an approach for a wider CFR on general contract law issues going beyond the consumer protection field;

4. Underlines that, besides the work on revision of the consumer *acquis*, the work on a wider CFR should go on; calls on the Commission to proceed, in parallel with the work on revision of the consumer *acquis*, with the project for a wider CFR; ...

The new European Commission, Commission Barosso II, responded to this call of the European Parliament. In its 'Action Plan implementing the Stockholm Programme' a legislative proposal on the Common Frame of Reference was planned for 2011.[33]

To achieve this, the European Commission set up an Expert Group on a Common Frame of Reference in the area of European contract law in April 2010.[34] Its task was:[35]

Commission Decision of 26 April 2010   **3.13 (EU)**

Article 2 Task

The group's task shall be to assist the Commission in the preparation of a proposal for a Common Frame of Reference in the area of European contract law, including consumer and business contract law, and in particular in:

(a) selecting those parts of the Draft Common Frame of Reference which are of direct or indirect relevance to contract law; and

---

[29] On the SGECC and the Acquis group, see pp 54–55 above. See also Micklitz et al (eds) (n 10 above) 158 ff and the *Projet de cadre commun de référence*, referred to in the list of Further Reading at the end of this chapter).

[30] Principles, Definitions and Model Rules of European Private Law, Draft Common Frame of Reference (DCFR), Interim Outline Edition, Prepared by the Study Group on a European Civil Code, Research Group on EC Private Law (Acquis Group), based in part on a revised version of C von Bar, et al (eds), *Principles of European Contract Law* (Munich: Sellier, 2008).

[31] For details see below, 3.2.C.

[32] European Parliament Resolution on European contract law, P6_TA (2006)0352.

[33] Communication from the Commission to the European Parliament, the Council, the European Economic and Social Committee and the Committee for the Regions, Delivering an area of freedom, security and justice for Europe's citizens, Action Plan Implementing the Stockholm Programme, Brussels 20 April 2010, COM(2010) 171 final, 25.

[34] Commission Decision of 26 April 2010 setting up the Expert Group on a Common Frame of Reference in the area of European Contract Law (2010/233/EU), OJ L105/2010, p 109.

[35] ibid.

(b) restructuring, revising and supplementing the selected contents of the Draft Common Frame of Reference, taking also into consideration other research work conducted in this area as well as the Union acquis.

However, a legislative proposal for a Common Frame of Reference was never drafted, because the European Commission changed its instruction. Rather than to help the European Commission in drafting a Common Frame of Reference in the area of contract law, it was to draft a text which could serve as an optional instrument.[36] The optional instrument will be discussed in Section 3.2.D.

3.2.C THE DRAFT COMMON FRAME OF REFERENCE (DCFR)

So far the CFR has been explained. However, a distinction must be made between an Academic CFR or Draft CFR (DCFR) on the one hand and a political CFR on the other. The European Commission stated with respect to the DCFR and the CFR:

European Commission   **3.14 (EU)**

Once we have real first findings from the CFR work and the researchers have delivered their draft CFR, the Commission, which means all involved Commissioners and their services, will need to select very carefully the parts which correspond to the common legislative objectives.

It is already clear that only a part of the research draft will correspond to these conditions. For example the parts dealing with unjust enrichment or benevolent intervention at the moment do not appear strictly speaking necessary for our policy-making purposes…

An interim outline of the Draft Common Frame of Reference (DCFR) was presented to the European Commission by the CoPECL-Network in December 2007.[37] A final outline edition of the DCFR was presented to the European Commission by the CoPECL-Network in the autumn of 2009.[38]

As to the content of the CFR, the document *The Way Forward* stated that it should contain 'principles, definitions and model rules'. In the Introduction to the interim outline of the DCFR the meaning of 'principles, definitions and model rules' in the DCFR is explained:[39]

---

[36] M Király, 'The Rise and Fall of Common European Sales Law' ELTE Law Journal 2015/2, 41.

[37] DCFR Interim Outline Edition (n 30 above).

[38] Principles, Definitions and Model Rules of European Private Law, Draft Common Frame of Reference (DCFR), Outline Edition, Prepared by the Study Group on a European Civil Code, Research Group on EC Private Law (Acquis Group), based in part on a revised version of C von Bar, et al (eds), *Principles of European Contract Law* (Munich: Sellier, 2009) (hereafter DCFR 2009). The full edition (which contains Comments and Comparative Notes, and consists of six volumes) was published by Sellier in the autumn of 2009.

[39] DCFR 2009 (n 38 above) no. 9.

Draft Common Frame of Reference **3.15 (INT)**

9. ... The DCFR contains 'principles, definitions and model rules'. The title of this book follows the scheme set out in the European Commission's communications ... and in our contract with the Commission. The notion of 'definitions' is reasonably clear. The notions of 'principles' and 'model rules' ... require some explanation.

10. ... The European Commission's communications concerning the CFR do not elaborate on the concept of 'principles'. The word is susceptible to different interpretations. It is sometimes used, in the present context, as a synonym for rules which do not have the force of law. This is how it appears to be used, ..., in the 'Principles of European Contract Law' (PECL) ... In this sense the DCFR could be said to consist of principles and definitions. ...

...

23. ... 'Definitions' have the function of suggestions for the development of a uniform European legal terminology. ...

24. ... The greatest part of the DCFR consists of 'model rules'. The adjective 'model' indicates that the rules are not put forward as having any normative force but are soft law rules of the kind contained in the Principles of European Contract Law and similar publications. ...

The table of contents of the model rules which are included in the DCFR is as follows:

Draft Common Frame of Reference **3.16 (INT)**

Book I: General provisions
Book II: Contracts and other juridical acts
    Chapter 1: General provisions
    Chapter 2: Non-discrimination
    Chapter 3: Marketing and pre-contractual duties
    Chapter 4: Formation
    Chapter 5: Right of withdrawal
    Chapter 6: Representation
    Chapter 7: Grounds of invalidity
    Chapter 8: Interpretation
    Chapter 9: Contents and effects of contracts
Book III: Obligations and corresponding rights
    Chapter 1: General
    Chapter 2: Performance
    Chapter 3: Remedies for non-performance
    Chapter 4: Plurality of debtors and creditors
    Chapter 5: Transfer of rights and obligations
        Section 1: Assignment of rights
        Section 2: Substitution of new debtor
        Section 3: Transfer of contractual position
    Chapter 6: Set-off and merger
    Chapter 7: Prescription

Book IV: Specific contracts and the rights and obligations arising from them
    Part A. Sales
    Part B. Lease of goods
    Part C. Services
    Part D. Mandate
    Part E. Commercial agency, franchise and distributorship
    Part F. Loans
    Part G. Personal security
Book V: Benevolent intervention in another's affairs
Book VI: Non-contractual liability arising out of damage caused to another
Book VII: Unjustified enrichment
Book VIII: Acquisition and loss of ownership of goods
Book IX Proprietary security rights in movable assets
Book X: Trusts
Annex: Definitions

From this table of contents it is obvious that the scope of the DCFR goes beyond contract law.

3.2.D THE OPTIONAL INSTRUMENT

In addition to the CFR, an optional instrument was mentioned as a measure in the European Commission's Action Plan. The European Commission wrote in its Action Plan:[40]

European Commission   **3.17 (EU)**

92. The Commission will examine whether non-sector-specific-measures such as an optional instrument may be required to solve problems in the area of European contract Law. It intends to launch a reflection on the opportuneness, the possible form, the contents and the legal basis for possible action of such measures. As to its form one could think of EU wide contract law rules in the form of a regulation or a recommendation, which would exist in parallel with, rather than instead of national contract laws. This new instrument would exist in all Community languages. It could either apply to all contracts, which concern cross-border transactions or only to those which parties decide to subject to it through a choice of law clause. The latter would give parties the greatest degree of contractual freedom. They would only choose the new instrument if it suited their economic or legal needs better than the national law which would have been determined by private international law rules as the law applicable to the contract.

93. It is the opinion of the Commission that contractual freedom should be one of the guiding principles of such a contract law instrument. Restrictions on this freedom should be envisaged where this could be justified for good reasons. Therefore it should be possible for the specific rules of such a new instrument, once it has been chosen by the contracting parties as the applicable law to their contract, to be adapted by the parties according to their needs.

---

[40] Action Plan (n 1 above) pp 15, 16.

94. Only a limited number of rules within this body of rules, for example rules aiming to protect the consumer, should be mandatory, if the new instrument applies to the contract. The reflection would have to include, *inter alia*, the question whether the optional instrument (if it were a binding instrument) could exclude the application of conflicting mandatory national provisions for areas which are covered thereby. Such an instrument would, accordingly, ensure freedom of contract in two ways: firstly, when the parties choose this instrument as the applicable law and secondly, as they are able, as a matter of principle, to modify the respective rules.

The basis for such an optional instrument would be the CFR:[41]

64. … Finally the common frame of reference should also form the basis for further reflection on an optional instrument in the area of European contract law.
…
95. It is clear that in reflecting on a non-sector-specific instrument, the Commission will take into account the common frame of reference. The content of the common frame of reference should then normally serve as a basis for the development of the new optional instrument. Whether the new instrument would cover the whole scope of the common frame of reference or only parts thereof, or whether it would cover only general contract law rules or also specific contracts, is at present left open.

In April 2007, the Justice and Home Affairs Council came to the conclusion that further reflection on an optional instrument was necessary:[42]

Justice and Home Affairs Council   **3.18 (EU)**

It was also felt that further reflection was necessary on the need for non-sector specific measures, for example an optional instrument in the area of European contract law. The Commission should pursue this reflection, in close collaboration with Member States and taking due account of the principle of contractual freedom …

The new European Commissioner, Barroso II, and in particular Viviane Reding, the Commissioner for Justice, Fundamental Rights and Citizenship favoured an optional instrument. Already in speeches in early 2010, she supported an optional instrument in contract law:[43]

Speech Viviane Reding, 24 February 2010   **3.19 (EU)**

Making the most of the Internal Market: Concrete EU Solutions to Cut Red Tape and to Boost the Economy

---

[41] ibid, pp 12, 16.

[42] 2794th Council Meeting, Justice and Home Affairs, Luxembourg, 19–20 April 2007, Council of the European Union, 8364/07 (Presse 77).

[43] Speech Viviane Reding 11 January 2010, Opening remarks at the European Parliament Hearing in the Legal Affairs Committee (JURI), Speech/10/; Speech Viviane Reding 24 February 2010, Making the most of the Internal Market: Concrete EU Solutions to Cut Red Tape and to Boost the Economy, Speech/10/42.

Business-to-consumer relations are complicated by 27 different regimes for contractual regimes. (…) The EU needs to do better. A possible solution is to have a 28th regime for contracts. Such a European Contract Law would exist in parallel to the national contract laws (…).

The European Commission set up an Expert Group on a Common Frame of Reference in the area of European contract law in April 2010.[44] However, during its work the European Commission changed the instruction of the Expert Group. Rather than to help the European Commission to draft a Common Frame of Reference in the area of contract law, it was to draft a text which could serve as an optional instrument.[45]

In July 2010 the European Commission issued the Green Paper on policy options for progress towards a European Contract Law for consumers and businesses, in which it asked what was the best way to proceed:[46]

European Commission   **3.20 (EU)**

An instrument of European Contract Law should respond to the problems of diverging contract laws identified above, without introducing additional burdens or complications for consumers or businesses. In addition it should ensure a high level of consumer protection. In the area it covers, the instrument should be comprehensive and self-standing, in the sense that references to national laws or international instruments should be as much as possible reduced. Several options have been identified, in respect of the legal nature, the scope of application and the material scope of the future instrument.

    Option 1: Publication of the results of the Expert Group
    Option 2: An official "toolbox" for the legislator
    Option 3: Commission Recommendation on European Contract Law
    Option 4: Regulation setting up an optional instrument of European Contract Law
    Option 5: Directive on European Contract Law
    Option 6: Regulation establishing a European Contract Law
    Option 7: Regulation establishing a European Civil Code

On 3rd May 2011 the European Commission published 'A Feasibility Study for a future instrument in European Contract Law' carried out by the Expert Group.[47] The European Commission used this Feasibility Study for a Proposal for a Regulation on a Common European Sales Law (CESL), which was published on 11th October 2011.[48]

The Proposal for a Regulation on CESL consists of three parts: an explanatory memorandum, a draft regulation and an annex which contains the substantive rules (CESL).

In the explanatory memorandum to the Proposal, the European Commission explained why a CESL was chosen:[49]

---

[44] Commission Decision of 26 April 2010 (n 34 above).
[45] M Király (n 36 above) 41. Mrs Reding said to the Expert Group that the DCFR provided a sufficient 'toolbox'.
[46] Green Paper from the Commission on policy options for progress towards a European Contract Law for consumers and businesses, Brussels, July 2010, COM(2010) 348 final, p 7.
[47] The Feasibility Study is no longer available on the website of the European Commission.
[48] See n 18 above. The evolution of the articles from the PECL through the DCFR to the CESL is analyzed in detail in N Jansen and R Zimmermann (eds), *Commentaries on European Contract Laws* (Oxford University Press, 2018).
[49] Proposal for a Regulation on a Common European Sales Law (CESL) (n 18 above) p 10.

Proposal for a Regulation on a Common European Sales Law   **3.21 (EU)**

A non-binding instrument such as a toolbox for the EU legislator or a Recommendation addressed to Member States would not achieve the objective to improve the establishment and functioning of the internal market. A Directive or a Regulation replacing national laws with a non-optional European contract law would go too far as it would require domestic traders who do not want to sell across borders to bear costs which are not outweighed by the cost savings that only occur when cross-border transactions take place. In addition, a Directive setting up minimum standards of a non-optional European contract law would not be appropriate since it would not achieve the level of legal certainty and the necessary degree of uniformity to decrease the transaction costs.

The provisions of the Regulation determine when and how CESL can be chosen as the applicable law to a contract. In order to make a choice for CESL, the conflict rules which determine which legal system governs an international contract, must refer a contract to a legal system of an EU Member State. In that case, parties have the possibility of choosing CESL rather than the national legal system to govern their contract, provided all the other criteria, included in the provisions of the Regulation, are met:[50]

Proposal for a Regulation on a Common European Sales Law   **3.22 (EU)**

Article 3: Optional nature of the Common European Sales Law
    The parties may agree that the Common European Sales Law governs their cross-border contracts for the sale of goods, for the supply of digital content and for the provision of related services within the territorial, material and personal scope as set out in Articles 4 to 7.

Article 4: Cross-border contracts
    1. The Common European Sales Law may be used for cross-border contracts.
    2. For the purposes of this Regulation, a contract between traders is a cross-border contract if the parties have their habitual residence in different countries of which at least one is a Member State.
    3. For the purposes of this Regulation, a contract between a trader and a consumer is a cross-border contract if:
        (a) either the address indicated by the consumer, the delivery address for goods or the billing address are located in a country other than the country of the trader's habitual residence; and
        (b) at least one of these countries is a Member State.
    4. ...
    5. ...
    6. ...

Article 5: Contracts for which the Common European Sales Law can be used
    The Common European Sales Law may be used for:
        (a) sales contracts;
        (b) contracts for the supply of digital content whether or not supplied on a tangible medium which can be stored, processed or accessed, and re-used by the user,

---

[50] Proposal for a Regulation on a Common European Sales Law (CESL) (n 18 above).

irrespective of whether the digital content is supplied in exchange for the payment of a price.

(c) related service contracts, irrespective of whether a separate price was agreed for the related service.

Article 6: Exclusion of mixed-purpose contracts and contracts linked to a consumer credit. …

Article 7: Parties to the contract

1. The Common European Sales Law may be used only if the seller of goods or the supplier of digital content is a trader. Where all the parties to a contract are traders, the Common European Sales Law may be used if at least one of those parties is a small or medium-sized enterprise ('SME').

2. For the purposes of this Regulation, an SME is a trader which

(a) employs fewer than 250 persons; and

(b) has an annual turnover not exceeding EUR 50 million or an annual balance sheet total not exceeding EUR 43 million, or, for an SME which has its habitual residence in a Member State whose currency is not the euro or in a third country, the equivalent amounts in the currency of that Member State or third country.

Article 8: Agreement on the use of the Common European Sales Law

1. The use of the Common European Sales Law requires an agreement of the parties to that effect. The existence of such an agreement and its validity shall be determined on the basis of paragraphs 2 and 3 of this Article and Article 9, as well as the relevant provisions in the Common European Sales Law.

2. In relations between a trader and a consumer the agreement on the use of the Common European Sales Law shall be valid only if the consumer's consent is given by an explicit statement which is separate from the statement indicating the agreement to conclude a contract. The trader shall provide the consumer with a confirmation of that agreement on a durable medium.

3. In relations between a trader and a consumer the Common European Sales Law may not be chosen partially, but only in its entirety.

…

The Common European Sales Law itself is contained in the Annex to the Regulation:

Annex 1 Common European Sales Law

Part I: Introductory provisions

 Chapter 1: General principles and application

  Section 1: General principles

  Section 2: Application

Part II: Making a binding contract

 Chapter 2: Pre-contractual information

  Section 1: Pre-contractual information to be given by a trader dealing with a consumer

  Section 2: Pre-contractual information to be given by a trader dealing with another trader

  Section 3: Contracts to be concluded by electronic means

  Section 4: Duty to ensure that information supplied is correct

  Section 5: Remedies for breach of information duties

 Chapter 3: Conclusion of contract

Section 2: Interest on late payments: general provisions
Section 3: Late payments by traders
Part VII: Restitution
  Chapter 17: Restitution
Part VIII: Prescription
  Chapter 18: Prescription
    Section 1: General provision
    Section 2: Periods of prescription and their commencement
    Section 3: Extension of periods of prescription
    Section 4: Renewal of periods of prescription
    Section 5: Effects of prescription
    Section 6: Modification by agreement

It should be noted that CESL does not deal with all issues of a sales contract.[51] In those instances the applicable law of a Member State will govern those issues.[52]

The European Parliament adopted this proposal with a number of amendments.[53] The main amendment concerned its scope. The Regulation would only apply to distance contracts, in particular contracts which are concluded through internet.

Despite the European Parliament's adoption, the proposal met severe criticism from different angles. The Council did not adopt the proposal. It was too controversial for many Member States. The Commission Work Programme 2015, 'A New Start', listed the proposal for a Common European Sales Law as one of the proposals that would be withdrawn.[54] The new European Commission ('the Juncker Commission') set new priorities for its policy, one of which is the creation of a digital single market as will be discussed in the next section.

Although it was withdrawn, the CESL is of interest as the most recent iteration of a 'European' contract law, at least on the topics that it covered.

3.2.E EUROPEAN CONTRACT LAW AND A DIGITAL SINGLE MARKET

Communication A Digital Single Market Strategy for Europe[55]   **3.23 (EU)**

A Digital Single Market is one in which the free movement of goods, persons, services and capital is ensured and where individuals and businesses can seamlessly access and exercise online activities under conditions of fair competition, and a high level of consumer and personal data protection, irrespective of their nationality or place of residence. Achieving

---

[51] Proposal for a Regulation on a Common European Sales Law (CESL) (n 18 above) p 6. Eg, it did not deal with precontractual liability nor with contracts that were illegal or otherwise contrary to public policy.

[52] Proposal for a Regulation on a Common European Sales Law (CESL) (n 18 above) p 8.

[53] European Parliament legislative Resolution of 26 February 2014 on the proposal for a Regulation of the European Parliament and of the Council on a Common European Sales Law (COM(2011)0635—C7-0329/2011— 2011/0284(COD)), P7_TA(2014)0159.

[54] Annex II: List of withdrawals or modifications of pending proposals, Annex to the Communication from the Commission, Commission Work Programme 2015, A New Start, Strasbourg, 16.12.2014 COM(2014) 910 final, no. 60, p 12.

[55] Communication from the Commission, A Digital Single Market Strategy for Europe, Brussels, 6.5.2015, COM(2015) 192 final, pp 3 ff.

a Digital Single Market will ensure that Europe maintains its position as a world leader in the digital economy, helping European companies to grow globally.

(…)

The Digital Single Market Strategy will be built on three pillars:

Better access for consumers and businesses to online goods and services across Europe—this requires the rapid removal of key differences between the online and offline worlds to break down barriers to cross-border online activity (…).

2. BETTER ONLINE ACCESS FOR CONSUMERS AND BUSINESSES ACROSS EUROPE

(…)

2.1. Cross-border e-commerce rules that consumers and business can trust

One of the reasons why consumers and smaller companies do not engage more in cross-border e-commerce is because the rules that apply to these transactions can be complex, unclear and may differ between Member States. Having 28 different national consumer protection and contract laws discourages companies from cross-border trading and prevents consumers from benefitting from the most competitive offers and from the full range of online offers.

In a Single Market, companies should be able to manage their sales under a common set of rules. Some aspects of consumer and contract law have already been fully harmonised for online sales (…). However, other aspects of the contract (…) are only subject to EU rules providing minimum harmonisation, with the possibility for Member States to go further. When it comes to remedies for defective digital content purchased online (such as e-books) no specific EU rules exist at all, and only few national ones.

(…)

The Commission will make an amended proposal before the end of 2015 (i) covering harmonised EU rules for online purchases of digital content, and (ii) allowing traders to rely on their national laws based on a focused set of key mandatory EU contractual rights for domestic and cross-border online sales of tangible goods.

In 2015, the European Commission published proposals for two directives which are the Proposal for a Directive on certain aspects concerning contracts for the online and other distance sales of goods[56] and a Proposal for a Directive on certain aspects concerning contracts for the supply of digital content.[57] Both are limited to consumer contracts, and both would require full harmonisation of the laws of the Member States. Following the conclusions of the Dutch presidency in 2016, priority was given to the proposal for a Directive on digital content.[58] At the time of writing it seems likely that this Directive will be adopted, subject to amendments to be agreed between the Parliament and the Council. The Directive on online sales, in contrast, ran into opposition, partly because of its call for full harmonisation (which would again result in a reduction of consumer protection in some Member States, whereas few Member States have specific legislation on the supply of digital content, so they would have 'little to lose'), and partly because it would mean traders have to deal with different regimes, one for online and distance

---

[56] Proposal for a Directive of the European Parliament and of the Council on certain aspects concerning contracts for the online and other distance sales of goods, Brussels, 9.12.2015, COM(2015) 635 final.

[57] Proposal for a Directive of the European Parliament and of the Council on certain aspects concerning contracts for the supply of digital content, Brussels 9.12.2015, COM(2015) 634 final. See above, ch 1.2.A.2.

[58] Outcome of the Council Meeting, 3546th Council meeting Justice and Home Affairs Luxembourg, 8, 9 June 2017, 10136/17.

sales and another for other sales (which would remain covered by the existing Directive on consumer sales).[59] The Commission has responded by amending the proposal on online sales so that it would require full harmonisation of the law on all sales of goods to consumers.[60]

3.2.F EUROPEANISATION OF CONTRACT LAW, A CONTROVERSIAL ENTERPRISE

The plans of the European Commission with respect to European contract law were welcomed by some but criticised by others. In what follows we discuss some of this criticism, which differs in nature. Although the European Commission stressed in its Communications that it is not its intention to establish a European Civil Code, some authors conceived this to be the plan of the Commission. They opposed a European Civil Code, since they considered the cultural differences between the different Member States too large. Others criticised the way the European Commission has presented the project. Others again had a different opinion.

One of the fiercest opponents of a European Civil Code was Pierre Legrand, who argued:[61]

— There is an array of reasons, largely historical and psychological, explaining why a legal community is (or is not) attracted to a particular genre of cultural product. It is clear, however, that the specific cultural form that is retained—such as a civil code—has significant connections with the wider social order within which a legal community operates …
— The civil law and common law must, therefore, be seen as two discrete epistemological formations … These epistemologies are conditioned by, and constantly reinforced in their turn, deeply embedded worldviews within the societies in which they have developed to the point where there can be found … a pattern of congruence between a legal culture and a culture tout court.[62]
— The point of a European Civil Code, then, becomes the taming of international tensions or, to put it more bluntly, the attenuation of the risk of war. The desire to assimilate the common law tradition is thus linked, for civilians, to the fact that nationalist forms, which are associated with a territory, terrify.[63]
— To promote the adoption of a European Civil Code is arrogant, for it suggests that the civilian representation of the world is more worthy than its alternative and is, in short, so superior that it deserves to supersede the common law's worldview.[64]

---

[59] Directive 1999/44/EG of the European Parliament and of the Council of 25 May 1999 on certain aspects of the sale of consumer goods and associated guarantees, OJ L 171/1999.

[60] Amended proposal of 31 October 2018 for a Directive of the European Parliament and of the Council on certain aspects concerning contracts for the online and other distance sales of goods, amending Regulation (EC) No. 2006/2004 of the European Parliament and of the Council and Directive 2009/22/EC of the European Parliament and of the Council and repealing Directive 1999/44/EC of the European Parliament and of the Council, COM(2017) 637 final.

[61] P Legrand, 'Against a European Civil Code' (1997) 60 MLR 44.

[62] ibid, 48.

[63] ibid, 53.

[64] ibid, 56.

— A European Civil Code reveals a utopian enterprise, for it suggests that legal cultures which purport to give normative strength to forms of behaviour developed in historically different contexts can be unified.[65]

French authors also expressed themselves against a European Civil Code:[66]

... the Code civil is a monument of French law, one of our primordial reference points ... The first question is linguistic (and cultural)... It is impossible to think of the French code, as it is drafted, being in anything but French, our unique tongue... Our language is our mother. There is no European language. French law can only be the daughter of the French language ... Another reason goes to the structure of our law. We hear the phrases 'European Civil Code' and 'European Contract Code' used indifferently. Does this mean that a Contract Code would be a title within this so-called Civil Code? In France, the Code civil is a unity. ...

Another argument made against a European Civil Code or a codification of contract law on a larger scale was that it does not leave any room for new experiments:[67]

A general European civil code, contract code or consumer code—at least if it would comprise not merely a minimal code—would probably be too static an instrument to allow sufficient space for a welfarist,[68] more scattered and decionistic, improvement of the rules. Welfarism requires a constantly learning law. This view rather speaks for a process of Europeanisation through a free movement of legal ideas and doctrines, across the borders, as well as between the national and EC levels, than for a once and for all codification of broad areas of private law.

The Study Group on Social Justice in European Private Law was rather critical of the approach which the European Commission adopted in its Action Plan. In 'Social Justice in European Contract Law: a Manifesto', the group wrote:[69]

The Action Plan for the future of European contract law sets an agenda concerned with vindicating the free market, and never mentions broader issues concerning social justice and European identity. The Action Plan is presented as a series of technical measures to deal with some technical problems, namely subtle barriers to trade caused by diversity in national private law systems. It is almost completely silent about the important political choices to be made with respect to social justice and European identity. These are issues that the Commission does not want to raise, because they reveal that the agenda of European Contract law concerns political questions, which stray far beyond the details of measures concerned with negative integration.

The DCFR was also subjected to fierce criticism. A group of German scholars came to the following conclusion:[70]

It is certainly an immense achievement for the participating academic groups to have produced such a comprehensive body of rules in such a short time. None the less, the verdict on the

---

[65] ibid, 60.

[66] eg G Cornu, 'Un Code civil n'est pas un instrument communautaire' D 2002, 351.

[67] T Wilhelmsson, 'Varieties of Welfarism in European Contract Law' (2004) 10 ELJ 712, 733.

[68] Wilhelmsson describes welfarism as 'reflect[ing] the intrusion of the values of the welfare state into the market oriented structure of traditional contract law' (n 67 above) 713.

[69] The Study Group on Social Justice in European Private Law, 'Social Justice in European Contract Law: a Manifesto' (2004) 10 ELJ 661, 662.

[70] H Eidenmüller, F Faust, HC Grigoleit, N Jansen, G Wagner and R Zimmermann, 'The Common Frame of Reference for European Private Law—Policy Choices and Codification Problems' (2008) OJLS 659, 706–07.

published Draft must be negative. The text suffers from a great number of serious shortcomings. These include unresolved or unconvincing policy decisions as much as ill-adjusted and inconsistent sets of rules. Especially alarming is the fact that the Draft paves the way for a massive erosion of private autonomy which goes far beyond existing tendencies to 'materialize' private law. Good faith and fair dealing are no longer merely taken to guide the interpretation of contracts and the process of determining issues which the contracting parties have failed to regulate. Rather, the content of what the parties to a contract may agree upon appears to be placed under the general proviso of good faith, fair dealing and general usage. Moreover, to a considerable extent, contract law is no longer conceived as providing rules which the parties may or may not choose to accept as suitable for their transaction, but as regulatory *ius cogens*.

FURTHER READING

Association Henri Capitant (ed), *The integration of European business law: Acquis and Outlook* (Paris: LGDJ, 2016).

von Bar, C, 'Coverage and Structure of the Academic Common Frame of Reference' (2007) 3 European Review of Contract Law 350–61.

Basedow, J, 'Codification of Private Law in the European Union: the making of a Hybrid' (2001) 9 European Review of Private Law 35–49.

Beale, H, 'The European Commission's Common Frame of Reference Project: a progress report' (2006) 2 European Review of Contract Law 303–14.

Common Market Law Review 50 (2013) issue 1/2 [a special issue concerning various aspects of the Commission's Proposal for a Regulation on a Common European Sales Law (CESL) and mostly from a law-and-economics perspective].

Dannemann, G and Vogenauer, S (eds), *The Common European Sales Law in Context: Interactions with English and German Law* (Oxford University Press, 2013).

Eidenmüller, H et al, 'Der Gemeinsame Referenzrahmen für das Europäische Privatrecht' (2008) 63 Juristenzeitung 529–50, as translated in 'The Common Frame of Reference for European Private Law—Policy Choices and Codification Problems' (2008) 28 Oxford Journal of Legal Studies 659–708.

Eidenmüller, H et al, 'Der Vorschlag für eine Verordnung über ein Gemeinsames Europäisches Kaufrecht—Defizite der neuesten Textstufe des Europäischen Vertragsrechts' (2012) 67 Juristenzeitung 269–89, as translated in 'The Proposal for a Regulation on a Common European Sales Law: Deficits of the Most Recent Textual Layer of European Contract Law' (2012) 16 Edinburgh Law Review 301–57.

Fauvarque-Cosson, B, 'The Need for Codified Guiding Principles and Model Rules in European Contract Law' in R Brownsword, H-W Micklitz, L Niglia and S Weatherill (eds), *The Foundations of European Private Law* (Oxford: Hart Publishing, 2011).

Grundmann, S, 'The Structure of the DCFR—Which Approach for Today's Contract Law?' (2008) 4 European Review of Contract Law 225–47.

Hartkamp, AS et al, *Towards a European Civil Code* (4th edn, Dordrecht: Kluwer International, 2011).

Jansen, N and Zimmermann, R (eds), *Commentaries on European Contract Laws* (Oxford University Press, 2018).

Király, M, 'The Rise and Fall of Common European Sales Law' (2015) ELTE Law Journal 31–42.

Lando, O, 'The Structure and the Legal Values of the Common Frame of Reference (CFR)' (2007) 3 European Review of Contract Law 245–66.

Projet de cadre commun de référence, Terminologie contractuelle commune 2008; Projet de cadre commun de référence, Principes contractuels communs, Association H Capitant et Société de législation comparée (eds) (Paris: Société de législation comparée, 2008), as partly translated in European Contract Law Materials for a Common Frame of Reference: Terminology, Guiding Principles, Model Rules, Fauvarque-Cosson, B and Mazeaud, D (eds), Association H Capitant et Société de législation comparée (Munich: Sellier, 2008).

Schmidt-Kessel, M (ed), *Ein einheitliches europäisches Kaufrecht? Eine Analyse des Vorschlags der Kommission* (Munich: Sellier, 2012).

Schulte-Nölke, H, 'EC Law on the Formation of Contract—from the Common Frame of Reference to the Blue Button' (2007) 3 European Review of Contract Law 332–49.

Schulte-Nölke, H et al (eds), *Der Entwurf für ein optionales europäisches Kaufrecht* (Munich: Sellier, 2012).

Schulze, R (ed), *Common Frame of Reference and Existing EC Contract Law* (Munich: Sellier, 2008).

Schulze, R and Stuyck, J (eds), *Towards a European Contract Law* (Munich: Sellier, 2011).

The Study Group on Social Justice in European Private Law, 'Social Justice in European Contract Law: a Manifesto' (2004) 10 European Law Journal 653–74.

Vogenauer, S, 'Common Frame of Reference and UNIDROIT Principles of International Commercial Contracts: Coexistence, Competition or Overkill of Soft Law' (2010) 6 European Review of Contract Law 143–83.

Vogenauer, S (ed), *Commentary on the UNIDROIT Principles of International Commercial Contracts (PICC)* (2nd edn, Oxford University Press, 2015).

Whittaker, S, 'The 'Draft Common Frame of Reference', an Assessment', commissioned by the Ministry of Justice (UK, November 2008).

CHAPTER 4
NATIONAL CONTRACT LAWS IN A EUROPEAN CONTEXT

4.1 THE CIVIL AND COMMON LAW TRADITIONS

As has been seen in Chapters 1–3 of this book, although the mass of international treaties and European legislation is growing, each nation State has its own contract law. The idea that this should be changed has gained considerable ground, particularly in Europe where, during the 1990s, leading academics paved the way for a European private law, even if only a minority of them had in mind, as a final goal, the enactment of a European Civil Code or even the adoption of a Common Frame of Reference. Many historians and comparatists have been deeply involved in the resurgence of a *ius commune* for Europe.[1] This has raised new interest in European legal history.[2] After highlighting some of the main differences but also resemblances between the civil and common law traditions, this chapter examines the place and sources of national contract laws.

The civil law tradition originates in the rediscovery of ancient Roman law in Italy, in the late eleventh century. The beginning of a European legal science was based on the study of the compilation of Roman law promulgated by the Byzantine Emperor Justinian (529–65), the *Corpus Iuris Civilis*, and on canon law texts. This European study of both Roman and canon law is known as the *ius commune*. It provided a common core upon which national legal systems and national codifiers were able to build. If modern proponents of a European contract law refer to a *ius commune* this reflects an intention to build on the achievements of this period which continued even after the first codifications and the corresponding 'nationalisation' of the European private laws. After examining the main sources of the civil and common law traditions, this section considers the place of contract law, within a wider category called 'the law of obligations'.

---

[1] See, eg, R Zimmermann, *The Law of Obligations: Roman Foundations of the Civilian Tradition* (Oxford University Press, 1996).

[2] R Lesaffer, *European Legal History: A Cultural and Political Perspective* (Cambridge University Press, 2009).

4.1.A SOURCES

Civil law was received in continental Europe as a *ius commune*, ie as a 'common law' applicable either by default or to a varying extent in substitution for the local law. Quite naturally, English lawyers saw this phenomenon as the hallmark of the civil law/ continental systems. As Barry Nicholas explained:

> French and German law belong to the Civil law because their methods of thought, their attitudes to law and its sources, derive from the centuries in which the *ius commune*, Romanistic but not Roman, was created out of the materials in the *Corpus Iuris*.[3]

Barry Nicholas further showed how these methods and attitudes are different from those of the English common law and summarises the major divide in those terms:

> The heart of the matter is that the *ius commune* is a law of the book, elaborated in universities, whereas the Common law is a law of the case, created by the courts … In short, for the common law, the beginning is the case, whereas for the *ius commune* the beginning is the book.[4]

The name, civil law, has been criticised, especially by civil lawyers who point out that 'it refers to only one element in the tradition which unites those systems'[5] and the expression 'continental law' is often used to designate that family of legal systems to which the name of civil law was traditionally attached. This having been said, the legal significance of Roman law has lost much of its importance due to centuries of intense legal activity, through codification, judicial decisions and legal doctrine. Yet civil law systems still share fundamental common aspects, among which is their civil codes.

4.1.A.1 CIVIL CODES OR CASES?

French, German and Dutch law, as well as many others not examined in this book, belong to the continental law or civil law tradition. In a vast majority of modern civil law systems, private law is based on general rules of law contained in a civil code. This is, for example, the Code civil in France, Belgium, Luxembourg, Italy (Codice civile), the Bürgerliches Gesetzbuch in Germany and the Burgerlijk Wetbook in the Netherlands. In civil law countries:

> law is primarily and characteristically a body of rules enacted by the state, to be found in the codes, and, in ever-increasing measure, in legislation supplementary to the codes.[6]

The different approaches of civil and common law legal systems towards codification (defined as legislation drafted as part of a larger whole) is one of the main differences between them. Codification, when conceived and structured as a whole, takes a global view of all the interests involved. It regulates matters in general, for reasons of legal certainty and consistency. This, however, does not preclude rules focusing on the protection of specific interests from being incorporated in the larger whole.

---

[3] B Nicholas, *The French Law of Contract* (2nd edn, Oxford: Clarendon Press, 1992) 2.
[4] Nicholas (n 3 above) 4; see also J Cartwright, *Contract Law: An Introduction to the English Law of Contract for the Civil Lawyer* (3rd edn, Oxford: Hart Publishing, 2016) 15–16.
[5] Nicholas (n 3 above) 1.
[6] Nicholas (n 3 above) 5.

Contract law codifications provide for a set of rules for the conduct of life and business. Most of these rules are not mandatory. This means that the parties may deviate from the codified model that is offered to them, in spite of it being carved in a civil code. It happens, however, that some contract rules are mandatory. This characteristic may be provided for in the rule itself (for instance, with an expression such as 'the parties may not otherwise agree') or, subsequently, a court may decide that a provision is mandatory. A court will do so according to the content of the provision and also based on the context of the case. This illustrates how even in civil law countries, establishing the law of contract is an ongoing process in which judges—and also commentators[7]—play a part.

By contrast, common lawyers have no Civil code. They start from the case and the facts; they then look into the various sources of law (legislation or case law) to find the proper solution. In the absence of contrary binding precedent, the courts create the law. The courts do not have the power to remove or amend statutes, but they can interpret them. While the courts usually interpret statutory law restrictively, they sometimes derive a general principle from earlier cases.[8]

4.1.A.2 THE GROWING IMPORTANCE OF CASE LAW IN CIVIL LAW COUNTRIES

Case law develops in civil law countries, incrementally, when problems come to light in respect of the pleas submitted. Although case law has no precedential effect, at least as a matter of principle, some cases are considered as settling the law.

The French Court of cassation ('Cour de cassation') thus plays a vital role in the development of French contract law. When a code or a statute does not cover a specific aspect of a case, the Cour de cassation may either apply existing texts to the situation that has not been foreseen by the legislator or refer to general principles (such as for example the *fraus omnia corrumpit* (fraud negates everything) rule, the theory of unjust enrichment, etc) insofar as they do not conflict with a statutory provision. Besides, when the interpretation of the wording of a legal provision (article of the Code civil or provision of an Act) has become questionable due to various developments, the Cour de cassation may deviate from it. The wide range of questions submitted to the Cour de cassation enables it to provide a balanced and consistent reply to the majority of potential questions raised concerning the interpretation of the law. Many of the new solutions adopted by the courts have been codified in 2016: for example, the new provisions on 'stipulation on behalf of a third party' (contracts for the benefit of a third party) were derived from the interpretation by the courts of former Article 1121 Cciv.[9]

German courts have also been strongly involved in the task of making the German Civil Code workable throughout the century following its enactment in 1900. By interpreting it, sometimes even against its letter, and by filling gaps, they created a vast body of case law. Some of these rules were codified in the major reform of the Code in 2001.

---

[7] C Pérès, 'Mandatory and Non-mandatory Rules in the New Law of Contract' in J Cartwright and S Whittaker (eds), *The Code Napoléon Rewritten: French Contract Law after the 2016 Reforms* (Oxford: Hart Publishing, 2017) 167.

[8] Cartwright (n 4 above) 19.

[9] See below, ch 31.

Throughout this book we will encounter many examples, such as the various mechanisms for the policing of unfair standard terms and the judge-made doctrines of precontractual liability (*culpa in contrahendo*), 'contracts with protective effect for third parties' and the 'collapse of the basis of the transaction' (*Wegfall der Geschäftsgrundlage*).[10]

Both French and German lawyers today generally acknowledge that case law, while not being legally binding, is a '*de facto* source of law' to the extent that the lower courts will normally follow the decisions of the higher courts.

Supreme courts develop the law by adapting it to the political, social and economic context. In civil law countries, they are not bound by their own precedents and are free to give another meaning to the law over time in line with changes in society. They are also expected to fill a legal vacuum in substantive law. In France, for instance, Article 4 of the Code civil prohibits a court from declining to hear a case on the grounds that a code or statute does not cover a specific aspect of the case, or that it is ambiguous or inadequate. As in common law countries, developments in case law are made either by way of distinctions from earlier case law or by a precedent being overturned. In all systems, the need to adapt the law to changes in society stands in opposition to the need of coherence and stability, and judges are concerned with laying down a stable case law which serves as a yardstick for the lower courts, the litigants and their counsel. It is therefore only after careful consideration that a precedent is overturned (insofar as it calls into question the practices which it condemns, it has retroactive effect).

There are major differences between France, Germany and the UK concerning the way judgments are rendered. The length of decisions varies considerably from one country to another, the longest being those of common law courts.

The most difficult cases to read, for a non-native lawyer, are probably those of the French Cour de cassation. This is due to their brevity, which is itself permitted by a very specific technique of cassation. In order to understand a French case of the Cour de cassation, the reader should be aware of how the Court's interpretation of a rule of law is laid down throughout the replies given to the pleas submitted and in particular to pleas which allege a breach of law. There is indeed a *technique de cassation* which is characteristic of French law and can only be understood in light of the specific mission of the Cour de cassation and of its organisation. This book reproduces extracts of cases or entire cases of various court decisions and explains them but it does not give the keys for understanding the technique of cassation.[11]

While the possibility to publish huge quantities of court decisions online has increased the visibility and importance of judge-made law, the availability of vast repositories hampers easy access to those decisions that reflect important legal developments. As a consequence, the utility of legal doctrine cannot be but increasing as these developments need to be identified and ascertained.

---

[10] See below, ch 13.

[11] There is a recent move towards a 'democratisation' of the Cour de cassation's decisions which have become more explicit and longer. Explanation and details on this new trend can be found on the Cour de cassation's official website: www.courdecassation.fr. An example of this in contract law is: Cass mixte 24 February 2017, no. 15-20411. See also, C Jamin, 'Juger et motiver, Introduction comparative à la question du contrôle de proportionnalité en matière de droits fondamentaux' RTD civ 2015, 263.

4.1.B THE LAW OF CONTRACT AS PART OF THE LAW OF OBLIGATIONS

The concept of contract under English law is not precisely the same as in Germany or France, as we will see in Chapter 5 of this book.[12] Contract law is studied separately in England, whereas in the two other countries it forms part of the study of the law of obligations. The reference to the law of obligations is rare in England, although not totally absent: 'English law is thus concerned with contracts as a source of obligations. The basic principle which the law of contract seeks to enforce is that a person who makes a promise to another ought to keep this promise'.[13] Interestingly, Lord Diplock's statement refers only to contractual obligations.

English contract law has developed on the basis of the means afforded to the disappointed creditor. English lawyers therefore tend to think in terms of, 'Where there is a remedy, there is a right'.[14] There are few attempts to construct a logical and coherent contract law theory in English law, as can be seen from the 23 chapters of the leading text book, *Treitel on the Law of Contract*, which discuss the various doctrines of contract law without a major attempt at further systematisation. In the US reference is even made to 'contracts' in the plural as if there were no single uniform concept.[15]

4.2 THE PLACE AND SOURCES OF NATIONAL CONTRACT LAWS

Where is contract law to be found? For each of the laws covered in this book, the reply throws light on the foundations of those laws.

The differences of methods and perceptions that constitute the main divide between common and civil law jurisdictions have been reinforced by the wave of national recodifications of the general law of contract that took place within various civil codes, all over continental Europe (as will be seen further in this chapter, German contract law was the subject of a major revision in 2002 and French contract law was recodified in 2016).

4.2.A FRENCH LAW (CIVIL CODE, 2016 AND 2018 REFORMS)

The general principles of contract are essentially contained in the Code civil, but this is supplemented by the rules on consumer contracts in the Consumer Code (Code de consommation),[16] by certain rules from the Code de commerce and by a number of other pieces of specific legislation.

---

[12] See below, p 93–120.

[13] See Lord Diplock in *Moschi v Lep Air Services Ltd* [1973] AC 331 (reproduced in the second edition of this book, 3.3 (EN)).

[14] See below, p 103.

[15] See the Restatement (Second) of the Law of Contracts, published by the American Law Institute in 1981 and EA Farnsworth, *Contracts* (4th edn, New York: Aspen Law & Business, 2004). Compare the English practitioners' work, *Chitty on Contracts*, vol I, *The General Part*, and vol II, *Specific Contracts*, 33rd edn by H Beale (gen ed) (London: Sweet & Maxwell/Thomson Reuters, 2018).

[16] This is a major difference with German law which has inserted the consumer acquis within the BGB.

Book III of the Code civil is about the different ways in which property may be acquired. We find the rules on contract law in Book III, Title III. In 1804, Title III was entitled 'of contracts and of contractual obligations in general', from which it may be inferred that the general rules on obligations are set out with regard to contract. This demonstrated the primacy of obligations freely entered into above all others. The courts apply by analogy to all legal acts the rules laid down in relation to contracts.[17]

Until 2016, these provisions of the French Code had been altered relatively little, but since their terms were generally flexible, the courts were able to mould them to changing circumstances. The Cour de cassation created new rules where there were none (eg, for precontractual negotiations, offer and acceptance, duties of information), modernised others and sometimes even consecrated academic concepts, notably the distinction (which was not codified in the new Code civil) between *obligation de moyens* and *obligation de résultat*.[18]

In 1804, the rules on contracts were inspired by the ideas of individualism and liberalism, reflecting the spirit of the Enlightenment and of the newly gained freedom and equality. Contractual fairness and equilibrium became important concerns later. Thus many rules governing French contracts were developed outside the Code (either in case law, ie in *la jurisprudence*, in specific codes or in statutory provisions not inserted in the Code civil). This stood in sharp contrast with the fact that, in France, codification is considered a source of accessibility and legal certainty. However, interestingly, the main incentive for reforming French law in 2016 came from the European and international models, notably from the Principles of European Contract Law (PECL), the work of the Commission chaired by Ole Lando, and the UNIDROIT Principles of International Commercial Contracts (UNIDROIT PICC).[19] It is noteworthy that the idea of drafting an academic project for reform, the so called *Avant-projet Catala*, came after a colloquium which discussed in parallel French law and the PECL.[20]

Two French academic projects gave a major impulse to the French reform. In 2006, an *Avant-projet de réforme du droit des obligations et de la prescription*[21] (Draft Bill reforming the law of obligations and of prescription) was submitted to the French Minister of Justice by Pierre Catala, the chairman of a group of more than 30 academics (hence its name, the *Avant-projet Catala*).[22] Another project, frequently referred to as the

---

[17] This is made explicit in new Art 1100-1 of the Cciv (see below).

[18] This distinction inspired the UNIDROIT PICC (obligation of best efforts or specific results, Arts 5.1.4 and 5.1.5).

[19] For a European and historical perspective (a sort of 'travaux préparatoires'), see F Ancel, B Fauvarque-Cosson and J Gest, *Aux sources de la réforme du droit des contrats* (Paris: Dalloz, 2017).

[20] P Rémy-Corlay and D Fenouillet (eds), *Les concepts contractuels français à l'heure des principes du droit européen des contrats* (Paris: Dalloz, 2003). This is reported by P Catala himself in his 'Présentation générale de l'avant-projet' in *Avant-projet de réforme du droit des obligations et de la prescription: Rapport remis au garde des Sceaux* (Paris: Documentation Française, 2006) 11; translated in J Cartwright, S Vogenauer and S Whittaker (eds), *Reforming the French Law of Obligations* (Oxford: Hart Publishing, 2009) 465, also available on www.justice.gouv.fr/art_pix/rapportcatatla0905-anglais.pdf.

[21] P Catala (ed), *Projet de réforme du droit des obligations et de la prescription* (Paris: La Documentation Française, 2006).

[22] The Catala project was translated into English by J Cartwright and S Whittaker (see note 20 above) and it was also translated into English by A Levasseur (Louisiana), www.henricapitant.org/sites/default/files/

Projet Terré, was subsequently prepared by another academic group,[23] under the aegis of the *Académie des sciences morales et politiques*. It took much inspiration from the PECL and the UNIDROIT PICC.

In 2006, the Ministry of Justice (more precisely the 'Division des affaires civiles et du sceau' (DACS)), started its own project.[24] From thereon, a wide-ranging and lively debate took place in France.[25] A first draft issued in July 2008 was debated.[26] It provoked numerous reactions, as it appeared to many observers to be too far from the French tradition, more akin to the scheme used for international treaties than to that of a codification of internal law.[27] For example, the concept of 'interest in the contract', which had been introduced to replace the concept of *cause*, succeeded in attracting the joint opposition of both 'causalists' and 'anti-causalist' authors. It was later abandoned.

New political impulse was given when, finally, after much difficulty, the *Assemblée Nationale* empowered the Government to reform this area by means of Ordonnance.[28]

The French Ordonnance was adopted on 10 February 2016.[29] A Report to the President of the French Republic was published on the same day as the Ordonnance: in a way, it serves as *travaux préparatoires*, since the ordinary legislative process was not followed.[30] It is easily accessible on Légifrance and explains the context of the reform,

Traduction_definitive_Alain_Levasseur.pdf. It is interesting to compare and contrast the two translations. See B Fauvarque-Cosson and D Mazeaud, 'L'avant-projet de réforme du droit des obligations et du droit de la prescription' (2006) 11 Uniform Law Review 103. In spite of the fact that its authors stressed the need to take account of the surrounding international and European legal environment, this Avant-projet paid tribute to the French tradition, with little space for European and international innovations.

[23] F Terré (ed), *Pour une réforme du droit des contrats* (Paris: Dalloz, 2008). The group, chaired by F Terré, was composed of academics but also representatives of the legal professions and lawyers from business circles.

[24] See B Fauvarque-Cosson, 'The French Contract Law Reform and the Political Process' (2017) 13 ERCL 337.

[25] This debate went far beyond academic circles. Prominent professional organisations such as the Barreau de Paris (the Paris Bar Association), Medef (the French employers' organisation), the Chamber of Commerce of Paris and the notaries launched their own working groups and made critical observations to the Ministry of Justice.

[26] In 2008, the *Draft Common Frame of Reference* (DCFR) had already been published: *Principles, Definitions and Model Rules of European Private Law: Draft Common Frame of Reference (DCFR), Outline Edition* (above, ch 3.2.C) The *Terminologie contractuelle commune* (Paris: Société de législation comparée, 2008) and *Principes contractuels communs* (Paris: Société de législation comparée, 2008), elaborated under the aegis of the Association Henri Capitant and the Société de législation comparée, also inspired the Ministry of Justice.

[27] The draft issued by the *Chancellerie* in 2008 proposed to establish a separate chapter to affirm the guiding principles of the French law of contract (contractual freedom, binding force and good faith). It also envisaged the substitution of the notion of 'interest in the contract' for that of 'cause'. However, the emphasis which had been placed on a chapter entitled 'Guiding Principles' gave rise to considerable reservations, both among academics and certain business representatives. All feared that these principles could be interpreted broadly by the courts or that they would be difficult to coordinate with the special rules. These principles did not disappear but they were made less visible, since they are no longer identified as such and come in a chapter neutrally titled 'Disposition liminaires'.

[28] *Ordonnances* are issued by the Council of Ministers, after seeking the opinion of the Conseil d'État. They come into force on publication, but lapse in the event of failure to bring before Parliament the Bill to ratify them by the date set by the enabling legislation. They may be ratified only expressly. At the end of the period referred to in the first paragraph of this article, *Ordonnances* may be amended only by legislation in those areas that are within the sphere of statute law.

[29] Ordonnance no. 2016-131, later ratified by Loi no. 2018-287.

[30] Rapport au Président de la République relatif à l'ordonnance no. 2016-131 du 10 février 2016 portant réforme du droit des contrats, du régime général et de la preuve des obligations, Journal Officiel de la République française du 11 février 2016, text no. 25.

its purposes and its content, although many authors have cast doubts about its authority. An interesting comparison can be drawn with the new Code civil of Québec: the new code was published with commentaries from the Ministry of Justice; year after year, the Commentaries' authority decreased and they are barely considered today. The translation into English of the new provisions was officially requested by the Director of the *Direction des Affaires Civiles et du Sceau* of the Ministry of Justice.[31]

The reform which came into force on 1 October 2016 is not limited to contract law and has an impact on Title III, Title IV and Title IV *bis* of Book III of the Code civil.[32]

The Code civil has the following structure:

— Title III of Book III, 'Of sources of obligations', has three subtitles for the three main sources of obligations.
Subtitle I: *Le contrat*, now reformed.
Subtitle II: *La responsabilité extracontractuelle* (non-contractual liability), not included in the 2016 reforms—reform is still pending.[33]
Subtitle III: *Les autres sources des obligations* (The other sources of obligations). This includes *gestion d'affaires* (management of another's affairs), *paiement de l'indu* (undue payment) and *enrichissement injustifié* (unjustified enrichment), now reformed.

— Title IV, also reformed in 2016, deals with the *régime général des obligations* (a systematic presentation of the general principles of obligations and how they relate to each other). It contains, for instance, texts on conditional obligations, plural obligations, extinction of obligations (by performance, set-off, impossibility of performance, release of debts, merger) and provisions on assignment of rights, debts and contracts, on novation and delegation, and on restitution.

— Title IV *bis*, also reformed in 2016, deals with proof of obligations.

The 2016 Ordonnance needed to be subsequently ratified by Parliament. Most commentators thought that the latter would merely approve the Ordonnance without any change. However, members of the Senate and of the National Assembly were eager to recover the legislative power they had been deprived of. The ratification process gave rise to important discussions and resulted in the amendment of the law of contract that had been effective since 1 October 2016. Some amendments are somewhat minor and purport to correct formal errors spotted in the Ordonnance. Others are substantial and clearly illustrate Parliament's willingness to contest the Government's work. The French literature is

---

[31] The new provisions of the Code civil created by Ordonnance no. 2016-131 of 10 February 2016 translated into English, www.legifrance.gouv.fr/Traductions/en-English/Translations-from-institutional-websites. This task was officially entrusted to John Cartwright and Simon Whittaker, who had previously translated the *Avant-projet Catala*, as well as to Bénédicte Fauvarque-Cosson who had been involved in the elaboration of the reform, at the Ministry of Justice, from 2016–18. Other translations, in other languages, have subsequently been made, notably under the auspices of the *Fondation pour le droit continental*.

[32] Historically, the Code civil had only 3 books. Books IV and V are recent and are on securities and 'rules applicable to Mayotte'.

[33] See JS Borghetti, 'Un pas de plus vers la réforme de la responsabilité civile: présentation du projet de réforme rendu public le 13 mars 2017' D 2017, 770.

quite divided when it comes to the appraisal of what is now known as the 'reform of the reform': while some are keen to note that the law of contract is now sounder, others stress the fact that the intervention of Parliament resulted in a more complex law of contract. Indeed, it is worth noting that courts are now expected to apply three laws of contract: the law before the 2016 reform (contracts concluded before 1 October 2016), the law from the latter reform to the ratification (contracts concluded between 1 October 2016 and 1 October 2018) and the law resulting from the ratification (contracts concluded after 1 October 2018). Besides, special provisions of the ratification provide for specific commencement dates for some modifications.[34] The present book was mainly written before the ratification of the Ordonnance but it takes into account the major amendments made by Parliament.

Contrary to the UNIDROIT PICC or the PECL, each and every article does not have a specific title. Yet, thanks to the many divisions and subdivisions (chapters, sections, subsections), it is easy to understand what each provision is about.

4.2.B GERMAN LAW

The most important legislative provisions of German contract law are contained in the Bürgerliches Gesetzbuch (BGB).

The BGB has the following elaborate structure:

	BGB	4.1 (DE)
Book 1. General Part		
Division 1. Persons		§§ 1–89
Title 1. Natural persons, consumers, entrepreneurs		
Title 2. Legal persons		
Division 2. Things and animals		§§ 90–103
Division 3. Legal transactions [*Rechtsgeschäfte*]		§§ 104–185
Title 1. Capacity to contract		
Title 2. Declaration of intention [*Willenserklärung*]		
Title 3. Contract		
Title 4. Conditions and specification of time		
Title 5. Agency and authority		
Title 6. Consent and ratification		

---

[34] For a survey: D Mazeaud, 'Quelques mots sur la réforme de la réforme du droit des contrats' D 2018, 912; M Mekki, 'La loi de ratification de l'ordonnance du 10 février 2016—Une réforme de la réforme?' D 2018, 900.

Title 10. Brokerage contract

Title 11. Promise of a reward

Title 12. Mandate, contract for management of the affairs of another
and payment services

Title 13. Agency without specific authorisation

Title 14. Safekeeping

[Titles 15–25. Various types of contract and other obligations]

Title 26. Unjustified enrichment

Title 27. Delicts

Book 3. Law of Property

Book 4. Family Law

Book 5. Law of Succession

The somewhat rigidly systematic approach of the BGB does not always make it obvious where to find the rules applicable to a particular contract. The part headed 'Contractual obligations', ie Section 3 of Book 2, merely contains a relatively small number of the relevant rules. This Section is embedded in a wider set of rules applicable to all obligations which are contained in the first seven Sections of Book 2, which is generally referred to as the 'general part of the law of obligations'. Various particular types of contract are then covered in detail in some of the Titles in Section 8 of Book 2, the so-called 'special part of the law of obligations'.

Matters are complicated further by the fact that the drafters of the BGB decided to precede the other Books of their Code with a 'General Part'. This first Book of the BGB contains certain basic institutions and doctrines common to the whole of private law, and thus applicable in the areas of obligations, property, family law and the law of succession alike. Many of them are highly relevant for contractual relationships. This holds particularly true for Section 3 of the 'General Part', which even contains a separate Title on 'Contract', with rules on formation and interpretation. Other Titles of this Section deal with matters such as capacity, mistake, deceit, duress, (again) interpretation, conditions and agency.

With its high level of abstraction, terminological precision and accuracy, the BGB is a highly consistent and coherent codification. Its internal economy avoids repetitions and allows trained lawyers to locate the rules governing a given transaction quickly. Beginners, however, are bewildered by the fact that these rules are often scattered across very different parts of the Code. A simple contractual claim arising from the delivery of defective goods to the buyer, for instance, will not only require application of the specific rules on remedies in the law of sales which are contained in the 'special part of the law of obligations' (§§ 433–453 BGB), but it will also involve recourse to the 'General Part' in order to establish whether a contract has been validly concluded in the first place, and at least some provisions on contractual remedies in the 'general part of the law of obligations' will have to be drawn on. These include the general rules on specific performance

(§ 241(1) BGB), damages (§§ 249–255 BGB) and termination (§ 323 BGB). The proprietary consequences, if any, of the delivery of defective goods are mostly determined by Book 3 of the Code—which deals with the law of property and, once again, has to be read against the background of the 'General Part'.

German contract law, finally, is not fully reflected in the legislative provisions of the BGB. These are supplemented by case law and legal writings. Since the coming into force of the BGB in 1900, courts and legal academics did major work in adapting the Code to evolving circumstances and in filling gaps. Some examples of *de facto* law-making by the courts have been mentioned above.[35]

Some of these doctrines were codified and incorporated into the BGB by the 2001 Act to Modernise the Law of Obligations (*Schuldrechtsmodernisierungsgesetz*) that entered into force on 1 January 2002.[36] The Act also provided for the integration of a few pieces of consumer protection legislation into the BGB which had originally been enacted as freestanding statutes in order to implement European directives. This major reform also required a renumbering of many of the existing BGB provisions. These changes were not meant to change the substance of the law, so that many of the pre-2002 cases that are reproduced in this book remain good law even if they rely on judge-made doctrines or cite legislative provisions that have now been superseded. However, the 2001 Act also introduced major substantial changes, particularly in the area of remedies for non-performance. The new law is set out in detail in Part 5 of this book.

4.2.C ENGLISH LAW

In English law the general law of contract is not chiefly based on legislation but on the 'common law'—that is, the law developed by the courts. It is true that there are very important pieces of legislation dealing with contracts—for example, the Misrepresentation Act 1967, the Unfair Contract Terms Act 1977 and the Contracts (Rights of Third Parties) Act 1999. The law governing a few types of specific contract was also 'codified' in the English sense of being put into statutory form in the nineteenth century. The best-known example was the Sale of Goods Act 1893 (now replaced by the Sale of Goods Act 1979, which has itself been amended several times). More recently, many of the provisions dealing with consumer contracts (including much that formerly was governed by the Sale of Goods Act) have been set out in the Consumer Rights Act 2015. However, the greatest part of general contract law remains to be found in the accumulation of decided cases or 'precedents' that constitute the common law.

Within the common law in this broad sense there is a narrower meaning of the common law: rules developed by the normal or common law courts, which were supplemented or sometimes modified by rules developed by the courts of equity. The distinction in English law between common law and equity, and between legal and equitable remedies, goes back to the Middle Ages, when a party who complained about

---

[35] See above, p 80.

[36] For an overview, see R Zimmermann, *The New German Law of Obligations: Historical and Comparative Perspectives* (Oxford University Press, 2005).

the rigidity of a rule at common law might appeal to the Chancellor (representing the King) for relief on the basis of 'equity'. In particular, if the common law did not provide an adequate remedy, the Chancellor (sitting later in the Court of Equity) might grant one. Thus equity was a supplementary jurisdiction which would in effect supersede the common law rule. It became settled that the equitable rule would prevail, but until the nineteenth century the plaintiff would have to bring a separate action in the courts of equity; the common law courts would then defer. Since the nineteenth century Judicature Acts, the same courts administer both sets of rules, always giving the final say to the rule of equity, but the two sets of rules remain largely distinct.[37] The rules applicable to contracts in general are primarily rules of common law in the narrower sense but they are frequently supplemented or attenuated by the rules of equity.

Owing to the fact that it is judge-made law, the English law of contract is less structured than codified laws. This is all the more so since a general theory of contract law emerged progressively and only belatedly. Different textbook writers explained the law in different ways, and though there is increasing uniformity in the way the law is presented, significant differences remain. Recently a distinguished academic author has produced a *Restatement of the English Law of Contract*[38] which attempts to set out English law in a series of articles (or 'sections'). This provides a very valuable summary and we will refer to it, but it represents only the view of the author. The *Restatement* may turn out to be influential[39] but that will be because of the respect in which the author's work is held, not because the *Restatement* has any official status.

It should also be noted that contract law is generally studied separately and not in the context of the law of obligations, the latter being a concept that has only recently emerged in the writings of some English academics[40] and occasional judgments.[41] It is still not the way in which most English lawyers analyse the law. This is borne out by a comparison between the titles of the current textbooks in the different jurisdictions.[42]

Furthermore, contract law was not influenced so directly by Roman law and by its commentators, and the so-called will theory that became widespread in the eighteenth and nineteenth centuries did not penetrate English law as profoundly as it did on the continent. It is through the intermediary of foreign authors that the principle of autonomy of intent has influenced English law, albeit modestly. Pothier, an author who inspired many provisions of the French Civil Code and was translated into English at the end of the eighteenth century, was frequently cited by English judges in the nineteenth century.[43]

---

[37] See further, JH Baker, *Introduction to English Legal History* (4th edn, London: Butterworths, 2002) 105–15.

[38] A Burrows, *A Restatement of the English Law of Contract* (Oxford University Press, 2016).

[39] It has already been cited extensively in the Supreme Court in *Patel v Mirza* [2016] UKSC 42, though the Court did not accept its analysis in full, see at [82]–[107].

[40] J Cooke and D Oughton, *The Common Law of Obligations* (3rd edn, Oxford University Press, 2000).

[41] See *Moschi v Lep Air Services Ltd* (n 13 above).

[42] See D Looschelders, *Schuldrecht: Allgemeiner Teil* (15th edn, Cologne: Heymanns, 2017); P Malaurie, L Aynès and P Stoffel-Munck, *Droit des obligations* (9th edn, Paris: LGDJ, 2017); *Treitel on the Law of Contract*, 14th edn by E Peel (London: Sweet & Maxwell, 2015).

[43] AWB Simpson, 'Innovation in Nineteenth Century Contract Law' (1975) 91 LQR 247. For an example, see *Taylor v Caldwell* (28.9 (EN)) below, p 1188.

To some extent English contract law was developed, and is still discussed, on the basis of the notion of a 'promise'. In certain contexts—particularly when the doctrine of consideration is being discussed—the contract is considered as the juxtaposition of two promises.

Brexit will have a very limited impact on English contract law, save in respect of consumer, agency and other special contracts which were governed by EU legislation. However, some indirect consequences may result from the attitude the courts will take towards the EU and particularly the ECJ cases: will they look at what the ECJ is doing or will they prefer not to, and thereby reinforce the contrast between the civil/European and the common law traditions?

Whereas France and Germany have, to various degrees, remodelled their basic contract laws to fit the European model on the occasion of the transposition of some directives (notably, the 'Consumer Sales Directive'[44]) in the UK the impact of the directives has been pretty much limited to the required subject matter. In particular consumer law, unfair terms and agency contracts, while the remainder of the law has been left unaffected. In any event, for the time being at least the secondary legislation that enacts EU Directives, and the EU Regulations, will be preserved as UK law.

A major influence on some English academic writers has been exerted by US law (see, in particular, the publications of PS Atiyah). The impact of US law on the English common law itself appears to have been much less important. In England, academic writings are not themselves treated as a source of law, though nowadays they are cited by judges with increasing frequency. Thus some of the academic commentary on English law must be treated with care.

4.3 CONCLUSION

International and European initiatives have fostered convergences between national codifications. However, mainly for historical reasons, there still is a fairly considerable gulf between the civil law systems of law based on Roman law and the common law. Care should be exercised not to be taken in by superficial similarities as many of these may be misleading.

FURTHER READING

Cartwright, J, *Contract Law: An Introduction to the English Law of Contract for the Civil Lawyer* (3rd edn, Oxford: Hart Publishing, 2016).

Farnsworth, EA, 'Comparative contract law' in Reimann, M and Zimmermann, R (eds), *Oxford Handbook of Comparative Law* (Oxford University Press, 2006) 899–935.

Kötz, H, *European Contract Law* (2nd edn, Oxford University Press, 2017).

---

[44] See ch 19.

Markesinis, BS, Unberath, H and Johnston, A, *The German Law of Contract* (2nd edn, Oxford: Hart Publishing, 2006) 55–81.

Nicholas, B, *The French Law of Contract* (2nd edn, Oxford, Clarendon Press, 1992).

Zweigert, K and Kötz, H, *Introduction to Comparative Law* (3rd edn, Oxford: Clarendon Press, 1998).

On the French reform

Ancel, F, and Fauvarque-Cosson, B, *Le nouveau droit des contrats: Guide bilingue à l'usage des praticiens/The new French contract law: A bilingual guide for practitioners (Ordonnance du 10 février 2016 – Loi du 20 avril 2018)* (Paris: Lextenso, forthcoming in 2019).

Ancel, F, Fauvarque-Cosson, B, and Gest, J, *Aux sources de la réforme du droit des contrats* (Paris: Dalloz, 2017).

Cartwright, J and Whittaker, S (eds), *The Code Napoléon Rewritten: French Contract Law after the 2016 Reforms* (Oxford: Hart Publishing, 2017).

Catala, P (ed), *Projet de réforme du droit des obligations et de la prescription* (Paris: La Documentation Française, 2006).

Chénedé, F, *Le nouveau droit des obligations et des contrats: Consolidations, innovations, perspectives* (Paris: Dalloz, 2016).

Deshayes, O, Genicon, T and Laithier, YM, *Réforme du droit des contrats, du régime général et de la preuve des obligations, Commentaire article par article* (Paris: LexisNexis, 2016).

Dissaux, N and Jamin, C, *Réforme du droit des contrats, du régime général et de la preuve des obligations* (Paris: Dalloz, 2016).

Fauvarque-Cosson, B and Wicker, G (eds), 'The reform of French Contract Law' (2017) 6 Special issue of the Montesquieu Law Review.

Fauvarque-Cosson, B, 'The French Contract Law Reform and the Political Process' (2017) ERCL 337–54.

Mekki, M, 'La loi de ratification de l'ordonnance du 10 février 2016—Une réforme de la réforme?' D 2018, 900–11.

Latina, M and Chantepie, G, *La réforme du droit des obligations: Commentaire théorique et pratique dans l'ordre du Code civil* (Paris: Dalloz, 2016).

Muir Watt, H and Grundmann, S (eds), 'The New French Code Civil—In a Broader Context' (2017) 13 Special Issue of the ERCL 335–490.

Rowan, S, 'The new French law of Contract' (2017) 66 ICLQ 805–31.

Séjean, M, 'The French Reform of Contracts: An opportunity to Tie Together the Community of Civil Lawyers' (2016) 76 Louisiana Law Review 1151–61.

Simler, P, *Commentaire de la réforme du droit des contrats et des obligations* (Paris: LexisNexis, 2016).

Smits, J and Calomme, C, 'The Reform of the French Law of Obligations: *Les Jeux Sont Faits*' (2016) 23 MJ 1040–50.

Terré, F, *La réforme du droit des obligations* (Paris: Dalloz, 2016).

CHAPTER 5
NOTIONS OF CONTRACT

'Contract' is a concept which has evolved over time and which, from a comparative point of view, does not take the form of a uniform model. A contract under common law is not exactly the same as a contract under the German or French legal systems. For that reason, we begin this chapter with a study of the definitions (5.1) and the basic elements of a contract (5.2) found in the main legal systems with which we are concerned, in order to work out what the various concepts found in those systems have in common. We then consider various traditional categories of contract found in the different systems (5.3).

5.1 DEFINITIONS OF CONTRACT

Draft Common Frame of Reference　　　　　　**5.1 (INT)**

Article II-1:101
(1) A contract is an agreement which is intended to give rise to a binding legal relationship or to have some other legal effect. It is a bilateral or multi-lateral juridical act.
(2) A juridical act is any statement or agreement, whether express or implied from conduct, which is intended to have legal effect as such. It may be unilateral, bilateral or multilateral.

Common European Sales Law　　　　　　**5.2 (INT)**

Article 2 Definitions
For the purpose of this Regulation, the following definitions shall apply:
(a) 'contract' means an agreement intended to give rise to obligations or other legal effects;
(b) ...
(y) 'obligation' means a duty to perform which one party to a legal relationship owes to another party.

What does one understand by the terms *contrat*, 'contract' or *Vertrag*? It is doubtful whether this term is identical in the different legal systems of Europe. Unless careful comparisons are made, it may even be that the term is misleading.

In searching for definitions, we need to look at legislation, if there is legislation which proves a definition, and also, where appropriate, at case law and academic legal literature. It is apparent from such an analysis that the definitions differ according to the particular legal system in which they appear. In addition, there are two specific questions on which the various national legal systems differ from one another. The first is whether voluntary obligations[1] are always based on agreement: can an obligation also arise from a unilateral promise to which the other party has not even agreed, for example (in some systems) a promise of a reward? (The Principles of European Contract Law (PECL) call this a 'promise intended to be binding without acceptance'.)[2] If so, how do such 'unilateral juridical acts' fit with contract? The second question is whether a contract necessarily involves some kind of exchange—or, to put the question another way, whether promises of gifts *inter vivos* constitute contracts.

5.1.A AGREEMENTS AND UNILATERAL JURIDICAL ACTS

Some legal systems treat voluntary obligations as depending on contract and contract as depending on agreement. They either do not mention 'promises intended to be binding without acceptance' or treat them as exceptional. Others have incorporated such promises into their structure and categorise them as a particular type of 'juridical act', as they do with contracts.

Code civil 1804   **5.3 (FR)**

Article 1101: A contract is an agreement (*convention*) by which one or several persons bind themselves, towards one or several others, to transfer, to do or not to do something.[3]

The revised Code civil sets forth a revised definition in its Article 1101. This provision is placed in a new Subtitle 1 of Title III, which is itself preceded by provisions which differentiate between 'juridical acts' (*actes juridiques*) and 'juridically significant facts' (*faits juridiques*).

---

[1] As opposed to obligations imposed by law as the result of a person's conduct (as in tort: see below, p 94) or because they have received a benefit (as with restitutionary liability: see below, p 158).

[2] PECL Art 2:107 (see below, p 101), cf DCFR Art II-1:103.

[3] In French law, contract was long defined in terms of 'convention' (agreement); in order to simplify, the word 'contract' now replaces the word 'convention'. According to G Cornu and Association Henri Capitant (eds), *Vocabulaire juridique* (12th edn, Paris: PUF, 2018), see the entry 'Convention' which signifies 'any agreement intended to produce legal effects'.

Code civil 2016   **5.4 (FR)**

TITLE III THE SOURCES OF OBLIGATIONS

Article 1100: Obligations arise from juridical acts, juridically significant facts[4] or from the sole authority of legislation.

They can arise from the voluntary performance or from the promise of performance of a moral duty towards another person.

Article 1100-1: Juridical acts are manifestations of will intended to produce legal effects. They may be based on agreement or unilateral.

As far as is appropriate, they are subject, both as to their validity and as to their effects, to the rules governing contracts.

Article 1100-2: Juridically significant facts consist of behaviour or events to which legislation attaches legal consequences.

Obligations which arise from a juridically significant fact are governed, according to the circumstances, by the sub-title relating to extra-contractual liability or the sub-title relating to other sources of obligations.

SUB-TITLE I CONTRACT
CHAPTER I INTRODUCTORY PROVISIONS

Article 1101: A contract is a concordance of wills of two or more persons intended to create, modify, transfer or extinguish obligations.[5]

The Dutch Civil Code also treats contract as a species of juridical act. Its definition served as a model for Article II-1:101 DCFR (above, 5.1 (INT)):

BW   **5.5 (NL)**

Article 3:33: A juridical act requires an intention to produce juridical effects, which intention has manifested itself by a declaration.

Article 6:213: A contract in the sense of this title is a multi-lateral juridical act whereby one or more parties assume an obligation towards one or more other parties.

The drafters of the German BGB were averse to textbook style definitions of concepts that they regarded as settled. The code therefore has no definition as such of contract (*Vertrag*) although it uses the term and a number of interrelated concepts liberally.

---

[4] The translators note: 'There is a difficulty in translating "*le fait*" as sometimes it refers to a person's action and sometimes more broadly to fact. We have therefore translated it differently according to context.'

[5] On the two debates underlying the choice that was finally made in the 2016 reform, see F Ancel, B Fauvarque-Cosson and J Gest, *Aux sources de la réforme du droit des contrats* (Paris: Dalloz, 2017) nos. 21.41–21.46.

§ 241: Duties arising from an obligation

(1) By virtue of an obligation an obligee is entitled to claim performance from the obligor. The performance may also consist in forbearance.

(2) An obligation may also, depending on its contents, oblige each party to take account of the rights, legal interests and other interests of the other party.

§ 311: Obligations created by legal transaction and obligations similar to legal transactions

(1) In order to create an obligation by legal transaction and to alter the contents of an obligation, a contract between the parties is necessary, unless otherwise provided by statute.

...

Notes

(1) § 311(1) BGB merely explains that contracts are a species of the broader category of 'legal transactions' (*Rechtsgeschäfte*). The purpose of the provision is not to set forth an abstract definition of the term 'contract', but implicitly to clarify that unilateral promises are not binding, unless otherwise provided by statute.[6]

(2) The BGB does not define the highly abstract notion of 'legal transaction' (*Rechtsgeschäft*) either, although it is central to the understanding of German private law. A 'legal transaction' is generally understood to be an act consisting of at least one 'declaration of intent' which creates an effect acknowledged by the law. Contracts are the most important example. They require at least two 'declarations of intent', offer and acceptance, to create legal effects. However, a single declaration of intent may suffice: such 'unilateral legal transactions' include the avoidance of a contract for mistake or fraud, the giving of notice to terminate a contract, the granting of authority to an agent, and the making of a will. As the last example shows, legal transactions may also occur outside the law of contract and, indeed, the law of obligations. For this reason, the rules pertaining to them (§§ 104-185 BGB) are to be found in the General Part of the Code. This, it may be remembered, sets forth the provisions that apply across all the subject matters dealt with in the other books of the BGB, ie, obligations, property, family law and the law of succession.[7]

(3) A contract, then, is generally defined as 'a legal transaction consisting of the corresponding declarations of intent, made with a view to each other, of at least two persons' or, more broadly, a meeting of the minds (literally, an 'agreement of wills' (*Willenseinigung*)).[8]

(4) The commonly used definitions of 'legal transaction' and 'contract' presuppose another central legal concept that is not defined in the BGB, ie, that of 'declaration of intent'. This is generally acknowledged to be any manifestation of the internal

---

[6] For the most important statutory exception, see § 657 BGB, p 119 below.
[7] For an explanation of the structure of the BGB, see pp 85–89 above.
[8] H Brox and WD Walker, *Allgemeiner Teil des BGB* (41th edn, Munich: Vahlen, 2017) para 77.

will that is directed at creating a legal effect. Two elements are therefore essential: the internal will of the person in question to create a legal effect ('intention') and its manifestation by words or other conduct ('declaration'). Note that in the case of a 'unilateral legal transaction' a single declaration of intent amounts to a legal transaction, so the two concepts are conflated.

(5) Clearly, many unilateral legal transactions are relevant in the law of contract, and often the same rules on, say, validity or interpretation are suitable for both contracts and unilateral legal transactions. In order to avoid spelling out the same rules twice, most contract laws set forth rules for contracts and stipulate that these rules apply with appropriate adaptations to unilateral acts. Article 1100-1(2) of the revised Code civil (above, 5.4 (FR)) is a particularly clear example, and the recent European and transnational model codes mostly adopt the same legislative technique.[9] English contract lawyers follow a similar approach without even discussing it. German law is different. The BGB takes the declaration of intent as its starting point and sets forth a number of rules on the validity and interpretation of such declarations in its 'General Part' (§§ 116–144). Since these rules apply, among others, to any contractual offer and acceptance they ultimately also affect any contract that the parties wish to bring about. However, this is just seen as the logical consequence of the contract being the product of two corresponding declarations of intent. Thus, many of the most important rules for contracts are framed as rules on declarations of intent in the BGB. For example, if there is a mistake or fraud, the relevant question under §§ 119 and 123 BGB is not whether the 'contract' is affected, but rather whether one of the 'declarations of intent' is voidable. As ever so often with German private law, this solution is doctrinally coherent but excessively complex and removed from the realities of everyday life. As a result, the 'doctrine of legal transactions' (*Rechtsgeschäftslehre*) is almost inaccessible for those not trained in the law, including the parties to contracts.[10]

(6) As is clear from § 311(1) BGB, a *Rechtsgeschäft*, normally a contract, is one of the mechanisms of creating an obligation (the other being legislation which prescribes the emergence of an obligation from certain facts or conduct, as in the law of delict). The conclusion of a contract therefore creates what German lawyers call a 'contractual relationship of obligation' (*vertragliches Schuldverhältnis*). This relationship, sketched out in § 241(1) BGB, comprises all the mutual rights and obligations of the parties flowing both from the terms of the contract itself and from the codified and judge-made rules of contract law. Its legal effects may even extend to the post-contractual phase, ie, after the performance of the contract.[11]

(7) There is no agreement on how to translate the concepts of *Rechtsgeschäft* and *Willenserklärung* because they have no full equivalents in other legal languages. Obviously there is an overlap with the French notions of *acte juridique* and *manifestation de volonté* which the 2016 reforms inserted in Articles 1100 and 1100-1 Code

---

[9] See, eg, Art 1:107 PECL, Art 3.2.17 PICC and Art II.-1:104(3), II.-8:202 DCFR. For a different model, see, eg, Art 4.2 PICC. See below, pp 98–99.

[10] For a scathing critique of this aspect of the legislative technique of the BGB, see K Zweigert and H Kötz, *An Introduction to Comparative Law* (3rd edn, Oxford: Clarendon Press, 1998) 146–47.

[11] eg, post-contractual duties of loyalty.

civil. However, what is regarded as a *Rechtsgeschäft* or a *Willenserklärung* under German law will not always qualify as an *acte juridique* or a *manifestation de volonté* by French lawyers, and vice versa. In English law, these concepts do not even have a remote equivalent because the categories as such are not acknowledged, as we will see below. Therefore, the translation into English is somewhat arbitrary, and *Rechtsgeschäft* has also been translated as 'legal act', 'act-in-law', 'juristic act' or 'juridical act'; *Willenserklärung* also as 'declaration of intent' or 'declaration of will'. In this book we normally follow the translations used in the English translation of the BGB that can be accessed through the website of the German Ministry of Justice, and for this reason we use the terms 'legal transaction' and 'declaration of intent'.[12]

In English law there is no legislative definition of contract either, and we must look to academic writing. Here it is common to see contractual liability as based on agreement, though less emphasis is put on the contract as a source of obligations than on the point that a contract is something which, if not performed, gives rise to remedies. Thus, a leading author, Treitel, defines contract as 'an agreement giving rise to obligations which are enforced or recognised by law'.[13]

English law does not employ the concept of juridical act. It tends to treat contracts as the principal source of obligations, and does not have a formal category for other forms of act that may change the actor's legal relationship. But even if it does not employ the phrase 'juridical act', it recognises that in some circumstances a voluntary unilateral action may have legal effects. For example, a unilateral promise made by deed may be binding on the party executing the deed irrespective of whether the beneficiary of the deed even knows about it;[14] and a unilateral notice by one party to the other may be effective to avoid or terminate a contract.

Indeed, every system recognises at least some of these 'unilateral juridical acts', for example, notices given under a contract. It is simply that they are not always given a formal place in the acknowledged categories of contract or of obligation.

Curiously, other than to say that a contract includes a promise intended to be binding without acceptance, the PECL do not contain a definition of contract. It seems that the meaning was regarded as self-evident. In the PECL, a promise that is 'intended to be binding without acceptance' may be binding.[15] Equally the PECL provide that unilateral notices of avoidance[16] or termination[17] may have legal effects. But rather than refer to

---

[12] Available at www.gesetze-im-internet.de/englisch_bgb/englisch_bgb.html#p1013. Even this translation is inconsistent and uses 'declaration of intent' and 'declaration of intention' interchangeably.

[13] *Treitel on the Law of Contract*, 14th edn by E Peel (London: Sweet & Maxwell, 2015) para 1-001. A Burrows, *A Restatement of the English Law of Contract* (Oxford University Press, 2016) (see above, p 89), s 2, defines a contract as an agreement that is legally binding because the agreement meets the various requirements of English law, such as consideration, certainty and completeness, is intended to be legally binding and meets any form requirements needed to make it binding.

[14] See below, pp 118, 128.

[15] PECL Art 2:107 (see below, p 101); cf DCFR Art II.-1:103(2).

[16] PECL Art 4:112; cf DCFR Art II.-7:209.

[17] PECL Art 9:303(1); cf DCFR Art III.-3:507(1).

'unilateral acts', the PECL merely provide that the Principles 'apply with appropriate modifications to agreements to modify or end a contract, to unilateral promises and other statements and conduct indicating intention'.[18] The UNIDROIT Principles for International Commercial Contracts (UNIDROIT PICC) do not recognise promises binding without acceptance. However, they explicitly refer to certain unilateral acts: they provide that the provisions on validity 'apply with appropriate adaptations to any communication of intention addressed by one party to the other', ie 'unilateral declarations', and they make provision for the interpretation of 'statements and other conduct'.[19]

Ultimately, it seems that the definition of 'contract' is a conceptual matter on which the systems differ; but the more important question is whether they reach different results in concrete cases. As we examine the laws more closely, it will become apparent that sometimes they do reach different results, but that there is not always a direct connection between the results and the conceptual structure.

5.1.B GRATUITOUS PROMISES AND GRATUITOUS CONTRACTS

Code civil **5.7 (FR)**

Article 1107: A contract is onerous where each of the parties receives a benefit from the other in return for what he provides.

It is gratuitous where one of the parties provides a benefit to the other without expecting or receiving anything in return.

As mentioned in the introduction to Section 5.1, there is a further question pertaining to the definition of what a contract is: does it require some kind of exchange, or can we also speak of a 'contract' if no such exchange is present?

Under all European contract laws, an agreement is binding and enforceable in the courts if both parties have given or promised something in return for what they receive. In a contract of sale, the buyer promises money for the goods and the seller promises delivery of the goods in return. Goods are exchanged for money. Because such contracts place a burden on each party they are called 'onerous'.

Divergences between legal systems appear when one of the parties does something or promises to do something under the agreement without receiving something in return. Such an agreement or promise is called 'gratuitous' (*gratuit*) or 'unilaterally binding' (*einseitig verpflichtend*). In the continental laws, gratuitous agreements qualify as 'contracts' (*contrats gratuits, einseitig verpflichtende Verträge*),[20] and they will be enforced by the courts. The classic example is the acceptance of an offer to donate a sum of money. Under French and German law, such an agreement is a contract of donation

---

[18] PECL Art 1:107. The DCFR has no direct equivalent, providing separately for unilateral juridical acts. See further below, p 62.

[19] UNIDROIT PICC Arts 3.2.17, 4.2. See also the rule on 'Unilateral statements and conduct' in CESL Art 12.

[20] Under German law, *einseitig verpflichtende Verträge* (unilaterally binding contracts) are distinguished from *einseitige Rechtsgeschäfte* (unilateral legal transactions; see above, p 96). The former require two declarations of intent, the latter only one.

which is, provided certain formalities are observed, as binding and enforceable as an onerous contract: the donee may sue the donor for performance.

In contrast, English law does not enforce gratuitous promises. This follows from the doctrine of consideration that we will discuss in greater detail in Chapter 11 of this book. An agreement will therefore not amount to an enforceable contract unless it involves some kind of exchange or 'bargain'. That sounds like an exchange of promised benefits—which may appear to exclude all but synallagmatic contracts (ie contracts under which each party undertakes obligations[21]). We will see that the notion of contract in English law includes more than synallagmatic contracts, though it seems to exclude agreements under which the other party has neither promised to do, nor actually done, anything in exchange.[22] As a result it has been argued that Treitel's definition of contract cited above, ie, as an agreement that the law will enforce, is misleading because English law does not enforce gratuitous promises.[23]

In contrast to Treitel, the US Second Restatement defines contract in terms which seem to include unilateral promises:

Restatement 2d on Contracts[24]   **5.8 (US)**

§1: A contract is a promise or a set of promises for the breach of which the law gives a remedy or the performance of which the law in some way recognises as a duty.

Notes

(1) The lack of emphasis on agreement may be linked to the fact that in the US[25] the law has moved away from always requiring consideration for a contract: a party who has suffered a loss by relying on another person's promise may have a remedy, which is not normally the case in English law. It may be that the emphasis on promise in the Restatement 2d definition reflects this move. The result is that for English law the Restatement 2d definition can be misleading, first since English law still seems to place more emphasis on agreement and secondly since a greater range of promises are enforceable under US law than are under English law. (The US definition's greater emphasis on the existence of a 'promise' seems awkward to apply to the normal synallagmatic contract, as it appears to involve the superimposition of two 'promises',[26] rather than any single, all-embracing transaction.[27])

(2) The Restatement of the Law, Contracts 2d, is one of nine Restatements of the Law produced by the American Law Institute. In the US, contracts are governed by

[21] See below, p 116.
[22] See below, p 250.
[23] *Chitty on Contracts*, 33rd edn by H Beale (gen ed) (London: Sweet & Maxwell/Thomson Reuters, 2018) para 1-019.
[24] Second Restatement of the Law, Contracts 2d (1981), vol 1.
[25] See further below, p 364.
[26] There may also be a contract in English law if there is an exchange of a promise for an action: see below, p 347.
[27] The role played by the notion of 'reliance' will be examined below, ch 11.2.B. See also D Harris and D Tallon (eds), *Contract Law Today: Anglo-French Comparisons* (Oxford: Clarendon Press, 1989) 380–82.

State law, so that there is not one but 50 contract laws. The Institute was founded in 1923 'to promote the clarification and simplification of the law'; its membership includes judges, practitioners and law professors. The final draft of the first Restatement of contracts was approved in 1932. The Reporter, Williston, stated that 'the endeavour in the Restatement is to restate the law as it is, not as new law' (3 *ALI Proceedings* 159), but several of its sections were remarkable innovations, as we shall see later. As a statement of law, it has no binding force, but it has been extremely influential, many of its sections being adopted by State courts as representing the law. A revised version was begun in 1962 and was published in final form in 1981 as the Restatement Second; its Reporters were Braucher and later Farnsworth.

For the time being we will adopt our own 'working definition' of a contract as an agreement which the law will enforce.

5.2 BASIC ELEMENTS

Principles of European Contract Law **5.9 (INT)**

Article 2:101: Conditions for the Conclusion of a Contract
 (1) A contract is concluded if:
  (a) the parties intend to be legally bound, and
  (b) they reach a sufficient agreement without any further requirement.
 (2) A contract need not be concluded or evidenced in writing nor is it subject to any other requirement as to form. The contract may be proved by any means, including witnesses.

Article 2:102: Intention
 The intention of a party to be legally bound by contract is to be determined from the party's statements or conduct as they were reasonably understood by the other party.

Article 2:103: Sufficient Agreement
 (1) There is sufficient agreement if the terms:
  (a) have been sufficiently defined by the parties so that the contract can be enforced, or
  (b) can be determined under these Principles.
 (2) However, if one of the parties refuses to conclude a contract unless the parties have agreed on some specific matter, there is no contract unless agreement on that matter has been reached.

Article 2:107: Promises Binding without Acceptance
 A promise which is intended to be legally binding without acceptance is binding.

These Articles from the Principles of European Contract Law[28] express the Lando Commission's view of the common principles that underlie the creation of a contract

---

[28] CESL Art 30 is broadly similar to PECL Arts 2:101 and 2:102. For an explanation of these instruments, see above, ch 3.1 and ch 3.2.D.

in the many different legal systems of Europe—or, perhaps, the principles which they think *ought* to underlie any European law. While it is true that the elements of 'sufficient agreement' and 'intention to be legally bound' are found in all the systems and thus clearly represent part of the 'common core', it is not true that contracts are made everywhere 'without any further requirement', as is suggested by PECL Article 2:101(1) (b): English law requires in addition that there be 'consideration'. Moreover, French law used to require that there be *cause* but this has been changed by the recent reform. These additional elements will be considered in detail in Chapter 11. The question of formal requirements, referred to by PECL Article 2:101(2), will be taken up in Chapter 12.

What the PECL stress are the two elements of agreement and intention to create a contract. In this chapter we look at them one after the other. However, in practice the two questions are interlinked. Sometimes it is clear that the parties have agreed but there is a question whether or not they intended their agreement to have the force of a contract; in other cases a party's intention is relevant to whether there was any agreement between them.

5.2.A AGREEMENT

In none of the legal systems being considered will there be a contract unless there has been some measure of agreement between the parties. Besides, the agreement must not be so vague or incomplete that it is not possible to determine (if necessary, with the help of supplemental rules of law which the parties may be taken to have agreed to, unless they indicated otherwise—the so-called 'default rules'), what the obligations of the parties are to be.

When in Chapters 8–11 we consider the ways in which the different systems analyse whether or not an agreement has been reached, we will see that they have a great deal in common, in particular on two points. First, in each system it is usually asked whether there has been an 'offer' by one party and an 'acceptance' of the same offer by another. Secondly, we will also see that it is not enough that the parties have reached an agreement, if it is not clear what obligations they have agreed upon. As PECL Article 2:101 puts it, the agreement must be 'sufficient'.[29] In all the systems the point seems to be that the agreement will not be treated as a contract unless the parties have agreed on enough of the elements of the contract, and have done so in sufficiently certain terms, so that the court can enforce it.

In the present section we deal with agreement, and ask the basic point: when will a person be treated as having 'agreed' to something? When we say that in each system there must be 'some measure of agreement' before there will be a contract, this is because the systems may differ on the extent to which the parties to the contract must 'actually' (or 'subjectively', this may deserve some explanation because the two adverbs are not synonymous) have been in agreement.

Suppose A says or does something which seems to show to B that A intends to make a contract—in other words, A appears to make an offer or to accept an offer that has been

---

[29] See further below, ch 9.

made by B—when A in fact had no such intention. If B expresses his or her agreement also (eg B 'accepts' A's apparent 'offer'), does a contract result therefrom?[30]

The question may be illustrated with reference to the classic German 'textbook' example of the Trier wine auction.[31] In this (hypothetical) case, a person from another part of Germany visits the somewhat remote city of Trier. He attends a wine auction, spots a friend and waves across the room. Unbeknownst to him, by custom his waving his arm indicates that he is bidding on the wine presently being auctioned. As a result he finds that the wine in question has been 'knocked down' to him. Has there been 'agreement' between him and the auctioneer? Certainly not if the question has to be answered with reference to the subjective (or actual) intentions of the parties. However, if the question has to be answered with reference to what an external observer would reasonably infer from the objective circumstances, an agreement has been reached. Legal systems diverge on this issue, with some basing obligations on the 'subjective' intention of the party obliged ('voluntarism') and others favouring a more objective approach.

You may have noticed this difference reflected in the different definitions of contract quoted earlier. Whereas the continental definitions speak of obligations created by the agreement or juridical act of the parties, the common law definitions put emphasis on whether the law provides a remedy. Much of this may be accounted for by history. On the Continent, Roman law (disseminated above all by the universities) had a major influence, even in those countries where Roman law was at no point formally brought into force as positive law. This influence was carried on by the canon lawyers and then by the school of natural law, leading to voluntarism, the notion that contractual obligations depended on the will of the parties. The leading lights of voluntarism in seventeenth and eighteenth-century France were Jean Domat and Robert Joseph Pothier. The French Civil Code is based on their views. German nineteenth-century lawyers also subscribed to the subjective approach. However, during the early twentieth century, German law shifted to an objective theory of contract. The discussion centred on the concept of 'declaration of intent' which was introduced earlier in this chapter: was it the internal will of a party ('intention') or was it its outward manifestation ('declaration') that created legal effects? Gradually, the theory of declaration prevailed over the theory of intention or 'will theory'.

In England, Roman law had less influence. Moreover, it took longer for a general notion of contract to be worked out than on the Continent. During the late nineteenth century, English lawyers briefly flirted with the idea of voluntarism, but it went into an almost immediate decline.[32] Rather, they tend to stress that contractual liability may arise not only when the party intended to create it but also sometimes when it was not intended: in other words, it may be imposed by law because of the way in which the party had behaved.[33] The decline of voluntarism in English academic writing at least was

---

[30] If there is a contract, it may be that A can escape from it on the grounds of mistake. We consider this in detail in ch 14.

[31] H Isay, *Die Willenserklärung im Thatbestande des Rechtsgeschäfts nach dem Bürgerlichen Gesetzbuch für das Deutsche Reich* (Jena: Fischer, 1899) 25.

[32] PS Atiyah, *The Rise and Fall of Freedom of Contract* (Oxford: Clarendon Press, 1990) esp chs 14 and 21.

[33] cf above, p 89.

hastened by the analyses of US writers, particularly following a famous article by Fuller and Perdue[34] which based the contractual obligations of a party on the reasonable belief, induced by the conduct of the other party, in the existence of agreement. This view protects a party's reasonable expectation in the existence and content of a contract. Some US scholars went as far as proclaiming the 'death of contract', the essential argument being that contractual liability does not depend on the intentions of the parties at all but on the consequences the law attaches to their actions, as (arguably) happens in the law of tort.[35]

To this day, the different balances struck between these two fundamental views of contractual liability—liability that is voluntarily self-imposed and liability that is imposed by law—account for many of the divergences between the laws of contract in Europe. We will return to it frequently throughout this book.

In French law, the starting point is that the creation of the contract requires an agreement in a subjective sense—the parties must actually intend the same thing.

Cass com, 15 February 1961[36] **5.10 (FR)**

Wine to Algiers

Where one party intends one price and the other another, the mistake prevents there being an effective agreement and no contract is formed.

Facts: The parties were negotiating the sale of a large quantity of wine. Originally it was envisaged that the wine would be delivered at Cherchell but the buyers, Orazzi, refused this, and offered to share in the cost of transport to Algiers. The sellers, Tirat, demanded the sum of 60 francs per hectolitre. The buyers were not willing to pay this sum and sent a telegram intending to offer 30 francs per hectolitre but in fact offering 300 francs. The sellers accepted this, delivered the wine and billed the buyers accordingly and the buyers paid, but later they realised the mistake and demanded repayment. The Cour d'appel of Montpellier gave judgment for the buyers and the sellers appealed, arguing (1) that the error was one of value not one of substance;[37] (2) that the contract was valid until annulled, so that the buyers could not claim that the payment was invalid; and (3) that when the buyers paid the 300 francs they were accepting an offer from the sellers.

Held: The appeal was dismissed.

Judgment: — Whereas it is apparent from the statement of facts in the contested judgment (Montpellier, 16 October 1957) and from the introductory part thereof, Marius Tirat et Cie ('Tirat') was to deliver 2,000 hectolitres of Algerian wine FOB to the purchaser, Orazzi et Fils ('Orazzi'); as it was envisaged that delivery would take place at Cherchell, but this was refused by Orazzi which offered to share the cost of haulage from Cherchell to Algiers; this offer was set out in a telegram agreeing to pay 300 francs a hectolitre; as after acceptance and delivery by Tirat, Orazzi claimed that the figure of 300 francs was the result of material error and that the true figure was 30 francs; accounts which were drawn up on the basis of the first figure were in the end reduced to 335,162 francs and

---

[34] LL Fuller and WR Perdue, 'The Reliance Interest in Contract Damages' (1936) 46 Yale LJ 52.
[35] G Gilmore, *The Death of Contract* (Columbus, OH: Ohio State University Press, 1974).
[36] Cass com 15 February 1961, no. 58-10828, Bull civ IV no. 91.
[37] On the relevance of this, see Note (2) after the case.

Orazzi drew a bill of exchange on Tirat for that amount, which was dishonoured and protested.

— Whereas Tirat then sued the purchasers for damages for the loss caused by a bill of exchange improperly presented and then protested, whereupon Orazzi counter-claimed for payment of the bill; as subsequently, the court of first instance in its contested judgment recognised that a mistake had been made and dismissed the claim in the main proceedings and upheld Orazzi's counterclaim.

— Whereas the appellant challenges the judgment inasmuch as it held that the agreement as to haulage charges was invalid by reason of a substantial mistake, on the ground that it incorrectly showed the sum of 300 francs instead of 30 francs, whereas, it argues, first, a mistake as to value is not a material mistake and in any event the court failed to explain its reasoning concerning the claims made by Tirat on that point; as second, a voidable act remains valid until declared void by the court and there was consequently no legal basis for the bill of exchange, which was presented before any annulment and, finally, as it was possible to remedy the curable nullity arising from a mistake, the findings in the judgment establish that Orazzi had confirmed the contract by accepting without demur the agreement reached on the offer of 300 francs and the accounts presented.

— Whereas however, it is stated in the judgment that, for the reasons set out, the figure of 300 francs per hectolitre in Orazzi's telegram could only be the result of a material mistake; as Orazzi proposed or believed it was proposing 30 francs, that is to say half of what Tirat had asked for; there was no agreement as to the amount of the consideration; 'that, since the parties' intentions differed as a result of a misunderstanding, it was not possible for an agreement to be formed'; as accordingly the Court, first, did not have to declare a contract void for a mistake as to the properties of its subject matter and was not required to answer any arguments put forward on that point; as second, having found that no agreement had been concluded concerning the division of haulage costs, it could not find that there was no legal basis for the bill of exchange which was based on market terms and the abovementioned offer of 30 francs.

...

On those grounds, the Court dismisses the appeal against the judgment of the Cour d'appel of Montpellier, of 16 October 1957.

Notes

(1) This case seems to have been decided on the basis of *erreur-obstacle*, ie that the error prevented the formation of a contract, just as in the cases of *dissensus* discussed earlier. In the traditional analysis, to quote Planiol, 'it is a misunderstanding, not a contract'.[38] In practice, French courts will often give relief in such cases on the basis of error as to the substance,[39] as in the next case.

(2) A contract may be avoided under Article 1110 Cciv (new Article 1132 Cciv) only if it involves a substantial quality of the thing sold, and a mistake as to value is not one of substance.[40] By holding that the mistake prevented any contract ever being made, the court avoids these restrictions.

---

[38] M Planiol, *Traité élémentaire de droit civil*, vol II (4th edn, Paris: LGDJ, 1951) no. 1052.
[39] As to which see below, pp 526–35.
[40] See below, pp 506–7, 530.

(3) Presumably the sellers should have been aware that the telegram from the buyers contained an error, as the sellers had already made an offer at 60 francs, one-fifth of the price offered in the telegram, but the buyers had rejected it. However, nothing is made of this point and it seems that the result would have been the same even if the buyers had had no reason at all to suspect the sellers had made a mistake.

Cass com, 14 January 1969[41] **5.11 (FR)**

Old francs, new francs

Where each party in its offer or acceptance intends the contract price to be in a different currency, there is a mistake as to the substance which justifies annulment of the contract.

Facts: See the judgment.

Held: When the parties are at cross-purposes as to the currency in which the price is to be paid, there is an error as to substance and the contract may be avoided.

Judgment: The Court:—On the sole ground of appeal—Whereas as stated in the judgment under appeal (Trib Com Versailles, 5 October 1966), la Société Blanchisserie de la Bièvre were invited in April 1964 to place an advertisement in the municipal newsletter of the community of Isgny, edited by the Agence company for regional official publications, and sent an order to the agency at a price of 1,000 francs but then, the next day, informed the agency that in signing the order they had thought they were committing themselves to paying 1,000 old francs and refused to pay 1,000 new francs;

— Whereas the ground of appeal is that the judgment stated that an error as to value cannot constitute a vice of consent, nor a ground for nullity of the agreement, except in the case of fraudulent conduct, which was not alleged in this case;

— But seeing that, according to the contested judgment, the laundry when making the agreement thought they were engaging themselves to pay 1,000 old francs; that the tribunal, within its power of appreciation, found that the error of fact made was the determining cause of the agreement given by the laundry to the agency's invitation; and that as this error was to the substance of the performance promised by the laundry to the other party, namely the monetary units by which the price was measured, the tribunal could decide that 'the consent (of the laundry) was vitiated from the start by a fundamental error' and so could annul the agreement and dismiss the agency's claim for 1,000 new francs; so the ground of appeal is not well founded;

For these reasons, the appeal is dismissed.

Notes

(1) The Court bases its decision on the doctrine of mistake. However, the note to the case by Pédamon points out that, instead of applying the doctrine of mistake, the Court could simply have held that there was no agreement on the amount to be

---

[41] Cass com 14 January 1969, no. 67-10920, Bull civ IV no. 13, D 1970, 458, annotated by M Pédamon.

paid: one meant 1,000 old francs, the other 1,000 new francs, so there was no meeting of the minds. Therefore there was no contract.

(2) Again there was no attempt to ask how it was reasonable for the other party to have interpreted the offer. In English law, by contrast, the court would first enquire whether one party's interpretation was objectively reasonable but not the other's, in which case the contract would be on the objectively reasonable meaning. Only if the two interpretations were equally plausible would there be no contract—on the ground that the agreement was too uncertain to enforce.[42]

(3) The way in which mistakes of this kind are treated is discussed in more detail in Chapter 14.

These cases, and the note by Pédamon, suggest that French law still places considerable importance on autonomy of the will, requiring subjective agreement in order for a contract to come into existence. However, frequently the French courts will find ways of protecting the reasonable expectations of the other party. We will see that sometimes delictual liability under Article 1240 (former Article 1382) Cciv may be imposed where in other systems the court would say simply that there is contractual liability.[43] Or good faith may be invoked. So later we will see an example where a party created the impression that she had given up her right to money under a contract, and was prevented from terminating the contract on the ground that the money had not been paid on the basis that to do so would be contrary to good faith.[44] One can see in this a glimmer of the idea of 'reliance': the attitude of the promisee had instilled in the promisor 'the firm belief that payment of the annuity would never be claimed'. It must be pointed out that there is no exact equivalent in French for the term 'reliance'; the closest phrase is perhaps *confiance légitime* (legitimate expectation).

English law, as a general rule, follows another approach. Thus, subjective agreement is not required for a contract to come into existence: it suffices that one party reasonably thinks that the other party has agreed. A classic statement of the 'objective principle' is that of Blackburn J in *Smith v Hughes*:[45]

> If whatever a man's real intention may be, he so conducts himself that a reasonable man would believe that he was assenting to the terms proposed by the other party, and that other party upon that belief enters into the contract with him, the man thus conducting himself would be equally bound as if he had intended to agree to the other party's terms.

Thus if the Trier wine auction case discussed earlier had to be decided under English law there would be a contract, provided the auctioneer reasonably believed that the buyer was bidding on the wine and accepted the bid in that belief.

---

[42] See below, p 504.
[43] See below, ch 6.2.B, pp 141–57.
[44] Cass civ (3) 8 April 1987, no. 85-17596, Bull III no. 88.
[45] (1871) LR 6 QB 597, 607 (QB). See 14.41 (EN) below, p 567.

House of Lords **5.12 (EN)**

***The Hannah Blumenthal*[46]**

The intention of a party should be judged by how it reasonably appeared to the other party.

Facts: A contract for the sale of a vessel contained an arbitration clause. After a dispute had arisen, arbitration proceedings were started in 1972 but they were pursued only sporadically. For a long period, neither party did anything. In 1980 the buyer proposed that a date be fixed for the hearing. The seller sought a declaration that the arbitration agreement no longer subsisted.

Held: The House of Lords declined to grant the declaration sought either on the basis that the agreement to arbitrate had been repudiated by one party and the repudiation had been accepted by the other[47] or on the basis of frustration.[48] It then considered whether the contract had been abandoned and held that it had not.

Judgment: LORD DIPLOCK: … Abandonment of a contract ("the former contract") which is still executory, i.e., one in which at least one primary obligation of one or other of the parties remains unperformed, is effected by the parties entering into a new contract ("the contract of abandonment") …

To the formation of the contract of abandonment, the ordinary principles of the English law of contract apply. To create a contract by exchange of promises between two parties where the promise of each party constitutes the consideration for the promise of the other, what is necessary is that the intention of each *as it has been communicated to and understood by the other* (even though that which has been communicated does not represent the actual state of mind of the communicator) should coincide. That is what English lawyers mean when they resort to the Latin phrase consensus ad idem and the words that I have italicised are essential to the concept of consensus ad idem, the lack of which prevents the formation of a binding contract in English law.

Thus if A (the offeror) makes a communication to B (the offeree) whether in writing, orally or by conduct, which, in the circumstances at the time the communication was received, (1) B, if he were a reasonable man, would understand as stating A's intention to act or refrain from acting in some specified manner if B will promise on his part to act or refrain from acting in some manner also specified in the offer, and (2) B does in fact understand A's communication to mean this, and in his turn makes to A a communication conveying his willingness so to act or to refrain from acting which mutatis mutandis satisfies the same two conditions as respects A, the consensus ad idem essential to the formation of a contract in English law is complete.

The rule that neither party can rely upon his own failure to communicate accurately to the other party his own real intention by what he wrote or said or did, as negativing the consensus ad idem, is an example of a general principle of English law that injurious reliance on what another person did may be a source of legal rights against him. I use the broader expression "injurious reliance" in preference to "estoppel" so as to embrace all circumstances in which A can say to B: "You led me reasonably to believe that you were assuming particular legally enforceable obligations to me," of which promissory or *High Trees* estoppel [*Central London Property Trust Ltd v High Trees House Ltd*][49] affords

---

[46] [1983] 1 AC 854.
[47] On 'repudiation' and 'acceptance of repudiation' (ie termination), see below, p 1024.
[48] ie impossibility: see below, p 1185.
[49] [1947] KB 130 (KBD); see 11.10 (EN) below, p 367.

another example; whereas "estoppel", in the strict sense of the term, is an exclusionary rule of evidence, though it may operate so as to affect substantive legal rights inter partes.

LORD BRIGHTMAN: The basis of "tacit abandonment by both parties," to use the phraseology of the sellers' case is that the primary facts are such that it ought to be inferred that the contract to arbitrate the particular dispute was rescinded by the mutual agreement of the parties. To entitle the sellers to rely on abandonment, they must show that the buyers so conducted themselves as to entitle the sellers to assume, and that the sellers did assume, that the contract was agreed to be abandoned sub silentio. The evidence which is relevant to that inquiry will consist of or include: (1) What the buyers did or omitted to do to the knowledge of the sellers. Excluded from consideration will be the acts of the buyers of which the sellers were ignorant, because those acts will have signalled nothing to the sellers and cannot have founded or fortified any assumption on the part of the sellers. (2) What the sellers did or omitted to do, whether or not to the knowledge of the buyers. These facts evidence the state of mind of the sellers, and therefore the validity of the assertion by the sellers that they assumed that the contract was agreed to be abandoned. The state of mind of the buyers is irrelevant to a consideration of what the sellers were entitled to assume. The state of mind of the sellers is vital to a consideration of what the sellers in fact assumed.

[LORDS BRANDON, ROSKILL and KEITH concurred].

Appeal allowed. Cross appeal dismissed.

Notes

(1) The same point is illustrated by the cases on whether there was an offer and acceptance, such as *Kleinwort Benson Ltd v Malaysia Mining Corp Bhd*[50] and *Carlill v Carbolic Smoke Ball Company*,[51] which look almost exclusively at what the parties said rather than what they may have intended.[52]

(2) The possibility of relief on the ground of mistake will be considered later,[53] but it is worth noting that there would probably be no relief in English law. The rules of English law on mistakes of this kind seem simply to be restatements of the original position: that what reasonably appears to the other party to be an offer or an acceptance, and which the other believes to be such, is binding.[54]

(3) The purpose of holding a party to the 'objective meaning' of its words understood by the other party is to protect the latter's reasonable reliance. However, it will be seen that as English law holds the first party to the apparent contract, it protects the second party's expectations as well as its reliance interest.[55]

---

[50] [1989] 1 WLR 179 (CA); see 10.14 (EN) below, p 323.

[51] [1893] 1 QB 256 (CA); see 8.8, 10.1 and 11.4 (EN) below, pp 217, 301, 348.

[52] It is also illustrated by a parody of English law based on another famous parody of English manners, *Alice in Wonderland* by Lewis Carroll (the pen-name of the mathematician CL Dodgson): you may like to look at this in GL Williams 'A Lawyer's Alice' (1946) 9 CLJ 171, 171–72.

[53] See below, p 501.

[54] See below, p 518.

[55] See *Hartog v Colin & Shields* [1939] 3 All ER 23 (KBD); see 14.21 (EN) below, p 511.

German commentators discussing the Trier wine auction scenario originally took the position that the person waving at his friend lacked the awareness of making a legally relevant declaration of intent (*Erklärungsbewusstsein*) and therefore could not make such a declaration which would constitute an offer.[56] However, for a long time German doctrine and case law have taken a more objective approach: a reasonable observer would have understood the waving of hands as a bid. If the auctioneer reasonably believed that the buyer was bidding on the wine and accepted the bid in that belief, a contract was concluded.

BGH, 7 June 1984[57]   **5.13 (DE)**

The bank guarantee

To form a valid contract, it does not matter whether the party communicating an intention to be bound by a contract actually had the will to make, or was even conscious of making, a declaration aimed at a legal transaction.

Facts: A savings bank wrote to the claimants, a firm of steel contractors, stating that it had undertaken to guarantee the debts of one of the firm's customers. The firm subsequently sought to enforce the guarantee on the basis that a contract had been formed. The defendant bank admitted that by stating that it had given a guarantee it had made an incorrect statement of fact because at the time of writing it had wrongly assumed that a guarantee had been undertaken at an earlier stage. The bank claimed that its letter to the claimants was only supposed to confirm the existence of the guarantee, but there had been no intention to make a (new) undertaking to provide a guarantee: because all that was intended was to give a representation of factual circumstances the bank lacked any awareness of making a legally relevant declaration of intent.

Held: The BGH held that the letter could be understood objectively as constituting the undertaking itself, and that a contract had been formed. Normally the defendants could have sought avoidance for mistake under § 119(1) BGB and they would also have been liable to pay the claimants reliance damages under § 122 BGB.[58] However, the Court held that they had lost this right because of undue delay in claiming it.

Judgment (majority of references omitted):
a) The view that the awareness of making a legally relevant declaration of intent (*Erklärungsbewusstsein*) is a constitutive element of a declaration of intent (*Willenserklärung*), so that its absence makes the declaration void even without the defendant claiming avoidance ... is particularly expounded by Enneccerus/Nipperdey, *Allgemeiner Teil des bürgerlichen Rechts*, 15th edn, vol. I/2, pp 901 *et seq*; ... The opinion that a declaration made without such awareness, but which the recipient could reasonably understand to be aimed at a legal transaction, is valid in the first place, although it can avoided like an error of declaration under §§ 119(1), 120, 121 BGB, is mostly held by Larenz, *Methode der Auslegung des Rechtsgeschäfts*, pp 82 *et seq*; ...

---

[56] On this approach, avoidance on the ground of mistake under § 119(1) BGB would not be an issue in this case, since there is in effect nothing to avoid. Furthermore there would be no obligation on the 'mistaken' party to make compensation under § 122 BGB. See the following case of *The bank guarantee* and below, p 499.

[57] BGHZ 91, 324. Translation based on a translation by G Dannemann, used with his kind permission.

[58] The German rules on mistake are discussed in detail in ch 14 below, pp 499–520.

So far, the Bundesgerichtshof has not conclusively decided on this issue. ...

b) This present Senate ... has arrived at the conclusion that, in order for the obligation to provide a guarantee to be valid, it does not matter whether or not those representing the defendant, when signing and dispatching their letter of 8 September 1981, actually had the will to make, or were even conscious of making, a declaration aimed at a legal transaction. In conformity with the view expressed by Bydlinski (JZ 1975, 1) and Kramer (*Münchener Kommentar* § 119 paras 81 *et seq*), the following considerations are decisive for this result: the concept of declaration of intent is not defined in §§ 116 *et seq* BGB. More particularly, the wording of § 119 BGB does not provide an argument against the view advanced by the present Senate. That a party did not wish to make 'a declaration of this content' is not only true for a party which intended a legal transaction with a different content, but also for a party which did not want to make any declaration aimed at a legal transaction at all. It cannot be concluded from § 118 BGB [see Note (1) after this case] that a lack of awareness of making a legally relevant declaration of intent (or the lack of will to do business) will always make a declaration void without any need for a rescission. If a party consciously makes a declaration, but without wanting to be bound, while expecting that this would be recognized (as is presupposed by § 118 BGB), voidness corresponds with the intention of this party. There is no need to grant to this party a choice, ie either to uphold the declaration with corresponding rights and obligations, or to rescind the declaration under § 119(1) BGB. This situation cannot be compared to a declaration which was made without the awareness that it could be understood as constituting a legal transaction. Such a declaration is much more similar to a declaration which is affected by a mistake, but which was aimed at a legal transaction. A party who declares to buy, but who actually means to sell, is in a situation very similar to that of a person who gives a signal which commonly indicates purchase, but who does not even think of buying. In both situations, it seems adequate to leave the choice to the party making the declaration, as to whether it wants to rescind under § 119(1) BGB and compensate for reliance damage under § 122 BGB, or else to let his declaration stand and receive any counter-performance which might be due, and which might make the situation more profitable to him than a one-sided obligation to compensate for reliance damage.

This choice also does away with the concern that, without awareness of making a legally relevant declaration, there is no self-determined shaping of one's party autonomy, which cannot simply be replaced by a person's responsibility for his acts. The law on declarations of intent is not built on self-determination by subjects of legal rights alone. In §§ 119, 157 BGB, it also protects the reliance of the recipient of the declaration, as well as certainty in trade, by binding the declaror to consequences which he had not intended, as well as—and this should be dealt with in a similar fashion—to legal consequences which he had not been conscious of instigating. By granting the declaror, who in both situations did not intend the legal consequences which were actually expressed by his declaration, the right to either destroy these consequences ab initio by way of rescission (§ 142(1) BGB), or else to uphold them, the idea of self-determination is given sufficient weight ...

However, in cases where the awareness of making a legally relevant declaration is absent, a declaration of intent exists only if it can as such be attributed to the party who actually makes the declaration. In order for the declaration to be attributed to a party it is necessary that this party, if he had exercised the care which is required in the course of business, could have realised, and avoided, that his declaration or conduct should have been understood by the recipient as a declaration of intent in accordance with good faith and with due regard to trade practice ...

Notes

(1) § 118 BGB provides:

Lack of seriousness. A declaration of intent not seriously intended which is made in the expectation that its lack of serious intention will not be misunderstood is void.

(2) The Court makes clear that, while there is a contract under German law, the mistaken party may be able to avoid the contract. In Chapter 14 we will see that there are major differences between the English and German systems as to when a party may be able to escape from a contract on the grounds of mistake.

(3) There is a significant difference in German law between holding that there is no contract and that there is a contract that may be avoided for mistake. In the latter case, the party who avoids the contract may have to compensate the other party for its reliance loss under § 122 BGB.[59]

BW   **5.14 (NL)**

Article 3:33: A juridical act requires an intention to produce juridical effects, which intention has manifested itself by a declaration.

Article 3:35: The absence of intention in a declaration cannot be invoked against a person who has interpreted another's declaration or conduct, in conformity with the sense which he could reasonably attribute to it in the circumstances, as a declaration of a particular tenor made to him by that other person.

Note

Articles 3:33 and 3:35 BW should be read together. Within Dutch literature, three doctrines are distinguished: voluntarism, the declaration doctrine, which seems to be comparable to the English approach, and the reliance doctrine. There is no agreement of opinion as to which doctrine to adopt.[60] The legislator has adopted none of them, but has combined all three approaches. One commentator puts it as follows: the declaration of the will involves not only the declaration of the real will, but also the expectations on which the other party reasonably could have relied, taking into account all the relevant facts and circumstances of the case.[61] So, as a result of reliance, there may be a contract even though subjectively the parties were not in agreement.

---

[59] See further below, 499–500.
[60] See for an overview of the discussion in Dutch literature: AS Hartkamp & CH Sieburgh, *Mr. C. Assers Handleiding tot de beoefening van het Nederlands Burgerlijk Recht. 6. Verbintenissenrecht. Deel III. Algemeen overeenkomstenrecht* (Deventer: Kluwer 2014) nos. 121 ff.
[61] ibid, nos. 125 ff.

Court of Appeal's Hertogenbosch, 22 January 2008[62]   **5.15 (NL)**

Stichting Postwanorder v Otto BV

Although a contract may be made when one party accepts what reasonably appears to be an offer by the other party, no contract will come into existence if what was said could not reasonably have been understood to be the offer.

Facts: Otto BV (hereafter Otto), a mail order company, had a website on which consumers could order items. From 20 October 2006 onwards, Otto offered a 80 centimetre wide flat-screen television for €99.90. Three days later Otto changed the price to €99.00. In the media, a discussion was started concerning this offer. After six days of discussion, Otto made a statement in the media that the price was a mistake; it should have been much higher. On 26 October 2006 Otto withdrew the offer from its website.

Approximately 12,000 consumers had ordered a 80 cm flat screen television via Otto's website for the price of either €99.00 or €99.90.

After having ordered the television via the website, consumers who had placed the order received a message on their computer screens, according to which an email would be sent to them, which would include the confirmation of the order and the price of the object ordered. Subsequently, Otto sent a letter dated 27 October 2006, to its customers, in which it stated that no contract was concluded and that all orders were cancelled.

In November 2006, a foundation to protect the interests of consumers who had bought a flat-screen television, *Stichting Postwanorder*, was established. This foundation represented approximately 850 customers. After the refusal by Otto to deliver the televisions to the customers for the price of either €99.00 or €99.90, Stichting Postwanorder started interim proceedings against Otto and asked for performance of the sales contracts. In first instance, the Court dismissed the claim. The foundation lodged an appeal.

Held: The decision of the court of first instance was upheld.

Judgment: [4.7] The parties disagree as to whether a contract of sale was concluded between Otto and the consumers. A contract is entered into by an offer and an acceptance thereof (Article 6:217(1) BW).

...

[4.8] On the basis of Article 3:33 BW, in order to be valid both an offer and an acceptance require that the will and the declaration of the offeror and the acceptor are in agreement. It is not disputed that the consumers validly accepted the offer. The essence of this dispute is whether Otto made a valid offer. Only when it is plausible that that there is a valid offer, can the offer's acceptance result in the conclusion of a contract of sale and Otto be required to perform.

[4.9] Contrary to what the Stichting argued, Otto has proven sufficiently, according to the preliminary judgment of the Court of Appeal, that Otto made a mistake. In this respect, Otto has proven sufficiently that, due to a failure in its computer system, the price of a wall-mounting bracket was mistakenly shown as the price of the LCD TV ... In deciding, it is presumed that Otto's offer to sell the LCD TV for the price of either €99.90 or €99.00 does not correspond to the will of Otto.

[4.10] The legislator does not attach the remedy of either voidness or avoidance to a declaration that does not correspond to the will. When a declaration lacks a corresponding will, according to Article 3:33 BW there is no valid juristic act, which implies that there is no valid offer.

...

[62] Gerechtshof's-Hertogenbosch, 22 January 2008, C0700350, LJN: BC2420.

[4.14] On the basis of what is stated above, no valid contract of sale is concluded on the basis of Article 3:33 BW, since it is clear that Otto's declaration does not correspond to its will.

[4.15] However, despite the lack of a declaration that corresponds to its will, Otto is bound by the declaration ... in the case of a justified reliance by the consumers (Article 3:35 BW). The question to be addressed is whether the consumers when they accepted the offer, could reasonably assume that it concerned a correct/proper offer considering all the circumstances of the case. If the answer is in the affirmative, then a contract is entered into on the basis of justified reliance (Article 3:35 BW).

[4.16] In order to answer this question, the starting point is the average consumer, that is to say an average well-informed consumer. It can be expected from a consumer who intends to buy a LCD television that he acquaints himself roughly of the prices. When this consumer, subsequently, sees for sale on Otto's website:

a) a HD ready broad screen LCD television
b) of Philips brand
c) with screen width of 80 centimetres
d) for the price of either €99.00 or €99.90,
e) that is stated in capitals to be NEW
f) whereas, it appears that it does not concern a stunt offer, a loss-leader or any other type of special offer, in that situation the consumer must understand that there has been a mistake. The average well-informed consumer knows or at least should know that the prices of comparable LCD televisions vary from €700.00 to approximately €1,300.00.

[4.17] Insofar as it was not obvious to the consumer from the start that it concerned a mistake, then the consumer should have had some doubts, given that the difference in price was considerable. In the case of doubt concerning the correctness of the price, the consumer should conduct further research (Article 3:11 BW). This will not result in chaos on the internet, as the Foundation argues. Generally, the prices given by the service supplier can be trusted. This applies only in the case when further research is required, which is not problematic. It is the opposite. One of the advantages of the internet is that a consumer can discover relatively easily at which prices other suppliers offer the same or similar televisions. It also would have been enough to call the customer services of Otto, which would have confirmed that the price was not the correct one. In case the consumer fails to do the research, he is treated as being aware of the facts to which the research would have led. In short, also in the case of doubt, the consumers could and should have known that the price stated by Otto was a mistake.

[4.18] In order to assess whether there is justified reliance, it does not matter that Otto left the offer for the sale of the televisions on the website for seven days, originally for the price €99.90 which changed after three days to a price of €99.00. This does not alter the fact that it should have been clear that there had been a mistake, taking into account the considerable price difference.

[4.19] Also the fact that Otto sent an order confirmation twice is not relevant to assess the justified reliance. The consumer's trust must be based on the circumstances present at the moment of acceptance. The confirmation is received at a later moment. ...

[4.20] Considering the above, the preliminary conclusion of the Court of Appeal is that the acceptance of the offer by the consumers does not result in the fact that Otto is bound. ...

Notes

(1) This decision concerns a preliminary judgment both in first instance and in appeal. Remarkably, within its decision the Court of Appeal holds that in a procedure on the merits a judge will probably not decide differently.

(2) The result would almost certainly be the same under English law; the court would probably hold that the consumers must have known that there was a mistake.[63] That was the outcome in the Singapore case of *Chwee Kin Keong v Digilandmall Com Pte Ltd*,[64] where the facts were very similar to those of *Stichting Postwanorder v Otto BVI*. One of the claimants noticed that the defendants were advertising colour laser printers on the internet at Singapore $66. A normal price would have been between $3,500 and $4,000 (the defendants' list price at the time was $3,854). He alerted a number of his friends and, between them, they placed orders over the Internet for 1,606 printers. The defendants' computer went through the appropriate motions to complete the deals. All of the transactions took place in the early hours of a Singapore morning. When the defendants became aware of the transactions when business opened, they immediately repudiated them and the claimants brought an action for breach of contract. The Singapore Court of Appeal held that the action failed because the claimants knew that the defendants did not intend to sell at $66.

5.2.B INTENTION TO CREATE LEGAL RELATIONS

The second element required to make a contract under the PECL is an intention to be legally bound. At least in principle, an intention to create legal relations—a contract—is required in each system, though again what is required varies. We will consider the intention to create legal relations in detail in Chapter 10. Here it suffices to make a number of introductory points.

The first is that in all the systems it will be assumed that an agreement made in a commercial context is assumed to be intended to create legal relations. In English law, for example, there is a presumption that such an agreement was meant to be legally binding. This presumption does not apply, however, when the agreement was a 'social' or 'domestic' arrangement, nor when it was a 'collective bargaining agreement' between an employer and a trade union.

Secondly, in each system it is possible for the parties to agree that their agreement should not have legal consequences. Thus, as a general rule, there will be no contract where the agreement expressly indicates that it is not to be legally binding.

Thirdly, the question whether a legally binding contract was 'intended' is linked to the question discussed in the previous section. In English law, for example, whether a party intended to be legally bound will be judged not by their subjective intention but objectively, by how it reasonably appeared to the other party. The other laws may place more emphasis on the parties' subjective intentions to create a contractual obligation.

---

[63] Compare the case of *Hartog v Colin & Shields*, see 14.21 (EN) below, p 511.
[64] [2005] 1 SLR 502.

5.3 SYNALLAGMATIC AND UNILATERAL CONTRACTS

Probably the majority of contracts involve each of the parties having one or more obligations. This is the case with contracts under which one party must deliver goods or provide services and the other must pay for them. This includes contracts for the sale or supply of goods and contracts for services (which include banking contracts, construction contracts, insurance contracts, transport contracts and many others). However, there may also be contracts in which the party who has made a promise either (1) seems to be getting nothing in return; or (2) is not being promised anything in return—it is left up to the other party whether or not to perform, and only if they do will the promisor's obligation come into effect. We have dealt with the first issue, that of 'gratuitous' contracts, in Section 5.1.B above and have seen that different systems adopt different categorisations in this regard. This is also true for the second issue, that of 'unilateral' contracts, where we will see that the same word or phrase (particularly 'unilateral contract') may mean rather different things in different systems.

5.3.A THE DISTINCTION IN GENERAL

The concept of synallagmatic contract is significant in continental and common law countries. After some discussion, the revised French Code civil kept it although the category seems to overlap with that of onerous contracts.

Code civil   **5.16 (FR)**

Article 1106: A contract is synallagmatic where the parties undertake reciprocal obligations in favour of each other.

It is unilateral where one or more persons undertake obligations in favour of one or more others without there being any reciprocal obligation on the part of the latter.

Article 1107: A contract is onerous where each of the parties receives a benefit from the other in return for what he provides.

It is gratuitous where one of the parties provides a benefit to the other without expecting or receiving anything in return.

Article 1108: A contract is commutative where each of the parties undertakes to provide a benefit to the other which is regarded as the equivalent of what he receives.

It is aleatory where the parties agree that the effects of the contract— both as regards its resulting benefits and losses—shall depend on an uncertain event.

Notes

(1) In French law, unilateral contracts are those where only one party has obligations. Unilateral are opposed to synallagmatic contracts, where the parties undertake reciprocal obligations in favour of each other. A contract which imposes an obligation on one party and does not require anything of the other party (in the sense that it does not put any reciprocal obligation on the part of the latter) is a unilateral contract when it is based on an agreement. In this respect, it differs from a unilateral juridical act

(Article 1100-1 Cciv). Typical examples of unilateral contracts in French law are the pre-emption agreement or *pacte de préférence* (under which a party agrees that if he decides to sell a piece of property, he will give the other the right of first refusal at whatever price he is going to sell: Article 1123 Civ) and the *promesse de vente* (under which one party gives the other an option to purchase the property at an agreed price—although such promises are more frequently bilateral than unilateral since the parties usually agree on the payment of an *indemnité d'immobilisation* by the beneficiary of the promise).

(2) The gratuitous contract referred to in Article 1107 is logically opposed to the onerous contract where each of the parties receives a 'benefit from the other in return for what he provides'. It is not the existence of 'reciprocal obligations' (as for synallagmatic contracts) but of reciprocal 'benefits' which characterises onerous contracts. The word 'obligations' puts emphasis on the contractual link while the word benefit emphasises the advantages received from one another. However, in actual practice, the distinction between synallagmatic and onerous contracts will often be hard to make (all synallagmatic contracts are onerous contracts).

(3) Some authors argue that this distinction which French law inherited from Pothier (while Domat only made one classification) could have been abandoned and that a unitary approach would have been more in line with some foreign laws,[65] but others argue that the distinction is useful and that the English notion of 'unilateral contract' (to which we will turn shortly) highlights the difference.[66] The new definitions in the Code civil show that a synallagmatic contract is always onerous and that there may be onerous unilateral contracts. Conversely, a gratuitous contract is always unilateral, but a unilateral contract may be onerous.[67] We will see below that English law also recognises synallagmatic contracts (though it is more usual to refer to them as 'bilateral' contracts).

The definition of synallagmatic contract given by the French Code civil corresponds to the definition in Dutch law which applies by way of analogy 'to other juridical relationships intended for the reciprocal performance of prestations':

BW   **5.17 (NL)**

Article 6:261: (1) A contract is synallagmatic if each of the parties assumes an obligation to obtain the prestation to which the other party, in exchange, obligates himself toward him.

(2) The provisions respecting synallagmatic contracts apply mutatis mutandis to other juridical relationships intended for the reciprocal performance of prestations, to the extent that this is not incompatible with the nature of those juridical relationships.

---

[65] F Chénedé, *Le nouveau droit des obligations et des contrats: Consolidations, innovations, perspectives* (Paris: Dalloz, 2016) no. 21.53.

[66] M Fabre-Magnan, *Droit des obligations*, t. 1, *Contrat et engagement unilatéral* (4th edn, Paris: PUF, 2016) no. 172.

[67] ibid.

The BGB does not define the concept of synallagmatic contract, but it contains an entire set of rules that is dedicated to the performance and non-performance of such agreements in particular. These provisions (§§ 320–326) are placed under the heading 'reciprocal contract' (*gegenseitiger Vertrag*). There is no such a thing as a unilateral contract under German law, although, as we have seen, 'unilateral legal transactions' are recognised in the context of contract law (notices of termination) and beyond (wills, promises of reward).[68]

In English law, there will normally be no contractual obligation on one party unless the other provides 'consideration'. As we will see in more detail in Chapter 11, this may be an obligation undertaken in return (when the contract will of course be synallagmatic or 'bilateral') or it may be some action which the other party is not *obliged* to do but nonetheless has carried out.[69] This is called a unilateral contract; a classic example is the celebrated judgment in *Carlill v Carbolic Smoke Ball Co Ltd*.[70] In that case, as we will see below, the Carbolic Smoke Ball Company promised to pay £100 to anyone who used the company's product for three weeks yet still caught influenza. Mrs Carlill used the smoke ball as directed and caught the' flu. The Court of Appeal held that the Company was contractually obliged to pay her £100. It is obvious that Mrs Carlill was not undertaking anything in that case—not even to use the smoke ball, let alone to catch 'flu. But if she used it and caught the' flu, the company would have to perform its (conditional) promise to pay the £100. Unilateral contracts are not uncommon in English law. For example, often the arrangement between a person who wishes to sell a house and an estate agent who may help to find a buyer will be in the form of a unilateral contract: the estate agent will not undertake to do anything (not even to advertise the house) but if the agent finds a buyer and the sale goes through, the seller will have to pay an agreed commission to the agent. The seller relies on the incentive that the arrangement gives the agent to find a buyer.

The question whether a unilateral promise to which the promisee has not expressed agreement may give rise to an obligation, in the absence of any specific legislative provision, is very controversial. Each system recognises that some 'unilateral juridical acts' can have legal effects—for example, a will that has not been revoked when the testator dies will confer rights (possibly of a proprietary nature) on the beneficiaries. But what about a simple unilateral promise or contract-like undertaking?

The answer appears to be that in each system there are some situations in which a unilateral promise or similar juridical act will create obligations. We have just seen an example from English law, the deed.[71] A deed requires a high degree of formality, but sometimes unilateral obligations may be created without formality. Thus in Chapter 8 we will see that in some systems an offer accompanied by a fixed period for acceptance cannot be revoked within that period.

---

[68] See above, p 96 and below, p 119.

[69] For a very careful analysis of synallagmatic (or 'bilateral') contracts and unilateral contracts in English law, see the judgment of Diplock LJ in *United Dominions Trust Ltd v Eagle Aircraft Services Ltd* [1968] 1 WLR 74, 82 (CA).

[70] See 8.8 (EN) below, p 217.

[71] See above, p 98.

5.3.B PROMISES OF REWARD

In many systems the promise of a reward is regarded as a classic example of a unilateral act. Under the BGB, a promise of reward (*Auslobung*) is binding simply because it was made to the public.

BGB	**5.18 (DE)**

§ 657: Binding promise
   A person who by public notice announces a reward for the performance of an act in particular for the production of a result, is bound to pay the reward to any person who has performed the act, even if he did not act with a view to the promise of reward.

§ 658: Revocation
   (1) The promise of reward may be revoked until the act has been performed. The revocation is effective only if is made known in the same manner as the promise of reward, or by special notice.
   (2) The revocability may be waived in the promise of reward; in case of doubt a waiver is presumed from the fact that a period of time has been fixed for the performance of the act.

> *Note*
>
>   § 657 BGB is placed in Book II of the BGB which deals with the law of obligations, right between different types of contract. The promise of reward is, however, not categorised as a contract but as a 'unilateral legal transaction' (*einseitiges Rechtsgeschäft*).[72] The drafters of the BGB deliberately deviated from the previously-held German view that the promise was to be regarded as an offer to indeterminate persons *(ad incertas personas)* which could be accepted by performing the act.[73]

In contrast, the analysis of 'reward' cases under English law is contractual. At first sight it may be difficult to see how the question can arise, because there can be no binding promise in the absence of consideration, something 'exchanged for' the promise.[74] However, very much like in German law before 1900, the promise of reward is treated as an offer which is accepted by the performance of an act. Doing the act also provides consideration, as it did in *Carlill v Carbolic Smoke Ball Company*.[75] But where the recipient did not know of the promise of reward at the outset or was not motivated by the offer, there will be no contract under the common law.[76]

---

[72] For the concept of 'legal transaction', see above, p 96.
[73] Münchener Kommentar/Sieber § 657 para 4.
[74] See further below, ch 11.2.A, pp 344–65.
[75] [1893] 1 QB 256 (CA), described above, p 118; and see further 8.8 (EN) below, p 217.
[76] *R v Clarke* (1927) 40 CLR 227 (High Court of Australia).

In Dutch law, a reward is also considered to be an offer which must be accepted by the other party in order to create a contract.[77] However, if the recipient did not know of the promise of the reward, the recipient is entitled to the reward, but no contract is created.[78]

In French law, there has been considerable academic debate on the promise of a reward (*promesse de récompense*). The courts have decided that if the conditions are fulfilled, the reward must be paid. In other words, the promisor is precluded from going back on his undertaking even though the claimant did not at the time make any agreement with the promisor. Some authors argue that the *promesse de récompense* is essentially contractual, others that it takes effect as a unilateral engagement (so that a person who returns the lost dog without knowing of the reward would qualify for the reward). The 2016 reform does not expressly deal with promises of reward but new Article 1100-1 expressly recognises the existence and validity of unilateral acts.[79]

5.4 CONCLUSION

In this chapter, we have seen that the notions of contract differ from one legal system to the other. While it is everywhere acknowledged that only agreements which the law will enforce qualify as contracts, there are diverging views as to what exactly constitutes an agreement and when exactly an agreement is enforceable in law. In some legal systems, the parties will only be taken to have reached agreement if they have ('subjectively') intended the same thing; in others, if their statements and other conduct ('objectively') mean the same thing. In English law, an agreement is only enforceable in law if it constitutes an exchange which places some burden on each party and is thus onerous; in contrast, continental laws also enforce gratuitous agreements, under which one of the parties does not receive anything in return for its performance. In some legal systems, obligations may also be created voluntarily without the agreement of both parties, ie, by way of a unilateral promise that the promisor intended to be legally binding. Yet, such obligations are regarded as exceptional.

FURTHER READING

Cartwright, J and Whittaker, S (eds), *The Code Napoléon Rewritten: French Contract Law after the 2016 Reforms* (Oxford: Hart Publishing, 2017), see esp. Whittaker, S, 'Contracts, Contract Law and Contractual Principle' 29–55.

Kötz H, *European Contract Law* (2nd edn, Oxford University Press, 2017).

Nicholas, B, *The French Law of Contract* (2nd edn, Oxford: Clarendon Press, 1992) 61–69.

Sacco, R, 'Formation of Contracts' in A Hartkamp et al, *Towards a Civil Code* (4th edn, Nijmegen: Ars Aequi, 2011) 483–92.

Zweigert, K and Kötz, H, *Introduction to Comparative Law* (3rd edn, Oxford: Clarendon Press, 1998) 356–64.

---

[77] *Asser/Hartkamp & Sieburgh 6-III* 2014/171 (n 60 above).

[78] ibid.

[79] See above, p 95; see also the discussion and sources cited in Fabre-Magnan (n 66 above) no. 741. For example, if an employer makes an announcement to its employees, it may be held to its word by those employees who relied on the announcement, even if they did not 'accept' the employer's promise.

CHAPTER 6
CONTRACT AND ADJOINING AREAS

In this chapter we consider the place that contract law occupies in each of the three main systems we are looking at by considering how it relates to adjoining areas of law. We focus on the law of property, the law of tort (or delict) and the law of restitution (or unjustified enrichment).

6.1 CONTRACT AND PROPERTY

6.1.A GENERAL CONSIDERATIONS

Exchange has long been considered the 'mainspring of any economic system that relies on free enterprise'.[1] Today, exchanges are frequently about services, particularly in the digital economy.[2] Historically, however, sales contracts featured most prominently in contract law. Therefore contract and property, the branch of law that governs the various forms of ownership, have close links.

The division of property into real and personal represents in a great measure the division into immovables and movables incidentally recognised in Roman law and generally adopted since. The law of personal property is particularly important for commercial law and insolvency. Property in land is the domain of the law of real property.

The French Code civil pays great attention to property. As already noted in Chapter 4, contract is dealt with in Title III of Book III of the Code civil, under the rubric 'Amongst the different ways in which property may be acquired'. This says much about the spirit of the Civil Code of 1804, sometimes described as 'the owners' code'. This Code was among the first to introduce the notion of absolute ownership.

In Germany, the place of property law in private law is slightly different from France. As has been seen in Chapters 4 and 5, German law is similar to French law in that it

---

[1] A Farnsworth, 'Comparative Contract Law' in M Reimann and R Zimmermann (eds), *Oxford Handbook of Comparative Law* (Oxford University Press, 2006) 899, 905.
[2] See ch 1.

also categorises contract law as a part of the law of obligations. However, the German Bürgerliches Gesetzbuch (BGB) draws a clearer dividing line between the law of obligations and the law of property which are dealt with in Books II and III of the Code, respectively. As a result, a transfer of property that is effected by a contract is regarded as legally distinct from the contract itself. This will be discussed in more detail in the following section. Like in France, the property law rules concerning movables differ from those concerning land.

In England, property law encompasses four main topics: land law, or the law of 'real property', the law of trusts, the law of personal property and intellectual property law. The latter has also become enormously important in French and German law, but is beyond the scope of this book.

In this section, we shall first look at how the various systems deal with the passing of ownership from one person to another.

6.1.B TRANSFER OF PROPERTY

6.1.B.1 PROPERTY PASSES BY SIMPLE AGREEMENT

In French law, property may be transferred by simple agreement. This purely 'consensual approach' applies to property in moveables and immoveables alike, unless otherwise provided for by statue or agreed upon by the parties.[3] The consensual approach is now codified in the revised Code civil, both in the preliminary section, in Article 1109 which defines three types of contract, and in a section dedicated to the 'form of contract', in Article 1172 which states that 'On principle, contracts require only the consent of the parties'.

Code civil **6.1 (FR)**

Article 1109: A contract is consensual where it is formed by the mere exchange of consents, in whatever way they may be expressed.

A contract is solemn[4] where its validity is subject to form prescribed by legislation.

A contract is real where its formation is subject to the delivery of a thing.

Note

It follows from the consensual system that if the contract is invalid or is avoided (for example for fraud), the property will either never transfer to the buyer or will revest in the seller (unless an innocent third party has acquired rights over the property[5]).

English law also adopts a consensual system to the passing of property in goods.

---

[3] This is particularly so for contracts for the sale of land where notarisation is usually required; this is also the case in Germany (§ 311b BGB), while in England, according to the Law of Property (Miscellaneous Provisions) Act 1989, s 2(1), 'a contract for the sale or other disposition of an interest in land can only be made in writing'. For more detail, see below, ch 12.

[4] Here, 'solemn' refers to a particular class of contracts where formality is required, the so-called *contrats solennels*.

[5] This may happen readily under Art 2276 Cciv, according to which 'as far as moveables are concerned, possession equals title', (*en fait de meubles, la possession vaut titre*).

Section 17: Property passes when intended to pass

(1) Where there is a contract for the sale of specific or ascertained goods the property in them is transferred to the buyer at such time as the parties to the contract intend it to be transferred.

(2) For the purpose of ascertaining the intention of the parties regard shall be had to the terms of the contract, the conduct of the parties and the circumstances of the case.

Section 18: Rules for ascertaining intention

Unless a different intention appears, the following are rules for ascertaining the intention of the parties as to the time at which the property in the goods is to pass to the buyer.

Rule 1:—Where there is an unconditional contract for the sale of specific goods in a deliverable state the property in the goods passes to the buyer when the contract is made, and it is immaterial whether the time of payment or the time of delivery, or both, be postponed.

...

Notes

(1) Other forms of agreement may also pass proprietary rights in goods, for example an agreement for a mortgage or charge.

(2) Equally, if the contract is avoided for fraud, the property will re-vest in the seller.

6.1.B.2 TRANSFER OF TITLE AND THE ABSTRACTION PRINCIPLE

German law has a different approach to the relationship between contract and proprietary rights. It does not adopt the 'consensual' approach of French and English law. A contract may create an obligation to transfer property or to create another *right in rem*. Another act, separate from the contract, is then required to effect the transfer or to create the right:

BGB   **6.3 (DE)**

§ 433: Standard obligations in contracts of sale

(1) By a contract of sale the seller of a thing is bound to hand over the thing to the buyer and to transfer to him ownership of the thing. The seller must procure the thing for the buyer in a state that is free from defects as to quality and defects of title.

(2) The buyer is bound to pay to the seller the agreed price and to take delivery of the thing purchased.

§ 929: Agreement and delivery

For the transfer of ownership of a movable thing, it is necessary that the owner of the thing deliver it to the acquirer and that both agree that the ownership be transferred. If the acquirer is in possession of the thing, the agreement on the transfer of ownership is sufficient.

A contract of sale thus merely creates an obligation to transfer property to the purchaser (§ 433). According to the 'principle of separation' (*Trennungsprinzip*), this transfer is not brought about by the contract of sale (or, indeed, by any other contractual obligation), but only by an additional and separate agreement, the so-called 'real' or 'proprietary agreement' (*dingliche Einigung*) between the transferor and the transferee, also referred to as a 'real contract' (*dinglicher Vertrag*). For the sale of moveables this is set out in § 929(1) BGB: '… it is necessary … that both agree that the ownership be transferred'. This provision also stipulates another requirement for the transfer of property: the goods must be delivered for the property to pass to the buyer.

Invalidity of the underlying contractual obligation does not necessarily entail the invalidity of the real contract since the latter transaction is independent, or 'abstract', from the former (*Abstraktionsprinzip*).[6]

The principles of separation and abstraction are fundamental tenets of German private law, and they have been upheld ever since the coming into force of the BGB. As a matter of legal policy, however, they are by no means uncontroversial. They have been criticised as unnecessarily complex, excessively conceptual and completely remote from everyday life. But the principles have been defended on grounds of both analytical clarity and legal policy.

As a matter of legal policy, the principle of abstraction is defended since it facilitates commerce by upholding transfers of real rights and thereby sustaining the ordinary flow of goods. The good faith transferee will acquire the right regardless of the validity of the underlying contractual obligation. He then has the power of disposition and can validly transfer the right to a third party. As a result, the third party will acquire good title and need not be concerned about the contractual relationship between the original transferor and transferee.

Other legal systems, where the transfer of the real right follows immediately from the contract, have found answers to questions such as acquisition by an innocent third party without relying on the principles of separation and abstraction, and usually these answers are satisfactory. They are, however, forced to merge the criteria for the transfer of property into the discussion of the scope of the parties' contractual obligations. English law, for instance, attaches different proprietary consequences to different kinds of contractual mistakes. As opposed to this, the transfer of property under German law is not affected by the mere fact that one or both parties have entered the contract under some kind of mistake. The existence of the principle of abstraction may thus explain why German law can afford to be fairly generous in accepting that mistakes set a contract aside, whilst English law adopts a much narrower doctrine of mistake.[7] The principle also has repercussions outside the laws of contract and property. It explains the comparatively great relevance and sophistication of unjustified enrichment in German law.

A 1925 decision of the Reichsgericht,[8] shows how the doctrine operates and also why German lawyers have referred to the law of unjustified enrichment as the 'child of the principle of abstraction'. A deceased man had transferred property to a married woman who was his mistress. This gift (which is treated by German law as a type of contract) was held to be contrary to good morals (§ 138 BGB) and therefore invalid. This did not

---

[6] See p 125 below.
[7] See below, ch 14.
[8] RG 25 June 1925, RGZ 111, 152.

invalidate the transfer. However, the man's widow was entitled to claim restitution under § 817 BGB. Under German law, the deed of transfer remains valid in accordance with the principle of abstraction and recourse must be had to the doctrine of unjustified enrichment in order to secure restitution. The mistress 'unjustifiably enriched' herself at the expense of the lawful wife.[9]

Zweigert and Kötz[10]   **6.4 (DE)**

Now if a legal system not only makes this distinction between the contract of sale and the real contract in this sense, but also makes the validity of each independent of the validity of the other, it accepts the doctrine of the 'abstract real contract'. By virtue of this doctrine, once a purchaser has made a 'real' contract with his vendor and has received delivery of the purchased property from him, in principle he obtains ownership in the thing even if the contract of sale was void from the beginning, or is subsequently rescinded or is invalid in any other way: the real agreement is thus 'abstract' because, given delivery or constructive delivery, it transfers the property even if no valid contract of sale was concluded or if the contract of sale was originally valid but has subsequently lapsed. Of course in such a case the purchaser is not entitled to retain the property; he has become owner, but has done so in the absence of a valid contract of sale, that is, 'without legal cause', and is therefore bound to retransfer the property to the vendor as an 'unjustified enrichment' pursuant to § 812 BGB.

These rules apply in German law not only when property is sold but also when it is donated or given in exchange, or when it is transferred to a creditor as security for a loan or to a trustee for purposes of administration: in all these cases a distinction is drawn between the 'basic transaction' or 'causal transaction' (namely the contract of sale, or the declaration of gift, security or trust) and the 'completion transaction' or 'performance transaction', namely the transfer of property; the 'abstract' completion agreement may be valid notwithstanding the invalidity of the basic transaction and thus the purchaser, the donee, the creditor or the trustee will have become owner. This is true not only in the case of things, moveable or immoveable, but also in the case on the transfer of a claim; here too the assignee may become owner of the claim which has been assigned, even if the 'basic transaction'—namely the contract of sale, agency or security—was invalid in some way. Furthermore the same is true when a limited real right, such as a right of hypothec, is to be transferred; here too the law treats as independent the contractual agreement to give security and the 'real contract' which creates the hypothec.

In English law, if a contract of sale of goods is avoided (for example on the ground of fraud) title to the goods revests in the seller, who can then recover the goods or their value from the buyer or anyone to whom the buyer has sold them.[11] It may seem odd that in

---

[9] For a comparison with French law, see A Rieg, *Le rôle de la volonté dans l'acte juridique en droit civil français et allemand* (Paris: LGDJ, 1961) nos. 278–82.

[10] K Zweigert and H Kötz, *Introduction to Comparative Law*, vol I, *The Framework* (Amsterdam/New York/Oxford: North-Holland Publishing, 1977) 178–79 (the passage was dropped from the second edition onwards).

[11] There are limited exceptions when the second buyer is a good faith purchaser; see Sale of Goods Act 1979, s 25 and *Newtons of Wembley Ltd v Williams* [1965] 1 QB 560 (CA). Curiously, English law does not provide the owner of goods with a simple proprietary action by which to recover them. Instead, the owner must bring an action in the tort of conversion to recover the value of the goods; sometimes the court will make an order that the actual goods must be returned.

English law, despite the recognition of a consensual system of transfer of property, the reasoning on the facts of the case of the gift to the mistress would be closer to German law than to French law. This is because it is accepted that a contract which is contrary to public policy, though unenforceable, may nonetheless be effective to pass property. Any claim to recover it would have to be by way of restitution.[12] However, the result would be different to that under German law. If the property given to the mistress belonged to the man, there is no basis in English law on which his widow could recover it.

It should be noted that German law uses the notion of 'abstract' obligations in yet another sense. Certain contracts create such an obligation because they do not contain the motivation for their conclusion (the *causa*) in themselves. Whilst a contract of sale, for instance, is concluded in order to acquire property or to obtain the purchase price, some other contracts are not similarly self-sufficient. Thus a promise to fulfil an obligation, defined in § 780 BGB as 'a contract by means of which performance is promised in such a way that the mere promise is intended to establish the obligation', is usually made in order to affirm the existence of another contractual obligation. Its validity does not, however, depend on the validity of this other obligation. In a similar fashion a bill of exchange or a cheque is 'abstract' from an underlying contract of sale. The bill may be enforced despite the invalidity of the underlying contract. English and French law both also recognise similar categories of separable or 'abstract' acts which may be detached from the underlying transaction. Such acts are valid irrespective of whether there is a valid underlying transaction. But this is an exceptional category, confined to certain transactions, such as exchange transactions or first-call guarantees.

6.1.C GIFTS

We have already noted in Chapter 5 that both French and German law will enforce a promise to make a gift but that special formal requirements may have to be complied with, if only for tax reasons. In English law, though normally a promise will not be enforceable (and thus there will be no contract) unless there was consideration for the promise, consideration is not required if the promise is made by deed. The main issue to be considered in this section is different: what amounts to a completed gift and what is its nature—is it a transfer of property or is it a specific type of contract? However, since the legislative texts sometimes deal simultaneously with both issues—the conditions under which a promise to make a gift may be enforced, as well as its nature—we will deal with them both at the same time.

As for gifts, the Code civil appears to treat them as a type of contract which will be enforceable only if formal requirements are met.

Code civil **6.5 (FR)**

Article 931: All acts containing an inter vivos gift shall be executed before *notaires*, in the ordinary form of contracts; and there shall remain the original of them, on pain of annulment.

---

[12] This is explored in more detail when we consider illegal contracts, below, p 712.

Article 932: An inter vivos gift is binding upon the donor and produces effect only from the day when it is accepted in express terms.

Acceptance may be made during the lifetime of the donor, by a subsequent and authentic instrument of which the original shall remain; but then the gift has effect, with regard to the donor, only from the day when he has been given notice of the instrument which establishes that acceptance.

Article 938: A gift duly accepted is complete by the sole consent of the parties; and ownership of the articles donated is transferred to the donee without need of any other delivery.

Notes

(1) Between living persons (*inter vivos*; testamentary promises are outside the scope of this book) a promise of a future gift is effective only if it has been notarised, and if it has been accepted by the donee. The French courts have put aside the requirements of Article 931 Cciv for *dons manuels*, which are constituted by handing over the thing or by a payment made into the donee's bank account (thus considered as *don manuel*). In both cases, the transfer of ownership is regarded as a sufficient formality. A person who is disposing of its asset by handing it over is normally conscious of what he or she is doing.

(2) The notarised form serves to ensure that the donor's intention is real and that the donor is well informed. This is important because of the close connection between gifts and anticipated legacies for which the donee may have to account for on claiming his or her right of succession. This is so because, in French law, the *réserve héréditaire* gives close relatives a right to inherit and the law must prevent lifetime gifts which would frustrate this right.

(3) In French law a promise of a gift may rank as a contract and transfer the property in the thing promised. However, a mere promise does not necessarily suffice to transfer ownership to the donee. In some cases, it will do so only if two conditions are satisfied. First, the undertaking must be notarised. Second, the promise must be accepted. In contrast, if the item is effectively delivered to the donee, the *don manuel* transfers the property.

(4) New Article 931-1 (formerly Articles 1339 and 1340) Cciv was inserted in the Code civil by Ordonnance no. 2016-131 on contract law (the other provisions on gifts were not affected by this reform). The provision sets out the consequences of the violation of a formal requirement: the gift cannot be confirmed and must be remade, with the appropriate legal form, unless it is done by the heirs, after the promisor's death.

(5) French law also recognises indirect gifts. An indirect gift may be an act of giving carried out by means of a 'neutral' transaction such as the remission of a debt or a waiver. It may even be a disguised gift, ie one concealed within a transaction purporting to be for valuable consideration, such as a sale in which it is understood that payment of the purchase price will not be demanded.

English law also recognises that the delivery of an item of personal property with the intention of making a gift will transfer ownership to the recipient. Delivery is not seen as a contract but as an act of property transfer. The delivery may be symbolic, eg by handing over the keys to a car or to the warehouse where the goods are stored.

A simple promise to make a gift will not be binding, for reasons that we explained above, and it will not operate to transfer property. However, it is possible for the parties to transfer property by way of gift without delivery by means of a deed. This too is seen as a form of property transfer independent of contract. Until 1989, the deed had to be 'under seal', but this is no longer required since the Law of Property (Miscellaneous Provisions) Act 1989, s 1. This is less stringent than the notarisation required in French law: the deed need only be signed and witnessed and then 'delivered' to the other party or to a third party to hold for the time being. Thus in practice English law reaches the same results as the other systems: a gift may be executed by delivery, or by deed, and a 'gift promise' is legally enforceable provided certain form requirements are met.

In contrast, on this point, German law has a different conceptual structure to both English and French law. On the one hand, it differs from English law, in that it views a gift—even the simple handing over of a thing with both parties being in agreement that a gratuitous disposition be made—as a form of contract. On the other hand, it differs from French law, in that neither the agreement to make a gift nor the actual handing over of the gift as such have the effect of transferring the property in the goods. Because of the 'principle of separation' discussed above, a legally distinct 'real' or 'proprietary agreement' is required to achieve this result and thus meet the obligation from the contract of donation.

BGB   **6.6 (DE)**

§ 516: Concept of donation

(1) A disposition by means of which someone enriches another person from his own assets is a donation if both parties are in agreement that the disposition occurs gratuitously.

(2) If the disposition occurs without the intention of the other party, the donor may, specifying a reasonable period of time, request him to make a declaration as to acceptance. Upon expiry of the period of time, the donation is deemed to be accepted if the other party has not previously rejected it. In the case of rejection, return of what has been bestowed may be demanded under the provisions on the return of unjust enrichment.

§ 518: Form of promise of donation

(1) For a contract by which performance is promised as a donation to be valid, notarial recording of the promise is required. ...

(2) A defect of form is cured by rendering the performance promised.

Notes

(1) § 518 BGB imposes on a gift promise the formal requirement of an officially or notarially recorded instrument; but note that, under § 518(2) BGB, the lack of formalities no longer matters if the promise is performed. This requires that the donor has effected a transfer of the property in question, typically by a 'proprietary agreement' to effect the transfer, combined with the goods promised being delivered or the money promised being paid. Thus a completed *don manuel* is effective without formalities.

(2) § 518(2) BGB provides that lack of form is cured by performance of the promise. In France, we have seen above that Article 931-1(2) Cciv provides that voluntary performance cures the lack of form of a donative promise if the performance is by the *heirs* of the promisor. Moreover, the courts held that, provided the donor was acting spontaneously and with donative intention in making the transfer, his handing over of the thing pursuant to an informal promise can constitute a valid *don manuel*.[13]

(3) In England, the doctrine of consideration leads to the same result since the informal 'gift promise' is only unenforceable, not void.[14]

6.1.D BAILMENT

Before we leave the interface of contract and the law of property, we need to note a unique doctrine of English law which will appear in some of the contract cases. This is the law of bailment. Bailment is the lawful holding of an item by a person who is not the owner thereof with the owner's consent—for example, under a contract of deposit—or without the owner's consent—for example, the finder of lost property. Bailment gives rise to a legal duty to conserve and give up the item. Where the bailment is with the owner's consent, the rules on bailment may overlap with those of contract. However, the rules on bailment sometimes differ considerably from the rules applicable to contract. For example, there is no requirement of consideration and the privity rules do not apply. Equally the rules on bailment overlap with the law of tort. However, a bailee may come under obligations that would not apply but for the bailment. Thus in English law generally there is no obligation to prevent (or, put another way, no liability for failing to prevent) another person's goods being damaged or stolen. But if the goods have been bailed to the defendant, the defendant will have such an obligation. Whether the defendant is liable in tort or on the independent basis of bailment is a matter of some debate.[15]

A classic description of bailment was given by Diplock LJ in *Morris v CW Martin & Sons Ltd*:[16]

> … Duties at common law are owed by one person to another only if there exists a relationship between them which the common law recognises as giving rise to such duty. One of such

---

[13] CA Dijon 26 April 1932, DH 1932, 339. Furthermore, the scope of Art 931 Cciv is significantly restricted by the fact that the courts in France regard a *donation déguisée* (dissimulated gift) as valid without any formality. Such a dissimulated gift occurs if the parties deliberately agree to clothe the gift in the guise of a sale, as by the 'seller' giving the 'buyer' a fictive receipt for the 'price' or where the price is risibly low, even as low as one franc (Cass civ (1) 29 May 1980, no. 79-11378, Bull I no. 164, D 1981, 273, annotated by I Najjar). Such decisions are clearly an evasion of Art 931, but are justified on the ground that the seriousness of the donor's intention to be bound is demonstrated by the trouble the parties have gone to in order to disguise the nature of their transaction. See T Debenest, 'Art 931 Code civil: Donations entre vifs, Fasc. A' in *Juris-classeur civil* (LexisNexis) no. 164: 'L'effort que le donateur doit accomplir pour dissimuler son intention libérale et masquer la donation sous l'apparence d'un contrat à titre onéreux atteste que l'opération a été mûrement réfléchie.'

[14] H Kötz, *European Contract law* (2nd edn, Oxford University Press, 2017) 55.

[15] See WVH Rogers, *Winfield & Jolowicz on Tort* (17th edn, London: Sweet & Maxwell, 2006) paras 1–12.

[16] [1966] 1 QB 716 (CA).

recognised relationships is created by the voluntary taking into custody of goods which are the property of another. … The legal relationship of bailor and bailee of a chattel can exist independently of any contract, for the legal concept of bailment as creating a relationship which gives rise to duties owed by a bailee to a bailor is derived from Roman law and is older in our common law than the legal concept of parol contract as giving rise to legal duties owed by one party to the other party thereto. The nature of those legal duties, in particular as to the degree of care which the bailee is bound to exercise in the custody of the goods and as to his duty to redeliver them, varies according to the circumstances in which and purposes for which the goods are delivered to the bailee. … While most cases of bailment today are accompanied by a contractual relationship between bailee and bailor which may modify or extend the common law duties of the parties that would otherwise arise from the mere fact of bailment, this is not necessarily so—as witness gratuitous bailment or bailment by finding …

One of the common law duties owed by a bailee of goods to his bailor is not to convert them, i.e. not to do intentionally in relation to the goods an act inconsistent with the bailor's right of property therein. … This duty, which is common to all bailments as well as to other relationships which do not amount to bailment, is independent of and additional to the other common law duty of a bailee for reward to take reasonable care of his bailor's goods. Stealing goods is the simplest example of conversion …

To a certain extent, bailment resembles what French law terms as real contract (*contrat réel*). A contract is real 'where its formation is subject to the delivery of a thing' (Article 1109(3) Cciv). This delivery may then give rise to an obligation to return the thing. This category includes *contrats de dépôt* (deposit), *de prêt à usage* (loan for use), *de gage* (pledge) and probably also *don manuel* (this is a contested issue since a *don manuel* results in a transfer of the ownership). It is usually considered that a mere promise of a *contrat réel* does not give rise to specific performance and, to circumvent this rule, French courts have sometimes considered a *contrat réel* as a *contrat consensuel* depending on the quality of the party; thus, for the *prêt d'argent* (money loan) between a consumer and a bank, the Cour de cassation held that the contract was consensual.[17] Some authors think that *contrat réel* is not a useful category and that a *contrat réel* is a consensual contract, the handing over of the thing being the first act of performance of this contract.

In German law, cases of voluntary bailment would be dealt with in the law of contract, mostly as deposits or loans. Cases of involuntary bailment would normally give rise to delictual and proprietary actions. Sometimes there would be a claim arising from the highly specific doctrine of 'owner-possessor-relationship' (*Eigentümer-Besitzer-Verhältnis*) (§§ 987–1003 BGB).

6.2 CONTRACT AND TORT (OR DELICT)

Contract and tort (or delict) stand side by side and sometimes overlap. Non-performance of a contract, like a tort, may cause damage to another person, either the other party or a third person. After setting out the most relevant basic texts, we consider the respective

---

[17] Cass civ (1) 27 May 1998, no. 96-17312, Bull civ I no. 186.

domains of contract and tort before going on to show why we may need to distinguish them. It is not the purpose of this section to give an account of the law of tort (or delict) in each system, but rather to show that the various systems draw the boundary between tort and contract in different places to the effect that the respective domains of contract and tort may vary from one legal system to another.

6.2.A BASIC SOURCES OF THE LAW OF TORT (OR DELICT)

It is often thought that there is a traditional and still significant schism between the continental laws of delict and the common law of tort. There is indeed a fundamental difference in style and structure—the general principles of the codes stand in sharp contrast to the approach of the law of tort in English law: the English system has long been based on a closed system of nominate torts; the tort of negligence is however increasing in importance over other types of tort, providing a wide scope of protection. Eventually 'there is much less diversity in the outcomes than one would expect'.[18] This can also be seen from the fact that different groups of scholars have been able to devise common sets of 'Principles of European Tort Law'. This being said, we set out here only the continental code provisions and the English cases on delict (tort) that are most relevant to contractual liability, and give (we hope) just enough commentary to enable the reader to follow the cases and discussion which will follow later in this section. Full treatment of tort law will be found elsewhere.[19]

A major French tort law reform is under discussion at the time of writing. A reform bill on civil liability was presented on 13 March 2017 by the Minister of Justice, following a public consultation undertaken between April and July 2016.[20] Meanwhile, the effect of the 2016 reform of the Code civil on the law of delict is mainly formal: the famous Articles 1382 to 1384 are now to be found in Articles 1240 to 1242.

Code civil   **6.7 (FR)**

Article 1240: Any act whatever of man, which causes damage to another, obliges the one by whose fault it occurred, to compensate it.

Article 1241: Everyone is liable for the damage he causes not only by his intentional act, but also by his negligent conduct or by his imprudence.

Article 1242: A person is liable not only for the damages he causes by his own act, but also for that which is caused by the acts of persons for whom he is responsible, or by things which are in his custody.

...

---

[18] G Wagner, 'Comparative Tort Law', in M Reimann and R Zimmermann (eds) (n 1 above) 1003.

[19] See in particular the casebook in this series, W van Gerven, P Larouche and J Lever, *Ius Commune Casebooks on the Common Law of Europe: Cases, Materials and Text on Tort Law* (Oxford: Hart Publishing, 2000).

[20] This Bill was translated into English by S Whittaker, in consultation with JS Borghetti. The translation, supplemented by notes written by the translator, is available on www.textes.justice.gouv.fr/textes-soumis-a-concertation-10179/projet-de-reforme-de-la-responsabilite-civile-traduit-en-anglais-30553.html.

Notes

(1) The effect of Articles 1240 and 1241 is, in very broad terms, to create liability for any loss caused intentionally or by negligence. French law does not distinguish between types of loss. Thus damages may be recovered not only in respect of physical harm or damage but also for purely financial loss ('pure economic loss'), provided that it is shown that the harm was caused by the defendant's intentional or negligent act. Nor is there any distinction in principle between negligent acts (or omissions) and negligent words.

(2) Liability is limited to some extent by the need to show that there was 'adequate' causation.

(3) Under what is now Article 1242 Cciv, the courts have developed 'liability for things' (also called *responsabilité objective* or *sans faute*) to impose strict liability. The leading case in this respect is the famous *arrêt Jand'heur*.[21] It is emblematic of the power of French judges who converted a rather insignificant provision (ex-Article 1384(1) (now Article 1242) was not initially meant to have such an ambit) into a general clause for strict liability. The tortfeasor must compensate all losses, even those that are unpredictable or impossible to avoid at reasonable cost. This explains the rise of insurance during the twentieth century both in the form of private liability insurance and social insurance. Since French law has a form of strict liability *sui generis*, regardless of whether the thing is dangerous (ex-Article 1384(1), now Article 1242), some French authors subsequently advocated the abolition of delictual liability in some areas, where insurance is compulsory (notably for traffic road accidents, since the Law of 5 July 1985 on improving the situation of the victims of traffic accidents).[22] A noteworthy development is the creation of a 'third' right of action, neither in tort nor in contract. This applies to product liability: a producer is liable for harm caused by a defect in his product, whether or not he is bound by a contract with the victim (see now Article 1245 Cciv, introduced by the Act of 19 May 1988 which was adopted in pursuance of a European directive).[23]

BGB   **6.8 (DE)**

§ 823: Liability in damages

(1) A person who, intentionally or negligently, unlawfully injures the life, body, health, freedom, property or another right of another person is liable to make compensation to the other party for the damage arising from this.

(2) The same duty is held by a person who commits a breach of a statute that is intended to protect another person. If, according to the contents of the statute, it may also be breached without fault, then liability to compensation only exists in the case of fault.

[21] Cass réun 13 February 1930, Bull no. 34.

[22] G Viney, P Jourdain and S Carval, *Traité de droit civil: Les régimes spéciaux et l'assurance de responsabilité* (4th edn, Paris: LGDJ, 2017).

[23] Council Directive 85/374/EEC of 25 July 1985 on the approximation of the laws, regulations and administrative provisions of the Member States concerning liability for defective products, OJ L 210/1985, p 29. Article 13 of the Directive states that it does 'not affect any rights which an injured person may have according to the rules of the law on contractual or non-contractual liability or a special liability system …'

§ 826: Intentional damage contrary to public policy

A person who, in a manner contrary to public policy, intentionally inflicts damage on another person is liable to the other person to make compensation for the damage.

§ 831: Liability for vicarious agents

(1) A person who uses another person to perform a task is liable to make compensation for the damage that the other unlawfully inflicts on a third party when carrying out the task. Liability in damages does not apply if the principal exercises reasonable care when selecting the person deployed and, to the extent that he is to procure devices or equipment or to manage the business activity, in the procurement or management, or if the damage would have occurred even if this care had been exercised.

(2) The same responsibility is borne by a person who assumes the performance of one of the transactions specified in subsection (1) sentence 2 for the principal by contract.

Notes

(1) There will be liability under § 826 BGB for any kind of harm that was caused intentionally and is contrary to public policy. For example, there is liability for damage caused by fraud[24] but a person is not liable for losses caused by legitimate competition, since that is not contrary to public policy.

(2) In contrast, under § 823(1) BGB, there will only be liability for harm caused intentionally or negligently if the harm is to the life, body, health, freedom, property or another right of another person—in other words, the harm is to one of the claimant's 'protected interests' which are enumerated in the provision. Moreover, the courts have consistently refused to interpret the concept of 'another right' broadly. They have required such rights to be as 'absolute' as those enumerated in the preceding list of incidences, ie, they have to be rights that can be interfered with by everyone and that can be asserted against everyone. This means that the scope of delictual liability under German law is comparatively narrow, and in particular there is not liability under § 823 BGB for pure economic loss (though the boundaries between this and 'harm to property' is drawn in a different place to, for example, English law).

(3) Another rule contributing to the narrow scope of the German law of delict is § 831 BGB. It severely restricts the delictual liability of an employer for damage caused by his employee. The employee's fault is not simply attributed to the employer. The employer is only liable for his or her fault in selecting or supervising the employee. While employers are presumed to have been at fault, they can normally rebut the presumption by showing that they took reasonable care in selecting, instructing and training their employees. As a result, delictual actions under German law can often not be brought against the well-off employers but only against their impecunious staff.

(4) The restrictive features of the law of delict are absent from German contract law. If the defendant is liable in contract he has, as a general rule, to compensate for the claimant's pure economic loss and is responsible for the fault of his employee, to the same extent as for his own fault (§ 278 BGB).[25] Because of these differences, the

---

[24] See further below, p 433.
[25] For § 278 BGB, see below, p 145; for a good example of the provision at work, see the *Falling roles of lino* case (6.12 (DE)), p 144.

> courts have sometimes been tempted to assume the existence of a contract in order to award liability to a seemingly deserving claimant, although this required some stretching of the notion of 'contract'. We shall encounter a number of such cases throughout this book.

English law does not have a single law of tort; rather, it recognises a large number of distinct torts, for example defamation (publishing falsehoods about a person), nuisance (unreasonable interference with private property or public access) and trespass (wrongful interference with the person, goods or land). The only tort that we need to consider in this book is the most important one, the tort of negligence. This tort was only conceptualised in its modern form in 1932.

House of Lords (Scotland)   **6.9 (EN)**

Donoghue v Stevenson[26]

A manufacturer who negligently creates a product which is likely to injure a user, and which the user will not be able to see is defective before they use it, is liable to the person injured; and any person who can foresee that if they do not exercise reasonable care they may cause physical harm to another person will be liable if they fail to take that care and the harm results.

Facts: The appellant alleged that she and a friend had visited Minchella's cafe in Paisley, where the friend had ordered some ginger beer for the appellant. The ginger beer, which was in an opaque glass bottle, was opened by Minchella, who poured part of it over some ice cream in a tumbler. The appellant drank part of the mixture and then poured out the remaining ginger beer. The decomposed remains of a snail floated out with the ginger beer. The appellant suffered shock and gastric illness as the result of drinking the ginger beer, and sued the manufacturer of the ginger beer for negligence. The respondent manufacturer pleaded that these allegations disclosed no cause of action; his plea was rejected by the Lord Ordinary. On appeal, the Second Division dismissed the appellant's action, holding that a manufacturer does not owe any duty to anyone with whom he does not have a contract, unless the article is inherently dangerous or the manufacturer actually knows that it is in a dangerous condition. The appellant appealed to the House of Lords.

Held: A manufacturer who makes a product negligently with the result that a consumer of the product is foreseeably injured is liable to the consumer.

Judgment: LORD ATKIN: … [I]n English law there must be, and is, some general conception of relations giving rise to a duty of care, of which the particular cases found in the books are but instances. The liability for negligence, whether you style it such or treat it as in other systems as a species of 'culpa', is no doubt based upon a general public sentiment of moral wrongdoing for which the offender must pay. But acts or omissions which any moral code would censure cannot in a practical world be treated so as to give a right to every person injured by them to demand relief. In this way rules of law arise which limit the range of complainants and the extent of their remedy. The rule that you are to love your neighbour becomes in law, you must not injure your neighbour; and the lawyer's question, Who is my neighbour? receives a restricted reply. You must take reasonable care to avoid acts or omissions which you can reasonably foresee would be likely to injure your

---

[26] [1932] AC 562.

neighbour. Who, then, in law is my neighbour? The answer seems to be—persons who are so closely and directly affected by my act that I ought reasonably to have them in contemplation as being so affected when I am directing my mind to the acts or omissions which are called in question. ...

My Lords, if your Lordships accept the view that this pleading discloses a relevant cause of action you will be affirming the proposition that by Scots and English law alike a manufacturer of products, which he sells in such a form as to show that he intends them to reach the ultimate consumer in the form in which they left him with no reasonable possibility of intermediate examination, and with the knowledge that the absence of reasonable care in the preparation or putting up of the products will result in an injury to the consumer's life or property, owes a duty to the consumer to take that reasonable care. It is a proposition which I venture to say no one in Scotland or England who was not a lawyer would for one moment doubt. It will be an advantage to make it clear that the law in this matter, as in most others, is in accordance with sound common sense. I think that this appeal should be allowed.

LORD MACMILLAN: ... It humbly appears to me that the diversity of view which is exhibited in [the] cases ... is explained by the fact that in the discussion of the topic which now engages your Lordships' attention two rival principles of the law find a meeting place where each has contended for supremacy. On the one hand, there is the well established principle that no one other than a party to a contract can complain of a breach of that contract. On the other hand, there is the equally well established doctrine that negligence apart from contract gives a right of action to the party injured by that negligence—and here I use the term negligence, of course, in its technical legal sense, implying a duty owed and neglected. The fact that there is a contractual relationship between the parties which may give rise to an action for breach of contract, does not exclude the co-existence of a right of action founded on negligence as between the same parties, independently of the contract, though arising out of the relationship in fact brought about by the contract. Of this the best illustration is the right of the injured railway passenger to sue the railway company either for breach of the contract of safe carriage or for negligence in carrying him. And there is no reason why the same set of facts should not give one person a right of action in contract and another person a right of action in tort.

Where, as in cases like the present, so much depends upon the avenue of approach to the question, it is very easy to take the wrong turning. If you begin with the sale by the manufacturer to the retail dealer, then the consumer who purchases from the retailer is at once seen to be a stranger to the contract between the retailer and the manufacturer and so disentitled to sue upon it. There is no contractual relation between the manufacturer and the consumer; and thus the plaintiff, if he is to succeed, is driven to try to bring himself within one or other of the exceptional cases where the strictness of the rule that none but a party to a contract can found on a breach of that contract has been mitigated in the public interest, as it has been in the case of a person who issues a chattel which is inherently dangerous or which he knows to be in a dangerous condition. If, on the other hand, you disregard the fact that the circumstances of the case at one stage include the existence of a contract of sale between the manufacturer and the retailer, and approach the question by asking whether there is evidence of carelessness on the part of the manufacturer, and whether he owed a duty to be careful in a question with the party who has been injured in consequence of his want of care, the circumstance that the injured party was not a party to the incidental contract of sale becomes irrelevant, and his title to sue the manufacturer is unaffected by that circumstance. ... I have no hesitation in affirming that a person who for gain engages in the business of manufacturing articles of food and drink intended for consumption by members of the public in the form in which he issues them is under a duty to take care in the manufacture of these articles. That duty, in my opinion, he owes to those whom he intends to consume his products. He manufactures his commodities for human consumption; he intends and contemplates that they shall be consumed. By reason of that very fact he places himself in a relationship with all the potential consumers of his commodities, and that relationship which he assumes and desires for his own ends imposes upon him a duty to take care to avoid injuring them. He owes them a duty not to convert by his own carelessness an article which he issues to them as wholesome and innocent into an article which is dangerous to life and health.

LORD THANKERTON delivered a judgment to the same effect; LORDS BUCKMASTER and TOMLIN dissented.

Appeal allowed.

Notes

(1) Like many famous tort cases to be found in 'English' law, this case originated in Scotland. Scotland has its own, distinctive, legal system. Its law of contract is quite different to English law, being a 'mixed system' derived in large part from the Roman tradition. However, its law of tort is less different and the tort of negligence in particular applies both sides of the border.

(2) This case illustrates one reason why a claimant may need to sue in tort rather than in contract. The claimant (the appellant; technically the 'pursuer', as claimants are called in Scots law) had been given the ginger beer by her friend who had bought it from Minchella. In neither Scottish nor English law would this give her a contractual right against her friend, nor would she have had the right to sue on the contract between her friend and Minchella, since she was not a party to it. Therefore she had to bring an action in tort against the only person who seemed to be at fault, the manufacturer.

(3) Before this case the scope of liability for negligence was unclear. In particular it was thought that a manufacturer who negligently put a defective product into circulation was liable only to the person to whom he sold it (which would be contractual liability) or if the product was 'inherently dangerous', like a gun. This case established the basic principle that persons are under a duty of care to avoid causing harm to those they can foresee may be injured by their negligence—Lord Atkin's 'neighbour principle'.

(4) Nowadays the claimant would not have to sue the manufacturer in negligence because she would have a claim under the Consumer Protection Act 1987, the Act which implements the Product Liability Directive.[27] This imposes more stringent liability on the manufacturer.[28] Were the facts to occur again in England, the claimant might also attempt to assert rights as a 'third party beneficiary' of the contract between the friend and Minchella. This is the result of the Contracts (Rights of Third Parties) Act 1999, discussed in Chapter 31. However, such an attempt would normally not be successful.

(5) *Donoghue v Stevenson* involved a negligent act leading to physical injury. The decision was about the liability of manufacturers for defective products, but later the courts came gradually to accept Lord Atkin's 'neighbour principle' as a guideline to

---

[27] Council Directive 85/374/EEC (n 23 above).
[28] For detail, see van Gerven et al (n 19 above) ch 6.3.2.

be applied in deciding whether or not there should be a 'duty of care' in novel situations. In *Home Office v Dorset Yacht Co Ltd*[29] the question was whether the Home Office was responsible when its officers negligently allowed the escape of some young offenders who stole and damaged the plaintiff's yacht. Lord Reid said:[30]

> In later years there has been a steady trend towards regarding the law of negligence as depending on principle so that, when a new point emerges, one should ask not whether it is covered by authority but whether recognised principles apply to it. *Donoghue v Stevenson* may be regarded as a milestone, and the well-known passage in Lord Atkin's speech should I think be regarded as a statement of principle. It is not to be treated as if it were a statutory definition. It will require qualification in new circumstances. But I think that the time has come when we can and should say that it ought to apply unless there is some justification or valid explanation for its exclusion.

It is now generally the case in English law that a defendant who has acted carelessly and has caused physical injury or property damage directly to a plaintiff will be liable, provided, firstly, that it was foreseeable that the plaintiff might be injured in the way that occurred, and secondly, that there is nothing in the relationship between the parties, or in a network of contracts in which they are both taking part, to suggest that the normal duty should not apply.[31]

Where the defendant's negligence consisted of a careless statement, and where it caused only financial loss rather than physical damage to person or property, it was long thought that there was no liability in tort; the plaintiff could only recover if it could be shown that the defendant had broken a contract under which he was obliged to use care in giving information, or possibly if he owed a 'fiduciary duty' to the claimant (like the duty a trustee owes to beneficiaries of the trust). However, in 1963, the House of Lords held in *Hedley Byrne v Heller* that there might be liability in tort for negligent misstatement if there was a sufficiently close relationship between the parties.

House of Lords   **6.10 (EN)**

Hedley Byrne & Co Ltd v Heller & Partners Ltd[32]

A party who gives advice or information which he knows or should realise that someone else is likely to rely on, when he knows or should realise that the other person will suffer loss if the information is incorrect, will be liable if he fails to take reasonable care and the person suffers loss, even if the loss is 'purely economic', unless he has disclaimed responsibility for the advice.

Facts: Hedley Byrne, an advertising agency, asked its bank to obtain a credit reference on Easipower Ltd. The bank enquired of Easipower's bankers, Hellers, and was told, in confidence and 'without responsibility', that Easipower was 'good for its ordinary business engagements'. Relying on this information, Hedley Byrne

---

[29] [1970] AC 1004.

[30] ibid, 1026–27.

[31] eg if the insurance arrangements show that it was intended that each party should bear its own losses: *Norwich City Council v Harvey* [1989] 1 WLR 828 (CA).

[32] [1964] AC 465.

booked advertising time and space for Easipower on the basis that it was personally responsible to the television and newspaper companies concerned, and when Easipower went into liquidation, Hedley Byrne lost over £17,000 on these contracts.

Held: McNair J held Hellers was negligent, but that it owed no duty of care to Hedley Byrne. The Court of Appeal agreed with the latter point. The House of Lords held that it was unnecessary to decide whether Hellers was negligent, because it was not liable in the light of its disclaimer. However, the House of Lords said that, in some circumstances, there might be liability for negligent advice or misrepresentation if responsibility were not disclaimed.

Judgment: LORD REID: … [A] negligently made article will only cause one accident, and so it is not very difficult to find the necessary degree of proximity or neighbourhood between the negligent manufacturer and the person injured. But words can be broadcast with or without the consent or the foresight of the speaker or writer. It would be one thing to say that the speaker owes a duty to a limited class, but it would be going very far to say that he owes a duty to every ultimate 'consumer' who acts on those words to his detriment. It would be no use to say that a speaker or writer owes a duty but can disclaim responsibility if he wants to. He, like the manufacturer, could make it part of a contract that he is not to be liable for his negligence: but that contract would not protect him in a question with a third party, at least if the third party was unaware of it.

So it seems to me that there is good sense behind our present law that in general an innocent but negligent misrepresentation gives no cause of action. There must be something more than the mere misstatement. I therefore turn to the authorities to see what more is required. The most natural requirement would be that expressly or by implication from the circumstances the speaker or writer has undertaken some responsibility, and that appears to me not to conflict with any authority which is binding on this House. Where there is a contract there is no difficulty as regards the contracting parties: the question is whether there is a warranty. The refusal of English law to recognise any *jus quaesitum tertii*[33] causes some difficulties, but they are not relevant, here. Then there are cases where a person does not merely make a statement but performs a gratuitous service. I do not intend to examine the cases about that, but at least they show that in some cases that person owes a duty of care apart from any contract, and to that extent they pave the way to holding that there can be a duty of care in making a statement of fact or opinion which is independent of contract … [Lord Haldane in *Robinson v National Bank of Scotland Ltd*] did not think that a duty to take care must be limited to cases of fiduciary relationship in the narrow sense of relationships which had been recognised by the Court of Chancery as being of a fiduciary character. He speaks of other special relationships, and I can see no logical stopping place short of all those relationships where it is plain that the party seeking information or advice was trusting the other to exercise such a degree of care as the circumstances required, where it was reasonable for him to do that, and where the other gave the information or advice when he knew or ought to have known that the inquirer was relying on him. I say 'ought to have known' because in questions of negligence we now apply the objective standard of what the reasonable man would have done.

A reasonable man, knowing that he was being trusted or that his skill and judgment were being relied on, would, I think, have three courses open to him. He could keep silent or decline to give the information or advice sought: or he could give an answer with a clear qualification that he accepted no responsibility for it or that it was given without that reflection or inquiry which a careful answer would require: or he could simply answer without any such qualification. If he chooses to adopt the last course he must, I think, be

---

[33] Right of a third party beneficiary to sue. See below, p 1264.

held to have accepted some responsibility for his answer being given carefully, or to have accepted a relationship with the inquirer which requires him to exercise such care as the circumstances require.

LORDS MORRIS, HODSON, DEVLIN and PEARCE delivered speeches to the same effect.

LORD DEVLIN ... I think that there is ample authority to justify your Lordships in saying now that the categories of special relationships which may give rise to a duty to take care in word as well as in deed are not limited to contractual relationships or to relationships of fiduciary duty, but include also relationships which in the words of Lord Shaw in *Nocton v Lord Ashburton* are 'equivalent to contract', that is, where there is an assumption of responsibility in circumstances in which, but for the absence of consideration, there would be a contract.

Notes

(1) Note that in this case the plaintiff also had to resort to suing in tort because, in English law, there was no contract—the information had been provided free of charge, so there was no contract because there was no consideration.

(2) Both Lord Reid and Lord Devlin seem to explain the imposition of liability for economic loss caused by a negligent misstatement by the fact that the defendant had assumed responsibility to the plaintiff. Subsequent cases have emphasised that it is not sufficient for it to be foreseeable that the claimant or someone else in the same position might rely on the information the defendant put out. An essential ingredient of liability for negligent misstatement is that the defendant gives the incorrect information knowing, at least in general terms, by whom the information will be acted on and for what purpose. This was made clear by the decision of the House of Lords in *Caparo Industries Ltd v Dickman* in 1990.[34] In that case, it was alleged that auditors who, as required by statute, had audited the annual accounts of a company had negligently allowed the company to appear more profitable than was actually the case. On a preliminary issue, it was held by the House of Lords that the auditors were not under a duty of care either to investors who purchased shares, or to existing shareholders who increased their holdings in reliance on the accounts. The auditors were responsible only to the company for which the accounts had been audited. Note that in *Hedley Byrne* Lord Devlin regarded the situation as '"equivalent to contract", that is, where there is an assumption of responsibility in circumstances in which, but for the absence of consideration, there would be a contract.'

(3) In contrast to the *Caparo* case, in *Morgan Crucible Co plc v Hill Samuel Bank Ltd*[35] the Court of Appeal held that if financial advisors to a company which was the target of a takeover bid were to make express representations about its affairs to the bidder, it was reasonably arguable that the advisors would be under a duty of care to the bidder.

The differences between *Hedley Byrne* and *Donoghue v Stevenson* are twofold. First, *Hedley Byrne* involved a statement, not an act, and secondly, the plaintiff had not suffered

[34] [1990] 2 AC 605.
[35] [1991] Ch 295.

physical injury or damage, only financial loss. In contract, it is immaterial whether the plaintiff's loss is physical or financial, and in *Hedley Byrne* Lord Devlin[36] said that he could see no logical distinction between the two. But his has been a lone voice. The courts have treated cases of negligent misstatement as an exception to the rule that pure economic loss is not recoverable in tort and have said that, where the negligence consisted of an action or omission, pure economic loss is not normally recoverable.[37] Negligent misstatement apart, the tort of negligence compensates only for physical harm and any financial consequences flowing directly from it, such as loss of earnings after an injury or loss of the earning capacity of equipment that has been physically damaged.[38]

This position was not clear immediately after the decision in *Hedley Byrne*, however. There was a series of cases in which the plaintiff had bought a house that had been built negligently and was defective. The plaintiffs sued not the builder (who was probably not worth suing) but the local authority, which had a statutory power to inspect the house while it was being built to ensure that the construction was in compliance with regulations. In *Anns v Merton London Borough Council*[39] the House of Lords held that, as the purpose of the statutory powers was to ensure that houses were built in compliance with the regulations, the council would be liable for the cost of any repairs necessary to remove any danger to health and safety of the occupants through non-compliance if negligence on the part of the council or its employees were shown. It was also said that the builder would be liable. However, even at the time, not all judges agreed on the last point. For example, in *Dutton v Bognor Regis UDC*,[40] Stamp LJ said:

> … [A] distinction has been drawn between constructing a dangerous article and constructing one which is defective or of inferior quality. I may be liable to one who purchases in the market a bottle of ginger beer which I have carelessly manufactured and which is dangerous and causes injury to person or property; but it is not the law that I am liable to him for the loss he suffers because what is found inside the bottle and for which he has paid money is not ginger beer but water. I do not warrant, except to an immediate purchaser, and then by the contract and not in tort, that the thing I manufacture is reasonably fit for its purpose.

> … the distinction between the case of the manufacturer of a dangerous thing which causes damage and that of a thing which turns out to be defective and valueless lies I think not in the nature of the injury but in the character of the duty. I have a duty not carelessly to put out a dangerous thing which may cause damage to one who may purchase it, but the duty does not extend to putting out carelessly a defective or useless or valueless thing.

In other words, someone who makes a thing that does not work or who builds a house that has defects should not be liable if the defect has not caused personal injury or damage to property. The point seems to be simply that the claimant is really claiming only economic loss—having spent good money on a worthless item. Such a loss is compensable in contract but not in tort.

---

[36] [1964] AC 465, 517.
[37] For an exception, see below, p 1324.
[38] eg *Spartan Steel and Alloys Ltd v Martin & Co (Contractors) Ltd* [1973] QB 27 (CA).
[39] [1978] AC 728.
[40] [1972] 1 QB 373, 414–15 (CA).

Essentially the same argument was later adopted by the House of Lords, which in *Murphy v Brentwood District Council*[41] (in an unusual move) overruled its previous decision in *Anns v Merton London Borough Council*.[42] In *Murphy* the House of Lords held that neither the builder of a house which, because of the negligence of the builder, has defects nor a local authority, because of whose negligence the building work was allowed to proceed, is liable in tort to a subsequent owner of the house who bought it not knowing of the defects. The case marked the end of the idea that a builder of a defective house, or the manufacturer of defective goods, may be made liable in tort in English law when the defect has not caused the claimant any physical injury or damage to his property (other than to the item itself). The principal reason is that the claimant's loss is purely economic and should be recoverable, if at all, only in contract. It would then, of course, be subject to any clauses in the contract excluding or restricting the defendant's liability. Unless the ultimate purchaser is a party to the contract under which the builder does the work, or is a third party beneficiary of that contract, this means they will have no claim. The rule is subject to two general exceptions. One is where the defect makes the property dangerous to the public. The other exception will be explored later in the book:[43] the courts have held that in exceptional circumstances, a builder (on the facts, a subcontractor of the main builder) may be liable for the pure economic loss if he or she undertook a 'voluntary assumption of responsibility' to the claimant sufficient to bring the case within the principle of *Hedley Byrne v Heller*. This will never be the case unless there has been some form of direct negotiation between the claimant and the builder or manufacturer, even if they did not enter into a direct contractual relationship.

6.2.B THE RESPECTIVE DOMAINS OF CONTRACT AND TORT

The demarcation line must be drawn in terms of time (pre- and post-contractual situations) and then in terms of persons—parties to the contract as against third parties.

6.2.B.1 PRE- AND POST-CONTRACTUAL SITUATIONS

It is important to determine precisely when the contract begins and ends because before and afterwards only liability in tort is possible, whereas during the currency of the contract both contractual and tortious liability may apply. The issue is one of pre-contractual or post-contractual liability.

Pre-contractual liability, which is dealt with in Chapter 13 in relation to formation of the contract, is treated differently in English and French law on the one hand, and German law and the other legal systems following the German notion of *culpa in contrahendo* on the other. Under German law, pre-contractual conduct may lead to delictual liability, but it often also triggers a specific category of liability originally developed by the courts under the general duty of good faith (§ 242 BGB) and now codified in the Code's section on contractual obligations (§ 311(2) and (3) BGB).[44]

---

[41] [1991] 1 AC 398.
[42] [1978] AC 728.
[43] See below, p 1324.
[44] See below, p 1324.

In French and English law matters occurring before the future parties have concluded their contract are matters for the law of tort.

Code civil   **6.11 (FR)**

Article 1112: The commencement, continuation and breaking-off of precontractual negotiations are free from control. They must mandatorily satisfy the requirements of good faith.

In case of fault committed during the negotiations, the reparation of the resulting loss is not calculated so as to compensate neither the loss of benefits which were expected from the contract that was not concluded nor the loss of the chance of obtaining these benefits.

Notes

(1) New Article 1112 is the first provision of an important new sub-section 1 on negotiations which is inserted in a new section of the Code civil on the conclusion of contracts

(2) Article 1112 does not specify that liability is in tort. In other words, it makes no reference to *responsabilité extracontractuelle*. The reason for this is that 'contractual liability' should not be excluded when, in commercial contracts, parties have reached some agreement before the final contract. If the parties have made a pre-contract during the negotiations (for instance, a non-disclosure agreement), and one party fails to comply with it, liability is contractual.[45]

We have seen that in French and English law, matters occurring before the future parties have concluded their contract are matters for the law of tort. The same is true after the end of the contract. A good example of this in French law is afforded by the contract for the transport of persons which is subject to a contractual regime imposing an *obligation de sécurité*. The French courts were hesitant. After a period in which they distinguished between three phases, namely before the transport proper (for example, a rail traveller who falls at the entrance to the platform), during transport and after it (the traveller who falls at the exit), the courts limited the domain of contract to the actual transport proper.

Cass civ (1), 7 May 1989[46]   **6.12 (FR)**

Icy platform

The obligation of security applies only from the moment a passenger boards the train to the moment he leaves it; but if the station premises are dangerous the railway may be liable in delict.

---

[45] F Chénedé, *Le nouveau droit des obligations et des contrats: Consolidations, innovations, perspectives* (Paris: Dalloz, 2016) no. 22.12.

[46] No. 87-11493, Bull I no. 118, D 1991, 1, annotated by P Malaurie.

Facts: On 17 January 1982 Mr Valverde was found on the track alongside a platform of Pierrefitte station. His legs had been cut off by the wheels of a train. Mr Valverde brought proceedings against SNCF for a declaration and damages, alleging that, after alighting from a carriage, he had slipped on the icy platform; in this connection he claimed breach of contract by the transport undertaking which had neglected to clear an icy patch.

Held: The cour d'appel dismissed the claim. The Cour de cassation upheld this decision on the contractual claim but allowed the plaintiff's delictual claim.

Judgment: THE COURT: ... *On the first appeal ground:*—Whereas Mr Valverde submits that the cour d'appel wrongly dismissed his claim on the grounds that it was common ground that the accident occurred after the traveller had finished alighting from the train and that therefore the transport undertaking was no longer bound by the duty to secure a safe outcome; —Whereas, it was argued, the contract of carriage by train and the duty of care attached thereto commences when the traveller having validated his ticket gains access to the platform of the station of departure and terminates at the exit of the station of destination when it is no longer possible to exercise supervision by means of checks; —Whereas thus by determining that the duty of care ancillary to the contract of carriage ceased to subsist after the passenger alighted from the train, when Mr Valverde was still walking on the platform of the station at which he had arrived, the judgment appealed against infringed Article 1147 [see now Article 1231-1] of the Civil Code;

— Whereas, however, contrary to what was claimed on appeal, the duty of care in conducting the traveller safely to his destination imposed by Article 1147 of the Civil Code is borne by the transport undertaking only during the implementation of the contract of carriage, that is to say from the time when the traveller begins to embark on the carriage until he has completely alighted from it; —Whereas the appeal ground is therefore unfounded.

On the second appeal ground on a pure point of law:—Under Article 1384(1) [see now Article 1242] of the Civil Code, whereas outside the performance of the contract, the transport undertaking's liability to the traveller is governed by the rules on tortious liability; —Whereas in dismissing the claim, the judgment appealed against (Paris, 17th Chamber A, 4 November 1986) also states 'that is for Mr Valverde to show that the SNCF by committing an error in this case by omitting to remove the icy patches from the platform has failed to fulfil its obligation to provide adequate means'; and that in the present case Mr Valverde has not adduced proof that he fell on the platform after slipping on an icy patch allegedly left by the transport undertaking on the platform; —Whereas it is therefore not established that SNCF committed any fault in connection with the accident;

— Whereas in so holding, although the accident occurred when the train from which the traveller had alighted, and which was under the control of SNCF, started, the court of appeal infringed the above-mentioned provision.

On those grounds and without there being any need to give a decision on the third plea, the Cour de cassation refers the case to the cour d'appel Versailles.

Notes

(1) The contractual scenario is well described in the judgment; it covers the time from the moment when the traveller begins to climb into the carriage until the moment when he has completely alighted from it. Outside that period of time, liability is only in delict, and it was for misapplying the rules on delictual liability that the appeal judgment was set aside.

(2) It will be noted that, as the court considers that the transport undertaking was in charge of the train or the platform, full liability is incurred under ex-Article 1384(1) (now 1242) Cciv which will generate the same outcome as if contractual liability was applied, namely to entitle the claimant to damages. Before this case, the Cour de cassation held that there was an *obligation de sécurité* and also made a distinction between (i) the harm caused during the transportation *stricto sensu* (*obligation de sécurité de résultat*) and (ii) the harm not caused during the transportation *stricto sensu* (ie the platform; *obligation de sécurité de moyens*). By turning to liability under the law of delict, the Cour de cassation, in this case, showed its willingness to rule in favour of the victim (had it followed its previous case law, the victim would have had to prove the SNCF's fault, because the *obligation de sécurité* was *de moyens*.

(3) During the transport there is a duty to ensure a safe outcome—ie, the *obligation de sécurité* during the actual carriage is an *obligation de résultat,* as opposed to a mere *obligation de moyens.*[47]

A typical scenario that illustrates the way in which the regimes of contractual and delictual liability interact in German, French and English law is that of a customer in a shop who has not as yet made a purchase and suffers harm. Is the liability during this pre-contractual phase delictual or contractual?

German law extends the scope of contractual liability to the pre-contractual phase.

RG, 7 December 1911[48]   **6.13 (DE)**

Falling rolls of lino

When a customer enters a shop intending to make a purchase, the shop is under a duty 'similar to contract' to take care towards her.

Facts: A shop's customer was injured by the fall of a linoleum roll incorrectly moved by the sales assistant who was showing the merchandise.

Held: The Berlin Court of Appeal held that the trader was liable for the negligence of the sales assistant (§ 278 BGB). The Supreme Court upheld the decision.

Judgment: According to the findings of the Court of Appeal the plaintiff, after making several purchases in the defendant company's department store, went to the linoleum department to buy linoleum floor-cover. She mentioned this to W, the sales assistant who served there, and looked through the patterns which he displayed for her to make a choice. W, in order to pull out the roll she pointed to, put two others aside. They fell, hit the plaintiff and her child, and struck both of them to the floor. The purchase of the linoleum was not completed because, in the plaintiff's words, she became seriously disturbed by the fall. The Court of Appeal rightly attributed the plaintiff's accident to W's fault, on the ground that he had put the rolls, which were not stable enough because of their relatively small bulk, insecurely on one side, instead of furnishing them with lateral protection or leaning them against the wall, and this even though he could have foreseen that the plaintiff, as usually happens with the buying public, would approach the place where the

---

[47] P Malaurie, L Aynès and P Stoffel-Munck, *Droit des obligations* (9th edn, Paris: Defrénois, 2017) no. 950.
[48] RGZ 78, 239.

goods she had asked to be displayed were stored. The Court of Appeal's view is confirmed by the simple conclusion that the rolls would not have fallen if W had placed them carefully and regularly on one side. The Court of Appeal's opinion that the defendant company is liable for W's fault under § 278 BGB cannot, in spite of the appellant's contention, be rightly objected to; and it conforms to the case-law of this Senate. W was acting for the defendant company (§ 164 BGB, § 54 HGB) when he entered into negotiation with the plaintiff. The plaintiff had asked for a piece of linoleum to be laid out for inspection and purchase. W had acceded to her request in order to make a sale. The proposal and its acceptance had for their purpose the conclusion of a sale, and therefore the production of a legal transaction. That was no mere factual proceeding, like a mere act of courtesy, but a legal relationship came into existence between the parties in preparation for a purchase; it bore a character similar to a contract and produced legal obligations in so far as both seller and prospective buyer came under a duty to observe the necessary care for the health and property of the other party in displaying and inspecting the goods. The judgments of this Senate have already proceeded on similar grounds…, and it has been recognized in several decisions of the Reichsgericht that duties of care for the life and property of the other party can arise from contracts and other obligations, which have nothing to do with the legal nature of the obligation in a narrower sense, but nevertheless follow from its factual character… The defendant company made use of W's services for the fulfilment of the aforesaid obligation to the prospective purchaser, and is therefore answerable for his fault. This is in line with the idea expressed in § 278 BGB, that whoever himself owes a performance that he must carry out with the required amount of care must, when he makes use of an employee to this effect, answer for the careful performance of the employee, and that accordingly the other person to whom the performance is due must not be put in a worse position because the first person does not do it himself but commits it to an employee. It would be contrary to the general feeling of justice if in cases where the person in charge of the business of displaying or laying out goods for exhibition, sampling, trial, or the like carelessly injures a prospective purchaser, the proprietor of the business—with whom the prospective purchaser wished to make a purchase—should be answerable only under § 831 BGB and not unconditionally, so that the injured person should, if the proprietor succeeds in exonerating himself, be referred to the usually impecunious employee. There is no need to go here into the legally questionable view of the Court of Appeal that the mere entry into a department store of a prospective purchaser or even a visitor without any intention of buying creates a contractual relation between him and the proprietor, including the previously discussed duties of care …

Notes

(1) According to § 278 BGB, '[t]he obligor is responsible for fault on the part of his legal representative, and of persons whom he uses to perform his obligation, to the same extent as for fault on his own part.'

(2) The decision represents an extension of contractual liability to the pre-contractual phase. Under German law, it is assumed that there exists a preliminary contractual relationship between the customer and the vendor in order to prepare the sale. Certain contractual rights and obligations apply already during this phase. The case law to this effect was codified in the 2001 reforms—see the new § 311(2) BGB. It is to be noted that this relationship does not extend to persons entering the shop with no intention of making a purchase. These issues will be discussed in more detail in Chapter 13. At this

stage it is important to note that extending the contractual relationship to pre-contractual situations enables the Court to impose on the shop vicarious responsibility for the act of its employee, which in German law would not exist if the liability were purely delictual, because § 831 BGB imposes liability on the employer for a wrong done by the employee only when the employer was at fault in choosing or managing the employee.[49]

The situation of a customer in a shop prior to any purchase is dealt with differently in French and English law, on the basis of tortious (or delictual) liability alone.[50]

Cass Civ (1), 7 November 1961[51]   **6.14 (FR)**

A fatal fall

A customer who suffers an unexplained injury which is not the result of any non-performance of the contract he was contemplating has no contractual claim.

Facts: A prospective customer fell in a trader's storage area; the reason is not known.

Held: The cour d'appel declined to hold the trader liable and the Cour de cassation dismissed the appeal.

Judgment: THE COURT: *On the first appeal ground:*—Whereas Garibal went to the Balard Establishments in order to purchase some galvanized sheets and was taken into a shop installed on the unloading platform of the factory's own railway track; as at a certain moment for a reason which has remained unclear he fell onto the track situated 3.50 metres below and was killed;

— Whereas the judgment appealed against (Montpellier, 13 November 1959) is criticised for declining to render contractually liable a trader who had authorised a customer to gain access to a storage area although, irrespective of any contract of sale, the fact of inviting, with a view to profit, customers on to premises for which one is responsible in itself constitutes a contract which may give rise to a duty of care;

— Whereas however the cour d'appel was right to hold that in order for contractual liability to be incurred it is not sufficient for damage to have been caused in connection with a contract but the damage must arise from non-performance of one of the obligations imposed by the contract; —Whereas the sales contract does not give rise to any duty of care towards the purchaser; —Whereas it is pleaded in the appeal but to no avail that, independently of any sale, the trader assumes a duty of care in regard to any person gaining access to the commercial premises and who may be a potential purchaser. In such a case it is only the rules on tortious liability which play a role. The plea is therefore unfounded.

Note

The Cour de cassation affirms that the fall has no direct connection with the sales contract—not yet entered into—and that moreover the sales contract gives rise to no duty of care towards the purchaser. Moreover, there is no preliminary contractual relationship, unlike under German law, with the result that liability can only be

---

[49] For the text of § 831 BGB see above, p 133.

[50] For further cases involving liability for injury which occurred when goods were being bought, see below, p 1203.

[51] Cass civ (1) 7 November 1961, no. 60-10459, Bull no. 509, D 1962, 146, annotated by P Esmein.

delictual.[52] However, in cases where the facts are similar to the *Fatal fall* case, both contractual and delictual liability are excluded. The reason for this is that there was no fault and the thing (here, the ground) played no active role in the accident.[53]

The route taken in English law is also that of tort.

Court of Appeal   **6.15 (EN)**

Ward v Tesco Stores Ltd[54]

A shop is under a duty to take reasonable care to ensure that customers are not injured by dangerously slippery substances spilt on the floor of the shop.

Facts: The plaintiff went round the store, carrying a wire basket, as shoppers are expected to do in supermarkets. She was doing her shopping at the back of the store when she felt herself slipping. She appreciated that she was slipping on something which was sticky. She fell to the ground, and sustained minor injuries. She had not seen what had caused her to slip. It was not suggested that she had in any way been negligent in failing to notice what was on the floor as she walked along doing her shopping. When she was picking herself up she appreciated that she had slipped on some pink substance which looked to her like yoghurt. It was yoghurt. Later, somebody on the defendants' staff found a carton of yoghurt in the vicinity which was two-thirds empty.

Held: The trial judge held that in the absence of any other explanation he was entitled to infer that the defendants had failed to take reasonable care to clear up the spillage. The Court of Appeal (by a majority) upheld this decision.

Judgment: LAWTON LJ: This is an appeal by the defendants from a judgment of his Honour Judge Nance given in the Liverpool County Court ... whereby he adjudged that the plaintiff should recover against the defendants £178.50 damages and her costs ... for personal injuries said to have been caused by the negligence of the defendants in the maintenance of the floor in their supermarket at Smithdown Road, Liverpool. [He stated the facts and continued:] That is all the plaintiff was able to prove, save for one additional fact. About three weeks later when she was shopping in the same store she noticed that some orange squash had been spilt on the floor. She kept an eye on the spillage for about a quarter of an hour. During that time nobody came to clear it up. The trial judge was of the opinion that the facts which I have related constituted a prima facie case against the defendants. I infer that this case, which involves only a small amount of damages, has been brought to this court because the defendants are disturbed that any judge should find that a prima facie case is established merely by a shopper proving that she had slipped on a supermarket floor. At the trial the defendants called some evidence. ... The defendants did not call any evidence as to when the store floor had last been brushed before the plaintiff's accident. It follows that there was no evidence before the court as to whether the floor had been brushed a few moments before the accident, or an hour, or possibly an hour and a half. The court was left with out any information on what may have been an

---

[52] It may be noted in passing that in French law the guardian of property may be held responsible for injury caused by it under Art 1242 (ex-1384) Cciv. However, in the present case no recourse may be had to full liability on this basis because the property—ie the premises—played only a passive role.

[53] G Viney, P Jourdain and S Carval, *Traité de droit civil: Les conditions de la responsabilité* (4th edn, Paris: LGDJ, 2013) no. 500-1; Cass civ (1) 29 May 1996, no. 94-16820, Bull I no. 227.

[54] [1976] 1 WLR 810.

important matter. … In this case the floor of this supermarket was under the management of the defendants and their servants. The accident was such as in the ordinary
course of things does not happen if floors are kept clean and spillages are dealt with as
soon as they occur. If an accident does happen because the floors are covered with spillage, then in my judgment some explanation should be forthcoming from the defendants
to show that the accident did not arise from any want of care on their part; and in the
absence of any explanation the judge may give judgment for the plaintiff. Such burden
of proof as there is on the defendants in such circumstances is evidential, not probative.
The trial judge thought that prima facie this accident would not have happened had the
defendants taken reasonable care. In my judgment he was justified in taking that view
because the probabilities where that the spillage had been on the floor long enough for
it to have been cleaned up by a member of the staff …

[Megaw LJ agreed with Lawton LJ. Ormerod LJ dissented on the ground that, as it had
not been proven that the yoghurt had been on the floor for a significant length of time,
an essential element of negligence had not been proven.]

> *Note*
>
> In this case, discussion turned essentially on the issue of proof of negligence on the
> part of the trader. It was not even alleged that there could have been a contract.

6.2.B.2 CONCURRENT LIABILITY IN CONTRACT AND TORT

Suppose that a breach of contract also amounts to a tort against the other party—for
example, a contracting party's performance is negligent and it causes injury to the other
party or damages his property. Can the injured party choose whether to sue in contract or
tort, or is he confined to one of those actions? This is the question of *cumul* or *non cumul*,
as it is put in French law.

(i) The interests at issue

Why does it matter whether the claimant can sue in tort rather than in contract? The interests at stake are rather variable since the rules on tort differ considerably from the rules
on contract. That is frequently the case as regards prescription, whether the period is laid
down by law or has been contractually agreed. For example, in French law there used to
be a sharp contrast between the short period allowed for a contractual action on a warranty for latent defects and the prescription period of ten years for actions in tort.[55] This
has now become less dramatic, as on the one hand consumers have been given greater
rights in respect of defects in goods they have bought (see Chapter 27 below) and, on the
other, recent reforms of the law of prescription[56] have shortened and largely harmonised
the periods of legal prescription (the standard period is five years from the date of knowledge, subject to a longstop of 20 years[57]). Similar changes have taken place in Germany.[58]
However, there may still be differences between the periods that apply in contract and tort.

---

[55] See former Arts 1648 and 2270(1) Cciv. Similarly under pre-2002 German law, see former § 477 BGB.
[56] See Arts 2219–2279 Cciv, introduced by Loi de 17 juin 2008.
[57] Art 2226 Cciv.
[58] See §§ 194–218 BGB; cf B Markesinis, H Unberath and A Johnston, *The German Law of Contract*
(2nd edn, Oxford: Hart Publishing, 2006) 486–91.

It has been pointed out above that whether or not there can be 'concurrent liability' in both tort and contract is significant in English law not only because the limitation periods for the two claims may differ but also because certain types of loss are not normally recoverable in tort but may be recovered in contract.[59]

Also to be considered is the application of exemption clauses. An issue may be the question of whether liability in tort can be excluded by means of a contractual clause. Below we consider some cases involving exemption clauses which illustrate the possible effects of allowing or disallowing the claimant to choose between suing in tort or in contract. But first we consider whether or not each of the laws allows the choice.

(ii) Concurrent liability (*cumul* or *non-cumul*)

When the preconditions of a right of action in tort and in contract are both met, there is no need to explain that there can be no right to double compensation. But is there a possible option between the two rights of action? Each right of action may have its own advantages. Without legislative backing but on the basis of settled case law, French law has the principle of *non-cumul* of the two *ordres de responsabilités* (contractual and delictual). It should be noted that the expression *non-cumul* can be misleading, insofar as it may suggest that, even if one cannot claim under both regimes, one may at least choose which to invoke. That is not the case. 'The rule is really one that there is no choice, as the victim of harm that occurred in the context of a contract may not rely on delictual responsibility'.[60]

Cass civ (1), 11 January 1989[61]   **6.16 (FR)**

Dishonest insurance agent

The creditor of a contractual obligation cannot rely, as against the debtor of that obligation, on the rules of delictual liability, even where there is an interest in doing so.

Facts: An insured person brought an action against the insurance company and its local agent for payment for compensation which he alleged was payable to him under the law on insurance.

Held: The court trying the case on its merits found the company liable on the basis of the principal's responsibility for the acts of its agent (who had misappropriated the funds), a delictual action based on Article 1384(5) (now 1242(5)) Cciv.

Judgment: On the second branch of the first appeal ground:—Under Articles 1134 [new Article 1103] of the Civil Code and L 114–1 of the Code des assurances, the creditor of a contractual obligation cannot rely, as against the debtor of that obligation, on the rules of delictual liability, even where there is an interest in doing so;

— Whereas Mr Bejottes was unable to obtain the compensation following two accidents causing physical injury to which he was entitled under the life and invalidity insurance policies which he had taken out with the insurance company La Protectrice; as Mr Bejottes therefore brought proceedings against the insurer and also against its local

---

[59] See above, pp 148–49. For a comparison between English law and French law, see D Tallon 'Remedies: French Report' in D Harris and D Tallon (eds), *Contract Law Today: Anglo-French Comparisons* (Oxford: Clarendon Press, 1989) 263, 275–76, nos. 23–25.

[60] A Bénabent, *Droit des obligations* (16th edn, Paris: Montchrestien, 2017) no. 510.

[61] No. 86-17323, Bull I no. 3, JCP 1989.II.21326, annotated by C Larroumet.

agent Mr Loustau who was criticised for not repaying to the insured the sums which he had received for that purpose from the company;

— Whereas in ordering La Protectrice to pay the amounts claimed by Mr Bejottes whilst at the same time declaring the action for payment brought by him against the company on the basis of the insurance company under the insurance contracts to be time-barred under Article L 114-1 of the law of insurance, the judgment appealed against notes that the line of argument against the overlapping of contractual and delictual liability is inadequate since the claim against the insurer is also based on the delict committed by Mr Loustau, deemed to be an agent of the company, who is therefore liable under Article 1384(5) [new 1242(5)] of the Civil Code;

— Whereas in so deciding, whereas the fault imputed to Mr Loustau did not enable Mr Bejottes to bring an action against La Protectrice in conditions other than those afforded to him by the insurance contract, the cour d'appel infringed the above-mentioned laws.

On those grounds the judgment given on 18 June 1986 between the parties by the Pau cour d'appel is set aside in that it ordered La Protectrice jointly and severally with Mr Loustau to pay to Mr Bejottes the principal sum of 50,160 Francs and 5,000 Francs under Article 700 of the new Code of Civil Procedure and the matter is referred to the Bordeaux cour d'appel for a fresh judgment.

> *Note*
>
> This case is a good illustration of the principle of *non-cumul*: the victim of harm that occurred in the context of a contract may not rely on the rules of delictual liability, even where there is an interest in doing so. Contract law therefore predominates; delictual liability is limited to cases which do not concern a breach of contract.

German law and English law allow the claimant to choose between an action in contract and an action in delict (or tort). In German law the two actions are said to be 'competing'; the general rule is that there is a 'competition of claims' (*Anspruchskonkurrenz*).

This issue used to arise in an acute form where the buyer could claim damages for breach of contract in respect of damage caused by a defect in the item sold and also on the basis of the law of delict. Under the prescription periods prevailing before the major reform of the German BGB, the action in delict was time-barred after three years, whereas for actions in contract based on a warranty, a six-months prescription period applied. The Bundesgerichtshof held that the claimant could bring whichever action was more favourable to him.[62] Since 2002, the standard limitation period of three years (§ 195 BGB) equally applies to most delictual claims and most claims for breach of contract. Claims for defects in goods sold, however, are subject to a two-year limitation period (§ 438(1) no. 3; for land it is five years: § 438(1) no. 2). So the problem may still arise.

English law also often applies different limitation periods to claims in contract and claims in tort.[63] In English law it has always been possible for a claimant to sue in either

---

[62] BGH 24 May 1976, BGHZ 66, 315 (extract in the first edition of this book, p 70).

[63] For an account of the differences, see The Law Commission, *Limitation of Actions* (Consultation Paper), Law Com CP No 151 (London: The Stationery Office, 1998). This is available at www.bailii.org/ew/other/EWLC/1998/c151.pdf. The Law Commission's Report No 270 (2001) recommended adoption of a unified 'core regime' that would apply to most types of claim but the recommendations have not been implemented. The report is available at www.lawcom.gov.uk/docs/lc270(2).pdf.

contract or tort if both claims can be made out. As Oliver J said in *Midland Bank & Trust Co Ltd v Hett, Stubb & Kemp*:[64]

> There is not and never has been any rule of law that a person having alternative claims must frame his action in one or the other. If I have a contract with my dentist to extract a tooth, I am not thereby precluded from suing him in tort if he negligently shatters my jaw.[65]

Similarly, a passenger who has been injured through the negligence of a carrier can sue in either contract or tort. However, it must be remembered that the English law of tort does not, in general, impose liability for 'pure economic loss', which is often what is being claimed in an action for breach of contract.[66] And even when on the facts it might be possible to find the defendant liable for pure economic loss on the basis of a voluntary assumption of responsibility, the courts have been reluctant to recognise new duties of care in tort solely in order that the claimant may take advantage of procedural advantages such as a longer limitation period. In *Tai Hing Cotton Mill Ltd v Liu Chong Hing Bank Ltd* Lord Scarman said:[67]

> Their Lordships do not believe that there is anything to the advantage of the law's development in searching for a liability in tort where the parties are in a contractual relationship. This is particularly so in a commercial relationship. Though it is possible as a matter of legal semantics to conduct an analysis of the rights and duties inherent in some contractual relationships including that of banker and customer either as a matter of contract law when the question will be what, if any, terms are to be implied or as a matter of tort law when the task will be to identify a duty arising from the proximity and character of the relationship between the parties, their Lordships believe it to be correct in principle and necessary for the avoidance of confusion in the law to adhere to the contractual analysis: on principle because it is a relationship in which the parties have, subject to a few exceptions, the right to determine their obligations to each other, and for the avoidance of confusion because different consequences do follow according to whether liability arises from contract or tort, e.g. in the limitation of action.

However, in the important case of *Henderson v Merrett Syndicates Ltd*[68] the House of Lords distinguished the *Tai Hing* case as dealing not with concurrent liability but with the separate question of whether, as between contracting parties, 'a tortious duty of care could be established which was more extensive than that which was provided for in the relevant contract'.[69] The House held that where the duty in contract and the alleged duty of care in tort to avoid causing economic loss were the same, there would be concurrent liability. After an extensive discussion of the cases, Lord Goff—with whom all other members of the House agreed—said:[70]

> My own belief is that, in the present context, the common law is not antipathetic to concurrent liability, and that there is no sound basis for a rule which automatically restricts the claimant to either a tortious or a contractual remedy. The result may be untidy; but, given that the tortious duty is imposed by the general law, and the contractual duty is attributable to the will of the parties, I do not find it objectionable that the claimant may be entitled to take advantage of the

---

[64] [1979] Ch 384 (ChD).
[65] *Edwards v Mallan* [1908] 1 KB 1002 (CA) [footnote in original].
[66] See above, p 148.
[67] [1986] AC 80, 107 (PC).
[68] [1995] 2 AC 145 (HL).
[69] Per Lord Goff, ibid, 186.
[70] ibid, 194.

remedy which is most advantageous to him, subject only to ascertaining whether the tortious duty is so inconsistent with the applicable contract that, in accordance with ordinary principle, the parties must be taken to have agreed that the tortious remedy is to be limited or excluded.

The result was that investors were permitted to sue their managing agents in tort when actions against the managers for breach of contract would have been barred by limitation. In an analogous case, French law would allow full recovery in contract (but would limit it to foreseeable damage: Article 1251-3 Cciv) There would be no choice of suing in delict.

6.2.B.3 *CUMUL* AND EXEMPTION CLAUSES

The issue of concurrent liability in contract and tort often arises in relation to the effect of clauses which purport to exclude or limit liability.

Cass civ (2), 17 February 1955[71]   **6.17 (FR)**

Fire spreads to warehouse

A clause cannot exclude liability which, were an action brought in delict, could not be excluded.

Facts: By a contract dated 1 July 1945 SNCF let to Lafond a warehouse at Lyon station. It was stipulated that the lessee undertook to assume all the risks to which any items or goods stored in the warehouse might be exposed and also to indemnify SNCF against any judgments against it. On 6 August 1948 a container wagon of fuel caught fire close to the warehouse. The fire spread to the warehouse and to the goods stored there.

Judgment: THE COURT:—Whereas it is pleaded on appeal that the contested judgment was wrong to uphold the claim by the insurance company against SNCF for repayment of the amounts paid by the insurance company to Lafond, and to have declared null and void the abovementioned clauses, even though an exemption clause is valid, even in the event of delictual liability, provided that it is not a serious fault equivalent to fraud, which is not so in this case. —Whereas the indemnity clause has a different purpose from that of an exemption clause, nullity of the latter clause could not, where the law was silent, entail nullity of the former;

— Whereas clauses exempting or restricting liability in matters of delict are null and void. Articles 1382 and 1383 [now Articles 1240 and 1241] of the Civil Code are a matter of public policy and their application cannot be neutralised in advance by way of agreement; —Whereas the court properly considered that the two clauses inserted in the same article of the lease agreement 'could not arbitrarily be separated.'—Whereas the terms employed 'clearly showed assimilation as between abandonment of any action and liability on the indemnity, the latter appearing to extend the former and the nullity affecting abandonment in regard to the current dispute also entails nullity of the indemnity';

— Whereas it follows that the pleas on appeal are unfounded.

On those grounds the appeal is dismissed.

Notes

(1) The justification given in this case for asserting the general principle that 'clauses exempting or restricting liability in matters of delict are null and void' is that former

---

[71] No. 55-02810, Bull civ II no. 100, D 1956, 17, annotated by P Esmein.

Articles 1382 and 1383 (now Articles 1240 and 1241) Cciv are a matter of public policy and their application cannot be neutralised in advance by way of agreement. The mandatory nature of former Articles 1382 and 1383 Cciv has been criticised, especially as the courts sometimes upheld clauses limited to the application of ex-Articles 1384 and 1385 Cciv (now Articles 1242 and 1243) dealing with liability for products and the acts of other persons.

(2) The justification given in this case has been challenged by the fact that specific statutes, such as those on liability for defective goods and on transport, recognise the validity of these types of clauses. The predominant view in France is now that such clauses should be valid, subject to at least two major exceptions in the case of a *faute dolosive* (fraud) or personal injury.

Reform Bill on Civil Liability (March 2017)   **6.18 (FR)**

SECTION 1: Contract terms excluding or limiting liability

Article 1281: Contract terms whose object or effect is to exclude or to limit liability are in principle valid, in contractual as well as in extra-contractual matters. However, in the case of personal injury, liability cannot be limited or excluded by contract.

Article 1282: In contractual matters, contract terms limiting or excluding liability have no effect in the case of gross or dishonest fault. They are deemed not written where they deprive the debtor's essential obligation of its substance.

Article 1283: In extra-contractual matters, a person cannot exclude or limit his liability for fault.

Notes

(1) The French 2017 bill establishes a general principle of validity of contract terms excluding or limiting liability in a new Chapter V on 'contract terms concerning liability' which should in the future apply to contractual as well as extra-contractual matters (draft Article 1281). This principle of validity is subject to two important exceptions: the case of personal injury liability (draft Article 1281(2)) and that of 'gross or dishonest fault' (draft Article 1282). The general rule set forth in the second sentence of draft Article 1281 (in the case of personal injury, liability cannot be limited or excluded by contract) is new. The French Cour de cassation had never laid it down (it could have done so, on the basis of Article 16-1 Cciv which preserves the right of each individual to its body[72]) and previously, it had only been admitted by specific texts, in specific situations, one of the most important being consumer law (see Article R 132-1 of the Code de la consommation).[73]

---

[72] G Viney, P Jourdain and S Carval, *Traité de droit civil: Les effets de la responsabilité*, (4th edn, Paris: LGDJ, 2017) no. 342.

[73] In favour of such a general prohibition, see ibid no. 342.

(2) With regard to liability for defective goods,[74] Article 1245-14 of the Code civil, as amended in 2016, states: 'Contract terms which seek to exclude or limit liability for defective products are forbidden and deemed not written. However, as regards harm caused to property which is not used by the victim mainly for his own private use or consumption, contract terms agreed between persons acting in the course of a business or profession are valid'.

(3) French courts have recently widened the possibility for third parties to a contract to bring a contractual claim.[75]

BGH, 9 May 1957[76]   **6.19 (DE)**

Stolen suitcase

Where there are claims in both contract and delict, the plaintiff may rely on either; special provisions limiting liability only affect the specific claim to which they apply.

Facts: On 19 April 1946 the applicant handed over a suitcase at the main station in W to the defendant company for onward transmission to K. In addition to clothing, the suitcase contained a collection of stamps and a ring. On registration the suitcase was stolen by an employee of the defendant company known as P. The theft was one of a series of such thefts recorded at the station of K between February and September 1946, when P was employed. A part of the value of the stolen stamps was reimbursed and a part in poor condition was returned. Under the railway regulations, the defendant merely paid the sum of 2,868 Reichsmarks (that is to say RM 200/kg).

Held: According to the Bundesgerichtshof, the defendant company was liable in delict, but not in contract.

Judgment: … The applicant sought full and complete restitution of his loss, relying on the provisions on delictual liability (§§ 823(1), 831,[77] 839 BGB). In his view the company had been careless in its choice of employee and had not adequately supervised him.

The defendant company submits that the provisions of the Commercial Code and of the Railway regulations preclude the application of the provisions of the Civil Code on delictual liability. Moreover, it claims that it chose carefully and duly supervised the employee. Finally, the applicant's right to damages ought to be precluded owing to the applicant's contributory negligence. …

As the Bundesgerichtshof has held [on a different set of facts], there is a genuine competition between contractual and delictual claims where a contractual breach and an unlawful act coexist side by side. Whereas the law of delict covers breaches of statutory and *generally* applicable legal obligations backed up by an obligation to pay damages, contract law concerns the *specific* obligations of two parties which are only created by their consensus ad idem and which entail certain legal consequences in case of breach, as provided for by statute.

According to the law of delict, it is only the infringement of a statutory provision which creates an obligation (namely the obligation to afford compensation), whereas in contractual matters a pre-existing obligation is transformed, in the event of its breach, into an obligation to pay damages. When an act or an omission infringes both a general legal

---

[74] On the specific nature of this liability regime, see above, p 132.
[75] See below, ch 31.2.B.
[76] BGHZ 24, 189.
[77] For the text of §§ 823 and 831 BGB, see above, p 133.

obligation and a contractual obligation, the provisions concerning tortious and contractual liability must both be considered in determining the legal consequences. Both may give rise to claims for damages, which are subject to distinct sets of legal rules with regard to their requirements, their content and their realisation.

Of course, a statute can conclusively provide for the legal consequences of a given set of facts and thereby make it clear that the facts are not to be assessed under a different legal regime. However, this is not the case with regard to the transport of goods and persons by rail... The Railway regulations which were enacted on the basis of the enabling provision in § 458 Commercial Code do not contain a rule which excludes recourse to delictual liability. ...

The provisions of the Railway regulations which limit the liability [to RM 200/kg] apply, as is already clear from their literal meaning, exclusively to the contractual liability of the carrier. ... The requirements for contractual and delictual liability are different. Under the [regulations' regime for the] contract of carriage, the carrier is liable for the loss of the transported goods, whether there is fault on his part or not ..., even for contingencies, unless there is a case of *force majeure*; it is strictly liable for its employees, regardless of whether they are involved in the transport of the goods and whether they are at fault. ... For the sake of the standardisation and speed of mass transport, this far-reaching liability is somewhat schematic; this is set off by the limitations of liability provided for in the Railway regulations (and in international conventions) which are similarly standardised. ... The requirements for liability under the delict provisions are very different. Here the carrier is liable if one of its organs, intentionally or negligently, unlawfully injures the property of another person (§§ 81, 89, 823 BGB); it is also liable if it cannot show that it is not at fault in selecting and supervising a vicarious agent who has unlawfully inflicted damage (§ 831 BGB). Here the duties of the railway are neither more nor less extensive than those of any other business; it is answerable for the reliability of its organs and for the necessary care when selecting and supervising the persons deployed. Neither the size of its business nor the fact that operating a railway necessarily entails frequent contact with property belonging to others would justify to exempt the railway form the generally applicable delictual provisions. ...

Therefore the railway cannot invoke the restriction of contractual liability, as provided for in the Railway regulations, if it is has committed a delict ...

[The court then establishes that the requirements of §§ 823(1), 831 BGB are met.]

Note

The competition of claims allows the claimant to choose between the two causes of action. Each action follows its own rules. However, German law recognises that delictual liability may have to be modified in the light of a contractual clause. Thus, if the parties have agreed on a clause limiting liability (as opposed to the statutory limitation of contractual liability which applied in the decision of the Reichsgericht above), a purposive interpretation of the clause may show that it is meant to limit both contractual and delictual liability. Furthermore, some statutory provisions which limit the liability of one party to a specific type of contract (such as the lender or the donor) are also applied to competing delictual claims; these statutory limitations would normally be nugatory if the delictual liability were to apply according to the general rules.[78]

---

[78] D Looschelders, *Schuldrecht: Allgemeiner Teil* (15th edn, Munich: Vahlen, 2017) para 23.

In English law a clause may exclude liability both in contract and in tort (subject to various statutory restrictions which we will consider later when we deal with unfair contract terms).[79] A question of interpretation arises: does the clause relate to both rights of action or to one of them only and, if so, to which one?

Subject to the statutory restrictions mentioned, it is possible to exclude liability for tort, for example liability in negligence, as well as liability for breach of contract. However, to exclude liability for negligence, clear words must be used. For example, in *White v John Warwick & Co Ltd*[80] a contract for the hire of a bicycle provided that 'Nothing in this agreement shall render the owners liable for any personal injuries …'. The plaintiff was thrown from the bicycle and injured when the saddle tilted as he was riding it. This was due to negligent maintenance of the bicycle by the defendants. The Court of Appeal held that the defendants were liable for negligence; the clause quoted excluded any liability for injuries caused by a breach of contract, but they were also under a duty in tort to take reasonable care and the clause did not cover that.

White v John Warwick was a case in which, but for the clause, there would have been both liability in tort for negligence and strict liability for breach of contract. Some thought that this meant that if there was only a duty to take care—whether in tort or contract—a similar clause must exclude all liability as otherwise it would be of no effect. However, in *Hollier v Rambler Motors (AMC) Ltd*[81] a garage which took the plaintiff's car for servicing negligently allowed it to be destroyed by fire. A clause in its standard conditions provided that 'the company is not liable for damage caused to customers' cars on the premises'. It argued that, as its only duty was to take reasonable care of the car, this clause must be effective to exclude that duty, otherwise it would have no effect. The Court of Appeal disagreed: a reasonable customer might interpret the clause as a warning that the company would not be liable for fires which started by accident. To exclude liability it thus may be necessary either to refer to negligence expressly or to use some synonym such as 'damage howsoever caused'.

To conclude, the question whether or not the rules of one liability system need to be protected from being put aside by concurring actions depends on an evaluation of both liability regimes. As Schlechtriem wrote:[82]

> The circumvention of one liability system by relying on concurring actions, which thereby gain factual priority over the other system, might be welcome and therefore not be regarded as a problem at all. This is true especially if the superseded rules of liability are outdated, inadequate and need correction. … Where, however, the rules of one liability system are regarded as adequate, well-balanced and just, there is a need to protect them from being pushed aside by concurring actions. This is especially the case if tort law uses broad general clauses, protecting even purely economic interests (in contrast to such tangible goods as life, health and property) and thereby (theoretically) allowing tort actions for every interest violated by a breach of contract.

---

[79] See below, p 838.
[80] [1953] 1 WLR 1285 (CA).
[81] [1972] 2 QB 71 (CA).
[82] P Schlechtriem, 'The Borderland of Tort and Contract' (1988) 21 Cornell International Law Journal 468.

6.2.B.4 LIABILITY TO PERSONS WHO ARE NOT PARTIES TO THE CONTRACT

In principle, only the parties to a contract may be affected by it or rely on its terms. In French law this is known as the principle of 'relative effect'. The Code civil has a specific and new section on 'The Effects of Contracts as regards Third Parties' and new Article 1199 (formerly Article 1165) Cciv states that 'A contract creates obligations only as between the parties'.[83]

The relative effect of contracts has two aspects. The first is that, generally speaking, a contract cannot impose obligations on, or reduce the rights of, a third person who is not a party to it. Of course, the effect of the contract may be to transfer property rights from one party to another, and the buyer's rights must be respected by third parties, but that does not impose new duties on the third party, it merely changes to whom the duties are owed. Third parties may even have to respect the fact that there is a contract between other parties. English law recognises a special tort of 'inducing a breach of contract'[84] and such conduct may lead to delictual liability in German law as well (§ 826 BGB).[85]

Secondly, normally only the parties to a contract may enforce it or take benefits under it. In Chapter 31 we will see that this rule is now heavily qualified. All the laws make it possible for a contract to confer enforceable rights upon a person who is not a party to it.[86] However, under each law there may be cases in which a third person does not acquire enforceable rights or the benefit of the contract terms. We will see that some courts are ready to extend 'contractual liability' for the benefit of the third person who has suffered the loss; other courts are less willing, but they apply liability in tort in some of these situations, especially in English law.

A particular issue is that of the third party involved in non-performance of the contract: for example, a person who is not a party to the contract but whose actions cause the non-performance. We saw above that where this is done deliberately there may be liability in tort, eg for inducing breach of contract. Much more commonly, the third party will merely have been careless. In such a case the liability of the third party may again only be in tort. Here there is often an overlap with the type of case discussed in the previous paragraph, because the third party was performing a contract in the same chain of contracts, but a contract to which the claimant was not a party. The claimant will be able to recover on the basis of contractual liability if this contract is seen as extending to him. Again we will see that some laws are more ready to make this extension than others. In those systems that are not so ready to treat the contract as extending to those who are not parties to it, there have been attempts to use the law of tort as the basis for a claim. Here we encounter again two issues. The first is *non cumul*. The second affects liability in tort: the question of when 'economic loss' can be recovered in tort is a question which does not arise in French law, but does in both English and German law. The issues involved are difficult and we will not deal with them here but in Chapter 31, where we discuss the effect of contracts on third parties.

---

[83] See ch 31. See also Art 1203 Cciv: 'A person is not able to undertake engagements in his own name except for himself.'

[84] *Lumley v Gye* (1853) 2 E & B 216 (QB).

[85] Münchener Kommentar/Wagner § 826 paras 66-78. For § 826 BGB, see p 133 above.

[86] Equally the contract may now confer a 'negative benefit', such as an exclusion or restriction of what would otherwise be the liability of the third person should he cause an accident: see ch 31.1.

6.3 CONTRACT AND RESTITUTION (QUASI-CONTRACT, UNJUSTIFIED ENRICHMENT)

It is now time to delimit the sphere of contract from that of a third source of obligations, that is to say 'quasi-contract' (according to the traditional French terminology, inherited from Roman law), 'restitution' (as it is frequently referred to in English terminology, though recent usage tends to distinguish between claims for 'unjust enrichment' and 'restitution' as an alternative, gain-based remedy for a wrong[87]) or 'unjustified enrichment' (as it is called in the BGB).

This kind of liability may arise as between parties who are not in any kind of contractual relationship, for example when by mistake A pays money to B which he does not owe to B but to C. In this book we are concerned with a narrower range of cases, where there may be 'restitutionary' liability 'in a contractual context'. We have in mind four principal types of case.

First, where the parties expected to make a contract and began performing, but either no contract was ever concluded or the contract they made turned out to be ineffective (for example because one of the parties had no power to make it).

Secondly, where the contract was made but it has been avoided on some ground of invalidity, such as fraud or duress.

Thirdly, where the contract was made and partly performed, but before performance on each side had been completed the contract was terminated for non-performance. We include in this category cases in which according to English law the contract is discharged by frustration.[88]

Fourthly, cases in which the defendant has received a benefit as the result of the claimant performing a contract with a third party, and the third party has failed to pay the claimant.

6.3.A THE NOTIONS OF QUASI-CONTRACT, RESTITUTION OR UNJUSTIFIED ENRICHMENT

We must start by noting the differences in terminology.

English law used to refer to quasi-contracts, but nowadays all the cases mentioned are treated under the general heading of restitution. However, there are a number of different grounds on which restitution may be claimed rather than a general principle that a benefit received should be returned unless the recipient has a justification for retaining it.[89]

The Draft Common Frame of Reference (DCFR) contains a Book on unjustified enrichment,[90] which applies in most of the situations outlined above. However, when dealing with the recovery of benefits that have been transferred under a contract which has subsequently been terminated, it has a separate set of rules on restitution.[91] This

---

[87] See the change in title of the classic English work, *Goff and Jones*, from *The Law of Restitution* to (in the 8th and 9th editions, by C Mitchell, P Mitchell and S Watterson, 2011 and 2017), *The Law of Unjust Enrichment*.

[88] See below, p 1185.

[89] See further below, p 161.

[90] Book VII DCFR.

[91] See Arts III.-3:510 to III.-3:514 DCFR.

legislative technique follows the BGB which, apart from the rules on unjustified enrichment in §§ 812-822 has a separate set of rules on the unwinding of failed contracts in §§ 346–354.[92]

Expressions such as 'quasi-contract' and 'restitution' are somewhat ambiguous when examined from the standpoint of a comparative lawyer. They may occasionally pose in the guise of false friends: quasi-contracts are not always akin to contracts. And a contract may give rise to liability which in practice is similar to restitution, such as contracts involving the restitution of property (*contrat réel*); the same applies in the case of bailment.[93] It will be helpful therefore to form an overall view of the notion of the subject prior to contrasting it with that of contract.

6.3.B CIVIL LAW JURISDICTIONS

Unjustified enrichment or quasi-contract is regarded as a source of obligations, namely the obligation to afford restitution of an item of value unduly obtained. It is in that light that the French Civil Code presents the matter and then distinguishes between three varieties of quasi-contracts.

Code civil   **6.20 (FR)**

Article 1300: Quasi-contracts are purely voluntary actions which result in a duty in a person who benefits from them without having a right to do so, and sometimes a duty in the person performing them towards another person.

The quasi-contracts governed by this sub-title are management of another's affairs, payment of a debt which is not due, and unjustified enrichment.

Notes

(1) Title III of Book III of the Code civil is on 'Sources of obligations'. It has three subtitles, one on contract, one on extra-contractual liability and one on other sources of obligations. Article 1300 opens Subtitle III which itself deals with 'management of another's affairs' (benevolent intervention), 'undue payment' and 'unjustified enrichment'. The list is not exhaustive. Article 1300(2) may be interpreted as opening the door to other quasi-contracts, not named (*innommés*) in the sense that they do not have their own denomination in the Code civil.[94]

(2) The third species of quasi-contracts mentioned in revised Article 1300(2) Cciv is a codification of previous case law: based on Articles 1371–1382 of the 1804 Code civil, the courts elaborated a general doctrine of unjust enrichment, first enunciated in the landmark *Patureau* judgment[95] and underpinned by 'an equitable principle which

---

[92] In Book II, Division 3, Title 1, Sub-title 1 ('Revocation'). See further below, pp 985–86, 1050–51.
[93] See above, pp 129–30.
[94] For examples, see Chénedé (n 45 above) no. 31.31: *créances et récompenses matrimoniales* and *indemnité d'accession*.
[95] Cass civ 15 June 1892, S 1893.1.281, annotated by JE Labbé.

prohibits a person from enriching himself to another's detriment'. Subsequent decisions refined the conditions under which a right of action to recover property (*in rem verso*) might arise.[96]

The trilogy of *gestion d'affaires*, recovery of sums wrongly paid and unjustified enrichment is found in some modern codes, but with differences in presentation and in different places. Thus, the German Code devotes two unconnected titles in Division 8 ('Particular types of obligations') in Book 2 ('Law of Obligations') to the law of unjustified enrichment which includes recovery of sums wrongly paid (Title 26: §§ 812–822 BGB) and what it calls 'managing another's affairs without mandate' (Title 13: §§ 677–687 BGB).[97]

Unjustified enrichment plays a major role in German law because of the principle of separation.[98]

BGB   **6.21 (DE)**

§ 812: Claim for restitution

(1) A person who obtains something as a result of the performance of another person or otherwise at his expense without legal grounds for doing so is under a duty to make restitution to him. This duty also exists if the legal grounds later lapse or if the result intended to be achieved by those efforts in accordance with the contents of the legal transaction does not occur.

(2) Performance also includes the acknowledgement of the existence or non-existence of an obligation.

The BGB does not use the concept of quasi-contract. Nor does the Netherlands Civil Code (BW).[99]

BW   **6.22 (NL)**

Article 6:212: (1) A person who has been unjustifiably enriched at the expense of another must, to the extent this is reasonable, make reparation for the damage suffered by that other person up to the amount of his enrichment.

(2) A decrease in the enrichment is not taken into consideration to the extent that it results from a cause which cannot be imputed to the enriched person.

(3) A decrease in the enrichment during the period in which the enriched person did not reasonably have to foresee the existence of an obligation to make reparation for damage, is not imputed to him. In determining this decrease, the expenses which would not have been made had there been no enrichment, are also taken into account.

It appears that unjust enrichment constitutes the essential feature, not to say the sole justification, of what we will call restitution.

---

[96] See, eg cases 3.27 (FR) and 3.28 (FR), extracted in the second edition of this book, pp 126 and 127.

[97] The official translation of the Ministry of Justice speaks of 'Agency without specific authorisation'.

[98] See above, pp 123–24.

[99] Nor does the Italian Civil Code, which devotes a title to each of the three doctrines, the latter in Title 4 to Book 6: 'Obligations arising from sources other than unlawful act or contract' and governs them in three sections (Arts 198–212).

6.3.C ENGLISH LAW

English law is vaguer and more ambiguous in its terminology. It used to refer to quasi-contract and now speaks of restitution or unjust enrichment,[100] but does not always accord the same meaning to those terms.

At the outset it may be noted that English law is unfamiliar with the trilogy known to civil lawyers: *gestion d'affaires* does not exist. It seems that this is because of a fear of encouraging untimely intervention by third parties in the business of other persons.[101] English lawyers therefore have to use the Roman law term *negotiorum gestio* in order to describe the doctrine that is absent from their law. English books at one time commonly referred to quasi-contract but now the recovery of money that was not due and other forms of unjust enrichment are treated under the general heading of 'restitution'. It is only quite recently that the courts have come to recognise general principles of restitution. As recently as 1978, Lord Diplock said that:[102]

> there is no general doctrine of unjust enrichment recognised in English law. What it does is to provide specific remedies in particular cases of what might be classified as unjust enrichment in a legal system that is based on the civil law.

However, it has been claimed that the later decision of the House of Lords in *Lipkin Gorman v Karpnale Ltd*[103] shows that a principle against unjust enrichment has been recognised by English law: 'not only did their Lordships use the language of unjust enrichment but, more specifically, the defence of change of position was accepted for the first time and that defence can only be rationalised through unjust enrichment reasoning'.[104]

In what follows we will adopt the modern approach of referring to 'restitution' or 'unjust enrichment' generally, rather than to 'quasi-contract' or to separate categories of recovery of money not due and unjust enrichment.

It should be noted that the law of restitution in England, at least on the traditional analysis, does not recognise a broad principle that a party who has been enriched must compensate the party at whose expense it occurred unless it can be shown that the enrichment was justified. Instead, restitution is available only in specific cases—as it is often said, when one of a list of 'unjust factors' is present. Unjust factors include grounds such as fraud, mistake, duress or undue influence—and also that the party conferring the benefit expected something in return but has not received it ('failure of consideration' or, as some prefer to say, 'failure of basis').[105]

---

[100] See above, p 158.

[101] See SL Stoljar, 'Negotiorum Gestio' in *International Encyclopedia of Comparative Law* (Tübingen: Mohr Siebeck, 1987), vol X, ch 17; J Kortmann, *Altruism in Private Law: Liability for Nonfeasance and negotiorum gestio* (Oxford University Press, 2005).

[102] *Orakpo v Manson Investments Ltd* [1978] AC 95, 104.

[103] [1991] 2 AC 548.

[104] A Burrows, E McKendrick and J Edelman, *Cases and Materials on the Law of Restitution* (2nd edn, Oxford: Clarendon Press, 2007) 35–39. These authors provide extracts and an extensive discussion on the competing views on the question to which extent English law recognises a general principle of restitution.

[105] See A Burrows, *Law of Restitution* (3rd edn, Oxford University Press, 2011) 86–116, comparing the alternative 'absence of basis' theory at 95 ff.

6.3.D RESTITUTION IN THE CONTRACTUAL CONTEXT

Apart from terminological and conceptual difficulties, there is one point in common: restitution applies where there is no contract or there is no longer any contract.

Until the 2016 reform, the French Civil Code had no general rules on restitution. The provisions contained in new Articles 1352 to 1352-9 are a useful clarification of the law. They constitute a 'general theory' of restitution, whatever the origin of the restitution (nullity, termination, *caducité*, undue payment). They have been inserted at the very end of the amended provisions (after the provision on *Régime général des obligations* and before the provisions on proof of obligations), in a specific chapter on restitution. Some of them are a novelty. There is no provision which deprives the person whose 'hands are not clean' from his right to claim restitution; however, the general principle *nemo auditur propriam suam turpitudinem allegans* may yet apply, all the more so that the Cour de cassation has long applied it to bar a person whose motivation was immoral from his restitutionary claim.[106]

Code civil

6.23 (FR)

Article 1352: Restitution of a thing other than a sum of money takes place in kind or, where this is impossible, by value assessed at the date of the restitution.

In German law the contract may also constitute the legal justification of the enrichment and thus debar the action. In that case, the contract in fact constitutes the legal ground justifying the enrichment (§ 812(1) BGB).

OLG Hamm, 9 January 1974[107]

6.24 (DE)

Car repairs

A car owner is not unjustly enriched by repairs to her car which were ordered by her now-bankrupt husband.

Facts: The applicant was the owner of a car repair workshop. The defendant was the owner of a Ford vehicle. The applicant claimed payment of the balance due for repairs carried out on the defendant's car. On 1 August 1970, following an accident, the defendant's husband towed the vehicle to the applicant's garage and continued his journey to Denmark. From Denmark he sent a letter dated 3 August 1970 to confirm the request for repairs to be carried out. He also informed the applicant that he would pay by a cheque drawn on the savings bank of the town X. He asked the applicant to contact that bank and said he would come back for his car on 8 August 1970. The applicant therefore went ahead and ordered spare parts and, on starting the repairs, he found that the damage to the vehicle was greater than at first thought.

On 3 September 1970 the defendant and her husband collected the vehicle which had been repaired. No invoice had been prepared as the applicant's computerised system had gone down. Nevertheless, the vehicle was handed over against payment of DM 2,000 (DM 500 in cash and DM 1,500 by cheque).

On 4 September 1970 the applicant sent the defendant an invoice for DM 4,765.15. The defendant asked for time to study the invoice. Following an exchange of correspondence the defendant alleged that she had not given her consent to the repairs. As she was refusing to pay, the applicant proceeded against the defendant's

---

[106] Chénedé (n 45 above) no. 22.12.
[107] NJW 1974, 951.

husband for payment of the amount remaining outstanding, namely DM 2,765.15 in the Hamburg Regional Court. By a default judgment dated 29 March 1971 he was ordered to pay the sum of DM 2,765.15.

However, execution proved fruitless since the husband had neither liquid assets nor mortgageable property. Accordingly, the applicant once again demanded payment from the defendant of the sum remaining outstanding and brought proceedings on the debt.

Held: The Regional Court ordered the defendant to pay the sum of DM 500 and dismissed the remainder of the applicant's claim. Both parties appealed against the decision. The applicant's appeal was dismissed whereas the defendant's appeal was allowed.

Summary of the Judgment:
I—The applicant has no right of action on the debt against the defendant.

(1) Absence of contractual relationship between the parties. Since the defendant's husband did not act as his wife's representative, there could be no ratification of the contract entered into between him and the applicant. The mere indication of the name of a third party on a registration document is not sufficient in order to establish agency. The defendant did not acknowledge the debt.

(2) No action based on managing another's affairs without mandate. Certainly the intention to manage another's affairs may be presumed even where that other person performs an act of their own. In the present case an inference of this kind may be drawn from the statement of the defendant's name and the sending to her of an invoice. But it is important to ask the question whether the repairs were objectively in the defendant's interests. Here, according to a witness statement, it appears that the defendant no longer wished to have major repairs carried out. Consequently, it may be inferred therefrom that an investment of that kind would no longer have seemed appropriate to her. In addition, the management of affairs was not ratified within the meaning of the second sentence of § 684 BGB.

(3) No action for enrichment under the first sentence of § 684 and §§ 812 *et seq* BGB. In the case of unauthorized managing another's affairs there is a right to recovery of the unjust enrichment. But the first sentence of § 684 BGB only applies in bilateral relations. In the present case such an action cannot succeed. In fact, the applicant performed a service on the basis of a genuine contract with the husband, that is to say on the basis of a legal ground. Thus, he cannot at the same time plead unjust enrichment under the first limb of § 812(1)(1) BGB on the basis of a contractual right against the defendant's husband.

Note

The Court points out successively that the applicant has no claim because there was (i) no agency of one spouse on behalf of the other, (ii) no management of another's affairs without mandate because it was not established that the repair was beneficial, and (iii) no unjust enrichment because there was a legal ground justifying it, namely the contract entered into with the husband, although this became worthless as a result of the husband's insolvency.[108]

The question whether there is a contract underlying the enrichment has also arisen in English law. Restitutionary claims 'in the context of contracts' arise frequently when the parties have conferred benefits on one another but either they had failed to conclude a

---

[108] For a Franco-German comparison, see Rieg (n 9 above).

contract or the contract was for some reason ineffective, for example, because one party had no power to conclude such a contract.

Queen's Bench Division[109]

6.25 (EN)

British Steel Corporation v Cleveland Bridge and Engineering Co Ltd

Where one party asks another to supply goods and the other does so although there is no contract between them because the terms of the proposed contract are still under active discussion, the recipient is liable in restitution for the value of the goods actually received.

Facts: The plaintiff (BSC) was in negotiations with the defendant (CBE) for the supply of nodes, for a construction project. During the negotiations a letter of intent was issued by CBE asking BSC to start the work and, with negotiations still under way. nearly all the nodes were delivered. Delivery of the final item was delayed by a strike and the nodes were not paid for. BSC claimed payment for the nodes on the basis of their reasonable value, in the absence of a contract. CBE counter-claimed for damages greater than that value for late delivery.

Held: BSC's claim was upheld on the basis of unjust enrichment.

Judgment: ROBERT GOFF J ... I now turn to the first issue in the case, which is concerned with the legal basis for BSC's claim for payment, and in particular whether there was any binding contract between BSC and CBE and, if so, what were its terms. As I have already indicated, it is the contention of CBE that there was such a contract; whereas BSC contends that they are entitled to payment in quasi contract ...

Now the question whether in a case such as the present any contract has come into existence must depend on a true construction of the relevant communications which have passed between the parties and the effect (if any) of their action pursuant to those communications. There can be no hard and fast answer to the question whether a letter of intent will give rise to a binding agreement: everything must depend on the circumstances of the particular case. In most cases, where work is done pursuant to a request contained in a letter of intent, it will not matter whether a contract did or did not come into existence, because, if the party who has acted on the request is simply claiming payment, his claim will usually be based on a *quantum meruit*,[110] and it will make no difference whether that claim is contractual or quasi-contractual. Of course, a *quantum meruit* claim (like the old action for money had and received and for money paid) straddles the boundaries of what we now call contract and restitution, so the mere framing of a claim as a *quantum meruit* claim, or a claim for a reasonable sum, does not assist in classifying the claim as contractual or quasi contractual. But where, as here, one party is seeking to claim damages for breach of contract, the question whether any contract came into existence if of crucial importance. As a matter of analysis the contract (if any) which may come into existence following a letter of intent may take one of two forms: either there may be an ordinary executory contract, under which each party assumes reciprocal obligations to the other; or there may be what is sometimes called an 'if' contract, i.e. a contract under which A requests B to carry out a certain performance and promises B that, if he does so, he will receive a certain performance in return, usually remuneration

---

[109] [1984] 1 All ER 504.
[110] Literally, a claim for 'how much the work was worth', ie its reasonable value.

for his performance. The latter transaction is really no more than a standing offer which, if acted on before it lapses or is lawfully withdrawn, will result in a binding contract.

The former type of contract was held to exist by Mr Edgar Fay QC, the official Referree, in *Turriff Construction Ltd v Regalia Knitting Mills Ltd*, and it is the type of contract for which counsel for CBE contended in the present case. Of course, as I have already said, everything must depend on the facts of the particular case; but certainly, on the facts of the present case (and, as I imagine, on the facts of most cases), this must be a very difficult submission to maintain. It is only necessary to look at the terms of CBE's letter of intent in the present case to appreciate the difficulties. In that letter, the request to BSC to proceed immediately with the work was stated to be 'pending the preparation and issuing to you of the official form of sub-contract', being a sub-contract which was plainly in a state of negotiation, not least on the issue of price, delivery dates, and the applicable terms and conditions. In these circumstances, it is very difficult to see how BSC, by starting work, bound themselves to any contractual performance. No doubt it was envisaged by CBE at the time they sent the letter that negotiation had reached an advanced stage, and that a formal contract would soon be signed; but, since the parties were still in a stage of negotiation, it is impossible to say with any degree of certainty what the material terms of that contract would be. I find myself quite unable to conclude that, by starting work in these circumstances, BSC bound themselves to complete the work. In the course of argument, I put to counsel for CBE the question whether BSC were free at any time, after starting work, to cease work. His submission was that they were not free to do so, even if negotiations on the terms of the formal contract broke down completely. I find this submission to be so repugnant to common sense and the commercial realities that I an unable to accept it. It is perhaps revealing that, on 4 April 1979, BSC did indeed state that they were not prepared to proceed with the contract until they had an agreed specification, a reaction which, in my judgment, reflected not only the commercial, but also the legal, realities of the situation.

I therefore, reject CBE's submission that a binding executory contract came into existence in this case. There remains the question whether, by reason of BSC carrying out work pursuant to the request contained in CBE's letter of intent, there came into existence a contract by virtue of which BSC were entitled to claim reasonable remuneration; i.e. whether there was an 'if' contract of the kind I have described. In the course of argument, I was attracted by this alternative (really on the basis that, not only was it analytically possible, but also that it could provide a vehicle for certain contractual obligations of BSC concerning their performance, e.g. implied terms as to the quality of goods supplied by them). But the more I have considered the case, the less attractive I have found this alternative. The real difficulty is to be found in the factual matrix of the transaction, and in particular the fact that the work was being done pending a formal sub-contract the terms of which were still in a state of negotiation. It is, of course, a notorious fact that, when a contract is made for the supply of goods on a scale and in circumstances such as the present, it will in all probability be subject the standard terms, usually the standard terms of the supplier. Such standard terms will frequently legislate, not only for the liability of the seller for defects, but also for the damages (if any) for which the seller will be liable in the event not only of defects in the goods but also of later delivery. It is a commonplace that a seller of goods may exclude liability for consequential loss, and may agree liquidated damages for delay. In the present case, an unresolved dispute broke out between the parties on the question whether CBS's or BSC's standard terms were to apply, the former providing no limit to the seller's liability for delay and the latter excluding such liability altogether. Accordingly, when, in a case such as the present, the parties are still in a state of negotiation, it is impossible to predicate what liability (if any) will be assumed by the seller for, e.g. defective goods or late delivery, if a formal contract should be entered into. In these circumstances, if the buyer asks the seller to commence work 'pending' the parties entering into a formal contract, it is difficult to infer from the buyer acting on that request that he is assuming any responsibility for his performance, except such responsibility as will rest on him under the terms of the contract which both parties confidently anticipate they will shortly enter into. It would be an extraordinary result if, by acting on such a request in such circumstances, the buyer were to assume an unlimited liability for his contractual performance, when he would never assume such liability under any contract which he entered into.

For these reasons, I reject the solution of the 'if' contract. In my judgment, the true analysis of the situation is simply this. Both parties confidently expected a formal contract to eventuate. In these circumstances, to expedite performance under that anticipated contract, one requested the other to commence the contract work, and the other complied with that request. If thereafter, as anticipated, a contract was entered into, the work done as requested will be treated as having been performed under that contract; if, contrary to their expectation, no contract was entered into, then the performance of the work is not referable to any contract the terms of which can be ascertained, and the law simply imposes an obligation on the party who made the request, such an obligation sounding in quasi contract or, as we now say, in restitution. Consistently with that solution, the party making the request may find himself liable to pay for work which he would not have had to pay for as such if the anticipated contract had come into existence, e.g. preparatory work which will, if the contract is made, be allowed for in the price of the finished word (cf. *William Lacey (Hounslow) Ltd v Davis*). The solution moreover accords with authority: see the decision in *Lacey v David*, the decision of the Court of Appeal in *Sander & Forster Ltd v A Monk & Co Ltd*, though that decision rested in part on a concession, and the crisp dictum of Parker J in *OTM Ltd v Hydranautics*, when he said of a letter of intent that 'its only effect would be to enable the defendants to recover on quantum meruit for work done pursuant to the direction' contained in the letter. I only wish to add to this part of my judgment the footnote that, even if I had concluded that in the circumstances of the present case there was a contract between the parties and that that contract was of the kind I have described as an 'if' contract, then I would still have concluded that there was no obligation under that contract on the part of BSC to continue with or complete the contract work, and therefore no obligation on their part to complete the work within a reasonable time. However, my conclusion in the present case is that the parties never entered into any contract at all.

Judgment for the plaintiffs. The counter-claim was dismissed.

Notes

(1) The Court found there was no contract. The letter of intent did not constitute a bilateral contract and there was also no conditional or 'if' (unilateral) contract. Accordingly, there was a claim in restitution.

(2) We shall see that many continental courts may impose precontractual liability in damages when they think that one party has acted improperly in failing to reach an agreement, or in misleading the other into acting in reliance on an agreement being

reached (see Chapter 13 on pre-contractual good faith). However, on the facts of the *BSC* case, there does not seem to have been any conduct which would give rise to liability of this kind. It is simply that no contract was ever concluded. Probably again there would be only liability to pay for the benefits that were received, eg under § 812 BGB.

English law may also grant restitution when the parties have purported to enter a contract which in fact is void: see *Westdeutsche Landesbank Girozentrale v Islington London Borough Council*.[111] In that case a local authority and a bank had entered an 'interest rate swap' contract which was later held to be *ultra vires* the local authority (ie outside its legal power to make). The bank was permitted to recover payments it had made. In contrast, if the contract is illegal, restitution may well be denied on the basis that, as between two guilty parties, the possessor has the better position or, as in French law, by the adage *nemo auditur propriam turpitudinem allegans*, limited in French law, it is true, to contracts for an immoral purpose. This is discussed in Chapter 17. If the parties have concluded a binding contract, then in English law the parties may not claim in restitution unless the contract has been avoided on one of the grounds of invalidity (see Chapters 14–16), has been discharged under the doctrine of frustration, for example because it has become impossible (see Chapter 28),[112] or has been terminated on the ground of fundamental non-performance (see Chapter 25).[113] 'Before a party can claim restitution for failure of consideration, he must establish that he has no contractual obligation to confer the relevant benefit on the defendant: the relevant contract must be ineffective.'[114] This rule seems to play a broadly similar role to the subsidiarity principle in French law, to prevent the use of unjust enrichment as a way of evading what was agreed in the contract.

The requirement of an 'unjust factor' in English law[115] means that cases such as the German *Car repairs*[116] will not arise in English law. The claimant would be unable to point to any relevant unjust factor as between himself and the defendant.

6.3.E CONCLUDING REMARKS ON CONTRACT AND RESTITUTION

Unlike what was found to be the case with regard to the contract/tort relationship, and in spite of the differences in the classification of types of quasi-contract, there do not appear to have been major difficulties in drawing the demarcation line between the sphere of contract and that of restitution in the legal systems covered in this book.

---

[111] [1994] 1 WLR 938 (CA) and [1996] AC 669 (HL).
[112] Restitution after the discharge is considered below, p 1124.
[113] Restitution after termination is considered below, p 980.
[114] Burrows (n 105 above) 323.
[115] See above, p 161.
[116] 6.24(DE) above, p 162.

FURTHER READING

von Bar, C, *The Common European Law of Torts*, 2 vols (Oxford University Press, 1998 and 2000).

Beatson, J and Schrage, E (eds), *Ius Commune Casebooks on the Common Law of Europe: Cases, Materials and Texts on Unjustified Enrichment* (Oxford: Hart Publishing, 2003).

Borghetti, JS, 'The Effects of Contracts and Third Parties' in Cartwright, J and Whittaker, S (eds), *The Code Napoléon Rewritten: French Contract Law after the 2016 Reforms* (Oxford: Hart Publishing, 2017) 227–53.

Johnston, D and Zimmermann, R (eds), *Unjustified Enrichment: Key Issues in Comparative Perspective* (Cambridge University Press, 2002).

van Dam, C, *European Tort Law* (2nd edn, Oxford University Press, 2013).

van Erp, S and Akkermans, B (eds), *Ius Commune Casebooks on the Common Law of Europe: Cases, Materials and Texts on Property Law* (Oxford: Hart Publishing, 2012).

van Gerven, W, Larouche, P and Lever, J, *Ius Commune Casebooks on the Common Law of Europe: Cases, Materials and Texts on Tort Law* (Oxford: Hart Publishing, 2000).

Wagner, G, 'Comparative Tort Law' in M Reimann and R Zimmermann (eds), *Oxford Handbook of Comparative Law* (Oxford University Press, 2006) 1003–41.

Zweigert, K and Kötz, H, *Introduction to Comparative Law* (3rd edn, Oxford: Clarendon Press, 1998) 537–708.

CHAPTER 7
CATEGORISATION OF CONTRACTS ACCORDING TO PARTIES

7.1 INTRODUCTION: WAYS OF CATEGORISING CONTRACTS

Within each legal system there are many different types of contract, and many different ways of categorising contract and contract law. For example, each system recognises rules for 'specific contracts', such as sale of goods, contracts for services and contracts for insurance, as well as rules that in principle apply to contracts of all types unless displaced by a specific rule—what may be called 'general contract law'.

Code civil	**7.1 (FR)**

Article 1105: Whether or not they have their own denomination, contracts are subject to general rules, which are the subject of this sub-title.
  Rules particular to certain contracts are laid down in the provisions special to each of these contracts.
  The general rules are applied subject to these particular rules.

The degree to which each system has specific legislation, or has developed judge-made rules, for specific contracts or specific categories of contracting parties, varies considerably. Generally speaking, the common law has fewer rules for specific contracts than do the civil law systems; instead the parties are required to reach a more detailed agreement,[1] and much of the English case law on specific contracts seems to consist of decisions on how the agreements that are used should be interpreted.[2] In this book we are primarily concerned with general contract law, but from time to time we will consider rules governing specific contracts.[3]

---

[1] See B Nicholas, 'Rules and Terms—Civil Law and Common Law' (1974) 48 Tulane Law Review 946.
[2] eg, construction contracts: see, *Chitty on Contracts*, 33rd edn by H Beale (gen ed) (London: Sweet & Maxwell/Thomson Reuters, 2018) ch 37.
[3] See in particular chs 19 and 27 below, which deal with non-conformity and remedies for non-conformity in sale of goods contracts.

There are other ways in which contracts may be categorised. We have already dealt with the distinctions between 'onerous' and 'gratuitous contracts' and between 'synallagmatic' and 'unilateral contracts' in Chapter 5. It is also possible to distinguish between contracts that provide for performance in successive parts ('severable contracts', *contrats à exécution successive, Dauerschuldverhältnisse*) and contracts that are made once-and-for all ('entire contracts', *contrats à execution instantannée*). This is particularly relevant to the effects of termination. We will consider such distinctions as and when they are relevant to the discussion.

In this chapter we are primarily concerned with categories of contract that depend on the status of the contracting parties. Ordinary contracts between individuals who are not contracting for the purposes of business fall within the scope of general contract law (referred to as the *droit commun* in France). Such contracts are sometimes called 'peer to peer' (P2P) or 'private'[4] contracts. We will refer to them as 'consumer to consumer' (C2C) contracts, as has become customary in European private law. In contrast, contracts between parties who are not on an equal footing may justify the application of specific rules rather than that of the general ones. This is notably the case for contracts concluded between traders on the one hand and 'consumers' ('business to consumer' (B2C) contracts) or non-profit organisations on the other, and for contracts made by administrative bodies. But some systems also have particular rules for contracts between traders ('business to business' (B2B) contracts).

7.2 CIVIL AND COMMERCIAL CONTRACTS: A GENERAL OVERVIEW

The general law of contract applies to C2C contracts, though there is seldom explicit reference to this category of contracts in legislation, let alone an agreed name for it. We will see later that when neither party is acting in the course of a business there are fewer legislative controls over the terms of the contract than there are over B2C or even B2B contracts.[5]

To quite some extent, the general law of contract also applies to B2B contracts. However, this is subject to some modifications which vary from one legal system to another. Both French law and German law distinguish between civil law and commercial law. This distinction is highlighted by the fact that there are two separate Codes and that cases on commercial contracts are heard at first instance by specialised courts (*tribunaux de commerce*), composed of elected business people or specialised chambers in the ordinary courts, also with participation of business people (*Handelskammern*). By contrast, Dutch law now does not distinguish between commercial and other contracts; they are all dealt with in the BW.

---

[4] The phrase 'private contracts' was used in the draft legislation on unfair terms proposed by the English and Scottish Law Commissions: *Unfair Terms in Contracts*, Law Com No 292, Scot Law Com No 199 (London: The Stationery Office, 2005) Draft Bill cl 13.

[5] See ch 21, below, esp at pp 855–87.

However, one should not overestimate the importance of this distinction. As regards French law, which seems to have the sharpest divide, it would be wrong to believe that *contrats civils* have their own legal regime in the Code civil, and *contrats commerciaux* another one in the Code de commerce. In actual practice, the category *contrats commerciaux* does not exist as such: any type of contract can either be *civil*, *commercial* or *mixte*. The characterisation thus depends on the status and intentions of the parties. Book III, Title III of the Code civil (reformed in 2016) contains the general rules applicable both to civil and commercial contracts. The influence of customs and usages is generally accepted in the Code civil (see Article 1194) even if, traditionally, customs and usages play a larger role in commercial contracts. There are, in the Code de commerce, in other Codes and even in the Code civil, chapters and specific provisions applicable to specific contracts but there is no general theory for commercial contracts, distinct from the Code civil.[6] This does not mean that the Code de commerce has no relevance. The Code de commerce has specific provisions for some specific categories of contract (eg carriers or commercial agents). More importantly, some of its rules have a wide scope of application, notably those which limit party autonomy and guard against inequality of bargaining power. So if a dispute about a B2B contract is brought before the specialised jurisdiction of the commercial courts, Article L 442-6, I of the Code de commerce provides remedies against unfair contractual terms and practices that are roughly parallel to the protection provided for consumers.[7]

German law also draws a distinction between the general 'civil law' (*Zivilrecht*) and 'commercial law' (*Handelsrecht*). The former is mostly governed by the Civil Code, the Bürgerliches Gesetzbuch (BGB), which has already been referred to in the previous chapters; the latter by the Commercial Code, the Handelsgesetzbuch (HGB). Both codes were closely co-ordinated and entered into force on the same day, 1 January 1900. The HGB presupposes the existence of the general rules of private law contained in the Civil Code and only stipulates provisions where different or special rules are appropriate for contracts between business people, or 'merchants' (*Kaufleute*). It is also known as the 'special private law for merchants'. Its rules therefore do not apply because of the nature of the contract in question but because of the status of the contracting parties.[8]

The interplay between the two codes can be seen, for example, in the law on formalities. While normally a surety has to be in writing to be valid (§ 766 BGB),[9] merchants can provide sureties and similar security without the observance of any prescribed form (§ 350 HGB). Differences between the general civil law and commercial law may even exist without a special rule in the Commercial Code. An example is provided by the

---

[6] The Code civil contains rules that are applicable to specific contracts, such as sales contracts or services contracts (named 'contrat de louage de services' or 'contrat d'entreprise'). The 2016 reform concerned the general rules of contracts and a reform of the rules applicable to specific contracts is now envisaged.

[7] See Art L 212-1 of the Code de la consommation below, p 846. But see now also Art 1171 Cciv, below p 848, which applies to B2B contracts.

[8] Somewhat confusingly, according to §§ 343, 345 HGB, contracts between a merchant and a non-merchant are also categorised as ('unilateral') commercial contracts (*einseitige Handelsgeschäfte*). As a result, a contract between a merchant and a consumer can in certain circumstances be a consumer contract (below, p 176) and a commercial contract at the same time which may lead to inconsistencies between consumer law and commercial law.

[9] See below, p 403.

slightly diverging rules on the formation of contracts. While silence cannot amount to acceptance in a C2C contract, there is a commercial usage, according to which the terms of a commercial letter of confirmation, or 'confirmation of order' (*Kaufmännisches Bestätigungsschreiben*) may be incorporated in a commercial contract even if the recipient of the letter does not react to them.[10] As in French law, however, there are relatively few 'special' rules for commercial contracts,[11] so the significance of the commercial/civil divide should not be overestimated.

English law does not have a formal category of commercial or B2B contracts. Rather, the general law of contract, which is frequently modified when the contract is a consumer contract, applies to B2B or commercial contracts without many modifications. Thus the relatively few formal requirements—for example, the requirements of writing for sales of land and for guarantees[12]—apply equally to C2C and B2B contracts.

However, there are a number of English statutory provisions which have the effect that, when both parties are businesses, a different regime applies from that which would apply where one or both parties are not acting for business purposes. For example, in a sale of goods contract, if the buyer is another business, the seller may exclude or restrict its liability for breach of the various implied terms as to description and quality (non-conformity) under the Sale of Goods Act 1979,[13] but only if the exclusion or restriction is fair and reasonable.[14] If the seller is a trader and the buyer is a consumer, any restriction of the equivalent obligations under the Consumer Rights Act 2015 is ineffective.[15] If neither party is a trader (C2C), the seller has fewer obligations under the Sale of Goods Act[16] and the parties have more freedom to exclude or restrict the seller's liability.[17]

Equally there are no special procedural requirements for commercial cases in English law.[18] The vast bulk of contract litigation in English courts, at least in the higher courts, is 'commercial litigation'. The cost of litigation means that cases between individual parties[19] are seldom fought in court, and then usually only in the county courts.

Even if there is no formal difference between B2B and C2C contracts, we will see that one of the most important questions in several of the laws is whether the contract was on standard terms of business or was negotiated.[20] The distinction has important

---

[10] See below, pp 254–55.

[11] Most importantly, the rules on unfair standard terms apply not only to consumer contracts but, at least in principle, also to commercial contracts; see below, pp 851–52.

[12] See below, pp 405–08.

[13] ss 13–15. See below, pp 785–86.

[14] Unfair Contract Terms Act 1977, s 6(1A).

[15] Consumer Rights Act 2015, s 31. See below, p 842.

[16] See below, 19.12 (EN), p 785, and the following Notes.

[17] See Unfair Contract Terms Act 1977, 21.16 (EN), below, p 838, and the follwing Notes.

[18] England does have a specialised Commercial Court, but this is just a part of the Queen's Bench Division of the High Court.

[19] Sometimes a consumer organisation will support a consumer, or a number of consumers, in bringing an action: see for example the recent case of *Beavis v ParkingEye Ltd* [2015] UKSC 67, discussed below, 26.50 (EN), p 1122. There have also been important cases on the unfair terms legislation involving actions brought by the Office of Fair Trading to prevent traders using unfair terms. See further below, 21.30 (EN), p 861.

[20] § 305b BGB distinguishes 'individually agreed' and 'standard business *terms*'. In 2016, Art 1110 Cciv introduced the distinction between negotiated and non-negotiated *contracts* into the Code civil, by expressly defining bespoke contracts (*contrats de gré à gré*) and non-negotiated contracts (*contrats d'adhésion*).

consequences, for example as regards unfair terms[21] and the interpretation of the contract.[22] Though a C2C contract may be made on a standard set of terms (perhaps bought from a stationer's shop or downloaded from the internet), the use of standard terms is much more common in B2B contracts.

The distinction between general contract law and commercial contract law is also relevant in transnational contract law. A number of international conventions are only applicable to certain international B2B contracts; the most important one is the United Nations Convention on Contracts for the International Sale of Goods (CISG).[23] EU law usually does not distinguish between civil and commercial contracts.[24] For example, civil and commercial contracts are all governed by the same rules on choice of law (Rome I Regulation)[25] and choice of jurisdiction (Brussels I bis Regulation).[26] There is some EU legislation that applies only to B2B contracts, eg the Commercial Agents Directive[27] and the Late Payments Directive.[28] However, in EU law, as in most national contract laws today, the major distinction lies elsewhere: in the distinction between consumers and businesses.

7.3 CONSUMER CONTRACTS

One of the most important and pervasive distinctions, both within general contract law and often within the rules on specific contracts, is that between consumer contracts and non-consumer contracts—as we have seen in the introduction to this chapter, the latter are typically contracts between businesses, but also contracts between parties none of whom are businesses. For example, the Draft Common Frame of Reference (DCFR) and the Common European Sales Law (CESL), like many legal systems, suggested different rules on unfair terms according to whether the contract is a B2B contract, a B2C contract or one between parties neither of whom are making the contract in connection with a business (C2C). Similarly, in each national system in Europe there are many rules that apply only to consumer contracts. To quite some extent, this is a result of the harmonisation of contract law by the EU. As indicated in Chapter 2, the greater part of

---

[21] See below, pp 833–54.

[22] See below, pp 756–64, 826–29.

[23] See above, pp 28–30, 35.

[24] Nor do the PECL. In contrast, the UNIDROIT PICC only apply to commercial contracts.

[25] Regulation (EC) No 593/2008 of the European Parliament and of the Council of 17 June 2008 on the law applicable to contractual obligations, OJ L 177/2008, p 6: see above, p 25.

[26] Council Regulation (EC) No 44/2001 on jurisdiction and the recognition and enforcement of judgments in civil and commercial matters ('Brussels I Regulation'), OJ L 12/2001, p 1, dated 22 December 2000 and revised in 2012 (Regulation (EU) No 1215/2012, OJ L 351/2012, p 1) ('Brussels I bis Regulation'): see above, p 25.

[27] Council Directive 86/653/EEC of 18 December 1986 on the coordination of the laws of the Member States relating to self-employed commercial agents, OJ L 382/1986, p 17.

[28] Directive 2011/7/EU of the European Parliament and of the Council of 16 February 2011 on combating late payment in commercial transactions, OJ L 48/2011, p 1.

the existing EU contract law (what used to be called the *acquis communautaire* or now simply the *acquis*) is concerned largely or exclusively with contracts between businesses and consumers.

We first look at the various definitions of the notion of 'consumer' and then consider where in each system consumer law will be found.[29]

7.3.A THE DEFINITIONS OF CONSUMER

Consumer legislation applies only where one party is a consumer and the other is a trader. The main question is how consumer should be defined. Definitions have changed over time and also varied from one Member State to another. As we shall see, some unification has now been achieved through EU law, but it is far from complete.

7.3.A.1 TYPICAL DEFINITIONS IN EARLY EU LAW

The definition of consumer used in the 1993 Directive on Unfair Terms in Consumer Contracts[30] is typical of EU consumer legislation. The Directive requires each Member State to ensure that its law provides the rights enshrined in the Directive, so that wherever they make contracts in the EU consumers will have the right to challenge 'non-individually negotiated terms' on the ground that the term is unfair. It is a 'minimum harmonisation directive',[31] so Member States can keep existing law, or create new law, that gives consumers greater rights. Equally importantly, even when a directive requires full harmonisation for consumer contracts,[32] Member States may extend similar protection to other contracts, although these are outside the scope of application of the directive. We will return to these points below.

We will examine the Directive on Unfair Terms in detail in Chapter 21. Here we look at its definitions, to see what types of contract it covers.

Unfair Terms Directive **7.2 (EU)**

Article 1: 1. The purpose of this Directive is to approximate the laws, regulations and administrative provisions of the Member States relating to unfair terms in contracts concluded between a seller or supplier and a consumer. ...

Article 2: For the purposes of this Directive:

(a)   ...;

(b)   'consumer' means any natural person who, in contracts covered by this Directive, is acting for purposes which are outside his trade, business or profession;

---

[29] See below, p 186.
[30] Council Directive 93/13/EEC of 5 April 1993 on unfair terms in contracts entered into with consumers OJ L 95/1993, p 29.
[31] Art 8.
[32] Compare the Consumer Rights Directive (n 40 below) (Art 4 requires full harmonisation).

(c)   'seller or supplier' means any natural or legal person who, in contracts covered by this Directive, is acting for purposes relating to his trade, business or profession, whether publicly owned or privately owned.

Other directives contain slightly different definitions of consumer. Thus the Consumer Sales Directive[33] defines a consumer as 'any natural person who, in the contracts covered by this Directive, is acting for purposes which are not related to his trade, business or profession.' It is unclear whether this is intended to mean something different from the definition in the Unfair Terms or other Directives. One of the aims of the revision of the consumer *acquis* discussed in Chapter 2 was to align the definitions as far as possible. We will assume that there is no real difference between these definitions.

7.3.A.2 'CONSUMER': QUESTIONS OF INTERPRETATION AND OF DEFINITIONS

The definition of consumer in the Unfair Terms Directive, and the linked definition of the trader as a seller or supplier who is acting for purposes related to his trade, etc, may seem to be straightforward. In fact it raises some difficult questions of both interpretation and policy.

    Moreover, the definition of consumer is complicated because it may vary between EU and national legislation. The idea of protecting weaker parties generally is certainly not new—for example, from the late nineteenth century there was case law in Germany[34] and legislation and case law in France[35] that clearly aimed to protect weaker parties, though these developments were not confined to consumer contracts in the strict sense—and the category of consumer contracts did not originate with the EU. In the last 30 years, in each of the national systems covered in this book, specific legislation has been enacted to protect the consumer by making consumer contracts subject to special rules. For example, each law had legislation aimed at protecting consumers and others from unfair terms (or at least certain types of unfair terms) well before the adoption of the EU Directive in 1993. Some of the national legislations differentiated between consumer and other contracts, using definitions that were different to those found in the Directives. Further, in some countries the definition used was wider and the wider definitions may continue to apply for some purposes.[36] We will see that though in some respects there has been a tendency to move in the direction of the 'autonomous EU definition', this is by no means always the case.

    Sometimes national law had to be changed in order to implement the Directive of 1993. For example, the English Unfair Contract Terms Act 1977 originally provided that a contract came within the provisions protecting consumers only if the parties had the required status (for this purpose, trader and consumer)[37] and also, if the contract was

---

[33] Directive 1999/44/EC of the European Parliament and of the Council of 25 May 1999 on certain aspects of the sale of consumer goods and associated guarantees, OJ L 171/1999, p 12.

[34] eg, judgments applying § 138 BGB (undue advantage) and § 242 BGB (good faith): see below, p 829.

[35] eg, holding a professional commercial vendor to be irrebuttably presumed to have knowledge of a defect in an item sold (Art 1645 of the 1804 Cciv), and see Cass civ 10 May 1909, DP 1912.1.16.

[36] On earlier definitions, see the previous edition of the book. See in particular, in the second edition, pp 142–155.

[37] For complications in this respect, see below, p 853.

for the supply of goods, if the goods supplied were of a type ordinarily supplied for private use and consumption.[38] But when the Consumer Sales Directive[39] had to be implemented, it required Member States to treat the buyer of goods as a consumer whatever the type of goods, and the last part of the definition had to be removed from the Act.

German law also changed its definition a number of times, the last time in 2014, in order to take into account the requirements of the Consumer Rights Directive.[40] Similarly, the definition of the other party to a consumer contract—the 'business', 'trader' or, as it is sometimes referred to, 'entrepreneur'—has changed over time. At the time of writing, the text of the BGB is as follows:

BGB   **7.3 (DE)**

§ 13: Consumer
A consumer means every natural person who enters into a legal transaction for purposes that predominantly are outside his trade, business or [independent][41] profession.

§ 14: Entrepreneur
(1) An entrepreneur means a natural or legal person or a partnership with legal personality who or which, when entering into a legal transaction, acts in exercise of his or its trade, business or profession.
(2) A partnership with legal personality is a partnership that has the capacity to acquire rights and to incur liabilities.

Note

In a case decided by the Bundesgerichtshof on 30 September 2009,[42] the claimant was a lawyer who ordered three lamps from an internet seller. She intended to use them for her private flat but she provided the address of her law firm as the delivery and invoice address. The confirmation of the order did not provide the exact information on the withdrawal rights of the purchaser that is required for consumer contracts under the BGB. The claimant argued that she had acted as a consumer, exercised her right of withdrawal and claimed repayment of the purchase price. The BGH held that someone who is in fact making the purchase for private purposes must be treated as a consumer, even if that was not made clear to the trader, unless 'the circumstances of which the contractual partner can be aware clearly and unequivocally suggest that the natural person acted in pursuit of its trade, business or independent profession'.

In French law, the definition of a consumer at least for the purposes of legislation on unfair terms has evolved over the years. To implement the Directive on Unfair Terms,

---

[38] Unfair Contract Terms Act 1977, s 12(1)(c).

[39] 1999/44/EC (n 33 above).

[40] Directive 2011/83/EU of the European Parliament and of the Council of 25 October 2011 on consumer rights, OJ L 304/2011, p 64. See above, p 58.

[41] This word is missing from the English translation provided by the Ministry of Justice. We are grateful to Professor Christopher Bisping for drawing this omission to our intention.

[42] BGH 30 September 2009, NJW 2009, 3780.

a preliminary provision was introduced in the Consumer code.[43] It differs from the German and English texts. Article L 132-1 of the Code de la consommation, as amended in 2016[44] and further in 2017[45] applies to contracts made between 'professionals' (*professionnels*) and 'non-professionals or consumers'. In an 'Article liminaire' (the first of the legislative part) of the Code de la consommation, the concepts of consumer, non-professional and professional are defined. The non-professional, a category introduced by the Ordonnance no 2016-301 of 14 March 2016, is now defined as 'any legal person not acting for professional purposes'.[46]

For the application of the present code, one understands under:

— consumer: any natural person not acting in a commercial, industrial, craft, independent or agricultural activity;
— non-professional: any legal person not acting for professional purposes;
— professional: any natural or legal person, public or private, acting for its commercial, industrial, craft, independent[47] or agricultural activity, including when it acts in the name or on behalf of another professional.

Thus, under French law, a legal person can benefit from the qualification as non-professional (unlike the consumer). However, the non-professional will not benefit from all the provisions of the Consumer Code but from those which expressly designate it. In actual practice, it is not always easy to attribute the quality of consumer, non-professional or professional. The Court of Cassation has given some indications in two judgments of 29 March 2017.

In the first case, where a union of co-owners relied on Article L 136-1 of the Consumer Code (now L 215-1 et seq.)—a provision that protects consumers and non-professionals against tacit renewal of contracts—the Court of Cassation recalled the existence of the category 'non-professional'. In this case, the union could rely on this status and thus legitimately benefit from the protection against tacit renewals. In the second case, a *comité d'établissement* which offered expeditions to its members was not entitled to benefit from the financial guarantee provided for in Article L 211-18, II, a, of the Code of Tourism.[48] This text benefits the 'clients' and the Court de cassation held that only 'consumers', and therefore individuals and not legal persons, can benefit from it.[49]

We will return to the various national definitions below.

The problem faced by English law was that the definition of consumer in the original version of the Unfair Contract Terms Act 1977 was *narrower* than that required by the Consumer Sales Directive. What if the national legislation used a *broader* definition of consumer?

---

[43] See the Loi no. 2014-344 of 17 March 2014.
[44] Ordonnance no. 2016-301 of 14 March 2016.
[45] See below, n 46.
[46] Code de la consommation, Article liminaire (modified by Loi no. 2017-203 of 21 February 2017 which ratifies the Ordonnance).
[47] The French word here is 'libéral' and it designates a professional, acting as an 'independent professional' rather than as an employee.
[48] Cass Civ (1) 29 March 2017, no. 16-10007, Bull. 2017, I, no. 79.
[49] Cass Civ (1) 29 March 2017, no. 15-26766, Bull. 2017, I, no. 85.

As we will see below, some countries have implemented various directives by 'copying out' the texts into national legislation, eg the UK's former Unfair Terms in Consumer Contracts Regulations 1999 and, though to a lesser extent, Part 2 of the Consumer Rights Act 2015, which replaced the 1999 Regulations. However, as we noted earlier,[50] Member States are not prevented from using a more expansive definition of consumer.

First, 'minimum harmonisation' directives expressly enable Member States to adopt or retain measures that give consumers a higher degree of protection than is required by the Directive, provided that the protection is compatible with the EU Treaty.[51] Many Member States have adopted or kept legislation that provides more protection than is required by minimum harmonisation directives.[52]

Secondly, even with 'maximum' or 'full harmonisation' Directives (the 2011 Consumer Rights Directive falls within this category), which require that all Member States give the same protection, neither more nor less, the requirement for full harmonisation applies only within the scope of application of the relevant Directive.[53] For example, an extension of protection against unfair terms to small businesses would be outside the field of application of the Directive on Unfair Terms in Consumer Contracts. Some Member States have taken advantage of this.

So there is still significant variation in the degree of protection afforded in the various jurisdictions, and differences between national and EU legislation, some of which depend on who is to count as a 'consumer' for the purposes of the legislation. We will consider six questions: (1) what if the buyer wants the goods for both business and non-business purposes, or the purpose is not specified? (2) If a trader purchases something to use in connection with the business but the item is not essential for the business and not something the trader regularly buys, is the buyer a consumer? (3) If legislation states that it applies to consumers without specifying that the other party is a trader, does the legislation apply when the other party is not a trader? (4) Can a not-for-profit organisation or an unincorporated association count as a consumer? (5) Are auction sales different? (6) What about consumers who supply goods or services to a trader?

(1) No stated purpose or mixed purpose contract

What if what is supplied under the contract can be used for either business or non-business purposes; or if goods bought are to be used partly for business and partly for other purposes?

We saw that the Unfair Terms Directive and other directives define a consumer as 'a person acting for purposes which are outside his trade, business or profession'.[54] Does this mean that any possible use in connection with the individual's business has the result

---

[50] See ch 2.

[51] eg Directive on Unfair Terms in Consumer Contracts (n 30 above) Art 8. The higher protection must be compatible with the 'four freedoms', see above, p 30; P Craig and G de Búrca, *EU Law, Text, Cases, and Materials* (6th edn, Oxford University Press, 2015) 626.

[52] See H Schulte-Nölke, C Twigg-Flesner and M Ebers (eds), *EC Consumer Law Compendium* (Munich: Sellier, 2008) Part 2C.

[53] Craig and de Búrca (n 51 above) 626.

[54] See similarly the Brussels I (bis) Regulation, Art 17 (n 26 above) and the Rome I Regulation, Art 6 (n 25 above).

that the individual no longer counts as a consumer? In *Costea v Volksbank România*[55] the Court of Justice held that Article 2(b) of Directive 93/13/EEC has to be interpreted as meaning that a natural person who practised as a lawyer and who concluded a credit agreement with a bank, in which the purpose of the credit was not specified, might be regarded as a consumer within the meaning of that provision, provided that the agreement was not linked to that lawyer's profession.[56] The fact that the debt that arose out of the same contract was secured by a mortgage taken out by that person in his capacity as representative of his law firm, and involved property intended for the exercise of that person's profession, such as a building that belonged to that firm, was not relevant in that regard. However, the Court of Justice went on to hold that a contract which is clearly partly for business purposes—a mixed purpose contract—falls outside the definition. In *Gruber v Bay Wa AG*[57] a farmer bought roof tiles for a building that was partly his home and partly a farm building. The Court held that the farmer did not count as a consumer within the meaning of the Brussels I Regulation on jurisdiction.

Subsequently, however, there was a change. The Directive on Consumer Rights of 2011[58] still defines the consumer in its Article 2 as 'any natural person who, in contracts covered by this Directive, is acting for purposes which are outside his trade, business, craft or profession', but Recital (17) of the Consumer Rights Directive states: 'The definition of consumer should cover natural persons who are acting outside their trade, business, craft or profession. However, in the case of dual purpose contracts, where the contract is concluded for purposes partly within and partly outside the person's trade and the trade purpose is so limited as not to be predominant in the overall context of the contract, that person should also be considered as a consumer'.

It seems extraordinary that such an important change is not mentioned in the body of the Directive, as it actually means that in the case of dual purpose contracts (where the contract is concluded for purposes partly within and partly outside the person's trade, and the trade purpose is so limited as not to be predominant in the overall context of the contract), that person 'should also be considered as a consumer' (Recital 17). This is in line with the DCFR, which defines a consumer as 'any natural person who is acting primarily for purposes which are not related to his or her trade, business or profession.'[59] It is different, however, from the definition in earlier Directives and Regulations.

What to do? Some Member States have decided simply to use the 'predominant purpose' definition found in Recital (17) of the Consumer Rights Directive, so that more parties will fall within the legislation. Thus the UK Consumer Rights Act 2015 defines a consumer as 'an individual acting for purposes which are wholly or mainly outside that individual's trade, business, craft or profession'.[60] In German law, the problem was

[55] C-110/14, 3 September 2015, ECLI:EU:C:2015:538.
[56] ibid.
[57] C-464/01, *Gruber*, 20 January 2005, ECLI:EU:C:2005:32.
[58] 2011/83/EU (n 40 above).
[59] DCFR Art I-1:106(1).
[60] Consumer Rights Act 2015, s 2(3). See also Consumer Contracts (Information, Cancellation and Additional Charges) Regulations 2013 (SI 2013/3134), and Consumer Protection (Amendment) Regulations 2014 (SI 2014/870).

solved by changing the wording of the definition of a consumer in § 13 BGB.[61] Where it used to require 'a legal transaction for purposes outside his trade, business or profession' it is now satisfied with a 'legal transaction for purposes that predominantly are outside his trade, business or profession'.[62] It remains to be seen under which conditions French judges will apply the distinction between 'professionals and non-professionals or consumers' (such as defined by the Article liminaire of the Code de la consommation)[63] in case of mixed contracts.

It is possible that these definitions go further than EU law, according to whether or not one interprets the recent recital as a guide to interpretation of the definitions used in EU legislation. However, applying consumer legislation to mixed contracts may be justified on one of two grounds. Where the national legislation is implementing a minimum harmonisation directive, it can be justified on the grounds that it is simply conferring greater rights on consumers.[64] Even where the directive is a full harmonisation directive, applying the implementing legislation to mixed contracts can be justified on the ground that mixed contracts are outside the scope of the directive.

(2) Trader purchases something to use in connection with, but not essential for, the business

This issue arose under the laws of some Member States who previously had not limited the definition of consumer to natural persons. Suppose someone who for some purpose is a trader buys an item which was only incidental to the business and not something he or she regularly buys, eg a lawyer who buys a coffee maker for her office or something for her home in connection with her business.

Under earlier legislation in France, protection against abusive clauses applied to 'non-professionals' (*non-professionels*). In Cass civ (1) 28 April 1987[65] Pigranel SA, an estate agency, bought an alarm system from Abonnement Téléphonique SA. The alarm never functioned well. The contract contained an exclusion clause regarding the responsibility of Abonnement Téléphonique. The Cour de cassation held that Pigranel SA was a *non-professionnel*, on the ground that the contract 'fell outside the ambit of the latter's professional competence; as Pigranel, as a company engaged in the business of estate agency, was unfamiliar with the highly specialised technology of alarm systems and was therefore as ignorant about the contents of the contract in issue as any other consumer would have been.' Somewhat similarly, in the UK Unfair Contract Terms Act 1977, until 2015 a consumer contract was defined as one between a person who was making the contract in the ordinary course of business and one who was not.[66] In *R&B Customs Brokers Ltd v United Dominions Trust Ltd*[67] an import-export company bought a car for the personal use of its managing director. The Court of Appeal held that the company

---

[61] See above, p 176.
[62] C-110/14, *Costea v Volksbank România*, 3 September 2015, ECLI:EU:C:2015:538.
[63] See above, p 177.
[64] cf above, ch 2.
[65] No. 85-13674, Bull I no. 134, D 1988, 1, annotated by P Delebecque.
[66] Unfair Contract Terms Act 1977, s 12.
[67] [1988] 1 WLR 321 (CA).

was acting as a consumer, as the purchase of the car was neither integral to the business nor a regular part of it.

However, neither of these two decisions still represents the law. The Cour de cassation has subsequently held[68] that the relevant legislation does not apply to contracts for the supply of goods or services having a direct relationship to the business carried on by the other contracting party. The English and Scottish Law Commissions[69] thought that neither non-natural persons nor persons acting for purposes connected to a business should count as consumers. (They recommended that small businesses should also be protected, though at a lower level than consumers; this has not been implemented).[70] As a result, in England the relevant part of the Unfair Contract Terms Act 1977 has been repealed and replaced by the Consumer Rights Act 2015. This limits the definition of consumer to, first, 'a natural person' and secondly, one who is acting for purposes that are 'outside his trade, business, craft or profession'—as in the normal EU definition. This seems to exclude contracts that are in any substantial way connected to the person's business. In *Di Pinto*[71] the Court of Justice held that traders who made contracts to advertise their businesses for sale were not acting 'outside the course of [their] business' for the purposes of former Directive 85/577/EEC, a directive to protect the consumer in respect of contracts negotiated away from business premises.[72]

(3) Can an individual count as a consumer if the other party is not a trader?

This question can only arise if the directive in question does not specify that it applies only when one party is a consumer and the other a trader. So the point is a narrow one, but the judgment of the Court of Justice on this point in the *Walter Vapenik* case brings new interesting elements into the general debate:

Court of Justice, 5 December 2013[73] **7.4 (EU)**

Walter Vapenik v Thurner

A piece of EU legislation aimed at protecting consumers, even if it does not expressly say that the other party must be a trader, is not applicable when the other party is not a trader.

Facts: The creditor, who was domiciled in Austria, brought an action in Austria seeking an order that the debtor, who was domiciled in Belgium, pay a debt resulting from a loan agreement which the parties had previously concluded. Neither party had been engaged in commercial or professional activities at the time when the contract had been concluded or when the action had been brought. An Austrian district court gave judgment in default and the debtor did not appeal against that judgment, which therefore became final and enforceable.

---

[68] Cass civ (1) 30 January 1996, no. 93-18684, Bull I no. 55, D 1996, 228, annotated by G Paisant.

[69] See their Joint Report *Unfair Terms in Contracts* (n 4 above).

[70] See their Joint Report, ibid, paras 8.4–8.5 and 8.55–8.69. The Law Commissions' recommendation that small businesses should be protected was accepted by Government but it has never been implemented.

[71] C-361/89, *Di Pinto*, 14 March 1991, ECLI:EU:C:1991:118.

[72] Directive 85/577/EC has been replaced by the Consumer Rights Directive 2011/83/EU (n 40 above).

[73] C-508/12, 5 December 2013, ECLI:EU:C:2013:790.

The creditor subsequently applied to that court for the certification of that judgment as a European enforcement order in accordance with Council Regulation (EC) No 805/2004.

The Landesgericht Salzburg (Regional Court, Salzburg) referred the following question to the Court of Justice for a preliminary ruling: 'Is Article 6(1)(d) of Regulation … No 805/2004[74] to be interpreted as applying only to contracts between business persons as creditors and consumers as debtors, or is it sufficient for at least the debtor to be the consumer for the provision also to apply to claims of a consumer against another consumer?'

Held: Special protection for consumers will only be available under Article 6(1)(d) of the Regulation if the party contracting with the consumer is a professional.

Judgment:

22 By its question, the referring court asks essentially whether Article 6(1)(d) of Regulation No 805/2004 must be interpreted as meaning that it also applies to contracts concluded between two persons not engaged in commercial or professional activities.

23 The Court has consistently held that it follows from the need for uniform application of European Union law and from the principle of equality that the terms of a provision of that law which makes no express reference to the law of the Member States for the purpose of determining its meaning and scope must normally be given an autonomous and uniform interpretation throughout the Union, having regard to the context of the provision and the objective pursued by the legislation in question (see, inter alia, Case C-320/12 *Malaysia Dairy Industries* [2013] ECR, paragraph 25 and the case law cited).

24 It is clear from the wording of Article 6(1)(d) of Regulation No 805/2004 that a consumer is a person who has concluded a contract for a purpose which can be regarded as being outside his trade or profession. That provision does not state whether or not the status of professional of the consumer's contracting party plays a role in defining the other party as a 'consumer'. Neither does the status of a consumer's contracting party arise from the other provisions of that regulation and, in the absence of a reference in that provision to the law of the Member States, the meaning and scope of the concept of 'consumer' laid down in Article 6(1)(d) must be determined in the light of the context in which it appears and the objective pursued by Regulation No 805/2004.

25 In that connection, and in order to ensure compliance with the objectives pursued by the European legislature in the sphere of consumer contracts, and the consistency of European Union law, account must be taken, in particular, of the definition of 'consumer' in other rules of European Union law. Having regard to the supplementary nature of the rules laid down by Regulation No 805/2004 as compared with those in Regulation No 44/2001, the provisions of the latter are especially relevant.

26 Thus, it must be stated at the outset that the system of protection implemented by Council Directive 93/13/EEC of 5 April 1993 on unfair terms in consumer contracts (OJ 1993 L 95, p. 29) is based on the idea that the consumer is in a weak position vis-à-vis the seller or supplier, as regards both his bargaining power and his level of knowledge (see, inter alia, Case C-618/10 *Banco Español de Crédito* [2012] ECR, paragraph 39; Case C-92/11 *RWE Vertrieb* [2013] ECR, paragraph 41; and Case C-488/11 *Asbeek Brusse and Man Garabito* [2011] ECR, paragraph 31).

27 Furthermore, the specific system instituted, in particular, by the provisions of Regulation No 44/2001 relating to jurisdiction over consumer contracts is intended, as is clear

[74] Regulation (EC) No 805/2004 of the European Parliament and of the Council of 21 April 2004 creating a European Enforcement Order for uncontested claims, OJ L 143/2004, p 15.

from recital 13 in the preamble thereto, to ensure adequate protection for the consumer as the party deemed to be economically weaker and less experienced in legal matters than the other party to the contract.

28 In that context, the Court has repeatedly stated that Article 15(1) of Regulation No 44/2001, which mentions 'consumer[s]', refers only to the private final consumer, not engaged in trade or professional activities (see, to that effect, Case C-419/11 *Česká spořitelna* [2013] ECR, paragraph 32).

29 Finally, as is clear from recitals 23 and 24 in the preamble to Regulation No 593/2008, the requirement of protection of weaker parties, including consumers, in contracts is also recognised for the purpose of determining the law applicable to consumer contracts. Article 6(1) thereof provides to that effect that contracts concluded between a consumer and a professional are to be governed by the law of the country where the consumer has his habitual residence.

30 Those legal instruments thereby recognise the need to protect the weaker party to a contract where it has been concluded between a person not engaged in commercial or professional activities and a person who is engaged in such activities.

31 Taking account of the objective of protecting consumers laid down by the above-mentioned provisions of European Union law, which aim to compensate for the imbalance between parties in contracts concluded between a consumer and a professional, their application cannot be extended to persons with respect to whom that protection is not justified.

32 Thus, the Court has already held that the rules of special jurisdiction over consumer contracts cannot be applied to contracts concluded between two persons engaged in commercial or professional activities (see, to that effect, Case C-89/91 *Shearson Lehmann Hutton* [1993] ECR I-139, paragraphs 11 and 24).

33 It must be stated that there is also no imbalance between the parties in a contractual relationship such as that at issue in the main proceedings, namely that between two persons not engaged in commercial or professional activities. Therefore, that relationship cannot be subject to the system of special protection applicable to consumers contracting with persons engaged in commercial or professional activities.

34 That interpretation is supported by the structure and broad logic of the rules of special jurisdiction over consumer contracts laid down in Article 16(1) and (2) of Regulation No 44/2001, which provides that the courts for the place where the consumer is domiciled are to have jurisdiction with respect to actions brought by and against him. It follows that that provision is applicable only to contracts in which there is an imbalance between the contracting parties.

35 Furthermore, account must be taken of the supplementary nature of the rules laid down by Regulation No 805/2004 as compared with those on recognition and enforcement of decisions laid down by Regulation No 44/2001.

36 In that connection, it must be stated that, although certification as a European enforcement order under Regulation No 805/2004 of a judgment with respect to an uncontested claim enables the enforcement procedure laid down by Regulation No 44/2001 to be circumvented, the absence of such certification does not exclude the possibility of enforcing that judgment under the enforcement procedure laid down by the latter regulation.

37 If, in the context of Regulation No 805/2004, a definition were to be adopted, which is wider than that in Regulation No 44/2001, that might lead to inconsistencies in the application of those two regulations. The derogation laid down by Regulation No 805/2004 might lead to refusal of certification as a European enforcement

order of a judgment, whereas it could still be enforced under the general scheme laid down by Regulation No 44/2001 since the circumstances in which that scheme allows the defendant to challenge the issue of an enforcement order, on the ground that the jurisdiction of the courts for the State in which the consumer is domiciled has not been respected, would not be satisfied.

38 It follows from all of the foregoing that the definition of 'consumers' within the meaning of Article 6(1)(d) of Regulation No 805/2004 refers to a person who concludes a contract for a purpose which can be regarded as being outside his trade or profession with a person who is acting in the exercise of his trade or profession.

39 Therefore, the answer to the question referred is that Article 6(1)(d) of Regulation No 805/2004 must be interpreted as meaning that it does not apply to contracts concluded between two persons who are not engaged in commercial or professional activities.

Note

The need for uniform application of EU law, the necessity to give an autonomous and uniform interpretation throughout the Union and the consistency of EU law are not particularly well ensured as far as the notion of consumer is concerned.

(4) Contracts between traders and not-for-profit organisations or unincorporated associations

The Directives and Regulations cited above all specify that the consumer must be a natural person. That would therefore exclude from the legislation contracts between a trader and a not-for-profit organisation or unincorporated association. But national law, even if it does not protect traders who make contracts that are not central to their business,[75] might define consumer so as to include not-for-profit organisations or unincorporated associations. The case of not-for-profit organisations or unincorporated associations provides a good illustration of how national laws may go beyond EU law.

In German law the definition of 'consumer' in § 13 BGB[76] explicitly refers to natural persons only.[77] However, the courts have extended the notion, so as to cover some entities established under private law rules that are not natural persons, such as an association of condominium owners.[78]

We saw earlier that in French law, the Code de la consommation defines 'non-professional' as 'any legal person not acting for professional purposes'.[79] Thus while a non-profit organisation may not claim to be a consumer, it could be considered to be a non-professional as long as it does not act for the purposes of commerce.[80] For instance, the Cour de cassation held that a co-ownership association was acting as a non-professional when it concluded a contract with a professional for a cleaning and

---

[75] See above, pp 180–81.
[76] See above, p 176.
[77] For the text of § 13 BGB, see above p 176.
[78] BGH 25 March 2015, BGHZ 204, 325.
[79] See above, p 177.
[80] P Malaurie, L Aynès and P Stoffel-Munck, *Droit des obligations* (9th edn, Paris: LGDJ, 2017) no. 422.

maintenance service.[81] When it comes to the actual benefit of the provisions contained in the Code de la consommation, one just has to check that they are applicable to non-professionals (for instance, provisions on unfair terms are applicable to contracts concluded by non-professionals with professionals—Article L 212-2 of the Code). As we have already seen, in the two cases of 29 March 2017, the Cour de cassation exercised its control on the definitions and the applicability of the specific provisions.[82]

In the UK, the definition of a consumer in the Consumer Rights Act 2015 is limited to an 'individual'.[83] The case for applying the protections of the Act to not-for-profit organisations or unincorporated associations does not appear to have been debated.

(5) Auction sales

Another difficult issue is auction sales. Some of the EU legislation that applies to contracts, particularly the Consumer Sales Directive,[84] does not apply to auction sales of second hand goods. Other EU legislation, in particular the requirements of the Consumer Rights Directive that the trader must give pre-contract information to the consumer, and the rules on the time for delivery and the passing of risk apply even to auction sales. This can lead to considerable complexity. Thus the UK Consumer Rights Act 2015 provides:

(5) For the purposes of Chapter 2,[85] except to the extent mentioned in subsection (6), a person is not a consumer in relation to a sales contract if—
(a) the goods are second hand goods sold at public auction, and
(b) individuals have the opportunity of attending the sale in person.

(6) A person is a consumer in relation to such a contract for the purposes of—
(a) sections 11(4) and (5), 12, 28 and 29, and
(b) the other provisions of Chapter 2 as they apply in relation to those sections.

Not a model of clarity! However it reflects the complexity of the EU law, and if you work through the sections of the Act referred to, you will find the provision implements the EU requirements to the letter.

(6) Consumers as suppliers

The 'normal' consumer contract involves a business supplying goods or services to a consumer. Sometimes, however, it is the other way round: for example, if a private motorist sells a car to a car dealer, or if a person gives a bank a guarantee of a third person's debt. Is the consumer still protected by the relevant legislation? The English version of the Directive refers to the business party to the contract as the 'seller or supplier', which might suggest that only the supply of goods or services by a trader to a consumer is covered. However, the Court of Justice has held that the Directive on Unfair Terms can

---

[81] Cass civ (1) 23 June 2011, no. 10-30645, Bull I no. 122.
[82] See above, p 177.
[83] s 2(3).
[84] 1999/44/EC (n 33 above).
[85] Chapter 2 is the chapter of the Act that deals with the supply of goods to consumers. Sections 11(4) and (5) and s 12 deal with information; ss 28 and 29 with delivery times and risk. The result is hardly a model of clarity.

apply to such a case, so that a natural person who guarantees payments owed by a commercial company to a banking institution under a credit agreement is to be regarded as a consumer provided 'he acted for purposes of a private nature' and not 'for purposes relating to his trade, business or profession or because of functional links he has with that company, such as a directorship or non-negligible shareholding'.[85a]

7.3.B THE PLACE OF CONSUMER LAW

A different issue is where in each system consumer law is to be found.

7.3.B.1 GERMAN LAW

In German law, legislative measures for consumer protection, like the 1894 Act concerning Instalment Sales, were not integrated into the BGB when the latter came into force in 1900.[86] Subsequent measures were also kept outside the BGB and enacted as separate statutes, such as the 1976 Distance Teaching Act or the 1976 Act on Standard Terms and Conditions in Business (AGBG). The latter applied not only to consumer contracts, but also to contracts concluded between two businesses. It was slightly modified in 1996 in order to make it compatible with the Unfair Contract Terms Directive. This was primarily achieved by inserting a new § 24a AGBG which provided for an increased level of protection, in certain respects, for consumers who were faced with terms not individually negotiated when engaging in a contract with a business. Further statutes enacted for the purpose of implementing Directives of the European Community concerning consumer contracts included the 1986 Revocation of Doorstep Contracts Act, the 1990 Consumer Credit Act and the 1996 Timeshare Agreements Act.

With the implementation in 2000 of Directive 97/7/EC on Distance Contracts, the piecemeal approach to incorporating EC measures continued, and a special statute relating to distance contracts was enacted. At the same time, a new pattern of incorporation emerged with the introduction of two new provisions into the BGB. They were inserted into the Title on rescission in the General Part of the Law of Obligations, and attempted to unify the various regimes of the right of revocation granted to consumers by different directives. More importantly, the precursors of the two fundamental definitions of 'consumer' and 'business' ('entrepreneur') quoted earlier were introduced into the General Part.[87]

Finally, a fundamental change of the German law of consumer protection was brought about by the 2001 Act on Modernising the Law of Obligations which was triggered by the need to transpose Directive 1999/44/EC on certain aspects of the sale of consumer goods and associated guarantees. This concerned a core area of the law of obligations, so it was implemented by amending the BGB's provisions on the law of sales (see now

---

[85a] C-74/15, *Tarcău v Banca Comercială Intesa Sanpaolo România SA*, 19 November 2015, ECLI:EU:C:2015:772 [29].

[86] For a comprehensive account of the developments outlined in the following paragraphs, see R Zimmermann, *The New German Law of Obligations: Historical and Comparative Perspectives* (Oxford University Press, 2005) 159–228.

[87] For the text of §§ 13, 14 BGB, see above, p 176.

§§ 474–479 BGB) and the General Part of the Law of Obligations. At the same time, the legislator integrated most of the special statutes enacted for the purpose of protecting consumers in the 1970s, 1980s and the 1990s into the second Book of the BGB. The provisions of the 1996 Timeshare Agreements Act, for instance, were slotted in as §§ 481–487 BGB, the 1990 Consumer Credit Act was integrated into the BGB Title on the contract of loan (§§ 488–506 BGB), and the 1976 Act on General Terms and Conditions in Business was inserted with some minor modifications into a new section in the General Part of the Law of Obligations (§§ 305–310 BGB).[88]

7.3.B.2 FRENCH LAW

In 1993 the Consumer Code, the Code de la consommation, was promulgated and it has been regularly revised since. New EU directives and regulations which concern consumer rights are implemented in this code.

The Code de la consommation gathers together a wide range of statutes, all aimed at protecting the consumer in his relationship with professional parties. It also contains much 'subordinate legislation' such as the Ordonnance no. 2016-301 du 14 mars 2016 quoted earlier.[89] The Code is of the utmost importance in the field of formation of contracts, where it imposes some form requirements. It also prohibits unfair clauses.[90] Consumer law also affects the performance of contracts, and the Code de la consommation includes provisions aimed at dealing with situations of *surendettement* (over-indebtedness). In spite of its increasing importance, and despite the fact that it has inspired a number of proposed changes to the Civil Code (eg on duties of disclosure,[91] rights of withdrawal[92] and unfair terms) consumer law is still regarded as a distinct—and perhaps also peripheral—subject, rather technical and unclear.

7.3.B.3 ENGLISH LAW

English law obviously does not face the question of whether consumer law should be incorporated into a civil code. It has faced a parallel but slightly different issue. This is whether EC directives protecting consumers should be implemented by radical amendment to legislation that is already in existence, by adding to it, or simply by separate legislation. Until 2015, implementation has normally not been by means of primary legislation (ie not by means of a new Act of Parliament). The European Communities Act 1972, section 2, allowed the government to implement directives by 'secondary legislation' and, to save time in Parliament, most directives were implemented in this way. The secondary legislation can either be free-standing or amend existing primary legislation. Practice on this has varied.

The Directive on Unfair Terms in Consumer Contracts was first implemented by a free-standing set of regulations which largely 'copy out' (repeat word for word) the

---

[88] See below, ch 21.
[89] See above, p 177.
[90] See below, ch 21.
[91] See below, pp 488, 573–76.
[92] See below, pp 277, 1134–35.

Directive. This approach is easy for the drafters and reduces the chances that a mistake will mean that the UK has not implemented the Directive correctly, but it was unsatisfactory because it meant that there was an overlap with the older Unfair Contract Terms Act 1977. After many complaints from both consumers and businesses that have to comply with both regimes, the Department of Trade and Industry referred the question to the English and Scottish Law Commissions. The Law Commissions recommended unifying the two regimes into a single piece of legislation.[93]

The Consumer Sales Directive was implemented by Regulations that amended the Sale of Goods Act 1979, so that at least all the rules were to be found in one place. However, the principal changes, which were to give consumers new remedies, were achieved by simply adding new provisions to what existed before. The result is that a consumer may have remedies under both the old and the new provisions, subject to different conditions. Again both consumers and businesses found this very confusing, and again the Department (it is now called the Department of Business, Energy and Industrial Strategy) referred the matter to the Law Commissions, which issued a Report[94] on the subject.

In 2015 the UK government implemented the Law Commissions' recommendations at least in part by securing the passage of the Consumer Rights Act 2015. This brings together much of the legislation that applies to consumer contracts, as well as introducing a number of new consumer protection measures. Thus in Part I, Chapter 2 of the Act there is now a single set of provisions governing the supply of goods (whether by sale, hire or in some other way). These deal mainly with the conformity of the goods and the consumer's remedies in the event of breach of contract by the seller. Chapter 3 applies similar provisions to contracts for the supply of digital content, which was not previously regulated by legislation. Chapter 4 does something similar for contracts under which a trader is to supply services to a consumer (replacing in part the Supply of Goods and Services Act 1982). Part 2 of the Act implements the Directive on Unfair Terms in Consumer Contracts.

Even now, however, not all consumer issues are dealt with in the one UK Act. First, some issues that arise under consumer contracts, for example the trader's rights and obligations and the passing of property between seller and buyer, are still governed by the Sale of Goods Act 1979. Secondly, the trader's duties to give precontractual information and the consumer's right to withdraw from a distance or off-premises contract are governed by a set of Regulations[95] which more-or-less copy out the wording of the Consumer Rights Directive. There are also separate Regulations[96] that implement the Unfair Commercial Practices Directive[97] and that, making use of the freedom to adopt

---

[93] Joint Report *Unfair Terms in Contracts* (n 4 above).

[94] The Law Commission and The Scottish Law Commission, *Consumer Remedies for Faulty Goods*, Law Com No 317, Scot Law Com No 216 (London: The Stationery Office, 2009).

[95] Consumer Contracts (Information, Cancellation and Additional Charges) Regs 2013, SI 2013/3134.

[96] Consumer Protection from Unfair Trading Regulations 2008 (SI 2008/1277).

[97] Directive 2005/29/EC of the European Parliament and of the Council of 11 May 2005 concerning unfair business-to-consumer commercial practices in the internal market, OJ L 149/2005, p 22. A useful summary of the Directive and its impact will be found in C Twigg-Flesner, 'Deep impact? The EC Directive on unfair commercial practices and domestic consumer law' (2005) 121 LQR 386.

consumer protection measures that are outside the scope of the Directive,[98] give remedies to individual consumers who have been the victims of certain kinds of unfair commercial practice.[99]

7.4 CONTRACTS ENTERED INTO BY PUBLIC AUTHORITIES: ADMINISTRATIVE CONTRACTS

Over the last several decades, there has been a contractualisation of government action which entails a rise of the use of contracts, in particular to provide services to the public. In continental legal systems, the wide variety of contracts entered into by public authorities forms the category of 'administrative contracts', which is of great importance. They are not governed by ordinary contract law, but are subject to supervision by the administrative courts. Accordingly, there are a number of exceptional rules—quite apart from the question of jurisdiction. By contrast, in England, contracts entered into by public authorities with individuals are in principle governed by the ordinary law both as regards the rules of law applicable to them and the courts having jurisdiction to hear disputes arising out of them.

The increasingly diverse forms of public action have led the EU to harmonise rules, notably on public procurement (a concept that refers to the process by which public authorities, such as government departments or local authorities, purchase work, goods or services from companies) and concessions. Every year, over 250,000 public authorities in the EU spend around 14% of GDP on the purchase of services, works and supplies.

Before examining the national traditions, some recent EU law developments need therefore to be mentioned.

7.4.A CONTRACTS ENTERED INTO BY PUBLIC AUTHORITIES: EU LEGISLATION

EU legislation does not refer to a category of 'administrative contracts' but rather uses distinctions based on contracting parties.

In 2014, EU law set out minimum harmonised rules for public procurement and concessions[100] which had to be transposed into national legislations in 2016. These rules are

---

[98] See above. The UCPD, which is a full harmonisation Directive, is primarily concerned with policing unfair commercial practices and is 'without prejudice to contract law and, in particular, to the rules of validity, formation or effect of a contract': Art 3(1).

[99] See the new Part 4A of the 2008 regulations, added by Consumer Protection (Amendment) Regulations 2014 (SI 2014/870). Consumers whose decisions have been affected by misleading statements or aggressive trade practices have the right to 'unwind' the transactions or get a discount off the price, and to claim damages for further loss. For details, see *Chitty* (n 2 above) paras 38-157 ff.

[100] Directive 2014/24/EU of the European Parliament and of the Council of 26 February 2014 on public procurement, OJ L 94/2014, p 65; Directive 2014/25/EU of the European Parliament and of the Council of 26 February 2014 on procurement by entities operating in the water, energy, transport and postal services sectors,

primarily about the process of selecting a contractor. They apply to tenders whose monetary value exceeds a certain amount. For tenders of lower value, national rules apply.[101] Nevertheless, the national rules also have to respect the general principles of EU law. The award of public contracts by or on behalf of Member States' authorities has to comply with the principles of the Treaty on the Functioning of the European Union (TFEU), and in particular the free movement of goods, freedom of establishment and the freedom to provide services, as well as the principles deriving from the aforementioned directives. The core principles of these directives are transparency, equal treatment, open competition and sound procedural management. They are designed to achieve a procurement market that is competitive, open and well regulated.

The directives apply when one of the parties is a body 'governed by public law', a notion that has been examined repeatedly in the case law of the Court of Justice of the EU and is also defined in the directives. According to Article 2(1) of Directive 2014/24/EU on public procurement: '"contracting authorities" means the State, regional or local authorities, bodies governed by public law or associations formed by one or more such authorities or one or more such bodies governed by public law'. By contrast, a 'body which operates in normal market conditions, aims to make a profit, and bears the losses resulting from the exercise of its activity should not be considered as being a "body governed by public law" since the needs in the general interest, that it has been set up to meet or been given the task of meeting, can be deemed to have an industrial or commercial character' (Recital (10) of the Directive).

7.4.B ADMINISTRATIVE CONTRACTS IN NATIONAL LEGAL SYSTEMS

7.4.B.1 FRENCH LAW: THE ADMINISTRATIVE CONTRACT

Specific rules for administrative contracts have been established by some leading cases of the Conseil d'État, which in its case law has elaborated special rules to take account of the fact that the public interest is at stake.[102] The Conseil d'État cases are all the more famous and easy to remember as they are referred to by the name of one of the parties, in contrast to the private law cases of the Cour de cassation, which are in principle anonymous.[103] Among these specific rules, some of the most famous are: the right of the public authority unilaterally to withdraw from the contract or to amend it, subject to compensating the other party recognition of the doctrine of *imprévision* which may lead to the amendment of the contract in the case of an unforeseen event (a doctrine that became applicable to

---

OJ L 94/2014, p 243; Directive 2014/23/EU of the European Parliament and of the Council of 26 February 2014 on the award of concession contracts Text with EEA relevance, OJ L 94/2014, p 1.

[101] Directive 2014/24/EU on public procurement only applies to certain to procurements with a value net of value added tax (VAT) estimated to be equal to or greater than certain thresholds, set out in Art 4(a) of the directive and revised every two years.

[102] The Conseil d'État is the highest administrative jurisdiction—and as such, it is the final arbiter of cases relating to executive power, local authorities, independent public authorities, public administration agencies or any other agency invested with public authority.

[103] The practice of the Conseil d'État may change due to the ongoing anonymisation of cases.

civil contracts only as a result of the reforms of 2016);[104] power to enforce remedies without prior judicial authorisation; and subsequent judicial review of remedies. The objective was to ensure that specific rules apply whenever contract law rules emanating from the Civil code (such as strict compliance with the contract) are inadequate for the organisation and functioning of the public service. The 2016 French reform of contract law did not deal with administrative contracts. This might appear quite surprising since, at some point, the draft Ordonnance went through the Conseil d'État. It testifies for the fact that administrative contracts are considered a specific kind of contracts.[105]

Brisson on the impact of Civil Code reform
on administrative contracts[106]   **7.5 (FR)**

Different but not indifferent: this is the position of French administrative contract law with regard to the Civil Code. Different, for there is a "general theory of administrative contracts" with principles "applicable to all administrative contracts". Not indifferent, however, as the notion of administrative contracts, if not its "general theory", was constructed in reference to the Civil Code: the administrative courts drawing on the general categories of contract law for their conceptual and theoretical apparatus and using, where necessary, the technical solutions therein, sometimes even without the slightest consideration for the autonomy of administrative law.

The notion of contract is unitary in French law. Attempts made in public law jurisprudence to establish a different definition of the contract have failed in the face of the attitude of the administrative courts to a conventional reading of the Civil Code, unless otherwise stated. Administrative law and civil law share the fundamental principles of contract law: contractual freedom, consensualism, the binding force of the contract and the rule of relative effect. And while the administrative court agrees to make an exception, it is to take into account either rules of public law deemed incompatible, or the specific purpose of administrative contracts.

Note

Insofar as administrative law and civil law share the fundamental principles of contract law, assessing the differences between the Civil Code and administrative contracts is an exercise with a symbolic dimension for administrative law. It establishes its autonomy.

It remains important to be aware of the manner in which an administrative contract is defined. The Conseil d'État has progressively elaborated two alternative criteria.

The first is taken from a celebrated judgment of the Conseil d'État of 31 July 1912 in the case of *Granits Porphyroïdes des Vosges* concerning exorbitant clauses. A contract is governed by private law where it is entered into in accordance with the rules and

---

[104] See below, ch 29.

[105] Y Gaudemet, 'Des oubliés de la réforme? Le nouveau droit des contrats et les contrats de l'Administration' (2016) RDC 641.

[106] J-F Brisson, 'The Impact of Civil Code Reform on Administrative Contracts' (2017) 6 Montesquieu Law Review 164.

conditions applicable to contracts between individuals, that is to say without any exorbitant clauses in favour of the public authority.

Conseil d'État, 31 July 1912[107]   **7.6 (FR)**

Société des Granits Porphyroïdes des Vosges

A contract for supply of goods is not a public works contract subject to the jurisdiction of the administrative courts.

Facts: This was a contract for the supply of paving stones to the town of Lille in the context of which the refusal of the town to reimburse a contractual penalty is challenged.

Held: The brief answer by the Conseil d'Etat is that the contract is a private law contract because it was entered into in accordance with the conditions applicable under the ordinary contract law. The reference to works to be carried out may be accounted for by the fact that public works contracts are governed by special rules.

Judgment:— Whereas the claim by the Société des Granits Porphyroïdes des Vosges is for payment of the sum of 3,436.20 francs retained by way of penalty by the municipality of Lille from the price payable for a supply of paving stones, owing to delayed delivery.

— Whereas the contract entered into between the municipality and the company did not include any works to be carried out by the company and solely concerned supplies to be made in accordance with the terms and conditions of contracts between individuals;

— Whereas accordingly, the claim raises an issue which it is not for the Administrative Court to determine;

— Whereas consequently, the company's claim is inadmissible and must be dismissed.

The second criterion, which is more recent, concerns contracts entrusting the performance of a public service to private persons. Such contracts are subject to administrative law even if there are no 'exorbitant clauses', that is to say clauses that are sufficiently unusual to exclude the contract from application of the ordinary law. This is known as the '*Epoux Bertin*' doctrine, after a case of 1956.

Conseil d'État, 20 April 1956[108]   **7.7 (FR)**

Epoux Bertin

A contract to provide meals for refugees until repatriation is a public service contract.

Facts: See the judgment.

Held: The verbal contract between the parties was a public service contract. However, the Court dismissed the application against the refusal of the Minister for Veterans and Victims of War to pay the additional bonus alleged to have been provided for in the couple's supplementary undertaking.

Judgment: On jurisdiction:— Whereas the judicial investigation shows that by an oral contract entered into with the public authorities on 24 November 1944 the Bertin couple undertook in consideration of the payment of a lump sum of Ff 30 per man and per day,

---

[107] No. 30701, Rec 909; D 1916.3.35, opinion by L Blum.
[108] No. 98637, Rec 167; D 1956, 433, annotated by A de Laubadère.

to feed the Soviet nationals sheltered at the Meaux repatriation centre pending their return to Russia; as that contract was intended to entrust the Bertin couple with the task of performing a public service which was to ensure the repatriation of foreign refugees then on French soil;

— Whereas that fact is in itself sufficient to enable the contract in question to be classified as an administrative contract;

— Whereas it follows that, without there being any need to investigate whether the contract included clauses exempting it from the ordinary law, the litigation, which turns on an additional undertaking to that contract whereby the authorities granted to the Bertin couple an additional bonus of Ff 7.50 per man and per day in consideration of the inclusion of new foodstuffs in the rations served, comes within the jurisdiction of the administrative courts;

On the merits:— Whereas the Bertin couple has not adduced evidence of the existence of the above-mentioned additional undertaking;

— Whereas under those conditions it is not possible to uphold their claim for the setting aside of the decision of 1 June 1949 whereby the Minister for Veterans and Victims of War refused to pay to them the additional bonuses alleged to have been provided for in that undertaking;

Application dismissed with costs.

Notes

(1) The jurisdiction of the administrative courts was upheld because under the contract for looking after the Soviet nationals the Bertin couple became involved in the public service of ensuring the repatriation of the foreign refugees.

(2) The French contract law reform only applies to civil and commercial contracts. The fact that the reform did not deal with administrative contracts has been criticised as a disruption of the normative process in France.[109] The reform can hardly claim to be exhaustive when no actual consideration was given to doctrines developed in administrative law such as the one on supervening events.[110] Further, it is worth noticing that there is a significant number of contracts concluded by public authorities that are governed by private contract law. It would have been wiser to pay more attention to the consequences of some rules in cases involving public authorities. At the end of the day, this clearly illustrates the strength of the private/public law divide in France.[111]

Administrative law cannot ignore developments in civil law: the unity of the French legal order means that civil and administrative contracts are of the same essence. For instance, the abolition of the *cause* which has raised intense debates will undoubtedly be extended

---

[109] Gaudemet (n 105 above).
[110] See below, ch 29.
[111] Brisson (n 106 above).

to administrative law, and particularly on the matter of whether, when the Conseil d'Etat refers to the *cause* in administrative contracts, it is to the *cause* as defined in the old Civil Code or a meta-legal principle outside the Civil Code.

7.4.B.2 ADMINISTRATIVE CONTRACTS IN ENGLISH LAW

English law does not have a separate body of rules for administrative contracts. The position is usefully summarised in an Anglo-French comparative study:

Harris and Tallon on Contract Law Today[112]   **7.8 (EN)**

(ii) Contracts governed by public law compared with those governed by private law

French law adopts a dualistic approach in contrast to the unitary approach of English law, which has not developed an independent body of law for administrative contracts. In principle, English law takes the view that the rules of contract law apply to all contracts whether the parties are private individuals or public bodies.[113] In practice, however, the position is very different, because the public interest is recognized in England and special rules have been developed in the practice of public authorities. Thus, administrative contracts contain clauses which are completely unknown in commercial contracts and which lead to the result that the ordinary legal principles are subdivided or even abrogated.

In England, some general considerations have led to some special legal rules for contracts with public authorities. It has been decided that such bodies cannot bind themselves for the future by undertaking contractual obligations which are contrary to the purposes for which the bodies were granted their powers. This rule permits them, in spite of general contractual theory, unilaterally to release themselves from their obligations. The same position applies to administrative contracts in France. In many contracts in England, such as those by which the Government buys goods and services, the fact that one party is a public body leads to the adoption of standard terms in specifying the details of the agreement. All these contracts include virtually the same clauses, which are imposed by the public body, and which obviously favour it. Sometimes, the standard clauses even permit the public body to pursue a different public interest from that directly pursued by the contract in question. In this way, a kind of customary law on purchasing by public authorities has been created through the almost automatic practice of including standard clauses. The regular use of these clauses is different from the application of general principles laid down in a body of administrative law, but they are used so regularly that we

---

[112] D Harris and D Tallon, 'Conclusions' in D Harris and D Tallon (eds), *Contract Law Today: Anglo-French Comparisons* (Oxford: Clarendon, 1989) 379, 382–83.

[113] In both France and England, certain matters fall outside the scope of contract. The reasons for this are completely different in each country and cannot be reconciled. French law has decided that in certain areas public authorities should unilaterally determine the content of some legal relationships, which are therefore not subject to negotiation by the parties. Moreover, the public authorities cannot be prevented by the existence of acquired contractual rights from modifying or abrogating contractual obligations. So the following topics fall outside the scope of contract: arrangements for public services, for taxation, and for financial and administrative regulation. In England, the delivery of mail is not a matter of contract: there is no particular reason for this rule, which is simply a matter of traditional law. It was laid down that the Post Office does not enter into a contract when it carries mail (see *Treifus & Co v Post Office* [1957] 2 QB 352).

can say that they should be properly analysed as rules of general application. The practical result is the same as if there were special legal rules for administrative contracts, although it is achieved by a different route.

English law permits the court neither to grant certain remedies against the Crown, nor to take certain enforcement measures against the Crown. For instance, an injunction cannot be granted against the Crown, nor can an order for specific performance be granted. If an award of damages is made against the Crown, there is no possibility of enforcing payment nor of any other form of execution. So the judge cannot issue orders to the Crown. In France, the problem is rather different because the Administration has its own judge. Nevertheless, many similar results are found. The administrative judge cannot grant an injunction against a public authority: only an award of damages may be given against it (although the remedy of *astreinte* is now available against it).

So the legal approach of the two systems is different because English law does not recognize a separate body of administrative law administered by special courts; but despite the fact that the two systems use legally distinct machinery, in both countries the scope and the contents of administrative contracts are often similar.[114] The theoretical differences between English and French law in this area can mainly be attributed to the clear, fundamental and all-pervasive distinction between private law and public law in France that, until fairly recently, was vividly rejected in England.

7.4.B.3 ADMINISTRATIVE CONTRACTS IN GERMAN LAW

German law also knows a rigid distinction between these two major areas of law, so the relationships between administrative authorities and citizens are in principle governed by administrative law and not by private law, the latter normally being only concerned with relationships among citizens. As a general rule therefore, an authority has to use one of the recognised types of administrative activity, such as administrative decisions, in establishing legal relationships with citizens, and it cannot conclude contracts with them. There are, however, four exceptions to this rule.

The first exception concerns situations where the authority acts exactly like a private entity by running a profit-making business. In the age of privatisation, such arrangements have become increasingly rare, but they continue to exist in traditional domains of State enterprise, such as breweries or porcelain manufactures. Contracts concluded by such businesses are completely—and exclusively—governed by private law. Disputes arising from them are adjudicated by the civil courts.

The second exception applies where an authority obtains the goods and services necessary for performing its public duties, even if the ultimate aim of these activities is to serve the public interest. Thus an agreement for the supply of surgical goods to a State health service,[115] the clearance of rubble from a public space[116] or the manufacture of

---

[114] [For more information on this, reference should be made to: B Nicholas, *The French Law of Contract* (2nd ed, Oxford: Clarendon Press, 1992) 25 ff; Y Gaudemet, *Droit administratif* (21st edn, Paris: LGDJ, 2015) 297 ff; and also to the Code on public contracts (*Code des Marchés publics*), which governs contracts entered into with public authorities.]

[115] BGH 26 October 1961, BGHZ 36, 91, 93–96.

[116] BVerwG 7 November 1957, BVerwGE 5, 325, 326–27. CE 31 July 1912 (*Granits Porphyroïdes des Vosges*), see above 7.6 (FR), p 160, would thus not be decided differently under German law.

weapons to be used by the police forces is regarded as an ordinary private law contract of sale, of work or for the delivery of works, all of which are falling into the jurisdiction of the civil courts.

The third exception arises when an authority provides a benefit for the public, such as transport, gas, water or the collection of waste. It can then choose whether it wishes to establish a relationship based on public law or on private law. In the first case the authority will enact a bye-law and levy a charge for procuring the service. In the second case it will conclude a contract with the citizen concerned. Such contracts are also governed by private law and fall into the jurisdiction of the civil courts. They are, however, subject to certain rules and principles of public law which impose constraints on the authority. The authority may not, for example, act ultra vires, but has to act within the limits of the competences conferred upon it. It has to respect the principle of proportionality. Most importantly, it is directly bound by the fundamental rights enshrined in the Basic Law. Thus a lease of several neighbouring plots of land to different citizens who are to construct houses on them with the expectation of having the land and the houses conveyed to them is subject to the general principle of equality.[117] Similarly, if a local authority establishes a public limited company in order to provide city transport it has to ensure equal treatment of all schoolchildren if it introduces a concessionary scheme for school travel.[118] All these restrictions of the authority's freedom of contract are meant to prevent the authority from 'escaping into private law': it should not be able to unilaterally enlarge its powers and do things it is not authorised to do by simply choosing to subject a particular relationship to private law. The result in these cases is an overlap of private law and public law rules that is called 'administrative private law' (*Verwaltungsprivatrecht*).

The fourth exception, finally, concerns 'administrative contracts' proper. These may be concluded by the authorities instead of using one of the types of administrative activity recognised in public law. Originally, such contracts were not regarded as admissible because it was thought that it is inherent to the notion of contract that the parties to it are on an equal footing. As opposed to this, the appropriate form of action in the relationship between authorities and citizens, characterised by superiority and subordination, was considered to be the administrative decision. But the second half of the twentieth century saw a change of attitude in this respect. The admissibility of administrative contracts was first postulated by legal scholars and later recognised by the courts. This development was codified in the 1976 Code on Administrative Procedure (*Verwaltungsverfahrensgesetz*), which provides a statutory definition of 'public law contracts', a term which is generally understood to be confined to administrative contracts:

German Code on Administrative Procedure   **7.9 (DE)**

§ 54: *Admissibility of a contract under public law*

A legal relationship in the area of public law can be established, modified or repealed by contract (public law contract) in so far as this is not contrary to legal provisions. In

---

[117] BGH 10 December 1957, BGHZ 29, 76, 80–82.
[118] BGH 23 September 1969, BGHZ 52, 325, 328.

particular, the authority may, instead of issuing an administrative decision, conclude a public law contract with the person to whom it otherwise would address the administrative decision.

Whether a contract is classified as an administrative contract or not has nothing to do with the status of the parties. Such contracts can, at least in principle, also be concluded between two authorities or two private parties. The decisive factor is rather the subject matter and the nature of the contract: a contract has an administrative law character if at least one of the contractual obligations relates to a matter governed by administrative law. A typical example would be the grant of a building permission in exchange for the promise to contribute towards the provision of a number of houses for social housing, a playground or the provision of car parking in the neighbourhood. An agreement to refund money paid to a civil servant for the pursuit of further studies in case he quits the civil service would also be qualified as an administrative contract. §§ 55–61 of the 1976 Code on Administrative Procedure provide a rudimentary statutory framework for administrative contracts which has to be supplemented by an analogous application of the provisions of the BGB if needed (§ 62 of the 1976 Code). These contracts always fall into the jurisdiction of the administrative courts, even in those cases where provisions of the BGB are applied analogously.

The requirements for concluding a valid administrative contract are stricter than in the case of private law contracts. In addition to an agreement reached in conformity with the respective provisions of the BGB (§§ 145 ff), a number of further criteria have to be met. All of these are designed to protect individual citizens and, ultimately, the rule of law against the authorities circumventing public law restrictions imposed on their activities by choosing to act by way of contract. Thus, whilst ordinary contracts are, as a general rule, not subject to formal requirements, all administrative contracts have to be in writing, unless an even more stringent formal requirement has to be met (§ 57 of the 1976 Code). If an administrative contract infringes upon the rights of third parties the consent of such parties must be obtained in writing (§ 58(1) of the 1976 Code). The authorities have to obtain approval, ratification or consent of another authority if this had been required, had they chosen to make an administrative decision instead of concluding a contract (§ 58(2) of the 1976 Code). A stricter standard also applies with respect to the legality of the contract. Ordinary contracts are only 'illegal' if they explicitly or implicitly contradict a legal provision prohibiting a certain type of contract or permitting it only subject to an official license or consent (§ 134 BGB).[119] In addition to this, an administrative contract is also 'unlawful' whenever it does not meet the formal and substantive requirements of lawfulness in administrative law. The authority is therefore, as in the aforementioned area of 'administrative private law', subject to the formal limits of its competence, the fundamental rights of the Constitution, the principle of proportionality and other administrative law standards. Furthermore, the authority has to comply with the statutory provision authorising it to act in the particular area in question, so that freedom as to the actual content of the contractual terms in effect exists only in as much as this statutory provision confers discretion on the authority. Finally, further special

---

[119] See below, pp 705 and 708.

requirements have to be met for some particular kinds of administrative contracts, such as compromise agreements between authorities and citizens (§ 55 of the 1976 Code), or contracts which, albeit not necessarily synallagmatic in the sense defined above,[120] confer obligations on both parties. In the latter instance, the citizen's obligation must be agreed for a specific purpose, it has to serve the authority in discharging itself of its public duties, it must be adequate or reasonable (*angemessen*) in the light of all the circumstances, and it has to be intrinsically connected with the contractual performance promised by the authority (§ 56 of the 1976 Code).

The effects of administrative contracts also differ to some extent from those of private law contracts. The 1976 Code of Administrative Procedure, for instance, contained a special provision on hardship arising from supervening events, long before this doctrine was codified in private law:[121]

German Code on Administrative Procedure   **7.10 (DE)**

§ 60: Adaptation and termination in special cases

(1) If the circumstances which were material for determining the content of the contract have changed so substantially since the conclusion of the contract that one party to the contract cannot reasonably be expected to adhere to the original terms of the contract, this party may demand that the content of the contract be adapted to the changed circumstances or, inasmuch as an adaptation is impossible or cannot reasonably be expected of the other party, may terminate the contract. The authority may also terminate the contract in order to avoid or eliminate grave harm to the public good.

(2) Termination must be in writing, except where the law requires another form. Reasons for termination must be stated.

The authority's right to unilaterally terminate the contract as set out in § 60(1)(2) of the 1976 Code does not have an equivalent in the private law context. However, it may only be invoked in cases of extreme necessity, and the other party usually will have a claim for damages for the loss arising from the termination. One of the most important differences between administrative and private law contracts concerns the consequences of illegality. In principle, administrative contracts are void ab initio if one of the grounds for invalidating contracts set out in the BGB applies (§ 59(1) of the 1976 Code). Whilst this is not in doubt for cases of incapacity, immorality, impossibility, mistake or representation without proper authority, unlawful administrative contracts are only void if the illegality is sufficiently serious[122] to outweigh the public interest in upholding the contract. As a consequence, some illegal administrative contracts are not void and the parties have to perform their contractual obligations. There is considerable doubt as to whether this is compatible with the principle of legality of administrative action and, ultimately, with the Rule of Law. Finally, § 59(2) of the 1976 Code enumerates a number of additional grounds of invalidity for administrative contracts concluded between an authority and a citizen which do not apply to private law contracts.

---

[120] See above, p 116.
[121] See also below, p 1230.
[122] BVerwG 3 March 1995, BVerwGE 98, 58, 63.

7.4.B.4 ADMINISTRATIVE CONTRACTS UNDER DUTCH LAW

Traditionally in Dutch law there was a strict distinction between private law and public law. However, the dividing line between these two areas of law has become blurred.[123] Generally three types of contract are distinguished when a public authority enters into a contract with an individual.[124] The first is when a public authority acts as a regular market actor/private party,[125] for instance, a public authority buys a batch of pencils. In that situation, the contract is regarded as a private law contract and the rules included in the Dutch Civil Code are applicable. However, a public authority is also bound by the general principles of good management (Article 3:14 BW), which are rules of administrative law.[126] A dispute concerning this type of contract is heard by a private law court rather than by an administrative law court.[127]

Secondly, there is the contract in which a public authority makes arrangements with respect to the powers which are attributed to it by public law (*bevoegdhedenovereenkomst*).[128] Such a contract can be entered into with other public authorities, but also with private parties. For example, a city council makes arrangements with a private party (such as a soccer association) about police action. These contracts are, in principle, governed by administrative law.[129] However, insofar as administrative law does not provide any rules, the rules laid down in Book 6 of the Civil Code may apply by way of analogy.[130] As to the issue whether an administrative or a civil law court has competence with respect to this type of contract, a very detailed body of case law had been developed.[131] In some instances, it is the administrative court that has competence; in others, it is a civil law court.

Finally, there are the mixed contracts.[132] They are a blend of the two types of contract which have just been described. For instance, a public authority sells a plot of land and at the same time it enters into agreements about the use of the land and the licenses it will grant concerning the use of the land. Since contracts of this type are a mix, they are governed by either private law or administrative law depending on the predominant element of the transaction.[133]

---

[123] AS Hartkamp & CH Sieburgh, *Mr. C. Assers Handleiding tot de beoefening van het Nederlands Burgerlijk Recht. 6. Verbintenissenrecht. Deel III. Algemeen overeenkomstenrecht* (Deventer: Kluwer 2014) no. 36.

[124] M Scheltema and MW Scheltema, *Gemeenschappelijk recht* (Deventer: Kluwer, 2013) 205 ff.

[125] *Asser/Hartkamp & Sieburgh 6-III* 2014/36 (n 123 above); Scheltema and Scheltema (n 125 above) 206 ff; cf Van Wijk/Konijnenbelt & Van Male, *Hoofstukken van bestuursrecht* (16th edn, Deventer: Kluwer, 2014) 411 ff.

[126] *Asser/Hartkamp & Sieburgh 6-III* 2014/36 (n 123 above); Scheltema and Scheltema (n 125 above) 208.

[127] Scheltema and Scheltema (n 124 above) 227.

[128] ibid, 209 ff; Van Wijk/Konijnenbelt & van Male (n 125 above) 242 ff.

[129] *Asser/Hartkamp & Sieburgh 6-III* 2014/36 (n 123 above); Scheltema and Scheltema (n 124 above) 209 ff; Van Wijk/Konijnenbelt and van Male (n 125 above) 242 ff.

[130] *Asser/Hartkamp & Sieburgh 6-III* 2014/36 (n 123 above); Scheltema and Scheltema (n 124 above) 195; Van Wijk/Konijnenbelt and van Male (n 125 above) 243 ff.

[131] See about this case law: Scheltema and Scheltema (n 124 above) 206 ff; Van Wijk/Konijnenbelt and van Male (n 126 above) 245 ff.

[132] Scheltema and Scheltema (n 125 above) 224 ff.

[133] ibid.

FURTHER READING

Brisson, J-F, 'The Impact of Civil Code Reform on Administrative Contracts' (2017) 6 Montesquieu Law Review 154–70.

Häcker, B, 'La Troisième Jeunesse du Code Civil: A German Lawyer Looks at the Reform of French Contract Law' in J Cartwright and S Whittaker (eds), *The Code Napoléon Rewritten: French Contract Law after the 2016 Reforms* (Oxford: Hart Publishing, 2017) 387–407.

Whittaker, S, 'Contracts, Contract Law and Contractual Principle' in J Cartwright and S Whittaker (eds), *The Code Napoléon Rewritten: French Contract Law after the 2016 Reforms* (Oxford: Hart Publishing, 2017) 29–55.

PART 2
FORMATION

CHAPTER 8
OFFER AND ACCEPTANCE

8.1 INTRODUCTORY NOTE

The agreement (*consensus ad idem*) required to form a contract is traditionally analysed as an offer made by one party (the offeror) followed by an acceptance of that offer by the other party (the offeree).[1] The meeting of the offer and the acceptance constitutes the agreement. As it is now stated in the French Code civil:[2]

Code civil   **8.1 (FR)**

Article 1113: A contract is formed by the meeting of an offer and an acceptance by which the parties demonstrate their will to be bound. This may stem from a person's declaration or unequivocal conduct.

This analysis is essentially common to the different jurisdictions studied in this book. Indeed, this may be one area in which the common law borrowed directly from the civil law, and in which the writings of Ulpian, Pufendorf and Pothier were influential in shaping English law.[3]

    This schematic representation of the formation of a contract has proved to be very useful for creating rules covering the formation phase. This chapter considers a number of important issues which arise in relation to the formation of contracts: how to

---

[1] See P Malaurie, L Aynès and P Stoffel-Munck, *Droit des obligations* (9th edn, Paris: LGDJ, 2017); B Nicholas, *The French Law of Contract* (2nd edn, Oxford: Clarendon Press, 1992) 61–69; F Terré, P Simler and Y Lequette, *Les obligations* (12th edn, Paris: Dalloz, 2013) 98; *Treitel on the Law of Contract*, 14th edn by E Peel (London: Sweet & Maxwell, 2015) paras 2-001 ff; E McKendrick, *Contract Law* (12th edn, Basingstoke: Palgrave Macmillan, 2017) 26; K Larenz and M Wolf, *Allgemeiner Teil des Bürgerlichen Rechts* (9th edn, Munich: CH Beck, 2004) 516; K Zweigert and H Kötz, *Introduction to Comparative Law* (3rd edn, Oxford: Clarendon Press, 1998) 356–57; AT von Mehren, 'The Formation of Contract' in AT von Mehren (ed), *International Encyclopedia of Comparative Law*, vol VII *Contracts* (Leiden: Brill, 1992) ch 9, 63.

[2] On the new French law of offer and acceptance, see S Whittaker, 'Contracts, Contract Law and Contractual Principles' and R Sefton-Green, 'Formation of Contract: Negotiation and Process of Agreement' in J Cartwright, and S Whittaker (eds), *The Code Napoléon Rewritten* (Oxford: Hart Publishing, 2017) 29–55 and 59–78.

[3] See AWB Simpson, 'Innovation in Nineteenth Century Contract Law' (1975) 91 LQR 247, 259.

distinguish offers from dealings which are merely preliminary to the conclusion of a contract (8.2.A), whether an offer may be revoked before it is accepted (8.2.B), when an offer will lapse (8.2.C); and then the form which an acceptance may take (8.3.A), whether an acceptance must be communicated to the offeror in order to take effect (8.3.B) and what the consequences are where the acceptance deviates from the offer (8.3.C). Indeed, in this final section, we will see that in some cases a contract may be concluded where it is difficult to identify a clear offer and acceptance between the parties, suggesting that the offer-and-acceptance model may be too simple to account for all varieties of contract.

The different legal systems impose some minimum requirements as to the content of a declaration in order to qualify it as an offer that can ripen into a contract by acceptance. This issue, 'Sufficiency of Agreement', is sufficiently complex that it is treated separately in Chapter 9.

We saw in Chapter 5[4] that there are differences over whether subjective consensus (a true 'meeting of the minds') is required in order for a contract to come into existence, or whether it suffices that one party reasonably believes that the other is agreeing to contract, the 'objective' approach. The distinction was discussed in Chapter 5 because the subjective and objective approaches reflect fundamentally different conceptions of 'contract'. The most obvious practical effect of the distinction—when one party says or writes something that he does not mean—is discussed further in Chapter 14, which deals with mistake. In the present chapter we will see that these differences are also reflected in some of the rules of 'offer and acceptance' of each system.

8.2 OFFER

8.2.A DISTINCTION BETWEEN PRELIMINARY DEALINGS AND OFFERS TO ENTER CONTRACT

8.2.A.1 OFFERS

Principles of European Contract Law   8.2 (INT)

Article 2:201: Offer
  (1) A proposal amounts to an offer if:
    (a) it is intended to result in a contract if the other party accepts it, and
    (b) it contains sufficiently definite terms to form a contract.
  (2) An offer may be made to one or more specific persons or to the public.
  (3) A proposal to supply goods or services at stated prices made by a professional supplier in a public advertisement or a catalogue, or by a display of goods, is presumed to be an offer to sell or supply at that price until the stock of goods, or the supplier's capacity to supply the service, is exhausted.

---

[4] See above, pp 102 ff.

Article 2:103: Sufficient Agreement

(1) There is sufficient agreement if the terms:

(a) have been sufficiently defined by the parties so that the contract can be enforced or

(b) can be determined under these Principles.

(2) However, if one of the parties refuses to conclude a contract unless the parties have agreed on some specific matter, there is no contract unless agreement on that matter has been reached.

> *Note*
>
> DCFR Articles II.-4:201 and II.-4:103 follow the PECL provisions with only very minor changes of wording; CESL Article 31 was even closer to the PECL. UNIDROIT PICC Articles 2.1.2 and 2.1.13 are to the same effect as the PECL articles. CISG Article 14 is very similar to PECL Article 2:201.

In English law there has been some difference of opinion as to whether it is necessary to show an offer and its acceptance, or whether the judge may adopt a more 'impressionistic' approach.

Court of Appeal and House of Lords **8.3 (EN)**

***Gibson v Manchester City Council*[5]**

A letter that indicates only that a party may be prepared to enter a contract with the other party, and that does not contain or refer to the detailed terms that one would normally expect to find in the type of contract concerned, does not amount to an offer.

Facts: In 1970, the city council, then in the control of the Conservative party, adopted a policy of selling council houses to its tenants. It circulated printed forms that tenants could send in to obtain details. The form read in part:

> Please inform me of the price of buying my council house. I am interested in obtaining a mortgage from the Corporation to buy the house. Please send me the details.

Gibson sent in a form and received a letter from the city treasurer stating (in part):

> *The Corporation may be prepared to sell the house to you at the purchase price of £2,725 less 20% = £2,180* (freehold).
>
> Maximum mortgage the Corporation may grant: £2,177 repayable over 20 years.
>
> …
>
> This letter should not be regarded as a firm offer of a mortgage.
>
> *If you would like to make a formal application to buy your council house, please complete the enclosed application form and return it to me as soon as possible.*

(Emphasis supplied.)

Gibson completed the application form except for the price and returned it; after being told that the Corporation would not lower the price as he had requested, he wrote:

> I would be obliged if you will carry on with the purchase as per my application already in your possession.

---

[5] [1978] 1 WLR 520 (CA); [1979] 1 WLR 294 (HL).

Thereafter, the house was removed from the council's maintenance list and placed on their house purchase list—but before the contracts had been exchanged, control of the council passed to the Labour Party and it was resolved to discontinue sales of council houses except in cases where there was a binding contract to sell. Gibson was notified that the council would not be proceeding with the sale to him, and he brought an action seeking specific performance of the agreement he alleged had been made. The county court judge held that there was a concluded contract and ordered specific performance. The Court of Appeal, by a majority (Lord Denning MR and Ormrod LJ; Geoffrey Lane LJ dissenting), agreed.

Held: In the Court of Appeal, Lord Denning MR held that on his reading of the correspondence the council's letter was an offer. He continued:

Judgment: Lord Denning MR: ... We have had much discussion as to whether Mr Gibson's letter of March 18, 1971, was a new offer or whether it was an acceptance of the previous offer which had been made. I do not like detailed analysis on such a point. To my mind it is a mistake to think that all contracts can be analysed into the form of offer and acceptance. I know in some of the text books it has been the custom to do so: but, as I understand the law, there is no need to look for a strict offer and acceptance. You should look at the correspondence as a whole and at the conduct of the parties and see therefrom whether the parties have come to an agreement on everything that was material. If by their correspondence and their conduct you can see an agreement on all material terms—which was intended thenceforward to be binding—then there is a binding contract in law even though all the formalities have not been gone through: see *Brogden v Metropolitan Railway Co.*[6]

It seems to me that on the correspondence I have read—and, I may add, on what happened after—the parties had come to an agreement in the matter which they intended to be binding. [Ormrod LJ also considered that the Council's letter amounted to an offer. Geoffrey Lane LJ dissented arguing that the Council's letter did not amount to an offer.] The words used, such as 'may be prepared to sell', were not a definite offer; and it did not refer to the terms and conditions on which the Council would always insist.

The House of Lords allowed the appeal by the Council.

Lord Diplock: My Lords, this is an action for specific performance of what is claimed to be a contract for the sale of land. The only question in the appeal is of a kind with which the courts are very familiar. It is whether in the correspondence between the parties there can be found a legally enforceable contract for the sale by the Manchester Corporation to Mr Gibson of the dwelling house of which he was the occupying tenant at the relevant time in 1971. That question is one that, in my view, can be answered by applying to the particular documents relied upon by Mr Gibson as constituting the contract, well-settled, indeed elementary, principles of English law. This being so, it is not the sort of case in which leave would have been likely to be granted to appeal to your Lordships' House, but for the fact that it is a test case ...

Lord Denning MR rejected what I have described as the conventional approach of looking to see whether upon the true construction of the documents relied upon there can be discerned an offer and acceptance. One ought, he said, ... to 'look at the correspondence as a whole and at the conduct of the parties and see therefrom whether the parties have come to an agreement on everything that was material.' This approach ... led him however to the conclusion that there should be imported into the agreement to be specifically performed additional conditions, against use except as a private dwelling house and

---

[6] (1876–77) LR 2 App Cas 666 (HL); 8.31 (EN) below, p 249.

against advertising and a restriction not to sell or lease the property for five years. These are conditions which would not be implied by law in an open contract for the sale of land. The reason for so varying the judge's order was that clauses in these terms were included in the standard form of 'Agreement for Sale of a Council House' which, as appears from the earlier case of *Storer v Manchester City Council* [1974] 1 WLR 1403, was entered into by the corporation and council tenants whose applications to purchase the freehold of their council house reached the stage at which contracts were exchanged. There was, however, no reference to this standard form of agreement in any of the documents said to constitute the contract relied on in the instant case, nor was there any evidence that Mr Gibson had knowledge of its terms at or before the time that the alleged contract was concluded …

My Lords, there may be certain types of contract, though I think they are exceptional, which do not fit easily into the normal analysis of a contract as being constituted by offer and acceptance; but a contract alleged to have been made by an exchange of correspondence between the parties in which the successive communications other than the first are in reply to one another, is not one of these. I can see no reason in the instant case for departing from the conventional approach of looking at the handful of documents relied upon as constituting the contract sued upon and seeing whether upon their true construction there is to be found in them a contractual offer by the corporation to sell the house to Mr Gibson and an acceptance of that offer by Mr Gibson. I venture to think that it was by departing from this conventional approach that the majority of the Court of Appeal was led into error …

My Lords, the words I have italicised [see the statement of facts above] seem to me, as they seemed to Geoffrey Lane LJ, to make it quite impossible to construe this letter as a contractual offer capable of being converted into a legally enforceable open contract for the sale of land by Mr Gibson's written acceptance of it. The words 'may be prepared to sell' are fatal to this; so is the invitation, not, be it noted, to accept the offer, but 'to make formal application to buy' upon the enclosed application form. It is, to quote Geoffrey Lane LJ, a letter setting out the financial terms on which it may be the council will be prepared to consider a sale and purchase in due course.

Both Ormrod LJ and the judge in the county court reaching the conclusion that this letter was a firm offer to sell the freehold interest in the house for £2,180, attached importance to the fact that the second paragraph, dealing with the financial details of the mortgage of which Mr Gibson had asked for particulars, stated expressly, 'This letter should not be regarded as a firm offer of a mortgage.' The necessary implication from this, it is suggested, is that the first paragraph of the letter is to be regarded as a firm offer to sell despite the fact that this is plainly inconsistent with the express language of that paragraph. My Lords, with great respect, this surely must be fallacious. If the final sentence had been omitted the wording of the second paragraph, unlike that of the first, with its use of the indicative mood in such expressions as 'the interest rate will change,' might have been understood by council tenants to whom it was addressed as indicating a firm offer of a mortgage of the amount and on the terms for repayment stated if the council were prepared to sell the house at the stated price. But whether or not this be the explanation of the presence of the last sentence in paragraph 2, it cannot possibly affect the plain meaning of the words used in paragraph 1. …

My Lords, the application form and letter of March 18, 1971, were relied on by Mr Gibson as an unconditional acceptance of the corporation's offer to sell the house; but this cannot be so unless there was a contractual offer by the corporation available for acceptance, and, for the reason already given I am of opinion that there was none.

It is unnecessary to consider whether the application form and Mr Gibson's letters of March 3 and 18, 1971, are capable of amounting to a contractual offer by him to purchase the freehold interest in the house at a price of £2,180 on the terms of an open contract, for there is no suggestion that, even if it were, it was ever accepted by the corporation. Nor would it ever have been even if there had been no change in the political control of the council, as the policy of the corporation before the change required the incorporation in all agreements for sale of council houses to tenants of the conditions referred to by Lord Denning MR in his judgment and other conditions inconsistent with an open contract.

I therefore feel compelled to allow the appeal. One can sympathise with Mr Gibson's disappointment on finding that his expectations that he would be able to buy his council house at 20 per cent. below its market value in the autumn of 1970 cannot be realised. Whether one thinks this makes it a hard case perhaps depends upon the political views that one holds about council housing policy. But hard cases offer a strong temptation to let them have their proverbial consequences. It is a temptation that the judicial mind must be vigilant to resist.

Lord Edmund-Davies: [Lord Edmund-Davies agreed that the Council's letter could not amount to an offer on its wording. He then quoted the words of Lord Denning above and continued:]

[Lord Denning MR's] second ground was that, in the belief that a contract to sell would emerge, the plaintiff did much work in repairing and improving his house and premises. But no evidence was called as to when such work had been done, and it appears from the correspondence that, although as far back as June 1970 Mr Gibson had inquired whether he might proceed to improve the property, '… to the mutual benefit of the city and myself until such time as my case comes up for consideration,' the corporation's reply in the following October gave no encouragement to the tenant to execute any improvements, and concluded, 'If at any time you decide to withdraw your application I should be obliged if you would let me know.' It is therefore impossible to conclude that improvements were executed on the basis that the corporation had already committed themselves to sell. Nor, with respect to Lord Denning MR, can it be material that, entirely unknown to Mr Gibson, the corporation at one stage took 174 Charlestown Road off the list of houses being maintained by them and put it on the list of 'pending sales,' for that action had been taken in February 1971 in relation to all cases where the Direct Works Department had been notified that sales were 'proceeding.' And it has to be observed that this alteration in the list was effected a month earlier than the time when, according to the plaintiff's pleaded case, he accepted the corporation's 'offer' to sell. And, finally, the town clerk's letter to Councillor Goldstone already referred to, cannot in my judgment have relevance to the matter of consensus ad idem. I have already sought to show that, read as a whole its wording is equivocal; and, even were it clear, the proper question is not whether the town clerk considered that a contract had been concluded but whether this was so in fact and in law.

My Lords, there are further difficulties in Mr Gibson's way. It is common ground that, had the corporation not altered its policy, the parties would in the ordinary way have entered into a standard 'Agreement for Sale of a Council House,' such as that concluded in *Storer v Manchester City Council* [1974] 1 WLR 1403. That agreement contained a provision that:

> 'Deeds of conveyance or transfer and mortgage to be in the corporation's standard forms including conditions against use except as a private dwelling house and against advertising and a restriction not to sell or lease the property for five years.'

But in the instant case no such agreement was ever prepared or referred to, and it is not suggested that Mr Gibson ever had knowledge of any special conditions, and still less that he assented to them. And as these special conditions are not such as may be implied in an open contract for the sale of land, their introduction would create—from his point of view—the difficulty of non-compliance with section 40 of the Law of Property Act 1925 and therefore unenforceability. I am accordingly in respectful disagreement with Lord Denning MR.

[Lords FRASER and KEITH agreed with Lord Diplock; Lord RUSSELL gave a brief speech also in favour of allowing the appeal.]

Appeal allowed.

Notes

(1) This case illustrates the 'objective' approach used in English law to decide whether an offer has been made by one party and accepted by the other. The speeches in the House of Lords look primarily to the words used, holding that the Council's statement that it 'may be prepared to sell' was not an offer. Note that they do not ask what the parties' subjective intentions were, and Lord Edmund Davies states that it does not matter what the Town Clerk thought, but rather the legal effect of the words used.

(2) The court looks at the words used in their context, to determine whether or not it seems correct to interpret the words as an offer. It would be very unusual to sell a house on an 'open contract', ie one without detailed terms, which is one reason that Lord Edmund-Davies (like Geoffrey Lane LJ in the Court of Appeal) held that the Council's letter did not amount to an offer that Mr Gibson could accept. Lord Denning in the Court of Appeal had attempted to get over this problem by holding that the offer was implicitly subject to the Council's standard terms of sale, but their Lordships point out that this is impossible because Mr Gibson did not know of the standard terms.

(3) It would also be difficult to argue that the standard terms were incorporated because statute (the Law of Property Act 1925, s 40, now repealed and replaced by the Law of Property (Miscellaneous Provisions) Act 1989, s 2[7]) imposed formal requirements which were not satisfied in this case.

(4) There have been other cases in which the courts have relied on the absence of detailed terms as evidence showing that a letter did not amount to an offer in law, even though the letter said: 'I … am prepared to offer you … my … estate for £600,000': see *Clifton v Palumbo*.[8] Lord Greene MR remarked that 'words like "agree", "offer", "accept", when used in relation to price, are not to be read necessarily as indicating an intention to make, then and there, a contract or an offer as the case may be. Whether they do or do not must depend entirely on the construction of the particular document.'

(5) On the other hand, if the court finds other evidence that the parties really did intend to be bound, they will hold that there is an offer despite the absence of detailed terms: see *Bigg v Boyd-Gibbins Ltd*.[9]

(6) The party alleged to have made an offer may have intended simply to answer a question from the other party, as was the case in *Harvey v Facey*,[10] where the plaintiffs

[7] See above, p 122, n 3.
[8] [1944] 2 All ER 497 (CA).
[9] [1971] 1 WLR 913 (CA).
[10] [1893] AC 552 (PC).

telegraphed to the defendants 'Will you sell us Bumper Hall Pen? Telegraph lowest cash price'. The defendants telegraphed in reply, 'Lowest price for Bumper Hall Pen, £900'. It was held by the Privy Council that the price statement was not an offer, but only an answer to the second question in the first telegram.

(7) For a summary of the 'rules' of offer and acceptance in English law see A Burrows, *A Restatement of the English Law of Contract*, s 7.

A statement that indicates a willingness to negotiate but which does not amount to an offer is often referred to as an 'invitation to treat' (ie to negotiate, compare the noun 'treaty'). The distinction between an offer and a mere invitation to make an offer or to negotiate is also made in German law[11] and in French law,[12] where it is now stated explicitly in the Code civil:

Code civil   **8.4 (FR)**

Article 1114: An offer, whether made to a particular person or to persons generally, contains the essential elements of the envisaged contract, and expresses the will of the offeror to be bound in case of acceptance. Failing this, there is only an invitation to enter into negotiations.

As in English law, the conclusive criterion is the intention with which a statement is made. The question to be asked is whether a statement has the purport to enable its addressee to conclude a contract by accepting it, or merely shows the intention of the person making the statement to be put in the position to conclude a contract.[13]

8.2.A.2 OFFERS 'SUBJECT TO CONFIRMATION'

In *Gibson*,[14] the Council's statement that it 'may be prepared to sell' did not amount to an offer because the words indicated that the Council was reserving the right to change its mind. Equally, if an 'offer' is stated to be 'subject to confirmation', it is not normally treated as an offer. Equally an 'agreement' that is not to be binding 'until signed on behalf of the seller' is merely an offer by the buyer, not a concluded contract.

Cass com, 6 March 1990[15]   **8.5 (FR)**

Hugin Sweda

A company which is selling goods but which indicates that its proposal is not definitive and must subsequently be approved or accepted by itself will not be held to have made an offer.

---

[11] H Kötz, *Vertragsrecht* (2nd edn, Tübingen: Mohr Siebeck, 2012) para 88; W Flume, *Allgemeiner Teil des bürgerlichen Rechts*, vol II, *Das Rechtsgeschäft* (3rd edn, Berlin: Springer, 1979) 636.

[12] Terré et al (n 1 above) no. 108. See also Dutch law: *Hofland v Hennis*, HR 10 April 1981, NJ 1981, 532; J Hijma, *Mr. C. Assers handleiding tot de beoefening van het Nederlands Burgerlijk Recht. 7. Internationaal Privaatrecht. Deel 1** (Deventer: Kluwer, 2013) no. 163 ff.

[13] Flume (n 11 above) 637.

[14] 8.3 (EN), above, p 205.

[15] No. 88-12477, Bull civ IV no. 74, JCP 1990.II.21583, annotated by B Gross.

Facts: Mr Borde ordered certain equipment from Messrs Hugin Sweda for the purposes of his business; that company had stated, in the general conditions of sale featuring in its order forms, that its offers did not become definitive, and did not constitute a binding commitment, until they were approved by it, and, moreover, that an order would not be regarded as definite until it had been accepted by the company. Before his order was accepted by Hugin Sweda, Mr Borde changed his mind and withdrew it.

Held: Mr Borde had not accepted an offer, but had himself made an offer which had been withdrawn before it was accepted.

Judgment: — Under articles 1134 and 1583 of the Civil Code;—Whereas between traders, a proposal to enter into a contract constitutes an offer only if it states an intention on the part of the person making it to be bound by it in the event of its acceptance; …

— Whereas in dismissing Mr Borde's claim for repayment of the sum paid by him on account, the cour d'appel held that the order form constituted 'a firm purchase on the terms proposed by Hugin Sweda', and that the clause appearing in that form constituted a condition having suspensory effect which was intended solely for the benefit of the vendor and which did not entitle the purchaser to withdraw from a sale which had been definitively concluded by agreement between the parties as to the subject matter and the price;

— Whereas in so ruling, despite the fact that, by complying with the proposal contained in the order form, Mr Borde had merely made an offer to purchase which he remained at liberty to withdraw until such time as the sale became definitive by acceptance on the part of the vendor, the cour d'appel infringed the legislation referred to above; …

Notes

(1) An offer 'subject to confirmation' is not in reality an offer but only an invitation to make an offer (or 'invitation to treat'), because it does not show the necessary intention to be bound by mere acceptance. Thus, when a buyer signs a seller's order form containing a condition that makes the seller's offer subject to confirmation of the latter, then the signing of the order form, and not the order form itself, constitutes the first offer. The decision reached in the present case would therefore have been the same if it had been given by an English court; the English case of *Robophone Facilities v Blank*[16] is precisely on point. As we will see, under German law the seller's 'offer subject to confirmation' would not be regarded as an offer either, but the outcome on the facts of *Hugin Sweda* would be different because in that case *the buyer* had made an offer and in German law that offer would not be revocable.[17]

(2) The Cour de cassation limits the applicability of the rule to contracts between merchants but the definition of an offer it gives is valid for every offer.[18]

(3) To prevent a prospective buyer from withdrawing between his signing of the order form and the confirmation of the seller, order forms sometimes contain a provision stipulating that the buyer will be bound definitively. Conditions of this nature are potentially valid in French law, but the Commission des clauses abusives (Commission for Unfair Terms) has recommended that these clauses—and similar conditions—should

---

[16] [1966] 1 WLR 1428 (CA).
[17] See below, p 228.
[18] See the annotations by B Gross, JCP 1990.II.21583 and J Mestre, RTD civ 1999, 464.

be eliminated from contracts between consumers and professionals.[19] (We will see that such a clause would not be effective in English law, though for different reasons.)[20]

(4) The Cour de cassation seems to state as a general rule that an offer is revocable. As will be seen in 8.2.C, this rule is subject to major restrictions in French law. That no restriction was placed on the revocability of the buyer's offer in the present case may be explained by the fact that it was the seller who had taken the first initiative to enter into a contract.[21]

In contrast, in German law an offer is not normally revocable. As a result, parties who think they may want to withdraw the offer often state that it is 'without engagement' (*freibleibend*). The next case explores the effect of doing so.

BGH, 8 March 1984[22]   **8.6 (DE)**

The Aeroplane Charter

*The use of the words 'without engagement' [*freibleibend*] will not necessarily prevent a communication from constituting an effective offer.*

Facts: The plaintiff, a tour company wishing to charter an aircraft for a flight planned for the 1979 summer season, sent a telex on 2 August 1978 to Messrs L, in which it requested that firm to submit an offer. It stated that it would prefer the departure day to be 'if possible a Friday, Saturday or Sunday, but that is not an absolute condition'. Since Messrs L did not have an aircraft available for the period requested, it passed the telex on to the defendant. The plaintiff, on being informed of this, sent a telex to the defendant on 4 August 1978, in which it referred to the telex sent to Messrs L and requested the defendant 'if possible, to make that offer … by return'. The defendant replied in writing on 4 August 1978, referring to the plaintiff's telex to Messrs L and stating that it was willing, 'without engagement, and subject to availability', to offer a Caravelle SE 210 for one-day flights at a price of DM 18,016 per flight, inclusive of all ancillary costs but without commission. The plaintiff replied in writing on 11 August 1978, stating that it was interested in the offer and requesting the reservation of a Caravelle SE 210. The defendant sent a further telex to the plaintiff on 1 September 1978, in which it informed the latter of the flight operations permit issued to it; thereafter, by telex of 10 October 1978, it stated that, having completed its planning for the summer 1979 season, it had 'no availability'. The plaintiff was then obliged to charter another aircraft having greater passenger capacity. It claimed from the defendant compensation for the damage suffered by it, in the sum of DM 120,000.

Held: The plaintiff's claim succeeded.

Judgment: 1. The appellate court correctly found that the defendant's communication to the plaintiff of 4 August 1978 constituted an effective offer. It was not rendered ineffective by the proviso 'without engagement, and subject to availability' contained therein. Moreover, the content of the offer—in conjunction with the telex from the plaintiff to Messrs L of 2 August 1978, to which reference was made—was adequately specified.

(a) The legal meaning of the phrase 'without engagement', when used in an offer, is disputed. The Reichsgericht (Supreme Court of the German Reich) has taken the view that an 'offer without engagement' does not constitute an offer within the meaning of § 145 BGB, but rather a request made to the other party, asking it to submit a contractual

---

[19] On the Commission, see below, p 846.
[20] See below, p 233.
[21] See D 1991, 317.
[22] NJW 1984, 1885.

offer. However, it held, in accordance with the principle of good faith, that a party making a request in such terms is obliged forthwith to comment on the application for an 'offer without engagement' contained in the answer. If a party making an 'offer without engagement' fails to fulfil that obligation to provide an answer, his silence will be regarded as constituting acceptance of the offer (see RGZ 102, 227 [229 et seq]; 103, 312 [313]; 105, 8 [12]; RG, JW 1921, 393; 1926, 2674 [2675]) …

The case-law of the Reichsgericht has been partially accepted by academic legal authors, who have likewise regarded an 'offer without engagement' as constituting merely a request for the submission of an offer, which is in turn deemed to be accepted in the event of silence on the part of the party making the request. … However, such an offer may also amount to a proposal within the meaning of § 145 BGB which, by reason of the revocation proviso expressly stated in the clause in question, may be revoked at any time *up to* acceptance by the other party. … By contrast, a different view has been expressed, to the effect that an 'offer without engagement' constitutes not merely a request for the submission of an offer but, invariably, a proposal the binding effect of which is excluded and which can still be revoked forthwith even *after* notice of its acceptance has been received. …

(b) The Bundesgerichtshof (Federal Court of Justice) has not yet expressed any definitive view concerning the legal meaning of the qualification 'without engagement'. In its judgment published at BGH, NJW 1958, 1628, it merely stated (*obiter*) that the use of such a qualification indicated a desire on the part of the seller not to be bound in any way. However, it did not rule on the question whether a statement subject to such a qualification constitutes merely a request for the submission of an offer or whether it amounts to an offer in its own right. It is not necessary in the present case to determine whether an 'offer without engagement' must *invariably* be regarded merely as a request for the submission of an offer, since, in the circumstances of this case, the defendant's statement that it was willing to offer an aircraft 'without engagement, *and subject to availability*' constituted in any event an effective *offer* within the meaning of § 145 BGB.

(aa) Both in its telex of 2 August 1978, addressed to Messrs L but forwarded to the defendant, and in its telex sent direct to the defendant on 4 August 1978, the plaintiff asked the defendant to submit an *offer*. In so doing—as the appellate court correctly points out—it did not merely make an enquiry of the defendant for the purposes of obtaining information; instead, it expressly requested the submission of an offer. Consequently, even though the response to that request, contained in the defendant's written answer of 4 August 1978, was qualified by the words 'without engagement', it cannot be regarded as constituting, in turn, a request for the submission of an offer. On the contrary, that response amounted to 'more than a mere request for an offer' (see Flume, § 35 I 3c, with comments in support), since the plaintiff was entitled to expect the defendant to make a specific offer in response to its enquiry. The defendant likewise had necessarily to assume that its reply, in which it expressly 'offered' to provide a specific service, would be understood as constituting an offer. On the basis of those facts—as the appellate court correctly found—the use by the defendant of the qualifying words '…' could only be understood as amounting to the reservation of a right of revocation, by which the defendant declined, in a permissible manner, to be bound by the application made to it (see § 145 BGB). In those circumstances, there are no grounds for treating its response as an acceptance of a mere request for the submission of an offer. The appellate court was unable to discern the existence of any contrary trade practice.

2. By its written communication of 11 August 1978, the plaintiff accepted the defendant's offer.

…

3. There is no need to determine whether—as the appellate court found—the reservation of the right of revocation contained in the phrase 'without engagement, and subject to availability' ceased to have effect upon the coming into existence of the contract, or whether—in accordance with the view expressed by academic legal authors, as mentioned in 1(a) above—the defendant could still have revoked its offer even after receiving the confirmation of its acceptance. This is because the defendant did not decline the plaintiff's acceptance of its offer immediately after receiving that acceptance on 11 August 1978. On the contrary, it was not until it sent its telex of 10 October 1978 that it informed the plaintiff that it had 'no availability'. By that time, revocation by the defendant had ceased to be possible under any circumstances.

4. Consequently—as the appellate court rightly held—an effective contract came into existence between the parties.

Notes

(1) This case illustrates that, in German law, the words used by the parties must be interpreted by reference to the intentions of the parties. The fact that the telex was sent in response to a request for an offer indicated that the intended purpose of the telex was to make an offer rather than an invitation to treat or the mere provision of information. On that basis, the disputed words could be interpreted only as reserving a right of revocation, and on the facts of the case that right had not been exercised.

(2) The legal meaning of the word *freibleibend* (free of engagement) in an offer has generated some controversy in German law. Three possible views are mentioned by the Bundesgerichtshof. The first view is that such an offer is not a real offer but only an invitation to make an offer—this view had been adopted by the Reichsgericht, for example in the *Alcohol for Sale* case.[23] The second view is that it is a real offer, but one that can be revoked until its acceptance, whereas the general rule in German law is that an offer cannot be revoked.[24] The third view is that it is a real offer, but one that is revocable even immediately after its acceptance. The Bundesgerichtshof in the present case avoided choosing between the three views, because the statement of the firm was not made without any commitment (*freibleibend*) in general, but without any commitment and 'subject to availability' and, moreover, it was not revoked immediately after it had been accepted. Anyway, the practical meaning of the difference between the first and the third view is small, especially when it is assumed that an offer, that has been made on invitation of the offeree, may be accepted by silence.[25] On both views the person who used the term *freibleibend* is bound to a contract if he does not revoke his proposal immediately after the addressee has agreed to it.

8.2.A.3 PUBLIC ADVERTISEMENTS

It is sometimes not just the words used but also the context in which the statement is made which determines whether or not an offer has been made. For example, in English law it is firmly established that an advertisement 'offering' to sell goods (or land) at

---

[23] 8.35 (DE), below, p 253.
[24] See below, p 228.
[25] For acceptance by silence, see below, pp 252 ff.

stated prices does not amount to an offer in the legal sense: *Grainger & Son v Gough*[26] (wine merchant's price list does not amount to an offer). This is not an absolute rule,[27] but it is a very strong presumption against the statement being an offer.[28] In *Partridge v Crittenden*[29] a notice in a periodical advertising 'Bramblefinch cocks and hens, 25s each' was held not to be an offer. Lord Parker stated the general rule in English law:

> I think that when one is dealing with advertisements and circulars … there is business sense in their being construed as invitations to treat and not offers for sale.

The reason given in *Grainger & Son v Gough* was that the merchant has a limited stock and, if the price list were treated as an offer and too many buyers 'accepted', the merchant would be unable to meet its contractual obligations. However, the same approach is normally taken even with an advertisement 'offering' a single item for sale.[30] On this, not all systems take the same approach.

Cass civ (3), 28 November 1968[31]   **8.7 (FR)**

Land for sale

An offer to the public at large is not merely an invitation to treat and is capable of being accepted so as to give rise to a contract.

Facts: Maltzkorn, having become aware of an advertisement published in the newspaper *L'Ardennais* on 23 May 1961, offering for sale a certain plot of land at a price of FF25,000, informed the owner, Mr Braquet, that he accepted his offer; however, Braquet claimed that he was not bound by Maltzkorn's offer to buy.

Held: Maltzkorn's claim failed, but this decision was overturned by the Cour de cassation.

Judgment: —Under article 1589 of the Civil Code;—Whereas an offer made to the public at large binds the offeror vis-à-vis the first person who accepts it, in the same way as an offer made to a specific person;

— Whereas the grounds for dismissal of Maltzkorn's claim for an order requiring the sale to be completed, as set out in the contested judgment, state that 'an offer made in a newspaper for the sale of an asset which can only be purchased by one person cannot be equated with an offer made to a specific person; it constitutes merely an invitation to treat addressed to potential purchasers, and cannot therefore bind the person by whom it is made vis-à-vis a person who accepts it';

— Whereas in making that general ruling, despite its finding that Braquet, upon receiving notice of the acceptance, had stated that 'the farm has not yet been sold', and without mentioning any factor which could have prompted it to infer that the advertisement constituted merely an invitation to enter into negotiations or that Braquet's offer was

---

[26] [1896] AC 325 (HL).

[27] cf below, p 219.

[28] See *Chitty on Contracts*, 33rd edn by H Beale (gen ed) (London: Sweet & Maxwell/Thomson Reuters, 2018) paras 2-014–2-017.

[29] [1968] 1 WLR 1204 (DC).

[30] This may be because of another rule of English law, namely that an offer can be accepted until either it has been revoked or it has lapsed through time (see below, pp 231 ff). Thus if the advertisement amounted to an offer, more than one buyer might 'accept' it even though there is only one item.

[31] No. 67-10935, Bull civ III no. 507, Gaz Pal 1969.1.95, JCP 1969.II.15797.

subject to any qualification, the cour d'appel failed to establish any legal basis for its decision; ...

Notes

(1) This case illustrates that, in French law, an offer to the public is no less a valid offer than an offer to a particular person. A statement that is made to the public at large by means of an advertisement in a newspaper is therefore a 'real' offer that is susceptible of being accepted.

(2) The French Court speaks generally of 'offers to the public'. Later in this section, we discuss another case which would be treated in this way by the French courts: the display of priced goods in a shop.[32]

(3) According to French authors and case law of the lower courts, if the offer relates to the conclusion of a contract for which the person of the other party is of particular interest to the offeror (*intuitus personae*), an exception is allowed to the rule laid down by the Cour de cassation concerning offers to the public.[33] The examples mentioned by these authors are employment contracts, credit agreements,[34] the rent of a flat and certain types of partnerships. In such cases, the offeror can be said to have made a reservation with regard to the person of the other party.

(4) It should be noted that particularly for the sale of real estate, the offer can contain some implied or express reservations or restrictions (for instance if it is made in consideration to the person—*intuitus personae*).[35]

(5) The approach of the French courts certainly contrasts with that of the English court in *Clifton v Palumbo*,[36] in which the court took into account the seriousness of a sale of land when construing a letter as merely preliminary to a binding contract.

(6) Both German and English law regard the advertisement as a mere invitation to treat.[37] In support of this analysis, some German authors[38] have argued that a statement addressed to an indefinite number of persons can never be meant as an offer, because the person making the statement cannot perform the proposed contract an infinite number of times.

The 'limited stock' argument is not convincing: the offer to the public could be seen as implicitly including a clause which limits the validity of the offer to the exhaustion of the offeror's stock. The offer would therefore lapse when the offeror's stock is finished. The stronger reason to deny an advertisement the character of an offer seems to be that the person placing the advertisement wishes to reserve to himself the final decision whether to conclude a contract, and therefore the proposal does not show the intention to be bound in case of acceptance. This will generally be the case for proposals

[32] See the English case of *Pharmaceutical Society v Boots*, 8.9 (EN), below, p 219.
[33] Malaurie et al (n 1 above) no. 468; Terré et al (n 1 above) para 108.
[34] Cass com 31 January 1966, no. 63-10813, Bull civ IV no. 64, D 1966, 537, annotated by M Cabrillac and J Rives-Lange.
[35] Malaurie et al (n 1 above) no. 468.
[36] Above, p 209.
[37] *Treitel* (n 1 above) para 2-011; McKendrick (n 1 above) 31.
[38] eg D Medicus and S Lorenz, *Schuldrecht I: Allgemeiner Teil* (21th edn, Munich: CH Beck, 2015) 135.

intuitus personae ('with an eye to the person'); other considerations may also lead to the assumption that, unless otherwise indicated, a proposal to the public at large is only an invitation to make an offer. This is the view promoted by some French authors and lower courts.[39] The Dutch Supreme Court has used the *intuitus personae* argument, holding that an advertisement in which a specific thing, such as a house (as opposed to a generic thing), is offered for a certain price, has to be taken by prospective buyers, in principle, as an invitation to enter into negotiations, in which not only the price and other conditions of the sale but also the person of the prospective buyer can be of interest.[40]

There are some transactions which can only be analysed as contractual if one party is treated as making an offer to 'the world at large'. In the common situation of an automatic car park with a ticket machine, it was said by Lord Denning in *Thornton v Shoe Lane Parking*[41] that the offer is made when the proprietor of the machine holds it out as being ready to receive the money, and the acceptance takes place when the customer puts his money into the slot. The same view is generally adopted with regard to all slot machines in German law.[42] German authors point out, however, that the offer is necessarily limited to the content of the machine: when the machine is empty, no contract comes into existence by putting money in. There may also be other situations in which a public advertisement amounts to an offer.

Court of Appeal   **8.8 (EN)**

Carlill v Carbolic Smoke Ball Co[43]

An advertisement setting up a unilateral contract constitutes an offer rather than an invitation to treat.

Facts: The Carbolic Smoke Ball Company, proprietor of a medical preparation called 'The Carbolic Smoke Ball', inserted in some newspapers the following advertisement: '100l [£100] reward will be paid by the Carbolic Smoke Ball Company to any person who contracts the increasing epidemic influenza, colds, or any disease caused by taking cold, after having used the smoke ball three times daily for two weeks according to the printed directions supplied with each ball. 100l is deposited with the Alliance Bank, Regent Street, shewing our sincerity in the matter.' Mrs Carlill on the faith of the advertisement bought one of the balls, and used it in the manner and for the period specified, but nevertheless contracted influenza and claimed the 100l.

Held: In purchasing and using the smoke ball, Mrs Carlill had accepted the company's offer to pay 100l should she contract influenza.

Judgment: LINDLEY LJ: … Then it is contended that it is not binding. In the first place, it is said that it is not made with anybody in particular. Now that point is common to the words of this advertisement and to the words of all other advertisements offering rewards. They are offers to anybody who performs the conditions named in the advertisement, and anybody who does perform the condition accepts the offer. In point of law this

---

[39] See Note (3) to the *Land for Sale* case, above, p 216. See also PECL Art 2:201, 8.2 (INT), above, p 204 and the comments on that provision under C.

[40] *Hofland v Hennis*, HR 10 April 1981, NJ 1981, 532, annotated by CJH Brunner.

[41] [1971] 2 QB 163, 169 (CA).

[42] Larenz and Wolf (n 1 above) 518; Flume (n 11 above) 636.

[43] [1893] 1 QB 256.

advertisement is an offer to pay 100l to anybody who will perform these conditions, and the performance of the conditions is the acceptance of the offer ...

BOWEN LJ: ... It was also said that the contract is made with all the world—that is, with everybody; and that you cannot contract with everybody. It is not a contract made with all the world. There is the fallacy of the argument. It is an offer made to all the world; and why should not an offer be made to all the world which is to ripen into a contract with anybody who comes forward and performs the condition? It is an offer to become liable to anyone who, before it is retracted, performs the condition, and, although the offer is made to the world, the contract is made with that limited portion of the public who come forward and perform the condition on the faith of the advertisement. It is not like cases in which you offer to negotiate, or you issue advertisements that you have got a stock of books to sell, or houses to let, in which case there is no offer to be bound by any contract. Such advertisements are offers to negotiate—offers to receive offers—offers to chaffer, as, I think, some learned judge in one of the cases has said. If this is an offer to be bound, then it is a contract the moment the person fulfils the condition.

That seems to me to be sense, and it is also the ground on which all these advertisement cases have been decided during the century; and it cannot be put better than in Willes, J's, judgment in *Spencer v Harding*. 'In the advertisement cases,' he says, 'there never was any doubt that the advertisement amounted to a promise to pay the money to the person who first gave information. The difficulty suggested was that it was a contract with all the world. But that, of course, was soon overruled. It was an offer to become liable to any person who before the offer should be retracted should happen to be the person to fulfil the contract, of which the advertisement was an offer or tender. That is not the sort of difficulty which presents itself here. If the circular had gone on, "and we undertake to sell to the highest bidder", the reward cases would have applied, and there would have been a good contract in respect of the persons.' As soon as the highest bidder presented himself, says Willes, J, the person who was to hold the vinculum juris on the other side of the contract was ascertained, and it became settled.

AL SMITH LJ: ... It was then said there was no person named in the advertisement with whom any contract was made. That, I suppose, has taken place in every case in which actions on advertisements have been maintained, from the time of *Williams v Carwardine*, and before that, down to the present day. I have nothing to add to what has been said on that subject, except that a person becomes a persona designata and able to sue, when he performs the conditions mentioned in the advertisement.

[*The Company was held liable.*]

Notes

(1) As discussed above,[44] the general rule in English law is that advertisements are invitations to treat. However, exceptions to the English rule may occur, as illustrated by *Carlill v Carbolic Smoke Ball Co*. As we have seen in Chapter 5, in English law a distinction is made between so-called unilateral contracts and bilateral contracts. In summary, a unilateral contract can be characterised as a contract where only one party comes under an obligation: the party who made the offer will be obliged to fulfil his undertaking if the offeree fulfils the conditions of the offer, but the offeree, even if she accepts, is under no obligation to act. The advertiser in *Carlill v Carbolic Smoke Ball Co* did not

---

[44] Above, p 216, Note (6).

intend to create an obligation on anyone's part to use the smoke ball three times daily for two weeks, but indicated his intention to become bound to anybody who performed that act. Advertisements of unilateral contracts may be treated as offers in English law, as is shown by the present case, provided that they sufficiently show the offeror's willingness to be bound in the case of acceptance and that they are sufficiently clear as to the required performance.

(2) In France, the putting up of a reward or prize, which is of course an offer to the public, is considered a 'real' offer in accordance with the general rule set out above.[45]

(3) In German law, offering a reward is dealt with in a different way. The advertisement of the reward is not regarded as an offer to make a contract but as what the Draft Common Frame of reference (DCFR) terms a 'unilateral juridical act' (the German term is *einseitiges Rechtsgeschäft*). In the case of rewards, the reward may be withdrawn at any time before the act has been performed: see §§ 657–661 BGB.[46] This 'non-contractual' analysis means that the reward may be claimed by someone who was unaware of it at the time they did the stipulated act: § 657 BGB, which is not the case in English law.[47]

(4) Will English courts ever treat advertisements for bilateral contracts as offers? In the US case of *Lefkowitz v Great Minneapolis Surplus Store*,[48] a shop had published the following advertisement: 'Saturday 9 AM Sharp 3 Brand New Fur Coats Worth to $100.00 First Come First Served $1 Each'. The plaintiff was the first to present himself at the seller's store and demanded the coat as advertised, indicating his readiness to pay the sale price of $1. The shop refused to sell the coat to the plaintiff, stating that it was not bound by the advertisement. The Court stated that the question whether, in any individual instance, a newspaper advertisement is an offer rather than an invitation to treat depends on the legal intention of the parties and the surrounding circumstances. The Court held that the offer of the sale of the fur coat was clear, definite and explicit, and left nothing open for negotiation, and that the plaintiff was entitled to performance. It is not clear whether the English courts would have decided this case in the same way as the American court but it would certainly be possible for them to do so. There is no absolute rule that an advertisement proposing a bilateral contract cannot amount to an offer, though there is a strong presumption against it.[49]

8.2.A.4 DISPLAYS IN SHOPS

Court of Appeal   **8.9 (EN)**

Pharmaceutical Society v Boots[50]

Placing goods on a shop shelf merely constitutes an invitation to treat. No contract is therefore concluded when a customer takes the goods from the shelf to pay for them at the cash desk.

---

[45] Above, p 216, Notes (1) and (2).
[46] See 5.18 (DE), above, p 119.
[47] See *R v Clarke* (1927) 40 CLR 277 (Australian High Court) (plaintiff admitted that when he did the act he had forgotten about the offer; held, no acceptance of it).
[48] 251 Minn 188; 86 NW 2d 689 (1957).
[49] See above, p 215.
[50] [1953] 1 QB 401.

Facts: A chemist's 'self-service' shop comprised one room around whose walls were shelves on which were laid out certain drugs and medicines specified in Part I of the Poisons List compiled under section 17(1) of the Pharmacy and Poisons Act 1933. These preparations were wrapped in packages and containers with the prices marked on them. A customer entering the shop took a wire basket, selected any articles he required from the shelves, placed them in the basket, and carried them to a cashier at one of the two exits. The cashier then examined the articles the customer wished to purchase, stated the total price and accepted payment. At this stage a registered pharmacist, who was authorised by the chemist to prevent the customer from buying any article if he thought fit, supervised the transaction. In order to decide whether the transaction took place 'under the supervision of a registered pharmacist' as required by the provisions of section 18(1)(a)(iii) of the Pharmacy and Poisons Act 1933, a question arose as to when the contract was concluded.

Held: The sale took place under the supervision of a registered pharmacist.

Judgment: SOMERVELL LJ: ... Is a contract to be regarded as being completed when the article is put into the receptacle, or is this to be regarded as a more organized way of doing what is done already in many types of shops—and a bookseller is perhaps the best example— namely, enabling customers to have free access to what is in the shop, to look at the different articles, and then, ultimately, having got the ones which they wish to buy, to come up to the assistant saying "I want this"? The assistant in 999 times out of 1,000 says "That is all right," and the money passes and the transaction is completed. I agree with what the Lord Chief Justice has said, and with the reasons which he has given for his conclusion, that in the case of an ordinary shop, although goods are displayed and it is intended that customers should go and choose what they want, the contract is not completed until, the customer having indicated the articles which he needs, the shopkeeper, or someone on his behalf, accepts that offer. Then the contract is completed. I can see no reason at all, that being clearly the normal position, for drawing any different implication as a result of this layout.

The Lord Chief Justice, I think, expressed one of the most formidable difficulties in the way of the plaintiffs' contention when he pointed out that, if the plaintiffs are right, once an article has been placed in the receptacle the customer himself is bound and would have no right, without paying for the first article, to substitute an article which he saw later of a similar kind and which he perhaps preferred. I can see no reason for implying from this self-service arrangement any implication other than that which the Lord Chief Justice found in it, namely, that it is a convenient method of enabling customers to see what there is and choose, and possibly put back and substitute, articles which they wish to have, and then to go up to the cashier and offer to buy what they have so far chosen ...

Notes

(1) The decision given in the present case was repeated in *Fisher v Bell*.[51] Thus, in the common situation of goods displayed in a shop and marked with a price, the intention of the seller is determined by means of a general rule:[52] the exhibition of goods in a shop-window or inside a shop—even a self-service shop—with a price attached does not constitute an offer to sell, but is merely an invitation to treat. However, exceptions to the general rule may follow from the special terms of a display or the circumstances in which it is made, and this may lead to the conclusion that the offeror intended to make a real offer.

[51] [1961] 1 QB 394 (DC).
[52] See *Treitel* (n 1 above) para 2-009; McKendrick (n 1 above) 30; A Burrows, *A Restatement of the English Law of Contract* (Oxford University Press, 2016) s 7(5).

(2) The reason for this rule given in the present case is that the consequence of the opposite view, in which the picking up of an article by a customer amounts to an acceptance, is undesirable, because the customer could not, on that view, change his mind and put the article back and substitute it with another. But this is not a valid reason for denying the display of priced goods the character of an offer to sell, because the acceptance of the buyer could be situated at a later moment in time, when he presents himself at the cash desk and pays for the things he has chosen.[53] The better reason to assume that the seller does not make a firm offer by displaying goods is that he wants to reserve the right to refuse to sell when a customer asks for the displayed thing, for example because the thing displayed in the shop-window was the last specimen (this argument has in turn been criticised as having no real application in the vast superstores of today[54]) or possibly because it is thought that shopkeepers should be entitled to refuse to serve people with whom they simply do not wish to do business. Some of the older English cases[55] seem to involve forms of discrimination which today would be unlawful. However, the rule of contract law remains unchanged.

In French law, it has been held that the display of goods in a supermarket or the mere fact of sitting in the driver's seat in a car parked in a dedicated rank for taxis constitutes an offer.[56] The same was held in a self-service store; consequently, the customer made the contract by placing the goods selected in the basket provided, even though she did not have to pay for the goods until she left the store. Therefore, the customer subsequently injured by the goods had a contractual claim against the store. However, insofar as it may be more favourable to the victim to sue in delict (eg under Article 1240 Cciv), judges have sometimes permitted this.[57] There is no specific provision on these points in the revised Civil Code and, as far as consumers are concerned, these should be looked for in the Code de la consommation.

Cour d'appel de Paris, 14 December 1961[58]   **8.10 (FR)**
and *Cass civ (1), 20 October 1964*[59]

Exploding lemonade bottle

A customer in a self-service store makes the contract by placing the goods selected in the basket provided, even though she does not have to pay for the goods until she leaves the store; and if she is subsequently injured by the goods her claim against the store will be in contract.[60] *The manufacturer of the goods will not be liable if the accident was caused by the way the goods had been treated by the store, not by a defect in the goods.*

[53] *Treitel* (n 1 above) para 2-009.
[54] McKendrick (n 1 above) 29–30.
[55] eg *Timothy v Simpson* (1834) 6 C&P 499.
[56] Cass civ (1) 2 December 1969, D 1970, 104 n. CGM; see Malaurie et al (n 1 above) para 465; A Bénabent, *Droit civil, Les obligations* (12th edn, Paris: Montchrestien, 2010) no. 58.
[57] Malaurie et al (n 1 above) nos. 1006 ff.
[58] Gaz Pal 1962.1.135, JCP 1962.II.12547.
[59] DS 1965, 62.
[60] NB: the principle of *non cumul* in French law then prevents the shop being liable in delict.

Facts: Mme Dehen went to Supermag-Rennes' self-service store, and, having taken a basket provided by the store, put in it various items, including a bottle of beer and a bottle of 'Vittel Delices'. She then went to the checkout, where an employee of the supermarket took the items out of the basket. While Mme Dehen waited for her total bill to be rung up she placed the items in her own bag. At this point the bottle of 'Vittel-Delices' bumped gently against the bottle of beer and exploded, and either the bottle cap or a piece of glass struck Mme Dehen in the right eye. She sued the supermarket and the producers of the lemonade, Vittel, in delict.

Held: Mme Dehen could recover from Supermag Rennes in contract but not against Vittel on the basis of former Articles 1382–1384 [now Articles 1240–1242].

(a) Cour d'appel de Paris

Judgment: THE COURT: ... — Whereas ... Mme Dehen has brought an action against Supermag-Rennes and Vittel ... on the basis of [former] Articles 1382, 1383 and 1384 Code civil, and on the basis of Articles 1641 *et seq*

— Whereas Mme Dehen is perfectly entitled to sue Supermag-Rennes but the latter's responsibility can only be contractual, even though the price is payable when the customer leaves the store.

— Whereas when goods are purchased in a self-service store, the sale takes place as soon as the customer, seeing an item marked with a price the client is prepared to accept, places the item in the basket or bag made available to her and which she is required to use until the goods are checked out by the employee at the till ...

(b) Cour de cassation

Judgment: THE COURT:— Whereas however, seeing that, after pointing out correctly that the responsibility of Supermag-Rennes to the victim could only be contractual, the lower court held that the bottle of lemonade, which Mme Dehen had taken from the shelf into her control, exploded when she placed it in her bag, where it bumped gently into a bottle of beer which was already in the bag;

— Whereas the lower court held that the bottle was 'abnormally warm' and that 'the supermarket had failed to foresee, as it should have done, that fizzy drinks left carelessly near a heat source, could constitute a danger'; as against Vittel, the cour d'appel stated that the explosion could be accounted for by the circumstances in which Supermag-Rennes had made the sale, thereby implicitly but necessarily excluding both the goods being dangerous in themselves and the theory that there was some defect in the bottle;

— Whereas on the basis of its findings of fact, the cour d'appel was entitled to allow the principal claim and reject the claim based on the *garantie*.

The appeal fails on both points, for these reasons, the appeal is dismissed.

Notes

(1) Tunc[61] makes the same objection to the reasoning of the Court as led Somervell LJ in the *Boots* case to hold that the contract was not made until the checkout.

(2) If the claim was in contract, the store would be liable unless it could show a *cause étrangère*. Could it be that the Court wanted to find a contract and that the reasoning is result-orientated?

---

[61] RTD civ 1962, 305.

(3) It seems to have been argued that there was no contract until the goods were paid for. This would mean that the customer could refuse to pay for any of the goods even if they had been rung up on the till. At what precise moment did Somervell LJ in the *Boots* case think the contract was made? Would this analysis not have provided a solution to the French case also?

(4) In German law, variations on the common situation discussed above[62] may be treated differently. The display of priced goods in a shop-window, the display of price lists in a shop and the distribution of price lists are all regarded as a request to interested persons to make an offer.[63] There are no cases in German law, but there is academic controversy about whether the display of goods in a self-service shop constitutes an offer. Some authors regard this as an offer that is accepted by the customer by presenting himself with the desired item at the cash desk; others regard the customer who presents himself at the cash desk with the item he wants to buy as the person making the offer, because they want to reserve to the shop owner the right to refuse to conclude a contract. In Germany, it has been argued that, if these situations are not treated as 'invitations to treat', there will be the risk of more acceptances than there are goods for sale.[64] As was observed above[65] in relation to the advertisement cases, this argument is not very strong, since such an offer may be assumed to implicitly contain a clause 'as long as supplies/stock lasts'. Indeed, in the case of a self-service shop, there is no risk that the goods on display are not in stock.

(5) In the PECL the display of goods is presumed to be an offer. Article 2:201 provides:

> (3) A proposal to supply goods or services at stated prices made by a professional supplier in a public advertisement or a catalogue, or by a display of goods, is presumed to be an offer to sell or supply at that price until the stock of goods, or the supplier's capacity to supply the service, is exhausted.

In the CESL, however, this rule was dropped because business representatives argued that it was too uncertain to be workable. What, for example, would count as a trader's 'stock' when the trader was a large company with many branches?

In another common situation, the sale on an auction, it was decided by the English Court of Appeal in *Payne v Cave*[66] that the bidding of a buyer is an offer that is accepted by the auctioneer when he knocks down the hammer. The same view is adopted in French and German law. The BGB provides:

> **§ 156**: Entry into contracts at auctions.
>
> At an auction, a contract is not entered into until the fall of the hammer. A bid lapses if a higher bid is made, or if the auction is closed without the fall of the hammer.[67]

---

[62] See above, Note (1) on p 220.
[63] BGH 16 January 1980, NJW 1980, 1388; Larenz and Wolf (n 1 above) 518; Flume (n 11 above) 636.
[64] Kötz (n 11 above) para 88.
[65] Above, p 216.
[66] (1789) Term R 148, 100 ER 502.
[67] For internet auctions, see below, p 224.

However, the two laws differ in at least one respect. As we will see below, in English law, because the bid is only an offer, it may be withdrawn before the hammer has fallen, whereas in German law the rule is the opposite.

Nowadays there are many 'auction' sites on the internet. A brief and unscientific scan of some suggests they operate in a variety of different ways. In some cases, the site states that the highest bidder will not necessarily get the goods: the vendor may then negotiate with the highest bidder. Others prohibit the bidder from withdrawing a bid even before the time for submitting bids has expired. Moral: before you use an internet auction site to sell or buy goods, read the small print!

8.2.A.5 FINAL REMARKS

The problem of the distinction between the precontractual and the contractual phase is dealt with theoretically in the same way in the three legal systems. A distinction is made between statements constituting offers and statements that merely invite negotiations. First, in order to constitute an offer, the proposal must show the intention of the party who makes it to be bound in the case of acceptance. If that party makes a reservation as to his final decision to enter into a contract—eg 'subject to confirmation'—then in general his proposal is not an offer. In other words, a proposal must be sufficiently definite. (In addition, as we will see in the next chapter, it must contain the essential elements of the contract.)

In certain common situations the intention of the party making the proposal is determined by way of general rules which may differ between legal systems. Thus, for example, in French law an advertisement offering to sell a certain thing for a certain price is regarded as an offer, whereas in German and in English law such an advertisement is deemed an invitation to make an offer.

All three legal systems leave the final decision concerning the conclusion of the contract to the parties themselves in that no contract is concluded as long as elements that are considered essential by the parties or by one of them have not yet been agreed upon.

8.2.B REVOCABILITY OF OFFER

In this section we consider whether, or in what circumstances, an offer that has been made may be revoked before the offeror has received an acceptance. We will see that the laws differ significantly on this issue. The Principles of European Contract Law (PECL) and UNIDROIT Principles of International Commercial Contracts (UNIDROIT PICC) also differ.

Principles of European Contract Law   **8.11 (INT)**

Article 1:303: Notice
(1) Subject to paragraphs (4) and (5), any notice becomes effective when it reaches the addressee ...

...

(5) A notice has no effect if a withdrawal of it reaches the addressee before or at the same time as the notice.

Article 2:202: Revocation of an Offer

(1) An offer may be revoked if the revocation reaches the offeree before it has dispatched its acceptance or, in cases of acceptance by conduct, before the contract has been concluded under Article 2:205(2) or (3).

(2) An offer made to the public can be revoked by the same means as were used to make the offer.

(3) However, a revocation of an offer is ineffective if:

(a) the offer indicates that it is revocable; or

(b) it states a fixed time for its acceptance; or

(c) it was reasonable for the offeree to rely on the offer as being irrevocable and the offeree has acted in reliance on the offer.

UNIDROIT Principles   **8.12 (INT)**

Article 2.1.3: Withdrawal of offer

(1) An offer becomes effective when it reaches the offeree.

(2) An offer, even if it is irrevocable, may be withdrawn if the withdrawal reaches the offeree before or at the same time as the offer.

Article 2.1.4: Revocation of offer

(1) Until a contract is concluded an offer may be revoked if the revocation reaches the offeree before it has dispatched an acceptance.

(2) However, an offer cannot be revoked

a. if it indicates, whether by stating a fixed time for acceptance or otherwise, that it is irrevocable; or

b. if it was reasonable for the offeree to rely on the offer as being irrevocable and the offeree has acted in reliance on the offer.[68]

> *Notes*
>
> (1) The texts quoted draw a distinction between withdrawing an offer that has not yet become effective, for example because it has not yet been communicated to the offeree, and revoking an offer that has been made.
>
> (2) Both allow for the withdrawal of an offer if the withdrawal is communicated before or at the same time as the offer is communicated.
>
> (3) Both provide also that generally an offer may be withdrawn before the offeree has dispatched its acceptance; but also that in some circumstances an offer may be irrevocable. The formulation in PECL Article 2:202(3) is perhaps a little more precise than that in UNIDROIT PICC Article 2.1.4(2).
>
> (4) Both provide that the offer can no longer be revoked once the offeree has dispatched an acceptance.

The revised French Code civil also distinguishes between withdrawal of an offer that has not yet reached the offeree and withdrawal of one that has:

---

[68] See also CISG Arts 15 and 16, which are identical to these provisions.

Code civil   **8.13 (FR)**

Article 1115: An offer may be withdrawn freely as long as it has not reached the person to whom it was addressed.

Article 1116: An offer may not be withdrawn before the expiry of any period fixed by the offeror or, if no such period has been fixed, the end of a reasonable period.

...

Notes

(1) The Code civil does not adopt the PECL's use of the words 'withdrawal' and 'revocation' to differentiate the two situations; in both it uses the word '*rétractée*'.

(2) Article 1115 Cciv does not mention whether the withdrawal must be communicated.

(3) Article 1115 Cciv is subject to the important exception of Article 1116. We will return to points (2) and (3) below.[69]

8.2.B.1 WHEN IS AN OFFER COMMUNICATED?

A preliminary issue is, at what point is an offer 'communicated' to the offeree? The same issue can rise with other communications such as the withdrawal or the revocation of an offer.

The German Civil Code contains a general provision on the moment any declaration directed to an absent person becomes effective:

BGB   **8.14 (DE)**

§ 130: Effectiveness of a declaration of intent to absent parties

(1) A declaration of intent that is to be made to another becomes effective, if made in his absence, at the point of time when his declaration reaches him. It does not become effective if a [withdrawal[70]] reaches the other previously or at the same time.

(cf BW Article 3:37(3)). The question whether an effective offer has been made is of more importance in German law, where the normal rule is that an offer cannot be revoked, than it is in systems under which the offer remains revocable until accepted.

RG, 25 October 1917[71]   **8.15 (DE)**

Delivery to a housemaid

An effective offer cannot be withdrawn. An offer which has been received by the offeree's employee is effective, and cannot therefore be withdrawn, even if it has not come to the attention of the offeree.

---

[69] See below, pp 229 ff.

[70] According to the terminology adopted here. The Ministry of Justice translation refers to this as a 'revocation'.

[71] RGZ 91, 60.

Facts: On 19 and 20 November 1915 the plaintiff requested, by way of newspaper advertisements, the submission of offers for the supply of military drill textiles. In response, Messrs B on 20 November offered him 'without engagement or obligation', according to sample, pure linen drill approximately 84 cm in width at a price of 0.80 marks per metre, 'pure net, prompt cash, approximately 20,000 m available for immediate delivery'. The plaintiff replied on 22 November, having on that day received Messrs B's letter, stating that he accepted the offer of 20,000 m and requesting confirmation by telegram. Messrs B wired him at 5.15 pm on the same day in the following terms: 'Organised only on the basis of telegraphic transfer of 1,000 marks today, balance payable cash on delivery'. That telegram was delivered at 7 pm to the plaintiff's residence, the plaintiff being out at the time. However, Messrs B then came to a different decision and asked the telegraph office to return their telegram. The telegraph office sent an official wire to the St office, requesting the latter to stop the telegram sent to the plaintiff. However, since that telegram had already been delivered, it arranged for the telegraph messenger to get the housemaid of the plaintiff, who was still out of the house, to hand it back.

Held: The defendant was not entitled to withdraw the offer.

Judgment: 2. The decision in the present case is founded on the import of § 130 BGB. The telegram sent by Messrs B, which was subsequently taken back, contained a contractual offer made to the plaintiff, and thus a declaration of intent which had to be received in order to be effective. It became effective, and the offer thus became binding (§§ 145, 146 BGB), at the moment in time when it reached the plaintiff. A statement contained in a letter, to which a telegraphic communication must be regarded as equivalent, is deemed to reach its recipient upon being delivered to the latter's address, even where it is handed to a member of the recipient's family or to a domestic servant, and irrespective of whether the recipient is at home or not; he is thereby given the opportunity of taking cognisance of its contents, this being an essential element of the concept of a communication 'reaching' its recipient (RGZ, Vol 50, p 191, 194, Vol 56, p 262, Vol 60, p 334). It does not matter, therefore, whether it actually comes to the knowledge of the recipient; what matters is that it is placed at his disposal, so that he is given the opportunity of taking cognizance of it. It is for that reason, as stated in the decision of the court below, that the second sentence of § 130(1) additionally provides that the withdrawal of a declaration of intent needing to be received by its addressee will be effective only if it reaches the recipient before or at the same time as the initial declaration of intent; in such circumstances, the time at which the communication actually comes to the knowledge of its recipient is wholly immaterial. According to those principles, the offer made in the present case by Messrs B to the plaintiff reached him when it was handed, in his absence, to his housemaid, with the result that the party by whom the telegram was sent was bound by his contractual offer on the terms contained therein. The withdrawal contained in the second telegram was too late, since at the time when it was delivered, or rather could and should have been delivered, that is to say, when the telegraph messenger arrived at the plaintiff's residence bearing the withdrawal telegram, the proposal concerning implementation of the contract had already reached the plaintiff.

In opposition to this, the appellant relies, nevertheless, on the view occasionally advanced by certain academic legal authors, which the Landgericht [Regional Court] has likewise seen fit to adopt in its judgment, to the effect that it would be contrary to the principle of good faith if the recipient of a contractual offer were able to rely on that offer to his benefit, and could derive rights from it, notwithstanding that the contractual offer, despite having reached him earlier, only actually came to his knowledge at the same time as the withdrawal of that offer. However, that view is not compatible with the clear provision contained in the second sentence of § 130(1), which cannot be excluded. The sole decisive factor, as regards both the sender and the recipient, is the time at which the communication reached the latter; by contrast, the time at which it actually came to his knowledge is immaterial, as regards both the offer and the withdrawal thereof ...

Notes

(1) This German case is concerned with the question when an offer made to an absent person becomes effective. This question is of relevance under German law because, although generally an offer once made is not revocable, any declaration, including an offer, may be retracted before it has become effective. In accordance with the terminology of the PECL, CISG and the UNIDROIT PICC, such a retraction will be described as a 'withdrawal'. The term 'revocation' can thus be reserved for retraction of the offer *after* it has become effective, also in accordance with PECL, CISG and the UNIDROIT PICC. The question of the revocability of an offer that is made orally to a present person or over the telephone does not arise, since such an offer is generally assumed to lapse if it is not accepted immediately[72]—unless the offeror intended it to remain valid for a longer time. Of greater importance is the question of the revocability of an offer when a contract is to be concluded *inter absentes*.

(2) In the case the Reichsgericht states that, in accordance with the concept of *zugehen* (reaching), it is not necessary that the offeree has actually been informed of the offer; it is sufficient that the letter or telegram containing the offer has been delivered at his house. Until that moment, the offer can be withdrawn by retracting it from the post or by sending a second letter or telegram that reaches the offeree before or at the same time as the offer; after that moment withdrawal is no longer possible, even if the offeree is informed of the withdrawal at the same moment as of the offer itself. The same decision was given in RG 8 February 1902.[73]

(3) At least for offers and communications in general, most laws hold that the communication can be effective once the message is available to the recipient, whether or not he or she has actually read it: see eg PECL Article 1:103 and the English case of *Holwell Securities Ltd v Hughes*.[74] Some laws, as we will see, apply a different rule to postal acceptances; others require communication in this case also. For example, the CSIG states:

> Art 24: For the purposes of this Part of the Convention, an offer, declaration of acceptance or any other indication of intention "reaches" the addressee when it is made orally to him or delivered by any other means to him personally, to his place of business or mailing address or, if he does not have a place of business or mailing address, to his habitual residence.

(4) When does 'communication' take place in the case of email? According to CISG Advisory Council Opinion No. 1, Electronic Communications under CISG (August 15, 2003), Opinion on Article 24:

> The term "reaches" corresponds to the point in time when an electronic communication has entered the addressee's server, provided that the addressee expressly or impliedly has consented to receiving electronic communications of that type, in that format, and to that address.

---

[72] Zweigert and Kötz (n 1 above) 364.
[73] RGZ 50, 191.
[74] [1974] 1 WLR 155 (CA).

(5) The possibility of *withdrawal* of an offer is of particular importance in German law, because once the offer has reached the offeree, it cannot in principle be revoked: under § 145 BGB, an offeror is bound by his offer unless he has excluded this engagement (see the next note).

8.2.B.2 REVOCATION OF AN OFFER

In German law, although the main rule is that an offeror is bound by his offer, the offeror may exclude the binding force of the offer under § 145 BGB. He may do this by using terms such as *freibleibend, ohne obligo* or *Zwischenverkauf vorbehalten*.[75] As has been seen in 8.2.A,[76] there is some uncertainty about the legal effect of such terms. It is certain, however, that a statement containing such terms may be revoked before it is accepted. However, if the offer is irrevocable, any purported revocation is simply ineffective; the offer may be accepted by the offeree and a binding contract will result. That is not the case in every law.

Cass civ, 17 December 1958[77]   **8.16 (FR)**

Chalet for sale

Where it is expressly or implicitly understood that an offer is to remain open for a certain period, the offer cannot be withdrawn within that period without incurring liability.

Facts: By letter of 11 August 1954, Isler informed Chastan that he was willing to sell to the latter a chalet owned by him, at a price of FF2,500,000. From the judgment, it appears that Chastan had written to Isler, saying that he planned to visit the chalet on the 15 or 16 August, and that Isler apparently approved this arrangement in his letter. Having visited the chalet four days later, Chastan notified Isler by telegram the following day that he accepted that offer. On 17 August 1954 he confirmed that acceptance by letter, stating that he was willing to pay the purchase price in cash upon the signing of the transfer deed. Chastan served formal notice on Isler on 6 September 1954, requiring the latter to accept the purchase price and to hand over the keys; Isler did not comply with that notice, whereupon Chastan brought legal proceedings. In the proceedings, Isler alleged that he could not have sold the chalet to the plaintiff on 11 August 1954, since, as at that date, he had already sold it to Puy. Puy intervened in the proceedings, stating that the sale of the property to him had been concluded at the beginning of August and that it had been formally completed by a private contract in writing on 14 August 1954, that act having been accompanied by a payment on account of one million francs.

Held: Chastan succeeded in his claim.

Judgment: … —Whereas whilst an offer may in principle be revoked at any time prior to its acceptance, that is not the position where the person making it has expressly or impliedly undertaken not to revoke it before a certain date;

— Whereas in the present case, the contested judgment, having acknowledged that the letter of 11 August 1954 constituted 'merely an offer to sell' which could 'in principle be revoked at any time prior to being accepted', goes on to state: 'however, Isler, knowing from a letter from Chastan dated 9 August that the latter was proposing to visit the

---

[75] Kötz (n 11 above) para 88; Flume (n 11 above) 642.
[76] See the *Aeroplane Charter* case, 8.06 (DE), above, p 212.
[77] D 1959.1.33.

chalet on 15 or 16 August, and having authorised him to do so in his reply of 11 August, tacitly undertook to keep his offer open during the period thus envisaged, that is to say, until after the proposed visit had taken place', and that Isler could not therefore have withdrawn from the transaction on 14 August without 'incurring liability' …

— Whereas it follows that the contested judgment did not infringe the legislation referred to in the appellant's pleadings and is justified in law.

Cass civ (3), 7 May 2008[78]   **8.17 (FR)**

Buyer's attempt to revoke

A party who makes an offer that must be accepted by a fixed date is undertaking not to revoke the offer before that date.

Facts: On 24 June 2000, a buyer made an offer to purchase the seller's property leaving three days for the seller to accept it. The buyer revoked its offer on 26 June 2000. However, on 27 June 2000, the real estate agent sent a letter to the buyer informing him that the seller had already accepted the offer.

Held: The cour d'appel held that the offer was already revoked (26 June) when the seller sent its letter of acceptance (27 June).

Judgment: In so ruling, whereas if an offer to buy or sell can in principle be revoked so long as it has not been accepted, it is otherwise if the person who made the offer undertook not to withdraw it before a certain time, and whereas it had noted that [the sellers] had a deadline until 27 June 2000 to give their agreement, and that it resulted that [the buyer] had undertaken to maintain its offer until that date, the cour d'appel violated [Article 1103 of the Code civil].

Notes

(1) In French law, the starting point was that an offer is revocable. The Cour de cassation held in a decision of Cass civ (1), 3 February 1919:[79]

> As an offer is not in itself binding on the offeror, it may in general be revoked so long as it has not been validly accepted.

In practice, revocability may lead to insecurity and injustice. The addressee of an offer may incur costs in reliance on the offer (eg travelling costs to examine the property on offer), turn down other offers or change his position, for example by resigning from his job or by terminating his tenancy. French case law has therefore strongly mitigated the principle of revocability and, in some situations, has reversed it. As mentioned above and cited again on the following page, the revised Code civil in its Article 1116(1), provides that an 'offer may not be withdrawn before the expiry of any period fixed by the offeror or, if no such period has been fixed, the end of a reasonable period'.

…

---

[78] No. 07-11690, Bull civ III no. 79.
[79] Cass civ (3) 7 May 2008, no. 07-11690, Bull III no. 79, DP 1923.I.126.

(2) So if the offer expressly contains a period within which it has to be accepted (*offre avec délai*), the offeror is obliged to keep the offer open during that period.[80] Further, as the *Chalet for Sale* case shows, if the offer does not expressly contain a period for its acceptance, it may be implied that the offeror tacitly promised to keep his offer open during a certain period.[81] This now stems directly (without having recourse to an implied term) from Article 1116, see below.

(3) It followed from the *Chalet for Sale* case that, in French law, the consequence of the obligation to keep the offer open during a certain period is not that a revocation of the offer lacks effect, but that the offeror is liable to pay damages for the loss the offeree has suffered from the untimely revocation. This stands in sharp contrast with the situation where an option to buy has been granted, see Article 1124, below.[82]

(4) It also followed that in French law even an offer to a particular individual can be effectively revoked as long as it has not been accepted without communicating the fact of the revocation to the offeree:[83] for example, an offer to sell goods will be effectively revoked through a sale of the goods to a third party whether or not the offeree knows of the sale. This rule, which may be linked to the subjective nature of the notion of agreement in French law,[84] is, as we will see, in contrast to German law and English law. But it should be noted that even before 2016 it seemed the offeror might be liable under former Article 1382 CCiv (ie in delict) for intentionally or carelessly misleading the offeree.

These points are now confirmed by the revised Article 1116, which we have referred to earlier but now consider in full.

Code civil   **8.18 (FR)**

Article 1116: An offer may not be withdrawn before the expiry of any period fixed by the offeror or, if no such period has been fixed, the end of a reasonable period.

The withdrawal of an offer in contravention of this prohibition prevents the contract being concluded.

The person who thus withdraws an offer incurs extra-contractual liability under the conditions set out by the general law, and has no obligation to compensate the loss of profits which were expected from the contract.

Notes

(1) In a case like *Chalet for Sale*, the offer (once communicated to the offeree) now cannot be withdrawn for a reasonable period, which presumably will include the time needed for the prospective purchaser to inspect the property as has been agreed. This now stems directly (without having recourse to an implied term) from Article 1116,

---

[80] See, eg, Cass civ (3) 10 May 1968, no. 66-13187, Bull civ III no. 209.
[81] See also the French cases mentioned below, pp 245–46.
[82] See 10.22 (FR), below, p 340.
[83] Cass civ (3) 17 September 2014, no. 13-21824, Bull civ III no. 108.
[84] See above, p 104.

which prevents an offer that has reached the offeree from being revoked for a 'reasonable period'.

(2) However, it now seems that it is not necessary for there to be some arrangement between the offeror and the offeree to give the offeree time to consider the offer: the rule that the offer cannot be revoked for 'reasonable time' applies to all offers.

(3) The damages provided for by the third paragraph play an important role in compensating losses arising from the revocation of an offer.

It will be seen that the irrevocability of an offer in French law does not lead to the same results as in German law. In German law, the consequence of the binding force of an offer is that its purported revocation has no effect: the offeree can still accept and thus conclude a contract. The same is true, it would seem, under the PECL, CISG and the UNIDROIT PICC. In French law, we have seen that the consequence of the obligation to keep the offer open during a certain period is not that a revocation of the offer lacks effect, but that the offeror is liable to pay damages for the loss the offeree has suffered from the untimely revocation. However, the 2016 version of the Code civil contains a new sub-section on pre-emption agreements and unilateral promises, which contains the following:

Code civil

8.19 (FR)

Article 1124: A unilateral promise is a contract by which one party, the promisor, grants another, the beneficiary, a right to have the option to conclude a contract whose essential elements are determined, and for the formation of which only the consent of the beneficiary is missing.

Revocation of the promise during the period allowed to the beneficiary to exercise the option does not prevent the formation of the contract which was promised.

A contract concluded in breach of a unilateral promise with a third party who knew of its existence, is a nullity.

Notes

(1) Thus it is possible in French law to create, by way of a pre-emption agreement or a unilateral promise, what is in effect an offer that cannot be revoked and which the offeree can accept and turn the option into a binding contract.

(2) The other article in the new subsection is Article 1123, which allows the parties to enter a 'pre-emption agreement'. This is an agreement that if one party (A) decides to enter a contract, he will make the first proposal for that contract to the other party (B). If A makes a contract with a third person without first offering it to B, B may recover his loss; or, if the third party knew of the pre-emption agreement, B may demand that he is substituted for the third party.

Dutch law is a mixture of German and French law. As in German law, an offer can be withdrawn. This rule is provided in the section on unilateral juristic acts (Article 3:37(5) BW). In addition, an offer can be revoked unless the offer contains a period within which it should be accepted or a notice concerning the acceptance of the offer has been sent (Article 6:219 BW). To this extent, Dutch law is similar to French law. However, the withdrawal or revocation must normally be communicated to the offeree to be effective (Article 3:37) and it seems that an uncommunicated or wrongful revocation is simply ineffective, so the offer can still be accepted. Article 6:219(1) BW states:

> An offer may be revoked, unless it includes a term for acceptance, or irrevocability results otherwise from the offer.

The position in English law is similar to German law in that if A has made an offer to B, B can accept it and create a contract unless A has communicated its revocation of the offer, or at least B knows that A no longer wants to proceed. But in another respect, English law is very different to the other laws: the offer may be revoked, even if the offeror promised that it would be kept open for a certain period.

Court of Appeal   **8.20 (EN)**

Dickinson v Dodds[85]

An offer to sell property may be revoked before acceptance even if the offeror had agreed to keep the offer open until a later time, and the revocation may be effective without any formal notice to the person to whom the offer is made. It is sufficient if that person has actual knowledge that the person who made the offer has done some act inconsistent with the continuance of the offer, such as selling the property to a third person.

Facts: The defendant, the owner of property, signed a document which purported to be an agreement to sell the property to the plaintiff at a fixed price. But a postscript was added, which he also signed: 'This offer to be left over until Friday 9 AM.' In the afternoon of the Thursday, the plaintiff was informed by a Mr Berry that the defendant had been offering or agreeing to sell the property to Thomas Allan. Thereupon the plaintiff, at about half-past seven in the evening, went to the house of Mrs Burgess, the mother-in-law of the defendant, where he was then staying, and left with her a formal acceptance in writing of the offer to sell the property. According to the evidence of Mrs Burgess, this document never in fact reached the defendant, she having forgotten to give it to him.

On the following (Friday) morning, at about seven o'clock, Berry, who was acting as agent for the plaintiff, found the defendant at the Darlington railway station, and handed to him a duplicate of the acceptance by the plaintiff, and explained to the defendant its purport. He replied that it was too late, as he had sold the property. A few minutes later the plaintiff himself found the defendant entering a railway carriage, and handed him another duplicate of the notice of acceptance, but the defendant declined to receive it, saying, 'You are too late. I have sold the property'. The plaintiff claimed there was a contract and sought specific performance.

Held: The document amounted only to an offer, which might be revoked at any time before acceptance, and that a sale to a third person which came to the knowledge of the person to whom the offer was made was an effectual revocation of the offer.

Judgment: JAMES LJ: The document, though beginning 'I hereby agree to sell,' was nothing but an offer, and was only intended to be an offer, for the Plaintiff himself tells us that he required time to consider whether he would enter into an agreement or not. Unless both parties had then agreed there was no concluded agreement then made; it was in effect and substance only an offer to sell. The Plaintiff, being minded not to complete the

---

[85] (1876) 2 Ch D 463.

bargain at that time, added this memorandum—'This offer to be left over until Friday, 9 o'clock AM, 12th June, 1874.' That shews it was only an offer. There was no consideration given for the undertaking or promise, to whatever extent it may be considered binding, to keep the property unsold until 9 o'clock on Friday morning; but apparently Dickinson was of opinion, and probably Dodds was of the same opinion, that he (Dodds) was bound by that promise, and could not in any way withdraw from it, or retract it, until 9 o'clock on Friday morning, and this probably explains a good deal of what afterwards took place. But it is clear settled law, on one of the clearest principles of law, that this promise, being a mere nudum pactum, was not binding, and that at any moment before a complete acceptance by Dickinson of the offer, Dodds was as free as Dickinson himself. Well, that being the state of things, it is said that the only mode in which Dodds could assert that freedom was by actually and distinctly saying to Dickinson, 'Now I withdraw my offer.' It appears to me that there is neither principle nor authority for the proposition that there must be an express and actual withdrawal of the offer, or what is called a retractation. It must, to constitute a contract, appear that the two minds were at one, at the same moment of time, that is, that there was an offer continuing up to the time of the acceptance. If there was not such a continuing offer, then the acceptance comes to nothing. Of course it may well be that the one man is bound in some way or other to let the other man know that his mind with regard to the offer has been changed; but in this case, beyond all question, the Plaintiff knew that Dodds was no longer minded to sell the property to him as plainly and clearly as if Dodds had told him in so many words, 'I withdraw the offer.' This is evident from the Plaintiff's own statements in the bill.

The Plaintiff says in effect that, having heard and knowing that Dodds was no longer minded to sell to him, and that he was selling or had sold to someone else, thinking that he could not in point of law withdraw his offer, meaning to fix him to it, and endeavouring to bind him, 'I went to the house where he was lodging, and saw his mother-in-law, and left with her an acceptance of the offer, knowing all the while that he had entirely changed his mind. I got an agent to watch for him at 7 o'clock the next morning, and I went to the train just before 9 o'clock, in order that I might catch him and give him my notice of acceptance just before 9 o'clock, and when that occurred he told my agent, and he told me, you are too late, and he then threw back the paper.' It is to my mind quite clear that before there was any attempt at acceptance by the Plaintiff, he was perfectly well aware that Dodds had changed his mind, and that he had in fact agreed to sell the property to Allan. It is impossible, therefore, to say there was ever that existence of the same mind between the two parties which is essential in point of law to the making of an agreement. I am of opinion, therefore, that the Plaintiff has failed to prove that there was any binding contract between Dodds and himself.

Bill for specific performance dismissed.

Notes

(1) English law is completely opposite to German law with respect to the revocability of offers: offers are freely revocable. Further, unlike French case law, English case law holds that offers are revocable regardless of whether they contain a time limit for their acceptance or even an express promise that the offer will not be revoked for a certain period. This is because of the English doctrine of consideration.[86] No binding

---

[86] On which see ch 11.

obligation can arise for the offeror to keep his offer open, even if he expressly fixes a period during which his offer may be accepted, since there is no consideration from the other party for such a promise. As Best CJ said in *Routledge v Grant*:[87]

> Here is a proposal by the Defendant to take property on certain terms; namely that he should be let into possession in July. In that proposal he gives the plaintiff six weeks to consider; but if six weeks are given on one side to accept an offer, the other has six weeks to put an end to it.

(2) It should be noted that an offer can be made irrevocable by an agreement between offeror and offeree in English law; the agreement is often called an 'option'. The option will normally be granted by deed to overcome the problem of consideration,[88] or the promise to keep the offer open will be expressly stated to be for nominal consideration such as £1.[89] In this case the offeree may accept the offer despite any purported revocation by the offeror: *Mountford v Scott*.[90] Such 'option agreements' are not uncommon with sales of land.

(3) US law goes further. UCC § 2-205 provides that if written offers relating to commercial sale contracts are stated to be binding, they may not be withdrawn during the prescribed period or, if no period is prescribed, for a reasonable period not exceeding three months.[91] The English Law Commission at one point considered recommending a similar rule but the project was not taken forward.[92]

(4) The more general question of when the offer becomes effective may also arise in English law, for example, where there is an issue whether the period of time for acceptance of an offer has expired, so that the offer has lapsed.[93] In English law, the two options are (a) the moment that the offer was dispatched and (b) the moment it was received by the offeree.[94] The answer is the same as that under German law: the offer is effective when it reaches the offeree, or at least when it is delivered to his house.[95] If the offer and a withdrawal of it arrive simultaneously, there is no effective offer.[96]

(5) The CISG and the UNIDROIT PICC distinguish between the moment the offer becomes effective[97] and the moment at which a period for acceptance begins to run.[98] In French law these questions do not seem to be of much practical importance.

---

[87] (1828) 4 Bing 653, 660.

[88] For the effect of a deed as a substitute for consideration, see below, p 351; and for the requirements, see 12.7 (EN), below, p 405.

[89] On 'nominal consideration' see below, p 351.

[90] [1975] Ch 258 (CA).

[91] See 11.5 (US), below, p 352.

[92] See The Law Commission, *Firm Offers* (Consultation Paper), Law Com CP No 60 (London: Her Majesty's Stationery Office, 1975). For an appraisal of the proposals which considers practice in the building industry, see R Lewis, 'Contracts between Businessmen: Reform of the Law of Firm Offers' (1982) 9 British Journal of Law & Society 153. An extract from this article will be found below, p 240.

[93] *Treitel* (n 1 above) para 2–015; see further below, p 243.

[94] See the similar problem, but of more practical importance, as to the moment at which the acceptance becomes effective, see below, p 256.

[95] cf *Holwell Securities Ltd v Hughes* [1974] 1 WLR 155 (CA) (acceptance of offer which required notice to the offeror, despite the 'postal rule', on which see below, pp 260 ff said to be effective on delivery through offeror's letter box).

[96] cf *Countess of Dunmore v Alexander* (1830) 9 S 190 (a Scottish case).

[97] See Art 15 CISG and Art 2.1.3 UNIDROIT PICC.

[98] Art 20 CISG and Art. 2.1.8 UNIDROIT PICC.

> (6) Like German law, and in contrast to French law, English law is to the effect that an offer can be revoked only through communication of the revocation to the offeree.[99]

The net result is that under English law it is risky for the offeree to rely on the offer; he should not assume that it will not be withdrawn unless he has secured an 'option' and therefore should not act on a simple offer. Sometimes this rule can cause hardship, however, particularly where the offer is one for a unilateral contract in the English sense—an offer like the one in *Carlill v Carbolic Smoke Ball Co Ltd*[100] which is to be accepted by performing. What happens if the offeree starts to perform only to receive notice of revocation before he has managed to complete his performance?

Court of Appeal   **8.21 (EN)**

Daulia v Four Millbank Nominees[101]

A unilateral contract cannot be revoked once the offeree has completed performance of the unilateral condition; and it may be irrevocable once he has begun to perform.

Facts: The defendants were mortgagees of a portfolio of properties which, the mortgagor being in default, they were entitled to sell. The plaintiffs were anxious to purchase the properties and made several unsuccessful offers. However, on 21 December 1976, the parties agreed terms and further agreed to exchange contracts the next day. When the plaintiffs attended the defendant's offices on 22 December to exchange contracts the defendants, who had in the meantime found another purchaser at a substantially increased price, refused to complete the sale. The plaintiffs brought an action against the defendants claiming damages for breach of contract. The plaintiffs alleged that on 21 December an agent of the defendants' had promised the plaintiffs that if the plaintiffs procured a banker's draft for the deposit, attended at the defendants' offices at 10 o'clock the next morning and there tendered to the defendants the plaintiff's part of the contract engrossed and signed together with the banker's draft, the defendants would enter into a contract ('the written contract') with the plaintiffs for the sale of the properties. The plaintiffs further alleged that the agent's promise and the plaintiffs' performance of the conditions stipulated constituted a contract ('the oral contract') and that by refusing to accept the plaintiffs' tender of the engrossed and signed contract and banker's draft the defendants were in breach of the oral contract.

Held: The plaintiff's argument on this point succeeded. [However, the court held that the contract was one for the disposition of an interest in land and the necessary formal requirements[102] had not been complied with, so it was not enforceable. This aspect of the judgments is not included below.]

Judgment: GOFF LJ: … The concept of a unilateral or "if contract" is somewhat anomalous, because it is clear that, at all events until the offeree starts to perform the condition, there is no contract at all, but merely an offer which the offeror is free to revoke.

Doubts have been expressed whether the offeror becomes bound so soon as the offeree starts to perform or satisfy the condition, or only when he has fully done so.

In my judgment, however, we are not concerned in this case with any such problem, because in my view the plaintiffs had fully performed or satisfied the condition when they presented themselves at the time and place appointed with a banker's draft for the

---

[99] See *Byrne v Van Tienhoven*, 8.45 (EN), below, p 261.
[100] 8.8 (EN), above, p 217.
[101] [1978] Ch 231.
[102] See below, ch 12.

deposit, and their part of the written contract for sale duly engrossed and signed and there tendered the same, which I understand to mean proffered it for exchange. ...

Whilst I think the true view of a unilateral contract must in general be that the offeror is entitled to require full performance of the condition which he has imposed and short of that he is not bound, that must be subject to one important qualification, which stems from the fact that there must be an implied obligation on the part of the offeror not to prevent the condition becoming satisfied, which obligation it seems to me must arise as soon as the offeree starts to perform. Until then the offeror can revoke the whole thing, but once the offeree has embarked on performance it is too late for the offeror to revoke his offer.

Buckley LJ: ... I agree with Goff LJ that the defendants could not withdraw their offer once the plaintiffs had embarked upon those acts.

In my opinion, the re-amended statement of claim is capable of supporting a conclusion that a contract was made on December 22, 1976, under which the first defendants became bound to enter into a written agreement of sale of the properties to the plaintiffs upon the terms which, as alleged in paragraph 7 of the re-amended statement of claim, had been finally agreed on the previous day.

Notes

(1) Because the principle of free revocability in English law may cause particular hardship to an offeree who has partly performed the act required under a unilateral contract,[103] English courts have decided that in some such cases the offeror can no longer revoke once the offeree has started to perform. *Daulia v Four Millbank Nominees* contains dicta to this effect (the Court held that on the facts the offeree had completed the required performance). Another example is *Errington v Errington*.[104] A father had bought a house for his son and daughter-in-law, paying part of the price (£250) in cash and borrowing the rest (£500) from a building society on the security of the house, the loan being repayable with interest by instalments over a period. The father told the daughter-in-law that the £250 was a present to her and her husband, handed the building society book to her, and said that if and when she and her husband had paid all the instalments the house would be their property. The daughter-in-law paid the instalments as they fell due. Then the father died and his widow claimed the house. It was held that the father's promise was a unilateral contract, a promise of the house in return for the young couple's act of paying the instalments. The promise could not be revoked by him once the couple entered on performance of the act, but it would cease to bind him if they left their side of the bargain incomplete and unperformed. Lord Denning said that the father expressly promised the couple that the property should belong to them as soon as the mortgage was paid, and impliedly promised that, so long as they paid the instalments to the building society, they should be allowed to remain in possession. Thus, the obligation not to revoke was regarded as stemming from an implied promise not to revoke.

(2) The English courts will not imply a term preventing the offeror revoking the offer, however, if they think that the offeree was taking, or should take, the risk that the

---

[103] See for the notion of a unilateral contract the discussion of *Carlill v Carbolic Smoke Ball Co*, above, p 118.
[104] [1952] 1 KB 290 (CA).

offer might be revoked. Thus, in *Luxor (Eastbourne) Ltd v Cooper*[105] an estate agent was promised a large commission if he found a buyer who purchased two cinemas from the defendants for at least £185. The agent introduced a buyer who was willing to pay that price but, before the sale could be completed, the defendants decided to withdraw the cinemas from the market. The House of Lords refused to imply a term that the defendants would not prevent the plaintiff from earning his commission by withdrawing the properties from the market. Lord Russell said that the agent took the risk 'in the hope of a substantial remuneration for comparatively small exertion' and continued, sardonically: 'A sum of £10,000, the equivalent of the remuneration of a year's work by a Lord Chancellor, for work done within a period of 8 or 9 days is no mean reward, and one well worth a risk.'[106]

(3) Some English writers prefer a different explanation of why the offeror is not free to revoke the offer once the offeree has begun to perform. This is that the offer is accepted when the offeree begins to perform, though obviously he must complete the performance before the other party will become liable to make the promised counter-performance.[107] On this view, *Luxor (Eastbourne) Ltd v Cooper*[108] is explained as a case in which the parties implicitly agreed that there should be a *locus poenitentiae* (ie either party should be free to withdraw) until the sale had been completed.[109]

It is instructive to compare English and US law on the revocability of offers. In US law the principle of free revocability used to prevail as in English law.[110] US law, as English law, also allows an exception to the main rule in the case of unilateral contracts. The Restatement 2d of Contracts provides:

> § 45: If an offer for a unilateral contract is made, and part of the consideration requested in the offer is given or tendered by the offeree in response thereto, the offeror is bound by a contract, the duty of immediate performance of which is conditional on the full consideration being given or tendered within the time stated in the offer, or, if no time stated therein, within a reasonable time.

In contrast, if an offer for a bilateral contract is revoked even after the offeree has relied on it, in English law there is unlikely to be any protection (unless the offer is a binding option, as described earlier).[111] However, in US law even the possibly harsh effects of the rule of free revocability in relation to bilateral contracts appear to have been mitigated. In *Drennan v Star Paving Co*,[112] a general contractor, who was preparing to compete for the award of a construction contract, solicited bids from various subcontractors for the paving work to be done on the project. A subcontractor submitted the lowest bid and the

---

[105] [1941] AC 108 (HL).
[106] Ibid 126.
[107] See *Treitel* (n 1 above) paras 2-051–2-053; *Chitty* (n 28 above) para 2-084; Burrows' *Restatement* (n 52 above) s 7(14).
[108] [1941] AC 108 (HL).
[109] *Chitty* (n 28 above) para 2-089.
[110] See *James Baird Co v Gimbel Bros Inc* 64 F.2d 344 (2d Cir. 1933); see also the Restatement 2d of Contracts, § 35.
[111] See also ch 13 on precontractual negotiations.
[112] 51 Cal 2d 409, 333 P 2d 757 (1958).

general contractor relied upon it in computing his own bid for the entire project. After the contract had been awarded to the general contractor, the subcontractor revoked his bid, claiming it had made an error in computation. The Court held that the offeree's reasonably foreseeable change of position in reliance upon an offer for a bilateral contract provides a basis for implying a subsidiary promise by the offeror not to revoke the offer, and that the promise became binding (even though there was no consideration for it), under the 'reliance doctrine', otherwise known as promissory estoppel.[113] Of this case, it has been written:

Note, (1959) Columbia L Rev 355   **8.22 (US)**

'*Subcontractor's offer for bilateral contract held irrevocable because of contractor's foreseeable reliance*'

Williston concludes that an offer is also a promise, albeit a conditional one, and that therefore the doctrine of promissory estoppel is applicable, presumably to make the offer irrevocable until the offeree has had a reasonable opportunity to accept it. On the other hand, in *James Baird Co v Gimble Bros, Inc*, a case not factually dissimilar to the instant one, it was held that promissory estoppel is not applicable to an offer for a bilateral contract. Although the court stated that 'an offer … is not meant to become a promise until a consideration has been received', it would seem that a better statement of the rationale for holding the doctrine of promissory estoppel inapplicable to offers is that an offer, being a promise conditional upon acceptance, is not reasonably relied upon until that condition has occurred.

Even if the doctrine of promissory estoppel is held not applicable to the offer itself, an offer can be irrevocable because of an enforceable express or implied subsidiary promise not to revoke. As to offers for unilateral contracts, which offers may not be capable of being accepted by the offeree without substantial preparation, Section 45 of the *Restatement of Contracts* states in effect that, upon partial performance by the offeree, the offer becomes irrevocable during the time stated in the offer or, if no time is stated therein, for a reasonable time. Although comment (b) to this section suggests that the offer is irrevocable because of a subsidiary promise not to revoke for which the consideration is the offeree's partial performance, the comment's reference to section 90 raises the possibility that the promise not to revoke may be a gratuitous promise which becomes enforceable by virtue of the doctrine of promissory estoppel.

The court in the instant case, analogising from the *Restatement* rule relating to offers for unilateral contracts, stated that the offeree's reasonably foreseeable change of position in reliance upon an offer for a bilateral contract provides a basis for implying a subsidiary promise by the offeror not to revoke the offer. While noting that detrimental reliance upon an offer for a bilateral contract differs from reliance upon an offer for a unilateral contract in that the latter reliance usually manifests itself in part performance which serves as consideration for the implied promise not to revoke, the court stated that the reference made to section 90 in section 45 of the Restatement indicated that a promise not to revoke could be considered gratuitous and enforceable by virtue of the doctrine of promissory estoppel. Since, in the instant case, the contractor could reasonably have been expected to rely upon the offer of the subcontractor and did so rely, as corroborated

---

[113] On this, see below, p 367.

by the fact that he included the name of the subcontractor in the submission of his bid for the main contract, the court held the subcontractor bound by an implied promise to give the contractor a reasonable opportunity to accept the offer.

This development in American case law is reflected in § 87 paragraph 2 of the Restatement 2d, which states that an offer is to be regarded as irrevocable if, as the offeror should reasonably have expected, it induces action or forbearance of a substantial character on the part of the offeree. In such a case the offer is to be regarded as binding only 'to the extent necessary to avoid injustice'. Like French law, American law therefore uses the idea of an implicit promise not to revoke as the basis for liability, but imposes liability on the basis of an estoppel rather than a tort.

On this issue, the approach of the PECL,[114] CISG[115] and the UNIDROIT Principles[116] strongly resembles the solution adopted in French and US case law: revocability is the main rule, but the exceptions seem to be more important than the rule itself—although, as noted, the practical results under French law and the various Principles are different.[117]

In summary, the German system (irrevocability as a main rule) and the English system (revocability as a main rule) hold opposite views on the revocability issue. The French system is in its practical outcome very near to the German system. In the PECL, CISG and in the UNIDROIT PICC, both views have been established: revocability as the main rule and irrevocability as the exception that, in practice, plays a more important part than the main rule itself.

The following excerpt from Zweigert and Kötz contains a strong argument for the binding force of an offer.[118]

> The critic is forced to conclude that on this point the German system is best. It is true that in practice the differences between the German system and the Common Law are slighter than might at first glance appear. ... Even so, the German system is superior. Experience shows that its results are practical and equitable; the offeree can act with assurance in the knowledge that his acceptance will bring about a contract. It also makes sense to put the risk of any changes in supplies and prices on the offeror: it is he who takes the initiative, it is he who invokes the offeree's reliance, and so it must be for him to exclude or limit the binding nature of his offer, failing which it is only fair to hold him bound.

However, the following extract, which summarises the results of an empirical survey of construction contractors operating under English law, might be thought to support the common law position. The scenario being discussed is that of the subcontractor (the 'sub') who offers a tender for a subcontract and later withdraws it, but not before the general contractor (the 'general') has entered into a binding contract with the employer on the basis of the tender—the very scenario which occurred in *Drennan v Star Paving Co:*

> The infrequency of the problem of withdrawal undoubtedly influences attitudes towards the introduction of legal sanctions to control it. But it may be that the informal control methods that already exist make legal regulation unnecessary. At least it is important to observe that

---

[114] See Art 2:202(3), 8.11 (INT) above, p 225.
[115] See Art 16.
[116] See Art 2.4.1.
[117] See also Art 6:219(1) BW, see above, p 233.
[118] Zweigert and Kötz (n 1 above) 362–63.

the potential which exists for making use of the legal system has not been exploited. Generals have either not devised standard tender forms or allow subs to ignore them. They do not use option contracts or bid bonds and they do not close a deal as soon as possible so as to create a contract and threaten legal sanction to prevent withdrawal. Resort to a court to determine rights and liabilities was not mentioned as a possible remedy. Instead the sanctions discussed were informal: re-negotiation and applying economic pressure; arbitration by a third party such as a quantity surveyor or architect; and as an ultimate deterrent, the severing of trade relations between the respective firms. … [The] legal solutions were rejected either as impractical, easily avoided and difficult to enforce, or as unfair and too inflexible in not making allowance for the several excuses which contractors recognised as good reasons for non-performance.[119]

If the reality is as this extract suggests, there would appear to be a strong argument in favour of the US solution: in general, offers are not binding, but the courts have the power (through the doctrine of estoppel) to correct an injustice in the particular case. On the other hand, for reasons we will see in Chapter 11, it seems that the doctrine of estoppel would not extend to provide a remedy in this scenario under English law, for it can be invoked as a defence to a claim but not as a cause of action. The doctrine of estoppel is therefore an important area in which the different common law jurisdictions have reached different conclusions.[120]

8.2.C LAPSE OF OFFER

Principles of European Contract Law   **8.23 (INT)**

Article 2:203: Rejection
When a rejection of an offer reaches the offeror, the offer lapses.

Article 2:206: Time Limit for Acceptance
(1) In order to be effective, acceptance of an offer must reach the offeror within the time fixed by it.
(2) If no time has been fixed by the offeror acceptance must reach it within a reasonable time.
(3) In the case of an acceptance by an act of performance under Article 2:205(3), that act must be performed within the time for acceptance fixed by the offeror or, if no such time is fixed, within a reasonable time.

Article 2:207: Late Acceptance
(1) A late acceptance is nonetheless effective as an acceptance if without delay the offeror informs the offeree that he treats it as such.
(2) If a letter or other writing containing a late acceptance shows that it has been sent in such circumstances that if its transmission had been normal it would have reached the offeror in due time, the late acceptance is effective as an acceptance unless, without delay, the offeror informs the offeree that it considers its offer as having lapsed.

---

[119] Lewis (n 92 above).
[120] This issue will be considered also in ch 13, see below, pp 443 ff.

Note

The PECL articles will also be found in the DCFR, Articles II.-4:203, 4:206 and 4:207, and in CESL Articles 33, 36 and 37, with only minor changes of wording. UNIDROIT PICC Articles 2.1.5 and 2.1.7–2.1.9 and CISG Articles 17, 18 and 21 have provisions that are broadly similar to the PECL, but UNIDROIT PICC Article 2.1.7 and CISG Article 18(3) add that 'An oral offer must be accepted immediately unless the circumstances indicate otherwise.' This rule may reflect German law, for which the rule is important because offers are normally irrevocable.

Code civil   **8.24 (FR)**

Article 1117: An offer lapses on the expiry of the period fixed by the offeror or, if no period is fixed, at the end of a reasonable period.

It also lapses in the case of the incapacity or death of the offeror, or the death of the offeree.

Cass civ (3), 10 May 1972[121]   **8.25 (FR)**

Lopez v Le Baste

Where an offer is not accepted within ten months and within that time the offeree has communicated with the offeror in terms inconsistent with an intention to accept the offer, the offer will not be capable of acceptance.

Facts: Lopez had purchased from the 'Le Baste' property company an apartment forming part of a block of flats constructed by that company. On 17 May 1967 Lopez made an offer to the manager of the company, to the effect that he was willing 'to surrender his rights in consideration of the sum of 3,725 francs'. The company accepted that offer on 16 March 1968. In a letter dated 17 August 1968, Lopez stated that he was revoking his offer to surrender his rights.

Held: The offer was not capable of acceptance in March 1968.

Judgment:— Whereas the court hearing the case at second instance, which has unfettered discretion in assessing whether an offer is implicitly made on the basis that it is to be accepted within a reasonable period, states: 'given the rapidity with which the parties habitually replied to each other's correspondence … Lopez could not reasonably have foreseen that the manager of the property company would delay for ten months before responding to the letter containing his most recent demands, notwithstanding that he had stated that he looked forward to receiving a prompt reply … as regards the negotiations concerning the repurchase of Lopez' rights, it would have been understandable for Le Baste to have asked for an extended period to think the matter over if Lopez' demands concerning the repurchase price had differed substantially from the proposals which had been made to him'.

— 'Whereas in actual fact, Lopez had only demanded an additional sum of forty thousand old francs; as, moreover, having received no response within a reasonable period to his two letters, Lopez was legitimately entitled to infer, upon receiving from the property company in December 1967 a communication, signed by the manager, inviting

---

[121] No. 71-11393, Bull civ III no. 297.

him to attend the general meeting of the company with a view to the regularisation of the allotment of the participating shares, that the counter-proposal made by him on 17 May 1967 had simply been rejected and that the invitation addressed to him constituted an unequivocal confirmation of that rejection'; lastly, on a date subsequent to 16 March 1968, Le Baste offered Lopez, by letter and by communication served by a process-server, a 'type F 5' apartment;

— Whereas the cour d'appel considered therefore, without distorting the meaning of the documents submitted to it, that the acceptance dated 16 March 1968 'appeared nugatory and worthless'; ...

Cass civ (3), 20 May 2009[122] **8.26 (FR)**

Land in the French Alps

An offer that is not subject to an express time limit will lapse after a reasonable time

Facts: The Haute-Savoie department offered to sell a portion of land to a buyer in 1995. The buyer accepted in 2001. However, the department argued that the offer had lapsed.

Held: The cour d'appel held that the offer, which did not have any deadline, had not lapsed and that, as a result, the buyer could accept it six years later. The Cour de cassation referred the case back to the cour d'appel.

Judgment: In so ruling, without checking whether the acceptance had been made within the reasonable deadline necessarily contained in any sale offer that does not provide for a specific time limit, the cour d'appel failed to give legal grounds to its decision.

Chancery Division **8.27 (EN)**

Manchester Diocesan Council v Commercial Investments[123]

Where an offer is made in terms which fix no time limit for acceptance, the offer must be accepted within a reasonable time. 'Reasonableness' should be assessed in the light of both the circumstances existing at the time of the offer and the circumstances arising thereafter.

Facts: A freehold property was vested in the plaintiff, a diocesan council for education. Part of the property was vested in the plaintiff under a scheme whereby the property could be sold subject 'to the approval of the purchase price' by the Secretary of State for Education and Science. In February 1963 the plaintiff's surveyor and the defendant company's surveyor started negotiations for the sale of the property by the plaintiff to the defendant company. Late in 1963 the plaintiff decided to sell the property by tender. Particulars and conditions of sale were prepared and these incorporated a form of tender. The conditions required, inter alia, that tenders be sent to the plaintiff's surveyor by 27 August 1964 and stipulated that the sale was subject to the approval of the purchase price by the Secretary of State. Clause 4 provided: 'The person whose tender is accepted shall be the purchaser and shall be informed of the acceptance of his tender by letter sent to him by post addressed to the address given in the tender ...'. On 25 August 1964 the defendant company completed the form of tender and stated thereon: 'and we agree that in the event of this offer being accepted in accordance with the above conditions ... we will pay the said purchase price and carry out and complete the purchase in accordance with the said conditions ...'. This was sent on the following day to the plaintiff's surveyor. On 1 September the plaintiff's surveyor informed the defendant company's surveyor that he would recommend acceptance of the defendant company's offer and that he would write again as soon as he had formal instructions.

---

[122] No. 08-13230, Bull. 2009, III, no. 118.
[123] [1970] 1 WLR 241.

243

On 14 September the defendant company's surveyor replied to the effect that he looked forward to receiving formal acceptance of the offer and he named the solicitors acting for the defendant company. This letter was acknowledged by the plaintiff's solicitor on 15 September when he also stated that the 'sale has now been approved' by the plaintiff and that instructions had been given to obtain the approval of the Secretary of State. The approval of the Secretary of State was obtained on 18 November. On 23 December the plaintiff's solicitors wrote to the defendant company's solicitors and, after reciting that the offer by tender had been accepted by the plaintiff subject to the consent of the Secretary of State, added that the consent had been forthcoming and they concluded therefore that the contract was binding on both parties. The defendant company's solicitors replied that they did not agree that there was any subsisting binding contract. On 7 January 1965 the plaintiff's solicitors wrote to the defendant company at the address given by it in the form of tender giving formal notification of acceptance of its offer.

Held: The plaintiff succeeded in its claim that a valid contract had been formed.

Judgment: Buckley J: … [The judge held first that the offer had been accepted by the plaintiff's surveyor's letter of 15 September.[124] He continued:]

If I am right in thinking that there was a contract on September 15, 1964, that disposes of the case but, in case I should be held to be wrong in that view, I will now consider the other point in the case and will for this purpose assume that no contract was made at that date. On this basis no contract can have been concluded before January 7, 1965. The defendant contends that, as the tender stipulated no time within which it must be accepted, it was an implied term of the offer that it must be accepted, if at all, within a reasonable time. It is said that acceptance on January 7 was not within a reasonable time.

It has long been recognised as being the law that, where an offer is made in terms which fix no time limit for acceptance, the offer must be accepted within a reasonable time to make a contract. … There seems, however, to be no reported case in which the reason for this is explained. There appear to me to be two possible views on methods of approaching the problem. First, it may be said that by implication the offer is made upon terms that, if it is not accepted within a reasonable time, it must be treated as withdrawn. Alternatively, it may be said that, if the offeree does not accept the offer within a reasonable time, he must be treated as having refused it. On either view the offer would cease to be a live one upon the expiration of what, in the circumstances of the particular case, should be regarded as a reasonable time for acceptance. The first of these alternatives involves implying a term that if the offer is not accepted within a reasonable time, it shall be treated as withdrawn or lapsing at the end of that period, if it has not then been accepted; the second is based upon an inference to be drawn from the conduct of the offeree, that is, that having failed to accept the offer within a reasonable time he has manifested an intention to refuse it. If in the first alternative the time which the offeror is to be treated as having set for acceptance is to be such a time as is reasonable at the date of the offer, what is reasonable must depend on circumstances then existing and reasonably likely to arise during the continuance of the offer; but it would be not unlikely that the offeror and offeree would make different assessments of what would be reasonable, even if, as might quite possibly not be the case, they based those judgments on identical known and anticipated circumstances. No doubt a court could resolve any dispute about this, but this approach clearly involves a certain degree of uncertainty about the precise terms of the offer. If, on the other hand, the time which the offeror is to be treated as having set for acceptance is to be such a time as turns out to be reasonable in the light of circumstances then existing and of circumstances arising thereafter during the continuance of the offer, whether foreseeable or not, an additional element of

---

[124] On this point, see further below, p 249.

uncertainty is introduced. The second alternative, on the other hand, involves simply an objective assessment of facts and the determination of the question whether on the facts the offeree should, in fairness to both parties, be regarded as having refused the offer.

It does not seem to me that either party is in greater need of protection by the law in this respect than the other. Until his offer has been accepted it is open to the offeror at any time to withdraw it or to put a limit on the time for acceptance. On the other hand, the offeree can at any time refuse the offer or, unless he has been guilty of unreasonable delay, accept it. Neither party is at a disadvantage. Unless authority constrains me to do otherwise, I am strongly disposed to prefer the second alternative to the first. …

I have dealt with this part of the case at some length because, if the first alternative were the correct view of the law and if what is reasonable had to be ascertained as at the time of the offer, the subsequent conduct of the parties would be irrelevant to the question how long the offer should be treated as remaining open. In my opinion, however, the subsequent conduct of the parties is relevant to the question, which I think is the right test, whether the offeree should be held to have refused the offer by his conduct.

In my judgment, the letter of September 15, 1964, excludes the possibility of imputing to the plaintiff a refusal of the offer. If that letter does not itself constitute an effective acceptance, it clearly discloses an intention to accept from which there is nothing to suggest a departure before January 7, 1965. Accordingly, if no contract was formed earlier, I am of opinion that it was open to the plaintiff to accept it on January 7 and that the plaintiff's letter of that date was effectual to bind the defendant contractually.

BGB   **8.28 (DE)**

§ 146: Expiry of an offer

An offer expires if a refusal is made to the offeror, or if no acceptance is made to this person in good time in accordance with sections 147 to 149.

§ 147: Period of acceptance

(1) An offer made to a person who is present may only be accepted immediately. This also applies to an offer made by one person to another using a telephone or another technical facility.

(2) An offer made to a person who is absent may be accepted only until the time when the offeror may expect to receive the answer under ordinary circumstances.

§ 148: Fixing a period for acceptance

If the offeror has determined a period of time for the acceptance of an offer, the acceptance may only take place within this period.

Notes

(1) In French law, as in the other laws, an offer will lapse if it is rejected by the offeree, even during the period fixed for acceptance.[125] In the *Lopez v La Baste* case, the cour d'appel had not only decided that a reasonable period for the acceptance had expired before the offer was accepted, but also that a rejection of the offer had taken place before the acceptance. This could in itself have been a sufficient ground for its decision. Similarly, for English law, see the reasoning of Buckley J in the *Manchester*

---

[125] See Malaurie et al (n 1 above) no. 471.

Diocesan Council case;[126] the case of *Hyde v Wrench*[127] illustrates that a counter offer will be treated as a rejection for this purpose. For German law, see § 146 BGB.

(2) Before the reforms of 2016, the questions whether and when an offer lapses if it has been neither accepted nor revoked were dealt with by the French courts analogously to the question of the revocability of an offer. If the offer expressly contained a period for acceptance, the offer would lapse when that period has expired without an acceptance taking place. An acceptance after the expiration of the period had no effect. If the offer did not expressly state a time for its acceptance, a reasonable time was implied either from the tacit will of the offeror or from other circumstances of the case.[128] What amounts to a reasonable period for acceptance is decided by the lower courts under marginal supervision of the Cour de cassation.

(3) This is a point on which the different jurisdictions studied have reached similar results. In English law, an offer that contains a time limit for its acceptance lapses if it has not been accepted within that time,[129] and an offer that does not fix a time limit for its acceptance lapses if it has not been accepted within a reasonable period.[130] What is a reasonable period depends on the circumstances of the case, and the *Manchester Diocesan Council* case held that this should take into account not only the circumstances at the time the offer is made, but also what happened after the offer was made. This is because one crucial factor is whether the offeree has rejected the offer, and this can only take place after the offer has been made. In the present case, because of his conduct in the period between the making of the offer and the final acceptance (the writing of several letters indicating his willingness to accept), the offeree could not be regarded as having silently rejected the offer.

(4) German law contains more detailed rules. For example, neither of the other systems has provisions about offers made face-to-face or on the telephone (§ 147(1) BGB). In German law these provisions are needed to protect the offeror; they are not necessary in systems in which an offer can be revoked freely. Often, however, the French or English courts would reach similar results on the ground that a reasonable time for acceptance has expired. German law on the position when the parties are not communicating instantaneously is governed by §§ 146, 147(2) and 148 BGB. § 149 BGB deals with the situation where the acceptance has been dispatched in time and normally would have reached the offeror in time, but as the result of a delay has reached the offeror after the period for acceptance has expired. In such a situation the offeror must give notice of the delay to the acceptor, who would otherwise rely on his acceptance being in time. If the offeror fails to give such notice, the late acceptance will be regarded as timely.

(5) German case law has extended this notion to cases in which the acceptance is slightly late for other reasons. Normally the late acceptance will be treated as a fresh offer (this is stated in § 150(1) BGB), which the recipient would be free to accept or

---

[126] See also *Treitel* (n 1 above) paras 2-062 ff and McKendrick (n 1 above) 44.
[127] 8.49 (EN), below, p 265.
[128] See Terré et al (n 1 above) para 189.
[129] *Treitel* (n 1 above) para 2-064; McKendrick (n 1 above) 44.
[130] *Treitel* (n 1 above) para 2-064.

to ignore just like a normal offer (eg BGHZ 18, 212). If, however, the acceptance is only slightly late, the courts have held that the recipient must notify the new offeror quickly if he does not wish to be treated as accepting it (RGZ 103, 11, 13). This rule is not found in English law nor is it codified in the French Code civil but it has been adopted by the various restatements, eg PECL Article 2:207, see above.

(6) The opportunity to put a time limit on the validity of an offer is important in German law, where an offer is irrevocable until it lapses. In French law, although the offeror may limit the period of validity of his offer by fixing a time for acceptance and thus protect himself against unreasonably late acceptances, this period for acceptance will serve at the same time as a 'no revocation period' (to be more precise: if the offer is revoked, liability is incurred, the contract is not formed; this explicitly results from Article 1116(2)).[131] In view of the broad freedom to revoke in English law, there seems to be less need than in other systems for the protection of the offeror against unreasonably late acceptances, and the *Manchester Diocesan Council* case shows that an acceptance is not easily considered to be late.

(7) At an auction sale, the offer made by each bidder lapses as soon as a higher bid is made, so that the auctioneer can no longer accept the next highest bid if a higher bid is made and revoked.[132]

As a result of the traditional view that the offer cannot exist without the will of the offeror, the French courts used to decide that an offer also lapses if the offeror dies. The Cour de cassation then began to have doubts about this point of view. In 1983 it gave a decision to the opposite effect in the case of the death of the offeror.[133] In 1989, the Cour de cassation returned to the former point of view and decided that an offer for a sale had lapsed as a consequence of the death of the offeror. However, in 1997 the Cour de cassation came back to the 1983 solution: the offer does not lapse if the offeror dies.[134] This question is now settled by new Article 1117(2) Cciv, which provides that an offer lapses in the case of the incapacity or the death of the offeror, and was completed by the 2018 ratification which added that it also lapses if the recipient dies. The solution provided by the revised Code civil has legitimately attracted criticism from commentators suggesting that in principle (i) the offeror has expressed some sort of will which is not within his power anymore and that (ii) the offeree may perfectly pass to his heirs and beneficiaries the offer. One must note finally that an offeror can specify that Article 1117(2) Cciv is not applicable to his offer.

The consequences of the death of the offeror remain unclear in English law. In *Dickinson v Dodds*,[135] discussed above, Lord Mellish stated that it is admitted law that, if a man who makes an offer dies, the offer cannot be accepted after he is dead. However, this has been doubted as the correct result except where the contract would be personal

---

[131] As has been seen above, p 231.

[132] See *Treitel* (n 1 above) para 2-008; see also § 156 BGB, above, p 223.

[133] Cass civ (3) 9 November 1983, no. 82-12996, Bull civ III no. 222, JCP 1984.IV.24, D 1984 IR174.

[134] Cass civ (3) 10 December 1997, no. 95-16461, Defr 1998, 336, annotated by D Mazeaud, D 1999, Somm 9, annotated by P Brun.

[135] [1876] 2 Ch D 463, 475 (CA).

and so discharged by the death of either party;[136] and it has been held that a continuing guarantee of a bank overdraft is not terminated merely by the death of the guarantor.[137]

French Article 1117(2) Cciv also provides that an offer also lapses if the offeror becomes incapable. In German law the opposite view is adopted as the main rule:

§ 153: Death or incapacity to contract of the offeror.

The coming into existence of the contract is not prevented by the offeror dying or losing capacity to contract before acceptance, unless a different intention of the offeror is to be presumed.[138]

The same is stated in Article 6:222 of the Dutch Civil Code. In English law, the supervening incapacity of the offeror prevents the offer being accepted if the offeree is aware of the change, or if the offeror's property has been made subject to the control of the court.[139]

8.3 ACCEPTANCE

In relation to the doctrine of acceptance, there is again a central requirement that a communication be intended to operate as an acceptance. As it is put in the new Code civil:

Code civil **8.29 (FR)**

Article 1118: An acceptance is the manifestation of the will of the offeree to be bound on the terms of the offer. As long as the acceptance has not reached the offeror, it may be withdrawn freely provided that the withdrawal reaches the offeror before the acceptance.

An acceptance which does not conform to the offer has no effect, apart from constituting a new offer.

In this section, we focus on three issues: the form in which an acceptance may be made, whether the acceptance must be communicated to the offeror in order to take effect, and whether the terms of the acceptance must mirror those of the offer exactly.

8.3.A FORM OF ACCEPTANCE

An acceptance need not take any particular form of words. Indeed, an acceptance may be by conduct alone[140] or, exceptionally, by silence. It is with these last two situations with which we are concerned in this subsection.

Principles of European Contract Law **8.30 (INT)**

Article 2:204: Acceptance
(1) Any form of statement or conduct by the offeree is an acceptance if it indicates assent to the offer.
(2) Silence or inactivity does not in itself amount to acceptance.

---

[136] *Treitel* (n 1 above) para 2-067.
[137] *Bradbury v Morgan* (1862) 1 H & C 249.
[138] cf von Mehren and Gordley (n 67 above) 193.
[139] *Chitty* (n 28 above) para 2-110.
[140] See *Treitel* (n 1 above) para 2-018; McKendrick (n 1 above) 35–36; Larenz and Wolf (n 1 above) 530 ff; Kötz (n 11 above) paras 113–18.

Article 2:205: Time of Conclusion of the Contract

...

(3) If by virtue of the offer, of practices which the parties have established between themselves, or of a usage, the offeree may accept the offer by performing an act without notice to the offeror, the contract is concluded when the performance of the act begins.

> *Note*
>
> DCFR Articles II.-4:204 and II.-4:206(3) and CESL Articles 34 and 35(3) follow the PECL very closely. UNIDROIT PICC Articles 2.1.6(1) and (3) are to the same effect; and similarly CISG Article 18.

8.3.A.1 PRESCRIBED MEANS OF ACCEPTANCE

An offer may state that it should be accepted in a certain way. Whether such a prescription of the mode of acceptance is exclusive and prevents a contract from being completed by an acceptance in any other form, or whether other equally effective means of communication will suffice, is a question of construction of the offer in the light of the circumstances of the case. In *Manchester Diocesan Council v Commercial Investments*[141] the tender for the purchase of property contained the condition that the company making the tender had to be informed of an acceptance of its tender by letter sent to it by post addressed to the address given in the tender, which was the address of the company. The owner of the property sent a letter of acceptance to the company's surveyor. Buckley J said:

> It may be that an offeror, who by the terms of his offer insists on acceptance in a particular manner, is entitled to insist that he is not bound unless acceptance is affected or communicated in that precise way, although it seems probable that, even so, if the other party communicates his acceptance in some other way, the offeror may by conduct or otherwise waive his right to insist on the prescribed method of acceptance. Where, however, the offeror has prescribed a particular method of acceptance, but not in terms insisting that only acceptance in that mode shall be binding, I am of opinion that acceptance communicated to the offeror by any other mode which is no less advantageous to him will conclude the contract.

8.3.A.2 ACCEPTANCE BY CONDUCT

House of Lords   **8.31 (EN)**

Brogden v Directors of The Metropolitan Railway Company[142]

The conduct of two parties may establish a binding contract between them, although the agreement has not been formally executed by either.

Facts: B had for some years supplied the M Railway Company with coals. It was eventually suggested by B that a contract should be entered into between them. After their agents had met together the terms of agreement were drawn up by the agent of the M Company and sent to B. B filled up certain parts of it which had been left

---

[141] 8.27 (EN), above, p 243.
[142] (1878–77) LR 2 App Cas 666.

in blank, and introduced the name of the gentleman who was to act as arbitrator in case of differences between the parties, wrote 'approved' at the end of the paper, and signed his own name. B's agent sent back the paper to the agent of the M Company, who put it in his desk, and nothing farther was done in the way of a formal execution of it. Both parties for some time acted in accordance with the arrangements mentioned in the paper, coals were supplied and payments made as stated therein. When some complaints of inexactness in the supply of coals, according to the terms stated in the paper, were made by the M Company, there were explanations and excuses given by B, and the 'contract' was mentioned in the correspondence, and matters went on as before. Finally, disagreements arose, and B denied that there was any contract which bound him in the matter.

Held: These facts, and the actual conduct of the parties, established the existence of such a contract, and there having been a clear breach of it B must be held liable upon it.

Judgment: Lord Blackburn: I have always believed the law to be this, that when an offer is made to another party, and in that offer there is a request express or implied that he must signify his acceptance by doing some particular thing, then as soon as he does that thing, he is bound. If a man sent an offer abroad saying: I wish to know whether you will supply me with goods at such and such a price, and, if you agree to that, you must ship the first cargo as soon as you get this letter, there can be no doubt that as soon as the cargo was shipped the contract would be complete, and if the cargo went to the bottom of the sea, it would go to the bottom of the sea at the risk of the orderer. So again, where, as in the case of *Ex parte Harris*, a person writes a letter and says, I offer to take an allotment of shares, and he expressly or impliedly says, If you agree with me send an answer by the post, there, as soon as he has sent that answer by the post, and put it out of his control, and done an extraneous act which clenches the matter, and shews beyond all doubt that each side is bound, I agree the contract is perfectly plain and clear. But when you come to the general proposition which Mr Justice Brett [the judge at first instance] seems to have laid down, that a simple acceptance in your own mind, without any intimation to the other party, and expressed by a mere private act, such as putting a letter into a drawer, completes a contract, I must say I differ from that. It appears from the Year Books that as long ago as the time of Edward IV, Chief Justice Brian decided this very point … I take it, my Lords, that that, which was said 300 years ago and more, is the law to this day, and it is quite what Lord Justice Mellish in *Ex parte Harris* accurately says, that where it is expressly or impliedly stated in the offer that you may accept the offer by posting a letter, the moment you post the letter the offer is accepted. You are bound from the moment you post the letter, not, as it is put here, from the moment you make up your mind on the subject.

But my Lords, while, as I say, this is so upon the question of law, it is still necessary to consider this case farther upon the question of fact. I agree, and I think every Judge who has considered the case does agree, certainly Lord Chief Justice Cockburn does, that though the parties may have gone no farther than an offer on the one side, saying, Here is the draft,—(for that I think is really what this case comes to,)—and the draft so offered by the one side is approved by the other, everything being agreed to except the name of the arbitrator, which the one side has filled in and the other has not yet assented to, if both parties have acted upon that draft and treated it as binding, they will be bound by it. When they had come so near as I have said, still it remained to execute formal agreements, and the parties evidently contemplated that they were to exchange agreements, so that each side should be perfectly safe and secure, knowing that the other side was bound. But, although that was what each party contemplated, still I agree (I think the Lord Chief Justice Cockburn states it clearly enough), 'that if a draft having been prepared and agreed upon as the basis of a deed or contract to be executed between two parties, the parties, without waiting for the execution of the more formal instrument, proceed to act upon the draft, and treat it as binding upon them, both parties will be bound by it. But it must be clear that the parties have both waived the execution of the formal instrument and have agreed expressly, or as shewn by their conduct, to act on the informal one.' I think that is quite right, and I agree with the way in which Mr Herschell in his argument stated it, very truly and fairly. If the parties have by their conduct said, that they act upon the draft which has been approved of by Mr Brogden, and which if not quite approved of by the railway company, has been exceedingly near it, if they indicate by their conduct that they accept it, the contract is binding.

Cass civ (3), 1 February 2005[143]   **8.32 (FR)**

The corrected rent

An offer may be accepted by conduct, but the conduct must be unequivocal.

Facts: A landlord made an offer to rent a flat for 1,800 francs per month. This offer was made through a public housing scheme. The landlord then sent a corrected version of the contract crossing out the amount and replacing it with 1,930 francs to the tenant. The tenant argued that it was not bound by the corrected amount.

Held: The court below found that, by staying in the premises for some time while it had the corrected version of the contract, the tenant accepted to be bound by the corrected amount.

Judgment: in so ruling, while the implied acceptance of a rent of 1,930 francs per month by the tenant could only result from acts manifesting his will in an unequivocal way, the court violated [Articles 1101 and 1128 of the Code civil].

Notes

(1) The speech of Lord Blackburn indicates that in English law there is a general requirement that an acceptance must be communicated to the offeror before it is effective. Thus a merely 'private act', such as putting a letter in a drawer, without any communication to the other party, will not suffice. It also shows that an act which is known to the other party, such as an act of performing the alleged contract, may also constitute acceptance.

(2) Lord Blackburn's speech also indicates that there are exceptions to the need for communication or knowledge of the acceptance, where the offer implicitly waives any need for communication and the offeree does an act which shows that it is irrevocably committed to the contract.[144] This issue is discussed further below.[145] In relation to unilateral contracts, acceptance will normally be by performance.

(3) Similarly, in French law, acceptance may be implied by the offeree's conduct (*acceptation tacite*). As shown by the *Corrected rent* case, the case law requires unequivocal behaviour of the offeree showing a clear acceptance.

---

[143] No. 03-19354, unpublished.
[144] See below, p 257.
[145] See below, pp 254 ff.

8.3.A.3 ACCEPTANCE BY SILENCE

Code civil   **8.33 (FR)**

Article 1120: Silence does not count as acceptance except where so provided by legislation, usage, business dealings or other particular circumstances.

Cass civ, 25 May 1870[146]   **8.34 (FR)**

The accidental investor

Silence on the part of a person alleged to be bound by an obligation cannot suffice, in the absence of any other factor, to constitute proof that he is bound by the alleged obligation.

Facts: The banking firm Robin et Cie was instructed to procure from investors subscriptions for shares in the Société des Raffineries Nantaises. It entered in the list of subscribers the name of Mr Guilloux, a customer of the bank, assigning twenty shares to him. Robin et Cie do not appear to have received from Mr Guilloux any formal order to that effect; but they wrote to him a letter in the following terms: 'Dear Sir, we have debited you the sum of 2,500 francs by way of initial payment for the twenty shares in Raffineries Nantaises for which you have subscribed; please find enclosed the vouchers relating thereto.' No reply to that letter was received. The Société des Raffineries Nantaises brought proceedings against Mr Guilloux and the—by that stage—insolvent firm of Robin et Cie, claiming payment of the outstanding sums due in respect of the twenty shares subscribed for.

Held: The Société's claim failed.

Judgment: —Whereas the contested judgment, in which it was held that the appellant was bound by the subscription undertaken in his name for twenty shares in the Société des Raffineries Nantaises, was based solely on the fact that the appellant did not reply to the letter by which Robin et Cie, acting on instructions to place the shares, had advised him that his name had been entered in the list of subscribers and that they had effected on his behalf the initial payment due in respect of the total amount of those shares;

— Whereas in law, silence on the part of a person alleged to be bound by an obligation cannot suffice, in the absence of any other factor, to constitute proof that he is bound by the alleged obligation;

— Whereas in ruling to the contrary, the contested judgment infringed the above-mentioned provisions of the Code Napoléon; ...

> **Note**
>
> As a rule, silence or inactivity does not amount to acceptance,[147] even when the offer states that it may be accepted by silence (subject to Article 1120). In English law, this is established by the case of *Felthouse v Bindley*.[148] The obvious justification for this is that an offeree should not be forced by an offer to take trouble and incur expense to reject it so as to avoid being bound. Compare UNIDROIT PICC Article 2.1.6(1) and CISG Article 18(1).[149]

---

[146] DP 1870.1.257, S 1870.1.341. F Terré and Y Lequette, *Grands arrêts de jurisprudence civil*, vol 2, *Obligations, Contrats spéciaux, Sûretés* (12th edn, Paris: Dalloz, 2008) no. 146.

[147] See for English law, *Treitel* (n 1 above) para 2-043; McKendrick (n 1 above) 38 and for German law, see Kötz (n 11 above) 119; Flume (n 11 above) 660.

[148] (1862) 11 CB (NS) 869.

[149] Both state that silence or inactivity does not in itself constitute acceptance.

However, in each legal system there are exceptions.

RG, 1 February 1926[150]   **8.35 (DE)**

Alcohol for sale

Where an offer is made in terms which accord with an offeree's prior proposal, the offer can be accepted by silence.

Facts: On Wednesday, 10 December 1924, the claimant sent a telegram to the defendant in the following terms: '(We) offer, without engagement, ready for shipment, 3,300 litres of alcohol, neutral, high-proof, 4.55 [marks] per litre of alcohol free on rail, payment to be made in cash in advance by telegraphic transfer. Sample on its way by express delivery. Reply by wire.' The defendant replied by wire on the same day: 'Bank already closed. Settlement will be made tomorrow. (We) await express sample.'

Held: The defendant's reply constituted an offer, and the contract had been accepted by the claimant's silence.

Judgment: The Landgericht [Regional Court] found that the first telegram contained an offer made by the claimant and that the second telegram constituted acceptance of that offer. The contested judgment draws attention, by contrast, to the qualifying words 'without engagement'. According to the prevailing view of the law, the effect of that qualification is such that the statement made constitutes not an offer but a request addressed to the other party, asking it to communicate an offer containing and setting out certain specific matters, which must be accepted in order to be effective.

... The appellate court concurred with that view. It regarded the defendant's telegram as amounting merely to an offer which still needed to be accepted by the claimant. However, it took the view that, in the present case, such acceptance could also take place tacitly, by silence on the part of the claimant. That court considered that such tacit acceptance had taken place by virtue of the fact that the claimant raised no objection of any kind to the offer during the period in which the defendant might under normal circumstances have expected to receive an answer from the claimant (§ 147(2) BGB). The appellate court held that, since the only appropriate method of replying was by wire, the period in question expired at 12.00 noon on Thursday, 11 December. It considered that the contract came into existence at that time on that day. There are no grounds in law for doubting the correctness of that finding. The defendant's offer read: 'Bank already closed. Settlement will be made tomorrow.' According to the interpretation applied by the appellate court, that meant that the purchase price would be remitted telegraphically on the following day. That interpretation, which was already advocated by ... in the proceedings at first instance, is in itself entirely feasible. It does not appear to be vitiated by any error of law, and is consequently binding on the court hearing the appeal on a point of law. According to the interpretation in question, the defendant may logically be deemed to have replied to the claimant to the following effect: 'we agree to your proposal in every respect. Consequently, we hereby make to you the offer that you want, and will tomorrow remit the purchase price telegraphically—without first waiting to receive from you confirmation that it is accepted. We would have remitted the purchase price today, but the bank was already closed.' The appellate court could even have inferred from this that the defendant was waiving the obligation on the part of the claimant requiring the latter to state that

---

[150] JW 1926, 2674.

it accepted the offer (first sentence of § 151 BGB). Still less can there be said to be any grounds for doubting that the contested judgment concerns one of those cases in which an offer is accepted by silence. The particular factors justifying such deemed acceptance are to be found in the fact that the defendant's offer accorded in every respect with the non-binding proposal previously put forward by the claimant, together with the urgency attaching—according to both parties—to the transaction, and the unconditional assurance given by the defendant in its telegram that it would transmit the purchase price telegraphically on the following day. It follows that the defendant needed to send a wire only if it agreed that the claimant, instead of sending any answer, should proceed without delay with the packing and shipment of the goods …

Notes

(1) In all three legal systems there are exceptions to the rule that silence cannot constitute an acceptance,[151] the most important ones being the existence of a course of dealing between the parties or a usage according to which silence amounts to acceptance[152] and the situation in which the offer has been solicited by the offeree—as in the *Alcohol for Sale* case (and see also BGH, 8 April 1957[153]). In English law it may be that the offeror who has said that the offer may be accepted by silence is bound if the offeree remains silent, but the offeree will not be bound in this case.[154] The same is also true in French law and is now well shown by Article 1120 of the French Civil Code. Before the introduction of this provision on silence in the Code civil, this solution was inferred from the case of *The accidental investor* (above), which is the leading case.[155] It results from this case that, more generally in French law, there is a whole series of exceptional cases in which silence can amount to an acceptation (it is sometimes referred to as *silence circonstancié*[156]): for instance, when this was provided for by the parties in a former contract; when parties had a usual course of business and the new contract offered by one of them is of the same nature as the previous ones; when there are some 'usages' in this respect; or when the offer is in the *intérêt exclusif* of the offeree, a situation now encompassed in the last words of Article 1120 which refer to 'other particular circumstances'.

(2) A further example in German law is where merchants have been in oral negotiations and afterwards one of them sends the other a 'confirmation of order' which sets out terms which the sender believes were part of the contract even though they were not referred to in negotiations. If the recipient does not act quickly to reject the terms, he will be bound by what is stated in the confirmation, whether the oral

---

[151] See *Treitel* (n 1 above) para 2-044; Terré et al (n 1 above) no. 124, who provide for a long list of exceptions under French law (some exceptions are statutory and others originate in case law); for Dutch law, see *Asser/Hijma 7-1** 2013/181 (n 12 above) 138 ff.

[152] For a US case in point, see *Ammons v Wilson* 176 Miss 645, 170 So 227 (1937).

[153] NJW 1957, 1105 (translation in B Markesinis, H Unberath and A Johnston, *The German Law of Contract* (2nd edn, Oxford: Hart Publishing, 2006) 567).

[154] *Treitel* (n 1 above) para 2-046.

[155] Terré and Lequette (n 146 above) no. 146.

[156] Malaurie et al (n 1 above) no. 475.

negotiations amounted to a contract or not.[157] This does not seem to have any direct equivalent in the other systems. It is reflected in the PECL Article 2:210, but that applies only when the oral agreements had led to a contract. So it is considered when conflicting terms are dealt with, below.[158]

(3) The comment on Article 2.1.6 of the UNIDROIT PICC makes it clear that the exception in cases of an existing course of dealing or usage also apply under paragraph 1 of that Article—where only the main rule is set forth; cf the words 'in itself' in the second sentence of that paragraph. Compare also the US Restatement 2d:

Restatement 2d of Contract **8.36 (US)**

§ 69: (1) Where an offeree fails to reply to an offer, his silence and inaction operate as an acceptance in the following cases only:

— where an offeree takes the benefit of offered services with reasonable opportunity to reject them and reason to know that they were offered with the expectation of compensation;

— where the offer has stated or given the offeree reason to understand that assent may be manifested by silence or inaction, and the offeree in remaining silent or inactive intends to accept the offer;

— where, because of previous dealings or otherwise, it is reasonable that the offeree should notify the offeror if he does not intend to accept.

The principle stated in Restatement 2d § 69(1)(a) certainly reflects English law and French law, in which the use of the goods will be classified as a 'tacit acceptance' that falls within the last words of Article 1120 Cciv (see above). This probably reflects also the other laws considered in this book: a party who knows that goods are being offered for sale and uses them will be held to have accepted the other to sell. It follows that if a business sends goods to a person who has not asked for them, and it is clear that the business wants to be paid for the goods, the person may be held to have accepted the business's offer, certainly if they use the goods and possibly if they simply retain them. This leads to what is called 'inertia selling'. Inertia selling to consumers is now forbidden and the consumer cannot be made to pay for the goods.

Consumer Rights Directive **8.37 (EU)**

Inertia selling

Article 27: The consumer shall be exempted from the obligation to provide any consideration in cases of unsolicited supply of goods, water, gas, electricity, district heating or digital content or unsolicited provision of services, prohibited by Article 5(5) and point 29 of Annex I to Directive 2005/29/EC. In such cases, the absence of a response from the consumer following such an unsolicited supply or provision shall not constitute consent.

---

[157] See Markesinis et al (above n 153) 76–77 and translated cases nos. 16–18. See above, p 172.
[158] See below, p 267.

Note

These provisions replace Article 9 of the Distance Selling Directive.[159] Article 5(5) of Directive 2005/29/EC (the Unfair Commercial Practices Directive) provides that the practices listed in Annex I 'shall in all circumstances be regarded as unfair'. Point 29 of Annex I lists:

Demanding immediate or deferred payment for or the return or safekeeping of products supplied by the trader, but not solicited by the consumer except where the product is a substitute supplied in conformity with Article 7(3) of Directive 97/7/EC (inertia selling).

8.3.B A REQUIREMENT OF COMMUNICATION?

8.3.B.1 ACCEPTANCES IN GENERAL

Principles of European Contract Law   **8.38 (INT)**

Article 2:205: Time of Conclusion of the Contract
   (1) If an acceptance has been dispatched by the offeree the contract is concluded when the acceptance reaches the offeror.
   (2) In the case of acceptance by conduct, the contract is concluded when notice of the conduct reaches the offeror.
   (3) If by virtue of the offer, of practices which the parties have established between themselves, or of a usage, the offeree may accept the offer by performing an act without notice to the offeror, the contract is concluded when the performance of the act begins.

UNIDROIT Principles   **8.39 (INT)**

Article 2.1.6: (Mode of acceptance)
   (1) …
   (2) An acceptance of an offer becomes effective when the indication of assent reaches the offeror.

Article 2.1.4: (Revocation of offer)
   (1) Until a contract is concluded an offer may be revoked if the revocation reaches the offeree before it has dispatched an acceptance.
   (2) …

Article 2.1.10: (Withdrawal of acceptance)
   An acceptance may be withdrawn if the withdrawal reaches the offeror before or at the same time as the acceptance would have become effective.

CISG   **8.40 (INT)**

Article 23: A contract is concluded at the moment when an acceptance of an offer becomes effective in accordance with the provisions of this Convention.

---

[159] Directive 97/7/EC of the European Parliament and of the Council of 20 May 1997 on the protection of consumers in respect of distance contracts, OJ L144/19.

Article 16: Until a contract is concluded an offer may be revoked if the revocation reaches the offeree before he has dispatched an acceptance.[160]

The general rule is that an acceptance must be communicated in order to be effective. We saw earlier that this does not mean that the offeror must actually know of it: it may suffice, for example, that a message has been delivered to his house. Thus we saw that in German law the issue is dealt with as a part of a more general question: when does a declaration of intention that is directed to another person (*empfangsbedürftige Willenserklärung*) become effective?[161] According to § 130(1) BGB, a declaration of intention that is directed to an absent person becomes effective when it 'reaches' that person. This provision applies to offers,[162] revocations of offers, acceptances and other declarations.[163] Thus, in German law the contract is concluded when the acceptance 'reaches' the offeror. On the concept of reaching (*zugehen*), see the *Delivery to a housemaid* case;[164] as that case illustrates, a communication may reach a person without being communicated to them. Zweigert and Kötz suggest that the limits of the concept of reaching can be determined by reference to the idea of a 'sphere of influence'; for example, a man may not prevent an acceptance from reaching him by refusing to collect it from his mail box, for it has already reached his 'sphere of influence'.[165]

The general rule in English law is also that an acceptance must be communicated to the offeror. However, where an offer invites acceptance by conduct, as in the example of shipping cargo given by Lord Blackburn in *Brogden*, the offer often expressly or impliedly waives the requirement that acceptance must be communicated,[166] so it suffices that the offeror has done the thing indicated by the offer, such as shipping the goods. Where acceptance takes place by performance of a unilateral contract, communication of acceptance is hardly ever required.[167] In *Carlill v Carbolic Smoke Ball Co*, Lindley LJ said:

> Unquestionably, as a general proposition, when an offer is made, it is necessary in order to make a binding contract, not only that it should be accepted, but that the acceptance should be notified. But is that so in cases of this kind? I apprehend that they are an exception to that rule, or, if not an exception, they are open to the observation that the notification of the acceptance need not precede the performance. This offer is a continuing offer. It was never revoked, and if notice of acceptance is required ... the person who makes the offer gets the notice of acceptance contemporaneously with his notice of the performance of the condition. If he gets notice of the acceptance before his offer is revoked, that in principle is all you want. I, however, think that the true view, in a case of this kind, is that the person who makes the offer shews by his language and from the nature of the transaction that he does not expect and does not require notice of the acceptance apart from the notice of the performance.

---

[160] Art 22 CISG is identical to Art 2.1.10 UNIDROIT PICC.

[161] cf Dutch law: Article 3:37(3) BW; AS Hartkamp & CH Sieburgh, *Mr. C. Assers Handleiding tot de beoefening van het Nederlands Burgerlijk Recht. 6. Verbintenissenrecht. Deel III. Algemeen overeenkomstenrecht* (Deventer: Kluwer 2014) nos. 99 ff.

[162] In relation to offers, see the *Delivery to a housemaid* case, 8.15 (DE), above, p 226.

[163] Dutch law provides a similar rule in Art 3:37(3) BW.

[164] Discussed above p 228.

[165] See also Kötz (n 11 above) para 99; Flume (n 11 above) 657.

[166] See *Chitty* (n 28 above) para 2-046.

[167] *Treitel* (n 1 above) para 2-028; McKendrick (n 1 above) 42.

Bowen LJ added:

> If I advertise to the world that my dog is lost, and that anybody who brings the dog to a particular place will be paid some money, are all the police or other persons whose business is to find lost dogs to be expected to sit down and write me a note saying that they have accepted my proposal? Why, of course, they at once look after the dog, and as soon as they find the dog they have performed the condition. The essence of the transaction is that the dog should be found, and it is not necessary under such circumstances, as it seems to me, that in order to make the contract binding there should be any notification of acceptance.

A different outcome would probably be reached under the UNIDROIT Principles. According to the comment on Article 2.1.6, an acceptance by mere conduct becomes, just as any other acceptance, effective only when notice thereof reaches the offeror. The comment states that in cases where the conduct will of itself give notice of acceptance to the offeror within a reasonable period of time, special notice to this effect is not necessary. However, the use of the smoke ball in *Carlill v Carbolic Smoke Ball Co* would not have sufficed for this purpose. Compare the American Restatement 2d:

Restatement 2d of Contracts **8.41 (US)**

§ 54: (1) Where an offer invites an offeree to accept by rendering a performance, no notification is necessary to make such an acceptance effective unless the offer requests such a notification.

(2) If an offeree who accepts by rendering a performance has reason to know that the offeror has no adequate means of learning of the performance with reasonable promptness and certainty, the contractual duty of the offeror is discharged unless

    (a) the offeree exercises reasonable diligence to notify the offeror of acceptance, or

    (b) the offeror learns of the performance within a reasonable time, or

    (c) the offer indicates that notification of acceptance is not required.

8.3.B.2 ACCEPTANCE BY POST OR OTHER NON-INSTANTANEOUS COMMUNICATION

If the parties conclude the contract in each other's presence, normally no question arises with regard to the need for communication of the acceptance. The same is true when the parties are in different places and use an instantaneous means of communication, such as the telephone. But if the parties use a slower means of communication, such as the post, these two moments are necessarily separated by a period of time. These cases therefore raise a question whether the acceptance must be communicated to the offeree.

The question whether the acceptance must have reached the offeree is also of crucial importance for another purpose: to determine the moment at which the acceptance becomes effective and thus at which moment the contract comes into being. This issue can be of importance in several respects, for example, if a new Act has come into force or to determine the beginning of periods eg of prescription (limitation). An important consequence of the conclusion of a sale contract in French law is the transfer of the ownership and the risk of the thing sold. The moment at which the acceptance becomes effective therefore also affects the point at which risk in the goods is transferred to the buyer.

In the case law, the question at which moment the acceptance takes effect arises in most of the cases for the purpose of determining whether the offer has lapsed by that time[168] or to determine the moment from which the offeror can no longer revoke his offer.[169]

Four possible moments have been suggested for the conclusion of a contract when the acceptance takes place by letter: (a) the moment the letter containing the acceptance is written (externalisation theory); (b) the moment at which the letter of acceptance is posted (expedition or dispatch theory); (c) the moment the letter is received by the offeror (reception theory); and (d) the moment the offeror is informed of the content of the letter (actual-notice theory). The externalisation theory and the actual-notice theory are rather impractical: it is often impossible to establish at which the moment the letter of acceptance was written or read. We have seen that in other contexts each of these theories has been rejected.[170] Moreover, when the actual-notice theory is followed the offeror could postpone the conclusion of the contract by leaving the letter of acceptance unopened. Italian law seems to have adopted the actual-notice theory in Article 1326 of the Italian Civil Code. This provides that the contract is made at the moment at which the party who has made the offer knows of the other party's acceptance. However, in practice receipt is regarded as knowledge in Italian law unless the offeror can prove that 'without his fault, he was prevented from taking notice' (Articles 1328, 1334, 1335 of the Italian Civil Code).

On the other hand, the time of dispatch and the time of receipt can be determined objectively. Which should be taken as the moment at which the contract is concluded?

Cass com, 7 January 1981[171] **8.42 (FR)**

L'Aigle v Comase

An acceptance by letter is effective upon dispatch, and not upon receipt.

Facts: On 10 June 1975 Messrs L'Aigle sent a purchase offer, valid for 30 days, to Messrs Comase. The latter company accepted it on 3 July, but was unable to prove that its acceptance reached the offeror before 10 July. Having failed to fulfil its obligations, L'Aigle sought to avoid the liability which it had incurred, by maintaining that the contract had not been concluded. It argued that a contract became definitive and binding only upon receipt by the offeror of acceptance of his offer; since it had not been proved by its opponent that such acceptance had indeed taken place within the time-limit stipulated in the offer, that offer had lapsed and it had not been possible for the contract to come into existence.

Held: A contract had been concluded.

Judgment: ... —Whereas the appellant, Société L'Aigle, contests the judgment of the cour d'appel ordering it to pay damages to Société Comase by way of compensation for the loss suffered by the latter as a result of the wrongful termination by the said Société L'Aigle of the abovementioned agreement, on the ground that Société Comase had accepted the offer made within the time-limit laid down;

---

[168] See above, pp 241 ff.
[169] See, eg below, p 261.
[170] See above, p 228.
[171] No. 79-13499, Bull civ IV no 14, RTD civ 1981, 849, annotated by F Chabas.

— Whereas according to the appellant, it is for the party seeking performance of an obligation to prove the same, and it is therefore for Société Comase to furnish evidence showing that it communicated its acceptance to Société L'Aigle before 10 July 1975; as the appellant further argues that, by basing its decision solely on its consideration of a letter from Société Comase dated 3 July 1975 (produced to the court in evidence), which could not have reached Société L'Aigle until after 10 July, the cour d'appel reversed the burden of proof, and that it was for Société Comase to prove that the letter was received before the time-limit expired, and not for Société L'Aigle to prove the contrary; as the appellant additionally maintains that, by failing, moreover, to investigate whether the letter reached its addressee by 10 July, the cour d'appel robbed its decision of any legal basis;

— Whereas however, in the absence of any stipulation to the contrary, the written communication of 10 June 1975 was intended to become definitive and binding not upon receipt by Société L'Aigle of Société Comase's acceptance but upon the despatch of that acceptance by Société Comase; the appellant's plea to the contrary is unfounded; ...

In the past, the French Cour de cassation had in a large number of decisions adopted the view that the point at which a contract is effective is a matter of fact that is purely within the discretion of the lower courts: eg Cass civ, 21 December 1960.[172] In the *L'Aigle v Comase* case, the Cour de cassation expressly adopted the dispatch theory.[173] However, the recent case law seemed to move towards the application of the receipt theory.[174] This evolution was confirmed by the 2016 reform, which provides that acceptance is effective only from the moment the offeror receives it:

Code civil **8.43 (FR)**

Article 1118: ... As long as the acceptance has not reached the offeror, it may be withdrawn freely provided that the withdrawal reaches the offeror before the acceptance.
...

Article 1121: A contract is concluded as soon as the acceptance reaches the offeror. It is deemed to be concluded at the place where the acceptance has arrived.
...

King's Bench **8.44 (EN)**

Adams v Lindsell[175]

An acceptance by post is effective when it is sent, not when it is received.

Facts: The defendants by letter offered to sell to the plaintiffs certain specified goods, receiving an answer by return of post; the letter containing the offer being misdirected, the answer notifying the acceptance of the offer arrived two days later than it ought to have done; on the day following that when it would have arrived if the original letter had been properly directed, the defendants sold the goods to a third person. The defendants

---

[172] D 1961.I.417, annotated by Ph Malaurie.
[173] Terré et al (n 1 above) no. 171.
[174] Cass civ (3) 16 June 2011, no. 09-72679, Bull. III, no. 103 and Cass civ (3) 17 September 2014, no. 12-22112.
[175] (1818) 1 B & Ald 681, 106 ER 250.

contended that until the plaintiffs' answer was actually received, there could be no binding contract between the parties; and before then, the defendants had retracted their offer, by selling the goods to other persons.

Held: A contract had been concluded between the plaintiffs and the defendants.

Judgment: The court said that if that were so, no contract could ever be completed by the post. For if the defendants were not bound by their offer when accepted by the plaintiffs till the answer was received, then the plaintiffs ought not to be bound till after they had received the notification that the defendants had received their answer and assented to it. And so it might go on ad infinitum. The defendants must be considered in law as making, during every instant of the time their letter was travelling, the same identical offer to the plaintiffs; and then the contract is completed by the acceptance of it by the latter. Then as to the delay in notifying the acceptance, that arises entirely from the mistake of the defendants, and it therefore must be taken as against them, that the plaintiff's answer was received in course of post.

Common Pleas Division   **8.45 (EN)**

Byrne v Van Tienhoven[176]

An offer is effectively revoked when the fact of the withdrawal is communicated to the offeree, and the mere posting of a notice of revocation will not suffice for this purpose. Once an offer has been accepted by dispatch of a letter of acceptance, the offer cannot be revoked.

Facts: By letter of 1 October the defendants wrote from Cardiff offering goods for sale to the plaintiffs in New York. The plaintiffs received the offer on the 11th and accepted it by telegram on the same day, and by letter on the 15th. On 8 October the defendants had posted to the plaintiffs a letter withdrawing the offer. This letter reached the plaintiffs on the 20th.

Held: The offer had not effectively been revoked before it had been accepted, and a binding contract had therefore been formed.

Judgment: LINDLEY J: There is no doubt that an offer can be withdrawn before it is accepted, and it is immaterial whether the offer is expressed to be open for acceptance for a given time or not: *Routledge v Grant*. For the decision of the present case, however, it is necessary to consider two other questions, viz: 1. Whether a withdrawal of an offer has any effect until it is communicated to the person to whom the offer has been sent? 2. Whether posting a letter of withdrawal is a communication to the person to whom the letter is sent?

It is curious that neither of these questions appears to have been actually decided in this country. As regards the first question, I am aware that Pothier and some other writers of celebrity are of opinion that there can be no contract if an offer is withdrawn before it is accepted, although the withdrawal is not communicated to the person to whom the offer has been made. The reason for this opinion is that there is not in fact any such consent by both parties as is essential to constitute a contract between them. Against this view, however, it has been urged that a state of mind not notified cannot be regarded in dealings between man and man; and that an uncommunicated revocation is for all practical purposes and in point of law no revocation at all. This is the view taken in

---

[176] (1880) 5 CPD 344.

the United States: see *Tayloe v Merchants Fire Insurance Co* cited in *Benjamin on Sales*, pp 56–58, and it is adopted by Mr Benjamin. The same view is taken by Mr Pollock in his excellent work on *Principles of Contract*, ed ii, p 10, and by Mr Leake in his *Digest of the Law of Contracts*, p 43. This view, moreover, appears to me much more in accordance with the general principles of English law than the view maintained by Pothier. I pass, therefore, to the next question, viz, whether posting the letter of revocation was a sufficient communication of it to the plaintiff. The offer was posted on the 1st of October, the withdrawal was posted on the 8th, and did not reach the plaintiff until after he had posted his letter of the 11th, accepting the offer. It may be taken as now settled that where an offer is made and accepted by letters sent through the post, the contract is completed the moment the letter accepting the offer is posted: *Harris' Case; Dunlop v Higgins*, even although it never reaches its destination. When, however, these authorities are looked at, it will be seen that they are based upon the principle that the writer of the offer has expressly or impliedly assented to treat an answer to him by a letter duly posted as a sufficient acceptance and notification to himself, or, in other words, he has made the post office his agent to receive the acceptance and notification of it. But this principle appears to me to be inapplicable to the case of the withdrawal of an offer. In this particular case I can find no evidence of any authority in fact given by the plaintiffs to the defendants to notify a withdrawal of their offer by merely posting a letter; and there is no legal principle or decision which compels me to hold, contrary to the fact, that the letter of the 8th of October is to be treated as communicated to the plaintiff on that day or on any day before the 20th, when the letter reached them. …

Before leaving this part of the case it may be as well to point out the extreme injustice and inconvenience which any other conclusion would produce. If the defendants' contention were to prevail no person who had received an offer by post and had accepted it would know his position until he had waited such a time as to be quite sure that a letter withdrawing the offer had not been posted before his acceptance of it. It appears to me that both legal principles, and practical convenience require that a person who has accepted an offer not known to him to have been revoked, shall be in a position safely to act upon the footing that the offer and acceptance constitute a contract binding on both parties …

Judgment for the plaintiffs.

Notes

(1) In English law, an acceptance by letter becomes effective the moment the letter is posted. Apart from the two cases cited above, this was also confirmed in *Henthorn v Fraser*.[177] Similarly, an acceptance by telegram takes effect when the telegram is communicated to a person authorised to receive it for transmission to the addressee.[178] The 'postal rule' applies only when it is reasonable to use the post as a means of communicating acceptance (*Henthorn v Fraser*);[179] and the offeror can explicitly or implicitly exclude the 'postal rule' in his offer.[180] The 'postal rule' in English law applies for the purposes of determining whether an offer can still be revoked, whether

---

[177] [1892] 2 Ch 27 (CA).

[178] *Treitel* (n 1 above) para 2-030; see *Brinkibon v Stahag Stahl* [1983] 2 AC 34 (HL).

[179] [1892] 2 Ch 27 (CA).

[180] eg by requiring 'notice' of the offeree's decision to accept: *Holwell Securities Ltd v Hughes* [1974] 1 WLR 155 (CA). See *Treitel* (n 1 above) para 2-033; McKendrick (n 1 above) 42.

a contract has been concluded if the acceptance is lost or delayed in the post[181]— this consequence is criticised by, for example, McKendrick—and whether the contract takes priority over another contract relating to the same subject matter. English case law does not provide examples of other consequences that might be drawn from the rule. In particular, it has never been decided whether an acceptor can withdraw his acceptance after it has been posted, for example by sending a telex message that reaches the offeror earlier than or at the same time as the letter of acceptance.

(2) In English law, an important function of the 'postal rule' is that it limits the offeror's power to revoke:[182] once the letter containing the acceptance is posted, the offeror can no longer revoke, since at that moment a contract has been concluded. This function of the rule is reinforced by the rule that the revocation of an offer becomes effective only when it has reached the offeree.[183] Thus, a revocation will come too late to prevent the contract from being completed if it reaches the offeree after he has posted his letter or telegram of acceptance. In the comment on Article 2.1.4 of the UNIDROIT PICC it is said that this solution may cause some inconvenience to the offeror who will not always know whether or not it is still possible to revoke the offer, but that it is justified in view of the legitimate interest of the offeree in the time available for revocation being shortened.

The problem of an offer being revoked after the offeree has tried to accept it by posting an acceptance does not necessarily have to be dealt with in the way it is in English law. Different issues—termination of the offeror's power to revoke, loss or delay of the acceptance in the post, withdrawal of acceptance, etc—may be treated separately. For example, under the PECL the contract is not formed until the acceptance is received but under Article 2:202,[184] once an acceptance has been dispatched the offer may no longer be revoked. This solution is also found in the UNIDROIT PICC[185] and the CISG.[186] One effect is that, while the offeror cannot revoke once the letter of acceptance has been posted, if the letter never arrives there will be no contract.

In contrast, English law seems to treat the contract as made when the letter is posted, so that not only can the offeror no longer revoke the offer once an acceptance has been dispatched but there will be a contract even if the letter never arrives. (It is not completely certain what the all the consequences of the English 'postal rule' are[187]—for example, if the letter of acceptance is not properly addressed and is therefore delayed.)

In summary, this issue is approached differently in the different jurisdictions studied. It can be seen that the moment at which an acceptance is effective is not the subject of clear rules in French law. English law establishes a general requirement of communication, but that requirement is subject to important exceptions, and the law thus takes

---

[181] *Household Fire and Carriage Accident Insurance Co Ltd v Grant* (1879) 4 Ex D 216 (CA).
[182] See *Treitel* (n 1 above) para 2–031; McKendrick (n 1 above) 41.
[183] See *Byrne v Van Tienhoven*, 8.45 (EN), above, p 261.
[184] See 8.11 (INT), above, p 225.
[185] Arts 2.1.4 and 2.1.6 UNIDROIT PICC: see 8.12 (INT), above, p 225.
[186] See Arts 16(1) and 18(2).
[187] See above, p 262.

an essentially pragmatic stance ultimately not dissimilar from the French position. In German law, on the other hand, one orderly approach is followed with regard to all related questions: an acceptance becomes effective upon receipt.

These different approaches can be traced back to the rules on revocability of offers. In English law, the dispatch rule is justified because, in combination with the receipt rule for the revocation of offers, it provides the offeree with some protection against revocation of the offer. In German law, where offers are, as a main rule, irrevocable,[188] there is less need to advance the moment at which the acceptance becomes effective.

8.3.C ACCEPTANCE THAT DEVIATES FROM THE OFFER

8.3.C.1 COUNTER-OFFERS

Principles of European Contract Law   **8.46 (INT)**

Article 2:208: Modified Acceptance[189]

(1) A reply by the offeree which states or implies additional or different terms which would materially alter the terms of the offer is a rejection and a new offer.

(2) A reply which gives a definite assent to an offer operates as an acceptance even if it states or implies additional or different terms, provided these do not materially alter the terms of the offer. The additional or different terms then become part of the contract.

(3) However, such a reply will be treated as a rejection of the offer if:

(a) the offer expressly limits acceptance to the terms of the offer; or

(b) the offeror objects to the additional or different terms without delay; or

(c) the offeree makes its acceptance conditional upon the offeror's assent to the additional or different terms, and the assent does not reach the offeree within a reasonable time.

UNIDROIT Principles   **8.47 (INT)**

Article 2.1.11 (Modified acceptance):

(1) A reply to an offer which purports to be an acceptance but contains additions, limitations or other modifications is a rejection of the offer and constitutes a counteroffer.

(2) However, a reply to an offer which purports to be an acceptance but contains additional or different terms which do not materially alter the terms of the offer constitutes an acceptance, unless the offeror, without undue delay, objects to the discrepancy. If the offeror does not object, the terms of the contract are the terms of the offer with the modifications contained in the acceptance.

CISG   **8.48 (INT)**

Article 19: (1) A reply to an offer which purports to be an acceptance but contains additions, limitations or other modifications is a rejection of the offer and constitutes a counter-offer.

---

[188] See above, p 228.
[189] cf Article II.-4:208 DCFR: Modified acceptance.

(2) However, a reply to an offer which purports to be an acceptance but contains additional or different terms which do not materially alter the terms of the offer constitutes an acceptance, unless the offeror, without undue delay, objects orally to the discrepancy or dispatches a notice to that effect. If he does not so object, the terms of the contract are the terms of the offer with the modifications contained in the acceptance.

(3) Additional or different terms relating, among other things, to the price, payment, quality and quantity of the goods, place and time of delivery, extent of one party's liability to the other or the settlement of disputes are considered to alter the terms of the offer materially.[190]

Note

DCFR Article II.-4:208 is in similar terms to the PECL provision. CESL Article 38 adds a new paragraph which is modeled on CISG Article 19(3):

(2) Additional or different contract terms relating, among other things, to the price, payment, quality and quantity of the goods, place and time of delivery, extent of one party's liability to the other or the settlement of disputes are presumed to alter the terms of the offer materially.

Rolls Court **8.49 (EN)**

Hyde v Wrench[191]

A counter-offer amounts to a rejection of the original offer, and the original offer cannot thereafter be accepted.

Facts: The defendant on 6 June offered in writing to sell his farm for £1,000, but the plaintiff offered £950, which the defendant on 27 June, after consideration, refused to accept. On the 29th the plaintiff wrote accepting the original offer of £1,000. The plaintiff brought an action for specific performance; the defendant admitted the facts but denied liability.

Held: No contract had been formed.

Judgment: LORD LANGDALE: Under the circumstances stated in this bill, I think there exists no valid binding contract between the parties for the purchase of the property. The defendant offered to sell it for £1000, and if that had been at once unconditionally accepted, there would undoubtedly have been a perfect binding contract; instead of that, the plaintiff made an offer of his own, to purchase the property for £950, and he thereby rejected the offer previously made by the defendant. I think that it was not afterwards competent for him to revive the proposal of the defendant, by tendering an acceptance of it; and that, therefore, there exists no obligation of any sort between the parties.

Queen's Bench Division **8.50 (EN)**

Stevenson, Jaques & Co v McLean[192]

A mere inquiry whether the offeror would accept particular terms does not amount to a counter-offer and thus a rejection of the original offer.

---

[190] Note the similarity of Art 19(1) and (2) CISG and Art 2.1.11 UNIDROIT PICC.
[191] (1840) 3 Beav 334.
[192] (1880) 5 QB 346.

Facts: The defendant, being possessed of warrants for iron, wrote from London to the plaintiffs in Middlesborough asking whether they could get him an offer for the warrants. Further correspondence ensued, and ultimately the defendant wrote to the plaintiffs fixing 40s per ton, net cash, as the lowest price at which he could sell, and stating that he would hold the offer open until the following Monday. The plaintiffs on the Monday morning at 9.42 telegraphed to the defendant: 'Please wire whether you would accept forty for delivery over two months, or if not, longest limit you could give.' The defendant sent no answer to this telegram, and after its receipt on the same day he sold the warrants. At 1.25 pm he telegraphed to plaintiffs that he had done so. Before the arrival of his telegram to that effect, the plaintiffs, having at 1 pm found a purchaser for the iron, sent a telegram at 1.34 pm to the defendant stating that they had secured his price. The defendant refused to deliver the iron, and thereupon the plaintiffs brought an action against him for non-delivery thereof.

Held: The plaintiffs' enquiry did not have the effect of rejecting the defendant's offer, which the plaintiffs had later accepted.

Judgment: LUSH J: ... It is apparent throughout the correspondence, that the plaintiffs did not contemplate buying the iron on speculation, but that their acceptance of the defendant's offer depended on their finding some one to take the warrants off their hands. All parties knew that the market was in an unsettled state, and that no one could predict at the early hour when the telegram was sent how the prices would range during the day. It was reasonable that, under these circumstances, they should desire to know before business began whether they were to be at liberty in case of need to make any and what concession as to the time or times of delivery, which would be the time or times of payment, or whether the defendant was determined to adhere to the terms of his letter; and it was highly unreasonable that the plaintiffs should have intended to close the negotiation while it was uncertain whether they could find a buyer or not, having the whole of the business hours of the day to look for one. Then, again, the form of the telegram is one of inquiry. It is not 'I offer forty for delivery over two months,' which would have likened the case to *Hyde v Wrench*, where one party offered his estate for 1000l., and the other answered by offering 950l. Lord Langdale, in that case, held that after the 950l. had been refused, the party offering it could not, by then agreeing to the original proposal, claim the estate, for the negotiation was at an end by the refusal of his counter proposal. Here there is no counter proposal. The words are, 'Please wire whether you would accept forty for delivery over two months, or, if not, the longest limit you would give.' There is nothing specific by way of offer or rejection, but a mere inquiry, which should have been answered and not treated as a rejection of the offer ...
Judgment for the plaintiffs

BGB **8.51 (DE)**

§ 150: Late and altered acceptance
   (1) ...
   (2) An acceptance with expansions, restrictions or other alterations is deemed to be a rejection combined with a new offer.[193]

Code civil **8.52 (FR)**

Article 1118: ...
   (3) An acceptance which does not conform to the offer has no effect, apart from constituting a new offer.

[193] For Dutch law, see Art 6:225 BW, which contains a similar provision.

Notes

(1) A statement that purports to be an acceptance but changes the terms of the offer is in reality a counter-offer: for example, an offer to supply goods that is 'accepted' by an order for their supply and installation.[194] The rule according to which the terms of the acceptance must correspond to those of the offer is referred to in the common law as the 'mirror-image rule'. *Hyde v Wrench* shows that a counter-offer is regarded in English law as a rejection of the original offer.[195] *Stevenson, Jaques & Co v McLean* shows that whether a communication is a counter-offer or a mere request for information depends on the intention with which it was made, objectively assessed.

(2) The 'mirror-image rule' is also to be found in Article 1326 of the Italian Civil Code and Section 59 of the US Restatement 2d. It is also to be found in French law where the general rule is that there must be an *acceptation pure et simple*. However, for the statement to be a 'counter-offer' and not an acceptance, it is necessary that the modifications show some point of disagreement and do not amount to mere specifications without altering the *objet* of the *contrat*.[196] The same solution applies in the PECL. Under Article 2:208, an acceptance need not mirror the offer precisely, but it must not 'materially alter the terms of the offer' of the offer. Paragraph C of the Comment on the Article explains that 'a term is material if the offeree knew or as a reasonable person in the same position as the offeree should have known that the offeror would be influenced in its decision as to whether to contract or as to the terms on which to contract'. See also UNIDROIT PICC Article 2.1.11 and CISG Article 19,[197] and Article 6:225(2) of the Dutch Civil Code.

8.3.C.2 THE 'BATTLE OF THE FORMS'

Principles of European Contract Law **8.53 (INT)**

Article 2:209: Conflicting General Conditions[198]

(1) If the parties have reached agreement except that the offer and acceptance refer to conflicting general conditions of contract, a contract is nonetheless formed. The general conditions form part of the contract to the extent that they are common in substance.

(2) However, no contract is formed if one party:

(a) has indicated in advance, explicitly, and not by way of general conditions, that it does not intend to be bound by a contract on the basis of paragraph (1); or

(b) without delay, informs the other party that it does not intend to be bound by such contract.

(3) General conditions of contract are terms which have been formulated in advance for an indefinite number of contracts of a certain nature, and which have not been individually negotiated between the parties.

---

[194] *Treitel* (n 1 above) para 2-019; see also McKendrick (n 1 above) 36.

[195] With the result that the original offer lapses, as has been seen above, pp 264–65.

[196] Terré et al (n 1 above) no. 121.

[197] 8.48 (INT), above, p 265.

[198] cf DCFR Art II.-4:209: Conflicting standard terms. The definition of standard terms in the DCFR is in the Annex of Definitions, cf PECL Art 2:209(3).

UNIDROIT Principles   **8.54 (INT)**

Article 2.1.22: Battle of forms

Where both parties use standard terms and reach agreement except on those terms, a contract is concluded on the basis of the agreed terms and of any standard terms which are common in substance unless one party clearly indicates in advance, or later and without undue delay informs the other party, that it does not intend to be bound by such a contract.

> *Note*
>
> See also DCFR Article II.-4:209 and CESL Article 39.

Court of Appeal   **8.55 (EN)**

Butler Machine Tool Co Ltd v Ex-cell-O Corpn Ltd[199]

On one approach to the battle of the forms, it is not necessary to look only at an offer and an acceptance when considering whether a contract has been agreed. As an alternative, all of the relevant documentation should be construed together to discern whether a harmonious interpretation can be achieved.

Facts: On 23 May 1969, in response to an enquiry by the buyers, the sellers made a quotation offering to sell a machine tool to the buyers for £75,535, delivery to be in 10 months' time. The offer was stated to be subject to certain terms and conditions which 'shall prevail over any terms and conditions in the Buyer's order'. The conditions included a price variation clause providing for the goods to be charged at the price ruling on the date of delivery. On 27 May the buyers replied by placing an order for the machine. The order was stated to be subject to certain terms and conditions, which were materially different from those put forward by the sellers and which, in particular, made no provision for a variation in price. At the foot of the buyers' order there was a tear-off acknowledgement of receipt of the order stating that 'We accept your order on the Terms and Conditions stated thereon'. On 5 June the sellers completed and signed the acknowledgement and returned it to the buyers with a letter stating that the buyers' order was being entered 'in accordance' with the sellers' quotation of 23 May. When the sellers came to deliver the machine they claimed that the price had increased by £2,892. The buyers refused to pay the increase in price and the sellers brought an action claiming that they were entitled to increase the price under the price variation clause contained in their offer. The buyers contended that the contract had been concluded on the buyers' rather than the sellers' terms and was therefore a fixed-price contract. The judge upheld the sellers' claim on the ground that the contract had been concluded on the basis that the sellers' terms were to prevail since they had stipulated that in the opening offer and all subsequent negotiations had been subject to that. The buyers appealed.

Held: A contract had been concluded by the parties on the buyers' terms.

Judgment: LORD DENNING MR: ... If those documents are analysed in our traditional method, the result would seem to me to be this: the quotation of May 23, 1969, was an offer by the sellers to the buyers containing the terms and conditions on the back. The order of May 27, 1969, purported to be an acceptance of that offer in that it was for the same machine at the same price, but it contained such additions as to cost of installation, date of delivery and so forth that it was in law a rejection of the offer and constituted a counter-offer. That is clear from *Hyde v Wrench* (1840) 3 Beav 334. As Megaw J said in *Trollope & Colls Ltd v Atomic Power Constructions Ltd* [1963] 1 WLR 333, 337: '... the counter-offer kills the original offer.' The letter of the sellers of June 5, 1969, was an

[199] [1979] 1 WLR 401.

acceptance of that counter-offer, as is shown by the acknowledgment which the sellers signed and returned to the buyers. The reference to the quotation of May 23 referred only to the price and identity of the machine ...

In many of these cases our traditional analysis of offer, counter-offer, rejection, acceptance and so forth is out of date ... The better way is to look at all the documents passing between the parties—and glean from them, or from the conduct of the parties, whether they have reached agreement on all material points—even though there may be differences between the forms and conditions printed on the back of them. As Lord Cairns said in *Brogden v Metropolitan Railway* Co (1877) 2 App Cas 666, 672:

> '... there may be a *consensus* between the parties far short of a complete mode of expressing it, and that *consensus* may be discovered from letters or from other documents of an imperfect and incomplete description; ...'

Applying this guide, it will be found that in most cases when there is a 'battle of forms', there is a contract as soon as the last of the forms is sent and received without objection being taken to it. That is well observed in *Benjamin's Sale of Goods*, 9th ed (1974), p 84. The difficulty is to decide which form, or which part of which form, is a term or condition of the contract. In some cases the battle is won by the man who fires the last shot. He is the man who puts forward the latest terms and conditions: and, if they are not objected to by the other party, he may be taken to have agreed to them. Such was *British Road Services Ltd v Arthur V Crutchley & Co Ltd* [1968] 1 Lloyd's Rep 271, 281–282, per Lord Pearson; and the illustration given by Professor Guest in *Anson's Law of Contract*, 24th ed, pp. 37, 38 when he says that 'the terms of the contract consist of the terms of the offer subject to the modifications contained in the acceptance.' In some cases the battle is won by the man who gets the blow in first. If he offers to sell at a named price on the terms and conditions stated on the back: and the buyer orders the goods purporting to accept the offer—on an order form with his own different terms and conditions on the back—then if the difference is so material that it would affect the price, the buyer ought not to be allowed to take advantage of the difference unless he draws it specifically to the attention of the seller. There are yet other cases where the battle depends on the shots fired on both sides. There is a concluded contract but the forms vary. The terms and conditions of both parties are to be construed together. If they can be reconciled so as to give a harmonious result, all well and good. If differences are irreconcilable—so that they are mutually contradictory—then the conflicting terms may have to be scrapped and replaced by a reasonable implication.

In the present case the judge thought that the sellers in their original quotation got their blow in first: especially by the provision that 'these terms and conditions shall prevail over any terms and conditions in the buyer's order.' It was so emphatic that the price variation clause continued through all the subsequent dealings and that the buyers must be taken to have agreed to it. I can understand that point of view. But I think that the documents have to be considered as a whole. And, as a matter of construction, I think the acknowledgment of June 5, 1969, is the decisive document. It makes it clear that the contract was on the buyers' terms and not on the sellers' terms: and the buyers' terms did not include a price variation clause. ...

LAWTON LJ: The modern commercial practice of making quotations and placing orders with conditions attached, usually in small print, is indeed likely, as in this case to produce a battle of forms. The problem is how should that battle be conducted? The view taken by Thesiger J was that the battle should extend over a wide area and the court should do its best to look into the minds of the parties and make certain assumptions. In my judgment, the battle has to be conducted in accordance with set rules. It is a battle more on classical

18th century lines when convention decided who had the right to open fire first rather than in accordance with the modern concept of attrition.

The rules relating to a battle of this kind have been known for the past 130-odd years. They were set out by Lord Langdale MR in *Hyde v Wrench*, 3 Beav 334, 337, to which Lord Denning MR has already referred; and, if anyone should have thought they were obsolescent, Megaw J in *Trollope & Colls Ltd v Atomic Power Constructions Ltd* [1963] 1 WLR 333, 337 called attention to the fact that those rules are still in force ...

[Lawton LJ then applied the ordinary rules for counter-offers. This meant that the order of 27 May constituted a counter-offer because it referred to the general conditions of the buyers which were materially different from those used by the sellers. This counter-offer of the buyers was accepted by the sellers by the acknowledgement and letter of 5 June; the reference to the original offer served only to identify the transaction and not to reintroduce the terms of the sellers. Therefore a contract was concluded on the terms and conditions of the buyers. Bridge LJ also delivered judgment allowing the appeal on the basis of the 'classical doctrine'.]

Appeal allowed.

Note

Lord Denning indicates briefly three approaches to resolving the problem of the so-called 'battle of forms'. The traditional approach, which was adopted by Lawton and Bridge LJJ, is to consider the communications between the parties as offers and counter-offers, in accordance with the 'mirror-image rule'.[200] Each communication in which a party refers to its own standard terms and conditions operates as a rejection of the other party's standard terms and conditions, and as a counter offer. In this approach the party who has made the last reference to its own terms and conditions often wins the battle—the 'last shot-doctrine'—because its counter-offer is accepted by the conduct of the other party when that party carries out the contract, for example by taking delivery, or possibly by shipping the ordered goods. The traditional approach was also applied by the Court of Appeal in the later case of *Tekdata Interconnections Ltd v Amphenol Ltd*.[201]

BGH, 26 September 1973[202]   **8.56 (DE)**

The heat-retaining silo

Whilst particular terms and conditions may not be incorporated into a contract following a battle of the forms, the parties may be estopped from denying that a contract has in fact been concluded.

Facts: On 1 December 1969 the defendant, using its own order form which referred in the standard way to its 'terms and conditions of purchase' printed overleaf, ordered a heat-retaining silo to be delivered by 15 April 1970. Clause 1 of the terms and conditions of purchase provided as follows:

Orders given by us ... are placed on the basis of our terms and conditions of purchase. Where the contractor's standard-form terms and conditions provide otherwise, they shall be valid only if they are confirmed by us in writing.

---

[200] See above, p 267.
[201] [2009] EWCA Civ 1209, [2010] 1 Lloyd's Rep 357.
[202] BGHZ 61, 282.

The essence of clause 3 of the terms and conditions of purchase was that the statutory rules were to apply decisively to any claim for compensation for failure to comply with the deadline for delivery. Thereafter, on 5 January 1970, the plaintiff sent the defendant a detailed 'confirmation of order', in which—likewise referring in the standard way to its attached 'terms and conditions of sale and delivery'—it accepted the order on the basis that delivery was to be effected by no later than 'middle to end April 1970'. However, according to the plaintiff's terms and conditions of sale and delivery, the particulars concerning the delivery deadline were only approximate and non-binding; liability to pay compensation for late delivery was excluded.

By letter of 22 April 1970, the defendant, referring expressly to its order form, gave the plaintiff formal notice of default by the latter and announced that, in the event of failure by the plaintiff to effect delivery by 30 April 1970, it would claim compensation. The equipment was delivered at the end of June 1970 and put into operation by the defendant. The defendant withheld from the agreed purchase price of approximately DM 90,000 the sum of DM 27,450 by way of recompense for the damage caused by the delay.

Held: The defendant had not accepted the plaintiff's terms and conditions in passively receiving the conditions set out in the plaintiff's confirmation of order or in acceptance of delivery, but a contract had nevertheless been concluded between the parties.

Judgment: (a) As is apparent inter alia from § 362 HGB, silence does not in principle constitute consent, even in legal dealings between commercial traders (BGHZ 1, 353, 355). In particular, in a settled line of case-law—relating, it is true, to disputes which did not concern letters of confirmation passing between commercial traders, the Bundesgerichtshof has declined to construe the mere passive receipt, without objection, of a modified confirmation of order as constituting tacit acceptance thereof (BGHZ 18, 212, 216; judgment of 12 February 1952—I ZR 98/51 = LM BGB § 150, 2; judgment of 14 March 1963—VII ZR 257/61 = WM 1963, 528 = LM BGB § 150, 6) …

2. It follows that the plaintiff's terms and conditions of sale and delivery were not incorporated into the contract merely by virtue of the passive receipt by the defendant, without objection, of the confirmation of order dated 5 January 1970. Nor, however, is the plaintiff entitled to rely in that connection on the fact that the defendant subsequently accepted the equipment and put it into operation. It is true that, in certain circumstances, where a modified confirmation of order is sent and the purchaser takes delivery of the goods without raising any objection, that may be regarded as constituting tacit acceptance by the purchaser of the modified contract (§ 150(2) BGB), with the result that he is deemed to have consented to the seller's general terms of business, as referred to—particularly where the seller has clearly stated at a previous juncture that he is prepared to effect delivery only on his own terms (see the judgment of the BGH of 17 September 1954—I ZR 18/53 = LM BGB § 150, 3 = BB 1954, 882, and the judgment of 14 March 1963—VII ZR 257/61 = WM 1963, 528 = LM BGB § 150, 6 = NJW 1963, 1248). The present case does not, however, involve any passive receipt, taking place without any objection being raised, which could be construed as amounting to tacit acceptance. On the contrary, the defendant gave notice by letter of 22 April 1970, in which it referred to its written order of 1 December 1969, that it proposed to claim compensation for failure to comply with the delivery deadline …

3. The fact that, because the plaintiff accepted the defendant's order of 1 December 1969 only in a modified form and the defendant did not accept the new terms proposed by the plaintiff at all, neither the defendant's terms and conditions of purchase nor the plaintiff's terms and conditions of sale and delivery were therefore incorporated into the contract does not mean, however, that no contract came into existence. The application of § 150(2) BGB is subject to the principle of good faith (judgment of the BGH of 12 February 1952—I ZR 98/51, cited above). In the present case, neither of the parties has at any time called in question, either before or during the dispute, the fact that a legally

effective purchase contract was concluded. They performed the contract—the plaintiff by delivering the equipment and the defendant by accepting delivery of it and by paying at least part of the purchase price, although it was already quite clear at that point that there was a dispute as to whose terms of business had been incorporated into the contract. In so doing, they made it clear that, as far as they were concerned, the determination of the matter in issue did not affect the existence of the contract itself. Consequently, in accordance with the principle of good faith, both parties must be deemed to be estopped from pleading that the contract never came into existence (judgment of the Chamber of 25 June 1957—VIII ZR 257/56 = WM 1957, 1064, not reproduced in that respect in LM BGB § 150, 5; Krause BB 1952, 996, 998).

BGH, 20 March 1985[203]   **8.57 (DE)**

Oven-timing clocks

Where a contract has been concluded but the parties each seek to rely on their standard terms, and the court is seeking to identify the terms of the contract, a party is not necessarily bound by a term which does not conflict with his own terms.

Facts: On 27 October 1980 the bankrupt debtor ordered from the plaintiff, on the terms and conditions of purchase printed on the reverse side of the order form, certain time-switch clocks to be installed in electric ovens. Clause 16 of those terms and conditions of purchase was in the following terms:

> Diverging terms of business. By accepting our order, the supplier declares that he consents to these terms and conditions of purchase. In the event that our order is confirmed by the supplier on terms which diverge from our terms and conditions of purchase, the latter shall nevertheless apply, even where we do not raise any objection. Consequently, divergent terms shall apply only where they have been expressly acknowledged by us in writing. If the supplier does not consent to the foregoing way of proceeding, he shall be obliged forthwith to indicate his disagreement in a specific letter to that effect. In such cases, we reserve the right to cancel the order, without thereby entitling the supplier to make any claim whatever against us. Our terms and conditions shall also apply to future transactions, even where no express reference is made to them, provided solely that they have already been received by the customer.

On 11 February 1982 the bankrupt debtor placed a supplementary order with the plaintiff for the supply of further energy-regulating devices. The plaintiff confirmed the order, referring to its General Terms and Conditions of Delivery and Payment, which provided that the transaction was to be governed exclusively by its written confirmation of order in conjunction with the said General Terms and Conditions of Delivery and Payment. Clause 7 of those Terms and Conditions contained an extended and wide-ranging retention of title provision in respect of delivered goods.

Held: Whilst a contract had been concluded, it was not possible to conclude that the bankrupt debtor intended, by means of its preventive clause, to exclude only those of the plaintiff's terms and conditions of sale which conflicted with its own terms and conditions of purchase, and not also to exclude the plaintiff's additional clauses.

Judgment: ... The appellate court further concluded, correctly, that the bankrupt debtor did not declare, even tacitly, that it consented to the global incorporation into the contract of the plaintiff's General Terms and Conditions. A finding that the bankrupt debtor tacitly submitted to be bound by the plaintiff's terms and conditions of sale would conflict with the unequivocal statement contained in its own terms and conditions of purchase, to the effect that it contracted solely on its own terms and that it was to be deemed to have agreed to the application of divergent conditions appearing in the confirmation of order

---

[203] NJW 1985, 1838.

only if it had acknowledged in writing that those divergent conditions were to apply. ... In view of the anticipatory objection by the bankrupt debtor, clearly expressed in the preventive clause contained in its terms and conditions, to the application of the plaintiff's General Terms and Conditions, such a change of mind on the bankrupt debtor's part cannot, in the absence of any new supervening circumstances, be held to have taken place and cannot, in particular, be inferred from the fact that the bankrupt debtor raised no fresh objection to the plaintiff's terms and conditions of sale and accepted delivery of the goods without reservation—as the appellate court rightly accepted, that point not having been challenged in the appeal on a point of law (see the judgment of the Chamber, WM 1977, 451 [452]) ...

(aa) Where—as in the present case—a contract has come into existence without any agreement being reached as to the application of the general terms and conditions of either of the parties, that does not mean that, in such circumstances, the corresponding default rules of contract law are to apply in their entirety, and without exception, in place of the rules and stipulations laid down in the general terms and conditions in question (see Bunte, ZIP 1982, 449 [450], setting out the relevant opinions on the issue; Wolf, in Wolf–Horn–Lindacher, *AGB-Gesetz*, § 2, para 77; Ulmer, in Ulmer–Brandner–Hensen, *AGB-Komm*, 4th edition, § 2, para 101; Erman–Hefermehl, *BGB*, 7th edition, § 2 AGB-Gesetz, para 48). On the contrary, the parties may be deemed to have intended to apply those stipulations diverging from or supplementing the default rules which were contained in the general terms and conditions of both the parties, which were framed in similar or identical forms of wording and which both parties accordingly wished to see incorporated into the contract.

(bb) However, such a manifest consensus is lacking where the general terms and conditions of one of the parties contain 'additional' stipulations which are not matched by corresponding, equivalent provisions contained in the terms and conditions of the other party, eg—as in the present case—a retention of title clause. The question whether, in such a case, it is possible to infer—even where no consensus is manifestly apparent from the general terms and conditions of both of the parties—that one of the parties tacitly agreed to the inclusion in the contract of the additional stipulations unilaterally laid down by the other party will depend on the wishes of the party opposing those stipulations, which are to be ascertained in the light of the other circumstances of the case (see Ulmer, § 2, para 104; Löwe–Graf von Westphalen–Trinkner, *AGB-Gesetz*, § 2, para 47). In the present case, however, it is not possible to conclude that the bankrupt debtor intended, by means of its preventive clause, to exclude only those of the plaintiff's terms and conditions of sale which conflicted with its own terms and conditions of purchase, and not also to exclude the plaintiff's additional clauses ...

Notes

(1) According to the Bundesgerichtshof in the *Heat Retaining Silo* case, the mere fact that A clearly believes a contract has been concluded, for example by sending a reminder, does not establish that the terms and conditions of the party that 'fired the last shot' have been accepted by the other party. Rather, the Bundesgerichtshof requires that the other party actually performs its part of the contract or takes delivery of the goods ordered. However, since in that case the dispute about the terms of the contract had already arisen at the moment of delivery, the buyer's taking delivery could not operate as an acceptance of the seller's terms and conditions. Furthermore, as is shown by the *Oven Timing Clocks* case, if A's standard terms and conditions

include a condition fending off B's terms and conditions, A's performance cannot be construed as an acceptance of B's terms and conditions. Thus, in German law an acceptance by conduct of the terms and conditions of the party who 'fired the last shot' is not easily assumed—compare also BGH, 10 June 1974.[204]

(2) An objection raised to the 'last shot-doctrine' is that it is arbitrary to give precedence to the terms and conditions of the party that happens to have 'the last word' in the process of concluding the contract.

(3) Another way to resolve the problem could be to let the terms and conditions of the offeror prevail, unless they are expressly rejected by the acceptor: the 'first blow' rule. This is the rule which is laid down in the Dutch Civil Code (Article 6:225(3) BW).[205] The underlying idea is that the party making the last communication has the last chance to clear up the matter; if he does not do this and enters into the contract without making his acceptance expressly conditional on acceptance of his own terms and conditions, he knowingly takes the risk of being bound to the other party's terms and conditions.[206] The German Bundesgerichtshof has followed this approach more than once. In this approach, in which an exception is made to the 'mirror image' rule, the question remains on what terms and conditions the contract is concluded.

(4) An objection that is raised to both of the two approaches mentioned above is that one party should not be given control where, in reality, the parties are in disagreement on relevant terms.[207]

(5) This objection is met by a third approach, according to which the terms and conditions of both parties insofar as they can be reconciled are included in the contract, whereas the conflicting terms and conditions are left out—the 'knock-out rule', adopted by Article 2.1.22 of the UNIDROIT PICC,[208] and by § 2-207(3) of the US UCC.[209] Any gaps in the contract will have to be filled by suppletive rules of law, usage, trade practices, etc. This approach was followed by the Bundesgerichtshof in the second of the two German cases here cited, where, as has been noted, the 'last-shot doctrine' could not be applied in the absence of an acceptance by conduct. While applying the 'knock-out rule', the BGH had to decide, however, not about a *conflicting* term, but about the inclusion in the contract of an *additional* term of the seller about reservation of property after delivery, and which was not dealt with at all in the terms and conditions of the buyer. The BGH held that the inclusion in the contract of additional terms of one party depended on the will of the other party, which had to be determined having regard to the circumstances. One of those circumstances was that the buyer's conditions fended off any deviating terms and conditions of the other party, and from this condition, the BGH deduced that the buyer did not assent to the incorporation of any other term, whether or not it conflicted with the buyer's own terms. It would seem more logical, however, to say that a condition that is different

---

[204] BB 1974, 1136.
[205] *Asser/Hartkamp & Sieburgh 6-III* 2014/478 (n 161 above).
[206] See von Mehren (n 1 above) 96.
[207] ibid, at 100.
[208] 8.54 (INT), above, p 268.
[209] 8.58 (US), below, p 275.

from the suppletive rules that would apply in its absence conflicts with the terms of the offer if the offer does not address the subject in question.

(6) The case law of the BGH shows a tendency towards an innovative and more realistic approach to the battle-of-forms problem. Instead of giving precedence to the terms and conditions of one party, the BGH is prepared to place the terms and conditions of both parties on an equal footing and substitute the conflicting terms by suppletive rules of law.

(7) French case law adopted the German solution: when they enter into conflict the terms and conditions of both parties are neutralised.[210] This is now provided in the revised Code civil: Article 1119(2) provides that:

> In case of inconsistency between general conditions relied on by each of the parties, incompatible clauses have no effect.

Article 1119(3) adds:

> In case of inconsistency between general conditions and special conditions, the latter prevail over the former.

Gaps in the contract will then have to be filled by suppletive rules of law, usage, trade practices, etc, according to Article 1194 of the Code civil. Before the reform the Commercial chamber of the Cour de cassation had already ruled, in a case of March 1995,[211] that two conflicting jurisdiction clauses neutralised one another and that the rules provided by Articles 42 and 46 of the Code de Procédure civile were applicable. One important exception may result, for sales contracts, from Article L 441-6 of the Commercial code which states that 'General conditions of sale form the sole basis of commercial negotiation.' As this provision refers to 'general conditions of *sale*', it appears to mean that any inconsistency between the general conditions of the seller and the general conditions of the buyer should be resolved by the seller's general conditions prevailing, unless the parties have specified otherwise.[212]

In the US, § 2-207 of the UCC (Uniform Commercial Code), which is applicable only to sale contracts, constitutes a departure from the traditional rule that offer and acceptance have to be a mirror image of one another. The rationale of § 2-207 is that a rigid application of the 'mirror-image rule' with regard to sale contracts is contrary to practice, because of the increasing use of standard forms with pre-printed terms and conditions. However, the provision requires a creative construction in order to reach the 'knock out' result:

Uniform Commercial Code   **8.58 (US)**

§ 2-207:

(1) A definite and reasonable expression of acceptance or a written confirmation which is sent within a reasonable time operates as an acceptance even though it states

---

[210] Terré et al (n 1 above) no. 122; Malaurie and Aynés (n 1 above) no. 772.

[211] No 83-15956.

[212] See F Chénedé, *Le nouveau droit des obligations et des contrats: Consolidations, innovations, perspectives* (Paris: Dalloz, 2016) no. 22.122.

terms additional to or different from those offered or agreed upon, unless acceptance is expressly made conditional on assent to the additional or different terms.

(2) The additional terms are to be construed as proposals for addition to the contract. Between merchants such terms become part of the contract unless:

(a) the offer expressly limits acceptance to the terms of the offer;

(b) they materially alter it; or

(c) notification of objection to them has already been given or is given within a reasonable time after notice of them is received.

(3) Conduct by both parties which recognises the existence of a contract is sufficient to establish a contract for sale although the writings of the parties do not otherwise establish a contract. In such case the terms of the particular contract consist of those terms on which the writings of the parties agree, together with any supplementary terms incorporated under any other provisions of this Act.

Notes

(1) By virtue of subsection (1), a contract may be concluded in spite of a 'battle of the terms' without a contrived 'acceptance by conduct' of the 'last-shot' terms and conditions of the other party. Even an acceptance that does not truly mirror the offer can conclude the contract, unless the acceptor has made his acceptance expressly conditional on the offeror's assent to his additional and different terms. On the other hand, subsection (2) seems to adopt the 'first-blow' rule, according to which the offeror's terms and conditions prevail; only terms and conditions contained in the acceptance and that do not materially alter the offer become part of the contract (subsection 2(b)). Moreover, under subsections 2(a) and (c), the offeror has the power to reject additional terms contained in the acceptance. The provision does not therefore remove the objection that it is unrealistic and undesirable to give one party control where the parties are not agreed as to the terms and conditions.

(2) The supporters of the 'knock-out rule' have tried to construe subsection (2) in a more innovative way.[213] They say that, since this subsection mentions only 'additional terms' and not 'conflicting' terms of the acceptance, the latter are not covered by the subsection. Therefore, if the acceptance contains conflicting terms, the offeror's terms do not prevail. In such a case the conflicting terms and conditions contained in offer and acceptance knock each other out, and gaps in the contract must be filled by suppletive rules of law (the 'knock-out rule'). This innovative reading of subsection (2) was applied in *Daitom Inc v Pennwalt Corp*.[214]

(3) The knock-out rule is adopted expressly in subsection (3) of the UCC provision. However, the provision applies only when no contract has been concluded on the basis of subsection (1), because there was no 'definite and reasonable expression of acceptance' or because the acceptance was expressly made conditional on the offeror's assent to the additional and conflicting terms in the acceptance. In English law, Lord Denning made an effort to introduce an approach very similar to the knock out rule in the *Butler Machine Co* case,[215] but his Lordship's preference for looking at the

---

[213] See von Mehren (n 1 above) 97–99.
[214] 741 F 2d 1569 (10 Cir 1984).
[215] 8.55 (EN), above, p 268.

documentation as a whole was rejected by the House of Lords in *Gibson v Manchester CC*[216] and in battle of the forms cases, the English courts continue to apply the traditional 'mirror image' approach: see *Tekdata Interconnections Ltd v Amphenol Ltd*.[217]

8.4 RIGHTS OF WITHDRAWAL

In all Member States, the classical position, that once there has been an offer and acceptance on terms that are sufficiently precise (see Chapter 9) there will be a binding contract, has been altered radically as far as consumer contracts are concerned. There is no general right of withdrawal but in certain cases, particularly in the field of consumer law, such a right does exist; and a generalisation has sometimes been envisaged.

In the French Civil Code, for example, there was no general right of withdrawal. Such a right has been consecrated by the legislator, in the Code de la consommation, for consumer contracts and also in the Code de la construction et de l'habitation, in the case of promises for the sale of land (Article L 2371-1, Loi no 2006-872, 13 July 2006). The new version of the Civil Code acknowledges that other legislation or the contract itself, may give a right of withdrawal:

> **Article 1122:** Legislation or the contract may provide for a period for reflection, which is a period within which the offeree cannot give his acceptance, or a period for withdrawal, which is a period within which a party may withdraw his consent.

Although this provision does no more than acknowledge that rights of withdrawal may exist elsewhere, it has an important pedagogical effect, notably as it recalls the priority of consumer law over the Code civil.

Book II of the DCFR contains a full chapter (Chapter 5) on the right of withdrawal. Articles II.-5:101 to II.-5:106, which form Section I, entitled 'Exercise and Effect', are applicable for the purposes of 'any rule in Books II to IV' where 'a party has a right to withdraw from a contract within a certain period'. At first sight, this appears as a typical example of generalisation drawn from the 'acquis communautaire'. However, in practice, Books II–IV mention no other rights of withdrawal than those which apply in the contexts of the two directives specifically dealt with in a second section of Book V, entitled 'Particular Rights of Withdrawal' ('door step' sales and 'distance' selling).[218]

Consumers have been granted rights of withdrawal or cancellation—often called a 'cooling-off period'—in certain types of contract. Full details will be found in the *Casebook on Consumer Law*,[219] but this phenomenon is so important that it must be mentioned here. The principal rights of withdrawal applied originally to 'door step' sales

---

[216] [1979] 1 WLR 294.

[217] [2009] EWCA Civ 1209, [2010] 1 Lloyd's Rep 357.

[218] See S Whittaker's study, commissioned by the Ministry of Justice of the United Kingdom, 'The "Draft Common Frame of Reference": an Assessment', November 2008, para 4; see also S Whittaker, 'A Framework of Principles for European Contract Law?' (2009) 125 LQR 616.

[219] H-W Micklitz, J Stuyck and E Terryn, *Ius Commune Casebooks on the Common Law of Europe: Consumer Law* (Oxford: Hart Publishing, 2010) ch 4.1. A new edition is in preparation.

and 'distance' selling, under the Doorstep Selling Directive[220] and the Distance Selling Directive.[221] In 2011 these two Directives were replaced by the Consumer Rights Directive, which covers both 'distance contracts' and what are now called 'off-premises contracts'.

Consumer Rights Directive[222]   **8.59 (EU)**

Article 2

Definitions

...

(7) 'distance contract' means any contract concluded between the trader and the consumer under an organised distance sales or service-provision scheme without the simultaneous physical presence of the trader and the consumer, with the exclusive use of one or more means of distance communication up to and including the time at which the contract is concluded;

(8) 'off-premises contract' means any contract between the trader and the consumer:

(a) concluded in the simultaneous physical presence of the trader and the consumer, in a place which is not the business premises of the trader;

(b) for which an offer was made by the consumer in the same circumstances as referred to in point (a);

(c) concluded on the business premises of the trader or through any means of distance communication immediately after the consumer was personally and individually addressed in a place which is not the business premises of the trader in the simultaneous physical presence of the trader and the consumer; or

(d) concluded during an excursion organised by the trader with the aim or effect of promoting and selling goods or services to the consumer;

...

Article 9

Right of withdrawal

(1) Save where the exceptions provided for in Article 16 apply, the consumer shall have a period of 14 days to withdraw from a distance or off-premises contract, without giving any reason, and without incurring any costs other than those provided for in Article 13(2) and Article 14.

---

[220] Council Directive 85/557/EEC of 20 December 1985 to protect the consumer in respect of contracts negotiated away from business premises, OJ L372/31.

[221] Directive 97/7/EC of the European Parliament and of the Council of 20 May 1997 on the protection of consumers in respect of distance contracts, OJ L144/19.

[222] Directive 2011/83/EU of the European Parliament and of the Council of 25 October 2011 on consumer rights, amending Council Directive 93/13/EEC and Directive 1999/44/EC of the European Parliament and of the Council and repealing Council Directive 85/577/EEC and Directive 97/7/EC of the European Parliament and of the Council, OJ 2011 L304 p 64.

(2) Without prejudice to Article 10, the withdrawal period referred to in paragraph 1 of this Article shall expire after 14 days from:

(a) in the case of service contracts, the day of the conclusion of the contract;

(b) in the case of sales contracts, the day on which the consumer or a third party other than the carrier and indicated by the consumer acquires physical possession of the goods or:

(i) in the case of multiple goods ordered by the consumer in one order and delivered separately, the day on which the consumer or a third party other than the carrier and indicated by the consumer acquires physical possession of the last good;

(ii) in the case of delivery of a good consisting of multiple lots or pieces, the day on which the consumer or a third party other than the carrier and indicated by the consumer acquires physical possession of the last lot or piece;

(iii) in the case of contracts for regular delivery of goods during defined period of time, the day on which the consumer or a third party other than the carrier and indicated by the consumer acquires physical possession of the first good;

(c) in the case of contracts for the supply of water, gas or electricity, where they are not put up for sale in a limited volume or set quantity, of district heating or of digital content which is not supplied on a tangible medium, the day of the conclusion of the contract.

(3) The Member States shall not prohibit the contracting parties from performing their contractual obligations during the withdrawal period. Nevertheless, in the case of off-premises contracts, Member States may maintain existing national legislation prohibiting the trader from collecting the payment from the consumer during the given period after the conclusion of the contract.

Article 10

Omission of information on the right of withdrawal

(1) If the trader has not provided the consumer with the information on the right of withdrawal as required by point (h) of Article 6(1), the withdrawal period shall expire 12 months from the end of the initial withdrawal period, as determined in accordance with Article 9(2).

(2) If the trader has provided the consumer with the information provided for in paragraph 1 of this Article within 12 months from the day referred to in Article 9(2), the withdrawal period shall expire 14 days after the day upon which the consumer receives that information.

...

Notes

(1) Article 6(1) of the Directive requires a trader making a distance or off-premises contract with a consumer to give the consumer specified information, which include:

...

(h) where a right of withdrawal exists, the conditions, time limit and procedures for exercising that right in accordance with Article 11(1), as well as the model withdrawal form set out in Annex I(B);

(i)   where applicable, that the consumer will have to bear the cost of returning the goods in case of withdrawal and, for distance contracts, if the goods, by their nature, cannot normally be returned by post, the cost of returning the goods;

(j)   that, if the consumer exercises the right of withdrawal after having made a request in accordance with Article 7(3) or Article 8(8), the consumer shall be liable to pay the trader reasonable costs in accordance with Article 14(3);

(k)   where a right of withdrawal is not provided for in accordance with Article 16, the information that the consumer will not benefit from a right of withdrawal or, where applicable, the circumstances under which the consumer loses his right of withdrawal; ...

(2) The consumer has no right of withdrawal in a number of cases, which are listed in Article 16. These include, for instance, where the goods supplied are made to the consumer's specifications or clearly personalised, or are sealed audio or sealed video recordings or sealed computer software which were unsealed after delivery; and there are many more kinds of contract to which the Directive as a whole does not apply, see Article 3.

(3) Article 16 also exempts service contracts after the service has been fully performed, if the performance was begun with the consumer's prior express consent, and with the acknowledgement that he will lose his right of withdrawal once the contract has been fully performed by the trader.

(4) Broadly speaking, if the consumer withdraws, the trader has 14 days to refund the price plus normal delivery costs, see Article 13; and the consumer has 14 days to send the goods back to the trader or hand them over to someone authorised to collect them: Article 14.

(5) CESL Chapter 4, Right to withdraw in distance and off-premises contracts between traders and consumers, replicated the Directive.

In addition, the Consumer Rights Directive tries to ensure that a consumer who makes a contract via a trader's website appreciates that they are making a commitment. Article 8 provides:

2. If a distance contract to be concluded by electronic means places the consumer under an obligation to pay, ...

The trader shall ensure that the consumer, when placing his order, explicitly acknowledges that the order implies an obligation to pay. If placing an order entails activating a button or a similar function, the button or similar function shall be labelled in an easily legible manner only with the words 'order with obligation to pay' or a corresponding unambiguous formulation indicating that placing the order entails an obligation to pay the trader. If the trader has not complied with this subparagraph, the consumer shall not be bound by the contract or order.

FURTHER READING

Christandl, G, 'Offer and Acceptance' in N Jansen and R Zimmermann (eds), *Commentaries on European Contract Laws* (Oxford University Press, 2018) 294–347.
Illmer, M, 'Contract (Formation)' in J Basedow, K Hopt and R Zimmermann (eds), *Max Planck Encyclopedia of European Private Law* (Oxford University Press, 2012) 378–83.

Kötz, H, *European Contract Law* (2nd edn, Oxford University Press, 2017) 17–39.

Markesinis, BS, Unberath, H and Johnston, A, *The German Law of Contract* (2nd edn, Oxford: Hart Publishing, 2006) 55–81.

Sacco, R, 'Formation of Contracts' in A Hartkamp et al, *Towards a European Civil Code* (4th edn, Alphen aan den Rijn: Wolters Kluwer, 2011) 483–92.

Zweigert, K and Kötz, H, *Introduction to Comparative Law* (3rd edn, Oxford: Clarendon Press, 1998) 356–64.

CHAPTER 9
SUFFICIENCY OF AGREEMENT

9.1 INTRODUCTION

In English and German law it is generally assumed that, in addition to the 'intention requirement', an offer must contain the essential elements of the contract.[1] If it does not, then even if the other party accepts, there will not be what the Principles of European Contract Law (PECL) term a 'sufficient' agreement.[2] What is 'sufficient' is defined as follows:

Principles of European Contract Law   **9.1 (INT)**

Article 2:103: Sufficient Agreement
  (1) There is sufficient agreement if the terms:
      (a) have been sufficiently defined by the parties so that the contract can be enforced or
      (b) can be determined under these Principles.
  (2) However, if one of the parties refuses to conclude a contract unless the parties have agreed on some specific matter, there is no contract unless agreement on that matter has been reached.

Notes

(1) The question of the essential minimum that a proposal should include in order to make it an offer should be distinguished from the fact that, in some cases, a failure to specify enough terms will indicate that no final agreement has been reached.[3] As we saw in Chapter 9, sometimes the lack of detail in a proposal will lead the court to conclude that it was not intended to be an offer.[4]

---

[1] W Flume, *Allgemeiner Teil des bürgerlichen Rechts*, vol II, *Das Rechtsgeschäft* (3rd edn, Berlin: Springer, 1979) 635; F Terré, Y Lequette and F Chénedé, *Grands arrêts de jurisprudence civile,* vol 2, *Obligations, Contrats spéciaux, Sûretés,* (13th edn, Paris: Dalloz, 2015); F Terré, P Simler and Y Lequette, *Les obligations* (11th edn, Paris: Dalloz, 2013); M Latina and G Chantepie, *La réforme du droit des obligations: Commentaire théorique et pratique dans l'ordre du Code civil* (Paris: Dalloz, 2016) nos. 408–22; E McKendrick, *Contract Law* (12th edn, Basingstoke: Palgrave Macmillan, 2017) ch 4; *Treitel on the Law of Contract*, 14th edn by E Peel (London: Sweet & Maxwell, 2015) paras 2-078–2-097.
[2] PECL Art 2:201, see 8.11 (INT), above, p 225.
[3] cf *May & Butcher v The King*, 9.4 (EN), below, p 285.
[4] This was one reason why in *Gibson v Manchester City Council* (8.3 (EN), above, p 205) the city treasurer's letter was held not to amount to an offer.

> (2) Moreover, one party may indicate that it is only prepared to agree a contract if an agreement is reached on a certain issue. This is dealt with in Article 2:103(2) PECL. Similarly, according to French case law, if one of the parties makes it clear that he does not want to enter into a binding agreement before a term of the contract is settled in a satisfactory manner, a contract does not come into existence before this additional matter is agreed upon.[5]

In effect, there appears to be a similar requirement of 'sufficiency' in French law, but as we will see, traditionally the question has been put in somewhat different terms, namely, whether the contract has a determinable *objet*[6] and whether the price has been determined.

Under the original code one of the four conditions for a contract to be validly concluded was that the contract had an *objet* (*un objet certain qui forme la matière de l'engagement*, as former Article 1108 Code civil put it). This requirement is no longer stated as one of the requirements for a contract[7], which are now listed as:

Code civil

9.2 (FR)

Article 1128: The following are necessary for the validity of a contract:
1. the consent of the parties;
2. their capacity to contract;
3. content which is lawful and certain.

We will see that the notion of *objet* appears to re-surface in the guise of the 'content' that is required for a contract, but the requirements of the former law seem to have been relaxed.

The issue of determination of price has led to considerable debate and major cases. This question was long been linked to the issue of validity of contract; more recently, it was also considered to be closely related to the performance of contract (the court's control is then a control of any *abus* in determining the price). French law will be dealt with after English and German law.

9.2 ENGLISH LAW

In English law the essential questions are whether the parties intend to be bound without further negotiation, and, if so, whether the court can determine what each of them is to do, if necessary by resorting to imposing obligations that appear reasonable in the circumstances.

---

[5] Terré, Simler and Lequette (n 1 above) no. 188; see also Cass req 1 December 1885, Terré, Lequette and Chénedé (n 1 above) no. 145.

[6] See the brief discussion of former Art 1108 Cciv 5.6 (FR), above, p 116. Terré, Lequette and Chénedé (n 1 above) no. 145; Terré, Simler and Lequette (n 1 above) nos. 104 ff.

[7] Dutch law is similar to French law. Art 6:227 BW requires that the obligation must be determinable. See AS Hartkamp & CH Sieburgh, *Mr. C. Assers Handleiding tot de beoefening van het Nederlands Burgerlijk Recht. 6. Verbintenissenrecht. Deel III. Algemeen overeenkomstenrecht* (Deventer: Kluwer 2014) nos. 284 ff.

Sale of Goods Act 1979   **9.3 (EN)**

Section 8: Ascertainment of price

(1) The price in a contract of sale may be fixed by the contract, or may be left to be fixed in a manner agreed by the contract, or may be determined by the course of dealing between the parties.

(2) Where the price is not determined as mentioned in subsection (1) above the buyer must pay a reasonable price.

(3) What is a reasonable price is a question of fact dependent on the circumstances of each particular case.

House of Lords   **9.4 (EN)**

May & Butcher v The King[8]

If the parties have left an essential element of the contract to be agreed, that will normally be interpreted as showing that they have not concluded a contract.

Facts: The Disposals Board had been set up after the First World War to dispose of unused materials. The plaintiffs (appellants) alleged that the Controller of the Disposals Board had agreed to sell them tentage (tent material) on terms contained in a letter, as follows:

(1) The Commission agrees to sell and [the appellants] agree to purchase the total stock of old tentage …

(3) The price or prices to be paid, and the date or dates on which payment is to be made by the purchasers to the Commission for such old tentage shall be agreed upon from time to time between the Commission and the purchasers as the quantities of the said old tentage become available for disposal, and are offered to the purchasers by the Commission. …

(10) It is understood that all disputes with reference to or arising out of this agreement will be submitted to arbitration in accordance with the provisions of the Arbitration Act 1889.

Held: The appellants argued that there was a contract to sell them the tentage either at a reasonable price or at a price that could be determined by an arbitrator. The Disposals Board contended that there was no binding contract, and the House of Lords upheld this view.

Judgment: VISCOUNT DUNEDIN: … This case arises upon a question of sale, but in my view the principles which we are applying are not confined to sale, but are the general principles of the law of contract. To be a good contract there must be a concluded bargain, and a concluded contract is one which settles everything that is necessary to be settled and leaves nothing to be settled by agreement between the parties. Of course it may leave something which still has to be determined, but then that determination must be a determination which does not depend upon the agreement between the parties. In the system of law in which I was brought up, that was expressed by one of those brocards of which perhaps we have been too fond, but which often express very neatly what is wanted: "Certum est quod certum reddi potest." Therefore, you may very well agree that a certain part of the contract of sale, such as price, may be settled by some one else. As a matter of the general law of contract all the essentials have to be settled. What are the essentials may vary according to the particular contract under consideration. We are here dealing with sale, and undoubtedly price is one of the essentials of sale, and if it is left still to be agreed between the parties, then there is no contract. It may be left to the determination of a certain person, and if it was so left and that person either would not or could not act,

---

[8] The case was decided in 1929 but was reported only in [1934] 2 KB 17n.

there would be no contract because the price was to be settled in a certain way and it has become impossible to settle it in that way, and therefore there is no settlement. No doubt as to goods, the Sale of Goods Act, 1893, says that if the price is not mentioned and set-tled in the contract it is to be a reasonable price. The simple answer in this case is that the Sale of Goods Act provides for silence on the point and here there is no silence, because there is a provision that the two parties are to agree. As long as you have something cer-tain it does not matter. For instance, with regard to price it is a perfectly good contract to say that the price is to be settled by the buyer. I have not had time, or perhaps I have not been industrious enough, to look through all the books in England to see if there is such a case; but there was such a case in Scotland in 1760, where it was decided that a sale of a landed estate was perfectly good, the price being left to be settled by the buyer himself. ... Here there was clearly no contract. There would have been a perfectly good settlement of price if the contract had said that it was to be settled by arbitration by a certain man, or it might have been quite good if it was said that it was to be settled by arbitration under the Arbitration Act so as to bring in a material plan by which a certain person could be put in action. The question then arises, has anything of that sort been done? I think clearly not. The general arbitration clause is one in very common form as to disputes arising out of the arrangements. In no proper meaning of the word can this be described as a dispute arising between the parties; it is a failure to agree, which is a very different thing from a dispute.

[Lords BUCKMASTER and WARRINGTON gave judgments to the same effect, and the appeal was dismissed.]

Court of Appeal   9.5 (EN)

British Bank for Foreign Trade v Novinex Ltd[9]

If the parties left the price to be agreed but one party had actually performed what would be required by the contract, they would be treated as implicitly agreeing that the contract should be binding and the other party should pay a reasonable price.

Facts: The plaintiffs had arranged for P to supply a consignment of oilskins to the defendants, who had not had any previous contact with P, and the defendants wrote confirming that they had agreed to pay the plaintiffs a commission for this. The letter continued:

> We also undertake to cover you with an agreed commission on any other business transacted with your friends [P]. In return for this, you are to put us in direct touch with your friends.

The plaintiffs put the defendants in direct contact with P, and the defendants entered into further transactions with P, but they refused to pay the plaintiffs any commission on them. The plaintiffs' action was dismissed by Denning J, and they appealed.

Held: The plaintiffs were entitled to a reasonable commission.

Judgment: COHEN LJ: ... Is this an enforceable agreement? A number of authorities have been cited to us, to which I do not propose to refer in detail, because, in my view, the effect of the authorities is stated correctly in the learned judge's judgment where he said:

> 'The principle to be deduced from the cases is that if there is an essential term which has yet to be agreed and there is no express or implied provision for its solution, the result in point of law is that there is no binding contract. In seeing whether there is an implied provision for its solution, however, there is a difference between

---

[9] [1949] 1 KB 623.

an arrangement which is wholly executory on both sides, and one which has been executed on one side or the other. In the ordinary way, if there is an arrangement to supply goods at a price "to be agreed", or to perform services on terms "to be agreed", then although, while the matter is still executory, there may be no binding contract, nevertheless, if it is executed on one side, that is if the one does his part without having come to an agreement as to the price or the terms, then the law will say that there is necessarily implied, from the conduct of the parties, a contract that, in default of agreement, a reasonable sum is to be paid.'

With that statement of the principle of law, I respectfully agree. My difference with the learned judge is only on the question whether he has correctly applied that statement of principle to the facts of this case. ...

Then the judge continued on what, I think, is the principal issue:

'And what is the amount of the commission to be? If there is no usual or customary commission, how can anyone say what is a reasonable commission for a follow-up transaction or a repeat transaction? That appeared quite clearly from the evidence which showed that when parties are negotiating for the price they are going to pay, they take account of any commission they have to pay to agents.'

Denning J went on to say that this showed that the agreement was too vague to be enforced. But the agreement had said in terms, instead of by implication: 'we also undertake to cover you with a reasonable commission on any other business transacted with your friends'. Denning J seems to have regarded that condition as being too vague to be enforceable. I cannot agree with this view. I think that a court should take the view that a jury properly directed would be able to arrive at a proper conclusion as to what in the circumstances of this case is a reasonable commission.

[His Lordship then considered what would be a reasonable commission in respect of the transactions and concluded that it would not exceed 1/4d per skin.]

BUCKNILL and SINGLETON LJJ agreed.

Notes

(1) *May & Butcher v The King* is a case in which the Court decided that the parties did not intend to be bound unless and until agreement had been reached on the price. It is not always obvious whether this is the case or whether they intended there to be a binding agreement at, for example, a reasonable price. In the Court of Appeal, Scrutton LJ, a very experienced commercial lawyer, had dissented; he held that the parties had meant to be bound. The House of Lords took the opposite view. Some years later Scrutton LJ said:

I am afraid I remain quite impenitent. I think I was right and that nine out of ten business men would agree with me. But of course I recognise that I am bound as a judge to follow the principles laid down by the House of Lords. But I regret that in many commercial matters the English law and the practice of commercial men are getting wider apart, with the result that commercial business is leaving the courts and is being decided by commercial arbitrators with infrequent reference to the courts.[10]

---

[10] *Hillas Ltd v Arcos Ltd* (1931) 40 Ll L Rep 307, 311 (CA).

(2) *May & Butcher v The King* was a case in which an essential term had been left 'to be agreed'. In contrast, in many cases the terms of the contract, such as the price, will not be determined but the contract itself will provide a mechanism for determining the price: for example, that it is to be fixed by a third person. Under Sale of Goods Act 1979, section 9, such an agreement will be binding but will cease to be binding if the third person fails to fix the price. That is not the only possible outcome. The court might hold that the mechanism in the contract for determining the price was only a mechanism for determining a fair price and, if the machinery fails, the court can decide the price.[11] But, as *May & Butcher v The King* demonstrates, the fact that there is an arbitration clause does not provide a mechanism for this if the parties' words and conduct show that they have yet to agree on essential terms.

(3) If the conduct of the parties shows that they must have meant to be bound, and particularly if one party has actually performed, the court will, if it can, 'fill in the gaps', for example by determining what it would be reasonable to pay for the goods or services. The court will consider the prices normally charged for the relevant goods or services, any relevant trade customs and also previous dealings between the parties.[12]

(4) If the parties have begun performance, leaving obligations that are to be performed in the future 'to be agreed', the court might hold that the contract is binding only so far as it has actually been performed. However, if the court thinks that the parties meant the contract as a whole to be binding, it will also do its best to find a way to determine the future obligations. For example, if there is an arbitration clause in the contract, it may say that the future obligations should be determined by the arbitrator.[13]

(5) As we will see later, an 'agreement to agree' is not itself a binding contract in English law, basically because it is considered to be too uncertain.[14]

(6) Thus, in English case law the question whether an agreement is a binding contract depends primarily on the intention of the parties and inferences on this intention may be drawn from the importance of a matter left over for further agreement. This was illustrated by the *Gibson* case,[15] where the fact that detailed terms had not been set out was used as evidence that the Council's letter did not amount to an offer. See also *Clifton v Palumbo*.[16] The extent to which the parties have acted on the agreement is also relevant.[17]

(7) Sometimes, however, even though the court thinks the parties intended to be bound, it will conclude that is not possible to determine what the obligations should

---

[11] See *Sudbrook Trading Estate Ltd v Eggleton* [1983] 1 AC 444 (HL).
[12] For an example, see *Hillas & Co Ltd v Arcos Ltd* (1932) 147 LT 503 (HL).
[13] eg *Foley v Classique Coaches Ltd* [1934] 2 KB 1 (CA); *F & G Sykes (Wessex) Ltd v Fine Fare Ltd* [1967] 1 Lloyd's Rep 53 (CA) where it was held that the quantities of goods to be supplied after the first six months of operation had been left 'to be agreed' but the contract must have been intended to last more than six months because that was the only way the plaintiffs could recoup their initial investment.
[14] See below, p 336.
[15] See 8.3 (EN) above, p 205.
[16] [1944] 2 All ER 497 (CA); above, p 209.
[17] *Treitel* (n 1 above) para 4-021.

be. For example, in *Scammell Ltd v Ouston*,[18] the parties agreed that the respondents should buy a new lorry from the appellants, trading in an old lorry and paying the balance of the agreed purchase price 'on hire-purchase terms' over two years. The precise terms of the hire-purchase agreement were not settled. The appellants subsequently refused to go ahead, alleging that there was no contract. The House of Lords held the phrase 'on hire-purchase terms' was too vague for there to be an enforceable contract, as too many questions were left open. Were the appellants to hire the lorry to the respondents themselves, or (as often happens) arrange to sell the lorries to a finance company which would then hire them to the respondents? And were the respondents to pay a cash deposit, as was often required at that time?

9.3 GERMAN LAW

German law seems to take a broadly similar approach to English law. If the parties have not agreed on an essential element, there will be no binding contract.

BGB[19]   **9.6 (DE)**

§ 154: Overt lack of agreement; lack of notarial recording

(1) As long as the parties have not yet agreed on all points of a contract on which an agreement was required to be reached according to the declaration even of only one party, the contract is, in case of doubt, not entered into. An agreement on individual points is not legally binding even if they have been recorded.

(2) If notarial recording of the contract contemplated has been arranged, the contract is, in case of doubt, not entered into until the recording has taken place.

§ 155: Hidden lack of agreement

If the parties to a contract which they consider to have been entered into have, in fact, not agreed on a point on which an agreement was required to be reached, whatever is agreed is applicable if it is to be assumed that the contract would have been entered into even without a provision concerning this point.

RG, 8 April 1929[20]   **9.7 (DE)**

Precontract without price

A 'precontract' which merely fixes a maximum price is not binding.

Facts: On 24 March 1919, the parties entered a 'precontract' (*Vorvertrag*) before a notary, by Clause II of which the plaintiff, at any time on the defendant's demand, undertook to enter a contract of sale with the

---

[18] [1941] AC 251 (HL).
[19] See also below, p 293.
[20] RGZ 124, 81.

defendant so as to vest in him ownership in house no 49 in P 'with all contents'. It was agreed and ordered that an entry should be made in the land register to secure this future claim. By Clause III 'the precise terms and conditions of the sale are to be finalised on the drawing up of the sales contract, the price of house and contents not to exceed M40,000.' By Clause IV the plaintiff's undertaking was to last until 24 March 1920. The relevant entry in the land register was made on the defendant's behalf on 28 March 1919. On 12 March 1920 the defendant gave the plaintiff one week to perform his obligations but the plaintiff did nothing, in the belief that the contract was void because the parties' agreement regarding the price was inaccurately recorded. He sought a declaration to that effect, and an injunction requiring the defendant to consent to the erasure of the entry in his favour in the land register. The defendant counter-claimed for an injunction that the plaintiff transfer house and contents for M40,000 and agree to a change of ownership in the land register. The lower court rejected the claim and gave judgment on the counter-claim. On the plaintiff's appeal the counter-claimant cross-appealed for a judgment that the plaintiff sell him the property on the terms of the Landgericht judgment. Judgment in the Oberlandesgericht was in the defendant's favour.

Held: The plaintiffs appeal was allowed because the alleged 'precontract' was void.

Judgment: On the substance of the matter, the appellant rightly insisted on a point which he raised below, namely that the 'precontract' of 24 March 1919 is invalid for want of content.

It is familiar law that a precontract must meet not only the formal requirements (which is here the case—§ 313(1) BGB [now § 311b(1) BGB][21]), but the substantive requirements of the main contract. In particular, the duties undertaken by the parties in the precontract must be certain or at least ascertainable, so that a court can determine the content of the ultimate contract (RGZ 66, 121; 72, 385; see also RGZ 106, 177). No such certainty or ascertainability exists in the 'precontract' of 24 March 1919. A sales contract, and consequently a precontract to a sale, requires agreement of the parties not only on the thing or right which constitutes the object of the contract but also on the price (§ 433 BGB[22]). We need not ask whether the seller's duty with regard to the contents was sufficiently certain or ascertainable under the contract of 24 March, since in any case the buyer's counterpart, the price, is left uncertain; the only thing fixed about the price is its upper limit, viz M40,000. The plaintiff could not on the basis of such a pre-contract have insisted on going through with a sales contract, let alone at a price of M40,000; nor can the defendant, even if he offers the highest sum mentioned. On the price alone, the agreement of 24 March lacks the quality of a precontract; it is simply a draft or sketch, not binding on either party, and capable at the very most of use in the interpretation of a subsequent precontract or main contract, if one were to be made. But there is the further point that the parties specifically agreed to postpone making the detailed terms of sale until the time of the later contract (compare § 154(1) BGB). It therefore depended on the free decision of both parties what these detailed terms should be, and such a decision could not conceivably be replaced or amplified by a judicial decision. Neither the Landgericht nor the Oberlandesgericht made any such attempt: both simply took M40,000 as the purchase price without even adverting to the matter or revalorisation, which they should have raised *proprio motu* (RGZ 106, 422; 107, 19, 129, 150; 109, 69).

The plaintiff's claim for a declaration that the contract of 24 March 1919 was void is therefore justified.

---

[21] See below, p 399.
[22] See 19.5 (DE), below, p 789.

Furniture

If it is clear that the parties regarded themselves as bound because they had gone ahead with performance, it will be presumed that they are agreeing that a fair price should be paid.

Facts: By notarial contract the plaintiff sold the defendants a plot of land on which a single family house, designed for occupation by the plaintiff and his wife, had recently been erected. While the house was being built, and long before entering into the contract of sale, the plaintiff had purchased a large quantity of furniture and fittings, at a total price of about 20,000 DM, much of it being custom made, such as cupboards and kitchen cabinets. The furniture and fittings were installed in the house, but the plaintiff never occupied it, so he was eager to sell them with the property, as he had no real use for them. The defendants started using the furniture as soon as they moved into the house, and are still using it today. They gave the plaintiff a cheque for 2,000 DM, but the plaintiff contended that a sale price of 20,000 DM had been agreed, and sued for 18,000 DM. The defendants denied that there was ever any contract about the furniture, as no agreement about the price ensued from the negotiations. The Landgericht gave judgment for the plaintiff.

Held: The defendant's appeal was mainly unsuccessful because the parties had made a valid contract of sale.

Judgment: I. The plaintiff has a claim for 18,000 DM under § 433 BGB. A contract for the sale of these fitments did come about between the parties.

1. The evidence does not make it absolutely clear that the parties expressly agreed on a price of 20,000 DM.

2. But under the special circumstances of this case the failure to agree on the price is not fatal to the formation of a contract of sale. It emerges from the whole evidence that the parties concluded a contract of sale with the peculiarity that it should be left for further negotiations to determine a fair price.

(a) It is true that in a case of doubt parties are held not to have made a contract until they have agreed on all the points which need agreement (§ 154 BGB), and both parties here realised that there should be agreement on the price. But this principle applies only 'in case of doubt' (§ 154 BGB), that is, it only gives rise to a presumption which is capable of being rebutted. It does not prevent the parties from entering into legal obligations although certain details of the transaction are still unregulated which one or both parties wish clarified. ... The principle of freedom of contract requires that people should be able to leave even essential points open, such as the purchase price in the present case (see BGH, NJW 1964, 1617), without impairing the contractual obligation which the parties wish to achieve.

(b) In the present case there was an agreement of this kind. It is common ground that the plaintiff wanted to sell the furniture along with the land, and as the defendants themselves say, they were in principle ready to take over the furniture, even if they had a somewhat different price in mind. It is not to be supposed that in such circumstances the plaintiff gave the defendants possession of the furniture, with all the risk of wear and tear, without there being any legal obligation between the parties at the time. Doubtless it would not have been easy for the plaintiff to sell the new furniture very favourably elsewhere, but he could hardly sell it at all once it was used. The plaintiff's letting

---

[23] NJW 1976, 1212. The following provisions of the BGB which are referred to in this case are cited at other places in this book: §§ 133 and 157 (see 18.4 (DE) and 18.7 (DE), below, pp 724–25), § 147 (see 8.28 (DE), above, p 245), §§ 315 and 316 (9.9 (DE), below, p 293), § 433 (19.15 (DE), below, p 789).

the defendants possess and use the furniture before there was any agreement as to the price must, in good faith, be treated as an offer for sale at a price which remained to be determined, and the defendants accepted this offer by beginning to use the furniture. The circumstances were all well-known to them. They could not reasonably suppose that the plaintiff was selling them the house without any agreement about the furniture, or that he was letting them use it without any obligation to buy it at a price still to be fixed. It is worth noting that the price mentioned for these items was quite small in relation to the price of the house, only about 5%.

Under these circumstances the defendants' taking possession of the furniture and making use of it is conduct which ranks as an acceptance of the plaintiff's offer (§ 133 BGB). If this was not the defendants' intention, it was for them to make this clear to the plaintiff, and they did not do so. Any secret reservation the defendants may have had about buying the furniture when they took possession of it can be disregarded (§ 116 BGB).

The court has also considered whether the agreement might be merely a precontract with an obligation to conclude the sales contract later, but such a construction overlooks the point that the plaintiff has already performed one of the seller's essential obligations by putting the defendants in possession and giving them use of the chattels being sold.

The defendants can obtain no assistance from § 147 BGB, whereby an offer made to a person actually present must be accepted forthwith. The offeror may extend the period for acceptance at any time, and may do so implicitly ... On a reasonable construction, the plaintiff's offer to sell the furniture to the defendants before any price was fixed was to last at least until the defendants moved into the house which had the furniture in it; proper acceptance duly took place. The view that a contract of sale was formed is further strengthened by the fact that the defendants have paid 2,000 DM. This may not show that any price was agreed, but it does show that the parties agreed that the defendants be bound to buy the furniture at a price yet to be hit upon.

(c) It is actually in the interests of both parties that the defendants should keep the furniture and pay a price still to be fixed. The defendants have often said that they were ready to keep the furniture, and the plaintiff cannot put it to any economic use. If no sales contract exists, the defendants will not only have to give up the furniture but also, after being credited with the 2,000 DM they have paid, pay the plaintiff the value of the use of the furniture, which in the case of new furniture is very high, until such time as they call upon him to remove it; furthermore, they will need to buy new furniture although, as has been said, they are quite happy with what they have. Both parties are experienced people and it must have been clear to them that unreasonable consequences of this kind would ensue if the furniture were used without there being any contract about it. This confirms the conclusion that the possession was handed over definitively and pursuant to a contract of sale.

3. There having been proof of the price which the defendants are thus bound to pay, it must be filled in by apt contractual construction (§ 157 BGB; ...). The parties must, as reasonable people, have intended to agree on a fair price. There is nothing to suggest that either party was to have a right of determination under § 315 BGB. As the defendant unanswerably argued, the purchase price was to be agreed, not laid down, especially not laid down by the plaintiff (§ 316 BGB). If the parties do not agree, and if neither party nor any third party has a right of determination, the determination of the fair purchase price which the defendants are bound to pay can only be made by the court.

Appeal dismissed.

Notes

(1) These cases seem to draw the same distinction as in English law. If the parties have left something to be agreed, and there is nothing to show that they meant to be bound, there will be no offer that can be accepted to make a binding contract: *Precontract without price*. In contrast, according to the *Furniture* case, if it is clear that the parties regarded themselves as bound because they had gone ahead with performance, it will be presumed that they are agreeing that a fair price should be paid.

(2) As in English law, the position depends primarily on the intentions shown by the words and conduct of the parties. Even if the court could determine a fair price or other term, it will not hold that there is a contract if the conduct of one or both parties showed that they did not intend to be bound until they had agreed on the relevant matter. This is clearly provided in § 154(1) BGB. Compare also Article 2:103(2)[24] of the PECL and Article 2.1.13 of the UNIDROIT Principles of International Commercial Contracts (UNIDROIT PICC).

(3) Where there clearly is meant to be a contract, but some element of the obligation is left to the discretion of one party, § 315 BGB applies.

BGB	**9.9 (DE)**

§ 315: Specification of performance by one party

(1) Where performance is to be specified by one of the parties to the contract, then in case of doubt it is to be assumed that the specification is to be made at the reasonably exercised discretion of the party making it.

(2) The specification is made by declaration to the other party.

(3) Where the specification is to be made at the reasonably exercised discretion of a party, the specification made is binding on the other party only if it is equitable. If it is not equitable, the specification is made by judicial decision; the same applies if the specification is delayed.

§ 316: Specification of [counter-performance][25]

If the extent of the [counter-performance] promised for an act of performance is not specified, then in case of doubt the party that is owed the [counter-performance] is entitled to make the specification.

9.4 FRENCH LAW

9.4.A *OBJET*

French law, as mentioned earlier, used to see the issue of 'sufficient agreement' at least in part as a question of whether there is an *objet*, one of the four elements that were necessary under former Article 1108 of the Civil Code to create a contract. An *objet* is no

---

[24] See 9.1 (INT), above, p 283.
[25] The official translation of the Ministry of Justice uses the term 'consideration' instead.

longer a constituent part of a contract under new Article 1128; what is required is that the 'content' of the contract be 'certain'. However, the reference to the *objet* ('subject matter') comes back in Article 1163 of the revised Code. The subsequent articles relate to the price and to the quality of the act of performance.

Code civil   **9.10 (FR)**

Article 1163: An obligation has as its subject matter [*pour objet*] a present or future act of performance.

The latter must be possible and determined or capable of being determined.

An act of performance is capable of being determined where it can be deduced from the contract or by reference to usage or the previous dealings of the parties, without the need for further agreement.

Article 1165: In contracts for the supply of services, in the absence of an agreement by the parties in advance of their performance, the price may be fixed by the creditor, subject to the latter's providing a reason for its amount if it is challenged. In the case of abuse in the fixing of the price, the court may hear a claim for damages and, where appropriate, termination of the contract.

Article 1166: Where the quality of the act of performance is not determined or capable of being determined under the contract, the debtor must offer an act of performance of a quality which conforms to the legitimate expectations of the parties taking into account its nature, usual practices and the amount of what is agreed in return.

Article 1167: Where the price or any other element of a contract is to be determined by reference to an index which does not exist or has ceased to exist or to be available, the index is replaced by the index which is most closely related to it.

Notes

(1) It was pointed out[26] that in the original version of the Code civil, *objet* was used in these texts to refer to (a) the purposes of the contract;[27] (b) the performance (*prestation*) that is required of each party;[28] and (c), where the performance required is delivery of a tangible item, the item itself.[29] In the revised Code, 'content' is the key word. It is certainly used in both the first sense (as in new Article 1128(3), 'content which is lawful') and the second sense (as in new Article 1163).[30]

(2) On the issue that we are considering, whether the content is sufficiently certain, what seems to matter is that each party's obligation, the *prestation* required, must be

---

[26] Eg B Nicholas, *The French Law of Contract* (2nd edn, Oxford: Clarendon Press, 1992) 114–15; also Terré, Simler and Lequette (n 1 above) no. 265.

[27] As in former Art 1126 first phrase.

[28] As in the second phrase of Art 1126.

[29] As in former Art 1128.

[30] L Aynès, 'The Content of Contracts: *Prestation*, *Objet* but No Longer *la Cause*?' in J Cartwright and S Whittaker (eds), *The Code Napoléon Rewritten: French Contract Law after the 2016 Reforms* (Oxford: Hart Publishing, 2017) 137.

determinable. And on the face of it, Article 1163(3) suggests that if the court decides that the parties did intend to create a binding contract even though their agreement was not complete, it will fill gaps in the contract using the same kind of criteria as the English courts use.[31]

(3) However, there still seem to be differences between the laws. A clear example of this is the question of whether the price must be fixed, or determinable from the contract, the usage or previous dealings of the parties.

9.4.B DETERMINATION OF PRICE

Whereas both English and German law say that if the parties have not agreed a price or it cannot be determined from the contract, the buyer must pay a reasonable price, this solution is not allowed by French law as a general rule. In particular, in the case of a sale of goods, Articles 1583 and 1591 Code civil provide that:

Code civil   **9.11 (FR)**

Article 1583: It is complete between the parties, and ownership is acquired as of right by the buyer with respect to the seller, as soon as the thing and the price have been agreed upon, although the thing has not yet been delivered or the price paid.

Article 1591: The price of a sale must be determined and stated by the parties.

Notes

(1) These articles are not affected by the reform in 2016. This means that it is necessary to reach agreement on both the item to be sold and the price to be paid before the contract can be complete.

(2) Article 1583 Code civil makes it easy to identify the essential elements of a sales contract. It is not always so easy, particularly as regards innominate contracts (contracts which are not classified in a well-established category: see revised Article 1105).[32]

There is unlikely to be a problem as far as what is to be supplied or done is concerned; it is hard to see that there can be a contract under any of the systems if the parties have not agreed on that. More problematic are cases in which the performance, unknown to the parties, is impossible or where it is illicit. Both these are considered later.[33]

Cases in which the parties have not fixed the price, nor agreed on a means of determining it, have caused difficulty. Traditional case law reflected a concern to ensure that the price was fair by requiring that either it be agreed by the parties or be determinable by some mechanism over which neither party would have any influence. Thus, the price might be determinable by a third person[34] or from an index or market price; but an

---

[31] See above, p 288.
[32] For some guidance on this point, see Terré, Lequette and Chénedé (n 1 above) no. 143.
[33] See chs 28 and 17, respectively.
[34] Art 1592 Cciv.

agreement to sell at the seller's list price at the date for delivery would be invalid and so would an agreement to sell at the 'market price' if in fact the seller controlled the price. This requirement of an agreed or determinable price was applied not only to sales but also to leases, hire, contracts for work, insurance and loan agreements.[35] Some other types of contract, however, in particular contracts for services, were not subjected to this rule, partly because of the practical difficulty of fixing a price in advance for these contracts.[36]

The contracts that gave rise to greatest difficulties, however, were distributorship contracts, such as those between petrol companies and filling stations. The petrol company would supply petrol to be re-sold by the filling station, and it would also provide advertising, signs and training; the filling station would agree not to re-sell the products of other companies. In these so-called 'framework contracts' (since they envisage other contracts being made within the framework of the distributorship agreement) it is almost impossible to fix the prices to be paid for the petrol at some time in the future. For a while the courts were regularly holding distributorship contracts invalid for want of a fixed or objectively determinable price. Their decisions were based on former Article 1129 Code civil, a general provision on *objet*. This provision then became a tool providing an easy way for distributors to walk out of a bad bargain. In order to avoid this, the Cour de cassation took a different approach. On 29 November 1994, in two cases, known as the *Alcatel* decisions,[37] it ruled that the requirement was satisfied, provided that a reference is made to a '*tarif*' (price of the vendor, fixed with objective elements). These cases entitled one party to unilaterally fix the price, subject to judicial control.

In 1995, in a series of four decisions,[38] the Assemblée plénière of the Cour de cassation took yet another approach. The Assemblée plénière held that former Article 1129 Code civil was not in principle applicable to the determination of price and thus decided that a framework contract was not invalidated by the fact that the price of some of the services that might be called for had not been fixed and could not be determined.[39] However, the supplier was required not to abuse his position to demand excessive prices. If he did so, though it did not affect the validity of the contract, the other party had remedies of termination or damages. The question which arose was whether or not these decisions stated a general rule for all contracts, unless expressly otherwise provided by legislation. Following these cases, the Cour de cassation expanded the solution it had adopted for framework and franchising contracts to other types of contract. Until the reform, the law was unsettled and incoherent.[40] It is now much clearer. The revised Code civil only permits unilateral determination of the price within strict limits:

---

[35] Terré, Lequette and Chénedé (n 1 above) no. 286.
[36] ibid, no. 287.
[37] Cass civ (1) 29 November 1994, no. 91-21009, Bull civ I no. 348.
[38] Ass plén 1 December 1995, nos. 91-15578, 91-15999, 93-13688 and 91-1965, Bull AP nos. 7–9. All four cases are reported in Terré, Lequette and Chénedé (n 1 above) nos. 152–55.
[39] Art 1111 Cciv now provides a definition of framework contracts: 'A framework contract is an agreement by which the parties agree the general characteristics of their future contractual relations. Implementation contracts determine the modalities of performance under a framework contract.'
[40] On this discussion, see Terré, Lequette and Chénedé (n 1 above) nos. 152–55.

Code civil   **9.12 (FR)**

Article 1164: In framework contracts it may be agreed that the price will be fixed unilaterally by one of the parties, subject to the requirement that the latter must provide the reason for the amount if it is challenged.

In the case of an abuse in the fixing of a price, a court may hear a claim for damages and, in an appropriate case, for the termination of the contract.[41]

Notes

(1) Unilateral determination of the price by one of the parties is possible in services contracts (see Art 1165 Cciv below) and in framework contracts which is where the greatest difficulties have arisen. It must have been agreed between the parties.

(2) Moreover, the party who fixes the price must be able to justify the amount if it is challenged. This clearly identified obligation to state the reason for the amount is an innovation compared to the Assemblée plénière's decisions mentioned earlier.

(3) Finally, if the price is fixed abusively, the party owing the price is expressly given the right to damages and, in an appropriate case, to terminate the contract. Contrary to what was provided in the final draft of the provision that was circulated for consultation, the court, though having to consider the question, does not have power to fix the price or revise a price that has been fixed unilaterally.

Another remarkable change (again contrary to the final draft[42]) relates to contracts for services, in which the pre-2016 case law had allowed the court to fix the price:[43]

Code civil   **9.13 (FR)**

Article 1165: In contracts for the supply of services, in the absence of an agreement by the parties in advance of their performance, the price may be fixed by the creditor, subject to the latter's providing a reason for its amount if it is challenged. In the case of abuse in the fixing of the price, the court may hear a claim for damages and, where appropriate, termination of the contract.

Notes

(1) The new French law departs from the approach adopted by numerous foreign laws, which provide that in the absence of a fixed or determinable price, the price will

---

[41] The French version says '*résolution*', which has been translated by 'termination': see below, p 988.

[42] The draft provided: 'In contracts for services, in the absence of agreement between the parties before performance, the price may be fixed by the creditor; it is for the creditor to justify the amount. In the absence of agreement, the debtor may request a judge to fix the price in the light of usage, market prices and other legitimate interests of the parties' (Art 1164, Bill of the Ordonnance).

[43] Cass civ (1) 15 June 1973, no. 72-12062, Bull civ I no. 202, according to which: 'prior agreement on the exact amount of remuneration due in a contract for work is not an essential element for the validity of the contract; therefore the amount may be fixed by the court taking into account all the circumstances.' This solution was extended by the Cour de cassation to all contracts involving obligations to do (cf Cass com 29 January 1991, no. 89-16446, Bull IV no. 43).

be fixed according to current market prices. That approach applies in German law to contracts of employment and contracts for work (§§ 612, 632 BGB). In England, as we have seen,[44] the price to be paid in the absence of a fixed or determinable price is a 'reasonable price'. That is also the solution adopted by the PECL (Article 6:101), the UNIDROIT PICC (Article 5.1.7) and the Vienna Convention on Contracts for the International Sale of Goods (CISG) (Article 55); likewise the Draft Common Frame of Reference (DCFR) (Article II.-9:104). The Code civil thus differs from all these laws and Principles, and gives the court power to fix the price only in the extreme case of change of circumstance (*imprévision*).[45]

(2) The solutions in new Articles 1164 and 1165 Code civil only concern framework and services contracts. For instance, in a lease agreement,[46] the fixing of the new rent may only result from the agreement of the parties. The Cour de cassation thus decided that:

> having rightly ruled … that the fixing of the new rent may only result from the agreement of the parties and that the office of the judge is limited to acknowledging this agreement, if it existed, and having acknowledged the lack of such an agreement on the fixed part of the rent, the cour d'appel rightly inferred that it had to reject the request of the lessor and of the lessee to have the rent fixed for the renewed lease.[47]

(3) The 2016 reform does not deal with the revision of the price in contracts where 'fees' (*honoraires*) are to be paid[48]. Before the reform, the courts held that when those fees were fixed *ab initio*, the debtor could require the court to reduce them when they were excessive compared to the service received. This claim, which had to be brought before any payment occurred, could be introduced against all sorts of professionals (accountants, lawyers etc). After the reform, some authors suggested that this was no longer good law because it was not codified, in contrast to other rules on the price in contracts for the supply of services, which are codified in Article 1165. This argument is not convincing because (i) Article 1165 has a different scope (fixation and reduction of the price *a posteriori*, or termination of the contract if necessary since the 2018 reform), and (ii) courts do not need any legal provision to develop their judicial power and may continue to do so provided it does not contradict a legal provision.

(4) Before the ratification of the Ordonnance (2018), new Article 1165 of the Code civil did not specify that abusive fixing of the price could result in the contract's termination (contrary to what Article 1164 Code civil provided for framework contracts). However, this certainly would not have prevented the courts from applying this general remedy in such a situation—the recent amendment to Article 1165 has solely an aesthetic purpose.

---

[44] Above p 285.

[45] F Ancel, B Fauvarque-Cosson and J Gest, *Aux sources de la réforme du droit des contrats* (Paris: Dalloz, 2017) nos. 25-151 and 25-161. For the doctrine of *imprévision*, see below, ch 29.

[46] A lease is defined under Art 1709 Cciv as 'a contract by which one of the parties binds himself to have the other enjoy a thing during a certain time, and at a charge of a certain price which the latter binds himself to pay him.'

[47] Cass civ (3) 7 May 2002, no. 00-18153, Bull civ III no. 94.

[48] A Bénabent, *Droit des contrats spéciaux civils et commerciaux* (12th edn, Paris: LGDJ, 2017) no. 572.

FURTHER READING

Christandl, G, 'Sufficient Agreement' in N Jansen and R Zimmermann (eds), *Commentaries on European Contract Laws* (Oxford University Press, 2018) 268–71.

Illmer, M, 'Contract (Formation)' in J Basedow, K Hopt and R Zimmermann (eds), *Max Planck Encyclopedia of European Private Law* (Oxford University Press, 2012) 378–83.

Kötz, H, *European Contract Law* (2nd edn, Oxford University Press, 2017) 41–47.

Kötz, H, 'Indicia of Seriousness' in J Basedow, K Hopt and R Zimmermann (eds), *Max Planck Encyclopedia of European Private Law* (Oxford University Press, 2012) 863–65.

CHAPTER 10
INTENTION TO CREATE LEGAL RELATIONS

10.1 INFORMAL ARRANGEMENTS

With some arrangements it is legitimate to ask whether the arrangement can give rise to legal obligations, because it is difficult to discern whether the parties intended to bind themselves to legal obligations. To this category belong acts of courtesy, social commitments including family arrangements, informal offers of help and many other situations.

10.1.A THE NOTION OF INTENTION TO CREATE LEGAL RELATIONS

The doctrine of 'intention to create legal relations' in English law made its first appearance in the case involving an advertisement for a 'quack' medicine:[1]

Court of Appeal   **10.1 (EN)**

Carlill v Carbolic Smoke Ball Co[2]

A statement in an advertisement for a patent cure that, if the cure did not work, a large payment would be made was meant as a contractual promise.

Facts: The defendants, the proprietors of a medical preparation called 'The Carbolic Smoke Ball,' issued an advertisement in which they offered to pay 100l [£100] to any person who contracted the influenza after having used one of their smoke balls in a specified manner and for a specified period. The plaintiff on the faith of the advertisement bought one of the balls, and used it in the manner and for the period specified, but nevertheless contracted the influenza.

Held: Affirming the decision of Hawkins J that the above facts established a contract by the defendants to pay the plaintiff 100l in the event which had happened.

---

[1] For the background to the case, and a discussion of its innovation in terms of doctrine, see AWB Simpson, *Leading cases in the Common Law* (Oxford University Press, 1996) ch 10.
[2] [1893] 1 QB 257; for other aspects of this case, see 8.8. (EN), above, p 217 and 11.4 (EN), below, p 348.

Judgment: LINDLEY LJ: We are dealing with an express promise to pay 100l in certain events. Read the advertisement how you will, and twist it about as you will, here is a distinct promise expressed in language which is perfectly unmistakable—

'100l reward will be paid by the Carbolic Smoke Ball Company to any person who contracts the influenza after having used the ball three times daily for two weeks according to the printed directions supplied with each ball.'

We must first consider whether this was intended to be a promise at all, or whether it was a mere puff which meant nothing. Was it a mere puff? My answer to that question is No, and I base my answer upon this passage: '1000l is deposited with the Alliance Bank, shewing our sincerity in the matter.' Now, for what was that money deposited or that statement made except to negative the suggestion that this was a mere puff and meant nothing at all? The deposit is called in aid by the advertiser as proof of his sincerity in the matter—that is, the sincerity of his promise to pay this 100l in the event which he has specified. I say this for the purpose of giving point to the observation that we are not inferring a promise; there is the promise, as plain as words can make it …

BOWEN LJ: I am of the same opinion. We were asked to say that this document was a contract too vague to be enforced.

The first observation which arises is that the document itself is not a contract at all, it is only an offer made to the public. The defendants contend next, that it is an offer the terms of which are too vague to be treated as a definite offer, inasmuch as there is no limit of time fixed for the catching of the influenza, and it cannot be supposed that the advertisers seriously meant to promise to pay money to every person who catches the influenza at any time after the inhaling of the smoke ball. It was urged also, that if you look at this document you will find much vagueness as to the persons with whom the contract was intended to be made—that, in the first place, its terms are wide enough to include persons who may have used the smoke ball before the advertisement was issued; at all events, that it is an offer to the world in general, and, also, that it is unreasonable to suppose it to be a definite offer, because nobody in their senses would contract themselves out of the opportunity of checking the experiment which was going to be made at their own expense. It is also contended that the advertisement is rather in the nature of a puff or a proclamation than a promise or offer intended to mature into a contract when accepted. But the main point seems to be that the vagueness of the document shews that no contract whatever was intended. It seems to me that in order to arrive at a right conclusion we must read this advertisement in its plain meaning, as the public would understand it. It was intended to be issued to the public and to be read by the public. How would an ordinary person reading this document construe it? It was intended unquestionably to have some effect, and I think the effect which it was intended to have, was to make people use the smoke ball, because the suggestions and allegations which it contains are directed immediately to the use of the smoke ball as distinct from the purchase of it. It did not follow that the smoke ball was to be purchased from the defendants directly, or even from agents of theirs directly. The intention was that the circulation of the smoke ball should be promoted, and that the use of it should be increased. The advertisement begins by saying that a reward will be paid by the Carbolic Smoke Ball Company to any person who contracts the increasing epidemic after using the ball. It has been said that the words do not apply only to persons who contract the epidemic after the publication of the advertisement, but include persons who had previously contracted the influenza. I cannot so read the advertisement. It is written in colloquial and popular language, and I think that it is equivalent to this: '100l will be paid to any person who shall contract the increasing epidemic after having used the carbolic smoke ball three times daily for two weeks.' And it seems to me that the way in which the public would read it would be this, that if anybody, after the advertisement was published, used three times daily for two weeks the carbolic smoke ball, and then caught cold, he would be entitled to the reward …

AL Sᴍɪᴛʜ LJ gave a judgment to the same effect.

Appeal dismissed.

As we will see in cases that follow, a similar doctrine—that some agreements are not meant to be legally binding—is recognised in French and German law.

Code civil   **10.2 (FR)**

Article 1100: Obligations arise from juridical acts, juridically significant facts[3] or from the sole authority of legislation.

They can arise from the voluntary performance or from the promise of performance of a moral duty towards another person.

Article 1100-1: Juridical acts are manifestations of will intended to produce legal effects. They may be based on agreement or unilateral.

BGB   **10.3 (DE)**

§ 118: Lack of seriousness

A declaration of intent not seriously intended which is made in the expectation that its lack of serious intention will not be misunderstood is void.

> *Note*
>
> The Bürgerliches Gesetzbuch (BGB) does not address the question of intention to create legal relations directly. Nonetheless § 118 BGB recognises that not all promises are meant to give rise to a legal commitment; and the cases later in this chapter indicate that the courts will interpret a party's words and conduct to determine whether the party reasonably appeared to be undertaking a legal obligation.

10.1.B LIFT-SHARING

Cass civ (1), 6 April 1994[4]   **10.4 (FR)**

Shared business trip

Facts: An agreement to share the costs of a business trip is not sufficient to establish a contract.

The parties went on a business trip to Italy together, using Mr Spinelli's car, and agreed to share the costs. They had an accident while Mr Spinelli was driving and Mr De Stephano was injured.

---

[3] Translator's note: 'There is a difficulty in translating '*le fait*' as sometimes it refers to a person's action and sometimes more broadly to fact. We have therefore translated it differently according to context.'

[4] No. 91-21047, Bull civ I no. 136, RTD civ 1994, 866, annotated by P Jourdain.

Judgment: THE COURT: *On the sole appeal ground:*— Whereas Mr De Stephano claims that the lower court (Besançon, judgment of 17 September 1991) ought not to have declared the Hague Convention of 4 May 1971 (on the law applicable to non-contractual liability resulting from a road traffic accident) applicable to the accident in Italy in which he was the passenger of a vehicle driven by Mr Spinelli and sustained injuries; as the appeal court, it is submitted, ought not to have applied the Italian law of the place of the accident and ought to have attributed to the facts at issue their proper classification by seeking to determine whether the agreement entered into between Mr De Stephano and Mr Spinelli to share the costs of using the latter's vehicle for a business trip, constituted, if not a contract of carriage, then at least an agreement excluding the application of the above-mentioned Convention;

— Whereas however, the appeal court was correct to hold that the existence of an agreement to share the costs of the trip was not sufficient to establish between the parties a link such as to give rise to liability in contract founded on the duty of the driver to ensure the safety of his passenger;

— Whereas thus, in holding that there was no contract of carriage, the appeal court's decision was soundly based in law, Mr Spinelli's liability being only non-contractual and thus coming within the sphere of the Hague Convention of 4 May 1971;

— Whereas the appeal ground is therefore unfounded;

On those grounds the appeal must be dismissed.

Notes

(1) In this case concerning the application of the Hague Convention on the law applicable to non-contractual liability in respect of road traffic accidents,[5] the question arose whether an agreement between two persons to share the use of one person's car for a trip, and to share the costs, constituted an agreement excluding the application of the Convention. The Cour de cassation considered that the agreement related only to the cost-sharing arrangement but that there was no agreement giving rise to any contractual liability to ensure the safety of the other party. The parties did not intend to enter into a genuine contract of carriage.

(2) An agreement is necessary to create a contract. However, new Article 1100-1 of the Code civil shows that French law is evolving towards a wider recognition of a general theory of *engagement unilateral*.[6]

In English law, on similar facts, the courts have differed over whether lift-sharing arrangements were legally binding.

Court of Appeal   **10.5 (EN)**

Coward v Motor Insurers' Bureau[7]

A lift-sharing arrangement was not intended to create legal relations and so the vehicle was not being used for 'hire or reward'.

[5] Convention of 4 May 1971 on the Law Applicable to Traffic Accidents.
[6] See above, pp 119 ff.
[7] [1963] 1 QB 259.

Facts: Coward was killed in an accident caused by the negligence of Cole, on whose motorbike Coward was a pillion passenger. Cole was also killed. Coward's widow brought an action against Cole's personal representatives and was given judgment, but the judgment was unsatisfied because Cole's insurance did not cover pillion passengers and his estate had no other assets. The widow then sued the Motor Insurers' Bureau, which had an obligation to pay unsatisfied judgments in respect of a 'liability which is required to be covered by a policy ...' under the Road Traffic Act 1930, claiming that Cole was bound to insure as he was carrying Coward for 'hire or reward'. The Court of Appeal thought it was necessary to decide whether there was a contract between Cole and Coward (in *Albert v Motor Insurers' Bureau*, below, the House of Lords held by a majority that this question need not be answered after all).

Held: There was no contract between Cole and Coward.

Judgment: Upjohn LJ (delivering the judgment of the court) [The Lord Justice first considered whether statements made by the two dead men could be heard in evidence, and held that they could. He continued:]

This, however, does not determine the question whether this arrangement contemplated that the parties would enter into a legal relationship enforceable in the courts of this country. Upon this point the fact that both parties are dead, we believe, matters little, for if the question had been posed to Coward or Cole: 'Did you intend to enter into a legal relationship?' each would probably have answered 'I never gave it a thought.'

The practice whereby workmen go to their place of business in the motor-car or on the motor-cycle of a fellow-workman upon the terms of making a contribution to the costs of transport is well known and widespread. In the absence of evidence that the parties intended to be bound contractually, we should be reluctant to conclude that the daily carriage by one of another to work upon payment of some weekly (or it may be daily) sum involved them in a legal contractual relationship. The hazards of everyday life, such as temporary indisposition, the incidence of holidays, the possibility of a change of shift or different hours of overtime, or incompatibility arising, make it most unlikely that either contemplated that the one was legally bound to carry and the other to be carried to work. It is made all the more improbable in this case by reason of the fact that alternative means of transport seem to have been available to Coward.

House of Lords   **10.6 (EN)**

Albert v Motor Insurers' Bureau[8]

A vehicle being used for carrying fellow workers was being used for 'hire or reward' even if there was no contract between the parties; but (per Lord Cross) a lift-sharing arrangement may be legally binding even if neither party would ever sue on it.

Facts: A stevedore with the name of Quirk drove some other stevedores to the place where they worked and it was agreed that they would pay him 5 to 10 shillings per week. Sometimes, he was also satisfied with cigarettes or beers; it sometimes happened that he did not ask for anything when the person carried had run out of money.

Held: The majority held that a vehicle was used to carry passengers for hire or reward if the driver was, on a systematic basis, going beyond acts of social kindness, even if there was no contract between the owner and the passengers. Quirk's vehicle had been so used.

---

[8] [1972] AC 301.

Judgment: LORD CROSS [differing from the majority, held it was necessary to determine whether there was a contract, and continued]: I think that the judge was wrong in holding that the facts which he found warranted the inference that there were no legally binding agreements between Quirk and any of his passengers. It is not necessary in order that a legally binding contract should arise that the parties should direct their minds to the question and decide in favour of the creation of a legally binding relationship. If I get into a taxi and ask the driver to drive me to Victoria Station it is extremely unlikely that either of us directs his mind to the question whether we are entering into a contract. We enter into a contract not because we form any intention to enter into one but because if our minds were directed to the point we should as reasonable people both agree that we were in fact entering into one. When one passes from the field of transactions of an obviously business character between strangers to arrangements between friends or acquaintances for the payment by the passenger of a contribution towards expenses the fact that the arrangement is not made purely as a matter of business and that if the anticipated payment is not made it would probably never enter into the head of the driver to sue for it disposes one to say that there is no contract, but in fact the answer to the question 'contract' or 'no contract' does not depend on the likelihood of an action being brought to enforce it in case of default.

Suppose that when one of Quirk's fellow workers got into touch with him and asked him whether he could travel in his car to Tilbury and back next day an 'officious bystander' had asked: 'Will you be paying anything for your transport?' the prospective passenger would have answered at once: 'Of course I will pay.' If the 'officious bystander' had gone on to ask Quirk whether, if he was not paid, he would sue the man in the county court, Quirk might well have answered in the words used by the driver in *Connell's case* [1969] 2 QB 494: 'Not bloody likely.' But the fact that if default was made Quirk would not have started legal proceedings but would have resorted to extra-judicial remedies does not mean that an action could not in theory have been brought to recover payment for the carriage. If one imagines such proceedings being brought a plea on the part of the passenger that he never meant to enter into a contract would have received short shrift and so, too, would a plea that the contract was void for uncertainty because no precise sum was mentioned. If the evidence did not establish a regular charge for the Tilbury trip the judge would have fixed the appropriate sum.

Note

According to Lord Cross, it is not necessary that the parties had consciously wanted to create a legal relationship for a contract to come into existence. One might ask whether there was a contract to pay for lifts that had been taken but no contract to give lifts in the future; or possibly that there was no contract but that the driver would have a claim in restitution against the other workers carried.[9] The House of Lords did not consider these points.

The German courts distinguish between the possible types of arrangement.

[9] cf *BSC v Cleveland Bridge*, 6.25 (EN) above, p 164.

Regular lift-sharing arrangement and a one-off lift

A regular lift-sharing arrangement amongst colleagues against payment normally amounts to a contract, whereas a single, gratuitous lift for a colleague who is unwell during work hours normally does not.

Facts: The defendant and S were employed in the same business. They had a regular lift-sharing arrangement, according to which S picked the defendant up at home in the morning and dropped her off again after work. The defendant made a monthly contribution of DM30 towards S's expenses. In the morning of 28 October 1987, the defendant came to work but felt unwell. S drove her home during the morning break, using the plaintiff's car. On her way back she had an accident and suffered major injuries. The car was a total loss. S assigned any claims she might have to the plaintiff who claimed damages. In the later proceedings she only acted as a witness. The first instance court awarded damages, the appellate court reversed the decision.

Held: The Bundesgerichtshof upheld the decision of the appellate court. No contract had been made between the defendant and S because they had no intention to be legally bound.

Judgment: 1. The appellate court held that the action based on the claims assigned by witness S had no merit because there was no contract between the defendant and witness S concerning the ride to the defendant's home during the work break on 28 October 1987, but merely a relationship of generosity (*Gefälligkeitsverhältnis*).

It held that the regular lift-sharing arrangement between witness S and the defendant which existed at the time was irrelevant with regard to the issue of the legal bindingness of the courtesy lift in question; the regular lift-sharing arrangement had only concerned joint trips to the place of work and back, not an intermittent drive during work hours which happened exclusively for the benefit of the defendant. The appeal against this decision is unsuccessful.

2. It depends on the circumstances of each individual case whether declarations or other conduct bring into existence a relationship of mandate or whether what occurs is merely an act of generosity …

a) The appeal court has not erred in law by holding that the willingness of witness S to drive the defendant home during the morning break is, as such, a typical act of generosity of every day life which is not legally binding.

aa) A legal transaction only exists if those involved had the intention to incur obligations of a legal nature and to be able to impose such obligations. Only then is it possible to speak of a contract of mandate within the meaning of § 662 BGB (BGHZ 56, 208 = NJW 1971, 1404 = LM § 662 BGB no. 11). Whether there is an intention to be legally bound (*Rechtsbindungswille*) is not to be assessed on the basis of the internal will, which has not outwardly manifested itself, of the person rendering performance. It rather has to be ascertained on the basis of whether the person receiving performance had to infer the existence of such an intention in the given circumstances, according to good faith and having regard to customary practice. It depends on how an objective observer would view the actions of the person rendering performance. Contractual bindingness will have to be affirmed in particular if it is apparent that significant interests of an economic kind

---

[10] NJW 1992, 498.

are at stake for the person receiving performance and he relies on the assurance made, or if the person rendering performance has a legal or economic interest in the matter. In contrast, if this is not the case, the actions of those involved can only be assumed to have been made with the intention to be legally bound if there are special circumstances. As a general rule, therefore, it will not be possible to assume an intention to be bound with regard to so called acts of generosity of everyday life (*Gefälligkeitshandeln des täglichen Lebens*), assurances in the context of social intercourse or similar instances (this Senate, BGHZ 88, 373 (382) = NJW 1984, 1533 …). Moreover, it must have been reasonable to expect of the person who acted that he would assume a legal obligation and the corresponding risk of being liable in damages (BGH, NJW 1974, 1705 = LM § 762 BGB no. 4).

bb) The appellate court bases its reasoning on these principles. It does not err in law when it views the giving of a lift home by an employee to a colleague who is incapable of working because she grieves the death of her grandfather and therefore asks her employer to release her from work as an act of camaraderie, an act of goodwill which is to be assessed differently from, for example, driving someone to an urgently required medical assistance (cf OLG Hamm, MDR 1974, 312). In the latter case there may be an urgent interest which is apparent to the helper to have him legally bound and make him adhere to his readiness to act out of generosity, to the extent that this is legally possible. As opposed to this, the appellate court does not believe that it would be justified to impose on witness S an obligation to proceed with the lift from which she would only have been able to escape in the aggravated circumstances set forth in § 671 BGB …

b) The appellant wrongly complains that the appellate court did not recognise the relationship between the lift in question and the existing regular and binding lift-sharing arrangement. The appellate court saw a potential connection and explained that the lift-sharing arrangement only concerned joint trips to the place of work and back, not an intermittent drive during work hours which happened exclusively for the benefit of the defendant. This cannot be seen as erroneous in law.

The circumstances in this case might militate in favour of the existence of a relationship of mandate between those involved with regard to the joint trips to their place of work and back. According to the requirements which are, as the appellate court has correctly stated, relevant for distinguishing a relationship of generosity at the merely social level from an equally gratuitous but legally binding mandate as contract of generosity, the daily lift provided to the defendant in the car of witness S potentially went beyond mere kindness and a mere non-binding assurance. A contract of mandate within the meaning of § 662 BGB exists if both sides had the intention to incur obligations of a legal nature and to be able to impose such obligations and if this intention can be ascertained in accordance with objective criteria (this Senate, BGHZ 88, 373 (382) = NJW 1984, 1533 = LM § 661 BGB no. 5); this may be particularly assumed if it is apparent that significant interests of an economic kind are at stake for the person receiving performance and he relies on the assurance made (cf BGHZ 56, 204 (210) = NJW 1971, 1404 = LM § 662 BGB no. 11). Given that witness S regularly picked up the defendant at home and dropped her off after work in exchange for a contribution of DM30 towards S's expenses, and given that the defendant had to rely on this because she was liable towards her employer to show up at work on time, everything points towards an intention on the part of witness S to be legally bound to this extent (cf OLG Frankfurt, VersR 1978, 745 (746); OLG Stuttgart, MDR 1959, 388 …).

The appellate court assessed the facts without erring in law to the extent that the drive of witness S on 28 October 1987 occurred outside the existing obligation towards the defendant which results from the lift-sharing arrangement and amounted to an (additional) mere courtesy which was not legally binding.

Even if, therefore, witness S was under a duty to pick up the defendant in time before work hours, take her with her to her place of employment and drop her off after work on her way back home, there is no reason to doubt the assessment of the appellate court that the present particular and special lift which was exclusively in the interest of the defendant was not included in what witness S was legally bound to do, but that witness S rather wished to bring her colleague home during the morning break as an act of compassion. This assessment also corresponds to general experience of life. It may be the case that witness S felt more compelled than other co-employees to do the defendant a favour and drive her home because she knew the way home and was connected to her in a lift-sharing agreement. This, however, does not militate against the witness having merely acted in an accommodating fashion, rather than her having acted in performance of a legal obligation, the more so as the defendant could also have gotten home in a different manner.

Notes

(1) German law distinguishes contracts from 'relationships of generosity, kindness or good will' (*Gefälligkeitsverhältnisse*). The former require two corresponding declarations of intent,[11] each of which has to be made with the intention to be legally bound (*Rechtsbindungswille*).[12] If any of the parties lacks such an intention because it simply wishes to engage in an 'act of generosity' ('act of kindness or good will') (*Gefälligkeit*), its words or conduct do not amount to a declaration of intent in the legal sense and cannot, therefore, constitute an offer to contract or an acceptance of such an offer.

(2) The test for ascertaining the *Rechtsbindungswille* is usually objective because in most cases it is impossible to know whether the parties subjectively intended to be legally bound. The court will therefore embark on an enquiry of the hypothetical intention of the parties which it will infer from the objective circumstances of the case, most importantly the typical interests of the parties in the kind of scenario that falls to be decided. These will depend on the kind of transaction in question, its economic and legal relevance for the parties and the risk that the parties would incur if they were to enter into a legal rather than a merely social relationship.[13] A typical example of the latter is where someone waters the garden and looks after the house of his neighbours while they are on holiday.[14]

(3) If someone agrees to do something gratuitously this is, as such, not sufficient to assume that he intended it to be an act of generosity: as was seen in Chapter 6, German law acknowledges the existence of gratuitous contracts.[15] It is therefore particularly difficult to distinguish a *Gefälligkeitsverhältnis* from a contract of mandate (*Auftrag*), under which one party, the mandatary, agrees to gratuitously carry out a transaction entrusted to him by the other party, the mandatory, for the benefit of that party (§ 662 BGB).

---

[11] For the notion of 'declaration of intent', see above, pp 96 ff.

[12] For the second constitutive part of the declaration of intent, the awareness of making a legally relevant declaration (*Erklärungsbewußtsein*), see the discussion of the *Trier wine auction* case, above, p 103.

[13] D Looschelders, *Schuldrecht: Allgemeiner Teil* (15th edn, Munich: Vahlen, 2017) para 95; Münchener Kommentar/Schäfer § 662 para 24.

[14] BGH 26 April 2016, NJW-RR 2017, 272 at [8].

[15] See above, p 128.

(4) The leading case on the distinction between contracts and acts of generosity concerned an arrangement between three haulage companies.[16] The claimant company was unable to do a job for the sister company of the defendant company because the claimant's driver had suffered a fatal injury. The defendant therefore agreed at short notice to gratuitously make available to the claimant one of its drivers who would carry out the trip with the claimant's truck. During the trip the truck broke down. It had to be repaired and could not be used for six weeks. The claimant alleged negligence on the part of the defendant's driver and sued the defendant for damages and lost profits in contract. The Bundesgerichtshof held that the defendant had not been under any obligation to provide a driver and had acted altruistically and unselfishly in order to help the claimant out in an emergency. However, an act of generosity might have

> ... the character of a legal transaction if the person rendering performance has the intention that his actions should ... create a legally binding relationship ... and the recipient has received performance in that sense. ... Whether there was or was not an intention to be legally bound is not to be determined on the basis of the internal will, which has not outwardly manifested itself, of the person rendering performance. It rather has to be ascertained on the basis of whether the person receiving performance had to infer the existence of such an intention in the given circumstances, according to good faith and having regard to customary practice. The answer therefore depends on how the actions of the person rendering performance appear to an objective observer (RG, JW 1915, 19).
>
> An act of generosity can be raised above the level of pure factual events by the type of the act; its ratio and purpose; its economic and legal relevance, particularly for the recipient of the performance; the circumstances in which the act is provided; and the interests of the parties. These criteria must therefore be considered in order to decide whether there was an intention to be bound and to determine the nature of the legal transaction, if any, that resulted from the act. Acts of generosity in everyday life will normally be outside the realm of legal transactions. The same holds true for acts of generosity that are rooted in purely social relationships (RGZ 128, 39, 42). An intention to be legally bound may be inferred from the value of an item that has been entrusted to a person, the economic significance of the matter, the apparent interest that the beneficiary of an act of generosity has in benefitting from the act and the danger that he is in if performance is defective—which may not be apparent to him but to the person rendering performance ... If the person rendering performance has himself a legal or economic interest in helping out the beneficiary of the act, this will normally militate in favour of an intention to be legally bound ...

In the case at hand, the defendant company had not been under any legal obligation to help out the claimant. However, the favour it had been asked for related to the business activities of both parties. Had the defendant not made its driver available the claimant would have incurred costs to perform his obligations towards its contracting party. It was apparent to the defendant that the claimant only would have accepted the provision of a reliable driver, not least because the truck represented one of the claimant's major assets and a major source of its income. Therefore the claimant could

---

[16] BGH 22 June 1956, BGHZ 21, 102, translated in B Markesinis, H Unberath and A Johnston, *The German Law of Contract* (2nd edn, Oxford: Hart Publishing, 2006) 597–600.

> reasonably rely on the defendant making available a reliable driver, and the defendant was not allowed to disappoint this reliance. These circumstances alone were sufficient to assume that the defendant had an intention to be legally bound. The defendant was therefore under a contractual duty to choose a reliable driver.

10.1.C JOINT BETTING

A further borderline situation may arise in connection with joint gaming or betting, where several persons take part and the prize is won. How is it to be shared out, given that there may, at best, have been merely an informal agreement? The German and English examples referred to below involved, in particular, the question whether there was a contract.

BGH, 16 May 1974[17]   **10.8 (DE)**

Betting syndicate

An agreement to place a bet each week does not create a legal obligation to the effect that the person who had agreed to place it would be liable if the bet had won.

Facts: The claimants and the defendant, as a group, placed bets in the State lottery on a regular basis. Each week they wagered the sum of DM50, that is to say DM10 per person. The wagers were paid by the defendant who filled out and handed in the lottery ticket in his own name. For the draw on 23 October 1971 the defendant neglected to hand in the ticket with the figures agreed. Yet at this draw those were the winning figures giving entitlement to a prize of DM10,550. Accordingly, the claimants demanded the sum of DM2,110 per head, together with interest and damages. It was contended on the defendant's behalf that he was under no legal obligation as to his conduct. He claimed that for work reasons he was unable to hand in the ticket as agreed. Quite unexpectedly, he had been unable to leave his place of work before a quarter to six and, on his arrival at the betting office, he discovered that the last bet had been taken an hour before. Therefore, instead of filling out the agreed ticket, he placed other bets totalling DM450.

Held: The lower courts trying the case on its merits dismissed the claim for damages and interest. The Bundesgerichtshof dismissed the appeal on a point of law.

Judgment: I—The appellate court dismissed the claim under § 762 BGB. Under that provision gambling debts and wagers cannot form the subject matter of legal proceedings. However, that provision was held not to apply in this case. Taking responsibility to place a wager on behalf of a gaming association is not in itself a wager but an ancillary act enabling the wager to proceed. Moreover, according to settled case-law, § 762 applies only where a person invites another to participate in gaming which is not authorised by the public authorities.

II—The second question was whether the task entrusted to the defendant by the claimants constituted an act legally binding on the defendant and giving rise to an obligation on his part.

1—As a general rule, there are legal relations between the members of a group who place joint bets in the weekly lottery. It is common ground that where one of them places a wager within the remit of his instructions, he is required to share any resulting winnings.

---

[17] NJW 1974, 1705.

2—Even if the existence of certain legal relations is assumed in the present case, the question remains whether and to what extent a legally enforceable obligation arises on the part of the person who has gratuitously undertaken to carry out transactions for others. It is normally impossible to resolve this question by reference to the express or implied intentions of the participants. Therefore, it has to be answered with reference to the typical interests of each of the parties, in light of the requirements of good faith and customary practice. On the one hand, it has to be asked whether significant interests of those persons who assign a task to another are at play, particularly economic interests, such as the loss to be expected if the task is not properly performed. On the other hand, it must be taken into account whether it can be reasonably expected of the person undertaking the task that he would assume a legal obligation and, in the event of its breach, the risk of being liable in damages.

In the present case, upon weighing the interests at stake, it had to be decided that undertaking the task of gratuitously filling out and handing in a lottery ticket for a group of players does not normally give rise to a legal obligation to complete these tasks. To find in favour of the existence of any such obligation would be too onerous on the person assuming the job. The risk of making a minor error in selecting the numbers or of missing the deadline for handing in the lottery ticket on time is relatively high. Although this risk will rarely materialize in an actual loss, where such loss is incurred, it can be particularly serious. Thus, if the person acting on behalf of the others were to incur damages these might result in his total financial ruin. Such a scenario would have been totally beyond the imagination of those who, after all, simply wanted to engage in a game. If those involved had considered and discussed the issue in advance, none of them would have been willing to assume such a risk, and none of them would have expected the others to assume it. Thus it cannot be presumed that the parties intended to create legally binding relations.

Notes

(1) Since this case involved betting in the State lottery it did not trigger the rule that any debt incurred in the process of private gaming and betting creates but an 'imperfect obligation': such a debt is not enforceable in law; however, if the debtor has performed his obligation he will not be able to reclaim his performance in the courts either (eg § 762 BGB and Articles 1965 and 1967 of the French Civil Code).

(2) The question was rather whether there was a contractual relationship between the players. The BGH clearly considered that a legal relationship had been formed, but declined to reach a conclusion based on any express or tacit intention shared by the participants, which would of necessity be a fiction. As in the lift-sharing cases discussed further above, it preferred to approach the matter from the standpoint of the weighing and balancing of interests. To impose a legal obligation on the person delegated to act on behalf of the participants would be inequitable, since this could result in that person facing ruin if, for example, he made a mistake in filling out the lottery ticket and, but for that mistake, the winnings would have been sizeable. The only legal commitment given to the other members of the group was the obligation to share the winnings if the ticket was correctly filled out in accordance with the numbers jointly agreed on by the participants. Thus an objective approach was adopted by the Court, similar to the approach found in the English case law, which, on account of its specific characteristics, in particular the doctrine of consideration, provides rather different illustrations.

Simpkins v Pays[18]

An agreement between a house-owner, her granddaughter and a lodger to enter competitions and share any winnings may be intended to be legally binding.

Facts: Since 1950 the plaintiff had been living as a lodger in the house of the defendant, an elderly woman, in circumstances which had some element of a family circle. Each of the parties used to compete separately in newspaper competitions. From about the beginning of May 1954, for a period of seven or eight weeks, the plaintiff, the defendant and the defendant's granddaughter each sent in, each week, a separate entry on one coupon to the fashion competition of a Sunday newspaper. Each of the three contributed one forecast, and the coupon was filled in by the plaintiff but was made out in the defendant's name. The costs of postage and entry were informally shared, being sometimes paid by one and sometimes by another. When the question of sharing winnings first came to be considered between the plaintiff and defendant, the latter said that they would 'go shares'. The granddaughter was not present on that occasion but the plaintiff and the defendant both knew that she would join in the arrangement. The coupon sent in for 27 June 1954 was successful, the correct forecast being that of the defendant's granddaughter, and a prize of £750 was paid to the defendant. The defendant refused to pay a third of the prize money to the plaintiff, claiming, among other things, that the arrangement to share the winnings was arrived at in a family context and was not intended to give rise to legal consequences, and that, accordingly, there was no contract.

Held: There was an enforceable contract, because there was a mutuality in the arrangement between the parties, and, therefore, the plaintiff was entitled to payment of a third share of the prize money.

Judgment: Sellers J ... When the plaintiff made out the coupon she put down the forecasts in the way I have indicated, and entered in the appropriate place on the coupon the name of Mrs Pays, 11, Trevor Street, Wrexham, and so with each coupon in those seven or eight weeks as if they had been the defendant's. In fact there were three forecasts there, and when the matter first came to be considered, I accept the plaintiff's evidence that what was said, when they were going to do it in that way, was: 'We will go shares' or words to that effect. 'Shares' was the word used, and I do not think anything very much more specific was said. Whether it was said by the plaintiff or the defendant does not really matter. I think that was the basis, and it may well be that the plaintiff is right when she said, in her evidence, that the defendant said: 'You're lucky, May, and if we win we will go shares.'

...

On the finding that the plaintiff's evidence is right as to what was said about the shares, and rejecting the incidental evidence given by the witnesses as to what occurred afterwards, counsel for the defendant not unnaturally said:

'Even if that is so, the court cannot enforce this contract unless the arrangement made at the time was one which was intended to give rise to legal consequences.'

It may well be there are many family associations where some sort of rough and ready thing is said which would not, on a proper estimate of the circumstances, establish a contract which was contemplated to have legal consequences, but I do not so find here. I think there was here a mutuality in the arrangement between the parties. It was not very formal, but certainly in effect it was agreed that every week the forecast should go in in the name of the defendant, and that if there was success, no matter who won, all should share equally. That seems to be the implication from or the interpretation of what was

---

[18] [1955] 1 WLR 975.

said, that this was in the nature of a very informal syndicate so that they should all get the benefit of success. It would be equally wrong, I think, to say from what was arranged that because the granddaughter's forecast was the one which was successful of those submitted by the defendant that the plaintiff and the defendant were to get nothing. Although she was not a party before the court and I have not had the benefit of her evidence, as far as I can see, on this arrangement she would be as entitled to the third share as the others, certainly, so far as the plaintiff is concerned. Esme was not, apparently, present when this bargain was made, but both the others knew, at any rate soon after the outset, that she was coming in. It is possible, of course, although the plaintiff is not concerned in it, that the granddaughter's effort was only to assist the defendant, her grandmother. She may accept that, but it makes no difference, so far as I can see, to the fact that the plaintiff and the defendant entered into an agreement to share. The plaintiff does not seek to say: 'Esme was only aiding Mrs Pays,' in asking for half the shares, but she was entitled to one-third, and I so find and give judgment to the amount of £250.

Note

This case clearly raises a problem of interpretation: what was it that the parties had agreed? And there is a further problem, concerning characterisation: in what way did the agreement fall to be analysed? The Court considered that there had been something cautiously characterised by it as an 'arrangement' which the parties had intended to have legal consequences. It even accepted that an 'informal syndicate' was involved. The upshot was the same: the plaintiff was entitled to one third of the prize. The decision appears to have been given on the basis of what seems a 'fair' interpretation of what took place between the parties.

It is apparent from a comparison of the judgments that, in cases of this kind involving similar circumstances, the courts have been at something of a loss to find any legal basis for the conclusion reached by them. They have taken the view that it is difficult to determine what the parties really intended where joint gaming has gone wrong, and have had problems in deciding whether, on the one hand, to order payment of a proportion of the winnings or whether, on the other, to dismiss the claim for payment. A French judgment[19] on similar facts speaks of the transformation of a moral obligation into an obligation in law, non-performance of which entails a legal sanction (see new Article 1100 Code civil, mentioned in Chapter 5[20]), whilst the English and German courts refer to the interests in issue. This is without doubt an area lying at the very fringes of contract law.

In part the problem may be that to say there is or is not a contract may seem to be an all-or-nothing solution, when justice may require a more nuanced approach. Thus it seems fair enough to make a defendant who has won the bet and taken the winnings to have to share them; while it may be much less fair to make a party who has failed to place the agreed bet pay his collaborators what they would have won out of his own pocket. Indeed, the parties themselves might have agreed that the two situations should be treated differently. Under French law, when a contract has been concluded in view of a participation

---

[19] Cass civ (1) 16 October 1995, no. 93-20300, Bull civ I no. 352, D 1995, 155, annotated by G Pignarre.
[20] See 5.4 (FR), above, p 95.

to some bet or game, parties must share the gains or losses; refusal to do so could even amount to an *abus*. Under French law, it has been considered that players involved in the same bet or game have created some sort of company (*société de participation*) and that refusal to share the gains or losses amounts to breach of trust (*abus de confiance*).[21]

We now turn, finally, to a judgment showing the special nature of English law in relation to family arrangements, the effectiveness of which in other European legal systems is open to debate.

Court of Appeal   **10.10 (EN)**

***Balfour v Balfour*[22]**

An agreement between a husband and wife that he will pay her an allowance, made while they were still on amicable terms, does not create a legal obligation.

Facts: A couple returned to England from Ceylon. When his leave was over, the husband went back alone, his wife remaining in England for health reasons. She maintained that before his departure her husband had promised to pay her the monthly sum of £30. Subsequently, the couple separated and the wife brought an action for the maintenance payments to be continued to be paid to her.

Held: The claimant was successful at first instance, but the defendant was successful on appeal.

Judgment: ATKIN LJ: The defence to this action on the alleged contract is that the defendant, the husband, entered into no contract with his wife, and for the determination of that it is necessary to remember that there are agreements between parties which do not result in contracts within the meaning of that term in our law. The ordinary example is where two parties agree to take a walk together, or where there is an offer and an acceptance of hospitality. Nobody would suggest in ordinary circumstances that those agreements result in what we know as a contract, and one of the most usual forms of agreement which does not constitute a contract appears to me to be the arrangements which are made between husband and wife. It is quite common, and it is the natural and inevitable result of the relationship of husband and wife, that the two spouses should make arrangements between themselves—agreements such as are in dispute in this action—agreements for allowances, by which the husband agrees that he will pay to his wife a certain sum of money, per week, or per month, or per year, to cover either her own expenses or the necessary expenses of the household and of the children of the marriage, and in which the wife promises either expressly or impliedly to apply the allowance for the purpose for which it is given. To my mind those agreements, or many of them, do not result in contracts at all, and they do not result in contracts even though there may be what as between other parties would constitute consideration for the agreement. The consideration, as we know, may consist either in some right, interest, profit or benefit accruing to one party, or some forbearance, detriment, loss or responsibility given, suffered or undertaken by the other. That is a well-known definition, and it constantly happens, I think, that such arrangements made between husband and wife are arrangements in which there are mutual promises, or in which there is consideration in form within the definition that I have mentioned. Nevertheless they are not contracts, and they are not contracts because the parties did not intend that they should be attended by legal

---

[21] Cass crim 20 May 1985, no. 84-92803, Bull crim no. 189.
[22] [1919] 2 KB 571.

consequences. To my mind it would be of the worst possible example to hold that agreements such as this resulted in legal obligations which could be enforced in the Courts. It would mean this, that when the husband makes his wife a promise to give her an allowance of 30s or 2l a week, whatever he can afford to give her, for the maintenance of the household and children, and she promises so to apply it, not only could she sue him for his failure in any week to supply the allowance, but he could sue her for non-performance of the obligation, express or implied, which she had undertaken upon her part. All I can say is that the small Courts of this country would have to be multiplied one hundredfold if these arrangements were held to result in legal obligations. They are not sued upon, not because the parties are reluctant to enforce their legal rights when the agreement is broken, but because the parties, in the inception of the arrangement, never intended that they should be sued upon. Agreements such as these are outside the realm of contracts altogether. The common law does not regulate the form of agreements between spouses. Their promises are not sealed with seals and sealing wax. The consideration that really obtains for them is that natural love and affection which counts for so little in these cold Courts. The terms may be repudiated, varied or renewed as performance proceeds or as disagreements develop, and the principles of the common law as to exoneration and discharge and accord and satisfaction are such as find no place in the domestic code. The parties themselves are advocates, judges, Courts, sheriff's officer and reporter. In respect of these promises each house is a domain into which the King's writ does not seek to run, and to which his officers do not seek to be admitted. The only question in this case is whether or not this promise was of such a class or not. For the reasons given by my brethren it appears to me to be plainly established that the promise here was not intended by either party to be attended by legal consequences. I think the onus was upon the plaintiff, and the plaintiff has not established any contract. The parties were living together, the wife intending to return. The suggestion is that the husband bound himself to pay 30l a month under all circumstances, and she bound herself to be satisfied with that sum under all circumstances, and, although she was in ill-health and alone in this country, that out of that sum she undertook to defray the whole of the medical expenses that might fall upon her, whatever might be the development of her illness, and in whatever expenses it might involve her. To my mind neither party contemplated such a result. I think that the parol evidence upon which the case turns does not establish a contract. I think that the letters do not evidence such a contract, or amplify the oral evidence which was given by the wife, which is not in dispute. For these reasons I think the judgment of the Court below was wrong and that this appeal should be allowed.

[Warrington and Duke LJJ delivered judgments to same effect.]

Appeal allowed.

Notes

(1) The first question was as to the existence of consideration, an issue that will be discussed in depth in the next chapter. Atkin LJ took the view that there was indeed consideration, but that there was no intention to enter into a legally enforceable contract. The underlying idea is that this kind of family arrangement falls outside the purview of the law. It is not certain that the solution would have been the same in other countries. In short, in order to specify that there is intention to be bound a lot depends on judicial interpretation of the will of the parties.

(2) It is not uncommon in England for persons who are about to marry to enter a 'pre-nuptial' agreement as to who should receive property or income in the event that the marriage breaks down. There seems no doubt that these agreements are intended to be legally binding; and an agreement made by the parties when they separate is also normally binding.[23] The major question in English law has been whether 'pre-nups' are unenforceable as being contrary to public policy[24]—and whether the courts should nonetheless take them into account when exercising their discretion as to matrimonial property after divorce.

It is not always easy to determine whether the parties, or the persons claiming to be parties, intended to establish legal relations and, what is more, contractual relations. Borderline situations exist affording the courts a relatively wide discretion. Two trends may be discerned. First, in contrast to the situation prevailing in certain legal systems and at certain times in the past, the courts are somewhat reluctant to engage in artificial enquiries into questions of intention, preferring to steer clear of a subjective approach. Instead, as will be noted, they tend to have recourse to the concept of the balance of interests, as favoured by Ihering. Secondly, this objective approach is, unsurprisingly, influenced by notions of what seems 'fair'.

10.2 AGREEMENTS IN HONOUR, 'GENTLEMEN'S AGREEMENTS'

This situation is closely related to the previous one, but with one slight difference: the parties deliberately include a clause stating that the agreement shall not be legally binding, in reliance on each other's good faith. Is it possible for the courts to acquiesce in what might seem to be an ouster of their jurisdiction?

Court of Appeal and House of Lords   **10.11 (EN)**

Rose & Frank Co v JR Crompton Bros[25]

Although commercial agreements are usually assumed to be legally binding, the parties may agree that the arrangement shall not be legally binding.

Facts: The parties agreed to extend a supply contract for a predetermined period at prices to be fixed every six months. The agreement contained the following clause: 'This arrangement is not entered into nor is this memorandum written, as a formal or legal agreement, and shall not be subject to legal jurisdiction in the law courts either of the United States or England, but is only a definite expression and record of the purpose and intention of the three parties concerned, to which they each honourably pledge themselves in the fullest confidence—based on past business with each other—that it will be carried through by each of the three parties with mutual loyalty and friendly co-operation.' Nonetheless, one of the parties repudiated the arrangement.

[23] *Merritt v Merritt* [1970] 1 WLR 1211 (CA).
[24] Public policy is discussed in ch 17, see below, p 669.
[25] [1923] 2 KB 261 and [1925] AC 445.

317

The other brought an action for breach of contract and non-delivery of the goods that they had ordered before the repudiation. The Court of Appeal took the view that the arrangement quoted was not a binding contract, and (by a majority) nor was the acceptance of an order placed by the plaintiffs.

Held: The House of Lords agreed with the view that the arrangement described above was not a binding contract, but agreed with the dissenting judge in the Court of Appeal that the acceptance of the specific order did create a contract (this part of the judgments is omitted).

Judgment: SCRUTTON LJ: In 1913 the parties concurred in signing a document which gives rise to the present dispute. I agree that if the clause beginning 'This arrangement' were omitted, the Courts would treat the rest of the agreement as giving rise to legal relations, though again of great vagueness. An agreement that Messrs Brittain & Crompton 'will subject to unforeseen circumstances and contingencies do their best, as in the past, to respond efficiently and satisfactorily to the calls of Messrs Rose & Frank Co for deliveries both in quantity and quality,' is not very helpful or precise. But the clause in question beginning 'This arrangement' is not omitted and reads as follows:

> 'This arrangement is not entered into, nor is this memorandum written, as a formal or legal agreement, and shall not be subject to legal jurisdiction in the Law Courts either of the United States or England, but it is only a definite expression and record of the purpose and intention of the three parties concerned to which they each honourably pledge themselves with the fullest confidence, based upon past business with each other, that it will be carried through by each of the three parties with mutual loyalty and friendly co-operation.'

The judge below thinks that by itself this clause 'plain as it is' means that the parties shall not be under any legal obligation to each other at all. But coming to the conclusion that without this clause the agreement would create legal obligations, he takes the view that the clause must be rejected as repugnant to the rest of the agreement. He also holds that if the clause merely means to exclude recourse to the Law Courts as a means of settling disputes, it is contrary to public policy as ousting the jurisdiction of the King's Courts.

In my view the learned judge adopts a wrong canon of construction. He should not seek the intention of the parties as shown by the language they use in part of that language only, but in the whole of that language. It is true that in deeds and wills where it is impossible from the whole of the contradictory language used to ascertain the true intention of the framers, resort may be had, but only as a last expedient, to what Jessel MR called 'the rule of thumb' in *In re Bywater* of rejecting clauses as repugnant according to their place in the document, the later clause being rejected in deeds and the earlier in wills. But before this heroic method is adopted of finding out what the parties meant by assuming that they did not mean part of what they have said, it must be clearly impossible to harmonize the whole of the language they have used. Now it is quite possible for parties to come to an agreement by accepting a proposal with the result that the agreement concluded does not give rise to legal relations. The reason of this is that the parties do not intend that their agreement shall give rise to legal relations. This intention may be implied from the subject matter of the agreement, but it may also be expressed by the parties. In social and family relations such an intention is readily implied, while in business matters the opposite result would ordinarily follow. But I can see no reason why, even in business matters, the parties should not intend to rely on each other's good faith and honour, and to exclude all idea of settling disputes by any outside intervention, with the accompanying necessity of expressing themselves so precisely that outsiders may have no difficulty in understanding what they mean. If they clearly express such an intention I can see no reason in public policy why effect should not be given to their intention …

[ATKIN LJ agreed on this point but was the only judge in the Court of Appeal who held that the actual orders which had been placed and accepted amounted to contracts.]

The House of Lords held that the accepted orders did amount to contracts, but they agreed that the arrangements quoted by SCRUTTON LJ did not amount to a contract.

LORD PHILLIMORE: ... I was for a time impressed by the suggestion that as complete legal rights had been created by the earlier part of the document in question, any subsequent clause nullifying those rights ought to be regarded as repugnant and ought to be rejected. This is what happens for instance in cases where an instrument inter vivos purports to pass the whole property in something either real or personal, and there follows a provision purporting to forbid the new owner from exercising the ordinary rights of ownership. In such cases this restriction is disregarded. But I think the right answer was made by Scrutton LJ. It is true that when the tribunal has before it for construction an instrument which unquestionably creates a legal interest, and the dispute is only as to the quality and extent of that interest, then later repugnant clauses in the instrument cutting down that interest which the earlier part of it has given are to be rejected, but this doctrine does not apply when the question is whether it is intended to create any legal interest at all. Here, I think, the overriding clause in the document is that which provides that it is to be a contract of honour only and unenforceable at law.

Notes

(1) The House of Lords considered that it was not contrary to public policy to agree in advance that the agreement should not be legally binding and that such a stipulation was to be observed by the parties. However, what the parties cannot do is to create a legally binding agreement and then seek to exclude the court's jurisdiction over points of law relating to the contract. That is known as an ouster of the jurisdiction of the court and in English law is contrary to public policy.[26] So, for example, a provision in an insurance policy that in certain circumstances the policy is to be 'incontestable' is ineffective to prevent a court holding that the policy is legally invalid for want of an insurable interest.[27] The parties may, of course, provide that disputes under the contract are to go to arbitration rather than to court; the court retains a supervisory jurisdiction.[28]

(2) In France, a leading author, Bruno Oppetit, has stressed that gentlemen's agreements are not within the legal sphere.[29] However, in French commercial law, gentlemen's agreements are usually considered by the courts as having the same binding nature as a normal contract and French courts do not give effect to the parties' agreement to exclude the court's jurisdiction over points of law relating to the contract.[30] Thus in Cass com 23 January 2007[31] the Camaieu company was held liable for having copied the design of a tee-shirt produced by Créations Nelson in breach of an agreement not to do so, even though the agreement was stated to be 'a purely moral undertaking of which no

[26] See *Treitel on the Law of Contract*, 14th edn by E Peel (London: Sweet & Maxwell, 2015) para 11-047.
[27] *Anctil v Manufacturers' Life Insurance Co* [1899] AC 604.
[28] *Treitel* (n 26 above) paras 11-050–11-053.
[29] B Oppetit, 'L'engagement d'honneur' D 1979 chron 107.
[30] P Malaurie, L Aynès and P Stoffel-Munck, *Droit des obligations* (9th edn, Paris: LGDJ, 2017) no. 440; Cass com 23 January 2007, no. 05-13189, Bull civ IV no. 12, Defr 2007, 1027, annotated by E Savaux.
[31] No. 05-13189, Bull IV no. 12.

breach should be considered a breach of the remainder of the agreement'. The Cour de cassation simply remarked that the undertaking by Camaieu was unequivocal and deliberate and therefore was binding on them.

(3) In German law, the use of the term 'gentleman's agreement' does not necessarily imply that the parties have no intention to be legally bound, even if it was so construed in the following case.

BGH, 22 January 1964[32]   **10.12 (DE)**

Priority treatment

A gentleman's agreement for priority treatment may be of no effect but good faith may be involved.

Facts: The plaintiff was a manufacturer and distributor of pumps. It concluded with the defendant, a shipbuilding company, an agreement by which the defendant stated that the plaintiff would be given 'priority treatment' for the purposes of the acceptance of tenders for the supply of pumps for the defendant's vessels. The plaintiff formed the view that the defendant had ceased to afford it the agreed treatment when ordering consignments of pumps. It demanded to be supplied with information in relation to all the pumps ordered by the defendant, as well as details concerning the defendant's other suppliers and the prices charged by its competitors.

Held: The Landgericht and the Oberlandesgericht ordered the defendant to supply the information, apart from the names of the suppliers. On appeal by the defendant, the plaintiff's action was dismissed.

Judgment: I. The parties described their agreement as a 'gentlemen's agreement'. That term was not recognised by the court. According to the works of academic legal authors, a gentlemen's agreement is a statement made without any intention of giving rise to any consequences in law, since the result which it seeks to achieve must be based on trust in the word of the other contracting party, or 'respect for morality' (meaning, in this context, the practices followed by business persons). Such an agreement may be discerned not only in the case of an agreement which is contrary to mandatory laws but also, and above all, in matters in which the parties merely enter into a simple agreement the detailed implementation of which is left to the sense of 'morality' of the business persons concerned, without this conferring on the parties any legally enforceable rights. The Hamburg Oberlandesgericht accepted that this type of agreement is frequently entered into by business persons; and it described a gentlemen's agreement as a unilateral or bilateral guarantee governed by the goodwill and sense of morality of business persons, stating that—subject to the parties' intentions—such an agreement did not confer any legally enforceable rights. It observed that this interpretation, which was recognised by the courts, was in line with the view taken by the great majority of business persons. Since the use by the parties of the somewhat unusual term 'gentlemen's agreement' must have been intended to have a particular meaning, it was necessary to conclude that all that could be expected of the defendant in the present case was that it should act in a gentlemanly way, without being legally bound to do so.

However, it is not possible to lay down any general rule to the effect that, whenever the parties call their agreement a 'gentlemen's agreement', this necessarily means that they have no intention to be legally bound by it and, consequently, that they may rely

---

[32] DB 1964, 475.

only on their goodwill and sense of morality as business persons. Irrespective of the term applied to the agreement, it is necessary instead to examine, in accordance with the general rules of contractual interpretation, whether the parties meant to bind themselves in law by creating legally enforceable rights, and if so, to what extent. The name given to the agreement may, within those parameters, form a starting-point for an analysis of the intention of the parties.

II. The existence of an extensive obligation to provide information was not apparent, either as a principal obligation or as an ancillary obligation, from the contents of the agreement. Nor could it be generally inferred from the principle of good faith. The existence of a contractual obligation to provide information has been upheld by case law where, in the light of all the circumstances, the person concerned was not in a position to determine on his own the existence and scope of the right vested in him and that right could therefore be enforced, in accordance with the principle of good faith, against the other party, who alone was in a position to provide him with the information in question. In the present case, the facts were not such as to admit of any such presumption. Instead, the making of what was termed a 'gentlemen's agreement' showed that the parties merely intended to arrange for a system of amicable cooperation between them, enabling them to waive the need to carry out regular checks on all the information relating to the defendant.

In the present case, however, it was necessary for the court to examine whether, even in the absence of a proven breach of contract by the defendant, a request for information could be justified by the fact that the defendant had fed suspicions of the plaintiff by virtue of the way in which the clause providing for priority treatment had hitherto been implemented … In such circumstances, it may be inferred from the principle of good faith (§ 242 BGB), which governs the whole of the law of obligations, that, in order for a plaintiff to invoke a right to be supplied with information, he simply needs to claim that he has reason to believe that the defendant has ceased to fulfil the criteria of amicable cooperation and mutual trust on the basis of which the contract was originally concluded.

Note

The definition by the BGH of a 'gentlemen's agreement' is noteworthy as not being entirely free from confusion with an 'agreement in principle' (on which see below). In actual fact, a gentlemen's agreement may be quite detailed. What is most interesting is the affirmation of the existence of an ancillary obligation of good faith which must be observed and upheld, to an extent, by the law. In order to be entitled to demand the information, the plaintiff in the present case had to show that it had grounds for doubting the defendant's good faith.

Cass civ (2), 27 November 1985[33]   **10.13 (FR)**

Alimony agreement

A promise by a divorcing person that she will not seek variation of an alimony order is not necessarily not binding.

[33] No. 84-13971, Bull civ II no. 178.

Facts: When a husband and wife were divorced the husband agreed to pay the wife alimony, and also promised that he would not seek to have the amount payable altered in the future. Later he applied to have the amount reduced and the cour d'appel reduced it.

Held: The Cour de cassation held that it was wrong for the lower court to do so without taking into account the husband's earlier promise and remitted the case.

Judgment: THE COURT: *On the second branch of the second appeal ground*:— Under Article 282 of the Civil Code;

— Whereas the judgment appealed against reduced, upon application by Mr A, the amount of alimony which he had been ordered to pay to Mrs de R de F, his ex-wife, by the decision declaring the parties divorced on the ground of a breakdown of their marriage;

— Whereas in doing so, that judgment disregarded the commitment in honour entered into by the promisor on the occasion of the divorce, to waive the right to seek a subsequent alteration in the amount of the alimony, merely stating that such waiver was not legally enforceable as against the person making it;

— Whereas in so deciding, without stating the grounds of fact or of law on which it based its decision, the cour d'appel deprived its decision of any basis in law;

On those grounds and without giving a decision on the other appeal grounds, the Cour de cassation sets aside and annuls the *inter partes* judgment given on 23 January 1984 by the Paris cour d'appel and consequently restores the cause and the parties to the state in which they found themselves before that judgment and, for a determination in accordance with the law, refers the case to the Amiens cour d'appel.

> *Note*
>
> The waiver of the right to seek an alteration in the amount of alimony was indeed described by the parties as a commitment in honour. The judgment of the cour d'appel was quashed for not stating the grounds 'of fact or of law' on which the held the waiver to be unenforceable. Thus, in principle a waiver of that kind may be legally binding, which was not obvious before. This judgment may be contrasted with the judgment in *Balfour v Balfour*,[34] where there was no commitment binding in honour or gentlemen's agreement.

10.3 LETTERS OF PATRONAGE OR OF COMFORT

These are often ambiguous assurances, under various different guises and designations, whereby a person, generally a parent company, gives an assurance to a third party, for example a bank, that it will lend financial support to another, often its subsidiary. Depending on the case, that might be a genuine legal commitment, for example a guarantee, or a simple declaration of intent without any specific legal consequence. All turns on the interpretation to be given of the intention of the author of the letter.

---

[34] 10.10 (EN), above, p 315.

Court of Appeal **10.14 (EN)**

Kleinwort Benson Ltd v Malaysia Mining Corp Bhd[35]

A statement to a lender by a parent company, stating that the parent company intends that its subsidiary, which is the borrower, should be able to meet its debts, may not amount to a guarantee that the subsidiary will pay.

Facts: A broker in the tin market, MMC Metals Ltd, obtained a bank loan, and its parent company sent the bank letters of assurance. In the critical letter, paragraph 2 stated: 'We confirm that we will not reduce our current financial interest in MMC Metals Ltd until the … facilities have been repaid'; paragraph 3 stated: 'it is our policy to ensure that the business of MMC Metals is at all times in a position to meet its liabilities to you under the loan facility arrangements'. Following a collapse in the tin market, MMC Metals was placed in liquidation without repaying the loans. The bank sought repayment from the signatory of the letters.

Held: The judge held that paragraph 3 amounted to a contractual commitment that the defendants would ensure that MMC could meet its commitments. The decision was reversed on appeal.

Judgment: RALPH GIBSON LJ: … The central question in this case, in my judgment, is that considered in *Esso Petroleum Co Ltd v Mardon*, upon which Mr Waller relied in this court but which was not cited to Hirst J. That question is whether the words of paragraph 3, considered in their context, are to be treated as a warranty or contractual promise. Paragraph 3 contains no express words of promise. Paragraph 3 is in its terms a statement of present fact and not a promise as to future conduct. I agree with Mr Stamler's submission that, in this regard, the words of paragraph 3 are in sharp contrast with the words of paragraph 2 of the letter: 'We confirm that we will not [etc].' The force of this point is not limited, as Hirst J stated, to the absence from paragraph 3 of the words 'We confirm.' The real contrast is between the words of promise, namely, 'we will not' in paragraph 2, and the words of statement of fact 'it is our policy' in paragraph 3. Hirst J held that, by the words of paragraph 3, the defendants gave an understanding that now and at all times in the future, so long as Metals should be under any liability to the plaintiffs under the facility arrangements, it is *and will be* the defendants' policy to ensure that Metals is in a position to meet its liabilities. To derive that meaning from the words it is necessary to add the words underlined, namely, 'and will be,' which do not appear in paragraph 3. In short, the words of promise as to the future conduct of the defendants were held by Hirst J to be part of the necessary meaning of the words used in paragraph 3. The question is whether that view of the words can be upheld.

The absence of express words of warranty as to present facts or the absence of express words of promise as to future conduct does not conclusively exclude a statement from the status of warranty or promise.

The evidence does not show that the words used in paragraph 3 were intended to be a promise as to the future conduct of the defendants but, in my judgment, it shows the contrary.

The concept of a comfort letter was, as Mr Stamler acknowledged, not shown to have acquired any particular meaning at the time of the negotiations in this case with reference to the limits of any legal liability to be assumed under its terms by a parent company.

---

[35] [1989] 1 WLR 379.

A letter, which the parties might have referred to at some stage as a letter of comfort, might, after negotiation, have emerged containing in paragraph 3 in express terms the word used by Hirst J to state the meaning which he gave to paragraph 3. The court would not, merely because the parties had referred to the document as a comfort letter, refuse to give effect to the meaning of the words used. But in this case it is clear, in my judgment, that the concept of a comfort letter, to which the parties had resort when the defendants refused to assume joint and several liability or to give a guarantee, was known by both sides at least to extend to or to include a document under which the defendants would give comfort to the plaintiffs by assuming, not a legal liability to ensure repayment of the liabilities of their subsidiary, but a moral responsibility only. Thus, when the defendants by Mr Green in June 1984 told the plaintiffs that Mr Green would recommend that credit lines for Metals be covered by a letter of comfort rather than by guarantee, the response of Mr Irwin, before any draft of a comfort letter had been prepared, was 'that a letter of comfort would not be a problem, but that we would probably have to charge a higher rate.' The comfort letter was drafted in terms which in paragraph 3 do not express any contractual promise and which are consistent with being no more than a representation of fact. If they are treated as no more than a representation of fact, they are in that meaning consistent with the comfort letter containing no more than the assumption of moral responsibility by the defendants in respect of the debts of Metals. There is nothing in the evidence to show that, as a matter of commercial probability or common sense, the parties must have intended paragraph 3 to be a contractual promise, which is not expressly stated, rather than a mere representation of fact, which is so stated.

Next, the first draft of the comfort letter was produced by the plaintiffs. Paragraph 1 contained confirmation that the defendants knew of and approved of the granting of the facilities in question by the plaintiffs to Metals, and paragraph 2 contained the express confirmation that the defendants would not reduce their current financial interest in Metals until (in effect) the facilities had been paid or the plaintiffs consented. Both are relevant to the present and future moral responsibility of the defendants. If the words of paragraph 3 are to be treated as intended to express a contractual promise by the defendants as to their future policy, which Hirst J held the words to contain, then the recitation of the plaintiffs' approval and the promise not to reduce their current financial interest in Metals, would be of no significance. If the defendants have promised that at all times in the future it will be the defendants' policy to ensure that Metals is in a position to meet its liabilities to the plaintiffs under the facility, it would not matter whether they had approved or disapproved, or whether they had disposed of their shares in Metals. Contracts may, of course, contain statements or promises which are caused to be of no separate commercial importance by the width of a later promise in the same document. Where, however, the court is examining a statement which is by its express words no more than a representation of fact, in order to consider whether it is shown to have been intended to be of the nature of a contractual promise or warranty, it seems to me to be a fact suggesting at least the absence of such intention if, as in this case, to read the statement as a contractual promise is to reduce to no significance two paragraphs included in the plaintiffs' draft, both of which have significance if the statement is read as a representation of fact only. That point can be made more plainly thus: if paragraph 3 in its original or in its final form was intended to contain a binding legal promise by the defendants to ensure the ability of Metals to pay the sums due under the facility, there was no apparent need or purpose for the plaintiffs, as bankers, to waste ink on paragraphs 1 and 2.

As I have said, the absence of express words of promise does not by itself prevent a statement from being treated as a contractual promise. The example given in argument by Mr Waller, namely, of the shop stating by a notice that it is its policy to accept, within 14 days of purchase, the return in good condition of any goods bought, and to refund the price without question, seems to me to be a case in which a court would be likely to hold that the notice imported a promise that the policy would continue over the 14-day period. It would be difficult on those facts to find any sensible commercial explanation for the notice other than a contractual promise not to change the policy over the 14-day period. It would not be satisfactory or convincing to regard the notice as no more than the assumption of a moral responsibility by the shop giving such a notice to its customers. In such a case, and in the absence of any relevant factual context indicating otherwise, it seems to me that the court would probably hold that the statement was shown to have been intended to be a contractual promise.

In the present case, however, the opposite seems to me to be clear ... If my view of this case is correct, the plaintiffs have suffered grave financial loss as a result of the collapse of the tin market and the following decision by the defendants not to honour a moral responsibility which they assumed in order to gain for their subsidiary the finance necessary for the trading operations which the defendants wished that subsidiary to pursue. The defendants have demonstrated, in my judgment, that they made no relevant contractual promise to the plaintiffs which could support the judgment in favour of the plaintiffs. The consequences of the decision of the defendants to repudiate their moral responsibility are not matters for this court. I would allow this appeal.

[NICHOLLS and FOX LJJ agreed.]

Appeal allowed.

Note

The letter of intent did not contain any formula limiting the scope of the commitment in the way one finds them in a gentlemen's agreement. However, on the basis of the deliberately vague wording, it may be asked whether there is indeed a legal commitment. In the present case the Court of Appeal considered there to be only a statement of intention, which can be changed without incurring liability—in other words, a moral responsibility and no legal liability.

In other circumstances, the courts may regard a letter of comfort as a genuine obligation, or even as a guarantee.

BGH, 30 January 1992[36] **10.15 (DE)**

Letter of patronage

A letter of patronage (Patronatserklärung) may amount to a guarantee.

Facts: The plaintiff, a Viennese bank, maintained business relations with a company, S GmbH, a wholly-owned subsidiary of P GmbH whose share capital was wholly-owned by the defendant company. The plaintiff granted S GmbH a loan of 25 million Austrian schillings. A 'letter of patronage' from the defendant was to be provided by way of guarantee for the capital increases. In August 1986 the defendant company sent such a letter to the plaintiff, in which it agreed to guarantee a loan exceeding, by 10 million schillings, the

---

[36] NJW 1992, 2093.

sum of 30 million schillings, with a view to 'constraining' the affiliated company 'to fulfil its obligations'. … Following negotiations between S GmbH and the plaintiff, the defendant on 10 November 1986 sent a second letter of patronage to the bank, the contents of which were as follows:

> It has come to our notice that S GmbH, which is affiliated to P, has entered into a business relationship with you, and we are agreeable to this. P GmbH is affiliated to our company as to 100%, and holds 100% of the capital of S GmbH. For as long as the above-mentioned business relationship continues to exist, or any debts are due to you from our affiliated company, we will maintain our participation at the same level. In the event that we intend to alter this state of affairs in any way, we will contact you in good time beforehand with a view to resolving the situation on an amicable basis. In addition, we irrevocably accept the obligation to exert our influence on our affiliated company throughout the period during which it has not yet repaid the loan in full, and to procure for it the requisite finance enabling it at all times to fulfil the obligations, present or future, which it owes to you. This declaration is governed by Austrian law.

On 28 December 1987 proceedings for court-supervised recovery were initiated against S GmbH. The plaintiff bank called in the loan and established the balance due at AS 18,545,418.99. Those proceedings were terminated by a compulsory settlement under which the bank was to have its claim satisfied as to 25%. On 30 December 1997 like proceedings were brought against the defendant company. Under a settlement dated 6 October 1989 these proceedings were brought to an end. The compulsory settlement provided for the payment, in three tranches, of a 35% proportion. On the basis of the letter of patronage of 10 November 1986 the bank registered its claim in the amount of AS 3,110,453.03 which was disputed by the official receiver. In addition, under the settlement of 6 October 1989, the bank demanded payment of 35% of its claim in three tranches.

Held: The action for payment brought by the bank was upheld by the courts trying the case on its merits which ordered the defendant to pay AS 6,490,896. The appeal on a point of law was dismissed by the Bundesgerichtshof.

Judgment:

1 The existence of a letter of patronage:

As the Oberlandesgericht acknowledged, the defendant is liable to pay damages pursuant to § 902 ABGB (the Austrian Civil Code) for failure to comply with its obligations as described in the (second) letter of patronage which it agreed to give and which it sent to the bank. According to the terms of that letter, the defendant undertook to provide S GmbH (the principal debtor) with finance enabling it to honour its debt to the plaintiff. That offer was accepted by the plaintiff in accordance with § 863 ABGB. According to that provision, acceptance may also be signified by 'such conduct as, having regard to all the circumstances, affords no valid reason for doubting an intention to accept'. In the proceedings at first instance, the plaintiff relied on the argument that its conduct had been conclusive, as was borne out by the fact that it had continued to abide by its commitment to provide credit to S GmbH. In the proceedings at second instance, it argued that, according to the defendant's letter of patronage, the latter had not expected any express acceptance of the terms of that letter. Silence in response to a contractual document corresponding to the matters agreed in oral negotiations was sufficient to constitute acceptance. In the present case, the Oberlandesgericht held that the (second) letter of patronage enured to the benefit of the plaintiff alone. Unlike the first letter, dated 4 August 1986, it was not limited as to the amount of the guarantee. Moreover, it was formulated in more precise terms than the first letter and more clearly imposed an obligation on the party issuing it. Neither in Austrian law nor in German law could one expect to find a letter of patronage having greater force than that issued in November 1986. In the present case, all those matters give rise to a very strong presumption that the second letter of patronage was firmly accepted.

2 The effects of the letter of patronage

A letter of patronage such as that in the present case is generally comparable to a form of security such as a suretyship or declaration of guarantee. In the event of the insolvency of the creditor, those two instruments acquire, in principle, the binding force of a guarantee having equal rank. In the case of a suretyship, this results from § 773(1) no 3 BGB, and, in the case of an ordinary guarantee (not governed by the Code), from the general legal principles of entitlement to damages, to which it is subject. According to the general rules, the obligation to pay damages means not only that damages are payable in the event of default by the debtor but also that compensation is payable for the entire loss suffered, where appropriate on a joint and several basis with other persons owing an obligation. If, in the present case, the defendant parent company had properly fulfilled its obligations arising from the letter of patronage, the loan would have been repaid by the due date. However, in the event of wrongful failure to perform, a party undertaking to guarantee the performance of the contractual obligation of another is in principle fully liable to pay the debt due from the principal debtor, jointly and severally with the latter.

Outcome

In the present case the letter of patronage, as widened, must be regarded as a genuine suretyship under § 773(1) no 3 BGB or a guarantee governed by the general principles of liability. Accordingly, full restitution of the loss suffered by the Bank must be afforded. The defendant, the promisor under the letter of patronage, is jointly liable for non-performance of the contractual obligations which the principal debtor was bound to perform.

> *Note*
>
> This is a declaration known as a *Patronatserklärung*, or letter of patronage. Again a problem of interpretation arises. The Court considers there to have been a legally binding commitment notwithstanding the absence of express acceptance, since silence here amounts to acceptance. There was, therefore, a genuine assumption of liability under a suretyship or an ordinary promise of guarantee.

In French law, in actual practice, letters of comfort are used mainly for commercial purposes to fix the elements of contractual negotiations on which the parties have agreed, before they agree on the final contract. However, there is also another specific use of the letter of comfort (or letter of intent).[37] It serves as a substitute to a guarantee (*cautionnement*), usually as between the *société commercial mère*, its *filiale* and a bank—in other words, in the same situation as in the *Kleinwort Benson* case above. The effect of the letter of comfort depends on the terms in which it was drafted and the case law is rather unclear.

Cass com, 17 May 2011[38]   **10.16 (FR)**

Emball'iso's letter

A party may undertake that another party will be in a position to meet its obligations to a creditor without the obligation amounting to a guarantee to the creditor that the debtor will perform.

---

[37] Cass com 17 May 2011, Bull civ IV no. 78; Malaurie et al (n 30 above) no. 440.
[38] No. 09-16186, Bull IV no. 78.

Facts: A company provided a letter of comfort to the bank for its subsidiary (which then went insolvent). According to this letter, the defendant company would unconditionally and irrevocably make sure that its subsidiary would meet its obligations. The lower courts held that while the defendant company had not intended to subscribe a guarantee (*cautionnement*) for its subsidiary, it had undertaken an obligation to make sure that the subsidiary would meet its obligations and that the wording of the letter indicated that the said obligation was *de résultat*.

Held: The Cour de cassation upheld the judgment.

Judgment: But whereas it had held that the contract of loan of €200,000 provided for, by way of guarantee, a letter of comfort in the amount of €200,000, the judgment held that if the Emball'iso Company had not intended to give a guarantee, it had undertaken an obligation to do, by undertaking to ensure that its subsidiary was in a position to meet the obligations that from time to time it owed to the bank, and moreover to put at its subsidiary's disposition the funds necessary to repay its debt and to ensure that the funds were used for this purpose; and that the cour d'appel had deduced from the terms of this letter that the obligation undertaken by the company was an obligation of result.

> *Note*
>
> This judgment of the Cour of cassation is a warning to contract drafters to take care. Even if in principle the case law considers that a letter of comfort may have a variety of meanings, it has clearly decided that an obligation to do of this kind can be analysed as an obligation of result and still be distinguished from a letter of guarantee.[39] What is the difference? When there is a guarantee, the guarantor will stand in the debtor's shoes if the said debtor fails to perform his obligation. On the other hand, when a letter of comfort has been issued, the author of this letter will engage his contractual liability when the debtor fails to perform his obligation. The situations are governed by two different sets of rules.

Since a 2006 Ordinance which reforms 'the law of suretyship', Article 2322 of the Code civil defines a *lettre d'intention* as 'an undertaking to do or not to do to support a debtor in the performance of his obligation to his creditor' and Article 2287-1 of the Code civil states that it is, along with *cautionnement* and *garantie autonome*, a species of personal security (*sûreté personnelle*). It differs from the *cautionnement* as the author of the letter will not take the place of the debtor if the latter fails to meet his obligations, though he will be liable from a contractual perspective if the author fails to meet his obligation to do or not to do. The extent of his liability depends on how the letter is phrased: it can be an *obligation de résultat* or a mere *obligation de moyen*.

In the final analysis, here again, it is all a question of interpretation which is all the more difficult to resolve since frequently the parties involved are careful not to be too specific in regard to the commitments which they are undertaking. The ambiguity is often intentional.

---

[39] See also Cass com 18 April 2000, no. 97-19043, Bull IV no. 78; Cass com 26 January 1999, no. 97-10003, Bull IV no. 31.

10.4 AGREEMENT IN PRINCIPLE (*ACCORD DE PRINCIPE*)

This is another intermediate situation. The parties are in agreement on the most important part of the contract, so much so that it may legitimately be asked whether the contract has been created or not. We already encountered a situation of this kind in *British Steel Corp v Cleveland Bridge and Engineering Co Ltd* (1984)[40] where it was found that, contrary to expectations, a definitive contract was never agreed. This situation may arise where negotiations are protracted and complicated and the contract is negotiated in successive stages. But what if the parties go further and state that they are agreed in principle? In a declaration of principle there is more than mere negotiation but less than a definitive contract. It has to be fleshed out. Does that mean to say that it is of no effect?

We should start by distinguishing such cases from cases in which the parties, though in negotiations with each other, do not intend there to be any legal commitment. In German law, if there is doubt as to whether the words and conduct of the parties can be understood as amounting to an offer and a corresponding acceptance the Civil Code provides two specific rules of interpretation. First, if the parties have agreed—or, indeed, if only one of the parties has flagged up—that a particular aspect still needs to be resolved, the court has to presume that a contract has not come into existence (§ 154(1) BGB). Similarly, if the parties have agreed that their agreement should be notarised or otherwise put in writing, the court has to presume that a contract has not been made as long as the agreed formality has not been complied with (§ 154(2) BGB).[41] However, it is important to remember that these rules only apply in 'cases of doubt', ie if the interpretation of the words and conduct of the parties remains inconclusive. If the interpretation leads the court to conclude that the parties obviously intended to be contractually bound, despite not having resolved the relevant aspects or not having complied with the agreed form, the court will conclude that the parties made a contract. This is normally the case if the parties have started performance.[42]

In English law, it is common to find cases in which the parties have deliberately indicated that their negotiations are not intended to commit them, by stating that any agreement is 'subject to contract'. This phrase has acquired a standard meaning: that any agreement is subject to the preparation and signing of a formal contract and, until that has taken place, neither is committed. Thus when parties agree to the sale and purchase of a house 'subject to contract', neither party is bound until each has signed his part of the contract and they have 'exchanged contracts'.[43]

Such situations must be distinguished from those to be considered in this section, where there are agreements which may give rise to *avant-contrats* or *Vorverträge* (pre-contracts), unilateral promises to enter into a contract and options. In most legal systems these are recognised, not of course as the full, final contract (which has yet to be agreed) but as a form of preliminary contract intended to serve as a preparatory step towards a definitive contract.

---

[40] See 6.25 (EN), above, p 164.
[41] For the text of § 154 BGB, see 9.6 (DE), above, p 289.
[42] Palandt/Ellenberger § 154 para 2.
[43] *Eccles v Bryant* [1948] Ch 93 (CA).

In French law, an *accord de principe* is not yet a contract, unless the issues which remain to be discussed are totally non-essential; but it may require the parties to continue the negotiations in good faith. If all elements essential to the contract are settled in the *accord de principe*, and if only secondary elements remain to be agreed upon, the contract can be concluded. In contrast, if elements that are missing are not purely secondary elements, there cannot be any binding contract (it is not possible for the parties to agree that an essential element of the contract is downgraded into a non-essential one: 'an agreement under which the parties would qualify as essential certain elements of the contract and would put aside, as ancillary, all other elements, including those traditionally qualified as essential, cannot amount to the conclusion of the final contract'[44]). In that case, there is only a preparatory document, by virtue of which the parties indicate the questions on which their mutual consent is reached and agree to further continue discussing the issues on which consent is not reached. This preparatory document is nothing but 'a step in the discussions'. This step requires the parties to continue their discussions under the general principle of good faith, subject to liability based upon delict and upon fault in case they do not comply with this obligation. But it does not by any means necessarily lead to the conclusion of the contract.[45]

Cass com, 4 February 1986[46]   **10.17 (FR)**

Maize driers

A short agreement may be binding if it contains the necessary elements of a contract. Whether it does so is a matter for the appreciation of the court.

Facts: Company S, in a letter dated 9 August 1977, stated to Mr B: 'We confirm the agreements reached during your visit and grant you sole rights for the whole of France for our maize driers.' The cour d'appel took the view that this was merely a declaration of principle and not a genuine contract.

Held: The Cour de cassation doubted this reasoning but refused to interfere.

Judgment: THE COURT: *On the first appeal ground taken in its three branches:*— Whereas it appears from the findings contained in the judgment appealed against (Bordeaux, 2nd Chamber, 9 May 1984) that Mr Betat bought from Mr Berger a business trading under the name of Italfrance (later Euromat) and that possession was to be given on completion before a notary, and that a deposit on account of the purchase price had been paid; as subsequently, Mr Betat sought to rescind the purchase, to recover the payment on account together with damages on the ground that he had been the victim of fraud, since the contract mentioning an exclusive distributorship agreement in respect of Pedrotti goods in France was, in Mr Betat's submission, entirely imaginary;
— Whereas the Berger couple criticise the judgment appealed against for upholding that claim since, as stated in the appeal, under Article 1101 of the Civil Code [still Article 1101 after the 2016 reforms] a contract is an agreement under which one or more

---

[44] F Terré, P Simler and Y Lequette, *Les obligations* (11th edn, Paris: Dalloz, 2013) no. 188.
[45] Malaurie et al (n 30 above) no. 441.
[46] Annexed to I Najjar, 'L'accord de principe' D 1991 chron 67.

persons enter into obligations towards one or more other persons to give, to do or not to do something;

— Under Article 1108 [see now Article 1128] of the Civil Code such a contract is valid once the subject matter is determined with certainty, the cause is lawful and the party assuming obligations has legal capacity to enter into contractual relationships and has given his unvitiated consent;

— Whereas in the present case, the letter from the Pedrotti company of 9 August 1977 expressly stated to Mr Berger: 'We confirm the agreements reached during your visit and grant you sole rights for the whole of France for our maize driers'; as that letter in which Pedrotti, whose capacity and consent were not in issue, undertook to give Mr Berger exclusive sales rights in France in respect of its maize driers, did constitute a firm, precise and definitive contract granting exclusive rights.

— Whereas by holding that it was merely an 'agreement in principle' and not a contract, the cour d'appel infringed Articles 1101 and 1108 of the Civil Code by misapplying them and by holding that the exchange of correspondence between the parties, in which Pedrotti stated clearly and unequivocally: 'We confirm the agreements reached during your visit and grant you sole rights for the whole of France for our maize driers', was too vague to constitute a genuine contract but merely amounted to an agreement in principle, the cour d'appel distorted the plain evidence of that letter and consequently was in breach of Article 1134 [now Article 1104] of the Civil Code, since it was in the end not disputed by any of the parties to the proceedings that since 1977 Pedrotti had in fact been granting exclusive rights to Mr Berger to sell its maize driers; as by holding, however, that 'the 1977 agreement was not followed up', the cour d'appel placed reliance on a matter of fact extraneous to the proceedings, thereby infringing new Article 7 of the Code of Civil Procedure;

— Whereas however, in the exercise of its sovereign power to appraise the evidence, the cour d'appel held that no contract conferring exclusive rights had been entered into between Pedrotti and Mr Berger;

— Whereas none of the branches of the appeal ground is therefore well founded …

Note

(1) The Cour de cassation relies on the appeal court's sovereign power to appraise the evidence in order to dismiss the appeal. The cour d'appel had found that the agreement did not constitute a 'precise, firm and definitive contract'. Too many important matters—duration, remuneration etc—had been left unsettled.[47]

(2) In the final analysis, the subject matter (*objet*) of the agreement was not sufficiently clear (see old Article 1108 of the Code civil; since 2016 this would be regarded as an issue of the 'content' of the contract, Article 1128).[48]

The notion of the agreement in principle was also used in slightly different circumstances in the following judgment.

---

[47] cf the English case of *Scammell v Ouston*, above, p 289.
[48] See 9.2 (FR), above, p 289.

Agreement to consider re-employment

A letter stating that an employer will consider re-employing an ex-employee if business improves imposes no commitment.

Facts: Marchal had been employed until 19 December 1940 by Renault. After the liberation he asked to be reinstated. Renault sent him the following letter in reply: 'Although we would wish to accede to your request, our reply to your request in which you mention the status which you acquired in the Resistance is that the current operational activity of our works and the organisation of our departments which are already very busy whilst production remains slack, prevent us from giving you for the moment a favourable reply'. The lower court interpreted this as a commitment by Renault to reinstate Marchal as soon as the post corresponding to his former duties had been recreated as a result of a recovery in the economic situation.

Held: Renault had not given an undertaking to reinstate the employee; at most the letter amounted to an undertaking to consider the possibility of reinstating him.

Judgment: THE COURT: ... *On the sole appeal ground*:— Under Article 1134 [now Article 1104] of the Civil Code;

— Whereas under this provision, contracts created in accordance with the law have the force of law as regards those who have entered into them;

— Whereas although it is indeed for the courts to interpret agreements, this is on condition that they do not distort the plain meaning of their clear and unambiguous provisions;

— Whereas the judgment appealed against finds that Marchal had been employed until 19 December 1940 by Renault; as after the liberation he asked to be reinstated by registered letter dated 4 December 1944; as on 19 January 1945 he was sent the following letter in reply: 'Although we would wish to accede to your request, our reply to your request in which you mention the status which you acquired in the Resistance is that the current operational activity of our works and the organisation of our departments which are already very busy whilst production remains slack, prevent us from giving you for the moment a favourable reply'; as on 24 March 1945 a reply along the same lines was sent to a third party who had intervened in Marchal's favour: 'Following a fresh examination of the question I can inform you that our intentions as regards Mr Marchal have not changed and that, as soon as the resumption of car manufacturing permits, we will once again study the possibility of reinstating him in the Company';

— Whereas the lower courts inferred from those letters that Renault had given an undertaking to reinstate Marchal as soon as the post corresponding to his former duties had been recreated as a result of a recovery in the economic situation; as it was for the Company itself to advise Mr Marchal as soon as a suitable post became vacant, and it mattered little that Mr Marchal delayed until 18 May 1951 before reiterating his request;

— Whereas by holding that the abovementioned letters contained a firm undertaking on the part of Renault to reinstate Marchal, as soon as the first post fell vacant, the judgment appealed against distorted the meaning and scope of the clear and unambiguous terms in which those letters were couched; as under those terms Renault, desirous of acceding to Marchal's request, would, depending on the state of prosperity and development of the undertaking, study the possibility of reinstating him, which amounted only to an agreement in principle;

---

[49] JCP 1958.II.10868, annotated by J Carbonnier.

— Whereas it followed that the judgment appealed against had no legal basis;

On those grounds, the Cour de cassation set aside the judgment delivered on 23 March 1956 by the Tribunal Civil de la Seine and referred the case to the Tribunal Civil de Versailles.

Notes

(1) The interpretation of this judgment is finely balanced. The Cour de cassation took the view that the lower court, in holding there to be a firm commitment on the part of Renault to reinstate Marchal as soon as a post fell vacant, distorted the meaning and scope of the clear and unambiguous terms in which the letters to Marchal were couched, so setting a limit to the court's untrammelled power of appraisal. In fact the lower courts appear to have stretched the meaning of those letters. Does that mean that the agreement in principle found by the Cour de cassation is a formula having no legal effect? One cannot make such an assertion, since the Cour de cassation used this form of words deliberately. Accordingly, it may reasonably be supposed that, though Renault was not required to give Marchal the first job that came up, it was under an obligation to re-examine his situation when the situation of the undertaking so permitted.

(2) In the field of labour law, the Cour de cassation has, in some cases, resorted to the concept of *engagement unilateral* to create a binding commitment on the employer and it is not sure that the Chambre sociale would still reach the same solution today.

Under French law, the *accord de principe* is a key notion which is sometimes used as a generic term to designate all sorts of conventions which are non-binding and yet are not deprived of any legal effect. The notion had been included in the various French proposals for reform, in the section dedicated to negotiations. The Avant-projet Catala was the first to name and attempt to define the *accord de principe* in its section on negotiations:

Avant-projet Catala **10.19 (FR)**

§1 Negotiations[50]

Article 1104: The parties are free to begin, continue and break off negotiations, but these must satisfy the requirements of good faith.

A break-down in negotiations can give rise to liability only if it is attributable to the bad faith or fault of one of the parties.

Article 1104-1: The parties may, by an agreement in principle, undertake to negotiate at a later date a contract whose elements are still to be settled, and to work in good faith towards settling them.

Article 1104-2: The rules governing agreements which are intended to provide for the conduct or breaking-off of negotiations are subject to the provisions of this sub-title.

---

[50] For a commentary on these texts, see B Fauvarque-Cosson, 'Negotiation and Renegotiation: A French Perspective' in J Cartwright, S Vogenauer and S Whittaker (eds), *Reforming the French Law of Obligations* (Oxford: Hart Publishing, 2009) 33.

However, nothing resembling Articles 1104-1 or 1104-2 of the Catala draft was adopted in the recent reform, so there has been no legislative endorsement of the *accord de principe*.[51]

The solution adopted by the German Bundesgerichtshof also results in giving some kind of legal effect to an agreement in principle, but in a slightly different way.

BGH, 8 June 1962[52]   **10.20 (DE)**

Consulting his lawyer

A preliminary contract may not be binding as to its precise terms but it creates the obligation to conclude a definitive principal contract along similar lines in the near future.

Facts: On 3 September 1958 the parties had a discussion and agreed to settle their differences concerning a licensing agreement entered into on 4 October 1950. A written settlement was drawn up on 30 September 1958 under which the parties signed a preliminary contract with a view to concluding a definitive agreement. However, the defendant wished to show the preliminary contract to his legal advisor in order to amend certain formal clauses and to ascertain the financial implications of what he was letting himself in for. Yet there was no provision to this effect in the preliminary contract. The plaintiff sought conclusion of the definitive contract, whilst the defendant resisted this. The plaintiff therefore brought an action for specific performance against the defendant whose defence to this claim was that he had never sought to commit himself contractually since he wished to consult his legal advisor. The appellate court decided that a binding preliminary contract had been concluded and ordered the defendant to agree to the conclusion of a definite principal contract on the same terms.

Held: The parties had concluded a binding preliminary contract which created an obligation to conclude a definite principal contract. However, this did not have to be exactly on the same terms as the preliminary contract. The case was therefore referred back to the appeal court.

Judgment: The Oberlandesgericht took the view that it had been established that the parties had agreed, in the course of the discussion which took place on 3 September 1958 between the plaintiff and WB, the co-tenant and manager of the defendant, that the differences between them concerning the licence of 4 December 1950 were to be settled in the form agreed, as set out in the memorandum of the meeting held on 3 September 1958. It regarded that agreement as a preliminary contract drawn up with a view to achieving a written settlement on the same terms as those set out in the memorandum. According to the Oberlandesgericht, such a contract may be concluded orally, even though it is agreed between the parties that the definitive contract is to be in writing. It is true to say that WB, in stating that he wished first of all to show the contract to a lawyer, gained for the defendant the opportunity of altering the forms of wording chosen, the scope of which he was unable to appreciate without the advice of a lawyer, whilst at the same time preserving the essential scheme of the contract. However, the draft contract did not contain such wording. As an experienced businessman, WB was aware of the general scope of that agreement, and was in a position to evaluate it without consulting a lawyer. In response to the plaintiff's statement that there was an agreement and that they should not part without agreeing the wording, he replied: 'Of course, of course, we've got an agreement'; consequently, that reply cannot have meant, as the defendant asserts, that it was an agreement without legal force. Instead, it was an agreement which

---

[51] The reform has new important provisions on confidential information: Art 1112-2. See 13.42 (FR), below, p 477.

[52] NJW 1962, 1812.

was intended to impose obligations on the two parties, since they had not wished to part without reaching an agreement and had intended to be bound. Moreover, the agreement thus reached by both sides had been cemented by a handshake. Thus the conduct of both parties, as it would have been understood by an objective observer, clearly indicated that they intended to be bound.

The appeal on a point of law criticized the judgments of the lower courts for analysing the agreement as a genuine preliminary agreement. In this regard, the Bundesgerichtshof points out that academic writers and judicial precedents are at one in considering that a preliminary agreement may give rise to a genuine contractual relationship under which the parties are bound to enter into a subsequent principal contract in the near future.

The Bundesgerichtshof observes that the conditions governing the validity of a preliminary agreement are the same as those applicable to contracts in general. Most importantly, the contents of the principal contract must be adequately definite. In cases involving preliminary contracts, it is necessary to examine very carefully whether the parties really intended to conclude such a preliminary contract or whether they intended to make the definitive principal contract right away. The intention to conclude a mere preliminary contract will especially be assumed if there are *de facto* or *de jure* obstacles preventing the parties from concluding the principal contract at the time of making the agreement, but the parties nevertheless wish to be bound from the outset, with a view to reaching the ultimate goal at a later stage. These conditions were fulfilled in the present case. Above all, the essential contents of the contract had been sufficiently determined in the terms of the agreement. Thus the Oberlandesgericht's categorisation of the agreement as a preliminary contract cannot be contested on legal grounds.

However, the order of the Oberlandesgericht requiring the defendant to conclude the contract cannot be upheld. The Bundesgerichtshof finds that the preliminary contract pleaded by the plaintiff was not the definitive contract; it merely obliged the parties to conclude a contract having the same general scope. This did not mean that the definitive contract had to be exactly on the terms of the preliminary contract. After all, the very reason for assuming that the agreement of the parties did not amount to a definitive contract was the expressed intention of WB to have the exact formulations assessed by a lawyer. Therefore the appellate court should not have ordered the defendant to make the principal contract on the exact terms of the precontract. It rather should have searched for a wording that would have expressed what the parties had intended with a view to their economic situation and that would have precluded any further dispute as conclusively as possible. Moreover, the contract to be concluded on the basis of the preliminary contract can take effect only from the time at which the decision ordering the defendant to enter into it acquires the force of *res judicata* (§ 894 ZPO). Consequently, in determining the content of the principal contract, the appellate court should also have taken account of the factual changes which had taken place since the conclusion of the preliminary contract. The terms of the principal contract should have been those which the parties would have determined in light of these changes.

Notes

(1) The first question was to decide whether there was merely a pre-contract or an actual contract. The Bundesgerichtshof found that the conduct of the parties indicated their intention to be legally bound, so there was a binding preliminary contract. This required the parties to conclude a definitive principal contract in the near future.

(2) The second question was to determine the precise terms on which the principal contract would have to be concluded. The Bundesgerichtshof held that, while the terms of the principal contract would have to be broadly along the same lines as those of the preliminary contract, they did not necessarily have to be identical. Thus, if a court ordered the parties to conclude a principal contract in order to fulfil their obligations from the preliminary contract it could not simply order them to make the principal contract on the exact terms of the preliminary contract. It should rather search 'for a wording that would express what the parties had intended with a view to their economic situation' and that would take into account any changes in the circumstances of the parties since the conclusion of the preliminary contract. Can you reconcile this decision with what you believe to be the proper role of the courts in contract law?

What is the position in English law if the parties make an 'agreement in principle', or even agree expressly that they will negotiate a contract, but then one of them breaks off negotiations? It is usually said that a 'contract to negotiate' imposes no obligations. This was confirmed in a case in the House of Lords in which one party agreed that it would not negotiate with anyone else.

House of Lords   **10.21 (EN)**

Walford v Miles[53]

A contract not to negotiate with a third party for an unspecified time is unenforceable for a lack of certainty, and it is not possible to make good that uncertainty by implying into the agreement a duty to conduct precontractual negotiations in good faith. An agreement to negotiate in good faith is itself too uncertain to be enforceable and would be repugnant to the adversarial position of the parties during the negotiations.

Facts: In 1986, the respondents, the Miles, decided to sell their photographic processing business and premises. The appellants, Walford, entered into negotiations with the respondents, and reached an agreement in principle for the sale of the business. The parties also made a 'lock-out' agreement, under which the respondents agreed to terminate and/or to refuse to enter into negotiations with any other party for the sale of the business, if the appellants provided a letter from their bank confirming that the bank would provide them with a loan to facilitate the purchase, which they duly did. The respondents nevertheless sold the business to a third party, and the appellants brought an action against the respondents for breach of the lock-out agreement. The appellants alleged that the lock-out agreement was a collateral contract, the consideration for which was the provision of the letter and the continuation of negotiations. However, in arguing that there was a lock-out agreement the appellants faced the difficulty that the agreement had no time-limit. Clearly it could not last forever, so how long would it last? Moreover, even successful agreement on all the terms would not necessarily lead to there being a contract, since the documents were 'subject to contract'. In an attempt to overcome these difficulties, the appellants argued that to give business efficacy to the agreement, or in other words to make the agreement workable,[54] it must have contained an implied term that, so long as the respondents desired to sell the business and the premises, the respondents would continue to negotiate in good faith with the appellants. The appellants claimed that the business was in fact worth £1 million more than they had agreed to pay, and claimed damages for the difference in value between the price agreed and the true value.

---

[53] [1992] 2 AC 128.
[54] On the English law of implied terms and the 'business efficacy test', see below, p 799.

Held: The trial judge held that there was a collateral agreement (a separate contract that runs alongside any main agreement for sale) and that this collateral agreement had been repudiated by the respondents. He therefore ordered that the damages for the alleged loss of opportunity be assessed. He also awarded £700 damages for wasted expenditure arising from precontractual misrepresentations. A majority of the Court of Appeal upheld the award of £700, but reversed the decision on the collateral contract point, holding that the agreement alleged was no more than an agreement to negotiate and was therefore unenforceable. The House of Lords upheld the decision of the Court of Appeal.

Judgment: LORD ACKNER: The justification for the implied term ... was that in order to give the collateral agreement 'business efficacy', Mr Miles was obliged to 'continue to negotiate in good faith.' It was submitted to the Court of Appeal and initially to your Lordships that this collateral agreement could not be made to work, unless there was a positive duty imposed upon Mr Miles to negotiate. It was of course conceded that the agreement made no specific provision for the period it was to last. It was however contended, albeit not pleaded, that the obligation to negotiate would endure for a reasonable time, and that such time was the time which was reasonably necessary to reach a binding agreement. It was however accepted that such a period of time would not end when negotiations had ceased, because all such negotiations were conducted expressly under the umbrella of 'subject to contract'.[55] The agreement alleged would thus be valueless if the alleged obligation to negotiate ended when negotiations as to the terms of the 'subject to contract' agreement had ended, since at that stage the Miles would have been entitled at their whim to refuse to sign any contract.

Apart from the absence of any term as to the duration of the collateral agreement, it contained no provision for the Miles to determine the negotiations, albeit that such a provision was essential.

It was contended by Mr Naughton [counsel for the appellants] that a term was to be implied giving the Miles a right to determine the negotiations, but only if they had 'a proper reason'. However in order to determine whether a given reason was a proper one, he accepted that the test was not an objective one—would a hypothetical reasonable person consider the reason a reasonable one? The test was a subjective one—did the Miles honestly believe in the reason which they gave for the termination of the negotiations? Thus they could be quite irrational, so long as they behaved honestly.

Mr Naughton accepted that as the law now stands and has stood for approaching 20 years, an agreement to negotiate is not recognised as an enforceable contract. This was first decided in terms in *Courtney and Fairbairn Ltd v Tolaini Brothers (Hotels) Ltd* [1975] 1 WLR 297. ... The decision in *Courtney's* case was followed by the Court of Appeal in *Mallozzi v Carapelli SpA* [1976] 1 Lloyd's Rep 407. ... The decision that an agreement to negotiate cannot constitute a legally enforceable contract has been followed at first instance in a number of relatively recent cases; ...

Before your Lordships it was sought to argue that the decision in *Courtney's* case was wrong. Although the cases in the United States did not speak with one voice your Lordships' attention was drawn to the decision of the United States' Court of Appeal [sic], Third Circuit, in *Channel Home Centers, Division of Grace Retail Corporation v Grossman* (1986) 795 F 2d 291 as being 'the clearest example' of the American cases in the appellants' favour. That case raised the issue whether an agreement to negotiate in good faith, if supported by consideration, is an enforceable contract. I do not find the decision of any assistance. While accepting that an agreement to agree is not an enforceable contract, the

---

[55] For the effect of this phrase see above, p 329.

Court of Appeal appears to have proceeded on the basis that an agreement to negotiate in good faith is synonymous with an agreement to use best endeavours and as the latter is enforceable, so is the former. This appears to me, with respect, to be an unsustainable proposition. The reason why an agreement to negotiate, like an agreement to agree, is unenforceable, is simply because it lacks the necessary certainty. The same does not apply to an agreement to use best endeavours. This uncertainty is demonstrated in the instant case by the provision which it is said to be implied in the agreement for the determination of the negotiations. How can a court be expected to decide whether, *subjectively*, a proper reason existed for the termination of negotiations? The answer suggested depends upon whether the negotiations have been determined 'in good faith'. However the concept of a duty to carry on negotiations in good faith is inherently repugnant to the adversarial position of the parties when involved in negotiations. Each party to the negotiations is entitled to pursue his (or her) own interest, so long as he avoids making misrepresentations. To advance that interest he must be entitled, if he thinks it appropriate, to threaten to withdraw from further negotiations or to withdraw in fact, in the hope that the opposite party may seek to reopen the negotiations by offering him improved terms. Mr Naughton, of course accepts that the agreement upon which he relies does not contain a duty to complete the negotiations. But that still leaves the vital question—how is a vendor ever to know that he is entitled to withdraw from further negotiations? How is the court to police such an 'agreement?' A duty to negotiate in good faith is as unworkable in practice as it is inherently inconsistent with the position of a negotiating party. It is here that the uncertainty lies. In my judgment, while negotiations are in existence either party is entitled to withdraw from those negotiations, at any time and for any reason. There can be thus no obligation to negotiate until there is a 'proper reason' to withdraw. Accordingly a bare agreement to negotiate has no legal content.

Notes

(1) *Walford v Miles* affirms that under English law there is no such thing as a general duty to negotiate in good faith. The point arose by virtue of the appellants' submission that the lock-in agreement could be rendered sufficiently certain by the implication of a duty to continue the negotiations in good faith. The House of Lords took the occasion to make clear by a single speech in very strong terms that English law does not know an obligation to negotiate in good faith.[56] This decision has met with criticism in England[57] and abroad.[58] On the other hand, there is quite wide agreement that it would not have been appropriate to allow the appellant's claim for £1 million lost profit in full. We will consider this issue in Chapter 13 when we explore precontractual good faith.[59] It may also be that some courts would think the respondents' conduct in this case was consistent with good faith. They had agreed to give a warranty that the annual profits for the first year after the sale would reach £300,000. They were concerned that their employees and the intending purchaser

---

[56] See further on this case below, pp 427 ff.

[57] See, eg, E McKendrick, *Contract Law* (12th edn, Basingstoke: Palgrave Macmillan, 2017) 52, [62]; contrast, however, *Treitel* (n 26 above), who finds it entirely appropriate on the facts: para 2-099.

[58] See, eg, S van Erp, 'The Pre-contractual Stage' in A Hartkamp et al (eds), *Towards a European Civil Code* (4th edn, Alphen aan den Rijn: Wolters Kluwer, 2011) 493.

[59] See pp 457 ff.

might not get on well, key staff might leave and the profit figure might not be met. So they may have had a good reason to back out of the negotiations.

(2) In *Petromec Inc v Petroleo Brasiliero SA* [2005] EWCA Civ 891, [2006] 1 Lloyd's Rep 121 Longmore LJ said that an express agreement to negotiate contained within a contract that was itself binding might well be binding despite *Walford v Miles*. He said:

> [119] ... the ... objection that is likely to give rise to the greatest problem [is] that the concept of bringing negotiations to an end in bad faith is somewhat elusive. But the difficulty of a problem should not be an excuse for the court to withhold relevant assistance from the parties by declaring a blanket unenforceability of the obligation ...

> [120] The authority chiefly relied on by Mr Hancock in support of blanket unenforceability was the decision of the House of Lords in *Walford v Miles*, which (of course) binds us for what it decides ... Lord Ackner (with whom the rest of their Lordships agreed) said: '... while negotiations are in existence either party is entitled to withdraw from those negotiations, at any time and for any reason. There can be thus no obligation to continue to negotiate until there is a 'proper reason' to withdraw. Accordingly, a bare agreement to negotiate has no legal content.'

> [121] ... [The relevant clause, which provided for negotiation in good faith of certain extra costs that might be payable,] is not a bare agreement to negotiate. It is not irrelevant that it is an express obligation which is part of a complex agreement drafted by City of London solicitors ... It would be a strong thing to declare unenforceable a clause into which the parties have deliberately and expressly entered. I have already observed that it is of comparatively narrow scope. To decide that it has 'no legal content' to use Lord Ackner's phrase would be for the law deliberately to defeat the reasonable expectations of honest men ...

(3) Lord Ackner said that a lock-out agreement for a definite period would be enforceable. That dictum was applied by the Court of Appeal in *Pitt v PHH Asset Management Ltd* [1994] 1 WLR 327. Such an agreement merely prohibits the parties from negotiating with anyone else during the agreed period.

10.5 PRE-EMPTION AGREEMENTS, OPTIONS AND UNILATERAL PROMISES

We have seen that in German law the parties may make a binding contract to make a contract. Alternatively, they may make an option contract (*Optionsvertrag*) under which one party has the right, if he chooses to exercise the option, to force the other into a contractual relationship.[60]

Likewise, in English law, even though a promise to negotiate is probably not binding,[61] it is possible to create an option contract (the buyer has to provide consideration or it must be by way of deed). Exercise of the option gives the buyer the right to enforce the contract.[62] Equally, it is possible to give a party a 'right of first refusal' at the same price that has been offered by or to a third person.

---

[60] Markesinis, Unberath and Johnston (n 16 above) 78.
[61] See *Walford v Miles*, 10.21 (EN), above, p 336.
[62] See *Mountford v Scott*, noted above, p 234.

French contract law has developed various sorts of *avant-contrats*: the parties can conclude a unilateral promise (*promesse unilatérale*) or a synallagmatic promise (*promesse synallagmatique*). If the promise is unilateral, this means that it is binding on the seller only, whereas if it is synallagmatic, both parties are bound and, in reality, the sales contract is already formed (as expressed by Article 1589 of the Code civil: '*promesse de vente vaut vente*'). However, synallagmatic promises are useful when the sale requires some formalities to be accomplished (for instance, a notarised act): this means that if the sale is not concluded, this may be due to external events but no longer at the parties' will, since both of them are bound by the promise.

Promises to sell or buy are an important subject in French law but until 2016 there were no provisions in the Code civil. The major issue regarding these *avant-contrats* is whether or not they should lead to the forced formation of contract. Prior to the reform there had been a move towards this solution in French case law as regards *pactes de préférence*, but not as regard unilateral promises. The recent reforms address this issue:

Code civil   **10.22 (FR)**

Sub-section 3[63]

Pre-emption Agreements and Unilateral Promises

Article 1123: A pre-emption agreement is a contract by which a party undertakes that, in the event that he decides to enter into a contract, he will make the first proposal for that contract to the beneficiary of the pre-emption agreement.

Where a contract has been concluded with a third party in breach of a pre-emption agreement, the beneficiary of that agreement may obtain reparation of the loss that he has suffered. Where the third party knew of the existence of the pre-emption agreement and of the beneficiary's intention to take advantage of it, the beneficiary may also sue for nullity or may ask the court to substitute him for the third party in the contract that has been concluded.

The third party may give written notice to the beneficiary requiring him to confirm, within a period which the former fixes and which must be reasonable, the existence of a pre-emption agreement and whether he intends to take advantage of it. Such a written notice must state that if he does not reply within that period, the beneficiary of the pre-emption agreement will no longer have the right to claim either to be substituted in any contract concluded with the third party, or nullity of the contract.

Article 1124: A unilateral promise is a contract by which one party, the promisor, grants another, the beneficiary, a right to have the option to conclude a contract whose essential elements are determined, and for the formation of which only the consent of the beneficiary is missing.

Revocation of the promise during the period allowed to the beneficiary to exercise the option does not prevent the formation of the contract which was promised.

A contract concluded in breach of a unilateral promise with a third party who knew of its existence, is a nullity.

---

[63] Sub-section 3 is placed in Section I on the 'Conclusion of contract', after Sub-section 1 on 'Negotiations' and Sub-section 2 on 'Offer and Acceptance'.

Notes

(1) Before 2016 a number of cases had held, controversially, that a party who had made a unilateral promise to enter a contract (for instance a contract for the sale of goods) but had changed his mind and no longer wanted to conclude the contract could withdraw his promise and pay damages only.[64] These cases were harshly criticised by most French authors because they denied value to the unilateral promise. The reformed Code civil takes an opposite view: such a withdrawal is deprived of any effect and the contract will proceed (Article 1124(2)).

(2) Regarding the violation of a *pacte de préférence*, Article 1223(2) of the reformed Code civil has included to a great extent the solution the Cour de cassation adopted in cases of breach of this *pacte*.[65] According to this provision, the beneficiary can request the annulment of the contract concluded between the promisor and the third party *or* ask to replace the third party in this contract. The latter remedy is somewhat similar to specific performance—as it is the primary remedy in French law—but is still different as the beneficiary will have to pay the price the third party negotiated with the promisor while no such price was agreed upon in the initial *pacte de préférence*. One must note however that beneficiaries are not very likely to obtain this efficient remedy as they need to establish the third party's bad faith (ie, according to case law, his knowledge of the *pacte de préférence* and his knowledge of the beneficiary's intent to rely on this *pacte*).

(3) To prevent cases of contracts concluded in breach of a *pacte de préférence*, Article 1123(3) of the Code civil has created an '*action interrogatoire*'. This action allows the third party to ask a person he thinks to be the beneficiary of a *pacte de préférence* whether he is indeed a beneficiary and whether he intends to rely upon this *pacte*. This relatively new kind of action was also implemented in other areas of contract law: nullity and agency. Authors have casted doubts about the efficiency of the mechanism as third parties—who are little favoured, if one considers the remedies when the *pacte* is violated—may not be willing to use this.

(4) A new question is whether all these provisions can be altered by the parties in their contract. For instance is a clause excluding specific performance in the situation considered by Article 1124(2) of the Code civil valid? While the Code civil does not provide an answer to this question, one might suggest that parties will perfectly be able to exclude specific performance as long as they provide for another remedy—for instance damages, especially contained in a penalty clause.

10.6 CONCLUSION

The intention to enter into a binding undertaking is a necessary precondition to a contract, but it is not always easy to discern. There are situations which are not free from doubt and where the laws reach different solutions, for example *accords de principe* and

---

[64] Cass civ (3) 15 December 1993, no. 91-10199, Bull III no. 174. See Terré et al (n 44 above) nos. 191 ff.
[65] Cass mixte 26 May 2006, nos. 03-19376 and 03-19494, Bull no. 4, D 2006, 1861, annotated by PY Gautier.

contracts to negotiate. There are no provisions on these in the PECL, but equally there is nothing in the PECL to prevent either type of agreement being given effect.

Remember that intention to create legal relations is not enough. There must also be a sufficient agreement, together with any additional requirement which is imposed by the different systems—most importantly, consideration in English law.[66]

FURTHER READING

Christandl, G, 'Intention' in N Jansen and R Zimmermann (eds), *Commentaries on European Contract Laws* (Oxford University Press, 2018) 266–67.

Illmer M, 'Contract (Formation)' in J Basedow, K Hopt and R Zimmermann (eds), *Max Planck Encyclopedia of European Private Law*, vol I (Oxford University Press, 2012) 378–83.

Kötz, H, 'Indicia of seriousness' in J Basedow, K Hopt and R Zimmermann (eds), *Max Planck Encyclopedia of European Private Law*, vol I (Oxford University Press, 2012) 863–65.

Sautonie-Laguionie, L, 'The Creation of a Legal Theory of the Conclusion of the Contract' (2017) 6 Montesquieu Law Review 45.

Whittaker, S, 'Contracts, Contract Law and Contractual Principle', in J Cartwright and S Whittaker (eds), *The Code Napoléon Rewritten: French Contract Law after the 2016 Reforms* (Oxford: Hart Publishing, 2017) 29–55.

---

[66] See below, ch 11.

CHAPTER 11
CAUSE AND CONSIDERATION

11.1. INTRODUCTION

In Chapters 8 and 10 we saw that all the systems require agreement and intention to create legal relations in order to create a contract. Some laws have no additional requirements for contracts in general (though nearly all systems have formal requirements, such as that the contract be in writing, for certain types of contract: see Chapter 12). For instance, there is no other general requirement in German or Dutch law, nor in the international restatements. The Principles of European Contract Law (PECL) state explicitly that there is no other requirement:

Principles of European Contract Law[1] **11.1 (INT)**

Article 2:101: Conditions for the Conclusion of a Contract
   (1) A contract is concluded if:
      (a) the parties intend to be legally bound, and
      (b) they reach a sufficient agreement without any further requirement.
   (2) A contract need not be concluded or evidenced in writing nor is it subject to any other requirement as to form. The contract may be proved by any means including witnesses.

Other systems impose additional requirements for any contract to be enforceable. Thus in English law a contractual obligation must be for good consideration, or must be contained in a deed. In the second part of this chapter we explore these requirements.

In the part on consideration we also discuss the extent to which in the common law a promise that is without consideration may be enforceable for other reasons, particularly when the promisee has acted in reliance on the promise ('reliance').

---

[1] See similarly DCFR Art II-4:101.

Until the 2016 contract law reform, French law required that the contract have a *cause* and this requirement still applies to contracts concluded before 1 October 2016. We explore the idea of *cause* in the third part of this chapter. However, one case in which a contract may not be enforceable in French law is where the *cause* is unlawful. We leave that aspect of *cause* to be considered in detail in Chapter 17, where we deal with contracts that involve illegality or are contrary to public policy.

At the end of the chapter we have a short part on Dutch and German law, to indicate how those laws solve the issues that are dealt with by consideration and *cause*.

11.2. CONSIDERATION (AND RELIANCE)

Consideration, which is a requirement additional to agreement and intention, is unique to the common law; there is no direct equivalent in European continental laws.[2] As is often the case in the common law, it is a product of history. It will not be possible in the confines of this work to dissect the doctrine of consideration in detail.[3]

In some circumstances a promise for which the promisee gave no consideration may nonetheless be binding because the promisee has relied on the promise. This doctrine, which is often known as 'reliance' or 'promissory estoppel', plays only a limited role in English law, in relation to a promise by one party not to enforce its contractual rights. The doctrine is much more highly developed in the laws of the US, where reliance is an alternative to consideration as the basis on which a promise may be enforced. However, English law does recognise that a promise to transfer an interest in property may confer rights on a promisee who has relied on the promise ('proprietary estoppel').

11.2.A CONSIDERATION

The early history of consideration as an essential component of a simple contract binding in law is obscure. It seems to have become a requirement in the sixteenth century for bringing an action of *assumpsit*, which at that time was being developed as the principal action for non-performance of a contract. The action was so-called because the writ by which it was begun (which was written in Latin) would begin, 'Whereas the defendant undertook (*assumpsit*) to ...'. Roughly speaking, consideration consists in the requirement of a counterpart in exchange for a promise. It may have been introduced to prevent any bare promise, however informal, creating a contractual obligation—this link between

---

[2] For a comparative viewpoint, see R, David, 'Cause et Consideration' in *Mélanges offerts à Jacques Maury, vol II: Droit comparé, Théorie générale du droit et Droit privé* (Paris: Dalloz Sirey, 1961) 111; AG Chloros, 'The Doctrine of Consideration and the Reform of the Law of Contract' (1968) 17 ICLQ 137; B Markesinis, 'Cause And Consideration: A Study In Parallel' (1978) 37 CLJ 53; H Kötz, *European Contract Law* (2nd edn, Oxford University Press, 2017) 53–54.

[3] In this connection reference is made to the standard works: *Treitel on the Law of Contract*, 14th edn by E Peel (London: Sweet & Maxwell, 2015) paras 3-001 ff; E McKendrick, *Contract Law* (12th edn, Basingstoke: Palgrave Macmillan, 2017) 66 ff.

form and consideration will be encountered again[4] and is a characteristic of English law. However, the restriction is not on the face of it a formal one; rather, it looks to the reason for the promise. Originally it may have meant something closer to *cause*, that there must be a 'good reason' for making the promise. Thus a promise to settle property on a child who was getting married was treated as binding, the marriage being 'the consideration'.[5] But during the nineteenth century, if not earlier, the doctrine was narrowed to cases where there was some kind of exchange.[6] The contract is upheld when the interests of business so demand, that is to say when there is a 'bargain'[7] but in the absence of a bargain an informal promise (ie one not made by deed)[8] would not be enforceable. This development was not uncontested, but attempts made by Lord Mansfield in the seventeenth century to replace 'consideration' with the 'sovereignty' of the will, or at least to mitigate the effects of consideration, all failed.[9] Similarly, the proposal by the Law Reform Committee in 1937 to abolish the requirement of consideration, or at least its worst effects, also came to grief.[10] Only in the US has this happened, at least in part, in particular in the Restatement 2d on Contracts[11] and, to some extent, in the Uniform Commercial Code concerning sales.

11.2.A.1 DEFINITIONS OF CONSIDERATION

There is no precise or agreed definition of consideration. Each definition, whether by academic writers or by the courts, places the emphasis on particular aspects of the doctrine.

> A valuable consideration, in the sense of the law, may consist either in some right, interest, profit or benefit accruing to one party or some forbearance, detriment, loss or responsibility, given, suffered or undertaken by the other.

(*Currie v Misa* (1875) LR 10 Exch 153, 162)

> Consideration means something which is of some value in the eye of the law, moving from the plaintiff; it may be some detriment to the plaintiff or some benefit to the defendant, but at all events it must be moving from the plaintiff.

(Patteson J in *Thomas v Thomas* (1842) 2 QB 851, 859)

> An act of forbearance of the one party, or the promise thereof, is the price for which the promise of the other is bought, and the promise thus given for value is enforceable.

(F Pollock, *Principles of Contract*,[12] approved by Lord Dunedin in *Dunlop v Selfridge* (1915))[13]

---

[4] See below, p 351.
[5] See AWB Simpson, *A History of the Common Law of Contract* (Oxford University Press, 1975) 418–21.
[6] See PS Atiyah, 'Consideration: a Restatement' in idem, *Essays on Contract* (Oxford: Clarendon Press, 1986) 184–87.
[7] See above, p 100.
[8] See above, p 98.
[9] JH Baker, *Introduction to English Legal History* (4th edn, London: Butterworths, 2003) 352.
[10] For details see *Treitel* (n 3 above) para 3-175.
[11] See above, p 101.
[12] F Pollock, *Principles of Contract* (13th edn, London: Stevens and Sons, 1950) 133.
[13] [1915] AC 847 (HL). See 31.5 (EN) below, p 1262.

Restatement 2d of Contracts, Section 71   **11.2 (US)**

§ 71: Requirement of Exchange; Types of Exchange

(1) To constitute consideration, a performance or a return promise must be bargained for.

(2) A performance or return promise is bargained for if it is sought by the promisor in exchange for his promise and is given by the promisee in exchange for that promise.

(3) The consideration may consist of

(a) an act other than a promise, or

(b) a forbearance, or

(c) the creation, modification or destruction of a legal relation.

Burrows, *A Restatement of the English Law of Contract*[14]   **11.3 (EN)**

8 Consideration

(1) To be legally binding, an agreement, unless made by deed, must be supported by consideration.

(2) 'Consideration' means that, in exchange for a promise by one party, a counter-promise or performance is given by the other party.

(3) The consideration need not be adequate and may be merely nominal.

(4) Past consideration (where A makes a promise to B in return for what B has already done) is not good consideration.

(5) If —

(a) B owes a pre-existing duty to A under the general law or under a contract with C or under a contract with A, and

(b) A makes a promise to B in exchange for B's promise to perform, or performance of, that pre-existing duty,

B's promise to perform, or performance of, that pre-existing duty is good consideration for A's promise although the contract may in certain circumstances be voidable for duress (see section 37) or unenforceable as being contrary to public policy (see section 44).

(6) B's promise to perform a part, or part performance, of a pre-existing duty (for example, part payment of a pre-existing debt) owed by B to A is not good consideration for A's promise to forgo the remaining part of the performance owing (for example, to forgo the balance of the pre-existing debt owed) although the law on promissory estoppel (see section 12) may operate to protect B.

Notes

(1) Even the definition in the Restatement of the American Law Institute is not complete for the purposes of English law, for it does not state that certain promises or acts, even if done in exchange for the promise to be enforced, are not 'sufficient' because they seem to involve no additional detriment to the promisee or benefit to the promisor. The same is true of section 8(2) of Burrows' Restatement. This looks like a definition but it is in effect qualified by a number of exceptions, particularly

---

[14] A Burrows, *A Restatement of the English Law of Contract* (Oxford University Press, 2016).

paras (3), (5) and (6) which also go to the 'sufficiency' of consideration. On this see further below.

(2) Much of the recent English case law on consideration has involved changes ('variations') to an existing contract rather than the formation of a new contract. Originally the courts required an agreement to vary an existing contract to be supported by consideration for a variation just as for a new contract, but (as section 8(5) of Burrows' Restatement indicates) there has been a considerable change in this respect— even since Burrows' Restatement was published. The American Restatement also relaxes the consideration rule in connection with amendments to the contract.

(3) The US definition of consideration in section 71 must be read alongside another provision, section 90. Section 90 creates liability when a promise made without consideration has reasonably been relied on by the promisee. At present this has only a very limited counter-part in English law. We return to each of these issues below.[15]

(4) The central point of both Restatements' definition of consideration continues to be the notion of 'bargain', the notion that there must be a counterweight to a promise. It is consideration, rather than a consensus of intentions, which brings two promises together in a relationship of dependency. The American Restatement indicates that the return promise or counter-performance may be a benefit conferred or some act of forbearance; and the definition requires that it must be 'sought by the promisor in exchange for his promise and ... given by the promisee in exchange for that promise.' This seems to mean that each must consciously have regarded the return promise or consideration as what they wanted from the exchange. Bargain also seems to be central to English law, but there may be a difference in emphasis. We will see that the English courts will sometimes treat the parties as making a bargain which can be enforced as a contract even though it is not clear that the parties were consciously bargaining for each other's performance. This gives the English doctrine a degree of flexibility. It may mean that English courts can find consideration in some cases which in the US would be treated under the 'reliance' doctrine of section 90. We explore this later.

Many of the English definitions emphasise the need for a benefit to the promisor and/or a detriment to the promisee. Evidently in the normal synallagmatic contract, such as a contract for the sale of goods or the supply of services, there will be both. The consideration for the seller or supplier's promise to deliver or supply will be the buyer's promise to pay the price and vice versa.

It may at first seem more difficult to discover consideration in what are known in English law as 'unilateral contracts', that is to say, contracts which come into existence by virtue of the performance of an act.[16] The question was discussed and resolved positively in the judgment in *Carlill v Carbolic Smoke Ball Co*, another aspect of which was discussed earlier.[17]

---

[15] See below pp 365 and 370.
[16] See above, pp 116 ff.
[17] See 8.8 (EN), above, p 217.

Carlill v Carbolic Smoke Ball Co[18]

There will be consideration for a promise if the promisee incurs inconvenience in exchange for it, or if the promisee's action results in a benefit to the promisor.

Facts: The Carbolic Smoke Ball Company had advertised that it would pay £100 to any person who used the Smoke Ball for two weeks and nonetheless caught influenza. Mrs Carlill purchased a Smoke Ball from a third party and used it as directed. She caught flu but the company refused to pay. The court of first instance held the Company liable and the Company appealed.

Held: The Company's promise was for good consideration.

Judgment: BOWEN LJ: A further argument for the defendants was that this was a nudum pactum—that there was no consideration for the promise—that taking the influenza was only a condition, and that the using of the smoke ball was only a condition, and that there was no consideration at all; in fact, that there was no request, express or implied, to use the smoke ball. Now, I will not enter into an elaborate discussion upon the law as to requests in this kind of contracts. I will simply refer to *Victors v Davies* (12 M & W 758) and Sergeant Manning's note to *Fisher v Pyne* (1 M & G 265), which everybody ought to read who wishes to embark in this controversy. The short answer, to abstain from academical discussion, is, it seems to me, that there is here a request to use involved in the offer. Then as to the alleged want of consideration. The definition of 'consideration' given in Selwyn's *Nisi Prius*, 8th edn, p 47, which is cited and adopted by Tindal CJ in the case of *Laythoarp v Bryant* (3 Scott 238, 250), is this: 'Any act of the plaintiff from which the defendant received a benefit or advantage, or any labour, detriment, or inconvenience sustained by the plaintiff, provided such act is performed or such inconvenience suffered by the plaintiff, with the consent, either express or implied, of the defendant'. Can it be said here that if the person who reads this advertisement applies thrice daily, for such time as may seem to him tolerable, the carbolic smoke ball to his nostrils for a whole fortnight, he is doing nothing at all—that it is a mere act which is not to count towards consideration to support a promise (for the law does not require us to measure the adequacy of the consideration). Inconvenience sustained by one party at the request of the other is enough to create a consideration. I think therefore, that it is consideration enough that the plaintiff took the trouble of using the smoke ball. But I think also that the defendants received a benefit from this user, for the use of the smoke ball was contemplated by the defendants as being indirectly a benefit to them, because the use of the smoke ball would promote their sale … if you once make up your mind that there was a promise made to this lady who is the plaintiff, as one of the public—a promise made to her that if she used the smoke ball three times daily for a fortnight and got the influenza, she should have £100, it seems to me that her using the smoke ball was sufficient consideration. I cannot picture to myself the view of the law on which the contrary could be held when you have once found who are the contracting parties. If I say to a person, 'If you use such and such a medicine for a week I will give you £5', and he uses it, there is ample consideration for the promise.

LINDLEY and AL SMITH LJJ delivered concurring judgments. *Appeal dismissed.*

---

[18] [1893] 1 QB 257; see also 8.8 (EN) above, p 217.

Notes

(1) Bowen LJ states that either a detriment to the promisee (using the smoke ball) or a benefit to the promisor (increased sales) will suffice. Usually the same facts will give rise to both. However, there may be cases in which there is a detriment to the promisee with no apparent benefit to the promisor. For example, if A gives a bank a guarantee of the loan that the bank plans to make to C, the detriment to the bank in advancing the money to C is consideration for A's promise even though A seems to get nothing out of the arrangement. (It is much harder to find convincing examples of a benefit to the promisor without a corresponding detriment to the promisee.)[19]

(2) However, Bowen LJ begins by stressing a different but equally important point: the action must have been done in exchange for the promise. The normal way of showing this is to show that the promisor was requesting the promise to act as he did. The request may be express or implicit.[20]

(3) Bowen LJ says that it was argued that catching the flu and using the smoke-ball were 'only conditions'. Clearly the company's promise to pay £100 was not unconditional—Mrs Carlill would have no claim if she never caught the flu. But was use of the smoke ball only a condition, or was it something the company was (at least implicitly) asking her to do? Sometimes a promise is made which is conditional but the promisor is clearly not asking the promisee to fulfil the condition. Byles J once gave a nice example: 'Suppose a defendant promise to a plaintiff, "I will give you £500 if you break your leg." Would that detriment to the plaintiff, should it happen, be any consideration? ... I conceive the promise would not be binding, for want of a previous request by the [promisor].'[21]

(4) It may be wondered whether there is not a certain artificiality in the discovery of consideration in the *Carlill* case. It is widely accepted that sometimes the courts 'discover' consideration that may not have been the parties' conscious reason for the contract.[22] This landmark case is also controversial on other points.[23] However, the case does fit the classical English doctrine: in a unilateral contract, there is consideration for the promise if, in exchange for it, the claimant has incurred a detriment or has done something which benefits the promisor.

Thus in a 'bilateral' (synallagmatic) contract the consideration for each party's promise is the other's promise; in an English-style unilateral contract, it is the act done in exchange.[24]

---

[19] See H Beale, W Bishop and M Furmston, *Contract: Cases and Materials* (5th edn, Oxford University Press, 2008) 99.

[20] See *Shadwell v Shadwell* (1860) CB(NS) 159 (Common Bench); and *Combe v Combe* [1951] 2 KB 215 (CA).

[21] *Shadwell v Shadwell* (1860) 9 CBNS 159 (Common Bench). In that case the question was whether an uncle who promised to pay money to his nephew if the nephew married and went to the Bar was requesting the nephew to do those things. The majority held that it was; Byles J dissented.

[22] See further below, p 350.

[23] See pp 217 and 257. For a fascinating account of the background to the case, see AWB Simpson, 'Quackery and Contract Law: The Case of the Carbolic Smoke Ball' (1985) 14 Journal of Legal Studies 345.

[24] The notion of consideration has a different meaning in the law of restitution (or unjust enrichment) on the ground of 'failure of consideration'. This means not that there was no consideration and thus no contract,

Not any act, nor a promise to do any act, will suffice, however. The act or promised act must, at least according to traditional analysis, be something of economic benefit to the promisor, or at least of economic detriment to the promisee. Thus, the fact that as a result of the agreement the promisee might feel some sense of moral or even commercial obligation to the promisor ('I owe you one …') will not suffice to provide consideration for an otherwise gratuitous agreement.[25] ('Moral consideration is no consideration.') This is presumably why it is often said that consideration must have some economic value[26] but, as Burrows states, 'a counter-promise or counter-performance of no clear economic value counts'.[27]

Similarly, the traditional analysis is that there will be no consideration if what the promisee is doing in exchange is simply to perform something he is already under an obligation to do under the general law. Thus it was held that a promise to pay a person to come to court as a witness was held to be made without consideration since the witness, once 'subpoenaed' (ie ordered to appear), was obliged to attend.[28] Likewise, the traditional analysis was that there will be no consideration if the promisee is merely doing something he is already obliged to do under an existing contract with the promisor. So traditionally a promise by one party to an existing contract to pay the other an extra amount if the other will actually get on and perform the contract was not binding for want of consideration, even if the promisor made the new arrangement thinking it would be beneficial to himself. The same problem arises with promises to release a party from an existing contractual obligation. We will see below that this rule has proved commercially inconvenient and in recent years it has been modified to such an extent that it may be doubted whether consideration is really required in these cases.[29]

The discussion shows that 'consideration' is an essentially objective concept; it does not include psychological motivations such as a desire to help another person, as did the doctrine of *cause* under French law.[30] On the other hand, the objective nature of the enquiry makes it possible for the court to 'find' consideration quite readily. This is particularly so in English law, where the courts may point to the fact that the parties have in fact made an exchange of some kind and hold that they have therefore made an agreement supported by consideration, even if the parties were perhaps not conscious of so doing—for example, in *de la Bere v Pearson*.[31] In that case, a newspaper offered financial advice to readers who wrote in asking for it. The advice given to the plaintiff was negligent and he lost money. It was held that the newspaper had a contractual duty (ie had promised) to use care, the consideration being that the defendants had the right to

---

but that one party has not received what he bargained for. When there has been a total failure of consideration in this sense, an action in restitution lies to recover money paid. See *Fibrosa Spolka Akcyjna v Fairbairn Lawson Comber Barbour Ltd* [1943] AC 32 (HL). See also McKendrick (n 3 above) 287. This idea of failure of consideration is close to *enrichement sans cause* in French law and *Bereicherung ohne Rechtsgrund* in German law (see below, p 392).

[25] See, eg, *The Atlantic Baron*, 15.6 (EN) below, p 602.

[26] eg, *Treitel* (n 3 above) para 3-027.

[27] Burrows (n 14 above) 65.

[28] *Collins v Godefroy* (1831) 1 B & Ald 950. However, the courts readily find that the promise has done more than the law required.

[29] See below, pp 356 ff.

[30] See below, pp 374–75.

[31] [1908] 1 KB 280 (CA).

publish the reader's letter to the newspaper. It is difficult to imagine that the parties had this exchange in mind as the purpose of the contract. The US Restatement, section 71, is more subjective, as it requires that each party sought for the other's counter-promise or performance; however, as we will see in more detail below, section 71 is supplemented by section 90, which would cover cases such as *de la Bere v Pearson*.

It is important to note that consideration applies only to simple contracts, that is to say, contracts that are oral or in an informal writing. Consideration is not necessary in the case of contracts made by deed. In other words, the form replaces the requirement of consideration. But the requirement of consideration means that English contract law disregards gratuitous promises which are not in the form of a deed, since by definition they are unsupported by consideration.[32]

It is also possible to argue that consideration itself is little more than a formal requirement because there is no requirement that the consideration—for example, money which is to be paid or property which is to be delivered in exchange for the promise—need be equivalent in value to the promise. As it is traditionally put, there must be consideration but it need not be adequate.[33] A standard way of making a gratuitous contract of lease is to agree that it will be at 'peppercorn rent'. In theory there is an obligation on the lessee to deliver one peppercorn—an item which has some but clearly minimal economic value—to the lessor each year. It seems obvious that the 'peppercorn rent' is being used as an alternative to a deed, in order to make a binding contract out of an agreement that is in reality gratuitous and thus would otherwise lack consideration. However, it is probably not correct to say that consideration is 'just' a requirement of form. The core of the doctrine seems to be the notion that only bargains should count as contracts. Cases in which the bargain and the consideration are only 'nominal' seem rather to be a by-product of the rule that the court will not (in the absence of other factors such as unconscionable conduct by one party)[34] investigate whether the performances to be exchanged were of equal value ('whether the consideration was adequate').

11.2.A.2 CONSEQUENCES OF THE DOCTRINE OF CONSIDERATION

It is clearly impossible here to provide an in-depth analysis of all the extremely complex aspects of the concept of consideration. Suffice it here to refer to major textbooks. We will confine our remarks to the main consequences and to those which are of most interest from a comparative point of view.

11.2.A.2.1 'Irrevocable' Offers

First of all, in English law an offer may be freely revoked, even if it is a firm offer expressed to be open for a specified period, because the undertaking not to revoke the offer within the period was unsupported by consideration.[35] This solution has been criticised and US law has disavowed it to an extent in the Uniform Commercial Code.

---

[32] See above, p 100.
[33] And see Burrows' Restatement (n 14 above) s 8(3), 11.3 (EN), above, p 346.
[34] See below, p 651.
[35] See *Dickinson v Dodds*, 8.20 (EN) above, p 233.

§2-205: Firm Offers

An offer by a merchant to buy or sell goods in a signed writing which by its terms gives assurance that it will be held open is not revocable for lack of consideration, during the time stated or if no time is stated for a reasonable time, but in no event may such period of irrevocability exceed three months; but any such term of assurance on a form supplied by the offeree must be separately signed by the offeror.

Note

The requirement that there be consideration is attenuated by § 2-205 only to a limited degree. The offer must be by a 'merchant', the offer must be contained in a signed document and there is a preclusive time-limit of three months.

To create a binding offer in English law, it would be necessary either for the offeror to make the promise to keep the offer open by deed or for the offeree to pay for the offer to be kept open—since the doctrine of consideration does not require that the exchange be of things of equivalent value, a nominal sum such as £1 would suffice. The agreement so created is often referred to as an 'option'.[36]

11.2.A.2.2 'Past Consideration'

An act which the promisee had already performed cannot, in the traditional view, amount to consideration because the act cannot have been done in exchange for the promise. A US case, *Harrington v Taylor*,[37] provides a graphic example. The defendant had assaulted his wife, who took refuge in the plaintiff's house. The next day, the defendant gained access to the house and began another assault on his wife. The wife knocked down the defendant with an axe and was on the point of cutting his head open or decapitating him while he lay on the floor when the plaintiff intervened, catching the axe as it descended. The defendant's life was saved but the plaintiff's hand was badly mutilated. The defendant subsequently promised to pay the plaintiff her loss, but after paying a small sum failed to pay any more. The Supreme Court of North Carolina held that the promise was without consideration. This is in line with old English authority.[38]

Most of the discussion of 'past consideration' in recent cases has focused on an apparent exception: the case where the promise is made in respect of something that has already been done (eg to pay for a service already performed) when it was always understood that what was done was in some way to be 'paid for', though what was to be done in exchange (eg the price to be paid for the service) had not been agreed.

---

[36] Compare Art 1124 of the French Code civil (*promesse de vente*).

[37] 225 NC 690, 36 SE 2d 227 (1945).

[38] *Eastwood v Kenyon* (1840) 11 Ad & El 438, 113 ER 482; see also *Re McArdle* [1951] Ch 669 (CA). In the US, the courts have sometimes departed from this rule in deserving 'rescue' cases, eg *Webb v McGowin*, 27 Ala App 82, 168 So 196 (1935). See also the *donation rémunératoire* in French Law.

Privy Council (on appeal from Hong Kong)   11.6 (EN)

Pao On v Lau Yiu Long[39]

The fact that the alleged consideration was an act which took place before the promise to pay for it was made does not render the promise without consideration if it was always understood that the act was to be paid for.

Facts: Pao assigned his shares in SO to SO, of which the Laus were the principal shareholders, in exchange for FC shares. There was a risk that if Pao resold substantial numbers of FC shares quickly, the price of the shares would fall, so Pao undertook not to resell the FC shares until at least 12 months after acquiring them. But to safeguard himself against the shares falling in value for other reasons during the 12 months, in an ancillary agreement Pao secured an agreement that 60% of his shares would be bought back by the Laus before the end of the year at $2.50 per share. Pao then realised that this arrangement would mean that if the value of the shares *rose* during the 12 months, he would not get the benefit. So Pao refused to perform the main agreement unless the Laus agreed to cancel the buy-back arrangement and replace it with an indemnity providing for compensation if the 60% of shares retained fell below the value of $2.50 each. A new agreement was made on 4 May 1973; it stated that the indemnity by the Laus was 'in consideration of your having at our request agreed to sell all your shares' in SO. At the end of the 12 months the shares were worth less than $2.50 but the Laus refused to pay.

Held: At first instance Pao was unsuccessful, but the judgment was reversed on appeal. On appeal to the Privy Council the judgment at first instance was reinstated. The Privy Council found that the agreement was not contrary to public policy, was not signed under duress[40] and above all was supported by consideration.

Judgment: The opinion of the Privy Council was delivered by LORD SCARMAN:

... The first question is whether upon its true construction the written guarantee of May 4, 1973, states a consideration sufficient in law to support the defendants' promise of indemnity against a fall in value of the Fu Chip shares.

Mr Neill, counsel for the plaintiffs before their Lordships' Board but not below, contends that the consideration stated in the agreement is not in reality a past one. It is to be noted that the consideration was not on May 4, 1973, a matter of history only. The instrument by its reference to the main agreement with Fu Chip incorporates as part of the stated consideration the plaintiffs' three promises to Fu Chip: to complete the sale of Shing On, to accept shares as the price for the sale, and not to sell 60 per cent. of the shares so accepted before April 30, 1974. Thus, on May 4, 1973, the performance of the main agreement still lay in the future. Performance of these promises was of great importance to the defendants, and it is undeniable that, as the instrument declares, the promises were made to Fu Chip at the request of the defendants. It is equally clear that the instrument also includes a promise by the plaintiffs to the defendants to fulfil their earlier promises given to Fu Chip.

The Board agrees with Mr Neill's submission that the consideration expressly stated in the written guarantee is sufficient in law to support the defendants' promise of indemnity. An act done before the giving of a promise to make a payment or to confer some other benefit can sometimes be consideration for the promise. The act must have been done at the promisors' request: the parties must have understood that the act was to be remunerated either by a payment or the conferment of some other benefit: and payment, or the conferment of a benefit, must have been legally enforceable had it been promised in advance. All three features are present in this case. The promise given to Fu Chip under

[39] [1980] AC 614.
[40] On the duress point, see below, p 619.

the main agreement not to sell the shares for a year was at the first defendant's request. The parties understood at the time of the main agreement that the restriction on selling must be compensated for by the benefit of a guarantee against a drop in price: and such a guarantee would be legally enforceable. The agreed cancellation of the subsidiary agreement left, as the parties knew, the plaintiffs unprotected in a respect in which at the time of the main agreement all were agreed they should be protected.

Mr Neill's submission is based on *Lampleigh v Brathwait* (1615) Hobart 105. In that case the judges said, at p 106:

> 'First … a mere voluntary courtesie will not have a consideration to uphold an assumpsit. But if that courtesie were moved by a suit or request of the party that gives the assumpsit, it will bind, for the promise, though it follows, yet it is not naked, but couples itself with the suit before, and the merits of the party procured by that suit. which is the difference.'

The modern statement of the law is in the judgment of Bowen LJ in *In re Casey's Patents* [1892] 1 Ch 104, 115–116; Bowen LJ said:

> 'Even if it were true, as some scientific students of law believe, that a past service cannot support a future promise, you must look at the document and see if the promise cannot receive a proper effect in some other way. Now, the fact of a past service raises an implication that at the time it was rendered it was to be paid for, and, if it was a service which was to be paid for, when you get in the subsequent document a promise to pay, that promise may be treated either as an admission which evidences or as a positive bargain which fixes the amount of that reasonable remuneration on the faith of which the service was originally rendered. So that here for past services there is ample justification for the promise to give the third share.'

Conferring a benefit is, of course, an equivalent to payment: see *Chitty on Contracts*, 24th edn (1977), vol 1, para 154.

Mr. Leggatt, for the defendants, does not dispute the existence of the rule but challenges its application to the facts of this case. He submits that it is not a necessary inference or implication from the terms of the written guarantee that any benefit or protection was to be given to the plaintiffs for their acceptance of the restriction on selling their shares. Their Lordships agree that the mere existence or recital of a prior request is not sufficient in itself to convert what is prima facie past consideration into sufficient consideration in law to support a promise: as they have indicated, it is only the first of three necessary preconditions. As for the second of those preconditions, whether the act done at the request of the promisor raises an implication of promised remuneration or other return is simply one of the construction of the words of the contract in the circumstances of its making. Once it is recognised, as the Board considers it inevitably must be, that the expressed consideration includes a reference to the plaintiffs' promise not to sell the shares before April 30, 1974—a promise to be performed in the future, though given in the past—it is not possible to treat the defendants' promise of indemnity as independent of the plaintiffs' antecedent promise, given at the first defendant's request, not to sell. The promise of indemnity was given because at the time of the main agreement the parties intended that the first defendant should confer upon the plaintiffs the benefit of his protection against a fall in price. When the subsidiary agreement was cancelled, all were well aware that the plaintiffs were still to have the benefit of his protection as consideration for the restriction on selling. It matters not whether the indemnity thus given be regarded as the best evidence of the benefit intended to be conferred in return for the promise not to sell, or as the positive bargain which fixes the benefit on the faith of which the promise was given—though where, as here, the subject is a written contract, the better analysis is probably that of the 'positive bargain.' Their Lordships, therefore, accept the submission that the contract itself states a valid consideration for the promise of indemnity.

This being their Lordships' conclusion, it is unnecessary to consider Mr. Neill's further submission (also raised for the first time before the Board) that the option given the defendants, if called upon to fulfil their indemnity, to buy back the shares at $2.50 a share was itself a sufficient consideration for the promise of indemnity. But their Lordships see great force in the contention. The defendants promised to indemnify he plaintiffs if the market price of Fu Chip shares fell below $2.50. However, in the event of the defendants being called on to implement this promise they were given an option to take up the shares themselves at $2.50. This on the face of it imposes on the plaintiffs in the circumstances envisaged an obligation to transfer the shares to the defendants at the price of $2.50 if called on to do so. The concomitant benefit to the defendants could be a real one—for example, if they thought that the market, after a temporary set-back, would recover to a price above $2.50. The fact that the option is stated in the form of a proviso does not preclude it being a contractual term or one under which consideration moves.

[His Lordship went on to hold that there was good consideration for the promise of indemnity despite the fact that the primary consideration was the promise given by the plaintiff to the Laus to perform their contract with FC: a promise to perform, or the performance of, a pre-existing contractual obligation to a third party can be a valid consideration.]

> *Note*
>
> The efforts made by the Privy Council to circumvent the 'past consideration' rule should be noted.

The three conditions of 'implied assumpsit' are not in fact always easy to satisfy. It is certainly the case that the requirement that there be consideration (whether a return promise yet to be performed—'executory' consideration—or an act which has been performed—'executed' consideration) may cause arrangements which are otherwise perfectly reasonable to founder. In addition to the implied assumpsit exception (if it is really an exception) the courts have developed a number of other exceptions to the doctrine of consideration which need not be explained here.[41]

11.2.A.2.3 Privity of Contract

There is a third consequence, which stems from another traditional rule: 'the consideration must move from the promisee'. Until the reforms introduced by the Contracts (Rights of Third Parties) Act 1999, this rule prevented a third person (a 'third party beneficiary') being given rights under a contract to which he or she was not party. This will be discussed in more detail in Chapter 31 below; the rule still applies when a case is not covered by this or other legislation. For the purposes of the present chapter, it is sufficient to refer to the judgment in *Dunlop Pneumatic Tyre Co Ltd v Selfridge & Co Ltd*.[42]

---

[41] See *Treitel* (n 3 above) paras 3-153 ff.
[42] [1915] AC 847 (HL), 31.5 (EN), below, p 1262.

This shows that the prohibition of such agreements arose out of the combination of two rules: the rule that the consideration must come from the promisee and the rule that only the parties to a contract may sue on it, and the result is the same in both cases.[43]

11.2.A.2.4 Agreements to Modify a Contractual Obligation

We mentioned earlier that a party who is merely performing, or promising to perform, its existing contractual duty was not, on the traditional analysis, providing consideration.[44] In other words, the traditional doctrine of consideration precludes the gratuitous amendment of a contract or the waiving of a debt.

(a) The traditional approach

King's Bench   **11.7 (EN)**

Stilk v Myrick[45]

A promise to pay an additional sum if the other party will perform his existing contractual duty is not binding for want of consideration.

Facts: The sailors on a ship had undertaken to the Master (the captain of the ship) to sail the ship from London to Cronstadt, a port in the Baltic, and back. At Cronstadt two sailors deserted the ship and the Master promised to divide their wages among the rest of the crew if the ship was sailed back to London. When the ship returned to London the Master failed to pay the plaintiff's wages or the additional amount promised.

There are two reports of this case.

The Espinasse report

This was an action brought by the plaintiff, a private sailor, to recover the amount of his wages, on a voyage from London to the Baltick and back.

The sum claimed was partly for monthly wages, according to articles which he had signed, and a further sum claimed under these circumstances.

Two sailors, part of the crew, had deserted the ship, and the master (the defendant), not being able to supply their places at Cronstadt, promised to divide among the crew, in addition to their wages, the wages due to the two men who had deserted.

Upon this being claimed, it was objected, That any engagement by the master for a larger sum than was stipulated for by the articles was void, and the case of *Harris v Watson*, … cited.

It was answered, That this case was very different from the case cited: that this engagement was made before the ship sailed on her voyage home; it was made under no coercion, from the apprehension of danger, nor extorted from the captain; but a voluntary offer on his part for extraordinary service.

Judgment: Lord Ellenborough ruled, That the plaintiff could not recover this part of his demand. His Lordship said, That he recognized the principle of the case of *Harris v Watson* as founded on just and proper policy. When the defendant entered on board the ship, he stipulated to do all the work his situation called upon him to do. Here the voyage was to the Baltick and back, not to Cronstadt only; if the voyage had then terminated, the sailors might have made what terms they pleased. If any part of the crew had died, would not the remainder have been forced to work the ship home? If that accident would

---

[43] See McKendrick (n 3 above) 125–27.
[44] Above, p 350.
[45] (1809) 2 Camp 317, 170 ER 1168; 6 Esp 129, 170 ER 851.

have left them liable to do the whole work without any extraordinary remuneration, why should not desertion or casualty equally demand it?

Campbell's report

LORD ELLENBOROUGH: I think *Harris v Watson* was rightly decided; but I doubt whether the ground of public policy, upon which Lord Kenyon is stated to have proceeded, be the true principle on which the decision is to be supported. Here, I say, the agreement is void for want of consideration. There was no consideration for the ulterior pay promised to the mariners who remained with the ship. Before they sailed from London they had undertaken to do all that they could under all the emergencies of the voyage. They had sold all their services till the voyage should be completed. If they had been at liberty to quit the vessel at Cronstadt, the case would have been quite different; or if the captain had capriciously discharged the two men who were wanting, the others might not have been compellable to take the whole duty upon themselves, and their agreeing to do so might have been a sufficient consideration for the promise of an advance of wages. But the desertion of a part of the crew is to be considered an emergency of the voyage as much as their death; and those who remain are bound by the terms of their original contract to exert themselves to the utmost to bring the ship in safety to her destined port. Therefore, without looking to the policy of this agreement, I think it is void for want of consideration, and that the plaintiff can only recover at the rate of £5 a month.

Verdict accordingly.

Note

The explanation of the case given by Campbell's report is now the one generally accepted.[46]

Thus the traditional position in English law is that if one party promises the other an additional payment, if the other completes its performance of the contract, the promise is not binding. If, on the other hand, the other party promises to do something additional (to perform some extra work, for example) or to perform when it was not bound to do so, there will be consideration. So in *Hartley v Ponsonby*[47] it was held that a ship master's promise to pay the crew an additional sum to sail the ship home was binding because so many of the crew had deserted the ship that the remaining crew would have been justified in refusing to sail it home.

A parallel rule was applied in cases in which the promise was not to pay the other party extra, but to release the other party from part of its obligation if it would perform the balance. Thus in *Foakes v Beer*[48] Dr Foakes owed money to Mrs Beer, who obtained a judgment against him. She agreed that he could pay by instalments. When he had paid the agreed instalments, she claimed interest from the date of the judgment. He claimed that she had promised not to claim interest. The House of Lords held that even if she had made such a promise (on which their Lordships were divided), her promise was not binding. The House of Lords confirmed longstanding authority (going back at least to

---

[46] See G Gilmore, *The Death of Contract* (Columbus, OH: Ohio State University Press, 1974) 22–28.
[47] (1857) 7 El & Bl 872.
[48] (1883–84) LR 9 App Cas 605 (HL).

Lord Coke in the seventeenth century) that if a creditor promised to release a debtor from part of a debt if the debtor would pay the rest, the creditor's promise was not binding. If, on the other hand, the debtor agreed to pay the sum before it was due under the existing contract, or instead to provide the creditor with a promissory note, or with goods worth the same amount, there would be consideration, as the debtor would be doing something he or she was not previously bound to do.

Lord Blackburn noted that this made the rule look artificial, and that the basic rule was not in accordance with business practice. He said:

> What principally weighs with me in thinking that Lord Coke made a mistake of fact is my conviction that all men of business, whether merchants or tradesmen, do every day recognise and act on the ground that prompt payment of a part of their demand may be more beneficial to them than it would be to insist on their rights and enforce payment of the whole. Even where the debtor is perfectly solvent, and sure to pay at last, this often is so. Where the credit of the debtor is doubtful it must be more so. I had persuaded myself that there was no such long-continued action on this dictum as to render it improper in this House to reconsider the question. I had written my reasons for so thinking; but as they were not satisfactory to the other noble and learned Lords who heard the case, I do not now repeat them nor persist in them.

> I assent to the judgment proposed, though it is not that which I had originally thought proper.[49]

The inconvenience caused by these applications of the doctrine of consideration to subsequent amendments to contracts has led the courts to seek ways to avoid or subvert it.

The story at this point becomes complex, because until very recently the courts have treated the case of a promise to be satisfied with part payment (as in *Foakes v Beer*) differently from the case of additional payments (as in *Stilk v Myrick*). The new approach to part payment did not involve changing the law on consideration but avoiding its effect by means of a separate doctrine now known as 'promissory estoppel'. This will be described in the next section. For reasons which will appear, it could not be used to deal with the 'additional payment' cases. But some years later, an additional payment case was considered by the Court of Appeal, which adopted a very different interpretation of consideration to that in *Stilk v Myrick*.

(b) A new approach: 'practical benefit'

Court of Appeal

11.8 (EN)

Williams v Roffey Bros & Nicholls (Contractors) Ltd[50]

A promise to pay the other party an additional sum if it performs its existing contractual duty is made for consideration if it was not the result of extortion (duress) by the other party and it produces a practical benefit for the promisor.

Facts: The defendants were building contractors who had agreed to refurbish 27 flats for a housing association under a contract that contained a 'penalty clause' for late completion (ie a clause stating that the defendants

---

[49] (1883–84) LR 9 App Cas 605, 622–23 (HL).
[50] [1991] 1 QB 1.

would pay so much for every week that they were late).[51] The defendants employed the plaintiff, a carpenter, as a subcontractor to do the necessary carpentry for £20,000. There was nothing in the contract about how the plaintiff was to be paid, but in fact he was paid as the work progressed. By April 1986, he had been paid some £16,000 and he had done some work on all the flats, but he had completed only nine of them and he was in financial difficulties. These were caused partly by his failure to supervise his workmen properly but largely because, as the defendants agreed, the original price for the work was too low. The defendants therefore promised to pay him an extra amount of £10,300, to be paid at the rate of £575 per completed flat. The plaintiff completed work on eight further flats but the defendants paid only £1,500 more and the plaintiff stopped work and brought this action for payment. The Recorder awarded him £3,500 (8 × £575 plus a proportion of the original £20,000 less the £1,500 paid and various deductions for defects). The defendants appealed.

Held: The promise to pay the extra amount for each flat completed was binding.

Judgment: GLIDEWELL LJ

... The judge quoted and accepted the evidence of [the defendants' surveyor] to the effect that a main contractor who agrees too low a price with a subcontractor is acting contrary to his own interests. He will never get the job finished without paying more money. The judge therefore concluded:

> 'In my view where the original subcontract price is too low, and the parties subsequently agree that additional moneys shall be paid to the subcontractor, this agreement is in the interests of both parties. This is what happened in the present case, and in my opinion the agreement of 9 April 1986 does not fail for lack of consideration.'

In his address to us, [counsel for the defendants] outlined the benefits to his clients, the defendants, which arose from their agreement to pay the additional £10,300 as: (i) seeking to ensure that the plaintiff continued work and did not stop in breach of the subcontract; (ii) avoiding the penalty for delay; and (iii) avoiding the trouble and expense of engaging other people to complete the carpentry work.

However, [counsel] submits that, though his clients may have derived, or hoped to derive, practical benefits from their agreement to pay the "bonus," they derived no benefit in law, since the plaintiff was promising to do no more than he was already bound to do by his subcontract, ie, continue with the carpentry work and complete it on time. Thus there was no consideration for the agreement. [Counsel] relies on the principle of law which, traditionally, is based on the decision in *Stilk v Myrick* (1809) 2 Camp 317. ...

There is, however, another legal concept of relatively recent development which is relevant, namely, that of economic duress. Clearly if a subcontractor has agreed to undertake work at a fixed price, and before he has completed the work declines to continue with it unless the contractor agrees to pay an increased price, the subcontractor may be held guilty of securing the contractor's promise by taking unfair advantage of the difficulties he will cause if he does not complete the work. In such a case an agreement to pay an increased price may well be voidable because it was entered into under duress. Thus this concept may provide another answer in law to the question of policy which has troubled the courts since before *Stilk v Myrick*, 2 Camp 317, and no doubt led at the date of that decision to a rigid adherence to the doctrine of consideration.

This possible application of the concept of economic duress was referred to by Lord Scarman, delivering the judgment of the Judicial Committee of the Privy Council in *Pao On v Lau Yiu Long* [1980] AC 614 ... It is true that Pao On is a case of a tripartite

---

[51] The phrase seems to be used in a non-technical sense of agreed damages for delay. We will see later that English law allows what it calls 'liquidated damages' but it will not enforce a 'penalty' clause which attempts to impose on the party in breach a penalty beyond the loss that is likely to occur: below, p 1120.

relationship that is, a promise by A to perform a pre-existing contractual obligation owed to B, in return for a promise of payment by C. But Lord Scarman's words, at pp 634–635, seem to me to be of general application, equally applicable to a promise made by one of the original two parties to a contract.

... [The] present state of the law on this subject can be expressed in the following proposition: (i) if A has entered into a contract with B to do work for, or to supply goods or services to, B in return for payment by B; and (ii) at some stage before A has completely performed his obligations under the contract B has reason to doubt whether A will, or will be able to, complete his side of the bargain; and (iii) B thereupon promises A an additional payment in return for A's promise to perform his contractual obligations on time; and (iv) as a result of giving his promise, B obtains in practice a benefit, or obviates a disbenefit; and (v) B's promise is not given as a result of economic duress or fraud on the part of A; then (vi) the benefit to B is capable of being consideration for B's promise, so that the promise will be legally binding.

As I have said, [counsel for the defendants] accepts that in the present case by promising to pay the extra £10,300 his client secured benefits. There is no finding, and no suggestion, that in this case the promise was given as a result of fraud or duress. If it be objected that the propositions above contravene the principle in *Stilk v Myrick*, 2 Camp 317, I answer that in my view they do not; they refine, and limit the application of that principle, but they leave the principle unscathed eg where B secures no benefit by his promise. It is not in my view surprising that a principle enunciated in relation to the rigours of seafaring life during the Napoleonic wars should be subjected during the succeeding 180 years to a process of refinement and limitation in its application in the present day ... It is therefore my opinion that on his findings of fact in the present case, the judge was entitled to hold, as he did, that the defendants' promise to pay the extra £10,300 was supported by valuable consideration, and thus constituted an enforceable agreement.

...

For these reasons I would dismiss this appeal.

RUSSELL LJ ...

I find [the] argument relating to consideration much more difficult ... whilst consideration remains a fundamental requirement before a contract not under seal can be enforced, the policy of the law in its search to do justice between the parties has developed considerably since the early 19th century when *Stilk v Myrick*, 2 Camp 317 was decided by Lord Ellenborough CJ. In the late 20th century I do not believe that the rigid approach to the concept of consideration to be found in *Stilk v Myrick* is either necessary or desirable. Consideration there must still be but, in my judgment, the courts nowadays should be more ready to find its existence so as to reflect the intention of the parties to the contract where the bargaining powers are not unequal and where the finding of consideration reflect the true intention of the parties.

...

For my part I wish to make it plain that I do not base my judgment upon any reservation as to the correctness of the law long ago enunciated in *Stilk v Myrick*. A gratuitous promise, pure and simple, remains unenforceable unless given under seal. But where, as in this case, a party undertakes to make a payment because by so doing it will gain an advantage arising out of the continuing relationship with the promisee the new bargain will not fail for want of consideration. As I read the judgment of the assistant recorder this was his true ratio upon that part of the case wherein the absence of consideration was raised in argument. For the reasons that I have endeavoured to outline, I think that the assistant recorder came to a correct conclusion and I too would dismiss this appeal.

[PURCHAS LJ also gave a judgment dismissing the appeal]

Appeal dismissed.

Note

This decision seems to 'sidestep' the rule in *Stilk v Myrick* by holding that there will be consideration if the promisor will get a practical benefit from the promisee's actual performance of its original contractual obligation. The reasoning seems to ignore the facts that the promisee is incurring no detriment by performing what he was already obliged to do, and that the promisor should have received those benefits anyway. So the logic of the decision is questionable.[52] However there is little doubt that it makes good sense in commercial terms.

Until very recently it was unclear whether *Foakes v Beer* would be 'reinterpreted' in the same way that *Stilk v Myrick* was reinterpreted in the *Williams v Roffey Bros* case. In *Re Selectmove Ltd*[53] the Inland Revenue was petitioning to wind up Selectmove on the basis of non-payment of taxes, although Selectmove was meeting the payments due under an agreement reached with a tax official that it could pay by instalments. The Court of Appeal said that it was bound by *Foakes v Beer* and could not apply *Williams v Roffey Bros* to a promise to release part of a debt. Instead, as we noted earlier, in the *Foakes v Beer* situation the courts seem to have changed the law by another route—not by finding consideration, as did the Court in *Williams v Roffey Bros*, but by the separate doctrine known as 'promissory estoppel'. This will be discussed in the next section.

In 2016, however, the Court of Appeal decided that the approach in *Williams v Roffey Bros* could also apply to promises to accept part payment of a debt, or payment of it by instalments, if that would bring practical benefits to the promisor. When the case went on appeal to the Supreme Court, the appeal was allowed on a different ground; but (obiter) the Court doubted whether not only the Court of Appeal's decision but also *Williams v Roffey* can stand with *Foakes v Beer*. At the same time, however, it suggested that the traditional rule may need to be reconsidered:

Court of Appeal[54] *and Supreme Court*[55]   **11.9 (EN)**

MWB Business Exchange Ltd v Rock Advertising Ltd

A promise to accept payment of an overdue debt in instalments may be binding on the promisor if it will produce practical benefits to the promisor, even though the promisee is merely performing part of its original contractual obligation.

Facts: Office premises managed by the claimants (MWB) were occupied by the defendants (Rock) under a licence agreement between themselves and the claimants. The agreement contained a clause requiring any

---

[52] The correctness of the reasoning in *Williams v Roffey Bros* was doubted by Colman J in *South Carribean Trading Co Ltd v Trafigura Beheer* [2004] EWHC 2676 (Comm), [2005] 1 Lloyd's Rep 128 [107]–[109].

[53] [1995] 1 WLR 474 (CA), annotated by E Peel (1994) 110 LQR 353.

[54] [2016] EWCA Civ 553, [2017] QB 604.

[55] [2018] UKSC 24, [2018] 2 WLR 1603.

variation to the contract terms to be in writing. The defendants fell into arrears and the parties agreed orally to vary their original licence agreement by 're-scheduling' the payments, so as in effect to give the defendants extra time to pay. The defendants made the first of the re-scheduled payments (of £3,500) on the same day, but shortly afterwards the claimants exercised their right under the original contract to lock the defendants out of the premises. The claimants then gave notice terminating the (original) agreement, and sued for arrears of licence fees and damages. The defendant counter-claimed for damages for wrongful exclusion from the premises. The trial judge allowed the claim, holding that the agreement to vary the original agreement was not binding and dismissed the counter-claim. Rock appealed.

Held: The Court of Appeal held that the clause did not make the oral variation ineffective, as their agreement had the effect of varying that clause as well as the terms of payment (this aspect of the judgments is omitted); and that the promise to allow the tenants extra time to pay was made for good consideration, so they had been excluded wrongfully.

Judgment: KITCHIN LJ: ...

46 Founding himself on these authorities [*Foakes v Beer* and *In re Selectmove*], Mr Darton [counsel for the claimants] submitted that it is clear that the judge was wrong to find that Rock's payment of the £3,500 and its agreement to comply with the other terms of the revised payment schedule amounted to good consideration. The benefits conferred on MWB were, said Mr Darton, just the kind of practical benefits which Lord Blackburn in *Foakes v Beer* and this court in *In re Selectmove* recognised might flow from an agreement for the payment of a debt by instalments to accommodate the debtor, yet in both cases they were held not to amount to good consideration. Further, he continued, if the rule in *Williams v Roffey* is to be extended to the circumstances governed by *Foakes v Beer*, it must be by (what is now) the Supreme Court or by Parliament.

47 I have to say that I was initially much attracted by these submissions. However, upon reflection, I have come to the conclusion that they fail to take proper account of the full extent of the factual findings of the judge. He was clearly of the view that the oral variation agreement would have a number of beneficial consequences for MWB. First, MWB would recover some of the arrears immediately and would have some hope of recovering them all in due course. But secondly and importantly, Rock would remain a licensee and continue to occupy the property with the result that it would not be left standing empty for some time at further loss to MWB.

48 There has been no suggestion that MWB was at any material time operating under any kind of duress. Rather, acting by Miss Evans, it had for some time been trying to find a way to accommodate Rock's financial difficulties. There was, so it seems to me, a commercial advantage to both MWB and Rock in reaching an agreement if that could be achieved. MWB would receive an immediate payment of £3,500, it would be likely to recover more from Rock than it would by enforcing the terms of the original agreement and it would also retain Rock as a licensee. Rock would remain in occupation of the property, continue its business without interruption and have an opportunity to overcome its cash flow difficulties. Accordingly this is not a case in which the only benefits conferred on MWB by the oral variation agreement were benefits of a kind contemplated by Lord Blackburn in *Foakes v Beer* and by this court in *In re Selectmove*. MWB derived a practical benefit which went beyond the advantage of receiving a prompt payment of a part of the arrears and a promise that it would be paid the balance of the arrears and any deferred licence fees over the course of the forthcoming months. This is therefore a case where, as in *Williams v Roffey*, Rock's immediate payment of £3,500 and its agreement to perform its obligations under the revised payment schedule conferred a practical benefit on MWB which amounted to good consideration, so rendering the oral variation agreement enforceable.

49 I conclude that the judge was right to find that the payment by Rock of the £3,500 and its promise to make further payments in accordance with the revised payment schedule conferred upon MWB a benefit which constituted sufficient consideration to support the oral variation agreement. In my judgment the oral variation agreement thereupon became binding upon MWB and it would remain binding for so long as Rock continued to make payments in accordance with the revised payment schedule. I would add that I agree with the judgment of Lady Justice Arden on this issue at [69] to [87] below. ...

ARDEN LJ: ...

80 Professor G.H. Treitel at paragraph 4-070 of *Chitty on Contracts*, vol 1, 32nd edition sums up the modern state of the law in relation to consideration for agreements to perform obligations already due under the original contract in the following words, with which I respectfully agree:

> Where [the debtor's conduct did not constitute economic duress], and the promisee has in fact conferred a benefit on the promisor by performing the original contract, then the requirement of consideration is satisfied and there seems to be no good reason for refusing to enforce the new promise.

...

83 ... [In] *In re Selectmove*, this Court drew a distinction between obligations to perform work and obligations to pay money and it held that the practical benefit to the creditor of (my words) "a bird in the hand rather than two in the bush" did not mean that a contract to pay a lesser sum than originally agreed was enforceable. ...

84 In my judgment, *Selectmove* is distinguishable from the present case and decides only that the benefit which a creditor obtains from a promise to pay an existing debt by instalments is not good consideration in law. In that case, there was no finding by the trial judge that there was any extra benefit to the Inland Revenue in having an instalment agreement with the taxpayer. The question of practical benefit only arose in this Court in *Selectmove* because counsel for the taxpayer argued that there was consideration because the instalment agreement was beneficial to the Inland Revenue in the sense that it had a promise to make payments in discharge of the existing debt in accordance with an agreed schedule, which would obviate the need for it to take steps to enforce payment of the amount owed to it. It was that argument that Peter Gibson LJ rejected. Peter Gibson LJ could not reject the general principle that, where there was other consideration, which the law recognised was sufficient to support a contract, that was good consideration for a promise. There can be no coherent distinction between agreement to pay debts and agreements to do work in this context. The strength of that general principle may well explain why in *Roffey* this Court did not refer to *Foakes v Beer*.

85 My conclusion that *Selectmove* can be distinguished in this case is not inconsistent with *Foakes v Beer*, where the only suggested consideration was the debtor's promise to pay part of his existing debt ...

McCombe LJ agreed with both judgments.

The case was then appealed to the Supreme Court. The Supreme Court allowed the appeal on the ground that the clause requiring any variation to be in writing rendered the oral variation of no effect (again, this part of the decision is omitted). LORD SUMPTION, with whom three of the other four Justices agreed, continued:

18 That makes it unnecessary to deal with consideration. It is also, I think, undesirable to do so. The issue is a difficult one. The only consideration which MWB can be said to have been given for accepting a less advantageous schedule of payments was (i) the prospect

that the payments were more likely to be made if they were loaded onto the back end of the contract term, and (ii) the fact that MWB would be less likely to have the premises left vacant on its hands while it sought a new licensee. These were both expectations of practical value, but neither was a contractual entitlement. In *Williams v Roffey* the Court of Appeal held that an expectation of commercial advantage was good consideration. The problem about this was that practical expectation of benefit was the very thing which the House of Lords held not to be adequate consideration in *Foakes v Beer*: see, in particular … Lord Blackburn [quoted above]. There are arguable points of distinction, although the arguments are somewhat forced. A differently constituted Court of Appeal made these points in *In re Selectmove Ltd*, and declined to follow *Williams v Roffey*. The reality is that any decision on this point is likely to involve a re-examination of the decision in *Foakes v Beer*. It is probably ripe for re-examination. But if it is to be overruled or its effect substantially modified, it should be before an enlarged panel of the court and in a case where the decision would be more than obiter dictum.

Appeal allowed.

Notes

(1) Although in both *Williams v Roffey* and *MWB v Rock* the Court of Appeal emphasised that consideration is still required, not only for the *formation* of a contract but for variations to it, on the approach the Court takes towards variations it is hard to see what role the doctrine is left to play. The Court indicates that there will be consideration if the promisor will get a practical benefit from the promisee actually performing his obligation in response to the promise of extra payment. But will one party ever make a promise to pay extra for the performance if he will not get any practical benefit from the performance? It seems unlikely. And although in *Williams v Roffey* Glidewell LJ adds the requirement that B's promise must not be given 'as a result of economic duress or fraud on the part of A', that follows from the rules on economic duress and fraud, whether consideration is needed or not. So it can be argued that the decisions are tantamount to saying that consideration is not required for a variation of an exiting contract. This is the position taken by the US Uniform Commercial Code: § 2-209 states that 'An agreement modifying a contract within this article needs no consideration to be binding'.[56]

(2) A counter-argument is that there just might be cases in which the promisee will not get any practical benefit from obtaining performance other than the performance itself. So, A might agree to let B pay a debt by instalments, or to let B off paying part of the debt, not because there will be any benefit to A but simply in order to help B. (This seems to have been the view that the Court in *MWB v Rock* took of the facts in *Foakes v Beer* and *In re Selectmove*.). Perhaps in such a case the promise to accept payment in instalments or the lesser sum should not be binding, but this seems to be the point of distinction that Lord Sumption calls 'somewhat forced'.

---

[56] See also Restatement 2d of Contracts § 74.

(3) So if Lord Sumption's suggestion that it is time to reconsider the rule in *Foakes v Beer* is taken up in a later case, one possible outcome would be to say that consideration is still required, but that it will be presumed that the promisor is getting some sort of benefit from the variation unless the promisor can prove the contrary (a position that is very close to that taken by the Court of Appeal in the *MWB* case). Another would be to say simply that in the case of a promise to vary an existing contract, no consideration is required (as under the UCC).

(4) If the court were to adopt the first approach, there might still be cases in which there was no consideration for the variation because the promisor was deriving no practical benefit from it. But in such a case, allowing the promisor to go back on its promise to pay more or, as the case may be, to accept less than is owed, might leave the debtor worse off or be unfair for some other reason. This brings us to the discussion of promissory estoppel. But before considering how this might affect 'variation' cases, we must start with a discussion of the general question of gratuitous promises which have been relied on by the promisee.

11.2.B GRATUITOUS PROMISES THAT HAVE BEEN RELIED ON

English law does not in general recognise transactions unsupported by consideration as a category of contracts. Gratuitous promises are not enforceable, owing to the absence of consideration, unless they are incorporated in a deed. Thus, a promise to give money to a charity is not enforceable unless the need for consideration is avoided by the promise being made in a deed.[57] We saw earlier that it does not matter that there may have been a very good reason for making the promise—eg that the promisee has just saved the promisor's life. Even if the promisee was gravely injured in the process, the act of saving the promisor was done before the promise and thus cannot have been in exchange for it—a rule summarised in the rather confusing phrase, 'past consideration is no consideration'.[58]

Equally in principle it makes no difference that the promisee has assumed that the promise will be performed and has acted in such a way that, if the promise is not performed after all, he will be left worse off than before—so-called 'detrimental reliance'. Unless the promisor had asked the promisee to act as he did, the promisee's action was not done in exchange for the promise. The classic test is, did the promisor expressly or impliedly request the promisee to act as he did?[59]

In practice, when the promisee's actions have seemed reasonable and his case for compensation strong, English judges have sometimes striven to find a remedy. One approach has been hinted at earlier: it is to 'discover' a contract in which something done by the promisee is treated as consideration for the promise.[60] Another approach, widely adopted

---

[57] Above, p 345.
[58] See above, p 352.
[59] See above, p 349.
[60] See *de la Bere v Pearson* [1908] 1 KB 280 (CA), discussed above at p 350.

by judges in the US but also used in a limited way by English courts, has been to use a doctrine known as 'promissory estoppel'.

11.2.B.1 ESTOPPEL BY REPRESENTATION

In its traditional sense, estoppel is a principle known to many systems, some of which phrase it in terms of 'good faith';[61] it prevents a party from going back on what he has said or done (*venire contra proprium factum*). The traditional common law version of this (usually known as 'estoppel by representation')[62] is that if a party made a statement of fact which the other party relied on to his detriment—in other words, acted in such a way that if the fact were not true, he would be worse off than before—then the first party could not deny the fact. If the relying party would have had some right or remedy had the fact stated been true, he will have that right or remedy anyway.

For example, suppose a ship-owner receives goods for shipment and issues a bill of lading stating that the goods were received in 'good order and condition'. The shipper then sells the bill of lading representing the goods to a buyer. When the buyer takes delivery from the carrier, it finds the goods have been visibly damaged. The carrier will not be permitted to raise the defence that the goods were already damaged when he received them, even if he could prove that this was the case. As he had stated that the goods were in visibly good condition when he received them, he is 'estopped' from raising that defence.

Because estoppel often prevents a party from raising a defence that otherwise he would be able to employ, it is often said that traditional estoppel operates 'as a shield but not a sword'.[63] Estoppel by representation is also limited to cases in which the statement on which reliance has been placed was a statement of fact. Thus, in *Jorden v Money*,[64] Money was liable to Jorden on a bond (a written promise to pay). When Money was thinking of getting married and wanted to know his financial position, Jorden stated categorically that she would never enforce the bond. After Money had married, Jorden changed her mind and sought to enforce the bond after all. The House of Lords held that she was not estopped from doing so: her statement that she would not enforce the bond was not a statement of fact.[65]

---

[61] See 1.2 (EN), above, p 9 and p 12.

[62] It is also possible for the parties to agree to act on an assumed state of facts even though they both know that the facts may be different. (Eg, they may act on the shared assumption that a particular loan to be made by one of them will be covered by a guarantee given by the other, even if on its true meaning the guarantee does not apply.) Again, neither party will be allowed to assert the true facts. This is known as 'estoppel by convention'. See generally *Treitel* (n 3 above) paras 3-094–3-099 and 9-167–9-168.

[63] This should not be misinterpreted: either party (claimant or defendant) may rely on an estoppel. Thus a claimant may rely on the estoppel to complete the facts he needs to show in order for his action to succeed. Eg, a claimant may rely on the authority apparently given by the defendant to the representative with whom the claimant was dealing: see below, p 1369.

[64] See (1854) 5 HL Cas 185.

[65] There is a puzzle over this case: was there not a promise by Jorden not to enforce the bond if Money got married, so that there was a contract? It may be that it was thought that Money was not marrying at Jorden's request (see above, p 349). Alternatively, it may have been thought that there was a contract but that it was unenforceable because of the Statute of Frauds 1677, which (by a section repealed since 1854, when *Jorden v Money* was decided) required that contracts in consideration of marriage be evidenced in writing signed by the defendant. See Atiyah (n 6 above) 234–38.

11.2.B.2 PROMISSORY ESTOPPEL

During the nineteenth century, courts in the US started to use estoppel where a person had given a promise and the promisee had acted to his or her detriment on the promise. For example, in *Ricketts v Scothorn*,[66] Katie Scothorn was at work when her grandfather entered and gave her a piece of paper (technically a promissory note, to which absence of consideration is still a defence), which read:

> May 1st 1891. I promise to pay to Katie Scothorn on demand, $2,000, to be at 6 per cent per annum. J C Ricketts.

He said: 'I have fixed something that you have not got to work any more. None of my grandchildren work and you don't have to.' Miss Scothorn gave notice to her employer and left her job. Her grandfather paid her some interest but died without paying all the interest due or any of the principal sum. Miss Scothorn sued his executor. The Supreme Court of Nebraska held that she did not provide consideration by quitting her job as this was not bargained for by her grandfather. However, it held that he was 'estopped from denying that there was consideration' and therefore his executors must pay.[67]

This is inconsistent with the traditional English position, which is that estoppel does not apply to a promise, only to a statement of existing fact. Also, English law would give a remedy only if there would be a remedy if the fact stated had been true. The only statement made by the grandfather was that he would pay, but a promise to pay made without consideration would not give Katie an action. What was missing was the consideration. The US courts get round this by saying that the promisor 'was estopped from denying that there was consideration'.[68]

'Promissory estoppel' has appeared in England in cases involving gratuitous amendments to existing contracts—'*Foakes v Beer*-type' cases.[69] The subject is attended by some degree of uncertainty and this is not the place to enter into a detailed discussion of it. But it is worth examining the manner in which promissory estoppel intervenes to mitigate the rigours of consideration, by studying the landmark judgment in the *High Trees House* case.

King's Bench Division   **11.10 (EN)**

Central London Property Trust Ltd v High Trees House Ltd[70]

A landlord's promise to reduce a tenant's rent will be binding without consideration if the tenant has acted on the promise in such a way that it would be inequitable for the landlord to go back on the promise.

---

[66] 77 NW 365 (1898).

[67] See now Restatement 2d of contracts § 90, 11.11 (US), below, p 371.

[68] Which at least in *Ricketts v Scothorn* was a complete fiction since the grandfather, doubtless being quite innocent of the niceties of contract law, had not said anything about consideration (all he had said was, 'I have fixed something that you have not got to work any more. None of my grandchildren work and you don't have to.')

[69] See above, pp 357 ff.

[70] [1947] KB 130.

Facts: The plaintiff, Central London Property Trust, granted to High Trees House Ltd (a tenant company that would sub-let the flats to the actual occupiers) a 99-year lease on a block of flats, at a ground rent of £2,500 a year. The war supervened, making it hard for the tenants to sub-let the flats, and the lessor granted a reduction in rent of one-half to take account of circumstances. The reduced rent was paid regularly. By 1945 all the flats were again let and the lessor sought to recover ground rent at the full rate from the beginning of the term. It then reduced its claim to the difference with effect from the third quarter of 1945. Denning J (as he then was) allowed this claim.

Held: The Court gave judgment for the plaintiff company for the amount claimed.

Judgment: DENNING J. stated the facts and continued: If I were to consider this matter without regard to recent developments in the law, there is no doubt that had the plaintiffs claimed it, they would have been entitled to recover ground rent at the rate of £2,500 a year from the beginning of the term, since the lease under which it was payable was a lease under seal which, according to the old common law, could not be varied by an agreement by parol (whether in writing or not), but only by deed.

Equity, however stepped in, and said that if there has been a variation of a deed by a simple contract (which in the case of a lease required to be in writing would have to be evidenced by writing), the courts may give effect to it as is shown in *Berry v Berry* [1929] 2 KB 316. That equitable doctrine, however, could hardly apply in the present case because the variation here might be said to have been made without consideration. With regard to estoppel, the representation made in relation to reducing the rent, was not a representation of an existing fact. It was a representation, in effect, as to the future, namely, that payment of the rent would not be enforced at the full rate but only at the reduced rate. Such a representation would not give rise to an estoppel, because, as was said in *Jorden v Money* (1854) 5 HLC 185, a representation as to the future must be embodied as a contract or be nothing. But what is the position in view of developments in the law in recent years? The law has not been standing still since *Jorden v Money*. There has been a series of decisions over the last fifty years which, although they are said to be cases of estoppel are not really such. They are cases in which a promise was made which was intended to create legal relations and which, to the knowledge of the person making the promise, was going to be acted on by the person to whom it was made and which was in fact so acted on. In such cases the courts have said that the promise must be honoured. The cases to which I particularly desire to refer are: *Fenner v Blake* [1900] 1 QB 426, *In re Wickham* (1917) 34 TLR 158, *Re William Porter & Co, Ltd* [1937] 2 All ER 361 and *Buttery v Pickard* [1946] WN 25. As I have said they are not cases of estoppel in the strict sense. They are really promises—promises intended to be binding, intended to be acted on, and in fact acted on. *Jorden v Money* can be distinguished, because there the promisor made it clear that she did not intend to be legally bound, whereas in the cases to which I refer the proper inference was that the promisor did intend to be bound. In each case the court held the promise to be binding on the party making it, even though under the old common law it might be difficult to find any consideration for it. The courts have not gone so far as to give a cause of action in damages for the breach of such a promise, but they have refused to allow the party making it to act inconsistently with it. It is in that sense, and that sense only, that such a promise gives rise to an estoppel. The decisions are a natural result of the fusion of law and equity: for the cases of *Hughes v Metropolitan Ry Co* (1877) 2 App Cas 439, 448, *Birmingham and District Land Co v London & North Western Ry Co* (1888) 40 Ch D 268, 286 and *Salisbury (Marquess) v Gilmore* [1942] 2 KB 38, 51, afford a sufficient basis for saying that a party would not be allowed in equity to go back on such a promise. In my opinion, the time has now come for the validity of such a promise to be recognised. The logical consequence, no doubt is that a promise to accept a smaller sum in discharge of a larger sum, if acted upon, is binding notwithstanding the absence of consideration: and if the fusion of law and equity leads to this result, so much the better. That aspect was not considered in *Foakes v Beer* (1884) 9 App Cas 605. At this time of day however, when law and equity have been joined together for over seventy years, principles must be reconsidered in the light of their combined effect. It is to be noticed that in the Sixth Interim Report of the Law Revision Committee, pars. 35, 40, it is recommended that such a promise as that to which I have referred, should be enforceable in law even though no consideration for it has been given by the promisee. It seems to me that, to the extent I have mentioned that result has now been achieved by the decisions of the courts.

I am satisfied that a promise such as that to which I have referred is binding and the only question remaining for my consideration is the scope of the promise in the present case. I am satisfied on all the evidence that the promise here was that the ground rent should be reduced to £1,250 a year as a temporary expedient while the block of flats was not fully, or substantially fully let, owing to the conditions prevailing. That means that the reduction in the rent applied throughout the years down to the end of 1944, but early in 1945 it is plain that the flats were fully let, and, indeed the rents received from them (many of them not being affected by the Rent Restrictions Acts), were increased beyond the figure at which it was originally contemplated that they would be let. At all events the rent from them must have been very considerable. I find that the conditions prevailing at the time when the reduction in rent was made, had completely passed away by the early months of 1945. I am satisfied that the promise was understood by all parties only to apply under the conditions prevailing at the time when it was made, namely, when the flats were only partially let, and that it did not extend any further than that. When the flats became fully let, early in 1945, the reduction ceased to apply.

In those circumstances, under the law as I hold it, it seems to me that rent is payable at the full rate for the quarters ending September 29 and December 25, 1945.

If the case had been one of estoppel, it might be said that in any event the estoppel would cease when the conditions to which the representation applied came to an end, or it also might be said that it would only come to an end on notice. In either case it is only a way of ascertaining what is the scope of the representation. I prefer to apply the principle that a promise intended to be binding, intended to be acted on and in fact acted on, is binding so far as its terms properly apply. Here it was binding as covering the period down to the early part of 1945, and as from that time full rent is payable.

I therefore give judgment for the plaintiff company for the amount claimed.
Judgment for plaintiffs.

Note

On this judgment, which upheld the reduction of rent under a lease during the war, the equitable doctrine of promissory estoppel in English law was founded. Under that doctrine, promises to reduce sums owing under a contract must be regarded as valid even if they are unsupported by consideration, if they are intended to alter the legal relationship and to be acted upon by the parties, unless (subsequent cases have added)[71] it is equitable for the promisor to go back on his promise. In the context of promises to accept part payment of a debt, the doctrine has been accepted by the Court of Appeal.[72] However, even in this context it is not uncertain whether or to what extent promissory estoppel modifies *Foakes v Beer*—which is a decision of the House of Lords and therefore binding on lower courts until the highest court itself overrules it, or Parliament passes legislation to that effect. In the light of the Court of Appeal's decision in *MWB v Rock*, the issue may become moot—as in that case, the court may hold that the variation was made for good consideration, so that estoppel ceases to be relevant.

In *High Trees* the doctrine is used as a shield rather than a sword in the sense that it is applied to a promise to give up an existing contractual right, rather than to the creation of a new right. What about a gratuitous promise that is not purporting to modify an existing contract, but simply to create an obligation where none existed before, as in the US case of *Ricketts v Scothorn*? As the cases stand, English law would not reach the same result. It will be noted that in the *High Trees* case Denning J was careful to say that 'The courts have not gone so far as to give a cause of action for breach of such a promise, but they have refused to allow the party making it to act inconsistently with it'. That promissory estoppel cannot be used to make binding a promise to create a new right was confirmed by the Court of Appeal—including Denning LJ, as he had become by then—in *Combe v Combe*.[73] This limit on promissory estoppel seems to be derived from the notion mentioned earlier[74] that estoppel does not confer a cause of action, it only helps to complete some other cause of action which would otherwise be incomplete.

11.2.B.3 RELIANCE LIABILITY (PROMISSORY ESTOPPEL) IN THE US

In the US, since the decision in *Ricketts v Scothorn*, promissory estoppel has been adopted in many of the States as creating a new cause of action, so that a promise made without consideration may be binding if the promisee reasonably relies on it.

---

[71] *D & C Builders Ltd v Rees* [1966] 2 QB 617 (CA) where it was held that builders who had agreed to accept less than was due to them could go back on their promise because they had only agreed as the result of what would now be called economic duress: see below, pp 599 ff.

[72] See *Collier v P & MJ Wright (Holdings) Ltd* [2007] EWCA Civ, [2008] 1 WLR 643. In that case the Court of Appeal held that there was an arguable case of promissory estoppel when the debtor had paid all that the creditor had asked of him (in that case, that he pay 'his share' of a debt for which he and two others were jointly and severally liable, so that any one of them could be made to pay the full amount); it would be inequitable for the creditor to go back on its promise. In *MWB Business Exchange Centres Ltd v Rock Advertising Ltd* [2016] EWCA Civ 553, 11.9 (EN), above, p 361, promissory estoppel was considered as alternative ground for the decision. It was held that MWB would not have been estopped from withdrawing from the agreement because Rock had not made all the promised payments and also because Rock could be restored to its original position (at [63] and [67]). On this second ground it is not easy to reconcile the two decisions. For a discussion, see McKendrick (n 3 above) 104. (When the *MWB* case went to the Supreme Court, the issue of estoppel was not argued; presumably counsel thought Rock had a better chance of winning on the consideration, and decided not to risk damaging the case by 'playing a weak card'.).

[73] [1951] 2 KB 215 (CA).

[74] Above, p 366.

Restatement 2d of Contracts   **11.11 (US)**

§ 90: Promise reasonably inducing action or forbearance

(1) A promise which the promisor should reasonably expect to induce action or forbearance on the part of the promisee or a third person and which does induce such action or forbearance is binding if injustice can be avoided only by enforcement of the promise. The remedy granted or breached may be limited as justice requires.

(2) A charitable subscription or a marriage settlement is binding under sub-section (1) without proof that the promise induced action or forbearance.[75]

The English rule that promissory estoppel cannot be used to create a new contractual right has also now been abandoned in Australia.[76] It is not impossible that on this point matters might evolve even in English law.[77]

11.2.B.4 PROPRIETARY ESTOPPEL

Indeed, to some extent estoppel-type reasoning has already been adopted in England. In one particular context the strict English rule has been relaxed and a gratuitous promise which has been acted on will be enforced. This is where the promise is to confer an interest in land. In the nineteenth century case of *Dillwyn v Llewellyn*,[78] a father said that he had given a piece of land to his son and encouraged the son to build on the land, but in fact the father never transferred ownership of the land to the son. After the father's death, his estate tried to reclaim possession of the land, complete with the mansion the son had built on it. Rather than allow this injustice, the courts of equity compelled the father's personal representatives to complete the gift. The rule was gradually extended, first to cases in which the father said he *would give* the land and the son again built without the transfer having taken place,[79] and then, as the next case shows, to cases in which the promisee has not built on the land but has acted in some other way in reliance on the promise. The doctrine has come to be known as 'proprietary estoppel'.

Court of Appeal   **11.12 (EN)**

Crabb v Arun District Council[80]

A party who indicates that he will grant another a right in property and who encourages the other to act on that assumption in such a way that if the right is not granted, the other will be left worse off than before, will be compelled to do justice.

Facts: This was an action for a declaration that the plaintiff had a right of access over the defendants' land in order to reach his own land. The plaintiff and the defendants had owned adjoining plots by the side of a road. The defendants were developing their land and built a service road along the boundary between their land

---

[75] The second sub-section of § 90 appears to mean that a promise of a gift to a charity is simply binding.
[76] See *Waltons Stores (Interstate) Ltd v Maher* (1988) 164 CLR 387 (High Court), 13.20 (AU), below, p 452.
[77] See *Treitel* (n 3 above) para 3-175.
[78] (1862) 4 DeG, F & J 517.
[79] See *Inwards v Baker* [1965] 2 QB 29 (CA).
[80] [1976] Ch 179.

and the plaintiff's. They indicated that they would allow the plaintiff access to his land from the service road at two points, A and B, and they erected gates at these points. The plaintiff sold the front portion of his land (ie the part adjoining the old road) without reserving a right of way over it to the rear portion which he retained, thinking he would have access from the service road at point B. The defendants then removed the gate at point B and refused the plaintiff access unless he paid £3,000 for such a right. The plaintiff claimed that he would not have gone ahead with the sale of part of his property if the council representative had not given the clear impression in discussions that the plaintiff would be granted access from the Council's land at point B.

Held: The Court of Appeal granted the declaration.

Judgment: LORD DENNING MR: … When counsel for Mr Crabb said that he put his case on an estoppel, it shook me a little, because it is commonly supposed that estoppel is not itself a cause of action. But that is because there are estoppels and estoppels. Some do give rise to a cause of action. Some do not. In the species of estoppel called proprietary estoppel, it does give rise to a cause of action. …

The new rights and interests, so created by estoppel in or over land, will be protected by the courts and in this way give rise to a cause of action … The basis of this proprietary estoppel—as indeed of promissory estoppel—is the interposition of equity. Equity comes in, true to form, to mitigate the rigours of strict law. The early cases did not speak of it as 'estoppel'. They spoke of it as 'raising an equity' …

What then are the dealings which will preclude him from insisting on his strict legal rights? If he makes a binding contract that he will not insist on the strict legal position, a court of equity will hold him to his contract. Short of a binding contract, if he makes a promise that he will not insist upon his strict legal rights—even though that promise may be unenforceable in point of law for want of consideration or want of writing—and if he makes the promise knowing or intending that the other will act upon it, and he does act upon it, then again a court of equity will not allow him to go back on that promise: see *Central London Property Trust Ltd v High Trees House Ltd* and *Charles Rickards Ltd v Oppenheim*. Short of an actual promise, if he, by his words or conduct, so behaves as to lead another to believe that he will not insist on this strict legal rights—knowing or intending that the other will act on that belief—and he does so act, that again will raise an equity in favour of the other, and it is for a court of equity to say in what way the equity may be satisfied. The cases show that this equity does not depend on agreement but on words or conduct. In *Ramsden v Dyson* Lord Kingsdown spoke of a verbal agreement 'or what amounts to the same thing, an expectation, created or encouraged'. In *Birmingham and District Land Co v London and North Western Railway Co*, Cotton LJ said that '… what passed did not make a new agreement, but what took place … raised an equity against him' …

The question then is: were the circumstances here such as to raise an equity in favour of Mr Crabb? True the council on the deeds had the title to their land, free of any access at point B. But they led Mr Crabb to believe that he had or would be granted a right of access at point B …

The council actually put up the gates at point B at considerable expense. That certainly led Mr Crabb to believe that they agreed that he should have the right of access through point B without more ado …

The council knew that Mr Crabb intended to sell the two portions separately and that he would need an access at point B as well as point A. Seeing that they knew of his intention—and they did nothing to disabuse him, but rather confirmed it by erecting gates at point B—it was their conduct which led him to act as he did; and this raises an equity in favour against them …

[Lawton LJ delivered a concurring judgment.]

Scarman LJ: I agree that the appeal should be allowed … I think it is now well settled law that the court, having analysed and assessed the conduct and relationship of the parties, has to answer three questions. First, is there an equity established? Secondly, what is the extent of the equity, if one is established? And, thirdly, what is the relief appropriate to satisfy the equity? … Such therefore I believe to be the nature of the inquiry that the courts have to conduct in a case of this sort. In pursuit of that inquiry I do not find helpful the distinction between promissory and proprietary estoppel. This distinction may indeed be valuable to those who have to teach or expound the law; but I do not think that, in solving the particular problem raised by a particular case, putting the law into categories is of the slightest assistance …

[Lord Scarman held that on the facts an equity was clearly established, and continued:] I turn now to the other two questions—the extent of the equity and the relief needed to satisfy it. There being no grant, no enforceable contract, no licence, I would analyse the minimum equity to do justice to the plaintiff as a right either to an easement or to a licence upon terms to be agreed. I do not think it is necessary to go further than that. Of course, going that far would support the equitable remedy of injunction which is sought in this action. If there is no agreement as to terms, if agreement fails to be obtained, the court can, in my judgment, and must, determine in these proceedings upon what terms the plaintiff should be put to enable him to have the benefit of the equitable right which he is held to have …

Declaration and injunction to enforce the plaintiff's right of access granted.

Notes

(1) Proprietary estoppel is most often used in cases in which there was no definite agreement between the parties but the defendant must have known that the claimant believed that, at least if he acted in a particular way, he would get the property, and had acted accordingly. For example, in *Thorner v Major*,[81] a farmer informed his nephew that the farm would be his and in reliance on that understanding his nephew worked on it for years, only to find that his uncle, in his will, had left it to someone else. It was held that proprietary estoppel applied and the nephew was entitled to the farm.

(2) The doctrine of proprietary estoppel is now firmly established, though its boundaries are not wholly clear. Despite what Scarman LJ said, most judges see it as distinct from promissory estoppel. Proprietary estoppel will result in the claimant acquiring a new right, whereas promissory estoppel applies only when a party promises not to enforce an existing right (as in the *High Trees* case). But proprietary estoppel applies only when the defendant indicated that the claimant would receive an interest in property.

(3) On a strict interpretation, therefore, 'proprietary estoppel' is a doctrine of property law, not of contract. But the dividing line seems thin. Why should it make a difference that the defendant promised to confer a proprietary interest on the claimant rather than, say, promising to pay money to the claimant? Moreover, we have seen that

---

[81] [2009] UKHL 18, [2009] 1 WLR 776.

at least one commentator believes that the essence of English contract law too is really the protection of reliance.[82]

(4) We will see that there have been attempts to use proprietary estoppel in situations that in other laws might be covered by notions of precontractual liability—and that sometimes the argument has succeeded. This is explored in Chapter 13.[83]

Whatever the future may bring, it may be concluded that the doctrine of consideration is an additional feature which may prevent the enforcement of obligations that in other legal systems would be binding. There is disagreement among academics over whether the doctrine is needed and, if so, what its true scope should be.[84] One judge remarked that 'A defence of lack of consideration rarely has merit',[85] and (at least in commercial contexts), whenever possible, the courts seem to try to mitigate its worst effects.

11.3. THE DOCTRINE OF *CAUSE*

This is a complex theory, much debated in academic circles and still very significant as far as decisions of the courts are concerned. Following a general discussion, we shall examine first its traditional applications and then more recent trends.

11.3.A GENERAL DISCUSSION

The history of *cause* is complicated because it draws on both the Roman tradition and the Canonist tradition. This accounts for the two tendencies which are discernible in the notion of *cause*: first, the objective aspect which can be traced back, albeit somewhat tenuously, to Roman law, was expounded by Domat in the seventeenth century and is sometimes referred to as the '*cause* of the obligation'; and secondly, the subjective aspect, which is derived from the Canonist tradition with its unclear boundary between law and morality.

It should be stated, by way of simplification, that the 'objective *cause*' is always the same for the same class of contract. In synallagmatic contracts, it is the counter-performance or, to be more precise, the prospect of the counter-performance to be given by the other party (an English lawyer would say that this is the 'consideration').[86] In the case of gratuitous contracts, it is the unfettered, abstract intention to supply or provide something without demanding anything in return (in this case there would be no

---

[82] See P Atiyah, 'Promises, Obligations and the Law of Contract' in idem, *Essays on Contract* (Oxford: Clarendon Press, 1988) 33.

[83] See especially pp 433 ff.

[84] For opposing views in the debate, see A Burrows, 'Improving Contract and Tort' in A Burrows (ed), *Understanding the Law of Obligations* (Oxford: Hart Publishing, 1998) 164, 197 and M Chen-Wishart, 'In defence of consideration' (2013) 13 Oxford University Commonwealth Law Journal 209.

[85] Donaldson J in *Thoresen Car Ferries Ltd v Weymouth Portland Borough Council* [1977] 2 Lloyd's Rep 614, 619 (QBD).

[86] See above, pp 344 ff.

consideration under English law). In the case of a *contrat réel* (ie a contract which requires for its formation the effective delivery of the thing to which it refers, in addition to the agreement of the parties, such as a deposit or loan for use), it is the delivery of the thing in question. By contrast, the 'subjective *cause*' is the individual motive which prompted the party concerned to commit himself or herself: it is thus different for each contract.

The requirement that there be a *cause* is written into, for example, the contract laws of Italy and Quebec and many other national contract laws which drew their inspiration from French law. It is no longer explicitly laid down in the French Code civil, and this may result in other countries that currently employ the doctrine also abandoning it. Dutch law, which borrowed the French doctrine of *cause* for its 1838 Civil Code, abandoned it with the Burgerlijk Wetboek of 1992.

The objective *cause*, which is sometimes described as the financial *cause*, ensures that a contract will not be enforced without a reason justifying the transfer of value under the contract. As for the Quebec Civil Code of 1993, the first draft abolished the *cause*, at least under that name. It reappeared in the definitive text, alongside the 'object' of the contract. It would appear that this resulted from the realisation that certain functions fulfilled by the *cause* could not readily be performed without it.[87] The definition of *cause* given in Article 1410 of the Quebec Civil Code—the 'reason leading each of the parties to enter into the contract'—is consistent with the dual analysis of the *cause*.

11.3.B FRENCH LAW ON *CAUSE* BEFORE THE 2016 REFORM OF THE CODE CIVIL

11.3.B.1 *CAUSE* IN THE CODE CIVIL 1804

Before explaining the new French contract law, it is important to recall the former provisions of the Code civil, all the more so because they are still applicable to contracts entered into before 1 October 2016.

Code civil 1804   **11.13 (FR)**

Article 1108: Four requisites are essential for the validity of an agreement:
   The consent of the party who binds himself;
   His capacity to contract;
   A definite object which forms the subject-matter of the undertaking;[88]
   A lawful cause in the obligation

Art 1131: An obligation without cause or with a false cause, or with an unlawful cause, may not have any effect.

Art 1132: An agreement is nevertheless valid, although its cause is not expressed.

Art 1133: A cause is unlawful where it is prohibited by legislation, where it is contrary to public morals or to public policy.

---

[87] But see below, pp 389–91.
[88] For the requirement of *objet*, see above, p 293.

11.3.B.2 ANTICAUSALIST MOVEMENT IN THE TWENTIETH CENTURY

The doctrine of *cause* was vehemently criticised by Marcel Planiol at the end of the nineteenth century, but his arguments were refuted by the so-called 'neo-causalists', such as Henri Capitant and Jacques Maury. The doctrinal controversies related primarily to the importance to be attached to each of the two aspects of the *cause*, respectively. For some, they are two distinct concepts. These academic controversies had little impact in the courts.

Jean Carbonnier[89] explained this dual function of *cause* and suggested putting less emphasis on *cause* and more emphasis on the notion of 'interest':

> The twofold presentation of the doctrine (abstract *cause* and *cause* as motive) appears to have become a locus classicus (eg Flour-Aubert, no. 267; Larroumet, nos. 44 et seq; Malaurie and Aynès, no. 336). It is convenient but its scope must not be exaggerated. It may be that academic writers have attached too much significance to the illegal or immoral *cause* (in this connection, see M Defossez, 'Réflexion sur l'emploi des motifs comme cause des obligations', RT, 85, 231: an overly psychological approach is not possible). A concept such as that of interest, which might have been a more appropriate translation of *causa*, clearly brings out the unity of purpose underlying [ex-] Article 1131; an interest must exist, it must be serious and it must also be legitimate (that is what is professed where the law expounds the doctrine of interest, namely under the law of procedure, in regard to the maxim 'no interest, no action'). That may also serve to elucidate the relationship between the object and the *cause*: the latter is the interest of the promisor; the object (useful and lawful) is the interest of the promisee. The assumption made by the law is that any step taken by a reasonably prudent person is dictated by a financial interest (contracts for valuable consideration) or a moral interest (gratuitious acts).

Notes

(1) The first Project of the Ministry of Justice leading up to the 2016 reform followed Carbonnier's suggestion of retaining the concept of *intérêt* rather than that of *cause*; this was so strongly criticised, that the notion of 'interest' was subsequently deleted.

(2) There is a distinction between the concept of *cause* and that of 'object' (still referred to in the Code civil, though now called 'content', see new Article 1128) which must exist, be determined or determinable and lawful.[90] An obligation without a predetermined object renders the contract null and void in its entirety.

(3) What used to be dealt with under the concept of unlawful *cause* is now linked to illegality which is discussed in Chapter 17 below.

11.3.B.3 JUDICIAL APPLICATIONS OF THE CONCEPT OF *CAUSE*

In this chapter, illustrations of the use, by French courts, of the concept of *cause* all relate to the 'objective *cause*'. Since the reform does not apply to contracts concluded before

---

[89] J Carbonnier, *Droit Civil—Les obligations* (21st edn, Paris: PUF, 1998) no. 64.
[90] See further below, p 390.

1 October 2016 (the date when the reform entered into force), French judges may still, for all contracts concluded before this date, use the old articles of the Code civil, referring to the *cause*.[91]

The application of the objective *cause* in modern transactions is illustrated by the following case.

Cass com, 6 April 1993[92]   **11.14 (FR)**

Delay in crediting accounts

Bank charges for interest on the time between the date payments were shown as taken out of one account and the date the payment was shown as credited in another were without cause.

Facts: Under a well-established banking practice, customer remittances (payments to be credited to their account) are entered only after a certain period whereas payments from the account by the bank (debits) are entered with a date preceding the date of the transaction. This practice affects the calculation of interest, which is charged from the date on which the credit or debit is entered.

Held: The lower court decided that the bank was entitled to the full payment of interest. The Cour de cassation set this decision aside for absence of *cause*.

Judgment: THE COURT:—Whereas according to the judgment appealed against (Aix-en-Provence, 2nd Civil Chamber, 3 October 1990), the companies Major, Jean Major, Suren and Ambre (the companies) which held current accounts with the Banco Exterior France (the Bank) sued the Bank for recovery of fees charged; the Bank brought a counter-claim for an order that the companies should pay to it the amounts debited to their accounts;

[A second plea relating to former Article 1154 Cciv is omitted.]

On the first branch of the first plea:—Under [former] Article 1131 of the Civil Code;

— Whereas the companies claimed that their obligation to pay interest was in part unsupported by any *cause*, inasmuch as the amounts on which interest was calculated were increased, without justification, by the application of 'dates of valuation' to remittances in the form of cheques and cash and to withdrawals;

— Whereas in rejecting that claim, the lower court found that the practice of the Bank, which was condemned by the companies, was justified by the fact that 'a remittance for the credit of an account, like a withdrawal debited to an account, takes time to collect or pay out', and that 'the value of a cheque can be credited to an account only after collection which cannot be instantaneous';

— Whereas by so holding, although the transactions at issue, other than remittances of cheques for collection, did not involve, even for the purpose of calculating interest, the postponement or bringing forward of the dates on which such amounts were to be credited or debited, the cour d'appel infringed the abovementioned provision.

On those grounds the judgment is set aside and the case referred to the cour d'appel, Lyon.

---

[91] Actually, it seems to us that nothing would prevent judges from reviving the use of the word, although it is not in the Code (similarly, the distinction between *obligations de moyens* and *obligations de résultat*, though not in the Code civil, is used by the courts).

[92] No. 90-21198, Bull IV no. 138, JCP 1993.II.22062, annotated by J Stoufflet.

Notes

(1) As is borne out by the reference to former Article 1131 of the Code civil, the Cour de cassation is availing itself of the doctrine of *cause* in order to hold that amounts of interest received or paid are in part unsupported by any *cause*. It holds that, in the case of the remittance of cheques for collection, postponement of the date from which interest becomes payable is justified by the delay involved in collection. However, there is no such justification in the other cases—cash remittances, telegraphic transfers, etc. In such cases, the interest charged is unsupported by any *cause*.

(2) In Germany, the Bundesgerichtshof, in its decision of 17 January 1989,[93] provided a similar solution by ordering the deletion of a clause fixing the value date of a current account transaction at 24 hours after the transaction where it involved the remitting of funds or a bank transfer, since, in such circumstances, the deferment of the value debt cannot be regarded as a reimbursement of costs. In order to arrive at that conclusion, the BGH referred to the AGBG (Act on Standard Terms),[94] even though the clause in question only appeared on a leaflet. It considered that the customers were not given sufficient information and that there was a lack of transparency. It further stated that the fact that use of the clause was common practice in the banking sector could not operate to save it. The reasons given for the Court's decision were therefore of a technical nature and based on a particular form of wording, even though there was also a reference to *Treu und Glauben* (the principle of good faith and fair dealing) and, in addition, to the absence of any consideration. Bank charges in consumer banking contracts (in this case, charges for overdrawing the account) have been the subject of litigation in the UK, under the legislation that implements the Unfair Terms in Consumer Contracts Directive—but the challenge failed.[95]

Another example of the application of *cause* is provided by 'aleatory' contracts, ie 'risky' agreements whose performance depends on a contingency or another uncertain event that is beyond the control of either of the parties. For such contracts, the French courts held that, if the supposed chance is in fact bound to occur, the contract is without *cause*.

Cass civ (1), 18 April 1953[96]   **11.15 (FR)**

The genealogist

An agreement to do research to discover facts which are already known and readily available is without cause.

Facts: A genealogist was promised payment to provide information that was readily available.

Held: The obligation to pay was without *cause*.

---

[93] NJW 1989, 582.
[94] See now §§ 305–310 BGB. See above, p 186 and below, p 758.
[95] See 21.30 (EN), below, p 861.
[96] No. 53-06152, Bull civ I no. 218.

Judgment: THE COURT:—Whereas the facts and reasoning of the decision under review, Aix, 17 July 1950, a decision which affirmed the decision of the lower court, indicate that, Doctor M having died on September 8, 1944, B, a genealogist, was asked by the family notary on the day of M's death to perform research in order to discover the heirs of the deceased; as on November 26, 1944, B entered into a contract with Mrs P, the niece and sole heir of Doctor M, by virtue of which he promised to reveal an inheritance which was to come to her in exchange for a substantial share of that inheritance; as after the contract was signed, he informed her of the inheritance of Doctor M and of her status as heiress.

— Whereas the appeal objects that the court of appeal declared the contract invalid for absence of *cause* at the request of Mr and Mrs P even though Mrs P had been running the risk of ignorance of the existence of the inheritance and of her status as heiress and that without the intervention of the genealogist it would have been impossible to discover the name and address of the said heiress;

— Whereas however the decision, in its own conclusions and those adopted from the lower court decision, and having seen the documents of the case and the results of an inquest, found that the address of Mrs P was known to the friends of Doctor M and of the notary; as the notary had asked B to do research pointlessly, with too much haste, and without consulting the documents he had at hand and in his files, and as he had given B enough information to permit B to find Mrs P with nothing left to chance; as B had not rendered Mrs P any service and as he had not run any risk himself; as the existence of the inheritance would have come to the knowledge of the heiress in the normal course without the intervention of the genealogist; as on these facts the cour d'appel could infer that no secret had been revealed and that the contract of November 26, 1944 was without *cause* …;

For these reasons, the *pourvoi* is rejected.

Note

A contract of this type is normally aleatory because the genealogist is not certain to find an heir. However, in the present case, there was no risk because the notary was in possession of the heir's address. The service rendered was non-existent and the contract was therefore unsupported by any *cause*. Of course the genealogist in such a case has an action in the law of delict against the negligent notary if he (the genealogist) has suffered any loss.

The case of a unilateral promise to sell subject to a 'cancellation charge' affords an illustration of the role played by *cause* in this type of contract.

Cass com, 23 June 1958[97]   **11.16 (FR)**

Cancellation charge on option

The cause *of an undertaking by a purchaser who has reserved the right to buy a property to pay a cancellation charge is the advantage conferred on him by the promisor's undertaking not to assign the business to another person for a specified period.*

[97] D 1958, 581.

Facts: F granted B an option to purchase F's business; the option agreement stated that if B did not take up the option within a fixed period, he would be liable to pay F 400,000 francs. B did not take up the option and refused to pay the agreed amount to F.

Held: Although B was not obliged to purchase the business there was *cause* for the promise to pay the sum of 400,000 francs.

Judgment: THE COURT: *On the sole appeal ground*:—Under [former] Article 1131 of the Civil Code;

— Whereas according to the judgment appealed against (Orléans, 2 December 1953), Fisch, by a writing under hand dated 11 March 1952, promised to sell to Bellanger who reserved the right to acquire his bakery and confectionery business at the price of 3,500,000F, that promise to remain valid until 1 May 1952, the date fixed for the taking of possession; as it was stipulated that, should Bellanger not acquire the business within the period provided for, he would be obliged to pay to the vendor, by way of a fixed lump-sum cancellation charge, the sum of 400,000F; as on 20 March 1952 Bellanger informed Fisch that, for personal reasons, he would not be acquiring the business; as Fisch sought payment by Bellanger of the fixed cancellation charge and the judgment appealed against dismissed that action;

— Whereas the judgment appealed against was based on the fact that Bellanger, the promisee, could not be ordered to pay any sum to the promisor Fisch since, not having himself promised to acquire the business but having merely reserved an option to do so, he remained free to decide;

— Whereas consequently, the insertion into a unilateral promise to sell of a clause providing for payment of a given sum by way of cancellation charge must be deemed not to have occurred because it is without *cause*;

— Whereas the *cause* of the undertaking by the likely purchaser to pay a cancellation charge was constituted by the advantage conferred on him by the promisor's undertaking not to assign the business to another person for a specified period;

— Whereas by holding this not to be the case, the cour d'appel misapplied and consequently infringed the provision referred to above;

On those grounds the Cour de cassation set aside the judgment of the cour d'appel.

Note

    The problem is to determine how to justify the payment of the 'cancellation charge', in other words to identify the *cause* in return for which the undertaking is offered. The Cour de cassation regards it as being constituted by the tying up of the property which the promisee can no longer dispose of, owing to his promise. The 'cancellation charge' is the price of the service rendered to the promisee. Alternatively, the party could validly undertake to make an immediate payment of a sum to be credited towards the price if the sale is completed, or to be retained by the other party if the option is not taken up.

Former Article 1131 Cciv also dealt with the false *cause*, where one party is mistaken as to the *cause*: either it does not exist or it is different from what the party believed. This is sometimes referred to as 'error as to the *cause*'. In actual fact, error as to the *cause* is to be distinguished from the false *cause* in that the latter is sanctioned irrespective of the error, which merely serves to explain how it happened. Unlike with mistake, there is no call for any study of psychological motives.[98]

Cass civ (1), 10 May 1995[99]   **11.17 (FR)**

Worthless services

A mistake as to the existence of the cause, *albeit inexcusable, warrants annulment of an undertaking given for that* cause.

Facts: Sominos had agreed to pay for services to be provided by SCET. It then discovered that the employee provided by SCET to deliver the services had been grossly incompetent.

Held: Even though Sominos was negligent in failing to supervise the employee, its obligation to pay was without *cause*.

Judgment:—Whereas according to the findings of the lower court, Sominos was set up in 1961 in order, in particular, to build and operate on land granted by the Loiret Department warehouses and office or shop buildings and to carry on the management of all the buildings that the Department might consider appropriate for purposes of economic development. As from 1962 Sominos had as directors general persons proposed by one of its shareholders, SCET; as on 28 June 1972 Sominos signed with SCET an agreement under which SCET undertook, in return for a lump-sum remuneration, to provide it with assistance in legal, fiscal, administrative, technical and financial matters, and in regard to financial management; as article 11 of the agreement provided that Sominos could call upon SCET to provide it with 'a qualified executive competent in the management of a mixed-economy company and capable of substituting in the absence or indisposition of the director'; as, as from 1 June 1980, Mr Pellerin was delegated by SCET to Sominos in order to perform the duties of the director; as after Sominos got into financial difficulties, La Fiduciaire de France was commissioned in December 1986 to carry out an audit of the company; it reported in 1987; as following the premature dissolution of Sominos in January 1988, SCET sought from Sominos payment of the sum of 212,881.74 francs representing the redemption of retirement points in favour of Mr Pellerin pursuant to an undertaking which it had entered into by letter dated 14 November 1986; as Sominos claimed that SCET had failed to fulfil its obligations, by providing it with an incompetent executive who was guilty of serious managerial errors; as it therefore sued for damages;

— Whereas the judgment appealed against (Orléans) dismissed the claim by Sominos and ordered it to pay to SCET the sum claimed. ...

On the second appeal ground:—Under [former] Article 1131 of the Civil Code;

— Whereas in ordering Sominos to pay to SCET the cost of redeeming retirement points in favour of Mr Pellerin, the court below was content merely to find that Sominos could not claim that the undertaking given in its letter of 14 November 1986 was vitiated by error, in light of the services rendered by Mr Pellerin, inasmuch as it was in ignorance at that time of the serious managerial mistakes of which Mr Pellerin was guilty; as it was for Sominos as principal to use its powers of supervision and authority over its chief executive;

---

[98] For avoidance of a contract on the ground of mistake, see below, ch 14.
[99] No. 92-10736, Bull civ I no. 194.

— Whereas by so holding, although the mistake as to the existence of the *cause*, albeit it was inexcusable, warrants annulment of the undertaking for lack of *cause*, the cour d'appel failed to give its decision any legal basis;

On those grounds, the Cour de cassation sets aside the cour d'appel's judgment (Orléans) of 20 November 1991 to the extent to which it orders Sominos to pay to SCET the sum of 212,881.74 francs; accordingly, restores the case and the parties to the status quo ante, and refers them to the Angers cour d'appel for a fresh determination.

Note

The *cause* of the undertaking to pay was constituted by the services rendered by the beneficiary. After the event, it was revealed that those services were negated by serious managerial mistakes. It might perhaps have been possible to discern some failure by Sominos to perform the contract. However, the Cour de cassation expressly confined itself to considering the matter in terms of '*cause*'. It clearly stated that there had been an error in that regard. Belief in the existence of the services rendered entails nullity of the undertaking, even though the error was inexcusable, a solution opposite to that which would have been reached in the case of consent vitiated by error.[100]

11.3.B.4 GENERAL TRENDS IN FRENCH CASE LAW BEFORE THE 2016 REFORM

Progressively, the French courts used the doctrine of *cause* in order to infuse contracts with greater ethical content. In so doing, they made the definition of *cause* more concrete in the sense that they were no longer satisfied with the existence of a contractual counter-performance of any nature, however slight its substance or significance, but required a 'real' contractual counter-performance which takes into account the interest which it represents. This is shown, notably, by phrases stating that the obligation undertaken by one of the parties did or did not constitute a 'real interest' for the other, 'a genuine counter-performance', a 'serious' counter-performance or a counter-performance which was not 'derisory'. The concept of *cause* also became more 'subjective' as it took into account the real interest presented by the contract in view of the precise individual goals pursued by the parties.[101] As a result, French courts employed the doctrine of *cause* in many ways and for various purposes. For instance, they used it to restore some sort of fairness by striking out unfair clauses.

The so-called *Chronopost* judgments constitute one of several examples of such a use of the *cause*. They relate to exemption clauses and were a source of inspiration for provisions introduced in the 2016 reform (see Note (5) below the following excerpt from the decision).

---

[100] For further discussion of error, see ch 14 below, esp at pp 526 ff.

[101] J Rochfeld, 'A Future for la cause? Observations of a French Jurist' in J Cartwright, S Vogenauer and S Whittaker (eds), *Reforming the French Law of Obligations* (Oxford: Hart Publishing, 2009) 73.

Cass com, 22 October 1996[102]

11.18 (FR)

Chronopost

Payment for the service of transporting goods is without cause *if the service provider did not perform the fundamental duty under the contract.*

Facts: Chronopost undertook to deliver a package by midday the next day but failed to do so, causing loss to the claimant. The contract contained a clause limiting the liability of Chronopost for late delivery.

Held: The clause was ineffective because it would deprive the contract of *cause.*

Judgment: THE COURT: *On the first appeal ground*:—Under [former] Article 1131 of the Civil Code;

— Whereas according to the judgment appealed against (Court of Appeal, Rennes, 1st Chamber B, 30 June 1993), the company Banchereau on two occasions handed to Chronopost, subrogated to the rights of SFMI, an envelope containing a bid in a tendering procedure; as those envelopes were not delivered before midday on the day following their despatch, as Chronopost had undertaken to do. Accordingly, Banchereau brought an action for damages against Chronopost in respect of the loss sustained by it; as Chronopost relied on the clause in the contract limiting compensation for delay to the cost incurred by it in transporting the packet;

— Whereas in dismissing Bandereau's claim, the court below found that, although Chronopost did not comply with its obligation to deliver the envelopes before noon on the day after despatch, its fault was not so serious as to preclude its reliance on the contractual clause limiting its liability;

— Whereas in so holding, the cour d'appel infringed the above-mentioned provision; as Chronopost, a specialist in swift transport guaranteeing the reliability and speed of its service, undertook to deliver the envelopes entrusted to it by Banchereau within a specified period; as owing to its failure to perform that fundamental duty, the contractual clause limiting liability, which contradicted the scope of the obligation entered into, was deemed not to have been incorporated (*réputée non écrit*) in the contract.

Notes

(1) Traditionally, the courts upheld the validity of exemption clauses and clauses limiting liability in contractual matters unless the non-performance was due to a serious fault or fraud (*dol* or *faute lourde*) of the debtor. The *Chronopost* judgment laid down a new limitation: the contract limited the undertaking's liability to reimbursement of the cost of transport, a derisory indemnity in relation to the loss actually suffered by the sender, namely the loss of the chance of obtaining major contracts. Non-performance was not due to the serious fault or fraud of *Chronopost*: it was caused by unknown factors. Yet, the Cour de cassation held that there had been a failure to perform a fundamental duty under the contract, which was not merely to convey the packet, but to do so within the period stated. By referring to former Article 1131 Cciv, the Cour de cassation based its reasoning on the

---

[102] Cass com 22 October 1996, no. 93-18632, Bull IV no. 261; F Terré, Y Lequette and F Chénédé, *Grands arrêts de jurisprudence civile*, vol 2, *Obligations, Contrats spéciaux, Sûretés* (13th edn, Paris: Dalloz, 2015) no. 157.

doctrine of *cause*. The doctrine was therefore made to apply at two distinct stages. The payment for the transport service is without *cause* because the transporter did not perform the fundamental duty under the contract, and also the *cause* is applied in the definition of the fundamental duty under the contract: it is that duty which was the *cause* of the promisee entering into the contract. In this 1996 *Chronopost* case, the Cour de cassation referred not only to the 'fundamental duty' ('*obligation essentielle*') but also to the fact that the clause limiting liability 'contradicted the scope of the obligation entered into'. The innovation as regards the penalty should also be noted: the clause was 'deemed not to have been incorporated' in the contract whereas the normal sanction would have been the absolute nullity of the contract.

(2) In 2006 the Cour de cassation again resorted to former Article 1131 Cciv in order to strike out the exemption clause invoked by *Chronopost* but its reasoning changed:[103]

> A cour d'appel has no legal basis for a decision based on [former] Article 1131 Code civil when it upholds the principle and detailed provisions of a clause limiting the indemnity payable in the event of loss of the parcel to be carried without enquiring, as the consignor argues, whether the limitation clause on which Chronopost relies, and which was not part of a standard-form contract approved by governmental decree, was not invalidated by the failure of the carrier to carry out an essential obligation under the contract.

In this 2006 case, the use of *cause* was linked to the concept of fundamental obligation (*manquement à une obligation essentielle*) and the exemption clause was not valid if it related to the non-performance of a fundamental obligation. The reference to the fact that the clause limiting liability 'contradicted the scope of the obligation entered into' disappeared. More specifically, this meant that all limitation clauses which applied to a fundamental obligation were ineffective, irrespective of whether or not they effectively contradicted the scope of the obligation entered into (in other words, even if they were reasonable in view of various factors, including the intention of the parties as to the allocation of the risks between themselves). Some French authors criticised this application of the *cause*, and there has been a move back to the approach of the 1996 *Chronopost* case. This issue is explored further in Chapter 21 where we discuss unfair terms.[104]

(3) It must also be noted that the sanction was not the nullity of the contract; it was merely the exemption clause which was disregarded (*reputée non écrite*). The contract survived and, if necessary, it would have been supplemented by some statutory non-mandatory provisions.[105]

(4) The *Chronopost* case is one among a series of cases in which the courts referred to the 'essential elements' of the contract, or its 'fundamental obligations'. Other examples may be found in cases where the Cour de cassation denied the lessor the

---

[103] Cass com 30 May 2006, no. 04-14974, Bull IV no. 132, D 2006, 1599, annotated by X Delpech and D Mazeaud.

[104] See especially Cass com 29 June 2010, no. 09-11841, Bull IV no. 115. See below, pp 821–22.

[105] See Cass com 22 October 1996, no. 93-18632, Bull IV no. 261; Terré et al (n 102 above) no. 157, esp. paras 21 ff.

possibility of exonerating himself through a term of the contract from the obligation of delivery set out in Article 1719(1) Cciv, or from the obligation of ensuring the quiet enjoyment of the premises. Thus, on 1 June 2005, the Cour de cassation affirmed that 'the lessor cannot, by means of a clause relating to the execution of works, free himself from his obligation to deliver the demised premises.'[106] Clauses creating such significant imbalance could also be sanctioned in all business to business (B2B) contracts, under the conditions set forth by Article L 442-6, I, 2° of the Code de commerce.[107]

(5) This control is now more generally provided by the Code civil in Articles 1170 and 1171, as introduced in 2016.[108] In line with the *Chronopost* case law, Article 1170, which applies to all contracts, provides that any contract term which deprives the debtor's essential obligation of its substance must be disregarded. Article 1171 introduces the same sanction for any term which creates a significant imbalance in the rights and obligations of the parties. However, following the further reform in 2018, it only applies to terms which were prepared in advance by one of the parties and could not be individually negotiated.[109]

(6) Courts in other systems might reach a similar result to the *Chronopost* case but would have to use a different route. There was a close parallel in the English doctrine of fundamental breach, but that doctrine is now discredited.[110] Now an English court could reach the same result only by one of two other routes. The first would be to hold that, as a matter of construction, the clause did not apply to the events which had occurred. On the facts of *Chronopost*, that seems unlikely. The second would be to hold the clause to be invalid under Unfair Contract Terms Act 1977, section 2(2), which invalidates clauses used by a business to limit its liability for negligence causing loss of property unless the clause is reasonable.[111] Likewise, a German court would employ the provisions of the BGB (§§ 305ff BGB) dealing with terms in standard conditions.[112] Indeed, the nullity of particular clauses which have not been the subject of individual negotiation, in cases where they create 'a significant imbalance in the parties' rights and obligations', can be compared with the control which used to be exercised through *cause* in French law. There is a major difference between German and French law, however, since the control exercised through *cause* in French law expanded to clauses which had been negotiated, even to those negotiated on an equal footing by the parties. The English Unfair Contract Terms Act 1977, section 2(2), also applies whether or not the clause was negotiated, though the courts are unlikely to hold that a clause that was negotiated is nonetheless unreasonable. However, the limitation of the scope of application of new Article 1171 Cciv by the further reform in 2018 brought French contract law closer to German law.

---

[106] Cass civ (3) 1 June 2005, no. 04-12200, Bull civ III no. 119, RTD civ 2005, 780, annotated by J Mestre and B Fages.

[107] On this provision, see above, p 171, and 21.22 (FR), below, p 848.

[108] For the text of new Arts 1170 and 1171 Cciv, see 11.21 (FR), below, p 390.

[109] On this provision, see below, p 848.

[110] See below, pp 823–26.

[111] See 21.16 (EN), below, p 838.

[112] See 21.15 (DE), below, p 835.

There was indeed, by the end of the twentieth century, a discernible trend in having recourse to the doctrine of *cause* to ensure that obligations and benefits were evenly distributed between the parties.[113] Traditionally, under French law, generally no account was taken of loss arising out of an imbalance in the obligations of the parties arising from a synallagmatic contract.[114] For a long time, case law privileged legal certainty and made a very narrow use of *cause* by demanding an '*absence de cause*'. French judges then started to use the *cause* in situations where the counterpart was useless and of no interest for one of the parties. This has been characterised as the 'subjectivisation of the *cause*'.

A good example of this is the so-called *Video club* case.

Cass civ (1), 3 July 1996[115]   **11.19 (FR)**

The video club

A contract made for a purpose which was known to both parties but which cannot possibly succeed is without cause.

Facts: With a view to setting up a video club at V, Mr and Mrs Pillet hired from DPM, a newly incorporated company, 200 video cassettes for a period of eight months subject to payment of the sum of 40,000 francs excluding taxes. DPM brought an action for payment in the first instance court which set aside the hire agreement on the ground that it was vitiated by a mistake. The cour d'appel preferred the absence of *cause* to mistake as the basis of the contract's nullity. In the words of the appeal court 'the *cause*, that is the determining motive for Mrs Pillet to enter into the contract, was the guaranteed distribution amongst her clientele of cassettes hired from DPM, which could not be achieved in V, a municipality numbering only 1,315 inhabitants'. On the basis of these findings, the cour d'appel held the hire agreement to be null and void for lack of *cause*. The appeal by DPM alleged that the appeal court had confused *cause* and motives without making any finding as to whether they had entered the ambit of the contract.

Held: The contract was set aside for lack of *cause*.

Judgment: THE COURT: *On the two branches of the sole appeal ground*:—Whereas DPM alleges that the court below (Court of Appeal, Grenoble, 17 March 1994) set aside for lack of any *cause* the contract for the setting up of a 'video club' and the hire of video cassettes entered into with Mr and Mrs Pillet; as it did this, it is submitted by finding the *cause*, namely the determining motive for the couple to enter into the contract, to be the guaranteed distribution of cassettes amongst their clientele, and further finding that the operation was doomed to failure in a community of just 1,315 inhabitants; as however, it was pleaded on appeal that in a synallagmatic contract the *cause* of one party's obligation is the obligation entered into by the other party; as applied to this case, the appellants submit, the *cause* of the Pillet couple's obligation was to be found in the making available to them of video cassettes, and determining motives cannot constitute the *cause* of the contract unless they have entered the ambit of the contract, which was not found to be the case by the cour d'appel;

— Whereas however, as the cour d'appel found, the contract was for the hire of video cassettes in order to operate a business; as performance of the contract according to the overall plan intended by the parties was impossible;

---

[113] For examples and for an analogy with competition rules, see Rochfeld (n 101 above) 90.
[114] For the very limited application of the notion of *lésion* in French law, see below, p 629.
[115] Cass civ (1) 3 July 1996, no. 94-14800, Bull civ I no. 286, D 1997, 499, annotated by P Reigne.

— Whereas therefore, the cour d'appel correctly inferred that the contract was unsupported by any *cause* once there was found to be no real consideration passing for the obligation to pay the price for the hire of the cassettes entered into by Mr and Mrs Pillet under an agreement for the setting up of a 'video club';

— Whereas the judgment was therefore sound in law;

— On those grounds the Cour de cassation dismissed the appeal.

Notes

(1) This innovative judgment imported a new idea into the doctrine of *cause*, at the same time quite deliberately declining to be swayed by the arguments drawn from traditional authors which were put forward on appeal. The *cause* of the contract was not merely the supply of the cassettes in consideration of the payment of the hire charge. The hirer knew the use to which the hire of the cassettes was to be put, namely the opening of a video centre which would in turn hire out the cassettes. The *cause* was to be inferred from the overall structure of the contract, including the actual motives of the parties. The Court accepted that it should consider the specific goal pursued by the contracting parties. As a result, it enlarged the control of *cause* to situations where a counter-performance or an interest for each of the contracting parties existed, but the advantages did not correspond to those which were sought. In this case, it proved impossible to achieve the objective pursued, owing to the small size of the community and the inadequate number of foreseeable rentals. The equilibrium sought by the parties was not achievable.

(2) The impact of this case was minimised by some authors who insisted on the fact that the Court had taken into account the overall and unrealistic plan intended by the parties. There was an *ensemble contractuel*: the main contract was the hire of video cassettes entered into with Mr and Mrs Pillet; it was linked to guaranteed distribution of cassettes amongst their customers, which was bound to fail in a community of just 1,315 inhabitants. Would the argument of lack of *cause* apply if there had not been such an overall plan? It should be noted that in a later, very similar case the Court refused to exercise a similar control: a businessman had entered into a contract with a company that hired out videos, intending to add video-rental to his principal activity which he pursued in a community of 160 inhabitants. Not being able to make a success of it, he sought a declaration that the contract was invalid for want of *cause*. The Commercial Chamber of the Cour de cassation[116] rejected this argument on the ground that:

> The cour d'appel accepts that there will be lack of *cause* only if performance of the contract on the business plan intended by the parties was impossible because there was no real counter-performance, and that Mr X …, who bore the burden of proving the case, had only shown facts that were insufficient to prove the alleged impossibility of being able to hire out video cassettes as an adjunct to his other business, when he himself had fixed the targets, as the context of having an established business enabled him to do; and that in these circumstances, the decision of the cour d'appel [that lack of *cause* was not shown] was legally justified …

---

[116] Cass com 27 March 2007, no. 06-10452, RDC 2008, 231, annotated by D Mazeaud.

The original *Video club* judgment paved the way for new cases in which French judges considered whether from the outset it was possible to reach specific objectives of viability. For example, the third Civil Chamber of the Cour de cassation was faced with a contract for the purchase of a 'hotel room' by a husband and wife, which was coupled with their signing up to the terms of a joint venture 'having as its object to share in the fruits and the costs of the hotel restaurant' which would be managed by another company.[117] The Court pronounced the nullity of the sale for absence of *cause*, stating that the counter-performance pursued by the 'purchasers' by means of this 'sale' lay not only in the assurance that their investment would generate a profit, but equally in the assurance and guarantee that they would never have to bear the losses of the hotel, these being borne by the seller by reason of a contract to stand surety. Absence of *cause* was found here as a result of the 'impossibility of realising a profit'.

(3) It is not clear how the other systems would approach a case like this, nor how French judges applying the new Code civil would now deal with similar situations. Article 1143 on duress introduces a new rule in the Code civil which draws inspiration from the UNIDROIT PICC (Article 3.2.7) as well as from the PECL and the DCFR (Article II.–7:207).

Code civil   **11.20 (FR)**

Article 1143. There is also duress where one party exploits the other's state of necessity or dependence on him and obtains an undertaking to which the latter would not have agreed in the absence of such constraint, and gains from it a manifestly excessive advantage.

Notes

(1) Courts could resort to this provision to sanction contracts that are not viable, but only in those cases where one party has forced the other party to enter into the agreement, using the other party's state of necessity or dependence on him.

(2) Conversely, Article 1143 does not apply where the contract has been freely entered into by each party.

In German law it is possible that the contract in the *Video Club* case would be regarded as sufficiently exploitative as to be void under § 138 BGB.[118] In English law it is conceivable that it would be held to be avoidable on the ground of unconscionability. That doctrine has not been applied in a business contract to date, but it has been suggested that it might be when the parties are unequal.[119] In the US the doctrine of unconscionability has been applied to contracts between sophisticated businesses and what are called 'Mom and Pop' outfits.[120] One may also think of Article 4:109 PECL. This allows a party

---

[117] Cass civ (3) 29 March 2006, no. 05-16032, Bull civ III no. 88, RDC 2006, 1072, annotated by D Mazeaud.
[118] See below, p 635.
[119] See *Alec Lobb (Garages) Ltd v Total Oil (Great Britain) Ltd* [1983] 1 WLR 87 (QBD); and below, pp 651 ff.
[120] See EA Farnsworth, *Contracts* (4th edn, New York: Aspen Publishers, 2004) para 4.28.

to avoid the contract or to adapt it where the excessive benefit or unfair advantage which leads to an imbalance in the contractual relationship is the result of an abuse by the other party based on the economic or intellectual dependence of the first party.[121]

In conclusion, the doctrine of *cause* in French law, as rejuvenated before the 2016 reform, showed the increasing interventionism of French courts in relation to contracts. As Judith Rochfeld put it:

> French courts have, over the course of the last twenty years, given back both strength and usefulness to the concept of *cause*. They have renewed the definition of *cause*, its use and its sanction—at least in relation to the control of the existence of *cause*, a control which … is to be distinguished from the control of the legality and the morality of the contract, which is also carried out in French law through the concept of *cause*. In doing so, the French courts have forged an instrument that is useful in the fight for the protection of the interests of each party in a contract, through the defence of the interest that each pursues in exchange for the sacrifice to which he consents. This instrument can be of assistance to anyone, irrespective of status—consumer, business and professional alike. Paradoxically, it would therefore appear that, more than ever before, surrounded by a universe which is unaware of it, French law has marked out a future for *cause*.[122]

It would be wrong to conclude that, by deleting the concept of *cause*, the legislator put an end to this new judicial trend. As was shown by some more recent cases, too far-reaching a recourse to the concept of *cause* is not appropriate as it creates much uncertainty. More clarity, more accessibility and thereby more predictability was necessary. Besides, a wider range of sanctions was equally necessary. For some time, the sanction of absence of *cause* had been absolute nullity. This was justified by the idea that a contract could not exist without a *cause*, one of its essential elements. Before the reform, the evolution of the various uses of the concept of *cause* had already called for new sanctions: mere termination, relative nullity (in order to protect one party) or the notion of *clause réputée non écrite* ('clause deemed not written'), as in the *Chronopost* case. Now that *cause* has in effect been replaced by a number of more specific articles a more nuanced and appropriate system of sanctions is available.

11.3.C THE CONCEPT OF *CAUSE* ABANDONED AND ITS FUNCTIONS REPLACED BY SPECIFIC PROVISIONS IN THE FRENCH REFORM OF CONTRACT

We have seen that some of the European countries (such as the Netherlands) that had used the concept of *cause* in the past have abolished it, and neither the PECL nor the UNIDROIT PICC refer to it. This was a strong argument, in spite of very fierce resistance, not to retain this concept in French law.

The various drafts that led to the 2016 reform clearly reveal that opposite approaches were taken by the various groups which drafted proposals for a reform of the Code civil. The debate was as vivid, if not more so, as the one which long ago opposed 'causalists' to

---

[121] For the text of PECL Art 4:109, see 16.4 (INT), below, p 635.
[122] Rochfeld (n 101 above) 73–74.

'non-causalists' and the legislator was greatly influenced by European and international trends.[123]

The *Avant-projet de réforme du droit des obligations et de la prescription*, drafted under the chairmanship of Professor Pierre Catala, maintained the concept of *cause* in its Article 1124. Although the proposal purported to give it a unitary definition, it could not avoid the divide between the two types of *cause* (objective and subjective *cause*). In contrast, the proposal drafted by the group led by Professor François Terré abandoned *cause*; this option was strongly supported by Terré himself.[124] The July 2008 draft of the Ministry of Justice also abolished the concept of *cause* and, drawing inspiration from Jean Carbonnier's suggestion (see above), replaced it by the concept of 'interest' which was in fact very close to that of *cause*. However, the uncertainty caused by the introduction of this new concept was strongly criticised. Consequently, both concepts (*cause* and 'interest') were abandoned. This, however, does not mean that the courts will no longer be able to control the legality of a contract, nor that they will no longer be able to eradicate an exemption clause or restore some form of contractual equilibrium.

The 2016 reform removed the notion of *cause* from the Code civil. Section 2 of the chapter on the formation of contracts (Chapter II) which is dedicated to the 'Validity of the Contract' begins with Article 1128; this provision makes clear that the *cause* has disappeared:

Code civil	**11.21 (FR)**

Article 1128: The following are necessary for the validity of a contract:
1. the consent of the parties;
2. their capacity to contract;
3. content which is lawful and certain.

Article 1162: A contract cannot derogate from public policy either by its stipulations or by its purpose, whether or not this was known by all the parties. …

Article 1168: In synallagmatic contracts, a lack of equivalence in the acts of performance of the parties is not a ground of nullity of the contract, unless legislation provides otherwise.

Article 1169: An onerous contract is a nullity where, at the moment of its formation, what is agreed in return for the benefit of the person undertaking an obligation is illusory or derisory.

Article 1170: Any contract term which deprives a debtor's essential obligation of its substance is deemed not written.[125]

---

[123] On this debate and on the new provisions of the Code civil, see L Aynès, 'The Content of Contracts: *Prestation, Objet* but No Longer *la Cause*?' in J Cartwright and S Whittaker (eds), *The Code Napoléon Rewritten: French Contract Law after the 2016 Reforms* (Oxford: Hart Publishing, 2017) 137.

[124] F Terré, 'La cause est entendue' JCP 2008, Actualités 609.

[125] cf the discussion of the *Chronopost* cases above, pp 383 ff; according to Aynès (n 123 above), this provision relates more to 'coherence' than 'cause'.

Article 1171: In a standard-form contract, any term which is non-negotiable and determined in advance by one of the parties and which creates a significant imbalance in the rights and obligations of the parties to the contract is deemed not written.

The assessment of significant imbalance must not concern either the main subject-matter of the contract nor to the adequacy of the price in relation to the act of performance.[126]

Note

(1) These provisions (and also Article 1143 quoted above) show that the various uses of the *cause* have been taken into account and even solidified by the legislator. This is further affirmed in the legislative materials: 'the formal abandonment of the notion of *cause*, which has given rise to much debate, will allow France to move closer to the legislation of many foreign countries, while introducing in the law the various functions, including the rebalancing of the contract, which had been assigned to the *cause* by the case-law'.[127]

(2) One might agree with Laurent Aynès that the requirement of a 'certain' content in new Article 1128 Cciv is rather meaningless: 'By definition, unless it is the work of madmen, every contract has a content that is certain! By "certain", do we mean "possible", or "capable of being determined", or "defined"? A regrettable confusion'.[128] However, the term 'content' is commonly used for example by the UNIDROIT PICC and the PECL. It did not occur in the Code civil until 2016 but the word 'object' had similar functions. As was explained in Chapter 9,[129] Article 1108 of the 1804 Code referred to the 'object' (*objet*) as one of the four essential conditions for the validity of a contract: (i) consent; (ii) capacity; (iii) a certain *objet*, forming the subject matter of the undertaking; and (iv) a lawful *cause* (*cause licite*) of the 'obligation'. New Article 1128 Cciv sets out three conditions: consent, capacity and a content which is lawful and certain. The *cause* as a condition of validity of the contract is thus abolished. Besides, the new provision no longer refers to the 'obligation' but to the 'contract'; this emphasis on the contractual relationship rather than an obligation highlights that 'the law has moved from debt to contracts'.[130]

(3) The content must also be 'lawful'. This is further required and explained in new Article 1162 of the Code civil which we will discuss in more detail in the context of illegality.[131]

---

[126] On these provisions, see ch 21 on unfair terms, especially at pp 822 and 848. Resort to the concept of 'economic violence' which may be found in all three projects can also be a useful means of fighting situations of disequilibrium which lead to contractual unfairness. In this respect, see Art 1143, 11.20 (FR), above, p 388.

[127] Report to the President (p 83 n 30 above).

[128] Aynès (n 123 above) 139.

[129] See above, p 293.

[130] Aynès (n 123 above) 138.

[131] See below, p 667.

11.4. GERMAN LAW AND DUTCH LAW

German and Dutch law have no requirement of either consideration or *cause*: they deal with the relevant issues through the concepts of agreement and intention to create legal relations. It is of course unsurprising that consideration, being a product of the common law alone, does not exist in German law. However, the doctrine of *cause*, with its Roman law origins, also plays no role in German law[132] or the systems of law that have been strongly influenced by German law, such as Swiss law and modern Dutch law.

German law directly reviews the immorality or illegality of the transaction in cases where French law used to ask whether the *cause* was immoral or unlawful.[133] However, as has been seen above, German law uses the notion of 'cause' (or *causa*) in a different context: German law attaches great importance to certain acts being abstracted from their underlying *causa*.[134] This includes all acts transferring property. As a result, the act of transfer may be valid although the underlying contract—the 'cause' of the transfer— is not. It is the doctrine of unjustified enrichment which is applied in order to restore equilibrium—although even in this context, the text of the BGB does not refer to the notion of 'cause'.[135]

BGB   **11.22 (DE)**

§ 812: A person who, through an act performed by another person or in any other manner, acquires something at the expense of the latter without legal justification is bound to return it to him. This liability in restitution is also incurred where the legal justification subsequently disappears or the objective pursued by means of the legal transaction does not materialise.

The 'objective pursued' is determined by the content of the transaction. Motives not forming part thereof are not taken into account. Thus, the German doctrine of unjust enrichment deals with issues that used to be classified as a failure of *cause* or a false *cause* under French law. Contracts as such do not have to be supported by a specific cause.

In the Netherlands, the 1992 Civil Code does not mention *cause* as a condition of the validity of a legal transaction: Article 3:33 requires merely that there be an intention to produce legal effects evidenced by a declaration. There is, however, at least a reflection of *cause* in Article 3:40, under which 'a legal transaction which by its content or scope is contrary to public policy or good morals shall be null and void'. This seems to echo the ideas of unlawful object ('content') and *cause* ('scope'). Likewise, the notion of objective *cause* seems to emerge between the lines of Article 6:229: 'A contract entered into

---

[132] For comparative references, see A Rieg, *La rôle de la volonté dans l'acte juridique en droit civil français et allemand* (Paris: LGDJ, 1961) 388; K Zweigert and H Kötz, *Introduction to Comparative Law* (3rd edn, Oxford: Clarendon Press, 1998) 388.

[133] See ch 17.

[134] See above, p 124.

[135] As opposed to French law which uses the notion of *enrichissement sans cause* for unjust(ified) enrichment.

in order to give effect to a legal relationship already existing between the parties may be annulled if that relationship fails to materialise'. Is this perhaps an application of the 'failure of *cause*'?

FURTHER READING

Aynès, L, 'The Content of Contracts: *Prestation, Objet* but No Longer *la Cause?*' in J Cartwright and S Whittaker (eds), *The Code Napoléon Rewritten: French Contract Law after the 2016 Reforms* (Oxford: Hart Publishing, 2017) 137–43.

Bénabent, A, *Les obligations* (16th edn, Paris: LGDJ, 2017) no. 200.

David, R, 'Cause et Consideration' in *Mélanges offerts à Jacques Maury*, vol II: *Droit comparé, Théorie générale du droit et Droit privé* (Paris: Dalloz Sirey, 1961) 111–38.

Deshayes, O, Genicon, T and Laithier, YM, 'La Cause a-t-elle réellement disparu du Droit français des Contrats?' (2017) 13 ERCL 418–30.

Ghestin, J, *Cause de l'engagement et validité du contrat* (Paris: LGDJ, 2006).

Illmer M, 'Contract (Formation)' in J Basedow, K Hopt and R Zimmermann (eds), *Max Planck Encyclopedia of European Private Law*, vol I (Oxford University Press, 2012) 378–83.

Kötz, H, 'Indicia of seriousness' in J Basedow, K Hopt and R Zimmermann (eds), *Max Planck Encyclopedia of European Private Law*, vol I (Oxford University Press, 2012) 863–65.

Malaurie, P, Aynès, L and Stoffel-Munck, P, *Droit des obligations* (9th edn, Paris: LGDJ, 2017) nos. 596–608.

Moore, B, 'International Perspectives on the French Reform: The Franco-Quebecois Paradox of the Cause' (2017) 6 Montesquieu Law Review 171–74.

Rochfeld, J, 'A Future for la *cause*? Observations of a French Jurist' in J Cartwright, S Vogenauer and S Whittaker (eds), *Reforming the French Law of Obligations: Comparative Reflections on the Avant-projet de reforme du droit des obligations et de la prescription* (Oxford: Hart Publishing, 2009) 73–100.

Rochfeld, J, 'The Abolition of the Cause: a Clean Slate and New Bases for Court Intervention (Standard-Form Contracts, Dependence, Error)?' (2017) 6 Montesquieu Law Review 55–67.

Sefton-Green, R, '*La cause* or the Length of the French Judiciary's Foot' in J Cartwright, S Vogenauer, and S Whittaker (eds), *Reforming the French Law of Obligations: Comparative Reflections on the Avant-projet de reforme du droit des obligations et de la prescription* (Oxford: Hart Publishing, 2009) 101–20.

CHAPTER 12
FORMAL REQUIREMENTS

12.1 INTRODUCTION

The doctrinal discussion is ancient: is a bare agreement (*nudum pactum*) sufficient to create a contract or must the parties' agreement be embodied in a special form?

For the consensualists, concurring intentions are sufficient. That is a consequence of the autonomy of the will, in contrast to the requirements of Roman law which refused to accord any value to a bare agreement. Formalism occurs where intent is not sufficient and the concurring intentions are required to take a specific form. Formalism may be intended to give effect to an act which, according to the general rules, would have no legal value: this is the function of a deed in English law, and of certain solemn acts in other legal systems; alternatively, it may involve an additional formality required in certain specific circumstances in order to give effect to an act which would be valid in other circumstances. This is the position in the case of certain consumer contracts, which would be valid under the ordinary law but which, being consumer contracts,[1] need in addition to comply with formal requirements.

Formalism may intervene at several stages. It may apply to the validity of the contract: *ad validitatem*. That is direct formalism. It may apply only to proof of the contract (*ad probationem*): the contract can be proved only in accordance with certain formal requirements, as opposed to a system in which there is freedom of proof. The contract is valid but, failing observance of the rules, it cannot be proved, save in exceptional circumstances. Or lack of form may render a contract unenforceable. In that case, if the contract is performed voluntarily, the contract may have the same effects as if it had been enforceable. There are also enabling formal requirements: to be effective the contract must receive the authorisation (*homologation*) of an administrative or judicial authority.

---

[1] See above, ch 7.3.

Finally, there are the formalities concerning publication and notification of the contract to third parties or the public at large—typically when the contact purports to confer a security right on one of the parties; the security right is often not fully effective unless it has been registered. Failure to observe those formalities in general means that the contract cannot be enforced as against third parties. In the case of 'real' contracts (*contrats réels*), the handing over of the item may also be regarded as a necessary formality for the validity of the contract. But this category is known to be controversial.[2]

The discussion will be confined to the formalities, properly so-called, which are required *ad validitatem*, or which are required for the contract to be enforceable. However, account must also be taken of the rules of evidence which are frequently difficult to distinguish from formal requirements in systems of law which have rules on proof laid down by law.

In the countries studied, the prevailing principle is that of consensualism; but formalism, even if it appears only exceptionally, occupies an important place, particularly in consumer law. The respective scope of consensualism and formalism may also vary according to the area of law in question. Thus, formal requirements *ad validitatem* or concerning public registration are normally laid down for risky or complex transactions, such as gifts or real estate transactions. The reciprocal advantages of both systems are much discussed. Formalism as a general rule precludes consent being given lightly and acts as a curb on disputes as to the existence and content of the contract. It also enables proof to be established in advance. For these reasons, formalism is often employed in the context of consumer contracts, for example consumer credit contracts, where not only may writing be required but legislation often lays down the contract's content and even the appearance of certain clauses.[3] Yet formalism is cumbersome and costly, and it may favour a party in bad faith, who may claim that a contract cannot be enforced against him on the pretext that there has been an error of form.

It would be useful to organise a discussion around the two opposing viewpoints set out below, both canvassed by *Jhering*.

50. Consensualism prevents "an honest man who is ignorant of affairs from being at the mercy of a wily and unscrupulous adversary, for the person who knows how to exploit formal requirements can make a noose out of them for the inexperienced person." ...

A sworn enemy of arbitrariness, formality is the twin sister of freedom. In fact, it serves as a counterweight to the tendency of liberty to degenerate into licence. It leads freedom on to a sure path where it can neither become dispersed nor go astray. It fortifies it within and protects it without. The fixed forms are discipline and order, consequently, freedom itself is a bulwark against external attacks. They yield but do not bend. Any people who has truly practised the cult of liberty has instinctively felt the value of formalism and known that in its formalities it possessed not something purely external but the bulwark of its liberty.[4]

---

[2] See above, ch 7.3.B.

[3] H-W Micklitz, J Stuyck and E Terryn, *Ius Commune Casebooks on the Common Law of Europe: Consumer Law* (Oxford: Hart Publishing, 2010) 185–88.

[4] R von Jhering, *Geist des römischen Rechts* (Leipzig: Breitkopf & Härtel, 1852–65) ch 50.

The principle of consensualism appears to be alive and kicking. It is reflected in the Principles of European Contract Law (PECL).

Principles of European Contract Law   **12.1 (INT)**

Article 2:101: Conditions for the Conclusion of a Contract
(1) A contract is concluded if:
(a) the parties intend to be legally bound, and
(b) they reach a sufficient agreement without any further requirement.
(2) A contract need not be concluded or evidenced in writing nor is it subject to any other requirement as to form. The contract may be proved by any means, including witnesses.

The PECL lay down only rules of general contract law, and this may be the reason why they contain no formal requirements. By contrast, the Draft Common Frame of Reference (DCFR) deals also with specific contracts and does lay down a few formal requirements. Most of them apply only to consumer contracts, however. Even the rules on guarantees (personal security) require form only when the guarantor is a consumer and the creditor is neither another consumer nor a legal entity over which the consumer has substantial influence (so that a director who gives a guarantee to a company he controls does not receive protection).[5]

This is not the place for a detailed study of the rules as to form and proof. Apart from a general presentation, attention will be paid to practical aspects and some examples will be given. In particular we will consider the rules relating to the form which a contract of suretyship (guarantee) must take in the three systems of law studied. In these systems suretyship is regarded as a risky transaction and formal requirements are laid down in order to protect persons against obligations entered into without due premeditation. But, in each system of law, the measures laid down and the sanctions are different, which makes it difficult to compare them, even if such measures all pursue the same objectives. The question is merely as to their respective effectiveness.

12.2 GERMAN LAW: MODERATE FORMALISM, FREEDOM AS TO PROOF

12.2.A GENERAL RULES

German law is the least stringent of the three systems of law studied. § 125 of the Bürgerliches Gesetzbuch (BGB) provides that legal acts which fail to comply with the formal requirements laid down by law are null and void. However, those formal requirements are rarely encountered. The principle is that of *Formfreiheit*. Also there are no rules governing the form which evidence must take for purposes of proof.

---

[5] See DCFR Arts IVG-4:101 and 4:104.

Evidence is assessed freely by the judge (*freie Beweiswürdigung*) under § 286 ZPO (Code of Civil Procedure). The formal requirement may be for a signed document, such as the contract of guarantee: § 766 BGB, discussed below, or consumer credit transactions (§ 492 BGB). Certain contracts require notarisation (*notarielle Beurkundung*): transfer of assets, marriage contracts, certain leases of real estate and gifts. Thus acquisition or transfers of real estate require notarisation under § 311b BGB (replacing former § 313 BGB; see 12.2(DE)). The role of the notary, the effectiveness of the act, and requirements as to form are governed by § 415 ZPO and by the Beurkundungsgesetz (Act on authentification of 28 August 1969). Finally, there is a public legalisation requirement (*öffentliche Beglaubigung*) in § 129 BGB which provides for the notarial authentication of a person's signature. It is necessary where a declaration has to be entered in a public register—land registry, or the registers of marriages, companies or business names.

The penalty attendant upon non-compliance with formal requirements is the nullity of the deed, which may be pronounced by the court even on its own motion (ie although the point has not been raised by either party).

12.2.B APPLICATIONS

It will be noted first and foremost that the courts tend to apply the legal requirements flexibly.

BGH, 7 May 1971[6]   **12.2 (DE)**

Notary left to complete contract

Facts: The parties appeared before a notary in order to enter into a sales contract relating to two pieces of real estate. The notarial deed dated 23 February 1966 was duly authenticated. The sales price amounted to DM 152,000. Payment was to be made partly by the constitution of three mortgages on the properties and partly in cash.

Since the parties were unaware of the amount of the liability secured under the mortgages, they authorised the notary to determine the amount with the creditors, and to complete the authenticated deed accordingly. After deductions, the balance to be paid, as inserted by the notary, amounted to DM 30,483.67. That additional clause was not read out to the parties.

The claimant contested that estimate and sought payment of DM 36,350. The defendants contended that the balance to be paid was DM 7,483.67. They further considered that they were not bound to pay that sum since there was no agreement on the price. Even if there had been agreement, the contract would be null and void for error or fraud.

The claimant (vendor) was unsuccessful. The regional court (LG) held that the contract was voidable for error. The higher regional court (OLG) held that the contract was voidable on the ground that it was vitiated by formal errors (former § 313; § 125 BGB). The Federal Supreme Court was to adopt the latter solution.

Judgment:

Reasoning

... The sales contract required as a matter of form the authentication provided for in [former] § 313 relating to real estate. The contract was not effectively authenticated on several grounds.

[6] BGHZ 56, 159.

The contract was not read out aloud, although that requirement also applied to the stipulations concerning the amount of the mortgage liability and the cash sum payable.

Whilst the notary was able to assess the amount of the mortgage liability and inform the parties thereof, he could not complete the contract without again complying with the requirements as to form.

However, it is correct that the additions made by the notary altered neither the vendor's obligation to give possession nor the purchasers' obligation to pay the purchase price. But the view to be taken must be that the question as to the method of financing is significant. That is why the claimant cannot plead that the additions made by the notary did not have to comply with the formal requirements under [former] § 313 on the ground that they did not give rise to new legal obligations.

Held: The view to be taken is that formal requirements are intended to afford evidence of the contractual obligations assumed. The contract entered into on 23 February 1966 before the notary does not perform this function, as is borne out by the dispute which has arisen over the determination of the sales price.

Notes

(1) Former § 313 BGB has been replaced by § 311b(1), which provides:

A contract by which one party agrees to transfer or acquire ownership of a plot of land must be recorded by a notary. A contract not entered into in this form becomes valid with all its contents if a declaration of conveyance and registration in the Land Register are effected.

(2) The Court considers that the additions to the contract made by the notary are not necessarily subject to the requirement of form if they do not create new obligations. However, in this case the additions were necessary for determining the price, that is to say for providing proof of the content of the contract. The judicial technique for saving the contract could not operate in this case. But there are other ways, notably through reference to good faith.

BGH, 18 October 1974[7]   **12.3 (DE)**

Contract never put in writing

It may be contrary to good faith to rely on a formal defence, but this depends on the party's conduct.

Facts: The claimant was the daughter of the defendants. Together with her husband she sought to enforce an oral contract entered into in 1968 under which she acquired title with her husband to a dwelling house, and her three sons jointly acquired title to another lodging in the defendants' house, for a total sum of about DM 150,000. She also sought damages.

Held: Following delivery by the Landgericht of a judgment in part finding in the claimant's favour, the Oberlandesgericht made an order against the defendant, based on the claimant's final ancillary claims and the defendant's consent to pay the sum of DM 121,520 plus interest, together with one half of the increase in the value of the two apartments between 1968 and 1972. However, it dismissed the main claims, which sought an order (1) for the partition of the property, the preparation of a plan for the dividing up of the house, the issue of a declaration of partition and guaranteed access to the land, and (2) acceptance of the purchase offers made

[7] WM 1974, 1224.

by the claimant and her three sons, together with a declaration that the defendant was obliged to transfer ownership of the two apartments in exchange for a payment of DM 2,900 (the latter claim being dismissed as inadmissible), alternatively for payment of the sum of DM 216,720, half of which was to be held by the claimant 'in her own hands' and one sixth by each of her three sons. The claimant's appeal on a point of law was dismissed.

Judgment: The appeal court dismissed the claim as ill founded because the formal requirements (authentication) laid down in the case of real estate transactions had not been met. The appeal on a point of law cannot be upheld. The agreement in question was required to be in notarised form (§ 4(3) Wohnugseigentumsgesetz; [former] § 313, 1 BGB). It was not. This defect was not cured by the transfer of property and by registration at the land registry ([former] § 313(2) BGB). Consequently, the agreement was null and void (§ 125 BGB).

However, the question is whether nullity on the ground of a formal defect (§ 125) contravenes the requirements of good faith (§ 242 BGB). As the Higher Regional Court (OLG) held, the reply must be in the negative.

It is settled case-law that an agreement for the sale of realty which is vitiated by a formal defect must be deemed to be valid in certain very specific cases, in particular where the consequences of nullity are incompatible with the requirements of good faith.

For such exceptions to be admitted strict conditions must be imposed in the interests of legal certainty. The mere fact that nullity harshly affects one of the parties does not suffice.

In the present case the Higher Regional Court (OLG) held that the financial consequences were harsh but not intolerable. From the point of view of good faith the present conduct of the defendants did not conflict with their past conduct. It was not established that the defendants left the claimants under a misapprehension and that before 1971 they were not prepared to comply with their obligations and that, finally, they provoked the dispute in 1971 in order to cause the contract to disappear.

In order to constitute a breach of the requirements of good faith it is not sufficient either that the defendants were from the start keen on the claimants' investing in the property.

The interpretation by the lower courts is free of any error in law, contrary to what was asserted in the appeal. The court made an overall assessment (§ 286 ZPO) and did not have regard only to the financial consequences but also envisaged the problem of the unlawful exercise of rights (abuse of rights) and, in particular, the contradiction between the defendants' past and current conduct. As regards the need for the contract to be authenticated, both parties were in error and therefore there was nothing significant which could be secured by the claimant.

The claim for damages

The claim was dismissed by the Higher Regional Court (OLG) because in such circumstances there must be a fault committed by the defendant. However, that condition is not satisfied in the present case. There cannot be an indemnity based on the principle of a breach of trust which presupposes a fault on the part of one of the parties during the negotiations which frustrates the expectations of the other party to the contract by failure to conclude a contract whose coming into being was expected and where, in reliance thereon, that party incurred expenditure. The case-law may be applied to the negotiation of contracts governed by the provisions as to form contained in [former] § 313 BGB.

The breaking off of contractual negotiations by one of the parties to the contract without there being any such initial fault may establish liability where the party responsible for breaking off the negotiations knew that the other party, in contemplation of the creation of the contract, had incurred considerable expenditure.

In its decision of 6 February 1969 the Second Civil Chamber of the BGH took the view that, by analogy with the case of rescission for mistake provided for in § 122, it was possible to obtain damages for refusal to enter into a projected contract, even where there was no initial fault, where there was a consensus between the parties as to the content of the future contract and the party refusing to proceed rejected the conclusion of the contract for no valid reason, although he had previously conducted himself in such a way as to lead the other party legitimately to expect that the contract would come into being, and thus to incur financial burdens. What must be borne in mind is the concept of liability for present or future repercussions.

However, according to the case-law of the BGH, there can be no such liability if there is no initial liability founded solely on a refusal at the outset to enter into the contract, where the law lays down a requirement as to the form to be taken by the contract, such as the requirement of authentication under [former] § 313 BGB, and that formal requirement is not met. In such a situation the precedents on rescission for mistake cannot be applied by analogy.

In fact, the purpose of the protection provided for by the rules as to formal requirements is to prevent any obligation from arising between the parties in connection with the actual subject matter of the contract, where the rules as to the formal requirements have not been observed. In the present case, as was held at first instance, no liability on the part of the defendants has been established.

Note

Here again is an illustration of good faith stepping in to mitigate the rigours of formalism. In the present case neither good faith nor reliance would avail because the German courts do not wish to compromise the security of transactions governed by rules as to formal requirements. The contract is void owing to the lack of formal authentication and the invalidity is not cured under former § 313 BGB. The courts will allow invalidity to stand against good faith only in certain specified cases: excessive financial hardship (not mere difficulties), and the past and current conduct of the party relying on nullity. It is to be noted that the concept of abuse of law (*abus de droit*) is considered in Germany more as a feature of bad faith than, as it is in France, a self-standing plea.

As regards the claim for damages, it is based on the detrimental reliance placed by the purchaser on the vendor's conduct. But, as far as the courts are concerned, the plea can succeed only if there was an initial fault by the vendor, which was not the case here. In other situations the courts have allowed good faith to intervene.

BGH, 21 April 1972[8]   **12.4 (DE)**

Defective house

It is contrary to good faith to rely on a formal defence if this would cause extreme hardship to the other party.

Facts: On 21 October 1963 the claimant (who was seeking to acquire a private residence) entered into negotiations with a co-operative society with a view to concluding a written sale/purchase contract with an option.

[8] NJW 1972, 1189.

The contract concerned the construction of a semi-detached house and the acquisition of two shares in the defendant co-operative society. The claimant paid the purchase price for the two shares (DM 1,000) and, in relation to the price of the house, which was provisionally estimated to amount to DM 78,500, the sum of DM 77,000 together with contributions in kind which he considered to be worth DM 2,000 and which the defendant considered to be worth DM 885.50. The claimant refused to pay the further sum of DM 7,047.58 which—in the light of the final construction cost of DM 83,900—was demanded by the defendant, pending the repair of certain defects found in the house. The claimant occupied the house from August 1965 onwards.

Held: The Landgericht and the Oberlandesgericht ordered the defendant to take the requisite formal steps to transfer ownership. The defendant appealed on a point of law.

Judgment: … Whilst the contract must be regarded, in accordance with § 313 [now § 311b(1)] BGB, as needing to be in a notarial form, and whilst, in the absence of compliance with that formal requirement, it must in principle be regarded as null and void (§ 125 BGB), nevertheless, such a result would be intolerably harsh as regards the claimant. Consequently, in the present case, the plea of nullity must, exceptionally, be rejected in favour of the need for the exercise of good faith ('*Treu und Glauben*', § 242 BGB). It is, however, settled case-law that such an exception may be made only in extraordinary cases and that the prospective purchaser of a private residence who, despite the absence of a contract executed before a notary, has nevertheless paid the purchase price and has lived in the house for a very long time is in principle entitled to claim only damages. … Be that as it may, such an exception, based as it is on the unacceptable nature of the situation, has previously been recognised in decided cases, since it involves criteria relating to the very existence of the party to the contract.

…

In the present case, the claimant, aged 63, was a small-scale craftsman (whereas the defendant was a lawyer). If he had not been totally sure of becoming the owner of the property, he would never have invested so much money in that house. The claimant bought that house with a view to spending the rest of his days in it. He used all his savings (approximately DM 80,000) in order to acquire that property and paid a very large proportion of the purchase price in cash, the balance being disputed in view of the defects in the house. The claimant trusted in the validity of the contract, which contained a clause by which the parties declared their wish to dispense with the need for it to be in notarial form.

If the formal requirements laid down in § 313 [now § 311b(1)] BGB were applied to the present case, the plaintiff would be obliged to vacate the building and to look for a new home. This would seriously prejudice his material circumstances. It follows that, in the light of the duty to act in good faith laid down by § 242 BGB, such obligations are intolerably harsh.

Note

There are two aspects here: the situation of the applicant buyer, which is particularly worthy of note, and 'reliance'. But, in contrast to earlier decisions, there is a lack of surefootedness in the choice and application of rules. Also worthy of note is the declared invalidity of the clause waiving the right to notarisation.

However, it is important to highlight the efforts made by the German courts to find a happy medium between the dictates of good faith and observance of the purpose of the rules as to formal requirements.

12.2.C FORMAL REQUIREMENTS GOVERNING SURETYSHIP

BGB **12.5 (DE)**

§ 766: Written form of the declaration of suretyship
For the contract of suretyship to be valid, the declaration of suretyship must be issued in writing. The declaration of suretyship may not be made in electronic form. If the surety discharges the main obligation, the defect of form is remedied.

Note

These formalities are not required in commercial transactions (§ 350 Handelsgesetzbuch (HGB)).

BGH, 28 January 1993[9] **12.6 (DE)**

Jeans

Facts: The claimant, a company incorporated according to English law whose registered office is situated in Gibraltar, entered into an agreement signed under hand with R, a textile company in Bavaria, for the supply of 3,000 pairs of jeans. The contract stipulated in particular that:

(11) R was obliged to pay DM 84,000 for the supply of the jeans, such sum to be payable within 60 days of the invoice date. ...

(13) The defendant acted as surety.

On 28 July 1989 the notary, Dr H, of B, authenticated the declaration made by the defendant, as director and sole manager of the company, by which the latter agreed to stand surety for the debt of DM 84,000. Subsequently, on 31 July 1989, he sent that declaration, with the defendant's consent, by fax to his client's address in Malaga. On 1 August 1989 the claimant's representatives wrote to R Co on the claimant's headed writing paper, accepting the order and the suretyship. Thereafter, 2,813 pairs of jeans were sent by the defendant; the invoices sent, totalling DM 78,764, were not paid by R Co.

The claimant relied on the authenticated declaration of 28 July 1989 and brought an action for payment against the surety in the sum of DM 79,551 (the amount of the invoice plus 1% interest).

Held: The claim was upheld by the lower courts. On appeal, the decision of those courts was set aside and the case was referred back for further determination.

Judgment:
1—German law was applicable.
2—Under German law, there was no valid contract of suretyship between the parties.
Under § 766(1) BGB, a suretyship must be accepted in writing. In the present case, the criteria laid down by § 350 HGB, according to which a contract of suretyship may be created in the absence of compliance with the formal requirements of § 766(1) BGB where it constitutes a commercial act on the part of the guarantor, were not fulfilled, despite the fact that the defendant was the sole manager of the company. The conditions prescribed by § 766(1) BGB were not met. The defendant had indeed had his declaration of suretyship

---

[9] NJW 1993, 1126.

authenticated by the notary, and had signed it himself; the declaration therefore fulfilled the formal requirements laid down by § 126(1) and (3) BGB. However, no formal delivery of the declaration had taken place. A declaration of suretyship is not formally delivered merely by reason of the deed having been signed. In order for it to be formally delivered, the deed had to be physically handed over to the creditor in such a way as to be held by the latter, even if only temporarily. That was not the position in this case.

(a) The transmission of the contents of the deed by fax could not be regarded as constituting formal delivery, in writing, of the declaration of suretyship.

According to § 126(1) BGB, the requirement of written form provided for by law is complied with only where the deed has been signed in his own hand by the person issuing it or initialled by him, such initialling being authenticated by the notary. A fax does not contain a holograph signature. Only the original bears such a signature, and that remains in the hands of the sender. Nor would it correspond to the objective of § 766(1) BGB to regard the fax transmission of a declaration of suretyship as constituting formal delivery in writing. The rationale for the formal requirement is to be found in the need to protect the guarantor, who must act with the greatest prudence and who must be protected against the consequences of any declaration made without sufficient forethought ... That objective precludes the application of a line of case-law which has developed with a view to making it possible to meet the time-limits for the commencement of proceedings by using modern telecommunications. ...

(b) The Oberlandesgericht took the view that case-law and academic authors had accepted that the transmission of a copy with the guarantor's knowledge and consent could be enough to constitute valid delivery of the contract of suretyship. It considered that, since the transmission of the wording of the deed by fax is equivalent to a copy, and since the notary had faxed the deed to the claimant with the defendant's consent, the latter had validly handed over his declaration. That argument cannot be accepted ... He (the defendant) had simply requested the notary to send the claimant a fax of the deed; he had not authorised him to send the claimant an official copy of the deed or to act in any other way on his behalf. In those circumstances, the requirements of § 766(1) BGB were not met.

Note

The BGH is showing itself to be demanding here in refusing to accept substitute formalities: a facsimile is not the same as a written document and authentication by a notary cannot cure the lack of signature by the surety.

This rigour may be contrasted with the solutions adopted by French and English law.[10]

German law remains attached to consensualism. It lays down certain obligations as to form which always go to validity, owing to the rule of unrestricted production of evidence. Particularly worthy of note are the efforts by the courts, aided by the concepts of good faith and reliance, to limit the unjust consequences of a strict application of the rule of nullity on the ground of a formal defect.

---

[10] See below, pp 407 and 413–19.

12.3 ENGLISH LAW: LIMITED FORMALISM; RULE OF ALMOST UNRESTRICTED PRODUCTION OF EVIDENCE

12.3.A GENERAL SURVEY

Formal requirements play a somewhat different role in English law. At common law they do not appear as an exception to the principle—unwritten—of consensualism but are often considered in relation to the doctrine of consideration.

According to McKendrick,[11] consideration and formal requirements are rules identifying types of agreement which must be treated as enforceable contracts. To that extent, form and substance are confounded. Proof of that fact is that a form, namely a deed, can replace the requirement of consideration. Thus, one may effect by deed transactions which would otherwise be unenforcable owing to a lack of consideration, eg gifts, unilateral undertakings and options.

12.3.B DEEDS

At common law a deed had to be 'sealed'. Traditionally this required a wax wafer to be attached to the document, but the requirement came to be satisfied by a mere printed mark indicating that the document should be considered to be sealed—eg the printed letters 'LS' (*locus sigilli*) would suffice. Nowadays it is an enactment of 1989 which regulates deeds.

Law of Property (Miscellaneous Provisions) Act 1989   **12.7 (EN)**

Section 1: Deeds and their exception

(1) Any rule of law which

(a) restricts the substances on which a deed may be written;

(b) requires a seal for the valid execution of an instrument as a deed by an individual; or

(c) requires authority by one person to another to deliver an instrument as a deed on his behalf to be given by deed,

is abolished.

(2) An instrument shall not be a deed unless

(a) it makes it clear on its face that it is intended to be a deed by the person making it or, as the case may be, by the parties to it (whether by describing itself as a deed or expressing itself to be executed or signed as a deed or otherwise); and

(b) it is validly executed as a deed by that person or, as the case may be, one or more of those parties.

---

[11] E McKendrick, *Contract Law* (12th edn, Basingstoke: Palgrave Macmillan, 2017) 66.

(3) An instrument is validly executed as a deed by an individual if, and only if

(a) it is signed

(i) by him in the presence of a witness who attests the signature; or

(ii) at his direction and in his presence and the presence of two witnesses who each attest the signature; and

(b) it is delivered as a deed by him or a person authorised to do so on this behalf.

(4) In subsection (2) and (3) above 'sign', in relation to an instrument, includes making one's mark on the instruments and 'signature' is to be construed accordingly.

...

(11) Nothing in this section applies in relation to instruments delivered as deeds before this section comes into force.

12.3.C REQUIREMENTS OF WRITING AND SIGNATURE

Even where there is consideration and thus no need for a deed, English law sometimes requires the contract to be reduced to writing: these are cases of real estate transactions[12] and certain consumer credit transactions.

12.3.C.1 CONSUMER CREDIT CONTRACTS

The Consumer Credit Act 1974, section 60 gives the relevant government minister power to make regulations as to the form that consumer credit agreements must take, and detailed regulations have been made. Section 61 imposes further requirements as to how the contract is to be executed, and section 65 provides that unless the agreement is properly executed (including being in the correct form) it is unenforceable except with the consent of a court.[13] We shall see that contracts of guarantee are subject to a different and older statute, which merely requires written evidence signed by the guarantor.

12.3.C.2 CONTRACTS FOR INTERESTS IN LAND

The formalities for land contracts are quite complex and date back to the Statute of Frauds 1677, which has been many times amended and now applies only to contracts of guarantee. The courts have sometimes developed ways to mitigate the rigour of this formalism.

The rationale of the original Statute of Frauds 1677 was to require written form for purposes of proof. In its original version, the Act used to provide:

Statute of Frauds 1677   **12.8 (EN)**

Section 4: No action shall be brought whereby to charge any executor or administrator upon any special promise to answer damages out of his own estate; or whereby to charge

---

[12] See below, p 407.

[13] For details, see *Chitty on Contracts*, 33rd edn by H Beale (gen ed) (London: Sweet & Maxwell/Thomson Reuters, 2018) paras 39-080 ff. Until amendments to the 1974 Act were made by the Consumer Credit Act 2006, an agreement that was not properly executed could not be enforced at all. See *Chitty* para 38-094.

the defendant upon any special promise to answer for the debt, default or miscarriage of another person; or to charge any person upon any agreement made upon consideration of marriage; or upon any contract or sale of lands, tenements or hereditaments, or any interest in or concerning them; or upon any agreement that is not to be performed within the space of one year from the making thereof; unless the agreement upon which such action shall be brought, or some memorandum or note thereof, shall be in writing and signed by the party to be charged therewith or some other person thereunto by him lawfully authorised.

All of section 4 has been repealed except the suretyship provision ('to charge the defendant upon any special promise to answer for the debt, default or miscarriage of another person'). A requirement concerning sales of goods of £10 and upwards (Statute of Frauds 1677, section 17, later replaced by Sale of Goods Act 1893, section 4) has also been abolished.

Until 1989, contracts for the sale or disposition of land, under the Law of Property Act 1925, section 40—a direct descendant of the Statute of Frauds—had to be evidenced in a writing signed by the party against whom the contract was to be enforced. As we will see in more detail later, The Law Reform (Miscellaneous Provisions) Act 1989, section 2, now requires such contracts to be in writing signed by both parties.

When the Law of Property Act 1925, section 40 or its predecessors were still in force, there were—needless to say—many cases in which the parties had not satisfied the requirements of the section but nonetheless had acted as if there were a binding contract, for example by the purchaser paying the price and being given possession of the land. A doctrine known as the doctrine of part-performance was used by the courts to mitigate the effects of the statute: see the speech of Lord Hoffmann in the next case and also *Wakeham v Mackenzie*.[14] The principle was that where one party has done acts in part performance of his own obligations under a contract which should have been evidenced in writing, then, even though there be no memorandum of the contract, equity would admit a decree of specific performance of the oral contract if the acts of part performance be such as to justify the admission of oral evidence of the agreement.

Under the 1989 Act this doctrine no longer applies. The Law Commission, on whose recommendations the 1989 Act is based, expected that the courts would deal with cases where the requirements of the 1989 Act would cause hardship, and which previously would have fallen under the doctrine of part performance, by using promissory estoppel.[15] However, while section 2(5) of the Act expressly states that it does not affect 'the creation or operation of resulting, implied or constructive trusts', it makes no exception for proprietary estoppels, and dicta by one judge in the House of Lords suggest that this doctrine cannot be relied on to cure a failure to comply with the Act's requirements.[16] This has left the law in some uncertainty.

One effect of the changes made in 1989 in relation to contracts for the sale of land is that all the terms of the contract must be in writing. If a party wishes to enforce some

---

[14] [1968] 1 WLR 1273 (ChD).

[15] See The Law Commission, *Transfer of Land: Formalities for Contracts for Sale etc. of Land*, Law Com No 164 (London: Her Majesty's Stationery Office, 1987) para 5.5. For proprietary estoppel, see above, pp 350, 371–74.

[16] *Cobbe v Yeomans Row Management Ltd* [2008] UKHL 55, [2008] 1 WLR 1752 [29]. See 13.19 (EN) below, p 446. For a discussion of the cases on whether proprietary estoppel can be used when s 2 of the Act has not been complied with, see *Chitty* (n 13 above) paras 5-039 ff.

undertaking by the other which was not included in the writing, he may find himself in a dilemma. It would seem that either he cannot say that the undertaking was part of the contract, so he cannot enforce it; or, if he proves that it was part of the contract, then the contract is no longer wholly in writing as required by the statute and thus the contract is wholly unenforceable! In fact the courts have mitigated this harsh result in two ways. First, they are sometimes prepared to accept that there was a second agreement between the parties, the contract for the sale of land and a so-called collateral contract containing the other undertaking—eg *De Lassalle v Guildford*[17]—or, in cases in which the term was omitted from the writing by mistake, they may order that the document be rectified[18] to bring it into line with what the parties intended. Whether giving rectification is really consistent with the purpose of the statute in requiring all the terms to be in writing might seem questionable, were it not that the statute specifically allows for it (section 2(4)).[19]

12.3.C.3 CONTRACTS OF SURETYSHIP

Statute of Frauds 1677

12.9 (EN)

4. Noe Action shall be brought ... whereby to charge the Defendant upon any speciall promise to answere for the debt default or miscarriages of another person ... unlesse the Agreement upon which such Action shall be brought or some Memorandum or Note thereof shall be in Writeing and signed by the partie to be charged therewith or some other person thereunto by him lawfully authorized.

Notes

(1) This is all that remains of the original section quoted in full earlier. It is quoted in the old-fashioned version provided by the government's statute law database.[20]

(2) All that the Act requires is that there be some written evidence of the guarantee, signed by the guarantor. It is not necessary that the guarantee be given in writing at the time—a later acknowledgement that it was given, eg in a letter, will suffice. Compare the current requirements for contracts for the sale of land discussed earlier.

Would it be possible to use the doctrine of part performance or estoppel in the case of a guarantee that was not in writing?

House of Lords

12.10 (EN)

Actionstrength Limited v International Glass Engineering InGlEn SpA[21]

A promise of a guarantee which is not evidenced in writing signed by the guarantor is not rendered enforceable merely because the promisee has acted in reliance on the promise.

Facts: See the speech of Lord Hoffmann.

---

[17] [1901] 2 KB 215.
[18] See below, p 503.
[19] See the discussion in *Chitty* (n 13 above) para 5-034.
[20] This is a useful free resource: see www.statutelaw.gov.uk/.
[21] [2003] UKHL 17, [2003] 2 AC 541.

Held: Any promise of guarantee that had been made was not enforceable as it was not in writing.

Judgment: LORD HOFFMAN

13 My Lords, the appellant ('Actionstrength') was a labour-only subcontractor providing services to the main contractor ('Inglen') in connection with the construction of a float glass factory in East Yorkshire for the respondent ('St-Gobain'). Action-strength has obtained a default judgment against Inglen for about £1.3m but Inglen is insolvent and there is unlikely to be a dividend. In these proceedings, Action-strength sues St-Gobain on an alleged oral guarantee of Inglen's liability. It says that the guarantee was given on behalf of St-Gobain by a Mr Watkinson on 11 February 2000, when Inglen owed Actionstrength about £197,000. Actionstrength was threatening that unless it was paid, it would withdraw its labour from the site. It alleges that to avoid this happening, Mr Watkinson promised that if he could not persuade Inglen to meet its obligations, St-Gobain would itself pay Actionstrength out of money withheld from what was due to Inglen under the main contract. Relying on this promise, Actionstrength went on providing labour to Inglen on credit for about another month until the indebtedness reached £1.3m.

14 St-Gobain, on the other hand, has a very different version of events. It agrees that Actionstrength was claiming to be unpaid and threatening to withdraw its labour and disrupt the contract in other ways. But it says that it told Actionstrength that this would be counter-productive. It said it had paid Inglen enough to enable it to meet its obligations to Actionstrength and offered to help try to resolve any dispute between Actionstrength and Inglen. That was enough to persuade Actionstrength to continue to perform the subcontract. But St-Gobain says that it certainly did not promise to pay Inglen's debts. On the contrary, it had made it clear that it would not make a direct payment to a subcontractor.

15 This is a fairly common dispute over who said what; in the ordinary way it would have been resolved by a judge hearing the witnesses and deciding which of them he believed. But St-Gobain says that a hearing is unnecessary because, even if Action-strength's version were to be accepted, the promise would be unenforceable by virtue of section 4 of the Statute of Frauds 1677: 'no action shall be brought ... whereby to charge the defendant upon any special promise to answer for the debt, default or miscarriages of another person ... unless the agreement upon which such action shall be brought, or some memorandum or note thereof, shall be in writing, and signed by the party to be charged therewith, or some other person thereunto by him lawfully authorised.'

16 So St-Gobain applied for summary judgment on the ground that the action had no real prospect of success ...

18 If one assumes that a judge would find that Actionstrength's version of events was right, to hold the promise unenforceable would certainly appear unfair. Action-strength would have supplied Inglen with services which were indirectly for the benefit of St-Gobain, because they enabled Inglen to perform the main contract, in reliance on St-Gobain's promise to pay for them. Morally, there would be no excuse for St-Gobain not keeping its promise. On the other hand, if one assumes that a judge would find that St-Gobain's version was right, the Statute enables it to dispose summarily of proceedings which should never have been brought.

19 In an application for summary judgment such as this, which is in the nature of a demurrer, one has to assume that Actionstrength's version is true. And that naturally inclines one to try to find some way in which the putative injustice can be avoided. It is, however, important to bear in mind that the purpose of the Statute was precisely to avoid the need to decide which side was telling the truth about whether or not an oral promise had been made and exactly what had been promised. Parliament decided that there had

been too many cases in which the wrong side had been believed. Hence the title, 'An Act for prevention of frauds and perjuries'. It is quite true, as Mr McGhee said, that the system of civil procedure in 1677 was not very well adapted to discovering the truth. For one thing, the parties to the action were not competent witnesses. But the question of whether the Act should be preserved in its application to guarantees was considered in 1953 by the Law Reform Committee (First Report, Statute of Frauds and Section 4 of the Sale of Goods Act 1893 (Cmd 8809)) and the recommendation of a very strong committee was to keep it.

20 The terms of the Statute therefore show that Parliament, although obviously conscious that it would allow some people to break their promises, thought that this injustice was outweighed by the need to protect people from being held liable on the basis of oral utterances which were ill-considered, ambiguous or completely fictitious. This means that while normally one would approach the construction of a statute on the basis that Parliament was unlikely to have intended to cause injustice by allowing people to break promises which had been relied upon, no such assumption can be made about the Statute. Although the scope of the Statute must be tested on the assumption that the facts alleged by Actionstrength are true, it must not be construed in a way which would undermine its purpose.

…

22 Very soon after the Statute of 1677, the courts introduced the doctrine of part performance to restrict its application to sales of land. It was held that a contract, initially unenforceable because of the statute, could become enforceable by virtue of acts which the plaintiff did afterwards. The doctrine was justified by a combination [of] two reasons. The first was a form of estoppel; as Lord Reid said in *Steadman v Steadman* [1976] AC 536, 540: 'If one party to an agreement stands by and lets the other party incur expense or prejudice his position on the faith of the agreement being valid he will not then be allowed to turn round and assert that the agreement is unenforceable.'

23 The second reason was that the acts done by the plaintiff could in themselves prove the existence of the contract in a way which could be an acceptable substitute for the note or memorandum required by the Statute. These two reasons did not cover the same ground: acts which satisfied the first might fail to satisfy the second. In Steadman's case the House of Lords gave priority to the first reason and relaxed the need for the acts of part performance to be probative of the contract. It was however still possible to adhere to the reconciliation of the Statute and the part performance doctrine which the Earl of Selborne LC gave in *Maddison v Alderson* (1883) 8 App Cas 467, 475–476:

'In a suit founded on … part performance, the defendant is really "charged" upon the equities resulting from the acts done in execution of the contract, and not (within the meaning of the Statute) upon the contract itself … The matter has advanced beyond the stage of contract; and the equities which arise out of the stage which it has reached cannot be administered unless the contract is regarded.'

24 The reconciliation thus draws a distinction between the executory contract, not performed on either side, and the effect of subsequent acts of performance by the plaintiff. The former attracted the full force of the Statute while the latter could create an equitable rather than purely contractual right to performance. The Statute and the doctrine of part performance could co-exist in this way because contracts for the sale of land almost always start by being executory on both sides and usually remain executory until completed by mutual performance.

25 What Mr McGhee submits in this case is that the estoppel principle which partly underpins the doctrine of part performance is wide enough to be applied to contracts of guarantee. On the facts presently alleged, it is also the case that, in Lord Reid's words, St-Gobain stood by and let Actionstrength prejudice its position, by extending credit to Inglen, on the faith of the guarantee being valid. There is authority for saying that estoppel is a principle of broad, not to say protean, application: see, for example *Taylors Fashions Ltd v Liverpool Victoria Trustees Co Ltd (Note)* [1982] QB 133. Although he cited no case in any jurisdiction in which estoppel had been applied to avoid the application of the Statute to a guarantee, Mr McGhee says that there is no argument of principle against it.

26 The difficulty which faces this submission is that while the nature of a sale of land is such that the contract and part performance can co-exist in their respective domains, no such co-existence is possible between the Statute and the estoppel for which Mr McGhee contends. It is in the nature of a contract of guarantee that the party seeking to enforce it will always have performed first. Unless he has advanced credit or forborne from withdrawing credit, there will be no guaranteed debt for which he can sue. It will always be the case that the creditor will have acted to his prejudice on the faith of the guarantor's promise. To admit an estoppel on these grounds would be to repeal the Statute.

27 Mr McGhee argues that the estoppel need not apply in every case. What makes this case different, he says, is that (a) Actionstrength continued to supply Inglen only because of St-Gobain's encouragement (b) St-Gobain knew that without such encouragement Actionstrength would not continue to perform its contract with Inglen (c) St-Gobain stood to suffer loss and delay if Actionstrength did not continue to perform and gave the guarantee to avoid this and (d) St-Gobain knew that if Actionstrength continued to perform, there was a real prospect that it would suffer substantial loss unless the guarantee was honoured.

28 In my opinion none of these features are different from those which attend the giving of every guarantee. If a creditor or prospective creditor asks for a guarantee, it is always a reasonable inference that without the guarantee he would not have extended or continued to extend credit. The guarantor may reasonably be expected to know this. It is frequently in the interest of the guarantor to give the guarantee; for example, when it secures the indebtedness of a company he controls, a business associate or even a spouse. And it must be obvious that the creditor may suffer loss if the guarantee is not honoured. No doubt in each case there will be differences in degree, but no distinctions that could be drawn without throwing the law into total confusion.

29 It is not necessary to consider whether circumstances may arise in which a guarantor may be estopped from relying upon the Statute. It is sufficient that in my opinion the estoppel which Actionstrength seeks to rely upon in this case would be inconsistent with the provisions of the Statute. I would therefore dismiss the appeal.

LORD WALKER: ...

50 Mr McGhee accepted that there appears to be no English case (indeed, so far as his researches have gone, no case in any jurisdiction) in which an oral contract of guarantee has been enforced through the medium of an estoppel. However, your Lordships' attention was drawn to two recent decisions which were put forward as offering some assistance. The first is *Bank of Scotland v Wright* [1991] BCLC 244. In that case a director of two companies (one a subsidiary of the other) had given the bank a written guarantee of the liability of the holding company (only); but under an 'interavailable' facility backed by cross-guarantees (by the companies) the holding company was liable for the subsidiary's indebtedness to the bank. When the bank sued the individual guarantor for the whole of the corporate indebtedness there were two issues, the construction of the guarantee

and (if the bank failed on that point) estoppel by convention. Brooke J decided the first point in favour of the bank, and said cautiously on the second …

> '… I would not exclude the possibility that circumstances might arise in which a guarantor might have acted in such a way as to create or influence the other party's mistaken belief in the effectiveness of his guarantee so that it would be unconscionable to allow him to rely on the Statute of Frauds. Such a finding would depend very much on the court's views, on the facts of any particular case, of the personalities and attributes of the two parties between whom the alleged estoppel was alleged to have arisen.'

I see no reason to disagree with those observations, but they presuppose some sort of representation by the guarantor, together with unconscionability; not just unconscionability on its own.

Appeal dismissed.

Notes

(1) This case shows that a contract of guarantee that does not satisfy the Statute of Frauds will not become enforceable simply because the contract has been partly performed, by the creditor doing the action (executing work or paying money) in exchange for which the guarantee was given. If the Court were to enforce the guarantee in such a case, it would undermine the Statute. It is possible, however, that the doctrine of estoppel may apply if the guarantor has represented to the creditor that the guarantee was enforceable and the creditor has acted accordingly.

(2) There is an interesting parallel with cases in which the parties have agreed that formality is required, for example, that no variation of the terms of the contract shall be effective unless it is set out in writing signed by both parties. In *MWB Business Exchange Centres Ltd v Rock Advertising Ltd*[22] the Supreme Court held that this meant that an oral agreement to change the terms of the contract was not binding; but the Court left open the possibility that one party's conduct, if relied on by the other, might lead to the first party being estopped from denying that the contract had been varied. Cf PECL Article 2:106, under which such a clause merely creates a presumption that the parties did not intend the informal variation to be binding.

12.3.D CONCLUSION

Except as regards consideration, formalism is limited in English law. It might be said that the common law is made by traders who do not need to be protected by formalities and those which existed have been progressively reduced, though, as in other systems, formalities are required for guarantees. However, in certain areas—consumer credit contracts and contracts for the sale of land—twentieth-century legislation has imposed strict formal requirements—and, when the law does impose a formal requirement, the courts do little to mitigate it.

[22] [2018] UKSC 24, [2018] 2 WLR 1603.

12.4 FRENCH LAW: A CERTAIN FORMALISM, MEANS OF PROOF LEGALLY CIRCUMSCRIBED

12.4.A GENERAL SURVEY

There is no doubt that the principle underlying French contract law is consensualism: this is clear from new Article 1128 of the Code civil, which does not mention form in the conditions governing the validity of contracts—consent, capacity, lawful and certain content. It is made even clearer by the new Section 3 (Chapter II of the Code civil) titled 'The Form of Contracts' which has two sub-sections: one containing the 'General Provisions' and another one setting out 'Special Provisions' governing contracts concluded by electronic means (Articles 1174–1177 Cciv). We will concentrate on the General Provisions.[23]

Code civil **12.11 (FR)**

Article 1172: On principle contracts require only the consent of the parties.

By way of exception, the validity of a solemn contract is subject to the fulfilment of formalities set by legislation, and their absence renders the contract a nullity except where it may be regularized.

Otherwise, legislation subjects the formation of certain contracts to the delivery of a thing.

Article 1173: Formal requirements imposed for the purposes of proof of a contract or setting up a contract against another person have no effect on the validity of the contract.

Note

Consensualism follows from the general acceptance of free will and the untrammelled formation of intent. Consensualism is fast and simple. However, the downside is that a party may give its consent without fully considering the consequences of such entering into the contract. By contrast, formalism provides some security as it forces parties to take time and weigh their options before committing.

This is why, for certain important contracts, formalism is required. Formalism can be only the exception. However, the principal feature of the French legal system is the marked effect of the rules on evidence whereby the respective value of each method of proof is laid down by the law, the written form being the preferred method. There is

---

[23] On the French law generally see A Bénabent, *Les obligations* (16th edn, Paris: LGDJ, 2017) nos. 116–56; F Chénedé, *Le nouveau droit des obligations et des contrats: Consolidations, innovations, perspectives* (Paris: Dalloz, 2016) nos. 23.381–23.383 and 50.01–53.113; P Malaurie, L Aynès and P Stoffel-Munck, *Droit des obligations* (9th edn, Paris: LGDJ, 2017) nos. 535–81; and M Latina and G Chantepie, *La réforme du droit des obligations: Commentaire théorique et pratique dans l'ordre du Code civil* (Paris: Dalloz, 2016) nos. 451–62 and 1080–243.

thus a certain evidentiary formalism which takes its place alongside formalism properly so-called. An important exception is provided by Article L 110-3 of the Code de commerce: subject to exception, proof of an *acte de commerce* may be freely made.[24] However, the rules of the Code civil and those of the Code de la consommation are applicable if proof is made against a party who is not a professional.

At the beginning of the nineteenth century there were only four solemn contracts—contract of marriage, gift,[25] mortgage on realty, subrogation agreed by the debtor—which had to be entered into before a notary—by authentic act which confers on the deed a particular significance. Since then, a number of provisions have laid down formal requirements governing validity, mostly by contract under hand signed by the parties. Examples of this are the contract of insurance, the contract of apprenticeship and consumer contracts. The penalty for non-compliance is not always nullity of the contract, and the contract is often required to contain particulars by way of information. The courts have frequently relaxed the legal requirements, in particular by construing them as mere requirements as to evidence.

Those requirements are laid down in new Title IV BIS on the 'Proof of Obligations', which has three chapters containing the general provisions—including some on electronic writing, the rules on admissibility of kinds of proof, and the rules on the different kinds of proof. This chapter is by far the longest one (Articles 1363 to 1386-1 Cciv).

12.4.B ADMISSIBILITY OF KINDS OF PROOF

Code civil   **12.12 (FR)**

Article 1358: Apart from cases for which legislation provides otherwise, proof may be established by any means.

Article 1359: A juridical act relating to a sum of money or value in excess of an amount fixed by decree must be proved by evidence in writing, whether privately signed or authenticated.[26]

No proof may be brought beyond or contrary to evidence in writing establishing a juridical act, even if the sum of money or value does not exceed this amount, except by other written evidence which is signed or contained in an authenticated instrument.

A person whose contractual right exceeds the threshold mentioned in the previous paragraph may not be dispensed from proving it by evidence in writing by reducing his claim.

The same rule applies to a person whose claim, even if lower than this amount, concerns the balance of a sum or a part of a right higher than this amount.

Article 1360: The rules provided by the preceding article find an exception in the case of physical or moral impossibility of the written evidence being obtained, if it is customary

---

[24] Art L 110-1 of the Code de commerce provides a list of *actes de commerce* (commercial acts).

[25] The French courts have freely accepted other forms of gift—disguised gifts, indirect gifts, gifts by transfer; for the latter the formal requirement is the handing over of the item.

[26] cf Arts 1369–1371 Cciv on authenticated instruments. An authenticated instrument is 'one which has been received, with the requisite formalities, by a public official having the power and the function to draw it up' (Art 1369 Cciv).

not to establish written evidence, or where the written evidence has been lost as a result of force majeure.

Article 1361: Evidence in writing may be supplemented by an admission in court, by a decisive oath, or by a beginning of proof by writing which is corroborated by another means of proof.

Article 1362: Any written evidence constitutes a beginning of proof by writing where it originates from the person who is challenging the act or a person whom he represents and renders what is alleged likely to be true.

A court may consider as equivalent to a beginning of proof by writing any statements made by a party in responding orally to the court's questions, his refusal to reply to the court's questions, or his failure to appear to respond to the court's questions.[27]

A reference to an authenticated writing or to a signed writing on a public register is equivalent to a beginning of proof by writing.

Notes

(1) The limit above which proof in writing is required is set at 1,500 euros. The requirement of writing is a tradition dating back to the Moulins Decree of 1556. The guiding principle is that it is of the first importance that there be pre-existing proof in order to avoid disputes. That rule is complemented by another, under which oral evidence is not admissible to vary or contradict a document, even where the amount at stake is less than 1,500 euros (for more detail, see below, ch 18.4.B, pp 752–54).

(2) The requirement of writing as proof is subject to significant exceptions. Thus Article 1360 of the Code civil provides an exception in the case of physical or moral impossibility of the written evidence being obtained, if it is customary not to establish written evidence, or where the written evidence has been lost as a result of *force majeure*. Besides, evidence by writing may be supplemented by other means of evidence (Article 1361) and these include 'a beginning of proof by writing which is corroborated by another means of proof', that is to say a written document which does not in itself constitute proof but which appears to bear out the veracity of the fact alleged.

(3) Among the different kinds of written evidence, the *acte sous signature privée contresigné par les avocats* makes its entry in the Code civil. It is an instrument countersigned by the legal counsel of each of the parties or by the legal counsel of all the parties; it was created in 2011.[28] Article 1374 states that it provides proof both of the writing and of the signature of the parties, equally as regards themselves and as regards their heirs or successors.

(4) There is also the 'formality of the duplicate', which provides that in the case of synallagmatic contracts there must be as many copies as there are parties (Article 1375 Cciv).

---

[27] This provision concerns various aspects of *la comparution personnelle*, which is a procedural mechanism for the collection of evidence available to a court and consists of the court putting questions orally to a party: see Arts 184–194 Code de procédure civile.

[28] Loi no. 2011-331 du 28 mars 2011 de modernisation des professions judiciaires ou juridiques et certaines professions réglementées.

(5) A further formal requirement is laid down in Article 1376 Cciv, that the amount of money due under a unilateral undertaking must be written by hand. That requirement only applies to unilateral acts which have, as their object, a sum of money or a *bien fongible*.[29] It is particularly important in connection with suretyship; this requirement does not apply in the commercial context (Article L 110-4 Code commercial).

12.4.C APPLICATIONS

The first question in connection with a requirement as to form laid down in a provision is of a practical nature: is it a formal requirement going to validity (*ad validatem*), that is to say, where non-compliance will be sanctioned by nullity, or is it a requirement as to proof (*ad probationem*), where a failure to comply will make it impossible or more difficult to prove the existence or terms of the document? Where the provision is not specific on this point, which is not infrequently the case, the courts tend to go for the second solution because of the greater flexibility which it offers.[30]

The second question, where formalism goes to the substance, is to determine the scope of the nullity: the nullity will be relative where the applicable rule seeks to protect the parties; and absolute if the public interest is at stake, according to the theory of nullity.[31]

Cass chambre mixte, 24 February 2017[32] **12.13 (FR)**

Notice of eviction

A tenant cannot seek the annulment of the notice she received from her landlord through an agent when the mandate does not satisfy a formal requirement, as this legal requirement solely protects the landlord and its violation results in relative nullity.

Facts: A landlord, through a real estate agency acting in the course of its mandate, gave notice to the tenant of an apartment as it was supposed to be sold. The tenant brought a claim in order to have the notice annulled.

Held: The tenant cannot obtain the annulment of the notice because, even though it might be voided by the landlord as a consequence of a formal irregularity, only the party protected by this formal requirement is entitled to ask for its enforcement and request the notice's annulment.

Judgment:— Whereas, according to the contested judgment (Aix-en-Provence—April 23, 2015), the SCI Lepante, represented by the SI Parnasse, real estate agent, has, on October 29, 2012, given notice to Mrs X, tenant since May 15, 2007, of a place of residence it owns, to leave the premises which were to be sold by May 14, 2013; Mrs X has brought a claim asking for the notice's annulment;

— Whereas Mrs X criticises the judgment for having rejected her claim and pronounced her eviction because, according to the appeal ground:

1/ the notice to leave the premises joined with an offer to buy being analysed as an offer to buy, the real estate agent must have a special mandate to deliver it; by

---

[29] Malaurie et al (n 23 above) no. 538.
[30] See below, 12.13 (FR).
[31] F Terré, P Simler and Y Lequette, *Les obligations* (11th edn, Paris: Dalloz, 2013) no. 139.
[32] No. 15-20411, Bull civ I 2017 no. 1.

simply stating that the SI Parnasse was mandated to proceed to the sale of the apartment because it received a management and operation mandate authorising it to deliver "all notices", without considering the existence of a special mandate to sell, the court of appeal deprived its judgment of legal basis pursuant to Arts 1 and 6 of the Act no 70-9 of January 2, 1970, and Art 72 of the Decree no 72-678 of July 20, 1972;

2/ the mandate to sell given to a real estate agent is only valid when it is written and when it specifies a length and a registration number; in order to reject Mrs X's claim for the notice's annulment and hold that the SI Parnasse was entitled to deliver a notice, the court of appeal based itself on a letter sent by the SCI Lepante to the SI Parnasse; in so deciding without considering, as it was requested, whether this complied with the formal requirements of a mandate to sell given to a real estate agent, and particularly whether it specifies a length and a registration number, the court of appeal deprived its judgment of legal basis pursuant to Arts 1 and 6 of the Act no 70-9 of January 2, 1970, and Art 72 of the Decree no 72-678 of July 20, 1972;

— Whereas, however, first, when considering that the SI Parnasse, holder of a management and operation mandate, with power to deliver all notices, and a letter dated October 12, 2012 specially mandating it to sell the premises occupied by Mrs X at the end of the lease agreement subject to a certain payment and to give her notice, the court of appeal has done the supposedly omitted research;

And whereas, secondly, pursuant to Arts 1 and 6 of the Act no 70-9 of January 2, 1970, and Art 72 of the Decree no 72-678 of July 20, 1972, the mandate must include a limitation of its temporal effects and the real estate agent must specify all the mandates by chronological order on a register continuously numbered in advance and bound, and report the registration number on the mandate's copy hold by the mandator; the Cour de cassation held until now that the violation of these provisions, which are matters of public policy, are punished by absolute nullity, and as such can be invoked by every party with an interest (Cass civ (1) 25 February 2003, no. 01-00461; Cass civ (3) 8 April 2009, no. 07-21610, Bull III no. 80);

The nullity is absolute where the rule that is violated has as its object the safeguard of the public interest, while the nullity is relative where the rule that is violated has as its object the safeguard of a private interest.

By the Act of January 2, 1970, regulating the exercise conditions of activities relative to certain operations on estate and commercial property, so called Hoguet Act, the legislator has intended, all at once, to regulate the real estate agent profession and protect its customer base; the Act no 2014-366 of March 24, 2014 for the access to housing and a renovated town planning, as is apparent from its impact study, and the Act no 2015-990 of August 6, 2015 for growth, activity and equal economic opportunities respond to the same concerns;

The Act no 89-462 of July 6, 1989 supervises the delivery of a notice for reason of sale to a tenant of a place of residence that is his principal residence, by notably laying conditions of delay, giving a right of pre-emption and imposing the delivery of an information leaflet with the notice;

The evolution of the Law of obligations, pursuant to the Ordinance no 2016-131 of February 10, 2016, leads to consider differently the objective pursued by the provisions on the formal requirements that a mandate must satisfy, the latter aiming to protect solely the mandator in his relation with the agent;

The existence of provisions protective of the tenant, that ensure a fair balance between the interests of the latter and those of the landlord, and the objective of the protection of the sole landlord in the rules set by to Art 7(1) of the Act no 70-9 of January 2, 1970, and Art 72(5) of the Decree no 72-678 of July 20, 1972, lead to change the case law and to hold that the violation of the above mentioned rules must be punished by a relative nullity;

Thus, the court of appeal was not required to proceed to an inoperative research on the mention of the mandate's length and on the report, on the mandate's copy held by the mandatary, of a registration number on the mandates' register.

Therefore the appeal ground is not well-founded;

For these reasons, dismiss the appeal.

Notes

(1) This decision, characterised by its highly developed motivation, illustrates a new practice used by the Cour de cassation,[33] especially in cases where it overturns its previous case law and in cases where it applies a proportionality test. In this case overturning one of its established case laws, the Cour de cassation quotes its own precedents and also other statutory sources. It is worth noticing that this decision is promised great publicity as it will be mentioned in the Court's annual report and because the Attorney-General's opinion and the report prepared by one of the judges on this case were published, along with an informative note.

(2) It is the first time that the Cour de cassation has made a reference to 'The evolution of the Law of obligations, pursuant to the Ordinance no 2016-131 of February 10, 2016' in order to interpret special provisions and justify overturning its case law.[34] It must be added that the judges made an anticipatory—and slightly altered—application of new Article 1179 of the Code civil.

(3) The Cour de cassation, which notes that the special mandate required for a real estate agent to deliver a notice to leave the premises about to be sold has been correctly characterised by the court of appeal, considers that the tenant, third party to the contract of mandate, is not entitled to rely on the violation of the statutory provisions mentioned in the case. To justify its decision, the Cour de cassation insists on the spirit of several statutory provisions (three Acts are quoted) which are designed to regulate the real estate agent profession and protect its customer base and, consequently, mix *ordre public de protection* with *ordre public de direction*. The Court then recalls that provisions for the protection of tenants already existed in the 1989 Act and that such provisions ensure 'a fair balance between the interests of the latter and those of the landlord'. For all these reasons, the Cour de cassation holds that 'the violation of the above-mentioned rules must be punished by a relative nullity'. This does not mean that a protective provision cannot be superimposed on another protective provision. Simply, the provision at stake, though of *ordre public*, protects a private interest and as such can only be relied on by the party it protects. The Cour de cassation's decision is in line with a general evolution of the law of obligations favourable to relative nullity,

---

[33] On this practice, see R Libchaber, 'Une motivation en trompe-l'oeil: les cailloux du Petit Poucet' JCP G 2016, 632.

[34] The Cour de cassation already had the occasion to refer to the Ordinance, but merely to note that the provisions it applies in the case are those of the former Code civil.

in spite of new Article 1179 which states 'Nullity is absolute where the rule that is violated has as its object the safeguard of the public interest. It is relative where the rule that is violated has as its *sole* object the safeguard of a private interest'.[35]

12.4.D FORMALISM AND SURETYSHIP

In the specific field of suretyship, after some hesitation, the Cour de cassation decided that the requirements as to the handwritten statement referred to were not mere rules on proof but pursued the objective of protecting the surety, thus entailing the penalty of nullity—relative because it is for the protection of the parties.[36] However, in 1989 the Court held that they were rules on proof (Cass civ (1) 15 November 1989) and this was subsequently reaffirmed.[37] Further judgments show that the contract is not null and void.

Cass civ (1), 15 October 1991[38]   **12.14 (FR)**

The surety

Irregularities in abiding by the requirements of a contract of suretyship do not render it null and void if there is prima facie written evidence of a clear undertaking between the parties.

Facts: See the judgment.

Held: The Cour de cassation rejected the argument of the appellant that the undertaking in the contract of suretyship was not genuine, as it did not satisfy the requirements of the Code civil.

Judgment: THE COURT: On the two branches of the single appeal ground:— Whereas according to the findings of the lower courts, the Del Giudice couple purchased from the Arbomonts a property by notarised deed dated 30 August 1982 which stipulated that the price of 1,400,000F was to be paid as to 750,000F in cash and, as to the remainder, by way of a loan for 650,000F; as by a document under hand signed on the same day, the purchasers acknowledged that they owed to the vendors the sum of 700,000F 'being the balance of the purchase price for the property', and undertook to 'return and reimburse' that amount within a one-year period; as a certain Mr Suma joined in the deed to act as surety for the liabilities of the Del Giudice couple; as the Arbomonts brought proceedings against the Del Giudices and Mr Suma, as well as the officiating notary, for payment of the sum of 700,000F remaining outstanding, according to them, on the purchase price, notwithstanding the receipt given in the deed;

— Whereas the confirmatory judgment appealed against (Aix-en-Provence, 3 October 1989) considered that proof of the debt in favour of the Arbomonts was established and ordered the Del Giudice couple and Mr Suma jointly and severally to pay the sum claimed; as Mr Suma maintains in his appeal on a point of law that the court below ought not to have found against him when, in the terms of the plea on appeal, he asked for the

---

[35] For a detailed commentary of this decision, see B Fauvarque-Cosson, 'Première influence de la réforme du droit des contrats: à propos de la nullité, relative ou absolue, du mandate de l'agent immobilier' D 2017, 793.

[36] Cass civ (1) 30 June 1987, no. 85-15760, Bull civ I no. 210.

[37] Malaurie et al (n 23 above) no. 572. See Cass civ (1) 5 October 1994, no. 92-17208, Bull civ I no. 269.

[38] No. 89-21936, JCP 1992.II.21923, annotated by P Simler.

judgment to be set aside on the ground that the contract of suretyship was null and void since it did not satisfy the requirements of [former] Article 1326 of the Civil Code;

— Whereas accordingly, the cour d'appel, in his submission, was not able to reach the determination which it did without infringing Article 4 of the new Code of Civil Procedure and Articles 1326 and 2015 of the Civil Code; as in his further submission, if the contract of suretyship did not satisfy the requirements of Article 1326 of the Civil Code it was not possible to infer from that document that the surety's undertaking was genuine;

— Whereas in deciding as it did, the cour d'appel failed to found its decision on a proper legal basis;

— Whereas however, the cour d'appel was correct in stating that, even though the absence of the handwritten particulars required under Article 1326 of the Civil Code in the contract of suretyship entered into by Mr Suma constituted an irregularity, that document was none the less prima facie written evidence which could be supplemented by other matters; as thus, the court below rejected rather than disregarded the submissions going to the nullity of the suretyship;

— Whereas, secondly, having taken note of the evidence adduced in addition to the document constituting prima facie written evidence of the contract of suretyship, the court below, acting within its jurisdiction, took the view that that additional evidence demonstrated that Mr Suma was aware of the nature and scope of his undertaking;

— Whereas the judgment of the cour d'appel was therefore sound in law, and none of the appeal grounds are well founded.

On those grounds, the appeal is dismissed.

Note

   This judgment reaffirms that the requirement that there be handwritten particulars is indeed a rule on proof. It also affirms that a document containing an irregularity is not null and void; it may constitute prima facie written evidence which may be supplemented by other matters. That will often be the case. This prevents favourable treatment from being accorded to the party acting in bad faith (this could also be achieved through the application of new Article 1104 which reaffirms the general principle of good faith and expands former Article 1134(3) insofar as it also mentions the formation of contracts).

Stringent solutions apply in order to protect consumers: they derogate from the general rules set forth in the Code civil and are in the Consumer Code.

12.4.E CONCLUSION

This conclusion must be a guarded one. The principle of consensualism appears to be well alive. Yet there is much talk of a re-emergence of formalism. The reason is that formal requirements, including those to do with proof, are a means of protecting the weaker or more naïve party. The same is also true with regard to the obligation of information (see especially new Article 1112-1 Cciv). It is for the courts to ensure that formal requirements are not misused to the advantage of the contracting party acting in bad faith.

FURTHER READING

Christandl, G and Hosemann, E, 'Conditions for the Conclusion of a Contract' in N Jansen and R Zimmermann (eds), *Commentaries on European Contract Laws* (Oxford University Press, 2018) 236–65.

Kötz, H, *European Contract Law* (2nd edn, Oxford University Press, 2017) 73–90.

Kötz, H, 'Indicia of seriousness' in J Basedow, K Hopt and R Zimmermann (eds), *Max Planck Encyclopedia of European Private Law*, vol I (Oxford University Press, 2012) 863–65.

Whittaker, S, 'Contracts, Contract Law and Contractual Principle' in J Cartwright and S Whittaker (eds), *The Code Napoléon Rewritten: French Contract Law after the 2016 Reforms* (Oxford: Hart Publishing, 2017) 29–55.

CHAPTER 13
PRECONTRACTUAL NEGOTIATIONS

13.1 INTRODUCTION

The formation of a contract is often preceded by lengthy negotiations. Especially with regard to major deals, rather than a contract being concluded quickly by one party accepting the other's offer, there is 'a gradual process in which agreements are reached piecemeal in several rounds with a succession of drafts'.[1] Most systems nowadays accept a general duty of precontractual good faith. For example, in most countries the brutal interruption of advanced negotiations is seen as the paradigmatic instance of negotiating contrary to good faith. However, the role of precontractual good faith is far from limited to that. In many systems the duty of precontractual good faith is also applied in several other situations.[2]

Rudolph von Jhering was the first to recognise that the classical rules on offer and acceptance appear to be insufficient to govern the process of formation of contract. In a famous article of 1861 he maintained that a party might be liable for fault in negotiations.[3] His view was that a party who induces another to rely on the conclusion of a valid contract could be liable for *culpa in contrahendo*. It is often thought that von Jhering proposed a liability for broken off negotiations. However, in that article he did not say a word about disappointing negotiations; he dealt exclusively with situations where at least one party thought that a valid contract was concluded.

The history of liability for broken off negotiations started in the shadow of Vesuvius. In 1906, the Neapolitan magistrate Gabriele Fagella published an article[4] in which he distinguished three stages in negotiations: the period before any offer has been drafted,

---

[1] EA Farnsworth, 'Precontractual Liability and Preliminary Agreements: Fair Dealing and Failed Negotiations' (1987) 87 Columbia Law Review 217.

[2] See below, p 424.

[3] R von Jhering, 'Culpa in contrahendo oder Schadensersatz bei nichtigen oder nicht zur Perfection gelangten Verträgen' (1861) 4 Jahrbücher für die Dogmatik des heutigen römischen und deutschen Privatrechts 1.

[4] G Fagella, 'Dei periodi precontrattuali e dell loro vera ed esatta costruzione scientifica' in *Studi giuridici in onore di Carlo Fadda*, vol III (Naples: L Pierro, 1906) 271.

the period during which an offer is drafted and the period after an offer has been made. The novelty of Fagella's theory was that he accepted that a negotiating party could be liable in all these stages, including the period before an offer is made. The importance of Fagella's theory was recognised by the French comparative lawyer Raymond Saleilles. In an article entirely dedicated to Fagella's theory he endorsed his ideas and elaborated them on some points.[5] Only a few years after the BGB came into force, the German Reichsgericht adopted a general doctrine of *culpa in contrahendo*, using it, however, to solve a very different problem from those for which von Jhering had proposed his theory.[6] The Italian Civil Code of 1942 was the first code to contain a specific provision on precontractual good faith.

This chapter will discuss the balance that the major European legal systems have found between the freedom to break off negotiations and respect for the interest of the other party in negotiations, or, more precisely, which behaviour during negotiations is considered to be contrary to good faith; whether it gives rises to liability; and what remedies are available to the aggrieved party. In this chapter, only a few specific instances of precontractual behaviour contrary to good faith will be dealt with, which are (a) negotiating without an intention to conclude a contract, (b) conducting parallel negotiations, (c) breaking off negotiations, (d) failing to comply with tendering procedures, (e) knowingly or carelessly entering into an invalid contract and (f) disclosing confidential information. One of the most important specific duties based on the general duty to negotiate in good faith is the duty that negotiating parties may have to inform each other adequately about the subject matter or the circumstances.[7] This, however, is discussed in Chapter 14.

Before these more detailed issues are discussed, first a few general remarks will be made with respect to a general duty of precontractual good faith.

13.2 A GENERAL DUTY OF PRECONTRACTUAL GOOD FAITH

The civil codes in many of the jurisdictions studied contain clear provisions establishing a general duty of precontractual good faith. A number of those provisions are set out below. However, there is an immediate contrast between the civil law jurisdictions and the common law, since the common law imposes no general duty of precontractual good faith.

Principles of European Contract Law   **13.1 (FR)**

Article 2:301: Negotiations Contrary to Good Faith[8]
    (1) A party is free to negotiate and is not liable for failure to reach an agreement.
    (2) However, a party who has negotiated or broken off contrary to good faith is liable for the losses caused to the other party.

---

[5] R Saleilles, 'De la responsabilité précontractuelle; à propos d'une étude nouvelle sur la matière' RTD civ 1907, 697.

[6] See below, p 426, and 6.13 (DE), above, p 144.

[7] See, eg, Comment to Art 2.1.15 UNIDROIT PICC.

[8] In Art II-3:301 of the DCFR a similar provision is included. However, after para (1) a new paragraph is included which states: '(2) A person who is engaged in negotiations has a duty to negotiate in accordance with

(3) It is contrary to good faith, in particular, for a party to enter into or continue negotiations with no real intention of reaching an agreement with the other party.

UNIDROIT Principles **13.2 (INT)**

Article 2.1.15: Negotiations in bad faith
(1) A party is free to negotiate and is not liable for the failure to reach an agreement.
(2) However, a party who negotiates or breaks off negotiations in bad faith is liable for losses caused to the other party.
(3) It is bad faith, in particular, for a party to enter into or continue negotiations when intending not to reach an agreement with the other party.

Note

Although these Articles deal only with negotiations contrary to good faith, the Comments[9] to both sets of rules explain that they, like many of the other rules, such as those imposing a duty to inform, are based on the general duty of good faith which applies not just during the contract but also at the precontractual stage.

Code civil **13.3 (FR)**

Article 1104: Contracts must be negotiated, formed and performed in good faith.
   This provision is a matter of public policy.

Sub-section 1

Negotiations

Article 1112: The commencement, continuation and breaking-off of precontractual negotiations are free from control. They must mandatorily satisfy the requirements of good faith.
   …

Notes

   (1) This provision is a codification of French case law and writings by French authors.[10]
   (2) The 1804 Code civil did not include a general duty of precontractual good faith. From Article 1134(3), which only related to good faith in the performance of contracts, a general duty of precontractual good faith was inferred by the courts and most contemporary French authors.

good faith and fair dealing. This duty may not be excluded or limited by contract.' (This is also included in PECL, but in the general provision on good faith: Art 1:201 PECL.) The CESL did not contain an article on negotiations, as it applied only when the parties had agreed on a contract using the CESL.
   [9] For PECL, see Comments A and B to Art 1:201 PECL.
   [10] See P Jourdain, 'Rapport Français' in *La bonne foi, Travaux de l'Association Henri Capitant*, vol XLIII, 1992 (Paris: Litec, 1994) 131; M Latina and G Chantepie, *La réforme du droit des obligations: Commentaire théorique et pratique dans l'ordre du Code civil* (Paris: Dalloz, 2016) nos. 168-79. D Mazeaud, 'Mystères et paradoxes de la période précontractuelle' in *Études offertes à J Ghestin* (Paris: LGDJ, 2001) 637; F Terré, P Simler and Y Lequette, *Les obligations* (11th edn, Paris: Dalloz, 2013) nos. 183 ff.

(3) There is a large body of case law on the question of precontractual liability under the 1804 Code civil. In brief, insofar as precontractual negotiations are concerned, French courts usually inferred three types of duties from this general obligation of good faith, which were a duty to inform, a duty of confidentiality and a duty not to behave inconsistently during the negotiations.

They have now been codified in the Articles 1112, 1112-1, 1112-2 Code civil, which will be considered below.[11]

BGB   **13.4 (DE)**

§ 311: Obligations created by legal transaction and similar obligations
...
(2) An obligation with duties in accordance with § 241(2) also arises as a result of
1. entry into contractual negotiations,
2. preparations undertaken with a view to creating a contractual relationship if one party permits the other party to affect his rights, his legally protected interest or other interests or entrusts them to that party, or
3. similar business contact.

§ 241: Duties arising out of the obligation
...
(2) An obligation may require each party to have regard to the other party's rights, legally protected interests and other interests.

Notes

(1) In Germany, before the original version of the BGB was adopted, the Reichsgericht had already accepted that, by taking up negotiations, parties enter into a legal relationship (*Rechtsverhältnis*), similar to a contractual relationship, that gives rise to several duties between the negotiating parties, for example, depending on the case, duties not to harm the other party's person or property, to provide her with certain types of information and not to break off very advanced negotiations. These duties will be discussed extensively in this chapter. The violation of such a duty makes a party liable for *culpa in contrahendo*.[12] The Bundesgerichtshof has proceeded on the same lines.[13] With regard to the dogmatic basis of these precontractual duties, several suggestions have been made by legal doctrine (eg *Treu und Glauben*; the *Vertrauensprinzip*) but none of them can be said to have been generally accepted. It has been argued that the cases dealt with by the doctrine of *culpa in contrahendo* are so disparate in character that they cannot be said to have a common basis.[14]

---

[11] See below, pp 433 and 458 (Art 1112), 477 (Art 1112-2) and 528 (Art 1112-1).
[12] See RG 7 December 1911 (6.13 (DE), above, p 144).
[13] See, eg, BGH 10 July 1970 (13.14 (DE), below, p 436).
[14] Münchener Kommentar/Emmerich § 311 paras 39–41.

(2) In the Netherlands the Hoge Raad has decided, in words very similar to those of the German Bundesgerichtshof, that parties starting negotiations enter into a legal relationship that is governed by good faith, which requires them to take each other's interests into account.[15] Although this was said in a case on mistake, the doctrine is now virtually always applied in cases concerning broken off negotiations.

(3) French law also imposes a duty to act in good faith during all the stages of the negotiations, recently codified at Article 1112 of the Code civil. Moreover, in French law, precontractual good faith is closely linked to the 'precontractual information duty', imposed on the negotiating parties pursuant to Article 1112-1.

In contrast, English law takes a very different position. *Walford v Miles* affirms that under English law there is no such thing as a general duty to negotiate in good faith.[16] The point arose by virtue of the appellants' submission that the lock-in agreement could be rendered sufficiently certain by the implication of a duty to continue the negotiations in good faith. The House of Lords took the occasion to make clear by a single speech in very strong terms that English law does not know an obligation to negotiate in good faith.[17]

13.3 CONDUCT CONTRARY TO PRECONTRACTUAL GOOD FAITH

This section will discuss what type of conduct is contrary to good faith. In particular, it will examine: (A) negotiating without intending to conclude a contract; (B) conducting parallel negotiations; (C) breaking off negotiations; (D) knowingly or carelessly concluding an invalid contract; and (E) disclosing confidential information.

13.3.A NO INTENTION TO CONCLUDE A CONTRACT

Principles of European Contract Law   **13.5 (INT)**

Article 2:301: Negotiations Contrary to Good Faith[18]

...

(3) It is contrary to good faith, in particular, for a party to enter into or continue negotiations with no real intention of reaching an agreement with the other party.

---

[15] See HR 15 November 1957, NJ 1958, 67. See AS Hartkamp & CH Sieburgh, *Mr. C. Assers Handleiding tot de beoefening van het Nederlands Burgerlijk Recht. 6. Verbintenissenrecht. Deel III. Algemeen overeenkomstenrecht* (Deventer: Kluwer 2014) nos. 191 ff.

[16] See 10.21 (EN), above, p 336. In *Yam Seng Pte Ltd v International Trade Corp Ltd* [2013] EWHC 111 (QB), [2013] Lloyd's Rep 526 Leggatt J said that a distribution agreement for branded goods contained an implied term of good faith in its performance, in particular that the supplier should not knowingly provide false information to the distributor about the availability of products. But subsequently the Court of Appeal has twice affirmed the absence of any general duty of good faith: see *Mid Essex Hospital Services NHS Trust v Compass Group UK and Ireland Ltd (t/a Medirest)* [2013] EWCA Civ 200, [2013] BLR 265 at [105] and see also at [150]; *MSC Mediterranean Shipping Co S.A. v Cottonex Anstalt* [2016] EWCA Civ 789 at [45].

[17] See above, p 338.

[18] A similar provision is included in Art II.-3:301(4) DCFR.

Article 2.1.15: Negotiations in bad faith

...

(3) It is bad faith, in particular for a party, to enter into or continue negotiations when intending not to reach an agreement with the other party.

Illustration No 1 to Article 2.1.15. A learns of B's intention to sell its restaurant. A, who has no intention whatsoever of buying the restaurant, nevertheless enters into lengthy negotiations with B for the sole purpose of preventing B from selling the restaurant to C, a competitor of A's. A, who breaks off negotiations when C has bought another restaurant, is liable to B, who ultimately succeeds in selling the restaurant at a lower price than offered by C, for the difference in price.

Notes

(1) In most European legal systems, it is held to be contrary to precontractual good faith to enter into negotiations without having any intention of making a contract. If a party, for example, enters into negotiations for the sole purpose of obtaining knowledge of business secrets of the other party or for the sole purpose of preventing him from contracting with a competitor of the first party, he is liable. In the latter case the liability will give rise to compensation for the lost opportunity to contract with the competitor (in such a case under German law liability can be based on § 826 BGB (*sittenwidrige vorsätzliche Schädigung;* see also Article 1112 of the French Code civil).

(2) At common law, the same result would be reached, but through the doctrine of fraud. In a US case the lessor conducted negotiations with the lessee for renewal of the lease in order to have the premises occupied during negotiations with a third party for their sale. Here damages for lost opportunities included the profits lost due to the loss of the lessee's principal customer, which would not have occurred had the lessee concluded a contract with a third party instead of entering into these deceiving negotiations.[19] In another US case the defendant had advertised for bids, although having already decided to give the contract to one candidate.[20] There is little doubt that English law is the same.

(3) Not only actual absence of intention to conclude a contract can lead to liability, but also negligence in beginning negotiations. See, for example, RGZ 143, 219, 19 January 1934, where a party entered into negotiations while knowing that he would not be able to comply with conditions put by the other party for concluding a new contract (ie providing sufficient securities) and thus provoked unnecessary expense for the other party. There is, however a general principle of freedom to contract which means that a party is free not to enter into the contract. Therefore, under French law, violation of good faith necessitates a fault or abuse of the right to negotiate.

(4) While a failure to agree on the price would constitute a legitimate reason for breaking off negotiations it is contrary to good faith to continue negotiations after having lost the intention to conclude the contract. A party who protracts negotiations

[19] *Markov v ABC Transfer & Storage Co*, 76 Wash. 2d 388, 457 P 2d 535 (1969).
[20] *Heyder Products Cov United States*, 140 F Supp. 409 (Ct.Cl.1956).

after having decided that he will not conclude any contract with this partner is liable for expenses and lost opportunities.[21]

(5) Although in some of the systems the liability discussed here is based on tort (fraud or negligence), in functional terms it seems to rest on the same principle as liability for inducing the other party into concluding a contract, while knowing that it will be invalid:[22] it is contrary to good faith to induce another party into negotiations on something one knows, or should know, to be incapable of realisation. Leading one party to believe that a contract will be concluded (for example, a loan) and in the end imposing new terms (such as additional guarantees in order to provide the loan) may also be contrary to good faith.[23]

13.3.B PARALLEL NEGOTIATIONS

Cour d'appel de Versailles, 5 March 1992[24]   **13.7 (FR)**

A French, a British and a Belgian Company

In the absence of a memorandum of exclusivity prohibiting the vendor from entering into parallel negotiations, a vendor is free to conduct parallel negotiations with other parties.

Held: Alvat's claim failed.

Judgment: On the alleged fault on the part of Gallay in the conduct of the negotiations:— Whereas the company Alvat België complains, first, that Gallay negotiated with other parties at the same time as it was conducting negotiations with Alvat and, second, that it wrongfully broke off the negotiations with the latter.

— Whereas it must be recalled, first of all, that Gallay never undertook not to conduct parallel negotiations with other parties concerning the transfer of the Rhod-arec shares.

— Whereas, if Alvat België had wished to negotiate on an exclusive basis, it could, as is normal in such matters, have insisted upon the signature of a memorandum of exclusivity prohibiting the vendor from negotiating with any other prospective purchaser pending a decision by Alvat.

— Whereas in the present case, not only was there no such agreement, but it is also clearly apparent from the documents produced by Alvat België that those documents were intended for any prospective purchaser.

— Whereas the note from Gallay dated 10 February 1989 is headed 'Search for a partner' and this establishes thus, at the very least, that the negotiations were open to any potential purchaser and that the appellant was not the victim of any unfair stratagem.

— Whereas nor was there any wrongful act on the part of Gallay in its discontinuance of the negotiations with Alvat België at the beginning of April 1989.

---

[21] See M Weber 'Haftung für in Aussicht gestellten Vertragsabschluß' (1992) 192 AcP 390, 396; Terré et al (n 10 above) no. 185; Cass com 26 November 2003, no. 00-10243, Bull IV no. 186; CJH Brunner, annotation under *Plas v Valburg*, HR 18 June 1982, NJ 1983, 723.

[22] See below, p 474.

[23] Cass com 31 March 1992, no. 90-14867, Bull civ IV no. 145.

[24] RTD civ 1992, 753, annotated by J Mestre; Bull Joly, 1992, 636, annotated by J Schmidt.

Cass Com, 26 November 2003[25]   **13.8 (FR)**

Manoukian

Conducting parallel negotiations itself does not result in delictual liability. However, these parallel negotiations must be conducted in good faith.

Facts: The company Alain Manoukian started negotiations with [X], who were shareholders in company Stuck, with a view to the transfer of the whole share capital of the Stuck Company to the Manoukian company in the spring of 1997. After several meetings and much exchange of correspondence a draft agreement was finalised on 24 September 1997. This was subject to several conditions, which had to be fulfilled prior to 10 October 1997; this was later deferred to 31 October 1997. On 16 October, after new discussions, Manoukian agreed to the transferors' request for modifications and proposed to defer the date for satisfaction of the conditions to 15 November 1997. X did not reply, but a new draft transfer agreement was presented to them on 13 November 1997. On 24 November 1997 Manoukian discovered that X had, on 10 November 1997, granted to the company Les Complices an option over the shares of Stuck. Manoukian claimed that X and Les Complices should be held liable to compensate the loss resulting from the culpable breaking off of the negotiations.

Held: The cour d'appel held X liable to pay Manoukian the sum of 400,000 FF by way of damages. The damages were limited to the loss suffered by Manoukian, ie to the expenses incurred in the negotiations and the surveys it had undertaken. The appeal was rejected.

Judgment:— But whereas the circumstances constituting fault in the exercise of the right unilaterally to break off precontractual negotiations are not the cause of the loss which comprises the lost chance of making the profits which one could expect from the conclusion of the contract;

— Whereas the Cour d'appel rightly decided that, in the absence of a firm and final agreement, the loss suffered by Alain Manoukian included only the expenses incurred in the negotiations and the surveys it had undertaken and not the profits that it could have hoped to make from the running of the business if the contract had been concluded, nor even the loss of the chance of making such profits; that the ground is not founded; ...

— But whereas the simple fact of contracting, even with full knowledge, with a person who has undertaken negotiations with a third party does not of itself, and unless it is driven by the intention to cause harm or is accompanied by fraudulent machinations, constitute fault of such a kind as to impose liability on its author.

— Whereas, having held that the clause of guarantee inserted in the share transfer option was not sufficient to establish that Les Complices had used disloyal practices to obtain the transfer of the share capital of Stuck, nor even that it had a precise knowledge of the state of advancement of the negotiations undertaken between Alain Manoukian and the sellers and the dishonesty of the latter with regard to the former, the Cour d'appel rightly held that this company was not liable to Alain Manoukian, regardless of the fact that it had in the end benefited from the disloyal machinations of X; that the ground is not founded; ...

Notes

(1) In most European legal systems conducting parallel negotiations is in itself not considered to be contrary to good faith. It is very common in practice, and essential to a market economy, to compare different proposals and to choose the most

---

[25] Nos. 00-10243 and 00-10949, Bull civ IV no. 186. See also 13.21 (FR), below, p 458.

advantageous one.[26] The *Manoukian* case shows that conducting parallel negotiations does not lead in itself to delictual liability under French law. This follows from the principle of freedom of contract (former Article 1134(1) Cciv, now Article 1102). However, the Cour de cassation upholds the decision of the cour d'appel when the latter finds that this freedom to negotiate with several potential parties must be exercised in good faith and must not lead to a situation where one party has the belief that a contract is to be concluded with her and is only informed that a contract has been concluded with a third party two weeks afterwards.

(2) Under French law, if a party wishes an exclusive right to negotiate with one other party excluding all others, she will have to bargain for it. See *A French, a British and a Belgian Company*.[27] In English law, clauses aimed at giving one party an exclusive right to negotiate are called 'lock out' clauses. In *Walford v Miles*,[28] the case in which the House of Lords said that an agreement to negotiate is unenforceable for lack of certainty, the House rejected the argument that a lock-out agreement without a time limit could be rendered sufficiently certain by implying that it was to last until such time as it became clear that the parties, negotiating in good faith, could not reach an agreement.[29] In a later case a lock-out agreement limited to a period of two weeks was held to be enforceable.[30] Note that a lock-out agreement merely prevents the parties from negotiating with anyone else during the relevant period; it does not impose a duty to negotiate.

(3) In principle, a party is not under an obligation to inform the other party spontaneously that he is also negotiating with others.[31] Therefore, in principle, a negotiating party cannot expect to be the only one dealing with his partner.

(4) However, it is contrary to good faith actually to lead the other party to believe that he is negotiating exclusively. In those laws that do not recognise precontractual duties of good faith, in this case there would again be a remedy on the ground of fraud.

(5) Of course, it is also contrary to good faith for a party who is conducting parallel negotiations to continue negotiations with one party after having decided to conclude the contract with another party. This follows from the rule, discussed above,[32] that it is contrary to good faith to continue negotiations with a party whilst no longer having the intention to conclude a contract with him.

13.3.C BREAKING OFF NEGOTIATIONS

No party is under a duty to reach an agreement. However, in exceptional cases a party may be liable for breaking off negotiations in a manner contrary to good faith. In this

---

[26] See, eg, *Asser/Hartkamp & Sieburgh 6-III* 2014/193 (n 15 above); Farnsworth (n 1 above) 279; Terré et al (n 10 above) no. 185.
[27] 13.7 (FR), above, p 429.
[28] 10.21 (EN), above, p 336.
[29] As suggested in the dissenting judgment of Bingham LJ in the Court of Appeal (1991) 62 P & CR 410, 421.
[30] See *Pitt v PHH Asset Management Ltd* [1994] 1 WLR 327 (CA). This seems to be in line with US law, where such clauses are accepted as long as they contain a time limit. See Farnsworth (n 1 above) 279.
[31] See CA Pau 14 January 1969, D 1969, 716.
[32] Above, pp 427–29.

section we discuss both the general freedom to break off negotiations and the cases in which liability is imposed for breaking off negotiations in bad faith. We also discuss the remedies available in cases of such liability.

13.3.C.1 THE FREEDOM TO BREAK OFF NEGOTIATIONS

Principles of European Contract Law   **13.9 (INT)**

Article 2:301: Negotiations Contrary to Good Faith[33]
  (1) A party is free to negotiate and is not liable for failure to reach an agreement.
  (2) …

UNIDROIT Principles   **13.10 (INT)**

Article 2.1.15: Negotiations in bad faith
  (1) A party is free to negotiate and is not liable for the failure to reach an agreement.
  (2) …

Note

  This freedom to break off negotiations is inherent to freedom of contract, which is essential to a market economy. If a party risks being held liable if negotiations do not lead to a contract he will be less willing to enter into negotiations.

Cass civ (1), 20 December 2012[34]   **13.11 (FR)**

The laboratories' failed merger

A company breaking off the negotiations initiated in view of a merger with another company merely exercises its freedom not to enter into a contract.

Facts: Two medical laboratories intended to merge but one of the companies (Company A) broke off the negotiations. The other company (Company B) claimed damages for the abusive breaking-off.

Held: The cour d'appel held that Company A did not commit any fault and rejected the claim. The Cour de cassation confirmed that judgment.

Judgment: But whereas the judgment notes that, after having rejected, in November 2007, a first draft of contract which stated, in the presence of Company B members, the conditions for the sale of the shares of his partner, whose retirement was imminent, M. X [Company A's officer], has, from 11 April 2008, notified his intention to stop the negotiations which had resumed in January 2008 in view of a merger of the two laboratories through an acquisition but which had only resulted in a draft of a partnership agreement, drawn up on 8 April on the basis of the financial conditions discussed the day before, and that Company B had prematurely initiated the preparatory steps and investments for an partnership whose principle was in no way agreed, could not invoke the bad faith of his partner during these unsuccessful attempts to reconcile; thus, the cour d'appel could, without verifying the reasons, decide that the breaking-off of the negotiations

---

[33] A similar provision is included in Art II.-3:301(1) DCFR.
[34] No. 11-27340, unpublished.

however sudden or disappointing it may have been, did not constitute a legal wrong on the part of Company A which had simply used the freedom which it had, at that point in the negotiations, not to enter into a contract.

Notes

(1) In exceptional circumstances a party who has broken off negotiations can be held liable.[35] This liability is sometimes conceived as an exception to the rule that a party is always free to break off.[36] However, the better view seems to be that liability of a party who has broken off negotiations in a manner contrary to good faith is liability not for breaking off—this would amount to *Kontrahierungszwang*, which means that parties are forced to enter into a contract—but for inducing the other party's reliance that a contract would be concluded. See, for example, the Italian author Bianca:[37]

> The conduct of the negotiations does not involve any obligation to contract. A party to those negotiations retains the power to withdraw any proposal which he may have made, or his acceptance of any proposal made to him, until such time as the contract is concluded, and the exercise of such power does not in itself constitute a breach of any obligation to behave in a given way. Instead, such liability as he may incur will derive from his having fraudulently or culpably led the other party to harbour a confident and reasonable belief that the contract would be concluded.

(2) Under French law, restrictions to the right to break off negotiations are, traditionally, considered as an exception to freedom of contract, which is justified by the abuse (*abus de droit*) of breaking off. The question is whether the breaking off itself constitutes an abuse or a fault. However, from *Manoukian* it follows that it is not the breaking off itself that constitutes a fault but the circumstances which lead to it. French courts usually perceive a fault—and therefore liability under tort law—when negotiations have reached an advanced stage and are suddenly broken off by one party.[38] As Article 1112 Code civil puts it, 'the commencement, continuation and breaking-off of precontractual negotiations are free from control, but this freedom is limited by the duty to act in good faith'. Thus, it is the bad faith that is sanctioned; not the breaking off of negotiations itself.

13.3.C.2 LIABILITY FOR BREAKING OFF NEGOTIATIONS CONTRARY TO GOOD FAITH

In most legal systems, there are exceptional cases in which a party who breaks off negotiations in a manner contrary to good faith may be liable. This liability is not conceived

---

[35] The circumstances in which this liability may arise will be discussed extensively in 13.2.C.2(i) below.

[36] See, eg, J Ghestin, G Loiseau and YM Serinet, *Traité de droit civil: La Formation du contrat*, Tome 1, (4th edn, Paris: LGDJ, 2013) nos. 727 ff; Terré et al (n 10 above) no. 185.

[37] CM Bianca, *Diritto Civile, 3, Il contratto* (2nd edn, Milano: Giuffrè, 2000 (rist. 2015)) para 79; See also, eg, K Larenz, *Lehrbuch des Schuldrechts*, vol I, *Allgemeiner Teil* (14th edn, Munich: CH Beck, 1987) 108; P Van Ommeslaghe, 'Rapport Général' in *La bonne foi, Travaux de l'Association Henri Capitant,* vol XLIII, 1992 (Paris: Litec, 1994) 25; BAG 7 June 1963, NJW 1963, 1843, JZ 1964, 324.

[38] P Malaurie, L Aynès and P Stoffel-Munck, *Droit des obligations* (9th edn, Paris: LGDJ, 2017) no. 468.

in the same way in all legal systems. Is a party who breaks off negotiations in a manner contrary to good faith liable in tort, in contract or should a *sui generis* liability be recognised? Moreover, the extent of the recovery varies among the systems. The question of the nature of liability for breaking off negotiations—tort, contract, *sui generis*—is relevant because most systems have different regimes for tort liability and contractual liability. For example, the periods of prescription (limitation) may vary.[39]

In what follows, we will first examine the general tests which are applied in the various systems for establishing liability below, under (i), then we will explain a fundamental distinction with regard to the extent of liability, the distinction between the reliance (negative) interest and the expectation (positive) interest under (ii). A comparison of the different approaches will be made and the availability of the remedy of specific performance in some jurisdictions will be dealt with under (iii) and (iv) respectively.

(i) The Test for Liability

Principles of European Contract Law   **13.12 (INT)**

Article 2:301: Negotiations Contrary to Good Faith[40]
(1) ...
(2) However, a party who has negotiated or broken off negotiations contrary to good faith is liable for the losses caused to the other party.

UNIDROIT Principles   **13.13 (INT)**

Article 2.1.15: Negotiations in bad faith
(1) ...
(2) However, a party who negotiates or breaks off negotiations in bad faith is liable for the losses caused to the other party.

Notes

(1) The comment on Article 2.1.15 of the UNIDROIT PICC says: 'even before [an offer is made], or in a negotiating process with no ascertainable sequence of offer and acceptance, a party may no longer be free to break off negotiations abruptly and without justification. When such a point of no return is reached, depends of course on the circumstances of the case, in particular the extent to which the other party, as a result of the conduct of the first party, had reason to rely on the positive outcome of the negotiations, and on the number of issues relating to the future contract on which the parties have already reached agreement'.

(2) Neither the wording of Article 2.1.15 of the UNIDROIT PICC and Article 2:301 PECL nor the comment on Article 2.1.15 of the UNIDROIT PICC

---

[39] See, eg, Cass it 11 May 1990, no. 4051, Foro it 1991.I.184.
[40] A similar provision is included in Art II.-3:301(3) DCFR.

indicates which regime is applicable to liability for breaking off negotiations. However, as said above, the application of the contractual regime seems inappropriate here and it is not stated that it concerns a tortious liability. Therefore, it seems, the most suitable solution would be here to adopt a *sui generis* liability for violation of the duty of precontractual good faith.

(3) However, within European private international law, precontractual liability is qualified as tortious. In *Tacconi*,[41] the Court of Justice held that it is 'a matter relating to tort, delict or quasi-delict within the meaning of Article 5(3) of the Convention of 27 September 1968 on Jurisdiction and the Enforcement of Judgments in Civil and Commercial Matters [now Article 7(2) of Brussels I recast Regulation] ...'. This is also reflected in the Rome I Regulation[42] and the Rome II Regulation:[43]

Recital 10 of Rome I
　Obligations arising out of dealings prior to the conclusion of the contract are covered by Article 12 of Regulation (EC) No 864/2007. Such obligations should therefore be excluded from the scope of this Regulation.

Recital 30 of Rome II
　(30) *Culpa in contrahendo* for the purposes of this Regulation is an autonomous concept and should not necessarily be interpreted within the meaning of national law. It should include the violation of the duty of disclosure and the breakdown of contractual negotiations. Article 12 covers only non-contractual obligations presenting a direct link with the dealings prior to the conclusion of a contract. This means that if, while a contract is being negotiated, a person suffers personal injury, Article 4 or other relevant provisions of this Regulation should apply.

Article 2 of Rome II
Non-contractual obligations
　1. For the purposes of this Regulation, damage shall cover any consequence arising out of tort/delict, unjust enrichment, negotiorum gestio or culpa in contrahendo. ...

Article 12 of Rome II
Culpa in contrahendo
　1. The law applicable to a non-contractual obligation arising out of dealings prior to the conclusion of a contract, regardless of whether the contract was actually concluded or not, shall be the law that applies to the contract or that would have been applicable to it had it been entered into. ...

---

[41] C-334/00, *Tacconi v Heinrich Wagner Sinto Maschinenfabrik GmbH (HWS)*, 17 September 2002, ECLI:EU:C:2002:499.
[42] Regulation (EC) No 593/2008 of the European Parliament and of the Council of 17 June 2008 on the law applicable to contractual obligations (Rome I), OJ L 177/2008, pp 6–16.
[43] Regulation (EC) No 864/2007 of the European Parliament and of the Council of 11 July 2007 on the law applicable to non-contractual obligations (Rome II), OJ L 199/2007, pp 40–49.

BGH, 10 July 1970[44]   **13.14 (DE)**

The letter

Once a party has induced or encouraged in another a confident expectation that a contract will be concluded, the breaking off of negotiations without good reason will give rise to liability to compensate the other for damage suffered as a result of his reliance on the expectation.

Held: The criteria governing liability for breaking off contractual negotiations were not satisfied in the case, and the decision of the appellate court was upheld.

Judgment:

1. Even at the stage when negotiations are being conducted with a view to the conclusion of contract, each party to those negotiations owes to the other party, in view of the relationship of trust created by the negotiations, which is analogous to that existing in a contractual relationship, a duty to have reasonable regard for the legitimate interests of that other party. This includes an obligation on each party not to break off the negotiations without good reason once that party has induced or encouraged in the other party a confident expectation that the contract will definitely come into existence. A culpable breach of that duty may give rise, on the basis of the doctrine of *culpa in contrahendo*, to liability to compensate the other party for the damage suffered by him as a result of his reliance on that expectation (judgments of the Chamber of 4.3.1955, V ZR 66/54, BB 55, 429; of 14.7.1967, V ZR 120/64, NJW 67, 2199, in each case with additional supporting material; see also the BGH judgment of 6.2.1969, LM No 28 re § 276 (Fa) BGB = WM 69, 595; OLG Munich, NJW 68, 651). Those principles also apply to negotiations concerning contracts for the sale of land, which must, in accordance with § 313 [now § 311b(1)] BGB, be judicially or notarially recorded in an official document. The fact that the parties had not yet agreed all the details of the contract to be concluded does not of itself preclude liability in damages (see the judgment of the Chamber of 4.3.1955, cited above).

2. However, the criteria giving rise to liability in damages on those grounds are not established in the present case. …

b) … Where, in the course of contractual negotiations, a person states that he is willing to conclude a contract containing detailed specific provisions and thereby arouses or promotes in the other party a firm expectation that the contract will definitely come into existence, that person is not bound by that statement for an unlimited period of time, even if, and in so far as, a claim may lie against him, as described above, on account of *culpa in contrahendo*. Not only *his* conduct, but also that of the *other party*, must be judged in the light of the principle of good faith (§ 242 BGB). In accordance with that principle, the other party must, in particular, obtain clarification from him within a reasonable time as to whether or not he intends, for his part, to conclude a contract containing the provisions proposed …

c) If, in accordance with the foregoing, the passage of time resulted in the plaintiff ceasing to be bound by the statement in her letter of 31.3.1965 that she was willing to conclude a contract, the fact that she may additionally have withdrawn from it for non-pertinent reasons is immaterial. In that respect too, it is necessary, however, to concur with the appellate court as regards the decisive points …

---

[44] LM § 276 (Fa) BGB no. 34, NJW 1970, 1840.

Notes

(1) The mere lengthy prolongation of the negotiations or the mere fact of knowing that the other party has already incurred significant expenses does not make a party liable for breaking off negotiations.[45]

(2) Under German law, only a party who by his fault has made the other party believe that a contract will certainly be concluded, but then without a good reason (*ohne triftigen Grund*) or from non-pertinent motives (*sachfremde Erwägungen*) breaks off the negotiations, is liable on the basis of the doctrine of *culpa in contrahendo* as it was developed by the German courts. On liability for the violation of a precontractual duty, especially the duty to take the interests of the other party into consideration and the duty to inform see the *Letter* case.[46]

(3) As for the nature of liability, in Germany liability for breaking off negotiations, like any liability for *culpa in contrahendo*, is dealt with by the rules of contractual liability (§§ 276 ff BGB).[47] As a matter of fact, the very reason why the courts have developed the doctrine of *culpa in contrahendo* lies in the shortcomings of German tort law.[48] Under tort law pure economic loss is not recoverable unless the damage is caused intentionally—see § 823(1) and § 826 BGB. For broken-off negotiations this implies that, in principle, recovery for expenditure or lost opportunities would be impossible. Moreover, in tort there is no real vicarious liability. Finally, the period of prescription for tort-based actions was rather short. On all these points contractual liability is much more favourable for the claimant. That is why the German courts developed the relationship of mutual trust, which is similar to a contractual relationship (*vertragsähnliches Vertrauensverhältnis*) and which allowed them to apply the contractual regime in the case of *culpa in contrahendo*. It should be remembered here that some scholars, followed by some senates of the Bundesgerichtshof, have argued that broken off negotiations are not a case of *culpa in contrahendo* but of protection of reliance. This view implies that § 123 BGB should be applied by analogy instead of the rules on contractual liability.

Cass com, 20 March 1972[49]   **13.15 (FR)**

The Hydrotile machine

Delictual liability for precontractual bad faith will be imposed where a party intentionally keeps another in a state of protracted uncertainty and then breaks off advanced negotiations without legitimate reason, knowing that the other has incurred considerable expense.

---

[45] See BGH 14 July 1967, NJW 1967, 2162 and earlier RG 24 February 1931, RGZ 132, 26, 28 (the cost of a draft contract made by a notary).

[46] See also, earlier, BGH 16 March 1954, LM § 276 (Fa) BGB no. 3, MDR 1954, 346; for a more recent example see BGH 21 September 1987, ZIP 1988, 88.

[47] Eg *The Letter* case.

[48] See A von Mehren, 'The Formation of Contract' in *International Encyclopedia of Comparative Law*, vol VII, *Contracts in General* (Tübingen: Mohr Siebeck, 1992) ch 9, para 121. See above, pp 133–34.

[49] No. 70-14154, Bull civ IV no. 93, JCP 1973.I.17543, annotated by J Schmidt, RTD civ 1972, 729, annotated by G Durry.

Facts: Société des Etablissements Gerteis entered into negotiations in April 1966 with Société Etablissements Vilber-Lourmat, the exclusive distributor in France of machines for the production of concrete pipes. The machines were manufactured by the American company Hydrotile Machinery Co. After a trip to the US by Robert Gerteis to see the machines in operation, Société Gerteis asked Société Vilber-Lourmat for further information before choosing one of various kinds of machines manufactured by Hydrotile. Société Vilber-Lourmat did not reply to that letter. Société Gerteis subsequently learned that the American manufacturer had sent an estimate on to Vilber-Lourmat but the latter had not forwarded it to Société Gerteis. Vilber-Lourmat subsequently sold a Hydrotile machine to a competitor of Société Gerteis, and that contract of sale contained a clause under which Vilber-Lourmat undertook not to sell a similar machine in an area including the east of France for a period of 42 months following delivery of the machine ordered by the company Les Tuyaux Centrifugés. Société Gerteis commenced proceedings for damages against Société Vilber-Lourmat.

Held: The Cour de cassation upheld the cour d'appel's decision in favour of Société Gerteis.

Judgment: On the two appeal grounds taken together:— Whereas the affirmative judgment now before this Court is criticised because it found against Société Vilber-Lourmat and upheld the accusations made against that company, whereas, according to the appeal, by referring to reciprocal commitments binding the two parties before negotiations were broken off, and to the fact that the discussions had progressed further than the precontractual stage, whilst at the same time affirming the decision of the lower court, which had held that the breaking off of negotiations by Société Vilber-Lourmat constituted a fault committed at the precontractual stage, falling within the scope of Article 1382 [now Article 1240] of the Civil Code, the Cour d'appel does not let it be known whether it considered that that company had incurred contractual liability or delictual liability; thus, by not clarifying the basis of its decision, the Cour d'appel did not provide it with a proper legal foundation, and, moreover, the affirmative judgment under appeal is not justified on the basis of either contractual liability or delictual liability; the Cour d'appel cannot, without distorting the terms of the dispute, base its decision on the contractual liability of Société Vilber-Lourmat, since Société Gerteis expressly confined itself to seeking an order against that company pursuant to Article 1382 of the Civil Code and, moreover, the grounds relied on by the court of first instance likewise do not justify the conclusion that the breaking off was improper; it is contradictory to say that negotiations were abruptly broken off whilst at the same time noting that Société Vilber-Lourmat was being dilatory, and that there was no legitimate reason for such breaking off, as likewise claimed, which has not been proved, since the Cour d'appel accepted as valid the exclusivity clause in the sale contract for a Hydrotile machine and did not respond to the submissions of Société Vilber-Lourmat, which contended that it had received a firm order for that high-technology machine, together with a payment on account from a company already specialising in the manufacture of concrete pipes;

— Whereas, however, the judgment under appeal, accepting submissions put to the court, noted that Société Vilber-Lourmat had deliberately not passed on the final estimate from the American manufacturer intended for Société Gerteis and, without legitimate reason, abruptly and unilaterally broken off the negotiations with that company which were at an advanced stage, and that company had already, to the other's knowledge, incurred considerable expense; it intentionally kept that company in a state of protracted uncertainty, thereby infringing the rules of good faith in commercial relations; the Cour d'appel, which certainly did not hold that Société Vilber-Lourmat had been in breach of contract, noted that Société Vilber-Lourmat had itself stated that, before committing itself to its other customer, it had made a last inquiry as to the intentions of Gerteis, but it did not produce the least proof of this, and in any event it was clear that such drawn-out negotiations could not be broken off by a mere telephone call;

— Whereas the court of first instance was therefore correct to declare that there had been 'an improper breaking off of negotiations' by Société Vilber-Lourmat; having regard to the foregoing, and without considering the other pleas, which need not be examined, the Cour d'appel, without erring in the manner alleged in the appeal, was entitled to find that Société Vilber-Lourmat had incurred delictual liability and the finding against that company was therefore justified;

— Whereas none of the grounds of appeal can therefore be upheld.

Cass civ (3), 3 October 1972[50]   **13.16 (FR)**

Monoprix

Liability for precontractual bad faith does not require negotiations to have been broken off with an intention to cause harm to the other party.

Facts: The building company 'Résidence Bonaparte' had a property complex built in Ajaccio which included, on the ground floor and in the basement, premises for commercial use. Société Anonyme des Monoprix expressed the intention to purchase those premises if the building company made certain alterations to them, and thus became involved in the construction and fitting out of the premises (by providing plans drawn up by its experts). The protracted discussions between the two companies were broken off by Monoprix as it established itself in other premises.

Held: Résidence Bonaparte's appeal before the Cour de cassation succeeded.

Judgment:— Under Articles 1382 and 1383 [now Articles 1240 and 1241] of the Civil Code; —Whereas Société Civile Immobilière Résidence Bonaparte seeks an order requiring Société des Monoprix to pay it damages for misusing the right to break off sales negotiations, and the contested judgment, in dismissing the application on the ground that it had not been alleged that the defendant company caused all or any of the alterations to be carried out solely for the purpose of causing harm, states as a principle of law that 'in the absence of a special agreement to the contrary, alterations to property by or with the authority of the owner thereof in the course of sales negotiations in order to render it suitable for the potential purchaser are carried out at the risk and peril of the owner. Consequently, even if there is no legitimate reason for it, a refusal by that potential purchaser to conclude the sale after the alterations have made it more difficult to sell the property to other persons does not cause him to incur quasi-delictual liability' and 'the position could be different only where those alterations were brought about by the potential purchaser solely with the intention of causing harm'.

— Whereas by giving judgment to that effect, even though delictual liability provided for in the above mentioned articles of the Civil Code may be held to exist in the absence of any intention to cause harm, the Cour d'appel infringed those provisions.

Notes

(1) Although both parties have the right to break off negotiations at any stage, a party who abuses that right can be liable in delict.[51]

---

[50] No. 71-12993, Bull civ III no. 491.
[51] cf for Belgian law: J Herbots, *Contract Law in Belgium* (Deventer-Boston/Bruxelles: Bruylant, 1995) para 190.

(2) In the *Monoprix* case,[52] the cour d'appel had declined liability, holding that the constructor had acted at his own risk and that, even though there was no valid ground which could justify Monoprix's breaking off, there was no abuse of right since it was not established that Monoprix had intended to harm the constructor. However, this harsh decision was reversed by the Cour de cassation, which held that for liability an intention to harm was not required. In a later case the Cour de cassation held that a prospective seller who eventually could not sell his land because he appeared not to be, as he thought, the sole owner would be liable only if he had intended to harm the prospective buyer or if he had been in bad faith.[53] The Cour de cassation also held that a party was liable because it had brutally and unilaterally broken off very advanced negotiations and had not respected a duty of good faith which prevails in international trade.[54] Increasingly French courts police whether the duty of good faith is respected.

(3) Most authors conclude from these cases that a party is liable for breaking off negotiations not only if he intended to harm the other party, but also if he acted in bad faith.

The position in English law is complicated by several issues. First, as we saw earlier, even if the parties had clearly agreed that neither would break off negotiations, it seems that English law will not enforce a contract to negotiate on the ground that it is too uncertain.[55]

Secondly, liability in tort is difficult in this type of case because the courts have been reluctant to award damages in tort when the claimant's loss is purely financial,[56] unless it can be shown that there was fraud. However, there is at least one case in which liability was imposed on one party after its employee negligently led the other party to believe that a contract would be concluded when the employee should have known that the deal would never be approved by his superiors.

Queen's Bench Division   **13.17 (EN)**

Box v Midland Bank Ltd[57]

A company whose employee indicates to an offeror that his offer will be accepted by the company, with the result that the offeror acts on the assumption that a contract will be forthcoming, when the employee should have known that the offer would not be accepted, may be liable to the offeror for the employee's negligence.

Facts: The plaintiff, Mr Box, was an engineer and surveyor. He was interested in supplying pylons to a nationalised concern in Manitoba in Canada, which looked like a very favourable contract. Mr Box sought

---

[52] 13.16 (FR) above, p 439.
[53] Cass civ (1) 12 April 1976, no. 74-11770, Bull civ I no. 122.
[54] Cass com 22 April 1997, no. 94-18953, RTD Civ 1997, 651, annotated by J Mestre.
[55] See *Walford v Miles*, 10.21 (EN), above, p 336.
[56] Above, pp 137–141.
[57] [1979] 2 Lloyd's Rep 391. An appeal on the question of costs only was allowed: [1981] 1 Lloyd's Rep 434.

the help of the Midland Bank. He had a very considerable overdraft already at the bank of about £20,000. But he wanted to extend that overdraft to finance these transactions. He applied to a branch manager in Wales, but without success. Then, in November 1974, he had a meeting with the manager at the Wells Branch in Somerset. He alleged that at that interview the manager, Mr Brokenshire, assured him that finance would be forthcoming, subject to the Export Credit Guarantee Department being satisfied. Also the manager said there might have to be permission from his head office for an increase of the loan. But he told Mr Box that there would be no difficulty about that. On the faith of the assurance Mr Box had been given, he proceeded to over-draw more money from the bank. He mortgaged his own house to the bank to secure the overdraft. But about a fortnight later he discovered that head office refused to grant him the loan because the Export Credit Guarantee Department would not give a policy of insurance to underwrite it—'there was not the slightest possibility' of the application being sanctioned.

Held: The Bank was liable to Mr Box for the manager's negligence.

Judgment: Lloyd J: The case was at one time, as I have already mentioned, a claim in con-tract, but that claim has been abandoned. The claim is now put in tort broadly on the basis of *Hedley Byrne v Heller & Partners* [1963] 1 Lloyd's Rep 485, [1964] 1 AC 465, and, in par-ticular, on the passage in Lord Devlin's speech at pp. 515–516 and 529, where he said this:

> I have had the advantage of reading all the opinions prepared by your Lordships and of studying the terms which your Lordships have framed by way of definition of the sort of relationship which gives rise to a responsibility towards those who act upon information or advice and so creates a duty of care towards them. I do not understand any of your Lordships to hold that it is a responsibility imposed by law upon certain types of persons or in certain sorts of situations. It is a responsibility which is voluntar-ily accepted or undertaken either generally, where a general relationship such as that of solicitor and client or banker and customer is created or specifically in relation to a particular transaction.

Mr Crawford also relied upon … *Esso Petroleum Co Ltd v Mardon* [1976] 2 Lloyd's Rep 305; [1976] QB 801 [where Esso was held liable to the lessee of one of its filling stations for a negligent overestimate of how much fuel the lessee would be able to sell]. He submit-ted that Mr Brokenshire was under a duty not to make careless statements about the availability of finance without first checking with the E.C.G.D. and his own regional head office. The matter was put well by Mr Box himself when he said, in the course of his cross-examination.

> … My claim is for the money I have lost through Mr Brokenshire not telling me that there was no hope of money being made available by the bank.

Mr Hoffman submits that the bank is not liable. His first argument is that this is not like a case where a customer goes to a bank for advice. Mr Box did not go for advice, but, as he himself said, to put a proposition. I think Mr Hoffman is right about that. … But the point does not carry the bank very far. The *Hedley Byrne* principle is not limited to negligent advice. It covers negligent statements generally including precontractual statements of the kind which grounded liability in *Esso Petroleum Co Ltd v Mardon*.

Mr Hoffman's second, and main, submission requires closer consideration. He submits that a statement by a party concerning the probability of his entering into a contract (in this case to lend £45,000) while reserving to himself the right not to enter into the con-tract, cannot ground an action in negligence. The reason is, he says, that the reservation of the right whether or not to enter into the contract is inconsistent with an assumption of legal responsibility; and without an assumption of responsibility there can be no liabil-ity under the *Hedley Byrne* principle. Alternatively, the reservation of the right whether to

441

enter into the contract or not is equivalent to saying to the other party that he must not rely upon any prediction of his as to the likelihood of a contract ensuing, but must make up his own mind. Mr Hoffman submits that that reasoning applies equally whether the contracting party is an individual or a corporation. In the case of a corporation the prediction may be made by one employee and the decision by another, but the reasoning, he says, is the same. It would, said Mr Hoffman, be absurd that the bank should incur liability in the present case by reason of a careless statement on the part of Mr Brokenshire, when Mr Brokenshire had himself made it clear—as I accept he did—that the ultimate decision in relation to the advance lay elsewhere. I see the force of that argument, but I cannot accept it. It seems to me that the *Hedley Byrne* principle ought not to be surrounded by too many limitations and qualifications. Of course if Mr Brokenshire had made clear that he was not accepting any responsibility for his prediction, then the bank would have escaped liability, just as the defendants escaped liability in *Hedley Byrne* itself. But that is not the present case. Mr Brokenshire never made clear that his prediction was without responsibility. He certainly never said so expressly and I refuse to draw that inference from what he did say, namely that the ultimate decision rested with regional head office. I can see no inherent inconsistency or self-contradiction, as Mr Hoffman argued, in one employee accepting responsibility for predicting the outcome of a decision by another employee. It seems to me that the duty of care was exactly the same here whether Mr Brokenshire was predicting the outcome of the application to E.C.G.D. or the outcome of the application to his own regional head office. Accordingly, I would reject Mr Hoffman's second submission.

I can … summarise my views as follows. First, Mr Brokenshire, as manager of the Wells branch, was not obliged to predict the outcome of his application to regional head office for a loan to Mr Box of up to £45,000. But if he did predict the outcome he was under a duty to take reasonable care, since he knew that his prediction would be relied on. Secondly, Mr Brokenshire failed to exercise reasonable care, that is to say the care to be expected of an ordinary competent bank manager—in that he gave Mr Box the impression, as he intended, that the granting of a facility up to £45,000 would be a mere formality once the E.C.G.D. policy had been obtained, whereas there was never the slightest prospect of the facility being made available, as Mr Brokenshire ought to have known. Thirdly, Mr Box did in fact rely on Mr Brokenshire's negligent prediction, in continuing to draw on his account between 18 November 1977, and 2 January 1978, thereby suffering damage. Accordingly, the bank is liable on the *Hedley Byrne* principle,

…

I now turn to the question of damages. As already mentioned, the damages claimed amount to just under £250,000. But a very large part of that represents the gains that the plaintiff would have made if the Manitoba contract had been successfully carried through and the Churchman Newton group saved. Once the claim in contract had been abandoned, Mr Box could not hope to recover for loss of his bargain and Mr Crawford, rightly, abandoned that part of the claim.

…

[T]he plaintiff would probably have saved £5,000 out of his eventual overdraft if it had not been for the negligent misstatement made by Mr Brokenshire on 18 November.

…

In the result there will be judgment for the plaintiff with damages under the first head amounting to £5,000. Everything else is disallowed.

Notes

(1) Although there have been no subsequent cases applying liability for negligent misstatement in the context of failed negotiations, and though later the House of Lords in *Caparo Industries Ltd v Dickman*[58] indicated a cautious approach to liability for negligently-induced economic loss, it is thought that *Box v Midland Bank Ltd* is still good law—the criteria laid down in *Caparo* for liability seem to be satisfied.

(2) But liability under the principle applied in *Box v Midland Bank Ltd* does depend on the defendant having made a negligent statement or forecast. That is not as far-reaching as liability for simply refusing to go ahead for no good reason.

What if the defendant has indicated that there definitely would be a contract but then breaks off negotiations without a good reason? Here we encounter a third problem in English law. Even if one party has promised that it would agree to a contract with the other, the promise may be unenforceable for lack of consideration, unless the promisee can show that it did or undertook to do something in return. As we saw earlier,[59] in cases in which the claimant relied on some promise or undertaking made by the other party without consideration, claimants have sought to rely on 'estoppel' as a substitute for consideration. Can the 'estoppel' principle help if one party has indicated to the other that a contract will definitely be concluded between them, and the other party has acted on this assumption, for example by incurring expenditure?

Claimants in this situation, who are in effect arguing that they are the victim of negotiations being broken off at a late stage, when they have relied on there being a contract, often also seek to rely on one or other form of estoppel. They have sometimes used what is called 'promissory estoppel'. Promissory estoppel is well developed in the US, but in English law it has a very limited role. It applies only when the promise was one not to enforce an existing right. As we saw earlier, generally, estoppel can be used only as a shield, not as a sword. In other words, the doctrine of estoppel cannot be used to create a new cause of action.

In contrast, in cases where the promise was to grant the claimant an interest in property, the courts have developed the doctrine known as 'proprietary estoppel', which can be used to create a new cause of action. On the basis of this doctrine, a promisee who to his detriment has relied upon the landowner's promise that the landowner will grant him an interest in the land can be entitled to be brought into the position he expected.[60]

We saw an example earlier: the case of *Crabb v Arun District Council*.[61] That was the case in which the District Council has indicated to the plaintiff that he would be given rights of access to his land from two gateways on its new service road but, after the plaintiff had sold off the front portion to its land without reserving a right of way over it to the rear portion, withdrew its consent unless the plaintiff paid £3,000. In effect the case is one of breaking off negotiations. The same principle was applied in the next case.

---

[58] [1990] 2 AC 605; see above, p 139.
[59] Above, pp 365 ff.
[60] See, eg, *JT Developments v Quinn* (1991) 62 P & CR 33 (CA), 13.18 (EN), below, p 444.
[61] [1976] Ch 179, 11.12 (EN), above, p 371.

J.T. Developments v Quinn[62]

The coffee shop

Renovation work done on the faith of an assurance by an agent of the lessor that a new lease would be granted to tenants was capable of giving rise to an estoppel, the appropriate remedy for which might be the grant of the new lease.

Facts: The defendants, Mr and Mrs Quinn, were the tenants of a coffee shop under a lease which was due to expire on 24 June 1989. In October 1988, their landlords served notice under section 25 of the Landlord and Tenant Act 1954 terminating the tenancy. The notice informed the tenants that if they did not wish to give up possession they could serve a counter-notice on the landlords within two months and apply to the court for a grant of a new tenancy which the landlords would not oppose. The defendants did not respond to this notice, and were not therefore entitled to apply to the court for a new tenancy. In November 1988, the landlords' surveyor, Mr Clayton, visited the shop. Mr Quinn told Mr Clayton that the Quinns were planning to make improvements to the kitchen. Subsequently in January 1989, there was a telephone conversation between Mr Clayton and Mr Quinn, in which Mr Clayton stated that his employers were prepared to grant a new tenancy to Mr Quinn on the same terms as those contained in a tenancy recently granted by the landlords to a Mr Maclucas in respect of a nearby shop. In January and February 1989, Mr Quinn carried out the kitchen improvements. Mr Clayton visited the property in February 1989, to measure the square footage to calculate the amount of rent under any new tenancy. In March 1989, Mr Clayton told Mr Quinn that the rent would be the same as that paid by Mr Maclucas. However, the landlords sold the shop to the plaintiffs on 23 June 1989. The plaintiffs issued proceedings for possession.

Held: The trial judge refused to grant an order for possession. He held that the telephone conversation in January 1989 constituted an oral agreement to grant a new tenancy on the same terms as the new tenancy granted to Maclucas. Alternatively, he held that the landlords had made a sufficiently clear representation that they would grant a new tenancy and the defendants had relied upon that representation by carrying out the kitchen work. The landlords were therefore estopped from going back upon that representation. The Court of Appeal dismissed the plaintiffs' appeal.

Judgment: RALPH GIBSON LJ: The issue of estoppel raised questions which I have found to be difficult. I have in the course of considering the case hesitated long before reaching a final conclusion and I have changed my mind as to what is the right conclusion more than once. ...

One distinction between promissory and proprietary or equitable estoppel, which has been regarded as established, is that a promissory estoppel cannot create any new cause of action where none existed before: see Halsbury's Laws of England: *Combe v Combe*. In this case, it is common ground that the defendants have asserted a right in equity by agreement or estoppel to a new lease of their shop and have not merely denied the plaintiffs' right to possession. It is clear that, by whatever name it is called, the defendants have set out to prove such an equity as gives rise to that cause of action. The defendants, in short, rely upon the principle, expounded and illustrated in the authorities considered by Lord Templeman in *Att-Gen of Hong Kong v Humphreys Estate* upon which a litigant, who is led to believe he will be granted an interest in land, and who acts to his detriment in that belief, is enabled to obtain that interest. The principle has generally been known in those authorities as proprietary or equitable estoppel.

---

[62] (1991) 62 P & CR 33.

The statement of the principle in a dissenting speech by Lord Kingsdown in *Ramsden v Dyson* has been held to state the law correctly: *Inwards v Baker* and was to the following effect:

> "The rule of law applicable to the case appears to me to be this: if a man, under a verbal agreement with a landlord for a certain interest in land, or, what amounts to the same thing, under an expectation created or encouraged by the landlord, that he shall have a certain interest, takes possession of such land, with the consent of the landlord, and upon the faith of such promise or expectation, with the knowledge of the landlord, and without objection by him, lays out money upon the land, a court of equity will compel the landlord to give effect to such promise or expectation. ..."

The law requires that a representation, if it is to provide the basis for an estoppel, be clear and unequivocal and that it be intended to be relied upon. The evidence of Mr Quinn, which the judge accepted, was that Mr Clayton said: "Mr Quinn would get a new tenancy on the same terms as Mr Maclucas." In one sense, there is nothing unclear or equivocal about that statement: it shows plainly the intention of the landlords. If I am right, however, in holding that no concluded agreement was made or intended to be made by the parties to that conversation, then the representation was, and would be understood as being, that Mr Quinn would get a new tenancy on the same terms as Mr Maclucas if, after Mr Quinn went and looked at the Maclucas lease, the parties were still in agreement to that effect. Nothing was said, it seems, about what was going to be done next or how long Mr Quinn would have to find out what he wanted to know about the Maclucas lease. The parties were, and knew that they were, negotiating the terms of a new lease which both sides probably expected would be completed. Nothing, however, was expressly stated to suggest that the parties had committed themselves in any way so as to deprive either side of the right to withdraw from the negotiations. On the judge's view, Mr Quinn's answer in the January conversation was equally plain: namely that he was in agreement that he would take the new lease. Each side, however, according to basic principles of our law of contract, was free to withdraw even if to his knowledge the other side believed that a binding contract would be made. The decisive question in this case, of course, is whether the landlords by what was said in the January conversation had imposed upon themselves the obligation of not departing from their statement of intention without giving notice to Mr Quinn and before Mr Quinn had within their knowledge acted to his detriment in reliance upon the statement made by Mr Clayton. ...

It must be asked, therefore, in this case first whether any representation made by Mr Clayton in the January conversation can fairly be held to have created or encouraged an expectation in Mr Quinn, before anything further was done towards the agreeing or granting of a new lease, and without any further acts on the part of the landlords, that he would have a new lease of the shop: and, secondly, whether the work done by Mr Quinn in the shop in January and February was done upon the faith of that expectation and with the knowledge of Mr Clayton.

As to the first question, I have been reluctant to accept that Mr Clayton's statements to Mr Quinn can properly be held to have been a clear and unequivocal assurance, which Mr Quinn was entitled to regard as intended by Mr Clayton to be acted upon by Mr Quinn, so as to provide the basis for an equitable estoppel. ... Secondly, my reluctance has been based upon the belief that there is a risk of injustice to a landlord if an unconfirmed and disputed statement in a telephone conversation, coupled with the expenditure of a sum of money upon premises of which the tenant is in occupation under an existing tenancy, can form the basis of a right to a new 18-year lease. I have reminded myself, however, that I have only read the papers and I have not had the benefit of seeing and hearing Mr Clayton and Mr Quinn. There is no suggestion, as I have said, that the judge misdirected himself in his approach to the primary issues of fact. If Mr Quinn spent £2,100 on the shop in reliance upon a clear promise made by Mr Clayton to him it would be unjust to let the landlords go back on that promise. Giving full effect, therefore, to the judge's findings of primary fact, and to the evidence of Mr Quinn upon which in particular Mr Rimer based his submissions, I have finally reached the conclusion that the assurance given by Mr Clayton was capable of providing the basis for the estoppel alleged. ...

The second and last question remains for consideration: was it open to the judge to hold that the work done in the shop by Mr Quinn in January and February 1989 was done upon the faith of that expectation and with the knowledge of Mr Clayton? ... The judge held, as I have said, that Mr Clayton, from what he had been told in November 1988, knew that the defendants would be staying and carrying out the works. With that knowledge he gave to Mr Quinn the assurance which, if I am right, was to the effect that the defendants could, if they wanted it, have a new lease on the Maclucas terms. Mr Quinn, as the judge found, proceeded to spend £2,100 in January and February 1989 in the belief, founded upon the assurance which he had been given, that he could have a new lease on those terms. I do not think that this case is so clear that this court should hold that the judge could not properly regard it as within the principle applied by the court in *Crabb v Arun District Council*.

I would dismiss the plaintiff's appeal.

Subsequently, however, the House of Lords decided the following case on proprietary estoppel, in which they seem to limit the doctrine in some important respects. It seems that the doctrine can apply only when (1) it is quite clear what property interest is to be granted to the claimant; (2) there is either no reservation such as 'subject to contract' or the defendant has clearly represented that he will not rely on the reservation. In *Quinn's* case it was clear what proprietary interest the claimants would get, and there was no reservation.[63] But also Lord Scott's speech in the House of Lords indicates (3) that proprietary estoppel may not be used to avoid the rule that contracts for the transfer of interests in land have to be in writing, under Law of Property (Miscellaneous Provisions) Act 1989, Section 2.

House of Lords   **13.19 (EN)**

Cobbe v Yeoman's Row Management Ltd[64]

A party cannot recover on the basis of promissory estoppels if the proprietary interest he is to receive is not certain, nor if he knows that the other party is not committed to the deal, for instance because both are aware that it is dependent on further negotiations.

Facts: The claimant, an experienced property developer, orally agreed with the third defendant, the sole director of the first defendant company, to purchase for £12 million a property comprising a number of flats, of which the first defendant was the registered freehold proprietor, for redevelopment into six town houses.

---

[63] Compare the next case.
[64] [2008] UKHL 55, [2008] 1 WLR 1752.

The arrangement was that the first defendant would obtain vacant possession of the property and the claimant would develop it and keep any profit subject to overage under which each party would have 50% of the gross proceeds of the property over £24 million. Acting in the belief, encouraged by the third defendant on behalf of the first defendant, that the property would be sold to him, the claimant spent the next 18 months, engaging architects and other professionals, in applying for planning permission. Immediately after the grant of planning permission the defendants withdrew from the agreement, demanded £20 million as the price for the sale of the freehold and suggested that the first defendant should receive 40% of the amount by which the gross proceeds exceeded £40 million. The claimant brought proceedings alleging, inter alia, that the defendants were estopped from denying that he had acquired a beneficial interest in the property because they had acted unconscionably in knowingly inducing and encouraging by their actions his belief, on which he had relied to his detriment, that the property would be sold to him and then refusing to honour the oral agreement, alternatively that there was a constructive trust in his favour.

Held: The judge found that the third defendant on behalf of the first defendant had encouraged the claimant's belief that if he succeeded in obtaining planning permission the oral agreement would be honoured and that she had taken an unconscionable advantage of him. He concluded that the claims in proprietary estoppel and constructive trust succeeded. The Court of Appeal dismissed the defendants' appeal, but a further appeal to the House of Lords was allowed.

Judgment: LORD SCOTT ...
[3] A number of possible bases for the grant of relief to B need to be considered. (i) First, there is proprietary estoppel. B has, with the encouragement of A, spent time and money in obtaining the planning permission and has done so, to the knowledge of A, in reliance on the oral agreement in principle and in the expectation that, following the grant of the planning permission, a formal written agreement for the sale of the property, incorporating the core financial terms that had already been agreed and any other terms necessary for or incidental to the implementation of the core terms, would be entered into. In these circumstances, it could be, and has been, argued, A should be held to be estopped from denying that B had acquired a proprietary interest in the property and a court of equity should grant B the relief necessary to reflect B's expectations. (ii) Second, there is constructive trust. In circumstances such as those described, equity can, it is suggested, give effect to the joint venture agreed upon by A and B by treating A as holding the property upon a constructive trust for himself and B, with A and B taking beneficial interests calculated to enable effect to be given to B's expectations engendered by the agreement in principle. (iii) Third, there is unjust enrichment. The grant of planning permission, obtained by B at his expense and through the deployment of his time and planning expertise, has increased the value of the property. So A has been enriched at the expense of B and, since it was A's repudiation of the oral agreement in principle that frustrated the basis upon which B had been relying, perhaps unjustly enriched.
[Lord Scott went on to outline a number of other issues that are not relevant to our discussion.]
...
[9] Mr Cobbe's claim, as originally pleaded, sought specific performance and damages for breach of contract, i.e. contractual relief. However, at the outset of the trial on liability, on 18 January 2005, these contractual claims were abandoned. Section 2(1) of the Law of Property (Miscellaneous Provisions) Act 1989 made them untenable: 'A contract for the sale or other disposition of an interest in land can only be made in writing ...' But section 2(5) of the 1989 Act says that 'nothing in this section affects the creation or operation of resulting, implied or constructive trusts', and Mr Cobbe, with the permission of Etherton J, amended his pleadings in order to substitute for the claims he had abandoned claims for declarations that the defendant company held the property on constructive

trust for itself and him and was estopped from denying that he had an interest in the property, with, in each case, consequential relief. He added, also, a claim for an inquiry into the time he had spent and expenditure he had incurred in obtaining planning permission and, following that inquiry, 'such restitution as the court considers just'.

...

[14] Both the judge and the Court of Appeal regarded the relief granted as justified on the basis of proprietary estoppel. I respectfully disagree. The remedy to which, on the facts as found by the judge, Mr Cobbe is entitled can, in my opinion, be described neither as based on an estoppel nor as proprietary in character. There are several important authorities to which I want to refer but I want first to consider as a matter of principle the nature of a proprietary estoppel. An 'estoppel' bars the object of it from asserting some fact or facts, or, sometimes, something that is a mixture of fact and law, that stands in the way of some right claimed by the person entitled to the benefit of the estoppel. The estoppel becomes a 'proprietary' estoppel—a sub-species of a 'promissory' estoppel—if the right claimed is a proprietary right, usually a right to or over land but, in principle, equally available in relation to chattels or choses in action. So, what is the fact or facts, or the matter of mixed fact and law, that, in the present case, the defendant company is said to be barred from asserting? And what is the proprietary right claimed by Mr Cobbe that the facts and matters it is barred from asserting might otherwise defeat?

[15] The pleadings do not answer these questions. The terms of the oral 'agreement in principle', the second agreement, relied on by Mr Cobbe are pleaded but it is accepted that there remained still for negotiation other terms. The second agreement was, contractually, an incomplete agreement. The terms that had already been agreed were regarded by the parties as being 'binding in honour', but it follows that the parties knew they were not legally binding. So what is it that the defendant company is estopped from asserting or from denying? It cannot be said to be estopped from asserting that the second agreement was unenforceable for want of writing, for Mr Cobbe does not claim that it was enforceable; nor from denying that the second agreement covered all the terms that needed to be agreed between the parties, for Mr Cobbe does not claim that it did; nor from denying that, pre-18 March 2004, Mr Cobbe had acquired any proprietary interest in the property, for he has never alleged that he had. And what proprietary claim was Mr Cobbe making that an estoppel was necessary to protect? His originally pleaded claim to specific performance of the second agreement was abandoned at a very early stage in the trial (see para 8 above) and the proprietary claims that remained were claims that the defendant company held the property on trust for itself and Mr Cobbe. These remaining proprietary claims were presumably based on the proposition that a constructive trust of the property, with appropriate beneficial interests for the defendant company and Mr Cobbe, should, by reason of the unconscionable conduct of Mrs Lisle-Mainwaring, be imposed on the property. I must examine that proposition when dealing with constructive trust as a possible means of providing Mr Cobbe with a remedy, but the proposition is not one that requires or depends upon any estoppel.

[16] It is relevant to notice that the amendments to Mr Cobbe's pleaded prayer for relief, made when the specific performance and damages for breach of contract claims were abandoned, include the following:

'(4) Alternatively, a declaration that [the defendant company and Mrs Lisle-Main waring] are estopped from denying that [Mr Cobbe] has such interest in the property and/or the proceeds of sale thereof as the court thinks fit.'

This is the only pleaded formulation of the estoppel relied on by Mr Cobbe and, with respect to the pleader, is both meaningless and pointless. Etherton J concluded, in para 85 of his judgment, that the facts of the case 'gave rise to a proprietary estoppel equity in favour of Mr Cobbe', but nowhere identified the content of the estoppel. Mummery LJ agreed (paras 60 and 61 of his judgment, concurred in by Dyson LJ (para 120) and Sir Martin Nourse (para 141)), but he, too, did not address the content of the estoppel. Both Etherton J and Mummery LJ regarded the proprietary estoppel conclusion as justified by the unconscionability of Mrs Lisle-Mainwaring's conduct. My Lords, unconscionability of conduct may well lead to a remedy but, in my opinion, proprietary estoppel cannot be the route to it unless the ingredients for a proprietary estoppel are present. These ingredients should include, in principle, a proprietary claim made by a claimant and an answer to that claim based on some fact, or some point of mixed fact and law, that the person against whom the claim is made can be estopped from asserting. To treat a 'proprietary estoppel equity' as requiring neither a proprietary claim by the claimant nor an estoppel against the defendant but simply unconscionable behaviour is, in my respectful opinion, a recipe for confusion.

...

[Lord Scott then moves to the point that the negotiations were 'subject to contract']

[26] Both Etherton J and Mummery LJ in the Court of Appeal recognised that, in cases where negotiations had been made expressly subject to contract and a contract had not in the end been forthcoming, it would be very difficult for a disappointed purchaser to establish an arguable case for a proprietary estoppel. Etherton J, having referred to the relevant authorities, accepted the improbability that in a subject-to-contract case a proprietary estoppel might arise (paras 119 and 120), but distinguished the present case on the footing that Mrs Lisle-Mainwaring had encouraged Mr Cobbe to believe that if he succeeded in obtaining planning permission the second agreement would be honoured even though not legally binding (para 123) and, also, I think, that nothing equivalent to a subject-to-contract reservation had ever been expressed (para 119) and that no issue likely to cause any difficulty had been raised in the negotiations that culminated in the second agreement: para 122. ...

[27] My Lords, I can easily accept that a subject-to-contract reservation made in the course of negotiations for a contract relating to the acquisition of an interest in land could be withdrawn, whether expressly or by inference from conduct. But debate about subject-to-contract reservations has only a peripheral relevance in the present case, for such a reservation is pointless in the context of oral negotiations relating to the acquisition of an interest in land. It would be an unusually unsophisticated negotiator who was not well aware that oral agreements relating to such an acquisition are by statute unenforceable and that no express reservation to make them so is needed. Mr Cobbe was an experienced property developer and Mrs Lisle-Mainwaring gives every impression of knowing her way around the negotiating table. Mr Cobbe did not spend his money and time on the planning application in the mistaken belief that the agreement was legally enforceable. He spent his money and time well aware that it was not. Mrs Lisle-Mainwaring did not encourage in him a belief that the second agreement was enforceable. She encouraged in him a belief that she would abide by it although it was not. Mr Cobbe's belief, or expectation, was always speculative. He knew she was not legally bound. He regarded her as bound 'in honour' but that is an acknowledgement that she was not legally bound.

[28] The reality of this case, in my opinion, is that Etherton J and the Court of Appeal regarded their finding that Mrs Lisle-Mainwaring's behaviour in repudiating, and seeking

an improvement on, the core financial terms of the second agreement was unconscionable, an evaluation from which I do not in the least dissent, as sufficient to justify the creation of a 'proprietary estoppel equity'. As Etherton J said, at para 123, she took unconscionable advantage of Mr Cobbe. The advantage taken was the benefit of his services, his time and his money in obtaining planning permission for the property. The advantage was unconscionable because immediately following the grant of planning permission she repudiated the financial terms on which Mr Cobbe had been expecting to be able to purchase the property. But to leap from there to a conclusion that a proprietary estoppel case was made out was not, in my opinion, justified. Let it be supposed that Mrs Lisle-Mainwaring were to be held estopped from denying that the core financial terms of the second agreement were the financial terms on which Mr Cobbe was entitled to purchase the property. How would that help Mr Cobbe? He still would not have a complete agreement. Suppose Mrs Lisle-Mainwaring had simply said she had changed her mind and did not want the property to be sold after all. What would she be estopped from denying? Proprietary estoppel requires, in my opinion, clarity as to what it is that the object of the estoppel is to be estopped from denying, or asserting, and clarity as to the interest in the property in question that that denial, or assertion, would otherwise defeat. If these requirements are not recognised, proprietary estoppel will lose contact with its roots and risk becoming unprincipled and therefore unpredictable, if it has not already become so. This is not, in my opinion, a case in which a remedy can be granted to Mr Cobbe on the basis of proprietary estoppel.

[29] There is one further point regarding proprietary estoppel to which I should refer. Section 2 of the 1989 Act declares to be void any agreement for the acquisition of an interest in land that does not comply with the requisite formalities prescribed by the section. Subsection (5) expressly makes an exception for resulting, implied or constructive trusts. ... Proprietary estoppel does not have the benefit of this exception. ... My present view ... is that proprietary estoppel cannot be prayed in aid in order to render enforceable an agreement that statute has declared to be void. The proposition that an owner of land can be estopped from asserting that an agreement is void for want of compliance with the requirements of section 2 is, in my opinion, unacceptable. The assertion is no more than the statute provides. Equity can surely not contradict the statute. As I have said, however, statute provides an express exception for constructive trusts.

[Lord Scott also dismissed the claim based on a constructive trust on the basis that there would be a constructive trust over the property only when it had been newly acquired for the purposes of a joint venture, not when (as here) the property already belonged to one party. However, the developer was allowed a claim based on unjust enrichment. The other Members of the House of Lords either agreed or delivered judgments to the same general effect.]

Notes

(1) Lord Scott sees three problems with the claimant's argument based on estoppel. The first seems to be that the terms of the proprietary interest to be granted to the claimant had not been agreed. He seems to indicate that the claimant must be making a proprietary claim which the defendant is not permitted to deny, and that this means the interest the claimant was to obtain must be certain. Compare the subsequent case of

Thorner v Major,[65] a case which did not involve a failed contract but reliance on a vaguer and non-bargain promise. A farmer indicated to his nephew that the farm would be his and in reliance the nephew worked on it for years, only to find that his uncle, in his will, had left it to someone else. It was held that the interest the nephew was to get—ownership of whatever land formed part of the farm at his uncle's death—was sufficient for proprietary estoppel.

(2) The second problem is that the negotiations were all subject to contract, which means that neither was committed[66]—so that the claimant was not justified in relying on getting the defendant's agreement. (See also the earlier Privy Council case of *A-G for Hong Kong v Humphreys Estate (Queens Gardens) Ltd.*[67])

(3) The third point is that Lord Scott doubts (obiter—this seems not to have been one of the main reasons for his decision) that the doctrine can be used to overcome the formal requirement that a contract for the disposition of an interest in land must be in writing. (On the third point see above.[68])

(4) It is possible to interpret *Cobbe's* case as making it very hard ever to use proprietary estoppels in the context of contract negotiations that have been broken off. It will frequently be the case that the interest the claimant is to receive is still subject to negotiation. Probably agreement on the essential elements will suffice, as it does for the making of a contract, but at least that seems to be required. Moreover, it seems that the claimant must have thought that the defendant was fully committed. This means that if the negotiations were subject to contract, the doctrine would not bite unless the defendant had represented that the 'subject to contract' reservation was being waived,[69] or perhaps if the defendant represented that the documents had been signed. On this see the next case.

A further restriction on the use of proprietary estoppel in England is that it may only be used by a claimant who relied on being granted an interest in land or other property. Thus it will not apply in all cases involving land, let alone cases in which property is not the subject matter of the contract.[70]

We have said that there is also a doctrine known as promissory estoppel, under which a party who has made a promise without consideration may be prevented from going back on it if the promisee has acted in reasonable reliance on the promise; but that in English law this only applies when the promise is one not to enforce existing contractual rights.[71]

In Australia, these restrictions have been abandoned, in a case which involved precontractual negotiations.

---

[65] [2009] UKHL 18, [2009] 1 WLR 776.
[66] See above, p 329.
[67] [1987] AC 114.
[68] See above, p 407.
[69] Compare *RTS Flexible Systems Ltd v Molkerei Alois Müller GmbH & Co KG (UK Production)* [2010] UKSC 14, [2010] 1 WLR 753.
[70] See above, p 443.
[71] See above, p 370.

Waltons Stores (Interstate) Ltd v Maher[72]

Where one party represents that he will let the other party know if there is any obstacle to the two parts of the contract being signed and exchanged,[73] and encourages the other in the meantime to take steps towards performance, then even if the contract is never signed by the first party he may be estopped from denying that there is a binding contract.

Facts: In September 1983 Waltons Stores (Interstate) Ltd and the Mahers entered into negotiations with a view to Waltons leasing the Mahers' property at Nowra. The property required considerable work in order to be suitable for Waltons' purposes, and it was intended that the Mahers would carry out this work by 5 February 1984. In October 1983, Waltons' solicitor sent a form of lease to the Mahers' solicitor, and the Mahers' solicitor subsequently informed Waltons' solicitor on November 1 that the Mahers had begun to demolish the old building on the site. On 7 November, the Mahers' solicitor told Waltons' solicitor that, if Mr Maher was to have sufficient time to make the necessary preparations for Waltons' takeover, it was essential that the agreement be concluded within the next day or so. The Mahers' solicitor also said that Mr Maher did not want to demolish a new brick part of the old building until it was clear that there were no problems with the lease. Waltons' solicitor sent the Mahers' solicitor an amended lease with a covering letter stating that he would let Mr Maher know the next day whether Waltons disagreed with any of the amendments incorporated in the redraft. Neither on the next day nor at all did Waltons' solicitor inform the Mahers' solicitor that Waltons disagreed with any of the amendments. On 11 November the Mahers' solicitor forwarded to Waltons' solicitor 'by way of exchange' the lease executed by the Mahers. Thereafter the Mahers began to demolish the new part of the old building. On or about 21 November Waltons had second thoughts about proceeding with the lease, and having ascertained from its solicitors that for want of an exchange of parts it was not bound to proceed, instructed them to 'go slow'. On 10 December Waltons became aware that the demolition had commenced. The Mahers began the building work in accordance with plans approved by Waltons in early January, but on 19 January, their solicitor received a letter from Waltons' solicitor saying that Waltons did not intend to proceed with the lease. The building was by then about 40% complete. Between 11 November 1983 and 19 January 1984 Waltons' solicitor had not communicated with the Mahers' solicitor, and retained the copy of the lease signed by the Mahers. The Mahers commenced proceedings in the Supreme Court of New South Wales for a declaration that there was in existence a valid and enforceable agreement for a lease, an order for specific performance and alternatively damages in lieu thereof.

Held: Kearney J gave judgment for the Mahers for damages in lieu of specific performance, and Waltons' appeal to the Court of Appeal (Glass, Samuels and Priestley JJ A) was dismissed (1986) 5 NSWLR 407. Waltons appealed, by special leave, to the High Court, where the appeal was dismissed.

Judgment: MASON CJ and WILSON J:

20. This brings us to the doctrine of promissory estoppel on which the respondents relied in this Court to sustain the judgment in their favour. ...

30. One may ... discern in the cases a common thread which links them together, namely, the principle that equity will come to the relief of a plaintiff who has acted to his detriment on the basis of a basic assumption in relation to which the other party to the transaction has 'played such a part in the adoption of the assumption that it would be unfair or unjust if he were left free to ignore it': per Dixon J in *Grundt*, at p 675;

---

[72] (1988) 164 CLR 387.

[73] This is a reference to the normal procedure for making a contract for the sale of land or granting a lease in both Australia and England: the vendor and the purchaser each sign a copy of the contract and then exchange copies. For an explanation of the procedure see *Eccles v Bryant* [1948] Ch 93.

see also *Thompson*, at p 547. Equity comes to the relief of such a plaintiff on the footing that it would be unconscionable conduct on the part of the other party to ignore the assumption. ...

32. Because equitable estoppel has its basis in unconscionable conduct, rather than the making good of representations, the objection, grounded in *Maddison v Alderson*, that promissory estoppel outflanks the doctrine of part performance loses much of its sting. ...

34. The foregoing review of the doctrine of promissory estoppel indicates that the doctrine extends to the enforcement of voluntary promises on the footing that a departure from the basic assumptions underlying the transaction between the parties must be unconscionable. As failure to fulfil a promise does not of itself amount to unconscionable conduct, mere reliance on an executory promise to do something, resulting in the promisee changing his position or suffering detriment, does not bring promissory estoppel into play. Something more would be required. *Humphreys Estate* [in which a claim for proprietary estoppels failed because all the dealings between the parties were subject to contract[74]] suggests that this may be found, if at all, in the creation or encouragement by the party estopped in the other party of an assumption that a contract will come into existence or a promise will be performed and that the other party relied on that assumption to his detriment to the knowledge of the first party. *Humphreys Estate* referred in terms to an assumption that the plaintiff would not exercise an existing legal right or liberty, the right or liberty to withdraw from the negotiations, but as a matter of substance such an assumption is indistinguishable from an assumption that a binding contract would eventuate. ...

36. All this may be conceded. But the crucial question remains: was the appellant entitled to stand by in silence when it must have known that the respondents were proceeding on the assumption that they had an agreement and that completion of the exchange was a formality? The mere exercise of its legal right not to exchange contracts could not be said to amount to unconscionable conduct on the part of the appellant. But there were two other factors present in the situation which require to be taken into consideration. The first was the element of urgency that pervaded the negotiation of the terms of the proposed lease. As we have noted, the appellant was bound to give up possession of its existing commercial premises in Nowra in January 1984; the new building was to be available for fitting out by 15 January and completed by 5 February 1984. The respondents' solicitor had said to the appellant's solicitor on 7 November that it would be impossible for Maher to complete the building within the agreed time unless the agreement were concluded 'within the next day or two'. The outstanding details were agreed within a day or two thereafter, and the work of preparing the site commenced almost immediately.

37. The second factor of importance is that the respondents executed the counterpart deed and it was forwarded to the appellant's solicitor on 11 November. The assumption on which the respondents acted thereafter was that completion of the necessary exchange was a formality. The next their solicitor heard from the appellant was a letter from its solicitors dated 19 January, informing him that the appellant did not intend to proceed with the matter. It had known, at least since 10 December, that costly work was proceeding on the site.

---

[74] See n 76 below.

38. It seems to us, in the light of these considerations, that the appellant was under an obligation to communicate with the respondents within a reasonable time after receiving the executed counterpart deed and certainly when it learnt on 10 December that demolition was proceeding. It had to choose whether to complete the contract or to warn the respondents that it had not yet decided upon the course it would take. It was not entitled simply to retain the counterpart deed executed by the respondents and do nothing: cf. *Thompson*, at p 547; *Olsson v Dyson* (1969) 120 CLR 365, at p 376. The appellant's inaction, in all the circumstances, constituted clear encouragement or inducement to the respondents to continue to act on the basis of the assumption which they had made. It was unconscionable for it, knowing that the respondents were exposing themselves to detriment by acting on the basis of a false assumption, to adopt a course of inaction which encouraged them in the course they had adopted. To express the point in the language of promissory estoppel the appellant is estopped in all the circumstances from retreating from its implied promise to complete the contract. ...

BRENNAN J: ...

23. Parties who are negotiating a contract may proceed in the expectation that the terms will be agreed and a contract made but, so long as both parties recognise that either party is at liberty to withdraw from the negotiations at any time before the contract is made, it cannot be unconscionable for one party to do so. Of course, the freedom to withdraw may be fettered or extinguished by agreement but, in the absence of agreement, either party ordinarily retains his freedom to withdraw. It is only if a party induces the other party to believe that he, the former party, is already bound and his freedom to withdraw has gone that it could be unconscionable for him subsequently to assert that he is legally free to withdraw. ...

25. The unconscionable conduct which it is the object of equity to prevent is the failure of a party, who has induced the adoption of the assumption or expectation and who knew or intended that it would be relied on, to fulfil the assumption or expectation or otherwise to avoid the detriment which that failure would occasion. The object of the equity is not to compel the party bound to fulfil the assumption or expectation; it is to avoid the detriment which, if the assumption or expectation goes unfulfilled, will be suffered by the party who has been induced to act or to abstain from acting thereon. ...

27. But there are differences between a contract and an equity created by estoppel. A contractual obligation is created by the agreement of the parties; an equity created by estoppel may be imposed irrespective of any agreement by the party bound. A contractual obligation must be supported by consideration; an equity created by estoppel need not be supported by what is, strictly speaking, consideration. The measure of a contractual obligation depends on the terms of the contract and the circumstances to which it applies; the measure of an equity created by estoppel varies according to what is necessary to prevent detriment resulting from unconscionable conduct. ...

29. ... There is no logical distinction to be drawn between a change in legal relationships effected by a promise which extinguishes a right and a change in legal relationships effected by a promise which creates one. Why should an equity of the kind to which *Combe v Combe* refers be regarded as a shield but not a sword? The want of logic in the limitation on the remedy is well exposed in Mr David Jackson's essay 'Estoppel as a Sword' in (1965) 81 *Law Quarterly Review* at pp 241–243.

30. Moreover, unless the cases of proprietary estoppel are attributed to a different equity from that which explains the cases of promissory estoppel, the enforcement of promises to create new proprietary rights cannot be reconciled with a limitation on the enforcement of other promises. If it be unconscionable for an owner of property in certain

circumstances to fail to fulfil a non-contractual promise that he will convey an interest in the property to another, is there any reason in principle why it is not unconscionable in similar circumstances for a person to fail to fulfil a non-contractual promise that he will confer a non-proprietary legal right on another? It does not accord with principle to hold that equity, in seeking to avoid detriment occasioned by unconscionable conduct, can give relief in some cases but not in others. ...

32. The qualifications proposed bring the principle closer to a principle the object of which is to avoid detriment occasioned by non-fulfilment of the promise. But the better solution of the problem is reached by identifying the unconscionable conduct which gives rise to the equity as the leaving of another to suffer detriment occasioned by the conduct of the party against whom the equity is raised. Then the object of the principle can be seen to be the avoidance of that detriment and the satisfaction of the equity calls for the enforcement of a promise only as a means of avoiding the detriment and only to the extent necessary to achieve that object. So regarded, equitable estoppel does not elevate non-contractual promises to the level of contractual promises and the doctrine of consideration is not blown away by a side-wind. Equitable estoppel complements the tortious remedies of damages for negligent mis-statement or fraud and enhances the remedies available to a party who acts or abstains from acting in reliance on what another induces him to believe. ...

35. ... Having elected to allow Mr Maher to continue to build, it was too late for Waltons to reclaim the initial freedom to withdraw which Waltons had in the days immediately following 11 November. As the Mahers would suffer loss if Waltons failed to execute and deliver the original Deed, an equity is raised against Waltons. That equity is to be satisfied by treating Waltons as though it had done what it induced Mr Maher to expect that it would do, namely, by treating Waltons as though it had executed and delivered the original Deed. It would not be appropriate to order specific performance if only for the reason that the detriment can be avoided by compensation. The equity is fully satisfied by ordering damages in lieu of specific performance. The judgment of Kearney J is supported by the first basis of estoppel. ...

Notes

(1) It will be recalled that in *Walford v Miles*,[75] the House of Lords took the approach that either party is entitled to withdraw from negotiations, at any time and for any reason.[76]

(2) In the traditional view, where a party has gone back on his word, relief on the basis of estoppel is restricted to cases where the promisee is induced to believe that he will acquire rights in the promisor's land, so that 'proprietary' estoppel can apply. In the *Waltons Stores* case this doctrine could not apply because Waltons Stores were not proposing to grant the Mahers an interest in land but to take a lease from the Mahers. In English law promissory estoppel is limited to cases in which one party has promised that it will give up, or not enforce, an existing right.[77] This restriction was not applied in *Waltons Stores* either.

---

[75] 10.18 (EN), above, p 336.
[76] See also *Att-Gen of Hong Kong v Humphreys Estates (Queen's Gardens)* [1987] 1 AC 114, where the Privy Council gave much weight to the fact that the agreement in principle was 'subject to contract' and that none of the parties had given up their right to withdraw from the negotiations.
[77] See above, p 370.

(3) It has been argued that the restrictions imposed by English law cannot be justified.[78] The only possible objection to accepting a cause of action in a case of detrimental reliance upon other promises is that it would be irreconcilable with the doctrine of consideration. However, in *Waltons Stores* Brennan J argued that allowing promissory estoppel to give rise to a cause of action does not necessarily undermine the doctrine of consideration. The reason for this is that the object of the principle of promissory estoppel is not to make a promise binding, which would require consideration, but to avoid a detriment. In other words, since the doctrine of promissory estoppel protects only the reliance interest and not the expectation interest, no consideration is required.[79] When could the promissory estoppel come into play? Mere reliance on a promise to do something, resulting in the promisee changing his position or suffering detriment, is not sufficient. Something more is required. According to Mason CJ and Wilson J in *Waltons Stores*, this 'may be found, if at all, in the creation or encouragement by the party estopped in the other party of an assumption that a contract will come into existence or a promise will be performed and that the other party relied on that assumption to his detriment to the knowledge of the first party'.

(4) In US law the doctrine of promissory estoppel is well established.[80] It has been applied in a case of broken off negotiations by the Supreme Court of Wisconsin.[81] It should, however, be added that this case seems to be rather isolated in US law.[82]

(5) McKendrick has argued that an eventual introduction of a cause of action based on promissory estoppel into English law following the example of US and Australian law would not undermine the doctrine of consideration because this action would give a right to recovery only of the reliance interest. This would follow from the object of the principle of estoppel, which is to prevent a detriment.[83] This view seems indeed to be confirmed by the US case, *Hoffman v Red Owl Stores*,[84] where the plaintiff merely got relief for the expenses he had incurred. However, the result of *Waltons Stores* seems to be different. Although the Australian High Court adopted the view that the object of the equity was to avoid detriment, the Court held that the appellant was estopped from retreating from its implied promise to complete the contract and awarded damages in lieu of specific performance. It is clear that the interest protected here is the expectation interest, since protection of the reliance interest would have been limited to recovery of the expenses made in demolishing the old building and in building 40% of the new one.

(6) Whether the English courts will ever be persuaded to follow the Australian lead and allow promissory estoppels in 'pre-contract' cases of this type may be doubted,

---

[78] See E McKendrick, *Contract Law* (12th edn, Basingstoke: Palgrave Macmillan, 2017) 108–13; contrast *Treitel on the Law of Contract*, 14th edn by E Peel (London: Sweet & Maxwell, 2015) paras 3-088 and 3-150.

[79] See McKendrick (n 78 above) 95–97.

[80] See, eg, s 90 of the Restatement 2d of Contracts.

[81] *Hoffman v Red Owl Stores* 26 Wis 2d 683, 133 NW 2d 267 (1965).

[82] See Farnsworth (n 1 above) 238; von Mehren (above n 48) para 124.

[83] Above, pp 365–70.

[84] Above, n 81.

particularly in the light of *Cobbe's* case.[85] That decision, together with *Walford v Miles*, suggests that the English courts are not in favour of trying to protect parties who incur expenditure before there is a contract (unless they have been positively misled by being given incorrect information, as the judge held was the case in *Walford v Miles*). In other words it is possible to take a variety of attitudes towards the Waltons Stores scenario. One is that the claimants were hard done by and should be given a remedy. Another is that they took a foolish risk in starting demolition before they had a contract. Perhaps they should sue their own lawyers for not warning them. For a study of different possible approaches to the *Waltons Stores* case, see Drahos and Parker, 'Critical Contract Law in Australia'.[86]

(ii) Nature and Extent of Liability

With regard to damages, a distinction is generally drawn between what some legal systems refer to as the reliance (negative) interest and the expectation (positive) interest.[87] Recovery of the expectation interest gives the claimant the financial equivalent of what he would have had, had a valid contract been concluded, including the profit he would have made with that contract. Recovery of the reliance interest means that the claimant is put back into the position he would have been in, insofar as is possible via damages, if no negotiations had taken place. Thus he can recover the expenses he incurred—travelling, drafting the contract etc. But reliance damages are not limited to that. Farnsworth has emphasised that they may also include recovery for lost opportunities, ie the loss a party made by not concluding an alternative contract with a third party due to the fact that he was engaged in negotiations with this party.[88] For example, in the Swiss case of *Escophon AG v Bank in Langenthal*,[89] the claimant could recover two months' profit which it would have made had it concluded the credit agreement with another bank. Similarly, in the US case of *Markov*,[90] lost opportunities included the profits lost due to the leaving of his principal customer, which would not have occurred had the plaintiff concluded a contract with a third party instead of entering into deceptive negotiations. An Italian case, *The Giuliana*,[91] shows that the lost opportunity to conclude a contract with a third party does not necessarily have to be an opportunity to conclude a contract of the same type.[92]

---

[85] 13.19 (EN), above, p 446.

[86] (1990) 3 Journal of Contract Law 30.

[87] See on this problem below, ch 26.2, pp 1060–66.

[88] Farnsworth (above n 1) 225 ff. See, earlier, von Jhering (n 3 above) 21, with regard to liability for concluding an invalid contract; cf *Asser/Hartkamp & Sieburgh 6-III* 2014/197 (n 15 above). There is no English case directly in point but it is established that the victim of fraud may recover damages for lost opportunities to make alternative arrangements: *East v Maurer* [1991] 1 WLR 461.

[89] Swiss Bundesgericht 6 February 1979, BGE 105 II 75.

[90] Above, p 428 n 19.

[91] Cass it 12 March 1993, no. 2973, Foro it 1993.I.956, reproduced at p 402 of the second edition of this book.

[92] See, eg, Cass it 20 August 1980, no. 4942, Mass Foro it 1980, 78.

Cass com, 26 November 2003[93]   **13.21 (FR)**

Manoukian

*In the case of breaking off negotiations in bad faith, only the expenses incurred in the nego-
tiations and the surveys that the innocent party had undertaken can be recovered. Neither
positive interest nor the loss of the chance of making such profits can be recovered.*

Facts: see 13.8 (FR), above, p 430.

Held: The appeal was rejected.

Judgment:— But whereas the circumstances constituting fault in the exercise of the right
unilaterally to break off precontractual negotiations are not the cause of the loss which
comprises the lost chance of making the profits which one could expect from the conclusion of the contract;

— Whereas the Cour d'appel rightly decided that, in the absence of a firm and final
agreement, the loss suffered by Alain Manoukian included only the expenses incurred in
the negotiations and the surveys it had undertaken and not the profits that it could have
hoped to make from the running the business if the contract had been concluded, nor
even the loss of the chance of making such profits; that the ground is not founded; ...

Code civil   **13.22 (FR)**

Article 1112: ...
   In the case of fault committed during the negotiations, the reparation of the resulting
loss is not calculated so as to compensate the loss of benefits which were expected from
the contract that was not concluded nor the loss of the chance of obtaining these benefits.

Notes

   (1) In *Manoukian*, the Cour de cassation held that there was no causal link between
the abuse in breaking off the negotiations and the loss of a chance to make a profit
(a causal link is one of the three elements required for liability in delict; the two other
elements are fault and prejudice).

   (2) Since *Manoukian*, it has become increasingly difficult to recover the loss of the
gain expected from the contract, and Article 1112(2) of the Code civil is along the
same line. It is justified by the general rule that the parties are free to break off negotiations in French law. This freedom would be illusory if the courts awarded damages
which included the recovery of the expectation interest. In that case the victim of the
legal wrong would be in the same position as if the contract had been concluded.

   (3) Article 1112(2) upholds the solution adopted in *Manoukian*. This provision
expressly excludes the loss of profits expected from contract and the loss of a chance
of obtaining these, had the contract been concluded. The recoverable loss is thus
limited to the loss actually incurred, such as the expenses related to the feasibility
study, the organisation of the negotiations, etc. The refusal to compensate the loss of
a chance to make a profit was specified by the ratification of the 2016 Ordonnance.

---

[93] Nos. 00-10243 and 00-10949, Bull civ IV no. 186; 13.8 (FR), above, p 430.

If breaking off itself became unlawful at a certain point in the negotiations, this might imply that the party who breaks off at that point should compensate the expectation interest, since the damage caused by the breaking off (the unlawful act) consists in the non-conclusion of the contract and, as a consequence, in the loss of the profit and the chance to obtain it that would have been made with it.[94] Such an extensive liability, however, is generally rejected by the legal systems.[95] An exception is Dutch law, where the Hoge Raad has accepted that there is a point in the negotiations from which parties are no longer free to break off in *Plas v Valburg* and subsequent decisions and where, in principle, expectation damages can be recovered.[96]

Hoge Raad, 18 June 1982[97]   **13.23 (NL)**

Plas v Valburg

If a party was justified in relying on the expectation that some sort of contract would in any event result from the negotiations, the act of the other party in breaking them off may in itself be regarded as contrary to good faith. In such a situation, an obligation to pay compensation in the positive interest may exist.

Facts: At a meeting in June 1974, the Municipal Council of Valburg decided on the construction of an indoor swimming pool and resolved to make HFL 1,312,000 available for the building costs. Plas submitted an offer for the construction of an indoor swimming pool. A Council committee then decided to examine Plas's offer, along with offers submitted by three other contractors. Thereafter, the committee requested one of the three previous tenderers and Plas to adapt their plans and to submit priced tenders. In December 1974, Plas submitted an adapted offer priced in the sum of HFL 1,300,000. At a meeting of the Mayor and the Council held on 9 January, the Mayor stated on behalf of the Municipal Executive that Plas's tender was the lowest, that his plan was acceptable to the Municipality, that the Council should make a decision about it and that a few adjustments still needed to be made concerning various points of detail. At the close of a subsequent meeting of the Council at which the construction of the swimming pool was not an item appearing on the agenda, a councillor stated that Arns BV had a plan for the construction of the swimming pool which was HFL 156,000 cheaper than Plas's plan, and distributed documentation concerning the Arns plan to those present. The Arns plan was adopted by the Council at a meeting in March 1975. Plas brought an action, seeking, as his principal claim, performance of an agreement which he submitted had come into existence; in the alternative, he claimed damages for default; and in the further alternative, he claimed damages for the breaking off of negotiations.

Held: The Rechtbank (District Court) allowed his claim, but the Gerechtshof (Regional Court of Appeal) set that judgment aside and dismissed all his claims. Plas appealed to the Hoge Road (Court of cassation) and his appeal was allowed.

Judgment:
     3. Findings in relation to the plea advanced:
     ... 3.4 The fourth part of the plea is also well founded. In the fourth of its grounds of judgment, the Regional Court of Appeal based its findings on the legal rule that the obligation to pay compensation on account of conduct in precontractual dealings which

---

94   See Bianca (n 37 above) para 79; Terré et al (n 10 above) no. 185.
95   See below, pp 463 ff. See eg for Italian law Cass it 20 August 1980, no. 4942, Mass Foro it 1980, 78.
96   See *Asser/Hartkamp & Sieburgh 6-III* 2014/197 ff (n 15 above).
97   NJ 1983, 723, annotated by CJH Brunner; (1983) 32 Ars Aequi, 758, annotated by P van Schilfgaarde.

does not accord with the duty to act in good faith 'extends no further than a requirement to make good the costs and damage incurred which the other party would not have suffered if the precontractual relationship had not arisen', and that it cannot therefore include an obligation to compensate for lost profits. However, the law generally affords no support for such a rule. It is not impossible that negotiations concerning a contract may reach such an advanced stage that the act of breaking them off must in itself be regarded, in the prevailing circumstances, as a breach of good faith, on the basis that the parties may be assumed mutually to have relied on the expectation that some sort of contract would in any event result from the negotiations. In such a situation, it may also be legitimate to find that an obligation exists to pay compensation for lost profits.

3.5 The fifth and sixth parts of the plea are directed against the fifth and sixth grounds of the judgment appealed against, in which the Regional Court of Appeal held that no compensation was payable in respect of the costs and damage incurred by Plas prior to the discussion on 9 January 1975, because it followed from Plas' arguments that the precontractual relationship on which his claim for compensation was based arose in the course of, and as a result of, that discussion, and because Plas never maintained that the Council was not free, prior to that date, to withdraw from the negotiations. The objections to this which are advanced in the fifth and sixth parts of the plea are well founded (286 NJ 1983, 723, annotated by Brunner; AA 32,1983, 758, annotated by Van Schilfgaarde). The Regional Court of Appeal's finding that Plas at no time asserted that the Council was not free, prior to 9 January 1975, to withdraw from the negotiations must be considered in conjunction with the District Court's ruling that, following the discussion on that date, the Council was no longer entitled to break off the negotiations. In omitting to deal with the objection raised against that ruling by the Council, the Regional Court of Appeal clearly assumed that the ruling in question was correct. However, if the Council was no longer able, after 9 January 1975, to withdraw from the negotiations, it is impossible to see why a breach of its obligations should not result in the Council being required to make good costs which had already been incurred before 9 January 1975 in the context of the negotiations held prior to that date. Such a requirement to pay compensation might even arise if the negotiations had not yet reached the stage at which the Council was no longer able in good faith to break them off but had nevertheless already advanced to the point that the act of breaking them off resulted, in the circumstances, in its no longer being free to walk away from them without assuming responsibility, wholly or in part, for the expenses incurred by Plas.

Hoge Raad, 12 August 2005[98]   **13.24 (NL)**

CBB v JPO

Each party is free to break off the negotiations, unless this would be unacceptable because the other party had reasonably believed that a contract would be concluded or other circumstances would render it unacceptable. The way and the extent to which the party who breaks off the negotiations, contributed to this belief as well as the reasonable interests of that party must be considered.

---

[98] NJ 2005, 467, ECLI:NL:HR:2005:AT7337.

Facts:[99] Centraal Bureau Bouwtoezicht (CBB) and JPO negotiated about the development of an office for CBB in Arnhem. Part of the deal was that JPO bought a plot of land from the city of Arnhem, where the office was to be built and that the land was sold partly to CBB. JPO negotiated about the sale of the land with the City of Arnhem. In March 2000 JPO wrote to CBB that preparations for the sale of the land were in the final stage. In reaction, CBB asked in writing when the plot of land was to be conveyed. JPO did not answer that question. In addition, parties debated the fee which CBB had to pay and other conditions of the cooperation. Subsequently, after one year and one month, CBB broke off the negotiations with JPO and CBB bought the plot of land directly from the City of Arnhem.

CBB started proceedings against JPO. In a counterclaim, JPO asked for a declaration that CBB had acted unlawfully, since the negotiations had reached their final stage, while there were reasonable expectations that an agreement would have been reached. In addition, JPO also asked for a declaration that JPO was entitled to expectation interest, which was to be calculated in a different procedure.

The court in first instance allowed the counterclaim. The Gerechtshof (Regional Court of Appeal) set aside that judgment insofar as it concerned JPO's counterclaim. It held, though, that CBB had acted unlawfully by breaking off the negotiations and that CBB had to pay half of the expectation interest, which was to be determined in a different procedure. CBB appealed to the Hoge Raad.

Held: The Hoge Raad quashed the decision of the Court of Appeal and referred the case to another court of appeal.

Judgment: 3.6 Assessing these pleas, it must be put first that the yardstick to assess whether there is a duty to pay damages after breaking off negotiations, each party, ... is free to break off the negotiations, unless this would be unacceptable because the other party had reasonably believed that a contract would be concluded or other circumstances would render it unacceptable. The way and the extent to which the party who breaks off the negotiations, contributed to this belief as well as the reasonable interests of that party must be considered. It may also be relevant that during the negotiations unforeseen circumstances occurred. If, however, in spite of these unforeseen circumstances, the negotiations are continued over a long period of time, the belief that a contract would be concluded must be judged at the moment of the breaking off of the negotiations in the light of all the negotiations.

3.7 The pleas concerned are well founded.

The Court of Appeal ... had to rule upon JPO's claim, which, in essence, concerned the reimbursement of damage, which is referred to in the plea as expectation interest, because no contract was concluded between the parties.

The challenged considerations do not show that the Court of Appeal ... used this yardstick, which is strict and requires restraint.

If the Court of Appeal failed to assess whether the breaking off of the negotiations by CBB was unacceptable and whether JPO reasonably could believe that a contract, ..., would have been concluded considering all the circumstances of this case, the Court of Appeal misunderstood the yardstick and misconceived the law.

If the Court of Appeal intended to apply the proper yardstick, ... its decision is not sufficiently motivated. The arguments, which the Court of Appeal use, show that CBB was not allowed to break off the negotiations at that moment in the opinion of the Court of Appeal, because ... CBB was not allowed to presume that agreement with JPO was not to be expected in the short run. However, these arguments do not show why the breaking off was unacceptable and why JPO could reasonably believe that contract would

---

[99] See the opinion by Advocate General AS Hartkamp, 12 August 2005, NJ 2005, 457, ECLI:NL:PHR:2005:AT7337.

have been concluded, had the negotiations been continued. Consequently, a sufficient reasoning is missing to allow a claim for damages resulting from the fact that no contract was concluded.

Notes

(1) Since the *Plas/Valburg* case,[100] the Dutch courts distinguish three stages in the negotiating process. At the first stage both parties are entirely free to break off negotiations. At the second stage a party is still free to break off negotiations, but if he does so he has to pay the expenses the other party has incurred. Finally, at a third stage parties are no longer free to break off negotiations. This is the case where the other party may reasonably believe that some contract of the type the parties were negotiating will be concluded or if other circumstances of the case make breaking off unacceptable.[101] If a party breaks off at that third stage, he is liable in damages, which may even amount to the expectation interest.[102] He may also be ordered to continue negotiations.[103] However, in later cases, the Hoge Raad seems to have introduced a new test to determine whether a party is entitled to expectation interest in the third stage.[104] The Hoge Raad limited its *Plas/Valburg* doctrine. In *CBB* v *JPO* it held that the other party is not liable in all cases where a party was justified in expecting the imminent conclusion of a contract, because that other party's interests must also be taken into account. Moreover, a change of circumstances during the negotiations may provide a justification for breaking off as well. If in the case of changed circumstances the negotiations have been continued, the moment of breaking off the negotiations is decisive to determine whether one is entitled to expectation damages.

(2) In the third stage breaking off is in itself contrary to good faith. In other words, in opposition to other systems, under Dutch law the advanced stage of negotiations can actually make a party lose his right to break off negotiations. Thus Dutch law has replaced the clear-cut distinction between contract and no-contract by a gradual process where at a very advanced stage of negotiations a party can claim to be put financially into the position as if a contract were concluded.[105]

(3) As regards the nature of liability: the Dutch Hoge Raad has based its 'three stages rule' on tort and good faith alternatively, and sometimes on both.[106] Especially in the most recent cases the Hoge Raad has based liability directly on good faith.[107] The drawback of such a 'third way' approach to liability would in most systems be that the code provides for only two regimes of liability (contract and tort) and therefore

---

[100] See 13.23 (NL), above, p 459. For the most recent developments, see: RPJL Tjittes, 'De aansprakelijkheid voor afgebroken onderhandelingen—een kritisch overzicht' Rechtsgeleerd Magazijn Themis 2016, no. 5, p 237.

[101] See *VSH v Shell,* HR 23 October 1987, NJ 1988, 1017, annotated by CJH Brunner.

[102] See above, p 459.

[103] See below, p 467.

[104] *De Ruiterij v Ruiters,* HR 14 June 1996, NJ 1997, 481, annotated by HJ Snijders; *CBB v JPO,* HR 12 August 2005, NJ 2005, 467.

[105] See Van Schilfgaarde, annotation under *Plas v Valburg,* above, n 97.

[106] For a decision based on tort, see eg *Heesch v Reijs,* HR 13 February 1981, NJ 1981, 456, annotated by CJH Brunner. See *Asser/Hartkamp & Sieburgh 6-III* 2014/201 ff (n 15 above).

[107] See, eg, HR 16 June 1995, NJ 1995, 705, annotated by PA Stein.

acceptance of a new third regime by the courts would lead to considerable uncertainty. However, in the Netherlands this approach is possible since the Dutch code provides for a single regime for any type of liability—see Articles 6:95 ff and 3:310 BW.

(4) As regards the extent of liability, if a party breaks off negotiations in the so-called second stage, as said above, he must reimburse the other party's expenses. A party who breaks off negotiations in the third stage, where breaking off is no longer allowed, is liable for the expectation interest. This was first accepted in the *Plas/Valburg* case.[108] However, it should be added that there are nearly no cases where expectation damages actually were awarded.[109] The Dutch rule can be explained by the fact that in Dutch law in the so-called third stage, which begins at the moment the other party could reasonably expect that a contract will be concluded,[110] breaking off itself is unlawful—contrary to good faith. The damage caused by this unlawful act— ie the breaking off—is the non-conclusion of the contract, since at that stage of the negotiations the contract would have been concluded if the negotiations had not been broken off. Thus the fact that Dutch courts accept expectation damages when negotiations are broken off in the third stage is just a logical consequence of considering their breaking off itself at a certain point unlawful—contrary to good faith. The *Plas/Valburg* case has been commented upon by several foreign authors, like Farnsworth, Sacco, Van Ommeslaghe. Most of them disapprove of the Dutch rule.[111]

(5) At this point it is appropriate to think again about the English case of *Walford v Miles*. Although the decision has met with criticism,[112] there is quite wide agreement that it would not have been appropriate to allow the appellant's claim for £1 million lost profit in full.[113] Just possibly a claim limited to the plaintiff's wasted expenditure would have been received more favourably. In fact, the plaintiff DID recover £700 reliance loss, on the basis of a misrepresentation by the defendants that they were not negotiating with anyone else—a finding by the trial judge that was not appealed. Although the point of departure is very different, as it relates to the general principle of good faith, eventually, is there much difference between this and the solution that French courts would have adopted, after the *Manoukian* case and would now adopt on the basis of Article 1112?

(iii) Comparison

(1) Comparing the rules of the Principles, Germany, France and the Netherlands, the test for liability for breaking off negotiations appears to be the same. The two decisive elements are: (a) the negotiations have come to a point where the other party, induced by the defendant, could reasonably expect that a contract would be concluded; (b) there is no

---

[108] See 13.23 (NL), above, p 459.
[109] *Asser/Hartkamp & Sieburgh 6-III* 2014/198 (n 15 above). See for empirical research with respect to case law of lower courts on this point: L Smeehuijzen and M van Oosten, 'Plas/Valburg: veel rechtsonzekerheid en ondermaats resultaat in de feitenrechtspraak' (2015) 64 Ars Aequi 72.
[110] See above, p 462.
[111] See, eg, Van Ommeslaghe (n 37 above) 34.
[112] See above, p 338.
[113] See below, p 469.

good reason for breaking off. In England, a party who breaks off negotiations is not liable unless he made a misrepresentation, or the negotiations involved a representation that the claimant would be granted an interest in land or other property.[114] Thus the opportunities in which the court can impose some form of precontractual liability are more limited. However, the Australian (*Waltons Stores*) and US (*Hoffman v Red Owl Stores*) examples show that the English position is not the only one possible under common law. The test applied in *Waltons Stores* is similar to the one applied in continental European systems. We will also see below that the other restrictions on the doctrine in English law are very similar to those found in the continental laws. In most European systems liability for breaking off negotiations is based on tort and in most systems liability is limited to the reliance interest.

(2) As regards the first element of the test (the provocation of reliance), the mere hope for a contract is not sufficient.[115] First, the other party must have relied on the conclusion of the contract. In Germany it is even necessary that the other party believed that the conclusion of the contract was certain.[116] The period in which a party can rely on the expectation provoked by the other is not unlimited in time, because he himself is also under a duty to behave according to good faith. Therefore, he has to make clear within a reasonable time what he intends to do.[117] Secondly, the reliance must have been justified in the circumstances. Thirdly, the reliance must have been induced by a representation, silence or conduct of the other party, for example, by telling him that he can give up his current position,[118] by asking him to prepare a tender which requires more costs than are normal in that field of business, or by inviting or allowing him to start to perform the prospective contract without warning him about the risk that the contract will eventually not be concluded.[119] See, as examples, BGH 19 October 1960,[120] where a negotiating party allowed the other party to start to rebuild premises destroyed during the war on the land which he expected to lease, the French *Monoprix* case[121] and the English proprietary estoppel cases.[122]

It should be noted that in many cases objective circumstances, like the long duration of the negotiations or the very advanced stage they had reached, seem to be decisive.[123] Earlier English cases, such as *Crabb v Arun DC*,[124] suggested that the doctrine of proprietary estoppel might apply even though it was not wholly clear on what terms the interest in property would be granted, but after *Cobbe's* case it seems that the proprietary interest

---

[114] It is a different question whether the plaintiff may have a restitutionary (*quantum meruit*) claim based on work done in anticipation of a contract: see, eg, *British Steel Corp v Cleveland Bridge Co*, 6.25 (EN), above, p 164.

[115] See, eg, Cass it 28 January 1972, no. 199, Foro it 1972.I.2088. See also, with regard to proprietary estoppel, *Att-Gen of Hong Kong v Humphreys Estates* (n 76 above) 264.

[116] See, eg, BGH 14 July 1967, NJW 1967, 2162.

[117] BGH 10 July 1970, 13.14 (DE), above, p 436.

[118] See BAG 7 June 1963 (n 37 above).

[119] See BGH 8 June 1978, BGHZ 71, 386.

[120] LM BGB § 276 (Fa) no. 11, NJW 1961, 169.

[121] 13.16 (FR) above, p 439.

[122] Above, pp 443–51.

[123] See, eg, CA Rennes 29 April 1992, JCP G 1993.IV.1520; CA Riom 10 June 1992. See also the Comment to Art 2.1.15 UNIDROIT PICC.

[124] 11.12 (EN), above, p 371.

must have been precisely defined. Conversely, the German Bundesgerichtshof does not require agreement on all essential points.[125]

(3) As regards the second element, a good reason for breaking off will readily be accepted. A better offer from a third party can be sufficient.[126] The disloyal behaviour of the other party, for example his unexpectedly raising new unjustified conditions, can also justify termination of the negotiations, even if they were in a very advanced stage. However, reasons that have nothing to do with the negotiations cannot justify the breaking off.[127] Saleilles held that breaking off must 'be possibly justified by an economic interest'.[128] In English law, it has not been discussed whether such factors can be taken into account in deciding whether or not there is a proprietary estoppel, but since the remedy is often seen as resting on equity or the need to prevent unconscionable conduct, it seems likely that they can.[129] It may also be that some courts would think the respondents' conduct in *Walford v Miles* was consistent with good faith. They had agreed to give a warranty that their annual profits for the first year after the sale would reach £300,000. They had become concerned that their employees and the intending purchaser might not get on well, key staff might leave and the profit figure might not be met.

(4) Can a party ever be liable for breaking off negotiations if the negotiations were conducted in view to a formal contract? A formal contract is a contract which is binding only if a certain formal requirement is met. A statutory provision may for example require a certain type of contract to be concluded in writing. See, for example, in England, for the sale of land, section 2 of the Law of Property (Miscellaneous Provisions) Act 1989. Sometimes a form requirement may also consist of authentication by a notary. See, for example, in Germany, for the sale of land, § 311b BGB, and, for the foundation of a company, § 2 GmbHG. It has been suggested that breaking off negotiations over such a contract can never make a party liable because the other party is never justified in relying on the imminent conclusion of such a contract, since he should know that there will be no binding contract before the formal requirement is met. Moreover, it has been argued that liability would undermine the purpose of the form requirement, which is often protection of a party from his own over-hasty decisions. However, the German BGH has held that a party who breaks off negotiations can be liable even if the contract could be effective only after complying with a formal requirement.[130] The reason is that the party who broke off is not liable for the breaking off itself but for inducing the other party to act on the belief that a contract would be concluded. Therefore liability does not undermine the form requirement.[131] Medicus has disapproved of these decisions in very

---

[125] See BGH 10 July 1970, 13.14 (DE), above, p 436; see also the US case of *Hoffman v Red Owl Stores* (above, p 456), where agreement on all essential details was not held to be necessary for liability on the basis of promissory estoppel.

[126] See Cour d'appel de Liège, 20 October 1989, Revue de droit commercial belge 1990, 521; see also Saleilles (n 5 above).

[127] See BGH 7 February 1980, BGHZ 76, 343–51, NJW 1980, 1683.

[128] Saleilles (n 5 above) 718–19.

[129] Compare promissory estoppel, which clearly does take such factors into account.

[130] See, eg, with regard to negotiations about the sale of land, BGH 10 July 1970 (n 125 above) and, with regard to negotiations concerning the foundation of a company, BGH 21 September 1987, ZIP 1988, 88, WM 1988, 163.

[131] See BGH 14 July 1967, NJW 1967, 2162.

strong terms.[132] He suggests that in cases where the result would be really unbearable § 242 BGB could bring a solution. Under English law, it is unclear whether the statutory provision which requires most contracts for the sale or disposition of an interest in land to be made in writing (section 2 of the Law of Property (Miscellaneous Provisions) Act 1989) excludes the operation of the doctrine of proprietary estoppel, but the most recent dicta suggests that it does.[133] In other countries this question does not seem to have led to any disputes yet.[134]

(5) Is liability for breaking off negotiations possible if the person who by his statements or conduct caused the reliance had no power to conclude a binding contract on behalf of the party, for example a company or a municipality, that he represented in the negotiations? The German Bundesgerichtshof has decided that lack of power of an agent does not exclude liability. Again the explanation lies in the character of liability for broken off negotiations. The fault lies in inducing reliance, not in refusing to conclude the contract.[135] Therefore, although the defendant cannot be bound by a person who has no power to conclude a contract on his behalf, this does not exclude his responsibility for the fault of those conducting negotiations on his behalf (§ 278 BGB).[136] In the Swiss case of *Escophon AG v Bank in Langenthal*,[137] it was exactly the circumstance that neither the head office nor the branch had ever informed the claimant that any contract would require the head office's approval which made their eventual breaking off contrary to good faith.

(6) In English law, where there may be liability in tort, the employer may be liable for the employee's negligence in misleading the claimant even though the claimant knows that the employer, or some higher-ranked employee, would have to approve any contract.[138]

(7) In France, if both negotiating parties are professionals, breaking off will lead to liability only in exceptional cases, because the costs of unsuccessful negotiations are supposed to be part of the parties' general expenses, which they can incorporate in the price in contracts resulting from other, successful negotiations.[139] We have seen that in *Cobbe's* case the English court took into account the fact that the claimant was a highly experienced property developer, but this seems to have been relevant principally on the question whether he had been misled by the other party.

(iv) Order for Specific Performance

In some systems liability in damages is not the only remedy. A party can be ordered to continue negotiations or even to conclude the contract.

---

[132] D Medicus, *Verschulden bei Vertragshandlungen: Gutachten and Vorschläge zur Überarbeitung des Schuldrechts,* vol I (Cologne: Heymanns, 1981) 192, 499.

[133] In addition to *Cobbe's* case, 13.19 (EN) above, p 446, see *Dudley Muslim Association v Dudley MBC* [2015] EWCA Civ 1123, [2016] 1 P & CR 10 at [33].

[134] On liability for concluding an invalid contract, see 13.3.E.

[135] See Medicus (n 132 above) 501.

[136] See, eg, BAG 7 June 1963 (n 37 above), and BGH 20 September 1984, BGHZ 92, 164, NJW 1985, 1779.

[137] Above, p 457, n 89.

[138] *Box v Midland Bank Ltd*, 13.17 (EN), above, p 440.

[139] See Ghestin et al (n 36 above). See, however, Cass com 22 April 1997, no. 94-18953, RTD Civ 1997, 651, annotated by J Mestre.

De Ziener

The duty of precontractual good faith may give rise to a duty to continue negotiations, and where that duty is not complied with, a court may order that the relevant negotiations should take place.

Facts: On 12 October 1983, the film director Du Mee wrote to the widow of Simon Vestdijk expressing the wish to make a film of Vestdijk's novel *De Ziener*. Mrs Vestdijk granted Du Mee an option expiring on 1 June 1984. Following the expiry of the option period, Du Mee sent his initial script of *De Ziener* to Mrs Vestdijk. Mrs Vestdijk wrote to Du Mee, informing him that a number of matters relating to the script needed to be resolved, and referred him to the publishing house De Bezige Bij in relation to these matters. In April 1985 the director of De Bezige Bij wrote to Du Mee informing him that he had been granted a further option for the film rights to De Ziener until 2 April 1986. The letter stated 'We will be pleased, towards the end of the option period, to enter into more specific consultations with you concerning the contract and related matters of detail'. In March 1986, Du Mee requested a one year extension of the option period, in view of the fact that he had not succeeded in arranging finance for the film. By a letter dated 24 April, De Bezige Bij stated that Mrs Vestdijk had not given a positive reaction to the request for an extension and that she was willing to give him until 15 May 1986 to produce a modified plan. On 11 May, Du Mee sent Mrs Vestdijk a new version of the script. However, on 27 May 1986, Mrs Vestdijk wrote to Du Mee informing him that the modified plan had not inspired in her any confident expectation that an extension of the option would lead to acceptable results. She was therefore unwilling to extend the option and stated that it had terminated with effect from 15 May 1986. Du Mee brought proceedings, seeking (a) an order restraining the defendants from taking steps to prevent him from filming *De Ziener* and from carrying out the preparatory work required for the filming, (b) an order prohibiting the defendants from entering into negotiations concerning the filming of *De Ziener* with any person other than Du Mee and/or from giving any third party the right to film *De Ziener*, and (c) an order requiring the defendants, or at least De Bezige Bij, within two days after service of the judgment to enter into reasonable consultations with Du Mee with a view to bringing into existence an agreement concerning the filming of *De Ziener*. The President of the Amsterdam Rechtbank (District Court) dismissed the claims.

Held: On appeal, Du Mee succeeded in his claims under (b) and (c) above.

Judgment: ... 4.5 The fourth plea is likewise well founded. As discussed in 4.3 above, Du Mee was entitled to assume, when seeking an extension of the option period, that, in the event of that request being refused, he would be given an opportunity to hold discussions with regard to a definitive contract taking immediate effect. De Bezige Bij did not give him that opportunity, choosing instead the middle course of confirming, by letter of 29 April 1986, the information, already given earlier in oral form, that Mrs Vestdijk had 'not given a positive reaction' to Du Mee's request for an extension, and giving Du Mee, on behalf of Mrs Vestdijk, the opportunity of submitting a 'modified plan or scenario' before 15 May 1986. Du Mee proceeded on that basis. De Bezige Bij's conduct was not in itself contrary to the principle of good faith.

4.6 However, following receipt of the second script, Mrs Vestdijk again indicated that she was 'unable to give a positive reaction' to Du Mee's request for an extension of the option in respect of the film rights. She gave two reasons for this. First, she was not satisfied with either the first or the second version of the script. The second reason given by her was stated to be Du Mee's conduct in relation to the statement made by Mr Hamming of De Bezige Bij in his letter of 24 April 1986 that Mrs Vestdijk regarded it as most important that Du Mee should in the near future hold an exchange of views with her. There existed no obligation per se on the second and third defendants to extend the term of the option.

[140] NJ 1988, 430.

However, the reasons given in Mrs Vestdijk's letter of 27 May 1986, as described above, did not justify the refusal, implicitly expressed in that letter and subsequently maintained, to negotiate with regard to the materialisation of a definitive contract. The first reason was inadequate, since Mrs Vestdijk, as is apparent from her letter of 2 April 1983, had already accepted the first script and, according to the contents of her letter of 27 May 1986, the second script differed from the first only in so far as one or two things in it had been altered, added or omitted. The second reason was inadequate ... [because] given that the defendants were aware of the considerable importance which Du Mee attached to the conclusion of a definitive contract, the second and third defendants were under a duty to act in good faith by proceeding to enter into reasonable consultations with the appellant to that end.

4.7 It follows from the considerations set out above that the judgment appealed against must be set aside. The claim should be allowed. The Court considers in that regard that the first version of the script was accepted by Mrs Vestdijk, so that there can be no further debate concerning the script beyond what the appellant has stated in the second complete paragraph on p 6 of his statement of grounds of appeal. The claim made under (b) falls to be allowed in the manner hereinafter set out.

The claim made under (a) cannot be allowed, since no definitive contract ever materialised. In view of the relative significance of the matter to the parties, the Court proposes to limit the penalty to HFL 200,000[141] per breach.

Notes

(1) Under Dutch law a party who breaks off negotiations at a stage where this is no longer allowed[142] can be ordered to continue negotiations.[143] In *De Ziener*, the widow of a writer was ordered to continue negotiations concerning the right to make a film on the basis of a famous novel.[144] According to some scholars, a party may even be ordered actually to conclude the contract.[145]

(2) In England, in a case of proprietary estoppel, the landowner may actually be compelled to grant the right in his land he has led the other party to expect he will obtain. See, for example, *Humphreys Estate* (per Lord Templeman),[146] where the Privy Council held that there was no difficulty in the court devising an order for specific performance provided that HKL was estopped from withdrawing from the negotiations. In the case the Privy Council held that no estoppel could be established since the government had failed to show that HKL had encouraged a belief that they would not withdraw from the agreement in principle and that the government had relied on that belief. The Privy Council gave much weight to the fact that the agreement in principle was 'subject to contract' and that none of the parties had given up their right to withdraw from the negotiations. Compare also *Cobbe's* case, above.[147]

---

[141] Approximately €100,000 per breach.
[142] See, on this so-called third stage, above, p 462.
[143] See *Asser/Hartkamp & Sieburgh* 6-III 2014/195 ff (n 15 above).
[144] See also Gerechtshof Arnhem 14 November 1983, NJ 1984, 499 (negotiations concerning the takeover of a company).
[145] See Van Schilfgaarde, annotation to *Plas v Valburg* (1983) 32 Ars Aequi, 758.
[146] See above, p 455 n 76.
[147] See 13.19 (EN) above, p 446.

In contrast, in *JT Developments v Quinn*,[148] where no such words had been used, proprietary estoppel was found. In view of these cases, it seems likely that in *Walford v Miles* specific performance could have been sought on the basis of proprietary estoppel if the appropriate detrimental reliance could have been established—improvement to the promisor's land or conferment of some other benefit on him is, however, not a necessary condition.[149]

(3) In most other systems, like in France, the remedies for broken off negotiations are limited to damages. In Germany, the Bundesgerichtshof has held that a party who has broken off negotiations in a manner contrary to good faith cannot be ordered to continue negotiations or actually made to conclude the contract.[150] Medicus finds German law inconsistent. He raises the question why a party at a certain point of the negotiations may rely on the conclusion of a contract but is denied the right to claim the actual conclusion of the contract or to claim expectation damages.[151]

13.3.D FAILING TO COMPLY WITH TENDERING PROCEDURES

BGH, 25 November 1992[152]   **13.26 (DE)**

Oolitic stones

A party is entitled to compensation in the measure of the positive interest if he can establish that, had the correct tendering procedure been followed, he would certainly have been awarded the contract.

Facts: The claimant was engaged in the extraction and sale of natural stones. The defendant, represented by the HM waterways authority, invited the claimant, in the context of a call for tenders limited to six tenderers, to submit, in compliance with certain regulations, an offer for the supply of stones for hydraulic structures. According to the 'practical directions' contained in the regulations, the contracting authority was to proceed in accordance with the Terms and Conditions for the Award of Contracts (VOL/A). The invitation to tender provided that the material to be used was to be rubble for use in hydraulic structures consisting of basalt, greywacke or hard sandstone. The claimant submitted a tender for the supply of basalt stones at a price of DM 237,430.65.

Apart from the claimant, two other tenderers responded to the invitation to tender. Messrs B submitted an offer for the supply of oolitic stones not corresponding with the requirements of the invitation to tender at a price of DM 118,349.10, together with an expert's report on the testing of such stones to establish their suitability for their intended purpose, and a third company made an incomplete offer. Messrs B were awarded the contract. The claimant brought proceedings against the defendant for breach of precontractual obligations claiming compensation for loss of profits. The claimant asserted that the defendant was bound to adhere to the provisions of the VOL/A and that it should have awarded the contract to the claimant.

Held: The Bundesgerichtshof upheld the appellate court's finding that the claimant was entitled to compensation in the measure of the positive interest.

---

[148] (1991) 62 P & CR 33 (CA), 13.18 (EN), above, p 443.
[149] See *Treitel* (n 78 above) paras 3-130–3-131.
[150] See BGH 19 October 1960, LM BGB § 276 (Fa) no. 11, NJW 1961, 169, MDR 1961, 49.
[151] Medicus (n 132 above) 498.
[152] NJW 1993, 520.

Judgment: ... This Court concurs with the appellate court's finding that the claimant is entitled to claim compensation in respect of its positive interest if it would definitely have won the contract had the procedure for awarding it been properly followed ... It is true that the burden of proof rests on the tenderer, who must show that it would have been awarded the contract had it not been for the breach by the contracting entity of its obligations. However, in cases such as the present one, that burden is discharged by the claimant if it can show that, had the terms of the invitation to tender been adhered to, and had the award been properly made in accordance with § 25(3) VOL/A, the contract would have been concluded with the claimant (see, by way of example, OLG Düsseldorf BauR 1986, 107, 111; Feber BauR 1989, 553, 557). On that basis, this Court, hearing the appeal on a point of law, must find in favour of the claimant: neither of the other two tenderers should have been taken into account in the procedure which followed. Messrs B should have been left out of consideration on account of its having submitted an ancillary offer excluded by § 25(1)(1)(g) VOL/A, and the third company should have been turned down on account of the absence of material price details as required by § 25(1)(1)(a) VOL/A. ... There can be no question of taking into consideration any other circumstances precluding consideration of the claimant's offer.

Note

    As for the extent of liability, in German law a party who breaks off negotiations in a manner contrary to precontractual good faith duties is liable to repair the reliance interest.[153] In practice, in most cases reliance damages consist in expenses, but lost opportunities may be recovered as well. See, for example, BAG 7 June 1963, NJW 1963, 1843, JZ 1964, 324, where the claimant could recover the wages he would have had if he had not given up his current position in justified reliance on the successful outcome of negotiations for a new job. Expectation damages are not awarded because a negotiating party is under no duty to contract.[154] A different rule would amount to *Kontrahierungszwang*.[155] In some *culpa in contrahendo* cases other than those concerning broken-off negotiations positive damages have been awarded. This was so in the *Oolitic Stones* case,[156] in the field of public bidding, where it was certain that a contract would have been concluded had the employer who invited the tenders not violated its precontractual duties;[157] also in a case where an insurer had failed to inform the insured correctly about which countries were covered by its insurance;[158] and in a case where a party had not informed the other party about a form requirement. In these cases the expectation interest was justified by the purpose of the duty concerned.[159] Compare the English case of *Blackpool & Fylde Aero Club v Blackpool Borough Council*.[160]

---

[153] See, eg, BGH 10 July 1970, 13.14 (DE), above, p 436.
[154] See, eg, Palandt/Grüneberg § 311 para 55, eg BGH 6 February 1969, LM § 276 (Fa) BGB no. 28, WM 1969, 595.
[155] See Münchener Kommentar/Emmerich § 311 para 164.
[156] See 13.26 (DE) above, p 469.
[157] See also BGH 16 November 1967, BGHZ 49, 77; contrast the American case *Heyder Products* (n 20 above).
[158] BGH 4 July 1989, BGHZ 108, 200.
[159] BGH 29 January 1965, NJW 1965, 812.
[160] [1990] 1 WLR 1995.

Blackpool and Fylde Aero Club Ltd v Blackpool Borough Council[161]

An organisation that invites offers by way of tender that must follow stated requirements is impliedly promising that it will consider every tender that is properly submitted.

Facts: The council owned and managed an airport, and raised revenue by granting a concession to an air operator to operate pleasure flights from the airport. The plaintiff club was granted the concession in 1975, 1978 and 1980. Shortly before the last concession was due to expire in 1983, the council sent invitations to tender to the club and six other parties, all of whom were connected with the airport. The invitations to tender stated that tenders were to be submitted in the envelope provided and were not to bear any name or mark that would identify the sender, and that tenders received after the date and time specified, namely 12 noon on 17 March 1983, would not be considered. Only the club and two other tenderers responded to the council's invitation. The club's tender was put in the town hall letterbox at 11am on 17 March, but the letterbox was not cleared by council staff at noon that day as it was supposed to be. The club's tender was recorded as being received late and was not considered. The club brought an action against the council claiming damages for breach of contract, contending that the council had warranted that if a tender was received by the deadline it would be considered and that the council had acted in breach of that warranty. The judge held that the council was liable in damages to the club for breach of contract and negligence. The council appealed.

Held: The judge held that the council was liable in damages to the club for breach of contract and negligence. The appeal by the council was dismissed.

Judgment: BINGHAM LJ

... The judge resolved the contractual issue in favour of the club, holding that an express request for a tender might in appropriate circumstances give rise to an implied obligation to perform the service of considering that tender. Here, the council's stipulation that tenders received after the deadline would not be admitted for consideration gave rise to a contractual obligation (on acceptance by submission of a timely tender) that such tenders would be admitted for consideration. In attacking the judge's conclusion on this issue, four main submissions were made on behalf of the council. Firstly, it was submitted that an invitation to tender in this form was well established to be no more than a proclamation of willingness to receive offers. Even without the first sentence of the council's invitation to tender in this case, the council would not have been bound to accept the highest or any tender. An invitation to tender in this form was an invitation to treat, and no contract of any kind would come into existence unless or until, if ever, the council chose to accept any tender or other offer. For these propositions reliance was placed on *Spencer v Harding* and *Harris v Nickerson*.

Secondly, counsel submitted that on a reasonable reading of this invitation to tender the council could not be understood to be undertaking to consider all timely tenders submitted. The statement that late tenders would not be considered did not mean that timely tenders would. If the council had meant that it could have said it. There was, although counsel did not put it in these words, no maxim exclusio unius, expressio alterius. Thirdly, the court should be no less rigorous when asked to imply a contract than when asked to imply a term in an existing contract or to find a collateral contract. A term would not be implied simply because it was reasonable to do so: *Liverpool City Council v Irwin*. In order to establish collateral contracts, 'Not only the terms of such contracts but the existence

---

[161] ibid.

of an animus contrahendi on the part of all the parties to them must be clearly shewn': see *Heilbut Symons & Co v Buckleton* [1913] AC 30 at 47. No lower standard was applicable here and the standard was not satisfied. Fourthly, counsel submitted that the warranty contended for by the club was simply a proposition 'tailor-made to produce the desired result' (to quote Lord Templeman in *CBS Songs Ltd v Amstrad Consumer Electronics plc* [1988] 2 All ER 484 at 497) on the facts of this particular case. There was a vital distinction between expectations, however reasonable, and contractual obligations: see *Lavarack v Woods of Colchester Ltd* [1966] 3 All ER 683 at 690 per Diplock LJ. The club here expected its tender to be considered. The council fully intended that it should be. It was in both parties' interests that the club's tender should be considered. There was thus no need for them to contract. The court should not subvert well-understood contractual principles by adopting a woolly pragmatic solution designed to remedy a perceived injustice on the unique facts of this particular case. In defending the judge's decision counsel for the club accepted that an invitation to tender was normally no more than an offer to receive tenders. But it could, he submitted, in certain circumstances give rise to binding contractual obligations on the part of the invitor, either from the express words of the tender or from the circumstances surrounding the sending out of the invitation to tender or (as here) from both. The circumstances relied on here were that the council approached the club and the other invitees, all of them connected with the airport, that the club had held the concession for eight years, having successfully tendered on three previous occasions, that the council as a local authority was obliged to comply with its standing orders and owed a fiduciary duty to ratepayers to act with reasonable prudence in managing its financial affairs and that there was a clear intention on the part of both parties that all timely tenders would be considered. If in these circumstances one asked of this invitation to tender the question posed by Bowen LJ in *Carlill v Carbolic Smoke Ball Co* 'How would an ordinary person reading this document construe it?', the answer in the submission of counsel for the club was clear: the council might or might not accept any particular tender; it might accept no tender; it might decide not to award the concession at all; it would not consider any tender received after the advertised deadline; but if it did consider any tender received before the deadline and conforming with the advertised conditions it would consider all such tenders.

I found great force in the submissions made on behalf of the council and agree with much of what was said. Indeed, for much of the hearing I was of opinion that the judge's decision, although fully in accord with the merits as I see them, could not be sustained in principle. But I am in the end persuaded that the argument proves too much. During the hearing the following questions were raised: what if, in a situation such as the present, the council had opened and thereupon accepted the first tender received, even though the deadline had not expired and other invitees had not yet responded? or if the council had considered and accepted a tender admittedly received well after the deadline? Counsel answered that although by so acting the council might breach its own standing orders, and might fairly be accused of discreditable conduct, it would not be in breach of any legal obligation because at that stage there would be none to breach. This is a conclusion I cannot accept, and if it were accepted there would in my view be an unacceptable discrepancy between the law of contract and the confident assumptions of commercial parties, both tenderers (as reflected in the evidence of Mr Bateson) and invitors (as reflected in the immediate reaction of the council when the mishap came to light). A tendering procedure of this kind is, in many respects, heavily weighted in favour of the invitor. He can invite tenders from as many or as few parties as he chooses. He need not tell any of them who else, or how many others, he has invited. The invitee may often, although not here, be put to considerable labour and expense in preparing a tender, ordinarily without recompense if he is unsuccessful. The invitation to tender may itself, in a complex case, although again not here, involve time and expense to prepare, but the invitor does not commit himself to proceed with the project, whatever it is; he need not accept the highest tender; he need not accept any tender; he need not give reasons to justify his acceptance or rejection of any tender received. The risk to which the tenderer is exposed does not end with the risk that his tender may not be the highest (or, as the case may be, lowest). But where, as here, tenders are solicited from selected parties all of them known to the invitor, and where a local authority's invitation prescribes a clear, orderly and familiar procedure (draft contract conditions available for inspection and plainly not open to negotiation, a prescribed common form of tender, the supply of envelopes designed to preserve the absolute anonymity of tenderers and clearly to identify the tender in question and an absolute deadline) the invitee is in my judgment protected at least to this extent: if he submits a conforming tender before the deadline he is entitled, not as a matter of mere expectation but of contractual right, to be sure that his tender will after the deadline be opened and considered in conjunction with all other conforming tenders or at least that his tender will be considered if others are. Had the club, before tendering, inquired of the council whether it could rely on any timely and conforming tender being considered along with others, I feel quite sure that the answer would have been 'of course'. The law would, I think, be defective if it did not give effect to that. It is of course true that the invitation to tender does not explicitly state that the council will consider timely and conforming tenders. That is why one is concerned with implication. But the council does not either say that it does not bind itself to do so, and in the context a reasonable invitee would understand the invitation to be saying, quite clearly, that if he submitted a timely and conforming tender it would be considered, at least if any other such tender were considered.

I readily accept that contracts are not to be lightly implied. Having examined what the parties said and did, the court must be able to conclude with confidence both that the parties intended to create contractual relations and that the agreement was to the effect contended for. It must also, in most cases, be able to answer the question posed by Mustill LJ in *Hispanica de Petroleos SA v Vencedora Oceanica Navegacion SA, The Kapetan Markos NL (No 2)* [1987] 2 Lloyd's Rep 321 at 331: 'What was the mechanism for offer and acceptance?' In all the circumstances of this case (and I say nothing about any other) I have no doubt that the parties did intend to create contractual relations to the limited extent contended for. Since it has never been the law that a person is only entitled to enforce his contractual rights in a reasonable way *(White & Carter (Councils) Ltd v McGregor* [below, p 950] per Lord Reid), counsel for the club was in my view right to contend for no more than a contractual duty to consider. I think it plain that the council's invitation to tender was, to this limited extent, an offer, and the club's submission of a timely and conforming tender an acceptance. Counsel's fourth submission on behalf of the council is a salutary warning, but it is not a free-standing argument: if, as I hold, his first three submissions are to be rejected, no subversion of principle is involved. I am, however, pleased that what seems to me the right legal answer also accords with the merits as I see them. ...

I would accordingly dismiss the appeal. The practical consequences of deciding the contractual issue on liability in the club's favour must, if necessary, be decided hereafter.

Stocker LJ gave judgment to the same effect and Farquharson LJ agreed.

Appeal dismissed.

Note

The Court did not determine what damages were payable, but it seems clear that they would be on the contractual measure, ie they would include loss of expectation, as in the *Oolitic Stones* case.

13.3.E KNOWINGLY OR CARELESSLY ENTERING AN INVALID CONTRACT

A party who knows or should know that a contract will be invalid but nevertheless concludes it without warning the other party may be liable to pay reliance damages. This liability differs from liability for breaking off negotiations[162] in that here an agreement is reached.[163]

In the approach of the German Bundesgerichtshof[164] the fault lies in the violation of a duty to inform.

UNIDROIT Principles   **13.28 (INT)**

Article 2.1.15: Illustration No 2 to Article 2.1.15

A, who is negotiating with B for the promotion of the purchase of military equipment by the armed forces of B's country, learns that B will not receive the necessary export licence from its own governmental authorities, a pre-requisite for permission to pay B's fees. A does not reveal this fact to B and finally concludes the contract, which, however, cannot be enforced by reason of the missing licences. A is liable to B for the costs incurred after A had learned of the impossibility of obtaining the required licences.

Note

In systems which are not, like German law, influenced by the will theory, contracts are less threatened with invalidity for defect of consent.[165] In those systems the use of the doctrine of *culpa in contrahendo* is, therefore much more limited. In Germany a party who has concluded a contract under mistake can avoid it independently of whether the other party knew better. That other party when he relied on the validity of the contract is protected by an action for reliance damages or, under, for example, the UNIDROIT PICC, the other party's reliance would make the contract incapable of being

---

[162] Above 13.3.C.
[163] See also Medicus (n 132 above) 504.
[164] See below p 476.
[165] See on this below, ch 14.

avoided (Article 3.2.15 UNIDROIT PICC). Therefore, in these systems this liability would, if ever, at most be of use in the case of invalidity for illegality or lack of form. The second illustration to Article 2.1.15 of the UNIDROIT PICC[166] shows a case where a party who knows that the contract will be unenforceable and does not inform the other party about this fact acts contrary to good faith and is, therefore, liable.

RG, 5 April 1922[167]   **13.29 (DE)**

Two sellers

A party who negligently expresses himself in such a way as to bring about misunderstanding in the mind of the other party and which prevents a contract from coming into existence may bear the burden of liability for the loss and damage suffered as a result.

Facts: Two parties had been so inept in their telegraphic communications with each other that a contract appeared to have been concluded for the purchase of 100 kg of tartaric acid. It subsequently transpired that each of them wished to sell the goods.

Held: Overturning the decision of the Oberlandesgericht (Court of Appeal), the Reichsgericht held that the claimant was not entitled to compensation for his loss of profit as a result of the defendant's failure to purchase the acid.

Judgment: This case therefore involves a real absence of *consensus ad idem*. Each of the parties used words which appeared to suit the other party's purposes, but they attached to those words a meaning which prevented any agreement from being reached. Consequently, no purchase agreement came into existence. ... It follows that the claimant cannot claim performance of the contract.

The question arises, however, whether the circumstances of the case, as described, are such as to allow a claim for compensation to be made. ... In the event that a contract fails to materialise, the statute permits a claim to be made, in a good many factual instances, with regard to the negative contractual interest (for damage suffered on account of reliance on a declaration, known as *Vertrauensschaden*): that is the position, for example, under § 122 (avoidance of a declaration of intent on account of mistake), § 179 (absence of power of representation on the part of an ostensible representative), § 307 (an intentional or reckless promise to do something which cannot be done), and § 309 (conclusion of an illegal contract). The question whether those principles can be extended to cover similar cases is the subject of controversy and disagreement. ...

On those grounds, and out of considerations of fairness and certainty in dealings between parties, it is justifiable to apply the same principles to the present case, involving what may be termed a hidden lack of consent. This because it is indeed in accordance with the concept of fairness, and with the requirements of certainty in dealings with other parties, to impose upon a party who negligently expresses himself in such a way as to bring about misunderstanding in the mind of the other party the burden of liability for the loss and damage suffered as a result.

---

[166] 13.28 (INT), above, p 474.
[167] RGZ 104, 205.

Notes

(1) In the BGB, von Jhering's theory[168] was not codified as such. Instead, the BGB contained several specific provisions on liability in many of the situations in relation to which von Jhering developed his *culpa in contrahendo* theory. See, for example, § 122; reliance on a contract that is invalid as a result of *Mangel der Ernstlichkeit* (§ 118); *Irrtum* (§ 119); *falsche Übermittlung* (§ 120); § 179, reliance on a contract concluded by an agent who had no power of agency. These provisions give the party that relied innocently on the validity of the contract the right to reliance damages, which are limited to the extent of the expectation interest. However, under the BGB, in some of these cases—see, for example, § 122—fault is not required. There the underlying principle is no longer the doctrine of *culpa in contrahendo*, but the reliance principle. The Reichsgericht, first, and the Bundesgerichtshof, later, have expanded fault liability for concluding an invalid contract to other ineffective contracts.[169] By now a general rule can be formulated: 'Where a party culpably fails to inform the other party about facts and matters which prevent the valid implementation of the transaction, that party is liable in respect of the negative interest, as limited by the positive interest'.[170]

(2) The Bundesgerichtshof has in particular held that under certain circumstances, most often relating to the qualities of the parties, a negotiating party might have a duty to disclose the presence of a form requirement. Liability for *culpa in contrahendo* here might extend to the expectation interest if, in the absence of violation of this duty a valid contract would have been concluded. However, damages *in natura* leading to a duty to conclude a valid contract or even to transfer property are inadmissible because this would undermine the form requirement. See, for example, BGH 29 January 1965,[171] where it was held that a common use flats company should inform the buyer about the formal requirement (§ 311b(1)). Most legal scholars reject this decision, because awarding expectation damages implies compulsion to contract and because, in their view, it equally undermines the form requirement.[172] In addition to this, in cases of extreme hardship, ie in cases where upholding the formal requirement would lead to an unbearable result (*unertragbares Ergebnis*), invocation of the invalidity of the contract is held to amount to an abuse of right, contrary to good faith (§ 242 BGB), and is therefore inadmissible. See, for example, BGH 27 October 1967,[173] where the claimant knew of the formal requirement but had been convinced by his former boss that his signature had the same value.

(3) The question, discussed here, whether a party who concludes a contract which he knows will be invalid for lack of form is liable, differs from the question, whether

---

[168] See above, p 423.
[169] See the leading case of *Two sellers*, 13.29 (DE), above, p 475.
[170] See Medicus (n 132 above) para 108.
[171] NJW 1965, 813.
[172] See, eg, Larenz (n 37 above) 114; see also D Medicus and J Petersen, *Bürgerliches Recht* (26th edn, Munich: Vahlen, 2017) para 185, who for this reason reject any liability for *culpa in contrahendo* in this type of cases; see earlier von Jhering (n 3 above).
[173] BGHZ 48, 396.

a form requirement can exclude liability for breaking off negotiations.[174] Here the negotiations have not been broken off but the parties have reached an agreement. However, the same argument invoked there for explaining that a form requirement for the conclusion of the contract does not exclude liability for breaking off negotiations, ie that liability would not frustrate the scope of the form requirement, is used here by the Bundesgerichtshof to justify liability.

(4) The duty to inform may include a duty to be informed oneself in order to be able to inform. Note BGH 29 January 1965,[175] where it was held that a common-use flats company should inform the buyer about the formal requirement, its own ignorance not serving as an excuse.

13.3.F DUTY OF CONFIDENTIALITY

Principles of European Contract Law **13.30 (INT)**

Article 2:302: Breach of Confidentiality[176]
If confidential information is given by one party in the course of negotiations, the other party is under a duty not to disclose that information or use it for its own purposes whether or not a contract is subsequently concluded. The remedy for breach of this duty may include compensation for loss suffered and restitution of the benefit received by the other party.

UNIDROIT Principles **13.31 (INT)**

Article 2.1.16: Duty of Confidentiality
Where information is given as confidential by one party in the course of negotiations, the other party is under a duty not to disclose that information or use it improperly for its own purposes, whether or not a contract is subsequently concluded. Where appropriate, the remedy for breach of that duty may include compensation based on the benefit received by the other party.

Code civil **13.32 (FR)**

Article 1112-2: A person who without permission makes use of or discloses confidential information obtained in the course of negotiations incurs liability under the conditions set out by the general law.[177]

---

[174] See above, p 466.
[175] NJW 1965, 813.
[176] A similar provision is included in Art II.-3:302(1) and (4) DCFR.
[177] The 'general law' (translating *le droit commun*) refers here to the general law of extra-contractual liability for fault under Arts 1240–1241 Cciv, except where the parties made contractual arrangements during negotiations.

Notes

(1) In the course of negotiations a party may have an interest in disclosing certain information regarding the object of the transaction, such as technical details, to the other party in order to convince him to conclude the contract. If these details are related to an idea which is protected by a patent, there is no risk for him in doing so since any infringement of his patent would make the other party liable. If, however, the information is not protected by such a right, he has an interest in concluding an agreement of confidentiality. In a situation where a party expressly declares that the given information is to be considered as confidential, receiving the information can be regarded as implicitly agreeing to treat it as confidential. In such a case disclosing it or using it for one's own purposes would constitute breach of contract.[178]

(2) In the absence of a patent or an agreement a party, in principle, is under no obligation to treat information obtained during negotiations as confidential. However, under certain circumstances it can be contrary to good faith for the receiving party to disclose information given by the other party, or to use it for his own purposes. In other words, the duty of precontractual good faith can imply a duty to treat information obtained during negotiations as confidential.[179] Such a duty of confidentiality is recognised in most countries. See, for example, the *Seager v Copydex* case in England[180] and the *Maine Tunnel* case in France.[181] In some systems this duty is based on the general duty of precontractual good faith;[182] in English law it is based on a principle of equity.[183]

The introduction of Article 1112-2 into the Code civil can be viewed both as a specific application of good faith and as a general application of delictual liability based in fault. Indeed, the 'general law' (*le droit commun*) can be understood as a reference to the general law of extra-contractual liability for fault (Articles 1240–1241 Cciv) except where the parties made contractual arrangements during negotiations on the very issue of confidentiality.

(3) Under what circumstances does such a duty of confidentiality exist? According to the Comment on Article 2.1.16 of the UNIDROIT PICC, the particular nature of the information or the professional qualifications of the parties can give rise to a duty of confidentiality. Instances of potentially confidential information which can be obtained during negotiations are: know-how; commercial strategies; lists of clients or suppliers; balance sheets which are more elaborate than those available to the public; and the results of an audit or a due diligence investigation.[184] As regards the qualification of the parties, the main reason for a duty of confidentiality is, of course, them (or the third party, in case of disclosure) being (potential) competitors.

---

[178] See Comment on Art 2.1.16 UNIDROIT PICC.
[179] ibid.
[180] [1967] 1 WLR 923 (CA).
[181] Cass com 3 October 1978, no. 77-10915, Bull civ IV no. 208.
[182] See Comment on Art 2.1.16 UNIDROIT PICC; Van Ommeslaghe (n 37 above) para 15; P Malaurie, L Aynès and P Stoffel-Munck, *Droit des obligations* (9th edn, Paris: LGDJ, 2017) no. 468.
[183] See Lord Denning in *Seager v Copydex* [1967] 1 WLR 923 (CA).
[184] See Van Ommeslaghe (n 37 above) para 15.

(4) There are essentially two distinct ways in which a party can violate his duty of confidentiality: first, by divulging the information to the public; secondly, by using it for his own purposes. The latter was the case in both the *Seager v Copydex* and the *Maine Tunnel* cases.[185]

(5) The principal remedy for violation of this duty is damages. Article 2.1.16 UNIDROIT PICC and Article 2:302 PECL say that damages may include recovery of the benefit the other party received by breaching his duty. The Comment on Article 2.1.16 of UNIDROIT PICC says that such a compensation may be awarded even if the injured party has not suffered any loss. Furthermore, the injured party may also seek an injunction.[186]

(6) If a party enters into negotiations for the sole purpose of obtaining knowledge of another company's secrets, he not only is liable for an eventual breach of a duty of confidentiality, but he also has to reimburse the other party for the expenses incurred in negotiating.[187] The claimant's lost opportunities then will often be identical to the losses caused by the defendant's violation of his duty of confidentiality.

FURTHER READING

Babusiaux, U, 'Liability for Negotiations' in N Jansen and R Zimmermann (eds), *Commentaries on European Contract Laws* (Oxford University Press, 2018) 348–82.

Cartwright, J and Hesselink, WH (eds), *Precontractual Liability in European Private Law* (Cambridge University Press, 2008).

von Hein, J, 'Culpa in Contrahendo' in J Basedow, K Hopt and R Zimmermann (eds), *Max Planck Encyclopedia of European Private Law* (Oxford University Press, 2012) 430–33.

Kästle-Lamparter, D, 'Pre-contractual Information Duties' in N Jansen and R Zimmermann (eds), *Commentaries on European Contract Laws* (Oxford University Press, 2018) 383–504.

Sefton-Green, R, 'Formation of Contract: Negotiation and the Process of Agreement' in J Cartwright and S Whittaker (eds), *The Code Napoléon Rewritten: French Contract Law after the 2016 Reforms* (Oxford: Hart Publishing, 2017) 59–78.

Sautonie-Laguionie, L, 'The Creation of a Legal Theory of the Conclusion of the Contract' (2017) 6 Montesquieu Law Review 45–54.

Zuloaga, I, *Reliance in the Breaking Off of Contractual Negotiations: Trust and Expectation in a Comparative Perspective* (Cambridge et al, Intersentia, 2019).

---

[185] See nn 180 and 181 above.
[186] See above, n 178.
[187] See above, p 477.

PART 3
FRAUD, ABUSE, IMMORALITY

CHAPTER 14
FRAUD, MISTAKE AND MISREPRESENTATION

14.1 GENERAL INTRODUCTION

This chapter and Chapter 15 deal with topics which in many European legal systems are linked together under the general heading of 'defects of consent'. According to the legal and moral theory dominant on the continent in the nineteenth century, the parties to an agreement could be bound only to the extent that they had so willed.[1] Explaining the nature of this 'willing', Kant stated that:

> Through a contract I obtain the promise of the other party (but not that which is promised), and yet something does accrue to my possessions; I become the possessor, through acquisition, of an active obligation upon the freedom and capability of the other party.[2]

The preconditions of such a valid alienation of individual freedom are, consistent with the notion of human freedom itself, voluntariness and adequate knowledge. In the absence of these features the consent of the contracting party is unacceptably flawed or simply non-existent. At least in the civilian systems, this theory remains at the core of the rules defining and delimiting the impediments to contract formation represented by error and fraud. Under the German Bürgerliches Gesetzbuch (BGB), an individual's engagement in *Rechtsgeschäfte* (legal transactions) is an emanation of that individual's private autonomy. Thus, a declaration of intent is voidable where the party making the declaration has done so under the influence of a mistake (§ 119 BGB) or where he has been

---

[1] See K Zweigert and H Kötz, *Introduction to Comparative Law* (3rd edn, Oxford: Clarendon Press, 1998) 401.

[2] I Kant, *Die Metaphysik der Sitten: Erster Theil—Methaphysische Anfangsgründe der Rechtslehre* (Königsberg: 1797) para 20.

deceived by the other party or certain third persons (§ 123 BGB). Similarly the former French Code civil provided:

> **Article 1109:** There is no valid consent, where the consent was given only by error, or where it was extorted by duress or abused by deception.

The reformed Code civil states:

Code civil

14.1 (FR)

Article 1130: Mistake, fraud and duress vitiate consent where they are of such a nature that, without them, one of the parties would not have contracted or would have contracted on substantially different terms.

Their decisive character is assessed in the light of the person and of the circumstances in which consent was given.

Article 1131: Defects in consent are a ground of relative nullity of the contract.

English law does not have an overarching structure linking the equivalent topics of mistake, duress and misrepresentation, but we will see that in practice the courts frequently treat them as parallel doctrines to the extent that a solution derived from one doctrine is applied by analogy to another.

However, in each of the three systems there are other doctrines which impinge on what, in functional terms, seem to be cases of fraud or mistake. The first point is that some of the grounds giving rise to a defect in consent are also civil wrongs. Which rule applies depends on the remedy the claimant is seeking. If she has been tricked into making a contract and has suffered losses as a result, she may seek to avoid the contract on the ground of fraud and also seek damages. In French or German law, whereas nullity/*avoidance* would be given on the basis of one of the provisions referred to above, *damages* would be available under the general provisions on tortuous (delictual) responsibility (Article 1240 (formerly Article 1382) of the Code civil; § 826 BGB). In English law, fraud is both a ground for rescission of a contract and a tort which gives rise to damages.

Secondly, in each system the rules on defects of consent occupy only part of the ground. This is particularly so in cases where there has been a mistake but no fraud. We shall see that the fact that a 'mistake' of some sort has been made by one or both parties may mean, not that the mistaken party may avoid the contract, but that there is no contract at all because they never reached an agreement—as it is put in French, there is an *erreur-obstacle*—or that the agreement is void for impossibility. Further, we will see that in English law the doctrine of mistake is very narrow, but it is supplemented by a liberal doctrine of misrepresentation.

Thirdly, a very common situation is that property sold is not what the parties thought it would be—for example, goods unexpectedly turn out to be defective. These cases might be treated as cases of mistake—and sometimes the buyer will indeed seek to avoid the contract on this ground[3] —but the buyer will often have other remedies under the law of sales. The seller may be held liable for the defect under the French *garantie des*

---

[3] See below, p 564.

vices cachés, the German sales law or the English Sale of Goods Act 1979[4] or Consumer Rights Act 2015.[5] This issue will be discussed when we come to liability for breach.[6]

Returning to the central notion of defects of consent, it would be incorrect to seek the origins of the various current rules on error and fraud in subjectivist, will-centred theories alone. The nature and extent of remedies available in these cases are also determined by an objective evaluation of the needs of a functioning market and, thus, of the wider society. Especially in the case of errors confined to one of the parties, an unlimited right to rescind the contract would pose an unacceptable threat to the security of transactions and the functioning of the market. In English law, which notably privileges objective over subjective interpretation and external over internal phenomena as relevant to the creation of contractual obligations, very little ground has been conceded to doctrines of unilateral mistake where this has not resulted from the conduct of the other party.

It would be wrong to suggest that the continental systems are monolithically subjectivist and the common law objectivist. Elements of each approach are to be found in each system. This is nowhere more evident than in the BGB rules on interpretation. Thus § 133 BGB states that the party's true intention must be sought without regard to the literal meaning of his declaration, which seems to be pure will theory; but § 157 BGB says that contracts shall be interpreted according to the requirements of good faith. § 157 seems to favour what is called the declaration theory—ie the expectations reasonably engendered by the declaration should be protected.[7] Somewhat similarly, Article 1188 of the reformed French Code civil[8] provides that a contract is to be interpreted according to the common intention of the parties, but that where this intention cannot be discerned, the contract should be interpreted in the sense that a reasonable person in the same situation would give to it.

Similarly, in civilian systems only certain types of error are deemed sufficiently potent and significant in law to lead to the annulment of the contract. Thus Fabre-Magnan remarks:

> Not only must there be consent, it must be full. Full consent is free and fully informed, in other words one that is not vitiated.

But she continues:

> The case law developed on the basis of the vices of consent is subtle, because a balance must always be struck between concern for the protection of the victim and legal security, which would be threatened if the contract could be challenged too readily for some subjective reason peculiar to one of the parties.[9]

Indeed it has been said that a theory of defects of consent is not only old-fashioned, representing a nineteenth-century view of contract law, but is also politically wrong because

---

[4] eg, s 14(2), implied term that goods will be of satisfactory quality.
[5] See s 9, consumer contract to be treated as including term that quality of goods will be satisfactory.
[6] See below, p 564.
[7] See ch 18 below.
[8] See 18.3 (FR), below, p 723.
[9] M Fabre-Magnan, *Droit des obligations*, vol 1, *Contrat et engagement unilatéral* (4th edn, Paris: PUF, 2016) no. 337.

it assumes that the binding force of contract rests on party autonomy whereas the binding force of contract is also based on solidarity.[10] The extent to which this is true is something you may want to consider as you read this chapter.

Although requiring as a causal element the error of one of the contracting parties, cases of fraud—like cases of violence[11]—are dealt with separately from and more severely than cases of mistake. In this regard, continental law adopts the same general position as English law in premising relief not solely upon the state of mind of the party who is making a mistake, but also upon the conduct of the other party. The 'victim' in such cases benefits from the sanctioning of his fraudulent opponent. This may be a reflection of the serious moral harm embodied in the manipulative use of another for one's own ends. A more instrumental justification would highlight the real threat posed by fraud and the fraudulent to the operation of the market.

The strength of the latter argument within the legal discourse of a particular jurisdiction will also be seen to determine the extent to which the legal system demands that one party take positive steps to disclose relevant information to the other party. A system which wishes to encourage the production of valuable information may be reluctant to define silence as fraudulent conduct. Other systems seem to place a greater weight on the moral issues involved in keeping silent when the other party is ignorant of some crucial fact, notably by recognising that fraud may be committed by remaining silent[12] and by imposing duties of disclosure.[13]

14.2 FRAUD

Principles of European Contract Law   **14.2 (INT)**

Article 4:107: Fraud

(1) A party may avoid a contract when it has been led to conclude it by the other party's fraudulent representation, whether by words or conduct, or fraudulent nondisclosure of any information which in accordance with good faith and fair dealing it should have disclosed.

(2) A party's representation or non-disclosure is fraudulent if it was intended to deceive.

(3) In determining whether good faith and fair dealing required that a party disclose particular information, regard should be had to all the circumstances, including:

    (a) whether the party had special expertise;

    (b) the cost to it of acquiring the relevant information;

    (c) whether the other party could reasonably acquire the information for itself; and

    (d) the apparent importance of the information to the other party.

---

[10] R Sefton-Green (ed), *Mistake, Fraud and Duties to Inform in European Contract Law* (Cambridge University Press, 2005) 4.

[11] See ch 15.

[12] See below, p 570.

[13] Section 14.4, below, pp 566 ff.

Article 4:117: Damages

(1) A party who avoids a contract under this Chapter may recover from the other party damages so as to put the avoiding party as nearly as possible into the same position as if it had not concluded the contract, provided that the other party knew or ought to have known of the mistake, fraud, threat or taking of excessive benefit or unfair advantage.

(2) If a party has the right to avoid a contract under this Chapter, but does not exercise its right or has lost its right under the provisions of Articles 4:113 or 4:114, it may recover, subject to paragraph (1), damages limited to the loss caused to it by the mistake, fraud, threat or taking of excessive benefit or unfair advantage. The same measure of damages shall apply when the party was misled by incorrect information in the sense of Article 4:106.

(3) In other respects, the damages shall be in accordance with the relevant provisions of Chapter 9, Section 5, with appropriate adaptations.

Note

In the Draft Common Frame of Reference (DCFR) and the Common European Sales Law (CESL), the equivalent provisions on fraud (DCFR Article II.-7:205, CESL Article 49)) refer in the first paragraph also to information that should have been provided under an information duty[14] and paragraph (2) is expanded to read:

(2) A misrepresentation is fraudulent if it is made with knowledge or belief that the representation is false and is intended to induce the recipient to make a mistake. A non-disclosure is fraudulent if it is intended to induce the person from whom the information is withheld to make a mistake.

The DCFR Article on damages, II.-7:214, has been re-drafted but without any major changes of substance. CESL Article 55 (Damages for Loss) is similar but shorter:

A party who has the right to avoid a contract under this Chapter or who had such a right before it was lost by the effect of time limits or confirmation is entitled, whether or not the contract is avoided, to damages from the other party for loss suffered as a result of the mistake, fraud, threats or unfair exploitation, provided that the other party knew or could be expected to have known of the relevant circumstances

14.2.A FRAUD AS A GROUND FOR AVOIDANCE OF A CONTRACT

Code civil **14.3 (FR)**

Article 1137: Fraud is an act of a party in obtaining the consent of the other by scheming or lies.

The intentional concealment[15] by one party of information, where he knows its decisive character for the other party, is also fraud.

Nevertheless, it is not fraud for a party not to reveal to the other contracting party his assessment of the value of the act of performance.

---

[14] See below, pp 592 ff.

[15] The Article uses the word '*dissimulation*'. This is translated as 'concealment' but that does not imply active concealment. As we will see later (p 571), in French law merely keeping silent may amount to fraud.

Article 1138: Fraud is equally established where it originates from the other party's representative, a person who manages his affairs, his employee [*préposé*] or one standing surety for him.

It is also established where it originates from a third party in collusion.

Article 1139: A mistake induced by fraud is always excusable. It is a ground of nullity even if it bears on the value of the act of performance or on a party's mere motive.

Notes

(1) Article 1137 should be read in the light of the more general Article 1130, quoted above,[16] which provides that fraud vitiates consent where it is of such a nature that, without it, one of the parties would not have contracted or would have contracted on substantially different terms; and that the decisive character of the fraud must be assessed in the light of the person and of the circumstances in which consent was given. The provision was amended on the occasion of the 2018 ratification as its original wording was the cause of a lively debate over the non-disclosure of the value of the other party's performance; we examine this specific question below.

(2) These provisions confirm the existing law, notably in that the definition of fraud includes not only inducing the other party's consent by lies or tricks but also simply keeping silent with the intention that the other party contracts on the basis of information that is incorrect. We consider this later.[17]

(3) A simple failure to perform a duty to give information does not amount to fraud that will be sanctioned by the right to avoid the contract and damages. To establish fraud, it must be shown that the information that was not revealed was 'determinant' and that the non-disclosure was intentional. Duties to give information are also considered later.[18]

BGB   **14.4 (DE)**

§ 123: Voidability on the grounds of deceit or duress

(1) A person who has been induced to make a declaration of intent by deceit or unlawfully by duress may avoid his declaration.

(2) If a third party committed this deceit, a declaration that had to be made to another may be avoided only if the latter knew of the deceit or ought to have known it. If a person other than the person to whom the declaration was to be made acquired a right as a direct result of the declaration, the declaration made to him may be avoided if he knew or ought to have known of the deceit.

The classic definition of fraud in English law is found in the judgment of Lord Herschell in *Derry v Peek*:[19]

I think the authorities sustain the following propositions: First, in order to sustain an action of deceit, there must be proof of fraud, and nothing short of that will suffice. Secondly,

---

[16] See 14.1 (FR), above, p 484.
[17] See below, p 489.
[18] See below, p 566.
[19] (1889) 14 App Cas 337, 374 (HL).

fraud is proved when it is shown that a false representation has been made (1) knowingly, or (2) without belief in its truth, or (3) recklessly, careless whether it be true or false. Although I have treated the second and third as distinct cases, I think the third is but an instance of the second, for one who makes a statement under such circumstances can have no real belief in the truth of what he states. ... Third, if fraud be proved, the motive of the person guilty of it is immaterial. It matters not that there was no intention to cheat or injure the person to whom the statement was made.

Derry v Peek was an action for damages for the tort of deceit, rather than for rescission of the contract. At common law 'rescission' (avoidance) was also available where there had been fraud in the sense defined in the case. We will see later[20] that the rule in equity was that rescission might be given for even 'innocent', ie non-fraudulent, misrepresentation.[21]

It should be noted that in some systems[22] fraud is seen as a particular kind of mistake, but one which has been provoked deliberately so that some of the normal restrictions on avoidance for mistake do not apply.

14.2.B PARTICULAR ISSUES IN FRAUD

14.2.B.1 THE REQUIREMENT OF DISHONESTY

Fraud requires an intention to deceive the other party.[23] In none of the three systems does it seem to be a requirement for rescission that the fraudulent person intended to cause loss to the other.[24]

14.2.B.2 POSITIVE MISSTATEMENTS AND 'FRAUD BY SILENCE' ('*DOL PAR RÉTICENCE*')

In the continental systems, in many cases of fraud the victim would also be able to avoid the contract for mistake because in those systems a serious mistake by one party may be a ground for avoidance. This may be one reason why, in the continental systems, the kind of conduct which may be fraudulent is broadly defined (eg the French Code civil speaks of *manoeuvres*, translated above as 'scheming'). Although in French and German law the starting point was that there was no duty to disclose facts that the other

---

[20] See below, p 558.

[21] On the distinction between common law and equity, see above, pp 88–89.

[22] eg, French law: see Art 1139 Cciv.

[23] England: *Derry v Peek* (1889) LR 14 App Cas 337; France: P Malaurie, L Aynès and P Stoffel-Munck, *Droit des obligations* (9th edn, Paris: Defrénois, 2017) no. 508. In French law, intention to deceive is the criterion which enables judges to draw a line between the failure to comply with a duty to inform (non-disclosure; as we will see at p 570 below, this may give rise to liability in damages in French law) and 'reticence dolosive', which is a ground for nullity of an agreement if an intention to deceive is proved and if this failure has caused a material mistake. See Cass com 28 June 2005, no. 03-16794, Bull civ IV no. 140; Germany: H Kötz, *Vertragsrecht* (2nd edn, Tübingen: Mohr Siebeck, 2012) para 336.

[24] England: *Brown Jenkinson & Co Ltd v Percy Dalton (London) Ltd* [1957] 2 QB 621 (CA); France: F Terré, P Simler and Y Lequette, *Les obligations* (11th edn, Paris: Dalloz, 2013) no. 234; Germany: BGH 21 June 1974, NJW 1974, 1505; Kötz (n 23 above) para 338.

party did not know,[25] it is now established that keeping silent about some matter of which you know the other party is ignorant may in some circumstances amount to fraud. This is now stated in the French Code civil, see Article 1137(2). In contrast, we will see that in English law a mistake by one party (other than a mistake in declaration[26]) is not normally a ground for avoidance, though relief could be given if the mistake was induced by the other party's misrepresentation; and it is still the case that only the making of a false representation of fact amounts to fraud. This includes false representations by conduct—gestures such as 'a nod or a wink or a shake of the head or a smile',[27] or covering up defects[28]—but there must be some positive action: in English law mere failure to disclose a fact cannot be fraud.

This difference is so fundamental, and seems to lead to such different results, that it is explored in a separate subsection on non-disclosure.[29] In the rest of this section we will assume that the fraud consisted of a positive representation, such as a false statement of fact.

14.2.B.3 THE APPARENT IMPORTANCE OF THE MATTER TO WHICH THE FRAUD RELATES

Because of the moral opprobrium which attaches to fraud—in all the systems, fraud is in many situations a criminal offence—contracts may be avoided on this ground under much less strict conditions than on the other grounds. Accordingly, the rules which follow should be contrasted with those for mistake.[30]

Thus, French and German law each have a general rule that a contract may not be avoided because of a mistake which is only as to the value of the thing bought or sold. This rule does not apply when the mistake has been brought about by fraud.[31]

Another restriction on relief for mistake is that it will not be given if the mistake is not in some way central to the contract. For example, in German law, relief on the ground of mistake is usually not granted in cases of errors of motive, unless the error is as to some characteristic of the subject matter which is regarded as essential; in French law, it is not granted where errors are not as to an 'essential' substance of the subject matter.[32] In contrast, in all the systems relief will be given for any fraudulent statement even if it was only as to a matter of motive.[33] It is necessary only that the person fraudulently given the wrong information was mistaken as a result and was influenced by her mistake in entering the contract.[34]

---

[25] Malaurie et al (n 23 above) no. 510; B Markesinis, H Unberath and A Johnston, *The German Law of Contract* (2nd edn, Oxford: Hart Publishing, 2006) 305.

[26] See 14.3.B, below, p 501.

[27] *Walters v Morgan* (1861) 3 De GF & J 718, 723.

[28] *Baglehole v Walters* (1811) 3 Camp 154.

[29] See 14.4, below, p 566.

[30] See below, pp 497 ff.

[31] Article 1139 Cciv; Malaurie et al (n 23 above) no. 511.

[32] Articles 1132 and 1133 Cciv; 14.9 (FR), below, p 498.

[33] See, eg, RG 22 November 1912, RGZ 81, 13; Art 1139 Cciv. See also H Kötz, *European Contract Law* (2nd edn, Oxford: Clarendon Press, 2017) 173.

[34] ibid; Malaurie et al (n 23 above) no. 511.

However, all the laws exclude general commendation, 'mere puffs', from counting as fraud. See, for example, Dutch law:

BW **14.5 (NL)**

Article 3:44: ...

(2): ... Representations in general terms, even if they are untrue, do not as such constitute fraud.

Presumably this is because it is felt that no reasonable person would be influenced by such sales talk. In some English cases sellers got away with quite misleading claims (for example, stating that land was 'fertile and improvable' when it was in fact a useless marsh,[35] or that silver-plated spoons were 'equal to Elkington's "A"'—a well-known brand of good quality—when in fact they were of much inferior quality).[36]

In one type of case, however, the German courts have not been willing to allow avoidance on grounds of fraud notwithstanding the importance of the statement, and the deceitful intention of the other party in making it. Where an employee is pregnant at the time of an interview it has been held that she may withhold this information from her prospective employer and may even respond untruthfully if questioned about it.[37] This 'right to lie' is clearly conceded to job applicants on grounds of policy and in particular in implementation of EU law on sex discrimination.[38]

14.2.B.4 THE INFLUENCE OF THE FRAUD

No relief will be given if the false information did not influence the recipient, for example because she did not read it or knew the true facts.[39] But at least in English[40] and German law it need not have been the only factor which influenced the decision to enter into the contract.[41]

In French law a distinction has sometimes been drawn between determinant fraud (*dol principal*) and incidental fraud (*dol incident*). The idea seems to be that if the victim of the fraud would have entered the contract anyway, though on different terms, this was only *dol incident* and the victim may not avoid the contract but only claim damages. However, the distinction is no longer as clear cut as it used to be. Indeed, it is now rare

---

[35] *Dimmock v Hallett* (1866) LR 2 Ch App 21.

[36] *R v Bryan* (1857) 7 Cox's Crim Cas 312.

[37] BAG 15 October 1992, NJW 1993, 1154.

[38] See C-177/88, *Dekker v VJV Centrum*, 8 November 1990, ECLI:EU:C:1990:383.

[39] In England it has been held that a party may avoid a contract for fraud even if it strongly suspected that the statement was untrue but could not prove it at the time: *Hayward v Zurich Insurance Co plc* [2016] UKSC 48, [2017] AC 142.

[40] *Edgington v Fitzmaurice* (1885) 29 ChD 459. For a claim for damages to succeed it is necessary that the claimant would not have entered the contract 'but for' the fraud; but rescission will be allowed if the fraud merely had some effect on the claimant's mind, even if he might have entered the contract anyway. This rule is aimed at deterring fraud. See *Chitty on Contracts*, 33rd edn by H Beale (gen ed) (London: Sweet & Maxwell/ Thomson Reuters, 2018) paras 7-039–7-040.

[41] RG 15 November 1911, RGZ 77, 309.

that French courts refuse to grant the victim the right to avoid the contract on the ground that it was merely a *dol incident* which only gives rise to damages.[42]

14.2.B.5 AVOIDANCE

As mentioned above,[43] the victim of fraud can usually avoid the contract and recover damages; alternatively, she may claim damages without avoidance. In some systems—for example, German law—avoidance for mistake etc must be claimed within a short time.[44] With fraud, the seriousness of the conduct is seen as a reason for not prejudicing the victim. Thus avoidance will not be prevented simply through the lapse of time until after the fraud has been discovered.

Thus in German law, § 124(1) and (2) BGB provide specifically that avoidance must take place within one year of the discovery of the fraud; under § 124(3) BGB, there is an upper limit of 10 years from the date of the relevant declaration of intent. Note that avoidance is effected by notice (a further 'declaration of intent') to the fraudulent party, § 143 BGB. In practice, in Germany relief may be sought on the basis of *culpa in contrahendo* (§§ 280(1), 241(2), 311(2) BGB) even when there has been fraud.[45] This gives rise to problems over the period for avoidance.

In France, fraud gives rise to a right to claim nullity by means of a court procedure.[46] The period in which to make the claim is five years from the date of discovery,[47] except that the defence of nullity is not subject to prescription if it relates to a contract which neither party has performed.[48] However, once the fraud has been discovered, an innovative article of the reformed Code civil gives the fraudulent party the right to demand in writing whether the victim wishes to claim nullity or to affirm the contract; if the victim does not proceed with an action of nullity within six months, he loses the right to do so.[49] This procedure is called the *action interrogatoire*.[50]

In English law the right to avoid the contract for fraud will not be lost before the fraud has come to light,[51] whereas the right to avoid because of non-fraudulent misrepresentation (which covers many of the cases which on the continent would be dealt with under mistake) can be lost a reasonable time after the misrepresentee received performance, even if they were unaware that they had been misled.[52]

---

[42] Malaurie et al (n 23 above) no. 512. The reforms to the Code civil do not address this issue.
[43] See above, p 484.
[44] See below, p 539.
[45] See below, p 494.
[46] See further below, pp 513–15.
[47] Art 2224 Cciv.
[48] Art 1185 Cciv.
[49] Art 1183 Cciv (applicable to all cases of nullity).
[50] It remains to be seen whether or not it will be possible to rely on this in consumer cases, where agreements over prescription are not normally allowed (Art L 218-1 Cconsom).
[51] See *Chitty* (n 40 above) para 7-137.
[52] *Leaf v International Galleries* [1950] 2 KB 86 (CA); but doubts about this decision have been expressed by later judges, see *Chitty* (n 40 above) para 7-137.

14.2.B.6 FRAUD BY THIRD PERSONS

So far we have assumed that the fraud was committed by the other party to the contract. A recurring problem is that a fraud by a third party has induced the claimant to make a contract with the defendant. Where there is a relationship of principal and agent between the defendant and the fraudulent third party, the former will be responsible for the latter's acts according to normal principles of agency; relief will also be given where they were accomplices. To solve this problem, Article 1138(2) of the Code civil now states that 'fraud is also established where it originates from a third party in collusion'.

This does not meet all the problems, however, as the fraud may have been committed by a third person who was not an agent of either party nor an accomplice. As this problem also arises in relation to other kinds of invalidity, such as duress and unfair advantage-taking, it is dealt with later.[53]

14.2.C DAMAGES FOR FRAUD

We have already noted[54] that in all three systems fraud is a ground of tortious or delictual liability, as well as a ground for avoidance of a contract.

Code civil   **14.6 (FR)**

Article 1240: Any human action whatsoever which causes harm to another creates an obligation in the person by whose fault it occurred to make reparation for it.

BGB   **14.7 (DE)**

§ 823: Liability in damages
    (1) A person who, intentionally or negligently, unlawfully injures the life, body, health, freedom, property or another right of another person is liable to make compensation to the other party for the damage arising from this.
    (2) The same duty is held by a person who commits a breach of a statute that is intended to protect another person. If, according to the contents of the statute, it may also be breached without fault, then liability to compensation only exists in the case of fault.

§ 826: Intentional damage contrary to public policy
    A person who, in a manner contrary to public policy, intentionally inflicts damage on another person is liable to the other person to make compensation for the damage.

For English law, see *Derry v Peek*.[55] See also Article 4:117 PECL.[56] In all three national laws, fraud may give rise to liability even if it did not result in the conclusion of a contract.[57]

---

[53] See ch 15.
[54] See above, p 484.
[55] See above, p 488.
[56] See 14.2 (INT), above, p 487.
[57] This was considered in ch 13 on pre-contractual negotiations: see eg above, p 428.

Generally, fraud which gives a right to avoid the contract will also give rise to liability in damages. In English and French law the damages are clearly tortious or delictual. In German law, such damages cannot strictly be contractual because avoidance makes the contract void *ab initio*. However, the reliance interest can frequently be claimed under the doctrine of *culpa in contrahendo* (§§ 311(2) with §§ 280(1), 241(2) BGB)[58] because the fraudulent conduct normally occurred during the pre-contractual relationship of the parties. A party seeking damages as well as avoidance on grounds of fraud may also bring a claim in delict. If—as usual in cases of fraud—the claimant seeks recovery of pure economic loss, she will not be able to rely on the general rule for delictual liability in § 823(1) BGB. However, because of the defendant's intention to deceive which is one of the requirements of fraud the claimant may be able to seek relief under two other provisions in the law of delict. First, under § 823(2) BGB[59] in connection with § 263 StGB (German Penal Code), damages may be sought for loss resulting from the violation of a protective statute, in this case the criminal code provision on fraud. The latter offence does not only require simple intention but also the offender's qualified intention to selfishly enrich himself. Secondly, damages may be sought under § 826 BGB[60] for harm inflicted *contra bonos mores*, and this has to be wilfully done, ie with the qualified intention specifically to cause harm or loss. Oblique intention suffices—ie it suffices that the maker of the statement knew there was a possibility that harm would result and made the statement nonetheless. Naturally, the intention to cause harm includes the lesser intention to deceive the other party.

14.2.C.1 CONCURRENCE OF ACTIONS

A buyer who has been induced by fraud to buy defective goods may also have a remedy for latent defect or non-performance. There may also be an overlap between the grounds for such remedies and mistake.[61] German law provides that in cases of a mistake concerning the characteristic features of the goods (§ 119(2) BGB)—not in cases where the mistake pertains to the content or to the making of the declaration of intent (§ 119(1) BGB)—the buyer is confined to the remedies for latent defects (§§ 434 ff BGB) where the risk has already passed (§ 446 BGB).[62] By contrast, in cases of fraud the buyer may choose between on the one hand avoidance under § 123 BGB and damages under §§ 823, 826 BGB, and on the other hand the remedies for latent defects.[63] French law allows a choice between avoidance or damages; it also allows the victim to claim for both if this is justified (ie when the loss is not entirely compensated for by the invalidity). Moreover, French law allows a party to choose between an action on the ground of hidden defects (in the case of a sales contract) and one on the ground of fraud, when the facts could lead to both types of actions. As a result, there is no need to worry about the short statutory

---

[58] See 13.4 (DE), above, p 426.
[59] See 6.8 (DE), above, p 132; 14.7 (DE), above, p 493.
[60] See 6.8 (DE), above, p 133; 14.7 (DE), above, p 493.
[61] See below, pp 564–65.
[62] See Markesinis et al (n 25 above) 498.
[63] RG 24 June 1919, RGZ 96, 156.

limitation of action to act on the ground of hidden defects (two years: Article 1648 Cciv). English law allows a victim to claim damages whether or not the contract is rescinded; rescission, which will normally result in the victim recovering the price he paid, may affect the amount of loss the victim has to claim by means of action for damages.

14.2.C.2 THE MEASURE OF DAMAGES

Because fraud is an intentional wrong, many systems of law provide more generous damages than for unintentional wrongs. For example, in English law, the normal rule which limits damages to losses which were foreseeable (the 'remoteness' rule) does not apply to fraud (*Doyle v Olby*);[64] and contributory negligence is not a defence (*Alliance & Leicester Building Society v Edgestop Ltd*).[65] Similarly in German law contributory negligence does not apply to fraud.[66] Other rules on damages may also apply differently to actions for fraud than they do in actions based on negligence.[67]

While French law has no special rules on the way in which damages for fraud are to be calculated, leaving it to the proper appreciation of the judge, English and German law provide that the damages are to be calculated in a different way from damages for breach of contract. In German law a claim for damages arising from fraud must be based on the delict provisions of the Civil Code, §§ 823(2), 826 BGB. The measure of damages is therefore the negative interest. A party must be put in the position in which he would have been had he not relied on the other party's statement(s). Generally he may not seek to be put in the position in which he would have been if the other party's statements had been true, ie recovery of the positive/expectation interest.[68] Exceptionally, a buyer may recover the expectation interest where the ground for seeking avoidance under § 123 BGB was a fraud of the seller as to the quality of the goods.[69] In English law it is also established that in an action for damages for fraud the victim's damages are to be measured by her negative interest. As Collins MR put it in *McConnel v Wright*:[70]

> It is not an action for breach of contract, and, therefore, no damages in respect of prospective gains which the person contracting was entitled to expect to come in, but it is an action of tort—it is an action for a wrong done whereby the plaintiff was tricked out of certain money in his pocket; and therefore, prima facie, the highest limit of his damages is the whole extent of his loss and that loss is measured by the money which was in his pocket …

In *Doyle v Olby (Ironmongers) Ltd*[71] the Court of Appeal cited this statement with approval and pointed out that the plaintiff in a fraud case may recover for consequential 'out of pocket' losses—in that case, money wasted trying to run a business which the fraud led him to buy but which was not in fact viable.

---

64 [1969] 2 QB 158 (CA). For the remoteness rule see below, p 1072.
65 [1993] 1 WLR 1462 (ChD).
66 BGH NJW 1978, 2240.
67 See *Chitty* (n 40 above) paras 7-056 ff.
68 Münchener Kommentar/Oetker § 249 para 129.
69 RG 10 November 1921, RGZ 103, 154, 160.
70 [1903] Ch 546, 554 (CA).
71 [1969] 2 QB 158 (CA).

In *East v Maurer*[72] the defendants owned two hair salons in Bournemouth. The plaintiff agreed to buy one of them for £20,000 after the defendant had stated that he would be opening another salon abroad and had no intention of working at the other salon in Bournemouth save in cases such as staff shortages caused by illness. This was untrue and he in fact worked full-time at the other Bournemouth salon. The plaintiffs found the business at the salon they had bought fell away very rapidly and, though they worked hard and made various investments in new equipment, they did not manage to make it profitable. Ultimately they sold the salon for £7,500. The court of first instance found that the defendant had committed fraud. The Court of Appeal held that the out-of-pocket losses could include the profit which the plaintiffs would have made if they had not bought the business which was the subject of the fraud but had bought another business of a similar kind in the same area. The plaintiffs should not, however, be awarded the profits they would have made if the false information they had been given was in fact true.

14.2.C.3 MISLEADING ADVERTISING

In all the systems, additional controls have been placed on false or misleading advertising. These may take the form of criminal prohibitions or administrative sanctions, or operate via competition law. An example of the latter is the Misleading and Comparative Advertising Directive,[73] whose purpose is to protect traders against misleading advertising and the unfair consequences thereof and to lay down the conditions under which comparative advertising is permitted.[74] The Unfair Commercial Practices Directive[75] requires Member States to prohibit, and to provide 'adequate and effective' means to combat, unfair commercial practices. These are defined so as to include misleading actions[76] (which will in turn include misleading advertising) and misleading omissions.[77] The Directive does not provide civil remedies for individual consumers who are the victims of unfair commercial practices within the meaning of the Directive, as the Directive is 'without prejudice to contract law and, in particular, to the rules of validity, formation or effect of a contract'.[78] However, some Member States have provided consumers who have been the victim of certain types of unfair commercial practice with individual remedies. Thus in the UK, a consumer who has been influenced by a misleading action or an aggressive trade practice may 'unwind the contract' or have a discount off the price, in addition to damages for any further loss caused by the unfair commercial practice.[79]

---

[72] [1991] 1 WLR 461 (CA).

[73] Directive 2006/114/EC of the European Parliament and of the Council of 12 December 2006 concerning misleading and comparative advertising (codified version), OJ L 376/2006, p 21.

[74] Art 1.

[75] Directive 2005/29/EC of the European Parliament and of the Council of 11 May 2005 concerning unfair business-to-consumer commercial practices in the internal market, OJ L 149/2005, p 22. A useful summary of the Directive and its impact will be found in C Twigg-Flesner, 'Deep impact? The EC Directive on Unfair Commercial Practices and domestic consumer law' (2005) 121 LQR 386.

[76] Directive 2005/29/EC Art 6.

[77] Directive 2005/29/EC Art 7.

[78] Directive 2005/29/EC Art 3(1).

[79] Consumer Protection from Unfair Trading Regulations 2008 (SI 2008/1277), Pt 4A, inserted by Consumer Protection (Amendment) Regulations 2014 (SI 2014/870).

Typically these laws take a broad definition of the type of statements which may mislead consumers. For example, Article 2 of the Unfair Commercial Practices Directive[80] defines advertising as:

> ... the making of a representation in any form in connection with a trade, business, craft or profession in order to promote the supply of goods or services, including immovable property, rights and obligations.

Note

Does this enactment set a higher standard for statements made to consumers? Compare the English cases of 'puffs' considered earlier[81] and Cass crim, 21 May 1984:[82] advertisement showing suitcase being run over by a bulldozer not likely to mislead consumers as to their strength.

14.3 MISTAKE

14.3.A MISTAKE IN GENERAL

This section deals with a variety of situations which have in common the fact that one or both parties have entered the contract under some 'mistake', using that word in the broadest sense—some misapprehension about the subject matter of the contract or the circumstances, or as to the terms of the contract. It is important to note that there may be a mistake in this broad sense even if the case would not be dealt with by the relevant legal system under that rubric. As we will see, sometimes relief for 'mistake' will be given on some other ground and sometimes relief will be refused altogether even though one or both parties have made a mistake.

To get a picture of what is covered in this part of the chapter, it may help to look at the most relevant articles of the PECL.

Principles of European Contract Law **14.8 (INT)**

Article 4:103: Fundamental Mistake as to Facts or Law[83]

(1) A party may avoid a contract for mistake of fact or law existing when the contract was concluded if:

    (a) (i) the mistake was caused by information given by the other party; or

        (ii) the other party knew or ought to have known of the mistake and it was contrary to good faith and fair dealing to leave the mistaken party in error; or

        (iii) the other party made the same mistake, and

---

[80] Directive 2005/29/EC.

[81] Above, p 491.

[82] No. 83-92070, Bull crim no. 185, RTD com 1985, 379.

[83] Compare DCFR Art II.-7:201, which in (1) refers to mistakes caused by breaches of information duties (see below, p 592) and which has been slightly re-drafted from the PECL to make it clearer.

(b) the other party knew or ought to have known that the mistaken party, had it known the truth, would not have entered the contract or would have done so only on fundamentally different terms.

(2) However a party may not avoid the contract if:

(a) in the circumstances its mistake was inexcusable, or

(b) the risk of the mistake was assumed, or in the circumstances should be borne, by it.

Article 4:104: Inaccuracy in Communication[84]

An inaccuracy in the expression or transmission of a statement is to be treated as a mistake of the person who made or sent the statement and Article 4:103 applies.

In addition to English, French and German law, this section considers Dutch law, which has a different approach from that of the others.

Each of the four systems has a doctrine of mistake which plays a central role in such situations. The three civil codes have rules on mistake:

Code civil

14.9 (FR)

Article 1132: Mistake of law or of fact, as long as it is not inexcusable, is a ground of nullity of the contract where it bears on the essential qualities of the act of performance owed or of the other contracting party.

Article 1133: The essential qualities of the act of performance are those which have been expressly or impliedly agreed and which the parties took into consideration on contracting.

Mistake is a ground of nullity whether it bears on the act of performance of one party or of the other.

Acceptance of a risk about a quality of the act of performance rules out mistake in relation to this quality.

Article 1134: Mistake about the essential qualities of the other contracting party is a ground of nullity only as regards contracts entered into on the basis of considerations personal to the party.

Notes

(1) These articles are also subject to the more general Article 1130, quoted above,[85] which provides that fraud, mistake and duress vitiate consent where they are of such a nature that, without them, one of the parties would not have contracted or would have contracted on substantially different terms; and that the decisive character of the fraud, mistake or duress must be assessed in the light of the person and of the circumstances in which consent was given.

(2) Article 1133 defines the 'essential qualities' which the mistake must affect if the contract is to be nullified, guiding the judge in order to restrain judicial control,

---

[84] Compare DCFR Art II.-7:202.
[85] See 14.1 (FR), above, p 484.

specifying that they must be 'those which have been expressly or impliedly agreed and which the parties took into consideration on contracting'.

BGB   **14.10 (DE)**

§ 119: Voidability for mistake

(1) A person who, when making a declaration of intent, was mistaken about its contents or had no intention whatsoever of making a declaration with this content, may avoid the declaration if it is to be assumed that he would not have made the declaration with knowledge of the factual position and with a sensible understanding of the case.

(2) A mistake about such characteristics of a person or a thing as are customarily regarded as essential is also regarded as a mistake about the content of the declaration.

§ 122: Liability in damages of the person declaring avoidance

(1) If a declaration of intent is void under section 118, or avoided under sections 119 and 120, the person declaring must, if the declaration was to be made to another person, pay damages to this person, or failing this to any third party, for the damage that the other or the third party suffers as a result of his relying on the validity of the declaration; but not in excess of the total amount of the interest which the other or the third party has in the validity of the declaration.

(2) A duty to pay damages does not arise if the injured person knew the reason for the voidness or the voidability or did not know it as a result of his negligence (ought to have known it).

BW   **14.11 (NL)**

Article 6:228: (1) A contract which has been entered into under the influence of error and which would not have been entered into had there been a correct assessment of the facts, can be annulled:

(a) if the error is imputable to information given by the other party, unless the other party could assume that the contract would have been entered into even without this information;

(b) if the other party, in view of what he knew or ought to know regarding the error, should have informed the party in error;

(c) if the other party in entering into the contract has based himself on the same incorrect assumption as the party in error, unless the other party, even if there had been a correct assessment of the facts, would not have had to understand that the party in error would therefore be prevented from entering into the contract.

(2) The annulment cannot be based on an error as to an exclusively future fact or an error for which, given the nature of the contract, common opinion or the circumstances of the case, the party in error should remain accountable.

English law too recognises 'mistake', but it divides mistake up into several categories, each with different rules: *unilateral* mistake, where one party enters the contract under a misapprehension; *common* mistake,[86] where the parties share the misapprehension; and

---

[86] Though (confusingly) this used sometimes to be referred to as 'mutual mistake': see, eg, below, p 525.

mutual mistake, where the parties simply misunderstand one another's proposals—what on the continent is often referred to as *dissensus*. It also treats mistakes over what the terms of the agreement are (we will refer to these as 'declaration mistakes') differently to mistakes about the facts, such as the substance of what is being sold. The relevant cases will be excerpted or described in the sections that follow.

There are very significant differences even between the civil law doctrines. For example, the BW makes it clear that the mistake must be serious if the contract is to be annulled, and the former French Code civil required that it go 'to the very substance of the object of the agreement' (ex-Article 1110); this expression generated much discussion and the case law is very rich regarding the interpretation of this text. In contrast, the German BGB contains no such restriction. However, the liberality of § 119 is counterbalanced by § 122, under which the avoiding party may have to compensate the other for his reliance losses.

There are even greater differences between the civil law doctrines and the common law. The doctrines of mistake in English law have a much narrower application. While the English rules concerning mistakes and misunderstandings about what are the terms of the contract (declaration mistakes) apply in a reasonably broad fashion,[87] in relation to other mistakes, such as mistakes as to the qualities of the subject matter or the circumstances surrounding the contract, the doctrines are confined to cases in which the mistake was 'common', ie shared by the parties.[88] However, English law has a highly developed doctrine of *misrepresentation*. This is a development of the doctrine of fraud and permits a party to avoid a contract when she has been misled by what the other party has told her, even if the other party acted without fault. In practice this covers many of the cases which on the continent are dealt with as mistake.

Another major difference we noted earlier: a mere failure to disclose information cannot amount to fraud or misrepresentation in English law. The combination of this rule and the fact that mistakes as to the subject matter are relevant in English law only if they are shared (ie 'common')[89] means that English law is very unlikely to give relief when one party has entered a contract under a self-induced misapprehension (even if it was excusable) as to the subject matter or the circumstances and the other party does not make the same mistake.

This difference does not seem to be just the result of technique, but also to reflect the differences mentioned in the introduction to this chapter.[90] The common law places great emphasis on the appearance of agreement, in order to protect the reasonable expectations of the other party. We shall see that it tends to confine relief to situations in which the other party's beliefs were not reasonable or where to some extent he himself caused the misapprehension. Continental systems have traditionally placed more emphasis on the will of the contracting party and are sometimes prepared to give relief when the resulting contract does not reflect what the party willed, though this liberality may be counterbalanced by greater willingness to award damages—on a delictual or other basis—to a party who incurs a loss as a result of a mistake which was the other party's fault, or which was not the first party's fault.

---

[87] For details see 14.3.B, below, p 501.
[88] See 14.3.D.5, below, p 553.
[89] See below, p 542.
[90] See above, pp 483–86.

The comparison of the different laws is made even more difficult by the already mentioned fact that, in each system, situations which fall within the general heading of 'mistake' are actually dealt with not just by doctrines of mistake (and in English law misrepresentation) but by other doctrines also. We shall see that there is a complex interplay involving, for example, rules of *objet*, *cause*, impossibility, *culpa in contrahendo*, offer and acceptance, interpretation, and responsibility for defects. This makes it essential to adopt a functional approach, in which we take characteristic situations rather than doctrines as our starting point.

We will start by considering cases in which there is, broadly speaking, some kind of communication problem between the parties so that one party is under a misapprehension as to what he or the other is agreeing to (14.3.B). Then we consider the related case in which a party is under a mistake as to the identity or attributes of the other party (14.3.C). Thirdly (14.3.D), we will turn to look at cases where the misapprehension relates to other aspects of the subject matter or the circumstances. For that purpose, it is helpful to divide up situations according to how the misapprehension arose and the state of mind of the other party. We therefore consider cases of (i) shared mistake, (ii) induced mistake and (iii) self-induced mistake.

14.3.B MISTAKES AND MISUNDERSTANDINGS AS TO THE TERMS

In this section we consider two types of case. The first is cases in which there is some kind of misunderstanding as to what the terms of the contract are. Under B.1(a) we consider cases in which the parties agree on the same thing, but use the wrong words to express their agreement, and, under B.1(b), cases in which they appear to agree but their agreement is only apparent, not real. Secondly, under B.2, we consider cases where one party appears to agree to contractual terms to which she does not in fact mean to agree.

In English, French and German law there is some uncertainty over how far any of the cases are to be dealt with under the rubric of mistake and how far by a combination of the rules of offer and acceptance and of interpretation, which we considered earlier.[91] This is most clear in the first category, misunderstandings.

14.3.B.1 MISUNDERSTANDINGS AS TO THE TERMS OF THE CONTRACT

(a) Shared misunderstanding as to the meaning of the words used in the contract

What if both parties are under the same misapprehension as to the meaning of their contract? For the continental systems this is really a case of interpretation of the agreement.

In French law, provisions on interpretation, in particular Article 1188 Cciv will apply:

Code civil   **14.12 (FR)**

Article 1188: A contract is to be interpreted according to the common intention of the parties rather than stopping at the literal meaning of its terms.

---

[91] See above, pp 102–15.

Where this intention cannot be discerned, a contract is to be interpreted in the sense which a reasonable person placed in the same situation would give to it.

German law also prefers the common subjective intentions of the parties to the objective meaning of the words used, where the subjective intention is discoverable.

RG, 8 June 1920[92]   **14.13 (DE)**

Shark meat

Where the parties are agreed on a particular obligation but use the wrong word to describe it, their common intention will prevail.

Facts: On 18 November 1916 the defendant sold the claimant approximately 214 barrels of '*haakjöringsköd*' shipped ex steamship *Jessica* at 4.30 marks per kilo cif Hamburg net cash against bill of lading and insurance policy. At the end of November the claimant paid the defendant, on delivery of the documents, the purchase price calculated in the provisional invoices. Upon arrival in Hamburg, the goods were distrained upon, and shortly thereafter taken over, by Zentral-Einkaufsgesellschaft mbH of Berlin. The claimant asserted that the goods had been sold to it as whale meat, whereas they were shark meat. As whale meat, they would not have been subject to distraint. It claimed that the defendant, which had delivered goods not in conformity with the contract, was consequently liable to reimburse to it the difference between the purchase price and the considerably lower price paid by the Zentral-Einkaufsgesellschaft upon taking over the goods. It sought payment of 47,515.90 DM.

Held: The Landgericht (Regional Court) held that there was a binding contract for the sale of whale meat and that the claimant could therefore claim the difference in price. The claimant's appeal to the Oberlandesgericht (Higher Regional Court) was rejected, as was his further appeal to the Reichsgericht.

Judgment: On those grounds:
    As the Oberlandesgericht (Higher Regional Court) rightly found, both parties errone-ously assumed, upon the conclusion of the contract of 18 November 1916, that the goods constituting the subject matter of the contract, and specified therein—namely, 214 bar-rels of haakjöringsköd loaded on board the steamship *Jessica*—were whale meat, whereas in reality they were shark meat and, as such, correctly described by the Norwegian word 'haakjöringsköd', the meaning of which the parties did not know. However, that find-ing does not justify the view that what had been sold, namely haakjöringsköd, was also what had been delivered, and that it was open to the claimant, following delivery to it of the goods in the form of the handing over of the bill of lading, to avoid the contract under § 119(2) BGB on account of mistake as to the essential commercial characteristics of the specific goods sold. On the contrary, it follows from that finding that both of the parties wished to contract in respect of whale meat, but that, in stating their contrac-tual intention, they had erroneously used the term 'haakjöringsköd', which did not cor-respond to that intention. Consequently, the legal relationship existing between them must be assessed in the same way as if they had used the expression 'whale meat', which did reflect their intention (RGZ 61, 265). Accordingly, what was to be delivered under the contract was whale meat, and the claimant, having received delivery of shark meat, was constrained to seek the remedies provided for in §§ 459 ff BGB [now § 433 ff BGB] (RGZ 61, 171). This is because the goods delivered did not possess the characteristic of being whale meat, and even though that characteristic was not, perhaps, 'warranted' within the meaning of § 459(2) BGB [now 'agreed' within § 434 BGB], it was nevertheless

---

[92] RGZ 99, 147.

so essential that its absence constituted a material defect within the meaning of § 459(1) BGB [now § 434 BGB]. Thus the claimant was justified in avoiding the contract and it is consequently entitled to claim from the defendant a sum—the amount of which remains to be determined—equivalent to the purchase price paid to the defendant less the price allowed to it by the Zentral-Einkaufsgesellschaft upon the goods being taken over by the latter (see §§ 467, 346 ff BGB [now §§ 323, 346 ff BGB]).

Notes

(1) Although '*haakjöringsköd*' meant shark meat, the Reichsgericht upheld the parties' shared but mistaken understanding that it meant whale meat. On the facts of the case, therefore, the defendants had failed to deliver whale meat and were liable to pay damages under the law of sale (§§ 459 ff BGB [now §§ 433 ff BGB]). The amount of damages here was the difference between the contract price and the price paid by the State board which had seized the meat—during the First World War.

(2) This case demonstrates clearly the persistence after the enactment of the BGB of the older principle of *falsa demonstratio non nocet*—'a false description does not vitiate if the thing or person has been sufficiently described'.

The result in English law would probably be the same. Even though it normally insists on an objective stance, it will not insist on upholding the letter of the contract against what the parties really meant. This is clearest with written documents, which can be 'recti-fied'. Rectification is a remedy usually used when the parties have reached an agreement and have then incorporated it into a written document, but by mistake the written docu-ment does not record accurately what they had agreed. In order to protect themselves for the future—for example, if the mistake is in a lease, which might be assigned to another tenant who would not know what the original agreement was—a party may apply to the court for correction, or 'rectification', of the document.[93] However, the English Court of Appeal has held that the fact that each party had the same intention is irrel-evant for the purposes of interpretation if neither had disclosed this to the other: *New Hampshire Insurance Co v MGN Ltd*.[94] Likewise, on current authority, rectification will not be ordered on the basis of the parties' common intention unless there was an 'outward expression of accord'.[95] So the outcome in the *Sharkmeat* case would depend on whether or not the parties had expressed their understanding of *haakjöringsköd* outwardly.

Principles of European Contract Law   **14.14 (INT)**

Article 5:101: General Rules of Interpretation[96]

(1) A contract is to be interpreted according to the common intention of the parties even if this differs from the literal meaning of the words.

---

[93] See *Treitel on the Law of Contract*, 14th edn by E Peel (London: Sweet & Maxwell, 2015) paras 8-059–8-068.

[94] *The Times*, 25 July 1995.

[95] See *Chitty* (n 40 above) para 3-065; but this view is questioned, ibid.

[96] Compare DCFR Art II.-8:101(1).

(b) Misunderstandings/*dissensus*/mutual mistake

Court of Exchequer   **14.15 (EN)**

Raffles v Wichelhaus[97]

Where the parties to an agreement each hold equally reasonable but different understandings as to a term of the contract, no binding contract will come into existence.

Facts: See the report.

Held: The court appears to have held that the misunderstanding between the parties was such that no contract resulted. But see the Notes.

Judgment: Declaration: For that it was agreed between the plaintiff and the defendants to wit, at Liverpool, that the plaintiff should sell to the defendants, and the defendants buy of the plaintiff, certain goods, to wit, 125 bales of Surat cotton, guaranteed middling fair merchant's Dhollorah, to arrive ex 'Peerless' from Bombay; and that the cotton should be taken from the quay, and that the defendants would pay the plaintiff for the same at a certain rate, to wit, at the rate of 17¼d per pound, within a certain time then agreed upon the arrival of the said goods in England. Averments: that the said goods did arrive by the said ship from Bombay in England to wit, at Liverpool, and the plaintiff was then and there ready, and willing and offered to deliver the said goods to the defendants, &c. Breach: that the defendants refused to accept the said goods or pay the plaintiff for them.

Plea. That the said ship mentioned in the said agreement was meant and intended by the defendants to be the ship called the 'Peerless', which sailed from Bombay, to wit, in October; and that the plaintiff was not ready and willing and did not offer to deliver to the defendants any bales of cotton which arrived by the last mentioned ship, but instead thereof was only ready and willing and offered to deliver to the defendants 125 bales of Surat cotton which arrived by another and different ship, which was also called the 'Peerless', and which sailed from Bombay, to wit in December.

Demurrer,[98] and joinder therein.

Milward [counsel for plaintiff], in support of the demurrer. The contract was for the sale of a number of bales or cotton of a particular description, which the plaintiff was ready to deliver. It is immaterial by what ship the cotton was to arrive, so that it was a ship called the 'Peerless'. The words 'to arrive ex 'Peerless',' only mean than if the vessel is lost on the voyage, the contract is to be at an end. [POLLOCK CB. It would be a question for the jury whether both parties meant the same ship called the 'Peerless'.[99]] That would be so if the contract was for the sale of a ship called the 'Peerless'; but it is for the sale of cotton on board a ship of that name. [POLLOCK CB. The defendant only bought that cotton which was to arrive by a particular ship. It may as well be said, that if there is a contract for the purchase of certain goods in warehouse A, that is satisfied by the delivery of goods of the same description in warehouse B.] In that case there would be goods in both warehouses; here it does not appear that the plaintiff had any goods on board the other 'Peerless'. [MARTIN B. It is

---

[97] (1864) 2 H & C 906.

[98] A 'demurrer' was a form of pleading by which one party responded to the other's case by saying that, even if what the other party alleged were true, it would not give him a cause of action or have the legal effect he claimed.

[99] The square brackets indicate interruptions of counsel's argument by one of the judges.

imposing on the defendant a contract different from that which he entered into. POLLOCK CB. It is like a contract for the purchase of wine coming from a particular estate in France or Spain, where there are two estates of that name.] The defendant has no right to contradict by parol evidence a written contract good upon the face of it. He does not impute misrepresentation or fraud, but only says that he fancied the ship was a different one. Intention is of no avail, unless stated at the time of the contract. [POLLOCK CB. One vessel sailed in October and the other in December.] The time of sailing is no part of the contract.

Mellish [opposing counsel] (Cohen with him), in support of the plea. There is nothing on the face of the contract to shew that any particular ship called the 'Peerless' was meant; but the moment it appears that two ships called the 'Peerless' were about to sail from Bombay there is a latent ambiguity, and parol evidence may be given for the purpose of shewing that the defendant meant one 'Peerless' and the plaintiff another. That being so, there was no consensus ad idem, and therefore no binding contract. He was then stopped by the Court.

Per Curiam [THE COURT]: There must be judgment for the defendants.

Notes

(1) There is in fact a good deal of debate over the exact ground on which this case was decided, as the Court did not give reasons. The Court did not accept the seller's argument that the mistake was of no relevance; it simply decided that 'parol evidence'—ie evidence from outside the document—could be admitted to see what the intention was. If the parties meant the same ship, the contract would be for cotton from that ship; if they meant different ships, then presumably the Court thought there would be no contract because, as counsel for the defendants argues, there would be no *consensus ad idem*. That suggests that the Court was thinking that a subjective *consensus ad idem* was needed for a contract; but, as we shall see in more detail later, this is not the approach now taken by the common law, which looks primarily at the objective appearance of agreement.[100]

(2) Even though the common law now takes an objective approach, it seems the result might well be that there was no contract. If each party takes a different view of which ship was meant and if neither view was unreasonable, there is no reason to prefer one party's view to the other. The contract is too ambiguous to be enforced.

(3) The case also suggests the fluidity of the borderline between mistake and other doctrines. English textbooks usually deal with this case under the rubric of mistake; but it is equally plausible to say that the contract is simply void for uncertainty.

Dutch law would deal with such a case in the same way as English law:

BW **14.16 (NL)**

Article 3:33: A juridical act requires an intention to produce juridical effects, which intention has manifested itself by a declaration.

Article 3:35: The absence of intention in a declaration cannot be invoked against a person who has interpreted another's declaration or conduct in conformity with the sense which

---

[100] See G Gilmore, *The Death of Contract* (Columbus, OH: Ohio State University Press, 1974) 35–44.

he could reasonably attribute to it in the circumstances, as a declaration of a particular tenor made to him by that other person.

> *Note*
>
> Applying these Articles, if neither party's view was unreasonable, there is no reason to permit one party to rely on what he understood by the other's declaration, so there is no contract.

Cass civ (1), 28 November 1973[101]   **14.17 (FR)**

Bottle-openers

A contract of sale will not come into existence if the parties have a misunderstanding over the price.

Facts: The sellers intended to sell bottle-openers at 550 FF per thousand, the buyers to buy at 55 FF per thousand. The buyers refused to pay the higher price.

Held: The lower court held the buyers liable but the Cour de cassation referred the case back for re-hearing, which should consider the argument that there was no agreement between the parties.

Judgment: THE COURT: *On the first branch of the appeal ground*:—Under Article 7 of the Law of 20 April 1810 applicable to the case;—Whereas the Régie communale des Sources Nessel has been sued by Messrs Eurogadget for payment in respect of 60,000 bottle openers which, according to the plaintiff, were sold to the defendant at a price of 0.55 francs each, ie 550 francs per thousand.

— Whereas the defendant asserted that its consent had been vitiated by an error in respect of the basic price agreed, and contended that the contract should be declared void; as it was nevertheless ordered to pay the sum claimed from it, on the ground, in particular, that an error as to the price cannot be relied on in support of a plea that the contract should be annulled.

— Whereas however, in the claims advanced by it in the appeal proceedings, the Régie maintained that it had been induced into the erroneous belief that the agreed price was 55 francs per thousand and that a 'fundamental misunderstanding' had thus arisen between the parties;

— Whereas in not dealing with that ground, the appellate court (cour d'appel, Colmar, 11th Chamber, 23 December 1971) failed to fulfil the requirements of the abovementioned provision. On those grounds, the Court sets aside the contested judgment and refers the case back to the cour d'appel de Colmar for a rehearing before a differently composed bench.

From the Annotation by Rodière

Speaking of error on the identity of the object, Planiol said: 'There is no consent because there is no agreement; it is a misunderstanding not a contract (*Traité élémentaire de droit civil*, vol 2, para 1052) …

(1) This judgment does not question in the least what authors traditionally teach and what the Cour de cassation has traditionally admitted without question, that an error of

---

[101] No. 72-12521, D 1975, 21 annotated by R Rodière.

value has no effect on the validity of a contract save in those very limited circumstances when the law allows a party to demand rescission on the ground of *lésion*.[102]

This judgment does not contradict that. The error here related to the *chose*, on the performance due from the party who under the agreement was the buyer. ...

(2) Our judgment does not involve [former] Art 1110 Code civil and, even if the Court does not point to the text which the judges should base their decision on, it in fact based its censure not on [former] Art 1110 but on [former] Art 1108 Code civil:

> 'Four conditions are needed for a valid agreement: The consent of the party who undertakes an obligation ...'

Before enquiring into the validity of consent one must ask whether it existed (Planiol, op cit, para 1047; Carbonnier, para 12). Also Planiol, before noting that there are immaterial errors, recognises, in addition to the error envisaged by [former] Art 1110 which affects the validity of consent, that there may be *erreurs-obstacles* which mean that there is no consent (see also L Josserand, *Cours de droit civil positif*, vol 2, para 61)...

Despite the argument in the note that this decision is based simply on the absence of agreement and therefore of any contract, we will see below that the French courts have frequently treated cases of *erreur-obstacle* as if there were a contract which should be set aside for mistake. This approach was followed by the Avant-projet Catala.[103] The reformed Code civil does not deal with the issue, so presumably the old case law remains relevant.

RG, 5 April 1922[104]   **14.18 (DE)**

Two Sellers

[See 13.39 (DE), above, p 475]

Notes

(1) The *Two Sellers* case which we considered earlier is also an example of 'total *dissensus*'. The Reichsgericht held that the parties had, on an objective interpretation, been at cross-purposes in their offers and that no contract had therefore been formed between the parties.

(2) Interestingly, the BGB provides for cases in which the parties have agreed on some points but not others (see above, p 289):

§ 155: Hidden lack of agreement
If the parties to a contract which they consider to have been entered into have, in fact, not agreed on a point on which an agreement was required to be reached, whatever is agreed is applicable if it is to be assumed that the contract would have been entered into even without a provision concerning this point.

§ 155 BGB allows enforcement of the contract only where the parties had reached agreement on the *essentialia negotii*. This was clearly not the situation in the *Two Sellers* case.

(3) The *Two Sellers* case is also a leading case on *culpa in contrahendo*. The claimants were allowed to recover damages for losses suffered in reliance upon the

---

[102] See 16.2, below, p 629.
[103] Avant-projet Catala Art 1109-1.
[104] RGZ 104, 265.

existence of a contract, since the defendants were found to have been more at fault for the misunderstanding which arose.[105]

(4) How much difference to the outcome of such cases does it make whether a subjective or an objective approach is taken? It may make a difference when one party's interpretation was objectively unreasonable. In cases in which each party's interpretation was equally reasonable, there is mutual misunderstanding and there is no contract whichever approach is taken.

The *dissensus* situation does not seem to be discussed in the PECL or the UNIDROIT Principles, nor in the DCFR or the CESL, but it is thought that the result would be same as in the national laws: no contract would be formed.

14.3.B.2 MISTAKE BY ONE PARTY

At this point the difference between the legal systems remarked on earlier[106] becomes more significant. In French law, the starting point is that the creation of the contract requires an agreement in a subjective sense—the parties must actually intend the same thing. In English law this is not required: it suffices that one party reasonably thinks that the other party has agreed. A classic statement of the 'objective principle' is that of Blackburn J in *Smith v Hughes*:[107]

> If whatever a man's real intention may be, he so conducts himself that a reasonable man would believe that he was assenting to the terms proposed by the other party, and that other party upon that belief enters into the contract with him, the man thus conducting himself would be equally bound as if he had intended to agree to the other party's terms.

Compare BW Article 3:35.[108]

German law adopts an intermediate position, favouring a complex solution over the 'bright line rule' of English law. As has been seen,[109] there is a tension in the BGB between objective and subjective standards of interpretation. This is, however, largely resolved in favour of the objective approach. Thus, even under § 133 BGB, the 'intention' to be established is the communicated intention. Accordingly, in legal writing and in the cases, the 'declaration theory' predominates over the 'will theory' in relation to the formation and interpretation of contracts. However, this reliance-based liability may seem to be undercut, even if only in a qualified manner, by the relatively wide possibility of avoiding for mistake contracts held—objectively—to have been formed. But the objectivist position is again partially restored by obliging the party seeking avoidance of the contract under § 119 BGB to pay reliance damages to the other party under § 122 BGB, at least where the latter was unaware of the mistake.[110]

---

[105] See above, p 475.
[106] See above, pp 102–15.
[107] (1871) LR 6 QB 597, 607. See 14.41 (EN), below, p 567.
[108] 14.16 (NL), above, p 505.
[109] See above, p 110 and also below, p 724.
[110] For analysis of these rules in terms of the allocation of risk, see Hart in *Alternativkommentar zum Bürgerlichen Gesetzbuch* (Neuwied: Luchterhand, 1987) §119 paras 1-6.

The PECL seem to take an objective approach. First, intention is to be judged objectively:

Principles of European Contract Law   **14.19 (INT)**

Article 2:102: Intention

The intention of a party to be legally bound by contract is to be determined from the party's statements or conduct as they were reasonably understood by the other party.

Secondly, Articles 4:103 and 4:104,[111] which between them apply to this situation, limit relief to cases in which:

(a) (i) the mistake was caused by information given by the other party; or

(ii) the other party knew or ought to have known of the mistake and it was contrary to good faith and fair dealing to leave the mistaken party in error; or

(iii) the other party made the same mistake …

In this section, we focus on the following situations:

(a) cases in which one party had no intention of contracting at all, for example the classic hypothetical case of the person who visits a wine auction in Trier, waves to a friend and finds that by customary usage his wave indicated that he was bidding on the wine being auctioned and that the wine in question has been 'knocked down' to him;

(b) Where a contract was intended but:

(i) there was a 'slip of the pen'—for example you write £103 when you meant £130; or

(ii) you used the wrong word—for example the tourist in Cologne who orders a 'halver Hahn', meaning thereby a half chicken, when in Cologne a 'halver Hahn' is a kind of cheese sandwich.

We will see that, whilst two situations dealt with under (b) are generally treated in the same way, in German law a distinction is drawn between them. Cases in which you sign a document which omits terms that you thought would be included, or which includes terms that you thought would not be included, are also dealt with in the same way as the cases under (b).

(a) The mistaken party did not intend to enter any transaction at all: *The Trier Wine Auction* Case

It follows from what was stated on p 508 above that in the *Trier Wine Auction* situation no contract would result in French law, as there was no intention to enter any legal act. In contrast, in English law, provided the auctioneer reasonably believed that the buyer was bidding on the wine and accepted the bid in that belief, there would be a contract; and there would probably be no relief even on the ground of mistake, since the rules of English law on mistakes of this kind seem simply to be restatements of the original

---

[111] See 14.8 (INT), above, p 498.

position: that what reasonably appears to the other party to be an offer or acceptance, and which the other believes to be such, is binding. This is illustrated by the cases on offer and acceptance such as *Kleinwort Benson Ltd v Malaysia Mining Corp Bhd*[112] and *Carlill v Carbolic Smoke Ball Company*,[113] which look almost exclusively at what the parties said rather than what they may have intended to say.[114]

The *Trier Wine Auction* case is a famous 'textbook' example in Germany.[114a] Commentators originally took the position that there was no subjective intention to perform a juristic act (*Erklärungsbewusstsein*) and therefore no legally significant declaration of intention which could go to constitute a contract. Avoidance would not be an issue in this case, since there is in effect nothing to avoid. Furthermore, there would be no obligation on the 'mistaken' party to make compensation under § 122 BGB. However, recent doctrine and case law have taken a more objective approach. The case extracted earlier is worth repeating:

BGH, 7 June 1984[115]   **14.20 (DE)**

The bank guarantee

To form a valid contract, it does not matter whether the party communicating an intention to be bound by a contract actually had the will to make, or was even conscious of making, a declaration aimed at a legal transaction.

[Please read again the judgment in this case, which is printed at 5.13 (DE), above, p 110.]

Note

This case shows the BGH taking an 'objective' approach to interpreting what one party said. The question in the case was whether there was any contract at all; but the same approach would apply if a party made a mistake in stating the terms that he or she intended. In other words, the contract would be on the terms that the other party reasonably thought were being offered. However, the mistaken party would be able to avoid the contract under § 119(1) BGB; but he or she might be liable to pay damages to the non-mistaken party for the latter's reliance loss (§ 122 BGB).

(b) The mistaken party intended to enter a contract but stated the terms he intended incorrectly ('slips of the pen' and the *Halver Hahn* cases)

Declaration errors of this type are also known as communication errors. The party concerned fails to convert his intentions into the sign or formulation which he wished to use

---

[112] [1989] 1 WLR 179, 10.14 (EN), above, p 323.
[113] [1893] 1 QB 256, 10.1 (EN), above, p 301.
[114] See above, p 107. It is also illustrated by a parody of English law that is based on another famous parody of English manners, *Alice in Wonderland* by Lewis Carroll (the pen-name of the mathematician CL Dodgson): you may like to look at this in GL Williams, 'A Lawyer's Alice' (1946) 9 CLJ 171, 171–72.
[114a] See above, pp 103, 109–10.
[115] BGH 7 June 1984, BGHZ 91, 324.

as a means of communication. He, for example, mistypes, misspells, enters relevant figures in the wrong column or misunderstands the terms which he uses. The consequences of such errors will vary depending on whether or not the other party was aware of the mistake.

(i) The other party is aware of what was actually intended

It is easiest to start with the simple case in which you write offering to sell your hi-fi for £103, when you meant to write £130. If the other party knew that there had been an error and also knew what you meant—for example, if the other party knew you meant £130, but tried to take advantage of the slip by accepting your offer without pointing out the error—it is probable that, in all three systems, there would be a contract at £130.

In German law this case would be treated like one of *falsa demonstratio non nocet*— 'false description does not vitiate if the thing is sufficiently described'.[116] The other party was not misled and there is a good contract for £130. The situation seems not to be discussed in French law in either case law or doctrine, but the result is probably the same: as a matter of interpretation it can be said that the parties had a common intention to deal at £130 and it would be bad faith for the non-mistaken party to try to argue that the price was less than this. The result in English law is less clear, but may well be the same despite what is said in the case which follows.

King's Bench Division   **14.21 (EN)**

Hartog v Colin & Shields[117]

Where a party takes up an offer which he or she knows has been made in error, he or she will not be able to claim on the apparent contract.

Facts: The defendants offered to sell the plaintiff a quantity of Argentine hare skins at 10¼d per lb. This was an error for 10¼d per piece. In the trade, such skins were always sold by the piece; and there are about three pieces to the pound, so that the defendants' offer was the equivalent of 3¾d per piece, whereas three weeks earlier the quoted price had been 10¾d per piece. The plaintiff purported to accept the offer and, when the defendants refused to deliver, brought this action.

Held: The plaintiff's claim was dismissed.

Judgment: Singleton J: In this case, the plaintiff, a Belgian subject, claims damages against the defendants because he says they broke a contract into which they entered with him for the sale of Argentine hare skins. The defendants' answer to that claim is: 'There really was no contract, because you knew that the document which went forward to you, in the form of an offer, contained a material mistake. You realised that, and you sought to take advantage of it.'

Counsel for the defendants took upon himself the onus of satisfying me that the plaintiff knew that there was a mistake and sought to take advantage of that mistake. In other words, realising that there was a mistake, the plaintiff did that which James LJ in *Tamplin v James* described as 'snapping up the offer'. It is important, I think, to realise that in the

---

116 Münchener Kommentar/Armbrüster § 119 para 59.
117 [1939] 3 All ER 233.

511

verbal negotiations which took place in this country, and in all the discussions there had ever been, the prices of Argentine hare skins had been discussed per piece, and later, when correspondence took place, the matter was always discussed at the price per piece, and never at a price per pound. ...

I am satisfied ... from the evidence given to me, that the plaintiff must have realised, and did in fact know, that a mistake had occurred. ...

There was an absolute difference from anything which had gone before—a difference in the manner of quotation, in that the skins are offered per pound instead of per piece.

I am satisfied that it was a mistake on the part of the defendants or their servants which caused the offer to go forward in that way, and I am satisfied that anyone with any knowledge of the trade must have realised that there was a mistake. ...

The offer was wrongly expressed, and the defendants by their evidence, and by the correspondence, have satisfied me that the plaintiff could not reasonably have supposed that that offer contained the offerers' real intention. Indeed, I am satisfied to the contrary. That means that there must be judgment for the defendants.

Notes

(1) '10¼d' and '10¾d' were English currency before decimalization ('d' means pence, from *denarii*). 'lb' means an imperial pound in weight (from *librum*; 1 lb = 454 grams).

(2) The judge seems to accept the argument that there was no contract; but in fact all that he had to decide was that there was no enforceable contract at 10¾d *per lb*. Whether there was a binding contract at 10¾d *per piece* is unclear; but cases involving the equitable remedy of rectification suggest there was one. In addition to the cases discussed earlier in which the written document does not reflect the common agreement of the parties,[118] rectification can also be obtained when the document does not reflect what one party intended and the other party knows this but does not point it out: *Thomas Bates & Son Ltd v Wyndham's (Lingerie) Ltd*.[119] This presupposes that the underlying contract is valid.

(ii) The other party knows the offer contains a mistake but not what is meant

It is conceivable that the other party knows that you have made a slip, and again tries to take advantage by accepting the offer you appeared to make, without knowing what you meant—£113? £123? In English law there is no authority on this point, but the probable result is that there is no contract: the other party cannot reasonably rely on what you have said, but there is no other basis for determining the terms. Dutch law appears similar: see BW Article 3:35.[120] The same result would follow in French law simply on the basis that there was no consensus (compare the case in the next sub-section). In German law this point has not been fully clarified. What commentary there is prefers to dispose of the question under §§ 119, 122(2) BGB.[121] Examples of such cases follow in the next sub-section.

---

[118] See above, p 503.
[119] [1981] 1 WLR 505 (CA).
[120] See 14.16 (NL), above, p 505.
[121] See Münchener Kommentar/Armbrüster § 122 para 21.

So in the situations considered so far, the results generally seem to be in line with the PECL:

Principles of European Contract Law **14.22 (INT)**

Article 5:101: General Rules of Interpretation[122]

(1) A contract is to be interpreted according to the common intention of the parties even if this differs from the literal meaning of the words.

(2) If it is established that one party intended the contract to have a particular meaning, and at the time of the conclusion of the contract the other party could not have been unaware of the first party's intention, the contract is to be interpreted in the way intended by the first party.

...

(iii) The other party is unaware of the mistake

It is in this case that the legal systems seem to differ considerably.

Cass com, 15 February 1961[123] **14.23 (FR)**

[Please look again at the judgment in this case, which is printed at 5.10 (FR), above, p 104.]

Notes

(1) Presumably the sellers should have been aware that the telegram from the buyers contained an error, as the sellers had already made an offer at 60 francs, one-fifth of the price offered in the telegram. However, nothing is made of this point and it seems that the result would have been the same even if the buyers had had no reason at all to suspect a mistake.

(2) This case seems to have been decided on the basis of *erreur-obstacle*, ie that the error prevented the formation of a contract, just as in the cases of *dissensus* discussed earlier. In the traditional analysis, to quote Planiol again, 'it is a misunderstanding, not a contract'.[124] In practice, despite what Rodière wrote in his note of 1975,[125] French courts will often give relief in such cases on the basis of error as to the substance.[126] Thus there will be an *action en nullité relative* and not an *action en nullité absolue*. The reason for this is that only private interests are at stake and not the concept of *intérêt général* which justifies and gives rise to the *action en nullité absolue*.

(3) The principal differences between absolute and relative nullity are now set out in new Articles 1178 to 1185 of the Code civil:

(i) relative nullity may be invoked only by the other party to the contract,[127] whereas the absolute nullity of a contract may be invoked by a third party also,

---

[122] cf DCFR Art II.-8:101.
[123] No. 58-10828, Bull civ III no. 91.
[124] See above, p 105.
[125] See 14.17 (FR), above, p 506.
[126] As to which, see below, pp 526 ff.
[127] Art 1181 Cciv.

provided that they have a direct interest connected to the nullity (eg they are claiming property which the defendant claims to have acquired in good faith under a contract with a third person; if the contract is an absolute nullity, for example it has an illegal purpose (see now Article 1128(3) Cciv), the claimant may invoke the nullity to defeat the defence). Absolute nullity may also be claimed by the *ministère public*.[128]

(ii) the party entitled to rely on relative nullity may confirm the contract,[129] whereas a contract that is absolutely null cannot be confirmed;[130] and

(iii) the prescription period for relative nullity is five years, but for claiming absolute nullity used to be 30 years. However, the new French law of prescription (Articles 2219 ff Cciv[131]) no longer makes such a distinction and the general period is that of five years. Article 2224 sets a time limit of five years from the date of discovery of the error.

The question whether a defect in the contract renders it absolutely or only relatively null tends to be determined by the interests at stake rather than by classification of the nature of the defect. Thus, while *erreur-obstacle* might be thought to mean simply that there is no contract at all, the courts apply relative nullity in this case.[132] The reformed Code civil does not mention the issue, so presumably the case law remains relevant and the likely solution the same.

(4) French law used not to admit unilateral avoidance for relative nullity. This meant that, if the parties were not in agreement as regards avoidance of the contract, the party who claimed for avoidance necessarily had to go to court: nullity was *judiciaire*.[133] If the conditions for nullity were established, the court was bound to grant the nullity (compare the case of *résolution* for non-performance[134]). The contrast to English law, German law and the system of PECL (and also the DCFR), under which a party entitled to avoid a contract may do so by giving notice of avoidance to the other party, and French law was sharp. The French reform adopted an intermediate approach. A unilateral notification of nullity may be effective, provided it is not contested. This results from new Article 1178, which notably provides that 'Nullity must be declared by a court, unless the parties establish it by mutual agreement' and also from the fact that a 'mutual agreement' need not be formal, nor even express (as a result of the principle of consensualism). Both the Avant-projet Catala and the projet Terré had provisions which expressly recognised the validity of such a mutual agreement and it is a matter of regret that the reform has not made this clearer. Indeed, commentators' views diverge on the interpretation of Article 1178. What is certain, and this is where French law still differs from the other models mentioned above, is that if there is

---

[128] Art 1180 Cciv.
[129] Art 1181(2) Cciv.
[130] Art 1180(2) Cciv.
[131] Law no. 2008-561, 17 June 2008.
[132] See generally B Nicholas, *The French Law of Contract* (2nd edn, Oxford: Clarendon Press, 1992) 77–79.
[133] Art 1178 Cciv.
[134] See below, pp 996 ff.

no agreement between the parties, it is for the party who claims for nullity to go to the judge; on the contrary, in the other systems, it is for the party who contests the avoidance to go to court and prove that the conditions for avoidance were not satisfied. But notice the new *action interrogatoire*, noted earlier.[135]

LG Hanau, 30 June 1978[136]   **14.24 (DE)**

Toilet paper

Where in a written statement of offer a technical term is incorrectly used, the declaration of intention may be avoided; a claim for performance of the contract will not be upheld.

Facts: The defendant assistant principal of a girls' secondary school ordered from the claimant, as the school's representative, '25 Gros Rollen' (25 gross rolls) of toilet paper. In that connection, the defendant signed an order form filled out by the claimant's representatives, which contained, amongst other detailed provisions, the indication 'Gros = 12×12'. When the claimant sought to deliver the goods, the girls' school refused to accept the overwhelming majority of them. The claimant then claimed against the defendant and served a default summons on her, which she contested. In addition, she gave notice of avoidance of the transaction. She denied having been aware of the meaning of the quantitative term 'Gros'. Instead, she maintained that she had ordered only 25 double packs of toilet paper, which the school had, moreover, accepted and paid for. Admittedly, the term 'Gros' had been specified when the order was placed. However, the claimant's representatives had referred to that term in the context of the measurement specification 12×12, relating to the manner of packaging.

Held: The claimant's claim for payment of the price of the toilet paper was unsuccessful.

Judgment: ...

The claimant has no claim against the defendant under § 179 BGB. It is true that the school represented by the defendant did not authorise the greater part of the transaction. However, the defendant is under no obligation to perform the contract, because it was effectively avoided by the defendant. In expressing her intention, the defendant committed an error consisting of what she actually said (§ 119(1) BGB). On no account did she wish to buy $25 \times 12 \times 12 = 3,600$ rolls of toilet paper, merely 25 large (*große*) rolls. Although the claimant maintains that the defendant had known exactly what meaning was to be attached to her statement, that cannot be assumed as a fact. It runs totally counter to normal experience of life that a person representing a school which can only be described as a small institution should in one fell swoop order 3,600 rolls of toilet paper each containing 1,000 sheets—a quantity which would have met the school's requirements for a period of several years. Quite apart from the fact that this is scarcely conceivable for reasons relating to the budgetary accounts, which are normally compiled annually, the difficulty of storing such a quantity of goods alone necessitates the conclusion that there can be no question of any conscious intention to proceed in that manner. Nor does the argument that the defendant must, as a teacher, have been familiar with the meaning of the unit of quantity used necessarily indicate that she was aware of its meaning. Quite apart from the fact that it has not been established which subjects she taught, the quantitative term 'Gros' is nowadays completely uncommon and obsolete, with the result that it can no longer be regarded as definitely falling within the ambit of the curriculum. Nor does the indication 'Gros = 12×12' provide any clarification in that regard, since it

---

[135] Above, p 492.
[136] NJW 1979, 721.

does not necessarily enable the number of rolls to be identified but may quite easily be intended to signify other units of measurement, particularly having regard to the spelling mistakes made by the claimant's representatives on the order form.

Notes

(1) § 119(1) BGB does not require that the recipient of the mistaken declaration knows or has any reason to know of the mistake. Where he does not, the mistaken party who avoids will have to compensate him under § 122(1) BGB.[137] Having regard to the findings of the Court in the above case it can be assumed that the seller of the toilet rolls did have reason to know of the mistake. Accordingly he would have been precluded from claiming reliance damages (§ 122(2) BGB).

(2) The above judgment and the example of the man who ordered a *halver Hahn* in Cologne[138] are cases where the declarants clearly intended to make the declaration which they made, but were mistaken as to its meaning. German doctrine refers to this as an *Inhaltsirrtum* and it is specifically provided for in § 119(1) BGB, first alternative, which allows avoidance by a 'person who, when making a declaration of intent, was mistaken about its contents'.

(3) By contrast, where there is a 'slip of the pen', such as occurred in the French 'bottle-openers' case,[139] the party making the declaration 'had no intention whatsoever of making a declaration with this content' (§ 119(1) BGB, second alternative). This is referred to as an *Erklärungsirrtum* and it will equally lead to avoidance. A modern example is provided by OLG Hamm, 8 January 1993,[140] in which a slip in filling in a computerised version of a life insurance contract resulted in a sum, which was intended to be paid as a single lump sum, being stated to be payable annually.

Court of Appeal   **14.25 (EN)**

Centrovincial Estates plc v Merchant Investors Assurance Co Ltd[141]

The offeror under a bilateral contract cannot withdraw an unambiguous offer, after it has been accepted in the manner contemplated by the offer, merely because he has made a mistake which the offeree neither knew nor could reasonably have known at the time when he accepted it.

Facts: The plaintiffs had let some floors of an office building to the Food, Drink and Tobacco Industry Training Board (FDTITB), which had in turn underlet one floor to the defendants at a rental of £68,320 per year. The underlease contained provisions for increasing the rent after four years to the then current market value; if the parties could not reach agreement on what this figure should be the matter would be referred to the assessment of an independent surveyor. Later FDTITB intended to surrender its lease so that the defendants would become direct tenants of the plaintiffs. A firm of solicitors, acting on behalf of both the plaintiffs and FDTITB, wrote to the defendants inviting the defendants to accept £65,000 as the current market value for the purpose of the review. The defendants wrote back agreeing. The solicitors then claimed that their letter had contained a mistake and the figure they had intended was £126,000.

---

[137] See 14.10 (DE), above, p 499.
[138] See above, p 509.
[139] See 14.17 (FR), above, p 506.
[140] NJW 1993, 2321; Markesinis et al (n 25 above) 297, 776.
[141] [1983] Com LR 158 (CA).

It was disputed whether the defendants knew or ought to have known that the figure of £65,000 was a mistake. This could only be resolved by a full trial, but the plaintiffs sought a declaration that no agreement had been reached and asked for summary judgment (ie claimed that they were entitled to the declaration even without proving the defendant knew or should have known of the mistake).

Held: An offer that has been accepted by the offeree is binding if the offeree did not know and had no reason to know that the offer contained a mistake.

Judgment: SLADE LJ: ... On the face of it, the letter of the 22nd June 1982 constituted a formal, unequivocal and unambiguous offer made to the defendants on behalf of the plaintiffs, with an intent to create legal relations, to agree that the 'current market rental value' of the demised premises, for the purpose of sub-paragraph A of the rent review provision, was £65,000 per annum. On the face of it, the letter of the 23 June 1982 constituted a formal, unequivocal and unambiguous acceptance of that offer by the defendants. The plaintiffs' solicitors indeed assert that they erroneously inserted the figure of £65,000 in the letter of the 22 June 1982 in substitution for the figure of £126,000, which they had intended to insert; and like the learned Judge we are prepared to accept the truth of this assertion for the purpose of dealing with the present application. But in the absence of any proof, as yet, that the defendants either knew or ought reasonably to have known of the plaintiffs' error at the time when they purported to accept the plaintiffs' offer, why should the plaintiffs now be allowed to resile from that offer? It is a well-established principle of the English law of contract that an offer falls to be interpreted not subjectively by reference to what has actually passed through the mind of the offeror, but objectively, by reference to the interpretation which a reasonable man in the shoes of the offeree would place on the offer. It is an equally well-established principle that ordinarily an offer, when unequivocally accepted according to its precise terms, will give rise to a legally binding agreement as soon as acceptance is communicated to the offeror in the manner contemplated by the offer, and cannot thereafter be revoked without the consent of the other party. Accepting, as they do, that they have not yet proved that the defendants knew, or ought reasonably to have known, of their error at the relevant time, how can the plaintiffs assert that the defendants have no realistic hope of establishing an agreement of the relevant nature by virtue of the two letters of the 22 and 23 June 1982? Mr Richard Scott in answer has submitted an argument to the following effect. The 'agreement' envisaged by sub-paragraphs A and B of the rent review provision is a genuine agreement, a real meeting of the minds. In the present case there was no real meeting of the parties' minds because of the plaintiffs' error. True it is that their intentions would have fallen to be judged objectively, according to their external manifestation, if the defendants had not only purported to accept the offer but had further altered their position as a result. However, so the argument runs, the general rule that the intentions of an offeror must be judged objectively is based on estoppel. Accordingly, if the person who has accepted the offer has not altered his position in reliance on the offer, no such estoppel arises. In the present case, it is submitted, the critical fact is that the figure of £65,000 was lower than the rent currently payable under the Lease immediately before the 25 December 1982. In these circumstances, it is said, the defendants in agreeing that figure, did not alter their position in any way. Because of sub-paragraph E of the rent review provision, the current rent of £68,320 would have continued to be payable after the 25 December 1982, notwithstanding the agreement. In all the circumstances, it is submitted, the plaintiffs, having proved their error at the relevant time, were at liberty to withdraw the offer contained in the letter of the 22 June 1982, even after it had been accepted, and they duly did so at the end of June 1982. We understand from the learned Judge's judgment that an argument on much the same lines was submitted to him on behalf of the plaintiffs and that, though he regarded it as novel and surprising, he was in the end convinced by it.

[SLADE LJ went on to explain that Mr Scott had accepted that this argument must fail if there was consideration for the agreement. As there was consideration, this concluded the question. He continued:]

Nevertheless, we should perhaps attempt to explain briefly (albeit *obiter*) why, quite apart from questions of consideration, we respectfully differ from the learned Judge on the question of mistake, as a matter of broad principle. The nature of the apparent contract concluded by the two letters of the 22 and 23 June 1982 is what is sometimes called a 'bilateral contract'. It was concluded by (a) an offer by the plaintiffs to treat £65,000 as the 'current market rental value' of the premises for the purpose of the Lease if the defendants would promise to accept that figure as that value, followed by (b) the giving of a promise by the defendants in those terms. Where the nature of an offer is to enter into a bilateral contract, the contract becomes binding when the offeree gives the requested promise to the promisor in the manner contemplated by the offer; the mutual promises alone will suffice to conclude the contract. In our opinion, … it is contrary to the well established principles of contract law to suggest that the offeror under a bilateral contract can withdraw an unambiguous offer, after it has been accepted in the manner contemplated by the offer, merely because he has made a mistake which the offeree neither knew nor could reasonably have known at the time when he accepted it. And in this context, provided only that the offeree has given sufficient consideration for the offeror's promise, it is nothing to the point that the offeree may not have changed his position beyond giving the promise requested of him. For these reasons we think that the plaintiffs' submissions based on mistake cannot, as matters stand, suffice to negative the existence of the apparent agreement of the parties to treat £65,000 as the current market rental value for the purpose of the Lease and to deprive the defendants of the right to defend this action on the basis of such agreement, though we are not, of course, saying that the plea of mistake as formulated in the statement of claim will not succeed at the trial.

… [We] have allowed this appeal and given the defendants unconditional leave to defend the action.

Notes

(1) Thus in English law a mistake in an offer or other contractual document is irrelevant where the other party had no reason to know of the mistake. This is an application of the objective principle, ie the mistaken party is simply bound by what he said or wrote.

(2) Slade LJ's dictum suggests that an offeree may not be able to rely on an offer which he ought to know contains a mistake, even though he was not in fact aware of that. Actual decisions in England do not go so far: in fact the rectification cases[142] have refused relief in cases on unilateral mistake unless the other party had actual knowledge of the error, or suspected it and took deliberate steps to prevent the mistaken party from noticing his own error (*Commission for New Towns v Cooper*

---

[142] See above, p 512.

(Great Britain) Ltd).[143] Canadian authority is more liberal, giving relief when the mistake should have been apparent: see *McMaster University v Wilchar Construction Ltd*.[144]

(3) Occasionally, a party who has made such a mistake is given some relief in that the court may refuse to grant specific performance against him, even if it is one of the (unusual) situations in which specific performance would normally be granted.[145] But the protection given to the mistaken party in this way is limited. First, there are many cases in which specific performance has been granted despite the mistake.[146] Secondly, even if it is refused, the party remains liable for damages for non-performance and there have been cases in which these have been claimed after specific performance was refused.[147]

(4) We saw above (the *Toilet Paper* case)[148] that in German law two situations— (a) using a word you did not intend and (b) using the word you intended but under a misapprehension as to its meaning—are distinguished. We noted also that § 119(1) BGB applies the same result to both—the mistaken party may avoid the contract. The two situations also seem to be treated in the same way by English law. For example, a typical rectification case is where the parties have written that one will pay the other '£1,000 free of tax' (which would mean that the payer pays £1,000 and the payee has to pay the tax), when what they meant is that the payer should pay such a sum that after deduction of tax will amount to £1,000—see *Van der Linde v Van der Linde*,[149] though in that case rectification was denied on other grounds. However, it must be noted that the discussion in Note (1), outlining the position where the other party has no knowledge of the mistake, also applies where the mistake is one as to the content of the declaration. Thus there is a fundamental difference between English and German law. In the *halver Hahn* case, the German buyer may avoid the contract even if the seller did not know of the mistake, whereas in England, rectification will be granted only if the change would give the document the meaning which was intended by both parties, or if it is what one party meant and the other knew that.[150]

(5) It should be noted that in English law a unilateral mistake which is known to the other party is a ground for relief only when the mistake relates to what the terms of the contract are. If the mistake is one as to motive, mistake is not relevant (though there may be relief for misrepresentation).[151] For cases showing this see *Smith v Hughes*[152] and *Statoil ASA v Louis Dreyfus Energy Services LP (The Harriette N)*.[153] In *The Harriette N*

---

[143] [1995] Ch 259 (ChD).

[144] (1971) 22 DLR (3d) 9, aff'd (1973) 69 DLR (3d) 400n.

[145] We will see later that in English law specific performance is rarely ordered except for contracts for the sale of land, below, p 910.

[146] eg *Tamplin v James* (1880) 15 Ch D 215. The circumstances in which it may be refused are discussed in *Stewart v Kennedy* (1890) 15 App Cas 75, 105 and *Treitel* (n 93 above) para 8-056.

[147] *Wood v Scarth* (1855) 2 K & J 33 and (1858) 1 F & F 293.

[148] See 14.24 (DE), above, p 515.

[149] [1947] Ch 306 (ChD).

[150] See above, pp 503 and 512.

[151] See above, p 500.

[152] See 14.41 (EN), below, p 567.

[153] [2008] EWHC 2257 (Comm), [2008] 2 Lloyd's Rep 685.

the parties to a charterparty had reached a compromise over the amount of demurrage due (ie the amount the charterer must pay the owner because of delays in loading the ship). One party had based its calculations on a mistaken assumption as to the date the ship had completed its unloading. The mistaken party was not entitled to relief even though the other party was aware of the mistake and decided to say nothing. It was not a term of the contract that discharge was completed on the date the claimant supposed.

(6) The different treatment given to mistakes which affect the terms of the contract—ie mistakes in declaration—and those which are merely as to the background facts—the motives—can produce nice distinctions. In the Canadian case of *Imperial Glass Ltd v Consolidated Supplies Ltd*[154] a glazing subcontractor put in a bid for a job at far too low a figure because an assistant had misplaced a decimal point in calculating the area of wall involved. The Court held that this was not a mistake about the terms of the contract, but only about the motives for it, so that the offeree could accept the bid even though he knew of the mistake. Presumably the result would have been different if the calculations had formed part of the subcontractor's bid. In the *McMaster* case cited in Note (2) above, the University could not accept a contractor's bid when it should have known that the contractor had by mistake omitted a price escalation clause. German law draws a similar distinction between errors in declaration and errors in motive, but it will allow relief for errors in motive that involve the essential characteristics of the subject matter as well as for mistakes in declaration.[155]

14.3.B.3 COMPARATIVE SUMMARY

Thus we find a good deal of common ground:

(a)   In cases in which the parties use the wrong word to express their common intention, the contract will be interpreted to give effect to their actual intention (at least in so far as they had expressed it to each other[156]).

(b)   In cases of *dissensus*, in which neither party's interpretation is more reasonable than the other's, there will be no contract.

(c)   Where there is either a slip of the pen, or the wrong word is used, by one party and the other party knows what was meant, the contract will again be interpreted as to give effect to the intention of the first party.

But if in either of the situations in (c) the other party does not know that there has been a mistake, the outcomes are rather different. In German law a party who by mistake understates the price, for example, may avoid the contract, whereas in English law the party is bound by what he wrote unless the other party actually knows that the offer contains a mistake. However, it must be remembered that in Germany the mistaken party will be liable under § 122 BGB to compensate the other party for her reliance losses unless the other party knew or ought to have known of the mistake. And, of course, the mistaken party will have to prove that it was mistaken, which will not always be easy. French law in

---

[154] (1960) 22 DLR (2d) 759, BC, CA.
[155] See above, p 499.
[156] See this caveat for English law, above, p 503.

this case seems different again, though perhaps closer to the German position than to the English. It does seem to discuss the case of *Inhaltsirrtum*, but in the case of *Erklärungs-irrtum* the result is that there is no contract because there is no consensus—though, as noted earlier, the courts in practice may avoid the contract under Article 1110 rather than rely on *erreur-obstacle*. In principle, the mistaken party who was careless might have to compensate the buyer on a delictual basis under Article 1240 of the Code civil.

The Principles of European Contract Law will enforce the contract in case (a). In case (b) there will not be a contract. In case (c)(i) there will be a contract on the terms intended by the mistaken party. In case (c)(ii) there will be a binding contract and it will not be avoidable on the grounds of mistake, since Article 4:103 limits relief to cases in which the other party either knew or ought to have known of the mistake, or shared it or caused it.

The DCFR provision follows the PECL ones. Before the CESL proposal was made an Expert Group was established to produce a first draft, which was published as a 'Feasibility Study'.[157] The Feasibility Study contained an article on mistake that was very similar to PECL Article 4:103[158] but added:

> (4) A party may not avoid a contract for mistake under this Article on the ground that one or both parties made a mistake over the terms of the contract.

This was because the Group took the view that problems over mistakes about the terms were adequately solved by applying the rules on formation (offer and acceptance, sufficiency of agreement, etc). However, paragraph (4) was not included in Article 48 of the final CESL proposal; and paragraph (3) indicates that mistakes in declaration were to be within the scope of Article 48:

> (3) An inaccuracy in the expression or transmission of a statement is treated as a mistake of the person who made or sent the statement.

14.3.C MISTAKE AS TO THE PERSON

A common problem is that a party is mistaken as to whom he is dealing with, or mistaken as to some attribute of that person—for example, whether he is credit-worthy. Consider the following examples.

(1) A wishes to sell his car privately for cash. He is approached by B, a rogue, who pretends that he is someone else (usually a well-known person whom A has heard of but never met), and so persuades A to let him take the car away against a cheque apparently drawn on the famous person's account. The cheque turns out to be worthless but, before the fraud is discovered, B has sold the car to an innocent third party, C.

(2) A wishes to employ the house painter, F Müller, who has previously proved himself to be a satisfactory tradesman. While searching the telephone book, he sees two painters of this name and chooses the wrong one, offering him the job.

---

[157] *A European contract law for consumers and businesses: Publication of the results of the feasibility study carried out by the Expert Group on European contract law for stakeholders' and legal practitioners' feedback* (May 2011); see above, p 66.

[158] See 14.8 (INT), above, p 497.

(3) Again A wishes to employ a certain painter, F Müller, and chooses the number correctly, offering him the job. He is mistaken in his belief, however, that it was F Müller who had previously done work for him. It was in fact P Müller.

(4) A meets a man on the street whom he erroneously believes to be the painter F Müller. He offers him the work.

The solutions to these examples are complex because more than one doctrine may come into play. First, the error may prevent any contract coming into existence at all because there is no sufficient agreement. Secondly, the mistake may be a ground on which the contract may be avoided on the ground of mistake as to the substance.

In English law, we shall see in the next part that the doctrine of mistake as to the substance plays a very limited role: it applies only to cases in which both parties make the same mistake—so-called 'common mistake'. It is possible to conceive of cases in which both parties might be mistaken as to the attributes of one of them—for example both employer and employee mistakenly think that the employee does not need a work permit—but there have been no such cases reported.

Even in English law, if one party entered a contract under a mistake as to the identity or attributes of the other, the contract may be avoided if the mistake results from a misrepresentation—for example fraud—by the non-mistaken party. Thus, in example (1), A would have been able to rescind the contract on the ground of fraud had he discovered the fraud and acted quickly, before the car had been sold by the rogue to a third person. But on the facts of the example, the acquisition of rights over the property by an innocent third party means that the right to rescind would have been lost and A cannot get back the car.

This result could be avoided if A could show that the contract was void for mistake. However, the only case in English law in which 'mistake as to the person' operates is one in which the mistake as to identity prevents a contract coming into existence. If A makes an offer which is open only to B, but mistakenly addresses it to C, C may not be able to accept it. However, under the objective principle used in English law, it will be necessary to show that C knew or should have known that the offer was not open to him to accept—see *Ingram v Little*.[159] Once again, there is doubt whether this is the result of a separate doctrine of mistake here or flows simply from the rules of offer and acceptance. It is possible that in example (1) A could show that B knew the offer was open only to the person A thought he was dealing with. When the parties are dealing with each other face to face, there is a strong presumption that A meant to deal with the person he was speaking to and that his mistake is not as to identity: *Lewis v Avery*.[160] However, in cases of contracts made by correspondence—for example, the old case of *Cundy v Lindsay*[161]—the House of Lords has held that the words of the documents are conclusive, so that there cannot be a contract with anyone except the party named in the document: *Shogun Finance Ltd v Hudson*.[162]

---

[159] [1961] 1 QB 31 (CA).
[160] [1972] 1 QB 198 (CA).
[161] (1878) 3 App Cas 459 (HL).
[162] [2003] UKHL 62, [2004] 1 AC 919.

In the remaining examples there would not be any relief in English law. The contract would not be voidable for fraud, since[163] English law does not recognise fraud except where one party has actively misled the other. In none of the remaining examples did the second party mislead A. Nor would the contract be void for mistake in English law, since in none of them did the non-mistaken party have any reason to think that A meant to deal with anyone else.

Article 1134 of the French Code civil allows mistake as to the person as a ground of nullity when the mistake is about the essential qualities of the other contracting party and the contract was 'entered into on the basis of considerations personal to the party'. Attributes as well as identity may be sufficiently fundamental. Mistake as to the identity of a third party can also be taken into account, provided it was *déterminante* of the consent.[164]

German law would deal with each of these sample situations differently. In example (1), the contract could be avoided for fraud under § 123 BGB; but further, in both examples (1) and (2), it might be avoided for mistake. But note that in example (1), the innocent party C would be protected by the rules on moveable property where he had acquired the item in good faith (§§ 929, 932 ff BGB). On an objective interpretation (§§ 133,157 BGB) the declaration of intent amounts to an offer to contract with the person in fact spoken to. There was, however, a divergence between this expression and A's actual intention. He made an error as to the content of his declaration of intention (*Inhaltsirrtum*). The latter may therefore be challenged under § 119(1), first alternative BGB. Assuming that the identity of the other party mattered to A, ie A would not have made this particular contract with any person other than the famous person, German law on agency offers an additional head of liability in example (1). B is then treated as if he were the unauthorised agent of the well-known person, with the consequence that the latter would be able to ratify the contract. If, as would be expected, the well-known person refuses to do so, A could elect to claim specific performance or damages from B, a person 'acting under an alien name' (*Handeln unter fremdem Namen*) (analogous application of §§ 177, 179(1) BGB).

In example (3), by contrast, A intended to contract with the person to whom the declaration of intent was addressed. There can, therefore, be no avoidance under § 119(1), first alternative BGB. A's error is merely one of motive: a mistake as to an attribute of the person with whom he contracted. What is an essential attribute within § 119(2) BGB? Personal attributes which are of direct relevance to the purpose of the transaction are likely to be held by German courts to be essential. For example, creditworthiness will not be an essential attribute in a contract of sale where payment is by cash. It will be, however, where payment is by cheque or a guarantee contract is at issue.[165] Given that the agreement in question was not a contract which particularly requires a mutual relationship of trust and confidence, it is doubtful whether there was such direct relevance in example (3).[166]

In the final case, it is generally held that there is no error under either § 119(1), first alternative BGB or § 119(2) BGB. The other party has been sufficiently identified

---

[163] As we saw earlier, p 489, and see further below, pp 570 ff.

[164] Cass com 19 November 2003, no. 01-01859, Bull civ IV no. 172; see Terré et al (n 24 above) no. 219.

[165] RG 29 September 1922, RGZ 90, 206.

[166] For the importance of trust and confidence in this context, see Palandt/Ellenberger § 119 para 26.

by his physical presence. There is no error as to the content of the declaration; A intends to contract with the person before him. It may be possible to seek avoidance under § 119(2) BGB if the person encountered on the street was not a painter, ie if there were an error as to an essential attribute of that person.

Dutch law treats mistaken identity or attributes as a kind of mistake falling under BW 6:228.

14.3.D MISTAKE AS TO THE SUBJECT MATTER OR CIRCUMSTANCES

In the last part we looked at cases in which the misapprehension or misunderstanding was about what was being agreed between the parties. In this part we look at cases in which the parties have agreed in the same terms, but one or each of them is under some misapprehension as to the nature of the subject matter of the contract, or some relevant circumstance. Under what conditions will this give rise to relief under the various systems?

In both French and German law, this is the central ground of the doctrine of mistake—although the relevant provision in the BGB appears rather as an afterthought, added in the second draft to qualify the rule that mistakes as to motive were never relevant, only mistakes as to declaration.[167] In each system, a party who has entered a contract under a mistake as to, for example, the essential qualities of the subject matter of the contract will be able to avoid the contract.

We also noted earlier that in each system there are complications, in that what seem in functional terms to be cases of mistake may be dealt with under other doctrines, for example absence of *cause* or impossibility. In principle, these will lead to the conclusion, not that the contract may be avoided (*nullité relative*) but that there never was a contract (*nullité absolue*). However, the French Cour de cassation has decided in favour of applying *nullité relative* in such cases. This solution is justified by the fact that the particular interest of the parties is concerned, not the *intérêt général*.[168]

Conversely, it may be that the legal system precludes any argument based on mistake by allocating the risk to one or other party. The typical example of this is where the seller of property is made responsible for defects in it, even if he did not know of the defect.

Leaving such complications aside for the moment and concentrating on avoidance for mistake, in the traditional code systems the key question is, as we suggested in the introduction, a subjective one: was the party claiming relief making the contract under a sufficiently serious misapprehension that the contract should be set aside? It is true that in neither French nor German law will a mistake give a right to avoidance unless both parties would have regarded the matter or the person (see Article 1132 Cciv) to which the mistake related (for example, the age of a piece of furniture sold) as being essential; but the questions of how the mistake arose—for example, was it through incorrect information given by the other party or was it self-induced?—and the situation of the other party—did she know of the mistake or did she share it?—are of lesser importance, at least as far as avoidance of the contract is concerned.

---

[167] See § 119(2) BGB, 14.10 (DE), above, p 499.
[168] Cass civ (1) 20 February 2001, no. 99-12574, Bull civ I no. 39.

The structure of English law is quite different. Mistake is a ground for relief only when (1) it is fundamental and (2) both parties make the same mistake (this book follows the modern custom of calling this 'common' mistake, though the leading case[169] refers to it as 'mutual' mistake). However, English law readily gives relief when one party has misled the other into entering the contract by giving incorrect information—even if this was done without fault. Relief is not under the doctrine of mistake but that of misrepresentation. In other words, the common law looks to the position of both parties and, with the limited exception of common mistake, insists on some misleading behaviour on the part of the other party before avoidance will be allowed (the 'objective approach').

We shall see that the international restatements take a 'mixed' approach: a shared mistake may give rise to avoidance but normally a mistake by one party alone will not do so unless the other party either caused the mistake (eg by giving incorrect information) or knew or should have known of it.

Even in the traditional civil law systems, however, much depends on the remedy sought. Avoidance is based on the claimant's subjective mistake; but if the claimant wants damages, she will normally have to show either (i) some fault on the other party's part (*culpa in contrahendo, responsabilité délictuelle*) or (ii) that the defendant is contractually liable—having expressly undertaken that what the claimant believed to be true would in fact be true, or being responsible under the general law (for example implied terms, *Garantie*) to the same effect.

In practice, these differing grounds do not always lead to differing remedies. In other words, even though either (i) fault on the defendant's part or (ii) the defendant's contractual liability is most often invoked in order that the claimant may claim damages, either ground can sometimes also lead to avoidance of the contract. First, in German law avoidance may on occasion be granted on the basis of *culpa in contrahendo* as well as on the ground of mistake. Secondly, the remedies under (ii) may well include avoidance or its functional equivalent (for example *action rédhibitoire, Rücktritt,* termination).

Again there are marked differences between the civil and common law systems. On (i), all systems recognise that there may be liability for fault. However, the civil law systems have for some time accepted that keeping silent may amount to fault where there is a duty to disclose. The common law is much more reluctant to impose duties on parties and has never recognised any general obligation to disclose pertinent facts. This difference seems so fundamental that it is considered in a separate section of the book, Section 14.4.[170] On (ii), in contract, the common law seems readier to hold that a party has expressly undertaken that something stated about the subject matter will be true, and also to impose more extensive contractual liabilities by the implication of terms into the contract.[171]

It will be obvious that this is a complex subject: in each system there is a variety of doctrines which overlap, while the concepts used differ markedly between civil and common law. To try to make the material simpler, we first give a general account of the law of mistake in French, German, English and Dutch law. This account will be interrupted by a note on various complications which affect French and German law, and one which

---

[169] *Bell v Lever Bros* [1932] AC 161, 14.33 (EN), below, p 543.
[170] See below, p 566.
[171] See below, ch 20.

has 'spilled over' into English law. We then set out one general exception to the rules on mistake, where relief on the basis of mistake is excluded because contractual liability is imposed on one party despite her mistake. After this, we compare the way in which two different species of mistake are dealt with in the different jurisdictions: (i) shared mistakes; and (ii) induced mistakes.

Following on from the discussion of mistake, we discuss the related issue of nondisclosure under 14.4 and the adaptation of contracts under 14.5. We end this chapter by comparing the treatment of mistake and the related doctrines in the national laws and in the international restatements under 14.6.

In all the cases to be discussed, the mistake has been about the facts—for example, the substance of the thing sold or the factual circumstances of the contract. In English,[172] French[173] and German[174] law the courts now recognise that relief may equally be given for a mistake about the law. For reasons of space we do not cover this point.

14.3.D.1 MISTAKE IN GENERAL: FRENCH AND GERMAN LAW

Look again at the principal texts: Code civil Articles 1132 to 1136, BGB §§ 119, 122; BW Article 6:228; PECL Article 4:103.[175]

Cass civ, 23 November 1931[176]   **14.26 (FR)**

The Villa Jacqueline

A party who has entered a contract under a mistake as to an essential quality of the thing sold may have the contract declared null. Essential qualities may include matters affecting the party's intended use of the property when this was known to the other party.

Facts: A villa which had been advertised as having grounds of 7,800 square metres was bought by the claimants, who (as the seller was aware) intended to divide the ground into separate lots and re-sell them. The buyers discovered that the true area was only 5,119 square metres, which was too little for their scheme to be practical, and they claimed that the contract was null on the ground of mistake.

Held: The lower courts held the contract void on the ground of mistake and the Cour de cassation agreed.

Judgment: THE COURT: … *On the sole appeal ground*:—Whereas on 13 June 1924 Mr Beltinissin sold to Mr and Mrs Crozillac by private document property known as the 'Villa Jacqueline', without mentioning the area, for FF36,000, payable by the end of July 1924 at the latest, subject to the condition that the sale would be set aside and a car, pledged as security, forfeited to the vendor if by that date the sale had not been confirmed by notarial act and the price paid in full.

— Whereas the appeal challenges the judgment (Bordeaux, 24 June 1926) in so far as, on the application of the purchasers, it declared the contract void on the ground of mistake as to area, regarded as an essential property of the thing sold.

---

[172] See *Brennan v Bolt Burden* [2004] EWCA Civ 1017, [2005] QB 303.
[173] See Terré et al (n 24 above) no. 224.
[174] See Palandt/Ellenberger § 119 para 15.
[175] See 14.8 (INT), above, p 497.
[176] DP 1932.1.129, annotated by L Josserand, Gaz Pal 1932.1.96.

— Whereas in accordance with Article 1619 of the Civil Code, deficiency in the area of a piece of land can give rise only to a reduction in price where the shortfall is greater than 5%, that is not the case where the deficiency in area makes the land unfit for its intended use, known to the parties, for the purpose of which it was purchased.

— Whereas in that case area actually becomes an essential property of the subject matter of the contract, and mistake as to such a property makes [former] Article 1110 of the Civil Code applicable; as it is clear from the grounds of the judgment that the information given by Mr Beltinissin to the agencies instructed to sell the villa or appearing in newspaper advertisements gave the area of the land sold as 7,800 square metres, whereas it was only 5,119 at most.

— Whereas for Mr and Mrs Crozillac, who purchased the property for the sole purpose (as the vendor was aware) of dividing it into lots and reselling it, the stated area was an essential condition of the contract.

— Whereas furthermore, the judgment notes that the vendor, deliberately and in bad faith, misled the purchasers and by so doing invalidated their consent. In those factual circumstances, the judgment, which interpreted the agreement in accordance with the intentions of the contracting parties and without distortion, could validly hold, without infringing the statutory provisions referred to in the ground of appeal, that the mistake went to the very essence of the thing which was the subject matter of the contract and declare the contract void.

On those grounds, the Court dismisses the appeal.

From the Note

On the facts the area of the land stated became, because of the buyer's plans (known to the seller), a substantial quality of the object of the contract; from that moment a mistake as to this quality brought into play [former] Article 1110: the contract must be annulled, at the buyer's request, for error as to the substance. In this way the Cour de cassation overcame the obstacle of Articles 1617 et seq. ...

1. Mistake leads to the nullity of the contract not only when it is as to the substance, in the strict sense of the word, as to the matter of which the object is composed, but, much more generally, when it relates to the substantial qualities, that is to say, essential qualities, in consideration of which the parties were dealing with one another ...

... These may be objective or subjective ...

Objective qualities are those which, without necessarily having a material character, without being 'substantial' in the etymological sense of the word, are nonetheless embodied in the object of the obligation and identified with it ... he who thinks he is buying a Corot and in fact is paying dear for a copy, is the victim of an error of substance ...

But it goes much further when we consider what we call error as to the subjectively substantial qualities. These are those, of infinite variety, which are attached to the object by the contracting party from such and such an angle, according to what he desires ...

2. Always, for a mistake to lead to nullity of the contract, the case law demands that another condition be fulfilled ... the seller must know that the buyer think she is buying a Corot ... on the facts of this case, the seller knew the use to which the buyers intended to put the land; the judgment stressed that point twice: the purpose 'was known to the two parties'; the buyer's purpose was known to the vendor. The mistake ... must be shared, 'agreed' or be error *ex pacto*. The formula is not rigorously precise, or at least, it could be made more precise: *the case law does not require that* the seller have fallen into the same error as the buyer; it is enough that he knew of the conditions in which the buyer thought he was dealing, the belief in which he is abused. This proven—and it is obviously for the buyer, who seeks annulment, to prove it—the vendor finds himself in a dilemma: either

he was himself in good faith, he thought the painting was a Corot, ...or that the land had the stated area, and so there is shared mistake ... and the contract must fall by virtue of [former] Article 1110; or the seller knew the truth, and in this case he has committed fraud by his silence, his failure to disclose, his misleading statements, actual fraud which justifies the application of [former] Article 1116.

Notes

(1) The Note by Josserand refers to Article 1617 Code civil, which provides:

> Article 1617: Where the sale of an immovable was made with indication of the capacity, at the rate of so much for a measure, the seller is obliged to deliver to the purchaser, if the latter so requires, the quantity stated in the contract; And if he cannot do so, or if the purchaser does not so require, the seller is obliged to suffer a proportionate reduction in price.

In the *Villa Jacqueline* case the seller could not deliver the area of land indicated, and a proportionate reduction in the price would not have been satisfactory for the buyers because the deficiency in area meant that the land was insufficient for the development they intended. Thus the deficiency in area went to 'the very substance of the object', as required by former Article 1110 (now see Article 1133, 'essential qualities'[177]). The case would presumably have been different if the buyers had intended simply to live in the villa. The error must have been *la considération déterminante* for the party seeking relief and a decision which failed to ask whether this was the case has been quashed.[178] See now Article 1130: the mistake must have been of such a nature that without it, the party seeking relief would not have contracted or would have contracted on substantially different terms.

(2) The Note indicates that some matters go to the substance in an objective sense, others only in a subjective way. The defendant was deemed to know the importance of a matter which went to the substance in an objective sense, whereas if the matter was only subjectively important to the particular buyer, the buyer might have to show that the defendant was aware of this (as in the *Villa Jacqueline* case). If a matter was determining and this was known to the other party (either because it is objectively substantial or because the importance of it was known to the other party), this sufficed to make it substantial for the purposes of former Article 1110. As the Avant-projet Catala put it:

> Article 1112: Mistake is a ground of nullity of the contract only where it is about the substance of the thing which is its subject-matter or about the person of the other contracting party. Article 1112-1: Mistake about the substance of the thing means that which bears its essential qualities which the two parties had in mind on contracting or, alternatively, which one of the parties had in mind to the knowledge of the other ...

The revised version of the Code civil puts it in different words:

> Article 1133: The essential qualities of the act of performance are those which have been expressly or impliedly agreed and which the parties took into consideration on contracting.

---

[177] 14.9 (FR), above, p 498.
[178] Cass civ 17 November 1930, S 1932.17, annotated by A Breton, DP 1932.1.161, annotated by JC Laurent, Gaz Pal 1930.2.1031.

It is likely that if some characteristic of the subject matter is essential to one party and the other knows that, it will be 'impliedly agreed'.

(3) The Note suggests that the seller was caught in a dilemma: either he had made the same mistake, so that relief is being given on the ground of shared (or 'common') mistake, or he knew of the mistake and therefore was guilty of fraud in not pointing it out to the buyer. On the facts of the case this seems correct, but in other situations there may be a third possibility. Suppose the seller had not stated the area of the land but the buyer had had it measured by a surveyor who had made a mistake. The seller would know that the area was important to the buyer but might not know that the buyer had been given an incorrect figure. It seems that in principle relief might be given. However, the court might take the line that the buyer was taking the risk. Thus it was held that there was no error of substance when a dressmaker who bought material discovered that what he had bought was furnishing fabric.[179] Even though the seller knew the buyer's purpose, the latter as a professional should have known the material was unsuitable and bought it *à ses risques et périls*. Article 1133(3) now provides that 'acceptance of a risk about a quality of the act of performance rules out mistake in relation to this quality'.

(4) If the mistaken party was seriously at fault, the error may be described as inexcusable and relief denied.[180]

(5) It must be shown that the error related to an essential characteristic of the thing sold, not merely to the motive for buying it.

> An error as to motive which is not, at the same time, an error as to the substantial qualities of the thing sold is inoperative, even if the motive was determining for one party and this was known to the other party. That is not enough to make it an element of the contract: for that there must be a common intention of the parties.[181]

However, it should be noted that the parties have always the choice to *essentialize* an element of the contract or of the contractual relationship by formally integrating the motivating element into the contractual scope. It does not seem sufficient that the other contracting party knows that something was a determining motive for the co-contractor; the reformed Code civil provides:

> Article 1135: Mistake about mere motive, extraneous to the essential qualities of the act of performance owed or of the other contracting party is not a ground of nullity unless the parties have expressly made it a decisive element of their consent.

The frontier between mistake as to the motive, which is not considered relevant, and mistake as to substantial qualities, which enables the party to avoid the contract, is sometimes difficult to identify.

---

[179] Cass com 4 July 1973, no. 72-11119, Bull IV no. 238, D 1974, 538, annotated by J Ghestin.

[180] See Art 1132 Cciv and Malaurie et al (n 23 above) no. 506.

[181] ibid, no. 505. See also Cass civ (1) 13 February 2001, no. 98-15092, Bull civ I no. 31, JCP 2001.I.330, annotated by J Rochfeld and Cass civ (3) 24 April 2003, no. 01-17458, Bull civ III no. 82, RDC 2003, 42, annotated by D Mazeaud: 'mistake on a motive to contract which is unrelated to the subject matter of the latter cannot, unless otherwise explicitly provided, lead to the nullity of the contract, even if this motive has been determining.' See also German law, below, p 537.

(6) A mistake simply as to the thing's value is not enough.

> Article 1136: A mistake as to value is not a ground of nullity where, in the absence of a mistake about the essential qualities of the act of performance, a contracting party makes only an inaccurate valuation of it.

As Malaurie, Aynès and Stoffel-Munck put it:

> A mistake as to value does not suffice to justify annulling the contract—otherwise, this would lead to rescission for general *lésion* (Article 1136 Cciv). In practice, an error as to substance may sometimes lead to a wrong estimation of the value; however it is on the former ground that the contract can been annulled.[182]

Hence the words in Article 1136: a mistake as to value is irrelevant only 'in the absence of a mistake about the essential qualities of the act...'. Moreover, the price may be relevant to what is to be expected and this in turn may amount to a substantial quality of the object, see Cass civ, 29 November 1968:[183] a holiday villa which was said to be comfortably equipped was let at 6,000FF a month; in fact it was in very poor repair and next to a noisy construction site; if held that the lessee was justified in assuming *un standing en rapport* with the high price, the finding of error of substance was justified.

(7) The effect of an operative mistake is of *nullité relative*: Article 1131. In other words, only the party whose consent was vitiated can rely on the error.[184]

(8) Cass civ, 29 November 1968[185] shows that where there is fault on the part of the non-mistaken party (or his agent), the mistaken party may recover damages. On the facts of the case, the owner and his agent 'could not have been ignorant of the bad state of the villa or of the construction site'. 'This is not a question of error as to the substance but one of responsibility' (ie liability).[186] The basis of liability is considered to be the same as that for precontractual fault.[187] This is confirmed in the reformed Code: Article 1178(3) provides:

> Irrespective of whether or not the contract is annulled, an injured party may claim reparation for any harm suffered under the conditions set out by the general law of extra-contractual liability.

If the loss were partly the victim's own fault, in principle the damages could be reduced.

(9) The Note to the *Villa Jacqueline* case goes on to suggest that if the party who has avoided the contract was mistaken through his own fault, he might be made liable in damages for any loss he has caused the other party.[188] This is the position taken by legal scholarship,[189] but in practice it seems that this sanction is not demanded and there is no reference to it in the reformed Code civil. Instead the normal sanction is to refuse annulation for error.

---

[182] Malaurie et al (n 23 above) no. 505.
[183] Cass civ 29 November 1968, Gaz Pal 1969.II.63.
[184] See above, pp 414–15.
[185] See Note (6) above.
[186] See Malaurie et al (n 23 above) no. 502.
[187] Nicholas (n 132 above) 110.
[188] cf § 122 BGB, under which the avoiding party may have to compensate the other party unless the latter knew or had reason to know of the mistake: see 14.10 (DE), above, p 499.
[189] See Terré et al (n 24 above) no. 227.

Cass civ, 13 December 1983[190] *and*
Cour d'appel de Versailles, 7 January 1987[191] **14.27 (FR)**

The Poussin

Where a party has been advised that a painting is not the work of a particular painter and therefore believes that the painting was painted by another, the party will be mistaken as to an essential attribute of the thing sold and will therefore be entitled to avoid the contract.

Facts: The St Arromans owned a painting of Olympus and Marsyas which family tradition held to be by Poussin; but they were advised by an art dealer that it was of the school of Carracci and worth only some 1,500FF. They sold it to a dealer for 2,200FF but the National Museum exercised its right of pre-emption and shortly afterwards exhibited the painting as a Poussin. The St Arromans sought to have the contract of sale set aside for mistake.

Held: In 1972, the St Arromans succeeded at first instance on the grounds that there was no meeting of minds on the thing to be sold, the sellers intending to sell a painting of the school of Carracci and the buyer intending to buy a Poussin (D 1973, 410, note J Ghestin and Ph Malinvaux). Advocate-General Gulphe later described this decision as a remarkable instance of ex-Article 1110 being applied to protect a seller rather than a buyer.

The cour d'appel of Paris reversed this decision on the ground that it was not proven that the painting was by Poussin and therefore the error had not been established (D 1976, 325, conclusions Cabannes; JCP 1976.II.18358, note Lindon). That decision was in turn quashed by the Cour de cassation on the basis that the court had not enquired whether the consent of the sellers was not vitiated by an erroneous conviction that the work *could not be* by Poussin. The case was remitted to the cour d'appel of Amiens.

The court at Amiens also found against the St Arromans, on the ground that at the time of sale the sellers had serious doubts whether the painting was by Poussin.

Before the Cour de cassation on its second consideration of the 'Poussin case', M Gulphe argued that the contract should be avoided. The authenticity of a painting is established as being a 'substantial quality' within former Article 1110 and

[i]n this case, the determining cause of the sale of the disputed picture, the substantial quality, as far as the sellers were concerned, has a negative quality. It is claimed that the contract is null because the picture was sold by its owners in the certainty that they were not dealing with a picture by [Poussin].

He noted that the court at Amiens had found that at least the seller's agents were convinced that the painting *could not be* by Poussin, and therefore the court should have considered the application of former Article 1110, but the court had not applied that Article on the ground that the attribution was not established at the time of sale. He noted:

'The Amiens judgment adopts the doctrinal theory that a seller cannot annul a sale because of an error he has made unless there is fraud on the part of the buyer.'

Once again the decision was reversed (see below), and in 1987 the sale was finally annulled by the Cour d'appel of Versailles (also below). The picture was returned to Mme St Arroman (her husband had died by this stage) and she refunded the 2,200FF. Later she sold the painting to a Swiss gallery for 7,400,000FF.

---

[190] No. 82-12237, Bull civ I no. 293, JCP 1984.II.20186.
[191] No. 298/85, Gaz Pal 1987, 34.

Cass civ, 13 December 1983

Judgment: On the sole appeal ground in law:—Under [former] Article 1110 of the Civil Code;— Whereas Mr and Mrs Saint-Arroman sold a painting by public auction through Messrs Maurice Rheims, Philippe Rheims and René Laurin which family tradition had it was the work of Nicolas Poussin; as however, Robert Lebel, the expert called in by the auctioneers attributed it to the school of Carracci, with the result that it was listed as such in the sale catalogue with the owners' consent and sold for FF2,000 on 21 February 1968;

— Whereas the Réunion des Musées Nationaux ('RMN') exercised its right of preemption and then exhibited the painting as an original work by Nicolas Poussin;

— Whereas Mr and Mrs Saint-Arroman brought an action to have the contract of sale set aside on the ground of mistake as to the essential property of the thing sold, but the cour d'appel, ruling after a previous judgment had been quashed and the case referred to it, rejected the claim on the grounds that, while at the time of the sale Mr and Mrs Saint-Arroman were convinced … that the painting at issue could not be by Poussin, neither the assignment of the painting in the Louvre to Poussin by order of 20 March 1968, nor the article by Mr Rosenberg in the *Revue du Louvre* which appeared in 1969, nor yet the fact that the painting was exhibited in the Louvre in the name of Poussin, gives rise to any implication or contains any evidence concerning the origin of the work either before or at the same time as the sale, and liable as such to influence the vendors' consent if at that time they or their agents had been aware of it.

— Whereas similarly, RMN observed in its pleadings that in short, and in spite of its own actions after acquiring the painting, there was no absolute certainty as to the origin of the work.

— Whereas the cour d'appel declared that 'it is irrelevant whether the Réunion des Musées Nationaux maintained, or subsequently corrected, its opinion concerning the attribution of the painting to Poussin, since the mistake must be determined on the day of sale'.

— Whereas by so deciding, and by denying Mr and Mrs Saint-Arroman the right to rely upon evidence subsequent to the sale in order to prove that there had been a mistake on their part at the time of the sale, the cour d'appel has infringed the abovementioned provision.

— Whereas the question of the validity of the sale and the question of the liability of the auctioneers and the expert are necessarily interdependent, the provision in the contested judgment concerning their liability must consequently be quashed, pursuant to Article 624 of the new Code of Civil Procedure.

On those grounds, the Court quashes the judgment given between the parties on 1 February 1982 by the cour d'appel, Amiens, and remits the matter to the cour d'appel, Versailles.

Cour d'appel de Versailles, 7 January 1987

Judgment:— Whereas where works of art are sold by public auction from a catalogue containing authentication by an expert, the attribution of the work is for both seller and buyer an essential property of the thing sold;

— Whereas the seller's conviction as to the attribution is determined on the basis of the information given in the sale catalogue which includes a definition of the essential features and real nature of the object he is selling;

— Whereas in this case, the painting sold on 21 February 1968 was described in the catalogue as follows: 'Carracci (school of), Bacchanalia. Large canvas. 1.03 m high, 0.87 m wide'; as this description, which thus defines the nature of the thing that is the subject matter of the contract, contains no allusion to the existence of a possible attribution of the work to Nicolas Poussin or even to his school, to his style or manner, whereas it is, however, the custom in cases of uncertainty as to the creator of a work of art to use terms such as 'signed by ... attributed to ... school of ... style ... *genre* ... manner'; as in the absence of any such expressions, to state merely 'School of Carracci', to which it is undisputed that Nicolas Poussin never belonged, excludes an attribution to the latter and leaves no doubt;

— Whereas accordingly it is proved that when the sellers concluded the contract they were convinced that the painting was not by Nicolas Poussin and were sure only that it was to be attributed to the school of Carracci.

— Whereas it is immaterial that in their documents Mr and Mrs Saint-Arroman acknowledged that an old family tradition attributed the work at issue to Nicolas Poussin since, on the one hand, it is only what they actually believed at the moment of the sale which must be taken into account and, on the other, laymen as they were, they could not be criticised for falling in with the decisive opinion given by Mr Lebel, a well-known expert, and confirmed by Maître Rheims, an auctioneer and valuer of high renown, or for allowing themselves to be persuaded that their family tradition was incorrect and that the work could not be by Nicolas Poussin;

— Whereas the assertion of the auctioneer and the expert that Mr and Mrs Saint-Arroman concealed that family tradition from them cannot be regarded as proved to be true. It is made by parties with an interest in the outcome of the dispute, it is entirely unsubstantiated and is not supported by any evidence; as moreover, it is scarcely probable that Mr and Mrs Saint-Arroman, in selling their painting at the best possible price, should not have told their agents of its attribution according to the family tradition, just as it strains credulity that the prudent professionals that the agents were should have failed to question the sellers about any knowledge they might have as to the painter of the work which they put into the hands of the agents to sell; as the plea alleging that Mr and Mrs Saint-Arroman were grossly negligent in failing to reveal to Maître Rheims and Mr Lebel what they knew of the painter has no factual basis;

— Whereas the authenticity of the painting's attribution to the artist Nicolas Poussin remains uncertain, in the light of opinions given by eminent experts which are as peremptory as they are contradictory, and while the Court, in the absence of decisive proof, cannot resolve that point, this division among the experts cannot mean, as the Minister for Culture argues, that Mr and Mrs Saint-Arroman's mistake is not allowable as it relates to certain persons' opinions concerning attribution and not to attribution itself;

— Whereas this divergence does not precisely make it impossible for the work to be 'a genuine Poussin', it supports Mrs Saint-Arroman's claim relying on the mistake which she and her husband made of selling the painting under the erroneous belief that it absolutely could not be the work of that painter, especially since at the same time, according to the evidence in the case, when the RMN exercised its right of pre-emption over the work it was, if not certain that the painting was by Poussin, at least persuaded that its origin was other than that stated in the catalogue; as if that were not so, it is inexplicable that the RMN, according to its own pleadings, was authorized to pay up to FF40,000 by way of pre-emption, a sum 25 times greater than the estimate of FF1,500 suggested by the expert, Mr Lebel;

— Whereas in addition, a fortnight after the sale an article by Jacques Thuillier, a Poussin specialist, was putting forward the painting as a work of Poussin's discovered by the Louvre's young conservation team, a view which the RMN shared at first instance but abandoned on appeal for the purposes of its own case;

— Whereas in order to resist (to no purpose) Mrs Saint-Arroman's action, the Minister for Culture objects that the mistake she pleads is in fact a mistake as to value and accordingly cannot render the sale void, because loss consisting of inadequate consideration cannot give rise to rescission of a contract for the sale of personal property; as the Minister argues that a distinction must be drawn between financial mistake arising from an incorrect economic assessment of correct facts, and mistake as to the qualitative value of the thing which, as in this instance, is only the result of a mistake as to an essential quality, in which case the mistake must be regarded as a mistake relating to the essential nature of the subject matter of the contract;

— Whereas there is no need otherwise to follow the parties into the details of their arguments; it must be held that in believing that they were selling a canvas of the school of Carracci, of indifferent quality, that is to say, under the mistaken conviction that it could not be a work by Nicolas Poussin, when it is possible that the work is his, Mr and Mrs Saint-Arroman made a mistake relating to the essential nature of the thing transferred which was crucial to their consent, which they would not have given if they had been aware of the facts; as accordingly, the contested judgment must be upheld in so far as it annulled the sale of 21 February 1968 on the basis of [former] Article 1110 Code civil and, in addition, it must be ordered that the painting be returned to Mrs Saint-Arroman and that her undertaking to refund the sum received of FF2,200 be formally recorded.

— Whereas Mrs Saint-Arroman's claim against Messrs Rheims and Laurin and the heirs of Mr Lebel is in the nature of a plea in the alternative, there is no need to adjudicate.

On those grounds, and having regard to the judgment of the Cour de cassation of 13 December 1983, the Court, in formal session in open court, confirms all the provisions of the judgment under appeal and, in addition, extends its effects to the Minister of Culture, orders the painting in dispute to be returned to Mrs Saint-Arroman, [and] formally records Mrs Saint-Arroman's undertaking to refund the proceeds of sale, that is to say, FF2,200 … [The court held that there was no need to give a ruling on an alternative claim against Messrs Rheims and Laurin and the heirs of Mr Lebel.]

The Court orders the Réunion des Musées Nationaux and the Minister of Culture to pay both the costs of the appeal incurred before the cours d'appel of Paris and Amiens and those incurred before the cour d'appel, Versailles, and also the costs of the judgments quashed …

Notes

(1) If the non-mistaken party's conduct can be described as *fautive*, the mistaken party may claim damages on the basis of Article 1240 Code civil as well as avoid the contract for error. Following the same solution and, again about a Poussin masterpiece, see Cass civ (1), 17 September 2003.[192]

(2) In German law this case might have been seen as a mere error of motive along the same lines as the error in the *Mozart Notebooks* case, below. Even if § 119(2)

---

[192] No. 01-15306, Bull civ I no. 183.

BGB had applied, the sellers would still have to pay damages under § 122 BGB unless the court's suspicions about the knowledge of the RMN's buyers crystallised into a definitive finding.

AG Coburg, 24 April 1992[193]   **14.28 (DE)**

Mozart notebooks

Where a party mistakenly includes in a lot for sale an item she had meant to reserve because of its value, there is no mistake as to the declaration under § 119(1) BGB and no mistake as to the essential characteristics of the thing sold under § 119(2) BGB.[194] *The buyer is not under an obligation to disclose the fact that the bundle includes a valuable item.*

Facts: The seller sold a bundle of miscellaneous notebooks for 10 DM, not realising that she had included in the bundle a notebook by Mozart. She had intended to set this aside and sold the bundle without knowing exactly what was in it.

Held: She could not avoid the contract nor recover compensation for fraud by the buyer.

Judgment: The parties are in dispute concerning the return of antiquarian music note-books. On 13 October 1991 the defendant acquired from the plaintiff in a public 'flea market', for the sum of 10 DM, various music note-books, sheets of music and musical periodicals. On 16/17 October 1991 the local press reported on a 'sensational Mozart find' having 'considerable rarity value' which the defendant had made in the flea market, whereupon the plaintiff declared, by letter dated 18 October 1991 which reached the defendant by 20 October at the latest, that she was avoiding, as against the defendant, the contract 'relating to the collection of manuscript sheet music (by, *inter alia*, Mozart) handed over to you on 13 October 1991, by reason of mistake' and demanded the return of the items handed over in return for reimbursement of the purchase price. The plaintiff maintains that on 12 October 1991, as the owner of a great many music note-books, including *inter alia* the note-books and sheets forming the subject matter of the claim, she sorted out and extracted from her stock the items produced prior to 1906, since these were not intended to be sold, and gathered all the rest together with a view to selling them in the flea market. She claims that, for inexplicable reasons, the items sorted out and extracted by her clearly got mixed up again with the items intended for sale, in some manner which she is unable to ascertain in detail, and that she was unaware on 13 October 1991 that the older items were included amongst the goods laid out on the stand in the flea market. When the defendant purchased the notebooks and other similar items from her, she was certainly aware that he was buying note-books, but she did not notice which particular note-books were involved. The defendant considers that the plaintiff's mistake is not one which justifies avoidance of the contract.

Grounds:

... II.1. The plaintiff's assertion that, for inexplicable reasons, the items initially sorted out and extracted by her got mixed up again with the items intended for sale is irrelevant in all the circumstances of the present case. The rules relating to transactions and declarations of intent are fundamentally inapplicable to the actual acts falling to be considered

[193] NJW 1993, 938.
[194] See 14.10 (DE), above, p 499.

in this matter, so that, for that reason alone, there can be no question of any avoidance of the contract. In so far as the contract and/or the transfer of ownership may have been indirectly influenced by this, avoidance of the contract and of the transfer of ownership on the ground of mistake cannot be legally justified, if only because the plaintiff's possible mistake or aberration could not have related to the declarations of intent themselves, but concerned only the circumstances surrounding the events leading up to the making of those statements.

2. There was patently no error made as regards the act of making the statements (§ 119(1) second alternative BGB). The plaintiff wished to bind herself under a sales contract and to transfer to the defendant ownership of the goods which were relinquished to him.

3. There was no question of any mistake as to the content of the statements (§ 119(1) first alternative BGB). The plaintiff was completely in the picture as to the meaning and legal consequences of the sales obligation into which she was objectively entering, and as to the transfer of ownership to the defendant. The subject matter of the transaction, in the eyes of the plaintiff and the defendant, was the notebooks handed over to the latter.

4. In so far as it was in fact open to the plaintiff to assume that the 'packets of note-books handed over to the defendant' contained only the 'flea market items' which she had got ready the day before, when they in fact also contained the notebooks at issue in the present case, the plaintiff cannot be said to have made a mistake, since according to her own statements she did not notice which particular note-books were involved; as a result of her conscious nonchalance in that regard, she made her contractual declaration, committing herself to the contract and to the transfer of ownership, in the conscious knowledge that she did not know precisely what inference was to be drawn from the objective circumstances (a contract of sale in respect of, and the transfer to the defendant of ownership in, certain note-books selected by the latter) as to the content of the items in question. Accordingly, the plaintiff cannot claim that, unknown to her, she was unaware of the actual facts asserted.

5. Nor can there be any question of an error as to ownership within the meaning of § 119(2) BGB. The characteristics of a thing or matter include the already existing factual or legal relationships and connections with the surrounding circumstances, in so far as these can be seen, upon consideration of the commercial aspects of the specific transaction in question, to have any significance as regards questions of valuation or usabililty, and in so far as they directly characterise the thing or matter. The value of the antiquarian note-books in terms of their origin, age, state of preservation and rarity, which emerges only indirectly from a consideration of the transaction, does not constitute a characteristic within the meaning of § 119(2) BGB; consequently, a possible mistake on the part of the plaintiff as to the actual value of the note-books handed over to the defendant for 10 DM is irrelevant in the present case.

6. Nor, lastly, can there be any question of avoidance of the contract and of the transfer of ownership pursuant to § 123(1) BGB. Even if the defendant had recognised the value of what the plaintiff claims to be the 'find', and had deliberately failed to disclose this to the plaintiff, the defendant cannot be said to have wilfully deceived the plaintiff, since the defendant was under no obligation to give the plaintiff any information or indication in relation to the fact not disclosed at the time (the tangible or intangible value of the note-books discovered). It is basically up to the parties to a contract to look after their own interests, and there exists no general duty, in the context of contractual or pre-contractual negotiations, to disclose all circumstances which might significantly affect the decision of the other party. Moreover, it is in the nature of a typical public flea market that anyone in

such a market—even a person possessing no commercial experience—can offer to buy or sell or acquire objects of every kind and degree of quality at prices which are not solely calculated to result in a profit. It follows that the principle of good faith does not require the attention of offerors who possibly lack commercial experience to be drawn to what may be the far greater value of an object offered for sale, in order to prevent such offerors from entering into what may, from a commercial standpoint, be a significantly disadvantageous transaction to which they have not given sufficient thought.

7. Nor, clearly, can there be said to have been a lack of consensus between the parties. The declarations of intent made by each of them, as described in the statement of facts provided by the plaintiff, tally with each other. The existence of a possible mutual mistake by the parties concerning the declaration made by the other party (possible hidden lack of agreement) has not been substantiated by the pleas advanced and is not otherwise apparent.

Notes

(1) In German law the class of mistakes as to the substance or attributes of some thing or person has been interpreted in two ways. According to the first, they normally amount to only insignificant errors of motive.[195] The nineteenth-century writings of Zitelmann have influenced this position. His analysis of the process of contracting posited a prior and necessarily distinct phase wherein the party was influenced by one or several motives. Only thereafter was an intention formed and communicated to the other party. A textbook example of this distinction is where a proud father purchases a ring in ignorance of the cancellation of his daughter's wedding. Zitelmann—and indeed most contemporary systems—would hold that the father cannot avoid since his mistake was as to a motivating factor. His intention to purchase this ring from this jeweller was in no way flawed by mistake. He intended to make a declaration of intent and one with this particular effect. He did this successfully. Errors as to the attributes, rather than the identity of a thing or person, are also made at the earlier stage and thus amount to errors of motive. According to this theory, § 119(2) BGB makes an exception to this where the mistake was as to an attribute considered essential in business. The distinction between significant and insignificant errors is therefore drawn on the basis of whether the attribute has a direct influence on the value of the item and is of special significance for contracts of that type—for example, the authenticity of a 'Ming vase'.[196] The definition in Section II.5 of the above judgment reflects this approach.

(2) The foregoing approach has been criticised on the basis that it does not yield clear criteria defining exactly which mistakes will actually lead to avoidance. As such, it threatens the security of transactions and unfairly puts the risk of (some) purely subjective errors of motive on the other party. A second, less objective, more context-dependent approach was therefore developed by Flume.[197] It is demonstrated in the reasoning of the following case.

---

[195] K Larenz and M Wolf, *Allgemeiner Teil des Bürgerlichen Rechts* (8th edn, München: CH Beck, 1997) § 36 paras 9, 45.

[196] RG 22 February 1929, RGZ 124, 115.

[197] See generally, W Flume, *Eigenschaftsirrtum und Kauf* (Darmstadt: Wissenschaftliche Buchgesellschaft, 1975).

The ultrasonic device

The buyer's purpose does not amount to an 'essential characteristic' of the goods within § 119(2) BGB unless it has been agreed between the parties.

Facts: A doctor bought an 'ultrasonic device' which had no technical defects but which was not suitable for its purpose. The seller sued for the contract price. The doctor claimed inter alia that he had been mistaken as to an essential characteristic of the device and that the contract could therefore be avoided.

Held: Both the lower courts upheld the claimant's claim. The BGH dismissed the defendant's appeal, holding that, as the device's suitability had not been 'raised to being an element of the contract', no challenge could be made under § 119(2) BGB.

Judgment: The claimant is claiming the sum of 6,367 DM, being the purchase price payable for an ultra-sound machine delivered to the defendant doctor in September 1949. The defendant used the machine and, by letter of 31 December 1949, placed it once again at the disposal of the seller. He contested the claim for the purchase price inter alia on the following ground: his personal experiences with the machine, which had been immediately confirmed by specialist colleagues, had shown that it in no way constituted a machine having any therapeutic value. It did not fulfil the full range of functions which it was claimed to possess. Even though the electro-physical machine revealed no technical defects, it was not suitable for its purpose as warranted; at any rate, treatment using the machine had produced results which were harmful and must be regarded as completely negative.

Grounds: …

2. The court hearing the appeal on a point of law also examined whether the defendant's objections were capable of substantiating a plea of avoidance on the ground of mistake. They are not …

According to settled case law, the value of an object cannot as such be deemed to constitute a characteristic of that object within the meaning of § 119(2) BGB. … Consequently, the possible commercial utilization of an object is not *per se*, and on its own, a characteristic of that object which is of the essence of the transaction. That concept covers only such factual and legal relationships as are capable of characterising the object itself, and does not include circumstances which can only indirectly affect an assessment of it. … Even if it were possible to assume that the fitness of the ultra-sound machine for treating certain types of illnesses constitutes an intrinsic element of the object itself, it could nevertheless only be regarded as an essential characteristic of the transaction if the conceptions entertained in that regard by the defendant or by both the contracting parties were elevated to the status of elements going to the very contents of the contract itself. It has not been shown, however, that that was the case.

Notes

(1) It is stated in the above case that an attribute is essential only where its presence was provided for in the contract itself. More recent case law has relaxed this requirement somewhat. The newer criterion is, thus, that the assumption must have been

---

[198] BGHZ 16, 54.

recognisably at the basis of the challenging party's entry into the agreement, without being necessarily contained in the contract.[199]

(2) It is stated in both of the above cases that the price or value of an item is not considered to be an essential attribute within § 119(2) BGB. Why, as a matter of common sense, might this be so?

(3) An assumption as to the course of future events will not be considered to be significant within § 119(2) BGB. Thus, it has been held that a declaration disclaiming an inheritance under a will in 1982 could not be avoided in 1990 because the declarant had mistakenly assumed that property mentioned in the will would remain under the control of the government of the German Democratic Republic.[200]

(4) The error must have been causative of the decision to enter into the contract such as it was. Causation in this regard is tested both subjectively—ie from the perspective of the mistaken party herself—and objectively. The latter allows courts to refuse avoidance of the contract where the mistaken facts would only have influenced a wilful or foolish individual. This requirement seems superfluous in cases coming within § 119(2) BGB.

(5) A declaration of intention which proceeded from an error and which it is sought to set aside must be challenged through a further declaration of intention directed to the other party to the contract (§ 143 BGB). The subsequent declaration of intention may be a notice to the other party, or be constituted by conduct which unequivocally indicates an intention to avoid. § 142(1) BGB provides that avoidance is of retrospective effect, ie the contract (or other juristic act) is void *ex tunc*. The German courts have made exceptions to this *ex tunc* rule, chiefly in the case of employment contracts and other ongoing contractual relationships, and ordered the contract avoided *ex nunc* only. This may be justified by the difficulty of making restitution of benefits on avoidance of such contracts.[201]

(6) A challenge to a declaration made under the influence of a mistake, within § 119 BGB, must be made 'without culpable delay' upon discovery of the grounds for challenge (§ 121 BGB). The period may be very short—in the *Bank Guarantee* case,[202] the right was lost in two weeks. How can this be rationalised on the basis of allocation of risk? In any case the right to challenge expires when ten years have elapsed from the date of the impugned declaration of intention (§ 121(2) BGB).

(7) The right to avoid under § 119 BGB (both sub-sections) is not lost by the mistaken party, even though contributory negligence has been shown on his part. However, as we have seen, the other party is afforded a measure of protection by § 122 BGB. He may thereby claim reliance damages (*negatives Interesse*) from the mistaken party where the latter opts to avoid. This right in its turn is conditional upon his having had no knowledge or possibility of knowing of the error. Thus the risk of 'accidental misapprehensions' is allocated to the party who was best placed to avoid it. In contrast, there is no such provision for compensation under § 123 BGB where there was fraud.

---

[199] BGH 22 September 1983, BGHZ 88, 240.
[200] See LG Berlin 6 December 1990, NJW 1991, 1238.
[201] The effects of termination of contracts in general is discussed below, pp 1044 ff.
[202] See 14.20 (DE), above, p 510.

It is interesting to compare French and German law to the mistake article of the Dutch BW, in particular because the BW has moved away from traditional concepts employed in the law of mistake, such as 'substance' or 'essential qualities'

BW   **14.30 (NL)**

Article 6:228: (1) A contract which has been entered into under the influence of error and which would not have been entered into had there been a correct assessment of the facts, can be annulled:

(a) if the error is imputable to information given by the other party, unless the other party could assume that the contract would have been entered into even without this information;

(b) if the other party, in view of what he knew or ought to know regarding the error, should have informed the party in error;

(c) if the other party in entering into the contract has based himself on the same incorrect assumption as the party in error, unless the other party, even if there had been a correct assessment of the facts, would not have had to understand that the party in error would therefore be prevented from entering into the contract.

(2) The annulment cannot be based on an error as to an exclusively future fact or an error for which, given the nature of the contract, common opinion or the circumstances of the case, the party in error should remain accountable.

Notes

(1) Article 6:228 seems generous in allowing relief even though the mistake is not as to the substance of the thing contracted for. It suffices that the mistake concerns facts or circumstances which are essential to the mistaken party (in the sense that he would not have entered the contract on the same terms or at all had he known the truth), even if the facts or circumstances are extrinsic to the contract. However, there is no relief if, at the time of the contract, the other party did not know and had no reason to know that the facts or circumstances were essential to the mistaken party.[203]

(2) However, it is narrower than French or German law in restricting the scope of error for which relief will be given by sub-paragraphs (1)(a)–(c).

(3) Article 3:49 provides:

Where a juridical act is subject to annulment, it can be annulled either by extrajudicial declaration or by judgment.

(4) The mistaken party may be able to claim damages from the other if the latter was at fault under the general rule relating to unlawful acts: Article 6:162. The damages will not include loss of expectation.

---

[203] See AS Hartkamp and MM Tillema, *Contract Law in the Netherlands* (The Hague/Boston: Kluwer, 1995) para 80.

14.3.D.2 COMPLICATIONS: ABSENCE OF *OBJET/CAUSE* AND IMPOSSIBILITY

At this stage we need to consider a complication. In at least French and German law there are a number of situations which involve a sort of mistake and in which the contract will be ineffective, but which are dealt with under doctrines other than mistake: for example lack of *objet*, lack of *cause* or impossibility. For example, suppose the parties agree to the sale of a car which, unknown to either party, has just been destroyed in a fire.

(a) Absence of *objet* or of *cause* in French law

In French law before the reforms, where there was a contract to sell specific goods which had ceased to exist, the contract would be void for lack of *objet* and so no question would arise of annulling it for mistake. This approach, which derives from Roman law, is also found in other systems, and is even reflected in English law.[204]

In a French case, M agreed with R (as was legally permissible) to do R's military service in R's place. Unknown to either of them, R was not liable for service. It was held that M's obligation lacked *objet* and R's lacked *cause*.[205]

Under the reformed Code civil the analysis may be different. An obligation must have a content which is licit and 'certain' (Article 1128(3)). Article 1163 further states that an obligation has as its subject matter a present or future act of performance and the latter must be possible and determined or capable of being determined. If one party's obligation is impossible the conditions set out in Article 1163 are not met.[206]

(b) Initial impossibility in German law

In the BGB before the reforms of 2002, mistakes as to the existence of the subject matter of the contract were dealt with not by §§ 119 ff BGB, but in the general part of the law of obligations under the rules on initial impossibility (*anfängliche Unmöglichkeit*): former §§ 306 ff BGB. Now cases of initial impossibility fall under § 275(1) BGB (which excludes a claim for actual performance by the obligor) and give the other party the right to terminate (§ 326(5) BGB) and a right to damages in lieu of performance if the first party was responsible for the impossibility.

In exceptional cases where performance, whilst being technically (or physically) possible, is so unacceptably burdensome as to be 'practically impossible' (for example, a contract to deliver a ring lost at the bottom of the ocean), the debtor may refuse performance (§ 275(2)).

(c) Cases where the goods have ceased to exist in English law

There is also a rule of English law that, if there is a contract to sell goods but, unknown to either party, the goods have already ceased to exist, the contract is void. The precise foundation of this rule, and its relationship to the rather limited doctrine of common mistake in English law, is not wholly clear.

---

[204] See below, pp 541–43.
[205] Req 30 July 1873, S 1873.1.448, D 1873.1.330.
[206] Under Arts 1224 ff; see 25.5 (FR), below, p 987.

The doctrine of common mistake in English law seems to be a relatively recent innovation, a nineteenth century importation from civil law.[207] During the first half of the century various cases which are now seen as involving common mistake were decided without invoking any such doctrine. Perhaps the best known is *Couturier v Hastie*.[208] A c&f contract had been made for a cargo of corn that both parties assumed was in existence. (A c&f contract is one in which the price covers the cost of the goods and the 'freight', ie the cost of carriage; unlike the more modern cif (cost, insurance and freight) contract, a c&f contract does not include insurance against loss of the goods.) In fact, the corn had begun overheating and the captain of the ship had unloaded and sold it (the normal practice). The sellers argued that the buyers must still take up the shipping documents and pay the price. If it had been the case that the goods had been damaged or lost after the contract had been made, then at least in modern law the buyer would indeed have been obliged to pay—the risk would have passed as from shipment and the buyer would be expected to claim on the insurance, if any. But the House of Lords affirmed the decision of the Exchequer Chamber that on the actual facts the buyer did not have to pay. The contract was one 'for the sale of a cargo supposed to exist', not 'for goods lost or not lost'. The word mistake does not occur in the judgments, nor is there any discussion of whether the contract was void—the only point decided was that the seller could not require the buyer to perform.

The most obvious source for the doctrine of mistake is *Kennedy v Panama, etc Royal Mail Co*.[209] The plaintiff had bought some shares relying on a statement that the company had obtained a valuable contract to carry mail for the New Zealand government. This would now be treated as an innocent misrepresentation.[210] But the case was argued and decided on purely common law grounds, and the question was simply whether there had been a total failure of consideration so that the plaintiff could get his money back.[211] Again, this is something different from mistake, but in deciding that there had not been a total failure of consideration Blackburn J drew on Roman law principles. He referred to the Roman doctrine of error, under which a mistake as to substance would invalidate a contract but a mistake merely as to quality would not, and said that the misunderstanding about the shares went only to quality, so that there was no total failure of consideration. It is easy to see how this could be interpreted as saying that a mistake as to substance will make the contract void for mistake, as it did in Roman law. At any rate, by the end of the century *Couturier v Hastie* was considered to have been decided on the ground that the contract was void, and this solution was adopted by the Sale of Goods Act 1893, now replaced by the following provision:

Sale of Goods Act 1979   **14.31 (EN)**

Section 6: Where there is a contract for the sale of specific goods, and the goods without the knowledge of the seller have perished at the time when the contract is made, the contract is void.

---

[207] See Simpson (1975) 91 LQR 247, 269; and C MacMillan, *Mistakes in Contract Law* (Oxford: Hart Publishing, 2010).
[208] (1856) 5 HL Cas 673 (HL).
[209] (1867) LR 2 QB 580, 587 (QB).
[210] See below, p 558.
[211] See further below, p 1052.

This seems to be very close to the French rule that a contract of sale cannot be valid without an object. However, English law does not have the requirement of *objet*, and generally the problem of a contract about a non-existent item seems to have been treated by English courts as a question of mistake—for example, *Galloway v Galloway*,[212] in which a separation agreement between parties who mistakenly thought themselves validly married was held to be void for common mistake.

In contrast, more recent codes do not treat a contract as automatically void because it is impossible, for example in Dutch law the debtor can set aside the contract under BW Articles 6:265 ff.[213] See also the Greek Code civil, Articles 362–364 and the PECL:

Principles of European Contract Law[214]   **14.32 (INT)**

Article 4:102: Initial Impossibility

A contract is not invalid merely because at the time it was concluded performance of the obligation assumed was impossible, or because a party was not entitled to dispose of the assets to which the contract relates.

Nor do the PECL adopt a principle of *cause*.

14.3.D.3 MISTAKE IN GENERAL (RESUMED)—ENGLISH LAW

While the case of the contract for something which did not exist is thus covered in English law, there remain two questions: (1) Does English law have a general doctrine of mistake or is it limited to cases of *res extincta*? (2) Is a contract for specific goods which do not exist always void? But first we should consider the basic authorities on mistake as to the substance in English law.

House of Lords   **14.33 (EN)**

Bell v Lever Bros[215]

A common mistake which makes the subject matter of a contract essentially different from what the parties supposed renders the contract void.

Facts: Two company directors, D'Arcy Cooper and Bell, agreed to leave their posts early in exchange for generous compensation which was paid to them by the company. The company later discovered that the directors had committed certain breaches of duty which (though the directors did not appreciate this) meant that they could have been dismissed without notice or compensation. The company sought to recover the money paid to the directors, claiming that the money should be repaid and damages for fraud.

Held: The jury found that the directors were not guilty of fraud. The court of first instance held that the compensation agreement was void for what it called mutual mistake, and the Court of Appeal agreed. The House

---

[212] (1914) 30 TLR 531.
[213] See Hartkamp and Tillema (n 203 above) para 93.
[214] cf DCFR Art II.-7:102.
[215] [1932] AC 161.

of Lords reversed this decision. (There was an issue whether the plaintiffs had pleaded 'mutual' (ie common) mistake, or only unilateral mistake, which would not be a sufficient ground (see above, pp 500, 525). Lord Atkin held that this point need not be decided as the claim on mutual mistake failed in any event.)

Judgment: LORD ATKIN: … In the view that I take of the whole case it becomes unnecessary to deal finally with the appellants' complaint that the points upon which the plaintiffs succeeded were not open to them. I content myself with saying that much may be said for that contention.

Two points present themselves for decision. Was the agreement of March 19, 1929, void by reason of a mutual mistake of Mr D'Arcy Cooper and Mr Bell? … The rules of law dealing with the effect of mistake in contract appear to be established with reasonable clearness. If mistake operates at all it operates so as to negative or in some cases to nullify consent. The parties may be mistaken in the identity of the contracting parties, or in the existence of the subject matter of the contract at the date of the contract, or in the quality of the subject matter of the contract. These mistakes may be by one party, or by both, and the legal effect may depend upon the class of mistake above mentioned. Thus a mistaken belief by A that he is contracting with B, whereas in fact he is contracting with C, will negative consent where it is clear that the intention of A was to contract only with B. So the agreement of A and B to purchase a specific article is void if in fact the article had perished before the date of sale. In this case, though the parties in fact were agreed about the subject matter, yet a consent to transfer or take delivery of something not existent is deemed useless, the consent is nullified. As codified in the Sale of Goods Act the contract is expressed to be void if the seller was in ignorance of the destruction of the specific chattel. I apprehend that if the seller with knowledge that a chattel was destroyed purported to sell it to a purchaser, the latter might sue for damages for non-delivery though the former could not sue for non-acceptance, but I know of no case where a seller has so committed himself. This is a case where mutual mistake certainly and unilateral mistake by the seller of goods will prevent a contract from arising. Corresponding to mistake as to the existence of the subject-matter is mistake as to title in cases where, unknown to the parties, the buyer is already the owner of that which the seller purports to sell to him. The parties intended to effectuate a transfer of ownership: such a transfer is impossible: the stipulation is naturali ratione inutilis. This is the case of *Cooper v Phibbs*, where A agreed to take a lease of a fishery from B, though contrary to the belief of both parties at the time A was tenant for life of the fishery and B appears to have had no title at all. To such a case Lord Westbury applied the principle that if parties contract under a mutual mistake and misapprehension as to their relative and respective rights the result is that the agreement is liable to be set aside as having proceeded upon a common mistake. Applied to the context the statement is only subject to the criticism that the agreement would appear to be void rather than voidable. Applied to mistake as to rights generally it would appear to be too wide. Even where the vendor has no title, though both parties think he has, the correct view would appear to be that there is a contract: but that the vendor has either committed a breach of a stipulation as to title, or is not able to perform his contract. The contract is unenforceable by him but is not void.

Mistake as to quality of the thing contracted for raises more difficult questions. In such a case a mistake will not affect assent unless it is the mistake of both parties, and is as to the existence of some quality which makes the thing without the quality essentially different from the thing as it was believed to be. Of course it may appear that the parties contracted that the article should possess the quality which one or other or both mistakenly believed it to possess. But in such a case there is a contract and the inquiry is a different one, being whether the contract as to quality amounts to a condition or a warranty, a different branch of the law. The principles to be applied are to be found in two cases which, as far as my knowledge goes, have always been treated as authoritative expositions of the law. The first is *Kennedy v Panama Royal Mail Co*.

In that case the plaintiff had applied for shares in the defendant company on the faith of a prospectus which stated falsely but innocently that the company had a binding contract with the Government of New Zealand for the carriage of mails. On discovering the true facts the plaintiff brought an action for the recovery of the sums he had paid on calls. The defendants brought a cross action for further calls.

... The Court came to the conclusion in that case that, though there was a misapprehension as to that which was a material part of the motive inducing the applicant to ask for the shares, it did not prevent the shares from being in substance those he applied for.

The next case is *Smith v Hughes*, the well known case as to new and old oats [see 14.41 (EN), below, p 567]. ...

The Court ordered a new trial. It is not quite clear whether they considered that if the defendant's contention was correct, the parties were not ad idem or there was a contractual condition that the oats sold were old oats. In either case the defendant would succeed in defeating the claim.

In these cases I am inclined to think that the true analysis is that there is a contract, but that the one party is not able to supply the very thing whether goods or services that the other party contracted to take; and therefore the contract is unenforceable by the one if executory, while if executed the other can recover back money paid on the ground of failure of the consideration.

We are now in a position to apply to the facts of this case the law as to mistake so far as it has been stated. It is essential on this part of the discussion to keep in mind the finding of the jury acquitting the defendants of fraudulent misrepresentation or concealment in procuring the agreements in question. Grave injustice may be done to the defendants and confusion introduced into the legal conclusion, unless it is quite clear that in considering mistake in this case no suggestion of fraud is admissible and cannot strictly be regarded by the judge who has to determine the legal issues raised. The agreement which is said to be void is the agreement contained in the letter of 19 March 1929, that Bell would retire from the Board of the Niger Company and its Subsidiaries, and that in consideration of his doing so Levers would pay him as compensation for the termination of his agreements and consequent loss of office the sum of £30,000 in full satisfaction and discharge of all claims and demands of any kind against Lever Brothers, the Niger Company or its subsidiaries. The agreement which, as part of the contract was terminated, had been broken so that it could be repudiated. Is an agreement to terminate a broken contract different in kind from an agreement to terminate an unbroken contract, assuming that the breach has given the one party the right to declare the contract at an end? I feel the weight of the plaintiffs' contention that a contract immediately determinable is a different thing from a contract for an unexpired term, and that the difference in kind can be illustrated by the immense price of release from the longer contract as compared with the shorter. And I agree that an agreement to take an assignment of a lease for five years is not the same thing as to take an assignment of a lease for three years, still less a term for a few months. But, on the whole, I have come to the conclusion that it would be wrong to decide that an agreement to terminate a definite specified contract is void if it turns out that the agreement had already been broken and could have been terminated otherwise. The contract released is the identical contract in both cases, and the party paying for release gets exactly what he bargains for. It seems immaterial that he could have got the same result in another way, or that if he had known the true facts he would not have entered into the bargain. A buys B's horse; he thinks the horse is sound and he pays the price of a sound horse; he would certainly not have bought the horse if he had known as the fact is that the horse is unsound. If B has made no representation as to soundness and has not contracted that the horse is sound, A is bound and cannot recover back the price. A buys a picture from B; both A and B believe it to be the work of an old master, and a high price is paid. It turns out to be a modern copy. A has no remedy in the absence of representation or warranty. A agrees to take on lease or to buy from B an unfurnished dwelling-house. The house is in fact uninhabitable. A would never have entered into the bargain if he had known the fact. A has no remedy, and the position is the same whether B knew the facts or not, so long as he made no representation or gave no warranty. A buys a roadside garage business from B abutting on a public thoroughfare: unknown to A, but known to B, it has already been decided to construct a bypass road which will divert substantially the whole of the traffic from passing A's garage. Again A has no remedy. All these cases involve hardship on A and benefit B, as most people would say, unjustly. They can be supported on the ground that it is of paramount importance that contracts should be observed, and that if parties honestly comply with the essentials of the formation of contracts—ie, agree in the same terms on the same subject-matter—they are bound, and must rely on the stipulations of the contract for protection from the effect of facts unknown to them.

This brings the discussion to the alternative mode of expressing the result of a mutual mistake. It is said that in such a case as the present there is to be implied a stipulation in the contract that a condition of its efficacy is that the facts should be as understood by both parties—namely, that the contract could not be terminated till the end of the current term. The question of the existence of conditions, express or implied, is obviously one that affects not the formation of contract, but the investigation of the terms of the contract when made. A condition derives its efficacy from the consent of the parties, express or implied. They have agreed, but on what terms. One term may be that unless the facts are or are not of a particular nature, or unless an event has or has not happened, the contract is not to take effect. With regard to future facts such a condition is obviously contractual. Till the event occurs the parties are bound. Thus the condition (the exact terms of which need not here be investigated) that is generally accepted as underlying the principle of the frustration cases is contractual, an implied condition. Sir John Simon formulated for the assistance of your Lordships a proposition which should be recorded: 'Whenever it is to be inferred from the terms of a contract or its surrounding circumstances that the consensus has been reached upon the basis of a particular contractual assumption, and that assumption is not true, the contract is avoided: ie, it is void ab initio if the assumption is of present fact and it ceases to bind if the assumption is of future fact'.

I think few would demur to this statement, but its value depends upon the meaning of 'a contractual assumption,' and also upon the true meaning to be attached to 'basis,' a metaphor which may mislead. When used expressly in contracts, for instance, in policies of insurance, which state that the truth of the statements in the proposal is to be the basis of the contract of insurance, the meaning is clear. The truth of the statements is made a condition of the contract, which failing, the contract is void unless the condition is waived. The proposition does not amount to more than this that, if the contract expressly or impliedly contains a term that a particular assumption is a condition of the contract, the contract is avoided if the assumption is not true. But we have not advanced far on the inquiry how to ascertain whether the contract does contain such a condition. Various words are to be found to define the state of things which make a condition. 'In the contemplation of both parties fundamental to the continued validity of the contract,' 'a foundation essential to its existence,' 'a fundamental reason for making it,' are phrases found in the important judgment of Scrutton LJ in the present case. The first two phrases appear to me to be unexceptionable. They cover the case of a contract to serve in a particular place, the existence of which is fundamental to the service, or to procure the services of a professional vocalist, whose continued health is essential to performance. But 'a fundamental reason for making a contract' may, with respect, be misleading. The reason of one party only is presumedly not intended, but in the cases I have suggested above, of the sale of a horse or of a picture, it might be said that the fundamental reason for making the contract was the belief of both parties that the horse was sound or the picture an old master, yet in neither case would the condition as I think exist. Nothing is more dangerous than to allow oneself liberty to construct for the parties contracts which they have not in terms made by importing implications which would appear to make the contract more businesslike or more just. The implications to be made are to be no more than are 'necessary' for giving business efficacy to the transaction, and it appears to me that, both as to existing facts and future facts, a condition would not be implied unless the new state of facts makes the contract something different in kind from the contract in the original state of facts. Thus, in *Krell v Henry* [see 28.11 (EN), below, p 1189], Vaughan Williams LJ finds that the subject of the contract was 'rooms to view the procession': the postponement, therefore, made the rooms not rooms to view the procession. This also is the test finally chosen by Lord Sumner in *Bank Line v Arthur Capel & Co*, agreeing with Lord Dunedin in *Metropolitan Water Board v Dick Kerr*, where, dealing with the criterion for determining the effect of interruption in 'frustrating' a contract, he says: 'An interruption may be so long as to destroy the identity of the work or service, when resumed, with the work or service when interrupted.'

We therefore get a common standard for mutual mistake and implied conditions whether as to existing or as to future facts. Does the state of new facts destroy the identity of the subject matter as it was in the original state of fact?

To apply the principle to the infinite combinations of facts that arise in actual experience will continue to be difficult, but if this case results in establishing order into what has been a somewhat confused and difficult branch of the law it will have served a useful purpose.

I have already stated my reasons for deciding that in the present case the identity of the subject-matter was not destroyed by the mutual mistake, if any, and need not repeat them …

Notes

(1) Because the mistake made in this case seems serious, yet relief was denied, some commentators argued that English law still does not go beyond giving relief in the cases of *res extincta* and *res sua*, and that it does not have a general doctrine of mistake as to substance. Subsequent judicial opinion rejected this: see the judgment of Steyn J in *Associated Japanese Bank (International) Ltd v Crédit du Nord SA*,[216] preferring Lord Atkin's broader formula. The most recent full examination of the doctrine

[216] [1989] 1 WLR 255 (QBD).

was by the Court of Appeal in *Great Peace Shipping Ltd v Tsavliris Salvage (International) Ltd (The Great Peace)*.[217] In this case the Court favoured a different approach to Lord Atkin's. It preferred to approach the question of common mistake as a parallel to the doctrine of frustration.[218] '[T]he implication of a term of the same nature as that which was applied under the doctrine of frustration, as it was then understood … was a more solid jurisprudential basis for the test of common mistake that Lord Atkin was proposing.'[219] A mistake, including one as to some quality of the subject matter, will render a contract void only if the nonexistence of the state of affairs assumed by the parties rendered the contract or the contractual adventure impossible.[220]

According to the Court of Appeal in *The Great Peace*:

> the following elements must be present if common mistake is to avoid a contract: (i) there must be a common assumption as to the existence of a state of affairs; (ii) there must be no warranty by either party that that state of affairs exists; (iii) the non-existence of the state of affairs must not be attributable to the fault of either party; (iv) the non-existence of the state of affairs must render contractual performance impossible; (v) the state of affairs may be the existence, or a vital attribute, of the consideration to be provided or circumstances which must subsist if performance of the contractual adventure is to be possible.[221]

(2) Lord Atkin says that the mistake must make the thing 'essentially different', and the examples he gives make it clear that even under his somewhat broader approach, this is interpreted strictly. Many of the cases in which he says there will be no operative mistake are ones in which the mistake would be sufficiently serious to ground relief in French or German law. The same must be true of the narrower test preferred in *The Great Peace*, whether the mistake makes the contract or the contractual adventure impossible. This strictness may be the counterpart of the relative generosity of English law in allowing rescission under the doctrine of misrepresentation.[222]

(3) It may be that Lord Atkin was too restrictive in some of his examples. Treitel argues persuasively that in Lord Atkin's example of the contract for the picture which the parties mistakenly thought to be by an Old Master, the contract might be void for mistake, as the thing bought and sold would be essentially different from what the parties believed they were buying and selling.[223] The parties would not say they had just bought and sold 'a picture of …' but 'a Rembrandt'. However, Treitel accepts the other examples.

(4) In the last two large paragraphs extracted above, Lord Atkin seems to admit that English courts can reach the same results as under the doctrine of mistake by using the doctrine of implied conditions. The Court of Appeal in *The Great Peace* favoured an approach analogous to that used in frustration cases, which also depend on whether the agreement, correctly construed, applies in the changed circumstances. This again

---

[217] [2002] EWCA Civ 1407, [2003] QB 679.
[218] See below, pp 1185 ff.
[219] [2002] EWCA Civ 1407 at [61].
[220] [2002] EWCA Civ 1407 at [76].
[221] ibid.
[222] See below, pp 558 ff.
[223] *Treitel* (n 93 above) para 8-020.

seems to suggest that similar results may be reached by way of construction of the contract. It will be seen later that the English courts will imply into a contract terms which they consider the parties must have intended. Some implied terms place an obligation on one party (for example *The Moorcock*[224]), but others may be conditions—ie a term[225] to the effect that, unless and until something occurs, a contractual obligation will not come into effect.[226] In this context the argument would be that the operation of the contract was conditional on the facts being as the parties believed them to be. On occasions the courts decide what look like mistake cases without ever mentioning mistake but instead relying on an implied condition: for example, *Financings Ltd v Stimpson*, in which the Court of Appeal held that the defendant's offer to buy a car was conditional on the car remaining in substantially the same condition as when he had inspected it. As it had been damaged since then, the plaintiff could not accept the offer.[227] This raises two questions. The first is whether English law really recognises a separate doctrine of common mistake. It has been argued that the 'implied condition' approach leaves no room for an independent doctrine of mistake.[228] The second is that the implied condition approach gives the court greater flexibility: for example, in *Financings* the contract was found to be void for failure of an implied condition precedent even though the 'mistake' seems not to have been sufficiently serious to give relief under the doctrine of common mistake, compare eg, the examples in the previous Note.

(5) Lord Atkin does not discuss the question of what will happen if one party was at fault, in the sense that he ought to have known the truth. This problem arose graphically in the Australian case of *McRae v Commonwealth Disposals Commission*.[229] The Disposals Commission purported to sell to a salvage contractor the wreck of an oil tanker lying on the Jourmand Reef, the position of which was stated; but when the contractor's salvage expedition arrived it could find no reef at such a location, let alone a wreck, and the contractor sued for non-delivery. The Disposals Commission argued that the contract was void for mistake but the High Court rejected the argument. *Couturier v Hastie*[230] had not decided that a contract for non-existent goods was necessarily void, merely that the buyer did not have to pay; moreover, the Australian equivalent of the Sale of Goods Act, section 6 did not apply since the goods had never existed.

---

[224] See 14.20 (EN), below, p 799.

[225] Note that in English law 'term' is used in a quite different sense from *termes* in French law. The English terms may include both obligations and conditions, whereas a French *terme* is something which is bound to occur, like the passage of time and therefore excludes conditions which are not bound to occur. See Nicholas (n 132 above) 158–59.

[226] This would be a condition 'precedent'. It is also possible that the occurrence of the event will bring a contractual obligation to an end, in which case the condition is said to be 'subsequent'.

[227] [1962] 1 WLR 1184 (CA); see also P Atiyah, *Essays on Contract* (Oxford: Clarendon Press, 1986) ch 9. It is true that the case involved the offer, rather than a contract, being conditional, but it is not clear what difference that makes.

[228] See JC Smith 'Contracts—Mistake, Frustration and Implied Term' (1994) 110 LQR 400 and *Chitty* (n 40 above) para 6-014.

[229] (1950) 84 CLR 377 (Australian High Court).

[230] See above, p 542.

The Commission had contracted that there was a tanker in the location specified and was liable for non-delivery. In the *Associated Japanese Bank* case Steyn J said:[231]

> [There] is a requirement which was not specifically discussed in *Bell v Lever BrosLtd*. What happens if the party who is seeking to rely on the mistake had no reasonable grounds for his belief? An extreme example is that of the man who makes a contract with minimal knowledge of the facts to which the mistake relates but is content that it is a good speculative risk. In my judgment a party cannot be allowed to rely on a common mistake where the mistake consists of a belief which is entertained by him without any reasonable grounds for such belief: *McRae v Commonwealth Disposals Commission*. That is not because principles such as estoppel or negligence require it, but simply because policy and good sense dictate that the positive rules regarding common mistake should be so qualified. Curiously enough this qualification is similar to the civilian concept where the doctrine of *error in substantia* is tempered by the principles of *culpa in contrahendo*.

The similarity to civilian concepts noted by the judge should not be taken too literally, however. Suppose the parties agree to the sale of a picture which both parties believed, in each case based on their own judgement, to be by an artist 'of the school of Constable' but not by Constable himself; but the seller should know from documents he (but not the buyer) has seen that the picture is almost certainly by Constable himself and so worth much more than the sale price. In English law the effect is to prevent the seller avoiding the contract. In contrast, in German law the seller may avoid the contract but will have to compensate the buyer under § 122 BGB.

(6) In English law the doctrine of mistake as to the subject matter or as to the circumstances is strictly limited to 'common mistake', ie cases where both parties make the same mistake. 'Unilateral' mistake is recognised only when it is a mistake as to the terms of the contract which prevents there being a proper agreement.[232] However, a large number of contracts are set aside for what looks like a kind of mistake under the doctrine of misrepresentation.[233]

(7) At one time the rather narrow and inflexible doctrine of common mistake set out in *Bell v Lever Bros* was supplemented by a separate rule that a contract might be set aside for common mistake in equity, even though it would be valid at common law. The leading case was *Solle v Butcher*.[234] In that case, the defendant was the landlord of a flat which was let to the tenant at a rent which was controlled. The landlord made various improvements which would have given him the right to increase the rent from £140 to approximately £250, as long as he served a special notice. He did not do this because the parties both considered that the work done meant that the old rent for the flat would no longer apply as it would constitute a new flat within the meaning of the rent-control legislation. Instead he simply let the flat to the tenant for seven years at £250 a year. After some months of paying the new rent the tenant claimed that the flat was still subject to the old rent figure and demanded repayment of the difference. It was by then too late for the landlord to serve a notice of increase. The Court of Appeal

---

[231] [1989] 1 WLR 255, 268, see above, n 216.
[232] See above, p 511.
[233] See below, p 558.
[234] [1950] 1 KB 671 (CA).

held that the old rent did still apply but the contract had been entered under a shared fundamental mistake and could be set aside. The tenant was given the choice of leaving or paying £250 a year.

The correctness of this case was much discussed, since (i) the existence of a separate equitable doctrine was not mentioned in *Bell v Lever Bros* and (ii) it was far from clear when a mistake would be sufficiently 'fundamental' to give rise to relief in equity yet not make the thing contracted for 'essentially different' so that the contract is void at common law.[235] The principal point decided in *The Great Peace*[236] was that *Solle v Butcher* and subsequent cases decided on equitable grounds should not be followed in future.

(8) This undoubtedly simplifies English law. However, it leaves it rather inflexible. Under the common law rule of *Bell v Lever Bros* and *The Great Peace*, the contract is either valid or wholly void: the court has no power to adapt it, nor to apportion any losses that may have been suffered in reliance on the supposed contract. You may compare this to the result in *Solle v Butcher*, where the Court allowed rescission only 'on terms' that the tenant be given the option of staying on at the increased rent—which is a form of adaptation of the contract.[237] Ironically, in the very case that overruled the equitable doctrine, the Court said 'there is scope for legislation to give greater flexibility to our law of mistake than the common law allows'.[238]

14.3.D.4 LIMITS ON THE MISTAKE DOCTRINE: MISTAKES AND OBLIGATIONS IMPOSED BY LAW

In all the systems there are cases in which one or both parties entered the contract under some misapprehension about the subject matter, and might therefore be able to invoke error, but where the law also provides that one party has a particular responsibility under the contract which has been breached as a result of the mistake. A typical example of the problem arises with sale of goods when the goods turn out to be defective. Usually neither the buyer nor the seller will have known this fact, and the parties will both therefore be mistaken as to the condition of the goods. However, the laws of the jurisdictions studied each impose certain obligations on the seller of goods in relation to their condition.

Under French law, the seller is subject to the *garantie des vices cachés*; in German law, subject to § 434 BGB; in Dutch law, subject to BW Articles 6:74ff and 7:21ff; and in English law, provided the seller was selling in the course of a business, subject to the Sale of Goods Act (SGA) 1979, section 14 or the Consumer Rights Act 2015, section 9. These regimes are discussed further below.[239] However, for present purposes,

---

[235] See J Cartwright '*Solle v Butcher* and the Doctrine of Mistake in Contract' (1987) 103 LQR 594.
[236] [2002] EWCA Civ 1407, [2003] QB 679; above, p 548.
[237] See further 14.5, below, p 584.
[238] *The Great Peace* [2002] EWCA Civ 1407 at [161].
[239] See below, pp 783 ff. It should be remembered that there are significant differences between the regimes. Of particular relevance here are (i) the range of application, in that the French *garantie* and §§ 437, 434 BGB apply to sales of property generally while in English law the seller's liability is confined to sales of goods made in the course of a business (in sales of land the doctrine of caveat emptor applies); and (ii) the remedies available.

the question is how the claims of both the buyer and the seller on grounds of mistake interrelate with the particular obligations and liabilities of the seller.

German law had a rule that mistake does not apply to cases within what was § 459 BGB (now §§ 437, 434 BGB). In BGH, 14 December 1960,[240] the defendant had bought some property which he then discovered to be in the path of a planned bypass; when sued for the price he sought to avoid the contract under § 119(2) BGB. The BGH said:

> The starting-point in that regard is the case law of the Reichsgericht, as confirmed by the Bundesgerichtshof and extensively approved in the works of academic legal authors, according to which the provisions of § 459 ff. BGB constitute special rules precluding the application of §119(2) BGB. … That view is substantiated by the fact that the object aimed at by the rules on avoidance, which finds expression, in particular, in the short limitation periods laid down by § 477 BGB—namely, in the interests of securing the certainty needed in the dealings between the parties, to enable sale transactions to proceed smoothly and within a relatively short period of time—would not be achieved if, by reason of some defect in the subject matter of the sale within the meaning of § 459 ff. BGB constituting at the same time an essential characteristic of the transaction within the meaning of § 119(2) BGB, avoidance were possible under the latter provision.

Under the former § 477 BGB the limitation period for actions to enforce obligations as to quality in the sale of goods were six months after delivery in the case of moveable property and one year after transfer in the case of real property.[241] As the BGH states, this limitation period would have been undermined if avoidance for mistake under § 119(2) BGB were permitted, since the latter type of claim expired only thirty years after the relevant declaration of intent (ex-§ 121(2) BGB[242]).

In French law the disappointed buyer was for a long time allowed to choose between remedies on the *garantie* (Articles 1641–1649 Cciv), or for non-performance, and seeking to avoid the contract for error. This might give the plaintiff extra time in which to seek a remedy: claims on the *garantie* had to be brought originally within *un bref délai* (Article 1648 Cciv). Because this period of time gave rise to much litigation and was uncertain, Article 1648 was amended to fix the period at two years from the discovery of the vice. However, the Cour de cassation held that if there is a *vice caché*, this precludes an action on the ground of mistake, though not an action on the ground of fraud.[243]

Dutch law also allows the buyer a choice, but the rules on limitation are the same: BW 7:23. The question of choice does not seem to arise in English law since there would be no advantage in the buyer seeking a remedy for mistake rather than one for breach of the implied terms under the SGA; however, alternative claims for breach and misrepresentation are common.

The other possibility is that the seller tries to avoid liability on the *garantie* or for breach by arguing mistake. In German law, where it is the seller rather than the

---

In French and German law the disappointed buyer may claim only return of the price or a reduction of price, unless the seller knew of the defect or warranted its absence; whereas in English law the seller is liable for damages in all cases where Sale of Goods Act 1979, s 14 applies.

[240] BGHZ 34, 32.

[241] The 2002 reform abolished the extremely short limitation period: § 438 BGB.

[242] The limitation period under § 121(2) BGB is now ten years.

[243] Cass civ (1) 14 May 1996, no. 94-13921, Bull civ I no. 213; and other cases cited in Terré et al (n 24 above) no. 255.

buyer who is seeking to rely on § 119(2) BGB, the relationship of § 119(2) BGB with §§ 433 ff BGB is somewhat different. The seller will not be allowed to escape his obligations under the law of sale by claiming that he was in error as to the presence of an essential attribute of the object of sale if that attribute is one which he is taken by law to have guaranteed to the buyer. The existence of these obligations depends upon the continued existence of the contract, so if the seller could avoid the contract for mistake he could evade his obligations under §§ 433 ff. Only where the buyer is not seeking to rely on §§ 433 ff BGB will the seller be allowed to invoke § 119(2) BGB.[244] In English law it is thought that the court would hold that the defect could not make the performance essentially different as the risk of a defect is placed by law on the seller.

There is also the possibility of overlap between error and a remedy against the seller for non-performance of some express undertaking he gave.[245]

14.3.D.5 APPLICATION OF MISTAKE: SHARED MISTAKE

Suppose both the parties have entered the contract on an incorrect assumption about the subject matter or the circumstances ('common' mistake); neither has been influenced by incorrect information given by the other (this situation is considered under 14.3.D.6[246]). For example:

(a) A wants to sell an area of waste land to B, who wishes to subdivide it for building a housing development. As neither of them knows how much land there is, and thus whether B can build enough houses to make it profitable at the price A is asking, they agree to employ a surveyor who tells them that 50 houses can be built. B agrees to buy the land for €1 million. In fact the area is only enough for 40 houses and B would not have paid more than €750,000 had he known this.

(b) C sells D a picture of Salisbury Cathedral; both of them assume (from the previous history of the painting, etc) that it is by the famous artist John Constable. In fact, many years ago there was a wrong attribution and the painting is by one of Constable's sons, a much less gifted artist whose paintings command only very modest prices.

(c) E goes to an auction of the contents of a country house owned by F's estate. The auction is very informal. E bids on a picture which pleases her eye and buys it for €500. She then discovers that it is a lost Caravaggio and worth €10 million.

Can B, D or the executors of F's estate obtain relief under any of the systems of law we have considered?

In French law, case (a) closely resembles the case of the *Villa Jacqueline*,[247] save that here both parties share in the mistake. This would not affect the outcome. Case (b) also seems to be an instance of error as to the substance and relief that would be given.

---

[244] BGH 8 June 1988, NJW 1988, 2597; Kötz (n 23 above) paras 305a, 306.
[245] eg the English case of *Dick Bentley Productions Ltd v Harold Smith (Motors) Ltd* [1965] 1 WLR 623 (CA) (undertaking as to condition of car sold); see below, p 564.
[246] See below, p 558.
[247] See 14.26 (FR), above, p 526.

Case (c) might be treated differently; the seller's failure to discover the provenance of the picture might be treated as inexcusable and relief be denied on that ground.

In English law, it is doubtful whether the doctrine of mistake would apply in any of the three cases. In case (a), the error does not seem to make the thing contracted for 'essentially different' within the strict test laid down in *Bell v Lever Bros*.[248] Alternatively, it might be possible for the buyer to persuade the court that the contract as a whole was conditional on the area of land being adequate for 50 houses (see *Financings Ltd v Stimpson*[249]). The contract in case (b) might be void at common law, but there are dicta in *Bell v Lever Bros*[250] to the contrary: see Note (3) after *Bell v Lever Bros*.[251] Relief would not be given on the ground of misrepresentation in either case (a) or case (b), as neither party seems to have relied on anything stated by the other party, but on what they were told by a third party. The rules on misrepresentation are covered in the next subsection. In case (c) it seems likely that the court would say that F's estate, by selling without getting an expert opinion, was taking the risk that the picture might be an Old Master and thus refuse relief: see Note (5).[252]

In Dutch law it seems that relief would be given in cases (a) and (b) under BW 6:228(1)(c). In case (c) it is possible that the seller would be denied relief under Article 6:228(2), because, according to the *communis opinio*, the risk of a mistake relating to the value of a thing sold should be borne by the seller.[253] But this view is now disputed by Dutch authors, especially if the buyer is a professional and the seller is not.

In German law, the solution to the three examples given earlier might be as follows. In cases (a) and (b), relief could be given on the ground of mistake. B could probably claim that his mistake as to the capacity of the land was an error concerning a fundamental attribute which formed the basis of the contract. D could make a similar claim as regards case (b). However, in both cases the right to avoid under § 119(2) BGB would be superseded by the claims available under §§ 434 ff BGB. By contrast it is hard to see how F's estate can even claim that it was in error as to anything apart from the value of the painting. As an unexceptional error of motive (ie one which had not been made the basis of, much less part of the contract) it could not justify avoidance. F's case seems as little likely to succeed as the seller in the '*Mozart notebooks*' case.[254]

In German law many cases of shared mistake are dealt with under the doctrine of *clausula rebus sic stantibus* instead of § 119(2) BGB. This more flexible doctrine is rooted in § 242 BGB and is now codified in § 313 BGB. It has been used by German courts to allow for revision of contracts in the light of supervening circumstances fundamentally different from those envisaged or assumed by the parties at the time of contracting.[255] Revision is similarly permissible where circumstances assumed to be present at the time of formation were in fact absent. The basis of the contract, which is said in such cases to

---

[248] See 14.33 (EN), above, p 543.
[249] See above, p 549.
[250] See above, p 543.
[251] See above, p 548.
[252] See above, p 549.
[253] HR 19 June 1959, NJ 1960, 59.
[254] 14.28 (DE), above, p 535.
[255] See ch 28, below, esp pp 1222 ff.

have 'collapsed' or be 'absent', may be objective—external to the contract itself, as in the period of drastic inflation in the 1920s—or subjective—where the parties were both in error as to a fundamental fact at the time of contracting. The following case, involving a shared error, is an example of the absence of the subjective basis of a contract.

BGH, 13 November 1975[256]   **14.34 (DE)**

Match-fixing

A contract formed under a shared misapprehension which goes to the basis of the contract can be adapted or set aside having regard to the requirements of good faith.

Facts: On 24 June 1971 the defendant, a football club in the Bundesliga (Federal League), reached agreement with the claimant, a club in the Regionalliga (third division league), regarding the transfer of W, a semi-professional player. Unknown to either party, W had accepted a bribe on the occasion of the defendant's Bundesliga match against Arminia Bielefeld on 29 May 1971. At the beginning of August 1971 W, who had in the meantime played in three games for the claimant, made a confession. He was dismissed by the claimant without notice. The Deutscher Fußballbund (DFB = German Football Association) imposed a ban on him. The claimant, which had purported to avoid the transfer agreement, claimed from the defendant reimbursement of the transfer fee paid by it.

Held: The lower courts allowed the claim. The defendant's appeal to the BGH on a point of law was dismissed.

Judgment:

II.2(b) ... [W]here two football clubs, such as the parties in the present case, agree to the payment of a transfer fee in order to fulfil one of the mandatory conditions laid down by the rules of the DFB, namely the requirement that a player must obtain a licence to play for the club acquiring him, they are to be deemed, upon any reasonable assessment of their reciprocal interests, to be attaching to their willingness to contract the fundamental precondition that the player must possess no personal qualities which render him, on an objective basis, unfit for the grant of a player's licence.

3. The court hearing the appeal on questions of fact and law bore in mind the fact that not every impairment of the basis of the transaction is necessarily significant in legal terms. In view of the overriding importance attaching, under the law of contract, to the principle of contractual good faith, a plea alleging a fundamental violation of the basis of the transaction will only exceptionally be admissible, where it appears unavoidable in order to avoid a result which would be intolerable, incompatible with the requirements of law and equity and thus incapable, according to the principle of good faith, of being ascribed to the party concerned. ... Where a football player accepts a bribe whereby he is to 'fix' the result of a game, he commits a serious breach of the recognised rules of the sport and of the principles of sportsmanship. As a general rule, he ceases to be eligible to receive the authorisation to play issued in respect of DFB clubs. From a legal standpoint, the payment of a transfer fee ceases to be of any relevance ... [A]n agreement relating to the payment of a transfer fee can only be meaningful if the player fulfils the personal criteria which such an agreement necessarily entails, namely the condition that he is eligible, under the rules of the DFB, for the grant to him of the requisite player's licence. That condition is not, in principle, fulfilled in the case of a player who, in return for the

---

[256] NJW 1976, 565.

payment of a sum of money, has been prepared to act deceitfully in order to influence the results of sporting competitions.

Thus there can be no inherent legal justification for any compensatory adjustment of the financial position as between the clubs which were parties to the transfer agreement. From an objective standpoint, the player personally charged with such a serious offence is no longer of any value to his former club, since the discovery of his lack of entitlement to play results, to all intents and purposes, in his being ineligible to play for any club. According to the principle of good faith, there appears to be no justification for an order requiring the transferor club to be compensated for a loss which it would have suffered even if the player had not moved to another club, and imposing on the transferee club the corresponding burden of paying such compensation despite the fact that, in the absence of the requisite player's licence, it can have no further use for the player, either in sporting or financial terms. In those factual circumstances, the basis of the transaction has been frustrated in such a way that the club liable to pay can no longer be deemed to be bound by the transfer agreement, which was concluded in ignorance of the bribery. Nor can there be any doubt that, if the factual position in the present case had been known, not only would the plaintiff have refrained from concluding an agreement but so too would any other club.

4. The court hearing the appeal on questions of fact and law also acted correctly, from a legal standpoint, in determining the extent of the risks confronting each of the parties. As regards the legal consequences of the absence or extinction of the basis of the transaction, particular significance attaches to the way in which the risk fell to be apportioned, as the appellant has correctly pointed out. It is acknowledged in the relevant case law that circumstances which manifestly fall, in accordance with the purpose of the contract, within the ambit of the risks faced by only one of the parties do not in principle entitle that party to plead that the basis of the transaction has been impaired. … However, that is not the position in the present case.

…

(b) The court hearing the appeal on questions of fact and law recognised that any transfer agreement concluded in the field of professional football necessarily entails a certain element of risk. It referred to the general risk, applying in every case, that a player who has been 'bought' by a club may not live up to the expectations which it is hoped that he will fulfil—in particular, that his performance as a player may not be what is expected of him. Such conceptions and expectations basically fall outside the ambit of the circumstances which are capable of influencing a transfer agreement reached in accordance with the principle of good faith. The risk that the full extent and significance of an injury suffered by a player before his move to another club may not become clear until after that move may possibly be regarded as typical of that type of contract. Nowadays, participation in competitive sports, including, in particular, professional football, invariably involves, as experience has shown, the risk of an injury which only manifests itself fully at some later date. The prejudice attributable to such an injury, or the cessation of the footballer's ability to play which necessarily results from it, has a direct effect only on the *actual* employment of the player with his new club. This involves a risk which must normally be borne by the (new) employer. The question whether, in such cases, it is solely the transferee club which has to bear the risk of the possibly fruitless expenditure of the transfer fee does not need to be decided in the present case, any more than does the example, also given by the court below, of a player who commits a criminal act outside the context of his sports activities which initially remains undiscovered but which results, following his transfer to another club, in the loss of its player's licence.

…

(d) In determining the apportionment of the risk, the court below placed decisive emphasis on the extent to which the alleged misconduct of the player affects the essence of his intrinsic relationship with the club employing him. It considered that the obligation owed by a semi-professional player to his club is, in essence, such as to require him to play for his club and not against it, and accordingly placed the risk of breach of that obligation on the club employing him, even in the event that the player subsequently moves to another club. Those considerations are unimpeachable in law. The court below correctly placed the risk at the door of the defendant, as the club which, in the circumstances of this particular case, was 'closer to the situation' than the claimant. The bribery of the player W in the context of the defendant's Bundesliga match in Bielefeld on 27 May 1971, which constitutes the cause of the impairment of the contractual basis of the transfer agreement, falls within the ambit of the risks to be borne by the defendant, and not only because of the point in time at which it occurred. On the contrary, the player's misconduct is directly connected with his sports activities as an employee of the defendant. In view of that circumstance, there can be no question, applying the principle of good faith, of that risk being transferred to the claimant.

5. The court below held that the legal consequence of the absence of the basis of the transaction was such as to entitle the claimant to rescind the contract; accordingly, it allowed a claim for repayment in full of the transfer sum paid. That decision is similarly unimpeachable in law.

(a) However, the absence or extinction of the basis of a transaction does not automatically result in the total elimination of the contractual relationship. On the contrary, there can only be any question of one or both of the contracting parties being released from their contractual obligations in so far as this is required by the application of the principle of good faith. It follows that the primary question to be asked is whether the contract can be adapted to fit the actual facts of the situation in a form which takes into account the legitimate interests of both parties. ... The court below bore those principles in mind. No objection can be raised on legal grounds to its finding that, having regard to the worthlessness, in practical terms, of the consideration furnished by the defendant, namely the premature release of the player W, there could be no question of any adaptation of the contract, and, in particular, that, in view of the unambiguousness of the way in which the risk fell to be apportioned, there could be no question of both parties being ordered to bear the pecuniary loss proportionately between them.

Note

In this case the Court recognised a right in the purchasing club to withdraw from the contract and seek recovery of the transfer fee (§§ 327, 346 [now only § 346] BGB). The more usual remedy will be the adaptation of the agreement in the light of the changed circumstances (§ 313(1) BGB).[257]

Normally a mistaken party will have to seek avoidance under § 119 BGB rather than under § 313 BGB. The latter, and in particular the doctrine of collapse of the basis of the contract (§ 313 BGB), however, allows an adjustment of the rights and liabilities of the parties more in consonance with objective fairness and the allocation of risk under

---

[257] Adaptation and other remedies are discussed more fully in 14.5, below, p 584.

the contract than the regime of unilateral avoidance and (possible) compensation established by §§ 119, 122 BGB.

14.3.D.6 APPLICATION OF MISTAKE: INDUCED MISTAKE

In the jurisdictions studied, this situation may be dealt with under a variety of doctrines. We consider the different approaches in turn.

(a) Avoidance for mistake

In practice, many cases which in civil law are dealt with under the doctrine of mistake are ones in which one party has stated what he thinks to be the facts and the other has believed him; that is why the other party has entered the contract under a misapprehension. An example is the case of the *Villa Jacqueline*.[258] Of course, if the party making the statement knew that what he was saying was untrue and intended to deceive the other, there is fraud; but if he did not know, relief can be given for mistake. In German law, an error caused by the other party but without fraud may amount to an error as to an attribute considered essential in business within § 119(2) BGB, allowing the first party to avoid the contract. In each system, even if the seller had not stated the area, if he knew that it was crucial to the buyer there might be liability here on the basis of fraud by silence; and even if the seller did not intend his silence to deceive the buyer, the seller might well be under a duty of disclosure. Both these possibilities are dealt with later.[259]

(b) Rescission for misrepresentation

In principle, in English law the contract might be void for mistake in this situation if the error was sufficiently fundamental; but in practice this will not be argued. This is because it is so difficult to show that a contract is void for mistake, whereas there is an easily available remedy for misrepresentation.[260]

Court of Appeal **14.35 (EN)**

Redgrave v Hurd[261]

A contract that has been induced by a misrepresentation of fact made by the other party may be avoided, even if the misrepresentation was made without fraud and the representee could have discovered the truth had he made further enquiries.

Facts: The plaintiff, an elderly solicitor, advertised for a younger partner who would not object to buying the plaintiff's house as well as to joining the plaintiff in practice. The plaintiff told the defendant that the practice brought in about £300 a year. The plaintiff showed the defendant summary accounts showing business of about £200 a year and said that the rest related to other business not summarised but which was referred to in a bundle of other papers. This he pointed out to the defendant but the defendant did not examine it. In fact,

---

[258] 14.26 (FR), above, p 526.
[259] See below, pp 570 and 574.
[260] See *Chitty* (n 40 above) para 6-013.
[261] (1881) 20 ChD 1.

examination of these other papers would have revealed that there was almost no other business. The defendant signed an agreement to purchase the house; this agreement made no reference to the agreement over the practice. When the defendant discovered the truth about the practice he refused to complete the purchase of the house. The plaintiff brought an action for specific performance and the defendant counter-claimed for rescission and damages.

Held: Fry J held that the defendant, having had the opportunity to check the truth of what he had been told but not having taken it, must be taken not to have relied on the representations, and granted specific performance. The Court of Appeal reversed this decision. Although the defendant's counter-claim for damages must fail because he had not pleaded that the plaintiff knew that the statements he was making were untrue, he was still entitled to rescind the agreement on the ground of innocent misrepresentation.

Judgment: JESSEL MR: As regards the rescission of a contract, there was no doubt a difference between the rules of Courts of Equity and the rules of Courts of Common Law— a difference which of course has now disappeared by the operation of the Judicature Act which makes the rules of equity prevail. According to the decisions of Courts of Equity it was not necessary, in order to set aside a contract obtained by material false representation, to prove that the party who obtained it knew at the time when the representation was made that it was false. It was put in two ways, either of which was sufficient. One way of putting the case was, 'A man is not to be allowed to get a benefit from a statement which he now admits to be false. He is not to be allowed to say, for the purpose of civil jurisdiction, that when he made it he did not know it to be false; he ought to have found that out before he made it.' The other way of putting it was this: 'Even assuming that moral fraud must be shown in order to set aside a contract, you have it where a man, having obtained a beneficial contract by a statement which he now knows to be false, insists upon keeping that contract. To do so is a moral delinquency: no man ought to seek to take advantage of his own false statements.' The rule in equity was settled, and it does not matter on which of the two grounds it was rested. As regards the rule of Common Law there is no doubt it was not quite so wide. There were, indeed, cases in which, even at Common Law, a contract could be rescinded for misrepresentation, although it could not be shewn that the person making it knew the representation to be false. They are variously stated, but I think, according to the later decisions, the statement must have been made recklessly and without care, whether it was true or false, and not with the belief that it was true …

There is another proposition of law of very great importance which I think it is necessary for me to state, because, with great deference to the very learned Judge from whom this appeal comes, I think it is not quite accurately stated in his judgment. If a man is induced to enter into a contract by a false representation it is not a sufficient answer to him to say, 'If you had used due diligence you would have found out that the statement was untrue. You had the means afforded you of discovering its falsity, and did not choose to avail yourself of them.' I take it to be a settled doctrine of equity, not only as regards specific performance but also as regards rescission, that this is not an answer unless there is such delay as constitutes a defence under the Statute of Limitations. That, of course, is quite a different thing. Under the statute delay deprives a man of his right to rescind on the ground of fraud, and the only question to be considered is from what time the delay is to be reckoned. It had been decided, and the rule was adopted by the statute, that the delay counts from the time when by due diligence the fraud might have been discovered. Nothing can be plainer, I take it, on the authorities in equity than that the effect of false representation is not got rid of on the ground that the person to whom it was made has been guilty of negligence. One of the most familiar instances in modern times is where men issue a prospectus in which they make false statements of the contracts made before the formation of a company, and then say that the contracts themselves may be inspected at the offices of the solicitor. It has always been held that those who accepted those false statements as true were not deprived of their remedy merely because they neglected to go and look at the contracts. Another instance with which we are familiar is where a vendor makes a false statement as to the contents of a lease, as, for instance, that it contains no covenant preventing the carrying on of the trade which the purchaser is known by the vendor to be desirous of carrying on upon the property. Although the lease itself might be produced at the sale, or might have been open to the inspection of the purchaser long previously to the sale, it has been repeatedly held that the vendor cannot be allowed to say, 'You were not entitled to give credit to my statement'. It is not sufficient, therefore, to say that the purchaser had the opportunity of investigating the real state of the case, but did not avail himself of that opportunity.

… [T]he learned Judge came to the conclusion either that the Defendant did not rely on the statement, or that if he did rely upon it he had shown such negligence as to deprive him of his title to relief from this court. As I have already said, the latter proposition is in my opinion not founded in law, and the former part is not founded in fact; I think also it is not founded in law, for when a person makes a material representation to another to induce him to enter into a contract, and the other enters into that contract, it is not sufficient to say that the party to whom the representation is made does not prove that he entered into the contract, relying upon the representation. If it is a material representation calculated to induce him to enter into the contract, it is an inference of law that he was induced by the representation to enter into it, and in order to take away his title to be relieved from the contract on the ground that the representation was untrue, it must be shown either that he had knowledge of the facts contrary to the representation, or that he stated in terms, or showed clearly by his conduct, that he did not rely on the representation.

Notes

(1) This case is a leading example of the difference in English law between the rules of common law and the rules of equity, the latter of which would provide additional remedies when the common law appeared to be deficient.[262] As we saw earlier,[263] the common law permitted rescission in cases of fraud; but, as Jessel MR remarks, in the nineteenth century the common law courts started to insist on a narrow definition of fraud involving dishonesty. This may have been justified by the fact that at common law, fraud would also give rise to liability in damages. The Courts of Equity could only grant rescission and perhaps for that reason would allow a remedy even in cases of 'innocent' (ie non-fraudulent) misrepresentation.

(2) In other respects, the requirements for misrepresentation were the same as for fraud: the plaintiff must have entered the contract in reliance on a false statement of a material fact by the other party to the contract. (As we noted earlier, in English law there is no remedy for fraud or misrepresentation if a party merely keeps silent about a pertinent fact.)

[262] See above, p 88.
[263] See above, p 489.

(3) This meant that rescission for misrepresentation was very readily available: the incorrect information did not have to relate to a substantial matter so long as the reasonable person would see it as having some relevance, and it did not have to be the only thing the plaintiff relied on in deciding to enter into the contract.[264] Although equitable remedies are frequently given only at the court's discretion, it seems that, if the requirements set out in the previous Note were met, rescission for misrepresentation would always be given. Thus the buyer of a house who had been told by the seller that the drains were in good order would be able to rescind the contract even if only one drain was not in good order. This rule was potentially inconvenient and unjust. It was tempered by a rule that, when land or houses were sold, the right to rescind was lost when the 'completion'—ie the transfer of ownership, which in English practice would take place sometime after contract—had taken place. This rule was equally unjust and in 1967 both rules were changed by statute. The fact that the contract has been performed is no longer a bar to rescission (Misrepresentation Act 1967, section 1); but in cases other than fraud the court is given power to refuse rescission and award damages instead:

Misrepresentation Act 1967   **14.36 (EN)**

Section 2(2): Where a person has entered a contract after a misrepresentation has been made to him otherwise than fraudulently, and he would be entitled, by reason of the misrepresentation, to rescind the contract, then, if it is claimed, in any proceedings arising out of the contract, that the contract has been or ought to be rescinded, the court or arbitrator may declare the contract subsisting and award damages in lieu of rescission, if of opinion that it would be equitable to do so, having regard to the nature of the misrepresentation and the loss that would be caused by it if the contract were upheld, as well as to the loss that rescission would cause to the other party.

In *William Sindall Ltd v Cambridgeshire CC*[265] a land developer claimed rescission on the ground of an alleged misrepresentation about a sewer crossing the site. The court held that on the facts there had not been any misrepresentation; but it went on to say that it would have refused rescission, because the main reason for the developer seeking to rescind appeared to be that the value of the site had fallen by millions of pounds through a general slump in property values. The measure of damages in such a case is the subject of debate.[266]

(4) The right to rescind is not only subject to the court's discretion; it may be lost in a number of ways, including affirmation or the lapse of quite a short time, even if the fact that there had been a misrepresentation was not discovered within that period: see *Leaf v International Galleries Ltd*.[267] The case of *Bernstein v Pamson Motors Ltd*[268] suggests that the time may be only a few weeks from the making of the contract.[269]

---

[264] See above, p 491.
[265] [1994] 1 WLR 1016 (CA).
[266] See *Chitty* (n 40 above) paras 7-109–7-110.
[267] [1950] 2 KB 86 (CA).
[268] [1987] 2 All ER 220 (QBD).
[269] See further below, p 1146.

(c) Liability in tort or delict for damages

Principles of European Contract Law[270]　　　　　**14.37 (INT)**

Article 4:106: Incorrect Information
A party which has concluded a contract relying on incorrect information given it by the other party may recover damages in accordance with Article 4:117(2) and (3) even if the information does not give rise to a fundamental mistake under Article 4:103, unless the party which gave the information had reason to believe that the information was correct.

Misrepresentation Act 1967　　　　　**14.38 (EN)**

Section 2(1): Where a person has entered into a contract after a misrepresentation has been made to him by another party thereto, and as a result thereof he has suffered loss, then, if the person making the misrepresentation would be liable to damages in respect thereof had the misrepresentation been made fraudulently, that person shall be so liable notwithstanding that the misrepresentation was not made fraudulently, unless he proves that he had reasonable grounds to believe, and did believe up to the time the contract was made that the facts represented were true.

Notes

(1) Where one party has given misleading information to the other, and the party who gave the information, though not fraudulent, was at fault, English law provides for damages. The law on this point has developed relatively recently. For many years rescission was the only remedy available for innocent—ie non-fraudulent—misrepresentation. After the case of *Hedley Byrne & Co Ltd v Heller & Partners Ltd*.[271] it became arguable that, if the misrepresentor was shown to be negligent, the misrepresentee could recover damages in tort, though this was not confirmed until the case of *Esso Petroleum Co Ltd v Mardon*.[272]

(2) Even before the decision in *Esso Petroleum Co Ltd v Mardon*, the 1967 Act created liability in damages when the misrepresentor, though honest and therefore not guilty of fraud, had no reasonable grounds for believing that what he said was true. The drafting of section 2(1), with its 'fiction of fraud', seems very curious: it was probably written in this way in order to avoid having to state all the basic requirements for liability in misrepresentation.[273] The 'fiction of fraud' has some interesting consequences. First, the measure of damages is the same as for fraud, ie loss of expectation is not included.[274] Secondly, the rule that any loss caused by the fraud may be recovered, even if it was not foreseeable, applies also to what is essentially liability for negligence

---

[270]　cf DCFR Art II.-7:204; CESL Art 28 (14.60 (EU), below, p 594).
[271]　[1964] AC 465 (HL), 6.10 (EN), above, p 137.
[272]　[1976] 1 QB 801 (CA).
[273]　See above, Note (2) on p 560.
[274]　See above, p 495.

under this section, see *Royscott Trust Ltd v Rogerson*.[275] This consequence of the fiction of fraud may not have been intended, and the drafting has been criticised.[276]

Although statutory, liability under section 2(1) is essentially tortious. Other systems also provide—in addition to the possibility of avoidance for mistake—non-contractual remedies when one party has misled the other. In French law the general rule for delictual liability applies:

Code civil   **14.39 (FR)**

Article 1240: Any human action whatsoever which causes harm to another creates an obligation in the person by whose fault it occurred to make reparation for it.

Similarly in Dutch law: the fact that one party has given the other incorrect information is one of the heads under which the contract may be avoided under Article 6:228, and if there was fault damages may be recovered from the party at fault under Article 6:162.[277]

We noted earlier[278] that in German law an error caused by the other party but without fraud may amount to an error as to an attribute considered essential in business within § 119(2) BGB, allowing the first party to avoid the contract. Should this be the case, the avoiding party will be freed from his obligation to pay reliance damages to the other party under § 122 BGB if the other party knew or should have known of the mistake. The express provisions of the BGB give no right to avoid where an error which does not come within § 119 BGB has been caused by the mere negligence or 'innocent' conduct of the other party. Since, by definition, the actions of the other party will not be intentional so as to come within § 826 BGB,[279] the Code itself gives no right to damages in such cases. Moreover, there is no relevant protective law, violation of which would under § 823(2) BGB ground an action in delict.

The alternative for the erring party is to make out a case of *culpa in contrahendo* and to seek restoration of the *status quo ante* as per §§ 249, 280(1), 311 BGB. Liability in *culpa in contrahendo*, which has already been discussed,[280] is imposed in cases of harm done in the bargaining process, whether intentionally or carelessly (§ 276 BGB). Negligently caused error leading to entry into the contract is a clear example of such harm.

This may not be adequate, however, where a contract has in fact been formed. As well as seeking reliance damages, the misled party may raise the fault of the other party as a defence to an action for enforcement of the contract. He can thereby be freed from his unfairly burdensome contractual obligations.[281] Where the buyer—or contractor in the case of a work contract—wishes to retain the other party's performance, the BGH has on occasion ordered a reduction in the price payable corresponding to the negative interest.[282]

---

[275] [1991] 2 QB 297 (CA).
[276] See *Chitty* (n 40 above) para 7-080.
[277] See above, p 542.
[278] See above, pp 535 ff.
[279] For § 826 BGB, see 14.7 (DE), above, p 493.
[280] See above, p 426.
[281] BGH 31 January 1962, NJW 1962, 1196.
[282] BGH 8 December 1988, JZ 1989, 592.

A line must be drawn between cases in which the claimant may rely on *culpa in contrahendo* and cases covered by §§ 433 ff BGB. Since *culpa in contrahendo* is a 'supplementary' doctrine, it is relevant only where the Code itself provides no appropriate remedies. Such a claim may thus, for example, be precluded by the availability of remedies in the law of sales (§§ 434 ff BGB). As will be seen in the next subsection, these cover defects in the thing itself, including the absence of qualities the seller explicitly promised. Carelessly given information about other facts is, by contrast, not covered. In such cases it will be open to the claimant to raise a claim in *culpa in contrahendo*. As we have already noted,[283] a claim for avoidance on the ground of fraud under § 123 BGB is not precluded by the availability of remedies in the law of sales arising out of the same set of facts. This is because, by contrast with § 119 BGB, the policy of the law as embodied in § 123 BGB is of greater importance than the preservation of §§ 433 ff BGB as *lex specialis*.

(d) Liability for breach of contract

There is another possibility to consider. If one party has made a statement to the other about the subject matter of the contract, he may become liable for breach of contract (non-performance) if what he says turns out to be incorrect. Suppose that the seller of goods indicates that a particular item corresponds to the buyer's description of what he wants, or the seller's own description of what it is he is seeking to sell. If the goods do not correspond to the description, the seller will in French law be guilty of *inexécution* of the contract and the buyer may seek *résolution*. In German law there may be remedies under §§ 434ff BGB and in English law under the Sale of Goods Act 1979, section 13 or the Consumer Rights Act 2015, section 11. The EC Directive on certain aspects of the sale of consumer goods and associated guarantees of 25 May 1999 is in rather similar terms.[284]

The case of sale of goods is considered in more detail later in the book,[285] but in principle, if a party to a contract of any type made a statement that described the subject matter of the contract and the other party entered the contract relying on the statement, the statement may be treated as a contractual promise—a term of the contract—so that if it turns out to be incorrect, the party who made it will be liable for non-performance. The circumstances in which a statement will be held to amount to a contractual promise are more clearly defined in some laws than others. In English law, for example, a statement will amount to a contractual promise if it was clearly of importance to the other party and it was reasonable to rely on it because the party who made it was in a better position to know whether it was correct. See for example *Oscar Chess Ltd v Williams*[286] and *Dick Bentley Productions Ltd v Harold Smith Motors Ltd*.[287]

---

[283] See above, p 494.
[284] See 19.11 (EU), below, p 784.
[285] See ch 19.
[286] [1957] 1 WLR 370 (CA).
[287] [1965] 1 WLR 623 (CA).

Article 6:101: Statements Giving Rise to Contractual Obligations

(1) A statement made by one party before or when the contract is concluded is to be treated as giving rise to a contractual obligation if that is how the other party reasonably understood it in the circumstances, taking into account:

(a) the apparent importance of the statement to the other party;

(b) whether the party was making the statement in the course of business; and

(c) the relative expertise of the parties.

(2) If one of the parties is a professional supplier which gives information about the quality or use of services or goods or other property when marketing or advertising them or otherwise before the contract for them is concluded, the statement is to be treated as giving rise to a contractual obligation unless it is shown that the other party knew or could not have been unaware that the statement was incorrect.

(3) Such information and other undertakings given by a person advertising or marketing services, goods or other property for the professional supplier, or by a person in earlier links of the business chain, are to be treated as giving rise to a contractual obligation on the part of the professional supplier unless it did not know and had no reason to know of the information or undertaking.

(e) Comparison of the different remedies for mistake induced by the other party

What practical difference will it make whether the claimant seeks remedies on the basis of mistake, misrepresentation or non-performance? For example, a private motorist sells a car which is five years old but which he has owned for only two years. During the negotiations he tells the buyer that the car has travelled 50,000 miles. He believes this to be true; when he bought it, it had 20,000 miles on the odometer and he has done 30,000 more. The buyer pays £5,000 for the car. The car's engine is severely damaged when the timing chain breaks; the chain should have been changed after 60,000 miles. The buyer discovers that the car has done more like 130,000 miles but the first owner had turned the odometer back. A car of the relevant age which had done only 50,000 miles would have been worth £6,000; the actual car was worth only £2,000 when it was delivered and the engine will cost £1,500 to repair.

Remedies based on non-performance (which will include liability under §§ 434 ff BGB and the English Sale of Goods Act 1979, sections 13–15) would entitle the buyer to a car of the same make and age, but which had done only 50,000 miles, at the seller's expense—or at least to claim damages representing the extra cost of buying such a car. The precise remedies will be explained in Chapter 22; they vary from system to system, and in some systems depend on whether or not the buyer is a consumer.

Remedies based on mistake (in French law, or German law if the risk of destruction of the goods had not passed) or on misrepresentation (in English law) would probably allow the buyer to avoid the contract, but he would not recover the additional cost of buying a car which had done only 50,000 miles. Under German law the buyer in our

---

[288] cf DCFR II.-9:102; CESL Art 69.

example would have to pay the seller damages (§ 122 BGB) as the seller did not know of the mistake.

If the buyer were to keep the car—or if it was held that he had lost the right to avoid the contract, for example through the lapse of time—the question of his entitlement to damages for the cost of repairs to the engine would arise. If the buyer claims on the basis of mistake, *culpa in contrahendo* or misrepresentation, the outcome would normally depend on whether the seller was at fault. Arguably he was not at fault on the facts given.

Remedies under the special regimes applying to defects in goods sold in French law would lead to much the same results as remedies based on mistake or misrepresentation. In French law the buyer could recover the price. However, if the seller were not a private person but a professional, he would be presumed to know of the defect and therefore would be liable in damages.[289] The measure of damages is not established.

14.4 NON-DISCLOSURE

Suppose a party enters the contract on an assumption about the substance of the contract, or the circumstances, which is incorrect. This is not because he is relying on information given by the other party; his misapprehension is 'self-induced'. We have seen that in the civil law jurisdictions, the mistaken party may be able to avoid the contract on the basis of mistake, albeit that he or she may come under a duty to compensate the other party for losses resulting from his or her mistake—under, for example, Article 1240 of the Code civil or § 122 BGB. However, in this section we consider whether the result is any different where the other party either knows of the misapprehension but does not point it out or does not know that the first party is mistaken but should have known. We also consider the position under English law, where on the facts given there will be no remedy for mistake[290] or misrepresentation.

To some extent, all the systems indirectly place at least professional sellers under an obligation to disclose any defect in the goods of which they are aware—or be liable for it. Thus, in English law, a seller who is selling in the course of a business is liable under the Sale of Goods Act 1979, section 14(2)[291] if the goods are not of satisfactory quality—except as regards any defect which was drawn to the buyer's attention. In French law the *garantie* applies only to *vices cachés*, not to ones which were pointed out by the seller. Under § 442(1) no. 1 BGB a seller is not responsible for a defect in the thing sold if the purchaser knew of the defect at the time of entering the contract. Thus if the seller knows of a defect, he must point it out or be liable. Furthermore a seller will be liable to pay damages for a defect that the buyer should have known about where the seller fraudulently concealed the defect from the buyer (§ 442(1)(2) BGB).

---

[289] See below, p 1155.

[290] Unless both parties made the same mistake and it rendered the contract or the contractual venture impossible: see above, p 548.

[291] Or for sales by a trader to a consumer, Consumer Rights Act 2015, s 9.

These 'indirect' obligations of disclosure are fairly limited, in that they relate only to sale of property—in English law only to the sale of goods—and only to certain characteristics of the items sold. There may be many other facts which are crucial to a party's decision whether to enter into a contract for the purchase of goods, let alone other types of contract where there may not be similar obligations.

It is in relation to more general duties of disclosure that the various systems produce radically different solutions. We will see later that in French and German law various doctrines (and now a provision of the Code civil) supplement the doctrine of mistake to produce wide-ranging duties of disclosure. Thus in French law the claimant may be able to base a claim on *dol par réticence*, and it is argued that there is a general duty of disclosure. In German law, fraud and *culpa in contrahendo* are both possible bases of relief.

In contrast, under the common law, with its objective approach and its reluctance to impose duties to act on parties, there may be no remedy at all. We have seen that the common law does not recognise fraud by silence, and that mistake will not apply unless either (1) the mistake was about the terms of the contract, so that there was no agreement, or (2) it was shared. The following case shows that, under the objective approach of the common law, the seller is under no obligation to bring to the buyer's attention the fact that he has made a mistaken assumption as to the subject matter of the contract.

14.4.A COMMON LAW

Queen's Bench	**14.41 (EN)**

Smith v Hughes[292]

A seller of goods is under no duty to point out to the buyer that the latter is mistaken as to a characteristic of the goods sold (assuming that the goods are of satisfactory quality within what is now section 14 of the Sale of Goods Act 1979).

Facts: The plaintiff, a farmer, offered the defendant, a race horse trainer, a quantity of oats. The defendant's manager looked at a sample of the oats and agreed to buy them, but when the oats were delivered he refused to pay for them on the ground that he had been under the impression that the oats were 'old', ie last season's oats, whereas the oats delivered were 'green', ie this season's oats. The defendant had no use for green oats. There was a conflict of evidence on whether the word 'old' had been used in the negotiations.

Held: The trial judge directed the jury that if the word 'old' had been used they should find for the defendant; and also they should find for the defendant if nothing was said about the oats being old but if the plaintiff believed that the defendant believed that he was contracting for old oats. The jury found for the defendant and the plaintiff appealed. The Court of Appeal held that the first part of the judge's direction was correct (there would have been a contractual promise, or at least a representation, that the oats were old), but that the second part was incorrect. As it was not possible to tell on which ground the jury had found for the defendant, there must be a new trial.

---

[292] (1871) LR 6 QB 596.

Judgment: Cockburn CJ: ... [We] must assume that nothing was said on the subject of the defendant's manager desiring to buy old oats, nor of the oats having been said to be old; while, on the other hand, we must assume that the defendant's manager believed the oats to be old oats, and that the plaintiff was conscious of the existence of such belief, but did nothing, directly or indirectly, to bring it about, simply offering his oats and exhibiting his sample, remaining perfectly passive as to what was passing in the mind of the other party. The question is whether, under such circumstances, the passive acquiescence of the seller in the self-deception of the buyer will entitle the latter to avoid the contract. I am of opinion that it will not.

I take the true rule to be, that where a specific article is offered for sale, without express warranty, or without circumstances from which the law will imply a warranty—as where, for instance, an article is ordered for a specific purpose—and the buyer has full opportunity of inspecting and forming his own judgment, if he chooses to act on his own judgment, the rule caveat emptor applies. If he gets the article he contracted to buy, and that article corresponds with what it was sold as, he gets all he is entitled to, and is bound by the contract. Here the defendant agreed to buy a specific parcel of oats. The oats were what they were sold as, namely, good oats according to the sample. The buyer persuaded himself they were old oats, when they were not so; but the seller neither said nor did anything to contribute to his deception. He has himself to blame. The question is not what a man of scrupulous morality or nice honour would do under such circumstances. The case put of the purchase of an estate, in which there is a mine under the surface, but the fact is unknown to the seller, is one in which a man of tender conscience or high honour would be unwilling to take advantage of the ignorance of the seller; but there can be no doubt that the contract for the sale of the estate would be binding ...

Now, in this case, there was plainly no legal obligation on the plaintiff in the first instance to state whether the oats were new or old. He offered them for sale according to the sample, as he had a perfect right to do, and gave the buyer the fullest opportunity of inspecting the sample, which practically, was equivalent to an inspection of the oats themselves. What, then, was there to create any trust or confidence between the parties, so as to make it incumbent on the plaintiff to communicate the fact that the oats were not, as the defendant assumed them to be, old oats? If, indeed, the buyer, instead of acting on his own opinion, had asked the question whether the oats were old or new, or had said anything which intimated his understanding that the seller was selling the oats as old oats, the case would have been wholly different; or even if he had said anything which shewed that he was not acting on his own inspection and judgment, but assumed as the foundation of the contract that the oats were old, the silence of the seller, as a means of misleading him, might have amounted to a fraudulent concealment, such as would have entitled the buyer to avoid the contract. Here, however, nothing of the sort occurs. The buyer in no way refers to the seller, but acts entirely on his own judgment.

[The remainder of the judgment is concerned with the possibility that the seller intended to sell the oats as they were but knew that the buyer thought he was buying them with a warranty that they were old. In this case there would be a misunderstanding as to the terms of the contract and no contract might result.[293] This should have been explained to the jury (in the nineteenth century, it was still common for contract cases to be tried by jury) in clearer terms, and a new trial on this point was ordered.]

---

[293] See above, p 504.

Notes

(1) This case confirms the general principle that in English law a party who knows that the other party is entering the contract under some mistake, whether it be as to the nature of the subject matter or as to other circumstances, need not point out the mistake even though he also knows that the mistaken party would not enter the contract if he knew the true position. We saw a modern application of the principle in *Smith v Hughes* in *Statoil ASA v Louis Dreyfus Energy Services LP (The Harriette N)*.[294] The principle is now qualified when the law imposes responsibility on one party: for example, a person who sells goods in the course of a business is responsible for the goods being of satisfactory quality, except so far as he informs the buyer of any defect before the sale.[295]

(2) There are many situations in which the law does not impose responsibility on even a seller. Thus in sales of land the English rule is still *caveat emptor*—let the buyer beware!—and the seller need not reveal defects in the property. In practice, there are standard precontract enquiry forms for real property transactions.[296] If the seller gives wrong or misleadingly incomplete information, the buyer will have remedies for misrepresentation. There will also be a misrepresentation if the seller answers that it doesn't have information about something—say whether the property is affected by a dispute with neighbours—when the seller knows full well that it is.[297] For sales of residential property, things have gone even further. The National Conveyancing Protocols[298] aim at speeding up the process.[299] Standard enquiry forms provided by the buyer's solicitor have been replaced by lists of information about the property which the seller's solicitor should prepare as soon as he or she is instructed—and they should try to get instructions as soon as the seller puts the property on the market, so that unnecessary delays in exchanging contracts can be avoided. But there are gaps in the system, particularly for things no one thinks to ask about—'unknown unknowns'. In *Sykes v Taylor-Rose*[300] a couple who had bought a house discovered that it had been the site of a horrific murder—and that parts of the victim's body had never been recovered and might still be secreted about the property. The sellers were fully aware of this. On the facts, no blame could be attached to them; they had known nothing about the murder when they bought the house and, when they did find out, they were advised by their solicitor that neither the person who had sold it to them nor they themselves had any duty to disclose—as indeed the trial judge and the Court of Appeal held. Perhaps not surprisingly, the property information form does not ask the seller to declare that no gruesome crime has been committed on the premises!

(3) Cockburn CJ refers to the question of whether there was any relationship of trust between the parties. English law does recognise a duty to disclose when there

---

[294] [2008] EWHC 2257 (Comm), [2008] 2 Lloyd's Rep 685; above, pp 519–20.
[295] Sale of Goods Act 1979, s 14; see 19.12 (EN), below, p 785.
[296] eg LexisNexis, Encyclopedia of Forms and Precedents, Sale of Land, vol 36, B 'Preliminary questions to be asked of seller' no. 11, Preliminary enquiries: long form (freehold and leasehold).
[297] *Walker v Boyle* [1982] 1 WLR 495 (ChD).
[298] See Law Society Conveyancing Protocol (January 2011).
[299] See K Gray and S Gray, *Elements of Land Law* (5th edn, Oxford University Press, 2009) paras 8.1.11–8.1.13.
[300] [2004] EWCA Civ 299, [2004] 2 P & CR 30.

is a 'relationship of confidence' between the parties, for example where one party is the other's solicitor.[301] There are a limited number of other cases in which even according to the common law a party does have a duty to disclose in English law. The most obvious example was the exceptional case of the contract of insurance. This was described as a contract 'of the utmost good faith'; the insured had to disclose any fact which is material in the sense that it might influence the reasonable insurer in deciding whether or not to accept the risk or on what terms (the duty of disclosure has now been abolished in consumer insurance,[302] and in other types of insurance it has been replaced by a duty to make a fair presentation of the risk[303]). Similarly, there is a duty of disclosure in some family arrangements such as agreements over the division of a deceased family member's property; and sureties must be told of unusual risks related to the loan they are guaranteeing.[304] There are numerous examples of duties to disclose imposed by statute in particular situations, for example under the Consumer Credit Act 1974 and the Financial Services and Markets Act 2000.

In civil law systems the position is very different. There may be relief simply on the basis of the doctrine of mistake, in accordance with the rules set out above—see, for example, the *Poussin* case.[305] However, we have seen that even under the subjective approach of the civil law jurisdictions the doctrine of mistake operates within significant limits. It is therefore notable that relief may be available on two alternative bases. First, in contrast to the common law, it has been recognised that a failure to point out the mistake may amount to fraud if it is dishonest. Secondly, there is some recognition of a duty to disclose which may give rise to liability in damages even though there was no fraud.

14.4.B FRANCE

14.4.B.1 NON-DISCLOSURE AS FRAUD

At one time the French courts appeared to deny that a mere failure to disclose a pertinent fact to the other party could amount to fraud: for example, Cass civ, 30 May 1927.[306] But legal scholars were critical of this approach. As Breton argued in his note to that case, mere silence is capable of provoking an error; the fact that it is an 'absence of action' does not deprive it of causal effect, as in the context things would have been different if the party accused of fraud had spoken out. The word '*manoeuvre*' is capable of covering reticence and while an abstention, keeping silent, is often morally indifferent, it is not always so. He quotes Ripert:

> What is true is that in the majority of contracts there is a conflict of interests between the parties. Each has to look after his own interests and should therefore make himself informed.

---

[301] See below, pp 645 ff.
[302] Consumer Insurance (Disclosure and Representations) Act 2012.
[303] Insurance Act 2015, s 3(1).
[304] See *Chitty* (n 40 above) para 45-036.
[305] See 14.27 (FR), above, p 531.
[306] Gaz Pal 1927.2.338, S 1928.1.105, annotated by A Breton.

There is then nothing wrong with not giving the other party information he could have found for himself. But the situation changes and silence becomes culpable if one of the parties has an obligation in conscience to speak out rather than take advantage of the other's ignorance.

Cass civ (3), 2 October 1974[307]   **14.42 (FR)**

The pig farm

Deceit may take the form of silence on the part of a contracting party who conceals from the other party a fact which, had it been known by the latter party, would have caused him not to enter into the contract. Since the consent of the innocent party was induced by the error brought about by the deceit, that error can be taken into consideration, even if it does not go to the substance of the thing forming the subject matter of the contract.

Facts: By a simple contract of 6 October 1970, Marcel Jacob, acting as agent for Mr and Mrs Paul Jacob, purchased from Mr and Mrs Goutailler a dwelling-house and some land for the sum of 95,000 FF, of which he paid on account the sum of 10,000 FF. That agreement, which was subject, in particular, to the condition precedent of the grant to Mr and Mrs Jacob by a financial organisation of a loan of 60,000 FF, was to be drawn up in the form of a notarial deed by no later than 1 December 1970. It was stipulated that Mr and Mrs Jacob were to take the property subject to all servient easements of whatever kind which might encumber the land sold and that, in the event of default on the part of the purchasers, the vendors would be entitled to require completion of the sale or to retain the sum paid on account by way of penalty. On 22 April 1971 Marcel Jacob informed the notary that it had not been possible to obtain the loan envisaged and that, having just learned of the imminent establishment of a piggery containing 400 pigs within a distance of 100 metres from the house, he was withdrawing from the sale; he stated that, had he been informed of this, his son Paul would never have agreed to purchase such a country house, given the drawbacks and the unpleasant smells involved, especially during the holiday period at the height of the summer. That disagreement between the purchasers and the vendors remained unresolved, and the latter consequently sold the house and land to a third party for the sum of 80,000 FF.

Held: Mr and Mrs Goutailler were ordered to repay to Mr and Mrs Paul Jacob the sum of 10,000 FF paid on account. The Goutaillers' appeal was rejected.

Judgment: On the two appeal grounds taken together: [the Court stated the facts as above, and continued:]
— Whereas the contested judgment is challenged on the basis of an appeal ground that it renders inapplicable, on the ground of fraudulent non-disclosure on the part of the vendors, the clause in the contract excluding any guarantees in respect of the servient easements; as according to the appellants, no evidence was adduced establishing any wrongful intention on the part of the vendors;
— Whereas the appellants contend, moreover, that the non-disclosure, which was not accompanied by any stratagems designed to mislead the other party to the contract, does not constitute deceit within the meaning of [former] Article 1116 of the Civil Code, because the vendor's knowledge of the perfectly proper establishment of the piggery did not involve or signify the adoption of any such stratagems or any ignorance on the part of the purchaser, *a fortiori* since that piggery, which is located on neighbouring

---

[307] No. 73-11901, Bull civ III no. 330, D 1974, IR.252, RGLJ 1975, 569, annotated by Blanc.

571

land, does not constitute an easement and does not affect any substantial feature of the property sold;

— Whereas it is further argued that, by failing to rule on the question whether Mr and Mrs Jacob would have proceeded with the purchase if they had been aware of the situation, the court below did not examine whether the conduct imputed to the vendor had been the determining factor which caused them to sign the agreement, and did not establish any causal connection between the alleged fraudulent non-disclosure on the part of the vendor and the consent given by the purchasers.

— Whereas the contested judgment is further criticized on the ground that it refused to apply the clause in the contract whereby, in the event of default by the purchasers, the vendors were to be entitled to retain the sum paid on account by way of penalty; according to the appellants, the terms of the synallagmatic promise to sell the property … expressly provided that the purchasers were to take the property sold in its existing condition and subject to all servient easements of whatever kind which might encumber the property in question, and further that, in the event of default on the part of the purchasers, the vendors were to be entitled either to demand completion of the sale or to retain the sum paid on account by way of penalty.

— Whereas however, deceit may consist and take the form of silence on the part of a contracting party who conceals from the other party a fact which, had it been known by the latter party, would have caused him not to enter into the contract.

— Whereas the consent of the innocent party was induced by the error brought about by the deceit, that error can be taken into consideration, even if it does not go to the substance of the thing forming the subject matter of the contract.

— Whereas the cour d'appel observes that, upon being informed of the purchasers' objection regarding the establishment of the piggery, Mr Goutailler, far from protesting his own ignorance of it, pointed out the date of the prefectorial order authorizing its establishment and simply claimed that Mr Jacob 'was deemed to have been aware of it' and that the latter had agreed to buy subject to all servient easements encumbering the property sold; as the court below also found that Mr Goutailler, knowing of the proposed establishment of that noxious and insanitary undertaking, which was bound to have a seriously adverse effect on the enjoyment of a country house situated in the immediate vicinity, not only mentioned nothing about it to his purchaser but also took care to ensure, upon the conclusion of the contract of 6 October 1970, that it contained a clause excluding guarantees, the entire value of which lay 'in the fact that he was the only person aware of the situation'.

— Whereas on the basis of those findings, it was open to the cour d'appel, without falling foul of the criticisms raised by the appellants, to infer that the vendor's non-disclosure was fraudulent in nature and that it had induced the purchasers, who were city-dwellers seeking a house in the country, to make an error in relation to an element which determined the giving of their consent.

— Whereas that defective consent affected the validity of the contract, the court below was right to refuse to allow the vendors to profit from the terms of that contract, which they persisted in trying to apply to their advantage, with a view to attempting to secure for themselves the benefit of their own non-disclosure and to retain the payment on account made by the victims of their fraudulent conduct.

— Whereas it follows that, on the aforementioned grounds alone, the cour d'appel has justified its decision in law and that the appellant's grounds are unfounded.

On those grounds, this Court dismisses the appeal.

Notes

(1) The development of the notion of *dol par réticence* is described by Legrand[308] and Ghestin.[309]

(2) Fraud by silence is now incorporated into the Code civil. Article 1137(2) provides:

> The intentional concealment by one party of information, where he knows its decisive character for the other party, is also fraud.

(3) The essence of *dol* is an error, either created by the defendant or of which he takes deliberate advantage. Seeking a remedy for fraud rather than for mistake may be advantageous, however, for the reasons suggested earlier;[310] in particular, if the defendant was fraudulent the claimant will not have to show that the error went to the substance of the thing contracted for.

(4) In French law, fraudulent non-disclosure always makes the mistake that it has caused an 'excusable' mistake: Article 1139.[311]

(5) We saw earlier that a mistake merely as to the value of property being bought or sold is not sufficient; it is not a mistake as to the substantial qualities of the thing sold.[312] We also noted that this rule has traditionally not been applied where the mistake was brought about by fraud.[313] Therefore some courts took the line that deliberately not telling the seller that the property was worth much more than she was asking for it amounted to *dol par réticence*. However, legal scholars and the courts frequently link fraud by non-disclosure to a duty to disclose.[314]

(6) In the *affaire Baldus*[315] the Cour de cassation rejected the idea that not telling the seller the value of the property could amount to fraud. In that case, a non-professional sold photographs by the famous photographer Baldus to a buyer who knew them to be worth many times the price the seller was asking. The Court held that there is no *dol par réticence* unless the buyer has an obligation of information, and there is no such obligation in relation to mere value. This approach was followed by a second case in 2007.[316]

Article 1137(2) of the Code civil as it resulted from the 2016 Ordonnance generated a vivid debate within the French literature. Reading the provision along with Article 1139 of the same Code could result in the abandonment of the *Baldus* solution, ie non-disclosure of the value of the other party's performance might amount to fraud

---

[308] P Legrand 'Pre-Contractual Disclosure and Information: English and French Law Compared' (1986) 6 OJLS 322.

[309] J Ghestin, 'The pre-contractual obligation to disclose information, 1: French report' in D Harris and D Tallon (eds), *Contract Law Today: Anglo-French Comparisons* (Oxford: Clarendon Press, 1993) 151 ff. See also Terré et al (n 24 above) no. 233.

[310] See above, p 490.

[311] 14.3 (FR), above, p 488, adopting the position of Cass civ (3) 21 February 2001, no. 98-20817, Bull civ III no. 20, RTD civ 2001, 353, annotated by J Mestre and B Fages.

[312] Above, p 528.

[313] Above, p 490.

[314] On which see below, pp 574 ff.

[315] Cass civ (1) 3 May 2000, no. 98-1138, Bull civ I no. 131, RTD civ 2000, 566, annotated by J Mestre.

[316] Cass civ (3) 17 January 2007, no. 06-10442, Bull civ III no. 5, D 2007, 1051, annotated by D Mazeaud.

and lead to the annulment of the contract.[317] Technically, this would have meant that there might be fraudulent non-disclosure even where there is no pre-existing information duty pursuant to Article 1112-1 of the Code civil. While some authors argued that the courts were likely to follow the *Baldus* solution, others opted for the contrary solution, as it would be more in accordance with some sort of 'contractual justice'. Fortunately the 2018 ratification made clear that *Baldus* was still good law by adding to Article 1137 a third paragraph, according to which 'it is not fraud for a party not to reveal to the other contracting party his assessment of the value of the act of performance'. This way, *dol par réticence*, just like the pre-existing information duty (see Article 1112-1) does not include the matter of value, and the apparent paradox between the two notions is explicitly overcome.

Code civil **14.43 (FR)**

Article 1139: A mistake induced by fraud is always excusable. It is a ground of nullity even if it bears on the value of the act of performance or on a party's mere motive.

It seems that in the new Code, the notion of fraud by silence is generally de-coupled from the duty to disclose.[318]

14.4.B.2 A DUTY OF DISCLOSURE BEYOND CASES OF FRAUD?

French law has many examples of duties of disclosure imposed by statute[319] and of contractual—as opposed to precontractual—obligations to give information to the other party. Writers, notably Ghestin,[320] argued for the existence of a general duty to disclose independent of error or fraud. There were a number of cases in French law in which the courts imposed liability for non-disclosure without reference to either fraud or mistake.

Thus in Civ (1), 13 May 2003[321] it was held that a bank is in breach of its duty to contract in good faith and is liable for fraudulent non-disclosure if, 'whilst being aware of the debtor's irremediably jeopardised situation …, it does not make this fact known to the person who stands as a guarantee for the debtor.' However, there was no legal duty

---

[317] Chénédé explained that Art 1137 after the 2016 Ordonnance did not overrule *Baldus* and simply invited judges 'to be indulgent towards to contracting parties who were perhaps insufficiently curious or diligent but who nonetheless were the victims of the other party's malevolence.' He based his reasoning on the fact that, as explained by the Report to the President (p 83 n 39 above), Article 1139 has made the choice not to condition *réticence dolosive* to the existence of an information duty, so as to put more emphasis on sanctioning the *intention de tromper* (F Chénédé, *Le nouveau droit des obligations et des contrats: Consolidations, innovations, perspectives* (Paris: Dalloz, 2016) no. 23.112). This is a controversial issue and the numerous commentators of the reform have very different opinions: for an opposite view, see for instance B Fages, *Droit des obligations* (7th edn, Paris: LGDJ, 2017) no. 115.

[318] See O Deshayes, T Genicon and YM Laithier, *Réforme du droit des contrats, du régime général et de la preuve des obligations: Commentaire article par article* (Paris: LexisNexis, 2016) 202–04, 209–13.

[319] See a list of examples given by M Fabre-Magnan, 'Duties of Disclosure and French Contract Law' in J Beatson and D Friedmann (eds), *Good Faith and Fault in Contract Law* (Oxford: Clarendon Press, 1995) 99, 100.

[320] Ghestin (n 309 above) 151.

[321] No. 01-11511, Bull civ I no. 114, RTD civ 2003, 700, annotated by J Mestre and B Fages.

on a company to disclose the fact that it is under a judicial rehabilitation procedure for insolvency to the other party to contractual negotiations.

The duty of disclosure is now written into the Code civil to the effect that it has a broad and general scope.

Code civil　　　　　　　　　**14.44 (FR)**

Article 1112-1: The party who knows information which is of decisive importance for the consent of the other, must inform him of it where the latter legitimately does not know the information or relies on the contracting party.

However, this duty to inform does not apply to an assessment of the value of the act of performance.

Information is of decisive importance if it has a direct and necessary relationship with the content of the contract or the status of the parties.

A person who claims that information was due to him has the burden of proving that the other party had the duty to provide it, and that other party has the burden of proving that he has provided it.

The parties may neither limit nor exclude this duty.

In addition to imposing liability on the party who had the duty to inform, his failure to fulfil the duty may lead to annulment of the contract under the conditions provided by articles 1130 and following.

Notes

(1) This is one of the most controversial and criticised provisions of the reform. It has an important political resonance and for this reason it is interesting to know more about its background. This is described in considerable detail in F Ancel, B Fauvarque-Cosson, J Gest, *Aux sources de la réforme du droit des contrats*;[322] each of the three authors was heavily involved in the drafting of the reforms. The notes that follow draw on their account.

(2) Some disputed the need for a general provision on disclosure, given the special legislation already in place and the existing case law, arguing that it would be better to allow the law to develop incrementally than to adopt too broad a provision. However, the majority of professionals insisted that it would be better to place the law into a proper framework; and consumer representatives particularly supported adoption of a general duty of disclosure. Therefore, each draft of the reforms included a general duty; the principal discussions were over its place in the Code civil, its title, which debtors would owe a duty to which creditors, what information should be treated as 'determining' and the fit with the new Article 1137 on fraud.[323]

(3) There was debate over whether the Article should impose an obligation to disclose or a duty to do so, as in the PECL[324] and the DCFR[325] (which is very careful to

---

[322] F Ancel, B Fauvarque-Cosson and J Gest, *Aux sources de la réforme du droit des contrats* (Paris: Dalloz, 2017).
[323] ibid, no. 25.12.
[324] PECL Art 2:202.
[325] DCFR Art II.-3:101.

distinguish obligations, which give rise to the full range of contractual remedies, from duties, breach of which at most gives rise only to a remedy of damages[326]). The decision to refer to a duty had consequences for the place of the article, and it was only in the latest published version that it was placed in the section on precontractual negotiations.[327]

(4) The authors' discussion of the conditions of application are worth quoting *in extenso*, as they capture the intense disagreements that arose over this controversial piece of legislation.

Aux sources de la réforme du droit des contrats[328]   **14.45 (FR)**

Conditions of application. As indicated above, it was on the conditions of application that the observations were concentrated and in particular those weighed on the person of the debtor who might owe this duty of information. The text proposed by the Catala draft reform had resulted in many observations and fears on the part of the professional organizations such as the CCIP, the MEDEF or the FBF, which found it too broad. Other observers, to the contrary, had regretted a text which seemed to them to be in retreat from the case law since it required the creditor to be 'unable to inform himself' in order to benefit from this article, which seemed to them very restrictive. This is why the expression that the debtor should reveal information he 'should have known' was removed in 2008, as this formula appeared too broad and a source of legal uncertainty. This had been preferred to the more 'objective' formula according to which the debtor had to fulfill this duty at least when he was 'in a position to know' the required information. The technical group wanted to substitute an even more objective formula: the debtor would be under a duty when he 'could not be unaware' of the information, and the ministerial group reinforced this option by laying down an even stricter rule: the duty to provide information. is imposed on those who know or 'must know' the information. Conversely, the requirement that the creditor be unable to inform himself if he is to have a remedy for the breach of an information obligation was considered too restrictive, in particular by consumer associations, and has been removed. The project substituted the concept of legitimate ignorance and reliance on its counterparty, a derivation from the principle of good faith, which is also consecrated. It is sufficient that the creditor could legitimately be ignorant of the information or rely on his co-contractor (who he might think would have informed him spontaneously) for the creditor to avail himself of this duty of information. This precision makes it possible to maintain a degree of exigency towards the creditor, thus suggesting that it is up to the creditor to make at least minimal enquiries.

14.4.C GERMANY

German law also recognises that a party to a contract will be under an obligation to make disclosure of certain important facts to the other party. Obligations of this sort are imposed under § 123 BGB and under the doctrine of *culpa in contrahendo*. It should be

---

[326] See the DCFR's Annex of definitions.
[327] Ancel et al (n 322 above) nos. 25.21–25.22.
[328] Ancel et al (n 322 above) no. 25.31 (footnotes omitted).

remembered first, however, that if the fact which should have been disclosed was one relating to an essential attribute of a thing or person, it will be possible to avoid the contract under § 119(2) BGB. But, since the category of essential attributes is limited,[329] and having regard to the very brief period before the right to avoid is lost (§ 121 BGB), one of the aforementioned alternatives is often preferred.

14.4.C.1 NON-DISCLOSURE AS FRAUD

As we saw above, it is a requirement of any claim for avoidance under § 123 BGB that the challenging party has been deceived by the conduct of the other party or by certain further third parties. Silence will be sufficient as conduct where there was a duty to disclose. When will such a duty arise?

The German courts have been particularly keen to impose a duty to make disclosure in cases arising from the sale of used cars and other vehicles, as the following case shows:

BGH, 3 March 1982[330]   **14.46 (DE)**

The used lorry

A seller of a vehicle must disclose to the buyer the fact that the vehicle has suffered significant damage in an accident, but need not disclose that the vehicle has a replacement engine, nor the seller's doubts about the accuracy of the odometer reading.

Facts: On 8 November 1978 the plaintiff purchased from the defendant, for the sum of DM 54,880, a second-hand lorry which had been fitted with a replacement engine and a replacement gearbox by the person who had owned it prior to the vendor. The plaintiff took delivery of the lorry on 9 November 1978. The written sale contract, which was entitled 'Invoice' and which was not drawn up on the basis of a printed form, provided inter alia: 'bought as seen … guaranteed for 6 months or 100,000 km—kilometres covered: 421,861'. By a letter from his lawyer dated 16 March 1979, the plaintiff avoided the contract on the ground of wilful deceit, claiming that the vehicle had covered a greater number of kilometres than had been indicated.

Held: The Landgericht (Regional Court) dismissed the plaintiff's claim, by which he sought an order for repayment of the purchase price, compensation for expenditure incurred by him and the return of bills of exchange in respect of the purchase price which had not yet matured. The plaintiff's appeal to the Oberlandesgericht (Higher Regional Court), in which he also pleaded fraudulent non-disclosure of a rear-end collision, was likewise dismissed. The plaintiff's further appeal on a point of law resulted in the judgment of the court below being set aside and in the case being referred back to the lower court.

Judgment: … II.2.(a) According to the settled case law of the Bundesgerichtshof, where the seller of a second-hand lorry is aware of a defect or of an earlier accident, he is in principle under a duty to inform the buyer of it, even if the latter does not ask about it. If he fails to do so, he will be liable for wilful deceit. According to the findings of the appellate court, the husband of the proprietor of the defendant firm, who acted on behalf of the defendant in the sale, gave the plaintiff no such indication, although he was aware that during the course of being driven by the previous owner to the place where it was to be delivered to the defendant, the lorry had been involved in a rear-end collision in which the front bumper, at least, had been damaged and had had to be replaced.

---

[329] See above, p 537.
[330] NJW 1982, 1386.

(b) However, the duty of disclosure is not completely unlimited in its scope. Since its justification is founded on the special characteristics of the second-hand vehicle trade, and since the purchaser's knowledge of defects and accidents suffered by the vehicle in question has a decisive influence on his decision to buy, he does not need to be informed of an accident which was so slight that it could not, on any reasonable view, influence his decision to buy. However, in the case of cars, the adjudicating Senate has hitherto recognised as falling into that category of 'trifling damage' only very minor external (paintwork) damage, and has held that it does not include other (bodywork) damage, even where such latter damage had no far-reaching consequences and the repair cost amounted (as it did in a 1961 case) to only DM 332.55 (BGH NJW 1967, 1222).

(c) In the case of lorries, however, it is legitimate to treat even more extensive damage as 'trifling', since the undamaged condition of the vehicle, including its bodywork, and the external appearance which that lends to the vehicle, does not as a general rule matter so much with commercial vehicles as it does with cars. Nevertheless, the criterion applying in the case of load-carrying or commercial vehicles is that defects which amount to more than merely visible and external damage, and which affect the condition of the vehicle in a more far-reaching way, must be excluded from the 'trifling' category.

That is not the position in the present case. It is not necessary to decide whether the damage caused to the front bumper constitutes of itself a danger to other parts which necessarily renders the accident more than merely 'slight'. The appellant rightly complains that the court below failed to take full account of the plaintiff's assertions and of the summary of the evidence concerning the extent of the damage. In his grounds of appeal, the plaintiff had maintained that, as a result of the rear-end collision—which initially was untruthfully denied by the defendant—several of the blades of the viscosity ventilating fan [*Viskolüfter*] were missing. The husband of the proprietor of the defendant firm, who gave evidence as a witness to the accident, stated in that regard that, in the course of the rear-end collision which occurred during a transportation journey, damage had been sustained not only to the bumper but also to the ventilation fan and the radiator. The court below did not deal with that statement. If, in fact, parts of the engine such as the fan and the radiator were damaged, there can be no question, even in the case of a lorry, of mere 'trifling' damage which does not need to be disclosed, since the risk of further adverse consequences would be so considerable for any purchaser that the decision as to whether to inform the buyer of the accident and of the main aspects of the repairs can no longer be left to the discretion of the seller.

...

III.3.(b) [It is not] possible to accept the appellant's submission that the defendant should at least have disclosed his doubts regarding the conformity of the reading on the tachometer with the total distance actually covered by the vehicle and the installation of a replacement engine and a replacement gearbox. It is not necessary to decide whether an assertion of wilful deceit concerning the possibly material circumstances relating to the distance covered by a lorry necessarily falls to be rejected where the actual distance covered is not declared. At all events, the defendant has not breached any duty of disclosure in that regard. Even in the second-hand vehicle trade, the vendor is under no duty—save in so far as, exceptionally, he takes it upon himself to give advice to the purchaser, which was not the position in this case—to inform the other party to the contract of all facts and/or considerations affecting the value to be placed upon the vehicle. Depending on the ambit of those facts and/or considerations, his duty of disclosure is also conditioned by the extent to which the purchaser is himself capable of gaining knowledge of them, and also by the latter's conduct, particularly as regards any interest manifested by him in individual facts and matters. The plaintiff, who was not completely lacking in experience of transport vehicles, was (or should have been) as aware as the defendant that the tachometer reading did not necessarily provide a reliable indication of the distance which the lorry had actually covered. If he had regarded that distance as an important factor, then he should have asked about it. The same consideration applies as regards the replacement engine and the replacement gearbox, from the presence of which in the vehicle no convincing conclusions can be drawn as to its having covered a given number of kilometres where—as is not disputed between the parties—the date of, and the reason for, their installation in the lorry were not known. Even the appellant does not question the fact that the installation of such replacement parts does not in itself indicate the existence of any defects requiring to be disclosed.

Notes

(1) A party may expect disclosure in accordance with the requirements of good faith and fair practices in accordance with § 242 BGB. Both the circumstances of the concrete transaction and the type of contract involved will be relevant to the identification of such duties. The BGH refers to the 'special features of the used car market' as justifying an extensive duty of disclosure in these cases. It is not quite clear what these 'features' are—perhaps the difficulty for buyers of discovering defects in used vehicles.

(2) The drafters of the BGB avoided including any general rule on positive duties of disclosure. They preferred instead to leave precision of § 123 BGB in this sense to future courts on the basis of the good faith provision of § 242 BGB.[331] What are the advantages of such a solution? What are the disadvantages?

(3) In spite of this prescribed casuistry, some tendencies are evident in the case law:[332]

    (a) questions must be answered truthfully;

    (b) a partial concealment is as good as a lie;

    (c) an imbalance in skill or access to information leading to significant reliance on the part of the challenging party is likely to lead to a duty to disclose;

    (d) increasing complexity of the transaction is also likely to lead to such a duty.

(4) Not everything known to one party must be disclosed to the other, only those facts which would indicate to the other party that his purpose in entering into the contract is likely to be thwarted. Is there any reason of economic policy for denying a wider duty to disclose?

In certain cases, the German courts have found that there is no obligation to disclose information.

---

[331] See *Motive zu dem Entwurf eines Bürgerlichen Gesetzbuches für das Deutsche Reich*, vol I, *Allgemeiner Teil* (1888) 208.
[332] See Münchener Kommentar/Armbrüster § 123 para 30–35.

The doctor's practice

A doctor who sells his practice on the basis that it has a turnover of a certain amount is not required to disclose the type of patients which he had.

Facts: The defendant sold his doctor's practice to the plaintiff for 75,000 DM, of which the plaintiff had already paid half. In the advertisement of sale he had stated inter alia that the practice generated a turnover of about 465,000 DM per year and that it was very possible that this would increase in the future. After the plaintiff took over the business it soon became apparent that a significant proportion of the figure of 465,000 DM had been composed of the fees of a relatively small number of private, fee-paying patients. There was a risk in the future that these patients would desert the practice. The plaintiff claimed that the defendant had deceitfully concealed the patient profile of the practice. He accordingly sought to avoid the contract on the basis of § 123 BGB and the return of the 75,000 DM which he had paid.

Held: At first instance the Landgericht upheld the claim. This decision was upheld by the Oberlandesgericht. The defendant's appeal to the BGH was successful.

Judgment: I. The court hearing the appeal on the facts regarded the plaintiff's claim for payment as well founded in accordance with §§ 812, 818 and 123 of the BGB. It held that, upon the conclusion of the contract for the transfer of the practice, the defendant had fraudulently misrepresented to the plaintiff the extent of his income from his activities as a doctor in the private sector. It further ruled that the claim for a declaration was justified, since the defendant had made further, exaggerated representations.

... [T]he appellate court below exaggerated the scope of the obligations imposed by the duty to provide information. Such a duty, breach of which may constitute fraudulent misrepresentation, has been inferred by case law from the specific legal relations existing between negotiating parties in cases where, having regard in particular to the possible frustration of the purpose of the contract, non-disclosure of the facts would be contrary to the principle of good faith and where the party to whom the representations were made was entitled, according to the accepted view, to expect to be informed of the fact concealed. ... That principle also applies to negotiations for contracts of sale. However, it does not extend so far as to require the vendor, of his own accord, to enlighten the purchaser in relation to all facts and matters which may be of significance for the purposes of creating in the latter an intention to contract. On the contrary, it is necessary to have regard to the opposing principle that a person concluding a contract must satisfy himself as to whether or not that contract is advantageous to him. This is something to which the other party may adjust his conduct; consequently, he is not required to draw attention to facts and matters which he may expect to be asked about if any weight is attached to them by the first party. ...

The facts on which the appellate court below based its decision are insufficient to warrant any conclusion that the defendant was required to provide the plaintiff, without being asked, with information concerning the very substantial level of fees attributable to individual patients. The situation might be different if, for example, only two or three patients likely to pass away in the near future had accounted for an annual fee income of approximately DM 370,000, alternatively DM 270,000, out of a total of DM 465,000. ... Such an extreme situation has not been found to exist in the present

---

[333] NJW 1989, 763.

case; nor, indeed, has it been alleged. True, a practice with only a few patients individu-ally paying very high amounts in fees clearly involves greater risks for a purchaser than a practice based predominantly on patients whose care is funded by a health insurance scheme. If, in such circumstances, even just one patient withdraws his custom from the purchaser, this may in itself result in very considerable financial loss. However, it is for the prospective purchaser to obviate such risks. The vendor is entitled to assume that the purchaser reckons on being able himself to provide medical care in such a way as to retain the loyalty to the practice of the majority of the patients. A different assessment might be necessary if there existed, for example, certain specific links or ties (eg as a result of kinship or on account of particular indulgence shown to inveter-ate patients). No such finding was made by the appellate court below; nor did it find that there had been any contravention of the law relating to doctors' fees. It simply accepted, without making any corresponding findings of fact, that the defendant had received income which could not have been earned by a subsequent proprietor of the practice on the basis of compliance with the law relating to doctors' fees. Nor does the finding of the appellate court below that the defendant had not operated any proper medical filing system warrant any inference with regard to the duty to provide informa-tion. The appellate court below made that assessment on the basis of the testimony of the witness S, even though she had seen only about 100 of the total of 800 file index cards which existed. The information contained on the cards available related merely to prescription details and, at most, blood pressure levels; they did not, however, contain any proposals for treatment or results of analyses. It is not clear how the plaintiff could have gained any information concerning the very substantial levels of fees attributable to a small number of patients from a comprehensively maintained patient filing system as conceived by the appellate court below, even if he had inspected all of the files and index cards concerned. In order to gain a proper picture of the fee structure, the course of action which he should have taken was not to look through 800 file index cards but instead to pose the appropriate question to the defendant. The plaintiff has not asserted that he asked any such question.

3. Since the finding made by the appellate court below to the effect that the plaintiff had effectively avoided the contract on account of fraudulent misrepresentation con-cerning the fee structure cannot be valid, it follows that there can be no basis for its conclusion that the contract was consequently void in law, that the defendant should be ordered, pursuant to §§ 812 and 818 of the BGB, to repay the purchase price instalment of DM 75,000 which had already been paid and that he was not entitled to receive pay-ment of the balance of the purchase price … For the purposes of determining whether the defendant was obliged to provide the plaintiff with information concerning the fee structure, the rules applying to a claim in damages for *culpa in contrahendo* are the same as those applying under § 123 BGB to the application for a declaration of entitlement to avoid the contract.

14.4.C.2 *CULPA IN CONTRAHENDO*

As with § 123 BGB, there may be liability in *culpa in contrahendo* (§§ 280(1), 241(2), 311(2) BGB) where a contracting party has breached a duty to make disclosure as opposed to actively causing a mistake. We have already seen that fault in the contracting process may be constituted by negligent as well as fraudulent conduct. The instances recognised in the academic writing and case law as giving rise to a duty to disclose under *culpa in contrahendo* are largely similar to those under § 123 BGB.[334] The appropriate allocation of the risk of a particular eventuality is very often decisive in this matter. Although a tendency to expand the duty has been observed,[335] there is no general obligation to make disclosure. Only those things need be disclosed which are recognisably of crucial significance to the entry of the other party into the contract.

There will frequently be a duty (under both *culpa in contrahendo* and § 123 BGB) on the offeror, or those acting on his behalf, to advise the offeree of the true content and legal significance of his offer.

BGH, 16 January 1991[336]   **14.48 (DE)**

The tax advisors

The seller of a business is under no duty to disclose problems with an employee to a buyer where these problems lie in the past and where the buyer has made his own investigations of the matter.

Facts: The claimant bought from the defendant a company which specialised in tax advice. Among the employees of the company was one N, a former partner, who had been accused of unacceptable practices by the local chamber of tax advisors. Having had cause to dismiss N, the claimant sought alternatively reduction of the purchase price, damages under the law of sale or damages for *culpa in contrahendo* from the defendant. In relation to the latter the claimant claimed that the defendant should have disclosed N's tendency to criminal behaviour.

Held: The Landgericht rejected the claim. The Oberlandesgericht held for the claimant on the grounds that there had been a culpable failure to disclose. The defendant's appeal to the BGH was successful.

Judgment: II. The findings of the appellate court do not stand up to scrutiny in all respects. ... liability for *culpa in contrahendo* ... is eliminated because the defendant did not breach any duty of disclosure, so that the questions of causality and fault do not even arise. A duty of disclosure exists, also in negotiations with a view to the conclusion of a contract of sale, where the non-disclosure of facts would be contrary to the principle of good faith and the recipient of the statement was entitled, according to commercial practice, to expect to be informed of the non-disclosed fact (cf BGH NJW 1983, 2493 ...); this falls to be decided according to the specific circumstances of each particular case (BGHZ 96, 302, 311 ...). The appellate court links the duty of disclosure to the factual circumstances which prompted the defendant, some two years prior to the contractual negotiations with the claimant, to address a serious written warning to N ... and to advise him 'to give some thought, as soon as possible, to dissolve the employment relationship'. The appellate court makes no findings to the effect that, following the written warning ..., N would have given further cause for complaint or that he and the defendant would have come close to dissolving the employment relationship. If this is so, the very

---

[334] See 14.4 (DE), above, p 488.

[335] K Larenz, *Lehrbuch des Schuldrechts,* vol I, *Allgemeiner Teil* (14th edn, Munich: CH Beck, 1987) para 9 I.

[336] NJW 1991, 1223.

passage of time militates against any conclusion that the defendant was under a duty to provide information; *a fortiori* since the matter involved facts which in the event of their unsolicited disclosure would have raised issues concerning N's right to privacy. With regard to what the claimant was entitled to expect, it is relevant that, as a tax advisor, he is business savvy (cf BGHZ 96, 302, 311 ...). Moreover, this circumstance must be considered together with the fact that the claimant did not only take N on as an employee of the practice. He rather offered to sell him a share in the business when concluding the contract with the defendant ... The proposed association with N as co-owner should have prompted the claimant to take the initiative to seek information concerning N – be it by making enquiries of the defendant, by inspecting the documents made available to him or by requesting particulars – so that he was not entitled to rely on unsolicited disclosure by the defendant. Having regard to the specific circumstances which the appellate court did not assess, it cannot be said that there was a duty of information with regard to the formal warning letter.

Notes

(1) The German courts have identified duties of disclosure in certain cases coming under the following headings:

- where one party is or should be aware that the other is or may be under a misapprehension as to the content and legal and economic significance of the agreement which they are about to enter into;[337]
- where one party is aware of a formal requirement of validity of the contract or performance of the obligations thereunder which has not been satisfied;[338]
- where one party knows of circumstances which threaten his or her ability to meet his or her obligations;[339]
- where one party knows of circumstances which make it unlikely that the objective of the contract can be attained—although generally a buyer takes the risk of the thing sold not being suitable for his further purposes.[340]

(2) The usual consequence of a finding of *culpa in contrahendo* is an award of damages in the amount of the negative interest. Exceptionally the expectation interest may be awarded if it can be shown that the party claiming would have entered into a contract on better terms, as opposed to not entering into the contract at all. In addition, the contract may be adjusted to change terms which have resulted from the *culpa in contrahendo*.

---

[337] BGH 28 February 1968, NJW 1968, 986.
[338] BGH 20 June 1952, BGHZ 6, 330, 333; BGH 18 February 1955, BGHZ 16, 334, 336.
[339] RG 21 April 1931, RGZ 132, 305, 309; BGH 5 April 1971, BGHZ 56, 81, 88.
[340] BGH 12 November 1969, NJW 1970, 653, 655.

14.4.D THE NETHERLANDS

BW   **14.49 (NL)**

Article 6:228: (1) A contract which has been entered into under the influence of error and which would not have been entered into had there been a correct assessment of the facts, can be annulled: ...

(b) if the other party, in view of what he knew or ought to know regarding the error, should have informed the party in error; ...

14.5 ADAPTATION OF CONTRACTS

This part covers two related questions:

(1)   What is the outcome where one party offers to perform the contract in the way the other party had thought would be the case when he entered it?
(2)   If one party has a prima facie right to avoid the contract, but the court thinks it can reach a fair result by adjusting the terms of the contract, can it do so and refuse to permit avoidance?

The most obvious example of (1) is where there is a mistake over the terms of the contract: for example, I make a mistake and offer to sell you my house for £120,000 when I meant to write £130,000. Assuming I have a right to escape from the contract, should I still be entitled to escape if, when you hear that there has been a mistake, you offer to pay the larger amount?

The same sort of problem can arise where the mistake is about the circumstances: for example, a flooring contractor employed to floor a large building makes a fundamental mistake about the amount of work needed. This mistake should have been known by the other party so the contractor has the right to avoid the contract. The employer offers to release the contractor from the extra work without any reduction in the payment. Can the contractor avoid the contract?

Principles of European Contract Law[341]   **14.50 (INT)**

Article 4:105: Adaptation of Contract

(1) If a party is entitled to avoid the contract for mistake but the other party indicates that it is willing to perform, or actually does perform, the contract as it was understood by the party entitled to avoid it, the contract is to be treated as if it had been concluded as the that [sic] party understood it. The other party must indicate its willingness to perform, or render such performance, promptly after being informed of the manner in which the party entitled to avoid it understood the contract and before that party acts in reliance on any notice of avoidance.

(2) After such indication or performance the right to avoid is lost and any earlier notice of avoidance is ineffective.

---

[341] cf DCFR Art II.-7:203.

(3) Where both parties have made the same mistake, the court may at the request of either party bring the contract into accordance with what might reasonably have been agreed had the mistake not occurred.

In this situation English law seems to do nothing to prevent the mistaken party from relying on the mistake to escape the contract. In German law, if the other party offers to perform the contract in the manner intended by the mistaken party it is held that it would be contrary to good faith (§ 242 BGB) to allow the latter to avoid. The contract, as intended, remains valid and enforceable. Were the mistaken party to insist on avoidance, a defence of *venire contra factum proprium* could be raised against him, ie a party is estopped from enforcing a right if he would, thereby, be acting inconsistently with his previous conduct.[342]

In French law there is no explicit provision on adaptation of the contract that has been entered as the result of mistake. However, the general principle of good faith (Article 1104) could also apply if the other party offers to perform the contract in the manner intended by the mistaken party and the latter claims nullity.

Dutch law also has a specific provision:

BW	**14.51 (NL)**

Article 6:230: (1) The power to annul a contract on the basis of Articles 228 and 229 lapses when the other party timely proposes a modification to the effects of the contract which adequately removes the prejudice which the person entitled to the annulment suffers by the continuance of the contract.

In situation (2), some systems seem to have limited powers of adjustment. In German law, even where the relevant grounds are made out, avoidance may be viewed by the court as unfair having regard to § 242 BGB. As will be seen,[343] in such cases the contract may be adapted if its continued application would be in the interests of both parties. Accordingly, the performance required of either or both parties may be adjusted to reflect the 'true' basis of the contract. The remedies under *culpa in contrahendo* were also seen to be more flexible than that of avoidance under § 119 BGB. In relation to defects, the BGB provides that the buyer or the employer may reduce the contract price in proportion to the extent to which an item sold or work carried out is defective: § 441 BGB, § 634 BGB. This will include cases where the party seeking these remedies was in error as to the presence of the defect.[344]

BW	**14.52 (NL)**

Article 6:230: (2) Furthermore, instead of pronouncing the annulment the judge may, upon the demand of one of the parties, modify the effects of the contract so as to remove this prejudice.

---

[342] RG 12 April 1921, RGZ 102, 87. This is expressly provided for in relation to avoidance for mistake in the Swiss Code (Art 25(2) OR). See also Art 1432 of the Italian Codice civile.

[343] See below, pp 1222 ff.

[344] RG 10 November 1921, RGZ 103, 154, 159; BGH 18 March 1977, NJW 1977, 1538, 1539.

14.6 COMPARATIVE SUMMARY: MISTAKE AND THE INTERNATIONAL RESTATEMENTS

14.6.A THE LAWS

It is useful to compare the national laws we have considered with each other, and to the provisions of the international restatements of contract law, on the question of relief for mistake as (1) mistakes over the terms of the contract and (2) mistakes as to the subject matter or circumstance.

14.6.A.1 MISTAKES OVER THE TERMS OF THE CONTRACT

All the systems covered allow a party who has agreed a contract under a mistake about what was being agreed to avoid the contract, or sometimes to argue that the mistake prevented a contract being formed. However, the circumstances in which this will be permitted vary significantly. The systems all seem to reach the result that if the parties were in fact agreed on the terms but the words used in the contract did not express their agreement correctly, the true meaning of the contract will prevail.[345] At one end of the spectrum, French law takes a subjective view of the parties' intentions, so that in principle, if one party did not mean to enter a contract or if the parties were not agreed on the same terms, there would be an *erreur obstacle,* which prevents the formation of a contract. In practice, however, the French courts normally assume that there is a contract in the terms actually stated by the parties but allow a party who was mistaken to avoid it on the basis of mistake. This is certainly now the position under German law and Dutch law: whether a contract was formed and on what terms will be judged objectively, but a party who did not intend to contract or who did not intend to contract on the terms as objectively determined will be allowed to avoid the contract on the ground of mistake.[346] The avoiding party may have to compensate the other for any loss suffered in reliance on the contract. English law is the most restrictive. Whether party A intended to contract and on what terms depends on how the other party, B, reasonably understood A's words or conduct. If B knew that A did not intend to contract on the terms stated, or at all, B cannot hold A to what he said or wrote, and possibly this is also true if B should have known that A was making a mistake over the terms; but if B had no reason to know that A was mistaken, there will be a contract on the terms as B reasonably understood them and it cannot be avoided for mistake. The only other case in which the mistake may be relevant is if the expressions used were ambiguous and there is no reason to prefer B's understanding of them over A's or vice versa ('mutual mistake'), in which case the contract will be void for uncertainty—a result which is also reached by the other systems.

---

[345] See above, pp 501 ff. In English law this may not follow if there was no 'outward expression' of the parties' true meaning; in that case the words actually used would prevail.

[346] See above, pp 508 ff.

How does this compare to the international restatements? The PECL, the DCFR and the CESL all provide that the subjective intentions of the parties prevail over the literal meaning of the words used. So the PECL provide:

Article 5:101: General Rules of Interpretation

(1) A contract is to be interpreted according to the common intention of the parties even if this differs from the literal meaning of the words.

…

In other respects the restatements adopt a position that seems to be closer to the English solution than to any of the continental ones. First, as in all the systems except the French, a party's intentions (as to whether to contract or on what terms) are judged by how they reasonably appeared to the other party, eg PECL:

Article 2:102: Intention

The intention of a party to be legally bound by contract is to be determined from the party's statements or conduct as they were reasonably understood by the other party.

Article 5:101 continues:

…

(2) If it is established that one party intended the contract to have a particular meaning, and at the time of the conclusion of the contract the other party could not have been unaware of the first party's intention, the contract is to be interpreted in the way intended by the first party.

(3) If an intention cannot be established according to (1) or (2), the contract is to be interpreted according to the meaning that reasonable persons of the same kind as the parties would give to it in the same circumstances.

Secondly, while the restatements all contain an article allowing a contract to be set aside on the ground of mistake, and these are all applicable to mistakes as to the terms,[347] the circumstances in which relief can be obtained are significantly more limited than in the continental laws.

Principles of European Contract Law　　　　　**14.53 (INT)**

Article 4:103: Fundamental Mistake as to Facts or Law

(1) A party may avoid a contract for mistake of fact or law existing when the contract was concluded if:

    (a) (i) the mistake was caused by information given by the other party; or

        (ii) the other party knew or ought to have known of the mistake and it was contrary to good faith and fair dealing to leave the mistaken party in error; or

        (iii) the other party made the same mistake, and

    (b) the other party knew or ought to have known that the mistaken party, had it known the truth, would not have entered the contract or would have done so only on fundamentally different terms.

---

[347] See PECL Art 4:104.

(2) However a party may not avoid the contract if:

(a) in the circumstances its mistake was inexcusable, or

(b) the risk of the mistake was assumed, or in the circumstances should be borne, by it.

This is narrower than either Article 1132 Code civil or § 119(1) BGB, principally because a party who made a mistake over the terms of the contract will not obtain relief unless the other party either caused the mistake, knew or should have known of it, or shared it.

14.6.A.2 MISTAKES AS TO THE SUBJECT MATTER OR CIRCUMSTANCES

All four legal systems covered in this section allow a party to escape a contract which he has entered into on the ground of a mistake as to the subject matter or circumstances, but under rather different conditions and sometimes under doctrines other than mistake.

Thus, the mistake may prevent there being a contract at all under separate doctrines: in French law because the contract lacks a *contenu certain et licite*, such as it is required in Article 1128 Code civil (and previously because it lacked *objet* or *cause*, see ex-Article 1108); in former German law because it was objectively impossible.[348] English law probably reaches a similar result where the contract is for the sale of goods which have already ceased to exist. These rules are not reflected in the more recent Dutch BW, and they are explicitly rejected by PECL Article 4:102[349] and UNIDROIT PICC Article 3.1.3.

A contract may also be void on the ground of mistake as to the subject matter or circumstances under the English doctrine at common law. However, the mistake must be very serious—it must 'render the thing essentially different'[350] or even render the contract or the contractual venture impossible[351]—and the doctrine is very restrictive in that the mistake must be shared by both parties.

In contrast, the continental systems all permit a party who has entered a contract on the basis of a mistake to avoid it on more liberal bases.

First, it seems that the mistake does not need to be so fundamental. While in French law the mistake must relate to an essential quality of the subject matter, this notion seems to be applied less strictly than the common law's requirement that the mistake 'render the thing essentially different'. In German law the mistake must relate to a characteristic considered essential in business. It is hard to say whether this is wider or narrower than the French 'essential quality'. Any characteristic which affects the value of the property seems to be treated by the courts as falling within § 119(2) BGB, though this is balanced by the obligation to pay reliance damages under § 122 BGB. However, German law is certainly more liberal in giving relief for mistake than is English law. In addition, as we have seen, in German law relief for mistake is supplemented by liability for *culpa in contrahendo*,[352] and this may result in the mistaken party being freed from his obligations.

---

[348] See above, p 541.
[349] See 14.32 (INT), above, p 543.
[350] See above, p 544.
[351] See above, p 548.
[352] See above, ch 13.

Secondly, neither French nor German law requires that the mistake be shared. The matter to which the mistake relates must be something which, to use broad terms, both parties would recognise as being important;[353] but neither system requires that the defendant has to have made the same mistake.

Dutch law is also generous in that the circumstances about which one party is mistaken are broadly defined; but relief under BW Article 6:228 is precluded if the other party did not know and had no reason to know of the importance of the fact to the party seeking to avoid the contract.[354]

Nonetheless, the practical importance of these differences must not be exaggerated.

(a) Shared mistakes

In cases of shared ('common') mistake, while French and German law seem to allow avoidance more readily than English law and will find the contract void or voidable for mistake, we saw that English courts can avoid the requirement that the mistake be essential or fundamental by the device of the implied condition precedent, so that if the facts are not as assumed there is again no contract.[355] However, cases of 'pure' shared mistake are relatively rare. Much more frequent are cases where the parties do indeed share the same misapprehension, but this is because the claimant has relied on incorrect information given him—without fraud[356]—by the other party. Here the differences between the continental and common law systems are very slight. In the continental systems, the contract may be avoided for mistake; in England, it may be avoided for misrepresentation. Indeed, the doctrine of misrepresentation may be the more liberal, as the matter misrepresented need not be of particular importance, though the court now has power to refuse to permit rescission on this or other grounds.[357] Thus in this situation the chief difference between the common law and civil law systems is simply the ground on which avoidance is permitted: in the continental systems, mistake, in the common law, misrepresentation.

Both the PECL (Article 4:103[358]) and the UNIDROIT PICC (Article 3.2.2[359]) adopt the continental approach.

Where the party giving the incorrect information was at fault, even if the conditions for avoidance on the ground of mistake have not been met, all four systems will allow the recovery of damages.[360] PECL Article 4:106[361] is to the same effect.

---

[353] See above, pp 529 and 538.

[354] See above, p 540.

[355] The fact that this approach and the common law doctrine of mistake both lead to the contract being void rather than voidable seems to have little practical importance in the cases. The question is most likely to be relevant when a third party is affected, but none of the reported cases seems to involve third parties.

[356] Of course if the party giving the information was dishonest, in all systems the contract is voidable for fraud.

[357] Misrepresentation Act 1967, s 2(2); see 14.36 (EN), above, p 561.

[358] See 14.8 (INT), above, p 497.

[359] See 14.57 (INT), below, p 591.

[360] See above, pp 562–64.

[361] See 14.37 (INT), above, p 562.

The UNIDROIT PICC do not have a parallel provision; damages may be recovered only if the contract could have been avoided for mistake:

UNIDROIT Principles   **14.54 (INT)**

Article 3.2.16: Damages

Irrespective of whether or not the contract has been avoided, the party who knew or ought to have known of the ground of avoidance is liable for damages so as to put the other party in the same position in which it would have been if it had not concluded the contract.

Compare the rather more elaborate provision of the PECL:

Principles of European Contract Law   **14.55 (INT)**

Article 4:117: Damages

(1) A party who avoids a contract under this Chapter may recover from the other party damages so as to put the avoiding party as nearly as possible into the same position as if it had not concluded the contract, provided that the other party knew or ought to have known of the mistake, fraud, threat or taking of excessive benefit or unfair advantage.

(2) If a party has the right to avoid a contract under this Chapter, but does not exercise its right or has lost its right under the provisions of Articles 4:113 or 4:114, it may recover, subject to paragraph (1), damages limited to the loss caused to it by the mistake, fraud, threat or taking of excessive benefit or unfair advantage. The same measure of damages shall apply when the party was misled by incorrect information in the sense of Article 4:106.

(3) In other respects, the damages shall be in accordance with the relevant provisions of Chapter 9, Section 5, with appropriate adaptations.

The second paragraph is intended to prevent a party who has not avoided the contract from recovering damages that would pass to the other party the loss caused by a fall in value in the property transferred unrelated to the misrepresentation: see Comment C.

(b) Self-induced unilateral mistakes and general duties of disclosure

The cases in which real differences between the systems emerge are those in which one party has made a mistake which the other party does not share, but which is not the result of any untrue statement by the latter. Here we saw that French and German law will allow avoidance on the ground of mistake, provided that the normal conditions as to the importance of the mistake are satisfied. Further, if the defendant was aware of the claimant's mistake and does not point it out, he will be guilty of fraud if good faith requires that he say something, except for value in French reformed contract law. Also, in France and Germany there are general duties of disclosure in the absence of fraud. In contrast, English law does not give a remedy for mistake in these circumstances, does not recognise that keeping silent may amount to fraud and has only limited duties of disclosure.

Perhaps an even more striking difference between the systems lies in the case in which one party enters the contract under a self-induced misapprehension about which the other party does not know, and has no reason to know. Here there is no element of dishonesty or reproachable behaviour on the part of the second party, and there is no question of liability in damages under any of the systems; but in principle French and German law may each allow relief, provided that the mistake was one as to the substance or sufficiently essential. English law gives no relief.

However, it should be said that in both French and German law the statement that a mistake that is as to substance or is essential gives rise to relief needs qualification. In French law the mistaken party's error may be branded *inexcusable* (Article 1132 Code civil) and relief be denied altogether. In German law relief on the ground of mistake is precluded where the rules on defects in property sold (§§ 433 ff BGB) apply, and if relief is given the mistaken party who avoids the contract may have to pay negative interest damages to the other under § 122 BGB.

The Dutch BW is perhaps less clear on the question of mistakes that are not known to the other party. Article 6:228 limits relief to cases in which the mistake was caused by incorrect information, was shared or in which:

BW   14.56 (NL)

Article 6:228: (1)(b) ... the other party, in view of what he knew or ought to know regarding the error, should have informed the party in error; ...

This may at first sight seem to suggest that the other party must have known, or have had reason to know, of the mistake; but Hartkamp and Tillema[362] deny that this is necessary, though pointing out that knowledge would be relevant to a claim for damages under BW Article 6:162.[363]

It will be seen that the PECL limit relief for mistake under Article 4:103 to cases where:

(i) the mistake was caused by information given by the other party; or (ii) the other party knew or ought to have known of the mistake and it was contrary to good faith and fair dealing to leave the mistaken party in error; or (iii) the other party made the same mistake, ...

In other words, under the PECL a party who has made a mistake will not obtain relief unless the other party knew or ought to have known of the mistake. The corresponding provision of the UNIDROIT Principles takes the same approach but in one respect is slightly broader:

UNIDROIT Principles   14.57 (INT)

Article 3.2.2: Relevant mistake

(1) A party may only avoid the contract for mistake if, when the contract was concluded, the mistake was of such importance that a reasonable person in the same situation as the party in error would only have concluded the contract on materially

---

[362] Hartkamp and Tillema (n 203 above) para 80.
[363] See above, p 540.

different terms or would not have concluded it at all if the true state of affairs had been known, and

    (a) the other party made the same mistake, or caused the mistake, or knew or ought to have known of the mistake and it was contrary to reasonable commercial standards of fair dealing to leave the mistaken party in error; or

    (b) the other party had not at the time of avoidance reasonably acted in reliance on the contract.

(2) However, a party may not avoid the contract if

    (a) it was grossly negligent in committing the mistake; or

    (b) the mistake relates to a matter in regard to which the risk of mistake was assumed or, having regard to the circumstances, should be borne by the mistaken party.

Article 3.2.2(1)(b) permits avoidance by a party whose unilateral mistake was unknown to and not caused by the other party, provided that the latter has not relied on the contract. This has parallels in some European laws,[364] but was not adopted as part of the PECL.

    On the question of fraud by silence, the Principles of European Contract Law quite clearly reject the common law approach:

Principles of European Contract Law

14.58 (INT)

Article 4:107: Fraud

    (1) A party may avoid a contract when it has been led to conclude it by the other party's fraudulent representation, whether by words or conduct, or fraudulent nondisclosure of any information which in accordance with good faith and fair dealing it should have disclosed.

    (2) A party's representation or non-disclosure is fraudulent if it was intended to deceive.

    (3) In determining whether good faith and fair dealing required that a party disclose particular information, regard should be had to all the circumstances, including:

    (a) whether the party had special expertise;

    (b) the cost to it of acquiring the relevant information;

    (c) whether the other party could reasonably acquire the information for itself; and

    (d) the apparent importance of the information to the other party.

It will be noted that the article on mistake also requires a party to point out certain mistakes to the other.

    The Draft Common Frame of Reference and the Common European Sales Law (CESL)[365] both take the same approach as the PECL, but add a new element: the contract may also be avoided where one party's mistake was caused by the other's failure to comply with 'information duties'.[366] Chapter 2 of the CESL, for example, includes

---

[364] See Note 5 to PECL Art 4:103.

[365] For a study of the development of 'European' and transnational rules on mistake, see N Jansen and R Zimmermann, 'Contract Formation and Mistake in European Contract Law: A Genetic Comparison of Transnational Model Rules' (2011) 31 OJLS 625.

[366] DCFR Art II.-7:201(1)(b)(iii); CESL Art 48(1)(b)(ii).

information duties on traders dealing with consumers, replicating the information duties required by the Consumer Rights Directive[367] and also a general duty on a trader dealing with another trader:

Common European Sales Law   14.59 (EU)

[Article 23:] Duty to disclose information about goods and related services

(1) Before the conclusion of a contract for the sale of goods, supply of digital content or provision of related services by a trader to another trader, the supplier has a duty to disclose by any appropriate means to the other trader any information concerning the main characteristics of the goods, digital content or related services to be supplied which the supplier has or can be expected to have and which it would be contrary to good faith and fair dealing not to disclose to the other party.

(2) In determining whether paragraph 1 requires the supplier to disclose any information, regard is to be had to all the circumstances, including:

(a) whether the supplier had special expertise;

(b) the cost to the supplier of acquiring the relevant information;

(c) the ease with which the other trader could have acquired the information by other means;

(d) the nature of the information;

(e) the likely importance of the information to the other trader; and

(f) good commercial practice in the situation concerned.

It is also interesting to note the remedies provided. The Consumer Rights Directive (CRD) provides that where a trader making a distance or off-premises contract is required to give information to the consumer, the information given 'shall form an integral part of the contract';[368] so a consumer who has been given wrong information will have a remedy for non-conformity or other breach of contract.[369] But the CRD does not provide a remedy for if the trader fails to give the information,[370] other than to give the consumer who has not been given information about the right to withdraw[371] the right to withdraw until the information has been provided,[372] and a breach of the Unfair Commercial Practices Directive does not affect the contract at all.[373] The CESL provided for damages for

---

[367] Directive 2011/83/EU of 25 October 2011, Arts 5 and 6.

[368] CRD Art 6(5).

[369] For how this has been implemented in the UK, see Consumer Rights Act 2015, ss 11(4), 12 and 19(4).

[370] The UK gives the consumer a remedy of damages for this case: Consumer Contracts (Information, Cancellation and Additional Charges) Regulations 2013/3134, reg 18.

[371] CRD Art 6(1)(h).

[372] CRD Art 10. There is a cut-off after 12 months.

[373] Article 3(1).

failing to give information or giving incorrect information, and also for avoidance when the failure to inform gives rise to a mistake:

Common European Sales Law   **14.60 (EU)**

[Article 28:] Duty to ensure that information supplied is correct

(1) A party who supplies information before or at the time a contract is concluded, whether in order to comply with the duties imposed by this Chapter or otherwise, has a duty to take reasonable care to ensure that the information supplied is correct and is not misleading.

(2) A party to whom incorrect or misleading information has been supplied in breach of the duty referred to in paragraph 1, and who reasonably relies on that information in concluding a contract with the party who supplied it, has the remedies set out in Article 29.

(3) In relations between a trader and a consumer the parties may not, to the detriment of the consumer, exclude the application of this Article or derogate from or vary its effects.

[Article 29:] Remedies for breach of information duties

(1) A party which has failed to comply with any duty imposed by this Chapter is liable for any loss caused to the other party by such failure.

(2) Where the trader has not complied with the information requirements relating to additional charges or other costs as referred to in Article 14 or on the costs of returning the goods as referred to in Article 17(2) the consumer is not liable to pay the additional charges and other costs.

(3) The remedies provided under this Article are without prejudice to any remedy which may be available under Article 42 (2), Article 48 or Article 49.

(4) In relations between a trader and a consumer the parties may not, to the detriment of the consumer, exclude the application of this Article or derogate from or vary its effects.

CESL Article 48(1)(b)(ii) included as one of the situations in which a contract may be avoided (subject to the other conditions of the Article[374]) the case where the party caused the contract to be concluded by failing to comply with a precontractual information duty.

14.6.B DUTIES TO DISCLOSE: WHY SUCH DIFFERENCES?

Readers may be interested in considering two related questions. The first is why there are such differences in attitude towards non-disclosure in the common law and the continental systems. Is it simply an accident of history? Can it be explained by the typical cases which are heard by the courts in the different countries? English contract law is often dominated by cases between commercial businesses which were operating at arm's length, where perhaps good faith would not require disclosure; possibly the

---

[374] Which are the same as those of PECL Art 4:103, see 14.8 (INT), above, p 497.

English rule is aimed primarily at such cases, but is applied, too broadly, to all cases. Or may the difference reflect underlying philosophies about law and the role of the legal system?[375]

Secondly, what should the law on self-induced mistake and nondisclosure be?[376]

One argument made by Kronman and Rudden is an economic one.[377] Consider the example (somewhat out of date, perhaps, but the point is still valid) given by Cockburn CJ in his judgment in *Smith v Hughes*:[378] the buyer of land knows that there is coal (Cockburn CJ refers to 'a mine') under the land and also knows that the sellers do not know this. Should the buyer have to reveal its knowledge? An argument against imposing a duty of disclosure on the buyer is that it will have discovered the coal only through a costly investigation. If it has to reveal its information, it will lose its advantage and it will no longer be worthwhile investing in costly investigations. That would be inefficient.[379]

But even if the efficiency argument is accepted, should the coal company be allowed to buy the land at its normal agricultural value when it is worth so much more? Is the additional value of the land once it is known to contain coal in direct proportion to the cost of exploration? If the cost of exploration is less than the increased value, is there any way in which the court might allow the mining company some advantage, so as to encourage it to search for coal, yet have to pay something extra to X?

FURTHER READING

Aubert de Vincelles, C, 'Validity of Contract: *Dol, Erreur* and *Obligation d'Information*' in J Cartwright and S Whittaker (eds), *The Code Napoléon Rewritten: French Contract Law after the 2016 Reforms* (Oxford: Hart Publishing, 2017) 79–108.

Beale, H, 'The Europeanisation of Contract Law' in R Halson (ed), *Exploring the Boundaries of Contract Law* (Aldershot: Dartmouth, 1996) 23–47.

—— *Mistake and Non-disclosure of Facts: Models for English Contract Law* (Oxford University Press, 2012)

Cartwright, J, 'Defects of Consent in Contract Law', in A Hartkamp et al (eds), *Towards a European Civil Code* (4th edn, Alphen aan den Rijn: Wolters Kluwer, 2011) 537–54.

Eisenberg, M, 'Disclosure in Contract Law' (2003) 91 California Law Review 1645–92.

Ernst, W, 'Mistake' in J Basedow, K Hopt and R Zimmermann (eds), *Max Planck Encyclopedia of European Private Law* (Oxford University Press, 2012) 1175–79.

Fabre-Magnan, M, 'Duties of Disclosure and French Contract Law: Contribution to an Economic Analysis' in J Beatson and D Friedmann (eds), *Good Faith and Fault in Contract Law* (Oxford: Clarendon Press, 1995) 99–120.

---

[375] These issues are explored in H Beale, *Mistake and Non-disclosure of Facts: Models for English Contract Law* (Oxford University Press, 2012).

[376] Pieces worth reading include AT Kronman 'Mistake, Disclosure, Information and the Law of Contracts' (1978) 7 JLS 1; AT Kronman 'Contract Law and Distributive Justice' (1980) 89 Yale LJ 472; B Rudden 'Le juste et l'inefficace pour un non-devoir de renseignements' RTD civ 1985, 91; Fabre-Magnan (n 9 above) 99–120; Hart in *Alternativkommentar zum BGB* § 119 BGB paras 27–29; M Eisenberg, 'Disclosure in Contract Law' (2003) 91 California LR 1645.

[377] The economic arguments have been refined considerably since Kronman wrote. For a very helpful survey and conclusions, see Eisenberg (n 376 above).

[378] See 14.41 (EN), above, p 567.

[379] You may wish to look again at the description of the discussion that preceded the adoption of a precontractual duty of disclosure in the reformed French Code civil, above, p 575.

Fauvarque-Cosson, B, 'L'erreur en droit anglais' [2003] RDC 233–45.

Harris, D and Tallon, D (eds), *Contract Law Today: Anglo-French Comparisons* (Oxford: Clarendon Press, 1989) 151–93.

Hartkamp, A and Tillema, MM, *Contract Law in the Netherlands* (The Hague/Boston: Kluwer, 1995) paras 71–84.

Hellwege, P, 'Invalidity' in J Basedow, K Hopt and R Zimmermann (eds), *Max Planck Encyclopedia of European Private Law* (Oxford University Press, 2012) 990–94.

Jansen, N and Zimmermann, R, 'Contract Formation and Mistake in European Contract Law: A Genetic Comparison of Transnational Model Rules' (2011) 31 OJLS 625–62.

Kötz, H, *European Contract Law* (2nd edn, Oxford University Press, 2017) 149–89.

Kronman, A, 'Mistake, Disclosure, Information and the Law of Contracts' (1978) 7 JLS 1–34.

—— 'Contract Law and Distributive Justice' (1980) 89 Yale LJ 472–511.

Lohsse, S, 'Validity' in N Jansen and R Zimmermann (eds), *Commentaries on European Contract Laws* (Oxford University Press, 2018) 649–739.

MacMillan, C, *Mistakes in Contract Law* (Oxford: Hart Publishing, 2010).

Markesinis, BS, Unberath, H and Johnston, A, *The German Law of Contract*, 2nd edn (Oxford: Hart Publishing, 2006) 276–314.

Martens, S, 'Fraud' in J Basedow, K Hopt and R Zimmermann (eds), *Max Planck Encyclopedia of European Private Law* (Oxford University Press, 2012) 730–33.

Sefton-Green, R (ed), *Mistake, Fraud and Duties to Inform in European Contract Law* (Cambridge University Press, 2005).

Zweigert, K and Kötz, H, *Introduction to Comparative Law* (3rd edn, Oxford: Clarendon Press, 1998) 411–30.

CHAPTER 15
THREATS

15.1 INTRODUCTION

In the continental legal systems, both the doctrines of freedom of contract and sanctity of contract are closely linked with the notion of party autonomy, in that a person may conclude a contract if he so wishes and is legally bound to a contract if he so wills. However, a party's will may be defective in a number of ways, as in the case where the party was mistaken, or deceived or threatened by the other party (or a third person). These instances are known to civilian lawyers as the 'defects of consent' (*Willensmängel, vices du consentement*), which, in French, traditionally include *erreur, dol, violence*.[1] As a general rule, a defect of consent, existing at the moment of conclusion of the contract, affects the validity of the contract. As the previous chapter shows, even systems which do not recognise the will theory, such as the common law, accept that in some circumstances a party's consent may not have been validly given, though in such systems the focus may be more on the acts of the other party (for example that he gave inaccurate information) than on the subjective state of mind of the claimant.

The different approaches of French and German law on the one hand (concentrating on the will of the threatened party) and English law on the other (concentrating on the illegitimacy of the threat by the other party) produce rather different results in two types of case: (1) that in France, taking advantage of the claimant's predicament, not caused by the defendant, is seen as a kind of threat (in German law this seems to get swept into public policy under § 138 BGB), and (2) in cases where the threat emanates from a third person. That gives a right to avoidance under French and German law, but not under English law unless the defendant had notice of the threat.

This chapter first examines the question whether and, if so, under what conditions a contract may be avoided if a party entered into the contract under the influence of a threat (15.2). Clearly, not all threats are actionable in law as some threats are part of everyday (business) life. For instance, if A is negotiating to buy a car from B, who is a car dealer, and A threatens that if B does not reduce the price A will instead buy a car from C, and B does reduce the price, B cannot then avoid the contract with A on the ground of threat. In order to distinguish threats on the basis of which a contract may be avoided from

---

[1] cf H Kötz, *European Contract Law* (2nd edn, Oxford University Press, 2017) 173–89.

those which do not, legal systems give specific rules. Thus, the continental jurisdictions are concerned only with psychological constraints (15.2.A) but do not restrict their doctrines of threat to particular means or objects of pressure, as was traditionally the case in English law (15.2.B). All legal systems agree that a threat must be illegitimate in order to avoid a contract (15.2.C). Furthermore, the jurisdictions discussed require—in one way or another—that the threatened party entered into the contract as a result of the threat (15.2.D) and that the threat is sufficiently serious and imminent as to determine the will of a reasonable person or the party in question (15.2.E).

Lastly, it will be considered whether a contract can be avoided where it has been made as the result of a threat not by the other party to the contract, but by a third person (15.3).

15.2 THREATS

Article 4:108: Threats[2]
A party may avoid a contract when it has been led to conclude it by the other party's imminent and serious threat of an act:

(a) which is wrongful in itself, or

(b) which it is wrongful to use as a means to obtain the conclusion of the contract, unless in the circumstances the first party had a reasonable alternative.

Article 1140: There is duress where one party contracts under the influence of a constraint which makes him fear that his person or his wealth, or those of his near relatives, might be exposed to considerable harm.

Article 1141: A threat of legal action does not constitute duress, except where the legal process is deflected from its proper purpose or where it is invoked or exercised in order to obtain a manifestly excessive advantage.

Article 1142: Duress is a ground of nullity regardless of whether it has been applied by the other party or by a third party.

Article 1143: There is also duress where one contracting party exploits the other's state of dependence on him and obtains an undertaking to which the latter would not have agreed in the absence of such constraint, and gains from it a manifestly excessive advantage.

Article 1144: In the case of mistake or fraud the period for bringing an action for nullity runs only from the day when they were discovered, and in the case of duress the period runs only from the day when it ceased.

---

[2] cf Art II.-7:206 DCFR; Art 50 CESL: 'Threats. A party may avoid a contract if the other party has induced the conclusion of the contract by the threat of wrongful, imminent and serious harm, or of a wrongful act.'

Note

In the official translation of the provisions of the Code civil the word 'duress' is used instead of 'threat' (similarly § 123(I) BGB, below). Under the new Code civil there are two types of threat: threat by the other party or a third party (Articles 1140–1142) and one which concerns the exploitation of the other's state of dependence (Article 1143). The latter will be discussed in Chapter 16.[3]

BGB	**15.3 (DE)**

§ 123: Voidability on the grounds of deceit or duress
(1) A person who has been induced to make a declaration of intent by deceit or unlawfully by duress may avoid the declaration.

BW	**15.4 (NL)**

Article 3:44: (1) A juridical act may be annulled when it has been entered into as a result of threat, fraud or abuse of circumstances.
(2) A person who induces another to execute a certain juridical act by unlawfully threatening him or a third party with harm to his person or property, makes a threat. The threat must be such that a reasonable person would be influenced by it.

Note

In addition, in Dutch law, a business to consumer (B2C) contract which is induced by an aggressive commercial practice (Articles 6:193h, 6:193i BW) can be avoided under Article 6:193j(3) BW.

In English law it has long been established that a contract that was entered into because of a threat by one party to kill or injure the other party can be avoided by the threatened party (eg *Barton v Armstrong*[4]); some decisions also recognised duress if the threat was of wrongful seizure of the claimant's goods (eg *Astley v Reynolds*[5]) though others denied it (eg *Skeate v Beale*[6]). In the last century the courts accepted not only 'duress of goods' but also that a threat to cause the other party financial harm could amount to 'economic duress'.

---

[3] On threat see F Chénedé, *Le nouveau droit des obligations et des contrats: Consolidations, innovations, perspectives* (Paris: Dalloz, 2016) nos. 23.141–23.167; O Deshayes, T Genicon and YM Laithier, *Réforme du droit des contrats, du régime général et de la preuve des obligations, Commentaire article par article* (Paris: LexisNexis, 2016) 214–28; M Latina, M and G Chantepie, *La réforme du droit des obligations: Commentaire théorique et pratique dans l'ordre du Code civil* (Paris: Dalloz, 2016) nos. 331–43.
[4] [1976] AC 104, 15.10 (EN), below, p 614.
[5] (1731) 2 Str 915.
[6] (1841) 11 Ad & E 983.

Universe Tankships Inc of Monrovia v International Transport Workers Federation (The Universe Sentinel)[7]

Whether a threat is (il)legitimate depends on the nature of the threat and the nature of the demand.

Facts: The defendants had 'blacked' (refused to work on it) a ship owned by the plaintiffs, preventing it from leaving port. In order to obtain the lifting of the blacking, the plaintiffs agreed to comply to the defendants' demand to pay a contribution to a general welfare fund for sailors. The plaintiffs feared catastrophic financial consequences if they did not submit because the ship was off-hire under a time charter while the blacking continued.

Judgment: LORD SCARMAN [dissenting, though not on this point]: … It is, I think, already established law that economic pressure can in law amount to duress; and that duress, if proved, not only renders voidable a transaction into which a person has entered under its compulsion but is actionable as a tort, if it causes damage or loss: *Barton v Armstrong* [1976] AC 104 and *PaoOn v LauYiu Long* [1980] AC 614. The authorities upon which these two cases were based reveal two elements in the wrong of duress: (1) pressure amounting to compulsion of the will of the victim; and (2) the illegitimacy of the pressure exerted. There must be pressure, the practical effect of which is compulsion or the absence of choice. Compulsion is variously described in the authorities as coercion or the vitiation of consent. The classic case of duress is, however, not the lack of will to submit but the victim's intentional submission arising from the realisation that there is no other practical choice open to him. This is the thread of principle which links the early law of duress (threat to life and limb) with later developments when the law came also to recognise as duress first the threat to property and now the threat to a man's business or trade. The development is well traced in Goff and Jones, *The Law of Restitution*, 2nd ed (1978), chapter 9.

The absence of choice can be proved in various ways, e.g. by protest, by the absence of independent advice, or by a declaration of intention to go to law to recover the money paid or the property transferred: see *Maskell v Horner* [1915] 3 KB 106. But none of these evidential matters goes to the essence of duress. The victim's silence will not assist the bully, if the lack of any practicable choice to submit is proved. The present case is an excellent illustration. There was no protest at the time, but only a determination to do whatever was needed as rapidly as possible to release the ship. Yet nobody challenges the judge's finding that the owner acted under compulsion …

The real issue in the appeal is, therefore, as to the second element in the wrong duress: was the pressure applied by the ITF in the circumstances of this case one which the law recognises as legitimate? For, as Lord Wilberforce and Lord Simon of Glaisdale said in *Barton v Armstrong* [1976] AC 104, 121D: 'the pressure must be one of a kind which the law does not regard as legitimate.'

As the two noble and learned Lords remarked at p 121D, in life, including the life of commerce and finance, many acts are done 'under pressure, sometimes overwhelming pressure': but they are not necessarily done under duress. That depends on whether the circumstances are such that the law regards the pressure as legitimate.

[7] [1983] 1 AC 366.

In determining what is legitimate two matters may have to be considered. The first is as to the nature of the pressure. In many cases this will be decisive, though not in every case. And so the second question may have to be considered, namely, the nature of the demand which the pressure is applied to support.

15.2.A A PHYSICAL COMPULSION AS OPPOSED TO PSYCHOLOGICAL PRESSURE

In the jurisdictions of continental Europe a distinction is made between physical compulsion (*vis absoluta*) and psychological pressure (*vis compulsiva*). Where actual physical force is used to compel a party to enter into a contract, for example if one party takes the other party's hand and makes him sign a document, there is no freedom of choice and, as a consequence, no contract comes into being, or differently put, the contract is void. In the case of psychological pressure, on the other hand, the threatened party does have a choice, albeit between what he considers to be the lesser of two evils (*coactus volui, tamen volui*). However, his consent to enter into the contract is defective because of the pressure put on him: he consents because he fears the consequences of not entering into the contract. The contract can therefore be avoided by the threatened person.[8]

In English law the distinction between physical compulsion and psychological pressure appears to be unknown. The common law concept of duress to the person is said to consist of actual or threatened physical violence, but it seems that the references are normally just to different forms of psychological pressure. In either case the contract may be avoided.[9] It may be that the case of the person whose hand is literally forced would be dealt with under another doctrine, that of *non est factum* (the Latin phrase means literally: 'This is not my deed').[10] Under this doctrine a person can simply deny that they agreed to the document even though it bears their signature. If so, the contract would be void.

15.2.B THE MEANS OF COMPULSION

At one time the common law concept of duress was restricted to actual or threatened violence to, and unlawful constraint of, the person of the contracting party (duress to the person).[11] Unlawful detention of another's goods, or threats of such detention, did not constitute duress.[12] In *The Siboen and the Sibotre*,[13] Kerr J rejected this stern concept of duress. His opinion has been accepted in later cases, for instance in the decision below.

---

[8] See, eg, F Terré, P Simler and Y Lequette, *Les obligations* (11th edn, Paris: Dalloz, 2013) nos. 241 ff; K Zweigert and H Kötz, *Introduction to Comparative Law* (3rd edn, Oxford: Clarendon Press, 1995) 428.

[9] See *Treitel on the Law of Contract*, 14th edn by E Peel (London: Sweet & Maxwell, 2015) para 10-002; E McKendrick, *Contract Law* (12th edn, Basingstoke: Palgrave Macmillan, 2017) 318. Contrast: Restatement 2d of Contracts §174 ('When Duress by Physical Compulsion Prevents Formation of a Contract') and § 175 ('When Duress by Threat Makes a Contract Voidable').

[10] See *Chitty on Contracts*, 33rd edn by H Beale (gen ed) (London: Sweet & Maxwell/Thomson Reuters, 2018) para 8-007 and, on *non est factum*, paras 3-049 ff; *Treitel* (n 9 above) paras 8-079 ff.

[11] See, eg, *Barton v Armstrong* [1976] AC 104, 15.10 (EN), below, p 614.

[12] eg *Skeate v Beale* (1840) 11 Ad & E 983.

[13] [1976] 1 Lloyd's Rep 293 (QBD).

North Ocean Shipping Co Ltd v Hyundai Construction Co, Ltd
(The Atlantic Baron)[14]

An agreement to alter the terms of an existing contract entered into as the result of a threat by one party to break the terms of the existing contract if the alteration is not agreed to may be voidable on the grounds of duress if the party threatened had no practical alternative but to give in to the threat.

Facts: On 10 April 1972 a shipbuilding company agreed to build a ship (the *Atlantic Baron*) for the owners at a fixed price in US dollars, payable in five instalments. The shipbuilders opened a letter of credit by way of security for repayment of the instalments in the event of their default in the performance of the contract. After payment of the first instalment, the US dollar devalued by 10%. The shipbuilders threatened not to deliver the ship unless the owners would agree to increase the remaining instalments by 10%. The owners asserted that there was no legal ground for the shipbuilders' claim, but on 28 June 1973 they agreed (by telex) to pay the additional 10% 'without prejudice' to their rights, as they were afraid to lose a very lucrative contract for the charter of the ship, which at that time they were negotiating with Shell. In turn, the owners requested the shipbuilders to increase the letter of credit by 10%, which the shipbuilders did. The owners paid the remaining instalments, including the 10% increase, without protest and in November 1974 the shipbuilders delivered the ship. Some eight months later the owners claimed the return of the additional 10% paid on the last four instalments; they argued that they did not make the claim earlier because they feared that the delivery of the sister ship might be affected, but in arbitration this fear was found to be groundless. For their claim, the owners asserted that there had been no consideration for their promise to pay the extra 10% and that they had entered into that agreement under duress.

Held: It was held (1) that the shipbuilders had given consideration for the owners' promise to pay the additional 10% by increasing the letter of credit by corresponding percentage and (2) that the shipbuilders' threat to break the original contract unless the owners agreed to increase their payments amounted to economic duress. The agreement of 28 June 1973 was therefore voidable; it was found, however, that the owners, by paying the increased instalments without protest and by waiting for eight months before bringing their claim, had affirmed the agreement.

Judgment: MOCATTA J: … Having reached the conclusion that there was consideration for the agreement made on June 28 … 1973, I must next consider whether even if that agreement, varying the terms of the original shipbuilding contract of 10 April 1972, was made under a threat to break that original contract and the various increased instalments were made consequently under the varied contract, the increased sums can be recovered as money had and received [a restitutionary remedy for unjust enrichment].

[The judge then considered the English case law and literature, as well as a number of Australian cases, especially the judgment of Isaacs J in *Smith v William Charlick Ltd* (1924) 34 CLR 38, as to the question whether the doctrine of duress is limited to either duress to the person of the contracting party or to goods.]

Before proceeding further it may be useful to summarise the conclusions I have so far reached. First, I do not take the view that the recovery of money paid under duress other than to the person is necessarily limited to duress to goods falling within one of the categories hitherto established by the English cases. I would respectfully follow and adopt the broad statement of principle laid down by Isaacs J cited earlier and frequently quoted and applied in the Australian cases. Secondly, from this it follows that the compulsion

---

[14] [1979] 1 QB 705.

may take the form of 'economic duress' if the necessary facts are proved. A threat to break a contract may amount to such 'economic duress'. Thirdly, if there has been such a form of duress leading to a contract for consideration, I think that contract is a voidable one which can be avoided and the excess money paid under it recovered.

I think that the facts found in this case do establish that the agreement to increase the price by 10 per cent reached at the end of June 1973 was caused by what may be called 'economic duress'. The Yard [ie the respondent shipbuilders] were adamant in insisting on the increased price without having any legal justification for so doing and the owners realised that the Yard would not accept anything other than an unqualified agreement to the increase. The owners might have claimed damages in arbitration against the Yard with all the inherent unavoidable uncertainties of litigation, but in view of the position of the Yard vis-à-vis their relations with Shell it would be unreasonable to hold that this is the course they should have taken: see *Astley v Reynolds* (1731) 2 Str 915. The owners made a very reasonable offer of arbitration coupled with security for any award in the Yard's favour that might be made, but this was refused. They then made their agreement, which can truly I think be said to have been made under compulsion, by the telex of 28 June without prejudice to their rights. I do not consider the Yard's ignorance of the Shell charter material. It may well be that had they known of it they would have been more exigent.

If I am right in the conclusion reached with some doubt earlier that there was consideration for the 10 per cent increase agreement reached at the end of June 1973, and it be right to regard this as having been reached under a kind of duress in the form of economic pressure, then what is said in *Chitty on Contracts*, 24th ed (1977), vol 1, para 442, p 207 ... is relevant, namely, that a contract entered into under duress is voidable and not void:

> '... consequently a person who has entered into a contract under duress, may either affirm or avoid such contract after the duress has ceased; and if he has so voluntarily acted under it with a full knowledge of all the circumstances he may be held bound on the ground of ratification, or if, after escaping from the duress, he takes no steps to set aside the transaction, he may be found to have affirmed it ...'

On the other hand, the findings of fact in the special case [arbitration] present difficulties whether one is proceeding on the basis of a voidable agreement reached at the end of June 1973, or whether such agreement was void for want of consideration, and it were necessary in consequence to establish that the payments were made involuntarily and not with the intention of closing the transaction.

I have already stated that no protest of any kind was made by the owners after their telex of June 28, 1973, before their claim in this arbitration on 30 July 1975, shortly after in July of that year the *Atlantic Baroness*, a sister ship of the *Atlantic Baron*, had been tendered, though, as I understand it, she was not accepted and arbitration proceedings in regard to her are in consequence taking place. There was therefore a delay between 27 November 1974, when the *Atlantic Baron* was delivered and 30 July 1975, before the owners put forward their claim.

The owners were, therefore, free from the duress on 27 November 1974, and took no action by way of protest or otherwise between their important telex of 28 June 1973, and their formal claim for return of the excess 10 per cent paid of 30 July 1975, when they nominated their arbitrator. One cannot dismiss this delay as of no significance, though I would not consider it conclusive by itself. I do not attach any special importance to the lack of protest made at the time of the assignment, since the documents made no reference to the increased 10 per cent. However, by the time the *Atlantic Baron* was due for delivery in November 1974, market conditions had changed radically, as is found in paragraph 39 of the special case [the decision of the arbitrators] and the owners must have been aware of this. The special case finds in paragraph 40, as stated earlier, that the owners did not believe that the Yard would have refused to deliver the vessel or the *Atlantic Baroness* and had no reason so to believe ... after careful consideration, I have come to the conclusion that the important points here are that since there was no danger at this time in registering a protest, the final payments were made without any qualification and were followed by a delay until 31 July 1975, before the owners put forward their claim, the correct inference to draw, taking an objective view of the facts, is that the action and inaction of the owners can only be regarded as an affirmation of the variation in June 1973 of the terms of the original contract by the agreement to pay the additional 10 per cent. In reaching this conclusion I have not, of course, over-looked the findings in paragraph 45 of the special case, but I do not think that an inten-tion on the part of the owners not to affirm the agreement for the extra payment not indicated to the Yard can avail them in the view of their overt acts. As was said in *Deacon v Transport Regulation Board* [1958] VR 458, 460 in considering whether a payment was made voluntarily or not: 'No secret mental reservation of the doer is material. The ques-tion is—what would his conduct indicate to a reasonable man as his mental state.' I think this test is equally applicable to the decision this court has to make whether a voidable contract has been affirmed or not, and I have applied this test in reaching the conclusion I have just expressed ...

Notes

(1) Today, duress to the person, and duress to goods or economic duress may entitle a party to avoid a contract.[15]

(2) Economic duress had earlier been recognised in US law.[16]

(3) *The Siboen and the Sibotre*[17] was a case of economic compulsion as the plain-tiffs exerted commercial pressure on the defendants by threatening them with breach of contract—yet the plea of duress failed because the pressure was acceptable and had not vitiated the defendant's consent.[18] Another example of economic duress can be found in the case of *Universe Tankships Inc of Monrovia v International Transport Workers Federation* (*The Universe Sentinel*),[19] where the defendants had 'blacked' (had refused to work on) a ship owned by the plaintiffs, preventing it from leaving port. In order to obtain the lifting of the blacking, the plaintiffs agreed to comply with the defendants' demand to pay a contribution to a general welfare fund for sailors. The plaintiffs feared catastrophic financial consequences if they would not submit because the ship was off-hire under a time charter while the blacking continued.

---

[15] *Dimskal Shipping Co SA v ITF (The 'Evia Luck')* [1992] 2 AC 152, 165 (HL). See McKendrick (n 9 above) 318.

[16] See, eg, Dawson 'Economic Duress—An Essay in Perspective' (1947) 45 Mich LR 253.

[17] [1976] 1 Lloyd's Rep 293 (QBD).

[18] See also *The Atlantic Baron* 15.6 (EN), above; *Pao On v Lau Yiu Long* [1980] AC 614 (PC).

[19] [1983] AC 366, 15.5 (EN), above, p 600 and 15.9 (EN), below, p 612.

The civil law systems take a rather broad view of the means and object of threat. The nature of the threatened harm may be physical, moral or pecuniary.[20] The only restriction is that 'A threat of legal action does not constitute duress' (Article 1140 Code civil). § 123(1) BGB does not mention the means or object of threat, but, according to some authors,[21] any kind of harm, material or immaterial, may suffice.[22]

Like the civil law jurisdictions, Article 4:108 of the PECL does not restrict threat to any particular means.[23] Comment A to Article 4:108 PECL reads:

> It is not only threats of physical violence or damage to property which constitute wrongful threats. A threat to inflict economic loss wrongfully, e.g. by breaking a contract, can equally constitute duress.

> *Illustration 2*: X owes a large debt to Y. Knowing that Y desperately needs the money, X tells Y that he will not pay it unless Y agrees to sell X a house which Y owns at a price well below its market value. Faced with bankruptcy, Y agrees. X then pays the debt. Y may avoid the contract to sell the house.

In practice the threat of a breach of contract is often used in an attempt to secure renegotiation of the same contract. In this case the renegotiation agreement may be avoided.

> *Illustration 3*: C has agreed to build a ship for D at a fixed price. Because of currency fluctuations which affect various subcontracts, C will lose a great deal if the contract price is not changed and it threatens not to deliver unless D agrees to pay 10% extra. D will suffer serious harm if the contract is not performed. D pays the extra sum demanded by C. D may recover the extra sum paid.

Under Article 4:108 PECL, a threat may consist of an act or omission.[24]

A contract can be avoided on the ground of threat if the pressure was directed against a third person under French law.[25] Equally, in German law, a threat against a third person may constitute a threat in the sense of § 123(1) BGB.[26] The English courts have held that pressure directed against a third person may amount to (actual) undue influence (see, for example, *Williams v Bayley*,[27] in which there was a threat to prosecute the son of the contracting party, and *Kaufman v Gerson*,[28] where there was a threat to prosecute the husband of the contracting party). It is generally accepted that these cases should now be seen as examples of economic duress.[29] Some English authors are of the opinion that the

---

[20] See Terré et al (n 8 above) no. 244; P Malaurie, L Aynès and P Stoffel-Munck, *Droit des obligations* (9th edn, Paris: Defrénois, 2017) no. 516.

[21] Palandt/Ellenberger § 123 BGB para 15.

[22] For a French and a Dutch case of economic threat, see Cass com 28 May 1991, no. 89-17672, Bull civ IV no. 180, D 1992, 166 annotated by P Morvan; HR 27 March 1992, NJ 1992, 377.

[23] See also Art 3.2.6 UNIDROIT PICC.

[24] cf Art 3.2.6 UNIDROIT PICC.

[25] cf for the Netherlands: Art 3:44(2) BW; AS Hartkamp & CH Sieburgh, *Mr. C. Assers Handleiding tot de beoefening van het Nederlands Burgerlijk Recht. 6. Verbintenissenrecht. Deel III. Algemeen overeenkomstenrecht* (Deventer: Kluwer, 2014) no. 260.

[26] See Palandt/Ellenberger § 123 para 15. See, eg, BGH 23 September 1957, BGHZ 25, 217 (threat to prosecute the husband of the contracting party), 15.8 (DE), below, p 608.

[27] (1866) LR 1 HL 200 (HL).

[28] [1904] 1 KB 591 (CA).

[29] See A Burrows, *Law of Restitution* (3rd edn, London: Butterworths, 2011) 280–81.

third person need not necessarily be related to the contracting person, and that the third person may even be a total stranger to him.[30]

15.2.C THREAT MUST BE ILLEGITIMATE

All legal systems recognise that a threat must be illegitimate in order to avoid a contract.[31]

Cass civ (1), 3 November 1959[32]   **15.7 (FR)**

The inexperienced widow

A threat of exercising a right is illegitimate if the person threatening is doing so to achieve a goal, such as the conclusion of a contract, which was not the purpose for which his right is given.

Facts: On 15 March 1947 Mrs Y, a widow, successfully bid at auction to acquire the house in which she had always lived. Two days later Mr X, a business agent, obtained from Mrs Y her agreement to withdraw from her acquisition of the property, in the form of a mandate in his favour authorising a declaration that she had been acting in the auction on his behalf. Mr X thus took her place as the successful bidder. Mrs Y sought to avoid her declaration on the ground of threat: she had given in to Mr X's threat that he would exercise his right *de surenchérir* (see below, Note 1). The contested judgment was challenged by Mr X on the ground that it annulled the said declaration as having been vitiated by threat despite the fact that the cour d'appel had not established the existence of coercion on the part of Mr X, that it had not taken into account the true statement that he had the right to make a higher bid and that Mrs Y, a capable woman in possession of her faculties, had freely signed an advantageous agreement.

Held: The Cour de cassation upheld the decision of the cour d'appel to annul the declaration on the ground of threat and dismissed the appeal on a point of law.

Judgment:—Whereas the appellate court noted the unremitting steps taken by Mr X in relation to Mrs Y, together with his repeated threats that he would outbid her and that, having successfully bid for the property, he would immediately evict her if she did not agree to withdraw and let him take her place as the successful bidder in return for a promise to provide her with accommodation for a further two years and to pay her 25,000 francs; as it found that on 17 March, in the course of one of his final visits to the home of Mrs Y, whom he found alone, Mr X at last succeeded in overcoming her resistance and got her to sign the document which he had brought with him, already prepared, under pressure of the same threats which he had previously used, in order to instil in that inexperienced woman 'such fear as to rob her of her free will and to override her consent, which she would not otherwise have given' to an act which would deprive her of a house which she had acquired only in order to be able to continue living in it.

---

[30] See *Chitty* (n 10 above) para 8-012; H McGregor, *Contract Code (Drawn up on behalf of the English Law Commission)* (London: Sweet & Maxwell, 1994) 221 (Comment to s 562). See also Restatement 2d of Contracts, Comment to § 176 and Illustration 5.

[31] Kötz (n 1 above) 185–89.

[32] D 1960.2.187, annotated by G Holleaux, RTD civ 1960, 295, annotated by H and L Mazeaud.

— Whereas the contested judgment further states that, although Mr X undoubtedly had the right to submit a higher bid and, in the event of his bid being successful, to institute eviction proceedings, the existence of that right 'was nevertheless incapable of rendering the compulsion exerted by him lawful, since Mr X, who had no right or entitlement capable of justifying his claim to require the signature of a declaration that Mrs Y had been acting on his behalf or her withdrawal in his favour, was not seeking to assert a legitimate right'.

— Whereas having regard to those absolute findings and assessments, the contested judgment, which contains a sufficient statement of reasons, constitutes justification in law for the decision of the appellate court.

Notes

(1) In this case, X had a right *de surenchérir*, ie a right to outbid others at auction. This right may be exercised even within 10 days after the last and highest bid has been made (in this case by Y).[33] If X had asserted that right, he would have been legally entitled to force Y to leave the house. However, X threatened Y that he would exercise his right *de surenchérir* in order to obtain from Y a declaration that she had been acting in the auction on X's behalf (which X in fact did obtain, thus depriving Y of her own rights in the house). As the right *de surenchérir* is not given for this purpose, X was guilty of abuse of right, rendering the threat illegitimate.[34]

(2) Threats of physical violence are always illegitimate; threats of exercise of a right (for example legal action), on the other hand, are legitimate, unless the exercise of a right amounts to abuse of right. The Cour de cassation thus ruled:[35]

[T]he threat of recourse to legal action constitutes violence within the meaning of Articles 1111 [now Articles 1140] et seq only if there is an abuse of the right to resort to such action, either because it is exercised for a purpose other than the achievement of its proper objective or because it is used in order to obtain a promise or an advantage which is unrelated or disproportionate to the essential obligation owed.

For instance, a woman who was caught shoplifting at Monoprix was made to agree to pay 5,000 francs to the firm to refrain from taking proceedings against her.[36] As the 5,000 francs was far greater than the amount of the firm's loss, the Court held that there was abuse of right.

(3) Apart from abuse of right, a threat to exercise a right may also be illegitimate if it is accompanied by illegitimate means of pressure, for instance a threat of a strike coupled with (threats of) physical violence.[37]

---

[33] See P Malaurie, L Aynès and PY Gautier, *Droit des contrats spéciaux* (9th edn, Paris: Defrénois, 2017) no. 166.

[34] cf the note by Holleaux: 'The objective pursued by the perpetrator of the violence was an objective other than the normal purpose to be achieved by exercising the right which he may have possessed. There was thus an abuse.'

[35] Cass civ (3) 17 January 1984, no. 82-15753, Bull civ III no. 13.

[36] CA Paris 31 May 1966, Gaz Pal 1966.2.194, RTD civ 1967, 147, annotated by J Chevallier.

[37] See Cass soc 8 November 1984, no. 82-14816, Bull civ V no. 423.

BGH, 23 September 1957[38] **15.8 (DE)**

The threatened wife

*If the means and the purpose of the exerted pressure are in themselves legitimate, the threat may nevertheless be illegitimate, depending on whether the person threatening has a legitimate interest in achieving the result he is after, and whether, according to all right-minded persons, the threat constitutes a reasonable means to achieve that result. Furthermore, a threat is illegitimate only if the person making the threat knows or should know the facts rendering the threat to be contrary to morality (*contra bonos mores*).*

Facts: The claimant bank had business dealings with the firm H, the proprietor of which was the defendant's husband; the defendant had an interest in the undertaking by virtue of having invested in it. On 11 November 1953 the claimant concluded an agreement with the firm. The defendant acted as guarantor for the performance of the obligations owed by the firm to the claimant. After composition proceedings had been instituted in respect of the assets of the firm H, a settlement was duly reached; however, it was not performed by the defendant's husband. The claimant then brought an action against the defendant under the guarantee. The defendant pleaded in her defence that the guarantee she had provided was a nullity, since she allegedly had avoided it pursuant to § 123 BGB. She argued that the deputy director of the claimant had threatened that criminal proceedings for 'kite flying' (jobbing in bills) would be brought against her husband unless she guaranteed his debts; as a result, she had been induced into signing the deed of guarantee.

Held: The Bundesgerichtshof set aside the decision of the appellate court, dismissing the claimant's claim, because it had applied a wrong standard in deciding whether the threat, which was lawful in its means and object, was illegitimate. The Bundesgerichtshof formulated the test which should have been applied and referred the case back to the appellate court.

Judgment: (a) The answer to the question as to the criteria which must be fulfilled in order to render a threat unlawful where the means and the objective of the pressure exerted are in themselves permissible cannot be made to depend solely on whether the party making the threat is legally entitled to require the threatened person to provide the declaration in question. If he is so entitled, the threat will not normally be tainted by unlawfulness; however, there are also cases in which, notwithstanding the absence of such legal entitlement, the threat cannot be held to be unlawful. The contrary view, regularly expressed in the past and still found even today in the works of certain academic jurists, according to which a threat must invariably be unlawful in the absence of such entitlement, must be rejected, as has been shown in later decisions of the Reichsgericht ... and in decisions of the Bundesgerichtshof ... The Senate concurs with that conclusion.

According to those decisions, it is necessary first of all to examine whether the person making the threat has a legitimate interest in achieving the result sought after by him and whether, in the view of all fair-minded and right-minded persons, the threat constitutes a reasonable means of achieving that result ... In the assessment which those decisions require to be carried out, it is necessary to have regard to all circumstances which characterize the events which occur. It is true that these include, most importantly, the question whether the person making the threat has a right to the objective which he is seeking to achieve. Even where he does not possess such a right, however, his conduct may appear justified in the particular circumstances of the case. This may be taken into account inter alia where, despite the fact that the legal order does not confer on the creditor any enforceable right, considerations of public policy indicate that the debtor should fulfil his

---

[38] BGHZ 25, 217.

obligations. Where, in such circumstances, the means employed by the creditor in making the threat are in themselves permissible, his conduct will still be capable, in the absence of any other aggravating factors, of being regarded as compatible with public policy and hence as not unlawful.

(b) Those principles also apply to a threat to lay an information leading to a criminal prosecution which—in the opinion of the creditor, at any rate—is justified.

A creditor cannot be debarred from requiring the debtor to make good the damage done to him by the latter's criminal act on the basis that, unless the debtor does so, he may expect such information to be laid … Such a threat must be regarded as a reasonable means of achieving its purpose; its justification is to be found in the relationship between the criminal act and the claim asserted.

That assessment is not altered by the fact that the case may involve a relationship between the creditor and a third party. Even where the creditor has no legal claim against that third party in substitution for his claim against the debtor, the threat may neverthe-less, depending on the circumstances of the case, be regarded as permissible. That will be the position, for example, where the third party has participated, in a manner which does not fall foul of the criminal or civil law, in the criminal act giving rise to the damage suffered, or where he has gained some advantage from it. The question of illegitimacy cannot be answered solely by reference to the concerns of the person threatened; the interests of the creditor also have to be taken into account. From the creditor's point of view, it may seem morally justifiable in such a case for him to threaten the third party—by whom he may also feel himself to have been prejudiced, or whom he may consider to have profited from the criminal act—with the laying of an information against the person who committed that act unless the third party also takes reasonable steps to make good the damage suffered.

Thus it is invariably necessary to weigh up all the circumstances in their entirety. The possibility cannot be excluded, even in a case such as that described by way of example above, that a threat to procure the institution of criminal proceedings may be unlawful. It is true that this will most frequently be the case where there exists an inherent connection between the criminal act and the claim asserted by the creditor; however, it is possible to envisage other situations involving competing interests in which such a threat may be justified.

… The criminal acts allegedly committed by the husband in the present case are said to have consisted of the issue and acceptance of what are known as 'kites' (fictitious bills), by means of which, it is claimed, he sought to obtain capital for his firm. The defendant's involvement in the firm was not insignificant; she had placed DM 36,000 at the disposal of the firm H and had entered into a deficiency guarantee in favour of the firm H in the sum of DM 24,000. Given those circumstances, there may be grounds for thinking that she too benefitted, even if only indirectly, from the conduct in which her husband is alleged to have engaged and from the discounting of the bills by the plaintiff, to its detri-ment. In accordance with the statements made above, that factor should not be left out of account in the assessment of the question whether the threat was unlawful; it should at least have been discussed.

[About the material requirements of applicability of § 123 BGB:]

(b) … As has already been mentioned above, it is also necessary, in considering whether the avoidance was permissible pursuant to § 123 BGB on the ground of the issue of a threat, to have regard to the interests of both parties. The primary considera-tion must of course be the need to protect the freedom of decision of the person to whom the threat is made; however, the fact that that person may have been prevented from exercising such freedom by the acts of another is not enough to render § 123 BGB applicable ... There must also exist, on the part of the creditor, some intrinsic attitude of a particular kind which necessarily characterises his conduct as an unlawful threat within the meaning of § 123 BGB.

It is on that basis that the Reichsgericht arrived at its decision. It pointed out, first of all, that the person issuing the threat must be conscious of the pressure exerted by him, and that his intention must be to compel the performance of an act by bending the will of the other party ... There appears to be no dispute in that regard ...

It must not be forgotten that avoidance pursuant to § 123 BGB on account of the issue of a threat is permissible only where there also exist, in relation to the unlawfulness of that threat, certain intrinsic elements underlying and prompting the conduct of the person by whom the threat is made.

As has been emphasised above, it is not only the interests of the person whose freedom of action has been taken away that must be taken into consideration; the question must always be asked as to whether, and to what extent, the person issuing the threat also deserves protection. He should unreservedly be given that protection where his attitude in the matter accords with the principles established by the legal order ...

It follows that a creditor will be protected against avoidance where, in issuing his threat, he proceeds without fault on the basis of facts which do not appear to render his conduct impermissible. By contrast, such protection must invariably be denied, having regard to what amounted at the time to the overriding interests of the person threatened, where the person exerting the pressure correctly appreciated the facts but drew the wrong legal conclusions from them. In such circumstances, the person issuing the threat will have deviated in his intentions from the fundamental requirements which the law imposes on all persons, and will consequently be forced to accept a finding that his conduct was impermissible and thus unlawful ...

It follows that it is necessary to adhere to the following rule: in order for a finding of unlawfulness to be made within the meaning of § 123 BGB, it must be established that the creditor is, or should be, aware of the facts characterising his threat as contrary to morality; culpable ignorance is thus equivalent to knowledge of the facts. Under no circumstances can the illegitimacy of the threat be precluded by an incorrect legal assessment of the facts on the part of the creditor ...

The judgment must therefore be set aside, and the case must be referred back to the appellate court.

Notes

(1) In accordance with § 123(1) BGB, a contract can be avoided if a party was illegitimately induced, by a threat, to enter into the contract. The emphasis is thus on the illegitimate nature of the inducement. It could be argued, however, that if the inducement is illegitimate, the threat itself is also illegitimate. In any event, it is not unusual for German courts and legal authors to relate the requirement of illegitimacy to the threat.[39]

---

[39] See Palandt/Ellenberger § 123 para 19; BGH 23 September 1957, BGHZ 25, 217, 219; BGH 4 November 1983, NJW 1983, 384.

(2) The illegitimacy of the threat may arise from the means of the pressure (ie the threatened harm), its purpose or the relation between means and purpose of the pressure.[40] The threat is always illegitimate if the means of the pressure is illegitimate, even though the purpose of the pressure may well be legitimate, for example if a promisee is threatened with physical violence by his promisor to pay his debt. Vice versa, the threat is also illegitimate if the purpose of the pressure is illegitimate, although the means of the pressure may be legitimate, for example if A threatens B with legal action (to which A is legally entitled) in order to induce B to enter into an illegal or immoral contract. In this type of case, however, the contract will generally be void on the ground of illegality (§ 134 BGB) or immorality (§ 138 BGB).[41] Finally, in the case of *Widerrechtlichkeit der Mittel-Zweck-Relation* (also known as *Inadäquanz von Mittel und Zweck*), both the means and the purpose of the pressure are legitimate, yet the threat is illegitimate because it is illegitimate to use this particular means to this particular end. The Bundesgerichtshof has repeatedly held that the decisive test is:

> ... whether the person issuing the threat has a legitimate interest in achieving the result sought after by him and whether, in the view of all right-minded persons [or: in accordance with the principle of good faith], the threat constitutes a reasonable means of achieving that result, taking into consideration all the circumstances of the case, especially the interests of both parties.[42]

If A, who suffered damage as a result of a criminal act by B, threatens B with criminal prosecution to compensate him for his injury, the threat is not illegitimate as it does not constitute an *unangemessenes Mittel*. The position will be different, however, if A threatens B with criminal prosecution to make B pay a debt which B indeed owes to A, but which is wholly unrelated to B's criminal act. In this case the threat does constitute an *unangemessenes Mittel*.[43]

The question whether the exerted pressure must be illegitimate in order to avoid the contract on the ground of duress was originally of no great importance in English law, as the only form of duress recognised was that to a person,[44] where the threat is in its nature illegitimate. In the early cases of 'economic duress' the test applied by the courts was whether there was a 'coercion of the victim's will' such as to 'vitiate his consent',[45] but

---

[40] See W Flume, *Allgemeiner Teil des Bürgerlichen Rechts*, vol II, *Das Rechtsgeschäft* (4th edn, Berlin: Springer, 1992) 535 ff; B Markesinis, H Unberath and A Johnston, *The German Law of Contract* (2nd edn, Oxford: Hart Publishing, 2006) 316–17.

[41] See BGH 23 September 1957, BGHZ 25, 217, 220–22.

[42] cf BGH 14 June 1951, BGHZ 2, 287, 297, 15.11 (DE), below, p 615; BGH 23 September 1957, BGHZ 25, 217, 220, 221, 15.8 (DE), above, p 608; BGH 6 May 1982, NJW 1982, 2301, 2302; BGH 4 November 1983, NJW 1983, 384, 385.

[43] See BGH 23 September 1957, BGHZ 25, 217, 220–22; further see above at p 609, also dealing with the question whether there can be *Inadäquanz von Mittel und Zweck* if the threat with criminal prosecution is directed against a third party.

[44] See above, p 601.

[45] See, eg, Kerr J in *The Siboen and the Sibotre* [1976] 1 Lloyd's Rep 293 (QBD).

this was not consistent with the explanation of duress given in cases in which duress was argued as a defence to a criminal charge.[46] Therefore the 'vitiation of consent' test met with strong disapproval,[47] and several authors have argued that, instead, greater emphasis should be placed upon the nature of the pressure.[48]

House of Lords **15.9 (EN)**

Universe Tankships Inc of Monrovia v International Transport Workers Federation (The Universe Sentinel)[49]

[See 15.5 (EN), above, p 600]

Notes

(1) The approach in this case forces the courts to distinguish between legitimate and illegitimate pressures. Lord Scarman held that a threat may be illegitimate either because what is threatened is unlawful, such as a threat to commit a tort or a crime, or because the threat is unlawful in its demand (purpose), even though the thing threatened may be lawful, such as a blackmailer's threat to report a person's criminal conduct to the police to make him enter into a contract.[50] As a general rule, threats to enforce contractual rights are not illegitimate. For example, in *CTN Cash and Carry Ltd v Gallaher Ltd*,[51] it was held that the defendants' threat to withdraw the plaintiffs' credit facilities—as the defendants were entitled to—did not amount to duress, even though the withdrawal would have seriously prejudiced the plaintiffs' business.

(2) Threats of a breach of contract may amount to illegitimate pressure. When they do so has been a topic of debate in England. There seems to be widespread agreement that it is not always enough that the party's agreement was procured by the other threatening to break the contract, but it is not clear what else must be shown. First, it was suggested that the threat must be the 'predominant' cause of the ensuing contract. However, this would amount to a special rule of causation for economic duress, and the idea seems to have been rejected by later cases.[52] Secondly, it may be that if the party who threatened not to perform unless he is paid extra will be genuinely unable to perform if he does not receive the extra payment, he will be seen as giving a

---

[46] See the speeches of Lord Wilberforce and Lord Simon of Glaisdale in *Lynch v DPP for Northern Ireland* [1975] 1 All ER 913, 926, 938 (HL).

[47] See, in particular, Atiyah, 'Economic Duress and the Overborne Will' (1982) 98 LQR 197.

[48] See, eg, McKendrick (n 9 above) 318–20.

[49] [1983] AC 366.

[50] See J Cartwright, *Unequal Bargaining: A Study of Vitiating Factors in the Formation of Contracts* (Oxford, Clarendon Press, 1991) 165–66; *Treitel* (n 9 above) para 10-002; McKendrick (n 9 above) 320–22. cf Dutch law Art 3:44(2) BW and HR 8 January 1999, NJ 1999, 342; *Asser/Hartkamp & Sieburgh 6-III* (n 25 above) 2014/259.

[51] [1994] 4 All ER 714 (CA).

[52] See *Chitty* (n 10 above) paras 8-025–8-037.

warning rather than as issuing a threat.[53] Thirdly, if the party could perform but would genuinely be in difficulties if he is not paid extra and there is some commercial justification for his demand, it is possible that the threat will not been seen as illegitimate. Some authors argue that a threat to break a contract constitutes illegitimate pressure only if the threat was made in bad faith.[54]

(3) Article 4:108 PECL recognises that not every threat to break a contract is illegitimate. Comment B to the Article reads:

> Not Every Warning of Non-performance Amounts to a Threat: If one party genuinely cannot perform the contract unless the other party promises to pay an increased price and the first party simply informs the second of this fact, the second party cannot later avoid any promise it makes to pay a higher price. The first party's statement was merely a warning of the inevitable; there is no threat within the meaning of this Article.

> *Illustration 4*: A employs B to build a road across A's farmland at a fixed price. A finds that the land is much wetter than either party had realised and A will literally be bankrupt before it has performed the contract at the original price. A informs B of this and B agrees to pay an increased price. Although B had no real choice, it cannot avoid the agreement to pay the increased price.

(4) Subjective requirements concerning the party making the threat are unknown to most legal systems. Yet the Bundesgerichtshof held that, under § 123 BGB, a threat is illegitimate only if the party exerting the pressure knows that his conduct amounts to a threat.[55] It also held: 'In order for a finding of unlawfulness to be made within the meaning of § 123 BGB, it must be established that the creditor is, or should be, aware of the facts characterizing his threat being contrary to morality ...'[56] On this point, however, the decision has been strongly criticised by many authors. They argue that § 123 BGB aims at protecting the free decision of the will (*freie Willensentschließung*) of the threatened party, irrespective of the other party's good faith.

15.2.D CAUSATION

In this section it will be discussed to what extent a causal link between the threat and the contract that a party wishes to avoid, is required. A party will not be permitted to avoid a contract on the ground of threat unless she was in fact influenced by the threat—in other words, unless there was some causal link between the threat and the contract which the claimant seeks to set aside.

---

[53] *Chitty* (n 10 above) para 8-041.
[54] See, eg, Birks, *An Introduction to the Law of Restitution* (Oxford: Clarendon Press, 1994) 183. For an extensive discussion of the 'legitimacy of the demand', see *Chitty* (n 10 above) paras 8-038–8-045. See also Restatement 2d of Contracts § 176 ('When a Threat is Improper') and the Comments and Illustrations; McGregor (n 30 above) Comment to s 562 ('Improper pressure').
[55] BGH 23 September 1957, BGHZ 25, 217, 223–25.
[56] See, eg, Flume (n 40 above) 539.

Barton v Armstrong[57]

A party who entered into a contract after he was threatened with death by the other party may avoid the contract for duress unless the other party shows that the threat was of no influence on the first party's decision to make the contract.

Facts: Barton, a managing director of a public company, executed on its behalf a deed by which the company agreed to pay $140,000 to Armstrong, its chairman, and to purchase Armstrong's shares in the company for $180,000, in order to get Armstrong off the board of the company. It was established that Barton acted as he did partly for commercial reasons, but the court also found that Armstrong had threatened Barton with having him killed if he did not make the arrangements. Barton later tried to avoid the deed for duress.

Held: The Court of Appeal of New South Wales held that the onus was on Barton to show that he would not have signed the deed but for the threats, and Barton had failed to discharge that onus. The Privy Council, by a majority, recommended that an appeal be allowed.

Judgment: LORD CROSS OF CHELSEA [delivering the majority judgment]: Their Lordships turn now to consider the question of law which provoked a difference of opinion in the Court of Appeal Division. It is hardly surprising that there is no direct authority on the point, for if A threatens B with death if he does not execute some document and B, who takes A's threat seriously, executes the document it can be only in the most unusual circumstances that there can be any doubt whether the threats operated to induce him to execute the document. But this is a most unusual case and the findings of fact made below do undoubtedly raise the question whether it was necessary for Barton in order to obtain relief to establish that he would not have executed the deed in question but for the threats ... There is an obvious analogy between setting aside a disposition for duress or undue influence and setting it aside for fraud ...

'Once make out that there has been anything like deception, and no contract resting in any degree on that foundation can stand': per Lord Cranworth LJ in *Reynell v Sprye* (1852) 1 De GM & G 660, 708 ... Their Lordships think that the same rule should apply in cases of duress and that if Armstrong's threats were 'a' reason for Barton's executing the deed he is entitled to relief even though he might well have entered into the contract if Armstrong had uttered no threats to induce him to do so ... If Barton had to establish that he would not have made the agreement but for Armstrong's threats, then their Lordships would not dissent from the view that he had not made out his case. But no such onus lay on him. On the contrary it was for Armstrong to establish, if he could, that the threats which he was making and the unlawful pressure which he was exerting for the purpose of inducing Barton to sign the agreement and which Barton knew were being made and exerted for this purpose in fact contributed nothing to Barton's decision to sign. The judge has found that during the 10 days or so before the documents were executed Barton was in genuine fear that Armstrong was planning to have him killed if the agreement was not signed. His state of mind was described by the judge as one of 'very real mental torment' and he believed that his fears would be at end when once the documents were executed. It is true that the judge was not satisfied that Vojinovic had been employed by Armstrong but if one man threatens another with unpleasant consequences if he does not act in a particular way, he must take the risk that the impact of his threats may be accentuated by extraneous circumstances for which he is not in fact responsible. It is true that on the

---

[57] [1976] AC 104.

facts as their Lordships assume them to have been Armstrong's threats may have been unnecessary; but it would be unrealistic to hold that they played no part in making Barton decide to execute the documents. The proper inference to be drawn from the facts found is, their Lordships think, that though it may be that Barton would have executed the documents even if Armstrong had made no threats and exerted no unlawful pressure to induce him to do so the threats and unlawful pressure in fact contributed to his decision to sign the documents and to recommend their execution by Landmark and the other parties to them. It may be, of course, that Barton's fear of Armstrong had evaporated before he issued his writ in this action but Armstrong—understandably enough—expressly disclaimed reliance on the defence of delay on Barton's part in repudiating the deed.

[LORD WILBERFORCE and LORD SIMON OF GLAISDALE (dissenting on the ground that it was not open to the court to review findings of fact made in the courts below)]: The next necessary step would be to establish the relationship between the illegitimate means used and the action taken. For the purposes of the present case (reserving our opinion as to cases which may arise in other contexts) we are prepared to accept, as the formula most favourable to the appellant, the test proposed by the majority, namely, that the illegitimate means used was a reason (not *the* reason, nor the *predominant* reason nor the *clinching* reason) why the complainant acted as he did. We are also prepared to accept that a decisive answer is not obtainable by asking the question whether the contract would have been made even if there had been no threats because, even if the answer to this question is affirmative, that does not prove that the contract was not made because of the threats.

BGH, 14 June 1951[58]   **15.11 (DE)**

The young mother

For a juristic act to be voidable on the ground of threat it must be shown that the threat was a decisive factor for the threatened party to make the declaration.

Facts: On 4 March 1948 the claimant had given birth to a child, fathered on her by a married man. The man was already father of three legitimate children. As early as on the day after the birth the claimant's mother sought to persuade her that she should give up the child, reproaching her for having brought shame on the family by having a relationship with a married man. The claimant's mother further told her that her father had expressed thoughts of suicide and that she could only return to the family home if she were to part from the child. On 20 March the claimant signed a document (*Einwilligungserklärung*) giving the child up for adoption. Nine months later the claimant sought to avoid the *Einwilligungserklärung* on the ground of, among other things, the threat exercised by her mother.

Held: Considering the claimant's age, her financial independence, the fact that she had had independent advice and that two weeks had passed before she signed the document, there was no causal link between the mother's threat and the claimant's decision to give up her child for adoption.

Judgment: In order for the claimant's declaration to be voidable on the ground of an unlawful threat, the claimant must have given her consent under pressure from her mother. The threat must have caused her to make the declaration. Thus it is necessary to show that, in the absence of the threat, the claimant would not have provided the declaration, or that she would not have provided it at the time when she did, or that she would have provided it in a different form. It is sufficient in that regard for the threat

---

[58] BGHZ 2, 287.

to have been a decisive factor in conjunction with other motivating factors (Palandt § 123 paras 21f, with supporting arguments).

As regards this point, the following findings of the appellate court are of significance: it is stated, in the context of the unlawfulness of the threat, that the claimant's mother had not shielded her from all external influences. The officials working in the youth welfare office in M, namely the witnesses B and H, had allegedly had the opportunity of exerting an influence on the claimant, and had stated that, in their view, she should not give up the child. The claimant was old enough and financially independent, so that she was not constrained, by virtue of having no choice in the matter, to accede to the wishes of her mother; and she may, in making her decision, have taken into account the views which had been expressed by the witnesses. If, notwithstanding the counter-effect exerted by the statements of both the witness S and the two officials, she acted in accordance with her mother's wishes in the matter, that can only mean, according to the court below, that she preferred to come to an understanding with her parents and to provide her child with the opportunity of a future without the stigma of illegitimacy caused by adultery than to sacrifice her feelings, as a daughter, for her mother. Those statements signify that, taking into consideration the claimant's age and financial independence, and having regard to the influence exerted by the abovementioned witnesses, the pressure which her mother brought to bear on the claimant no longer influenced her decision, and, by contrast, that the claimant reached her decision to agree to the adoption of her child after herself weighing up the pros and cons of the matter. That means, however, that there can be no causal connection between the threat made by the claimant's mother and the decision made by the claimant, particularly having regard to the fact that a period of some two weeks elapsed between the issue of the threat by the mother and the signature of the declaration by the claimant. If the threat ceased to constitute one of the deciding factors which led the plaintiff to give her consent, and if, instead, she decided of her own free will between continuing to live with her parents and continuing to live with her child, then there can be no possibility in law of avoiding that consent. The element of unlawful manipulation of the will of the person making the declaration, constituting a necessary criterion for the application of § 123(1) BGB, is lacking.

Notes

(1) The threat must have induced the threatened party to conclude the contract. In other words, if the contract is to be avoided on the ground of threat, the requirement of causation has to be met. This rule applies in all legal systems. In the French Code civil the requirement follows from the wording of the relevant provisions and this is also the case in other codifications.[59]

(2) The problem of causation does not often arise where the threat is of violence. One explanation is that if the threat were of a serious and imminent nature it would be only in rare cases that the threat would not induce the threatened party to enter into the contract.[60] But we will see that English law's recognition of 'economic duress'— which

---

[59] See, eg, § 123(1) BGB; Art 3:44(1) and (2) BW ('A juridical act … entered into as a result of threat'; 'A person who induces another to execute a certain juridical act by unlawfully threatening him'); Art 3.2.6 UNIDROIT PICC ('led to conclude the contract by … threat') and Art 4:108 PECL.

[60] See the speech of Lord Cross of Chelsea in *Barton v Armstrong* [1976] AC 104, 118, above, p 614.

in most of the cases has involved a threat not to perform a contract unless it is renegotiated in favour of the threatening party—has led to tricky questions of whether
the other party really agreed to the adjustment because of the threat or for other (eg
commercial) reasons.

(3) In German textbooks, the issue of the serious nature of the threat tends to
merge into a discussion of the requirement of causation. In establishing the causative
link between the threat and the conclusion of the contract, the German courts apply a
subjective test.[61] In the decision provided it was held that the claimant had not signed
the document as a result of her mother's threats.[62] The BGH took into consideration
the claimant's age and economic independence, the fact that she had had independent
advice and that she had taken two weeks to make her decision. Also the Court stated
as a general rule that the requirement of causation is met if the threatened party would
not have concluded the contract at all, or would have done so at another moment, or
on different terms, but for the threat. The same rule applies in Dutch law.[63]

In the decision cited above the BGH furthermore held that it suffices if the threat
was a motive for the threatened party to conclude the contract.[64]

(4) In *Barton v Armstrong*,[65] which was a case of duress to the person, the Privy
Council also held that the threat need be only a reason (not even the predominant or
clinching reason) for the conclusion of the contract. In cases of economic duress, in
contrast, the English courts will seem to apply a different rule.[66] In *Dimskal Shipping
CoSA v ITF (The Evia Luck)*,[67] Lord Goff said that the illegitimate economic pressure need have been 'a significant cause'. Lord Goff's statement has been interpreted
to mean that the 'minimum' for relief is that the claimant would not have entered
the contract (or the renegotiated terms) 'but for' the threat.[68] It is possible that even
more is required, for example that the threat was the 'predominant' reason; but that is
doubtful. In practice the court will ask, did the claimant have a reasonable alternative,
which seems to be essentially another way of asking whether the claimant would have
agreed but for the threat.[69]

(5) Which party has to prove whether the threat induced the conclusion of the
contract? In most jurisdictions, the general rule is that the onus of proof rests with the
party seeking to avoid the contract.[70] In *Barton's* case the onus of proof was placed on

---

[61] cf RG 29 October 1928, JW 1929, 242.
[62] BGH 14 June 1951, BGHZ 2, 287.
[63] See *Asser/Hartkamp & Sieburgh 6-III* (n 25 above) 2014/260.
[64] See Palandt/Ellenberger § 123 para 24.
[65] [1976] AC 104, see above, 15.10 (EN).
[66] See Cartwright (n 50 above) 168. §175 of the Restatement 2d of Contracts appears to be less generous
than the rule laid down in *Barton*, since Comment c reads: 'A party's manifestation of assent is induced by
duress if the duress substantially contributes to his decision to manifest his assent'.
[67] [1992] 2 AC 152, 165 (HL).
[68] See *Huyton SA v Peter Cremer GmbH* [1998] EUHC 1208 (Comm), [1999] 1 Lloyd's Rep 620, 636.
[69] See *Chitty* (n 10 above) paras 8-025–8-037.
[70] See for French law, eg Terré et al (n 8 above) no. 250; G Marty and P Raynaud, *Traité de droit civil*, Tome
1 (2nd edn, Paris: Sirey, 1988) no. 169; for German law, eg Palandt/Ellenberger § 123 para 30; BGH 13 May
1957, NJW 1957, 988.

the party who had made the illegitimate threats (ie Armstrong). It is not clear whether this is the general rule in English law. In this particular case, however, there was much to be said for placing the onus on Armstrong. Cartwright[71] explains: 'Once it is shown that the defendant acted wrongly in applying unlawful pressure, he ought to have the (very difficult) burden of disproving the causal relationship between the pressure and the contract; the law favours the innocent party over the wrongdoer'. As suggested in Note (4) above, this very stringent rule of English law may not apply outside duress to the person.[72]

15.2.E SERIOUS AND IMMINENT THREAT

Some civil codes of the European continent provide that a threat must be imminent and serious. This is no longer the case in the new French Code civil while, before the reform, Article 1112(1) of the Code civil required *un mal considérable et présent*. However, this was interpreted as requiring that the threat, considering its seriousness and imminence, must have determined the consent of the threatened party to conclude the contract,[73] and very much resembled the causation requirement (see above): did the threat cause the threatened party to enter into the contract?[74]

Cass com, 30 January 1974[75]

15.12 (FR)

The former shop director

A contract cannot be avoided on the ground of threat if the threat was not sufficiently serious to determine the threatened party's consent.

Facts: Ms Ceytère, a former shop director, entered into a contract with M and Mme Tournaire, owners of the shop, whereby Ms Ceytère agreed to pay a debt to Etablissements Claritex for the supply of goods she had ordered in her capacity as shop director. Mrs Tournaire had made it clear in a letter that if Ms Ceytère did not settle the debt, criminal proceedings would be undertaken against her on account of her improper behaviour as a shop director.

Held: The appellate court had dismissed Ms Ceytère's claim for avoidance of the contract on the ground of *violence* (ie the threat with criminal prosecution), because the court was of the opinion that Ms Ceytère had not been influenced by the threat, having regard to, among other things, her experience as a business woman and her age. The Cour de cassation upheld that decision.

Judgment:— Whereas first, the cour d'appel found that Mlle Ceytère, confronted by Mme Tournaire's letter of 3 October 1969 with the option either of settling the Claritex debt herself or of facing criminal and civil proceedings on account of irregularities discovered in her managerial activities, possessed sufficient experience of business matters, and was

---

[71] Cartwright (n 50 above) 155.
[72] See *Chitty* (n 10 above) paras 8-025–8-028.
[73] See, eg, Terré et al (n 8 above) no. 249; Marty and Raynaud (n 70 above) no. 164.
[74] See, eg, Terré et al (n 8 above) no. 249; Marty and Raynaud (n 70 above) no. 165.
[75] D 1974, 382.

old enough, to resist intimidation and to avoid succumbing to irrational fears of criminal prosecution;

— Whereas the judgment further observes that that letter made so little impression upon her that she waited for three months before replying to it, and that she was so sure of having the upper hand that she attached precise terms to her acceptance of the arrangement by giving Mme Tournaire a deadline of forty eight hours in which to confirm her final agreement; as Mlle Ceytère therefore gave her undertaking with full knowledge of the facts and in a state of total lucidity.

— Whereas on those grounds, the cour d'appel considered, in the exercise of its sovereign discretion, that Mlle Ceytère's consent had not been vitiated by any constraint ...

On those grounds, this Court dismisses the appeal.

Note

Whether the threat was sufficiently serious to determine the threatened party's consent can be established in two different ways: by applying either a subjective test—did the threat in fact constrain this person?—or an objective test—was the threat such as to constrain a reasonable person? In practice, the courts will also look at the fact the particular claimant had reason to fear, which seems to be the same question with which the English and German courts deal under causation.

It has already been noted[76] that in English law it is unclear what is the causal requirement in cases of economic duress: need the threat have been merely one factor, as in duress to the person,[77] or must it have had some greater influence? In *The Universe Sentinel*[78] Lord Scarman identified two elements of the concept of duress, one of which was the 'pressure amounting to compulsion of the will of the victim'. There is compulsion of the victim's will, still according to Lord Scarman, if the pressure was so great that it gave the victim no other choice but to act as he did.[79] In establishing whether the pressure was so great as to leave the victim no other choice, the English courts take a number of factors into consideration: whether the party alleged to have been coerced did or did not protest; whether he did or did not have an alternative course open to him, such as an adequate legal remedy; whether he was independently advised; and whether after entering into the contract he took steps to avoid it.[80] These factors seem to imply that the test applied is an objective, rather than a subjective, one. But contrast *Scott v Sebright*,[81] a case of duress to the person in which Butt J held:[82]

It has sometimes been said that in order to avoid a contract entered into through fear, the fear must be such as would impel a person of ordinary courage and resolution to yield to it. I do not think that is an accurate statement of the law.

---

[76] See 15.2.D.

[77] See *Barton v Armstrong*, 15.10 (EN), above, p 614.

[78] Extracted see above, p 600.

[79] See Cartwright (n 50 above) 163.

[80] See *Pao On v Lau Yiu Long* [1980] AC 614, 635 (PC); *The Siboen and the Sibotre* [1976] 1 Lloyd's Rep 293 (QBD).

[81] (1886) 12 PD 21.

[82] ibid at 24.

Butt J then applied a subjective test, taking into account the sex, age, mental condition and inexperience of the threatened person.[83]

§ 123(1) BGB does not provide that the threat must be imminent and serious. However, this does not mean that the seriousness and the imminence of the threat are irrelevant in German law. A leading commentator explains:[84]

> However, the gravity of the threatened harm must also have been sufficient, in accordance with § 123, to place the person making the declaration in a position of constraint, since otherwise, by virtue of the lack of a causal link, there will exist no ground for upholding a submission that the contract has been avoided.

The test to establish the causal link between the threat and the conclusion of the contract is a subjective one.[85] As for the imminent nature of the threat, it could be argued that it is also a requirement in German law since *Drohung* is defined as 'An announcement of the prospect of some future harm …; not, however, the exploitation of some existing harm'.[86]

Under Article 3.2.6 UNIDROIT PICC, the threat must have been so imminent and serious as to leave the threatened party no reasonable alternative but to conclude the contract on the terms proposed by the other party. As in English law, probably the availability of an adequate legal remedy will qualify as a reasonable alternative, as will, for instance, the availability on the market of the goods or services bargained for.[87] The Comment to Article 3.2.6 UNIDROIT PICC does not discuss 'reasonable alternative'; but it does state that the 'imminence and the seriousness of the threat must be evaluated by an objective standard, taking into account the circumstances of the individual case'. It is not surprising that the test to be applied is an objective one since the UNIDROIT PICC lay down general rules for 'international' commercial contracts, which are generally concluded between parties who have been negotiating at arm's length. An objective test, being stricter than a subjective test, therefore seems more appropriate.

Under Article 4:108 PECL, the threat must also have been imminent and serious—though it is not clear from the wording of Article 4:108 whether the test to be applied is a subjective or an objective one; further, the contract may not be avoided if the complaining party had a reasonable alternative.[88]

15.3 THREATS BY THIRD PERSONS

Can a contract between A and B be avoided on the ground that B entered into the contract under a threat or abuse of circumstances exercised by C, a third person who is not a party to the contract?

---

[83] See *Chitty* (n 10 above) para 8-034.
[84] Soergel/Hefermehl § 123 BGB para 41.
[85] See above, p 613.
[86] cf BGH 14 June 1951, BGHZ 2, 287, 295, 15.11 (DE), above, p 615.
[87] See also Restatement 2d of Contracts § 175, Comment b and the Illustrations.
[88] Comment E to Art 4:108 PECL.

Code civil   **15.13 (FR)**

Article 1142: Duress is a ground of nullity regardless of whether it has been applied by the other party or by a third party.

Note

In French law, B may avoid a contract on the ground of a threat exercised by C, regardless of whether A was in good faith, ie whether A knew or ought to have known of the threat or abuse by C.[89]

In German law, too, B is entitled to avoid the contract in a case where C exerted a threat, even though A was in good faith.[90] The position taken by French and German law was thus explained by Kötz:[91]

> German law and the Romanistic systems regard the contractor's will as more strongly vitiated by duress than by deceit, so allow avoidance even as against a party in good faith.

The BGH also held that a father (C) had acted *contra bonos mores* by having his daughter (B) provide security for his debts in favour of a bank (A). The BGH stated that the guarantee (*Bürgschaft*) may be void under § 138(1) BGB if the bank knew that the main debtor had *contra bonos mores* and illegally influenced the personal guarantee or if the bank had in full knowledge endorsed such behaviour.[92]

BW   **15.14 (NL)**

Article 3:44: (5) If a declaration has been made as a result of threat, fraud or abuse of circumstances on the part of a person who is not party to the juridical act, this defect cannot be invoked against a party to the juridical act who had no reason to assume its existence.

Note

Under Article 3:4(5) BW, B is not entitled to avoid the contract if A was in good faith.

---

[89] Art 1142 Cciv; see C Kennefick, '*Violence* in the Reformed Napoleonic Code: the Surprising Survival of Third Parties' in J Cartwright and S Whittaker (eds), *The Code Napoléon Rewritten: French Contract Law after the 2016 Reforms* (Oxford: Hart Publishing, 2017) 109.

[90] See Palandt/Ellenberger § 123 para 18 (with reference to BGH 6 July 1966, NJW 1966, 2399); K Larenz and M Wolf, *Allgemeiner Teil des Bürgerlichen Rechts* (9th edn, Munich: CH Beck, 2004) 688 (§ 37 para 17).

[91] Kötz (n 1 above) 189.

[92] BGH 24 February 1994, NJW 1994, 1341, 1343. See also the passage on the constitutionalisation of contract law, above pp 14 ff.

Barclays Bank plc v O'Brien[93]

A creditor which takes a security from a surety whom he knows is in a relationship with the debtor such that undue influence or some other wrong by the debtor is a substantial risk, and where the giving of the security is on its face not to the surety's financial advantage, will be treated as having constructive notice of any threat, misrepresentation or undue influence by the debtor unless the creditor has warned the surety to take independent advice.

Facts: The defendants, Mr and Mrs O'Brien, who were husband and wife, agreed to execute a mortgage of their matrimonial home as security for overdraft facilities extended by the plaintiff bank to the husband's company. The branch manager of the bank had sent the documents to another branch with the instruction to make sure that both defendants were fully aware of the nature of the documents and that, if in doubt, they should consult their solicitor before signing. This instruction was neglected and the wife signed without reading the document. She relied on her husband's false representation that the security was limited to £60,000 and would last only three weeks. When the company's overdraft exceeded £154,000 the bank sought to enforce the security. The wife claimed the avoidance as against the bank of the security transaction on the ground of the misrepresentation by her husband.

Held: The wife's claim was dismissed by the judge in first instance, but allowed by the Court of Appeal. The House of Lords dismissed the bank's appeal holding that, given the circumstances of the case (see below), the bank had had constructive notice of the husband's misrepresentation.

Judgment: LORD BROWNE-WILKINSON:

Undue influence, misrepresentation and third parties

Up to this point I have been considering the right of a claimant wife to set aside a transaction as against the wrongdoing husband when the transaction has been procured by his undue influence. But in surety cases the decisive question is whether the claimant wife can set aside the transaction, not against the wrongdoing husband, but against the creditor bank. Of course, if the wrongdoing husband is acting as agent for the creditor bank in obtaining the surety from the wife, the creditor will be fixed with the wrongdoing of its own agent and the surety contract can be set aside as against the creditor. Apart from this, if the creditor bank has notice, actual or constructive, of the undue influence exercised by the husband (and consequentially of the wife's equity to set aside the transaction) the creditor will take subject to that equity and the wife can set aside the transaction against the creditor (albeit a purchaser for value) as well as against the husband: see *Bainbrigge v* Browne (1881) 18 Ch D 188 and *Bank of Credit and Commerce International SA v Aboody* [1990] 1 QB 923, 973. Similarly, in cases such as the present where the wife has been induced to enter into the transaction by the husband's misrepresentation, her equity to set aside the transaction will be enforceable against the creditor if either the husband was acting as the creditor's agent or the creditor had actual or constructive notice.

[Lord Browne-Wilkinson then discussed cases decided on the basis of a 'special equity' in favour of wives derived from the Privy Council case of *Turnbull v Duval* [1902] AC 429]

Conclusions

Wives …

In my judgment, if the doctrine of notice is properly applied, there is no need for the introduction of a special equity in these types of cases. A wife who has been induced to

---

[93] [1994] 1 AC 180.

stand as a surety for her husband's debts by his undue influence, misrepresentation or some other legal wrong has an equity as against him to set aside that transaction. Under the ordinary principles of equity, her right to set aside that transaction will be enforceable against third parties (e.g. against a creditor) if either the husband was acting as the third party's agent or the third party had actual or constructive notice of the facts giving rise to her equity. Although there may be cases where, without artificiality, it can properly be held that the husband was acting as the agent of the creditor in procuring the wife to stand as surety, such cases will be of very rare occurrence. The key to the problem is to identify the circumstances in which the creditor will be taken to have had notice of the wife's equity to set aside the transaction …

Therefore, in my judgment a creditor is put on inquiry when a wife offers to stand surety for her husband's debts by the combination of two factors: (a) the transaction is on its face not to the financial advantage of the wife; and (b) there is a substantial risk in transactions of that kind that, in procuring the wife to act as surety, the husband has committed a legal or equitable wrong that entitles the wife to set aside the transaction.

It follows that, unless the creditor who is put on inquiry takes reasonable steps to satisfy himself that the wife's agreement to stand surety has been properly obtained, the creditor will have constructive notice of the wife's rights.

What, then are the reasonable steps which the creditor should take to ensure that it does not have constructive notice of the wife's rights, if any? Normally the reasonable steps necessary to avoid being fixed with constructive notice consist of making inquiry of the person who may have the earlier right (i.e. the wife) to see if whether such right is asserted. It is plainly impossible to require of banks and other financial institutions that they should inquire of one spouse whether he or she has been unduly influenced or misled by the other. But in my judgment the creditor, in order to avoid being fixed with constructive notice, can reasonably be expected to take steps to bring home to the wife the risk she is running by standing as surety and to advise her to take independent advice. As to past transactions, it will depend on the facts of each case whether the steps taken by the creditor satisfy this test. However for the future in my judgment a creditor will have satisfied these requirements if it insists that the wife attend a private meeting (in the absence of the husband) with a representative of the creditor at which she is told of the extent of her liability as surety, warned of the risk she is running and urged to take independent legal advice. If these steps are taken in my judgment the creditor will have taken such reasonable steps as are necessary to preclude a subsequent claim that it had constructive notice of the wife's rights. I should make it clear that I have been considering the ordinary case where the creditor knows only that the wife is to stand surety for her husband's debts. I would not exclude exceptional cases where a creditor has knowledge of further facts which render the presence of undue influence not only possible but probable. In such cases, the creditor to be safe will have to insist that the wife is separately advised …

Other persons

I have hitherto dealt only with the position where a wife stands surety for her husband's debts. But in my judgment the same principles are applicable to all other cases where there is an emotional relationship between cohabitees. The 'tenderness' shown by the law to married women is not based on the marriage ceremony but reflects the underlying risk of one cohabitee exploiting the emotional involvement and trust of the other. Now that unmarried cohabitation, whether heterosexual or homosexual, is widespread in our society, the law should recognise this. Legal wives are not the only group which are now exposed to the emotional pressure of cohabitation. Therefore if, but only if, the creditor is aware that the surety is cohabiting with the principal debtor, in my judgment the same principles should apply to them as apply to husband and wife.

In addition to the cases of cohabitees, the decision of the Court of Appeal in *Avon Finance Co Ltd v Bridger* [1985] 2 All ER 281 shows (rightly in my view) that other relationships can give rise to a similar result. In that case a son, by means of misrepresentation, persuaded his elderly parents to stand surety for his debts. The surety obligation was held to be unenforceable by the creditor inter alia because to the bank's knowledge the parents trusted the son in their financial dealings. In my judgment that case was rightly decided: in a case where the creditor is aware that the surety reposes trust and confidence in the principal debtor in relation to his financial affairs, the creditor is put on inquiry in just the same way as it is in relation to husband and wife.

Summary

I can therefore summarise my views as follows. Where one cohabitee has entered into an obligation to stand as surety for the debts of the other cohabitee and the creditor is aware that they are cohabitees: (1) the surety obligation will be valid and enforceable by the creditor unless the suretyship was procured by the undue influence, misrepresentation or other legal wrong of the principal debtor; (2) if there has been undue influence, misrepresentation or other legal wrong by the principal debtor, unless the creditor has taken reasonable steps to satisfy himself that the surety entered into the obligation freely and in knowledge of the true facts, the creditor will be unable to enforce the surety obligation because he will be fixed with constructive notice of the surety's right to set aside the transaction; (3) unless there are special exceptional circumstances, a creditor will have taken such reasonable steps to avoid being fixed with constructive notice if the creditor warns the surety (at a meeting not attended by the principal debtor) of the amount of her potential liability and of the risks involved and advises the surety to take independent legal advice …

The decision of this case

Applying those principles to this case, to the knowledge of the bank Mr and Mrs O'Brien were man and wife …

Unfortunately Mr Tucker's [the branch manager of the bank] instructions were not followed and to the knowledge of the bank (through the clerk at the Burnham branch) Mrs O'Brien signed the documents without any warning of the risks or any recommendation to take legal advice. In the circumstances the bank (having failed to take reasonable steps) is fixed with constructive notice of the wrongful misrepresentation made by Mr O'Brien to Mrs O'Brien. Mrs O'Brien is therefore entitled as against the bank to set aside the legal charge on the matrimonial home securing her husband's liability to the bank.

For these reasons I would dismiss the appeal with costs.

[The other members of the House agreed.]

Notes

(1) In English law, in a case where undue influence has been exerted by C, equity will not grant relief to B against A if A, at the moment of conclusion of the contract, was in good faith and gave value.[94] As a general rule, however, equity will grant relief if A had actual or constructive 'notice'—knowledge—of the undue influence

---

[94] See, eg, *Coldunell Ltd v Gallon* [1986] QB 1184 (CA); *Treitel* (n 9 above) para 10-037.

exercised by C, or if C acted as an agent for A. See for example *Bank of Credit and Commerce International SA v Aboody*.[95] The above-cited case of *O'Brien* elaborates and extends the point of constructive knowledge.

(2) In *CIBC Mortgages Plc v Pitt*,[96] which was heard with *O'Brien's* case, the husband had exercised undue influence. Although the Court held that in a case of actual undue influence it was not necessary for the claimant to show manifest disadvantage in order to be able to set aside a transaction as against the party (her husband) who had used the undue influence, the position vis-à-vis the bank was different. The bank would be put on notice, and therefore would have to give a warning, only if the arrangement on its face appeared to be disadvantageous to her. In that case the arrangement was a loan to the husband and wife. In fact, the husband used the money for speculating on the stock market, but on its face it was a loan to the couple to enable them to buy a holiday home, so it was apparently advantageous to the wife. For a case of undue influence by an employer over his employee and where constructive notice of the bank was accepted along the lines set out in *O'Brien*, see *Crédit Lyonnais Bank Nederland NV v Burch*.[97]

(3) *O'Brien* was a case of misrepresentation by the husband, *Pitt* one of undue influence. In a case of duress exercised by C, B may avoid the contract if he proves that A knew or had constructive notice of the duress.[98]

(4) In *Etridge's* case, the House of Lords developed the principle underlying the decision in *O'Brien's* case. The Court of Appeal in *Etridge*[99] had read Lord Browne-Wilkinson as saying that the bank need only make an enquiry when (a) the transaction was on its face disadvantageous to the wife and (b) there was a substantial risk that the husband had committed a wrong. The House of Lords disagreed: the bank should make enquiries whenever a wife offers to stand surety for her husband's debts[100] or, indeed, 'whenever the relationship between the surety and the debtor is non-commercial'.[101] Lord Nicholls said:

> I do not understand Lord Browne-Wilkinson to have been saying that, in husband and wife cases, whether the bank is put on inquiry depends on its state of knowledge of the parties' marriage, or of the degree of trust and confidence the particular wife places in her husband in relation to her financial affairs. That would leave banks in a state of considerable uncertainty in a situation where it is important they should know clearly where they stand. The test should be simple and clear and easy to apply in a wide range of circumstances. I read (a) and (b) as Lord Browne-Wilkinson's broad explanation of the reason why a creditor is

---

[95] [1990] 1 QB 923, 971–73 (CA); see above p 622.

[96] [1994] 1 AC 200 (HL).

[97] [1997] 1 All ER 144 (CA), 3.3.4.C. see 16.10 (EN), below, p 651. Contrast *Barclays Bank plc v Coleman* [2001] QB 20 (CA). See further *Treitel* (n 9 above) paras 10-036–10-042; Cartwright (n 50 above) 188–92. See also Restatement 2d of Contracts § 177(3) and Comment c.

[98] eg *Talbot v Von Boris* [1911] 1 KB 854 (CA); *Kesarmal s/o Letchman Das v Valliappa Chettiar (NKV) s/o Nagappa Chettiar* [1954] 1 WLR 380 (PC); see also Restatement 2d of Contracts §175(2), Comment e and Illustrations 10 and 110, or if the conditions laid down in *O'Brien* are satisfied.

[99] [1998] 4 All ER 705, 719 (CA).

[100] [2001] UKHL 44 (for extracts from this case on what amounts to undue influence, see 16.9 (EN), below, p 645).

[101] [2001] UKHL 44 at [87], per Lord Clyde.

put on inquiry when a wife offers to stand surety for her husband's debts. These are the two factors which, taken together, constitute the underlying rationale.

Lord Nicholls went on to set out in detail the steps a bank should take to try to ensure that there has not been improper conduct. In summary:[102]

a bank satisfies these requirements if it insists that the wife attend a private meeting with a representative of the bank at which she is told of the extent of her liability as surety, warned of the risk she is running and urged to take independent legal advice. In exceptional cases the bank, to be safe, has to insist that the wife is separately advised.

In practice, the bank will seek a letter from a solicitor stating that the wife has been advised by the solicitor. The steps that the bank and the solicitor should take are set out in detail by Lord Nicholls in what comes close to a judicially imposed code of conduct.[103]

Principles of European Contract Law **15.16 (INT)**

Article 4:111: Third Persons[104]

(1) Where a third person for whose acts a party is responsible, or who with a party's assent, is involved in the making of a contract: …

(d) makes a threat, …

remedies under this Chapter will be available under the same conditions as if the behaviour or knowledge had been that of the party itself.

(2) Where any other third person:

…

(c) makes a threat, …

remedies under this Chapter will be available if the party knew or ought to have known of the relevant facts, or at the time of avoidance it has not acted in reliance on the contract.

Notes

(1) Article 4:111 PECL—and Article 3.2.8 UNIDROIT PICC, which is a very similar provision—appears to be influenced by US law as it makes a distinction between cases where A is responsible for C—C acting as an 'agent' for A—and cases where A is not responsible for C.[105]

(2) For cases in which the party is not responsible for the third person, the PECL comment:

B. *Remedies Where Fraud, etc by a Third Person for Whom Party is not Responsible.* A party cannot be fixed with the consequences of improper or careless behaviour of a third person

---

[102] [2001] UKHL 44 at [50], per Lord Nicholls.
[103] [2001] UKHL 44 at [64]–[67].
[104] cf Art II.7:208 DCFR.
[105] cf above and Restatement 2d of Contracts §175(2), Comment e.

for whom it is not responsible and who does not fall into the other categories mentioned in Comment A. But it should not be allowed to enforce a contract which it knows or should know was concluded only through such behaviour by a third person, if, had it behaved in the same way itself, the other party to the contract could have a remedy under the provisions of this chapter.

Illustration 2: A bank lends money to a husband's business on the strength of a charge, signed by the wife, over the family home. The charge is very much against the wife's interest and the husband has procured the wife's signature by duress. The bank ought to know that it is most unlikely that the wife would sign voluntarily and the bank cannot enforce the charge. It should have made enquiries to ensure that the wife was acting freely. The party should also be liable for damages under Article 4:117 if it knows of the ground for avoidance, or if it knows that the other party has been given incorrect information by a third person but does not inform the other party that the information is incorrect.

(3) Also, the element of reliance in Article 4:111 PECL (and paragraph (2) of Article 3.2.8 UNIDROIT PICC) appears to be borrowed from US law.[106] According to Comment 2 to Article 3.2.8(2) UNIDROIT PICC, the exception to the rule that B may avoid the contract only if A is in good faith is justified because if A has not acted in reliance on the contract A does not need protection.

FURTHER READING

Cartwright, J, 'Defects of consent in Contract Law, ch 23' in AS Hartkamp et al (eds), Towards a European Civil Code (4th edn, Alphen aan den Rijn: Wolters Kluwer, 2011) 537–554.

Dawson, JP, 'Economic Duress—An Essay in Perspective' (1947) 45 Mich LR 253–90.

Drobnig, U, 'Substantive Validity' (1992) 40 Am J Comp L 635–44.

Enman, SE, 'Doctrines of Unconscionability in Canadian, English and Commonwealth Contract Law' (1987) 16 AALR 191–219.

Kennefick, C, '*Violence* in the Reformed Napoleonic Code: the Surprising Survival of Third Parties' in J Cartwright and S Whittaker (eds), *The Code Napoléon Rewritten: French Contract Law after the 2016 Reforms* (Oxford: Hart Publishing, 2017) 109–33.

Lohsse, S, '*Validity*' in N Jansen and R Zimmermann (eds), *Commentaries on European Contract Laws* (Oxford University Press, 2018) 649–739.

---

[106] See Restatement 2d of Contracts § 175(2) and § 177(3).

CHAPTER 16
ABUSE OF CIRCUMSTANCES

16.1 INTRODUCTION

This chapter will focus on the question of whether a contract can be avoided if one party took an excessive advantage by abusing the situation in which the other party found himself. This situation is also referred to as qualified *laesio enormis* or excessive benefit or unfair advantage, which is the heading of the relevant provision in PECL (Article 4:109). We will discuss the general doctrines under continental law and subsequently deal with the situation under English law. Then, other abuses of circumstance will be discussed, for instance, is an excessive advantage or a gross disproportion in the mutual performances required, and, finally, abuse of circumstances by third parties.

However, we will start by discussing *laesio enormis*, which refers to the situation where there is simply a gross disproportion between the mutual performances. Can a contract be avoided on that ground?

16.2 *LAESIO ENORMIS*

In this section the focus will be on the question as to whether a contract can be avoided on the ground of *laesio enormis*, simply because there is a gross disproportion between the mutual performances.

Code civil **16.1 (FR)**

Article 1674: Where a seller has suffered a loss greater than seven-twelfths of the price of an immovable, he is entitled to apply for the rescission of the sale, even though he may have expressly renounced in the contract the faculty of applying for that rescission and have declared to donate the surplus.

Article 1675: In order to ascertain whether there has been a loss of the seven-twelfths, the immovable must be appraised according to its condition and its value at the time of the sale.

  (Act of 28 Nov 1949) In the case of a unilateral promise of sale, the loss is appraised on the day of its execution.

Notes

(1) Article 1674 Code civil is a specific provision, which applies to sales contracts only and is not affected by the French reform which concerns general contract law. This provision only applies where the seller of an immovable (there is no similar right for the buyer) suffered a loss greater than seven-twelfths of the price of the property.

(2) Article 1677 sets an additional condition regarding the establishment and the proof of the *lésion*. The only way is by a judgment. It has been held by the courts that the test is purely objective in that *lésion* is a ground for rescission 'in and by itself, independently of the circumstances which may have accompanied it or given rise to it'.[1]

(3) None of Dutch, English or German laws recognises a disparity in value alone as a ground of 'rescission' (the term used in Article 1674 of the Code civil) or invalidity.[2]

BGH, 24 January 1979[3]   **16.2 (DE)**

The pool/billiards equipment

A (gross) disparity in value between the performances does not in itself render the contract void for being contrary to public policy (§ 138 BGB).

Facts: On 24 January 1973 the claimant and the defendant, who at that time was running a hotel and restaurant business, concluded an agreement headed 'Rental Agreement' in respect of pool/billiards equipment. Under that agreement, the defendant was required, with effect from a date four weeks after the installation of the equipment, to pay a monthly rental sum of DM 285 plus value added tax at the rate applying from time to time. The agreement contained the following clause: 'After 42 months the equipment becomes the property of the hirer'. In total, the defendant had to pay DM 13,386.70 (42 × DM 285 plus 11% VAT). Upon the installation of the equipment on 1 February 1973, the defendant received a crossed cheque for DM 2,000. Altogether, the claimant was obliged to provide the equipment, which had a market value of DM 3,252.30, and to make a cash payment of DM 2,000 (adding up to DM 5,242.30). There was therefore a disparity between the value of the defendant's performance and the claimant's of almost 250%. By letter of 14 February 1973 the defendant declared that he regarded the contract as void under § 138 BGB.

Held: According to the Bundesgerichtshof, the appellate court rightly held that, despite the disparity in value between the performances, the agreement was not contrary to *bonos mores* (public policy), since there was no usury in the sense of § 138(2) BGB nor a reprehensible motive on the part of the plaintiff which, coupled with the disparity, could have rendered the agreement void under § 138(1) BGB.

Judgment: I. The court hearing the appeal on questions of law and fact examined whether the contract was contrary to public policy and consequently void pursuant to § 138 BGB.

1. The appellate court correctly ruled that the circumstances of the case did not amount to usury. The defendant did not plead necessity or carelessness on his part; moreover, the

---

[1] Req 28 December 1932, S 1933.1.377, annotated by D Torat, DP 1933.1.87, rapport Dumas; see B Nicholas, *The French Law of Contract* (2nd edn, Oxford: Clarendon Press, 1992) 139; J Ghestin, G Loiseau and YM Serinet, *Traité de droit civil: La formation du contrat,* Tome 2 (4th edn, Paris: LGDJ, 2013) nos. 412 ff.
[2] See below pp 632–33. However, §§ 934, 935 of the Austrian ABGB include a doctrine of *laesio enormis*; see H Kötz, *European Contract Law* (2nd edn, Oxford University Press, 2017) 111.
[3] NJW 1979, 758.

Landgericht, to whose statements the higher appellate court referred, rightly found that there had been no carelessness. Nor could the defendant's submission that he lacked experience of life generally and business matters in particular be regarded as a valid plea of 'inexperience'. Even if he did not possess adequate specialist knowledge in relation to the market price and profitability of the billiards equipment, that did not mean that a finding of inexperience on the part of the defendant was appropriate, since, as the appellate court rightly stated, such inexperience cannot be held to exist where the party to the contract in issue merely lacks experience and business knowledge of a specific area of life or commercial activity …

2. The appellant on a point of law wrongly considers that the difference in value between the billiards equipment and the consideration to be furnished by the defendant is so disproportionate that § 138(1) BGB must necessarily be applicable. The view is unanimously expressed in the case-law of the Reichsgericht (RGZ 150, 1 [4]; 165, 1 [14]) and of the Bundesgerichtshof (Senate, NJW 1957, 1274 = LM § 138 [Ba] BGB no. 2; BGH WM 1969, 1256 et seq) that, in the case of an obvious disproportion between consideration and performance in a contract, that contract is void as contrary to public policy where the motives of the party benefitting from the contract are shown to have been reprehensible, particularly in the event of conscious exploitation of the predicament of the other party (see BGH, WM 1971, 857 et seq). In that regard, the fact that the relationship between consideration and performance is particularly disproportionate may necessarily prompt the conclusion that there has been conscious or grossly negligent exploitation of some factual circumstance restricting the freedom of action of the other party to the contract (RGZ 150, 1 [6]; Senate, WM 1969, 1256 et seq; WM 1966, 832 [835]). The appellate court did not misconstrue or misapply those principles. Its refusal to conclude, solely on the basis of the disproportion which it found to exist between the consideration to be furnished by the defendant and the performance incumbent on the claimant (the value of the former being some two and a half times as great as that of the latter), that the claimant's motives were reprehensible fell within the scope of its discretion as the court adjudicating on the facts …

The appellant on a point of law is admittedly correct in his submission that it was not open to the court hearing the appeal on questions of fact and law to proceed, in its examination of the disproportionate relationship between consideration and performance, on the basis of the loan amount specified in the loan application. Instead, it is necessary to have regard to the objective value (market value: BGH, LM § 138 [Ba] BGB no. 1) of all the obligations to be fulfilled by the parties pursuant to the rental agreement of 24 January 1973, rather than those obligations which in fact subsequently fell to be performed (BGH, WM 1977, 399). Accordingly, the defendant was required to pay DM 13,286.70 in 42 monthly instalments of DM 285 each plus 11% value added tax, whilst the claimant for his part was obliged in return to make a cash payment of DM 2,000 and to provide equipment having, according to the findings made in another connection by the court hearing the appeal on questions of fact and law, a market value of DM 3,252.30. It follows, therefore, that the court hearing the appeal on questions of fact and law was correct in its assessment of the respective values in question, notwithstanding that it left out of account the fact—working in the claimant's favour—that the obligation to be performed by the defendant was spread over a period of 42 months and that, to a considerable extent, allowance should therefore be made for this.

The question whether, in the event of a disparity of some 250% between the value of the consideration and that of the performance, it must be concluded that the motives of the party benefitting from the transaction must necessarily be reprehensible cannot be mechanically determined solely by reference to the degree of disparity in terms of the figures involved. The answer will depend on the facts of each individual case. In this connection, the court hearing the appeal on questions of fact and law was not bound to find that the claimant's motives had been reprehensible and, in particular, to conclude that the claimant had been actuated by an unscrupulous and exaggerated pursuit of profit since it has not been shown that the profit is purely and simply reflected in terms of the expense factors contained in the net cash price of DM 6,850 calculated by the claimant. As far as what may be termed the subjective aspect of the matter is concerned, the answer will depend not so much on the objective market value to be ascertained by means of experts' reports as on the value of the performance from the claimant's point of view (see Senate, judgment of 2.2.1960—VIII ZR 200/59, p 16) and on the profit-reducing expense factors needing to be taken into account.

The court hearing the appeal on questions of fact and law was also correct in rejecting the argument that, regardless of whether he was driven by a censurable pursuit of profit, the claimant was actuated by reprehensible motives because he exploited the defendant's troublesome predicament. Nor has the appellant indicated that that was the position. The defendant was clearly prompted to enter into the transaction by a possible exaggerated expectation of profit—which was not subsequently fulfilled—without undertaking (as, being a businessman, he could quite easily have done) an examination of the objective relationship between the value of the consideration and that of the performance. Where it is open to the adversely affected party himself to calculate the advantages and disadvantages of the transaction, and he nevertheless enters into it (particularly where his reasons for doing so are speculative) without properly protecting his interests, notwithstanding that he should necessarily have been expected to weigh those interests up, then there cannot be said to have been any exploitation of a factor restricting the freedom of action of the other party to the contract. Nor has it been shown that an exaggerated expectation of profit on the part of the defendant was brought about by any particular incorrect statement made by the claimant. Moreover, the defendant's further submission in this regard, that the events relating to the cheque for DM 2,000 should not have been left out of account, fails to fulfil the specific criteria governing the application of § 138(1) BGB, since, according to the findings of the court hearing the appeal on questions of fact and law, which deal correctly, from a legal standpoint, with the issue of avoidance on the ground of wilful deceit, and which have not been individually challenged by the appellant, it cannot be assumed that the defendant was misled concerning his obligation to repay that sum in the context of the monthly rental payments.

Note

In German law, an obvious disproportion between the performance and counter-performance does not in itself render a contract void under § 138(1) BGB (nor, of course, under § 138(2) BGB, as paragraph (2) expressly requires the exploitation of one of the enumerated weaknesses in addition to the obvious inequality).[4] In the

---

[4] Palandt/Ellenberger § 138 para 7; the *Pool/billiards equipment* case; and BGH 25 May 1983, BGHZ 87, 309, 317, 318.

Disproportionate loan agreement[5] the BGH decided that not even a particularly gross disparity can in itself void the contract. For the contract to be contrary to public policy under § 138(1) BGB, a further requirement has to be met, which is a subjective one. On several occasions, the BGH has held that, if there is an obvious disparity in the mutual performances, the contract is contrary to public policy and therefore void under §138(1) BGB if the advantaged party displayed a reprehensible attitude, for example by deliberately exploiting the disadvantaged party's weaker economic position.[6] However, the terms of the contract alone may 'suffice ... to indicate a transaction in the nature of exploitation which is contrary to public policy'.[7] Thus, the reprehensible attitude may be inferred from the contractual imbalance.[8] In Section 16.3.A this will be elaborated.

Equally English law has no doctrine of *laesio enormis*. In order for there to be a contract in English law, there must be consideration of some economic value, but this is satisfied without the consideration being 'adequate'.[9] Inadequacy of consideration is a ground for relief, but only when coupled with other factors such as undue influence or unconscionable behaviour. These doctrines are dealt with in the next section.[10] As with German and Dutch law, it must be said that on occasion the additional requirements which have to be met for the doctrine of unconscionability to be satisfied may be inferred from the gross undervalue.[11]

The nearest English law comes to *laesio enormis* is that under Sections 140A–140B of the Consumer Credit Act 1974 (as amended by Consumer Credit Act 2006: these sections replace former Sections 137–40, which dealt with 'extortionate' credit bargains) the English courts may reopen a credit agreement if they determine that the relationship between the creditor and the debtor is unfair to the debtor.

Consumer Credit Act 1974[12]   **16.3 (EN)**

Section 140A: Unfair relationships between creditors and debtors

(1) The court may make an order under section 140B in connection with a credit agreement if it determines that the relationship between the creditor and the debtor arising out of the agreement (or the agreement taken with any related agreement) is unfair to the debtor because of one or more of the following—

(a) any of the terms of the agreement or of any related agreement;

(b) the way in which the creditor has exercised or enforced any of his rights under the agreement or any related agreement;

---

[5] BGH 12 March 1981, BGHZ 80, 153, 16.6 (DE), below, p 635. This decision overruled OLG Stuttgart, NJW 1979, 2409.

[6] cf eg, BGH 24 January 1979, NJW 1979, 758, 16.2 (DE), above, p 630.

[7] BGH 12 March 1981, BGHZ 80, 153, 16.6 (DE), below, p 635; cf the *Pool/billiards equipment* case (above).

[8] cf. Dutch law: Art 3:44(4) BW.

[9] See above, p 351.

[10] See below, pp 645 ff and 651 ff.

[11] See below, pp 641–42 (Note (3)).

[12] New sections inserted by the Consumer Credit Act 2006, ss 19–20.

(c) any other thing done (or not done) by, or on behalf of, the creditor (either before or after the making of the agreement or any related agreement).

(2) In deciding whether to make a determination under this section the court shall have regard to all matters it thinks relevant (including matters relating to the creditor and matters relating to the debtor).

...

Section 140B: Powers of court in relation to unfair relationships

(1) An order under this section in connection with a credit agreement may do one or more of the following—

(a) require the creditor, or any associate or former associate of his, to repay (in whole or in part) any sum paid by the debtor or by a surety by virtue of the agreement or any related agreement (whether paid to the creditor, the associate or the former associate or to any other person);

(b) require the creditor, or any associate or former associate of his, to do or not to do (or to cease doing) anything specified in the order in connection with the agreement or any related agreement;

(c) reduce or discharge any sum payable by the debtor or by a surety by virtue of the agreement or any related agreement;

(d) direct the return to a surety of any property provided by him for the purposes of a security;

(e) otherwise set aside (in whole or in part) any duty imposed on the debtor or on a surety by virtue of the agreement or any related agreement;

(f) alter the terms of the agreement or of any related agreement;

(g) direct accounts to be taken, or (in Scotland) an accounting to be made, between any persons.

...

(9) If, in any such proceedings, the debtor or a surety alleges that the relationship between the creditor and the debtor is unfair to the debtor, it is for the creditor to prove to the contrary.

> *Note*
>
> Normally it will be the overall circumstances which will make the relationship unfair; but it seems that in an extreme case the court may find the relationship to have been unfair solely on the ground that the price charged under the agreement is excessive.

In accordance with the jurisdictions discussed above, an (excessive) benefit does not in itself seem to suffice to avoid a contract under Article 4:109 PECL.[13] The provision requires that the one party knew or ought to have known of the other party's weak bargaining position and, in addition, that he abused that position by either taking advantage of it in a grossly unfair manner or by taking an excessive benefit. This will be discussed in the next section.

[13] See 16.4 (INT), below, p 635.

16.3 ABUSE OF CIRCUMSTANCES AND EXCESSIVE BENEFIT: QUALIFIED *LAESIO ENORMIS*

Can a contract be avoided on the ground of what is here called qualified *laesio enormis*, ie if the one party took an excessive advantage by abusing the situation in which the other party found himself?

Principles of European Contract Law   **16.4 (INT)**

Article 4:109: Excessive Benefit or Unfair Advantage[14]
(1) A party may avoid a contract if, at the time of the conclusion of the contract:

(a) it was dependent on or had a relationship of trust with the other party, was in economic distress or had urgent needs, was improvident, ignorant, inexperienced or lacking in bargaining skill, and

(b) the other party knew or ought to have known of this and, given the circumstances and purpose of the contract, took advantage of the first party's situation in a way which was grossly unfair or took an excessive benefit.

(2) Upon the request of the party entitled to avoidance, a court may if it is appropriate adapt the contract in order to bring it into accordance with what might have been agreed had the requirements of good faith and fair dealing been followed.

(3) A court may similarly adapt the contract upon the request of a party receiving notice of avoidance for excessive benefit or unfair advantage, provided that this party informs the party which gave notice promptly after receiving it and before that party has acted in reliance on it.

16.3.A GENERAL DOCTRINES: CONTINENTAL LAW

BGB   **16.5 (DE)**

§ 138:   Transactions contrary to public policy; usury
(1) A transaction which is contrary to public policy is void.
(2) In particular, a transaction by which a person exploits the position of constraint in which another person finds himself, or the inexperience, lack of discernment or substantial weakness of will of that other person, in order, for his own benefit or that of a third party, to procure the promise of, or to obtain, a pecuniary advantage in return for the provision of a service which is markedly disproportionate to such provision, is void.

BGH, 12 March 1981[15]   **16.6 (DE)**

The disproportionate loan agreement

If there is a marked disproportion between the mutual performances and if the advantaged party had the intention—which may be inferred from the circumstances of the case—to

---

[14] cf Art 3.2.7 UNIDROIT PICC, Art II.7:207 DCFR, Art 51 CESL.
[15] BGHZ 80, 153.

635

exploit the disadvantaged party's economically weaker position, a contract is contrary to public policy and void (under § 138(1) BGB).

Facts: The defendant was 'jointly liable' for the repayment of a loan taken out in March 1976 by her then fiancé, through a credit broker, with B Bank. The 'total loan' amounted to DM 20,325.70. That sum was made up of the following:

1.	Sum paid out	12,000.00 DM
2.	Credit broker's commission	600.00 DM
3.	Extraneous expenses, inquiries, etc	50.00 DM
4.	Insurance premium covering inability to pay the residual debt due in the event of death or incapacity	1,210.00 DM
5.	Monthly loan charges amounting to 0.95% of the 'amount financed' (DM 13,860, representing the sum of items 1 to 4), totalling	6,188.50 DM
6	2% handling charge, application fee, collection expenses arising from the 'amount financed'	277.20 DM
		20,325.70 DM

The total sum was repayable in 47 monthly instalments from 1 May 1976. The debtors fell into arrears with the repayment instalments. The claimant applied for an order requiring the defendant to pay the sum of money due under the contract. The defendant applied for the claim to be dismissed, asserting that the loan contract was contrary to public policy.

Held: The contract is void for being contrary to public policy (§ 138(1) BGB) because there is not only an obvious disproportion between the performances given. For one thing, the monthly loan charge of 0.95% exceeded the predominant market rate of 0.33% considerably, but there was also an intention on the part of the lender to exploit the borrower's weaker financial position. This reprehensible attitude of the lender can be inferred from the circumstances of this case, such as the disparity between the mutual performances.

Judgment: The judgment given in the appeal on questions of fact and law stands up to the test applied to it in the appeal on a point of law. The loan agreement on which the claimant bases its claims against the defendant as a jointly liable party is contrary to public policy and void (§ 138(1) BGB).

I. 1. However, it is not possible in law to uphold the view expressed by the appellate court, to the effect that a loan agreement providing for part payment or payment by instalments will only be contrary to public policy on the ground of a 'particularly serious disparity' between consideration and performance where the effective annual interest rate demanded by the bank exceeds the normal market rate of interest by more than 100%.

(a) It is true that § 138 BGB imposes restrictions on contractual freedom, particularly as regards the way in which the contract is formulated, with a view to preventing abuse of that freedom. However, § 138 is not designed to restrict the subjective assessment by the parties to the contract of the equilibrium between consideration and performance by rendering such assessment subject to the application of objective 'standard prices' established by the courts, such as the fixing of a maximum interest rate applicable to consumer credit transactions. ...

(b) The appellate court is incorrect in its attempts to draw support for its findings from the rules contained in a foreign system of law, namely Austrian law (§ 934 ABGB), and to establish a connection with legal principles which have applied in the past (the *ius commune* concept of *laesio enormis*). The legislature was aware of the provisions of Austrian law and the *ius commune* when it decided against the adoption of a statutory rule whereby, in the absence of abuse of contractual freedom, particularly as regards the way in which the contract is formulated, a contract is rendered contrary to public policy by the existence of an objective disparity, albeit a substantial disparity, between consideration and performance. ... Thus it has also been acknowledged in the relevant case-law that, in order for a transaction to be held contrary to public policy within the meaning of § 138(1) BGB, there must also exist, in addition to a marked objective disparity between consideration and performance, a subjective factual element, in particular a reprehensible motive on the part of the creditor (BGH NJW 1951, 397; 1957, 1274). Otherwise, the concept of *laesio enormis*, which was eliminated by the BGB, would find itself being reintroduced. ...

(c) It is likewise apparent from the way in which the law has developed since the entry into force of the Civil Code that credit transactions which provide for a rate of interest in excess of a given rate are not to be regarded as contrary to public policy solely because of the high level of interest charged, and that regard must also be had to the other circumstances of the case ...

It is true that, according to the current view of the law, the function of § 138 BGB is to secure compliance not only with the moral principles underlying the assessment of legal and social issues but also with the essential principles and basic norms of the law relating to abuse of contractual freedom (see BGHZ 68, 1, 4). It is not possible, however, even taking into account the notions of consumer protection expressed in the various different rules, to infer from the prevailing legal order any principles or norms suggesting that a credit transaction must be held contrary to public policy pursuant to § 138 BGB solely because it provides for a high rate of interest, and without having any regard to the other circumstances of the case ...

2. Moreover, as the appellant has rightly argued, the alternative grounds advanced in support of its judgment by the appellate court, to the effect that the criteria laid down by § 138(2) BGB in respect of usury are fulfilled, are erroneous in law.

The appellate court bases its alternative reasoning on the argument that the factual criteria established by a rule such as that contained in § 138(2) BGB, involving 'factual elements varying as to the limits imposed on them', are fulfilled even where one of the elements in question (in the present case, the marked disparity between consideration and performance) is 'abundantly fulfilled' but another element which is equally essential (in this case, the inexperience of the party contracting with the lender) is 'insufficiently fulfilled' or fulfilled 'only to a limited extent' (the so-called 'heap of sand' proposition).

That view, which has also been the subject of criticism in the works of academic legal authors ..., cannot be upheld. A transaction will be usurious within the meaning of § 138(2) BGB only if *all* of the factual elements constituting usury are fulfilled. It is true that a serious disparity between consideration and performance may provide compelling grounds for supposing that the party benefitting from that objective disparity between consideration and performance has consciously, or with gross negligence, exploited, contrary to public policy, some factor restricting the freedom of action of the other party (see BGH WM 1969, 1255, 1257). However, the appellate court made no findings of fact justifying the conclusion that—assuming there to have been a substantial disparity between consideration and performance—the claimant did actually exploit any youthful inexperience on the part of the defendant, who was not yet 20 years old at the time when the contract was concluded. It is apparent even from the significance attached by the court below to what it found to have been 'artful deceit' in respect of the interest rate that there are no grounds for finding that a usurious transaction took place within the meaning of § 138(2) BGB. The question is therefore whether the findings of fact arrived at by the appellate court are sufficient to establish the existence of a transaction in the nature of usury which is contrary to public policy pursuant to § 138(1) BGB.

II. 1. In its case-law, the adjudicating Senate has assessed credit agreements providing for the grant of loans at a high rate of interest, and for part payment or payment by instalments, in the light of the principles governing transactions in the nature of usury as contemplated by § 138(1) BGB. According to those principles, a loan agreement is void, as the Senate has previously held on a number of occasions (*inter alia* in its judgment of 9 November 1978—III ZR 21/77 = NJW 1979, 805, and, most recently, in its judgment of 10 July 1980—III ZR 177/78 = NJW 1980, 2301, accompanied in each case by supporting arguments), if there exists a marked disparity between the consideration provided by the lender and the obligations imposed on the borrower in consequence of the unilateral formulation of the contract, and if the lender consciously exploits to his own advantage the economically weaker position of the borrower and the latter's inferior bargaining power at the time when the terms and conditions of the loan are fixed. The same considerations apply where the lender, acting in a manner which, from an objective standpoint, is contrary to public policy, irresponsibly closes his eyes to the fact that the borrower is agreeing to terms and conditions which will place a heavy burden on him only because he is in a financially weaker position. The contents and purpose of the loan agreement, together with all the other circumstances surrounding the transaction, must be assessed as a whole. That overall assessment must take into account the consideration and performance obligations laid down by the contract, together with any other rules by which it is governed, including the lender's standard terms and conditions of business (BGH judgment of 25 October 1979—III ZR 182/77 = NJW 1980, 445, 446). Particular weight must be given in that regard to the relationship between the consideration for the loan, the interest payable and the main service provided by the lender, namely the transfer, for a given period of time, of the ability to utilize a capital sum.

2. Those principles underlying the assessment of such cases do not preclude the possibility that the relationship between consideration and performance which is found to exist by the court examining the facts will suffice on its own to indicate a transaction in the nature of exploitation which is contrary to public policy. The Bundesgerichtshof has previously considered, in individual cases concerning commercial loans, the question whether a given rate of interest justifies the conclusion that the transaction is in the nature of exploitation and contrary to public policy. It has confirmed, in relation to transactions involving a particularly high interest rate (rates of 40% or more, for example, and certainly in the case of rates of 50% or more), that such contracts are contrary to public policy. ... In so doing, it has taken into account, to a considerable extent, the risk incurred by the lender in handing over the money ...

3. (a) A comparison of market rates represents an appropriate means of examining, in accordance with the requirements referred to above (II 1), whether there exists a marked disparity between consideration and performance; by means of such a market comparison, it is possible to ascertain what constitutes the customary and economically acceptable consideration which is normally to be provided in return for a loan, and to compare that norm with the credit agreement in issue, in order to verify whether the latter is contrary to public policy (judgments of the Senate of 10 July 1980, *loc cit*, of 17 April 1980—III ZR 96/78 = NJW 1980, 2076, and of 10 April 1980—III ZR 59/79 = NJW 1980, 2074). In that connection, the adjudicating Senate has hitherto not concentrated solely

on the interest rates charged by the finance houses but has also taken into account the whole of the market for loans repayable in instalments involving the lending of comparable sums for comparable periods (judgments of 10 April 1980 and 17 April 1980, *loc cit*, with supporting arguments). That was also the basis on which the court below proceeded. It considered, for the purposes of comparison, the 'predominant' rate of interest indicated in the monthly reports of the Deutsche Bank, which covers not only the rates charged by the finance houses but also those charged by the general clearing banks. The use of such material for comparative purposes by courts adjudicating on the facts has previously been approved by this Senate (see the judgments of 17 April 1980, *loc cit*, and 10 July 1980, *loc cit*) …

III. 1. According to the findings of the court below, the loan repayable in instalments to which the defendant committed herself constituted a loan *arranged through an intermediary* which provided for *insurance cover* in respect of the outstanding residue in the event of the death or incapacity of the borrower. For the purposes of assessing whether the transaction is contrary to public policy, and in the context of the market comparison to be carried out to that end, that circumstance must be taken into account, in accordance with the requirement that all the circumstances of the matter be weighed generally in the balance. The fact that a legally independent brokerage agreement may exist between the intermediary negotiating the loan and the borrower and, in particular, the fact that, in the present case, the insurance contract covering residual indebtedness which was concluded between the claimant and the insurer was legally independent of the loan agreement, is not decisive. For the purposes of assessing whether a credit agreement constitutes a transaction in the nature of exploitation which is contrary to public policy and infringes § 138(1) BGB, the terms and conditions imposed by, and attributable to, the lender must be taken into account, together with 'all the objective circumstances' in which the transaction came to be effected. … The requirement that regard must be had to all the circumstances characterizing the contract involves, in essence, consideration of the purpose and economic significance of the individual acts of consideration and performance in the relationship between the parties, rather than of the outward legal form which the lending bank chooses to attach to the standard commercial operations involved.

In accordance with the requirement that an overall assessment be carried out, proper weight must be given in the market comparison, first of all, to the remuneration payable by borrowers in consideration of the placing of capital sums at their disposal for utilization by them, together with the interest and/or credit charges payable, in credit transactions involving the lending of comparable sums for comparable periods. Other credit charges imposed on the borrower by the lender, such as application fees, must also be included in the assessment. It is true that such costs do not constitute interest charges in the legal sense of the term; they are not a *quid pro quo* for the use of the capital sum in the sense of being dependent on, and referable to, the term of the loan and constituting monetary consideration. However, the fact that the lender may include those costs relating to the provision and grant of the loan as part of the interest constituting the consideration for the use of the capital sum, and that they place a burden on the borrower similar to that imposed by credit charges, conclusively indicates that they must be taken into account. For the bank, interest and credit charges are in a certain sense 'interchangeable'. For the borrower, higher interest payments and lower credit charges (or *vice versa*) may ultimately mean, depending on the way in which the other terms of the contract are formulated, that he is required to bear the same financial burden for a loan of the same amount (see the judgments of the Senate of 10 July 1980, *loc cit*, and of 10 April 1980, *loc cit*, accompanied in each case by supporting arguments).

2. The *arrangement fees* imposed on the borrower and financed by the bank, which were clearly indicated by the latter in the loan agreement, likewise constitute remuneration for the procurement or grant of the sum loaned, and are not, therefore, interest charges within the private law meaning of the term. They must be included as a factor in the overall assessment of the matter, in order to ascertain the total cost of the loan to the borrower. According to the past case-law of the Senate, regard must be had in that context to the purpose which they serve and the advantage which they are intended to give to one or other of the contracting parties (see the judgments of the Senate of 9 November 1978, *loc cit*, of 11January 1979—III ZR 119/77 = NJW 1979, 808, and of 29 June 1979, *loc cit*; ...) ...

3. As the Senate has previously held, the cost imposed on the borrower of the *insurance cover in respect of residual indebtedness* arranged for him by the plaintiff must also be taken into account in the overall assessment of all the circumstances of the matter, and likewise in the comparison of the terms and conditions of the various different credit institutions (see the judgments of the Senate of 11 January 1979, 29 June 1979, 10 April 1980, 17 April 1980 and 10 July 1980, cited above) ...

IV. The findings of the court below and the uncontested facts of the case are such as to justify a conclusive decision in the matter.

The 'predominant' rate of interest shown in the monthly reports of the Deutsche Bank, which the court below took into account in its assessment of the case, represents the average rate of interest, disregarding the top 5% of the credit institutions charging the highest rates and the bottom 5% charging the lowest rates. At the time when the contract was concluded, the predominant rate was 0.33% per month, whilst the monthly rate charged by the plaintiff was 0.95% of the original amount of the loan. That rate diverges considerably—indeed, markedly—from the rate charged by the majority of credit institutions, and thus, in addition, from the normal rate payable for loans repayable in instalments which are not negotiated through an intermediary. The fact that the loan at issue in the present case was of an amount higher than, and was granted for a term longer than, the loans covered by the monthly reports of the Deutsche Bank is immaterial in that regard. The normal commercial interest rate for such a loan might well be lower on account of the reduced administrative expense of granting a larger loan for a longer term. Even if the cost burden imposed on the borrower, particularly in respect of the charges for the negotiation of the loan through an intermediary, which were clearly indicated to him, and the cost of the insurance cover in respect of residual indebtedness, represented the normal commercial remuneration payable for the service rendered by the credit broker and for the insurance protection provided by the insurer, there would still be a marked disparity between consideration and performance as regards the cost of the loan by comparison with the cost of loans from other credit institutions. The general reference made to increased refinancing costs and administrative expenses is not enough to invalidate the indication, suggested by the circumstances of the case, that the transaction involved a marked disparity.

There are in addition further elements which indicate that the transaction constituted exploitation contrary to public policy within the meaning of § 138(1) BGB, namely an unreasonable accumulation of excessive cost burdens imposed in the event of the borrower falling into arrears. In anticipation of such an event, the claimant sought, even at the time when the transaction was held to be contrary to public policy, to impose on the borrowers corresponding charges payable in arrears situations, including a fee, described by the claimant itself as a 'contractual penalty', of 5% due in the event of its having to assert its claims by the institution of legal proceedings, and agreement to a default fee of 1.5% per month over and above the credit charges, without there having been at the time any tacit agreement, as is normally the case in the sector concerned, providing for the reimbursement of unused credit charges in the event of the loan falling due. The imposition of a charge analogous to a penalty in the event that it becomes necessary to resort to legal proceedings is liable not only to place an excessive burden on the borrowers but also to deter them from seeking to safeguard their rights by allowing matters to reach the stage of a lawsuit.

Where a borrower is in a weaker financial position, contractual terms providing for the situation which is to apply in the event of his falling into arrears assume considerable significance. The danger exists that, upon falling into arrears, and faced with the mounting claims of the lender, he will fall into even heavier debt. This also applies with regard to the defendant, who, following her apprentice's final examination, worked as an assistant in a photographic laboratory and who, by assuming responsibility for the repayment of the loan, took on what was for her the substantial commitment of monthly instalment payments in excess of DM 400.

As a result of the form which it took, the entire contract is in the nature of a transaction contrary to public policy, and is void (see the judgment of the Senate of 9 November 1978, *loc cit*, accompanied by supporting arguments) ...

Notes

(1) As has already been noted in 16.2, a contract is void under § 138(2) BGB for being contrary to public policy if one of the weaknesses enumerated in that provision has been exploited and if, in addition, the contract entailed an obvious disproportion between the performance and the counter-performance. This type of case is commonly known as usury. Whether or not the requirement of an obvious disproportion has been met in a particular case must be decided by comparing the objective (market) value of the mutual performances at the moment of conclusion of the contract and by taking into account all the relevant circumstances of the individual case.

(2) As regards the obvious nature of the inequality, Larenz and Wolf[16] write: 'There may only be said to be a "striking" disparity where the disparity is so great that it patently goes beyond the limits of what is justifiable in all the circumstances.'[17]

(3) *Ausbeutung* is the exploitation of a weakness, enumerated in § 138(2) BGB, on the part of the other party. The party exploiting the weakness must have had knowledge of the weakness and of the obvious disparity. Constructive knowledge does not suffice, nor is an intention to exploit required.[18] The weaknesses enumerated in § 138(2) BGB are discussed in detail by commentary writers.[19] If in a particular case the requirements of § 138(2) BGB have not been fulfilled, the contract may be void under §138(1)

---

[16] K Larenz and M Wolf, *Allgemeiner Teil des Bürgerlichen Rechts* (9th edn, Munich: CH Beck, 2004) 749 (§ 41 para 58).

[17] See also Palandt/Ellenberger § 138 para 67; for a *Ratenkreditvertrag*, extensively, BGH 12 March 1981, 16.6 (DE), above, p 635.

[18] See, eg, BGH, 8 July 1982, NJW 1982, 2767, 2768; see also Palandt/Ellenberger § 138 para 74; Larenz and Wolf (n 16 above) 750 (§ 41 para 64).

[19] See eg Soergel/Hefermehl § 138 BGB paras 78–81.

BGB, which lays down the general rule on juristic acts contrary to public policy, as a usury-like contract. The courts have held that a contract is void under § 138(1) BGB if there is an obvious disproportion between the mutual performances and the advantaged party displayed a reprehensible attitude by either deliberately exploiting the weaker economic position of the disadvantaged party or by grossly negligently failing to realise that the disadvantaged party entered into the contract only because of his predicament.[20] It should be noted, however, that the subjective requirement of a reprehensible attitude is in a sense fictitious[21] since the courts are prepared to infer the reprehensible attitude from the objective circumstances of the individual case— especially from (the extent of) the disparity.[22] As the courts have brought the 'usury-like contract' under the sphere of application of § 138(1) BGB, § 138(2) BGB has lost much of its practical importance.

Code civil   **16.7 (FR)**

Article 1143: There is also duress where one contracting party exploits the other's state of dependence on him and obtains an undertaking to which the latter would not have agreed in the absence of such constraint, and gains from it a manifestly excessive advantage.

Article 1144: In the case of mistake or fraud the period for bringing an action for nullity runs only from the day when they were discovered, and in the case of duress the period runs only from the day when it ceased.

Notes

(1) In the revised Code civil the notion of *violence* relates to two situations. It should be noted that in both instances, *violence* is translated as 'duress' in the official translation of the Code civil. The first instance concerns the situation, which this book refers to as threat and was discussed in the previous chapter (Articles 1140–1142). The other type of *violence* concerns the exploitation of the other's state of dependence (Article 1143). This chapter will focus on Article 1143.[23]

(2) The notion of the exploitation of the other's state of dependence existed already in French case law and some cases were based on *violence*, in particular *violence économique*.[24] The revised Code emphasises the abuse of the other's state of dependence and the manifestly excessive advantage it grants to the party who is exerting *violence* (duress).

(3) The Terré project had a provision on *lésion qualifiée*, which was inspired by comparative law. However, it has not become law.

---

[20] See, eg, BGH 12 March 1981, 16.6 (DE), above, p 635.
[21] See Münchener Kommentar/Armbrüster § 138 para 129.
[22] cf eg, BGH 24 January 1979, 16.2 (DE), above, p 630; BGH 12 March 1981, 16.6 (DE), above, p 635.
[23] See also: J Ghestin et al, *Traité de droit civil: La formation du contrat*, Tome 1 (4th edn, Paris: LGDJ, 2013) nos. 1498–1511; F Terré, P Simler and Y Lequette, *Les obligations* (11th edn, Paris: Dalloz, 2013) no. 248.
[24] Cass civ (1) 3 April 2002, no. 00-12932, Bull civ I no. 108.

Cass soc, 5 July 1965[25] **16.8 (FR)**

A pressing need for money

A (labour) contract which is disadvantageous for one party may be avoided on the ground of violence *if that party's consent to enter into the agreement is not freely given because of his urgent need for money.*

Facts: Under a contract dated 22 January 1959, Mr Maly was engaged for six months on a probationary basis as a salesman by Frameco, a manufacturer of concrete products, on terms whereby he was to receive a 3% commission on the net price of direct and indirect sales. As he had to move from Paris to Grenoble, he resigned on 21 September 1959. At that time Mr Maly was in urgent need of money to provide medical treatment for his sick child. On 12 October 1959 he entered into a new agreement with IMAC, a firm, whereby he was, with the authorization of Frameco, to sell the same product as an independent operator and was to receive a commission of 1.5% on direct sales only; this arrangement was to have retroactive effect. On 17 February 1960 Mr Maly sued IMAC, seeking an order requiring that company to pay commission on the basis on the agreement of 22 January 1959.

Held: The Cour de cassation upheld the decision of the appellate court that the contract of 12 October 1959 was to be declared void on the ground of duress as Mr Maly's consent, given, among other things, his pressing need of money, had been constrained.

Judgment:—Whereas the contested judgment is challenged in that (a) it declared the agreement of 12 October 1959 void on the ground that it was vitiated by 'violence', (b) it held that the relationship between the parties continued to be governed by the agreement of 22 January 1959 and (c) it appointed an expert to calculate the commission due, on the grounds that Maly had had certain doubts as to the enforceability against IMAC of the agreement entered into with Frameco and that Maly had only agreed to accept the conditions laid down in the agreement of 12 October 1959 because of the constraint in which he found himself.

— Whereas according to the appellant, it is patently clear that Maly at all times worked on behalf of IMAC, that it was that company which paid him his commission and which he sued for payment of the commission provided for under the original agreement, and that he could not therefore have been unaware that that agreement could if necessary be enforced against IMAC; as furthermore, the legal status of a salesman is such that he is required to exercise his profession on an exclusive and steadfast basis, and the contested judgment, which did not examine the question whether, as is contended by IMAC, Maly had sold goods for a competitor, provided no legal basis for the decision delivered by the court below; as lastly, the appellant contends that the findings in the contested judgment do not adequately establish, first, that the rate of commission was not reduced in pursuance of an agreement between the parties and, second, that the contract of 12 October 1959 was entered into in circumstances of compelling constraint amounting to 'violence'.

— Whereas the contested judgment found, however, that, at the time of his resignation, Maly, who was required to leave Paris and take up residence in Grenoble with a sick child, was in pressing need of money, that his employer refused to perform the obligations imposed by the initial contract, that he was faced with the alternative of either bringing what might prove to be protracted proceedings or agreeing to the immediate receipt of a reduced sum by consenting to pursue his activities on draconian terms which involved a considerable reduction in the rate of commission and the renunciation of social benefits, etc, one of those terms being unlawful and their provisions as a whole being

---

[25] Bull civ V no. 545.

inequitable; as the complaint that Maly had effected sales for a competitor undertaking—which Maly contested, stating that the company had agreed to his carrying out such operations on an occasional basis—was not levelled against him by the company at the time of his departure, the company having, on the contrary, expressed its regret at seeing him go, and was only raised in the course of the proceedings; as moreover, he had not exerted any influence on the signature of the second agreement.

— Whereas in inferring from this that Maly's consent had been vitiated by intellectual 'violence' [*violence morale*] and that the contract of 12 October 1959 was void, the contested judgment provided a legal basis for the decision therein contained.

Note

French case law had been struggling with the question of whether or not a contract may be avoided on the ground of *violence* when the constraint of the will did not arise from a threat but from the external circumstances in which one party found himself, such as a state of necessity or economic dependence. The courts referred to *violence morale*—arising from a state of necessity and required that the other party had gained an excessive advantage by abusing the state of necessity. *The Rolf* illustrates this position: the Cour de cassation upheld the decision of the appellate court that the agreement could be avoided because of *violence (morale)* as the captain of the *Rolf*, in danger of being lost unless it was pulled off the sandbank, agreed to pay an excessive price.[26] However, French case law was not well settled. In 2002, the Cour de cassation refused to consider that economic dependence could, as such, constitute *violence* and set the rule that the strong party must have unduly made use of an economic dependence situation, to take advantage of the fear of a party whose legitimate interests are directly jeopardised, insomuch as making illegitimate the economic pressure.[27] Based on this, new Article 1143 sets three conditions: one party exploits the other's state of dependence on him, he obtains an undertaking to which the latter would not have agreed in the absence of such constraint and he gains from it a manifestly excessive advantage.

Interestingly, the Belgian courts and legal authors have developed a doctrine of qualified *lésion* based on the doctrine of *cause licite*[28] or the doctrine of *culpa in contrahendo*. On this Belgian doctrine of qualified *lésion*, Jacques Herbots writes:[29]

The doctrine requires two elements: first a serious disproportion between the terms of the contract. But this is not sufficient. Moreover there must be an exploitation of one of the parties, a

[26] Req 27 April 1887, D 1888.1.263; S 1887.1.372; cf the English salvage case of *The Port Caledonia and the Anna* [1903] P 184, see below, p 653.

[27] Cass civ (1) 3 April 2002, no. 00-12932, Bull civ I no. 108: this case is about an employee of Larousse, who, after having been dismissed, argued that her intellectual property rights had been infringed while she was working there, as she allegedly had to agree with terms offered by her employer, out of fear of being dismissed. The Cour de cassation quashed the lower court's decision, as the employee failed to establish that her job was indeed threatened and that her employer would have used this threat as an argument.

[28] cf Cass Civ (1) 3 July 1996, no. 94-14800, Bull civ 1996 I no. 286, D 1997, 499, annotated by P Reigne (*The video club*), 11.19 (FR), above, p 386.

[29] J Herbots, *Contract Law in Belgium* (Deventer/Boston/Brussels: Kluwer Law and Taxation/Bruylant, 1995) 129.

taking advantage of the needs, weaknesses, emotions or ignorance of one of the parties, or an abuse of a dominant position.[30]

In Dutch law, in a case of qualified *laesio enormis*, the contract may be avoided under Article 3:44(4) BW as there has been an abuse of circumstances and the excessive disadvantage should have prevented the one party from prompting the other party to enter into the contract.[31]

16.3.B SPECIFIC DOCTRINES: UNDUE INFLUENCE IN ENGLISH LAW

It is in English law that it is least clear whether there is any equivalent to what is here called qualified *laesio enormis*. Certainly there are certain doctrines which lean in that direction, notably undue influence and the rules on unconscionable bargains. However, the former is distinctly limited in its application while the latter, though of ancient origin, is of uncertain scope in modern law. As we will see later, an attempt by Lord Denning MR to formulate a broad doctrine of inequality of bargaining power was firmly rejected by the House of Lords.[32]

House of Lords	**16.9 (EN)**

Royal Bank of Scotland v Etridge (No 2)[33]

Undue influence may be proven by evidence that one party abused a relationship of emotion or trust between them. If the parties were in a relationship of trust and confidence and the claimant entered a transaction that requires explanation, it will be presumed that this resulted from undue influence unless the other party shows that this was not the case.

Facts: see the judgment.

Judgment:

LORD NICHOLLS OF BIRKENHEAD ...

[5] My Lords, before your Lordships' House are appeals in eight cases. Each case arises out of a transaction in which a wife charged her interest in her home in favour of a bank as security for her husband's indebtedness or the indebtedness of a company through which he carried on business. The wife later asserted she signed the charge under the undue influence of her husband. ... Seven of the present appeals are of this character. In each case the bank sought to enforce the charge signed by the wife. The bank claimed an order for possession of the matrimonial home. The wife raised a defence that the bank was on notice that her concurrence in the transaction had been procured by her husband's undue influence. The eighth appeal concerns a claim by a wife for damages from a solicitor who advised her before she entered into a guarantee obligation of this character.

---

[30] With references to Cass 25 November 1977, Arr Cass 1978, 343 and Comm Brussels 16 April 1974, BRH 1974, 229.

[31] See below, pp 657–58.

[32] Below, pp 655–56.

[33] [2001] UKHL 44, [2002] AC 773.

UNDUE INFLUENCE

[6] The issues raised by these appeals make it necessary to go back to first principles. Undue influence is one of the grounds of relief developed by the courts of equity as a court of conscience. The objective is to ensure that the influence of one person over another is not abused. In everyday life people constantly seek to influence the decisions of others. They seek to persuade those with whom they are dealing to enter into transactions, whether great or small. The law has set limits to the means properly employable for this purpose. To this end the common law developed a principle of duress. Originally this was narrow in its scope, restricted to the more blatant forms of physical coercion, such as personal violence.

[7] Here, as elsewhere in the law, equity supplemented the common law. Equity extended the reach of the law to other unacceptable forms of persuasion. The law will investigate the manner in which the intention to enter into the transaction was secured: 'how the intention was produced', in the oft repeated words of Lord Eldon LC, from as long ago as 1807 (*Huguenin v Basely* (1807) 14 Ves Jun 273 at 300). If the intention was produced by an unacceptable means, the law will not permit the transaction to stand. The means used is regarded as an exercise of improper or 'undue' influence, and hence unacceptable, whenever the consent thus procured ought not fairly to be treated as the expression of a person's free will. It is impossible to be more precise or definitive. The circumstances in which one person acquires influence over another, and the manner in which influence may be exercised, vary too widely to permit of any more specific criterion.

[8] Equity identified broadly two forms of unacceptable conduct. The first comprises overt acts of improper pressure or coercion such as unlawful threats. Today there is much overlap with the principle of duress as this principle has subsequently developed. The second form arises out of a relationship between two persons where one has acquired over another a measure of influence, or ascendancy, of which the ascendant person then takes unfair advantage …

[9] In cases of this latter nature the influence one person has over another provides scope for misuse without any specific overt acts of persuasion. The relationship between two individuals may be such that, without more, one of them is disposed to agree a course of action proposed by the other. Typically this occurs when one person places trust in another to look after his affairs and interests, and the latter betrays this trust by preferring his own interests. He abuses the influence he has acquired …

[10] The law has long recognised the need to prevent abuse of influence in these 'relationship' cases despite the absence of evidence of overt acts of persuasive conduct. The types of relationship, such as parent and child, in which this principle falls to be applied cannot be listed exhaustively. Relationships are infinitely various. Sir Guenter Treitel QC has rightly noted that the question is whether one party has reposed sufficient trust and confidence in the other, rather than whether the relationship between the parties belongs to a particular type (see Treitel, *The Law of Contract* (10th edn, 1999) pp 380–381). For example, the relation of banker and customer will not normally meet this criterion, but exceptionally it may (see *National Westminster Bank plc v Morgan* [1985] AC 686, at 707–709).

[11] Even this test is not comprehensive. The principle is not confined to cases of abuse of trust and confidence. It also includes, for instance, cases where a vulnerable person has been exploited. Indeed, there is no single touchstone for determining whether the principle is applicable. Several expressions have been used in an endeavour to encapsulate the essence: trust and confidence, reliance, dependence or vulnerability on the one hand

and ascendancy, domination or control on the other. None of these descriptions is perfect. None is all embracing. Each has its proper place.

[12] In *CIBC Mortgages plc v Pitt* [1994] 1 AC 200 your Lordships' House decided that in cases of undue influence disadvantage is not a necessary ingredient of the cause of action. It is not essential that the transaction should be disadvantageous to the pressurised or influenced person, either in financial terms or in any other way. However, in the nature of things, questions of undue influence will not usually arise, and the exercise of undue influence is unlikely to occur, where the transaction is innocuous. The issue is likely to arise only when, in some respect, the transaction was disadvantageous either from the outset or as matters turned out.

BURDEN OF PROOF AND PRESUMPTIONS

[13] Whether a transaction was brought about by the exercise of undue influence is a question of fact. Here, as elsewhere, the general principle is that he who asserts a wrong has been committed must prove it. The burden of proving an allegation of undue influence rests upon the person who claims to have been wronged. This is the general rule. The evidence required to discharge the burden of proof depends on the nature of the alleged undue influence, the personality of the parties, their relationship, the extent to which the transaction cannot readily be accounted for by the ordinary motives of ordinary persons in that relationship, and all the circumstances of the case.

[14] Proof that the complainant placed trust and confidence in the other party in relation to the management of the complainant's financial affairs, coupled with a transaction which calls for explanation, will normally be sufficient, failing satisfactory evidence to the contrary, to discharge the burden of proof. On proof of these two matters the stage is set for the court to infer that, in the absence of a satisfactory explanation, the transaction can only have been procured by undue influence. In other words, proof of these two facts is prima facie evidence that the defendant abused the influence he acquired in the parties' relationship. He preferred his own interests. He did not behave fairly to the other. So the evidential burden then shifts to him. It is for him to produce evidence to counter the inference which otherwise should be drawn.

...

[17] The availability of this forensic tool in cases founded on abuse of influence arising from the parties' relationship has led to this type of case sometimes being labelled 'presumed undue influence'. This is by way of contrast with cases involving actual pressure or the like, which are labelled 'actual undue influence' (see *Bank of Credit and Commerce International SA v Aboody* [1990] 1 QB 923 at 953. ... This usage can be a little confusing. In many cases where a plaintiff has claimed that the defendant abused the influence he acquired in a relationship of trust and confidence the plaintiff has succeeded by recourse to the rebuttable evidential presumption. But this need not be so. Such a plaintiff may succeed even where this presumption is not available to him; for instance, where the impugned transaction was not one which called for an explanation.

[18] The evidential presumption discussed above is to be distinguished sharply from a different form of presumption which arises in some cases. The law has adopted a sternly protective attitude towards certain types of relationship in which one party acquires influence over another who is vulnerable and dependent and where, moreover, substantial gifts by the influenced or vulnerable person are not normally to be expected. Examples of relationships within this special class are parent and child, guardian and ward, trustee and beneficiary, solicitor and client, and medical advisor and patient. In these cases the law presumes, irrebuttably, that one party had influence over the other. The complainant

need not prove he actually reposed trust and confidence in the other party. It is sufficient for him to prove the existence of the type of relationship.

[19] It is now well established that husband and wife is not one of the relationships to which this latter principle applies …

INDEPENDENT ADVICE

[20] Proof that the complainant received advice from a third party before entering into the impugned transaction is one of the matters a court takes into account when weighing all the evidence. The weight, or importance, to be attached to such advice depends on all the circumstances. In the normal course, advice from a solicitor or other outside advisor can be expected to bring home to a complainant a proper understanding of what he or she is about to do. But a person may understand fully the implications of a proposed transaction, for instance, a substantial gift, and yet still be acting under the undue influence of another. Proof of outside advice does not, of itself, necessarily show that the subsequent completion of the transaction was free from the exercise of undue influence. Whether it will be proper to infer that outside advice had an emancipating effect, so that the transaction was not brought about by the exercise of undue influence, is a question of fact to be decided having regard to all the evidence in the case.

MANIFEST DISADVANTAGE

[21] As already noted, there are two prerequisites to the evidential shift in the burden of proof from the complainant to the other party. First, that the complainant reposed trust and confidence in the other party, or the other party acquired ascendancy over the complainant. Second, that the transaction is not readily explicable by the relationship of the parties.

[22] Lindley LJ summarised this second prerequisite in the leading authority of *Allcard v Skinner*, where the donor parted with almost all her property. Lindley LJ pointed out that where a gift of a small amount is made to a person standing in a confidential relationship to the donor, some proof of the exercise of the influence of the donee must be given. The mere existence of the influence is not enough. He continued:

> 'But if the gift is so large as not to be reasonably accounted for on the ground of friendship, relationship, charity, or other ordinary motives on which ordinary men act, the burden is upon the donee to support the gift.' (See (1887) 36 ChD 145 at 185.)

…

[30] I return to husband and wife cases. I do not think that, in the ordinary course, a guarantee of the character I have mentioned is to be regarded as a transaction which, failing proof to the contrary, is explicable only on the basis that it has been procured by the exercise of undue influence by the husband. Wives frequently enter into such transactions. There are good and sufficient reasons why they are willing to do so, despite the risks involved for them and their families. They may be enthusiastic. They may not. They may be less optimistic than their husbands about the prospects of the husbands' businesses. They may be anxious, perhaps exceedingly so. But this is a far cry from saying that such transactions as a class are to be regarded as prima facie evidence of the exercise of undue influence by husbands.

[31] I have emphasised the phrase 'in the ordinary course'. There will be cases where a wife's signature of a guarantee or a charge of her share in the matrimonial home does call for explanation. Nothing I have said above is directed at such a case.

A CAUTIONARY NOTE

[32] I add a cautionary note, prompted by some of the first instance judgments in the cases currently being considered by the House. It concerns the general approach to be adopted by a court when considering whether a wife's guarantee of her husband's bank overdraft was procured by her husband's undue influence. Undue influence has a connotation of impropriety. In the eye of the law, undue influence means that influence has been misused. Statements or conduct by a husband which do not pass beyond the bounds of what may be expected of a reasonable husband in the circumstances should not, without more, be castigated as undue influence. Similarly, when a husband is forecasting the future of his business, and expressing his hopes or fears, a degree of hyperbole may be only natural. Courts should not too readily treat such exaggerations as misstatements.

[33] Inaccurate explanations of a proposed transaction are a different matter. So are cases where a husband, in whom a wife has reposed trust and confidence for the management of their financial affairs, prefers his interests to hers and makes a choice for both of them on that footing. Such a husband abuses the influence he has. He fails to discharge the obligation of candour and fairness he owes a wife who is looking to him to make the major financial decisions.

[Further extracts from this case, dealing with the position of the banks, will be found above.[34]]

[The other Law Lords each gave a speech. There are some minor differences between them but Lord Bingham said (at [3]) that Lord Nicholls's opinion 'commands the unqualified support of all members of the House'.]

Notes

(1) The *Etridge* case is now the leading exposition of the doctrine of undue influence. A contract may be avoided by a party (for the purposes of this Note, we will assume the claimant is a woman, the other party a man) who shows that she was the victim of undue influence. She may prove undue influence directly: for example, by showing that she was the victim of improper pressure or coercion, or that she is a vulnerable person who has been exploited (see Lord Nicholls's speech at [11]), or that she left her affairs in the hands of the other party, who abused her trust by preferring his interests to hers (see at [8]–[9]). Lord Nicholls points out that undue influence in the form of coercion such as unlawful threats may now be treated as duress, as we noted earlier.[35]

(2) More frequently, the claimant will not prove directly that they were the victim of undue influence. Instead she will rely on the evidential presumption created by the fact that she placed trust and confidence in the other party and that the transaction between the parties is one 'that calls for explanation' (see at [14]).

(3) In some situations, it will be irrebuttably presumed that there was a relationship of trust and confidence between the parties, for example, where he is her solicitor and she is his client (see above at [18]). In other cases the claimant will have to show that

---

[34] pp 625–26.
[35] Above, p 605.

she placed trust and confidence in the other party. But in neither case will an evidential presumption that there has been undue influence unless there is a transaction 'which calls for explanation.'

(4) Lord Nicholls preferred that phrase to one which had been used in previous cases, 'manifest disadvantage'. In a passage not reproduced above, Lord Nicholls points out that the:

> manifest disadvantage test is hard to apply to cases in which a wife guarantees her husband's business debts—in a narrow sense, having to give the guarantee is a disadvantage to her but overall it may be a perfectly sensible thing for her to do, and one that will help them both, so it does not always require explanation.

(5) In some of the cases before *Etridge*, the judges (following the example of Slade LJ in *Bank of Credit and Commerce International SA v Aboody*[36]) divided the cases up into classes. Class A were cases where actual undue influence was shown; in class 2A cases there was a presumption that there was a relationship of trust and confidence (see Note (3) above); and class 2B cases were ones in which a relationship of trust and confidence was actually shown. But Lord Nicholls does not use this classification and some of the other lords doubted its usefulness.[37]

(6) The presumption of undue influence, once it has arisen, may be rebutted by showing that the plaintiff acted independently of any influence. The most usual way of rebutting the presumption is to show that the plaintiff had independent and competent advice before entering into the contract.[38]

(7) An example of undue influence where the claimant proved a relationship of trust and confidence is provided by *Lloyd's Bank Ltd v Bundy*.[39] In that case the defendant was an elderly farmer who was not well versed in business matters. His son formed a plant hire company. Father, son and the company were customers of the same plaintiff bank. The son's company was in financial difficulties. The defendant had already given a guarantee and a charge for £7,500 over his farmhouse (his only asset) to secure the company's overdraft. On that occasion the defendant had been advised by his solicitor that this was the most he could afford to commit to his son's business. The company's affairs got worse and an assistant bank manager and the son went to see the defendant. The assistant manager told the defendant that the bank could allow the company's overdraft to increase only if the defendant increased the guarantee and charge to £11,000. The defendant signed the form of guarantee and charge. There was evidence that the assistant manager knew that the defendant was relying on him for advice and that the house was the defendant's only asset; he did not explain the company's position in full to the defendant. The plaintiff bank proceeded to enforce the

---

[36] [1990] 1 QB 923, 953 (CA).

[37] See [2001] UKHL 44, [2002] AC 773 at [105]–[107], [158]–[162].

[38] For further details, see *Treitel on the Law of Contract*, 14th edn by E Peel (London: Sweet & Maxwell, 2015) paras 10-027–10-028; J Cartwright, *Unequal Bargaining: A Study of Vitiating Factors in the Formation of Contracts* (Oxford: Clarendon Press, 1991) 185–87. See also H McGregor, *Contract Code (Drawn up on behalf of the English Law Commission)* (London: Sweet and Maxwell, 1994) s 563, paras 3 and 223.

[39] [1975] 1 QB 326; see also 16.11 (EN), below, p 653.

charge and sought possession of the farmhouse. The majority of the Court of Appeal decided that the defendant could set aside the charge on the basis of presumed undue influence by the bank. It should have been obvious to the bank that the defendant was trusting the manager to advise him and so a confidential relationship had been shown on the facts.[40]

(8) Undue influence renders a contract voidable,[41] although the courts and legal doctrine tend to speak of 'granting relief' or 'setting aside the contract'. The contract is avoided by the influenced party giving notice to the other within a reasonable time after the influence comes to an end.

16.3.C SPECIFIC DOCTRINES: UNCONSCIONABILITY AND OTHER RULES IN ENGLISH LAW

Court of Appeal **16.10 (EN)**

Crédit Lyonnais Bank Nederland NV v Burch[42]

For a bank to take as security for a business's debts a charge over a flat belonging to a junior employee of the company with no stake in the business, knowing that the employee had refused to take independent advice, may be unconscionable conduct entitling the employee to set aside the charge.

Facts: The defendant, Miss Burch, had given a guarantee and charged her flat to secure the borrowings of her employer's company. She was a junior employee of the company with no stake in its future. She had been advised by the bank to seek independent advice, but had said she had no need of it.

Held: The charge could be set aside on the ground of undue influence by the employer of which the bank had constructive notice (on this point see below, 3.3.6). The court also said that the charge might also have been set aside on the basis of unconscionable conduct by the bank, except that this argument had not been put to the trial court.

Judgment: NOURSE LJ: On that state of facts it must, I think, have been very well arguable that Miss Burch could, directly against the bank, have had the legal charge set aside as an unconscionable bargain. Equity's jurisdiction to relieve against such transactions, although more rarely exercised in modern times, is at least as venerable as its jurisdiction to relieve against those procured by undue influence. In *Fry v Lane, re Fry, Whittet v Bush* (1889) 40 ChD 312 at 322, [1886–90] All ER Rep 1084 at 1089, where sales of reversionary interests at considerable undervalues by poor and ignorant persons were set aside, Kay J, having reviewed the earlier authorities, said:

'The result of the decisions is that where a purchase is made from a poor and ignorant man at a considerable undervalue, the vendor having no independent advice, a Court of Equity will set aside the transaction. This will be done even in the case of property in possession, and a fortiori if the interest be reversionary. The circumstances of poverty and ignorance of the vendor, and absence of independent advice, throw upon the purchaser,

---

[40] Extracts from Lord Denning MR's judgment in this case will be found below, pp 653–65.
[41] See Cartwright (n 38 above) 192; see also Restatement 2d of Contracts §177(2).
[42] [1997] 1 All ER 144.

when the transaction is impeached, the onus of proving, in Lord Selbome's words, that the purchase was 'fair, just, and reasonable'.'

Lord Selborne LC's words will be found in *Earl of Aylesford v Morris* (1873) LR 8 Ch App 484 at 491, [1861–73] All ER Rep 300 at 303. The decision of Megarry J in *Cresswell v Potter* [1978] 1 WLR 255 at 257 where he suggested that the modern equivalent of 'poor and ignorant' might be a 'member of the lower income group ... less highly educated', demonstrates that the jurisdiction is in good heart and capable of adaptation to different transactions entered into in changing circumstances. See also the interesting judgment of Balcombe J in *Backhouse v Backhouse* [1978] 1 All ER 1158 at 1165–6, [1978] 1 WLR 243 at 250–252, where he suggested that these cases may come under the general heading which Lord Denning MR referred to in *Lloyds Bank Ltd v Bundy* [1974] 3 All ER 757 at 765, [1975] QB 326 at 339 as 'inequality of bargaining power'.

A case based on an unconscionable bargain not having been made below, a decision of this court cannot be rested on that ground ...

Notes

(1) Outside the doctrine of undue influence, equity can give relief against what are often called 'unconscionable bargains' in cases in which the one party, being in a strong position, has exploited a weakness of the other party. One category of these cases involves transactions at (considerable) undervalue by poor and ignorant persons[43]; another, expectant heirs.[44]

(2) So far, the courts have failed to define the basis of their jurisdiction in this area and it is therefore not exactly clear which requirements have to be met if relief is to be granted.[45] Cartwright, however, emphasises:[46] 'that neither an unfair bargain, nor an inequality between the parties' bargaining positions, of themselves, vitiate a contract. What is required is an abuse of that inequality, which may be shown by the existence of an unfair bargain'. See Lord Brightman in *Hart v O'Connor*,[47] who held:

Equity will relieve a party from a contract which he has been induced to make as a result of victimisation. Equity will not relieve a party from a contract on the ground only that there is contractual imbalance not amounting to unconscionable dealing.[48]

(3) In *Boustany v Piggott*[49] the Privy Council set aside a lease on the ground of unconscionability. Lord Templeman, delivering the judgment of the Privy Council, agreed in general terms with the submissions of counsel for the appellant:[50] (i) there must be unconscionability in the sense that objectionable terms have been imposed on the weaker party in a reprehensible manner; (ii) 'unconscionability' refers not only to the

---

[43] See, eg, *Fry v Lane* (1888) 40 ChD 312 (ChD); *Cresswell v Potter* [1978] 1 WLR 255 (ChD).
[44] See, eg, *Earl of Aylesford v Morris* (1873) 8 Ch App 484. For the other categories of cases, see HG Beale, WD Bishop and MP Furmston, *Contract: Cases and Materials* (5th edn, Oxford University Press, 2008) 803 ff.
[45] See E McKendrick, *Contract Law* (12th edn, Basingstoke: Palgrave Macmillan, 2017) 328.
[46] Cartwright (n 38 above) 215.
[47] [1985] AC 1000, 1017–18 (PC).
[48] cf. also *Alec Lobb v Total Oil GB Ltd* [1985] 1 WLR 173 (CA). Equity thus seems to focus primarily on the unconscionable conduct of the stronger party ('procedural unfairness').
[49] (1995) 69 P & CR 298.
[50] (1995) 69 P & CR 298, 303.

unreasonable terms but to the behaviour of the stronger party, which must be morally culpable or reprehensible; (iii) unequal bargaining power or objectively unreasonable terms are no basis for interference in equity in the absence of unconscionable or extortionate abuse where, exceptionally and as a matter of common fairness, 'it is unfair that the strong should be allowed to push the weak to the wall'; (iv) a contract will not be set aside as unconscionable in the absence of actual or constructive fraud or other unconscionable conduct; and (v) the weaker party must show unconscionable conduct, in that the stronger party took unconscientious advantage of the weaker party's disabling condition or circumstances.

(4) In *Crédit Lyonnais Bank Nederland NV v Burch*[51] Millett LJ pointed out that it would be necessary to show that the bank had imposed the objectionable terms in a morally objectionable manner, but said that impropriety might be inferred from the terms of the transaction itself in the absence of an innocent explanation.

(5) It is unclear whether the doctrine of unconscionable bargains will cover the case where the defendant took advantage of the claimant's state of necessity to drive a very hard bargain.[52] English law does have a special rule allowing agreements for salvage to be adjusted if the salvor has charged an extortionate fee: *The Port Caledonia and The Anna*.[53] This rule is not one of common law but of admiralty law, which in turn came from the Roman *ius commune*. Possibly an English court would extend this to give relief against exploitation of the claimant's difficult circumstances in truly exceptional circumstances.[54]

(6) As noted previously, English legislation allows the re-opening of credit agreements in circumstances which amount to qualified *laesio enormis*: see the Consumer Credit Act 1974, Sections 140A–140B.[55]

16.3.D AN ATTEMPT AT A GENERAL DOCTRINE IN ENGLISH LAW

Court of Appeal **16.11 (EN)**

Lloyds Bank v Bundy[56]

[For the decision of the majority of the Court of Appeal, namely that the defendant could set aside the charge on the ground of presumed undue influence by the bank, see above.[57] Lord Denning reached the same conclusion but on broader grounds. What follows here is Lord Denning's heroic (but ultimately unsuccessful) attempt to infer from the case law a general principle that English law grants relief in cases of 'inequality of bargaining power'.]

---

[51] [1997] 1 All ER 144, 153.
[52] See A Burrows, *Law of Restitution*, (3rd edn Oxford: University Press, 2011) 306–07.
[53] [1903] P 184; cf the French case of *The Rolf*, above, p 644, n 26.
[54] See A Burrows, *A Restatement of the English Law of Contract* (Oxford, University Press, 2016), 210.
[55] 16.3 (EN), above, p 633.
[56] [1975] 1 QB 326.
[57] Above, pp 650–51.

Judgment: LORD DENNING MR: …

The general rule

Now let me say at once that in the vast majority of cases a customer who signs a bank guarantee or a charge cannot get out of it. No bargain will be upset which is the result of the ordinary interplay of forces. There are many hard cases which are caught by this rule. Take the case of a poor man who is homeless. He agrees to pay a high rent to a landlord just to get a roof over his head. The common law will not interfere. It is left to Parliament. Next take the case of a borrower in urgent need of money. He borrows it from the bank at high interest and it is guaranteed by a friend. The guarantor gives his bond and gets nothing in return. The common law will not interfere. Parliament has intervened to prevent moneylenders charging excessive interest. But it has never interfered with banks.

Yet there are exceptions to this general rule. There are cases in our books in which the court will set aside a contract, or a transfer of property, when the parties have not met on equal terms—when the one is so strong in bargaining power and the other so weak—that, as a matter of common fairness, it is not right that the strong should be allowed to push the weak to the wall. Hitherto those exceptional cases have been treated each as a separate category in itself. But I think the time has come when we should seek to find a principle to unite them. I put on one side contracts or transactions which are voidable for fraud or misrepresentation or mistake. All those are governed by settled principles. I go only to those where there has been inequality of bargaining power, such as to merit the intervention of the court.

The categories

The first category is that of 'duress of goods'. A typical case is when a man is in a strong bargaining position by being in possession of the goods of another by virtue of a legal right, such as by way of pawn or pledge or taken in distress. The owner is in a weak position because he is in urgent need of the goods. The stronger demands of the weaker more than is justly due: and he pays it in order to get the goods. Such a transaction is voidable. …[58]

The second category is that of the 'unconscionable transaction'. A man is so placed as to be in need of special care and protection and yet his weakness is exploited by another far stronger than himself so as to get his property at a gross undervalue. The typical case is that of the 'expectant heir'. But it applies to all cases where a man comes into property transferred to him: see *Evans v Llewellin* (1787) 1 Cox 333 …[59]

This second category is said to extend to all cases where an unfair advantage has been gained by an unconscientious use of power by a stronger party against a weaker: see the cases cited in Halsbury's *Laws of England*, 3rd ed, vol 17 (1956), p 682 and, in Canada, *Morrison v Coast Finance Ltd* (1965) 55 DLR (2d) 710 and *Knupp v Bell* (1968) 67 DLR (2d), 256. The third category is that of 'undue influence' usually so called. …[60]

The fourth category is that of 'undue pressure'. The most apposite of that is *Williams v Bayley* (1866) LR 1 HL 200…[61]

Other instances of undue pressure are where one party stipulates for an unfair advantage to which the other has no option but to submit. As where an employer—the stronger party—has employed a builder—the weaker party—to do work for him. When the builder

---

[58] For duress of goods, cf above, p 599.
[59] On unconscionable bargains, see above, p 651.
[60] On undue influence, see above, p 645.
[61] On salvage agreements, see above, p 653.

asked for payment of sums properly due (so as to pay his workmen) the employer refused to pay unless he was given some added advantage. Stuart V-C said: 'Where an agreement, hard and inequitable in itself, has been exacted under circumstances of pressure on the part of the person who exacts it, this court will set it aside': see *Ormes v Beadel* (1860) 2 Giff 166, 174 (reversed on another ground, 2 De GF & J 333) and *D & C Builders Ltd v Rees* [1966] 2 QB 617, 625.

The fifth category is that of salvage agreements...[62]

The general principles

Gathering all together, I would suggest that through all these instances there runs a single thread. They rest on 'inequality of bargaining power'. By virtue of it, the English law gives relief to one who, without independent advice, enters into a contract upon terms which are very unfair or transfers property for a consideration which is grossly inadequate, when his bargaining power is grievously impaired by reason of his own needs or desires, or by his own ignorance or infirmity, coupled with undue influences or pressures brought to bear on him by or for the benefit of the other. When I use the word 'undue' I do not mean to suggest that the principle depends on proof of any wrongdoing. The one who stipulates for an unfair advantage may be moved solely by his own self-interest, unconscious of the distress he is bringing to the other. I have also avoided any reference to the will of the one being 'dominated' or 'overcome' by the other. One who is in extreme need may knowingly consent to a most improvident bargain, solely to relieve the straits in which he finds himself. Again, I do not mean to suggest that every transaction is saved by independent advice. But the absence of it may be fatal. With these explanations, I hope this principle will be found to reconcile the cases.

Notes

(1) Lord Denning's new doctrine did not find favour with other judges and was rejected by the House of Lords in *National Westminster Bank Plc v Morgan*.[63] Lord Scarman said:

> Lord Denning MR believed that the doctrine of undue influence could be subsumed under a general principle that English courts will grant relief where there has been 'inequality of bargaining power'. He deliberately avoided reference to the will of one party being dominated or overcome by another. The majority of the court did not follow him; they based their decision on the orthodox view of the doctrine as expounded in *Allcard v Skinner*, 36 ChD 145. The opinion of the Master of the Rolls, therefore, was not the ground of the court's decision, which was to be found in the view of the majority, for whom Sir Eric Sachs delivered the leading judgment.
>
> Nor has counsel for the respondent sought to rely on Lord Denning MR's general principle: and, in my view, he was right not to do so. The doctrine of undue influence has been sufficiently developed not to need the support of a principle which by its formulation in the language of the law of contract is not appropriate to cover transactions of gift where there has been no bargain. The fact of an unequal bargain will, of course, be a relevant feature in

---

[62] [1985] 1 AC 687 (HL).
[63] [1980] AC 614, 634–35; *Treitel* (n 38 above) paras 10-049–10-051.

> some cases of undue influence. But it can never become an appropriate basis of principle of
> an equitable doctrine which is concerned with transactions 'not to be reasonably accounted
> for on the ground of friendship, relationship, charity, or other ordinary motives on which
> men act' (Lindley LJ in *Allcard v Skinner*, at p 185). And even in the field of contract I ques-
> tion whether there is any need in the modern law to erect a general principle of relief against
> inequality of bargaining power. Parliament has undertaken the task—and it is essentially a
> legislative task—of enacting such restrictions upon freedom of contract as are in its judg-
> ment necessary to relieve against mischief: for example, the hire-purchase and consumer
> protection legislation, of which the Supply of Goods (Implied Terms) Act 1973, Consumer
> Credit Act 1974, Consumer Safety Act 1978, Supply of Goods and Services Act 1982 and
> Insurance Companies Act 1982 are examples. I doubt whether the courts should assume the
> burden of formulating further restrictions.

See also Lord Scarman's speech in *Pao On v Lau Yiu Long*.[64] Some authors, on the
other hand, have shown not to be dismissive and do seem to favour a general doctrine
of inequality of bargaining power or unconscionability.[65] Whether any general doctrine in this field will be recognised in English law in the near future is uncertain. Until
then, English law will pursue its piecemeal treatment of this type of case.

(2) There is little doubt that in the nineteenth century the English courts gave relief
more readily than they do today.[66]

(3) A general doctrine of unconscionability has made its way into Australian and
Canadian law.[67]

(4) A doctrine of unconscionability, based on eighteenth-century English cases but
now very much broader, is well established in the US.

Uniform Commercial Code   **16.12 (US)**

§ 2-302: Unconscionable Contract or Clause

(1) If the court as a matter of law finds the contract or any clause of the contract to
have been unconscionable at the time it was made the court may refuse to enforce the
contract, or it may enforce the remainder of the contract without the unconscionable
clause, or it may limit the application of any unconscionable clause as to avoid any unconscionable result ...

Restatement of the Law (Second), Contracts 2d   **16.13 (US)**

§ 208: Unconscionable Contract or Term

If a contract or term thereof is unconscionable at the time the contract is made a court
may refuse to enforce the contract, or may enforce the remainder of the contract without

---

[64] [1980] AC 614, 634 (PC). See further McKendrick (n 45 above) 331–32; D Capper 'Undue Influence
and Unconscionability: a Rationalisation' (1998) 114 LQR 479.

[65] See above, p 653.

[66] See S Waddams, 'Good Faith, Good Conscience, and the Taking of Unfair Advantage' in A Dyson,
J Goudkamp and F Wilmot-Smith (eds), *Defences in Contract* (Oxford: Hart Publishing, 2017) 63.

[67] See, eg, Enman, 'Doctrines of Unconscionability in Canadian, English and Commonwealth Contract Law'
(1987) 16 AALR 191; the Australian case of *Commercial Bank of Australia Ltd v Amadio* (1983) 151 CLR 447.

the unconscionable term, or may so limit the application of any unconscionable term as to avoid any unconscionable result …

16.3.E CAUSATION

The undue influence, *violence morale* or 'abuse of circumstances' exercised by the one party must have caused the other party to enter into the contract. In French and Dutch law the general test of causation applied in cases of threat[68] is also applicable in cases of *violence morale* and 'abuse of circumstances'. In English law, in the case of presumed undue influence, the party presumed to have exercised the influence must show that his conduct did not cause the contract to be concluded—rebuttal of the presumption. As regards the case of actual undue influence, the Court of Appeal has held that the test of causation applied in cases of duress to the person—that it is enough if the undue influence had some causal affect—is also applicable in a case of actual undue influence.[69]

It seems that in German law causation is not a separate requirement under § 138 BGB (at least, it is not discussed as such in the textbooks and commentaries on § 138 BGB). Apparently, for instance in the case of *Wucher*, the requirements of *Ausbeutung* and *auffälliges Mißverhältnis* suffice to render a contract contrary to public policy.

Under Article 4:109 PECL, the words 'takes advantage of' seem to imply that there must be a causal connection.

16.4 OTHER ABUSE OF CIRCUMSTANCES

Can a contract be avoided in a case where the one party has abused the situation in which the other party found himself, but (a) where the contract is not excessively disadvantageous to the latter party, ie there is no gross disproportion in the mutual performances, or (b) where the disadvantage is of a nature other than financial, or (c) where there is no disadvantage at all?

In Dutch law, a contract may be avoided for abuse of circumstances in the sense of Article 3:44(4) BW[70] if the one party promotes the conclusion of the contract even though he knows or ought to know that the other party enters into the contract because of the circumstances he finds himself in, which should have prevented the first party from promoting the conclusion of the contract. It is not required that the contract is grossly disadvantageous to the other party. In fact, the Hoge Raad held that disadvantage is not a constituent element whatsoever.[71] This decision is in tune with the wording of Article 3:44(4) BW, which does not mention disadvantage—and it could be argued that to require disadvantage is unnecessary because the fact that the consent of the abused

---

[68] See 15.2.D at pp 616–17.
[69] *UCB Corporate Services Ltd v Williams* [2002] EWCA Civ 555, [2003] 1 P & CR 12 [86]; see *Chitty on Contracts*, 33rd edn by H Beale (gen ed) (London: Sweet & Maxwell/Thomson Reuters, 2018) para 8-074.
[70] See 15.4 (NL), above, p 599.
[71] HR 5 February 1999, NJ 1999, 652, annotated by PA Stein.

party has been constrained by the abuse itself should suffice to render the contract voidable.[72] Even though excessive disadvantage is not a constituent element, it may be taken into account in establishing whether or not the one party should have refrained from promoting the conclusion of the contract—he should have if he knew or ought to have known that the contract is disadvantageous to the other party.[73] In the context of abuse of circumstances, disadvantage is to be understood in the broad sense of the word: it not only includes material or financial disadvantage, but also immaterial—subjective—disadvantage.[74] Article 3:44(4) BW does not give an exhaustive account of the circumstances which may be abused; thus, an abuse of someone's economic dependence may also render the contract voidable.

In English law, the decision by the Court of Appeal in *Bank of Credit and Commerce International SA v Aboody*[75] that even in actual undue influence cases the claimant must show what was then called[76] manifest disadvantage was overruled by the House of Lords in *CIBC Mortgages Plc v Pitt*.[77] Lord Browne-Wilkinson said:

Whatever the merits of requiring a complainant to show manifest disadvantage in order to raise a Class 2 presumption of undue influence, in my judgment there is no logic in imposing such a requirement where actual undue influence has been exercised and proved. Actual undue influence is a species of fraud. Like any other victim of fraud, a person who has been induced by undue influence to carry out a transaction which he did not freely and knowingly enter into is entitled to have that transaction set aside as of right. No case decided before [*National Westminster Bank Ltd v Morgan*[78]] was cited (nor am I aware of any) in which a transaction proved to have been obtained by actual undue influence has been upheld nor is there any case in which a court has even considered whether the transaction was, or was not, advantageous. A man guilty of fraud is no more entitled to argue that the transaction was beneficial to the person defrauded than is a man who has procured a transaction by misrepresentation. The effect of the wrongdoer's conduct is to prevent the wronged party from bringing a free will and properly informed mind to bear on the proposed transaction which accordingly must be set aside in equity as a matter of justice.

I therefore hold that a claimant who proves actual undue influence is not under the further burden of proving that the transaction induced by undue influence was manifestly disadvantageous: he is entitled as of right to have it set aside.

I should add that the exact limits of the decision in *Morgan* may have to be considered in the future. …

---

[72] See Lord Browne-Wilkinson in *Pitt's* case, see below.

[73] See AS Hartkamp & CH Sieburgh, *Mr. C. Assers Handleiding tot de beoefening van het Nederlands Burgerlijk Recht. 6. Verbintenissenrecht. Deel III. Algemeen overeenkomstenrecht* (Deventer: Kluwer 2014) no. 267.

[74] See HR 29 May 1964, NJ 1965, 1.104; HR 13 June 1975, NJ 1976, 98; *Asser/Hartkamp & Sieburgh 6-III* 2014/267.

[75] [1990] 1 QB 923, 953 (CA).

[76] See above p 650.

[77] [1994] 1 AC 200 (HL).

[78] Above, p 646, at [10].

As to manifest disadvantage not needing to be shown in 'abuse of confidence cases',[79] Article 4:109 PECL[80] does not require abuse of circumstances to have resulted in manifest disadvantage in the sense of 'excessive benefit', as the Article states that the other party must have taken advantage of the complaining party's situation 'in a way which was grossly unfair or took an excessive benefit' (emphasis supplied). The Comment states:

E. Grossly Unfair Advantage

The Article may apply even if the exchange is not excessively disparate in terms of value for money, if grossly unfair advantage has been taken in other ways. For example, a contract may be unfair to a party who can ill afford it even if the price is not unreasonable.

Illustration 5: X, a widow, lives with her many children in a large but dilapidated house which Y, a neighbour, has long wanted to buy. X has come to rely on Y's advice in business matters. Y is well aware of this and manipulates it to his advantage: he persuades her to sell it to him. He offers her the market price but without pointing out to her that she will find it impossible to find anywhere else to live in the neighbourhood for that amount of money. X may avoid the contract.

16.5 ABUSE OF CIRCUMSTANCES BY THIRD PERSONS

Can a contract between A and B be avoided on the ground that B entered into the contract under duress or abuse of circumstances exercised by C, a third person who is not a party to the contract?

Code civil   **16.14 (FR)**

Article 1142: Duress is a ground of nullity regardless of whether it has been applied by the other party or by a third party.

Article 1143: There is also duress where one contracting party exploits the other's state of dependence on him and obtains an undertaking to which the latter would not have agreed in the absence of such constraint, and gains from it a manifestly excessive advantage.

As stated before, the official French translation uses the word 'duress' rather than 'abuse' of circumstances' to refer to the situation that a contracting party abuses the other's state of dependence. Under Article 1143 of the Code civil, duress only occurs if a contracting party exploits the other's state of dependence on him. In other words, if a contracting party exploits the other's state of dependence on a third party—for instance a close friend or a family member—the contract could not be avoided. While this amendment does

---

[79] See also McKendrick (n 45 above) 325–26 and Comment b to Restatement 2d of Contracts § 177 (the unfairness of the transaction is only a factor to be taken into account in determining whether there was unfair persuasion but it is not in itself 'controlling').

[80] See 16.4 (INT), above, p 635.

serve legal certainty, arguably it creates a dissonance with Article 1142 and the general aim of contractual justice.

The Bundesgerichtshof also held that a father (C) had acted contrary to public policy by having his daughter (B) provide security for his debts in favour of a bank (A). The BGH stated that the guarantee (*Bürgschaft*) may be void under § 138(1) BGB if the bank knew that the main debtor had contrary to public policy and illegally influenced the personal guarantee or if the bank had in full knowledge endorsed such behaviour.[81]

BW   **16.15 (NL)**

Article 3:44: (5) If a declaration has been made as a result of threat, fraud or abuse of circumstances on the part of a person who is not party to the juridical act, this defect cannot be invoked against a party to the juridical act who had no reason to assume its existence.

> *Note*
>
>   Under Article 3:44(5) BW, B is not entitled to avoid the contract if A was in good faith and C abused the circumstances.

In English law the same rule applies as in cases of duress: a party who has entered a contract as the result of undue influence by a third person can avoid the contract only if the other party to the contract knew of the undue influence or, since the decision of the House of Lords in *Barclays Bank plc v O'Brien*,[82] had constructive notice of it.[83]

Principles of European Contract Law   **16.16 (INT)**

Article 4:111: Third Persons[84]

(1) Where a third person for whose acts a party is responsible, or who with a party's assent, is involved in the making of a contract:

...

(e) takes excessive benefit or unfair advantage,

remedies under this Chapter will be available under the same conditions as if the behaviour or knowledge had been that of the party itself.

(2) Where any other third person:

...

(d) takes excessive benefit or unfair advantage,

remedies under this Chapter will be available if the party knew or ought to have known of the relevant facts, or at the time of avoidance it has not acted in reliance on the contract.

---

[81] BGH 24 February 1994, NJW 1994, 1341, 1343. See also the section on constitutionalisation of contract law, above, pp 14 ff.

[82] [1994] 1 AC 180, 15.15 (EN), above, p 622.

[83] Please refer to ch 15.

[84] cf Art II.-7:208 DCFR.

Notes

(1) Article 4:111 PECL appears to be influenced by US law as it makes a distinction between cases where A is responsible for C—C acting as an 'agent' for A—and cases where A is not responsible for C.[85]

(2) For cases in which the party is not responsible for the third person, the PECL comment:

B. *Remedies Where Fraud, etc by a Third Person for Whom Party is not Responsible.* A party cannot be fixed with the consequences of improper or careless behaviour of a third person for whom it is not responsible and who does not fall into the other categories mentioned in Comment A. But it should not be allowed to enforce a contract which it knows or should know was concluded only through such behaviour by a third person, if, had it behaved in the same way itself, the other party to the contract could have a remedy under the provisions of this chapter.

Illustration 2: A bank lends money to a husband's business on the strength of a charge, signed by the wife, over the family home. The charge is very much against the wife's interest and the husband has procured the wife's signature by duress. The bank ought to know that it is most unlikely that the wife would sign voluntarily and the bank cannot enforce the charge. It should have made enquiries to ensure that the wife was acting freely. The party should also be liable for damages under Article 4:117 if it knows of the ground for avoidance, or if it knows that the other party has been given incorrect information by a third person but does not inform the other party that the information is incorrect.

(3) Also, the element of reliance in Article 4:111 PECL appears to be borrowed from US law.[86] According to Comment 2 to Article 3.2.8(2) UNIDROIT PICC, the exception to the rule that B may avoid the contract only if A is in good faith is justified because if A has not acted in reliance on the contract A does not need protection.

FURTHER READING

Capper, D, 'Undue Influence and Unconscionability: A Rationalisation' (1998) 114 LQR 479–504.

Cartwright, J, *Unequal Bargaining: A Study of Vitiating Factors in the Formation of Contracts* (Oxford: Clarendon Press, 1991).

Deshayes, O, 'The Search for a Global and Lasting Contractual Balance: the Content of the Contract and the Change of Circumstances' (2017) 6 Special issue of the Montesquieu Law Review 68–76.

Drobnig, U, 'Substantive Validity' (1992) 40 Am J Comp L 635–44.

---

[85] cf Art 3.2.8 UNIDROIT PICC and Restatement 2d of Contracts §175(2), Comment e.

[86] cf Art 3.2.8(2) UNIDROIT PICC. See Restatement 2d of Contracts § 175(2) and § 177(3).

Enman, SE, 'Doctrines of Unconscionability in Canadian, English and Commonwealth Contract Law' (1987) 16 AALR 191–219.

Kennefick, C, '*Violence* in the Reformed Napoleonic Code: the Surprising Survival of Third Parties' in Cartwright, J and Whittaker, S (eds), *The Code Napoléon Rewritten: French Contract Law after the 2016 Reforms* (Oxford: Hart Publishing, 2017) 109–33.

Lohsse, S, 'Validity' in N Jansen and R Zimmermann (eds), *Commentaries on European Contract Laws* (Oxford University Press, 2018) 649–739.

CHAPTER 17
IMMORAL AND ILLEGAL CONTRACTS

17.1 INTRODUCTION

Illegality is recognised in each system, but the extent of the control over what the parties may do and its technical rules vary from one jurisdiction to another.

A contract may be invalid or unenforceable despite the fact that it was made freely and voluntarily by parties who knew what they were doing. If a mafia boss hires a hit-man to kill the police chief, no judge will order the hit-man to perform the contract specifically or the mafia boss to pay the agreed price, even though the parties' agreement was based on a serious intention to be bound and was not tainted by fraud, duress, misrepresentation or mistake.

A contract may involve illegality either in the strict sense of infringing a statutory rule or in the broader sense involving some infringement of public order or morality. Where a statute expressly prohibits a party from making a contract of a certain description it is clear that no court will uphold it. In most cases, however, the bounds of the permissible are not clearly defined, and it is then for the judge to test the circumstances of the case in order to discover whether, by the current standards of morality and public policy, a claim under the contract should be enforced or not. All legal systems reserve the right to declare a contract void or unenforceable, whether totally or partially, if it is legally or morally offensive, contrary to public policy or *ordre public*, or involves the commission of an unlawful act.

Principles of European Contract Law   **17.1 (INT)**

Article 15:101: Contracts Contrary to Fundamental Principles
   A contract is of no effect to the extent that it is contrary to principles recognized as fundamental in the laws of the Member States of the European Union.

Article 15:102: Contracts Infringing Mandatory Rules
   (1) Where a contract infringes a mandatory rule of law applicable under Article 1:103 of these Principles, the effects of that infringement upon the contract are the effects, if any, expressly prescribed by that mandatory rule.
   (2) Where the mandatory rule does not expressly prescribe the effects of an infringement upon a contract, the contract may be declared to have full effect, to have some effect, to have no effect, or to be subject to modification.

(3) A decision reached under paragraph (2) must be an appropriate and proportional response to the infringement, having regard to all relevant circumstances, including:
  (a) the purpose of the rule which has been infringed;
  (b) the category of persons for whose protection the rule exists;
  (c) any sanction that may be imposed under the rule infringed;
  (d) the seriousness of the infringement;
  (e) whether the infringement was intentional; and
  (f) the closeness of the relationship between the infringement and the contract.

Notes

(1) The effects of illegality (partial ineffectiveness, restitution, damages) are dealt with in Articles 15:103–105. The Draft Common Frame of Reference (DCFR) also deals with illegality (Articles II.-7:301, II.-7:302). Arguably for good reasons (how should illegality be defined at an international level?), the first two editions of the UNIDROIT Principles of International Commercial Contracts (UNIDROIT PICC) did not contain rules on illegality; however, such rules were inserted into the third edition UNIDROIT PICC 2010 (see now fourth edition. 2016). They form a Section 3, entitled 'Illegality', of Chapter 3 of UNIDROIT PICC on validity. This section has two articles, one entitled 'Contracts infringing mandatory rules' and one dealing with 'restitution' where there has been performance under a contract infringing a mandatory rule. In the Common European Sales Law (CESL), illegality was left to national laws (see Recital 27).

(2) For the purpose of Article 15:102 PECL, mandatory rules are those applicable under Article 1:103 of the Principles, that is to say those applicable according to the relevant rules of private international law. Article 1:103 distinguishes between two types of mandatory rules: (1) those national mandatory rules which may be rendered inapplicable by the parties' choice of the Principles to govern their contract, where this is allowed by the law which would otherwise be applicable; (2) those rules which are applicable regardless of the law governing the contract according to the relevant rules of private international law. It is infringement of the latter which may trigger the application of Article 15:102.

Continental judges get little help from the words of the civil codes. In most cases the codes simply provide that contracts offending against a statutory prohibition or public policy are void (§ 138 Bürgerliches Gesetzbuch (BGB)) or of no or limited effect. It is noteworthy that Swiss law draws a distinction between contracts which are illegal or immoral—Article 20 of the Swiss Law of Obligations—and those which are in breach of Article 27(2) of the Swiss Civil Code, which provides that 'no one may alienate his liberty or restrict it to a degree inconsistent with law or morals'.

In the majority of cases, the reason that the contract is objectionable is that, like the contract to murder just mentioned, its performance would injure a third party or society at large. On occasion, however, contracts are held to be contrary to public policy because the contract involves some form of exploitation of one party by the other. The link between the two is shown clearly in the BGB, in which the two aspects are dealt with in the separate paragraphs of § 138.¹

BGB   **17.2 (DE)**

§ 134: Statutory prohibition
   A legal transaction that violates a statutory prohibition is void, unless the statute leads to a different conclusion.

§ 138: Legal transaction contrary to public policy; usury
   (1) A legal act that is contrary to public policy is void.
   (2) In particular, a legal transaction is void by which a person, by exploiting the predicament, inexperience, lack of sound judgment or considerable weakness of will of another, causes himself or a third party, in exchange for an act of performance, to be promised or granted pecuniary advantages which are clearly disproportionate to the performance.²

BW   **17.3 (NL)**

Article 3:40: (1) A juridical act which by its content or necessary implication is contrary to good morals or public order is null.
   (2) Violation of an imperative statutory provision entails nullity of the juridical act; if, however, the provision is intended solely for the protection of one of the parties to a multilateral juridical act, the act may only be annulled; in both cases this applies to the extent that the necessary implication of the provision does not produce a different result.
   (3) Statutory provisions which do not purport to invalidate juridical acts contrary to them are not affected by the preceding paragraph.

Code civil of 1804   **17.4 (FR)**

Article 6: Statutes relating to public policy and morals may not be derogated from by private agreements.

Article 1128: Only things which may be the subject matter of legal transactions between private individuals may be the object of agreements.

Article 1131: An obligation without *cause* or with a false *cause*, or with an unlawful *cause*, may not have any effect.

Article 1132: An agreement is nevertheless valid, although its *cause* is not expressed.

Article 1133: A *cause* is unlawful where it is prohibited by legislation, where it is contrary to public morals or to public policy.

---

¹ See also the English cases on restraint of trade, 17.13 (EN) and 17.16 (EN), below, pp 684 and 691.
² § 138(2) was already analysed in chs 15 and 16.

Note

Under Article 6 of the French Code civil, which has been maintained by the 2016 reform, the parties are forbidden to derogate by way of an agreement from laws concerning public order or good morals. A contract is contrary to 'public order' if it violates statutory or judge-made rules protecting the political, social and economic order of the State. Overall, the term 'good morals' is given a more restricted meaning in France than in Germany and other countries since a contract will be invalid as offending the *bonnes moeurs* only when it tends to promote sexual immorality or is inconsistent with basic principles of family life. In a more comprehensive view, good morals may also relate to corruption or improper influence, although these are usually dealt with by specific statutes[3] and also constitute criminal offences.

Before the 2016 reform of French contract law, Article 1128 of the Code civil drew a line between two categories of 'things': those which 'may be the subject matter of legal transactions' (*dans le commerce*) and those which may not (*hors du commerce*). The courts held that a wide variety of transactions was covered by the latter concept, among them the sale of medical clientele (assignment of such a clientele is no longer prohibited),[4] political investiture, fundamental rights attached to the person such as honour, products of the human body, surrogate motherhood, tombs and family 'souvenirs'.

The Code civil also linked the problem of illegality to the concept of *cause*. In fact, the Section dedicated to *cause* (ex-Articles 1131–1133) contained two out of the three provisions which referred to 'illicit' *cause*. This explains the dual role of *cause* in French contract law.[5] The control of the existence of *cause* was distinguished from the control of the legality and the morality of the contract, but that was also carried out in French law through the concept of *cause*. In the latter function, *cause* provided a mechanism for the annulment of contracts whose subject matter may have been perfectly valid (for instance, a lease) but which one of the parties entered for reasons which were objectionable (for instance, prostitution) and thus rendered the contract illicit. In order to control whether the contract was illicit or immoral, the courts looked at the motivation and purpose of the parties, in other words, at the *cause impulsive et déterminante*. This approach was said to be 'subjective'. However, the use of this adjective is misleading, in the light of the evolution of case law. As explained in Chapter 11, the control of the existence of *cause* became an instrument for the protection of the interest that each pursues in exchange for what he agrees to, irrespective of status—consumer, business and professional alike. *Cause* was then used in situations where there was not a total lack of counter-performance but where the counter-performance was of no interest for one party. This analysis of one party's own specific interest has been characterised as the 'subjectivisation of the *cause*'. A good example is the *Video club* case.[6]

---

[3] See, eg, the Bribery Act which was passed on 9 April 2010. See The Law Commission, *Reforming Bribery*, Law Com No 313 (London: The Stationery Office, 2008), superseding a 1998 report on Corruption, Law Com No 248.

[4] Cass civ (1) 7 November 2000, no. 98-17731, Bull civ I no. 283.

[5] See above, ch 11.

[6] See above, 11.19 (FR), p 386.

The concept of *cause* has always generated a lot of debate in France and, mainly due to the confusion it raised, some doubted whether the concept as such should be maintained in French law. Strong views were expressed on the occasion of various draft reform projects.

The concept was abandoned by the 2016 reform. Yet, it is unlikely that the absence of *cause* in the new Code civil will change the way that illegality and immorality will be treated in the future by the case law. Although the word *cause* has been deleted, the main applications of the concept introduced by case law have been maintained.

Code civil **17.5 (FR)**

Article 1128: The following are necessary for the validity of a contract:

...

3. content which is lawful and certain.

Article 1162: The contract cannot derogate from public policy either by its stipulations, or by its purpose, whether or not this was by all the parties.

A contract may be illicit simply in view of the parties' purpose in making the contract. For instance, the lease of a property is perfectly licit as long as it is not concluded for an illegal purpose.

Under French law, a contract concluded for an illegal purpose is *nul* even if the party's illicit intent was not known to the other party.[7] A different solution used to be adopted, but it was highly criticised on the ground that nullity is *absolue* and that it should therefore be invoked by either party. In order to protect the innocent party's interests, judges will hold the other party liable in tort law or they will freeze restitution by resorting to *nemo auditur*.

In English law, the courts have generally allowed the innocent party to enforce the contract where he had no knowledge of the illegality (see the judgment of Pollock in *Pearce v Brooks* (1866) LR 1 Ex 213 (Ex)), while the guilty party was not allowed to do so. It may be said in support of this rule that the innocent party must be protected. However, this is persuasive only in cases in which the innocent party relies on the validity of the contract. If, on the contrary, the innocent party wants to annul the contract, the contract should still be treated as invalid. As a result, English law allows the party to withdraw from the contract and claim restitution of any performance it has rendered.

The texts of the civil codes on contracts which conflict with good morals, public order or legal prohibitions are all couched in very broad terms and need to be fleshed out by reference to court decisions. Writers who try to put the cases into some sort of order invariably add that the categories they adopt are neither exhaustive nor mutually exclusive. Among the contracts that are potentially invalid as illegal or immoral are bargains harmful to the administration of justice, contracts intended to defraud third parties, agreements inducing a party to breach its contract with another or to commit an unlawful act, and many others.

---

[7] Cass civ (1) 7 October 1998, no. 96-14359, Bull I no. 285; F Terré, Y Lequette and F Chénedé, *Grands arrêts de jurisprudence civile*, vol 2, *Obligations, Contrats spéciaux, Sûretés* (13th edn, Paris: Dalloz, 2015) no. 158.

English law likewise refuses to enforce some contracts that involve an illegal act and contracts that are contrary to public policy for other reasons (some writers prefer to treat both categories of forms of illegality).[8] Thus a contract which involves the commission of a crime or a serious civil wrong[9] may be unenforceable.[10] For such cases the Supreme Court has recently adopted a flexible approach, under which the court must decide whether or not it would be appropriate to enforce the claim being made, taking into account two basic principles: (1) that the claimant should not profit from their own wrong and (2) that the law should act consistently. In deciding whether enforcing a claim would be inconsistent with the rest of the law the court should look at the underlying purpose of the prohibition and any other relevant policies.[11] There are many other categories of contracts which have been held to be unenforceable in English law for reasons of public policy.[12]

In this chapter we shall deal only with cases involving agreements adversely affecting basic principles of family life and sexual morality (17.2), contracts which improperly restrict a person's economic liberties and are therefore in 'restraint of trade' (17.3) and contracts allegedly invalid as being in breach of an express or implied statutory prohibition, or some other crime or civil wrong (17.4). Normally, the invalidity of a contract will be pleaded as a defence to an action for the payment of the contractually agreed price or for damages resulting from the breach of a contractual duty. A quite different question, discussed below in Section 17.5, is whether a party to an illegal or immoral contract must give back what he received under it.

17.2 CONFLICTS WITH PRINCIPLES OF SEXUAL MORALITY AND FAMILY LIFE

The ideas of what is immoral change over the course of time. Behaviour which would have been regarded as utterly repulsive 20 years ago may be tolerated with equanimity, if not eagerly endorsed, by the law today.

---

[8] *Treitel on the Law of Contract*, 14th edn by E Peel (London: Sweet & Maxwell, 2015) ch 11.

[9] See below, ch 17.4.

[10] We use the word unenforceable rather than void (even some English texts speak of contracts void for public policy) because, as will be seen later (below pp 695–705) in English law an illegal contract may have some effect: eg, if it is a contract of sale and the goods are actually delivered, the ownership of the goods will pass from seller to buyer despite the illegality.

[11] See below, p 702.

[12] See *Treitel* (n 8 above) paras 11-032–11-062 listing agreements by married persons to marry; agreements in contemplation of divorce; agreements inconsistent with parental responsibility; agreements in restraint of marriage; marriage brokage contracts; contracts promoting sexual immorality; contracts interfering with the course of justice; contracts purporting to oust the jurisdiction of the courts; contracts to deceive public authorities; the sale of offices and honours; lobbying and bribery; trading with the enemy; contracts which involve doing an illegal act in a friendly foreign country; and contracts restricting personal liberty. In addition, contracts in restraint of trade may be unenforceable.

In the Australian case of *Andrews v Parker*, Stable J said:[13]

> Surely, what is immoral must be judged by the current standards of morality of the community. What was apparently regarded with pious horror when the cases were decided would, I observe, today hardly draw a raised eyebrow or a gentle 'tut-tut' ... George Bernard Shaw's Eliza Doolittle (circa 1912) thought the suggestion that she have a bath in private with her clothes off was indecent, so she hung a towel over the bathroom mirror.[14] One wonders what she would have thought and said to the suggestion that she wear in public one of today's minuscule and socially accepted bikinis, held miraculously in place apparently with the aid of providence, and, possibly, glue.

Public policy and good morals have indeed evolved. For instance, in contracts which relate to love affairs, notions of immorality have constantly retreated over the years.

Contracts which are prejudicial to the institution of marriage were considered contrary to public policy. It is now questionable whether many of the English cases which traditionally fall within the categories of 'contracts contrary to good morals' or 'prejudicial to family life' are still good law. There has been litigation on the effect of a 'prenuptial agreement' under which parties who are getting married agree what their rights should be in the event that the marriage breaks down.[15] The Court of Appeal[16] held that a 'pre-nup' is still contrary to public policy as tending to undermine marriage, but that the court should take what was agreed into account when exercising its wide jurisdiction to adjust the property rights of the spouses on divorce.[17] The case of *Radmacher v Granatino* was appealed to the Supreme Court, where the majority disagreed that a pre-nup is still contrary to public policy.[18] The majority quoted the words of Baroness Hale in an earlier decision[19] on the question whether a 'post-nuptial' agreement might be binding, Baroness Hale had said:

> 38. Leaving aside the usual contractual reasons, such as misrepresentation or undue influence, the only other such reason might be the old rule that agreements providing for a future separation are contrary to public policy. But the reasons given for that rule were founded on the enforceable duty of husband and wife to live together. This meant that there should be no inducement to either of them to live apart ... There is no longer an enforceable duty upon husband and wife to live together. The husband's right to use self-help to keep his wife at home has gone. He can now be guilty of the offences of kidnapping and false imprisonment if he tries to do so: ... The decree of restitution of conjugal rights, disobedience to which did for a while involve penal sanctions, has not since the abolition of those sanctions been used to force the couple to live together: ... It was abolished by the Matrimonial Proceedings and Property

---

13 [1973] Qd R 93, 104 (Queensland Supreme Court).

14 *Pygmalion* (1913) is a play by George Bernard Shaw based on the Greek myth of the same name. It tells the story of Henry Higgins, a professor of phonetics, who makes a bet with his friend Colonel Pickering that he can successfully pass off a Cockney flower girl, Eliza Doolittle, as a refined society lady by teaching her how to speak with an upper class accent and training her in etiquette. The play led to a series of adaptations, among them *My Fair Lady* (1964).

15 In France and Germany, agreements made by a couple will, to a certain extent, be ruled by the law of 'matrimonial regimes'.

16 *Radmacher v Granatino* [2009] EWCA Civ 649, [2009] 2 FLR 1181.

17 The power is conferred by Pt II of the Matrimonial Causes Act 1973.

18 *Radmacher v Granatino* [2010] UKSC 42, [2011] 1 AC 534.

19 *MacLeod v MacLeod* [2008] UKPC 64, [2010] 1 AC 298; Baroness Hale was delivering the opinion of the Board of the Privy Council.

Act 1970, at the same time as the Law Reform (Miscellaneous Provisions) Act 1970 abolished all the common law actions against third parties who interfered between husband and wife.

39. Hence the reasoning which led to the rule has now disappeared. It is now time for the rule itself to disappear …

The majority in *Radmacher v Granatino* continued:

52. We wholeheartedly endorse the conclusion of the Board, in paras 38 and 39, that the old rule that agreements providing for future separation are contrary to public policy is obsolete and should be swept away, for the reasons given by the Board. But … this should not be restricted to post-nuptial agreements. If parties who have made such an agreement, whether ante-nuptial or post-nuptial, then decide to live apart, we can see no reason why they should not be entitled to enforce their agreement.

However, the Supreme Court held that the court's power to make financial adjustment on divorce cannot be taken away by an agreement; though the court should give effect to a nuptial agreement which was freely entered into by each party with a full appreciation of its implications unless in the circumstances prevailing it would not be fair to hold the parties to the agreement, the agreement might turn out to be nugatory. Baroness Hale gave a vigorous dissent, arguing that the decision whether to treat pre-nups as binding should be decided by Parliament. The matter was referred to the Law Commission, which responded:

The Supreme Court, in *Radmacher v Granatino*, has gone as far as it is possible for the courts to go in endorsing the validity of marital property agreements without an amendment of the statutory framework; only legislation can enable parties to enforce agreements without involving the courts' discretionary jurisdiction under the Matrimonial Causes Act 1973. We recommend that legislation be enacted to introduce "qualifying nuptial agreements". These would be a new form of contract, subject to requirements as to their formation including the provision of legal advice and financial disclosure. They would enable couples to make contractual, and truly enforceable, arrangements about the financial consequences of divorce or dissolution. Qualifying agreements could not, however, be used to enable one or both parties to contract out of any responsibility to meet each other's financial needs.[20]

In 2018, a final response from the government was still awaited.[21]

Similar difficulties arise in other countries. For example, in 1986, the French Cour de cassation held that *a gift* to a woman who was at the time the donor's mistress but whom he intended to marry, and later did marry, after his first marriage had been dissolved, was not illicit,[22] and in 1999 a further step was taken: the gift made with the purpose of maintaining an adulterous relationship is no longer considered as immoral.[23]

Another example is prostitution. In the past, a prostitute's claim for the agreed price was regarded as unenforceable in most, if not all, legal systems. Nowadays, many legal

---

[20] The Law Commission, *Matrimonial Property, Needs and Agreements*, Law Com No 343 (London: The Stationery Office, 2014) para 1.35.

[21] In the 2016–17 Parliamentary session, Baroness Deech (Crossbench) introduced a Private Member's Bill intended to make provision, among other things, for binding pre-nuptial and post-nuptial agreements, subject to specified requirements. The Bill had its Second Reading but did not make any further progress.

[22] Cass civ (1) 11 February 1986, no. 84-15521, Bull I no. 21.

[23] Cass civ (1) 3 February 1999, no. 96-11946, Bull I no. 43.

systems would allow it, and other contracts made by prostitutes for the known purpose of furthering their business will also be viewed with more tolerance. In Germany, the government changed the law in an effort to improve the legal situation of prostitutes. Before 2002, German courts repeatedly ruled that prostitution offended against good morals (*verstößt gegen die guten Sitten*) and that contracts were void (therefore, prostitutes could not sue for payment and they could lose their leases). In 2002 a one-page law, the Prostitutionsgesetz (Act on Prostitution) sponsored by the Green Party, was passed by Parliament. It removed the general prohibition on furthering prostitution and allowed prostitutes to obtain regular work contracts. The Act carefully avoids saying that 'Prostitution is not immoral within § 138(1) BGB' or similar, so it is still possible to maintain, as most writers do, that prostitution is immoral. However, the Act in effect overrules the previous case law on that provision by stipulating that a legally enforceable claim follows from a prostitution agreement.

Good morals and public policy are still very prominent in the field of surrogate motherhood. However, there are recent signs of possible evolutions.

Cass Ass plén, 31 May 1991[24]   **17.6 (FR)**

Surrogate motherhood: France I

The wife of a childless couple who arranges that another should bear the husband's child and hand it over on birth is not permitted to adopt the child.

Facts: In order to remedy their childlessness, a married couple had recourse to the Alma Mater association, since wound up. In accordance with a well-established practice, that association put the couple in touch with a woman who agreed to bear a child on their behalf. That child was conceived by artificial insemination, using the husband's sperm. The child, a girl, was declared as having been born on 7 February 1988 to LG, her biological father, who acknowledged her as his progeny. The name of the mother was not stated, her biological mother having given birth to her under the name of X. The wife of LG then lodged an application for full adoption.

Held: The Paris Tribunal de Grande Instance dismissed that application on 26 June 1989. Its decision was overturned by the Paris Cour d'appel (15 June 1990, JCP 1991.II.21563). An appeal to the Cour de cassation was lodged by the Procureur Général (Attorney General) on the ground that a point of law of general interest was in issue. The Cour de cassation quashed the decision of the Paris Cour d'appel and ruled that the adoption of the child by the intended mother was not permitted.

Judgment: The Court:— *As regards the appeal brought before the Cour de cassation by the Procureur Général on a point of law of general interest*—Under Articles 6 and [former] 1128 of the Code civil, together with Article 353 thereof;

— Whereas an agreement whereby a woman undertakes, whether or not free of charge, to conceive and bear a child, with a view to abandoning it on its birth, is contrary both to the public policy principle of the inalienability of the human body and to that of the inalienability of a person's status. According to the contested judgment (Paris, 1re Ch C., 15 June 1990), which overturned the decision of the court below, Mme X …, the wife of M. Y …, was incurably sterile, and her husband therefore gave his sperm to another woman who, after being artificially inseminated, bore and produced the child thus con-

---

[24] Ass plén 31 May 1991, no. 90-20105, Bull AP no. 4.

671

ceived; as upon being born, that child was declared as being the child of Y ..., without its maternal affiliation being stated.

— Whereas in the context of pronouncing the adoption of the child by Mme Y ..., the [contested] judgment states that, as matters currently stand with regard to scientific practice and morality, surrogate motherhood must be regarded as lawful and as not contrary to public policy, and that that adoption is in accordance with the interests of the child, who has been accepted and brought up in the home of M. and Mme Y ... practically since its birth.

— Whereas in so ruling, notwithstanding that the adoption was merely the final stage in an entire process designed to enable a couple to receive into their home a child conceived pursuant to a contract involving its abandonment at birth by its mother, and that that process, which violated the principles of the inalienability of the human body and of personal status, thus constituted an abuse of the institution of adoption, the cour d'appel infringed the abovementioned legislative provisions.

On those grounds, the Court quashes the contested judgment ... but only in the interests of establishing the law and without referring the case back for further adjudication.

Note

In December 2008,[25] the Cour de cassation quashed a cour d'appel decision in a case which concerned the transcription on the civil registers of the birth documents of two children born after a surrogacy contract was made and duly executed, in conformity with Californian law. The cour d'appel had rejected a claim based on public policy, introduced by the public prosecutor. The Cour de cassation held that since statements on the civil registers could only result from a surrogacy contract, the public prosecutor had an interest in bringing an action in nullity of the transcriptions. The Cour de cassation reversed its position by a decision taken in Plenary session on 3 July 2015.[26]

Cass Ass Plén, 3 July 2015[27]   **17.7 (FR)**

Surrogate motherhood: France II

The transcription on civil registers of the birth documents of two children born from a surrogate mother under a foreign surrogate contract is not contrary to public policy. The transcription can only be challenged when the birth certificates are unlawful or forged.

Facts: The birth certificate of the applicant, born in Moscow, had been produced by the Russian authorities. The document designated as parents his father, a French citizen, as well as his mother, the Russian citizen who gave birth to him. The applicant requested that his birth certificate be transcribed into the birth register of the French Consulate. The French Public Prosecutor, however, objected to this request by alleging that the birth was the result of a surrogate motherhood agreement between the French father and the Russian mother.

Held: The cour d'appel ruled that the birth was the result of a fraudulent process, including a surrogate motherhood agreement. This decision was quashed by the Cour de cassation.

[25] Cass civ (1) 17 December 2008, no. 07-20468, Bull I no. 289, D 2009, 1285.
[26] Ass plén 3 July 2015, nos. 14-21323 and 15-50002, Bull. 2015 no. 4.
[27] No. 14-21323, Bull. 2015 no. 4.

Judgment: With respect to the first ground of appeal before the Court: Considering Article 47 of the Code civil and Article 7 of the French Decree of August 3, 1962 amending certain civil status rules, considered in the light of Article 8 of the European Convention for the Protection of Human Rights and Fundamental Freedoms;

Whereas it results from the first two of the foregoing texts that the birth certificate of a French citizen, entered in a foreign country and drawn up in conformity with the forms used in the said country, is transcribed into French Birth Registers, unless other deeds or documents held, external data or information based on the very birth certificate demonstrate, after making all useful verifications, if necessary, that the birth certificate is unlawful or forged or that the facts declared therein do not correspond to reality;

Whereas, according to the ruling under appeal before this Court, K X ..., who was acknowledged by Mr X ... on March 10, 2011, was born on [...] in Moscow; his birth certificate, drawn up in Russia, designates Mr Dominique X ..., a citizen of France, as the father, and Mrs Kristina Z ..., a citizen of Russia who gave birth to the child, as the mother; the Public Prosecutor objected to Mr X ...'s request aiming at having the birth certificate transcribed into a birth register kept by the French Consulate, by alleging the existence of a surrogate motherhood agreement entered into by and between Mr X ... and Mrs Z ...;

Whereas, in order to deny transcription, the ruling holds that there is a number of pieces of evidence likely to establish the existence of a fraudulent process including a surrogate motherhood agreement entered into by and between Mr X ... and Mrs Z ...;

Whereas by ruling as it did, while it had not found that the birth certificate was unlawful or forged or that the facts declared therein did not correspond to reality, the cour d'appel violated the aforementioned texts ...

Notes

(1) The decision of the Cour de cassation to authorise the transcription into French birth registers of the foreign birth certificate of a child born abroad from a surrogate mother is the consequence of the rulings of the European Court of Human Rights (ECtHR). Before 2015, French case law prohibited the transcription of foreign birth certificates into the French birth registers, based successively on two grounds. At first, the Cour de cassation held that such transcription was contrary to public policy, as it violated the principle of unavailability (*indisponibilité*) of personal status.[28] Subsequently, the Cour de cassation refused to allow such transcription on the ground that obtaining a birth certificate in a country in which surrogate motherhood agreements are lawful and then trying to have it transcribed into French registers amounted to fraud.[29]

(2) On 26 June 2014, the ECtHR held, in the *Mennesson v France*[30] and *Labassée v France*[31] cases, that the refusal of the French authorities to transcribe foreign birth

---

[28] Cass Civ (1) 6 April 2011, nos. 09-17130, 09-66486 and 10-19053, Bull I nos. 70, 71 and 72.
[29] Cass civ (1) 13 September 2013, nos. 12-30138 and 12-18315, Bull I no. 176. See also Cass civ (1) 19 March 2014, no. 13-50005, Bull I no. 45.
[30] Case no. 65192/11.
[31] Case no. 65941/11.

certificates into the French registers, on the basis that the children were born as a result of a surrogate motherhood agreement, was contrary to the children's right to respect for their private life. The Court considered that the lack of transcription of the children's birth certificates was undermining the children's identity within French society (*Mennesson v France*, paragraphs 87–95; *Labassée v France*, paragraphs 75–80). The Court thus found that the French position was contrary to Article 8 of the European Convention of Human Rights, which sets forth a right to respect for private life. After the ECtHR ruling, the Cour de cassation reversed its case law on 3 July 2015 and now allows the transcription of foreign birth certificates into French registers regardless of whether the birth certificates result from a surrogate motherhood agreement. Unless the birth certificate is unlawful or forged, or the facts declared in the birth certificate do not correspond to reality, the transcription of the birth certificate can no longer be refused. As a result, the surrogate motherhood agreement alone cannot justify the refusal to transcribe into French birth registers the foreign birth certificate of a child who has one French parent.[32] Finally one must note that the two aforementioned cases—*Mennesson* and *Labassée*—will be heard again by the Cour de cassation as a result of a newly created procedure[33] which has been set up by the Act no. 2016-1547 for the modernisation of Justice: when a decision of the ECtHR holds that a judgment of the Cour de cassation in civil matters did violate a provision of the European Convention, the parties may request a second hearing of their case before the Assemblée plénière of the Cour de cassation.

(3) A similar reasoning has been applied to the adoption of a child born of a surrogate motherhood agreement by the husband of his biological father. The Cour de cassation held, on 5 July 2017, that a surrogate motherhood agreement concluded abroad does not, in itself, prevent a man from adopting his husband's child, born as a result of the surrogate motherhood agreement.[34]

OLG Hamm, 2 December 1985[35]   **17.8 (DE)**

Surrogate motherhood: Germany

An arrangement for surrogate motherhood is illicit and the money paid to the surrogate mother is not recoverable even if the surrogate mother's husband succeeds in claiming the child as his own.

Facts: No children had been born to the applicant and his wife. By written agreements dated 29 November and 18 December 1981, the applicant undertook to pay the respondent DM 27,000 if she was to carry a child procreated by him to full term and hand it over, following its birth, for adoption by the applicant and his wife. After the respondent had been inseminated with the applicant's sperm, she bore a child, which was immediately handed over to the applicant and his wife. Since the respondent was also married, the adoption could not

---

[32] For a recent confirmation of the solution, see Cass civ (1) 29 November 2017, no. 16-50061.
[33] Cass 16 February 2018, nos. 17RDH001 and 17RDH002.
[34] Cass civ (1) 5 July 2017, nos. 16-16455, 16-16901, 15-28597 and 16-20052.
[35] NJW 1986, 781.

proceed until the illegitimacy of the child had been established in proceedings brought by the respondent's husband. Those proceedings were duly brought by the husband—as likewise agreed between the parties—but they were dismissed, since it was established with virtually 100 per cent certainty that the child was his own. The applicant thereupon claimed repayment of the DM 27,000 together with reimbursement of the further costs incurred by him. He applied for legal aid in order to bring his action.

Held: The Landgericht rejected the application for legal aid. The applicant's recourse to the Oberlandesgericht was successful because the action to be brought was sufficiently meritorious (whether or not ultimately successful).

Judgment: ... 2. Furthermore, the action intended by the applicant has also sufficient prospect of success, as far as the applicant seeks repayment of the DM 27,000 paid. The applicant substantiated that he has a claim for repayment based on unjustified enrichment under § 812(1)(1) or (2) BGB; it does not seem to be impossible that he will be able to prove the factual requirements of such a claim.

a) ... The Senate tends towards holding that the promise of payment of 29 November 1981 is void because it is *contra bonos mores*, so that the applicant's payment of DM 27,000 to the respondent lacked a legal base (§ 812(1)(1) BGB).

aa) In commercial terms, the agreement of 29 November 1981, despite being separate from a legal perspective, was only a part of what the parties intended to be one single contractual set of transactions. The parties intended from the outset that the respondent would conceive and give birth to a child procreated by the applicant. Both the agreement of a 'voluntary payment' of 29 November 1981 and the contract of 18 December 1981 which fleshed out the detail served to achieve this aim. ...

It may well be that this single contractual set of transactions is *contra bonos mores* and thus void (§ 138(1) BGB). It is commonly held in the case law that a legal transaction is *contra bonos mores* if it violates the common perception as to decency, shared by all those having reasonable and just views [*das Anstandsgefühl aller billig und gerecht Denkenden*] (Palandt-Heinrichs, BGB, 44th edn, § 138 para 1 b, with further references). Regard must be had to the moral views that are recognised by society; the concept of good morals is filled with content by recourse to the prevailing legal and social morality (Larenz, BGB AT, 6th edn, § 22 III a). In doing this, it is particularly the system of values embodied in the Basic Law [Grundgesetz] that informs private law via § 138 BGB (BVerfGE 7, 198, 206 = NJW 1958, 257; BGHZ 70, 313, 324 = NJW 1978, 943). Using this yardstick, there are serious concerns with regard to the validity of the contractual set of transactions under consideration.

aaa) The Senate does not fail to see that the parties may have had commendable subjective motives. The marriage of the applicant and his wife was not crowned by the birth of their own child. ...

bbb) However, ultimately these subjective features are not decisive. According to the prevailing view in legal scholarship and in the case law, the contractual partners do not need to be aware of their conduct being *contra bonos mores* in order for a contract that cannot be reconciled with the fundamental value judgments of the legal and moral order to be *contra bonos mores*. In the case that falls to be decided much can be said in favour of finding such a fundamental violation of the legal and moral order.

The ethical and legal questions thrown up by modern gene technology are, to some extent, not yet settled, and, to some extent, they are controversially discussed in legal writings. ...

The Senate does not have to decide which of the views ought to prevail. The contractual set of transactions that falls to be considered is particularly *contra bonos mores* because it makes the desired child an object of a bargain and thereby, as it were, degrades it to a commercial good; the contract highly endangers the welfare of the child. As stated above, the agreements of 29 November and 18 December 1981 form an economic whole. The entire scheme of the contract exhibits the characteristics of a contract for work and services: the respondent was to carry to term and give birth to a child engendered by the applicant. He for his part was to pay her a sum by way of remuneration; although this was described as a 'voluntary payment', it was, from an economic standpoint, in the nature of consideration. The payment was clearly not intended merely to compensate the respondent for additional expenditure incurred by her during her pregnancy; the arrangement that the agreed sum was not to be paid until the child was handed over shows in itself that it was intended to represent contractual consideration. Contracts of this kind are rightly described as 'trading in human lives at prices equivalent to the cost of a medium-range car' (Lauff-Arnold, Zeitschrift für Rechtspolitik 1984, 282). The form taken by the contract concealed the critical danger that the child, after being handed over, would continue—even though that may not have been the intention—to retain the characteristics of an item of merchandise. As far as the respondent was concerned, the child was not a wished-for or heaven-sent relative and future member of her family and household, but someone who was to be removed immediately by the applicant. Within the respondent's household, therefore, there was no prospect of any real human devotion of the kind on which a tiny child is dependent from the start of its existence; on the contrary, the respondent had to take care, as far as possible, to avoid building up any deep-seated emotional bond with the child, so as to be able to separate herself from it quickly and painlessly. On the other hand, there was no guarantee that the child would be accepted into the applicant's family as if it were, genetically, their own offspring. It is true that the agreement of 18 December 1981 expressly stated—along the lines of an exclusion of warranty—that 'the child [could] not, as a matter of principle, be rejected'. Notwithstanding that, there were grounds for fearing that the child's prospects of development might from the outset be jeopardised if it failed, wholly or partially, to live up to the applicant's expectations, since it is natural that a child who has been 'acquired' for a considerable financial outlay may be regarded differently from a child who is genetically one's own, whether or not its arrival in this world is a wished-for event. It was impossible to rule out the danger that the child might form the subject of a price/performance comparison. Moreover, the fact of taking the child over might possibly give rise to problems in the applicant's marriage, which could in turn adversely affect the child. It is impossible to foresee, for example, whether the state of the marriage and the emotional condition of the other spouse would be such as to enable her in the long term to put up with the existence in the family of a child who was not her own without any conflict or severe emotional upset occurring; moreover, it is uncertain what effects on the husband's attitude to the marriage might result from his consciousness of sharing the genetic parenthood with another woman (see in that regard BGHZ 87, 169 = NJW 1983, 2073).

Nor was there any certainty with regard to the destiny of the child from a legal standpoint. It is true that the respondent undertook in the agreement of 18 December 1981 to make 'an irrevocable declaration of renunciation following the establishment of pregnancy, releasing the child for adoption'. However, that declaration, quite apart from being void under § 138 BGB, was in any event ineffective, since consent to adoption cannot be given until the child is eight weeks old (§ 1747(3)(1) BGB). Conversely, even if a valid and effective consent to the adoption had been given, there was no guarantee that the applicant and his wife would adopt the child as their own. The decision as to whether an adoption is to take place lies with the Vormundschaftsgericht [Guardianship Court] (§ 1752(1) BGB). An adoption order may only be made if it is in the interests of the child and if there are grounds for anticipating the development of a parent-child relationship between the adoptive parent and the child (§ 1741(1) BGB). Thus there can be no certainty in advance that the intended adoption will take place. …

bb) If the contractual set of transactions is shown to be *contra bonos mores* the applicant can probably claim repayment of the DM 27,000 paid to the respondent.

Surrogate motherhood now tends to be dealt with by the legislator. In France, there is a intense political debate in view of the revision of the law on bioethics. This Statute was enacted in 1994 (Act no. 94-653); it was revised in 2004 and in 2011 (Act no. 2011-814). Although a working group of the Senate had expressed itself in favour of an authorisation, in strictly defined conditions,[36] the 2011 law upheld the prohibition of surrogacy contracts.

In German law, contracts for surrogate motherhood were explicitly made illegal in 2001 by the insertion of § 13a–d in the Adoptionsvermittlungsgesetz of 1976 (Act on the Facilitation of Adoptions).

In England, the prohibition is limited to commercial transactions. Section 1A of the Surrogacy Arrangements Act 1985, as amended by section 36 of the Human Fertilisation and Embryology Act 1990, provides that 'No surrogacy arrangement is enforceable by or against any of the persons making it' and section 2 forbids 'Negotiating surrogacy arrangements on a commercial basis'. The Act, which is aimed at avoiding the commercialisation of surrogacy, prohibits organisations, and people other than intended parents or surrogate mothers themselves, from undertaking certain activities relating to surrogacy on a commercial basis. In 2008, further amendments were made to allow bodies that operate on a not-for-profit basis to receive payment for providing some surrogacy services, by exempting them from the prohibition in the current law. Changes were also made in relation to advertising by non-profit making bodies.[37] Under the 1985 Act, section 3, it is an offence to publish or distribute an advertisement that someone may be willing to enter into a surrogacy arrangement, that anyone is looking for a surrogate mother or that anyone is willing to facilitate or negotiate such an arrangement, but in 2008 the Act was amended so that this prohibition does not apply to an advertisement placed by or on behalf of a non-profit-making body, provided that the advertisement only refers to activities which may legally be undertaken on a commercial basis. This means that a not-for-profit body can advertise that it held a list of people seeking surrogate mothers and a list of people willing to be involved in surrogacy, and that it could bring them together for discussion. But it would remain illegal for anyone to advertise that they wanted a surrogate mother or to be a surrogate mother.[38]

---

[36] In 2008, a working group of the Senate published a Report (Sénat, 'Rapport d'information par le groupe de travail sur la maternité pour autrui, au nom de la commission des affaires sociales et de la commission des Lois', presented by M André, A Milon and H de Richemont, 25 June 2008) advocating for an autorisation, in strictly defined conditions, of surrogacy contracts. Later on that year, the Office parlementaire d'évaluation des choix scientifiques et technologiques of the Assemblée nationale took an opposite view (OPECST, Rapport sur l'évaluation de l'application de la loi du 6 août 2004 relative à la bioéthique). Currently, French law prohibits such contracts, even if they are gratuitous. In 2018, the Etats Généraux de la bioéthique were held (https://etatsgenerauxdelabioethique.fr/blog/le-rapport-des-etats-generaux-de-la-bioethique-2018-est-en-ligne), and a legislative reform which will notably deal with these issues is currently being contemplated.

[37] Human Fertilisation and Embryology Act 2008, s 59.

[38] The Human Fertilisation and Embryology Act came into force on 6 April 2010.

When no statute deals with surrogacy agreements, national judges may refer to fundamental rights, particularly to rights protecting the interests of the child, such as Article 7 of the Convention on the Rights of the Child (right to know and be cared for by one's parents). However, fundamental rights can be used in both ways, either to invalidate or to authorise such contracts. In Italy, for example, courts have applied fundamental rights (Articles 2 and 32 of the Italian Constitution) both to protect the interests of the child and to protect the interests of the intended parents.[39] The Italian legislator then intervened to forbid surrogacy contracts expressly (Act no. 40 of 2004).

Contracts about human body parts are also more and more dealt with by statutes, together with some general provisions of the Codes, when they exist (for instance, former Article 1128 Cciv). For instance, in France, gratuitous contracts on human body parts are authorised within the conditions set forth in the Code de la santé publique. In Germany, dealing with human organs and human tissue is a criminal offence under § 17 of the 1997 Act on Transplantations (Transplantationsgesetz). Contracts with a view to dealing in such objects are therefore illegal and void under § 134 BGB.

To the extent that entering or putting an end to a marriage can be considered juridical acts which are contracts, developments on illegality in this branch of the law are also relevant. In a decision *B and L v United Kingdom*, the ECtHR[40] stated that an impediment on marriages between daughter-in-law and father-in-law is contrary to the right to marry and found a family if it impairs the very essence of the right. The Cour de cassation applied the ECtHR case law and held that the restriction set out in Article 161 of the Code civil was an unjustified interference with the daughter-in-law's right to marry and found a family (Cass civ (1), 4 December 2013). When would a restriction be considered as a justified interference? This question was partly answered in another decision:[41] a man had married his daughter-in-law, who was the daughter of his ex-wife. The appellate court held that the marriage was void. Although the father-in-law and daughter-in-law had no blood connection, the daughter-in-law 'had lived, when she was minor, for six years, with the one whom she subsequently married, and who represented for her, when she was a child, a paternal reference, at least on a symbolic point of view'. The Cour de cassation confirmed that position and affirmed the prohibition on marrying relatives in direct line. Interestingly, in this case, the Cour de cassation, borrowing from the ECtHR's methodology, made a concrete application of the proportionality test. The judges first noted that the restriction set out in Article 161 of the Code civil has 'a legitimate purpose as it aims at safeguarding the integrity of the family and preserving the children from consequences resulting from a change in the family structure'. The Court, however, pointed out that the judge must carry out a case-to-case analysis of the facts, to verify whether or not the restriction at stake causes an unjustified interference to the party's right to marry and found a family. The Court then applied the proportionality test. Based on the facts that the daughter-in-law and father-in-law had no children, that they had been married for only eight years and that the father-in-law represented a paternal reference for the daughter-in-law, the appellate court had rightly considered that, in this

---

[39] C Mak, 'Harmonising Effects of Fundamental Rights in Contract Law' (2007) Erasmus Law Review 59.
[40] ECtHR 13 September 2005, *B. and L. v United Kingdom*, no. 36536/02.
[41] Cass civ (1) 8 December 2016, no. 15-27201, Bull 2016 no. 248.

case, the nullity of the marriage was not a disproportionate interference: the prohibition to marry relatives in direct line 'does not amount to a disproportionate interference with the right to respect for private and family life of [the daughter-in-law]'. In this ruling, the Cour de cassation confirmed that the principle of nullity of marriages between daughter-in-law and father-in-law still holds, although this nullity may be lifted when it is deemed to cause an unjustified interference with the rights of the parties.

In the last decades, the use of illegality in the field of family law has been reduced dramatically. Traditionally, contracts relating to adulterous relationships were avoided because of the illegality of their *cause*. Under Article 212 of the Code civil, spouses owe each other an obligation of fidelity. A contract based on adultery would be deemed to be in violation of this provision and, as a result, would be declared null and void. In 1999, however, the Cour de cassation decided for the first time that a donation made by a married man to his mistress was not null for illegality.[42] This decision was then confirmed by the Plenary Assembly of the Cour de cassation, which held, as a principle, that a donation made in the context of an adulterous relationship is not null for a *cause* contrary to morality.[43] In the same vein, it was decided in 2011 that a contract of 'matrimonial agency' in which one party organised meetings where the other party could meet women is not null.[44] More recently, the promotion and advertising of adultery by websites organising meetings between married individuals was held lawful. The Tribunal de Grande Instance of Paris held that 'the reference to infidelity by the defendant in its adverting materials, on its website or its blog, cannot be characterised as an unlawful act, since the violation of the obligation of fidelity, which belongs to the public order of protection, does not necessarily constitute a fault.'[45]

17.3. CONTRACTUAL RESTRICTIONS ON FREEDOM TO CONDUCT BUSINESS

Contracts or contractual terms (clauses) unduly fettering a person's freedom in the future to carry on his trade, business or profession will be struck down by the courts as being 'in restraint of trade' or contrary to public policy.

A particularly relevant provision in this respect is Article 101 of the Treaty on the Functioning of the European Union (TFEU).

Article 101 TFEU **17.9 (EU)**

1. The following shall be prohibited as incompatible with the internal market: all agreements between undertakings, decisions by associations of undertakings and concerted

---

[42] Cass civ (1) 3 February 1999, no. 96-11946, Bull I no. 43.
[43] Ass plén 29 October 2004, no. 03-11238, Bull AP no. 12.
[44] Cass civ (1) 4 November 2011, no. 10-20114, Bull I no. 191.
[45] TGI Paris 9 February 2017, no. 15/07813. In the same vein, the Cour de cassation held that the mere disclosure of one's unfaithfulness could not amount to libel per se (Cass civ (1) 17 December 2015, no. 14-29549, Bull 2015 no. 334).

practices which may affect trade between Member States and which have as their object or effect the prevention, restriction or distortion of competition within the internal market, and in particular those which:

(a) directly or indirectly fix purchase or selling prices or any other trading conditions;

(b) limit or control production, markets, technical development, or investment;

(c) share markets or sources of supply;

(d) apply dissimilar conditions to equivalent transactions with other trading parties, thereby placing them at a competitive disadvantage;

(e) make the conclusion of contracts subject to acceptance by the other parties of supplementary obligations which, by their nature or according to commercial usage, have no connection with the subject of such contracts.

2. Any agreements or decisions prohibited pursuant to this Article shall be automatically void.

3. The provisions of paragraph 1 may, however, be declared inapplicable in the case of:

— any agreement or category of agreements between undertakings,

— any decision or category of decisions by associations of undertakings,

— any concerted practice or category of concerted practices, which contributes to improving the production or distribution of goods or to promoting technical or economic progress, while allowing consumers a fair share of the resulting benefit, and which does not:

(a) impose on the undertakings concerned restrictions which are not indispensable to the attainment of these objectives;

(b) afford such undertakings the possibility of eliminating competition in respect of a substantial part of the products in question.

The Commission Regulation (EU) No. 330/2010 of 20 April 2010 on the application of Article 101(3) TFEU to categories of vertical agreements and concerted practices lays down block exceptions.[46]

Some of the cases reported in the following pages as leading cases on the application of the doctrine of restraint of trade would most probably nowadays fall within the scope of Article 101. Even if they now play a secondary role, national cases are still interesting insofar as they show what sort of responses national judges are willing to give to clauses unduly fettering a person's freedom in the future to carry on his trade, business or profession.

Very frequently, the objectionable restraint of trade is only part of a larger agreement— for example, it may be an agreement between the seller and the buyer of a business that the seller will not compete with the buyer, or between an employer and employee that after the end of the employment the employee will not compete with the employer. In such cases it is commonly the case that the offending clause will be void or unenforceable, but that the rest of the contract is not affected. In this respect, the rule set out in the Principles of European Contract Law (PECL) Article 15:103 is in accordance with most legal systems.

---

[46] No. 330/2010; in addition, see the Guidelines on Vertical Restraints (OJ C 130/2010, p 1).

Principles of European Contract Law **17.10 (INT)**

Article 15:103: Partial ineffectiveness

(1) If only part of a contract is rendered ineffective under Articles 15:101 or 15:102, the remaining part continues in effect unless, giving due consideration to all the circumstances of the case, it is unreasonable to uphold it.

We shall here focus on contracts which may be void not only because they are inimical to the public interest in freedom of trade and unfettered competition but also in order to protect an economically weaker or inexperienced party against unconscionable contract terms.

In English law, exclusive dealing agreements fall within the doctrine of restraint of trade, as shown by the cases of *Schroeder* and *Esso Petroleum* below. English courts adopt a flexible approach and were generally willing to find a legitimate interest with exclusive dealing agreements. As already mentioned above, nowadays this case law plays a secondary role in the regulation of anti-competitive practices as the primary role is played by statute (the Competition Act 1998) and by European law (Article 101 TFEU).

House of Lords **17.11 (EN)**

Schroeder Music Publishing Co v Macaulay[46a]

A contract which binds a young songwriter to a publisher, giving the latter an exclusive right to publish the composer's songs for a long period but imposing no duty to promote them is void as being in restraint of trade.

Facts: An unknown songwriter, aged 21, entered into an agreement with music publishers in their 'standard form' whereby the publishers engaged his exclusive services during the term of the agreement and the songwriter assigned to the publishers the full copyright for the whole world in all his musical compositions during the term. If the total royalties during the term exceeded £5,000, the agreement was automatically extended for a further five years; otherwise, the agreement was to remain in force for five years. The publishers could terminate the agreement at any time by one month's written notice but no such right was given to the songwriter. The publishers had the right to assign the agreement, but the songwriter agreed not to assign his rights under the agreement without the publishers' prior written consent. The songwriter brought an action claiming, inter alia, a declaration that the agreement was contrary to public policy and void.

Held: Plowman J made the declaration sought, and his judgment was affirmed by the Court of Appeal and the House of Lords.

Judgment: LORD REID: ... The public interest requires in the interests both of the public and of the individual that everyone should be free so far as practicable to earn a livelihood and to give to the public the fruits of his particular abilities. The main question to be considered is whether and how far the operation of the terms of this agreement is likely to conflict with this objective. The respondent is bound to assign to the appellants during a long period the fruits of his musical talent. But what are the appellants bound to do with those fruits? Under the contract nothing. If they do use the songs which the respondent composes they must pay in terms of the contract. But they need not do so. As has been said they may put them in a drawer and leave them there.

[46a] [1974] 1 WLR 1308.

No doubt the expectation was that if the songs were of value they would be published to the advantage of both parties. But if for any reason the appellants chose not to publish them the respondent would get no remuneration and he could not do anything. Inevitably the respondent must take the risk of misjudgment of the merits of his work by the appellants. But that is not the only reason which might cause the appellants not to publish. There is no evidence about this so we must do the best we can with common knowledge. It does not seem fanciful and it was not argued that it is fanciful to suppose that purely commercial consideration might cause a publisher to refrain from publishing and promoting promising material. He might think it likely to be more profitable to promote work by other composers with whom he had agreements and unwise or too expensive to try to publish and popularise the respondent's work in addition. And there is always the possibility that less legitimate reasons might influence a decision not to publish the respondent's work

...

Any contract by which a person engages to give his exclusive services to another for a period necessarily involves extensive restriction during that period of the common law right to exercise any lawful activity he chooses in such manner as he thinks best. Normally the doctrine of restraint of trade has no application to such restrictions: they require no justification. But if contractual restrictions appear to be unnecessary or to be reasonably capable of enforcement in an oppressive manner, then they must be justified before they can be enforced.

In the present case the respondent assigned to the appellants 'the full copyright for the whole world' in every musical composition 'composed created or conceived' by him alone or in collaboration with any other person during a period of five or it might be 10 years. He received no payment (apart from an initial £50) unless his work was published and the appellants need not publish unless they chose to do so. And if they did not publish he had no right to terminate the agreement or to have copyrights re-assigned to him. I need not consider whether in any circumstances it would be possible to justify such a one-sided agreement. It is sufficient to say that such evidence as there is falls far short of justification. It must therefore follow that the agreement so far as unperformed is unenforceable.

I would dismiss this appeal.

[The other law lords delivered judgments to the same effect.]

Note

In this case the great disparity in bargaining power between the parties explains the interventionist approach of the House of Lords. Suppose that there exists fierce competition in the UK between music publishing companies and yet that, despite this competition, all agreements made with young and unknown songwriters have for many years been couched in terms quite similar to those before the court in *Schroeder's* case. Would it not follow from the House of Lords' holding that music publishing companies will refrain in the future from making any contracts with young songwriters, so that the latter will be worse off than if the agreement had been upheld?[47]

---

[47] For an interesting discussion of *Schroeder's* case from the viewpoint of the economic analysis of law, see M Trebilcock, 'An Economic Approach to Unconscionability' in B Reiter and J Swan (eds), *Studies in Contract Law* (Toronto: Butterworths, 1980) 379.

BG, 23 May 1978[48]   **17.12 (CH)**

The jazz singer

A 'management contract' under which a young singer places her entire career in her manager's hands for a period which the manager can extend indefinitely is an excessive restriction on the singer's personal freedom and contrary to Article 27 ZGB.

Facts: The defendant was a young woman who, after having been trained by the claimant for seven months in the art of singing jazz and popular songs, had entered into a 'management contract' with her. In an action brought by the claimant for the payment of a contractually agreed penalty, the defendant argued that the management contract was void under Article 27(2) of the Swiss Civil Code (ZGB), which provides that an agreement is void by which a person 'divests himself of, or restricts, his liberty to an extent contrary to the law or morality'.

Held: The contract was void.

Judgment: ... The defendant assigned to the claimant ... the right to conclude, on the latter's own responsibility, contracts relating to appearances and the release of records, to delegate to a recognized agency responsibility for arranging appearances of all kinds, and for the claimant to collect fees and royalties herself. The defendant covenanted not to appear in public without the claimant's consent, not to enter into any contracts relating to artistic matters, to comply with all instructions given by the claimant, to accept all titles offered, to perform contracts relating to appearances, to meet deadlines and to remain sufficiently independent as to be in a position to make herself available when required. She further covenanted to notify the claimant of enquiries and offers received by her and not to conduct any negotiations in relation thereto, as well as to give immediate notice of any absence lasting several days and of any change of address. Her right to share in decision-making concerning appearances was limited to matters regarding the repertoire, which was to be determined jointly; in the event of any difference of opinion, however, the decision was to lie with the claimant alone. Thus the defendant placed herself, as regards her plans to carve out a career as a pop singer, entirely in the hands of the claimant, and relinquished all power to make her own decisions. She was required to submit to restrictions not only in the sphere of her artistic activities but also with regard to the entire way in which she led her life, since she had to be available whenever the claimant needed her. Consequently, her freedom to lead a meaningful private life was substantially restricted, and her ability to engage in any other occupational activity or training was rendered, if not non-existent, at least fraught with extreme difficulty.

Clearly, the continuation of such a commitment against the defendant's wishes infringed her personal rights. The contract provided for its premature termination within the first two years only if both parties consented thereto and only in the event that the defendant's artistic abilities proved insufficient for the achievement of a 'positive success', in particular if the efforts to secure a recording contract within that period failed to bear fruit. In addition, the contract could be terminated if the defendant permanently discontinued her artistic activities. In both cases, however, the defendant was required to pay the claimant 'all costs relating to expenditure of money and time by the management since the commencement of the contract', which would potentially impose a severe financial burden on the defendant.

---

[48] BGE 104 II 108.

Even after the fixed contractual term of five years had elapsed, the defendant did not automatically win unqualified freedom. In the event that notice to terminate the contract was not given six months prior to its expiry date, it was to be tacitly extended for a further year. And if, at the end of the contract, the defendant were offered a more favourable contract by a third party, the claimant was to have the preferential right 'to conclude within 14 days an equivalent contract'.

The imposition of such a mass of obligations on a 22-year-old, who could hardly yet have formed any clear ideas as to her future professional and artistic career, amounts to a severe restriction of personal freedom and is thus incompatible with Article 27 ZGB.

Note

If a trader agrees to buy certain goods he thereby necessarily limits or restricts his freedom to enter into another contract buying the same goods from somebody else. Clearly, this agreement is not invalid as being in restraint of trade. But suppose that the same trader agrees to buy certain goods from a seller and to refrain from buying them from anybody else for a term of 5, 10 or 20 years? Should this 'exclusive dealing agreement' be struck down as an undue fetter on the trader's freedom to carry on his business as he pleases? What if the seller shows good reasons why a 'tie' of a certain duration is needed for the commercial viability of the operation?

House of Lords   **17.13 (EN)**

Esso Petroleum Co Ltd v Harper's Garage (Stourport) Ltd[49]

A contract between a petrol company and a filling station which binds the latter to selling the company's fuel for five years is reasonable but one for 21 years is void as being in restraint of trade.

Facts: The respondents, the owners of two filling stations, agreed to purchase their total requirements of motor fuels exclusively from the appellants at their list prices in force on the date of delivery. The agreement for Mustow Green Garage was to remain in force for four years and five months, the one for Corner Garage for 21 years. The appellants had lent the respondents £7,000 for the purpose of acquiring the land on which the 'Corner Garage' was being operated and of carrying out constructional work thereon. When the respondents started to sell another brand of petrol at their filling stations the appellants sought injunctions restraining the respondents from buying or selling motor fuels other than those of the appellants.

Held: The solus agreement in respect of Mustow Green garage was upheld, but in respect of Corner Garage the agreement was held to be void.

Judgment: LORD REID: ... It is I think well established that the court will not enforce a restraint which goes further than affording adequate protection to the legitimate interests of the party in whose favour it is granted. This must I think be because too wide a restraint is against the public interest. It has often been said that a person is not entitled to be protected against mere competition. I do not find that very helpful in a case like the

---

[49] [1968] AC 269.

present. I think it better to ascertain what were the legitimate interests of the appellants which they were entitled to protect and then to see whether these restraints were more than adequate for that purpose.

What were the appellant's legitimate interests must depend largely on what was the state of affairs in their business and with regard to the distribution and sale of petrol generally. And those are questions of fact to be answered by evidence or common knowledge.

When petrol rationing came to an end in 1950 the large producers began to make agreements, now known as solus agreements, with garage owners under which the garage owner, in return for certain advantages, agreed to sell only the petrol of the producer with whom he made the agreement. Within a short time three-quarters of the filling stations in this country were tied in that way and by the dates of the agreements in this case over 90 per cent had agreed to ties. It appears that the garage owners were not at a disadvantage in bargaining with the large producing companies as there was intense competition between these companies to obtain these ties. So we can assume that both the garage owners and the companies thought that such ties were to their advantage. And it is not said in this case that all ties are either against the public interest or against the interests of the parties. The respondents' case is that the ties with which we are concerned are for too long periods.

The advantage of the garage owner is that he gets a rebate on the wholesale price of the petrol which he buys and also may get other benefits or financial assistance. The main advantages for the producing company appear to be that distribution is made easier and more economical and that it is assured of a steady outlet for its petrol over a period. As regards distribution, it appears that there were some 35,000 filling stations in this country at the relevant time, of which about a fifth were tied to the appellants. So they only have to distribute to some 7,000 filling stations instead of to a very much larger number if most filling stations sold several brands of petrol. But the main reason why the producing companies want ties for five years and more, instead of ties for one or two years only, seems to be that they can organise their business better if on the average only one-fifth or less of their ties come to an end in any one year. The appellants make a point of the fact that they have invested some £200 millions in refineries and other plants and that they could not have done that unless they could foresee a steady and assured level of sales of their petrol. Most of their ties appear to have been made for periods of between five and 20 years. But we have no evidence as to the precise additional advantage which they derive from a five-year tie as compared with a two-year tie or from a 20-year tie as compared with a five-year tie.

The Court of Appeal held that these ties were for unreasonably long periods. They thought that, if for any reason the respondents ceased to sell the appellants' petrol, the appellants could have found other suitable outlets in the neighbourhood within two or three years. I do not think that that is the right test. In the first place there was no evidence about this and I do not think that it would be practicable to apply this test in practice. It might happen that when the respondents ceased to sell their petrol, the appellants would find such an alternative outlet in a very short time. But, looking to the fact that well over 90 per cent. of existing filling stations are tied and that there may be great difficulty in opening a new filling station, it might take a very long time to find an alternative. Any estimate of how long it might take to find suitable alternatives for the respondents' filling station could be little better than guesswork.

I do not think that the appellants' interest can be regarded so narrowly. They are not so much concerned with any particular outlet as with maintaining a stable system of distribution throughout the country so as to enable their business to be run efficiently and economically. In my view there is sufficient material to justify a decision that ties of less than five years were insufficient, in the circumstances of the trade when these agreements were made, to afford adequate protection to the appellants' legitimate interests.

But the Corner Garage agreement involves much more difficulty. Taking first the legitimate interests of the appellants, a new argument was submitted to your Lordships that, apart from any question of security for their loan, it would be unfair to the appellants if the respondents, having used the appellant's money to build up their business, were entitled after a comparatively short time to be free to seek better terms from a competing producer. But there is no material on which I can assess the strength of this argument and I do not find myself in a position to determine whether it has any validity. A tie for 21 years stretches far beyond any period for which developments are reasonably foreseeable. Restrictions on the garage owner which might seem tolerable and reasonable in reasonably foreseeable conditions might come to have a very different effect in quite different conditions: the public interest comes in here more strongly. And, apart from a case where he gets a loan, a garage owner appears to get no greater advantage from a 20-year tie than he gets from a five-year tie. So I would think that there must at least be some clearly established advantage to the producing company—something to show that a shorter period would not be adequate—before so long a period could be justified. But in this case there is no evidence to prove anything of the kind.

LORD WILBERFORCE: ... The doctrine of restraint of trade (a convenient, if imprecise, expression which I continue to use) is one which has throughout the history of its subject-matter been expressed with considerable generality, if not ambiguity. The best-known general formulations, those of Lord Macnaghten in *Nordenfelt* and Lord Parker of Waddington in *Adelaide*, adapted and used by Diplock LJ in the Court of Appeal in the *Petrofina* case, speak generally of all restraints of trade without any attempt at a definition. Often we find the words 'restraint of trade' in a single passage used indifferently to denote, on the one hand, in a broad popular sense, any contract which limits the free exercise of trade or business, and, on the other hand, as a term of art covering those contracts which are regarded as offending a rule of public policy. Often, in reported cases, we find that instead of segregating two questions, (i) whether the contract is in restraint of trade, (ii) whether, if so, it is 'reasonable', the courts have fused the two by asking whether the contract is in 'undue restraint of trade' or by a compound finding that it is not satisfied that this contract is really in restraint of trade at all but, if it is, it is reasonable. A well-known text book describes contracts in restraint of trade as those which 'unreasonably restrict' the rights of a person to carry on his trade or profession. There is no need to regret these tendencies: indeed, to do so, when consideration of this subject has passed through such notable minds from Lord Macclesfield onwards, would indicate a failure to understand its nature. The common law has often (if sometimes unconsciously) thrived on ambiguity and it would be mistaken, even if it were possible, to try to crystallise the rules of this, or any, aspect of public policy into neat propositions. The doctrine of restraint of trade is one to be applied to factual situations with a broad and flexible rule of reason. ...

This does not mean that the question whether a given agreement is in restraint of trade, in either sense of these words, is nothing more than a question of fact to be individually decided in each case. It is not to be supposed, or encouraged, that a bare allegation that a contract limits a trader's freedom of action exposes a party suing on it to the burden of justification. There will always be certain general categories of contracts as to which it can be said, with some degree of certainty, that the 'doctrine' does or does not apply to them. Positively, there are likely to be certain sensitive areas as to which the law will require in every case the test of reasonableness to be passed: such an area has long been and still is that of contracts between employer and employee as regards the period after the employment has ceased. Negatively, and it is this that concerns us here, there will be types of contract as to which the law should be prepared to say with some confidence that they do not enter into the field of restraint of trade at all.

How, then, can such contracts be defined or at least identified? No exhaustive test can be stated—probably no precise non-exhaustive test. But the development of the law does seem to show that judges have been able to dispense from the necessity of justification under a public policy test of reasonableness such contracts or provisions of contracts as, under contemporary conditions, may be found to have passed into the accepted and normal currency of commercial or contractual or conveyancing relations. That such contracts have done so may be taken to show with at least strong prima force that, moulded under the pressures of negotiation, competition and public opinion, they have assumed a form which satisfies the test of public policy as understood by the courts at the time, or, regarding the matter from the point of view of the trade, that the trade in question has assumed such a form that for its health or expansion it requires a degree of regulation. Absolute exemption for restriction or regulation is never obtained: circumstances, social or economic, may have altered, since they obtained acceptance, in such a way as to call for a fresh examination: there may be some exorbitance or special feature in the individual contract which takes it out of the accepted category: but the court must be persuaded of this before it calls upon the relevant party to justify a contract of this kind.

Some such limitation upon the meaning in legal practice of 'restraints of trade' must surely have been present in to the minds of Lord Macnaghten and Lord Parker. They cannot have meant to say that any contract which in whatever way restricts a man's liberty to trade was (either historically under the common law, or at the time of which they were speaking) prima facie unenforceable and must be shown to be reasonable. They must have been well aware that areas existed, and always had existed in which limitations of this liberty were not only defensible, but were not seriously open to the charge of restraining trade. Their language, they would surely have said, must be interpreted in relation to commercial practice and common sense.

[LORDS MORRIS, HODSON and PEARCE agreed that the shorter agreement was valid but the longer one void.]

BGH, 31 March 1982[50] **17.14 (DE)**

The German solus agreement

An exclusive distribution agreement between a petrol company and a filling station which gives the former the effective right to renew the contract indefinitely is void as contrary to public policy.

Facts: In 1952 the defendants, owners of a filling station, had agreed to purchase all their requirements of motor fuels exclusively from the claimant. The agreement was to remain in force until 31 December 1977, ie for 25 years. Clause 9 provided that, while the defendants were free to buy motor fuels from other sources for the period commencing on 1 January 1978, the claimant had an option to enter into a contract on the same terms as any agreement that might be offered to the defendants by another supplier. When the defendants, having terminated the agreement with effect from 31 December 1977, made a contract with another supplier without giving the claimant an opportunity to enter into a contract on the same terms, the claimant brought an action for damages against them.

[50] BHGZ 83, 31, NJW 1982, 1692.

Held: The contract was held to be void by the Bundesgerichtshof.

Judgment: … a) The appellate court correctly approached the case on the basis that Clause 9 of the contract results in the imposition on the defendants of a commitment *vis-à-vis* the claimant which is unlimited in time, since it makes it impossible for the defendants to terminate their contractual relationship with the claimant against the latter's will. It is true that the parties fixed a date—31 December 1977—on which the contract was to expire, provided notice to terminate it had been given in good time. However, as regards the defendants' commitment to the claimant, that arrangement was decisively restricted by Clause 9 of the contract, since the power irrevocably conferred on the claimant by that clause, enabling it to intervene in any offer made by a third party and to continue the contractual relationship on the terms contained in that offer, make it impossible for the defendants to break free from the claimant, despite having given a valid and effective notice to terminate the contract. Accordingly, the defendants are bound to the claimant for an unlimited period of time—possibly extending over 30, 40 or 50 years—as long as the claimant wishes to continue the contractual relationship, albeit on terms offered by third parties.

b) A contract of that sort, whereby the continuation of the contractual relationship is dependent on the wishes of the oil company alone and the filling-station owner is precluded in perpetuity from breaking free from a specific contracting party, constitutes an unjustifiable restriction on the economic freedom of movement and autonomy of the filling-station owner in the choice of a new contracting party following the expiry of the term of the contract; it thus results, as the appellate court correctly states, in the filling-station owner being bound to the oil company in a manner incompatible with the concept of fair business dealings. Thus Clause 9 of the contract is contrary to public policy (§ 138 BGB) and to the fundamental ideas on which the law is based, which must be respected in the present case. The Bundesgerichtshof has in the past been prepared to confirm the validity of long term contracts for the lease of a filling station pursuant to which—as in the present case—the filling-station operator makes the site available for the sale of the company's petroleum products and the company assumes responsibility for the construction of the filling-station buildings, the procurement of petrol pumps and the acquisition of other technical equipment, even where the duration of the contract in question has been 10, 20 or 25 years … However, even in contracts of that duration, it is impossible to justify an arrangement such as that in the present case, which completely excludes the possibility of breaking free from a commitment to a specific contracting party. Recognition of the validity of long-term filling-station contracts having a duration of 10, 20 or 25 years … is based on the consideration that oil companies invest substantial amounts of capital over many years in setting up and fitting out the filling-station, whether it is the company itself which effects the necessary installations and places the filling-station at the disposal of the person operating it, or whether it grants the latter a long-term loan in order to set up the filling-station. In all such cases, the intention is, as a general rule, that the capital invested should gradually be repaid from the receipts of the filling-station's business. That necessitates a long-term commitment by the filling-station operator to the contract and to the oil company, since it is only on that basis that the company can be sure that its capital will, over time, yield interest and be amortised from the profits of the filling-station. If the commitment were to last only for a few years, oil companies would no longer be willing, as a general rule, to make long-term capital investments—to the detriment of filling-station operators, who have an interest in concluding such contracts. As a general rule, therefore, there can be no objection in principle to an arrangement whereby the parties to a filling-station contract declare that the matters agreed between them are to be incapable of termination throughout the duration of a reasonable period fixed by reference to amortisation considerations—which, in the present case, having regard to the contractual term stipulated by the claimant itself, should not extend beyond 31 December 1977. Where the filling-station owner is bound to the oil company for any longer period, as per Clause 9 of the contract in the present case, there can be no inherent grounds for such a commitment, since it cannot be justified either from the standpoint of reasonable amortisation or on the basis of any other considerations. Such a tie rather violates the underlying policy of § 624 BGB (although this provision is not directly applicable to contracts for the lease of a filling station) which provides for the possibility to terminate long-term contractual relationships after the expiry of a certain period of time in order to protect employees against an inappropriate restriction of their personal and professional liberty. The parties cannot derogate from this rule. Similarly, with regard to pub owners' obligations to accept supplies resulting from contracts on the supply of beer it is established case law that ties to one contractual partner for an unlimited period of time after the expiry of the original agreement cannot be valid, even if the breweries provide particular consideration for such ties (RG JW 1927, 119; …). It is true that the courts have upheld the validity of contracts of this kind which bind pub owners to breweries for a longer period, even for 15 and 20 years. However, in these cases, too, the courts have declined to accept the validity of unlimited ties because those who undertake such an obligation are frequently unable to assess the risks and the dangers of the obligations they undertake and because such unlimited ties in themselves, with regard to their long duration, have the consequence that they impermissibly restrict the economic liberty and the independence of those undertaking such obligations (BGHZ 68, 1, 5; …). This is equally true for contracts for the lease of a filling station which—as in the present case—impose obligations to respect options and thus deprive the owner of the filling station of his liberty to decide to look out for a new contractual partner after expiry of the agreed duration of the contract—here: after 25 years … the economic independence and the professional liberty of the contractual partner of a petrol company would be unacceptably restricted if he were permanently bound to this company only. On the other hand, it is not unacceptable for a petrol company like the claimants if the owner of the filling station terminates the contractual relationship after the expiry of the duration of the contract which the company itself had stipulated and after amortisation of the capital which the company had invested.

Note

A question arising frequently in this group of cases is whether a restraint which is invalid for excessive duration may be cut down to size by the court. The same problem must be solved in cases where there is a clause in a contract for the sale of a business under which the seller promises not to engage in competition with the buyer, or a clause in an employment contract under which or the employee promises not to compete with the former employer after the end of the employment. If the clause as written is found unlawful as regards its duration, geographical area and/or subject matter, must the court strike it down *in toto* or has it a power to reduce the clause to its reasonable scope and then to apply it in that form? Judges now tend to reduce the clause to its reasonable duration or scope.

The sugar broker

A clause which places an excessive restriction on an ex-employee competing with his old firm may nonetheless be enforced to prevent him from working for a direct competitor situated in the same town as his ex-employer.

Facts: Mermilliod was engaged in October 1951 by the firm of Borione & Cie, sugar brokers, without any particular job title, to visit sugar factories and refineries and, generally, to devote himself to the satisfactory operation and development of the business of that firm. The contract between the parties contained a non-competition clause which provided that, in the event of its termination by either of the parties, for whatever reason, Mermilliod, who acknowledged that he had hitherto had no knowledge of that business sector, would refrain for a period of 10 years following his departure from joining any competitor of Messrs Borione and from operating in competition with that firm. Messrs Borione brought an action for damages against Mermilliod, who, having resigned, joined the firm of Berger & Cie, sugar agents.

Held: The lower court held that the clause was completely ineffective. The Cour de cassation held that the clause was ineffective only insofar as it was too wide in time or geographical coverage and could be enforced to prevent the employee going to work, immediately after his employment, for a direct competitor.

Judgment: On the sole appeal ground:— Under Article 1134 of the Code civil [now Article 1103] and Article 7 of the Law of 20 April 1810;—Whereas according to the wording of the first of those provisions, agreements legally entered into are to be binding on the persons concluding them.

— Whereas it appears from the recitals and grounds set out in the contested judgment that Mermilliod was engaged in October 1951 by the firm of Borione & Cie, sugar brokers, without any particular job title, to visit sugar factories and refineries and, generally, to devote himself to the satisfactory operation and development of the business of that firm; as the contract between the parties contained a non-competition clause which provided that, in the event of its termination by either of the parties, for whatever reason, Mermilliod, who acknowledged that he had hitherto had no knowledge of that business sector, would refrain for a period of ten years following his departure from joining any competitor of Messrs Borione and from operating in competition with that firm.

— Whereas Messrs Borione brought an action for damages against Mermilliod who, having resigned, joined the firm of Berger & Cie, sugar agents.

— Whereas the court below considered, in holding that the employment contract was void and ineffective, and in dismissing Messrs Borione's claim, that the non-competition clause was unlawful, since it did not limit geographically the prohibition agreed to by Mermilliod, and further ruled that the promise made to Mermilliod by one of the partners in Messrs Borione, to the effect that the clause would not be enforced against him, constituted a fraudulent practice which had invalidated his consent.

— Whereas however, a non-competition clause is in principle lawful and should be annulled only in so far as it impairs freedom to work on account of its temporal and geographical scope and as regards the nature of the activities of the person to whom it applies.

---

[51] No. 59-40160, Bull civ V no. 912, JCP 1960.II.11886 (first case).

— Whereas in the present case, the clause in issue was capable of being held valid at least in so far as it prohibited Mermilliod, in consideration of the apprenticeship of which he had had the benefit, from placing himself, on the day following his departure, at the service of a direct competitor of his former employer, established in the same city. …

— Whereas in declaring the non-competition clause unlawful, and in holding the employment contract to be void and ineffective, the contested judgment consequently misapplied and thus infringed the legislative provisions referred to above, and the court below failed to provide any legal basis for its decision.

On those grounds, the Court quashes and annuls the judgment delivered by the Tribunal Civil de la Seine and refers the case back to the Tribunal de Grande Instance de Versailles.

Note

French judges have developed their control over the *engagements de non-concurrence*. Such commitments must not only be limited in time and space but must also be justified by a legitimate interest, remain proportionate in view of the 'object' of the contract and, more concretely, must not prevent the party bound by such a term to find a new job; moreover, when they are inserted in a *contrat de travail*, they must give rise to a specific indemnity (*contrepartie*).[52]

As will be seen in the next case, English judges also check that a clause preventing an ex-employee from working for any firm carrying on a similar business to the employer's will not, in practice, completely prevent the employee from working close by. If it is, it will not be enforced, or at least not enforced in full. In *Goldsoll v Goldman*,[53] the Court of Appeal held that a 'clause which is unreasonably broad but which contains distinct restrictions, some of which are reasonable and some unreasonable, may be severed and the reasonable parts enforced'. However, a powerful argument against the technique of cutting objectionable restraints down to size has been made by the House of Lords in the following case.

House of Lords   **17.16 (EN)**

***Mason v Provident Clothing & Supply Co Ltd*[54]**

A clause preventing an ex-employee from working for any firm carrying on a similar business to the employer's within 25 miles of London was unreasonable when the employee had worked only in one branch. The clause was completely ineffective and the employee could not be prevented from working for a competitor close by.

---

[52] A Bénabent, *Droit des obligations* (16th edn, Paris: LGDJ, 2017) no. 189.
[53] [1915] 1 Ch 292 (CA).
[54] [1913] AC 724.

Facts: The respondent, a clothing and supply company, entered into an employment contract with the appellant employee as a 'canvasser' (salesman). The contract provided that he should not within three years after the termination of his engagement 'enter into any employment with other firms carrying on a business similar to that of the plaintiffs within 25 miles of London'. The appellant was attached to the respondent's Islington branch and, after having been dismissed by it, entered into an employment contract with another company based in Islington which carried on a similar business. The respondent brought an action against the appellant for liquidated damages as provided in the agreement. It was argued on its behalf that even if the clause were found to be too wide in its geographical scope it surely covered the situation at hand in which the defendant had taken up employment with a competitor doing business around the corner.

Held: The House of Lords rejected the appellant's argument.

Judgment: VISCOUNT HALDANE LC: ... The test is now settled. The law is summed up in Lord Macnaghten's judgment in *Nordenfelt v Maxim Nordenfelt Guns and Ammunition Co.*[55] After pointing out, as Lord Watson had already done, that the standard of public policy must be the standard of the day, and that what was laid down as to public policy a long time ago may be of little use in settling what the actual standard is, he says:

> 'The true view at the present time, I think, is this: The public have an interest in every person's carrying on his trade freely: so has the individual. All interference with individual liberty of action in trading, and all restraints of trade of themselves, if there is nothing more, are contrary to public policy, and therefore void. That is the general rule. But there are exceptions: restraints of trade and interference with individual liberty of action may be justified by the special circumstances of a particular case. It is a sufficient justification, and, indeed, it is the only justification, if the restriction is reasonable—reasonable, that is, in reference to the interests of the parties concerned and reasonable in reference to the interests of the public, so framed and so guarded as to afford adequate protection to the party in whose favour it is imposed, while at the same time it is in no way injurious to the public.'

My Lords, the respondents have to shew that the restriction they have sought to impose goes no further than was reasonable for the protection of their business. But even assuming the construction most favourable to them, that which makes the words introducing the twenty-five miles limit apply to every branch of the restrictive language, I think that they fail to shew this. I have examined the evidence as to the character of the business and the document which sets out particularly the duties of these canvassers. I can find nothing to lead me to think that the canvasser could become possessed of any special knowledge of the kind recognized as a trade secret. I doubt whether there were any secrets in this business. The success of the canvasser depended, as I have already said, mainly on his natural aptitude. No doubt he might acquire, in the course of his employment, lists of actual or possible customers in the district in which he had canvassed. I think that under a properly limited clause the employers would have been entitled to restrain him from canvassing such customers. But that is not the clause which the respondents in this case did frame. They have chosen to try to bind the appellant to an extent which might be necessary for their protection if they had been carrying on a business of a different kind.

The reported cases afford instances of varying descriptions in which restriction over a wide area is necessary for the protection of the employer. But in the case of a business which is local, and which is carried on simply by canvassing, it is hardly possible for an employer to justify an area with a twenty-five-mile radius, and I do not think it has been justified here. It is no doubt as a general rule wise to leave adult persons to make their

---

[55] [1894] AC 535, 565 (HL).

own agreements and take the consequences, but in the present class of case considerations of public policy come in and make it necessary for the Court to scrutinize agreements like the one before your Lordships jealously. The practice of putting into these agreements anything that is favourable to the employer is one which the Courts have to check, and the judges have to see that Lord Macnaghten's test is carefully observed. As I do not think that clause 8 complies with that test, I am of opinion that it was void altogether.

LORD MOULTON: ... It was suggested in the argument that even if the covenant was, as a whole, too wide, the Court might enforce restrictions which it might consider reasonable (even though they were not expressed in the covenant), provided they were within its ambit. My Lords, I do not doubt that the Court may, and in some cases will, enforce a part of a covenant in restraint of trade, even though taken as a whole the covenant exceeds what is reasonable. But, in my opinion, that ought only to be done in cases where the part so enforceable is clearly severable, and even so only in cases where the excess is of trivial importance, or merely technical, and not a part of the main purport and substance of the clause. It would in my opinion be *pessimi exempli* if, when an employer had exacted a covenant deliberately framed in unreasonably wide terms, the Courts were to come to his assistance and, by applying their ingenuity and knowledge of the law, carve out of this void covenant the maximum of what he might validly have required. It must be remembered that the real sanction at the back of these covenants is the terror and expense of litigation, in which the servant is usually at a great disadvantage, in view of the longer purse of his master. It is sad to think that in this present case this appellant, whose employment is a comparatively humble one, should have had to go through four Courts before he could free himself from such unreasonable restraints as this covenant imposes, and the hardship imposed by the exaction of unreasonable covenants by employers would be greatly increased if they could continue the practice with the expectation that, having exposed the servant to the anxiety and expense of litigation, the Court would in the end enable them to obtain everything which they could have obtained by acting reasonably. It is evident that those who drafted this covenant aimed at making it a penal rather than a protective covenant, and that they hoped by means of it to paralyse the earning capabilities of the man if and when he left their service, and were not thinking of what would be a reasonable protection to their business, and having so acted they must take the consequences.

I am of the opinion, therefore, that the appeal should be allowed and the action dismissed ...

Notes

(1) Note the tests laid down in the *Maxim Nordenfelt* case, and applied by the House of Lords here: the covenant must be both reasonable as between the parties and reasonable relative to the public interest. This shows the dual operation of the doctrine of public policy referred to earlier.[56] The courts have traditionally been much readier to strike down 'no competition clauses' in contracts between employer and employee than similar clauses agreed to by the seller of a business. If the seller of a business cannot agree not to compete with the buyer, the 'good will' of the business would be reduced in value.

---

[56] Above p 663.

(2) In *Atwood v Lamont*,[57] the appellant, who had been employed as a tailor's cutter, entered a covenant not to act in any one of a long list of trades, including that of a tailor. It was argued that the Court should simply strike out the references to the other trades and enforce the covenant against him acting as a tailor. The Court refused to do so on the ground that in reality this was not a series of separate covenants but a single covenant which should stand or fall as a whole. As it was much too wide it was wholly unenforceable.

(3) The reason for not 'cutting the clause down to size' is that it seems unfair for an employer to be able to use a clause which is much too severe and yet be able to enforce those parts of it which would be reasonable. A similar issue has arisen with exclusion or limitation of liability clauses that are drafted in unreasonably broad terms.[58]

(4) In Germany, judges tend to adjust the length of a tie. In a case which would now fall within the scope of EU Law, the BGH held that a tie on a restaurant requiring it to purchase all its beer from the plaintiff for 24 years was excessive, but a 16-year tie would have been reasonable and the penalty for breach of the tie should be adjusted accordingly.[59]

17.4 CONTRACTS WHICH INVOLVE PROHIBITED CONDUCT

The cases in this section deal with contracts which involve prohibited conduct alleged to be invalid or unenforceable. In most cases, the conduct will be prohibited by statute. The question then is whether the statute renders the contract unenforceable. But there can also be broader questions: what if the contract involves the commission of a crime or of a civil wrong of some kind?

No serious problem arises in cases in which the statute explicitly makes some contract illegal and unenforceable; or, conversely, provides that a contract shall not be unenforceable on the ground that there was some breach of the statute. The more frequent and more difficult cases are those where a statute merely prohibits some activity, requires a licence for those wishing to engage in that activity or prescribes a certain manner in which the activity must be carried out but says nothing on the validity of a contract performed in a way prohibited by the statute. Thus if, contrary to a statutory prohibition, a carrier overloads his lorry or a quack gives legal advice without being duly licensed as an attorney, he may be punished. But it is a wholly different question whether the contracts should be held unenforceable so that the carrier and the quack would be unable to sue for the agreed price, and the other parties to the contracts unable to claim damages for a breach of the contract.

Most of the time, statutes create offences without alluding to the question whether contracts formed in violation of their provisions are valid or not. There is a particular

---

[57] [1920] 3 KB 571 (CA).
[58] See below, ch 21.2.D, p 826.
[59] See the reference to these cases in BGHZ 83, 31, 17.14 (DE), p 687 above.

problem when only one of the parties is breaking the law by entering the contract, or when only one of the parties can know the facts that make the performance illegal—for example, only the seller knows that he does not have the necessary authorisation to make the sale.

French courts have annulled contracts whose purpose was to achieve a prohibited conduct.

Cass Civ (1), 29 October 2014[60]   **17.17 (FR)**

'Our Body' exhibition

Facts: The company Encore Events organised an exhibition of human corpses called 'Our body' in Paris. Two associations brought an action against the company before the Tribunal de Grand Instance de Paris to stop the exhibition. The Tribunal held that the exhibition was illegal and prohibited it. Subsequently, the company brought an action against its insurer to obtain compensation. The cour d'appel held that the insurance contract was null and void because its *cause* was illegal.

Held: The Cour de cassation confirmed the appeal decision. As the contract's object was 'to guarantee the consequences of the cancellation of an exhibition using human corpses and organs for commercial purposes, the cour d'appel correctly deduced that … the contract at stake had an illegal *cause*'.

Note

The ground for annulment was the illegality or immorality of the *cause*. This solution should therefore not be affected by the abandonment of the *cause* in the 2016 reform. Indeed, Articles 16-1 and 16-1-1 of the Code civil provide that the human body is 'inviolable' and that the respect due to it does not cease after death. The first instance judges held that the exhibition was contrary to these rules of public policy (see Article 6 of the Code civil, on public order).

In English law a distinction is drawn between 'statutory illegality', where the making or performance of a contract involves the breach of a statutory prohibition, and a separate doctrine of the common law that a contract that involves something illegal may be unenforceable.

In cases of statutory illegality, English courts have sometimes felt obliged by the wording of the statute to hold that the contract is unenforceable. In *Re Mahmoud v Ispahani*,[61] the Court of Appeal held that, where statute forbids the making of a contract without a licence and one party does not have the required licence, the contract is unenforceable by or against him, even if he has told the other party that he does have a licence. This kind of result has sometimes been reached even when the outcome is manifestly inconvenient.

---

[60] No. 13-19729, Bull I no. 178.
[61] [1921] 2 KB 716 (CA).

In *Phoenix General Insurance Co of Greece SA v Adas*,[62] Kerr LJ described the test to be used in cases of a 'unilateral prohibition' as follows:

> Where a statute merely prohibits one party from entering into a contract without authority and/or imposes a penalty on him if he does so (ie a unilateral prohibition) it does not follow that the contract itself is impliedly prohibited so as to render it illegal and void. Whether or not the statute has this effect depends on considerations of public policy in the light of the mischief which the statute is designed to prevent, its language, scope and purpose, the consequences for the innocent party, and any other relevant considerations.

In that case, however, the relevant statute prohibited the 'business of effecting or carrying out of contracts of insurance' without authorisation. The Court of Appeal, obiter, accepted the correctness of an earlier decision[63] that this meant that neither party could enforce any contract of insurance made without authorisation. The result was, of course, very dangerous for the insured, who would be left without cover, and it was later reversed by statute: Financial Services Act 1986, section 132.

English lawyers usually think of the *Phoenix* solution as 'out of line' with the modern trend, which is to hold that such statutes merely create offences but do not invalidate the contract: see the next case.

The next case also explains the 'rules' that traditionally were applied to determine whether a contract will be unenforceable in English law not because it infringes a statutory provision but as a matter of common law because it involves a crime or a tort. We will see later that this 'rules-based' approach has recently been abandoned in favour of a flexible approach.

Queen's Bench Division   **17.18 (EN)**

St John Shipping Corp v Joseph Rank Ltd[64]

The fact that a shipowner has overloaded the ship does not entitle the owner of goods carried to refuse to pay the freight, at least if it was not intended when the contract was made that the ship should be overloaded.

Facts: The defendants chartered the plaintiff's ship to carry grain from the USA to the UK. During the voyage the ship was overloaded in contravention of the Merchant Shipping (Safety and Load Line Conventions) Act 1932. On arrival in the UK the Master was convicted and fined the maximum fine of £1,200. The defendants paid part of the freight but withheld a sum equivalent to the extra freight earned by the overloading. They argued that the plaintiffs could not recover the freight as they had performed the charter party illegally.

Held: The defendants must pay the freight in full.

Judgment: DEVLIN J: ... It is a misfortune for the defendants that the legal weapon which they are wielding is so much more potent than it need be to achieve their purpose. Believing, rightly or wrongly, that the plaintiffs have deliberately committed a serious infraction of the Act and one which has placed their property in jeopardy, the defendants wish to do no more than to take the profit out of the plaintiff's dealing. But the principle which

---

[62] [1987] 2 All ER 152, 176 (CA).
[63] *Bedford Insurance Co Ltdv Instituto de Ressurgos do Brasil* [1985] QB 966 (CA).
[64] [1957] 1 QB 267.

they invoke for this purpose cares not at all for the element of deliberation or for the gravity of the infraction, and does not adjust the penalty to the profits unjustifiably earned. The defendants cannot succeed unless they claim the right to retain the whole freight and to keep it whether the offence was accidental or deliberate, serious or trivial. The application of this principle to a case such as this is bound to lead to startling results. Mr Wilmers does not seek to avert his gaze from the wide consequences. A shipowner who accidentally overloads by a fraction of an inch will not be able to recover from any of the shippers or consignees a penny of the freight. ... Carriers by land are in no better position; again Mr Wilmers does not shrink from saying that the owner of a lorry could not recover against the consignees the cost of goods transported in it if in the course of the journey it was driven a mile an hour over its permitted speed. If this is really the law, it is very unenterprising of cargo owners and consignees to wait until a criminal conviction has been secured before denying their liabilities. A service of trained observers on all our main roads would soon pay for itself. An effective patrol of the high seas would probably prove too expensive, but the maintenance of a corps of vigilantes in all principal ports would be well worth while when one considers that the smallest infringement of the statute or a regulation made there-under would relieve all the cargo owners on the ship from all liability for freight.

Of course, as Mr Wilmers says, one must not be deterred from enunciating the correct principle of law because it may have startling or even calamitous results. But I confess I approach the investigation of a legal proposition which has results of this character with a prejudice in favour of the idea that there may be a flaw in the argument somewhere. ...

There are two general principles. The first is that a contract which is entered into with the object of committing an illegal act is unenforceable. The application of this principle depends upon proof of the intent, at the time the contract was made, to break the law; if the intent is mutual the contract is not enforceable at all, and, if unilateral, it is unenforceable at the suit of the party who is proved to have it. This principle is not involved here. Whether or not the overloading was deliberate when it was done, there is no proof that it was contemplated when the contract of carriage was made. The second principle is that the court will not enforce a contract which is expressly or impliedly prohibited by statute. If the contract is of this class it does not matter what the intent of the parties is; if the statute prohibits the contract, it is unenforceable whether the parties meant to break the law or not. A significant distinction between the two classes is this. In the former class you have only to look and see what acts the statute prohibits; it does not matter whether or not it prohibits a contract; if a contract is deliberately made to do a prohibited act, that contract will be unenforceable. In the latter class, you have to consider not what acts the statute prohibits, but what contracts it prohibits; but you are not concerned at all with the intent of the parties; if the parties enter into a prohibited contract, that contract is unenforceable. ...

Two questions are involved. The first—and the one which hitherto has usually settled the matter—is: does the statute mean to prohibit contracts at all? But if this be answered in the affirmative, then one must ask: does this contract belong to the class which the statute intends to prohibit? For example, a person is forbidden by statute from using an unlicensed vehicle on the highway. If one asks oneself whether there is in such an enactment an implied prohibition of all contracts for the use of unlicensed vehicles, the answer may well be that there is, and that contracts of hire would be unenforceable. But if one asks oneself whether there is an implied prohibition of contracts for the carriage of goods by unlicensed vehicles or for the repairing of unlicensed vehicles or for the garaging of unlicensed vehicles, the answer may well be different. The answer might be that collateral contracts of this sort are not within the ambit of the statute.

The relevant section of the Act of 1932, section 44, provides that the ship 'shall not be so loaded as to submerge' the appropriate loadline. It may be that a contract for the loading of the ship which necessarily has this effect would be unenforceable. It might be, for example, that the contract for bunkering at Port Everglades which had the effect of submerging the loadline, if governed by English law, would have been unenforceable. But an implied prohibition of contracts of loading does not necessarily extend to contracts for the carriage of goods by improperly loaded vessels. Of course, if the parties knowingly agree to ship goods by an overloaded vessel, such a contract would be illegal; but its illegality does not depend on whether it is impliedly prohibited by the statute, since ... there is an intent to break the law. The way to test the question whether a particular class of contract is prohibited by the statute is to test it in relation to a contract made in ignorance of its effect.

In my judgment, contracts for the carriage of goods are not within the ambit of this statute at all. A court should not hold that any contract or class of contracts is prohibited by statute unless there is a clear implication ... that the statute so intended. If a contract has as its whole object the doing of the very act which the statute prohibits, it can be argued that you can hardly make sense of a statute which forbids an act and yet permits to be made a contract to do it; that is a clear implication. But unless you get a clear implication of that sort, I think that a court ought to be very slow to hold that a statute intends to interfere with the rights and remedies given by the ordinary law of contract. Caution in this respect is, I think, especially necessary in these times when so much of commercial life is governed by regulations of one sort or another, which may easily be broken without wicked intent. Persons who deliberately set out to break the law cannot expect to be aided in a court of justice, but it is a different matter when the law is unwittingly broken. To nullify a bargain in such circumstances frequently means that in a case—perhaps of such triviality that no authority would have felt it worth while to prosecute—a seller because he cannot enforce his civil rights, may forfeit a sum vastly in excess of any penalty that a criminal court would impose; and the sum forfeited will not go into the public purse but into the pockets of someone who is lucky enough to pick up the windfall or astute enough to have contrived to get it. It is questionable how far this contributes to public morality.

Notes

(1) Devlin J's first 'general principle' deals with the effect of illegality at common law.[65] He says that 'a contract which is entered into with the object of committing an illegal act is unenforceable'. Devlin J is here referring to the common law doctrine. He says it does not apply on the facts, as when the contract was made neither party contemplated performing it in an illegal way. We will return to the common law doctrine in a moment.

(2) Devlin J's second 'general principle' refers to contracts that somehow involve breaking a statutory prohibition. Here the effect depends on what the statute provides,

---

[65] A survey and critique of the English law will be found in The Law Commission, *The Illegality Defence: A Consultative Report*, Law Com CP No 189 (London: The Stationery Office, 2009).

expressly or by implication. On occasion the courts have reached the conclusion that the Act renders the contract illegal merely because the performance involved breaking the statute,[66] but that is rare. Much more often the courts hold, as in the *St John Shipping* case, that the statute does not affect the contract.

The common law doctrine of illegality to which Devlin J refers to as the 'first general principle' has been much trickier to explain. The cases seemed to lay down 'rules' as to when the doctrine would apply—for example, Devlin J said that 'a contract which is entered into with the object of committing an illegal act is unenforceable'—but the cases were unclear and no two writers seemed to explain the cases in the same way. One way of explaining them would be to say that a contract might be unenforceable in three types of case.

(1) Where the contract does not involve doing anything illegal of itself but where the purpose of the parties is unlawful. Thus a contract to sell a knife to enable the buyer to murder his wife with it would be unenforceable—if this was the objective of both the seller and the buyer, it would be unenforceable by either party; if it was only the buyer's objective, the seller could enforce the contract but not the buyer.[67]

(2) Where the contract requires the commission of an illegal act (like a contract to murder, or a contract to sell something that requires the buyer to have a licence to an unlicensed buyer). In this case, it is usually said that neither party may enforce the contract.[68] However, it has been suggested that where one party did not know of the facts that made the performance illegal (for example, did not know that the vehicle in which the goods were required to be carried did not have the required licence), that innocent party should be able to enforce the contract.[69]

(3) Where at the outset it was intended to perform the contract in an unlawful way—for example, to carry the goods by overloading the ship. Again, if both parties had this intention, neither may enforce the contract; if only one did, that party may not enforce it but the other may.

In contrast, if the purpose of the contract was not unlawful, its performance did not involve illegality and when it was made neither party intended to perform unlawfully, the mere fact that some unlawful act was committed during the course of performance will not make it illegal. Thus, if you notice that a taxi in which you are riding is breaking the speed limit, you cannot refuse to pay the fare on the ground that the contract is illegal. This at least is the principle generally stated. In practice, the courts have sometimes held that a contract is illegal because it has been performed in an illegal manner, eg where an employee has agreed to be paid his wages without income tax being deducted first, as the law requires.[70]

---

[66] As in the *Mahmoud* and *Phoenix* cases, above pp 695–96.
[67] cf *Fielding & Platt Ltd v Najjar* [1969] 1 WLR 357 (CA).
[68] eg *J M Allan (Merchandising) Ltd v Cloke* [1963] 2 QB 340 (CA).
[69] *Archbolds (Freightage) Ltd v S Spanglett Ltd* [1961] 1 QB 374, 387 (CA).
[70] See the discussion in Law Commission (n 65 above) paras 3.27 ff.

If the contract was held to be unenforceable, could either party claim restitution of any money or other benefits it had transferred under the unenforceable contract? Here the starting point appeared to be that restitution would not be allowed—*in pari delicto, potior est conditio possidentis*. This is taken up below.[71]

There was also a common law principle that a party cannot claim under a contract where his claim would involve relying on his own unlawful act—*ex turpi causa non oritur actio*. In particular the 'no reliance' rule was applied when a party tried to argue that the defendant held property 'on trust' for the claimant (in other words, that the claimant had an 'equitable interest' in the property). Thus, in *Tinsley v Milligan*[72] Tinsley and Milligan were in a same-sex relationship. They each contributed to the price of a house, which was put into the name of Tinsley alone so that Milligan could say she had no assets for the purpose of claiming social security. Later Milligan confessed and paid back the social security payments that she had received. Her relationship with Tinsley broke down and she tried to recover her half share in the house. A minority in the House of Lords said she could not do so because of the illegality of the scheme, but the majority held that she could demonstrate the resulting trust simply by showing that she had contributed to the purchase price; she did not need to 'rely on' the illegality. Thus her claim was enforceable.

The way that English courts are to approach the question of whether the fact that a contract that involves a crime or a serious civil wrong renders the contract unenforceable at common law, has now changed dramatically as the result of a recent decision of the Supreme Court. This followed a period of intense debate about how to deal with illegality, as the law was widely considered to be unsatisfactory. The principal problems were, first, that the results of the cases did not always fit the rules, or could not be explained without significant qualifications and exceptions; and that, secondly, the rules sometimes produced results that seemed arbitrary. For example, compare *Tinsley v Milligan* to *Collier v Collier*[73] in 2002. In *Collier* a father had paid for a property, which was put into the name of his daughter to hide it from the father's creditors. When a father transfers property to his child there is a presumption that it was meant as a gift, and the only way in which the father could show that it was not meant as a gift, but should be held in trust for him, was by revealing the fact that the transfer was made for an illegal purpose. Thus he was not able to recover although he did not seem to have been guilty of a more serious offence than the offence committed by Milligan.

In an attempt to make the law of illegality more rational, in the 1990s the Court of Appeal abandoned the 'rules-based' approach and instead applied the test, 'would enforcement of the claim shock the public conscience?'[74] It applied this test in *Tinsley v Milligan*.[75] The House of Lords in that case were unanimous in rejecting the public conscience test as giving judges an unacceptable discretion. Instead some judges called for the doctrine to be reviewed by the Law Commission, and the government referred the question to that body.

---

[71] See below, ch 17.5, pp 712–18.
[72] [1994] 1 AC 340 (HL).
[73] [2002] EWCA Civ 1095.
[74] eg *Euro-Diam Ltd v Bathurst* [1990] 1 QB 1 (CA).
[75] [1992] Ch 310 (CA).

The Law Commission worked on illegality for a long time and produced no less than three consultation papers[76] as well as a report.[77] The first consultation paper in 1999[78] provisionally proposed that whenever a contract or trust involved illegality, the court should have a statutory discretion whether or not to enforce the contract. This would not be an open discretion like the 'public conscience' test; it would be 'structured'. The court should take into account a range of factors such as the seriousness of the illegality; the knowledge and intention of the claimant; whether to deny relief would deter this kind of illegal activity; whether denying relief will further the purpose of the rule; and whether to deny relief would be proportionate.

However, after consultation the Commission decided that it was too difficult to legislate on this matter, principally because it was very hard to define when the discretion should apply. Rather the Commission thought that the courts were already taking a more flexible and open approach, and recommended that illegality in contract should be left to judicial development. It recommended[79] that in contract cases:

> ... the courts should consider in each case whether the application of the illegality defence can be justified on the basis of the policies that underlie that defence. These include:
>
> (a) furthering the purpose of the rule which the illegal conduct has infringed;
> (b) consistency;
> (c) that the claimant should not profit from his or her own wrong;
> (d) deterrence; and
> (e) maintaining the integrity of the legal system.
>
> Against those policies must be weighed the legitimate expectation of the claimant that his or her legal rights will be protected ...

The Law Commission also said that:

> ... the courts should consider whether illegality is a defence to the particular claim brought by the particular claimant, rather than whether the contract is 'illegal' as a whole.[80]

There followed a period in which there was considerable uncertainty. Two cases in the Court of Appeal[81] and arguably one in the Supreme Court[82] adopted the approach advocated by the Law Commission; but in a second case in the Supreme Court[83] the majority rejected the Law Commission approach—without referring to its earlier decision. This enabled Lord Toulson, who had been in a minority of one in the second case, to argue in a third case[84] that the Supreme Court had contradicted itself. The majority in the third

---

[76] The Law Commission, *Illegal Transactions: The Effect of Illegality on Contracts and Trusts* (Consultation Paper), Law Com CP No 154 (London: The Stationery Office, 1999); The Law Commission, *The Illegality Defence in Tort: A Consultation Paper*, Law Com CP No 160 (London: The Stationery Office, 2001); The Law Commission (n 65 above). The documents are available via the Law Commission's website.

[77] The Law Commission, *The Illegality Defence*, Law Com No 320 (London: The Stationery Office, 2010).

[78] The Law Commission, *Illegal Transactions* (n 76 above).

[79] The Law Commission (n 65 above) para 3.142, confirmed in The Law Commission (n 77 above) para 3.41.

[80] The Law Commission (n 65 above) para 3.144, similarly confirmed.

[81] *Les Laboratoires Servier v Apotex* [2012] EWCA Civ 593, [2013] Bus LR 80 and *ParkingEye v Somerfield* [2012] EWCA Civ 1338, [2013] 1 QB 840.

[82] *Allen v Hounga* [2014] UKSC 47, [2014] 1 WLR 2889.

[83] *Les Laboratoires Servier v Apotex* [2014] UKSC 55, [2015] 1 AC 430.

[84] *Jetivia SA v Bilta (UK) Ltd* [2015] UKSC 23, [2016] AC 1.

case agreed that the law needed a full review but held that it was not necessary to review it in that case itself. The opportunity for review came in a fourth Supreme Court case. In view of its importance and the fact that the court was being asked to overrule the House of Lords decision in *Tinsley v Milligan*, the panel consisted of nine judges.

Supreme Court   **17.19 (EN)**

Patel v Mirza [85]

Whether the court should allow a claim under a contract which has an illegal purpose or involves one or both parties in doing an illegal act, and (if the contract cannot be enforced) whether a claim in restitution to recover any benefits transferred, depends on a balancing of factors. These include (a) the underlying purpose of the prohibition which has been transgressed and whether that purpose will be enhanced by denial of the claim, (b) any other relevant public policy on which the denial of the claim may have an impact, and (c) whether denial of the claim would be a proportionate response to the illegality, bearing in mind that punishment is a matter for the criminal courts.

Facts: Patel had paid money to Mirza in order for Mirza to place bets, on Patel's behalf, on the future price of Royal Bank of Scotland shares. At the time RBS shares were owned by the Government and the parties expected to be able to use insider information about the Government's intentions when deciding what bets to place. This would have constituted the criminal offence of insider trading. In fact the insider information never became available and the bets were never placed. The question was whether Patel could recover his money, or was his claim was barred because of the illegal purpose.

Held: The trial judge held the claim was barred; the Court of Appeal, for varying reasons, allowed it. In the Supreme Court, Lord Toulson, speaking for the majority, took the opportunity to review the common law of illegality as a whole. He quoted extensively from Professor Andrew Burrows' *Restatement of the English Law of Contract*, in which the author criticises the 'rules-based approach' and suggested instead a 'factors-based' approach not far removed from the Law Commission's. Lord Toulson rejected a rule-based approach as having failed to produce certainty. After explaining the difficulties of a rule-based approach and considering many of the previous cases, he continued:

Judgment: LORD TOULSON: 99. … there are two broad discernible policy reasons for the common law doctrine of illegality as a defence to a civil claim. One is that a person should not be allowed to profit from his own wrongdoing. The other, linked, consideration is that the law should be coherent and not self-defeating, condoning illegality by giving with the left hand what it takes with the right hand. …

109. The courts must obviously abide by the terms of any statute, but I conclude that it is right for a court which is considering the application of the common law doctrine of illegality to have regard to the policy factors involved and to the nature and circumstances of the illegal conduct in determining whether the public interest in preserving the integrity of the justice system should result in denial of the relief claimed. I put it in that way rather than whether the contract should be regarded as tainted by illegality, because the question is whether the relief claimed should be granted. …

120. The essential rationale of the illegality doctrine is that it would be contrary to the public interest to enforce a claim if to do so would be harmful to the integrity of the legal system (or, possibly, certain aspects of public morality, the boundaries of which have

---

[85] [2016] UKSC 42, [2017] AC 467.

never been made entirely clear and which do not arise for consideration in this case). In assessing whether the public interest would be harmed in that way, it is necessary (a) to consider the underlying purpose of the prohibition which has been transgressed and whether that purpose will be enhanced by denial of the claim, (b) to consider any other relevant public policy on which the denial of the claim may have an impact and (c) to consider whether denial of the claim would be a proportionate response to the illegality, bearing in mind that punishment is a matter for the criminal courts. Within that framework, various factors may be relevant, but it would be a mistake to suggest that the court is free to decide a case in an undisciplined way. The public interest is best served by a principled and transparent assessment of the considerations identified, rather [than by] the application of a formal approach capable of producing results which may appear arbitrary, unjust or disproportionate.

Appeal Dismissed

Notes

(1) *Patel v Mirza* was a claim for restitution of the payment that had been made in order for an illegal contract to be carried out, not a claim to enforce a contract. All the justices agreed that, save in exceptional circumstances, it would be appropriate to restore any benefits that had been transferred under an illegal contract, as this would merely be putting the parties back into the position they were in before the contract was made.[86] Lord Toulson did not explain in detail how he thought claims to enforce a contract that involved illegality should be dealt with. Lord Neuberger raised a question about how the new approach should be applied in such a case, saying:

> I have difficulties in seeing how a court could order specific performance of a contract which necessarily involved one or other of the parties committing a crime (even a minor crime) ... [or] how a court could normally award damages for breach of such a contract. ... [to do so] would seem to infringe the principle of consistency. ...[87]

It is clear, however, that Lord Toulson's approach applies equally to claims to enforce a contract, as he referred to it in the *ParkingEye* case,[88] which was a claim for Somerfield's breach of a contract under which ParkingEye were to manage a parking lot for Somerfield and to collect payments from motorists who stayed longer than allowed. It was held ParkingEye's claim was enforceable even though one of the terms required ParkingEye to send errant motorists letters that contained false statements.

(2) The Supreme Court was unanimous that *Tinsley v Milligan*[89] had reached the right result but for the wrong reason. Lord Toulson said simply:

> ... [E]ven if Miss Milligan had not owned up and come to terms with the DSS, it would have been disproportionate to have prevented her from enforcing her equitable interest in the property and conversely to have left Miss Tinsley unjustly enriched.[90]

---

[86] See further below, pp 715–16.
[87] [2016] UKSC 42 [160].
[88] *ParkingEye v Somerfield* [2012] EWCA Civ 1338, [2013] 1 QB 840.
[89] See above, p 700.
[90] [2016] UKSC 42 [112].

(3) Lord Toulson's judgment makes it clear that when the question is whether to enforce a claim on the ground that it involved breach of a statutory prohibition, the question remains one of interpreting the statute.[91]

(4) In *Les Laboratoires Servier v Apotex*[92] Lord Sumption, speaking for the majority, held that:

> [25] The ex turpi causa principle is concerned with claims founded on acts which are contrary to the public law of the state and engage the public interest. The paradigm case is, as I have said, a criminal act. In addition, it is concerned with a limited category of acts which, while not necessarily criminal, can conveniently be described as "quasi-criminal" because they engage the public interest in the same way. Leaving aside the rather special case of contracts prohibited by law, which can give rise to no enforceable rights, this additional category of non-criminal acts giving rise to the defence includes cases of dishonesty or corruption, which have always been regarded as engaging the public interest even in the context of purely civil disputes; some anomalous categories of misconduct, such as prostitution, which without itself being criminal are contrary to public policy and involve criminal liability on the part of secondary parties; and the infringement of statutory rules enacted for the protection of the public interest and attracting civil sanctions of a penal character, such as … competition law …

On the facts of that case the alleged illegality was the infringement of a patent granted in Canada, and the Supreme Court held that this was not a sufficiently serious form of illegality to bring the *ex turpi causa* doctrine into play. The majority in *Patel v Mirza* did not mention any such restriction of the doctrine but it seems consistent with their general approach: it would be disproportionate to deny the claim in a case of minor illegality.

There is an interesting intersection between the doctrine of illegality and EU competition law. On the basis of the cases of *Courage Ltd v Crehan*[93] and *Manfredi*,[94] it is generally accepted in the competition law literature that there is a *sui generis* action to obtain damages in the case of a violation of Article 101 [ex-Article 81, and before that Article 85] of the European Treaty (now the TFEU). In *Manfredi* the claim was by a third party but in *Courage Ltd v Crehan* the claim was by a publican whose rental contract required that he buy all his beer from Courage Ltd. Crehan had failed to pay for the beer and when Courage started proceedings, he counter-claimed for damages, since Courage sold its beer to independent publicans for a much lower price than the fixed one included in the rent contract. This price difference reduced the profitability of tied tenants and drove them out of business. However, it was thought at the time that according to English law a party to an illegal contract could not claim damages from the other party. The Court of Appeal asked the ECJ a preliminary question as to whether this bar to claim damages

---

[91] [2016] UKSC 42 [109].
[92] [2014] UKSC 55 (above n 83).
[93] C-453/99, 20 September 2001, ECLI:EU:C:2001:465.
[94] Joined Cases C-295/04, 296/04, 297/04, 298/04, *Vincenzo Manfredi v Lloyd Adriatico Assicurazioni SpA, Antonio Cannito v Fondiaria Sai SpA, Nicolò Tricarico, Pasqualina Murgolo v Assitalia SpA*, 13 July 2006, ECLI:EU:C:2006:461.

was contrary to Community law and in particular contrary to [former] Article 85 EC. The Court of Justice held that a party to a contract liable to restrict or distort competition within the meaning of [former] Article 85 of the Treaty can rely on the breach of that Article to obtain relief from the other contracting party; that [former] Article 85 of the Treaty precludes a rule of national law under which a party to a contract liable to restrict or distort competition within the meaning of that provision is barred from claiming damages for loss caused by performance of that contract on the sole ground that the claimant is a party to that contract; and that Community law does not preclude a rule of national law barring a party to a contract liable to restrict or distort competition from relying on his own unlawful actions to obtain damages where it is established that that party bears significant responsibility for the distortion of competition. Thus a blanket rule that a party to an illegal contract cannot recover damages would be contrary to EU law. This situation is unlikely to arise ever again, as there is no longer a rigid rule that a party to an illegal contract cannot enforce it. Under the new approach to illegality adopted by the Supreme Court in *Patel v Mirza*,[95] the court is required

(a) to consider the underlying purpose of the prohibition which has been transgressed and whether that purpose will be enhanced by denial of the claim, (b) to consider any other relevant public policy on which the denial of the claim may have an impact …

It seems that in considering (b), the court would take into account the principle of effectiveness referred to by the ECJ and allow the publican to claim damages.

In German law, if a statute prohibits both parties from concluding a contract and makes both parties liable to penalties, the contract itself will normally be viewed as impliedly forbidden and void. However, in exceptional cases, a court may come to the conclusion that it would be unjust to allow a party to rely on the invalidity. This position was taken by the Bundesgerichtshof in the following case.

BGH, 23 September 1982[96] **17.20 (DE)**

Illegal building labour

A contract under which the parties agree to use illegal labour and which has been carried out may be enforced by one party to the extent of recovering excess charges paid to the other.

Facts: By a contract of 16 January 1978 the defendant had agreed to build a house for the claimant for a price of DM 146,949.50. After the completion of the house it turned out that the claimant, who had paid DM 143,000, to the defendant, was liable for another DM 45,087.50 to various suppliers of building materials with whom the defendant had placed orders on behalf of the claimant. In a suit brought by the claimant the defendant moved for a dismissal on the ground that the contract of 16 January 1978 was invalid. He relied on the fact that the house had been built, as was known to both parties, with the help of clandestine workers, which was forbidden by a statute.

Held: The claimant could recover from the defendant builder the amount which the claimant had become liable to pay the suppliers.

---

[95] See above, 17.19 (EN), p 702.
[96] BGHZ 85, 39, NJW 1983, 109.

Judgment: 1. ... b) The appeal court correctly held that the contract of 16 January 1978 violates the Act on the combating of clandestine labour, in the amended version of 31 May 1974. It is therefore directed against a statutory prohibition and void according to § 134 BGB.

aa) The question whether the commission, in the context of a transaction, of a breach of a statutory prohibition renders the transaction void falls to be determined in accordance with the object and purpose of the prohibition concerned (cf BGHZ 37, 258, 261; ...). Where the Act does not make express provision in that regard, the answer will depend on whether it would be incompatible with the object and purpose of the prohibiting legislation to accept without demur the legal effects of the transaction and to allow it to stand (cf BGHZ 65, 368, 370; ...).

The Act on the combating of clandestine labour ... contains no provision *expressly* prohibiting clandestine labour. However, the object and purpose of the statute, together with the penalties in the form of fines provided for in §§ 1 and 2 thereof, indicate that the statute constitutes a statutory prohibition and that a transaction which infringes it is to be regarded as void under § 134 BGB.

The Act on the combating of clandestine labour is intended to combat the high level of unemployment in many occupational sectors, to prevent businesses, especially craft trades, from being jeopardised by wage and price undercutting and to protect customers who place contracts against loss and damage resulting from the provision of low-quality services and the improper use of raw materials. In addition, the statute is designed to prevent a diminution in tax revenues and a detrimental effect on the level of contributions received by the social insurance and unemployment insurance authorities (cf the Explanatory Statement to the Draft Bill, Printed Papers of the Bundestag, 2nd legislative period 1111, pp 3–4). ...

§§ 1and 2 of the Act provide, subject to certain conditions, for the imposition of fines on both persons engaging in clandestine work and those commissioning it. In so providing, the statute seeks, to all intents and purposes, to prohibit clandestine working and generally to prevent the exchange of services between the person commissioning the work and the unregistered person performing it (cf OLG Düsseldorf, BauR 1978, 412). Thus, the prohibition of clandestine working is aimed not only at the person by whom the work is carried out but also at the person who commissions it. The fines provided for in §§ 1 and 2 of the Act provide in themselves significant grounds for supposing that it is the intention of the legal order to refuse to recognise the validity of a contract which disregards the prohibition of clandestine working (cf BGHZ 37, 363, 365, on forbidden games). Above all, the *aim* of the Act, namely to prevent clandestine working, can only be achieved if contracts which infringe it are regarded as invalid in law.

bb) The appeal court was also correct in holding that *both* parties violated the Act on the combating of clandestine labour when concluding the contract of 16 January 1978. ...

2. ... *Exceptionally*, however, the invalidity of the contract under § 134 BGB does not, in the present case, mean that the claimant has no claim against the defendant for indemnification in respect of the sums due to the suppliers of materials which exceeded the fixed price agreed, since the defendant's plea that the contract was invalid violates, in the particular circumstances of the present case, the principle of good faith (§ 242 BGB).

a) [The Court pointed out that the contract price of DM 146,949.50 was a guaranteed price and that the defendant had given an implied promise to save the claimant any extra expense.]

b) It is true that the court must *ex officio* take account of the illegality of a legal transaction. However, the principle of good faith which dominates the entire legal life is also valid in the context of void legal transactions (BGH NJW 1981, 1439, with further references; …). Therefore, relying on the nullity of a contract can, in very exceptional cases, constitute an abusive exercise of rights (BGH NJW 1981, 1439, with further references; …).

This is also true in the present case.

The defendant arranged for the claimant's building project, apart from the garage and the fitting of the doors, to be carried out to a large extent by clandestine workers, as the parties had planned. The claimant paid the agreed 'fixed price', apart from a sum of DM 3,949.50, corresponding more or less to the value of the garage and the uninstalled doors. Thus the contract was almost performed in its entirety *by both parties*. Moreover, neither of the parties wishes the restitution of the consideration furnished by them. Were the defendant, in this situation, to succeed with his plea alleging the nullity of the contract, he would be able to shift onto the claimant the risk, assumed by him in the contract, of his being able to adhere to the agreed 'fixed price'. He would thus free himself, at the claimant's expense, from an obligation pertaining to him, notwithstanding that the contract has, for the rest, been performed by both parties who wish not to disturb what has been achieved. He would thereby be able unilaterally to exploit the nullity of the contract to his advantage, even though, in concluding it, he likewise infringed the Act on the combatting of clandestine labour.

Furthermore, the claimant, instead of the defendant, would not only have to assume the risk of adhering to the fixed price but would not even be able to check whether the defendant expended the whole of the sum paid over to him on the construction of the house. Clandestine workers do not, as a general rule, issue invoices and receipts. That was the position here. In cases of this kind, the person commissioning the building works would therefore have to rely, as regards the amounts paid to the clandestine workers, on the information provided by the person dealing with them. The latter could secure additional advantages by making false statements. Nor would it be possible to subject the value of the work carried out by the clandestine workers to an evaluation, since there are no 'usual' prices for the labour of clandestine workers. The person commissioning the works would be in an almost completely unprotected position *vis-à-vis* the person to whom they were entrusted.

All in all, therefore, the claimant would be placed at an intolerable disadvantage, and the defendant would be unjustifiably better off, if the latter were allowed to succeed with his defence that the contract was invalid, notwithstanding the fact that *both* parties acted unlawfully in agreeing that clandestine labour was to be used for the construction works, and despite the fact that the offence committed by the defendant is rather more heinous than that of the claimant. The object of the Act on the combating of clandestine labour, namely to protect businesses engaged in craft trades and consumers by preventing work and services from being provided by clandestine labour, is not such as to require that the claimant be denied, in the particular circumstances of this case, the right to indemnification. The services of the clandestine workers have already been provided. Consequently, it is no longer possible, in the present case, to satisfy the protective purpose which the statute is designed to serve. Settlement of the outstanding aspects of the (void) contract, namely payment of the sums due for the materials supplied and indemnification of the claimant in respect of claims by the suppliers of those materials, can no longer jeopardise the protection of craft trades which the Act on the combating of clandestine labour is intended to ensure. The present case is not concerned with assessing the consequences arising from the prohibited use of clandestine labour but with settling the outstanding aspects of a void legal relationship, which is not essentially different from the settlement of matters under a valid contract.

3. It follows that the defendant cannot rely, by way of defence against the claimant's claims, on the nullity of the contract. He must be ordered to repay to the claimant the sum which the latter has expended, or has yet to expend, in settlement of invoices rendered by the suppliers of materials or other firms. ...

Note

If it was the policy of the statute to deter owners and building contractors from entering into such agreements, the best deterrent would have been to deprive the claimant of a contractual claim for the extra expense. Do you agree?

BGH, 26 November 1980[97]   **17.21 (DE)**

Pre-auction bid

A statute forbidding auctioneers to take bids made before the auction begins unless they are in writing and signed by the buyer is designed to prevent fraud by the auctioneer and if the auctioneer wrongly allows a bid which was sent in by unsigned telegram that does not render the contract of sale illegal.

Facts: A German statute forbids auctioneers to take into consideration bids submitted by a party not physically present at the auction unless the pre-auction bid is in writing and signed by the bidder. A painting was knocked down by the claimant auctioneer to the defendant on the basis of a pre-auction bid which had been sent by telegram only and did not comply with the statutory form requirement. The defendant bidder argued that there was no contract, his bid being invalid under the statute.

Held: The claim was dismissed and the contract upheld.

Judgment: 1. Even if the conduct of the defendant had infringed § 34b(6) no. 3 of the Trade Regulations [Gewerbeordnung] the contract of the claimant with the defendant who auctioned in his own name was not void because of a violation of a statutory prohibition (§ 134 BGB) since the prohibition under consideration is only directed against the defendant.

a) Under § 134 BGB, a transaction which breaches a statutory prohibition is void only if the statute does not provide otherwise. It follows, according to settled case-law, that the question whether the breach renders the prohibited transaction void depends on the object and purpose of the prohibiting legislation. If the prohibition applies only to one of the contracting parties, the transaction will not, as a general rule, be void. However, in certain particular cases, a breach of even a unilateral prohibition will render the transaction void, especially where it would otherwise be impossible to achieve the protection aimed at by the statute in question, as is regularly the case with violations of the Act on the provision of legal services or repeated violations of the prohibition of private

---

[97] NJW 1981, 1204 (citations omitted).

procurement of job offers. Even in such cases, though, the importance and the extent of the violation must be taken into account.

b) aa) § 34b(6) no. 3 of the Trade Regulations expressly prohibits 'the auctioneer' from bidding or purchasing auctioned items on behalf of another person unless there exists a written offer made by that other person. Thus, the only person to whom the prohibition is addressed is the auctioneer; in the event of an infringement, it is solely on him that a fine may be imposed (§ 144(3) and (4) of the Trade Regulations).

bb) The statutory prohibition in issue does not prohibit the auctioneer from acting on behalf of third parties under any circumstances whatever; it only prohibits him from so acting in the absence of evidence of authority in the form of a written offer which is accordingly verifiable in the context of the auction. Consequently, the object and purpose of the provision in question is not to exclude bidders who are not physically present at the auction from participating in it. On the contrary, the aim of the provision is merely, in the interests of ensuring the transparency of the auction, to prevent the auctioneer from secretly taking part in it himself—as he is in any case prohibited from doing by § 34b(6) no. 1 of the Trade Regulations—or from feigning the existence of bids by third parties in order to push up the price. There is nothing in the legislation to suggest, as the applicant maintains and as the appellate court accepted, that, in addition, bidders who are not present are to be protected against the consequences of over-hasty bidding; nor does that contention correspond to the particular circumstances of an auction. The course taken by an auction is frequently such as to force absent bidders to make rapid decisions which need to be given oral expression, for example, where the question arises as to whether to exceed the upper limit which one had intended to place on of one's own bids. Such circumstances do not, however, provide any grounds for accepting that the purpose of the statute is to protect absent bidders against oral bidding instructions. The protection which the prohibition laid down by the legislation is intended to provide is not such as to give rise in such circumstances to the inference that, because the offer made was unwritten, the bid, and its acceptance on the fall of the hammer, must necessarily be void: if the aim of the legislation is merely to prevent the auctioneer from participating in the auction himself and from feigning the existence of offers from absent bidders, there is no need, for the purposes of protecting either the principal on whose behalf the bid is made or the other bidders, to invalidate bidding instructions which actually exist but which have merely not been given in writing.

Adequate sanctions are available against the auctioneer, in the form of the imposition of fines (§ 144(3) and (4) of the Trade Regulations) and the suppression or suspension of auctions held in breach of the statutory prohibition (§ 34b(8) no. 1d of the Trade Regulations ...). In those circumstances, there is no need to determine the question whether that result would already have been justified because there existed in the present case a telegram containing the name, address and intended offer of the bidder, so that the breach of the prohibition related at most to a matter of external form—namely, the absence of a personal signature—whereas the protective purpose of the statute was fully satisfied. ...

Note

Likewise, in French law, when the contract has involved a breach of a statutory regulation, the question is whether the aim of the law can be achieved by simply applying the sanctions expressly laid down in it or whether the contract should be invalidated. In order to find the answer, French judges must construe the statute and find out whether it impliedly meant that contracts formed in breach of it would be valid or not. In doing so, French courts ask whether these rules merely impose penalties in the form of disciplinary measures or whether, beyond the discipline measure, the public interest (*intérêt général*) is involved and, thereby, some form of professional public order mainly aimed at protecting the other party. Only if this is the case, will the courts invalidate the contract.

Cass civ (1), 15 February 1961[98]   **17.22 (FR)**

The bailiff's commission

Although it was a disciplinary offence for a bailiff to accept a fee for arranging a sale, the contract to pay the fee was not illegal.

Facts: L, a bailiff, arranged for property to be sold to M, who gave the bailiff a promissory note in payment of commission. Arranging a sale would constitute a commercial act by the bailiff, and bailiffs were at the time prohibited from engaging in commercial activity. M argued that the promissory note was unenforceable on the grounds of illegality.

Held: The cour d'appel held that the obligation was founded on an illegal basis, but the Cour de cassation quashed this decision.

Judgment: On the first branch of the first appeal ground:— Whereas it appears from the statements contained in the contested judgment that on 30 January 1954 Lancroux sold to Mabru, through the intermediary of L …, bailiff, of Souillac, a hotel/restaurant business situated in that locality; as on the same day, Mabru handed to L …, as remuneration for his services and by way of commission, a promissory note by which he undertook to pay to the bearer of that note the sum of 162,500 francs.

— Whereas the appellant's complaint concerns the declaration by the cour d'appel that the obligation thus accepted and assumed was void on the ground of illegality; as according to the appellant, at the time when that obligation came into being, bailiffs were not prohibited from acting as brokers in the sale of businesses, which is not in any event a commercial activity.

— Whereas first of all, however, the fifth paragraph of Article 632 of the Commercial Code provides that all brokerage operations are deemed to constitute commercial acts; as second, it is clear from Articles 39, 40 and 41 of the Decree of 14 June 1813, which was in force at the material time, that bailiffs are prohibited from engaging in any commercial activity, whether because that prohibition results from the actual wording of the aforementioned Article 41 or because such activities are regarded as incompatible with the professional dignity of such ministerial officers.

— Whereas the appeal ground is consequently unfounded as regards the first branch thereof.

— Whereas the first branch of the first appeal ground must therefore be rejected.

As to the second branch of that appeal ground, however:

— Under Articles 39, 40 and 41 of the Decree of 14 June 1813;

---

[98] No. 58-11914, Bull civ I no. 105.

— Whereas although those articles prohibit bailiffs from engaging in any commercial activity, they merely state that such activities are incompatible with the duties of a bailiff, and provide only for the imposition of penalties in the form of disciplinary measures.

— Whereas the cour d'appel considered, as the grounds for its declaration that the obligation assumed by Mabru in favour of the bailiff L … on 30 January 1954 was void, that that obligation was founded on an illicit *cause*.

— Whereas however, the brokerage operation in issue, which consisted of bringing the parties together and providing for L … to be remunerated for his expenses and efforts, was not in itself, and on that account alone, founded on any illicit *cause*; it merely rendered that ministerial officer liable to the imposition of the disciplinary sanctions provided for in such cases.

— Whereas in ruling as it did, the cour d'appel infringed the legislative provisions referred to above.

…

Notes

(1) In this French case, very little is said about the reasons which led the Court to its conclusion. It is quite clear, however, from this silence, that the 'disciplinary measures' are not considered by the Court as forming part of the 'professional public order'.[99] Some more explanation for such a solution is given in Cass civ (1) 5 November 1991:[100]

> Rules based on professional ethics (*règles de déontologie*) which set forth the obligations of members of a specific profession only give rise to disciplinary measures which do not, as such, give rise to the nullity of contracts formed in violation of these rules.

(2) It is for French courts to hold that in the light of the meaning and purpose of the statury rule, according to which certain conduct is illegal, a contract must be held void even if only one of the parties broke the law. Courts will do so by asking themselves whether public order is violated by such a contract. The dividing line between mere disciplinary measures and measures aimed at protecting some form of professional public order is a difficult one. The line is not always clear-cut. For instance, the question arose as to whether contracts concluded with an organisation providing credit which had no authorisation for this were valid or null. The First Civil Chamber of the Cour de cassation held that it was valid[101] but the Commercial Chamber then held that it was null, of absolute nullity. The Plenary Assembly of the Cour de cassation took the view that it was valid:[102] the mere violation, by a bank, of the requirement of an authorisation as required by the law (Article 15, Act no. 84-46 of 24 January 1984, which became Articles L511–10, L511–14 and L612–2 of the Code monétaire et financier) does not lead to the nullity of the contracts it has concluded.

---

[99] On this concept, see F Terré, P Simler and Y Lequette, *Les obligations* (11th edn, Paris: Dalloz, 2013) no. 381.

[100] No. 89-15179, Bull I no. 297.

[101] Cass civ (1) 30 March 1994, no. 92-16797, Bull I no. 125, RTD civ 1995, 100, annotated by J Mestre.

[102] Ass plén 4 March 2005, no. 03-11725, Bull AP no. 2, RTD civ 2005, annotated by J Mestre and B Fages.

17.5 RESTITUTION OF BENEFITS CONFERRED UNDER AN IMMORAL OR ILLEGAL CONTRACT

If an agreement is immoral or illegal and therefore void no party can sue on it either for specific performance or for damages resulting from a breach. But suppose that the agreement has been performed: is a party entitled to recover the money paid or the property delivered under it? In cases where the claimant is guilty of clearly outrageous or shocking behaviour, the traditional answer is no. Many such cases were discussed even in Roman law. Thus, it was held that a person cannot reclaim a bribe paid to a judge or witness, hush-money paid to a person who caught him *in flagranti* or the price paid for an immoral act. The general rule was that money cannot be recovered if both the payor and the payee, by paying and accepting the money, have contravened elementary principles of morality: *in pari delicto potiorem esse possessorem*.[103]

Principles of European Contract Law **17.23 (INT)**

Article 15:104: Restitution

(1) When a contract is rendered ineffective under Articles 15:101 or 15:102, either party may claim restitution of whatever that party has supplied under the contract, provided that, where appropriate, concurrent restitution is made of whatever has been received.

(2) When considering whether to grant restitution under paragraph (1), and what concurrent restitution, if any, would be appropriate, regard must be had to the factors referred to in Article 15:102 (3).

(3) An award of restitution may be refused to a party who knew or ought to have known of the reason for the ineffectiveness.

(4) If restitution cannot be made in kind for any reason, a reasonable sum must be paid for what has been received.

Note

The DCFR operates by way of *renvoi* to the rules on unjustified enrichment or to the rules on the transfer of property (Article II-7:303: Effects of nullity or avoidance).

The problem is discussed in the context of the law of restitution. While a performance made under a void contract is generally recoverable as not being based on a valid *causa*, such restitutionary claim will be barred when the performance was made and accepted for an immoral purpose or in contravention of a rule of public policy. A codified version of the maxim is to be found in the second sentence of § 817 BGB.[104] In France the courts invoke the principle *nemo turpitudinem suam allegans auditur* and in England the principle is that *ex turpi causa non oritur actio* or—in the words of Lord Mansfield—that

---

[103] Papinian Digest 12.5.7 pr. For a historical and comparative view, see H Kötz, *European Contract Law* (2nd edn, Oxford University Press, 2017) 125–29.

[104] See also Art 2033 of the Italian Civil Code, Art 66 Swiss Law of Obligations, Art 6:211 Dutch Civil Code.

'no court will lend its aid to a man who founds his cause of action upon an immoral or illegal act'.[105]

This principle makes sense in cases involving serious crimes and other grave infringements of the moral code. But it is very doubtful whether all claims in restitution should be denied in cases in which the agreement, forbidden though it is, runs counter merely to one of the many modern, morally indifferent statutory prohibitions. Indeed, the rule is not appropriate.

In France, the scope of the rule *nemo auditur* is limited. First, the rule *nemo auditur* only applies to claims for restitution and is used as a defence to an action for restitution. It does not apply to a claim of nullity, a claim in tort or a claim in resolution of a contract.[106] Secondly, it usually applies only if the agreement is immoral (*convention immorale*)[107] and not if it is merely illegal (*convention seulement illicite*).[108]

Cour d'appel Aix, 28 March 1945[109]   **17.24 (FR)**

Potage créole

A sum paid in performance of an obligation void for illegality may be recovered.

Facts: D sold C 150,000 cases of Potage Créole, a new food product which had not been approved by the authorities. C sought to recover the money it had paid.

Held: The price paid by the buyer could be recovered.

Judgment:— Whereas it is necessary and appropriate to adopt the grounds set out in the judgment of the court adjudicating at first instance, which correctly applied the principles of law to the facts of the case; as it is not denied by either of the parties that the sale of the 150,000 cases of 'Potage Créole' was void, since it was contrary to the Law of 17 June 1942, which prohibits the sale of any new product intended for human consumption before that product receives official approval;

— Whereas the 'Potage Créole' has never been officially approved and its sale was unlawful.

— Whereas Société Soprodis, Pichon & Guimard and Établissements Bancey have no basis for their argument that the claim for restitution should be disallowed because payment for the goods was made in full knowledge of the circumstances and without any error on the part of the payor.

— Whereas the payment in question was made in performance of an unlawful obligation which was, as such, void; as such a payment, made on an invalid basis, operates, irrespective of any error, to vest in Société Nationale the right to claim restitution.

---

[105] *Holman v Johnson* (1775) 1 Cowp. 341, 98 ER 1120.

[106] P Malaurie, L Aynès and P Stoffel-Munck, *Droit des obligations* (9th edn, Paris: LGDJ, 2017) no. 727.

[107] See, eg, Cass com 27 April 1981, no. 80-11200, Bull no. 187, DS 1982, 51, annotated by Ph Le Tourneau: 'The purchaser of a bar who knew when she bought it that it had been used for immoral purposes and that criminal investigations were under way had no action against the vendor when the authorities closed the establishment down and withdrew its licence.'

[108] Malaurie et al (above n 106) no. 727; Ph Le Tourneau, *La règle nemo auditur* (Paris: LGDJ, 1970); Ph Le Tourneau, 'La spécificité et la subsidiarité de l'exception d'indignité' D 1995, chr 298.

[109] Gaz Pal 1945.2.12.

— Whereas nor is it possible to accept the appellants' submission that Société Nationale should be refused the right to bring its claim in the courts on the ground that it participated in the illicit sale in full knowledge of the circumstances.

—Whereas it is true that the case-law on which they rely does indeed debar a person who claims that an agreement is void for immorality from bringing an action on that agreement, the position is not the same where the agreement is merely prohibited by law or contrary to public policy, as the case may be, and not actually immoral.

—Under Articles 1131 and 1133 of the Code civil [now Article 1162], a person who has paid sums in pursuance of obligations which are void for illegality may bring proceedings for their repayment.

—Whereas a sum of money paid in performance of a void obligation is not due, and moneys which have been paid without being due may be the subject of proceedings for restitution …

On those grounds, the court confirms the contested judgment.

Notes

(1) To support the conclusion of the Court in the preceding judgment one might also have argued that the prohibition was primarily directed to the defendant who, as a producer and seller of foodstuffs, was under a clear statutory duty to obtain the governmental authorisation prior to marketing his products, while the claimant, as buyer, was not equally to blame though he knew or had reason to know about the defendant's breach of his statutory duty. Indeed, many courts have held that restitution should be denied only if the parties are *in pari delicto*. If it was primarily the defendant who was guilty of the illegality or immorality, the relatively innocent claimant should be allowed to reclaim. This principle is used in several different types of case. For example, a claimant is not *in pari delicto* with the defendant if he was induced to enter the agreement by the defendant's representation that it was lawful, nor if the defendant has exploited his difficulty, simplicity or inexperience, and the same is true if the prohibitory law which renders the contract invalid was designed to protect a special class of persons which includes the claimant.

(2) Compare this case with the proposed rule that was contained in a new section of the Avant-projet Catala entirely dedicated to restitution (Article 1162-3): 'Restitution may be refused to a person who has knowingly violated public policy, public morality, or more generally any mandatory rule.' If enacted, would the distinction between immoral and illegal contracts still be relevant as regards restitution? Should such a rule be adopted?

By contrast with the Avant-projet Catala, the 2016 reform of French contract law does not deal with the question of restitution in case of illegality or immorality. The general rule, laid down in Article 1178 of the new Code civil, is that the nullity of the contract gives rise to the restitution of the acts of performance previously carried out.

Article 1178: A contract which does not satisfy the conditions required for its validity is a nullity. Nullity must be declared by a court, unless the parties establish it by mutual agreement.

An annulled contract is deemed never to have existed.

Acts of performance which have been carried out give rise to restitution under the conditions provided by articles 1352 to 1352-9. ...

As the lawfulness of the contract is a condition of its validity, the illegality of the contract is sanctioned by nullity, and the acts of performance carried out before the declaration of nullity must give rise to restitution. Neither Article 1178 nor the regime of restitution, set out in Articles 1352 to 1352-9 of the new Code civil, make an exception in events of illegality or immorality. Therefore, under the 2016 reform, it seems that the illegality or immorality of a contract will not prevent a party from obtaining restitution, even if that party is the one who created the illegality or immorality, unless the courts decide otherwise, by application of the adage *nemo auditur propriam suam turpitudinem*, as they have done in the past.

In English law a party is not entitled to restitution merely because the contract is illegal. Rather, illegality may be used as a defence by either party to any action for restitution by the other, on the principle *in pari delicto potior est conditio possidentis* referred to earlier. That rule used to be the starting point, but there were exceptions: for example, where the purpose of the rule making the conduct illegal was to protect the claimant;[110] where the claimant had repented and no longer wished the contract to go ahead;[111] and, in more recent cases, where the contract was not going to be carried out because there was no longer any point in doing so.[112] One case at least had suggested the courts were taking a more flexible approach to restitution. In *Mohammed v Alaga*[113] the Court of Appeal allowed a translator who had done work for a firm of solicitors under an illegal fee-sharing agreement to recover a reasonable amount for his services. Robert Walker LJ said that it was not necessary for the claimant to show that he was completely blameless. To establish a *quantum meruit* claim, it would be enough if the claimant established at trial 'that he was not culpable, or was significantly less culpable, than the defendant solicitors'. But if the plaintiff could not bring himself within one of these exceptions his claim would fail. For example, in *Parkinson v College of Ambulance Ltd* [1925] 2 KB 1 the plaintiff made a donation to a charity in order to secure a knighthood. When the honour failed to materialise he sued for the return of his money. The claim was rejected.

In *Patel v Mirza*,[114] the case in which the claimant had paid money to the defendant to place illegal bets but the bets had never been placed, all the Justices in the Supreme Court agreed that Patel should be able to recover the money. Lords Mance, Sumption, Clarke and Neuberger argued that a restitution claim should always, or at least nearly always, be allowed, as this would not enable the claimant to profit from his own wrong nor make the law inconsistent, as the contract was not being enforced. Speaking for the majority, Lord Toulson said:

> 115. In the present case I would endorse the approach and conclusion of Gloster LJ [in the Court of Appeal]. She correctly asked herself whether the policy underlying the rule which

---

[110] *Kiriri Cotton Co Ltd v Dewani* [1960] AC 192 (PC) (landlord had demanded an illegal premium to allow tenant to occupy flat; tenant allowed to recover the premium).

[111] See *Palaniappa Chettiar v Arunasalam Chettiar* [1962] AC 294 (PC).

[112] *Tribe v Tribe* [1996] Ch 107 (CA).

[113] [1999] 3 All ER 699 (CA).

[114] [2016] UKSC 42; see above, p 702.

made the contract between Mr Patel and Mr Mirza illegal would be stultified if Mr Patel's claim in unjust enrichment were allowed. After examining the policy underlying the statutory provisions about insider dealing, she concluded that there was no logical basis why considerations of public policy should require Mr Patel to forfeit the moneys which he paid into Mr Mirza's account, and which were never used for the purpose for which they were paid. She said that such a result would not be a just and proportionate response to the illegality. I agree. It seems likely that Lord Mansfield CJ would also have agreed: see *Walker v Chapman* (1773) Lofft 342. Mr Patel is seeking to unwind the arrangement, not to profit from it.

116. It is not necessary to discuss the question of locus poenitentiae which troubled the courts below, as it has troubled other courts, because it assumed importance only because of a wrong approach to the issue whether Mr Patel was prima facie entitled to the recovery of his money. In place of the basic rule and limited exceptions to which I referred at para 44 above, I would hold that a person who satisfies the ordinary requirements of a claim in unjust enrichment will not prima facie be debarred from recovering money paid or property transferred by reason of the fact that the consideration which has failed was an unlawful consideration. I do not exclude the possibility that there may be particular reason for the court to refuse its assistance to the claimant, applying the kind of exercise which Gloster LJ applied in this case, just as there may be a particular reason for the court to refuse to assist an owner to enforce his title to property, but such cases are likely to be rare. (At para 110 I gave the example of a drug trafficker.) In *Tappenden v Randall* (1801) 2 B & P 467, 471, a case of a successful claim for the repayment of money paid for an unenforceable consideration which failed, Heath J said obiter that there might be "cases where the contract may be of a nature too grossly immoral for the court to enter into any discussion of it; as where one man has paid money by way of hire to another to murder a third person". The case was mentioned by the Law Commission (Consultation Paper 189), para 4.53, but there is a dearth of later case law on the point. This is hardly surprising because a person who takes out a contract on the life of a third person is not likely to advertise his guilt by suing. But as a matter of legal analysis it is sufficient for present purposes to identify the framework within which such an issue may be decided. No particular reason has been advanced in this case to justify Mr Mirza's retention of the monies beyond the fact that it was paid to him for the unlawful purpose of placing an insider bet.

117. In support of his argument that this purpose was sufficient to disentitle Mr Patel from obtaining the return of his money, Mr Collings relied on cases such as *Parkinson v College of Ambulance Ltd* [1925] 2 KB 1. In that case the plaintiff made a donation to a charity to secure a knighthood. When the honour failed to materialise he sued for the return of his money. The claim was rejected.

118. Bribes of all kinds are odious and corrupting, but it does not follow that it is in the public interest to prevent their repayment. There are two sides to the equation. If today it transpired that a bribe had been paid to a political party, a charity or a holder of public office, it might be regarded as more repugnant to the public interest that the recipient should keep it than that it should be returned. We are not directly concerned with such a case but I refer to it because of the reliance placed on that line of authorities.

119. Since criticism was made of the Court of Appeal's decision in *Mohamed v Alaga & Co* ..., I would affirm its correctness and reject the view that it should somehow be confined to its own peculiar facts ...

Thus the traditional English approach to claims for restitution of money or other benefits transferred under an illegal contract seems to have been reversed; under the new approach, restitution will generally be allowed, as to put the parties back into the position they were in before the illegal transaction does not enable the claimant to profit from his wrong, nor is it seen to be harmful to the integrity of the legal system.

BGH, 23 November 1959[115]

17.25 (DE)

The struggling fur trader

A borrower who has taken out an illegal loan which he is then required to repay may set off by way of restitution the interest he has paid to the lender, unless he has committed a wilful breach of public policy.

Facts: The defendant had got into serious financial trouble. He had applied for and received various loans from the claimant at an exorbitant interest rate which rendered the agreements void under § 138(2) BGB. When the claimant brought an action the defendant sought to set off a counterclaim for the restitution of the interest paid.

Held: The lower court dismissed the defendant's counterclaim on the ground that he knew or ought to have known that his financial breakdown was inevitable and than an artificial prolongation of his struggle might harm other unsuspecting creditors. The Bundesgerichtshof disagreed and allowed the defendant's counterclaim.

Judgment (citations omitted): ... Those statements do not bear legal scrutiny. It may be doubtful whether the defendant objectively infringed the rules relating to public policy ... However, there is no need to adjudicate on that issue, since, in any event, the subjective criteria laid down by the second sentence of § 817 BGB are not fulfilled. That provision divests a creditor of his right to claim, or at least to enforce a claim, based on the general rules relating to unjustified enrichment. It may be the case that the justification for this rule lies in the fact that the creditor should be punished for his contravention of public policy and morality, or the rule may be regarded as justified on the ground that the State should deny the creditor the protection of the law because the State must itself be protected against abusive recourse to the courts by persons who have broken the law. The fact remains that it is always necessary, on account of the severe and harsh consequences for the creditor, that he must have committed a wilful breach of public policy. Such reprehensibility cannot generally be said to exist where a borrower has, out of necessity, taken out a loan at an excessively high rate of interest and has paid that interest in order, once again for reasons of necessity, to receive a further loan at an excessively high interest rate. ... The defendant had got into serious financial difficulties, arising primarily, according to the findings of the appellate court, from the fact that he owned a large warehouse at a time when there was a fall in prices in the fur trade of some 25 to 30 per cent. The defendant was no longer able to obtain a bank loan, but was dependent on credit. He hoped to be able to overcome the difficulties affecting his business by means of the loan granted by the claimant. He did not manage to do so; in the spring of 1955 an out-of-court settlement was concluded, and the defendant has stated that his business undertaking has since then been the property of a bank. However, where a trader has been forced by financial difficulties to take out a loan at an excessively high rate of interest in order thereby to avoid the collapse of his business, even where that hope is not essentially fulfilled, and his recourse to the loan increases the risk of collapse of the business or

---

[115] LM § 817 BGB no. 12, MDR 1960, 111.

operates to make the extent of the losses flowing from its possible collapse even greater, he does not generally act in deliberate contravention of public policy or morality; consequently, he should not be punished by a refusal to allow him to claim restitution of the interest paid on an unlawful basis or denied the legal protection afforded by the State, as if he had wilfully broken the law. Nor can there be any objective justification for allowing a lender who has granted a loan on unethical or usurious terms to retain, as a matter of principle, the interest paid to him by a borrower who took out that loan because he was in severe financial difficulties.

FURTHER READING

Hellwege, P, 'Invalidity' in J Basedow, K Hopt and R Zimmermann (eds), *Max Planck Encyclopedia of European Private Law* (Oxford University Press, 2012) 990–94.

Kötz, H, 'Die Ungültigkeit von Verträgen wegen Gesetzes- und Sittenwidrigkeit' (1994) 58 RabelsZ 209–31.

Kötz, H, *European Contract Law* (2nd edn, Oxford University Press, 2017) 109–29.

Kötz, H, 'Illegality of Contracts' in J Basedow, K Hopt and R Zimmermann (eds), *Max Planck Encyclopedia of European Private Law* (Oxford University Press, 2012) 847–49.

MacQueen, H and Cockrell, A, 'Illegal Contracts' in R Zimmermann, D Visser and K Reid (eds), *Mixed Legal Systems in Comparative Perspective: Property and Obligations in Scotland and South Africa* (Oxford University Press, 2004) 143–75.

Meier, S, 'Illegality' in N Jansen and R Zimmermann (eds), *Commentaries on European Contract Laws* (Oxford University Press, 2018) 1887–1930.

Zweigert, K and Kötz, H, *Introduction to Comparative Law* (3rd edn, Oxford: Clarendon Press, 1998) 380–87.

PART 4
CONTENT OF CONTRACTS

CHAPTER 18
INTERPRETATION

Words are not always understood as intended. The meaning of a verbal statement depends essentially on what the parties making and receiving it think it means, but since what people think depends on their personal knowledge, experience, preferences, concerns and interests, the author of the statement and its addressee can easily think it means different things. If the statement forms part of a contract, it must be given a single meaning binding on both parties. The process of educing such a meaning is called interpretation. We will deal with it in this chapter, and we will see that it cannot always be neatly distinguished from other issues, such as mistake, formation of contracts, formal requirements and questions of proof. Different legal systems have different views on what is a question of contractual interpretation and what is not. As a general rule, the English concept is narrower than its civil law counterparts: some situations that are perceived to be falling within the domain of contractual 'interpretation' in France or Germany have traditionally been understood as related, but more or less independent, doctrines of contract law by English contract lawyers.

This can be seen in cases where the parties have failed to provide for a contingency which they would have covered had they thought of all the problems which might arise as the contract proceeded. Contracts are almost always incomplete in this sense. Different legal systems employ different techniques to fill the resulting gaps. Some of them are comfortable with using the language of 'interpretation' in this context. After all, in these cases the content and the meaning of a contract must be ascertained, too. Others insist that the 'supplementation' of terms which are not written in the contract is an exercise that differs from the ordinary process of interpretation. We will see how judges deal with this issue in Chapter 20.

Frequently, however, omissions in contracts can be remedied by the application of 'default rules' which the legal system has developed for the very purpose of filling such gaps. The most important of these rules will be dealt with in Chapter 19.

18.1 'OBJECTIVE' AND 'SUBJECTIVE' INTERPRETATION

If contracting parties are agreed on what they said or wrote but differ on what it means, the process of interpretation may be guided by two different approaches. On one view, precedence is given to the subjective 'will of the parties'. This is consistent with the principle of party autonomy, according to which legal obligations arise from, and are justified by, the free will of the individual. The other view gives precedence to the external fact of the words in which the will has been objectively expressed. After all, social and commercial intercourse requires that reliance be protected, and people rely on what others actually say, not on what they meant to say. Most modern contract law regimes hover between 'objective' and 'subjective interpretation':

Principles of European Contract Law   **18.1 (INT)**

Article 5:101: General Rules of Interpretation[1]
(1) A contract is to be interpreted according to the common intention of the parties even if this differs from the literal meaning of the words.
(2) If it is established that one party intended the contract to have a particular meaning, and at the time of the conclusion of the contract the other party could not have been unaware of the first party's intention, the contract is to be interpreted in the way intended by the first party.
(3) If an intention cannot be established according to (1) or (2), the contract is to be interpreted according to the meaning that reasonable persons of the same kind as the parties would give to it in the same circumstances.

One often comes across the statement that English law, in the interest of commercial convenience and the security of transactions, looks to the external appearance of consent and is therefore based on what has been called the 'expression theory', while the civil law, following the 'will theory', is inclined to favour the true state of mind of the parties.[2]

House of Lords   **18.2 (EN)**

Ashington Piggeries Ltd v Christopher Hill Ltd[3]

A party's intentions are to be determined not by what the party may have intended subjectively but by how his words and conduct would be interpreted by a reasonable person in the same position as the other party.

Facts: The plaintiffs, Hill, who were feeding-stuff compounders, contracted with the defendants, Udall, who were mink-breeders, to compound for and deliver to them an animal foodstuff known as 'King Size'. The contract provided as to quality and description that it was to be 'fair average quality of the season, expected to analyse not less than 70 per cent protein, not more than 12 per cent fat and not more than 4 per cent salt'. The foodstuff supplied under the contract caused thousands of mink to die because an ingredient, Norwegian

---

[1] A slightly amended rule can be found in Art II-8:101 DCFR.
[2] See above, pp 89, 103–04.
[3] [1972] AC 441, 502.

herring meal, contained a toxic agent, a chemical which, however, was not unfit for animals other than mink. The plaintiffs sued the defendants for sums due in respect of the supply of the foodstuff. The defendants counter-claimed. (This extract concerns only the 'objective' interpretation' point.)

Judgment: LORD DIPLOCK: ... In each of the instant appeals the dispute is as to what the seller promised to the buyer by the words which he used in the contract itself and by his conduct in the course of the negotiations which led up to the contract. What he promised is determined by ascertaining what his words and conduct would have led the buyer reasonably to believe that he was promising. That is what is meant in the English law of contract by the common intention of the parties. The test is impersonal. It does not depend upon what the seller himself thought he was promising, if the words and conduct by which he communicated his intention to the seller would have led a reasonable man in the position of the buyer to a different belief as to the promise; nor does it depend upon the actual belief of the buyer himself as to what the seller's promise was, unless that belief would have been shared by a reasonable man in the position of the buyer. The result of the application of this test to the words themselves used in the contract is 'the construction of the contract'.

... the question of law for the court should be: What, if any, responsibility as to the characteristics of the goods to be supplied under the contract would the seller reasonably understand that the buyer believed that he, the seller, was accepting? Or, put in the obverse form: What responsibility as to the characteristics of the goods to be supplied would the buyer reasonably believe that the seller was accepting by entering into the contract? And in the circumstances of the present case that question of law can be reduced to this: Would Hill's reasonable understanding and Udall's reasonable belief be that Hill was accepting responsibility to deliver feeding-stuffs characterised by their being compounded in accordance with the formula provided by the appellants and composed of ingredients of the kinds specified and of a quality suitable for use in compound feeding-stuffs for domestic animals and poultry? Or were their respective reasonable understanding and belief that Hill was accepting an additional responsibility that feeding-stuffs so compounded and composed would be suitable for feeding to mink?

Note

There is an exception to which Lord Diplock does not refer: if the buyer actually knows that the normal meaning of the words is not what the seller intends, and accepts the seller's offer without pointing out the seller's mistake, the buyer will not be able to hold the seller to the normal meaning of the words. If the contract is in writing, the seller may be able to get it rectified to accord with his actual intention, as known to the buyer.[4]

Code civil   18.3 (FR)

Article 1188: (1) A contract is to be interpreted according to the common intention of the parties rather than stopping at the literal meaning of its terms.

---

[4] Under the PECL, this scenario would be dealt with by Art 5:101(2), see p 722 above. See above, pp 408, 503, 512, 519.

§ 133: Interpretation of a declaration of intent
In interpreting a declaration of intent the real intention is to be ascertained without clinging to the literal meaning of the declaration.

Looking more closely, however, it is apparent that the civilian codes do not require that the parties' 'common' or 'real' intention is the only aspect to be taken into account. The element of intention is rather balanced against other factors which have nothing to do with the subjective state of mind of the parties.

Article 1189: (1) All the terms of a contract are to be interpreted in relation to each other, giving to each the meaning which respects the consistency of the contract as a whole.

Thus in France, courts and writers have long agreed that interpretation must seek the 'common intention' of the parties. However, they have also accepted that in the normal case where no real common intention of the parties can be established the task of the judge is to ascertain what must, in the light of all the circumstances, be taken to be what the parties must reasonably have intended. The revised Code civil of 2016 reflects this dual approach:

Article 1188: (1) A contract is to be interpreted according to the common intention of the parties rather than stopping at the literal meaning of its terms.
(2) Where this intention cannot be discerned, a contract is to be interpreted in the sense which a reasonable person placed in the same situation would give to it.

The Dutch Burgerlijk Wetboek of 1992 does not contain rules on contractual interpretation but the respective provisions of the old Dutch Civil Code of 1838 resembled those of the Code civil of 1804. When they were still in force the Hoge Raad, in the *Haviltex* case, developed a test that is frequently referred to as a 'subjective–objective approach':

> How a written contract regulates the relationship between the parties and whether that contract leaves a gap that must be supplemented, cannot be determined on the basis of a purely literal interpretation of the provisions of the contract. To answer that question, it is necessary to have regard to the meaning that the respective parties in the circumstances could have reasonably attached to these provisions and to that which in that respect they could reasonably have expected from each other. In this process, the parties' social position and the knowledge of the law that may be expected of such parties may be of significance.[5]

The foundation of this test, as the Court later clarified, is that 'all the circumstances of the individual case, assessed in accordance with the requirements of good faith, are of

---

[5] HR 13 March 1981, NJ 1981, 635. Translation by N Kornet, *Contract Interpretation and Gap-filling: Comparative and Theoretical Perspectives* (Antwerp: Intersentia, 2006) 31.

decisive importance'.[6] The element of good faith is also central to the German approach to the interpretation of contracts.

BGB   **18.7 (DE)**

§ 157: Interpretation of contracts
   Contracts are to be interpreted in accordance with the dictates of good faith taking into account normal commercial practice.

BGH, 12 March 1992[7]   **18.8 (DE)**

Demand guarantee

A guarantee given by a layperson cannot be interpreted as a 'demand guarantee', even if that is what was asked of her, if the party seeking the guarantee must have known that the layperson would not understand the meaning of the phrase.

Facts: The defendant was the wife of a man whose business partner had borrowed money from the plaintiff company. In order to secure the loan her husband had persuaded her to give the plaintiff a 'demand guarantee' (*Bürgschaft auf erstes Anfordern*), which is generally understood in the export trade to mean that the guarantor must pay immediately on demand and can raise defences to the claim only in a subsequent action for restitution. The defendant argued that she had no experience in the export or banking business and had therefore believed the guarantee to be a 'simple' guarantee.

Held: The defendant's appeal was allowed; 'guarantee' must be interpreted as 'simple' guarantee.

Judgment: ... a) In interpreting the declaration of the guarantee of 27 July 1987, the appellate court has violated §§ 133, 157 BGB ... The final appellate court has the power to control the interpretation of an individually negotiated agreement with regard to the violation of established principles of interpretation, statutory rules of interpretation, the rules of logic or experience and with regard to whether important materials which are relevant in the process of interpretation have been overlooked (settled case law, cf ...). ...

   b) The interpretation of the declaration has to be made according to what was the recognisable intention from the perspective of the person to whom the declaration was addressed (BGHZ 36, 30, 33 ...). This principle applies to declarations of intent that must be received in order to take effect, and it also applies to the unilaterally binding contract of guarantee (BGH NJW 1986, 1681, 1683 ...). As the declaration of the guarantee is directed to the creditor, it is relevant how the latter had to understand the declaration according to good faith and commercial practice (BGH, ibid ...).

   The interpretation depends primarily on the content of the deed of guarantee (BGHZ 76, 187, 189 ...). Even assuming that the plaintiff company, in formulating its terms, deliberately chose a form of wording which is regularly used by banks for 'demand' guarantees, it was not entitled, on that ground alone, to presume, upon receiving the declaration of guarantee, that the defendant intended to go so far as to shoulder liability under such a 'demand' guarantee. From the point of view of the creditor, who arranged for the declaration of guarantee to be given and formulated its wording, the intention of the guarantor

---

[6] HR 20 February 2004, NJ 2005, 493.
[7] NJW 1992, 1446.

725

can only have been in accordance with what she understood the wording submitted to her to mean. Consequently, the plaintiff company must accept the declaration of guarantee as having the meaning which, having regard to the circumstances which it could be aware of, it must on an objective basis be understood as possessing (cf BGH NJW 1983, 1903, 1904 …).

However, the wording of the agreement in issue ('The guaranteed sum shall become payable forthwith upon demand or upon this deed being first produced …') corresponds to the standard wording which has come to be used in banking transactions for 'demand guarantees'. Such accessory circumstances, lying outside the ambit of the declaratory act, may be taken into account for the purposes of interpretation, in so far as they allow the recipient of the declaration to draw a conclusion as to its meaning (BGH, WM 1971, 39, 42 …). That is not the position in the present case, since the plaintiff could not assume that the defendant knew or recognised the meaning attaching to the wording of the agreement in banking operations. It is only since the end of the 1970s that the concept of a 'demand guarantee'—designed to meet the needs of an export-oriented economy—has been judicially recognised; it is used primarily as a means of security in foreign trade. In domestic transactions, it has acquired practical significance mainly in the context of the financing of groups of companies (Heinsius, in: *Festschrift für Merz*, 1992, pp 177, 181). A demand guarantee is a typical type of banking transaction. It is little known outside banking circles. The plaintiff has not sought to argue that the defendant possessed any knowledge or experience with respect to credit security generally or in relation to areas in which demand guarantees are to be encountered in particular; nor has it submitted that the defendant, before assuming the guarantee obligation, was informed of the special characteristics of demand guarantees.

A person who possesses no particular knowledge of the field of credit security and who is, in particular, ignorant of the legal character of a demand guarantee cannot infer from the agreement an intention that the guarantor should be under a provisional payment obligation which cannot be contested on the basis of any objection or defence arising from the principal debtor-creditor relationship … Appeal allowed.

Notes

(1) The interpretation of a guarantee or any other contract is therefore 'objective' to the extent that a specific meaning which is only known to one of the parties cannot determine the meaning.

(2) However, the objective approach of German law is qualified if the parties chose to use words in a distinctive sense, different from their usual meaning. In this case, it is their intention rather than their expression that counts: *falsa demonstratio non nocet*. Thus it was held that if buyer and seller both use the word *Haakjöringsköd* to signify 'whalemeat' when it properly denotes 'sharkmeat', the contract is for whalemeat, and if the seller tenders sharkmeat the buyer can claim damages for non-performance.[8]

(3) If the contract is in writing English law reaches a similar result by way of an action for rectification.[9] The court will rectify the error and order specific performance

---

[8] RG 8 June 1920, RGZ 99, 147; see above, 14.13 (DE), p 502.
[9] For the most recent exposition of the doctrine, see *Chartbrook v Persimmon Homes Ltd* [2009] UKHL 38, [2009] 1 AC 1101 [48], [59]–[66]. See above, pp 408, 503, 512, 519, 723.

of the contract as rectified. This is a separate doctrine which has traditionally not been related to questions of interpretation.[10]

(4) Cases where the words used do not adequately reflect the *common* intention of the parties would be covered by Article 5:101(1) of the Principles of European Contract law (PECL).[11] But they are exceptional. In most other cases the contract has to be interpreted 'according to the meaning that reasonable persons of the same kind as the parties would give to it in the same circumstances': Article 5:101(3) PECL.

Today, the distinction between 'subjective' and 'objective' interpretation is therefore largely irrelevant in practice, particularly since it is well established that the same criteria must be employed in establishing both the 'subjective' intention of the parties and the 'objective' understanding of reasonable persons:

Principles of European Contract Law **18.9 (INT)**

Article 5:102: Relevant Circumstances

In interpreting the contract, regard shall be had, in particular, to:

(a) the circumstances in which it was concluded, including the preliminary negotiations;

(b) the conduct of the parties, even subsequent to the conclusion of the contract;

(c) the nature and purpose of the contract;

(d) the interpretation which has already been given to similar clauses by the parties and the practices they have established between themselves;

(e) the meaning commonly given to terms and expressions in the branch of activity concerned and the interpretation similar clauses may already have received;

(f) usages; and

(g) good faith and fair dealing.

Note

This list is not exhaustive. In interpreting contracts, regard is also had to other factors, for example policy arguments, considerations of equity and the desire to achieve consistency with national statute law and supra-national instruments.[12] The most important 'circumstance' is not even enumerated. It is the language of the contract, the words employed by the parties.

18.2 AMBIGUOUS CLAUSES

It is widely agreed that recourse to the relevant circumstances is to be had if the wording of a contractual clause is ambiguous. Furthermore, all legal systems rely on a number of

---

[10] For the modern relationship of the two doctrines, see A Burrows, 'Construction and Rectification' in A Burrows and E Peel (eds), *Contract Terms* (Oxford University Press, 2007) 77.

[11] Above, p 722.

[12] See ECtHR, *Pla and Puncerneau v Andorra*, Application no. 69498/01, 13 July 2004, [46], [51]–[62] for the interpretation of a private instrument (a will) in conformity with Art 14 ECHR.

long established and widely accepted interpretative precepts that have traditionally been phrased as maxims.

Principles of European Contract Law[13]   **18.10 (INT)**

Article 5:105: Reference to Contract as a Whole
  Terms are to be interpreted in the light of the whole contract in which they appear.

Article 5:106: Terms to Be Given Effect
  An interpretation which renders the terms of the contract lawful, or effective, is to be preferred to one which would not.

Code civil   **18.11 (FR)**

Article 1189: (1) All the terms of a contract are to be interpreted in relation to each other, giving to each the meaning which respects the consistency of the contract as a whole.

Article 1191: Where a contract term is capable of bearing two meanings, the one which gives it some effect is to be preferred to the one which makes it produce no effect.

> *Notes*
>
> (1) Prior to 2016, the Code civil contained a whole raft of provisions of this kind. However, according to the Cour de cassation, the former Articles 1156–1164 Cciv were merely 'pieces of guidance for the judges as to the interpretation of contracts, rather than rigorous and mandatory rules from which they are not permitted to depart under any circumstances, even the most extreme'.[14] Most of these rules were abolished in the course of revising the Code civil.
>
> (2) The drafters of the BGB deliberately refrained from the codification of such rules. They regarded them as 'nothing but rules of logic … which do not claim to have any substantive legal content'. However, these interpretative maxims are still used by German courts.

Queen's Bench Division   **18.12 (EN)**

Vitol BV v Compagnie européenne des pétroles[15]

Words which are unclear or ambiguous must be given the interpretation which makes most sense in the light of the agreement as a whole and the circumstances.

Facts: Clause 7 of a contract for the sale of 500,000 barrels of crude oil provided that the parties were to agree, as to each month, on the range of days when the oil was to be lifted by the buyers ('lifting range'). Under clause 8 the buyers had to pay $36.75 per barrel. However, if the 'official price' were to decrease by more than

---

[13] Similar rules are contained in Arts 4.4 and 4.5 UNIDROIT PICC and in Arts II-8:105 and II-8:106 DCFR.
[14] Req 18 March 1807, S 1807.1.361.
[15] [1988] 1 Lloyd's Rep 574.

$0.75 per barrel the buyers had to pay the lower price (minus $0.10). The term 'official price' was defined as 'the price in force 7 days before the [first] day of the confirmed and agreed upon laydays'. Laydays are the days permitted for the charterer to have the ship loaded; they begin to run once the ship has arrived and the charterer has been notified that she is ready to load. In early February the lifting range had been agreed by the parties to commence on 15 February. The buyers' ship arrived in the port of loading on 23 February, and this day was therefore the first layday. The 'official price' had been reduced on 9 February to $35.25, ie by more than $0.75. The sellers now invoiced the buyers at $36.75 on the ground that the terms 'the confirmed and agreed upon laydays' referred to the agreed lifting range commencing on 15 February so that the price drop on 9 February had come too late to affect the shipment. The buyers contended that the clause referred to 'laydays' so that the price change had occurred more than 7 days before the first layday (23 February).

Held: The arbitrators held that the clause must refer to the laydays, but the Queen's Bench Division held that it referred to the days of the 'lifting period'.

Judgment: Saville J: The approach of the English law to questions of the true construction of contracts of this kind is to seek objectively to ascertain the intentions of the parties from the words which they have chosen to use. If those words are clear and admit of only one sensible meaning, then that is the meaning to be ascribed to them—and that meaning is taken to represent what the parties intended. If the words are not clear and admit of more than one sensible meaning, then the ambiguity may be resolved by looking at the aim and genesis of the agreement, choosing the meaning which seems to make the most sense in the context of the contract and its surrounding circumstances as a whole. In some cases, of course, having attempted this exercise, it may simply remain impossible to give the words any sensible meaning at all, in which case they (or some of them) are either ignored, that is to say, treated as not forming part of the contract at all, or (if of apparent central importance) treated as demonstrating that the parties never really made an agreement at all, that is to say, had never truly agreed upon the vital terms of their bargain. In any of these cases, if it can be demonstrated that the parties were in fact agreed upon the terms of their bargain, but by mistake wrote them down wrongly, then the law allows the contract to be rectified so as to accord with what was in fact agreed.

Applying this approach to the present case, I take the view that the words in question themselves do not admit of only one clear or sensible meaning—for, while the word 'laydays' would *prima facie* seem to refer to the laytime provisions of the contract, the words 'confirmed and agreed upon' can hardly do so and seem instead to be referring to something that has to be settled between the parties as the contract progresses, the obvious candidate being the lifting range period in cl 7.

The arbitrator appears to have concluded that, since the word 'laydays' could only be a reference to the laytime provisions of the contract, the other words had simply to be ignored—to be treated, as he put it, as 'surplus'. However, if the phrase is read as a whole, I am of the view that this conclusion does not necessarily follow. The words 'confirmed and agreed upon' qualify the word 'laydays'. *Prima facie*, therefore, the phrase is referring to laydays that are to be confirmed and agreed upon. That is not the case with the laytime provisions of the contract (that have already been agreed and are not subject to confirmation)—and it is much more in line with the days that are to be agreed or 'reconfirmed' under cl 7 for the period during which the vessel is to load. In short, reading the phrase as a whole, I see no undue difficulty in treating the qualifying words as altering the meaning that would ordinarily, in the absence of those words, be given to the word 'laydays'. That is not to say, of course that this meaning is thus automatically to be preferred to that adopted by the arbitrator; what is now to be done is to see which meaning makes most sense in the context of the contract and its surrounding circumstances as a whole.

On this aspect of the case it seems to me that the most sensible construction is that contended for by the sellers. The pricing provisions give the sellers an additional option if there is a certain fall in the official price; indeed, the arbitrator found that at the time the contract was made it was well known in the market that the official price was likely to fall. The parties were agreed that the option given to the sellers could only be exercised if the official price of Ekofisk was reduced by more than $0.75 seven days or more before the relevant date.

If the relevant date is the first day of the loading range, then as soon as this is settled the sellers will know that any official price reduction less than seven days before will be irrelevant, and can decide what to do with regard to any earlier price reduction of more than $0.75. If, on the other hand, the relevant date is the first day of laytime, the exercise of counting back cannot be done until after that uncertain date has arrived, so that for a period the sellers could be effectively deprived of their contractual right through simply not knowing whether or not it was or would be available to them.

In my view, the latter would not be as sensible a construction as the former, and accordingly I consider that the ambiguity in the phrase under discussion should be resolved in favour of the sellers. It follows, therefore, that I allow the appeal from this award.

In rare cases it happens that a clause is utterly ambiguous in the sense that, despite one's best efforts at interpretation, no single meaning can be given to it, since a reasonable man would find either of two meanings equally plausible. If such a clause relates to an essential point of the transaction, the contract fails for want of agreement. In the famous English case of *Raffles v Wichelhaus*[16] the plaintiff had sold the defendant 125 bales of cotton 'to arrive ex Peerless from Bombay', and tendered cotton which arrived in Liverpool in December on a vessel of that name. The defendant refused to accept it and, when the seller claimed damages, offered evidence that he had in mind a quite different vessel also called *Peerless* which had sailed from Bombay and arrived in Liverpool in October. The Court held that this would be a good defence and allowed the proof to be brought. The outcome of the case is unknown, but if one accepts that in the light of the actual evidence the reasonable observer would have been unable to determine which of the vessels the parties had agreed on, it would be right to hold that no contract had come about.

It is important, though, that a court should take all the relevant circumstances into account before concluding that the ambiguity cannot be resolved. This can be seen from the following decision of the Bundesgerichtshof.

BGH, 23 February 1956[17]   **18.13 (DE)**

Contradictory words

Judgment: The appellate court states in detail, on the basis of the wording of the contract of 23 February 1949, that the meaning of the contract is rendered so contradictory by those words that it is impossible to ascertain what the contracting partners intended. According to the appellate court, it must be concluded from this that the contract never came into existence, since its contradictory contents do not permit any construction to be placed on the intention of the parties.

---

[16] (1864) 2 H & C 906. For further details of this case, see above, 14.15 (EN), p 504.
[17] BGHZ 20, 109, NJW 1956, 665. The facts of the case are not relevant, and they are unpublished.

The appellant contests those statements, contending that, in making them, the appellate court wrongly stuck to the letter of the contract and failed to ascertain the meaning which the contracting parties intended to give to the contract.

It is settled case law, laid down at the highest judicial level, that a court may not stick, for the purposes of interpreting a contract, solely to its wording. That is the position, in any event, where the wording of the contract is not clear and unambiguous. In such a case, the court is required, in order properly to fulfil its interpretative task, to take into account all the circumstances which may be material for the purposes of construing the content of what is *stated* in the contract as well as the content that is *intended* by the parties thereto. This involves consideration not only of the intended economic purpose of the contract but also of the meaning which the contracting parties themselves attached to the individual formulations which they chose to employ. To this effect, it is, as a general rule, necessary to proceed in accordance with the principle, derived from experience, that, even in the case of a contract couched in inadequate or contradictory terms, the contracting parties, in concluding the contract, were envisaging and pursuing a specific economic objective, and that they wished to express their intention by means of the words chosen by them.

Consequently, it is only in quite exceptional circumstances that the interpretation of a contract may be regarded as impossible by reason of its totally contradictory or non-sensical content. For the purposes of interpreting a contract, the meaning of its wording becomes wholly immaterial where the contracting parties have attached to a congruous, specific idea an incomplete, incorrect or even nonsensical term or expression which is not covered, either at all or without being supplemented, by the wording in question (Enneccerus-Nipperdey, *Lehrbuch des Bürgerlichen Rechts, Allgemeiner Teil*, pp 896, 709, with further references). In such a case, the content of the contract is deemed, regardless of the wording chosen, to be what the contracting parties actually intended. Given that this is the law as it stands, the substantive law regarding the principles of contractual interpretation will be violated if the trial court, faced with a contract which is unclear or contradictory, purports to interpret it by considering and assessing only its written terms, thereby completely disregarding other circumstances which are material in the interpretation of contracts.

Only if the contradiction inherent in the wording remains unclarified and unresolved even after those further circumstances have been taken into consideration will it be legitimate for the court in its final judgment to conclude, in exceptional cases, that an interpretation of the contract is impossible on account of its contradictory or nonsensical content.

18.3 'UNAMBIGUOUS CLAUSES': 'LITERAL' AND 'CONTEXTUAL' INTERPRETATION

The interpretative factors or circumstances may point in different directions. The nature and purpose of the contract may, for example, indicate a meaning that differs from the practices which the parties have established between themselves. The court then has to balance the different factors in order to determine the meaning of the contractual clause that is in question. The most difficult conflict arises if the supposedly clear and unambiguous language of the contract is contradicted by other elements.

The traditional 'literalist' or 'formalist' approach accords absolute priority to the wording of the contract, according to the 'literal rule', the 'rule of unambiguity'

(*Eindeutigkeitsregel*) or the 'doctrine of clear and precise terms' (*doctrine des termes clairs et précis*). A literal approach was accepted in all the major European jurisdictions in the nineteenth and early twentieth centuries.

Court of Exchequer **18.14 (EN)**

Mallan v May[18]

Facts: In an agreement of 1835, 'Edward Mallan and James Mallan, of No 32, Great Russell-street, Bloomsbury-square, in the county of Middlesex' agreed to instruct Leon May from Edinburgh in the business of surgeon-dentist for a term of four years. The articles of agreement further stipulated that May should not, without the consent of the Mallans, practice as a surgeon-dentist 'in London' and certain other places in Britain after the expiry of these four years. The City of London is an ancient city and county of itself. It was (and still is) bounded by known and defined limits and boundaries, and Great Russell-street is more than half a mile, in a direct line, from any part of the City of London. Once the four year period had expired, May practiced as principal surgeon-dentist from No 32, Great Russell-street without the consent of the Mallans. The Mallans sued May for damages for breach of performance of the stipulation.

Held: May is not liable to an action for damages.

Judgment: POLLOCK CB: … The question turns upon the construction of the articles of agreement of December, 1835, by which the defendant stipulated that he would not carry on the business of a surgeon-dentist in *London*, or any of the towns or places in England or Scotland, where the plaintiffs might have been practising before the expiration of his term of service; and the point to be decided is, whether Great Russell-street, in the county of Middlesex, be within *London*, as it is to be understood in this indenture. We must apply the ordinary rules of construction to this instrument; and though, by so doing, we may, in some instances, probably in this, defeat the real intention of the parties, such a course tends to establish a greater degree of certainty in the administration of the law. One of these rules is, that words are to be construed according to their strict and primary acceptation, unless from the context of the instrument, and the intention of the parties to be collected from it, they appear to be used in a different sense, or unless, in their strict sense, they are incapable of being carried into effect; and subject always to the observation, that the meaning of a particular word may be shewn by parol [ie oral] evidence, to be different in some particular place, trade, or business, from its proper and ordinary acceptation. In applying this rule to the present case, we find nothing in the context to prevent us from construing the word 'London' in its proper sense, as the city of London. The description of Great Russell-street, *Middlesex*, rather justifies the argument that London is to be understood in its proper sense, by shewing that Middlesex and London were meant to be distinguished: and though it is probable, from the nature of the contract, that the plaintiffs would mean to exclude the defendant from practising in Middlesex, that object would be accomplished as well by the provision that the defendant was not to practise in any place in which the plaintiffs might have practised during the term, as by holding London to include Great-Russell street; …

Nor is there any difficulty in carrying this instrument into effect, by understanding the word 'London' in its strict sense: and there is no parol evidence of any understanding of the word in a different sense, in the trade or business to which this contract relates.

---

[18] (1844) 13 M & W 511, 517–18.

The statement in the case, that London has a popular and colloquial sense, in which Great Russell-street would be understood to be within its limits, is by no means sufficient for the purpose of causing us to put a different construction on that word in this instrument.

We are therefore of the opinion, that the proper sense of the word 'London' is that in which it is to be construed in this instrument.

Notes

(1) Which are the principal arguments for and against literalism?

(2) Do you think the judges were influenced by the type of contract that fell to be interpreted in the present case?[19]

RG, 28 October 1911[20]   **18.15 (DE)**

Sale of redemption funds and reserve funds

Judgment: § 2 of the contract does not permit any interpretation at all. There is only scope for the interpretation of a contractual document if the document itself suffers from an ambiguity and gives rise to doubts as to what has been truly declared, particularly where there is an ambiguous contractual clause. But there is no opportunity whatsoever for an interpretation if the wording of the instrument is absolutely clear and unambiguous and does not leave room for doubt as to the meaning of what is declared therein; in such a case an interpretation cannot be permitted; the clear wording always imposes a limit on the interpretative liberty. Now, in the present case the wording of the clause, according to which 'all the redemption funds and reserve funds which have been accrued ... with regard to the eventual loan of the estates are deemed to be sold and to be taken into account for the purchase price', is so clear and unambiguous that it could not be clearer and more explicit; no doubt as to the meaning of the clause can arise; in particular the wording, according to which '*all* ... redemption funds' are sold, is indeed irreconcilable with the holding of the appeal court that this phrase somehow expresses a restriction of the sale to a *part* of the redemption funds, viz to the part that has been accrued since 1 July 1904.

Note

Compare the wording of § 133 BGB.

In France, the 'doctrine of clear and precise terms' is primarily of procedural relevance. The Cour de cassation does not normally review the trial courts' interpretation of a contract.[21] The interpretation is held to be within 'the sovereign power of assessment'

---

[19] For contracts in restraint of trade, see above, ch 17.3, pp 679–94.

[20] JW 1912, 69. The facts of the case are not relevant, and they are unpublished.

[21] Cass réun 2 February 1808 (arrêt Lubert), S 1808.1.480, F Terré, Y Lequette and F Chénedé, *Grands arrêts de jurisprudence civil*, vol 2, *Obligations, Contrats spéciaux, Sûretés* (13th edn, Paris: Dalloz, 2015) no. 160.

of the latter (*le pouvoir d'appréciation souverain des juges de fond*). But it is otherwise where there is a clause which in the view of the Cour de cassation is *claire et précise*, for then the Court will quash decisions of the lower courts which give it any other meaning, even on the ground of a supposed common intention of the parties. This rule was first laid down in 1872.

Cass civ, 15 April 1872[22]　　　　　　　　　　　**18.16 (FR)**

Discretionary bonuses

An employee has no enforceable right to a promised bonus if the bonus was clearly stated to be discretionary.

Facts: The defendants had publicly announced that they would pay their employees a premium if certain conditions were met. When they discontinued the practice of paying the premium, relying on a clause in the announcement which gave them a power to do so, an employee brought an action.

Held: The Conseil des prud'hommes de Flers [Flers Labour Court] held that the employee had a right to the bonus, but the Cour de cassation quashed the decision.

Judgment: THE COURT: Having regard to [former] Article 1134 [now Article 1103] Cciv ... That article provides: 'An agreement which is legally created shall bind the parties by whom it is made as if its terms were laid down by legislation'. Where the wording of an agreement is clear and precise, a court may not misconstrue the obligations resulting from it or modify the stipulations which it contains. The clause relied on by the appellants in cassation as justifying their refusal to pay the premiums claimed by Pringault, pursuant to a management notice posted up in the factory of Messrs Veuve Foucauld & Colombe, expressly states: 'it is understood that, whatever the circumstances may be, payment of the premium shall be and remain optional and discretionary'. That clause, by which the company stipulates that it shall not be bound to pay the premium, is express and can be validly relied on in every case as against the workers in the factory. The Conseil des prud'hommes de Flers, in seeking to justify the non-application of the clause at issue to the dispute before it, relied, first, on the fact that Pringault had carried out his work in accordance with the notice in question and, second, on the fact that he had previously been paid premiums. In paying those premiums, and in subsequently refusing to award them to Pringault, the appellants exercised the discretion which they had reserved unto themselves by the abovementioned clause, and of which they could avail themselves or decline to avail themselves as they wished. It follows that, in ordering Messrs Veuve Foucauld & Colombe to pay the premiums claimed by Pringault, the contested judgment formally infringed the provisions of [former] Article 1134 Cciv.

On those grounds, the Court quashes the judgment of the Conseil des prud'hommes de Flers of 4 March 1870.

> *Note*
>
> Which provision of the Civil Code does the Court rely on? Compare the wording of Article 1188(1) (ex-Article 1156) Cciv.

[22] DP 1872.1.176; Terré, Lequette and Chénedé (n 21 above) no. 161.

Codfish

An agreement which gave the seller a right to reduce the amount it had to deliver if a clearly stated event had occurred entitled the seller to rely on the clause even if the circumstances which gave rise to the stated event were not what had been anticipated.

Facts: The plaintiff had agreed to buy a certain quantity of codfish, subject to reduction by the seller if the fishmongers' association so decided. The association did so decide, and in accordance with that decision the seller delivered only half the quantity originally agreed. The buyer sued for damages on the basis that the seller, who had sufficient codfish in stock, could have delivered the full amount.

Held: The lower courts twice gave judgment for the buyer, apparently because the parties had originally assumed that a reduction would be authorised only if there were a drop in the catch, not just because of a sudden a rise in demand, as was the case. The Cour de cassation quashed both decisions, and the buyer's claim was dismissed. The clause in question being unambiguous, further investigation of the intention of the parties was excluded.

Judgment: THE COURT: Rovida brought proceedings against Vimeney for termination of the contract on the ground that it had not been performed in its entirety. The courd'appel rightly acknowledged that 'the clause in issue is sufficiently clear and precise, and plainly affords the vendor the right to impose on the purchaser a reduction in the quantities fixed by the contract, in reliance on the decision taken by the abovementioned Association'. Nevertheless, it proceeded to award Rovida the damages claimed, on the following grounds: (a) that 'it is necessary to determine the common intention of the parties from the facts and documents in the case'; (b) that the spirit of the clause is such as to shift from the vendor to the purchaser the burden of proof regarding impossibility of performance, and consequently to restrict the exercise of the right to cases in which performance is impossible; (c) consequently, that Rovida had established the lack of justification for the Association's decision by supplying proof that the fishing catch in 1928 was inadequate only in the light of the increase in consumer demand, and not in terms of the average catch during the previous five years; and (d) that Vimeney could have performed the Rovida contract by accepting Rovida's priority and by declining fresh orders from other customers at a substantially higher price. However, it was not possible for the cour d'appel, without contradicting itself, to rule that the clause in issue was clear, precise and lawful and at the same time to refuse to apply it in its exact terms. The courts below acknowledged that Vimeney was entitled to impose on the purchaser, in line with the fishing yield, a reduction in the unsecured contractual quantity, by reference to the 'decision' of the Association, taken pursuant to the power of assessment vested in it by the contract, declaring a deficit in the 1928 fishing catch on the basis that it was insufficient to meet the increase in consumer demand; [yet the lower courts found for the buyer] on the pretext that the spirit of the clause, despite the general way in which it was formulated, was such as to permit a reduction only in the event of performance being absolutely impossible, and did not concern the loss which the fishing yield might cause the vendor to suffer. Since the clause was clear and required no interpretation, it was not open to the courts below to seek to justify their refusal simply to apply its terms by relying on a letter sent by Vimeney to its broker after the conclusion of the sale, in which it acknowledged that the Association's decision must be justified by a fishing deficit; that letter does not

---

[23] D 1944.12, annotated by P Lerebours-Pigeonnière.

state how a 'deficit' is to be defined, and the contested judgment formally acknowledges that Vimeney did not waive any of its rights in its correspondence. It follows that, in ruling as it did, the cour d'appel infringed the legislation referred to above.

On those grounds, the Court quashes the contested judgment and refers the case back to the cour d'appel de Poitiers.

Code civil **18.18 (FR)**

Article 1192: Clear and unambiguous terms are not subject to interpretation as doing so risks their distortion.

> *Note*
>
> This provision was introduced by the 2016 reform of the Code. It is meant to codify the previous case law.

In the course of the twentieth century, particularly since the 1960s, European contract laws gradually abandoned literalism and shifted to a more 'contextual' or 'purposive' approach.

Vogenauer on interpretation of contracts[24] **18.19 (INT)**

The Cour de cassation continued to uphold the doctrine of *clauses claires et précises* throughout the twentieth century, although strong objections were raised by a number of legal writers. It has even found its way into a recent proposal for a major overhaul of the parts of the Civil Code concerned with the law of obligations.[25] But, once again, the abstract and general interpretative doctrine does not tell the full story. In practice, its apparent harshness has been considerably softened by the Cour de cassation. The final arbiter as to whether a clause is clear or obscure is the Supreme court itself. In making this decision, it does not always stick to the wording of the terms, but takes into account the context of the contract and the aims pursued by the parties. As a result, a term that is clear and precise on the surface can turn out to be merely 'apparently clear'. It is then open to interpretation and may be interpreted even against its wording in order to bring it in line with the (presumed) intention of the parties.[26] The prohibition of *dénaturation* thus does not exclude all deviations from the literal meaning, but only those which are badly reasoned: it enables the Cour de cassation 'to curb arbitrary decisions of certain lower courts. Thanks to it, the lower judges know that they cannot indulge in the most far-fetched interpretations'.[27]

---

[24] S Vogenauer, 'Interpretation of Contracts: Concluding Comparative Observations' in A Burrows and E Peel (eds) (n 10 above) 123, 133–34.

[25] Art 1138 of the Avant-projet de réforme du droit des obligations et de la prescription [now, with slight reformulations: Art 1192 Code civil].

[26] See the references provided by J Voulet, 'Le grief de dénaturation devant la Cour de cassation' JCP 1971.1.2410, no. 15.

[27] F Terré, P Simler and Y Lequette, *Les obligations* (9th edn, Paris: Dalloz, 2005 [now 11th edn, 2013]) no. 459.

In Germany, the rule that the interpreter is not supposed to deviate from the apparently unambiguous meaning of the words of the contract saw its heyday during the late eighteenth and the nineteenth century. The rule was subject to severe criticism by legal scholars, and, although the Supreme Court only broke with it for good in the 1980s,[28] the courts themselves did not adhere to it strictly. They seemed to rely on it when the result yielded was convenient, but they were ready to ignore it if this was not the case.

In sum, today both French law and German law attach great weight to the wording of the contract, but they are willing to deviate from it if other circumstances strongly militate in favour of a different result. This is neither pure 'literalism' nor pure 'contextualism'. It is rather a rebuttable presumption in favour of the contractual language, according only a prima facie priority to the text of the contract vis-à-vis the other interpretative factors.

House of Lords   18.20 (EN)

Investors Compensation Scheme Ltd v West Bromwich Building Society[29]

Contracts are to be interpreted in the way that the words would be understood by a reasonable person in the particular context, even if this is against the natural meaning of the words.

Facts: The Investors Compensation Scheme Ltd (ICS) brought an action against West Bromwich Building Society (WBBS). ICS purported to rely on rights which had been assigned to them by investors who had made a claim against WBBS. WBBS and the investors objected that no valid assignment of the investors' rights against WBBS had taken place. The dispute concerned the interpretation of the assignment clause used in the ICS claim form. The clause required the investors to assign to the Scheme any claims they had against the parties involved, subject to a reservation of certain rights which an investor might have against the building society. The reservation, spelt out in section 3(b) of the claim form, concerned 'any claim (whether sounding in rescission for undue influence or otherwise) that you have or may have against the West Bromwich Building Society'.

Held: The House of Lords, Lord Lloyd dissenting, decided the point of construction in favour of ICS. Therefore the assignment of the investors' rights against WBBS was valid.

Judgment: LORD LLOYD (dissenting): On this occasion … a single clause in the claim form which investors are required to sign when making a claim for compensation [is in issue]; and the problem arises not from any obscurity of language (the meaning is, I think tolerably clear) but from slovenly drafting. …

I now return to section 3(b). It provides for an exception in respect of third party claims assigned under paragraph 6 of section 4. Mr. Vos on behalf of ICS submits that the exception is confined to claims against WBBS for rescission. Mr. Oliver, on behalf of WBBS and Mr. Strauss on behalf of the investors submit that the exception covers all claims against WBBS whether for rescission or not …

The Court of Appeal agreed with Evans-Lombe J. that the investors' construction accords with the natural meaning of the words. But unlike the judge they did not regard the result as commercially ridiculous. Leggatt LJ who gave the leading judgment said: 'There is simply no warrant for limiting the rights retained to claims for or consequent upon rescission.' I find myself in complete agreement with the Court of Appeal.

---

[28] BGH 10 July 1981, NJW 1982, 31. In Switzerland it took even longer: the turning point was BG 5 July 2001, BGE 127 III 444, 445.

[29] [1998] 1 WLR 896.

The question of construction

A useful starting point for ascertaining the meaning of section 3(b) of the claim form is to put oneself in the position of the ordinary investor to whom the claim form is addressed …

… the position would be that he, the investor, would retain his right to sue WBBS for a reduction of the mortgage debt, but ICS would obtain the right to sue … 'third parties' other than WBBS … This would strike the investor as fair and reasonable. At this stage our hypothetical investor would feel that he understood his rights and obligations well enough and would sign …

Is there, then, any reason why the courts should not give section 3(b) and the claim form as a whole, the same meaning as the investor? (I shall refer to this as 'the plain meaning'.) The objections fall into two groups. The first group of objections relate to the language of section 3(b); the second group of objections relate to the legal and commercial consequences of adopting a plain meaning. I suspect that none of these objections would occur to anyone other than a lawyer.

The meaning of language

The objection to the plain meaning is the inclusion of the words 'for undue influence' after 'rescission;' for any lawyer would know that there are other grounds on which the investor might claim rescission, for example, on the ground of misrepresentation. Why, therefore, should the draftsman have specifically included one of the grounds on which the investor might claim rescission, but not others?

We do not know the answer to this question. It may be that if one had access to the preliminary drafts of the claim form, or to the mind of the draftsman himself, the answer would emerge clearly enough. It may be that a claim for rescission on the ground of undue influence was, for some reason, uppermost in the draftsman's mind; so he put the words in. But we cannot go into the draftsman's mind. We having (sic) nothing to go on but the words he has used. The inclusion of undue influence is odd, but not so odd as to obscure the meaning … The drafting is slovenly. But I do not have any great difficulty with the meaning. …

What are the alternatives? Mr. Vos submits that section 3(b) means 'any claims sounding in rescission (whether for undue influence or otherwise) in which you claim an abatement …' I agree with Evans-Lombe J. that such a construction does violence to the language. I know of no principle of construction … which would enable the court to take words from within the brackets, where they are clearly intended to underline the width of 'any claim,' and place them outside the brackets where they have the exact opposite effect. As Leggatt LJ said in the Court of Appeal, such a construction is simply not an available meaning of the words used; and it is, after all, from the words used that one must ascertain what the parties meant. Purposive interpretation of a contract is a useful tool where the purpose can be identified with reasonable certainty. But creative interpretation is another thing altogether. The one must not be allowed to shade into the other.

So with great respect to those taking a different view, I do not regard the present case as raising any question of ambiguity, or of choosing between two possible interpretations. The construction advocated by the investors, though it gives rise to the oddity which I have mentioned, is a permissible construction of the words used. The ICS's construction is not.

The legal and commercial consequences

If Evans-Lombe J is right that the investors' construction is the more natural meaning of section 3(b) and if, a fortiori, the Court of Appeal is right that the ICS's construction is not even a possible meaning of the language used, then it would take a very strong case indeed before I would reject the former meaning in favour of the latter. ...

What then are the consequences of the investors' construction which are said to be so extraordinary, or so 'unreasonable' ... and which Evans-Lombe J described as producing a ridiculous result? ...

I agree with Mr. Vos that there are theoretical anomalies on the investors' construction, though how likely they would be to arise in practice is another question. Where I disagree with him is in his evaluation of these anomalies. In my judgment they fall far short of the sort of absurdity which would justify the rejection of what I have called the plain meaning of section 3(b). They do not prompt the comment 'whatever else the parties may have had in mind, they cannot have meant *that*'. ...

For the above reasons I would hold that on the true construction of the claim form the investors' claims against WBBS have been retained by the investors, and have not been assigned to ICS.

LORD HOFFMANN: ... My Lords, I start with the construction of section 3(b). Evans-Lombe J followed his own decision in the earlier Cheltenham and Gloucester case and I shall first summarise his reasoning and then that of Leggatt LJ in the Court of Appeal. Evans-Lombe J focused on the words 'any claim (whether sounding in rescission for undue influence or otherwise) that you have ... against the ... society in which you claim an abatement of sums which you would otherwise have to repay to that society ...' According to ordinary rules of syntax, 'any claim' is the antecedent of 'that you have' and the words 'or otherwise' in the adjectival parenthesis mean that it does not limit the breadth of 'any claim'. It follows that claims of any description are reserved as long as they amount to claims for an 'abatement' of what is owing to the Society. There are various ways in which the amount owing might be abated but one would be on account of a set-off against the society's liability for damages. Thus the syntax of the words following 'any claim' points to a wide meaning of 'abatement' which includes the effect of cross-claims.

Evans-Lombe J then turned to the background against which the language in the claim form had been used. Two features seemed to him odd. First, the building society and the solicitors were the only solvent parties against which the investors were likely to have any claim. As between the building society and the solicitors, the former would certainly be the prime target. It had profited from the home income plans by lending money at enhanced rates of interest on safe security (maximum of 50 per cent of value) at a time when lenders were falling over themselves to lend as much money as possible. One might expect that ICS, having paid compensation to the investor, would take over his claim against the building society. If not, the investor might well be overcompensated. Other provisions of the form, like clause 7, seemed to assume that ICS would do the suing and account to the investor for the net recovery in excess of the compensation paid. But there was no provision for the investor having to pay anything back to ICS. This pointed to ICS being entitled to any recoverable damages.

Secondly, the parenthesis seemed very strange against the background of the law. If it was exhaustive, why was 'sounding in rescission for undue influence' singled out? What about rescission on other grounds, or claims for breach of statutory or common law duty? It was rather like providing in a lease of a flat that the tenant should not keep 'any pets (whether neutered Persian cats or otherwise).' Something seemed to have gone wrong.

Considerations of this kind led the judge to conclude ... that the wider construction of 'any claim' and 'abatement' led to a 'ridiculous commercial result which the parties to the claim forms were quite unlikely to have intended' and that it was clear that 'the drafting of the second paragraph of section 3(b) was mistaken.' He therefore concluded that the meaning intended by the parties was that the investor should retain any claim for an abatement of his debt which arose out of a claim for rescission, whether for undue influence or otherwise. ... But the learned judge seems to have had some misgivings about his interpretation: he said that was doing violence to the natural meaning of the words and altering the drafting of the paragraph in a way 'more appropriate to rectification than the process of construction.' In the present case, however, the judge adhered to his construction and gave some additional reasons. ...

My Lords, I will say at once that I prefer the approach of the learned judge. But I think I should preface my explanation of my reasons with some general remarks about the principles by which contractual documents are nowadays construed. ... The principles may be summarised as follows.

Holding

(1) Interpretation is the ascertainment of the meaning which the document would convey to a reasonable person having all the background knowledge which would reasonably have been available to the parties in the situation in which they were at the time of the contract.

(2) The background was famously referred to by Lord Wilberforce as the 'matrix of fact,' but this phrase is, if anything, an understated description of what the background may include. Subject to the requirement that it should have been reasonably available to the parties and to the exception to be mentioned next, it includes absolutely anything which would have affected the way in which the language of the document would have been understood by a reasonable man.

(3) The law excludes from the admissible background the previous negotiations of the parties and their declarations of subjective intent. They are admissible only in an action for rectification. The law makes this distinction for reasons of practical policy and, in this respect only, legal interpretation differs from the way we would interpret utterances in ordinary life. The boundaries of this exception are in some respects unclear. But this is not the occasion on which to explore them.

(4) The meaning which a document (or any other utterance) would convey to a reasonable man is not the same thing as the meaning of its words. The meaning of words is a matter of dictionaries and grammars; the meaning of the document is what the parties using those words against the relevant background would reasonably have been understood to mean. The background may not merely enable the reasonable man to choose between the possible meanings of words which are ambiguous but even (as occasionally happens in ordinary life) to conclude that the parties must, for whatever reason, have used the wrong words or syntax: see *Mannai Investments Co Ltd v Eagle Star Life Assurance Co Ltd* [1997] AC 749.

(5) The 'rule' that words should be given their 'natural and ordinary meaning' reflects the common sense proposition that we do not easily accept that people have made linguistic mistakes, particularly in formal documents. On the other hand, if one would nevertheless conclude from the background that something must have gone wrong with the language, the law does not require judges to attribute to the parties an intention which they plainly could not have had. Lord Diplock made this point more vigorously when he said in *Antaios Compania Naviera SA v Salen Rederierna AB* [1985] AC 191, 201 'if detailed semantic and syntactical analysis of words in a commercial contract is going to lead to a conclusion that flouts business commonsense, it must be made to yield to business commonsense.'

If one applies these principles, it seems to me that the judge must be right and, as we are dealing with one badly drafted clause which is happily no longer in use, there is little advantage in my repeating his reasons at greater length. The only remark of his which I would respectfully question is when he said that he was 'doing violence' to the natural meaning of the words. This is an over-energetic way to describe the process of interpretation. Many people, including politicians, celebrities and Mrs. Malaprop, mangle meanings and syntax but nevertheless communicate tolerably clearly what they are using the words to mean. If anyone is doing violence to natural meanings, it is they rather than their listeners.

I shall, however, make four points supplemental to those of the judge … Finally, on this part of the case, I must make some comments upon the judgment of the Court of Appeal. Leggatt LJ said that his construction was 'the natural and ordinary meaning of the words used'. I do not think that the concept of natural and ordinary meaning is very helpful when, on any view, the words have not been used in a natural and ordinary way. In a case like this, the court is inevitably engaged in choosing between competing unnatural meanings. Secondly, Leggatt LJ said that the judge's construction was not an 'available meaning' of the words. If this means that judges cannot, short of rectification, decide that the parties must have made mistakes of meaning or syntax, I respectfully think he was wrong.

Note

The dissenting judgment of Lord Lloyd shows that the use of 'purposivism' to override what seems to be clear and unambiguous language is not uncontroversial.[30] However, the approach of the *ICS* case was followed in subsequent decisions and for a while seemed to be firmly established.[31]

House of Lords   18.21 (EN)

***Chartbrook Ltd v Persimmon Ltd*[32]**

If it is evident from the context that the parties must have used the wrong words to achieve what they wanted, and it is clear what the parties had agreed on, the court may interpret the contract in that sense.

Facts: Chartbrook owned a piece of land. They agreed with Persimmon that Persimmon should obtain planning permission, construct a mixed residential and commercial development on the land and sell the properties. Persimmon would receive the proceeds from these sales and pay Chartbrook an agreed price for the land. In addition, Persimmon would pay a balancing payment, referred to as the 'Additional Residential Payment' (ARP) which was a term defined in the contract. Planning permission was granted and the development was built. The dispute arose because both parties had a different understanding of the term which defined how the ARP had to be calculated. According to the interpretation advanced by Chartbrook, Persimmon had to pay £4,484,862. According to the construction favoured by Persimmon, the amount due was £897,051. The first instance judge and the Court Appeal decided in favour of Chartbrook. The majority of the Court of Appeal, Collins LJ dissenting, based its decision on its view that the term defining the ARP was 'clear, certain and unambiguous'. The Court also held that material from the precontractual negotiations was not admissible for the purposes of construing a contract although it pointed very strongly in favour of Persimmon's interpretation.

---

[30] See C Staughton, 'How do the Courts Interpret Commercial Contracts?' (1999) 58 CLJ 303, and a number of Court of Appeal decisions referred to therein.

[31] Apart from the *Chartbrook* decision, below, see *Rainy Sky v Kookmin Bank* [2011] UKSC 50, [2011] 1 WLR 2900.

[32] [2009] UKHL 38, [2009] 1 AC 1101.

Persimmon appealed. It argued that the contract should be interpreted in a different way which would make commercial sense and it invited the House of Lords to take account of the precontractual negotiations.

Held: The House of Lords upheld the construction suggested by Persimmon on the basis that it made commercial sense. It did so without having regard to the precontractual negotiations.

Judgment: LORD HOFFMANN: ... 14. There is no dispute that the principles on which a contract (or any other instrument or utterance) should be interpreted are those summarised by the House of Lords in *Investors Compensation Scheme Ltd v West Bromwich Building Society* [1998] 1 WLR 896, 912–913. They are well known and need not be repeated. It is agreed that the question is what a reasonable person having all the background knowledge which would have been available to the parties would have understood them to be using the language in the contract to mean. The House emphasised that 'we do not easily accept that people have made linguistic mistakes, particularly in formal documents' (similar statements will be found in *Bank of Credit and Commerce International SA v Ali* [2002] 1 AC 251, 269, *Kirin-Amgen Inc v Hoechst Marion Roussel Ltd* [2005] 1 All ER 667, 681–682 and *Jumbo King Ltd v Faithful Properties Ltd* (1999) 2 HKCFAR 279, 296) but said that in some cases the context and background drove a court to the conclusion that 'something must have gone wrong with the language'. In such a case, the law did not require a court to attribute to the parties an intention which a reasonable person would not have understood them to have had.

15. It clearly requires a strong case to persuade the court that something must have gone wrong with the language and the judge and the majority of the Court of Appeal did not think that such a case had been made out. On the other hand, Lawrence Collins LJ thought it had. It is, I am afraid, not unusual that an interpretation which does not strike one person as sufficiently irrational to justify a conclusion that there has been a linguistic mistake will seem commercially absurd to another: compare the *Kirin-Amgen* case [2005] All ER 667, 684–685. Such a division of opinion occurred in the *Investors Compensation Scheme* case itself [1998] 1 WLR 896. The subtleties of language are such that no judicial guidelines or statements of principle can prevent it from sometimes happening. It is fortunately rare because most draftsmen of formal documents think about what they are saying and use language with care. But this appears to be an exceptional case in which the drafting was careless and no one noticed.

16. I agree with the dissenting opinion of Lawrence Collins LJ because I think that to interpret the definition of ARP in accordance with ordinary rules of syntax makes no commercial sense. [Lord Hoffmann then goes on to explain why this is the case.] ...

20. ... the striking feature of this case is ... that the provisions as interpreted by the judge and the Court of Appeal ... make the structure and language of the various provisions of Schedule 6 appear arbitrary and irrational, when it is possible for the concepts employed by the parties to be combined in a rational way.

21. ... When the language used in an instrument gives rise to difficulties of construction, the process of interpretation ... is to decide what a reasonable person would have understood the parties to have meant by using the language which they did. The fact that the court might have to express that meaning in language quite different from that used by the parties ('12th January' instead of '13th January' in *Mannai Investment Co Ltd v Eagle Star Life Assurance Co Ltd* [1997] AC 749; 'any claim sounding in rescission (whether for undue influence or otherwise)' instead of 'any claim (whether sounding in rescission for undue influence or otherwise)' in *Investors Compensation Scheme Ltd v West Bromwich Building Society* [1998] 1 WLR 896) is no reason for not giving effect to what they appear to have meant. ...

25. ... All that is required is that it should be clear that something has gone wrong with the language and that it should be clear what a reasonable person would have understood the parties to have meant. In my opinion, both of these requirements are satisfied.

Note

More recently, it appears that the Supreme Court is retreating from the wider and more flexible approach. In *Arnold v Britton* [2015] UKSC 36, [2015] AC 1619 and in *Wood v Capita Insurance Services* Ltd [2017] UKSC 24, [2017] AC 1173, it applied a meaning that fitted best with the words although the outcome was apparently commercially nonsensical or arbitrary. Influential judges have called for an end of 'the looser approach to the construction of contractual documents' ushered in by the *ICS* case.[33] However, neither that case nor *Chartbrook* were overruled or even questioned as a matter of principle in the recent case law. It seems as if individual judges have different views as to the permissible limits of recourse to 'business common sense' beyond the letter of the contract as a matter of principle, and that they are willing to adapt these views in light of the circumstances of individual cases.

18.4 PRELIMINARY NEGOTIATIONS

Frequently, one of the parties argues that the court should interpret the contract in the light of prior negotiations and should therefore admit evidence on what took place during such negotiations. The rules on the admissibility of such evidence vary depending on whether the court perceives the contractual words to be ambiguous or not.

18.4.A RECOURSE TO PRELIMINARY NEGOTIATIONS FOR THE PURPOSES OF INTERPRETATION

If a continental court perceives the contractual words to be ambiguous it fully admits recourse to the preliminary negotiations. Article 5:102 PECL adopts a similar approach.[34] By contrast, English judges do not admit such evidence.

House of Lords	18.22 (EN)

Chartbrook Ltd v Persimmon Ltd[35]

Evidence of precontractual negotiations is admissible in an action for rectification.

Facts: The facts of the case are stated above, p 741.

---

[33] Lord Sumption, 'A Question of Taste: The Supreme Court and the Interpretation of Contracts' (2017) 17 Oxford University Commonwealth Law Journal 301.

[34] Above, p 727.

[35] [2009] UKHL 38, [2009] 1 AC 1101. The decision in *Prenn v Simmonds* [1971] 1 WLR 1381, which is referred to in the speech of Lord Hoffmann was reproduced in the first edition of this book, at pp 565–66.

Held: Evidence of precontractual negotiations is not admissible for the purposes of interpreting a contract. However, an action for rectification can be brought if, by a common mistake, the contract does not reflect what an objective observer would have thought the intentions of the parties to be.

Judgment: LORD HOFFMANN: ... [In the first part of his speech, Lord Hoffmann interpreted the contract in a way that made commercial sense but did not correspond to the literal meaning of the words.]

27. If your Lordships agree with this conclusion about the construction of the contract, the appeal must be allowed. There is no need to say anything more. But Persimmon advanced two alternative arguments of very considerable general importance and I think it is appropriate that your Lordships should deal with them. The first was that (contrary to the unanimous opinion of the judge and the Court of Appeal) the House should take into account the pre-contractual negotiations, which in the opinion of Lawrence Collins LJ, at para 132, were determinative confirmation of Persimmon's argument on construction. The second was that the judge and the Court of Appeal had misunderstood the principles upon which rectification may be decreed and that if Persimmon had failed on construction, the agreement should have been rectified. ...

30. To allow evidence of pre-contractual negotiations to be used in aid of construction would ... require the House to depart from a long and consistent line of authority, the binding force of which has frequently been acknowledged: ...

31. In *Prenn v Simmonds* [1971] 1 WLR 1381, 1384–1385 Lord Wilberforce said by way of justification of the rule:

'The reason for not admitting evidence of these exchanges is not a technical one or even mainly one of convenience, (though the attempt to admit it did greatly prolong the case and add to its expense). It is simply that such evidence is unhelpful. By the nature of things, where negotiations are difficult, the parties' positions, with each passing letter, are changing and until the final agreement, though converging, still divergent. It is only the final document which records a consensus. If the previous documents use different expressions, how does construction of those expressions, itself a doubtful process, help on the construction of the contractual words? If the same expressions are used, nothing is gained by looking back: indeed, something may be lost since the relevant surrounding circumstances may be different. And at this stage there is no consensus of the parties to appeal to. It may be said that previous documents may be looked at to explain the aims of the parties. In a limited sense this is true: the commercial, or business object, of the transaction, objectively ascertained, may be a surrounding fact. Cardozo J thought so in the *Utica Bank* case [*Utica City National Bank v Gunn* (1918) 118 NE 607]. And if it can be shown that one interpretation completely frustrates that object, to the extent of rendering the contract futile, that may be a strong argument for an alternative interpretation, if that can reasonably be found. But beyond that it may be difficult to go: it may be a matter of degree, or of judgment, how far one interpretation, or another, gives effect to a common intention: the parties, indeed, may be pursuing that intention with differing emphasis, and hoping to achieve it to an extent which may differ, and in different ways. The words used may, and often do, represent a formula which means different things to each side, yet may be accepted because that is the only way to get 'agreement' and in the hope that disputes will not arise. The only course then can be to try to ascertain the 'natural' meaning. Far more, and indeed totally, dangerous is it to admit evidence of one party's objective—even if this is known to the other party. However strongly pursued this may be, the other party may only be willing to give it partial recognition, and in a world of give and take, men often have to be satisfied with less than they want. So, again, it would be a matter of speculation how far the common intention was that the particular objective should be realised.'

32. Critics of the rule, such as Thomas J in New Zealand (*Yoshimoto v Canterbury Golf International Ltd* [2001] 1 *NZLR* 523, 538–549) Professor David McLauchlan ('Contract Interpretation: What is it About?' (2009) 31:5 *Sydney Law Review* 5–51) and Lord Nicholls of Birkenhead ('My Kingdom for a Horse: The Meaning of Words' (2005) 121 *LQR* 577–591) point out that although all this may usually be true, in some cases it will not. Among the dirt of aspirations, proposals and counter-proposals there may gleam the gold of a genuine consensus on some aspect of the transaction expressed in terms which would influence an objective observer in construing the language used by the parties in their final agreement. Why should the court deny itself the assistance of this material in deciding what the parties must be taken to have meant? Mr Christopher Nugee QC, who appeared for Persimmon, went so far as to say that in saying that such evidence was unhelpful, Lord Wilberforce was not only providing a justification for the rule but delimiting its extent. It should apply only in cases in which the pre-contractual negotiations are actually irrelevant. If they do assist a court in deciding what an objective observer would have construed the contract to mean, they should be admitted. I cannot accept this submission. It is clear from what Lord Wilberforce said and the authorities upon which he relied that the exclusionary rule is not qualified in this way. There is no need for a special rule to exclude irrelevant evidence.

33. I do however accept that it would not be inconsistent with the English objective theory of contractual interpretation to admit evidence of previous communications between the parties as part of the background which may throw light upon what they meant by the language they used. The general rule, as I said in *Bank of Credit and Commerce International SA v Ali* [2002] 1 AC 251, 269, is that there are no conceptual limits to what can properly be regarded as background. Prima facie, therefore, the negotiations are potentially relevant background. They may be inadmissible simply because they are irrelevant to the question which the court has to decide, namely, what the parties would reasonably be taken to have meant by the language which they finally adopted to express their agreement. For the reasons given by Lord Wilberforce, that will usually be the case. But not always. In exceptional cases, as Lord Nicholls has forcibly argued, a rule that prior negotiations are always inadmissible will prevent the court from giving effect to what a reasonable man in the position of the parties would have taken them to have meant. Of course judges may disagree over whether in a particular case such evidence is helpful or not. In *Yoshimoto v Canterbury Golf International Ltd* [2001] 1 *NZLR* 523, Thomas J thought he had found gold in the negotiations but the Privy Council said it was only dirt. As I have said, there is nothing unusual or surprising about such differences of opinion. In principle, however, I would accept that previous negotiations may be relevant.

34. It therefore follows that while it is true that, as Lord Wilberforce said, inadmissibility is normally based in irrelevance, there will be cases in which it can be justified only on pragmatic grounds. I must consider these grounds, which have been explored in detail in the literature and on the whole rejected by academic writers but supported by some practitioners.

35. The first is that the admission of pre-contractual negotiations would create greater uncertainty of outcome in disputes over interpretation and add to the cost of advice, litigation or arbitration. Everyone engaged in the exercise would have to read the

correspondence and statements would have to be taken from those who took part in oral negotiations. Not only would this be time-consuming and expensive but the scope for disagreement over whether the material affected the construction of the agreement (as in the Yoshimoto case) would be considerably increased. As against this, it is said that when a dispute over construction is litigated, evidence of the pre-contractual negotiations is almost invariably tendered in support of an alternative claim for rectification (as in *Prenn v Simmonds* [1971] 1 WLR 1318 and in this case) or an argument based on estoppel by convention or some alleged exception to the exclusionary rule. Even if such an alternative claim does not succeed, the judge will have read and possibly been influenced by the evidence. The rule therefore achieves little in saving costs and its abolition would restore some intellectual honesty to the judicial approach to interpretation.

36. There is certainly a view in the profession that the less one has to resort to any form of background in aid of interpretation, the better. The document should so far as possible speak for itself. As Popham CJ said in the *Countess of Rutland's Case* (1604) 5 Co Rep 25, 25b, 26a:

> 'it would be inconvenient, that matters in writing made by advice and on considera-
> tion, and which finally import the certain truth of the agreement of the parties should
> be controlled by averment of the parties to be proved by the uncertain testimony of
> slippery memory.'

37. I do not think that these opinions can be dismissed as merely based upon the fallacy that words have inherent or 'available' meanings, rather than being used by people to express meanings, although some of the arguments advanced in support might suggest this. It reflects what may be a sound practical intuition that the law of contract is an institution designed to enforce promises with a high degree of predictability and that the more one allows conventional meanings or syntax to be displaced by inferences drawn from background, the less predictable the outcome is likely to be. ...

38. ... statements in the course of pre-contractual negotiations will be drenched in subjectivity and may, if oral, be very much in dispute. It is often not easy to distinguish between those statements which (if they were made at all) merely reflect the aspirations of one or other of the parties and those which embody at least a provisional consensus which may throw light on the meaning of the contract which was eventually concluded. But the imprecision of the line between negotiation and provisional agreement is the very reason why in every case of dispute over interpretation, one or other of the parties is likely to require a court or arbitrator to take the course of negotiations into account. ...

39. Supporters of the admissibility of pre-contractual negotiations draw attention to the fact that Continental legal systems seem to have little difficulty in taking them into account. Both the *UNIDROIT Principles of International Commercial Contracts* (1994 and 2004 revision) and the *Principles of European Contract Law* (1999) provide that in ascertaining the 'common intention of the parties', regard shall be had to prior negotiations: Articles [4.3] and [5:102] respectively. The same is true of the United Nations Convention on Contracts for the International Sale of Goods (1980). But these instruments reflect the French philosophy of contractual interpretation, which is altogether different from that of English law. ... One cannot in my opinion simply transpose rules based on one philosophy of contractual interpretation to another, or assume that the practical effect of admitting such evidence under the English system of civil procedure will be the same as that under a Continental system.

40. In his judgment in the present case [2007] 1 All ER (Comm) 1083, Briggs J thought that the most powerful argument against admitting evidence of pre-contractual negotiations was that it would be unfair to a third party who took an assignment of the contract or advanced money on its security. Such a person would not have been privy to the negotiations and may have taken the terms of the contract at face value. There is clearly strength in this argument, but it is fair to say that the same point can be made (and has been made, ...) in respect of the admissibility of any form of background. ... The law has sometimes to compromise between protecting the interests of the contracting parties and those of third parties. But an extension of the admissible background will, at any rate in theory, increase the risk that a third party will find that the contract does not mean what he thought. How often this is likely to be a practical problem is hard to say. In the present case, the construction of the agreement does not involve reliance upon any background which would not have been equally available to any prospective assignee or lender.

41. The conclusion I would reach is that there is no clearly established case for departing from the exclusionary rule. The rule may well mean, as Lord Nicholls has argued, that parties are sometimes held bound by a contract in terms which, upon a full investigation of the course of negotiations, a reasonable observer would not have taken them to have intended. But a system which sometimes allows this to happen may be justified in the more general interest of economy and predictability in obtaining advice and adjudicating disputes. It is, after all, usually possible to avoid surprises by carefully reading the documents before signing them and there are the safety nets of rectification and estoppel by convention. ...

42. The rule excludes evidence of what was said or done during the course of negotiating the agreement for the purpose of drawing inferences about what the contract meant. It does not exclude the use of such evidence for other purposes: for example, to establish that a fact which may be relevant as background was known to the parties, or to support a claim for rectification or estoppel. These are not exceptions to the rule. They operate outside it. ...

47. ... There are two legitimate safety devices which will in most cases prevent the exclusionary rule from causing injustice. But they have to be specifically pleaded and clearly established. One is rectification. The other is estoppel by convention ...: see *Amalgamated Investment & Property Co Ltd v Texas Commerce International Bank Ltd* [1982] QB 84. If the parties have negotiated an agreement upon some common assumption, which may include an assumption that certain words will bear a certain meaning, they may be estopped from contending that the words should be given a different meaning. Both of these remedies lie outside the exclusionary rule, since they start from the premise that, as a matter of construction, the agreement does not have the meaning for which the party seeking rectification or raising an estoppel contends.

48. The last point is whether, if Chartbrook's interpretation of the agreement had been correct, it should have been rectified to accord with Persimmon's interpretation. The requirements for rectification were succinctly summarized by Peter Gibson LJ in *Swainland Builders Ltd v Freehold Properties Ltd* [2002] 2 EGLR 71, 74, para 33:

'The party seeking rectification must show that: (1) the parties had a common continuing intention, whether or not amounting to an agreement, in respect of a particular matter in the instrument to be rectified; (2) there was an outward expression of accord; (3) the intention continued at the time of the execution of the instrument sought to be rectified; (4) by mistake, the instrument did not reflect that common intention.'

49. To explain how the claim for rectification arose, I must summarise the relevant pre-contractual exchanges between the parties. [Lord Hoffmann then went on to analyze the extensive correspondence between the parties.]

59. Until the decision of the Court of Appeal in *Joscelyne v Nissen* [1970] 2 QB 86 there was a view, based upon dicta in 19th and early 20th century cases, that rectification was available only if there had been a concluded antecedent contract with which the instrument did not conform. …

60. Now that it has been established that rectification is also available when there was no binding antecedent agreement but the parties had a common continuing intention in respect of a particular matter in the instrument to be rectified, it would be anomalous if the 'common continuing intention' were to be an objective fact if it amounted to an enforceable contract but a subjective belief if it did not. On the contrary, the authorities suggest that in both cases the question is what an objective observer would have thought the intentions of the parties to be. Perhaps the clearest statement is by Denning LJ in *Frederick E Rose (London) Ltd v William H Pim Jnr & Co Ltd* [1953] 2 QB 450, 461:

> 'Rectification is concerned with contracts and documents, not with intentions. In order to get rectification it is necessary to show that the parties were in complete agreement on the terms of their contract, but by an error wrote them down wrongly; and in this regard, in order to ascertain the terms of their contract, you do not look into the inner minds of the parties—into their intentions—any more than you do in the formation of any other contract. You look at their outward acts, that is, at what they said or wrote to one another in coming to their agreement, and then compare it with the document which they have signed. If you can predicate with certainty what their contract was, and that it is, by a common mistake, wrongly expressed in the document, then you rectify the document; but nothing less will suffice.'

66. … In this case there was no suggestion that the prior consensus was based on anything other than the May letter. It is agreed that the terms of that letter were accepted by Chartbrook and no one gave evidence of any subsequent discussions which might have suggested an intention to depart from them. It follows that (on the assumption that the judge was right in his construction of the ARP definition) both parties were mistaken in thinking that it reflected their prior consensus and Persimmon was entitled to rectification.

67. Since, however, I think that the judge and the majority of the Court of Appeal were wrong on the question of construction, I would allow the appeal on that ground.

Notes

(1) This passage is, as is clear from the first paragraph cited, an *obiter dictum*.

(2) What are the arguments in favour of the 'exclusionary rule'? Are they sound?

(3) Do you agree with Lord Hoffmann's view that Article 5:102 PECL reflects 'the French philosophy of contractual interpretation'?

(4) In paragraph [47] of *Chartbrook*, Lord Hoffmann refers to rectification as a 'safety device' mitigating the otherwise harsh consequences of the exclusionary rule. To what extent does the existence of this doctrine undermine the case for the exclusionary rule? Note that there is debate over whether rectification can be awarded only

when there has been some 'outward expression' of the shared intention, or whether unexpressed but identical intentions would be a sufficient basis.

(5) Continental laws do not need a doctrine of rectification. German law can apply the maxim *falsa demonstratio non nocet*.[36] French lawyers can simply refer to Article 1188 (1) Cciv.[37]

18.4.B RECOURSE TO PRELIMINARY NEGOTIATIONS IN ORDER TO ADD TO, VARY OR CONTRADICT A WRITTEN CONTRACT

The positions of European legal systems with regard to preliminary negotiations are more similar in cases where reference to such negotiations is not sought to elucidate which of two or more possible meanings of a clause should be followed, but rather when the question is whether a particular statement or promise formed part of the contract. When the contract is oral, that is usually explained as being just a matter of interpreting what the parties said (and possibly their conduct): what was their final agreement? But when there is a written document, and one party claims there was also some term, not in the writing, which would add to, vary or contradict the written document, the position is more complicated. The mechanisms employed in the different jurisdictions vary.

The traditional English response to this problem is the so-called 'parol evidence rule'. Once a contract has been reduced to writing, neither party can rely on extrinsic evidence of terms alleged to have been agreed, ie on evidence not contained in the document. The classic formulation of the rule was made by Tindal LCJ in *Shore v Wilson*, giving advice to the judges of the House of Lords:[38]

> The general rule I take to be, that where the words of any written instrument are free from ambiguity in themselves, and where external circumstances do not create any doubt or difficulty as to the proper application of those words to claimants under the instrument, or the subject-matter to which the instrument relates, such instrument is always to be construed according to the strict, plain, common meaning of the words themselves; and that in such case evidence dehors the instrument, for the purpose of explaining it according to the surmised or alleged intention of the parties to the instrument, is utterly inadmissible. If it were otherwise, no lawyer would be safe in advising upon the construction of a written instrument, nor any party in taking under it; for the ablest advice might be controlled, and the clearest title undermined, if, at some future period, parol evidence of the particular meaning which the party affixed to his words, or of his secret intention in making the instrument, or of the objects he meant to take benefit under it, might be set up to contradict or vary the plain language of the instrument itself.

He set out certain exceptions to the rule, and continued:

> But whilst evidence is admissible in these instances for the purpose of making the written instrument speak for itself, which without such evidence would be either a dead letter, or would use a doubtful tongue, or convey a false impression of the meaning of the party, I conceive the exception to be strictly limited to cases of the description above given, and to evidence of the

---

[36] See above, pp 726–27.

[37] For a comprehensive discussion, see Vogenauer (n 24 above) 139–46.

[38] (1839) 9 Clark & Fin 355, 565 and 567.

nature above detailed; and that in no case whatever is it permitted to explain the language of a deed by evidence of the private views, the secret intentions, or the known principles of the party to the instrument, whether religious, political, or otherwise, any more than by express parol declarations made by the party himself, which are universally excluded; for the admitting of such evidence would let in all the uncertainty before adverted to; it would be evidence which in most instances could not be met or countervailed by any of an opposite bearing or tendency, and would in effect cause the secret undeclared intention of the party to control and predominate over the open intention expressed in the deed.

The case concerned the construction of a will. However, the language used by Tindal LCJ also covers other legal instruments, such as contracts.

Chancery Division **18.23 (EN)**

Jacobs v Batavia and General Plantations Ltd[39]

Parol evidence may not be admitted to add to, vary or contradict a written contract.

Facts: The plaintiff bought profit sharing deposit notes of the defendant company. He relied on a prospectus which the defendants had issued and in which they promised, in the event of a sale of their estates on the Rio Bravo, to set aside a sum sufficient to pay off the outstanding deposit notes. After they had sold the estates, the defendants refused to perform their promise contained in the prospectus. The plaintiff brought an action to have liability of the defendants established and for an injunction to restrain them from dealing with the proceeds of sale without in the first place setting aside a sum sufficient to pay off the outstanding notes.

Held: The plaintiff was entitled to relief.

Judgment: PO LAWRENCE J: It is firmly established as a rule of law that parol evidence cannot be admitted to add to, vary or contradict a deed or other written instrument. Accordingly, it has been held that (except in cases of fraud or rectification and except, in certain circumstances, as a defence in actions for specific performance) parol evidence will not be admitted to prove that some particular term, which had been verbally agreed upon, had been omitted (by design or otherwise) from a written instrument constituting a valid and operative contract between the parties: see, eg, …

[T]he agreement in the present case directly affects the terms upon which the principal moneys mentioned in the deposit notes are secured, and does in fact both add to and vary those terms by conferring additional rights on the deposit holders in the event of the sale of the Rio Bravo estates and by modifying, in that event, both the covenant to pay the principal moneys … Had the promise which the plaintiff seeks to enforce in this action been merely a verbal promise, I should have felt constrained to hold that the rule of law, to which I have referred, was applicable and that evidence of such promise was inadmissible. The strength of the plaintiff's case, in my judgment, lies in the fact that the promise is incorporated in the written contract signed by the parties.

The real point which, in my opinion, has to be determined here is, whether the deposit notes issued to the plaintiff do, in fact, express the whole bargain which was come to between him and the Trust, or, whether they only express part of such bargain, and the promise which the plaintiff seeks to enforce constitutes the rest of the bargain and still remains operative. If the latter be the correct view, the promise would, in my opinion, be enforceable on one or other of the following grounds, either because the entire contract

---

[39] [1924] 1 Ch 287; affirmed [1924] 2 Ch 329 (CA).

between the parties is contained in two written instruments which this Court will construe together, that is, the deposit notes and so much of the preliminary written contract as has not been superseded by the deposit notes; or else, because the promise is a written collateral contract, the consideration for which was the entering into by the plaintiff of the contract to take the deposit notes. That such a written collateral contract is capable of strict proof without coming into conflict with any rule of law or procedure, although it operates to add to or vary another contemporaneous written contract, cannot, I think, be disputed; it is altogether outside the rule of law relating to the inadmissibility of parol evidence to add to, vary or contradict the terms of a written instrument. ...

The introductory sentence of the paragraph containing the promise obviously refers to the sixth condition indorsed on the specimen deposit note and, in my opinion, the true meaning of that paragraph is that, notwithstanding that by the sixth condition the Trust retains the right of redemption therein mentioned, the Trust promises that, in the event of the Rio Bravo estates being sold before the deposit notes are redeemed, the directors will, etc. ... The promise was inserted in the prospectus to make the issue more attractive to the public, and such insertion would have been quite meaningless and highly misleading if, as now pleaded, the promise was to have no effect after the deposit notes had been issued.

In the result, I hold that the promise constitutes a binding operative contract which was not superseded by the issue of the deposit notes; and that the latter do not contain the whole contract between the parties, but that the entire contract is compounded of two documents, that is, the deposit note and the written collateral promise, which two documents the Court will construe together, or, alternatively, that the promise constitutes a binding collateral contract in writing which the plaintiff is entitled to enforce. Treating the two documents as together constituting the entire contract, there is no difficulty in construing the promise, just as if it had been inserted in the deposit notes as a proviso to come into operation, if and when the Rio Bravo estates were sold ...

Notes

(1) The parol evidence rule has been likened to the Holy Roman Empire (which, it will be recollected, was neither holy, nor Roman, nor an Empire), in that none of the three stated elements was correct. First, the rule does not apply to 'parol' (an old word meaning, originally, a statement not in a deed and, later, every oral statement), but rather to all 'extrinsic' evidence. It thus covers both oral agreements and agreements contained in a separate document (eg a letter) which is not referred to in the written contract. Secondly, it is not a rule of evidence—if the rule applies it does not matter in the slightest that there is ample other evidence of the additional term; the written document will still be treated as conclusive of what has been agreed as the contract. Thirdly, it can hardly be said to be a 'rule' because so many exceptions to it have been acknowledged that a court that is convinced that the oral or other extrinsic promise was in fact made will always be able to rely on one of the exceptions to take the evidence into account.

(2) The decision of the Chancery Division is a good example for two of the most far-reaching exceptions:[40] (a) even where extrinsic evidence cannot be used to add to,

---

[40] See *Treitel on the Law of Contract*, 14th edn by E Peel (London: Sweet & Maxwell, 2015) paras 6-015–6-031.

vary or contradict the terms of a written agreement, it may be possible to show that the parties made two related contracts, one written, and an oral or written 'collateral agreement' which may contradict the first contract; (b) if a written agreement was not intended to set out all the terms on which the parties had actually agreed, extrinsic evidence is admissible.

(3) Under the second exception, instead of treating an oral promise as a collateral contract, the courts so find that the contract was partly written and partly oral. In *J Evans Ltd v Andrea Merzario Ltd* the defendant forwarding agents had frequently arranged for the carriage of goods of the claimants, who were importers of machinery. They now suggested that the goods should in future be transported in containers, rather than in crates or trailers which were always shipped under deck. The defendants gave an oral assurance that machines shipped for the claimants in containers would also not be carried on deck. No written provision to this effect was included in the printed standard contract form used by the parties. The Court of Appeal held that the assurance was enforceable although this 'was not a collateral contract in the sense of an oral agreement varying the terms of a written contract. It was a new express term which was to be included thereafter in the contracts between the plaintiffs and the defendants':[41] the contract was 'partly oral, partly in writing, and partly by conduct', and in these circumstances the parol evidence rule did not apply, so that the Court was entitled to look at extrinsic evidence in order to determine the content of the bargain.[42]

(4) It has frequently been argued that these and other exceptions totally undermine the parol evidence rule and that it should be abolished[43] or consigned to the dustbin of history.[44] A formal overruling or abolition has not yet occurred in England, but most commentators seem to agree that the 'rule' is no more than a rebuttable presumption that the writing contains all the terms of the contract. There is, incidentally, less hostility to the rule in some of the US jurisdictions, in Australia and in New Zealand.

The parol evidence rule and its exceptions may be seen as an attempt to strike a balance between the desire to achieve legal certainty on the one hand and a materially 'right' outcome on the other. French law is similarly reluctant to admit that the wording of a contract concluded in writing can be overridden by other factors. The following extract discusses the ambit and effect of Article 1359(1) and (2) (ex-Article 1341) Cciv, and it mentions the English Statute of Frauds. Both provisions have already been reproduced and discussed above, in the section on formalities.[45]

---

[41] [1976] 1 WLR 1078, 1084, per Geoffrey Lane LJ.
[42] ibid, 1083, per Roskill LJ. On the analysis of Lord Denning MR (ibid, 1081), the assurance was binding as a collateral warranty.
[43] The Law Commission, *Law of Contract: The Parol Evidence Rule* (Consultation Paper), Law Com CP No 70 (London: Her Majesty's Stationery Office, 1976). In 1986, The Law Commission, *Law of Contract: The Parol Evidence Rule*, Law Com No 154 (London: Her Majesty's Stationery Office, 1986) concluded that there was in fact no rule left that could be abolished.
[44] See the first edition of this book, p 167.
[45] See above, pp 406–08, 414–15.

Vogenauer on interpretation of contracts[46]   **18.24 (INT)**

In France, art 1341(1) [now: art 1359 (1) and (2)] Cciv, a provision which can be traced back to the Royal Edict of Moulins of 1566 and very much resembles s 4 of the 1677 Statute of Frauds, determines that contracts can only be proved by means of a signed or notarised document if the sum or value involved exceeds €1,500, and 'no evidence by witnesses against and outside of the content of instruments is allowed, nor as to what is alleged to have been said before, at the time of, or after the instruments'. The evidence excluded can be identified in three ways. First, as to the kind of evidence, art 1341(1) only mentions evidence obtained by witnesses. It can, however, be inferred from art 1347 [now: art 1361] Cciv that art 1341(1) also extends to written evidence which does not consist in a signed or notarised document. Such written material, for instance a photo-copy, a cheque, a revoked will, or a newspaper article, can at best constitute 'a beginning of written proof' for the purposes of art 1347 [now: art 1361], one of the exceptions to art 1341(1) which I will discuss in the paragraph after next, but it is excluded as admissible evidence under art 1341(1). Secondly, with respect to the facts to be proved, art 1341(1) excludes both evidence of mistakes or omissions which occurred at the stage of negotiat-ing and drafting and proof of modifications of the contract subsequent to its formation. Thirdly, as far as the relationship between these facts and the written document is con-cerned, extrinsic evidence will not be admitted if one party alleges that the writing does not correspond to what has been agreed ('evidence against') or does not capture the entirety of the agreement ('evidence outside'). Extrinsic evidence can, however, be used for the purposes of interpreting a written document that contains internal contradictions or is otherwise unclear.[47]

Article 1341(1) Cciv therefore, like the parol evidence rule, prohibits the admission of extrinsic evidence for the purpose of varying or contradicting a written document. It differs from the English rule, though, in that it is not regarded as a substantive rule of interpretation. It only concerns proof of the existence of a contractual obligation, ie that the contract has been concluded in the first place. If the parties disagree about an essential requirement for the validity of the contract, for instance the purchase price, art 1341(1) Cciv excludes extrinsic evidence inconsistent with the writing.[48] But as long as the existence of the contract is not contested and the parties only disagree about the extent of their contractual obligations because the terms of the contract are in need of interpretation, the rule does not prohibit extrinsic evidence from being adduced for this purpose.[49]

Finally, the scope for the exclusion of extrinsic evidence for the proof of the exist-ence of financially important transactions is substantially reduced by a number of excep-tions which have been understood in the broadest possible sense by the courts. Oral evidence is, for instance, admitted if there exists 'a beginning of written proof', which is defined as any written act emanating from the defendant which makes it probable that the alleged fact is true, art 1347 [now: art 1361] Cciv. Such evidence is further allowed whenever it was 'materially or morally' impossible for a party to obtain written evidence

[46] Vogenauer (n 24 above) 135–37.

[47] Terré, Simler and Lequette (n 27 above) no. 153; F Terré, *Introduction générale au droit* (7th edn, Paris: Dalloz, 2006) no. 638 [now (10th edn, 2015) no. 563]; J Ghestin and G Goubeaux, *Traité de droit civil: introduction générale* (4th edn, Paris: LGDJ, 1994) nos. 663–64.

[48] Cass civ (1) 27 April 1977, no. 74-13897, Bull civ I no. 192, D 1977.2.413; CA Reims 27 May 1980, Gaz Pal 1980.2.554.

[49] Cass civ 31 May 1948, no. 37604, S 1949.1.127.

or the written document has gone lost because of *'force majeure* or accident', art 1348 [now: art 1360] Cciv. Most importantly, all contracts governed by commercial law can be proved 'by any means', see art 1341(2) Cciv [now reformulated in art 1359] and art 110-3 of the Commercial code.

German law has developed yet another set of mechanisms to deal with the problem that US lawyers refer to as the 'protection of the integrity of the writing'. We can again observe an amalgam of questions of contractual interpretation, formal requirements and evidence.

Vogenauer on interpretation of contracts[50]   **18.25 (INT)**

Eighteenth and nineteenth century German law knew a prohibition on extrinsic evidence which, in substance, resembled the parol evidence rule. The Civil Codes of Prussia, Baden and Austria, for instance, excluded any proof of oral agreements made before or during the conclusion of a written contract and contradicting the text of the instrument. The courts, however, slowly subverted these rules by altering their character. They permitted evidence of collateral oral agreements, but only if it could be proved that these had been meant to be valid besides the written contract. This reasoning was based on a presumption that the writing accurately reflected the totality of the contract at the time of its conclusion. As a result, the prohibition turned into a mere presumption against the admissibility of evidence. The presumption of the written agreement being complete was not included in the Civil Code, but mentioned approvingly in the *travaux préparatoires*. Thus, the courts continued to apply it after 1900, and today it is regarded as customary law. The presumption can be rebutted by evidence to the contrary, but the courts profess to impose 'the strictest requirements' for such proof. In a recent case, the state of the law was summarised as follows: 'The presumption of completeness and accuracy of the written instrument is valid if the text of the instrument, according to its wording and internal context and taking into account commercial practice, is a manifestation of a particular content of the transaction. In order to rebut the presumption criteria of interpretation external to the instrument can be referred to (concomitant circumstances, declarations of the parties external to the document, etc.)'.[51]

Admitting interpretative material from outside the four corners of the document, however, does not necessarily entail that such material has to be controlling. It is important not to confuse *admissibility* and *weight*. Whilst no barriers as to admissibility are erected, external factors will not usually carry much weight if they conflict with the text of the instrument. In practice, the previous negotiations and the subsequent conduct, leave alone a party's statements of subjective intent, will extremely rarely be used to add to, vary or contradict the text of the instrument. …

It may be added that German law even strengthens the presumption of the completeness and accuracy of written contracts in cases where the parties used writing because of a mandatory formal requirement. In such cases German courts engage in a two step process which, once more, is not mentioned anywhere in the Civil Code.[52] In a first step, they determine the content of the contract. In doing so, they apply the general rules of

---

[50] Vogenauer (n 24 above) 137–39.
[51] BGH 5 July 2002, NJW 2002, 3164 (headnote of the court).
[52] See, eg, BGH 17 February 2000, NJW 2000, 1569.

interpretation. As has been seen, these include the presumption of completeness and accuracy, but there is no limitation as to the circumstances that may be drawn upon in order to attribute a meaning to the document. In rare cases, the consideration of external circumstances may lead to a rebuttal of the presumption and thus to a result that does not correspond to the literal meaning of the document. In a second step, then, it has to be established whether the contract is valid with this particular content. It might, after all, be argued that the formal requirement has not been adhered to if the content of the contract cannot be established from the written words. This will only be the case if the (true) content of the contract has found some articulation in the text itself. According to the so-called 'theory of indication' (*Andeutungstheorie*) this requires that the content is 'at least somehow, maybe even imperfectly indicated', 'reflected', or 'alluded to' in the written text. This, the Supreme Court holds, will certainly not be the case if the document does not contain the slightest hint that its content might differ from the text. The contract will than be void because the formal requirement has been violated.

The 'theory of indication' tries to strike a balance. On the one hand there are the basic principles of construction which aim to answer interpretative questions according to the meaning a reasonable person in the position of the parties would have given to the contract, even if this requires a deviation from the letter of the instrument. On the other hand there is a need to uphold the function of the statutory formal requirements which aim to protect the general public's faith in the evidential value of formal records of transactions and the individual party's reliance on a certain declaration which has been reduced to writing. Still, the test remains notoriously vague, and it is attacked time and again by legal scholars. There are reasons to suspect that the courts will find an 'indication' if they need to refer to external circumstances in order to achieve a desired result which contradicts or adds to the instrument.

Notes

(1) We have seen that it is frequently argued that the English parol evidence rule should be understood as a (mere) presumption that a document which looks like a contract is the whole contract.[53] The German experience shows that such a presumption makes it possible to reach adequate and balanced interpretative results.

(2) English lawyers who wish to retain at least the remnants of the traditional parol evidence rule are concerned that the courts might otherwise be inundated with irrelevant documents or with spurious allegations as to what the parties had intended. This is not the German experience. There, the admission of all relevant background material in combination with the presumption has proved perfectly workable. If irrelevant evidence is introduced, the experienced judge can quickly dismiss and ignore it. The admission of contextual evidence leads neither to intolerable delays nor to excessive costs.

The parties may reinforce the presumption that the written document contains the entire contract by inserting into their contract a so-called 'entire agreement clause' or 'merger clause'.

---

[53] See above, p 752.

Article 5:105: Merger clause

(1) If a written contract contains an individually negotiated clause stating that the writing embodies all the terms of the contract (a merger clause), any prior statements, undertakings or agreements which are not embodied in the writing do not form part of the contract.

(2) If the merger clause is not individually negotiated it will only establish a presumption that the parties intended that their prior statements, undertakings or agreements were not to form part of the contract. This rule may not be excluded or restricted.

(3) The parties' prior statements may be used to interpret the contract. This rule may not be excluded or restricted except by an individually negotiated clause.

(4) A party may by its statements or conduct be precluded from asserting a merger clause to the extent that the other party has reasonably relied on them.

Notes

(1) The courts in European jurisdictions tend to respect these clauses and do not permit the parties to adduce additional evidence to add to, vary or contradict the written contract.

(2) However, despite such a clause, recourse to extrinsic evidence is allowed for the purposes of interpretation, see Article 5:105(3) PECL.

18.5 THE *CONTRA PROFERENTEM* RULE

The maxim that ambiguous clauses in a contract must be interpreted against the person who drafted them—*in dubio contra proferentem*—goes back to the Middle Ages, and it has roots in Roman law. The rule is widely acknowledged today, and it has been codified in many European jurisdictions. However, it has a slightly diverging scope in different contract laws.

Unfair Terms Directive[54]   **18.27 (EU)**

Article 5: ... Where there is doubt about the meaning of a term, the interpretation most favourable to the consumer shall prevail. ...

Court of Justice, 10 May 2001   **18.28 (EU)**

European Commission v Netherlands[55]

The contra proferentem *rule applies even when it has not been codified.*

---

[54] Council Directive 93/13/EEC of 5 April 1993 on unfair terms in consumer contracts, OJ L 95/29. On this Directive, see below, ch 21.

[55] C-144/99, ECLI:EU:C:2001:257.

Facts: The Dutch BW of 1992 did not codify rules of contractual interpretation, so it did not contain the *contra proferentem* rule. The government of the Netherlands did not enact a corresponding rule in order to implement Directive 93/13. The Commission applied for a declaration that, by failing to adopt the legislation necessary for the full transposition into Dutch law of Article 5 of the Directive, the Kingdom of the Netherlands had failed to fulfil its obligations under what is now Article 288 TFEU. The Dutch government argued that specific implementing measures were not required because Dutch law already secured the aims pursued by the Directive by way of some provisions of the BW which could be interpreted in such as a way as to confer sufficient protection upon consumers and because of 'the unwritten rules of law' acknowledged in the legal system, such as the principle *interpretatio contra proferentem.*

Held: The Kingdom of the Netherlands has failed to fulfil its obligations.

Judgment: ... 17. It should be borne in mind, in that connection, that, according to settled case-law, whilst legislative action on the part of each Member State is not necessarily required in order to implement a directive, it is essential for national law to guarantee that the national authorities will effectively apply the directive in full, that the legal position under national law should be sufficiently precise and clear and that individuals are made fully aware of their rights and, where appropriate, may rely on them before the national courts (Case C-365/93 *Commission v Greece* [1995] ECR I-499, paragraph 9).

18. As the Court has already made clear, the last-mentioned condition is of particular importance where the directive in question is intended to accord rights to nationals of other Member States (Case C-365/93, cited above, paragraph 9). That is the position in the present case, it being one of the aims of the Directive, according to the sixth recital in its preamble, 'to safeguard the citizen in his role as consumer when acquiring goods and services under contracts which are governed by the laws of Member States other than his own'.

19. However, for the reasons given by the Advocate General in points 25 and 26 of his Opinion, it appears that the Kingdom of the Netherlands has been unable to show that its legal system contains provisions equivalent to Articles 4(2) and 5 of the Directive.

20. Given that the Netherlands Government has stated that the aims sought by the Directive could be attained through a schematic interpretation of the provisions of Netherlands law, it is enough to point out that, for the reasons set out by the Advocate General in points 26 to 31 of his Opinion, the results intended by the Directive cannot be attained by applying Netherlands law as it stands at present.

21. As regards the argument advanced by the Netherlands Government that, if the Netherlands legislation were interpreted in such a way as to ensure conformity with the Directive—a principle endorsed by the Hoge Raad der Nederlanden (Netherlands)— it would be possible in any event to remedy any disparity between the provisions of Netherlands legislation and those of the Directive, suffice it to note that, as the Advocate General explained in point 36 of his Opinion, even where the settled case-law of a Member State interprets the provisions of national law in a manner deemed to satisfy the requirements of a directive, that cannot achieve the clarity and precision needed to meet the requirement of legal certainty. That, moreover, is particularly true in the field of consumer protection.

Note

The rule is now codified in Article 6:238(2)(2) BW.

Code de la consommation[56] **18.29 (FR)**

Article L 133-2(2): In case of doubt, [contractual clauses proposed by professionals to consumers or non-professionals] are interpreted in the sense most favourable to the consumer or the non-professional. ...

> *Note*
>
> As opposed to the provisions on contractual interpretation in the Code civil,[57] this rule is regarded as a mandatory rule of law and not merely as a simple 'piece of guidance' to the judges.[58]

Code civil[59] **18.30 (FR)**

Article 1190: In case of ambiguity, a bespoke contract is interpreted against the creditor and in favour of the debtor, and a standard-form contract is interpreted against the person who put it forward.

BGB[60] **18.31 (DE)**

§ 305c: Surprising and ambiguous clauses

...

(2) In case of doubt, standard business terms are interpreted against the user.

§ 310: Scope of Application

...

(3) In the case of contracts between a businessperson and a consumer (consumer contracts) the rules in this section apply subject to the following provisions:

1. ...;

2. §§ 305c (2) and §§ 306, 307 to 309 of the present Act and Article 29a of the Introductory Act to the Civil Code apply to pre-established conditions of contract even if they are intended for use only once and in so far as, because they are pre-established, the consumer could not influence their content.

---

[56] The provision was introduced in the 1995 revision of the Code de la consommation which implemented the EC Directive 93/13 in France, see below, p 847.

[57] See above, p 778.

[58] Cass civ (1) 21 January 2003, nos. 00-13342 and 00-19001, Bull civ I no. 19, D 2003, 693; Cass civ (2) 13 July 2006, no. 05–18104, Bull civ II no. 214, D 2006, 2848.

[59] The provision was introduced by the 2016 reform of the Code civil. It replaced ex-Art 1162 Cciv: 'In case of doubt, an agreement shall be interpreted against the one who has stipulated, and in favour of the one who has contracted the obligation'; see CA Colmar, 25 January 1963, GazPal 1963.I.277 (below, p 762).

[60] Previously § 5 AGBG. For the 1976 AGBG, its revision in 1996 and its integration into the BGB in 2002, see below, p 835.

Consumer Rights Act 2015[61]   **18.32 (EN)**

Section 69: Contract terms that may have different meanings
   (1) If a term in a consumer contract, or a consumer notice, could have different mean-ings, the meaning that is most favourable to the consumer is to prevail.
   (2) Subsection (1) does not apply to the construction of a term or a notice in proceed-ings on an application for an injunction or interdict under paragraph 3 of Schedule 3.

UNIDROIT Principles   **18.33 (INT)**

Article 4.6: Contra proferentem rule
   If contract terms supplied by one party are unclear, an interpretation against that party is preferred.

Principles of European Contract Law   **18.34 (INT)**

Article 5:103: Contra Proferentem Rule
   Where there is doubt about the meaning of a contract term not individually negoti-ated, an interpretation of the term against the party who supplied it is to be preferred.

Draft Common Frame of Reference   **18.35 (INT)**

Article II-8:103: Interpretation against supplier of term or dominant party
   (1) Where there is doubt about the meaning of a contract term not individually negoti-ated, an interpretation of the term against the party who supplied it is to be preferred.
   (2) Where there is doubt about the meaning of any other term, and that term has been established under the dominant influence of one party, an interpretation of the term against that party is to be preferred.

Notes

   (1) Note the different scopes of these provisions. Which types of contract and which types of term does the rule apply to?
   (2) The rule that unclear terms must be construed against the party who drafted them is usually justified on the basis that the risk of ambiguity should be borne by the party who could more cheaply avoid it, and this is usually the party who selected or drafted the clause rather than the party to whom it was presented. More recent variants of the rule rather rely on the rationale of consumer protection or protection of the 'weaker party'.

Traditionally, the *contra proferentem* rule was mostly applied in the interpretation of exemption, limitation and penalty clauses, ie clauses that were specifically drafted in order to improve the position of the drafter and to weaken the position of the other party.

---

[61] This replaces Unfair Terms in Consumer Contracts Regulations 1999, SI 1999/2083, Reg 7. For the Regulations and the 2015 Act, see below, p 838.

Gold Coast cocoa

A clause which is unclear in its scope will be interpreted against the party who was responsible for drafting the contract.

Facts: The plaintiffs had bought from the defendant sellers 105 tons Gold Coast cocoa. The confirmation note was on a form supplied by the sellers' agents. It provided as follows:

Delivery:	ex quay Hamburg (inserted with typewriter). The risk of transport is borne by the seller …
Packaging:	in sacks (inserted with typewriter). I expressly reserve the right to use another appropriate kind of packaging for the delivery …
Time of delivery:	25 tons in each of the months of July, August and September 1954 (inserted with typewriter). Subject to the goods being properly and punctually delivered to, and safely received by, the sellers from their own suppliers, and subject to any official measures taken by the authorities.
Payment:	net cash against invoice … (inserted with typewriter).
Special terms & conditions:	…

The sellers argued that they were relieved from their duties to perform the contract under the clause 'Subject to the goods being properly and punctually delivered to, and safely received by, the sellers from their own suppliers', since their own suppliers had become insolvent and failed to deliver the cocoa. The buyers brought an action for damages. In their view the clause was applicable only in the event of delay.

Held: The BGH held for the buyers.

Judgment: In accordance with the case law (OHZ 1, 178 …) and legal writings …, the appeal court understood the clause 'Subject to the goods being properly and punctually delivered to, and safely received by, the sellers from their own suppliers', taken in isolation, to the effect that the seller intends to free himself of any liability whatsoever for non-delivery, in the event that his supplier does not render performance for whatever reason. …

The appeal court holds that the clause can have this meaning only in the present case although it is placed after the phrase 'Time of delivery'. It explicates that there is no connection between the terms behind the entry 'Time of delivery' and the very entry itself which is made in the margin. …

The interpretation made by the appeal court also violates the principle, derived from experience, that, like rubrics, entries in the margin are meant to make it easier for the reader to find his way round the document, and they are also meant to structure and to summarise long statements which have a material inner connection. … The indented clauses are therefore allocated to particular marginal entries, very much like the text which has been inserted in the free spaces with the help of a typewriter. …

---

[62] BGHZ 24, 39. For another example (interpretation of a contractual release), see BGH 18 October 1972, NJW 1973, 39 (see below, 33.24 (DE), p 1409).

The court of final appeal thus ... follows the opinion of the court of first instance that in this case the subject-to-delivery clause ... only expresses a reservation with regard to the consequences of late delivery. ...

Moreover, it has always been a settled rule, established by the case law relating to exemption clauses, that a seller who wishes to make his obligation to make delivery subject to reservations of a more or less extensive nature must signal his intention in a clear and unambiguous manner (RGZ 102, 227, 229). As the Reichsgericht has pointed out, a clause rendering the transaction conditional on the seller himself taking delivery of the goods constitutes, and is regarded as, an exceptional phenomenon (RGZ 103, 180, 182). The defendant's sale confirmation note provided an opportunity of giving clear expression to such an exception, and of securing total exoneration from the delivery obligation, by inserting the appropriate reservation either next to the entry 'Delivery', or under the rubric 'Special terms and conditions', or in the standard terms and conditions of the contract, for example, after the word 'sells'. Instead, it was inconspicuously inserted under the entry 'Time of delivery' after the statement '25 tons in each of the months of July, August and September 1954'. The effect of this is to leave the buyer—whatever the circumstances, and even if he carefully scrutinizes the contract—in a state of uncertainty as to the scope of the intended exclusion of liability, which, providing as it purports to do for exoneration from the entire contractual risk in the event of non-performance by the seller's supplier, was not something that the buyer should have expected to encounter at that point in the extensive confirmation document. The existence of any reasonable doubt as to the scope of such an exemption—which, as is generally recognised, must always be narrowly construed—will necessarily result in its being interpreted against the party using such standard forms, since that party is easily able, by arranging the layout of the document in an appropriate manner and by duly highlighting any wording requiring emphasis, to give clear expression to an agreement which is so far-reaching in its scope and which affects the entire contractual obligation (BGHZ 5, 111, 115). It follows that the defendants must accept the more obvious—and, from their point of view, less favourable—interpretation of their ambiguously framed conditions (RGZ 142, 353, 356).

Court of Appeal **18.37 (EN)**

Houghton v Trafalgar Insurance Co Ltd[63]

A clause which is unclear in its scope will be interpreted against the party who was responsible for drafting the contract.

Facts: A policy of insurance covering a motor-car contained a provision excluding liability for damage 'caused or arising whilst the car is conveying any load in excess of that for which it was constructed'. At the time of the plaintiff's accident six persons were being conveyed in the car, although seating accommodation was only provided for five persons, and the insurers denied liability on the ground that a load in excess of that for which the car was constructed was being carried.

Held: At first instance, Gorman J decided against the insurers' contention and gave judgment for the plaintiff. The insurers appealed, but the appeal was dismissed.

Judgment: SOMERVELL LJ: If there is any ambiguity, since it is the defendants' clause, the ambiguity will be resolved in favour of the assured. In my opinion, the words relied on

---

[63] [1954] 1 QB 247.

'any load in excess of that for which it was constructed', only clearly cover cases where there is a weight load specified in respect of the motor-vehicle, be it lorry or van. I agree that the earlier words in the clause obviously are applicable to an ordinary private car in respect of which there is no such specified weight load. But there was—and I think that it would have been inadmissible—no evidence whether this was a form which was used for lorries as well as for ordinary private motor-cars. I do not think that that matters. We have to construe the words in their ordinary meaning, and I think that those words only clearly cover the case which I have put. If that is right, they cannot avail the insurance company in the present case.

I would only add that the present suggestions of their application is, to me, a remarkable one. I think that it would need the plainest possible words if it were desired to exclude the insurance cover by reason of the fact that there was at the back one passenger more than the seating accommodation. All sorts of obscurities and difficulties might arise. I would like to add that if this or any other insurance company wishes to put forward a policy which will be inapplicable when an extra passenger is carried, I hope that they will print their provision in red ink so that the assured will have it drawn to his particular intention. For these reasons, in my opinion, this appeal should be dismissed.

[DENNING LJ and ROMER LJ concurred.]

Cour d'appel de Colmar, 25 January 1963[64]   **18.38 (FR)**

Late completion of dwelling

A clause which is unclear in its scope will be interpreted against the party who was responsible for drafting the contract.

Facts: The defendant builder had undertaken to construct a house with three flats. Clause 13 of the contract gave him 50 days for the job, and clause 14 provided for the payment of a penalty in the case of delay. The words used were not clear as to whether the 50-day period was to apply for the construction of just one flat or of the whole building. The parties also disagreed on the relevance of an instruction by the employer's architect extending the time for the whole building to 75 days.

Held: The clause applied to the completion of just one dwelling; the attempt to order completion of the whole project within 75 days was contrary to good faith.

Judgment: THE COURT: As to the law: whereas having regard to Article 1134 [now cf Article 1104 Code civil], according to which agreements are to be carried out in good faith, and Article 1162 [now cf Article 1190], which provides that 'in case of doubt, an agreement shall be interpreted against the one who has stipulated, and in favour of the one who has contracted the obligation' ... Whereas the second of those provisions is applicable with particular strictness to standard-form contracts, such as a detailed specification of works, which is not the outcome of free negotiation but comprises a whole series of stipulations imposed on a contractor. Whereas a penalty clause included in a specification of works is especially subject to that rule of interpretation, which is reinforced in such cases by the principle *odia restringenda*.

Whereas the penalty clause relied on by the respondent is ambiguous, since the phrase 'in relation to a dwelling-house', contained in the annex, may be interpreted as meaning

---

[64] Gaz Pal 1963.I.277 (citations omitted).

that the time allowed is to be multiplied by the number of individual dwellings. Whereas the wording in issue is as follows: 'Art 14: In the event of the works not being completed within the period prescribed, and without there being any need for the prior service of any formal default notice, there shall be deducted from the total due the sum of 5,000 old francs for each working day that the works remain uncompleted ...—Annex to Art 13. Time allowed for carrying out the works: the periods hereinafter specified shall in each case run from the time when instructions are given in accordance with the building trade practice. The table appearing below applies in relation to a dwelling-house: completion of fabric of building ... 50 working days. ...'

Whereas in view of Article 1162 Cciv [now cf Article 1190], the uncertainty resulting from the poor-quality drafting of the specification of works, which was prepared by the respondent's representative, must be removed by the adoption of an approach favouring the contractor against whom the clause is to operate. Whereas it is immaterial that an instruction subsequently given by the architect expressly fixed a time-limit, this time of 75 days, for completion of the entire fabric; an instruction does not constitute an agreement since it is, by definition, a unilateral act. Whereas it can acquire the nature of an agreement only once it is expressly accepted by the party to whom it is addressed.

As to the facts: whereas, far from accepting the instruction in question, Gentner raised a protest, which was such as to preclude the signature which he appended to the document before returning it from being construed as an acceptance; whereas that signature appears, in all probability, to have been no more than an acknowledgement of receipt.

Whereas the claim made by Roesch or by his representative, alleging that the contractor was under an obligation to construct the fabric of three individual dwellings in 75 working days, is of a draconian nature. Whereas it amounts to an invitation to carry out the work perfunctorily and to ignore the established rules of construction, which are modelled on the requirements of nature; whereas according to those requirements, a house in the course of construction must be given the time to settle; in particular, the site must be left to stand over the winter, in order to allow the frost to draw the moisture out from the walls, which are saturated with it. Whereas a person who disregards those rules is acting like a motorist who drives a new car at top speed without bothering with the essential business of running it in. Whereas to require the work to be carried out with excessive haste is contrary to the precepts inherent in a conscientious professional approach. It follows that such a claim is vitiated by bad faith ...

Notes

(1) It is not altogether obvious that the clauses in the three previous cases were 'ambiguous'. The judgments rather show a general hostility to the substance of the particular clauses. In many cases, the courts, instead of striking down clauses as unfairly prejudicial to the customer, preferred to achieve the same result by way of interpretative devices, such as the *contra proferentem* rule. In doing so they could avoid having to articulate the reasons for their hostility.[65]

(2) Now that special legislation on unfair contract terms has been enacted in nearly all European countries,[66] there is no need to use the *contra proferentem* rule in order

---

[65] See the statement by Lord Denning MR in *George Mitchell (Chesterhall) Ltd v Finney Lock Seeds Ltd* [1983] QB 284 (CA) quoted below, p 827.
[66] See below, ch 21.3, pp 833–50.

to do indirectly what is better done directly by controlling the substance of contract terms. However, the rule will retain its potential in cases to which the legislation does not apply, as do other mechanisms for restoring the 'contractual equilibrium' in the face of exclusion and limitation clauses.[67]

FURTHER READING

Canaris, C-W and Grigoleit, HC, 'Interpretation of Contracts' in A Hartkamp et al (eds), *Towards a European Civil Code* (4th edn, Alphen aan den Rijn: Wolters Kluwer, 2011) 587–618.

Ferreri, S, 'The Interpretation of Contracts From a European Perspective' in R Schulze et al (eds), *Informationspflichten und Vertragsschluss im Acquis communautaire* (Tübingen: Mohr Siebeck, 2003) 117–39.

Herbots, JH, 'Interpretation of Contracts' in J Smits (ed), *Elgar Encyclopedia of Comparative Law* (2nd edn, Cheltenham: Elgar, 2012) 421–48.

Kaczorowska, A, 'Règles uniformes d'interprétation d'un contrat international' (1991) 68 Rev dr int dr comp 294–313.

Kaufmann, S, *Parol Evidence Rule und Merger Clauses im Internationalen Einheitsrecht* (Frankfurt/Main: Lang, 2004).

Kornet, N, *Contract Interpretation and Gap Filling: Comparative and Theoretical Perspectives* (Antwerp: Intersentia, 2006).

Kötz, H, *European Contract Law* (2nd edn, Oxford University Press, 2017) 91–108.

Lüderitz, A, *Auslegung von Rechtsgeschäften: Vergleichende Untersuchung anglo-amerikanischen und deutschen Rechts* (Karlsruhe: CF Müller, 1966).

McMeel, G and Grigoleit, HC 'Interpretation of Contracts' in G Dannemann and S Vogenauer (eds), *The Common European Sales Law in Context: Interactions with English and German Law* (Oxford University Press, 2013) 341–72.

Vogenauer, S, 'Interpretation of Contracts: Concluding Comparative Observations' in Burrows, A and Peel, E (eds), *Contract Terms* (Oxford University Press, 2007) 123–50.

Vogenauer, S, 'Interpretation of Contracts' in Basedow, J et al (eds), *The Max Planck Encyclopedia of European Private Law* (Oxford University Press, 2012) 973–77.

Vogenauer, S, 'Interpretation' in N Jansen and R Zimmermann (eds), *Commentaries on European Contract Laws* (Oxford University Press, 2018) 740–85.

Wolgast, A, *Die Auslegung von Rechtsgeschäften im französischen Recht, im deutschen Recht und im Common law* (Diss, Hamburg, 1965).

Zuppi, AL, 'The Parol Evidence Rule: a Comparative Study of the Common Law, the Civil Law Tradition, and *Lex Mercatoria*' (2007) 35 Georgia Journal of International and Comparative Law 233–76.

---

[67] See, eg, Cass com 22 October 1996, no. 93-18632, Bull IV no. 261, D 1997.121 (above, 11.18 (FR), p 383).

CHAPTER 19
THE OBLIGATIONS OF THE PARTIES: SALES
AND SERVICES CONTRACTS

19.1 INTRODUCTION

Even when one has ascertained the meaning of what the parties actually said, there may be situations in which the parties' rights and obligations are not stated: while the contract is under way, a problem may arise for which the parties have provided no solution, either because they did not foresee the problem at all, or they foresaw it and failed to deal with it. The question is how to fill this gap in the contract.

19.1.A DEFAULT RULES

In this situation the continental judge looks first to the civil and commercial codes and any special laws which contain rules intended to be applied by the court in the absence of a contractual agreement by the parties. The starting point will normally be statutory rules, but these must be considered along with the glosses added by the courts. Thus when parties to a sale in France have said nothing about the seller's liability for latent defects, the courts apply Article 1645 of the Code civil, which renders the seller who knows of the defect liable for all consequential loss due to it, and also the judge-made rule which imputes such knowledge to all commercial distributors such as manufacturer, wholesaler and retailer.[1] These gap-filling rules are called in France *règles supplétives*, in Germany *dispositives Recht*. This is because in most cases 'suppletive' rules are ones which will apply only if the parties have not expressly agreed something different—they are what are often now called 'default rules'. However, it must be remembered that in each system (and in particular in consumer contracts) there are some rules which the parties are not permitted to contract out of, ie mandatory rules.

---

[1] See below, p 1155.

In England, too, gaps in agreed contractual structures are made good by recourse to general rules which apply unless the parties have provided otherwise, depending on the type of contract in issue. Traditionally these are referred to as 'implied terms' since, as a matter of principle, they are regarded as what the parties intended to be part of their agreement but did not express. When the law (statute or case law) sets out terms which will normally apply to contracts of a certain type, the terms are said to be 'implied in law'; they will apply unless the parties have expressly or impliedly agreed otherwise.[2] The Consumer Rights Act 2015, however, takes a different approach. Partly because in a consumer contract the obligations and remedies cannot be excluded or restricted, and partly because it was thought that consumers would not understand the concept of an 'implied' term, the Act adopts a different formulation. The relevant terms are 'treated as included' in the contract.[3] Whether the change in formulation makes the Act easier for consumers to understand is doubtful!

Most of these terms were developed originally by the courts, and many important terms are still 'implied by law' into particular kinds of contract: for example, in a contract of employment there is a general implied duty to preserve the trust and confidence that an employee should have in his or her employer.[4] However, many of the terms are now enshrined in statute. For example, the Sale of Goods Act 1979 and the Supply of Goods and Services Act 1982 reflect rules which were developed originally at common law. They set out, for instance, the seller or supplier's obligations as to the kind and quality of goods to be supplied[5] (ie the obligations relating to conformity of the goods[6]). Thus these statutory implied terms perform the same role for contracts of sale and services as the corresponding suppletive rules in the continental civil codes. The starting point is that implied terms are also 'default rules', but, as mentioned, some of them have become mandatory in that (particularly in consumer contracts) the parties are no longer permitted to contract out of them.

One thing we do in this chapter is to survey some of the more important rules that apply to some common kinds of contract: contracts for the supply of goods and services, construction contracts and contracts for the transport of persons and goods. It may be objected that this belongs more properly to the law of specific contracts than to a book on general contract law, but there is of course no such thing as a contract in general: every contract is for something specific, whether it falls within one of a series of recognised

---

[2] Compare 'terms implied in fact', which are terms implied only in the circumstances of the particular contract in order to make it work. These are discussed in the next chapter.

[3] eg Consumer Rights Act 2015, s 9(1): 'Every contract to supply goods is to be treated as including a term that the quality of the goods is satisfactory.' and s 31(1) ('(1) A term of a contract to supply goods is not binding on the consumer to the extent that it would exclude or restrict the trader's liability arising under any of these provisions—

(a) Section 9 (goods to be of satisfactory quality); ...'

[4] *Courtaulds Northern Textiles Ltd v Andrew* [1979] IRLR 84 (EAT); *Post Office v Roberts* [1980] IRLR 347 (EAT); *Woods v WM Car Services Ltd* [1981] ICR 666 (EAT); *Bliss v South East Thames RHA* [1987] ICR 700 (CA). See *Chitty on Contracts*, 33rd edn by H Beale (gen ed) (London: Sweet & Maxwell/Thomson Reuters, 2018) para 40-151. On implied terms in employment contracts see further below, pp 770 ff.

[5] See 19.12 (EN), below, p 785.

[6] cf below, p 790.

types (sale, services, etc) or is *sui generis*, a 'one-off' contract. The aim is to give the reader an idea of how general contract law has to be supplemented by specific rules.

A good illustration of the differing approaches is provided by legislation and cases on a point about leases of real property. When several tenants have to use 'common parts' of a building, such as stairways and lifts, is the landlord obliged to keep the common parts clean and in working order? France and Germany have statutory provisions which apply.

Code civil   **19.1 (FR)**

Article 1719: A lessor is bound, by the nature of the contract, and without need of any particular stipulation:

1° To deliver the thing leased to the lessee 'and, where the main dwelling of the latter is concerned, a decent lodging' (Act no 2000-1208 of 13 Dec 2000);

2° To maintain that thing in order so that it can serve the use for which it has been let;

3° To secure to the lessee a peaceful enjoyment for the duration of the lease;

4° (Act no 46-682 of 13 April 1946) To secure also the permanence and quality of plantings.

Article 1720: A lessor is bound to deliver the thing in good repair of whatever character. He must, during the term of the lease, make all the repairs which may become necessary, other than those incumbent upon lessees.

Note

Under Article 1719(2) Cciv, the owner is under 'an obligation to maintain certain common parts' (in the case, to keep the stairs clean): Cass soc 6 February 1958.[7]

BGB   **19.2 (DE)**

§ 536: Rent reduction for material and legal defects

(1) The lessee is entitled to withhold the rent, wholly or in part, if at the time when the thing leased is handed over to the lessee, it is vitiated by a defect which is such as to nullify or reduce its fitness for its intended use under the contract, or if such a defect comes into existence during the course of the lease …

Notes

(1) The rental of a flat includes the rental of those parts of the building which are necessary for access to and use of the flat (such as stairs, lifts), and the landlord is obliged to ensure that they are fit for their contractual purpose and can be safely used.[8]

(2) § 536a BGB entitles the lessee to claim damages if a defect as defined in § 536 exists at the time when the thing is handed over to him or if such defect develops

---

[7] Cass soc 6 February 1958, D 1958, 271, JCP 1959.II.11115, annotated by B Starck (in this case the owner had contracted out the performance of his duties to a third person).

[8] Palandt/Weidenkaff § 535 paras 16, 34, 36, 38, 60.

during the lease. However, in the latter case, the lessee must show that the damages were caused by the lessor's negligent failure to take the care that would be expected from a reasonable lessor under the circumstances.

In England, the equivalent case depended on whether a term could be 'implied' into the lease:

House of Lords   **19.3 (EN)**

Liverpool City Council v Irwin[9]

When a flat is in a tower block, the landlord is under an implied obligation to use reasonable care to keep the common areas, such as stairways, lifts and rubbish chutes, in good repair.

Facts: The appellants were tenants of an apartment on the ninth floor of a 15 storey block containing some seventy dwelling units erected and owned by the respondents, a municipal corporation. Owing in part to vandalism, in part to non-cooperation by the tenants and in part to inaction by the local authority, serious defects in the common parts of the building developed, including a continual failure of the lifts, lack of lighting on the stairs, dangerous condition of the staircase with unguarded holes giving access to the rubbish chutes, etc. The tenancy agreement imposed a number of obligations on the tenants but said nothing concerning the obligations of the respondents. When the appellants refused to pay rent the respondents sought an order for possession of their apartment, and the appellants counterclaimed alleging that the respondents had been in breach of an implied duty to keep the common parts of the block in repair and the lights in working order.

Held: The landlords were under an implied obligation to take reasonable care to keep the common areas, such as stairways, lifts and rubbish chutes, in good repair; but there was no evidence that they had failed to use reasonable care.

Judgment: LORD WILBERFORCE: [After stating that the written tenancy agreement contained nothing on the obligations of the respondents:] We have then a contract which is partly, but not wholly, stated in writing. In order to complete it, in particular to give it a bilateral character, it is necessary to take account of the actions of the parties and the circumstances. As actions of the parties, we must note the granting of possession by the corporation and reservation by it of the 'common parts'—stairs, lifts, chutes etc. As circumstances we must include the nature of the premises, viz a maisonette for family use on the ninth floor of a high block, one which is occupied by a large number of other tenants, all using the common parts and dependent on them, none of them having any expressed obligation to maintain or repair them.

To say that the construction of a complete contract out of these elements involves a process of 'implication' may be correct: it would be so if implication means the supplying of what is not expressed. But there are varieties of implications which the courts think fit to make and they do not necessarily involve the same process. Where there is, on the face of it, a complete, bilateral contract, the courts are sometimes willing to add terms to it, as implied terms; this is very common in mercantile contracts where there is an

---

[9] [1977] AC 239, 253–56.

established usage; in that case the courts are spelling out what both parties know and would, if asked, unhesitatingly agree to be part of the bargain. In other cases, where there is an apparently complete bargain, the courts are willing to add a term on the ground that without it the contract will not work ... This is, as was pointed out by the majority in the Court of Appeal, a strict test—though the degree of strictness seems to vary with the current legal trend, and I think that they were right not to accept it as applicable here. There is a third variety of implication, that which I think Lord Denning MR favours, or at least did favour in this case, and that is the implication of reasonable terms. But though I agree with many of his instances, which in fact fall under one or other of the preceding heads, I cannot go so far as to endorse his principle; indeed, it seems to me, with respect, to extend a long, and undesirable, way beyond sound authority.

The present case, in my opinion, represents a fourth category or, I would rather say, a fourth shade on a continuous spectrum. The court here is simply concerned to establish what the contract is, the parties not having themselves fully stated the terms. In this sense the court is searching for what must be implied. [His Lordship then stated the parties' legal positions and continued:]

My Lords, in order to be able to choose between these, it is necessary to define what test is to be applied, and I do not find this difficult. In my opinion such obligation should be read into the contract as the nature of the contract itself implicitly requires, no more, no less; a test in other words of necessity. The relationship accepted by the corporation is that of landlord and tenant; the tenant accepts obligations accordingly, in relation, *inter alia*, to the stairs, the lifts and the chutes. All these are not just facilities, or conveniences provided at discretion; they are essentials of the tenancy without which life in the dwellings, as a tenant, is not possible. To leave the landlord free of contractual obligation as regards these matters, and subject only to administrative or political pressure, is, in my opinion, totally inconsistent with the nature of this relationship. The subject-matter of the lease (high-rise blocks) and the relationship created by the tenancy demands, of its nature, some contractual obligation on the landlord ...

It remains to define the standard. My Lords, if, as I think, the test of the existence of the term is necessity the standard must surely not exceed what is necessary having regard to the circumstances. To imply an absolute obligation to repair would go beyond what is a necessary legal incident and would indeed be unreasonable. An obligation to take reasonable care to keep in reasonable repair and usability is what fits the requirement of the case. Such a definition involves—and I think rightly—recognition that the tenants themselves have their responsibilities. What it is reasonable to expect of a landlord has a clear relation to what a reasonable set of tenants should do for themselves.

[The other Law Lords delivered speeches to the same effect.]

Notes

(1) Lord Wilberforce distinguishes different types of implied terms. We will consider the details of these categories, and in particular terms that are implied 'on the ground that without it the contract will not work' (or, as they are sometimes called, 'terms implied in fact') in the next chapter. For the moment it suffices to note that Lord Wilberforce states clearly that, in this case, 'The court here is simply concerned to establish what the contract is, the parties not having themselves fully stated the terms. In this sense the court is searching for what must be implied.' Since what was

held to be implied here would presumably apply (unless the parties agreed something different) to every lease of a building with common parts, this 'fourth category' (as Lord Wilberforce puts it) is usually classified as a term implied in law, as opposed to terms that would apply only to the particular contract, which are called 'terms implied in fact'. Terms implied in fact will be considered in the next chapter.

(2) Note the balancing of the interests of (typical) landlords and (typical) tenants in the last paragraph cited from the judgment. It is such a balanced outcome that parties would presumably have intended.

A second example of the difference in approach is from contracts of employment. In employment contracts the obligations of the parties are left undefined in many cases and, in English law, are settled by the courts through the device of the implied term. Thus it has been held that the employee is under an implied duty to use proper care in the performance of his duties, not to enter into competition with his employer, not to divulge or improperly use confidential information acquired in the course of his employment and, within certain limits, to disclose to the employer information harmful to the employer's interest. It has also been held that employees engaging in 'go slow' or 'work to rule' action are in breach of an implied duty to serve their employers faithfully with a view of promoting their commercial interests.[10] On the other hand, an employer is bound by an implied duty to take all reasonable care for the safety of the employee in the course of his or her work.[11] Again, a similar duty is codified in German law:

BGB   **19.4 (DE)**

§ 618: Duty to undertake protective measures

(1) An employer has to fit up and maintain rooms, equipment and apparatus which he has to provide for the performance of the service, and so to regulate services which are to be performed under his orders or his direction, that the employee is protected against danger to life and health as far as the nature of the service permits.

Traditionally, English judges tended to be more reluctant in implying employers' duties than continental courts. However, in recent years employment contracts have become a fertile breeding ground for the judicial development of implied terms.

House of Lords   **19.5 (EN)**

Malik v Bank of Credit and Commerce International SA[12]

In a contract of employment there is an implied obligation on each party not to act, without reasonable and proper cause, in a manner that is likely to destroy or seriously damage the relationship of confidence and trust between employer and employee.

---

[10] See *Secretary of Employment v ASLEF* [1972] 2 QB 455, 498, 508 (CA), and BGH 31 January 1978, BGHZ 70, 277.

[11] *Wilsons & Clyde Coal Co v English* [1938] AC 57 (HL).

[12] [1997] UKHL 23, [1998] AC 20.

Facts: Mr Malik and Mr Mahmud worked for the Bank of Credit and Commerce International (BCCI). BCCI went insolvent due to massive fraud, connection with terrorists, money-laundering, extortion and other criminal activity on a global scale. Malik and Mahmud lost their jobs When they sought employment elsewhere they could not find jobs. They sued BCCI for their loss of job prospects, alleging that their failure to secure new jobs was due to the reputational damage they had suffered from working with the bank. However, there was no express term in their employment contracts according to which they were entitled to claim damages for loss of reputation caused by a breach of contract by his employer. Neither does English law have an established head of action for such 'stigma compensation'.

Held: Malik and Mahmud were entitled to damages against BCCI.

Judgment: LORD STEYN: It will be convenient first to examine the legal position regarding the implied term relied on by the employees. ...

The implied term of mutual trust and confidence

The employees do not rely on a term implied in fact. They do not therefore rely on an individualised term to be implied from the particular provisions of their employment contracts considered against their specific contextual setting. Instead they rely on a standardised term implied by law, that is, on a term which is said to be an incident of all contracts of employment: *Scally v Southern Health and Social Services Board* [1992] 1 AC 294, 307B. Such implied terms operate as default rules. The parties are free to exclude or modify them. But it is common ground that in the present case the particular terms of the contracts of employment of the two employees could not affect an implied obligation of mutual trust and confidence.

The employer's primary case is based on a formulation of the implied term that has been applied at first instance and in the Court of Appeal. It imposes reciprocal duties on the employer and employee. Given that this case is concerned with alleged obligations of an employer I will concentrate on its effect on the position of employers. For convenience I will set out the term again. It is expressed to impose an obligation that the employer shall not:

> '... without reasonable and proper cause, conduct itself in a manner calculated and likely to destroy or seriously damage the relationship of confidence and trust between employer and employee.'

See *Woods v WM Car Services (Peterborough) Ltd* [1981] ICR 666, 670 (Browne-Wilkinson J.), approved in ... A useful anthology of the cases applying this term, or something like it, is given in *Sweet and Maxwell's Encyclopedia of Employment Law* (loose leaf ed) Vol 1, para 1.507, pp 1467–1470. The evolution of the term is a comparatively recent development. The obligation probably has its origin in the general duty of co-operation between contracting parties: BA Hepple, *Employment Law*, 4th ed (1981), paras 291–292, pp 134–135. The reason for this development is part of the history of the development of employment law in this century. The notion of a 'master and servant' relationship became obsolete. Lord Slynn of Hadley recently noted 'the changes which have taken place in the employment and employee relationship, with far greater duties imposed on the employer in the past, whether by statute or judicial decision, to care for the physical, financial and even psychological welfare of the employee': *Spring v Guardian Assurance Plc* [1995] 2 AC 296, at 325B. A striking illustration of this change is *Scally* to which I have already referred where the House of Lords implied a term that all employees in a certain category had to be notified by an employer of their entitlement to certain benefits. It was the change in legal culture which made possible the evolution of the implied term of trust and confidence.

There was some debate at the hearing about the possible interaction of the implied obligation of confidence and trust with other more specific terms implied by law. It is true that the implied term adds little to the employee's implied obligations to serve his employer loyally and not to act contrary to his employer's interests. The major importance of the implied duty of trust and confidence lies in its impact on the obligations of the employer: Douglas Brodie, 'Recent cases, Commentary, The Heart of the Matter: Mutual Trust and Confidence' (1996) 25 *ILJ* 121. And the implied obligation as formulated is apt to cover the great diversity of situations in which a balance has to be struck between an employer's interest in managing his business as he sees fit and the employee's interest in not being unfairly and improperly exploited.

The evolution of the implied term of trust and confidence is a fact. It has not yet been endorsed by your Lordships' House. It has proved a workable principle in practice. It has not been the subject of adverse criticism in any decided cases and it has been welcomed in academic writings. I regard the emergence of the implied obligation of mutual trust and confidence as a sound development.

Notes

(1) Lord Steyn is very explicit about using the mechanism of implied terms as a vehicle for the development and modernisation of English employment law. Employment law is a politically sensitive matter. Imposing (implied) obligations on employers will increase production costs and ultimately make British goods less competitive in a global market. Should judges make such decisions?

(2) We have noted elsewhere that English contract law is hostile to the idea of an overarching principle of good faith.[13] How does *Malik* fit in?

19.1.B NATURE OF THE DEBTOR'S OBLIGATION

As is shown by the decision in *Liverpool CC v Irwin*[14]—that the landlords were only obliged to take reasonable steps to keep the lifts, etc in working order—we must consider the nature of the obligation that the debtor has in each situation. In particular, is the debtor undertaking that a particular outcome will be brought about, or only that he will use reasonable efforts (or perhaps his best efforts—there are many possibilities) to bring it about? We will see, for example, that normally a seller of goods is obliged to deliver goods of the correct quality by the date for delivery, and if it fails—if the goods are not of the correct quality or are delivered late—the seller will not have performed its obligations and the buyer will have a remedy for non-performance. But the fact that the creditor has not obtained what she hoped for does not always mean that the debtor has failed to perform. In many contracts for services the supplier's obligation is only to use reasonable care and skill to seek to bring about the desired result. Under a contract for medical treatment the doctor's contractual obligation is normally one to act with reasonable care and skill, and if the doctor has done so the contractual obligation will have been fulfilled

---

[13] See above, p 10.
[14] 19.3 (EN), above, p 768.

even if the patient has not been cured. The patient who has been treated with reasonable care and skill but who has not been cured will have a remedy only if she can show that the doctor had undertaken some stricter obligation—which is possible but would be very unusual[15]—and has not fulfilled this stricter obligation.

In French law this difference is expressed by asking whether the obligation is one of result (*de résultat*) or to use reasonable care (*de moyens*). German law recognises similar distinctions in the categorisation of different types of contracts. English law also recognises the distinction between obligations to achieve a particular result and obligations merely to use reasonable care. The basic rule is often said to be that contractual liability is 'strict'. In *Raineri v Miles*,[16] Lord Edmund-Davies said:

> In relation to a claim for damages for breach of contract, it is, in general, immaterial why the defendant failed to fulfil his obligations and certainly no defence to plead that he had done his best.[17]

It is true that if the defendant has failed to perform its obligation, it is no defence that its failure was 'not its fault', but it has first to be asked: what was the debtor's obligation? If the obligation in question was the seller's obligation under a contract of sale to deliver the correct goods on time, it is true that the reason why the goods were not of the correct quality or were delivered late is immaterial. This is often referred to as 'strict liability'. But under a contract for services the debtor is normally only obliged to carry out the service with reasonable care and skill.[18]

The distinction between an obligation to achieve a particular result and obligation to use 'best efforts' is found in the UNIDROIT Principles of International Commercial Contracts (UNIDROIT PICC).

UNIDROIT Principles   **19.6 (INT)**

Article 5.1.4: Duty to achieve a specific result. Duty of best efforts
  (1) To the extent that an obligation of a party involves a duty to achieve a specific result, that party is bound to achieve that result.
  (2) To the extent that an obligation of a party involves a duty of best efforts in the performance of an activity, that party is bound to make such efforts as would be made by a reasonable person of the same kind in the same circumstances.

Article 5.1.5: Determination of kind of duty involved
  In determining the extent to which an obligation of a party involves a duty of best efforts in the performance of an activity or a duty to achieve a specific result, regard shall be had, among other factors, to
  (a) the way in which the obligation is expressed in the contract;
  (b) the contractual price and other terms of the contract;
  (c) the degree of risk normally involved in achieving the expected result;
  (d) the ability of the other party to influence the performance of the obligation.

---

[15] See below, p 782.
[16] [1981] AC 1050 (HL).
[17] ibid, 1086.
[18] See below, p 781.

Note

The Principles of European Contract Law (PECL) do not contain any provisions on the distinction between *obligations de moyens* and *obligations de résultat*. It was thought that there can be a great variety of types of obligation (for example, there are different standards of care; or the duty may be to use 'best efforts' rather than 'reasonable care'). So, it was considered that it was not possible to lay down useful general rules on which obligation would apply in which circumstances. But the distinction is discussed in the Comment to Article 6:102, where it is suggested that the relevant factors are exactly the same as those listed in Article 5.1.5 of UNIDROIT PICC.

We will explore the distinction between obligations to achieve a particular result and lesser obligations, such as to use reasonable care, in Section 19.2. First, however, we need to make a further introductory point.

19.1.C RELATIONSHIP TO IMPOSSIBILITY OF PERFORMANCE

A further point by way of introduction is that, even where the obligation is one 'of result', or in English law there is 'strict' liability, the debtor's obligation is seldom completely unqualified or its liability absolute. The fact that the debtor has not achieved the promised outcome does not necessarily mean that the debtor is in breach of contract and will be subject to a full panoply of remedies that are made available in cases of breach (see Part Five of this book). This is because each system recognises that in certain circumstances the debtor may be excused from its obligation. In Chapter 28 of this book we will see that in each system, if without the fault of either party it becomes impossible to perform the contract, the debtor may be excused. None of the systems will attempt to make a debtor actually perform an obligation that has become impossible; nor, generally, will the debtor be liable in damages for non-performance if the debtor did not cause the impossibility. The mechanisms by which this is achieved differ from system to system. Broadly speaking, in German law, unless he has undertaken a stricter liability, the debtor will not normally be liable in damages if he was not at fault.[19] In French law, if performance of an obligation has become impossible because of an event which was 'irresistible, unforeseeable and external to the debtor', the debtor may raise the defence of *cause étrangère* or *force majeure*.[20] In English law, the debtor may be excused under the doctrine of 'frustration' if unforeseeable events have unavoidably made it permanently impossible to perform the substance of the contract.

The effect of supervening impossibility is viewed differently between the systems. So, in the continental systems, the excuse—for example, *cause étrangère*, *nachträgliche*

---

[19] See below, pp 896 ff. In addition the doctrine of *Wegfall der Geschäftsgrundlage*, based on the principle of good faith in the performance of contractual obligations (§§ 313 and 242 BGB), may exceptionally be applicable to allow relief of the debtor from obligations which have become disproportionately burdensome due to supervening circumstances. See below, pp 1222 ff.

[20] See below, pp 1173 ff.

Unmöglichkeit (subsequent impossibility for which the debtor is not responsible)—is usually seen as affecting the remedies available to the creditor; the creditor may not seek specific performance or damages, but in principle it retains the choice whether to terminate the contract or not. In the common law, the doctrine of frustration discharges the obligations of both parties automatically, and the only remedies available will be by way of restitution or under the Law Reform (Frustrated Contracts) Act 1943, which provides restitution-like remedies.[21]

It is worth noting that the English doctrine of frustration is narrower than its continental counterparts, particularly when the impossibility is only temporary.[22] Thus, for example, unless the parties have agreed otherwise, a seller of goods is liable for late delivery even if this was caused by an Act of God or industrial action; a builder is liable for failure to complete the work on time even if the delays were caused by unforeseeably bad weather; and so on. *Force majeure*, which is not sufficiently serious to frustrate the contract, is not a defence.[23] The narrowness of the doctrine of frustration may explain why English lawyers continue to refer to contract liability as 'strict' when in reality it is subject to this defence.

Cases of impossibility will be considered in detail in Chapter 28. At this stage, we merely need to note that in each system there are cases in which the law does not permit a debtor to rely on a defence of 'not my fault' even though the debtor's failure to perform was in fact not his fault, or on a defence of impossibility even though in a non-legal sense the reason for the impossibility might be viewed as something the debtor could not have avoided. Thus in German law there are some instances of liability without fault. These cases are seen as exceptional to the basic rule, but they are wide in scope. For example, absence of fault is no defence to liability for defects in goods sold and in services rendered under a work contract (*Werkvertrag*) if the seller or contractor has given a guarantee to this effect, nor to a seller's failure to supply generic goods if the seller has assumed the risk of procurement.[24] In such cases the debtor may be said to have 'guarantee liability'. Likewise, in neither French nor English law is an inability to obtain generic goods treated as, respectively, *cause étrangère* or frustration, and the debtor will be liable for non-performance even in such cases. Likewise, it is very doubtful whether a seller who has supplied non-conforming goods can ever rely on *cause étrangère* or frustration as a defence. Again this seems to create a form of 'guarantee' liability.

In German law, even where the debtor has undertaken a stricter form of liability than liability for intention or negligence,[25] the defence of subsequent impossibility may provide an excuse. Again, however, there are some situations in which impossibility is not accepted as a defence to a claim for damages.[26] For example, it is considered that impossibility is never an excuse for failing to pay.[27]

---

[21] See 28.15 (EN), below, p 1205.
[22] See below, p 1206.
[23] See below, p 1199.
[24] §§ 276(1)(1), 443, 639 BGB; cf Palandt/Grüneberg § 276 paras 29–33; Palandt/Sprau § 634 paras 35–38.
[25] See above, p 774.
[26] Compare below, p 1185.
[27] Though in some cases where there has been an extreme change of circumstances, the court may hold that the contract must be adjusted. See below, pp 1222 ff.

The net result seems to be that each of the three laws works with three categories. In French law, (1) if the obligation is one *de moyens*, the debtor is obliged only to use reasonable care; (2) if the obligation is one *de résultat*, the debtor will be liable if the result was not achieved, unless the debtor can show it was prevented from achieving the result by a *cause étrangère*; and (3) in certain situations of *obligation de garantie*, even a *cause étrangère* is no defence. In English law, (1) if the obligation is one to use reasonable care and skill, there will be no liability unless a failure to use care and skill is shown; (2) if liability is strict, the debtor will be liable if the result promised has not been achieved, unless the debtor can prove discharge by frustration; and (3) there are certain types of obligation to which the doctrine of frustration seems not to apply, so that in effect liability is absolute.

19.2 OBLIGATIONS TO ACHIEVE A RESULT AND LESSER OBLIGATIONS

19.2.A FRENCH LAW

Does it suffice for a creditor who has not received what she expected to show simply that, or must she show also that this was due to the imprudence, negligence or bad faith of the debtor? In French law, this depends on whether the debtor's obligation was one of result (*de résultat*) or to use reasonable care (*de moyens*). The distinction is accepted in doctrine and case law[28] but it is not set down explicitly in the Code civil even after the 2016 reforms.[29] However, it can be seen in the following texts:

Code civil   **19.7 (FR)**

Article 1197: An obligation to deliver a thing entails an obligation to look after it until delivery, taking all the care of a reasonable person in doing so.

Article 1231-1: A debtor is condemned, where appropriate, to the payment of damages either on the ground of the non-performance or a delay in performance of an obligation, unless he justifies this on the ground that performance was prevented by force majeure.

> *Note*
>
> The first impression is that these texts are contradictory. Article 1197 presupposes that liability requires proof of fault. In contrast, Article 1231-1 only refers to non-performance and does not mention the necessity of a fault, but denies liability in the

---

[28] See B Nicholas, *The French Law of Contract* (2nd edn, Oxford: Clarendon Press, 1992) 50–56.

[29] In contrast, Art 1364 of the *Avant-projet Catala* provided: 'Where a debtor undertakes to procure a result within the meaning of article 1149, non-performance is established from the mere fact that the result is not achieved, unless the debtor justifies this failure by reference to an external cause … In all other situations, a debtor must make reparation only if he has failed to use all necessary care.'

case of *force majeure*. There was a similar contradiction in the former version of the Code Civil between Article 1137 (which required a party who was to safeguard a thing to use 'the care of a prudent administrator') and former Article 1147 (the precursor to new Article 1231-1).[30] In order to overcome this contradiction, the following interpretation has been set forth, both by case law and authors: that the mere non-performance of an obligation does not suffice to give rise to the debtor's liability—a contractual fault is needed. However, while such a fault was presumed in former Article 1147, it had to be proven in former Article 1137.[31] This combined interpretation of Articles 1137 and 1147 gave support to the major distinction between *obligations de moyens* and *obligations de résultat*.

In 1925 René Demogue wrote that contractual responsibility always presupposes proof of fault, but that the proof was more or less easy according to whether the obligation was one of *moyens* or one of result.[32] For him this distinction was not a *summa divisio* of obligations. It became that under the influence of Henri and Léon Mazeaud,[33] though using different terminology (obligation of prudence and *obligation déterminée*); then a third category was added, so that nowadays there are three: *obligations de moyens, de résultat* and *de garantie*. (An example of *garantie* liability in French law is the case of a defect in goods sold, mentioned earlier;[34] this is considered in detail in Section 3.A of this chapter.) The distinction was rapidly adopted by the case law, which continues to refer to it despite the criticism which it has attracted.

The fundamental idea that lies behind this distinction is that one must scrutinise both what has been promised and what can reasonably be expected. If a precise result is promised (for instance, delivery of goods at a certain date), it is an *obligation de résultat*; if, on the contrary, one promises to use all appropriate means in order to achieve a result (for instance, in order to cure a patient), it is an *obligation de moyens*.

In fact, the distinction is more complex than it first appears. Some *obligations de résultat* are *allégées*: the debtor can free himself from his liability by proving that he has committed no fault (see, for instance, Article 1732 Cciv on the lessee's obligations). Some *obligations de résultat* are *aggravées*: it may well happen that the debtor cannot free himself by proving that non-performance is due to a *cause étrangère*; it is then considered an *obligation de garantie*.

We have already seen an example of the distinction between *moyens* and *résultat*, in the case of the exploding bottle of lemonade.[35] In comparison, the occupier of business

---

[30] P Malaurie, L Aynès and P Stoffel-Munck, *Droit des obligations* (9th edn, Paris: LGDJ, 2017) nos. 939–41.

[31] F Terré, P Simler and Y Lequette, *Les obligations* (11th edn, Paris: Dalloz, 2013) nos. 571 ff; M Fabre-Magnan, *Droit des obligations*, vol 1, *Contrat et engagement unilatéral* (4th edn, Paris: PUF, 2016) no. 213.

[32] Demogue, *Traité des obligations*, vol V (Paris: A Rousseau, 1925) nos. 1237 ff.

[33] H Mazeaud, L Mazeaud and A Tunc, *Traité théorique et pratique de la responsabilité civile contractuelle et délictuelle*, vol I (6th edn, Paris: Montchrestien, 1965) nos. 103–2 ff.

[34] Above, p 775.

[35] See 8.10 (FR) above, p 221.

premises is usually held to be under an obligation to take only reasonable care for the safety of its customers.[36] A single contract may contain different obligations, some of which are *de résultat* and others *de moyens*.

Nicholas made the point that it is hard to know when the French courts will characterise the obligation as *de moyens* and when as *de résultat*.[37] As he said, it is hard to see why a cinema owner and other occupiers are usually under only the first obligation while the operator of 'dodgem' cars at a fairground is bound by an obligation of result in relation to the safety of customers, so that a customer who was injured by the shock of a collision with another dodgem car could recover damages without showing fault on the part of the operator.[38] In practice, in order to distinguish between the *obligations de résultat* and *de moyens*, French judges have over the years had recourse to the criterion of the *aléa*. The test is the extent to which the result depends on external circumstances (or *aléas*). If these are predominant, the obligation is only *de moyens*, while if they are merely accessory, the obligation is *de résultat*. Modern French doctrine points out that this distinction lacks rigour.[39] But to some extent, it at least forces the judge to decide precisely what kind of obligation the debtor has. It is generally considered that obligations to transfer property (*de donner*) and obligations not to do something (*de ne pas faire*) are obligations *de résultat* while obligation to do something (*de faire*) are either *de moyens* or *de résultat*. If they relate to the safety of the person, they tend to be *obligations de résultat*.[40] This solution has long been established by case law as regards the carriage of persons and now tends to be extended to all sorts of contractual obligations, such as obligations to give information or advice, which also concern persons and their safety. (For instance, an association was held responsible for physical harm to a person who was injured while visiting a ruined castle.[41])

The question of *obligations de résultat* and *de moyens* is connected to a wider debate taking place in France as regards 'contractual responsibility'.[42] The French legal system distinguishes between delictual liability (*responsabilité délictuelle*) and contractual liability (*responsabilité contractuelle*).[43] ('Civil liability' includes both contractual and delictual liability.) Among those who favour retaining the distinction between contractual and delictual liability (a vast majority of authors[44]), different views are set forth.

---

[36] See Cass civ 17 March 1947, D 1947.1.269: a cinema owner is only obliged to use measures of prudence and reasonable care for the safety of spectators.

[37] Nicholas (n 28 above) 54.

[38] K Zweigert and H Kötz, *Introduction to Comparative Law* (3rd edn, Oxford: Clarendon Press, 1998) 501 ff.

[39] Terré et al (n 31 above) no. 586, who remarked that the distinction, based as it is on the criterion of *aléa* (if the *aléa* is strong, the obligation is *de moyens*), is in fact sometimes used to further judicial policy (*à des fins de pure politique jurisprudentielle*). Thus the courts may hold that one party is under an obligation of result when they think that the other party to the relevant type of contract needs to be protected: see below the example of contracts for the carriage of persons.

[40] A Bénabent, *Droit des obligations* (16th edn, Paris: LGDJ, 2017) no. 414.

[41] The same idea inspires, in the French Code pénal, Art 223-1 which creates the *délit de risque causé à autrui*.

[42] Among the opponents, see D Tallon, 'L'inexécution du contrat: pour une autre présentation' RTD civ 1994, 223; add P Rémy, 'La 'responsabilité contractuelle', histoire d'un faux concept, RTD civ 1997, 323.

[43] See above, p 148.

[44] See, ie, C Larroumet, 'Pour la responsabilité contractuelle' in *Le droit privé à la fin du XXe siècle: Études offertes à Pierre Catala* (Paris: Litec, 2001) 543; G Viney, 'La responsabilité contractuelle en question' in *Études offertes à Jacques Ghestin: Le contrat au début du XXIe siècle* (Paris: LGDJ, 2001) 921. On this

According to a leading author in the field of civil liability, Viney, the specificity of the contractual liability should be reduced to a minimum and delictual liability should serve as the model. This approach was followed in the Catala project. The *exposé des motifs* of the Catala draft explains the current debate and justifies the position of the group directed by Viney.[45] The *Reform Bill on Civil Liability* above, p 149 (March 2017)[46] goes further in this direction, with a Chapter II on the Conditions of liability, starting with a Section I entitled 'Provisions common to contractual and extra-contractual liability' (these provisions would, if adopted, become Articles 1235ff of the Code civil). After some vivid debate among the members of the working group, the Bill maintained the *non-cumul* principle, with an important exception in favour of victims of physical injury.[47] Indeed, the fact that there is a distinction between the two sorts of liability (delictual and contractual) explains the *non-cumul* principle (in French law, a different regime still applies to each of them).[48]

19.2.B GERMAN LAW

BGB   **19.8 (DE)**

§ 611: Typical contractual duties in a service contract

(1) By means of a service contract, a person who promises services is obliged to perform the services promised, and the other party is obliged to grant the agreed remuneration.

(2) The subject-matter of a service contract can be services of any kind.

§ 631: Typical contractual duties in a contract for works

By means of a contract for works, the contractor is obliged to produce the work promised, and the customer is obliged to grant the agreed remuneration.

The subject matter of a contract for works can be the production or alteration of a thing, as well as another result to be achieved by work or by a service.

Fikentscher and Heinemann on the law of obligations[49]   **19.9 (DE)**

The distinction between a service contract and a contract for works is particularly difficult because in both types of contract the debtor is obliged to render a service to the creditor.

---

debate and its current implications, particularly with regard to the concept of fault, see Malaurie et al (n 30 above) nos. 933 ff.

[45] Avant-projet Catala, *Exposé des motifs* written by G Viney, p 161, see Art 1341 of this draft. On 15 July 2009, the Senate published a Report in view of the reform of the law of civil liability. A proposition was deposited at the Senate in July 2010. After a comparative survey and an analysis of all the arguments that have been developed by French authors, it recommended keeping the distinction between contractual and delictual liability: French Senate, *Rapport d'information* no. 558 (2008–09) de MM A Anziani and L Béteille, www.senat.fr/rap/r08-558/r08-558_mono.html.

[46] www.textes.justice.gouv.fr/textes-soumis-a-concertation-10179/projet-de-reforme-de-la-responsabilite-civile-traduit-en-anglais-30553.html, see above, pp 131, 153.

[47] AG Castermans, D Dankers-Hagenaars, AD de La Batie, JS Borghetti, C De Cabarrus et al, 'Regards Comparatistes sur la Réforme de la Responsabilité Civile' RIDC 2017, 5. Interestingly, although it is based on the same provisions of the Code civil, Belgian law does not have the 'non-cumul' rule, as noted by Bénabent (n 40 above) no. 510.

[48] Bénabent (n 40 above) no. 510. See 6.2.B.2(ii), above, pp 149–54.

[49] W Fikentscher and A Heinemann, *Schuldrecht Allgemeiner und Besonderer Teil* (11th edn, Berlin: de Gruyter, 2017) paras 1129–31.

Usually, the distinction is made according to the set phrase that in a *service contract* the obligation is the *provision* of a service as such, ie the mere *performance of a particular activity* and therefore the labour as such, while in a *contract for works* the debtor is obliged to *effect a result* or outcome precisely by way of his activity. The decisive criterion is therefore whether the debtor is paid for his merely becoming active or only for a certain result.

This distinction is frequently *not very helpful*, though, because in a service contract, too, the activity is normally sought with regard to a certain result which, however, the obligor cannot guarantee or does not want to guarantee. For example, the doctor's patient wants to be healthy and the participants of a lawyers' cram school want to perform well in their exams. However, in these cases the person obliged to render the service cannot promise the results strived for, and indeed he does not intend to do so, because their achievement is beyond his sphere of influence. It follows that a contract is not turned into a contract for works simply because the person to whom the service is owed has an interest in the successful rendering of the services. On the other hand, the pursuit of the activity itself can be the result which is relevant for a contract for works, without a need for the achievement of a further result. For example, in the case of a theatre performance all that is owed is the performance of the play; a further result, such as a positive response of the audience, is not owed.

It is therefore helpful to pay *attention to the legal consequences*: does the obligor intend to be answerable for the result? Which of the two types of contract is more in tune with the interests of the parties? For these purposes, the allocation of liability is very important: in the case of a contract for works, the obligor is liable for the realisation of the result that is to be achieved; performance is only achieved once the result is achieved. If the result is not achieved the contractor cannot claim the agreed remuneration even if he has orderly rendered his services. He therefore bears the risk … In contrast, the person obliged by a service contract is not burdened with this risk, ie he can claim the agreed remuneration even if the result aimed at by conducting the activity is not realised. The question therefore is always whether, according to the views of the parties, the obligor is meant to bear the *risk for achieving the result*. Whether one or the other is true must be decided by interpretation, having regard to all the circumstances of the individual case. …

Moreover, there are certain indicia which can facilitate the classification of the transaction as falling under §§ 611ff or 631ff respectively. For example, it points towards the existence of a contract for works if the parties are very specific in determining the task to be fulfilled and the scope of the works or if the remuneration agreed is so high that it may be inferred that it was meant to cover the risk of failing to achieve the result. As opposed to this, a general and ongoing activity is characteristic for a service contract. Furthermore, for the most part, there will be a service contract if the realisation of the result does not only depend on the efforts and skills of the obligor, but also on circumstances which are beyond his control (eg those lying in the person of the creditor). If the obligor performs under instructions of, and shares responsibilities with the obligee there will also mostly be a service contract. In many cases, the classification of a particular contract as a service contract or as a contract for works simply depends on usage or tradition.

Typical examples of service contracts are ordinary, salaried employment contracts (*Arbeitsverträge*) and so-called 'free' service contracts, eg contracts with solicitors, tax advisors, doctors and hospitals. Contracts for works include contracts for the construction of buildings, for the repair of movables and for the production of artworks and other non-corporeal items (eg drafting an expert opinion or writing of a casebook).

The classification of a transaction as one or the other contract matters because the BGB has different default rules and, to a lesser extent, mandatory rules for each type of contract. As we will see in the relevant chapters, the ancillary obligations, the rules on termination and, most importantly, the other remedies for non-performance of service contracts and of contracts for works differ. However, when the issue is whether the debtor is liable in damages, the two types of contract do *not* differ with regard to the burden of proof required, as is the case in French law. As already noted,[50] and as we will see in more detail in Chapter 26 on damages, unless the debtor has given specific guarantees or has undertaken a particular risk, he is only liable for intentional and negligent conduct (§ 276 BGB), but the fault of the debtor does not have to be proved by the creditor; rather, it is for the debtor to show that he has not been at fault if he wishes to escape liability (reversed burden of proof according to § 280(1)(2) BGB). The general rules on the burden of proof in contract apply to all kinds of contract.

19.2.C ENGLISH LAW

We have already noted that for English lawyers the starting point tends to be that contractual liability is 'strict', but that in reality the debtor's obligation is often only one to use reasonable care and skill. This is the general rule in contracts for services, as is provided by Supply of Goods and Services Act 1982, section 13.[51]

Supply of Goods and Services Act 1982   **19.10 (EN)**

Section 13: Implied term about care and skill
In a contract for the supply of a service where the supplier is acting in the course of a business, there is an implied term that the supplier will carry out the service with reasonable care and skill.

Notes

(1) It would perhaps be more accurate to say that the obligation is one to see that reasonable care and skill are taken. This is because, if the debtor delegates performance to another, for instance to a subcontractor (as is permissible unless the performance involves a personal element or the contract prohibits delegation), and the subcontractor or other person to whom the work is delegated fails to use reasonable care and skill, the debtor will be liable, even though the debtor used reasonable care in selecting the subcontractor.

(2) Although the duty in contracts of service is usually only that described in section 13, it is possible that the debtor will be held to have warranted that it will achieve a particular result.[52] This is unusual. For example, the English Court of Appeal

---

[50] Above, p 775.
[51] For consumer contracts, see the equivalent provision in Consumer Rights Act 2015, s 49.
[52] For an example, see below, p 792.

781

refused to find that a doctor who performed an operation to sterilise a man was promising that the man would be rendered permanently sterile, even though the doctor told the patient that the operation was 'irreversible'. Thus the doctor was not liable when the operation, which had been carried out properly, reversed itself naturally, and as a result the man's wife became pregnant.[53] But in the next section we will see a case in which the Court of Appeal held that the designer of a building was under an obligation to ensure that the building would meet certain performance specifications.[54]

However, it is the case with many types of obligation in English law that liability to achieve what was promised is 'strict' and thus it is no defence to show that the non-performance was caused by something outside the debtor's control—unless, as suggested earlier, the event makes it permanently impossible to perform the substance of the contract, so that it is frustrated. Lesser kinds of impossibility, let alone the mere absence of fault, are no excuse. So, for example, a seller of goods is liable for late delivery even if this was caused by an Act of God or industrial action; a builder is liable for failure to complete the work on time even if the delays were caused by unforeseeably bad weather; and so on. *Force majeure*, which is not sufficiently serious to frustrate the contract, is not a defence.[55]

However, two points must be noted. The first is that contracts very commonly contain clauses altering the general rule. Thus sale contracts frequently contain *force majeure* clauses excusing late delivery for reasons outside the seller's control; building contracts frequently contain 'extension of time clauses' under which the employer must allow the contractor additional time for delays caused by bad weather, etc.[56]

The second point is that occasionally the courts have mitigated the normal rule (for the type of obligation) that the debtor is liable even in the absence of fault, by holding that, as a matter of interpretation of the particular contract (rather than as a rule of law), a non-performance caused by something not the debtor's fault provides an excuse. The result is that the debtor is not liable in damages, even though the contract is not frustrated. The most common case is where an employee or person due to perform personal services is prevented from doing so temporarily by illness.[57] The result is clearly close to the French doctrine of *cause étrangère*.

Conversely, as was mentioned earlier,[58] there are cases in which there may appear to be absolute liability because the doctrine of frustration will not apply. Thus, under the Sale of Goods Act 1979 the seller who sells in the course of a business is responsible for the goods being of satisfactory quality.[59] If the goods are not satisfactory, not only is it

---

[53] *Thake v Maurice* [1986] QB 644 (CA); on the facts, however, the doctor was held liable for negligence in failing to give the patient a warning of this possibility.

[54] *Greaves v Baynham Miekle*, 19.16 (EN), below, p 792.

[55] See further below, pp 1199 ff.

[56] See E McKendrick, *Force Majeure and Frustration of Contract* (2nd edn, London: Lloyd's of London Press, 1995) and G Treitel, *Frustration and Force Majeure* (3rd edn, London: Sweet & Maxwell, 2014).

[57] See, eg, *Poussard v Spiers & Pond* (1875–76) LR 1 QBD 410.

[58] See above, p 776.

[59] s 14 (as amended by the Sale and Supply of Goods Act 1994). See further below, p 785.

no defence that the seller was not at fault, it is also no defence that the defect could not have been discovered by any amount of skill and care.[60]

19.2.D CONCLUSION ON THE NATURE OF THE DEBTOR'S OBLIGATION

It might be argued that, though the systems have different starting points, the practical results reached are surprisingly similar. There is truth in this; and it is certainly the case that one system is in principle capable of reaching the same results as another. All three systems recognise both obligations to produce a result and obligations to use reasonable care. But the hesitation of the Commission on European Contract Law[61] to lay down general rules on *obligation de moyens* and *obligation de résultat* seems justified when it is seen that the systems by no means always categorise obligations in the same way—so the actual results even in everyday cases may be startlingly different. Two examples of these divergences will be seen when we consider the parties' obligations under particular types of contract in the next section of this chapter.

19.3 OBLIGATIONS IN TYPICAL CONTRACTS

In this section we look at some of the main obligations on a selection of typical contracts to see what the obligations are and whether they are obligations to achieve a particular result or merely to use best efforts or reasonable care. We will see that the systems sometimes reach very different conclusions on the latter question.

19.3.A SALE: THE SELLER'S OBLIGATIONS AS TO THE KIND AND QUALITY OF THE GOODS

In this sub-section we look at contracts for the sale of goods and ask what obligations the seller is under in respect of the kind and quality of goods that it must deliver. (The question of what remedies the buyer will have if the goods are not of the correct kind or quality is considered in Chapter 27.)

Traditionally the systems approached these questions in rather different ways. The relevant English law was (and remains) largely contained in the Sale of Goods Act 1979, but until 2002 the provisions of the Act were a very close reflection of general principles: a seller who delivers defective goods is breaking the contract and the usual remedies apply.

In contrast, both French and German law had special regimes for defects. The special regimes seem to reflect the Roman law notion (developed in relation to specific goods but later applied also when goods were sold by a generic description) that the seller had performed his obligation under the contract of sale if he delivered the goods

---

[60] *Frost v Aylesbury Dairy* [1905] 1 KB 608 (CA); *Kendall v Lillico* [1969] 2 AC 31, 84 (HL).
[61] See above, p 774.

contracted for; liability for defects was a separate matter.[62] In the case of German law the regime was treated as exclusive (ie the buyer could not rely on general contract law as an alternative). In French law, the remedies were cumulative if the buyer had not accepted the goods. If he had accepted them, his only remedy would be under Articles 1641 ff of the Code Civil. However, as interpreted by the courts, this special regime provides remedies against a wider range of defendants than does general contract law, because the buyer is permitted to bring an *action directe* against any previous seller of the goods.

All three regimes have been amended as a result of the Directive 99/44/EC,[63] often called the Consumer Sales Directive.

Consumer Sales Directive[64]   **19.11 (EU)**

Article 2: Conformity with the contract

1. The seller must deliver goods to the consumer which are in conformity with the contract of sale.

2. Consumer goods are presumed to be in conformity with the contract if they:

    (a) comply with the description given by the seller and possess the qualities of the goods which the seller has held out to the consumer as a sample or model;

    (b) are fit for any particular purpose for which the consumer requires them and which he made known to the seller at the time of conclusion of the contract and which the seller has accepted;

    (c) are fit for the purposes for which goods of the same type are normally used;

    (d) show the quality and performance which are normal in goods of the same type and which the consumer can reasonably expect, given the nature of the goods and taking into account any public statements on the specific characteristics of the goods made about them by the seller, the producer or his representative, particularly in advertising or on labelling.

3. There shall be deemed not to be a lack of conformity for the purposes of this Article if, at the time the contract was concluded, the consumer was aware, or could not reasonably be unaware of, the lack of conformity, or if the lack of conformity has its origin in materials supplied by the consumer.

4. The seller shall not be bound by public statements, as referred to in paragraph 2(d) if he:

    — shows that he was not, and could not reasonably have been, aware of the statement in question,

    — shows that by the time of conclusion of the contract the statement had been corrected, or

    — shows that the decision to buy the consumer goods could not have been influenced by the statement.

5. Any lack of conformity resulting from incorrect installation of the consumer goods shall be deemed to be equivalent to lack of conformity of the goods if installation forms part of the contract of sale of the goods and the goods were installed by the seller or under his responsibility. This shall apply equally if the product, intended to be installed

---

[62] See R Zimmermann, *The New German Law of Obligations* (Oxford University Press, 2005) 80.

[63] Directive 1999/44/EC of the European Parliament and of the Council of 25 May 1999 on certain aspects of the sale of consumer goods and associated guarantees, OJ L171/1999, p 12 ('the Directive').

[64] ibid.

by the consumer, is installed by the consumer and the incorrect installation is due to a shortcoming in the installation instructions.

Article 3: Rights of the consumer
    1. The seller shall be liable to the consumer for any lack of conformity which exists at the time the goods were delivered.
    ...

We will see that the substance of the seller's obligations are very similar in the three systems, at least where the seller is a business and the buyer is a consumer. It is interesting to compare how the legislators in the three jurisdictions decided to implement the changes. In the UK, the Directive was implemented initially principally by adding new sections to the Sale of Goods Act 1979.[65] As the existing law on the seller's obligations (implied terms) was already close to the requirements of the Directive, only slight additions (applicable only to consumer contracts) were needed. The additions, together with a re-drafted version of the provisions that existed before the Directive, were then transferred to the Consumer Rights Act 2015[66] and removed from the Sale of Goods Act 1979; so that the Sale of Goods Act 1979 is now back to where it was before the Directive, but now the sections on implied terms apply only to non-consumer sales. French law introduced a separate regime for consumer sales and permits consumers to pursue the old or the new regime. This means that the French consumer or business buyer still has a wider range of possible defendants against whom to claim. The German legislator decided to adopt the 'Directive regime' for all sales.

19.3.A.1 ENGLISH LAW

Sale of Goods Act 1979 (as amended)   **19.12 (EN)**

Section 13: Sale by description
    (1) Where there is a contract for the sale of goods by description, there is an implied term that the goods will correspond with the description.
    (1A) As regards England and Wales and Northern Ireland, the term implied by subsection (1) above is a condition.
    (2) If the sale is by sample as well as by description it is not sufficient that the bulk of the goods corresponds with the sample if the goods do not also correspond with the description.
    (3) A sale of goods is not prevented from being a sale by description by reason only that, being exposed for sale or hire, they are selected by the buyer.
    ...

Section 14: Implied terms about quality or fitness
    (1) Except as provided by this section and section 15 below and subject to any other enactment, there is no implied term about the quality or fitness for any particular purpose of goods supplied under a contract of sale.

---

[65] When we consider the remedies we will see that Parliament added new sections to the Act which applied only to consumer (B2C) sales. The previous law remained in place, and not only for business-to-business (B2B) sales but also for B2C sales—so that a consumer could select whether to pursue the 'old' or the 'new' remedies. These provisions have also been replaced by the Consumer Rights Act 2015.
[66] Consumer Rights Act 2015, ss 9–11, 13–15.

(2) Where the seller sells goods in the course of a business, there is an implied term that the goods supplied under the contract are of satisfactory quality.

(2A) For the purposes of this Act, goods are of satisfactory quality if they meet the standard that a reasonable person would regard as satisfactory, taking account of any description of the goods, the price (if relevant) and all the other relevant circumstances.

(2B) For the purposes of this Act, the quality of goods includes their state and condition and the following (among others) are in appropriate cases aspects of the quality of goods—

(a) fitness for all the purposes for which goods of the kind in question are commonly supplied,

(b) appearance and finish,

(c) freedom from minor defects,

(d) safety, and

(e) durability.

(2C) The term implied by subsection (2) above does not extend to any matter making the quality of goods unsatisfactory—

(a) which is specifically drawn to the buyer's attention before the contract is made,

(b) where the buyer examines the goods before the contract is made, which that examination ought to reveal, or

(c) in the case of a contract for sale by sample, which would have been apparent on a reasonable examination of the sample.

(3) Where the seller sells goods in the course of a business and the buyer, expressly or by implication, makes known—

(a) to the seller, or … any particular purpose for which the goods are being bought, there is an implied[term] that the goods supplied under the contract are reasonably fit for that purpose, whether or not that is a purpose for which such goods are commonly supplied, except where the circumstances show that the buyer does not rely, or that it is unreasonable for him to rely, on the skill or judgment of the seller …

(4) An implied term about quality or fitness for a particular purpose may be annexed to a contract of sale by usage.

(5) The preceding provisions of this section apply to a sale by a person who in the course of a business is acting as agent for another as they apply to a sale by a principal in the course of a business, except where that other is not selling in the course of a business and either the buyer knows that fact or reasonable steps are taken to bring it to the notice of the buyer before the contract is made.

(6) As regards England and Wales and Northern Ireland, the terms implied by subsections (2) and (3) above are conditions.

…

Notes

(1) These provisions of the Sale of Goods Act 1979 are what govern sales other than sales by a trader to a consumer, which are covered by Consumer Rights Act 2015. That Act includes the additional provisions required by the Directive.

(2) Note the characteristic technique of English law that the obligations of the seller are expressed as implied terms of the contract. In other words, they are in principle based on the (implicit) agreement of the parties. This meant originally that the

sections would not apply if the parties had agreed otherwise—either expressly, for example if the seller were to insert a clause stating that he was under no obligation to deliver goods of satisfactory quality, or implicitly, where other circumstances showed that the parties did not mean the normal term to be implied.[67] As we will see in Chapter 21, however, under the Unfair Contract Terms Act 1977, section 6, these obligations can now be excluded, or the seller's liability limited, in a business to business (B2B) sale only if the exclusion or restriction is reasonable.[68] In a consumer sale, the consumer's rights (which are not described as 'implied terms'[69]) and the trader's liabilities under the equivalent provisions of the Consumer Rights Act cannot be excluded or restricted at all.[70]

(3) Section 13 of the Sale of Goods Act requires the goods to correspond to the description. It has been pointed out that to impose an implied term to this effect may be unnecessary.[71] If the seller has promised to supply a particular kind of goods (either because that is how he has described them to the buyer or because the buyer has said what he wants and the seller has supplied the goods to meet this requirement) it will normally be an express term of the contract that the goods are to be of the type described.

(4) Section 13 applies to all contracts for the sale of goods. (The same is true of section 15, which states that where a sale is by sample, the goods must correspond to the sample, etc; section 15 is omitted for reasons of space.) In contrast, section 14, which requires that the goods must be of satisfactory quality and (under stated conditions) fit for the buyer's purpose, applies only to sales in the course of a business. A business which sells something it does not normally sell, as when a fisherman sold his old boat, is nonetheless a sale in the course of a business.[72]

(5) The odd numbering system of section 14 ((2A), (2B) etc) is because the 1979 Act has been amended. First, an Act of 1994 introduced the requirement that the goods be of satisfactory quality, and a list of the factors to be taken into account (section 14(2)–14(2C)). This replaced the previous requirement (taken from the first Sale of Goods Act of 1893 but ultimately derived from the common law) that goods supplied in the course of a business must be 'of merchantable quality'.

(6) In contrast, the Consumer Sales Directive introduced remedies which were completely new to English law. These were included in new sections 48A–F, and are now in the Consumer Rights Act, sections 19 ff. They will be considered in Chapter 21.

---

[67] eg, *Gloucestershire CC v Richardson* [1969] 1 AC 480 (HL) (building contract: parties cannot have intended contractor to be responsible for quality of materials employer had instructed contractor to buy and use when contractor was given no right to object to the limited-liability terms on which the manufacturer made the materials available).

[68] See 21.16 (EN), below, p 838.

[69] See above, p 766.

[70] Consumer Rights Act 2015, s 31; see 21.17 (EN), below, p 842.

[71] C Twigg-Flesner, R Canavan and H McQueen, *Atiyah and Adams' Sale of Goods* (13th edn, Harlow: Pearson, 2016) 124.

[72] *Stevenson v Rogers* [1999] QB 1028 (CA).

19.3.A.2 FRENCH LAW

Code civil **19.13 (FR)**

Article 1641: A seller is bound to a warranty on account of the latent defects of the thing sold which render it unfit for the use for which it was intended, or which so impair that use that the buyer would not have acquired it, or would only have given a lesser price for it, had he known of them.

Article 1642: A seller is not liable for defects which are patent and which the buyer could ascertain for himself.

Article 1643: He is liable for latent defects, even though he did not know of them, unless he has stipulated that he would not be bound to any warranty in that case.

> *Note*
>
> Any buyer, including a consumer,[73] may rely on these provisions, but they will be of most use to non-consumer buyers, since consumer buyers will have stronger rights under the Code de la consommation, below.

Code de la consommation **19.14 (FR)**

Article L 211-4: The seller is required to deliver a product which conforms to the contract and is held liable for any lack of conformity which exists upon delivery.

He is also held liable for any lack of conformity caused by the packaging or the assembly instructions, or the installation if he assumed responsibility therefor or had it carried out under his responsibility.

Article L 211-5: To conform to the contract, the product must:

1. — Be suitable for the purpose usually associated with such a product and, if applicable:

— correspond to the description given by the seller and have the features that the seller presented to the buyer in the form of a sample or model;

— have the features that a buyer might reasonably expect it to have considering the public statements made by the seller, the producer or his representative, including advertising and labelling;

2. Or have the features defined by mutual agreement between the parties or be suitable for any special requirement of the buyer which was made known to the seller and which the latter agreed to.

Article L 211-6: The seller is not bound by the public statements of the producer or his representative if it is established that he was unaware of them and could not rightfully be expected to have been aware of them.

...

Article L 211-8: The buyer is entitled to demand that the product conform to the contract. He may nevertheless not contest its conformity by invoking a defect that he was

---

[73] See Code de la consommation, Art L 211-13, below, p 1158.

aware of, or could not have been unaware of, when he entered into the contract. The same shall apply when the defect originates from materials he has supplied himself.

Note

These provisions of the Code de consommation are also closely modeled on the words of the Directive, though the obligations set out in Article L 211-5 are set out in a slightly different fashion.

19.3.A.3 GERMAN LAW

BGB   **19.15 (DE)**

§ 433: Standard obligations in contracts of sale

(1) By a contract of sale the seller of a thing is bound to hand over the thing to the buyer and to transfer to him ownership of the thing. The seller must procure the thing for the buyer in a state that is free from defects as to quality and defects of title.

(2) The buyer is bound to pay to the seller the agreed price and to take delivery of the thing purchased.

§ 434: Defects as to quality

(1) The thing is free from defects as to quality if, upon the passing of the risk, the thing is in the agreed quality. If the quality has not been agreed, the thing is free from defects as to quality

    1. if it is fit for the use specified in the contract, and otherwise

    2. if it is fit for the normal use and its quality is such as is usual in things of the same
    kind and can be expected by the buyer by virtue of its nature.

For the purposes of sentence 2, No. 2, above, quality includes features which the buyer may expect by virtue of public statements concerning the thing's features that are made by the seller, the producer (§ 4 (1) and (2) of the Product Liability Act) or persons assisting him, in particular in advertisements or in connection with labelling, unless the seller was not aware of the statement nor ought to have been aware of it, or at the time of the conclusion of the contract it had been corrected by equivalent means, or it could not influence the decision to purchase the thing.

(2) There is a defect as to quality also where the agreed assembly of the thing has not been properly performed by the seller or persons employed by him for that purpose. Moreover, there is a defect as to quality of a thing intended to be assembled if the assembly instructions are defective, save where the thing has been assembled correctly.

(3) Delivery by the seller of a different thing or of a lesser amount of the thing is equivalent to a defect as to quality.

§ 442: Awareness of the buyer

(1) The buyer has no rights in respect of a defect if he is aware of the defect upon conclusion of the contract. If, owing to gross negligence on his part, the buyer is unaware of a defect, he may assert rights in respect of that defect only if the seller fraudulently concealed the defect or guaranteed the quality of the thing.

(2) …

Notes

(1) The articles above apply to all sales, including both B2B and business to consumer (B2C) sales. Thus, the provisions on statements made by the producer, etc apply in German law even when the buyer is a business.

(2) German law distinguishes legal and material defects. The latter seems to comprise any form of non-conformity other than a defect of title—so goods are regarded as having a material defect if they are of good quality but not suitable for the purpose intended by the buyer and agreed with the seller.

(3) Under German law the buyer who has received defective goods can only proceed under these rules and cannot bring an action for non-performance under the more general provisions of the BGB described earlier. The purpose of § 434(3) is to prevent the buyer being able to avoid this restriction by the *aliud* argument—that is, by arguing that the goods were so defective that there has been no performance at all, so that the case would come within the general rules.

19.3.B CONTRACTS OF CARRIAGE

An example in which the systems reach more varied results concerns contracts of carriage. In all systems, a carrier has an obligation to carry the passenger or the goods to the destination, and has some responsibility to avoid injuring the passenger or damaging the goods. What is the carrier's obligation, its liability if the things or persons carried are damaged or injured? As we saw earlier when we considered the interface between contract and tort (delict), French judges have established the principle that the safety of passengers is an *obligation de résultat*, so that the carrier will be liable for any injury unless it is shown to have resulted from a *cause étrangère*.[74] To be more precise, in carriage of persons, there is an *obligation de sécurité* which is treated as an *obligation de résultat* during the transport itself (it is sometimes called an '*obligation de sécurité de résultat*'), that is to say between the moment the person enters the vehicle and the moment they complete leaving it. If the accident does not take place during the transport itself but, for instance, on the platform of the railway station, the liability is delictual and not contractual and normally it must be shown that the carrier was at fault[75] or that some other ground of delictual liability exists.[76] The *obligation de résultat* has been extended to loss of or damage to the luggage carried by the passenger.[77]

English law has the reverse rule. At common law a carrier is under an obligation only to take reasonable care to prevent injury to passengers. Even more curiously, the

---

[74] See 6.12 (FR), above, p 142.

[75] As required by Art 1382 Cciv.

[76] eg, if the passenger is injured by a thing under the carrier's control: Art 1384 Cciv. See W van Gerven, P Larouche and J Lever, *Ius Commune Casebooks on the Common Law of Europe: Tort Law* (Oxford: Hart Publishing, 2000) 556 ff.

[77] Cass civ (1) 26 September 2006, no. 03-13726, Bull civ I no. 418, RDC 2007, 391, annotated by P Delebecque.

old common law rule[78] was that a common carrier of goods was strictly liable for damage unless he could show that it was caused by one of a series of exceptions such as Acts of God or acts of a third party—a rule that seems very close to the French obligation of result. It is no doubt facile to suggest the difference between the two laws says something about the relative importance given to persons and possessions in the two countries!

German law seems to be most protective of the creditor (passenger or goods owner) in contracts of carriage, a contract for works (§ 631 BGB).[79] If the carrier does not fulfil his collateral duty of care (*Nebenpflicht: Obhuts- und Fürsorgepflicht*) and damage to persons or goods occurs, he will normally be liable under the general rules of §§ 280ff BGB, unless he can prove that his conduct was neither intentional nor negligent.

19.3.C CONSTRUCTION CONTRACTS

We find differences also in construction contracts. Take, for example, contracts to build or to design and construct a building.

In English law, the builder is strictly liable for the quality of the materials used. This was established as a matter of common law. Thus, in *Young & Marten v McManus Childs*,[80] a building contractor was building houses and subcontracted the roofing to the appellants, instructing them to use a particular brand of roofing tile. The appellants in turn sub-subcontracted the work to Acme, who bought the tiles from the manufacturers. The batch of tiles supplied was not of satisfactory quality. It was held that the appellants were responsible, and liable to pay damages to cover the cost of re-roofing the houses, even though they were in no way at fault and had no choice as to which kind of tile to use. The Sale and Supply of Goods Act 1982, sections 1–5, now implies into contracts for the transfer of property in goods other than sale[81] terms that are almost word for word the same as the terms implied into contracts under the Sale of Goods Act 1979, sections 13–15.[82]

In contrast, the contractor is liable for defective *work* only if it failed to use reasonable care and skill in virtue of section 13 of the Supply of Goods and Services Act 1982.[83] Similarly, an architect who designs the building will not be in breach of contract simply because the design is in some way defective; it must normally be shown that the architect was negligent. The designer will only be strictly liable in exceptional circumstances.

---

[78] See *Coggs v Bernard* (1703) 2 Ld Raym 918; *Forward v Pittard* (1785) 1 TR 27. In practice carriers no longer hold themselves out as willing to accept any goods for carriage and therefore no longer qualify as common carriers.

[79] §§ 407 ff and 453 ff of the Commercial Code (HGB) and a number of statutory instruments contain important rules for contracts of carriage which may displace the general regime of §§ 631 ff BGB.

[80] [1969] 1 AC 454 (HL).

[81] And hire-purchase, into which similar terms are implied by a separate piece of legislation, Supply of Goods (Implied terms) Act 1973. The provisions mentioned in the text do not apply to B2C contracts, for which see Consumer Rights Act 2015, ch 2.

[82] See 19.12 (EN), above, p 785. If the contract is one between a trader and a consumer, the quality of the materials used is covered by Consumer Rights Act 2015, s 9 ff: ch 2 of the Act applies not just to sale but to all contracts under which goods are supplied by a trader to a consumer.

[83] See 19.10 (EN), above, p 781. If the employer is a consumer, Consumer Rights Act 2015, s 49 applies instead.

Court of Appeal **19.16 (EN)**

Greaves & Co (Contractors) Ltd v Baynham, Miekle & Partners[84]

Engineers employed by a contractor to design a building to meet a specified performance, as required by the 'design and build' contract between the contractor and the employer, are liable even without fault if the design of the building fails to meet the specification.

Facts: A firm of contractors entered a 'design and build package deal' contract with an oil company to provide the company with a warehouse for storing large drums of oil. The defendants were employed by the contractors to design the warehouse. The oil drums were very heavy and would be moved around by forklift trucks. The warehouse was to be built in accordance with a new system of construction. The British Standards Institution had issued a circular warning designers of the effect of vibrations in such buildings, but the defendants read this as a warning merely about vibrations in general and did not allow for the random impulses set up by the forklift trucks. After a year the floor of the warehouse cracked and repairs costing £100,000 were required. The contractors were liable to bear this cost and brought an action seeking a declaration that the defendants were liable to reimburse them.

Held: The trial judge held that the defendants were in breach of an implied term that the design would be fit for its purpose. The defendants appealed. The Court of Appeal agreed that on the facts of the case the defendants were strictly liable, though it also decided that they had failed to use reasonable care and skill in designing the building without allowing for the random impulses.

Judgment: Lord Denning: ... The law does not usually imply a warranty that he will achieve the desired result, but only a term that he will use reasonable care and skill. The surgeon does not warrant that he will cure the patient. Nor does the solicitor warrant that he will win the case. But when a dentist agrees to make a set of false teeth for a patient, there is an implied warranty that they will fit his gums: see *Samuels v Davis* [1943] KB 526.

What then is the position when an architect or an engineer is employed to design a house or a bridge? Is he under an implied warranty that, if the work is carried out to his design, it will be reasonably fit for the purpose? Or is he only under a duty to use reasonable care and skill? This question may require to be answered some day as a matter of law. But in the present case I do not think we need answer it. For the evidence shows that both parties were of one mind on the matter. Their common intention was that the engineer should design a warehouse which would be fit for the purpose for which it was required. That common intention gives rise to a term implied in fact.

Appeal dismissed

Notes

(1) Lord Denning is using the word 'warranty' in the sense of a contractual promise. (We will see later that the word can also have a narrower meaning.[85])

(2) He explains the decision that the engineer gave a warranty as a term 'implied in fact'. As we will see in the next chapter, this means a term that the parties meant to include in a particular contract although it is not one of the normal default rules for that kind of contract.[86]

---

[84] [1975] 3 All ER 99.
[85] See below, p 972.
[86] See below, p 800.

(3) This case has been interpreted as meaning that a professional who is given a specification of what is required is strictly responsible for achieving that specification.[87] However, the *Greaves* case has been treated by the courts as depending on its special facts, in particular the fact that the contractors who had employed the engineer were themselves working under a 'package deal' contract under which they may have been obliged to produce a building that was fit for the employer's purposes.[88]

(4) An architect is often responsible for both designing the building and supervising its construction. Even if elements of the design work may involve strict liability, as the *Greaves* case may be interpreted as suggesting, the supervisory duties are—unless agreed otherwise—only duties to take reasonable care.

In French Law the result is different. Construction contracts form part of a wider category of *contrats d'entreprise* (services contracts). While some *contrats d'entreprise* only give rise to *obligations de moyens* (for instance, a doctor or a lawyer only promise to do their best efforts; they do not promise success), the construction contract gives rise to an obligation of result in relation to the work as well as to the materials used.[89] For construction contracts there is now specific legislation which covers both builders and designers of buildings.

Code civil[90] $\qquad$ **19.17 (FR)**

Article 1792: Any builder of a work is liable as of right, towards the building owner or purchaser, for damages, even resulting from a defect of the ground, which imperil the strength of the building or which, affecting it in one of its constituent parts or one of its elements of equipment, render it unsuitable for its purposes.

Such liability does not take place where the builder proves that the damages were occasioned by an extraneous event.

Article 1792-1: Are deemed builders of the work:

1 Any architect, contractor, technician or other person bound to the building owner by a contract of hire of work;

2 Any person who sells, after completion, a work which he built or had built;

3 Any person who, although acting in the capacity of agent for the building owner, performs duties similar to those of a hirer out of work.

In German law a builder's obligations are determined in the first instance by the provisions of the BGB relating to contracts for works (*Werkverträge*). The rules governing work contracts are very similar to those governing the sale of goods in relation to remedies for defects.[91] In both cases the availability of certain remedies is dependent on whether the debtor was at fault or not.

---

[87] See G Treitel, *Remedies for Breach of Contract* (Oxford: Clarendon Press, 1988) 27–30, para 27.

[88] See *Hawkins v Chrysler (UK) Ltd and Burne Associates* (1986) 38 BLR 36 (CA).

[89] H Périnet-Marquet, 'La Cour de cassation et la responsabilité des constructeurs' in *Le monde du droit: Écrits rédigés en l'honneur de Jean Foyer* (Paris: Economica, 2008) 757.

[90] Act no. 78-12 of 4 January 1978.

[91] See above, p 789.

§ 633: Material defects and legal defects

(1) The contractor must procure the work for the customer free of material defects and legal defects.

(2) The work is free of material defects if it is of the agreed quality. To the extent that the quality has not been agreed, the work is free from material defects

    1. if it is suitable for the use envisaged in the contract, or else

    2. if it is suitable for the customary use and is of a quality that is customary in works of the same type and that the customer may expect in view of the type of work.

It is equivalent to a material defect if the contractor produces a work that is different from the work ordered or too small an amount of the work.

(3) The work is free of legal defects if third parties, with regard to the work, either cannot assert any rights against the customer or can assert only such rights as are taken over under the contract.

§ 634: Rights of the customer in the case of defects

If the work is defective, the customer, if the requirements of the following provisions are met and to the extent not otherwise specified, may

    1. under section 635, demand cure,

    2. under section 637, remedy the defect himself and demand reimbursement for required expenses,

    3. under sections 636, 323 and 326(5), withdraw from the contract or under section 638, reduce payment, and

    4. under sections 636, 280, 281, 283 and 311a, demand damages, or under section 284, demand reimbursement of futile expenditure.

Notes

(1) The builder is obliged to produce work that is free from defects (including being suitable for the employer's purpose if that was envisaged by the contract). If the work is not suitable, the employer can demand cure, or can have the work done again at the builder's expense, even if the builder was not at fault.

(2) However, consistently with general principle, the builder will be liable in damages only if he was responsible, either because he was at fault or because he had undertaken a stricter liability (§ 276). The burden of disproving fault is on the debtor (§ 280(1)).

(3) Thus the obligation in work contracts is one of result. In this no distinction is made, unlike in English law, between liability for defective materials and liability for defective work. Work contracts are distinguished in this respect from service contracts (*Dienstverträge*). Under the latter the debtor is obliged to perform tasks, but does not bear the risk of the desired result not being achieved. Thus, both contracts of employment (*Arbeitsverträge*) and contracts with most professionals are classified as service contracts.[92] German law also accepts mixed types of work and service contracts

---

[92] See above, pp 779–80.

(for example where a party agrees to supply machinery and then to maintain it for a certain period). Then the applicability of work and/or service contract rules is in general determined by the interpretation of the main obligation of the contract.[93]

(4) Contracts with architects form an exception to the foregoing. The architect's liability in relation to the drafting of the plan for a building is clearly strict. The supervisory tasks of the architect during the construction phase, on the other hand, seem to amount to service type obligations. Nonetheless, the BGH and academic commentators have long held that the result-orientation of the planning stage predominates throughout. There has been agreement, therefore, that the architect's contract is a work contract with corresponding liability for failure to achieve the result of a defect-free building in accordance with the plans.[94] This classification was confirmed when the legislator introduced specific provisions on the architect's contract for the first time in 2018 (§ 650q BGB). Note that the architect will not only be liable for defects caused by his work. He will also be liable, jointly and severally with the builder, if he has not properly performed his supervision tasks (§ 650t BGB).

FURTHER READING

Martens, S and Rüfner, T, 'Sale of Goods' in N Jansen and R Zimmermann (eds), *Commentaries on European Contract Laws* (Oxford University Press, 2018) 1961–2072.

Willems, C, 'Obligations of the Parties to a (related) Service Contract' in N Jansen and R Zimmermann (eds), *Commentaries on European Contract Laws* (Oxford University Press, 2018) 2073–2120.

---

[93] Münchener Kommentar/Busche § 631 paras 16–19.
[94] ibid, para 198.

CHAPTER 20
SUPPLEMENTATION AND IMPLICATION OF TERMS

In Chapter 18 we have seen how different legal systems ascertain the meaning of contractual terms by interpreting what the parties actually said. We have also noted that sometimes the parties did not make any provision at all on a given issue. If such an issue arises, an answer is often provided by the default rules of the contract law concerned. These rules provide standard solutions for problems that typically arise in contractual relationships of a certain nature. In Chapter 19 we have seen how they operate as gap-filling devices. But what to do if, in a given case, no such rule is available?

A continental court will proceed to examine the possibility of a 'supplementary', 'constructive' or 'creative interpretation' of the contract. It will ascribe a meaning to an agreement which has precisely *not* spoken on the issue in question, and it will do so by employing the general rules and principles of interpretation. English judges are in general more reluctant to speak for parties who have not spoken for themselves, and if they do so they do not perceive this as an exercise in contractual interpretation. They rather speak of the 'implication' of a contractual term. However, since the established default rules do not provide an answer in these cases, such implications only result in 'implied terms in fact', not 'in law'.

The recent instruments which are meant to prepare the international harmonisation of contract law oscillate between the English model of 'implied terms' and the continental technique of 'supplementary interpretation'.

Principles of European Contract Law   **20.1 (INT)**

Article 6:102: Implied Terms
In addition to the express terms, a contract may contain implied terms which stem from

    (a) the intention of the parties,

    (b) the nature and purpose of the contract, and

    (c) good faith and fair dealing.

Common European Sales Law   **20.2 (INT)**

Article 68: Contract terms which may be implied
(1) Where it is necessary to provide for a matter which is not explicitly regulated by the agreement of the parties, any usage or practice or any rule of the Common European Sales Law, an additional term may be implied, having regard in particular to:

    (a) the nature and purpose of the contract;

(b) the circumstances in which the contract was concluded; and

(c) good faith and fair dealing.

(2) Any contract term implied under paragraph (1) is, as far as possible, to be such as to give effect to what the parties would probably have agreed, had they provided for the matter.

(3) Paragraph (1) does not apply if the parties have deliberately left a matter unregulated, accepting that one or other party would bear the risk.

UNIDROIT Principles   **20.3 (INT)**

Article 4.8: Supplying an omitted term

(1) Where the parties to a contract have not agreed with respect to a term which is important for a determination of their rights and duties, a term which is appropriate in the circumstances shall be supplied.

(2) In determining what is an appropriate term regard shall be had, among other factors, to

(a) the intention of the parties;

(b) the nature of the contract;

(c) good faith and fair dealing;

(d) reasonableness

Article 5.1.1: Express and implied obligations

The contractual obligations of the parties may be express or implied.

Article 5.1.2: Implied obligations

Implied obligations stem from

(a) the nature and purpose of the contract;

(b) practices established between the parties and usages;

(c) good faith and fair dealing;

(d) reasonableness.

Notes

(1) Article 4.8 of the UNIDROIT Principles of International Commercial Contracts (UNIDROIT PICC) is in Chapter 4 of the instrument ('Interpretation'); Article 5.1.2 is in Chapter 5 ('Content and Third Party Rights').

(2) Look at the factors that must be taken into account in the implication of terms or in 'supplementary' interpretation in the various instruments. To what extent do they differ from each other? To what extent do they differ from the factors that must be taken into account in 'simple' interpretation?

We will now look at the different approaches of national contract laws.

Court of Appeal **20.4 (EN)**

The Moorcock[1]

A term will be implied into a contract if the term is necessary in order to give 'business efficacy' to the contract.

Facts: The defendants had agreed to let the plaintiff unload his ship at the defendant's jetty on the Thames. When the tide went out the ship inevitably settled and was holed because the river bed was uneven.

Held: The court of first instance and the Court of Appeal both decided that a term must be implied that the berth was safe or that, if it was not, the defendant would warn the shipowner.

Judgment: BOWEN LJ: The defendants in this case are the owners of a wharf and jetty attached in the river Thames, and the only use to which it is put is holding out to ships facilities for loading and unloading alongside of it. There is only one berth where the ships can lie, and that is close alongside the jetty. The question which arises in this case is whether, when a contract is made to let the use of this jetty to a ship which can only use it, as is known to both parties, by her taking the ground, there is any implied warranty on the part of the wharfingers, and if so what is the extent of that warranty.

An implied warranty, or as it is called a covenant in law, as distinguished from an express contract or express warranty, really is in every instance founded on the presumed intention of the parties and upon reason. It is the implication which the law draws from what must obviously have been the intention of the parties, an implication which the law draws with the object of giving efficacy to the transaction and preventing such a failure of consideration as cannot have been within the contemplation of either of the parties. I believe that if one were to take all the instances, which are many, of implied warranties and covenants in law which occur in the earlier cases it will be seen that in all these cases the law is raising an implication from the presumed intention of the parties with the object of giving to the transaction such efficacy as both parties must have intended it should have. If that is so the reasonable implication which the law draws must differ according to the circumstances of the various transactions, and in business transactions what the law desires to effect by the implication is to give such business efficacy to the transaction as must have been intended by both parties; not to impose on one side all the perils of the transaction or to emancipate one side from all the burdens, but to make each party promise in law as much, at all events, as it must have been in the contemplation of both parties that he should be responsible for.

What did each party in the present case know? Because, if we are examining into their presumed intention, we must examine into their minds as to what the transaction was. Both parties knew that the jetty was let for the purpose of profit, and knew that it could only be used by the ship taking the ground and lying on the ground. They must have known that it was by grounding that she would use the jetty. They must have known, both of them, that unless the ground was safe the ship would be simply buying an opportunity of danger and buying no convenience at all, and that all consideration would fail unless the ground was safe. In fact, the business of the jetty could not be carried on unless, I do not say the ground was safe, it was supposed to be safe. The master and crew of the ship could know nothing, whereas the defendants or their servants might, by exercising reasonable care, know everything. The defendants or their servants were on the

---

[1] (1889) 14 PD 64.

spot at high and low tide, morning and evening. They must know what had happened to the ships that had used the jetty before, and with the slightest trouble they could satisfy themselves in case of doubt whether the berth was safe or not safe. The ship's officers, on the other hand, had no means of verifying the state of the berth, because, for ought I know, it might be occupied by another ship at the time the Moorcock got there.

The question is how much of the peril or the safety of this berth is it necessary to assume in order to get the minimum of efficacy to the business consideration of the transaction which the ship consented to bear, and which the defendants took upon themselves. Supposing that the berth had been actually under the control of the defendants, they could, of course, have repaired it and made it fit for the purpose of loading and unloading. It seems to me that Mersey Docks Trustees v Gibbs shows that those who own a jetty, who take money for its use, and who have under their control the locus in quo, are bound to take all reasonable care to prevent danger to those using the jetty, either to make the berth good or else not to invite ships to go to the jetty, ie either to make it safe or to advise ships not to go there. But there is a distinction between that case and the present. The berth here was not under the actual control of the defendants …

Applying that modification, which is a reasonable modification, to this case, it may well be said that the law will not imply that the defendants, who had not control of the place, ought to have taken reasonable care to make the berth good, but it does not follow that they are relieved from all responsibility, a responsibility which depends not merely on the control of the place, which is one element as to which the law implies a duty, but on other circumstances. The defendants are on the spot. They must know the jetty cannot be safely used unless reasonable care is taken. No one can tell whether reasonable safety has been secured except themselves, and I think that, if they let out their jetty for use, they at all events imply that they have taken reasonable care to see that the berth, which is the essential part of the use of the jetty, is safe, and, if it is not safe, and if they have not taken such reasonable care, it is their duty to warn persons with whom they have dealings that they have not done so …

[F_RY LJ agreed. Appeal dismissed.]

Notes

(1) *The Moorcock* case is regarded as an example of 'term implied in fact', ie a term that is implied on the basis of the particular facts of the case at hand. This is to be distinguished from a 'term implied in law' which will be implied in all contracts of a particular type, as in *Liverpool City Council v Irwin*.[2]

(2) Since *The Moorcock* there have been a number of judicial attempts to describe the tests for implying terms in fact. One which is often quoted is the 'officious bystander test' of MacKinnon LJ in *Shirlaw v Southern Foundries*:[3]

Prima facie that which in any contract is left to be implied and need not be expressed is something so obvious that it goes without saying. Thus, if, while the parties were making their bargain, an officious bystander were to suggest some express provision for it in their agreement, they would testily suppress him with a common: Oh, of course.

---

[2] [1977] AC 239, 253–56, above, 19.3 (EN), p 768.
[3] [1939] 2 KB 206, 227 (CA).

In *Liverpool City Council v Irwin* Lord Wilberforce seemed to equate the 'business efficacy' test (which is also often referred to as a test of 'necessity') with the 'officious bystander' test. He further stated that for the implication of a term it was sufficient that the term be a reasonable one.

(3) It is not necessary to discuss these terminological niceties in detail. However, it should be noted that all types of 'terms implied in fact' are somehow related to the 'presumed intentions' of the parties (a term used three times in the excerpt of Bowen LJ's judgment). The question is what the parties would have agreed had they been put on notice at the time of contracting that there was a gap in their agreement. Now, if it can be presumed that they would have agreed with the solution implied by the term, they would have chosen an efficient solution, would have said 'yes of course' and would have agreed that it is 'necessary' and 'reasonable' to adopt this solution. Remember the balancing of the interests of (typical) landlords and (typical) tenants in the last paragraph cited from *Liverpool City Council v Irwin* (on p 769 above). As we have seen, we may presume that the parties would have intended such a balanced outcome.

(4) Similarly, as we will see below, the German courts will supply a missing term by resorting to what is described as the 'hypothetical' or 'presumed' intention of the parties. It is arguable that the judges cling to this terminology only to cloak the fact that they are simply developing the rule which provides a reasonable and appropriate solution to the dispute.

In a more recent case, Lord Hoffmann, delivering the advice of the Board of the Privy Council, attempted to inject some consistency in the law on implied terms.

Privy Council	**20.5 (EN)**

Attorney General of Belize v Belize Telecom Ltd[4]

The implication of a term into a contract is part of the process of interpretation.

Facts: The articles of association of Belize Telecommunications Ltd entitled the company to appoint two 'special directors' and empowered the holder of a 'special share' (the government) to remove these directors. Two special directors were in fact appointed. Later, the company defaulted, with the result that no holder of a special share existed anymore. The company sought to remove the directors. The judge granted a declaration that the company had the right to do so but the Court of Appeal of Belize reversed that decision.

Held: The company has the power to remove the directors because the articles contained an implied term providing that the special directors would automatically cease to hold office in such circumstances.

Advice of the Board: LORD HOFFMANN: ... 16. Before discussing in greater detail the reasoning of the Court of Appeal, the Board will make some general observations about the process of implication. The court has no power to improve upon the instrument which it is called upon to construe, whether it be a contract, a statute or articles of association.

---

[4] [2009] UKPC 10, [2009] 1 WLR 1988.

It cannot introduce terms to make it fairer or more reasonable. It is concerned only to discover what the instrument means. However, that meaning is not necessarily or always what the authors or parties to the document would have intended. It is the meaning which the instrument would convey to a reasonable person having all the background knowledge which would reasonably be available to the audience to whom the instrument is addressed: see *Investors Compensation Scheme Ltd v West Bromwich Building Society* [1998] 1 WLR 896, 912–913.[5] It is this objective meaning which is conventionally called the intention of the parties, or the intention of Parliament, or the intention of whatever person or body was or is deemed to have been the author of the instrument.

17. The question of implication arises when the instrument does not expressly provide for what is to happen when some event occurs. The most usual inference in such a case is that nothing is to happen. If the parties had intended something to happen, the instrument would have said so. Otherwise, the express provisions of the instrument are to continue to operate undisturbed. If the event has caused loss to one or other of the parties, the loss lies where it falls.

18. In some cases, however, the reasonable addressee would understand the instrument to mean something else. He would consider that the only meaning consistent with the other provisions of the instrument, read against the relevant background, is that something is to happen. The event in question is to affect the rights of the parties. The instrument may not have expressly said so, but this is what it must mean. In such a case, it is said that the court implies a term as to what will happen if the event in question occurs. But the implication of the term is not an addition to the instrument. It only spells out what the instrument means.

19. The proposition that the implication of a term is an exercise in the construction of the instrument as a whole is not only a matter of logic (since a court has no power to alter what the instrument means) but also well supported by authority. …

21. It follows that in every case in which it is said that some provision ought to be implied in an instrument, the question for the court is whether such a provision would spell out in express words what the instrument, read against the relevant background, would reasonably be understood to mean … this question can be reformulated in various ways which a court may find helpful in providing an answer—the implied term must 'go without saying', it must be 'necessary to give business efficacy to the contract' and so on—but these are not in the Board's opinion to be treated as different or additional tests. There is only one question: is that what the instrument, read as a whole against the relevant background, would reasonably be understood to mean? …

27. The Board considers that this list [of tests] is best regarded, not as series of independent tests which must each be surmounted, but rather as a collection of different ways in which judges have tried to express the central idea that the proposed implied term must spell out what the contract actually means, or in which they have explained why they did not think that it did so. The Board has already discussed the significance of 'necessary to give business efficacy' and 'goes without saying'. As for the other formulations, the fact that the proposed implied term would be inequitable or unreasonable, or contradict what the parties have expressly said, or is incapable of clear expression, are all good reasons for saying that a reasonable man would not have understood that to be what the instrument meant.

---

[5] See above, 18.20 (EN), p 737.

28. The Board therefore turns to consider the question raised by the articles of association. Two things are immediately apparent. The first is that the board has been constructed so that its membership will reflect the interests of the various participants in the company: ... The second is that the powers which the articles confer upon the Government (or its successor as special shareholder acting upon its written instructions: ...

30. ... The Board considers that, if one considers the role of the Government Appointed Directors and the policy of giving the Government the power to require redemption of the special share, namely, to enable it to relinquish its influence over the conduct of the company's business, the articles cannot reasonably mean that the Government Appointed Directors should remain in office after the special share has ceased to exist. They must be read as providing by implication that when the special share goes, the Government Appointed Directors go with it. In the opinion of the Board it is no answer to say that the special shareholder could have thought of the problem in advance and removed the Government Appointed Directors before redemption. No doubt he could, but the question is what the articles mean in the situation in which he has not done so. Nor is it relevant that the articles could be amended. They must be construed as they stand.

31. If, as the Board thinks, it would plainly be necessary to imply such a term in relation to the Government Appointed Directors, it must follow that upon the redemption of the special share, the special C directors will also cease to hold office ...

Appeal allowed

Notes

(1) A few years ago, the Supreme Court rejected the idea that *Belize* had actually changed the law on implied terms. In *Marks and Spencer* it made clear that Lord Hoffmann had not suggested that mere reasonableness is a sufficient ground for implying a term, so that it might be easier to imply terms than in the past. Instead the traditional tests of 'business efficacy' and 'officious bystander' were still to be applied.[6]

(2) Lord Hoffmann links the doctrine of implied terms firmly to contractual interpretation. In *Marks and Spencer*, the judges were not in agreement as to whether this was correct or whether 'the process of implication involves a rather different exercise from that of construction'.[7] However, taken to its logical conclusions, Lord Hoffmann's approach would render the doctrine superfluous and align English law to continental systems.

This can be seen if we turn to German law. German judges, as has been mentioned at the outset of this chapter, fill gaps in a contract without resorting to a mechanism of implying terms. Rather, they proceed to give the contract a so-called 'supplementary'

---

[6] *Marks and Spencer v BNP Paribas Securities Services Trust Company (Jersey) Ltd* [2015] UKSC 72, [2016] AC 742 [23]–[24], per Lord Neuberger.
[7] For the contrasting views, see ibid, [25]–[30], per Lord Neuberger, and [71], per Lord Carnwath.

or 'constructive interpretation' (*ergänzende Vertragsauslegung*). The formula generally used is this: where the parties have omitted to say something, no default rule being supplied by a statute, the judge must discover and take into account what, in the light of the whole purpose of the contract, the parties, as reasonable and fair-minded persons, would have said if they had provided for the point in question, acting according to the requirements of good faith and good commercial practice.

BGH, 18 December 1954[8]   **20.6 (DE)**

Exchange of doctors' practices

If it emerges that the contract does not provide for the situation which has occurred, including a situation which the parties had not considered, the court will fill the lacuna by supplementary interpretation, supplying a term which the parties would have agreed had they considered the point.

Facts: The parties were two doctors who had agreed to exchange practices. The defendant found his new place of work not to his liking and intended to return and set up a new practice in his old town only nine months later. The claimant feared that the defendant's patients would flock back to him and sought an injunction. Since there was nothing in the contract on a 'right to return', the question arose whether a term disallowing such return could be read into it.

Held: The defendant had no unqualified right to return to compete in private practice with the claimant. The case was sent back to the lower court to take further evidence on the local conditions, the type of the parties' patients, etc and then to rule on the precise limits, as to time and location, of the defendant's right to return.

Judgment: § 157 BGB provides that in the interpretation of contracts due consideration is to be given to the principle of good faith and the prevailing practice. It is true that, according to that provision, the interpretation must be based—having regard to the purpose of the contract, the principle of good faith and the prevailing practice—on the discernible states of mind of the parties at the time when the contract was concluded. However, § 157 BGB requires the court to ascertain the entire content of the contract according to objective criteria. That task will be fulfilled only if the court also establishes the content of the contract as regards those points which have not been agreed by the parties, irrespective of whether they consciously dispensed with any detailed stipulations, whether the lacuna in the matters agreed existed from the outset or whether it only manifested itself at a later stage, as a result of subsequent developments. It may therefore also be necessary, in undertaking a supplementary interpretation of the contract, to ascertain and take into account matters which the parties did not clarify but which, in view of the purpose of the contract as a whole, they would have clarified had they also settled the outstanding point when reaching their agreement, thereby observing, at the same time, the dictates of good faith and of the prevailing practice. This is conditional on the existence, within the actual context of the contract, of a lacuna needing to be filled, that is to say, one which is essential for the purposes of securing the purpose of the contract.

---

[8] BGHZ 16, 71.

In the present case, the criteria for a supplementary interpretation of the contract are fulfilled. According to the findings of the appellate court, the parties, when agreeing the terms on which the practices were to be exchanged, did not contemplate the possibility that one of them might soon return to the area in which he formerly practised; and they made no particular provision for that eventuality. Yet the facts of the case are clearly such that it needed to be catered for. Even if one concurs with the appellate court's view that the actual purpose of the exchange contract was limited to affording the possibility of carrying on the other party's practice by taking over that party's patient clientèle, there can be no serious doubt that such a possibility would be considerably impaired by the return of the former owner of the practice, if he were unable, either at all or at any rate immediately, to secure readmission to practise under a health insurance scheme. There is no need to determine the question whether, as the claimant maintained, a medical practice is generally speaking viable only if it produces income from the treatment of private patients as well as patients who are members of a health insurance scheme. It is indisputable that the parties both practised on a private basis and accordingly intended to continue to do so. However, there is bound to be a diminution in the income from the private practice if the patients within that practice are once again given the opportunity of going for treatment to the former owner of the practice, with whom they have built up, in some cases over a period of many years, a relationship of trust. Thus, the entire purpose of the contract would be substantially jeopardised if one of the parties were to return, only a short while after its conclusion, to the place in which he had formerly practised … In those circumstances, the appellate court should not simply have taken as the starting-point for its interpretation the mere fact that there was no agreement between the parties regarding the possible return by one of them to the place in which he had previously practised. Instead, it should have examined whether, and if so to what extent, the parties would have included in the contract a clause prohibiting them from returning to their former practice area if they had given any thought to that eventuality at the time. The contractual lacuna existing in that regard falls within the effective scope of the arrangements made between the parties. We are concerned here not with the creation of an additional obligation going beyond the essential content of the contract for the exchange of practices, but merely with the concrete enunciation of a collateral obligation which is closely connected with the purpose of the contract. Consequently, the filling of that lacuna would not result in an impermissible extension of the content of the contract …

The supplementary interpretation of the contract which is possible—and, indeed, necessary—in the light of the above can in principle be provided by this Court itself, applying the objective criteria laid down in § 157 BGB. On the basis of the foregoing considerations, this interpretation must be that, upon a reasonable assessment of the purpose for which the practices were to be exchanged, the parties—had they given any thought in advance to the possibility of one of them returning to the immediate vicinity of his former practice—would have agreed to prohibit such a return within a given period of, say, two to three years following completion of the exchange of practices. This is because it is not generally possible, within such a period, for the successor to a practice to consolidate his relations with his predecessor's patients to such an extent that he need no longer fear any significant loss or damage as a result of the latter's return. Within those parameters, therefore, the contract must in any event be deemed to include a stipulation prohibiting a return.

BGH, 25 June 1980[9]   **20.7 (DE)**

Redecoration

A term will be supplied by supplementary interpretation only if not to do so would produce a result at odds with the purpose of the contract as agreed by the parties.

Facts: The parties had entered into an agreement for the lease of a restaurant providing that, upon its termination, the lessee was bound to carry out at his expense certain repair work designed to restore the premises to good condition. The lessee had failed to do so. The lessor then decided to rebuild the premises, and there was no dispute that the rebuilding would have destroyed the repair work if it had been carried out by the lessee. The lessor sued the lessee for the value of the repair work. The lessee's defence was that his failure to carry out the contractually agreed repair work had caused no loss to the lessor. Since the contract was silent on whether the lessor was to have a pecuniary entitlement in these circumstances, the question was whether such a term could be implied.

Held: The lessor was not entitled to require the tenant to perform the obligation; at most he could claim the saving to the tenant through not having to do the work.

Judgment: The claimant's claim may … be substantiated if a supplementary interpretation of the contract shows that the presumed intention of the parties must have been to allow the claimant, in the event of the demised premises being rebuilt, a pecuniary claim instead of an accrued entitlement to demand performance …

The parties agreed that the lessee was to carry out the decorative repairs. The contract is silent on the question whether the lessor was to be entitled to compensation in the event that, upon the lessee failing at the end of the lease to carry out the outstanding decorative repairs, the lessor were immediately to rebuild the demised premises in accordance with a decision which—as the appellate court found—he had already made prior to the termination of the lease, and the rebuilding resulted in the destruction of any decorative repairs which might have been carried out. There is, to that extent, a lacuna in the contract.

However, not every point which a contract omits to provide for is susceptible of resolution by means of a supplementary interpretation. Where the parties to a contract make no stipulation regarding a given matter, it may generally be assumed that they are content to let the form which their contractual relationship is to take be governed by the provisions enshrined in legislation. A contractual lacuna needing to be filled by interpretation exists only where the contract requires to be supplemented within its established framework or within the ambit of the matters on which the parties actually intended to agree. A judicial interpretation may not have the effect of extending the subject matter of the contract, and must be supported by the contents of the contract. It must follow cogently and self-evidently from the entire context of the matters agreed, in such a way that, if the contract were not thus supplemented, the result would be manifestly at odds with the matters which, according to the contents of the contract, were actually agreed between the parties.

That may possibly be the position in the present case. It would be absurd for the lessor, having firmly decided to rebuild, to be stuck with having to demand the performance by the lessee of the latter's obligation to carry out the decorative repairs, as laid down in the contract, notwithstanding that, upon that obligation being performed, the work

---

[9] BGHZ 77, 301 (citations omitted).

done would immediately be destroyed. On the other hand, however, it would clearly be at variance with the content of the contract—as a general rule, in any event—if the lessee were to be released from his obligation without having to pay any compensation in lieu, since the lessee's obligation, laid down in the lease, requiring him to carry out the decorative repairs represents, generally at any rate, part of the consideration due from the lessee in return for performance by the lessor ... Consequently, in accordance with the principle of good faith and the prevailing practice, the intention of the contracting parties must be presumed to have been that the lessor should have a corresponding pecuniary entitlement in lieu of the right to require the decorative repairs to be carried out, which had become economically pointless (§ 157 BGB). That pecuniary entitlement consists of an amount equivalent to what the lessee would have had to spend in carrying out the requisite decorative repairs. The corresponding sum is payable by the lessee to the lessor.

The amount of such pecuniary entitlement will depend on the circumstances of each individual case. In particular, significance may attach to the question whether, according to the presumed intention of the parties, the lessor would have had to accept the decorative repairs being done by the lessee personally or by relatives or acquaintances of the lessee. If so, the sum due to the lessor may be less substantial than it would have been if the lessor could have insisted on the repair works being done by a professional workman.

'Supplementary interpretation' is also used by German courts in cases where a clause in a standard form contract is struck down as unfair and the question arises how the resulting gap is to be filled. Thus it was held in an action brought by a consumer organisation against Daimler-Benz AG that the defendants, as sellers of new cars, could not validly reserve a power to charge their buyer the price in force at the time of delivery regardless of the time that would elapse between the date of the contract and the time of delivery. In order to fill the gap the court supplied a term which upheld the sellers' right to charge the list price in force at the time of delivery but added a right for the buyer to cancel the contract if the difference between the two prices 'substantially exceeds' the increase in the general costs of living between the two relevant dates.[10] Writers have criticised this decision on the ground that it is in conflict with a rule laid down in other German cases according to which courts cannot rewrite a clause, only strike it out *in toto*.[11]

French courts do not use the concept of 'supplementary interpretation', although they actually decide in much the same way. Sometimes they say that the term to be implied is based on what the courts, exercising the *pouvoir souverain des juges de fond*, think has been the 'common intention of the parties'. Sometimes they rely on the Code civil which expressly authorises such an approach. In the Code civil of 1804 there were even two overlapping provisions to this effect (ex-Articles 1135 and 1160). The second of these, referring to the supplementation of non-expressed 'terms which are customary'

---

[10] See BGH 1 February 1984, BGHZ 90, 69.
[11] There is authority for this rule in England too; see *Stewart Gill Ltd v Horatio Myer & Co Ltd* [1992] QB 600 (CA) and the discussion in H Kötz, *European Contract Law* (2nd edn, Oxford University Press, 2017) 143–45.

was abolished as redundant in the 2016 reform. The first was maintained in a slightly reformulated fashion:

Code civil   **20.8 (FR)**

Article 1194: Contracts create obligations not merely in relation to what they expressly provide, but also to all the consequences which are given to them by equity, usage or legislation.

Important examples of duties implied by the French courts are dealt with in other parts of this book, notably the so-called 'obligations of security' and 'information',[12] but there are other examples which have not developed into more or less freestanding legal doctrines.

Cour d'appel de Rouen, 29 November 1968[13]   **20.9 (FR)**

Delayed building work

A clause will be implied into a contract on the basis of Article 1160 [cf now Article 1194] Code Civil only if the parties must have intended it to apply but omitted it unintentionally.

Facts: The parties had entered into a contract in 1957 under which the claimant building contractor had agreed to carry out certain work for a price. For various reasons, the work was not completed before 1967. The contractor asked the employer to pay a higher price computed on the price revision mechanism known in the industry as the 'MRL method'. The employer paid only what had been agreed in the 1957 contract.

Held: The lower court gave judgment for the claimant contractor on the ground that a clause entitling him to a price revision was to be implied on the basis of Article 1160 [cf now Article 1194] Cciv, which empowers the court to read into a contract *les clauses qui y sont d'usage, quoiqu'elles n'y soient pas exprimées*. The defendant appealed. The appeal was allowed.

Judgment: Whereas Article 1160 [cf now Article 1194] Cciv authorises the implied inclusion in contracts of clauses which, although not expressly set out therein, are of the type customarily contained in such contracts. Whereas however, the sole purpose and effect which that provision can have is to modify the scheme of the contract by introducing into it, where the parties have said nothing on the point, a clause which alters the main elements of their rights and obligations. Whereas a clause may be said to be 'customary' within the meaning of the abovementioned provision only if, first, its omission must be presumed to have been unintentional and the parties must be deemed to have intended in any event to apply it and, second, if it can be applied without the court having to stipulate factual matters the choice and determination of which lay with the parties alone and with regard to which the court may not substitute its own ideas of what the parties intended for those of the parties themselves. Whereas the omission of the price revision clause in the agreement between Guéry and Druart does not appear to be the result of mere inadvertence, since it has not been established, or even alleged, that Guéry enjoyed, in his contractual relations with his clients, the benefit of the possibility of a revision of the price. Whereas furthermore, in order for such a clause to be applied, it would be

---

[12] See above, pp 142 and 790.
[13] D 1969, 146.

necessary to determine the revision dates and the matters capable of being revised, and to choose between the various possible methods of revision. Whereas it follows that, as a matter of law, there exists no basis on which Article 1160 of the Civil Code can apply. Whereas the court adjudicating at first instance believed that it could infer that adherence to the fixed prices had been abandoned in November 1957 from the fact that, by letter of 14 February 1959, Druart, without alluding to those initially agreed prices, proposed new prices, referring to 'our meeting on 12 February 1959'. Whereas however, the 1957 prices and the 1959 prices do not relate to the same works; the 1957 prices concern works in connection with flooring and skirting-boards, whilst the 1959 prices concern stairs and risers. Whereas consequently, the fixing in 1959 of prices relating to matters not provided for in 1957 does not signify any abandonment of the prices previously agreed. Whereas since no price revision was provided for, notwithstanding that it was clearly going to be a long time before the works were completed, the conclusion reached by the court below, based on the length of time which elapsed between the prices being agreed and the works being completed, is wholly invalid. Whereas if Société Druart had intended to take precautions against a change in economic circumstances, it could have provided either for a maximum period for completion of the works or for the possibility of revision; but it did not at any juncture suggest a price revision, proceeding without reservation to carry out the works at Saint-Étienne-du-Rouvray whilst none the less reserving the right to include VAT in its final account. Whereas it was only when that account was drawn up (on 4 March 1960) that it applied the simplified method of revision published by the Seine-Maritime MRL, which Guéry was unwilling to accept, since, despite the numerous demands made by Druart, it was not until 2 December 1961 that a bill of exchange for 3,452.70 francs was accepted, representing settlement of 95% of the price of the works; the difference of 5% did not correspond to the normal retention sum and does not explain the dispute regarding a possible revision. It follows that Druart's claim is unfounded and that the court below was wrong to allow it.

Cass civ (3), 15 February 1972[14]   **20.10 (FR)**

Wage scale no longer published

Where the price in a contract is to be determined by reference to a price index which, during the course of the contract, ceases to be published, the court will substitute a closely equivalent scale.

Facts: Premises were sold to the appellants at a price payable over five years and to be adjusted by reference to a wage scale for a particular class of skilled workers. This scale ceased to be published.

Held: According to the court of Caen, the price should be adjusted by reference to the closest equivalent wage scale. The buyers' appeal was dismissed.

Judgment: THE COURT: As to the first plea advanced.—Whereas by a notarial act dated 28 February 1964, Mr and Mrs Couasse purchased a property for residential use and for use as premises in which to carry on a motor mechanic's business. Whereas the price was 85,000 francs, payable over five years. Whereas they are appealing against the ruling in the contested judgment (Caen, 3 June 1970) that the indexation clause provided for in the contract should apply, on the ground that the court below, having found that it was

---

[14] No. 70-13280, Bull civ III no. 100, D 1973, 147, annotated by J Ghestin.

not possible to apply the literal terms of the clause in question, nevertheless proceeded arbitrarily to alter its terms by inserting 'particulars other than those by reference to which the parties had contracted'. Whereas however, having noted that the parties had taken as the indexation basis the index for a grade OP4 skilled worker as published from time to time in the lists of standard occupational wages, the cour d'appel observed that that index did not exist and that no such lists of standard occupational wages were published. Whereas in seeking to determine the common intention of the parties by means of the requisite interpretation of the wording of the deed, the cour d'appel found that it was apparent from the evidence in the case that the contracting parties had intended, from the outset of their dealings, that the purchase price, payable over a term of years, should be coupled with, and subject to, a price adjustment clause linked to increases in the salary of a skilled worker in the highest grade, that a reference to a grade three skilled mechanic came closest to reflecting that occupational category, and that reference should be made to the written wording in which the variations in the index chosen appeared. Whereas in so ruling, the cour d'appel were merely exercising their unfettered discretion. The first plea must therefore be rejected.

Note

The Cour de cassation, under cover of the *pouvoir souverain* of the lower court, gives a bold interpretation of the indexation clause, in order to save it. The case shows the considerable power that courts can give themselves by interpreting contracts 'creatively'. As far as indexation clauses are concerned, the solution is now codified by new Article 1167 Cciv.

FURTHER READING

Dedek, H, 'Implied Terms' in N Jansen and R Zimmermann (eds), *Commentaries on European Contract Laws* (Oxford University Press, 2018) 801–13.

Grobecker, W, *Implied Terms und Treu und Glauben: Vertragsergänzung im englischen Recht in rechtsvergleichender Perspektive* (Berlin: Duncker & Humblot, 1999).

Hadžimanovié, N, *Auslegung und Ergänzung von Verträgen: Vertragliche Nebenpflichten im englischen und schweizerischen Recht* (Zurich: Schulthess, 2006).

See also the literature referred to above, at the end of Chapter 18.

CHAPTER 21
UNFAIR CLAUSES

21.1 INTRODUCTION

The principle of 'freedom of contract' has traditionally been of paramount importance in the different countries considered in this book, but it no longer has an exclusive hold over the law of contract across Europe. Since the 1960s, and perhaps earlier, contract law has been seen to reflect a new principle, described by Zweigert and Kötz as 'contractual justice'.[1] Contractual justice is not confined to *procedural* fairness (the way in which the conclusion of the contract took place), but also relates to *substantive* fairness— the very content of the contract.[2] One of the most obvious ways to foster contractual justice is the protection of a contracting party against unfair clauses, and particularly exclusion and limitation clauses. Exclusion (sometimes called exemption) clauses and limitation clauses are terms of a contract which exclude some right which one of the parties would otherwise have had under the law, or which reduce the remedies available to him.[3] The need for control is particularly pressing when these contractual provisions are part of 'standard term' contracts which have not been negotiated by the parties in the particular case.

---

[1] K Zweigert and H Kötz, *Introduction to Comparative Law* (3rd edn, Oxford: Clarendon Press, 1998) 331.
[2] See A von Mehren, *International Encyclopedia of Comparative Law*, vol VII, *Contracts in General* (Tübingen: Mohr Siebeck, 1982) ch 1: The Formation of Contracts, para 72.
[3] See for a survey of the different clauses: H Beale, W Bishop and M Furmston, *Contract: Cases and Materials* (5th edn, Oxford University Press, 2008) 975.

In order to control contract terms, the courts used, at least until recently, a number of general doctrines of private law. First, the doctrine of 'offer and acceptance' has been used, whereby a party is required to show that the (standard) terms in question have been incorporated into the contract in the particular case.[4] Secondly, an unfair clause may be vitiated by misrepresentation.[5] Thirdly, the courts in some countries have developed doctrines to prevent such clauses applying where a contract has been breached in a particular way.[6] Fourthly, rules of construction or interpretation can be used, for example the rule that ambiguous clauses are to be construed against the party putting them forward (the *contra proferentem* rule).[7] Finally, the content of a contract term may conflict with 'public policy', 'good morals' or 'reasonableness and equity', and may therefore be inapplicable.[8]

However, more overt forms of review of unfair terms have also developed in both the civil law and common law countries. Originally, in several civil law jurisdictions (such as Germany and the Netherlands), the general requirement of contractual 'good faith' was invoked as the basis of review. Today, the review of unfair contract terms is often based upon specific statutory provisions. Since 1993, Directive 93/13/EEC on Unfair Terms in Consumer Contracts has provided for common minimum standards across the Community in the control of unfair terms in consumer contracts;[9] and even before 1993 all the laws described in this book had some legislative provisions on certain types of unfair term. Thus, in contrast to the other parts of this book, this section deals to a large extent with statutory materials.[10] However, the general doctrines discussed above remain applicable in this context, and are of particular importance when the statutory rules do not apply (for example, where the subject matter of the contract, the nature of the clause or the status of the parties involved takes it outside the statutory schemes).

This chapter follows a more or less historical sequence, starting with the 'indirect' controls through the general law; then considering selected national legislation; next, the impact of the Directive on Unfair Terms in Consumer Contracts will be considered; and, finally, some key features of the protection now available against unfair terms in the different countries studied will be considered. The chapter thus traces the development of controls on unfair contract terms in Europe, and shows that there was in fact considerable convergence between the different systems even before the Directive on Unfair Terms in Consumer Contracts was introduced; but differences remain, especially in B2B contracts.

---

[4] See below, p 813. On offer and acceptance generally see ch 8.
[5] See below, p 819.
[6] See below, p 820.
[7] See below, p 826. On interpretation generally, see ch 18.
[8] See ch 12; but contrast the position of English law, see below, p 814.
[9] Council Directive 93/13/EEC of 5 April 1993 on unfair terms in consumer contracts, OJ L 95/1993, p 29.
[10] See for a survey of legislative developments with regard to unfair contract terms in consumer transactions before the harmonisation in the EC by the Directive: E Hondius, *Unfair Terms in Consumer Contracts* (Utrecht: Molengraaf Institute for Private Law, 1987).

21.2 CONTROLS UNDER THE GENERAL LAW

21.2.A INCORPORATION TESTS

Court of Appeal   **21.1 (EN)**

Interfoto Picture Library Ltd v Stiletto Visual Programmes Ltd[11]

A party who wishes to rely on a clause in standard conditions of contract which have not been signed by the other party must give the other reasonable notice of the existence of the terms at or before the time the contract is made and, if the term is unusual or onerous, must take steps to bring the particular term to the other party's attention.

Facts: The plaintiffs ran a photographic transparency lending library. Following a telephone inquiry by the defendants, the plaintiffs delivered to them 47 transparencies together with a delivery note containing nine printed conditions. Condition 2 stipulated that all the transparencies had to be returned within 14 days of delivery; otherwise a holding fee of £5 a day plus VAT would be charged for each transparency retained thereafter. The defendants, who had not used the plaintiffs' services before, did not read the conditions and returned the transparencies four weeks later, whereupon the plaintiffs invoiced the defendants for £3,783.50. The defendants refused to pay and the plaintiffs brought an action to recover that sum. The judge gave judgment in favour of the plaintiffs for the amount claimed.

Held: Allowing the appeal, the Court of Appeal held that the plaintiffs were not entitled to rely on Condition 2 of the contract because (per Dillon LJ) Condition 2 had never been made a term of the contract or (per Bingham LJ) the defendants were relieved of any liability under the clause. The plaintiff was therefore entitled only to an award assessed *quantum meruit*.

Judgment: DILLON LJ: ... There was never any oral discussion of terms between the parties before the contract was made. In particular there was no discussion whatever of terms in the original telephone conversation when Mr. Beeching made his preliminary inquiry. The question is therefore whether condition 2 was sufficiently brought to the defendants' attention to make it a term of the contract which was only concluded after the defendants had received, and must have known that they had received, the transparencies and the delivery note.

This sort of question was posed, in relation to printed conditions, in the ticket cases, such as *Parker v South Eastern Railway Co* (1877) 2 CPD 416, in the last century. At that stage the printed conditions were looked at as a whole and the question considered by the courts was whether the printed conditions as a whole had been sufficiently drawn to a customer's attention to make the whole set of conditions part of the contract; if so the customer was bound by the printed conditions even though he never read them.

More recently the question has been discussed whether it is enough to look at a set of printed conditions as a whole. When for instance one condition in a set is particularly onerous does something special need to be done to draw customers' attention to that particular condition? In an obiter dictum in *J Spurling Ltd v Bradshaw* [1956] 1 WLR 461, 466 (cited in *Chitty on Contracts*, 25th ed (1983), vol 1, p 408) Denning LJ stated:

---

[11] [1989] QB 433.

'Some clauses which I have seen would need to be printed in red ink on the face of the document with a red hand pointing to it before the notice could be held to be sufficient.'

Then in *Thornton v Shoe Lane Parking Ltd* [1971] 2 QB 163 both Lord Denning MR and Megaw LJ held as one of their grounds of decision, as I read their judgments, that where a condition is particularly onerous or unusual the party seeking to enforce it must show that that condition, or an unusual condition of that particular nature, was fairly brought to the notice of the other party. ...

[W]hat their Lordships said was said by way of interpretation and application of the general statement of the law by Mellish LJ in *Parker v South Eastern Railway Co*, 2 CPD 416, 423–424 and the logic of it is applicable to any particularly onerous clause in a printed set of conditions of the one contracting party which would not be generally known to the other party.

Condition 2 of these plaintiffs' conditions is in my judgment a very onerous clause. The defendants could not conceivably have known, if their attention was not drawn to the clause, that the plaintiffs were proposing to charge a 'holding fee' for the retention of the transparencies at such a very high and exorbitant rate.

At the time of the ticket cases in the last century it was notorious that people hardly ever troubled to read printed conditions on a ticket or delivery note or similar document. That remains the case now. In the intervening years the printed conditions have tended to become more and more complicated and more and more one-sided in favour of the party who is imposing them, but the other parties, if they notice that there are printed conditions at all, generally still tend to assume that such conditions are only concerned with ancillary matters of form and are not of importance. ...

In the present case, nothing whatever was done by the plaintiffs to draw the defendants' attention particularly to condition 2; it was merely one of four columns' width of conditions printed across the foot of the delivery note. Consequently condition 2 never, in my judgment, became part of the contract between the parties.

BINGHAM LJ: In many civil law systems, and perhaps in most legal systems outside the common law world, the law of obligations recognises and enforces an overriding principle that in making and carrying out contracts parties should act in good faith. This does not simply mean that they should not deceive each other, a principle which any legal system must recognise; its effect is perhaps most aptly conveyed by such metaphorical colloquialisms as 'playing fair,' 'coming clean' or 'putting one's cards face upwards on the table.' It is in essence a principle of fair and open dealing. In such a forum it might, I think, be held on the facts of this case that the plaintiffs were under a duty in all fairness to draw the defendants' attention specifically to the high price payable if the transparencies were not returned in time and, when the 14 days had expired, to point out to the defendants the high cost of continued failure to return them.

English law has, characteristically, committed itself to no such overriding principle but has developed piecemeal solutions in response to demonstrated problems of unfairness. Many examples could be given. Thus equity has intervened to strike down unconscionable bargains. Parliament has stepped in to regulate the imposition of exemption clauses and the form of certain hire-purchase agreements. The common law also has made its contribution, by holding that certain classes of contract require the utmost good faith, by treating as irrecoverable what purport to be agreed estimates of damage but are in truth a disguised penalty for breach, and in many other ways.

The well known cases on sufficiency of notice are in my view properly to be read in this context. At one level they are concerned with a question of pure contractual analysis, whether one party has done enough to give the other notice of the incorporation of a term in the contract. At another level they are concerned with a somewhat different question, whether it would in all the circumstances be fair (or reasonable) to hold a party bound by any conditions or by a particular condition of an unusual and stringent nature. ...

The tendency of the English authorities has, I think, been to look at the nature of the transaction in question and the character of the parties to it; to consider what notice the party alleged to be bound was given of the particular condition said to bind him; and to resolve whether in all the circumstances it is fair to hold him bound by the condition in question. This may yield a result not very different from the civil law principle of good faith, at any rate so far as the formation of the contract is concerned. ...

The crucial question in the case is whether the plaintiffs can be said fairly and reasonably to have brought condition 2 to the notice of the defendants. ... In my opinion the plaintiffs did not do so. They delivered 47 transparencies, which was a number the defendants had not specifically asked for. Condition 2 contained a daily rate per transparency after the initial period of 14 days many times greater than was usual or (so far as the evidence shows) heard of. For these 47 transparencies there was to be a charge for each day of delay of £235 plus value added tax. The result would be that a venial period of delay, as here, would lead to an inordinate liability. The defendants are not to be relieved of that liability because they did not read the condition, although doubtless they did not; but in my judgment they are to be relieved because the plaintiffs did not do what was necessary to draw this unreasonable and extortionate clause fairly to their attention. I would accordingly allow the defendants' appeal and substitute for the judge's award the sum which he assessed upon the alternative basis of *quantum meruit*.

Notes

(1) The 'reasonable notice test' was laid down by the Court of Appeal in *Parker v South Eastern Railway Co Ltd*.[12] It is not sufficient that the plaintiff knew that there was writing on a ticket or notice (in that case, a ticket was given when luggage was deposited in a left-luggage office and a notice was located outside the office); according to the majority,[13] he must know or have been given reasonable notice that the writing contained conditions. Thus, if the plaintiff might reasonably have thought that a ticket given to him was simply a receipt for his payment, he is not bound by the terms in the ticket: see *Chapelton v Barry UDC*[14] (plaintiff was given a ticket when he hired a deckchair; he was not bound by the conditions on the ticket). The *Interfoto* case confirmed earlier suggestions that it may not suffice to give the plaintiff general notice that the contract contains conditions; if the conditions contain any term which is particularly onerous, the plaintiff may have to be given fair notice of the existence of that term.

(2) In the *Interfoto* case, Dillon LJ held that, in the light of the plaintiff's failure to give the defendants reasonable notice of the onerous term, the term had not been incorporated into the contract. Bingham LJ stated the same, but related this to a notion of fairness.

[12] (1877) 2 CPD 416.
[13] Bramwell LJ dissented on this point.
[14] *Chapelton v Barry* UDC [1940] 1 KB 532 (CA).

(3) Under the 'reasonable notice' test, it follows that the notice must be given before the contract is made.[15]

(4) Terms in notices, tickets, etc, may also be incorporated by a previous course of dealing on those terms, even if on the occasion in question the terms were not referred to.[16] However, for this purpose there must have been a course of previous dealing between the parties[17] and the terms in question must have been used consistently in previous contracts.[18]

(5) In contrast, if the condition has been brought to the plaintiff's attention, it will be incorporated into the contract. The same is true if the plaintiff has signed the contract, even if she has not read the document and the clause was in 'regrettably small print'; in the absence of fraud, misrepresentation or possibly mistake, the clause will form part of the contract.[19] We will see that some other laws apply a different rule to signed documents.

Cass civ (1), 4 July 1967[20] **21.2 (FR)**

Tragic flying lesson

A limitation of liability clause not contained in a written contract will be binding on the other party only if it is shown that he knew of it.

Facts: At the end of a flying lesson provided by the aeroclub, the instructor gave the pupil a demonstration of low-level flying. The aircraft touched a high-tension electricity line and crashed, killing both pupil and pilot. The pupil's widow brought an action against the aeroclub. The club argued that its liability was limited by a statute of 2 March 1957 applicable to aerial transport, or by a notice which referred to the limitation of liability set out in this law and which therefore became part of the contract.

Held: By the cour d'appel, that this was not a contract of transport by air, as it was not intended to convey the pupil from one place to another; that the pupil was still not a regular passenger even if the tuition had ended; and that the club had failed to prove that the pupil knew of the notice. The Cour de cassation agreed with the cour d'appel. On the notice point it said:

Judgment: THE COURT:—Whereas it is complained that the lower court, by requiring that the Aeroclub prove that the victim knew of the notice referring to the law of 1957, reversed the burden of proof ...

— Whereas however by seeing that the limitation of liability clause must have been intended by the parties, under the normal rules of formation of agreements; and thus it

---

[15] See *Thornton v Shoe Lane Parking Ltd* [1971] 2 QB 163 (CA).

[16] See *Henry Kendall & Sons v William Lillico & Sons Ltd* (appeals from *Hardwick Game Farm v Suffolk Agricultural and Poultry Producers Assoc*) [1969] 2 AC 31 (HL).

[17] See *Hollier v Rambler Motors (AMC) Ltd* [1972] 2 QB 71 (CA) (three or four times over a period of five years not sufficient).

[18] *McCutcheon v David MacBrayne Ltd* [1964] 1 WLR 165 (HL).

[19] *L'Estrange v Graucob Ltd* [1934] 2 KB 394 (CA): the legibility of the clause will be relevant if it can be challenged under legislation as unfair or unreasonable, see below, pp 838 ff.

[20] No. 65-11954, Bull civ I no. 248, JCP 1967.II.15234.

was for the club or its insurer to prove the agreement between the parties on which they seek to rely …

… — [The] ground of appeal must be struck out …

Cass civ (1), 3 June 1970[21]   **21.3 (FR)**

Air passenger in a hole

A regular passenger on an airline that has always publicised its conditions of carriage will be taken to know of them.

Facts: M Maché travelled with Air France from Orly to Palma de Majorca where, with the other passengers, he was directed by an Air France employee to make his way by a short cut to the airport building. On the way he caught his foot on a broken paving stone and fell into a shaft, injuring himself seriously. He sued Air France.

Held: By the lower court, that the employee had been negligent in not checking that the short cut he had directed passengers to take was safe; but that the company was protected by the limitation of liability clause in its general conditions. On these points the Cour de cassation agreed.

Judgment: THE COURT: On the first appeal ground, taken in its various branches:—Whereas the findings of the judgment appealed against were that Maché, who had flown on 29 March 1958 with Air France from Orly to Palma de Majorca, had been directed with the other passengers from the de-boarding area to the airport buildings by an employee of the company; as in the course of this walk, Maché caught his foot on a broken paving stone and fell into a shaft, injuring himself seriously; as the cour d'appel had found that the accident had resulted from 'the carelessness of the employee of Air France who, contrary to his employer's instructions, had pointed out a short cut without first having reconnoitred it', so that the victim 'could bring himself within the provisions of Article 1147 [now 1231-1], Code civil'; as it had however held that the carrier could 'invoke the limitation of liability clause contained in its general conditions of carriage of passengers'; as it is complained that the court so decided when, on the one hand, it had not answered the various points made by Maché showing that he could not have accepted the purported limitation of liability clause without knowing of it; and as, on the other hand, according to the judgment, since it accepted that Maché had never been in the places in which the carrier displayed the conditions, the judgment appealed against could not, without contradicting itself and reversing the burden of proof, justify its decision that he knew of them and accepted them;

— Whereas, however, the lower court held that the report of a judicial officer that, 'since it was first set up', the company Air France had always displayed its conditions for the carriage of passengers in public places; that the limitation of liability clause is referred to under para 2(b) of the conditions for contracts of transport; that as the general conditions themselves state, in para 3, the liability of the carrier for injury is limited to 125,000 gold francs, or the equivalent; that it stressed the fact that Maché was a frequent air traveller;

— Whereas, without contradicting itself or reversing the burden of proof, and taking into account the points supposedly ignored, the cour d'appel had been within its powers to decide that Maché 'could not have been ignorant of the existence of the clause concerned';

— Whereas therefore the first appeal ground must be rejected.

…

---

[21] No. 67-12789, Bull civ I no. 190, D 1971, 373.

Notes

(1) In French law, in principle it is for the party which wishes to rely on the clause to show that the other party accepted it, ie knew of it at the time the contract was made. The 2016 reform has codified this rule. Article 1119(1) Code civil states that 'General conditions put forward by one party have no effect on the other party unless they have been brought to the latter's attention and that party has accepted them.'

(2) However, as the second case shows, the party's knowledge may be deduced from the circumstances, particularly from prior dealings between the parties.

BGH, 4 June 1970[22]   **21.4 (DE)**

Greedy accountant

A standard term which strongly deviates from the statutory default rules and operates exclusively to the benefit of the supplier is not one that the other party need anticipate and will not form part of the contract.

Facts: The defendant transferred all his tax matters to the claimant under a mandate. The claimant subsequently confirmed the oral agreement in writing, pointing to his standard terms of business with regard to the carrying out of his duties and the calculation of his remuneration. The standard terms incorporated a clause saying that the standard terms of trade agreed by the profession ('ALLGO') would apply unless there was agreement to the contrary. The defendant did not react to this letter; however, he sought to revoke the mandate before the claimant had completed his work under it. The claimant claimed payment of the entire amount which had been agreed for his full performance. He pointed to one of the standard terms of ALLGO which was to the effect that the principal who revoked a mandate prematurely 'without good reason' was liable to pay in full, incompleteness of the work notwithstanding.

Held: A clause which makes a contracting partner liable to payment in full for premature revocation of a mandate, without regard to the service actually provided, is contrary to good faith and is consequently, as it was not part of the individually negotiated contract but merely incorporated by reference, ineffective.

Judgment: ... It is settled case law that the person who relies on standard terms assumes for himself control over the general freedom of contract as far as the content of the contract is concerned. He is therefore obliged at the stage of drafting those standard terms to look to the reasonable protection of the interests of his future contractual partners. If he brings to bear his own interests only, he abuses the freedom of contract which to this extent is limited by § 242 BGB. Standard terms can therefore lose their legal force, insofar as they contain disproportionate, surprising terms, in which the abusive furthering of one-sided interests at the expense of the other party is apparent and which, when the interests of those usually taking part in such transactions are weighed up, offend principles of fairness and equity (BGH NJW 1969, 230 ...).

Statutory default rules are based not only on the facilitation of transactions, but also on an immanent principle of fairness. Thus there must be a justification for standard terms departing from the default rules and calling into question the principle of justice on which the default rules are based, while at the same time passing themselves off as being in accordance with principles of law and fairness in the field they regulate. The degree to which the default rules framed by the legislator embody principles of justice can vary.

[22] BGHZ 54, 106, NJW 1970, 1596.

The stronger it is, the more stringently the court must scrutinise whether deviations from default rules stipulated in standard terms are compatible with the principle of good faith. The requirements of day-to-day legal transactions, which are meant to take place under the dominance of standard terms, demand that these terms stay within the boundaries of what fair and just-minded individuals would think reasonable. The contracting party, who has submitted himself to the standard terms unilaterally prepared by the other party, can be held to have agreed only to such terms as one can reckon with as a matter of fairness and justice (BGHZ 41, 151, 154; 38, 183, 185; 33, 216, 219; 22, 90, 94; …).

The provision which falls to be considered in the present case, § 17 ALLGO, does not satisfy these requirements which have been worked out by the VIIIth and IInd Civil Senates and which the present [VIIth] Senate has adopted (compare, for instance, BGHZ 48, 264, 268; 52, 171, 178; NJW 1963, 1148).

[Further extracts from this case, on the question of whether the substance of the clause was in conformity with good faith, will be found below.[23]]

> *Note*
>
> This principle of 'unfairly surprising clauses' is now included in § 305c BGB.[24]

21.2.B MISREPRESENTATION ETC

In the English case of *Curtis v Chemical Cleaning and Dyeing Co Ltd*,[25] the plaintiff took a wedding dress to be cleaned by the defendants. She was asked to sign a document which exempted the defendants from liability 'for any damage howsoever arising'. The plaintiff asked why she had to sign and was told that it was because the defendants could not accept responsibility for damage to beads or sequins on the dress. The plaintiff then signed the document. The dress was returned to her with a stain on it that had not been there before, and the defendants denied liability, relying on the clause. The Court of Appeal held that the statement made to the plaintiff misrepresented the effect of the clause and therefore the defendants could not rely on the clause.[26] A similar result would have been reached in France and Germany, but on the basis of the plaintiff's (subjective) mistake.[27]

Whilst *Curtis* is a straightforward application of the doctrine of misrepresentation, one can readily envisage that parties will fail accurately to explain the effect of their exclusion or limitation clauses, and that the doctrine may therefore assume particular importance in this context.

---

[23] 21.11 (DE), below, p 829.
[24] See below, p 836.
[25] [1951] 1 KB 805 (CA).
[26] It has been pointed out that the judges gave somewhat different reasons for this result. Lord Denning MR said that the defendants could not rely on the clause except as to damage to beads or sequins, but the other two judges seem to have held that although the clause was contained in a document signed by the plaintiff, because its effect had been misrepresented it never formed part of the contract. See *AXA Sun Life Services Plc v Campbell Martin Ltd* [2011] EWCA Civ 133, [2011] 2 Lloyd's Rep 1 at [100]–[105].
[27] See above, pp 501 ff.

21.2.C NATURE OF THE BREACH OF CONTRACT

As mentioned above, legal controls on the use of unfair terms have been particularly concerned with the use of exclusion and limitation clauses. The type of control considered in this section applies particularly where one party is in breach of contract and seeks to rely on a limitation or exclusion clause to reduce his liability.

Cass com, 15 June 1959[28]   **21.5 (FR)**

Rotting vegetables

*A clause seeking to exclude liability for breach of contract will be disregarded where the relevant breach of contract occurred intentionally (*dol*) or resulted from gross negligence (*faute lourde*).*

Facts: SICOMA contracted with Cherenque to import and transport some fresh vegetables from Spain to France. For the transport, Cherenque contracted a refrigerated car from STEF. All of the mentioned parties were companies. On arrival, the temperature was more than 40°C and the goods were damaged. Cherenque sought recovery for the damages they had to pay to SICOMA. The contract between Cherenque and STEF contained an exclusion clause with regard to the temperature in the refrigerated car, especially insofar as the condition of the goods on delivery are concerned.

Held: The judgment of the cour d'appel, to the effect that the clause should be disregarded, was set aside.

Judgment: THE COURT:—Under [former] Article 1134 of the Civil Code;
— Whereas where a party seeks to avoid liability by relying on a clause exempting him from liability which is contained in the contract and accepted by the other party, that clause is inapplicable only if there has been intentional fault or gross negligence on the part of the party invoking it;
— Whereas in merely stating, as a ground for disregarding the clause in question, that the contract was badly performed, without making any finding of intentional fault or gross negligence on the part of STEF, the cour d'appel failed to provide a legal basis for its decision;
On those grounds, and without there being any need to examine any of the other aspects of the appeal grounds advanced, this Court hereby sets aside the judgment appealed against ...

Notes

(1) An exemption clause cannot be invoked by a contractor who is guilty of intentional fault or gross negligence (*dol ou faute lourde*). The other contractor must prove intentional fault or gross negligence of the party that invokes the exemption clause. Gross negligence consists in negligence of an extreme gravity, which shows an inability to accomplish the task agreed upon. To assess whether there is gross negligence, two approaches are possible. The 'subjective approach' consists in assessing the defaulting party's behaviour: there is a *faute lourde* when there is a gross negligence. The

---

[28] No. 57-12362, Bull com no. 265; F Terré, Y Lequette and F Chénedé, *Grands arrêts de jurisprudence civile*, vol 2, *Obligations, Contrats spéciaux, Sûretés* (13th edn, Paris: Dalloz, 2015) no. 167.

other approach, called the 'objective approach', consists in examining the importance of the non-performance in relation to the contractual obligations.[29] In other words, non-performance with respect to an *obligation essentielle* amounts to a *faute lourde*, irrespective of the defaulting party's behaviour (mere negligence or lack of care suffices). For years, this objective approach prevailed. In practice, this opened the way for systematically invalidating exemption clauses which affected the *obligation essentielle*, independently of any *faute lourde*. The *faute lourde* test was only relevant when the exemption clause concerned an ancillary obligation, as opposed to an *obligation essentielle*. In 2005, a Chambre mixte of the Cour de cassation, decided, in two important cases, to return to the subjective approach of the *faute lourde*, meaning that such a fault was effectively required. The concept of *faute lourde* remains relevant when the exemption clause concerns a non-fundamental obligation. In that case, it is used in a subjective manner (provided there is not only a non-performance but negligence of an extreme gravity, akin to fraud).[30] This new definition of *faute lourde* has no direct relevance as regards exemption clauses which affect the *obligation essentielle* because the *Chronopost* case, which was based on the lack of a *cause*, has led to the systematic invalidation of exemption clauses which affected the *obligation essentielle*, independently of any scrutiny of the defaulting party's behaviour. The 2016 reform does not aim to reform the rules on damages arising from non-performance of a contract, therefore the 'intentional fault or gross negligence' limitation to the validity of exemption clauses is still good law. Further, Article 1282 of the reform bill on civil liability published in March 2017 states that 'In contractual matters, contract terms limiting or excluding liability have no effect in the case of gross or dishonest fault.'

(2) In 1996, in the *Chronopost* decision, the Cour de Cassation held that even in the absence of intentional fault or gross negligence, a clause that excludes liability for failure of performance of an obligation which constitutes the essence of the contract (*obligation essentielle*) can be avoided.[31] The Cour de cassation relied on the notion of *cause* to avoid the exemption clause.[32] *Chronopost* was followed by other decisions which rephrased *the test*. In *Chronopost*, it had been held that the exemption clause affected the *obligation essentielle* and that it 'contradicts the scope of the obligation entered into'. In a later decision the latter phrase was omitted.[33] This seemed to imply that any exemption clause which affected an *obligation essentielle* was ineffective, irrespective of whether it contradicted the scope of the contract entered into (in other words, even if they are reasonable in view of various

---

[29] F Terré, P Simler and Y Lequette, *Les obligations* (11th edn, Paris: Dalloz, 2013) no. 575.
[30] Cass mixte 22 April 2005, no. 03-14112, Bull No. 4, RDC 2005, annotated by D Mazeaud. This only applies to exemption clauses which are included in the contract and not to those which are included in a decree, Cass com 21 February 2006, no. 04-20139, Bull IV no. 48, RTD civ 2006, 322, annotated by P Jourdain; Cass com 13 June 2006, no. 05-12619, Bull IV no. 143.
[31] Cass com 22 October 1996, no. 93-18632, Bull IV no. 261; Terré, Lequette and Chénedé (n 28 above) no. 157.
[32] See 11.18 (FR), above, p 383.
[33] Cass com 30 May 2006, no. 04-14974, Bull IV no. 132, D 2006, 1599, annotated by D Mazeaud.

factors, including the parties' intent as to the allocation of the risks between them).[34] As observed by French authors, this rather radical solution did not seem compatible with the notion of *cause*, which required a careful examination of the clause to decide if it excluded any form of liability, either by stating that clearly or by stating such a low financial compensation that it is derisory.[35] The Cour de cassation finally returned to a more nuanced approach. Decisions just before the 2016 reform referred to the fact that the clause limiting liability 'contradicted the scope of the obligation entered into'.[36] Undoubtedly, the *Chronopost* saga has contributed to the abandonment of *cause* in French contract law as it established how versatile this concept was—and thus dangerous for the contract's integrity. As put by some authors: 'The *Chronopost* case sparked a vivid debate the roughness of which is explained, it seems, less by the solution in itself than the fact that it relied on the theory of *cause* to found it'.[37] This certainly explains why the solution drawn from the *Chronopost* saga was partly codified by the 2016 reform.

(3) Since *cause* was abandoned by the 2016 reform, the notion of *cause* cannot be used to avoid an exemption clause. However, to achieve the same result as under the notion of *cause*, a party may invoke the new Article 1170 Code civil.

Code civil   **21.6 (FR)**

Article 1170: Any contract term which deprives a debtor's essential obligation of its substance is deemed not written.

Notes

(1) Although Article 1170 of the Code civil applies not only to exemption clauses, but to any contract term, it probably will be invoked by a party wishing to avoid an exemption clause. In practice, (i) the essential obligation of the contract at stake must be determined and (ii) the extent to which the exemption clause deprives an essential obligation of its substance. This will be the case when the limitation is too important and when the creditor has not obtained a discount for accepting such a limitation. If an exemption clause infringes Article 1170, it is not null but deemed not to have been incorporated in the contract. This does not differ from the solution previously reached by the French courts.

(2) In addition to this limitation of exemption clauses, there are specific limitations. First, the case of a creditor who suffers a personal injury must be considered. Neither a statutory provision nor case law states expressly that an exemption clause is invalid in the case of personal injury. However, this limitation is widely accepted. They are

---

[34] cf Cass civ (3) 1 June 2005, no. 04-12200, Bull civ III no. 119, RTD civ 2005, 780, annotated by J Mestre and B Fages.

[35] D Mazeaud, 'Clauses limitatives de réparation: les quatre saisons' D 2008, 1776, 1779.

[36] Cass com 18 December 2007, no. 04-16069, Bull IV no. 265; Cass com 4 March 2008, no. 06-18893, RDC 2008, 292, annotated by G Viney. This has been made very clear in *Faurecia*, Cass com 29 June 2010, no. 09-11841, Bull IV no. 115, D 2010, 1832, annotated by D Mazeaud.

[37] Terré et al (n 29 above) no. 618.

deemed not to have been incorporated in the contract (i) if they are wholly exclusive of liability, as they would deprive the debtor's essential obligation of its substance, or (ii) if the contract at stake is a consumer contract (Article L 132-1 Code de la consommation), or (iii) if the contract is one of transportation (by air, boat or car) etc. In these scenarios, a court would probably avoid an exemption clause, since it most likely violates the *ordre public*.[38] Secondly, it is commonly accepted that an exclusion of liability arising from the law of delict is void because, as recently held by the Cour de cassation: 'Articles 1382 and 1383, now 1240 and 1241 of the Code civil, are of public policy'.[39] Criticising this decision, authors have doubted its application to cases of liability without fault (mainly based on new Article 1242 Code civil).

(3) The reform bill on civil liability in extra-contractual matters has opted for the validity of exemption clauses only for liability without fault.[40]

(4) Clauses excluding liability for hidden defects, such a contractual exemption clauses used by a professional seller are void under Article 1643 of the Code civil (because a professional seller is presumed to have knowledge of the hidden defect) *unless* the buyer himself knew of the defect or is himself a merchant dealing in goods of that kind and does not therefore need protection.[41]

Court of Appeal   **21.7 (EN)**

***Karsales v Wallis*[42]**

A breach which goes to the root of the contract disentitles the party from relying on the exempting clause [NB no longer the law!].

Facts: A buyer agreed to buy a Buick car on credit terms. The buyer had seen the car at a dealer's at which time it was in good condition. Under the credit arrangement, the car was sold by the dealer to a finance company who in turn agreed to sell it to the defendant. When it was delivered by the dealer, it was in very poor condition and was incapable of self-propulsion. The finance company, which was quite unaware of what had happened and had never seen the car, claimed the price from the buyer, relying on a clause in the contract which stated that it was not responsible for the condition of the car.

Held: Overturning the decision at first instance, the Court of Appeal held that the finance company was not entitled to rely on the exemption clause and therefore was responsible for the car being fit to drive; so it could not claim the price. The majority held simply that the clause did not apply when the thing supplied 'could not be described as a car'. Lord Denning reasoned differently.

Judgment: ... DENNING LJ: [T]he law about exempting clauses has been much developed in recent years, at any rate about printed exempting clauses, which so often pass unread.

---

[38] In the reform bill on civil liability of March 2017, Art 1281(2) states that 'However, in the case of personal injury, liability cannot be limited or excluded by contract.' Thus, it confirms the widely shared idea that one cannot limit one's liability when another has sustained a personal injury.

[39] Cass civ (1) 16 May 2017, no. 16-13407, unpublished. See also Cass civ (2) 17 February 1955, no. 55-02810, Bull II no. 100; Terré, Lequette and Chéndé (n 28 above) no. 185.

[40] See Art 1283 of the reform bill on civil liability: 'In extra-contractual matters, a person cannot exclude or limit his liability for fault.'

[41] On conformity in contract for the sale of goods, see above pp 783 ff.

[42] [1956] 1 WLR 936. See also p 828 below, at n 53.

Notwithstanding earlier cases which might suggest the contrary, it is now settled that exempting clauses of this kind, no matter how widely they are expressed, only avail the party when he is carrying out his contract in its essential respects. He is not allowed to use them as a cover for misconduct or indifference or to enable him to turn a blind eye to his obligations. They do not avail him when he is guilty of a breach which goes to the root of the contract. The thing to do is to look at the contract apart from the exempting clauses and see what are the terms, express or implied, which impose an obligation on the party. If he has been guilty of a breach of those obligations in a respect which goes to the very root of the contract, he cannot rely on the exempting clauses …

The principle is sometimes said to be that the party cannot rely on an exempting clause when he delivers something 'different in kind' from that contracted for, or has broken a 'fundamental term' or a 'fundamental contractual obligation,' but these are, I think, all comprehended by the general principle that a breach which goes to the root of the contract disentitles the party from relying on the exempting clause. In the present case the lender was in breach of the implied obligation that I have mentioned. When the defendant inspected the car before signing the application form, the car was in excellent condition and would go: whereas the car which was subsequently delivered to him was no doubt the same car, but it was in a deplorable state and would not go. That breach went, I think, to the root of the contract and disentitles the lender from relying on the exempting clause.

Notes

(1) Denning's judgment is an example of the so-called 'substantive' doctrine of fundamental breach that he and some other English judges developed to try to deal with exclusion and limitation of liability clauses which they thought were unfair (the other LJJ decided the case on interpretation of the clause). The result of this doctrine was that a person who committed a breach of a 'fundamental term'—apparently meaning a condition of the contract[43]—or a 'fundamental breach'—apparently meaning a serious breach of an innominate term[44]—was precluded from relying on any exemption clause.[45]

(2) There is no known link between the two developments, but the substantive doctrine of fundamental breach had similarities to the use of *cause* by the French courts described earlier (and see now Article 1170 Cciv, above).

(3) In *Suisse Atlantique v NV Rotterdamsche Kolen Centrale*[46] (discussed further below) this doctrine was disapproved by both the Court of Appeal and the House of Lords, but some doubts about its validity remained until the decision in *Photo Production Ltd v Securicor Transport Ltd.*

---

[43] See below, p 972.

[44] See below, p 999.

[45] See on the doctrine of fundamental breach, *Chitty on Contracts*, 33rd edn by H Beale (gen ed) (London: Sweet & Maxwell/Thomson Reuters, 2018) paras 15-023–15-027; *Treitel on the Law of Contract*, 14th edn by E Peel (London: Sweet & Maxwell, 2015) paras 7-023–7-025.

[46] [1967] 1 AC 361.

Photo Production Ltd v Securicor Transport Ltd[47]

The questions whether, and to what extent, an exclusion clause is to be applied to a fundamental breach are simply a matter of interpretation of the contract.

Facts: While carrying out a night patrol at the factory of Photo Production, an employee of Securicor, a security company, deliberately lit a small fire which got out of hand. The factory and stock inside, together valued at £615,000, were completely destroyed. Photo Production sued Securicor for damages on the ground that they were liable for the act of their employee. Securicor pleaded, *inter alia*, an exemption clause in the contract, to the effect that Securicor was not responsible for damage caused by its employee unless that damage could have been avoided through due diligence on the part of the company or the employee had been acting in the course of his employment when he or she caused the damage.

Held: In the Court of Appeal, Lord Denning held that Securicor were in fundamental breach of contract, and that they were not therefore entitled to rely on the exclusion clause. In doing so, his Lordship stated that he was applying the decision of the House of Lords in *Suisse Atlantique*. Allowing the appeal, the House of Lords held that Securicor were entitled to rely on the exclusion clause.

Judgment: LORD WILBERFORCE: My Lords, whatever the intrinsic merit of [the] doctrine [of fundamental breach], ... it is clear to me that so far from following this House's decision in the *Suisse Atlantique* it is directly opposed to it and that the whole purpose and tenor of the *Suisse Atlantique* was to repudiate it ...

I have no second thoughts as to the main proposition that the question whether, and to what extent, an exclusion clause is to be applied to a fundamental breach, or a breach of a fundamental term, or indeed to any breach of contract, is a matter of construction of the contract. Many difficult questions arise and will continue to arise in the infinitely varied situations in which contracts come to be breached—by repudiatory breaches, accepted or not, by anticipatory breaches, by breaches of conditions or of various terms and whether by negligent, or deliberate action or otherwise. But there are ample resources in the normal rules of contract law for dealing with these without the superimposition of a judicially invented rule of law.

... The doctrine of 'fundamental breach' in spite of its imperfections and doubtful parentage has served a useful purpose. There was a large number of problems, productive of injustice, in which it was worse than unsatisfactory to leave exception clauses to operate. Lord Reid referred to these in the *Suisse Atlantique* case [1967] 1 AC 361, 406, pointing out at the same time that the doctrine of fundamental breach was a dubious specific. But since then Parliament has taken a hand: it has passed the Unfair Contract Terms Act 1977. This Act applies to consumer contracts and those based on standard terms and enables exception clauses to be applied with regard to what is just and reasonable. It is significant that Parliament refrained from legislating over the whole field of contract. After this Act, in commercial matters generally, when the parties are not of unequal bargaining power, and when risks are normally borne by insurance, not only is the case for judicial intervention undemonstrated, but there is everything to be said, and this seems to have been Parliament's intention, for leaving the parties free to apportion the risks as they think fit and for respecting their decisions.

---

[47] [1980] 1 AC 827.

> *Note*
>
> Whilst the *Securicor* case is clear authority that there is no place for the doctrine of fundamental breach in English law, this is true only of the *substantive* doctrine (ie the doctrine that, whatever the clause said, it could not protect a party who was in fundamental breach of contract). As we will see in the next section, a particular rule of *construction* remains applicable to breaches of fundamental terms, and will be of significance if, for example, the statutory controls on unfair terms do not apply to the disputed clause.

21.2.D INTERPRETATION

The interpretation—or construction—of unfair clauses is the most important mechanism for controlling the effect of these terms under general contract law. The principal rule of construction in the systems studied is the *contra proferentem* rule: a clause is, on the face of it, expressed clearly and without ambiguity and yet it will be held so as not to apply in the particular circumstances.[48]

An exclusion or limitation clause may in effect deprive one party of any benefit under the contract, as where a term purports to exclude all liability for breach of contract.

This inconsistency between the primary contractual obligation and the exclusion clause can be resolved using the *contra proferentem* rule, as illustrated by English law. Whilst the House of Lords in the *Suisse Atlantique* case ruled out the 'substantive' doctrine of fundamental breach,[49] they ruled that the *contra proferentem* rule should be applied to fundamental breaches of contract as follows: the more serious the breach, the less likely it is that the parties intended to exclude or limit liability for that breach.[50] There are still cases where the rules on interpretation are important, particularly when the clause is not one covered by the Unfair Contract Terms Act 1977 (UCTA) or the Consumer Rights Act 2015.[51]

Nevertheless, as illustrated by the following case, there remains a key difference between the 'substantive' and 'construction' doctrines of fundamental breach; under the latter, but not the former, a clearly worded exclusion or limitation clause may apply even to very serious breaches of the contract:

Court of Appeal and House of Lords **21.9 (EN)**

George Mitchell (Chesterhall) Ltd v Finney Lock Seeds Ltd[52]

Where an exclusion or limitation clause clearly applies to a given situation, it is not open to the courts to put a strained interpretation on that clause so as to diminish its effects.

Facts: George Mitchell (Chesterhall) Ltd ordered a quantity of Dutch winter cabbage seeds from Finney Lock Seeds Ltd, a company of seed merchants. Owing to errors by the suppliers and employees of Finney Lock

---

[48] See also above, p 756.

[49] See n 46 above.

[50] See also the accounts of Lord Denning and Lord Bridge in the *George Mitchell* case, below.

[51] J Cooke and D Oughton, *The Common Law Of Obligations* (London: Butterworths, 1993) 400. On the UCTA see below, pp 838–42.

[52] [1983] QB 284, [1983] 2 AC 803.

Seeds, the seeds were in fact not of this variety but were autumn cabbage seeds. The resulting crop proved to be worthless. In an action by the farmer for wasted expenditure and loss of anticipated profits, the sellers of the seeds relied on a clause in their standard conditions of sale which provided that, if the seeds sold or agreed to be sold did not comply with the express terms of the contract or proved defective in varietal purity, the sellers' liability was limited to the replacement of the seeds or a refund of the price paid.

Held: In the Court of Appeal, a majority (Oliver and Kerr LJJ, Lord Denning dissenting on this point) held that, properly construed, the limitation clause did not protect the sellers from the consequences of their own negligence because the wrong kind of seed had been supplied (hence the reference below to 'peas and beans'). The House of Lords overturned the decision of the Court of Appeal, holding that the limitation clause clearly applied to the breach of contract which had occurred.

Judgment of the Court of Appeal: Lord Denning *The heyday of freedom of contract*: None of you nowadays will remember the trouble we had—when I was called to the Bar—with exemption clauses. They were printed in small print on the back of tickets and order forms and invoices. They were contained in catalogues or timetables. They were held to be binding on any person who took them without objection. No one ever did object. He never read them or knew what was in them. No matter how unreasonable they were, he was bound. All this was done in the name of 'freedom of contract'. But the freedom was all on the side of the big concern which had the use of the printing press. No freedom for the little man who took the ticket or order form or invoice. The big concern said, 'Take it or leave it'. The little man had no option but to take it. The big concern could and did exempt itself from liability in its own interest without regard to the little man. It got away with it time after time. When the courts said to the big concern, 'You must put it in clear words,' the big concern had no hesitation in doing so. It knew well that the little man would never read the exemption clauses or understand them.

It was a bleak winter for our law of contract …

The secret weapon: Faced with this abuse of power—by the strong against the weak—by the use of the small print of the conditions—the judges did what they could to put a curb upon it. They still had before them the idol, 'freedom of contract.' They still knelt down and worshipped it, but they concealed under their cloaks a secret weapon. They used it to stab the idol in the back. This weapon was called 'the true construction of the contract.' They used it with great skill and ingenuity. They used it so as to depart from the natural meaning of the words of the exemption clause and to put upon them a strained and unnatural construction …

Fundamental breach: No doubt has ever been cast thus far by anyone. But doubts arose when in this court—in *Karsales (Harrow) Ltd v Wallis* [1956] 1 WLR 936—we ventured to suggest that if the big concern was guilty of a breach which went to the 'very root' of the contract—sometimes called a 'fundamental breach'—or at other times a 'total failure' of its obligations—then it could not rely on the printed clause to exempt itself from liability. This way of putting it had been used by some of the most distinguished names in the law. Such as Lord Dunedin in *WS Pollock Co v Macrae*, 1922 SC(HL) 192; by Lord Atkin and Lord Wright in *Hain Steamship Co Ltd v Tate Lyle Ltd* (1936) 41 Com Cas 350, 354 and 362–363 respectively and by Devlin J in *Smeaton Hanscomb Co Ltd v Sassoon I Setty, Son & Co (No 1)* [1953] 1 WLR 1468, 1470. But we did make a mistake—in the eyes of some—in elevating it—by inference—into a 'rule of law.' That was too rude an interference with the idol of 'freedom of contract.' We ought to have used the secret weapon. We ought to have said that in each case, on the 'true construction of the contract' in that case, the exemption clause did not avail the party where he was guilty of a fundamental breach or a breach going to the root. That is the lesson to be learnt from the 'indigestible' speeches in *Suisse Atlantique Société d'Armement Maritime SA v NV Rotterdamsche Kolen Centrale* [1967] 1 AC 361.

Judgment of the House of Lords: LORD BRIDGE OF HARWICH: … In his judgment, Lord Denning MR traces, in his uniquely colourful and graphic style, the history of the courts' approach to contractual clauses excluding or limiting liability … My Lords, in considering the common law issue, I will resist the temptation to follow that fascinating trail, but will content myself with references to the two recent decisions of your Lordships' House commonly called the two Securicor cases: *Photo Production Ltd v Securicor Transport Ltd* [1980] AC 827 ('Securicor 1') and *Ailsa Craig Fishing Co Ltd v Malvern Fishing Co Ltd* [1983] 1 WLR 964 ('Securicor 2').

Securicor 1 gave the final quietus to the doctrine that a 'fundamental breach' of contract deprived the party in breach of the benefit of clauses in the contract excluding or limiting his liability. Securicor 2 drew an important distinction between exclusion and limitation clauses. This is clearly stated by Lord Fraser of Tullybelton, at p 105:

> 'There are later authorities which lay down very strict principles to be applied when considering the effect of clauses of exclusion or of indemnity: see particularly the Privy Council case of *Canada Steamship Lines Ltd v The King* [1952] AC 192, 208, where Lord Morton, delivering the advice of the Board, summarised the principles in terms which have recently been applied by this House in *Smith v UMB Chrysler (Scotland) Ltd*, 1978 SC(HL) 1. In my opinion these principles are not applicable in their full rigour when considering the effect of conditions merely limiting liability. Such conditions will of course be read contra proferentem and must be clearly expressed, but there is no reason why they should be judged by the specially exacting standards which are applied to exclusion and indemnity clauses.'

In my opinion, this is not a 'peas and beans' case at all. The relevant condition applies to 'seeds'. Clause 1 refers to seeds 'sold' and 'seeds agreed to be sold'. Clause 2 refers to 'seeds supplied'. As I have pointed out, Oliver LJ concentrates his attention on the phrase 'seeds agreed to be sold'. I can see no justification, with respect, for allowing this phrase alone to dictate the interpretation of the relevant condition, still less for treating clause 2 as 'merely a supplement' to clause 1. Clause 2 is perfectly clear and unambiguous. The reference to 'seed agreed to be sold' as well as to 'seeds sold' in clause 1 reflects the same dichotomy as the definition of 'sale' in the Sale of Goods Act 1979 as including a bargain and sale as well as a sale and delivery. The defective seeds in this case were seeds sold and delivered, just as clearly as they were seeds supplied, by the appellants to the respondents. The relevant condition, read as a whole, unambiguously limits the appellants' liability to replacement of the seeds or refund of the price.

[The House of Lords went on to hold that the decision of the Court of Appeal, that in this case the clause did not apply because the sellers supplied something completely different from what they were supposed to supply, was wrong.[53]]

Notes

(1) Having held that the clause, properly interpreted, did apply in the instant case, the House of Lords went on to consider whether the clause satisfied the statutory controls on unfair terms. This aspect of the decision is considered below.[54]

(2) Whilst exemption clauses are construed strictly under English law, the House of Lords has emphasised that, since there are now statutory controls on unfair contract

---

[53] See *Karsales v Wallis*, 21.7 (EN), above, p 823.
[54] 21.41 (EN), below, p 885.

terms, there is no justification for placing a strained and artificial meaning upon the language of a clear and unambiguous clause so as to avoid the exclusion or restriction of liability contained in it. The *George Mitchell* case is an example of this. The House of Lords thus rejected an approach evident in some of the earlier case law (as described by Lord Denning in the extract above) and which had developed in the absence of substantive controls on contractual terms.[55]

(3) In a case after *Photo Production*,[56] the House of Lords ruled that a distinction should be drawn between the interpretation of clauses which *exclude* liability altogether and those which only *limit* liability to a certain sum. Exclusion clauses are subjected to the strictest standards of *contra proferentem* interpretation, whereas limitation clauses are construed less strictly, for the reason that a party is more likely to have agreed to a limitation of his legal right than the complete exclusion of it.[57]

21.2.E GOOD FAITH AND PUBLIC POLICY POLICING SUBSTANCE

We saw earlier that the German courts held that, as a matter of good faith, one party will not be able to rely on a clause which is 'surprising' unless he drew it to the other party's attention when the contract was made. In this section we consider the extent to which the courts in Germany and the Netherlands are empowered under the general law to review the terms of contracts simply on the basis of their substance—so that even a clause that was pointed out to the other party may not be effective.

BGB   21.10 (DE)

§ 138: Transactions contrary to public policy; usury
  (1) Any transaction which is contrary to public policy is void.
  (2) In particular, a transaction by which a person exploits the position of constraint in which another person finds himself, or the inexperience, lack of discernment or substantial weakness of will of that other person, in order, for his own benefit or that of a third party, to procure the promise of, or to obtain, a pecuniary advantage in return for the provision of a service, is void.

§ 242: Performance in accordance with the principle of good faith
  The debtor must perform his obligation in accordance with the requirements of good faith, taking into account the prevailing practice.

BGH, 4 June 1970[58]   21.11 (DE)

Greedy accountant

A clause allowing an accountant to charge the full fee when the client cancels his mandate before the accountant has done the work is contrary to good faith.

---

[55] See also *Chitty* (n 45 above) para 15-007.
[56] 21.8 (EN), above, p 825.
[57] See *Ailsa Craig Fishing Co Ltd v Malvern Fishing Co Ltd* [1983] WLR 964, 970 (see above, p 828).
[58] BGHZ 54, 106, NJW 1970, 1596.

[For the facts of this case, see 21.4 (DE), above, p 818.]

Judgment: ... The provision which falls to be considered in the present case, § 17 ALLGO, does not satisfy these requirements which have been worked out by the VIIIth and IInd Civil Senates and which the present [VIIth] Senate has adopted (compare, for instance, BGHZ 48, 264, 268; 52, 171, 178; NJW 1963, 1148).

It is true that it is not unacceptable *as such* that, according to the substance of § 17 ALLGO, the agent can and should retain the *complete* remuneration in the event of an early revocation of the agency agreement 'without good reason'. The law in force is by no means averse to taking this idea as a starting point when making provision for the present conflict of interests, as is precisely shown by § 649 BGB [now § 648 BGB] that was used by the appeal court, and also by § 615 BGB in the context of contracts of employment; though with the limitations contained in the second half sentence of § 649 BGB [now § 648 BGB] and in the second sentence of § 615 BGB, respectively. Therefore, according to this principle, the clause which falls to be assessed is not inherently contrary to the case law outlined above.

The clause does not, however, accord with the principle of good faith, because in setting the level of the remuneration claim of the agent in the case of early revocation of the mandate it pays no attention at all to the extent to which services have actually been provided at that point, but instead gives full remuneration even in the case where he has performed minimal or even no services at all, that is to say when the agreed payment bears absolutely no relation to the actual performance by the agent. A provision which makes such an outcome possible is contrary to equity and represents an abusive pursuit of the self interest of one contractual partner at the expense of the other whose justifiable needs are insufficiently taken into account.

§ 628(1)(1) BGB, relating to partial remuneration in the case of premature termination of a contract for the provision of services is to be read in the context of the exceptional rights to termination stipulated in §§ 626 and 627 BGB, the operation of which it seeks to facilitate. In this case, § 627 BGB only is of interest (which is not affected by ALLGO). With this provision the legislator clearly takes account of the fact that, according to general experience, the remuneration payable to the service provider who has been given notice of termination and the exercise of the right to terminate in itself are closely interrelated. Termination under § 627 BGB is disproportionately impeded if the remuneration which is payable in spite of the premature and voluntary termination of the contract for services bears absolutely no relation to the actual services performed at that point. Assuming that this is the case, the basic idea underlying that provision is called into question, i.e. to bind a person, who can demand services of a more sophisticated nature from an independent third party on the basis of a special fiduciary relationship, to the agreement arrived at only for so long as the relationship of trust underlying this agreement continues to exist, irrespective of whether there is a good reason for an eventual loss of trust or not.

It is therefore not at all the case that the statutory solution in § 628(1)(1) BGB is totally based on considerations of mere practicality. It is rather meant to strike a *just* balance between the conflicting interests of the parties in the dispute at issue. The claimant cannot argue that in the tax advisory professions special conditions obtain, which require the *complete* disapplication of the statutory provision in favour of the agent and which would make it appear that only this is indeed the just outcome in the instant case. Rather, there is no sufficient reason in evidence which would justify that standard terms departing from statutory provisions would put to one side the principles of justice inherent in § 628(1)(1) BGB and would completely disregard the justifiable interests of the principal.

Consequently, in order to be in accordance with good faith, a provision contained in standard terms which diverges from a statutory default rule must protect the interests of the principal in case of premature termination of the mandate to the minimum extent which corresponds to the idea of justice underlying the statutory provision. This includes that the relation between the level of remuneration and the actual services provided must be within a spectrum which can still be described as proportionate and as acceptable for the principal with a view to the exceptional right of termination granted by § 627 BGB. It is of lesser importance in which way this is achieved, whether by adding a clause which contains a general and appropriate limitation of the basic principle requiring full remuneration, or by means of a sensible sliding scale or breakdown of payments which is agreed from the start, applies across the board and more or less mirrors the various services to be performed. ...

It is not possible to give § 17(1) ALLGO an unambiguous content which would be in conformity with the requirements of the case law outlined above by way of (supplementary) interpretation under § 157 BGB: the possibilities of determining the level of remuneration payable in the case of a mandate terminated prematurely 'without good reason' are too many and varied; on the one hand one has to start from the original agreement that full remuneration should be paid, on the other hand the actual performance must adequately be taken into account. The clause must therefore be ineffective in its entirety, without any judgment being made as to the effectiveness of the remaining provisions of the ALLGO, which is not at issue in the present case, let alone as to the validity of the entire contract between the parties (BGHZ 51, 55, 57; 22, 90, 92). Instead, the statutory rule in § 628(1)(1) BGB, which was meant to be displaced but—as was shown above—was not in fact displaced by a different term, simply takes the place of the contractual term which ceases to exist.

Note

The German legal system was one of the first to develop a comprehensive and successful system of judicial review of standardised contracts.[59] The courts based their intervention on general principles of German contract law, such as the rule prohibiting contracts contrary to good morals (§ 138 BGB), which are held void, and the general requirement of good faith (§ 242 BGB).

BW   **21.12 (NL)**

Article 6:2: (1) A creditor and debtor must, as between themselves, act in accordance with the requirements of reasonableness and equity.

(2) A rule binding upon them by virtue of law, usage or a juridical act does not apply to the extent that, in the given circumstances, this would be unacceptable according to criteria of reasonableness and equity.

Article 6:248: (2) A rule binding upon the parties as a result of the contract does not apply to the extent that, in the given circumstances, this would be unacceptable according to criteria of reasonableness and equity.

---

[59] See von Mehren (n 2 above) para 79.

Hoge Raad, 19 May 1967[60]   **21.13 (NL)**

Saladin v HBU

Whether a clause satisfies the requirements of 'reasonableness and equity' should be assessed by reference to criteria including those referred to in the judgment below.

Facts: After being advised by the Hollandsche Bank-Unie, a bank, Mr Saladin, a layman in financial affairs, bought shares in a Canadian company. The advice proved to be too optimistic. Saladin had to bear a loss of Dfl80,000. The bank pleaded an exemption clause for negligent information and advice.

Held: In the circumstances of the case, the bank could successfully invoke the exemption clause.

Judgment: ... The answer to the question as to the circumstances in which a party—such as the Bank in the present case—is debarred from relying on a term in a contract excluding him from liability for certain conduct, even where that conduct wrongfully prejudices the other party, may depend on the assessment of numerous factors, such as: the gravity of the fault, taking into account the nature and substance of the interests affected by the conduct in question, the nature and other contents of the agreement containing the term in issue, the social position of the parties and their mutual relationship, the way in which the term came into existence, and the extent to which the other party was aware of the effect of the term ...

Notes

(1) In Dutch law a contract term does not apply to the extent that, in the given circumstances, this would be unacceptable according to criteria of reasonableness and equity (Articles 6:2 and 6:248(2) BW). An interpretation of the relevant circumstances is given in the *Saladin v HBU* case.

(2) These general rules of 'good faith' may be invoked when Section 6.5.3 BW (standard term contracts[61]) is not applicable, particularly where a term is not part of standard terms or when the other party is a 'large company' within the meaning of Article 6:235 BW.

We will also see that in France the Cour de cassation granted the civil courts the autonomous power to annul unfair contract terms.[62] This decision built upon the existing statutory controls on unfair contract terms, but at that time the statutory controls were extremely limited. As we will see, the decision of the Cour de cassation transformed the nature of the controls under French law from a mere public law power, given effect through abstract review, to a power to declare unfair contract terms null and void in the course of civil proceedings. However, this decision is better considered in the following section, in conjunction with the relevant legislation.

In England there was a single-handed attempt by Lord Denning to develop the overt review of unfair contract terms at common law. In *Gillespie Bros & Co Ltd v Roy Bowles*

---

[60] NJ 1967, 261 with a note by GJ Scholten.
[61] This is broadly similar in substance to §§ 305 ff BGB.
[62] 21.19 (FR), below, p 846; cf also Cass civ (1) 26 May 1993, no. 92-16327, Bull I no. 192, D 1993, 568, annotated by G Paisant. See B Starck, H Roland and L Boyer, *Les Obligations,* vol II: *Contrat* (5th edn, Paris: Litec, 1993) nos. 671 ff; Terré et al (n 29 above) nos. 319 ff.

Transport Ltd,[63] his Lordship had previously suggested that the courts had the power to review contract terms on a yet more open-ended basis. In the *Securicor Transport* case in the Court of Appeal he summarised his view:[64]

> Thus we reach, after long years, the principle which lies behind all our striving: the court will not allow a party to rely on an exemption or limitation clause in circumstances in which it would not be fair or reasonable to allow reliance on it; and, in considering whether it is fair and reasonable, the court will consider whether it was in a standard form, whether there was equality of bargaining power, the nature of the breach, and so forth.

The House of Lords implicitly rejected this in deciding, in the same case, that whether a clause applies is a matter of construction. Later, in *Lloyds Bank Ltd v Bundy*,[65] Lord Denning expressed the view that English law contains a general doctrine of 'inequality of bargaining power'. That was explicitly rejected by the House of Lords in a later case.[66]

21.3 LEGISLATIVE CONTROLS

In each of the three countries to be discussed in this section (England, France and Germany), controls developed by the courts at common law or under general provisions of the civil codes have been supplemented by legislation aimed specifically at unfair terms of various kinds.[67] The legislation varies significantly both in the scope and the means of control employed. In this respect, it must be noted that Directive 93/13 on Unfair Terms in Consumer Contracts came into force and had to be implemented no later than 31 December 1994 in the national legal systems (Article 10(1) of the Directive).[68] In this section, the different statutory regimes with respect to unfair terms will be discussed and the effect of the Directive on Unfair Terms in Consumer Contracts on these national legal systems.

Unfair Terms Directive[69]   **21.14 (EU)**

Article 1: 1. The purpose of this Directive is to approximate the laws, regulations and administrative provisions of the Member States relating to unfair terms in contracts concluded between a seller or supplier and a consumer.

2. ...

Article 2: For the purpose of this Directive:

(a) 'unfair terms' means the contractual terms defined in Article 3;

(b) 'consumer' means any natural person who, in contracts covered by this Directive, is acting for purposes which are outside his trade, business or profession;

---

[63] *Gillespie Bros & Co Ltd v Roy Bowles Transport Ltd* [1973] 1 QB 400, 416 (CA).

[64] *Photo Production Ltd v Securicor Transport Ltd* [1978] 1 WLR 856, 865 (CA). For the facts of this case, see the excerpt from the House of Lords decision, 21.8 (EN), above, p 825.

[65] *Lloyds Bank Ltd v Bundy* [1975] QB 326 (CA), 16.11 (EN), above, p 653 (a case of undue influence).

[66] See *National Westminster Bank Ltd v Morgan* [1985] AC 686, above, p 655.

[67] See also, H-W Micklitz, J Stuyck and E Terryn (eds), *Ius Commune Casebooks on the Common Law of Europe: Consumer Law* (Oxford: Hart Publishing, 2010) 279 ff.

[68] See on the Directive also: Micklitz et al (n 67 above) 280 ff.

[69] Council Directive 93/13/EEC of 5 April 1993 on unfair terms in consumer contracts, OJ L 95/1993, p 29.

(c) 'seller or supplier' means any natural or legal person who, in contracts covered by this Directive, is acting for purposes relating to his trade, business or profession, whether publicly owned or privately owned.

Article 3: 1. A contractual term which has not been individually negotiated shall be regarded as unfair if, contrary to the requirement of good faith, it causes a significant imbalance in the parties' rights and obligations arising under the contract, to the detriment of the consumer.

2. A term shall always be regarded as not individually negotiated where it has been drafted in advance and the consumer has therefore not been able to influence the substance of the term, particularly in the context of a pre-formulated standard contract.

The fact that certain aspects of a term or one specific term have been individually negotiated shall not exclude the application of this Article to the rest of a contract if an overall assessment of the contract indicates that it is nevertheless a pre-formulated standard contract.

Where any seller or supplier claims that a standard term has been individually negotiated, the burden of proof in this respect shall be incumbent on him.

3. The Annex shall contain an indicative and non-exhaustive list of the terms which may be regarded unfair.

Article 4: 1. Without prejudice to Article 7, the unfairness of a contractual term shall be assessed, taking into account the nature of the goods or services for which the contract was concluded and by referring, at the time of conclusion of the contract, to all the circumstances attending the conclusion of the contract and to all the other terms of the contract or of another contract on which it is dependent.

2. Assessment of the unfair nature of the terms shall relate neither to the definition of the main subject matter of the contract nor to the adequacy of the price and remuneration, on the one hand, as against the services or goods supplied in exchange, on the other, in so far as these terms are in plain, intelligible language.

Article 5: [see above, p 756, and below, p 874].

Article 6: 1. Member States shall lay down that unfair terms used in a contract concluded with a consumer by a seller or supplier shall, as provided for under their national law, not be binding on the consumer and that the contract shall continue to bind the parties upon those terms if it is capable of continuing in existence without the unfair terms.

2. ...

Article 7: 1. Member States shall ensure that, in the interests of consumers and of competitors, adequate and effective means exist to prevent the continued use of unfair terms in contracts concluded with consumers by sellers or suppliers.

2. ...

Notes

(1) The Directive has a minimum character, which means that it allows Member States to grant consumers a higher level of protection than the Directive (Article 8). As we will see, some Member States have retained features of the pre-existing statutory controls on unfair terms, or have since adopted wider provisions, and as a result offer protection wider in scope than that required by the Directive.

(2) The subject matter of the Directive is *standard terms* only; that is, terms in contracts that have not been individually negotiated (Article 3(1)). The Directive does not apply to non-contractual notices.

(3) The standard for review is the 'unfairness' of a clause. A contractual term is 'unfair' if it causes a *significant imbalance* in the parties' rights and obligations arising under the contract to the *detriment of the consumer* contrary to the requirement of *good faith* (Article 3(1)). Moreover, it follows from the Court of Justice's case law that a clause is also unfair if it does not meet the transparency requirements as laid down in Article 5 of the Directive.[70] Whether a term is 'unfair' depends on all the circumstances attending the conclusion of the contract (Article 4(1)). The Annex to the Directive contains an *indicative* and non-exhaustive list of the terms which *may be regarded* as unfair (Article 3(3)).[71] The unfairness of a contract term shall not be assessed with regard to the core provisions of the contract, such as the subject matter or the price (Article 4(2)), provided those terms are in plain and intelligible language.

(4) When a contractual term is regarded as 'unfair', the term is not binding (Article 6(1)).

(5) Article 7 of the Directive requires that the Member States must ensure adequate and effective means to prevent the continued use of unfair terms in consumer contracts. These means have to include individual actions by persons or 'class actions' by organisations having a legitimate interest under national law in protecting consumers, and which may be heard by (civil) courts or by competent administrative bodies.[72] The review in a collective action has an 'abstract' character; the judicial control is thus exercised independently of the validity of a term in any particular contract.

21.3.A GERMANY: BGB

In Germany, the case law concerning unfair contract terms was first codified in the 1976 Unfair Contract Terms Act (Gesetz zur Regelung des Rechts der Allgemeinen Geschäftsbedingungen—AGBG). The Unfair Terms Directive only required minor amendments to the Act, which were duly implemented. Finally, the Act to Modernise the Law of Obligations (Schuldrechtsmodernisierungsgesetz), which came into force on 1 January 2002, incorporated most of the AGBG provisions in the BGB, with only minor amendments having been made. The procedural provisions concerning consumer injunctions were moved to a new Act on Actions for Injunctions (Unterlassungsklagengesetz—UklaG).

BGB   **21.15 (DE)**

§ 305: Incorporation of standard business terms into the contract

(1) Standard business terms are all contract terms pre-formulated for more than two contracts which one party to the contract (the user) presents to the other party upon the

---

[70] C-26/13, *Árpád Kásler and Hajnalka Káslerné Rábai v OTP Jelzálogbank Zrt*, 30 April 2014, ECLI:EU:C:2014:282; see 21.32 (EU), below, p 868.

[71] C488/11, *DF Asbeek Brusse, K de Man Garabito v Jahani BV*, 30 May 2013, ECLI:EU:C:2013:341.

[72] See below, ch 21.5.

entering into of the contract. It is irrelevant whether the provisions take the form of a physically separate part of a contract or are made part of the contractual document itself, what their volume is, what typeface or font is used for them and what form the contract takes. Contract terms do not become standard business terms to the extent that they have been negotiated in detail between the parties.

(2) Standard business terms only become a part of a contract if the user, when entering into the contract, refers the other party to the contract to them explicitly or, where explicit reference, due to the way in which the contract is entered into, is possible only with disproportionate difficulty, by posting a clearly visible notice at the place where the contract is entered into, and gives the other party to the contract, in an acceptable manner, which also takes into reasonable account any physical handicap of the other party to the contract that is discernible to the user, the opportunity to take notice of their contents, and if the other party to the contract agrees to their applying.

(3) The parties to the contract may, while complying with the requirements set out in subsection (2) above, agree in advance that specific standard business terms are to govern a specific type of legal transaction.

§ 305a: Incorporation in special cases

Even without compliance with the requirements cited in section 305 (2) nos. 1 and 2, if the other party to the contract agrees to their applying the following are incorporated,

1. the tariffs and regulations of the railways issued with the approval of the competent transport authority or on the basis of international conventions, and the terms of transport approved under the Passenger Transport Act [Personenbeförderungsgesetz], of trams, trolley buses and motor vehicles in regular public transport services,

2. the standard business terms published in the gazette of the Federal Network Agency for Electricity, Gas, Telecommunications, Post and Railway [Bundesnetzagentur für Elektrizität, Gas, Telekommunikation, Post und Eisenbahnen] and kept available on the business premises of the user,

> a) into transport contracts entered into off business premises by the posting of items in postboxes,
>
> b) into contracts on telecommunications, information services and other services that are provided direct by the use of distance communication and at one time and without interruption during the supply of a telecommunications service, if it is disproportionately difficult to make the standard business terms available to the other party before the contract is entered into.

§ 305b: Priority of individually agreed terms

Individually agreed terms take priority over standard business terms.

§ 305c: Surprising and ambiguous clauses

(1) Provisions in standard business terms which in the circumstances, in particular with regard to the outward appearance of the contract, are so unusual that the other party to the contract with the user need not expect to encounter them, do not form part of the contract.

(2) Any doubts in the interpretation of standard business terms are resolved against the user.

§ 306: Legal consequences of non-incorporation and ineffectiveness

(1) If standard business terms in whole or in part have not become part of the contract or are ineffective, the remainder of the contract remains in effect.

(2) To the extent that the terms have not become part of the contract or are ineffective, the contents of the contract are determined by the statutory provisions.

(3) The contract is ineffective if upholding it, even taking into account the alteration provided in subsection (2) above, would be an unreasonable hardship for one party.

§ 306a: Prohibition of circumvention

The rules in this division apply even if they are circumvented by other constructions.

§ 307: Test of reasonableness of contents

(1) Provisions in standard business terms are ineffective if, contrary to the requirement of good faith, they unreasonably disadvantage the other party to the contract with the user. An unreasonable disadvantage may also arise from the provision not being clear and comprehensible.

(2) An unreasonable disadvantage is, in case of doubt, to be assumed to exist if a provision

1. is not compatible with essential principles of the statutory provision from which it deviates, or

2. limits essential rights or duties inherent in the nature of the contract to such an extent that attainment of the purpose of the contract is jeopardised.

(3) Subsections (1) and (2) above, and sections 308 and 309 apply only to provisions in standard business terms on the basis of which arrangements derogating from legal provisions, or arrangements supplementing those legal provisions, are agreed. Other provisions may be ineffective under subsection (1) sentence 2 above, in conjunction with subsection (1) sentence 1 above.

Notes

(1) As regards the subject matter, these provisions of the BGB apply only to standard terms (§ 305(1) BGB). Individually negotiated contracts have priority over standard terms (§ 305b BGB).

(2) According to the general clause of § 307(1) BGB, a contract clause is not binding (*unwirksam*, ie void) when the other party suffers an 'undue advantage' to such an extent as to be incompatible with good faith.

(3) § 309 BGB contains a 'black list', a list of terms which are deemed to be not binding, and § 308 BGB contains a 'grey list', the terms of which are not binding if they contain disproportionate elements.[73] Only consumers can directly invoke these lists (§ 310(1) BGB). However, as we will see, the lists may be applied indirectly to commercial contracts.[74]

(4) According to §§ 1 and 3 Unterlassungsklagengesetz (see above, p 835, and below, p 888), an action to review a standard term cannot only be brought to a district court by an individual, but also by consumer groups or associations. The review in such a 'class action' has an abstract character.

(5) See also Articles 6:231, 6:233, 6:236, 6:237; 6:240; 6:241, 6:243 of the BW, which are to similar effect.[75]

---

[73] These provisions are set out below, 21.28 (DE), p 856.

[74] See below, pp 882 ff.

[75] See in this respect: AS Hartkamp & CH Sieburgh, *Mr. C. Assers Handleiding tot de beoefening van het Nederlands Burgerlijk Recht. 6. Verbintenissenrecht. Deel III. Algemeen overeenkomstenrech* (Deventer: Kluwer 2014) ch 17.

21.3.B ENGLAND: THE UNFAIR CONTRACT TERMS ACT 1977 AND THE CONSUMER RIGHTS ACT 2015

English law contains two separate schemes for the regulation of unfair contract terms, which are the Unfair Contract Terms Act 1977 (UCTA) and the Consumer Rights Act 2015 (CRA).

Originally, the Directive was transposed in the Unfair Terms in Consumer Contracts Regulations 1994. These were replaced by the Unfair Terms in Consumer Contracts Regulations 1999 (UCCTR);[76] the principal change was to allow a wider range of bodies to challenge the use of unfair terms, but the opportunity was taken to make the wording of the Regulations nearly identical to the Directive itself. Both sets of Regulations left the UCTA unamended. This meant that there was a significant degree of overlap between the UCTA, on the one hand, and the Regulations, on the other; and, to make matters even more confusing for consumers and also businesses, the two pieces of legislation used different terms and concepts and applied to consumer contracts in different circumstances. The matter was referred to the English and Scottish Law Commissions, which in 2005 recommended that both pieces of legislation be replaced by a single statute. Although the government accepted this recommendation in principle, nothing was done until the passing of the Consumer Rights Act 2015. The effect of the 2015 Act is that controls over unfair terms in consumer contracts are contained in the Act, and UCTA is amended so as no longer to apply to consumer contracts. Some sections are therefore amended, others that applied only to consumer contracts are repealed entirely.

Unfair Contract Terms Act 1977   **21.16 (EN)**

Introductory

Section 1: Scope of Part I

...

(3) In the case of both contract and tort, sections 2 to 7 apply (except where the contrary is stated in section 6(4)) only to business liability, that is liability for breach of obligations or duties arising—

(a) from things done or to be done by a person in the course of a business (whether his own or another's); or

(b) from the occupation of premises used for business purposes;

and references to liability are to be read accordingly ...

Avoidance of liability for negligence, breach of contract, etc

Section 2: Negligence liability

(1) A person cannot by reference to any contract term or to a notice given to persons generally or to particular persons exclude or restrict his liability for death or personal injury resulting from negligence.

---

[76] The 1999 Regulations are considered in detail in *Chitty* (n 45 above) paras 38-211 ff.

(2) In the case of other loss, or damage, a person cannot so exclude or restrict his liability for negligence except in so far as the term or notice satisfies the requirement of reasonableness.

(3) Where a contract term or notice purports to exclude or restrict liability for negligence a person's agreement to or awareness of it is not of itself to be taken as indicating his voluntary acceptance of risk.

(4) ...

Section 3: Liability arising in contract

(1) This section applies as between contracting parties where one of them deals on the other's written standard terms of business.

(2) As against that party, the other cannot by reference to any contract term—

(a) when himself in breach of contract, exclude or restrict any liability of his in respect of the breach; or

(b) claim to be entitled—

(i) to render a contractual performance substantially different from that which was reasonably expected of him, or

(ii) in respect of the whole or any part of his contractual obligation, to render no performance at all,

except in so far as (in any of the cases mentioned above in this subsection) the contract term satisfies the requirement of reasonableness.

(3) ...

Section 6: Sale and hire-purchase

(1) Liability for breach of the obligations arising from—

(a) section 12 of the Sale of Goods Act 1979 (seller's implied undertakings as to title, etc);

(b) section 8 of the Supply of Goods (Implied Terms) Act 1973 (the corresponding thing in relation to hire-purchase),

cannot be excluded or restricted by reference to any contract term.

(1A) Liability for breach of the obligations arising from

(a) section 13, 14 or 15 of the 1979 Act (seller's implied undertakings as to conformity of goods with description or sample, or as to their quality or fitness for a particular purpose),

(b) section 9, 10 or 11 of the 1973 Act (the corresponding things in relation, to hire-purchase),

cannot be excluded or restricted by reference to any contract term except in so far as the term satisfies the requirement of reasonableness.

(4) The liabilities referred to in this section are not only the business liabilities defined by section 1(3), but include those arising under any contract of sale of goods or hire-purchase agreement.

(5) ...

Section 7: Miscellaneous contracts under which goods pass

(1) Where the possession or ownership of goods passes under or in pursuance of a contract not governed by the law of sale of goods or hire-purchase, subsections (2) to (4) below apply as regards the effect (if any) to be given to contract terms excluding or restricting liability for breach of obligation arising by implication of law from the nature of the contract.

(1A) Liability in respect of the goods' correspondence with description or sample, or their quality or fitness for any particular purpose cannot be excluded or restricted by reference to any such term except in so far as the term satisfies the requirement of reasonableness.

3(A) Liability for breach of the obligations arising under section 2 of the Supply of Goods and Services Act 1982 (implied terms about title etc in certain contracts for the transfer of the property in goods) cannot be excluded or restricted by references to any such term.

(4) Liability in respect of—

(a) the right to transfer ownership of the goods, or give possession; or

(b) the assurance of quiet possession to a person taking goods in pursuance of the contract,

cannot (in a case to which subsection (3A) above does not apply) be excluded or restricted by reference to any such term except in so far as the term satisfies the requirement of reasonableness.

(4A) ...

Other provisions about contracts

Section 10: Evasion by means of secondary contract

A person is not bound by any contract term prejudicing or taking away rights of his which arise under, or in connection with performance of, another contract, so far as those rights extend to the enforcement of another's liability which this Part of this Act prevents that other from excluding or restricting.

Explanatory provisions[77]

Section 13: Varieties of exemption clause

(1) To the extent that this Part of this Act prevents the exclusion or restriction of any liability it also prevents—

(a) making the liability or its enforcement subject to restrictive or onerous conditions;

(b) excluding or restricting any right or remedy in respect of the liability, or subjecting a person to any prejudice in consequence of his pursuing any such right or remedy;

(c) excluding or restricting rules of evidence or procedure;

and (to that extent) sections 2 and 5 to 7 also prevent excluding or restricting liability by reference to terms and notices which exclude or restrict the relevant obligation or duty.

(2) But an agreement in writing to submit present or future differences to arbitration is not to be treated under this Part of this Act as excluding or restricting any liability.

Section 14: Interpretation of Part I

In this Part of this Act:

'business' includes a profession and the activities of any government department or local or public authority;

...'goods' has the same meaning as in the Sale of Goods Act 1979;

'hire-purchase agreement' has the same meaning as in the Consumer Credit Act 1974;

'negligence' has the meaning given by section 1(1);

---

[77] Section 11, which defines 'fair and reasonable', and Sch 2, which sets out guidelines on reasonableness, are extracted below, p 884. Section 12, which defines 'dealing as a consumer', was discussed at pp 175–76.

'notice' includes an announcement, whether or not in writing, and any other communication or pretended communication; and

'personal injury' includes any disease and any impairment of physical or mental condition.

Notes

(1) The Unfair Contract Terms Act 1977 applies not only to contract terms, but also to non-contractual notices which purport to exclude or restrict liability in tort. Nevertheless, the Act is concerned mainly with contractual liability. The Act does not seek to control unfair contract terms in general. For the most part, it applies only to exclusion and limitation clauses.

(2) The pattern of control exercised by the Act is very complex. With regard to the Act, Zweigert and Kötz[78] remarked: 'This very complex enactment is hard enough for the English lawyer, let alone the foreigner, to understand'. It is only slightly simpler now that the Act does not apply to contracts or notices between a trader and a consumer (see below). The three principal divisions of control—which may overlap[79]—are:

(a) contract terms which exclude or restrict liability for negligence;[80]

(b) contract terms which exclude or restrict liability for breach of certain terms implied by statute or common law in contracts of sale of goods, hire-purchase and in other contracts for the supply of goods; and

(c) contract terms contained in a party's written standard terms of business, and which exclude or restrict liability for breach of contract, or which purport to entitle one of the parties to render a contractual performance substantially different from that reasonably expected of him, or to render no performance at all.

(3) The exclusion or restriction of liability may be rendered absolutely ineffective, or effective only insofar as the term satisfies the requirement of reasonableness:

(a) *Absolutely ineffective*: contract terms and notices excluding and limiting a business's liability for death or personal injury resulting from negligence (section 2(1)); and excluding or restricting liability for breach of Sale of Goods Act 1979, section 12 (seller's obligations as to title, etc.);

(b) *Requirement of reasonableness*: for example, contract terms excluding or limiting liability for harm other than death or personal injury caused by negligence (section 2(2)); clauses in standard form contracts (section 3); clauses in contracts for supply of goods to businesses purporting to exclude or limit the supplier's liability if the goods are not of the right type or quality (sections 6(1A) and 7(1A)); clauses excluding liability for misrepresentation (section 8, which amends section 3 of the Misrepresentation Act 1967).

(4) Section 6 of the Act was not new legislation but replaced similar provisions in the Supply of Goods (Implied Terms) Act 1973. The only significant change from the 1973 legislation is that the 'reasonableness' test has been changed from the test

---

[78] K Zweigert and H Kötz, *Introduction to Comparative Law* (2nd edn, Oxford: Clarendon Press, 1987) 366 (omitted from 3rd edn).

[79] See *Chitty* (n 45 above) para 15-067.

[80] See s 1(1).

of 'whether it was reasonable for a party to rely on the clause' to the test of 'whether or not the clause was a fair and reasonable one to be included in the contract'.[81] (The *George Mitchell* case[82] was decided under the 1973 Act.)

(5) As stated above, the Directive was transposed in English law by the Unfair Terms in Consumer Contracts Regulations.[83] Consequently, the UTCC Regulations 1994 and then 1999 operated alongside the Unfair Contract Terms Act 1977. Now the 1999 Regulations and the parts of UCTA that applied to consumer contracts have been replaced by the Consumer Rights Act 2015.

Consumer Rights Act 2015 **21.17 (EN)**

Section 31: Liability that cannot be excluded or restricted

(1) A term of a contract to supply goods is not binding on the consumer to the extent that it would exclude or restrict the trader's liability arising under any of these provisions—

(a) section 9 (goods to be of satisfactory quality);

(b) section 10 (goods to be fit for particular purpose);

(c) section 11 (goods to be as described);

(d) section 12 (other pre-contract information included in contract);

(e) section 13 (goods to match a sample);

(f) section 14 (goods to match a model seen or examined);

(g) section 15 (installation as part of conformity of the goods with the contract);

(h) section 16 (goods not conforming to contract if digital content does not conform);

(i) section 17 (trader to have right to supply the goods etc);

(j) section 28 (delivery of goods);

(k) section 29 (passing of risk).

(2) That also means that a term of a contract to supply goods is not binding on the consumer to the extent that it would—

(a) exclude or restrict a right or remedy in respect of a liability under a provision listed in subsection (1),

(b) make such a right or remedy or its enforcement subject to a restrictive or onerous condition,

(c) allow a trader to put a person at a disadvantage as a result of pursuing such a right or remedy, or

(d) exclude or restrict rules of evidence or procedure.

(3) The reference in subsection (1) to excluding or restricting a liability also includes preventing an obligation or duty arising or limiting its extent.

(4) An agreement in writing to submit present or future differences to arbitration is not to be regarded as excluding or restricting any liability for the purposes of this section.

(5) Subsection (1)(i), and subsection (2) so far as it relates to liability under section 17, do not apply to a term of a contract for the hire of goods.

---

[81] UCTA, s 11, 21.40 (EN), below, p 884.
[82] See both 21.9 (EN), above, p 826, and 21.41 (EN), below, p 885.
[83] See above, p 838. The 1999 Regulations are considered in detail in *Chitty* (n 45 above) paras 38-211 ff.

(6) But an express term of a contract for the hire of goods is not binding on the consumer to the extent that it would exclude or restrict a term that section 17 requires to be treated as included in the contract, unless it is inconsistent with that term (and see also section 62 (requirement for terms to be fair)).

(7) See Schedule 3 for provision about the enforcement of this section.

Section 57: Liability that cannot be excluded or restricted

(1) A term of a contract to supply services is not binding on the consumer to the extent that it would exclude the trader's liability arising under section 49 (service to be performed with reasonable care and skill).

(2) Subject to section 50(2), a term of a contract to supply services is not binding on the consumer to the extent that it would exclude the trader's liability arising under section 50 (information about trader or service to be binding).

(3) A term of a contract to supply services is not binding on the consumer to the extent that it would restrict the trader's liability arising under any of sections 49 and 50 and, where they apply, sections 51 and 52 (reasonable price and reasonable time), if it would prevent the consumer in an appropriate case from recovering the price paid or the value of any other consideration. (If it would not prevent the consumer from doing so, Part 2 (unfair terms) may apply.)

(4) That also means that a term of a contract to supply services is not binding on the consumer to the extent that it would—

(a) exclude or restrict a right or remedy in respect of a liability under any of sections 49 to 52,

(b) make such a right or remedy or its enforcement subject to a restrictive or onerous condition,

(c) allow a trader to put a person at a disadvantage as a result of pursuing such a right or remedy, or

(d) exclude or restrict rules of evidence or procedure.

(5) The references in subsections (1) to (3) to excluding or restricting a liability also include preventing an obligation or duty arising or limiting its extent.

(6) An agreement in writing to submit present or future differences to arbitration is not to be regarded as excluding or restricting any liability for the purposes of this section.

(7) See Schedule 3 for provision about the enforcement of this section.

Section 62: Requirement for contract terms and notices to be fair

(1) An unfair term of a consumer contract is not binding on the consumer.

(2) An unfair consumer notice is not binding on the consumer.

(3) This does not prevent the consumer from relying on the term or notice if the consumer chooses to do so.

(4) A term is unfair if, contrary to the requirement of good faith, it causes a significant imbalance in the parties' rights and obligations under the contract to the detriment of the consumer.

(5) Whether a term is fair is to be determined—

(a) taking into account the nature of the subject matter of the contract, and

(b) by reference to all the circumstances existing when the term was agreed and to all of the other terms of the contract or of any other contract on which it depends.

(6) A notice is unfair if, contrary to the requirement of good faith, it causes a significant imbalance in the parties' rights and obligations to the detriment of the consumer.

(7) Whether a notice is fair is to be determined—

(a) taking into account the nature of the subject matter of the notice, and

(b) by reference to all the circumstances existing when the rights or obligations to which it relates arose and to the terms of any contract on which it depends.

(8) This section does not affect the operation of—

(a) section 31 (exclusion of liability: goods contracts),

(b) section 47 (exclusion of liability: digital content contracts),

(c) section 57 (exclusion of liability: services contracts), or

(d) section 65 (exclusion of negligence liability).

Section 65: Bar on exclusion or restriction of negligence liability

(1) A trader cannot by a term of a consumer contract or by a consumer notice exclude or restrict liability for death or personal injury resulting from negligence.

(2) Where a term of a consumer contract, or a consumer notice, purports to exclude or restrict a trader's liability for negligence, a person is not to be taken to have voluntarily accepted any risk merely because the person agreed to or knew about the term or notice.

(3) In this section "personal injury" includes any disease and any impairment of physical or mental condition.

(4) In this section "negligence" means the breach of—

(a) any obligation to take reasonable care or exercise reasonable skill in the performance of a contract where the obligation arises from an express or implied term of the contract,

(b) a common law duty to take reasonable care or exercise reasonable skill,

(c) the common duty of care imposed by the Occupiers' Liability Act 1957 or the Occupiers' Liability Act (Northern Ireland) 1957, or

(d) the duty of reasonable care imposed by section 2(1) of the Occupiers' Liability (Scotland) Act 1960.

(5) It is immaterial for the purposes of subsection (4)—

(a) whether a breach of duty or obligation was inadvertent or intentional, or

(b) whether liability for it arises directly or vicariously.

(6) This section is subject to section 66 (which makes provision about the scope of this section).

Notes

(1) Section 31(1) replaces the former section 6(2) of UCTA, which prevented a trader who was selling goods to a consumer from excluding or restricting its liability to the consumer for breaches of the relevant obligations as to conformity, etc; section 31(2) and (3) are the equivalent of UCTA, section 13.

(2) Section 47 of the CRA 2015, not reproduced here, has parallel provisions for contracts under which a trader supplies digital content to a consumer.

(3) Section 57 applies to contracts to supply services to a consumer. Here, UCTA, section 2(2) used to provide that an exclusion or restriction of liability could be valid if it satisfied the requirement of reasonableness. The new section provides consumers with additional protection in that the trader cannot limit its liability to below the amount the consumer has paid; any further limit must be fair under section 62.

(4) The Unfair Contract Terms Act used to provide that a number of types of term in a consumer contract—mainly varieties of exclusion or restriction of the trader's liability—and also notices affecting the trader's liability to the consumer in tort would be effective only if the term or notice satisfied the requirement of reasonableness. The relevant provisions have all been replaced by Consumer Rights Act 2015, section 62, which imposes a general requirement that the terms in a consumer contract, and notices affecting the trader's liability to consumers, be fair.

21.3.C FRANCE: THE LOI SCRIVENER, CODE DE LA CONSOMMATION, THE 2009 DECREE, CODE DE COMMERCE AND CODE CIVIL

Loi Scrivener[84] **21.18 (FR)**

Article 35: (1) In contracts between professionals and non-professionals or consumers, a decree of the Conseil d'État made on the advice of the Commission established by Art L 132–2, may, taking into account the nature of the goods or services concerned, forbid, limit or regulate any clause dealing with a determined or determinable price, or its payment, with the quality of the thing or its delivery, with the allocation of risks, or with termination or modification of the agreement, where such clauses appear to be imposed on the non-professional or consumer by an abuse of economic power by the other party and to give the other party an excessive advantage.

(2) Such abusive clauses, stipulated contrary to the preceding article, are to be treated as of no effect.

Note

In France, in contrast to most other legal systems in Europe, the overt examination of contract terms by civil courts is a relatively recent development. Until recently the French civil courts had no general statutory mandate to examine the reasonableness of terms in (standard) contracts. The control had an administrative, public law character. Article 35 of the Loi Scrivener of 10 January 1978 empowered the government to issue decrees prohibiting specific clauses in contracts between professionals and consumers. For a long time, the only decree ever issued was decree no. 78-464 of 24 March 1978. Its effect was, in fact, limited to two sorts of clauses: clauses in sales contracts, which restrict the buyer's right to damages if the seller is in breach, and clauses in any type of contract which enable a professional to modify unilaterally the characteristics of the product or service promises, unless such modification is linked to technical factors and does not affect the price.

After a long period without policing contract terms, the civil courts decided to react: after giving an extensive interpretation to the 1978 decree, they simply got rid of the necessity of a decree for a clause to be declared unfair, as shown in the following case which was at that time considered a real *coup d'état jurisprudentiel*.

---

[84] Loi no. 78-23, 10 January 1978.

Minit France

The civil courts are entitled to apply Article 35 of the Loi Scrivener to unfair contract terms in the course of civil proceedings, and to hold that an unfair term is null and void.

Facts: A consumer took his slides to a branch of Minit France, a photography shop, in order to get them printed as photographs. The slides were lost. The receipt contained an exclusion clause.

Held: The Cour de cassation held that the cour d'appel was right in considering the clause void.

Judgment: ... —Whereas having observed that the clause appearing on the deposit receipt exonerated the laboratory from all liability in the event of loss of the slides, the court below, whose contested judgment indicates that a clause of that kind conferred an excessive advantage on Minit France and that that company was able, on account of its economic position, to impose it on its customers, rightly decided that that clause was unfair and must be deemed null and void;

— Whereas neither part of the appeal ground can therefore be upheld;

Notes

(1) In this decision, the Cour de cassation took the view that the civil courts were entitled to invoke the ground of review set out in Article 35 of the Loi Scrivener to render unfair clauses inapplicable in the course of civil disputes. The decision therefore transformed the nature of the control on unfair contract terms under French law.

(2) The Loi Scrivener also set up a Commission des clauses abusives (CCA) with an advisory task towards the government and a task to make (non-binding) recommendations in order to suppress or to modify terms which the Commission regards as unreasonable. The CCA is an independent authority under the wing of the minister responsible for consumer affairs. It includes, on a parity basis, representatives of professionals and consumers, judges, and specialists in contract law (law professors, lawyers). The CCA recommendations are a guide enabling consumers to identify unfair terms and to single out the best contracts, or again to renegotiate contracts, by inviting the professional to review his terms on the basis of the recommendations. In the event of a dispute, CCA recommendations can be relied upon in actions seeking the injunction of unfair terms brought before the civil courts by individual consumers or by consumer organisations.

Code de la consommation **21.20 (FR)**

Article L 212-1: Any clause contained in a contract concluded between a professional and a consumer shall be regarded as unfair if its object or effect is to create, to the detriment of that person or consumer, a significant imbalance in the rights and obligations of the parties to the contract.

---

[85] No. 89-20999, Bull I no. 153, D 1991, 449, annotated by J Ghestin.

Without prejudice to the rules of construction laid down in Articles 1188, 1189, 1191 and 1192 of the Civil Code, the unfairness of a clause shall be assessed by reference, at the time of conclusion of the contract, to all the circumstances attending the conclusion of the contract and to all the other terms of the contract. It shall also be assessed in the light of the clauses contained in another contract where the conclusion or performance of each of those two contracts is legally dependent on the conclusion or performance of the other.

Assessment of the unfair nature of any clause within the meaning of the first paragraph shall relate neither to the definition of the main subject-matter of the contract nor to the adequacy of the price or remuneration as against the goods sold or the service offered, as long as the clause is drafted in plain, intelligible language.

A Council of State decree issued upon the advice of the Commission des clauses abusives determines the type of clauses which, in view of the extent to which such clauses affect the equilibrium of the contract, must be considered, irrebuttably, as unfair according to the first paragraph.

A decree adopted by the Council of State under the same conditions as above determines a list of clauses that must be regarded as unfair; in case of disagreement concerning a contract with such a clause, the professional must prove that the clause is unfair.

These provisions shall be applicable irrespective of the form of the contract or the medium in which it appears. The foregoing shall apply inter alia to any purchase order, invoice, guarantee, delivery note or delivery order, ticket or coupon containing stipulations, whether or not the same have been freely negotiated, or references to general conditions drawn up in advance.

Article L 212-2: The provisions of Article L 212-1 are also applicable to contracts concluded between professionals and non-professionals.

Article L 212-3: The provisions of this Chapter are a matter of public policy.

Notes

(1) The rules to police unfair terms in B2C contracts were amended in 1995 to meet the requirements of the Directive on Unfair Terms in Consumer Contracts and more recently by Loi no. 2008-776, Loi no. 2014-344 and the 2016 Ordonnance.

(2) According to these rules, a consumer—or a non-professional[86]—may strike down an unfair term either by establishing (i) that the term creates a significant imbalance in the rights and obligations of the parties to the contract, or (ii) that the term belongs to the list of unfair terms adopted by decree.

(3) According to Loi no. 2008-776, a Decree was adopted which established two lists of unfair terms: a black list of terms which are unfair, and a grey list of terms which are presumed to be unfair. These lists can be found respectively in Articles R 212-1 and R 212-2 of the Code de la consommation. For instance, exemption clauses are included in the black list and are invalid if they are incorporated in a consumer contract.

---

[86] On this notion, see above ch 7.

Perhaps the most controversial change of the French contract law reform is the expansion of the control of unfair terms in B2B contracts in the Code civil itself, which is laid down in the following provisions:

Code civil   **21.21 (FR)**

Article 1104: Contracts must be negotiated, formed and performed in good faith.
   This provision is a matter of public policy.

Article 1110: ...
   A standard-form contract[87] is one which comprises a collection of non-negotiable terms which are determined in advance by one of the parties without negotiation.

Article 1119: General conditions put forward by one party have no effect on the other party unless they have been brought to the latter's attention and that party has accepted them.
   ...

Article 1171: In a standard-form contract, any term which is non-negotiable and determined in advance by one of the parties and which creates a significant imbalance in the rights and obligations of the parties to the contract is deemed not written.
   The assessment of significant imbalance must not relate either to the main subject-matter of the contract nor to the adequacy of the price in relation to the act of performance.

Code de commerce   **21.22 (FR)**

Article L 442-6: I.—Any producer, trader, manufacturer or person recorded in the trade register who commits the following offences shall be held liable and obliged to make good the damage caused:
   ...
   2° Subjecting or seeking to subject a trading partner to obligations that create a significant imbalance in the rights and obligations of the parties; ...

Notes

   (1) In addition to Article L 442-6, I and the rules in the Code de la consommation, the new provisions of the Code civil police standard form contracts. In 2015 a draft of the contract law reform was published by the Chancery. It was criticised because the control of unfair terms concerned both negotiated and non-negotiated terms. As a consequence, in the 2016 reform, the control was limited to standard form contracts (*contrats d'adhésion*) (Article 1171 of the Code civil). This restriction did not end

---

[87] 'Standard-form contract' translates *contrat d'adhésion*, more literally 'a contract to which one adheres' and whose conclusion therefore involves no or little choice as to the terms – 'take it or leave it'. As to the 2016 reforms, see F Chénedé, *Le nouveau droit des obligations et des contrats: Consolidations, innovations, perspectives* (Paris: Dalloz, 2016) nos. 23.321–23.375; O Deshayes, T Genicon and Y-M Laithier, *Réforme du droit des contrats, du régime général et de la preuve des obligations: Commentaire article par article* (Paris: LexisNexis, 2016) 292–310; M Latina and G Chantepie, *La réforme du droit des obligations: Commentaire théorique et pratique dans l'ordre du Code civil* (Paris: Dalloz, 2016) nos. 436–49.

the debate, particularly with regard to the definition and scope of the *contrat d'adhésion*. Under the 2016 Ordonnance, a *contrat d'adhésion* was defined as 'one whose general conditions are determined in advance by one of the parties without negotiation'. However, this definition was criticised because French law is unfamiliar with it. As a consequence, the 2018 ratification amended both Article 1110(2) and Article 1171 of the Civil code to refer to 'non-negotiable' terms. In spite of these changes, the crucial issue will still be whether a term has been negotiated. Answers to many other questions are still open, for instance where the burden of proof lies.

(2) According to Article 1171, a term which creates a significant imbalance in the rights and obligations of the parties to the contract is deemed unwritten. At the time of writing, it is unclear which test the courts will develop to determine whether a term creates a significant imbalance. Hopefully, case law will soon determine if the test to be applied is similar to the test already used by the courts with respect to the abovementioned specific controls. In general, there are many doubts about the future application of Article 1171 and, consequently, parties are more likely to rely on the specific controls when available.

(3) The aforementioned Loi no. 2008-776 also created a legislative control of unfair terms in B2B contracts which is included in Article L 442-6, I, 2° of the Code de commerce. While this provision includes neither a grey nor a black list, the test which must be applied is rather similar to the test with respect to unfair terms in B2C contracts. It must be established whether an obligation creates a significant imbalance in the rights and obligations of the parties to the contract in order to have the clause struck down. Two aspects of this control are worth noting: (i) the claim can be brought by one of the party to the contract and also by the Minister in charge of the Economy, (ii) the mere attempt to subject the other party to an unfair term is actionable.

(4) These different provisions in different codes raise the issue as to whether they can be invoked at the same time or whether they are mutually exclusive. There is no provision precluding a party subject to a specific control to rely on Article 1171 of the Code civil. However, it is very likely that a consumer will use the Code de la consommation to have an unfair term struck down since this specific control is well established and easier to invoke because of the grey and black lists. Similarly, a business is more likely to invoke the specific control of the Code de commerce because it does not require the contract at stake to be a *contrat d'adhésion*.[88]

Principles of European Contract Law **21.23 (INT)**

Article 4:110: Unfair Terms not Individually Negotiated[89]

(1) A party may avoid a term which has not been individually negotiated if, contrary to the requirements of good faith and fair dealing, it causes a significant imbalance in the parties' rights and obligations arising under the contract to the detriment of that party, taking

---

[88] In commercial contracts, one might rely on Art 1171 of the Code civil in order to avoid the specific procedural rules applicable to Art L 442-6, I, 2° of the Code de commerce. Pursuant to the latter, a claim based on this provision can only be brought in front of eight special courts, and appeal can only be heard by the Cour d'appel de Paris.

[89] cf Art II.-9:102 DCFR: terms not individually negotiated; Arts 79–86 CESL.

into account the nature of the performance to be rendered under the contract, all the other terms of the contract and the circumstances at the time the contract was concluded.

(2) This Article does not apply to:[90]

(a) a term which defines the main subject matter of the contract, provided the term is in plain and intelligible language; or to

(b) the adequacy in value of one party's obligations compared to the value of the obligations of the other party.

Article 8:109: Clause Excluding or Restricting Remedies

Remedies for non-performance may be excluded or restricted unless it would be contrary to good faith and fair dealing to invoke the exclusion or restriction.

UNIDROIT Principles   **21.24 (INT)**

Article 2.1.19: Contracting under standard terms

(1) Where one party or both parties use standard terms in concluding a contract, the general rules on formation apply, subject to Articles 2.1.20–2.1.22.

(2) Standard terms are provisions which are prepared in advance for general and repeated use by one party and which are actually used without negotiation with the other party.

Article 2.1.20: Surprising terms

(1) No term contained in standard terms which is of such a character that the other party could not reasonably have expected it, is effective unless it has been expressly accepted by that party.

(2) In determining whether a term is of such a character regard shall be had to its content, language and presentation.

Article 2.1.21: Conflict between standard terms and non-standard terms

In case of conflict between a standard term and a term which is not a standard term the latter prevails.

21.4 KEY ISSUES IN UNFAIR CONTRACT TERMS LEGISLATION

In this section we will discuss crucial issues with respect to any unfair terms legislation. This will not merely be restricted to Directive 93/13 on Unfair Terms in Consumer Contracts.

21.4.A CONSUMERS AND NON-CONSUMERS

The 'status' of the parties to a contract generally determines whether the courts are empowered to review its terms for unfairness (or the extent of the courts' powers of review).

---

[90] cf Art II.-9:406(2) DCFR; Art 80(2) CESL. For a comparison of the PECL and UNIDROIT PICC provisions, see H Beale, '"Surprising" or "Unfair"? Controls over Standard Terms' in UNIDROIT (ed), *Eppur si muove: The Age of Uniform Law – Essays in honour of Michael Joachim Bonell* (Rome: UNIDROIT, 2016), 975.

In a contractual relationship between two equally powerful commercial parties, there is widespread agreement that they can look after themselves. According to Whittaker:[91]

> It can reasonably be argued that, in many commercial contracts where both parties are of equal bargaining power, such exclusion or restriction of liability does no more than apportion the risk between the parties, in respect of which one party will be expected to insure.

A different view is taken of the review of terms in contracts concluded between a professional seller or supplier and a consumer-purchaser. Given the inferior bargaining power of the consumer, the courts are inclined to redress the contractual imbalance by protecting the consumer against onerous clauses. (Of course, controls on unfair contract terms generally respond to some substantive unfairness in the terms of the contract rather than simply an inequality of bargaining power.)

However, whilst consumers may require particular protection, a small business may also find itself dealing with a much more powerful and experienced party, as where the manager of a petrol station deals with an oil company. These small businessmen arguably need the same protection as consumers. On the other hand, the need for consumer protection in certain situations is questionable: for example, where the consumer can be regarded as an expert in a certain field or where they enjoy professional advice.

In Chapter 7 the notions of a consumer contract and business to business contract were discussed. Hereafter, the focus will be on the extent to which the control of unfair clauses is restricted to consumer contracts or whether it also applies to business to business contracts.

It must be remembered that the Directive on Unfair Terms in Consumer Contracts is applicable only to consumer contracts, that is to say contracts between a (professional) seller or supplier and a consumer (Article 1(1)).[92] A consumer can only be a natural person and not a legal person. Furthermore, he or she must act outside his trade, business or profession.

BGB **21.25 (DE)**

§ 310: Scope of application

(1) Section 305(2) and (3) and sections 308 and 309 do not apply to standard business terms which are used in contracts with an entrepreneur, a legal person under public law or a special fund under public law. Section 307(1) and (2) nevertheless apply to these cases in sentence 1 to the extent that this leads to the ineffectiveness of the contract provisions set out in sections 308 and 309; reasonable account must be taken of the practices and customs that apply in business dealings. [The remaining paragraphs of § 310 state that the provisions on standard terms do not apply to certain types of transaction.]

Notes

(1) As regards the parties covered, §§ 305 ff apply whenever standard terms have been used, even if both parties are merchants. According to § 310(1) BGB, transactions between merchants are exempted from certain provisions of the Act, such as the 'grey

---

[91] In *Chitty* (n 45 above) para 15-001.
[92] See above, pp 174 ff, 833.

list' of § 308 BGB and the 'black list' of § 309 BGB, with their automatic invalidation of standard terms of the specified types. These lists can be directly invoked by
consumers only. However, the general clause—§ 307 BGB—remains applicable in
business transactions.

(2) The decision in the *Foam Insulation* case, which will be discussed later,[93] shows
that the general clause in § 307 BGB also applies in B2B contracts. In addition, as a
general rule, when a merchant uses a clause which falls within one of the prohibited
categories of §§ 308 and 309 BGB, the court will invoke § 307 BGB in order to hold
it invalid. The black and grey lists provide an indication that the contract terms contained therein are invalid (the so-called *Indizwirkung*).

BW   **21.26 (NL)**

Article 6:235: (1) The grounds of annulment referred to in articles 233 and 234 cannot
be invoked by:

a. a legal person as referred to in article 360 of Book 2 who, at the time of entering into the contract, has lastly made public its annual account, or a legal person
in respect of whom, at that time, article 403 paragraph q of Book 2 has lastly been
applied;

b. a party to whom the provision of sub-paragraph a does not apply, if at the aforementioned time, fifty or more persons work there or if, at that time, a declaration
pursuant to article 17a of the *Handelsregisterwet* shows that fifty or more persons
work there.

(2) The ground of annulment referred to in article 233 *sub* a can also be invoked by
a party for whom the general conditions have been used by a procurator, provided that
the other party enters repeatedly into contracts to which the same or almost the same
general conditions apply.

(3) The grounds of annulment referred to in articles 233 and 234 cannot be invoked
by a party who uses the same or almost the same general conditions in its contracts
repeatedly.

(4) The period referred to in article 52 paragraph 1 *sub* d of Book 3 commences upon
the beginning of the day following the one on which the stipulation has been invoked.

Article 6:244: (1) A person acting in the course of a profession or business may not invoke
a stipulation in a contract with a party who, using general conditions, has entered into
contracts with its clients concerning the goods or services to which that contract applies,
to the extent that invoking that stipulation would be unreasonable because of its close
connection with a stipulation contained in the general conditions which, pursuant to this
section, has been annulled or has been affected by a decision as referred to in Article 240
paragraph 1.

(2) Where an action as referred to in article 240 paragraph 1 has been instituted against
the user, he is entitled to implead that person in order to have it judicially declared that
invoking a stipulation as referred to in the preceding paragraph would be unreasonable.
Article 241 paragraphs 2, 3 *sub* c, 4 and 5, as well as Articles 68, 69 and 73 of the Code
of Civil Procedure apply *mutatis mutandis*.

---

[93] See 21.38 (DE), below, p 882.

(3) Article 242 applies *mutatis mutandis* to the decision.

(4) Paragraphs 1–3 apply *mutatis mutandis* to earlier contracts pertaining to the afore-mentioned goods and services.

(See also Article 6:236 and Article 6:237 BW (the black and grey lists), not set out here for reasons of space.)

Notes

(1) In principle, the BW protects both consumers and merchants against unduly onerous clauses (Article 6:233). Large legal persons (companies, associations, governmental bodies) are not protected by this rule (Article 6:235 BW). However, they may invoke the general rules of reasonableness and equity (Articles 6:2(2) and 6:248(2) BW), which apply to all contracts.[94]

(2) Under Articles 6:236 and 6:237 BW, only consumers can profit directly from the special protection of the black and the grey lists. The notion of consumer in Articles 6:236 and 6:237 BW is a narrow one, and applies only to 'a contract between a user and the other party, where the latter is a natural person not acting in the course of a business or profession'. However, the explanatory commentaries to the new Civil Code indicate that even in cases between merchants the court may be inspired by the fact that a clause is mentioned in the black list or the grey list when considering whether a clause is unreasonably onerous (see Article 6:233), and courts do so.[95] On the limits on the protection afforded to merchants, see the decision in *The Shipyard De Schelde* case, below.[96]

(3) A particular kind of protection of small businessmen is provided by Article 6:244 BW. It affords some protection to a dealer (retailer) who uses standard contract terms annulled or prohibited according to the previous articles, but which are closely related to (general) conditions which he himself has been 'forced' to accept by his seller, for example a producer. This seller in the previous link of the distribution chain is not allowed to invoke his contract terms insofar as this would be unreasonable for the retailer because of such a connection.[97]

In Chapter 7 we saw that under English law there were two different definitions of a consumer.[98] The UCTA's consumer protection provisions applied when a party to a contract 'dealt as a consumer' as defined in section 12. This applied when one party made the contract in the course of a business and the other party did not. In *R&B Customs Brokers Ltd v United Dominions Trust Ltd*[99] the Court of Appeal held that a company which bought an item of a kind that it did not regularly buy, and which was not integral to the business, might be dealing as a consumer. The Unfair Terms in Consumer Contracts

---

[94] See above, p 831; *Asser/Hartkamp & Sieburgh 6-III* 2014/484.
[95] J Hijma, *Algemene voorwaarden* (Deventer: Kluwer 2016) nos. 31 ff.
[96] See 21.39 (NL), below, p 883.
[97] See *Asser/Hartkamp & Sieburgh 6-III* 2014/508.
[98] See above, pp 175–76.
[99] [1988] 1 WLR 321; above, p 180.

Regulation 1999, which operate in parallel to the Act, adopt the narrower definition of a consumer set out in the Directive.[100] The Consumer Rights Act now adopts the 'standard' definition of consumer in EU law, which includes only natural persons who are buying for purposes that are predominantly outside that individual's trade, business, craft or profession.[101]

Something similar can be perceived in French law, as was explained in Chapter 7.[102] Initially the Cour de cassation employed a broad notion of consumer.[103] However, the Cour de cassation has aligned its interpretation of Article L 212-1 of the Code de la consommation with the definition of the Directive; it now excludes all professionals from the scope of the protection, even when there is no direct relationship between the contract matter and the professional activities of the buyer or client.[104] However, under the Code de la consommation some protective provisions also apply to certain legal persons, ie the non-professional that is defined as any legal person who does not act for professional purposes (non-profit organisations etc.).

21.4.B NEGOTIATED AND NON-NEGOTIATED TERMS

As we have seen above, the distinction between negotiated and non-negotiated terms is important for the control of unfair terms.[105]

In France, Article L 212-1 of the Code de la consommation applies to all contract terms, whether in individually negotiated or in standard term contracts. However, the new rules in the Code civil (Article 1171) only apply to non-negotiated terms.

In England, the Unfair Contract Terms Act 1977 was also for the most part not limited to non-negotiated terms. Under the 1977 Act in its original form, the controls over clauses excluding or restricting liability for negligence (section 2 and, in guarantees, section 5), those dealing with similar clauses in contracts for the supply of goods (sections 6 and 7) and those dealing with indemnity clauses (section 4) and clauses excluding or restricting liability for misrepresentation (section 8) all applied whether the clause was negotiated or not. On the other hand, section 3 (on general liability for breach of contract) applied only to clauses in a party's written standard terms of business and in consumer contracts (where the vast majority of such clauses will in any event have been non-negotiated). The Consumer Rights Act 2015 applies to all terms whether they were negotiated or not. This is true not only where the relevant liability cannot be excluded or restricted at all, as under sections 31, 47, 57 and 65, but also for the 'general' requirement of fairness

---

[100] See above, p 178.

[101] CRA 2015, s 2, quoted above, p 179.

[102] See above, p 180.

[103] See Cass civ (1) 28 April 1987, no. 85-13674, Bull I no. 134, above, p 180.

[104] See A Bénabent, *Droit des obligations* (16th edn, Paris: LGDJ, 2017) no. 29; Terré et al (n 29 above) no. 74–1.

[105] Code de la Consommation, Art L 212-1; Code civil, Arts 1110, 1171; see also the Directive on Unfair Terms in Consumer Contracts, Art 3; and the language of §§ 305 ff BGB and the BW generally. See on this issue also: Micklitz et al (n 67 above) 287 ff.

under section 62. The reason for this change can be gathered from a Consultation Paper and a report of the Law Commissions that preceded the Act:[106]

> ... [F]or any negotiations to be meaningful, the customer must genuinely understand the proposed term and must be able to assess its possible impact. Where the customer is a consumer, there are likely to be few cases in which she will have the necessary knowledge (except in relation to the "core" terms such as the subject matter of the contract and the price).

The Law Commissions therefore proposed that, unlike the UTCCR, the new legislation should apply to both negotiated and non-negotiated terms. In their report they confirmed this recommendation, saying:

> A large majority of consultees agreed with our proposal. They gave three main reasons. First, there is considerable uncertainty over when a term is individually negotiated. Second, a consumer may not realise the implications of negotiating. Third, the proposal would make the legislation simpler, while affecting very few cases. The OFT also gave evidence that firms are currently exploiting the fact that the UTCCR do not apply to individually negotiated terms.

Article 3 of the Directive, by contrast, makes clear that the Directive is to apply only to non-negotiated terms in contracts. The language of §§ 305 ff BGB and the BW is worded so as to apply the relevant controls only to 'standard terms' and 'general conditions' respectively. However, under Dutch law the definition of a standard term differs (Article 6:231 BW).

French consumer law and UK law are therefore wider in scope than the legislation in Germany and the Netherlands, and also than the Directive (all of which are confined to standard terms). However, the Directive does cover non-negotiated terms which are not in writing—for instance, if a consumer is told of standard conditions when making a booking over the telephone.

21.4.C BLACKLISTS, GREY AND INDICATIVE LISTS

The Directive and the national legal systems provide for lists of clauses in their legislations. However, the character of those lists differ as will be shown in the discussion below.

Unfair Terms Directive[107]   **21.27 (EU)**

Article 3(3): The Annex shall contain an indicative and non-exhaustive list of the terms which may be regarded unfair.

ANNEX
Terms referred to in Article 3(3)

The list of terms is not set out here for reasons of space.

---

[106] The Law Commission and The Scottish Law Commission, *Unfair Terms in Contracts: A Joint Consultation Paper*, Law Com CP No 166, Scot Law Com DP No 119 (London: The Stationery Office, 2002) para 4.50; Report, Law Com No 292, para 3.52.
[107] Council Directive 93/13/EEC (n 9 above). See also Micklitz et al (n 67 above) 291.

The precise meaning of the list is unclear. In *Aziz* the Court of Justice held:[108]

> 70 In that regard, it should be recalled that the annex, to which Article 3(3) of the directive refers, contains only an indicative and non-exhaustive list of terms which may be regarded as unfair. …

However, two months later, in *Asbeek Brusse*, the Court of Justice held:[109]

> 55 … The Court has held in that regard that, while the content of that annex does not suffice in itself to establish automatically the unfair nature of a contested term, it is nevertheless an essential element on which the competent court may base its assessment as to the unfair nature of that term (Case C-472/10 *Invitel* [2012] ECR, paragraph 26).

In short, the items included in the list are an element that is to be taken into account to determine whether a clause is unfair.

BGB **21.28 (DE)**

§ 308: Prohibited clauses with the possibility of evaluation

In standard business terms the following are in particular ineffective

1. (Period of time for acceptance and performance)

a provision by which the user reserves to himself the right to unreasonably long or insufficiently specific periods of time for acceptance or rejection of an offer or for rendering performance; this does not include the reservation of the right not to perform until after the end of the period of time for revocation or return under sections 355 (1) and (2) and 356;

2. (Additional period of time)

a provision by which the user, contrary to legal provisions, reserves to himself the right to an unreasonably long or insufficiently specific additional period of time for the performance he is to render;

3. (Reservation of the right to withdraw)

the agreement of a right of the user to free himself from his obligation to perform without any objectively justified reason indicated in the contract; this does not apply to continuing obligations;

4. (Reservation of the right to modify)

the agreement of a right of the user to modify the performance promised or deviate from it, unless the agreement of the modification or deviation can reasonably be expected of the other party to the contract when the interests of the user are taken into account;

5. (Fictitious declarations)

a provision by which a declaration by the other party to the contract with the user, made when undertaking or omitting a specific act, is deemed to have been made or not made by the user unless

> a) the other party to the contract is granted a reasonable period of time to make an express declaration, and

> b) the user agrees to especially draw the attention of the other party to the contract to the intended significance of his behaviour at the beginning of the period of time;

---

[108] C-415/11, *M Aziz v Caixa d'Estalvis de Catalunya, Tarragona i Manresa (Catalunyacaixa)*, 14 March 2013, ECLI:EU:C:2013:164, see 21.36 (EU), below, p 878.
[109] C-488/11, *Asbeek Brusse*, 30 May 2013, ECLI:EU:C:2013:341. For this case, see below, p 881.

this does not apply to contracts in which the whole of Part B of the Award Rules for Building Works [Verdingungsordnung für Bauleistungen] are incorporated;

6. (Fictitious receipt)

a provision providing that a declaration by the user that is of special importance is deemed to have been received by the other party to the contract;

7. (Reversal of contracts)

a provision by which the user, to provide for the event that a party to the contract withdraws from the contract or gives notice of termination of the contract, may demand

a) unreasonably high remuneration for enjoyment or use of a thing or a right or for performance rendered, or

b) unreasonably high reimbursement of expenses;

8. (Unavailability of performance)

the agreement, admissible under no. 3, of the reservation by the user of a right to free himself from the duty to perform the contract in the absence of availability of performance, if the user does not agree to

a) inform the other party to the contract without undue delay, of the unavailability, and

b) reimburse the other party to the contract for consideration, without undue delay.

§ 309: Prohibited clauses without the possibility of evaluation

Even to the extent that a deviation from the statutory provisions is permissible, the following are ineffective in standard business terms:

1. (Price increases at short notice)

a provision providing for an increase in payment for goods or services that are to be delivered or rendered within four months of the entering into of the contract; this does not apply to goods or services delivered or rendered in connection with continuing obligations;

2. (Right to refuse performance)

a provision by which

a) the right to refuse performance to which the other party to the contract with the user is entitled under section 320, is excluded or restricted, or

b) a right of retention to which the other party to the contract with the user is entitled to the extent that it is based on the same contractual relationship, is excluded or restricted, in particular made dependent upon acknowledgement of defects by the user;

3. (Prohibition of set-off)

a provision by which the other party to the contract with the user is deprived of the right to set off a claim that is uncontested or has been finally and non-appeal-ably established;

4. (Warning notice, setting of a period of time)

a provision by which the user is exempted from the statutory requirement of giving the other party to the contract a warning notice or setting a period of time for the latter to perform or cure;

5. (Lump-sum claims for damages)

the agreement of a lump-sum claim by the user for damages or for compensation of a decrease in value if

a) the lump sum, in the cases covered, exceeds the damage expected under normal circumstances or the customarily occurring decrease in value, or

b) the other party to the contract is not expressly permitted to show that damage or decrease in value has either not occurred or is substantially less than the lump sum;

6. (Contractual penalty)

a provision by which the user is promised the payment of a contractual penalty in the event of non-acceptance or late acceptance of the performance, payment default or in the event that the other party to the contract frees himself from the contract;

7. (Exclusion of liability for injury to life, body or health and in case of gross fault)

a) (Injury to life, body or health) any exclusion or limitation of liability for damage from injury to life, body or health due to negligent breach of duty by the user or intentional or negligent breach of duty by a legal representative or a person used to perform an obligation of the user;

b) (Gross fault) any exclusion or limitation of liability for other damage arising from a grossly negligent breach of duty by the user or from an intentional or grossly negligent breach of duty by a legal representative of the user or a person used to perform an obligation of the user;

letters (a) and (b) do not apply to limitations of liability in terms of transport and tariff rules, authorised in accordance with the Passenger Transport Act [Personenbeförderungsgesetz], of trams, trolley buses and motor vehicles in regular public transport services, to the extent that they do not deviate to the disadvantage of the passenger from the Order on Standard Transport Terms for Tram and Trolley Bus Transport and Regular Public Transport Services with Motor Vehicles[110] of 27 February 1970; letter (b) does not apply to limitations on liability for state-approved lotteries and gaming contracts;

8. (Other exclusions of liability for breaches of duty)

a) (Exclusion of the right to free oneself from the contract) a provision which, where there is a breach of duty for which the user is responsible and which does not consist in a defect of the thing sold or the work, excludes or restricts the right of the other party to free himself from the contract; this does not apply to the terms of transport and tariff rules referred to in No. 7 under the conditions set out there;

b) (Defects) a provision by which in contracts relating to the supply of newly produced things and relating to the performance of work

aa) (Exclusion and referral to third parties) the claims against the user due to defects in their entirety or in regard to individual parts are excluded, limited to the granting of claims against third parties or made dependent upon prior court action taken against third parties;

bb) (Limitation to cure) the claims against the user are limited in whole or in regard to individual parts to a right to cure, to the extent that the right is not expressly reserved for the other party to the contract to reduce the purchase price, if the cure should fail or, except where building work is the object of liability for defects, at its option to withdraw from the contract;

cc) (Expenses for cure) the duty of the user to bear the expenses necessary for the purpose of cure according to section 439(2) and (3) or section 635(2) is excluded or limited;

---

[110] Verordnung über die Allgemeinen Beförderungsbedingungen für den Straßenbahn- und Obusverkehr sowie den Linienverkehr mit Kraftfahrzeugen.

dd) (Withholding cure) the user makes cure dependent upon prior payment of the entire fee or a portion of the fee that is disproportionate taking the defect into account;

ee) (Cut-off period for notice of defects) the user sets a cut-off period for the other party to the contract to give notice of non-obvious defects which is shorter than the permissible period of time under double letter (ff) below;

ff) (Making limitation easier) the limitation of claims against the user due to defects in the cases cited in section 438 (1) no. 2 and section 634a (1) no. 2 is made easier, or in other cases a limitation period of less than one year reckoned from the beginning of the statutory limitation period is attained; this does not apply to contracts to which the whole of Part B of the Award Rules for Building Works [Verdingungsordnung für Bauleistungen] is incorporated;

9. (Duration of continuing obligations)

in a contractual relationship the subject matter of which is the regular supply of goods or the regular rendering of services or work performance by the user,

a) a duration of the contract binding the other party to the contract for more than two years,

b) a tacit extension of the contractual relationship by more than one year in each case that is binding on the other party to the contract, or

c) a notice period longer than three months prior to the expiry of the duration of the contract as originally agreed or tacitly extended at the expense of the other party to the contract; this does not apply to contracts relating to the supply of things sold as belonging together, to insurance contracts or to contracts between the holders of copyright rights and claims and copyright collecting societies within the meaning of the Act on the Administration of Copyright and Neighbouring Rights [Gesetz über die Wahrnehmung von Urheberrechten und verwandten Schutzrechten];

10. (Change of other party to contract) a provision according to which in the case of purchase or service agreements or agreements to produce a result a third party enters into, or may enter into, the rights and duties under the contract in place of the user, unless, in that provision,

a) the third party is identified by name, or

b) the other party to the contract is granted the right to free himself from the contract;

11. (Liability of an agent with power to enter into a contract) a provision by which the user imposes on an agent who enters into a contract for the other party to the contract

a) a liability or duty of responsibility for the principal on the part of the agent himself, without any explicit and separate declaration to this effect, or

b) in the case of agency without authority, liability going beyond section 179;

12. (Burden of proof) a provision by which the user modifies the burden of proof to the disadvantage of the other party to the contract, in particular by

a) imposing on the latter the burden of proof for circumstances lying in the sphere of responsibility of the user, or

b) having the other party to the contract confirm certain facts; letter (b) does not apply to acknowledgements of receipt that are signed separately or provided with a separate qualified electronic signature;

13. (Form of notices and declarations)
a provision by which notices or declarations that are to be made to the user or a third party are tied to a more stringent form than written form or tied to special receipt requirements.

> *Note*
>
> § 309 BGB contains a list of clauses which are always invalid; § 308 BGB contains a list which is 'prohibited subject to evaluation'.

In France, Decree no. 2009-302 of 18 March 2009 concerning the application of Article L 212-1 of the Consumer Code, which follows the Loi de modernisation de l'économie (LME) of 4 August 2008, changed the protection of consumers considerably. It established a black list of 12 clauses which are unfair. In addition it also includes a grey list of clauses which are presumed to be unfair. In that case, the professional must prove that the clause is fair. See now Articles R 212-1 and R 212-2 of the Code de la consommation.

This Decree was an important change, since previously, a term could only be declared unfair in the light of the overall economic circumstances surrounding the disputed contract. Since the legal definition of an unfair term is very open-ended, the courts used to rely upon the guidelines on unfair terms as included in the Annex to the Directive (which is also an annex to the Consumer Code) and of the recommendations issued by the Commission des Clauses Abusives. These guidelines were grey lists and they gave mere guidance to the courts.

With respect to English law, we have seen that sections 31, 47, 57 and 65 of the Consumer Rights Act 2015 render some clauses completely invalid whilst others may be valid if they are fair under section 62.[111] Where a term in a B2B contract is subject to a requirement of reasonableness, the Unfair Contract Terms Act explicitly places the burden of proof on the party claiming that a contract term or notice satisfies the requirement of reasonableness (section 11(5)). This used to apply also to consumer contracts but the Consumer Rights Act 2015 follows the wording of the Directive so that it is not clear who has the burden of proof. Schedule 2 of the 2015 Act contains the list of terms contained in the Annex to the Directive.

When we discuss the *Aziz* case, the question may arise to what extent the grey lists are still grey or should they be considered black?

21.4.D 'CORE TERMS'

Under the Directive on Unfair Terms in Consumer Contracts, a core term is not subject to the fairness control, if it is drafted in plain and intelligible language (Article 4(2) of the Directive). In 2014 the Court of Justice answered a preliminary question as to the definition of a core term and whether it was subject to the fairness control. Prior to that decision,

---

[111] See 21.17 (EN), above, p 842.

national courts had already rendered decisions as to the fairness control of core terms. These national decisions will be discussed before the decision of the Court of Justice.

House of Lords, 25 October 2001   **21.29 (EN)**

Director General of Fair Trading v First National Bank[112]

A standard term, under which (on enforcement of an overdue debt) interest was to continue to accrue at the contractual rate until payment 'after as well as before any judgment (such obligation to be independent of and not to merge with the judgment)', is not unfair.

(For the facts and the judgments, see 21.34 (EN), below, p 874)

Note

A term which only applies on default can be reviewed and is not considered a core term.[113]

Supreme Court, 25 November 2009[114]   **21.30 (EN)**

The Office of Fair Trading v Abbey National plc & Others (Appellants)[115]

Relevant charges in the form of unpaid item charges, paid item charges, overdraft excess charges and guaranteed paid item charges levied when a customer gives instructions or undertakes a transaction without having sufficient funds to back it are regarded as being part of the agreed price or remuneration in exchange for which the banks undertook to provide their whole package of services and therefore fall outside the scope of The Unfair Terms in Consumer Contracts Regulations 1999.

Facts: Contracts between the eight defendant banks and their consumer customers provided that consumers might overdraw their accounts, but if they did so without prior authorisation the consumer would have to pay a significant charge (eg £30) to the bank. The Office of Fair Trading claimed that these and other charges made by the banks were unfair within the meaning of the Directive. The banks collected so much in charges that they were able to provide free banking to customers who kept their accounts in credit.

Held: The charges made formed part of the price of the services provided by the banks and their amount was not subject to review under the Regulations.

Judgment: ...
LORD MANCE
[94]. Council Directive 93/13/EEC of 5 April 1993 and The Unfair Terms in Consumer Contracts Regulations 1999 (SI No 2083), which implement the Directive domestically, both relate to 'unfair terms in contracts concluded between a seller or [a] supplier and a consumer'. They make the validity of 'a contractual term which has not been individually

---

[112] [2001] UKHL 52, [2002] 1 AC 481. See also about core terms: C-484/08, *Caja de Ahorros y Monte de Pié-dad de Madrid v Asociación de Usuarios de Servicios Bancarios (Ausbanc)*, 3 June 2010, ECLI:EU:C:2010:309.
[113] See on core terms also Micklitz et al (n 67 above) 292 ff.
[114] Note that the functions of the Judicial Committee of the House of Lords were transferred to the new Supreme Court in October 2009.
[115] [2009] UKSC 6, [2010] 1 AC 696.

negotiated' subject generally to the criterion of fairness (defined by reference to whether 'contrary to the requirement of good faith, it causes a significant imbalance in the parties' rights and obligations arising under the contract, to the detriment of the consumer'). This appeal concerns the exception to this rule, provided in Article 4(2) of the Directive and Regulation 6(2). It is not suggested that there is any material difference between these two provisions. As Regulation 6(2) puts it:

'In so far as it is in plain intelligible language, the assessment of fairness of a term shall not relate:

(a) to the definition of the main subject matter of the contract, or

(b) to the adequacy of the price or remuneration, as against the goods or services supplied in exchange.'

'Adequacy' (the word also used in the Directive) means appropriateness or reasonableness (in amount).

[95]. This appeal is concerned with Relevant Charges in the form of unpaid item charges, paid item charges, overdraft excess charges and guaranteed paid item charges levied when a customer gives instructions or undertakes a transaction without having sufficient funds to back it. The Office of Fair Trading (OFT) has written to various banks expressing concerns about the fairness of the terms agreed by the banks with their customers so far as they provide for payment of Relevant Charges. The question for decision is whether the OFT would be entitled to challenge the fairness of such terms under Regulation 12. It is now accepted that such terms are not individually negotiated within Regulation 5(1). But it is also common ground (except in the case of four banks in certain specific and minor respects) that they are in 'plain intelligible language' within regulation 6(2). The issue is whether the Relevant Charges or the agreement to pay them constitute 'price or remuneration' in exchange for the supply of services within Regulation 6(2). If they do, then any challenge to their fairness based on their appropriateness in relation to such services is excluded under Regulation 6(2). Any assessment based on matters not relating to the appropriateness in amount of the price or remuneration is not excluded by regulation 6(2)(b). ...

[96]. The parties have in their written cases and oral submissions identified two broad issues for determination. The first concerns the proper interpretation of Regulation 6(2)(b), the second whether the Relevant Charges fall within the scope of that regulation, properly interpreted. The first issue is one of European law. As to the second, however, no question of European law is involved in the determination of the relevant circumstances. The parties also agree that no such question is in this case involved in applying the regulation, properly interpreted, to the circumstances—including identifying the price or remuneration in exchange for which goods or services are to be supplied. ...

[97]. Since the Directive and Regulations are concerned with terms in contracts, it is first of all necessary to identify the relevant contracts. This is a matter about which the judge, Andrew Smith J, and the Court of Appeal took different views, although again it is not suggested that it raises on the facts of this case any particular issue of European law. The banks' primary case is that the relevant contracts are the contracts for an overall package of banking facilities made by the banks with their customers. Andrew Smith J rejected this analysis as unnatural: payments by way of Relevant Charges could not be said to be paid in exchange for services supplied when an account is in credit; and the description 'free-if-in-credit' connoted that there was no price to be paid when an account was in credit (paras 398–9). Furthermore, if the relevant contract was taken to be the overall package, the Relevant Charges would represent no more than part of the price or remuneration, and an assessment of the fairness of such charges as against the package of

services would be 'beside the point' and 'would not intrude upon the essential bargain' intended to be protected from assessment (para 400).

[98]. There is in my opinion a flaw in this reasoning. It is not comparing like with like. Viewing the matter at the level of the banking contracts, the comparison is between, on the one hand, the package of services offered by the banks (some or all of which may or may not be used by any particular customer) and, on the other, the customer's commitment to pay such charges as may arise from whatever facilities he does use. At this level, the banks' case is that price or remuneration is or includes the customer's potential liability for charges, rather than the payments which he or she has actually to make if and when such charges are incurred. In my opinion the Court of Appeal was right in para 97 of its judgment to identify the relevant contract as being in the first instance the banking contract for an overall package of facilities. That is the contract in which the Relevant Charges appear and were agreed.

[99]. Further, any challenge to the fairness of a term must be to its fairness in the context of the relevant contract in which it appears. It is 'beside the point' if it is not. If, on a proper analysis, the customer's potential liability for the Relevant Charges is the or part of the 'price or remuneration' in exchange for which the overall package of banking services is supplied, and it is challenged on the ground that it makes such price or remuneration disproportionate overall, then Regulation 6(2)(b) excludes the challenge. If there is no challenge to the overall proportionality of the overall price or remuneration of the package, then I fail to see how a challenge to the proportionality of the Relevant Charges in relation to the cost of providing particular services in isolation can be admissible or relevant. A term which is proportionate in context cannot become disproportionate viewed out of context.

[100]. It is true that Relevant Charges are only incurred when a customer, either deliberately or inadvertently, gives an instruction or enters into a transaction, by which as a matter of law and contract he or she requests the bank to provide overdraft facilities. So, each time such a request is made and acted upon (even if only with the result that the request is declined), it is possible to identify a more developed contractual relationship as arising. Under that relationship, the Relevant Charges become payable in respect of the request (although not, the judge thought, in exchange for any services provided in consequence of the request). I do not however consider that this relationship can be the contract to which the Directive and Regulations refer. If the agreement to incur the Relevant Charges is part of an overall package contract, its vulnerability to challenge and, if permissible, any assessment of its fairness under the Directive and Regulations must, as I have said, depend upon an analysis of such agreement as part of the package contract.

Otherwise, as Mr Sumption pointed out, a customer could challenge each separate part of a package in isolation, although as a whole the price or remuneration charged was unchallengeable.

[101]. Issues arise under two heads: the first, the proper interpretation of Article 4(2) and Regulation 6(2) (I shall for convenience generally refer only to the latter); and the second, the application on the facts of whatever is that proper interpretation. As to the first, it is common ground that not every provision for payment contained in a contract for the supply of goods or services is rendered immune from scrutiny under Regulation 6(2). There can be payments which do not constitute either 'price or remuneration' of goods or services supplied in exchange. Further, payments which do constitute price or remuneration in this sense can be challenged as unfair on grounds which do not relate to their appropriateness in amount as against the goods or services supplied in exchange.

Heads (d), (e), (f) and (l) in the grey list of terms set out in Schedule 2 to the Regulations fall within one or both categories. *Director-General of Fair Trading v First National Bank plc* [2002] 1 AC 481 provides another example.

...

[104]. In accordance with general European legal principle, Article 4(2) and regulation 6(2) are as exceptions to be construed narrowly. Nevertheless, the concepts of 'price or remuneration' must, I think, be capable in principle of covering, under a banking contract, an agreement to make a payment in a particular event. The language of Regulation 6(2)(b) is on its face therefore capable of covering a customer's commitment, under the package contracts put before the House, to pay the Relevant Charges in the specified events. There is no reason why a customer should not be given free services in some circumstances, but, as a quid pro quo, be expected to pay for them in others.

...

[106]. The OFT's case, essentially accepted by the Court of Appeal, is that the agreement to pay the Relevant Charges is not price or remuneration, because Regulation 6(2)(b) is confined in scope to payments in exchange for sales or supplies on which payments the consumer can be taken to have focused and to which he can be taken truly to have consented. The Court of Appeal encapsulated this conclusion as 'import[ing] the notion of essential bargain into the construction of Article 4(2) and into both paragraphs (a) and (b) of Regulation 6(2)' (para 86). It added that 'the concept of the essential bargain flows naturally' from the structure and purpose of the Directive because not every payment that a consumer makes falls within Regulation 6(2)(b), and such a construction 'prevents Regulation 6(2)(b) being construed too widely'. It considered that its conclusion reflected 'the reasoning both in the travaux préparatoires and in the *First National Bank* case', which it interpreted as indicating that ancillary or incidental payment terms were not intended to be exempt from assessment for their 'adequacy' under Regulation 6(2) (paras 64, 69 and 86).

...

[108]. One difficulty about the Court of Appeal's reasoning lies in its reliance on the concept of negotiation or indeed bargain, as in para 90(iii)(a) and (b) above—and elsewhere, repeatedly, in its judgment: see paras 64, 87, 107 and 109 (negotiation) and 86, 90, 94–95 and 106 (bargain). The Court of Appeal suggested that the absence of any negotiation or bargain or of any ability to negotiate or bargain militated strongly against a conclusion that a particular charge constituted (part of) the price or remuneration. However, the Directive and Regulations are only concerned with contractual terms which have not been individually negotiated. Another difficulty is that the Court of Appeal's broad test, and the sliding scale of relevant considerations introduced by para 90, convert the apparently simple language of Regulation 6(2)(b) (or Article 4(2)) into a complex and uncertain value judgment. This is rendered even more complex by the Court of Appeal's further conclusion that the judgment should be made by the court through the eyes of 'the typical consumer' (para 91). This led to considerable argument before the House as to who might be regarded as the typical consumer. Was it relevant to look at the whole body of customers, or at those who would or might be likely to incur Relevant Charges? Before the House Mr Crow for the OFT summarised three main considerations on which the OFT relied to determine whether a payment was part of the essential bargain, namely whether the payment was (a) ancillary, (b) readily recognisable or visible by a typical customer and (c) one arising in the normal performance of the contract.

[Lord Mance then considered the legislative history of the Directive, and concluded:]

[112]. The legislative history shows therefore an extensive process of development, during which the original proposal was replaced by an amended proposal which was itself very largely amended. The measure ultimately agreed was confined to non-negotiated terms. It stressed the need for transparency ('plain, intelligible language') in relation to all such terms. But, provided such transparency existed, any assessment of the fairness of such terms was excluded in relation to 'the definition of the main subject-matter of the contract' and 'the adequacy of the price and remuneration ... as against the services or goods supplied in exchange ...'. The general approach and the rationale as explained in the Council's Reasons match those of Brandner and Ulmer in their article cited above. It would re-write the legislation to read Article 4(2) of the Directive or Regulation 6(2) as if they introduced as the test a complex enquiry as to whether or how far consumers had actually exercised contractual freedom when agreeing upon a price or remuneration stated in plain and intelligible language in a contract into which they entered. Article 4(2) and Regulation 6(2) can loosely be described as being concerned with the assessment of 'core terms' (see e.g. *First National Bank*). But that is on the basis that price and remuneration always fall within them. The Court of Appeal erred in introducing a yet further restriction, whereby it would be only 'essential core terms' which could attract immunity.

...

[115]. Taking the view that I do of the meaning of both the Directive and the Regulations, the question arises whether it is nevertheless incumbent on us to refer the interpretation of the Directive to the Court of Justice. Under *CILFIT v Ministry of Health* (Case 283/81; [1982] ECR 3415) and in the absence of any prior Court of Justice authority, this depends upon (a) whether the question is relevant to the outcome of the case and (b) 'whether the correct application of Community law is so obvious as to leave no scope for reasonable doubt'. In the latter connection we have to ask ourselves whether the answer we consider correct would be equally obvious to the courts of other Member States and to the Court of Justice itself; and in this regard we have to bear in mind the fact that Community legislation is drafted in different languages which may convey different meanings to different readers, that the Community concepts it uses (here 'price and remuneration') are autonomous concepts and that every provision of Community law must be placed in the context of Community law as a whole. In the present case, we are concerned with a relatively simple sentence, using simple and basic concepts, and the scope for different readings of different language texts seems very limited. The complex and unpredictable value judgment involved in the Court of Appeal's approach was based in large measure upon a clear error, in treating the existence or absence of negotiation as significant in a context dealing by definition only with non-negotiated terms. The suggested test of what is 'not ... ancillary to the main bargain' involves a restatement of the language of the Directive and Regulations; that language treats the 'price or remuneration' as axiomatically part of the core bargain and so immune from scrutiny for reasonableness. Bearing in mind the general Community aim of legal certainty, the likelihood of the Court of Justice (or any other Member State's courts) accepting the Court of Appeal's approach to the interpretation of Article 4(2) seems to me remote indeed. I would regard the position as acte clair and not as requiring a reference.

[116]. However, if one takes a different view on whether the position is acte clair, there remains the question of relevance. Eliminating the Court of Appeal's clear error in introducing as part of the test whether the relevant term had been 'directly negotiated', and

assuming that the Court of Appeal was generally right in adopting as a test whether the term was 'not ... ancillary to the main bargain', the question would be whether the Court was right to treat the terms of the package contracts relating to the Relevant Charges as ancillary terms, rather than as part of the agreed price or remuneration in exchange for which the banks undertook to provide their whole package of services. That question would involve the application of the Directive and Regulations, which is, as I have said, a matter for domestic, not European, law. [Lord Mance concluded that even if the Court of Appeal's approach on the law had been right, it had misapplied it on the facts; the charges for overdrawing were not outside what the normal consumer would expect to incur.]

Note

After this case there was considerable disquiet and the government referred the matter to the Law Commissions. They advised that a 'core' term should not be exempt from review for fairness unless, in addition to being in plain and intelligible language, it is 'prominent'. This requirement was included in the Consumer Rights Act 2015, which provides:

Section 64 Exclusion from assessment of fairness

(1) A term of a consumer contract may not be assessed for fairness under section 62 to the extent that—

(a) it specifies the main subject matter of the contract, or

(b) the assessment is of the appropriateness of the price payable under the contract by comparison with the goods, digital content or services supplied under it.

(2) Subsection (1) excludes a term from an assessment under section 62 only if it is transparent and prominent.

(3) A term is transparent for the purposes of this Part if it is expressed in plain and intelligible language and (in the case of a written term) is legible.

(4) A term is prominent for the purposes of this section if it is brought to the consumer's attention in such a way that an average consumer would be aware of the term.

(5) In subsection (4) "average consumer" means a consumer who is reasonably well-informed, observant and circumspect.

(6) This section does not apply to a term of a contract listed in Part 1 of Schedule 2.

Sections 64(3) and (5) give a definition of a transparent term. If this definition is compared to what the Court of Justice held in *Kásler*[116] as to the meaning of terms in plain and intelligible language, the question arises whether this definition in Section 64(3) can be upheld. The Court of Justice held inter alia that the consumer can foresee, on the basis of clear, intelligible criteria, the economic consequences for him.

Hoge Raad, 21 February 2003[117]   **21.31 (NL)**

Heir Weevers Stous v Stichting Parkwoningen

A clause in an apartment sale contract which stated that, in the case of the buyer's death or departure from the apartment, the original seller was entitled to repurchase it for the price

---

[116] See *Kásler*, 21.32 (EU), below, p 868, especially at [73] (on p 872 below).
[117] NJ 2004, 567, annotated by J Hijma.

for which it had sold it, is considered to be an ancillary term and falls within the scope of the controls of unfair terms.

Facts: Stichting Parkwoningen (hereafter also the Foundation) is a foundation that developed, owned and sold apartments to elderly people. The Foundation sold an apartment to Weevers Stous. In the sales contract it was stated that, in the case of death or in the case of leave, the Foundation was entitled to repurchase the apartment for the price for which it had sold the apartment (a certain type of indexation was provided for). It was a settled policy of the Foundation to include such a clause in the sales contracts of the apartments.

Weevers Stous died and his heir argued that the repurchase clause was void on the basis of Article 6:233 first phrase sub a BW. Stichting Parkwoning argued that this provision did not apply, because it was a clause concerning the core of the contract (*kernbeding*) and therefore fell outside the scope of Article 6:233 BW.

Held: Both the court of first instance and the court of appeal rejected the claim. The decision of the court of appeal was quashed.

Judgment: ... 3.4.2. First, it must be stated, ..., that in order to consider whether a clause concerns the core of the contract, it is not decisive that a clause concerns an important issue for either the drafter of the terms or for both parties. Further, the concept of a clause concerning the core of the contract must be construed as narrowly as possible; as a rule of thumb, it can be stated that such a clause will concur with the 'essentialia of a contract' without which a contract cannot be created, because the contract lacks determination (*bepaalbaarheid*) (HR 19 September 1997, NJ 1998, 6).

Where in the Explanatory Legislative Commentaries, it is stated that it is decisive whether a clause is so fundamental that without that clause the contract cannot be created or without that clause there is no agreement as to the essence of the contract, this must be interpreted in an objective sense and it cannot be inferred that the subjective views of both parties or of any of them could be relevant. The question as to whether parties can determine which clauses concern the core of a contract must be answered in a negative way; the mandatory character of the rules opposes all clauses that aim at frustrating the protection provided by the law.

3.4.3 As follows from what is stated in 3.4.2, the Court of Appeal gave the wrong opinion with respect to the notion of a clause concerning the core of the contract as included in Article 6:231, sub a, BW by deciding that the clause at stake concerns a clause concerning the core of the contract. Neither by the circumstance, mentioned by the Court of Appeal, that the Foundation only could achieve its aims continuously by means of these clauses, nor by its decision that the right of preference in tandem with the clause concerning the price was such an essential part of the contract for the Foundation that, without it, it would not have entered into the contract, nor the circumstance that the Foundation had indicated already during the precontractual negotiations that there was no negotiation possible about this clause, made that the clause was a clause that concerned the core of the contract. ...

Notes

(1) In this decision the Hoge Raad held that the notion of a clause that concerns the core of the contract must be interpreted as narrowly as possible.[118] Moreover, it must be interpreted in an objective way. The intentions of the parties are not relevant, nor is the aim of the contract.

---

[118] See on core obligations: *Asser/Hartkamp & Sieburgh 6-III* 2014/467 ff.

> (2) In this case the Hoge Raad referred to an earlier decision of 19 September 1997 (*Assoud v SNS*),[119] in which the Court had referred explicitly to Article 4(2) of the Directive, which was one of the arguments that led to the conclusion that the notion of clause concerning the core of the contract must be interpreted as narrowly as possible.

In France, as we have seen above, a general control of unfair terms is included in Article 1171(2) of the Code civil.[120] According to this, 'the assessment of significant imbalance must not concern either the main subject matter of the contract nor the adequacy of the price in relation to the act of performance.'

Court of Justice, 30 April 2014[121]   **21.32 (EU)**

Árpád Kásler, Hajnalka Káslerné Rábai v Otp Jelzálogbank Zrt

A core term of the contract concerns an essential obligation of that agreement which characterises it. Under the transparency principle included in Article 4(2) and Article 5, a term must be both grammatically correct and the consumer must be able to foresee the economic consequences for him on the basis of clear, intelligible criteria.

Facts: On 29 May 2008, Mr and Mrs Kásler, the borrowers, concluded an agreement for a 'mortgage loan denominated in foreign currency secured by a mortgage' with Jelzálogbank. Under Clause I/l of the agreement, Jelzálogbank advanced to the borrowers a loan amounting to 14,400,000 Hungarian forints (HUF). Under this clause: 'the amount of the loan in foreign currency will be determined at the buying rate for the foreign currency applied by the bank on the date of advance of the funds' and 'after the funds have been advanced, the amount of the loan, the related interest, the administration fees and default interest and other charges will be determined in the foreign currency'.

The amount lent was fixed at 94,240.84 Swiss francs at the buying rate of exchange applied by Jelzálogbank on the date of advance of the funds. Mr and Mrs Kásler had to repay that sum over 25 years, by monthly instalments. Under Clause II of the agreement, the loan was subject to a nominal interest rate of 5.2% which, together with administration fees of 2.04% resulted in an annual percentage rate of charge (APR) of 7.43% as at the date of conclusion of the agreement. Under Clause III/2 of that agreement, 'the lender is to determine the amount in HUF of each of the monthly instalments due by reference to the selling rate of exchange for the foreign currency applied by the bank on the day before the due date.'

The borrowers brought an action against Jelzálogbank claiming that Clause III/2 was unfair. In last resort, the Hungarian Supreme Court referred preliminary questions to the Court of Justice concerning inter alia the issues which clauses have to be regarded as a core term and when such a clause is not drafted plainly and intelligibly.

Held:— the expression the 'main subject matter of a contract' covers a term, incorporated in a loan agreement denominated in foreign currency concluded between a seller or supplier and a consumer and not individually negotiated, ..., pursuant to which the selling rate of exchange of that currency is applied for the purpose of

---

[119] NJ 1998, 6.
[120] See 21.21 (FR), above, p 848.
[121] C-26/13, 30 April 2014, ECLI:EU:C:2014:282.

calculating the repayment instalments for the loan, only in so far as it is found, ..., that that term lays down an essential obligation of that agreement which, as such characterises it;

— such a term, in so far as it contains a pecuniary obligation for the consumer to pay, in repayment of instalments of the loan, the difference between the selling rate of exchange and the buying rate of exchange of the foreign currency, cannot be considered as 'remuneration' the adequacy of which as consideration for a service supplied by the lender cannot be the subject of an examination as regards unfairness under Article 4(2) of Directive 93/13.

— Article 4(2) of Directive 93/13 must be interpreted as meaning that ... the requirement that a contractual term must be drafted in plain intelligible language is to be understood as requiring not only that the relevant term should be grammatically intelligible to the consumer, but also that the contract should set out transparently the specific functioning of the mechanism of conversion for the foreign currency to which the relevant term refers and the relationship between that mechanism and that provided for by other contractual terms relating to the advance of the loan, so that that consumer is in a position to evaluate, on the basis of clear, intelligible criteria, the economic consequences for him which derive from it.

Judgment:

36 By its first question, the referring court asks essentially whether Article 4(2) of Directive 93/13 must be interpreted as meaning that the expressions 'the main subject-matter of the contract' and 'the adequacy of the price and remuneration on the one hand, as against the services or goods supplied, on the other' cover a term, incorporated into a credit agreement denominated in a foreign currency, concluded between a seller or supplier and a consumer and not individually negotiated, ..., pursuant to which the selling rate of exchange of that currency applies for the purpose of calculating the loan repayment instalments.

37 According to settled case-law, the need of the uniform application of EU law and the principle of equality require that the terms of a provision of EU law which makes no express reference to the law of the Member States for the purpose of determining its meaning and scope must normally be given an autonomous and uniform interpretation throughout the European Union, which must take into account the context of that provision and the purpose of the legislation in question. ...

38 The same is true for the terms in Article 4(2) of Directive 93/13, since that provision does not contain any express reference to the law of the Member States for the purpose of determining its meaning and scope.

39 Moreover, the Court has consistently held that the system of protection introduced by Directive 93/13 is based on the idea that the consumer is in a position of weakness vis-à-vis the seller or supplier, as regards both his bargaining power and his level of knowledge, a situation that leads to his agreeing to terms drawn up in advance by the seller or supplier without being able to influence the content of those terms. ...

40 As regards such a position of weakness, Directive 93/13 requires Member States to provide for a mechanism ensuring that every contractual term not individually negotiated may be reviewed in order to determine whether it is unfair. In that context, it is for the national court to determine, taking account of the criteria laid down in Articles 3(1) and 5 of Directive 93/13, whether, having regard to the particular circumstances of the case, such a term meets the requirements of good faith, balance and transparency laid down by that directive. ...

41 However, Article 4(2) of Directive 93/13, read in conjunction with Article 8 thereof, allows the Member States [to] provide, in the legislation transposing that directive, that an '[a]ssessment of the unfair nature' is not to apply to the terms to which that provision relates, on condition that they are drafted in plain, intelligible language. It follows from that provision that the terms to which it refers are not the subject of an assessment of their unfairness, but, as the Court stated, come within the area covered by that directive. ...

42 Article 4(2) of Directive 93/13 thus laying down an exception to the mechanism for reviewing the substance of unfair terms, such as that provided for in the system of consumer protection put in place by that directive, that provision must be strictly interpreted.

43 That exception covers, in the first place, terms that concern the 'main subject-matter of the contract'.

44 In the case in the main proceedings, the referring court is unsure whether Clause III/2, in that it provides that the selling rate of exchange of a foreign currency is to apply for the purposes of calculating the repayment instalments of a loan denominated in that currency, falls within the 'main subject-matter' of the loan agreement, within the meaning of that provision.

...

46 The Court has already held that Article 4(2) of the Directive is intended solely to establish the detailed rules and the scope of the substantive assessment of contract terms that have not been individually negotiated and that describe the essential obligations of contracts concluded between a seller or supplier and a consumer. ...

47 The fact that a term has been negotiated by the co-contracting parties, in the context of their contractual freedom and of market conditions, cannot constitute a criterion making it possible to assess whether that term falls within the 'main subject-matter of the contract' within the meaning of Article 4(2) of Directive 93/13.

48 As is clear from Article 3(1) of that directive and the twelfth recital in the preamble thereto, terms ... individually negotiated do not, as a matter of principle, fall within the scope of that directive. Therefore, the question whether they are excluded from the scope of Article 4(2) does not arise.

49 However, taking account also of the fact that Article 4(2) of Directive 93/13 represents a derogation and the ensuing necessity of its being interpreted strictly, contractual terms falling within the notion of the 'main subject-matter of the contract', within the meaning of that provision, must be understood as being those that lay down the essential obligations of the contract and, as such, characterise it.

50 By contrast, terms ancillary to those that define the very essence of the contractual relationship cannot fall within the notion of the 'main subject-matter of the contract' within the meaning of Article 4(2) of Directive 93/13.

51 It is for the referring court to determine, having regard to the nature, general scheme and the stipulations of the loan agreement, and its legal and factual context, whether the term setting the exchange rate for the monthly repayment instalments constitutes an essential element of the debtor's obligations, consisting in the repayment of the amount made available by the lender.

52 In the second place, Article 4(2) of Directive 93/13 covers the terms relating to 'the adequacy of the price and remuneration on one hand, as against the services or goods supplied, on the other' or, in accordance with the nineteenth recital in the preamble to that directive, the terms 'which describe ... the quality/price ratio of the goods or services supplied'.

53 In the case in the main proceedings, the referring court wishes to know whether Clause III/2, in so far as it provides that the selling rate of exchange of a foreign currency is applicable for the purpose of calculating the repayment instalments of a loan while, according to other terms of the loan agreement, the amount advanced is converted into national currency on the basis of the buying rate of exchange of the foreign currency, contains a pecuniary obligation for the consumer, that is to say, the obligation to pay, in the context of the repayment instalments of the loan, the difference between the selling and buying rates of the foreign currency, which may be treated as 'remuneration' for the

service supplied, the adequacy of which may not be examined as regards unfairness under Article 4(2) of Directive 93/13.

54 In that connection, it is clear from the wording of Article 4(2) of Directive 93/13 that the second category of terms that cannot be examined as regards unfairness is limited in scope, for that exclusion concerns only the adequacy of the price or remuneration as against the services or goods supplied in exchange.

55 As the Advocate General has observed in point 69 of his Opinion, the exclusion of a review of contractual terms as to the quality/price ratio of a supply of goods or services is explained by the fact that no legal scale or criterion exists that can provide a framework for, and guide, such a review.

56 In that context, the Court has previously held that that exclusion does not apply to a term concerning a mechanism for amending the prices of the services provided to the consumer. ...

57 In the circumstances, it must be stated, in addition, that the exclusion of the assessment of the unfairness of a term being limited to the adequacy of the price and the remuneration on one hand as against the services or goods supplied on the other, it cannot apply where there is a challenge to the variation between the selling rate of exchange of a foreign currency, which must be used in accordance with that term in order to calculate the repayment instalments, and the buying rate of exchange of that currency, which must be used in accordance with other terms of the loan agreement in order to calculate the amount of the loan advanced.

58 Moreover, that exclusion cannot apply to terms that, like Clause III/2, merely determine the conversion rate of the foreign currency in which the loan agreement is denominated, in order to calculate the repayment instalments, without however any foreign exchange service being supplied by the lender in making that calculation and do not, therefore, constitute 'remuneration', the adequacy of which as consideration for a service supplied by the lender could be assessed to determine its unfairness pursuant to Article 4(2) of Directive 93/13.

...

Transparency

60 By its second question, the referring court asks essentially whether Article 4(2) of Directive 93/13 must be interpreted as meaning that the requirement that a contractual term must be drafted in plain intelligible language must be understood as requiring not only that the relevant term should be grammatically clear and intelligible to the consumer, but also that the economic reasons for using that term and its relationship with other contractual terms should be clear and intelligible to him.

61 If the referring court were to consider that, having regard to the answer given to the first question, Clause III/2 falls within the 'main subject-matter of the contract', within the meaning of Article 4(2) of Directive 93/13, an assessment of the unfairness of that term may be avoided only if it is drafted in clear and intelligible language.

62 In order to safeguard in practice the objectives of consumer protection pursued by the Directive, any transposition of Article 4(2) must be complete, with the result that the prohibition of the assessment of the unfairness of the terms relates solely to those which are drafted in plain, intelligible language. ...

63 However, it is apparent from the order for reference that Article 209(4) of the [Hungarian] Civil Code, a provision intended to transpose Article 4(2) of Directive 93/13 into national law, did not lay down that requirement that contractual terms be drafted in clear intelligible language.

64 In that connection, it must be recalled that a national court, when hearing a case between individuals, is required, when applying the provisions of domestic law, to consider the whole body of rules of national law and to interpret them, so far as possible, in the light of the wording and purpose of the directive in order to achieve an outcome consistent with the objective pursued by the directive. ...

65 In that context, the Court has also stated that this principle of interpreting national law in conformity with EU law has certain limits. Thus, the obligation for a national court to refer to the content of a directive when interpreting and applying the relevant rules of domestic law is limited by general principles of law and cannot serve as the basis for an interpretation of national law contra legem. ...

66 If, taking account of that principle of consistent interpretation thus defined, the referring court were to consider that the national provision intended to transpose Article 4(2) of that directive may be understood as meaning that it includes the requirement that contractual terms are to be drafted in plain intelligible language, the question arises of the scope of that requirement.

67 In that connection, it must be held that that requirement appears in Article 5 of Directive 93/13, which provides that contractual terms in writing must 'always' be drafted in plain, intelligible language. The twentieth recital in the preamble to Directive 93/13 states in that regard that the consumer should actually be given an opportunity of examining all the terms of the contract.

68 It follows that that requirement of plain, intelligible language applies in all cases, including that in which a term falls within Article 4(2) of Directive 93/13 and therefore avoids the assessment of its unfairness referred to in Article 3(1) thereof.

69 It also follows that that requirement as it appears in Article 4(2) of Directive 93/13 has the same scope as that referred to in Article 5 of that directive.

70 As regards Article 5, the Court has already held that information, before concluding a contract, on the terms of the contract and the consequences of concluding it is of fundamental importance for a consumer. It is on the basis of that information in particular that he decides whether he wishes to be bound by the terms previously drawn up by the seller or supplier. ...

71 The requirement of transparency of contractual terms laid down by Directive 93/13 cannot therefore be reduced merely to their being formally and grammatically intelligible.

72 On the contrary, as has already been recalled out in paragraph 39 of this judgment, the system of protection introduced by Directive 93/13 being based on the idea that the consumer is in a position of weakness vis-à-vis the seller or supplier, in particular as regards his level of knowledge, the requirement of transparency must be understood in a broad sense.

73 As regards a contractual term, such as Clause III/2, which allows the seller or supplier to calculate the level of monthly repayment instalments owed by the consumer in accordance with the selling rate of exchange of the foreign currency applied by that seller or supplier, which has the effect of increasing the costs of the financial service at the consumer's expense, apparently without an upper limit, it follows from Articles 3 and 5 of Directive 93/13 and Points 1(j) and (l) and 2(b) and (d) of the annex thereto, that it is of fundamental importance for the purpose of complying with the requirement of transparency, to determine whether the contract sets out transparently the reason for and the particularities of the mechanism for converting the foreign currency and the relationship between that mechanism and the mechanism laid down by other terms relating to the advance of the loan, so that the consumer can foresee, on the basis of clear, intelligible criteria, the economic consequences for him which derive from it. ...

74 As regards the particularities of the mechanism for conversion of the foreign currency such as those set out in Clause III/2, it is for the referring court to determine whether, having regard to all the relevant information, including the promotional material and information provided by the lender in the negotiation of the loan agreement, the average consumer, who is reasonably well informed and reasonably observant and circumspect, would not only be aware of the existence of the difference, generally observed on the securities market, between the selling rate of exchange and the buying rate of exchange of a foreign currency, but also be able to assess the potentially significant economic consequences for him resulting from the application of the selling rate of exchange for the calculation of the repayments for which he would ultimately be liable and, therefore, the total cost of the sum borrowed.

Notes

(1) In this case the Court of Justice defines a core term (para 49). However, this definition is not very helpful, since the Court of Justice uses the words 'essential obligations' without saying how these should be defined.

(2) A core term falls within the scope of the Directive; however, it is not subject to the fairness test insofar as it is drafted in plain and intelligible language (transparency principle).

(3) The Court of Justice also elaborated on the transparency principle. A clause is drafted in plain and intelligible language if it is formally and grammatically comprehensible. However, a consumer must also be able to foresee the economic consequences of such a clause on the basis of clear, intelligible criteria.

The transparency tests included in Article 4(2) and in Article 5 are the same. The transparency test is part of the fairness test, as will be discussed in Section 21.4.E.1.

21.4.E THE TEST OF 'UNFAIRNESS'

In this section we will discuss which test must be applied to determine whether a term is unfair. First, we will deal with the test which is applied with respect to B2C contracts and subsequently which test is applied with respect to B2B contracts.

21.4.E.1 UNFAIRNESS TEST IN B2C CONTRACTS

Unfair Terms Directive[122] **21.33 (EU)**

Article 3: 1. A contractual term which has not been individually negotiated shall be regarded as unfair if, contrary to the requirement of good faith, it causes a significant imbalance in the parties' rights and obligations arising under the contract …

Article 4: 1. Without prejudice to Article 7, the unfairness of a contractual term shall be assessed, taking into account the nature of the goods or services for which the contract

---

[122] Directive 93/13/EEC (n 9 above). See also above, pp 833–34.

was concluded and by referring, at the time of conclusion of the contract, to all the circumstances attending the conclusion of the contract and to all the other terms of the contract or of another contract on which it is dependent. ...

Article 5: In the case of contracts where all or certain terms offered to the consumer are in writing, these terms must always be drafted in plain, intelligible language. Where there is doubt about the meaning of a term, the interpretation most favourable to the consumer shall prevail. This rule on interpretation shall not apply in the context of the procedures laid down in Article 7 (2).

House of Lords, 25 October 2001 **21.34 (EN)**

Director General of Fair Trading v First National Bank[123]

A standard term, under which (on enforcement of an overdue debt) interest was to continue to accrue at the contractual rate until payment 'after as well as before any judgment (such obligation to be independent of and not to merge with the judgment)', is not unfair.

Facts: First National Bank plc ('the bank') is licensed to carry on consumer credit business and is a major lender in the market, that has lent large sums to borrowers under credit agreements regulated under the Consumer Credit Act 1974. Such agreements are made on its printed form, which contains a number of standard terms. The Director General of Fair Trading ('the Director'), in exercising powers conferred on him by regulation 8 of the Unfair Terms in Consumer Contracts Regulations 1994 (SI 1994/3159) ('the regulations'), sought an injunction to restrain use of or reliance on one such standard term, under which (on enforcement of an overdue debt) interest was to continue to accrue at the contractual rate until payment 'after as well as before any judgment (such obligation to be independent of and not to merge with the judgment)', on the ground that it was unfair.

The bank resisted the Director's application on two grounds. The first, rejected by Evans-Lombe J at first instance ([2000] 1 WLR 98) and the Court of Appeal (Peter Gibson, Waller and Buxton L JJ) ([2000] QB 672), was that the fairness provisions of the regulations did not apply to the term in question. The second, accepted by the judge but partially rejected by the Court of Appeal, was that the term in question was not unfair. In the appeal to the House of Lords, the bank relied on both arguments. The Director sought to uphold the decision of the Court of Appeal but contended that the term was more fundamentally unfair than the Court of Appeal held it to be.

Held: The House of Lords allowed the appeal: the clause was subject to review but was not unfair.

Judgment: LORD STEYN: ...

[34]. ... It would be a gaping hole in the system if such clauses were not subject to the fairness requirement. For these further reasons I would reject the argument of the bank that regulation 3(2), and in particular 3(2)(b), take clause 8 outside the scope of the regulations.

[35]. Given these conclusions the attack on the merger principle mounted by the bank was misplaced. In any event, I am not willing to uphold criticism by the bank of the well tried and tested principle of merger. I would therefore reject the bank's submissions under this heading.

---

[123] [2001] UKHL 52, [2002] 1 AC 481.

[36]. It is now necessary to refer to the provisions which prescribe how it should be determined whether a term is unfair. Implementing article 3(1) of the directive regulation 4(1) provides:

'"unfair term" means any term which contrary to the requirement of good faith causes a significant imbalance in the parties' rights and obligations under the contract to the detriment of the consumer.'

There are three independent requirements. But the element of detriment to the consumer may not add much. But it serves to make clear that the directive is aimed at significant imbalance against the consumer, rather than the seller or supplier. The twin requirements of good faith and significant imbalance will in practice be determinative. Schedule 2 to the Regulations, which explains the concept of good faith, provides that regard must be had, amongst other things, to the extent to which the seller or supplier has dealt fairly and equitably with the consumer. It is an objective criterion. Good faith imports, as Lord Bingham has observed in his opinion, the notion of open and fair dealing: see also *Interfoto Picture Library Ltd v Stiletto Visual Programmes Ltd* [1989] QB 433. And helpfully the commentary to the 2000 edition of Principles of European Contract Law, prepared by the Commission of European Contract Law, explains that the purpose of the provision of good faith and fair dealing is 'to enforce community standards of fairness and reasonableness in commercial transactions': at 113; A fortiori that is true of consumer transactions. Schedule 3 to the Regulations (which corresponds to the Annex to the directive) is best regarded as a check list of terms which must be regarded as potentially vulnerable. The examples given in Schedule 3 convincingly demonstrate that the argument of the bank that good faith is predominantly concerned with procedural defects in negotiating procedures cannot be sustained. Any purely procedural or even predominantly procedural interpretation of the requirement of good faith must be rejected.

[37]. That brings me to the element of significant imbalance. It has been pointed out by Hugh Collins that the test 'of a significant imbalance of the obligations obviously directs attention to the substantive unfairness of the contract': 'Good Faith in European Contract Law' (1994), 14 *Oxford Journal of Legal Studies* 229, 249. It is however, also right to say that there is a large area of overlap between the concepts of good faith and significant imbalance.

[38]. It is now necessary to turn to the application of these requirements to the facts of the present case. The point is a relatively narrow one. I agree that the starting point is that a lender ought to be able to recover interest at the contractual rate until the date of payment, and this applies both before and after judgment. On the other hand, counsel for the Director advanced a contrary argument. Adopting the test of asking what the position of a consumer is in the contract under consideration with or without clause 8, he said that the consumer is in a significantly worse position than he would have been if there had been no such provision. Certainly, the consumer is worse off. The difficulty facing counsel, however, is that this disadvantage to the consumer appears to be the consequence not of clause 8 but of the County Courts (Interest on Judgment Debts) Order 1991. Under this Order no statutory interest is payable on a county court judgment given in proceedings to recover money due under a regulated agreement: see regulation 2. Counsel said that for policy reasons it was decided that in such a case no interest may be recovered after judgment. He said that it is not open to the House to criticise directly or indirectly this legal context. In these circumstances he submitted that it is not legitimate for a court to conclude that fairness requires that a lender must be able to insist on a stipulation designed

875

to avoid the statutory regime under the 1991 Order. Initially I was inclined to uphold this policy argument. On reflection, however, I have been persuaded that this argument cannot prevail in circumstances where the legislature has neither expressly nor by necessary implication barred a stipulation that interest may continue to accrue after judgment until payment in full.

[39]. For these reasons as well as the reasons given by Lord Bingham I agree that clause 8 is not unfair and I would also make the order which Lord Bingham proposes.

> *Note*
>
> Thus, the House of Lords held that the clause at stake was a default clause, which falls within the scope of the Directive. The House of Lords did not consider the clause unfair, since the clause did not constitute a significant imbalance to the detriment of the consumer.

BGH, 8 March 2005[124] **21.35 (DE)**

Bank charges

An internal letter of the bank to its branches cannot be regarded as standard business terms. However, the rules on standard business terms apply by way of analogy, insofar as the letter is intended to circumvent the rules on standard business terms. Bank charges for return of debit are ineffective under the rules concerning standard business terms.

Facts: A bank (the defendant) had sent a letter dated 4 May 1998 to all its branches in Germany, in which it gave instructions how to deal with the return of debit because of a lack of cover. According to this letter, the branches had to charge its customers a fee in the case of return of debit because of lack of cover. The account statements of the customers concerned included a debit notice of '6.00 return of debit'. Upon the complaints of the account holders concerned, the bank argued that it was entitled to claim damages for non-performance of the customers, since they had not met their duty of cover of the account.

A consumer association started proceedings against the bank, and it argued that the bank's practice to charge the fee in the whole of Germany should be considered a standard business term and was ineffective, because of violation of the rules on standard business terms.

The first instance court (LG Köln) granted the claim. On appeal the claim was dismissed. There was further appeal before the BGH.

Held: The decision of the Court of Appeal was quashed and replaced with the decision of the first instance.

Judgment: ...

II.1. The view of the Court of Appeal that the practice of the defendant, introduced by letter of 4 May 1998, was not a standard business term within the meaning of § 305(1) BGB is without any legal error.

(a) The concept of standard business terms presupposes, in accordance with § 305(1)(1) BGB, a clause, ie a declaration, of the user that it provides for the content of the contract (BGHZ 99, 374 [376] = NJW 1987, 1634; BGHZ 133, 184 [187] = NJW 1996, 2574). ...

(b) On that score, there is no standard business term in the present case. Neither the internal instruction of 4 May 1998 nor the debit notices nor the letters to

---

[124] NJW 2005, 1645.

complaining customers can be classified as standard business terms. An internal bank instruction given by the defendant to its employees is not addressed to the account holders and is not made available to them. It therefore does not aim to establish a contractual arrangement, but rather aims at coordinating a factual situation (Borges, ZIP 2005, 185 [187]). It cannot create the impression in the account holders that it concerned a contractual arrangement. …

(c) This is also not contradicted by 1(i) of the Annex to Article 3 of Directive 93/13/EEC concerning unfair terms. … The Directive also presupposes a contract clause, which was not there.

2. However, the court of appeal was wrong in denying a violation of the circumvention prohibition in § 306a BGB.

(a) According to this provision, the rules on standard business terms also apply when they are circumvented by other arrangements. According to the unambiguous wording of the BGB, this does not only apply to §§ 308 ff BGB (Stoffels, AGB-Recht, 2003 para 92), but to all provisions of Title 2 of Book 2 of the BGB (cf. Soergel/ Stein, BGB, 12th edn, § 7 AGBG para 2). …

(b) There is an infringement of the prohibition of circumvention according to § 306a BGB, when a legal arrangement which is ineffective as a standard business term is meant to be achieved by another legal arrangement … the only purpose of which can be to circumvent the statutory prohibition (Palandt/Heinrichs, § 306a para 2; Borges, ZIP 2005, 185 [187]). [The court then shows that the requirements of § 306a BGB are met.]

3. Given that there is an infringement of the prohibition of circumvention, the content can be policed according to §§ 307–309 BGB (Basedow, in: MünchKomm, 4. Aufl., § 306a para 4), which also can be invoked in collective proceedings according to § 1 of the Act on Actions for Injunctions [UKlaG]. The defendant's conflicting instruction which is in dispute and the commercial practice based thereupon fall short of this standard. A similar term in standard terms, by which the user has the payment of a fixed sum concerning damages in the case of a debit because of lack of cover promised to himself, is incompatible with essential basic principles of the legal order (§ 307(2) no 1 BGB) and constitutes a disproportionate disadvantage of customers concerned (§ 307(1) BGB).

(a) A fixed amount of damages presupposes that the requirements for a claim for damages are met (Erman/Roloff, BGB, 11th edn, § 309 para 44). The fundamental conceptions of the default rules in private law include the idea that contractual damages may only be claimed when the debtor is responsible for the non-performance (§ 280(1) BGB).

(aa) In the decisions of this Senate of 21 October 1997 … the question whether the contract establishing a current account obliges the customer of a bank to provide sufficient cover on his account, so that direct debits which have been authorized will not be returned, did not fall to be decided

(bb) In the lower courts and in legal writings it has partly been answered in the affirmative (AG Neuss, WM 1998, 2021; AG Erkelenz, WM 1999, 2403 [2405] …).

(cc) This Senate associates itself with the latter opinion with regard to the cases at issue where direct debit payments must be returned because of a lack of cover against the authorized amount. The customer of a bank is not obliged to his bank to provide cover for the direct debit payments he authorizes. There is only an obligation of the debtor to hold enough cover to the debtor on the basis of the agreement to provide direct debit.

The debtor's bank does not become active on the basis of the instruction of the debtor, but upon the instruction of the creditor's bank without any instruction of its own customer. The debtor's bank carries the risk in the relationship with its customers that there is not sufficient cover on the account or that the customer objects to the debiting. ...

Note

In this case, the BGH held that a bank's letter that is intended to circumvent the rules on standard business terms under German law is governed by way of analogy by those rules on standard business terms. In contrast to the UK Supreme Court's decision, the BGH held that the bank charge was unfair.

Court of Justice, 14 March 2013[125]   **21.36 (EU)**

Aziz

The test to determine whether a term is contrary to good faith in Article 3(1) of the Unfair Terms Directive implies that it must be assessed whether the seller or supplier, dealing fairly and equitably with the consumer, could reasonably assume that the consumer would have agreed to the term concerned in individual contract negotiations.

To assess whether there is a 'significant imbalance' in the parties' rights and obligations to the detriment of the consumer in Article 3(1), it must be evaluated to what extent the term places the consumer in a worse position than would have been the situation under the relevant national law in the absence of that term.

Facts: In July 2007, Mr Aziz concluded a loan agreement for the amount of €138,000 secured by a mortgage on Mr Aziz's family home with Catalunyacaixa, a bank.

The loan agreement entered into with Catalunyacaixa provided, in clause 6, for annual default interest of 18.75%, automatically applicable to sums not paid when due, without the need for any notice. In addition, clause 6a of that agreement conferred on Catalunyacaixa the right to call in the totality of the loan on expiry of a stipulated time-limit where the debtor failed to fulfil his obligation to pay any part of the principal or of the interest on the loan. Finally, clause 15 of that agreement, concerning the agreement on determination of the amount due, stipulated not only that Catalunyacaixa had the right to bring enforcement proceedings to reclaim any debt but also, for the purposes of those proceedings, that it could immediately quantify the amount due by submitting an appropriate certificate indicating that amount.

Mr Aziz stopped paying the instalments from June 2008 onwards. On 11 March 2009 Catalunyacaixa instituted enforcement proceedings against him before a Spanish court seeking recovery of the sums of €139,674 in respect of the loan, €90 in respect of accrued interest and €41,902 in respect of interest and costs. The court ordered enforcement and Mr Aziz was then sent an order for payment but he neither complied with it nor objected to it. Finally, the bank sold Aziz's property for 50% of its value and Mr Aziz was evicted from his home. Shortly before that occurrence, on 11 January 2011, Mr Aziz had started proceedings, in which he claimed the unfairness of the clauses in the contract with the bank before another Spanish court. This court referred preliminary questions to the Court of Justice inter alia as to how the unfairness test in Article 3 should be applied.

[125] C-415/11, *M. Aziz v Caixa d'Estalvis de Catalunya, Tarragona i Manresa (Catalunyacaixa)*, 14 March 2013, ECLI:EU:C:2013:164.

Held: Article 3(1) of Directive 93/13 must be interpreted as meaning that:

— the concept of 'significant imbalance' to the detriment of the consumer must be assessed in the light of an analysis of the rules of national law applicable in the absence of any agreement between the parties, in order to determine whether, and if so to what extent, the contract places the consumer in a less favourable legal situation than that provided for by the national law in force. To that end, an assessment of the legal situation of that consumer having regard to the means at his disposal, under national law, to prevent continued use of unfair terms, should also be carried out;

— in order to assess whether the imbalance arises 'contrary to the requirement of good faith', it must be determined whether the seller or supplier, dealing fairly and equitably with the consumer, could reasonably assume that the consumer would have agreed to the term concerned in individual contract negotiations.

Judgment: 65 By its second question, the referring court seeks, essentially, to obtain clarification of the constituent elements of the concept of 'unfair term', in the light of Article 3(1) and (3) of the directive, and of the annex thereto, in order to assess whether the terms which are the subject of the main proceedings and relate to acceleration in long-term contracts, setting of default interest rates and the agreement on quantification are or are not unfair.

66 In that regard, according to settled case-law, the relevant jurisdiction of the Court extends to the interpretation of the concept of 'unfair term' used in Article 3(1) of the directive and in the annex thereto, and to the criteria which the national court may or must apply when examining a contractual term in the light of the provisions of the directive, bearing in mind that it is for that court to determine, in the light of those criteria, whether a particular contractual term is actually unfair in the circumstances of the case. It is thus clear that the Court must limit itself to providing the referring court with guidance which the latter must take into account in order to assess whether the term at issue is unfair. ...

67 That being so, it should be noted that, in referring to concepts of good faith and significant imbalance in the parties' rights and obligations arising under the contract, to the detriment of the consumer, Article 3(1) of the directive merely defines in a general way the factors that render unfair a contractual term that has not been individually negotiated. ...

68 As stated by the Advocate General in point 71 of her Opinion, in order to ascertain whether a term causes a 'significant imbalance' in the parties' rights and obligations arising under the contract, to the detriment of the consumer, it must in particular be considered what rules of national law would apply in the absence of an agreement by the parties in that regard. Such a comparative analysis will enable the national court to evaluate whether and, as the case may be, to what extent, the contract places the consumer in a legal situation less favourable than that provided for by the national law in force. To that end, an assessment should also be carried out of the legal situation of that consumer having regard to the means at his disposal, under national legislation, to prevent continued use of unfair terms.

69 With regard to the question of the circumstances in which such an imbalance arises 'contrary to the requirement of good faith', having regard to the sixteenth recital in the preamble to the directive and as stated in essence by the Advocate General in point 74 of her Opinion, the national court must assess for those purposes whether the seller or supplier, dealing fairly and equitably with the consumer, could reasonably assume that the consumer would have agreed to such a term in individual contract negotiations.

70 ...

71 Furthermore, pursuant to Article 4(1) of the directive, the unfairness of a contractual term is to be assessed taking into account the nature of the goods or services for which the contract was concluded and by referring, at the time of conclusion of the

contract, to all the circumstances attending the conclusion of it. ... It follows that, in that respect, the consequences of the term under the law applicable to the contract must also be taken into account, requiring consideration to be given to the national legal system. ...

72 It is in the light of those criteria that the Juzgado de lo Mercantil No 3 de Barcelona must assess whether the terms referred to in the second question are unfair.

73 In particular, with regard, first, to the term concerning acceleration, in long-term contracts, on account of events of default occurring within a limited specific period, it is for the referring court to assess in particular, as stated by the Advocate General in points 77 and 78 of her Opinion, whether the right of the seller or supplier to call in the totality of the loan is conditional upon the non-compliance by the consumer with an obligation which is of essential importance in the context of the contractual relationship in question, whether that right is provided for in cases in which such non-compliance is sufficiently serious in the light of the term and amount of the loan, whether that right derogates from the relevant applicable rules and whether national law provides for adequate and effective means enabling the consumer subject to such a term to remedy the effects of the loan being called in.

74 Second, regarding the term concerning the fixing of default interest, it should be recalled that, in the light of paragraph 1(e) of the annex to the Directive, read in conjunction with Articles 3(1) and 4(1) of the directive, the national court must assess in particular, as stated by the Advocate General in points 85 to 87 of her Opinion, first, the rules of national law which would apply to the relationship between the parties, in the event of no agreement having been reached in the contract in question or in other consumer contracts of that type and, second, the rate of default interest laid down, compared with the statutory interest rate, in order to determine whether it is appropriate for securing the attainment of the objectives pursued by it in the Member State concerned and does not go beyond what is necessary to achieve them.

75 With regard, finally, to the term concerning the unilateral determination by the lender of the amount of the unpaid debt, linked to the possibility of initiating mortgage enforcement proceedings, it must be held that, taking into account paragraph 1(q) of the annex to the directive and the criteria contained in Articles 3(1) and 4(1) thereof, the referring court must in particular assess whether and, if appropriate, to what extent, the term in question derogates from the rules applicable in the absence of agreement between the parties, so as to make it more difficult for the consumer, given the procedural means at his disposal, to take legal action and exercise rights of the defence.

Notes

(1) In this case the Court of Justice formulated inter alia a test to determine whether a clause is contrary to good faith. The situation in which a consumer negotiated the term, must be compared with the situation in which the consumer did not negotiate it. If a consumer would not have accepted a term, had he negotiated it, the term is considered contrary to good faith.

(2) The Court of Justice also formulated a test to determine whether a clause causes a 'significant imbalance' in the parties' rights and obligations arising under the contract, to the detriment of the consumer. In that case, the clause must be compared with the rules under national law which would have applied in the absence of the clause in the contract. If the clause deviates from national law to the detriment of the consumer, there is an indication that there is a significant imbalance in the parties' rights and obligations.

(3) In both instances, all the circumstances at the time of the conclusion must be taken into consideration (Article 4(1) Unfair Terms Directive).

(4) This decision differs from *Freiburger Kommunaulbauten*, where the Court of Justice had held that the fairness of a clause must be considered according to the national law applicable to the contract.[126]

(5) From later case law, it follows that the transparency test is also part of the unfairness test of the Directive on Unfair Terms in Consumer Contracts.[127]

(6) Two months after *Aziz*, the Court of Justice answered a preliminary question by a Dutch court on a penalty clause which was included in the general conditions of a rental contract in *Asbeek Brusse*.[128] Under the clause, the tenant had to pay a penalty every day he failed to pay the rent. The referring court of appeal asked whether it could reduce the amount of the penalty, which is possible according to Article 6:94 BW. The Court of Justice held that this penalty clause fell within item (e) of the Annex to the Directive, which states: 'requiring any consumer who fails to fulfil his obligation to pay a disproportionately high sum in compensation.'[129] As a result, it was unfair. Since it concerned an unfair clause which is not binding according to Article 6 of the Directive, it was not possible to reduce the penalty.

(7) In 2015, in *ParkingEye Ltd v Beavis*, a majority of the UK Supreme Court (5-1) held that a penalty clause in a parking contract was fair after applying the good faith test, as formulated by the Advocate General in *Aziz*.[130] The penalty amounted to £85, if a consumer overstayed the allowed parking time of two hours. This penalty was clearly visible in the parking lot. None of the judges referred to the decision in *Asbeek Brusse* and explained why this case differed. Would the bank charge cases of the House of Lords and the Supreme Court be decided in the same way if *Aziz* and *Kásler* are taken into account?

Under French law, the standard for review in the renewed Article L 212-1 of the Code de la consommation is similar to the one in the European Directive. A contractual term is unfair if it causes a significant imbalance in the parties' rights and obligations arising under the contract, to the detriment of the non-professional or consumer. Under the former Article 35 of the Loi Scrivener, an 'abuse of economic power' by the professional (*abus de puissance économique*) was required. However, the change is rather insignificant, because the Cour de cassation held that an abuse of economic power of a professional is inherent in standard terms in a B2C contract.[131] In contrast to the Directive, the provision in the French Code does not mention the requirement of good faith, since this vague concept was thought to have no additional value.[132] Whether a term is 'unfair' depends on all the circumstances at the moment of conclusion of the contract (Article L 212-1(2) Cconsomm). The issue which arises is whether this is in line with the case law of the Court of Justice.

---

[126] C-237/02, *Freiburger Kommunalbauten*, 1 April 2004, ECLI:EU:C:2004:209.
[127] See *Kásler*, 21.32 (EU) above, p 868.
[128] C-488/11, *Asbeek Brusse*, 30 May 2013, ECLI:EU:C:2013:341 (n 109 above).
[129] See on the Annex to the Directive on Unfair Terms in Consumer Contracts: 21.4.C above.
[130] [2015] UKSC 67, [2016] AC 1172.
[131] Cass civ (1) 6 January 1994, no. 91-19424, Bull I no. 8, D 1994, 209, annotated by P Delebecque.
[132] See G Paisant, D 1995, 100.

§ 307: Test of reasonableness of contents

(1) Provisions in standard business terms are ineffective if, contrary to the requirement of good faith, they unreasonably disadvantage the other party to the contract with the user. An unreasonable disadvantage may also arise from the provision not being clear and comprehensible.

(2) An unreasonable disadvantage is, in case of doubt, to be assumed to exist if a provision is not compatible with essential principles of the statutory provision from which it deviates, or limits essential rights or duties inherent in the nature of the contract to such an extent that attainment of the purpose of the contract is jeopardised.

(3) Subsections (1) and (2) above, and sections 308 and 309 apply only to provisions in standard business terms on the basis of which arrangements derogating from legal provisions, or arrangements supplementing those legal provisions, are agreed. Other provisions may be ineffective under subsection (1) sentence 2 above, in conjunction with subsection (1) sentence 1 above.

A series of ECJ cases held that a court should not wait for an individual consumer to raise the question whether a term of the contract is unfair: the court should take the initiative and, provided it has the necessary information, determine whether or not the term is fair.[133] This requirement is replicated in the UK's Consumer Rights Act 2015, section 77. However, this provision seems to be out of date—subsequently the Court of Justice has held that the same applies to any EU consumer protection legislation.[134]

21.4.E.2 UNFAIRNESS TEST IN B2B CONTRACTS

BGH, 8 March 1984[135] **21.38 (DE)**

Foam insulation

Professional parties are in general equally prejudiced by terms shortening the generally applicable limitation period in relation to proceedings for breach of a construction contract, and are thus able to complain that such a term is contrary to § 9 AGBG [now § 307 BGB].

Facts: A company charged a building company with the job of insulating two tanks, containing hot liquids, with polyether-foam. After a while the foam bubbled and cracked. The building company's standard terms included a provision that shortened the statutory limitation of the action based on quality and fitness for the purpose. A question arose whether, in the light of § 24(2) AGBG [now § 310(1) BGB], that Act applies to a limitation clause in a standard contract concluded between professionals.

---

[133] Joined Cases *Océano Grupo Editorial SA v Roció Murciano Quintero* (C-240/98), *Salvat Editores SA v José M. Sánchez Alcón Prades* (C-241/98), *José Luis Copano Badillo* (C-242/98), *Mohammed Berroane* (C-243/98) and *Emilio Viñas Feliú* (C-244/98), 27 June 2000, ECLI:EU:C:2000:346; C-473/00, *Cofidis SA v Jean-Louis Fredout*, 21 November 2002, ECLI:EU:C:2002:705; C-168/05, *Elisa María Mostaza Claro v Centro Móvil Milenium SL*, 26 October 2006, ECLI:EU:C:2006:675; C-243/08, *Pannon GSM Zrt. v Erzsébet Sustikné Gyorfi*, 4 June 2009, ECLI:EU:C:2009:350; C-227/08, *Eva Martín Martín v EDP Editores SL*, 17 December 2009, ECLI:EU:C:2009:792. For a more elaborate account of this issue, see Micklitz et al (n 67 above) 299; AS Hartkamp, CH Sieburgh, W Devroe, *Cases, Materials and Text on European Law and Private Law* (Oxford: Hart Publishing, 2017) ch 7 II C.

[134] See, ie with respect to Council Directive 87/102/EEC on consumer credit as amended by Directive 98/7/EC: C-429/05, *M Rampion and M-J Rampion v Franfinance SA and K par K SAS*, 4 October 2007, ECLI:EU:C:2007:575; C-497/13, *Faber v Autobedrijf Hazet Ochten BV*, 4 June 2015, ECLI:EU:C:2015:357.

[135] NJW 1984, 1750.

Held: The company was entitled to complain that the term was contrary to the AGBG.

Judgment: ... The customs and usages applying in commercial dealings to which reasonable regard must (under § 24(2) AGBG) be paid in the context of the application of
§ 9 AGBG [now § 307 BGB] are not such as to permit the determination of this case in a
way which diverges from § 11 no 10ff AGBG [now § 309 no 8bff BGB]. Where a stipulation used in dealings with non-business people falls within one of the prohibitions laid
down in § 11 AGBG, that indicates that, even if used in dealings between business people,
it will place the party on whom it is imposed at an unreasonable disadvantage, unless,
exceptionally, it is capable of being regarded as reasonable on account of the particular
interests and requirements inherent in commercial business dealings. ... However, the
essential idea underlying the statutory rule diverged from (§ 9(2) no 1 AGBG), namely
that the relatively short periods prescribed by §§ 477, 638 [now cf §§ 438, 634a] BGB for
bringing breach of warranty claims take reasonable account of the periods within which
defects usually appear, and that any (further) shortening of the limitation periods would
unreasonably prejudice the customer as regards defects which initially remain hidden,
also applies in commercial dealings. ...

In carrying on their trade or profession, business people are no less affected than non-
business people by construction defects. The particular interests and requirements inherent in commercial business dealings, and the standards applying in such dealings, are
irrelevant as regards the risk to which the customer is typically exposed where construction works are concerned. A business person is not generally in a position to detect hidden
construction defects any earlier than a nonbusiness person. It follows that, as a general
rule, business people engaged in carrying on their trade or profession are also unreasonably prejudiced, in their capacity as customers, by a stipulation contained in standard terms
and conditions which shortens the five-year limitation period (commencing on acceptance
of the works) for bringing breach of warranty claims in respect of works done under a
construction contract, and this is contrary to the requirements of good faith (§ 9 AGBG).

Hoge Raad, 31 December 1993[136]   **21.39 (NL)**

The Shipyard De Schelde

*In agreements between businesses in related industries, it is not unreasonable wholly or
partially to exclude liability for serious fault on the part of subcontractors.*

Facts: Matatag cs, the owners of a ship, sought to hold the shipyard De Schelde responsible for the damage
caused by an employee of its subcontractor. The shipyard referred to an exclusion clause in the contract. The
shipowners for their part argued that the clause was not applicable, because that would be unacceptable according to criteria of reasonableness and equity (Articles 6:2(2) and 6:248(2) BW).

Held: The clause was not unreasonable.

Judgment: ... 3.2. For the purposes of assessing the plea advanced, the following must
be taken into consideration.

This case concerns an agreement between two businesses—a ship-owning company and a shipyard—operating in industrial sectors which regularly have dealings with
each other and in which the standardisation of agreements by the inclusion therein of

---

[136] NJ 1995, 389, annotated by CJH Brunner.

general terms and conditions incorporating exclusion of liability clauses is an everyday phenomenon. ...

After all, in the case of agreements of the type at issue here, concluded between business entities as indicated above, it cannot be said to be unacceptable, according to the criteria of reasonableness and fairness, to incorporate in the applicable general terms and conditions stipulations which wholly or partially exclude liability, even for serious fault on the part of persons engaged to carry out the work who are not members of the management of the business concerned, and then to rely on that exclusion in the event of loss or damage as suffered in the present case.

Unfair Contract Terms Act 1977   **21.40 (EN)**

Explanatory Provisions

Section 11: The 'reasonableness' test

(1) In relation to a contract term, the requirement of reasonableness for the purposes of this Part of this Act, section 3 of the Misrepresentation Act 1967 and section 3 of the Misrepresentation Act (Northern Ireland) 1967 is that the term shall have been a fair and reasonable one to be included having regard to the circumstances which were, or ought reasonably to have been, known to or in the contemplation of the parties when the contract was made.

(2) In determining for the purposes of section 6 or 7 above whether a contract term satisfies the requirement of reasonableness, regard shall be had in particular to the matters specified in Schedule 2 to this Act; but this subsection does not prevent the court or arbitrator from holding, in accordance with any rule of law, that a term which purports to exclude or restrict any relevant liability is not a term of the contract.

(3) In relation to a notice (not being a notice having contractual effect), the requirement of reasonableness under this Act is that it should be fair and reasonable to allow reliance on it, having regard to all the circumstances obtaining when the liability arose or (but for the notice) would have arisen.

(4) Where by reference to a contract term or notice a person seeks to restrict liability to a specified sum of money, and the question arises (under this or any other Act) whether the term or notice satisfies the requirement of reasonableness, regard shall be had in particular (but without prejudice to subsection (2) above in case of contract terms) to—

> (a) the resources which he could expect to be available to him for the purpose of meeting the liability should it arise; and

> (b) how far it was open to him to cover himself by insurance.

SCHEDULE 2
'GUIDELINES' FOR APPLICATION OF REASONABLENESS TEST

The matters to which regard is to be had in particular for the purposes of sections 6(3), 7(3) and (4), 20 and 21 are any of the following which appear to be relevant—

> (a) the strength of the bargaining positions of the parties relative to each other, taking into account (among other things) alternative means by which the customer's requirements could have been met;

> (b) whether the customer received an inducement to agree to the terms, or in accepting it had an opportunity of entering into a similar contract with other persons, but without having to accept a similar term;

(c) whether the customer knew or ought reasonably to have known of the existence and extent of the term (having regard, among other things, to any custom of the trade and any previous course of dealing between the parties);

(d) where the term excludes or restricts any relevant liability if some condition is not complied with, whether it was reasonable at the time of the contract to expect that compliance with that condition would be practicable;

(e) whether the goods were manufactured, processed or adapted to the special order of the consumer.

Note

The Guidelines contained in Schedule 2 of the Act are brought forward from the earlier Supply of Goods (Implied Terms) Act 1973. Technically they apply only to cases falling within sections 6 and 7 (see section 11(2)), but the courts also take these factors into account in other cases: for example, *Rees Hough Ltd v Redland Reinforced Plastics Ltd*,[137] *Phillips Products Ltd v Hyland*.[138]

Court of Appeal and House of Lords **21.41 (EN)**

George Mitchell (Chesterhall) Ltd v Finney Lock Seeds Ltd[139]

The following factors are relevant in assessing whether it is reasonable to rely on a limitation clause: (i) the fact that the supplier in practice pays compensation to some customers who have suffered the same loss as the purchaser, irrespective of the clause; (ii) the fact that the supplier could insure against such losses without materially increasing the price of the goods; (iii) the fact that the goods supplied were of no value to the purchaser.

Facts: See above.[140]

Held: In addition to finding that the seller was not entitled to rely on the clause, the Court of Appeal unanimously found that it was not reasonable for the sellers to rely on the clause under the Supply of Goods (Implied Terms) Act 1973. Having overturned the decision of the Court of Appeal on the first point, the House of Lords upheld the decision on the reasonableness point.

Judgment in the House of Lords:

LORD BRIDGE: … This is the first time your Lordships' House has had to consider a modern statutory provision giving the court power to override contractual terms excluding or restricting liability, which depends on the court's view of what is 'fair and reasonable.' The particular provision of the modified section 55 of the Act of 1979 which applies in the instant case is of limited and diminishing importance. But the several provisions of the Unfair Contract Terms Act 1977 which depend on 'the requirement of reasonableness,' defined in section 11 by reference to what is 'fair and reasonable,' albeit in a different context, are likely to come before the courts with increasing frequency. It may, therefore, be appropriate to consider how an original decision as to what is 'fair and reasonable' made in the application of any of these provisions should be approached by an appellate court. It would not be accurate to describe such a decision as an exercise of discretion. But a decision under any of the provisions referred to will have this in common with the

---

[137] (1984) 27 Building LR 136 (QBD).
[138] [1987] 2 All ER 620 (CA).
[139] [1983] 2 AC 803.
[140] 21.9 (EN), above, p 826.

exercise of a discretion, that, in having regard to the various matters to which the modi-fied section 55(5) of the Act of 1979, or section 11 of the Act of 1977 direct attention, the court must entertain a whole range of considerations, put them in the scales on one side or the other, and decide at the end of the day on which side the balance comes down. There will sometimes be room for a legitimate difference of judicial opinion as to what the answer should be, where it will be impossible to say that one view is demonstrably wrong and the other demonstrably right. It must follow, in my view, that, when asked to review such a decision on appeal, the appellate court should treat the original decision with the utmost respect and refrain from interference with it unless satisfied that it proceeded upon some erroneous principle or was plainly and obviously wrong.

... [I]t is common ground that the onus was on the respondents to show that it would not be fair or reasonable to allow the appellants to rely on the relevant condition as limit-ing their liability. It was argued for the appellants that the court must have regard to the circumstances as at the date of the contract, not after the breach. ... But, in any event, the language of subsections (4) and (5) of that section is clear and unambiguous. The question whether it is fair or reasonable to allow reliance on a term excluding or limiting liability for a breach of contract can only arise after the breach. The nature of the breach and the circumstances in which it occurred cannot possibly be excluded from 'all the cir-cumstances of the case' to which regard must be had.

My Lords, ... I turn to the application of the statutory language to the circumstances of the case. Of the particular matters to which attention is directed by paragraphs (a) to (e) of section 55(5), only those in (a) to (c) are relevant. As to paragraph (c), the respondents admittedly knew of the relevant condition (they had dealt with the appellants for many years) and, if they had read it, particularly clause 2, they would, I think, as laymen rather than lawyers, have had no difficulty in understanding what it said. This and the magni-tude of the damages claimed in proportion to the price of the seeds sold are factors which weigh in the scales in the appellants' favour.

The question of relative bargaining strength under paragraph (a) and of the oppor-tunity to buy seeds without a limitation of the seedsman's liability under paragraph (b) were inter-related. The evidence was that a similar limitation of liability was universally embodied in the terms of trade between seedsmen and farmers and had been so for very many years. The limitation had never been negotiated between representative bodies but, on the other hand, had not been the subject of any protest by the National Farmers' Union. These factors, if considered in isolation, might have been equivocal. The decisive factor, however, appears from the evidence of four witnesses called for the appellants, two independent seedsmen, the chairman of the appellant company, and a director of a sister company (both being wholly-owned subsidiaries of the same parent). They said that it had always been their practice, unsuccessfully attempted in the instant case, to negotiate settlements of farmers' claims for damages in excess of the price of the seeds, if they thought that the claims were 'genuine' and 'justified.' This evidence indicated a clear recognition by seedsmen in general, and the appellants in particular, that reliance on the limitation of liability imposed by the relevant condition would not be fair or reasonable.

Two further factors, if more were needed, weight the scales in favour of the respond-ents. The supply of autumn, instead of winter, cabbage seeds was due to the negligence of the appellants' sister company. Irrespective of its quality, the autumn variety supplied could not, according to the appellants' own evidence, be grown commercially in East Lothian. Finally, as the trial judge found, seedsmen could insure against the risk of crop failure caused by supplying the wrong variety of seeds without materially increasing the price of seeds.

My Lords, even if I felt doubts about the statutory issue, I should not, for the reasons explained earlier, think it right to interfere with the unanimous original decision of that issue by the Court of Appeal. As it is, I feel no such doubts. If I were making the original decision, I should conclude without hesitation that it would not be fair or reasonable to allow the appellants to rely on the contractual limitation of their liability.

I would dismiss the appeal.

Note

This case was decided not under UCTA 1977, but under the Supply of Goods (Implied Terms) Act 1973 (now superseded by UCTA). The earlier Act did not use the test of whether it was reasonable to incorporate the clause into the contract, but of whether it was reasonable for the seller to rely on the clause.

21.5 PUBLIC LAW CONTROLS

Unfair Terms Directive   **21.42 (EU)**

Article 7: 1. Member States shall ensure that, in the interests of consumers and of competitors, adequate and effective means exist to prevent the continued use of unfair terms in contracts concluded with consumers by sellers or suppliers.

2. The means referred to in paragraph 1 shall include provisions whereby persons or organisations, having a legitimate interest under national law in protecting consumers, may take action according to the national law concerned before the courts or before competent administrative bodies for a decision as to whether contractual terms drawn up for general use are unfair, so that they can apply appropriate and effective means to prevent the continued use of such terms.

3. With due regard for national laws, the legal remedies referred to in paragraph 2 may be directed separately or jointly against a number of sellers or suppliers from the same economic sector or their associations which use or recommend the use of the same general contractual terms or similar terms.

It has already been noted that the French *Loi Scrivener* was originally designed, not to affect the private rights of parties *inter se*, but to prohibit the use of abusive clauses. The Commission on Abusive Clauses has been retained under the amended legislation. Under the following provisions of the Code de la consommation, consumer associations also have the right to challenge unfair terms in civil proceedings:

Code de la consommation[141]   **21.43 (FR)**

Article L 621-7: The associations mentioned in Article L 621-11 and organisations able to provide proof of their inclusion in the list published in the Official Journal of the European

---

[141] The two provisions were first introduced in 1993 and 2001, respectively, and last revised in 2016.

Union in application of Article 4 of directive 2009/22/CE of the European Parliament and Council dated 23 April 2009 and amended relating to actions for an injunction to stop in matters of protection of consumers' interests, can bring a claim before the civil courts in order to stop or prohibit any illicit action in respect of the provisions transposing the directives mentioned in Article 1 of the aforementioned directive.

Article L 621-8: When he is hearing a case pursuant to Article L 621-7, the judge may order, where appropriate subject to a fine, the deletion of an illicit or abusive clause in any contract or standard contract offered to, or intended for, the consumer or in a contract being performed.

The associations and organisations mentioned in Article L 621-7 can also ask the judge to declare that this clause is deemed unwritten in all identical contracts concluded by the same professional with consumers, and to require the professional to inform at his own expenses the concerned consumers by all appropriate means.

§ 13 AGBG of 1976 also created a public law control on the use of unfair standard terms in addition to the civil law control. This provision was incorporated in §§ 1 and 3 of the 2002 Act on Actions for Injunctions (UKlaG (Unterlassungsklagengesetz)). Consumer organisations are thus empowered to act under the Unterlassungsklagengesetz. They can obtain a written assurance from the business and take proceedings if the assurance is broken. This has proven to be an extremely effective control.[142]

In England there was no equivalent to these procedures before 1994, even for the limited range of unfair clauses[143] falling within the Unfair Contract Terms Act 1977. There were only very limited powers under the Fair Trading Act 1973 (Part II) (now repealed) for the Director-General of Fair Trading to issue regulations banning the use of clauses if they amounted to 'consumer trade practices which adversely affect the interests of consumers'. When the Directive on Unfair Terms was first implemented in the UK, the power to take action was given only to the Director-General of Fair Trading. Regulation 11 of and Schedule 1 to the 1999 Regulations now give the power to take action to a much wider range of authorities (including local trading standards officers) and to the Consumers Association. Later the Director-General of Fair Trading's powers were transferred to the Office of Fair Trading (OFT), and then to the Competition and Markets Authority (CMA), which now exercises it powers under the Consumer Rights Act 2015.[144] The OFT and the CMA have been very active in obtaining assurances that unfair terms in contracts will be removed by the businesses responsible for them; and they have also published helpful guidance to businesses.[145]

---

[142] See H-W Micklitz, 'La Loi Allemande Relative Au Régime Juridique des Conditions Générales des Contrats du 9 Décembre 1976—Bilan de 11 Années d'Application' RIDC 1989, 101; E Hondius, *Unfair Terms in Consumer Contracts* (Utrecht: Molengraaf Institute for Private Law, 1987) 184.

[143] Primarily exclusion and limitation of liability clauses, see above, p 841.

[144] CRA 2015, Sch 3.

[145] See, eg, OFT, *Unfair Standard terms*, OFT 143, Annexe B (available from: www.oft.gov.uk/shared_oft/business_leaflets/unfair_contract_terms/oft143.pdf). This has been adopted without changes by the Competition and Markets Authority.

21.6 CONCLUDING REMARKS

One of the most important and innovative developments in private law in the last century has been the judicial review of unfair contract terms. Although the principle of freedom of contract remains of paramount importance, this freedom is subject to restrictions. This is especially true where the freedom of contract is monopolised by one of the contracting parties with a stronger bargaining position and for that reason may easily lead to contractual injustice. Nowadays this role of the courts is commonly accepted, even in countries such as France, where the protection of weaker parties against unfair terms effectively imposed by stronger parties was traditionally a feature of administrative law.

The use by the courts of open-ended concepts, such as good morals or good faith, has in some countries been replaced by legislation which specifically empowers the courts to review unfair contract terms. This legislation is sometimes of general application and is sometimes restricted to standard terms or particular contracts (such as sale of goods or insurance contracts). In this story, the Directive on Unfair Terms, which has given rise to a partial harmonisation of the laws in the Member States and thus created a minimum level of consumer protection against unfair clauses in standard terms, is very important. In the EU, the review of unfair standard terms may occur through an individual action before the civil courts, and also through a public action (England and France) or collective action (Germany, France and the Netherlands). The collective or public review of contract terms has an inevitably abstract character.

Clauses that are individually negotiated and clauses in contracts between professional parties are outside the scope of the Directive. The availability of review for such clauses therefore remains a matter for the Member States. We have seen that, in addition to general concepts such as good faith, a number of other general doctrines of contract law are used to control the effect of unfair contract terms, notably the law relating to the formation of contracts and the rules on interpretation. In the application of these more general contract law rules, the courts in any Member State may derive inspiration from particular legislation (the so-called *Indizwirkung* of the indicative list of unfair clauses for contracts between large companies and small businessmen) as well as, evidently, from case law in other Member States.

However, some Member States, notably Germany, France, The Netherlands and the UK, do have legislative controls over unfair clauses used in contracts between businesses, and under both UCTA 1977 and CRA 2015 and Article L 442-6, I, 2° of the French Code de commerce the control is not limited to standard contractual terms.

The PECL subject any term which has not been individually negotiated to a test of good faith and fair dealing (Article 4:110) and provide that any clause exempting or limiting liability, negotiated or not, may be relied on only if it is not contrary to good faith to do so (Article 8:109).[146]

---

[146] In the CESL different tests are included with respect to unfair terms in B2C contracts (Art 83 ff CESL) and in B2B contracts (Art 86 CESL).

FURTHER READING

Baum, M, 'Penalty Clauses' in J Basedow, K Hopt and R Zimmermann (eds), *Max Planck Encyclopedia of European Private Law* (Oxford University Press, 2012) 1259–63.

Collins, H (ed), *Standard Contract Terms in Europe: A Basis for and a Challenge to European Contract Law* (Alphen aan Den Rijn: Kluwer Law International, 2008).

Gerstenberg, O, 'Constitutional Reasoning in Private Law: The Role of the CJEU in Adjudicating Unfair Terms in Consumer Contracts' (2015) 21 ELJ 599–621.

Hellwege, P, 'Standard Contract Terms' in J Basedow, K Hopt and R Zimmermann (eds), *Max Planck Encyclopedia of European Private Law* (Oxford University Press, 2012) 1588–92.

Hesselink MW, 'Unfair terms in contracts between businesses' in R Schulze and J Stuyck (eds), *Towards a European contract law* (Munich: Sellier European Law Publishers, 2011) 131–47.

Jansen, N, 'Unfair Contract Terms' in N Jansen and R Zimmermann (eds), *Commentaries on European Contract Laws* (Oxford University Press, 2018) 919–94.

Leveneur-Azémar, M, *Étude sur les clauses limitatives ou exonératoires de responsabilité* (Paris: LGDJ, 2017).

Loos, MBM, 'Transparency of Standard Terms under the Unfair Contract Terms Directive and the Proposal for a Common European Sales Law' (2015) 23 ERPL 179–93.

Micklitz H-W and Reich N, 'The Court and Sleeping Beauty: the Revival of the Unfair Contract Terms Directive (UCTD)' (2014) 51 CMLRev 771–808.

Rutgers, JW, 'Unfair Terms in Consumer Contracts' in *English and European Perspectives on Contract and Commercial Law: Essays in Honour of Hugh Beale* (Oxford: Hart Publishing, 2014) 279–90.

Stoffel-Munck, P, 'The Revolution in Unfair Terms' in L Gullifer and S Vogenauer (eds), J Cartwright and S Whittaker (eds), *The Code Napoléon Rewritten: French Contract Law after the 2016 Reforms* (Oxford: Hart Publishing, 2017) 145–65.

PART 5

REMEDIES FOR NON-PERFORMANCE

CHAPTER 22
THE RANGE OF REMEDIES FOR BREACH OF CONTRACT

In this Part (Chapters 22–27), we consider the remedies which are available to one party when the other party is in 'breach of contract', ie it has failed to perform its contractual obligations and the non-performance is not excused under one of the doctrines concerning 'Supervening Events'.[1] The remedies covered by the chapters are specific enforcement; withholding of performance; termination (and restitutionary claims which may be available after termination); and damages. The remedy of reduction of the price is also covered. These remedies are available in all the systems at least in some circumstances.

22.1 THE POSSIBLE REMEDIES

The modern trend is to provide a list of the possible remedies as a form of sign-post to the reader. Thus the 2016 reform of French contract law sets out a broadly drafted list of the available remedies in case of non-performance of a contract and so codifies what had been admitted by the case law and the doctrine for a long time.

Code civil   **22.1 (FR)**

Article 1217: A party towards whom an undertaking has not been performed or has been performed imperfectly, may

— refuse to perform or suspend performance of his own obligations;
— seek enforced performance in kind of the undertaking;
— request a reduction in price;
— provoke the termination of the contract;
— claim reparation of the consequences of non-performance.

Sanctions which are not incompatible may be combined; damages may always be added to any of the others.

---

[1] See ch 28 below.

Somewhat similarly, for sales and work and materials contracts, the reformed Bürgerliches Gesetzbuch (BGB) sets out the remedies available where there is a non-conformity:

BGB   **22.2 (DE)**

§ 437: Rights of buyer in the case of defects

If the thing is defective, the buyer may, provided the requirements of the following provisions are met and unless otherwise specified,

1. under section 439, demand cure,

2. withdraw from the agreement under sections 440, 323 and 326(5) or reduce the purchase price under section 441, and

3. under sections 440, 280, 281, 283 and 311a, demand damages, or under section 284, demand reimbursement of futile expenditure.

§ 634: Rights of the customer in the case of defects

If the work is defective, the customer, if the requirements of the following provisions are met and to the extent not otherwise specified, may

1. under section 635, demand cure,

2. under section 637, remedy the defect himself and demand reimbursement for required expenses,

3. under sections 636, 323 and 326(5), revoke the contract or under section 638, reduce payment, and

4. under sections 636, 280, 281, 283 and 311a, demand damages, or under section 284, demand reimbursement of futile expenditure.

Similarly, the UK Consumer Rights Act 2015, Sections 19, 42 and 54 list the remedies that are available to the consumer if the goods, digital content or services do not comply with the various statutory terms as to description, quality and so on.[2]

However, we will see that the various remedies are not always equally available to the creditor. There are two questions to bear in mind at this stage: (i) the relationship between enforcing actual performance (which we will call 'specific performance') by the debtor and the other remedies; and (ii) whether the non-performance was excused eg, if through no fault of the debtor the contract became impossible to perform. We will consider each in turn, but the structure of the Codes makes it difficult to keep them entirely separate.

22.2 SPECIFIC PERFORMANCE AND OTHER REMEDIES

Thus in English law specific performance will only be ordered in exceptional circumstances; in effect, the claim for damages is given priority. In French law specific performance and damages are equivalent: providing that specific performance is an available remedy, the creditor may choose between them freely.

German law, in contrast, puts the emphasis the opposite way to English law: it is assumed that the creditor will seek literal enforcement. The BGB then sets out what

---

[2] See below, ch 27.

should happen if literal enforcement is not available for various reasons, or if the creditor opts for another remedy. Because the relevant sections of the BGB are complex, though very logically structured, it will be helpful to set them out here.

The BGB deals separately with whether a debtor can actually be made to perform and whether the debtor who does not perform, or who does so late or defectively in some other way, is liable in damages.[3] It then has separate provisions governing the right to damages in various situations. We set out most of the relevant texts in full here, although detailed consideration of most of them will be left until Chapter 23, on specific performance, and Chapter 26, on damages.

BGB **22.3 (DE)**

§ 241: Duties arising from an obligation
(1) By virtue of an obligation the obligee is entitled to claim performance from the obligor. Performance may also consist in forbearance.
(2) An obligation may also, depending on its contents, oblige each party to take account of the rights, legal interests and other interests of the other party.

§ 275: Exclusion of the duty of performance
(1) A claim for performance is excluded to the extent that performance is impossible for the obligor or for any other person.
(2) The obligor may refuse performance to the extent that performance requires expense and effort which, taking into account the subject matter of the obligation and the requirements of good faith, is grossly disproportionate to the interest in performance of the obligee. When it is determined what efforts may reasonably be required of the obligor, it must also be taken into account whether he is responsible for the obstacle to performance.
(3) In addition, the obligor may refuse performance if he is to render the performance in person and, when the obstacle to the performance of the obligor is weighed against the interest of the obligee in performance, performance cannot be reasonably required of the obligor.
(4) The rights of the obligee are governed by sections 280, 283 to 285, 311a and 326.

§ 276: Responsibility of the obligor
(1) The obligor is responsible for intention and negligence, if a higher or lower degree of liability is neither laid down nor to be inferred from the other subject matter of the obligation, including but not limited to the giving of a guarantee or the assumption of a procurement risk. The provisions of sections 827 and 828 apply with the necessary modifications.
(2) A person acts negligently if he fails to exercise reasonable care.
(3) The obligor may not be released in advance from liability for intention.

§ 280: Damages for breach of duty
(1) If the obligor breaches a duty arising from the obligation, the obligee may demand damages for the damage caused thereby. This does not apply if the obligor is not responsible for the breach of duty.

---

[3] cf Dutch law: Arts 3:296 ff BW deal with performance in *natura*; Arts 6:74 ff BW deal with damages for non-performance.

(2) Damages for delay in performance may be demanded by the obligee only subject to the additional requirement of section 286.

(3) Damages in lieu of performance may be demanded by the obligee only subject to the additional requirements of sections 281, 282 or 283.

§ 281: Damages in lieu of performance for non-performance or failure to render performance as owed

(1) To the extent that the obligor does not render performance when it is due or does not render performance as owed, the obligee may, subject to the requirements of section 280(1), demand damages in lieu of performance, if he has without result set a reasonable period for the obligor for performance or cure ...[4]

§ 282: Damages in lieu of performance for breach of a duty under section 241(2)

If the obligor breaches a duty under section 241(2), the obligee may, if the requirements of section 280(1) are satisfied, demand damages in lieu of performance, if he can no longer reasonably be expected to accept performance by the obligor.

§ 283: Damages in lieu of performance where the duty of performance is excluded

If, under section 275(1) to (3), the obligor is not obliged to perform, the obligee may, if the requirements of section 280(1) are satisfied, demand damages in lieu of performance. Section 281(1) sentences 2 and 3 and (5) apply with the necessary modifications.

§ 311a: Obstacle to performance when contract is entered into

(1) A contract is not prevented from being effective by the fact that under section 275(1) to (3) the obligor does not need to perform and the obstacle to performance already exists when the contract is entered into.

(2) The obligee may, at his option, demand damages in lieu of performance or reimbursement of his expenses in the extent specified in section 284. This does not apply if the obligor was not aware of the obstacle to performance when entering into the contract and is also not responsible for his lack of awareness. Section 281 (1) sentences 2 and 3 and (5) apply with the necessary modifications.

Notes

(1) It may be helpful to consider a number of questions in turn. The first is whether a debtor who has not performed can be made to do so, or one who has performed incorrectly can be made to perform correctly. The right to performance is set out in § 241, but it is qualified by § 275 BGB. § 275(1) provides that performance cannot be enforced when it is impossible either in a subjective sense, in that the particular debtor is unable to perform, or objectively ('impossible for the obligor or for any other person'). § 275(2) and (3) apply further restrictions.[5] § 275(4) refers to other provisions that deal with the debtor's possible liability in damages.

(2) In probably the majority of cases, even if the debtor was not at fault for its failure to date (eg the seller failed to deliver on time because of a strike by the carrier, or the goods delivered were found to be defective because of a hidden defect in manufacture), it will still be possible to perform in the future and performance can still be

---

[4] The remainder of (1) and (2)–(5) is omitted.
[5] These are considered below, pp 919 ff.

enforced. But even if the creditor ultimately obtains performance, it may have suffered a loss from the initial non-performance for which it may wish to claim damages.

(3) We will see later that, even if performance by the debtor can be enforced, the creditor does not have to enforce it. Instead, the creditor may (after giving a suitable warning) 'go over' to damages (§ 281 BGB). (Alternatively, the creditor may be entitled to terminate the contract under § 323 BGB; again, the creditor may be entitled to claim damages, see § 325 BGB.[6])

(4) The availability of damages depends on showing that the debtor is responsible within § 276(1) BGB. The starting point is that the debtor is responsible only if his actions or omissions were intentional or negligent. However, § 276 recognises that the parties may agree on a stricter standard, as explained earlier.[7]

(5) If the debtor is responsible, its obligation to compensate the creditor is governed by separate provisions, depending on which obligation has been broken and the nature of the breach. The basic provision is § 280(1). This provides for the debtor to be liable in damages unless he is not responsible for the breach of duty—note the reference back to § 276. (In other words, the debtor will be liable in damages if his act or omission was intentional or negligent, or if the parties had agreed on a stricter standard.) It will apply when the failure to perform the principal obligations of the contract led directly to a loss—for example, if a taxi booked to take a customer to the airport runs out of fuel on the way and the customer misses the flight. Damages for delay are dealt with by § 280(2). Damages under § 280 may also be claimed for breach of ancillary duties under § 241(2), see § 282.

(6) An alternative scenario is that under § 275(1) the debtor cannot be made to perform because performance is impossible, or to enforce it would involve the debtor in disproportionate expense, see § 275(2). The fact that the debtor cannot be made to perform does not necessarily mean that he will escape liability in damages. For example, if it was his own actions after the contract was made which made it impossible to perform, he may well be liable; and equally if performance of the contract was always impossible and the debtor should have known this. One of the provisions referred to in § 275(4) is § 311a, which provides that when a debtor cannot be made to perform because performance was impossible from the outset (§ 275), the contract is not necessarily ineffective, and the debtor may be liable for the non-performance unless he did not know of the impossibility and was not responsible for his ignorance.

22.3 NON-PERFORMANCE NOT EXCUSED

In this Part we make two assumptions. The first is that the debtor has failed to perform. We explained in Chapter 19 that, before we can say whether there has been a non-performance, it may first have to be determined what was the nature of the debtor's obligation. If, for example, the debtor was only obliged to use reasonable care and skill,

---

[6] See 25.6 (DE), below, p 990.
[7] Above, p 776.

the creditor will not have a remedy for non-performance unless it shows that the debtor did not in fact use reasonable care and skill. In contrast, if the debtor had undertaken to achieve a particular result and has not done so, that will be a non-performance.

The second assumption is that there has been breach of contract: or, to use the language of the Principles of European Contract Law (PECL), there has been a non-performance which was not excused, for example by *force majeure* (or, in English law, the contract has not been discharged under the doctrine of frustration). 'Excused non-performance' is considered in Part 7. However, excused and non-excused non-performance cannot be separated completely, because in French and German law the remedies of withholding performance, termination and price reduction of contract apply also in cases where the non-performance was excused, whereas the other remedies (literal enforcement and damages) apply only in cases of breach.

As mentioned earlier,[8] the effects of whether the debtor is responsible for the non-performance or is excused is viewed in rather different terms in the continental and common law traditions. In the continental systems, the question is thought of primarily in terms of what remedies are available against the debtor.[9] For example, as we will see in Chapter 28,[10] if the debtor is excused because of some supervening event, the creditor will be able to withhold his own performance and (provided that the impossibility is not merely temporary) to terminate the contract, but he will not be able to claim damages for non-performance. This is also the approach of PECL:

Principles of European Contract Law[11]   **22.4 (INT)**

Article 8:101: Remedies Available

(1) Whenever a party does not perform an obligation under the contract and the non-performance is not excused under Article 8:108, the aggrieved party may resort to any of the remedies set out in Chapter 9.

(2) Where a party's non-performance is excused under Article 8:108, the aggrieved party may resort to any of the remedies set out in Chapter 9 except claiming performance and damages.

(3) A party may not resort to any of the remedies set out in Chapter 9 to the extent that its own act caused the other party's non-performance.

In the common law, in contrast, the question of the debtor's responsibility is viewed as substantive: has there been a breach of contract? There may be no breach for one of two reasons. The first possibility is that the debtor has done all that he undertook to do—the doctor who has used all reasonable care and skill in treating the patient will normally have performed the contract and so the patient will have no remedy even if she has not been cured. The second possibility is that performance of the debtor's obligation has

---

[8] See above, p 772.

[9] See G Treitel, *Remedies for Breach of Contract* (Oxford, Clarendon Press, 1988) 7–8, para 8; R Zimmermann, *The New German Law of Obligations* (Oxford University Press, 2005) 49–51.

[10] See below, pp 1174 ff.

[11] See also DCFR, Art III.-3:101.

become impossible. If that happens, the normal result is that the contract is 'frustrated' and both parties are automatically released. None of the normal remedies will apply.[12]

At first sight, the approach taken by the PECL and the continental systems may seem simple: unless the non-performance was excused, the debtor can be made to perform and will be liable in damages. In fact, it is not so simple. First, we will see in Chapter 23 that specific performance will sometimes be refused even if the debtor has no excuse. Secondly, while the PECL render the debtor liable in damages for non-performance unless there was an excuse, the German system is different: the starting point is that the debtor is liable for damages only if he was at fault.[13] In most cases this may produce the same results, but it is not clear that it does so in every case. We will consider this in more detail in Chapter 26, when we deal with damages.

FURTHER READING

Fontaine, M and Viney, G, *Les sanctions de l'inexécution des obligations contractuelles: Etudes de droit comparé* (Bruxelles: Bruylant, 2001).

Kleinschmidt, J, Martens, S and Rüfner, T, 'Non-Performance and Remedies in General' in N Jansen and R Zimmermann (eds), *Commentaries on European Contract Laws* (Oxford University Press, 2018) 1074–1184.

Le Tourneau, P, *Droit de la responsabilité et des contrats* (7th edn, Paris: Dalloz, 2008).

Markesinis, BS, Unberath, H and Johnston, A, *The German Law of Contract* (2nd edn, Oxford: Hart Publishing, 2006).

Ogus, A and Tallon, D, 'Remedies' in D Harris and D Tallon (eds), *Contract Law Today: Anglo-French Comparisons* (Oxford: Clarendon Press, 1989) 243–300.

Tallon, D, 'Breach of Contract and Reparation of Damage', in *Towards a European Civil Code*, (1st edn, Nijmegen: Ars Aequi Libri, 1994) 223–35.

Treitel, G, *Remedies for Breach of Contract* (Oxford: Clarendon Press, 1988).

Zimmermann, R, *The New German Law of Obligations* (Oxford University Press, 2005).

Zweigert, K and Kötz, H, *Introduction to Comparative Law* (3rd edn, Oxford: Clarendon Press, 1998) 470–515.

---

[12] See below, pp 1185 ff.

[13] cf Dutch law, Art 6:74 BW. However, according to this provision, the non-performance must be attributable to the debtor, rather than that the debtor being at fault. Fault is just one of the circumstances in which non-performance may be attributed to the debtor (Art 6:75 BW). AS Harkamp & CH Sieburgh, *Mr. C. Assers Handleiding tot de beoefening van het Nederlands Burgelijk Recht. 6. Verbintenissenrecht. Deel II*. De verbintenis in het algemeen* (Deventer: Kluwer 2009) nos. 1 ff.

CHAPTER 23
SPECIFIC PERFORMANCE

23.1 INTRODUCTION

In this chapter on specific performance (enforcement *in natura*) of obligations we deal with both the enforcement of claims to money, such as a claim for the price, and the enforcement of other obligations, such as to transfer property, to do something or not to do something. The difference between the two types of claim is significant in the common law; it seems to be of less importance in the other systems, but the distinction between the two is reflected in the Principles of European Contract Law and other international instruments.[1]

Principles of European Contract Law	**23.1 (INT)**

Article 9:101: Monetary Obligations[2]

(1) The creditor is entitled to recover money which is due.

(2) Where the creditor has not yet performed its obligation and it is clear that the debtor will be unwilling to receive performance, the creditor may nonetheless proceed with its performance and may recover any sum due under the contract unless:

    (a) it could have made a reasonable substitute transaction without significant effort or expense; or

    (b) performance would be unreasonable in the circumstances.

---

[1] See Unidroit Principles of International Commercial Contracts, Arts 7.2.1 and 7.2.2; Draft Common Frame of Reference, Arts III.-3:301 and III.-3:302. On Dutch law, see MB Beekhoven van den Boezem, *De dwangsom in het burgerlijk recht*, Serie Burgerlijk Proces & Praktijk (Deventer: Kluwer, 2006); on French law, A Bénabent, *Les obligations* (16th edn, Paris: LGDJ, 2017) nos. 374–77; F Chénedé, *Le nouveau droit des obligations et des contrats: Consolidations, innovations, perspectives* (Paris: Dalloz, 2016) nos. 28.71–28.122; O Deshayes, T Genicon and YM Laithier, *Réforme du droit des contrats, du régime général et de la preuve des obligations: Commentaire article par article* (Paris: LexisNexis, 2016) 485–92; M Latina and G Chantepie, *La réforme du droit des obligations: Commentaire théorique et pratique dans l'ordre du Code civil* (Paris: Dalloz, 2016) 632–40; P Malaurie, L Aynès and P Stoffel-Munck, *Droit des obligations* (9th edn, Paris: LGDJ, 2017) nos. 879–81; B Nicholas, *The French Law of Contract* (2nd edn, Oxford: Clarendon Press, 1992) 216–24; on German law, see B Markesinis, H Unberath and A Johnston, *The German Law of Contract* (2nd edn, Oxford: Hart Publishing, 2006) chs 8 and 9.

[2] cf DCFR Art III.-3:301: Monetary obligations.

Article 9:102: Non-monetary Obligations

(1) The aggrieved party is entitled to specific performance of an obligation other than one to pay money, including the remedying of a defective performance.

(2) Specific performance cannot, however, be obtained where:

(a) performance would be unlawful or impossible; or

(b) performance would cause the debtor unreasonable effort or expense; or

(c) the performance consists in the provision of services or work of a personal character or depends upon a personal relationship, or

(d) the aggrieved party may reasonably obtain performance from another source.

(3) The aggrieved party will lose the right to specific performance if it fails to seek it within a reasonable time after it has or ought to have become aware of the non-performance.

Article 9:103: Damages Not Precluded[3]

The fact that a right to performance is excluded under this Section does not preclude a claim for damages.

We start with obligations other than those to pay money; claims for money due are dealt with in Section 23.3 of this chapter.

23.2 NON-MONETARY OBLIGATIONS

23.2.A INTRODUCTORY NOTE

Each of the systems will in some circumstances ensure that the plaintiff gets the performance it has bargained for, rather than getting a substitute such as damages. The exact conditions under which this remedy will be given vary, as we will see. First we must note that the notion of 'enforcement *in natura*' itself differs as between the systems. In the civil law systems, this phrase is used to cover not only the case in which the defendant is compelled to perform itself but also the case where the plaintiff is entitled to obtain performance by a third party at the defendant's expense. The common law recognises only the first situation as one of specific performance. If the plaintiff wants to get performance by a third party, the plaintiff is expected to terminate the original contract and to recover the cost of obtaining performance by a third party by way of a claim for damages. This is one reason why the common law remedy of specific performance appears to be much more limited than literal enforcement of performance in continental systems. We will see other differences between what is regarded as literal enforcement and what is regarded as a form of damages.

23.2.B THE BASIC RULES

Code civil

23.2 (FR)

Article 1221: A creditor of an obligation may, having given notice to perform, seek performance in kind unless performance is impossible or if there is a manifest disproportion between its cost to the debtor in good faith and its interest for the creditor.

---

[3] cf. DCFR Art III.-3:303: Damages not precluded.

Article 1222: Having given notice to perform, a creditor may also himself, within a reasonable time and at a reasonable cost, have an obligation performed or, with the prior authorisation of the court, may have something which has been done in breach of an obligation destroyed. He may claim reimbursement of sums of money employed for this purpose from the debtor.

He may also bring proceedings in order to require the debtor to advance a sum necessary for this performance or destruction.

Notes

(1) In the previous chapter we saw how contractual liability operates in French law. While contractual liability gives rise to damages which compensate for the loss caused by the breach of contract, literal enforcement does not aim at compensating for a loss but leads to performance of the contract itself. In French law, these two aspects are well distinguished by the expressions *réparation* (repairing or compensating for a loss) and *exécution* (performing the contract). Literal enforcement is a key principle of French contract law. Literal enforcement is often linked to the binding force of contract (Article 1103 of the new Code civil). It is usually considered that, if deprived of such a remedy, a contract has less binding force.[4]

(2) Article 1221 of the new Code civil sets out the principle that the creditor may demand performance in kind.[5] There are only two exceptions to that principle: (i) when performance in kind is impossible; (ii) when there is a manifest disproportion between its costs to the bona fide debtor and its interest for the creditor. In these cases, the creditor may only request performance through payment of damages. The 2018 ratification added that the debtor must be in good faith. This requirement was surely implied in the 2016 wording of Article 1221 as good faith is a general principle of French contract that judges are keen to apply. Still, the forthcoming case law will have to establish when a debtor is not in good faith.

(3) Before 2016, the wording of former Article 1142 was misleading. Article 1142 read: 'any obligation to do or not to do resolves itself in *damages* in case of non-performance on the part of the obligor-debtor'. Inspired by Roman law, it reflected the general principle that the law should not force individuals to perform a specific act, and it appears at first sight to adopt the approach of the common law. But it contradicted

---

[4] For a critical analysis of such a correlation, see YM Laithier, *Étude comparative des sanctions de l'inexécution du contrat* (Paris: LGDJ, 2004) 39 ff. For a general view of this question, see *Exécution du contrat en nature ou par équivalent*, special issue, RDC 2005. For a comparative overview on these questions, see S Whittaker, 'Un droit à la prestation plutôt qu'un droit à l'exécution? Perspectives anglaises sur l'exécution en nature et la réparation' RDC 2005, 49; F Bellivier and R Sefton-Green, 'Force obligatoire et exécution en nature du contrat en droits français et anglais: bonnes et mauvaises surprises du comparatisme' in *Le contrat au début du XXIe siècle: Études offertes à Jacques Ghestin* (Paris: LGDJ, 2001) 91; B Fauvarque-Cosson, 'Regards comparatistes sur l'exécution forcée en nature' RDC 2006, 529.

[5] For a comparison of the new French law with the state of the law before the 2016 reform, see YM Laithier 'Exécution Forcée en Nature' in J Cartwright and S Whittaker (eds), *The Code Napoléon Rewritten: French Contract Law after the 2016 Reforms* (Oxford: Hart Publishing, 2017) 257; H Boucard, 'Penalties for Contractual Non-Performance: The Art of Doing Something New with Something Old, and Vice Versa' (2017) 6 Montesquieu Law Review 103.

former Article 1184(2) (see below),[6] which stated that 'The party towards whom the undertaking has not been fulfilled has the choice either to compel the other to fulfil the agreement when it is possible, or to request its avoidance (*résolution*) with damages.' That puts enforced performance on the same level as *résolution*. Over the years, French judges had reversed the principle stated in Article 1142: enforcement *in natura* became the basic principle. Each time that the obligation to do something could be performed, performance *in natura* had to be ordered if it was asked for. The only exception was when the performance was impossible.[7]

(4) The new Article 1221 upheld the case law established under former Article 1142, by providing that performance *in natura* may be refused on the ground of impossibility. According to the case law (which is expected to be followed under the new Article 1221), the exception of impossibility is threefold. First, it can be a *practical* impossibility, when, for instance, a specific thing that a debtor had to deliver has been destroyed. Second, it can be *moral* impossibility, when the performance sought has a clearly personal character. This type of impossibility is further considered below.[8] Third, it can be a *legal* impossibility, when the performance is barred by a law or a regulation.

(5) Beside impossibility, the 2016 reform added a second exception to the availability of performance in kind. Performance in kind may be refused when there is a 'manifest disproportion between its costs to the debtor in good faith and its interest for the creditor'. This new exception contradicts a recent decision of the Cour de cassation, which held that the 'exorbitant amount' required from the debtor for the performance in kind was no reason for refusing the specific performance.[9] Through this new exception, the legislator wants to put an end to some extreme consequences of the performance *in natura*. An example of such extreme consequence is to be found in a case in which a builder was asked to build a house but he did not conform with the contract specifications: part of the house's height was 0.33 meters shorter than what was contracted for. The Cour de cassation, contrary to the Cour d'appel, ruled that specific performance could be ordered.[10] This would most probably no longer be the case under the reformed Code civil, except where the construction is encroaching on the neighbour's property, thus violating the neighbour's fundamental right, protected by First Protocol of the European Court of Human Rights (ECHR).[11]

(6) For the creditor to have right to claim performance in kind, it must have given prior notice to perform (*mise en demeure*) to the debtor. This is another departure from the former rule. Before 2016, the creditor did not need to serve a prior notice to the debtor to obtain enforcement *in natura*. The obligation to serve prior notice only applied to damages.

---

[6] See p 988.
[7] See below, p 919.
[8] See p 932.
[9] Cass civ (3) 16 June 2015, no. 14-14612, unpublished.
[10] ibid.
[11] Cass civ (3) 21 December 2017, no. 16-25406: 'every proprietor is entitled to obtain the demolition of a work encroaching upon his funds, without his action being liable to fault or abuse', and referring to the First Protocol.

(7) The creditor has a choice between enforcement *in natura* and contractual liability which gives rise to damages. A major difference between contractual liability and enforcement *in natura* is that in the latter case the creditor does not need to show that it has suffered a loss as a result of the breach of contract. It is sufficient that there has been a breach of contract for him to be entitled to this remedy. Indeed, all contractual obligations can give rise to enforcement *in natura*, whatever the contractual violation. In particular, it must be noted that the seriousness of the violation does not affect the right for a creditor to obtain enforcement in kind.[12]

(8) As for the debtor, not only must he be "in good faith" (2018 reform) but he cannot impose performance on the creditor by insisting on performing itself, since that would deprive the creditor of its choice of remedy.[13]

Cass civ, 20 January 1953[14]   **23.3 (FR)**

Equivalent goods

Where the defendant is obliged to deliver specified goods to the plaintiff but is unable to do so, the court may order him to deliver equivalent goods.

Facts: The plaintiff, Plissonnier, had obtained an order that the defendant, Ailloud, should deliver various goods to the plaintiff, their owner. The defendant claimed that he was unable to do so.

Held: The court of first instance had ordered the defendant to deliver goods of the same kind and value instead. The Cour de cassation rejected his appeal.

Judgment: THE COURT: ... *On the second appeal ground:*—Whereas by reason of Ailloud's alleged inability to deliver certain chattels as required by the judgment of 20 January 1947, it is asserted in the appeal that reparation of the resulting loss suffered by Plissonnier, their owner, should take the form of damages;

— Whereas the appellant submits that, in ordering him to deliver goods of the same kind and value, the contested judgment therefore infringed [former] Article 1142 of the Civil Code.

— Whereas however, that provision is applicable only in the case of non-compliance with a personal obligation to do or refrain from doing something; it follows from the findings contained in the contested judgment that the fault giving rise to the loss consists, quite simply, in the unjustified retention of goods belonging to another;

— Whereas consequently, the provision relied on in the appeal is inapplicable in the present case, and in ruling that the delivery of equivalent, commonly available goods of the same kind is the best way of making good the loss, the cour d'appel was merely exercising its absolute discretionary power.

— Whereas it follows that the appeal ground is unfounded.

On those grounds, the Court dismisses the appeal.

[12] Cass civ (3) 22 May 2013, no. 12-16217.
[13] Cass civ (3) 28 September 2005, no. 04-14586, Bull civ III no. 180, RDC 2006, 818, annotated by G Viney: 'the business responsible for the problems of construction cannot impose repair of the harm done on its victim'.
[14] JCP 1953.II.7677, annotated by P Esmein.

Notes

(1) In the case of an obligation to deliver a specific item, the contract may have the effect of transferring the ownership to the creditor.[15] If so, the creditor has a right to take the property, and the court may make an order for possession to be enforced by an official. If transfer of ownership requires the execution of a formal document, the court's order will act as a substitute for this document.[16]

(2) The Code civil provisions on literal enforcement are supplemented by those on procedure. The law of 9 July 1991 on the reform of civil enforcement procedures states in its first article (now codified as Article L 111-1 of the Code of civil enforcement procedures) that 'any creditor may, under the conditions laid down by law, constrain the defaulting debtor to carry out his obligations'. It is also necessary to consider the texts on *astreinte* (see below).[17]

BGB

§ 241: Duties arising out of the obligation

(1) By virtue of the obligation the obligee is entitled to claim performance from the obligor. The performance may also consist in forbearance.

(2) An obligation may also, depending on its contents, oblige each party to take account of the rights, legal interests and other interests of the other party.

§ 249: Nature and extent of damages

(1) A person who is liable in damages [*Schadensersatz*] must restore the position that would exist if the circumstance obliging him to pay damages had not occurred.

(2) Where damages are payable for injury to a person or damage to a thing, the obligee may demand the required monetary amount in lieu of restoration. When a thing is damaged, the monetary amount required under sentence 1 only includes value-added tax if and to the extent that it is actually incurred.

§ 275: Exclusion of the duty of performance

(1) A claim for performance is excluded to the extent that performance is impossible for the obligor or for any other person.

(2) The obligor may refuse performance to the extent that performance requires expense and effort which, taking into account the subject matter of the obligation and the requirements of good faith, is grossly disproportionate to the interest in performance of the obligee. When it is determined what efforts may reasonably be required of the obligor, it must also be taken into account whether he is responsible for the obstacle to performance.

(3) In addition, the obligor may refuse performance if he is to render the performance in person and, when the obstacle to the performance of the obligor is weighed against the interest of the obligee in performance, performance cannot be reasonably required of the obligor.

(4) The rights of the obligee are governed by sections 280, 283 to 285, 311a and 326.

---

[15] See Art 1196 of the new Code civil.

[16] See F Terré, P Simler and Y Lequette, *Les obligations* (11th edn, Paris: Dalloz, 2013) no. 1117; *Colloque Exécution en nature ou par équivalent*, 14 October 2004, special issue, RDC 3 (2005).

[17] See below, p 911.

Zivilprozessordnung (ZPO) (German Code of Civil Procedure) **23.5 (DE)**

§ 887: Actions that may be taken by others

(1) Should the debtor fail to meet his obligation to take an action, where such action can be taken by a third party, the creditor is to be authorised by the court of first instance hearing the case, upon his having filed a corresponding petition, to have this action taken by a third party at the costs of the debtor.

(2) Concurrently, the creditor may file the petition that the court sentence the debtor to make advance payment of the costs that will result from having a third party so take the action, notwithstanding the right to any supplementary claim.

(3) The above rules are not to be applied to any compulsory enforcement serving to obtain the surrender or provision of objects.

§ 888: Actions that may not be taken by others

(1) Where an action that depends exclusively on the will of the debtor cannot be taken by a third party, and where a corresponding petition has been filed, the court of first instance hearing the case is to urge the debtor to take the action in its ruling by levying a coercive penalty payment and, for the case that such payment cannot be obtained, by coercive punitive detention, or by directly sentencing him to coercive punitive detention. The individual coercive penalty payment may not be levied in an amount in excess of 25,000 euros. The stipulations of Chapter 2 regarding detention shall apply mutatis mutandis to coercive punitive detention.

(2) No warning shall be issued regarding the coercive measures.

(3) These rules shall not be applied in those cases in which a person is sentenced to provide services under a service agreement.

Notes

(1) § 241(1) BGB refers only to the actual performance promised.[18] However, as § 887 ZPO provides, this primary obligation may be enforced by judicially sanctioned performance by a third party. § 241(2) BGB refers to ancillary obligations which the debtor may be subject to, for example, not to damage the other party's property while carrying out the contract.

(2) The creditor is never confined to the remedy of specific performance. § 893(1) ZPO provides that the right of the creditor to seek damages instead of enforced performance is not limited by the provisions governing the latter.[19] Note that under § 281(1) BGB the creditor who wishes to claim damages for non-performance from the debtor may first have to serve a notice demanding performance by a certain date (*Nachfrist:* § 281(1) BGB). When the date has passed without performance the creditor can still choose between performance and damages in lieu of performance. Yet, as soon as he opts for damages he is no longer entitled to demand the actual performance (§ 281(4)).[20] One of the major principles of the new German law of

[18] cf for Dutch law: Art 3:296(1) BW; CH Sieburgh, *Mr. C. Assers Handleiding tot de beoefening van het Nederlands Burgerlijk Recht. 6. Verbintenissenrecht. Deel II. De verbintenis in het algemeen, tweede gedeelte* (Deventer: Wolters Kluwer, 2017) nos. 343 ff.

[19] cf for Dutch law: CH Sieburgh, *Mr. C. Assers Handleiding tot de beoefening van het Nederlands Burgerlijk Recht. 6. Verbintenissenrecht. Deel I. De verbintenis in het algemeen, eerste gedeelte* (Deventer: Wolters Kluwer 2016) nos. 380 ff.

[20] See below, pp 1012 ff.

obligations of 2002 is that the debtor has a right to be given a notice period by the creditor during which he can (try to) perform *in natura* if he either failed at performing or did not even start to perform in the first place. This is often referred to as the 'right to a second chance to perform' (*Recht der zweiten Andienung*). Exceptions apply, for instance when the debtor explicitly refuses to perform at all (§ 281(2)).[21]

(3) If there is a fixed date for performance (ie if the contract involves a *relatives Fixgeschäft*)[22] and, at the same time, it is a commercial contract under § 343 HGB (*Handelsgeschäft*), the presumption is in favour of damages or termination. Therefore, the creditor must put the debtor on notice of his intention to claim performance *in natura* immediately (§ 376(1)(2) HGB).

(4) § 249 BGB defines the nature of the obligation to make compensation (*Schadensersatz*). According to this, restoration of the *status quo ante* and not money damages is the normal rule. Thus an obligation to supply replacement goods, for example, would be characterised as compensation within § 249 BGB although, as Treitel notes, lawyers in other systems might understand this as a form of enforced performance.[23] § 249 refers to compensation (*Schadensersatz*) for damage. Treitel notes that it is tempting for a common lawyer to contrast *Schadensersatz* to judgments for performance and to translate *Schadensersatz* as 'damages',[24] but the first sentence of § 249 BGB makes it clear that the primary duty on the debtor is to bring things back to the state of affairs before the damage occurred, a duty often called *Naturalherstellung*. Only if that is not done in good time will the creditor obtain money compensation.

(5) German law allows a creditor to choose between compensation *in natura*—as per § 249(1) BGB—and money damages, or more exactly to 'go over' to damages in certain cases, viz, where a person is injured or physical property is damaged (§ 249(2) BGB); after a notice period has expired (§ 250 BGB); or where performance *in natura* is insufficient to compensate the creditor (§ 251(1) BGB). In cases of delay the claim for performance is extinguished on expiry of the notice period and the only remedies available are damages for non-performance or *Rücktritt*: § 326(1), second sentence BGB. If the creditor has set a notice under § 250 but the debtor has not performed within the time set, the creditor may only claim damages: § 250, second sentence.[25] It should be emphasised that §§ 249–251 BGB are general rules that apply only as long as the creditor is entitled to demand damages in the first place. As seen above, this usually requires a notice demanding performance by a certain date.

In English law, the common law courts at a very early date ceased to order the defendant to perform a contract literally and gave only monetary remedies such as damages. The courts of equity would grant specific performance, but only as a supplementary remedy when the remedy at common law was thought to be inadequate.

---

[21] See below, p 991, on the need to give a notice period.
[22] See below, p 1012.
[23] G Treitel, *Remedies for Breach of Contract* (Oxford: Clarendon Press, 1988) 51, para 44.
[24] ibid.
[25] See 26.4 (DE), below, p 1062.

Vice-Chancellor's Court **23.6 (EN)**

Falcke v Gray[26]

Where there is a contract to sell goods which are unique, specific performance may be ordered.

Facts: The defendant let her house to the plaintiff for six months, and gave him the option of purchasing at the end of the term certain articles of furniture at a valuation. Among the articles were what counsel described as 'a couple of large Oriental jars, with great ugly Chinese pictures upon them'. The valuer admitted that he was ignorant of the value of the vases, but a sum of £40 was eventually agreed on, although the defendant said in her evidence that she had been left the jars by a lady who had, she understood, been offered £100 for them by King George IV. The defendant was later offered £200 for the jars by a purchaser, to whom she had explained what had happened, and she accepted that offer. The plaintiff obtained an *ex parte* injunction against the defendant and the second purchaser, and then sought specific performance.

Held: The Vice-Chancellor expressed himself willing to grant specific performance, except for the fact that the price the purchaser had agreed to pay was inadequate. [This part of the decision would probably not be followed today.][27]

Judgment: THE VICE-CHANCELLOR (SIR RT KINDERSLEY) [after stating the facts above]: The first ground of defence is that, this being a bill for the specific performance of a contract for the purchase of chattels, this Court will not interfere. But I am of opinion that the Court will not refuse to interfere simply because the contract relates to chattels, and that if there were no other objection the contract in this case is such a contract as the Court would specifically perform.

What is the difference in the view of the Court between realty and personality in respect to the question whether the Court will interfere or not? Upon what principle does the Court decree specific performance of any contract whatever? Lord Redesdale in *Harnett v Yeilding* says: 'Whether Courts of Equity in their determinations on this subject have always considered what was the original foundation for decrees of this nature I very much doubt. I believe that from something of habit, decrees of this kind have been carried to an extent which has tended to injustice. Unquestionably the original foundation of these decrees was simply this, that damages at law would not give the party the compensation to which he was entitled; that is, would not put him in a situation as beneficial to him as if the agreement were specifically performed'. So that the principle on which a Court of Equity proceeds is this. A Court of law gives damages for the non-performance, but a Court of Equity says, 'that is not sufficient—justice is not satisfied by that remedy'; and, therefore, a Court of Equity will decree specific performance because a mere compensation in damages is not a sufficient remedy and satisfaction for the loss of the performance of the contract.

Now why should that principle apply less to chattels? If in a contract for chattels damages will be a sufficient compensation, the party is left to that remedy. Thus if a contract is for the purchase of a certain quantity of coals, stock &c, this Court will not decree specific performance, because a person can go into the market and buy similar articles and get damages for any difference in the price of the articles in a Court of law. But if damages would not be a sufficient compensation, the principle, on which a Court of Equity decrees specific performance, is just as applicable to a contract for the sale and purchase of chattels, as to a contract for the sale and purchase of land.

---

[26] (1859) 4 Drew 651.
[27] See I Spry, *The Principles of Equitable Remedies* (9th edn, London: Sweet & Maxwell, 2014) 196–97.

In the present case the contract is for the purchase of articles of unusual beauty, rarity and distinction, so that damages would not be an adequate compensation for non-performance; and I am of opinion that a contract for articles of such a description is such a contract as this Court will enforce; and, in the absence of all other objection, I should have no hesitation in decreeing specific performance.

Notes

(1) An order of specific performance is to force the defendant to perform an obligation to do something positive, eg to transfer land or to deliver goods. In the case of an obligation not to do something, the court may order an injunction. If it is merely an order not to do something in the future, it is termed a 'prohibitory'; if it also requires the defendant to undo something which he has done in breach of contract, it is known as a 'mandatory' injunction.

(2) Neither specific performance nor a mandatory injunction will be granted if damages would be an adequate remedy. This is because these are in origin equitable remedies and the Lord Chancellor would normally grant a remedy only when the remedy at common law seemed inadequate.[28] However, with prohibitory injunctions the courts do not always insist on this. Where the defendant has undertaken expressly not to do a certain thing, the injunction may be issued even without showing that the breach is causing the plaintiff any loss at all.[29] The difference must not be exaggerated. First, even in the case of an express negative promise, the court will not make an order if this would have the practical effect of forcing the defendant to perform a contract which is not otherwise specifically enforceable.[30] Secondly, the court will not hold that the contract 'impliedly' forbids a particular act, and then grant an injunction against doing that act, if the effect would also be to coerce performance.[31]

Thus in English law specific performance is a relatively unusual remedy, as normally if the plaintiff obtains damages it will be able to make a substitute transaction with a third party and be compensated for any other losses. The only case in which specific performance has regularly been granted is in contracts for interests in land. This may be because each piece of land was regarded as unique, so that the plaintiff cannot go out and buy an equivalent.[32] However, as the result of developments following the adoption of the Consumer Sales Directive,[33] the court may also order specific performance when a consumer has been supplied with non-conforming goods, digital content or services.

[28] See above, pp 88–9.
[29] *Marco Productions Ltd v Pagola* [1945] 1 KB 111 (express promise not to perform in competing theatre).
[30] See below, pp 931 ff.
[31] See *Chitty on Contracts*, 33rd edn by H Beale (gen ed) (London: Sweet & Maxwell/Thomson Reuters, 2018) paras 27-088–27-089.
[32] Nowadays, whatever its origin, the rule is inextricably linked to the notion of 'equitable interests' in property, which result in a person who has merely agreed to take an interest in property being regarded for many purposes as the owner, even though there has been no conveyance of the property.
[33] Directive 1999/44/EC of the European Parliament and of the Council of 25 May 1999 on certain aspects of the sale of consumer goods and associated guarantees, OJ L 171/1999, Art 3(3), which requires that the consumer buyer should have the right to have non-conforming goods repaired or replaced.

The court may order the trader to repair or replace goods or digital content, or to do work again. This is considered below.[34]

23.2.C MAKING THE DEFENDANT HIMSELF PERFORM

In French law, if a defendant refuses to obey a court order to perform, the public authorities will only employ force to recover a piece of movable property or to evict the defendant from an immovable one—and even then the authorities may exercise a discretion to refuse to act. More usually the court will order an *astreinte*, a monetary penalty for noncompliance.[35] Originally, the *astreinte* was a 'praetorian' creation of case law, which treated it as derived from the authority of the judge. The *astreinte* was validated by legislation in 1972, and reformed by the law No. 91-650 of 9 July 1991.[36] It was subsequently codified in the Code of Civil Enforcement Procedures.

Code des procédures civiles d'exécution[37] **23.7 (FR)**

Article L 131-1: Any court may, of its own motion or otherwise, order the payment of a penalty (*astreinte*) in order to ensure compliance with its decision.

A court implementing such compliance may attach an order for payment of a penalty (*astreinte*) to a decision made by another court, if it appears necessary in the circumstances so to do.[38]

Article L 131-2: Penalties (*astreinte*) are independent of damages.

A penalty (*astreinte*) shall be provisional or definitive. It shall be regarded as provisional unless it is expressed to be definitive by the court imposing it.

No order shall be made imposing a definitive penalty (*astreinte*) until an order has first been made imposing a provisional penalty (*astreinte*) for such period as the court shall determine. In the event of non-compliance with any of the foregoing requirements, the penalty (*astreinte*) shall be levied on a provisional basis.

Article L 131-3: A penalty (*astreinte*), whether provisional or definitive, shall be levied by the court implementing compliance with the decision, save where the court which ordered its imposition remains seized of the case or has reserved to itself the power to levy the same.

Article L 131-4: Regard shall be had, in levying the amount of a provisional penalty (*astreinte*), to the conduct of the party to whom the order is addressed and to any difficulties encountered by that party in complying therewith.

The amount of a definitive penalty (*astreinte*) may not be altered upon the same being levied.

A provisional or definitive penalty (*astreinte*) shall be lifted, either wholly or in part, where it is established that the non-compliance, or delay in compliance, with the court's order results wholly or in part from some extraneous cause.

---

[34] For services contracts, see p 1167; for contracts for the supply of goods, see ch 27.

[35] cf for Dutch law: Art 611a Code of Civil Procedure (Wetboek van Burgerlijke rechtsvordering).

[36] See above, p 906.

[37] Code of Civil Enforcement Procedures.

[38] Contra Dutch law, under which a court cannot order an *astreinte* of its own motion, it must be requested by one of the parties (Art 611a Code of Civil Procedure).

Notes

(1) The *astreinte* condemns the debtor to pay a sum of money if he does not perform. It is often fixed at so much per day of delay. It does not give the creditor a direct right against the debtor; the creditor has to apply to the court to obtain the money. The *astreinte* is at first provisional, in the sense that when the defendant has performed, the judge may adjust the sum payable. If the defendant fails to perform, the *astreinte* may be made definitive; in this case there is no power to adjust it later.

(2) The money is payable to the plaintiff.[39] Since 1972 the *astreinte* has had a legislative basis which makes it clear that it is not compensation but a penalty payable to the plaintiff. The plaintiff may also recover damages.

Zivilprozessordnung (ZPO)[40]   **23.8 (DE)**

§ 890: Forcing the debtor to cease and desist from actions, or to tolerate actions

(1) Should the debtor violate his obligation to cease and desist from actions, or to tolerate actions to be taken, the court of first instance hearing the case is to sentence him for each count of the violation, upon the creditor filing a corresponding petition, to a coercive fine and, for the case that such payment cannot be obtained, to coercive detention or coercive detention of up to six (6) months. The individual coercive fine may not be levied in an amount in excess of 250,000 euros, and the coercive detention may not be longer than a total of two (2) years.

(2) The sentence must be preceded by a corresponding warning that is to be issued by the court of first instance hearing the case, upon corresponding application being made, unless it is set out in the judgment providing for the obligation.

(3) Moreover, upon the creditor having filed a corresponding petition, the debtor may be sentenced to creating a security for any damages that may arise as a result of future violations, such security being created for a specific period of time.

§ 894: Fiction of a declaration of intent having been made

Where the debtor has been sentenced to make a declaration of intent, such declaration shall be deemed to have been made as soon as the judgment has attained legal force. Where the declaration of intent depends on counter-performance being made, this effect shall occur as soon as an enforceable execution copy of the final and binding judgment has been issued in accordance with the stipulations of sections 726 and 730.

Notes

(1) By contrast to the *astreinte* procedure in French law, any fines levied under §§ 887, 888 ZPO are paid into court, not to the creditor.

(2) Detailed provisions are laid down in the ZPO in relation to the duration of custody where committal is ordered and prohibiting this measure where the health of the debtor would be endangered thereby (§§ 802g–802j ZPO).

---

[39] cf for Dutch law: Art 611c Code of Civil Procedure (Wetboek van Burgerlijke Rechtsvordering).
[40] German Code of Civil Procedure. See also §§ 887, 888 ZPO, 23.5 (DE), above, p 907.

In English law the debtor who fails to obey an order of specific performance or an injunction will be in contempt of court. He may be imprisoned or fined; and if the defendant is a company, its assets may be sequestered and its directors imprisoned or fined. In cases of transfer of land, the court will simply order that the land be transferred, and will if necessary execute any documents itself. The ease of this, compared to the harshness of the sanction for contempt of court which might have to be employed in other cases, may explain why specific performance is given readily in land cases but so rarely in other situations.

23.2.D PERFORMANCE BY A THIRD PARTY

As an alternative to seeking performance in kind before the courts, a creditor may himself have an obligation performed by a third party.

Code civil	**23.9 (FR)**

Article 1222: Having given notice to perform, a creditor may also himself, within a reasonable time and at a reasonable cost, have an obligation performed or, with the prior authorisation of the court, may have something which has been done in breach of an obligation destroyed. He may claim reimbursement of sums of money employed for this purpose from the debtor.

He may also bring proceedings in order to require the debtor to advance a sum necessary for this performance or destruction.

Notes

(1) Article 1222 Cciv provides for the debtor's obligation to be performed by a third party at the debtor's expense. This may involve performing in the debtor's place, or destroying something that the debtor should not have done.

(2) Until the 2016 reform, French law required the creditor first to obtain a court order, except if the matter was urgent.[41] However, the prior authorisation of the court became optional in Article 1222 of the new Code civil.

(3) The system set out in Article 1222 can be divided into three steps. First, the creditor must give notice to perform to the debtor. Second, if the debtor fails to carry out its obligation, the creditor may have the debtor's obligation performed by a third party. Third, the creditor may claim reimbursement of the costs spent for the enforcement from the debtor.

(4) This faculty of 'replacement'[42] is subject to three conditions: (i) giving prior notice to the debtor; (ii) leaving a reasonable time for the debtor to carry out his obligations; and (iii) having the obligation performed at a reasonable cost and within a reasonable time. By contrast with former Article 1144 of the Code civil, new Article 1222 does not make prior authorisation of the court mandatory. Yet, in the event where a creditor would not seek prior authorisation of the court, the court may still exercise a control *a posteriori*.

---

[41] Cass civ (1) 28 June 1988, no. 87-11898, Bull I no. 208.
[42] P Malaurie, L Aynès and P Stoffel-Munck, *Droit des Obligations* (9th edn, Paris: LGDJ, 2017) no. 881.

A similar system exists in German law. However, the faculty to have a third party perform the debtor's obligation is subject to the prior authorisation of the court.

Zivilprozessordnung (ZPO)   **23.10 (DE)**

§ 887: Actions that may be taken by others
  (1) Should the debtor fail to meet his obligation to take an action, where such action can be taken by a third party, the creditor is to be authorised by the court of first instance hearing the case, upon his having filed a corresponding petition, to have this action taken by a third party at the costs of the debtor. ...

> *Notes*
>
>   (1) In German law, as in French law, a set notice period must have expired—ie the debtor must be in delay—before the creditor is entitled to have a third party remove the defect.[43]
>
>   (2) In addition, German law requires the creditor to obtain a court order authorising performance by a third party (§ 887 ZPO—'*der Gläubiger [ist] von dem Prozessgericht ... auf Antrag zu ermächtigen*').[44]

As explained earlier, English law does not know this form of specific performance. Instead, the creditor is expected to terminate the contract, employ the third party to perform in place of the debtor and bring an action for damages for any additional cost or other loss. Even in consumer contracts, the remedies of 'repair or replacement' refer only to repair or replacement by the trader itself, not by a third party employed by the consumer at the trader's expense. Both the PECL and the DCFR are the same as English law in this respect.

This means that a court order is not a requirement of English law. For example, if a builder has committed a serious breach of contract, the employer may terminate the contract by a simple notice to the builder.[45] The employer may then employ another builder to do the work and can recover any additional expense as damages. However, most building contracts of any complexity will contain provisions which in effect require the employer to give the contractor an opportunity to correct any defect before terminating the contract on this ground.

23.2.E PRACTICAL EXAMPLES

23.2.E.1 A SELLER FAILS TO DELIVER

A striking example of the differences between the civil law systems on the one hand and the common law on the other is provided by the case of a sale of goods contract under which the seller refuses to deliver the goods.

---

[43] Contra Dutch law: *Asser/Sieburgh 6-II* 2017/343, 353 (n 18 above).

[44] cf Dutch law: Art 3:299(2) BW; CH Sieburgh, *Mr. C. Assers Handleiding tot de beoefening van het Nederlands Burgerlijk Recht. 6. Verbintenissenrecht. Deel II*. *De verbintenis in het algemeen* (Deventer: Kluwer 2009) nos. 352 ff.

[45] See below, p 984.

Code civil   **23.11 (FR)**

Article 1610: Where the seller fails to make delivery within the time agreed upon between the parties, the purchaser may, at his choice, apply for avoidance of the sale, or for his being vested with possession, if the delay results only from an act of the seller.

> *Note*
>
> The court may impose an *astreinte* on the seller until the property is delivered.[46]

BGB   **23.12 (DE)**

§ 433: Typical contractual duties in a purchase agreement
   (1) By a purchase agreement, the seller of a thing is obliged to deliver the thing to the buyer and to procure ownership of the thing for the buyer. The seller must procure the thing for the buyer free from material and legal defects. …

> *Note*
>
> Performance of this primary obligation may be demanded in accordance with § 241(1) BGB.[47] It is enforceable under the provisions of § 883 ZPO, which allow for the seizure of movable property.

In England, contracts for the sale of goods are specifically enforced only if the goods are unique or unobtainable. The rule is strictly applied. Thus in *Société des Industries Métallurgiques SA v The Bronx Engineering Co Ltd*[48] the sellers of a machine tool wrongly refused to deliver it, threatening to sell it instead to a third party. The Court of Appeal said that specific performance would not be available even though it would be nine months before the buyers could obtain a similar machine from any other supplier. However, it has been accepted that a contract for the sale of goods may be specifically enforced if a temporary shortage means that they are practically unavailable from any other source: *Sky Petroleum Ltd v VIP Petroleum Ltd*.[49]

23.2.E.2 A BUILDER FAILS TO COMPLETE THE WORK

If a builder fails to complete work under a construction contract, or fails to rectify defects in the work, it is common in French or German law for the employer to obtain enforcement *in natura*.[50] Either the employer may obtain an order that the builder shall do the work or, more usually, it may have the necessary work done by a third party at the original

---

[46] Cass com 12 December 1966, no. 64-13748, Bull civ IV, 478 (car) and Req 18 November 1907, S 1913.386 (land), both cited in K Zweigert and H Kötz, *Introduction to Comparative Law* (3rd edn, Oxford: Clarendon Press, 1998) 476, who point out that alternatively a *huissier* could be ordered to execute the judgment.

[47] See 22.3 (DE), above, p 895.

[48] [1975] 1 Lloyd's Rep 465 (CA).

[49] [1974] 1 WLR 576 (ChD) (during an oil crisis the defendants threatened to refuse to supply the plaintiffs, who would not be able to get oil from any other source; the court gave an injunction prohibiting the defendants from selling the oil to anyone else, thereby effectively forcing them to supply to the plaintiffs).

[50] For examples, see the cases extracted below, pp 919–29.

builder's expense. In German law there are specific provisions dealing with *Werkverträge* where the builder's work is defective.

BGB   **23.13 (DE)**

§ 634: Rights of the customer in the case of defects

If the work is defective, the customer, if the requirements of the following provisions are met and to the extent not otherwise specified, may

(1) under section 635, demand cure,

(2) under section 637, remedy the defect himself and demand reimbursement for required expenses,

(3) under sections 636, 323 and 326(5), revoke the contract or under section 638, reduce payment, and

(4) under sections 636, 280, 281, 283 and 311a, demand damages, or under section 284, demand reimbursement of futile expenditure.

§ 637: Self-help

(1) If there is a defect in the work, the customer may, after the expiry without result of a reasonable period specified by him for cure, remedy the defect himself and demand reimbursement of the necessary expenses, unless the contractor rightly refuses cure.

(2) Section 323(2) applies with the necessary modifications. A period of time need not be specified even if cure has failed or cannot reasonably be expected of the customer.

(3) The customer may demand from the contractor advance payment of the expenses necessary to remedy the defect.

> *Note*
>
> These provisions do not apply when the problem is simply that the builder has not completed the work, but in such a case the employer has similar rights under the general provisions of the BGB. The right of self-help under § 637 is available only for defective work, but it will be seen that in practice it is very similar to getting a third party to perform at the debtor's expense, the principal difference being that in cases that fall under § 637 a court order is not required.

Again, there is a contrast with English law. In consumer contracts, if the service element of the contract has not been carried out properly, the consumer has the right to 'a repeat performance', which can be ordered by the court:

Consumer Rights Act 2015   **23.14 (EN)**

Section 55: Right to repeat performance

(1) The right to require repeat performance is a right to require the trader to perform the service again, to the extent necessary to complete its performance in conformity with the contract.

(2) If the consumer requires such repeat performance, the trader—

(a) must provide it within a reasonable time and without significant inconvenience to the consumer; and

(b) must bear any necessary costs incurred in doing so (including in particular the cost of any labour or materials).

(3) The consumer cannot require repeat performance if completing performance of the service in conformity with the contract is impossible.

(4) Any question as to what is a reasonable time or significant inconvenience is to be determined taking account of—

(a) the nature of the service, and

(b) the purpose for which the service was to be performed.

Section 58: Powers of the court

(1) In any proceedings in which a remedy is sought by virtue of section 19(3) or (4), 42(2) or 54(3), the court, in addition to any other power it has, may act under this section.

(2) On the application of the consumer the court may make an order requiring specific performance or, in Scotland, specific implement by the trader of any obligation imposed on the trader by virtue of section 23, 43 or 55.

English courts will not usually grant specific performance of other kinds of building contract; apart for anything else,[51] damages are treated as providing an adequate remedy. The employer is expected to terminate the contract, get the work put right by another builder and sue the first builder for any extra costs incurred as a result.

However, the contrast between the common law and the continental systems may be more apparent than real. First, as suggested earlier, in English law the employer may terminate the contract, employ another builder to do the work and then claim any extra cost incurred from the original builder in an action for damages. This is functionally equivalent to execution by a third party. The provision for self-help in work contracts which have been performed defectively (§ 637 BGB, above) reduces the differences between German and English law still further. Secondly, even if a French court orders the builder to finish the work on pain of an *astreinte*, the builder does not have to do the work himself; he can arrange for a third person to do it. Thus the principal difference between this and English law is as to who has to organise the replacement builder. Thirdly, there is one situation in which even in England a building contract which is not a consumer contract may be specifically enforced. This is where the work is to be done on the defendant's own land, so that the plaintiff cannot simply employ another builder or do the work himself because that would involve trespassing on the defendant's land. Damages would not be an adequate remedy.[52]

A further example which shows the practical differences between the systems is the case of the seller who delivers defective goods. Here we encounter both the special regimes which, as mentioned earlier,[53] apply in French and German law to defects in goods and the impact of the Directive on certain aspects of the sale of consumer goods. This material is complex and is therefore treated separately in Chapter 27.

23.2.F COMPARATIVE SUMMARY ON BASIC RULES AND THE INTERNATIONAL RESTATEMENTS

Because of the differences in what is understood in the various systems by the phrase 'specific performance', the differences between the systems may be less than appears

---

[51] On the issue of supervision of the work, see below, pp 939 ff.

[52] See *Wolverhampton Corp v Emmons* [1901] 1 KB 515 (CA).

[53] See above, pp 788 ff.

at first sight. Nonetheless, the point remains that in French and German law specific enforcement is seen as a normal remedy for non-performance, while in the common law it is seen as exceptional—save in contracts for land. However, it is thought that practice, at least in Germany, reduces the differences still further, in that a creditor will not seek an order for performance if it is feasible to find a substitute but will claim damages instead.[54]

The Convention on Contracts for the International Sale of Goods (CISG) appears to follow the continental approach. Article 46(1) allows a buyer to require performance by the seller of his obligations subject only to the buyer not having resorted to any remedy which would be inconsistent with this.[55]

The PECL, in contrast, take a more compromising approach which is thought to be more generous towards specific performance than the common law but more in line with practice on the continent, at least in the German system.

Principles of European Contract Law   **23.15 (INT)**

Article 9:102: Non-monetary Obligations

(1) The aggrieved party is entitled to specific performance of an obligation other than one to pay money, including the remedying of a defective performance.

(2) Specific performance cannot, however, be obtained where …

(d) the aggrieved party may reasonably obtain performance from another source.[56]

On this point, however, the Draft Common Frame of Reference (DCFR) took a different view. Rather the creditor should be able to obtain performance unless doing so would be unreasonable because it would in fact increase his loss (for example, because of the delay involved). Therefore (d) was deleted and a new paragraph (5) was inserted:[57]

(5) The creditor cannot recover damages for loss or a stipulated payment for non-performance to the extent that the creditor has increased the loss or the amount of the payment by insisting unreasonably on specific performance in circumstances where the creditor could have made a reasonable substitute transaction without significant effort or expense.

This does not deny the creditor the right to specific performance but makes it clear that the creditor, not the debtor, will bear the additional costs. It seems much closer than the PECL to the continental position. The CESL is also closer to the continental provision; the buyer may not require performance where it is impossible or unlawful, or where 'the burden or expense of performance would be disproportionate to the benefit that the buyer would obtain' (Article 110(3)).

---

[54] See Zweigert and Kötz (n 46 above) 484.

[55] According to Art 28 CISG: 'If, in accordance with the provisions of this Convention, one party is entitled to require performance of any obligation by the other party, a court is not bound to enter a judgment for specific performance unless the court would do so under its own law in respect of similar contracts of sale not governed by this Convention.' This text has tried to reconcile both tradition but it is only a half success since, in doing so, it renounces real unification and opens the way for the application of the law of the forum.

[56] Art 7.2.2(c) UNIDROIT PICC is in similar terms.

[57] DCFR Art III.-3:302.

23.2.G LIMITATIONS ON SPECIFIC PERFORMANCE

23.2.G.1 IMPOSSIBILITY

In none of the systems will the court make an order for performance when that is no longer possible, even if that was the debtor's fault.

In French law, Article 1221 of the Code civil provides that specific performance shall not be awarded when performance in kind is impossible.[58] Impossibility can be moral, legal or practical.

The case of impossibility is also expressly provided for in German law.[59]

BGB	**23.16 (DE)**

§ 275: Exclusion of the duty of performance

(1) A claim for performance is excluded to the extent that performance is impossible for the obligor or for any other person. ...

[For the rest of this section see below].[60]

In English law, specific performance is a discretionary remedy. It will not be ordered if it is impossible for the defendant to perform,[61] or if it will be impossible to enforce the order because the defendant is not in the jurisdiction and has no assets in the UK.[62]

23.2.G.2 DISPROPORTIONATE EXPENSE

BGB	**23.17 (DE)**

§ 275: Exclusion of the duty of performance

...

(2) The obligor may refuse performance to the extent that performance requires expense and effort which, taking into account the subject matter of the obligation and the requirements of good faith, is grossly disproportionate to the interest in performance of the obligee. When it is determined what efforts may reasonably be required of the obligor, it must also be taken into account whether he is responsible for the obstacle to performance. ...

§ 439: Supplementary performance

...

(4) Without prejudice to § 275(2) and (3), the seller may refuse the form of supplementary performance chosen by the buyer if such performance is possible only with unreasonable expense. In that connection, it is necessary to have regard in particular to the value of the thing when free from defects, the significance of the defect and the question whether the defect could be remedied by the other form of supplementary performance without

---

[58] See 23.2 (FR), above, p 902; see Laithier (n 5 above) 257.
[59] cf Dutch law: Art 3:296(1) BW; *Asser/Sieburgh 6-II* 2017/344 (n 19 above).
[60] Above, p 858.
[61] *Forrer v Nash* (1865) 33 Beav 167, 171: see *Treitel on the Law of Contract*, 14th edn by E Peel (London: Sweet & Maxwell, 2015) para 21-034.
[62] *The Sea Hawk* [1986] 1 WLR 657, 665.

material detriment to the buyer. The buyer's claim is restricted in this case to the other form of supplementary performance; the seller's right to refuse also that supplementary performance under the conditions laid out in sentence 1 above is unaffected.

§ 635: Supplementary performance

...

(3) The contractor may refuse supplementary performance, without prejudice to section 275(2) and (3), if it is only possible at disproportionate cost. ...[63]

BGH, 10 October 1985[64]   **23.18 (DE)**

Insulated windows

A claim for performance of a contractor's obligation to remedy a defect complained of may be brought, even after acceptance of the work, if that is the only way in which such a defect or defects can be permanently eliminated.

Facts: In 1977 the plaintiff commissioned the defendant to install aluminium-framed windows and doors in the former's single-family residence at a cost of DM 21,607.04. Since the plaintiff required the smallest possible loss of heat (calorific value), the defendant proposed for the frames a construction having a calorific value of between 2.4 and 2.6. That proposal, together with the defendant's terms and conditions of supply and payment, formed the basis of the contract; for the rest, Part B of the VOB (*Verdingungsordnung für Bauleistungen* = contracting rules for the award of public works contracts) was to apply. By way of guarantee, Clause 9 of the terms and conditions of supply and payment provided inter alia: 'Duly established defects shall be repaired or replaced free of charge; a reasonable time shall be deemed to be agreed for completion of the work required in that regard. All further claims, eg for damages, are excluded.'

In 1977 the works carried out by the defendant were accepted. It subsequently became apparent that the actual calorific value of the window-frame and door-frame parts used was 3.8 (value per square metre). The plaintiff brought an action for an order requiring the defendant to perform his contractual obligation by replacing *all* the frames and casements of the windows and doors with new ones having a calorific value of between 2.4 and 2.6 and by carrying out all necessary ancillary work.

Held: The Landgericht in Berlin and the Kammergericht decided that the cost of replacing the windows was not disproportionate and that the work should be done. An appeal to the BGH was dismissed.

Judgment: ... In support of his claim, [the plaintiff] pointed out that the inferior thermal insulation meant that additional heating was needed, and that it was giving rise to slight condensation on the profiles of the windows and doors which had resulted *inter alia* in the formation of mould on the wallpaper and plastering. ...

The defendant opposed the claim on the grounds that the replacement of all the windows and doors would require it to incur disproportionate and unreasonable expense, involving a cost price of approximately DM 22,000. In practical terms, this would mean carrying out the work again from scratch, which it was no longer obliged to do, the works having been accepted. Moreover, the state of technological development in 1977 was in fact such that a calorific value of between 2.4 and 2.6 for the frames could not at that time have been achieved. It maintained that the value and fitness of the windows and doors had suffered only an insignificant reduction as a result of the failure to conform to the calorific value indicated to the plaintiff in the offer made to the latter. The risk of slight

---

[63] See DCFR III.-3:302(3), (5), above, p 918.
[64] BGHZ 96, 111, NJW 1986, 711.

condensation arose only when the outside temperature was between –5 and –10 degrees centigrade—thus only on a few days in the year …

On those grounds: …

III.2. The Chamber proposes to depart from its previous case-law, and henceforth to determine the point of law in issue, which is crucial to the outcome of, *inter alia*, the present case, by ruling that a claim for performance of a contractor's obligation which seeks an order requiring the works to be carried out again from scratch may invariably be brought if that is the only way in which the defects can be permanently eliminated, irrespective of whether the contract for the work is governed solely by the rules laid down in the Bürgerliches Gesetzbuch or whether Part B of the *Verdingungsordnung für Bauleistungen* applies to it.

(a) In the judgments previously given, excessive attention has in general been paid to (what may be supposed to be) notional distinctions between the carrying out of the works again from scratch [*Neuherstellung*] and the making good of defects following completion of the works [*Nachbesserung*]. Insufficient regard has been had, by contrast, to the *purpose* of the elimination of defects, which occupies such a prominent place in the law relating to building contracts.

The word '*Nachbesserung*' does not appear in the relevant legislation or Part B of the *Verdingungsordnung für Bauleistungen*; instead, they merely speak of the elimination of a defect, for which a demand may be made (§§ 633, 634 BGB; §§ 4(7), 13 VOB/B). However, the *elimination* of defects, considered in terms of its natural meaning, merely signifies that defective workmanship must be replaced by workmanship which is free from defects, *in so far* as that is *necessary* in order to give rise *as a whole* to a work which is free from defects. The more far-reaching the defect, the greater the scope of the remedial work which may be demanded. Consequently, the comprehensive elimination of defects is intrinsically and *a priori* such that it may even necessitate the total replacement of previously defective workmanship by new, defect-free workmanship where that is the only way of successfully achieving the goal sought after by the elimination of the defects. In such a situation, and depending on the circumstances, the carrying out of the works again from scratch [*Neuherstellung*] means no more than the remedying of post-completion defects [*Nachbesserung*] on the largest possible—but also the requisite—scale. The remedying of post-completion defects which is such as to leave intact only a—possibly minimal—residual part of the work originally carried out frequently shifts seamlessly into the carrying out of the works again from scratch, where even that part of the work which has most recently been carried out needs to be replaced or done again. The distinction between such measures for the elimination of defects is one of scope, not of substance. To render the contractor's obligation to eliminate defects dependent on whether such elimination involves *Neuherstellung* or merely *Nachbesserung* entails problems of demarcation which cannot easily be overcome, and constitutes an approach which leads not infrequently to purely haphazard and thus unsatisfactory results …

The only proper approach to adopt is to treat the elimination of defects as covering *all* measures which are *necessary* in order to produce a work which, *taken as a whole*, is in conformity with the contract and is free from defects, even if that entails the total replacement of works which have already been carried out. In that connection, the amount which it costs to eliminate the defects by carrying out of the works again from scratch cannot constitute a material factor. It can be very expensive even to remedy individual defects by means of *Nachbesserung*; depending on the extent and scope of such defects, the cost of doing so may frequently far exceed the remuneration payable for the work as a whole. By contrast, it may be substantially cheaper for the contractor to carry out all of the work again from scratch than to remedy defects in the majority of the individual parts. Consequently, it must from the outset be open to the contractor, in accordance, at the very least, with the principle of good faith, to choose to remedy defects by carrying out the work again from scratch, provided that, in the circumstances prevailing, that is not unreasonable from the point of view of the client …

(e) … For the purposes of weighing up the interests of the parties in circumstances involving the elimination of defects, priority must be given to the interest of the client/customer in the production of an end result which is free from defects and which it is the responsibility of the contractor to provide. The latter's interest in restricting his involvement in the matter, following acceptance of the works, to the construction as accepted by the client, and in being required only to remedy defects appearing in individual parts thereof, must take second place. Compared to the success of the project, which he is contractually bound to ensure, his own interest in the matter is less deserving of protection. It follows that the interest of the client/customer in the production of a work which is *free from defects* must prevail even where—indeed, particularly where—the nature, gravity and significance of the defects is such that the only way in which that objective can be achieved is by starting again from scratch and completely replacing all of the works which have already been carried out [*Neuherstellung*].

In those circumstances, the contractor is by no means deprived of all means of protecting himself against a demand by the client that he should carry out all the work again from scratch. Thus, he is only required to take such action if it is really *necessary* in order permanently to eliminate the defects, that is to say, if the remedying of defects in individual parts of the completed work would not suffice. Even where such remedial steps would suffice, the scope of his obligation to take those steps will depend on, and be restricted to, such measures as are necessary in order to produce an end result which is free from defects.

Where the client demands that the contractor should eliminate the defects by carrying out of the works again from scratch [*Neuherstellung*], that demand is subject to the further qualification that the contractor may refuse to eliminate a defect if it would be disproportionately expensive to do so.

That restriction likewise applies to all claims for the remedying of post-completion defects [*Neuherstellung*] (§ 633(2)(2) [now § 635(3)] BGB; § 13(6) VOB/B, first sentence). It is sufficient, as a general rule, to prevent inequitable results in individual cases …

3. In the present case, it is undeniable that the thermal insulation guaranteed by the defendant to the plaintiff in relation to the door-frames and window-frames can be achieved only by their total replacement (including the panes). That is tantamount to carrying out the work again from scratch. When the construction works were at the planning stage, the plaintiff set particular store by the provision of above-average insulation. Consequently, it was of decisive importance to him that the window-frames and door-frames should provide a high level of heat insulation. By contrast, the court below found, on the basis of an expert's report, that the windows and doors installed in the premises constituted, in terms of the insulation of the premises as a whole, 'a significant weakness compromising the thermal insulation of the property to a considerable degree'. In those circumstances, the plaintiff should not have to settle for the remedying of individual defects; instead, it will only be possible for the defendant to fulfil its obligation to produce an end result corresponding to the standard guaranteed by it, that is to say, work which is free from defects, if the windows and doors are replaced in their entirety. The plaintiff is entitled to demand that; in particular, he should not have to settle for a reduction in the price payable for the work. There is no need to examine the question of the extent of any entitlement which he may have to damages.

4. The court below rightly found, moreover, that the defendant was not entitled to refuse to take the remedial action demanded (in this instance, the carrying out of the works again from scratch) on the ground that it would involve disproportionate expense (§ 13(6) VOB/B). It would only have been open to the defendant to refuse to take remedial action if, weighing up all the circumstances, the expense involved in eliminating the defects bore no reasonable relationship to the prospects of successfully eliminating them. That issue depends not solely on the amount of the costs arising, but on the relationship which such expense bears to the benefit accruing to the client as a result of the elimination of the defects. On that basis, the improvement to be achieved in the calorific value constituted a significant benefit for the plaintiff, since it would remove a substantial 'weakness' in the thermal insulation of the building. The plaintiff wished, by means of the high level of thermal insulation sought after by him, inter alia to eliminate the long-term risk of slight condensation during periods of frosty weather; consequently, the average number of days per year on which such condensation is likely to form with the frames originally installed is not a material consideration.

Furthermore, as regards the resulting increase in heating costs, the plaintiff runs the risk, in the event of significant unexpected increases in those costs, of incurring a corresponding loss. It follows that, having regard to all the circumstances, the replacement of the windows and doors with new ones possessing the guaranteed calorific value is by no means out of all reasonable proportion to the expense to the defendant, which is calculated to involve a cost price of DM 22,000.

Notes

(1) Both the right to have full performance and the right to demand a cure are limited by the proportionality requirement of § 635 BGB, the former implicitly and the latter explicitly.

(2) The question of 'disproportionality' depends not only on the amount of time or money required for the work but on other factors, such as the interests of the client that were explicitly stated at the time of making the contract.

The disproportion point rarely arises in relation to specific performance in English law because specific performance is so seldom granted; but it arises in relation to the measure of damages.

House of Lords   **23.19 (EN)**

Ruxley Electronics and Construction Ltd v Forsyth[65]

When building work has been done defectively the plaintiff will not recover damages based on the cost of correcting the defect, even if he undertakes to use the damages to this end, if to do so would be unreasonable.

Facts: The defendant had contracted for a swimming pool 7 feet 6 inches deep. In breach of contract the finished pool was only 6 feet deep and when the contractors sued for the price the defendant counter-claimed for

---

[65] [1996] AC 344.

the cost of deepening it. This would have involved total reconstruction. Before the Court of Appeal the defendant offered an undertaking to use any damages awarded on this basis for correcting the defect.

Held: The trial judge held that the depth was perfectly adequate for the-off-the-side diving which was all that was intended and that it would be unreasonable to reconstruct the pool. The plaintiff was therefore entitled only to damages for any difference in value between a 6 foot pool and a 7 foot 6 inches one, plus £2,500 for loss of amenity. The Court of Appeal by a majority reversed this decision. The defendant could not reasonably mitigate the loss, for example by buying another house with a deeper pool. The reasonableness of his desire to reconstruct the pool was irrelevant if that was the only way in which the defendant could get what he had contracted for (Staughton LJ); or reconstruction was not unreasonable (Mann LJ). The House of Lords restored the first instance judgment.

Judgment: LORD JAUNCEY: ... Mr McGuire for the appellants argued that the cost of reinstatement was only allowable where (1) the employer intended as a matter of probability to rebuild if damages were awarded, and (2) that it was reasonable as between him and the contractor so to do. Since the judge had found against the respondent on both these matters the appeal should be allowed. Mr. Jacob on the other hand maintained that reasonableness only arose at the stage when a real loss had been established to exist and that where that loss could only be met by damages assessed on one basis there was no room for consideration of reasonableness. Such was the case where a particular personal preference was part of the contractual objective—a situation which did not allow damages to be assessed on a diminution of value basis ...

Damages are designed to compensate for an established loss and not to provide a gratuitous benefit to the aggrieved party from which it follows that the reasonableness of an award of damages is to be linked directly to the loss sustained. If it is unreasonable in a particular case to award the cost of reinstatement it must be because the loss sustained does not extend to the need to reinstate. A failure to achieve the precise contractual objective does not necessarily result in the loss which is occasioned by a total failure ...

I take the example suggested during argument by my noble and learned friend, Lord Bridge of Harwich. A man contracts for the building of a house and specifies that one of the lower courses of brick should be blue. The builder uses yellow brick instead. In all other respects the house conforms to the contractual specification. To replace the yellow bricks with blue would involve extensive demolition and reconstruction at a very large cost. It would clearly be unreasonable to award to the owner the cost of reconstructing because his loss was not the necessary cost of reconstruction of his house, which was entirely adequate for its design purpose, but merely the lack of aesthetic pleasure which he might have derived from the sight of blue bricks. Thus in the present appeal the respondent has acquired a perfectly serviceable swimming pool, albeit one lacking the specified depth. His loss is thus not the lack of a useable pool with consequent need to construct a new one. Indeed were he to receive the cost of building a new one and retain the existing one he would have recovered not compensation for loss but a very substantial gratuitous benefit, something which damages are not intended to provide.

What constitutes the aggrieved party's loss is in every case a question of fact and degree. Where the contract breaker has entirely failed to achieve the contractual objective it may not be difficult to conclude that the loss is the necessary cost of achieving that objective. Thus if a building is constructed so defectively that it is of no use for its designed purpose the owner may have little difficulty in establishing that his loss is the necessary cost of reconstructing. Furthermore in taking reasonableness into account in determining the extent of loss it is reasonableness in relation to the particular contract and not at large. Accordingly if I contracted for the erection of a folly in my garden which shortly thereafter suffered a total collapse it would be irrelevant to the determination of my loss to argue that the erection of such a folly which contributed nothing to the value of my house was a crazy thing to do. As Oliver J said in *Radford v De Froberville* [1977] 1 WLR 1262, 1270:

'If he contracts for the supply of that which he thinks serves his interests—be they commercial, aesthetic or merely eccentric—then if that which is contracted for is not supplied by the other contracting party I do not see why, in principle, he should not be compensated by being provided with the cost of supplying it through someone else or in a different way, subject to the proviso, of course, that he is seeking compensation for a genuine loss and not merely using a technical breach to secure an uncovenanted profit.'

However where the contractual objective has been achieved to a substantial extent the position may be very different.

It was submitted that where the objective of a building contract involved satisfaction of a personal preference the only measure of damages available for a breach involving failure to achieve such satisfaction was the cost of reinstatement. In my view this is not the case. Personal preference may well be a factor in reasonableness and hence in determining what loss has been suffered but it cannot per se be determinative of what that loss is.

My Lords, the trial judge found that it would be unreasonable to incur the cost of demolishing the existing pool and building a new and deeper one. In so doing he implicitly recognised that the respondent's loss did not extend to the cost of reinstatement. He was, in my view, entirely justified in reaching that conclusion. It therefore follows that the appeal must be allowed.

It only remains to mention two further matters. The appellant argued that the cost of reinstatement should only be allowed as damages where there was shown to be an intention on the part of the aggrieved party to carry out the work. Having already decided that the appeal should be allowed I no longer find it necessary to reach a conclusion on this matter. However I should emphasise that in the normal case the court has no concern with the use to which a plaintiff puts an award of damages for a loss which has been established. Thus irreparable damage to an article as a result of a breach of contract will entitle the owner to recover the value of the article irrespective of whether he intends to replace it with a similar one or to spend the money on something else. Intention, or lack of it, to reinstate can have relevance only to reasonableness and hence to the extent of the loss which has been sustained. Once that loss has been established intention as to the subsequent use of the damages ceases to be relevant.

The second matter relates to the award of £2,500 for loss of amenity made by the trial judge. The respondent argued that he erred in law in making such award. However as the appellant did not challenge it, I find it unnecessary to express any opinion on the matter.

LORD MUSTILL: My Lords, I agree that this appeal should be allowed for the reasons stated by my noble and learned friends, Lord Jauncey of Tullichettle and Lord Lloyd of Berwick. I add some observations of my own on the award by the trial judge of damages in a sum intermediate between, on the one hand, the full cost of reinstatement, and on the other the amount by which the mal-performance has diminished the market value of the property on which the work was done: in this particular case, nil. This is a question of everyday practical importance to householders who have engaged contractors to carry out small building works, and then find (as often happens) that performance has fallen short of what was promised. I think it proper to enter on the question here, although there is no appeal against the award, because the possibility of such a recovery in a suitable case sheds light on the employer's claim that reinstatement is the only proper measure of damage.

The proposition that these two measures of damage represent the only permissible bases of recovery lie at the heart of the employer's case …

In my opinion there would indeed be something wrong if, on the hypothesis that cost of reinstatement and the depreciation in value were the only available measures of recovery, the rejection of the former necessarily entailed the adoption of the latter; and the court might be driven to opt for the cost of reinstatement, absurd as the consequence might often be, simply to escape from the conclusion that the promisor can please himself whether or not to comply with the wishes of the promise which, as embodied in the contract, formed part of the consideration for the price. Having taken on the job the contractor is morally as well as legally obliged to give the employer what he stipulated to obtain, and this obligation ought not to be devalued. In my opinion however the hypothesis is not correct. There are not two alternative measures of damage, at opposite poles, but only one; namely, the loss truly suffered by the promisee. In some cases the loss cannot be fairly measured except by reference to the full cost of repairing the deficiency in performance. In others, and in particular those where the contract is designed to fulfil a purely commercial purpose, the loss will very often consist only of the monetary detriment brought about by the breach of contract. But these remedies are not exhaustive, for the law must cater for those occasions where the value of the promise to the promisee exceeds the financial enhancement of his position which full performance will secure. This excess, often referred to in the literature as the 'consumer surplus' (see for example the valuable discussion by Harris, Ogus and Philips (1979) 95 LQR 581) is usually incapable of precise valuation in terms of money, exactly because it represents a personal, subjective and nonmonetary gain. Nevertheless where it exists the law should recognise it and compensate the promisee if the misperformance takes it away. The lurid bathroom tiles, or the grotesque folly instanced in argument by my noble and learned friend, Lord Keith of Kinkel, may be so discordant with general taste that in purely economic terms the builder may be said to do the employer a favour by failing to install them. But this is too narrow and materialistic a view of the transaction. Neither the contractor nor the court has the right to substitute for the employer's individual expectation of performance a criterion derived from what ordinary people would regard as sensible. As my Lords have shown, the test of reasonableness plays a central part in determining the basis of recovery, and will indeed be decisive in a case such as the present when the cost of reinstatement would be wholly disproportionate to the nonmonetary loss suffered by the employer. But it would be equally unreasonable to deny all recovery for such a loss. The amount may be small, and since it cannot be quantified directly there may be room for difference of opinion about what it should be. But in several fields the judges are well accustomed to putting figures to intangibles, and I see no reason why the imprecision of the exercise should be a barrier, if that is what fairness demands. My Lords, once this is recognised the puzzling and paradoxical feature of this case, that it seems to involve a contest of absurdities, simply falls away. There is no need to remedy the injustice of awarding too little, by unjustly awarding far too much. The judgment of the trial judge acknowledges that the employer has suffered a true loss and expresses it in terms of money. Since there is no longer any issue about the amount of the award, as distinct from the principle, I would simply restore his judgment by allowing the appeal.

[LORDS KEITH, BRIDGE and LLOYD delivered concurring judgments.]

In French law, before the 2016 reform, specific performance could not be refused simply on the ground that the inconvenience caused to the creditor by the non-performance was slight. This was well illustrated by the decision of 17 January 1984 involving a swimming pool built with three steps instead of four, as contractually agreed. The Cour de cassation held that the mere fact that the defect had not been shown to cause any inconvenience was not an adequate ground for refusing the order of specific performance.

Cass civ (3), 17 January 1984[66]   **23.20 (FR)**

The French swimming pool

Specific performance should not be refused simply on the ground that the inconvenience caused to the creditor by the non-performance is slight.

Facts: A contract for a swimming pool required it to be provided with four steps. It was built with only three. The employer sought an order that the defect should be corrected.

Held: The cour d'appel refused an order on the ground that it had not been shown that having only three steps caused any inconvenience. This decision was quashed by the Cour de cassation.

*Judgment: In the matter of the appeal lodged by Mr Maurice Abou ... seeking the setting aside of a judgment delivered ... by the Aix-en-Provence cour d'appel (8th Chamber) in favour of Mr François Alessandra ...:—*Whereas by his first appeal ground, Mr Abou complains of the dismissal by the contested judgment of his application for an order requiring Mr Alessandra to carry out the necessary works and to make the swimming pool and its appurtenances correspond with the contractual quotation of 26 December 1977, in particular as regards the number of steps providing access to the swimming pool in question, the said application having been dismissed on the ground that no evidence had been adduced showing that that deviation from the contract would render access to the pool more difficult and that the claim should not therefore be upheld.

— Whereas the appellant asserts that the cour d'appel refused to apply the terms of the contract signed by the two parties ... and that, in the light of Article 1134 [now Article 1104] of the Civil Code, its decision thus has no legal basis ...

— Whereas [former] article 1184 of the Civil Code provides that where a party is owed an obligation which is not performed, that party may require the other party to perform the agreement where such performance is possible;

— Whereas in dismissing the application by the party who had commissioned the works for an order requiring the swimming pool to be fitted with four steps in conformity with the contract, instead of the three steps installed therein, the contested judgment found that no evidence had been adduced showing that that deviation from the contract would render access to the pool more difficult;

---

[66] Cass civ (3) 17 January 1984, no. 82-15982, unpublished; surprisingly, it is impossible to find this decision on Legifrance under this *numéro de pourvoi* or with keywords. But on Dalloz, the *numéro de pourvoi* leads to the decision. The relevant part of the original decision was annotated by J Mestre, RTD civ 1994, 711; it is quoted in O Kahn Freund, B Lévy and B Rudden, *A Source Book on French Law* (3rd edn, Oxford University Press, 1991) 500-1. Another part of the decision was published and annotated in Actualité juridique de propriété immobilière 1985, 25. Compare Cass mixte 26 May 2006, above, p 341, which is interpreted as not requiring the creditor to prove that he has suffered any loss before being able to enforce performance.

— Whereas in so ruling, without examining whether or not the installation could be altered so as to conform with the contract, the cour d'appel provided no legal basis for its decision.

On those grounds, the Court quashes and sets aside the contested judgment.

Notes

(1) The case appears to suggest that correction of the defect should be ordered unless it is impossible; the mere fact that the defect has not been shown to cause any inconvenience is not an adequate ground for refusing the order of specific performance.[67] In spite of its rigour for the debtor, this solution was firmly established; it was based on Article 1103 of the Code civil (former 1134(1)), that sets the principle of the binding force of the contract. This solution was rather extreme.

(2) Symmetrically, if an obligation not to do something was violated, and even though this had caused no prejudice whatsoever to the creditor, the Cour de cassation adopted the same solution. It did so in a case of 10 May 2005.[68] In that case, a party had violated a term of the contract restricting the exercise of a professional activity. However, since the other party was not capable of exercising that activity, such a violation did not prejudice it. The appeal court had therefore ruled that there was no prejudice and hence no *réparation*. The Cour de cassation reversed this judgment on the basis of former Article 1145 of the Code civil, which stated that 'Where there is an obligation not to do, he who violates it owes damages by the mere fact of the violation.' Some commentators had tried to limit the ambit of this case and thus explained that it concerned 'forced performance' and not '*réparation en nature*'. Indeed, traditionally, the very concept of *réparation* necessitates that there is a prejudice.[69] However, two years later, the Cour de cassation ruled, once again, that in spite of there being no prejudice, a remedy was available at that time, and that the remedy that had been claimed was damages.[70] Just like in English law in certain circumstances,[71] damages could hereby be granted even though there was no prejudice.[72]

The 2016 reform put an end to this rigorous case law. Article 1221 of the new Code civil now provides that performance in kind may be refused not only when the performance is impossible but also when 'there is a manifest disproportion between its cost to the debtor and its interest for the creditor'. This provision introduces a cost-benefit analysis in the availability of performance in kind. Although this provision brings some uncertainty as it gives new power to the court, it prevents the extreme consequences which resulted from the former case law. In applying Article 1221, the French courts are likely to resort to a proportionality test similar to the one used under German law. Some questions still

---

[67] See also Cass civ (3) 16 June 2015, no. 14-14612, cited above, p 904.
[68] Cass civ (1) 10 May 2005, no. 02-15910, Bull I no. 201, RTD civ 2005, 594, annotated by J Mestre and B Fages.
[69] See annotation by J Mestre and B Fages in RTD civ 2005, 594.
[70] Cass civ (1) 31 May 2007, no. 05-19978, Bull I no. 212, D 2007, 2784, annotated by C Lisanti.
[71] See below, p 1114.
[72] For a comparative analysis of this case and of its implications, see B Fauvarque-Cosson, D 2007, 2974.

remain to be solved, notably that of its mandatory or non-mandatory nature—can the parties agree to exclude its application by a term which prevents a party from invoking this disproportion?[73]

Thus at least now there is a general principle that specific performance, or in English law, damages based on the cost of obtaining full performance, should not be ordered if it would involve the debtor in expense or difficulty which would be disproportionate to the benefit the creditor would gain thereby. The PECL provide:

Principles of European Contract Law **23.21 (INT)**

Article 9:102: Non-monetary Obligations
(1) The aggrieved party is entitled to specific performance of an obligation other than one to pay money, including the remedying of a defective performance.
(2) Specific performance cannot, however, be obtained where: ...
(b) performance would cause the debtor unreasonable effort or expense; or ...[74]

23.2.G.3 EFFECTS ON THIRD PERSONS OR THE PUBLIC

Cass civ, 17 December 1963[75] **23.22 (FR)**

Too many storeys

A housing shortage does not justify refusing to order the destruction of a building which has been built in breach of planning laws.

Facts: The defendant lessees had built more storeys on their apartment building than was permitted by the lease they had been granted. The owners demanded the demolition of the extra storeys.

Held: The cour d'appel of Montpellier refused their demand, in the light of the interests of the tenants living there, and awarded damages instead. The owners appealed and the earlier decision was quashed.

Judgment: THE COURT: ... *On the first branch of the second appeal ground*: ...
— Under [former] Article 1143 of the Civil Code;
— Whereas the sole application made to the court adjudicating on the substance of the case was for an order requiring Parena and the Société Civile Immobilière La Rabelais to demolish the storeys of the building which they had constructed in breach of a provision contained in the specifications governing the erection of constructions on the land.
— Whereas although the contested judgment found that that provision had indeed been breached, it refused to order the demolition of the extra storeys and awarded the plaintiffs compensatory damages on the ground that it was necessary to safeguard the interests of the tenants living in those storeys.
— Whereas the cour d'appel acknowledged that it would not be impossible to enforce the order for specific performance applied for, and that the plaintiffs had an interest

---

[73] Although contract law provisions in the Code civil are, in principle, of a non-mandatory character, Art 1221 may be considered mandatory for two sorts of reasons: preventing abuse of rights and 'judicial activism of recent times'; see C Pérès, 'Mandatory and Non-Mandatory Rules in the New Law of Contract' in Cartwright and Whittaker (n 5 above) 167, esp at 180.
[74] See also DCFR III.-3:302(3)(b) and also UNIDROIT PICC Art 7.2.2(b).
[75] JCP 1964.II.13609, annotated by CH Blaevoet.

in obtaining such an order, but nevertheless refused to make the order in question, for reasons relating to the interests of third parties; in so doing, it infringed the legislative provision referred to above.

[On those grounds, and without there being any need to rule on the second part of that plea, the Court quashes and sets aside the contested judgment.]

[From the note:] The facts are very simple. Parena and the Société Immobilière Le Rabelais had constructed on a parcel of land a building comprising more storeys than permitted by the specifications relating to that land. The owners of certain lots brought proceedings against them for an order requiring them to demolish the surplus storeys. The Montpellier cour d'appel, before which the case was brought, found that the provisions contained in the specifications had indeed been infringed, but refused to order the demolition sought and awarded the plaintiffs compensatory damages on the ground that it was necessary to safeguard the interests of the tenants of the dwellings located in those storeys. It is that judgment which is contested.

The 1st Civil Chamber of the Cour de cassation, ruling on the plea relating to Article 1143 of the Civil Code, held that the cour d'appel had infringed that article: although the cour d'appel acknowledged that it would not be impossible to enforce the order sought, and that the plaintiffs had an interest in obtaining such an order, it nevertheless refused to make the order in question, for reasons relating to the interests of third parties.

However, certain cours d'appel were in the habit of restricting the relief granted by them to awards of damages. In so doing, those courts invoked various considerations, such as the fact that 'a demolition order would be disproportionate to the loss suffered', the fact that the permitted height of the building had not been significantly exceeded, the general need, in dealing with construction cases, to have regard to the crisis in the housing sector and, in certain cases, the fact that the builder had acted in good faith … The strict approach adopted by the Civil Chamber in applying the Civil Code is commendable, since it accords with the concern of the legislature to preserve the salubrity of certain premises by providing, in the town planning rules enacted by it, for the imposition of severe penalties for infringements of those rules.

Notes

(1) Before this case, some French appeal courts used to grant only damages in situations similar to this one. In so doing, those courts invoked various considerations, such as the fact that 'a demolition order would be disproportionate to the loss suffered', the fact that the permitted height of the building had not been significantly exceeded, the general need, in dealing with construction cases, to have regard to the crisis in the housing sector and, in certain cases, the fact that the builder had acted in good faith.

(2) The strict approach adopted by the Civil Chamber in applying the Code civil accords with the concern of the legislature to preserve the salubrity of certain premises by providing, in the town planning rules enacted by it, for the imposition of severe penalties for infringements of those rules. It seems that the 2016 reform will not trigger any change in the case law on this point. In this respect, it must be noted that the 'disproportion exception' of Article 1221 of the new Code civil only applies in the relationship between the debtor and the creditor. This provision does not allow courts to take into accounts the effect that specific performance would have on third parties or the public.

(3) In the English case of *Wrotham Park Estates Co v Parkside Homes*,[76] developers acquired land subject to a restrictive covenant limiting the number of houses which could be built. In ignorance of the restriction, they built more houses than they were allowed to. Brightman J refused a mandatory injunction ordering destruction of the houses, as that would be 'an unpardonable waste of much needed housing', and awarded damages instead.[77]

(4) Such factors are not referred to in the international restatements.

23.2.G.4 CONTRACTS INVOLVING PERSONAL SERVICES

The fact that a contract is for services does not prevent the court from granting execution *in natura*. First, in French or German law it may be possible for the contract to be performed by a third person at the defendant's expense. Examples are the building contract cases (these are contracts for services and materials) and the contract to publish, which can be performed by a third party in certain circumstances.[78] Secondly, in both those systems, and even in English law on the rare occasions in which a contract for services and materials is specifically enforceable, the courts will not be concerned if the defendant can get someone else to do the work. It will be different if the defendant is the only person who can perform the contract.[79]

Cass civ, 14 March 1900[80]   **23.23 (FR)**

Lady Eden's portrait

Specific performance of a contract involving artistic or other personal services will not be granted.

Facts: Sir William Eden had commissioned James McNeill Whistler to paint a portrait of Lady Eden. The painting had been completed and exhibited, and Eden had tendered payment for it; but the parties fell out. Whistler refused to deliver the picture and painted the head of another woman in place of Lady Eden's. Mr Eden appealed to the Cour de cassation against the judgment delivered by the cour de Paris on 2 December 1897, reported in S and P 1900.2.201. The sole plea advanced by the appellant alleged infringement of [former] Articles 1136, 1138, 1583, 1584, 1603 et seq, 1787 and 1788 Cciv, misapplication of Article 1142 of the Civil Code, the absence of any legal basis, a lack of reasons and infringement of Article 7 of the Law of 20 April 1810 in that, although the contested judgment acknowledged that Whistler had contracted with Sir William Eden to paint the portrait of Lady Eden, and that he had painted and completed that portrait, it refused to order that the portrait be delivered to the plaintiff, on the ground that the contract concluded between the parties had given rise only to a mere obligation to perform an act the remedy for the non-performance of which lay in damages; the appellant asserted that that contract in fact constituted an agreement for the sale of an object to be created in the future or for the provision of services in the form of work requiring the provider of those services to deliver the result of his labours, or, at the very least, that the contract imposed an obligation to hand something over, the effect of which was automatically to transfer ownership of the portrait to the plaintiff as soon as it was completed, or at least upon its being approved by Sir Eden, prior to delivery

---

[76] [1974] 1 WLR 798 (ChD).
[77] On the way the judge calculated the damages, see 26.43 (EN), below, p 1110.
[78] eg OLG München 31 May 1955, MDR 1955, 682.
[79] cf for Dutch law: *Asser/Sieburgh* (n 18 above) 6-II 2017/344.
[80] S 1900.1.489.

thereof; the plaintiff further claimed that, even if Mr Whistler's obligation was merely to perform an act, the court adjudicating on the substance of the case should nevertheless have ordered specific performance, since the obligation in question was susceptible of specific performance and did not impose any constraint on the freedom of the party by whom it was owed.

Held: In the lower courts the plaintiff's action for delivery of the painting was dismissed, and an appeal was rejected.

Judgment: THE COURT:—Whereas an agreement whereby a painter undertakes to paint a portrait for an agreed sum constitutes a contract of a special kind, pursuant to which property in the picture does not pass to the person commissioning it until the artist presents that picture to his client and the picture is approved by the latter; as until that stage is reached, the painter retains control over his work, although he may not lawfully keep it for himself or dispose of it as a portrait to a third party, since the right to reproduce the features of the sitter has only conditionally been conferred on him with a view to completion of the contract and in the event of failure by the artist to fulfil his obligations, he will incur liability in damages.

— Whereas as is indicated in the findings made in the contested judgment, Whistler undertook to paint a portrait of Lady Eden but refused throughout to make that portrait available to the plaintiff, who had commissioned it; having exhibited the picture at the *Salon du Champ-de-Mars*, he made radical changes to the painting, replacing the head of Lady Eden with that of another person.

— Whereas it was held in the contested judgment, first, that, since the plaintiff had not become the owner of the picture, he was not entitled to require it to be delivered to him in its existing state and, second, that Whistler was liable, by way of damages, to return the price paid in advance and in addition, the contested judgment prohibited Whistler from making any use whatever of the canvas until such time as he had altered its appearance in such a way as to render it unrecognisable, in so ruling, the contested judgment, which is accompanied by a statement of reasons, did not infringe the legislative provision referred to by the appellant; on the contrary, it correctly applied the same.

[On those grounds, the Court dismissed the appeal.]

Note

French case law added another limit, which appears to be upheld by Article 1221 of the new Code civil. It relates to orders for performance: performance may not be ordered if the subject matter of the obligation has a clearly personal character, or if it would necessitate coercion compromising 'the debtors' personal liberty or dignity'. Such a limit should fall within the scope of the 'impossibility to perform', as a *moral* impossibility.

We will see that in English law a 'contract for service' (ie a contract of employment) will not be enforced specifically.[81] A contract that requires one party to perform services of a personal nature, such as to paint a picture or to write a book, will also not be enforced specifically. An agreement between an author and a publisher to publish a book was held not to be specifically enforceable, on the ground that co-operation between

---

[81] See below, p 933.

the parties would be necessary: *Malcolm v Chancellor, Masters and Scholars of the University of Oxford.*[82]

§ 888(3) ZPO[83] precludes the enforcement of personal service obligations under a contract of service (*Dienstvertrag*), but it is notable that the carrying out of work under a contract for work (*Werkvertrag*) is not similarly excluded. Thus, as long as such an obligation could not be performed by a third party and is dependent solely on the will of the debtor it could be enforced. This raises the possibility that in German law, unlike in English or French law, an artist could be compelled to paint a picture under a contract for work. Of course the practical difficulties and the probably unsatisfactory nature of the end product has meant that such enforcement is rarely sought.

Principles of European Contract Law **23.24 (INT)**

Article 9:102: Non-monetary Obligations
(2) Specific performance cannot, however, be obtained where: ...
(c) the performance consists in the provision of services or work of a personal character or depends upon a personal relationship ...[84]

The DCFR takes a slightly different approach. Specific performance may be granted of an obligation to perform personal services unless the services are of such a personal character that it would be unreasonable to enforce it.[85] According to the Comments, this is to enable performance to be ordered where the services are in a sense personal but the performance can be delegated to another, rather than being services that only the defendant can properly perform (like an artist's obligation to produce a portrait).

23.2.G.5 EMPLOYMENT CONTRACTS

The traditional rule is that a contract of employment cannot be enforced specifically.

Zivilprozessordnung (ZPO) **23.25 (DE)**

§ 888: Actions that may not be taken by others
...
(3) These rules shall not be applied in those cases in which a person is sentenced to provide services under a service agreement.

In England, the traditional position is that a contract of employment will not be specifically enforced at the suit of either party—not against the employee because of the interference with liberty, and not against the employer on the ground that an employer should not have to employ anyone against its will. Now the Trade Union and Labour Relations (Consolidation) Act 1992, Section 236 provides that no court shall compel an employee to do any work by ordering specific performance of a contract of employment or by

---

[82] *The Times*, 19 December 1990.
[83] See 23.25 (DE), below.
[84] UNIDROIT PICC Art 7.2.2(d) excludes enforcement of an obligation which requires 'performance of an exclusively personal character'.
[85] DCFR Art III.-3:302.

restraining the breach of such contract by injunction. The case law has turned around two questions.

The first is whether it is possible to restrain an employee who is threatening to do something forbidden by the contract, such as working for a competitor. In English law the answer rests on whether this would be tantamount to giving specific enforcement, since preventing the employee from working for any other employer might prevent them from having any income unless they came to work for the plaintiff.[86] In German law the HGB provides for the agreement of such restrictive clauses in certain employment contracts (at §§ 74–75d) and the Federal Labour Court (BAG) has applied these to all employment contracts. These statutory rules and the case law of the BAG indicate a policy of confining and ameliorating the effects of such clauses. This is because the *Grundgesetz* (GG) guarantees freedom to choose and exercise one's profession or calling and to choose where to do so (Article 12 GG). Thus such clauses must be in writing; they must serve a legitimate business interest of the employer; they must not unfairly limit the scope for professional development of the employee; they may last no longer than two years; and the employer must pay compensation to the employee during the relevant period. The enforcement of such clauses through the agreement of penalties is also subject to review by the courts (§§ 339–345 BGB). While the employment contract subsists, the employee is of course subject to a *Nebenpflicht* not to compete.[87]

The second question is whether employers can be restrained from dismissing employees wrongfully when in fact the employers—or at least the employees' immediate superiors who will have to work with them—still have trust in the employees and are themselves willing to employ them. As just stated, the traditional attitude was that neither specific performance nor an injunction would be given against the employer any more than it would be against the employee. But in each jurisdiction the courts have sometimes been willing to order that an employee who is still trusted by those with whom they will have to work should be reinstated. Thus in *Powell v Brent London Borough Council*[88] the employer was perfectly willing to continue employing the plaintiff but it threatened to dismiss her wrongfully as the result of pressure from a trade union. The Court of Appeal held that an injunction should be issued to restrain the dismissal. This case is exceptional in the sense that the employer had confidence in the employee and was bowing to union pressure. However, this is (or at least was) not an uncommon situation in England.[89]

In somewhat similar vein, in Cass soc, 14 June 1972[90] the court held that an employer which wrongly dismisses an employee without using the proper procedures should be ordered to reinstate the employee.

The German courts seem to have gone further, ordering reinstatement even when this would not be acceptable to the employer or the employee's immediate superior.

---

[86] See *Lumley v Wagner* (1852) 1 De GM & G 604 (which involved the opera singer Johanna Wagner), *Warner Bros v Nelson* [1937] 1 KB 209 (KBD) (which involved the film star Bette Davis) and *Page One Records Ltd v Britton* [1968] 1 WLR 157 (ChD) (which involved 'The Troggs'). In addition the clause must not be in unreasonable restraint of trade: see above at pp 679 ff.

[87] See generally Münchener Kommentar/Müller-Glöge § 611 para 1100; Palandt/Weidenkaff § 611 paras 42–43c.

[88] [1987] IRLR 466.

[89] See also *Hill v CA Parsons* [1972] Ch 305.

[90] Cass soc 14 June 1972, no. 71-12508, D 1973, 114, annotated by N Catala, JCP 1972.1.17275, annotated by G Lyon-Caen.

The Radiologist

An employer may be ordered to reinstate an employee who has been wrongly dismissed, even if this will require the employer to organise its operations in such a way as to provide her with work.

Facts: The plaintiff was a consultant radiologist who was appointed head of the X-ray department. After a reorganisation of the department she was dismissed, the employer claiming that she did not fit the requirements of head of the new department.

Held: The Landesarbeitsgericht granted her an order for continuation of her employment as head of department and damages for loss suffered as the result of the employer's actions. An appeal to the Bundesarbeitsgericht was dismissed.

Judgment: The plaintiff had been a specialist in internal medicine since 1933 and a specialist in radiology and radiotherapeutics since 1937. From 1933 onwards she worked as an assistant doctor, and from 1943 onwards as a senior consultant, in the X-ray department of the R Hospital. On 1 November 1947, having already worked for a long period as the acting chief physician in the absence of the incumbent of that post, she was appointed to the position of chief physician in charge of that department. In the course of the reconstruction of the R Hospital, the X-ray department was accommodated in a newly constructed building, in the medical aspects of the design and organization of which the plaintiff participated to a considerable extent. On 10 December 1953 she was given notice of dismissal with effect from 30 June 1954, on the ground that she did not satisfy the requirements needed of the head of the newly completed radiology institute.

The plaintiff considered that her dismissal was unjustified, and brought proceedings for a declaration that the employment relationship was not terminated by the notice in question. She further claimed an order for the continuation of her employment as chief physician in charge of the radiology and radiotherapeutics department of the R Hospital, together with a declaration that the defendant was liable to compensate her for all damage suffered by her as a result of the refusal to allow her to continue her activities as head of that department. The Landesarbeitsgericht (Higher Labour Court) allowed those claims. The defendant's appeal on a point of law against the judgment of the Landesarbeitsgericht was dismissed.

On those grounds: ... II. It is also necessary to concur with the finding of the Landesarbeitsgericht that, according to recent developments in the law, there exists in principle an obligation on employers to give their employees work to do. An employment relationship is a mutual relationship conferring personal rights which does not merely involve the provision of specified individual services—as in the case of a contract for services entered into by a self-employed person or a contract imposing similar obligations—but extends to cover the employee's entire being, and thus substantially shapes and dictates that employee's life and personality. Moreover, the respect and approval due to an employee as a human being are based not merely on the commercial value of his/her services (reflected in the amount of his/her remuneration) but also, to a considerable extent, on the manner in which he/she fulfils the tasks which he/she is called upon to perform. In the sphere of a person's working life, it is that, above all, which decisively confers on that person his/her value as a human being. It follows that the employer is obliged, not merely on the basis of his duty to act in good faith but also, and above all, in accordance with the

---

[91] NJW 1956, 359.

obligation imposed on all persons by Articles 1 and 2 of the Grundgesetz (Basic Law), to refrain from any act which might be detrimental to the value of the employee and the free development of his/her personality. Both of those aspects of the employee's fundamental rights would be impaired were he/she expected, not merely on a temporary basis but possibly for years on end, to draw his/her salary without being able to carry on the activity pertaining to his/her previous profession. That would be tantamount to compelling the employee concerned to do nothing, and would result in his/her ceasing in any way to be a full member of the professional community and of society. Not only the general public, but also the overwhelming majority of employees who are conscious of their abilities and achievements, regard it as contemptible to draw a wage which has not been earned by the provision of corresponding services. Moreover, such a situation would mean that an employee who was prohibited, during the existing employment relationship, from offering his labour to anyone else would be prevented from continuing his/her professional activities and from maintaining and improving his professional skills—in other words, from developing his/her personality. The foregoing applies in particular in the case of senior employees or others fulfilling particularly important tasks, since a lengthy period with no work to do creates the impression that the services previously rendered by the employee must have been so inferior that the employer prefers to spend money than to be provided with those services.

Consequently, the employer's right, during the course of the existing contract, and subject to the continued payment of the employee's salary, to give the latter nothing to do must be restricted, unless the employee agrees, to a temporary period only, possibly amounting to the length of a notice period. In other cases, there must exist special reasons justifying such a regime, which must be subjected to careful scrutiny.

In the present case, however, there is no need to enquire further into the findings made in that regard by the Landesarbeitsgericht, since the defendant's contention that its refusal to provide the plaintiff with work is justified by overriding interests cannot be considered further. That contention merely repeats, in essence, the assertion, given as a reason for the plaintiff's dismissal, that, following the changes arising from the reconstruction of the X-ray department, she was no longer acceptable to the hospital. In the event, however, of its being definitively established that the employment relationship continues to exist, and that the plaintiff is entitled to continue her activities as chief physician in charge of the X-ray department of the R. Hospital, the defendant will be unable to escape from its obligation in that regard; it will be required, in those circumstances, to organize its operations in such a way as to enable the plaintiff to continue to carry on her activities. Only if that subsequently proves de facto to be impossible, for unforeseeable reasons which are not attributable to the defendant, will it be possible, in proceedings instituted on the basis of a fresh notice of dismissal, to examine the situation anew.

Note

Although this decision was rendered more than 60 years ago it is still frequently cited by other courts and legal writers. Karl Larenz writes:[92]

In a rejection of his services the employee may suffer a personal rejection or a setback, including a disadvantage in respect of his professional development. If, for example, an actor is engaged to act by the management of a theatre, it would have a serious impact on

---

[92] K Larenz, *Lehrbuch des Schuldrechts*, vol II/1: *Besonderer Teil* (13th edn, Munich: CH Beck, 1986) 325.

him if he were denied any acting roles. It is thus clear that many contracts of service have a "personal" character from the perspective of the employee. In such cases, the refusal of services offered would be a breach of the duty of good faith of the employer, unless it were justified for special reasons. Put positively, this means that the employer can, in certain circumstances be obliged under BGB § 242 to take up the services offered to him and to engage the employee in an appropriate way. Thus in essence an "obligation to engage (*Beschäftigungspflicht*)" is now accepted.

English law seems the most restrictive of the three laws, granting reinstatement to the employee only in exceptional circumstances, and even then taking a very mercenary attitude to the employment, so that the employee needs to be protected only against financial loss. The international restatements (PECL, UNIDROIT) say nothing about employment contracts specifically.

23.2.G.6 OBLIGATIONS REQUIRING THE INVOLVEMENT OF THIRD PARTIES

Zivilprozessordnung (ZPO) **23.27 (DE)**

§ 888: Actions that may not be taken by others
(1) Where an action that depends exclusively on the will of the debtor cannot be taken by a third party, and where a corresponding petition has been filed, the court of first instance hearing the case is to urge the debtor to take the action in its ruling by levying a coercive penalty payment and, for the case that such payment cannot be obtained, by coercive punitive detention, or by directly sentencing him to coercive punitive detention. The individual coercive penalty payment may not be levied in an amount in excess of 25,000 euros. The stipulations of Chapter 2 regarding detention shall apply mutatis mutandis to coercive punitive detention.
...

OLG Hamm, 10 October 1972[93] **23.28 (DE)**

The Mom and Pop Shop

Where the debtor will not be able to perform the contract without the co-operation of third parties who are not before the court, specific performance cannot be ordered.

Facts: The lease of a small shop required the tenants to carry on a grocery and dairy business. The lessor sought to enforce this obligation.

Held: By judgment of the Amtsgericht (local court) the defendants were ordered, on pain of the imposition by the court of such legally permissible fine or detention order as it might decide upon, to carry on their grocery and dairy produce business in S. Upon the continued refusal by the defendants to carry on the business in question, the plaintiff applied to the Amtsgericht in S for an order for the enforcement of the judgment in accordance with § 890 ZPO; the court imposed on the defendants, jointly and severally, a fine in the sum of DM 2,000. On appeal by the defendants the Landgericht overturned this decision. The plaintiff's appeal to the Oberlandesgericht was rejected.

[93] NJW 1973, 1135.

Judgment: ... in the circumstances of the case, the plaintiff's further special appeal cannot be allowed. The defendants' non-compliance with the obligation imposed on them by the judgment of the Amtsgericht in S, requiring them to carry on a grocery and dairy produce business, can be penalized by enforcement measures only if that obligation involves an act to be performed by the defendants in person and is exclusively dependent on the will of the defendants, or alternatively if the claim is capable, like a claim to compel a person from refraining from doing something, of being enforced. Neither of those conditions is satisfied in the present case.

In the Senate's view, the obligation to carry on a grocery and dairy produce business in specified premises must be regarded as involving an act to be performed by the defendants in person. An act is fungible only if it is capable of being performed by a third party. That will be the position where, from the point of view of the party to whom the obligation is owed, it is commercially immaterial whether the act is performed by the other party himself or by a third person, and where, from the point of view of the party by whom the obligation is owed, the performance of the act is legally permissible. In the present case, it is doubtful whether the identity of the person carrying on the grocery business in her premises is commercially immaterial to the plaintiff. In the tenancy agreement, she expressly imposed on the defendants the obligation to carry on the grocery and dairy produce business. Furthermore, the operation of a grocery and dairy produce business involves so many different acts, such as buying, selling, the acquisition of advertising material and the maintenance of the shop premises, that, for that reason also, there can scarcely be any question of a third party being able to fulfil that obligation. Moreover, even if performance by another person were ordered, the operation of the business by a third party would conflict with the plaintiff's obligation to permit the defendants to use the premises. Consequently, the obligation to carry on a grocery and dairy produce business in premises let by the plaintiff to the defendants involves an act which may not be performed by another, within the meaning of § 888 ZPO. That does not mean, however, that enforcement is therefore possible under § 888 ZPO. That provision further stipulates that the performance of the act must be dependent exclusively on the will of the party obliged to perform it. The operation of a grocery and dairy produce business involves the conclusion of contracts with suppliers who deliver the goods to be sold in the business. Consequently, the operation of the business not only requires willingness on the part of the defendants to run it but also involves the conclusion of contracts with the suppliers, who must be willing to contract with the defendants. Even if the suppliers are willing to enter into the relevant contracts, the operation of the business is dependent on circumstances which are not contingent solely upon the will of the defendants.

Nor, accordingly, can there be any question of the imposition of a penalty under § 890 ZPO. The judgment ordering the defendants to operate a grocery and dairy produce business constitutes a decision requiring the defendants to perform an act. It is true that, in its judgment of 4 June 1962 the Oberlandesgericht Hamm considered that a claim for performance of an act pursuant to a long-term obligation was enforceable. However, that view is not shared by the Senate in the present case. The wording of § 890 ZPO does not cover the imposition of a penalty on the basis of a right to demand performance. § 890 ZPO is concerned only with claims for injunctive relief in the form of an order restraining a person from doing something. Enforcement of an order requiring a person, in mandatory terms, to perform an act is never permissible under § 890 ZPO; such an order may be enforced only pursuant to §§ 887 and/or 888 ZPO. The Oberlandesgericht Hamm purported, in its aforementioned decision, to have identified a lacuna in the legislation, consisting of the impossibility of applying any pressure in the form of a penalty to procure compliance with an order for the performance of an act incapable of being performed by anyone else, which is unenforceable under § 888 ZPO; in the Senate's view, however, that earlier finding does not justify the application of § 890 ZPO by analogy to claims for mandatory injunctive relief. It cannot be assumed in that regard that there exists any latent lacuna in the legislation which is capable of being filled by case-law. In providing, in § 888 ZPO, that a claim for the performance of an act may be enforced by the imposition of a penalty only where such performance is exclusively dependent on the will of the party required to perform it, the legislature was seeking to achieve a rational objective. A decision imposing a penalty under § 888 ZPO is not conditional on the existence of fault. Such a penalty constitutes an enforcement measure falling within the ambit of the civil law. By contrast, a penalty imposed under § 890 ZPO is in the nature of a criminal sanction. It is for the party to whom the obligation is owed, when instituting the proceedings, to have regard to the different enforcement possibilities. Where a claim for performance of an act is not enforceable by the imposition of a penalty, it is not the task of the court seised of the enforcement application to make that claim enforceable by treating it, by analogy, as if it were a claim to restrain a person from doing something. If enforcement of a claim for performance of an act cannot be ordered under § 888 ZPO, the only remedy available to the party to whom the obligation is owed is an award of damages pursuant to § 893 ZPO.

Note

It is not clear to what extent other systems regard the co-operation of third parties as a problem. For example, compare the English cases in the next section.

23.2.G.7 PROBLEMS WITH SUPERVISING LONG-TERM CONTRACTS

In English cases it used frequently to be said that it is not possible to order specific performance of an obligation which is to be performed over a period of time, as the court has no mechanism for supervising the performance. Thus in *Ryan v Mutual Tontine Westminster Chambers Association*[94] the court refused to order specific performance of a contract to provide portering services to an apartment. However, the cases have not been consistent; for example, contracts for building work have on occasion been enforced specifically if damages would not be an adequate remedy.[95]

In *Giles Co v Morris*,[96] Megarry J ordered the defendant to appoint a person to provide the services. The judge said:

One day, perhaps, the courts will look again at the so-called rule that contracts for personal services or involving the continuous performance of services will not be specifically enforced. Such a rule is plainly not absolute and without exception, nor do I think that it can be based on any narrow consideration such as difficulties of constant superintendence by the court. Mandatory injunctions are by no means unknown, and there is normally no question of the court having to send its officers to supervise the performance of the order of the court. Prohibitory injunctions are common, and again there is no direct supervision by the court. Performance of each type of injunction is normally secured by the realisation of the person enjoined that he is

---

[94] [1893] 1 Ch 116 (CA).
[95] See above, p 917.
[96] [1972] 1 WLR 307, 318 (ChD).

liable to be punished for contempt if evidence of his disobedience to the order is put before the court; and if the injunction is prohibitory, actual committal will usually so long as it continues, make disobedience impossible. If instead the order is for specific performance of a contract for personal services, a similar machinery of enforcement could be employed, again without there being any question of supervision by any officer of the court. The reasons why the court is reluctant to decree specific performance of a contract for personal services (and I would regard it as a strong reluctance rather than a rule) are, I think, more complex and more firmly bottomed on human nature. If a singer contracts to sing, there could be no doubt be proceedings for committal if, ordered to sing, the singer remained obstinately dumb. But if instead the singer sang flat, or sharp, or too fast, or too slowly, or too loudly, or too quietly, or resorted to a dozen of the manifestations of temperament traditionally associated with some singers, the threat of committal would reveal itself as a most unsatisfactory weapon: for who could say whether the imperfections of performance were natural or self-induced? To make an order with such possibilities of evasion would be vain; and so the order will not be made. However, not all contracts of personal service or for the continuous performance of services are as dependent as this on matters of opinion and judgment, nor do all such contracts involve the same degree of the daily impact of person upon person. In general, no doubt, the inconvenience and mischief of decreeing specific performance of most of such contracts will greatly outweigh the advantages, and specific performance will be refused. But I do not think that it should be assumed that as soon as any element of personal service or continuous services can be discerned in a contract the court will, without more, refuse specific performance. Of course, a requirement for the continuous performance of services has the disadvantage that repeated breaches may engender repeated applications to the court for enforcement. But so may many injunctions; and the prospects of repetition, although an important consideration, ought not to be allowed to negative a right. As is so often the case in equity, the matter is one of the balance of advantage and disadvantage in relation to the particular obligations in question: and the fact that the balance will usually lie on one side does not turn this probability into a rule. The present case, of course, is *a fortiori*, since the contract of which specific performance has been decreed requires not the performance of personal services or any continuous series of acts, but merely procuring the execution of an agreement which contains a provision for such services or acts.

House of Lords　　　　　　　　　　　　　　**23.29 (EN)**

Co-operative Insurance Society Ltd v Argyll Stores (Holdings) Ltd[97]

A tenant will not be ordered to 'keep open' a business.

Facts: The appellant defendants, Argyll Stores (Holdings) Ltd ('Argyll'), decided in May 1995 to close their Safeway supermarket in the Hillsborough Shopping Centre in Sheffield because it was losing money. This was a breach of a covenant in their lease, which contained in clause 4(19) a positive obligation to keep the premises open for retail trade during the usual hours of business. Argyll admitted the breach. The landlords, Cooperative Insurance Society Ltd ('CIS'), brought an action.

Held: The trial judge refused to order specific performance and the defendants consented to an order for damages to be assessed. The Court of Appeal [1996] Ch 286, reversing the trial judge, ordered that the covenant be specifically performed. It made a final injunction ordering Argyll to trade on the premises during the remainder of the term (which would expire on 3 August 2014) or until an earlier subletting or assignment. The Court of Appeal suspended its order for three months to allow time for Argyll to complete an assignment which by that

---

[97]　[1998] AC 1.

time had been agreed. After a short agreed extension, the lease was assigned with the landlord's consent. In fact, therefore, the injunction never took effect. The appeal to the House of Lords was substantially about costs, but the issue remained of great importance to landlords and tenants under other commercial leases.

Judgment: LORD HOFFMANN: My Lords,

1. The issue—

In 1955 Lord Goddard CJ said:

No authority has been quoted to show that an injunction will be granted enjoining a person to carry on a business, nor can I think that one ever would be, certainly not where the business is a losing concern: *Attorney-General v Colchester Corporation* [1955] 2 QB 207, 217.

In this case his prediction has been falsified … [His Lordship stated the facts as above.]

4. The settled practice

There is no dispute about the existence of the settled practice [of refusing to make an order to carry on a business] to which the judge referred …

But the practice has never, so far as I know, been examined by this House and it is open to CIS to say that it rests upon inadequate grounds or that it has been too inflexibly applied.

Specific performance is traditionally regarded in English law as an exceptional remedy, as opposed to the common law damages to which a successful plaintiff is entitled as of right. There may have been some element of later rationalisation of an untidier history, but by the 19th century it was orthodox doctrine that the power to decree specific performance was part of the discretionary jurisdiction of the Court of Chancery to do justice in cases in which the remedies available at common law were inadequate. This is the basis of the general principle that specific performance will not be ordered when damages are an adequate remedy. By contrast, in countries with legal systems based on civil law, such as France, Germany and Scotland, the plaintiff is prima facie entitled to specific performance. The cases in which he is confined to a claim for damages are regarded as the exceptions. In practice, however, there is less difference between common law and civilian systems than these general statements might lead one to suppose. The principles upon which English judges exercise the discretion to grant specific performance are reasonably well settled and depend upon a number of considerations, mostly of a practical nature, which are of very general application. I have made no investigation of civilian systems, but a priori I would expect that judges take much the same matters into account in deciding whether specific performance would be inappropriate in a particular case.

The practice of not ordering a defendant to carry on a business is not entirely dependent upon damages being an adequate remedy. In *DowtyBoulton Paul Ltd v Wolverhampton Corporation* [1971] 1 WLR 204, Sir John Pennycuick V-C refused to order the corporation to maintain an airfield as a going concern because: 'It is very well established that the court will not order specific performance of an obligation to carry on a business': see p 211. He added: 'It is unnecessary in the circumstances to discuss whether damages would be an adequate remedy to the company:' see p 212. Thus the reasons which underlie the established practice may justify a refusal of specific performance even when damages are not an adequate remedy.

The most frequent reason given in the cases for declining to order someone to carry on a business is that it would require constant supervision by the court. In *JC Williamson Ltd v Lukey and Mulholland* (1931) 45 CLR 282, 297–298, Dixon J said flatly: 'Specific performance is inapplicable when the continued supervision of the court is necessary in order to ensure the fulfilment of the contract.'

There has, I think, been some misunderstanding about what is meant by continued superintendence. It may at first sight suggest that the judge (or some other officer of the court) would literally have to supervise the execution of the order. In *CH Giles & Co Ltd v Morris* [1972] 1 WLR 307, 318 Megarry J said that 'difficulties of constant superintendence' were a 'narrow consideration' because:

> 'there is normally no question of the court having to send its officers to supervise the performance of the order ... Performance ... is normally secured by the realisation of the person enjoined that he is liable to be punished for contempt if evidence of his disobedience to the order is put before the court ...'

This is, of course, true but does not really meet the point. The judges who have said that the need for constant supervision was an objection to such orders were no doubt well aware that supervision would in practice take the form of rulings by the court, on applications made by the parties, as to whether there had been a breach of the order. It is the possibility of the court having to give an indefinite series of such rulings in order to ensure the execution of the order which has been regarded as undesirable.

Why should this be so? A principal reason is that, as Megarry J pointed out in the passage to which I have referred, the only means available to the court to enforce its order is the quasi-criminal procedure of punishment for contempt. This is a powerful weapon; so powerful, in fact, as often to be unsuitable as an instrument for adjudicating upon the disputes which may arise over whether a business is being run in accordance with the terms of the court's order. The heavy-handed nature of the enforcement mechanism is a consideration which may go to the exercise of the court's discretion in other cases as well, but its use to compel the running of a business is perhaps the paradigm case of its disadvantages and it is in this context that I shall discuss them.

The prospect of committal or even a fine, with the damage to commercial reputation which will be caused by a finding of contempt of court, is likely to have at least two undesirable consequences. First, the defendant, who ex hypothesi did not think that it was in his economic interest to run the business at all, now has to make decisions under a sword of Damocles which may descend if the way the business is run does not conform to the terms of the order. This is, as one might say, no way to run a business. In this case the Court of Appeal made light of the point because it assumed that, once the defendant had been ordered to run the business, self-interest and compliance with the order would thereafter go hand in hand. But, as I shall explain, this is not necessarily true.

Secondly, the seriousness of a finding of contempt for the defendant means that any application to enforce the order is likely to be a heavy and expensive piece of litigation. The possibility of repeated applications over a period of time means that, in comparison with a once-and-for-all inquiry as to damages, the enforcement of the remedy is likely to be expensive in terms of cost to the parties and the resources of the judicial system.

This is a convenient point at which to distinguish between orders which require a defendant to carry on an activity, such as running a business over or more or less extended period of time, and orders which require him to achieve a result. The possibility of repeated applications for rulings on compliance with the order which arises in the former case does not exist to anything like the same extent in the latter. Even if the achievement of the result is a complicated matter which will take some time, the court, if called upon to rule, only has to examine the finished work and say whether it complies with the order ...

This distinction between orders to carry on activities and orders to achieve results explains why the courts have in appropriate circumstances ordered specific performance of building contracts and repairing covenants: see *Wolverhampton Corporation v Emmons*

[1901] 1 KB 515 (building contract) and *Jeune v Queens Cross Properties Ltd* [1974] Ch 97 (repairing covenant). It by no means follows, however, that even obligations to achieve a result will always be enforced by specific performance. There may be other objections, to some of which I now turn.

One such objection, which applies to orders to achieve a result and *a fortiori* to orders to carry on an activity, is imprecision in the terms of the order. If the terms of the court's order, reflecting the terms of the obligation, cannot be precisely drawn, the possibility of wasteful litigation over compliance is increased. So is the oppression caused by the defendant having to do things under threat of proceedings for contempt. The less precise the order, the fewer the signposts to the forensic minefield which he has to traverse. The fact that the terms of a contractual obligation are sufficiently definite to escape being void for uncertainty, or to found a claim for damages, or to permit compliance to be made a condition of relief against forfeiture, does not necessarily mean that they will be sufficiently precise to be capable of being specifically enforced. So in *Wolverhampton Corporation v Emmons,* Romer LJ said, at p 525, that the first condition for specific enforcement of a building contract was that 'the particulars of the work are so far definitely ascertained that the court can sufficiently see what is the exact nature of the work of which it is asked to order the performance' ...

Precision is of course a question of degree and the courts have shown themselves willing to cope with a certain degree of imprecision in cases of orders requiring the achievement of a result in which the plaintiffs' merits appeared strong; like all the reasons which I have been discussing, it is, taken alone, merely a discretionary matter to be taken into account: see Spry, *Equitable Remedies*, 4th edn (1990), p 112. It is, however, a very important one ...

There is a further objection to an order requiring the defendant to carry on a business, which was emphasised by Millett LJ in the Court of Appeal. This is that it may cause injustice by allowing the plaintiff to enrich himself at the defendant's expense. The loss which the defendant may suffer through having to comply with the order (for example, by running a business at a loss for an indefinite period) may be far greater than the plaintiff would suffer from the contract being broken ...

It is true that the defendant has, by his own breach of contract, put himself in such an unfortunate position. But the purpose of the law of contract is not to punish wrongdoing but to satisfy the expectations of the party entitled to performance. A remedy which enables him to secure, in money terms, more than the performance due to him is unjust. From a wider perspective, it cannot be in the public interest for the courts to require someone to carry on business at a loss if there is any plausible alternative by which the other party can be given compensation. It is not only a waste of resources but yokes the parties together in a continuing hostile relationship. The order for specific performance prolongs the battle. If the defendant is ordered to run a business, its conduct becomes the subject of a flow of complaints, solicitors' letters and affidavits. This is wasteful for both parties and the legal system. An award of damages, on the other hand, brings the litigation to an end. The defendant pays damages, the forensic link between them is severed, they go their separate ways and the wounds of conflict can heal.

The cumulative effect of these various reasons, none of which would necessarily be sufficient on its own, seems to me to show that the settled practice is based upon sound sense. Of course the grant or refusal of specific performance remains a matter for the judge's discretion. There are no binding rules, but this does not mean that there cannot be settled principles, founded upon practical considerations of the kind which I have discussed, which do not have to be re-examined in every case, but which the courts will apply in all but exceptional circumstances ...

6. Conclusion: I think that no criticism can be made of the way in which Judge Maddocks exercised his discretion. All the reasons which he gave were proper matters for him to take into account. In my view the Court of Appeal should not have interfered and I would allow the appeal and restore the order which he made.

Appeal allowed

> *Note*
>
> Compare this to German law, in which the requirement of certainty of performance relates in the first instance to the creditor's application seeking enforcement. Thus, the court will refuse enforcement under §§ 887, 888, 890 ZPO if the application is not sufficiently specific. However, the question of whether this application is sufficiently specific or not only arises when specific performance has been awarded in the first place. This is so because the claimant must already ask for a specific remedy at the time of bringing an action to court. There are many cases where he or she has to decide between seeking either specific performance or damages. The lawsuit has to state explicitly what the claimant demands, and the judgment is rendered accordingly.

23.2.G.8 HARDSHIP AND OTHER FACTORS

Zivilprozessordnung (ZPO) **23.30 (DE)**

§ 765a: Protection from execution

(1) Upon a corresponding petition being filed by the debtor, the court responsible for execution may reverse a measure of compulsory enforcement in its entirety or in part, may prohibit it, or may temporarily stay such measure if, upon comprehensively assessing the creditor's justified interest in protection, the court finds that the measure entails a hardship that due to very special circumstances is immoral (contra bonos mores). ... Should the measure concern an animal, the execution court is to consider, in weighing the matter, the responsibility that the person has for the animal.

> *Notes*
>
> (1) § 765a ZPO applies to all forms of execution. In practice, however, it has been most frequently invoked where eviction under a lease agreement is sought.
>
> (2) It is assumed that, apart from in the most drastic and exceptional circumstances, the creditor's interest in having the judgment enforced should prevail. Mere inconvenience or purely financial hardship on the part of the debtor will not be sufficient.
>
> (3) In every case, even where the debtor claims that their life or health is at risk, the court must weigh up the interests on both sides. The Federal Constitutional Court has held on a number of occasions that, having regard to the right to life of the debtor (Article 2(2)(1) GG), lower courts must take into account suicide threats and the risks to old people from their infirmity where execution is sought.[98]

---

[98] BVerfG 3 October 1979, BVerfGE 52, 214, NJW 1979, 2607; BVerfG 21 September 1991, BVerfGE 84, 345, NJW 1991, 3207.

We have already noted above[99] that, as regards compensation in German law, there is a presumption that this will be *in natura* (§ 249 BGB) and that such compensation *qua* replacement can be viewed as the functional equivalent of enforcement in other systems. Two exceptions are made to this presumption.

BGB **23.31 (DE)**

§ 251: Damages in money without the specification of a period of time
(1) To the extent that restoration is not possible or is not sufficient to compensate the obligee, the person liable in damages must compensate the obligee in money.
(2) The person liable in damages may compensate the obligee in money if restoration is only possible with disproportionate expenses. ...

OLG Hamm, 11 December 1946[100] **23.32 (DE)**

Shortage of horses

In considering whether restitution in kind would be a disproportionate burden upon the debtor a court should have regard to the fact that money damages would not adequately compensate the creditor.

Facts: Towards the end of March 1945 the third company of the Becker combat group was located in G. On 24 March 1945 it needed horses for the purposes of a sortie which it was to make in the direction of Wesel. At the instigation of the company commander and the sergeant-major, the witness Sp, who at that time was a non-commissioned officer in that unit of the German armed forces, procured from the plaintiff a dark chestnut mare belonging to the latter, which was harnessed to a wagon belonging to the company. On 26 March 1945 that mare was returned, but on 27 March it was once again requisitioned by the company, since the company was being forced to retreat by virtue of the military situation. On 27 March the mare was again collected from the plaintiff by the witness Sp, and was harnessed, along with a horse belonging to the witness Th, to an ammunition cart belonging to the company.

On 30 March 1945 the witness Sp appeared, together with a severely lame mare, whose hind legs were not shod, at the defendant's farm. Sp requested the latter to exchange that horse for a horse belonging to the defendant. The defendant stated that he was willing to do so. The defendant's horse was harnessed up, and Sp departed with the wagon, leaving the lame mare at the defendant's farm.

Neither the plaintiff nor the defendant recovered the horses which they had made available for use by the army. In the autumn of 1945, the horse which Sp had left at the defendant's farm died from meningitis at the defendant's sister's farm in Münster-St Mauritz, whither the defendant had arranged for it to be taken.

The plaintiff pleaded in the proceedings as follows: in May 1945 he had made a total of three visits to the defendant's farm. Initially, after the plaintiff had described his horse to the defendant, the latter had stated that no such horse had ever been in his possession. Later on, the defendant had admitted that such a horse had been left by the army at his farm. However, that horse had been taken away again by a group of Poles. The defendant had produced in that regard a certificate signed by one of the Poles. The defendant refused to allow the plaintiff access to his stables. The plaintiff had therefore been forced to desist from making any further enquiries regarding the horse. It was not until January 1946 that he learned from a conversation with Sp that his horse had in fact come to the defendant's farm.

Since, in his view, it appeared certain that the mare would have survived if the defendant had handed her over to him, the plaintiff claimed that the defendant was liable to compensate him for all the loss which he had suffered. According to the plaintiff, the horse in question had been a particularly

---

[99] See above, p 908.
[100] MDR 1947, 100.

945

valuable, five- to six-year-old breeding mare of a special class, the standard price for which was 2,600 Reichsmarks. The plaintiff claimed that the defendant was therefore liable to supply him with a horse of equivalent value, belonging to that special class, which should, as far as possible, be capable of use for breeding purposes. He also claimed that the defendant could render compensation in the form of the supply of a horse in that condition, since the defendant kept on his farm three load-bearing horses and a one-and-a-half-year-old foal. The plaintiff claimed to have suffered further loss by reason of the fact that he had had to dispense with the horse's services in the context of the work to be carried out in the sowing season and at harvest time. In addition, he had invariably possessed three working horses on his farm, which was significantly larger than that of the defendant. Despite the most strenuous efforts, he had been unable to procure a replacement horse. He had had to spend the sum of 145 Reichsmarks just for the use of a tractor for mowing purposes—a course of action to which he had had to resort as a result of the loss of the horse.

The plaintiff therefore claimed *inter alia* that the defendant should be ordered to supply to him a working horse, if possible a mare, of equivalent value to the heavy dark chestnut mare, aged between five and six years, belonging to the plaintiff, which had died in the defendant's custody in autumn 1945 (an animal of a special class for which the standard price was 2,600 Reichsmarks).

The defendant denied the plaintiff's account of the facts and contended that the claim should be dismissed.

Held: The Landgericht (Regional Court) found in favour of the plaintiff and made an order against the defendant in the terms sought. The Oberlandesgericht (Higher Regional Court) dismissed as unfounded the defendant's appeal against that judgment. In the grounds for its decision, it stated that the horse which had died was the plaintiff's horse and that the plaintiff had remained the owner of it. It further stated that the defendant was liable to compensate the plaintiff pursuant to §§ 990 and 826 BGB. The issue of the form which such compensation should take was dealt with as follows in the grounds of the judgment.

Judgment: § 249 BGB provides that a person liable to provide compensation must in principle be required to restore the situation to that which would have existed if the circumstance giving rise to such liability had not arisen. Thus the legislation lays down the principle that compensation is to take the form of restitution in kind, and it is only as an alternative measure, provided for by § 251 BGB, that it may be permitted, subject to the fulfilment of special conditions, to take the form of pecuniary damages. In accordance with the principle laid down by § 249 BGB, the plaintiff is therefore entitled to claim from the defendant restitution in kind, provided that that is at all feasible in the present case. However, restitution in kind does not mean that the situation must literally be restored to that which previously existed; it suffices for that situation to be restored in economic terms. Even though the horse does not constitute something which is capable of being replaced by exactly the same thing, nevertheless, it is not inconceivable that, where such a thing has been lost, restitution in kind, in the form of the provision of something of equivalent value, may be an appropriate remedy. In the present case, that must *a fortiori* be the position, since the defendant is himself a farmer and the owner of horses. He undeniably possesses four horses, whereas the plaintiff, whose farm is at least as large as that of the defendant, currently has only two horses at his disposal. If, however, the defendant is liable to furnish compensation, the means of discharging his liability must extend to cover the things which he has on his own farm. That must *a fortiori* be the position as matters currently stand, since in the present circumstances the payment of a sum of money cannot satisfy the plaintiff's entitlement. The defendant cannot rely on the fact that delivery of the horse would involve him in disproportionate expense. According to the tenor of § 251(2) BGB, regard may be had to the interests of a debtor only where that does not prejudice the legitimate interests of the creditor. It follows that § 251(2) BGB cannot be applicable where the needs of the debtor are opposed by corresponding needs of the creditor.

The approach taken by the legislation is in principle that the debtor is obliged to provide compensation for the totality of the loss in the form of restitution in kind. He is only entitled to provide compensation in the form of money where restitution which does not prejudice the interests of the creditor is only possible at disproportionate expense. There is no need to consider the question whether an order for restitution in kind may also be made where the debtor does not possess a thing capable of being supplied as a replacement; in the present case, the defendant possesses horses and can supply the plaintiff with one of those horses as a replacement for the latter's deceased mare. It may well be that the defendant normally keeps, and needs, four horses on his farm. However, since the plaintiff only has two horses on his farm at present, and that farm is at least as big as that of the defendant, it is entirely appropriate to require the defendant to compensate the plaintiff by providing the latter with one of his own horses. In so far as he cannot procure another horse elsewhere, he will have to make do with three horses; moreover, the Senate is convinced in that regard that, if he makes sufficient effort, he will be in a position to do so. The defendant's objection that it will not be possible for him to comply with the judgment given is unfounded; the judgment is to be enforced immediately by the removal of one of the defendant's horses.

Notes

(1) The substantive action here was clearly in property and tort, but the remedial question was decided under § 251(2) BGB, which is applicable to contractual, as well as delictual liability.

(2) The decision of the claimant to opt for compensation *in natura* was almost certainly motivated by the inadequacy of almost any damages award, given the great scarcity of livestock in the immediate post-war period.[101]

(3) We have already noted above that, as regards damages in German law, the general rule is that the creditor is entitled to compensation *in natura* (§ 249(1) BGB). In cases of injury to a person or damage to a thing, an important exception applies and the creditor may demand damages instead of compensation *in natura* (§ 249(2) BGB). Only if compensation *in natura* is not possible at all, § 251(1) BGB applies. In this case, the creditor is exclusively entitled to damages. Yet another situation is provided for in § 251(2) BGB: if compensation *in natura* is possible, but only with disproportionate expenses, the debtor may choose to compensate the creditor with money. The ratio of § 251(2) BGB is to protect the debtor.

Court of Appeal   **23.33 (EN)**

Patel v Ali[102]

Specific performance of a contract may be refused where, as the result of events since the contract was made and not attributable to the plaintiff, the order would cause hardship to the defendant.

Facts: The vendor of a house had, since the sale (the performance of which had been much delayed for reasons not the fault of either party), become disabled and heavily dependent on her neighbours for help. If the vendor

---

101 See Zweigert and Kötz (n 46 above) 472.
102 [1984] Ch 283.

was forced to relinquish the house she would have to leave the neighbourhood as she could no longer afford to buy another property in the area (prices had risen), so she would lose her neighbours' support.

Held: Specific performance would not be granted against her.

Judgment: GOULDING J: … It is not in dispute that, like other equitable relief, the specific performance of contracts is a discretionary remedy; but, in the ordinary case of a sale of land or buildings, the court normally grants it as of course and withholds it only on proof of special facts. The textbooks and reported decisions have long recognised hardship as one ground on which, in a proper case, a purchaser or vendor may be refused specific performance and be left to his right to damages for breach of contract at law. The difficulty is to determine within what limits hardship to a defendant can properly be said to justify this exercise of judicial discretion. There is no doubt that, in the majority of cases, the hardship which moves the court to refuse specific performance is either a hardship existing at the date of the contract or a hardship due in some way to the plaintiff. In the present case, neither of those conditions being satisfied, the plaintiffs rely strongly on that principle or practice, which is stated in varying terms in all the well-known textbooks. It is sufficient for me to cite a passage from *Fry on Specific Performance*, 6th ed. (1921), p 199:

'It is a well-established doctrine that the court will not enforce the specific performance of a contract, the result of which would be to impose great hardship on either of the parties to it; and this although the party seeking specific performance may be free from the least impropriety of conduct. The question of the hardship of a contract is generally to be judged of at the time at which it is entered into: if it be then fair and just and not productive of hardship, it will be immaterial that it may, by the force of subsequent circumstances or change of events, have become less beneficial to one party, except where these subsequent events have been in some way due to the party who seeks the performance of the contract. For whatever contingencies may attach to a contract, or be involved in the performance of either part, have been taken upon themselves by the parties to it. It has been determined that the reasonableness of a contract is to be judged of at the time it is entered into, and not by the light of subsequent events, and we have already seen that the same principle applies in considering the fairness of a contract.'

However, the principle so stated cannot be erected into a fixed limitation of the court's equitable jurisdiction. It is recognised, both by Fry LJ in his book and in the argument of Mr Simpkiss for the plaintiffs in the present action, that the court has sometimes refused specific performance because of a change of circumstances supervening after the making of the contract and not in any way attributable to the plaintiff. One such case is *City of London v Nash* (1747) 1 Ves Sen 11, 12 …

The important and true principle, in my view, is that only in extraordinary and persuasive circumstances can hardship supply an excuse for resisting performance of a contract for the sale of immovable property. A person of full capacity who sells or buys a house takes the risk of hardship to himself and his dependants, whether arising from existing facts or unexpectedly supervening in the interval before completion. This is where, to my mind, great importance attaches to the immense delay in the present case, not attributable to the defendant's conduct. Even after issue of the writ, she could not complete, if she had wanted to, without the concurrence of the absent Mr Ahmed.

Thus, in a sense, she can say she is being asked to do what she never bargained for, namely to complete the sale after more than four years, after all the unforeseeable changes that such a period entails. I think that in this way she can fairly assert that specific performance would inflict upon her 'a hardship amounting to injustice' to use the phrase employed by James LJ, in a different but comparable context, in *Tamplin v James* (1880) 15 ChD 215, 221. Equitable relief may, in my view, be refused because of an unforeseen change of circumstances not amounting to legal frustration, just as it may on the ground of mistake insufficient to avoid a contract at law.

In the end, I am satisfied that it is within the court's discretion to accede to the defendant's prayer if satisfied that it is just to do so. And, on the whole, looking at the position of both sides after the long unpredictable delay for which neither seeks to make the other responsible, I am of opinion that it *is* just to leave the plaintiffs to their remedy in damages if that can indeed be effective.

I have come to this conclusion without taking into account the welfare of the defendant's children except as involved in her own personal hardship. I much doubt whether, even in the present atmosphere of opinion on which Mr Briggs dwelt in his address, the interests of the children are material in their own right …

> *Note*
>
> It seems likely that on these facts a German court would also refuse to enforce performance, but on the basis that to do so would be disproportionate to the creditors' interest in performance, § 275(2) BGB.

23.3 MONETARY OBLIGATIONS

In all the systems, a sum of money—typically the price—due under the contract may be recovered once it is due. Thus if the plaintiff has delivered goods to the defendant or performed services for him and has not been paid the agreed price by the time she should have received it, she may simply sue for the sum due. The mechanisms for enforcement differ, but this question is procedural and outside the scope of this book.

Where the systems seem to differ is over the case in which the party who is ultimately to pay indicates, before he has received the other's performance and before the price is due, that he no longer wishes to receive the performance.

In the continental systems, it appears that the creditor may normally require the debtor to pay; whether he wishes to receive the services or take the goods in exchange is a matter for the debtor. This follows from the principle that the creditor can normally require performance. For example, under French law, the creditor of a sum of money may require the performance of the payment even when it is entitled to damages, though the payment due may be higher.[103] In English law, however, we have seen that the creditor is not normally able to make an unwilling debtor perform an obligation. Is it different if the obligation is simply one to pay money? The question will not arise if the defendant has to do something else before the creditor can 'earn' the price. For example, if the creditor is to paint the debtor's house, with payment due on completion, and the defendant refuses the creditor admission to the house, the creditor cannot earn the price without gaining

---

[103] Cass civ (1) 9 July 2003, no. 00-22202, unpublished: 'the creditor of a contractual obligation to pay a sum of money which remained unperformed is always entitled to prefer the payment of the price to damages or to the termination of the contract'.

admission—and if, as in English law, he will normally not get an order that the creditor must admit him, he will in practice be unable to sue for the price. Instead he will have to sue for damages,[104] and he will be expected to take reasonable steps to mitigate his loss, for example by finding other work.

What if the creditor is able to perform without the debtor having to co-operate further?

House of Lords   **23.34 (EN)**

White & Carter (Councils) Ltd v McGregor[105]

Despite a repudiation of the contract by one party, the other may continue performance of his obligations under the contract if he is able to do so without the first party's co-operation and then claim the payment due on completion.

Facts: The plaintiffs made bins for litter, which they supplied free of charge to local authorities; they made their money by placing advertisements on the bins. The defendants' sales manager entered into a contract for the defendant's business to be advertised in this way for three years. The same day the defendant repudiated the agreement, but the plaintiffs displayed the advertisements nonetheless and then claimed the price, which, under an 'acceleration clause' stating that in the event of delay in payment the whole sum would become due immediately, was then due.

Held: The lower court held that the plaintiffs could not recover the full price, but the House of Lords (by a majority, LORDS REID, HODSON and TUCKER) reversed this decision.

Judgment: LORD REID: ... The general rule cannot be in doubt. It was settled in Scotland at least as early as 1848 and it has been authoritatively stated time and again in both Scotland and England. If one party to a contract repudiates it in the sense of making it clear to the other party that he refuses or will refuse to carry out his part of the contract, the other party, the innocent party, has an option. He may accept that repudiation and sue for damages for breach of contract, whether or not the time for performance has come; or he may if he chooses disregard or refuse to accept it and then the contract remains in full effect ...

I need not refer to the numerous authorities. They are not disputed by the respondent but he points out that in all of them the party who refused to accept the repudiation had no active duties under the contract. The innocent party's option is generally said to be to *wait* until the date of performance and then to claim damages estimated as at that date. There is no case in which it is said that he may, in face of the repudiation, go on and incur useless expense in performing the contract and then claim the contract price. The option, it is argued, is merely as to the date as at which damages are to be assessed. Developing this argument, the respondent points out that in most cases the innocent party cannot complete the contract himself without the other party doing, allowing or accepting something, and that it is purely fortuitous that the appellants can do so in this case. In most cases by refusing co-operation the party in breach can compel the innocent party to restrict his claim to damages. Then it was said that, even where the innocent party can complete the contract without such co-operation, it is against the public interest that he should be allowed to do so. An example was developed in argument. A company might engage an expert to go abroad and prepare an elaborate report and then repudiate the

---

[104] As we will see in more detail below, ch 26.
[105] [1962] AC 413.

950

contract before anything was done. To allow such an expert then to waste thousands of pounds in preparing the report cannot be right if a much smaller sum of damages would give him full compensation for his loss. It would merely enable the expert to extort a settlement giving him far more than reasonable compensation.

The respondent founds on the decision of the First Division in *Langford Co Ltd v Dutch*. There an advertising contractor agreed to exhibit a film for a year. Four days after this agreement was made the advertiser repudiated it but, as in the present case, the contractor refused to accept the repudiation and proceeded to exhibit the film and sue for the contract price. The Sheriff-Substitute dismissed the action as irrelevant and his decision was affirmed on appeal. In the course of a short opinion Lord President Cooper said:

> 'The pursuers could not force the defender to accept a year's advertisement which she did not want, though they could of course claim damages for her breach of contract. On the averments the only reasonable and proper course, which the pursuers should have adopted, would have been to treat the defender as having repudiated the contract and as being on that account liable in damages, the measure of which we are, of course, not in a position to discuss.'

The Lord President cited no authority and I am in doubt as to what principle he had in mind ...

We must now decide whether that case was rightly decided. In my judgment it was not. It could only be supported on one or other of two grounds. It might be said that, because in most cases the circumstances are such that an innocent party is unable to complete the contract and earn the contract price without the assent or co-operation of the other party, therefore in cases where he can do so he should not be allowed to do so. I can see no justification for that. The other ground would be that there is some general equitable principle or element of public policy which requires this limitation of the contractual rights of the innocent party. It may well be that, if it can be shown that a person has no legitimate interest, financial or otherwise, in performing the contract rather than claiming damages, he ought not to be allowed to saddle the other party with an additional burden with no benefit to himself. If a party has no interest to enforce a stipulation, he cannot in general enforce it: so it might be said that, if a party has no interest to insist on a particular remedy, he ought not to be allowed to insist on it. And, just as a party is not allowed to enforce a penalty, so he ought not to be allowed to penalise the other party by taking one course when another is equally advantageous to him. If I may revert to the example which I gave of a company engaging an expert to prepare an elaborate report and then repudiating before anything was done, it might be that the company could show that the expert had no substantial or legitimate interest in carrying out the work rather than accepting damages: I would think that the de minimis principle would apply in determining whether his interest was substantial, and that he might have a legitimate interest other than an immediate financial interest. But if the expert had no such interest then that might be regarded as a proper case for the exercise of the general equitable jurisdiction of the court. But that is not this case. Here the respondent did not set out to prove that the appellants had no legitimate interest in completing the contract and claiming the contract price rather than claiming damages; there is nothing in the findings of fact to support such a case, and it seems improbable that any such case could have been proved. It is, in my judgment, impossible to say that the appellants should be deprived of their right to claim the contract price merely because the benefit to them, as against claiming damages and re-letting their advertising space, might be small in comparison with the loss to the respondent: that is the most that could be said in favour of the respondent. Parliament has on many occasions relieved parties from certain kinds of improvident or oppressive contracts, but the common law can only do that in very limited circumstances. Accordingly, I am unable to avoid the conclusion that this appeal must be allowed and the case remitted so that decree can be pronounced as craved in the initial writ.

LORD MORTON OF HENRYTON [dissenting]: ... It is well established that repudiation by one party does not put an end to a contract. The other party can say 'I hold you to your contract, which still remains in force.' What then is his remedy if the repudiating party persists in his repudiation and refuses to carry out his part of the contract? The contract has been broken. The innocent party is entitled to be compensated by damages for any loss which he has suffered by reason of the breach, and in a limited class of cases the court will decree specific implement [the Scottish equivalent of specific performance]. The law of Scotland provides no other remedy for a breach of contract and there is no reported case which decides that the innocent party may act as the appellants have acted.

The present case is one in which specific implement could not be decreed, since the only obligation of the respondent under the contract was to pay a sum of money for services to be rendered by the appellants. Yet the appellants are claiming a kind of inverted specific implement of the contract. They first insist on performing their part of the contract, against the will of the other party, and then claim that he must perform his part and of pay the contract price for unwanted services. In my opinion, my Lords, the appellants' only remedy was damages, and they were bound to take steps to minimise their loss, according to a well-established rule of law. Far from doing this, having incurred no expense at the date of the repudiation, they made no attempt to procure another advertiser, but deliberately went on to incur expense and perform unwanted services with the intention of creating a money debt which did not exist at the date of the repudiation ...

LORD HODSON: ... It is settled as a fundamental rule of the law of contract that repudiation by one of the parties to a contract does not discharge it ...

It follows that if, as here, there was no acceptance, the contract remains alive for the benefit of both parties and the party who has repudiated it can change his mind but it does not follow that the party at the receiving end of the proffered repudiation is bound to accept it before the time for performance and is left to his remedy in damages for breach ...

The true position is that the contract survives and does so not only where specific implement is available ...

[LORD TUCKER agreed with the reasoning of LORD HODSON.]

Notes

(1) This case arose in Scotland, but this is an area of law in which Scotish and English law were treated by the House of Lords as being the same.

(2) The minority held that the repudiation by the defendant was a breach of contract which gave the plaintiff a right to damages but also a duty to take reasonable steps to mitigate the loss—presumably by finding other clients to take the advertising space.[106] The plaintiff could not recover more than he would have had he so mitigated.

(3) The majority decision was much criticised in England as being wasteful. If the plaintiffs had been claiming damages, they would have been under a duty to mitigate

---

[106] See further below, pp 1081 ff.

their loss by seeking other advertisers to take the space.[107] It seems wrong that they should be able to evade this requirement by performing and then suing for the price. In effect, this amounts to giving specific performance of a type of contract which, in English law, would not normally be specifically enforceable.

(4) Lord Reid qualifies his decision by saying that the plaintiff must have a substantial and legitimate interest in claiming damages. Technically this was an *obiter dictum*, and neither of the other members of the majority mentioned it; but subsequent cases have adopted it.[108] In the *Clea Shipping* case, time-charterers of a ship stated that they had no use for her services, but the owners ignored this repudiation and kept the vessel anchored off Piraeus with a full crew and ready to sail as soon as the charterers gave an order.[109] The charterers refused to pay the hire. The owner's action to recover it was rejected by Lloyd J, who held that the owners should have terminated the contract and sought alternative employment for the ship. But subsequent cases have shown that the courts are reluctant to fetter the innocent party's choice. In *The Aquafaith* case, after a full review of the authorities referred to in the last paragraph, Cooke J., concluded that:[110]

> [t]he effect of the authorities is that an innocent party will have no legitimate interest in maintaining the contract if damages are an adequate remedy and his insistence on maintaining the contract can be described as "wholly unreasonable", "extremely unreasonable" or, perhaps, in my words, "perverse".

This seems to be equivalent to saying that the innocent party may continue performance unless to do so would be an abuse of right.

(5) In any event, the principle of *White & Carter* applies only when the plaintiff can perform without the defendant's co-operation. If he cannot and the defendant refuses to co-operate, the outcome will depend on whether the plaintiff can get an order of specific performance. If this is not available (as it will usually not be, except in cases of sales of land: see above), the plaintiff will in practice have no choice but to terminate and sue for damages—in which case he will be under a duty to mitigate his losses. The courts have taken a narrow view of when a contract may be performed without the other party's cooperation; thus in the *Clea Shipping* case Lloyd J suggested, without deciding, that the owners of a ship cannot perform a time-charter without the co-operation of the charterer.[111]

---

[107] ibid.

[108] See *Attica Sea Carriers Corp v Ferrostaal Poseidon Bulk Reederei GmbH (The Puerto Buitrago)* [1976] 1 Lloyd's Rep 250 (CA); *The Odenfeld* [1978] 2 Lloyd's Rep 357, 374 (QBD); *Clea Shipping Corp v Bulk Oil International Ltd (The Alaskan Trader)* [1984] 1 All ER 129 (QBD); *MSC Mediterranean Shipping Co SA v Cottonex Anstalt* [2016] EWCA Civ 789; and *Cavendish Square Holding BV v Makdessi* and *ParkingEye Ltd v Beavis* [2015] UKSC 67, [2016] AC 1172 at [29].

[109] *Clea Shipping Corp v Bulk Oil International Ltd (The Alaskan Trader)* [1984] 1 All ER 129.

[110] *Isabella Shipowner SA v Shagang Shipping Co Ltd (The Aquafaith)* [2012] EWHC 1077 (Comm), [2012] 2 Lloyd's Rep 61 at [44]. The judge went on to hold that that the exception did not apply on the facts of the case, where the owner would be left 'in a difficult market where a substitute time charter was impossible, and trading on the spot market very difficult' (at [56]).

[111] ibid.

(6) English law is not wholly consistent on this point. We have seen that normally a contract for the sale of goods is not specifically enforceable against the seller. By reason of the principle of mutuality, the seller cannot get an order of specific performance against the buyer. However, the Sale of Goods Act 1979 (SGA 1979), section 49(1) provides:

> Where, under a contract of sale, the property in the goods has passed to the buyer and he wrongfully neglects or refuses to pay for the goods according to the terms of the contract, the seller may maintain an action against him for the price of the goods.

The property in the goods may pass to the buyer before they have been delivered: Sale of Goods Act 1979, section 18, rule 1. This means that the seller may sue for the price even though the buyer has not yet received the goods and does not want them. The rule is criticised by English writers.[112]

(7) Continental European legal systems do not at first sight seem to have equivalent restrictions upon claims for payment. However, there are a number of situations in which the same practical result, that the aggrieved party cannot carry on regardless of the other's desires, is reached by specific provisions. Thus in German law, in a *Werkvertrag* the customer is entitled to cancel the contract on payment of the agreed payment less the expenses saved by the other party (§ 648 BGB). In a *Dienstvertrag*, however, § 615 BGB provides that an employer who does not let the employee perform his contractual obligations still has to pay the agreed sum, even though the employee did not actually perform and is not obliged to perform anymore. More generally, § 314 BGB allows a party to terminate a contract requiring recurring performance 'for an important reason', but will then have to compensate the other party for any loss.

BGB **23.35 (DE)**

§ 314: Termination, for good cause, of contracts for the performance of a recurring obligation

(1) Either party may terminate a contract for the performance of a recurring obligation on notice with immediate effect if there is good cause for doing so. There is good cause if, having regard to all the circumstances of the specific case and balancing the interests of both parties, the terminating party cannot reasonably be expected to continue the contractual relationship until the agreed termination date or until the end of a notice period.

(2) If the good cause consists in the infringement of a duty under the contract, the contract may be terminated on notice only after a specified period for remedial action has expired or notice of default has been given to no avail. § 323(2) applies mutatis mutandis.

(3) The person entitled may terminate only if he gives notice of termination within a reasonable period after becoming aware of the cause for termination.

(4) The right to claim damages is not precluded by the termination.

---

[112] eg C Twigg-Flesner, R Canavan and H McQueen, *Atiyah and Adams' Sale of Goods* (13th edn, Harlow: Pearson, 2016) 420–22.

In French law the employer can cancel a *contrat d'entreprise* unilaterally upon payment of damages to the other party (Article 1794 Cciv).[113]

Principles of European Contract Law **23.36 (INT)**

Article 9:101: Monetary Obligations

(1) The creditor is entitled to recover money which is due.

(2) Where the creditor has not yet performed its obligation and it is clear that the debtor will be unwilling to receive performance, the creditor may nonetheless proceed with its performance and may recover any sum due under the contract unless

> (a) it could have made a reasonable cover transaction without significant effort or expense; or
>
> (b) performance would be unreasonable in the circumstances.

Note

Article 9:101(2)(a) was designed to reflect English law, but in fact seems to be more restrictive than the more recent English cases. It has been argued persuasively that English courts should simply say that a party faced with a wrongful repudiation should have a duty to mitigate their losses, even if that requires electing to terminate the contract.[114]

FURTHER READING

Cohen, N, and McKendrick, E (eds), *Comparative Remedies for Breach of Contract* (Oxford: Hart Publishing, 2005).

Kleinschmidt, J, 'Right to Performance' in N Jansen and R Zimmermann (eds), *Commentaries on European Contract Laws* (Oxford University Press, 2018) 1185–1275.

Kleinschmidt, J, 'Specific Performance' in J Basedow, K Hopt and R Zimmermann (eds), *Max Planck Encyclopedia of European Private Law* (Oxford University Press, 2012) 1581–85.

Kötz, H, *European Contract Law* (2nd edn, Oxford University Press, 2017) 197–214.

Laithier, YM, '*Exécution Forcée en Nature*' in J Cartwright and S Whittaker (eds), *The Code Napoléon Rewritten: French Contract Law after the 2016 Reforms* (Oxford: Hart Publishing, 2017) 257–89.

Pérès, C, 'Mandatory and Non-mandatory Rules in the New Law of Contract' in J Cartwright, and S Whittaker (eds), *The Code Napoléon Rewritten: French Contract Law after the 2016 Reforms* (Oxford: Hart Publishing, 2017) 167–86.

Rowan, S, *Remedies for Breach of Contract* (Oxford University Press, 2012).

Rowan, S, 'Termination for Contractual Non-performance' in J Cartwright and S Whittaker (eds), *The Code Napoléon Rewritten: French Contract Law after the 2016 Reforms* (Oxford: Hart Publishing, 2017) 317–35.

Treitel, G, *Remedies for Breach of Contract* (Oxford: Clarendon Press, 1988) 43–74.

Zweigert, K and Kötz, H, *Introduction to Comparative Law* (3rd edn, Oxford: Clarendon Press, 1998) 470–85.

---

[113] See G Treitel, *Remedies for Breach of Contract* (Oxford: Clarendon Press, 1988) 126–28, para 107.

[114] J Morgan, 'Smuggling mitigation into *White & Carter v McGregor*: time to come clean?' [2015] LMCLQ 575.

CHAPTER 24
WITHHOLDING PERFORMANCE

In this chapter and Chapter 25 we consider the remedies of withholding performance and termination of the contract. By 'withholding of performance' we mean a party's right to refuse to perform some or all of its outstanding obligations until the other party has performed its obligations, or at least until it is willing to perform them. 'Termination' means the right to refuse to accept further performance by the other party, and to refuse to perform one's own counter-obligations, on a permanent basis, or (where the other party has already performed, at least in part) to return what has been transferred—in other words, to escape from the contract.[1] In most of the systems considered, the two remedies are linked.

Including the right to withhold performance until the other party has performed (*exceptio non adimpleti contractus*) in this chapter involves a broad definition of 'remedies'. Not all of the systems would define the right to withhold performance as a remedy, but rather as a question of when performance is due. We deal with it in this chapter because it seems to us to fulfil a function as a temporary remedy.

We describe the remedies of withholding performance and termination as 'linked' for at least two reasons.[2] First, withholding performance is usually a prelude to seeking some other remedy, and (especially in those systems in which specific performance is not readily granted) very often that other remedy will be termination. When party A has not performed its part of a contract, frequently party B will withhold its performance as a temporary measure; then, if A's default continues, B will terminate the contract. Secondly, in some legal systems the two remedies are linked conceptually, in that the justification for allowing B to withhold its performance is partly the same as that given for

---

[1] There is a marked lack of consistency over the correct terminology in the English cases and doctrine. Some judges and authors refer to 'refusal to perform' or 'repudiation', some to 'rescission', some to 'termination'. We prefer to describe the process of ending a contract because of a non-performance by the other party as 'termination'. This is to avoid confusion. 'Refusal to perform' and 'repudiation' are also used to mean *wrongful* refusals to perform a contract. 'Rescission' is also used to describe the process of avoiding a contract on the grounds of invalidity (eg for fraud), which in English law (and some other laws) has a different effect from termination for breach.

[2] cf for Dutch law: AS Hartkamp & CH Sieburgh, *Mr. C. Assers Handleiding tot de beoefening van het Nederlands Burgerlijk Recht. 6. Verbintenissenrecht. Deel III. Algemeen overeenkomstenrecht* (Deventer: Kluwer 2014) nos. 712 ff.

ultimately allowing B to terminate the contract—though for B to be entitled to terminate, additional factors, such as the expiry of the time for performance, will have to be present.

In other systems there is more of a contrast between the two sets of rules. This is particularly so in French law. Traditionally, under French law termination (*résolution*) was, by nature, a judicial act (former Article 1184 of the Code civil). In contrast, if the necessary grounds existed, withholding of performance could be done unilaterally by the creditor. Before the 2016 reform, there was no general legislative text, only specific ones; but the right to withhold performance was well-established by case law.[3] The new reforms have not only allowed termination by notice to the other party,[4] but have put withholding performance onto a legislative footing, see below. However, even in French law the two 'remedies' are seen as linked, as the performances due from each side are interdependent, each being the cause of the other.

In German law, termination is an act of the creditor rather than of the court, but it is frequently necessary for the creditor to give formal notice before termination, allowing the debtor a further chance to perform, whereas formal notice is not required for withholding of performance.[5] In English law both withholding of performance and termination may be exercised unilaterally and, in most cases, without prior warning.

Another theme that may be worth considering throughout this chapter on withholding of performance and Chapter 25 on termination is the extent to which the rules are influenced by what each legal system seems to consider as the 'primary remedy' for breach of contract.[6] It is arguable that the conceptual 'primacy' of specific performance in the civil law systems has a considerable impact on the rules to be considered now.

24.1 BASIC RULES

In this section we start by considering when party A will have a right to withhold performance because party B has not performed his obligations under a straightforward synallagmatic contract—ie a contract in which each party's obligations are exchanged for the other, as expressed by the maxim *do ut des*.[7] Later we consider related rights, such as the *droit de rétention, Zurückbehaltungsrecht* or the lien, which may apply within individual non-synallagmatic contracts or, indeed, to situations involving several contracts or none at all.

As Carbonnier wrote of French law:[8]

> It is a principle recognised in case-law that in synallagmatic contracts both obligations must be performed at the same time. Each party may demand performance of the obligation due to him only if he offers to perform his side of the bargain. Conversely, he may withhold performance

---

[3] eg Cass com 2 May 1990, no. 88-18313, Bull civ IV no. 129.

[4] See below, p 988. See generally F Chénedé, *Le nouveau droit des obligations et des contrats: Consolidations, innovations, perspectives* (Paris: Dalloz, 2016) nos. 28.41–28.62; M Latina and G Chantepie, *La réforme du droit des obligations: Commentaire théorique et pratique dans l'ordre du Code civil* (Paris: Dalloz, 2016) nos. 627–31.

[5] cf for Dutch law: Arts 6:262–6:264 BW.

[6] See above, p 894.

[7] See the definitions in Art 1106 Cciv. The same idea is expressed in the phrases *trait pour trait, Zug um Zug*.

[8] J Carbonnier, *Droit civil*, vol IV, *Les obligations* (22nd edn, Paris: PUF, 2000) no.194.

if his contractual partner does not offer performance. This refusal is manifested by an exception—in the procedural sense of the term—namely that of non-performance of the contract (*exceptio non adimpleti contractus*). It stems from the interdependence of the obligations under a synallagmatic contract. Furthermore, it is not always easy to distinguish this objection from the right of retention which comes under the law of credit (a kind of guarantee whereby the creditor who holds or possesses an asset belonging to the debtor may refuse to give it up as long as he has not been paid) …

The withholding of performance as a general defence against non-performance was introduced in the French Code civil by the 2016 reform.

Code civil **24.1 (FR)**

Article 1219: A party may refuse to perform his obligation, even where it is enforceable, if the other party does not perform his own and if this non-performance is sufficiently serious.

Article 1220: A party may suspend the performance of his obligation as soon as it becomes evident that his contracting partner will not perform his obligation when it becomes due and that the consequences of this non-performance are sufficiently serious for him. Notice of this suspension must be given as quickly as possible.

Notes

(1) Before 2016, the defence (*'exception'*) of non-performance was provided for only in a few miscellaneous texts—for example, Articles 1612 and 1653 of the Code civil. Now, the new Articles 1219 and 1220 of the Code civil set out a general principle according to which a party may withhold his performance when the other party fails or is very likely to fail to perform his own obligation.

(2) The courts allowed the defence of non-performance in a large number of cases (for example, a tenant may refuse to pay rent if he does not have free enjoyment of the rented premises; the lessor may refuse to carry out repairs if rents are not paid to him). It is the notion of the synallagmatic contract which determines the scope of this principle: the objection is admissible in the case of all genuine synallagmatic contracts, and even in imperfectly synallagmatic contracts (argued from Article 1948). The exception is further extended to the converse synallagmatic case of the parties when a contract has been avoided or terminated: the two obligations to make restitution must be performed *trait pour trait*. Article 1219 of the new Code civil seems to codify the approach taken by the case law. This provision only allows a party to withhold performance if the other party has not complied with its own obligation. Withholding performance thus requires that each party is obliged towards the other party. The *avant projet Catala* went even further, stating that the defence applied only in synallagmatic contracts.

(3) The courts dismissed the defence where it appeared to them to be invoked in cases where it is contrary to the obligation of good faith binding the contracting parties. For example, a tenant may not refuse to pay his rent on the pretext that the landlord has failed to carry out necessary repairs to the building. It would not be in

keeping with the principle of good faith to object to non-performance of a relatively secondary obligation (and, moreover, one which is not clear in its extent) in order to escape from a fundamental obligation. Only obligations of an equivalent importance must be performed on a reciprocal basis.

(4) This link to good faith dates back to canon law, according to which it was contrary to good faith for a party to require performance when it did not comply with its own obligations.[9] Malaurie and Aynès say:[10]

> For the exception to be relied on there must be a serious non-performance and good faith on the part of the party invoking it.

(5) So in a lease, the tenant, by virtue of the fact that he is in enjoyment of the rented premises, already benefits from performance sufficient to balance his obligation to pay the rent and French courts have developed a specific set of rules to protect the other party when the defence is relied on by tenants.[11] A tenant cannot normally withhold rent on the ground of the landlord's failure to carry out repairs, but may do so if the defects prevent the premises being used safely.[12]

(6) The new Article 1219 lays down one main condition for the application of the defense of non-performance. The other party's failure to perform must be '*sufficiently serious*'. The purpose of this condition, which amounts to a proportionality test, is to avoid the disproportionate application of this defense. According to the Report to the President on the 2016 reform of contract law, the use in bad faith of the exception of non-performance against an insignificant non-performance constitutes an abuse or at least a fault, which may trigger contractual liability.

(7) Beside the classical approach embodied in Article 1219, the 2016 reform introduced another form of defense for non-performance in Article 1220. Under this provision, a party may withhold performance if it has become 'evident that his contracting partner will not perform his obligation'.

(8) Although Articles 1219 and 1220 do not expressly mention it, the defence of non-performance should apply only to the case where the two parties are due to perform simultaneously. If party A is to perform before party B, B may refuse to until A has done so simply because B's performance is not yet due; B need not resort to the defence.

(9) French authors used to point out that this defence is a self-help remedy, not directly subject to control of the court but which enables the creditor to put pressure on the debtor.[13] Articles 1219 and 1220 codify the '*exception d'inexécution*', and it is no longer necessary to look for a legal basis such as good faith, *cause* or *connexité* (where obligations are connected so that, for instance, one debt may be set off against another) outside these provisions.[14]

---

[9] F Terré, P Simler and Y Lequette, *Les obligations* (11th edn, Paris: Dalloz, 2013) no. 631.

[10] P Malaurie, L Aynès and P Stoffel-Munck, *Droit des obligations* (9th edn, Paris: LGDJ, 2017) no. 861.

[11] On the *droit de rétention* referred to by Carbonnier see Art 1613 Cciv.

[12] Malaurie et al (n 10 above) no. 859; B Nicholas, *The French Law of Contract* (2nd edn, Oxford: Clarendon Press, 1992) 215, citing Cass civ 21 February 1927, DH 1928, 82 and Cass soc 10 April 1959, no. 57-11590, D 1960, 61.

[13] Malaurie et al (n 10 above) no. 873.

[14] See ch 11.3, above.

(10) Carbonnier refers to the coercive effect of the exception. All the systems in some circumstances allow a party who has received a performance which is defective and therefore worth less than it should have been, to reduce the price that he agreed to pay for the performance.[15] Equally, if the non-performance causes a loss, the creditor may be able to deduct the damages to which he is entitled from any payment due. In a way these solutions look like withholding performance; but they are different. They provide a permanent solution rather than just a temporary one, and the creditor is entitled to reduce the price only in proportion to the reduction in value of the performance he has received, or to deduct the actual amount of his loss. If he is entitled to withhold performance, however, he may be entitled to withhold the whole of his performance. It is this which gives withholding of performance its coercive effect. Restrictions on the amount the creditor may withhold will be considered later.[16]

BGB

24.2 (DE)

§ 320: Defence of failure to perform the contract

(1) Unless the contract requires him to perform first, a person bound by a synallagmatic contract may refuse to perform his part until the other party effects counter-performance. If performance is to be made to several persons, the part due to one of them can be refused until the entire counter-performance has been effected. The rule in § 273(3) does not apply.

(2) If one party has partially performed, counter-performance may not be refused if, under the circumstances, in particular on account of the relative insignificance of the part not performed, the refusal would constitute bad faith.

§ 322: Order to perform concurrently

(1) If a party under a synallagmatic contract brings an action for performance and the other party asserts his right to refuse to perform until he receives counter-performance, the only effect of that assertion is that the other party must be ordered to perform concurrently.

(2) If the party bringing the action must perform his part first, he may, if the other party is in default through non-acceptance, bring an action for performance after receipt of counter-performance.

(3) The rule in § 274 (2) applies to execution of the judgment.

Notes

(1) German law distinguishes between the 'genetic' and the 'functional' synallagma. It is functional synallagma which we are concerned with here, where under a valid contract one party's obligation to perform is contingent upon the other's readiness and willingness to do likewise. ('Genetic synallagma' denotes the fact that A's obligations under the contract will fall away if B's obligation is held not to exist, for example, where B's declaration of intent is avoided.)

---

[15] See below, ch 27.
[16] See below, pp 967 ff.

(2) It may seem that the basis of the exceptio in § 320 BGB is simply that no duty to perform has yet arisen (*Einwendung*). The prevailing view, however, is that it is a defence (*Einrede*) which must be raised by the party against whom judgment is sought for the performance of the corresponding obligation.[17]

(3) The BGB has a separate paragraph, § 273, on the right of retention (*Zurückbehaltungsrecht*).[18]

(4) § 321 BGB allows a party who is to perform first to refuse to perform if it becomes apparent that the other party will not be able to perform his part when the time comes. This is dealt with below.[19]

English law explains the right to withhold performance in terms of conditional obligations.

King's Bench   **24.3 (EN)**

***Kingston v Preston*[20]**

A contractual obligation may be independent of the other party's obligation; or one party's obligation may be a condition precedent to, or a concurrent condition of, the other's obligation.

Facts: The plaintiff agreed to serve the defendant for a year and a quarter in the defendant's business as a silk-mercer, and the defendant agreed that at the end of the period he would convey the business and the stock in trade to the plaintiff and the defendant's nephew. The stock in trade was to be paid for over a period of time, and the plaintiff agreed to provide security for these payments. The plaintiff claimed that the defendant had failed to convey the business; the defendant pleaded that the plaintiff had failed to provide the promised security.

Held: The giving of the security was a condition precedent to the defendant's obligation to convey the business.

Judgment: Lord Mansfield: There are three kinds of covenants:

1. Such as are called mutual and independent, where either party may recover damages from the other, for the injury he may have received by a breach of the covenants in his favour, and where it is no excuse for the defendant, to allege a breach of the covenants on the part-of the plaintiff.

2. There are covenants which are conditions and dependant, in which the performance of one depends on the prior performance of another, and, therefore, till this prior condition is performed, the other party is not liable to an action on his covenant.

3. There is also a third sort of covenants, which are mutual conditions to be performed at the same time; and, in these, if one party is ready, and offered, to perform his part, and the other neglected, or refused, to perform his, he who was already, and offered, has fulfilled his engagement, and may maintain an action for the default of the other; though it is not certain that either is obliged to do the first act.

[His Lordship then proceeded to say that the dependence, or independence, of covenants was to be collected from the evident sense and meaning of the parties, and that,

---

[17] G Treitel, *Remedies for Breach of Contract* (Oxford: Clarendon Press, 1988) 316–17, para 238. See generally J Gernhuber, *Handbuch des Schuldrechts*, vol VIII, *Das Schuldverhältnis* (Tübingen: Siebeck, 1989).

[18] This is considered in more detail below, p 978.

[19] See 25.23 (DE), below, p 1029.

[20] (1773) 2 Doug KB 689.

however transposed they might be in the deed, their precedence must depend on the order of time in which the intent of the transaction requires their performance. In the case before the Court, it would be the greatest injustice if the plaintiff should prevail: the essence of the agreement was that the defendant should not trust to the personal security of the plaintiff, but, before he delivered up his stock and business, should have good security for the payment of the money. The giving of such security, therefore, must necessarily be a condition precedent. Judgment was accordingly given for the defendant, because the part to be performed by the plaintiff was clearly a condition precedent.]
  Judgment for the defendant

Sale of Goods Act 1979   **24.4 (EN)**

Section 28: Payment and delivery are concurrent conditions
  Unless otherwise agreed, delivery of the goods and payment of the price are concurrent conditions, that is to say, the seller must be ready and willing to give possession of the goods to the buyer in exchange for the price and the buyer must be ready and willing to pay the price in exchange for possession of the goods.

Note
  As said above, English law explains the right to withhold performance in terms of conditional obligations. Although it is possible for the two parties' obligations to be entirely independent of each other, so that each party must perform irrespective of the other's failure, this is uncommon. Party A is only obliged to perform when B has not yet done so only if that is what was agreed (and we will see below that even then there may be cases in which A is excused). If A and B are to perform simultaneously, party A need perform only when party B is ready and willing to do so too (the performances are 'concurrent conditions' of each other). Thus in a contract of sale, as Section 28 states, the buyer need not pay until the seller has the goods ready and the seller need not deliver until the buyer is ready to pay.[21] If party B is to perform first, A need perform only when B has done so (B's performance is a 'condition precedent' to A's obligation).

It is important to note that to say that B's performance is a condition precedent to A's obligation to perform, or a concurrent condition of it, is different from saying that the operation of the contract, or of one of its terms, is conditional on the occurrence of some event which is—wholly or partly—outside the control of the parties. The latter is sometimes called a 'suspensive' condition. An example would be a contract which is to come

---

[21] There is a complication, however, caused by the fact that in the English law of sale property may pass before the goods are delivered, so that the goods belong to the buyer even though they remain in the seller's possession. The seller may still refuse to deliver the other party's property until the buyer tenders the price for the goods (unless the seller has agreed to deliver on credit). The Sale of Goods Act 1979, s 39 describes this as the seller's 'lien or right to retain the goods'. If the buyer's default continues the seller may, after giving notice to the buyer, resell the goods: s 48(3). This has the effect of terminating the contract of sale and re-vesting the property in the seller: *RV Ward v Bignall* [1967] 1 QB 534 (CA). English law recognises liens in other situations also. Thus, a person who has been employed to repair goods may refuse to redeliver them to their owner until he has been paid for the work done ('the repairer's lien': see *Goode on Commercial Law*, 5th edn by E McKendrick (London: Penguin, 2017) para 22.66).

into effect only if the government grants an export licence. The difference is that, in the example just given, neither party will be liable to the other if the condition fails to occur because the licence is refused (though there may be liability if one party brings about the refusal of the licence by, for example, not submitting a proper application). In the cases we are considering in this chapter, although B's performance is a condition of A's obligation, B is *obliged* to perform. If he fails, he will normally be in breach of contract and liable for damages. To make this clear, sometimes this type of condition is called 'promissory', whereas the type of condition involved in the case of the contract dependent on the grant of the licence is termed 'contingent'.[22]

Principles of European Contract Law   **24.5 (INT)**

Article 9:201: Right to Withhold Performance

(1) A party which is to perform simultaneously with or after the other party may withhold performance until the other has tendered performance or has performed. The first party may withhold the whole of its performance or a part of it as may be reasonable in the circumstances.

(2) A party may similarly withhold performance for as long as it is clear that there will be a non-performance by the other party when the other party's performance becomes due.[23]

24.2 THE ORDER OF PERFORMANCE

24.2.A INTRODUCTORY NOTE

In the simplest cases the right to withhold performance is the simple result of the order of performance—either an order which was agreed expressly in the contract or one which is applicable to the contract under the relevant rules of law. Thus if a sales contract provides for payment in cash on delivery, it seems self-evident that the seller does not have to deliver unless he is going to be paid. The right not to deliver follows simply from the fact that the seller is not obliged to perform until the buyer does so. A fortiori, in the case where, under the contract, A is to perform first; B is not obliged to perform until A has done so. On a simple reading, § 320 BGB, the French jurisprudence referred to by Carbonnier,[24] and the English doctrine of conditions are no more than reflections of this.

This seems to be confirmed by the details of the doctrine. Thus, in German law, § 320 BGB does not apply simply because the contract as a whole involves an exchange of undertakings. It is necessary that the obligation performance of which is to be withheld be synallagmatic with the obligation which the other party has not yet performed.

---

[22] See *Treitel* (n 17 above) 259–61, para 198. For a case which turned on which type of condition was involved, see *Trans-Trust SPRL v Danubian Trading Co Ltd* [1952] 2 QB 297 (CA).

[23] See for Dutch law: Art 6:262 BW.

[24] See above, p 958.

We will consider one example of this later, when we see that a minor obligation of the contract may not be synallagmatic with other obligations under the same contract—so that non-performance of the minor obligation does not justify withholding performance of the rest.[25] Another example of non-synallagmatic obligations can be found in a contract of mandate. The mandatory may be obliged to render accounts to the principal and the principal may have to indemnify the mandatory for expenses incurred; but, under German law, it has been held that the two obligations are not synallagmatic, so that the mandatory cannot refuse to account because he has not been paid his expenses.[26] There may, however, be a 'right of retention' even in this case.[27]

The English notion that some 'covenants' may be 'independent' of each other also seems to reflect the same idea that, if there is to be a right to withhold performance of one obligation because of non-performance of the other, the obligations must be synallagmatic. Thus, in *Taylor v Webb*,[28] du Parcq J held that a landlord must repair the leased premises even if the tenant was in arrears with the rent, as the two obligations were independent.

24.2.B ESTABLISHING THE ORDER OF PERFORMANCE

In order to apply such principles to decide whether party A is entitled to withhold its performance until B has performed, it will first be necessary to determine the order in which the parties are to perform.

The order of performance will determine the extent to which one party will have to extend credit to the other. If the performances can be exchanged simultaneously, no extension of credit by either will be necessary. This may be why, when the parties have not expressly agreed the order of performance, the three systems seem to have some presumption in favour of simultaneous exchange. This is clear in the common law,[29] and may be deduced in French and German law.[30] However, all three systems depart from this when simultaneous performance would be impractical—for example, in a contract for building work it would hardly be sensible to require the employer to pay the builder as each brick is laid. In such cases it will have to be decided which party is to perform first.

'Work first, payment later' is the norm in service contracts and work contracts. This is explicit in the BGB (§§ 614, 641). Frequently, however, there are contrary customs—such as for contracts to see theatre performances. In addition, the parties may, of course,

---

[25] See below, pp 967 ff.

[26] See Münchener Kommentar/Seiler § 662 para 17. Note however that the French Cour de cassation held that the mandatory may withhold performance if the principal fails to reimburse the expenses incurred by the mandatory for the performance of its obligation: Cass com 16 June 1981, no. 79-16204, Bull civ IV no. 276; JCP G 1981.IV.318.

[27] See 24.15 (DE), below, p 978.

[28] [1937] 2 KB 283.

[29] See *Treitel* (n 17 above) 279–81, para 214.

[30] ibid para 220.

contract out of or reverse legal rules or customary stipulations in favour of advance performance.[31]

Article 6:110: Order of performance

(1) To the extent that the performances of the parties can be rendered simultaneously, the parties are bound to render them simultaneously unless the circumstances indicate otherwise.

(2) To the extent that the performance of only one party requires a period of time, that party is bound to render its performance first, unless the circumstances indicate otherwise.

> *Note*
>
> It will also be necessary to decide how much of one party's performance is due before the other's obligation arises—must the first party perform the whole of his obligation, or is he entitled to the counter-performance 'bit by bit'?

In English law the question is put thus: is the obligation entire or severable? Again, to reduce the amount of credit that must be advanced, there is a presumption in favour of severability. Thus, unless agreed otherwise, a contract for employment is treated as severable by the day, so that at the end of each day the employee will have earned a day's pay.[32] However, if there is no way of apportioning the price to the various tasks to be carried out under the contract, it will be treated as entire. Thus a builder's obligation under a simple contract for building work where the price is stated as a single ('lump') sum is entire, so that the builder is not entitled to any payment until the work is finished.[33]

---

[31] See the discussion of this in Gernhuber (n 17 above) 354–57.

[32] See Apportionment Act 1870, s 2; in practice, it is usually agreed that payment will be deferred until the end of the week or month.

[33] *Sumpter v Hedges* [1898] 1 QB 673, 25.36 (EN), below, p 1053. In practice, builders cannot afford to extend this much credit to employers, and therefore in England large building contracts usually provide for the value of the work carried out to be certified at monthly intervals. The employer must pay the value of these 'interim certificates', less previous payments and a 'retention percentage', within 30 days of the date of the certificate. In the 1990s a scheme was provided by statute: see Housing Grants, Construction and Regeneration Act 1996, ss 109–13. German law and practice on building contracts have developed in a rather similar fashion. § 641(1) BGB states that payment in a contract for work is to be made on acceptance of the completed work. But if the work is accepted in parts, then payment must be made on each separate acceptance. Furthermore, advance, instalment and completion payments on presentation of certificates attesting to the progress of building work are provided for specifically in Part B of the General Conditions for Construction Works (Verdingungsordnung für Bauleistungen) which may be adopted into the contract by the parties; see W Lorenz, *International Encyclopaedia of Comparative Law*, vol VIII, *Specific Contracts* (Tübingen: Mohr, 1971) ch 8: Contracts for Work on Goods and Building Contracts, paras 6–7. Similarly, in leases the basic rule is that the rent is to be paid at the end of the period of the lease, or at the end of such time intervals as the rent is calculated by (*Coomber v Howard* (1845) 1 CB 440), though very frequently the parties agree on payment in advance. In Germany, this only applies to pieces of land and moveables (§ 579(1) BGB), but no longer to flats and commercial property (§§ 556b and 579(2), as opposed to the former § 551 BGB).

24.3 WITHHOLDING BECAUSE OF DEFECTIVE OR PARTIAL PERFORMANCE

Evidently, a party may be entitled to withhold its performance even if the other has not totally failed to perform, provided that the non-performance is of some essential obligation and the breach is significant. Thus if a seller tenders goods which are obviously defective, the buyer need not take them or pay for them. Does *any* failure to perform by party A justify party B in withholding his performance, or must the failure be a serious one?

In German law two principles apply. The first deals with the case in which a particular obligation has not been performed and looks at its importance. The second considers rather the case in which an obligation has been performed defectively.

On the first, German law employs a number of tests in order to distinguish obligations which are synallagmatic from those which are not. First, the main obligations (*Hauptpflichten*) for the contract type will be taken to be in a synallagmatic relationship. These are the obligations which are considered essential to the existence of a contract of the particular type. Thus, in contracts of sale, the obligation of the seller to supply the buyer with the goods (§ 433(1) BGB) and the obligation of the buyer to pay the purchase price (§ 433(2) BGB) are *Hauptpflichten*. In contrast, the obligation of the buyer to take delivery is not normally a main obligation but a collateral obligation (*Nebenpflicht*).[34] Further, protective duties (*Schutzpflichten*), as implied by the law on positive breach of contract, will not be in synallagmatic relationship. The agreement of the parties may make an obligation a main one, even where it is not typically so.[35]

On the second idea, § 320(2) BGB is explicit:

> If one party has partially performed, counter-performance may not be refused if, under the circumstances, in particular on account of the relative insignificance of the part not performed, the refusal would constitute bad faith.

Notes

(1) The German courts understand the *exceptio* as a means of compelling performance and, therefore, interpret § 320(2) BGB narrowly.[36] They take account of the fact that it is often where the outstanding performance, or the size of the defect, is quite small that the other party is least willing to make up the difference. There is no sense therefore in which the performance withheld must be equivalent (in value or otherwise) to the performance outstanding.[37]

---

[34] The obligation of the lessor to allow the use of the property to the lessee (§ 535(1) BGB) and the obligation of the lessee to pay rent (§ 535(2) BGB) are *Hauptpflichten*. By contrast, neither the obligation of the lessor to make good any expenditure by the lessee on the property (§§ 536a(2), 539(1) BGB) nor that of the lessee to return the property at the end of the lease (§ 546(1) BGB) is a main obligation. As merely collateral obligations (*Nebenpflichten*), they are not, therefore, in synallagmatic relationship.

[35] See Gernhuber (n 17 above) 322–25.

[36] See BGH 6 February 1958, NJW 1958, 706.

[37] See Gernhuber (n 17 above) 343–46.

> (2) It is accepted that defective performance is tantamount to part performance within the terms of § 320(2) BGB.
>
> (3) Apart from the breach itself, in determining the requirements of good faith, a court may consider the general circumstances of the case, including the length of the delay in performing and the deterioration of relations between the parties. Even if § 320(2) BGB is applicable A may withhold a part of his own performance sufficient to compel B to perform.

Under French law, the principle is that a party may withhold performance if the other party failed to perform and if this non-performance is 'sufficiently serious' (Code civil of 2016, Article 1219). The 'sufficiently serious' test is a codification of the case law.

Cass com, 30 January 1979[38] **24.7 (FR)**

Defective computer

The lessee of defective equipment is entitled to suspend payment of rentals only if the breach committed by the lessor is of a sufficient magnitude.

Facts: According to the judgment appealed against (Paris, 25 March 1977), SEFCO, an IT company working on accounting and management, used equipment hired or sold by the company, Honeywell Bull, which maintained that equipment subject to a monthly payment. By letters of 26 September and 30 October 1968 containing an exclusivity clause, Honeywell Bull agreed that SEFCO could rescind the contract in the event that a Honeywell installation were used by an IT company located in the same geographical area as SEFCO. In spite of difficulties in regard to monthly payments, and although SEFCO alleged that Honeywell Bull equipped a competing company, SEFCO nevertheless on 31 December 1971 entered into a contract under which Honeywell Bull sold it a computer which to be operational depended on hired equipment; it was provided that that contract was to replace all earlier contracts. In 1972 fresh difficulties led Honeywell Bull to rescind the maintenance and leasing contract in respect of which periodic payments had not been paid and to sue SEFCO on 4 October 1972 for payment of the sums due. SEFCO counterclaimed for damages and interest in respect of the loss which it alleged it had suffered owing to the need to reconvert its equipment.

Held: The defects in the equipment were not serious enough to justify withholding of the rental payments.

Judgment: ... Whereas the judgment appealed against is also criticised for ordering SEFCO, the lessee of two magnetic disc units which it considered to be defective, to pay the entirety of the rentals; whereas, according to the appeal, the objection of non-performance applies to defective performance in the same way as it does to total non-performance; as the lessee of defective equipment is therefore, it is submitted, entitled to suspend payment of rentals, especially where, as in the present case, it ceased payments only a long time after noting the difficulties that had occurred.

Whereas in finding that the H1200 unit and discs, although not a brilliant performer, had shown itself to be viable for SEFCO which used it until 1973, the court of appeal made clear that, although defective performance of the contract allowed that undertaking to raise the objection of non-performance, the deficiencies found were not, however, sufficient to warrant withholding performance even if that withholding occurred only after a long period of difficulties; and therefore the plea is unfounded ...

[38] No. 77-13151, Bull civ IV no. 41.

On those grounds: The appeal against the judgment delivered on 25 March 1977 by the court of appeal, Paris, is dismissed.

Notes

(1) The 'sufficiently serious' condition amounts to a proportionality test.[39] French courts verify, on a case by case basis, whether the decision to withhold performance was the proportionate response to the failure to perform.[40]

(2) In applying this test of proportionality, French courts have two options. They can opt for a broad test of proportionality and consider all the aspects of the contractual relationship; or they can opt for a restrictive test based only on the two breaches at stake. The two approaches are illustrated by the decisions of the cour d'appel and the Cour de cassation in a case involving the French national lottery.[41] The French national lottery games operator, *Française des jeux* (FDJ), concluded a contract with the Mikha company under which Mikha was entitled to organise lottery games and had to transfer a portion of the sums paid by the bettors to FDJ. Mikha failed to pay the sums to FDJ. Consequently, FDJ decided to withhold performance of its own obligation. Mikha argued that FDJ was liable for abusively breaching the contract. The court of appeal held that Mikha had failed to perform its obligation but that 'the immediate suspension of the contract was disproportionate, with regard to the length of the contractual relationship and the lack of any prior information'. However, the Cour de cassation quashed the appeal decision and held that there was no disproportion between the *exception d'inexécution* and the failure to perform by Mikha. The Cour de cassation thus opted for the second approach.

(3) The *exception of inexecution* is also closely linked to the concept of risk. A party which decides to withhold performance takes a risk because its decision to withhold will be subject to the control of the judge *a posteriori*. For example, a tenant who decides to stop paying its rent because of the landlord's failure to grant peaceful enjoyment of the premises takes the risk that its decision not to pay may subsequently be characterised as a breach of contract.[42]

In English law the question of how serious a non-performance must be to justify the other party withholding performance, and the closely related question of how serious a breach of contract must be to entitle the innocent party to terminate the contract, have caused great difficulty and complexity. Different (though related) rules have been developed in different contractual situations. In contracts for work in which one party is to perform the work in advance of payment, and has not completed it or has done some of it defectively, the courts have applied a doctrine known as the doctrine of substantial performance.

[39] O Deshayes, 'L'exception d'inexécution doit-elle être proportionnée?' RDC 2016, 654.
[40] eg, in Cass civ (1) 12 Mai 2016, no. 15-20834, see next note.
[41] Cass civ (1) 12 Mai 2016, no. 15-20834, D 2016 1076, and 2365, annotated by A Rabreau.
[42] Cass civ (3) 19 November 2015, no. 14-24612; J-B Seube, 'Le risque au cœur de l'exception d'inexécution' RDC 2016, 249.

Court of Appeal   **24.8 (EN)**

Hoenig v Isaacs[43]

Once building work has been substantially completed the employer must pay the contract price but may deduct damages, including the cost of having any defects in the work put right.

Facts: The defendant employed the plaintiff to decorate and furnish the defendant's flat for £750. The work was finished bar some defects in a bookcase and a wardrobe, which would cost about £55 to rectify, and the defendant moved into the flat, but he refused to pay the outstanding balance of the contract price.

Held: The court of first instance held that the balance of the price must be paid subject to any counter-claim for damages. The Court of Appeal dismissed the employers' appeal.

Judgment: SOMERVELL LJ: Each case turns on the construction of the contract. In *Cutter v Powell* the condition for the promissory note sued on was that the sailor should proceed to continue and do his duty as second mate in the ship from Jamaica to the port of Liverpool. The sailor died before the ship reached Liverpool and it was held his estate could not recover either on the contract or on a quantum meruit. It clearly decided that his continuing as mate during the whole voyage was a condition precedent to payment. It did not decide that if he had completed the main purpose of the contract, namely, serving as mate for the whole voyage, the defendant could have repudiated his liability by establishing that in the course of the voyage the sailor had, possibly through inadvertence, failed on some occasion in his duty as mate whereby some damage had been caused.

The learned official referee regarded *H Dakin & Co Ltd v Lee* laying down that the price must be paid subject to set-off or counterclaim if there was a substantial compliance with the contract. I think on the facts of this case where the work was finished in the ordinary sense, though in part defective, this is right. It expresses in a convenient epithet what is put from another angle in the Sale of Goods Act. 1893. The buyer cannot reject if he proves only the breach of a term collateral to the main purpose. I have, therefore, come to the conclusion that the first point of counsel for the defendant fails.

The learned official referee found that there was substantial compliance. Bearing in mind that there is an appeal on fact, was there evidence on which he could so find? The learned official referee having, as I hold, properly directed himself, this becomes, I think, a question of fact. The case on this point was, I think, near the border line, and if the finding had been the other way I do not think we could have interfered ...

DENNING LJ: This case raises the familiar question: Was entire performance a condition precedent to payment? That depends on the true construction of the contract. In this case the contract was made over a period of time and was partly oral and partly in writing, but I agree with the official referee that the essential terms were set down in the letter of 25 April, 1950. It describes the work which was to be done and concludes with these words:

'The foregoing, complete, for the sum of £750 net. Terms of payment are net cash, as the work proceeds: and balance on completion.'

The question of law that was debated before us was whether the plaintiff was entitled in this action to sue for the £350 balance of the contract price as he had done. The defendant said that he was only entitled to sue on a quantum meruit. The defendant was anxious to insist on a quantum meruit, because he said that the contract price was

---

[43] [1952] 2 All ER 176.

unreasonably high. He wished, therefore, to reject that price altogether and simply to pay a reasonable price for all the work that was done. This would obviously mean an inquiry into the value of every item, including all the many items which were in compliance with the contract as well as the three which fell short of it. That is what the defendant wanted. The plaintiff resisted this course and refused to claim on a quantum meruit. He said that he was entitled to the balance of £350 less a deduction for the defects.

In determining this issue the first question is whether, on the true construction of the contract, entire performance was a condition precedent to payment. It was a lump sum contract, but that does not mean that entire performance was a condition precedent to payment. When a contract provides for a specific sum to be paid on completion of specified work, the courts lean against a construction of the contract which would deprive the contractor of any payment at all simply because there are some defects or omissions. The promise to complete the work is, therefore, construed as a term of the contract, but not as a condition. It is not every breach of that term which absolves the employer from his promise to pay the price, but only a breach which goes to the root of the contract, such as an abandonment of the work when it is only half done. Unless the breach does go to the root of the matter, the employer cannot resist payment of the price. He must pay it and bring a cross-claim for the defects and omissions, or, alternatively, set them up in diminution of the price. The measure is the amount which the work is worth less by reason of the defects and omissions, and is usually calculated by the cost of making them good: see *Mondel v Steel*; *H Dakin & Co Ltd v Lee* and the notes to *Cutter v Powell* in *Smith's Leading Cases*, 13th edn, vol 2, pp 19–21. It is, of course, always open to the parties by express words to make entire performance a condition precedent. A familiar instance is when the contract provides for progress payments to be made as the work proceeds, but for retention money to be held until completion. Then entire performance is usually a condition precedent to payment of the retention money, but not, of course, to the progress payments. The contractor is entitled to payment pro rata as the work proceeds, less a deduction for retention money. But he is not entitled to the retention money until the work is entirely finished, without defects or omission … But … I think this contract should be regarded as an ordinary lump sum contract. It was substantially performed. The contractor is entitled, therefore, to the contract price, less a deduction for the defects…

ROMER LJ: The position is, I think, in some respects analogous to a case where a man agrees to sell land and, before completion, finds that he is unable to make title to a small part of it which is of no great significance in relation to the whole. In such a case the vendor can substantially perform what he has agreed to do but cannot perform it wholly, and the Court of Chancery has never hesitated to grant specific performance at this instance against the purchaser subject to a proper and reasonable deduction being made in the purchase price. It would not, however, make such an order if it resulted in the purchaser getting something substantially less than or different from what he had bargained for. … I am, accordingly, of the opinion, as already indicated, that the learned official referee fell into no error of law and that this appeal fails.

Notes

(1) The effect of this rule is that exact performance is not a condition precedent to the employer's obligation to pay; the condition precedent is that the work be substantially completed. The employer may deduct from the price damages for the

builder's failure to complete. Usually the damages will be the cost of having the work finished by another builder, but for an exception see the *Ruxley* case.[44]

(2) As the judgment notes, the doctrine of substantial performance, that the price is earned once the work is substantially complete, is the general rule, but the parties may provide that the work must be done exactly as a condition precedent to payment.

(3) In *Hoenig v Isaacs* the employer had offered to pay a reasonable sum for the work done. If the employer had been right that the work had not been substantially completed, it seems that he would not have been *obliged* to pay anything at all.[45]

(4) There is some debate in English law whether the doctrine of substantial performance applies only when the work has been completed but some of it has been done defectively, or also when some of the work has not been done at all. Treitel explains *Hoenig v Isaacs* by saying that the obligation to complete the work was entire, but the obligation as to its quality was not. He continues:[46]

> In relation to "entire obligations", there is no scope for the doctrine of 'substantial performance'.

The courts have applied the doctrine in cases in which some element of the work had simply not been done.[47]

In English Law there is a second approach, which is applied to contracts in general. This is to ask whether the term which has not been performed was a 'condition', going 'to the root of the contract', or only a 'warranty'. In *Wallis, Son & Wells v Pratt & Haynes*,[48] Fletcher Moulton LJ explained the distinction thus:

> A party to a contract who has performed or is ready and willing to perform his obligations under that contract is entitled to the performance by the other contracting party of all the obligations which rest upon him. But from a very early period of our law it has been recognised that such obligations are not all of equal importance. There are some which go so directly to the substance of the contract, or, in other words, are so essential to its very nature, that their non-performance may fairly be considered by the other party as a substantial failure to perform the contract at all. On the other hand, there are other obligations which, though they must be performed, are not, so vital that a failure to perform them goes to the substance of the contract. Both clauses are equally obligations under the contract, and the breach of any one of them entitles the other party to damages. But in the case of the former class he has the alternative of treating the contract as being completely broken by the non-performance, and (if he takes proper steps) he can refuse to perform any of the obligations resting upon himself and sue the other party for a total failure to perform the contract.

---

[44] See 23.19 (EN), above, p 923.

[45] There are dicta in *Hoenig v Isaacs* to the effect that the employer would have to pay something on a restitutionary basis ('quantum meruit', meaning simply 'however much it is worth'). They are not extracted here and they seem to be inconsistent with the generally accepted rule in English law; see below, p 1054.

[46] See *Treitel on the Law of Contract*, 14th edn by E Peel (London: Sweet & Maxwell, 2015) para 17-040.

[47] eg *Dakin v Lee* [1916] 1 KB 566 (CA).

[48] [1910] 2 KB 1003 (CA). The actual question in this case was about whether an exclusion clause applied to a breach of condition. The clause excluded liability for any 'warranty'. Was it effective to exclude liability when the breach was one of a term stated by the Sale of Goods Act 1893, s 13, to be a condition, even though the buyers had accepted the goods and thus lost their right to terminate the contract? The majority held that it was, but the dissenting judgment of Fletcher Moulton LJ was approved by the House of Lords [1911] AC 394.

Notes

(1) Fletcher Moulton LJ uses the words 'refuse to perform' in the same sense as we have used 'terminate'. He refers to conditions as giving rise to a right to refuse to perform and to sue for damages for total failure to perform. He is assuming that the time for performance has expired. Before that time, the buyer would normally not be entitled to terminate, but it would be able to withhold payment until the seller was ready and willing to perform those terms which are conditions of the contract. It could not, however, withhold its performance merely because the seller had not performed a warranty.

(2) It will be seen that Fletcher Moulton LJ is using the word 'condition' meaning something slightly different to its use in the phrases 'condition precedent' (an obligation A must perform before B has to perform and 'concurrent condition' (an obligation A must be ready and willing to perform before B has to perform). He is using it to mean a term imposing on A an obligation that is sufficiently important that its non-performance will justify termination by B, even if B has already performed. (So if A sells goods to B, who takes delivery and pays for the goods before he discovers that they are seriously defective, B may still reject the goods and terminate the contract for breach of condition.)

The distinction between conditions and warranties is taken up in the Sale of Goods Act 1979:

Sale of Goods Act 1979   **24.9 (EN)**

Section 11: When condition to be treated as a warranty

… (2) Where a contract of sale is subject to a condition to be fulfilled by the seller, the buyer may waive the condition, or may elect to treat the breach of condition as a breach of warranty and not as a ground for treating the contract as repudiated.

(3) Whether a stipulation in a contract of sale is a condition, the breach of which may give rise to a right to treat the contract as repudiated, or a warranty, breach of which may give rise to a claim for damages but not to a right to reject the goods and treat the contract as repudiated, depends in each case on the construction of the contract; and a stipulation may be a condition, though called a warranty in the contract.

Notes

(1) Most of the implied terms as to conformity of the goods are stated to be conditions.[49]

(2) We will see that the English courts have found the distinction between conditions and warranties to be too rigid to produce satisfactory results in all cases. The decisions have all concerned attempts by one party to terminate the contract, and therefore we consider them in the next chapter.

---

[49] See above, p 785. In contrast, the Consumer Rights Act 2015 does not use the language of conditions and warranties: it states what remedies the consumer will have in each fact situation. See 27.3 (EN), below, p 1148.

The English law on withholding of performance seems to operate rather less subtly than the French or German rules. On the one hand, since there is no doctrine of good faith, a party may be able to withhold a performance worth a great deal more than the obligation that the other party has not performed.[50] On the other hand, the fact that English law decides whether a party may withhold its performance by the same criteria as whether it may, if the other's non-performance continues, termination of the contract may reduce the availability of withholding of performance in English law compared to the continental systems. A slight breach—ie one which is not a breach of condition, nor sufficiently serious to justify termination under the rules just mentioned—cannot give rise to a right to withhold performance. The good faith test of German law, and the requirement of sufficient seriousness in French law, seem more flexible.

Principles of European Contract Law   **24.10 (INT)**

Article 9:201: Right to Withhold Performance

(1) A party which is to perform simultaneously with or after the other party may withhold performance until the other has tendered performance or has performed. The first party may withhold the whole of its performance or a part of it as may be reasonable in the circumstances ...

COMMENT

...

B. Non-performance need not be fundamental

Where the obligations of the two parties are to be performed simultaneously a party's non-performance need not be fundamental in order to entitle the other party to withhold its own performance. But it is not necessarily appropriate for a party to be entitled to withhold the whole of its performance if the obligations not performed by the other party are not fundamental. In the common law countries the right to withhold performance is restricted to cases where the contract expressly or impliedly makes the obligations conditional upon one another and to cases of fundamental non-performance; in other cases the aggrieved party must perform its obligations in full (though if the non-performance is a breach it may have a claim for damages). Other systems are more flexible, permitting withholding of performance as a way of coercing the non-performing party even where the non-performance is minor, provided that the amount withheld is not wholly disproportionate and the withholding party acts in good faith. It is this approach which is adopted by this Article, which must be read together with Article 1:201 (Good Faith and Fair Dealing).

> *Illustration 3*: A agrees to buy a new car from B, a dealer. When A comes to collect the car he finds it has a scratch on the bodywork. He may refuse to accept the car or pay any part of the price until the car is repaired.

> *Illustration 4*: The same except that the car is to be shipped to A's home in another country, where B has no facilities. Since it would be unrealistic to expect B to repair the scratch, it would be contrary to good faith for A to withhold more than the cost of having the car repaired locally.

---

[50] The rules mentioned in the previous paragraph and to be described in more detail later, below, pp 931ff, were developed to deal with this and the parallel problem in the context of termination of a contract on the pretext of a slight breach.

In some cases the aggrieved party cannot practicably withhold part of its performance—for instance, many obligations to perform a service must realistically be performed in full or suspended in full. The aggrieved party may only withhold its performance in full if in the circumstances that is not unreasonable. However, it may be expressly provided in the contract that a performance is made reciprocal to the other performance.

A particular application of the right to withhold performance arises under a contract of sale when the buyer has been supplied with goods that do not conform to the contract. This is considered along with the other remedies the buyer may have in Chapter 27.

24.4 DEFAULT CAN BE ANTICIPATED

As set out in 24.2 above, the logic of the right to withhold performance may simply be that A's performance is not due until either B has performed—where B is to perform in advance—or is ready and willing to do so—where B is to perform simultaneously. But what of the case where it is A who is to perform in advance, but he is unwilling to do so because he believes that B will fail to reciprocate? The simple logic of *trait pour trait* or *Zug um Zug* will not assist here.

BGB **24.11 (DE)**

§ 321 Defence of insecurity
   A person bound by a synallagmatic contract to perform first may refuse to perform his part if after conclusion of the contract it becomes apparent that his claim for counter-performance is endangered by the other party's lack of ability to perform. The right to refuse to perform ceases if counter-performance is effected or security provided for it.

Notes

   (1) The deterioration referred to in § 321 BGB must have occurred after the formation of the contract. If it occurred before, then the appropriate remedy is rescission for mistake or fraud under §§ 119(2), 123 BGB,[51] where applicable. Only deterioration in the particular party's situation will be considered, not general deterioration in the economic climate, though the doctrine *of clausula rebus sic stantibus* may be invoked in such cases (§ 313 BGB).

   (2) The policy embodied in § 321 BGB has been summed up by one author as follows:[52]

   The undertaking of a duty to perform in advance represents a granting of credit. Whoever provides credit must rely upon the other party to a heightened degree. The law protects this reliance in cases of subsequent deterioration in the finances of the other party …

---

[51] See 14.10 (DE), p 499, and 14.4 (DE), p 488, above.
[52] K Larenz, *Lehrbuch des Schuldrechts*, vol 1: *Allgemeiner Teil* (14th edn, Munich: CH Beck, 1987) 207.

Neither English nor French law has a general provision, but in some cases they reach a similar result by a slightly different means. Both systems, and also German law, recognise, in addition to the right to withhold performance, a right of retention or lien. As we saw earlier, in some cases this operates in more or less the same way as the right to withhold performance: for example, the English Sale of Goods Act 1979, section 39.[53] In some ways, however, the seller's right of lien and retention may go beyond what would be possible under the simple notion of withholding performance. The situation we are considering, of the party who is to perform first but who anticipates a default by the other, is one of them.

Sale of Goods Act 1979

24.12 (EN)

Section 41: (1) Subject to this Act, the unpaid seller of goods who is in possession of them is entitled to retain possession of them until payment or tender of the price in the following cases:–

(a) where the goods have been sold without any stipulation as to credit;

(b) where the goods have been sold on credit but the term of credit has expired;

(c) where the buyer becomes insolvent …[54]

Code civil

24.13 (FR)

Article 1220: A party may suspend the performance of his obligation as soon as it becomes evident that his contracting partner will not perform his obligation when it becomes due and that the consequences of this non-performance are sufficiently serious for him. Notice of this suspension must be given as quickly as possible.

Note

This provision formally introduced the anticipated *exception d'inexécution* in French law.[55] A party will now be entitled to withhold performance if it believes that the other party will fail to perform. The standard seems to be very high, however. First, it must be evident that the other party will not perform when the obligation becomes due. This requirement may bring about a problem of proof, as a party will need to show on a case by case basis, that there was no doubt that the counterparty would not be able to perform. Second, the other party's failure to perform must be 'sufficiently serious'. Again, a party which withholds performance will need to prove that, had it not suspended performance of its obligation, it would have suffered a serious harm. Third, a party willing to apply this defence must serve the other party a notice beforehand.[56]

---

[53] See above, p 963.

[54] It will be noted that (c) applies even when the seller had agreed to deliver on credit.

[55] Although the anticipated *exception d'inexécution* had not been generally affirmed by the former case law, it seems that the Cour de cassation was favourable to this defence: see, eg, Cass com 11 February 2003, no. 00-11085, unpublished.

[56] This notification requirement is regarded as analogous to a requirement of a 'mise en demeure'; on this point, A Bénabent, *Les obligations* (16th edn, Paris: LGDJ, 2017) no. 372.

Article 9:201: Right to Withhold Performance

(1) ...

(2) A party may similarly withhold performance for as long as it is clear that there will be a non-performance by the other party when the other party's performance becomes due.

Article 8:105: Assurance of Performance[57]

(1) A party which reasonably believes that there will be a fundamental non performance by the other party may demand adequate assurance of due performance and meanwhile may withhold performance of its own obligations so long as such reasonable belief continues.

(2) Where this assurance is not provided within a reasonable time, the party demanding it may terminate the contract if it still reasonably believes that there will be a fundamental non-performance by the other party and gives notice of termination without delay.[58]

Note

The Notes to Article 8:105 PECL state: '... except for the UNITED STATES UCC § 2.609, no statutory provision is known which provides a general rule equivalent to Article 8:105'.

24.5 NON-PERFORMANCE OF OTHER CONTRACTS

A frequent practical problem is that there is a series of contracts between the parties, and A wishes to withhold performance under a contract it has not yet performed because B has not yet performed an earlier one, for example has not yet paid for goods received earlier. Is this permissible?

In German law, the right to withhold performance under § 320 BGB will not apply unless the obligations which, on the one side, have not been performed and, on the other, are consequently being withheld, are synallagmatic, ie exchanged one for the other. Thus § 320 BGB cannot be used in a number of situations. One is where the contract imposes obligations which are imperfectly synallagmatic.[59] Another, and this is the situation

---

[57] This provision is modelled on a rule found in the US Uniform Commercial Code § 2–609 on the 'right to adequate assurance of performance'.

[58] See further below, pp 1024 ff.

[59] We saw earlier (p 965) that in a contract of mandate, under which the agent is obliged to render accounts to the mandator and the mandator has to indemnify the mandatory for expenses incurred, it has been held that the two obligations are not synallagmatic, so that the mandatory cannot refuse to account because he has not been paid his expenses. It seems that the distinction in German law between synallagmatic obligations to which §§ 320–322 apply and non-synallagmatic is parallel to the English distinction between covenants which are conditions (concurrent or precedent) and 'independent' covenants: see above, p 963. There is no right to withhold your performance because the other party has not performed if his obligation is independent.

which is to be discussed here, is where the obligations in question arise under different contracts.

Although § 320 BGB does not apply to such cases, there is a general right of retention. This is described as a right of lien, but is a good deal wider since it is not limited to the withholding of the other party's property:

BGB **24.15 (DE)**

§ 273: Right of retention

(1) If the debtor has a matured claim against the creditor arising from the same legal relationship upon which his own obligation is based, he may, unless a contrary intention appears from the obligation, refuse to effect the performance due from him until the performance due to him is effected (right of retention).

(2) Whoever is obliged to hand over an object has the same right, if he has a claim due on account of disbursements incurred in connection with the object, or on account of any damage caused to him by it, unless he has acquired the object by an unlawful willful act.

(3) The creditor may avoid the exercise of the right of lien by giving security. The giving of security by way of guarantee is barred.

§ 274: Effects of right of retention

(1) As against the claims of the creditor the only effect of the enforcement of the right of retention is that the debtor is ordered to perform on receipt of the performance due to him (contemporaneous performance).

(2) By virtue of such a judgment the creditor may pursue his claim by means of compulsory execution without effecting the performance due from him if the debtor is in default with is acceptance.

Notes

(1) This allows a party to withhold performance of his obligation under one contract if the other party is in default under a separate contract, provided that there is a 'connection' between the two obligations. The BGH has stated fairly loosely that the latter should be 'a natural, internal economic connection, based upon a single factual relationship' such that 'to enforce one claim without regard to the other would be against good faith'.[60]

(2) If §§ 273–274 are compared to §§ 320–322, it will be seen that the procedure is different. §§ 320–322 look to performance, and the creditor whose claim is properly met by a defence that the debtor is withholding performance will get a judgment for performance conditional upon himself performing. Under § 273, in contrast, the creditor may defeat the debtor's right of retention either by performing or by giving

---

However, how different will the outcome be? Take the case referred to earlier, *Taylor v Webb* [1937] 2 KB 283, in which it was held that a landlord must repair the leased premises even if the tenant was in arrears with the rent, as the two obligations were independent. The tenant will not be able to get an order of specific performance against the landlord; he will have to claim damages for the cost of getting the repairs done by a third person and other loss. This may then be deducted from the rent due, as it is permissible to set off against one another counter-claims arising from the same transaction.

60 BGH 17 March 1975, BGHZ 64, 122, 124; BGH 22 February 1967, BGHZ 47, 157, 167.

> the debtor security—so that, at the end of the day, the debtor may have to be content with having a (secured) money claim against the creditor rather than having actual performance.

In French law, Articles 1219 and 1220 Cciv are more likely to be applied to performances under the same—synallagmatic—contract. However, the wording of these provisions might give a broader scope to the *exception d'inexécution*. Contrary to the Avant-projets Catala and Terré, the Ordonnance has not limited this remedy to synallagmatic contracts. Thus case law applying the *exception d'inexécution* to all the synallagmatic relationships, for instance when restitutions are to be performed after the annulment of a contract, might still be valid. The same goes for the case law holding that a party can withhold performance when the other party has not performed an obligation from another contract they have concluded, as long as there is a 'link' between those obligations.[61]

English law has no general rule allowing a party to withhold performance under a contract because another contract has not been performed. However, in English law a lawyer may exercise a lien over documents belonging to the client until the client has paid the lawyer's fees, even if the documents retained are not connected to the work for which the fee is due.[62] Furthermore, such a 'general lien' may be created expressly by contract and such clauses are common in sales.[63]

It should also be noted that all the systems, under differing conditions, allow claims arising out of the same or different contracts to be 'set off' against one another. This is particularly important when one party has become insolvent.[64]

FURTHER READING

Boosfeld, K, 'Withholding Performance' in N Jansen and R Zimmermann (eds), *Commentaries on European Contract Laws* (Oxford University Press, 2018) 1276–84.

Genicon, T, 'The *Exception d'Inexécution*' in J Cartwright and S Whittaker (eds), *The Code Napoléon Rewritten: French Contract Law after the 2016 Reforms* (Oxford: Hart Publishing, 2017) 291–315.

Treitel, G, *Remedies for Breach of Contract* (Oxford, Clarendon Press, 1988) 245–317.

---

[61] Cass com 12 July 2005, no. 03-12507, RJDA, no. 1316, p 1146, JCP G 2005.I.194, annotated by A Constantin.

[62] See *Goode* (n 21 above) para 22.66.

[63] eg: 'The Company shall be entitled, without prejudice to its other rights and remedies, either to terminate wholly or in part any or every contract between itself and you or to suspend any further deliveries under any or every such contract in any of the following events: (a) if any debt is due and payable by you to the Company but is unpaid; (b) … (c) if you have failed to take delivery of any goods under any contract between you and the Company otherwise than in accordance with your contractual rights.'

[64] Suppose A owes B £1,000 under contract no. 1 and B owes A £1,500 under contract no. 2. A becomes bankrupt. If there were no right of set-off, B would have to pay £1,000 to A and then prove in the bankruptcy for the £1,500. He will probably get only a small proportion of the amount. If he can set off the two debts, however, he may retain £1,000 and need only prove for the balance of what he is owed (£500). For English law, see L Gullifer, *Goode and Gullifer on Legal Problems of Credit and Security* (6th edn, London: Sweet & Maxwell, 2017) ch VII. In Germany set-off (*Aufrechnung*) is governed by §§ 387 ff BGB. In France set-off (*compensation*) is regulated by Arts 1289 ff Cciv; see Toledo, 'La compensation conventionnelle' RTD civ 2000, 265.

CHAPTER 25
TERMINATION

25.1 INTRODUCTION

The scope of this chapter is indicated by the following Articles of the Principles of European Contract Law (PECL):

Principles of European Contract Law   **25.1 (INT)**

Article 8:103: Fundamental Non-Performance

A non-performance of an obligation is fundamental to the contract if:

(a) strict compliance with the obligation is of the essence of the contract; or

(b) the non-performance substantially deprives the aggrieved party of what it was entitled to expect under the contract, unless the other party did not foresee and could not reasonably have foreseen that result; or

(c) the non-performance is intentional and gives the aggrieved party reason to believe that it cannot rely on the other party's future performance.

Article 8:106: Notice Fixing Additional Period for Performance

(1) In any case of non-performance the aggrieved party may by notice to the other party allow an additional period of time for performance.

(2) During the additional period the aggrieved party may withhold performance of its own reciprocal obligations and may claim damages, but it may not resort to any other remedy. If it receives notice from the other party that the latter will not perform within that period, or if upon expiry of that period due performance has not been made, the aggrieved party may resort to any of the remedies that may be available under chapter 9.

(3) If in a case of delay in performance which is not fundamental the aggrieved party has given a notice fixing an additional period of time of reasonable length, it may terminate the contract at the end of the period of notice. The aggrieved party may in its notice provide that if the other party does not perform within the period fixed by the notice the contract shall terminate automatically. If the period stated is too short, the aggrieved party may terminate, or, as the case may be, the contract shall terminate automatically, only after a reasonable period from the time of the notice.

Article 9:301: Right to Terminate the Contract
(1) A party may terminate the contract if the other party's non-performance is fundamental.
(2) In the case of delay the aggrieved party may also terminate the contract under Article 8:106(3).

Article 9:302: Contract to be Performed in Parts
If the contract is to be performed in separate parts and in relation to a part to which a counter-performance can be apportioned, there is a fundamental non-performance, the aggrieved party may exercise its right to terminate under this Section in relation to the part concerned. It may terminate the contract as a whole only if the non-performance is fundamental to the contract as a whole.

Article 9:303: Notice of Termination
(1) A party's right to terminate the contract is to be exercised by notice to the other party …

As mentioned earlier,[1] the legal systems differ in the means by which a contract may be terminated. This has a marked effect on the substance of the law: for example, English law, in which termination is an informal act of the aggrieved party, contains much more detailed rules on when termination is permitted than does French law, which even after the reforms of 2016 leaves a great deal to the appreciation of the judge.[2]

25.2 THE MEANING AND NATURE OF TERMINATION

Although in each system the basic notion of termination seems similar—as suggested at the start of Chapter 24,[3] the idea of escaping from the contract—there are quite significant differences not only in the mechanisms of termination but also in the detailed conceptions of what is involved. The principal difference in conception is whether the process is seen as essentially retrospective, that is, to undo what has taken place so far, or essentially only prospective, that is, for the future.

Traditionally, in French law, *résolution* was seen as retrospective; the contract was treated almost as if it had been annulled, triggering mutual restitution of benefits. Where

---

[1] Above, p 957.
[2] See further below, p 989.
[3] Above, p 957.

performance took place over a period of time (*contrat à exécution successive*, as opposed to a *contrat à execution instantanée*)[4] it was impractical to restore the benefits received and then the contract was simply terminated for the future. It was common to distinguish this process from *résolution* by calling it *résiliation*.[5] The 2016 reform of French contract law abandoned the retrospective character of the résolution. Authors who were closely involved with the process summarise the position taken by the 2016 reform:[6]

> The Ordonnance adopts a new approach that no longer makes an express reference to the retroactive nature of *résolution*, nor accounts for the effects of *résolution* by distinguishing between contracts to be performed successively and contracts to be performed instantaneously. This choice results from the criticisms of this distinction made by doctrine, which has demonstrated its inappropriateness since the material impossibility of making restitution does not occur only with regard to contracts for successive performance. This is why Article 1229 adopts a unitary conception of *résolution*. Abandoning the opposition between instantaneous and successive performance, the Ordonnance prefers a "teleological" analysis (according to the purpose). This leads to distinguishing the contracts whose performance find their utility and their justification in the full execution of the agreement, in which case the parties must return all of what they have procured to the other, and the contracts under which the benefits become fully useful and justified as and when they are performed, in which case there is no need for restitution for the period prior to the last benefit for which the counter-performance has not been received. Article 1229 specifies that in the latter situation the *résolution* is named *résiliation*.

Résolution is in principle a sanction for non-performance.[7] It is not necessary that the creditor has suffered a loss, nor that the debtor is at fault.[8] The breach need not be full and may be partial.[9] The question of restitution will be dealt in Section 25.9.C of this chapter.

---

[4] In the category *contrats successifs*, a distinction is sometimes made between *contrat à exécution successive* (one that creates a lasting set of obligations, such as a lease of goods or an employment contract) and *contrat à exécution échelonée* (which is to be performed in instalments); on this distinction, see F Terré, P Simler and Y Lequette, *Les obligations* (11th edn, Paris: Dalloz, 2013) no. 70.

[5] Authors agree that the term is misleading as *résiliation* also refers to the ability given to a party by the contract or by law to walk away from the contractual relationship.

[6] F Ancel, B Fauvarque-Cosson and J Gest, *Aux sources de la réforme du droit des contrats* (Paris: Dalloz, 2017) no. 25.171. This analysis is confirmed by the Report to the President (p 83 n 30 above), which clearly states at 34 that 'the Order abandons … the legal fiction of the retroactivity traditionally attached to *résolution* by the doctrine and the case-law, insofar as the retroactivity, in principle, has the effect of generating restitution … The question of restitution is henceforth formally detached from retroactivity, as refunds become an effect of the law.' On the new French law generally, see A Bénabent, *Les obligations* (16th edn, Paris: LGDJ, 2017) nos. 384-403; F Chénedé, *Le nouveau droit des obligations et des contrats: Consolidations, innovations, perspectives* (Paris: Dalloz, 2016) nos. 28.141–28.224; O Deshayes, T Genicon and YM Laithier, *Réforme du droit des contrats, du régime général et de la preuve des obligations; Commentaire article par article* (Paris: LexisNexis, 2016) 497–516; M Latina and G Chantepie, *La réforme du droit des obligations: Commentaire théorique et pratique dans l'ordre du Code civil* (Paris: Dalloz, 2016) nos. 646–73; P Malaurie, L Aynès and P Stoffel-Munck, *Droit des obligations* (9th edn, Paris: LGDJ, 2017) nos. 884–920.

[7] Nullity (eg, when the contract suffers from a vice of consent) also is retroactive and gives rise to restitution. However, there are important differences from the case of nullity: after *résolution* the aggrieved party will have an action for damages for breach of contract and may enforce a penalty clause against the other party.

[8] On this point, authors have various views, some of them consider that there should be fault and others do not; there is no such legal or judicial requirement.

[9] Case law even resorts to *résolution* when the case is one of impossibility: see further below, p 1180. This is criticised by doctrine, eg Terré et al (n 4 above) no. 650.

In contrast, in English law termination, which is effected by notice to the other party, is seen as essentially prospective: the aggrieved party is entitled to refuse to accept the other's performance in the future and itself to refuse to perform. Termination does not necessarily lead to a restitution of benefits transferred but, in practice, may lead to the undoing of what has been done. The aggrieved party must act consistently; it cannot, for example, both refuse to perform its part and keep the counter-performance it has received when it is able to return it. Thus, a buyer who has received defective goods and wishes to refuse to pay for them will normally have to reject them and allow the seller to take them away,[10] but a party who has received services before justifiably terminating the contract may simply refuse to pay. This is simply because the services cannot be returned. Thus, as we shall see in Section 25.9.C below,[11] in some circumstances the party in breach will not have a claim in restitution. The aggrieved party will usually claim damages, but he may be permitted instead, subject to quite stringent conditions, to claim in restitution for the value of the benefits he has conferred on the other party, though he may be subject to restitution in favour of the party in breach if the latter does have such a claim.[12]

German law[13] recognises termination in both senses. As in French law, if contractual obligations are to be performed over an extended period (*Dauerschuldverhältuis*), a party will in general be permitted to terminate only with effect for the future. This is known as *Kündigung*.[14]

BGB   **25.2 (DE)**

§ 314: Termination, for good cause, of contracts for the performance of a recurring obligation

(1) Either party may terminate a contract for the performance of a recurring obligation on notice with immediate effect if there is good cause for doing so. There is good cause if, having regard to all the circumstances of the specific case and balancing the interests of both parties, the terminating party cannot reasonably be expected to continue the contractual relationship until the agreed termination date or until the end of a notice period.

(2) If the good cause consists in the infringement of a duty under the contract, the contract may be terminated on notice only after a specified period for remedial action has expired or notice of default has been given to no avail. § 323(2) applies mutatis mutandis.

(3) The person entitled may terminate only if he gives notice of termination within a reasonable period after becoming aware of the cause for termination.

(4) The right to claim damages is not precluded by the termination.

---

[10] If the contract is for a number of goods of which only some are defective, the buyer may reject the whole quantity or keep the ones that are in accordance with the contract and reject the rest, in which case it must pay for the goods kept at the contract rate: Sale of Goods Act 1979, ss 30 and 35A (inserted by Sale and Supply of Goods Act 1994, s 3(1)).

[11] See below, p 1047.

[12] See below, p 1053.

[13] See on termination generally V Emmerich, *Das Recht der Leistungsstörungen* (6th edn, Munich: CH Beck, 2005); B Markesinis, H Unberath and A Johnston, *The German Law of Contract* (2nd edn, Oxford: Hart Publishing, 2006) ch 9.4.

[14] Formerly this applied only to certain types of contract: see §§ 542, 554(3) BGB—lease; §§ 620 ff BGB—contract of service; § 651e(2) BGB—travel contract.

However, even in the case where the creditor is only concerned with performances by the debtor that are already due, in German law there appear to be two mechanisms by which the creditor may in effect escape from his ties to the debtor. One is by a claim for damages for non-performance in place of performance itself; the other is by a declaration of termination (*Rücktritt*). The first is dealt with in the articles of the BGB dealing with performance, the second in the articles on termination.

BGB **25.3 (DE)**

§ 281: Compensation in lieu of performance because of failure to perform or failure to perform properly

(1) In so far as the obligor fails to perform when performance is due or fails to perform properly, the obligee may, subject to the requirements of § 280(1), demand compensation in lieu of performance if he has fixed to no avail a reasonable period within which the obligor is to perform or to effect supplementary performance. If the obligor has performed only in part, the obligee may demand compensation in lieu of full performance only if he has no interest in performance in part. If the obligor has failed to perform properly, the obligee may not demand compensation in lieu of performance if the breach of duty is immaterial.

...

§ 323: Termination for non-performance or for performance not in accordance with the contract

(1) If under a synallagmatic contract the obligor fails to effect performance when due or to perform in accordance with the contract, the obligee may terminate the contract, if he has fixed, to no avail, an additional period of time for performance.

...

§ 349: Declaration of termination

Termination is effected by declaration to the other party.

Both when damages are claimed in lieu of performance and when the creditor opts for termination, the main performance obligations of the contract are converted into 'secondary' obligations. In the case of the creditor opting for termination, these are obligations to make restitution of performance(s) already rendered under the contract. The BGB contains special rules (§§ 346–348) governing the 'winding down' of the contract in this manner. In the case of damages in lieu of performance, the debtor's main performance obligation is converted into an obligation to pay damages. The creditor is no longer obliged to perform and may claim damages in the amount of the difference between the value of the two parties' performance—the so-called 'difference theory'.[15] Alternatively, where the creditor has an interest in doing so, he may go ahead and perform his own obligations, in which case he can claim the full value of the other party's performance—the 'surrogation/exchange method'.[16]

Whether the creditor opts for *Rücktritt* or for damages, he may claim damages for breach of protective duties (*Schutzpflichten*, see § 241(2) BGB), as well as damages for delay not amounting to non-performance (§ 286(1) BGB), in addition to either restitution (in the case where he opts for *Rücktritt*) or damages for non-performance. Note that in the latter case the same harm or loss may not be counted twice in the process of calculating the damages.

It is interesting to compare with Dutch law. Dutch law allows termination (*ontbinding*) because of fundamental non-performance (Article 6:265 BW).[17] Theoretically *ontbinding* does not have retroactive effect—termination is said not to be retrospective (Article 6:269 BW)—but termination results in each party being liable to make restitution of any benefits received under the contract (Article 6:271 BW). This may be restitution of what was actually received or, if that is not possible—for example, because the buyer has before termination resold the goods to a third party—restitution of the value of the benefit received.[18] However, after termination the creditor may claim damages for non-performance (Article 6:277 BW).[19]

In the international restatements, termination is by notice and is prospective in effect:

Principles of European Contract Law   **25.4 (INT)**

Article 9:303: Notice of Termination

(1) A party's right to terminate the contract is to be exercised by notice to the other party.

(2) The aggrieved party loses its right to terminate the contract unless it gives notice within a reasonable time after it has or ought to have become aware of the non-performance.

(3) (a) When performance has not been tendered by the time it was due, the aggrieved party need not give notice of termination before a tender has been made. If a tender is later made it loses its right to terminate if it does not give such notice within a reasonable time after it has or ought to have become aware of the tender.

(b) If, however, the aggrieved party knows or has reason to know that the other party still intends to tender within a reasonable time, and the aggrieved party unreasonably

---

[15] See further below, p 1063.

[16] For an example see Markesinis et al (n 13 above) 455 (contract to barter piano for horse; creditor still wants to get rid of piano even though debtor has not delivered horse).

[17] Dutch law distinguishes between *ontbinding* because of fundamental non-performance (Art 6:265 BW) and *opzegging* (closest to *Kündigung*) in the case of long-term contracts. *Opzegging* is not included in the general rules on contract law, but mainly developed by case law. *Opzegging* does not require non-performance, but a notice period. If parties fail to observe a notice period damages must be paid.

[18] See AS Hartkamp & CH Sieburgh, *Mr. C. Assers Handleiding tot de beoefening van het Nederlands Burgerlijk Recht. 6. Verbintenissenrecht. Deel III. Algemeen overeenkomstenrecht* (Deventer: Kluwer 2014) nos. 699 ff.

[19] See ibid, no. 690.

fails to notify the other party that it will not accept performance, it loses its right to terminate if the other party in fact tenders within a reasonable time.

(4) If a party is excused under Article 8:108 through an impediment which is total and permanent, the contract is terminated automatically and without notice at the time the impediment arises.

Article 9:305: Effects of Termination in General

(1) Termination of the contract releases both parties from their obligation to effect and to receive future performance, but, subject to Articles 9:306 to 9:308, does not affect the rights and liabilities that have accrued up to the time of termination. (2) Termination does not affect any provision of the contract for the settlement of disputes or any other provision which is to operate even after termination.

25.3 BASIC RULES AND THE MEANS OF TERMINATION

25.3.A FRENCH LAW

French law on termination underwent thorough changes in 2016. On the one hand, the reform codified some of the evolution introduced by the case law, such as the admission of unilateral termination, making the judicial character of termination no longer as preeminent as it used to be. On the other hand, the reform introduced some innovations, such as the abandonment of the retroactive effect of termination.

Code civil **25.5 (FR)**

Sub-section 4

Termination

Article 1224: Termination results either from the application of a termination clause, or, where the non-performance is sufficiently serious, from notice by the creditor to the debtor or from a judicial decision.

Article 1225: A termination clause must specify the undertakings whose non-performance will lead to the termination of the contract.

Termination may take place only after service of a notice to perform which has not been complied with, unless it was agreed that termination may arise from the mere act of non-performance. The notice to perform takes effect only if it refers expressly to the termination clause.

Article 1226: A creditor may, at his own risk, terminate the contract by notice. Unless there is urgency, he must previously have put the debtor in default on notice to perform his undertaking within a reasonable time.

The notice to perform must state expressly that if the debtor fails to fulfil his obligation, the creditor will have a right to terminate the contract.

Where the non-performance persists, the creditor notifies the debtor of the termination of the contract and the reasons on which it is based.

The debtor may at any time bring proceedings to challenge such a termination. The creditor must then establish the seriousness of the non-performance.

Article 1227: Termination may in any event be claimed in court proceedings.

Article 1228: A court may, according to the circumstances, recognise or declare the termination of the contract or order its performance with the possibility of allowing the debtor further time to do so, or award only damages.

Article 1229: Termination puts an end to the contract.

Termination takes effect, according to the situation, on the conditions provided by any termination clause, at the date of receipt by the debtor of a notice given by the creditor, or on the date set by the court or, in its absence, the day on which proceedings were brought.

Where the acts of performance exchanged were useful only on the full performance of the contract which has been terminated, the parties must restore the whole of what they have obtained from each other. Where the acts of performance which were exchanged were useful to both parties from time to time during the reciprocal performance of the contract, there is no place for restitution in respect of the period before the last act of performance which was not reflected in something received in return; in this case, termination is termed resiling from the contract.[20]

Restitution takes place under the conditions provided by articles 1352 to 1352-9.

Article 1230: Termination does not affect contract terms relating to dispute-resolution, nor those intended to take effect even in the case of termination, such as confidentiality or non-competition clauses.

Notes

(1) Articles 1224 to 1230 of the new Code civil replace the former Articles 1183 and 1184. Article 1184 contained a strange contradiction. *Résolution* was presented as a form of resolutory condition, which would operate as a matter of law, but the text stated twice that *résolution* had a judicial character. Article 1184, which also affirmed the creditor's fundamental right to choose between enforcing performance and termination, was criticised as being a poorly conceived and badly placed text.[21]

(2) Although the former Code civil provided for the judicial character of termination, many exceptions were recognised. First, the judicial character of the remedy was sometimes removed by specific texts (eg Article 1657 for the sale of perishable goods; Article 1764 for lump sum building contracts). Second, express clauses which qualified or took away the judicial character of termination were recognised as valid. Third, case law recognised that in certain cases unilateral *résolution* was valid.

---

[20] The translators note that they translate '*la résiliation*' as 'resiling from a/the contract', so as to distinguish it from '*la résolution*' ('termination').

[21] D Tallon, 'L'article 1184 du Code civil, un texte à rénover?' in Université Panthéon-Assas (Paris II), *Clés pour la siècle* (Paris: Dalloz, 2000) 254; S Whittaker, 'Termination for Contractual Non-performance and its Consequences: French Law Reviewed in the Light of the Avant-projet de réforme' in J Cartwright, S Vogenauer and S Whittaker (eds), *Reforming the French Law of Obligations* (Oxford: Hart Publishing, 2009) 187.

(3) The new Code civil confirmed the decline of the judicial character of termination, already introduced by the case law.[22] Article 1224 now provides that termination can occur either by application of a clause, or through a unilateral decision in case of a serious breach, or by a judicial decision. Thus termination by a judicial decision is just one option. However, unilateral termination of a contract is still viewed with some caution. The drafters have therefore put in some restrictions. By contrast with unilateral termination, and also termination by application of a clause, which are subject to specific conditions, judicial termination may be claimed 'in any event' (Article 1227). The idea is that even though parties have included a termination clause in the contract, they can still seek judicial termination.

(4) The first restriction on the right to terminate unilaterally is that unless there is urgency, a party must give a notice of default to the other party, prior to the termination (Article 1226(1)). This notice must state expressly the consequence of a failure to perform, ie the termination of the contract (Article 1226(2)).

(5) Secondly, if the failure to perform persists, the party wishing to terminate must notify the other party of the termination of the contract and of the reasons on which it is based (Article 1226(3)). The obligation to give reasons for the decision to terminate is an innovation. The case law before 2016 did not require reasons to be given.

(6) Admitting unilateral termination has the advantages both of overcoming the slowness of the administration of justice and of bringing the French system into line with solutions of foreign legal systems that allow unilateral termination. There are doubts about the real improvement in terms of rapidity, and parties are still likely to opt for judicial termination for various reasons: in order to claim restitution, and also because, in line with the pre-existing case law, Article 1226 provides that the unilateral termination can only be made 'at the creditor's own risk'. This means that the creditor's decision to terminate is subject to judicial review, and the court may subsequently determine whether such termination was well founded. If the court rules that it was not justified, the party who unilaterally terminated the contract will have to pay damages to the other. When it is still possible, the other party may ask for the contract to be restored, that is to say, for specific performance of the contract. Before the ruling, if there is a serious disagreement as to the gravity of the breach, the other party may also obtain, from the *juge des référés*, an interim or conservatory measure (Articles 808 and 872 Code of civil procedure) to preserve the contract.[23]

25.3.B GERMAN LAW

Nor in German law is it necessary for the creditor to start court proceedings to have the contract terminated. Instead, in most cases he may have to set a notice period within

---

[22] The previous reform drafts already called for the introduction in the Code civil of unilateral termination. See: the Avant-Projet Catala, Arts 1158 and 1158-1; the Terré draft, Art 108; and the Chancellerie draft, Arts 165 ff. Each of these drafts has its own specificities in this respect.

[23] Cass civ (1) 7 November 2000, no. 99-18576, Bull civ I no. 286; for a discussion of Art 1158 of the Avant-Projet Catala and its successors, see in the volume by Cartwright et al (n 21 above): M Fabre-Magnan, ch 8; S Whittaker, ch 9 and L Miller, ch 7.

which the debtor must perform and, if the debtor does not comply, refuse performance thereafter. Exceptionally this notice period may be dispensed with.

25.3.B.1 *RÜCKTRITT*

BGB   **25.6 (DE)**

§ 323: Termination for non-performance or for performance not in accordance with the contract

(1) If under a synallagmatic contract the obligor fails to effect performance when due or to perform in accordance with the contract, the obligee may terminate the contract, if he has fixed, to no avail, an additional period of time for performance. (2) A period of time does not have to be fixed if

> 1. the obligor seriously and definitely refuses to perform,
>
> 2. the obligor fails to perform by a date specified in the contract or within a specified period and, in the contract, the obligee has linked the continuation of his interest in performance to the punctuality of that performance, or
>
> 3. special circumstances exist which, after each party's interests have been weighed, justify immediate termination.

(3) If the type of breach of duty is such that it is not feasible to fix a period for performance, a warning notice replaces it.

(4) The obligee may terminate the contract before performance becomes due if it is obvious that the preconditions for termination will be satisfied.

(5) If the obligor has performed in part, the obligee may terminate the entire contract only if he has no interest in partial performance. If the obligor has failed to perform in accordance with the contract, the obligee may not terminate the contract if there has been no more than an immaterial breach of duty.

(6) Termination is excluded if the obligee is solely or overwhelmingly responsible for the circumstance which would entitle him to terminate the contract or if a circumstance for which the obligor is not responsible materialises at a time when the obligee is in default through non-acceptance.

§ 324: Termination for breach of a duty under § 241(2)

If the obligor breaches some other duty under § 241(2) under a synallagmatic contract, the obligee may terminate the contract if he can no longer reasonably be expected to abide by the contract.

§ 325: Compensation and termination

The right to claim compensation in the case of a synallagmatic contract is not precluded by termination.

§ 326: Release from counter-performance, and termination where there is no duty to perform

(1) If, by virtue of § 275(1) to (3), the obligor is released from his obligation to perform, the claim for counter-performance lapses; in the case of part performance § 441(3) applies mutatis mutandis. Sentence 1 does not apply if the obligor under § 275(1) to (3)

990

does not have to effect supplementary performance in the event of a failure to perform in accordance with the contract.

(2) If the obligee is solely or overwhelmingly responsible for the circumstance releasing the obligor from the need to perform pursuant to § 275(1) to (3), or if the obligor is not responsible for that circumstance and this occurs at a time when the obligee is in default through non-acceptance, the obligor retains his claim for counter-performance. He must, however, allow a deduction for whatever he saves as a result of release from performance, he acquires through the utilisation of his labour elsewhere, or he maliciously fails to acquire.

(3) If, pursuant to § 285, the obligee demands the surrender of a substitute obtained for the object in respect of which the obligation is due or assignment of a substitute claim, he remains bound to effect counter-performance. Counter-performance is, however, reduced in accordance with § 441(3) in so far as the value of the substitute or of the claim for compensation is less than the value of the performance due.

(4) To the degree that counter-performance is effected although not due under this provision, whatever is effected may be reclaimed under §§ 346 to 348.

(5) If, by virtue of § 275(1) to (3), the obligor does not have to perform, the obligee may terminate; § 323 applies mutatis mutandis to the termination, except that it is not necessary to fix a period of time.

Notes

(1) Where the creditor seeks to terminate the contract under § 323, the starting point is that a notice period is required. (We will see below that the same is true if he seeks to claim damages in lieu of performance under § 281.) The purpose of the notice requirement is to allow the other party one last chance to fulfil his contractual obligations. In cases of non-performance, the debtor will be in delay. He may well already have been given notice (*Mahnung*) to perform under § 286 BGB. It is presumably possible, however, for the creditor to combine the notice putting the debtor into delay with a notice of refusal of performance, so that on expiry of the (single) notice period the creditor will be able to enforce one of his remedies under § 323 BGB. As indicated by § 323(2) no. 2, it is possible to fix agreed notice periods.[24]

(2) Clauses which purport to exclude the need for notice appear to be invalid if they are part of the creditor's standard conditions.[25] The BGB provides:

§ 309 Clauses whose invalidity is not subject to any appraisal

Even where derogation from the statutory provisions is permissible, the following are invalid in standard business terms: …

4. (notice, period for performance) a provision by which the user is relieved of the statutory requirement to give notice to the other party to perform or to fix a period for performance or supplementary performance by him; …

Clauses which allow the creditor to terminate after an unreasonably short period of notice do not seem to be regulated specifically, whereas clauses which fix an unreasonably

---

[24] See below, p 1011.
[25] cf above, pp 835 ff.

long period of notice before the creditor can terminate may be declared invalid under § 308(2) BGB.

(3) A warning notice before termination is not required in the cases set out in § 323(2) BGB. Note that § 323(2) no. 1 is dealing only with cases in which the debtor has already failed to perform in time. Refusal to perform before any performance is due ('anticipatory breach') is covered by § 323(4).[26] § 323(2) no. 2 is considered further below when we look at time stipulations.[27] It is not clear exactly what would or would not be covered by § 323(2) no. 3, but one case is where it would be wholly unreasonable to expect the creditor to accept performance, for example if the manner of an employee's non-performance has shown that he cannot be trusted.

(4) A warning notice is also not required where under § 275(1)–(3) there is no obligation actually to perform—for example, where it is impossible for the debtor to do so, or performance would involve disproportionate effort or expense. In these cases, § 326(5) provides that the notice can be dispensed with.

(5) In the same cases, § 326(1) provides that the creditor's obligation to perform (or, literally, the debtor's 'claim to counter-performance') comes to an end. However, here there is an exception for cases in which the non-performance took the form of non-conformity which because of § 275(1)–(3) the debtor cannot be required to cure. (Remember that 'cure' may be impossible without the contract as a whole being impossible and therefore ineffective.)[28] In such cases the contract should not be terminated automatically. The creditor might wish to keep the goods and claim a price reduction or (if applicable) damages. So, in this case, the creditor's option whether or not to terminate is preserved, but (as explained in (4) above) a warning notice need not be given.

(6) In cases in which the obligations do not come to an end automatically, termination is effected by a notice (if a warning notice is required, then a second notice) to the other party: § 349.

(7) § 323(3) provides that where setting a period of time is out of the question, a warning notice should be given instead. Since by definition it is too late for the debtor to do anything, the usefulness of this provision has been questioned.[29]

(8) If a right of termination is not exercised within any time agreed between the parties, or if no period has been agreed, within a reasonable time, it lapses: § 350.[30]

(9) Once the contract has been terminated, the parties come under mutual obligations to return any benefits received by performance.[31]

(10) § 325 provides that exercising the right to terminate does not prevent the creditor from claiming damages. This is in principle a change from the earlier law, under which the starting point was that claiming *Rücktritt* and claiming damages were

---

[26] See 25.20 (DE), below, p 1027.
[27] See below, pp 1011 ff.
[28] See above, p 919.
[29] R Zimmermann, *The New German Law of Obligations* (Oxford University Press, 2005) 71 n 176.
[30] See further below, p 1058.
[31] See further below, pp 1047 ff.

incompatible. However, in practice the creditor was allowed to claim in many cases. See the discussion in the first edition of this work.[32]

(11) It will be noted that the manner and seriousness of the non-performance may affect whether or not the creditor needs to give a notice (see § 323(2) no. 1), but, with two exceptions, it is not a prerequisite for termination under § 323 that the non-performance be of a particular seriousness. The two exceptions are contained in § 323(5): (i) where the debtor has effected partial performance (which we will see has a particular meaning)[33] and (ii) there is no right to terminate when the breach is trivial: § 323(5). We consider the issue in detail in the next section.

25.3.B.2 GOING OVER TO DAMAGES

BGB **25.7 (DE)**

§ 281: Damages in lieu of performance for non-performance or failure to render performance as owed

(1) To the extent that the obligor does not render performance when it is due or does not render performance as owed, the obligee may, subject to the requirements of section 280(1), demand damages in lieu of performance, if he has without result set a reasonable period for the obligor for performance or cure ...[34]

Notes

(1) In the previous section we noted that effects rather similar to termination may result from the creditor claiming damages in lieu of performance under § 281.[35] How close the analogy is depends on the circumstances.

(a) If the debtor has not performed at all, then (provided he has given the necessary warning to no avail) the creditor may simply claim damages for non-performance. As explained earlier,[36] the creditor is no longer obliged to perform and may claim damages in the amount of the difference between the value of the two parties' performance—the so-called 'difference theory'. Alternatively, where the creditor has an interest in doing so, he may go ahead and perform his own obligations, in which case he can claim the full value of the other party's performance—the 'surrogation/exchange method'.

(b) Equally in the case of partial performance, if the creditor has no interest in it (ie it is of no value to him), he may demand compensation instead of the whole performance. In this case it seems clear that the creditor need no longer perform himself, since § 281(5) provides that the debtor may recover back what

---

[32] H Beale, A Hartkamp, H Kötz and D Tallon, *Casebooks on the Common Law of Europe: Contract Law* (Oxford: Hart Publishing, 2002) 746–47.

[33] See below, p 1006.

[34] The remainder of (1) and (2)–(5) are omitted. On § 281(2) BGB, see below, p 1015.

[35] See above, p 985.

[36] Above, p 986 and below, p 1063.

he transferred under §§ 346–348. This makes sense only on the assumption that the debtor will not receive the counter-performance.

(c)   If the partial failure to perform is not substantial, § 281 seems to envisage that the creditor will claim damages in lieu of the unfulfilled obligations, but the contract will otherwise continue in effect. Thus the creditor will have to render the counter-performance originally due (eg to pay the full price) save that he may set off his claim for damages against the sum he owes himself.

The effect in cases (a) and (b) seems to be very similar to that where the contract is terminated: the creditor no longer has to perform, but instead gets damages for non-performance, while the debtor can reclaim the benefits he has transferred. However, there is a technical difference. Under § 281 the creditor cannot seek restitution of the benefits he has transferred; rather, he will claim damages based on the 'difference principle'.

(2) It should also be remembered that when the contract which has been broken was to be performed over a period of time, the creditor may bring it to an end for the future by means of *Kündigung* under § 314.[37] *Kündigung* will normally also require a period of notice, but this is made subject to the exceptions set out in § 323(2).

25.3.C ENGLISH LAW

In English law, a contract may be terminated if, within the time permitted under the contract, one party has failed to perform an obligation which is a condition of the contract. The distinction between a condition—breach of which gives rise to a right to terminate—and a warranty—breach of which does not give rise to a right to terminate but only to a claim for damages—was explained in Chapter 24.[38] However, in that chapter we were considering the right to withhold performance. We explained that if A has not performed a condition precedent to B's obligation to perform, or if A is unwilling to perform a concurrent condition, B need not perform until A performs or is ready to do so. If A's failure continues for long enough (see below), B may then terminate the contract. However, B may have a right to terminate the contract even if B has already performed, so that there can be no question of B withholding performance, if A commits a sufficiently serious breach. A term that is sufficiently important that breach of it gives such a right is also called 'a condition' (again, as opposed to a warranty; breach of a warranty will only give B a right to damages). The word 'condition' has thus come to have an extended meaning—it covers not only obligations that A has to perform before B's obligations or concurrently with them, but also terms that are so important that a breach by A gives B the right to terminate.[39] To give a simple example, A sells and delivers goods to B, who takes delivery and pays for the goods. B then finds that the goods do not correspond to the description. According to the Sale of Goods Act 1979, section 13,[40] A is in breach of

---

[37]   See 25.2 (DE), above, p 984.
[38]   See above, p 972.
[39]   See also above, p 973.
[40]   See 19.12 (EN), above, p 785.

an implied condition. B can reject the goods and terminate the contract.[41] Then B may either recover damages for non-performance or simply recover the price he has paid.

We will see in Section 25.4.B that a party will also have a right to terminate if the other party fails to perform an obligation that is not a condition, if the non-performance deprives the first party of the substance of what it was contracting for.

Thus, in English law the aggrieved party may not terminate the contract because of the other party's non-performance until the time for performance has expired.[42] A very important question is whether this happens as soon as the date for contractual performance has passed or whether the other party, though in breach of contract and thus liable for damages for delay, is allowed additional time for performance. This is considered below, when we consider termination for delay.[43]

25.3.D PECL

Principles of European Contract Law   **25.8 (INT)**

Article 8:103: Fundamental Non-performance
A non-performance of an obligation is fundamental to the contract if:
(a) strict compliance with the obligation is of the essence of the contract; or …

Article 8:106: Notice Fixing Additional Period for Performance
…
(3) If in a case of delay in performance which is not fundamental the aggrieved party has given a notice fixing an additional period of time of reasonable length, it may terminate the contract at the end of the period of notice. The aggrieved party may in its notice provide that if the other party does not perform within the period fixed by the notice the contract shall terminate automatically. If the period stated is too short, the aggrieved party may terminate, or, as the case may be, the contract shall terminate automatically, only after a reasonable period from the time of the notice.

Article 9:303: Notice of Termination
(1) A party's right to terminate the contract is to be exercised by notice to the other party.
…

Article 9:305: Effects of Termination in General
(1) Termination of the contract releases both parties from their obligation to effect and to receive future performance, but, subject to Articles 9:306 to 9:308, does not affect the rights and liabilities that have accrued up to the time of termination.

---

[41] At least if A cannot deliver goods of the right description within the time allowed: see below, p 1040. B's right to terminate is subject to s 15A (see 25.11 (EN), below, p 1005) and also to the rules on 'loss of the right to reject' in s 35 (see 27.2 (EN), below, p 1143).

[42] This is subject to an exception which we will consider below at p 1024. Sometimes there is in effect no question of time: for example, if a party promises not to do something and breaks the contract by doing the thing forbidden, the only question is whether the term broken was a condition.

[43] See below, pp 1011 ff.

(2) Termination does not affect any provision of the contract for the settlement of disputes or any other provision which is to operate even after termination.

Note

In the PECL, the rules on termination appear to follow the model of the common law. First, termination is by notice. Secondly, whether the aggrieved party has the right to terminate depends on the nature of the term broken or the effect of the breach, rather than on the discretion of the court. Thirdly, the contract may not normally be terminated until the time for performance has elapsed; and this depends on whether time was originally fundamental or the aggrieved party has subsequently given reasonable notice fixing a period for performance. Fourthly, it is (as we saw in the last section) prospective in effect[44] and, fifthly, it does not preclude a claim for damages. The provisions of the UNIDROIT Principles of International Commercial Contracts (UNIDROIT PICC) are broadly similar (see Articles 7.3.1, 7.3.2 and 7.3.5).[45] The Draft Common Frame of reference (DCFR) is different in one respect, as detailed below.[46]

25.4 THE SERIOUSNESS OF THE DEFAULT

25.4.A FRENCH LAW

Cass Civ (1), 22 September 2016[47]   **25.9 (FR)**

Horse rider

A serious breach of contract justifies the other party in terminating the contract unilaterally and without prior warning.

Facts: An equestrian club purported to cancel a member's subscription after he had behaved inappropriately towards other riders.

Held: The club's unilateral termination was justified by the seriousness of the member's breach of contract.

Judgment: Considering, according to the decision under appeal (Rouen, 5 March 2015), that on 6 September 2008, Mr. X ... renewed his annual registration at the equestrian center operated by the company Chevalerie de la Bretèque (the company); that by registered letter of 19 September 2008, the latter unilaterally terminated the contract and returned the subscription fee; that Mr X ... brought an action before the courts to cancel the termination and obtain the payment of damages.

Considering that Mr. X ... challenges the judgment for rejecting his requests, on the ground that:

1°/ that the unilateral and immediate resolution of the contract is justified only in the event of a breach by a party of its contractual obligations and provided that the

---

[44] Thus we will see that though after termination a party may return property it has received, there is only a right to restitution for benefits for which no counter-performance has been received, below, pp 1047 ff.

[45] The rules on restitution after termination are different: see Arts 7.3.6 and 7.3.7.

[46] Below, p 1055.

[47] No. 15-20614, unpublished.

breach is serious enough to justify such a sanction; that by merely stating that the documents submitted before the court established on the part of Mr. X ... an ambiguous behaviour towards female riders of the equestrian club and verbal violence towards Mrs. Y..., without checking, by reference to contractual documents, whether these facts contravened the obligations subscribed by M. X... at the time of his subscription, the court of appeal failed to give legal basis to its decision, with regard to [former] Article 1184 of the Code civil;

2°/ that only a serious breach by the contracting party of his obligations may justify the termination of the contract without notice and without compensation; that an ambiguous behaviour is by definition a behaviour whose meaning cannot be defined precisely; that the court of appeal, which stated that Mr. X... had had, with regard to young riders, "a behaviour whose ambiguity had a certain gravity", violated [former] Article 1184 of the Civil code by inferring that the unilateral termination decided by the company could not be sanctioned;

...

But considering that the decision notes that the altercation between Mr. X... and the father of a young rider took place within the premises of the equestrian center and that Mr. X... committed inadmissible verbal violence against a staff member; that the decision also points out that Mr. X... who preferred to rise a horse within a group composed exclusively of minors and especially young girls, offered them gifts, photographed them without their agreement, showed great interest in their conversations, and even sent them electronic messages close to harassment, and that was often aggressive against them; that the court of appeal, which thus characterised a serious breach on the part of Mr. X..., exactly inferred that the unilateral termination was justified.

...

On these grounds, the appeal is dismissed.

Notes

(1) When there is a total failure of performance, the court must certainly terminate the contract. It certainly will do so also when it considers that the creditor would not have contracted had he foreseen the breach. The discretion of the court to decide whether a non-performance is sufficiently serious to grant termination is wider when the obligation that is not performed is an accessory one or where non-performance of an essential obligation is only partial. The courts may take into account the economic context as well as the existence of a fault of the debtor. In the 'horse rider case', the Cour de cassation confirmed the unilateral termination, although the court of appeal had not clearly identified the obligation that was breached. The Cour de cassation found that the overall behaviour of the person amounted to a serious breach, which justified the termination.

(2) The judge may, if he refuses termination, take other measures. He can grant extra time for performance (a *délai de grâce*) (Article 1229; and see also Article 1343-5, which allows the court to allow extra time, up to two years, for money that is due to be paid).[48] He can also, of course, grant damages. He can also grant partial termination by, for instance, reducing the amount to be paid by the buyer of goods of an unsatisfactory quality. This amounts to a judicial modification of the contract and is justified

---

[48] This refers to payment of sums due. See further below, p 1042.

by the fact that good faith prevents one party from demanding total performance when partial performance can satisfy him. In commercial law, this is a well-known practice called *réfaction*: the judge can, under some conditions, modify the contract by adjusting the price.[49] In Cass civ, 27 November 1950,[50] the Court modified one party's obligation. The defendants had agreed to purchase the plaintiff widow's house in exchange for a *rente viagère* by which she would be provided with accommodation, food and care. The defendants failed to comply with their obligations and the plaintiff sought *résolution* of the agreement. The Court refused to allow the widow to terminate the agreement but decided to substitute a compensatory maintenance annuity in place of the positive obligation to care for the widow as provided for in the agreement. Some authors argued that it might be appropriate to extend the *réfaction* mechanism to other contracts than commercial contracts.[51] That was done by the 2016 reform by giving the creditor the option of price reduction. According to the new Article 1223 of the Code civil:

> In the case of imperfect performance of the act of performance, the creditor, having given notice to perform and where he has not yet paid for all or part of the act of performance, may notify the debtor as quickly as possible of his decision to reduce its price proportionally. Acceptance by the debtor of the creditor's decision to reduce the price must be made in writing. Where he has already paid, and in the absence of an agreement between the parties, the creditor may claim a reduction in price in court.

However, in this provision the possibility to reduce the price is given to the parties and not to the judge. It will not preclude the judge from reducing the price.

(3) When the court allows termination, it can decide that termination will only be granted after a period of time.[52] The court may also either award or refuse to award damages to the party who terminates (Article 1128).

25.4.B ENGLISH LAW

Because in English law termination is by act of the parties alone, the law must set criteria for when the non-performance is serious enough for the right to be exercised. We saw two such criteria in the last chapter on withholding of performance: in building contracts, the employer cannot withhold performance or terminate if there has been substantial performance; while more generally, a breach of condition entitles the aggrieved party to terminate while a breach of warranty does not.

The second approach involves classifying the terms of the contract as conditions or warranties a priori, rather than looking at how serious the actual breach is on the facts of the case. This gives rise to difficulties when the term is one that may be broken in a

---

[49] Req 23 May 1900, DP 1901.1.129: 'according to the trade usages that the contracting parties are deemed to apply in their commercial transactions, unless they exclude them by an express agreement …, the inferiority of quality, if not considerable, does not trigger the resolution of the conventions but only a reduction of the price.'

[50] Cass civ 27 November 1950, Bull civ I no. 237.

[51] Terré et al (n 4 above) no. 652.

[52] See further below, p 1042.

number of different ways, some of which will be serious but others not. If the contract does not specify the status of the term, should the court classify it as a condition because it *might* be broken in a very serious way? If this is done, there is a danger that a party who has indeed suffered a breach of the term by the other party will terminate the contract even though on the facts the breach caused little or no loss—the 'innocent' party's aim being to escape from a contract which has turned out unfavourably for other reasons, such as a fall in market prices since he entered the contract—remember that English law has no general doctrine of good faith or of abuse of rights. The problem is particularly acute when the contract is of a kind (often even on the same standard terms) that is frequently litigated—the court has to think about not just the case before it but also the impact of its decision on future disputes. A more flexible approach seems to be needed.

Court of Appeal **25.10 (EN)**

Hong Kong Fir Shipping Co Ltd v Kawasaki Kisen Kaisha[53]

The term that a chartered ship was to be fit in every way for cargo service was neither a condition nor a warranty. Whether breach of it gave rise to the right to terminate the contract depended on the consequences of the particular breach.

Facts: A 24 month time charter (which was on the 'Baltime 1939' form) provided that the vessel was to be delivered to the charterers at Liverpool, she being in every way fitted for 'ordinary cargo service'. The 'off-hire' clause provided that the charterers need not pay hire in respect of periods over 24 hours lost in carrying out repairs, and that such off-hire periods might, at the charterers' option, be added to the hire period. The vessel left for Newport News, to load a cargo of coal for carriage to Osaka. At the date of her delivery, the ship was unseaworthy because she had old engines which required careful supervision, whereas her engine-room staff was undermanned and inefficient. As a result, repairs had to be carried out on the way to Osaka and after her arrival there, and it took a total of 18 weeks to make her seaworthy. This left a period of 17 months during which she could be available to the charterers. There had been a steep fall in freight rates since the date of the charter, and the charterers purported to terminate.

Held: SALMON J held that the charterers had no right to terminate, and they appealed. The appeal was dismissed.

Judgment:
[SELLERS LJ held that there had been only a breach of warranty.]
UPJOHN LJ: ... Why is this apparently basic and underlying condition of seaworthiness not, in fact, treated as a condition? It is for the simple reason that the seaworthiness clause is breached by the slightest failure to be fitted 'in every way' for service. Thus, to take examples from the judgments in some of the cases I have mentioned above, if a nail is missing from one of the timbers of a wooden vessel, or if proper medical supplies or two anchors are not on board at the time of sailing, the owners are in breach of the seaworthiness stipulation. It is contrary to common sense to suppose that, in such circumstances, the parties contemplated that the charterer should at once be entitled to treat the contract as at an end for such trifling breaches. ...
It is open to the parties to a contract to make it clear either expressly or by necessary implication that a particular stipulation is to be regarded as a condition which goes to

---

[53] [1962] 2 QB 26.

the root of the contract, so that it is clear that the parties contemplate that any breach of it entitles the other party at once to treat the contract as at an end. That matter is to be determined as a question of the proper interpretation of the contract. Where … on the true construction of the contract, the parties have not made a particular stipulation a condition, it would be unsound and misleading to conclude that, being a warranty, damages is a sufficient remedy.

In my judgment, the remedies open to the innocent party for breach of a stipulation which is not a condition strictly so called, depend entirely on the nature of the breach and its foreseeable consequences. Breaches of stipulation fall, naturally, into two classes. First, there is the case where the owner by his conduct indicates that he considers himself no longer bound to perform his part of the contract: in that case, of course, the charterer may accept the repudiation and treat the contract as at an end. The second class of case is, of course, the more usual one, and that is where, due to misfortune such as the perils of the sea, engine failures, incompetence of the crew and so on, the owner is unable to perform a particular stipulation precisely in accordance with the terms of the contract try he never so hard to remedy it. In that case, the question to be answered is, does the breach of the stipulation go so much to the root of the contract that it makes further commercial performance of the contract impossible, or, in other words, is the whole contract frustrated? If yea, the innocent party may treat the contract as at an end. If nay, his claim sounds in damages only.

If I have correctly stated the principles, then, as the stipulation as to seaworthiness is not a condition in the strict sense, the question to be answered is, did the initial unseaworthiness as found by the learned judge, from which finding there has been no appeal, go so much to the root of the contract that the charterers were then and there entitled to treat the charterparty as at an end? The only unseaworthiness alleged, serious though it was, was the insufficiency and incompetence of the crew, but that surely cannot be treated as going to the root of the contract for the parties must have contemplated that, in such an event, the crew could be changed and augmented. In my judgment, on this part of his case counsel for the charterers necessarily fails.

I turn, therefore, to his second point: Where there have been serious and repeated delays due to the inability of the owner to perform his part of the contract, is the charterer entitled to treat the contract as repudiated after a reasonable time, or can he do so only if delays are such as to amount to a frustration of the contract? Some of my earlier observations on the remedy available for breach of contract are relevant here, but I do not repeat them. I agree with the conclusions reached by the learned judge and by Sellers LJ … Accordingly, I agree that this appeal must be dismissed.

DIPLOCK LJ: … Every synallagmatic contract contains in it the seeds of the problem: in what event will a party be relieved of his undertaking to do that which he has agreed to do but has not yet done? The contract may itself expressly define some of these events, as in the cancellation clause in a charterparty, but, human prescience being limited, it seldom does so exhaustively and often fails to do so at all. In some classes of contracts, such as sale of goods, marine insurance, contracts of affreightment evidenced by bills of lading and those between parties to bills of exchange. Parliament has defined by statute some of the events not provided for expressly in individual contracts of that class; but, where an event occurs the occurrence of which neither the parties nor Parliament have expressly stated will discharge one of the parties from further performance of his undertakings, it is for the court to determine whether the event has this effect or not. The test whether an event has this effect or not has been stated in a number of metaphors all of which I think amount to the same thing: does the occurrence of the event deprive the party who has further undertakings still to perform of substantially the whole benefit which it was the intention of the parties as expressed in the contract that he should obtain as the consideration for performing those undertakings? This test is applicable whether or not the event occurs as a result of the default of one of the parties to the contract, but the consequences of the event are different in the two cases. Where the event occurs as a result of the default of one party, the party in default cannot rely on it as relieving himself of the performance of any further undertakings on his part and the innocent party, although entitled to, need not treat the event as relieving him of the performance of his own undertakings. This is only a specific application of the fundamental legal and moral rule that a man should not be allowed to take advantage of his own wrong. Where the event occurs as a result of the default of neither party, each is relieved of the further performance of his own undertakings, and their rights in respect of undertakings previously performed are now regulated by the Law Reform (Frustrated Contracts) Act, 1943.

This branch of the common law has reached its present stage by the normal process of historical growth, and the fallacy in counsel for the charterers' contention that a different test is applicable when the event occurs as a result of the default of one party from that applicable in cases of frustration where the event occurs as a result of the default of neither party arises, in my view, from a failure to view the cases in their historical context. The problem: in what event will a party to a contract be relieved of his undertaking to do that which he has agreed to do but has not yet done? has exercised the English courts for centuries, probably ever since assumpsit emerged as a form of action distinct from covenant and debt, and long before even the earliest cases which we have been invited to examine: but, until the rigour of the rule in *Paradine v Jane* was mitigated in the middle of the last century by the classic judgments of Blackburn J in *Taylor v Caldwell* and Bramwell B in *Jackson v Union Marine Insurance Co*, it was in general only events resulting from one party's failure to perform his contractual obligations which were regarded as capable of relieving the other party from continuing to perform that which he had undertaken to do.

Once it is appreciated that it is the event and not the fact that the event is a result of a breach of contract which relieves the party not in default of further performance of his obligations, two consequences follow: (i) The test whether the event relied on has this consequence is the same whether the event is the result of the other party's breach of contract or not, as Devlin J pointed out in *Universal Cargo Carriers Corpn v Citati*. (ii) The question whether an event which is the result of the other party's breach of contract has this consequence cannot be answered by treating all contractual undertakings as falling into one of two separate categories: 'conditions', the breach of which gives rise to an event which relieves the party not in default of further performance of his obligations, and 'warranties', the breach of which does not give rise to such an event. Lawyers tend to speak of this classification as if it were comprehensive, partly for the historical reasons which I have already mentioned, and partly because Parliament itself adopted it in the Sale of Goods Act, 1893, as respects a number of implied terms in contracts for the sale of goods and has in that Act used the expressions 'conditions' and 'warranty' in that meaning. But it is no means true that of contractual undertakings in general at common law.

No doubt there are many simple contractual undertakings, sometimes express, but more often because of their very simplicity ('It goes without saying') to be implied, of which it can be predicated that every breach of such an undertaking must give rise to an event which will deprive the party not in default of substantially the whole benefit which it was intended that he should obtain from the contract. And such a stipulation, unless the parties have agreed that breach of it shall not entitle the non-defaulting party to treat the contract as repudiated, is a 'condition'. So, too, there may be other simple contractual undertakings of which it can be predicated that no breach can give rise to an event which will deprive the party not in default of substantially the whole benefit which it was intended that he should obtain from the contract; and such a stipulation, unless the parties have agreed that breach of it shall entitle the non-defaulting party to treat the contract as repudiated, is a 'warranty'. There are, however, many contractual undertakings of a more complex character which cannot be categorised as being 'conditions' or 'warranties' if the late nineteenth century meaning adopted in the Sale of Goods Act, 1893, and used by Bowen LJ in *Bentsen v Taylor, Sons & Co*, be given to those terms. Of such undertakings, all that can be predicated is that some breaches will, and others will not, give rise to an event which will deprive the party not in default of substantially the whole benefit which it was intended that he should obtain from the contract; and the legal consequences of a breach of such an undertaking, unless provided for expressly in the contract, depend on the nature of the event to which the breach gives rise and do not follow automatically from a prior classification of the undertaking as a 'condition' or a warranty'. For instance, to take the example of Bramwell B in *Jackson v Union Marine Insurance Co*, by itself breach of an undertaking by a shipowner to sail with all possible despatch to a named port does not necessarily relieve the charterer of further performance of his obligation under the charterparty, but, if the breach is so prolonged that the contemplated voyage is frustrated, it does have this effect.

As my brethren have already pointed out, the shipowner's undertaking to tender a seaworthy ship has, as a result of numerous decisions as to what can amount to 'unseaworthiness', become one of the most complex of contractual undertakings. It embraces obligations with respect to every part of the hull and machinery, stores and equipment and the crew itself. It can be broken by the presence of trivial defects easily and rapidly remediable as well as by defects which must inevitably result in a total loss of the vessel. Consequently, the problem in this case is, in my view, neither solved nor soluble by debating whether the owners' express or implied undertaking to tender a seaworthy ship is a 'condition' or a 'warranty'. It is, like so many other contractual terms, an undertaking one breach of which may give rise to an event which relieves the charterer of further performance of his undertakings if he so elects, and another breach of which may not give rise to such an event but entitle him only to monetary compensation in the form of damages. It is, with all deference to counsel for the charterers' skilful argument, by no means surprising that, among the many hundreds of previous cases about the shipowner's undertaking to deliver a seaworthy ship, there is none where it was found profitable to discuss in the judgments the question whether that undertaking is a 'condition' or a 'warranty': for the true answer, as I have already indicated, is that it is neither, but one of that large class of contractual undertakings, one breach of which may have the same effect as that ascribed to a breach of 'condition' under the Sale of Goods Act, 1893, and a different breach of which may have only the same effect as that ascribed to a breach of 'warranty' under that Act.

...

What the learned judge had to do in the present case as in any other case where one party to a contract relies on a breach by the other party as giving him a right to elect to rescind the contract, was to look at the events which had occurred as a result of the breach at the time at which the charterers purported to rescind the charterparty, and to decide whether the occurrence of those events deprived the charterers of substantially the whole benefit which it was the intention of the parties as expressed in the charterparty that the charterers should obtain from the further performance of their own contractual undertakings. One turns, therefore, to the contract, the Baltime 1939 Charter. Clause 13, the 'due diligence' clause, which exempts the shipowners from responsibility for delay or loss or damage to goods on board due to unseaworthiness unless such delay or loss or damage has been caused by want of due diligence of the owners in making the vessel seaworthy and fitted for the voyage, is in itself sufficient to show that the mere occurrence of the events that the vessel was in some respect unseaworthy when tendered or that such unseaworthiness had caused some delay in performance of the charterparty would not deprive the charterer of the whole benefit which it was the intention of the parties he should obtain from the performance of his obligations under the contract-for he undertakes to continue to perform his obligations notwithstanding the occurrence of such events if they fall short of frustration of the contract and even deprives himself of any remedy in damages unless such events are the consequences of want of due diligence on the part of the shipowner.

The question which the learned judge had to ask himself was, as he rightly decided, whether or not, at the date when the charterers purported to rescind the contract, namely 6 June, 1957, or when the owners purported to accept such rescission, namely 8 Aug, 1957, the delay which had already occurred as a result of the incompetence of the engine-room staff, and the delay which was likely to occur in repairing the engines of the vessel and the conduct of the owners by that date in taking steps to remedy these two matters, were, when taken together, such as to deprive the charterers of substantially the whole benefit which it was the intention of the parties they should obtain from further use of the vessel under the charter-party. In my view, in his judgment—on which I would not seek to improve—-the learned judge took into account and gave due weight to all the relevant considerations and arrived at the right answer for the right reasons.

Notes

(1) It will be noted that Diplock LJ takes a slightly different approach to Upjohn LJ. According to Diplock LJ, a term will be a condition only if the agreement itself, or statute, so provides, or 'if it can be predicated that every breach of [the term] must give rise to an event which will deprive the party not in default of substantially the whole benefit …'. Upjohn LJ states that it is open to the parties to make it clear that a term is a condition either expressly or 'by necessary implication'. This seems to allow terms to be classified as conditions even though not every breach of them would necessarily have serious consequences. The House of Lords has held that Upjohn LJ's approach is the correct one.[54]

(2) In *Cehave NV v Bremer Handelsgesellschaft mbH, The Hansa Nord*,[55] the more flexible approach adopted in the *Hong Kong Fir* case was applied to a term in a cost, insurance and freight (cif) sale contract that the goods be shipped 'in good condition'. A small quantity of the goods (citrus pulp pellets) had been damaged by overheating and the buyers rejected the whole cargo although the pellets were still perfectly good for the buyers' purpose—as was shown by the fact that, when the goods were

[54] See below, p 1019.
[55] [1976] QB 44 (CA).

auctioned on the orders of a court in Rotterdam after the sellers had refused to repay the price, the buyers bought the goods again at a knock down price and used them for their original purpose. The English trial judge considered that as the Sale of Goods Act (SGA) refers only to conditions and warranties, and a breach of the term that the goods were to be shipped in good condition *might* have serious consequences, it must be a condition. Thus he held that the buyers were within their rights to reject. The Court of Appeal held that the Sale of Goods Act 1979 did not exclude the rules of the common law, under which the term would not be a condition. Thus the buyer would be entitled to reject the goods only if the breach had deprived them of the substance of what they were contracting for, which was not the case. (The Court of Appeal also held that such a slight defect did not make the goods 'unmerchantable' within the words of SGA, section 14(2) as it then read. If the goods had been unmerchantable, the buyers *would* have had the right to reject, since Section 14(2) also stated that it was a 'condition' that the goods be of merchantable quality. The section now refers to 'satisfactory quality',[56] and almost certainly the goods would not have passed this test—but the buyers would still not have had a right to reject the goods because of the new section 15A, see below.)

We have seen that the Sale of Goods Act 1979, as amended by the Sale and Supply of Goods Act 1994, provides a number of terms relating to the description and quality of goods which are implied into contracts for the sale of goods.[57] Thus, where the sale is by description, the goods must correspond to the description (section 13(1)); and in sales in the course of a business, the goods must be of satisfactory quality, and may have to be fit for the buyer's particular purpose (section 14(2) and (3)). The Act provides explicitly that the relevant implied terms 'are conditions' (sections 13(1A) and 14(6)). However, the cases show that sometimes there may be a breach of one of these implied conditions which does not in fact have serious consequences for the buyer, yet the buyer takes advantage of the fact that there has been a breach of condition to escape from the contract for ulterior motives—typically because the market price for the goods has fallen since the date of the contract. On occasions the courts have seemed to strain the law to prevent this (for example in *The Hansa Nord*,[58] that the goods were merchantable despite being damaged); on other occasions they have allowed the buyer to terminate even though the buyer's conduct smacked of abuse of rights. An example is *Arcos Ltd v EA Ronaasen & Son*.[59] In that case a buyer was permitted to reject a consignment of barrel staves (strips of wood for making barrels) that did not correspond to the contractual description of half an inch thick, although they were only one-sixteenth of an inch too thick and were perfectly suitable for making barrels. (It will be recalled that English law does not have doctrines of good faith or abuse of rights.) To prevent these problems recurring, the Law

---

[56] See 19.12 (EN), above, p 785.
[57] ibid.
[58] Above, p 1003.
[59] [1933] AC 470 (HL).

Commission recommended that in commercial sales the law should be changed to prevent buyers from acting in this way:

Sale of Goods Act 1979[60]   **25.11 (EN)**

Section 15A: Modification of remedies for breach of condition in non-consumer cases

    (1) Where in the case of a contract of sale—

        (a) the buyer would, apart from this subsection, have the right to reject goods by reason of a breach on the part of the seller of a term implied by section 13, 14 or 15 above, but

        (b) the breach is so slight that it would be unreasonable for him to reject them, then, if the buyer does not deal as consumer, the breach is not to be treated as a breach of condition but may be treated as a breach of warranty.

    (2) This section applies unless a contrary intention appears in, or is to be implied from, the contract.

    (3) It is for the seller to show that a breach fell within subsection (1)(b) above.

Notes

(1) Before the Consumer Rights Act 2015, the Sale of Goods Act applied also to consumer sales, but this section did not apply 'if the buyer was dealing as a consumer'. It was thought that consumers should retain an absolute right of rejection, as a way of reducing the inequality between them and suppliers.[61] The Consumer Rights Act 2015 amended the 1979 Act to remove the reference to consumers. There is no equivalent to section 15A in the Consumer Rights Act.

(2) Section 15A looks like an introduction of a duty of good faith in exercising rights of termination. However, the change is very limited. Section 15A applies only to the kinds of breach listed. There is an equivalent section, section 30(2A), applying to cases where the wrong quantity of goods have been delivered. But there is no rule to restrict termination when the goods have been delivered late, and there is nothing equivalent to these sections for contracts other than sale of goods.[62]

The Consumer Rights Act 2015 contains special rules on when a consumer may reject the goods and terminate the contract because the goods are not in conformity with the contract. These do not use the language of 'condition' and 'warranty' but spell out the remedies available to the consumer in each case. We consider these consumer provisions in Chapter 27.

25.4.C GERMAN LAW

German law seems to present a contrast to the other systems considered. Look again at the texts set out earlier.[63] The creditor may not terminate if the non-performance is only

---

[60] As amended by Sale and Supply of Goods Act 1994 and Consumer Rights Act 2015.

[61] See The Law Commission and The Scottish Law Commission, *Sale and Supply of Goods*, Law Com No 160, Scot Law Com No 104 (London: Her Majesty's Stationery Office, 1987) paras 2.26, 4.1, 4.24 and 6.18–6.20.

[62] See below, p 1023.

[63] 25.3 (DE), p 985, and 25.6 (DE), p 990, above.

'immaterial' (*unerheblich*),[64] but apart from this there seems to be no requirement that the non-performance be particularly serious before the creditor may terminate under § 323. Rather, the creditor may terminate in any case of non-performance provided that the debtor has been given the necessary notice that it must perform within a reasonable time and thus a last chance to perform. The seriousness of any non-performance—(for example, whether it was a 'serious and final' refusal to perform, or the effect of the delay) seems to go to whether or not this notice to perform within a reasonable time (*Fristsetzung*) is required. Thus, under § 323(2) no. 3, a warning notice before termination is not required if there are special circumstances which justify an immediate withdrawal. (The other cases under § 323(2) are considered below.)[65]

In effect, § 323 deals separately with different types of non-performance—complete non-performance, late performance, partial performance and defective (ie non-conforming) performance. Not surprisingly, if the debtor completely fails to perform after being given any *Fristsetzung* that may be required, the creditor may terminate the contract. Late performance is considered in the next section. Here we need to concentrate on partial performance and defective performance.

The first sentence of § 323(5) states that 'If the obligor has performed in part, the obligee may withdraw from the whole contract only if he has no interest in part performance.' This may seem like a requirement of seriousness. However, § 323(5) BGB applies only if the contract is one under which the performances can naturally be severed into distinct units, and the question is whether or not the units already received can be rejected.[66] Thus, if goods are to be delivered or work is to be carried out in a series of separate instalments, the employer can terminate in respect of the whole only if he can show that because of the non-performance, the goods delivered or the work that has been done to date is of no value to him—for instance, because the services must conform to a particular format which other suppliers cannot provide. The employer (after giving any necessary warning) can, in effect, treat the contract as if it had never been performed at all. (The service provider will in theory have a claim for restitution of benefits under §§ 346–348, but if the work done was of no value this will fail.)

Cases in which a single performance is not completed is treated in the same way as performance which is defective; both fall within § 323(5), second sentence. This states: 'If the obligor has not performed in conformity with the contract, the obligee may not withdraw from the contract if the breach of duty is immaterial.' In other words, after giving any necessary warnings, the creditor may terminate unless the defect or non-performance was trivial. Thus, when a decorator uses the wrong paint, the employer may terminate (rather than opt to reduce the price)[67] unless the decorator can show that the non-conformity was 'immaterial'.

The case where the contract is for the sale of goods and the seller delivers too small a quantity is also treated as a case of non-conformity: § 434(3). Possibly this was done with the aim of allowing the buyer to terminate for short delivery unless the shortage was

---

[64] § 325(5)(2) BGB.
[65] On (i) see 25.20 (DE), below, p 1027 (anticipatory repudiation); on (ii) see pp 1011 ff (delay).
[66] Markesinis et al (n 13 above) 429, citing BGH NJW 1990, 3011, 3012.
[67] See above, p 992.

insignificant (this is the position under CISG),[68] but in fact it is controversial whether the second sentence of § 323(5) applies in this case.[69]

It seems that the restriction that the creditor may not terminate if the non-performance was only *unerheblich* was designed to reflect the provision in the Consumer Sales Directive, which permits Member States to exclude the consumer's right to terminate where the non-conformity was 'minor'.[70] Whether this is correctly translated as 'trivial' or 'immaterial' is an interesting question. It seems entirely possible that the Directive was intended to allow Member States to refuse termination in cases in which the non-conformity was certainly more than trivial but was something less than fundamental.[71]

Earlier we noted that, instead of seeking *Rücktritt* under § 323, the creditor may claim damages in lieu of performance under § 281. The two sections are very closely parallel and the rule for partial performance under § 281 mirrors that of § 323. Under § 281(1), in a case of partial performance of a contract to be performed in instalments, the creditor may claim damages in lieu of complete performance only if he has no interest in the part performance. In other cases he may 'go over to damages' unless the non-performance was immaterial.[72]

The net result seems to be that when we ask how serious must a non-performance be in substance, the answer may be that under German law the test is less demanding than under the other systems. However, against that must be set the rule that termination is not normally permitted until after the debtor has been given a *Fristsetzung*—and thus a further chance to perform. It is that rule—and its exceptions—which we consider next. We also need to consider the practical effects of termination.[73]

BGH, 13 November 1953[74]   **25.12 (DE)**

Ship not loaded

When a positive breach of contract is so serious that the aggrieved party cannot reasonably be expected to continue with the contract, he may terminate it without serving a notice requiring the other to perform.

Facts: Under a charter agreement a ship was to be ready to load in New York around 5 September. It arrived on 11 September. After repeated demands by the owners, the charterers named as responsible for loading a stevedore firm who were not in fact involved at all. The plaintiffs set 12 September as the date on which loading was to begin or for a bank guarantee to be given. This was not done, the charterers making only a vague offer of loading in New Orleans. On 13 September the plaintiffs. declared they were withdrawing from contract and reserving all damages claims. They claimed damages.

---

[68] See Art 49(1)(b); cf English Sale of Goods Act 1979, s 30.

[69] Markesinis et al (n 13 above) 428.

[70] Directive 1999/44/EC of the European Parliament and of the Council of 25 May 1999 on certain aspects of the sale of consumer goods and associated guarantees (OJ L 171/1999, p 12) Art 3(6). See Markesinis et al (n 13 above) 427–28.

[71] For a discussion of this point, see H Beale, 'Remedies for Breach of Contract in the Light of the Recent Changes to German Law, English Law and the DCFR' in U Blaurock and G Hager (eds), *Obligationenrecht im 21. Jahrhundert* (Baden Baden: Nomos, 2010) 115.

[72] § 281(1), last sentence.

[73] See below, pp 1044 ff.

[74] BGHZ 11, 80.

Held: The regional court dismissed the action. The appeal court declared the claim well founded. The defendant's appeal on a point of law was dismissed.

Judgment: On 30 August 1950 the plaintiff entered into a charterparty with the defendant in the form of the Gencon charter. Under that charterparty the plaintiff undertook to make its steamer 'Ouistreham' available around 5 September 1950 in New York.

On 11 September 1950 the 'Ouistreham' arrived in New York and notified its readiness to load to C Sh Co whose name had finally been given to it by the defendant after repeated requests to that effect. That firm again informed the plaintiff that it had nothing to do with loading. In fact the defendant had no one for loading. On the same day the plaintiff informed the defendant that it would consider itself released from its obligations under the charterparty if loading of the vessel was not started by not later than mid-day on 12 September 1950, or if the defendant did not provide a bank guarantee for performance of the charterparty. The defendant did not proceed to load, nor did it present the promised guarantees by the Federal Government and the Bank but merely pointed to the possibility of a loading in New Orleans. Thereupon, the plaintiff informed the defendant on 13 September 1950 that as a result of the defendant's default it considered that the charterparty had not been performed, was withdrawing the 'Ouistreham' and reserving all rights to damages arising out of the defendant's breach of contract.

According to the plaintiff, on the evening of 15 September 1950 the 'Ouistreham' was brought into another dock in New York and on 28 September 1950 again made ready for regular service.

In its application the plaintiff claims recovery of its costs for unnecessarily sending the vessel to New York. It bases its claim to damages expressly on Clause 13 of the Charterparty ('indemnity for non-performance of this charterparty, proved damages, not exceeding amount of freight').

The defendant contested the ground of action and the amount, contending that the plaintiff had not complied with § 577 HGB (Commercial Code).

The Regional Court dismissed the action. The appeal court declared the claim well founded. The defendant's appeal on a point of law was dismissed.

On those grounds:
In so far as the culpable breach does not involve impossibility of performance and delay specifically provided for in the Civil Code and occasions damage going beyond the interest in performance, such damage is to be made good in accordance with §§ 249ff BGB. That does not apply to unilateral obligations not dependent on counter-performance but only to synallagmatic contracts.

… In the case of synallagmatic contracts the injured party is not, however, limited to claiming such damage concerning the 'negative' (breach of faith or compensatory) interest. The contracting party affected by the positive breach of contract can under certain circumstances claim further rights which as to content correspond to the rights arising out of §§ 325, 326 BGB but have their legal basis in § 242 BGB. Where, as a result of the breach, the object of the contract is jeopardised to the extent that the party faithfully adhering to the contract cannot, in light of all the circumstances of the case and in good faith, be expected to continue the contract or to perform its obligations under the contract, it can for its part refuse to perform the contract and opt either for damages for non-fulfilment, that is to say the 'positive' interest in performance or indeed withdraw from the contract …

Whereas the claim for damages going beyond the interest in performance does not in principle affect performance of the contract, performance is precluded in the event of the 'unreasonable jeopardising of the object of the contract'. The party who may therefore withhold performance, is also entitled to withdraw from the contract or claim damages for non-performance. The subject matter of the present dispute is not loss going beyond the interest in performance. The claim for damages formulated in the action cannot, in the view of the Reichsgericht (Imperial Court), be founded merely on an application of § 276 BGB, as it may have seemed from the submissions of the plaintiff. The essential examination of whether, in light of the defendant's conduct, the plaintiff was entitled to withdraw prematurely from the contract depends upon whether the plaintiff in all the circumstances could in good faith still be expected to perform its obligations under the charterparty which were essentially to make the vessel available and to effect the carriage. According to general principles of law contained in the BGB—not the special provisions of the HGB—a party is released from those obligations where the charterer by his conduct culpably jeopardises the object of the contract to such an extent that the shipowner can no longer reasonably be expected to effect the performance stipulated by those obligations. The defendant is wrong in law to assert that the plaintiff, as the party required to effect performance first, was entitled to withhold performance only under the conditions set out in § 321 BGB. That provision only governs the special case of a significant deterioration occurring subsequently in the financial situation of the party receiving performance first, even in the absence of fault by that party. It does not, however, preclude further restrictions on the duty to effect performance from being justified in practice under the good faith requirement of § 242 BGB. Moreover, the prevailing opinion is that the party required to perform first is also entitled under § 242 BGB to withdraw from the contract if the party receiving performance first is not prepared to counteract the risk occurring to the object of the contract as a result of the deterioration in his financial situation by means of a step-by-step performance or by provision of security.

In the present case any default is sufficient in order to satisfy the definition of a positive breach of contract. Moreover, the decisive factor is merely whether the breach is so serious that not only the object of the contract is jeopardised but that, as a result of that risk, the injured party can no longer be expected to continue with the contract. ... Where in light of all the circumstances, in particular the nature of the agreement and the specific situations and interests of the contracting parties, the breach of contract is so fundamental that the party complying with the terms of the contract can no longer be expected to continue to do so, the fixing of a period on expiry of which performance will not be accepted is no longer a requirement, at least as a general rule. ... The party affected by the breach of contract may indicate the grounds which are decisive for him and withdraw from the contract straight away. In that connection the decisive grounds can only be those existing at the time of the party's declaration and stated as being significant in that connection. ... A subsequent alteration in the conduct or the views of the parties to the contract cannot affect the justification of the declaration to withdraw from the contract. ...

On the basis of these legal considerations the findings of the court a quo from the uncontested submissions of the parties entirely warrant the plaintiff's declared intention to withhold performance.

Although the defendant had no-one responsible for loading, on 7 September 1950 it gave the plaintiff the name of the non-existent Co. Sh. Co and on 8 September 1950 C Sh Co Inc. After the plaintiff had become suspicious of this repeatedly false information, the defendant sought to allay the plaintiff's suspicion on 9 September 1950 by stating that the A Bank had assumed responsibility for financing the transaction and had done so. This statement too turned out on immediate enquiry to be untrue. As a result of this conduct by the defendant the plaintiff must have had not only subjectively justifiable doubts as to the fulfilment of its interest in the proper performance of the charterparty but there was also the danger that the plaintiff's interests would be objectively frustrated in view of the defendant's culpable breach. Therefore, without erring in law, the court a quo found that even two days before arrival of the steamer in New York the situation had been such that the plaintiff must have had grave fears that the defendant would not fulfil the contract; the defendant repeatedly showed itself to be unreliable; even then its conduct would have justified the vessel's immediate withdrawal.

The duty incumbent on the shipowner to effect performance first generally entails a considerable financial risk which is only reasonable and tolerable if the charterer avoids anything which could undermine the basis of trust necessary for the carrying out of such a contract. On the undisputed facts of the case the defendant's unreliable conduct must have led the plaintiff seriously to doubt that the contract could properly be performed. Notwithstanding the undermining of the relationship of trust, the plaintiff did not straight away withdraw from the contract but gave the defendant a chance—in line with the provision contained in § 321 BGB—to remove the plaintiff's doubts and reservations as regards performance of the contract, by commencing loading or by providing a bank guarantee by 12 September 1950. By fixing this period the plaintiff did everything which could have been reasonably expected of it in accordance with the principle of good faith in order to preserve the interests of both contracting parties in the effecting of counter-performance. The defendant did not avail itself of the chance given to it. It did not fulfil conditions subject to which the plaintiff was prepared to continue with the contract. In that state of affairs the plaintiff, which is established abroad and could only have pursued its claims in Germany, could no longer be expected on account of the lack of certainty to expose itself to the continued risk of an ever-increasing loss occasioned by the vessel standing idle. The plaintiff's confidence in the defendant's adherence to the contract was thus finally so completely shaken that it could not be expected to continue to regard itself as bound by the contract. In such a case the initial jeopardising of interests is to be equated to frustration of interests. ... By telex of 13 September 1950 the plaintiff expressly substantiated the allegation of breach of contract against the defendant and its decision to withdraw the vessel and seek damages on the ground of the defendant's unreliable conduct ('... having been twice misled ...'). By that statement the plaintiff was finally released from its duty of performance under the contract and entitled to claim damages under clause 13 of the charter party.

Notes

(1) The Gencon charter is a form of voyage charter under which the owner is remunerated by the freight he earns through carrying the goods. Thus the owner has a very direct interest in being provided with a full cargo as quickly as possible. (Compare a 'time charter' under which the charterer pays the owner a monthly hire fee.)

(2) The references to the BGB in the case are to the pre-2002 version, but the discussion remains relevant.

(3) Whether the creditor must serve a Fristsetzung is now governed by § 323.[75] If the breach by the debtor is very serious, no Fristsetzung is required: § 323(2) no. 3. In other cases the creditor must first serve a Fristsetzung, § 323(1).

---

[75] See 25.6 (DE), above, p 990.

(4) Curiously, there is an English case, *Universal Cargo Carriers v Citati* [1957] 2 QB 401 with almost identical facts—the charterer under a voyage charter failed to provide a cargo. But the English court said the date for loading was *not* of the essence of the contract and the owner was entitled to terminate only when the delay became very serious (what the judge called a 'frustrating delay', though he did not mean that the contract was frustrated in the legal sense). He did not discuss 'making time of the essence' by serving a notice; it is thought that in modern law the owners would have such a right: see below.[76]

25.5 TERMINATION FOR DELAY IN PERFORMANCE

The question to be asked in this section is this. Suppose the debtor has not yet performed, or he has performed in a way that, in substance, departs from the contract seriously enough that termination might be justified (eg it is not just a minor non-performance). How long does the creditor have to wait before terminating? Can he terminate right away? Must he show that the delay is very serious? Or must he at least give the debtor a warning so that, in effect the debtor has a second chance?

We have seen that in French law, under Article 1228 of the new Code civil, the judge can grant an additional period of time for performance.[77] When termination is unilateral, a notice (*mise en demeure*) to perform is needed before termination can take place (Article 1226 of the Code civil).[78] The only exception to this obligation to serve a prior notice is when there is urgency. The new Code civil organises a rather demanding system for the creditor, inspired by the desire to protect the debtor against what is still viewed as a dangerous alternative to judicial termination. The creditor must first put the defaulting debtor on notice to fulfil his undertaking within a reasonable time. This notice must state expressly that if the debtor fails to fulfil his obligation, the creditor will be entitled to terminate the contract. After a while, if non-performance continues, he can then give notice that the contract is terminated and must specify on what grounds. Termination only takes effect at the time of receipt of that notice by the other party to the contract.[79]

It seems that, on paper, modern English and German law reach broadly similar results: in some cases the creditor may terminate as soon as the date for performance has passed,[80] in other cases he can terminate if he has given the debtor a reasonable warning and the debtor has still failed to perform. However, the two laws seem to start from opposite ends.

---

[76] Below, p 1019.

[77] 25.5 (FR), above, p 988.

[78] The case law before the reform already adopted this solution: Terré et al (n 4 above) no. 661.

[79] This system was widely inspired from the Avant-projet Catala, in Art 1158, see above, p 989. The Terré draft (Art 110) and the former Ministry of Justice draft (Art 168) also established a procedure of 'notification' with the view of protecting the debtor.

[80] Termination before the date for performance is considered in the next section.

BGB **25.13 (DE)**

§ 323: Termination for non-performance or for performance not in accordance with the contract

(1) If under a synallagmatic contract the obligor fails to effect performance when due or to perform in accordance with the contract, the obligee may terminate the contract, if he has fixed, to no avail, an additional period of time for performance.

(2) A period of time does not have to be fixed if

1. the obligor seriously and definitely refuses to perform,

2. the obligor fails to perform by a date specified in the contract or within a specified period and, in the contract, the obligee has linked the continuation of his interest in performance to the punctuality of that performance, or

3. special circumstances exist which, after each party's interests have been weighed, justify immediate termination.

(3) If the type of breach of duty is such that, it is not feasible to fix a period for performance, a warning notice replaces it.

HGB **25.14 (DE)**

§ 376: (1) If it is agreed that the performance of one of the parties should be rendered by a firmly set date or within a firmly set period, and if performance is not rendered by that date or within that period, the other party may terminate the contract or instead of performance, if the debtor is in delay, demand damages for non-performance. He may only demand performance if he notifies the other party of his insistence on performance immediately after the date has been passed or the period has expired. ...

BGH, 21 June 1985[81] **25.15 (DE)**

Nachfrist

If a Nachfrist is set for too short a period, the creditor may terminate after a reasonable period. What is reasonable is to be judged objectively and it is immaterial that the creditor may wish to escape the contract for other reasons.

Facts: In a contract for the sale of land, an instalment of the price due on 27 January had not been paid by 29 January. On that day the vendor gave a *Nachfrist*, set to run until 4 February with refusal of performance thereafter. Payment was not forthcoming until after that date and the vendor declared *Rücktritt* on 11 February. The purchasers sought to enforce the contract.

Held: The lower courts upheld the plaintiffs' claim on the ground that the period set in the *Nachfrist* was too short, but the BGH set aside their decision and referred the case back.

Judgment: By a notarial agreement of 22 December 1982 the plaintiffs bought from the defendant a housing plot which at that time was mortgaged to the Volksbank E. for DM 260,000. In regard to payment of the purchase price Article 4 of the agreement

---

[81] NJW 1985, 2640.

provided that the purchase price was DM 300,000. DM 100,000 was payable by 27 January 1983 and the remaining DM 200,000 by 15 February 1983. In case of non-payment interest was to be paid on the purchase price as from 28 January 1983 or as from 16 February 1983, as the case may be, at the rate of interest as calculated by the Volksbank E. for mortgages (III, 1, 2 and 3). The purchase price was to be paid to the vendor's account no 203392 with the Volksbank E. The vendor was to assign by way of priority the first part of the purchase price amounting to DM 260,000 to the Volksbank E. The plaintiffs intended to finance the whole purchase price by way of life insurance. The payment of the loan was dependent on an application being made to the Land Registry for registration of a charge in favour of the insurance company. The application was lodged by the notary on 31 January 1983. After the first instalment of the purchase price of DM 100.000 had not been paid into the defendant's account on 27 January 1983, the defendant on Saturday 29 January 1983 gave the plaintiff a further period expiring at 10 o'clock Friday 4 February 1983 and stated that after that date he would refuse to accept performance. By a telegraphic transfer of 8 February 1983 the defendant's account was credited on 10 February 1983, backdated to 9 February 1983, with an amount of DM 288,996.08. By letter of 11 February 1983 the defendant gave notice of termination from the sales agreement since the sum due had not by that time been received. The plaintiffs who in the meantime had been registered in the Land Registry as the owners brought an action for vacant possession and delivery up of the land.

The Landgericht (Regional Court) upheld the claim. During the appeal procedure the defendant vacated the property in order to avert a writ of execution. He lodged a counter-claim for conveyance and delivery up of the property. The Oberlandesgericht (Higher Regional Court) dismissed the defendant's appeal and counter-claim. On appeal by the defendant on a point of law the judgment of the lower court was set aside and the case referred back.

Judgment: II.1. The judgment of the court a quo cannot be upheld on those grounds.

(a) The court a quo ought to have taken into consideration that generally a further period of too short a duration generally sets in motion a reasonable period. ... It may exceptionally be otherwise where the creditor only sets a further period for the sake of appearance or has intimated that he will in no event accept performance even if effected within a reasonable period. ... The court a quo did not establish any such exceptional circumstance. It merely considered that the suspicion had not been allayed that the defendant only withdrew because he regretted having entered into the transaction in the first place. Therefore, the court a quo ought to have established what further period would have been reasonable in the circumstances of this case and whether the plaintiffs in fact paid the first instalment of the purchase price within that period. The court *a quo* failed to make this assessment. This court cannot substitute its assessment for that of the lower court because the assessment of reasonableness is in principle a matter for the court trying the case on its merits. ...

(b) The court hearing an appeal on a point of law can merely examine whether the court hearing the case on its merits applied lawful criteria. Nor judged against that yardstick can the judgment of the court below stand on the basis of the grounds given. The further period provided for by the law is intended to give the debtor a last chance properly to perform the contract. ... It is intended to enable him to complete performance which has already begun to be effected. ... What period of time is reasonable in that regard is determined in accordance with the circumstances of the case.

... In the case of periods within which payments are to be made it must be borne in mind that the debtor has to answer for his financial ability to pay. ... Just as difficulties in obtaining credit cannot put off the occurrence of default by the debtor, neither can they affect the length of the further period to be set under § 326 [now § 323] BGB.

An additional factor in that connection is that the court a quo also did not find that the further period was objectively too short. It merely found that the period was 'very tight in view of the specific nature of that real estate transaction', especially as the purchase price was not to be paid, as is usually the case, into the notary's client account but directly into the defendant's account with the Volksbank E. For that reason, the insurance company wished to make the loan available only after notification by the notary that he had applied for registration of the charge at the Land Registry and that there were no problems precluding registration. Evidently, the court a quo based its assessment that the further period had been too short on the suspicion that the defendant had only withdrawn because he regretted the whole transaction. That is wrong in law.

The reasonableness of a further period can only be assessed on objective criteria related to the stated purpose of the fixing of a further period in the event of default by the debtor. ... Indeed in that connection the creditor's special interest in performance as punctual as possible by the debtor can be taken into consideration. ... If, in spite of relevant factual submissions and evidence, the court a quo did not consider that the defendant had demonstrated any such special interest, it ought to have left that interest aside and appraised the reasonableness of the further period in the light of all the other circumstances. In that connection it should have formed a view on the plaintiffs' claim that, as borne out by the notarial confirmation of 3 February 1983, they could have managed to have the first instalment of the purchase price in the amount of DM 100,000 transferred by the insurance company, if the employee responsible for signing the payment order had not been away and only reachable again on 7 February 1983. If, however, the further period had been objectively adequate and also reasonable in the light of all other circumstances, the defendant's motives in setting that precise period and seeking to free himself from the contract would no longer be relevant ...

Notes

(1) § 323(1) lays down the starting point for German law, that the creditor cannot terminate without having first having given the debtor a warning in the form of a notice setting an additional time for performance (when the debtor has not performed, or has performed only in part) or a chance to cure (where the debtor's performance was defective).

(2) As the *Nachfrist* case shows, if too short a period is set, the creditor may terminate after a reasonable period. What is reasonable is to be judged objectively.

(3) § 323(2) then lays down exceptions were a warning is not required.

(4) The first exception (§ 323(2) no. 1) is where the non-performance is coupled with a categorical refusal to perform. In such a case the creditor is not required to seek enforced performance, even if that could be obtained under § 275(1)–(3). There is obviously a close parallel here to cases where the debtor announces in advance that he will never perform, which we consider in the next section.

(5) The second exception (§ 323(2) no. 2) is where the contract set a date on or by which performance had to be made and the contract contains words to the effect that

the creditor will not accept late performance. This constitutes what is known as a *Fixgeschäft*. In these cases the *Fixgeschäft* was termed relative—the performance, though delayed, is still held to be possible, but it is subject to the agreed right to terminate.

(6) In this respect § 376 HGB appears to be different. All that is stated to be required for commercial contracts that fall within the HGB is that the date on or by which performance is to be rendered be 'firmly set'. But as the case below shows, even a clause stating that a time is *fix* may be displaced by evidence from other circumstances that this was not really the agreement.

(7) The third exception (§ 323(2) no. 3) is very open-textured. Its most obvious applications are:

(a) where it is obvious that late performance will be of no value. This is what is known as an *absolutes Fixgeschäft*. These are contracts which, having regard to their essential purpose, cannot meaningfully be performed after a certain date. Examples would be the case of a taxi reserved to take a passenger to a certain aeroplane flight or the delivery of flowers on the day of a wedding. Once the relevant date has been passed, performance is viewed as being impossible and § 275 BGB applies; and

(b) where the non-performance which has occurred makes it unreasonable to expect the creditor to accept performance from the debtor in the future. In the stakeholders' meeting on the DCFR, an example given was where, some hours before the wedding feast, it is found that the food delivered by the caterer contains a dead mouse. Cure (replacement of the dish affected) would be possible and the caterer may be willing to deliver fresh food but the creditor surely doesn't have to accept it.

(8) Again, the creditor faced with a delay in performing by the debtor may either seek *Rücktritt* under the provisions just described or he may claim damages in lieu of performance under § 281. It might be expected that the provisions of § 281 would mirror those of § 323,[82] but on this occasion they differ. § 281(2) has a provision allowing the creditor to 'go over to damages' without first serving a warning in cases of a serious and final refusal by the debtor to perform, or if special circumstances justify it. It does not, however, contain a provision allowing it in the case of a *Fixgeschäft*. This has puzzled commentators and may be a drafting mistake.

BGH, 17 January 1990[83]   **25.16 (DE)**

Aluminium bottle caps

A clause included in general conditions to the effect that the dates and notice periods were 'fixed' is not enough of itself to make the contract into a Fixgeschäft if the circumstances showed differently.

---

[82] See 25.6 (DE), above, p 990.
[83] BGHZ 110, 88.

Facts: The plaintiff was a wine producer; the defendant carried on business as a supplier to wine cellars and vintners. By a written order of 15 January 1986 the plaintiff ordered from the defendant 350,000 aluminium bottle caps for sealing wine bottles. On 21 September 1987 it once again ordered various quantities of aluminium caps, that is to say, 400,000, 205,000 and 50,000, 'for delivery by 1.10.1987'. Both written orders contained a reference to the plaintiff's general terms and conditions of business printed on the back of the order form, in which it is stated inter alia:

(7) The delivery dates and periods agreed are mandatory and fixed (*fix*). In the event of any delay in delivery the person placing the order shall be entitled without needing to fix a further period to pursue all the legal consequences of delay …

The defendant delivered the caps covered by the first order on 29 January 1986, and the plaintiff paid the purchase price of DM 7,233.87. On 24 September 1987, when the plaintiff sought to use those caps, the joins in the caps came apart immediately after the capping process as a result of uneven gluing. Of the second order on 1 October 1987, the defendant delivered 400,000 and 205,000 caps. For the 400,000 caps, the defendant paid DM 8,664. After 5,000 of these caps had been used on 1 October 1987 the same defect as in the caps from the first order became apparent.

By letter dated 2 October 1987 the plaintiff complained to the defendant of the defectiveness of the caps, demanded repayment of the purchase price paid and gave notice that it would not accept delivery of the 50,000 caps undelivered as at 1 October 1987. The defendant confirmed that the uneven gluing of the joins constituted a latent defect, but refused to meet the plaintiff's claims and insisted on acceptance of the remaining 50,000 caps.

Held: The clause was not enough of itself to make the contract into a *Fixgeschäft* as the circumstances showed differently. (The clause was also invalid under §§ 3, 9(1) AGBG [now §§ 305c(1), 307 BGB].)

Judgment: On these grounds:

II.2 (b) It cannot avail the appellant that the regional court granted the defendant's counter-claim to the purchase price of DM 1,083 for the 50,000 caps ordered on 21 September 1987 delivery of which has not yet been accepted. The plaintiff did not effectively withdraw from the sales agreement relating to these 50,000 caps. The regional court held that there was no right to withdraw under § 326 [now § 323(2) no 2] BGB, which is not contested on appeal and is not vitiated by an error of law. Nor can the plaintiff derive any support for termination from the provision contained in § 376(1) HGB for there was in fact no agreement that this should be a mandatory and fixed transaction (*Fixgeschäft*).

(aa) The regional court was unable to find any support from the individual contractual provisions and the surrounding circumstances for the proposition that the parties were at one on the fact that, in the event of the delivery period not being observed, the sales agreement entered into could straight away be terminated by the plaintiff. On appeal it is erroneously sought to find support for the contrary proposition from the delivery date precisely laid down. A *Fixgeschäft* requires not only the laying down of a precise delivery date or period but also consensus of the parties that the contract is to stand or fall on compliance or non-compliance with the delivery date whereby, in case of doubt, a contract is assumed not to be a time bargain. … It does not follow solely from the agreement of a specifically laid down (final) delivery date (in this case, 'by 1.10.1987') that, in the event of non-compliance with that period, the plaintiff no longer has any interest in that transaction being effected. … That is borne out by the fact that the plaintiff used the caps delivered in January 1986 only twenty months later and gave no reason why observance of the delivery period in the case of the second order was of such great importance for it.

(bb) That appraisal is not altered by Clause 7(1) of the plaintiff's General Terms and Conditions of Business. It is true that the term *fix* used in that connection suggests that

a time bargain was intended, in the absence of persuasive factors to the contrary. ...
Where, however, the conditions of a time bargain and of the basis of an individual agreement to that effect are not met, a standard provision which none the less makes the
agreement appear to be in the nature of a time bargain is surprising in light of § 3 AGBG
[now § 305c(1) BGB] ... and unreasonable in light of § 9 thereof [now § 307(1) BGB] ...
For the contractual partner of the user, who did not agree with the latter that the transaction was to stand or fall with observance of the period, cannot reasonably be required
in the circumstances to reckon on the General Terms and Conditions of Business making
the transaction subject to strict adherence to the time limit. The unreasonable disadvantage within the meaning of § 9(1) of that legislation follows from the fact that by
means of clauses such as that now under consideration the user would in the result be
relieved of the obligation to fix a further period under § 326 BGB which, in commercial
transactions, may be agreed more effectively by means of standard clauses. ... For if
the clause were effective and it were sought—which may remain an open question—to
attach to it the significance that the contract could essentially be determined as being a
time bargain ..., § 376 HGB, which would be applicable, would have the effect of allowing the purchaser to withdraw even without fixing a further period for performance of
the other party's obligations and, in the event of delay by the seller, to claim damages.

Whether under §§ 3, 9 AGBG that appraisal would be different where, in sectors in
which time bargains are common, the standard form additional wording *fix* is used
directly in conjunction with the provision concerning the delivery period, does not need to
be decided. ... The clause is on the reverse side of the plaintiff's order form in the middle
of a number of other standard terms.

Furthermore, there is not the slightest indication that a time bargain is typically the
contractual objective of agreements such as the one now under consideration.

Notes

(1) The references to § 326 BGB and to the AGBG (Gesetz zur Regelung des
Rechts der Allgemeinen Geschäftsbedingungen—Act on Standard Terms) in this case
are, of course, out of date. Old § 326 has been replaced by the current § 323. The
relevant articles dealing with the validity of general conditions are now BGB §§ 305c
(surprising and ambiguous clauses), paragraph (1) and 307 (test of reasonableness of
contents).

(2) Note that a non-commercial creditor may, instead of terminating, demand performance (as long as it remains possible) at any time after the stipulated date. A commercial creditor must insist on this immediately.

(3) A very slight delay in performance of obligations after a *Nachfrist* has expired
or even under a *Fixgeschäft* may, for reasons of good faith (§ 242 BGB), be held insufficient to give rise to a right to terminate.

(4) If we compare the outcomes to English law, it seems that under German law
the court will not take the initiative of declaring that time for performance is 'of the
essence',[84] but the parties themselves may do so—provided that they spell out the

---

[84] cf below, p 1019.

consequences clearly. It seems unlikely that the court would accept that this was the implicit meaning of the contract even if the contract did not spell it out in so many words.

(5) If the contract is not a *Fixgeschäft*, and none of the other provisions of § 323(2) apply, it follows that the creditor must give the debtor a warning before terminating the contract.

In English law, when the question is whether a delay entitles the innocent party to terminate the contract, the courts ask whether the time 'was of the essence' of the contract. This means simply, is it a condition of the contract that performance be completed by the time stated? The contract may state this expressly—for an example, see *Lombard North Central v Butterworth*.[85] If the contract simply states a date for performance without stating whether or not it is of the essence, the question again becomes one of construction of the contract.

English law approaches this question in a similar way to breaches of other kinds: as a matter of interpretation of the contract, is the delay a breach of condition? If not, does the delay deprive the aggrieved party of the substance of what he was contracting for? If prompt performance is a condition, then it is said that 'time is of the essence' and the aggrieved party may terminate as soon as the date has passed. As was stated by McCardie J in *Hartley v Hymans*:[86]

> In ordinary commercial contracts for the sale of goods, the rule clearly is, that time is prima facie of the essence with respect to delivery.

This means that, if the seller is late in delivering the goods, the buyer may terminate the contract without further ado. This strict rule does not apply to all obligations, even in a contract of sale:

Sale of Goods Act 1979 **25.17 (EN)**

Section 10: Stipulations about time

(1) Unless a different intention appears from the terms of the contract, stipulations as to time of payment are not of the essence of a contract of sale.

If time is not of the essence, the aggrieved party may terminate if the delay is such that it frustrates the venture,[87] or if the other party repudiates the contract.[88]

However, in some situations where time is not of the essence, such as contracts for the sale of land and cases of the buyer failing to accept goods, English law has long recognised a procedure rather like the German *Nachfrist*. But now this procedure is generally applicable to all cases where time is not of the essence. On two occasions (*United Scientific Holdings Ltd v Burnley Borough Council*;[89] and in the next case) members

---

[85] See 25.27 (EN), below, p 1035.
[86] [1920] 3 KB 475, 484 (KBD).
[87] See the judgment of Devlin J in *Universal Cargo Carriers v Citati* [1957] 2 QB 401 (QBD).
[88] On this see below, pp 1024 ff.
[89] [1978] AC 904, 958 (HL).

of the House of Lords have approved the following passage from Halsbury's Laws of England:[90]

> The modern law, in the case of contracts of all types, may be summarised as follows. Time will not be considered to be of the essence unless: (1) the parties expressly stipulate that conditions as to time must be strictly complied with; or (2) the nature of the subject matter of the contract or the surrounding circumstances show that time should be considered to be of the essence; or (3) a party who has been subjected to unreasonable delay gives notice to the party in default making time of the essence.

It is important to know whether the time for performance is or is not 'of the essence'. In some situations, the answer, if not stated in the contract, is provided by established case law or by statute.[91] In other cases the court will have to decide as a matter of construction of the contract.

One question which lawyers discussed was whether the new, more flexible *Hong Kong Fir* approach[92] should apply to time stipulations, so that (unless expressly agreed), time would not be of the essence and whether the innocent party has the right to terminate would depend on whether or not the delay had serious consequences.

Court of Appeal and House of Lords   **25.18 (EN)**

Bunge Corp v Tradax SA[93]

A clause requiring the buyer under an FOB contract for bulk goods to give fifteen days' notice of the nominated vessel's readiness to load was a condition of the contract.

Facts: A contract for the purchase of 15,000 tons of soya FOB one US Gulf port (made on the GAFTA 119 form of contract) required the buyer to nominate a ship to collect the goods and to give the seller at least 15 days' notice of the ship's probable readiness to load. The sellers would then select which Gulf port to direct the ship to in order to load the goods. The buyers gave less than 15 days' notice and the sellers terminated the contract. They then claimed damages for non-performance by the buyers. The buyers argued that the sellers' purported termination was wrongful as the time for giving notice was not a condition but an intermediate term and the sellers had not shown that the delay caused them any difficulty.

Held: The arbitrator awarded damages to the sellers. On appeal to the Commercial Court the judge reversed that award, but the Court of Appeal allowed the sellers' appeal. An appeal by the buyers to the House of Lords[94] was dismissed. [In what follows, there is an extract from the judgment of the Court of Appeal, followed by another from the speeches in the House of Lords.]

Judgment: Megaw LJ: ... I come to the second main issue: is the term of the contract which has been broken by the buyers a condition or an intermediate term? The sellers have, before us, made it clear that the term is not a condition, but is an intermediate term, they will not seek to contend that they can discharge the burden of showing that they were entitled to treat the contract as having been repudiated by the buyers.

---

[90] As for delivery and payment in the sale of goods, see Sale of Goods Act 1979, s 28, 24.4 (EN), above, p 963.
[91] See above, p 963.
[92] See 25.10 (EN), above, p 999.
[93] [1981] 2 All ER 513 (CA), [1981] 1 WLR 711 (HL).
[94] See below, p 1023.

1019

The contract is, by its express terms, governed by English law. That is the effect of cl 25 of GAFTA 119.

It is an accepted principle of English law that in a mercantile contract for the sale of goods 'prima facie a stipulated time of delivery is of the essence'. This longstanding principle has recently been re-stated by Lord Diplock in *United Scientific Holdings Ltd v Burnley Borough Council* ...

In the present case, then, there can be no doubt but that the obligation of the sellers to deliver the soya bean meal not later than 30 June 1975 was a condition of the contract. They had an obligation to tender the contractual quantity of the goods at the ship's rail so that they could be loaded in accordance with the contractual provision as to rate of loading, on or before that date. If they failed, in breach of contract, to carry out that obligation, and if the buyers thereupon were treat the contract as having been wrongfully repudiated by the sellers, it would be no answer for the sellers to say that the buyers had not proved that they, the buyers, had suffered any loss or would suffer any loss, if loading were to take place on 1 July. It would be unreal to suggest that one day's lateness in delivery would necessarily be a matter of serious consequence to the buyers. The lateness might or might not have such consequences. But the buyers' right to treat the contract as repudiated, and to treat themselves as freed from the performance of any further contractual obligations which they would otherwise have been required to perform under the contact, does not depend on the buyers being able to prove any such thing.

In para 5 of the award the board of appeal, having said that the term means 'Buyers were to give at least 15 consecutive days' notice of probable readiness of vessel(s)', went on: 'Such a provision is customarily treated in the trade as being for the purpose of giving to sellers sufficient time to make necessary arrangements to get the goods to the port for loading on board the nominated vessel.' In other words, the parties have agreed, by acceptance of this term, that 15 days is 'the time which is reasonably required by the sellers for the purpose of this particular contract, to enable them to make the arrangements necessary for the fulfilment by them of their contractual to deliver the goods by the due time'. It would, in my view, be impossible for a court to hold that that was not the parties' intention in agreeing this term. There is no question here of the parties not being in an equal bargaining position. It would, in my opinion, be arrogant and unjustifiable for a court to substitute any view of its own for the view of the parties themselves as to what was a reasonable time for this purpose.

Unless there is some principle of law, or some authority binding on us, which leads necessarily to a contrary conclusion, it appears to me to follow that, just as the contractual time for delivery of the goods is a condition binding on the sellers, so that the contractual time by which the notice as to be given for the purpose of enabling the sellers to perform that condition should be regarded as a condition binding on the buyers. There is no more, and no less, reason to suppose that a breach of the time provision in the sellers' obligation will necessarily or probably lead to serious loss to the buyers than there is to suppose that a breach of the notice of readiness provision will necessarily or probably lead to serious loss to the sellers ...

I come back to the purpose of the notice of probable readiness term in the present contract. The commercial reasons why advance notice is required are, I think, obvious. The sellers have to nominate the loading port. Is loading going to be possible, and if possible convenient, at port A, or port B, or port C? Until the probable date of readiness is known, it may be impossible to answer those questions. Until they are answered, the sellers cannot perform their contractual duty of dominating the port. When the port is decided, arrangements have to be made to have the contract quantity (to be defined by the buyers by reference to '5% more or less') of the contract goods available when the vessel is ready. What is involved in making such arrangements? It may involve or include, buying goods, arranging for them to be moved by road, rail or water from wherever they may be; for warehousing them or moving them from one warehouse to another. Of course, in any given case, some or all of these tasks may be simply achieved, or their achievement may be possible in less than 15 days, in order to have the goods ready for loading where and when the vessel is ready for loading. It obviously cannot be predicated that 14 days' notice, instead of 15 days, would necessarily and in all circumstances cause sellers serious difficulties in respect of a contract containing these terms. What can and should be accepted is that the parties have agreed that, for the purpose of this contract, the reasonable time required to enable the sellers to perform their contractual obligations as to delivery of the goods is 15 days' notice of the probable readiness of the vessel to load ...

Apart from [a] particular reason, relating to the extension of shipment clause, Parker J was of the opinion that the term could not be a condition because of what he regarded as being 'the principles established in the *Hong Kong Fir* case' ... and *Cehave NV v Bremer Handelsgesellschaft mbH, The Hansa Nord*. In the latter case, Roskill LJ, while recognising that some terms of a contract of sale may be conditions, expressed the view that 'a court' should not be over ready, unless required by statute or authority so to do, to construe a term in a contract as a 'condition' ...

The passage in the *Hong Kong Fir* case, to which Parker J referred, was that where Diplock LJ said this ...

'No doubt there are many simple contractual undertakings, sometimes express, but more often because of their very simplicity ('It goes without saying') to be implied, of which it can be predicated that every breach of such an undertaking must give rise to an event which will deprive the party not in default of substantially the whole benefit which it was intended that he should obtain from the contract. And such a stipulation, unless the parties have agreed that breach of it shall not entitle the non-defaulting party to treat the contract as repudiated, is a condition.'

If that statement is intended to be a definition of the requirements which must always be satisfied, in all types of contract and all types of clauses, in order that a term may qualify as, a condition, I would very respectfully express the view that it is not a correct statement of the law. I am confirmed in the view that it was not so intended because of what was recently said by Lord Diplock in a passage ... from his speech in *United Scientific Holdings Ltd v Burnley Borough Council* in relation to time being 'of the essence' in certain commercial contracts ...

In the light of what was said by their Lordships in that case, I think it can fairly be said that in mercantile contracts stipulations as to time not only may be, but usually are, to be treated as being 'of the essence of the contract', even though this is not expressly stated in the words of the contract. It would follow that in a mercantile contract it cannot be predicated that, for time to be of the essence, any and every breach of the term as to time must necessarily cause the innocent party to be deprived of substantially the whole of the benefit which it was intended that he should have ...

In my opinion in the term with which we are concerned the provision as to time is of the essence of the contract. The term is a condition.

It is, I believe, a factor which is not without weight in that conclusion that, at least, it tends towards certainty in the law ... The parties, where time is of the essence, will at least know where they stand when the contractually agreed time has passed and the contract has been broken. They will not be forced to make critical decisions by trying to anticipate how serious, in the view of arbitrators or courts, in later years, the consequences of the breach will retrospectively be seen to have been, in the light, it may be, of hindsight.

I must, however, return to the *Hong Kong Fir* case … No one now doubts the correctness of that decision: that there are 'intermediate' terms, breach of which may or may not entitle the innocent party to treat himself as discharged from the further performance of his contractual obligation. No one now doubts that a term as to seaworthiness in a charterparty, in the absence of express provision to the opposite effect, is not a condition, but is an 'intermediate' term. The question arising on that case which I think we are compelled to examine in the present case is the test by which it falls to be decided whether a term is a condition.

I have previously quoted a passage from the judgment of Diplock LJ. In its literal sense, the condition, then the term with which we are here concerned would not pass the test. The view which I have expressed that it is a condition would necessarily be wrong.

There are various reasons why I do not think that this was intended to be a literal, definitive and comprehensive statement of the requirements of a condition: and also, if it were, why, with great respect, I do not think that it represents the law as it stands today.

First, if it were intended to cover terms as to time in mercantile contracts, how could the requirements be said to be met in respect of stipulations in contracts of types in which, as Lord Diplock has recently said, time may be of the essence: for example, in respect of a stipulated time for delivery? It could never be said, as I see it, in any real sense, that any breach of such a stipulation *must necessarily cause the innocent* party to be deprived of *substantially all the benefit*.

Second, and following on what I have just said, I do not see how any contractual term, whether as to time or otherwise, could ever pass the test. Conditions would no longer exist in the English law of contract. For it is always possible to suggest hypothetically some minor breach or breaches of any contractual term which might, without undue use of the imagination, be wholly insufficient to produce serious effects for the innocent party, let alone the loss of substantially all the benefit.

Third, English law does recognise as conditions contractual terms which do not pass that test. For example, *Bowes v Shand* and, I think a substantial number of other cases which are binding, at least on this court.

Fourth, it is clear law, reaffirmed by the House of Lords since *Hong Kong Fir* was decided, that where there has been a breach of a condition the innocent party is entitled to elect whether or not to treat the contracts as repudiated …

How could this right of election be anything other than a legal fiction, a chimera, if the election can arise only in circumstances in which, as a result of the breach, an event has happened which will deprive the innocent party of substantially the whole benefit which it was intended that he should receive? This test, it is to be observed, is regarded (*Hong Kong Fir*) … as applying also where the term is an intermediate term, except that you then look to what has actually happened in order to see if the innocent party has lost substantially all the benefit. So, again, if the test be right, the former principle of English law that the innocent party has the right to elect is no longer anything but an empty shadow. For a right to elect to continue a contract, with the result that the innocent party will be bound to continue to perform his own contractual obligations, when he will, by definition, have lost substantially all his benefit under the contract, does not appear to me to make sense.

Fifth, the same considerations as I have set out in the previous paragraph apply if the test be that a breach of contract gives a right to the innocent party to treat it as a repudiation only if the events which in fact have flowed from the breach would, if they had come about otherwise than by a breach of contract, amount to frustration of the contract …

I would allow the appeal and, subject to any questions of detail which may arise as to the form of the order, I would restore the decision of the board of appeal.

BROWNE LJ: I agree that this appeal should be allowed, for the reasons given by Megaw LJ, with which I entirely agree.

[BRIGHTMAN LJ concurred.]

The House of Lords affirmed the judgment of the Court of Appeal:

Judgment: LORD WILBERFORCE: The fundamental fallacy of the appellants' argument lies in attempting to apply this analysis to a time clause such as the present in a mercantile contract, which is totally different in character. As to such a clause there is only one kind of breach possible, namely, to be late, and the questions which have to be asked are, first, what importance have the parties expressly ascribed to this consequence, and secondly, in the absence of expressed agreement, what consequence ought to be attached to it having regard to the contract as a whole.

The test suggested by the appellants was a different one. One must consider, they said, the breach actually committed and then decide whether that default would deprive the party not in default of substantially the whole benefit of the contract. They invoked even certain passages in the judgment of Diplock LJ in the *Hong Kong Fir* case [1962] 2 QB 26 to support it. One may observe in the first place that the introduction of a test of this kind would be commercially most undesirable. It would expose the parties, after a breach of one, two, three, seven and other numbers of days to an argument whether this delay would have left time for the seller to provide the goods. It would make it, at the time, at least difficult, and sometimes impossible, for the supplier to know whether he could do so. It would fatally remove from a vital provision in the contract that certainty which is the most indispensable quality of mercantile contracts, and lead to a large increase in arbitrations. It would confine the seller—perhaps after arbitration and reference through the courts—to a remedy in damages which might be extremely difficult to quantify. These are all serious objections in practice. But I am clear that the submission is unacceptable in law. The judgment of Diplock LJ does not give any support and ought not to give any encouragement to any such proposition; for beyond doubt it recognises that it is open to the parties to agree that, as regards a particular obligation, any breach shall entitle the party not in default to treat the contract as repudiated. Indeed, if he were not doing so he would, in a passage which does not profess to be more than clarificatory, be discrediting a long and uniform series of cases—at least from *Bowes v Shand* (1877) 2 App Cas 455 onwards ...

Notes

(1) In this case, the House of Lords agrees that the most important thing is that the parties should know where they stand—ie that there should be certainty. Thus, the sellers were permitted to terminate the contract even though they had not shown that the buyer's delay had caused them any loss or difficulty. It may seem to go in precisely the opposite direction to the policy behind the addition (in 1994) of sections 15A and 30(2A) to the Sale of Goods Act 1979, considered earlier.[95] This may represent a change in policy, but it seems that the Law Commissions (which proposed the 1994 amendment) thought that time stipulations should be treated differently to stipulations

---

[95] Above, p 1005.

as to the conformity or quantity of goods: they said that 'in many commercial situations it would be normal to infer an intention that any breach of a time clause,
however, slight, would justify ... termination of the contract'.[96] Cases of late performance are therefore not affected by the 1994 amendments.

(2) It is not easy to predict when a court will interpret the date for performance
as being 'of the essence' (ie as a condition) and when not. For example, there were
conflicting dicta, and conflicting decisions at first instance, on whether the date for the
payment of the hire due under a time-charter was a condition or only an innominate
term. In *Grand China Logistics Holding (Group) Co Ltd v Spar Shipping AS* [2016]
EWCA Civ 982 the Court of Appeal held that prompt payment was NOT a condition.
Gross LJ distinguished *Bunge v Tradax* on the ground that in that case the parties'
obligations were independent: until the buyer had given the notice, the seller could
not arrange delivery of the cargo to the port. In contrast, in the Spar Shipping case,
'it could not be said that any failure to pay hire punctually in advance, no matter how
trivial, would derail Spar's performance under the charterparties.' (at [53]-[54]). On
the issue of certainty, Gross LJ remarked:

> [58] ... Certainty is plainly a consideration of major importance when construing com-
> mercial contracts such as the charterparties here. That it should be so is both a matter of
> legal principle and commercial common sense—having regard to the importance of the
> framework provided by commercial law for commercial decision-taking. In my judgment,
> it would be quite wrong to overlook commercial common sense, even recognising that its
> claims can be over-stated and its application vulnerable to the particular perspective of the
> party espousing them ...

> [59] The key question, however, is striking the right balance. Classifying a contractual pro-
> vision as a condition has advantages in terms of certainty; in particular, the innocent party
> is entitled to loss of bargain damages (such as they may be) regardless of the state of the
> market. Where, however, the likely breaches of an obligation may have consequences rang-
> ing from the trivial to the serious, then the downside of the certainty achieved by classifying
> an obligation as a condition is that trivial breaches will have disproportionate consequences.

> 62 To my mind, the real question lies not between certainty and no certainty but as to the
> degree of certainty best likely to achieve the right balance of which I have already made
> mention and to which Lord Roskill referred in *Bunge v Tradax*. ... I cannot conceive that
> the parties intended the withdrawal clause in cl.11 of the charterparties to operate so that a
> single payment of hire a few minutes late would entitle Spar to throw up a five- or three-year
> charterparty and claim loss of bargain damages.

25.6 TERMINATION BEFORE PERFORMANCE IS DUE

What if, before the date for performance, it is clear that the other party will not perform:
he has announced this, or has put it out of his power to perform? Clearly, once the date for
performance arrives, the innocent party will in all systems be able to terminate; but does

---

[96] The Law Commission and The Scottish Law Commission (n 61 above) para 4.24.

he have to wait until that date to do so? If so, he may be left in some uncertainty, because he may want to make other arrangements, yet there may be the possibility that the other party will perform after all. Can the innocent party somehow prevent this? English and German law reach a fairly similar solution in this regard: he may terminate the contract and bring an action for damages, either immediately (England) or after giving due notice (Germany). We shall see that French law takes quite a different approach.

Queen's Bench **25.19 (EN)**

Hochster v de la Tour[97]

Where a contractual obligation is renounced before the date on which performance is due, the innocent party is entitled to treat the contract as terminated immediately and can bring proceedings for breach of contract before the date on which performance would have been due.

Facts: The defendant hired the plaintiff to travel with him as his courier for the purposes of a journey, his employment to commence on a set date. Before the date on which the journey was due to commence, the defendant informed the plaintiff that he no longer required the plaintiff's services and the plaintiff sought to bring an action against the defendant for breach of contract. The date for performance of the contract had not yet been reached.

Held: The plaintiff was entitled to treat the contract as terminated even though the date for performance had not yet occurred.

Judgment: LORD CAMPBELL CJ: On this motion in arrest of judgment, the question arises, whether, if there be an agreement between A and B, whereby B engages to employ A on and from a future day for a given period of time, to travel with him into a foreign country as a courier and to start with him in that capacity on that day, A being to receive a monthly salary during the continuance of such service, B may, before the day, refuse to perform the agreement and break and renounce it so as to entitle A, before the day, to commence an action against B to recover damages for breach of the agreement, A having been ready and willing to perform it till it was broken and renounced by B.

The defendant's counsel very powerfully contended that, if the plaintiff was not contented to dissolve the contract and to abandon all remedy upon it, he was bound to remain ready and willing to perform it till the day when the actual employment as courier in the service of the defendant was to begin, and that there could be no breach of the agreement, before that day, to give a right of action. But it cannot be laid down as a universal rule that, where by agreement an act is to be done on a future day, no action can be brought for a breach of the agreement till the day for doing the act has arrived. If a man promises to marry a woman on a future day and before that day marries another woman, he is instantly liable to an action for breach of promise of marriage: *Short v Stone*. If a man contracts to execute a lease on and from a future day for a certain term, and, before that day, executes a lease to another for the same term, he may be immediately sued for breaking the contract: *Ford v Tiley*. So, if a man contracts to sell and deliver specific goods on a future day, and before the day he sells and delivers them to another, he is immediately liable to an action at the suit of the person with whom he first contracted to sell

---

[97] (1853) E & B 678.

and deliver them: *Bowdell v Parsons*. One reason alleged in support of such an action is that the defendant has, before the day, rendered it impossible for the plaintiff to perform the contract at the day, but this does not necessarily follow, for, prior to the day fixed for doing the act, the first wife may have died, a surrender of the lease executed might be obtained, and the defendant might have re-purchased the goods so as to be in a situation to sell and deliver them to the plaintiff. Another reason may be that where there is a contract to do an act on a future day there is a relation constituted between the parties in the meantime by the contract, and that they impliedly promise that in the meantime neither will do anything to the prejudice of the other inconsistent with that relation. As an example, a man and woman engaged to marry are affianced to one another during the period between the time of the engagement and the celebration of the marriage.

In the present case, of traveller and courier, from the day of the hiring till the day when the employment was to begin, the parties were engaged to each other, and it seems to be a breach of an implied contract if either of them renounces the engagement. This reasoning seems in accordance with the unanimous decision of the Exchequer Chamber in *Elderton v Emmens* which we have followed in subsequent cases in this court. The declaration in the present case, in alleging a breach, states a great deal more than a passing intention on the part of the defendant which he may repent of, and could only be proved by evidence that he had utterly renounced the contract or done some act which rendered it impossible for him to perform it. If the plaintiff has no remedy for breach of the contract unless he treats the contract as in force, and acts upon it down to June 1, 1852, it follows that, till then, he must enter into no employment which will interfere with his promise 'to start with the defendant on such travels on the day and year, and that he must then be properly equipped in all respects as a courier for a three months' tour on the continent of Europe.

But it is surely much more rational, and more for the benefit of both parties, that, after the renunciation of the agreement by the defendant, the plaintiff should be at liberty to consider himself absolved from any future performance of it, retaining his right to sue for any damage he has suffered from the breach of it. Thus, instead of remaining idle and laying out money in preparations which must be useless, he is at liberty to seek service under another employer, which would go in mitigation of the damages to which he would otherwise be entitled for a breach of the contract. It seems strange that the defendant, after renouncing the contract, and absolutely declaring that he will never act under it, should be permitted to object that faith is given to his assertion, and that an opportunity is not left to him of changing his mind. If the plaintiff is barred of any remedy by entering into an engagement inconsistent with starting as a courier with the defendant on June 1, he is prejudiced by putting faith in the defendant's assertion, and it would be more consonant with principle, if the defendant were precluded from saying that he had not broken the contract when he declared that he entirely renounced it.

Suppose that the defendant, at the time of his renunciation, had embarked on a voyage for Australia, so as to render it physically impossible for him to employ the plaintiff as a courier on the continent of Europe in the months of June, July and August, 1852. According to decided cases the action might have been brought before 1 June, but the renunciation may have been founded on other facts, to be given in evidence, which would equally have rendered the defendant's performance of the contract impossible. The man who wrongfully renounces a contract into which he has deliberately entered cannot justly complain if he is immediately sued for a compensation in damages by the man whom he has injured: and it seems reasonable to allow an option to the injured party, either to sue immediately or to wait till the time when the act was to be done, still holding it as prospectively binding for the exercise of this option, which may be advantageous to the innocent party, and cannot be prejudicial to the wrongdoer.

An argument against the action before 1 June is urged from the difficulty of calculating the damages, but this argument is equally strong against an action before 1 Sep, when the three months would expire. In either case, the jury in assessing the damages would be justified in looking to all that had happened, or was likely to happen, to increase or mitigate the loss of the plaintiff down to the day of trial.

We do not find any decision contrary to the view we are taking of this case …

If it should be held that, upon a contract to do an act on a future day, a renunciation of the contract by one party dispenses with a condition to be performed in the meantime by the other, there seems no reason for requiring that other to wait till the day arrives before seeking his remedy by action, and the only ground on which the condition can be dispensed with seems to be that the renunciation may be treated as a breach of the contract. Upon the whole, we think that the declaration in this case is sufficient. It gives us great satisfaction to reflect that, the question being on the record, our opinion may be reviewed in a court of error. In the meantime we must give judgment for the plaintiff.

BGB   **25.20 (DE)**

§ 323: Termination for non-performance or for performance not in accordance with the contract

…

(4) The obligee may terminate the contract before performance becomes due if it is obvious that the preconditions for termination will be satisfied.

Notes

(1) This provision was new in 2002 but it represents the position reached by case law. If, before performance was due the debtor refused to perform, either absolutely or only if some condition not justified by the contract were met, this amounted to a positive breach of contract: eg BGH, 21 March 1974.[98] In that case actual performance of building work was not yet due since planning permission had not yet been granted, but the contractor unjustifiably refused to continue excavation without a geological study.

(2) The BGB distinguishes between a refusal before the date on which performance is due and a refusal after that date. The former comes within § 323(4), the latter is a case in which the creditor may terminate without serving a warning: see § 323(1) and (2) no. 1.

(3) Where a contract is to be performed over a period of time, failures to perform in the early stages may give the creditor reason to doubt that the debtor will perform adequately in future. This may constitute a sufficiently 'important reason' to justify the creditor in serving a *Kündigung* without notice.[99]

---

[98] BGH NJW 1974, 1080.
[99] See 25.2 (DE), above, p 984.

French law, in contrast to English and German law, has no doctrine of anticipatory breach as such. In principle, it is impossible to seek *résolution* of the contract before the date on which performance is due. Thus Whittaker noted in 1996:[100]

> in French law the fact that a breach of contract has occurred before the time for performance does not in general affect when any remedy based on breach becomes available, but its deliberate nature may have considerable effects on any subsequent remedy.

However, the rule has sometimes been ignored by courts, notably when the dispute between the parties was such that it rendered pursuit of the contractual relationship between them impossible.[101] Besides, as Whittaker says, the fact that a debtor has either refused performance or been responsible for making performance impossible may enhance the remedies available to the creditor,[102] and there is a greater likelihood of resolution being granted after the due date.

The 2016 reform does not change the principle on this point. The new law on termination does not provide for termination for a breach that has not yet occurred. With respect to termination by effect of a clause and unilateral termination, the wording of Articles 1225 and 1226 seems to exclude that possibility. Indeed, before terminating the contract, the creditor must precisely identify the debtor's failure to perform. The position is less clear with judicial termination. Article 1228, a provision which deals exclusively with judicial termination, does not specify the circumstances in which a court may declare the termination. This provision's wording seems to leave an important discretion to the courts. However, Article 1224 specifies that:

> termination results either from the application of a termination clause, or, where the non-performance is sufficiently serious, from notice by the creditor to the debtor, or from a judicial decision.

Thus, it is likely that the courts will declare the termination before the breach only in very limited circumstances.

In contrast, the 2008 draft of the Ministry of Justice had introduced the right to terminate the contract when, before the date for performance, it becomes obvious that the other party will not be able to perform its essential obligations. (Article 1690 of the July 2008 draft). This reflected a PECL provision:

Principles of European Contract Law **25.21 (INT)**

Article 9:304: Anticipatory Non-Performance
Where prior to the time for performance by a party it is clear that there will be a fundamental non-performance by it, the other party may terminate the contract.

What if one party fears that the other may not perform but the second party has not clearly repudiated his obligations or put it out of his power to perform? We saw earlier

---

[100] S Whittaker, 'How Does French Law Deal with Anticipatory Breaches of Contract?' (1996) 45 ICLQ 662, 666.

[101] Cass civ (3) 29 April 1987, no. 84-17021, Bull III, no. 93.

[102] eg, the creditor may recover damages greater than those merely foreseeable: see below, p 1071.

that this may give rise to a right to withhold performance; BW Article 6:263 states this in general terms, as does CISG Article 71. Other laws apply it to limited circumstances, such as the other party's insolvency.[103] However, the PECL (following the UCC § 2-609 on this point)[104] go further; they allow the party who is uncertain to demand and assurance and, if he does not get it, to terminate.

Principles of European Contract Law   **25.22 (INT)**

Article 8:105: Assurance of Performance

(1) A party which reasonably believes that there will be a fundamental non-performance by the other party may demand adequate assurance of due performance and meanwhile may withhold performance of its own obligations so long as such reasonable belief continues.

(2) Where this assurance is not provided within a reasonable time, the party demanding it may terminate the contract if it still reasonably believes that there will be a fundamental non-performance by the other party and gives notice of termination without delay.

In German law before 2002 there was some suggestion that in similar circumstances termination might be possible.[105] Since 2002 the BGB follows the same approach as PECL:

BGB   **25.23 (DE)**

§ 321: Defence of insecurity

(1) A person bound by a synallagmatic contract to perform first may refuse to perform his part if after conclusion of the contract it becomes apparent that his claim for counter-performance is endangered by the other party's lack of ability to perform. The right to refuse to perform ceases if counter-performance is effected or security provided for it.

(2) The person required to perform first may specify a reasonable period within which the other party must, at his option, effect counter-performance or provide security concurrently with performance. If the period expires to no avail the person required to perform first may terminate the contract. § 323 applies mutatis mutandis.

25.7 AGREED RIGHTS OF TERMINATION

What if one party attempts to expand its right of termination to apply to cases in which the other has only committed what would normally be regarded as a minor breach? For example, we have seen that in English law the aggrieved party may terminate either if the breach is one which deprives it of the substance of what it was contracting for or if the breach was a condition. In principle, a condition is a term which is so important that

---

[103] See above, p 975.
[104] See above, p 977.
[105] BGH 21 October 1982, NJW 1983, 989; see V Emmerich, *Das Recht der Leistungsstörungen* (3rd edn, Munich: CH Beck, 1991) 198, 239.

'it goes to the root of the contract'. What happens if the parties agree that some minor, or even trivial, default shall give the creditor a right to terminate?

In principle, the systems seem to permit the parties to agree on such a right of termination by way of specific clauses, which in French law are called *clauses résolutoires*. However, whatever they may say, such clauses do not give an absolute power to terminate—or at least, deprive the termination of the normal consequences. In French and German law it seems that the right to terminate will still be subject to some judicial control, in that the right to terminate must be used in good faith. English law, having no general rule of good faith, has had to resort to less obvious means of control based on construction of the contract and, ultimately, a clearly drafted clause may give the creditor an unfettered right to terminate.

French law recognises the right of a party to insert a term giving an express right to terminate the contract, a *clause de résolution de plein droit*.

Code civil   **25.24 (FR)**

Article 1225: A termination clause must specify the undertakings whose non-performance will lead to the termination of the contract.

Termination may take place only after service of a notice to perform which has not been complied with, unless it was agreed that termination may arise from the mere act of non-performance. The notice to perform takes effect only if it refers expressly to the termination clause.

Notes

(1) A termination clause allows termination without judicial proceedings. It is widely used in contractual practice. Note that according to Article 1225, if the failure to perform falls within the undertakings listed in the clause, the creditor must first serve a notice to perform the obligation that has not been fulfilled; if the non-performance persists, the creditor may terminate.

(2) The obligation to serve a notice may be excluded by the agreement of the parties, for example if the clause provides that the mere act of non-performance is sufficient to trigger the termination.

(3) Now that unilateral termination is allowed by the Code civil itself, it might be thought that termination clauses have lost their purpose. In fact, this is not so, since such clauses may also be used to give the creditor a right to terminate in circumstances in which termination—be it judicial or unilateral—would not be permitted. Moreover, the existence of such a clause does not deprive the parties of the possibility of using judicial or unilateral termination.

(4) Termination clauses are efficient and make termination easy; for the other party, they are harsh and dangerous.[106] This is why Article 1225 requires that such clauses 'specify the undertakings whose non-performance will lead to the termination of the contract' and restricts the way it can be exercised.

---

[106] ibid.

(5) French courts will exercise control over the use of termination clauses. While, in principle, judges have no power to moderate the clause (there is no such power of revision like the one granted by the legislator in case of penalty clauses),[107] in practice, they exercise some control by resorting to a restrictive interpretation of these clauses and sometimes also through the concept of good faith. For instance, if the clause merely states that termination is possible in case of non-performance, French judges could decide that it is only a reminder of Article 1224 of the Code civil and that the clause is not one which enables a party to terminate the contract; the party should therefore either seek judicial termination or serve a prior notice of default and proceed to a unilateral termination. Similarly, a clause which merely provides that the termination results from the act of non-performance may be interpreted as only avoiding the need for judicial recourse, so that notice must still be served prior to the termination. In practice, the only clause which will certainly lead to automatic termination for breach is the one which states that termination is 'of right and without warning'. The next case, *Widow Thomas' rente viagère*, even though it pre-dates the 2016 reform, is still relevant as it illustrates how the courts will monitor the use of such clauses.

Cass civ (3), 8 April 1987[108]　　　　　　　**25.25 (FR)**

Widow Thomas' rente viagère

Where the terms of a contract have not been enforced over an extended period of time, and a party has been led to believe that the terms will not be enforced, it is not open to the other party to terminate the contract for a breach of those terms. In such a case, the termination clause is not relied upon in good faith.

Facts: Mr Thomas sold a house in 1970 to Mr and Mrs Andre-Renouvier. The sale contained an easement in favour of his wife and himself for a cash amount together with an annuity. After the death of Mr Thomas, his wife, invoking the termination clause in the contract for sale, gave formal notice to the debtors to pay the annuity which had never been claimed. Mr Andre and Mrs Renouvier refused to pay, and Mrs Thomas brought proceedings against them for repudiation of the sale.

Held: The creditors' claim for dissolution of the arrangement was dismissed on the basis that the termination clause was not relied on in good faith: by omitting for more than 10 years to claim the annuity payment from the debtors, the creditor, and later his wife, had led the debtors to believe that the annuity would never be claimed. The Cour de cassation upheld the judgment on appeal.

Judgment: THE COURT: *On the first three appeal grounds taken together* ... —Whereas Mrs Thomas criticises the judgment for dismissing her claim whereas, in the terms of her first appeal ground, the termination clause in the deed of sale of 17 December 1970 was entirely lawful and binding on the parties and the courts; as furthermore, in her submission, once the courts found that effect had not been given to the claims in the summons, they had no power other than to hold that the contract had been terminated; as by excusing non-payment of arrears on alleged grounds of equity, the judgment appealed against infringed Articles 1134 [now Article 1104], 1184 [repealed: see now Articles 1224 et seq.] and 1656 of the Civil Code;

---

[107] See below, pp 1119 ff.
[108] No. 85-17596, Bull III no. 88, Gaz Pal 1988.II.21037, annotated by Y Picod.

— Whereas under the second appeal ground it is submitted that, although the court may examine points of law of its own motion, it must first invite the parties to submit their observations; as in holding there to have been an abuse of her rights by Mrs Thomas to the detriment of her adversaries the judgment appealed against infringed Articles 12 and 16 of the new Code of Civil Procedure;

— Whereas finally, under the third plea it is submitted that the exercise of a right cannot degenerate into an abuse unless it is exercised with the intention of harming another person or constitutes a serious fault equivalent to deception to be established by the court; as that is argued not to be the case here since Mrs Thomas merely availed herself of a right which accrued to her only on the death of her husband some months earlier, and whose exercise could have been foreseen by the debtors;

— Whereas the judgment appealed against is therefore said to be without legal basis under Articles 1382 et seq (now Article 1240 et seq] of the Civil Code.

— Whereas the court of appeal found that, by omitting for more than 10 years to claim the annuity payment from the debtors the creditor then, after his death, his wife had led the debtors to believe that the annuity would never be claimed, the spouses having a particularly affectionate relationship with Mrs Renouvier, who was the foster sister of the creditor, and that the sudden change in the creditor's attitude which was solely due to dissension in Mrs Renouvier's daughter's family constituted a situation which was unforeseeable as far as the debtors were concerned, and prevented them from bringing themselves into conformity within the period allowed;

— Whereas the judgment is lawful on those grounds alone from which the court of appeal was entitled to infer, without infringing the principle of *audi alteram partem*, that the termination clause had not been relied on in good faith.

On the fourth appeal ground:— Whereas Mrs Thomas criticises the judgment for granting Mrs Renouvier a period of one year to pay the arrears accrued due. However, it is submitted on appeal that the court must confine itself to claims made before it, and Mrs Renouvier made no request for a period of grace;

— Whereas the judgment is therefore in breach of Article 5 of the new Code of Civil Procedure, since the grant of a period for payment of a debt is reserved to the debtor in difficulties and the courts trying the case on its merits must state the grounds relating to the debtor's situation on which it decides to grant the debtor a period of grace; as by stating no ground in that connection it is submitted that the judgment appealed against infringed [former] Article 1244[109] of the Civil Code and Article 455 of the new Code of Civil Procedure;

— Whereas however, since a judgment which gives a decision on matters in respect of which no request was made may be rectified as provided for in Articles 462 and 463 of the new Code of Civil Procedure, that plea is inadmissible.

On those grounds: The appeal is dismissed.

Notes

(1) In this case, Article 1134(3) of the Civil Code (now Article 1104) serves to mitigate the rigorous effects of the termination clause which derives its validity from Article 1134(1) (now Article 1103).

(2) While the good or bad faith of the party in breach is in principle irrelevant, good faith of the party who invokes the clause can be taken into account. This is so

---

[109] Art 1244 provided that a creditor was not obliged to accept part payment from the debtor.

particularly when that party serves a notice of default on his debtor in such conditions that the latter cannot possibly perform (for instance, while the lessee who has not paid his rent is on holiday).[110] It is also relevant when, as in this case, the creditor has omitted to claim his due for a long time.

(3) The Cour de cassation acknowledges that the courts are empowered to review whether the use of the termination clause complies with the principle of good faith. It is not always easy to discern the intention of the contracting parties. The court will have to scrutinise the intentions of the parties: if bad faith appears to guide the actions of the creditor, the court could prevent the creditor from relying on the termination clause.

(4) Subsequently, the Commercial Chamber of the Cour de cassation tried to refine the use of the good faith principle by introducing the following distinction: even if the rule by which contracts have to be performed in good faith permits the judge to sanction unfair use of a contractual power, it does not permit the reduction of the substance of the rights, if the rights are the result of the agreement between the parties.[111] In practice, this distinction is hard to apply. Indeed, if the judge deprives a termination clause of its effect, this amounts to a form of adaptation of the contract. Consequently, is there not a risk that the judge will reduce the substance of the rights?

In German law, as we have already noted, in cases of non-performance or defective performance, the creditor may be able to terminate under § 323 BGB, or to 'go over to damages' under § 281, even though the debtor's non-performance is slight.[112] This means that there is less need for a party who is concerned to have a right to terminate for even slight breaches to make express provision in the contract. Normally the creditor will have to give a warning before termination, but we also saw that this does not apply if the contract is a *Fixgeschäft*. However, to purport to terminate because of a very slight delay, even under a *Fixgeschäft*, would be contrary to good faith.[113]

As we suggested earlier, English law has no mechanism by which to prevent a party from inserting a clause that gives him the right to terminate even for a very minor breach of contract, and then exercising that right. However, the court may interpret the clause in a way that deprives the terminating party of the rights he would normally have after terminating for a serious breach.

Court of Appeal   **25.26 (EN)**

Financings Ltd v Baldock[114]

Where a hire-purchase contract provides that it may be terminated because the hirer has failed to pay every instalment on time, and the owner has exercised that right when the

---

[110] For various cases on such facts, see the references in Terré et al (n 4 above) no. 664.
[111] Cass com 10 July 2007, no. 06-14768, Bull IV no. 188, Droit & Patrimoine 2007, 94, annotated by P Stoffel-Munck.
[112] See above, pp 1006–07.
[113] See above, p 1017.
[114] [1963] 2 QB 104.

hirer has committed only a minor breach, the owner cannot claim damages for its full loss under the agreement. It may claim only for the instalments due at the date of termination.

Facts: A hire-purchase agreement provided:

> 8. Should the hirer fail to pay the initial instalment … or any subsequent instalment … within ten days after the same shall have become due or if he shall die … the owner may … by written notice … forthwith and for all purposes terminate the hiring.

Clause 11 provided that if the agreement were terminated under clause 8, the hirer would pay to the owner 'such further sum as with the total amount of any instalments previously paid hereunder will equal two-thirds of the total hiring cost …'. The hirer failed to pay the second and third instalments, and the owners gave notice of termination under clause 8 and repossessed the vehicle. Clause 11 was invalid as a penalty clause.[115] Therefore the owners claimed damages from the hirer for their full loss.

Held: The Court of Appeal held that they were entitled to the overdue instalments up to the date of repossession, but no more. The failure to pay one or two instalments on time would not justify termination of the contract under the general law,[116] and Clause 8 merely conferred a right to terminate the agreement without making the failure to pay a breach of condition. If the hirer's failure to pay had amounted to a repudiation, as in *Overstone Ltd v Shipway*,[117] the hirer would have been liable in damages, but here the owners could only claim money due at the date of termination and any payments required under the termination clause itself (none in this case).

Judgment: DENNING LJ: (On the effect of clause 8) It seems to me that when an agreement of hiring is terminated by virtue of a power contained in it, and the owner retakes the vehicle, he can recover damages for any breach up to the date of termination but not for any breach thereafter, for the simple reason that there are no breaches thereafter. … That principle is implicit in what Salter J said as long ago as 1926 in *Elacy & Co Ltd v Hyde*, an unreported case quoted by Jenkins LJ in *Cooden Engineering Co Ltd v Stanford*. Salter J took the very case:

> 'where the hire is determined by the owner, because the hirer is in arrear with his payments. It is proved that this is a breach of this contract, and it is proved that that breach, apart from any termination of the hirer, would give the owner a right to damages against the hirer. But what would those damages be? They would be interest on the amount unpaid and nothing more. The fact that the hirer is in arrear with his payments will not entitle the owner to any damages for depreciation of these things. The reason that they have suffered is that they have second hand goods put on their hands before they have received very much money in respect of them. That is not the result of the hirer's breach of contract, in being late in his payments, it is the result of their own election to determine the hiring. That passage is in my view good law: and Jenkins LJ seems to have accepted the reasoning in it as correct.'

DIPLOCK LJ: … [The hirer] was clearly in breach of his obligation to pay two instalments on the due dates but, in the absence of any express provision to the contrary in the

---

[115] The rules on penalty clauses are explained in greater detail below, pp 1118 ff. In essence, if the parties agree on a sum which is to be paid as damages if one of them breaks the contract, the clause will be valid if it is a genuine pre-estimate of the loss which the breach is likely to cause ('liquidated damages'). If it exceeds this figure the clause will be invalid as a 'penalty'. Clause 11 in the *Financings* contract was penal because the same amount had to be paid by the hirer irrespective of the value of the car repossessed.

[116] See above, p 1018.

[117] [1962] 1 All ER 52 (CA).

contract, these breaches of a contract of hire expressed to be for a duration of 24 months would not of themselves go to the root of the contract or evince an intention on the part of the hirer no longer to be bound by the contract. The owners' only remedy would have been to sue for the two instalments overdue and their measure of damages would have been the amount of these instalments, together with interest at the agreed rate of 10 per cent per annum. They would also have continued to be liable to perform their own obligations under the contract, viz, to continue to hire the van to the hirer: for again, in the absence of express provision to the contrary, the non-payment of two instalments would not be an event which relieved the owners from their undertaking to do what they had agreed to do but had not yet done ... Parties to a contract may incorporate in it provisions which expressly define the events, whether or not they amount to breaches of contract, which are to have this result. But such a provision of itself may do no more than define an event which of itself, or at the option of one or other of the parties, brings the contract to an end and thus relieves both parties from their undertakings further to perform their obligations thereunder. Whether it does more than this and confers any other rights or remedies on either party on the termination of the contract, depends upon the true construction of the relevant provision. If it does not, then each party is left with such causes of action, if any, as had already accrued to him at the date that the contract came to an end, but acquires no fresh cause of action as a result of the termination.

Court of Appeal **25.27 (EN)**

Lombard North Central plc v Butterworth[118]

Where timely payment is a condition of a contract, and that condition is breached, the other party is entitled to claim all outstanding instalments by way of compensation for breach of the condition.

Facts: The plaintiff, a finance company, leased a computer to the defendant for a period of five years on payment of an initial sum of £584.05 and 19 subsequent quarterly instalments of the same amount. Clause 2(a) of the hiring agreement made punctual payment of each instalment of the essence of the agreement and under clause 5 failure to make due and punctual payment entitled the plaintiffs to terminate the agreement. By clause 6 the plaintiffs were entitled on termination to all 'arrears of instalments and all future instalments which would have fallen due had the agreement not been terminated less a discount for accelerated payment'. Although the defendant paid the first two instalments promptly, the next three were paid very belatedly, and on four occasions payment made by direct debit was recalled by the bank. When the sixth instalment was six weeks overdue the plaintiffs wrote to the defendant terminating the agreement. Subsequently the plaintiffs recovered possession of the computer and sold it for only £172.88. The plaintiffs brought an action against the defendant claiming the amount of the unpaid sixth instalment and the 13 future instalments or, alternatively, damages for breach of contract. They then applied for and obtained summary judgment under RSC Ord 14 for damages to be assessed.

Held: In assessing the damages the master held that the defendant had by his conduct repudiated the contract and accordingly the plaintiffs were entitled to recover damages in respect of all future instalments less certain credits. The defendant appealed, contending that he ought not to be held liable for more than the amount due and unpaid at the date of termination. The appeal was dismissed.

---

[118] [1987] QB 527.

Judgment: Mustill LJ: ... The hire agreement contained the following material provisions: The LESSEE ... AGREES ...

2. (a) to pay to the lessor: (i) punctually and without previous demand the rentals set out in Part 3 of the Schedule together with Value Added Tax thereon punctual payment of each which shall be of the essence of this lease.

5. IN THE EVENT THAT (a) the Lessee shall (i) make default in the due and punctual payment of any of the rentals or of any sum of money payable to the Lessor hereunder or any part thereof ... then upon the happening of such event ... the Lessor's consent to the Lessee's possession of the Goods shall determine forthwith without any notice being given by the Lessor, and the Lessor may terminate this Lease either by notice in writing, or by taking possession of the Goods ...

6. IN THE EVENT THAT the Lessor's consent to the Lessee's possession of the goods shall be determined under clause 5 hereof *(a)* the Lessee shall pay forthwith to the Lessor: (i) all arrears of rentals; and (ii) all further rentals which would but for the determination of the Lessor's consent to the Lessee's possession of the Goods have fallen due to the end of the fixed period of this Lease less a discount thereon for accelerated payment at the rate of 5 per cent per annum; and (iii) damages for any breach of this Lease and all expenses and costs incurred by the Lessor in retaking possession of the Goods and/or enforcing the Lessor's rights under this Lease together with such Value Added Tax as shall be legally payable thereon: *(b)* the Lessor shall be entitled to exercise any one or more of the rights and remedies provided for in clause 5 and sub clause *(a)* of this clause and the determination of the Lessor's consent to the Lessee's possession of the Goods shall not affect or prejudice such rights and remedies and the Lessee shall be and remain liable to perform all outstanding liabilities under this Lease notwithstanding that the Lessor may have taken possession of the Goods and/or exercised one or more of the rights and remedies of the Lessor; *(c)* any right or remedy to which the Lessor is or may become entitled under this Lease or in consequence of the Lessee's conduct may be enforced from time to time separately or concurrently with any other right or remedy given by this Lease or now or hereafter provided for or arising by operation of law so that such rights and remedies are not exclusive of the other or others of them but are cumulative.

Three issues were canvassed before us. (1) Is cl 6 of the agreement to be disregarded, on the ground that it creates a penalty? (Strictly speaking, this issue does not arise, since the judgment was for damages to be assessed, but cl 6 was relied on by the plaintiffs before the master and in this court, without objection.) (2) Apart from cl 2(a) of the agreement, was the master correct in holding that the conduct of the defendant amounted to a wrongful repudiation of the contract, and that the sum claimed was recoverable in damages? (3) Does the provision in cl 2(a) of the agreement that time for payment of the instalments was of the essence have the effect of making the defendant's late payment of the outstanding instalments a repudiatory breach?

As to the first two issues, I need say only that I have had the advantage of reading in draft the judgment to be delivered by Nicholls LJ, and that I am in such entire agreement with his conclusions and reasons that it is unnecessary to add any observations of my own.

The reason why I am impelled to hold that the plaintiffs' contentions are well-founded can most conveniently be set out in a series of propositions. (1) Where a breach goes to the root of the contract, the injured party may elect to put an end to the contract. Thereupon both sides are relieved from those obligations which remain unperformed. (2) If he does so elect, the injured party is entitled to compensation for (a) any breaches which occurred before the contract was terminated and (b) the loss of his opportunity to receive performance of the promisor's outstanding obligations. (3) Certain categories of obligation, often called conditions, have the property that any breach of them is treated as going to the root of the contract. On the occurrence of any breach of condition, the injured party can elect to terminate and claim damages, whatever the gravity of the breach. (4) It is possible by express provision in the contract to make a term a condition, even if it would not be so in the absence of such a provision. (5) A stipulation that time is of the essence, in relation to a particular contractual term, denotes that timely performance is a condition of the contract. The consequence is that delay in performance is treated as going to the root of the contract, without regard to the magnitude of the breach. (6) It follows that where a promisor fails to give timely performance of an obligation in respect of which time is expressly stated to be of the essence, the injured party may elect to terminate and recover damages in respect of the promisor's outstanding obligations, without regard to the magnitude of the breach. (7) A term of the contract prescribing what damages are to be recoverable when a contract is terminated for a breach of condition is open to being struck down as a penalty, if it is not a genuine covenanted pre-estimate of the damage, in the same way as a clause which prescribes the measure for any other type of breach. No doubt the position is the same where the clause is ranked as a condition by virtue of an express provision in the contract. (8) A clause expressly assigning a particular obligation to the category of condition is not a clause which purports to fix the damages for breaches of the obligation, and is not subject to the law governing penalty clauses. (9) Thus, although in the present case cl 6 is to be struck down as a penalty, cl 2(a)(i) remains enforceable. The plaintiffs were entitled to terminate the contract independently of cl 5, and to recover damages for loss of the future instalments. This loss was correctly computed by the master.

These bare propositions call for comment. The first three are uncontroversial. The fourth was not, I believe, challenged before us, but I would in any event regard it as indisputable ...

The fifth proposition is a matter of terminology, and has been more taken for granted than discussed. That making time of the essence is the same as making timely performance if condition was, however, expressly stated by Megaw and Browne LJJ in *Bunge Corp v Tradax SA*[119] and the same proposition is implicit in the leading speeches of Lord Wilberforce and Lord Roskill in the House of Lords.

The sixth proposition is a combination of the first five. There appears to be no direct authority for it, and it is right to say that most of the cases on the significance of time being of the essence have been concerned with the right to the injured party to be discharged, rather than the principles on which its damages are to be computed. Nevertheless, it is axiomatic that a person who establishes a breach of condition can terminate and claim damages for loss of the bargain, and I know of no authority which suggests that the position is any different where late performance is made into a breach of condition by a stipulation that time is of the essence.

I return to the propositions stated above. The seventh is uncontroversial, and I would add only the rider that when deciding on the penal nature of a clause which prescribes a measure of recovery for damages resulting from a termination founded on a breach of condition, the comparison should he with the common law measure, namely with the loss to the promisee resulting from the loss of his bargain. If the contract permits him to treat the contract as repudiated, the fact that the breach is comparatively minor should in my view play no part in the equation.

---

[119] See 25.18 (EN), above, p 1019.

I believe that the real controversy in the present case centres on the eighth proposition. I will repeat it. A clause expressly assigning a particular obligation to the category of condition is not a clause which purports to fix the damages for breach of the obligation, and is not subject to the law governing penalty clauses. I acknowledge, of course, that by promoting a term into the category where all breaches are ranked as breaches of condition, the parties indirectly bring about a situation where, for breaches which are relatively small, the injured party is enabled to recover damages as on the loss of the bargain, whereas without the stipulation his measure of recovery would be different. But I am unable to accept that this permits the court to strike down as a penalty the clause which brings about this promotion. To do so would be to reverse the current of more than 100 years' doctrine, which permits the parties to treat as a condition something which would not otherwise be so. I am not prepared to take this step.

For these reasons I conclude that the plaintiffs are entitled to retain the damages which the master has awarded. This is not a result which I view with much satisfaction, partly because the plaintiffs have achieved by one means a result which the law of penalties might have prevented them from achieving by another and partly because if the line of argument under cl 2 had been developed from the outset, the defendant might have found an answer based on waiver which the court is now precluded from assessing, for want of the necessary facts. Nevertheless, it is the answer to which, in my view, the authorities clearly point. Accordingly, I would dismiss the appeal.

Notes

(1) Nicholls LJ (whose judgment is not extracted here) held that clause 6 was a penalty clause because it would allow the lessor (the finance company) to recover a greater amount than it would recover at common law. It seems odd that, if the lessor's terms state that in the event of the goods being repossessed, the lessor may recover its full loss, the clause is void as a penalty and the lessor can recover only the unpaid instalments; but that if the time for payment is stated to be of the essence, the lessor can recover the full loss.

(2) Quite an extensive case law on termination clauses in English law has developed. For a useful survey, see E Peel, 'The termination paradox' [2013] LMCLQ 519; and for an exhaustive discussion of the cases, see the judgment in *Phones 4U Ltd (in administration) v EE Ltd*.[120]

(3) Although the Court of Appeal held that the rules affecting penalty clauses did not apply to clause 2(a), such clauses in credit agreements are not completely uncontrolled in English law. First, where the credit agreement is for hire-purchase or conditional sale it may be regulated by the Consumer Credit Act 1974. (As the result of amendments made by the Consumer Credit Act 2006, this applies to many credit agreements made by individual consumers without any financial limit, and also to such agreements made by unincorporated businesses provided the agreement is for less than £25,000.)[121] This may mean that repossession is subjected to a formal

---

[120] [2018] EWHC 49 (Comm), [2018] 1 Lloyd's Rep 204, especially at [87] ff.
[121] Consumer Credit Act 1974 (as amended), s 8. There is an exception for 'high net worth' individuals and organisations, s 16A.

notice procedure, and that sometimes a court order is needed before the creditor may repossess the goods.[122] Secondly, this type of clause, if it were in a contract between a consumer and trader, would be subject to the requirement of fairness imposed by Consumer Rights Act 2015, section 62.[123]

(4) In order to make an obligation of minor importance into a condition, the parties will have to use clear language. In *L Schuler AG v Wickman Machine Tools Ltd*,[124] Wickman had been appointed sole distributor of Schuler's panel presses in the UK for a period of four-and-a-half years. Clause 7(b) of the agreement provided that:

> It shall be condition of this agreement that (i) [Wickman] shall send its representatives to visit [the (then) six large UK motor manufacturers] at least once in every week for the purpose of soliciting orders for panel presses …

Clause 11(a) provided that either party might determine the agreement by notice in writing if:

> (i) the other shall have committed a material breach of its obligations hereunder and shall have failed to remedy the same within sixty days of being required in writing so to do …

Wickman's representatives failed to make the weekly visit on a few occasions, and Schuler terminated the agreement immediately, claiming that Wickman was in breach of a condition under clause 7(b). The House of Lords held, by a majority, that the parties cannot have meant clause 7(b) to be a condition in the strict sense, because it would be unreasonable for Schuler to have a right to terminate for a minor breach which might not even be Wickman's fault, eg if the weekly visit was not made because the manufacturers were shut down for a holiday in the relevant week. Therefore Schuler could terminate only after giving a warning under clause 11. Lord Wilberforce, in a powerful dissenting speech, held that a draconian right to terminate was precisely what was intended.

25.8 A LAST CHANCE TO PERFORM

If the debtor has committed a breach of contract which seems serious enough to warrant termination by the creditor, does the debtor still have a last chance to perform—if he can—and thereby avoid the contract being terminated? Three issues require comment.

25.8.A RIGHT TO PERFORM BEFORE DUE DATE

If the time for performance has not yet expired, the debtor will normally still have the right to perform. The creditor can of course withhold performance until the debtor has performed, but—subject to the rules on anticipatory breach which exist in some systems[125]—the creditor cannot terminate before that date. In France, with respect

---

[122] Consumer Credit Act 1974, s 90.
[123] See 21.17 (EN), above, p 842.
[124] [1974] AC 235.
[125] See above, pp 1024 ff.

to judicial termination, the debtor may perform at any time before the court actually declares that the contract is terminated. We have already seen that a claim for *résolution* which is brought before the date on which performance is due will normally be dismissed as premature.[126] In English law the situation is usually much the same because of the fact that (unless there has been an anticipatory repudiation by the other party)[127] the innocent party is not entitled to terminate until the date for performance has passed. In the case of *Borrowman, Phillips & Co v Free and Hollis*[128] the sellers tendered documents representing the goods (which were in the course of shipment) that were not in accordance with the contract and which the buyers rejected. However, the contract period for delivery had not yet expired, and when within that period the sellers made a fresh tender of goods which did conform to the contract, the buyers had no right to reject the second tender. The result would be different in English law if there had been an anticipatory repudiation (see a case in which the first delivery was so defective that the court held that it amounted to a repudiation of the whole contract, which could be terminated right away: *Millar's Karri & Jarrah Co v Weddel, Turner & Co*).[129]

In German law it is clear that a seller of goods is entitled to cure removable defects or supply a substitute item at any time before performance was actually due.[130]

Principles of European Contract Law **25.28 (INT)**

Article 8:104: Cure by Non-Performing Party

A party whose tender of performance is not accepted by the other party because it does not conform to the contract may make a new tender and conforming tender where the time for performance has not yet arrived or the delay would not be such as to amount to a fundamental non-performance.

25.8.B REQUIREMENT OF NOTICE

As we have seen, in many systems a formal notice to the debtor is required before the debtor is treated as being in default. It operates to prevent sudden termination, as at least the debtor must first be put into default by serving the notice. For example, in French law the creditor must serve a notice called '*mise en demeure*'[131] on the debtor before having the right to unilaterally terminate the contract (Article 1226 of the Code civil). The same applies where there is a termination clause, unless this clause specifies that the termination may arise from the mere act of non-performance (Article 1225).[132] In principle, the prior notice requirement is also applicable to other remedies (except the

---

[126] See above, pp 1033 and 1028.
[127] See p 1025.
[128] (1878) 4 QBD 500 (CA).
[129] (1909) 100 LT 128 (KBD).
[130] See Münchener Kommentar/Ernst § 323 para 25.
[131] On the concept of *mise en demeure*, defined in Art 1344, see p 1011.
[132] See 25.24 (FR), above, p 1030.

exception d'inexécution). For instance, damages are due only if the debtor has previously been put on notice to perform his obligation (Article 1231). If the creditor is merely seeking judicial *résolution*, the notice of action will suffice.[133] German law requires a *Mahnung*, putting the debtor into delay (§ 286 BGB), and frequently a *Nachfrist* (§ 323 BGB), before the contract may be terminated. All these requirements give the debtor a chance to perform.

Even English law, which does not generally require any advance warning to the debtor, requires a 'default' notice before termination in certain cases, for example before termination of a consumer credit agreement (Consumer Credit Act 1974, Sections 87–89; see also Law of Property Act 1925, section 146 (leases)).

We will see later that, in contracts of sale of goods, consumer buyers (and in German law, buyers in general) often have to give the seller a chance to cure a non-conformity before the buyer can terminate the contract.[134]

Article 8:104 PECL applies only in cases in which the creditor had refused to accept a defective performance tendered by the debtor. This in effect acts only as a restraint on termination. The rule in consumer sales just mentioned, that the buyer may have to give the seller a chance to cure, applies not only when the buyer wants to terminate but also when he wants to reduce the price. When the PECL were being reconsidered as part of the DCFR, it was considered that this approach should apply not just to sales but also to other kinds of contract. The result is that under the DCFR there is now a general 'hierarchy of remedies', giving the debtor a right to cure before the creditor may terminate, reduce the price or claim damages other than for any loss caused by the debtor's initial or subsequent non-performance or the process of effecting cure.[135]

Draft Common Frame of Reference   **25.29 (INT)**

Section 2:
Cure by debtor of non-conforming performance

III.-3:201: Scope
This Section applies where a debtor's performance does not conform to the terms regulating the obligation.

III.-3:202: Cure by debtor: general rules
(1) The debtor may make a new and conforming tender if that can be done within the time allowed for performance.
(2) If the debtor cannot make a new and conforming tender within the time allowed for performance but, promptly after being notified of the lack of conformity, offers to cure it within a reasonable time and at the debtor's own expense, the creditor may not pursue any remedy for non-performance, other than withholding performance, before allowing the debtor a reasonable period in which to attempt to cure the nonconformity.

---

[133] ibid.
[134] See below, ch 27.
[135] DCFR II.-3:201–3:204.

(3) Paragraph (2) is subject to the provisions of the following Article. III-3:203: When creditor need not allow debtor an opportunity to cure

The creditor need not, under paragraph (2) of the preceding Article, allow the debtor a period in which to attempt cure if:

(a) failure to perform a contractual obligation within the time allowed for performance amounts to a fundamental non-performance as defined in III-3:502 (2);

(b) the creditor has reason to believe that the debtor's performance was made with knowledge of the non-conformity and was not in accordance with good faith and fair dealing;

(c) the creditor has reason to believe that the debtor will be unable to effect the cure within a reasonable time and without significant inconvenience to the creditor or other prejudice to the creditor's legitimate interests; or

(d) cure would be inappropriate in the circumstances.

III.-3:204: Consequences of allowing debtor opportunity to cure

(1) During the period allowed for cure the creditor may withhold performance of the creditor's reciprocal obligations, but may not resort to any other remedy.

(2) If the debtor fails to effect cure within the time allowed, the creditor may resort to any available remedy.

(3) Notwithstanding cure, the creditor retains the right to damages for any loss caused by the debtor's initial or subsequent non-performance or by the process of effecting cure.

Note

Although the DCFR provisions have a wider scope than Article 8:104 PECL, the practical difference may be slight. For example, though Article 8:104 does not affect the right to damages, if the seller offered to cure a non-conforming performance and the creditor unreasonably refused, the creditor would normally be unable to recover any additional loss he suffered as a result, under what is known as the mitigation rule.[136]

25.8.C COURT MAY GIVE ADDITIONAL PERIOD FOR PERFORMANCE

The court may have power to give the debtor an additional period to perform even if no notice is required, or if a notice has been given and has expired without the debtor performing.

Article 1228 of the French Code civil allows the court, according to the circumstances, to grant the debtor further time (*délai*), in other words, a last chance to perform. Traditionally this applied only to the judicial termination (*résolution judiciaire*). A *délai* may now also be granted by the judge where the creditor unilaterally terminates the contract and the debtor goes to court in order to contest the validity of such a unilateral act. In such a case, the court can—at least theoretically, for in practice this will not always be possible once a contract has been treated as terminated by the creditor—invalidate the termination and grant a *délai* for the party to perform.

---

[136] See further below, pp 1018 ff.

There is a debate on whether or not the provisions on *délai de grâce* can be used to temporarily paralyse a *clause résolutoire* (by granting a *délai de grâce* to the defaulting party). Since a *délai de grâce* only applies when a judicial decision orders performance of the contract, strictly speaking, it is not applicable in such a situation.[137]

The *délai* that may be granted under Article 1228 is different from the *délai de grâce* of Article 1343-5 of the Code civil, which may be given to every kind of debtor who is unable to pay money that is due, but only in a judicial decision which orders performance of the contract. The Article provides:

Code civil   **25.30 (FR)**

Article 1343-5: Taking into account the situation of the debtor and the needs of the creditor, a court may defer payment of sums that are due, or allow it to be made in instalments, for a period no greater than two years").

Note

Some authors consider that it would be logical that the effect of the termination clause may be postponed by virtue of Article 1343-5.[138]

English law does not as a general rule allow the debtor extra time. However, there are a number of exceptions by statute and at common law. Most involve situations in which the debtor stands to forfeit property, or the right to possess property, if the contract is terminated. For example, under the Consumer Credit Act 1974, if a debtor under a hire-purchase or conditional sale agreement has paid more than one-third of the total price when he defaults, the creditor may not repossess the goods without a court order (section 90), and the court may give the debtor extra time to pay (section 129). There are also provisions governing the forfeiture of leases of land for non-payment of rent (Common Law Procedure Act 1852, sections 210–12) and other breaches of covenant (Law of Property Act 1925, section 146). At common law, relief, in the form of extra time in which to pay before the other party will be allowed to terminate the contract, has been given to hirers of machines who were late in paying: *Barton, Thompson & Co Ltd v Stapling Machines Co*,[139] and *Transag Haulage Ltd v Leyland Daf Finance plc*.[140] But the House of Lords has held that this form of equitable relief against forfeiture is confined to cases where a proprietary or possessory right is to be forfeited. Thus, a time-charterer of a ship who has failed to pay the instalments of hire on time cannot invoke the jurisdiction to prevent the owner from withdrawing the ship under a clause which permits 'withdrawal' for late payment: *Scandinavian Trading Tanker Co AB v Flota Petrolera Ecuatoriana (The Scaptrade)*,[141] as a time-charter is a contract for services, not a contract giving the charterer any possessory rights. Equally, in *Union Eagle Ltd*

---

[137] Terré et al (n 4 above) no. 664.
[138] Bénabent (n 6 above) no. 398.
[139] [1966] Ch 499 (ChD).
[140] [1994] 2 BCLC 88 (ChD).
[141] [1983] 2 AC 694 (HL).

v Golden Achievement Ltd [1997] AC 514, when a buyer of a piece of land who was required by the contract to complete by 5pm on a particular day arrived with the money 10 minutes late, the Privy Council held that the seller could not be restrained from rescinding the contract.

In German law an extension of the debtor's period for performance beyond the *Nachfrist* can only be justified on the basis of § 242 BGB; that is where not to do so would seriously infringe the interests of the debtor against the requirements of good faith. Such cases are likely to be most exceptional.

25.9 EFFECTS OF TERMINATION

25.9.A THE EFFECT OF TERMINATION ON CLAIMS FOR DAMAGES FOR NON-PERFORMANCE

In French law the creditor may obtain both *résolution judiciaire* and damages for non-performance. Indeed, damages are based on the loss suffered and the non-performance may have caused loss which will not avoided by termination. When parties are both in breach, both of them may have to pay damages. (The judge can also grant damages when he considers that the breach is not sufficiently important to justify termination.) We have already seen that Article 1228 of the Code civil allows the court to award only damages instead of declaring the termination. Equally in English law, termination of the contract may be combined with an action for damages for non-performance.[142] In German law before 2002, a claim for *Rücktritt* could not be combined with a claim for damages for non-performance;[143] but now it is expressly provided that *Rücktritt* does not preclude a claim for damages: § 325 BGB.

25.9.B THE EFFECT ON ANCILLARY OBLIGATIONS

Although the process of termination is often likened to that of avoidance for invalidity— for example, for fraud—in all the systems there are at least two major differences. One is the point just referred to, that the creditor may generally claim damages for non-performance. The other is that, though the main obligations to perform come to an end, the contract may continue to be binding in other respects; in particular, the ancillary clauses of the contract will continue to apply.

Code civil   **25.31 (FR)**

Article 1230: Termination does not affect contract terms relating to dispute-resolution, nor those intended to take effect even in the case of termination, such as confidentiality or non-competition clauses

---

[142] *Johnson v Agnew* [1980] AC 367 (HL).
[143] See above, p 986.

Notes

(1) Article 1230 of the Code civil gives the examples of confidentiality or non-competition clauses. In addition to these examples, penalty clauses may also continue to apply (see Article 1231-5 of the French Code civil).[144]

(2) Similarly, if there is a contract to manufacture patented goods under licence and the contract is terminated by the licensor because of defaults by the licensee, clauses which forbid the licensee to divulge confidential information will still bind the licensee. The same applies to other clauses of the contract, such as arbitration clauses and clauses which limit one party's liability.

In English law this has long been accepted as far as arbitration clauses are concerned: for example *Heyman v Darwins Ltd*.[145] At one time the English Court of Appeal took a different approach to exclusion and limitation clauses, arguing that these did not survive termination of the contract—the so-called doctrine of 'fundamental breach'.[146] This was undoubtedly an attempt to control the use of such clauses, but it was rejected by the House of Lords both as a matter of principle and because it failed to distinguish between clauses which were unfair and those which represented a perfectly proper allocation of risks under the contract—see particularly the judgment of Lord Reid in *Suisse Atlantique*.[147] The doctrine of fundamental breach was finally laid to rest in *Photo Production Ltd v Securicor Ltd*.[148] In that case Lord Diplock explained the general principle underlying the effect of termination in English law.

House of Lords   **25.32 (EN)**

Photo Production Ltd v Securicor Ltd[149]

[For the facts of this case and other extracts, see 21.8 (EN), above, p 825].

LORD DIPLOCK: A basic principle of the common law of contract, to which there are no exceptions that are relevant in the instant case, is that parties to a contract are free to determine for themselves what primary obligations they will accept. They may state these in express words in the contract itself and, where they do, the statement is determinative; but in practice a commercial contract never states all the primary obligations of the parties in full; many are left to be incorporated by implication of law from the legal nature of the contract into which the parties are entering. But if the parties wish to reject or modify primary obligations which would otherwise be so incorporated, they are fully at liberty to do so by express words.

Leaving aside those comparatively rare cases in which the court is able to enforce a primary obligation by decreeing specific performance of it, breaches of primary obligations give rise to substituted or secondary obligations on the part of the party in default, and, in some cases, may entitle the other party to be relieved from further performance of

---

[144] Cass civ (3) 26 January 2011, no. 10-10376, Bull III no. 12.
[145] [1942] AC 356 (HL).
[146] See above, pp 823–26.
[147] [1967] 1 AC 361.
[148] See 21.8 (EN), above, p 825.
[149] [1980] AC 827.

his own primary obligations. These secondary obligations of the contract breaker and any concomitant relief of the other party from his own primary obligations also arise by implication of law—generally common law, but sometimes statute, as in the case of codifying statutes passed at the turn of the century, notably the Sale of Goods Act ... The contract, however, is just as much the source of secondary obligations as it is of primary obligations; and like primary obligations that are implied by law, secondary obligations too can be modified by agreement between the parties, although, for reasons to be mentioned later, they cannot, in my view, be totally excluded. In the instant case, the only secondary obligations and concomitant reliefs that are applicable arise by implication of the common law as modified by the express words of the contract.

Every failure to perform a primary obligation is a breach of contract. The secondary obligation on the part of the contract breaker to which it gives rise by implication of the common law is to pay monetary compensation to the other party for the loss sustained by him in consequence of the breach; but, with two exceptions, the primary obligations of both parties so far as they have not yet been fully performed remain unchanged. This secondary obligation to pay compensation (damages) for non-performance of primary obligations I will call the 'general secondary obligation.' It applies in the cases of the two exceptions as well.

The exceptions are: (1) Where the event resulting from the failure by one party to perform a primary obligation has the effect of depriving the other party of substantially the whole benefit which it was the intention of the parties that he should obtain from the contract, the party not in default may elect to put an end to all primary obligations of both parties remaining unperformed. (If the expression' fundamental breach' is to be retained, it should, in the interests of clarity, be confined to this exception.) (2) Where the contracting parties have agreed, whether by express words or by implication of law, that any failure by one party to perform a particular primary obligation ('condition' in the nomenclature of the Sale of Goods Act ...), irrespective of the gravity of the event that has in fact resulted from the breach, shall entitle the other party to elect to put an end to all primary obligations of both parties remaining unperformed. (In the interests of clarity, the nomenclature of the Sale of Goods Act ..., 'breach of condition' should be reserved for this exception.)

Where such an election is made (a) there is substituted by implication of law for the primary obligations of the party in default which remain unperformed a secondary obligation to pay monetary compensation to the other party for the loss sustained by him in consequence of their non-performance in the future and (b) the unperformed primary obligations of that other party are discharged. This secondary obligation is additional to the general secondary obligation; I will call it 'the anticipatory secondary obligation.'

In cases falling within the first exception, fundamental breach, the anticipatory secondary obligation arises under contracts of all kinds by implication of the common law, except to the extent that it is excluded or modified by the express words of the contract. In cases falling within the second exception, breach of condition, the anticipatory secondary obligation generally arises under particular kinds of contracts by implication of statute law; though in the case of 'deviation' from the contract voyage under a contract of carriage of goods by sea it arises by implication of the common law. The anticipatory secondary obligation in these cases too can be excluded or modified by express words.

When there has been a fundamental breach or breach of condition, the coming to an end of the primary obligations of both parties to the contract at the election of the party not in default, is often referred to as the 'determination' or 'rescission' of the contract or, as in the Sale of Goods Act ... 'treating the contract as repudiated.' The first two of these expressions, however, are misleading unless it is borne in mind that for the unperformed primary obligations of the party in default there are substituted by operation of law what I have called the secondary obligations.

The bringing to an end of all primary obligations under the contract may also leave the parties in a relationship, typically that of bailor and bailee, in which they owe to one another by operation of law fresh primary obligations of which the contract is the source; but no such relationship is involved in the instant case.

I have left out of account in this analysis as irrelevant to the instant case an arbitration or choice of forum clause. This does not come into operation until a party to the contract claims that a primary obligation of the other party has not been performed; and its relationship to other obligations of which the contract is the source was dealt with by this House in *Heyman v Darwins Ltd* [1942] AC 356.

In German law it is now agreed that termination of the contract, whether through making a declaration of *Rücktritt* (§ 323 BGB) or seeking damages for non-performance (§§ 280(1) and (3), 281 BGB), merely transforms or recasts the main performance obligations (*Hauptpflichten*) of the contract into obligations either to make restitution or to pay damages.[150] Logically this recasting of performance obligations can have no effect on the continued validity of the other contractual obligations. We have thus already referred to the fact that, notwithstanding his seeking *Rücktritt*, the creditor may also claim damages for delay in the performance of collateral obligations, for breach of protective obligations etc.[151]

25.9.C RESTITUTIONARY CLAIMS

Principles of European Contract Law **25.33 (INT)**

Article 4:305: Effects of Termination in General
   (1) Termination of the contract releases both parties from their obligation to effect and to receive future performance, but, subject to Articles 4:306, 4:307 and 4:308, does not affect the rights and liabilities accrued up to the time of termination.
   (2) Termination does not affect any provision of the contract for the settlement of disputes or any other provision which is to operate even after termination.

Article 4:306: Property Reduced in Value
   A party who terminates the contract may reject property previously received from the other party if its value to the first party has been fundamentally reduced as a result of the other party's non-performance.

Article 4:307: Recovery of Money Paid
   On termination of the contract a party may recover money paid for a performance which he did not receive or which he properly rejected.

---

[150] See Münchener Kommentar/Gaier Introduction to § 346 para 26.
[151] See above, p 986.

Article 4:308: Recovery of Property

On termination of the contract a party who has supplied property which can be returned and for which he has not received payment or other counter-performance may recover the property.

Article 4:309: Recovery for Performance that Cannot be Returned

On termination of the contract a party who has rendered a performance which cannot be returned and for which he has not received payment or other counter-performance may recover a reasonable amount for the value of the performance to the other party.

What if one or both parties has rendered some performance to the other before termination of the contract? Can the party who has performed claim restitution of what he transferred or, if there is nothing to be reclaimed *in specie*, its value?

From the point of view of the aggrieved party, it will not always matter much whether he can claim restitution: if he is left out of pocket, he can claim damages. However, there is one case in which it will be critical. If the debtor is bankrupt, it will be very important to know whether any property transferred by the aggrieved party can be recovered, either from the debtor or from anyone else who now has possession of it.

Obviously a party in breach who has transferred property to the aggrieved party, and who now finds the latter to be insolvent, may have a similar concern. However, the party in breach has a much greater interest in being able to claim in restitution even from a solvent aggrieved party, since the party in breach has no action for damages to fall back on.

Systems which regard termination as essentially retroactive seem to have little difficulty in allowing restitution as between the original contracting parties, in favour of either of them.[152]

25.9.C.1 FRANCE

The question of restitution after the termination of contract used to be a difficult one in French law, as it was not codified as such in the Code civil. It is now set out in the Code; Article 1229 and states that termination 'puts an end to the contract' and that 'Restitution takes place under the conditions provided by Articles 1352 to 1352-9.'

We saw earlier that the availability of restitution after the termination of a contract depends on the effects of termination in time, ie whether the termination has a retroactive effect or takes effect only for the future.[153]

If, pursuant to the rules presented above, termination gives rise to restitution, the general rules on restitution apply. A new regime of restitution is set out in Articles 1352 to 1352-9 of the new Code civil.

Code civil   **25.34 (FR)**

Article 1352: Restitution of a thing other than a sum of money takes place in kind or, where this is impossible, by value assessed at the date of the restitution.

---

[152] Various problems then arise when a creditor or other third party is interested (eg, a buyer in good faith). These (essentially proprietary) issues are not covered in this book.

[153] Above, pp 982 ff.

Article 1352-1: A person who makes restitution of a thing is responsible for any degradations or deteriorations which have reduced its value unless he was in good faith and these were not due to his fault.

Article 1352-2: A person who sells a thing which he received in good faith must make restitution only of the sale price.

If he received it in bad faith, he must pay the value at the date on which he makes restitution where that is higher than the price.

Article 1352-3: Restitution includes its fruits and the value of the enjoyment to which the thing has given rise.

The value of the enjoyment is to be assessed by the court as at the date of its decision.

Unless otherwise stipulated by the contracting parties, if the fruits no longer exist in kind, their restitution takes place, according to a value assessed at the date of reimbursement, on the basis of the condition of the thing at the date of satisfaction of the obligation.

Article 1352-4: Restitution owed by an unemancipated minor or by a protected adult is reduced to the profit which he has drawn from the act that has been annulled.

Article 1352-5: The amount of restitution is fixed taking into account for the party who owes restitution any necessary expenses incurred in the maintenance of the thing, and expenses which have increased its value, limited to the increase in value assessed at the date of restitution.

Article 1352-6: Restitution of a sum of money includes interest at the rate set by legislation and any taxes paid to the person who received it.

Article 1352-7: A party in receipt in bad faith owes interest, the fruits he has taken and the value of enjoyment from the moment of receipt of satisfaction. A party in receipt in good faith owes these only from the date when they are claimed.

Article 1352-8: Restitution in respect of a supply of a service takes place by value, assessed at the date at which the service was supplied.

Article 1352-9: Securities created for the satisfaction of an obligation are transferred by operation of law to the obligation to make restitution, although the guarantor does not lose the benefit of any time delay.

Notes

(1) Articles 1352 to 1352-9 form part of a new chapter of the Code civil, dedicated to restitution. It contains provisions designed to cover restitution in general, not just after termination of a contract for non-performance, and this explains why not all the provisions set out above are relevant to restitution after termination, eg Article 1352-4. The provisions on benefits received or actions taken in bad faith will seldom apply, as normally the parties to a contract will have received any benefits and have dealt with them in good faith.

(2) Normally a party who received property by the other party before the contract was terminated will have to return it or, where this cannot be done, pay its current value, unless he has sold it. In that case he must pay the price he obtained for the property. A party who was paid money will have to repay it with interest. A party who

received services will have to pay their value. It is not specified how the services are to be valued—for example, by the cost incurred by the service provider in rendering them, or by the benefit gained from them by the recipient?

25.9.C.2 GERMANY

German law was likewise greatly clarified by the reforms to the BGB.[154]

BGB

25.35 (DE)

§ 346: Effects of termination

(1) If one party to a contract has reserved a right to terminate the contract or if he has a statutory right of termination, then, if termination occurs, any performance received is to be returned, as are benefits derived from such performance.

(2) The obligor must pay compensation for value rather than effect a return, where

1. the return or surrender is excluded because of the nature of what has been acquired,

2. he has consumed, transferred, encumbered, processed or transformed the object received,

3. the object received has deteriorated or has been destroyed; any deterioration resulting from the proper use of the object for its intended purpose is, however, disregarded.

If the contract specifies a counter-performance, such counter-performance is to be taken as a basis for calculation of the compensation for value.

(3) There is no duty to pay compensation for value

1. if the defect which gives the right to termination became apparent only during the processing or transformation of the item,

2. in so far as the obligee is responsible for the deterioration or destruction or the damage would also have occurred in his hands,

3. if, in the case of a statutory right of termination, the deterioration or destruction has occurred in the hands of the person entitled even though he has taken the care which he usually takes in his own affairs.

Any remaining enrichment must be given up.

(4) The obligee may demand compensation, in accordance with §§ 280 to 283, for infringement of a duty under subsection (1) above.

§ 347: Benefits and expenditure after termination

(1) If, contrary to the rules of proper management, the obligor has failed to derive benefits even though it would have been possible to do so, he must compensate the obligee for their value. In the case of termination based on a statutory right, the person entitled must display with regard to the benefits only the standard of care which he usually takes in his own affairs.

(2) If the obligor returns the object, compensates the obligee for value, or if his duty to compensate for value is excluded pursuant to § 346 (3), nos 1 or 2, he must be reimbursed

---

[154] For the law before the reforms of 2001, see Beale et al (n 32 above) 801–03.

for necessary expenditure. Other expenditure is to be reimbursed in as much as the obligee is enriched by it.

§ 348: Concurrent performance

The obligations of the parties arising out of termination are to be performed concurrently. The provisions of §§ 320 and 322 apply mutatis mutandis.

Notes

(1) The restitution regime set out in §§ 346–348 applies when the law gives right to withdrawal (eg under § 323); when the parties have agreed on a right to withdrawal (see § 346(1)); when performance has been effected even though it was not owed (see § 326(4)); and when the creditor has claimed damages in lieu of the entire performance (see § 281(5)). Since the general provisions now apply also in cases of the delivery of non-conforming goods (see Chapter 27), the regime in effect also applies in that case if the buyer opts to terminate the contract.

(2) The starting point is that, if a creditor declares *Rücktritt*, both parties are under an obligation to return what they have received under the contract, unless this is not possible (see § 346(2)). The obligations are treated as synallagmatic duties (§ 348 BGB) and the normal remedies apply, so that if one party does not comply the other may either enforce the obligation or go over to damages (see § 346(3)). *Rücktritt* has no direct effect on the property rights of the parties themselves or of third parties. Only when the obligations of both parties to make restoration are performed will property pass back.

(3) The cases in which return of the performance is not required because it is no longer feasible are set out in § 346(2). It will be seen that in most cases the debtor must provide compensation instead, but § 346(3) lists a number of cases in which there will be no obligation to provide full compensation, generally because it was not the debtor's fault that he is unable to return the item.

(4) Note that under § 346(2) no. 2 it will normally not be a defence to a claim for compensation that the debtor no longer has the benefit he received.

(5) It does not seem that the accidental destruction of the thing delivered will prevent the creditor from terminating the contract. However, unless the destruction of the thing was not his fault, he may be obliged to pay the value of the thing by way of damages to the seller: § 346(3) BGB.

(6) The amount of compensation is normally to be calculated on the basis of the price for the benefit agreed in the contract: § 346(2), last paragraph.

25.9.C.3 ENGLAND

English law is much less favourable to the party seeking restitution. Termination of the contract, being prospective only, does not revest property transferred in the transferor. An unpaid seller of goods can repossess them only if he has made specific provision in the agreement to that effect, typically by reserving title to the goods sold. If he has done this, it will give him the right to repossess goods from the buyer if the buyer is insolvent.

Even then a sub-purchaser who has bought and paid for the goods without knowing of the seller's rights will normally get good title to them (Sale of Goods Act 1979, Section 25). If the seller has not reserved title, his only remedy is to sue for the price—and if the buyer is insolvent, the seller will probably get little or nothing. Even as between the original parties, English law is much more restrictive on the use of restitution. It is necessary to distinguish (a) between the aggrieved party and the party in breach and (b) between cases in which the benefit transferred was money and cases in which it was property or services which were performed.

(a) The Position of the Aggrieved Party in English Law

(i) Where Money has been Paid

English law allows recovery by the aggrieved party only where there has been 'a total failure of consideration', in the sense that the innocent party has received no part of what he contracted for,[155] or (in a contract for work and materials) the other party has not performed any part of the work.[156] In principle it remains the case that in a case of partial failure the aggrieved party cannot claim restitution. However, the courts are somewhat flexible in their application of the notion of 'total failure': thus, in *Ebrahim Dawood Ltd v Heath (Est 1927) Ltd*,[157] a buyer of steel sheets who had justifiably rejected part of a consignment of steel sheets was allowed to recover a proportionate part of the price, which was agreed at so much per ton. (In any event, the aggrieved party will have a claim for damages, which in most cases will serve to recoup the value of benefit conferred, though it may not so do if the value of what he was to receive is less than the amount he has paid.)

(ii) Where Goods have been Provided or Services Rendered

If the claiming party has completed its performance, or a severable part of it, the only remedy in English law is an action for the agreed price. In the situation of partial performance before the contract was terminated for breach, the aggrieved party may, as an alternative to claiming damages, claim a *quantum meruit*—ie recover a reasonable sum for the work done: see, for example, *Planché v Colburn*.[158] It seems that the amount that must be paid may exceed a proportionate part of the contract price,[159] and possibly even the total amount due under the contract if it had been properly performed.[160]

---

[155] *Fibrosa Spolka Akcyjna v Fairbairn, Lawson, Combe, Barbour Ltd* [1943] AC 32 (HL). The meaning of 'total failure of consideration' is discussed by A Burrows, *Law of Restitution* (3rd edn, London: Butterworths, 2011) 322 ff.

[156] See *Stocznia Gdanska SA v Latvia Shipping Co* [1998] 1 WLR 574 (HL) (shipbuilding contract; no total failure after work on ship started, even though nothing ever delivered to buyers).

[157] [1961] 2 Lloyd's Rep 512 (QBD).

[158] (1831) 8 Bing 14 (CP).

[159] See *Lodder v Slowey* [1904] AC 442 (PC), affirming (1900) 20 NZLR 321.

[160] This controversial point is discussed by Burrows (n 155 above) 347–50.

(b) The Position of the Party in Breach

(i) Money Paid

The party in breach may recover money paid for which he has received nothing in return, unless (a) the contract provides otherwise, for example by stating that the money was paid as a deposit,[161] or (b) broadly speaking, the money was a payment for work which has been done by the other party.[162]

(ii) Services Rendered

If the party who rendered the service, but who failed to perform the contract properly in some way, has substantially performed the contract,[163] there will of course be no right to terminate: the contract has been performed. But what if the party has performed only part of an entire obligation? The contract price will not be payable; and it has been held that the other party need not pay anything for benefits he received unless he could have returned them but decided not to.

Court of Appeal **25.36 (EN)**

Sumpter v Hedges[164]

A builder employed to construct a house for a lump sum and who completes only part of the work is not entitled either to the contract price or to restitution of the value of the work done. The owner must pay for loose materials left behind by the builder and subsequently used by the owner.

Facts: The plaintiff had contracted to do building works for a lump sum of £565. After doing some of the work he ran out of money and abandoned the job, leaving behind some materials which the owner later used to finish the works. The plaintiff claimed the value of the materials and of the work done.

Held: The trial judge allowed the claim for the reasonable value of the materials but awarded nothing in respect of the work done. An appeal failed.

Judgment: COLLINS LJ ... I think the case is really concluded by the finding of the learned judge to the effect that the plaintiff had abandoned the contract. If the plaintiff had merely broken his contract in some way so as not give the defendant the right to treat him as having abandoned the contract, and the defendant had then proceeded to finish the work himself, the plaintiff might perhaps have been entitled to sue on a quantum meruit on the ground that the defendant had taken the benefit of the work done. But that is not the present case. There are cases in which, though the plaintiff has abandoned the performance of a contract, it is possible for him to raise the inference of a new contract to pay

---

[161] On which see further below, pp 1133 ff.
[162] See *Hyundai Heavy Industries Co Ltd v Papadopoulos* [1980] 2 All ER 29 (HL); J Beatson, 'Discharge for Breach: The Position of Instalments, Deposits and Other Payments Before Completion' (1981) 97 LQR 389.
[163] See above, pp 969 ff.
[164] [1898] 1 QB 673.

for the work done on a quantum meruit from the defendant's having taken the benefit of that work, but, in order that that may be done, the circumstances must be such as to give an option to the defendant to take or not to take the benefit of the work done. It is only where the circumstances are such as to give that option that there is any evidence on which to ground the inference of a new contract. Where, as in the case of work done on land, the circumstances are such as to give the defendant no option whether he will take the benefit of the work or not, then one must look to other facts than the mere taking the benefit of the work in order to ground the inference of a new contract. In this case I see no other facts on which such an inference can be founded. The mere fact that a defendant is in possession of what he cannot help keeping, or even has done work upon it, affords no ground for such an inference. He is not bound to keep unfinished a building which in an incomplete state would be a nuisance on his land. I am therefore of opinion that the plaintiff was not entitled to recover for the work which he had done.

[AL SMITH and CHITTY LJJ delivered concurring judgments.]

Notes

(1) It may be argued that this case was wrongly decided, in that it seems to assume that the plaintiff can have restitution only if there was some agreement by the defendant to pay for what he had received. Whatever the strength of this argument, *Sumpter v Hedges* remains good law and a proposal to change it to allow restitution has been rejected. In 1983 the Law Commission, in its Report No 121, Pecuniary Restitution for Breach of Contract, recommended that the rule in *Sumpter v Hedges* be reversed, so that if, after taking into account any losses suffered by the owner, the work done left the owner with a net benefit, the builder should be entitled to a sum by way of restitution of that benefit. But one of the Commissioners dissented, pointing out that the present rule has a great advantage to the householder, who can say to the builder, 'Unless you come back and finish the job, I shan't pay you a penny'. The majority's recommendation was not accepted.

(2) In German law before 2002 the remedy of *Wandlung* was rarely sought in the case of building contracts. This was said to be primarily because the standard terms and conditions for building contracts (VOB/B) simply do not mention the remedy. The new § 634, which sets out the rights of the customer under a *Werkvertrag* in the case of defects, expressly refers to the customer's right to terminate. (The right will be subject to the normal requirements of notice, etc.)[165] *Rücktritt* would bring in § 346 and, as we have seen, the builder would be entitled to compensation based on the contract rates: § 346(2). The German builder would thus seem to be in a more favourable position than his English colleague, normally being able to cure as a matter of course and, even if not being entitled to cure, being entitled to something like a *quantum meruit*.

(3) It may be argued that the difference between the law in England and in Germany reflects the differing approaches to literal enforcement of the contract. It is evident that the dissenting Law Commissioner thought of the current English rule as a way of coercing the builder into finishing the job even though the court would not order specific performance.

---

[165] See above, p 1014.

(4) What is the position in English law if the benefit received cannot be returned? It is complex. If the destruction or damage was due to the fault of the buyer seeking to terminate, including a failure to look after the object properly, he will lose the right to terminate; but if the damage was due to an accident for which neither party was responsible, the buyer is still able to terminate.[166]

25.9.C.4 INTERNATIONAL SOLUTIONS

The PECL provisions on restitution after termination for non-performance were set out earlier.[167] These were considered by the CRT to be inadequate and the DCFR has adopted a more elaborate scheme.

Draft Common Frame of Reference **25.37 (INT)**

Article III.-3:511: Restitution of benefits received by performance
(1) On termination under this Section a party (the recipient) who has received any benefit by the other's performance of obligations under the contract is obliged to return it. Where both parties have obligations to return, the obligations are reciprocal.
(2) If the performance was a payment of money, the amount received is to be repaid.
(3) To the extent that the benefit (not being money) is transferable, it is to be returned by transferring it. However, if a transfer would cause unreasonable effort or expense, the benefit may be returned by paying its value.
(4) To the extent that the benefit is not transferable it is to be returned by paying its value in accordance with III-3:513 (Payment of value of benefit).
(5) The obligation to return a benefit extends to any natural or legal fruits received from the benefit.

Article III.-3:512: When restitution not required
(1) Restitution is not required where the performance was due in separate parts or was otherwise divisible and what was received by each party resulted from due performance of a part for which counter-performance was duly made.
(2) Paragraph (1) does not, however, apply if what was received by the terminating party was properly rejected under III-3:510 (Property reduced in value) or if the value of a non-transferable benefit received by the terminating party has been eliminated or fundamentally reduced as a result of the other party's non-performance.

Article III.-3:513: Payment of value of benefit
(1) The recipient is obliged to:
   (a) pay the value (at the time of performance) of a benefit which is not transferable or which ceases to be transferable before the time when it is to be returned; and
   (b) pay recompense for any reduction in the value of a returnable benefit as a result of a change in the condition of the benefit between the time of receipt and the time when it is to be returned.

---

[166] See *Benjamin's Sale of Goods*, 10th edn by M Bridge (ed) (London: Sweet & Maxwell, 2017) paras 12-059–12-061.
[167] See 25.33 (INT), above, p 1047.

(2) Where there was an agreed price the value of the benefit is that proportion of the price which the value of the actual performance bears to the value of the promised performance. Where no price was agreed the value of the benefit is the sum of money which a willing and capable provider and a willing and capable recipient, knowing of any non-conformity, would lawfully have agreed.

(3) The recipient's liability to pay the value of a benefit is reduced to the extent that as a result of a non-performance of an obligation owed by the other party to the recipient:

  (a) the benefit cannot be returned in essentially the same condition as when it was received; or

  (b) the recipient is compelled without compensation either to dispose of it or to sustain a disadvantage in order to preserve it.

(4) The recipient's liability to pay the value of a benefit is likewise reduced to the extent that it cannot be returned in the same condition as when it was received as a result of conduct of the recipient in the reasonable, but mistaken, belief that there was no non-conformity.

Article III.-3:514: Use and improvements

(1) The recipient is obliged to pay a reasonable amount for any use which the recipient makes of the benefit except in so far as the recipient is liable under III-3:513 (Payment of value of benefit) paragraph (1) in respect of that use.

(2) A recipient who has improved a benefit which the recipient is obliged under this Section to return has a right to payment of the value of improvements if the other party can readily obtain that value by dealing with the benefit unless:

  (a) the improvement was a non-performance of an obligation owed by the recipient to the other party; or

  (b) the recipient made the improvement when the recipient knew or could reasonably be expected to know that the benefit would have to be returned.

Article III.-3:515: Liabilities arising after time when return due

(1) The recipient is obliged to:

  (a) pay the value (at the time of performance) of a benefit which ceases to be transferable after the time when its return was due; and

  (b) pay recompense for any reduction in the value of a returnable benefit as a result of a change in the condition of the benefit after the time when its return was due.

(2) If the benefit is disposed of after the time when return was due, the value to be paid is the value of any proceeds, if this is greater.

(3) Other liabilities arising from non-performance of an obligation to return a benefit are unaffected.

Notes

(1) It will be seen that the basic scheme of the DCFR is broadly similar to that under German law. After termination, under Article III.-3:511 each party is obliged to return what it has received or, if that is not feasible, its value.

(2) The DCFR deals differently with contracts that are to be performed in separate parts and which have been partially performed. Under § 323 BGB, *Rücktritt* may apply to just the unperformed part of the contract; the creditor may withdraw from the whole contract only if he has no interest in the part performance. (Similarly with the

claim for damages under § 281.) In other words, termination may be partial or as to the whole. In the DCFR it seems that the contract as a whole will be terminated, but there will be no restitution in relation to the parts of the contract that were not affected by the non-performance. Thus the restriction applies at the stage of restitution rather than at the stage of termination. The net effect seems to be much the same.

(3) The CESL, Chapter 17, adopted a unique scheme drafted by an Expert Group. It was heavily criticised and is not reproduced here.

25.10 LOSS OF RIGHT TO TERMINATE

This section will deal with the various ways in which the right to terminate may be lost: for example, waiver; delay in termination; and impossibility of restitution.

25.10.A AFFIRMATION

Principles of European Contract Law   **25.38 (INT)**

Article 9:303: Notice of Termination

(1) A party's right to terminate the contract is to be exercised by notice to the other party.

(2) The aggrieved party loses its right to terminate the contract unless it gives notice within a reasonable time after it has or ought to have become aware of the non-performance …

A party who knows that the other's non-performance gives him the right to terminate, but announces that he will not exercise that right, may lose the right to terminate.

In German law the innocent party may renounce his right to terminate, either explicitly or implicitly, for example by accepting late performance. It appears that the innocent party must have known that there had been non-performance.[168]

In French law the right to *résolution* may be renounced, and the court may, as a matter of discretion, refuse *résolution* to a party who had appeared to waive his right.[169]

In English law a party who knows he has a right to terminate and announces that he will not exercise it will be bound by the so-called doctrine of 'election'. In addition, a party who gives the appearance of affirming the contract may be bound by the doctrine of estoppel[170] if the other party acts on the apparent affirmation, even if the first party did not know he had a right to terminate: see *The Kanchenjunga*.[171]

Loss of the right to terminate through affirmation is not mentioned explicitly in either PECL or the DCFR but it seems to be implicit.

---

[168] G Treitel, *Remedies for Breach of Contract* (Oxford: Clarendon Press, 1988) 397–400, para 290.

[169] See Cass civ (3) 8 April 1987, no. 85-17596, Bull III no. 88, *Widow Thomas' rente viagère*, 25.25 (FR) above, p 1031; Cass civ (3) 3 November 2011, no. 10-26203, Bull III no. 178. Contrast 'judicial waiver clauses' by which the parties may waive their right to termination in advance, which may be invalid, see ch 21.

[170] See above, p 366.

[171] [1990] 1 Lloyd's Rep 391, 399 (HL).

25.10.B LAPSE OF TIME

We need to distinguish two situations here: first, where the aggrieved party knows the facts that give it the right to terminate, and secondly where it does not.

In the first case, the only specific provision seems to be in German law. It applies where the debtor also knows of the creditors' right to terminate:

BGB **25.39 (DE)**

§ 350: Extinction of the right of withdrawal after a period of time has been specified

If a period of time has not been agreed for the exercise of the contractual right of withdrawal, then the other party may specify a reasonable period of time within which the person entitled to withdraw must exercise that right. The right of withdrawal is extinguished if withdrawal is not declared before the end of that period.

In other systems, the creditor's failure to declare termination might be treated as an affirmation. It will be seen that the PECL provision just cited would apply in this case.

What if the reason that a party does not try to terminate the contract for a considerable time after the other party has purportedly performed it is simply because the first party did not yet know that there was anything wrong? In none of the systems does a simple lapse of time prevent termination. However, in all three systems there are special rules in sale of goods cases which require a buyer who has received defective goods to exercise any right to terminate the contract within a short period—or lose the right to terminate. These are dealt with in Chapter 27.

FURTHER READING

Beale, H, 'Remedies for breach of contract in the light of the recent changes to German Law, English law and the DCFR' in U Blaurock and G Hager (eds), *Obligationenrecht im 21. Jahrhundert* (Baden Baden: Nomos, 2010) 115–46.

Fabre-Magnan, M, 'Termination of Contract: A Missed Opportunity for Reform' in J Cartwright, S Vogenauer and S Whittaker (eds), *Reforming the French Law of Obligations* (Oxford: Hart Publishing, 2009) 169–86.

Kleinschmidt, J and Hellwege, P, 'Termination of the Contract' in N Jansen and R Zimmermann (eds), *Commentaries on European Contract Laws* (Oxford University Press, 2018) 1285–1421.

Rowan, S, 'Termination for Contractual Non-performance' in J Cartwright and S Whittaker (eds), *The Code Napoléon Rewritten: French Contract Law after the 2016 Reforms* (Oxford: Hart Publishing, 2017) 317–35.

Rowan, S, *Remedies for Breach of Contract* (Oxford University Press, 2012) 70–106.

Treitel, G, *Remedies for Breach of Contract* (Oxford: Clarendon, 1988) 318–410.

Whittaker, S, '"Termination" for Contractual Non-performance and its Consequences: French Law Reviewed in the Light of the *Avant-projet de réforme*' in J Cartwright, S Vogenauer and S Whittaker (eds), *Reforming the French Law of Obligations* (Oxford, Hart Publishing, 2009) 187–204.

Zimmermann, R, *The New German Law of Obligations* (Oxford University Press, 2005).

CHAPTER 26
DAMAGES

26.1 INTRODUCTION

The general scope of this chapter is indicated by the provisions of the Principles of European Contract Law (PECL) set out below.

Principles of European Contract Law[1]   **26.1 (INT)**

Article 9:501: Right to Damages
  (1) The aggrieved party is entitled to damages for loss caused by the other party's non-performance which is not excused under Article 8:108.
  (2) The loss for which damages are recoverable includes:
    (a) non-pecuniary loss; and
    (b) future loss which is reasonably likely to occur.

Article 9:502: General Measure of Damages
  The general measure of damages is such sum as will put the aggrieved party as nearly as possible into the position in which it would have been if the contract had been duly performed. Such damages cover the loss which the aggrieved party has suffered and the gain of which it has been deprived.

Article 9:503: Foreseeability
  The non-performing party is liable only for loss which it foresaw or could reasonably have foreseen at the time of conclusion of the contract as a likely result of its non-performance, unless the non-performance was intentional or grossly negligent.

---

[1] cf Arts III.-3:701–III.-3:711 DCFR.

Article 9:504: Loss Attributable to Aggrieved Party

The non-performing party is not liable for loss suffered by the aggrieved party to the extent that the aggrieved party contributed to the non-performance or its effects.

Article 9:505: Reduction of Loss

(1) The non-performing party is not liable for loss suffered by the aggrieved party to the extent that the aggrieved party could have reduced the loss by taking reasonable steps.

(2) The aggrieved party is entitled to recover any expenses reasonably incurred in attempting to reduce the loss.

[For articles 9:506 and 9:507, see below.][2]

Article 9:508: Delay in Payment of Money

(1) If payment of a sum of money is delayed, the aggrieved party is entitled to interest on that sum from the time when payment is due to the time of payment at the average commercial bank short-term lending rate to prime borrowers prevailing for the contractual currency of payment at the place where payment is due. (2) The aggrieved party may in addition recover damages for any further loss so far as these are recoverable under this Section.

[For Article 9:509, see below][3]

26.2 THE BASIC MEASURE OF DAMAGES FOR BREACH OF CONTRACT

Code civil **26.2 (FR)**

SECTION 5

Sub-section 5

Article 1231-2: In general, damages due to the creditor are for the loss that he has incurred or the gain of which he has been deprived, with the following exceptions and qualifications.

Notes

(1) The 2016 reform of French contract law did not substantially modify the law on damages.[4] A bill on the reform of civil liability was submitted to the Ministry of Justice on 13 March 2017, containing provisions special to contractual liability (Articles 1250 to 1252 of the bill).[5] The Report to the President on the reform of

---

[2] 26.39 (INT), below, p 1103.

[3] 26.46 (INT), below, p 1118.

[4] See generally A Bénabent, *Les obligations* (16th edn, Paris: LGDJ, 2017) nos. 404–39; B Nicholas, *The French Law of Contract* (2nd edn, Oxford: Clarendon Press, 1992) 224–32; F Terré, P Simler and Y Lequette, *Les obligations* (11th edn, Paris: Dalloz, 2013) nos. 558–628; G Viney, P Jourdain and S Carval, *Traité de droit civil: Les effets de la responsabilité* (4th edn, Paris: LGDJ, 2017).

[5] Reform Bill on Civil Liability, March 2017, translated into English by S Whittaker in consultation with J-S Borghetti: www.textes.justice.gouv.fr/art_pix/reform_bill_on_civil_liability_march_2017.pdf.

contract law explains why the reform of contractual liability fits into the general reform of civil liability and not contract law:[6]

> Subsection 5, which deals with compensation for damage resulting from the non-performance of a contract, is a restatement of existing Section 4 of Chapter III of the current Title III of the Civil Code, with some formal adjustments. Contractual liability cannot be reformed in isolation from extra-contractual liability: it is generally accepted that, basically, these two forms of liability are mechanisms of the same nature, which are based on the existence of an event giving rise to liability, damage, and a causal link between the two. The only differences are founded essentially on the origin of the operative event in contractual matters, which the ordonnance does not change. The regime of contractual liability will therefore be modernized in the context of the future comprehensive reform of civil liability, which will set out the provisions common to both contractual and non-contractual liability and the provisions specific to each of the two regimes.

(2) French law adopts the principle of full compensation (*réparation intégrale*). The distinction between *damnum emergens* ('the loss he has suffered') and *lucrum cessans* ('the gain of which he has been deprived') dates from Roman law. If the creditor does not receive the goods promised and has to pay a higher price to buy substitute goods, this is *damnum emergens*, whereas if the creditor is prevented from making a profitable resale, this is *lucrum cessans*. From the principle of full compensation, the Code civil draws a number of rules on the assessment of damages, but it has been remarked that 'what principally strikes the English lawyer is that the French analysis is relatively underdeveloped'.[7] The same may appear true even after the reforms of 2016. For example, the distinction between expectation (positive interest) and reliance (negative interest) damages known to both English and German law seems not to be recognised in the articles quoted. One possible explanation for the lack of detailed rules is that the assessment of damages is within the full 'power of appreciation' of the court of first instance, though it has been pointed out that this is not a complete explanation, as the Cour de cassation in principle controls the question of the kinds of loss for which compensation may be paid.[8] But it must be noted that sub-section 5 is not an exhaustive statement of when damages may be available and how they should be calculated. For example, Article 1116 provides that damages for the wrongful withdrawal of an offer are not to include compensation of the loss of profits that were expected from the contract—in other words, the damages will be for reliance loss only.

(3) The reform bill on civil liability does not distinguish between the loss suffered and the gain missed. Rather, the bill adopts a general definition of the reparable harm, applying to both contractual and extra-contractual liability. Then, the bill specifies that, under contract law, a party is liable for every non-performance of the contract which has caused harm to the other party.

---

[6] Report to the President on the reform of contract (p 83 n 30 above) 35.
[7] Nicholas (n 4 above) 225.
[8] ibid.

Article 1235: Any certain loss is reparable where it results from harm and consists of an injury to a lawful interest, whether patrimonial or extra-patrimonial.

Article 1250: Every non-performance of a contract which has caused harm to the creditor gives rise to an obligation in the debtor to be liable for it.

BGB **26.4 (DE)**

§ 249: Nature and extent of damages

(1) A person who is obliged to make compensation shall restore the situation which would have existed if the circumstance rendering him liable to make compensation had not occurred.

(2) If the compensation is required to be made for injury to a person or damage to a thing, the creditor may demand, instead of restitution in kind, the sum of money necessary for such restitution. …

§ 250: Damages in money after the specification of a period of time

The creditor may fix a reasonable period for the restitution by the person liable to compensate with a declaration that he will refuse to accept restitution after the expiration of the period. After the expiration of the period the creditor may demand the compensation in money if the restitution is not effected in due time; the claim for restitution is barred.

§ 251: Damages in money without the specification of a period of time

(1) Insofar as restitution in kind is impossible or is insufficient to compensate the creditor, the person liable shall compensate him in money.

(2) The person liable may compensate the creditor in money if restitution in kind is only possible through disproportionate outlays. …

§ 252: Lost profits

The compensation shall also include lost profits. Profit is deemed to have been lost which could probably have been expected in the ordinary course of events, or according to the special circumstances, especially in the light of the preparations and arrangements made.

§ 284: Reimbursement for wasted expenditure

Instead of demanding compensation in lieu of performance, the obligee may demand reimbursement of the expenditure which he has incurred in reasonable reliance on the receipt of performance, save where the purpose of that expenditure would not have been achieved even if the obligor had not breached his duty.

Notes

(1) The circumstances under which the debtor will be liable in damages in German law, and the different provisions which apply to various types of non-performance, were discussed earlier.[9] The need for the creditor to serve a warning (*Mahnung*) is discussed further below.[10]

---

[9] Above, pp 779 and 895. On damages for breach of contract generally, see B Markesinis, H Unberath and A Johnston, *The German Law of Contract* (2nd edn, Oxford: Hart Publishing, 2006) ch 9.5.

[10] See below, p 1068.

(2) As we saw earlier,[11] German law adopts the distinction between the positive interest and the negative interest. In cases of breach of contract the creditor may claim the positive interest. In contrast, under § 122 BGB (compensation where party avoids a contract) only negative interest damages are recoverable. It is provided that these may not exceed the value to the other party if the contract had been valid, ie may not exceed the positive interest.

(3) In some cases of breach of contract the creditor is entitled to claim a form of negative interest damages in place of the normal positive interest, for instance if it is hard to prove what profit he would have made or of the venture was not a profit-making one. This is permitted by § 284 BGB. However, the negative interest damages may not exceed what he would have received under the positive interest measure.

(4) German law also recognises the distinction between 'abstract' assessments of damages, where the damages are measured by an abstract standard such as the market value of what the creditor would have received, and 'concrete' assessment by reference to the actual loss, for example the actual cost of obtaining substitute goods.[12] In certain circumstances the German Commercial Code (HGB) expressly provides for the abstract measure of damages:

HGB   **26.5 (DE)**

§ 430: (1) If a carrier is obliged by a contract of carriage to make compensation for the total or partial loss of the item carried, he must pay the value in the place where, and at the time when, delivery was to be made.

In German law it has sometimes been said that damages may be calculated according to the 'exchange (or "surrogation") theory' and sometimes according to the 'difference theory'.[13] Schlechtriem explained:[14]

There are two possible means of calculating the amount of compensation: the creditor can demand the whole value of the debtor's performance including all consequential loss and render his own performance in return. Damages are thus available for the full value of the debtor's performance, but in return for the whole of the (still possible) counter-performance of the creditor and are calculated accordingly ("surrogation" or "exchange" theory). The creditor can also, however, deduct the value of his performance from the amount of damages, but only if he has not yet rendered performance and wishes to retain it (the so-called limited-"difference" theory). Where he owes a sum of money, for example the price of purchase, the same result is reached through setting off this amount against the (total) amount of damages, leaving only the difference between the loss due to non-performance and the purchase price.

The "difference" theory, which allows the creditor to retain his own performance and to take it into account in calculating his damages, is based essentially on a combination of withdrawal from the contract and damages for non-performance. It is nevertheless allowed and regularly

---

[11] In ch 13, above, p 457 and ch 14, above, p 495.
[12] See below, pp 1101 ff.
[13] See also above, p 993.
[14] P Schlechtriem and M Schmidt-Kessel, *Schuldrecht Allgemeiner Teil* (6th edn, Tübingen: Mohr Siebeck, 2005) excerpts from paras 388–99.

used. The creditor may only demand the whole amount of damages under the 'surrogation' theory if for his part he has already performed (and he does not and cannot take back his performance) or if he has a particular interest in rendering his own performance.

English law has highly developed case law on damages.[15] At this point we will refer only to the basic rules.

Court of Exchequer   **26.6 (EN)**

Robinson v Harman[16]

[It is not necessary to set out the facts and decision in this case.]

Judgment: PARKE B: ... The rule of the common law is, that where a party sustains a loss by reason of a breach of contract, he is, so far as money can do it, to be placed in the same situation, with respect to damages, as if the contract had been performed. ...

Notes

(1) Until recently, English law did not distinguish openly between the positive and negative interests, but in practice it applied the two interests. Thus in breach of contract cases the plaintiff is to be put into the position he would have been in had the contract been performed, whereas in cases where liability is based on tort, such as for fraud, he is to be put back to the position he was in before the tort was committed.[17] However, the American author Fuller, in his famous article with Perdue,[18] adopted the parallel distinction between the expectation interest, the reliance interest and the restitution interest, and this terminology has now found its way, via the Canadian courts, into English case law: for example, *C & P Haulage v Middleton*.[19]

(2) Normally the plaintiff will, in effect, be compensated for all three interests. The plaintiff will be given damages representing the value of what he would have received if the contract had been performed, less any sums already paid and any savings made as a result of the breach. Thus, suppose a manufacturer agrees to deliver a custom-built machine and accessories to a buyer for a price of £1,000. In accordance with the contract, the manufacturer delivers some accessories worth £200 to the buyer and spends a further £500 in building the machine; meanwhile the buyer makes an advance payment of £250. Before the machine is finished the buyer repudiates the contract. The manufacturer would incur a further £100 in labour costs to finish the machine. The damages will be calculated as follows: from the total £1,000 the manufacturer would have received, one deducts the £250 already paid, the £100 needed to complete the machine (a saving) and also any scrap value of the machine (say £50); thus the seller will get £1,000 − £250 − £100 − £50 = £600. It will be seen that this sum, together with

---

[15] See *Chitty on Contracts*, 33rd edn by H Beale (gen ed) (London: Sweet & Maxwell/Thomson Reuters, 2018) ch 26.
[16] (1848) 1 Exch 850, 855.
[17] eg *East v Maurer* [1991] 1 WLR 461 (CA), see above, p 496.
[18] (1936) 46 Yale LJ 52.
[19] [1983] 1 WLR 1461 (CA).

the money already paid and the scrap value of the machine (which is still in the seller's hands), in effect gives the seller not only the value of the accessories delivered (£200, the restitution interest) plus the wasted expenditure (£500, the reliance interest), but also the profit it should have made (£200, the expectation interest).[20]

(3) On occasion the plaintiff will claim only the reliance loss, because, for example, the loss of profit is hard to prove. For example, in *Anglia TV v Reed*,[21] the plaintiff had, even before the contract, incurred expenses in assembling a crew to make a film. The principal actor refused at the last moment to take part and the project was abandoned. The plaintiff was allowed to recover expenses including those incurred before the actor had agreed to take part. On other occasions the court will hold that the plaintiff has failed to prove that he would have made a profit but allows recovery of reliance loss (for example, *McRae v Commonwealth Disposals Commission*).[22] However, the damages are in principle calculated by reference to the plaintiff's expectation; and if the profit he expected would not in fact have covered the reliance expenditure, so that he would have lost money anyway, the extra reliance loss is not recoverable: *C & P Haulage v Middleton*.[23] The court will assume that the plaintiff would have recovered his costs unless the defendant shows otherwise: *CCC Films (London) Ltd v Impact Quadrant Films Ltd*.[24]

(4) If the contract has been terminated for non-performance, the creditor may claim restitution instead of damages.[25] Normally this requires showing that the defendant (the debtor) received a benefit by the creditor's performance (as in *BSC v Cleveland Bridge*,[26] though that was not a case of non-performance)—in other words, these are cases of unjust enrichment 'by subtraction', where what the debtor gained was at the creditor's expense. Occasionally there have been cases in which a claimant has been allowed to claim the reasonable value of services performed (a *quantum meruit* claim) even though it does not seem that the defendant derived any benefit from the services.[27] Some authors prefer to regard this as an award of reliance damages.[28]

(5) We will see later that sometimes English law permits a different form of restitution, where the creditor is allowed to recover the profit the debtor made through his wrongdoing, even though there was no measurable loss to the creditor.[29]

Thus, in all three systems, where there has been a non-performance for which a debtor is responsible, the creditor may—subject to various limitations to be noted—be able to recover damages; and these will aim to give the creditor what she would have received. There seems to be no practical difference between the 'expectation' or 'positive interest'

---

[20] cf *Hydraulic Engineering Co Ltd v McHaffie* (1878) 4 QBD 670.
[21] [1971] 3 All ER 690 (CA).
[22] (1950) 84 CLR 377, (High Court of Australia). See above, p 549.
[23] [1983] 1 WLR 1461 (CA).
[24] [1984] 3 All ER 298 (QBD).
[25] See above, p 1052.
[26] See 6.25 (EN), above, p 164.
[27] eg *Planché v Colburn* (1831) 8 Bing 14 (author's work in writing chapters for a book though not apparently ever delivered to publisher).
[28] A Burrows, *Law of Restitution* (3rd edn, London: Butterworths, 2011) 346.
[29] See below, pp 1108 ff.

formulae of English and German law and the traditional formulation of French Code civil, Article 1231-2. The Principles of European Contract Law place both formulae in a single Article:

Principles of European Contract Law **26.7 (INT)**

Article 9:502: General Measure of Damages[30]
The general measure of damages is such sum as will put the aggrieved party as nearly as possible into the position in which it would have been if the contract had been duly performed. Such damages cover the loss which the aggrieved party has suffered and the gain of which it has been deprived.

The equivalent Article of UNIDROIT Principles of International Commercial Contracts (UNIDROIT PICC) speaks of 'full compensation':

UNIDROIT Principles **26.8 (INT)**

Article 7.4.2: Full compensation
(1) The aggrieved party is entitled to full compensation for harm sustained as a result of the non-performance. Such harm includes both any loss which it suffered and any gain of which it was deprived, taking into account any gain to the aggrieved party resulting from its avoidance of cost or harm ...

26.3 THE REQUIREMENT OF NOTICE

Normally the debtor will not become liable in damages until there has been a breach of contract—that is, until he has failed to perform by the date due, has made it impossible for himself to perform or has committed some other breach of contract. (Note that, in systems which recognise the doctrine of anticipatory breach or its functional equivalent,[31] the debtor who announces in advance that he will not perform or who is clearly going to be unable to do so may become liable for non-performance even before the date set for performance.) However, in some systems, particularly in cases of delay, the debtor's liability for damages may not arise until he has also been given a warning or a demand for performance by the creditor.

Code civil **26.9 (FR)**

Article 1231: Unless non-performance is permanent, damages are due only if the debtor has previously been put on notice to perform his obligation within a reasonable time.

Article 1344: A debtor is put on notice to perform by formal demand, by an act which gives sufficient warning, or, where this is provided for by the contract, by the mere fact that the obligation is enforceable.

---

[30] cf Art III.-3:701 DCFR.
[31] See above, pp 1024 ff.

Notes

(1) A formal demand (*sommation*) is a notice served by a *huissier* (bailiff).

(2) In principle a notice (*mise en demeure*) to inform the debtor that the creditor still requires performance is a prerequisite to any remedy except withholding of performance. If, however, the creditor seeks a judicial remedy (specific performance or judicial termination), commencement of the action may be sufficient.[32] The same will be true of an action for damages but, if the creditor has not served a notice earlier, the damages will run only from the date of commencement of the action.

(3) The fact that the original contract fixed a time within which the debtor must perform does not amount to an agreement to dispense with a notice within Article 1231 (assuming that performance is still possible). But the parties may agree to dispense with the need for a notice, and the courts have held that this may be implicit.[33]

(4) Where performance is no longer possible—for example, where an electricity company failed to supply power to a customer for a period of time that has now passed[34]—a notice is not required. In such a case the customer will be claiming compensation for the failure to perform (*dommages-intérêts compensatoires*) rather than for delay (*dommages-intérêts moratoires*). Like Article 1365 of the Avant-projet Catala, the recent reform bill on civil liability proposes to clarify the situations in which a notice is required.

Reform bill on civil liability **26.10 (FR)**

Article 1252: The reparation of loss resulting from delay in performance is premised on the prior giving of a notice to perform to the debtor. Notice to perform is not required for reparation of any other loss except where it is necessary in order to characterise the non-performance.

Notes

(1) The notice is only required where (i) there is a delay in performance and (ii) it is necessary in order to characterise the non-performance.

(2) It is not yet clear what is included in the expression 'where it is necessary in order to characterise the non-performance'.

A similar distinction between claims for loss that has already been caused and claims for delay will be found in German law.

BGB **26.11 (DE)**

§ 280: Compensation for breach of duty

(1) If the obligor fails to comply with a duty arising under the obligation, the obligee may claim compensation for the loss resulting from this breach. This does not apply if the obligor is not liable for the failure.

---

[32] See above, pp 904 and 987.
[33] CA Paris 28 March 1990, D 1990.IR.98; Cass mixte 6 July 2007, no. 06-13823.
[34] Nicholas (n 4 above) 239.

(2) The obligee may demand compensation for delay in performance only if the additional requirement in § 286 is satisfied.

(3) The obligee may demand compensation in lieu of performance only if the additional requirements of § 281, § 282 or § 283 are satisfied.

§ 286: Delay by the obligor

(1) If, after notice from the obligee to perform, such notice having been given after performance became due, the obligor fails to perform, that notice puts him in default. The bringing of an action for performance and the service of a demand for payment in summary debt proceedings is equivalent to a notice to perform.

(2) Notice to perform is unnecessary, if

1. a time for performance is determined according to the calendar,

2. an event must precede performance and an appropriate time for the performance is fixed in such a way that it can be calculated according to the calendar from the date of the event,

3. the obligor seriously and definitely refuses to perform,

4. having regard to each party's interests, special reasons justify the occurrence of default with immediate effect.

(3) ...

(4) The obligor is not put in default for as long as performance is not made because of a circumstance for which he is not responsible.

Notes

(1) In German law also the debtor is put into delay by the creditor serving a warning (*Mahnung*). This need not be in any particular form, provided that the debtor is warned that he is expected to perform. The warning is held to be subject to the same rules as an ordinary declaration of intent: for example, it must be communicated to the debtor.

(2) In order to claim damages for non-performance arising out of delay in the performance of a main obligation, if the loss is one which can still be prevented by the debtor performing, the creditor must normally provide a warning under § 286 BGB. Similarly, if he wishes to terminate the contract and claim damages for non-performance he must normally set a period (*Nachfrist*) with a further warning that he will refuse performance after that period (§ 281 BGB).[35] Both warnings may be combined in one declaration, however.

(3) Note that a *Nachfrist* is not necessary in a number of cases, including if the contract fixed a day for performance (*Fixgeschäft*).[36]

(4) In principle the parties can provide in the contract that no notice need be given, but this is not permissible in a standard form consumer contract: § 309 no 4 BGB.

(5) In contrast, if the loss is one which cannot be cured by the debtor, so that a warning would not be of any value, then the loss will be recoverable under § 280 and a *Mahnung* is not required. So, if the seller has delivered food with a hidden defect that made it unfit to eat and the buyer has already been made ill, the claim will be under § 280 and the seller will be liable unless he can show that he was not responsible.

---

[35] See above, pp 1011 ff.
[36] See above, p 1014.

> (This is a reference back to § 276. In other words, the debtor will be liable in damages if his act or omission was intentional or negligent, or if the parties had agreed on a stricter standard: see the discussion of the nature of the debtor's obligation in Chapter 19).[37]

English law does not have any requirement of a notice to put the debtor into default— save in exceptional cases in which the debtor cannot know that he is in default until told by the creditor, for example a tenant must notify the landlord if a repair is needed. In the case of delay, damages will run from the date on which the debtor should have performed. This date may be agreed in the contract. If it is not, the debtor must perform within a reasonable time and damages will run from the expiry of that time; the creditor does not need to serve a notice to start the damages running. (It will be recalled that notice is sometimes needed before termination is permitted.)[38]

26.4 RESTRICTIONS ON DAMAGES RECOVERABLE

This section deals with a number of rules which, in each system, limit the damages recoverable, so that the plaintiff may not in fact receive the measure of damages provided for under the general rules set out above.

26.4.A UNFORESEEABLE OR INDIRECT LOSSES

Code civil   26.12 (FR)

Article 1231-3: A debtor is bound only to damages which were either foreseen or which could have been foreseen at the time of conclusion of the contract, except where non-performance was due to a gross or dishonest fault.[39]

Article 1231-4: In the situation where non-performance of a contract does indeed result from gross or dishonest fault, damages include only that which is the immediate and direct result of non-performance.

Cass civ, 22 November 1893[40]   26.13 (FR)

Machine for peeling artichokes

A party who has failed to perform cannot be ordered to pay compensation for losses which were not envisaged, and could not have been envisaged, at the time the contract was made.

Facts: The defendant railway company, Compagnie Paris-Lyon-Méditerranée, delayed in delivering a package containing a machine for peeling artichokes to the plaintiffs, Benoit and Laurin, who were consequently

---

[37] Above, p 779.

[38] See above, p 1019.

[39] Translators' note: 'Gross or dishonest fault' translates *'une faute lourde ou dolosive'*. While we have translated *'faute dolosive'* as 'dishonest fault', dishonesty for this purpose must be understood in a broad way so as to include situations treated as bad faith in the debtor, notably, where the non-performance is deliberate.

[40] D 1894.1.358.

unable to use it in preparing vegetables for sale; the plaintiffs therefore had to employ manual labour and some of the vegetables perished. They claimed damages for losses of 1,200 FF.

Held: The court of first instance held that the losses suffered were unforeseeable, and were also not proven in full, so that only damages of 600 FF would be awarded. The Cour de cassation set aside the judgment.

Judgment of the Tribunal de Commerce: whereas Benoit and Laurin commenced proceedings against Compagnie Paris-Lyon-Méditerranée for an order requiring it to pay them FF1,200 by way of damages for the harm suffered by them following the said company's delay in delivering a machine to be used in their factory;

— whereas the railway company, without denying the delay of eight days in delivery of the packages despatched on an urgent basis and without denying liability, offers as compensation for the damage the sum of FF50, together with transport costs amounting to FF17;

— whereas the Company seeks to rely on Arts 1150 and 1151 of the Civil Code (now Articles 1231-3 and 1231-4), contending that carriers can be held liable only for loss envisaged or envisageable when the contract was concluded, but never for [other] damages.

— but whereas the harmful consequences suffered by the plaintiffs were not envisaged by the parties when concluding the contract; since the parties could not have foreseen them, the contract of carriage was concluded outside the scope of those articles; it follows that the loss suffered by Benoit and Laurin can be redressed only within the limits and scope of Article 1149 of the Civil Code (now Article 1231-2).

— Whereas it is not appropriate to assess the damage described by the Company as indirect damage, but rather, in accordance with the above-mentioned article, it is necessary to determine the loss incurred by the plaintiffs and the profit of which they were deprived;

— whereas the delayed package, containing a machine for peeling artichokes, should have reached the addressees on 4 June; at that time, they would have made arrangements to offer for sale a quantity of vegetables, using that machine; since the machine did not arrive, they were obliged to employ workers;

— whereas part of the goods deteriorated and the plaintiffs had to pay compensation of FF300 to their suppliers; but it has not been proved that their losses amount to the sum of FF1,200 and the Court considers that it must observe the requirements of Article 1149 of the Civil Code (now Article 1231-2), by setting the total damages at FF600;

— accordingly, it orders the Company to pay the sum of FF600 by way of damages.

APPEAL in cassation by Compagnie des chemins de fer de Paris-Lyon-Méditerranée, alleging infringement of Articles 97 and 104 of the Commercial Code and 1150 of the Civil Code (now Article 1231-3); misapplication of Article 1149 of the Civil Code (now Article 1231-2), in that the contested judgment ordered the Company to pay the respondents' damages, even though it was acknowledged that damages were not envisaged and could not have been when the contract was concluded.

Judgment of the Cour de cassation: THE COURT: *On the first appeal ground:*—Under Article 1150 of the Civil Code (now Article 1231-3);

— Whereas, as a matter of law, a debtor is required by law, in the event of breach of an obligation, to pay only the damages which were envisaged or were envisageable at the time when the contract was concluded;

— Whereas, as a matter of fact, Benoit and Laurin sought from Compagnie des Chemins de Fer de Paris-Lyon-Méditerranée redress for the loss caused them by the delay in delivery of a machine necessary for their business;

— Whereas, having found 'that the harmful consequences suffered by the plaintiffs were not envisaged by the parties when concluding the contract and the parties could not have foreseen them', the lower court nevertheless ordered the Company to pay the sum at which it set 'the *total*' damage suffered;

— Whereas, by giving judgment to that effect, on the ground that 'since the parties could not have foreseen the loss, the contract of carriage was concluded outside the scope of Article 1150 (now Article 1231-3) of the Civil Code', the judgment, formally, infringed that article;

On those grounds, and without its being necessary to adjudicate on the second ground of the appeal; the judgment is set aside …

Notes

(1) At one time the rule laid down in Article 1231-3 was seen as limiting the type of loss which would be recoverable, but not its extent. Now the rule is also often applied by the courts to the extent, so as to moderate the amount of damages in the light of what the claimant had anticipated.[41] It acts as a financial limit on the defendant's liability.

(2) The limitation of the debtor's liability to foreseeable losses will not apply in cases of gross (*dol*) or dishonest fault (*faute lourde*), nor will any limitation by way of a clause restricting the debtor's liability.[42] Under former Article 1150, the limitation to foreseeable loss was excluded only in cases of gross fault. However, the case law had extended it to dishonest fault.[43] New Article 1231-3 confirms the position of the case law by mentioning both the gross and the dishonest fault.

(3) Even in cases of gross or dishonest fault, the debtor will still be liable only for losses which followed 'immediately and directly' from the non-performance (Article 1231-4). The application of this directness test (also and more frequently applied in delict cases) is 'elusive'.[44] A classic explanation was given by Pothier:[45]

If a trader sells me a cow which he knows to be infected with a contagious disease and conceals that defect from me, that concealment constitutes a deceit on his part rendering him liable for the damage suffered by me, not only in respect of the cow itself, which forms the subject matter of his original obligation, but also with regard to any loss suffered by me in respect of any of my other livestock to which that cow has passed on the contagion—since it is as a result of that trader's deceit that I have suffered all of the damage in question. But is he liable for any other damage suffered by me which constitutes a more remote and less direct consequence of his deceit? For example, if the contagion passed to my cattle by the cow sold to me prevents me from cultivating my land, the damage which I suffer by reason of my land remaining uncultivated appears likewise to be a consequence of the deceit on the part of that trader, who has sold me an infected cow; but it is a more remote consequence than the loss which I have suffered in terms of my infected cattle. Is the trader liable for that damage? And what is the position if, by reason of the loss made by me on my cattle and the

---

[41] See Nicholas (n 4 above) 230–31; P Malaurie, L Aynès and P Stoffel-Munck, *Droit des obligations* (9th edn, Paris: LGDJ, 2017) no. 964.

[42] eg Cass req 24 October 1932, DP 1932, 176 annotated by EP.

[43] Cass com 26 September 2006, no. 04-18232, unpublished; Cass com 4 March 2008, no. 07-11790, Bull IV no. 53.

[44] Nicholas (n 4 above) 229.

[45] M Dupin, *Oeuvres de R-J Pothier* (Brussels: de Ode et Wadon, 1881) nos. 166–67.

damage suffered by me as a result of my inability to cultivate my land, I am prevented from paying my debts, so that my creditors attach my assets and sell them at a totally inadequate price? Is the trader also liable for that damage? ... The trader is not liable for the damage suffered by me in consequence of the attachment of my assets. That damage is nothing more than a very remote and indirect consequence of his deceit, and the requisite causal nexus does not exist, since, although the loss of my cattle which I have suffered as a result of his wrongful act may have had some influence on the upset in my financial position, that upset may have been caused by other factors. ... The loss which I have suffered as a result of the non-cultivation of my land appears to be a less remote consequence of the trader's deceit, but in my view he cannot be liable for it, or at least not for all of it. That non-cultivation is not a wholly necessary consequence of the loss of my cattle suffered by me as a result of the trader's deceit; despite that loss of cattle, I could avoid such non-cultivation by using other cattle to cultivate the land. ... Nevertheless, since, by having recourse to that expedient, I would not have made as great a profit from my land as I would have done if I had used my own cattle, the loss of which was caused by the trader's deceit, that factor may be taken into account in the context of the damages for which he is liable.

(4) Article 1251 of the reform bill on civil liability adopts the same position as Article 1231-3 of the Code civil.

Court of Exchequer   **26.14 (EN)**

Hadley v Baxendale[46]

Where two parties have made a contract that one of them has broken, the damages which the other party ought to receive in respect of such breach of contract should be such as may fairly and reasonably be considered either as arising naturally, i.e. according to the usual course of things from such a breach of contract itself, or such as may reasonably be supposed to have been in the contemplation of both parties, at the time they had made the contract, as the probable result of the breach of it.

Facts: The plaintiffs, the owners of a flour mill, sent a broken iron shaft to an office of the defendants, who were common carriers, to be conveyed by them, and the defendant's clerk, who attended at the office, was told [that the mill was stopped—see Note (1) below—and] that the shaft must be delivered immediately and that a special entry, if necessary, must be made to hasten delivery. The delivery of the broken shaft to the consignee, to whom it had been sent by the plaintiffs as a pattern by which to make a new shaft, was delayed by an unreasonable time. In consequence of this, the plaintiff did not receive the new shaft for some days after the time it ought to have received it and it was consequently unable to work its mill for want of the new shaft, and thereby incurred a loss of profits.

Held: Under the circumstances, such loss could not be recovered in an action against the defendants as common carriers.

Judgment: ALDERSON B: We think that there ought to be a new trial in this case; but in doing so we deem it to be expedient and necessary to state explicitly the rule which the Judge, at the next trial, ought, in our opinion to direct the jury to be governed by when they estimate the next damages ...

---

[46] (1854) 9 Exch 341.

Now we think the proper rule in such a case as the present is this:—Where two parties have made a contract where one of them has broken, the damages that the other party ought to receive in the respect of such a breach of contract should be such as may fairly and reasonably be considered either arising naturally, i.e. according to the usual course of things, from such breach of contract itself or such as may reasonably be supposed to have been in contemplation of the both parties, at the time that they made the contract, as the probable result of the breach of it. Now, if the special circumstances under which the contract was actually made were communicated by the plaintiffs to the defendants, and thus known to both parties, the damages resulting from the breach of such a contract, which they would reasonably contemplate, would be the amount of injury which would ordinarily follow from a breach of contract under these special circumstances so known and communicated. But, on the other hand, if these special circumstances were wholly unknown to the party breaking the contract, he, at the most could only be supposed to have had in his contemplation the amount of injury which would arise generally, and in great multitude of cases not affected by any special circumstances, from such a breach of contract. For, had the special circumstances been known, the parties may have specially provided for the breach of contract by special terms as to the damage in that case; and of this advantage it would be very unjust to deprive them. Now the above principles are those by which we think the jury ought to be guided in estimating the damages arising out of any breach of contract.

Now, in the present case, if we are to apply the above principles laid down, we find that the only circumstances here communicated by the plaintiffs to the defendants at the time of the contract was made, were, that the article to be carried was the shaft of a mill, and that the plaintiffs were millers of that mill. But how do these circumstances shew reasonably that the profits of the mill must be stopped by an unreasonable delay in the delivery of the broken shaft by the carrier to the third person? Suppose the plaintiffs had another shaft in their possession put up or putting up at the time, and that they only wished to send back the broken shaft to the engineer who made it; it is clear that this would be quite consistent with the above circumstances, and yet the unreasonable delay in the delivery would have no effect upon the intermediate profits of the mill. Or, again, suppose that, at the time of the delivery to the carrier, the machinery of the mill had been in other respects defective, then, also, the same results would follow. Here it is true that the shaft was actually sent back to serve as a model for a new one, and that the want, of a new one was the only cause of the stoppage of a mill, and that the loss of profits really arose from not sending down the new shaft in proper time, and that this arose from the delay in delivering the broken one to serve as a model. But it is obvious that, in a great multitude of cases of millers sending off broken shaft to the third persons by a carrier under ordinary circumstances, such consequences would not, in all probability, have occurred; and these special circumstances were here never communicated by the plaintiffs to the defendants. It follows, therefore, that the loss of profits here cannot reasonably be considered such a consequence of breach of contract as could have been fairly and reasonably contemplated by both the parties when they made this contract. For such loss would neither have flowed naturally from the breach of this contract in the greater multitude of such cases occurring under ordinary circumstances, nor were the special circumstances, which, perhaps, would have made it reasonable and natural consequence of breach of contract, communicated to or known by the defendants ... there must therefore be a new trial ...

Notes

(1) It has been said judicially that the headnote to the case, from which the statement of facts above is taken, actually gets the facts wrong: the words placed here in […] should have been omitted. If the plaintiffs *had* told the defendant's clerk that the mill was stopped, they would have recovered.[47]

(2) The words of Baron Alderson which are quoted in the summary are now known as 'the rule in *Hadley v Baxendale*'. The rule seems to have been derived from French sources.[48]

(3) It is said that the rule in *Hadley v Baxendale* restricts liability to the kind of loss that it was contemplated the claimant might suffer, not merely as to its extent. So if the loss was of the same kind but merely greater in amount, the rule should not prevent recovery.[49] Thus in *Balfour Beatty Construction (Scotland) Ltd v Scottish Power plc*[50] the plaintiffs had contracted for a continuous supply of power to enable them to make a 'continuous pour' of concrete to construct an aqueduct. As the 'pour' was being made, the power was interrupted; the plaintiffs had to demolish what had been done and start again. This could not have been contemplated by the defendants, but they were liable for the costs as they should have anticipated the necessity of some remedial work, such as cutting back the hardened concrete to form a joint with the new, and the difference was one of degree only.

(4) However, in practice the rule often works as a financial limit on the defendant's liability. In the *Victoria Laundry* case the buyers of a second-hand boiler wanted to use it immediately and suffered a loss of profits when the sellers delivered it late. The Court held that this should have been obvious to the sellers. What the sellers could not have known was that the buyers wanted the boiler not for their normal laundering business but to fulfil some much more profitable government dyeing contracts. The Court held that the sellers were not liable for these higher losses but only for the normal loss of profits on laundering—though of course if the buyers had received the boiler on time they would not have used it for laundering but for dyeing!

(5) Similarly, in English tort law a defendant is only liable for loss caused by his breach of duty only if the loss is of a foreseeable type. In the leading case of *The Wagon Mound (No 1)*,[51] it was held to be foreseeable that crude oil spilled in a harbour would cause damage to a dock company by fouling its slipways, but not that the oil would cause damage by catching fire. However, it seems that the defence will not apply if the kind of damage was foreseeable even as a remote possibility. In contract cases, however, the standard is different. It is not enough that the loss was foreseeable as a possibility. Alderson B spoke of the 'natural' or 'probable' results of the breach. The House of Lords has held that, to be recoverable under *Hadley v Baxendale*, the

---

[47] *Victoria Laundry (Windsor) Ltd v Newman Industries Ltd* [1949] 2 KB 528, 537–38 (CA).

[48] See AWB Simpson, 'Innovation in 19th Century Contract law' (1975) 91 LQR 247. For a fascinating account of the background to the case, see R Danzig, '*Hadley v Baxendale*: A Study in the Industrialization of the Law' (1975) 4 JLS 249.

[49] See *Treitel on the Law of Contract*, 14th edn by E Peel (London: Sweet & Maxwell, 2015) para 20-103.

[50] 1993 SLT 1005.

[51] [1966] 1 AC 188 (PC).

kind of loss must either have been known to the defendant or foreseeable by him as a substantial possibility: *The Heron II*.[52] The difference between the contract and tort rules has caused the courts some difficulty in those cases in which the defendant is liable in both contract and tort—there is no rule of *non cumul* in English law.[53]

(6) The fact that a loss was foreseeable even as a usual consequence may not suffice to make the defendant liable for it. Following the decision of the House of Lords in *Transfield Shipping Inc v Mercator Shipping Inc (The Achilleas)*,[54] it seems that a claimant will not recover even for losses that were not unlikely to occur in the usual course of things if the defendant cannot reasonably be regarded as assuming responsibility for losses of the particular kind suffered. This seems to be not merely an aspect of the circumstances in which the parties will be held to have 'had in contemplation' unusual kinds of loss, and so part of the remoteness rule, but to be an additional and separate element of the remoteness rule. The question was whether a time-charterer, who at the end of the charter period had redelivered the ship late, was liable just for the difference between the rate of hire under the charter and the higher rate the owner could have earned during the period of delay, or for the much greater loss the owner suffered when, because of the delay, it lost a 'follow-on' charter which it had concluded at favourable rates. The facts were very unusual: there were many judicial statements to the effect that the charterer would not be liable for the higher loss, and this was the general understanding in the industry. It was held that it was not reasonable to assume the charterer was accepting responsibility for the greater loss. Lord Hoffmann said:

11 The question of principle has been extensively discussed in the literature. Recent articles by Adam Kramer ('An Agreement-Centred Approach to Remoteness and Contract Damages' in *Comparative Remedies for Breach of Contract* (2005), eds Cohen & McKendrick, pp 249–286), Andrew Tettenborn ('Hadley *v* Baxendale Foreseeability: a Principle Beyond its Sell-by Date' in (2007) 23 Journal of Contract Law 120–147) and Andrew Robertson ('The Basis of the Remoteness Rule in Contract' (2008) 28 Legal Studies 172–196) are particularly illuminating. They show that there is a good deal of support in the authorities and academic writings for the proposition that the extent of a party's liability for damages is founded upon the interpretation of the particular contract; not upon the interpretation of any particular language in the contract, but (as in the case of an implied term) upon the interpretation of the contract as a whole, construed in its commercial setting. Professor Robertson considers this approach somewhat artificial, since there is seldom any helpful evidence about the extent of the risks the particular parties would have thought they were accepting. I agree that cases of departure from the ordinary foreseeability rule based on individual circumstances will be unusual, but limitations on the extent of liability in particular types of contract arising out of general expectations in certain markets, such as banking and shipping, are likely to be more common. There is, I think, an analogy with the distinction which Lord Cross of Chelsea drew in *Liverpool City Council v Irwin* [1977] AC 239, 257–258 between terms implied into all contracts of a certain type and the implication of a term into a particular contract.

---

[52] [1969] 1 AC 350 (HL).

[53] See above, p 151 and *H Parsons (Livestock) Ltd v Uttley Ingham & Co Ltd* [1978] QB 791 (CA); see also Bishop, 'The Contract-Tort Boundary and the Economics of Insurance' (1983) 12 JLS 241.

[54] [2008] UKHL 48, [2009] 1 AC 61.

12 It seems to me logical to found liability for damages upon the intention of the parties (objectively ascertained) because all contractual liability is voluntarily undertaken. It must be in principle wrong to hold someone liable for risks for which the people entering into such a contract in their particular market, would not reasonably be considered to have undertaken.

13 The view which the parties take of the responsibilities and risks they are undertaking will determine the other terms of the contract and in particular the price paid. Anyone asked to assume a large and unpredictable risk will require some premium in exchange. A rule of law which imposes liability upon a party for a risk which he reasonably thought was excluded gives the other party something for nothing. And as Willes J said in *British Columbia and Vancouver's Island Spar, Lumber and Saw-Mill Co Ltd v Nettleship* (1868) LR 3 CP 499, 508: 'I am disposed to take the narrow view, that one of two contracting parties ought not to be allowed to obtain an advantage which he has not paid for.'

14 In their submissions to the House, the owners said that the 'starting point' was that damages were designed to put the innocent party, so far as it is possible, in the position as if the contract had been performed: see *Robinson v Harman* (1848) 1 Exch 850, 855. However, in *Banque Bruxelles Lambert SA v Eagle Star Insurance Co Ltd (sub nom South Australia Asset Management Corpn v York Montague Ltd)* [1997] AC 191, 211, I said (with the concurrence of the other members of the House):

> I think that this was the wrong place to begin. Before one can consider the principle on which one should calculate the damages to which a plaintiff is entitled as compensation for loss, it is necessary to decide for what kind of loss he is entitled to compensation. A correct description of the loss for which the valuer is liable must precede any consideration of the measure of damages.

15 In other words, one must first decide whether the loss for which compensation is sought is of a 'kind' or 'type' for which the contract-breaker ought fairly to be taken to have accepted responsibility.

Because the facts were so unusual, it is hard to know what impact this decision will have.[55] However, it is interesting to compare the approach taken by the House of Lords in the *South Australia* case, and the German cases on 'the protective purpose of the norm', to be discussed below.[56]

In German law two approaches to the remoteness of the harm sustained as a result of a breach of contract are taken. The chief means of deciding this question is by asking whether there was adequate causation of the harm; alternatively, one may inquire about the scope of the protective purpose of the norm, here the contract. (The theory of the purpose of the norm is explored in the next sub-section.)

BGB **26.15 (DE)**

§ 254: Contributory negligence
(1) If any fault of the injured party has contributed to causing the damage, the omission to compensate the injured party and the extent of the compensation to be made

---

[55] See further *Chitty* (n 15 above) paras 26-137 ff.
[56] See below, p 1078.

depends upon the circumstances, especially upon how far the injury has been caused predominately by the one or the other party.

(2) This applies also if the fault of the injured party consisted only in an omission to call the attention of the debtor to the danger of unusually high damage which the debtor neither knew nor should have known, or in an omission to avert or mitigate the damage. The provision of § 278 applies *mutatis mutandis.*

Notes

(1) Schlechtriem wrote:[57]

The theory of adequate causation enables the exclusion from compensation of losses which were unforeseeable or highly improbable. The adequacy of causation is in particular judged from the perspective of an objective [or 'optimal'] observer having regard to the events which he could have foreseen in the circumstances. The theory of adequate causation is also applied through giving legal form to a judgment as to probability: whether as a result of the initial harm the probability of the subsequent harm occurring was significantly increased. As against this the theory of the 'purpose of the norm' or 'normative connection' (*Rechtswid-rigkeitszusammenhang*) requires a determination of whether the duty which was breached was supposed to protect the creditor from just the type of harm which in fact resulted.

(2) The requirement that possible loss, beyond that which is foreseeable, be notified to the debtor is expressly included among the rules governing contribution and mitigation (§ 254(2)(1) BGB). Since this rule is part of the general law of obligations, it applies inter alia to both contract and tort. We shall see[58] that there are specific rules governing the extent of recoverable damages in the law governing sales and work contracts.

Thus, in effect, all three systems normally limit the liability of the party who has failed to perform to losses which, at the time the contract was made, were probable or foreseeable or which he was warned might be caused if the contract were not to be performed properly. The French rule that this limit does not apply in cases of gross or dishonest fault (*dol* or *faute lourde*) does not appear in the other systems.[59] Nor does it appear in CISG[60] or the UNIDROIT Principles, but it is found in the Principles of European Contract Law.

Principles of European Contract Law   **26.16 (INT)**

Article 9:503: Foreseeability[61]
    The non-performing party is liable only for loss which it foresaw or could reasonably have foreseen at the time of conclusion of the contract as a likely result of its non-performance, unless the non-performance was intentional or grossly negligent.

---

[57] Schlechtriem and Schmidt-Kessel (n 14 above) paras 225–26.
[58] See below, pp 1100 ff.
[59] See G Treitel, *Remedies for Breach of Contract* (Oxford: Clarendon Press, 1988) 144–48, paras 123–26.
[60] See Art 74.
[61] cf Art III.-3:703 DCFR.

26.4.B THE PROTECTIVE PURPOSE OF THE NORM

OLG Köln, 8 July 1982[62]   **26.17 (DE)**

The bank which told the tax man

The loss for which compensation is sought must be within the protective purpose of the contract.

Facts: An official of the defendant bank gave information to the police concerning a number of bogus accounts held by the plaintiff customer. As a result, the plaintiff was convicted of tax evasion. She sued for damages.

Held: The lower court held that there could be no recovery. The plaintiff's appeal against this decision was rejected on the basis that the purpose of the contract between the customer and the bank was not to protect the former against such harm.

Judgment: Until mid-1986 the plaintiff and her husband maintained various accounts in various names with the D branch of the defendant bank. Towards the end of 1986, K, the manager of the branch, was summarily dismissed on account of his having committed serious criminal offences in the context of his employment. Upon being arrested on 10 December 1986, he was questioned by the police. He stated *inter alia*, in the light of documents comprised in a list of suspense accounts dated November 1986, that he had played a significant role in the setting up of an index of creditors. He had drawn to the attention of the customers, and also of the directors of the bank, the existence of accounts in respect of which the identity of the account-holder was not the same as that of the creditor. Those accounts included the accounts maintained in several different names by the plaintiff. The accounts had been closed in mid-1986.

In June 1987 the plaintiff and her husband were the subject of a preliminary investigation by the public prosecutor concerning suspected tax evasion. Following an examination of the tax returns of the plaintiff and her husband, the department charged with investigating suspected tax offences, which had been instructed in the matter on 29 September 1987, summoned K to give evidence. His evidence was taken on 20 November 1987. On that occasion, he provided further details regarding the accounts of the plaintiff and her husband. On 30 May 1988 the residence of Mr and Mrs D was searched. Since 1973 they had declared only part of their unearned income in their income tax returns, and had failed to submit any capital tax returns. The plaintiff was convicted of tax evasion. Proceedings are now pending before the fiscal courts for payment of arrears of tax. The plaintiff has pleaded that the defendant is liable in damages to her and her husband, because K was employed by the defendant in the performance of its obligations and breached, without justification, the bank's duty to maintain confidentiality. The plaintiff claims that, by reason of the statements made by K, she and her husband were prevented from availing themselves of the *Steueramnestiegesetz* (Law on tax amnesty) (Article 17 of the 1990 *Steuerreformgesetz* (Law on tax reform)), as they had firmly arranged to do at the end of 1987/beginning of 1988. Consequently, the loss and damage occasioned by the breach of contract included, according to the plaintiff, not only the fine and the legal costs but also the tax arrears payable up to and including 1985. She alleges that the defendant is additionally at fault since it was advised of K's breach of the duty of confidentiality but failed to inform the plaintiff and her husband of this. The Landgericht (Regional Court)

[62] BB 1992, 2174.

dismissed the claim for damages in relation to the fine, the legal costs and the arrears of tax payable. The plaintiff's appeal against that judgment was likewise dismissed.

Grounds: The … plaintiff's appeal must be dismissed, without there being any need for further investigation of the factual matters at issue between the parties . … Even if K. unlawfully breached the duty of confidentiality owed by the defendant, the plaintiff has not in any event suffered any loss for which compensation is payable. The defendant was under no duty to furnish information.

1. On 10 December 1986 K made a number of statements covered by the banking secrecy rules

…

2. The defendant remained under a duty to preserve banking secrecy following the closure of the accounts in 1986. Moreover, despite his dismissal, K remained the agent of the bank for the purposes of the fulfilment of its obligations, and the defendant is in principle answerable for his actions.

…

4. There can be seen to exist a causal link between the statements made by K and the pecuniary losses suffered by the plaintiff and her husband. There are grounds for supposing that, if it had not been for K.'s initial statement, there would have been no criminal proceedings and no liability to pay arrears of tax. That is a separate issue from the question whether the plaintiff would have availed herself of the tax amnesty legislation.

5. However, the claims for damages cannot be accepted as giving rise to liability to pay compensation. The prejudicial consequences of an offence which arise from a criminal conviction for that offence cannot, as a matter of principle, be shifted on to others. According to the relevant case law, the courts have hitherto been willing to accept the existence of a duty to pay compensation only where there was some special reason in law for restraining the offender from committing the offence or for affording him legal protection against punishment. … That is not the position in the present case. Banking confidentiality is not intended to enable offences to be committed or kept secret, and its breach gives rise to liability, even in contractual relations, only in so far as may be necessary in order to safeguard a rule of law. … The commission by the plaintiff of criminal acts was not an issue to be taken into account by the defendant and K. The statements made by K did not in themselves give rise to the suspicion of tax evasion; they had, moreover, already been superseded by the closure of the accounts.

The arrears of tax constitute an illegal pecuniary advantage which does not merit protection, and the plaintiff was not entitled to the continuance of that advantage.

No divergent conclusion can be drawn from the Steueramnestiegesetz, as regards either the criminal or the fiscal consequences of the matter. That statute, which entered into force in August 1988, lays down the way in which the plaintiff's loss could have been avoided, but does not affect the assessment of that loss.

Moreover, no special significance attaches to the fact that the point in time at which a criminal offence is discovered may produce effects as far as the person committing it is concerned, e.g. where it is no longer possible, subject to the detailed requirements laid down in that regard, to submit to the tax authorities a report of a false or incomplete tax declaration or to abandon the attempt to commit the offence, or where the running of the anticipated period of limitation for bringing a prosecution is interrupted. The fact that an offender is placed in the position in which he would have found himself if he had submitted a report of a false or incomplete tax declaration to the tax authorities or had abandoned his attempt to commit the offence, or if the limitation period had expired, in no way indicates whether a claim exists in contract.

Contrary to the view advanced by the plaintiff, the decisive factor which ultimately led to her exposure was the statement made by K in December 1996, and not the evidence given by him in November 1987. The argument that the preliminary investigation by the public prosecutor would have been discontinued if K, invoking banking confidentiality, had refused to make a statement is not convincing. On the contrary, there are compelling grounds for supposing that he would then have been formally examined in a manner precluding a refusal to give evidence (§ 286 ZPO).

However, that in no way alters the fact that the course of events whereby the plaintiff and her husband found themselves no longer able to submit any rectifying tax declarations is irrelevant to the substance of any liability in damages which the defendant may have incurred.

6. Even if, contrary to the observations set out above, liability in damages for the loss suffered were to attach to the defendant, the plaintiff's claim would fall foul of § 254 BGB and would be bound to fail. The facts disclosed by K. were in themselves unimportant, and had already been overtaken by events, whereas the plaintiff and her husband were primarily instrumental in bringing about the prejudice which subsequently arose, in that they engaged in a course of wilful conduct over a period of many years.

7. Nor, finally, can the defendant be criticised for having failed to inform the plaintiff of the initial statement made by K, assuming that it was aware of the content of that statement. In that regard also, the position is such that the matter did not manifestly involve any interest of the plaintiff. The fact that the public prosecutor's suspicions may have been increased cannot constitute a criterion governing the defendant's obligations to give consideration to the matter and to exercise care.

Consequently, there is no need to consider the point in time at which the plaintiff and her husband would still have been able to escape a criminal prosecution by submitting to the tax authorities a confession in relation to their false or incomplete tax declarations, or to examine the question whether, had they known of the content of the statement made by K on 10 December 1986, they would have decided to do so.

Notes

(1) The protective purpose of the norm approach is usually seen as limiting the recoverable harm to a greater extent than the theory of adequate causation. In other words, the debtor's breach of contract may have increased the probability that harm of the relevant type would occur, but such loss may still be held to be outside the purpose of the contractual norm. Thus, for example, in the case above it is very likely that a test of adequate causation would have applied in the plaintiff's favour.

(2) The precise scope of the protective purpose of the contract is a matter of fact to be determined in the light of all the circumstances, including especially the intentions of the parties. This gives judges considerable leeway. Tests applied in this connection take either an objective or subjective approach to intention.[63]

(3) It is doubtful whether any other legal systems would have permitted the plaintiffs to recover compensation for what was, in essence, the consequence of their own wrongdoing. There are alternative ways in which this could have been reached— for instance, by holding that the loss was caused primarily by their own actions;

[63] See H Lange, *Schadensersatz* (Tübingen: Mohr Siebeck, 1979) 79 ff.

contributory negligence; or a rule based on public policy denying compensation for the just desserts of criminal activity.[64]

(4) An approach which is rather similar to the purpose of the norm has been used in England to limit liability in cases which did not involve any criminal activity of any kind. The court was concerned to relieve the debtor of liability for a loss which was foreseeable, and which would not have occurred but for its negligence, but which it did not seem fair to lay at the debtor's door. In *South Australia Asset Management Corp v York Montague Ltd*[65] (the case referred to by Lord Hoffmann in *The Achilleas*),[66] valuers had been employed by lenders to value properties which the lenders were promising to accept as security, but had negligently overvalued the properties. Had the valuation been done properly, the lenders would not have accepted the security or made the loans. When the borrowers defaulted and the lenders tried to enforce the security it was found that they were worth much less than the amount owed, partly because of the overvaluation and partly because of a general fall in property values. The House of Lords held that the negligent valuers were not necessarily liable for a fall in market value. The purpose of the contract must be looked at, and it was not to protect the lenders against general falls in the market value. The valuers were liable for no more than the initial deficiency, ie the difference between the negligent over-valuation and what would have been a proper valuation at the time of the loan. However, if the same thing happens when the defendant was employed to give advice on the transaction as a whole, the defendant is liable for the full loss suffered by the claimant.[67]

26.4.C LOSSES WHICH MIGHT HAVE BEEN AVOIDED OR REDUCED BY THE CREDITOR

English law contains a very distinctive rule on damages, the so-called 'duty to mitigate'.

House of Lords **26.18 (EN)**

British Westinghouse Electric and Manufacturing Co Ltd v Underground Electric Railways Co of London Ltd[68]

[The facts of this case are not relevant at this point as the case did not in fact involve mitigation.]

VISCOUNT HALDANE LC: … In order to come to a conclusion on the question as to damages thus raised, it is essential to bear in mind certain propositions which I think are well established. In some of the cases there are expressions as to the principles governing the measure of general damages which at first sight seem difficult to harmonise. The apparent discrepancies are, however, mainly due to the varying nature of the particular

---

[64] Compare *Moore Stephens v Stone & Rolls Ltd (in liquidation)* [2009] UKHL 39, [2009] 1 AC 1391.
[65] [1997] AC 191 (HL).
[66] Above, pp 1075–76.
[67] *Hughes-Holland v BPE Solicitors* [2017] UKSC 21, [2018] AC 599.
[68] [1912] AC 673, 688–89.

questions submitted for decision. The quantum of damage is a question of fact, and the only guidance which the law can give is to lay down general principles which afford at times but scanty assistance in dealing with particular cases. The judges who give guidance to juries in these cases have necessarily to look at their special character, and to mould for the purposes of different kinds of claim the expression of the general principles which apply to them, and this is apt to give rise to an appearance of ambiguity. Subject to these observations I think that there are certain broad principles, which are quite well settled. The first is that, as far as possible, he who has proved a breach of a bargain to supply what he contracted to get is to be placed, as far as money can do it, in as good a situation as if the contract had been performed. The fundamental basis is thus compensation for pecuniary loss naturally flowing from the breach; but this first principle is qualified by a second, which imposes on a plaintiff the duty of taking all reasonable steps to mitigate the loss consequent on the breach, and debars him from claiming in respect of any part of the damage which is due to his neglect to take such steps …

Notes

(1) This dictum is probably the clearest statement of the English law on the 'duty to mitigate', as it is often called. In fact, it is not a duty, since a duty must be owed to someone else; rather, it is a rule that a party cannot recover a loss he could have avoided by taking reasonable steps. It is what in German is called an *Obliegenheit* (or requirement).

(2) The principle has two aspects. One is that the creditor should not act unreasonably in such a way as to risk making the loss worse—for example, by continuing to drive a car which he has bought if he knows it has defective brakes; the other is that he should take reasonable positive steps to reduce the loss, for example, by making a substitute contract.[69]

(3) The mitigation principle is so fundamental that it is often incorporated into statements of the damages recoverable. For example, the Sale of Goods Act 1979, section 51(3),[70] which sets out the damages recoverable by a buyer when the seller has failed to deliver, assumes that the buyer will normally mitigate by making a substitute purchase in the market. Likewise, section 50(3), the section dealing with the seller's damages for the buyer's failure to accept the goods, assumes the seller will sell the goods to another buyer in the market.

(4) The creditor is expected only to take steps which are reasonable. A buyer who, when the seller fails to deliver, faces loss of profitable sub-sales is expected to buy replacement goods to meet its needs if these are readily available, but it need not 'go hunting the globe' for goods which are not readily available: *Lesters Leather and Skin Co Ltd v Home and Overseas Brokers Ltd.*[71] An employee who, as the result of a partnership being dissolved, has been dismissed without proper notice but who is then offered immediate re-employment on the same terms by the new partners is expected to accept the offer: *Brace v Calder*,[72] whereas an employee who has had his

---

[69] See *Treitel* (n 49 above) para 20-115.
[70] See 26.36 (EN), below, p 1101.
[71] (1948) 64 TLR 569 (CA).
[72] [1895] 2 QB 253 (CA).

trust in his old employer destroyed need not accept an offer of re-employment: *Yetton v Eastwoods Froy Ltd.*[73]

(5) The creditor may recover the costs involved in mitigating, for example the costs of arranging a substitute sale or purchase. Sometimes what appeared to be a reasonable step to mitigate loss does not reduce the loss as much as some other action might have done; the cost of the action taken is recoverable nonetheless: *Gebrüder Metelmann GmbH v NBR (London) Ltd.*[74]

(6) Once the date for performance has passed, so that damages are payable, the creditor must take reasonable steps to mitigate her loss, and this may involve terminating the contract so as to make a substitute arrangement. It is not clear in what circumstances there may be a duty to mitigate before this date. If there has been an anticipatory breach of the contract and the creditor elects to terminate the contract right away, she comes under a duty to mitigate when she terminates; but if she does not so elect, it has been said that she is not under a duty to act: *Shindler v Northern Raincoat Co Ltd.*[75] See, however, the cases following *White & Carter v McGregor,*[76] which may qualify this statement to some extent.

(7) On the actual facts of the *British Westinghouse* case, the duty was not directly relevant but the case involved a closely-connected rule—that if after the breach the claimant acts in a way that reduces the loss (even if he had no 'duty' to act as he did), the resulting savings will be taken into account. The plaintiffs had supplied turbines to the defendants which did not perform as efficiently as required by the contract. After several years the defendants had installed newer, much more efficient turbines made by another manufacturer. The House of Lords said that this was more than could reasonably have been required of them by the duty to mitigate. The question was whether the defendants could set the cost of installing these second turbines against the—still unpaid—contract price. It was held that they could not, because in fact the new turbines were so much more efficient than the old ones would have been, even if they had conformed to the contract, that the new machines paid for themselves. In other words, the plaintiff's actions had resulted in a saving to them which should be taken into account in reducing their damages.

BGB	**26.19 (DE)**

§ 254: [See above.][77]

§ 326: Release from counter-performance, and termination where there is no duty to perform

…

(2) If the obligee is solely or overwhelmingly responsible for the circumstance releasing the obligor from the need to perform pursuant to § 275(1) to (3), or if the obligor is not responsible for that circumstance and this occurs at a time when the obligee is in default

---

[73] [1967] 1 WLR 104 (QBD).
[74] [1984] 1 Lloyd's Rep 614, 634 (CA).
[75] [1960] 1 WLR 1038 (CA).
[76] 23.34 (EN), above, p 950.
[77] 26.15 (DE), above, p 1076.

through non-acceptance, the obligor retains his claim for counter-performance. He must, however, allow a deduction for whatever he saves as a result of release from performance, he acquires through the utilisation of his labour elsewhere, or he maliciously fails to acquire.

[paras (1) and (3)–(5) omitted]

BGH, 7 May 1962[78] **26.20 (DE)**

The architect and the defective building

The responsibility of the creditor to mitigate may include the enforcement of rights against third parties.

Facts: The creditor of a building contract sued the architect responsible for the work for loss caused by defective work on the roof. The architect claimed in response that the creditor was first obliged to proceed against the craftsman who actually carried out the work by way of mitigating his loss.

Held: The Landgericht and the Oberlandesgericht upheld the creditor's claim. The architect's appeal to the BGH was successful.

Judgment: On the grounds:

...

II. The court below considers the head of claim to be substantiated under § 635 BGB.

Accordingly, it correctly assesses the contract for architectural services covering building plans, direction and on-the-spot supervision entered into between the plaintiff and the defendant's husband as a contract for the provision of works.

...

2. However, the defendant's argument is relevant on another ground. The defendant claims that her husband and, after his death, she herself could have had the roof defects removed at a much lower cost. There was no need for a new roof.

If that is true, the plaintiff's claim for damages may be reduced or nullified under § 254(2) BGB ...

IV. It is contended in the context of this appeal that the plaintiff culpably omitted to avert or mitigate the damage (§ 254(2) BGB), by not requiring the carpenter W., who assembled the roof structure, to carry out subsequent repairs (*Nachbesserung*, see § 633 BGB), thereby forfeiting his rights against the carpenter to the detriment of the defendant. This contention must be upheld and the case must be further examined under this aspect.

The court *a quo* did not decide the question whether the carpenter was jointly liable for the defects. Accordingly, for the purposes of the present proceedings there must be presumed to be joint liability with W.

It cannot be ruled out that the plaintiff was obliged first to require W to carry out subsequent repairs, prior to seeking damages from the defendant's husband under the contract for architectural services. It is true that it is in principle open to the person giving instructions in respect of the building works to seek redress for building defects from the undertakings responsible or from the architect. But this right to choose is subject to the principle of good faith, as enshrined in § 254 BGB.

The architect and the craftsman are not jointly and severally liable. Irrespective of the fact that their obligations stem from different contracts, they do not contemplate the same contractual performance. It will not, therefore, be possible for the architect to demand compensation directly from the craftsman, for example, under § 426 BGB.

---

[78] NJW 1962, 1499.

The person directing the works as the creditor may not ignore that fact. He will therefore as a matter of principle be bound by the principle of good faith in relation to the architect also to seek redress from the craftsman. In particular he is obliged to avail himself of his right to call for subsequent repairs by the craftsman in order in that way to mitigate the loss for which the architect is liable (§ 254(2) BGB), without, however, in this way being burdened by an unreasonable task.

He cannot be expected to embark on a protracted dispute with the craftsman the outcome of which way be in doubt. Should appreciable difficulties in enforcing these rights against the craftsman already be foreseeable or even have already arisen, the architect cannot require that procedure to be followed but must accept liability for the full extent of the damage.

None the less, it does not appear to be free from doubt whether the particular circumstances under which the plaintiff had to seek redress from the building company are present in this case, if W was required to adhere to the plans drawn up by the defendant's husband. However this requires further elucidation.

Notes

(1) Reasonable, rather than extraordinary, measures only need be taken in mitigation of harm. Thus, it has been held that a holidaymaker whose hotel becomes unavailable or unacceptable either before or during the trip may be required—under § 254(2) BGB—to accept a substitute offer from the travel company. However, the substitute must be largely compatible with the original in terms of location and quality, and it must be offered without delay after the problem becomes known. In any event, the requirement may not be imposed where the holidaymaker has lost all confidence in the company.[79]

(2) A disappointed buyer or seller is generally not required to enter into a cover transaction in mitigation of their loss unless the subject matter of the contract was perishable or its price is subject to frequent fluctuation.[80]

(3) However, the suggestion that the creditor should take action against one of two parties who are both liable before suing the other goes beyond anything found in English law. This is, however, a more general difference. For example, in German law a guarantor of a debt may not be sued by the creditor until the creditor has been unsuccessful in obtaining payment from the debtor, whereas in English law the creditor may recover from the guarantor as soon as the debtor is in default. The guarantor and the debtor are jointly and severally liable; if the guarantor pays, he may recover from the debtor—if the latter is solvent!

French law does not as such recognise the duty to mitigate.[81] However, a creditor who fails to warn the debtor that the contract is being broken and allows damages to mount up will not recover the additional loss, the loss being treated as his own fault: for example,

---

[79] See LG Frankfurt 17 March 1986, NJW 1986, 1616.
[80] See Lange (n 63 above) 369.
[81] Cass civ (3) 10 July 2013, no. 12-13851, unpublished: 'the person causing a damage must repair all the consequences and the victim has no obligation to limit its damage in the interest of the person responsible'.

Gatelier v Electricité de France.[82] The limitation of damages recoverable is usually considered as an application of the duty to perform the contract in good faith.[83]

Cour d'appel de Paris, 7 January 1924[84]   **26.21 (FR)**

Low gas pressure

A customer of the gas company is not entitled to a particular pressure, in the absence of any special agreement; but in any event it cannot recover damages for difficulties experienced over a period of time when it has not notified the gas company of the problem.

Facts: The plaintiff hospice sued for losses caused allegedly by inadequate gas pressure over a two-year period. It had not notified the gas company of the difficulty.

Held: The first instance court allowed the claim but the decision was reversed on appeal.

Judgment:—Whereas Viollette, as Chairman of the administrative committee of the Dreux hospice, commenced proceedings against Société du gaz de Maubeuge for an order requiring it to pay FF20,000 by way of damages, on the ground that from 1919 to 1921 the irregular and insufficient supply of gas disturbed the operation of the bath and sterilisation services; as since the hospice had no special arrangement guaranteeing minimum and constant pressure, it is necessary primarily to rely on the Company's terms and conditions; as those terms and conditions, it appears, do not require the concessionaire to observe any minimum pressure;

— Whereas it is therefore inappropriate to interpret a clause which does not exist and cannot be supplied; as the gas company, bound only by general contractual principles and the prevailing circumstance, was a fortiori entitled to moderate the pressure, varying it according to the times of day and corresponding needs;

— Whereas Article 1 of the Decree of 1 June 1917 required plants to interrupt supplies at times of low consumption, and Viollette does not even allege that that decree had been expressly repealed, except as regards Article 2 which limited the circulation of hot water in buildings; as it merely contends that it had fallen into desuetude and there had been no penalty; moreover, the expert's reports and other documents produced in the proceedings show that the alleged inadequacy was attributable above all to the malfunctioning of the installations, the maintenance of which is the responsibility of the hospice; as in any event, whatever the cause, that inadequacy should have been reported to the gas company as early as 1919, so that the latter could attend to repairing it;

— Whereas a person to whom a service is provided in a defective manner is not entitled to allow the loss to increase and possible damages to accumulate, without formally complaining or giving notice that the defective supply should be remedied promptly; as the gas company properly criticises Viollette for failing to serve any notice setting out his complaints before commencing proceedings;

— Whereas accordingly, this court sets aside the judgment of the Tribunal de Commerce, Dreux, of 6 January 1992, and directs that no interpretation, stay of proceedings or inquiry is appropriate.

Thus, although French law does not recognize the duty to mitigate, and though in German law the principle is not expressed in these terms, all three systems seem to reach

---

[82] Cass civ (1) 29 April 1981, no. 80-11289, Bull civ I no. 142, JCP 1982.II.19730, annotated by P Courbe.
[83] Malaurie et al (n 41 above) no. 963.
[84] DP 1924.2.143.

the result that the creditor will not recover damages for loss which could have been avoided had the creditor taken reasonable steps. This is how it is formulated in the international restatements.

Cass civ (3), 2 October 2013[85] **26.22 (FR)**

The broken boiler

A plaintiff will not recover damages to the extent that its losses that have been increased by its own inertia.

Facts: A landlord purchased a new boiler, which had to be rinsed before the first use. The installer did not comply with its obligation to rinse the boiler and the boiler broke down after a short time (October 2005). The landlord waited several years before informing the installer of the malfunction. The boiler was finally repaired in 2011. The landlord claimed damages for not being able to rent the property.

Held: The court of appeal awarded only a portion of the damages claimed.

Judgment ... whereas, the Court of appeal, having discretionarily assessed the extent of the harm suffered by [the landlord], found that the lack of heating contributed to make the property unfit for renting for the period of October 2005 to December 2007 and that the inertia of the [the landlord] had increased its damage, noting that if the rinsing had been performed in October 2005 the boiler would have worked and the embellishment work following the water damage could have been done and the property could have been leased in January 2007 ...

Notes

(1) In this case, the Cour de cassation dismissed the *pourvoi* and decided that it was for the court of appeal to assess the extent by which a party's non-performance may free the other party from its corresponding obligations.

(2) At the end of the day, the landlord could not claim damages for the 2007–2011 period as she had failed to avoid an increase of her losses.

The reform bill on civil liability includes a duty to mitigate.

Reform bill on civil liability **26.23 (FR)**

Article 1263: Except in the case of personal injuries, damages are reduced where the victim did not take safe and reasonable measures, notably having regard to his ability to pay, appropriate to avoid an increase in his own loss.

Principles of European Contract Law **26.24 (INT)**

Article 9:505: Reduction of Loss

(1) The non-performing party is not liable for loss suffered by the aggrieved party to the extent that the aggrieved party could have reduced the loss by taking reasonable steps.

[85] No. 12-19887, unpublished.

(2) The aggrieved party is entitled to recover any expenses reasonably incurred in attempting to reduce the loss.

26.4.D CONTRIBUTORY NEGLIGENCE

Damages may also be reduced or refused altogether because the damage was partly due to the creditor's own conduct. Obviously, this principle might explain some cases of mitigation, but there is a wider rule. The duty to mitigate does not apply until the creditor knows that the debtor has broken the contract; it is only then that he is expected to take reasonable steps to reduce the loss. Here we are concerned with the case in which the creditor's carelessness contributed to the damage in some other way.

Cass civ (1), 31 January 1973[86]   **26.25 (FR)**

The bad-tempered bear

A debtor whose non-performance has caused injury to the creditor should be liable in full for her injuries unless he is exonerated on the ground of force majeure or unless she contributed to her own injury through her own fault.

Facts: Mrs D fell against a barrier designed to keep visitors a safe distance from a cage in which there was a bear. The barrier collapsed and the bear put its muzzle through the bars and bit her. She sued the zoo company.

Held: The court of appeal reduced her damages on the ground that her fall was an external event, but without finding that the fall was either unforeseeable or unavoidable, nor that it was the creditor's fault. On appeal the decision was quashed.

Judgment: THE COURT: *On the sole appeal ground*:—Under Article 1147 of the Civil Code (now Article 1231-1);
— Whereas an act by the victim, which was neither unforeseeable nor inevitable, does not constitute grounds of partial exoneration for a person who entered into a specific obligation to ensure safety unless it involves fault;
— Whereas Mrs Dantony, who was visiting the zoo operated by Condour, fell against a barrier designed to keep visitors at a certain distance from the cage occupied by a bear; as the barrier collapsed under the weight of Mrs Dantony, and the bear stuck its muzzle through the bars of its cage and bit her arm;
— Whereas the cour d'appel (Lyon, 4 May 1971), having held that Condour was under an obligation to ensure safety vis-à-vis Mrs Dantony, exonerated it in part from its obligation on the ground that there was an external event, namely the victim's fall, when she lost her footing;
— Whereas by giving judgment to that effect, but not finding any fault on the part of Mrs Dantony, the court of second instance infringed the above-mentioned provision;
On those grounds, sets the judgment aside … and refers the matter back to the cour d'appel, Grenoble.

---

[86] No. 71-12953, Bull civ I no. 41, D 1973, 149, annotated by R Schmelck.

In English law the position is complicated by the fact that in 1945 a statute was passed to allow the courts to reduce the damages awarded to a plaintiff who had been contributorily negligent. The statute, the Law Reform (Contributory Negligence) Act 1945, was aimed primarily at tort cases; before the Act, contributory negligence was a complete defence to a claim in tort.

Law Reform (Contributory Negligence) Act 1945   **26.26 (EN)**

Section 1: Apportionment of liability in case of contributory negligence
(1) Where any person suffers damage as the result partly of his own fault and partly of the fault of any other person or persons, a claim in respect of that damage shall not be defeated by reason of the fault of the person suffering the damage, but the damages recoverable in respect thereof shall be reduced to such extent as the court thinks just and equitable having regard to the claimant's share in the responsibility for the damage:
    …

Section 4: Definition
    … "fault" means negligence, breach of statutory duty or other act or omission which gives rise to a liability in tort or would, apart from this Act, give rise to the defence of contributory negligence.

Notes

It has not been clear to what extent the Act also applies to cases of breach of contract. It is necessary to distinguish three cases: (i) where the defendant has broken a contractual duty of care and is concurrently liable in tort—remember that English law recognises concurrent liability in contract and tort;[87] (ii) where the defendant has broken a contractual duty of care but would not be liable in tort—for example, his carelessness has caused only purely economic loss, which is seldom actionable in tort in English law;[88] and (iii) where the defendant's obligation was a 'strict' obligation, even if in fact the defendant was negligent—but again he would not be liable in tort.

(i)   *Concurrent liability in tort.* It is established that the Act applies where the defendant's breach of contract was also a tort. Thus in *Sayers v Harlow UDC*[89]

---

[87] See above, p 151.
[88] See above, pp 136–41.
[89] [1958] 1 WLR 623 (CA).

a lady used a public lavatory, for which she had to pay a penny. When she had finished she found there was no way of opening the door from the inside and, being in a hurry to catch a bus, she tried to climb out by standing on the toilet paper holder. This rotated under her foot and she fell, injuring herself. The Court of Appeal reduced her damages on the ground of contributory negligence. See also *Forsikringsaktielskapet Vesta v Butcher*.[90]

(ii) *No liability in tort*. It seems likely that the Act does not apply when the defendant's breach of contract was not also a tort, even if it was a breach of a contractual duty to use reasonable care and skill: dicta in *Forsikringsaktielskapet Vesta v Butcher*.[91]

(iii) *Strict obligations*. Where the defendant's obligation was a strict one, neither the old doctrine of contributory negligence nor the 1945 Act applies—the Act refers to cases in which the damage was caused partly by the 'fault' of the defendant, and fault is defined in a way that excludes a breach of a strict contractual obligation.

The Law Commission recommended that the power to reduce the plaintiff's damages should be extended to case (ii), but that it should not apply to case (iii), in which the defendant's contractual obligation was a strict one.[92] It said:

> If the defendant commits himself to a strict obligation regardless of fault, the plaintiff should be able to rely on him fulfilling his obligation and should not have to take precautions against the possibility that a breach might occur.[93]

However, its recommendations were not accepted by the government, so it seems that the power to reduce the claimant's damages still applies only in case (i).

BGB   **26.27 (DE)**

§ 254: Contributory negligence
    (1) If any fault of the injured party has contributed to causing the damage, the omission to compensate the injured party and the extent of the compensation to be made depends upon the circumstances, especially upon how far the injury has been caused predominantly by the one or the other party.
    (2) ...

Kammergericht, 14 November 1984[94]   **26.28 (DE)**

The stolen double bass

A contract creditor who does not exercise reasonable care to avoid the occurrence of harm is liable to have an award of damages proportionately reduced.

Facts: The plaintiff was employed under a contract of service by the defendant, the arts department of a city district council, to give a recital with other musicians. After the recital he left his double bass unattended in another

---

[90] [1988] 2 All ER 43 (CA), affirmed on other grounds [1989] AC 852 (HL).
[91] ibid.
[92] The Law Commission, *Contributory Negligence as a Defence in Contract*, Law Com No 219 (London: Her Majesty's Stationery Office, 1993).
[93] ibid para 4.2.
[94] NJW 1985, 2137.

room while he changed. The instrument was stolen. He sued the department for breaching obligations of protection (positive breach of contract—see now § 241 BGB). The defendant claimed in turn that the plaintiff had been culpably careless in leaving the instrument unattended while there were still visitors in the building.

Held: The decision of the lower court (Landgericht) awarding damages but reducing them by 50% in accordance with § 254 BGB was upheld.

Judgment: 1. The Landgericht rightly approached the matter on the basis that a contract for services had been concluded between the parties (§ 611 BGB), whereby the plaintiff undertook to the defendant (the T arts directorate) to give a concert in the P concert hall on the evening of 2 June 1983 in return for the payment of a specified fee. Contrary to the view taken by the Landgericht, however, the defendant owed the plaintiff a duty, on the basis of the contractual relationship existing between them, to protect the plaintiff's property against reasonably foreseeable loss and damage. It is generally recognised in case-law and academic legal literature that such a duty of protection forms a part of every contractual relationship (see RGZ 78, 240; Roth, in: Münch Komm, § 242, para 182). Such duties of protection (or preservation) are intended to safeguard the party to whom they are owed not only against prejudice to his existing or future interest in the performance by the other party of the latter's obligations, but also against loss or damage to his other legally protected interests (as previously explained in detail by Stoll in *Die Lehre von den Leistungsstörungen*, 1936, p 27). The duties involved are those existing under the contract, breach of which gives rise, in accordance with the principles of positive violation of contractual obligations, to liability in damages. If the other party to the contract uses another person to assist him in the fulfilment of the protection obligations imposed on him under the contract, he will be equally liable, pursuant to § 278 BGB, for fault on the part of that assistant as for his own fault.

In the present case, the defendant had taken it upon itself, through the T arts directorate, to organise the performance of the concert featuring the plaintiff in the P concert hall. That organisational duty (that is to say, the duty to ensure that the concert proceeded smoothly) also encompassed the collateral duty owed to plaintiff to take appropriate organisational steps to protect not only the plaintiff's person but also his property against loss and damage. In particular, the T arts directorate was under an obligation to entrust one or more of its employees with the task of looking after the organisational aspects of the performance of the concert.

According to the facts, which were not contested in the proceedings before the appellate court below, the defendant only inadequately fulfilled that obligation, and this was the cause of the loss and damage suffered. It is common ground that two employees of the arts directorate were present during the concert, together with the caretaker employed by the horticultural department, who was entrusted with the task of unlocking and re-locking the doors. However, the event organised by the arts directorate did not finish at the end of the performance given by the artists; it continued until such time as the artists had left the auditorium and the neighbouring rooms. In view of this, it was possible and reasonable, and thus incumbent on the defendant, without incurring further expense, to ensure that one of its employees was continuously present in the auditorium, thereby performing the function of the organiser, until all the artists had departed. The defendant did not discharge that duty. It is common ground that the defendant's two employees left the building immediately after the end of the concert, that is to say, at a time when persons attending the concert had not yet left the auditorium. The task of the caretaker employed by the horticultural department was merely to be responsible for the unlocking and re-locking of the doors to the building. He had not been directed to take any measures connected with the actual organisation of the event. In those factual circumstances, either at least one of the defendant's employees should have remained present in the auditorium until the artists had left or the caretaker, who remained behind, should have been given the responsibility of seeing to the final completion of the event before himself leaving the building. The defendant has not asserted that any of its employees assigned the functions of the organiser to the caretaker in the manner described. Moreover, even if any such assignment of functions had taken place, the defendant would still have been liable, since the loss would in that event have been based on a failure by the caretaker to fulfil his duty of care as a person assisting in the performance of the contract (§ 278 BGB).

Since the defendant has failed, on account of negligence (§ 276(1) BGB) on the part of its executive bodies or persons employed by it in the performance of its obligations, to fulfil its contractual duty to protect the plaintiff, it is liable in damages to the plaintiff in accordance with the principles of positive violation of contractual obligations.

2. As it is, the Landgericht rightly found that, in the context of the occurrence of the damage consisting of the loss of the instrument, the plaintiff had been contributorily negligent (§ 254(1) BGB) and that, in consequence of that contributory negligence, the plaintiff was entitled to receive from the defendant damages representing only half of the loss sustained by him. According to § 254 BGB, a party suffering loss and/or damage will be [contributorily] negligent if he fails to fulfil the duty of care normally applied by an ordinary, reasonable person in order to avoid himself sustaining such loss and/or damage (RGZ 112, 284 [287]; BGHZ 9, 316 [318] = NJW 1953, 977). The plaintiff failed to fulfil that requirement obliging him to safeguard his own interests.

However, contrary to the view advanced by the defendant, the plaintiff cannot be said to have been contributorily negligent solely on account of the fact that, because of the circumstances relating to the space available, he did not take his musical instrument with him to the artists' dressing room immediately after the end of the concert, depositing it instead in a side room adjoining the auditorium. Nor does anything turn on the defendant's allegation, contested by the plaintiff, that the caretaker had indicated prior to the final rehearsal that it was risky to leave the instrument in the unsupervised, empty building. The plaintiff could not have inferred from that remark that the defendant would omit at the end of the concert to fulfil its contractual duty of protection. However, if (as the plaintiff himself stated in the proceedings before the Chamber) he deposited his valuable instrument in a side room adjoining the auditorium when he was aware that members of the public were still in the auditorium and the caretaker was just on the point of locking various doors to the auditorium, he should have made sure, by enquiring of the caretaker before going to the artists' dressing room, that his instrument would be watched over during his absence. Since, by that time, the employees of the arts directorate organising the event had already left the building, and the plaintiff did not in any event see that any employee of the defendant was still present when he deposited the double bass in the side room, there was no adequate basis on which he could be sure that a watch would be kept on his instrument, especially since the building was not designed for events of that kind. Accordingly, by failing to fulfil his own duty of care, the plaintiff was contributorily negligent and partially caused his own loss. Having regard to all the circumstances of the case, particularly the degree of causation and the extent of the fault attributable to each of the parties, the Chamber, applying § 287 ZPO (see BGH, NJW 1968, 985 et seq), considers each of the parties to have contributed in equal measure to the cause of the loss. Consequently, responsibility for the damage suffered by the plaintiff must be divided equally between the parties.

Principles of European Contract Law **26.29 (INT)**

Article 9:504: Loss Attributable to Aggrieved Party

The non-performing party is not liable for loss suffered by the aggrieved party to the extent that the aggrieved party contributed to the non-performance or its effects.

26.4.E NON-PECUNIARY LOSS (*PRÉJUDICE MORAL*)

Cass civ (1), 16 January 1962[96] **26.30 (FR)**

Lunus

Regardless of the material damage which it causes, the death of an animal may, for its owner, be the cause of subjective and affective harm, which may carry entitlement to compensation.

Facts: The first plaintiff's horse Lunus was hired to the second plaintiff, a trainer, and was placed by the latter in stables run by the defendant racecourse. Lunus bit through an electric cable and was electrocuted.

Held: The Cour d'appel of Poitiers held that not only should the owner be paid the market value of the horse but he should receive FF500,000, and the trainer FF75,000, for non-material damage. This decision was upheld, but its finding that various defendants were jointly liable was set aside.

Judgment: THE COURT: *On the first appeal taken in its two parts:*—Whereas in August 1952, Daille, the owner of the racehorse Lunus, hired it to the trainer Henri de Lotherie; the latter had the animal taken to Langon, where he was to take part on 26 and 27 July 1953 in races organised by Société hippique de Langon; as Fabre, the Chairman of that company, made available to the trainer a box in his stable to accommodate the horse; as on the morning of 27 July 1953, the animal grabbed between its teeth the wire of a mobile lamp known as a 'baladeuse' ('walkabout lamp') and was electrocuted.—Whereas Daille commenced proceedings against Société hippique de Langon, Fabre personally, and de Lotherie, seeking damages; the contested judgment (Bordeaux, 5 July 1956) attributed responsibility for the death of the horse Lunus to Fabre as to 50 per cent, to Société hippique de Langon as to 25 per cent and to de Lotherie as to 25 per cent; whilst refusing to compensate Daille for the loss of such profits as the horse might have generated in the future, the cour d'appel held that in addition to the market value of the animal, which it put at Ff 350,000, Daille should receive an additional sum for the undoubted harm which he suffered as a result of the death of Lunus, and set the total amount of damages payable to Daille at FF500,000, de Lotherie to receive the sum of FF75,000;

— Whereas that decision is criticised for awarding damages intended to compensate for nonmaterial damage suffered as a result of loss of the horse and for accepting that de Lotherie, under whose colours the horse was entered in the race, had himself suffered

[95] Markesinis et al (n 9 above) 476.
[96] Cass civ (1) 16 January 1962, no. 2531 civ 56, Bull no. 33, D 1962, 199, annotated by R Rodière, S 1962.281, JCP 1962.II.12447.

non-material damage, even though, first, such damage is conceivable only in respect of the loss of a cherished being, and there is nothing in common between the upset caused by the death of a person and that of an animal, and, secondly, it was allegedly for the court to prove, by reference to particular circumstances, the existence of damage which it merely affirmed but of which there was no evidence;

— Whereas regardless of the material damage which it entails, the death of an animal may, for its owner, be the cause of subjective and affective damage which may entail entitlement to redress; as in this case, the cour d'appel rightly considered that the harm suffered by Daille in respect of the death of his horse was not limited to the sum necessary to buy another animal having the same qualities, and that it was also necessary to bring into account, in calculating the damages, compensation intended to cover the harm suffered through loss of an animal to which he was attached; as regards de Lotherie, the court was also entitled to take note of the adverse effect on his interests as a trainer;

— Whereas it follows, that in giving judgment as it did, the court properly founded its decision; But on the second appeal ground:—Under Having regard to Article 1202 of the Civil Code (now Article 1309 and 1310);

— Whereas, whilst each of the joint authors of a fault committed by more than one person may be ordered to redress in its entirety the damage to whose occurrence they contributed, the joint and several liability provided for in Article 1202 of the Civil Code (now Article 1309 and 1310) can be declared against them only in the cases provided for by law.

— Whereas in finding Fabre, Société hippique de Langon, de Lotherle, and the insurance company, were jointly and severally liable vis-à-vis Daille and de Lotherie, the judgment merely notes that they shared the fault, but, having inferred from that finding alone that they were jointly and severally liable, the cour d'appel failed to indicate the legal basis of its decision;

On those grounds, the judgment is set aside ... but only as regards this ground of appeal, and refers the matter back to the cour d'appel, Poitiers.

Notes

(1) R. Rodière's Note on this case states (in part):

The press has done this judgment the honour of devoting attention to it. The owner of a horse is awarded damages for his hurt against those responsible for killing the animal— that is indeed something unusual enough to be worth recounting and a great outcry may be expected!

1. First of all, there are the moralists, who will compare this compassion with the parents' of the animal with the indifference of public opinion to the violence which we witness daily and who will think that the immunity granted to some is not offset by the award of damages against those who, without wishing to do so, have run over 'Mummy's little dog'. A facile subject.

The pedants, imitating Rabelais who satirised the period in which he lived, will recall all the historic examples of disproportionate love for animals and will not fail to mention the horse Incitatus which Caligula wished to appoint as Consul, adding that Caligula did not exactly serve as a model of mental equilibrium.

Lovers of quotations, drawing a moral from the case, will recall two verses by Victor Hugo in 'Les Contemplations':

'Les bêtes sont au Bon Dieu,
  Mais la bêtise est à l'homme',

without specifying to whom the second line refers.

Finally, lawyers will compare this decision with those which withhold any compensation from a fiancée overcome by the death of her loved one on the ground that she had no 'blood relationship or relationship by marriage' with him, and will irreverently ask the Cour de cassation what exactly is the relationship by blood or marriage between the deceased horse and its master …

Anticipating all these ironical comments, the undersigned thought that this judgment needed at least a 'Devil's advocate'. He took the risk, with his lawyer's hat on, of course, and he will respond to the criticisms. In truth, the result is not very conducive to the continuing reliability of the case-law of the Civil Chamber.

2. Indeed, it is only possible to defend the judgment if the Civil Chamber abandons the solution which it has so far accepted in regard to proceedings by fiancé(e)s. It is necessary to refer specifically to the 'Civil Chamber' since we know that the Criminal Chamber 'requires no relationship by blood or marriage', which enables it to uphold actions by fiancé(e)s (Crim 5 January 1956, D 1956, 216) and those by foster parents (Crim 30 January 1958, Gaz Pal 1958.1.367).

The refusal to grant compensation to those who were not related by blood or marriage to the deceased is even less comprehensible in view of the fact that, in matters of contract, redress for nonmaterial damage is quite usual, even though examples in the courts are not numerous.

Article 1382 [now Article 1240] requires any person who, by his fault, has caused damage to redress the same.

The courts must of course display circumspection and allow themselves to be convinced only on the basis of extensive evidence (R Rodière, Responsabilité civile, No 161 1) but a priori there is no obstacle. Any profound and real pain deserves compassion and the assistance that judges can bring may consist in making the order for financial compensation requested of them by the plaintiff. Why, then, not take account of the pain caused by the death of a horse, a tom cat or a parrot if its 'parents' were overcome by it …

The Devil's advocate rests his case. No need to say whether he himself is convinced.

(2) The notion of *prejudice moral* is a broad one, which goes as far as indemnifying the *prejudice d'affection*, including the harm suffered by the loss of an animal. This is criticised: 'Why should not an ecologist be able to obtain reparation for the mental suffering he is experiencing by losing the tree he loved? (…) *Prejudice moral* is the Pandora's box of tort law. The judges limit the expansion by repairing it only poorly'.[97]

---

[97] Malaurie et al (n 41 above) no. 248.

Court of Appeal   **26.31 (EN)**

Jarvis v Swans Tours[98]

Damages for mental distress (disappointment) can be recovered for a breach of contract where the purpose of the contract is to provide entertainment and enjoyment.

Facts: A solicitor booked a skiing holiday on the basis of a description in a brochure. The holiday failed to live up to the attractive terms in which it had been described.

Held: Overturning the first instance decision, the Court of Appeal awarded the plaintiff damages for mental distress and loss of enjoyment.

Judgment: LORD DENNING MR: … What is the legal position? I think that the statements in the brochure were representations or warranties. The breaches of them give Mr. Jarvis a right to damages. It is not necessary to decide whether they were representations or warranties: because since the Misrepresentation Act 1967, there is a remedy in damages for misrepresentation as well as for breach of warranty.

The one question in the case is: What is the amount of damages? The judge seems to have taken the difference in value between what he paid for and what he got. He said that he intended to give 'the difference between the two values and no other damages' under any other head. He thought that Mr. Jarvis had got half of what he paid for. So the judge gave him half the amount which he had paid, namely, £31.72. Mr. Jarvis appeals to this court. He says that the damages ought to have been much more.

What is the right way of assessing damages? It has often been said that on a breach of contract damages cannot be given for mental distress. Thus in Hamlin v Great Northern Railway Co (1856) 1 H & N 408, 411 Pollock CB said that damages cannot be given 'for the disappointment of mind occasioned by the breach of contract'. and in *Hobbs v London & South Western Railway Co* (1875) LR 10 QB 111, 122, Mellor J said that

> 'for the mere inconvenience, such as annoyance and loss of temper, or vexation, or for being disappointed in a particular thing which you have set your mind upon, without real physical inconvenience resulting, you cannot recover damages.'

The courts in those days only allowed the plaintiff to recover damages if he suffered physical inconvenience, such as having to walk five miles home, as in Hobbs' case; or to live in an over-crowded house, *Bailey v Bullock* [1950] 2 All ER 1167.

I think that those limitations are out of date. In a proper case damages for mental distress can be recovered in contract, just as damages for shock can be recovered in tort. One such case is a contract for a holiday, or any other contract to provide entertainment and enjoyment. If the contracting party breaks his contract, damages can be given for the disappointment, the distress, the upset and frustration caused by the breach. I know that it is difficult to assess in terms of money, but it is no more difficult than the assessment which the courts have to make every day in personal injury cases for loss of amenities. Take the present case. Mr. Jarvis has only a fortnight's holiday in the year. He books it far ahead, and looks forward to it all that time. He ought to be compensated for the loss of it.

A good illustration was given by Edmund Davies LJ in the course of the argument. He put the case of a man who has taken a ticket for Glyndebourne. It is the only night on which he can get there. He hires a car to take him. The car does not turn up. His damages

---

[98] [1973] QB 233.

are not limited to the mere cost of the ticket. He is entitled to general damages for the disappointment he has suffered and the loss of the entertainment which he should have had. Here, Mr. Jarvis's fortnight's winter holiday has been a grave disappointment. It is true that he was conveyed to Switzerland and back and had meals and bed in the hotel. But that is not what he went for. He went to enjoy himself with all the facilities which the defendants said he would have. He is entitled to damages for the lack of those facilities, and for his loss of enjoyment.

... I think the damages in this case should be the sum of £125. I would allow the appeal, accordingly.

Notes

(1) This was the first English case in which damages for disappointment were awarded in contract. It was followed by others in which similar 'moral damage' was recovered. For example, in *Heywood v Wellers*[99] a woman employed solicitors to obtain an injunction to prevent a man molesting her. The solicitors failed to take proper steps and the molestation continued. She was awarded damages for mental distress.

(2) In *Heywood* James LJ suggested[100] that damages for distress could be awarded whenever distress was a foreseeable consequence of the breach. However, in *Watts v Morrow*[101] this broad approach was rejected and it was said that, in contract, damages for disappointment or distress are recoverable only if the purpose of the contract was to provide enjoyment or peace of mind. In that case the plaintiffs bought a house in the country relying on a survey prepared by the defendant. The survey report had been prepared negligently and failed to reveal the need for major repairs. The trial judge included in the damages £8,000 for 'distress and inconvenience'. The Court of Appeal disallowed this, though it allowed £1,500 for 'physical discomfort'. Bingham LJ said:[102]

A contract-breaker is not in general liable for any distress, frustration, anxiety, displeasure, vexation, tension or aggravation which his breach of contract may cause to the innocent party. This rule is not, I think, founded on the assumption that such reactions are not foreseeable, which they surely are or may be, but on considerations of policy.

But the rule is not absolute. Where the very object of a contract is to provide pleasure, relaxation, peace of mind or freedom from molestation, damages will be awarded if the fruit of the contract is not provided or if the contrary result is procured instead. If the law did not cater for this exceptional category of case it would be defective. A contract to survey the condition of a house for a prospective purchaser does not, however, fall within this exceptional category.

In cases not falling within this exceptional category, damages are in my view recoverable for physical inconvenience and discomfort caused by the breach and mental suffering directly related to that inconvenience and discomfort. If those effects are foreseeably suffered during a period when defects are repaired I am prepared to accept that they sound in damages even

---

[99] [1976] QB 446 (CA).
[100] ibid, 461.
[101] [1991] 1 WLR 1421 (CA). See also *Farley v Skinner* [2001] UKHL 49, [2002] 2 AC 732.
[102] [1991] 1 WLR 1421, 1445.

though the cost of the repairs is not recoverable as such. But I also agree that awards should be restrained, and that the awards in this case far exceeded a reasonable award for the injury shown to have been suffered.

(3) Compare, however, the case of *Ruxley v Forsyth*.[103] This was a contract to build a swimming pool; the pool was less deep than the contract required though it was perfectly adequate for swimming and diving. The House of Lords seemed to accept that a similar award for 'loss of amenity', which must mean loss of enjoyment, as there was no physical inconvenience to the owner, was proper, though strictly speaking this was obiter, as the trial judge's award of £2,500 for loss of amenity was not appealed: see the last words of Lord Jauncey's speech.[104] This suggests that the courts may now be ready to find that a contract was intended to provide enjoyment as well as its primary purpose of providing work or goods.[105]

BGB **26.32 (DE)**

§ 253: Intangible damage
(1) For an injury which is not an injury to patrimony (*Vermögen*), compensation in money may be demanded only as provided by law.
...

Note

§ 253(1) BGB seems to imply that damages for non-patrimonial loss can only be awarded if there is specific statutory authorisation. However, German courts in fact allowed compensation in 'holiday' cases, similar to *Jarvis v Swan's Tours*,[106] by treating the plaintiff as having a patrimonial right to his holiday entitlement, and by holding that this right had been destroyed by the bad holiday.[107] The matter is now covered by a specific legislative provision.

BGB **26.33 (DE)**

§ 651f: Damages
(1) Notwithstanding any reduction of price or notice of termination, the traveller may demand damages for nonperformance unless the defect in the travel package resulted from a circumstance for which the travel organiser is not responsible. (2) If the travel package is made impossible or significantly impaired, then the traveller may also demand appropriate compensation in money for holiday leave spent to no avail.

---

[103] 23.19 (EN), above, p 923.
[104] See above, p 925.
[105] However, it is doubtful whether an employee who has been unfairly (but not wrongfully) dismissed can recover damages for humiliation or distress. The House of Lords held that in an unfair dismissal claim an employee cannot recover compensation for non-economic or non-pecuniary loss, such as distress, humiliation or loss of reputation: *Dunnachie v Kingston upon Hull City Council* [2004] UKHL 36, [2005] 1 AC 226 (interpreting s 123 of the Employment Rights Act 1996).
[106] 26.31 (EN), above, 1096.
[107] See BGH 10 December 1974, BGHZ 63, 98.

> *Note*
>
> Commentators agree that the parties can set aside the rule in § 253(1) BGB by agreement,[108] for example through inserting an agreed damages clause into their contract. Thus under German law the plaintiff in a case like *Heywood v Wellers* would be able to recover damages if she could show that the protection of her peace of mind was a purpose of her contract (*Schutzzweck des Vertrages*) with the lawyer.[109]

Court of Justice, 12 March 2002[109a] **26.34 (EU)**

Simone Leitner v TUI Deutschland GmbH & Co KG

Facts: The family of Simone Leitner, who was 10 at the time, booked a package holiday (all-inclusive stay) with TUI at the Pamfiliya Robinson club in Turkey for a fortnight in the summer of 1997, where they spent the entire holiday and they took all their meals. About a week after the start of the holiday, Simone Leitner showed symptoms of Salmonella poisoning. The poisoning was attributable to the food offered in the club. Her parents had to look after her until the end of the holiday. Many other guests in the club also fell ill with the same illness and presented the same symptoms. Two to three weeks after the end of the holiday a letter of complaint concerning Simone Leitner's illness was sent to TUI. Since no reply to that letter was received, Simone Leitner, through her parents, brought an action for damages in the sum of ATS 25,000. The court of first instance awarded the claimant only ATS 13,000 for the physical pain and suffering (*Schmerzensgeld*) caused by the food poisoning and dismissed the remainder of the application, which was for compensation for the non-material damage caused by loss of enjoyment of the holidays (*entgangene Urlaubsfreude*). That court considered that, if the feelings of dissatisfaction and negative impressions caused by disappointment must be categorised, under Austrian law, as non-material damage, they cannot give rise to compensation because there is no express provision in any Austrian law for compensation for non-material damage of that kind. The claimant appealed to the Landesgericht Linz, which concurs with the court of first instance so far as regards Austrian law, but considers that application of Article 5 of the Directive could lead to a different outcome and asks a preliminary ruling.

Held: Article 5 of Council Directive 90/314/EEC of 13 June 1990 on package travel, package holidays and package tours is to be interpreted as conferring, in principle, on consumers a right to compensation for non-material damage resulting from the non-performance or improper performance of the services constituting a package holiday.

Judgment: ...

14. By its question the national court seeks to ascertain whether Article 5 of the Directive must be interpreted as conferring, in principle, on consumers a right to compensation for non-material damage resulting from failure to perform or the improper performance of the obligations inherent in the provision of package travel. ...

19. The first subparagraph of Article 5(2) of the Directive requires the Member States to take the necessary steps to ensure that the holiday organiser compensates the damage resulting for the consumer from the failure to perform or the improper performance of the contract.

20. In that regard, it is clear from the second and third recitals in the preamble to the Directive that it is the purpose of the Directive to eliminate the disparities between the national laws and practices of the various Member States in the area of package holidays which are liable to give rise to distortions of competition between operators established in different Member States.

[108] BGH 12 July 1955, JZ 1955, 581.
[109] See Lange (n 63 above) 238.
[109a] Case C-168/00, ECLI:EU:C:2002:163.

21. It is not in dispute that, in the field of package holidays, the existence in some Member States but not in others of an obligation to provide compensation for non-material damage would cause significant distortions of competition, given that, as the Commission has pointed out, non-material damage is a frequent occurrence in that field.

22. Furthermore, the Directive, and in particular Article 5 thereof, is designed to offer protection to consumers and, in connection with tourist holidays, compensation for non-material damage arising from the loss of enjoyment of the holiday is of particular importance to consumers.

23. It is in light of those considerations that Article 5 of the Directive is to be interpreted. Although the first subparagraph of Article 5(2) merely refers in a general manner to the concept of damage, the fact that the fourth subparagraph of Article 5(2) provides that Member States may, in the matter of damage other than personal injury, allow compensation to be limited under the contract provided that such limitation is not unreasonable, means that the Directive implicitly recognises the existence of a right to compensation for damage other than personal injury, including non-material damage.

24. The answer to be given to the question referred must therefore be that Article 5 of the Directive is to be interpreted as conferring, in principle, on consumers a right to compensation for non-material damage resulting from the non-performance or improper performance of the services constituting a package holiday.

> *Note*
>
> Council Directive 90/314/EEC on package travel, package holidays and package tours[110] imposes on Member States the obligation to regulate contracts for these services, and to provide for liability in cases of personal injury. Compensation for other losses, including disappointment over spoiled holidays, may, however, be subject to reasonable limitation in the holiday contract.

Though French law is the only one of the three to offer compensation for *préjudice moral* whenever it is a foreseeable consequence of the non-performance, English and German law seem each to be moving towards allowing recovery of this kind of loss. The PECL allow recovery for 'non-pecuniary loss' (Article 9:501(2)(a)); the UNIDROIT PICC state that a party is entitled to full compensation for harm and that 'such harm may be non-pecuniary and includes, for instance, physical suffering and emotional distress' (Article 7.4.2(2)). The Comments to Article 7.4.2 do not give disappointment as an example of such loss, but it should be remembered that the UNIDROIT PICC are for international commercial contracts in which personal disappointment or distress is less likely to occur.

26.5 SOME TYPICAL CASES

In this section we look at how the three systems deal with two 'typical cases' situations that arise commonly in practice. These are where a seller fails to deliver goods and

---

[110] OJ L 158/1990, p 59.

where a debtor fails to carry out a contract for work or services correctly. A third situation, where a seller delivers goods that do not conform to the contract, is covered in Chapter 27.

26.5.A A SELLER OF GOODS FAILS TO DELIVER

Code civil **26.35 (FR)**

Article 1222: Having given notice to perform, a creditor may also himself, within a reasonable time and at a reasonable cost, have an obligation performed or, with the prior authorisation of the court, may have something which has been done in breach of an obligation destroyed. He may claim reimbursement of sums of money employed for this purpose from the debtor.

He may also bring proceedings in order to require the debtor to advance a sum necessary for this performance or destruction.

Notes:

(1) When the seller fails to deliver, a buyer may enter into another sale with a third party to replace the sale concluded with the first seller. If the contract price of the second sale is higher than the first, the buyer may claim reimbursement of the extra sums from the first seller. Article 1222 modifies former Article 1144 which required the authorisation of the judge. Now, the replacement can be a unilateral action by the buyer.

(2) Article 1222 is part of the section of the Code civil on specific performance (for a more detailed analysis, see Chapter 23).

Sale of Goods Act 1979 **26.36 (EN)**

Section 51: (1) Where the seller wrongfully neglects or refuses to deliver the goods to the buyer, the buyer may maintain an action against the seller for damages for non-delivery.

(2) The measure of damages is the estimated loss directly and naturally resulting, in the ordinary course of events from the seller's breach of contract.

(3) Where there is an available market for the goods in question the measure of damages is prima facie to be ascertained by the difference between the contract price and the market or current price of the goods at the time or times when they ought to have been delivered or (if no time was fixed) at the time of refusal to deliver.

BGB **26.37 (DE)**

§ 252: Lost profits

The compensation shall also include lost profits. Profit is deemed to have been lost which could probably have been expected in the ordinary course of events, or according to the special circumstances, especially in the light of the preparations and arrangements made.

§ 376: (1)[111] ...

(2) If the payment of damages for non-performance is demanded and the goods have a stock exchange or market price, the difference between the purchase price and the exchange or market price at the time and place of the performance owed may be demanded.

(3) The proceeds of a sale or purchase effected in a different way may, when the goods have a stock exchange or market price, be adopted as a basis of a claim for damages, only when the purchase or sale takes place immediately after the expiration of the stipulated time or period fixed for the performance. The sale or purchase, if not made by public auction, must be carried out at the current price by a commercial broker officially licensed for such sales or by a person who is an officially licensed auctioneer.

Notes

(1) Under the general law of sale in Germany, where the seller fails to deliver, the buyer may seek to enforce either the concrete or the abstract measure of damages. Under the concrete measure, the buyer will recover the difference between the cost of an actual cover purchase undertaken and the contract price. Where a cover purchase was not possible, he may recover the difference between the contract price and the price he would have obtained from selling the goods on to another party. Under the abstract measure, the buyer may recover the difference between the market price of the goods—known as the price of a hypothetical cover purchase—and the contract price. Alternatively he may claim the difference between the contract price and the market price of the goods had he been able to resell them—known as a hypothetical further sale. In both cases it is obvious that where the cover purchase price, the market price or the further sale price was below the actual contract price no damages are recoverable—for non-performance at least.

(2) An abstract calculation of damages amounts normally, in effect, to a lightening of the burden of proving loss which lies upon the creditor—here the seller. Thus, if the loss would have been caused in the normal course of events, it will be assumed that it was so caused in the particular case (see § 252, sentence 2 BGB). However, it is always open to the debtor to prove that the case did not involve a 'normal course of events'. Indeed, it is argued that, where the buyer is not in business, the abstract measure is not applicable at all since in these and related cases the seller will be able to prove that a further sale, for example, was improbable in the normal course of events.[112]

(3) The effect of § 376 HGB is to allow the seller or buyer, in the case of a commercial sale of goods, to claim damages where there is a delay in performance for which the other party is responsible. In such cases an abstract measure of damages is privileged over a concrete assessment by forcing the buyer to undertake a cover purchase immediately. It is in fact agreed that, whereas the abstract assessment in

---

[111] See 25.14 (DE), above, p 1012.
[112] cf, for English law, *Treitel* (n 59 above) 111–15, para 102.

ordinary sales cases is merely a rebuttable presumption, easing the buyer's burden of proof, as to the measure of damages, the principle for calculation laid down in § 376(2) HGB is an irrebuttable rule of law.[113]

When in French law the buyer/creditor is authorised to buy for himself the goods that the seller/debtor has failed to deliver, he will recover the actual cost of so doing—subject to it being shown that he acted in bad faith.

English law refers only to an 'abstract' method. The difference seems to depend on how the concrete measures are applied in practice. The English lawyer would defend the abstract principle by saying that if the buyer has paid more than the current market price for the replacement goods, he has not acted reasonably. If he has managed to get them for less, this is a profitable deal he would have been able to make anyway, so that he should keep any profit.

The international restatements provide both concrete and abstract methods.

Principles of European Contract Law **26.39 (INT)**

Article 9:506: Substitute Transaction

Where the aggrieved party has terminated the contract and has made a substitute transaction within a reasonable time and in a reasonable manner, it may recover the difference between the contract price and the price of the substitute transaction as well as damages for any further loss so far as these are recoverable under this Section.

Article 9:507: Current Price

Where the aggrieved party has terminated the contract and has not made a substitute transaction but there is a current price for the performance contracted for, it may recover the difference between the contract price and the price current at the time the contract is terminated as well as damages for any further loss so far as these are recoverable under this Section.

26.5.B A DEBTOR FAILS TO CARRY OUT WORK CORRECTLY

Under a contract for work, such as a building contract, suppose that the contractor does some of the work defectively and refuses to put the defect right. What remedy will the employer have? In the continental systems, one possibility is that the contractor will be ordered to do the work; another, that the employer can have the work done at the contractor's expense.[114] English law will not normally grant specific performance of a building contract;[115] rather, the normal remedy will be for the employer to engage another contractor to do the necessary work and to recover the cost from the defaulter in an action for damages. We have already pointed out that this is the functional equivalent of *exécution par un tiers*.[116]

---

[113] See Lange (n 63 above) 221.
[114] For these possibilities, see above, pp 913 ff.
[115] For this and an exception, see above, p 917.
[116] ibid.

However, what if the defect is not of great significance and repair would cost a disproportionate amount? We encountered this problem earlier, in Chapter 23 (Specific performance).[117] We considered three cases. One was a French case (Cass civ (3) 17 January 1984)[118] in which the cour d'appel had refused to give an order that a contractor should increase the number of the steps in a swimming pool from three to four, on the ground that it had not been shown that access with only three steps was more difficult. The Cour de cassation quashed the decision on the basis that, in deciding this without considering whether it was possible to make the pool conform to the contract, there was no legal basis for the decision. However, we pointed out that the courts should no longer take such a strict approach as the recent reform of contract law prevents a creditor to obtain specific performance if there is if 'there is a manifest disproportion between its cost to the debtor and its interest for the creditor' (Article 1221 of the new Code civil).[119] We compared a German case on replacement windows[120] in which the BGH upheld new performance—at great expense—where a cure would be ineffective. It was stated there that a proportionality requirement applied in relation to enforced performance in German law. We also considered the English case of *Ruxley Electronics and Construction Ltd v Forsyth*,[121] in which the House of Lords refused to award damages based on the cost of rebuilding a swimming pool to the correct depth on the ground that to rebuild it would be unreasonable when the pool was perfectly useable.

What if, as in *Ruxley*, the defect is so slight that it would be unreasonable to incur the cost of correcting it—or, indeed, that the employer will not in fact spend any damages obtained on doing so? In English law the position is now fairly clear: first, if the employer will not in fact have the defect corrected, he may not recover the cost of doing so; nor can he if to do so would be unreasonable. In each case he may recover only any difference in value between the property with and without the defect and possibly damages for 'loss of amenity'.[122] What about the other systems?

Cass civ, 11 April 1918[123]   **26.40 (FR)**

Wrong kind of wood

When a defect does not affect the usefulness or outward appearance of the finished work, the court may legitimately find that the employer has suffered no loss and award no damages, even if the material used is less expensive than that specified.

Facts: A shop-fitting contractor used a different kind of wood to that specified for furniture for a shop in Cairo. The usefulness and outward appearance of the finished furniture were not affected. The employer sought *résolution* of the contract and damages.

---

[117] See above, p 856.
[118] No. 82-15982, RTD civ 1984, 711, annotated by J Mestre. See 23.20 (FR), above, p 927.
[119] See ch 23.
[120] BGH 10 October 1985, BGHZ 96, 111. See 23.18 (DE), above, p 920.
[121] [1996] AC 344. See 23.19 (EN), above, p 923.
[122] See above, p 1098.
[123] S 1918.1.171.

Held: The Tribunal Consulaire in Cairo refused to grant the employer *résolution* and, though it held that the contract had been broken, refused damages on the ground that there was no loss.

Judgment: ... THE COURT: *On the first ground of appeal:*—Whereas from the introductory part and the grounds of the contested judgment, it appears that Francès brought an action against Collin and Courcier before the Tribunal Consulaire de France in Cairo for the cancellation of agreements concluded between them on 18 June and 12 July 1913 for the supply of furniture intended for the plaintiff's shops in Cairo, alleging in particular incomplete or incorrect compliance with the conditions laid down in the contract;

— Whereas the contested judgment, both adopting the grounds set out by the lower court and setting out its own grounds, examines the three complaints successively, and declares as follows:

1. The substitution of white Trieste pine for Swedish pine involves a significant price difference, but both woods can serve more or less the same purpose in the fitting out of a shop.

2. Although, according to the specification, the front of the furniture was to be of waxed oak and the interior of Swedish wood, the use of oak on only part of the external front side and Swedish wood inside was in conformity with cabinet-making usage, and a well-made veneer serves just as well as solid oak.

3. The bottom of the furniture was of the agreed thickness, and Collin and Courcier could not be criticised for reducing the thickness of the shelves by 0.02 mm; hence, the judgment concludes that Francès's complaints, of a secondary nature, did not relate to the essential qualities of solidity and elegance of the furniture sold, and could not there-fore entail rescission, but only the award of damages;

— Whereas where a synallagmatic contract contains no express cancellation clause, it is for the courts to decide, in the event of partial non-performance and having regard to the factual circumstances, whether such non-performance is so significant that cancella-tion must be declared immediately or whether it might not be sufficiently remedied by an order awarding damages; that power of appraisal is absolute;

— Whereas consequently, the contested judgment, which did not, as wrongly alleged in the appeal, substitute new stipulations for those of the actual agreement, falls outside the scope of the Court of Cassation's review; *On the third appeal ground:*—Whereas the appeal alleges finally that the contested judgment is vitiated by a contradiction in its grounds, because after recognising, as did the judgment which it upheld, the wrongful acts and negligence of which Collin and Courcier were guilty, it refused to grant Francès any right to damages, on the pretext that he did not suffer any loss;

— Whereas however, the only grounds taken over from the earlier decision are those which are not contrary to those of the judgment itself; the latter holds that, from all the facts, it is apparent that Francès had no grounds for complaining against the other par-ties, that he suffered no loss because of them, that the discount on the agreed prices will-ingly offered by Collin and Courcier constitutes adequate reparation, and that accordingly it is inappropriate to award higher damages;

— Whereas the finding as to the existence, extent or absence of loss falls within the absolutely unfettered powers of the trial court, and therefore the ground of appeal can-not be upheld;

— Whereas it thus follows that, by reaching the decision which it contains, the con-tested judgment did not infringe any of the articles referred to in the appeal;

The Court dismisses the appeal brought against the judgment delivered by the cour d'Aix, on 19 January 1916, etc.

§ 633: Defects as to quality and defects of title

(1) The contractor must procure the work for the customer free of defects as to quality and defects in title.

(2) The work is free of defects as to quality if it is of the agreed quality. In so far as the quality is not agreed, the work is free of defects as to quality

    1. if it is fit for the use required by the contract,

    2. otherwise for the usual use and is of a quality which is usual in work of a similar kind and which may be expected by the customer according to the kind of work.

If the contractor produces work different from the work ordered or work of a lesser amount than that ordered, that is equivalent to a defect as to quality.

(3) The work is free of defects in title if third persons cannot assert against the customer any rights in relation to the work or can assert only such rights as are assumed in the contract.

§ 634: Customer's rights in the case of defects

Where the requirements of the following provisions are satisfied and except as otherwise provided, if the work is defective, the customer may

    1. demand supplementary performance under § 635,

    2. remove the defect himself and demand reimbursement of the necessary expenditure under § 637;

    3. terminate the contract under §§ 636, 323 and 326(5) or reduce the remuneration under § 638; and

    4. claim compensation under §§ 636, 280, 281, 283 and 311a or reimbursement of wasted expenditure under § 284.

§ 637: Self-help

(1) If there is a defect if the work, the customer may remove the defect himself after the expiry to no avail of a reasonable period fixed by him for supplementary performance and claim reimbursement for the necessary expenditure, unless the contractor rightly refuses supplementary performance.

(2) § 323(2) applies mutatis mutandis. Nor does a period have to be fixed if supplementary performance has been unsuccessful or is unreasonable for the customer. (3) The customer may claim from the contractor advance payment of expenditure necessary to remove the defect.

Notes

(1) Thus the French courts seem to refuse to refuse to award damages when the goods delivered or materials used are just as good as those required by the contract.

(2) In German law, if the completed work is not in accordance with the contract requirements, this probably amounts to a defect within § 633(1) BGB, even where the nonconformity does not reduce the value of the work or its usefulness for purposes to which it would ordinarily be put or which were envisaged in the contract. Thus it seems that in German law the creditor will be entitled to have the work re-done at the debtor's expense under § 637 BGB or, provided the debtor was responsible, to damages under §§ 634(4) and 281 BGB for the cost of having the work

done again, at least if the creditor genuinely intended to have the non-conformity corrected. Possibly the creditor's right will be limited by the principle of good faith, but it has been said that in such cases the rights contained in §§ 634, 637 BGB— ie including the right to damages—will be limited by the principle of good faith only in 'extremely exceptional cases'.[124] Whether a German court would use this to decide a case with the same facts as the *Ruxley* case in the same way as the House of Lords did must be doubted: see further Note (6) below.

(3) Apart from cases where a promised quality is absent, unless the defect is trivial (§ 281(1), last sentence), the employer can, as an alternative to using self-help under § 673, reject the work, refuse to pay the remuneration—or demand repayment if it has already been paid—and seek damages for the loss sustained—the 'greater' damages claim. Alternatively the employer can retain the work and seek damages only for the reduction in the value of the work—the 'lesser' damages claim. In this case the amount of damages can be set off against the contractor's claim for remuneration.

(4) Neither a claim under § 637 nor a damages claim under § 634 BGB is subject to the 'disproportionality' restriction imposed upon the right to a cure by § 635(3) BGB.[125]

(5) Damages for non-performance recoverable under § 634(2) BGB may be calculated by reference to:

— the loss of profit of the employer;
— the reduction in the market value of the work (*merkantiler Minderwert*);
— the cost to the creditor of removing the defect.

(6) In relation to the last-mentioned means of calculating damages, in principle, the 'subjective' value, including the cost of securing conformity with the contract and not simply the difference in value, is to be paid. The decision of the English Court of Appeal in *Ruxley Electronics & Construction v Forsyth*—it will be recalled that the Court of Appeal had allowed the employer the cost of rebuilding the pool to the correct depth[126]—has been used to illustrate precisely this point of German law.[127]

(7) It is even the case that the employer will recover the cost of doing the work even though he has no intention of doing it.[128] In a number of tort cases it has been held that the owner of a car which has been damaged in an accident caused by the defendant's fault may recover the cost of hiring another car while his is being repaired even though he does not in fact hire a replacement.[129] The principle seems to be that what individuals do with their money/patrimony is their own business (*Privatautonomie*).

(8) By contrast, there is a personal injury case[130] in which the opposite result was reached. The plaintiff was left with scars after an accident. She was unable to recover

---

[124] See Münchener Kommentar/Busche § 636 para 9.
[125] Münchener Kommentar/Busche § 635 para 32.
[126] See above, p 932.
[127] See Schlechtriem and Schmidt-Kessel (n 14 above) para 206.
[128] See BGH 24 May 1973, BGHZ 61, 28; BGH 16 May 1974, BGHZ 62, 323.
[129] eg BGH 30 September 1963, BGHZ 40, 345; BGH 15 April 1966, BGHZ 45, 212 and other cases cited in Markesinis et al (n 9 above) 484.
[130] BGH 14 January 1986, BGHZ 97, 14; see Markesinis et al (n 9 above) 482.

the cost of an operation to remove the scars unless she had the operation. The BGH treated the personal injury as essentially and irreducibly injury to a different legal value (*Rechtsgut* or physical integrity or health). Damages compensate directly for this injury, for example, pain and suffering (*Schmerzensgeld*) (even for loss of earnings) and also money for an operation, but only if it is going to be used to restore the primary *Rechtsgut*, ie having a scarred face does not per se amount to being poorer, by contrast with having a scratched car.

Thus, on the one hand, English and French law seem to refuse the full cost of repair when this is greater than the loss of use or value of the property to the employer—at least if the employer does not in fact carry out the repair and probably also if it would be unreasonable to do so because the cost would be disproportionate to the benefits to be obtained. German law, on the other hand, seems prepared to award the full cost of repair in all cases. The international restatements do not address the question.

26.6 PLAINTIFF'S LOSS OR DEFENDANT'S GAIN

The cases in which work has been done incorrectly raise the possibility that, by breaking the contract, the defendant may make savings, or a profit, exceeding any loss to the plaintiff—though this does not seem to have been the situation in the *Ruxley* case. We encountered the question in the French case about the contractor who used a cheaper kind of wood than had been specified to complete the contract,[131] but there the contractor seems to have offered to pay the employer the amount saved. In principle, damages are to compensate for loss, so recovery of any additional profit or any savings made by the debtor would have to be by way of restitution.[132] But occasionally cases seem to award damages where the loss is at best notional. We saw one example earlier: the French case in which the court awarded damages for breach of a contract not to do something, even though there seemed to be no harm to the creditor.[133]

OLG Braunschweig, 26 January 1891[134] **26.42 (DE)**

The bread rolls

Where a party receives goods that are worth less than they should have been he may recover damages even though he sells the goods for the same price for which he would have sold conforming goods.

---

[131] 26.40 (FR), above, p 1104.
[132] See *Treitel* (n 59 above) 76–77, para 76.
[133] Above, p 928.
[134] Seuff A 46 no. 173.

Facts: A baker received quantities of dough from a bread dealer, to make into rolls for the customer. The baker kept some of the dough for himself but made the correct number of rolls, though they were smaller than they should have been. The bread dealer did not notice and re-sold the rolls for the normal price to his customers. He later claimed damages.

Held: The baker was liable.

Judgment: The plaintiff, a bread dealer, had had a business relationship with the defendant, a baker, in the context of which he had dough delivered daily to the defendant in containers and baked by the defendant. It was established by the evidence of a number of witnesses that for the whole of this period, if not daily very frequently, the baker removed quantities of the dough delivered to him of up to five pounds and more to the value of 10 Marks to the pound and kept them for himself. Since the defendant was unsuccessful in his testimony that this procedure was based on an arrangement, he was ordered to pay damages and the plaintiff was requested to give sworn testimony of the estimate of his losses. At second instance the defendant went on to raise the plea that the action of damages should be struck out because the plaintiff had in reality not suffered any damage as a result of removal of the relevant quantities of bread dough on the ground that the bread rolls made for him by the defendant had always been sold at the full price, in spite of the reduction of the raw material delivered for that purpose. That objection was turned down.

Just as the defendant undoubtedly enriched himself by the unlawful taking of those quantities for his own use by the value thereof, to the same extent was the plaintiff harmed by the fact that instead of the full number of bread rolls of full weight either a lesser quantity of bread rolls or rolls below full weight were delivered to him. It is irrelevant to the question of the occurrence of damage and the defendant's obligation to pay damages that the damage caused is imperceptible or subsequently balanced out on other grounds beyond the defendant's control—including the assertions made by him apparently at random and unsupported by evidence. Whilst the defendant's liability in damages is founded solely in the principles of the contract for the hire of services, which the court of first instance took sole cognisance of, there is no doubt concerning such liability under the principles of *condictio furtiva* the preconditions of which are all satisfied. For, according to these principles, the claim of the injured party is first to the return of the thing alienated together with all accessory rights or, if this is not possible, to its pecuniary value, even if a claim in respect of other damage may be made in addition (fr 3 S 13 de cond furt 18.1; fr 29 rer amot 25.2), without the plaintiff being obliged to prove, understandably, particularly to the defendant, that, had the items in question not been removed he would have had use of them according to their value, or to prove that he suffered loss and, it so, the extent thereof, by removal of the items.

Notes

(1) This case predates the introduction of the BGB in 1901 and so was decided in accordance with the *ius commune* or *gemeines Recht*.

(2) In a similar case a brewer had wasted several vats of beer, but had made up the loss by weakening the strength of later quantities, thereby in fact making a profit for his employers beyond what could normally be expected. The Reichsgericht held him

nonetheless liable—under the terms of his contract—to pay his employers for the wasted vats. The reasoning in these cases has been explained by Lange as follows:[135]

> In the brewery and bread roll cases a harm was undoubtedly suffered. The apparently purported elimination of the loss is not held to be sufficient because the defendant should not be able to derive any advantage from a further breach of the contract tending to damage the business interests of the plaintiff even more.
>
> (3) Although the bread roll and the brewery cases involved a breach of contract, they also involved misappropriation of the plaintiff's property. The defendant is made to pay for the property even though the plaintiff does not show that he has lost by being deprived of it.

English cases with similar facts, in that in breach of contract the defendant has misused the plaintiff's property, have applied a similar rule. Thus in *Penarth Dock Engineering Co Ltd v Pounds*[136] the defendant bought a pontoon which was on the plaintiffs' land and undertook to remove it. He failed to remove it until some months after the agreed date. The defendant was required to pay the plaintiffs damages based on what he would have had to pay to rent the land, although there was no evidence that the plaintiffs would either have rented or used the land themselves. Lord Denning MR applied a principle which he had stated in the earlier case of *Strand Electric and Engineering Co Ltd v Brisford Entertainments Ltd*:[137]

> If a wrongdoer has made use of goods for his own purposes, then he must pay a reasonable hire for them, even though the owner has in fact suffered no loss. It may be that the owner would not have used the goods himself or that he had a substitute readily available which he used without extra cost to himself. Nevertheless the owner is entitled to a reasonable hire. … The claim for a hiring charge is therefore not based on loss to the plaintiff but on the fact that the defendant has used the goods for his own purposes. It is an action against him because he has had the benefit of the goods. It resembles therefore an action for restitution, rather than an action for tort.

Lord Denning seems to regard this as a form of restitution, but the other members of the Court of Appeal in the *Strand Electric* case considered the damages to be compensatory. There has been much discussion in England in recent years about whether the plaintiff can seek 'restitution' of the savings or profit.

Chancery Division   **26.43 (EN)**

Wrotham Park Estate Co v Parkside Homes[138]

Where a breach of contract amounts to an invasion of the plaintiff's property right, the defendant may be liable for damages equalling the price the claimant might have charged to release the right.

---

[135] See Lange (n 63 above) 163 n 7.
[136] [1963] 1 Lloyd's Rep 359 (QBD).
[137] [1952] 2 QB 246 (CA).
[138] [1974] 1 WLR 798.

Facts: The predecessor in title of the plaintiffs had in 1935 sold some land to a predecessor in title of the defendants, subject to a restrictive covenant restricting building to a particular layout. That covenant was duly registered under the Land Charges Act 1925. In 1971 the land was sold to the defendants, who had no actual knowledge of the restrictive covenant and proceeded to build 14 houses on the land in breach of the covenant. In early 1972 the plaintiffs, as successors in title to the benefit of the covenant, issued their writ against the defendants claiming an injunction to restrain building in breach of the covenant, and demolition of anything built in breach. The plaintiffs made no application for an interim injunction. By the time the action came on for trial in July 1973, the 14 houses had all been completed and sold to purchasers with the benefit of indemnity insurance policies.

Held: Brightman J held that the plaintiffs were indeed entitled to the benefit of the covenant and the defendants were bound by it. However, he held that he could not shut his eyes to the fact that the houses existed and it would be an unpardonable waste of much needed houses to direct that they be pulled down, so he refused to grant a mandatory injunction. However, he awarded damages based on a share of the profit made by the defendants by building the extra houses in breach of contract.

Judgment: BRIGHTMAN J. I turn to the consideration of the quantum of damages. I was asked by the parties to assess the damages myself, should the question arise, rather than to direct an inquiry. The basic rule in contract is to measure damages by that sum of money which will put the plaintiff in the same position as he would have been in if the contract had not been broken. From that basis, the defendants argue that the damages are nil or purely nominal, because the value of the Wrotham Park Estate as the plaintiffs concede is not diminished by one farthing in consequence of the construction of a road and the erection of 14 houses on the allotment site. If, therefore, the defendants submit, I refuse an injunction I ought to award no damages in lieu. That would seem, on the face of it, a result of questionable fairness on the facts of this case. Had the offending development been the erection of an advertisement hoarding in defiance of protest and writ, I apprehend (assuming my conclusions on other points to be correct) that the court would not have hesitated to grant a mandatory injunction for its removal. If, for social and economic reasons, the court does not see fit in the exercise of its discretion, to order demolition of the 14 houses, is it just that the plaintiffs should receive no compensation and that the defendants should be left in undisturbed possession of the fruits of their wrongdoing? Common sense would seem to demand a negative answer to this question. A comparable problem arose in wayleave cases where the defendant had trespassed by making use of the plaintiff's underground ways to the defendant's profit but without diminishing the value of the plaintiff's property. The plaintiff, in such cases, received damages assessed by reference to a reasonable wayleave rent. This principle was considered and extended in *Whitwham v Westminster Brymbo Coal and Coke Co* [1896] 2 Ch 538. For six years the defendant wrongfully tipped colliery waste onto the plaintiff's land. At the trial the defendant was directed to cease tipping and give up possession. The question then arose what damages should be awarded for the wrongful act done to the plaintiff during the period of the defendant's unauthorised user of the land. The official referee found that the diminution in the value of the plaintiff's land was only £200, but that the value of the plaintiff's land to the defendant in 1888 for tipping purposes for six years was some £900. It was held that the proper scale of damages was the higher sum on the ground that a trespasser should not be allowed to make use of another person's land without in some way compensating that other person for the user.

A like principle was applied by the House of Lords in a Scottish case *Watson, Laidlaw & Co Ltd v Pott, Cassels and Williamson* (1914) 31 RPC 104. A patentee elected to sue an infringer for damages rather than for an account of profits. Part of the infringement had taken place in Java. There was evidence that the patentee could not have competed successfully in that island. It was submitted that no damages ought to be awarded in respect of the Java infringement. Lord Shaw said, at pp. 119–120:

'It is at this stage of the case, ... that a second principle comes into play. It is not exactly the principle of restoration, either directly or expressed through compensation, but it is the principle underlying price or hire. It plainly extends—and I am inclined to think not infrequently extends—to patent cases. But, indeed, it is not confined to them. For wherever an abstraction or invasion of property has occurred, then, unless such abstraction or invasion were to be sanctioned by law, the law ought to yield a recompense under the category or principle, as I say, either of price or of hire. If A, being a liveryman, keeps his horse standing idle in the stable, and B, against his wish or without his knowledge, rides or drives it out, it is no answer to A for B to say: 'Against what loss do you want to be restored? I restore the horse. There is no loss. The horse is none the worse; it is the better for the exercise.' I confess to your Lordships that this seems to me to be precisely in principle the kind of question and retort which underlay the argument of the learned counsel for the appellants about the Java trade. ... in such cases it appears to me that the correct and full measure is only reached by adding that a patentee is also entitled, on the principle of price or hire, to a royalty for the unauthorised sale or use of every one of the infringing machines in a market which the infringer, if left to himself, might not have reached. Otherwise, that property which consists in the monopoly of the patented articles granted to the patentee has been invaded, and indeed abstracted, and the law, when appealed to, would be standing by and allowing the invader or abstractor to go free.'

The same principle was applied in detinue in *Strand Electric and Engineering Co Ltd v Brisford Entertainments Ltd* [1952] 2 QB 246 ...

The point was further considered in *Penarth Dock Engineering Co Ltd v Pounds* ...

The facts of the cases I have mentioned are a long way from the facts of the case before me. Should I, as invited by the plaintiffs, apply a like principle to a case where the defendant Parkside, in defiance of protest and writ, has invaded the plaintiffs' rights in order to reap a financial profit for itself? In *Leeds Industrial Co-operative Society Ltd v Slack* [1924] AC 851 Lord Sumner said, at p 870:

'... no money awarded in substitution can be justly awarded, unless it is at any rate designed to be a preferable equivalent for an injunction and therefore an adequate substitute for it, ...'

This was said in a dissenting speech but his dissent did not arise in the context of that observation.

In the present case I am faced with the problem what damages ought to be awarded to the plaintiffs in the place of mandatory injunctions which would have restored the plaintiffs' rights. If the plaintiffs are merely given a nominal sum, or no sum, in substitution for injunctions, ii seems to me that justice will manifestly not have been done.

As I have said, the general rule would be to measure damages by reference to that sum which would place the plaintiffs in the same position as if the covenant had not been broken. Parkside and the individual purchasers could have avoided breaking the covenant in two ways. One course would have been not to develop the allotment site. The other course would have been for Parkside to have sought from the plaintiffs a relaxation of the covenant. On the facts of this particular case the plaintiffs, rightly conscious of their obligations towards existing resident, would clearly not have granted any relaxation, but for present purposes I must assume that it could have been induced to do so. In my judgment a just substitute for a mandatory injunction would be such a sum of money as might reasonably have been demanded by the plaintiffs from Parkside as a quid pro quo for relaxing the covenant. The plaintiffs submitted that that sum should be a substantial proportion of the development value of the land …

I think that in a case such as the present a landowner faced with a request from a developer which, it must be assumed, he feels reluctantly obliged to grant, would have first asked the developer what profit he expected to make from his operations. With the benefit of foresight the developer would, in the present case, have said about £50,000 for that is the profit which Parkside concedes it made from the development. I think that the landowner would then reasonably have required a certain percentage of that anticipated profit as a price for the relaxation of the covenant, assuming, as I must, that he feels obliged to relax it. In assessing what would be a fair percentage I think that the court ought, on the particular facts of this case, to act with great moderation. For it is to be borne in mind that the plaintiffs were aware, before the auction look place, that the land was being offered for sale as freehold building land for 13 houses, and they knew that they were not going to consent to any such development. They could have informed the Potters Bar Urban District Council of their attitude in advance of the auction, or could have given the like information to Parkside prior to completion of the contract for sale. In either event it seems highly unlikely that Parkside would have parted with its £90,000, at any rate unconditionally. I think that damages must be assessed in such a case on a basis which is fair and, in all the circumstances, in my judgment a sum equal to five per cent. of Parkside's anticipated profit is the most that is fair. I accordingly award the sum of £2,500 in substitution for mandatory injunctions. I think that this amount should be treated as apportioned between the 14 respective owners or joint owners of the plots and Parkside (as the owner of the road) in 1/15th shares, so that the damages awarded will be £166 odd in each case. In fact, I apprehend that by virtue of the arrangement between Parkside and the insurance office the entirety of the £2,500 will ultimately be recoverable from Parkside, so that the apportionment does not have any real significance. I will also grant a declaration in appropriate terms after I have heard submissions from counsel as to such terms.

Note

The *Wrotham Park* case was doubted in the Court of Appeal in *Surrey County Council v Bredero Homes Ltd*[139] but subsequently it was approved by the House of Lords in *A-G v Blake*, below. However, the Supreme Court has recently held that damages based on what the claimant could have demanded as the price of allowing the defendant to do what it did may be awarded (which the Court called 'negotiating damages') in two types of case only: (i) where the defendant has made use of the claimant's property without causing the claimant any other loss, and (ii) where the court could have awarded the claimant specific performance or an injunction but refuses to do so as a matter of discretion (as was the case in the *Wrotham Park* case).[140]

---

[139] [1993] 1 WLR 1361 (CA).
[140] *Morris-Garner v One Step (Support) Ltd* [2018] UKSC 20, [2018] 2 WLR 1353.

Attorney-General v Blake[141]

Restitutionary damages may be awarded in exceptional situations where profits are occasioned directly by a breach of contract and compensatory damages would be inadequate, because the plaintiff has a legitimate interest in preventing the defendant from doing what the defendant promised not to do though it causes the plaintiff no loss, or where the defendant has obtained his profit by doing the very thing he contracted not to do, and justice demands that he should retain no benefit from his actions.

Facts: The defendant was a former member of the Secret Intelligence Service (SIS) who in 1944 signed an undertaking not to divulge any official information gained as a result of his employment. Between 1951 and 1960 he disclosed valuable secret information to the Soviet Union. In 1961 he was convicted of spying and sentenced to 42 years' imprisonment, but in 1966 he escaped and went to live in Moscow, where he remained. In 1989 he wrote an autobiography substantial parts of which were based on information he had acquired in the course of his duties as an SIS officer. By section 1(1) of the Official Secrets Act 1989 it was an offence for a person who had been a member of the intelligence services without lawful authority to disclose any information relating to intelligence which was in his possession by virtue of his position as a member of those services. The defendant entered into a publishing contract with the third party under which he was to receive an advance of £50,000, a further £50,000 on delivery of the final manuscript and £50,000 on publication. The defendant neither obtained permission from the Crown nor submitted the manuscript for prior approval, and the Crown had no knowledge of the book until its publication was announced in the press. After he had already received some £60,000 from the third party, the Attorney-General brought a private law action against the defendant claiming damages for breach of fiduciary duty and payment of all moneys received and to be received by him from the third party on the ground that the defendant owed the Crown a fiduciary duty not to use his position as a former member of the SIS or make use of secret or confidential information acquired during his service so as to generate a profit for himself.

Held: The judge dismissed the action on the grounds that the lifelong duty owed by former members of the security services not to disclose secret or confidential information acquired during the course of their employment did not extend to information no longer secret or confidential and the disclosure of which would not damage the national interest, that the defendant had not expressly contracted not to publish any information relating to the intelligence service without the Crown's prior approval, nor could such an equitable obligation be implied, and that the breaches of section 1(1) of the Act of 1989 did not establish any breach of duty under the civil law for which the civil remedies sought could be claimed. The Attorney-General appealed, amending the statement of claim to raise issues of public law and claiming an injunction to restrain the defendant from receiving any payment or other benefit resulting from his criminal conduct.

On the appeal it was held, dismissing the appeal on the private law issues, that a fiduciary obligation did not continue after the determination of the particular relationship which gave rise to it; that a former employee did not owe a duty of undivided loyalty to his former employer nor was he under a duty to maintain the confidentiality of information which had ceased to be confidential; that, therefore, since the defendant's fiduciary relationship with the Crown had long since terminated and the information published in his autobiography was no longer confidential, the defendant was not in breach of any fiduciary duty to the Crown in publishing the information he obtained during his employment; but that by submitting the manuscript of his autobiography for publication without having first obtained clearance from the Crown the defendant was in breach of the express undertaking he signed when he joined the service of the Crown; that that obligation was not an unlawful restraint of trade since it did not exceed what was rendered unlawful by section 1(1) of the Official Secrets Act 1989; and that, accordingly, the defendant was in breach of contract, but, since the Crown had not sought an injunction to prevent publication, it could not establish loss and was therefore entitled to no more

---

[141] [2001] 1 AC 268.

than nominal damages. The House of Lords held that, as a matter of private law, the Crown was entitled to an account of the profit made by Blake.

Judgment: LORD NICHOLLS …

Breach of trust and fiduciary duty

Leaving aside the anomalous exception of punitive damages, damages are compensatory. That is axiomatic. It is equally well established that an award of damages, assessed by reference to financial loss, is not always "adequate" as a remedy for a breach of contract. The law recognises that a party to a contract may have an interest in performance which is not readily measurable in terms of money. On breach the innocent party suffers a loss. He fails to obtain the benefit promised by the other party to the contract. To him the loss may be as important as financially measurable loss, or more so. An award of damages, assessed by reference to financial loss, will not recompense him properly. For him a financially assessed measure of damages is inadequate.

The classic example of this type of case, as every law student knows, is a contract for the sale of land. The buyer of a house may be attracted by features which have little or no impact on the value of the house. An award of damages, based on strictly financial criteria, would fail to recompense a disappointed buyer for this head of loss. The primary response of the law to this type of case is to ensure, if possible, that the contract is performed in accordance with its terms. The court may make orders compelling the party who has committed a breach of contract, or is threatening to do so, to carry out his contractual obligations.

All this is trite law. In practice, these specific remedies go a long way towards providing suitable protection for innocent parties who will suffer loss from breaches of contract which are not adequately remediable by an award of damages. But these remedies are not always available. For instance, confidential information may be published in breach of a non-disclosure agreement before the innocent party has time to apply to the court for urgent relief. Then the breach is irreversible. Further, these specific remedies are discretionary. Contractual obligations vary infinitely. So do the circumstances in which breaches occur, and the circumstances in which remedies are sought. The court may, for instance, decline to grant specific relief on the ground that this would be oppressive.

An instance of this nature occurred in *Wrotham Park* … For social and economic reasons the court refused to make a mandatory order for the demolition of houses built on land burdened with a restrictive covenant. Instead, Brightman J made an award of damages under the jurisdiction which originated with Lord Cairns's Act. The existence of the new houses did not diminish the value of the benefited land by one farthing. The judge considered that if the plaintiffs were given a nominal sum, or no sum, justice would manifestly not have been done. He assessed the damages at 5% of the developer's anticipated profit, this being the amount of money which could reasonably have been demanded for a relaxation of the covenant.

In reaching his conclusion the judge applied by analogy the cases mentioned above concerning the assessment of damages when a defendant has invaded another's property rights but without diminishing the value of the property. I consider he was right to do so. Property rights are superior to contractual rights in that, unlike contractual rights, property rights may survive against an indefinite class of persons. However, it is not easy to see why, as between the parties to a contract, a violation of a party's contractual rights should attract a lesser degree of remedy than a violation of his property rights.

I turn to the decision of the Court of Appeal in *Surrey County Council v Bredero Homes Ltd* … This is a difficult decision. It has attracted criticism from academic commentators and also in judgments of Sir Thomas Bingham MR and Millett LJ in *Jaggard v Sawyer*

[1995] 1 WLR 269. I need not pursue the detailed criticisms … Suffice to say, in so far as the *Bredero* decision is inconsistent with the approach adopted in the *Wrotham Park* case, the latter approach is to be preferred.

The Wrotham Park case, therefore, still shines, rather as a solitary beacon, showing that in contract as well as tort damages are not always narrowly confined to recoupment of financial loss. In a suitable case damages for breach of contract may be measured by the benefit gained by the wrongdoer from the breach. The defendant must make a reasonable payment in respect of the benefit he has gained. In the present case the Crown seeks to go further. The claim is for all the profits of Blake's book which the publisher has not yet paid him. This raises the question whether an account of profits can ever be given as a remedy for breach of contract. The researches of counsel have been unable to discover any case where the court has made such an order on a claim for breach of contract …

There is a light sprinkling of cases where courts have made orders having the same effect as an order for an account of profits, but the courts seem always to have attached a different label …

These cases illustrate that circumstances do arise when the just response to a breach of contract is that the wrongdoer should not be permitted to retain any profit from the breach …

My conclusion is that there seems to be no reason, in principle, why the court must in all circumstances rule out an account of profits as a remedy for breach of contract. I prefer to avoid the unhappy expression "restitutionary damages". Remedies are the law's response to a wrong (or, more precisely, to a cause of action). When, exceptionally, a just response to a breach of contract so requires, the court should be able to grant the discretionary remedy of requiring a defendant to account to the plaintiff for the benefits he has received from his breach of contract. In the same way as a plaintiff's interest in performance of a contract may render it just and equitable for the court to make an order for specific performance or grant an injunction, so the plaintiff's interest in performance may make it just and equitable that the defendant should retain no benefit from his breach of contract.

The state of the authorities encourages me to reach this conclusion, rather than the reverse. The law recognises that damages are not always a sufficient remedy for breach of contract. This is the foundation of the court's jurisdiction to grant the remedies of specific performance and injunction. Even when awarding damages, the law does not adhere slavishly to the concept of compensation for financially measurable loss. When the circumstances require, damages are measured by reference to the benefit obtained by the wrongdoer. This applies to interference with property rights. Recently, the like approach has been adopted to breach of contract. Further, in certain circumstances an account of profits is ordered in preference to an award of damages. Sometimes the injured party is given the choice: either compensatory damages or an account of the wrongdoer's profits. Breach of confidence is an instance of this. If confidential information is wrongfully divulged in breach of a non-disclosure agreement, it would be nothing short of sophistry to say that an account of profits may be ordered in respect of the equitable wrong but not in respect of the breach of contract which governs the relationship between the parties. With the established authorities going thus far, I consider it would be only a modest step for the law to recognise openly that, exceptionally, an account of profits may be the most appropriate remedy for breach of contract. It is not as though this step would contradict some recognised principle applied consistently throughout the law to the grant or withholding of the remedy of an account of profits. No such principle is discernible.

The main argument against the availability of an account of profits as a remedy for breach of contract is that the circumstances where this remedy may be granted will be uncertain. This will have an unsettling effect on commercial contracts where certainty is important. I do not think these fears are well founded. I see no reason why, in practice, the availability of the remedy of an account of profits need disturb settled expectations in the commercial or consumer world. An account of profits will be appropriate only in exceptional circumstances. Normally the remedies of damages, specific performance and injunction, coupled with the characterisation of some contractual obligations as fiduciary, will provide an adequate response to a breach of contract. It will be only in exceptional cases, where those remedies are inadequate, that any question of accounting for profits will arise. No fixed rules can be prescribed. The court will have regard to all the circumstances, including the subject matter of the contract, the purpose of the contractual provision which has been breached, the circumstances in which the breach occurred, the consequences of the breach and the circumstances in which relief is being sought. A useful general guide, although not exhaustive, is whether the plaintiff had a legitimate interest in preventing the defendant's profit-making activity and, hence, in depriving him of his profit.

It would be difficult, and unwise, to attempt to be more specific.

…

Notes

(1) The government's claim was one for restitution of the profit made by Blake through breaking the contract. Note that this is quite different from the kind of restitution claim (common in contract cases) where a contract is avoided or terminated and a party then seeks restitution of property he had delivered or for other benefits transferred before the contract was brought to an end.[142]

(2) Thus in some cases the defendant will be made to pay the amount that the claimant might have demanded as the price for permitting the defendant to do what he did without permission, as in the *Wrotham Park* case; in other, more exceptional, cases the claimant will be entitled to an 'account' of the defendant's profit, ie to have the full amount of profit calculated and paid over to the claimant. The differing nature of the claims was considered by the Court of Appeal in *WWF-World Wide Fund for Nature v World Wrestling Federation Entertainment Inc*,[143] and by the Supreme Court in *Morris-Garner v One Step (Support) Ltd*[144]; in both cases the Wrotham Park-type claim was held to be a form of compensatory damages, whereas an account of profits is not.

(3) It is far from clear in what circumstances the claimant will be entitled to an account of profits. It is generally considered that it will not be appropriate when a commercial contract has been broken, though an account was ordered in *Esso Petroleum Co Ltd v Niad*.[145] Esso operated a 'Price Watch' scheme under which participating petrol stations agreed to sell petrol at the same low price. The defendant joined the scheme but in fact sold petrol at higher prices. This risked undermining motorists' confidence in the scheme but it was very hard for Esso to show what loss they suffered

---

[142] See above, pp 1047 ff.
[143] [2007] EWCA Civ 286, [2008] 1 WLR 445.
[144] [2018] UKSC 20, [2018] 2 WLR 1353.
[145] [2001] All ER (D) 324 (ChD).

as a result of the breach. The Court ordered the defendant to account to Esso for extra profit it had made by selling petrol at higher prices. The case has been criticised on the grounds that it did not involve exceptional facts like *A-G v Blake*, but in the light of a recent decision of the UK Supreme Court on penalty clauses,[146] the case may be upheld on the ground that this was the only measure of compensation that would ensure that petrol stations adhered to the scheme.[147]

(4) Lord Nicholls refers to 'punitive' damages. These (which are payable to the defendant) are sometimes awarded in English law, but not for breach of contract. The idea of punitive damages was included the *Avant-projet Catala*;[148] but the Reform Bill on civil liability, though allowing awards that are punitive, does not allow the 'victim' to benefit at all from these damages; as such, they cannot be considered as punitive damages. Rather, the bill introduced a 'civil penalty'.

Reform bill on civil liability **26.45 (FR)**

Article 1266-1: In extra-contractual matters, where the author of the harm has deliberately committed a fault with the view to making a gain or to saving money, a court may, at the request of the victim or the *ministère public* and by specially justified decision, condemn him to the payment of a civil penalty.

Such a penalty is proportionate to the seriousness of the fault committed, to the ability to pay of the author of the harm, and to any profits which he may have made from it.

The penalty cannot be higher than ten times the amount of any profit made.

If the person liable is a legal person, the penalty can be as high as 5% of the highest amount of its revenue excluding value-added tax realised in France in the course of one of the fiscal years ending after the fiscal year before the one in the course of which the fault was committed.

Such a penalty is allocated to the financing of a compensation fund related to the nature of the harm suffered or, if not, to the public Treasury.

It is not insurable.

26.7 AGREED DAMAGES AND FORFEITURE CLAUSES

Principles of European Contract Law **26.46 (INT)**

Article 9:509: Agreed Payment for Non-performance
(1) Where the contract provides that a party which fails to perform is to pay a specified sum to the aggrieved party for such non-performance, the aggrieved party shall be awarded that sum irrespective of its actual loss.

---

[146] *Cavendish Square Holding BV v Makdessi* [2015] UKSC 67, 26.50 (EN), below, p 1122.
[147] See below, p 1126.
[148] The Avant-projet Catala, Art 1371 provided that 'A person who commits a manifestly deliberate fault, and notably a fault with a view to gain, can be condemned in addition to compensatory damages to pay punitive damages, part of which the court may in its discretion allocate to the Public Treasury. A court's decision to order payment of damages of this kind must be supported with specific reasons and their amount distinguished from any other damages awarded to the victim. Punitive damages may not be the object of insurance.'

(2) However, despite any agreement to the contrary the specified sum may be reduced to a reasonable amount where it is grossly excessive in relation to the loss resulting from the non-performance and the other circumstances.

26.7.A THE VALIDITY OF AGREED DAMAGES CLAUSES

What if the parties agree on the amount that one party should pay if it breaks the contract—for example, a building contractor agrees to pay a sum of money for every day that it is late in completing the work, or a debtor agrees to pay a high rate of interest on any payment that is late? In particular, what if the amount payable is greater than the loss the other party suffers, so that the agreed sum operates as a penalty for breaking the contract?

In French law, the traditional position was that a penalty clause would be valid. The courts were then awarded the power to reduce or increase the penalty by Act no. 75-597 of 9 July 1975.[149] That was confirmed by the 2016 reform. The court's power to moderate is used mostly to reduce the amount of the penalty when it is manifestly excessive.

Code civil **26.47 (FR)**

Article 1231-5: Where a contract stipulates that the person who fails to perform shall pay a certain sum of money by way of damages, the other party may be awarded neither a higher nor a lower sum.

Nevertheless, a court may, even of its own initiative, moderate or increase the penalty so agreed if it is manifestly excessive or derisory.

Where an undertaking has been performed in part, the agreed penalty may be reduced by a court, even of its own initiative, in proportion to the advantage which partial performance has procured for the creditor, without prejudice to the application of the preceding paragraph.

Any stipulation contrary to the preceding two paragraphs is deemed not written.

Except where non-performance is permanent, a penalty is not incurred unless the debtor was put on notice to perform.

Cass com, 5 April 2016[150] **26.48 (FR)**

Clause in loan contract

A clause in a loan contract providing for a rise in the rate of interest payable in the event of the borrower failing to pay on time may be a penalty and may be adjusted if the default rate is excessive.

Facts: A bank granted several loans to a company. The loans contained a clause entitled 'delays', which provided that the interest rate would be increased by three percentage points in case of default.

---

[149] See Nicholas (n 4 above) 235–36.
[150] No. 14-20169, Bull 2016 no. 849, IV, no. 1206.

1119

Held: The court of appeal characterised the clause providing for an increase of the interest rate as a penalty. The court thus reduced the increase to one percentage point. The bank appealed from this decision, arguing that the clause was not a penalty clause and that, as such, the interest rate could not be reduced. The bank's appeal failed.

Judgment: Having rightly established that the clause increasing the rate of the contractual interest in case of default of the borrower must be analysed as a penalty clause that the judge can reduce… if it is manifestly excessive, the judgment considers that the increase of the rate in the range of 75%, or even 100%, compared to a standard contractual rate, significantly exceeds the refinancing cost of the bank and that it is disproportionate to the damage for the bank resulting from the late payment; having thus considered that the clause was manifestly excessive, the Court of Appeal reduced its amount; the claim is therefore unfounded.

Notes

(1) It must be noted that the power of moderation of penalty clauses is a kind of proportionality test. Whittaker[151] explains:

Article 1231-5's new provision on penalty clauses contains two elements of proportionality. First, following the former law, it grants courts a power to reduce an agreed penalty where 'it is manifestly excessive or derisory' and it adds that, without prejudice to this general power, where an undertaking has been performed in part, the court should reduce a stipulated penalty 'in proportion to the advantage which partial performance has procured for the creditor.'

(2) Normally an agreed sum by way of damages that is not a penalty will be payable whatever the actual loss suffered by the other party. It thus operates as both a minimum and a maximum. However, if the debtor is guilty of *dol* or *faute lourde*, the creditor may claim full damages and is not limited to the amount agreed in the clause.[152]

In English law, the approach is different. A clause which provides for a 'penalty' is invalid. The creditor may then sue only for the actual loss. If, in contrast, the clause was a genuine attempt to pre-estimate the loss, it is a valid 'liquidated damages' clause. In this case the creditor may recover the agreed amount even if the actual loss is less or even nil—see *Clydebank Engineering & Shipbuilding Co v Castaneda*.[153]

For many years it was assumed that there was a simple dichotomy: either the clause was a genuine pre-estimate of the loss (and valid) or it was a penalty and invalid. The courts did not insist that the pre-estimate be precise—but if the agreed sum was 'extravagant and unconscionable' in comparison to the loss, and particularly if it was not designed to compensate the innocent party but to punish the wrongdoer, or to act as a deterrent against breach, it would be treated as a penalty.

---

[151] S Whittaker, 'Contracts, Contract Law and Contractual Principle' in J Cartwright and S Whittaker (eds), *The Code Napoléon Rewritten: French Contract Law after the 2016 Reforms* (Oxford: Hart Publishing, 2017) 29, 52.
[152] eg Cass civ (1) 22 October 1975, no. 74-13217, Bull I no. 290, DS 1975, 151. This presupposes that the amount of the penalty is less than the actual damage.
[153] [1905] AC 6 (HL).

In a case decided in 2015, however, the Supreme Court decided that a clause that was clearly designed to deter breach—by requiring the payment of an agreed amount of damages, or by visiting other financially adverse consequences such as a reduction in the price payable, in the event of breach—would not be invalid as a penalty if the party who would benefit from the clause could show that it had a legitimate interest in obtaining performance rather than damages. Thus there now seem to be two bases for valid 'agreed damages' clauses in English law—'liquidated damages' and 'legitimate deterrent' clauses.

The traditional 'genuine pre-estimate' test is set out in an extract from the case of *Dunlop Pneumatic Tyre Co Ltd v New Garage & Motor Co Ltd*. We then give extracts from the new decision.

House of Lords **26.49 (EN)**

Dunlop Pneumatic Tyre Co Ltd v New Garage & Motor Co Ltd[154]

A clause which requires a party who has broken the contract to pay a sum which is extravagant in relation to the likely loss is invalid as a penalty, but a clause which represents a genuine pre-estimate of the likely loss is a valid liquidated damages clause. The clause may be valid even though the loss is hard to estimate.

Facts: The respondents had agreed, as part of a retail price maintenance scheme (not at the time considered to be anti-competitive), not to sell the appellants' tyres at less than the appellants' list prices; and, if they did, to pay the appellants £5 per tyre (including both 'covers' and inner tubes).

Held: The sum of £5 per tyre sold at below list price was liquidated damages and enforceable.

Judgment: LORD DUNEDIN: … I shall content myself with stating succinctly the various propositions which I think are deducible from the decisions which rank as authoritative:–

1. Though the parties to a contract who use the words 'penalty' or' liquidated damages' may prima facie be supposed to mean what they say, yet the expression used is not conclusive. The Court must find out whether the payment stipulated is in truth a penalty or liquidated damages. This doctrine may be said to be found passim in nearly every case.

2. The essence of a penalty is a payment of money stipulated as in terrorem of the offending party; the essence of liquidated damages is a genuine covenanted pre-estimate of damage (*Clydebank Engineering aid Shipbuilding Cov Don Jose Ramos Yzquierdo y Castaneda* [1905] AC 6).

3. The question whether a sum stipulated is penalty or liquidated damages is a question of construction to be decided upon the terms and inherent circumstances of each particular contract, judged of as at the time of the making of the contract, not as at the time of the breach (*Public Works Commissioner v Hills* [1906] AC 368 and *Webster v Bosanquet* [1912] AC 394).

4. To assist this task of construction various tests have been suggested, which if applicable to the case under consideration may prove helpful, or even conclusive. Such are:

> (a) It will be held to be penalty if the sum stipulated for is extravagant and unconscionable in amount in comparison with the greatest loss that could conceivably be proved to have followed from the breach. (Illustration given by Lord Halsbury in *Clydebank* case).

[154] [1915] AC 79.

(b) It will be held to be a penalty if the breach consists only in not paying a sum of money, and the sum stipulated is a sum greater than the sum which ought to have been paid (*Kemble v Farren* (1829) 6 Bing 141). This though one of the most ancient instances is truly a corollary to the last test. Whether it had its historical origin in the doctrine of the common law that when A promised to pay B a sum of money on a certain day and did not do so, B could only recover the sum with, in certain cases, interest, but could never recover further damages for non-timeous payment, or whether it was a survival of the time when equity reformed unconscionable bargains merely because they were unconscionable—a subject which much exercised Jessel MR in *Wallis v Smith* (1882) 21 ChD 243)—is probably more interesting than material.

(c) There is a presumption (but no more) that it is penalty when 'a single lump sum is made payable by way of compensation, on the occurrence of one or more or all of several events, some of which may occasion serious and others but trifling damage' (Lord Watson in Lord *Elphinstone v Monkland Iron and Coal Co* (1886) 11 App Cas 332).

On the other hand:

(d) It is no obstacle to the sum stipulated being a genuine pre-estimate of damage, that the consequences of the breach are such as to make precise pre-estimation almost an impossibility. On the contrary, that is just the situation when it is probable that pre-estimated damage was the true bargain between the parties (*Clydebank* Case, Lord Halsbury; *Webster v Bosanquet*, Lord Mersey).

Supreme Court   **26.50 (EN)**

Cavendish Square Holding BV v Makdessi and ParkingEye Ltd v Beavis[155]

A clause providing for a party to pay an agreed sum, or suffer a similar financial consequence, if the party breaks the contract, will be valid not only where it is not excessive in relation to a genuine pre-estimate of the loss that the other party will suffer but also where the other party has a legitimate interest in securing performance rather than damages and the amount payable is not disproportionate to the legitimate interest.

Facts: In the *Cavendish Square* case the contract was for the sale of a business. The seller entered various covenants not to compete with the buyers; and it was provided that if the seller broke the covenants, he would not be entitled to receive further instalments of the purchase price (clause 5.1) and could be required to transfer to the buyers shares that he would otherwise retain at a favourable price (clause 5.6), with the net result that the seller would lose millions of dollars. The Court of Appeal[156] took a more liberal view of the penalty clause rule than Lord Dunedin had done in the Dunlop case, arguing that a clause need not be a genuine pre-estimate of the loss if it was 'commercially justifiable; but it held that the clauses in this case were clearly designed to deter Makdessi from breaching his covenants and that deterrence could not be a commercial justification.

In *Parkingeye Ltd v Beavis* the claimants operated a car park at a retail park on behalf of the owners. Motorists were allowed to park free of charge for up to two hours but a 'failure to comply' would result in a parking charge of £85. The Court of Appeal[157] said the claimants would suffer no direct loss if the motorists overstayed the two hours; it had only an indirect commercial interest in that if it did not deliver the service required by the owners of the retail park it might lose its contract and its reputation. There was also a social

---

[155] [2015] UKSC 67, [2016] AC 1172.
[156] [2013] EWCA Civ 1539.
[157] [2015] EWCA Civ 402.

interest, in that consumers and retailers would benefit from having free parking for limited periods; and indeed legislative provisions suggested that Parliament considered that parking charges of this type should be recoverable. Although it was clear that the principal purpose of the parking charge was to deter motorists from overstaying, the judge at first instance had taken the correct approach when he held that the charge was neither improper in its purpose nor manifestly excessive in its amount, having regard to the level of charges imposed by local authorities and others for overstaying in public car parks. While in a purely commercial context a 'dominant purpose of deterrence' has been equated to extravagance and unconscionability, in the context of the *Parkingeye* case that was not the case. (The Court also held that the term was not unfair under the Unfair Terms in Consumer Contracts Regulations 1999. We considered this issue in Chapter 21.)

Both Cavendish Square and Beavis appealed to the Supreme Court, which heard the cases together, with a banc of seven Justices (because they were being invited to depart from previous decisions of the House of Lords).

On behalf of Cavendish Square counsel argued, first, that the penalty doctrine should simply be abolished, or at least should not apply when the parties were clearly of equal bargaining power. Secondly, if the doctrine is to retained, it should not apply to clauses that in substance set the price—one price if the seller complied with its covenants and another if it did not. Thirdly, the appellants argued that a clause should be valid if it was commercially justified, and that commercial justification should be treated more broadly than it had been treated in the Court of Appeal. The question should not be whether the clauses would in some way compensate the buyers for loss they might suffer and were extravagant in that sense: they represented the different values that the buyers placed on the business according to whether or not the seller was going to be competing with them, and value is not a question that the court should decide. In the *Beavis* case, counsel for the appellant (the motorist) argued that under the traditional approach the agreed sum must be a genuine pre-estimate of the loss and, that as it was accepted that Parkingeye suffered no direct loss at all if the motorist overstayed, the requirement to pay £85 was a penalty. Counsel for respondents, Parkingeye, did not (at least in oral argument) seek to challenge the whole doctrine of penalties. However, he argued that it was legitimate to take into consideration Parkingeye's interest in retaining its contract with the landowners, its general reputation as an efficient operator and the indirect interests of the landowner and users of the shopping centre in ensuring that parking was available.

Held: The Supreme Court was unanimous in holding that the clauses in each case would pass the legitimate interest test. Cavendish had a legitimate interest is preserving the good will for which it was paying such a large amount; it would be hard to prove the loss flowing from any breach of the non-competition covenants; and therefore it was legitimate to deter Makdessi from breach. Likewise, in the *ParkingEye* case there was clearly a legitimate interest in ensuring that motorists did not stay longer than two hours. Cavendish's appeal was allowed, Beavis's appeal was dismissed. (The majority, Lord Toulson dissenting, also held that the term in the *Parkingeye* case was not unfair under the 1999 Regulations.)

Most of the Justices gave an individual judgment but on the principal points of law the joint judgment of Lords Sumption and Neuberger reflects the view of them all.

Judgment LORD SUMPTION AND LORD NEUBERGER: ...

11 The penalty rule as it has been developed by the judges gives rise to two questions, both of which have a considerable bearing on the questions which arise on these appeals. In what circumstances is the rule engaged at all? And what makes a contractual provision penal?

In what circumstances is the penalty rule engaged?

12 In England, it has always been considered that a provision could not be a penalty unless it provided an exorbitant alternative to common law damages. This meant that it had to be a provision operating on a breach of contract. ... As a matter of authority the question is settled in England by the decision of the House of Lords in Export Credits Guarantee Department v Universal Oil Products Co [1983] 1 WLR 399 ("ECGD"). Lord Roskill, with whom the rest of the committee agreed, said, at p 403:

"perhaps the main purpose, of the law relating to penalty clauses is to prevent a plaintiff recovering a sum of money in respect of a breach of contract committed by a defendant which bears little or no relationship to the loss actually suffered by the plaintiff as a result of the breach by the defendant. But it is not and never has been for the courts to relieve a party from the consequences of what may in the event prove to be an onerous or possibly even a commercially imprudent bargain."

As Lord Hodge JSC points out in his judgment, the Scottish authorities are to the same effect.

13 This principle is worth restating at the outset of any analysis of the penalty rule, because it explains much about the way in which it has developed. There is a fundamental difference between a jurisdiction to review the fairness of a contractual obligation and a jurisdiction to regulate the remedy for its breach. Leaving aside challenges going to the reality of consent, such as those based on fraud, duress or undue influence, the courts do not review the fairness of men's bargains either at law or in equity. The penalty rule regulates only the remedies available for breach of a party's primary obligations, not the primary obligations themselves. …

…

What makes a contractual provision penal?

19 As we have already observed, until relatively recently this question was answered almost entirely by reference to straightforward liquidated damages clauses. It was in that context that the House of Lords sought to restate the law in two seminal decisions at the beginning of the 20th century, the Clydebank case in 1904 and the Dunlop case in 1915.

…

22 Lord Dunedin's speech in the Dunlop case achieved the status of a quasi-statutory code in the subsequent case law. Some of the many decisions on the validity of damages clauses are little more than a detailed exegesis or application of his four tests with a view to discovering whether the clause in issue can be brought within one or more of them. In our view, this is unfortunate. In the first place, Lord Dunedin proposed his four tests not as rules but only as considerations which might prove helpful or even conclusive "if applicable to the case under consideration". He did not suggest that they were applicable to every case in which the law of penalties was engaged. Second, as Lord Dunedin himself acknowledged, the essential question was whether the clause impugned was "unconscionable" or "extravagant". The four tests are a useful tool for deciding whether these expressions can properly be applied to simple damages clauses in standard contracts. But they are not easily applied to more complex cases. To deal with those, it is necessary to consider the rationale of the penalty rule at a more fundamental level. What is it that makes a provision for the consequences of breach "unconscionable"? And by comparison with what is a penalty clause said to be "extravagant"? Third, none of the other three Law Lords expressly agreed with Lord Dunedin's reasoning, and the four tests do not all feature in any of their speeches. For present purposes, the most instructive is that of Lord Atkinson, who approached the matter on an altogether broader basis.

23 Lord Atkinson pointed, [1915] AC 79 at pp 90–91, to the critical importance to Dunlop of the protection of their brand, reputation and goodwill, and their authorised distribution network. Against this background, he observed, at pp 91–92:

"It has been urged that as the sum of £5 becomes payable on the sale of even one tube at a shilling less than the listed price, and as it was impossible that the appellant company should lose that sum on such a transaction, the sum fixed must be a penalty. In the sense of direct and immediate loss the appellants lose nothing by such a sale. It is the agent or dealer who loses by selling at a price less than that at which he buys, but the appellants have to look at their trade in globo, and to prevent the setting up, in reference to all their goods anywhere and everywhere, a system of injurious undercutting. The object of the appellants in making this agreement, if the substance and reality of the thing and the real nature of the transaction be looked at, would appear to be a single one, namely, to prevent the disorganisation of their trading system and the consequent injury to their trade in many directions. The means of effecting this is by keeping up their price to the public to the level of their price list, this last being secured by contracting that a sum of £5 shall be paid for every one of the three classes of articles named sold or offered for sale at prices below those named on the list. The very fact that this sum is to be paid if a tyre cover or tube be merely offered for sale, though not sold, shows that it was the consequential injury to their trade due to undercutting that they had in view. They had an obvious interest to prevent this undercutting, and on the evidence it would appear to me impossible to say that that interest was incommensurate with the sum agreed to be paid."

...

31 In our opinion, the law relating to penalties has become the prisoner of artificial categorisation, itself the result of unsatisfactory distinctions: between a penalty and genuine pre-estimate of loss, and between a genuine pre-estimate of loss and a deterrent. These distinctions originate in an over-literal reading of Lord Dunedin's four tests and a tendency to treat them as almost immutable rules of general application which exhaust the field. ...

The real question when a contractual provision is challenged as a penalty is whether it is penal, not whether it is a pre-estimate of loss. These are not natural opposites or mutually exclusive categories. A damages clause may be neither or both. The fact that the clause is not a pre-estimate of loss does not therefore, at any rate without more, mean that it is penal. To describe it as a deterrent (or, to use the Latin equivalent, in terrorem) does not add anything. A deterrent provision in a contract is simply one species of provision designed to influence the conduct of the party potentially affected. It is no different in this respect from a contractual inducement. Neither is it inherently penal or contrary to the policy of the law. The question whether it is enforceable should depend on whether the means by which the contracting party's conduct is to be influenced are "unconscionable" or (which will usually amount to the same thing) "extravagant" by reference to some norm.

32 The true test is whether the impugned provision is a secondary obligation which imposes a detriment on the contract-breaker out of all proportion to any legitimate interest of the innocent party in the enforcement of the primary obligation. The innocent party can have no proper interest in simply punishing the defaulter. His interest is in performance or in some appropriate alternative to performance. In the case of a straightforward damages clause, that interest will rarely extend beyond compensation for the breach, and we therefore expect that Lord Dunedin's four tests would usually be perfectly adequate to determine its validity. But compensation is not necessarily the only legitimate interest that the innocent party may have in the performance of the defaulter's primary obligations. ...

Notes

(1) Thus a clause may be valid either on the basis that it is not excessive by comparison to a genuine pre-estimate of the loss that a breach of contract will cause, or because the party who will benefit from the clause has a legitimate interest in securing performance rather than damages and the sum payable (or other financial adjustment) is not disproportionate in amount to that interest.

(2) This makes it clear that 'proportionality' is now part of the test in English law also.[158]

(3) It is not wholly clear when the party who stands to benefit from the clause will be regarded as having a legitimate interest in securing performance rather than claiming damages. Lords Sumption and Neuberger give specific performance as an example of English law protecting a party's legitimate interest in performance rather than damages. This suggests that the party must show that for some reason damages would not be an adequate remedy (for example, because the loss would be hard to prove, or it is a third party or the public who will lose); or that the deterrent is part of a commercially-reasonable scheme, as in the *Beavis* case. A party probably does not have a legitimate interest in securing performance simply because he would prefer performance over damages.[159]

(4) The Court was unanimous in refusing to abolish the penalty clause rules, or to confine them to cases of unequal bargaining power. On this point you may like to look particularly at the judgment of Lord Mance.[160]

(5) In the *Cavendish Square* case, the penalty rules were held to be potentially applicable to clause 5.1 of the agreement, which would reduce the price that would otherwise be payable to the party in breach, and to clause 5.6, which required the seller, if he broke the contract, who to transfer assets to the other party at a low price.[161] But the Supreme Court held that neither clause was invalid, as neither was disproportionate to the buyer's legitimate interest in securing the seller's adherence to the 'noncompetition' covenants in the contract.

(6) Their Lordships were also unanimous that the penalty rules should not apply to sums that were payable on events other than a breach of contract. They declined to follow the decision of the Australian High Court in *Andrews v Australia and New Zealand Banking Group Ltd*[162] which had held that there is an equitable jurisdiction to relieve against any sufficiently onerous provision which was conditional on a failure to observe some other provision, whether or not that failure was a breach of contract.[163] In some situations this makes it rather easy to avoid the operation of the penalty rule. The eminent law professor the late Sir John Smith QC was asked by his university if the university could impose a penalty on students who did not pay their fees by the end of the first week of term. He answered that the university could not impose a penalty: but it could perfectly well stipulate that the fees would be £x if paid in the first week of term; £$x+y$ if paid in the second week, and so on. This seems to have been the effect of the terms used by the banks in the *Bank Charges* case, which

---

[158] cf above, p 1128.
[159] See *Chitty* (n 15 above), paras 26-213–26-225.
[160] [2015] UKSC 67 at [162]–[170].
[161] See, eg, [2015] UKSC 67 at [16].
[162] (2012) 247 CLR 205.
[163] See [2015] UKSC 67 at [41]–[42].

we considered when we looked at unfair terms[164]—customers were not forbidden to overdraw their accounts without the bank's prior agreement but customers who did overdraw would incur substantial charges.

(7) However, Lords Neuberger and Sumption (at [15] and [77]) and also Lord Hodge (at [258]) referred to 'disguised penalties'—in other words, they seem to suggest that a payment that on the face of it is not triggered by a breach but is payable if a party exercises an option under the contract may still fall within the doctrine. It is very hard to know when a sum payable if and when a party exercises a right under a contract will be treated as a disguised penalty. Possibly, the Justices were thinking of cases in which the 'price' of the option is so high that no one would exercise it willingly.

(8) Equally puzzling is the suggestion by Lords Neuberger and Sumption (with whom Lord Carnwath agreed) that the clauses in the *Cavendish Square* case, though 'triggered' by breaches of contract, were not within the penalty rules at all. They said:

> [73]…[C]lause 5.1 … is plainly not a liquidated damages clause. It is not concerned with regulating the measure of compensation for breach of the restrictive covenants. It is not a contractual alternative to damages at law. Indeed in principle a claim for common law damages remains open in addition, if any could be proved. The clause is in reality a price adjustment clause. Although the occasion for its operation is a breach of contract, it is in no sense a secondary provision.

They said something very similar about clause 5.6 of the agreement.[165] It is not easy to know when their Lordships thought that a payment or price reduction that comes into play only when the contract has been broken would not be a penalty at all. However, this view that clauses 5.1 and 5.6 were not subject to the penalty rules at all seems to be a minority view. The other four justices appeared to treat both clauses as potentially falling within the penalty doctrine, albeit valid because in each case the claimant had a legitimate interest in securing performance of the relevant terms of the contract.

(9) Thus English law now seems to be that an agreed damages clause, or a clause that requires a party in breach to forfeit a payment otherwise due or to transfer property, may be valid *either* if it is not extravagant in relation to a pre-estimate of the loss that is likely to follow from the breach of contract in question *or* if the other party has a legitimate interest in securing performance rather than receiving damages and the clause is not disproportionate to that interest.

BGB **26.51 (DE)**

§ 339: Payability of contractual penalty

If the debtor promises the creditor the payment of a sum of money as a penalty in case he does not perform his obligation or does not perform it in the proper manner, the penalty is forfeited if he is in default through delay. If performance due consists in a

---

[164] *Office of Fair Trading v Abbey National Plc* [2009] UKSC 6, [2010] 1 AC 696, 21.30 (EN), above, p 861.

[165] [2015] UKSC 67 at [79]–[88].

forbearance, the penalty is forfeited as soon as any act in contravention of the obligation is committed.

§ 340: Promise to pay a penalty for nonperformance

(1) If the debtor has promised the penalty for the case of his not fulfilling his obligation, the creditor may demand the forfeited penalty in lieu of performance. If the creditor declares to the debtor that he demands the penalty, the claim for performance is barred.

(2) If the creditor has a claim for compensation for non-performance, he may demand the forfeited penalty as the minimum amount of the damage. Proof of further damage is not inadmissible.

§ 341: Promise of a penalty for improper performance

(1) If the debtor has promised the penalty for the case of his not performing the obligation in the proper manner, in particular not at the stipulated time, the creditor may demand the forfeited penalty in addition to the performance.

(2) If the creditor has a claim for compensation on account improper performance, the provisions of § 340(2) apply.

(3) If the creditor accepts the fulfilment, he may demand the penalty only if on acceptance he reserves the right to do so.

§ 342: Alternatives to monetary penalty

If a performance other than the payment of a sum of money is promised as penalty, the provisions of §§ 339 to 341 apply; the claim for compensation is barred if the creditor demands the penalty.

§ 343: Reduction of the penalty

(1) If a forfeited penalty is disproportionately high, it may be reduced to a reasonable amount by judicial decree on the application the debtor. In the determination of reasonableness every legitimate interest of the creditor, not merely his property interest shall be taken into consideration. The claim for reduction is barred if the penalty has already been paid.

(2) The same rule applies also, apart from the cases provided for by §§ 339, 342, if a person promises a penalty for the case of his doing or forbearing some act.

§ 344: Ineffective promise of a penalty

If the law declares the promised performance invalid, an agreement made for a penalty for non-fulfilment of the promise is also invalid even if the parties knew of the invalidity of the promise.

§ 345: Burden of proof

If the debtor contests the forfeiture of the penalty on the ground of having performed his obligation, he is required to prove the performance unless the performance due from him consisted in a forbearance.

HGB

26.52 (DE)

§ 348: A contract penalty, promised by a merchant operating a commercial concern, cannot be reduced on the basis of the provisions of § 343 BGB.

[26.7.A]

OLG Köln, 24 April 1974[166]

Plastic windows

Even though a clause may formally appear to contain a pre-estimate of damages, it is none-theless open to be judged a penalty clause and to be subject to reduction under § 343 BGB.

Facts: A clause provided that 50% of the contract price be paid in the event of a customer cancelling a contract for the supply of windows. The customer, after various delays by the supplier, cancelled without giving proper notice, and the supplier claimed DM 3,000.

Held: The lower court granted the application, but on appeal the sum to be paid was reduced to DM 2,000, having regard to the fact that no work on the windows had yet been undertaken. Further, although the customer had unjustifiably cancelled the contract, the manufacturer had contributed to this by its delay and lack of clarity in specifying the time of delivery.

Judgment: The defendant instructed the firm G., whose claim is pursued by the plaintiff, to manufacture and fit plastic windows (contract value ca DM 21,000). Forming part of the contract were General Conditions of Sale and Delivery, clause 10 of which requires the purchaser to pay 50 per cent of the contract value as compensation for loss of profit and costs arising, should he give notice to terminate the contract prior to the manufacture of the goods ordered. For various reasons supply of the windows was delayed. Without prior notice of termination and without warning of refusal to accept delivery, the defendant withdrew from the contract. The Regional Court granted an application for an order that the defendant should pay to the plaintiff DM 3,000. The defendant's appeal was success-ful in part.

On the following grounds: II. In accordance with clause 10 of the General Terms and conditions in conjunction with §§ 339 ff BGB, §§ 398 ff BGB, the plaintiff is entitled only to DM 2,000 as against the defendant.

1. It may remain open whether it is justified to make a distinction between the agree-ment of a contractual penalty within the meaning of §§ 339 ff BGB and liquidated dam-ages (*Schadenspauschale*)

...

For, even on the basis of the principles developed by the BGH, it cannot be said that this is an agreement for liquidated damages. It is true that the wording of Clause 10 of the Conditions militates in favour of such an agreement when it speaks of an amount of '50 per cent of the contract value for loss of profit and costs arising.' The amount of the agreed damages, however, precludes such interpretation. For the significant factor is whether a serious attempt was made to estimate in advance the damage deemed pos-sible. Only in such a case may it be assumed that the provision is intended to be for the purposes of the simplified enforcement of the anticipated claim for damages. Where the agreed liquidated damages are unreasonably high, all the indications are that the primary intention is that pressure should be exerted on the contractual partner in order to hold him to performance of the contract.

In this case the agreed liquidated damages are unreasonably high. The seller is to receive 50 per cent of the contract value, even if the contract is terminated prior to manu-facture of the goods ordered. In the event that delivery is not taken of the goods already produced, the buyer was even obliged under Clause 10(1) of the General Conditions to

[166] NJW 1974, 1952.

pay the full price. 50 per cent as loss of profit is unreasonably high, even if one bears in mind that the firm G. has already incurred costs by instructing a fitter to re-measure [the windows]. A profit of this magnitude is not credible in light of the competitive situation in the building supplies market. Nor has it been demonstrated by the plaintiff that the firm G. works on such profit margins. It cannot therefore be assumed that the possible loss of profit was seriously calculated in advance. The plaintiff's submission that it works on a commission basis and therefore has an interest in performance of contracts also militates in favour of the construction of the clause as being in the nature of a contract penalty. Clause 10(2) of the General Conditions is therefore to be construed as a penalty clause. That is not altered by the fact that the plaintiff in its action is not claiming the full 50 per cent of the contract value, for the legal nature of an agreement cannot subsequently be altered by that fact.

2. The defendant is as a matter of principle obliged to pay the agreed penalty to the plaintiff. For it terminated the contract without notice prior to manufacture of the goods without good reason.

...

A contractual penalty in the amount of DM 2,000 is reasonable. The court has taken into account in determining that amount the fact that the plaintiff or the firm G. lost the profit on that contract and that it incurred expenditure in processing the contract and keeping the appointment for measurements. Expenditures incurred on partial or complete manufacture of the windows were not taken into account since, in the absence of submissions to the contrary, it may be assumed that G. had not yet started to manufacture the windows. Even if the loss of profit, together with the expenditure mentioned, reaches or even exceeds the amount claimed in the action, it does not appear to be justified to grant it in its full amount. For in assessing the contractual penalty account must also be taken of how it came about that the contract was terminated. It is true, as has already been stated, that the defendant unlawfully withdrew from the contract with G. Even though the conduct of G. did not justify termination without notice by the contractual partner, it did cause the defendant to hasten its decision. G's assurances as to dates were undesirably imprecise. It too could have taken steps, in the interests of avoiding ambiguities, in order to give the necessary clarity to the contractual arrangement.

Notes

(1) German law is like English law in distinguishing penalties from pre-estimates. It is like French law in allowing for the reduction of the amount of the penalty in cases of disproportionality. As in France, penalty clauses are viewed as having two functions: first, as an acceptable means of pressurising the debtor into performing—this is seen as a particularly useful tool where the debtor's obligation is one of omission, particularly obligations to refrain from unfair competition;[167] and secondly, to allow for a ready and expeditious calculation of damages. By contrast, a genuine pre-estimate has only the second function. The distinction between the two types of clause is not so readily ascertained in practice.[168]

---

[167] See BGH 7 October 1982, NJW 1983, 942.
[168] See Münchener Kommentar/Gottwald Introduction to § 339 para 7.

(2) The intention of the parties—was this clause meant to be a pre-estimate or meant to be a penalty?—is important in the classification of the clause. The difficulty is that the intention of the parties may be hard to discern. Therefore, as the above case demonstrates, the amount payable, and whether it is excessive or proportionate to the loss likely to be suffered, may be the best guide to the purpose of the clause.

(3) Although German law accepts the need for penalty clauses, their use is (under § 343 BGB) effectively limited by reference to their purpose. Clauses are suspect if they are actually aimed at enriching the proponent, abusing a dominant market position or maliciously impoverishing the other party. Other factors to be considered in this regard are: the interest which the creditor had in performance; the previous behaviour—for example, reliability—of the debtor; the economic position of the debtor; and the comparative fault of the parties. The absence of harm in a particular case is not decisive.[169]

(4) In BGH NJW 1954, 998, although § 348 HGB applied, it was held that the enforcement of the penalty clause could still amount to an exercise of contractual rights contrary to good faith. § 242 BGB may thus be applicable to allow for review of the amount of a penalty. In that case the parties estimated the value of the object of sale at more than DM 1 million. It was in fact much less than this. The basis of the contract (*clausula rebus sic stantibus*) had changed radically and the court could reduce the penalty for non-performance from DM 20,000 to DM 5,000. The basis of the contract—ie the parties' estimation of value—was a question prior to that of the proportionality of the penalty.

(5) Should the clause not be challenged under § 343 BGB, or should such a challenge fail, the penalty will be payable in case of breach regardless of whether loss has been suffered or not. Where there is a claim for damages this may not be claimed in addition to the penalty. Instead, the penalty may be claimed as minimum damages and any excess of loss may be claimed in addition.

German law also provides for the invalidity of certain clauses containing pre-estimates of damages and penalty clauses where these are contained in standard conditions of business.

BGB **26.54 (DE)**

§ 309: Prohibited clauses without the possibility of evaluation
Even to the extent that a deviation from the statutory provisions is permissible, the following are ineffective in standard business terms:
...
5. (Lump-sum claims for damages) stipulation of a lump-sum claim by the user for damages or for compensation for reduction in value, if
a) the lump sum in the cases in question exceeds the damage expected in the normal course of events or the reduction in value which normally occurs, or

---

[169] See Münchener Kommentar/Gottwald § 343 para 21.

b) the other party is not given the express right to prove that damage or reduction in value has not occurred or is materially lower than the lump sum agreed;

6. (Contractual penalty) a provision by which the user is promised the payment of a contractual penalty in the event of non-acceptance or late acceptance of performance, payment default or in the event that the other party to the contract frees himself from the contract …

Notes

(1) One purpose of pre-estimates in general conditions of business is to simplify the process of calculating damages. Hence the reference in § 309 no. 5a BGB to 'damage … to be expected in the ordinary course of events' replicates the wording of § 252 BGB, the general rule on the calculation of damages for lost profits. It could be said that a pre-estimate is an ex ante calculation of damages on an abstract basis. Where a pre-estimate clause is challenged under § 309 no. 5a BGB, the proponent is thus obliged to show that the amount set is not more than the loss to be expected in the particular branch of business should such a breach occur.[170]

(2) Should a court hold a pre-estimate clause invalid under § 309 no. 5a BGB, any damages will be calculated in the normal manner.[171]

(3) § 309 no. 6 BGB is not applicable in contracts between businesses. However, even if a clause is not caught by § 309 no. 6 BGB, for example due to the nature of the parties or the type of breach which gives rise to the penalty, it is still open to review under § 307 BGB—general good faith clause.

(4) A penalty clause impermissible under either § 307 or § 309 no. 6 BGB cannot be adapted to become a pre-estimate.[172]

(5) Thus the following distinctions can be made as between clauses providing for payment of a liquidated sum in the event of a breach of contract:

(a)   genuine pre-estimates;

(b)   invalid pre-estimates in general conditions of business beyond what is to be expected in the ordinary course of events (§ 309 no. 5 BGB);

(c)   acceptable penalties;

(d)   invalid penalties for specific types of breach contained in general conditions of business (§ 309 no. 6 BGB);

(e)   disproportionately high penalties (§ 343 BGB);

(f)   penalties the enforcement of which would, in the circumstances, be contrary to good faith (§ 242 BGB).

Thus there are significant differences in the way in which penalty clauses are treated in the national laws. In England they are simply invalid. In France and Germany a penalty clause may be valid, but is subject to reduction by the court—and also to being struck down under legislation on unfair terms. In England, liquidated damages clauses

---

[170] See Münchener Kommentar/Wurmnest § 309 no. 5 para 16.
[171] See ibid para 26.
[172] See OLG Frankfurt 15 June 1982, NJW 1982, 2564.

are frequently used—for example, for delay in building contracts—but cases in which clauses are found to be penalties, and therefore invalid, are rare.[173] In Germany it is said that penalty clauses are quite commonly used.

It may be suggested that by allowing penalty clauses German and French law are being consistent with their more generous approach to specific performance.[174] English law is being consistent with its hostile approach to specific performance by not allowing penalties. However, by controlling penalty clauses, continental systems are also recognising that there are limits to the coercion which may be employed to ensure performance. English law, by banning all penalties, avoids the difficult question of what penalties are acceptable and which are not—though the recent acceptance of 'legitimate deterrents' raises another set of questions.

The international restatements both adopt the continental approach of accepting that a penalty clause may be valid but subjecting unreasonably high penalties to reduction by the court. For PECL Article 9:509: Agreed Payment for Non-performance, see above. It appears that whether the sum agreed is excessive or not is to be judged in the light of the actual loss, as there is no reference to the circumstances envisaged at the time the contract is made: see Comment B. UNIDROIT Article 7.4.13 and its Comment are to the same effect.

26.7.B DEPOSITS AND FORFEITURE CLAUSES

Contracts often call for one party to pay a sum of money when the contract is made. What will be the position if one of the parties then withdraws from the contract or refuses to perform? This is a complex topic and one in which English, French and German law have rather different rules.

The three systems agree on the position if the payment is merely part of the price paid on account (*accomptes, Anzahlung*). If before the contract has been performed either party refuses to go on with it and it is then terminated by the other party, the sum paid will normally have to be returned; but the usual remedies for non-performance will apply. Thus, if a buyer pays part of the price in advance and then wrongly refuses to go with the contract, and the seller terminates the contract, the buyer may recover the sum paid but will be liable to the seller in damages for non-performance—and the seller will normally be entitled to set the damages off against the sum to be repaid.[175] If, however, the sum is paid as a deposit, or it is provided that it shall be forfeited, the position will depend on what the parties intended.

French law recognises a distinction between part payment and earnest money (*arrhes*), and also that the parties may have intended that either party should be able to withdraw from the agreement if they will forfeit the amount of the earnest money (*faculté de dédit*).

---

[173] Though see *Lombard North Central v Butterworth*, 25.28 (EN), above, p 968.
[174] See above, ch 23.
[175] See *Treitel* (n 59 above) 234–43, paras 182–86.

Article 1590: Where a promise to sell was made with an earnest, each contracting party is at liberty to withdraw.

The one who has given it, by losing it.

And the one who has received it, by returning twice the amount.

It has been held that the right to withdraw may be not exercised in bad faith, for example threatening to withdraw unless better terms are offered,[176] but this decision is described as an isolated one (*demeurée isolée*).[177] In consumer contracts there is a presumption that sums paid in advance by the consumer are earnest money: see Code de la consommation, Article L. 214 1. Thus the consumer may withdraw, but she will lose the *arrhes*; if the supplier were to withdraw, it would have to reimburse double the sum paid. However, it has been said by the Cour de cassation that Article 1590 merely 'supplements the will of the parties',[178] and it is possible that *arrhes* may be paid without there being a possibility to withdraw from the contract.

Where the *arrhes* are substantial there is a presumption that they were merely *acomptes*, not to be forfeited in the case of default; but it seems possible that the contract could provide for forfeiture of a substantial sum which would operate as a penalty. Nevertheless, the principle remains that a clause permitting withdrawal (often called a clause of *dédit*) on pain of forfeiting a sum that has been paid is not a penalty clause and thus cannot be reduced by the courts.

Cass civ (3), 15 February 2006[179]   **26.56 (FR)**

A clause in a contract of sale giving the buyer the right to withdraw from the contract on forfeiture of a sum of money (clause de dédit) is not subject to the court's power to reduce excessive penalties.

Facts: after the conclusion of a sale agreement concerning a villa, the purchasers failed to pay for the contract price and did not respond to the notices of default. As a result, the sellers sold the property to a third party. The sellers claimed payment from the purchasers of an indemnity of 140,000 francs, as provided by the contract in case of withdrawal from the contract.

Held: The court of appeal awarded the damages claimed, with interests at the legal rate. The purchasers appealed from the judgment, arguing that the clause providing for the payment of 140,000 francs in case of withdrawal from the sale was a penalty clause, whose amount should have been reduced by the court. The appeal failed.

Judgment: "Having established that the sale agreement specified that the purchasers undertook to pay an advance on the sale price of 140,000 francs within 19 days and the balance no later than 29 March 1987 in front of a real estate lawyer (*notaire*) and that in case of withdrawal on their part, the funds paid would remain the property of the seller,

---

[176] Cass civ (3) 11 May 1976, no. 75-10854, Bull III no. 199, D 1978, 269, annotated by J-J Taisne.

[177] Malaurie et al (n 41 above) no. 919. However, the decision may have been implicitly confirmed by the Cour de cassation in Cass civ (3) 15 February 2000, no. 98-17860, unpublished: 'having established, without any distortion of the facts, that the disputed clause constituted a clause of *dédit*, the cour d'appel found that the spouses X… did not prove that the spouses Z… had exercised, in bad faith, the faculty to withdraw arising from the clause'.

[178] Cass civ (1) 16 July 1956, D 1956, 609.

[179] No. 04-17595, Bull III no. 43.

the latter being obliged, in case of withdrawal, to pay twice that amount, the court of appeal, which considered, by a sovereign interpretation of the terms of the contract that their ambiguity made necessary, that this sum constituted an indemnity payable by the purchasers pursuant to Article 1590 of the Code civil to enable them to free themselves from their commitment, and which did not apply Article 1153-1 (now Article 1231-7) of the Code civil, rightly deduced that it was not a penalty clause liable to be reduced, that the indemnity could not be reduced and that the interests started running from the commencement of the proceedings".

Notes

(1) Contracts often include a term which imposes the payment of a lump sum. It is important to characterise this term. In France, there is much litigation on this question: is this term a *clause de dédit* or a *clause pénale* subject to judicial revision, according to Article 1152(2) Code civil?

(2) We saw above that Article 1231-5 applies to clauses which would be characterised as valid 'liquidated damages' clauses in English law. The important elements to determine whether this provision is applicable are: the contractual origin of the penalty; whether the person who fails to person is at fault by failing to perform (here lies the difference with the *clause de dédit*); and whether it is a sanction (*caractère comminatoire*).

German law distinguishes between a sum which is paid as earnest (*Draufgabe*) and a sum of money which is to be forfeited (or paid) as the price of exercising a right to withdraw from the contract (*Reugeld*).

BGB	**26.57 (DE)**

§ 336: Interpretation of earnest

(1) If, on entering into a contract, something is given as earnest, this is deemed to be proof of the conclusion of the contract.

(2) In case of doubt the earnest is not deemed to be a forfeit.

§ 338: Earnest in case of impossibility of performance for which giver of earnest is responsible

The holder of the earnest is entitled to retain it if the performance due from the giver becomes impossible because of a circumstance for which he is responsible, or if the rescinding of the contract is due to his fault. If the holder of the earnest demands compensation for non-performance, the earnest shall, in case of doubt, be credited or, if this cannot be done, shall be returned on payment of the compensation.

Note

§§ 336, 338 BGB seem to assume that the sum paid as *Draufgabe* is likely to be small. A very large *Draufgabe* is likely to be classed as a penalty clause and therefore to be subject to reduction under § 343 BGB, where it is held to be excessive as such.[180]

---

[180] See Münchener Kommentar/Gottwald § 338 para 1.

Unlike Article 1590 Cciv, the BGB does not provide for double the earnest money to be paid if the payee defaults. However, if the earnest money were paid by a consumer under a clause which was not individually negotiated, the absence of 'balance' might make it contrary to good faith. Compare the following provision, which includes on a 'grey' list of terms those:

Directive on Unfair Terms in Consumer
Contracts 93/13/EEC[181]   **26.58 (EU)**

Annex 1: Terms referred to in article 3(3)
1. Terms which have the object or effect of:
... (d) permitting the seller or supplier to retain sums paid by the consumer where the latter decides not to conclude or perform the contract, without providing for the consumer to receive compensation of an equivalent amount from the seller or supplier where the latter is the party cancelling the contract.

English law does not have any presumption that, when a party pays a sum of money in advance, he is entitled to withdraw from the contract on forfeiture of the sum paid, though such a right could be agreed expressly.[182] Deposits are paid frequently, for example for hotel bookings, and the sums are often substantial—in contracts for the sale of land, it is customary for the buyer to pay a 10% deposit on exchange of contracts. If the buyer defaults, the seller may—subject to what is said below—retain the deposit; if the seller defaults, the deposit must be returned, but there is no rule that double the sum should be paid.

The position of deposits in English law is not wholly clear. It seems that if a buyer pays a deposit of a customary amount, the seller may keep it if the buyer then defaults—even though in sale of land cases the deposit is customarily 10% of the price and the seller's loss may be much less. Deposits that are larger than is customary may be invalid as penalties.

Privy Council (on appeal from Jamaica)   **26.59 (EN)**

Workers Trust and Merchant Bank Ltd v Dojap Investments Ltd[183]

Where, for a particular kind of contract, there is a custom to pay a certain percentage of the price in advance as a deposit, to be forfeited if the buyer defaults, the seller will not be able to retain a greater deposit unless there was a good reason for requiring the larger sum.

Facts: A contract for the sale of land in Jamaica provided for a deposit of 25% of the purchase price. The purchaser paid the deposit but then defaulted. It claimed relief against forfeiture of the deposit by the vendor.

Held: The court of first instance (Zacca CJ) held that the deposit was reasonable. The Court of Appeal in Jamaica granted relief to the extent that the deposit exceeded 10%. Both parties appealed. The Privy Council dismissed the vendor's appeal and allowed the purchaser's cross-appeal.

---

[181] OJ L 95/1993, p 29.
[182] See the right to withdraw from a hire-purchase agreement on making the payment up to a minimum sum, often 2/3 of the total credit price. It seems that such a provision, even if it were to give the finance company much more than it would lose through the hirer's termination, is not subject to the penalty rules, as the latter apply only to sums payable upon breach of contract: see *Associated Distributors Ltd v Hall* [1938] 2 KB 83 (CA); *Bridge v Campbell Discount Co Ltd* [1962] AC 600 (HL); Consumer Credit Act 1974, ss 99, 100.
[183] [1993] AC 573.

Judgment: LORD BROWNE WILKINSON: ... In general, a contractual provision which requires one party in the event of his breach of the contract to pay or forfeit a sum of money to the other party is unlawful as being a penalty, unless such provision can be justified as being a payment of liquidated damages, being a genuine pre-estimate of the loss which the innocent party will incur by reason of the breach. One exception to this general rule is the provision for the payment of a deposit by the purchaser on a contract for the sale of land. Ancient law has established that the forfeiture of such a deposit (customarily 10 per cent. of the contract price) does not fall within the general rule and can be validly forfeited even though the amount of the deposit bears no reference to the anticipated loss to the vendor flowing from the breach of contract. This exception is anomalous and at least one textbook writer has been surprised that the courts of equity ever countenanced it: see Farrand, *Contract and Conveyance*, 4th edn (1983), p 204. The special treatment afforded to such a deposit derives from the ancient custom of providing an earnest for the performance of a contract in the form of giving either some physical token of earnest (such as a ring) or earnest money. The history of the law of deposits can be traced to the Roman law of *arra* and possibly further back still: see *Howe v Smith* (1884) 27 ChD 89, 101–102, per Fry LJ. Ever since the decision in *Howe v Smith*, the nature of such a deposit has been settled in English law. Even in the absence of express contractual provision, it is an earnest for the performance of the contract: in the event of completion of the contract the deposit is applicable towards payment of the purchase price; in the event of the purchaser's failure to complete in accordance with the terms of the contract, the deposit is forfeit, equity having no power to relieve against such forfeiture.

However, the special treatment afforded to deposits is plainly capable of being abused if the parties to a contract, by attaching the label 'deposit' to any penalty, could escape the general rule which renders penalties unenforceable ...

In the view of their Lordships ... [it] is not possible for the parties to attach the incidents of a deposit to the payment of a sum of money unless such sum is reasonable as earnest money. The question therefore is whether or not the deposit of 25 per cent. in this case was reasonable as being in line with the traditional concept of earnest money or was in truth a penalty intended to act in terrorem. Zacca CJ tested the question of 'reasonableness' by reference to the evidence before him that it was of common occurrence for banks in Jamaica selling property at auction to demand deposits of between 15 per cent. and 50 per cent. He held that, since this was a common practice it was reasonable. Like the Court of Appeal their Lordships are unable to accept this reasoning. In order to be reasonable a true deposit must be objectively operating as 'earnest money' and not as a penalty. To allow the test of reasonableness to depend upon the practice of one class of vendor, which exercises considerable financial muscle, would be to allow them to evade the law against penalties by adopting practices of their own. However although their Lordships are satisfied that the practice of a limited class of vendors cannot determine the reasonableness of a deposit, it is more difficult to define what the test should be. Since a true deposit may take effect as a penalty, albeit one permitted by law, it as hard to draw a line between a reasonable, permissible amount of penalty and an unreasonable, impermissible penalty. In their Lordships' view the correct approach is to start from the position that, without logic but by long continued usage both in the United Kingdom and formerly in Jamaica, the customary deposit has been 10 per cent. A vendor who seeks to obtain a larger amount by way of forfeitable deposit must show special circumstances which justify such a deposit ...

Their Lordships agree with the Court of Appeal that this evidence falls far short of showing that it was reasonable to stipulate for a forfeitable deposit of 25 per cent. of the purchase price or indeed any deposit in excess of 10 per cent.

The question therefore arises whether the court has jurisdiction to relieve against the express provision of the contract that the deposit of 25 per cent. was to be forfeited. Although there is no doubt that the court will not order the payment of a sum contracted for (but not yet paid) if satisfied that such sum is in reality a penalty, it was submitted that the court could not order, by way of relief, the repayment of sums already paid to the defendant in accordance with the terms of the contract which, on breach, the contract provided should be forfeit. ...

There is clear authority that in a case of a sum paid by one party to another under the contract as security for the performance of that contract, a provision for its forfeiture in the event of non—performance is a penalty from which the court will give relief by ordering repayment of the sum so paid, less any damage actually proved to have been suffered as a result of non-completion: *Commissioner of Public Works v Hills* [1906] AC 368.

Accordingly, there is jurisdiction in the court to order repayment of the 25 per cent. deposit. The Court of Appeal took a middle course by ordering the repayment of 15 per cent. out of the 25 per cent. deposit, leaving the bank with its normal 10 per cent. deposit which it was entitled to forfeit.

Their lordships are unable to agree that this is the correct order. The bank has contracted for a deposit consisting of one globular sum, being 25 per cent. of the purchase price. If a deposit of 25 per cent. constitutes an unreasonable sum and is not therefore a true deposit, it must be repaid as a whole. The bank has never stipulated for a reasonable deposit of 10 per cent: therefore it has no right to such a limited payment. If it cannot establish that the whole sum was truly a deposit, it has not contracted for a true deposit at all.

Notes

(1) You will have noted the difficulty that Lord Browne-Wilkinson had in squaring the 10% deposit in land sales with the general penalty rules.

(2) In a way, the *Worker's Trust* case was unusual. Had it been an English case, the court would have had power under the Law of Property Act 1925, section 49(2), to award the return of the deposit; and so the question of whether the clause was a penalty would not have arisen. But section 49(2) applies only to sale of land cases (and only in England and Wales).

(3) In the *Cavendish Square* case the Supreme Court was unanimous that an unreasonable deposit is subject to the penalty rules. For example, Lord Hodge said:[184]

... (a) a deposit which is not reasonable as earnest money may be challenged as a penalty and (b) where the stipulated deposit exceeds the percentage set by long established practice the vendor must show special circumstances to justify that deposit if it is not to be treated as an unenforceable penalty.

Probably the customary 10% deposit is now to be explained as reflecting the seller's legitimate interest in having performance rather than damages; but Lord Hodge described it as 'earnest money'—a phrase that is well known in other legal systems but which does not seem to have an established meaning in English law. 10% of the price seems rather large a sum to be mere earnest money.

---

[184] [2015] UKSC 67 at [238], 26.50 (EN), above, p 1122.

(4) So what is the position if the case is not one involving land and there is no customary amount for a deposit? Suppose a customer agrees to buy a new car from a dealer and pays a deposit of 10% of the purchase price, the balance to be paid in cash on delivery of the new car. The customer repudiates the agreement—perhaps she loses her job, or is offered a new job with a company car provided—and the dealer resells the car for a similar price to another customer. Since the demand for this model exceeds the supply, the dealer resells the car without any difficulty and its loss is much smaller than the deposit—see *Charter v Sullivan*[185] (car was re-sold with no loss to the dealer). Can the customer recover the deposit less the dealer's actual loss? The *Worker's Trust* case leaves the answer unclear.

(5) It is possible to infer from Lord Browne-Wilkinson's speech in the *Workers' Trust* case that he thought the use of deposits not related to the payee's loss is permitted *only* in the case of sales of land and that all other deposits must be genuine pre-estimates. This was one of the provisional solutions put forward by the Law Commission in its Working Paper No. 61, 'Penalty Clauses and Forfeiture of Monies Paid', but it does not represent the present law as it is generally understood to be.[186]

(6) In the working paper just cited, the Law Commission provisionally recommended that deposits and forfeiture clauses should be subjected to the penalty rules, and thus be valid only if they are genuine pre-estimates of the loss; but nothing further has been done.

(7) English law does not have provisions or cases dealing with clauses that, like the French *clause de dédit*, allow the party who has paid the sum to escape the contract on payment of the sum. Nonetheless, such clauses are quite common, for example when holidays are booked. The only case in which this problem was discussed is *Bridge v Campbell Discount Co Ltd*.[187] In that case a hire-purchase contract for a vehicle provided that if the hirer defaulted and the finance company repossessed the vehicle, or if the hirer exercised his right to return the vehicle and terminate the agreement, the hirer would remain liable to make payments up to two-thirds of the total price (a 'minimum payment' clause). This clause was clearly not a genuine pre-estimate of the finance company's loss, as the shorter the time the hirer had the vehicle, the less the company's loss would be but the more the hirer would have to pay—in Lord Radcliffe's words, 'it is a sliding scale of compensation, but a scale that slides in the wrong direction'. The hirer ceased paying and returned the vehicle. In the Court of Appeal, this was treated as an exercise of the hirer's option to return the goods, and the minimum payment provision was held enforceable because the penalty rules did not apply if the hirer merely exercised the option. The members of the House of Lords expressed conflicting views on whether this was correct; but the majority avoided the problem by holding that the hirer was not exercising his right, but breaking the contract—he had written to the finance company: 'I am very sorry but I will not be able to pay any more payments on the [vehicle]'; but why apologise if he was exercising a

---

[185] [1957] 2 QB 117 (CA).
[186] eg Working Paper No. 61, para 53.
[187] [1962] AC 600 (HL).

right? Therefore this was a case of breach and the penalty clause rules were applied and the clause was held to be unenforceable against the hirer. So that case left the law on options to cancel unclear. But subsequent cases strongly suggest that the sum could not be challenged, as it would not be a sum payable on breach of contract: see the *ECGD* case discussed in the judgments in *Cavendish Square*.[188] Fortunately such clauses are most commonly found in consumer contracts and can be controlled under the legislation that implements the Unfair Terms Directive,[189] or are effectively invalidated by the Consumer Credit Act 1974.[190]

The international restatements do not regulate deposits explicitly, either by giving a presumption that there is a right to withdraw on forfeiture of the deposit or by stating that substantial deposits are subject to the rules on penalty clauses. However, there is no doubt that those rules could be applied by analogy:

Principles of European Contract Law **26.60 (INT)**

Article 1:106: (2) Issues within the scope of these Principles but not expressly settled by them are so far as possible to be settled in accordance with the ideas underlying the Principles

...

FURTHER READING

Baum, M, 'Penalty Clauses' in J Basedow, K Hopt and R Zimmermann (eds), *Max Planck Encyclopedia of European Private Law* (Oxford University Press, 2012) 1259–63.

Bishop, W, 'The Contract–Tort Boundary and the Economics of Insurance' (1983) 12 JLS 241–66.

Cohen, N, and McKendrick, E (eds), *Comparative Remedies for Breach of Contract* (Oxford: Hart Publishing, 2005).

Whittaker, S, 'Contracts, Contract Law and Contractual Principle', in J Cartwright and S Whittaker (eds), *The Code Napoléon Rewritten: French Contract Law after the 2016 Reforms* (Oxford: Hart Publishing, 2017) 29–55.

Kötz, H, *European Contract Law* (2nd edn, Oxford University Press, 2017) 241–78.

Rowan, S, *Remedies for Breach of Contract* (Oxford University Press, 2012).

Treitel, G, *Remedies for Breach of Contract* (Oxford: Clarendon Press, 1988) 75–244.

Unberath, H, 'Reparation in Kind' in J Basedow, K Hopt and R Zimmermann (eds), *Max Planck Encyclopedia of European Private Law* (Oxford University Press, 2012) 1453–55.

Wurmnest, W, 'Damages' in J Basedow, K Hopt and R Zimmermann (eds), *Max Planck Encyclopedia of European Private Law* (Oxford University Press, 2012) 444–48.

Zimmermann, R, 'Damages and Interest' in N Jansen and R Zimmermann (eds), *Commentaries on European Contract Laws* (Oxford University Press, 2018) 1432–1556.

Zimmermann, R, *The New German Law of Obligations* (Oxford University Press, 2005) 49–60.

---

[188] 26.50 (EN), above, p 1122.
[189] See above, p 873.
[190] See Consumer Credit Act 1974, ss 99 and 100.

CHAPTER 27
REMEDIES FOR NON-CONFORMING GOODS AND SERVICES

27.1 INTRODUCTION

In this chapter we make two case-studies of remedies: first the remedies which the systems provide when goods supplied under a contract of sale are not in conformity with the contract, and secondly (more briefly) of those available when services provided are not in conformity. The conformity requirements were set out in Chapter 19.[1]

The reason for studying these situations is that they illustrate well how the various remedies available may relate to one another—and show that sometimes the buyer may have to seek one remedy before being allowed to pursue another. We will not go into the details of each remedy, for example, into the detailed rules governing damages. These were explained earlier.

For the sale of goods, all three regimes have been amended as a result of the Directive 99/44 on certain aspects of the sale of consumer goods and associated guarantees.[2] We start with this Directive. In contrast, the Directive does not apply to services and in principle the laws remain unharmonised. However, we will see that in the English Consumer Rights Act 2015, the remedies available to the consumer have been reformed to bring them closer to those available to a consumer who buys goods. This has also had the effect of reducing the differences between the three national systems.

Earlier we compared the ways in which the legislators in the three jurisdictions decided to implement the changes. The different methods are particularly obvious when it comes to the remedies. For example, whereas German law has a single new regime that applies to all contracts of sale, English law has implemented the directive by creating an additional set of remedies that apply only to consumer contracts. The result is not only that other sales contracts are subject to the previous regime, but also—since the remedies required by the Directive are not complete (the Directive leaves damages to national law)—the general legislation on sales is sometimes still relevant to consumers.

---

[1] See above, pp 781 and 783.
[2] Directive 1999/44/EC of the European Parliament and of the Council of 25 May 1999 on certain aspects of the sale of consumer goods and associated guarantees, OJ L 171/1999, p 12. Hereafter: the Directive.

27.2 REMEDIES IN SALE

27.2.A EUROPEAN LAW

Consumer Sales Directive[3]   **27.1 (EU)**

Article 3: Rights of the consumer

1. The seller shall be liable to the consumer for any lack of conformity which exists at the time the goods were delivered.

2. In the case of a lack of conformity, the consumer shall be entitled to have the goods brought into conformity free of charge by repair or replacement, in accordance with paragraph 3, or to have an appropriate reduction made in the price or the contract rescinded with regard to those goods, in accordance with paragraphs 5 and 6.

3. In the first place, the consumer may require the seller to repair the goods or he may require the seller to replace them, in either case free of charge, unless this is impossible or is proportionate.

A remedy shall be deemed to be disproportionate if it imposes costs on the seller which, in comparison with the alternative remedy, are unreasonable, taking into account:

— the value the goods would have if there were no lack of conformity,

— the significance of the lack of conformity, and

— whether the alternative remedy could be completed without significant inconvenience to the consumer.

Any repair or replacement shall be completed within a reasonable time and without any significant inconvenience to the consumer, taking account of the nature of the goods and the purpose for which the consumer required the goods.

4. The terms 'free of charge' in paragraphs 2 and 3 refer to the necessary costs incurred to bring the goods into conformity, particularly the cost of postage, labour and materials.

5. The consumer may require an appropriate reduction of the price or have the contract rescinded:

— if the consumer is entitled to neither repair nor replacement, or

— if the seller has not completed the remedy within a reasonable time, or

— if the seller has not completed the remedy without significant inconvenience to the consumer.

6. The consumer is not entitled to have the contract rescinded if the lack of conformity is minor.

Article 7: Binding nature

1. Any contractual terms or agreements concluded with the seller before the lack of conformity is brought to the seller's attention which directly or indirectly waive or restrict the rights resulting from this Directive shall, as provided for by national law, not be binding on the consumer.

...

---

[3] See n 2 above.

27.2.B ENGLISH LAW

We deal first with the remedies available to buyers under English law. It will be recalled that the Sale of Goods Act 1979, Sections 13–15,[4] set out various implied terms as to the description, quality and fitness for purpose of the goods; and that for consumer buyers, very similar terms (and some additional terms) are treated as included in the contract of sale.[5] The remedies available, in contrast, differ.[6]

27.2.B.1 NON-CONSUMER SALES

In the Sale of Goods Act, each implied term 'is a condition'.[7] As we saw earlier, this means that if the implied term is not complied with, the buyer may reject the goods and, once the relevant time for delivery has passed, terminate the contract.

Sale of Goods Act 1979   **27.2 (EN)**

Section 11: When condition to be treated as warranty.

...

(2) Where a contract of sale is subject to a condition to be fulfilled by the seller, the buyer may waive the condition, or may elect to treat the breach of the condition as a breach of warranty and not as a ground for treating the contract as repudiated.

(3) Whether a stipulation in a contract of sale is a condition, the breach of which may give rise to a right to treat the contract as repudiated, or a warranty, the breach of which may give rise to a claim for damages but not to a right to reject the goods and treat the contract as repudiated, depends in each case on the construction of the contract; and a stipulation may be a condition, though called a warranty in the contract.

(4) Subject to section 35A below, where a contract of sale is not severable and the buyer has accepted the goods or part of them, the breach of a condition to be fulfilled by the seller can only be treated as a breach of warranty, and not as a ground for rejecting the goods and treating the contract as repudiated, unless there is an express or implied term of the contract to that effect.

...

Section 35: Acceptance.

(1) The buyer is deemed to have accepted the goods, subject to subsection (2) below—

(a) when he intimates to the seller that he has accepted them, or

(b) when the goods have been delivered to him and he does any act in relation to them which is inconsistent with the ownership of the seller.

---

[4] See above, p 787.

[5] Consumer Rights Act 2015, ss 9–17.

[6] See *Atiyah and Adams' Sale of Goods*, 13th edn by C Twigg-Flesner, R Canavan and H MacQueen (Harlow: Pearson, 2016) ch 28; *Chitty on Contracts*, 33rd edn by H Beale (gen ed) (London: Sweet & Maxwell/Thomson Reuters, 2018) paras 38-512–38-525 (consumers: supply of goods) and paras 44-387–44-448 (non-consumer sales).

[7] Sale of Goods Act 1979, ss 13(1A), 14(6) and 15(3).

(2) Where goods are delivered to the buyer, and he has not previously examined them, he is not deemed to have accepted them under subsection (1) above until he has had a reasonable opportunity of examining them for the purpose—

> (a) of ascertaining whether they are in conformity with the contract, and
>
> (b) in the case of a contract for sale by sample, of comparing the bulk with the sample.

(3) …

(4) The buyer is also deemed to have accepted the goods when after the lapse of a reasonable time he retains the goods without intimating to the seller that he has rejected them.

(5) The questions that are material in determining for the purposes of subsection (4) above whether a reasonable time has elapsed include whether the buyer has had a reasonable opportunity of examining the goods for the purpose mentioned in subsection (2) above.

(6) The buyer is not by virtue of this section deemed to have accepted the goods merely because—

> (a) he asks for, or agrees to, their repair by or under an arrangement with the seller, or
>
> (b) the goods are delivered to another under a sub-sale or other disposition.

(7) Where the contract is for the sale of goods making one or more commercial units, a buyer accepting any goods included in a unit is deemed to have accepted all the goods making the unit; and in this subsection 'commercial unit' means a unit division of which would materially impair the value of the goods or the character of the unit.

Section 35A: Right of partial rejection.

(1) If the buyer—

(a) has the right to reject the goods by reason of a breach on the part of the seller that affects some or all of them, but

(b) accepts some of the goods, including, where there are any goods unaffected by the breach, all such goods,

he does not by accepting them lose his right to reject the rest.

(2) In the case of a buyer having the right to reject an instalment of goods, subsection (1) above applies as if references to the goods were references to the goods comprised in the instalment.

(3) For the purposes of subsection (1) above, goods are affected by a breach if by reason of the breach they are not in conformity with the contract.

(4) This section applies unless a contrary intention appears in, or is to be implied from, the contract.

Section 51: Damages for non-delivery.
[See above.][8]

---

[8] 26.36 (EN), above, p 1101.

Section 52: Specific performance.

(1) In any action for breach of contract to deliver specific or ascertained goods the court may, if it thinks fit, on the plaintiff's application, by its judgment or decree direct that the contract shall be performed specifically, without giving the defendant the option of retaining the goods on payment of damages.

(2) The plaintiff's application may be made at any time before judgment or decree.

(3) The judgment or decree may be unconditional, or on such terms and conditions as to damages, payment of the price and otherwise as seem just to the court.

Section 53: Remedy for breach of warranty.

(1) Where there is a breach of warranty by the seller, or where the buyer elects (or is compelled) to treat any breach of a condition on the part of the seller as a breach of warranty, the buyer is not by reason only of such breach of warranty entitled to reject the goods; but he may—

(a) set up against the seller the breach of warranty in diminution or extinction of the price, or

(b) maintain an action against the seller for damages for the breach of warranty.

(2) The measure of damages for breach of warranty is the estimated loss directly and naturally resulting, in the ordinary course of events, from the breach of warranty.

(3) In the case of breach of warranty of quality such loss is prima facie the difference between the value of the goods at the time of delivery to the buyer and the value they would have had if they had fulfilled the warranty.

(4) The fact that the buyer has set up the breach of warranty in diminution or extinction of the price does not prevent him from maintaining an action for the same breach of warranty if he has suffered further damage.

Notes

(1) The remedies available to the non-consumer buyer under the Sale of Goods Act 1979 (SGA 1979) are not all to be found in one part of the Act. The principal sections on damages and the section on specific performance are in a Part of the Act entitled 'Actions for Breach of Contract' but the rules on termination have to be gleaned from sections contained in Parts called 'Formation' and 'Performance' of the contract. This reflects the idea that the right to terminate depends upon the nature of the term broken.[9] (The remedies for consumers are explained below.)

(2) Section 52 gives the court a wide discretion to order specific performance, but it will be ordered only if damages would not be an adequate remedy.[10] This means in practice that it will be ordered only if the goods are unique or it is impossible to get replacement goods from another seller.[11]

(3) Section 11 refers to the right to treat the contract as repudiated, rather than to a right of termination. It means the same thing. If the buyer has this right, it can refuse to take the goods, can refuse to pay the price and can sue the seller for damages for non-performance.

---

[9] See above, pp 972–73.
[10] See above, pp 908–911.
[11] eg *Sky Petroleum Ltd v VIP Petroleum Ltd* [1974] 1 WLR 576 (QBD).

(4) Section 35A refers to the right to reject. The distinction between rejecting the goods and 'treating it as repudiated' is the distinction between withholding performance and terminating. If the goods tendered by the seller are defective, the buyer can refuse to take delivery of them or (provided it has not 'accepted' them within section 35) can 'reject' them. If there is still time (for example, if the date for delivery has not yet passed), the seller may be able to make a fresh tender of goods that do conform with the contract, and the buyer will normally[12] have to take them.[13]

(5) Whether the buyer has the right to reject the goods and (if the seller does not make a fresh tender in time) to terminate depends on the seriousness of the breach. However, as noted, the implied terms that the goods must correspond to the description and, when the seller is a business, be of satisfactory quality, etc, are stated to be conditions. In other words, the buyer has the right to reject the goods if the term is broken in any way. The only restriction is under section 15A, noted earlier.[14] This prevents a commercial non-consumer buyer rejecting for a slight breach of contract when it would be unreasonable to do so. (A consumer may, however, reject slight for any non-conformity, see below.)

(6) Under section 35(4), the right to reject may be lost after the expiry of a reasonable time, even if the buyer was not yet aware of the non-conformity. It has been held that this does not mean a reasonable time in which to discover the specific defect but simply a reasonable time to check the goods for apparent defects—and this may be quite short. In *Bernstein v Pamson Motors (Golders Green) Ltd*[15] the engine of a new car had seized up after only 140 miles. It was held that the car was not merchantable, but that, as the buyer had had the car for nearly a month, a reasonable time had elapsed under section 35 and he could no longer reject it. It made no difference that the defect could not have been discovered earlier or that for much of the month the buyer had been ill and unable to drive the car. Rougier J said:[16]

> [W]hat is a reasonable time in the circumstances? And here the 1979 Act ceases to be helpful. By s 59 "a reasonable time" is defined as a question of fact, no more, as if it could be anything else.

> The submission made on behalf of the defendants is that in the context of the sale of [a] new motor car a reasonable time must entail a reasonable time to inspect and try out the car generally rather than with an eye to any specific defect, and that to project the period further would be artificial and contrary to the general legal proposition that there should, whenever possible, be finality in commercial transactions. At first I regret to say this proposition got a hostile reception on the ground that a mere 140-odd miles, and some three weeks, part of which were occupied by illness, were not nearly enough to afford the plaintiff any opportunity of discovering this wholly latent defect.

> However … [i]n my judgment, the nature of the particular defect, discovered ex post facto, and the speed with which it might have been discovered, are irrelevant to the concept of

---

[12] There is an exception of the non-conforming delivery amounts to an anticipatory repudiation of the contract, eg it shows that the seller is incapable of performing properly. See above, p 1024.

[13] See *Borrowman, Phillips & Co v Free and Hollis* (1878) 4 QBD 500.

[14] See 25.11 (EN), above, p 1005.

[15] [1987] 2 All ER 220.

[16] ibid, at 230.

reasonable time in s 35 as drafted. That section seems to me to be directed solely to what is a reasonable practical interval in commercial terms between a buyer receiving the goods and his ability to send them back, taking into consideration from his point of view the nature of the goods and their function, and from the point of view of the seller the commercial desirability of being able to close his ledger reasonably soon after the transaction is complete. The complexity of the intended function of the goods is clearly of prime consideration here. What is a reasonable time in relation to a bicycle would hardly suffice for a nuclear submarine.

Subsequent cases have suggested that this decision may have been insufficiently generous to the buyer, but there has been no case setting out a clear approach.[17] Note that it is only the right to reject the goods (and thus to terminate the contract) which is lost. The buyer has the full normal limitation period (six years from the breach) in which to claim damages.

(7) Section 53(1) states that the buyer may 'set up against the seller the breach of warranty in diminution or extinction of the price'. This seems to be the only reference in the Act to anything like price reduction. However, the section seems to envisage simply that the buyer may deduct his loss from the amount he owes for the goods, which is not the way that price reduction works in the other systems or under the new consumer provisions.

(8) If the buyer rejects the goods and the seller does not replace them, the buyer will claim damages for non-delivery under section 51. If the buyer decides or is obliged to keep the goods, it is entitled to damages in accordance with section 53. Section 53(3) states that prima facie the damages will be the difference between the value of the goods at the time of delivery to the buyer and the value they would have had if they had fulfilled the warranty; but if the buyer decides to have the goods repaired, it may recover the cost of the repair even if this increases the damages, provided it is reasonable to have the goods repaired.

27.2.B.2 CONSUMER BUYERS

The requirements of the Directive for consumer remedies were first implemented in 2002 by new Sections 48A–48F being inserted into the Sale of Goods Act 1979. This allowed consumers a choice between the remedies provided (at that time) for all buyers—viz, to reject the goods and claim damages—and the 'new' remedies of demanding repair or replacement. This was rather confusing; but the question of how long consumers had to exercise the right to reject the goods (see above) was even more difficult. The matter was referred to the Law Commissions, which recommended that the right to reject under the Sale of Goods Act 1979 should be replaced by a short-term right to reject the goods and recover any payment in full; this right would be exercisable in the first 30 days after delivery.[18] This change was implemented, and the consumer's remedies were partly codified, in the Consumer Rights Act 2015 (CRA 2015).

---

[17] See *Chitty* (n 6 above) para 44-284.
[18] The Law Commission and The Scottish Law Commission, *Consumer Remedies for Faulty Goods*, Law Com No 317, Scot Law Com No 216 (London: The Stationery Office, 2009).

Section 19: Consumer's rights to enforce terms about goods

(1) In this section and sections 22 to 24 references to goods conforming to a contract are references to—

(a) the goods conforming to the terms described in sections 9, 10, 11, 13 and 14,

(b) the goods not failing to conform to the contract under section 15 or 16, and

(c) the goods conforming to requirements that are stated in the contract.

(2) But, for the purposes of this section and sections 22 to 24, a failure to conform as mentioned in subsection (1)(a) to (c) is not a failure to conform to the contract if it has its origin in materials supplied by the consumer.

(3) If the goods do not conform to the contract because of a breach of any of the terms described in sections 9, 10, 11, 13 and 14, or if they do not conform to the contract under section 16, the consumer's rights (and the provisions about them and when they are available) are—

(a) the short-term right to reject (sections 20 and 22);

(b) the right to repair or replacement (section 23); and

(c) the right to a price reduction or the final right to reject (sections 20 and 24).

(4) If the goods do not conform to the contract under section 15 or because of a breach of requirements that are stated in the contract, the consumer's rights (and the provisions about them and when they are available) are—

(a) the right to repair or replacement (section 23); and

(b) the right to a price reduction or the final right to reject (sections 20 and 24).

(5) If the trader is in breach of a term that section 12 requires to be treated as included in the contract, the consumer has the right to recover from the trader the amount of any costs incurred by the consumer as a result of the breach, up to the amount of the price paid or the value of other consideration given for the goods.

(6) If the trader is in breach of the term that section 17(1) (right to supply etc) requires to be treated as included in the contract, the consumer has a right to reject (see section 20 for provisions about that right and when it is available).

(7) Subsections (3) to (6) are subject to section 25 and subsections (3)(a) and (6) are subject to section 26.

(8) Section 28 makes provision about remedies for breach of a term about the time for delivery of goods.

(9) This Chapter does not prevent the consumer seeking other remedies—

(a) for a breach of a term that this Chapter requires to be treated as included in the contract,

(b) on the grounds that, under section 15 or 16, goods do not conform to the contract, or

(c) for a breach of a requirement stated in the contract.

(10) Those other remedies may be ones—

(a) in addition to a remedy referred to in subsections (3) to (6) (but not so as to recover twice for the same loss), or

(b) instead of such a remedy, or

(c) where no such remedy is provided for.

(11) Those other remedies include any of the following that is open to the consumer in the circumstances—

(a) claiming damages;

(b) seeking specific performance;

(c) seeking an order for specific implement;

(d) relying on the breach against a claim by the trader for the price;

(e) for breach of an express term, exercising a right to treat the contract as at an end.

(12) It is not open to the consumer to treat the contract as at an end for breach of a term that this Chapter requires to be treated as included in the contract, or on the grounds that, under section 15 or 16, goods do not conform to the contract, except as provided by subsections (3), (4) and (6).

(13) In this Part, treating a contract as at an end means treating it as repudiated.

(14) For the purposes of subsections (3)(b) and (c) and (4), goods which do not conform to the contract at any time within the period of six months beginning with the day on which the goods were delivered to the consumer must be taken not to have conformed to it on that day.

(15) Subsection (14) does not apply if—

(a) it is established that the goods did conform to the contract on that day, or

(b) its application is incompatible with the nature of the goods or with how they fail to conform to the contract.

Section 20: Right to reject

(1) The short-term right to reject is subject to section 22.

(2) The final right to reject is subject to section 24.

(3) The right to reject under section 19(6) is not limited by those sections.

(4) Each of these rights entitles the consumer to reject the goods and treat the contract as at an end, subject to subsections (20) and (21).

(5) The right is exercised if the consumer indicates to the trader that the consumer is rejecting the goods and treating the contract as at an end.

(6) The indication may be something the consumer says or does, but it must be clear enough to be understood by the trader.

(7) From the time when the right is exercised—

(a) the trader has a duty to give the consumer a refund, subject to subsection (18), and

(b) the consumer has a duty to make the goods available for collection by the trader or (if there is an agreement for the consumer to return rejected goods) to return them as agreed.

(8) Whether or not the consumer has a duty to return the rejected goods, the trader must bear any reasonable costs of returning them, other than any costs incurred by the consumer in returning the goods in person to the place where the consumer took physical possession of them.

[Sub-sections (9)–(18) (omitted) deal with the details of the right to a refund]

(19) It may be open to a consumer to claim damages where there is no entitlement to receive a refund, or because of the limits of the entitlement, or instead of a refund.

[Sub-sections (20) and (21) (omitted) deal with severable contracts]

Section 22: Time limit for short-term right to reject

(1) A consumer who has the short-term right to reject loses it if the time limit for exercising it passes without the consumer exercising it, unless the trader and the consumer agree that it may be exercised later.

(2) An agreement under which the short-term right to reject would be lost before the time limit passes is not binding on the consumer.

(3) The time limit for exercising the short-term right to reject (unless subsection (4) applies) is the end of 30 days beginning with the first day after these have all happened—

(a) ownership or (in the case of a contract for the hire of goods, a hire-purchase agreement or a conditional sales contract) possession of the goods has been transferred to the consumer,

(b) the goods have been delivered, and

(c) where the contract requires the trader to install the goods or take other action to enable the consumer to use them, the trader has notified the consumer that the action has been taken.

(4) If any of the goods are of a kind that can reasonably be expected to perish after a shorter period, the time limit for exercising the short-term right to reject in relation to those goods is the end of that shorter period (but without affecting the time limit in relation to goods that are not of that kind).

(5) Subsections (3) and (4) do not prevent the consumer exercising the short-term right to reject before something mentioned in subsection (3)(a), (b) or (c) has happened.

(6) If the consumer requests or agrees to the repair or replacement of goods, the period mentioned in subsection (3) or (4) stops running for the length of the waiting period.

(7) If goods supplied by the trader in response to that request or agreement do not conform to the contract, the time limit for exercising the short-term right to reject is then either—

(a) 7 days after the waiting period ends, or

(b) if later, the original time limit for exercising that right, extended by the waiting period.

(8) The waiting period—

(a) begins with the day the consumer requests or agrees to the repair or replacement of the goods, and

(b) ends with the day on which the consumer receives goods supplied by the trader in response to the request or agreement.

Section 23: Right to repair or replacement

(1) This section applies if the consumer has the right to repair or replacement (see section 19(3) and (4)).

(2) If the consumer requires the trader to repair or replace the goods, the trader must—

(a) do so within a reasonable time and without significant inconvenience to the consumer, and

(b) bear any necessary costs incurred in doing so (including in particular the cost of any labour, materials or postage).

(3) The consumer cannot require the trader to repair or replace the goods if that remedy (the repair or the replacement)—

(a) is impossible, or

(b) is disproportionate compared to the other of those remedies.

(4) Either of those remedies is disproportionate compared to the other if it imposes costs on the trader which, compared to those imposed by the other, are unreasonable, taking into account—

(a) the value which the goods would have if they conformed to the contract,

(b) the significance of the lack of conformity, and

(c) whether the other remedy could be effected without significant inconvenience to the consumer.

(5) Any question as to what is a reasonable time or significant inconvenience is to be determined taking account of—

(a) the nature of the goods, and

(b) the purpose for which the goods were acquired.

(6) A consumer who requires or agrees to the repair of goods cannot require the trader to replace them, or exercise the short-term right to reject, without giving the trader a reasonable time to repair them (unless giving the trader that time would cause significant inconvenience to the consumer).

(7) A consumer who requires or agrees to the replacement of goods cannot require the trader to repair them, or exercise the short-term right to reject, without giving the trader a reasonable time to replace them (unless giving the trader that time would cause significant inconvenience to the consumer).

(8) In this Chapter, "repair" in relation to goods that do not conform to a contract, means making them conform.

Section 24: Right to price reduction or final right to reject

(1) The right to a price reduction is the right—

(a) to require the trader to reduce by an appropriate amount the price the consumer is required to pay under the contract, or anything else the consumer is required to transfer under the contract, and

(b) to receive a refund from the trader for anything already paid or otherwise transferred by the consumer above the reduced amount.

(2) The amount of the reduction may, where appropriate, be the full amount of the price or whatever the consumer is required to transfer.

(3) Section 20(10) to (17) applies to a consumer's right to receive a refund under subsection (1)(b).

(4) The right to a price reduction does not apply—

(a) if what the consumer is (before the reduction) required to transfer under the contract, whether or not already transferred, cannot be divided up so as to enable the trader to receive or retain only the reduced amount, or

(b) if anything to which section 20(12) applies cannot be given back in its original state.

(5) A consumer who has the right to a price reduction and the final right to reject may only exercise one (not both), and may only do so in one of these situations—

(a) after one repair or one replacement, the goods do not conform to the contract;

(b) because of section 23(3) the consumer can require neither repair nor replacement of the goods; or

(c) the consumer has required the trader to repair or replace the goods, but the trader is in breach of the requirement of section 23(2)(a) to do so within a reasonable time and without significant inconvenience to the consumer.

(6) There has been a repair or replacement for the purposes of subsection (5)(a) if—

(a) the consumer has requested or agreed to repair or replacement of the goods (whether in relation to one fault or more than one), and

(b) the trader has delivered goods to the consumer, or made goods available to the consumer, in response to the request or agreement.

(7) For the purposes of subsection (6) goods that the trader arranges to repair at the consumer's premises are made available when the trader indicates that the repairs are finished.

(8) If the consumer exercises the final right to reject, any refund to the consumer may be reduced by a deduction for use, to take account of the use the consumer has had of the goods in the period since they were delivered, but this is subject to subsections (9) and (10).

(9) No deduction may be made to take account of use in any period when the consumer had the goods only because the trader failed to collect them at an agreed time.

(10) No deduction may be made if the final right to reject is exercised in the first 6 months (see subsection (11)), unless—

(a) the goods consist of a motor vehicle, or

(b) the goods are of a description specified by order made by the Secretary of State by statutory instrument.

...

Notes

(1) Section 19(3) sets out a 'road map' of the remedies available in most cases when the goods do not meet the statutory requirements, eg if the goods are not of satisfactory quality, or do not conform to an express requirement of the contract. (For some kinds of non-conformity, the remedies are more limited, see below.) The remedies implement the requirements of the Consumer Sales Directive,[19] which when first introduced in 2002[20] were quite revolutionary for English law.

(2) The traditional right to reject, which under the Sale of Goods Act 1979 follows from a breach of condition, is replaced by the short-term right to reject. Note that section 20(4) provides that the right to reject is also a right to terminate the contract. This means that the consumer is entitled to terminate the contract and demand his or her money back without giving the trader the chance to correct the problem, provided that the consumer exercises the short-term right to reject within the time limits set out in section 22.

[19] 19.11 (EU), above, p 784.
[20] See above, p 785.

Sections 20(9)–(12) and (15)–(19) set out how the right to refund is to work, in particular where the consumer has given the trader something in part exchange. Note that the remedies set out in the CRA 2015 are in addition to the right to damages (see section 19(11)), so that the buyer who rejects and terminates may still claim damages for non-performance.[21]

(3) The remedies now contained in the CRA 2015 sections 19(3) and 23, were also a major change, because they introduce a specifically enforceable right to repair or replacement of the goods. Under the general law, and under the Sale of Goods Act 1979 before the changes that were made in 2002, the court would not make such an order. Rather, the buyer would have to get the goods repaired at his own expense and claim damages to cover the cost, or reject the goods, buy substitute goods elsewhere and claim any additional cost by way of damages.

(4) Note the restrictions on the right to repair or replacement contained in section 23 CRA 2015. These reflect the Directive.

(5) If the buyer is not entitled to repair or replacement, or if he has demanded it but the seller has failed to provide it (and note that the trader is allowed only one attempt: section 24(5)(a)), the buyer may either claim a reduction in the price, or exercise the long-term right to reject: section 24.

(6) The buyer has a free choice between reducing the price and rejection; the right to reject is not excluded where the defect is only 'minor', as it is under the Directive.[22] (Remember that it is a 'minimum harmonisation' directive.)

(7) The rights apply no matter how long the consumer has had the goods, but if he exercises the final right to reject and terminates the contract he may have to make an allowance for the use he has made of the goods (section 24(8)). This applies only if the consumer has had the goods for more than six months or if they are a motor vehicle, though a power was reserved to extend the exceptions to other goods also.

(8) Where the trader is to install the goods as well as supplying them, the goods will not conform to the contract if they are not installed correctly. But in this case the consumer does not have a short-term right to reject: section 19(4). The consumer will have to demand repair or replacement and can exercise price reduction or the final right to reject and terminate only if this is impossible of the trader fails to do it.

(9) The Consumer Rights Directive[23] requires the trader to give the consumer certain information before the contract is made; and when the contract is a distance or off-premises contract, states that the information provided shall form an integral part of the contract.[24] The CRA 2015 implements this, and extends it to information required in on-premises contracts, in sections 11 and 12. If the information relates to the characteristics of the goods, section 11(4) treats it in the same way as other descriptions of the goods and the consumer will have the full range of remedies available for failure

---

[21] *Chitty* (n 6 above) para 38-453. If it is taken to mean avoidance *ab initio* (as with 'rescission' for misrepresentation), then rescission would be incompatible with a claim for damages for non-performance; but a number of English writers use 'rescission' in relation to breach as well as when a contract is avoided *ab initio*.

[22] Compare 27.1 (EU), above, p 1142.

[23] Directive 2011/83/EU of the European Parliament and of the Council of 25 October 2011 on consumer rights, OJ L 304/2011, p 64.

[24] CRD Art 6(5).

to comply with section 11. But if the information is actual information about other matters (such as the trader's address or the existence of a commercial guarantee[25]), though section 12 provides that the information will form part of the contract, the consumers' only remedy if the information is incorrect will be a claim for damages for up to the amount the consumer has paid: section 19(5).

(10) The options given by the Directive to limit the buyer's remedies to non-conformities that appear within two years of the time of delivery (Article 5(1)), and to those which were notified to the seller within two months of when the buyer discovered them (Article 5(2)) were not taken up by the UK.

(11) Article 7 of the Directive requires that the buyer's rights be mandatory. In English law this is achieved by CRA 2015, section 31.[26]

(12) The provisions of the CRA 2015 apply also to other types of contract under which a trader supplies goods to a consumer, eg contracts of hire-purchase. Chapter 3 provides for a consumer who has received digital content that does not conform to the contract to get it repaired or replaced; the remedies are slightly different from those for goods but space precludes covering them here.

27.2.C FRENCH LAW

Code civil   **27.4 (FR)**

Article 1643: He [the seller] is liable for latent defects, even though he did not know of them, unless he has stipulated that he would not be bound to any warranty in that case.

Article 1644: In the cases of Articles 1641 and 1643, the buyer has the choice either of returning the thing and having the price repaid to him or of keeping the thing and having a part of the price repaid to him, as appraised by experts.

Article 1645: Where the seller knew of the defects of the thing, he is liable, in addition to restitution of the price which he received from him, for all damages towards the buyer.

Article 1646: Where the seller did not know of the defects of the thing, he is only liable for restitution of the price and for reimbursing the buyer for the costs occasioned by the sale.

Notes

(1) In French law[27] the situation of non-conformity is complicated because the general law of contract is supplemented by several sets of rules: (i) on the non-conformity of the good *stricto sensu* (*obligation de délivrance conforme*, Articles 1604 ff Cciv): (ii) on hidden defects of the goods (*garantie des vices cachés*,

---

[25] See CRD Art 6(1).
[26] See 21.17 (EN), above, p 842.
[27] See generally A Bénabent, *Droit des contrats spéciaux civils et commerciaux* (12th edn, Paris: LGDJ, 2017) nos. 181–95, 231–59.

Articles 1641 ff Cciv); and (iii) on the non-conformity of the goods sold in consumer contracts (*garantie de conformité du droit de la consommation*, Articles L 217-9 Cconsom).

(2) For years, case law experienced difficulties to clearly distinguish the obligation de *délivrance conforme* from the *garantie des vices cachés*.[28] The confusion might seem surprising as the two concepts have different scopes: the obligation de *délivrance conforme* is applicable when the goods do not comply with the specifications agreed upon by the parties prior to the sale, while the *garantie des vices cachés* is applicable when the defects affect the 'normal' use of the goods and diminish their utility. Actually, this confusion was motivated by the necessity, for the buyer, to circumvent the short period (*bref délai*) allowed in which to exercise the action for hidden defects. During the 1990s, the Cour de cassation re-established the distinction between the two.[29] Thus in order to determine whether the obligation de *délivrance conforme* or the *garantie des vices cachés* is to be relied on, it might be helpful to ask the following question: non-conformity to what?[30] If there is a non-conformity to the specifications of the contract relating to the goods' characteristics[31] or use[32] set out in the contract, the buyer must rely on the *obligation de délivrance conforme*. If there is a non-conformity making the goods unfit for their normal use, the buyer must rely on the *garantie des vices cachés*.

(3) As indicated by its name, the *garantie des vices cachés* only applies when the good sold has hidden defects reducing its utility, either partially or completely. The buyer has two types of remedy available. He may choose to return the goods and recover the price (*action rédhibitoire*), which resembles termination of the contract, or he may choose to keep the goods and recover a part of the price (*action estimatoire*). On the other hand, when the buyer has to rely on the obligation de *délivrance conforme*, he can either ask for the termination of the contract or the specific performance of this obligation. We will later see that other remedies are available under special rules on consumer sales.

(4) Many rules governing the *garantie* are influenced by the seller's knowledge as to the defect. First, the restriction of the *garantie* by the parties (through a *clause de non-garantie*),[33] is allowed by Article 1643 but it is no longer effective if the seller knew that the goods had defects. Indeed, French case law has constantly reduced the validity of provisions excluding the *garantie*, especially when the seller is a professional, as he is deemed to have known the defect. It is now settled law that there is an irrebuttable presumption that a professional seller knew of the defect. Consequently, a *clause de non-garantie* is only valid when (i) the seller had no knowledge of the defect and (ii) this seller is a private individual, or is a professional dealing with another professional of the same field. Secondly, Article 1343 makes it clear that in the absence

---

[28] Cass civ (1) 20 March 1989, no. 87-18517, Bull I no. 140; see Bénabent (n 27 above) no. 186.
[29] Cass civ (1) 5 May 1993, no. 90-18331, Bull I no. 158.
[30] Bénabent (n 27 above) no. 187.
[31] Cass civ (1) 29 May 1996, no. 94-15263, Bull I no. 230.
[32] Cass civ (3) 7 June 1995, nos. 13-19945 and 13-27050, Bull III no. 15.
[33] Bénabent (n 27 above) no. 233.

of a disclaimer, ignorance of the defect is not a defence to liability under the *garantie*. Finally, regarding the award of damages alongside the *action estimatoire* (ie when the buyer chooses to pay a reduced price) or the *action rédhibitoire* (when the buyer chooses to return the thing and to recover the price),[34] knowledge of the defect is also paramount. Indeed, Articles 1645 and 1646 state that the seller is only liable to damages if he knew about the defect. Further, as there is an irrebuttable presumption that a professional seller knew about the defect, the professional seller will always be liable in damages if the buyer has sustained a loss.

(5) The *action rédhibitoire* appears to lead to the same results as termination for non-conformity. However, there is a difference as regards restitution, since the Cour de cassation, in a series of cases,[35] held that if the *action rédhibitoire* is granted, the seller must give back the price previously received and has no claim for compensation based upon the use of the goods or its depreciation due to that use. This exception to the general regime of restitution is worth noting even though authors have cast doubt on the validity of this solution after the 2016 reforms.[36] Moreover, in contrast to the position under the English Sale of Goods Act 1979, section 35 and CRA 2015, section 24,[37] a French buyer can claim cancellation on the basis of the *garantie des vices cachés* despite considerable use of the goods.

(6) Under Article 1648 Cciv, the buyer must bring his action within a two-year period (before 2005, the aforementioned provision required the buyer to sue the seller within a *bref délai*, a rather vague concept which was partly responsible for the blurring of the definition of the *obligation de délivrance conforme*). The period does not start from the date of sale or of delivery of the goods, but from the date at which the buyer discovered the defect—not only its existence, but also its impact. This means that, very often, the delay will start only after an expert has given a report.[38] This specific period is, however, subject to the general prescription period of five years (Law of 17 June 2008) which starts from the sale itself.[39]

(7) If the buyer brings an *action estimatoire* and thus asks for a reduction in the price, the amount of the reduction is to be adjudged by experts. More usually in civil law systems the price is reduced by the proportion that the value of the goods actually delivered bears to the value they should have had they not been defective, and this appears to be a restitutionary remedy rather than one measured by the buyer's loss. Once again, the price reduction does not prevent the buyer claiming for damages in addition.

(8) When the defect is both a hidden defect and a defect precluding the goods to comply with the contract specifications, is the buyer free to choose among the available actions?[40] The basic principle is that the buyer may choose among them, within certain limits.[41]

---

[34] Bénabent (n 27 above) no. 245.
[35] Cass civ (1) 21 March 2006, nos. 03-16075, 03-16307 and 03-16407, Bull I nos. 171, 172 and 173.
[36] Bénabent (n 27 above) no. 244.
[37] See above, p 1151.
[38] Bénabent (n 27 above) no. 242.
[39] ibid.
[40] ibid, no. 259.
[41] Bénabent (n 27 above) no. 244; Cass civ (3) 4 October 1995, no. 93-14879, Bull III no. 216.

(9) When the action based on the hidden defects is available to a buyer, the Cour de cassation held that the buyer cannot exercise an action based upon mistake.[42] The solution was duly criticised by French authors as inconsistent because there is no such hierarchy in the case of fraud[43] and as unfair because a buyer who fulfils the conditions of various actions should have a choice.[44] Moreover, in consumer sales, such a choice is allowed by Article L 217-13 of the Code de la consommation.

(10) Where the goods have been bought by the seller from a third party before being supplied to the buyer (who is thus a sub-buyer or *sous-acquereur*), the *garantie des vices cachés* may be the basis of an *action directe* by the sub-buyer against the original seller. If the goods have been the subject of a series of sales, for example by the manufacturer to a wholesaler and then by the wholesaler to the retailer who in turn sold to the sub-buyer, the sub-buyer may bring an action based on the *garantie des vices cachés* against any of the previous sellers. This will be particularly useful to sub-buyers if their immediate seller is insolvent or cannot be traced. The original seller's liability will be based on the terms of the contract under which they sold, including any valid clause limiting their liability, since it is considered that the action is transmitted together with the goods sold.[45]

Code de la consommation **27.5 (FR)**

Article L 217-9: In the event of lack of conformity, the buyer shall choose between repair and replacement of the product.

The seller may nevertheless elect not to proceed in accordance with the buyer's choice if that choice gives rise to a manifestly disproportionate cost compared with the other option given the value of the product or the seriousness of the defect. He is then required to proceed with the option not chosen by the buyer, unless this proves impossible.

Article L 217-10: If neither repair nor replacement of the product is possible, the buyer may return the product and obtain reimbursement of the price or keep the product and obtain reimbursement of a portion of the price.

He has the same option:

1. If the solution requested, proposed or agreed pursuant to Article L 211-9 cannot be implemented within one month of the buyer making his claim;

2. Or if that solution cannot be implemented without major inconvenience for the buyer given the nature of the product and his intended use.

The sale shall not be cancelled, however, if the lack of conformity is minor.

Article L 217-11: The provisions of Articles L 211-9 and L 211-10 shall be applied at no cost to the buyer.

Those same provisions shall not impede the awarding of damages.

---

[42] Cass civ (1) 14 May 1996, no. 94-13921, Bull I no. 213.

[43] Cass civ (3) 29 November 2000, no. 98-21224, Bull III no. 182.

[44] P Malaurie, L Aynès and P Stoffel-Munck, *Droit des obligations* (9th edn, Paris: LexisNexis, 2017), no. 497.

[45] The legal basis for such an *action directe* was much disputed; it lies in the transmission of the action 'à titre d'accessoires juridiques', Bénabent (n 27 above) no. 239 and no. 158.

Article L 217-12: Action resulting from lack of conformity lapses two years after delivery of the product.

Article L 217-13: The provisions of the present section do not deprive the buyer of the right to bring an action on account of latent defects as provided for in Articles 1641 to 1649 of the Civil Code or any other action of a contractual or extra-contractual nature to which he is entitled under the law.

Article L 217-14: An action for indemnity may be brought by the final seller against the successive sellers or intermediaries and the producer of tangible movable property, pursuant to the principles of the Civil Code.

Article L 241-5: Any agreement between the seller and the buyer which was entered into prior to the latter making a claim and which directly or indirectly nullifies or limits the rights Articles L 217-1 to L 217-20 concerning the guarantee of conformity of goods, commercial guarantee or after-sale services.

Notes

(1) Following the pattern set by the Directive, the Code provisions require a consumer buyer first to seek repair or replacement of the goods; he must not choose repair if that would be disproportionate compared to replacement or vice versa. Only if neither repair nor replacement is possible, or cannot be carried out within a month or without major inconvenience to the buyer, may the buyer claim price reduction or reimbursement of the price, and full reimbursement is not permitted if the defect is minor.

(2) These provisions are without prejudice to the buyer's right to damages for any loss he has suffered as the result of the non-performance (Article L 211-11).

(3) The buyer is not obliged to employ these provisions. He may equally claim under the *garantie* or simply sue for non-performance under the general rules (Article L 211-13). However, there will normally be little point in so doing when the buyer wants price reduction or damages. However, if he wants his money back, it seems that the remedies under the *garantie* may be slightly better because he does not have to give the seller the chance to cure the defect before he recovers the price. In neither case will he recover if the defect is not serious: under the *garantie*, the defect must be 'of a certain seriousness' while under Article L 211-10 he will not recover the price if the defect is minor.

27.2.D GERMAN LAW

The German law applicable when the buyer has received defective goods was changed radically from 1 January 2002.[46] Under the previous law, the seller's responsibility for defects in goods appeared to be absolute: the seller could not defeat a buyer's claim by showing that it was in no way his fault that the goods were 'defective'—for example,

---

[46] See B Markesinis, H Unberath and A Johnston, *The German Law of Contract* (2nd edn, Oxford: Hart Publishing, 2006) 493–520; R Zimmermann, *The New German Law of Obligations* (Oxford University Press, 2005) ch 3.

because no one could have discovered the defect. However, the buyer did not necessarily have the full range of remedies. In the absence of a promise that the goods have a particular quality or fraudulent concealment of a known defect (§ 463) the buyer's only remedies were cancellation (*Wandlung*) and price reduction (*Minderung*) (former §§ 459(1), 462 BGB). In 2001 it was decided to update the whole law of sales by adopting, broadly speaking, the model of the Directive on consumer sales for all sales and by making the remedies much closer to those available the general law.

BGB   **27.6 (DE)**

§ 437: Buyer's rights in the event of defects
    If the thing is defective, then, if the requirements of the following provisions are satisfied and save as otherwise provided, the buyer may
    1. demand supplementary performance under § 439;
    2. terminate the contract under §§ 440, 323, and 326(5), or reduce the purchase price under § 441; and
    3. claim compensation under §§ 440, 280, 281, 283 and 311a, or reimbursement for wasted expenditure under § 284.

§ 439: Supplementary performance
    (1) As supplementary performance, the buyer may, at his option, demand the removal of the defect or supply of a thing free from defects.
    (2) The seller must bear all expenditure required for the purposes of supplementary performance, in particular carriage, transport, labour and material costs.
    (3) If the buyer has fitted or attached the defective thing to other things according to their nature and their purpose, the seller is, within the regime of supplementary performance, under an obligation to compensate the buyer for the necessary expenditure for removing the defective thing or the fitting or the attachment of the improved or delivered thing that is free from defects. ...
    (4) Without prejudice to § 275(2) and (3), the seller may refuse the form of supplementary performance chosen by the buyer if such performance is possible only with unreasonable expense. In that connection, it is necessary to have regard in particular to the value of the thing when free from defects, the significance of the defect and the question whether the defect could be remedied by the other form of supplementary performance without material detriment to the buyer. The buyer's claim is restricted in this case to the other form of supplementary performance; the seller's right to refuse also that supplementary performance under the conditions laid out in sentence 1 above is unaffected.
    (5) If the seller delivers a thing free from defects for the purpose of supplementary performance, he may demand the return of the defective thing in accordance with §§ 346 to 348.

§ 440: Special provisions on withdrawal and damages
    Apart from in the cases set out in § 281(2) and § 323(2), it is also not necessary to specify a period of time if the seller has refused to carry out both kinds of cure under § 439 (4) or if the kind of cure that the buyer is entitled to receive has failed or cannot reasonably be expected of him. A repair is deemed to have failed after the second unsuccessful attempt, unless in particular the nature of the thing or of the defect or the other circumstances leads to a different conclusion.

§ 441: Price reduction

(1) Instead of terminating the contract, the buyer may, by declaration to the seller, reduce the price. The exclusion in § 323(5), sentence 2, does not apply.

(2) If the buyer or the seller consists of more than one person, price reduction may be declared only by or to all such persons.

(3) In the case of price reduction, the purchase price is reduced in the ratio which the value of the thing free of defects would, at the time of the conclusion of the contract, have had to the actual value. Where necessary, the price reduction is to be estimated.

(4) If the buyer has paid more than the reduced purchase price, the excess amount is to be refunded by the seller. § 346(1) and § 347(1) apply mutatis mutandis.

Notes

(1) The remedies available to the buyer who has received defective goods are in many ways very close to those available under the general law. First, under § 439 BGB, he may seek to enforce performance by having the goods repaired or replaced, subject to the restrictions that the kind of cure chosen (repair or replacement) must not be disproportionate to the other form, nor, as under the general law, must cure be disproportionate to his interest.

(2) If cure is not available or the seller fails to carry it out, then the buyer may either claim damages in lieu of performance (§ 281) or terminate (§ 323). The only special rule relates to warnings: if the seller has refused to cure or cure has failed, no warning is needed: § 440. Note the provision that repair is deemed to have failed after the second unsuccessful attempt.

(3) Where the sales provisions differ from the general rules of the BGB is in giving the buyer the right to reduce the price. This seems to be considered as a form of partial termination, hence the disapplication of § 323(5) second sentence, which normally prevents termination in cases of a minor non-performance.

(4) The remedies of cure, termination and price reduction apply whether or not the seller was at fault in any way. The buyer may also have the remedy of damages under either § 280 (simple damages) or § 281 (damages in lieu of performance). The right to damages depends on the seller being responsible. That in turn depends on the seller having acted intentionally or negligently, or having given a guarantee. Thus liability for damages is not very different to before the reforms.

(5) The remedies in case of non-conformity of goods sold are subject to a limitation period of two years from the date of delivery: § 438(1) no.3. This appears to reflect Article 5(1) of the Consumer Sales Directive, which requires that the consumer's rights must not be subject to a limitation period shorter than two years from the date of delivery. It does not seem that the buyer's right to terminate is otherwise affected by the lapse of time under the BGB, but under the HGB (Commercial code) there is a more general limitation.

HGB **27.7 (DE)**

§ 377: (1) If the sale is a commercial transaction for both parties, the buyer should examine the goods immediately after their delivery by the seller, to the extent that this is possible in the ordinary course of business, and if a defect is found he should without delay notify the seller.

(2) If the buyer fails to give notice, the goods are considered approved unless the defect was not one which was discernible upon examination.

This provision affects all the remedies. It has no counterpart in English or French law, nor in the Principles of European Contract Law (PECL). However, the Draft Common Frame of Reference (DCFR) has a similar provision. In addition to a rule requiring that notice of termination be given within a reasonable time of when the buyer knew or ought to have known of the non-performance,[47] and a general limitation period of three years[48] (which may be extended while the buyer did not know of the non-conformity),[49] a buyer who knows of a non-performance must notify the seller.

Draft Common Frame of Reference **27.8 (INT)**

Article III.-3:107: Failure to notify non-conformity

(1) If, in the case of an obligation to supply goods or services, the debtor supplies goods or services which are not in conformity with the terms regulating the obligation, the creditor may not rely on the lack of conformity unless the creditor gives notice to the debtor within a reasonable time specifying the nature of the lack of conformity.

(2) The reasonable time runs from the time when the goods are supplied or the service is completed or from the time, if it is later, when the creditor discovered or could reasonably be expected to have discovered the non-conformity.

(3) The debtor is not entitled to rely on paragraph (1) if the failure relates to facts which the debtor knew or could reasonably be expected to have known and which the debtor did not disclose to the creditor.

(4) This Article does not apply where the creditor is a consumer.

If the buyer terminates the contract because the seller fails (or is not required) to repair or replace the goods, the buyer will recover the price but have to make an allowance for the use he or she has had from the goods. Some companies took the position that the same should be true when the seller replaced an item which had been used with a new item. The ECJ disagreed.

Court of Justice, 17 April 2008 **27.9 (EU)**

***Quelle AG v Bundesverband der Verbraucherzentralen und Verbraucherverbände*[50]**

Article 3 of Directive 1999/44/EC of the European Parliament and of the Council of 25 May 1999 on certain aspects of the sale of consumer goods and associated guarantees precludes national legislation under which a seller who has sold consumer goods which are not in conformity may require the consumer to pay compensation for the use of those defective goods until their replacement with new goods.

---

[47] DCFR III-3:508.
[48] DCFR III-7:201.
[49] DCFR III-7:301.
[50] C-404/06, ECLI:EU:C:2008:231.

Facts: In August 2002, Quelle AG, a mail-order company, delivered a 'stove-set' to Ms Brüning for her private use. In early 2004, Ms Brüning noticed that the appliance was not in conformity. Since repair was not possible, Ms Brüning returned the appliance to Quelle, who replaced it with a new appliance. However, Quelle required Ms Brüning to pay €69.97 by way of compensation for the benefit which she had obtained from use of the appliance initially delivered. The Bundesverband der Verbraucherzentralen und Verbraucherverbände ('the Bundesverband'), an authorised consumers' association acting on behalf of Ms Brüning, demanded reimbursement to her of that amount. In addition, it applied for an order prohibiting Quelle, in cases where goods not in conformity with the contract of sale ('not in conformity') are replaced, from invoicing consumers for the use of those goods. The court at first instance granted the application for reimbursement, but dismissed the order not to invoice customers for the use of goods not in conformity. Both Quelle and the Bundesverband appealed this decision and both appeals were dismissed. Appeals on points of law were brought before the BGH. The BGH noted that, under section 439(4) [now 439(5)] of the BGB, read in conjunction with section 346(1) and (2)(1) thereof, the seller is entitled to payment by way of compensation for the benefits derived by the purchaser from the use of those goods until their replacement with new goods in cases where goods not in conformity are replaced. The BGH expressed doubts regarding the unilateral burden thus placed on the purchaser, and stated that it saw no way of correcting the national legislation by means of interpretation. An interpretation to the effect that the seller could not claim payment from the purchaser for use of the replaced goods would be at odds with the wording of the relevant provisions of the BGB and the clear intention of the legislature, and is prohibited by Article 20(3) of the Basic Law (Grundgesetz), according to which judicial authority is bound by legislation and by the law. Subsequently the BGH asked the ECJ a preliminary question concerning the transposition of Article 3 of the Directive in German law.

Held: Article 3 of Directive 1999/44/EC of the European Parliament and of the Council of 25 May 1999 on certain aspects of the sale of consumer goods and associated guarantees is to be interpreted as precluding national legislation under which a seller who has sold consumer goods which are not in conformity may require the consumer to pay compensation for the use of those defective goods until their replacement with new goods.

Judgment:

1 This reference for a preliminary ruling relates to the interpretation of Article 3 of Directive 1999/44/EC of the European Parliament and of the Council of 25 May 1999 on certain aspects of the sale of consumer goods and associated guarantees (OJ 1999 L171, p 12; 'the Directive').

Legal context

Community legislation

...

5 The 15th recital in the preamble to the Directive states that 'Member States may provide that any reimbursement to the consumer may be reduced to take account of the use the consumer has had of the goods since they were delivered to him; ... the detailed arrangements whereby rescission of the contract is effected may be laid down in national law'. ...

National legislation

8 Paragraphs 439 and 346 are among the provisions of the German Civil Code (Bürgerliches Gesetzbuch; 'the BGB') adopted in order to transpose the Directive into German domestic law. ...

10 Paragraph 346(1) to (3) of the BGB, entitled 'Effects of termination of the contract', states as follows:

'1. If one party to a contract has reserved the right to terminate the contract or if he has a statutory right of termination, then, if termination occurs, any performance received shall be returned, and the benefits derived from such performance shall be surrendered.

2. The debtor shall pay compensation for value, in lieu of restitution or surrender, where:

(1) restitution or surrender is excluded by virtue of the nature of what has been obtained;

(2) he has used up, transferred, encumbered, processed or transformed the object received;

(3) the object received has deteriorated or has been destroyed, any deterioration resulting from the proper use of the object for its intended purposes being disregarded.

If the contract specifies a counter-performance, such counter-performance shall be taken as a basis for calculation of the compensation for value; if compensation is to be paid for the benefit deriving from a loan, it shall be sufficient to show that the value of such benefit was lower.

3. No obligation to pay compensation for value shall arise:

(1) if the defect which gives the right to termination became apparent only during the processing or transformation of the object;

(2) in so far as the creditor is responsible for the deterioration or destruction, or in so far as the damage would also have occurred in his hands;

(3) if, in the case of a statutory right of termination, the deterioration or destruction has occurred in the hands of the person entitled, even though he has taken the care that he customarily exercises in relation to his own affairs.

Any remaining enrichment must be surrendered.'

11 Paragraph 100 of the BGB, headed 'Benefits', provides that:

'Benefits are the fruits of a thing or of a right, including the benefits arising from use of the thing or exercise of the right'. ...

The question referred

17 By its question, the national court essentially asks whether Article 3 of the Directive is to be interpreted as precluding national legislation under which a seller who has sold consumer goods which are not in conformity may require the consumer to pay compensation for the use of those defective goods until their replacement with new goods.

...

Substance

24 According to the Bundesverband, the Spanish and Austrian Governments and the Commission of the European Communities, Article 3(3) of the Directive clearly establishes that it is not only the repair of goods not in conformity that must be carried out for the consumer free of charge by the seller, but also—where appropriate—their replacement with goods which are in conformity. In all the situations covered by that provision, the 'free of charge' requirement applies as a whole and in full, being intended to protect the purchaser from the risk of financial burdens which might dissuade him from asserting his rights.

25 The German Government observes that the wording of the Directive gives no clear indication whether the seller may, in cases where goods not in conformity are replaced, claim payment for the use of those goods. It points out that, in terms of internal logic, the 15th recital in the preamble to the Directive sets out a very general principle of law, leaving the Member States entirely free to legislate on the question concerning the situations in which the consumer is required to pay compensation for the use of goods.

26 As a preliminary point, it should be borne in mind that, under Article 3(1) of the Directive, the seller is to be liable to the consumer for any lack of conformity in the goods at the time when they are delivered.

27 Article 3(2) of the Directive lists the rights which the consumer may rely on against the seller in cases where the goods delivered are not in conformity. Initially, the consumer has the right to require the goods to be brought into conformity. If that is not possible, he may subsequently require a reduction in the price or rescission of the contract.

28 As regards the bringing into conformity of the goods, Article 3(3) of the Directive states that the consumer is entitled to require the seller to repair the goods or to replace them—in either case free of charge—unless that is impossible or disproportionate.

29 The German Government argues that, in both Proposal 96/C 307/09 for a European Parliament and Council Directive on the sale of consumer goods and associated guarantees (OJ 1996 C 307, p 8) and Amended Proposal 98/C 148/11 for a European Parliament and Council Directive (OJ 1998 C 148, p 12), submitted by the Commission, the text merely referred either to a repair of the goods free of charge or to a replacement thereof. The fact that those proposals are silent as to the financial consequences of replacement goes to show that it was not intended that the Directive should govern the question of compensation for use.

30 However, that is entirely irrelevant since it is the expression 'in either case free of charge'—used in Common Position (EC) No 51/98, adopted by the Council on 24 September 1998 with a view to adopting the Directive (OJ 1998 C 333, p 46)—which was retained in the definitive text, thus reflecting the intention of the Community legislature to strengthen consumer protection.

31 The expression 'free of charge' is defined in Article 3(4) of the Directive as referring to 'the necessary costs incurred to bring the goods into conformity, particularly the cost of postage, labour and materials'. It follows from the use by the Community legislature of the adverb 'particularly' that that list is illustrative, not exhaustive.

32 The fact, relied upon by the German Government, that Press Release C/99/77 of the 'Parliament—Council' Conciliation Committee of 18 March 1999 on agreement on consumer guarantees gives a restrictive definition of the term 'free of charge' is irrelevant in that regard. It is settled case-law that, where a statement recorded in Council minutes is not referred to in the wording of a provision of secondary legislation, it cannot be used for the purpose of interpreting that provision (see, inter alia, Case C-292/89 *Antonissen* [1991] ECR I-745, paragraph 18, and Case C-402/03 *Skov and Bilka* [2006] ECR I-199, paragraph 42).

33 Thus it follows from the wording of the Directive, as well as from the related travaux préparatoires, that the Community legislature intended to make the 'free of charge' aspect of the seller's obligation to bring goods into conformity an essential element of the protection afforded to consumers by the Directive.

34 The 'free of charge' requirement attaching to the seller's obligation to bring the goods into conformity, whether by repair or replacement, is intended to protect consumers from the risk of financial burdens which, as the Advocate General observed in point 49 of her Opinion, might dissuade them from asserting their rights in the absence of such protection. The certain nature of the 'free of charge' aspect, which was intentional on the part of the Community legislature, means that the seller cannot make any financial claim in connection with the performance of its obligation to bring into conformity the goods to which the contract relates.

35 Support for that interpretation is to be found in the intention, manifested by the Community legislature in the third subparagraph of Article 3(3) of the Directive, to provide effective protection to consumers. That provision states that any repair or replacement is to be completed not only within a reasonable time but also without significant inconvenience to the consumer.

36 That interpretation is also consistent with the purpose of the Directive which, as stated in the first recital in the preamble thereto, is to ensure a high level of consumer protection. As follows from Article 8(2) of the Directive, the protection provided by it is minimal and, although Member States may adopt more stringent provisions, they may not undermine the guarantees laid down by the Community legislature.

37 The other arguments advanced by the German Government against that interpretation are not such as to call it into question.

38 As regards, first, the scope which must be accorded to the 15th recital in the preamble to the Directive, which permits account to be taken of the use the consumer has had of the goods not in conformity, it should be noted that the first part of that recital refers to a 'reimbursement' to be made to the consumer, whereas the second part mentions the 'detailed arrangements whereby rescission of the contract is effected'. Those expressions are identical to those used in the Common Position of the Council to which the German Government also referred.

39 That terminology makes it clear that the situation envisaged in the 15th recital is restricted to cases where the contract is terminated, as provided for in Article 3(5) of the Directive, and where, pursuant to the principle that the contracting parties must each give up the benefits they have received, the seller must reimburse to the consumer the selling price of the goods. Contrary to the contentions of the German Government, the 15th recital cannot, therefore, be interpreted as a general principle enabling the Member States to take account, in any situation they wish, including that of a mere request for replacement submitted pursuant to Article 3(3) of the Directive, of the use which the consumer has had of goods not in conformity.

40 As regards, secondly, the German Government's assertion that the fact that, by virtue of the replacement of goods not in conformity, the consumer has the benefit of new goods without having to make proper payment constitutes unjust enrichment, it should be borne in mind that Article 3(1) of the Directive makes the seller liable to the consumer for any lack of conformity which exists at the time the goods are delivered.

41 If a seller delivers goods which are not in conformity, it fails correctly to perform the obligation which it accepted in the contract of sale and must therefore bear the consequences of that faulty performance. By receiving new goods to replace the goods not in conformity, the consumer—who, for his part, paid the selling price and therefore correctly performed his contractual obligation—is not unjustly enriched. He merely receives, belatedly, goods in conformity with the specifications of the contract, which he should have received at the outset.

42 The fact remains that the seller's financial interests are protected, on the one hand, by the two-year time-limit laid down in Article 5(1) of the Directive and, on the other, by the fact that, under the second subparagraph of Article 3(3) of the Directive, it may refuse to replace the goods where that remedy would be disproportionate in that it would impose unreasonable costs on the seller.

43 In the light of all the foregoing, the answer to the question referred must be that Article 3 of the Directive is to be interpreted as precluding national legislation under which a seller who has sold consumer goods which are not in conformity may require the

consumer to pay compensation for the use of those defective goods until their replacement with new goods.

Note

The German legislator brought national sales law in line with this decision by inserting § 475(3) BGB.

27.2.E INTERNATIONAL RESTATEMENTS

Neither the PECL nor the UNIDROIT PICC have specific provisions on sale, presumably because sale was thought to be covered adequately by the Vienna Convention on International Sale of Goods (1980) (CISG). There is not space to cover the CISG in this book.[51] The DCFR contains a book on sales; readers with a particular interest in the remedies for non-conformity may wish to look at the provisions in Book IVA, Chapter 4. Sales are in general subject to the provisions on remedies noted earlier, but there are articles dealing with consumer sales and, for non-consumer sales, requirements of notification which are more demanding than under the general provisions. Likewise the proposed Common European Sales Law (now withdrawn)[52] dealt with both B2B and B2C sales.

27.3 SERVICES CONTRACTS

When a trader has contracted to provide services to a customer, and the services provided do not conform to the contract, the remedies available to the customer in French and German law[53] are the same whether or not the customer is a consumer. In French law, the *garantie* set in the Code de la consommation is only applicable to contracts for sale of moveable and material goods (Article L 217-1 Cconso), services contracts being excluded from its scope. Further, there is no set of rules establishing a similar *garantie* in the Code de la consommation for services contracts. Thus, if a customer thinks the service provided does not conform to the contract, he will have to rely both on the *droit commun* and on the text governing the specific contract at stake to obtain remedies. In English law, in contrast, the remedies available differ very much according to whether or not the claimant is a consumer. Non-consumers will very seldom be able to get specific performance against the trader.[54] If the non-conformity prevents there being substantial completion, they may be entitled to refuse to pay the price to the trader;[55] or if it is so serious that it deprives the customer of the substance of what he was contracting for, the

---

[51] See works such as P Schlechtriem and I Schwenzer, *Commentary on the UN Convention on the International Sale of Goods (CISG)* (4th edn, Oxford University Press, 2016).
[52] See above, p 70.
[53] On German law see Markesinis et al (n 46 above) 520–33.
[54] See ch 23 above, esp pp 910 and 914.
[55] See above, p 966.

customer may terminate the contract.[56] In any case the customer can claim damages. In effect, if the trader will not correct the non-conformity voluntarily, the consumer will have to employ someone else to do the work and claim damages for the extra cost. A customer who is a consumer, in contrast, now has the right to have the work done again by the trader, a right that can be enforced by an order of specific performance.[57]

Consumer Rights Act 2015   **27.10 (EN)**

Section 54: Consumer's rights to enforce terms about services

(1) The consumer's rights under this section and sections 55 and 56 do not affect any rights that the contract provides for, if those are not inconsistent.

(2) In this section and section 55 a reference to a service conforming to a contract is a reference to—

(a) the service being performed in accordance with section 49, or

(b) the service conforming to a term that section 50 requires to be treated as included in the contract and that relates to the performance of the service.

(3) If the service does not conform to the contract, the consumer's rights (and the provisions about them and when they are available) are—

(a) the right to require repeat performance (see section 55);

(b) the right to a price reduction (see section 56).

...

(6) This section and sections 55 and 56 do not prevent the consumer seeking other remedies for a breach of a term to which any of subsections (3) to (5) applies, instead of or in addition to a remedy referred to there (but not so as to recover twice for the same loss).

(7) Those other remedies include any of the following that is open to the consumer in the circumstances—

(a) claiming damages;

(b) seeking to recover money paid where the consideration for payment of the money has failed;

(c) seeking specific performance;

(d) seeking an order for specific implement;

(e) relying on the breach against a claim by the trader under the contract;

(f) exercising a right to treat the contract as at an end.

Section 55: Right to repeat performance

(1) The right to require repeat performance is a right to require the trader to perform the service again, to the extent necessary to complete its performance in conformity with the contract.

---

[56] See above, pp 969–72.
[57] See *Chitty* (n 6 above) paras 38-580–38-584 (consumers: services).

(2) If the consumer requires such repeat performance, the trader—

(a) must provide it within a reasonable time and without significant inconvenience to the consumer; and

(b) must bear any necessary costs incurred in doing so (including in particular the cost of any labour or materials).

(3) The consumer cannot require repeat performance if completing performance of the service in conformity with the contract is impossible.

...

FURTHER READING

Boosfeld, K, 'Price Reduction' in N Jansen and R Zimmermann (eds), *Commentaries on European Contract Laws* (Oxford University Press, 2018) 1422–31.

Martens, S and Rüfner, T, 'Obligations of Buyer and Seller, Remedies' in N Jansen and R Zimmermann (eds), *Commentaries on European Contract Laws* (Oxford University Press, 2018) 1973–2021.

Willems, C, 'Obligations of the Parties to a (related) Service Contract' in N Jansen and R Zimmermann (eds), *Commentaries on European Contract Laws* (Oxford University Press, 2018) 2073–2120.

PART 6
SUPERVENING EVENTS

CHAPTER 28
IMPOSSIBILITY OF PERFORMANCE

28.1 INTRODUCTION TO PART SIX

A contracting party may fail to perform even though the failure is not due to her fault or under her responsibility.[1] Supervening events may make performance impossible in a wide range of situations: destruction of the subject matter of the contract, its unavailability (for instance, if a ship or aircraft is requisitioned by the government), or the death or incapacity of a party who had undertaken a personal obligation. In this Part we consider cases in which the supervening event has occurred without the fault of the debtor (and the debtor is not responsible on some other basis, for example if the debtor has undertaken the risk that the event will not occur).[2]

A distinction is drawn between circumstances or events which render the performance of the contract impossible and those which merely make it more difficult or onerous. The position of French law on this question used to be clear-cut: it was all or nothing. Either there was total impossibility and the debtor was freed on the ground of *force majeure* (fortuitous event) or else he had to perform the contract, however onerous its performance had become. The new Code civil now recognises both impossibility (*force majeure*) (Articles 1231-1, 1351) and *imprévision*, which means that the judge is given the power to revise or terminate the contract if it has become excessively onerous for one of the parties and the parties are not able to agree on an adjustment (Article 1195 Cciv).[3] German law distinguishes various categories of impossibility and also allows the courts to adapt contracts in the event of change of circumstances. In English law, impossibility of performance includes the notion of that which renders the contract 'something radically different from that which was in the contemplation of the parties', which arguably goes further than *force majeure*. However, unlike French and German law, English law does not allow the courts to adapt contracts in the event of change of circumstances.

Chapter 28 will consider the consequences of impossibility of performance and Chapter 29 will deal with situations where performance of the contract has become much more onerous. In both situations, the rules of the various legal systems are not mandatory.

---

[1] See above, Part Five, for situations where non-performance is not excused.
[2] See below, ch 30.
[3] See below, pp 1173–80, 1211–19.

Most of the time, parties foresee such possibilities when entering the contract and make provision for the occurrence of unlikely events. Chapter 30 analyses contractual clauses by which the parties seek to anticipate the consequences of unforeseen events, for instance rent indexation clauses designed to overcome the consequences of monetary inflation, *force majeure* clauses or hardship clauses.

In the absence of such clauses, the first question is one of classification: is this a case of impossibility or has the contract merely become more onerous for one party to perform? From a legal point of view, the consequences are very different. If the situation is within the notion of impossibility, the debtor is discharged of his obligations. Should it merely fall within the other category ('more onerous'), the consequences vary according to the national laws and the debtor may still be bound to perform, if not the entire obligation, at least part of it. In practice, the distinction between the circumstances or events which render the performance of the contract impossible and those which merely make it more difficult or onerous is fluid. It operates differently in the national legal systems, which each have their own doctrines. These doctrines reflect the way each legal system deals with ever conflicting policy questions: an emphasis put on contractual certainty leads to narrow escape routes, while, in contrast, a search for contractual fairness suggests a more flexible approach which may even lead to judicial adaptation of the contract. It would be unjust to overwhelm the debtor by making him bear all the consequences of unforeseen events.

28.2 IMPOSSIBILITY

Chapter 28, on impossibility, deals with the consequences of an event which is not the fault or responsibility of the debtor and which prevents the debtor from performing the obligation. It is a commercially sensitive matter, both for internal and international contracts. A fairly wide divergence in national laws may be noted. It may be wondered whether the international instruments have succeeded in harmonising them.

The United Nations Convention on Contracts for the International Sale of Goods (CISG) of 11 April 1980, which has been adopted by nearly 90 States, provides for discharge as a result of impossibility of performance (Article 79). This text formed the point of departure for the Principles of European Contract law (PECL) and the Draft Common Frame of Reference (DCFR), as well as for the UNIDROIT Principles of International Commercial Contracts (UNIDROIT PICC).[4]

Principles of European Contract Law   **28.1 (INT)**

Article 8:108: Excuse Due to an Impediment

(1) A party's non-performance is excused if it proves that it is due to an impediment beyond its control and that it could not reasonably have been expected to take the impediment into account at the time of the conclusion of the contract, or to have avoided or overcome the impediment or its consequences.

---

[4] See Art 7.1.7 UNIDROIT PICC.

(2) Where the impediment is only temporary the excuse provided by this Article has effect for the period during which the impediment exists. However, if the delay amounts to a fundamental non-performance, the creditor may treat it as such.

(3) The non-performing party must ensure that notice of the impediment and of its effect on its ability to perform is received by the other party within a reasonable time after the non-performing party knew or ought to have known of these circumstances. The other party is entitled to damages for any loss resulting from the non-receipt of such notice.

The concept of impossibility of performance covers the doctrines of *force majeure*, frustration and 'excuse due to an impediment' (PECL, DCFR). In the UNIDROIT PICC the term *force majeure* was chosen for the title of Article 7.1.7 because it is widely known in international trade practice and many international contracts include '*force majeure* clauses'. However, the black letter rule, Article 7.1.7, resorts to the concept of 'impediment' and is very similar to the provisions of the PECL. The term 'impediment' covers every sort of event (such as natural occurrences, restraints of princes and acts of third parties).

Each national legal systems has its own doctrine: *force majeure* in French law (28.3), impossibility (*Unmöglichkeit*) in German law (28.4) and frustration in English law (28.5).

28.3 FRENCH LAW

The courts at first developed a theory of *force majeure* on the basis of two short articles of Section IV of the 1804 Code civil entitled 'Damages Resulting from Non-performance of an Obligation' (ex-Articles 1147 and 1148).[5] Since the 2016 reform, *force majeure* is defined in Article 1218 (see below) and stated as a defence in Articles 1351 and 1351-1 in Chapter V of the Code civil on the extinction of obligations.[6]

Code civil **28.2 (FR)**

SECTION 5

Impossibility of Performance

Article 1351: Impossibility of performing the act of performance discharges the debtor to the extent of that impossibility where it results from an event of *force majeure* and is definitive unless he had agreed to bear the risk of the event or had previously been given notice to perform.

Article 1351-1: Where the impossibility of performance is a result of the loss of the thing that is owed, the debtor who has been given notice to perform is still discharged if he proves that the loss would equally have occurred if his obligation had been performed.

He must, however, assign to the creditor his rights and claims attached to the thing.

---

[5] Cciv, Section IV of Ch 3 on the 'Effect of Obligations'.

[6] On the 2016 reforms, see F Chénedé, *Le nouveau droit des obligations et des contrats: Consolidations, innovations, perspectives* (Paris: Dalloz, 2016) nos. 28.11–28.34; O Deshayes, T Genicon and YM Laithier, *Réforme du droit des contrats, du régime général et de la preuve des obligations, Commentaire article par article* (Paris: LexisNexis, 2016) 477–79; M Latina and G Chantepie, *La réforme du droit des obligations: Commentaire théorique et pratique dans l'ordre du Code civil* (Paris: Dalloz, 2016) nos. 617–26.

> *Note*
>
> It is worth noting that these new provisions create a close link between impossibility and *force majeure*, as 'impossibility of performance' can only result from an event of *force majeure*. However, the relationship between the two notions is confusing.

Classically, the impossibility of performance is one of the main conditions of the *force majeure*. The case law has since long required that for an event to be qualified as *force majeure*, the event must render the performance of the obligation impossible.[7] This condition is known as the irresistibility of the event's effects (see below) and has been codified by the 2016 reform as one of the conditions of the *force majeure*. However, under Article 1351 of the new Code civil, the 'impossibility of performance' is also regarded as the consequence of the *force majeure*.

28.3.A THE DEFINITION OF *FORCE MAJEURE*

Traditionally, an event constituted *force majeure* if it satisfied three conditions: it had to be irresistible, unforeseeable and external to the debtor. The first two conditions are now set forth in the Code civil.

Code civil 28.3 (FR)

Article 1218: In contractual matters, there is *force majeure* where an event beyond the control of the debtor, which could not reasonably have been foreseen at the time of the conclusion of the contract and whose effects could not be avoided by appropriate measures, prevents performance of his obligation by the debtor.

If the prevention is temporary, performance of the obligation is suspended unless the delay which results justifies termination of the contract. If the prevention is permanent, the contract is terminated by operation of law and the parties are discharged from their obligations under the conditions provided by articles 1351 and 1351-1.

> *Notes*
>
> (1) Two cases of the *Assemblée plénière* of the Cour de cassation had defined *force majeure* as 'an event which is unforeseeable on conclusion of the contract and irresistible in its performance'.[8] The lack of reference to the externality led commentators to wonder whether the Cour de cassation had got rid of this third condition.[9] The new Article 1218 of the Code civil seems to settle the discussion: an event does not have to be external to be qualified as *force majeure*. However, the phrase

---

[7] Cass civ (1) 8 December 1998, no. 96-17811, Bull civ I no. 346.

[8] Ass plén 14 April 2006, nos. 04-18902 and 02-11168, Bull AP nos. 6 and 5.

[9] In a *communiqué* published on its website (a new and controversial practice) the Cour de cassation has drawn attention to the fact that these two cases do not do away with the condition of an external event.

'an event *beyond the control*' could mean that the externality can be used to evaluate the irresistibility of the event.[10]

(2) The definition of Article 1218 is in line with the meaning usually given to *force majeure* under common law. In common law systems, *force majeure* is not a case law or statutory concept but rather a generic description of the application of any clause in the contract that provides relief to a party that has been prevented from performing by events outside its control. Nonetheless, the definition of *force majeure* in common law contracts usually refers to 'an event beyond the control of the parties'.[11] The use of the same expression in Article 1218 illustrates one of the objectives of the 2016 reform, that is to make French contract law 'more legible and foreseeable... [which] constitutes a factor likely to attract foreign investors and operators wishing to base their contract upon French law'.[12]

These conditions allow a fairly large judicial power of appreciation; they must be assessed in view of what a reasonable person would have considered as such.[13] Moreover, unforeseeability must be examined at the time the promise was made and not at the time the event occurs. Parties may—provided they do not rule out the rules governing unfair terms and *obligations essentielles*—specify that they are not discharged in case of *force majeure* or that specific situations falling outside its legal scope must be considered as amounting to *force majeure*.[14]

The two conditions of unforeseeability and irresistibility are connected, and the following decisions provide interesting detail on this subject.

Cass civ (1), 9 March 1994[15]   **28.4 (FR)**

The Saint-Tropez robbery

Impossibility of resisting the event in itself constitutes force majeure where to foresee it does not enable its effects to be averted.

Facts: At around 5 o'clock in the morning of 27 July 1985, four wrongdoers managed to gain access to the hotel 'Résidence des Lices', Saint-Tropez, where they forced the staff under the threat of arms to open the safe, which they emptied. On 10 June 1986 Mr Montagnani, an Italian customer of the hotel, brought proceedings against the Hotel des Lices company ('the company') and the Concorde Group, its insurer, for recovery of the equivalent of LIT 32,850,000 and USD 1,030, which he said he had deposited in the hotel's safe.

Held: According to the findings of the lower court, the judgment appealed against (Aix-en-Provence, 9 April 1991), setting aside the lower court's decision, upheld that claim, taking the view that armed robbery of that

---

[10] P Malaurie, L Aynès and P Stoffel-Munck, *Droit des obligations* (9th edn, Paris: LGDJ, 2017) no. 956.

[11] *Chitty on Contracts*, 33rd edn by H Beale (gen ed) (London: Sweet & Maxwell/Thomson Reuters, 2018) para 15-153.

[12] Report to the President (p 83 n 30 above).

[13] Malaurie et al (n 10 above) no. 952.

[14] Malaurie et al (n 10 above) no. 953.

[15] Nos. 91-17459 and 91-17464, Bull civ I, 91, RTD civ 1994, 871, annotated by P Jourdain.

kind did not constitute a case of *force majeure* for the purposes of Article 1954(1) of the Civil Code. The Cour de cassation approved.

Judgment: ... The first two branches of the sole appeal ground by the company and the first branch of the first ground of appeal of the Concorde Group, taken together:

— Whereas the company and its insurer criticise the judgment appealed against for finding there to have been no case of *force majeure* whereas, according to the appeal grounds, the cour d'appel which found that no resistance could have been offered to the armed robbery, ought to have considered whether that impossibility of resistance did not of itself constitute a case of *force majeure*; as by holding that the *hôtelier* ought to have carried out stricter controls of entries and exits and ought to have drawn up an inventory, in the presence of the parties concerned, of the items deposited, after finding there to have been violence and armed threats, the court of second instance, giving judgment on inoperative grounds, deprived its decision of any legal basis under Article 1954(1) of the Civil Code; as unforeseeability is on the other hand a relative concept and not absolute in nature; as the judgment appealed against by considering that an armed robbery was not unforeseeable in a hotel in Saint-Tropez owing to its wealthy clientele, it did not attach sufficient weight to the normal unforeseeability of armed aggression carried out by ruse in the hotel, and again it deprived its decision of any legal basis under the aforementioned provision;

— Whereas, however, although impossibility to resist the event constitutes in itself a case of *force majeure* where to foresee it does not enable its effects to be averted, the defendant must still have taken all the precautions necessary in order to avoid the occurrence of the event; as having found that the *hôtelier* or his agents and employees did not carry out a strict control of entries since the night watchman himself let in one of the wrongdoers who claimed to have an appointment with one of the hotel's customers, the cour d'appel was right in taking the view that the armed robbery in question did not constitute a case of *force majeure*, since not all the possible precautions necessitated by its foreseeability had been taken; ...

Notes

(1) Article 1954(1) of the Civil Code, cited by the Court provides: 'Innkeepers or *hôteliers* shall not be liable in respect of thefts or injury occurring as a result of *force majeure* ...'.

(2) That judgment confirms and develops earlier case law: impossibility of resisting the event in itself constitutes *force majeure* where to foresee it does not enable its effects to be averted. The rule is logical: if the event is unavoidable, even if it could be foreseen, it constitutes in itself a case of *force majeure*. In this case the Court finds that armed robbery is impossible to resist but it was foreseeable and the possible precautions 'necessitated by its foreseeability' had not been taken. If those precautions had been taken, there would have been a case of *force majeure*, notwithstanding the foreseeability of the event. The test applied by the Cour de cassation brings foreseeability into connection with the negligent conduct of the defendant, which was negligent by virtue of the fact that he did not take the precautions required by the damage foreseeably likely to occur.

(3) What is the purpose of the unforeseeability test? In principle, nearly everything can be foreseen. In fact, this test serves to evaluate the conduct of the defendant

(and thus relates to the reasonableness test aforementioned). The condition of unforeseeability makes sense if appreciated at the time of the formation of contract. For, indeed, an event which was initially unforeseeable becomes foreseeable when it occurs. Some authors believe that it would be preferable to speak of inevitability rather than unforeseeability.[16]

(4) It is sometimes difficult to distinguish between *force majeure* and the absence of fault. According to prevailing opinion, failure to fulfil obligations is not imputed to the defendant if it is not his fault, or if he is not liable under a law or legal act.

(5) The defendant's illness or unemployment may constitute external events leading to the excuse of *force majeure*. As aforementioned, although new Article 1218 of the Code civil does not require the event to be 'external' to qualify as *force majeure*, it uses the phrase 'an event *beyond the control*' which means that externality can still be used to appreciate whether or not an event is 'irresistible'.[17] An event may thus not be 'irresistible' when it constitutes a failure on the part of persons for whom the defendant is liable or by materials used by him. A good example of this is strike action: depending on the circumstances, it may or may not constitute *force majeure*.

Cass civ (1), 24 January 1995[18]	**28.5 (FR)**

The EDF strike

A strike of a party's own workforce is an internal event except when it affects the public as a whole.

Facts: On 18 November 1992, the company Héliogravure Jean Didier entered into a contract with the French public utility Electricité de France (EDF) for the supply of high-tension electric current. Complaining of interruptions in the supply in January 1987 and in 1988, it brought proceedings against EDF claiming payment of the sum of FR 784,230 by way of compensation for the loss caused by those interruptions. EDF countered that those interruptions were the result of a strike led by part of its staff, constituting a case of *force majeure*. EDF counterclaimed for payment of the sum of FR 567,084.49, being the amount of its invoice for the month of January 1987.

Held: The judgment appealed against (Cour d'appel de Douai 14 May 1992) dismissed the claim for compensation for the interruptions in the supply in January 1987, holding that the conflict situation had given rise, as far as EDF was concerned, to a situation of constraint constituting a case of *force majeure*. As regards the interruptions in the supply in 1988, the cour d'appel considered that EDF had not adduced proof that these were interruptions within the meaning of Article XII(5) of the contract capable of being treated as cases of *force majeure*. It therefore calculated compensation in accordance with Article XII(3) which limited the amount of compensation to the user, save in the event of a finding of a serious fault, thus rejecting the arguments of Héliogravure Jean Didier that that clause should be deemed to be non-existent under Article 35 of Act 78-23 of 10 January 1978 and Article 2 of Order 78–464 of 24 March 1978. Finally, offsetting the compensation thus calculated with the sum of FR 70.891,72, the amount due from Héliogravure Jean Didier, which the latter did not contest, it ordered Héliogravure Jean Didier to pay the amount of FR 496,192.77, together with interest as from 7 June 1990. The Cour de cassation upheld the decision.

---

[16] See Jourdain (n 15 above).
[17] Malaurie et al (n 10 above) no. 956.
[18] No. 92-18227, Bull I no. 54, D 1995, 237, annotated by G Paisant.

Judgment: On the three branches of the first appeal ground:—Whereas Héliogravure Jean Didier criticises the contested judgment for deciding so, on the one hand, and according to the terms of the appeal ground, the cour d'appel infringed Article 16 of the NCPC [Nouveau Code de Procédure Civile] by taking cognisance, of its own motion, without first requesting the parties to submit their own observations, of the argument that the strike by EDF employees constituted an extraneous event, on the ground that 'when they collectively cease to render their services in pursuance of the right to strike conferred on them by the constitution and by legislation, they are no longer under the authority of the employer who has no means of compelling them to perform on his behalf the tasks necessary to satisfy users' needs'; as the fact that agents or employees take strike action does not in itself constitute an event extraneous to the undertaking necessary for a finding of *force majeure* such as to exempt the undertaking from liability; as by so deciding, the cour d'appel therefore infringed former Article 1147 of the Civil Code; as, moreover, a general large scale strike in a nationalised public service is far from constituting an unforeseeable event; as, therefore, by declaring *force majeure* to be inapplicable solely on account of the abovementioned characteristics of strike action without making any actual findings as to unforeseeability, the lower court reached its decision without any legal basis under the abovementioned provision;

— Whereas, however, EDF claimed in its pleadings served on 5 February 1992 that the strike had been called by the large trade unions in order to protest against the wages policy in the public and nationalised sector and that it was unable either to forbid its staff to take strike action or decide on requisition measures, or recruit sufficiently well qualified temporary staff; as irrespective of the taking cognisance of arguments of its own motion, the cour d'appel which examined the circumstances of the case thus described in order to determine whether they revealed the existence of *force majeure*, noted that that public utility was unable in January 1987 to provide a continuous supply of electric current, as it was contractually obliged to do, to Héliogravure Jean Didier owing to large-scale strike action affecting the whole of the public and nationalised sector, and thus extraneous to the undertakings, and that EDF could not have foreseen this action, or avert it by satisfying the claims of its employees, in view of government control on decisions concerning wages; nor from a technical point of view could it overcome the problems associated with such action; the appeal is therefore without any ground;

On the two branches of the second appeal ground:—Whereas Héliogravure Jean Didier criticises also on this ground the judgment for deciding the case as it did, on the one hand, according to the terms of the plea ground, by relying on the fact that that company had available to it staff competent in the legal sector, which had in no way been contended on behalf of EDF, the cour d'appel infringed Article 7 NCPC; whereas, on the other hand, a consumer is a person who enters into a contract outside his usual sphere of activities and specialities; as the contracts entered into with EDF are standard form contracts which cannot be negotiated owing to the monopoly exercised by that public utility, which places consumers, when they enter into contracts, in the position of a mere individual; as by considering that Héliogravure Jean Didier, a printing company, was a professional user of electricity not entitled to avail itself of the provisions of Act 78-23 of 10 January 1978, the cour d'appel infringed Article 35 of that Law and Article 2 of Order 78-464 of 24 March 1978.

— Whereas, however, the provisions of Article 35 of Act 78-23 of 10 January 1978—now Articles L 132-1 and L 133-1 of the Code de la consommation—and Article 2 of the Order of 24 March 1978 do not apply to agreements for the supply of goods and services directly related to the business carried on by the other contracting party; as on those alternative grounds, the decision is legally justified, On those grounds, the appeal is dismissed.

Notes

(1) A strike by employees of an undertaking does not normally constitute a case of *force majeure* even if it is unforeseeable and impossible to avert, because it is an internal event for which the head of the undertaking must be called to account. It is otherwise where the strike, as in this case, affects the whole of the public and nationalised sector. On that account it is extraneous to the undertaking. And it is certainly impossible to avert, since wages in that sector are determined by the government and not by the undertaking. It is to be noted that foreseeability—which could not be denied in this case—was not even raised because EDF could do nothing to avoid the strike.

(2) Another point of interest in this judgment is that it gave a new definition to the term business (*professionnel*) within the meaning of Article L 132-1 of the Code de la consommation, in the version contained in Act 95-96 of 1 February 1995, enacted under Directive 93/13/EEC of 5 April 1993 on Unfair Terms in Consumer Contracts.[19] This legislation amends the earlier system for reviewing unfair terms in 'contracts entered into between businesses and individuals or consumers'. In this case the EDF contract contained a clause concerning compensation in the event of power cuts during 1988—whereas that clause was not in existence for 1987 in respect of which the new definition of *force majeure* was given—and that clause could fall under the purview of the rules on unfair terms in contracts between a business and an individual or consumers. As we saw earlier in Chapter 7, a person who enters into a contract directly related to his business activities is not a consumer.[20]

(3) The act of a third party can discharge a party from its obligations if this act satisfies the conditions of *force majeure*. This is well illustrated by a recent judgment.[21] In this case, a person was stabbed on the train by another passenger. The analysis of the facts showed that the action of the third party was completely beyond the control of the train company, which was therefore discharged from its obligation of security. Indeed, the attacker came silently and without any sign of mental disorder and suddenly stabbed the other passenger. The victim's mother claimed damages against the train company, arguing that the latter had failed to comply with the obligation to maintain the passengers' security. The Cour de cassation upheld the cour d'appel's judgment which considered that, because of its irrational nature, the stabbing could not have been foreseen nor prevented by the personnel of the train company. The event was thus qualified as *force majeure*.

28.3.B EFFECTS OF *FORCE MAJEURE*

The effects of *force majeure* vary according to the circumstances. As stated in Article 1218 of the revised Code civil, when the impossibility is permanent, the parties are discharged

---

[19] On this Directive see above, ch 21 and pp 40–41, 174–75, 178–79, 756–57, 1136.
[20] On this issue see above, pp 176–77.
[21] Cass civ (1) 23 June 2011, no. 10-15811, Bull I no. 123.

from their obligations; conversely, when impossibility of performance is merely tempo-rary (for instance, due to the illness of the party) and if time is not of the essence of the contract, the contract is merely suspended; it resumes effect on the disappearance of the obstacle, provided that performance remains useful.[22] The suspension of the obligation in case of temporary *force majeure* is also provided at Article 1231-1 of the new Code civil.

Code civil   **28.6 (FR)**

Article 1231-1: A debtor is condemned, where appropriate, to the payment of damages either on the ground of the non-performance or a delay in performance of an obligation, unless he justifies this on the ground that performance was prevented by *force majeure*.

In the event of partial non-performance due to the *force majeure*, the debtor is relieved of his obligation only to the extent of the impossibility of performance, provided that performance of the remainder of the contract is still of sufficient interest to the creditor.[23] In the case of full impossibility to perform, the contract as a whole falls away and the other party is thus released from it owing to the interdependence of obligations.

The detailed rules governing such disappearance of the contract are, however, uncer-tain. Disappearance occurs automatically by operation of law: release of the debtor automatically entails cancellation of the contract, wholly or in part. This is affirmed in particular by the judgment of 28 April 1982[24] in light of former Article 1147 Code civil: 'An application for the judicial termination of the contract is not necessary in the case of impossibility of performance'. That solution is also expressly provided for in former Article 1722 Code civil with respect to leases.[25]

28.4 GERMAN LAW

German law distinguishes various categories of impossibility (*Unmöglichkeit*): initial, subsequent, objective, subjective, temporary, definitive, full or partial impossibility. Where impossibility is only temporary, the contract is normally suspended. German law also makes a distinction between impossibility attributable or not attributable to the debtor. What is of interest to us here is subsequent impossibility not attributable to the debtor.

After the recent reforms, the effects of supervening impossibility have to be gleaned from several provisions. First, § 275(1) of the Bürgerliches Gesetzbuch (BGB) provides for release of the debtor from any obligation actually to perform (in other words, the cred-itor cannot enforce literal performance by the debtor) where performance is impossible. Secondly, under § 280(1)(2), the debtor will normally not be liable in damages since the liability depends on intention or negligence unless the debtor has assumed some stricter liability (§ 276 BGB[26]). Thirdly, the creditor will normally have the right to terminate the

---

[22] See Cass civ 19 June 1923, DP 1923.I.94.

[23] The same reasoning as for the theory of partial nullity is applied in order to see if the various elements of the contract can be divided: A Bénabent, *Les obligations* (16th edn, Paris: LGDJ, 2017) no. 356.

[24] Cass com 28 April 1982, no. 80-16678, Bull civ IV no. 145.

[25] Which deals with the destruction of the property through *force majeure*.

[26] See above, p 895.

contract (*Rücktritt*) for non-performance under § 323 BGB even if the non-performance was not the debtor's fault. Lastly, unless the creditor was responsible for the impossibility, he will be released from the obligation to make counter-performance (§ 326 BGB).

BGB   **28.7 (DE)**

§ 275: Exclusion of the obligation to perform
   (1) A claim for performance cannot be made in so far as it is impossible for the obligor or for anyone else to perform.
   [(2)–(4) are omitted as they are not concerned with impossibility.]
   ...

§ 280: Compensation for breach of duty
   (1) If the obligor fails to comply with a duty arising under the obligation, the obligee may claim compensation for the loss resulting from this breach. This does not apply if the obligor is not liable for the failure.
   (2) The obligee may demand compensation for delay in performance only if the additional requirement in § 286 is satisfied.
   (3) The obligee may demand compensation in lieu of performance only if the additional requirements of § 281, § 282 or § 283 are satisfied.
   ...

§ 283: Compensation in lieu of performance where there is no duty to perform
   If, by virtue of § 275(1) to (3), the obligor does not have to perform, the obligee may, if the requirements of § 280(1) are satisfied, demand compensation in lieu of performance. § 281(1), second and third sentence, and (5) apply mutatis mutandis.
   ...

§ 285: Surrender of substitute
   (1) If, as a result of a circumstance under which § 275(1) to (3) relieves the obligor of the obligation to perform, the obligor obtains a substitute or a substitute claim for the object owed, the obligee may demand surrender of what has been received as substitute or an assignment of the substitute claim.
   (2) If the obligee may demand compensation in lieu of performance, then, if he uses the right laid down in subsection (1) above, the compensation is reduced by the value of the substitute or substitute claim he has obtained.
   ...

§ 326: Release from counter-performance, and termination where there is no duty to perform
   (1) If, by virtue of § 275(1) to (3), the obligor is released from his obligation to perform, the claim for counter-performance lapses; in the case of part performance § 441(3) applies mutatis mutandis. Sentence 1 does not apply if the obligor under § 275(1) to (3) does not have to effect supplementary performance in the event of a failure to perform in accordance with the contract.
   (2) If the obligee is solely or overwhelmingly responsible for the circumstance releasing the obligor from the need to perform pursuant to § 275(1) to (3), or if the obligor is not responsible for that circumstance and this occurs at a time when the obligee is in default through non-acceptance, the obligor retains his claim for counter-performance.

He must, however, allow a deduction for whatever he saves as a result of release from performance, he acquires through the utilisation of his labour elsewhere, or he maliciously fails to acquire.

(3) If, pursuant to § 285, the obligee demands the surrender of a substitute obtained for the object in respect of which the obligation is due or assignment of a substitute claim, he remains bound to effect counter-performance. Counter-performance is, however, reduced in accordance with § 441(3) in so far as the value of the substitute or of the claim for compensation is less than the value of the performance due.

(4) To the degree that counter-performance is effected although not due under this provision, whatever is effected may be reclaimed under §§ 346 to 348.

(5) If, by virtue of § 275(1) to (3), the obligor does not have to perform, the obligee may terminate; § 323 applies mutatis mutandis to the termination, except that it is not necessary to fix a period of time.

Notes

(1) § 275(1) BGB does not require the event to be unforeseeable, nor does it matter whether or not the debtor is at fault. This is because it is dealing with the question of whether or not the debtor can be made to perform, and if performance is impossible it should not be ordered, whatever the reason. Likewise, the cause of the impossibility is not relevant to termination under § 323 BGB. However, both are relevant to whether the debtor is liable in damages under §§ 280, 283 BGB.

(2) Thus, if it was the debtor who caused the impossibility, he will normally be liable in damages: §§ 280, 283 BGB. (The debtor has violated a duty under § 241 BGB.)[27] These are cases which in other systems might be labelled 'breach of contract' or (in the language of the PECL) 'non-excused non-performance'. In this book they are treated in Part Five. Here we are dealing only with cases in which the debtor was not responsible for the non-performance. In such cases the debtor will not be liable in damages: see § 283 BGB, which refers back to § 280(1) BGB. The second sentence of § 280(1) BGB excludes liability when the debtor is not responsible for the violation.

(3) The creditor may be entitled to terminate the contract under § 326 BGB whether or not the impossibility was caused by the debtor. Note that § 326(2) BGB deals with the case in which it was the creditor who caused the performance to become impossible; again, we are not concerned with this case here.

(4) Even if it has become impossible for the debtor to perform in a literal sense, if he is able to provide a substitute, he may be obliged to do so. Under § 285 BGB the creditor may demand surrender of what has been received as a substitute by the debtor, for example a claim against an insurer.

The following decision shows how the debtor is released and at the same time his side of the bargain can no longer be enforced or must be returned.

---

[27] See above, p 895.

OLG Düsseldorf, 30 December 1964[28] **28.8 (DE)**

The illuminated sign

Where contractual obligations become impossible to perform, the obligor is released from its obligations, and the other party may reclaim any payment made.

Facts: A trader desired to advertise the name of her undertaking by means of an illuminated sign. In October 1961 she contacted a company specialising in such signs. After several proposals she ordered a sign which was to be mounted on the roof of her factory. During negotiations both parties agreed that such an installation in a protected area needed an administrative authorisation which would not be easy to obtain. On 31 October 1961 the company confirmed the order at the price of DM 5,415.50. On the same day, the selling company sought in its name and on behalf of the trader the administrative authorisation required in order to install the sign. On 23 November 1961 the trader made an initial payment of DM 1,733. On 28 November 1961 the administrative authority refused the request for authorisation. The trader brought an action in order to obtain reimbursement of the amount of DM 1,733.

Held: At first instance and on appeal the trader was successful. The Bundesgerichtshof dismissed the further appeal.

Judgment: ... The provisions on subsequent impossibility must be applied. Performance by the selling company (namely manufacture and sale of the sign) became legally impossible as a result of the refusal of the request for authorisation which represents a permanent obstacle to the installation of the sign ... The impossibility of performance is not attributable to either of the two parties. ... The mere fact that the selling company sought authorisation on behalf of the trader does not mean that on that account the risk was transferred. First, the company sought authorization in the name of the trader and at the latter's request. Secondly, unless something to the contrary was explicitly agreed, the company is not liable for a failure of its actions for which it is not responsible if it simply seeks authorization on behalf of the trader. Nor is the impossibility to be borne by the trader on account of her refusal to change the sign and order another sign.

Thus ... the impossibility of performance is not to be borne by either of the parties. Consequently, the selling company is released from its obligations and loses its right to its side of the bargain. Furthermore, since the trader has made a payment of DM 1,733, she is entitled to claim reimbursement under [former] §§ 323(1) and (3) and 812 BGB.

Note

This decision illustrates the application of § 326 BGB and the interdependence of obligations under a synallagmatic contract. Performance by one of the parties has become impossible because of the refusal of administrative authorisation. Valuable consideration was paid—a payment on account. Recovery lies under § 326 and §§ 346 ff BGB (previously §§ 323 and 812 BGB).[29]

---

[28] NJW 1956, 761.
[29] Here again pre-2016 French law would have applied the notion of *cause:* the price of the ticket, the making of a payment on account lost their purpose (*cause*).

We have seen that, if performance of the contract becomes totally impossible without the debtor's fault, the creditor may terminate the contract and claim restitution of any benefits transferred. If the performance becomes partially impossible, the creditor has the right to terminate if performance of the remainder is of no interest to him, or he may claim performance of the balance. However, the German courts have long recognised that in such a case the debtor's remaining obligations are also qualified by the good faith principle.

RG, 3 February 1914[30]   **28.9 (DE)**

The bad harvest

One cannot be required to do more than one can reasonably perform, considering good faith requirements and exceptional circumstances.

Facts: In June 1909 the defendant sold to the plaintiff 20,000 kg of sugar beet seed in respect of each of the years 1910, 1911 and 1912 at the price of 26 Reichsmarks per 50 kg, to be delivered in February in each year. In February 1912 only 920 kg were delivered because in 1911, owing to the drought, only 933.35 quintals were harvested, instead of the 4,908 expected. Since the defendant was also committed to other purchasers he allocated the supplies of seeds on a pro rata basis to each of the customers ordering. The claimant disputed the allocation thus carried out (namely 46% of the contractually agreed quantity) and brought an action for performance of the contract and seeking judgment to be entered against the defendant for damages and interest.

Held: The Handelsgericht dismissed the claimant's action. The Oberlandesgericht set aside the judgment and upheld the claim. The defendant appealed to the Reichsgericht (RG) which quashed the appeal judgment.

Judgment: The RG approves the finding of the lower courts that the sugar beet seeds were generic. Consequently [former] § 279 BGB was to be applied.

It is important to note that the order was for quality seed from the defendant's own cultivation. Consequently, the lower courts misdirected themselves as to the action and the rights of the parties, when they considered that the defendant was entitled in the event of need to supply substitute seed of the same quality as that provided for in the contract. Pursuant to the agreement entered into, the claimant was entitled to call for seed from the defendant's own personal cultivation. Inability to perform the contract releases the defendant only where, on the one hand, performance has become totally impossible and, on the other hand, on condition as a *sine qua non* that no fault could be attributed to the defendant under [former] § 279 BGB.

The defendant is entitled to claim that in their appraisal of impossibility the Oberlandesgericht judges infringed the provisions of § 242.

It is common ground that the summer of 1911 was marked by a drought of such extraordinary severity that harvests were very bad. Consequently, in light of the requirements of good faith laid down in § 242 and the exceptional circumstances supervening in 1911, the defendant cannot be required to do more than he can reasonably perform. Thus he was entitled to treat his customers on an equal footing and to sell his seeds on a pro rata basis in accordance with quantities ordered by each of them.

[30] RGZ 84, 125.

It should be declared that the claimant's action is ill-founded and that the appeal in revision by the defendant should be granted.

Notes

(1) It is to be noted first of all that since the case involved a limited generic quantity—the seeds produced by the seller—there could be no question of purchasing a substitute in order to satisfy the order. The seller is released, according to the court, when performance is—reasonably—impossible and there is no fault. It therefore seems that, unlike French law, the concept of *force majeure* in German law is mingled with that of absence of fault. § 279 BGB was abolished in the 2002 reform; the facts of *The bad harvest* would now be covered by § 275(1) BGB.

(2) Reference is also made to good faith (§ 242 BGB). The defendant might have been able to supply enough seed to fill this one contract, but he had other buyers who would then have got nothing. So the court holds that it was right for him to deliver a pro rata quantity to each buyer. Compare the English case of *The Super Servant II*.[31]

28.5 ENGLISH LAW

28.5.A FRUSTRATION[32]

English law is less inclined to give relief than either the French and German systems. It is true that impossibility of performance may be perceived less narrowly than under French law, since it includes the notion of that which renders the contract 'something radically different from that which was in the contemplation of the parties', which seems to go further than *force majeure*. But unlike French and German law, English law declines to allow the courts to adapt contracts in the event of change of circumstances.[33]

A second difference is that English law takes an 'all-or-nothing' approach. Either the contract as a whole is frustrated and the parties are released, or they remain bound and liable for non-performance. There is no notion of partial frustration, nor of temporary impossibility which excuses performance for the time being. In this respect, there is a clear distinction between breach of contract and impossibility.

The system has been developed in successive cases and does not necessarily form a coherent whole. Moreover, the terminology is fluid. One may speak of frustration of the purpose, of impossibility, of act of God or of discharge by supervening illegality.[34]

The starting point is that a person who has undertaken obligations must perform them. Some old cases suggest that liability used to be strict,[35] though the courts always

---

[31] See below, 28.13 (EN), p 1199.

[32] On the doctrine of frustration generally, see E McKendrick (ed), *Force majeure and Frustration of Contract* (2nd edn, London: Lloyd's of London Press, 1995); G Treitel, *Frustration and Force majeure* (3rd edn, London: Sweet & Maxwell, 2014).

[33] See below, ch 29.

[34] See *Treitel on the Law of Contract*, 14th edn by E Peel (London: Sweet & Maxwell, 2015) paras 19-009–19-031.

[35] *Paradine v Jane* (1647) Aleyn 26, in which the lessee of property was held bound to pay the rent even though he was unable to occupy the premises because they were in the hands of 'the King's enemies'.

recognised that there must be some scenarios in which a party would be released from his obligations, eg by death. The modern doctrine is based on *Taylor v Caldwell*.

Queen's Bench   **28.10 (EN)**

Taylor v Caldwell[36]

Impossibility of performance resulting from the disappearance of the person or the thing releases the debtor in certain circumstances.

Facts: A hall was hired for a series of four concerts. Before the date set for the first concert, the hall was completely destroyed by a fire for which neither of the parties was responsible. The hirer sued for damages to cover the cost of wasted advertising.

Held: The contract had been discharged so that the defendant was not liable.

Judgment: BLACKBURN J: In this case the plaintiffs and defendants had, on the 27 May, 1862, entered into a contract by which the defendants agreed to let the plaintiffs have the use of the Surrey Gardens and Music Hall on four days then to come, viz, the 17 June, 15 July, 5 August and 19 August, for the purpose of giving a series of four grand concerts, and day and night fêtes at the Gardens and Hall on those days respectively; and the plaintiffs agreed to take the Gardens and Hall on those days, and pay £700 for each day.

The parties inaccurately call this a 'letting', and the money to be paid a 'rent'; but the whole agreement is such as to shew that the defendants were to retain the possession of the Hall and Gardens so that there was to be no demise of them, and that the contract was merely to give the plaintiffs the use of them on those days. Nothing however, in our opinion, depends on this. The agreement then proceeds to set out various stipulations between the parties as to what each was to supply for these concerts and entertainment, and as to the manner in which they should be carried on. The effect of the whole is to shew that the existence of the Music Hall in the Surrey Gardens in a state fit for a concert was essential for the fulfilment of the contract,—such entertainment as the parties contemplated in their agreement could not be given without it.

After the making of the agreement, and before the first day on which a concert was to be given, the Hall was destroyed by fire. This destruction, we must take it on the evidence, was without the fault of either party, and was so complete that in consequence the concerts could not be given as intended. And the question we have to decide is whether, under these circumstances, the loss which the plaintiffs have sustained is to fall upon the defendants. The parties when framing their agreement evidently had not present to their minds the possibility of such a disaster and have made no express stipulation with reference to it, so that the answer to the question must depend upon the general rules of law applicable to such a contract.

There seems no doubt that where there is a positive contract to do a thing, not in itself unlawful, the contractor must perform it or pay damages for not doing it, although in consequence of unforeseen accidents, the performance of his contract has become unexpectedly burdensome or even impossible. The law is so laid down in 1 Roll Abr 450, Condition (G), and in the note to *Walton v Waterhouse*, and is recognised as the general

---

[36] (1863) 3 B & S 826.

rule by all the Judges in the much discussed case of *Hall v Wright*. But this rule is only applicable when the contract is positive and absolute, and not subject to any condition either express or implied: and there are authorities which, as we think, establish the principle that where, from the nature of the contract, it appears that the parties must from the beginning have known that it could not be fulfilled unless when the time for the fulfilment of the contract arrived some particular specified thing continued to exist, so that, when entering into the contract, they must have contemplated such continuing existence as the foundation of what was to be done; there, in the absence of any express or implied warranty that the thing shall exist, the contract is not to be construed as a positive contract, but as subject to an implied condition that the parties shall be excused in case, before breach, performance becomes impossible from the perishing of the thing without default of the contractor.

There seems little doubt that this implication tends to further the great object of making the legal construction such as to fulfil the intention of those who entered into the contract. For in the course of affairs men in making such contracts in general would, if it were brought to their minds, say that there should be such a condition. ... There is a class of contracts in which a person binds himself to do something which requires to be performed by him in person; and such promises, eg promises to marry, or promises to serve for a certain time, are never in practice qualified by an express exception of the death of the party; and therefore in such cases the contract is in terms broken if the promisor dies before fulfilment. Yet it was very early determined that, if the performance is personal, the executors are not liable; *Hyde v The Dean of Windsor*. See 2 Wms Exors 1560 5th edn, where a very apt illustration is given. 'Thus', says the learned author, 'if an author undertakes to compose a work, and dies before completing it, his executors are discharged from this contract: for the undertaking is merely personal in its nature, and, by the intervention of the contractor's death, has become impossible to be performed.' For this he cites a dictum of Lord Lyndhurst in *Marshall v Broadhurst*, and a case mentioned by Patteson J in *Wentworth v Cock*. In *Hall v Wright*, Crompton J, in his judgment, puts another case. 'Where a contract depends upon personal skill, and the act of God renders it impossible, as, for instance, in the case of a painter employed to paint a picture who is struck blind, it may be that the performances might be excused.'

It seems that in those cases the only ground on which the parties or their executors, can be excused from the consequences of the breach of the contract is, that from the nature of the contract there is an implied condition of the continued existence of the life of the contractor, and, perhaps in the case of the painter of his eyesight. In the instances just given, the person, the continued existence of whose life is necessary to the fulfilment of the contract, is himself the contractor, but that does not seem in itself to be necessary to the application of the principle; as is illustrated by the following example. In the ordinary form of an apprentice deed the apprentice binds himself in unqualified terms to 'serve until the full end and term of seven years to be fully complete and ended', during which term it is covenanted that the apprentice his master 'faithfully shall serve', and the father of the apprentice in equally unqualified terms binds himself for the performance by the apprentice of all and every covenant on his part. (See the form, 2 Chitty on Pleading, 370, 7th ed by Greening.) It is undeniable that if the apprentice dies within the seven years, the covenant of the father that he shall perform his covenant to serve for seven years is not fulfilled, yet surely it cannot be that an action would lie against the father? Yet the only reason why it would not is that he is excused because of the apprentice's death.

These are instances where the implied condition is of the life of a human being, but there are others in which the same implication is made as to the continued existence of a thing. For example where a contract of sale is made amounting to a bargain and sale, transferring presently the property in specific chattels, which are to be delivered by the vendor at a future day; there, if the chattels, without the fault of the vendor, perish in the interval, the purchaser must pay the price and the vendor is excused from performing his contract to deliver, which has thus become impossible.

That this is the rule of the English law is established by the case of *Rugg v Minett*, where the article that perished before delivery was turpentine, and it was decided that the vendor was bound to refund the price of all those lots in which the property had not passed; but was entitled to retain without deduction the price of those lots in which the property had passed, though they were not delivered, and though in the conditions of sale, which are set out in the report, there was no express qualification of the promise to deliver on payment. It seems in that case rather to have been taken for granted than decided that the destruction of the thing sold before delivery excused the vendor from fulfilling his contract to deliver on payment.

This is also the rule in the civil law, and it is worth noticing that Pothier, in his celebrated *Traité du contrat de vente* (see Part 4, ss 307 et seq; and Part 2, ch 1, s 1 art 4, a1) treats this as merely an example of the more general rule that every obligation *de certo corpore* is extinguished when the thing ceases to exist. See Blackburn on the Contract of Sale, p 173. ...

It may, we think, be safely asserted to be now English law, that in all contracts of loan of chattels or bailments if the performance of the promise of the borrower or bailee to return the things lent or bailed, becomes impossible because it has perished, this impossibility (if not arising from the fault of the borrower or bailee from some risk which he has taken upon himself) excuses the borrower or bailee from the performance of his promise to redeliver the chattel.

The principle seems to us to be that, in contracts in which the performance depends on the continued existence of a given person or thing, a condition is implied that the impossibility of performance arising from the perishing of the person or thing shall excuse the performance; ... but that excuse is by law implied, because from the nature of the contract it is apparent that the parties contracted on the basis of the continued existence of the particular person or chattel. In the present case, looking at the whole contract, we find that the parties contracted on the basis of the continued existence of the Music Hall at the time when the concerts were to be given; that being essential to their performance.

We think, therefore, that the Music Hall having ceased to exist, without fault of either party, both parties are excused, the plaintiffs from taking the gardens and paying the money, the defendants from performing their promise to give the use of the Hall and Gardens and other things. Consequently the rule must be absolute to enter the verdict for the defendants.

Note

Taylor v Caldwell mitigates the rigor of the old principle by establishing the rule that, in contracts whose performance depends on the continued existence of a person (contracts *intuitu personae*) or of a thing, there is an implied condition that the impossibility of performance resulting from the disappearance of the person or the thing releases the debtor. Noteworthy in this connection is the reference to Pothier's *Traité du contrat du vente*—rather than to the Civil Code.[37]

The rule laid down in *Taylor v Caldwell* is limited but offers the means of extending it by application of the doctrine of implied terms (on which see Chapter 20, above), which can be and has been used for other contracts. We will see later that the 'implied term' has been abandoned as the explanation for 'frustration', in particular by the judgment in *Davis Contractors Ltd v Fareham* UDC.[38] Frustration was however, developed on the basis of the implied term to cover cases in which the implied 'foundation' of the contract has disappeared, particularly in the judgments in the so-called coronation cases given following postponement of the coronation of King Edward VII because of illness.

Court of Appeal   **28.11 (EN)**

Krell v Henry[39]

A contract may be frustrated when its essential feature no longer exists.

Facts: Henry hired a room in order to watch the passing of the coronation procession. The price agreed was £75. He paid £25 on account. Although the coronation was postponed, the hirer claimed payment of the remaining amount, that is £50. Henry counterclaimed for recovery of the payment on account, though he later abandoned this claim.[40]

Held: At first instance Henry was successful on both points. Krell's appeal was dismissed.

Judgment: VAUGHAN WILLIAMS LJ: ... The real question is the extent of the application in English law of the principle of the Roman law which has been adopted and acted on in many English decisions, and notably in the case of *Taylor v Caldwell* ...

English law applies the principle not only to cases where the performance of the contract becomes impossible by the cessation of existence of the thing which is the subject-matter of the contract, but also to cases where the event which renders the contract incapable of performance is the cessation or non-existence of an express condition or state of things, going to the root of the contract, and essential to its performance. It is said, on the one side, that the specified thing, state of things, or condition the continued existence of which is necessary for the fulfilment of the contract, so that the parties entering into the contract must have contemplated the continued existence of that thing, condition, or state of things as the foundation of what was to be done under the contract, is limited to things which are either the subject-matter of the contract or a condition or state of things, present or anticipated, which is expressly mentioned in the contract. But, on the other side, it is said that the condition or state of things need not be expressly specified, but that it is sufficient if that condition or state of things clearly appears by extrinsic evidence to have been assumed by the parties to be the foundation or basis of the contract, and the event which causes the impossibility is of such a character that it cannot reasonably be supposed to have been in the contemplation of the contracting

---

[37] See Art 1722 Cciv, above, p 1180.
[38] [1956] AC 696, see 28.11 (EN), below, p 1193.
[39] [1902] 2 KB 740.
[40] For the reasons, see below, p 1204 n 64.

parties when the contract was made. In such a case the contracting parties will not be held bound by the general words which, though large enough to include, were not used with reference to a possibility of a particular event rendering performance of the contract impossible. I do not think that the principle of the civil law as introduced into the English law is limited to cases in which the event causing the impossibility of performance is the destruction or nonexistence of some thing which is the subject-matter of the contract or of some condition or state of things expressly specified as a condition of it. I think that you first have to ascertain, not necessarily from the terms of the contract, but, if required, from necessary inferences, drawn from surrounding circumstances recognised by both contracting parties, what is the substance of the contract, and then to ask the question whether that substantial contract needs for its foundation the assumption of the existence of a particular state of things. If it does, this will limit the operation of the general words, and in such case, if the contract becomes impossible of performance by reason of the non-existence of the state of things assumed by both contracting parties as the foundation of the contract, there will be no breach of the contract thus limited. Now what are the facts of the present case? The contract is contained in two letters of 20 June which passed between the defendant and the plaintiff's agent, Mr Cecil Bisgood. These letters do not mention the coronation, but speak merely of the taking of Mr Krell's chambers, or, rather, of the use of them, in the daytime of 26 and 27 June, for the sum of £75, £25 then paid, balance £50 to be paid on 24 June. But the affidavits, which by agreement between the parties are to be taken as stating the facts of the case, shew that the plaintiff exhibited on his premises, third floor, 56A, Pall Mall, an announcement to the effect that windows to view the Royal coronation procession were to be let, and that the defendant was induced by that announcement to apply to the housekeeper on the premises, who said that the owner was willing to let the suite of rooms for the purpose of seeing the Royal procession for both days, but not nights, of 26 and 27 June. In my judgment the use of the rooms was let and taken for the purpose of seeing the Royal procession. It was not a demise of the rooms, or even an agreement to let and take the rooms. It is a licence to use rooms for a particular purpose and none other. And in my judgment the taking place of those processions on the days proclaimed along the proclaimed route, which passed 56A, Pall Mall, was regarded by both contracting parties as the foundation of the contract; and I think that it cannot reasonably be supposed to have been in the contemplation of the contracting parties, when the contract was made, that the coronation would not be held on the proclaimed days, or the processions not take place on those days along the proclaimed route; and I think that the words imposing on the defendant the obligation to accept and pay for the use of the rooms for the named days, although general and unconditional, were not used with reference to the possibility of the particular contingency which afterwards occurred. It was suggested in the course of the argument that if the occurrence, on the proclaimed days, of the coronation and the procession in this case were the foundation of the contract, and if the general words are thereby limited or qualified, so that in the event of the non-occurrence of the coronation and procession along the proclaimed route they would discharge both parties from further performance of the contract, it would follow that if a cabman was engaged to take some one to Epsom on Derby Day at a suitable enhanced price for such a journey, say £10, both parties to the contract would be discharged in the contingency of the race at Epsom for some reason becoming impossible; but I do not think this follows, for I do not think that in the cab case the happening of the race would be the foundation of the contract. No doubt the purpose of the engager would be to go to see the Derby, and the price would be proportionately high; but the cab had no special qualifications for the purpose which led to the selection of the cab for this particular occasion. Any other cab would have done as well.

Moreover, I think that, under the cab contract, the hirer, even if the race went off, could have said, 'Drive me to Epsom; I will pay you the agreed sum; you have nothing to do with the purpose for which I hired the cab,' and that if the cabman refused he would have been guilty of a breach of contract, there being nothing to qualify his promise to drive the hirer to Epsom on a particular day. Whereas in the case of the coronation, there is not merely the purpose of the hirer to see the coronation procession, but it is the coronation procession and the relative position of the rooms which is the basis of the contract as much for the lessor as the hirer; and I think that if the King, before the coronation day and after the contract, had died, the hirer could not have insisted on having the rooms on the days named. It could not in the cab case be reasonably said that seeing the Derby race was the foundation of the contract, as it was of the licence in this case. Whereas in the present case, where the rooms were offered and taken, by reason of their peculiar suitability from the position of the rooms for a view of the coronation procession, surely the view of the coronation procession was the foundation of the contract, which is a very different thing from the purpose of the man who engaged the cab—namely, to see the race—being held to be the foundation of the contract. Each case must be judged by its own circumstances. In each case one must ask oneself, first, what, having regard to all the circumstances, was the foundation of the contract? Secondly, was the performance of the contract prevented? Thirdly, was the event which prevented the performance of the contract of such a character that it cannot reasonably be said to have been in the contemplation of the parties at the date of the contract? If all these questions are answered in the affirmative (as I think they should be in this case), I think both parties are discharged from further performance of the contract. I think that the coronation procession was the foundation of this contract, and that the non-happening of it prevented the performance of the contract; and, secondly, I think that the non-happening of the procession, to use the words of Sir James Hannen in *Baily v De Crespigny*, was an event 'of such a character that it cannot reasonably be supposed to have been in the contemplation of the contracting parties when the contract was made, and that they are not to be held bound by general words which, though large enough to include, were not used with reference to the possibility of the particular contingency which afterwards happened.'

The test seems to be whether the event which causes the impossibility was or might have been anticipated and guarded against. It seems difficult to say, in a case where both parties anticipate the happening of an event, which anticipation is the foundation of the contract, that either party must be taken to have anticipated, and ought to have guarded against, the event which prevented the performance of the contract. In both *Jackson v Union Marine Insurance Co* and *Nickoll v Ashton* the parties might have anticipated as a possibility that perils of the sea might delay the ship and frustrate the commercial venture: in the former case the carriage of the goods to effect which the charterparty was entered into; in the latter case the sale of the goods which were to be shipped on the steamship which was delayed. But the Court held in the former case that the basis of the contract was that the ship would arrive in time to carry out the contemplated commercial venture, and in the latter that the steamship would arrive in time for the loading of the goods the subject of the sale.

I wish to observe that cases of this sort are very different from cases where a contract or warranty or representation is implied, such as was implied in *The Moorcock*, and refused to be implied in *Hamlyn v Wood*. But *The Moorcock* is of importance in the present case as shewing that whatever is the suggested implication—be it condition, as in this case, or warranty or representation—one must, in judging whether the implication ought to be made, look not only at the words of the contract, but also at the surrounding facts and the knowledge of the parties of those facts. There seems to me to be ample authority for this proposition. Thus in *Jackson v Union Marine Insurance Co*, in the Common Pleas, the question whether the object of the voyage had been frustrated by the delay of the ship was left as a question of fact to the jury, although there was nothing in the charterparty defining the time within which the charterers were to supply the cargo of iron rails for San Francisco, and nothing on the face of the charterparty to indicate the importance of time in the venture; and that was a case in which, as Bramwell B points out in his judgment at p 148, *Taylor v Caldwell* was a strong authority to support the conclusion arrived at in the judgment—that the ship not arriving in time for the voyage contemplated, but at such time as to frustrate the commercial venture, was not only a breach of the contract but discharged the charterer, though he had such an excuse that no action would lie ...

I myself am clearly of opinion that in this case, where we have to ask ourselves whether the object of the contract was frustrated by the non-happening of the coronation and its procession on the days proclaimed, parol evidence is admissible to shew that the subject of the contract was rooms to view the coronation procession, and was so to the knowledge of both parties. When once this is established, I see no difficulty whatever in the case. It is not essential to the application of the principle of *Taylor v Caldwell* that the direct subject of the contract should perish or fail to be in existence at the date of performance of the contract. It is sufficient if a state of things or condition expressed in the contract and essential to its performance perishes or fails to be in existence at that time. In the present case the condition which fails and prevents the achievement of that which was, in the contemplation of both parties, the foundation of the contract, is not expressly mentioned either as a condition of the contract or the purpose of it; but I think for the reasons which I have given that the principle of *Taylor v Caldwell* ought to be applied. This disposes of the plaintiff's claim for £50 unpaid balance of the price agreed to be paid for the use of the rooms. The defendant at one time set up a cross-claim for the return of the £25 he paid at the date of the contract. As that claim is now withdrawn it is unnecessary to say anything about it. I have only to add that the facts of this case do not bring it within the principle laid down in *Stubbs v Holywell Ry Co*; that in the case of contracts falling directly within the rule of *Taylor v Caldwell* the subsequent impossibility does not affect rights already acquired, because the defendant had the whole of 24 June to pay the balance, and the public announcement that the coronation and processions would not take place on the proclaimed days was made early on the morning of 24 June, and no cause of action could accrue till the end of that day. I think this appeal ought to be dismissed.

Notes

(1) *Krell v Henry* seems to expand the notion of 'destruction of the subject matter' to cover situations in which it seems that in a literal sense the parties could still perform but the change of circumstances means that the foundation of the contract has disappeared. As it is sometimes said, the 'contractual venture' has become impossible.[41]

---

[41] *Great Peace Shipping Ltd v Tsavliris Salvage (International) Ltd (The Great Peace)* [2002] EWCA Civ 1407, [2003] QB 679 [59]–[60].

(2) It is noteworthy that the courts are prepared to look at 'parol evidence' (in other words, to look beyond what is written in the contract documents[42]) to establish what the foundation of the contract was.

(3) In another 'coronation' case, *Herne Bay Steam Boat Co v Hutton*,[43] Hutton had chartered a boat to take a party to see the naval review which was to be held on the following day and to take them round the naval fleet. The naval review was cancelled but the fleet remained in the offing. Hutton did not use the boat and the shipowner sought payment of the amount due under the charter-party. The case was heard by the same judges as *Krell v Henry* but they reached a different outcome: the contract to charter the boat was held not to have been frustrated by the cancellation of the naval review. There has been considerable debate over the reason for the different result.[44] For Stirling LJ it seems to have been that it was still possible to view the fleet at anchor. But the majority do not mention this—nor do they mention an explanation offered by a modern commentator, that Henry was a consumer whereas Hutton, who intended to sell tickets for the trip on the boat, was not.[45] Vaughan Williams LJ likened the case to that of the cab hired to take someone to Epsom, which he discusses in his judgment in *Krell v Henry*. It is hard to follow the first part of his reasoning on this point: why does it matter that any other cab would have done as well? (Presumably any other room with a view of Pall Mall would have done as well for Henry.) But his second point may be the crux of the matter. Just like a cab, the boat in the *Hutton* case was regularly for hire and it was not of any particular concern to the owner what the purpose of the journey was. In contrast, the purpose was crucial to Krell. The owner of a flat is most unlikely to rent it out to strangers for the day unless there was something like the coronation procession going on.

House of Lords   **28.12 (EN)**

Davis Contractors Ltd v Fareham UDC[46]

For frustration to occur, there must be such a change in the significance of the obligation that the thing undertaken would, if performed, be a different thing from that contracted for.

Facts: A business contracted to build 78 houses for a local authority within a period of eight months. In actual fact 22 months were required for completion chiefly owing to the lack of labour. The business which was paid the contractual price sought additional compensation on the basis of unjust enrichment.

Held: The action was dismissed. There was no frustration.

Judgment: LORD REID: ... Frustration is regarded as depending on the addition to the contract of an implied term or as depending on the construction of the contract as it stands ...

I may be allowed to note an example of the artificiality of the theory of an implied term given by Lord Sands in *James Scott Sons Ltd v Del Sel:* 'A tiger has escaped from a

---

[42] See above, p 749–56.

[43] [1903] 2 KB 683 (CA).

[44] See *Treitel* (n 34 above) para 19-042.

[45] R Brownsword, 'Henry's Lost Spectacle and Hutton's Lost Speculation: A Classic Riddle Solved?' (1985) 129 Solicitors' Journal 860.

[46] [1956] AC 696.

travelling menagerie. The milk girl fails to deliver the milk. Possibly the milkman may be exonerated from any breach of contract; but, even so, it would seem hardly reasonable to base that exoneration on the ground that 'tiger days excepted' must be held as if written into the milk contract.'

I think that there is much force in Lord Wright's criticism in *Denny, Mott Dickson Ltd v James B Fraser Co Ltd*: 'The parties did not anticipate fully and completely, if at all, or provide for what actually happened. It is not possible, to my mind, to say that, if they had thought of it, they would have said: 'Well, if that happens, all is over between us.' On the contrary, they would almost certainly on the one side or the other have sought to introduce reservations or qualifications or compensations.'

It appears to me that frustration depends, at least in most cases, not on adding any implied term, but on the true construction of the terms which are in the contract read in light of the nature of the contract and of the relevant surrounding circumstances when the contract was made.

LORD RADCLIFFE: … Before I refer to the facts I must say briefly what I understand to be the legal principle of frustration. It is not always expressed in the same way, but I think that the points which are relevant to the decision of this case are really beyond dispute. The theory of frustration belongs to the law of contract and it is represented by a rule which the courts will apply in certain limited circumstances for the purpose of deciding that contractual obligations, ex facie binding, are no longer enforceable against the parties. The description of the circumstances that justify the application of the rule and, consequently, the decision whether in a particular case those circumstances exist are, I think, necessarily questions of law.

It has often been pointed out that the descriptions vary from one case of high authority to another. Even as long ago as 1918 Lord Sumner was able to offer an anthology of different tests directed to the factor of delay alone, and delay, though itself a frequent cause of the principle of frustration being invoked, is only one instance of the kind of circumstance to which the law attends (see *Bank Line Ltd v Arthur Capel Co*). A full current anthology would need to be longer yet. But the variety of description is not of any importance so long as it is recognised that each is only a description and that all are intended to express the same general idea. I do not think that there has been a better expression of that general idea than the one offered by Lord Loreburn in *FA Tamplin Steamship Co Ltd v Anglo-Mexican Petroleum Products Co Ltd*. It is shorter to quote than to try to paraphrase it: '… a court can and ought to examine the contract and the circumstances in which it was made, not of course to vary, but only to explain it, in order to see whether or not from the nature of it the parties must have made their bargain on the footing that a particular thing or state of things would continue to exist. And if they must have done so, then a term to that effect will be implied, though it be not expressed in the contract. … no court has an absolving power, but it can infer from the nature of the contract and the surrounding circumstances that a condition which is not expressed was a foundation on which the parties contracted.' So expressed, the principle of frustration, the origin of which seems to lie in the development of commercial law, is seen to be a branch of a wider principle which forms part of the English law of contract as a whole. But, in my opinion, full weight ought to be given to the requirement that the parties 'must have made' their bargain on the particular footing. Frustration is not to be lightly invoked as the dissolvent of a contract. Lord Loreburn ascribes the dissolution to an implied term of the contract that was actually made. This approach is in line with the tendency of English courts to refer all the consequences of a contract to the will of those who made it. But there is something of a logical difficulty in seeing how the parties could even impliedly have provided for something which ex hypothesi they neither expected nor foresaw; and the ascription of frustration to an implied term of the contract has been criticised as obscuring the true action of the court which consists in applying an objective rule of the law of contract to the contractual obligations that the parties have imposed upon themselves. So long as each theory produces the same result as the other, as normally it does, it matters little which theory is avowed (see *British Movietonews Ltd v London and District Cinemas Ltd*, per Viscount Simon). But it may still be of some importance to recall that, if the matter is to be approached by way of implied term, the solution of any particular case is not to be found by inquiring what the parties themselves would have agreed on had they been, as they were not, forewarned. It is not merely that no one can answer that hypothetical question: it is also that the decision must be given 'irrespective of the individuals concerned, their temperaments and failings, their interest and circumstances' (*Hirji Mulji v Cheong Yue Steamship Co Ltd*). The legal effect of frustration 'does not depend on their intention or their opinions, or even knowledge, as to the event.' On the contrary, it seems that when the event occurs 'the meaning of the contract must be taken to be, not what the parties did intend (for they had neither thought nor intention regarding it), but that which the parties, as fair and reasonable men, would presumably have agreed upon if, having such possibility in view, they had made express provision as to their several rights and liabilities in the event of its occurrence' (*Dahl v Nelson*, per Lord Watson).

By this time it might seem that the parties themselves have become so far disembodied spirits that their actual persons should be allowed to rest in peace. In their place there rises the figure of the fair and reasonable man. And the spokesman of the fair and reasonable man, who represents after all no more than the anthropomorphic conception of justice, is and must be the court itself. So perhaps it would be simpler to say at the outset that frustration occurs whenever the law recognises that without default of either party a contractual obligation has become incapable of being performed because the circumstances in which performance is called for would render it a thing radically different from that which was undertaken by the contract. *Non haec in foedera veni*. It was not this that I promised to do.

There is, however, no uncertainty as to the materials upon which the court must proceed. 'The data for decision are, on the one hand, the terms and construction of the contract, read in the light of the then existing circumstances, and on the other hand the events which have occurred' (*Denny, Mott Dickson Ltd v James B Fraser Co Ltd*, per Lord Wright). In the nature of things there is often no room for any elaborate inquiry. The court must act upon a general impression of what its rule requires. It is for that reason that special importance is necessarily attached to the occurrence of any unexpected event that, as it were, changes the face of things. But, even so, it is not hardship or inconvenience or material loss itself which calls the principle of frustration into play. There must be as well such a change in the significance of the obligation that the thing undertaken would, if performed, be a different thing from that contracted for.

I am bound to say that, if this is the law, the appellants' case seems to me a long way from a case of frustration.

Notes

(1) This judgment highlights the artificiality of the implied term doctrine in relation to frustration. Thus, Lord Radcliffe's formula should be borne in mind:

Frustration occurs whenever the law recognises that, without default of either party, a contractual obligation has become incapable of being performed because the circumstances in which performance is called for would render it a thing radically different from that which was undertaken by the contract.

(2) It may be wondered to what extent that formula differs from the definition in French law of *imprévision*[47] or from the German doctrine of *Wegfall der Geschäfts-grundlage*.[48] But note that Lord Radcliffe stressed that 'it is not hardship or inconvenience or material loss itself which calls the principle of frustration into play'. It is normally accepted by English lawyers that impossibility (including 'frustration of the contractual venture') must be distinguished from 'impracticability'; the latter is not within the doctrine of frustration.[49] We return to this point in the next chapter.[50]

(3) As Lord Radcliffe says, many different explanations of the juristic basis of the doctrine of frustration have been offered by the English courts. But Treitel writes:

> It is often asked whether the theoretical discussion has any practical significance. It seems to have none.[51]

Even if performance of a contract has become impossible, it will not be frustrated unless other conditions are fulfilled. It is sometimes said that the event must have been foreseen and the frustration must not have been 'self-induced'. These points need qualification or explanation.

Court of Appeal **28.13 (EN)**

Ocean Tramp Tankers Corp v VO Sovracht (The Eugenia)[52]

For a contract to be frustrated, the event must bring about a fundamentally different situation from the one contemplated by the parties.

Facts: Under charter-party the vessel *Eugenia* was to undertake a voyage to the Indies via the Black Sea. The parties were aware of the risk of closure of the Suez Canal but had made no express contractual provision in that regard. On 25 October the *Eugenia* left Odessa for the Indies via the Suez Canal, which had been declared a danger zone. The charterer did not prevent it from doing so and the vessel was blocked in the Canal. The charterer relied on frustration.

Held: The Court of Appeal held that the charterer could not plead frustration.

Judgment: DENNING LJ: The second question is whether the charterparty was frustrated by what took place. The arbitrator has held it was not. The judge has held that it was. Which is right? One thing that is obvious is that the charterers cannot rely on the fact that the *Eugenia* was trapped in the canal; for that was their own fault. They were in breach of the war clause in entering it. They cannot rely on a self-induced frustration, see *Maritime National Fish Ltd v Ocean Trawlers Ltd*. But they seek to rely on the fact that the canal

---

[47] See below, 29.7 (FR), p 1218.
[48] See below, pp 1222–32.
[49] See *Treitel* (n 34 above) paras 19-032–19-040.
[50] Below, pp 1219–21.
[51] *Treitel* (n 34 above) para 19-120.
[52] [1964] 2 QB 22.

itself was blocked. They assert that even if the *Eugenia* had never gone into the canal, but had stayed outside (in which case she would not have been in breach of the war clause), nevertheless she would still have had to go round by the Cape. And that, they say, brings about a frustration, for it makes the venture fundamentally different from what they contracted for. The judge has accepted this view …

This means that once again we have had to consider the authorities on this vexed topic of frustration. But I think the position is now reasonably clear. It is simply this: if it should happen, in the course of carrying out a contract, that a fundamentally different situation arises for which the parties made no provision—so much so that it would not be just in the new situation to hold them bound to its terms—then the contract is at an end.

It was originally said that the doctrine of frustration was based on an implied term. In short, that the parties, if they had foreseen the new situation, would have said to one another: 'If that happens, of course, it is all over between us.' But the theory of an implied term has now been discarded by everyone, or nearly everyone, for the simple reason that it does not represent the truth. The parties would not have said: 'It is all over between us.' They would have differed about what was to happen. Each would have sought to insert reservations or qualifications of one kind or another. Take this very case. The parties realised that the canal might become impassable. They tried to agree on a clause to provide for the contingency. But they failed to agree. So there is no room for an implied term.

It has frequently been said that the doctrine of frustration only applies when the new situation is 'unforeseen' or 'unexpected' or 'uncontemplated', as if that were an essential feature. But it is not so. The only thing that is essential is that the parties should have made no provision for it in their contract. The only relevance of it being 'unforeseen' is this: If the parties did not foresee anything of the kind happening, you can readily infer they have made no provision for it: whereas, if they did foresee it, you would expect them to make provision for it. But cases have occurred where the parties have foreseen the danger ahead, and yet made no provision for it in the contract. Such was the case in the Spanish Civil War when a ship was let on charter to the republican government. The purpose was to evacuate refugees. The parties foresaw that she might be seized by the nationalists. But they made no provision for it in their contract. Yet, when she was seized, the contract was frustrated, see *WJ Tatem Ltd v Gamboa*. So here the parties foresaw that the canal might become impassable: it was the very thing they feared. But they made no provision for it. So there is room for the doctrine to apply if it be a proper case for it. We are thus left with the simple test that a situation must arise which renders performance of the contract 'a thing radically different from that which was undertaken by the contract,' see *Davis Contractors Ltd v Fareham Urban District Council*, by Lord Radcliffe. To see if the doctrine applies, you have first to construe the contract and see whether the parties have themselves provided for the situation that has arisen. If they have provided for it, the contract must govern. There is no frustration. If they have not provided for it, then you have to compare the new situation with the situation for which they did provide. Then you must see how different it is. The fact that it has become more onerous or more expensive for one party than he thought is not sufficient to bring about a frustration. It must be more than merely more onerous or more expensive. It must be positively unjust to hold the parties bound. It is often difficult to draw the line. But it must be done. And it is for the courts to do it as a matter of law: see *Tsakiroglou & Co Ltd v Noblee Thorl GmbH* by Lord Simonds and by Lord Reid.

Applying these principles to this case, I have come to the conclusion that the blockage of the canal did not bring about a 'fundamentally different situation' such as to frustrate the venture. My reasons are these:

(1) The venture was the whole trip from delivery at Genoa, out to the Black Sea, there load cargo, thence to India, unload cargo, and redelivery. The time for this vessel from Odessa to Vizagapatam via the Suez Canal would be 26 days, and via the Cape, 56 days. But that is not the right comparison. You have to take the whole venture from delivery at Genoa to redelivery at Madras. We were told that the time for the whole venture via the Suez Canal would be 108 days and via the Cape 138 days. The difference over the whole voyage is not so radical as to produce a frustration.

(2) The cargo was iron and steel goods which would not be adversely affected by the longer voyage, and there was no special reason for early arrival. The vessel and crew were at all times fit and sufficient to proceed via the Cape.

(3) The cargo was loaded on board at the time of the blockage of the canal. If the contract was frustrated, it would mean, I suppose, that the ship could throw up the charter and unload the cargo wherever she was, without any breach of contract.

(4) The voyage round the Cape made no great difference except that it took a good deal longer and was more expensive for the charterers than a voyage through the canal.

Notes

(1) In his judgment Lord Denning deals with three questions. The first is that frustration cannot be relied on when it is self-induced, that is to say, it is the fault of the party relying on it. So the charterers could not rely on the fact that the ship was caught in the Suez Canal, since they should have known this was a risk and could have ordered the ship not to enter the canal. Instead, they argued that the blocking of the canal would have frustrated the contract. On the second question, Lord Denning adopted an original approach because he considered that frustration may apply even if the event is foreseeable, so long as the basic criterion of something fundamentally different from that which was in the parties' contemplation is satisfied. It does not appear that this dictum by Lord Denning is universally accepted.[53] Finally, he examines whether the alteration is sufficiently important in order to render the contract radically different.

(2) Frustration has no application when the contract as a whole is not radically different. So, if only a part of the contract becomes impossible, there is a difficulty. If the impossible part can be severed from the rest of the contract, then that alone may be frustrated. In *Howell v Coupland*,[54] the agreement was to sell a quantity of potatoes to be grown on a particular farm; the crop failed in part and the seller could only deliver part of the agreed quantity. He was not liable for the shortfall but, as was held in the later case of *Sainsbury Ltd v Street*,[55] he was still bound to deliver what he could. In *Sainsbury Ltd v Street* a grower contracted to sell 275 tonnes of barley from his holding, which, however, produced only 140 tonnes. The vendor was released in respect of 135 tonnes but had to deliver the 140 tonnes produced. If however,

---

[53] See *Treitel* (n 34 above) para 19-037.
[54] (1874) LR 9 QB 462 (1875–76), aff'd 1 QBD 258 (CA).
[55] [1972] 1 WLR 834 (Bristol Assizes).

the impossible part cannot be severed, and the contract as a whole is not radically different, the non-performing party will in principle be liable for breach even though he was not at fault. Similarly with temporary impossibility, if the delay is not serious enough to frustrate the contract. This leads the courts on occasion to imply terms in order to excuse the non-performing party.[56]

(3) Moreover, the doctrine will not apply if the non-performing party had any degree of choice.

Court of Appeal **28.14 (EN)**

***J Lauritzen A S v Wijsmuller B V (The Super Servant II)*[57]**

The English doctrine of frustration does not apply when the seller has a choice whether to perform either contract A or contract B.

Facts: By a contract dated 7 July 1980, the defendants (Wijsmuller) agreed to carry the plaintiffs' (Lauritzen's) drilling rig (*Dan King*) from the Hitachi shipyard at Aryake, Japan to a delivery location off Rotterdam. The drilling rig was to be delivered between 20 June 1981 and 20 August 1981 and was to be carried by using what the contract described as the 'transportation unit'. The unit was defined as meaning *Super Servant I* or *Super Servant II*. The contract provided in clause 17:

17. *Cancellation*

17.1. Wijsmuller has the right to cancel its performance under this Contract whether the loading has been completed or not, in the event of force majeur (sic), Acts of God, perils or danger and accidents of the sea, acts of war, warlike-operations, acts of public enemies, restraint of princes, rulers or people or seizure under legal process, quarantine restrictions, civil commotions, blockade, strikes, lockout, closure of the Suez or Panama Canal, congestion of harbours or any other circumstances whatsoever, causing extra-ordinary periods of delay and similar events and/or circumstances, abnormal increases in prices and wages, scarcity of fuel and similar events, which reasonably may impede, prevent or delay the performance of this contract.

On 29 January 1981 *Super Servant II* sank. The defendants had intended to use *Super Servant II* for this contract; they had entered into other contracts with other persons which they could only perform using *Super Servant I*. On or about 16 February 1981 the defendants informed the plaintiffs that they would not carry out the transportation of the drilling rig with either *Super Servant I* or *Super Servant II*. In the event a 'without prejudice' agreement was entered into in April 1981 under which the rig was transported on a barge towed by a tug. The plaintiffs claimed the losses they had suffered and the defendants counterclaimed in respect of the increased expenses they had incurred. The preliminary issues for decision were (1) whether the defendants were entitled to cancel the contract under clause 17 and/or (2) the contract was frustrated (a) if the loss of *Super Servant II* occurred without the negligence of the defendants and (b) if the loss was caused by the defendants' negligence. At first instance ([1989] 1 Lloyd's Rep 148), Hobhouse J held for the defendants on issue 1(a) (ie under clause 17, they were entitled to cancel the contract if the loss of the *Super Servant II* occurred without their negligence), but against them on the other issues. The defendants appealed against the decision on questions 1(a) and 2(a) and (b). The Court of Appeal agreed that clause 17 would protect the defendants if the loss had occurred without their or their servants' negligence.[58]

Held: The Court of Appeal dismissed the appeal.

---

[56] See H Beale, 'Partial and Temporary Impossibility in English and French Law' in *Mélanges Denis Tallon* (Paris: Société de legislation comparée, 1999) 19.

[57] [1990] 1 Lloyd's Rep 1.

[58] For discussion of *force majeure* clauses, see below, pp 1248–51.

Judgment:

[On the issue of frustration:]

BINGHAM LJ: Certain propositions, established by the highest authority are not open to question:

1. The doctrine of frustration was evolved to mitigate the rigour of the common law's insistence on literal performance of absolute promises ... The object of the doctrine was to give effect to the demands of justice, to achieve a just and reasonable result, to do what is reasonable and fair, as an expedient to escape from injustice where such would result from enforcement of a contract in its literal terms after a significant change in circumstances ...

2. Since the effect of frustration is to kill the contract and discharge the parties from further liability under it, the doctrine is not to be lightly invoked, must be kept within very narrow limits and ought not to be extended ...

3. Frustration brings the contract to an end forthwith, without more and automatically ...

4. The essence of frustration is that it should not be due to the act or election of the party seeking to rely on it ... A frustrating event must be some outside event or extraneous change of situation ...

5. A frustrating event must take place without blame or fault on the side of the party seeking to rely on it ... [citations omitted].

Question 2(a)

Mr Clarke for Wijsmuller submitted that the extraneous supervening event necessary to found a plea of frustration occurred when *Super Servant Two* sank on Jan 29, 1981. The *Dan King* contract was not, however, thereupon frustrated but remained alive until Wijsmuller decided a fortnight later that that contract could not be, or would not be, performed. There was, he submitted, factually, no break in the chain of causation between the supervening event and the non-performance of the contract ... For authoritative support Mr Clarke relied on cases dealing with the application of *force majeure* clauses in commodity contracts, and in particular on an unreported judgment of Mr Justice Robert Goff, as he then was, adopted with approval by the Court of Appeal in *Bremer Handelsgesellschaft mbH v Continental Grain Co*:[59]

'... the question resolves itself into a question of causation: in my judgment, at least in a case in which a seller can (as in the present case) claim the protection of a clause which protects him where fulfilment is hindered by the excepted peril, subsequent delivery of his available stock to other customers will not be regarded as an independent cause of shortage, provided that in making such delivery the seller acted reasonably in all the circumstances of the case. ...

... Thus, Mr Clarke urged, this was a case in which Wijsmuller could not perform all their contracts once *Super Servant Two* was lost: they acted reasonably (as we must assume) in treating the *Dan King* contract as one they could not perform; so the sinking had the direct result of making that contract impossible to perform.

Had the *Dan King* contract provided for carriage by *Super Servant Two* with no alternative, and that vessel had been lost before the time for performance, then assuming

---

[59] [1983] 1 Lloyd's Rep 269, 292 (CA).

no negligence by Wijsmuller (as for purposes of this question we must), I feel sure the contract would have been frustrated. The doctrine must avail a party who contracts to perform a contract of carriage with a vessel which, through no fault of his, no longer exists. But that is not this case. The *Dan King* contract did provide an alternative. When that contract was made one of the contracts eventually performed by *Super Servant One* during the period of contractual carriage of *Dan King* had been made, the other had not, at any rate finally. Wijsmuller have not alleged that when the *Dan King* contract was made either vessel was earmarked for its performance. That, no doubt, is why an option was contracted for. Had it been foreseen when the *Dan King* contract was made that *Super Servant Two* would be unavailable for performance, whether because she had been deliberately sold or accidentally sunk, Lauritzen at least would have thought it no matter since the carriage could be performed with the other. I accordingly accept Mr Legh-Jones' submission that the present case does not fall within the very limited class of cases in which the law will relieve one party from an absolute promise he has chosen to make.

But I also accept Mr Legh-Jones' submission that Wijsmuller's argument is subject to other fatal flaws. If, as was argued, the contract was frustrated when Wijsmuller made or communicated their decision on Feb. 16, it deprives language of all meaning to describe the contract as coming to an end automatically … it is in my view inconsistent with the doctrine of frustration as previously understood on high authority that its application should depend on any decision, however reasonable and commercial, of the party seeking to rely on it.

I reach the same conclusion as the Judge for the reasons which he lucidly and persuasively gave.

Question 2(b)

The issue between the parties was short and fundamental: what is meant by saying that a frustrating event, to be relied on, must occur without the fault or default, or without blame attaching to, the party relying on it?

Mr Clarke's answer was that a party was precluded from relying on an event only when he had acted deliberately or in breach of an actionable duty in causing it. Those conditions were not met here …

Wijsmuller's test would, in my judgment, confine the law in a legalistic strait-jacket and distract attention from the real question, which is whether the frustrating event relied upon is truly an outside event or extraneous change of situation or whether it is an event which the party seeking to rely on it had the means and opportunity to prevent but nevertheless caused or permitted to come about. A fine test of legal duty is inappropriate; what is needed is a pragmatic judgment whether a party seeking to rely on an event as discharging him from a contractual promise was himself responsible for the occurrence of that event.

Lauritzen have pleaded in some detail the grounds on which they say that *Super Servant Two* was lost as a result of the carelessness of Wijsmuller, their servants or agents. If those allegations are made good to any significant extent Wijsmuller would (even if my answer to Question 2(a) is wrong) be precluded from relying on their plea of frustration.

I would answer this question also as the Judge did and would therefore dismiss the appeal.

DILLON LJ gave judgment to the same effect.

Notes

(1) It is interesting to contrast this case with the German case of *The bad harvest*.[60] In each case the debtor was put into a situation in which he could not perform all his contractual commitments. It is true that the situations are not identical: in the bad harvest case, the seller could deliver some seed to each buyer, whereas in *The Super Servant II* Wijsmuller had to choose whether to perform the contract with Lauritzen or another contract. It is possible that on the facts of the German case the English court would have reached the same result and have held that the sellers could and should 'pro-rate'. However, the Court of Appeal's reasoning points the other way, since even pro-rating involves the seller in making a choice, and Bingham LJ says this precludes application of the doctrine of frustration. Note that the dictum of Robert Goff J quoted by Bingham LJ, though it seems to suggest that the seller can pro-rate, is qualified by the words: 'at least in a case in which a seller can (as in the present case) claim the protection of a clause which protects him where fulfilment is hindered by the excepted peril'.

(2) Bingham LJ also holds that negligence on Wijsmuller's part would be enough to prevent them relying on frustration. It is not quite clear how far this goes. If a soprano is unable to sing in a concert because she has a serious cold, would she be prevented from relying on frustration (and thus be liable in damages) if it were shown that she had caught the cold by carelessly sitting in a draught?

It seems that a third condition needs also to be satisfied: that neither party was taking the risk of the event that made performance impossible.

Court of Appeal **28.15 (EN)**

Edwinton Commercial Corp v Tsavliris Russ (Worldwide Salvage & Towage) Ltd (The Sea Angel)[61]

A contract will not be frustrated if one or other of the parties was taking the risk of the events that occurred. To decide the allocation of risk requires consideration of a range of factors, and in particular the justice of the outcome.

Facts: Tsavliris were employed by the owners of a tanker called The Tasman Spirit to clean up an oil spill caused when The Tasman Spirit went aground in the port of Karachi. To carry away oil from the wrecked vessel, Tsavliris chartered another small tanker, The Sea Angel, for 'up to 20 days', starting on 26 August 2003. The Sea Angel's work was completed on 9 September and Tsavliris gave notice that it would re-deliver the ship on 9 September; but the ship (and others being used by Tsavliris) was detained by the port authorities, who wanted to keep the vessels as security against possible pollution claims. Tsavliris and other parties involved tried to negotiate a solution. On 13 October the port authorities sent a fax which suggested that no compromise was possible. Ultimately negotiations and threats of legal action led to The Sea Angel being released 108 days late. Tsavliris paid no hire for the vessel after 18 September. The owners claimed hire. (There was a clause stating that if the vessel were detained in certain circumstances, it would be 'off-hire', ie the hire would not be due; but the clause did not cover the events here. There was also a provision in the salvage

---

[60] Above, 28.8 (DE), p 1184.
[61] [2007] EWCA Civ 547, [2007] 1 CLC 876.

agreement between Tsavliris and the owners of The Tasman Spirit (the 'SCOPIC provision') which had the effect that the owners would pay some of the costs of detention at least while the charter remained in force.) Tsavliris argued that the charter was frustrated on 13 October; or alternatively on 17 October, when it had to accept that the negotiating efforts so far had failed.

Held: The Court of Appeal held that in cases of delay it will sometimes be necessary to 'wait and see' how long the delay in likely to last; and that in the circumstances, taking into account a range of factors, it would not be just to hold that the contract was frustrated.

Judgment: Rɪx ʟJ: ... 110 In the course of the parties' submissions we heard much to the effect that such and such a factor 'excluded' or 'precluded' the doctrine of frustration, or made it 'inapplicable'; or, on the other side, that such and such a factor was critical or at least amounted to a prima facie rule. I am not much attracted by that approach, for I do not believe that it is supported by a fair reading of the authorities as a whole. Of course, the doctrine needs an overall test, such as that provided by Lord Radcliffe, if it is not to descend into a morass of quasi-discretionary decisions. Moreover, in any particular case, it may be possible to detect one, or perhaps more, particular factors which have driven the result there. However, the cases demonstrate to my mind that their circumstances can be so various as to defy rule making.

111 In my judgment, the application of the doctrine of frustration requires a multi-factorial approach. Among the factors which have to be considered are the terms of the contract itself, its matrix or context, the parties' knowledge, expectations, assumptions and contemplations, in particular as to risk, as at the time of contract, at any rate so far as these can be ascribed mutually and objectively, and then the nature of the supervening event, and the parties' reasonable and objectively ascertainable calculations as to the possibilities of future performance in the new circumstances. Since the subject matter of the doctrine of frustration is contract, and contracts are about the allocation of risk, and since the allocation and assumption of risk is not simply a matter of express or implied provision but may also depend on less easily defined matters such as 'the contemplation of the parties', the application of the doctrine can often be a difficult one. In such circumstances, the test of 'radically different' is important: it tells us that the doctrine is not to be lightly invoked; that mere incidence of expense or delay or onerousness is not sufficient; and that there has to be as it were a break in identity between the contract as provided for and contemplated and its performance in the new circumstances.

112 What the 'radically different' test, however, does not in itself tell us is that the doctrine is one of justice, as has been repeatedly affirmed on the highest authority. Ultimately the application of the test cannot safely be performed without the consequences of the decision, one way or the other, being measured against the demands of justice. Part of that calculation is the consideration that the frustration of a contract may well mean that the contractual allocation of risk is reversed. A time charter is a good example. Under such a charter, the risk of delay, subject to express provision for the cessation of hire under an off-hire clause, is absolutely on the charterer. If, however, a charter is frustrated by delay, then the risk of delay is wholly reversed: the delay now falls on the owner. If the provisions of a contract in their literal sense are to make way for the absolving effect of frustration, then that must, in my judgment, be in the interests of justice and not against those interests. Since the purpose of the doctrine is to do justice, then its application cannot be divorced from considerations of justice. Those considerations are among the most important of the factors which a tribunal has to bear in mind.

...

132 I have referred to this factor ['justice'] above. It is not an additional test, but it is a relevant factor which underlies all and provides the ultimate rationale of the doctrine. If one uses this factor as a reality check, its answer should conform with a proper assessment of the issue of frustration. If it does not appear to do so, it is probably a good indication of the need to think again. The question in this case is whether it would be just to relieve Tsavliris of the consequences of their bargain, or unjust to maintain the bargain, in a situation where they have assumed the general risk of delay, and have done so in a specific context where the risk of unreasonable detention is foreseeable and has at least in general been actually foreseen, as demonstrated by SCOPIC which, subject to the limits of frustration, protects the salvor from the financial consequences of the delay; where from the very beginning a solution was considered to be possible rather than impossible or hopeless, but only after a period of some three months, and where that solution, although not entirely or even mainly in Tsavliris's own control, was achievable with the co-operation of the owners of the casualty and their Club, known to be in principle available, and the assistance of legal action in the local courts; and where the outcome has confirmed the calculations of the objectively reasonable participants in the events.

133 In my judgment, the judge's conclusion, that the charter had not been frustrated by 13 or 17 October, shows the doctrine working justly, reasonably and fairly…

WALLER and HOOPER LJJ agreed. Appeal Dismissed

Note

Rix LJ's reference to 'the dictates of justice' does not imply that the courts have an absolving power. It is rather a reference to the courts' unwillingness to upset what they see as the contractual allocation of the risks of the venture.

28.5.B EFFECTS OF FRUSTRATION

Frustration causes the contract to disappear. The courts cannot alter the agreement. It is generally accepted that the disappearance of the contract is by operation of law: *Hirji Mulji v Cheong Yue SS Co Ltd*.[62] Nor is it a question of the party who is affected having an option; frustration occurs automatically or not at all.

When the contract is discharged, what is the position if the parties have already paid money or supplied goods or services under the contract, or if they have incurred expenditure in getting ready to perform?

Taking first the case where one party had made a payment to the other, the common law rule, as applied in particular in *Chandler v Webster*[63] (another coronation case) was that the parties were discharged for the future but any payments already made (or obligations to make payments that that were due) before the contract was frustrated were unaffected.[64] This excluded any restitution in respect of monies paid under the contract. In *Fibrosa Spolka Akcyjna v Fairbairn, Lawson, Combe, Barbour Ltd*[65] the House of

---

[62] [1926] AC 497 (PC).
[63] [1904] 1 KB 493 (CA).
[64] This is why in *Krell v Henry* (28.10 (EN) above, p 1189) Henry abandoned his claim for repayment.
[65] [1943] AC 32 (HL).

Lords held that this was incorrect; the fact that there had been a contract did not prevent the party getting restitution of the payment where there was a total failure of consideration. (The normal rule of English law is that payments can be recovered only where there has been a total failure of consideration in the sense that the payor has received nothing in exchange for his payment.[66]) Neither the old rule nor the new one was thought to be satisfactory: under the old rule, the payee might be unjustly enriched, but under the new one he might be left out of pocket if he had already incurred expenses in preparing to perform (in the *Fibrosa* case, the sellers had incurred costs in building the machinery which could not be delivered because of the Nazi occupation of Poland). Moreover, if the payer had received something in exchange, he would not recover any of the money paid, even if he had paid much more than the value of what he had received in return.

The position where goods and services had been supplied was also unsatisfactory. In *Appleby v Myers*[67] the contract was to install machinery in a factory; payment was due upon completion. The factory was destroyed by fire, with the result that the contract was frustrated, after only some of the machinery had been installed. It was held that the contractor was not entitled to any payment. The price was not due until all the machinery had been installed, and recovery would not be given on a restitutionary basis either. The Court reasoned that to allow recovery by way of restitution would be inconsistent with the express terms of the contract stipulating for payment only on completion.[68]

Therefore, the legislature intervened.

Law Reform (Frustrated Contracts) Act 1943   **28.16 (EN)**

Section 1: Adjustment of rights and liabilities of parties to frustrated contracts

(1) Where a contract governed by English law has become impossible of performance or been otherwise frustrated, and the parties thereto have for that reason been discharged from the further performance of the contract, the following provisions of the section shall, subject to the provisions of section two of this Act, have effect in relation thereto.

(2) All sums paid or payable to any party in pursuance of the contract before the time when the parties were so discharged (in this Act referred to as 'the time of discharge') shall, in the case of sums so paid, be recoverable from him as money received by him for the use of the party by whom the sums were paid, and, in the case of sums so payable, cease to be so payable:

Provided that, if the party to whom the sums were so paid or payable incurred expenses before the time of discharge in, or for the purpose of, the performance of the contract, the court may, if it considers it just to do so having regard to all the circumstances of the case, allow him to retain or, as the case may be, recover the whole or any part of the sums so paid or payable, not being an amount in excess of the expenses so incurred.

---

[66] See above, p 349 n 24.

[67] (1867) LR 2 CP 651.

[68] See also *Sumpter v Hedges* (25.36 (EN), above, p 1053), which applies a similar rule when the contract has been terminated because of a breach by the contractor.

(3) Where any party to the contract has, by reason of anything done by any other party thereto in, or for the purpose of, the performance of the contract, obtained a valuable benefit (other than a payment of money to which the last foregoing subsection applies) before the time of discharge, there shall be recoverable from him by the said other party such sum (if any), not exceeding the value of the said benefit to the party obtaining it, as the court considers just, having regard to all the circumstances of the case and, in particular:

(a) the amount of any expenses incurred before the time of discharge by the benefited party in, or for the purpose of, the performance of the contract, including any sums paid or payable by him to any other party in pursuance of the contract and retained or recoverable by that party under the last foregoing subsection, and

(b) the effect, in relation to the said benefit, of the circumstances giving rise to the frustration of the contract.

(4) In estimating, for the purposes of the foregoing provisions of this section, the amount of any expenses incurred by any party to the contract, the court may, without prejudice to the generality of the said provisions, include such sums as appears to be reasonable in respect of overhead expenses and in respect of any work or service performed personally by the said party.

(5) In considering whether any sum ought to be recovered or retained under the foregoing provisions of this section by any party to the contract, the court shall not take into account any sums which have, by reason of the circumstances giving rise to the frustration of the contract, become payable to that party under any contract of insurance unless there was an obligation to insure imposed by any express term of the frustrated contract or by or under any enactment.

(6) Where any person has assumed obligations under the contract in consideration of the conferring of a benefit by any other party to the contract upon any other person, whether a party to the contract or not, the court may, if in all the circumstances of the case it considers it just to do so, treat for the purposes of sub-section (3) of this section any benefit so conferred as a benefit obtained by the person who has assumed the obligations as aforesaid.

Notes

(1) The Act deals first with restitution of money (in section 1(2)) and then with claims for other benefits (in section 1(3)).

(2) Section 1(2) has the effect that any sum paid is to be repaid, but the court may allow the payee to retain some or all of the sum to cover expenses incurred in preparing to perform. If the money is due at the date of frustration but has not been paid, it ceases to be payable but the creditor may recover up to the amount of its expenses. The exact sum to be kept or recovered is in the court's discretion. Note that expenses that exceed the amount that was paid or payable in advance will not be compensable.

(3) Section 1(3) allows the court to award up to the value of the benefit conferred. It must take into account the effect of the frustrating circumstances—so if, as in *Appleby v Myers*, the work done has all been destroyed in the frustrating event, the recipient might be treated as having received no benefit and need pay nothing (whereas if the machinery were covered by insurance, it would seem that the recipient would still

be receiving a benefit). When deciding how much the recipient should pay, the court should also take into account any expenses the recipient incurred.

(4) For a case discussing and applying the Act, see *BP Exploration Co (Libya) Ltd v Hunt (No 2)*.[69]

FURTHER READING

Faust, F, 'Impossibility, Initial' in J Basedow, K Hopt and R Zimmermann (eds), *Max Planck Encyclopedia of European Private Law* (Oxford University Press, 2012) 849–52.

Kötz, H, *European Contract Law* (2nd edn, Oxford University Press, 2017) 205–26, 248–51.

Rüfner, T, 'Change of Circumstances' in N Jansen and R Zimmermann (eds), *Commentaries on European Contract Laws* (Oxford University Press, 2018) 899–911.

Treitel, G, *Frustration and Force Majeure* (3rd edn, London: Sweet & Maxwell, 2014).

Tunc, A, 'Force majeure et absence de faute en matière contractuelle' RTD civ 1939, 19.

---

[69] [1979] 1 WLR 783, aff'd [1982] 1 WLR 232 (CA) and [1983] 2 AC 352 (HL).

29.1. INTRODUCTION

The question of whether a party may be released from her obligations by supervening events which make the contract much more onerous is an important one. Many contracts last over a long period of time and frequently the circumstances that existed at the moment the contract was made are subsequently radically changed. This is all the more true in a period of economic instability. In practice, contracting parties often supplement the general rules of law with specific clauses, such as 'hardship' clauses; if they do not, the reasonable conclusion may be that one of them assumed the risk of a drastic change of circumstances. However, it is not always so; parties may just have forgotten to include such a clause. Most countries have introduced into their law some mechanism in order to deal with such situations. These mechanisms vary from one country to another. It is instructive to observe these differences as they reveal a lot about the general policies which underlie each legal system in the field of contracts. In spite of the differences between national laws, attempts have been made to harmonise the solutions at a European level. The prevailing view is that, when the contract becomes excessively onerous because of a change of circumstances, parties should renegotiate the agreement. If renegotiations fail, the court may then terminate the contract or adapt it. This judicial power granted to the court stands in sharp contrast with the more rigid approach that some jurisdictions, such as England, have retained.

Principles of European Contract Law   **29.1 (INT)**

Article 6:111: Change of Circumstances

(1) A party is bound to fulfil its obligations even if performance has become more onerous, whether because the cost of performance has increased or because the value of the performance it receives has diminished.

(2) If, however, performance of the contract becomes excessively onerous because of a change of circumstances, the parties are bound to enter into negotiations with a view to adapting the contract or terminating it, provided that:

(a) the change of circumstances occurred after the time of conclusion of the contract,

(b) the possibility of a change of circumstances was not one which could reasonably have been taken into account at the time of conclusion of the contract, and

(c) the risk of the change of circumstances is not one which, according to the contract, the party affected should be required to bear.

(3) If the parties fail to reach agreement within a reasonable period, the court may:

   (a) terminate the contract at a date and on terms to be determined by the court; or

   (b) adapt the contract in order to distribute between the parties in a just and equitable manner the losses and gains resulting from the change of circumstances. In either case, the court may award damages for the loss suffered through a party refusing to negotiate or breaking off negotiations contrary to good faith and fair dealing.

Notes

(1) Article III-1:110 of the Draft Common Frame of Reference (DCFR) ('Variation or termination by court on a change of circumstances') is similar to the Principles of European Contract Law (PECL). Both texts begin by recognising the principle that obligations must be performed even if performance turns out to be more onerous than anticipated. Thus, the point of departure is obviously observance of the binding force of the contract 'which has the force of law' as between those who entered into it and can be altered or dissolved prematurely only by common accord of the parties. However, these texts then refer to those situations where an exceptional change of circumstances, which could not reasonably have been taken into account, is so extreme that it would be manifestly unjust to hold the debtor to the obligation. In such situations, they provide a mechanism whereby, if certain rather demanding requirements are satisfied, a court may adapt the obligation to the changed circumstances or even terminate it altogether. Both texts encourage negotiated solutions to the problems caused by changes in circumstances. Article III-1:110 DCFR does not impose an obligation on the parties to negotiate. It simply requires that the debtor has attempted, reasonably and in good faith, to achieve a satisfactory negotiated adjustment.

(2) The UNIDROIT Principles of International Commercial Contracts (UNIDROIT PICC) contain similar provisions in a Section called Hardship (Articles 6.2.1, 6.2.2, 6.2.3). First, the party may request renegotiations (Article 6.2.3(1)); second, upon failure to reach an agreement within a reasonable time, 'either party may resort to the court' (Article 6.2.3(3)) and the court may, if reasonable, 'terminate the contract' or 'adapt it with a view to restoring its equilibrium' (Article 6.2.3(4)). However, in commercial arbitration cases, tribunals often refuse to modify the contract and the refusal to admit *révision pour imprévision* is considered as an element of the 'law of merchants' or *lex mercatoria*.

(3) The United Nations Convention on Contracts for the International Sale of Goods (CISG) has no rule on change of circumstances. Although there is some debate as to the proper interpretation of Article 79 (which deals with *force majeure*), the leading interpretation (which also stems from the preparatory works) is that the CISG has deliberately refrained from laying down (and not only omitted) any provision with regard to the change of circumstances. The Belgian Cour de cassation, however, has taken the view that this gap should be filled by general principles of international trade. In the case of *Scafom International BV v Lorraine Tubes SAS*,[1] the parties had concluded an agreement for the sale of steel tubes. After the conclusion of the contract

---

[1] Belgian Cour de cassation, 19 June 2009, *Scafom International BV v Lorraine Tubes SAS*; translation of the case and comments available at http://cisgw3.law.pace.edu/cases/090619b1.html.

and before delivery, the price of steel unexpectedly rose by about 70%. The seller tried to renegotiate a higher contract price, but the buyer refused and insisted on delivery of the goods at the price agreed upon. The decision of the court of first instance was overturned by the Court of Appeal in Antwerp. That court decided that the issue regarding economic hardship was not dealt with by the CISG and applied French domestic law in allowing the seller's counterclaim for an amount based on a higher price (whether or not French law does lead to this solution is arguable). The Cour de cassation rejected the application of French domestic law, holding that there was a gap in the CISG to be filled by general principles of international trade, according to Article 7(2) CISG. It then decided that:

> under these principles, as incorporated inter alia in the UNIDROIT Principles of International Commercial Contracts, the party who invokes changed circumstances that fundamentally disturb the contractual balance, as mentioned in paragraph 1, is also entitled to claim the renegotiation of the contract.

(4) On the occurrence of extraordinary events—economic crisis, war—it is for the legislature to intervene, as happened after the two world wars, by conferring on the courts a provisional power of revision; for example, the French Acts of 21 January 1918 and 22 April 1949 and the German Act on assistance to contracts of 1952 which relaxed the burden of debtors who were suffering from the consequences of the war and the transition to the new currency. (As time went by, the Act became obsolete and it was formally abolished in 2000.[2]) There are also specific statutory provisions for certain long-term transactions. It remains to be determined whether it is desirable to make this kind of provision permanent.

(5) A famous French judgment of principle refused to admit *révision pour imprévision* (it dates back to 1876).[3] Doctrinal controversy developed after the First World War and, following a famous German judgment of the 1920s,[4] judicial revision of the contract in the case of an unforeseen event has been allowed by the laws of several countries. In contrast, French (private law) and English law have refused, on grounds of principle, to give courts the power to adjust the original contract. However, modern French case law tried to find ways to partially circumvent this rule; and French law has now been modified.

29.2. FRENCH LAW

In 2016, Article 1195 of the Code civil introduced a major change into French law.[5] Until the 2016 reform of the Code civil, the landmark judgment for civil and commercial

---

[2] Gesetz über die richterliche Vertragshilfe (Vertragshilfegesetz) of 23 March 1952, BGBl. 1952 I 198; abolished by Art 9 Gesetz über Fernabsatzverträge und andere Fragen des Verbraucherrechts sowie zur Umstellung von Vorschriften auf den Euro of 27 June 2000, BGBl. 2000 I 897.

[3] Cass civ 6 March 1876, *Canal de Craponne*, D 1876.I.93; see F Terré, Y Lequette and F Chénedé, *Grands arrêts de jurisprudence civil*, vol 2, *Obligations, Contrats spéciaux, Sûretés* (13th edn, Paris: Dalloz, 2015) no. 165.

[4] See below, 29.8 (DE), p 1222.

[5] On the reforms see F Chénedé, *Le nouveau droit des obligations et des contrats: Consolidations, innovations, perspectives* (Paris: Dalloz, 2016) nos. 25.51–25.91; O Deshayes, 'The Search for a Global and Lasting

contracts was *Canal de Craponne* of 6 March 1876.[6] It concerned an agreement of 1567 which fixed a charge for water at a rate which three centuries later had become derisory. That judgment set aside the judgment of a cour d'appel which had readjusted the charge.

In contrast, in the field of administrative contracts, the administrative courts, since the landmark judgment of the Conseil d'État of 30 March 1916, *Gaz de Bordeaux*,[7] have allowed *révision pour imprévision* in the case of a contract whose 'structure is absolutely overturned owing to exceptional circumstances', provided that the event is not definitive. The public authorities are then liable to pay compensation so as to share equitably the exceptional burden. The ideas put forward to justify that stance are the following: first, the principle of the continuity of the public service (in the absence of an adjustment the public service secured under the contract would be interrupted); secondly, the right of the person contracting with the public authorities to expect financial equilibrium within the contract. It is debatable, however, whether these arguments effectively justified a difference between French private law and administrative law. On 12 March 1976, the Conseil d'État admitted that, even though the contract had already been terminated, the *concessionnaire* could benefit from the theory of *imprévision* and obtain compensation on this basis. This shows that what is at stake is not only the mere value of continuity, but also the right of the party to a certain equilibrium.[8] Besides, the opposition between public interest and private interest no longer appears sufficiently clear-cut to allow such a dichotomy between French private and administrative law as regards the theory of *imprévision*. Public interest is also concerned by contracts between private persons. This is proved by the development of mandatory rules, all throughout the twentieth century (with the diffusion of the concepts of *ordre public économique de direction* and *ordre public de protection*[9]). Moreover, administrative contracts are more and more 'privatised'. It is true that in the French system the concept of public service is very structured and distinctive, much more than in other countries; yet the major distinction between administrative law and private law, and also the separation between administrative and private law courts, is not always justified. The fact that French law had two opposite sets of rules regarding the question of supervening events gave the impression that, on this point, French law was limping.[10] The 2016 reform of French contract law removed this distinction between private and administrative law regarding the rules on supervening events; with the introduction of the *révision pour imprévision*, private law is now aligned with the position of the administrative courts. This does not mean that the topic is now settled in French contract law. Indeed, as many authors

Contractual Balance: the Content of the Contract and the Change of Circumstances' (2017) 6 Montesquieu Law Review 68; O Deshayes, T Genicon and YM Laithier, *Réforme du droit des contrats, du régime général et de la preuve des obligations, Commentaire article par article* (Paris: LexisNexis, 2016) 384–420; M Latina and G Chantepie, *La réforme du droit des obligations: Commentaire théorique et pratique dans l'ordre du Code civil* (Paris: Dalloz, 2016) nos. 522–30; P Malaurie, L Aynès and P Stoffel-Munck, *Droit des obligations* (9th edn, Paris: LGDJ, 2017) nos. 758–64.

[6] Cass civ, 6 March 1876 (n 3 above).

[7] S 1916.III.17, opinion by P Chardenet, annotated by M Hauriou.

[8] H Capitant, F Terré and Y Lequette, *Les grands arrêts de la jurisprudence civile, Tome 2, Obligations, contrats spéciaux, sûretés* (12th edn, Paris: Dalloz, 2008) no. 165.

[9] See ch 17 on immoral and illegal contracts.

[10] D Tallon, 'La révision du contrat pour imprévision au regard des enseignements récents du droit comparé' in *Mélanges à la mémoire d'Alain Sayag* (Paris: Litec, 1997) 403, 404; B Fauvarque-Cosson, 'Le changement de circonstances' RCD 2004, 67.

are still opposed to the *révision pour imprévision* and the Senate attempted to abolish the mechanism during the 2018 ratification process, the future application of Article 1195 of the Code civil will be anything but a long quiet river.

Cass civ, 6 March 1876[11]   **29.2 (FR)**

Canal de Craponne

The court has no power to adjust the terms of a contract that has proven onerous for one party to perform.

Facts: In contracts made in 1560 and 1567 a canal company undertook to supply water users with water at a fixed price of 3 sols per unit of water. Over time this sum had become derisory and the canal owners sought to increase the price.

Held: The terms of the contract could not be adjusted.

Judgment: The Cour d'appel of Aix gave the following judgment on 31 December 1873:
— On the increase in the watering charges:
— Whereas while contracts that are lawfully concluded hold the place of the law itself for those who have made them and while they may only be modified by mutual consent, the position is not the same in relation to contracts of a continuing nature;
— That it is recognised in law that these contracts, which are based upon periodic charges, can be modified by the courts when a fair relationship no longer exists between the charges on the one hand and the costs incurred on the other; that, in the present case, the sum owed by the waterers represents the use of the water of the canal, having for its counterpart the maintenance and expenses in respect of the canal; that from the day that this balance ceases to exist, the original law of the contract is broken and it is for the courts to re-establish the initial position of equality;
— Whereas, in fact, the contracts of 1560 and 1567 are of a continuing nature, that Craponne, in undertaking the obligation to provide water to the waterers of Pélisanne, stipulated, by way of compensation, for a set charge; that this charge of 3 sols[12] per unit of water, which could have been sufficient at that time, was no longer sufficient today as the costs of maintaining the canal had increased significantly; that one could not argue that Adam de Craponne had initially obtained particular benefits, which prevented his heirs from asking today for a fair increase in the charges;
— Whereas the judges of first instance, in setting this increase at 60 centimes per unit of water, had properly assessed the facts of the case, etc.
Appeal by the association of waterers—2nd ground of appeal: excess of power and violation of Article 1134 Civil Code in that on the pretext that the matter concerned a contract of a continuing nature, the court substituted a new price for that which resulted from the contract of the parties.
— On the second appeal ground: … etc;
— Rejects this appeal ground;
— But on the first appeal ground:
— Having considered Article 1134 Civil Code;
— Whereas the provisions of this Article are no more than a re-enactment of long-established principles which have constantly been followed as regards consensual

11 Cass civ 6 March 1876 (n 3 above).
12 Unit of money.

obligations, the fact that these contracts, the performance of which gives rise to this litigation, were concluded prior to the promulgation of the Civil Code cannot constitute an obstacle to the application of the said Article in this case;

— Whereas the rule that this Article consecrates is general, absolute and governs contracts whose performance extends to successive periods, just as it governs contracts of all other types;

— That under no circumstances is it for the courts, however fair their decision may appear to them to be, to take into account the time and the circumstances in order to substitute new terms for those which have been freely accepted by the contracting parties;

— That in deciding the contrary and in increasing the watering charges, which had been fixed at 3 sols by the contracts of 1560 and 1567, to 30 centimes from 1834–1874, then to 60 centimes from 1874 onwards, under the pretext that this charge no longer bore any relation to the costs of maintaining the canal de Craponne, the judgment under challenge had categorically violated Article 1134, which was considered above;

— Quashes in relation to the order increasing the watering charges, etc.

Notes

(1) *Canal de Craponne* is a leading case, in which the Cour de cassation categorically refused to revise the contract. It did so on the legal basis of former Article 1134 Cciv (now Article 1103).

(2) Various arguments were put forward by some French academics to justify the rule set out in *Canal de Craponne*, notably these two: (a) such an approach encourages the parties to make appropriate contractual provision; (b) the courts are not well placed to intervene.

(3) The position adopted by the Cour de cassation was upheld after the First World War in spite of monetary depreciation—500% price inflation. An example of this may be seen below in the judgment of the Civil chamber of the Cour de cassation of 6 June 1921, in factual circumstances very close to those of the contemporaneous judgment of the RG of 27 June 1922.[13] At the same time a doctrinal controversy sprang up which has lasted until the 2016 Ordonnance, as shown by the various of French contract law projects of reform.[14]

Cass civ, 6 June 1921[15]   **29.3 (FR)**

The rearing contract

No equitable consideration permits the courts to vary the contract.

Facts: Under a peculiar stock-rearing contract entered into in 1910, the farmer was required to leave the herd with capital of the same value as he had received, that value being fixed in the contract. The owner claimed a proportion of the added value resulting from monetary depreciation during the war.

Held: This claim was upheld by the cour d'appel. The judgment was set aside.

---

[13] See below, 29.9 (DE), p 1224.
[14] See below, pp 1216–18.
[15] D 1921.I.73, with the report of Colin, S 1921.I.193, annotated by L Hugueney.

Judgment: THE COURT:—By reference to Articles 1134 and 1826[16] of the Civil Code,

— Whereas agreements legally entered into have the force of law as regards those entering into them and that no consideration of equity allows the courts, where agreements are clear and precise, to amend on the pretext of interpretation the provisions contained therein;

— Whereas on 4 December 1910, Saint-Pé, a proprietor, entered into a stock-rearing contract with Bacou containing the following clause: 'The capital taken over by the farmer amounts to 3,000 FRF for the beasts and 2,425 FRF for the herd, and it is in respect of this amount in cash or in kind, as the proprietor shall decide, which the farmer shall account on expiry of the agreement'; as that precise and clear clause derogated from the rules of the Civil Code on stock leases containing an estimate of the condition of the animals, solely inasmuch as it gave the lessor the right to opt at the end of the lease between payment in cash or restitution in kind but for the rest left the parties subject to the ordinary law; as, accordingly, the stock account was to be governed by Article 1826 of the Civil Code;

— Whereas under that provision, the farmer at the end of the lease is required to leave stock 'equal in value to that which he received'; as, if there is a deficit he must pay it but any surplus belongs to him; as no distinction is made between the value added to the stock by the care and improvements of the farmer and that stemming from accidental circumstances; as it is apparent from Article 1826 read in conjunction with Article 1821 that the farmer shall 'leave beasts equal in value to the estimated price of those he received'; as secondly, the law had in contemplation the actual value of the stock and not its potential for commercial exploitation; as the judgment therefore erred in holding that Bacou should share the entirety of the added value acquired by the stock and by the herd, instead of awarding it to Bacou.

— Whereas the cour d'appel asserts in vain that, in entering into the contract, the parties could not have foreseen the extraordinary increase in animal prices as a result of the First World War but merely a normal rise, the maximum amount of which evidently corresponded to the highest price for stock during the period of the latest years prior to conclusion of the contract.

— Whereas by undertaking indeed to bear the risk of a future rise in prices of animals and herds, the counterpart of the risks likely to result from either a fall in those prices or fortuitous loss of the animals entrusted to the farmer, Saint-Pé imposed upon himself a law from which he could not exempt himself by alleging that his forecasts had been wrong; as it was for him to restrict his commitment to a given amount; as by inferring however such restriction from circumstances concerning which the lease was silent, the judgment appealed against merely substituted a presumed agreement for the agreement expressed by the contracting parties; as in that regard it infringed the abovementioned legislation;

On those grounds the judgment is set aside.

Notes

(1) This judgment essentially follows the judgment in *Canal de Craponne*. It sets aside the appeal decision, which had divided between the farmer and proprietor the added value resulting from the depreciation of the franc after the First World War, contrary to the clause in the contract which awarded that added value to the

---

[16] This provision was amended in 1941 and fixes now as the date at which the evaluation should take place the day on which the contract comes to an end.

farmer. It reaffirms the absolute nature of the contract as a 'law' as between the parties, even if the projections of one of the parties turn out to be wrong. No 'equitable consideration' permits the courts to vary the contract. It gives precedence to former Article 1134(1) Cciv (now Article 1103)—the binding force of the contract—over former Article 1134(3) (now Article 1104)—agreements are to be performed in good faith—and former Article 1135 (now Article 1194)—a contract is binding as regards all the effects to which by its nature equity, usage or the law the obligation gives rise.

(2) Note the link made in this judgment between the allocation of the risk of future rise in prices of animals and herds to one party and the impossibility for the judge to substitute a presumed agreement for the agreement expressed by the contracting parties. Is it not contrary to good faith and equity to impose the burden of unforeseen risks on one of the parties only?

(3) Later on, even more weight to this solution was given by the economic argument that, in chains of contracts, if the creditor is called upon to pay compensation in respect of an unforeseen event, a compensation indeed not foreseen by him, he in turn should be able to claim compensation from other contracting parties, and so on.

(4) Before the French reform took place, some authors advocated admission of a judicial power to revise the contract when circumstances have so altered this contract that its performance, although not impossible (impossibility would be *force majeure*), has become excessively onerous for one of the parties. The Cour de cassation itself started opening new routes, notably by referring to good faith (see former Article 1134(3) on good faith, now new Article 1104). Indeed, the Cour de cassation held that a party would not conform with its duty of good faith if it refuses to enter into renegotiations of the contract.[17] The Cour de cassation also relied on the concept of *cause*. In 2010, the Cour de cassation quashed an appeal judgment on the ground that the cour d'appel did not check whether the evolution of the economic circumstances, and in particular the increase of the cost of raw materials, had undermined the general equilibrium of the contract and deprived the contract from any actual counterparts, that is from its *cause*.[18]

The various projects which have preceded the French reform of the law of contract show how divided French opinion was on this question.

Avant-projet Catala   **29.4 (FR)**

Article 1135-1: In contracts whose performance takes place successively or in instalments, the parties may undertake to negotiate a modification of their contract where as a result of supervening circumstances the original balance of what the parties must do for each other is so disturbed that the contract loses all its point for one of them.

Article 1135-2: In the absence of such an express term, a party for whom a contract loses its point may apply to the President of the *tribunal de grande instance* to order a new negotiation.

---

[17] Cass civ (1) 16 March 2004, no. 01-15804, Bull I no. 86.
[18] Cass com 29 June 2010, no. 09-67369, unpublished.

Article 1135-3: Where applicable, these negotiations should be governed by the rules provided by Chapter I of the present Title.

In the absence of bad faith, the failure of the negotiations gives rise to a right in either party to terminate the contract for the future at no cost or loss.

Propositions de réforme du droit des contrats (F Terré) **29.5 (FR)**

Article 92: Parties are bound to fulfil their contractual obligations even if their performance has become more onerous.

However, the parties must renegotiate the contract with a view to adjusting it or ending it if performance becomes excessively onerous for one of them because of a change of circumstances which was unforeseeable and of which they did not take the risk at the time the contract was made.

If the parties do not reach an agreement within a reasonable time, the judge may adapt the contract taking into account the legitimate interests of the parties or end it under conditions that he may lay down.

French Ministry of Justice Project (July 2008) **29.6 (FR)**

Article 136: If an unforeseeable and unsurmountable change of circumstances makes performance excessively onerous for one party, and that party had not taken the risk, he may demand that the other party renegotiate the contract, but the first party must continue to perform during the re-negotiations.

If re-negotiations are refused or break down, the judge may adapt the contract if the parties so agree, or may put an end to it from a date and on conditions that he may fix.

Notes

(1) Initially, the Ministry of Justice did not wish to allow the courts to adapt the contract (compare for example the Catala project which would only have allowed for the parties to make a new contract), except in the rather rare case of a joint request by the parties ('the judge may adapt the contract if the parties so agree'). It was not until the end of 2015 that, due to the results of the consultations, the Ministry finally changed its view. New Article 1195 thus came as a surprise for many and was intensely debated, still after the Ordonnance was passed.

(2) The Report to the President of the Republic which accompanied the 2016 Ordonnance stressed the importance and influence of the European context for such a change: 'France is one of the last European countries not to recognize the theory of *imprévision* as a factor moderating the binding force of contracts. Such recognition, inspired by comparative law as well as by the European harmonisation projects, makes it possible to combat the major contractual imbalances which occur during performance, in accordance with the objective of contractual justice pursued by the *Ordonnance*'.[19]

---

[19] Report to the President (p 83 n 30 above).

Article 1195: If a change of circumstances that was unforeseeable at the time of the conclusion of the contract renders performance excessively onerous for a party who had not accepted the risk of such a change, that party may ask the other contracting party to renegotiate the contract. The first party must continue to perform his obligations during renegotiation.

In the case of refusal or the failure of renegotiations, the parties may agree to terminate the contract from the date and on the conditions which they determine, or by a common agreement ask the court to set about its adaptation. In the absence of an agreement within a reasonable time, the court may, on the request of a party, revise the contract or put an end to it, from a date and subject to such conditions as it shall determine.

Notes

(1) Article 1195 is the third article of Chapter IV on 'The Effects of Contracts', Section 1 on 'The Effects of Contracts between the Parties' and Subsection 1, 'Binding Force'. The principle of binding force has been moved up to the 'Introductory Provisions' of Chapter I (Article 1103: 'Contracts which are lawfully formed have the binding force of legislation for those who have made them'). Judicial revision has made a remarkable entrance into French general contract law but it is still too early to determine whether the courts will use the powers thus given to them. French judges are not in the best position to revise a contract which is supposed to be applicable over a long period of time.

(2) Article 1195 is evidence of the reluctance of the French legislator to depart from earlier solutions. Judicial termination or revision is a last resort remedy, which may only be resorted to after the refusal or the failure of renegotiations. Article 1195 also provides that 'the parties may agree to terminate the contract from the date and on the conditions which they determine, or by a common agreement ask the court to set about its adaptation'. Judicial termination or adaptation may thus result from a common agreement of the parties. It is only if there is no such agreement and if negotiations failed or could not take place that a party may unilaterally ask the court to 'revise the contract or put an end to it'.

(3) The legislator hoped that granting such powers to the courts would encourage the party that would have the greatest interest in maintaining the contract to renegotiate. Actually, not only adaptation but also termination gives extended powers to the judges since they can terminate the contract 'from a date and subject to such conditions'.

(4) The conditions for the operation of *force majeure* differ from those required for *imprévision*: performance of the obligation must be 'prevented' (and therefore impossible) and not simply 'excessively onerous' (see new Article 1218(1) of the Code civil). The effects of *force majeure* are also different from those of *imprévision*: *force majeure* permits the debtor not to perform his obligations and is thus a genuine exemption from liability for the debtor, whereas *imprévision* allows the revision of the contract by the courts.

(5) The non-mandatory nature of Article 1195 allows the parties to modify or exclude the application of their provisions. In contractual practice 'adaptation clauses'

and '*force majeure* clauses' are widely used (there is sometimes confusion between *force majeure* clauses and clauses relating to a change of circumstances which causes 'hardship'; on these clauses, see Chapter 30). The *Ordonnance* says nothing about the non-mandatory nature of Article 1195, but the Report to the President of the Republic does.[20] In principle clauses of this type are valid, but they must be drafted carefully, whether their aim is to exclude the operation of Article 1195 (for example, by a clause in which one of the parties formally assumes the risk of changes of circumstances, a possibility which the text of course envisages), or to exclude the possibility of suspending or releasing the obligations of one of the parties in the event of *force majeure* (the contracting party undertakes to fulfil its obligations even in the event of *force majeure*).

(6) A creditor who establishes non-performance by the other party may apply to the court for judicial termination, which will enable the court to decide whether or not there is a change in circumstances apt to trigger Article 1195, and, if so, to decide whether or not to refer it back to the parties to agree on its consequences. The creditor may also terminate the contract unilaterally by notice (Article 1224) at his own risk and in accordance with a procedure defined by Article 1226.

(7) The 2018 ratification slightly narrowed the scope of Article 1195: the provision is not applicable to obligations which result from the securities and financial contracts mentioned in Article L 211-1 of the Code monétaire et financier (see Article L 211-40-1 of the same Code).

29.3. ENGLISH LAW

English law in principle holds the parties to their bargain and so leaves it to them to make their own provision for events which may make performance more onerous.

The existence of a judicial power to adapt the contract has never been accepted, even in situations which undoubtedly constitute cases of *imprévision*, for example, the cases arising out of the closure of the Suez Canal. In the judgment in the *Davis Contractors* case,[21] Lord Radcliffe approved the dictum of Lord Loreburn:

> a court can and ought to examine the contract and the circumstances in which it was made, not of course to vary, but only to explain it, in order to see whether or not from the nature of it the parties must have made their bargain on the footing that a particular thing or state of things would continue to exist.

Even if no judicial power to adapt the contract is accepted, in certain situations, the doctrine of frustration may apply. In principle, the doctrine of frustration is applicable where, after the contract was concluded, events occur which make performance of the contract impossible, illegal or 'radically different' from what was envisaged by the parties at the time of the contract. In contrast to the French administrative doctrine of *révision pour imprévision*, English courts do not ask whether the execution of the contract would be

---

[20] C Pérès, 'Mandatory and Non-mandatory Rules in the New Law of Contract' in J Cartwright and S Whittaker (eds), *The Code Napoléon Rewritten: French Contract Law after the 2016 Reforms* (Oxford: Hart Publishing, 2017) 167.
[21] Above, 28.11 (EN), p 1193.

much more onerous, but whether performance of the contract in the altered circumstance would be 'fundamentally different' from what was envisaged at the time of the contract. The object of the test is the contract itself, not the cost of the contract. The relevant questions are (a) is the contractual venture now impossible and (b) was the risk of this allocated by the agreement?

In practice, English law has a strict approach and it is rare that frustration applies. The courts' reluctance is based on two reasons. First, the doctrine of frustration is 'not lightly to be invoked to relieve contracting parties of the normal consequences of imprudent bargains', as summed up by Lord Roskill in *The Nema*.[22] Secondly, contracting parties usually make provisions for the impact of unexpected circumstances and should do so themselves. One reason for the strict approach may be that the consequences of the application of the doctrine of frustration are drastic. Frustration brings the contract automatically to an end and discharges both parties. The court cannot impose upon the parties a duty to renegotiate, nor can it adjust the contract. Contrary to the position under German law, disappearance of the contractual basis entails disappearance of the contract and not its revision. The parties will have to negotiate a new contract.

However, occasionally the courts seem to have come close to allowing relief in cases of hardship. In *Staffordshire Area Health Authority v South Staffordshire Water Works Co*,[23] the facts were similar to those in the French *Canal de Craponne* judgment: the contract provided that water was to be supplied at a fixed price 'at all times hereafter'. The majority of the Court of Appeal allowed it to be ended by the water company on a construction of the parties' intentions that the contract was a contract for an indefinite period which could be brought to an end after a reasonable period of notice.[24] It seems a little unlikely that this was what the parties intended when they made the agreement, and the case suggests that English courts will in practice give a result that leads to the contract being renegotiated. Indeed, Lord Denning decided the case on a different ground.

Even though the two other Appeal Court judges did not follow Lord Denning's reasoning, it is worth quoting parts of his judgment:

> [I]t is possible to detect a new principle emerging as to the effect of inflation and the fall in the value of money. In the ordinary way this does not affect the bargain between the parties. As I said in *Treseder-Griffin v Co-operative Insurance Society Ltd* [1956] 2 QB 127, 144: "in England we have always looked upon a pound as a pound, whatever its international value ... Creditors and debtors have arranged for payment in our sterling currency in the sure knowledge that the sum they fix will be upheld by the law. A man who stipulates for a pound must take a pound when payment is made, whatever the pound is worth at that time." But times have changed. We have since had mountainous inflation and the pound dropping to cavernous depths. In the recent case of *Multi-service Bookbinding Ltd v Marden* [1978] 2 WLR 535, 544, Browne-Wilkinson J departed from some of the things I said in *Treseder-Griffin* for that very reason-because of 20 years' experience of continuing inflation. The time has come when we may have to revise our views about the principle of nominalism, as it is called. Dr FA Mann in his

---

[22] [1982] AC 724, 752 (HL).
[23] [1978] 1 WLR 1387 (CA).
[24] See *Treitel on the Law of Contract*, 14th edn by E Peel (London: Sweet & Maxwell, 2015) para 19-037.

book on *The Legal Aspect of Money*, 3rd edn (1971) said, at p 100: "If the trend" [of inflation] "which has clouded the last few decades continues some relief in the case of certain long-term obligations … will become unavoidable." That was written in 1971. Inflation has been more rampant than ever since that time. Here we have in the present case a striking instance of a long term obligation entered into 50 years ago. It provided for yearly payments for water supplies at seven old pence per 1,000 gallons. In these 50 years, and especially in the last 10 years, the cost of supplying the water has increased twenty-fold. It is likely to increase with every year that passes. Is it right that the hospital should go on forever only paying the old rate of 50 years ago? It seems to me that we have reached the point which Viscount Simon contemplated in *British Movietonews Ltd v London and District Cinemas Ltd* [1952] AC 166, 185. Speaking à propos of a depreciation of currency, he envisaged a situation where "a consideration of the terms of the contract, in the light of the circumstances existing when it was made, shows that they never agreed to be bound in a fundamentally different situation which has now unexpectedly emerged …" When such a situation emerges, he went on to say: "the contract ceases to bind at that point—not because the court in its discretion thinks it just and reasonable to qualify the terms of the contract, but because on its true construction it does not apply to the situation." That is the forerunner of the modern rule of construction.

So here the situation has changed so radically since the contract was made 50 years ago that the term of the contract "at all times hereafter" ceases to bind: and it is open to the court to hold that the contract is determined by reasonable notice.

Notes

(1) As already mentioned, this was a minority view of Lord Denning. Goff LJ and Cumming-Bruce LJ were not of the opinion that inflation should lead to a discharge of contract. Cumming-Bruce LJ clearly expressed his disagreement with Lord Denning's reasoning:

> I can find no authority which leads me to the view that the changing value of money has the effect in relation to domestic, as compared to international, contracts of giving rise to the operation of an implied term that the contract should only persist while money maintained the value or more or less the value it has at the date of the formation of the agreement.

The majority's solution was reached by construing the words 'at all times hereafter' as meaning that 'the obligations granted and accepted by the agreement were only intended to persist during the continuance of the agreement; and the agreement was determinable on reasonable notice at any time'.

(2) Lord Denning's approach has not prevailed,[25] but the case remains interesting because the majority seemed to have strained the natural meaning of the contract to reach the result that the water company could escape from it.

(3) French law also declines to bring a contract to an end on the grounds of inflation.[26] How do you explain such a reluctance to take inflation into account? How can the parties cope with inflation?

---

[25] eg *Treitel* (n 24 above) para 19-037.
[26] See above, p 1214.

29.4. GERMAN LAW

The point of departure used to be the same in German law as in French law: the contract must be performed, except in the case of absolute impossibility. This was the position of the drafters of the Bürgerliches Gesetzbuch (BGB) who deliberately refrained from inserting a provision that would enable the debtor to discharge his obligation if supervening events had made it too burdensome. The Reichsgericht followed this view[27] and maintained it even after the First World War had broken out. In a judgment of 4 May 1915[28] the Court held that it was not possible to terminate the hiring of a circus arena on account of the war, which prevented normal operations, where there was no express or implied provision to that effect in the contract, since 'good faith and commercial loyalty in no way justify transferring to the defendant the loss which the war has occasioned to the plaintiff'.

Towards the end of the war, the Reichsgericht softened its approach. Initially it conceptualised the respective cases as instances of 'economic impossibility' and held that the debtor was released from his obligation.[29] But in 1920, after the collapse of the Mark and in the wake of the ensuing hyperinflation, the Court for the first time invoked the unwritten *clausula rebus sic stantibus* ('term that matters should remain as they were') in order to adapt the price agreed in a contract for the delivery of vapour in the light of extraordinary war-related price increases for natural resources.[30] As the phrase *rebus sic stantibus* suggests, this doctrine makes the validity of the contract depend on the continuance of the circumstances established at the time of its formation.

Cases concerning consequences of inflation or devaluation of a currency present a particular difficulty. They not only raise issues with regard to the principle of the binding force of contract, but are also difficult to reconcile with the principle of monetary nominalism, that is to say, the principle that a monetary unit retains the same value for as long as it retains the same name, even if over time its real value (purchasing power) has changed. Since the debtor may discharge his obligations by means of a currency devalued to the extreme, the creditor alone bears the risk of devaluation. Nevertheless, a landmark judgment of 1922 paved the way for the development of what soon became known as the 'doctrine of the disappearance of the basis of the transaction' (*Lehre vom Wegfall der Geschäftsgrundlage*).

RG, 3 February 1922[31]   **29.8 (DE)**

The 1919 inflation

In the event of an exceptional change of circumstances, such as a considerable shift in the relative value of performance and counter-performance, the debtor may resile from the contract. However, before doing so he must give the other party the opportunity to

---

[27] RG 11 April 1902, RGZ 50, 255, 257.
[28] RGZ 86, 397.
[29] See RG 4 February 1916, RGZ 88, 71, 74; RG 15 October 1918, RGZ 94, 45, 47.
[30] RG 21 September 1920, RGZ 100, 129, 131.
[31] RGZ 103, 328.

preserve the contract by requesting the other party to increase his counter-performance by an amount that corresponds to the monetary depreciation.

Facts: W, the defendant, and B were joint owners of a partnership (*offene Handelsgesellschaft – oHG*) which operated a spinning mill. They each held an equal share in the business. W terminated the partnership agreement with effect from 31 May 1919. K, the claimant, intended to acquire the business once the partnership would be dissolved. The actual value of the business and thus the purchase price to be paid by K would be known only after the formal dissolution between the joint owners and the valuation of the assets that would be made in the course of the dissolution proceedings. W wanted to be sure to receive his full share upon the dissolution of the partnership and the subsequent sale of the business to K. He also wished to carry on as manager of the business.

W therefore entered into a notarised contract with K on 21 May 1919. According to the agreement, W would attempt to acquire the business upon its dissolution and then transfer it to K. If the acquisition was successful K would employ W as the manager of the business. Moreover, K would provide W with the purchase price, and the parties would subsequently settle their accounts 'on the basis of RM 600,000': if the actual purchase price was lower than RM 600,000, K would pay an extra sum to W (half of the difference between the price and RM 600,000) on top of the price; if the actual purchase price was higher than RM 600,000, W would pay an extra sum to B (half of the difference between RM 600,000 and the price). Under the terms of the contract, K regarded himself as bound to this agreement until 31 December 1919.

The dissolution of the business was delayed, and from autumn 1919 onwards Germany was gripped by hyperinflation. K brought an action for, among others, a declaration that the contract of 21 May 1919 continued to exist and that W continued to be bound by it. Opposing the action, W argued on a number of grounds that he was no longer bound, including that the contract had ceased to exist because of a change of circumstances.

Held: The Landgericht rejected W's arguments but the Oberlandesgericht set aside that decision. On further appeal, the Reichsgericht referred the case back to the Oberlandesgericht.

Judgment: ... the defence of the so-called *clausula rebus sic stantibus* has not been sufficiently taken into account. The appellate court contends itself with the observation that it would result in a complete state of lawlessness in the area of contract law if the defendant were to be accorded the right to rescind the contract because of a change of the economic circumstances. This concern is unfounded; all that is required is to be careful when delimiting the boundaries within which the defence deserves to be considered. In this regard, to the following extent the pleadings of the defendant can be regarded as correct without further proof: the sum of RM 600,000 which recurs in clauses 1 to 3 of the contract was based on the estimate of the price of the business at approximately this sum and that, therefore, the adequate price of the business share of the defendant amounted to RM 300,000. Moreover, the Court takes official notice of the depreciation of money which began in the autumn of 1919 and led to a rapid increase in the prices of land, machinery, provisions etc, many times over. ... As a general rule, to speak with Oertmann's *Geschäftsgrundlage* (1921), what is decisive is always whether the basis of the transaction, understood as the assumption of the parties with regard to the continuation of certain relevant circumstances, as evidenced at the time of making the contract, has ceased to exist. This may be the case as a result of a mere disturbance of the balance of values if the continuation of the equivalence of performance and counter-performance had been assumed. Whether this was the case on the present facts must be assessed ... As a general rule, it will be sufficient to take into account that the monetary depreciation, as it occurred in 1919, came as a surprise to the business world and could not have been foreseen. ...

Accordingly, the decision appealed against must be set aside, and the case must be referred back to the appellate court. However, ... if the appellate court were to hold ... that the basis of the transaction had collapsed ... it will be necessary to make an attempt to uphold the contract with an appropriate modification. ... before the debtor resiles from the contract or gives notice of termination because of a fundamental shift of the relative value of performance and counter-performance he has to request that the creditor should increase the counter-performance; only if the latter declines to do so is the debtor free. This follows from the provision of § 242 BGB, according to which the taking into account of good faith is to be the supreme yardstick of the contractual debtor. ... If the contract were to be modified the price would have to be increased in line with the current monetary depreciation in order to avoid the defendant resiling from the contract.

RG, 27 June 1922[32]   **29.9 (DE)**

The farmer's stocks

Where hyperinflation has rendered a literal application of the terms of the contract wholly inappropriate, the contract terms should be adjusted to reflect the original economic balance between the parties' obligations.

Facts: By notarial deed of 17 August 1894 the defendant gave a lease over land for a period expiring on 1 July 1922. With regard to stock, the contract expressly referred to the provisions of §§ 587–589 BGB.[33] The value of the whole of the stock for the purposes of valuation at the end of the contract was fixed at 113,802 RM. The defendant considered that the claimant was required at the end of the lease to sell the stock for consideration in kind and for its actual value. The estimate of the value of the stock merely served to describe the different elements and gave only an indication of the state of those assets. The claimant requested the court to declare that, on return of the stock, the component animals are to be assessed on the basis of their intrinsic value on the date of their return, and thus, if the estimated value is greater or less than the original amount, in the former case the defendant is obliged to compensate the claimant on account of enrichment and in the latter case the opposite solution must be adopted. The courts trying the case on its merits upheld that claim.

Held: LG and OLG took the view that liquidation of stock at the end of the lease was governed by § 589(3) BGB, without there being any need to take into consideration monetary depreciation which was foreseeable. The RG disapproved of this reasoning.

Judgment: The presumption made by the OLG that the lessor could refuse the valuation is without foundation and is based on a manifest disregard of § 589(3). Under that provision, the lessor may only refuse the taking into account by the farmer of elements of stock which are superfluous or have too high a value for the land. An increase in the value of the stock does not permit him to refuse the lease. Moreover, the decision of the OLG is equitable neither under §§ 587 to 589 nor in light of the situation caused by the unhappy outcome of the war and the terrible fall in the German currency.

§ 589 must be understood as follows. The pecuniary valuation of the stock undertaken at the beginning of the lease by the lessor and the farmer must be compared to the value of the stock on its return. The initial valuation is not intended solely to determine the assets comprising the stock but is also to facilitate establishment of the starting value and value at the end of the contract.

---

[32] RGZ 104, 394. The English translation is from von AT Mehren and JR Gordley, *The Civil Law System* (2nd edn, Boston, MA: Little Brown, 1977) 1080–85.

[33] These provisions have long been amended, but this does not really matter for the question of *rebus sic stantibus*. Under §§ 588 and 589(1) and (2), the stock belongs to the land and must remain there to determine the assets comprising the stock but is also to facilitate establishment of the starting value and value at the end of the contract.

Under §§ 588 and 589(1) and (2), the stock belongs to the land and must remain there. That is true not only of stock items at the beginning of the contract but also of items acquired by the farmer during the lease. The latter become the property of the lessor by virtue of their incorporation into the contract (§ 588(2). On the other hand, if the strict application of those provisions required the lessor to incur considerable expenditure for stock maintenance, they would have to be disapplied.

The collapse of the German currency is so major that governing lease arrangements according to the provisions of § 589(3) makes stock maintenance impossible. The gold mark which served as the basis for valuing the stock and the paper mark on the basis of which compensation is to be calculated are in no wise comparable, notwithstanding the financial parity established by the law.

Neither the legal provisions nor contractual provisions enable the dispute to be resolved. The courts must be creative and deliver a judgment which accords with equity. The guiding principle must be that an equitable adjustment of the interests at stake must be made. The motives of the parties in light of the pre-war economic situation must be taken into consideration. In the present case, the extent of the stock was not in itself altered (that is to say neither increased nor diminished). Thus the lessor may not be obliged to pay sums greater than one million RM on return of the stock solely on account of the impressive rise in prices. The value of the stock increased by only 2%. It is that added value in respect of which an obligation arises for the lessor. The economic and legal principles elaborated by the RG must be observed by the courts trying the issues of fact. A decision taking into account the interests of the parties must be adopted.

The case is referred back to the OLG to apply these principles of adjustment.

Note

These two decisions are the consequence of the devaluation of the Mark at the end of the First World War. The two judgments of the Reichsgericht recognise, on the one hand, judicial revision and consider that revision is preferable to rescission. The first judgment even encourages the parties to make appropriate contractual provision. On the other hand, those judgments are the first to openly acknowledge Oertmann's theory of the 'disappearance of the contractual basis' (*Wegfall der Geschäftsgrundlage*) as the basis for that revision. It would, then, be contrary to good faith to maintain the contract as it stands. The resemblance to the English doctrine of frustration is to be noted: the contract is no longer the same as that which the parties initially entered into. But the outcome is different: English law does not acknowledge revision of the contract, but merely, in a proper case, its disappearance; and it seems fairly certain that (despite Lord Denning's views) English law would not accept that inflation would give rise to frustration of the contract.

After the Second World War, the monetary consequences of the transition period in Germany were dealt with by the 1952 Act on assistance to contracts.[34] However, the courts continued to allow revision in cases not covered by the Act.

[34] See above, p 1211 n 2.

BGH, 16 January 1953[35]

The Berlin blockade

According to the theory of the disappearance of the contractual basis, judges seek to adapt the contract equitably, on the basis of the respective interests of the contracting parties.

Facts: The defendant, a company established in West Berlin which had for a long time conducted business relations with the claimant, ordered by letter dated 31 May 1948 600 drill hammers. It wished to take delivery of them as quickly as possible and said that it would organise a convoy to take delivery of the goods. Finally, it stated that payment would be made by its West German office. The drill hammers were ordered for the External Trade Administration in the Eastern zone for mining operations in that zone. That fact was known to the claimant. Between the issue and receipt of the order letter, the Berlin blockade occurred. It was to last from 24 June 1948 to 22 May 1949. Pursuant to the order, the claimant initially manufactured 200 drill hammers and proposed to deliver them under cover of an invoice dated 30 November 1948. It went on to manufacture 78 more hammers and started production of the remaining 326 hammers. The defendant neither took delivery of nor paid for those hammers. The claimant brought an action for payment under the order.

Held: The OLG ordered the defendant immediately to pay on delivery of the drill hammers. The defendant's appeal was dismissed.

Judgment: ... 1.— *Was delivery of the drill hammers a condition subsequent of the contract?*

In light of § 158 BGB neither the terms of the defendant's order nor acceptance by the plaintiff enable the view to be taken that validity of the contract depended on the possibility of delivery in the Eastern zone. In support of its claims the defendant contends that the hammers in question used old technology as far as the West German mining industry was concerned. When the claimant received the order the Berlin blockade had already occurred and it was impossible to determine when it would be lifted.

According to the claimant, to make the validity of the contract depend on that factual situation would have given rise to major and very heavy production costs. The claimant had no interest in making validity of the contract subject to the possibility of making deliveries in the Eastern zone.

It was not in the claimant's interest to know how the defendant intended to use the drill hammers.

Its sole interest in performance under the contract was in the taking of delivery of and payment for the hammers by the defendant under the terms of the contract. There is no expression of intention by the parties to make the purpose for which the hammers were to be used a condition subsequent entailing termination of the contract.

2.— *Performance of contractual obligations does not preclude specific legal provisions from prohibiting or limiting exports to the Eastern zone.*

To the extent to which an unlawful circumvention of any export ban had not been included in the contract and the defendant did not take delivery of the goods at the place of performance specified in the contract, the appeal in Revision based on the fact that performance is contrary to § 134 BGB is inadmissible and ill-founded. Furthermore, performance of its obligations by the defendant has not become impossible.

The question arose whether the theory of economic impossibility might apply where performance had been rendered more difficult after creation of the contract to such an

---

[35] MDR 1953, 282.

extent that foreseeable sacrifices were exceeded. That theory, which has been abandoned, was based on the legal consequences of impossibility. The RG then focussed on the contractual basis in light of § 242 BGB.

The problem remains that of the foreseeability of performance of the contract which falls to be resolved by taking into consideration the equity of the divergent interests of the parties in accordance with § 242 which allows the contract to be adapted to new circumstances, regard being had to the parties' interests and the principle of foreseeability.

The OLG correctly assessed foreseeability in regard to disappearance of the contractual basis under § 242 and in regard to economic impossibility.

Both the LG and the OLG considered that the contractual basis was the delivery and sale of the drill hammers. That analysis is legally questionable. Certainly the manufacturer will often know the purpose to which his products are to be put, but the purpose of the contract as far as the works contractor for buildings is concerned does not constitute the contractual basis as far as the two parties are concerned. Each party must bear the risk of the disappearance of the subjective purpose of the contract. The parties agreed, in spite of the existence of the blockade on the date when the contract was created, on the manufacture and delivery of drill hammers in the Eastern zone.

The expectation of the parties was not realised. The question arises whether the contractual basis existed on the creation of the contract. It was only after conclusion of the contract that it was agreed that the sale could not be realised. Consequently, that cannot entail nullity of the contract but its adaptation in accordance with the provisions of § 242.

Solution.—In order to adapt the contract, the contractual interests at stake must be determined.

The defendant is obliged to pay the cost of the work representing 1/4 of the amount due and provided for *expressis verbis* by the contract.

Note

This judgment takes up again the theory of the disappearance of the contractual basis described by Oertmann, which had been to some extent discarded in earlier decisions where the theory of economic impossibility was applied instead.[36] According to that theory, the courts had direct regard to the legal consequences of the occurrence of an economic event. According to the theory of disappearance of the contractual basis, the courts first seek to discern the initial basis of the contract and the parties' interests on creation of the contract. They will then seek, on the basis of the respective interests of the contracting parties, to adapt the contract equitably. (A comparison may be made with the dicta of Lord Radcliffe.[37]) The theory leads to adjustment of performance under the contract rather than termination.

A more recent example provided by the German reunification—which has given a boost to the theory—well illustrates the pre-eminence of adaptation over disappearance of the contract.

[36] See RG 23 February 1904, RGZ 57, 116; RG 15 October 1918, RGZ 94, 45; RG 16 April 1921, RGZ 102, 98.
[37] See above, 28.11 (EN), pp 1194–95.

The German reunification

The theory of the disappearance of the contractual basis should be implemented in order to save the contract, taking into account good faith requirements.

Facts: The parties are former state undertakings in East Germany which were transformed into private limited companies. Following an order by the predecessor in title of the claimant, VEB Berliner AE Fabrilx, and following confirmation on 10 January 1990 by the predecessor in title of the defendant, VEB E Export Import, a contract was entered into for the importation of a pressurised milling machine at an agreed price of 1,706,000 Ostmarks. Delivery of the machine was to form part of a reconstruction plan envisaged by the state. In respect of 1990, the financial needs for achievement of the plan were estimated at 7,675,000 Ostmarks, which were to be borne as to 50% by means of a subsidy and as to the remainder by a loan from the defendant. On 14 December 1989 the plan which provided, inter alia, for the acquisition of the machine in question was approved by the Council of Ministers and included in the economic plan. The machine supplied to the claimant by an Austrian manufacturer at a price of AS 2,644,259 was imported by the claimant on 27 March 1990, and the defendant took delivery of it on 26 April 1990. The Deutsche Aussenhandelsbank granted the defendant a loan of 1,706,000 Ostmarks. On 4 April 1990 the claimant called for payment of the agreed price. From April to June 1990 the defendant endeavoured to secure the financial aid provided for under the plan. It obtained only a part of the credit facility. On 27 June 1990 BS Bank AG advanced a loan of 376,806.90 Ostmarks. That sum was paid to the claimant on 29 June 1990. However, the defendant could secure no subsidy and was informed that it would not be receiving any additional credit facility. The claimant brought an action for payment of the price laid down in the contract, the defendant being liable in the amount of DM 664,597 (1,706,000–376,806.90 = 1,329,193.90 Ostmarks = DM 664,597, following monetary union on 1 June 1990). The defendant argued that it was not bound to pay the price inasmuch as the price was agreed before monetary union on the basis of state provisions. The Ostmark price could no longer be called for after entry into force of the Regulation of 25 June 1990. The initial price of the machine amounted to DM 376,806.90, the Deutschmark equivalent to the agreed price in Austrian schillings. The claimant's profit margin is 2.5% and the officially agreed exchange rate (*Richtungskoeffizienten*) 240%, which does not form part of the price but is an official conversion method and, as such, a typical tool used by a centralised, planned economy to manipulate prices.

Held: The Commercial Chamber of the Berlin Landgericht upheld the claim. On appeal, the Kammergericht set aside the decision at first instance and ordered the defendant to pay the amount of DM 451,346.55 together with interest at the rate of 28%. That decision was revised by the BGH.

Judgment: The BGH considers that the East German law cannot be applied inasmuch as the law on contracts was repealed on 1 July 1990.

The court below took the view that the defendant was entitled to a reduction in price under § 242 BGB which is applicable to contracts entered into before the entry into force of the BGB in the East German zone. It is of no relevance that the defendant was unable to secure credit. Certainly, it was provided in the contract that the acquisition would be financed as to 50% by a credit. However, a debtor may never plead refusal of a loan in support of financial difficulties. The decisive factor for the purposes of § 242 is that the defendant did not secure the subsidy provided for in the East German budget. Both parties had in mind on the creation of the contract that the acquisition of the machine formed part of an economic plan and that it would be financed as to 50% by a subsidy.

As a result of the failure of the plan at the time the contract was entered into and of the consequent impossibility of seeking the subsidy, the contractual basis disappeared. With the disappearance of the subsidy corresponding to 50% of the investment, performance of the contract at the agreed price constitutes an unforeseeable burden

---

[38] BGHZ 120, 10.

for the defendant. After transformation of the parties into share-capital companies, the requirements of good faith make it inappropriate to allow such a burden to be imposed on the defendant.

The BGH recalls that the contractual basis is constituted by the intentions of the two parties respectively. In this case the intention to enter into legal relations was dependent upon the economic plan. Whilst the BGH was entitled to consider that refusal of aid did not amount to disappearance of the contractual basis, it should be emphasised that the defendant had no freedom of choice and had to implement the plan. On the adjustment of the contract the requirements of good faith have to be taken into account. It is a question as a matter of principle of upholding the contract as far as possible and of adapting it in the interests of the parties to the new circumstances.

> *Note*
>
> The German reunification has given rise to numerous decisions of which the 1992 judgment is a very good example. It renews the theory of disappearance of the contractual basis, whilst at the same time having direct regard to the principle of good faith in § 242 BGB.

The notion of termination of the contract as the ultimate remedy, to be used only if an adjustment is not possible, had already been used by the BGH in a judgment of 11 February 1958:[39]

> Disappearance of the contractual basis must not lead systematically and as a matter of priority to cancellation of the contract but rather to an adaptation of the contractual obligations to the changed circumstances.

That stance had already been adopted in the 1922 judgments. The necessary adaptation may be made in various ways: lessening performance in kind, price reductions, postponement of due dates, or performance by instalments, compensation, etc.

The leading cases on the doctrine of disappearance of the basis of the transaction concern situations that occurred in the context of major political upheavals of twentieth-century Germany, such as wars, inflation and regime changes. However, the doctrine also applies to cases concerning far less dramatic changes of circumstances that do not have repercussions for society at large. This can be seen from the classical textbook example, which resembles the facts of *Krell v Henry*:[40] a carnival parade is cancelled, so that the basis of the rental of a balcony or a window overlooking the route of the procession has disappeared.

Contrary to fears expressed, particularly by French academic writers, judicial revision in the event of disappearance of the contractual basis is not a threat to legal certainty because the German courts use it conscientiously and with moderation. That is why the German model has been followed and codified in a number of national laws and adopted in certain harmonising instruments (PECL, DCFR, UNIDROIT PICC[41]) which, in this respect, distance themselves from the CISG.

---

[39] NJW 1958, 785.
[40] Above, 28.10 (EN), p 1189.
[41] Above, pp 1209–11.

While the German legislator only took this step in 2002, the solutions adopted by the German courts were codified in a number of European jurisdictions from the 1940s onwards.

Codice civile[42] **29.12 (IT)**

Article 1467: Synallagmatic contracts (*corrispettive*)
In continuing or periodic contracts, or where performance is deferred, if performance by one of the parties has become excessively onerous as a result of the occurrence of exceptional or unforeseeable events, the party liable for performance under such conditions may apply for termination of the contract which will entail the effects laid down in Article 1458.

Article 1468: Contract with obligations on one of the parties only
In the case mentioned in the preceding article, if the contract merely provides for performance by one of the parties, that party may apply for a lessening of performance or an alteration in the manner of performance which must be sufficient for the contract to proceed on an equitable basis.

Article 1469: Speculative contract (*contratto aleatorio*)
The provisions of the preceding articles shall not apply to contracts which are speculative in nature or according to the intentions of the parties.

BW[43] **29.13 (NL)**

Article 6:258: (1) Upon the demand of one of the parties, the judge may modify the effects of a contract, or he may set it aside in whole or in part on the basis of unforeseen circumstances which are of such a nature that the co-contracting party, according to criteria of reasonableness and equity, may not expect that the contract be maintained in an unmodified form. The modification or the setting aside of the contract may be given retroactive force.

(2) The modification or the setting aside of the contract is not pronounced to the extent that the person invoking the circumstances should be accountable for them according to the nature of the contract or common opinion.

(3) For the purposes of this article, a person to whom a contractual right or obligation has been transferred, is assimilated to a contracting party.

The doctrine was also incorporated into the BGB in 2002.

BGB **29.14 (DE)**

§ 313: Interference with the basis of the contract
(1) If circumstances upon which a contract was based have materially changed after conclusion of the contract and if the parties would not have concluded the contract or

---

[42] These Articles of the Italian Codice civile belong to Section III on *eccessiva onerosità* of Chapter XIV on 'Termination of Contracts'.

[43] See about Dutch law and further references: AS Hartkamp & CH Sieburgh, *Mr. C. Assers Handleiding tot de beoefening van het Nederlands Burgerlijk Recht. 6. Verbintenissenrecht. Deel III. Algemeen overeenkomstenrecht* (Deventer: Kluwer, 2014) nos. 436 ff.

would have done so upon different terms if they had foreseen that change, adaptation of the contract may be claimed in so far as, having regard to all the circumstances of the specific case, in particular the contractual or statutory allocation of risk, it cannot reasonably be expected that a party should continue to be bound by the contract in its unaltered form.

(2) If material assumptions that have become the basis of the contract subsequently turn out to be incorrect, they are treated in the same way as a change in circumstances.

(3) If adaptation of the contract is not possible or cannot reasonably be imposed on one party, the disadvantaged party may terminate the contract. In the case of a contract for the performance of a recurring obligation, the right to terminate is replaced by the right to terminate on notice.

Notes

(1) The provision is designed to codify the case law as it had developed since the 1920s. Thus old cases remain good law, particularly with regard to the concept of the 'basis of the transaction', which is not defined in § 313 BGB.

(2) Only § 313(1) BGB concerns supervening circumstances that interfere with the basis of the transaction. § 313(2) BGB concerns cases where both parties shared incorrect assumptions at the stage of contracting: for example, the parties contracted on the basis of the erroneous belief that a piece of land has a certain size, that the transaction would have particular tax consequences or that the expenses of one party would be covered by insurance.[44] Such a 'shared error in motive' constitutes an initial absence of the basis of the transaction that is treated similar to the subsequent failure or collapse of this basis.

(3) There is a debate as to whether § 313 BGB may only be invoked after the parties have unsuccessfully attempted to renegotiate the contract. The legislative materials show a degree of sympathy for such a requirement, and an earlier draft explicitly imposed an obligation to renegotiate on the parties. However, when § 313 BGB was finally enacted, this passage was dropped. Most commentators therefore believe that the parties are under no such obligation.[45]

(4) Adaptation of the contract is only one of the possible remedies under § 313 BGB, albeit the primary one. § 313(3) BGB provides for the possibility of termination in exceptional cases.

(5) There may be cases falling under both § 313 and § 275(2) BGB.[46] Usually there will be no overlap because the provisions have different requirements and provide for different remedies. However, if performance turns out to be exceptionally more burdensome for the debtor than originally envisaged, there may be a case of both interference with the basis of the transaction and 'practical impossibility'.

---

[44] BGH 30 January 2004, NJW-RR 2004, 735; BGH 24 September 1976, DB 1976, 2394; BGH 28 April 2005, NJW 2005, 2069, 2071. For this scenario, see above, pp 554–55.

[45] For a comprehensive overview, see HS Urich-Erber, *Äquivalenzstörungen und Leistungserschwernisse im deutschen und englischen Recht sowie in den Principles of European Contract Law* (Baden-Baden: Nomos, 2008) 95–107.

[46] See above, pp 547, 901, 912, 925.

Whilst some writers maintain that § 275(2) BGB should take precedence in such cases, others suggest that the claimant should be able to choose whether he wants to raise the § 275(2) BGB defence or whether he wants to claim adaptation of the contract under § 313 BGB.[47]

(6) Finally, it must be re-emphasised that § 313 concerns exceptional cases only. The basic principle is still that of the binding force of contract (*pacta sunt servanda*), and the requirements of § 313 BGB are stringent. The changed circumstances or the initial assumptions must have been 'material', the parties would not have concluded the contract if they had foreseen the supervening event, and binding one of the parties to the contract would be unreasonable.

FURTHER READING

Fauvarque-Cosson, B, 'Does Review on the Ground of *Imprévision* Breach the Principle of the Binding Force of Contracts?' in J Cartwright and S Whittaker (eds), *The Code Napoléon Rewritten: French Contract Law after the 2016 Reforms* (Oxford: Hart Publishing, 2017) 187–206.

Fauvarque-Cosson, B, 'Le changement de circonstances' RDC 2004, 67–92.

Hondius, E and Grigoleit, C (eds), *Unexpected Circumstances in European Contract Law* (Cambridge University Press, 2011).

Lutzi, Tobias, 'Introducing *imprévison* into French Contract Law – a Paradigm Shift in Comparative Perspective' in S Stijns and S Jansen (eds), *The French Contract Law Reform: a Source of Inspiration?* (Intersentia: Cambridge et al, 2011) 89–112.

Momberg Uribe, Rodrigo, *The Effect of a Change of Circumstances on the Binding Force of Contracts* (Intersentia: Cambridge et al, 2011).

Oppetit, B, 'L'adaptation des contrats internationaux aux changements de circonstances: la clause de hardship' (1974) JDI 794–814.

Rodière, R and Tallon, D (eds), *Les modifications du contrat au cours de son exécution en raison de circonstances monétaires* (Paris: Institut de droit comparé, 1986).

Rösler, H, 'Change of Circumstances' in J Basedow, K Hopt and R Zimmermann (eds), *Max Planck Encyclopedia of European Private Law* (Oxford University Press, 2012) 163–67.

Rösler, H, 'Hardship in German Codified Private Law: In Comparative Perspective to English, French and International Contract Law' (2007) 15 ERPL 483–513.

Tallon, D, 'La révision du contrat pour imprévision au regard des enseignements récents du droit comparé' in *Mélanges à la mémoire d'Alain Sayag* (Paris: Litec, 1997) 403–18.

Urich-Erber, HS, *Äquivalenzstörungen und Leistungserschwernisse im deutschen und englischen Recht sowie in den Principles of European Contract Law* (Baden-Baden: Nomos, 2008).

[47] Urich-Erber (n 45 above) 136–57.

CHAPTER 30
CLAUSES DEALING WITH SUPERVENING EVENTS

30.1 INTRODUCTION

The parties often make provision for situations arising from the occurrence of supervening events, despite the fact that they do not know whether those events will arise. Such situations include monetary depreciation, strikes, embargoes, etc. Clauses of this type are particularly useful in long-term contracts, in which the circumstances existing at the time when the contract is entered into may well alter during the course of its term. They may assist in the determination of conditions in which situations of *force majeure* or unforeseen circumstances are to be deemed to have arisen, since those conditions are frequently uncertain. They may also be designed to regulate the consequences which such situations are to have in relation to the contract, by providing either that it is to cease to be effective or that its terms are to be adjusted. They enable the parties, in principle, to avoid having recourse to the courts. They must be distinguished from clauses which define the scope of the performance or consideration originally agreed. By the same token, they are different from clauses excluding liability or penalty clauses, which are applicable only in the event of failure to perform on the part of the party from whom performance is due.

Clauses dealing with supervening events are to be found, in particular, in international contracts;[1] however, they have also found their way into domestic legal systems, in which they are on occasion the subject of specific qualifications and prohibitions. Of these, the strictest are usually requirements relating to public policy—or *ordre public*—for example, public policy in monetary matters.

Many of these clauses are introduced as standard terms and are subject to control with regard to unfairness. Some of them are drafted by international organisations such

---

[1] M Fontaine and F de Ly, *Drafting International Contracts: An Analysis of Contract Clauses* (Ardsley, NY: Transnational Publishers, 2006) chs 8 (*force majeure* clauses) and 9 (hardship clauses).

as the International Chamber of Commerce (ICC) and parties incorporate them in their contracts.

It is important to insist on the fact that clauses dealing with supervening events present many advantages. First, they provide a higher degree of certainty (this is the case, for instance, when the parties agree on a list of events which will constitute *force majeure* or 'hardship'). Secondly, they enable the parties to provide for more contractual equilibrium by agreeing that certain types of events will alter their obligations. Thirdly, they lead the parties to make their best endeavours to renegotiate and adapt the contract to the new circumstances. Parties thus circumvent the remedial rigidity of the doctrines of frustration or of *force majeure*.[2]

Amongst the numerous types of clause encountered in practice, those most often used are indexation clauses (30.2), *force majeure* clauses (30.3) and hardship or saving clauses (30.4).

30.2 INDEXATION CLAUSES

These clauses are designed to provide against future price changes, arising generally from disorders of a monetary nature. The circumstances arising have already been encountered in the context of unforeseen events. Numerous examples spring to mind, including the paper money (*assignats*) crisis in France during the Revolution, the plummeting of the German Mark in the aftermath of the First World War and the semi-permanent inflation which set in following the end of the Second World War. Exchange rate fluctuations may also be provoked by economic factors—as in the case of the oil crises—or political factors—such as the closure of the Suez Canal and the Gulf War.

Such circumstances make it very difficult to determine with any certainty the price to be paid—for goods, services, etc—under a long-term contract. The legal problems which may arise in relation to the determination of the price—involving, inter alia, the degree of certainty with which it can be determined, 'open price' clauses and subsequent unilateral price determination[3]—have already been considered.

In addition, it is necessary to have regard to monetary issues, such as the principle of monetary nominalism—a pound remains a pound, whatever its purchasing power may be. In addition, a distinction is universally drawn between the currency of account—which is used to evaluate the debt—and the currency of payment—which is used to discharge the debt.

Various clauses have been formulated in practice to provide for variations in the amount to be paid on the due date, depending on fluctuations in the price of gold, foreign exchange and economic indices, etc. Other, similar clauses provide for prices to vary in accordance with the most favourable terms offered by competitors or with terms agreed to by other customers—competitive offer clauses, most-favoured-customer clauses, etc.

The lawfulness of such clauses, and especially of what are known as 'monetary' clauses—linked to gold, gold values, foreign currencies, etc—will depend on the degree

---

[2] E McKendrick (ed), *Force Majeure and Frustration of Contract* (2nd edn, London: Lloyd's of London Press, 1995) para 14.9.
[3] See above, pp 295–98.

of importance attached to public policy concerning monetary matters in a given country. At international level, the importance of public policy requirements is diminished. As we will see, the rules relating to indexation clauses differ according to the laws under consideration.

30.2.A INDEXATION CLAUSES UNDER ENGLISH LAW

The validity of indexation clauses has been the subject of less debate than in other countries, doubtless because the pound sterling has proved to be a more stable currency than certain others. It is true that Lord Denning has stated that a 'gold clause' in a domestic contract 'is disturbing';[4] but his view was not shared by the other judges.

<table>
<tr><td>Chancery Division</td><td align="right">30.1 (EN)</td></tr>
</table>

Multiservice Bookbinding v Marden[5]

A clause linking the amount of capital and interest to be due under a loan agreement to the value of the Swiss franc is not contrary to public policy.

Facts: A mortgage was granted in 1966 to secure capital and interest payments in respect of a debt which was index-linked to the value of the Swiss franc. That debt was repayable at the end of a term of ten years. Repayment was demanded in 1976; the validity of the clause was challenged on the ground that the value of the pound had fallen from 12 Swiss francs in 1966 to four Swiss francs in 1976. Two defences were advanced: the first, adopting Lord Denning's arguments, asserted that the clause was contrary to public policy, and the second maintained that it was unlawful by reason of the usurious rate applied by it.

Held: The two defences were rejected. [Discussion of the second defence is omitted.]

Judgment: BROWNE-WILKINSON J: ... I deal fist with the question of public policy. The plaintiffs' case on this issue is based entirely on certain statements made by Denning LJ in *Treseder-Griffin v Co-operative Insurance Society Ltd* [1956] 2 QB 127. That case concerned the effect of a clause in a long lease which provided for the payment

'yearly during the said term either in gold sterling or Bank of England notes to the equivalent value in gold sterling the rent of £1,900 ... by equal quarterly payments ...'

The main point at issue was one of construction, which does not touch the present case. But in the Court of Appeal, Denning LJ said, at pp 144, 145:

'This is the first case, so far as I know, to come before our courts where the parties have inserted a "gold clause" in a domestic contract where all the parties are within our own country. In external transactions it is, of course, quite common for parties to protect themselves against a depreciation in the rate of exchange by means of a gold clause. But in England we have always looked upon a pound as a pound, whatever its international value. We have dealt in pounds for more than a thousand years—long before there were gold coins or paper notes. In all our dealings we have disregarded alike the debasement of the currency by kings and rulers or the depreciation of it by

---

[4] *Treseder Griffin v Cooperative Insurance Society* [1956] 2 QB 127 (CA).
[5] [1979] Ch 84.

the march of time or events. This is well shown by the *Case de Mixed Moneys* (1604) Davies's Rep 48. Creditors and debtors have arranged for payment in our sterling currency in the sure knowledge that the sum they fix will be upheld by the law. A man who stipulates for a pound must take a pound when payment is made, whatever the pound is worth at that time. Sterling is the constant unit of value by which in the eye of the law everything else is measured. Prices of commodities may go up or down, other currencies may go up and down, but sterling remains the same.'

Then after referring to an example of that principle:

'The principle which I have stated is so well established that it is disturbing to find a creditor inserting a gold clause in a domestic transaction. I am not altogether sure that it is lawful. In the United States gold clauses are declared by the joint resolution of Congress to be contrary to public policy: see *Rex v International Trustee for the Protection of Bondholders Aktiengesellschaft* [1937] AC 500. In Canada they are rendered inoperative by the Gold Clauses Act 1937: see *New Brunswick Railway Co v British and French Trust Corporation Ltd* [1939] AC 1. Many other countries have like legislation. In France, ever since the Franco-Prussian War, the Cour de Cassation has ruled that gold clauses are invalid in the case of internal contracts for payments in France by the French people; but they are valid in the case of international payments, that is, which involve a traffic across international frontiers. Those countries do it, I suppose, to protect their own currencies. If we are now to hold gold clauses valid in England for internal payments, we may be opening a door through which lessors and mortgagees, debenture holders and preference shareholders, and many others, may all pass. We might find every creditor stipulating for payment according to the price of gold; and every debtor scanning the bullion market to find out how much he has to pay. What, then, is to become of sterling? It would become a discredited currency unable to look its enemy inflation in the face. That should not be allowed to happen.'

Morris LJ who, with Denning LJ constituted the majority of the Court of Appeal on the construction point, expressed no view on the public policy point. Harman J, who dissented on the construction point, expressly said, at p 163, that such a clause was not unlawful even in a domestic contract.

Mr Nugee, who appeared for the plaintiffs, contended that the remarks of Denning LJ formed a separate ground of decision which was binding on me. I cannot think that that is right. Denning LJ prefaced the material passage by the words, and I quote, at p 145, "I am not altogether sure that it is lawful." These are not words of decision but of doubt. Therefore in my opinion Denning LJ's dictum is not strictly binding on me. But of course it carries great weight.

I have had the point elaborately argued before me by distinguished counsel, and after considering the arguments I do not feel that in 1977 I can declare that an index-linked money obligation is contrary to public policy. The reasons which lead me to this view are as follows: (1) If, as Denning LJ said, the evil to be guarded against is that sterling will become discredited, this evil will flow not only from indexing by reference to the price of gold or Swiss franc, but equally from any other form of indexing, for example an obligation quantified by reference to the cost of living index. The evil lies in the revalorisation of the pound sterling by reference to any other yardstick, not in the nature of the yardstick itself. (2) Today a large number of obligations originally expressed in pounds sterling are varied by reference to an external yardstick. Long-term commercial contracts frequently include index linked obligations: so do many contracts of employment. The rent payable under certain leases has for centuries been made variable dependent upon the price of corn. More important, Parliament itself has authorised the linking of public service pensions to the cost of living and the issue of Savings Bonds similarly linked. It would be strange if Parliament had authorised transactions contrary to public policy. (3) Denning LJ treated the process of index-linking as being a cause, not a symptom, of inflation. I know nothing of economics but it has been demonstrated to me that economists are not agreed that indexing has a deleterious effect in promoting inflation. It would, in my judgment, be wrong for the courts to declare that a particular class of transaction is against the public interest even though there is a body of better-informed opinion that takes the view that no harm is caused. It is for Parliament, with all its facilities for weighing the complex issues involved, to make a policy decision of this kind. (4) It seems to me that, even if there are good grounds for saying that indexing causes inflation, there may well be counter-availing considerations which would have to be weighed. In any economy where there is inflation there are few inducements to make long-term loans expressed in a currency the value of which is being eroded. It is at least possible that, unless lenders can ensure that they are repaid the real value of the money they advanced, and not merely a sum of the same nominal amount but in devalued currency, the availability of loan capital will be much diminished. This would surely not be in the public interest. (5) Shortly after 1956, the Cour de Cassation in France reversed its Policy referred to by Denning LJ and allowed index-linked obligations even in domestic contracts. Index-linked obligations were held valid by the High Court of Australia in *Stanwell Park Hotel Co Ltd v Leslie* (1952) 85 CLR 189.

Therefore I feel unable to follow the obiter dictum of Denning LJ. I need hardly say that I do so with considerable diffidence; but I receive some comfort from the fact that since he expressed his views, we have experienced 20 years of inflation and, on the somewhat analogous question whether a judgment of an English court can be expressed otherwise than in pounds sterling, he has departed from the nominalist principle which underlies his remarks in the *Treseder-Griffin* case [1956] 2 QB 127. In my judgment, clause 6 of the mortgage is not contrary to public policy ...

Notes

(1) See, to the same effect, also in relation to a mortgage loan, *National Building Society v Registry of Friendly Societies*.[6]

(2) In *Multiservice Bookbinding v Marden* the judge was prompted, not without some diffidence, to criticise Lord Denning. He considered that he was not bound by the latter's dictum, which was a statement of doubt and did not have binding force; and he took the view that there had been a change of circumstances over the course of 20 years. It is interesting to note the recourse had to comparative law, both by Lord Denning and by Browne-Wilkinson J. Reference is made not only to the common law systems—in the US, Canada and Australia—but also to the most recent French case law.[7]

(3) The judge considered that there was nothing to preclude the use of indexation clauses in general and, in particular, the use of a clause linked to the value of a foreign currency, such as that at issue in the case under consideration. He took the view that,

[6] [1983] 1 WLR 1226 (ChD).
[7] Browne-Wilkinson J cites indeed the 1957 reversal of precedent effected by the decision.

in 1977, public policy did not preclude such a clause, which had become necessary by reason of the depreciation in the value of the pound. He concluded, departing from the view expressed by Lord Denning, that index-linking was not a cause but a symptom of inflation. Moreover, it was hardly appropriate to condemn a practice which had become commonplace by virtue of general usage and which had even been adopted by the public authorities. In the judge's view, it was not for the courts—which maintain, in any event, a somewhat cautious approach to the extension of public policy by the creation of 'new heads'—to declare such a practice to be unlawful; that is a matter solely for Parliament, which alone possesses the facilities for weighing all the issues involved. And, by contrast with what happened in France, the UK Parliament has not intervened in the matter.

30.2.B INDEXATION CLAUSES UNDER GERMAN LAW

Germany has been the chief country to be hit by a wave of galloping inflation: it is this which has given rise to the formulation in German case law of the doctrine of *Wegfall der Geschäftsgrundlage* or disappearance of the contractual basis—sometimes referred to as the doctrine of *clausula rebus sic stantibus*—which entails the modification of the contract. Although the nominalist principle continues to be the underlying rule, it has been modified by that case law.

In Germany, therefore, indexation clauses are less important than elsewhere. However, the aftermath of the Second World War saw the enactment, on 20 June 1948, of the Currency Act (Währungsgesetz) of the Allied Forces,[8] which reformed the monetary system and provided for the replacement of the Reichsmark by the new Deutschmark (DM). Under that statute, indexation clauses were subjected to a system of control.

Währungsgesetz of 20 June 1948   **30.2 (DE)**

§3: Save where special authorisation is granted by the body empowered to control monetary policy, money-debts may not be contracted in any currency other than the German mark. The same rule shall apply to debts the amount of which in DM is to be linked to the exchange rate of another currency, to the price or quantity of fine gold or of other goods, or to the price of benefits or services.

According to the second sentence of the provision, an indexation clause was only valid if its use had been authorised by the Bundesbank. The Bank adopted a restrictive approach. In 1978, it published guidelines containing clauses for which authorisation was or was not required. Practitioners went to considerable lengths in their efforts to formulate clauses which circumvented the requirements laid down by the statute; they benefited from the courts' narrow construction of § 3, which was based on the view that the provision constituted a restriction on the principle of contractual freedom.[9]

---

[8] Gesetz no. 61 der Amerikanischen und der Britischen Militärregierung; Verordnung no. 158 d der Französischen Militärregierung.

[9] See BGH 17 September 1954, BGHZ 14, 306; BGH 3 July 1981, BGHZ 81, 135.

However, certain clauses that were regarded as excessively inflationary were not authorised under any circumstances; these included indexation clauses linked to obligations relating to money trading or the capital markets—loans, insurance, etc 'upwards only' clauses and clauses based on the price of gold, the purchasing power of the DM, average wage levels or average pension levels. Other clauses were held to circumvent the need for authorisation, depending on the classification applied to them.

BGH, 6 December 1978[10]   **30.3 (DE)**

Clause 'to be adjusted by court'

A rent-review clause which will require adjustment after a short period is invalid without authorisation. However, the parties may provide in the contract for the court to adjust it so as to validate it.

Facts: The claimant, who had constructed a building in 1972, let it to the defendant for commercial use until 31 December 1978. The parties agreed a rent of DM 80 per square metre. Clause 6 of the contract provided for indexation linked to the cost of living index. In addition, clause 20 contained a nullity provision, in the following terms:

> In the event that any stipulation contained in this contract proves to be invalid, it shall be adjusted and adapted in such a way as to enable the object which it seeks to achieve to be attained as far as possible. The contract shall in any event remain valid as regards the remaining stipulations contained therein, without the stipulation impugned.

The parties did not seek authorisation for the indexation clause. The reference index having risen by over 10 points, the claimant claimed a proportional increase in the rent from 1 April 1973 until 31 October 1974. In addition, the claimant applied for an order requiring the defendant to accept the transformation of the indexation clause into a 'performance proviso' clause.

Held: The Landgericht and the Oberlandesgericht declared the claim to be admissible and well founded. The defendant's appeal on a point of law was dismissed.

Judgment: In order to be valid, the indexation stipulation contained in clause 6 of the contract, providing as it did for a genuine graduated scale, required the grant of authorisation by the central bank pursuant to the third sentence of § 3 of the Währungsgesetz. That authorisation could not be taken for granted, since the lease had been concluded for a term of less than ten years.

In view of the fact that the indexation clause was not capable of being valid, the OLG correctly examined whether there might be grounds for considering, by means of a supplementing interpretation of the contract, that the parties had intended to provide for the substitution of an alternative clause. According to the appellant, such an interpretation could not be validly applied, since the parties knew that the clause was invalid and that there was no prospect of its being authorised. The BGH does not share that view.

According to the OLG, the parties wished to be able subsequently to alter the amount of the rent. There is nothing to indicate whether the parties knew that the same goal, more or less, could equally well be attained by using either an indexation clause or a 'performance proviso' clause, which did not require authorisation.

---

[10] NJW 1979, 2250.

The BGH considers, having regard to the objective aimed at by the contract, that the parties intended to provide for a clause other than the indexation clause which would safeguard their interests and which would be valid. The substitution of a clause not requiring authorisation in place of the indexation clause corresponds to the intentions of the parties, as is apparent from clause 20. The clause substituted by the OLG is in conformity with the interests of both parties, on the basis of a supplementing interpretation. It reflects the intention of the contracting parties as expressed in clause 6, and makes it possible for the rent to be varied in accordance with fluctuations in the cost of living index.

Inasmuch as the parties have been unable to reach agreement concerning the change to be made to the amount of the rent, the claimant is entitled to adjust it on the basis of the cost of living index (§§ 315, 316 BGB). Thus it should be adjusted having regard to equitable principles.

Note

It is interesting to note here the efforts made by the courts to save the contract. The initial indexation clause providing for a 'graduated scale' had not been authorised, and was incapable of being authorised in view of the insufficiently long term of the contract. However, the contract contained a clause providing for it to be salvaged in the event of the nullity of the clause at issue, and the courts applied to it a bold interpretation founded on equitable principles. One wonders, in the circumstances, what purpose was served by declaring the unauthorised clause to be null and void.

Another type of clause is the *Spannungsklausel*, otherwise known as a 'tension' clause or 'divergence' clause.

BGH, 25 May 1977[11]   **30.4 (DE)**

'Tension clause' (Spannungsklausel)

In the case of a continuing contract providing a 'tension clause', a modification of the equivalence between the service provided could be demanded only if there was an imbalance between the obligations which formed part of a long-term phenomenon.

Facts: In 1972 the claimants purchased from the defendant a single-occupation dwelling house. The supply of fuel for heating and hot water in the houses on the estate was provided by a business owned by the defendant. Paragraph L of the notarially recorded sale contract, dated 18 January 1972, provided: 'Water and heating is to be supplied from a thermal boiler plant. The price per calorific unit shall correspond to that charged by the municipal boiler undertaking.' The general terms and conditions of supply were to be such that the customer was not placed in a less advantageous position than if the supplies had been made from the municipal boiler, and were to be equivalent to the latter's terms. The prices charged for supplies were not to be higher than those charged by the municipal boiler undertaking. The municipal boiler undertaking supplied its customers with heating on the basis of a standard-form contract, at a price made up of a price relating to the annual provision of services and a price relating to the labour corresponding to the quantity of heat supplied. Each customer could choose one of two different tariffs. The standard-form contract contained a 'tension' clause geared to the price of coal, the transport cost and the hourly rate of the employees concerned.

The parties disagreed as to the price to be charged for the provision of supplies to the claimants' house.

[11] NJW 1977, 2262.

Held: The Landgericht ordered the defendant to supply the claimants, throughout the year, with hot water and heating at the rate charged by the municipality. The Oberlandesgericht upheld the judgment of the lower court and the appeal lodged on a point of law against its decision was dismissed. The BGH confirmed the decision.

Judgment: Under the contract concluded between the parties, the defendant is required to supply hot water and heating to the claimants at the price charged by the municipal boiler undertaking. The defendant may free himself from that obligation by pleading, on the basis of the principles of good faith (§ 242 BGB), that the circumstances underlying the contract have ceased to exist. In support of his arguments, the defendant maintains that the oil crisis has brought about an increase in the price of raw materials which has imposed a very heavy financial burden; he further claims that the municipality uses coal, not fuel oil. The appellate court rightly took the view that, when the crisis came to an end, the prices of coal and of fuel oil were similar to those prevailing at the commencement of the contractual relationship. In the case of a continuing contract, a modification of the equivalence between the service provided could be demanded only if there was an imbalance between the obligations which formed part of a long-term phenomenon. Variations in the relative prices of coal and of fuel oil fall within the sphere of activities of the undertaking concerned, which must bear the risk in that regard, since that risk is not highly unreasonable. It should be noted, moreover, that it is open to the defendant to choose between two sources of heat production.

Notes

(1) The contract, which was of a relatively complex nature, contained a 'tension' clause linking the price level to variations in the cost of similar goods or services: the 'tension' between the two—in this instance, coal and fuel oil—was to remain constant. It is interesting to note the link with the doctrine of *imprévision*, which was also pleaded in this case—to no avail.

(2) The liberal approach taken by the case law had the effect of restricting considerably the scope of those cases in which the authorisation of the Bundesbank was required.

§ 3 of the Currency Act was superseded by a statutory instrument based on the Act introducing the Euro in 1998.[12] The instrument more or less codified the Bundesbank guidelines for the authorisation of indexation clauses, although it removed some of the restrictions and transferred the power of authorisation to the Federal Office of Economics and Export Control. With a few exceptions, the case law on § 3 of the Currency Act remained good law.

A completely new regime was introduced by the 2007 Act on price clauses.[13] It abolished the requirement to obtain authorisation by an executive agency. Whether an indexation clause is valid or not follows directly from the Act. Invalidity can only be established by judicial decision. As a rule, indexation clauses remain prohibited under § 1(1). However, in § 1(2) and §§ 3–7, the Act provides an exhaustive list of exceptions that

---

[12] Preisklauselverordnung of 23 September 1998, based on § 2 Preisangaben- und Preisklauselgesetz of 3 December 1984, BGBl 1984 I 1429, as amended by the Euroeinführungsgesetz of 9 June 1998, BGBl 1998 I 1242.

[13] Preisklauselgesetz of 7 September 2007, BGBl 2007 I 2446.

mainly correspond to the exceptions recognised in the statutory instrument of 1998. Further exceptions that are enumerated in the Act concern indexation clauses in certain long-term contracts that are to run for at least 10 years or for the lifetime of one of the parties, contracts establishing a building lease (*Erbbaurechtsverträge*) for a duration exceeding 30 years, contracts in the money and capital markets (*Geld- und Kapitalmarktverkehr*), particularly consumer credit contracts, and contracts between businesses based in Germany and parties based in another country. For the validity of some of these clauses, § 2 of the Act requires that the clause is 'sufficiently certain' and does not 'place a party at an unreasonable disadvantage'.

30.2.C INDEXATION CLAUSES UNDER FRENCH LAW

The history of indexation clauses in France has been chaotic. In the aftermath of the paper money (*assignats*) crisis at the time of the French Revolution, the Code civil formulated the principle of monetary nominalism in relation to loans.

Code civil   **30.5 (FR)**

Article 1895: The obligation which results from a loan of money is always for the sum stated in the contract.

Where there is a rise or a fall in currency before the time of payment, the debtor must return the numerical sum loaned, and must do so only in the currency having legal tender at the time of the payment.

Nominalism has been extended by the case law to all money debts and the 2016 reform of French contract law has introduced it as a principle of the general law of contracts, in the new Code civil.

Code civil   **30.6 (FR)**

Article 1343: A debtor of a monetary obligation is discharged by payment of its nominal value.

The value of a sum due may vary as a result of indexation.

A person who owes a debt whose value is to be assessed is discharged by the payment of the sum of money which is identified by its assessment.

Notes

(1) As we have seen, French law does not countenance any re-evaluation by the courts to allow for monetary depreciation.[14]

(2) Article 1343(2) of the Code civil expressly allows variations of a monetary sum's value through the application of an indexation clause. But before the 2016 reform, the approach in relation to indexation clauses, whether or not linked to monetary factors, had fluctuated and varied over the years. The judgment in what has come to be known

---

[14] See above, p 1213.

as the *Matter* doctrine—named after the Advocate General who proposed the decision adopted in the court's decision—recognised the validity of clauses linked to gold in international contracts, subject to the possible application of exchange control rules. In French domestic law, by contrast, the position was different: whilst clauses linked to the value of gold and of foreign currencies were in principle considered to be contrary to public policy, clauses providing for a graduated scale were regarded as valid, subject to certain reservations the scope of which was sometimes uncertain, especially in cases involving the lending of sums of money.[15] Thereafter, the Cour de cassation, by a conscious reversal of precedent, lifted all restrictions.

Cass civ (1), 27 June 1957[16]　　　　　**30.7 (FR)**

Guyot

A clause in a domestic loan agreement indexing the amount to be repaid under a loan to the price of corn is valid.

Facts: A loan of a sum of money was index-linked to the price of corn prevailing as at the date on which the debt was to be repaid. The debtor pleaded that the indexation clause was void.

Held: The court of first instance upheld the creditor's claim; the debtor's appeal against the judgment was dismissed.

Judgment: THE COURT—*On the two appeal grounds considered together:*—Whereas Mr Praquin, a grain trader, lent the sum of 350,000 francs to Mr and Mrs Guyot, who were farmers; as, according to the contract, that sum corresponded, at the time when the contract was concluded, to the value of 500 quintals of corn, and the borrowers were required to discharge the debt in seven annual instalments, the first six of which each were to correspond to the value of 70 quintals of corn and the seventh of which was to correspond to the value of 80 quintals by reference to the price of corn prevailing at the date when the instalments respectively fell due or were paid;

— Whereas the price of corn subsequently rose, and Mr and Mrs Guyot refused to pay the sum of 693,000 francs which represented, in consequence of the price increase, the first four instalments; they pleaded that the clause providing for a graduated scale was void. The contested judgment upholding the claimant's claim declared the clause to be valid, on the ground that there existed no provision permitting the loan to fall outside the system of ordinary law, under which such a graduated scale is lawful, where, as in the present case, that scale may move upwards or downwards and is therefore incapable of frustrating the operation of the applicable monetary laws, evidencing instead merely the parties' intention to provide against economic instability.

— Whereas the appellants criticise the conclusion reached by the cour d'appel, arguing that it disregarded the *ordre public* consideration inherent in the rule laid down by Article 1895 of the Civil Code, which provides that a person borrowing a sum of money

---

[15] See Cass civ 3 June 1930, DP 1931.1.5, opinion by P Matter, annotated by R Savatier.

[16] No. 57-01212, Bull civ I no. 302, D 1957, 649, annotated by G Ripert. See, F Terré, Y Lequette and F Chénedé, *Grands arrêts de jurisprudence civil,* vol 2, *Obligations, Contrats spéciaux, Sûretés* (13th edn, Paris: Dalloz, 2015) no. 248.

is required only to repay, in numerical terms, the sum lent; they further maintain that the contested judgment infringes the monetary laws establishing the forced currency, since, in their submission, the clause in issue can only have been intended to frustrate the operation of those laws.

— Whereas, however, the clause at issue is not invalidated by the legislation in question;

— Whereas, first of all, the sole object of Article 1895 is to preclude, where the agreement is silent on the point, any revision by the courts of the terms on which the loan is to be repaid, in the event that application is made for such revision under Article 1892 on the ground that the 'quality' of the currency has changed.

— Whereas in the case of a loan of money, the *ordre public* does not actually require that the borrower should be protected against the free acceptance by him of the risk of an increase in the sum to be repaid, which is intended to preserve the purchasing power of the sum lent, on the basis that the sum repayable is to be assessed in relation to the cost of a commodity, since such borrowers are able to assume risks of similar magnitude when entering into other contracts.

— Whereas it is not possible to claim that the mandatory nature of Article 1895 is justified by monetary principles which dictate its application on account of some threat allegedly posed to the stability of the currency by clauses providing for such increases, since, as matters stand, the effect of such clauses appears to be too uncertain to justify their being found to be void on the ground that they seriously undermine the security of the savings and credit system.

— Whereas, lastly, alleged *ordre public* considerations can hardly be reconciled with the provisions of Article 1897, concerning loans of commodities, which, in the event of an increase in the price of the commodity lent, requires the borrower in every case to bear the consequences of that increase, irrespective of its cause.

— Whereas the clause in issue rendered is not void by any monetary laws currently in force, since those laws cannot prevent variations in the purchasing power of the currency, which varies with the price of commodities, and cannot preclude the lenders concerned, any more than other creditors, from taking variations in purchasing power into account.

— Whereas, leaving aside the reasons stated by the cour d'appel concerning the reciprocity of the clause and the intention of the parties, which are immaterial, and the criticism of which by the appellant is therefore irrelevant, the contested decision is consequently legally justified.

On those grounds, the appeal is dismissed …

Notes

(1) The position under the relevant case law had previously been somewhat uncertain as regards money loans, the indexation of which was in some instances regarded as running directly counter to the principle of monetary nominalism, as expressly laid down by the Code civil in relation to lending. The judgment in *Guyot* swept all those reservations aside. It construed Article 1895 on the basis that the provision is not of a mandatory nature. It further stated that the threat posed by such indexation clauses to the stability of the currency is not sufficiently serious. Some of the grounds of the judgment appealed against—concerning the reciprocity of the clause and the intention of the parties, which the Cour de cassation expressly disregarded—had been the subject of particular debate in the court below.

(2) The French legislature—which was authorised at that time to legislate in economic matters by way of orders—reacted immediately, by enacting Article 79-3 of the Order of 30 December 1958 (amended in 1959, 1970 and 1977), now codified at Article L 112-1 of the Code monétaire et financier. The purpose of the Order was to limit the freedom of indexation resulting from the *Guyot case.*

Code monétaire et financier[17] **30.8 (FR)**

Article L 112-1: Without prejudice to the provisions of the first paragraph of Article L. 112-2 and Articles L 112-3, L 112-3-1, and L 112-4, the automatic indexation of prices of goods or services shall be prohibited.

Any clause in a successive performance contract, including leases and rental agreements of any kind, which provides for an index variation period that is longer than the interval between each revision shall be deemed void.

In an agreement pertaining to a housing unit, any clause that provides that indexation must be linked to the "rents and charges" index on which are based the general retail price indexes shall be prohibited. The same applies to any clause according to which indexation would be linked to the statutory rates of increase determined in accordance with Act no. 48-1360 of 1 September 1948, unless the initial amount itself was set in accordance with the provisions of said Act and its implementing legislation.

Article L 112-2: With regard to company constitutional or contractual provisions, any clause shall be prohibited, where it stipulates that indexation must be linked to the guaranteed minimum wage, to the general level of prices or of wages, or to the price of goods, products, or services, and where it does not directly relate either to the object of the company constitutional documents or contract, or to the business of one of the parties. In order to be deemed to directly relate to the object of a contract with respect to a building, a clause shall stipulate that indexation must be linked to variations in the National Construction Cost Index published by the National Institute of Statistics and Economic Studies or, in the case of commercial activities defined as such by decree, that indexation must be linked to the variations in the Quarterly Commercial Rent Index published under the conditions set forth in said decree by the National Institute of Statistics and Economic Studies.

The provisions of the preceding paragraph shall not apply to company constitutional or contractual provisions relating to maintenance debts.

Life annuities arranged between individuals, including those arranged pursuant to the provisions of Article 759 of the Civil Code, shall be treated as maintenance debts.

Article L 112-3: As an exception to the provisions of Article L 112-1 and the first paragraph of Article L. 112-2 and subject to the terms and conditions laid down by decree, the following may be indexed to the general level of prices:

1° [Abolished]

2° *Livret A* savings accounts, as defined in Article L 221-1

3° *Livret d'Épargne Populaire* savings accounts, as defined in Article L 221-13

4° *Livret de Développement Durable* savings accounts, as defined in Article L 221-27

---

[17] Official translation by the Translation centre of the Ministries of the economy and finance, version of 2011 (on Legifrance website).

5° home-ownership savings accounts (*comptes d'épargne-logement*), as defined in Article L. 315-1 of the Building and Housing Code

6° *Livret d'Épargne-Entreprise* business savings accounts, as defined in Article 1 of the Economic Initiative Development Act 84-578 of 9 July 1984

7° *Livrets d'Épargne Institués au Profit des Travailleurs Manuels* savings accounts, as defined in Article 80 of the 1977 Budget Act (no. 76-1232 of 29 December 1976)

8° Loans granted to legal entities as well as to individuals for their professional activities.

9° Rents provided for under agreements pertaining to housing units or premises used for commercial activities and that fall within the decree referred to in the first paragraph of Article L 112-2. …

Article L 112-3-1: Notwithstanding any contrary legislative provision, the indexation of the debt instruments and financial contracts respectively referred to under paragraphs II,2 and III of Article L 211-1 shall be permitted.

Article L 112-4: The guaranteed minimum wage may be indexed according to the rules set forth in Articles L 3231-4 and L 3231-5 of the Labour Code.

It will be noted that, save in special cases outside the scope of this order—maintenance obligations—certain types of indexation are prohibited, whilst others are permissible where they are directly 'related to the object of the company constitutional documents or contracts, or to the business of one of the parties' (Code monétaire et financier, Article L 112-2, 2(1)). For example, in the Cour de cassation case of 12 January 1988,[18] a loan of a sum of money was index-linked to the Swiss franc. The Cour de cassation found that the loan was of a domestic nature, and thus subject to restrictions. The Court said:

> [S]ince it was accepted that the loan was of a domestic nature, the second-instance court rightly held that that contract was subject to Order 59-246 of 4 February 1959 amending the Order of 30 December 1958, which permits indexation only where the indexation in question is directly related to the subject-matter of the agreement or to the activity carried on by one of the parties and thus prohibits the fixing of the debt in a foreign currency, save where one of the contracting parties is a banker or financier. Consequently, the loan at issue could not validly relate to a sum of money expressed in Swiss francs. That loan is therefore unlawful as regards its subject-matter, and hence null and void.

The emphasis on the domestic character of the loan confirms that international contracts remain outside the scope of the legislation concerned—save that payment in France had to be made in French francs (this was before the euro), as the only currency in which obligations may be discharged, such clauses relating solely to the currency of account. The concept of international payment is also flexible, having been held to constitute a payment forming part of an international transaction.[19]

Consequently, the above judgment refused to countenance indexation based on a foreign currency—in the form of a foreign currency value clause—in a contract between

---

[18] Cass civ (1) 12 January 1988, no. 86-11966, Defr 1989, 169, annotated by P Malaurie.
[19] Cass civ (1) 13 May 1985, no. 83-16923, Bull civ I no. 146.

private persons, save where one of the contracting parties—in particular, the lender—is a banker or financier, because in the latter case the indexation is directly related to that party's business.[20]

Article L 112-1 to L 112-4 of the Code monétaire et financier do not specify the manner in which unlawful indexation is to be penalised—save in the second paragraph of Article L 112-1, which states that a clause in a successive performance contract providing for an index variation period that is longer than the interval between each revision 'shall be deemed to be void'. In the past, the nullity was generally regarded as absolute, since it was considered that public interest was primarily involved. Only the offending clause was deemed void, unless the inclusion of that unlawful clause was a determining factor in the conclusion of the contract.[21] As more emphasis was put on protection of one party, nullity has more and more often been merely 'relative'; nowadays, absolute nullity seems 'anachronistic'.[22]

Another significant change concerns the power of the judge. The traditional rule is that it is not open to the courts to substitute a valid index in place of an index which is invalid or no longer effective.[23] However, little by little, the Cour de cassation has admitted that judges could substitute an existing index for one which has disappeared, provided this corresponds to the parties' intent. Indeed, this has been done by means of interpretation of the parties' intent, on the basis of former Article 1134(1) (now Article 1103) of the Code civil (parties are thus presumed to have wanted to insert a valid clause).[24] The legislator had paved the way for this evolution in prescribing automatic substitution for leases of *habitations* (Act of 9 July 1970, modifying Article 79 of the 1958 Order). The 2016 reform codified the case law.

Code civil	**30.9 (FR)**

Article 1167: Where the price or any other element of a contract is to be determined by reference to an index which does not exist or has ceased to exist or to be available, the index is replaced by the index which is most closely related to it.

If an index does not exist or cannot be used, Article 1167 requires that judges apply the index which is most closely related to the original index. Although no express reference is made to the intent of the parties, looking at their intent seems to be the best way of finding the 'most closely related' index. In the event where the parties have not expressed any intention regarding the chosen index, the Cour de cassation held that the invalid index should be replaced by an index provided by statutory law.[25]

---

[20] See the judgment in *Multiservice Bookbinding v Marden*, above, 30.1 (EN), p 1235.

[21] Terré, Lequette and Chénedé (n 16 above).

[22] F Terré, P Simler and Y Lequette, *Les obligations* (11th edn, Paris: Dalloz, 2013) no. 1337.

[23] On the consequences arising from the invalidation of an indexation clause, see the passage relating to hardship clauses, and the judgment CA Paris 28 September 1976, 30.12 (FR) below. Compare with Cass civ (3) 15 February 1972, no. 70-13280, Bull III no. 100, 20.10 (FR) above, p 809, on the possibility to replace a wage scale no longer published, by way of interpretation of the clause.

[24] Cass civ (3) 12 January 2005, no. 03-17260, Bull III no. 4, RDC 2005, 101, annotated by D Mazeaud.

[25] ibid.

Beside the indexation clause, the 2016 reform has introduced the concept of 'debt of value', borrowed from the German doctrine of *Wertschuld*. Article 1343(3) of the revised Code civil provides that '[a] person who owes a debt whose value is to be assessed is discharged by the payment of the sum of money which is identified by its assessment.'

The debt of value imposes an obligation on the debtor other than the payment of a monetary sum. For example, the victim of a tort is entitled to compensation for the damage suffered, which has no monetary value until the assessment of the damage. As a result, from the time the victim suffers damage to the moment the damage is assessed, the victim has a debt of value. During this period, the debt is not subject to monetary depreciation. The debt of value is thus another protection from monetary fluctuations.

A comparative study of German, English and French law may raise questions of what is meant, first of all, by the concept of public policy.[26] Public policy in monetary matters provides a good illustration of the relativity attached to the concept at different times and in different places.

The question also arises whether the restrictive measures adopted by French law and German law have been effective, given that they have been watered down by case law and that practitioners have found ways of circumventing them,[27] and, more importantly, whether a national regulation, based upon the negative effect of indexation clauses for the economy, is still compatible with the adoption of the Euro.[28]

30.3 *FORCE MAJEURE* CLAUSES

In domestic legal systems, including France and Germany, it is generally accepted that the parties may by agreement modify the rules applying under the ordinary law to cases of *force majeure*, either by extending them or by restricting them, and that they may even provide that *force majeure* is not to have the effect of releasing them from their obligations. We have already come across a clause of that type, in the judgment of the French Cour de cassation of 24 January 1995.[29]

Force majeure clauses are generally inserted in contracts because the legal regime of *force majeure* or frustration operates very restrictively. Such modifications may relate to the definition of *force majeure*, particularly with a view to avoiding uncertainty concerning the circumstances in which it is to be deemed to exist, the procedure to be followed—for example, the notice to be given—and/or the effect which it is to have on the contract. For instance, while an abnormal increase in prices does not constitute a frustrating event in English law nor a case of *force majeure* under French law, a contractual clause may state that it shall constitute a *force majeure* event. Clauses are frequently used in

---

[26] See above, ch 17.

[27] See, by way of example in relation to French law, F Dion and C Thierache, 'Faut-il abroger les ordonnances de 1958 et 1959 sur les indexations?' D 1995, chron 55.

[28] Terré et al (n 22 above) no. 1336.

[29] Cass civ (1) 24 January 1995, no. 92-18227, Bull I no. 54; see also Cass com 8 July 1981, no. 79-15626, Bull civ IV no. 312.

English contracts to extend the circumstances in which a non-performance is excused. For instance, a short delay will seldom result in a contract being frustrated; rather, the party who is late will be in breach of contract, and liable in damages, unless the parties have agreed on a *force majeure* clause exonerating him from liability for delays that were outside his control.

Such clauses have been frequently used in international contracts, but they may also be found in domestic law, in which they appear to raise few problems save as regards to their interpretation.[30]

The model *force majeure* clause drawn up by the International Chamber of Commerce (Force majeure ICC 2003)—text and commentary—illustrates the issues raised by that type of clause.

ICC force majeure clause[31]   30.10 (INT)

[1] Unless otherwise agreed in the contract between the parties expressly or impliedly, where a party to a contract fails to perform one or more of its contractual duties, the consequences set out in paragraphs 4 to 9 of this Clause will follow if and to the extent that that party proves:

[a] that its failure to perform was caused by an impediment beyond its reasonable control; and

[b] that it could not reasonably have been expected to have taken the occurrence of the impediment into account at the time of the conclusion of the contract; and

[c] that it could not reasonably have avoided or overcome the effects of the impediment.

[2] Where a contracting party fails to perform one or more of its contractual duties because of default by a third party whom it has engaged to perform the whole or part of the contract, the consequences set out in paragraphs 4 to 9 of this Clause will only apply to the contracting party:

[a] if and to the extent that the contracting party establishes the requirements set out in paragraph 1 of this Clause; and

[b] if and to the extent that the contracting party proves that the same requirements apply to the third party.

[3] In the absence of proof to the contrary and unless otherwise agreed in the contract between the parties expressly or impliedly, a party invoking this Clause shall be presumed to have established the conditions described in paragraph 1 [a] and [b] of this Clause in case of the occurrence of one or more of the following impediments:

[a] war (whether declared or not), armed conflict or the serious threat of same (including but not limited to hostile attack, blockade; military embargo), hostilities, invasion, act of a foreign enemy, extensive military mobilisation;

---

[30] See, eg, *Pagnan SpA v Tradax Ocean Transportation SA* [1987] 3 All ER 564 (CA), which featured a combination of the provisions of the normal *force majeure* clause incorporating the general GAFTA conditions and of the clause making the vendor responsible for obtaining an export certificate.

[31] ICC Force Majeure Clause 2003, ICC Hardship Clause 2003, ICC Publication no. 650. This document is included in the CENTRAL Transnational Law Database website by kind permission of ICC Publishing.

[b] civil war, riot rebellion and revolution, military or usurped power, insurrection, civil commotion or disorder, mob violence, act of civil disobedience;

[c] act of terrorism, sabotage or piracy;

[d] act of authority whether lawful or unlawful, compliance with any law or governmental order, rule, regulation or direction, curfew restriction, expropriation, compulsory acquisition, seizure of works, requisition, nationalisation;

[e] act of God, plague, epidemic, natural disaster such as but not limited to violent storm, cyclone, typhoon, hurricane, tornado, blizzard, earthquake, volcanic activity, landslide, tidal wave, tsunami, flood, damage or destruction by lightning, drought;

[f] explosion, fire, destruction of machines, equipment, factories and of any kind of installation, prolonged break-down of transport, telecommunication or electric current;

[g] general labour disturbance such as but not limited to boycott, strike and lockout, go-slow, occupation of factories and premises.

[4] A party successfully invoking this Clause is, subject to paragraph 6 below, relieved from its duty to perform its obligations under the contract from the time at which the impediment causes the failure to perform if notice thereof is given without delay or, if notice thereof is not given without delay, from the time at which notice thereof reaches the other party.

[5] A party successfully invoking this Clause is, subject to paragraph 6 below, relieved from any liability in damages or any other contractual remedy for breach of contract from the time indicated in paragraph 4.

[6] Where the effect of the impediment or event invoked is temporary, the consequences set out under paragraphs 4 and 5 above shall apply only insofar, to the extent that and as long as the impediment or the listed event invoked impedes performance by the party invoking this Clause of its contractual duties. Where this paragraph applies, the party invoking this Clause is under an obligation to notify the other party as soon as the impediment or listed event ceases to impede performance of its contractual duties.

[7] A party invoking this Clause is under an obligation to take all reasonable means to limit the effect of the impediment or event invoked upon performance of its contractual duties.

[8] Where the duration of the impediment invoked under paragraph 1 of this Clause or of the listed event invoked under paragraph 3 of this Clause has the effect of substantially depriving either or both of the contracting parties of what they were reasonably entitled to expect under the contract, either party has the right to terminate the contract by notification within a reasonable period to the other party.

[9] Where paragraph 8 above applies and where either contracting party has, by reason of anything done by another contracting party in the performance of the contract, derived a benefit before the termination of the contract, the party deriving such a benefit shall be under a duty to pay to the other party a sum of money equivalent to the value of such benefit.

Although Article 1218 of the new Code civil now provides a statutory definition of the *force majeure*, the parties may still decide to insert a *force majeure* clause in their contract. The definition given by the Code civil is a general one, which may be subject to various interpretations. A *force majeure* clause allows the parties to determine more precisely what kind of events would qualify as *force majeure* and what would be the effects of such events. For instance, *force majeure* clauses often lay down a list of events which fall within the scope of *force majeure*. It must be highlighted that the validity of *force majeure* clauses inserted in contracts between professionals and consumers are subject to consumer law which prohibits clauses which create a significant imbalance between the rights and obligations of the parties in a consumer contract (see Article L 212-1 and 2 of the Code de la consommation). Accordingly, when drafting a *force majeure* clause in a contract between a professional and a consumer or a non-professional, the parties must ensure that the clause does not alter the equilibrium of the contract. For instance, if, for the same event, the *force majeure* clause discharges the professional from its obligation but not the consumer or non-professional, such a clause would be unfair.[32] And as we have seen in the chapter on Unfair terms, the protection of the weaker party has been extended: the Code civil prohibits the contractual clauses which significantly impair the equilibrium of the contract, even if it is concluded between two professionals.[33]

The drafting of *force majeure* clauses may be affected by these new provisions. Pursuant to Article 1170, the *force majeure* clause cannot be relied upon by a party in such a way that allows it to disregard its main obligation under the contract. For example, a transport company should not be able to use a clause that treats the failure of its trucks as a *force majeure* event; such a clause would deprive the transport company from its essential obligation. Article 1171 of the new Code civil goes further as it prohibits, in standard contracts, all clauses which create a significant imbalance between the parties. This provision may apply to *force majeure* clauses which allow one party only to rely on *force majeure* to be discharged from its obligation. The innovation is that Article 1171 applies to contracts concluded between professionals having the same bargaining power. The effect of this provision will depend on the interpretation of 'significant imbalance' by the courts. If the courts set a low threshold for the 'significant imbalance' to be charac-terised, this provision may force many economic operators to make their standard terms and conditions more even-handed.

30.4 HARDSHIP CLAUSES

The contracting parties usually envisage the occurrence of future events which disrupt the normal operation of the contract without rendering its performance impossible. Inter-national practitioners have likewise formulated a whole range of clauses dealing with such circumstances, to which different names have been applied—harshness clauses, saving clauses, renegotiation clauses, hardship clauses, unforeseeability clauses, etc—and which provide for different outcomes: renegotiation of the contract, intervention by a third party-ombudsman, conciliation, etc. Hardship clauses are frequently combined with arbitration clauses.

---

[32] Cass civ (1) 26 April 2017, no. 15-18970, Bull 2017, 1, no. 496: a consumer association claimed that the *force majeure* clause inserted in the standard terms and conditions of Air France benefited only the airline company. The cour d'appel, confirmed by the Cour de cassation, held that the *force majeure* clause did not create any imbalance between the rights and obligations of the parties as both the airline company and the consumers could rely on a *force majeure* event.

[33] See ch 21.

Hardship clauses are often found in international contracts. Such clauses generally define 'hardship' and lay down a procedure that parties must follow in the event such hardship occurs. Both parties must generally use their best endeavours to renegotiate the contract in good faith.

ICC hardship clause 2003   **30.11 (INT)**

[1] A party to a contract is bound to perform its contractual duties even if events have rendered performance more onerous than could reasonably have been anticipated at the time of the conclusion of the contract.

[2] Notwithstanding paragraph 1 of this Clause, where a party to a contract proves that:

> [a] the continued performance of its contractual duties has become excessively onerous due to an event beyond its reasonable control which it could not reasonably have been expected to have taken into account at the time of the conclusion of the contract; and that

> [b] it could not reasonably have avoided or overcome the event or its consequences, the parties are bound, within a reasonable time of the invocation of this Clause, to negotiate alternative contractual terms which reasonably allow for the consequences of the event.

[3] Where paragraph 2 of this Clause applies, but where alternative contractual terms which reasonably allow for the consequences of the event are not agreed by the other party to the contract as provided in that paragraph, the party invoking this Clause is entitled to termination of the contract.

Notes

(1) This hardship clause draws inspiration from by Article 1467 of the Italian Codice civile and Article 6.2.2 of the UNIDROIT PICC. A procedure for renegotiation is set out by paragraph 2; in case of failure of these renegotiations, the party who had relied on that clause can terminate the contract.

(2) The clause does not give authority to a third party to resolve the dispute. It is explained in the comments that the drafters wanted to encourage the parties to resort to a general dispute resolution clause (for instance, an ICC arbitration clause) rather than provide for a specific solution in such a situation.

(3) A specific clause which gives authority to a third party to resolve the dispute between the parties in case they have failed to reach an agreement once hardship has occurred is often named an 'intervener clause'.

Hardship clauses are also used in domestic law. German law considers them to be valid unless their application would seriously undermine the balance struck in § 313 BGB. They are also valid in French law and in English law where they may seem all the more necessary as the courts have no power to adjust the terms of a contract to meet changed circumstances. Indeed, not only does English law allow parties to adjust their bargain to meet changing circumstances, but, as noted by McKendrick, due to the strict application of the doctrine of frustration, 'contracting parties frequently include force majeure and hardship clauses in their contracts so that they can allocate the risk of the occurrence of such unforeseen events'.[34] The same applies in France where, until the 2016 reform, the courts could neither revise nor terminate contracts on the ground of a change of circumstances (see Chapter 29).

It is important that such clauses not only define when there is 'hardship' but also lay down a procedure to be adopted in the event that these circumstances occur.

Cour d'appel de Paris, 28 September 1976[35]   **30.12 (FR)**

Renegotiation of oil supply contract

A clause requiring the parties to consult one another in certain circumstances may be given effect by ordering negotiations under the supervision of a third party.

Facts: The indexation clause in a contract for the provision of oil concluded between EDF and Shell (France) was rendered inoperable (as the parties acknowledged) by the upheaval caused to the market by the oil crisis. The contract contained a saving clause, in the following terms: 'In the event of an increase of six francs per tonne in relation to the initial value, the parties shall consult one another with a view to considering the alterations, if any, to be made to the contract (as regards the price or any other clause)'. An attempt at conciliation failed.

Held: The Paris tribunal de commerce declared that the contract had become null and void (ie had lapsed) in consequence of the cessation of existence of the price. The cour d'appel reversed the judgment and ordered that further negotiations should take place.

Judgment: ... — Whereas the so-called 'saving' clause contained in the contracts provides that, in the event that the price of ordinary fuel oil delivered to its destination increases by more than six francs per tonne in relation to its initial value, the parties are to 'consult one another with a view to considering the alterations, if any, to be made to the contract (as regards the price or any other clause)'.

— Whereas it is not contested that prices have risen by more than the amount thus provided for. The contracting parties are therefore required, in accordance with the obligation entered into by them, to negotiate such modifications as may have become necessary.

— Whereas the failure of the attempt at conciliation which took place in 1974 did not put an end to that obligation, because, since that time and even now, the parties have manifestly declared their intention to continue to perform the agreements reached between them, the supplier by delivering fuel in return for sums 'on account' of the price, and EDF by accepting deliveries on the basis of that reservation concerning the subsequent determination of the new price.

— Whereas the attitude jointly adopted by the contracting parties clearly shows that, far from wanting the agreements to lapse, they simply wish to adapt them to the new circumstances. Consequently, for the purposes of calculating the price and the variations in that price, it falls to them to substitute, in place of a reference mechanism which has ceased to operate or has become inapplicable, a formula that will ensure that EDF benefits, in respect of each category of fuel, from a reduced purchase price reflecting the exceptional magnitude of the supplies made to it, in terms of their volume and duration

---

[34] E McKendrick, *Contract Law* (12th edn, Basingstoke: Palgrave Macmillan, 2017) 280.
[35] JCP 1979.II.18810, annotated by J Robert.

and taking into account the public service provided by that organisation, whilst leaving the oil company with an adequate profit margin; as before any ruling is given on the substance of the case, it is appropriate that the parties be ordered, in accordance with the obligation incumbent upon them, to conclude an agreement on that point, under the auspices of an observer; as only if those negotiations fail to bear fruit will the Court, in the knowledge of the solutions proposed, declare whether the formula which might possibly be suitable on a financial level (fundamentally) modifies the stipulations laid down by the contracts currently existing and therefore precludes the Court from imposing it, or whether, on the other hand, it is restricted, in accordance with the wishes of the parties, and without altering the basic scheme of the contracts, to adapting the price to the fluctuations in the market and can thus be substituted by the Court of its own motion.

On those grounds; the Court, before giving any ruling as to the substance of the case:

— orders the parties to negotiate with a view to determining, by consent, the new prices of the different categories of fuel oil supplied to EDF and the formula or formulae applicable to variations in those prices; instructs Stéphane Thouvenot, of 74 Rue ..., to attend the negotiations;

— and orders that, in the event of the failure of those negotiations to bear fruit, the case be referred back to the Court, within six months from the bringing of the proceedings before it, in order for a ruling to be given concerning the substance thereof;—costs reserved.

Notes

(1) This is a bold judgment—and it is a pity that the case was not brought before the Cour de cassation. The cour d'appel decided to order the parties to reopen the negotiations, which was not something for which the parties had applied, under the auspices of an observer, for which the contract had not provided. The cour d'appel even envisaged, not without a certain degree of inconsistency, the possibility of substituting, of its own motion, a formula limited 'without altering the basic scheme of the contracts, to adapting the price to the fluctuations in the market'. Two factors played a part: the fact that the parties were continuing to perform the contract and EDF's 'public service' function—which brings to mind the acceptance of revision, on account of unforeseen circumstances, of contracts concluded by administrative authorities[36]—notwithstanding that the case in question concerned a contract concluded under private law. The Paris cour d'appel justified its decision by interpreting the contract, thereby seeking to give effect to the real wishes of the parties. Ultimately the parties came to a settlement.

(2) As mentioned above,[37] the 2016 reform has introduced the *révision pour imprévision*. Even if the contract does not contain a hardship clause, Article 1195 of the new Code civil provides for a renegotiation process where a 'change in circumstances that was unforeseeable at the time of conclusion of the contract renders performance excessively onerous for a party who had not accepted the risk of such a change'. Parties are actually likely to continue to use hardship clauses in order to

---

[36] See above, p 1212.
[37] See above, pp 1211–18.

regulate every step of the process (they thus decide when there is hardship, how to renegotiate, which remedies are excluded, etc). Besides, parties might actually be interested in, for instance, excluding the judicial power to revise their contract while keeping the possibility to ask for termination.

Hardship clauses are also to be found in English contracts. However, they normally have to refer any issues that arise to be decided by a third person.[38] If the clauses provide for renegotiation between the parties, it might be unenforceable. As noted by John Cartwright,[39] in English law:

> the problem at the moment is that a strict reading of the cases—and the legacy of, in particular, *Walford v Miles*—means that even express hardship clauses may fail because the duty to renegotiate has not been accepted as having sufficient content that the operation of such a clause can be controlled by the courts. So parties are often left simply to negotiate their way out of serious supervening circumstances, unaided by the legal process even where they had sought to provide for it.

However, further development may be possible. In *Petromec Inc v Petroleo Brasilieiro SA*[40] Longmore LJ discussed (obiter) whether an express obligation to negotiate is enforceable. The contract contained a revisable price as well as a clause which imposed on the parties the duty to negotiate in good faith the 'reasonable extra costs' of the works which would be due in certain specified circumstances. According to Longmore LJ:

> The traditional objections to enforcing an obligation to negotiate in good faith are (1) that the obligation is an agreement to agree and thus too uncertain to enforce, (2) that it is difficult, if not impossible, to say whether, if negotiations are brought to an end, the termination is brought about in good or in bad faith, and (3) that, since it can never be known whether good faith negotiations would have produced an agreement at all or what the terms of any agreement would have been if it would have been reached, it is impossible to assess any loss caused by breach of the obligation.

However, Longmore LJ noted that, in that particular case, the Court could ascertain the 'reasonable costs' involved if the negotiations broke down (there was no real uncertainty); it would in fact be sufficiently clear in this case whether the parties had acted in bad faith in not concluding an agreement on the revised sums payable; and the Court could assess the losses which would flow from the breakdown of the negotiations.

FURTHER READING

Fontaine, M, 'Les clauses de hardship' [1976] Droit et pratique du commerce international 7–49.
Fontaine, M and de Ly, F, *Drafting International Contracts: an Analysis of Contract Clauses* (Ardsley/NY: Transnational Publishers, 2006).

---

[38] As in *Superior Overseas Development Corp v British Gas Corp* [1982] 1 Lloyd's Rep 262 (CA).
[39] J Cartwright, 'Negotiation and Renegotiation: An English Perspective' in J Cartwright, S Vogenauer and S Whittaker (eds), *Reforming the French Law of Obligations: Comparative Reflections on the Avant-projet de réforme du droit des obligations et de la prescription* (Oxford: Hart Publishing, 2009) 51, 66.
[40] [2005] EWCA Civ 891, [2006] 1 Lloyd's Rep 121.

Mann, F, *The Legal Aspect of Money* (7th edn, Oxford: Clarendon Press, 2012).

McKendrick, E (ed), *Force Majeure and Frustration of Contract* (2nd edn, London: Lloyd's of London Press, 1995).

van Ommeslaghe, P, 'Les clauses de force majeure et d'imprévision dans les contrats internationaux' (1980) Rev dr int dr comp 7–59.

Oppetit, B, 'L'adaptation des contrats internationaux aux changements de circonstances: la clause de hardship' (1974) JDI 794–814.

Rodière, R and Tallon, D (eds), *Les modifications du contrat au cours de son exécution en raison de circonstances monétaires* (Paris: Institut de droit comparé, 1986).

Treitel, G, *Frustration and Force Majeure* (3rd edn, London: Sweet & Maxwell, 2014).

Urich-Erber, HS, *Äquivalenzstörungen und Leistungserschwernisse im deutschen und englischen Recht sowie in den Principles of European Contract Law* (Baden-Baden, Nomos, 2008).

See also the literature referred to above, at the end of Chapters 28 and 29.

PART 7
THIRD PARTY CONSEQUENCES

CHAPTER 31
CONTRACTS FOR THE BENEFIT OF THIRD PARTIES

31.1 THE GENERAL POSITION

Principles of European Contract Law   **31.1 (INT)**

Article 6:110: Stipulation in Favour of a Third Party
(1) A third party may require performance of a contractual obligation when its right to do so has been expressly agreed upon between the promisor and the promisee, or when such agreement is to be inferred from the purpose of the contract or the circumstances of the case. The third party need not be identified at the time the agreement is concluded.
(2) …

Today, European legal systems broadly agree on two issues. First, a contract cannot create obligations in a third party, nor take away the rights of a third party without the consent of that party. Secondly, a contract may be concluded by the parties so as to create an enforceable right in a third person who is a stranger to the contract. This consensus is the result of a long historical process. Roman law adhered to the contrary rule: no one could validly contract for the benefit of another person who had not been party to the original contract (*alteri nemo stipulari potest*). It was only in the nineteenth century that the numerous restrictions on the use of the third-party beneficiary contract were whittled down and—in the continental systems at least—a general theory of the doctrine emerged. The economic force which fuelled this development was the enormous growth in the nineteenth century of insurance, particularly life insurance. Life insurance policies are frequently based on a contract between the insured and the insurance company whereby the latter promises upon certain conditions to pay money to a third-party beneficiary. It is clear that in this case the contracting party wishes the beneficiary to be able to sue on the policy and that the proceeds should belong to him, rather than to the estate of the insured.

The development of French law provides a good example of the movement away from the rigid prohibition of contracts for the benefit of third parties.[1] The Code civil of 1804

---

[1] See F Terré, P Simler and Y Lequette, *Les obligations* (11th edn, Paris: Dalloz, 2013) nos. 513–18.

contained two general provisions that restated and refined the maxim *alteri nemo stipulari potest*. As a general rule, contracts had 'relative effect' only: they did not create obligations for, or confer rights on, anyone but for the parties who concluded the contract (ex-Article 1165). Former Article 1119 reinforced the rule by providing that a promise that someone received for the benefit of another was not valid. Contracts for the benefit of a third party—or, as they are usually called in France, 'stipulations for another' (*stipulations pour autrui*)—were only allowed in two exceptional cases. These were set out in the first sentence of ex-Article 1121. If they were taken seriously, a beneficiary of a life insurance policy would acquire an enforceable right against the insurer (promisor) only if either the insured (promisee) were himself the beneficiary of a stipulation made for his benefit by the insurer or if the insurer had received something from the insured as a gift.

The courts, under pressure to recognise and enforce third party rights under insurance contracts, dismantled these restrictions. They held that the performance which the promisee must make to the promisor under ex-Article 1121 need not be a 'gift' in the technical sense; *any* performance, such as the payment of a premium, will suffice. The alternative requirement of ex-Article 1121, that the promisee must at the time of the contract always stipulate something for himself, was understood by the courts as being satisfied if any 'moral benefit' accrues to him as a result of the transaction. In the case of insurance, such a *profit moral* exists in the insured's certainty that the insured sum will be paid to the third party on the occurrence of the insured event. Thus, the limiting requirements of ex-Article 1121 were effectively struck out by the courts, since it is hardly conceivable that a promisee who intends to benefit a third party, by way of an insurance contract or any other agreement, does not derive at least a *profit moral* from the assurance that his intention will eventually be implemented.

The reinterpretation of ex-Article 1121 Cciv was part of a shift of attitude vis-à-vis contracts for the benefit of third parties that occurred in most continental jurisdictions towards the end of the nineteenth century. In France, it was finally recognised by the legislator in the 2016 reform of contract law.

Code civil **31.2 (FR)**

Article 1199: A contract creates obligations only as between the parties.
Third parties may neither claim performance of the contract nor be constrained to perform it, subject to the provisions of this section and those in Chapter III of Title IV.

Article 1203: A person is not able to undertake engagements in his own name except for himself.

Article 1205: A person may make a stipulation for another person.
One of the parties to a contract (the 'stipulator') may require a promise from the other party (the 'promisor') to accomplish an act of performance for the benefit of a third party (the 'beneficiary'). The third party may be a future person but must be exactly identified or must be able to be determined at the time of the performance of the promise.

Article 1206: The beneficiary is invested with a direct right to the act of performance against the promisor from the time of the stipulation.
...

Notes

(1) Revised Article 1199 still upholds the principle of 'relative effect' (ex-Article 1165), but the second paragraph of the provision clarifies that there are a number of exceptions. Revised Article 1203, modifying ex-Article 1119, reinforces the principle by prohibiting the creation of an obligation in a third party.

(2) Revised Article 1205 makes the possibility of creating a third party right much clearer than ex-Article 1121. Moreover, it helpfully defines the designations of the three parties involved and clarifies that even future persons may be beneficiaries of a third party right.

(3) The first paragraph of revised Article 1206 clarifies that the right of the beneficiary arises at the very moment when the stipulator and the promisor reach agreement. However, as the following provisions make clear, the stipulator may still revoke the stipulation as long as the beneficiary has not accepted it.[2]

Other modern codifications displayed an equally positive attitude to contracts for third parties much earlier. They allow the parties to conclude such contracts as a matter of course.

BGB **31.3 (DE)**

§ 328: Contract for the benefit of a third party
(1) A contract may stipulate performance for the benefit of a third party, so that the third party acquires the right directly to demand performance.
(2) …

BW **31.4 (NL)**

Article 6:253: (1) A contract creates a right for a third person to claim performance from one of the parties or to otherwise invoke the contract against any of them if the contract contains a stipulation to that effect and if the third person so accepts.
(2) …

English law resisted the recognition of contracts for the benefit of third parties longer than the other European jurisdictions. Even today, the technical position at common law is that rights of third parties flowing from such contracts can only be enforced in relatively limited circumstances; but legislation first created a number of specific exceptions for particular kinds of contract and then, in 1999, a general exception that the parties can confer rights on a third party if they make their intention to do so sufficiently clear in the contract.

There are two common law doctrines which make it difficult for someone to sue on a contract to which he is not a party. First, under the doctrine of privity, rights and duties can be created by way of contract only for and against those who are parties to the

---

[2] See below, p 1347.

agreement. Secondly, according to the doctrine of consideration,[3] promises are legally enforceable only if they are given in return for a 'consideration' from the promisee, ie some counter-promise or counter-performance. It follows that only the promisee can enforce a promise and even then must show that he, not someone else, has provided consideration for it.

House of Lords   **31.5 (EN)**

Dunlop Pneumatic Tyre Co Ltd v Selfridge & Co Ltd[4]

A person who is not a party to a contract cannot enforce it or any of its terms. Even if the person can show that one of the parties to the contract was acting as his agent, he will still be unable to enforce it if he has not provided consideration.

Facts: Dunlop had sold some of their tyres to Dew & Co (Dews) on terms that Dews would not resell at less than Dunlop's list prices and that, if they resold them to trade buyers, they would extract from them a similar undertaking. Dews resold the tyres to Selfridge, who agreed to observe the restrictions and 'to pay to the Dunlop Pneumatic Tyre Co Ltd the sum of £5 for each and every tyre … sold or offered in breach of this agreement, as and by way of liquidated damages'. Selfridge supplied tyres to two of their customers at below the list price, and Dunlop sought to recover two sums of £5 each.

Held: Upholding the decision of the Court of Appeal, the House of Lords held that Dunlop (the defendants) could not enforce the term as they were not parties to the contract; and even if Dews were acting as agents for Dunlop, Dunlop had not provided any consideration to Selfridge (the respondents).

Judgment: Viscount Haldane LC: My Lords, in the law of England certain principles are fundamental. One is that only a person who is a party to a contract can sue on it. Our law knows nothing of a jus quaesitum tertio arising by way of contract. Such a right may be conferred by way of property, as, for example, under a trust, but it cannot be conferred on a stranger to a contract as a right to enforce the contract in personam. A second principle is that if a person with whom a contract not under seal has been made is to be able to enforce it consideration must have been given by him to the promisor or to some other person at the promisor's request. These two principles are not recognized in the same fashion by the jurisprudence of certain Continental countries or of Scotland, but here they are well established. A third proposition is that a principal not named in the contract may sue upon it if the promisee really contracted as his agent. But again, in order to entitle him so to sue, he must have given consideration either personally or through the promisee, acting as his agent in giving it.

My Lords, in the case before us, I am of opinion that the consideration, the allowance of what was in reality part of the discount to which Messrs Dew, the promisees, were entitled as between themselves and the appellants, was to be given by Messrs Dew on their own account, and was not in substance, any more than in form, an allowance made by the appellants. The case for the appellants is that they permitted and enabled Messrs Dew, with the knowledge and the desire of the respondents, to sell to the latter on the terms of the contract of January 2, 1912. But it appears to me that even if this is so the answer is conclusive. Messrs Dew sold to the respondents goods which they had a title to obtain from the appellants independently of this contract. The consideration by way of

---

[3] See above, ch 11.2, pp 344–365.
[4] [1915] AC 847.

discount under the contract of January 2 was to come wholly out of Messrs Dew's pocket and neither directly nor indirectly out of that of the appellants. If the appellants enabled them to sell to the respondents on the terms they did, this was not done as any part of the terms of the contract sued on.

No doubt it was provided as part of these terms that the appellants should acquire certain rights, but these rights appear on the face of the contract as jura quaesita tertio, which the appellants could not enforce. Moreover, even if this difficulty can be got over by regarding the appellants as the principals of Messrs Dew in stipulating for the rights in question, the only consideration disclosed by the contract is one given by Messrs Dew, not as their agents, but as principals acting on their own account.

The conclusion to which I have come on the point as to consideration renders it unnecessary to decide the further question as to whether the appellants can claim that a bargain was made in this contract by Messrs Dew as their agents; a bargain which, apart from the point as to consideration, they could therefore enforce. If it were necessary to express an opinion on this further question, a difficulty as to the position of Messrs Dew would have to be considered. Two contracts—one by a man on his own account as principal, and another by the same man as agent—may be validly comprised in the same piece of paper. But they must be two contracts, and not one as here. I do not think that a man can treat one and the same contract as made by him in two capacities. He cannot be regarded as contracting for himself and for another *uno flatu*.

My Lords, the form of the contract which we have to interpret leaves the appellants in this dilemma, that, if they say that Messrs Dew contracted on their behalf, they gave no consideration, and if they say they gave consideration in the shape of a permission to the respondents to buy, they must set up further stipulations, which are neither to be found in the contract sued upon nor are germane to it, but are really inconsistent with its structure. That contract has been reduced to writing, and it is in the writing that we must look for the whole of the terms made between the parties. These terms cannot in my opinion consistently with the settled principles of English law, be construed as giving to the appellants any enforceable rights as against the respondents.

I think that the judgment of the Court of Appeal was right, and I move that the appeal be dismissed with costs.

LORD DUNEDIN: My Lords, I confess that this case is to my mind apt to nip any budding affection which one might have had for the doctrine of consideration. For the effect of that doctrine in the present case is to make it possible for a person to snap his fingers at a bargain deliberately made, a bargain not in itself unfair, and which the person seeking to enforce it has a legitimate interest to enforce. Notwithstanding these considerations I cannot say that I have ever had any doubt that the judgment of the Court of Appeal was right.

My Lords, I am content to adopt from a work of Sir Frederick Pollock, to which I have often been under obligation, the following words as to consideration: 'An act or forbearance of one party, or the promise thereof, is the price for which the promise of the other is bought, and the promise thus given for value is enforceable.' (*Pollock on Contracts*, 8th edn, p 175).

Now the agreement sued on is an agreement which on the face of it is an agreement between Dew and Selfridge. But speaking for myself, I should have no difficulty in the circumstances of this case in holding it proved that the agreement was truly made by Dew as agent for Dunlop, or in other words that Dunlop was the undisclosed principal, and as such can sue on the agreement. None the less, in order to enforce it he must show consideration, as above defined, moving from Dunlop to Selfridge.

In the circumstances, how can he do so? The agreement in question is not an agreement for sale. It is only collateral to an agreement for sale; but that agreement for sale is an agreement entirely between Dew and Selfridge. The tyres, the property in which upon the bargain is transferred to Selfridge, were the property of Dew, not of Dunlop, for Dew under this agreement with Dunlop held these tyres as proprietor, and not as agent. What then did Dunlop do, or forbear to do, in a question with Selfridge? The answer must be, nothing. He did not do anything, for Dew, having the right of property in the tyres, could give a good title to any one he liked, subject, it might be, to an action of damages at the instance of Dunlop for breach of contract, which action, however, could never create a *vitium reale* in the property of the tyres. He did not forbear in anything, for he had no action against Dew which he gave up, because Dew had fulfilled his contract with Dunlop in obtaining, on the occasion of the sale, a contract from Selfridge in the terms prescribed.

To my mind, this ends the case. That there are methods of framing a contract which will cause persons in the position of Selfridge to become bound, I do not doubt. But that has not been done in this instance; and as Dunlop's advisers must have known of the law of consideration, it is their affair that they have not so drawn the contract.

I think the appeal should be dismissed.

Notes

(1) The expression *ius quaesitum tertio* ('right acquired by a third party') refers to Scottish law where contracts for the benefit of third parties have long been recognised.[5]

(2) There are two main objections against giving the third party an enforceable right as against the promisor. One is that no promise was made by the promisor to the third party, and the other is that the third party did not provide consideration. The first objection can be overcome if one accepts Lord Dunedin's view that Dews made the agreement with Selfridge as an agent for Dunlop. Since this would make Dunlop a party to the agreement, Selfridge's promise could be viewed as having been made to Dunlop. To overcome the second objection the agreement between Dews and Selfridge would have to be framed so as to show that Dunlop provided some sort of consideration in return for Selfridge's promise to pay £5 to Dunlop in the event of a breach of the restrictions imposed by them.

(3) In *Beswick v Beswick*[6] a coal merchant of more than 70 years old made a written contract with his nephew: the merchant was to transfer his whole coal business to the nephew, and in return the nephew was to pay £6 per week to the coal merchant while he lived and, after his death, £5 per week to his widow. After the coal merchant died, the nephew refused to make the agreed payments to the widow, and she sued him both in her own right and as administratrix, ie as a person appointed by law to manage the estate of her deceased husband who had died intestate. The House of Lords held that the widow had no claim in her own right, English law knowing nothing of a *ius quaesitum tertio* by way of contract. It was only in her capacity as

---

[5] However, the law of Scotland was long considered to be unsatisfactory because many aspects of the *ius quaesitum tertio* were uncertain or impracticable. The Contract (Third Party Rights) (Scotland) Act 2017 achieved a major reform of this area of Scottish law.

[6] [1968] AC 58 (HL).

administratrix that the House of Lords was able to award her a decree ordering the nephew to perform the agreement specifically.

(4) Suppose in *Beswick v Beswick* the nephew had been the administrator, rather than the widow. Do you think it would have been fair to let the widow go away empty-handed? How could the agreement between the coal merchant and the nephew have been arranged so as to give the widow an indisputable right to the £5 per week?

(5) The unquestionable need to recognise the rights of third parties to a contract was, until 1999, only partially satisfied in English law by a number of isolated, albeit important, exceptions. Section 11 of the Married Women's Property Act 1882 provides that a husband or wife and/or their children may sue the insurance company on a life insurance policy made for their benefit by a spouse or parent. This Act does not apply if the insured intended another relative (eg a niece) or a charitable organisation to benefit from the policy. Other statutes provide that third parties may enforce marine and fire insurance policies, and this applies also to some other types of liability insurance, such as motor insurance. Insurance that is intended to benefit third parties is very common and insurance companies seldom 'took the privity point': it would probably mean commercial ruin for an insurance company to set up the privity rule as a defence against an otherwise indisputable claim by a beneficiary. However, if the insurer disputed whether the claim was valid or the amount that had been lost, it could prove difficult for a beneficiary whose claim did not fall within one of the statutory exceptions.[7] Further exceptions have been carved out at common law.[8]

(6) The rigid rule against enforcement of third party rights was frequently criticised. The following case provides a useful summary of the proposals for reform that were mooted throughout the twentieth century.

Court of Appeal   **31.6 (EN)**

***Darlington Borough Council v Wiltshier Northern Ltd*[9]**

Under the privity rule, a contract cannot be treated as having been made for the benefit of a third party so as to enable the latter to sue on it. Although there is a powerful case for reform of the rule, it can only be amended or abolished by statute or by resolution of the House of Lords in an appropriate case.

Facts: A borough council wanted to create a new recreational centre on land which the council already owned. The straightforward way of doing this would have been for the council to enter into a building contract with a construction company and to raise the money to pay for the work by borrowing. However, as there were restrictions on local authority borrowing, a finance company (Morgan Grenfell) entered into the contract with Wiltshier Northern Ltd, a construction company, to build the recreational centre. According to an agreement with the council, Morgan Grenfell then assigned to it all rights and causes of action against Wiltshier to which Morgan Grenfell was entitled under the contract.

---

[7] eg *Mulchrone v Swiss Life (UK) plc* [2005] EWHC 1808 (Comm).
[8] E McKendrick, *Contract Law* (12th edn, London: Palgrave, 2017) 137–52.
[9] [1995] 1 WLR 68.

Held: The Court of Appeal held that damages for loss caused by Wiltshier's breaches could be claimed by the council as assignee. The result was not straightforward because an assignee is not entitled to recover more than the assignor (Morgan Grenfell) could have recovered and, as a general rule, a claimant can only claim damages for his own loss. The first instance judge held that Morgan Grenfell would not have had a claim against them if the assignment had not taken place because they did not have a proprietary interest in the site and they did not suffer any loss. The Court of Appeal surmounted these hurdles. Steyn LJ noted that they would not exist if contracts for the benefit of third parties were recognised under English law.

Judgment: Steyn LJ: In order lawfully to avoid the financial constraints of the Local Government Act 1972 Morgan Grenfell acted as financier to the council in connection with the construction of the Dolphin Centre in Darlington. Morgan Grenfell entered into building contracts with Wiltshier for the benefit of the council. That is how the transaction was structured and that is how all three parties saw it. And it is, of course, manifest that the council, as the third party, accepted the benefit of the building contract. But for the rule of privity of contract the council could simply have sued on the contract made for its benefit.

The case for recognising a contract for the benefit of a third party is simple and straightforward. The autonomy of the will of the parties should be respected. The law of contract should give effect to the reasonable expectations of contracting parties. Principle certainly requires that a burden should not be imposed on a third party without his consent. But there is no doctrinal, logical or policy reason why the law should deny effectiveness to a contract for the benefit of a third party where that is the expressed intention of the parties. Moreover, often the parties, and particularly third parties, organise their affairs on the faith of the contract. They rely on the contract. It is therefore unjust to deny effectiveness to such a contract ...

While the privity rule was barely tolerable in Victorian England, it has been recognised for half a century that it has no place in our more complex commercial world. Indeed, as early as 1915, in *Dunlop Pneumatic Tyre Co Ltd v Selfridge & Co Ltd* [1915] AC 847, 855, when the House of Lords restated the privity rule, Lord Dunedin observed in a dissenting speech that the rule made.

> 'it possible for a person to snap his fingers at a bargain deliberately made, a bargain not in itself unfair, and which the person seeking to enforce it has a legitimate interest to enforce.'

Among the majority, Viscount Haldane LC asserted as a self-evident truth, at p 853, that 'only a person who is a party to a contract can sue on it.' Today the doctrinal objection to the recognition of a *stipulatio alteri* continues to hold sway. While the rigidity of the doctrine of consideration has been greatly reduced in modern times, the doctrine of privity of contract persists in all its artificial technicality.

In 1937 the Law Revision Committee in its Sixth Report (Cmd. 5449, para 41–48) proposed the recognition of a right of a third party to enforce the contract which by its express terms purports to confer a benefit directly on him. In 1967, in *Beswick v Beswick* [1968] AC 58, 72, Lord Reid observed that if there was a long period of delay in passing legislation on the point the House of Lords might have to deal with the matter. Twelve years later Lord Scarman, who as a former chairman of the Law Commission usually favoured legislative rather than judicial reform where radical change was involved, reminded the House that it might be necessary to review all the cases which 'stand guard over this unjust rule': *Woodar Investment Development Ltd v Wimpey Construction UK Ltd* [1980] 1 WLR 277, 300G. ... In 1983 Lord Diplock described the rule as 'an anachronistic shortcoming that has for many years been regarded as a reproach to English private law': *Swain v The Law Society* [1983] 1 AC 598, 611D.

But as important as judicial condemnations of the privity rule is the fact that distinguished academic lawyers have found no redeeming virtues in it: see, for example, Markesinis (1987) 103 *LQR* 354; Reynolds (1989) 105 *LQR* 1; Beatson (1992) 45 *CLP* 1 and Adams and Brownsword (1993) 56 *MLR* 722. And we do well to remember that the civil law legal systems of other members of the European Union recognise such contracts. That our legal system lacks such flexibility is a disadvantage in the single market. Indeed it is a historical curiosity that the legal system of a mercantile country such as England, which in other areas of the law of contract (such as, for example, the objective theory of the interpretation of contracts) takes great account of the interests of third parties, has not been able to rid itself of this unjust rule deriving from a technical conception of a contract as a purely bilateral vinculum iuris.

In 1991 the Law Commission revisited this corner of the law. In cautious language appropriate to a consultation paper the Law Commission has expressed the provisional recommendation that 'there should be a (statutory) reform of the law to allow third parties to enforce contractual provisions made in their favour': Privity of Contract: [Contracts] for the Benefit of Third Parties, Consultation Paper No 121, p 132. The principal value of the consultation paper lies in its clear analysis of the practical need for the recognition of a contract for the benefit of third parties, and the explanation of the unedifying spectacle of judges trying to invent exceptions to the rule to prevent demonstrable unfairness. No doubt there will be a report by the Law Commission in the not too distant future recommending the abolition of the privity of contract rule by statute. What will then happen in regard to the proposal for legislation? The answer is really quite simple: probably nothing will happen.

But on this occasion I can understand the inaction of Parliament. There is a respectable argument that it is the type of reform which is best achieved by the courts working out sensible solutions on a case by case basis, eg, in regard to the exact point of time when the third party is vested with enforceable contractual rights: see Consultation Paper No 121, para 5.8. But that requires the door to be opened by the House of Lords reviewing the major cases which are thought to have entrenched the rule of privity of contract. Unfortunately, there will be few opportunities for the House of Lords to do so. After all, by and large, courts of law in our system are the hostages of the arguments deployed by counsel. And Mr Furst for the council, the third party, made it clear to us that he will not directly challenge the privity rule if this matter should go to the House of Lords. He said that he is content to try to bring his case within exceptions to the privity rule or what Lord Diplock in *Swain v The Law Society* [1983] 1 AC 598, 611D, described as 'juristic subterfuges ... to mitigate the effect of the lacuna resulting from the non-recognition of a *jus quaesitum tertio* ...'.

Note

The report by the Law Commission mentioned by Steyn LJ was published in 1996.[10] It did indeed recommend the recognition of third party rights in limited circumstances, and it was implemented by the Contracts (Rights of Third Parties)

[10] The Law Commission, *Privity of Contract: Contracts for the Benefit of Third Parties*, Law Com No 242 (London: The Stationery Office, 1996).

Act 1999, which carves out substantial exceptions to the doctrine of privity of contract. Section 1 of the Act explicitly allows that, subject to a number of restrictions, 'a person who is not a party to a contract (a "third party") may in his own right enforce a term of the contract'. We will analyse this provision in the next section of this chapter.

31.2 REQUIREMENTS FOR THE CONFERRAL OF A RIGHT ON A THIRD PARTY

Once a legal system has recognised a third person's right to enforce a contract to which he is not a party, the further question arises under what conditions the third party will be accorded a right of action. There are many contracts whose performance will be of some benefit to a third person or persons. However, not every such contract should be enforceable by the third person, so it is necessary to establish standards and guidelines for the decision as to whether in a given case a third person can sue on a contract as a third-party beneficiary.

31.2.A AGREEMENT OF THE PARTIES IN GENERAL

As a general rule,[11] all that is required is that the parties to the contract must have agreed on the conferral of an enforceable *right*, as opposed to a mere benefit, on behalf of a third person. It is therefore not sufficient that a third party stands to benefit from performance of the contract. For example, if retailer A agrees with landowner B that it will open a large store in B's shopping centre,[12] C, the owner of a nearby café, might benefit very much from increased passing trade, but that will not be enough to give C the right to sue either A or B if the contract between them is not performed. Nor even will it suffice that the parties have provided that one or both of them may discharge his liability by rendering performance to someone else. If the buyer, at the seller's request, is to pay the price to the seller's creditor rather than to the seller himself, or if the seller is to deliver the goods to the buyer's order rather than to him personally, each party, in rendering performance to a third party, is performing an obligation which he owes only to his contractor and not to the third party. The seller's creditor cannot sue the buyer for the purchase price; the person designated by the buyer cannot successfully bring an action for delivery of the goods.

The situation is different where the parties have agreed that the third party is to be entitled not only to receive the promised performance, but to demand that performance from the promisor. This can be seen from the language of Article 6:110(1) of the Principles of

---

[11] For an exception, see Art 6:253(1) BW which, in addition to the agreement of the parties, requires acceptance by the third person, see above, p 1261. The third person is then 'deemed to be a party to the contract' (Art 6:254(1) BW). However, even under Dutch law, this requirement is in effect negated because the courts are willing to assume an 'acceptance' of the third party at the stage when the third party enforces its right flowing from the contract.

[12] cf above, p 940.

European Contract Law (PECL) ('may require performance') and Article 6:253(1) BW ('creates the right for a third person to claim a performance from one of the parties').[13] German and English law are equally explicit:

BGB   **31.7 (DE)**

§ 328: Contract for the benefit of a third party

(1) A contract may stipulate performance for the benefit of a third party, so that the third party acquires the right directly to demand performance.

(2) In the absence of express stipulation it is to be deduced from the circumstances, especially from the object of the contract, whether the third party shall acquire the right, whether the right of the third party shall arise forthwith or only under certain conditions, and whether any right shall be reserved to the contracting parties to take away or modify the right of the third party without his consent.

Contracts (Rights of Third Parties) Act 1999   **31.8 (EN)**

Section 1: Right of third party to enforce contractual term

(1) Subject to the provisions of this Act, a person who is not a party to a contract (a 'third party') may in his own right enforce a term of the contract if—

(a) the contract expressly provides that he may, or

(b) subject to subsection (2), the contract purports to confer a benefit on him.

(2) Subsection (1)(b) above does not apply if on a proper construction of the contract it appears that the parties did not intend the term to be enforceable by the third party.

(3) The third party must be expressly identified in the contract by name, as a member of a class or as answering a particular description but need not be in existence when the contract is entered into.

(4) ...

Both provisions recognise that the parties' agreement to confer an enforceable right on the third person can be either express or implied. In the absence of express agreement, the contract must be interpreted by looking at the relevant circumstances, such as the purpose of the agreement, the interests of the parties and the circumstances of the individual case. However, under the Contracts (Rights of Third Parties) Act 1999 the circumstances in which an intention to confer a right can be implied are much more limited than under the BGB provision. First, s 1(3) requires that the third party be expressly identified in the contract, though not necessarily by name. As has been said in the Court of Appeal, 'section 1(3), by use of the word "express", simply does not allow a process of construction or implication.'[14] And secondly, under s 1(2) the terms of the contract must purport

---

[13] The provisions are reproduced above, pp 1259 and 1261.

[14] *Avraamides v Colwill* [2006] EWCA Civ 1533 at [19], per Waller LJ. In that case the agreement by which A agreed to buy a company (B) that was in financial trouble provided that A would 'complete outstanding customer orders taking into account any deposits paid by customers as at 31 March 2003, and to pay in the normal course of time any liabilities properly incurred by the company.' A customer of the company tried to make A liable for earlier breaches by the company. The Court of Appeal held that the part of the contract that referred to 'liabilities' did not identify to whom the liability was owed and therefore s 1(3) of the Act was not satisfied.

to confer a benefit on C, which seems to require more than that C is merely mentioned in the contract.[15]

It is, however, important to note the specific interplay of sub-sections (1)(b) and (2) of section 1 of the 1999 Act. In the absence of express provision by the parties, a right of action will always be conferred on a party on whom the contract purports to confer a benefit, as long as the contract, as interpreted objectively, does not positively show that the parties did *not* intend that result. In other words, once it appears from the terms of the contract that C is to obtain a benefit under it, there is a strong 'presumption of enforceability' that can only be rebutted if the parties have expressly stated *not* to confer a right or if it is otherwise obvious from the circumstances that they did not wish to do so. This presumption was introduced in order to ensure that the courts would not unduly narrow down the scope of the Act by entertaining the argument that the parties could not possibly have intended to create an enforceable right in a third person unless they had expressly said so. The drafters of the BGB considered the enactment of a similar presumption, and they did so for similar reasons. However, in the end they trusted the interpretative skills of the courts. Therefore § 328(2) BGB requires that the contract, as interpreted objectively, positively shows that the parties *did* have a corresponding intention.

With or without guidance by a presumption, in many cases the outcome will be obvious. Where A contracts with B to erect an apartment building on B's land, the owner of the adjoining land (C) will not be permitted to enforce the contract against A or B even though he may run a department store on the adjoining land which will benefit from the construction of the building. On the other hand, where an insurance company promises the insured to pay an agreed sum to the insured's wife after his death there will be little doubt that the wife can enforce the policy by bringing a suit against the insurer in her own name. Between these two cases there is a large area in which the decision is more difficult.

The following cases provide examples of courts taking the entire factual and legal background into account when determining whether the parties have, albeit not expressly, agreed on conferring an enforceable right on a third party.

BGH, 17 January 1985[16]   **31.9 (DE)**

Airline charter

If a holiday tour operator charters from an airline seats on certain flights, a customer, after having booked one of those seats with the operator, is a third-party beneficiary of the charter agreement. The customer therefore has an independent right to sue the airline for damages if he was wrongfully denied his seat as booked.

Facts: The defendant, an airline company, agreed with T to provide a return charter flight from Frankfurt to Santa Lucia and back from 9 to 16 December 1980. A number of seats were assigned by T to O, a travel agency. On 15 December 1980, T suspended payments. On 16 December 1980, the defendant airline company refused Ms H, who had booked a journey to Santa Lucia, a place on the return flight to Frankfurt. The refusal

---

[15] On this see below, pp 1295–96.
[16] BGHZ 93, 271, NJW 1985, 1457. For this decision, see also below, p 1350.

was based on the fact that T had not paid for that flight. Ms H took a flight with another airline. The courts trying the case on the substantive issues ordered O to reimburse the sum of $1,783.60, together with interest. The claimant, an insurance company, repaid to O the sums incurred by it in legal proceedings and the sum which it was found liable to pay in the proceedings. The total amount was then claimed from the defendant by the claimant.

Held: The courts trying the case on the substantive issues upheld the claim in part and ordered the defendant to pay the sum of DM 4,579.69. The defendant's appeal on a point of law was dismissed.

Judgment: 1. On the basis of the travel contract concluded between Ms H and Company O as travel operator, Ms H had a claim against Company O for transport from Frankfurt/Main to Santa Lucia and back (§ 651a(1) BGB). This claim for transport also existed (as the appeal court rightly held) as against the defendant. It is correct that there were no contractual relationships between Ms H and the defendant. Most importantly, travel operator O did not act as an agent of the defendant. However, Ms H had booked two of the seats which the defendant had charted to Company T when she concluded the travel contract for herself and her companion. The charter contract concluded between the defendant and Company T is a contract for transport for the benefit of Ms H (cf BGHZ 52, 194, 201, 202; …).

a) Contrary to the submission of the appellant, it cannot be said that such a contract for the benefit of Ms H did not exist because the charter contract does not contain an agency clause, because the flight tickets had been issued by Company T, and not by the defendant, and because the defendant did not know the persons who had to be transported. Now it is true that BGHZ 52, 194, 202 and the legal writers supporting this decision … have held the existence of an 'agency' clause, according to which the charter contract is concluded both in the charterer's own name and for the benefit of the individual passengers who fall to be transported, to be particularly important for establishing whether a contract for the benefit of a third party has been concluded. However, such a clause is not the crucial factor for classifying the charter contract a contract for the benefit of third parties. Nor is it decisive whether the flight tickets are issued by Company T or by the defendant.

Under the charter contract, the chartered party is obliged to make available to the charterer seats on the flights organised by him. The chartered party is aware of the fact that the persons who fall to be transported are usually designated by the charterer or, as in this case, by a third person who has been authorised to do so only after the conclusion of the charter contract, on the basis of a package travel contract. It is therefore the purpose of the charter contract which is relevant under § 328(2) BGB to provide transport for air passengers who are identified to the chartered party by the charterer or by a third person by way of issuing a flight ticket in their name. It is the intention of the contracting parties to achieve this purpose. It is therefore appropriate to assume that the air passengers who would not usually be known at the time of the conclusion of the charter contract, and *in whose interests* the charter contract was concluded, have a direct contractual claim for transportation against the chartered party even if the charter contract does not contain an agency clause and the flight tickets have not been issued by the chartered party itself.

b) Contrary to the submission of the appellant, § 651a BGB does not preclude assuming a contract for the benefit of a third party either. Certainly, under § 651a BGB, the *contractual* partner of a traveller who has entered into a travel contract is, as a general rule, only the travel agent. The travel agent may use other persons to provide specific tour services as persons whom he uses to perform his obligation. However, § 651a BGB—which concerns the relationship between the travel agent and the traveller only—does not rule out that, as a consequence of the specific contractual arrangement, the traveller has claims against these other persons *in addition to* the claim against the travel agent. The prevailing opinion of legal writers is correct in assuming that it is possible to regard the contract between the travel agent and the person who provides specific tour services as a contract for the benefit of a third party which confers direct contractual claims against the service provider on the traveller (see Beuthien …).

c) Finally, the interests of the parties are only served if the charter contract is seen as a contract for the benefit of the traveller. In the case of air package tours in particular, the traveller depends, as can be seen from the present case, to a large extent on the services of the chartered party. The traveller's interest in a journey that is as free from trouble as possible therefore requires that he be able to make his claim for transportation not only against the travel agent but also against the airline. By contrast, the interests of the chartered party in only being obliged to render performance to the travel agent are of comparatively little weight.

Notes

(1) The Court held that the contract genuinely conferred a right on a third party, that is to say, it created a real contractual right in favour of a person not directly a party to the contract—in the present case, the traveller. The latter had a direct right of action in relation to the performance of the contract and, in addition, a right to claim damages.

(2) How would the case be decided under the Contracts (Rights of Third Parties) Act 1999 in England? It is thought that the outcome might be different. The German Court held that the traveller acquired rights under the charter agreement for the aircraft made between the defendant and T. However, it is not obvious that the charter—which probably referred only to providing an aircraft with a certain carrying capacity—'purported to confer a benefit' (the words of s 1(1)(b) of the 1999 Act) on the individual travellers. Possibly an English court might be able to find that a contract for the benefit of the traveller was made when the airline was notified of the names of the passengers and, by not rejecting any of them (eg on the grounds that they were suspected terrorists) implicitly agreed to carry them. (In practice the traveller would normally be refunded under a guarantee scheme. By law, every UK travel company which sells air holidays and flights is required to hold an ATOL, which stands for Air Travel Organiser's Licence, and this provides the guarantee. A further scheme is operated by the Association of British Travel Agents.)

(3) There are many other cases in which German courts have made use of the third-party beneficiary contract. If, for example, the lessor of a private clinic provides in the lease that a named specialist should have the right to reserve beds in it, the contract may be construed under § 328 so as to give the specialist an independent contractual right against the lessee.[17] The circumstances under which a person opens an account in a bank or savings bank, especially the name chosen for the account, may show that a third party should also have an immediate right to draw on the funds in the account.[18]

---

[17] BGH 16 November 1951, BGHZ 3, 385.
[18] BGH 25 June 1956, BGHZ 21, 148.

If a collective agreement between a trade union and an employers' federation contains a promise not to strike and the promise is broken, an individual employer may be able to claim damages in respect of the harm suffered by him, since the contract made by the employers' federation is to this extent a contract in favour of the individual employers who are its members.[19]

Cass civ (3), 4 February 1986[20]   **31.10 (FR)**

Selling bread

Where a landlord leases two neighbouring properties and inserts a clause into one lease restraining the lessee from using the property for the same purposes as the second property, that clause is made for the benefit of the lessee of the second property and cannot be deleted from the lease without his consent.

Facts: These were stated by the lower court (Bordeaux, 22 February 1984) as follows: '… Mr and Mrs Gomez are the owners of commercial premises situated in the same building which were let (a) to Mr Esteban for use as a shop for cakes and confectionery, subject to a restriction prohibiting their use for the sale of bread, and (b) to Mr Frappier for use as a baker's shop; by a rider to the lease granted to Mr Esteban, the restriction prohibiting the use of his premises for the sale of bread was removed with effect from 1 September 1978; Mr Frappier brought proceedings against Mr and Mrs Gomez and Mr Esteban, by which he sought an order restraining the use of the latter's premises for the sale of bread and, in addition, compensation for the loss suffered.'

Held: The cour d'appel held that Frappier could enforce the covenant given by Esteban to Gomez. The decision was upheld by the Cour de cassation.

Judgment: As regards the first two pleas, considered together: … —Whereas Mr and Mrs Gomez and Mr Esteban contest the judgment of the cour d'appel allowing those claims; as according to their appeal ground, they argue, 'first, that, on the one hand, it was not open to the cour d'appel, having itself ruled that a stipulation for the benefit of a third party must be express and that the absence of such an express stipulation in Mr Frappier's favour proved that the parties had not intended to confer a benefit on him, to go on to decide that, in the present case, despite the absence of any such form of wording, the parties had stipulated in favour of Mr Frappier; as, in so ruling, it is submitted that the cour d'appel infringed [former] Article 1121 Cciv; on the other hand, the clause permitting the lessee to "carry on the business of selling pastries, cakes and confectionery, dairy products and dietary products but excluding the sale of bread" does not constitute a provision for the benefit of a third party, being instead a clear, precise clause relating to the intended purpose of the premises which is binding solely on the lessee and the lessor; as, in so ruling, it is submitted that the cour d'appel infringed [former] Article 1121 Cciv; and, in addition, matters agreed in a contract take effect only as between the contracting parties; as in deciding that Mr Frappier, who was not a party to the contract and was not mentioned in it, should have been a party to the rider of 1 September 1978 deleting the clause at issue, it is submitted that the cour d'appel infringed [former] Article 1165 Cciv; and, moreover, and in any event, even if the clause at issue were capable of being construed as a stipulation for the benefit of a third party,

---

[19] BAG 10 February 1956, NJW 1957, 647.
[20] Gaz Pal 1986, 370, annotated by JD Barbier.

it could only vest in the baker an acquired right such that he could only be deprived of it without his consent if he had declared that he wished to avail himself of it; as in the absence of such a declaration, by ruling that the rider of 1 September 1978 deleting the clause in issue could not be relied on as against Mr Frappier, it is submitted that the cour d'appel infringed [former] Article 1121 Cciv. Secondly, ...'

— Whereas, however, in seeking to determine the common intention of the parties to the lease of the premises to be used as a shop for cakes and confectionery, the cour d'appel found, in its power of appreciation, that the clause prohibiting Mr Esteban from using the premises let to him for the sale of bread could only have been intended to benefit the lessee of the neighbouring baker's shop and that it constituted a stipulation, binding on the parties thereto, for the benefit of a third party; as the cour d'appel correctly held that, in order to be valid, the rider deleting that prohibition required the consent of Mr Frappier; on those grounds alone, it lawfully justified its decision in that regard; ...;

On those grounds, the Court dismisses the appeal ...

Cass civ (1), 21 November 1978[21]   **31.11 (FR)**

The Carrefour takings

A security company employed by a bank to collect takings from one of its customer's stores and which carried the takings in an ordinary car instead of the armoured vehicle stipulated is liable to the customer if the takings are stolen as a result.

Facts: On 8 March 1972 employees of the Société Parisienne de Surveillance (SPS) were engaged in loading into the boot of a Mercedes motor-car a trunk containing the takings of a Carrefour store operated by the Société des Grands Magasins Garonne-Adour (Sogara), with a view to transporting it to the head office of the Crédit Commercial de France (CCF) in Bordeaux, when armed raiders appeared, wounded one of the employees of SPS, seized the trunk and fled. Sogara brought legal proceedings for damages against SPS, which regularly transported funds to and from the store, and CCF under an agreement dated 28 June 1971 which had been concluded between CCF and SPS. The agreement obliged SPS to use armoured vehicles and to take out insurance. It also provided that Sogara would settle the invoices with SPS. Sogara claimed that SPS had failed to take all necessary precautions, and in particular that it had used an ordinary, unarmoured Mercedes motorcar.

Held: The cour d'appel found that the contract imposed a stipulation for the benefit of a third party, namely Sogara, on SPS, and since SPS had failed to fulfil its contractual obligations, ordered the latter to pay damages to Sogara. The Cour de cassation upheld this decision.

Judgment: THE COURT: *On the sole ground taken in its two branches:*—Whereas the appellant contests the decision of the second instance court, arguing, first, that a stipulation for the benefit of a third party cannot be said to exist merely by reason of the fact that the third party has an interest in the contract to which it was not a party; as a stipulation for the benefit of a third party can only exist where the contract creates a right in favour of the third party and does not impose an obligation on that third party; and, secondly, that the cour d'appel omitted to deal with SPS's submission that Sogara had been at fault because it had not objected to the transportation of the money in a Mercedes motorcar and that it had thus exonerated the carrier from liability;

— Whereas, however, the cour d'appel—adopting one of the grounds on which the decision of the first instance court had been based—held that SPS had undertaken in the

---

[21] No. 77-14653, Bull civ I no. 356, JCP 1980.I.19315, annotated by P Rodière.

agreement of 28 June 1971 to make armoured vehicles available to CCF and to provide teams of drivers and accompanying personnel with a view to ensuring the safe carriage of cash in consideration of the payment of a fixed-rate fee, and that it had further undertaken to take out insurance to cover the period from the time when the valuables were handed over to its personnel until the time when they were placed in the CCF's safe; as the cour d'appel could so consider that the contract created a right in favour of Sogara and could hold that this contract, which was concluded in the interests of both CCF and Sogara, contained a stipulation for the benefit of a third party, namely Sogara, the existence of a stipulation for the benefit of a third party not being excluded by the fact that the contract required Sogara to settle the invoices—a requirement which that company accepted; whereas, secondly, the cour d'appel—adopting, again, one of the grounds on which the decision of the first instance court had been based—found that it was not open to SPS to maintain that Sogara had authorised the use of the Mercedes motorcar, since Rolland, an employee of SPS, had admitted that the decision to use it had been taken by him alone and, in so concluding, the cour d'appel dealt with the submissions which the appellant had relied on; as none of the appeal grounds is consequently well-founded;

On those grounds, the Court dismisses the appeal lodged against the judgment delivered on 29 June 1977 by the cour d'appel, Bordeaux.

Notes

(1) The Cour de cassation holds that CCF and SPS concluded a contract for the benefit of Sogara although the contract does not expressly provide that Sogara should acquire an enforceable right. In doing so, the supreme court does not interpret the contract. It adopts the reasoning of the second instance court, the cour d'appel, which, in turn, relied on the grounds of the decision of the Court of first instance. Here we see again that the interpretation of a contract falls within the 'sovereign power of assessment' of the *juge du fond*. The higher courts will only review such a decision if it amounts to a 'distortion' (*dénaturation*) of a 'clear and unambiguous term' (*clause claire et précise*).[22] Therefore the lower courts enjoy considerable discretion to find the existence of contracts for the benefit of a third party on the basis of an alleged implied intention of the parties. In the *Selling Bread* case, above, the Cour de cassation also relied on 'the power of appreciation' of the lower instance court.[23]

Nevertheless, in both cases the Cour de cassation reproduced the reasons given by the lower courts for inferring the intention of creating an enforceable right in the third party. How convincing are these reasons?

(2) The first branch of the appeal ground invoked in *The Carrefour Takings* case relates to the principle of 'relative effect', as codified in Article ex-Article 1165 Cciv (now Article 1199). As has been seen above, the creation of a right in a third party by way of a *stipulation pour autrui* is one of the recognised exceptions to this principle.[24] However, the principle remains intact with regard to imposing *duties*, rather than

---

[22] See above, pp 733–36.
[23] Contrast Cass civ (2) 17 December 1954, Bull civ II no. 422, D 1955.269 (*Contaminated blood*), see below, p 1280.
[24] See above, p 1260.

rights on third persons. All legal systems agree that two parties cannot validly agree to create an *obligation* in a third person. In this case, however, the contract between the promisee (CFC) and the promisor (SPS) imposed an obligation on the third person, Sogara, namely to pay for the services rendered by SPS. The case note by Rodière refers to this point:

> If the burden imposed on the beneficiary were negligible or of a clearly secondary nature with regard to the benefit which he derives from the transaction, one could, unless one wants to be guilty of purism, agree to see in this transaction, globally, a stipulation for the benefit of a third party. But nothing like it in the present case: the obligation imposed on the beneficiary consists in paying the price of the transport from which he benefits— it is the exact consideration for the advantage which he derives from the promise. This is, therefore, squarely a synallagmatic contract made for a third person which is covered behind a stipulation for the benefit of a third party ... It can be seen how the *stipulation pour autrui* in the process of its formation is analogous to those other mechanisms which are so closely related to it—*negotiorum gestio* where the principal ratifies the intervention, and implied agency—and which also have the effect of binding another (someone other than those directly negotiating), whilst at the same time ensuring that he acquires rights. *Nothing more* is required to ensure that the third person is bound than what is required to make him a creditor: in both cases his acceptance is sufficient, his 'yes', which in both cases normally follows the same rules of consensual agreement. ... It is tempting to work on the hypothesis that this is a mandate. This works nicely on the facts of the case. We have already seen how the bank presents itself as a natural intermediary between the transporter of the money—a necessary accessory service for the business of the bank—and the person depositing funds with the bank. This position of a natural intermediary makes the bank the normal agent of the owner of the money, an agent found to act with regard to a transporter of money. Therefore one is moved towards the notion of an implied agency ...

Do you agree with the reclassification suggested by Rodière? What are the consequences following from it?

31.2.B 'IMPLIED STIPULATIONS FOR ANOTHER' AND 'CONTRACTS WITH PROTECTIVE EFFECT FOR THIRD PARTIES'

The agreement of the parties to create an enforceable right in the third person does not have to be express; nor, in either French or German law, does the third party have to be mentioned in the contract, as can be seen from the three previous cases. It is sufficient that, on an objective interpretation of the agreement, the parties agreed to create such a result. However, the courts in France and Germany have interpreted contracts boldly in a way that extends their scope to third parties, with no discernible reference to the intentions, the hypothetical intentions or sometimes even the typical interests of the parties involved. By using more or less fictitious implied agreements, they established contractual liability in cases where a third person suffers damage from the breach of a contractual duty of care owed by one party to the contract to the other party. German law, as we will see below, has abandoned the fiction and developed a freestanding doctrine to resolve cases of this type. French law still relies on the notion of an implied contract for the benefit of third parties although, for reasons discussed on pp 1281–82 below, there is increasingly less need to do so. In English law these cases have been addressed by other means, with different results; and as will be seen below, the cases would not fall within the Contracts (Rights of Third Parties) Act 1999.

We will discuss two types of case. The first concerns physical injury, the second pure economic loss.

31.2.B.1 PHYSICAL INJURY

31.2.B.1.1 France

An implied contract for the benefit of third parties or, more precisely, an 'implied stipulation for another' (*stipulation pour autrui implicite*) has been held to exist, for example, in contracts of carriage.

Cass civ, 6 December 1932[25]   **31.12 (FR)**

Fatal fall from train (I): wife and children

The obligation de securité *owed to a passenger is an implicit stipulation in favour of his wife and children.*

Facts: M Noblet had fallen from a train run by the defendant company. The victim's widow, acting on her own behalf and that of her minor children, sought compensation for the loss caused to them as a result of the accident. No fault on the part of the company was shown.

Held: The court of first instance held that the widow could recover without proving fault on the part of the railway, and an appeal was dismissed. The Cour de cassation dismissed the further appeal.

Judgment: THE COURT: *On the first appeal ground*:—Whereas Noblet, an infantry captain, had taken a seat in a carriage headed for Angers and he fell on to the track and his death was instantaneous; as the victim's widow, acting on her own behalf and that of her minor children, sought compensation for the loss caused to them as a result of the accident;

— Whereas since no fault on the part of the company was shown, the cour d'appel declined to apply [former] Article 1382; it none the less upheld the claim for damages pursuant to the rules on contractual liability and [former] Article 1147 Cciv;

— Whereas according to the appeal ground, widow Noblet and her minor children were unable to recover the damages awarded to them under [former] Article 1147 alone; as standing in the shoes of the victim, they were entitled under that article only to damages for the physical injury suffered by the deceased as a result of the accident, prior to his demise; since death was instantaneous, there was no injury of a kind to satisfy that provision; as thus, being unable to establish fault on the part of the company, widow Noblet and her minor children were not entitled to damages;

— Whereas, however, under the contract of carriage, the railway company assumes as regards the person to be conveyed an obligation to carry him safely to his destination; as in the event of a fatal accident occurring during the course of performance of the contract, there was a right to obtain compensation under [former] Article 1147 Cciv in favour of the victim's spouse and children for whose benefit also, and to the extent

---

[25] DP 1933.1.137, annotated by L Josserand.

of their interest, the victim struck the bargain, without there being any need to do so expressly. ...

— On those grounds the appeal against the decision of the cour d'appel of Angers of 13 May 1929 is dismissed.

Notes

(1) The Court held that, on taking his ticket, the traveller is also impliedly contracting on behalf of his spouse and children. The parties do not confer a right to claim performance on the third party but rather the right to claim damages for non-performance or defective performance of the obligation to provide safe carriage.[26] This gives the beneficiaries of such a *stipulation pour autrui* the advantage of a direct contractual action against the carrier.

(2) Had the Court not assumed the existence of an 'implied stipulation for another' the carrier would not have been liable to Noblet's widow and children. They could not bring an action in the law of delict or tort (either as the deceased's successors in title or in their own right) because they were not able to prove the defendant's negligence/fault (*faute*) under ex-Article 1382 Cciv. By contrast, in a contractual action under French law the burden of proof is on the defendant: he is required to show that no negligence on his part was involved in his non-performance or defective performance, but that it was rather due to *force majeure* (ex-Article 1147 Cciv). However, the claimants could not bring a contractual action as successors of Noblet: he himself would not have had a claim because his death had been 'instantaneous', and thus he had not suffered physical injury prior to his demise. Making the claimants a 'party' to the contract between Noblet and the defendant company was the only way of establishing liability. As we will see later in this chapter, judges would not have to find a way to create a contractual relationship between the wrongdoer and the deceased's successors today as the doctrine of liability for the action of things is now more lenient. Thus this case illustrates how contract rules develop in relation to their legal environment.

(3) In his annotation of the *Noblet* case, Josserand called the doctrine of the implied stipulation for the benefit of another a 'purely fictitious mental operation invented to satisfy the needs of the case'. Indeed, it cannot be seriously argued that every time a passenger buys a train or bus ticket he has the actual or implied intention of making a kind of testamentary disposition by stipulating, for his relatives, a right to sue the carrier in contract in case of a fatal accident. It may therefore be assumed that the underlying motive of the Cour de cassation's sidestepping the confines of tort law was the desire to further a strong social policy of granting maximum protection to the innocent dependants of fatally injured victims of accidents.

(4) The desire to benefit third parties like the widow Noblet is understandable. The downside of this solution is the potentially huge increase in claims for contractual damages, coupled with the near impossibility for parties to a contract to foresee their liability. The Court seems to have recognised this. Only a few months after the *Noblet* case it limited the circle of potential beneficiaries of an implied *stipulation pour autrui*.

---

[26] For the notion of *obligation de sécurité*, see above, pp 144 and 790.

Fatal fall from train (II): the sister

The railway's obligation de securité *is presumed to be a stipulation only in favour of those to whom the passenger owed a legal duty of support.*

Facts: A railway passenger fell to his death in unexplained circumstances. His sister, whom he had supported financially, brought a claim.

Held: The lower court dismissed the claim and this decision was upheld on appeal. The Cour de cassation dismissed the further appeal.

Judgment: THE COURT: *On the sole appeal ground:*—Whereas the appeal alleges that the contested judgment wrongly declined to award Miss Falduti damages for the injury occasioned to her as a result of the accidental death of her brother who provided for all her needs and who died following a fall from a moving train on the company's network from Paris to Lyon and the Mediterranean;

— Whereas, however, the judgment shows that the causes of the fatal fall remained unknown and that the claimant neither proved nor offered evidence to prove that it was owing to the carrier's fault; as although a traveller who is the victim of a fatal accident must be presumed to have contracted in favour of the persons to whom he was legally bound by a duty of support, such a presumption may not be extended to a case in which, as in the present case, a claimant is unable to set up in support of her action any such legal duty; from which it follows that on the facts as found in the judgment and notwithstanding the incorrect reasoning challenged in the appeal, there is sufficient warrant in law for the operative provision of the judgment.

— On those grounds the appeal against the decision of the cour d'appel of Paris of 11 July 1928 is dismissed.

Notes

(1) The Cour de cassation ties the conferral of a benefit on the third party to the existence of a duty of support owed by the victim to the claimant. The circle of potential beneficiaries is therefore limited to close relatives (spouses, parents and children).

(2) The Cour de cassation has been reluctant to extend the doctrine of implied contracts for the benefit of third parties to other types of contract. For example, in 2003 the Court confirmed a judgment that had rejected the notion of a holiday travel contract containing an 'implied stipulation' for the benefit of close relatives of persons who had been killed while being on an excursion abroad with a dugout canoe,[28] although it might be argued that the position of the travel agency does not differ materially from that of the carrier.

(3) However, the Court has consistently applied the doctrine to contracts for the supply of blood, as will be seen in the following case.

---

[27] DP 1933.1.137, annotated by L Josserand.
[28] Cass civ (1) 28 October 2003, nos. 00-18794 and 00-20065, Bull I no. 219, D 2004, 233, annotated by P Delebecque.

Cass civ (2), 17 December 1954[29] **31.14 (FR)**

Contaminated blood

A patient who receives a blood transfusion in a public hospital is a third-party beneficiary of a contract under which the National Blood Transfusion Centre supplies blood to hospitals and can thus recover if the blood is contaminated, unless the National Blood Transfusion Centre shows force majeure.

Facts: In the course of treatment at a hospital, the claimant was given a transfusion of blood which the hospital had obtained under a contract between the public services which were in charge of the hospital and the Centre National de Transfusion Sanguine (the National Blood Transfusion Centre). The blood was contaminated and the claimant was infected by it.

Held: The cour d'appel held that the claimant could recover even though no fault had been shown. The National Blood Transfusion Centre appealed against the decision but the Cour de cassation upheld it.

Judgment: THE COURT: *As regards the first two appeal grounds, considered together:—* Whereas it appears from the contested judgment that a blood transfusion was ordered in the course of treatment which Mrs L was undergoing at the Boucicaut Hospital; the staff of that establishment requested assistance from the Centre National de Transfusion Sanguine which nominated Miss V as the blood donor; the latter was affected by syphilis, and this illness was transmitted to Mrs L;

— Whereas it is complained in the appeal that the cour d'appel wrongly held, in an essentially contractual matter, that the Centre National de Transfusion Sanguine was liable in tort for the commission of a fault in relation to Mrs L, and that it based its assessment of the damage caused to her on matters of pure conjecture, notwithstanding that no fault of any kind whatsoever was proved to have been committed by the member of the medical staff concerned and that, according to the medical practices accepted and recognised at the time of the accident, no fault attached to anyone;

— Whereas whilst simultaneously applying to the administrative court for a declaration that the public services [which were in charge of the hospital] were liable for the acts of their own servants, Mrs L obtained from the civil courts, on the basis of [former] Article 1382, an order requiring the Centre National de Transfusion Sanguine to pay damages;

— Whereas it is, however, for the Cour de cassation to determine the true nature of the legal relationships inferred by the lower courts from the findings of fact made by it in its sovereign power of assessment;

— Whereas it is not disputed that the agreement concluded between the public services and the appellant Centre National de Transfusion Sanguine had the object of procuring for the hospitalised patient the assistance of a blood donor with a view to providing medical treatment which had been prescribed and that that agreement was thus accompanied by a stipulation for the benefit of a third party, made on behalf of Mrs L, who, although she was not a party to the original contract and was not in any way represented by an agent, was none the less meant to benefit from the contractual obligation entered into for her sake; as the non-performance of that obligation by the party by whom

---

[29] No. 2154, D 1955, 269, annotated by M Rodière, JCP 1955.II.8490, annotated by R Savatier. For a similar solution in more recent cases concerning the supply of blood contaminated with the HIV virus, see TGI Paris 1 July 1991, JCP 1991.II.21762, annotated by M Harichaux; Cass civ (2) 20 October 2005, no. 03-19420, Bull civ II no. 274, RTD civ 2006, 122, annotated by P Jourdain.

it was owed was consequently such as to make the latter directly liable for the resulting damage to the party to whom it was owed, by virtue of the combined effect of [former] Articles 1121 and 1135 Cciv;

— Whereas, moreover, against the background of the contractual relationship which it has itself pleaded, the appellant has neither proved nor even alleged that the breach of the obligation at issue arose, in accordance with [former] Article 1147 Cciv, as a result of some extraneous cause, such as *force majeure*, which cannot be attributed to it; as in making the factual finding that, in circumstances not involving any negligence of a medical nature, 'Mrs L was infected with contaminated blood', the court adjudicating on the substance of the case established that the Centre National de Transfusion Sanguine had failed to provide the proper service which Mrs L was entitled to expect, and it based on the fault thus committed a right to receive compensation; on that purely legal ground, which automatically supplants all others attacked in the appeal, it follows that the contested judgment is justified in law.

— On those grounds, the Court dismisses the appeal.

Notes

(1) As in its previous decisions on contracts of transport, the Court's reliance on a contract for the benefit of a third party was clearly motivated in this case by its desire to make up for what it felt to be a deficiency of tort law. The claimant had originally based her claim on tort but had not been able to prove the defendant's negligence under former Article 1382 Cciv (new Article 1240 Cciv). The device of putting into the claimant's hands one end of the contractual *vinculum iuris* made it possible for the Court to improve significantly her position: as has been seen before, on a contractual approach ex-Article 1147 Cciv (new Article 1231-1 Cciv) requires the defendant to prove that no negligence on his part was involved in passing on contaminated blood and that this was due to *force majeure*.

(2) There was no contract between the patient and the public hospital. The patient was a 'user of public services', and her relationship to the hospital was governed by administrative law.

(3) Contrast this case with the *Fatal fall from train* cases with regard to the position of the person who is suffering physical injury vis-à-vis the contract on which liability is based.

(4) Contrast this case with the *Selling bread* and *The Carrefour takings* cases[30] with regard to the reliance of the Cour de cassation on the findings of the lower courts.

(5) The extent to which the courts have been willing to imply a stipulation for the benefit of another has varied over the decades. It seems to have been on the wane whenever other mechanisms for achieving the desired liability of the party who did not perform its obligations were available. For example, the need for the dependants of victims of accidents occurred in the performance of a contract of carriage to sue as contract beneficiaries has declined. Since the 1930s French courts have improved the protection of tort law significantly. Under ex-Article 1384(1) (now Article 1242) Cciv

---

[30] See above, pp 1273–75.

the dependants must prove only that their relative was killed through the operation of a bus, train or other 'thing' under the control of the defendant at the time of the accident. It is then up to the defendant to show that the accident was caused by *force majeure* or by the act of a third person for which he was not responsible. Furthermore, from the 1960s onwards, a number of pieces of legislation were enacted (frequently in order to implement international conventions) which provide for contractual claims of the relatives of victims of transport accidents. The different limitation periods for contractual and delictual claims were aligned by the reform of the law of prescription in 2008. Finally, the implementation of the Product Liability Directive[31] in ex-Articles 1386-1 to 1386-18 (now Articles 1245 to 1245-17) Cciv provides for a regime of strict liability, whether contractual or delictual, which might have helped the claimant in the *Contaminated blood* case.

(6) Treating a third person as a party to the contract seems to give it additional rights. But what if the contract terms validly restrict the liability of the party who did not perform its contractual obligations, eg the carrier? In such a case, the Cour de cassation has allowed the third party to renounce the contract made for its benefit.

Cass civ (2), 23 January 1959[32]　　　　　　　　　**31.15 (FR)**

Drowning caused by negligence

The heirs of a deceased passenger may renounce the stipulation in their favour and sue in delict, thereby avoiding the effect of a contractual limitation of liability.

Facts: A passenger travelling under a contract which limited the defendant shipowners' liability was drowned through the negligence of the defendants' employees. His sons brought an action based on delict.

Held: The lower court allowed their claim in full, and on appeal this decision was confirmed. The Cour de cassation upheld the decision of the cour d'appel.

Judgment: THE COURT: ... *On the first two branches of the first appeal ground:*—Whereas it appears from the confirmatory judgment appealed against that Viaud-Grandmarais who had taken a passage on board the packet-boat 'Champollion' met his death in attempting to swim ashore after the vessel had foundered off the Lebanese coast; Bernard and Hervé Le Roterf, his heirs, brought proceedings under [former] Articles 1382 and 1384 Cciv against Commander Bourde, the ship's captain, and against Compagnie des Messageries Maritimes, the ship-owner, for damages for the loss suffered by them;

— Whereas the court below found that Commander Bourde had committed no fault and held that the death of Viaud-Grandmarais was attributable to a fault in the vessel for which the Compagnie des Messageries Maritimes was liable as the vessel's keeper;

— Whereas it is argued on appeal that the court below declined to have regard to a clause limiting liability included in the ticket, although the general obligation entered into by the passenger to limit his complaint to the amount stipulated (which was binding not

---

[31] Directive 1985/374/EEC of 25 July 1985 on the approximation of the laws, regulations and administrative provisions of the Member States concerning liability for defective products, [1985] OJ L210/29.
[32] No. 57-10063, Bull civ II no. 80, D 1959, 281, annotated by R Rodière.

only on him but also devolved with his estate on his successors in title) precluded those persons from bringing 'an action contrary to that obligation';

— Whereas, however, as Viaud-Grandmarais perished in the accident he was unable to transmit to the respondents the action in contract which would have been available to him if he had survived; and as the court below also found as a fact that the deceased's successors in title had renounced the alleged stipulation for another included for their benefit in the contract of carriage, and, consequently, there was nothing to prevent them from bringing an action in quasi-tort against Compagnie des Messageries Maritimes for compensation for the loss occasioned to them as a result of the death of their father, which would be a different action—with regard to both the legal basis and the quality of the parties—from that to which non-performance of the contract at issue could have given rise;

— Whereas in so deciding the cour d'appel violated none of the legislative provisions mentioned in the appeal. ...

— On those grounds the appeal in cassation is dismissed.

Note

If the contractual route is blocked by exemption clauses, the potential beneficiaries of an implicit stipulation for another are entitled to renounce the benefit. They may then, as the successors in title of the victim, claim in delict with regard to their own injury and not that suffered by the victim. They would, however, have to prove the defendant's negligence. The traveller himself would not be able to sue in delict because of the rule against the overlapping of remedies (*règle de non cumul*).[33] The successors are therefore not in a similar, but in a better position than the victim. This is difficult to justify and has been criticised as circumventing the rule of *non cumul*.

31.2.B.1.2 Germany

The German courts have also held that third persons can have 'contractual' rights in situations where it can hardly be said that the original parties did indeed agree to make a contract for the benefit of a third party. They did not do this in all the cases where French law invokes the 'implied stipulation for another'. Sometimes the German law of delict gives an appropriate remedy:

Strict Liability Act (Haftpflichtgesetz)[34]   **31.16 (DE)**

§ 1 (1) If in the operation of a railway or a tramway a human being is killed or suffers injury to body and health, or a thing is damaged, the undertaking operating the railway or tramway is bound to make good to the injured party the damage arising therefrom.

(2) The duty to make good is excluded if the accident was caused by *force majeure*.

(3) ...

---

[33] See above, p 149.
[34] Strict Liability Act of 4 January 1978, BGBl 1978 I 145, as amended on 19 July 2002, BGBl 2002 I 2674. The Act is based on the Imperial Strict Liability Act of 1871.

§ 5 (1) In cases where death is caused compensation (§§ 1, 2 and 3) must be made by making good the cost of the attempted cure as well as of the pecuniary damage which the deceased has suffered therefrom by having his earning capacity destroyed or decreased during the illness, or by having his personal needs increased.

The person liable in damages must reimburse the costs of a funeral to the person under a duty to bear these costs.

(2) If the person killed, at the time of the injury, stood in a relationship to a third party on the basis of which he was obliged or might become obliged by operation of law to provide maintenance for that person and if the third party has as a result of the death been deprived of his right to maintenance, then the person liable in damages must give the third party damages to the extent that the person killed would have been obliged to provide maintenance for the presumed duration of his life. Liability in damages also arises where the third party at the time of injury had been conceived but not yet born.

Notes

(1) The question to whom the deceased is obliged to provide maintenance is answered by specific provisions in the part of the BGB dealing with family law.

(2) §§ 1 and 5(2) of the Strict Liability Act, read together with these family law provisions, would have established the carrier's liability for the loss caused to the relatives of the victim in the first, but not in the second French *Fatal fall from train* case.[35]

(3) Third-party compensation claims for death are also provided for in the general law of delict, where § 844 BGB corresponds almost verbatim to § 5(1)(2) and (2) of the Strict Liability Act. However, § 844 BGB, read together with § 823(1) BGB, requires the claimant to prove the fault of the defendant.

Frequently, however, there is no claim in the law of delict, and the German courts extend contractual liability in order to provide a remedy for third parties. Originally they did so on the basis of § 328 BGB and the interpretation of the agreement between the original parties. As in France, the first case concerned a contract for the transport of persons:

RG, 7 June 1915[36] **31.17 (DE)**

Taxi collision

Relatives traveling together with a passenger derive contractual rights from the contract concluded between the passenger and the carrier.

Facts: Sch, together with his wife and his daughter, took a taxi which belonged to the first defendant. Due to negligence of the second defendant, the taxi driver, the taxi collided with a tram. The three passengers were injured.

Held: The taxi driver and the owner of the taxi are liable to all three passengers.

---

[35] See above, 31.12 (FR), p 1277.
[36] RGZ 87, 64.

Judgment: ... § 278 BGB was not misapplied, as the appellant contends. It is not necessary to decide whether one has to subscribe to the reasoning given by the appeal court which is not entirely above reproach, ie that in a case like this the taxi driver must regard all his passengers as contractors and thus must also claim the fare from each of them. In any event, government accountant Sch who boarded the taxi for the purposes of carriage at the same time as his wife and daughter must be regarded as a contracting party. It does not necessarily follow that only he can bring contractual claims arising from the contract of carriage. He rather concluded the contract of carriage also for the benefit of his wife and his daughter who were travelling with him, so that these were 'third persons' according to § 328, and, as such, directly acquired the right to demand performance, ie the proper and safe carriage. Therefore the findings of the appeal court, that the first defendant was liable to all three passengers under the contract of carriage and thus must answer for the fault of the second defendant, as its auxiliary under § 278 BGB, do not give cause for concern.

Notes

(1) The claimant in this case was the tram company, which was liable to the passengers, regardless of its fault, under the Imperial Strict Liability Act of 1871 (*Reichsha*ftpflichtgesetz).[37] The claimant sought a declaration that the first and second defendants were bound to indemnify them.

(2) The liability of the owner of the taxi for the negligence of the taxi driver follows from § 278 BGB.[38] This is a key provision which only applies in the contractual context: the debtor of a contractual obligation is responsible for the fault of persons whom he employs in the execution of this obligation, to the same extent as for fault on his own part. The taxi driver's negligence is thus directly attributed to the owner of the taxi who employed the driver. A similarly straightforward imputation of negligence is not possible in the law of delict. According to § 831 BGB, the defendant is only liable for his own negligence in selecting or supervising another person who he uses to perform a task.[39] Such a 'proof of exculpation' is relatively easy to achieve. In this case, we may expect that it would not have been difficult for the owner of the taxi to show that he exercised ordinary care in the selection and the supervision of the driver. The weak vicarious liability rule contained in § 831 BGB is sidestepped if an action can be brought in contract.

(3) Compare this case with the French *Fatal fall from train* cases.[40] To what extent is the position of the relatives of the contracting party different in this case? To what extent is their position different from that of the patient in the *Contaminated blood* case?[41]

(4) The judgment of the Reichsgericht gives the impression that its decision is a straightforward application of § 328 BGB and that the relatives are the beneficiaries

[37] The relevant provision can now be found in § 1(1) of the Strict Liability Act of 1978 (see above, p 1283).
[38] See above, pp 133, 145.
[39] The provision is reproduced above, p 133.
[40] See above, pp 1277–79.
[41] See above, p 1280.

of a 'genuine' contract made for the benefit of third parties. But is this true? Did the passenger and the taxi driver agree to create a right on the part of the relatives to enforce specific performance of the taxi driver's obligation to carry them from A to B? In fact, this ('primary') contractual obligation of the carrier is not at issue in this case. The question is rather whether the relatives should be entitled to enforce breaches of the taxi driver's ('secondary') contractual obligation to protect the physical integrity of his passengers.

RG, 10 February 1930[42]   **31.18 (DE)**

Leaking gas

An attendant who is not permanently employed by the tenant of a flat derives contractual rights from a contract for works made between the tenant and the contractor.

Facts: The claimant worked as an attendant for widow M from mid-April until the end of June of 1926. She accepted a job as a maid with someone else with effect from 15 August 1926. M was about to move into a new flat. She contracted with the defendant company to have the position of the gas meter in the new flat changed. In late July chief installer B, who was employed by B & R, the defendant company, made the changes. He negligently omitted to fix a screw. On 10 and 11 August 1926 the claimant helped Mrs M with moving into the new flat. On 11 August she smelled gas. In order to find the leak, she climbed a ladder in the bathroom and lit a match to have a look at the pipework. In doing so, she set the leaking gas alight. It exploded and the claimant suffered severe injuries. Her action against widow M was dismissed because of her predominant contributory negligence. The claimant then sued the defendant company and B for damages and an annuity.

Held: The first instance court and the appeal court awarded damages. The appeal court deducted 50% because of the claimant's contributory fault. The Reichsgericht dismissed the further appeal of the defendants, apart from a point concerning the duration of the annuity.

Judgment: The appeal court justifies the judgment against the defendants essentially as follows. On the basis of the contract for works that it concluded with Mrs M the defendant company was liable for the harm caused by B. It could not furnish proof of proper care and diligence in selecting the persons whom they employ in the execution of their contractual obligations. This contract included the defendants' duty to exercise, in carrying out the works, the care expected in daily affairs; in performing this duty, too, the defendant company used B as the person whom they employed in the execution of their contractual obligations, and therefore the defendant company had to take responsibility for him according to § 278 BGB. It was not only Mrs M who was, as the other party of the contract, entitled to have that care exercised and thus entitled to a claim to compensation of the damage caused by the neglect of the duty of care, but also the claimant because to this extent it had to be assumed that there was a contract for the benefit of third parties.

Whether the contractual intention was geared towards the effect spelt out in § 328(1) BGB, according to which the third person should acquire the right directly to demand the performance stipulated for him, had to be determined according to § 328(2) BGB,

---

[42] RGZ 127, 218.

in the absence of an express stipulation, from the circumstances of the individual case, especially from the purpose of the contract as it could be recognised by both parties to the contract. In conducting this exercise, the contractual purpose served as an objective yardstick for the determination of the content of the contract, to the effect that an agreement which the contracting parties would have made, had they envisioned an elaboration of the details in line with the contractual purpose, had to be assumed as having been covered by the contractual intention. It was not relevant whether the parties had actually been aware of this scope of their agreement. Having applied these legal principles it had to be assumed that there was a contract for the benefit of third parties in the present case. Where a contract for works was concluded which was to be executed in the employer's dwelling and which involved dangers for those using it, it was normally necessary to impute to the employer the intention—recognisable to the contractor—to have the interests at least of the relatives living with him respected as far as possible, and for this purpose to make available to them the same rights against the contractor which the employer himself would have for any damage caused by the execution of the works. For without such an extension of the contractor's contractual duties the relatives would be limited to extra-contractual claims in the case of damage incurred. To arrange the legal position of the employer and his relatives in such a different manner would run against a healthy sense of justice and would thus be out of step with the contractual intentions of the employer who, as the contractor would not have been able to ignore, would not have wished to place his relatives in a worse position than himself, as far as claims for compensation were concerned.

The domestic staff of the employer had to be treated similarly. Here, too, it was necessary to impute to him the intention—recognisable to the contractor—to respect the interests of the domestic staff who were required to work in the dwelling where the contractor performed his works and who would have had a claim against the employer to have their safety protected (§ 618 BGB). In cases where the employer concluded a contract for works which required him to carry out activities of a dangerous nature his intention, which was also recognisable to the contractor, was to have the activities carried out in a way that would not cause harm to either himself or his relatives or his domestic staff and also not to place himself with regard to such harm in a better position than the persons belonging to the community living in his household.

Now it was true that the claimant did not belong to the domestic staff but was only an attendant of Mrs M, and thus she had not been admitted into the domestic community living in the household. Nevertheless, it had to be assumed that it had been the intention of the master of the household—and this was equally capable of being recognised by the contractor—to provide the special protection of a personal claim to have the duties of care obeyed, over and above the circle of the relatives and the domestic staff mentioned above, to all those persons to whom the master of the household was liable for the protection of their health under § 618(1) BGB. This class included the attendant. However, this view had to be qualified to the extent that of the persons who had a right under § 618 BGB only those could be seen as deriving such a benefit whose relationship with the master of the household was of a certain duration, so that the master of the household was at least under a moral obligation to exercise increased care. For it could not simply be assumed that the master of the household intended to make a contract for the benefit of third parties in order to also benefit such persons whose activities in his dwelling was only of a casual and transitional nature and with whom he did not form close links, as they would have arisen from a longer use of their services and a more frequent contact, perhaps also from the establishment of more personal relationships. The claimant did not only have a transitional relationship with Mrs M because she had been employed by her for about a quarter of a year, and there had also been, as is shown more fully, a longstanding relationship between the claimant and Mrs M.

But even if that had not been the case anymore on 11 August 1926—the appellate decision says—there would still be a contract for the benefit of third parties with regard to the claimant. For during the days of the removal and the refurbishment of the new flat the dangers emanating from the furnishing were so much greater than in times of ordinary housekeeping that it had to be assumed that it had been the recognisable intention of the occupier to afford a particularly far-reaching level of protection to all the persons involved in the removal. It thus had to be assumed that, with regard to the duty of care owed, the contract for the benefit of third parties had extended to all the persons involved in the removal.

Against this, the appellants contend that in the case of a contract for works it cannot be assumed that it was agreed to protect all those who are constantly or transitionally present in a flat; the principles that have been developed for tenancy agreements cannot be applied to contracts for works.

This appeal cannot succeed, in particular because the appellate judge's interpretation of the contract of works concluded between the defendant company and Mrs M to the effect that the contract of works included a contract for the benefit of the claimant, too, is free from legal error, particularly as far as the application of §§ 133, 157, 328 BGB is concerned. It is not necessary to discuss whether the circle of the beneficiaries is always defined correctly in the judgment appealed against. For it certainly includes such persons to whom the employer of the contractor is liable for damages under § 618 BGB.

The fundamental considerations which serve as the appeal court's point of departure are correct and are settled case law of the Imperial Court (cf references in …). Most importantly, it is correct that a contract for the benefit of a third party can also be concluded impliedly and that the decision of the questions as to whether a contract must be assumed to have been concluded for the benefit of a third person also and whether the third person is meant to acquire from the contract immediate rights against the promisor depends essentially, in the absence of a specific contractual term, on an assessment of the factual circumstances in the individual case (RGZ 87, 292). In making such an assessment, regard must be had to the intention of the parties, the purpose of the transaction and trade usages (RGZ 64, 113; 65, 168); particular attention must be given to the issue of supplementary interpretation (Reichsgerichtsrätekommentar, para 1(2) to § 157 BGB) of the contract (RGZ 98, 213). The commercial purpose pursued by the parties is an objective criterion; it is therefore irrelevant whether the parties were at the time of contracting aware of the scope of their declarations (WarnRspr 1915, no 203). Finally, it is not necessary that the third person for whose benefit the contract is made is identified at the time of contracting; it is enough that he is identifiable (RGZ 106, 126; 117, 149).

On this basis, more recent judgments of the Imperial Court have further developed the earlier case law and have increasingly assumed that contracts for the benefit of third parties have been concluded in cases where a third person has suffered harm. In the judgment of 30 June 1910 it was still held that, as a general rule, the servant of a tenant who had suffered harm in the rented premises because of their irregular state was denied an immediate contractual claim against the landlord, and in RGZ 77, 101; 81, 200 (cf 81, 215) the tenant was awarded damages against the landlord to the extent that the tenant himself had suffered harm as a consequence of an accident which his wife had had in the rented flat. As opposed to this, in such cases the relatives of the tenant were awarded an immediate contractual claim for damages against the landlord based on § 328 BGB in the decisions RGZ 91, 24; 102, 232; WarnRspr 1921, no 96. [The court goes on to give a dozen or so examples from its case law over the previous two decades, including the *Taxi collision* case.[43]] This more recent case law is to be followed. It represents a perspective which is indeed healthy and which lives up to the contemporary living conditions and the general sense of justice.

If the present case is adjudicated on the basis of this case law the following conclusions are to be drawn. The claimant was in a long term employment relationship with widow M as her attendant. By virtue of this position the claimant was entitled and obliged, not only in order to sustain her own health but also to look after the interests of her employer, to enter the bathroom from which the smell of gas seemed to emerge. This room was therefore designated for her to provide services, and because the gas leaked from the pipe the room was not fit to protect her against dangers for life and limb; the unfitness was due to the grossly negligent performance of the task of changing the position of the gas meter, which had been given to the defendant company, by B, the person they employed in the execution of their contractual obligations. With regard to the protection of life and limb of the attendant, Mrs M was, according to § 618(1) BGB, under obligations which the legislator considered to be so essential that the parties may not exclude or limit them in advance (§ 619 BGB). These made her liable for damages to the claimant although there was no fault on her part. For liability under § 618 BGB is contractual, and therefore § 278 BGB is applicable (RGZ 77, 408; ...), so that Mrs M had to answer the claimant for the fault of the respondent company. ...

Now the purpose of the contract for works which was pursued by Mrs M and which was capable of being recognised by the defendant company was to have the position of the gas meter properly changed, and in particular to prevent that the performance of the task should cause danger to life and limb of either Mrs M or of such persons to whom she might become liable under § 618 BGB. Furthermore, no objection in law can be taken against the view of the appellate judge, gained from a supplementary interpretation of the contract according to § 157 BGB, that Mrs M and the defendant company would have agreed—if all those involved had contemplated such a possibility at the time of contracting—on the latter being directly liable for all damage which could arise for the persons which would be entitled to damages against Mrs M under § 618 BGB because of the improper changing of the position of the gas meter. For Mrs M would have made the assumption of such direct liability a term of the contract, and the defendant company would have agreed to accept the term to get the job, all the more so because the defendant company in any case had to deliver the works without any defects, and it did not make a significant difference for it whether it would be directly liable for damages to the employee of Mrs M or whether it would be subject to the recourse of the latter. ...

Notes

(1) § 618(1) BGB provides that the employer in a contract for services (here, Mrs M):

> has to fit up and maintain rooms, equipment and apparatus which he has to provide for the performance of the service, and so to regulate services which are to be performed under his orders or his direction, that the employee is protected against danger to life and health as far as the nature of the service permits.

---

[43] See above, p 1284.

(2) In this case, § 278 BGB is relevant in two legal relationships. With regard to the contract for services between Mrs M and the claimant, it provides that Mrs M is responsible for the fault of the defendant company. With regard to the contract for works between Mrs M and the defendant company, it ensures that the defendant company is responsible for its plumber, B.

(3) The Reichsgericht refers to the huge body of case law that had come into existence since the 1915 *Taxi collision* case. It acknowledges that these decisions did not concern situations where the agreement between the parties created a right to enforce performance in the third party but rather 'cases where a third person has suffered harm', ie where the non-performance or defective performance of the contract adversely affected the third person. However, the language of the Reichsgericht is still that of an application of § 328 BGB, the provision on contracts for the benefit of third parties in the strict sense.

(4) In the 1950s it was increasingly recognised that this approach was stretching the limits of § 328 BGB too far. Legal scholars suggested that the contract in cases like this should be treated as having 'protective effects' for the third person. Since then, actions like those in the *Leaking gas* case have been considered as being based on the 'doctrine of the contract with protective effect for third parties' (*Lehre vom Vertrag mit Schutzwirkung für Dritte*).

(5) The application of this doctrine has even been extended to the precontractual phase. It may be remembered that German law, under the doctrine of *culpa in contrahendo*, assumes contractual liability if a prospective buyer suffers physical damage during the negotiations.[44] The protective effect of the precontractual duty of care can also extend to third parties.

BGH, 28 January 1976[45]   **31.19 (DE)**

Vegetable leaf

A 14-year-old girl who accompanies her mother to a self-service store derives contractual rights from the precontractual relationship between her mother and the store.

Facts: The claimant, aged 14, and her mother went to a small self-service store which was a branch of the defendant company. Whilst her mother stood at the till, the claimant went around the till to the packing counter, fell and suffered an injury. She alleged that she had slipped on a vegetable leaf and sued the defendant for damages.

Held: The first instance court rejected the claim. The appeal court granted the claim on the basis of delictual liability, *culpa in contrahendo* and the doctrine of the contract with protective effect for third parties, but deducted 25% because of the claimant's contributory fault. The defendant's further appeal was unsuccessful.

Judgment: ... IV. These findings [of the appeal court] are legally sound—at least as far as the result is concerned.

---

[44] See above, 6.13 (DE), p 144 (*Falling rolls of lino*).
[45] BGHZ 66, 51, NJW 1976, 112.

However, there are concerns with regard to the main line of reasoning of the appeal court, according to which the defendant is directly liable to the claimant for fault in concluding a contract (*culpa in contrahendo*), without a need to rely on the doctrine of the contract with protective effect for third parties. In cases like the present, liability for *culpa in contrahendo* is significantly more favourable to the injured party than the general delictual liability for breach of the general duty of care towards third persons, for example in respect of the aggravated liability for persons who the debtor employs in the execution of his contractual obligations (§ 278 BGB, as opposed to § 831 BGB), the longer limitation period ([former] § 195 BGB, as opposed to [former] § 852 BGB) and the reversal of the burden of proof ([former] § 282 BGB). This head of liability is based on a legal relationship of obligation, developed in supplementation of the written law, which arises from the parties entering into negotiations and which is mostly independent of the actual conclusion or validity of the contract (BGHZ 6, 330, 333; settled case law; *cf* Larenz, *Schuldrecht*, 11th edn, vol I, pp 94, 96f, with further references) ... However, liability for *culpa in contrahendo* in contracts of sale like this always requires that the injured party has entered the business premises with the object of concluding a contract, or at least with the object of establishing 'business contacts' (thus Larenz, *Schuldrecht*, above, pp 94ff and MDR 1954, 515)—ie at least as a *potential* customer, albeit perhaps without a firm intention to make a purchase (*cf* BGH 26 September 1961 [NJW 1962, 31] ...) ... It may be difficult to draw the line in a given case, above all because the distinction refers to an internal intention which is hard to prove. However, in the present case it is beyond dispute that the claimant, from the start, did not intend to conclude a contract of sale with the defendant, but rather wished to accompany her mother and help her with making her purchases. A direct application of liability for fault in concluding a contract is therefore excluded.

V. Nevertheless, the appellate judgment is correct, as far as the result is concerned, because the appeal court's alternative line of reasoning supports the decision.

1. Had the mother of the claimant suffered an injury in the same way as her daughter, the liability of the defendant for *culpa in contrahendo* would be beyond doubt—the further appeal of the defendants evidently takes this for granted ... it is obvious that at the moment of the accident there was a legal relationship of obligation which justifies liability for *culpa in contrahendo* between the defendant and the mother of the claimant who had already made a definite selection of the goods to be purchased.

2. The claimant, too, can rely on this legal relationship of obligation to justify her contractual claim for damages. It is in line with long-established case law, particularly of this Senate, to hold that, in special circumstances, even external, third persons who were not involved in the formation of a contract can be included in its sphere of protection. As a result, they do not have a claim for performance of the primary contractual duty but they are entitled to the protection and care afforded by the contract and they can in their own name enforce claims for damages arising from the breach of these secondary duties (judgments of this Senate of 16 October 1963 ... = NJW 1964, 33; ...). There is no need in this case to delve into and decide on the theoretical question whether such a 'contract with protective effect for third parties' (*cf* Larenz, *Schuldrecht*, above, pp 183f and NJW 1960, 77f) is based on the supplementary interpretation of a contract that is, to this extent, incomplete (§§ 133, 157 BGB), as has been hitherto assumed by the courts, or whether direct, quasi-contractual claims derive from grounds independent of the hypothetical intention of the parties, such as custom or judicial development of the law, as is increasingly suggested by legal writers (see, eg, Palandt/Heinrichs, ...; Larenz, ...; Gernhuber, ...; Esser, ...; Canaris, ...). In any event, according to both views, the decisive factor is that the contract, according to its purpose and object, and taking into account

the requirements of good faith, requires an inclusion of the third person in its sphere of protection, and that one contractual party can honestly—and in a way that is recognizable for the other party—expect that the protection and care owed to him will similarly be afforded to the third person (*cf* BGHZ 51, 91, 96; …). There is no valid reason, as a general rule, to exclude contracts of sale from this kind of contractual arrangement which is legally possible—as is particularly shown by sales in shops, where the buyer potentially has to enter the seller's sphere of influence together with the third person. This has not been held by the Sixth Civil Senate, in the decision referred to above (BGHZ 51, 91, 96), either.

3. However, the inclusion of third persons in the protective sphere of the contract must be limited to narrowly confined instances if the difference in design between contractual and delictual liability, as established by the legislator, is not to be abandoned or blurred (BGH 25 April 1956 … = NJW 1956, 1193, …). It does not have to be decided whether the mere fact that the customer makes use of a third person in initiating and conducting the contract of sale in a self-service store is sufficient to justify the protective effect; in the present case there is the additional element that the mother of the claimant was, under her relationship with her, responsible for the wellbeing of her daughter (BGHZ 51, 91, 96). She could therefore, for this reason alone, reasonably—and in a way that was recognizable for the defendant—expect that her daughter who accompanied her would enjoy the same level of protection as she did. The courts have always seen such a close family law tie as a justification for the extension of the protective effect of a contract (BGH 16 May 1965 …).

4. It does not matter for the result that in the present case the contract of sale had not been concluded at the moment of the accident. Particularly if the duty of protection and care is regarded as the determinative element of the legal relationship of obligation which is established by the parties entering into negotiations, and if it is taken into account that the other party owes this duty of care to the same extent before and after the conclusion of the contract, it is only logically consistent to include in this legal relationship of obligation third persons who are equally worthy of protection (*cf* Larenz, *Schuldrecht*, above, p 188). Furthermore, there would be no reasonable justification to make the contractual liability contingent on the mere coincidence whether, at the moment of the injury, the contractual negotiations have led to the final conclusion of the contract or not; this is graphically shown by the present case where the 'negotiations for the sale' had been essentially completed and the conclusion of the contract was in any event, at the moment of the accident, imminent—possibly it was even delayed without the claimant's mother being responsible for this by her checking out at the till. The view raised by the defendants in their further appeal, ie that an accumulation of liability for '*culpa in contrahendo*' and 'inclusion of a third person in the protective effect of a contract' would lead to an unpredictable extension of the seller's risk, is in principle directed against the justification of both doctrines. Indeed, it cannot be dismissed out of hand that there is a danger of opening the floodgates. However, as it has been said before, the courts have always met this concern by subjecting the inclusion of a third person in the protective sphere of a contract to strict requirements. It may be the case that with regard to merely *pre*contractual legal relationships particular reluctance may be required. But in any event, even if the lines are drawn as narrowly as possible, there are no concerns against the extension of the protective effect if—as in the present case—the person causing the damage could not reasonably have objected at the outset to the request by the mother who led the negotiations to expressly grant her child which was later injured the same level of protection as herself. Finally, insofar as the defendants in their further appeal contend that the long limitation period—combined with the reversal of the burden of proof—would intolerably worsen

the evidentiary position of the person who is sued for causing damages, the doctrine of laches may provide an appropriate corrective mechanism although there is no indication that it would apply in the present case. ...

Notes

(1) Before the 2002 reform of the German law of obligations, the limitation period applicable to contractual claims was 30 years, compared with three years for delictual claims. Today, the period is three years in both cases (§ 195 BGB).

(2) According to the doctrine of laches (*Verwirkung*), which is mentioned at the end of the excerpt, a lapse of time in pursuing a right may lead to the premature extinction of that right if the creditor has created the impression that he would waive the right.

(3) For the 'supplementary interpretation' (*ergänzende Auslegung*) of contracts under § 157 BGB, see Chapter 20 above. Would it be possible in this case to base the right of the claimant on the interpretation of the contract between the mother and the shop owners?

(4) The daughter of the claimant did not intend to make a purchase. Imagine she had slipped on a vegetable leaf dropped by the defendant when she was walking past the defendant's store on her way to school. Should these cases be treated differently?

The *Vegetable leaf* case shows that the Bundesgerichtshof is not overly concerned with linking the doctrine of contracts with protective effect for third parties to a particular provision of the BGB. Various suggestions for a legal base have been made over the decades. Originally, these cases were seen as a straightforward application of § 328 BGB (*Taxi collision*)[46] or as based on an analogy of § 328 BGB. It was also suggested that they be derived from a 'supplementary interpretation' of the contract between the original parties (§ 133, 157 BGB) or simply from the general duty of the parties to act in good faith (§ 242 BGB). Gradually it was acknowledged that the action awarded in these cases was purely judge-made law. Today the 'doctrine of the contract with protective effect for third parties' has become a freestanding head of action with a number of requirements but without the need to have recourse to the notion of an implied contract for the benefit of a third party. The 2002 reform of the BGB by the Act to Modernise the Law of Obligations introduced § 311(3)(1) BGB, which is frequently said to be capable of providing a legal base:

BGB   **31.20 (DE)**

§ 311: Obligations created by legal transaction and similar obligations

...

(3) An obligation with duties under section 241(2) may also arise towards persons who are not intended to be parties to the contract. Such an obligation arises in particular if the third party by enlisting a particularly high degree of reliance materially influences the contractual negotiations or the conclusion of the contract.

---

[46] See above, p 1284.

Notes

(1) § 241(2) BGB, which was also introduced in the 2002 reform deals with the 'secondary obligations' of the parties: each party is required to have regard to the other party's rights, legally protected interests and other interests.[47]

(2) § 311(3)(2) BGB deals with the *liability* of third parties only. However, this sentence does not control the meaning of § 311(3)(1) BGB which is capable of covering the *rights* of third persons in cases where one of the contracting parties infringes a secondary obligation or protective duty.

(3) § 311(3)(1) BGB is silent with regard to the requirements for the inclusion of third persons in the protective sphere of contracts. These are still governed by pre-2002 case law.

Looschelders on Obligations[48]   **31.21 (DE)**

Requirements for the inclusion of third persons in the protective sphere

There is broad agreement in the case law and in legal writings that, as a general rule, the protective scope of the obligation may only be extended to third persons if *strict requirements* are met. The restrictive approach can be justified on the basis that the inclusion of third persons deviates from the principle of the *relativity* of duties in the law of obligations and extends the contractual debtor's risk of liability. It cannot be the case that everyone who incurs damage because of a violation by the debtor of a duty of protection may derive his own claim for damages from the contract between the contractual creditor and the debtor. The following criteria must be adhered to:

(a) Intended proximity of performance of the third person

First, the third person must, in normal circumstances, be close to the performance of the contractual debtor and must thus be exposed to the risks connected with the performance to a similar extent as the creditor (*proximity of performance* [*Leistungsnähe*]). This requirement is met, for example, if children accompany their parents who are shopping (cf the *Vegetable leaf* case) or if employees use machinery which has been leased or bought by the employer. … Intended proximity of performance also exists for the relatives of a tenant who live together with him under one roof. However, the visitors and guests of the tenant are not included in the protective sphere of the contract with the landlord.

(b) Legitimate interest of the creditor in protecting the third person

Secondly, the contractual creditor must have a legitimate interest in protecting the third person (*interest of the creditor* [*Gläubigerinteresse*]). For cases of physical injury and damage to property, the courts have developed the so-called 'wellbeing formula' [*Wohl-und-Wehe-Formel*]. According to this, the necessary interest in protecting the third person exists 'if the creditor shares, as it were, the responsibility for the well-being of the third person because any harm done to the third person also harms the creditor, the latter owing protection and care vis-à-vis the third person'. In the first instance, this formula covers personal relationships where there is a legal obligation to provide care, such as between parents and children, between spouses or between employer and employee.

---

[47] See above, pp 96–97, 426.
[48] D Looschelders, *Schuldrecht: Allgemeiner Teil* (15th edn, Munich: Franz Vahlen, 2017) paras 164–66, 168–69 (citations omitted).

[The following two paragraphs are reproduced below, pp 1303–04.]

(c) Foreseeability of the proximity of performance and of the interest of the creditor

Thirdly, the contractual debtor must have been *able to foresee* the proximity of per-formance and the interest of the creditor. Foreseeability [*Erkennbarkeit*] does not require that the debtor knows the names or the number of the third persons concerned. How-ever, since it must be possible to predict the risk of liability only a manageable and clearly defined group of persons may be included. Yet, in the case of a structural surveyor the Bundesgerichtshof held it to be sufficient that the surveyor knew that his survey would be relevant for a (potential) buyer.

(d) Third person's need of protection

Even if all the other requirements are met the inclusion of the third person can fail because he has no *need of protection*. The Bundesgerichtshof denies a need of protection if the injured person derives from the event that caused the damage a contractual claim of his own that is *of equal value*. As a result of this restriction, the sub-tenant is not included in the protective sphere of the contract between the landlord and the main tenant. Since the sub-tenant can enforce his own claim for damages under § 536a(1) [BGB] against his contractual partner—the main tenant—there is no reason to allow him, on top of this, a claim for damages under § 536a against the landlord, flowing from the doctrine of the contract with protective effect for third parties.

Note

Note the emphasis on restricting liability via the policy arguments of 'proximity' and 'foreseeability'. This is typical floodgate reasoning that is implicit in the French case law, too. We also encounter it when we turn to English law.

31.2.B.1.3 England

In English law the victims in the French and German cases reproduced in this section would not have a contractual claim. The early-twentieth-century case of *Cavalier v Pope*[49] is a good example. The owner and landlord of a dilapidated house contracted with his tenant to repair it, but failed to do so. The tenant's wife, who lived in the house, was injured by an accident caused by the want of repair. Under German law, the wife would have been included in the 'protective sphere' of the tenancy agreement between her husband and the landlord. As a consequence, she would have had a contractual rem-edy against the landlord. In contrast, the House of Lords held that the husband alone could sue for breach of contract in order to claim the damages he had incurred by reason of the accident of his wife. The wife did not have an action to claim for her injuries because there 'was but one contract, and that was made with the husband. The wife can-not sue upon it.'[50] The Contracts (Rights of Third Parties) Act 1999 would not provide a remedy for Mrs Cavalier either. Section 1(3) of the Act requires that the 'third party must

---

[49] [1906] AC 428 (HL).
[50] ibid, 430, per Lord James.

be expressly identified in the contract by name, as a member of a class or as answering a particular description'.[51]

Rather than expanding contractual liability, English law relegates third party victims in situations such as described in this section to tort law. Unless a more specific head of tort liability applies, they have to rely on the general tort of negligence.[52] This requires that the defendant owed a duty of care to the claimant and caused him damage by a breach of that duty. Crucially, the tort is premised on fault, so the claimant has to prove negligence to recover.

Furthermore, the relatively restrictive rules on 'vicarious liability' make it difficult to hold a person liable for a tort committed by someone who acted on his behalf. This will only be the case if the defendant was the 'employer' (or 'master') of the other person and if the other person was the defendant's 'employee' (or 'servant') under a contract of employment (or 'contract of service'). In contrast, the defendant will not be vicariously liable for torts committed by an independent contractor employed under a contract for services.

A tort action of third party victims will not always meet these requirements. The defendant's breach of his contractual duty owed to the other party to the contract does not always amount to a breach of his duty of care owed to the third party. In *Cavalier v Pope*,[53] for example, the House of Lords held that at common law a landlord was deemed to relinquish control to the tenant by virtue of the lease: even if the landlord let a house in a dangerous state he did not owe a duty of care to anyone apart from the tenant under the terms of the lease. Therefore Mrs Cavalier did not have a remedy in tort. In the 1950s, the legislator intervened by partly abrogating the immunity that this decision provided for landlords.[54] Today the relevant provision can be found in the Defective Premises Act 1972:

Defective Premises Act 1972 **31.22 (EN)**

Section 4: Landlord's duty of care in virtue of obligation or right to repair premises demised

(1) Where premises are let under a tenancy which puts on the landlord an obligation to the tenant for the maintenance or repair of the premises, the landlord owes to all persons who might reasonably be expected to be affected by defects in the state of the premises a duty to take such care as is reasonable in all the circumstances to see that they are reasonably safe from personal injury or from damage to their property caused by a relevant defect.

(2) ...

The common law was similarly reluctant to award tort liability in situations broadly resembling those in the French *Fatal Fall from Train* cases.[55] In *Clark v London General*

---

[51] See above, p 1269.
[52] See above, pp 134–41.
[53] [1906] AC 428, 430, per Lord James (HL).
[54] s 4(1) of the Occupiers Liability Act 1957.
[55] See above, pp 1277–79.

Omnibus Co Ltd[56] the unmarried daughter of the plaintiff was killed as a result of an accident with one of the defendant's omnibuses. Contractual liability was not in issue because, in contrast to the French cases, there was no contractual relationship between the victim and the defendant. The Court of Appeal held that there was no tortious liability either. At common law the father could not recover the cost of burying his daughter:

> ... no action lies in respect of death. ... In this case it seems to me that there is no duty towards the father which has been broken. There is no property of the father which has been injured, and no contract with the father which has been broken. Some breach of duty must be made out, and I can see no ground for any suggestion that there is any duty to the father that has been infringed, or any property of the father which has been injured. It seems to me that this case falls within that class ... where there are certain wrongful acts which may place persons in the position of spending money and yet will not involve a legal liability to make that expenditure good.[57]

Thus the death of a person as a result of a tort did not normally give rise to an independent cause of action in those who had suffered damage as a result of the death. This was particularly harsh in cases where the breadwinner of a family was killed and his dependants were not able to sue for an allowance or an annuity. However, the result can be explained on the basis that such claims are not for personal injury but for 'relational loss', ie loss caused as a consequence of an injury to someone else, and thus for a pure economic loss of the claimant, and the English tort rules for recovery of pure economic loss are, as we will see in the next section, very restrictive. Once again, statute law provided a limited remedy:

Fatal Accidents Act 1976   **31.23 (EN)**

Section 1: Right of action for wrongful act causing death

(1) If death is caused by any wrongful act, neglect or default which is such as would (if death had not ensued) have entitled the person injured to maintain an action and recover damages in respect thereof, the person who would have been liable if death had not ensued shall be liable to an action for damages, notwithstanding the death of the person injured.

(2) Subject to section 1A(2) below, every such action shall be for the benefit of the dependants of the person ('the deceased') whose death has been so caused.

(3) In this Act 'dependant' means—

(a) the wife or husband or former wife or husband of the deceased;

(b) any person who—

(i) was living with the deceased in the same household immediately before the date of the death; and

(ii) had been living with the deceased in the same household for at least two years before that date; and

(iii) was living during the whole of that period as the husband or wife of the deceased;

---

[56] [1906] 2 KB 648 (CA).
[57] ibid, 660, per Lord Alverstone CJ.

(c) any parent or other ascendant of the deceased;

(d) any person who was treated by the deceased as his parent;

(e) any child or other descendant of the deceased;

(f) any person (not being a child of the deceased) who, in the case of any marriage to which the deceased was at any time a party, was treated by the deceased as a child of the family in relation to that marriage;

(g) any person who is, or is the issue of, a brother, sister, uncle or aunt of the deceased.

(4) …

Section 1A: Bereavement

(1) An action under this Act may consist of or include a claim for damages for bereavement.

(2) A claim for damages for bereavement shall only be for the benefit—

(a) of the wife or husband of the deceased; and

(b) where the deceased was a minor who was never married—

(i) of his parents, if he was legitimate; and

(ii) of his mother, if he was illegitimate.

(3) Subject to subsection (5) below, the sum to be awarded as damages under this section shall be £10,000.

(4) …

Section 2: Persons entitled to bring the action

(1) The action shall be brought by and in the name of the executor or administrator of the deceased.

(2) …

Section 3: Assessment of damages

(1) In the action such damages, other than damages for bereavement, may be awarded as are proportioned to the injury resulting from the death to the dependants respectively.

(2) …

(5) If the dependants have incurred funeral expenses in respect of the deceased, damages may be awarded in respect of those expenses.

Notes

(1) The defendant is liable under section 1(1) if the deceased, had he not died, would have had an action against the defendant for damages. Thus liability is still predicated on the defendant's fault.

(2) If the action is successful the dependants are entitled to benefit from it (section 1(2)). However, the action can only be brought by the estate of the deceased, not by the dependants themselves (section 2(1)). Their action is thus not independent but derivative. As a result, the defendant may rely on any defence that would have been available against the deceased, such as that the deceased had willingly accepted the risk, or that the recovery should be reduced on the grounds of the deceased's contributory negligence.

(3) Damages are awarded for actual and expected pecuniary loss incurred by the dependants, eg loss of financial support or the value of services provided by the deceased. Under sections 1A(1) and 3(5), damages may also be awarded for bereavement and for funeral expenses.

(4) The class of dependants who may benefit from an action under the Act is limited; even more so in the case of a claim for bereavement.

(5) The widow and the sister in the French *Fatal fall from train* cases[58] would have been able to benefit from an action brought under section 1(3)(a) and (g). However, under these provisions, it would have been necessary to prove negligence.

31.2.B.2 PURE ECONOMIC LOSS

Many of the French and German cases reproduced in the previous section have in common that the extension of the domain of contract law makes good for some of the perceived weaknesses of delictual liability (difficulties of proof, short limitation periods, etc). They also share a second feature, ie that a person suffered physical injury. Therefore the law of delict was at least prima facie available with regard to the harm caused.

But what about cases where the availability of an action in delict or tort is itself in question because the harm caused does not normally trigger delictual or tortious liability? Should contractual liability be extended here as well? In other words, it may be justified to give a person a right which is flowing from a contract to which he was not a party in cases where he would have had an action in delict or tort, were it not for one of the peculiar (and, arguably, unreasonably narrow) requirements of delictual or tortious liability—but is this also justified where the third person could not conceivably have had any delictual or tortious action at all?

The question is particularly relevant where the victim suffered pure economic loss—ie financial loss that does not arise out of physical damage (personal injury or damage to the property) suffered by the claimant—and it is particularly relevant under German law.[59] English law, as we have seen, is reluctant to extend contractual liability even in cases of physical injury. Thus it would be surprising if it were to do so where pure economic loss is concerned. This is particularly so because English tort law has a relatively restrictive approach to liability for interfering with purely economic interests. French law may be expected to reach a similar result (no extension of contractual liability), albeit for another reason. Its law of delict is relatively generous in allowing recovery for pure economic loss, so there is less need to extend contractual liability. German law, however, does not mention economic interests amongst the protected rights (*Rechtsgüter*) listed in its general provision on delictual liability (§ 823(1) BGB).[60] It will therefore often be

---

[58] See above, pp 1277–79.

[59] For a comparative overview of the protection of economic interests in the law of delict or tort, see W van Gerven, J Lever and P Larouche, *Ius Commune Casebooks on the Common Law of Europe: Tort Law* (Oxford: Hart Publishing, 2000) 208–48.

[60] § 823(1) BGB is reproduced above, p 132.

incapable of establishing liability without extending either the law of contract or the law of delict.

The following three cases from France, Germany and England have a common theme: an expert enters into a contract with his client under which he is to render an expert opinion for a fee. Due to the expert's carelessness, his opinion is erroneous and misleading. If it is not the client but a third person who relies on the accuracy of the opinion, can that person bring a claim for damages against the expert? Does the action of the third party lie in contract or tort?

Cour d'appel de Paris, 18 June 1957[61]   **31.24 (FR)**

The 'Double de Genève'

A valuer who is employed by the seller of a rare stamp to give an expert opinion on it for the purpose of a sale and who fails to report that the stamp has been repaired is liable to a purchaser of the stamp who pays the value of an unrepaired stamp.

Facts: Cosnelle employed Busser to appraise a Swiss 'Double de Genève' stamp which he was hoping to sell to Fabre. Busser gave a certificate that the stamp had 'a fine appearance, authentic and not repaired'. Relying on this certificate, Fabre bought the stamp for 300,000 francs. When he came to sell it six years later, Fabre discovered that the stamp had been repaired and re-coated and was worth only some 100,000 francs. Fabre claimed from Busser the difference between this and the value the stamp would have had at the moment of the attempted sale if it had been in the condition stated by Busser.

Held: The first instance court dismissed Fabre's claim on the ground that there was no legal relationship between Fabre and Busser. The cour d'appel reversed this decision but remitted the case for further findings of fact.

Judgment:—Ruling on the appeal lodged by Fabre against a judgment delivered by the Tribunal de commerce de la Seine on 13 December 1954, declaring his claim inadmissible, alternatively unfounded, and dismissing the same;

— Whereas it is common ground that Busser, to whom Mr Cosnelle had submitted for examination a Swiss postage stamp dating from 1843 known as a 'Double de Genève', issued on 1 March 1947 an expert's certificate containing a description of the stamp and stating 'stamp having a fine appearance, authentic and not repaired', and further that, in early 1953, Fabre offered for sale, at a price of 600,000 francs, a 'Double de Genève' stamp accompanied by the aforementioned certificate;

— Whereas Fabre states that on 1 March 1947 he acquired the stamp in relation to which Busser had provided his expert's opinion, paying therefore the sum of 300,000 francs, and that in January 1953, just when he was putting it up for sale, that stamp was found to have been 'repaired and re-coated', its value in that condition being approximately 100,000 francs; as he maintains that Busser committed a fault or was negligent in his expert appraisal, and claims that he should be ordered to pay him the sum of 800,000 francs, representing the difference between the current value which the stamp in question would have had if it were in good condition and the value which it is actually recognised as having;

— Whereas in dismissing Fabre's claim, the court hearing the case at first instance considered that there was no legal relationship between Fabre and Busser and, moreover,

---

[61] JCP 1957.II.10134 (2nd case), annotated by R Lindon.

that it had not been established that the same stamp was involved or that the condition of the stamp in 1947 was the same as that which it was found to possess in 1953;

— Whereas it appears from the attestation made by Cosnelle on 11 May 1953 that on 1 March 1947 Fabre acquired a Swiss 'Double de Genève' (no 1) postage stamp dating from 1843 through the intermediary of Cosnelle, who had previously submitted the stamp in question to Busser for examination and expert appraisal by the latter;

— Whereas the expert appraisal was requested by Cosnelle and carried out by Busser on behalf (*pour le compte*) of the purchaser, namely Fabre; as Fabre was thus the beneficiary of a stipulation which was made for his benefit by Cosnelle and accepted by Busser and which created a direct contractual link between Busser and himself;

— Whereas the wording of the said attestation shows furthermore that Cosnelle acted in the circumstances as agent (*comme mandataire*) of Fabre and that both the expert appraisal of the stamp and its acquisition were organised by him in pursuance of that agency, so that Fabre, as the principal, was in a contractual relationship with Busser;

— Whereas in the event that any fault attributable to Busser became apparent, it would consequently establish the contractual liability of the latter to Fabre;

— Whereas however, the court does not have before it, as matters stand, sufficient evidence enabling it to assess the matter and to determine whether any fault was even committed or, if it was, to adjudicate on the quantum of damages; Whereas it is consequently necessary to order an expert appraisal on the terms hereinafter set out …

Notes

(1) It seems that the cour d'appel did not even consider delictual liability, as there were two alternative grounds for liability in contract. One was that Cosnelle made the agreement with Busser in his own name, but on behalf (*pour le compte*) of Fabre, and that Fabre could therefore be considered as a third-party beneficiary. The other ground was that Cosnelle made the agreement with Busser *comme mandataire* (as an agent) of Fabre (presumably acting in Fabre's name).

(2) In another case the Cour de cassation held that a corporate auditor who negligently certified factually inaccurate company accounts was liable in delict (ex-Article 1382 Cciv, now Article 1240 Cciv) to a shareholder who subscribed to an increase in the company's capital on the basis of the accounts.[62] This decision can be compared with the following two cases.

BGH, 26 November 1986[63] $\qquad$ **31.25 (DE)**

Inaccurate audit

A tax consultant employed by the owner of a company to prepare a balance sheet for use in selling the company may, if the balance sheet is inaccurate, be liable not only to the purchaser but also to the bank financing the purchase.

[62] Cass com 17 October 1984, no. 83-12414, Bull civ IV no. 269, JCP 1985.II.20458, annotated by A Viandier, translated in van Gerven et al (n 59 above) 241 (*Inaccurate corporate documents*).
[63] NJW 1987, 1758.

Facts: M was the sole shareholder and manager of a company, V-GmbH, which he wanted to sell. He requested the defendants, the company's tax consultants, to draw up an interim balance sheet. At the request of M, the defendants passed on two copies of this balance sheet to V as a potential purchaser of the company, and V in turn passed one on to his bank, the claimant, in support of an application for credit to finance the purchase price. The bank was duly impressed and lent V DM 500,000, taking a pledge on the company's shares as security. The bank lost all its money when shortly thereafter both V and his newly acquired company became insolvent and went into liquidation. The bank brought a claim for damages against the tax consultants. They had been negligent in over estimating the company's financial position.

Held: The court of first instance dismissed the claim, and the appeal court rejected the appeal. The Bundesgerichtshof remitted the case for further findings of fact. It held that a breach by the tax consultants of their contractual duty to use proper care in drawing up the balance sheet does not necessarily engender their contractual liability vis-à-vis their contractual partner alone. They may also be liable in contract to a third person who, as they knew or ought to have known, might rely on the accuracy of the balance sheet. This included not only V (and other potential purchasers of the company who might be shown the balance sheet), but also the bank to whom the balance sheet had been submitted by the purchaser in support of an application for a loan to finance the acquisition.

Judgment: … The appeal court correctly assumed that a contract to draw up an interim balance sheet was concluded between the firm of the defendants and the V-GmbH (or its manager and sole shareholder, M). However, it took the view that the claimant was not included in the sphere of protection of this contract: such an inclusion could only be assumed if the contractual partner of the defendant owed a duty of protection to the injured third person, and no such relationship existed between the V-GmbH (or its shareholder M) and the claimant. This legal assessment is not in line with the case law of the Bundesgerichtshof. It is true that in a number of decisions this court has made the inclusion of a third person in the sphere of protection afforded by a contract dependent on whether the contractual partner of the [defendant] was entrusted with the wellbeing of the third person (BGHZ 51, 91, 96; BGHZ 56, 269, 273; BGHZ 66, 51, 57; …). However, this case law may not be understood as establishing limits for the inclusion of third persons in the sphere of protection afforded by a contract. The court rather wanted to decide on the requirements for assuming an implied agreement of a duty of protection to a third person on the basis of the objective interests of the parties alone—ie without a specific indication to this effect in the express declarations of the parties or in their other conduct. According to § 328 BGB, the parties are free to create a right to demand performance for the benefit of a third person. In this regard, the freedom of the parties to arrange their affairs as they see fit is subject to no further limitations than those applying to all contracts (particularly §§ 134, 138 BGB). Similar considerations must apply to duties of protection. Therefore the parties are free to create a duty of protection also for the benefit of persons who are not entrusted to their welfare. Whether such an intention existed must be established by the court trying the merits of the case, according to the general principles of interpretation (BGH NJW 1984, 355; …).

The present case affords grounds for supposing that the contracting parties intended to include third parties within the sphere of protection afforded by the contract. As stated above, it cannot be assumed that the interim balance sheet was intended solely for the instruction of the defendants' client; on the contrary, it was meant to serve as the basis on which a third person—either the purchaser or a lender—might reach a decision. In such a case, it is fair to assume that the third person was meant to be included within the sphere of protection afforded by the contract. Against this it cannot be argued in the present case that the interests of the purchaser or lender, on the one hand, and of the tax consultant's client, on the other, ran counter to each other. Where a person instructs another person recognised by the State as possessing expert knowledge in a particular field (eg a publicly appointed expert, chartered or certified accountant, publicly appointed survey-ing engineer or tax consultant) to produce an expert's report or to give an expert opinion (eg an accountant's or tax consultant's attestation) to be used in dealings with a third person, the client generally has an interest in ensuring that the results of the work car-ried out have the requisite probative value. This can only be guaranteed, however, if the author of the report or opinion produces it on an objective basis and does so to the best of his knowledge and belief, and if he is also able to vouch for it vis-à-vis the third person.

The inclusion of the claimant within the sphere of protection afforded by the contract does not depend on whether the defendants were aware of the fact that the interim balance sheet was to be submitted to the claimant; it will suffice in that regard if the defendant realised, or ought to have realised, that the results of his work were intended either for a purchaser or for a lender (bank). The Bundesgerichtshof has previously held on numerous occasions that a duty of protection exists in cases in which the person owing that duty was aware neither of the number nor of the names of the persons entitled to such protection (BGHZ 26, 365, 367; …). This does not mean, however, that the group of persons to whom the duty of protection is owed may be extended ad infinitum; on the contrary, that duty must be restricted to a discernible, clearly circumscribed group of persons. Accordingly, it does not appear unacceptable to include within the sphere of protection afforded by the contract the person for whom the interim balance sheet was clearly intended to serve as the basis for a decision, since in this case the scope of such protection would extend to cover only the purchaser and whoever might lend money to the purchaser.

Notes

(1) The case was controversial for two reasons. First, it confirmed that a person included in the protective sphere of a contract with protective effect could sue for pure economic loss, as well as for personal injury suffered. Secondly, it abandoned the requirement that the contractual partner of the defendant had to be entrusted with the 'wellbeing' of the third person. Looschelders (n 48 above, at paras 167 and 167a) comments:

> The wellbeing formula only works if the contractual creditor and the third person have similar interests. However, in cases of pure *economic loss* the Bundesgerichtshof assumes that the requirements of a contract with protective effect for third parties are also met if the interests of the creditor and the third party are *contradictory*. Here the legitimate interest of the creditor in protecting the third person must be based on other factors. In particular, the protection extends to persons in whose interest, albeit among others, performance is to be made under the express or implied agreement of the parties. This is of particular practical relevance with regard to the liability of experts for surveys that are meant to be presented to a third person.

Example (BGHZ 127, 378):[64] Vendor V intends to sell his residential property. In order to prepare the transaction he commissions building surveyor B with the production of a report

---

[64] A full translation of this case can be found in BS Markesinis and H Unberath, *The German Law of Torts: A Comparative Treatise* (4th edn, Oxford: Hart Publishing, 2002) 280.

concerning the value of the property. In preparing the report B negligently overlooks that the roof structure displays significant damage caused by damp which requires a replacement of the structure. He therefore reaches the conclusion that no "noteworthy repairs" are required at this stage. V is aware of the damage. He nevertheless sells the property to the unsuspecting purchaser P after having produced the report. The contract excludes V's liability for "visible and hidden defects". Shortly thereafter P renovates the attic and realises the existence of the damage caused by damp.—The Bundesgerichtshof held that P had a contractual claim against B because P was included in the protective sphere of the contract to produce a survey concluded between V and B. V had a legitimate interest that B would answer for the correctness of the survey. For without such an obligation to be answerable it would not have been warranted that P relies on the survey and pays a corresponding purchase price. The fact that V was in effect not interested in having a correct survey must be disregarded as a hidden internal reservation.

According to the case law of the Bundesgerichtshof, the criteria developed for the restriction of the number of third persons who are protected—mostly the particular interest of the creditor in protecting the third person—may be disregarded in particular cases where the contract with protective effect for third parties does *not* lead to an *extension of the risk of liability*. In substance this concerns contracts on the production of audits intended for the use of loan creditors and capital investors. The specific feature of these cases is that, from the outset, the damage can only be incurred by the third person—the loan creditor and the capital investor—and not by the contractual creditor himself. It may be doubted, though, whether this consideration justifies the relaxation of the general requirements for a contract with protective effect for third parties. Since these are cases where the loss is merely reallocated legal writers suggest having recourse to the *doctrine of transferred loss* [see below, pp 1310–11]. However, the relevant basis of liability is the surveyor's taking advantage of particular personal reliance. Therefore a solution on the basis of the liability of persons enlisting a particularly high degree of reliance (§ 311(3)(2) [see above, pp 1293–94]) is preferable.

(2) Assume (a) that V had bought the company with his own money and had submitted the balance sheet to his bank in order to obtain a loan for other purposes; and (b) that V, by submitting the balance sheet to his suppliers, had persuaded them to make deliveries to the company on credit. Would the bank or the sellers be able to sue the tax consultants for breach of contract? Where does the ball stop rolling?

(3) The Court also held that, in the circumstances of the case, the provision of the inaccurate audit amounted to conduct *contra bonos mores* causing injury which triggers delictual liability under § 826 BGB. This provision allows, inter alia, for the recovery of pure economic loss, but it requires that the defendant acted intentionally. The Court made it clear that such an intention could probably be established in the present case but remitted the case to the appeal court for further findings of fact.[65] The case shows that contracts with protective effect for third parties can arise regardless of whether the third party has another claim in delict or not.

---

[65] This part of the judgment is translated in van Gerven et al (n 59 above) 234.

The approach of English tort law to liability for pure economic loss is also very restrictive. Originally, in cases concerning statements causing such loss, an action for damages only arose if actual fraud in making the statement could be proved or the parties were in a fiduciary relationship.[66] This was true for mere two-party situations and for cases where three persons were involved. In the 1950s, the Court of Appeal decided a case, the facts of which resembled those of the German *Inaccurate audit* case. In *Candler v Crane, Christmas & Co*[67] the plaintiff was a potential investor in a company for which the defendants were the auditors. The plaintiff requested to see the company accounts before making a decision. The manager of the company asked the auditors to prepare the accounts and discuss them with the plaintiff. On the basis of the accounts, the plaintiff decided to invest in the company, which was wound up within a year. The plaintiff lost his entire investment. It turned out that the defendants 'had been extremely careless in the preparation of the accounts'. They contained numerous false statements and gave a wholly misleading picture of the state of the company. By a majority of two to one the Court of Appeal rejected the plaintiff's claim for damages. Denning LJ dissented with regard to

> ... the great question in the case: did the accountants owe a duty of care to the plaintiff? If the matter were free from authority, I should have said that they clearly did owe a duty of care to him. They were professional accountants who prepared and put before him these accounts, knowing that he was going to be guided by them in making an investment in the company. On the faith of those accounts he did make the investment, whereas if the accounts had been carefully prepared, he would not have made the investment at all. The result is that he has lost his money. In the circumstances, had he not every right to rely on the accounts being prepared with proper care; and is he not entitled to redress from the accountants on whom he relied? I say that he is ...

> Before I consider [a case decided in 1893] I wish to say that, in my opinion, at the time it was decided current legal thought was infected by two cardinal errors. The first error was one which appears time and time again in nineteenth century thought, namely, that no one who is not a party to a contract can sue on it or on anything arising out of it. This error has had unfortunate consequences both in the law of contract and in the law of tort. So far as contract is concerned, I have said something about it in *Smith v River Douglas Catchment Board*.[68] So far as tort is concerned, it led the lawyers of that day to suppose that, if one of the parties to a contract was negligent in carrying it out, no third person who was injured by that negligence could sue for damages on account of it ...

Denning LJ suggested that English law of tort had moved on since the nineteenth century. He therefore held that the accountants' duty to use care in their statements is not only owed to their clients but also to any third person to whom they showed their accounts or to whom they knew their clients were going to show them, so as to induce him to invest money or take some other action on the accounts. The majority of the Court, however, held that, in the absence of fraud or of any contractual or fiduciary relationship between

---

[66] For the requirements of the tort of misrepresentation, see above pp 561–63.
[67] [1951] 2 KB 164 (CA).
[68] [1949] 2 KB 500, 514–17 (CA).

the parties, a false but careless statement did not give rise to liability on the part of the accountants.

For more than a decade thereafter the only special relationship that was recognised as giving rise to a duty to take care with regard to a statement was a fiduciary relationship. This restrictive approach was only dropped in 1963, in the leading case of *Hedley Byrne & Co Ltd v Heller & Partners Ltd.*[69] Since then it has been recognised that a person who is possessed of a special skill, such as an expert, a surveyor, a chartered accountant or a banker, and negligently makes an erroneous or misleading statement will be liable in damages to another who, as he knows or should know, has relied on the statement and suffered loss. Note, however, that in this case the liability of the professional person is based not on a breach of contract, but on the tort of negligence. Note, also, that *Hedley Byrne* involved a two-party situation, ie the defendant bankers had made a representation to the plaintiffs (or, more precisely, to the bank of the plaintiffs, which passed it on to the plaintiffs; but it was not a case where the defendants had made a representation to their own clients). It took more than a quarter of a century for the *Hedley Byrne* liability to be extended, so as to impose a duty on the maker of a statement in favour of a third-party recipient of that information:

House of Lords   **31.26 (EN)**

Smith v Eric S Bush[70]

A valuer who is employed by a building society to value a property on which a loan for the purchase price is to be secured will be liable to the purchaser/borrower if the property is negligently overvalued.

Facts: The plaintiff applied to a building society for a mortgage to assist her in purchasing a house. The building society instructed the defendants, a firm of surveyors and valuers, to carry out a visual inspection of the house and to report on its value and any matter likely to affect its value. The defendants' valuer who carried out the inspection was careless in failing to check whether the chimneys were adequately supported. He stated that the house needed no essential repairs. The building society supplied a copy of the report to the plaintiff, who purchased the house. The chimneys were not adequately supported and one of them subsequently collapsed. The plaintiff claimed damages from the defendants in negligence.

Held: The court of first instance upheld the claim. The Court of Appeal reversed this decision on the ground that the survey contained a disclaimer of responsibility which prevented the surveyor being liable. The House of Lords allowed the purchaser's appeal.

Judgment: LORD GRIFFITHS: … In the present case, the purpose of providing the report is to advise the mortgagee but it is given in circumstances in which it is highly probable that the purchaser will in fact act on its contents, although that was not the primary purpose of the report. I have had considerable doubts whether it is wise to increase the scope of the duty for negligent advice beyond the person directly intended by the giver of the advice to act upon it to those whom he knows may do so. …

---

[69] [1964] AC 465 (HL), above p 137.
[70] [1990] 1 AC 831.

I therefore return to the question in what circumstances should the law deem those who give advice to have assumed responsibility to the person who acts upon the advice or, in other words, in what circumstances should a duty of care be owed by the adviser to those who act upon his advice? I would answer—only if it is foreseeable that if the advice is negligent the recipient is likely to suffer damage, that there is a sufficiently proximate relationship between the parties and that it is just and reasonable to impose the liability. In the case of a surveyor valuing a small house for a building society or local authority, the application of these three criteria leads to the conclusion that he owes a duty of care to the purchaser. If the valuation is negligent and is relied upon damage in the form of economic loss to the purchaser is obviously foreseeable. The necessary proximity arises from the surveyor's knowledge that the overwhelming probability is that the purchaser will rely upon his valuation, the evidence was that surveyors knew that approximately 90 per cent. of purchasers did so, and the fact that the surveyor only obtains the work because the purchaser is willing to pay his fee. It is just and reasonable that the duty should be imposed for the advice [that] is given in a professional as opposed to a social context and liability for breach of the duty will be limited both as to its extent and amount. The extent of the liability is limited to the purchaser of the house—I would not extend it to subsequent purchasers. The amount of the liability cannot be very great because it relates to a modest house. There is no question here of creating a liability of indeterminate amount to an indeterminate class. I would certainly wish to stress that in cases where the advice has not been given for the specific purpose of the recipient acting upon it, it should only be in cases when the adviser knows that there is a high degree of probability that some other identifiable person will act upon the advice that a duty of care should be imposed. It would impose an intolerable burden upon those who give advice in a professional or commercial context if they were to owe a duty not only to those to whom they give the advice but to any other person who might choose to act upon it.

Notes

(1) Would it have made a difference if the building society had not shown the report to the plaintiff, but had simply offered him a mortgage? Would the House of Lords have awarded damages in tort to the plaintiff bank in the German *Inaccurate audit* case[71] if the test proposed by Lord Griffiths had been used?

(2) The House of Lords did not even discuss the possibility of a contractual claim against the surveyors. Even the tort claim was less straightforward than the short excerpt of the case suggests, as can be seen from the development of the case law outlined above this excerpt.

(3) In the first paragraph cited above, Lord Griffiths was anxious to point out that there must be limits with regard to the persons to whom the defendants' duty of care is owed. Otherwise the floodgates of liability would be opened. Only a few months later, in *Caparo Industries Plc v Dickman*,[72] the House of Lords decided that auditors are not liable to a third party if the audit has nothing to do with the transaction for

---

[71] See above, p 1301.
[72] [1990] 2 AC 605 (HL). The case is discussed in greater detail above, p 139.

which it was relied on. In that case, the audited accounts had only been produced to meet the company's statutory duty under the Companies Act 1985 to produce audited accounts in order to allow the shareholders to supervise the company. They had not been provided with a view to give potential investors information for their investment decisions. Lord Oliver held that *Smith v Eric S Bush*:

> although establishing beyond doubt that the law may attribute an assumption of responsibility quite regardless of the expressed intentions of the adviser, provides no support for the proposition that the relationship of proximity is to be extended beyond circumstances in which advice is tendered for the purpose of the particular transaction or type of transaction and the adviser knows or ought to know that it will be relied upon by a particular person or class of persons in connection with that transaction. …

> My Lords, no decision of this House has gone further than *Smith v Eric S Bush*, but your Lordships are asked by the respondents to widen the area of responsibility even beyond the limits to which it was extended by the Court of Appeal in this case and to find a relationship of proximity between the adviser and third parties to whose attention the advice may come in circumstances in which the reliance said to have given rise to the loss is strictly unrelated either to the intended recipient or to the purpose for which the advice was required. My Lords, I discern no pressing reason of policy which would require such an extension and there seems to me to be powerful reasons against it. …

> As I have already mentioned, it is almost always foreseeable that someone, somewhere and in some circumstances, may choose to alter his position upon the faith of the accuracy of a statement or report which comes to his attention and it is always foreseeable that a report—even a confidential report—may come to be communicated to persons other than the original or intended recipient. To apply as a test of liability only the foreseeability of possible damage without some further control would be to create a liability wholly indefinite in area, duration and amount and would open up a limitless vista of uninsurable risk for the professional man.[73]

In the previous cases the defendants provided information or advice on which a third party relied. What about the provision of services from which a third party may benefit? What if a professional carelessly fails to take the steps necessary to comply with his client's intention to benefit a third party? Will the professional be liable to the third party—even though a statement was neither made nor relied on? This problem is discussed in the next three judgments.

BGH, 11 January 1977[74] **31.27 (DE)**

Carelessly drafted divorce settlement

An attorney employed to draw up a divorce settlement which will benefit the children of the marriage but who fails to ensure that the settlement is adequate to protect those children may be liable to them.

---

[73] ibid, 641–43.
[74] NJW 1977, 2073. Translation by T Weir in BS Markesinis and H Unberath (n 64 above) 702.

Facts: The defendant was an attorney who had represented M in divorce proceedings. In January 1972 Mr and Mrs M met in the defendant's office, where they signed a divorce agreement drawn up by the defendant. It contained the following clause:

§ 6. As to the house, the parties agreed that the half belonging to Mrs M is to be transferred to the three children in equal parts. Mr M hereby agrees not to sell his half but to transfer it to his present legitimate children. An appropriate notarial contract to this effect is to be concluded immediately after the divorce is final. Mr M further promises that once the divorce is final he will indemnify Mrs M against any liabilities arising from the house or its construction …

A divorce decree was granted in February 1972, and the defendant, in the name of his client, waived any rights of appeal, as did Mrs M's attorney. Mrs M then refused to transfer her interest in the property to M's son and his siblings. The minor son, represented by his father as his statutory representative, thereupon claimed damages from the defendant on the ground that he had failed, before waiving his client's rights of appeal, to take the steps necessary to create, by way of a notarial contract, a legally binding obligation of Mrs M to transfer her interest in the house to the claimant and his siblings.

Held: The defendant had indeed acted carelessly and was liable to the claimant, even though there was no contract with him.

Judgment: … Nor is there anything wrong in law with the Court of Appeal's holding that although there was no contract between the claimant and the defendant, the claimant could sue the defendant for damages for his faulty breach of contract.

(a) The Court of Appeal found that there was here a contract with protective effect for third parties and that the claimant's claim arose therefrom. We do not have to decide whether this is so.

(aa) Certainly an important factor pointing in that direction is that the claimant was the son of the attorney's client and was entitled to care and protection from him (compare BGHZ 61, 227, 233). The usual problem in cases of contracts with protective effects for third parties is whether the victim was someone the debtor could expect to be harmed by a breach of the contract. That is not the problem here. The very words of § 6 of the divorce agreement drawn up by the defendant show that the children were its sole beneficiaries, the only people apt to suffer if the agreement proved invalid.

The only question here is how far the protective effect of this contract works in favour of the children, in particular whether they have any claim for damages for breach of contract in their own right. Now the contract between client and attorney is such, given its nature and structure, that it can only be very seldom, whether one interprets the contract extensively or invokes § 242 BGB (see BGHZ 56, 269, 273; NJW 1975, 977), that the duties it generates can be sued on by third parties, for the fiduciary relationship between client and attorney makes it strongly bilateral and self-contained [references omitted]. Thus the fact that third parties have an interest in what an attorney does will not normally lead to any extension of his liability, even if those persons are named or known to him. However, an exception must be made where a contract drafted by the attorney is designed to vest rights in third parties specified therein, especially third parties who, as in the present case, are represented by the client. It is true that most of the cases where the courts have granted third parties a claim for damages arising out of a contract to which they were not parties have involved personal injury or property damage and its consequences (BGHZ 49, 350, 355; NJW 1955, 257; [other references omitted]), but it is not impossible for a third party to have a personal claim for economic loss caused by breach of subsidiary contractual duties (NJW 1968, 1929; BGH NJW 1975, 344). In drawing the line here one must certainly apply an especially stringent test: the circle of persons to whom the protective effect of a contract extends is to be narrowly drawn, so as to avoid blurring the line between contractual and delictual liability in an unacceptable manner (BGHZ 66, 51, 57; NJW 1974, 1189). It must always be borne in mind, in claims for purely economic loss, that the debtor is not to be made liable for the mere ricochet effect of his conduct on third parties.

(bb) Despite this, we cannot, on the special facts of the present case, fault the Court of Appeal's holding that the claimant was drawn into the protective ambit of the attorney's contract. The respondent invokes a decision of this court of 6 July 1965 (NJW 1965, 1955), but this is not quite in point. The court there did allow the daughter of a client to sue the attorney although she was not herself a party to the contract, but the court was reluctant to categorise the contract as one with protective effect for third parties [references omitted]. Contracts with protective effect for third parties are concerned with breach of subsidiary duties by the contractor (see BGH NJW 1975, 344) whereas in that case the question was really whether the attorney could be made liable towards the client's daughter, the third party, for a breach of specific duties of performance [reference omitted].

Our case is clearly distinguishable.

(b) The claimant might also base his claim here on the concept of *Drittschadensliquidation*, a doctrine which borders on, if it does not actually overlap with, the area of application of the doctrine of contracts with protective effect for third parties (see BGHZ 49, 350, 355). It would have been quite proper for the defendant's client to indemnify his son, the claimant, for the harm he had suffered, and one could then infer from the fact that he brought the suit as his son's statutory representative that he was making an assignment of his own claim which the claimant, on the threshold of majority, could implicitly accept. But we need not pursue the matter here.

(c) In whatever legal or doctrinal category one puts the present litigated facts, the result must be that the claimant has a direct claim against the defendant attorney for compensation for the harm which he suffered as a result of the defendant's failure to tell his father of the need to implement the agreement in § 6 of the divorce document. Any other conclusion would be inconsistent with the meaning and purpose of the attorney's contract here and of the father-son relationship between the client and the claimant of which the defendant was well aware.

Note

The Bundesgerichtshof mentions that, apart from the doctrine of contracts with protective effect for third parties, the claimant might also have been able to rely on the doctrine of transferred loss (*Drittschadensliquidation*). This is yet another judge-made technique, developed without a statutory base on purely equitable grounds. It deals with cases in which A enters into a contract with B under which B is to store, guard, repair, manage or carry a chattel owned by C. If a breach of B's contractual duties results in damage to C's chattel, A has a contractual claim against B for the damages *sustained by* C, and C, as assignee, may then enforce that claim himself against B.[75] The same technique is used where a seller contracts with a carrier for the carriage of goods sold to a buyer and the goods are damaged or lost *in transitu* owing to the carrier's negligence. In these cases, as a result of the agreement between

---

[75] BGH 10 July 1963, BGHZ 40, 91, 100; BGH 10 May 1984, NJW 1985, 2411.

the seller and the buyer, the loss falls on, or is 'transferred' to, the buyer as he must pay the full price despite the fact that the goods were lost or destroyed. The buyer has no remedy against the carrier, either in contract as he is not a party to the contract of carriage, or in tort as title to the goods was in the seller at the time when the loss or damage occurred. In this situation German courts have held, first, that the seller has a contractual claim against the carrier for the loss suffered by the buyer, and, secondly, that there is an express or implied assignment under which the seller has assigned his claim for damages to the buyer so that the latter, as the real party in interest, has a right to sue of his own.[76] See also Lord Goff's discussion of *Drittschadensliquidation* in the following case. In French law, as we can see from the *The Carrefour takings* case,[77] *Drittschadensliquidation* is considered as a form of *stipulation pour autrui* and treated as such.

<table>
<tr><td>House of Lords</td><td>**31.28 (EN)**</td></tr>
</table>

White v Jones[78]

A solicitor who is employed by a testator to draw up a new will leaving property to the plaintiff but who negligently fails to prepare the will before the testator dies will be liable to the disappointed beneficiary.

Facts: The testator had been reconciled with his daughters and instructed a solicitor, Mr Jones, to draw up a new will, leaving £9,000 to each daughter, to replace an earlier will which left them nothing. The solicitor failed to prepare the will before the testator died.

Held: The first instance court dismissed the plaintiffs' action on the ground that the solicitor owed them no duty of care. This decision was reversed by the Court of Appeal. By a majority the House of Lords dismissed the solicitor's appeal.

Judgment: LORD KEITH OF KINKEL (dissenting): ... The contractual duty which Mr Jones owed to the testator was to secure that his testamentary intention was put into effective legal form promptly. The plaintiffs' case is that precisely the same duty was owed to them by Mr Jones in tort. If the intended effect of the contract between Mr Jones and the testator had been that an immediate benefit, provided by Mr Jones, should be conferred on the plaintiffs, and by reason of Mr Jones's deliberate act or his negligence the plaintiffs had failed to obtain the benefit, the plaintiffs would have had no cause of action against Mr Jones for breach of contract, because English law does not admit of jus quaesitum tertio. Nor would they have had any cause of action against him in tort, for the law would not, I think, allow the rule against jus quaesitum tertio to be circumvented in that way. To admit the plaintiffs' claim in the present case would in substance, in my opinion, be to give them the benefit of a contract to which they were not parties. ...

LORD GOFF OF CHIEVELEY: My Lords, in this appeal, your Lordships' House has to consider for the first time the much discussed question whether an intended beneficiary under a

---

[76] BGH 29 January 1968, BGHZ 49, 356, 360.
[77] See above, p 1274.
[78] [1995] 2 AC 207.

will is entitled to recover damages from the testator's solicitors by reason of whose negligence the testator's intention to benefit him under the will has failed to be carried into effect. In *Ross v Caunters* [1980] Ch 297, a case in which the will failed because, through the negligence of the testator's solicitors, the will was not duly attested, Sir Robert Megarry V-C held that the disappointed beneficiary under the ineffective will was entitled to recover damages from the solicitors in negligence. In the present case, the testator's solicitors negligently delayed the preparation of a fresh will in place of a previous will which the testator had decided to revoke, and the testator died before the new will was prepared. The plaintiffs were the two daughters of the testator who would have benefited under the fresh will but received nothing under the previous will which, by reason of the solicitor's delay, remained unrevoked. It was held by the Court of Appeal, reversing the decision of Turner J, that the plaintiffs were entitled to recover damages from the solicitors in negligence. The question which your Lordships have to decide is whether, in cases such as these, the solicitors are liable to the intended beneficiaries who, as a result of their negligence, have failed to receive the benefit which the testator intended they should receive. …

… it has been recognised on all hands that *Ross v Caunters* [1980] Ch 297 raises difficulties of a conceptual nature, and that as a result it is not altogether easy to accommodate the decision within the ordinary principles of our law of obligations. …

It is right however that I should immediately summarise these conceptual difficulties. They are as follows.

(1) First, the general rule is well established that a solicitor acting on behalf of a client owes a duty of care only to his client. The relationship between a solicitor and his client is nearly always contractual, and the scope of the solicitor's duties will be set by the terms of his retainer. But a duty of care owed by a solicitor to his client will arise concurrently in contract and in tort: see *Midland Bank Trust Co Ltd v Hett, Stubbs & Kemp* [1979] Ch 384, recently approved by your Lordships' House in *Henderson v Merrett Syndicates Ltd* [1995] 2 AC 145. But, when a solicitor is performing his duties to his client, he will generally owe no duty of care to third parties. …

As I have said, the scope of the solicitor's duties to his client are set by the terms of his retainer; and as a result it has been said that the content of his duties are entirely within the control of his client. The solicitor can, in theory at least, protect himself by the introduction of terms into his contract with his client; but, it is objected, he could not similarly protect himself against any third party to whom he might be held responsible, where there is no contract between him and the third party.

In these circumstances, it is said, there can be no liability of the solicitor to a beneficiary under a will who has been disappointed by reason of negligent failure by the solicitor to give effect to the testator's intention. There can be no liability in contract, because there is no contract between the solicitor and the disappointed beneficiary; if any contractual claim was to be recognised, it could only be by way of a ius quaesitum tertio, and no such claim is recognised in English law. Nor could there be liability in tort, because in the performance of his duties to his client a solicitor owes no duty of care in tort to a third party such as a disappointed beneficiary under his client's will.

(2) A further reason is given which is said to reinforce the conclusion that no duty of care is owed by the solicitor to the beneficiary in tort. Here, it is suggested, is one of those situations in which a plaintiff is entitled to damages if, and only if, he can establish a breach of contract by the defendant. First, the plaintiff's claim is one for purely financial loss; and as a general rule, apart from cases of assumption of responsibility arising under the principle in *Hedley Byrne & Co Ltd v Heller & Partners Ltd* [1964] AC 465, no action

will lie in respect of such loss in the tort of negligence. Furthermore, in particular, no claim will lie in tort for damages in respect of a mere loss of an expectation, as opposed to damages in respect of damage to an existing right or interest of the plaintiff. Such a claim falls within the exclusive zone of contractual liability; and it is contrary to principle that the law of tort should be allowed to invade that zone. ...

(3) A third, and distinct, objection is that, if liability in tort was recognised in cases such as *Ross v Caunters* [1980] Ch 297, it would be impossible to place any sensible bounds to cases in which such recovery was allowed. In particular, the same liability should logically be imposed in cases where an inter vivos transaction was ineffective, and the defect was not discovered until the donor was no longer able to repair it. Furthermore, liability could not logically be restricted to cases where a specific named beneficiary was disappointed, but would inevitably have to be extended to cases in which wide, even indeterminate, classes of persons could be said to have been adversely affected.

The fact that the problems which arise in cases such as the present have troubled the courts in many jurisdictions, both common law and civil law, and have prompted a variety of reactions, indicates that they are of their very nature difficult to accommodate within the ordinary principles of the law of obligations. It is true that our law of contract is widely seen as deficient in the sense that it is perceived to be hampered by the presence of an unnecessary doctrine of consideration and (through a strict doctrine of privity of contract) stunted through a failure to recognise a jus quaesitum tertio. But even if we lacked the former and possessed the latter, the ordinary law could not provide a simple answer to the problems which arise in the present case, which appear at first sight to require the imposition of something like a contractual liability which is beyond the scope of the ordinary jus quaesitum tertio. In these circumstances, the effect of the special characteristics of any particular system of law is likely to be, as indeed appears from the authorities I have cited, not so much that no remedy is recognised, but rather that the system in question will choose its own special means for granting a remedy notwithstanding the doctrinal difficulties involved.

We can, I believe, see this most clearly if we compare the English and German reactions to problems of this kind. Strongly though I support the study of comparative law, I hesitate to embark in an opinion such as this upon a comparison, however brief, with a civil law system; because experience has taught me how very difficult, and indeed potentially misleading, such an exercise can be. Exceptionally however, in the present case, thanks to material published in our language by distinguished comparatists, German as well as English, we have direct access to publications which should sufficiently dispel our ignorance of German law and so by comparison illuminate our understanding of our own.

I have already referred to problems created in the English law of contract by the doctrines of consideration and of privity of contract. These, of course, encourage us to seek a solution to problems of this kind within our own law of tortious negligence. In German law, on the other hand, in which the law of delict does not allow for the recovery of damages for pure economic loss in negligence, it is natural that the judges should extend the law of contract to meet the justice of the case. In a case such as the present, which is concerned with a breach of duty owed by a professional man, A, to his client, B, in circumstances in which practical justice requires that a third party, C, should have a remedy against the professional man, A, in respect of damage which he has suffered by reason of the breach, German law may have recourse to a doctrine called Vertrag mit Schutzwirkung für Dritte (contract with protective effect for third parties), the scope of which extends beyond that of an ordinary contract for the benefit of a third party: see Professor Werner Lorenz in *The Gradual Convergence*, edited by Markesinis (1994), pp 65, 68–72). This doctrine was invoked by the German Supreme Court in the *Testamentfall* case (BGH 6 July 1965, NJW 1965, 1955) which is similar to the present case in that the plaintiff, C, through the dilatoriness of a lawyer, A, (instructed by her father, B) in making the necessary arrangements for the father's will, was deprived of a testamentary benefit which she would have received under the will if it had been duly made. The plaintiff, C, was held to be entitled to recover damages from the lawyer, A. Professor Lorenz has expressed the opinion (p 70) that the ratio of that case would apply to the situation in *Ross v Caunters* itself. In these cases, it appears that the court will examine 'whether the contracting parties intended to create a duty of care in favour of' the third person (BGH NJW 1984, 355, 356), or whether there is to be inferred 'a protective obligation … based on good faith …' (BGHZ 69, 82, 85 et seq). (Quotations taken in each case from Professor Markesinis's article on 'An Expanding Tort Law—the Price of a Rigid Contract Law' (1987) 103 LQR 354, 363, 366, 368.) But any such inference of intention would, in English law, be beyond the scope of our doctrine of implied terms; and it is legitimate to infer that the German judges, in creating this special doctrine, were extending the law of contract beyond orthodox contractual principles.

I wish next to refer to another German doctrine known as Drittschadensliquidation, which is available in cases of transferred loss (Schadensverlagerung). In these cases, as a leading English comparatist has explained:

> 'the person who has suffered the loss has no remedy while the person who has the remedy has suffered no loss. If such a situation is left unchallenged, the defaulting party may never face the consequences of his negligent conduct; his insurer may receive an unexpected (and undeserved) windfall; and the person on whom the loss has fallen may be left without any redress.' See Markesinis, *The German Law of Torts*, 3rd edn (1994), p 56.

Under this doctrine, to take one example, the defendant, A, typically a carrier, may be held liable to the seller of goods, B, for the loss suffered by the buyer, C, to whom the risk but not the property in the goods has passed. In such circumstances the seller is held to have a contractual claim against the carrier in respect of the damage suffered by the buyer. This claim can be pursued by the seller against the carrier; but it can also be assigned by him to the buyer. If, exceptionally, the seller refuses either to exercise his right for the benefit of the buyer or to assign his claim to him, the seller can be compelled to make the assignment: see Professor Werner Lorenz in *Essays in Memory of Professor FH Lawson* (1986), pp 86, 89–90, and in *The Gradual Convergence*, pp 65, 88–89, 92–93; and Professor Hein Kötz in Tel Aviv University Studies in Law (1990), vol 10, pp 195, 209. Professor Lorenz (*Essays*, at p 89) has stated that it is at least arguable that the idea of *Drittschadensliquidation* might be 'extended so as to cover' such cases as the *Testamentfall* case, an observation which is consistent with the view expressed by the German Supreme Court that the two doctrines may overlap (BGH 19 [sic] January 1977, NJW 1977, 2073 =VersR 1977, 638: translated in Markesinis, *The German Law of Torts*, p 293). At all events both doctrines have the effect of extending to the plaintiff the benefit of what is, in substance, a contractual cause of action; though, at least as seen through English eyes, this result is achieved not by orthodox contractual reasoning, but by the contractual remedy being made available by law in order to achieve practical justice. …

It may be suggested that, in cases such as the present, the simplest course would be to solve the problem by making available to the disappointed beneficiary, by some means or another, the benefit of the contractual rights (such as they are) of the testator or his estate against the negligent solicitor, as is for example done under the German principle of Vertrag mit Schutzwirkung fur Dritte. Indeed that course has been urged upon us by Professor Markesinis, 103 *LQR* 354, 396–397, echoing a view expressed by Professor Fleming in (1986) 4 *OJLS* 235, 241. Attractive though this solution is, there is unfortunately a serious difficulty in its way. The doctrine of consideration still forms part of our law of contract, as does the doctrine of privity of contract which is considered to exclude the recognition of a jus quaesitum tertio. To proceed as Professor Markesinis has suggested may be acceptable in German law, but in this country could be open to criticism as an illegitimate circumvention of these long established doctrines; and this criticism could be reinforced by reference to the fact that, in the case of carriage of goods by sea, a contractual solution to a particular problem of transferred loss, and to other cognate problems, was provided only by recourse to Parliament. Furthermore, I myself do not consider that the present case provides a suitable occasion for reconsideration of doctrines so fundamental as these. ...

I therefore return to the law of tort for a solution to the problem. For the reasons I have already given, an ordinary action in tortious negligence on the lines proposed by Sir Robert Megarry V-C in *Ross v Caunters* [1980] Ch 297 must, with the greatest respect, be regarded as inappropriate, because it does not meet any of the conceptual problems which have been raised ... Even so it seems to me that it is open to your Lordships' House ... to fashion a remedy to fill a lacuna in the law and so prevent the injustice which would otherwise occur on the facts of cases such as the present. In the *Lenesta Sludge* case [1994] 1 AC 85, as I have said, the House made available a remedy as a matter of law to solve the problem of transferred loss in the case before them. The present case is, if anything, a fortiori, since the nature of the transaction was such that, if the solicitors were negligent and their negligence did not come to light until after the death of the testator, there would be no remedy for the ensuing loss unless the intended beneficiary could claim. In my opinion, therefore, your Lordship's House should in cases such as these extend to the intended beneficiary a remedy under the *Hedley Byrne* principle by holding that the assumption of responsibility by the solicitor towards his client should be held in law to extend to the intended beneficiary who (as the solicitor can reasonably foresee) may, as a result of the solicitor's negligence, be deprived of his intended legacy in circumstances in which neither the testator nor his estate will have a remedy against the solicitor. Such liability will not of course arise in cases in which the defect in the will comes to light before the death of the testator, and the testator either leaves the will as it is or otherwise continues to exclude the previously intended beneficiary from the relevant benefit. I only wish to add that, with the benefit of experience during the 15 years in which *Ross v Caunters* has been regularly applied, we can say with some confidence that a direct remedy by the intended beneficiary against the solicitor appears to create no problems in practice. That is therefore the solution which I would recommend to your Lordships. ...

Notes

(1) In a Dutch case where a notary had negligently delayed the making of a will, delictual liability to an intended beneficiary was established on the basis on Article 1401 of the old BW, which was strongly influenced by the French Code civil.[79]

[79] Hof van Beroep Amsterdam 31 January 1985, NJ 1985, 740. Since 1992 delictual liability would be based on Art 6:162 BW.

(2) The extension of tortious liability by the majority in *White v Jones* is very contentious, as can be seen from the powerful dissenting speech by Lord Mustill which we cannot set out in full because of its length. According to his view, the result of the majority could not be arrived at by an application of the existing authorities in tort law, and he did not consider it legitimate 'simply to create a specialist pocket of tort law ... sufficient to provide a remedy in the present case'. Lord Mustill expressed his 'instinctive preference for a contractual solution'. After all, it was the plaintiffs' 'only possible complaint ... that they failed to receive a benefit from the testator (via his estate) which they would have received if the solicitor had done his job'. The special feature of the case was that 'the conferring of the benefit on the plaintiff was to be done by the testator, not by the solicitor himself. The undertaking to do the work and the intended conferring of the benefit were therefore directed along two sides of a triangle'. Lord Mustill therefore explored 'whether whatever rights the plaintiff may possess can be derived in one way or another' from the contract. However, like Lord Keith, he ultimately rejected this approach: (i) the doctrine of transferred loss, even if transplanted to English law, would not give a remedy; (ii) it could not be said that the testator had acted as an agent for the intended beneficiary to make a contract between the solicitor and the beneficiary, with subsequent ratification by the beneficiary; and (iii):

> Nor is the proposition improved by implying into the contract of retainer an auxiliary promise by the solicitor to give the beneficiaries the rights which the testator had by contract secured for himself. English law may be inching towards the direct enforcement of contracts, or benefits intended to be conferred under them, by persons standing outside the mutual obligations created by the bargain. How far the courts will be able to go remains to be seen. This is not the occasion to find out, for no claim in contract is before the court. But even under a much expanded law of contract it is hard to see an answer to the objection that what the testator intended to confer on the new beneficiaries was the benefit of his assets after his death; not the benefit of the solicitor's promise to draft the will.[80]

(3) Would the plaintiffs in *White v Jones* have a claim after the coming into force of the Contracts (Third Party Rights) Act 1999?

English Law Commission **31.29 (EN)**

Report on Contracts for the Benefit of Third Parties[81]

7.19 In fixing the boundaries of our proposed reform, we have encountered most difficulty with the situation where a solicitor negligently fails properly to draw up a will thereby causing loss to the intended beneficiaries of the will. Should those beneficiaries have the right to sue the solicitor under a reform of privity? While we can certainly see

---

[80] *White v Jones* [1995] 2 AC 207, 281 (HL).
[81] For this Report, see n 10 above.

the force in allowing those beneficiaries a cause of action, we do not think that this is best rationalised as effecting the parties' intentions to confer that right. Moreover, as the House of Lords in *White v Jones* has now held that the prospective beneficiaries have an action in the tort of negligence against the solicitor, we see no pressing practical need to stretch our facilitative reform in order to achieve what is widely perceived to be the just solution.

7.20 The wording of our proposed reform is therefore not intended to include negligent will-drafting (and analogous) situations. The crucial words are that the promise must be one to confer a benefit on the third party. The solicitor's express or implied promise to use reasonable care is not one by which the solicitor is to confer a benefit on the third party. Rather it is one by which the solicitor is to enable the client to confer a benefit on the third party. ...

7.25 It is our view, therefore, that the negligent will-drafting situation ought to lie, and does lie, just outside our proposed reform. It is an example of the rare case where the third party, albeit expressly designated 'as a beneficiary' in the contract, has no presumed right of enforcement. Indeed it is arguable that, by merely adjusting the wording of the second limb to include promises that are 'of benefit to' expressly designated third parties, rather than those that 'confer benefits on' third parties, we would have brought the negligent will-drafting situation within our reform. But we believe that those words draw the crucial distinction between the situation where it is natural to presume that the contracting parties intended to confer legal rights on the third party and the situation where that presumption is forced and artificial. ...

7.27 However we must add that, while we consider that negligent will-drafting should fall outside our proposed reform, at a theoretical level we prefer the view that the right of the prospective beneficiaries more properly belongs within the realm of contract than tort. It is very difficult to explain the basis of the claim, which deals with an omission and pure economic loss, as being other than one to enforce the promise of the solicitor (albeit by a party who was not intended to have that right). Had *White v Jones* been decided against the potential beneficiaries, we would have seriously contemplated a separate provision—outside our general reform—giving prospective beneficiaries a right to sue the negligent solicitor for breach of contract. The primary basis of such a provision would have been that a right of action for the beneficiaries is the only way to ensure that the promisee's expectations engendered by the solicitor's binding promise are fulfilled. But given the decision in *White v Jones* the practical need for such a provision has been obviated.

Note

A footnote to paragraph 7.25 of the Report clarifies that:

our reform is based on a model of a contract for the benefit of third parties and does not seek to embrace the wider German concept of a contract with protective effects for third parties. We would be afraid of the uncertainty that the generalised legislative introduction of that German concept would create.

Is the Law Commission's intention sufficiently expressed in the wording of section 1 of the Contracts (Third Party Rights) Act 1999?

Cass civ (1), 14 January 1981[82]   **31.30 (FR)**

Right of pre-emption overlooked

A notary who draws up and notarises a contract for the sale of land without having regard to the existence of a third person's right of pre-emption will be liable to that person.

Facts: Mrs Rieu and her three daughters, Mrs Mellet, Mrs Martina and Mrs Fleudin, were joint proprietors of agricultural land. On 7 June 1960 they sold three pieces of land to the Compagnie Nationale d'Aménagement de la région du Bas-Rhône et du Languedoc (CNARBRL) by way of a notarised document, drawn up by notary Q. The contract contained a pre-emption clause in favour of the sellers: if the buyers were to sell the land or let it on lease they would give priority to the sellers on equal conditions. In 1961 the CNARBRL decided to sell the three pieces of land. They approached Q in order to have the sale arranged. Q replied by letter of 12 July 1961 and asked whether the sellers had waived their right of pre-emption. On 17 July 1961 the CNAR-BRL wrote back and requested Q to go ahead with the sale without replying to his question. On 18 January 1962 the CNARBRL sold the pieces of land to Mrs Bernavon by way of notarised document, drawn up by Q. In 1976, Mrs Mellet, who had meanwhile become the sole owner of the agricultural land holdings, sued the CNARBRL, Mr and Mrs Bernavon and Q. She demanded a declaration that the sale of 18 January 1962 did not affect her rights, as well as damages.

Held: The first instance court and the appeal court upheld the claim. The further appeal of the notary was dismissed.

Judgment: ... Whereas Q contests that the appeal court has upheld his liability to Mrs Mellet although, on the one hand, the notary is under a duty to give advice to the parties of a notarized transaction only and that this duty cannot be invoked by a third person ...;

Whereas, however, notaries are liable, even to third persons, for every fault causing harm which they commit in exercising their functions; they are particularly obliged to examine the correctness of documents which they are requested to draw up and not to notarize a contract which they know to be illegal because it is made by defrauding the rights of other interested parties; the appeal court held, both on its own findings and in adopting the findings of the first instance court, that Q who had known the right of pre-emption, which the CNARBRL had granted the Rieus by way of the document of 7 June 1960 that was correctly published, had abstained from making sure, before notarizing the contract of resale for the pieces of land, that the Rieus had waived that right, and that he had nevertheless notarized the contract of 18 June 1962 in violation of the rights of the beneficiaries of the right of preemption and in misunderstanding the legal provisions with regard to the publicity of land holdings; the appeal court could conclude from this that the notary, who had knowingly lent his official services to the drawing up of such a document and had contributed to the realization of harm caused to Mrs Mellet, had become liable to her; on those grounds alone, it lawfully justified its decision; ...

On those grounds, the court dismisses the appeal lodged against the judgment delivered on 3 May 1979 by the cour d'appel, Nîmes; ...

---

[82] No. 79-14687, Bull civ I no. 14, JCP 1982.II.19728, annotated by M Dagot.

31.2.B.3 DIRECT ACTIONS IN CHAINS OF CONTRACTS

The question whether a third person acquires an enforceable right of action against one of the parties to a contract also arises in cases where there is a chain of contracts. A typical example is that of a chain of contracts for the sale of goods. The producer sells the goods to a distributor. The distributor sells them to an intermediary, who sells them to the final seller, who in turn sells them to the final purchaser. In these cases it might be queried whether one of the contracts in the chain can be characterised as having been concluded, possibly by way of an implied agreement, for the benefit of a third person who is party to one of the other contracts 'further up' or 'further down' in the chain. Can the producer claim payment of the purchase price from the final purchaser or the final seller? Can the final purchaser sue the producer in contract if the item was defective from the outset?[83] Such 'direct actions' would be particularly useful for the claimant if one of the intermediaries in the chain is insolvent.

31.2.B.3.1 Claims for Performance

Legal systems in Europe do not normally acknowledge the right of the creditor of one of the contracts in the chain to enforce performance against the debtor of one of the other contracts. There are only a few legislative exceptions to this rule. For example, the Code civil and other pieces of French legislation have long acknowledged an *action directe* for payment in certain chains of contracts, especially an action of the owner/landlord against the sub-tenant or of the principal against the sub-agent (Articles 1753, 1994(2) Cciv).[84] The 2016 reform has recognised the *action directe* more explicitly:

Code civil   **31.31 (FR)**

Article 1341-3: In cases determined by legislation, a creditor may sue directly to obtain satisfaction from a debtor of his own debtor.

However, no similar action exists for the original producer or the distributor in a chain of contracts of sale, and revised Article 1341-3 is restricted to actions for payment. Other claims can only be brought if there is a guarantee or the law of delict applies.[85]

German law insists on the 'relative effect' of contracts in all such cases:

---

[83] On liability and remedies for defective goods in general, see above, ch 27.

[84] For similar rules in other legal systems, cf Art 1705(2) Codice civile, Art 1722 of the Spanish Código civil, Art 399(3) Swiss Law of Obligations.

[85] F Chénedé, *Le nouveau droit des obligations et des contrats: Consolidations, innovations, perspectives* (Paris: Dalloz, 2016) no. 43.31.

BGH, 13 December 1973[86]   **31.32 (DE)**

Direct invoices

*The fact that a contractor which has been directed to delegate certain work to a subcon-
tractor arranges that, in order to save VAT, the subcontractor will invoice the employer
directly does not give the subcontractor a right to be paid by the employer.*

Facts: From 1956 to 1958 the claimant carried out infrastructure works for the construction of a motorway
bridge. The defendant, BRD, entered into a contract for the building of this bridge with K subject to the proviso
that K would forward the plans for the infrastructure works to the claimant for the account of and on behalf
of the defendant. The defendant's order form to K dated 21 May 1956 fixed the total remuneration relating
to the bridge construction at DM 5,691,661.30, which excluded the claimant's offer relating to infrastructure
amounting to DM 2,728,621.50. On 24 August 1956 the claimant and K entered into an agreement for performance and settlement of the order for the bridge (internal contract). During the construction of the bridge
the services which the claimant was liable to perform were altered in relation to those which were originally
agreed, which were moreover contested from the point of view of their extent and the payment therefore. In
addition, the construction period was exceeded. The defendant paid the claimant's invoice in the amount of
DM 3,689,077.25, but the parties were in dispute concerning the claimant's additional claim amounting to
DM 300,000. The claimant brought proceedings for the payment of DM 300,000 together with interest. The
defendant invoked the penal clauses and price clauses concluded by it and K. The claimant claimed not to be
bound by those clauses.

Held: The Regional Court (LG) upheld the claim. On appeal, the question also arose as to whether there were
direct contractual relations as between the parties, as alleged by the claimant and denied by the defendant. The
Higher Regional Court (OLG) dismissed the claim on the ground that there was no right of action against the
owner. The appeal on a point of law was dismissed.

Judgment: The court of appeal considered that there was no contractual relationship
between the parties to the proceedings. The defendant did not instruct the claimant in
respect of the infrastructure works. Consequently, the claimant had no right of action to
recover from the defendant. It intervened in the carrying out of the infrastructure works
on the instructions of K and could recover from K. According to the appeal it was argued
that the claimant was not a subcontractor but a secondary undertaking to K, the main
undertaking, and that therefore there was a contractual relationship between the claimant and the defendant.

1—Transmission of the order by the defendant

It is for the claimant to prove that by the order of 7 May 1956 the defendant confirmed that the claimant was a secondary undertaking and not a subcontractor. Under
the additional contract of 16 May 1956 the defendant gave instructions to K as the sole
contractual partner, admittedly subject to the proviso that K would transmit the order to
the claimant in order to carry out the infrastructure works. The account given of the facts
highlights the fact that there is no contractual relationship between the parties to the
proceedings.

K's request to the defendant to place the order for infrastructure works directly with
the claimant in order to save VAT did not form part of the contract negotiations with the
defendant. Moreover, in the contractual document of 21 May 1956, reference is made
only to K, the contracting undertaking.

(a) The Higher Regional Court is not disregarding the difference between a secondary
undertaking who acts on the direct orders of the owner to carry out a portion of the

---

[86] WM 1974, 197.

works, and the subcontractor who assists in the performance of the contract by the principal undertaking without there being any contractual relationship between him (the subcontractor) and the owner.

(b) In the appeal it is argued that the term main contractor used both by the defendant and by K means nothing else than the general contractor (as opposed to secondary) and thus covers not only a subcontracting relationship but also that of a secondary undertaking.

(c) K entrusted the works to the claimant on behalf of the defendant in order to avoid double liability to VAT. At the outset the defendant wished to contract and deal only with K as the contractor for the whole of the works.

2—Transmission of the order to the claimant

The court of appeal also considers that no contractual link was created subsequently between the parties. If K was in fact obliged to transmit instructions to the claimant on behalf of the defendant, no evidence has been adduced of a delegation of authority to that effect or of a subsequent ratification. Moreover, the 1959 negotiations with regard to a possible set-off do not enable the view to be taken that a contract was created.

The court of appeal could not infer the existence of a delegated authority solely on the basis of an act indicative of an intention to enter into contractual relations.

The saving in terms of VAT benefits K, the main contractor. That benefit derives from an internal contract entered into between the claimant and K. Thus, the claimant made out its invoices directly to the defendant which paid the claimant direct. Those methods of deduction and payment do not alter the contractual relationships and give rise to no direct contractual relationship.

The changes in the services to be performed under the contract stem from the fact that K delegated the infrastructure works to the claimant. The payments by the defendant to the claimant should not lead one to think that there is a contract between them but rather may be analysed as mere payments in favour of a third party on the instructions of the person with a right of action for payment.

3—Unjustified enrichment

The Higher Regional Court dismissed the claim under that head. The claimant maintains that it carried out major and additional infrastructure works not provided for in the initial order. If those additional works were carried out in the absence of any contract with the defendant, then the defendant would have unjustly enriched itself. Those claims were to no avail. If the claimant carried out additional work the beneficiary thereof is K and not the defendant. It provided services under the contract with K and therefore did not do so for no consideration. Payment for those services is a matter for its contractual partner K and not for the defendant. The claimant mistook its defendant. On that ground its claims were dismissed.

Note

This was a case of subcontracting. The court confirms that there is no contractual relationship between the owner and the subcontractor even if the former became directly involved in the contractual process. Also worthy of note is the fact that there was no recourse to the doctrine of unjustified enrichment.

31.2.B.3.2 Claims for Non-Performance

Similarly, most legal systems in Europe reject the idea that a third person should be able to enjoy contractual remedies for non-performance of the primary obligation arising from a contract to which he was not a party. For example, they limit the contractual rights of the final purchaser to claims against the final seller.[87] The final seller can pursue his contractual remedies against his seller, and so on; only the first buyer can sue the producer in contract. Liability 'follows the contractual chain', and no 'shortcuts' can be made. This is seen as a straightforward application of the 'relative effect' of contracts[88] or the doctrine of privity of contract. This is illustrated by the following three cases from Germany and England, which concern building works.

BGH, 28 June 1979[89]   **31.33 (DE)**

Isolar glass

Where a manufacturer issues a guarantee in relation to goods sold to an intermediary, intending that guarantee to be enforceable by the ultimate consumer of the goods, the guarantee is treated as a contract made for the benefit of the consumer which can be enforced by the consumer directly against the manufacturer.

Facts: The claimant had asked the firm F to install panes of glass in his house. F bought panes described as 'ISOLAR-Glass' from the defendant. A letter in which the claimant's architect complained of the opaqueness of the panes was passed on by F to the defendant, and the defendant's answer of 8 November 1974 denying liability was passed on by F to the claimant. It was only from this letter that the claimant learned that the following statement was printed under the heading 'Guarantee' on prospectuses disseminated by the defendant for marketing purposes:

> The manufacturers of ISOLAR glass guarantee, for a period of 5 years calculated from the date of initial delivery, that under normal conditions the transparency of ISOLAR glass will not be impaired either by the formation of a film or by deposits of dust between the panes.

F denied all liability under its contract with the claimant. In an action for damages the defendant argued that he had no contract with the claimant. (A separate point was also raised that the five-year period had already run out; this argument was dismissed by the court in parts of the judgment not extracted here.)

Held: The claimant was the beneficiary of the warranty given by the defendant manufacturer.

Judgment: The appellate court took the view that no direct contractual relationship had come into existence between the defendant, as the manufacturer of the glass panes, and the claimant, as the ultimate purchaser thereof. There is no need to determine whether that view is correct. As it is, the contested judgment cannot be valid, since a guarantee

---

[87] For a comparative overview, see M Ebers, A Janssen and O Meyer (eds), *European Perspectives on Producers' Liability: Direct Producers' Liability for Non-conformity and the Sellers' Right of Redress* (Munich: Sellier, 2009).

[88] For Art 1199 Cciv, see above p 1260. For German law, see W Fikentscher and A Heinemann, *Schuldrecht Allgemeiner und Besonderer Teil* (11th edn, Berlin: de Gruyter, 2017) paras 64, 948.

[89] BGHZ 75, 75, NJW 1979, 2036.

agreement for the benefit of the claimant as the final consumer (ie a contract in favour of a third party) came into existence between the defendant and Messrs F.

(a) The appellate court also held that no such [guarantee] contract existed; it stated that, as a general rule, there could not be said to have been any intention on the part of either the manufacturer or the intermediate supplier, who did not enter into direct contractual relations with the final consumer, to create any rights benefiting the latter or to burden themselves with any obligations …

(b) The appellant rightly contests those arguments. The defendant's guarantee … took effect from the date of initial delivery, ie from the date when the glass was delivered to F. Clearly, therefore, the defendant intended to be contractually bound as from that date. This accorded with the interests of the intermediate supplier, which likewise benefited from the creation of the guarantee contract in favour of the final consumer, since, in the event of a defect arising which was covered by the guarantee, it would itself be absolved from liability *vis-à-vis* its customer, inasmuch as the manufacturer would for its part be obliged to make good the defect pursuant to the contractual guarantee. It follows that F must necessarily have wished the guarantee contract to be constituted as rapidly as possible, in order thereby to secure for itself the indirect exemption afforded by that guarantee and to extricate itself from involvement in any subsequent contingencies which might arise (concerning, eg, the question whether the final consumer, as a third party, acquired knowledge of the guarantee) …

(c) Thus, inasmuch as it was in the interests of all the parties concerned that the guarantee relating to a contract benefiting a third party should be constituted as quickly as possible (§ 328 BGB), it must also be assumed that the defendant and F intended such contractual relations to be established. This is also borne out by the fact that, according to the defendant's letter of 8 November 1974, it regarded F as its customer as far as the guarantee contract was concerned. Otherwise, the defendant would have referred not to a complaint about the glass made by Messrs F but to notification of a defect by the claimant, and would have argued the matter out primarily with the claimant, as the final consumer, and not with Messrs F.

That result is not affected by the fact that, in the contractual circumstances prevailing in the present case, the identity of the 'third party' had not yet been established at the time when the contract between the defendant and Messrs F was concluded. As far as the contracting parties were concerned, the identity of the future end consumer was at the outset immaterial. It was enough that they agreed that the third party beneficiary should be whoever was the final consumer. That agreement rendered the third party beneficiary sufficiently ascertainable.

Notes

(1) The right to sue did not arise from the contract of sale but from an (additional) guarantee contract which was held to benefit the claimant. Without such a guarantee he would not have had a remedy against the defendant. This can be seen from §§ 478(5) and 479(3) BGB. These provisions clearly imply that parties to a 'supply chain' can only sue their contractual partner, and cannot jump a link in the chain.

(2) English law has a similarly strict approach. This can be seen from a case that turned on very similar facts, but where no separate warranty had been given:

Simaan General Contracting Co v Pilkington Glass Ltd (No 2)[90]

A manufacturer of materials who was chosen by the employer to supply materials for a building being constructed for the employer and who supplies defective materials is not liable in tort to the contractor when the employer refuses to pay the contractor because of the defects in the material.

Facts: A contractor (Simaan) entrusted a subcontractor (Feal) with the installation of glass panes in a building under construction. The employer, a sheikh, required the glass to be obtained from the manufacturer, Pilkington Glass. The glass was defective in that it was not green (in the country where the building was being constructed, the colour of peace) but tinged with red. The contractor sought compensation from the manufacturer for the loss incurred by him as a result of the owner's refusal to pay based on the defects in the glass.

Held: At first instance Pilkington's defence was unsuccessful. An appeal against the judgment was allowed.

Judgment: BINGHAM LJ: I can, I think, state my conclusions fairly shortly.

(1) I accept without reservation that a claim may lie in negligence for recovery of economic loss alone. Were that not so the *Hedley Byrne* case [1964] AC 465 could not have been decided as it was.

(2) I am quite sure that the defendants owed the plaintiffs a conventional *Donoghue v Stevenson* [1932] AC 562 duty of care to avoid physical injury or damage to person or property. Suppose (however improbably) that the defendants manufactured the units so carelessly that they were liable to explode on exposure to strong sunlight and that one of the units did so explode, blinding an employee of the plaintiffs working in the building. I cannot conceive that such employee would fail in a personal injury action against the defendants for failure to prove a duty of care.

(3) There is no meaningful sense in which the plaintiffs can be said to have relied on the defendants. No doubt the plaintiffs hoped and expected that the defendants would supply good quality goods conforming with the contract specification. But the plaintiffs required Feal to buy these units from the defendants for one reason only, namely, that they were contractually obliged to do so and had no choice in the matter. There was no technical discussion of the product between the plaintiffs and the defendants.

(4) Where a specialist sub-contractor is vetted, selected and nominated by a building owner it may be possible to conclude (as in the *Junior Books* case [1983] 1 AC 520) that the nominated subcontractor has assumed a direct responsibility to the building owner. On that reasoning it might be said that the defendants owed a duty to the Sheikh in tort as well as to Feal in contract. I do not, however, see any basis on which the defendants could be said to have assumed a direct responsibility for the quality of the goods to the plaintiffs: such a responsibility is, I think, inconsistent with the structure of the contract the parties have chosen to make.

(5) The *Junior Books* case has been interpreted as a case arising from physical damage. I doubt if that interpretation accords with Lord Roskill's intention, but it is binding upon us. There is in my view no physical damage in this case. The units are as good as ever they were and will not deteriorate. I bridle somewhat at the assumption of defects

---

[90] [1988] QB 758.

which we are asked to make because what we have here are not, in my view, defects but failures to comply with Sale of Goods Act conditions of correspondence with description or sample, merchantability or (perhaps) fitness for purpose. It would, I think, be an abuse of language to describe these units as damaged. The contrast with the floor in the *Junior Books* case is obvious.

(6) I do not accept that the *Hedley Byrne* case [1964] AC 465, and such authorities as *Ross v Caunters* [1980] Ch 297, establish a general rule that claims in negligence may succeed on proof of foreseeable economic loss caused by the defendant even where no damage to property and no proprietary or possessory interest are shown. If there were such a general rule, the plaintiffs in the *Candlewood* case [1986] AC 1 and *Leigh and Sillavan Ltd v Aliakmon Shipping Co Ltd* [1986] AC 785 would not have failed on the ground they did and the causes of action in the Pirelli case [1983] 2 AC 1 and *London Congregational Union Inc v Harriss & Harriss* [1988] 1 All ER 15 would have been complete at an earlier date. However attractive it may theoretically be to postulate a single principle capable of embracing every kind of case, that is not how the law has developed. It would of course be unsatisfactory if (say) doctors and dentists owed their patients a different duty of care. I do not, however, think it unsatisfactory or surprising if, as I think, a banker's duty towards the recipient of a credit reference and an industrial glass manufacturer's duty towards a main contractor, in the absence of any contract between them, differ. Here, the plaintiffs' real (and understandable) complaint is that the defendants' failure to supply goods in conformity with the specification has rendered their main contract less profitable. This is a type of claim against which, if laid in tort, the law has consistently set its face.

(7) If, contrary to my view, these units can be regarded as damaged at all, the damage (or the defects) occurred at the time of manufacture when they were the defendants' property. I therefore think that the plaintiffs fail to show any interest in the goods at the time when damage occurred. I very much doubt if there was any time on site, whether in course of erection or after rejection, when the plaintiffs had a proprietary or possessory interest in the units, but I do not think it useful to pursue this, since neither was the time at which, if at all, physical damage occurred.

(8) I do not think it just and reasonable to impose on the defendants a duty of care towards the plaintiffs of the scope contended for. (a) Just as equity remedied the inadequacies of the common law, so has the law of torts filled gaps left by other causes of action where the interests of justice so required. I see no such gap here, because there is no reason why claims beginning with the Sheikh should not be pursued down the contractual chain, subject to any short-cut which may be agreed upon, ending up with a contractual claim against the defendants. That is the usual procedure. It must be what the parties contemplated when they made their contracts. I see no reason for departing from it. (b) Although the defendants did not sell subject to exempting conditions, I fully share the difficulty which others have envisaged where there were such conditions. Even as it is, the defendants' sale may well have been subject to terms and conditions imported by the Sale of Goods Act 1979. Some of those are beneficial to the seller. If such terms are to circumscribe a duty which would be otherwise owed to a party not a party to the contract and unaware of its terms, then that could be unfair to him. But if the duty is unaffected by the conditions on which the seller supplied the goods, it is in my view unfair to him and makes a mockery of contractual negotiation. I would accordingly allow the appeal and answer the question posed by the preliminary issue in the negative.

Note

The loss at issue is regarded as economic loss and therefore not in principle recoverable in tort. The plaintiff had an action in contract against the subcontractor. For unknown reasons (insolvency?) the plaintiff preferred to bring an action against the manufacturer with whom he had no contractual link. The Court of Appeal pointed out that the situation is different from that which gave rise to the judgment in *Junior Books Ltd v Veitchi Co Ltd*, discussed below and mentioned repeatedly in this judgment. Since the action is in tort, it was held in the judgment that, even if there was negligence, that does not allow recovery of damages for economic loss stemming from non-payment of the undertaking. For that it would have been necessary to retrace the chain of contracts link by link. However, in the *Junior Books* case a way had been found to avoid this difficulty.

House of Lords **31.35 (EN)**

Junior Books Ltd v Veitchi Co Ltd[91]

When an employer has nominated a particular firm to be employed by the main contractor to carry out a particular part of the work, there is a sufficient relationship between the employer and the nominated subcontractor to make the latter liable in tort if it does its work without proper care, even if the defective floor made by the subcontractor is not dangerous and has caused no physical injury.

Facts: An owner asked an undertaking to build a factory. A subcontractor appointed by the owner was to build a special concrete floor. There was no contract between the owner and the subcontractor but only between the main contractor and the subcontractor. Cracks appeared in the floor after only two years. The owner sued the subcontractor and asked for the floor to be replaced and for restitution of the economic loss resulting from closure of the factory for the duration of the works.

Held: The Scottish courts declared the action admissible and their decision was confirmed by the House of Lords.

Judgment: LORD ROSKILL: ... [I]n *Anns v Merton London Borough Council* [1978] AC 728, 751, Lord Wilberforce, approving the earlier decisions of the Court of Appeal in *Dutton v Bognor Regis Urban District Council* [1972] 1 QB 373 and *Sparham-Souter v Town and Country Developments (Essex) Ltd* [1976] QB 858, said of the trilogy of cases, *Donoghue v Stevenson, Hedley Byrne,* and *Dorset Yacht*:

'the position has now been reached that in order to establish that a duty of care arises in a particular situation, it is not necessary to bring the facts of that situation within those of previous situations in which a duty of care has been held to exist. Rather the question has to be approached in two stages. First one has to ask whether, as between the alleged wrongdoer and the person who has suffered damage there is a sufficient relationship of proximity or neighbourhood such that, in the reasonable contemplation of the former, carelessness on his part may be likely to cause damage to the

[91] [1983] 1 AC 520.

latter—in which case a prima facie duty of care arises. Secondly, if the first question is answered affirmatively, it is necessary to consider whether there are any considerations which ought to negative, or to reduce or limit the scope of the duty or the class of person to whom it is owed or the damages to which a breach of it may give rise: ...'

Applying those statements of general principle as your Lordships have been enjoined to do both by Lord Reid and by Lord Wilberforce rather than to ask whether the particular situation which has arisen does or does not resemble some earlier and different situation where a duty of care has been held or has not been held to exist, I look for the reasons why, it being conceded that the appellants owed a duty of care to others not to construct the flooring so that those others were in peril of suffering loss or damage to their persons or their property, that duty of care should not be equally owed to the respondents. The appellants, though not in direct contractual relationship with the respondents, were as nominated subcontractors in almost as close a commercial relationship with the respondents as it is possible to envisage short of privity of contract. Why then should the appellants not be under a duty to the respondents not to expose the respondents to a possible liability to financial loss for repairing the flooring should it prove that that flooring had been negligently constructed? It is conceded that if the flooring had been so badly constructed that to avoid imminent danger the respondents had expended money upon renewing it the respondents could have recovered the cost of so doing. It seems curious that, if the appellants' work had been so bad that to avoid imminent danger expenditure had been incurred, the respondents could recover that expenditure, but that if the work was less badly done so that remedial work could be postponed they cannot do so. Yet this is seemingly the result of the appellants' contentions ...

Turning back to the present appeal I therefore ask first whether there was the requisite degree of proximity so as to give rise to the relevant duty of care relied on by the respondents. I regard the following facts as of crucial importance in requiring an affirmative answer to that question. (1) The appellants were nominated sub-contractors. (2) The appellants were specialists in flooring. (3) The appellants knew what products were required by the respondents and their main contractors and specialised in the production of those products. (4) The appellants alone were responsible for the composition and construction of the flooring. (5) The respondents relied upon the appellants' skill and experience. (6) The appellants as nominated sub-contractors must have known that the respondents relied upon their skill and experience. (7) The relationship between the parties was as close as it could be short of actual privity of contract. (8) The appellants must be taken to have known that if they did the work negligently (as it must be assumed that they did) the resulting defects would at some time require remedying by the respondents expending money upon the remedial measures as a consequence of which the respondents would suffer financial or economic loss.

My Lords, reverting to Lord Devlin's speech in *Hedley Byrne & Co Ltd v Heller & Partners Ltd* [1964] AC 465, it seems to me that all the conditions existed which give rise to the relevant duty of care owed by the appellants to the respondents.

I then turn to Lord Wilberforce's second proposition. On the facts I have just stated, I see nothing whatsoever to restrict the duty of care arising from the proximity of which I have spoken. During the argument it was asked what the position would be in a case where there was a relevant exclusion clause in the main contract. My Lords, that question does not arise for decision in the instant appeal, but in principle I would venture the view that such a clause according to the manner in which it was worded might in some circumstances limit the duty of care just as in the *Hedley Byrne* case the plaintiffs were ultimately defeated by the defendants' disclaimer of responsibility. But in the present case the only suggested reason for limiting the damage (ex hypothesi economic or financial only) recoverable for the breach of the duty of care just enunciated is that hitherto the law has not allowed such recovery and therefore ought not in the future to do so. My Lords, with all respect to those who find this a sufficient answer, I do not. I think this is the next logical step forward in the development of this branch of the law. I see no reason why what was called during the argument 'damage to the pocket' simpliciter should be disallowed when 'damage to the pocket' coupled with physical damage has hitherto always been allowed. I do not think that this development, if development it be, will lead to untoward consequences. The concept of proximity must always involve, at least in most cases, some degree of reliance—I have already mentioned the words 'skill' and 'judgment' in the speech of Lord Morris of Borth-y-Gest in *Hedley Byrne* [1964] AC 465 at 503. These words seem to me to be an echo, be it conscious or unconscious, of the language of section 14 (1) of the Sale of Goods Act 1893. My Lords, though the analogy is not exact, I do not find it unhelpful for I think the concept of proximity of which I have spoken and the reasoning of Lord Devlin in the Hedley Byrne case involve factual considerations not unlike those involved in a claim under section 14 (1); and as between an ultimate purchaser and a manufacturer would not easily be found to exist in the ordinary everyday transaction of purchasing chattels when it is obvious that in truth the real reliance was upon the immediate vendor and not upon the manufacturer ...

[LORDS FRASER and RUSSELL agreed, LORD KEITH delivered a separate concurring judgment and LORD BRANDON dissented].

Notes

(1) On the very specific facts of this case the House of Lords held that a duty of care in tort exists between a contractor or subcontractor and an employer. The general rule, as can be seen from *Simaan*, is still that an action lies only for one chain of the contract.

(2) It is not easy to see exactly the facts that made *Junior Books* different. Lord Roskill explains that the case is different to the situation 'between an ultimate purchaser and a manufacturer ... in the ordinary everyday transaction of purchasing chattels' because 'it is obvious that in truth the real reliance was upon the immediate vendor and not upon the manufacturer.' With respect, that reasoning is simply implausible: many everyday purchases of branded goods are made in reliance on the manufacturer's reputation, not in reliance on the retailer's recommendation of the brand.

(3) Nonetheless, the contrast to the 'everyday purchase' may in fact explain why *Junior Books* was different. The manufacturer of goods normally has no direct contact with the purchaser and knows nothing about the purpose for which they are required. That case is analogous to *Caparo v Dickman*, which laid down a strict requirement for the recovery of economic loss caused by negligent misstatement.[92] In contrast, in *Junior Books* it is almost certain that the employer and the nominated subcontractor would have been in direct negotiations even though they did not contract with each

---

[92] See above, p 1308.

other, and the subcontractor would have known exactly what the floor was wanted for. The requirements for liability for pure economic loss set out in *Caparo* would have thus been satisfied. The only difference is that *Junior Books* was a case of negligent acts rather than negligent words.

A similar approach, denying liability of manufacturers as a general rule, prevails in most European jurisdictions. The notable exceptions are Belgium and, especially, France, where the courts have long recognised the existence of an *action directe* of the final purchaser against the distributor and the producer.[93] At first, the Cour de cassation did not give reasons for this result, which has no textual basis in the Code civil. A justification was only provided in a later case that did not concern a chain of contracts of sales but a chain of contracts of different types, involving sales and service contracts:

Cass Ass plén, 7 February 1986[94] $\qquad$ **31.36 (FR)**

Insulation not fit for purpose

Under a building contract, if material supplied by a manufacturer is not in conformity with the contract, the employer has a direct action against the manufacturer.

Facts: Insulating material supplied to a building contractor by MPI was not in accordance with the contract and caused water pipes to corrode. The employer brought a direct action against the manufacturer after expiry of the short time period in which it would have been necessary to make a claim for a latent defect.

Held: The lower court allowed the claim on the basis of delict. The Plenary Court upheld the decision on the basis of a direct contractual action.

Judgment: THE COURT: *On the first appeal ground*:—Whereas according to the findings of the judgment appealed against (Paris, 19th Chamber B, 14 June 1984) the Résidence Brigitte, insured by Union des Assurances de Paris (UAP), in 1969 entrusted the construction of a building to the architects Marty & Ginsberg (to whose rights the Ginsberg couple had succeeded), assisted by the consultants OTH and BEPET; as the company Petit which was responsible for the main structural work subcontracted to the company Samy the digging of trenches for the laying of services to be carried out by the company Laurent Bourillet; as Samy applied a product called Protexculate to those surfaces which was intended to ensure thermal insulation; as the product was sold to it by the Soc. commerciale de Matériaux pour la protection et insulation (MPI); as upon the occurrence of leaks of water the experts appointed at the interlocutory stage concluded in 1977 that there had been corrosion of the pipes caused by the Protexculate product which was aggravated by failings in the trench cutting;

---

[93] Cass civ 12 November 1884, DP 1885.1.357, S 1886.1.149; Cass civ (1) 9 October 1979, no. 78-12502, Bull civ I no. 241, translated in H-W Micklitz, J Stuyck and E Terryn (eds), *Ius Commune Casebooks on the Common Law of Europe: Consumer Law* (Oxford: Hart Publishing, 2010) 342 (*Defective Lamborghini*).

[94] No. 84-15189, Bull civ AP no. 2, D 1986, 232, annotated by A Bénabent; F Terré, Y Lequette and F Chénedé, *Grands arrêts de jurisprudence civile*, vol 2, *Obligations, Contrats spéciaux, Sûretés* (13th edn, Paris: Dalloz, 2015) no. 268.

— Whereas UAP brought proceedings against MPI, Petit, Samy, Laurent Bourillet and Messrs Marty & Ginsberg and the consultants for reimbursement of the compensation paid to the co-owners under an invoice giving rights of subrogation dated 30 October 1980;

— Whereas MPI argues that the court below was wrong to uphold that claim together with interest at the legal rate with effect from 30 October 1980 on the basis of liability in tort; as according to the appeal ground the employer (*maître de l'ouvrage*) has a right of action against the manufacturer of materials laid by an undertaking only as regards the guarantee against a latent defect affecting the item sold at the time of its manufacture; and that action, which is of necessity contractual, must be brought within a short period after the defect is discovered.

— Whereas thus, in the present case, by upholding the action brought on 28 January 1980 by UAP succeeding to the rights of the main contractor seeking a guarantee of a defect discovered by the court-appointed expert on 4 February 1977, and in respect of which compensation was paid by UAP on 30 October 1980, the cour d'appel which declined to examine whether the action ought to have been brought within a shorter time-frame misapplied and therefore infringed Article [former] 1382 of the Civil Code and, by failing to apply it, Article [former] 1648 of that Code;

— Whereas, however, the employer, in the same way as the sub-owner, enjoys all the rights and rights of action attaching to the item which belonged to the manufacturer;

— Whereas the employer therefore has a direct contractual right of action against the manufacturer based on the non-compliance of the item supplied;

— Whereas therefore, in finding that MPI had manufactured and sold under the name 'Protexculate' a product which was not fit for the use for which it was intended and which was the cause of the injury suffered by Résidence Brigitte, the employer, the cour d'appel which characterised this to have been a breach of contract, which UAP (succeeding to the rights of Résidence Brigitte) was entitled to rely upon in order to make a direct claim for compensation within the time limits applicable under the ordinary law, underpinned its decision with proper legal reasons; ...

On those grounds the appeal is dismissed.

Notes

(1) This judgment concerns a classic scenario: A produces and sells defective materials to B, who uses them for erecting a building on C's land. Does C have a contractual right of redress against the manufacturer? Or can he only enforce contractual rights against the builder, who in turn has contractual rights against the manufacturer? The solution of the Assemblée plenière avoids a multiplicity of suits resulting from pursuing liability through each link in the chain. In fact, there is a direct right of action based on non-conformity—or for a latent defect—because the remedies for non-performance are 'attached' to the goods transferred. Therefore, the Cour de cassation justifies the *action directe* with the accessory character of the rights flowing from the defects in the goods. It thereby rejects the different analyses that had been suggested, such as an implied stipulation for the benefit of the employer or an implied assignment of the builder's claim against the manufacturer. The manufacturer's liability is in fact an obligation *propter rem*, ie an obligation that runs with the product sold.

(2) This result is generally accepted today, although it flatly contradicts the letter of ex-Article 1165 (new Article 1199) Cciv:[95] a person who is not party to a particular contract is given the right to enforce remedies for non-performance flowing from this contract, which thereby 'confers a benefit' on him.

(3) We have already seen on a number of occasions that the distinction between contractual and non-contractual liability can matter for a variety of reasons. First, the claimant in a delictual action needs to prove fault while contractual liability in cases like this is strict. Secondly, the rule of *non cumul* prevents the bringing of a delictual action where the cause of action is the non-performance of a contractual obligation. Thirdly, in the case of contractual liability, the manufacturer will normally be able to raise against the final contracting party the exceptions and defences which he would have been entitled to raise against the intermediate contracting party,[96] such as clauses exempting the manufacturer from liability or periods of limitation, most contractual limitation periods traditionally being much shorter than those of the law of delict (many of these differences were abolished by the reform of the French law of prescription in 2008).[97]

In 1988, the first Civil Chamber of the Cour de cassation went even further and extended the contractual rights of third parties to cases where no property had been transferred, so that it was not possible to argue that any accessory rights whatsoever had passed with the goods. In its *Soderep* decision the Court held that:

> in a group of contracts liability in contract necessarily applies to claims for damages by all those who have suffered damage simply by virtue of the fact that they had some link with the initial contract; indeed, since in such a case the party liable to perform under the contract must have foreseen the consequences of his failure to perform according to the applicable rules of contract, the victim can have against him only a contractual action, although there is no contract between them.[98]

The ruling was strongly criticised by academic writers since it was difficult to determine its limits and because of the inherent vagueness of the notion of a 'group of contracts'. It was firmly rejected by the Assemblée plénière in the 1991 *Besse* decision:

Cass Ass plén, 12 July 1991[99]   **31.37 (FR)**

Bad plumbing

An employer does not have a direct contractual claim against a subcontractor for defective work.

---

[95] See above, p 1260.

[96] Cass civ (1) 7 June 1995, no. 93-13898, Bull I no. 249.

[97] Recently the Cour de cassation even held that the manufacturer is entitled to raise against the final contracting party a defence although this would normally be possible because of this party being a consumer: Cass civ (3) 3 November 2016, no. 15-18340, unpublished.

[98] Cass civ (1) 21 June 1988, no. 85-12609, Bull I no. 202, D 1989, 5, annotated by C Larroumet.

[99] No. 90-13602, Bull AP no. 5, Terré, Lequette and Chénedé (n 94 above) nos. 173–76.

Facts: Mr Besse asked Mr Alhalda, a builder, to construct a dwelling house. The builder subcontracted the plumbing work to Mr Protois. Since that work proved to be defective, Mr Besse brought an action based on delict against the subcontractor more than 10 years after the handover of the works.

Held: The Appeal Court of Nancy declared the action inadmissible on the basis that, where a party liable to perform a contractual obligation has entrusted performance of that obligation to another person, the other party to the bargain merely has a right of action in contract against that person to the same extent as regards rights and obligations as the substituted party that is primarily liable. (It thus applied the case law of the first Civil Chamber and, more particularly, the principles laid down in the judgment of 8 March 1988 whose reasoning it adopted.) An appeal was allowed.

Judgment: THE COURT: *On the sole appeal ground*:—With a view to [former] Article 1165 Cciv;
— Whereas agreements have effect only as between the parties to them;
— Whereas according to the contested judgment (Nancy, 1st Civil Chamber, 16 January 1990), more than ten years after the handover of the dwelling house which Mr Besse had asked Mr Alhalda, the main contractor, to build, and in which a subcontractor, Mr Protois, had carried out various items of plumbing work which turned out to be defective, Mr Besse brought proceedings against both of them for damages for losses sustained;
— Whereas in declaring inadmissible the claims against the subcontractor, the judgment notes that where a party liable to perform a contractual obligation has entrusted performance of that obligation to another person, the person to whom the first party is liable to perform merely has a right of action against that other person that is necessarily contractual, subject to the limits on his rights and on the obligations of the substituted party primarily liable; as it deduces therefrom that Mr Protois may set up against Mr Besse all the rights of defence based on the building agreement entered into by Mr Besse with the main contractor, as well as the legal provisions governing it, in particular the ten-year time-bar;
— Whereas in so deciding, where the subcontractor is not contractually bound to the owner who asked for the works to be carried out, the appeal court infringed the above-mentioned provision;
On those grounds the Court quashes the judgment of 16 January 1990 by the Nancy cour d'appel, but only to the extent to which it declared inadmissible the claim against Mr Protois …

Notes

(1) The action of the employer against the subcontractor could therefore only be in delict. As a result, the limitation period applicable was the delictual one of 10 years from the appearance of the damage[100] and not the strict contractual period applicable to builders (at that time 10 years from the non-performance of the contract[101]), as had been held by the cour d'appel.

(2) The *Besse* judgment did not overrule the decision in the *Insulation not fit for purpose* case:[102] in a number of subsequent decisions the Cour de cassation clarified

---

[100] ex-Art 2270-1 Cciv [now five years (Art 2224 Cciv) or 10 years if the victim suffers physical harm (Art 2226 Cciv)].

[101] ex-Arts 1792 and 2270 Cciv [now Arts 1792 to 1792-4-3].

[102] See above, p 1329.

that an *action directe* will still be acknowledged in those areas where it had been traditionally accepted, ie where there has been a transfer of property. As a result, the final purchaser in a chain of sales and the employer of a builder who used material supplied by a manufacturer enjoy a direct action against the manufacturer, while the employer of a builder who contracted for the services of a subcontractor (*Besse*) and the lessee of a commercial property which the lessor rented from the owner[103] do not have a direct action against the subcontractor and the owner, respectively. Bénabent argues that this is an 'absurdity' that cannot be justified.[104] Do you agree?

(3) The success of an action that Mr Besse might bring in delict depends above all on his ability to prove that Mr Protois's work constituted *faute* within the meaning of ex-Article 1382 (new 1240) Cciv. According to the traditional view of the Cour de cassation, the mere fact that the defendant's performance of a contractual obligation was defective was not sufficient because delictual liability required proof of an independent or 'specific delictual fault', ie a violation of the general duty not to inflict harm on anyone which was 'detached from the contract'. However, from the late 1990s onwards the Court gradually dropped this requirement and assimilated delictual and contractual fault to the extent that the defective performance of the contract in itself constituted delictual fault vis-à-vis a person who was not a party to the contract, no further proof of a violation of the general duty of care being needed. According to most commentators, the Assemblée plénière approved of this result in 2006.[105] Moreover, it seems that in a delictual action Mr Protois would be liable in full, even if the contract under which he was employed to do the work by Mr Alhalda had clauses excluding or limiting his liability. Finally, Mr Protois would not be able to invoke the contractual limitation period in case it would be shorter than the delictual one. Paradoxically, Mr Besse might therefore have been better off by being referred to delictual liability: on the one hand, he would have benefited from an action that was triggered by the defective performance of the terms of a contract to which he was no party without having to show delictual fault; on the other hand, he would not have been subject to any contractual limitations imposed on Mr Alhalda for the benefit of Mr Protois by the terms of this very contract or to any statutory limitation periods attached to contractual actions. This outcome has frequently been criticised as not being equitable: the third party to a contract, it has been said, would be allowed to have his cake and eat it, too.[106] Do you agree? And can the result be reconciled with the rule of *non cumul*?

The question of the liability of contractual parties towards third parties was one of the most pressing to be tackled in the reform of the law of obligations. However, in preparing the 2016 revision of the Code civil it was decided to leave the issue for the upcoming

[103] Ass plén 6 October 2006, no. 05-13255, Bull civ AP no. 9; Terré, Lequette and Chénedé (n 94 above) no. 177.

[104] A Bénabent, *Les obligations* (16th edn, Paris: LGDJ, 2017) nos. 271–72.

[105] Ass plén 6 October 2006, no. 05-13255, Bull civ AP no. 9; Terré, Lequette and Chénedé (n 94 above) no. 177.

[106] P Ancel, 'Faut il "faire avec"? À propos de l'arrêt de l'Assemblée plénière du 6 octobre 2006' RDC 2007, 538, 544.

reform of civil liability. At the time of writing the outcome of this reform is uncertain. Maybe it will be decided to quash the Assemblée plénière's solution in its entirety, as suggested by the Avant-projet Terré on contract law[107] and the first draft of the reform of civil liability published by the Chancery in 2016.[108] But probably a more nuanced solution will be reached in the end. While it has been suggested that the issue can be resolved by assuming the existence of an implicit stipulation for the benefit of the third person (the party who is liable to perform under the initial contract tacitly promises to the intermediary contractor that he will make good any damage which a third person who contracts with the intermediary might incur from the promisor's potential non-performance), it is more likely that the upcoming reform of civil liability will not have recourse to the doctrine of *stipulation pour autrui*. Indeed, it seems that the reform will give the third-party victim of the non-performance an option between contractual liability and delictual liability. If the third party chooses the former in order to prove easily the promisor's non-performance, he will be subject to all the conditions and limitations which the promisee is also subject to. On the other hand, if the third party chooses the latter he will not be subject to these conditions and limitations but will have to establish that the non-performance is *per se* a delictual conduct. This solution was adopted by Article 1342 of the Avant-projet Catala and by the reform bill on civil liability published in 2017:

Reform bill on civil liability **31.38 (FR)**

Article 1234: Where non-performance of a contract causes harm to a third party, the latter can claim reparation of its consequences from the debtor only on the basis of extra-contractual liability, and subject to that third party's establishing one of the actions giving rise to liability targeted by Section II of Chapter II.

Nevertheless, a third party who has a legitimate interest in the proper performance of a contract can equally invoke, on the basis of contractual liability, a contractual failing where the latter has caused him harm. The conditions and limitations on this liability which are applicable in the relations between the contracting parties may be set up against him. Any contract term which limits the contractual liability of a party to the contract in relation to a third party is deemed not written.

Notes

(1) This provision is very similar to Article 1342 of the Avant-projet Catala. However, from a formal perspective the two paragraphs of the latter provision are somewhat reversed in the reform bill, maybe to highlight that the general rule is that the third party must bring a delictual action rather than a contractual one. Another difference is to be noted from a substantive perspective: the third party can only bring a contractual claim when it 'has a legitimate interest in the proper performance of [the]

---

[107] F Terré (ed), *Pour une réforme du droit des contrats* (Paris: Dalloz, 2009) Art 125(2) : 'The mere existence of a harm sustained by a third party as the result of the non-performance of the contract by one of the parties does not engage the latter's delictual liability'.

[108] Art 1234 of the first reform draft was almost identical to Art 1234(1) of the 2017 reform bill; however, the provision in the reform bill added a second paragraph (see below, 31.38 (FR)).

contract.' Considered by an author as 'vague',[109] this requirement will hardly limit the scope of this contractual liability. Another substantial difference is the specification that the parties to the contract cannot stipulate clauses absolving them from any contractual actions brought by third parties.

(2) The vivid debate about whether the solution suggested by the reform bill on civil liability is appropriate will probably not be settled by case law. Despite two recent decisions that can hardly be reconciled with the 2006 decision[110] the Cour de cassation and legal scholars are not yet willing to say that the latter is not good law anymore. In the end one may legitimately hope that the reform bill will soon provide a definitive answer to the problem.

The EC Consumer Sales Directive explicitly refrains from providing a uniform solution to the question of the *action directe*. It does not oblige the Member States to harmonise this issue:

Sale of Consumer Goods Directive[111]   31.39 (EU)

Article 3: Rights of the consumer
(1) The seller shall be liable to the consumer for any lack of conformity which exists at the time the goods were delivered.
(2) …

Article 4: Right of redress
Where the final seller is liable to the consumer because of a lack of conformity resulting from an act or omission by the producer, a previous seller in the same chain of contracts or any other intermediary, the final seller shall be entitled to pursue remedies against the person or persons liable in the contractual chain. [T]he person or persons liable against whom the final seller may pursue remedies, together with the relevant actions and conditions of exercise, shall be determined by national law.

Article 12: Review
The Commission shall, not later than 7 July 2006, review the application of this Directive and submit to the European Parliament and the Council a report. The report shall examine, inter alia, the case for introducing the producer's direct liability and, if appropriate, shall be accompanied by proposals.

---

[109] JS Borghetti, 'La responsabilité des contractants à l'égard des tiers dans le projet de réforme de la responsabilité civile' D 2017, 1846. *Contra* M Leveneur, 'Une solution convaincante pour l'engagement de la responsabilité des contractants par les tiers. À propos de l'article 1234 du projet de réforme de la responsabilité civil' JCP G 2017, 1182.

[110] Cass com 18 January 2017, no. 14-16442, Bull no. 557; Cass civ (3) 18 May 2017, no. 16-11203, Bull no. 557. See also older cases giving rise to similar doubts: Cass civ (3) 22 October 2008, no. 07-15583, Bull civ III no. 160; Cass civ (1) 15 December 2011, no. 10-17691, unpublished.

[111] Directive 1999/44/EC of the European Parliament and of the Council of 25 May 1999 on certain aspects of the sale of consumer goods and associated guarantees, OJ L171/12.

> *Notes*
>
> (1) Some Member States, eg Finland, Lithuania, Latvia, Portugal, Spain and Sweden, introduced direct claims of consumers to have goods repaired or replaced against manufacturers after 1999.
>
> (2) Article 4 of the Directive accepts national choices. It probably requires that the national law give the ultimate seller (the retailer who has to provide a remedy to the consumer) some sort of recourse, but it would be adequate if the retailer could simply sue the person who supplied him (eg a wholesaler) and so on up the chain. It is probably also permissible for Member States to allow the wholesaler to limit its liability to the retailer.
>
> (3) However, it does not follow that the European Court of Justice (ECJ) simply follows a national solution, eg the French qualification of the *action directe* as being of a contractual nature, in other areas of law, such as in determining jurisdiction:

Court of Justice, 17 June 1992 **31.40 (EU)**

Jakob Handte & Co GmbH v Traitements Mécano-chimiques des Surfaces SA[112]

Facts: The French company Traitements Mécano-chimiques des Surfaces (TMCS) purchased two machines from a Swiss company. Into these machines a component was incorporated that was manufactured by the German firm Jakob Handte & Co, but sold and installed by the French company Handte France. TCMS sought compensation from Handte Germany for damage incurred because the equipment manufactured and sold did not comply with rules on hygiene and safety at work and was unsuitable for its intended purpose. The Tribunal de Grande Instance of Bonneville and the Cour d'appel of Chambéry held that the French courts had jurisdiction to rule on the claim under Article 5(1) of the 1968 Brussels Convention on jurisdiction and the enforcement of judgments in civil and commercial matters [now Article 7(1)(a) of Council Regulation (EU) No 1215/2012 of 12 December 2012], according to which a person domiciled in a Contracting State may, in another Contracting State, be sued 'in matters relating to a contract, in the courts for the place of performance of the obligation in question'. Handte Germany appealed against the decision of the cour d'appel. The Cour de cassation stayed the proceedings and requested a preliminary ruling from the ECJ.

Held: The phrase 'matters relating to a contract' in Article 5(1) of the Brussels Convention does not apply to an action between a sub-buyer of goods and the manufacturer, who is not the seller, relating to defects in those goods or to their unsuitability for their intended purpose.

Judgment: 10. In replying to the question from the national court, it should first be observed that the Court has consistently held that the phrase "matters relating to a contract" in Article 5(1) of the Convention is to be interpreted independently, having regard primarily to the objectives and general scheme of the Convention, in order to ensure that it is applied uniformly in all the Contracting States ... The phrase should not therefore be taken as referring to how the legal relationship in question before the national court is classified by the relevant national law.

11. Secondly, it should be noted that, according to the preamble to the Convention, one of its objectives is to 'strengthen in the Community the legal protection of persons therein established'. ...

[112] C-26/91, ECLI:EU:C:1992:268.

13. The Convention achieves that objective by laying down a number of jurisdictional rules which determine the cases, exhaustively listed in Sections 2 to 6 of Title II of the Convention, in which a defendant domiciled or established in a Contracting State may, under a rule of special jurisdiction, or must, under a rule of exclusive jurisdiction or prorogation of jurisdiction, be sued before a court of another Contracting State.

14. The rules on special and exclusive jurisdiction and those relating to prorogation of jurisdiction thus derogate from the general principle, set out in the first paragraph of Article 2 of the Convention, that the courts of the Contracting State in which the defendant is domiciled are to have jurisdiction. That jurisdictional rule is a general principle because it makes it easier, in principle, for a defendant to defend himself. Consequently, the jurisdictional rules which derogate from that general principle must not lead to an interpretation going beyond the situations envisaged by the Convention.

15. It follows that the phrase 'matters relating to a contract', as used in Article 5(1) of the Convention, is not to be understood as covering a situation in which there is no obligation freely assumed by one party towards another.

16. Where a sub-buyer of goods purchased from an intermediate seller brings an action against the manufacturer for damages on the ground that the goods are not in conformity, it must be observed that there is no contractual relationship between the sub-buyer and the manufacturer because the latter has not undertaken any contractual obligation towards the former.

17. Furthermore, particularly where there is a chain of international contracts, the parties' contractual obligations may vary from contract to contract, so that the contractual rights which the sub-buyer can enforce against his immediate seller will not necessarily be the same as those which the manufacturer will have accepted in his relationship with the first buyer.

18. The objective of strengthening legal protection of persons established in the Community, which is one of the objectives which the Convention is designed to achieve, also requires that the jurisdictional rules which derogate from the general principle of the Convention should be interpreted in such a way as to enable a normally well-informed defendant reasonably to predict before which courts, other than those of the State in which he is domiciled, he may be sued.

19. However, in a situation such as that with which the main proceedings are concerned, the application of the special jurisdictional rule laid down by Article 5(1) of the Convention to an action brought by a sub-buyer of goods against the manufacturer is not foreseeable by the latter and is therefore incompatible with the principle of legal certainty.

20. Apart from the fact that the manufacturer has no contractual relationship with the sub-buyer and undertakes no contractual obligation towards that buyer, whose identity and domicile may, quite reasonably, be unknown to him, it appears that in the great majority of Contracting States the liability of a manufacturer towards a sub-buyer for defects in the goods sold is not regarded as being of a contractual nature.

21. It follows that the answer to the question submitted by the national court must be that Article 5(1) of the Convention is to be understood as meaning that it does not apply to an action between a sub-buyer of goods and the manufacturer, who is not the seller, relating to defects in those goods or to their unsuitability for their intended purpose.

Notes

(1) For another decision where the ECJ did not follow a national qualification of an action as being 'contractual', see Case C-334/00 *Tacconi*.[113]

(2) The ECJ decision in *Handte* has not affected the position of the French Cour de cassation with regard to purely domestic chains of sales contracts. However, in a case of a contractual chain where the original sale was governed by the Convention on the International Sale of Goods (CISG) the Court held that the Convention cannot apply between the manufacturer and the final purchaser unless there is a contract of sale between these two. The Court did not uphold the decision of the cour d'appel, which had applied the CISG to the relationship between these two, based on the existence of an *action directe* of the final purchaser against the manufacturer.[114]

31.3 EXEMPTION CLAUSES AND OTHER DEFENCES FOR THE BENEFIT OF THIRD PARTIES

So far we have discussed cases in which a person acquires (or does not acquire) an enforceable right by virtue of a contract to which he is not a direct party. A similar problem arises in cases where a third party wishes to avail himself of an immunity, a limitation or exclusion of liability, or another defence which is based on a contract made by others but intended by them, either expressly or impliedly, to benefit the third party. In other words, can the benefit conferred on a third party to a contract consist not only of a sword, but also of a shield?

Draft Common Frame of Reference   **31.41 (INT)**

Article II-9:301: Basic rules

…

(3) The benefit conferred may take the form of an exclusion or limitation of the third party's liability to one of the contracting parties.

BGH, 7 December 1961[115]   **31.42 (DE)**

The patrolman and the stove

A clause which protects an employer from liability to its customer may be interpreted as also protecting the employees who carry out the contract on behalf of the employer.

Facts: A firm had entered into a contract with a security organisation under which the firm's plant was to be guarded by patrolmen during the night. A clause in the 'Special Conditions' of the contract provided that liability for damages resulting from negligence in guarding machines, stoves and heaters was excluded. When a fire occurred because of a patrolman's negligent failure to look after a stove, an action was brought by the

---

[113] See above, p 435.
[114] Cass civ (1) 5 January 1999, no. 96-19992, Bull I no. 6, D 1999, 383, annotated by C Witz.
[115] NJW 1962, 388.

firm's insurer, as subrogee of the firm's claims, against the patrolman in his personal capacity. His defence was that he was entitled to the protection of the exemption clause in his employers' contract with the claimants.

Held: The Oberlandesgericht held that the patrolman was protected by the clause, even though the clause did not refer to the liability of employees. The BGH agreed.

Judgment: ... Thus the decision [to be made in this case] depends on whether the defendant was included within the scope of protection afforded by the exemption clause agreed between the security firm and the company. The Chamber concurred with the OLG in answering that question in the affirmative.

However, the 'Special Conditions' contain no express provisions in that regard. Furthermore, it is correct to say that, where such stipulations are contained in general terms and conditions of business, they are to be interpreted narrowly and must, where doubt arises, be construed against the party who drafted them and whom they are intended to benefit (*contra proferentem*).

That is not, however, the sole decisive factor. It is not the wording of the exemption clause but its purpose, discernible to the other contracting party, which is decisive. Thus, where any doubt exists in that regard, it is not merely permissible but mandatory to take the appropriate steps to supplement the deficiency in accordance with § 157 BGB (citation omitted).

1. The security firm obviously intended that the protection afforded by the stipulation should extend to its employees, if only because it was arguably bound to secure such protection for them by virtue of its duty to have regard for their interests and welfare.

It had undertaken to perform the task of protecting the things which it was guarding against damage. It regarded the potential risk involved as so significant that it felt it had to limit its liability; indeed, as regards the task of guarding and attending to the stoves, it considered that it had to exclude even gross negligence on the part of its employees. As the Oberlandesgericht correctly states, it would have been inconceivable for it to have sought to shift the risk which it recognised in that connection off its own shoulders but to have intended that that risk should be borne by its employees. The employees were in an economically weaker position and even less able than their employer to bear the consequences of the negligent acts and omissions which, as human beings, they might perpetrate—*a fortiori* since, according to the findings made by the Oberlandesgericht, the employees in question were in many cases elderly persons whose mental faculties were beginning to wane.

In those circumstances, the duty incumbent on the security firm to have regard for the welfare and interests of its employees was in itself such as to require it to include those employees within the scope of the protection which it regarded as necessary. In the absence of any evidence indicating otherwise, it clearly intended to fulfil that duty by means of the exemption clause in issue. ...

3. However, the intention on the part of the security firm to include its employees within the scope of protection afforded by the exemption clause will only be of any consequence if it was sufficiently apparent to the other party to the contract. The Chamber has no hesitation in concurring, in this respect also, with the conclusion reached by the Oberlandesgericht and in finding that it was so apparent.

The company is itself an employer. Thus, like all other clients of the security firm finding themselves in a similar position, it was clearly aware of those considerations. It is inconceivable that a contracting party willing to accept limitations of liability as far-reaching as those agreed in the present case should intend to exonerate the well-to-do other party to the contract yet to insist that the economically weaker employees of that other party should assume the more onerous liability.

Notes

(1) This was a fairly clear case as there seemed to be little merit in a claim brought against an impecunious patrolman in order to circumvent an exemption clause to which the firm had agreed, knowing, no doubt, that its property was fully protected by insurance. Compare the following:

BW **31.43 (NL)**

Article 6:257: Where a contracting party can derive a defence from the contract against his co-contracting party to shield him from liability for conduct by his servant, the servant may also invoke this defence, as if he were a party to the contract, if he is sued by the co-contracting party on the basis of that conduct.

(2) Most cases in which the problem of 'vicarious immunity' arises deal with situations involving the carriage of goods where stevedores, warehousemen and other third parties seek to shield themselves behind exemption clauses contained in contracts of carriage to which they are not direct parties. It has been held in many German cases that they were allowed to do so, at least where the shipper knew or ought to have known that the goods were to be handled not only by the carrier himself but also by stevedores and other independent contractors.[116] The Dutch Civil Code has express provisions to this effect: see, for example, Articles 7:608 and 8:71 BW.

The issue of the stevedore's liability has also raised the enforceability of exemption clauses by third parties to the contract in English law. In *Adler v Dickson*[117] the plaintiff, as a passenger on board the *Himalaya*, suffered injuries caused by the negligence of the shipping company's crew. Since the contract of carriage exempted the company from all liability, a suit was brought by the passenger against the ship's master and boatswain. The Court of Appeal held that the defendants were not entitled to the protection of the exemption clause since its wording could not be construed so as to express an intention by the passenger to give up any claims against the shipping company's crew. According to the majority, even if the clause had expressly mentioned the employees, they would not have been protected by it because they were not parties to it. Clauses in contracts of carriage designed to extend its protections and immunities to the carrier's crew, agents and subcontractors have ever since been called 'Himalaya clauses' in the shipping industry.

House of Lords **31.44 (EN)**

Scruttons Ltd v Midland Silicones Ltd[118]

Stevedores to whom the task of unloading goods is subcontracted are not protected by a clause in the contract of carriage between the carrier and the owner of the goods which

---

[116] BGH 28 April 1977, VersR 1977, 717.
[117] [1955] 1 QB 158 (CA).
[118] [1962] AC 446.

limits the carrier's liability; and, because of the doctrine of privity, the stevedores would still not be protected even if the clause purported to apply to them.

Facts: The respondents were consignees and, at the material time, owners of a drum of chemicals consigned to them from America by ship under a bill of lading signed on behalf of the shipowners as carriers which exempted them from all liability for loss to the goods exceeding $500. The shipowners had asked the appellants, a firm of stevedores, to unload the ship's cargo in the port of London. In the course of their duties the appellants negligently dropped the drum, causing damage in excess of $500. They admitted negligence but contended that they were entitled to limit their liability to $500 by virtue of the main contract. The defence failed.

Held: The stevedores were not protected by the clause, nor would they have been protected even if the clause had expressly purported to limit their liability rather than just that of the shipowner.

Judgment: LORD REID: ... We were informed that questions of this kind frequently arise and that this action has been brought as a test case.

In considering the various arguments for the appellants, I think it is necessary to have in mind certain established principles of the English law of contract. Although I may regret it I find it impossible to deny the existence of the general rule that a stranger to a contract cannot in a question with either of the contracting parties take advantage of provisions of the contract, even where it is clear from the contract that some provision in it was intended to benefit him. That rule appears to have been crystallised a century ago in *Tweddle v Atkinson* and finally established in this House in *Dunlop Pneumatic Co Ltd v Selfridge & Co Ltd.* There are, it is true, certain well established exceptions to that rule—though I am not sure that they are really exceptions and do not arise from other principles. But none of these in any way touches the present case.

The actual words used by Lord Haldane in the *Dunlop* case were made the basis of an argument that, although a stranger to a contract may not be able to sue for any benefit under it, he can rely on the contract as a defence if one of the parties to it sues him in breach of his contractual obligation—that he can use the contract as a shield though not as a sword. I can find no justification for that. If the other contracting party can prevent the breach of contract well and good, but if he cannot I do not see how the stranger can. As was said in *Tweddle v Atkinson*, the stranger cannot 'take advantage' from the contract.

It may be that in a roundabout way the stranger could be protected. If A, wishing to protect X, gives to X an enforceable indemnity, and contracts with B that B will not sue X, informing B of the indemnity, and then B does sue X in breach of his contract with A, it may be that A can recover from B as damages the sum which he has to pay X under the indemnity, X having had to pay it to B. But there is nothing remotely resembling that in the present case.

The appellants say that through the agency of the carrier they were brought into contractual relation with the shipper and that they can now found on that against the consignees, the respondents. And they say that there should be inferred from the facts an implied contract, independent of the bill of lading, between them and the respondents. It was not argued that they had not committed a tort in damaging the respondents' goods.

I can see a possibility of success of the agency argument if (first) the bill of lading makes it clear that the stevedore is intended to be protected by the provisions in it which limit liability, (secondly) the bill of lading makes it clear that the carrier, in addition to contracting for these provisions on his own behalf, is also contracting as agent for the stevedore that these provisions should apply to the stevedore, (thirdly) the carrier has authority from the stevedore to do that, or perhaps later ratification by the stevedore would suffice, and (fourthly) that any difficulties about consideration moving from the stevedore were overcome. And then to affect the consignee it would be necessary to show that the provisions of the Bills of Lading Act, 1855, apply.

But again there is nothing of that kind in the present case. I agree with your lordships that the 'carrier' in the bill of lading does not include stevedore[s], and if that is so I can find nothing in the bill of lading which states or even implies that the parties to it intended the limitation of liability to extend to stevedores. Even if it could be said that reasonable men in the shoes of these parties would have agreed that the stevedores should have this benefit, that would not be enough to make this an implied term of the contract. And even if one could spell out of the bill of lading an intention to benefit the stevedore, there is certainly nothing to indicate that the carrier was contracting as agent for the stevedore in addition to contracting on his own behalf. So it appears to me that the agency argument must fail.

And the implied contract argument seems to me to be equally unsound. From the stevedores' angle, they are employed by the carrier to deal with the goods in the ship. They can assume that the carrier is acting properly in employing them and they need not know who the goods belong to. There was in their contract with the carrier a provision that they should be protected, but that could not by itself bind the consignee. They might assume that the carrier would obtain protection for them against the consignee and feel aggrieved when they found that the carrier did not or could not do that. But a provision in the contract between them and the carrier is irrelevant in a question between them and the consignee. Then from the consignees' angle they would know that stevedores would be employed to handle their goods, but if they read the bill of lading they would find nothing to show that the shippers had agreed to limit the liability of the stevedores. There is nothing to show that they ever thought about this or that if they had they would have agreed or ought as reasonable men to have agreed to this benefit to the stevedores. I can find no basis in this for implying a contract between them and the stevedores. It cannot be said that such a contract was in any way necessary for business efficiency.

Note

In the light of this decision, contract planners returned to the attack and produced *Himalaya* clauses by which the carrier is presented as being the stevedore's agent. A clause of this type to be included in a bill of lading may be worded as follows:

It is hereby expressly agreed that no servant or agent of the Carrier (including every independent contractor from time to time employed by the Carrier) shall in any circumstances whatsoever be under any liability whatsoever to the Shipper, Consignee or Owner of the goods or to any holder of this Bill of Lading for any loss or damage or delay of whatsoever kind arising or resulting directly or indirectly from any act neglect or default on his part while acting in the course of or in connection with his employment and, without prejudice to the generality of the foregoing provisions in this Clause, every exemption, limitation, condition and liberty herein contained and every right, exemption from liability, defence and immunity of whatsoever nature applicable to the Carrier or to which the Carrier is entitled hereunder shall also be available and shall extend to protect every such servant or agent of the Carrier acting as aforesaid and for the purpose of all the foregoing provisions of this Clause the Carrier is or shall be deemed to be acting

> as agent or trustee on behalf of and for the benefit of all persons who are or might be his servants or agents from time to time (including independent contractors as aforesaid) and all such persons shall to this extent be or be deemed to be parties to the contract in or evidenced by this Bill of Lading.

This clause was tested in *The Eurymedon*.[119] The Privy Council held that the terms of the bill of lading amounted to an offer by the shipper to the stevedores, made through the carrier as the stevedores' agent, that if the stevedores unloaded the goods, they should have the benefit of the exemption clause. This offer had been accepted, and consideration provided, by the stevedores through performing, or promising to perform, the agreement made with the carrier for the unloading of the cargo.

Privy Council   **31.45 (EN)**

New Zealand Shipping Co Ltd v AM Satterthwaite & Co Ltd (The Eurymedon)[120]

A third person who is not directly a party to the contract may be protected from liability in tort by clauses arranged on his behalf by one of the contracting parties.

Facts: A bill of lading contained a clause exempting the carrier from liability (see further above). The clause purported to protect independent contractors acting on behalf of the carrier. The carrier was said to make this arrangement as agent on their behalf and they were deemed to be parties to the contract. The defendants, independent stevedores, relied on the clause.

Held: The Privy Council, to which the case was referred by the New Zealand courts, upheld the claim of the defendants.

Judgment: Lord WILBERFORCE, delivering the judgment of the majority, quoted the part of Lord Reid's speech in the *Midland Silicones* case in which Lord Reid stated the prerequisites for success of the 'agency' argument:

'... [I]f (first) the bill of lading makes it clear that the stevedore is intended to be protected by the provisions in it which limit the liability, (secondly) the bill of lading makes it clear that the carrier, in addition to contracting for these provisions on his own behalf, is also contracting as agent for the stevedores that these provisions should apply to the stevedore, (thirdly) the carrier has authority from the stevedore to do that, or perhaps later ratification by the stevedore would suffice, and (fourthly) that any difficulties about consideration moving from the stevedore were overcome.'

[Lord Wiberforce continued:]
The question in this appeal is whether the contract satisfies these propositions.
Clause 1 of the bill of lading, whatever the defects in its drafting, is clear in its relevant terms. The carrier, on his own account, stipulates for certain exemptions and immunities: among these is that conferred by article III, rule 6, of the Hague Rules which discharges the carrier from all liability for loss or damage unless suit is brought within one year after delivery. In addition to these stipulations on his own account, the carrier as agent for, inter alios, independent contractors stipulates for the same exemptions.

---

[119] [1975] AC 154.
[120] ibid.

Much was made of the fact that the carrier also contracts as agent for numerous other persons; the relevance of this argument is not apparent. It cannot be disputed that among such independent contractors, for whom, as agent, the carrier contracted, is the appellant company which habitually acts as stevedore in New Zealand by arrangement with the carrier and which is, moreover, the parent company of the carrier. The carrier was, indisputably, authorised by the appellant to contract as its agent for the purposes of clause 1. All of this is quite straightforward and was accepted by all the judges in New Zealand. The only question was, and is, the fourth question presented by Lord Reid, namely that of consideration.

It was on this point that the Court of Appeal differed from Beattie J, holding that it had not been shown that any consideration for the shipper's promise as to exemption moved from the promisee, ie, the appellant company.

If the choice, and the antithesis, is between a gratuitous promise, and a promise for consideration, as it must be in the absence of a tertium quid, there can be little doubt which, in commercial reality, this is. The whole contract is of a commercial character, involving service on one side, rates of payment on the other, and qualifying stipulations as to both. The relations of all parties to each other are commercial relations entered into for business reasons of ultimate profit. To describe one set of promises, in this context, as gratuitous, or nudum pactum, seems paradoxical and is prima facie implausible. It is only the precise analysis of this complex of relations into the classical offer and acceptance, with identifiable consideration, that seems to present difficulty, but this same difficulty exists in many situations of daily life, eg, sales at auction; supermarket purchases; boarding an omnibus; purchasing a train ticket; tenders for the supply of goods; offers of rewards; acceptance by post; warranties of authority by agents; manufacturers' guarantees; gratuitous bailments; bankers' commercial credits. These are all examples which show that English law, having committed itself to a rather technical and schematic doctrine of contract, in application takes a practical approach, often at the cost of forcing the facts to fit uneasily into the marked slots of offer, acceptance and consideration.

In their Lordships' opinion the present contract presents much less difficulty than many of those above referred to. It is one of carriage from Liverpool to Wellington. The carrier assumes an obligation to transport the goods and to discharge at the port of arrival. The goods are to be carried and discharged, so the transaction is inherently contractual. It is contemplated that a part of this contract, viz discharge, may be performed by independent contractors—viz the appellant. By clause 1 of the bill of lading the shipper agrees to exempt from liability the carrier, his servants and independent contractors in respect of the performance of this contract of carriage. Thus, if the carriage, including the discharge, is wholly carried out by the carrier, he is exempt. If part is carried out by him, and part by his servants, he and they are exempt. If part is carried out by him and part by an independent contractor, he and the independent contractor are exempt. The exemption is designed to cover the whole carriage from loading to discharge, by whomsoever it is performed: the performance attracts the exemption or immunity in favour of whoever the performer turns out to be. There is possibly more than one way of analysing this business transaction into the necessary components; that which their Lordships would accept is to say that the bill of lading brought into existence a bargain initially unilateral but capable of becoming mutual, between the shipper and the appellant, made through the carrier as agent. This became a full contract when the appellant performed services by discharging the goods. The performance of these services for the benefit of the shipper was the consideration for the agreement by the shipper that the appellant should have the benefit of the exemptions and limitations contained in the bill of lading. The conception of a 'unilateral' contract of this kind was recognised in *Great Northern Railway Co v Witham* (1873) LR 9 CP 16 and is well established. This way of regarding the matter is very close to if not identical to that accepted by Beattie J in the [New Zealand] Supreme Court: he analysed the transaction as one of an offer open to acceptance by action such as was found in *Carlill v Carbolic Smoke Ball Co* [1893] 1 QB 256. But whether one describes the shipper's promise to exempt as an offer to be accepted by performance or as a promise in exchange for an act seems in the present context to be a matter of semantics. The words of Bowen LJ in *Carlill v Carbolic Smoke Ball Co* [1893] 1 QB 256, 268: 'why should not an offer be made to all the world which is to ripen into a contract with anybody who comes forward and performs the condition?' seem to bridge both conceptions: he certainly seems to draw no distinction between an offer which matures into a contract when accepted and a promise which matures into a contract after performance, and, though in some special contexts (such as in connection with the right to withdraw) some further refinement may be needed, either analysis may be equally valid. On the main point in the appeal, their Lordships are in substantial agreement with Beattie J.

The following points require mention. 1. In their Lordships' opinion, consideration may quite well be provided by the appellant, as suggested, even though (or if) it was already under an obligation to discharge to the carrier. (There is no direct evidence of the existence or nature of this obligation, but their Lordships are prepared to assume it.) An agreement to do an act which the promisor is under an existing obligation to a third party to do, may quite well amount to valid consideration and does so in the present case: the promisee obtains the benefit of a direct obligation which he can enforce. This proposition is illustrated and supported by *Scotson v Pegg* (1861) 6 H. & N. 295 which their Lordships consider to be good law.

2. The consignee is entitled to the benefit of, and is bound by, the stipulations in the bill of lading by his acceptance of it and request for delivery of the goods thereunder. This is shown by *Brandt v Liverpool, Brazil and River Plate Steam Navigation Co Ltd* [1924] 1 KB 575 and a line of earlier cases. The Bills of Lading Act 1855, section 1 (in New Zealand the Mercantile Law Act 1908, section 13) gives partial statutory recognition to this rule, but, where the statute does not apply, as it may well not do in this case, the previously established law remains effective.

3. The appellant submitted, in the alternative, an argument that, quite apart from contract, exemptions from, or limitation of, liability in tort may be conferred by mere consent on the part of the party who may be injured. As their Lordships consider that the appellant ought to succeed in contract, they prefer to express no opinion upon this argument: to evaluate it requires elaborate discussion.

4. A clause very similar to the present was given effect by a United States District Court in *Carle & Montanari Inc v American Export Isbrandtsen Lines Inc* [1968] 1 Lloyd's Rep 260. The carrier in that case contracted, in an exemption clause, as agent, for, inter alios, all stevedores and other independent contractors, and although it is no doubt true that the law in the United States is more liberal than ours as regards third party contracts, their Lordships see no reason why the law of the Commonwealth should be more restrictive and technical as regards agency contracts. Commercial considerations should have the same force on both sides of the Pacific.

In the opinion of their Lordships, to give the appellant the benefit of the exemptions and limitations contained in the bill of lading is to give effect to the clear intentions of a commercial document, and can be given within existing principles. They see no reason to strain the law or the facts in order to defeat these intentions. It should not be overlooked that the effect of denying validity to the clause would be to encourage actions against servants, agents and independent contractors in order to get round exemptions (which are almost invariable and often compulsory) accepted by shippers against carriers, the existence, and presumed efficacy, of which is reflected in the rates of freight. They see no attraction in this consequence.

Their Lordships will humbly advise Her Majesty that the appeal be allowed and the judgment of Beattie J restored. The respondent must pay the costs of the appeal and in the Court of Appeal.

Notes

(1) The solution arrived at might appear to connive at evasion of the doctrine of privity of contract because the exemption clause may validly be relied on by a person who was not a party to the contract. The justification given by Lord Wilberforce is largely pragmatic: to allow the stevedore the benefit of the clause is 'to give effect to the clear intentions of a commercial document and can be given within existing principles'. Indeed, the argument adopted (that the consignor was, through the agency of the carrier, making an offer to the stevedores that, if they unloaded the goods, they would be given the protection of the limitation of liability clauses contained in the bill of lading; and that the stevedores, by unloading the goods, both accepted the offer and provided consideration) is consistent with both the principles of agency and of consideration. The only disagreement between the members of the Privy Council was over interpretation, ie whether such an offer could be read into the wording of the *Himalaya* clause in the bill of lading.

(2) *Himalaya* clauses of this kind do not always work; for example, if the damage occurred before the unilateral offer had been accepted by unloading prematurely[121] or if the promisee was not authorised to act on the third party's behalf and the latter cannot ratify.[122]

These complications can now be avoided under English law:

Contracts (Rights of Third Parties) Act 1999   **31.46 (EN)**

Section 1(6): Where a term of the contract excludes or limits liability in relation to any matter references in this Act to the third party enforcing the term shall be construed as references to his availing himself of the exclusion or limitation.

In other words, if the term excluding or restricting liability purports to protect the third party by mentioning him or describing him, the third party will be protected by it.

31.4 MODIFICATION AND REVOCATION

A question to be answered by all legal systems recognising the third-party beneficiary contract is whether and up to what time the promisor and the promisee, or one of them,

---

[121] *Raymond Burke Motors v Mersey Docks and Harbour Co* [1986] 1 Lloyd's Rep 155 (QBD).
[122] *Southern Water Authority v Carey* [1985] 2 All ER 1077 (QBD).

may modify or revoke the contract without the beneficiary's consent. In one group of legal systems the actual or implied intention of the parties is the controlling factor. § 328(2) BGB provides that, in the absence of specific contractual provisions, it is to be inferred from the circumstances, and especially from the purpose of the contract, not only whether a third person is to acquire a right to enforce the contract at all, but also 'whether his right arises at once or only under certain conditions, and whether the contracting parties retain the power to annul or modify the right of the third party without his consent'. In ascertaining the parties' implied intention, the judge gets no help from the Code, except that § 331(1) BGB lays down a presumption if the performance to the third party is to take place after the promisee's death. In that situation, the third party shall, in case of doubt, acquire the right to performance only at the time of the promisee's death. It follows that, in the absence of stipulations to the contrary, the third party's position before the promisee's death amounts to a mere *nuda spes*.

The majority of Continental legal systems have followed the French solution laid down in the second sentence of ex-Article 1121 Cciv. According to this provision, the promisee's right of revocation ceased once the beneficiary had made it clear that he wished to avail himself of the benefit to be conferred on him by virtue of the contract. Similar provisions are Article 112(3) of the Swiss Code of Obligations, Article 1257(2) of the Spanish Civil Code, Article 412 of the Greek Civil Code, Article 6:253(2) BW. However, this aspect of contracts for the benefit of third parties was significantly revised by the 2016 reforms which implemented the previous case law of the Cour de cassation.

Code civil **31.47 (FR)**

Article 1206: The beneficiary is invested with a direct right to the act of performance against the promisor from the time of the stipulation.

Nevertheless, the stipulator may freely revoke the stipulation as long as the beneficiary has not accepted it.

The stipulation becomes irrevocable at the moment when the acceptance reaches the stipulator or the promisor.

Article 1207: Revocation may be effected only by the stipulator, or, after his death, by his heirs. The latter may do so only after a period of three months has elapsed from the date when they put the third party on notice to accept the benefit of the promise.

If it is not accompanied with the designation of a new beneficiary, the revocation benefits the stipulator or his heirs, as the case may be.

Revocation is effective as soon as the third party beneficiary or the promisor becomes aware of it.

Where it is made by testament, it takes effect from the moment of the testator's death.

The third party who was initially designated is deemed never to have benefited from the stipulation made for his benefit.

Article 1208: Acceptance may come from the beneficiary or, after his death, his heirs. It may be express or implied. It may take place even after the death of the promisee or the promisor.

Article 1411(2) of the Italian Civil Code follows the old French rule, but provides that, in cases in which the performance may be demanded by the third person only after the promisee's death, the promisee can revoke the benefit 'notwithstanding that such third person has declared that he intends to avail himself of it, unless, in this latter case, the promisee has waived in writing his power of revocation'. A very detailed and elaborate solution is to be found in section 2 of the Contracts (Rights of Third Parties) Act 1999.

Contracts (Rights of Third Parties) Act 1999   **31.48 (EN)**

Section 2: Variation and rescission of contract

(1) Subject to the provisions of this section, where a third party has a right under section 1 to enforce a term of the contract, the parties to the contract may not by agreement rescind the contract, or vary it in such a way as to extinguish or alter his entitlement under that right without his consent if—

    (a) the third party has communicated his assent to the term to the promisor,

    (b) the promisor is aware that the third party has relied on the term, or

    (c) the promisor can reasonably be expected to have foreseen that the third party would rely on the term and the third party has in fact relied on it.

(2) The assent referred to in subsection (1)(a) above—

    (a) may be by words or conduct, and

    (b) if sent to the promisor by post or other means, shall not be regarded as communicated to the promisor until received by him.

(3) Subsection (1) is subject to any express term of the contract under which—

    (a) the parties to the contract may by agreement rescind or vary the contract without the consent of the third party, or

    (b) the consent of the third party is required in circumstances specified in the contract instead of those set out in subsection (1)(a) to (c).

Consider also:

Principles of European Contract Law   **31.49 (INT)**

Article 6:110: Stipulation in Favour of a Third Party

   …

(3) The promisee may by notice to the promisor deprive the third party of the right to performance unless:

    (a) the third party has received notice from the promisee that the right has been made irrevocable, or

    (b) the promisor or the promisee has received notice from the third party that the latter accepts the right.

Draft Common Frame of Reference   **31.50 (INT)**

Article II-9:303: Rejection or revocation of benefit

   (1) …

(2) The contracting parties may remove or modify the contractual term conferring the right or benefit if this is done before either of them has given the third party notice that the right or benefit has been conferred. The contract determines whether and by whom and in what circumstances the right or benefit can be revoked or modified after that time.

(3) Even if the right or benefit conferred is by virtue of the contract revocable or subject to modification, the right to revoke or modify is lost if the parties have, or the party having the right to revoke or modify has, led the third party to believe that it is not revocable or subject to modification and if the third party has reasonably acted in reliance on it.

31.5 DEFENCES AVAILABLE TO THE PROMISOR

There is general agreement that if a claim is brought by the third party the promisor may rely on all defences, set-offs and counterclaims which would have been available to him in an action by the promisee: § 334 BGB, Article 1413 of the Italian Civil Code and Article 449 of the Portuguese Civil Code. The Contracts (Rights of Third Parties) Act 1999 provides in section 3 that, subject to any express terms to the contrary in the contract:

Contracts (Rights of Third Parties) Act 1999 **31.51 (EN)**

Section 3: Defences etc available to promisor
   (1) ...
   (2) The promisor shall have available to him by way of defence or set-off any matter that—
      (a) arises from or in connection with the contract and is relevant to the term and
      (b) would have been available to him by way of defence or set-off if the proceedings had been brought by the promisee.
...
(4) The promisor shall also have available to him—
      (a) by way of defence or set-off any matter, and
      (b) by way of counterclaim any matter not arising from the contract, that would have been available to him by way of defence or set-off or, as the case may be, by way of counterclaim against the third party if the third party had been a party to the contract.

Draft Common Frame of Reference **31.52 (INT)**

Article II-9:302: Rights, remedies and defences
   Where one of the contracting parties is bound to render a performance to the third party under the contract, then, in the absence of provision to the contrary in the contract:
      (a) the third party has the same rights to performance and remedies for non-performance as if the contracting party was bound to render the performance under a binding unilateral promise in favour of the third party; and
      (b) the contracting party may assert against the third party all defences which the contracting party could assert against the other party to the contract.

In a case decided by the Cour de cassation,[123] the buyer in a contract for the sale of a grain business had promised the seller to purchase a certain quantity of grain from C

---

[123] Cass com 25 March 1969, no. 66-14054, Bull civ IV no. 118.

at a stated price. When C, tendering the grain, sued the buyer for the price, the buyer asked the court to stay the proceedings until an action, brought by him against the seller of the business for rescission of the contract because of a breach by the seller, had been decided. The Cour de cassation held that the lower court was right in staying the proceedings since the agreement for the benefit of C 'constituted an agreement for the benefit of a third party whose validity was subordinated to that of the sales agreement on which it was based'.

On the other hand, there may be cases in which the promisor's right to raise certain defences vis-à-vis the third party has been excluded. In the *Airline charter* case,[124] the Bundesgerichtshof held that an airline was not allowed to deny a passenger a seat as booked on the ground that the tour operator (an intermediary) had not paid for the seats as provided in the charter agreement. We have also seen that, in the *Drowning caused by negligence* case,[125] the Cour de cassation allowed the potential beneficiaries of an implicit stipulation for the benefit of another to sidestep an exemption clause by renouncing the stipulation and suing in delict. And we have seen how Article 1234 of the French reform bill on civil liability of 2017 attempts to overcome the problems following from the exclusion of contractual liability in cases where the rule of *non cumul* applies.[126]

31.6 REMEDIES AVAILABLE TO THE PROMISEE

Normally the person mainly interested in enforcing the promise made for the benefit of a third party is the third party himself. There may be cases, however, in which the promisee has a strong interest in the promisor's performance or where enforcement by the third party is impractical. For example, in a case involving a service company's promise to a municipality to provide services to its residents, an action by one of the individual contract beneficiaries against the company may be unlikely or unreasonable because the cost of litigation is much higher than what the claimant may hope to recover. In such cases the municipality is clearly the more efficient claimant. Accordingly, all Continental jurisdictions recognising the third-party beneficiary contract allow the promisee not only to enforce the contract specifically for the benefit of the third party (as set out in § 335 BGB, Article 112 of the Swiss Code of Obligations, Article 6:256 BW and Article 1209 Cc), but also to claim damages from the promisor for breach of the promise.[127]

In contrast, English law has traditionally taken the position that the promisee may recover only his own losses, not those of the third party. Moreover, at the suggestion of the Law Commission,[128] this matter is not dealt with in the new Contracts (Rights of

---

[124] BGH 17 January 1985, BGHZ 93, 271 (see above, 31.9 (DE), p 1270).

[125] Cass Civ (2) 23 January 1959, Bull civ II no. 80 (see above, 31.15 (FR)).

[126] See above, 31.38 (FR).

[127] See, eg, Cass civ (1) 12 July 1956, no. 56-07052, Bull civ I no. 306, D 1956, 749 and Cass com 14 May 1979, no. 77-15865, Bull civ IV no. 153, DS 1980, 157. For criticism that revised Art 1209 Cciv failed to codify this issue, see O Deshayes, T Genicon and YM Laithier, *Réforme du droit des contrats, du régime général et de la preuve des obligations, Commentaire article par article* (Paris: LexisNexis, 2016) 447.

[128] Law Commission (n 10 above) para 5.11.

Third Parties) Act but is left to the common law to develop.[129] There have been a number of recent cases on the point, including *Linden Gardens Trust Ltd v Lenesta Sludge Disposals Ltd*,[130] *Darlington Borough Council v Wiltshier Northern Ltd*[131] and *Alfred McAlpine Ltd v Panatown Ltd*.[132] To summarise very briefly a complex and controversial discussion,[133] in the *Linden Gardens* case the House of Lords allowed the promisee to recover on one of two grounds, the 'narrower ground' and the 'broader ground'. The 'narrower ground' (see the speech of Lord Browne-Wilkinson, speaking for the majority) is that if the contract required something to be done to a property which the parties contemplated from the start would be transferred to a new owner, and the work is not done or not done correctly, causing loss to the new owner, the original owner (the promisee) can recover damages for the loss suffered by the new owner (the third party). The promisee will hold the sums recovered on trust for the third party. The broad ground (which was relied on by Lord Griffiths) is that if A contracts with B to have work done on property owned by C, and B does not do the work or does it badly, A himself suffers loss, in that he may have to pay someone else to do the work, and A can recover damages for that loss. In the *Panatown* case the House of Lords confirmed the basic rule that a party to a contract can recover damages only for the losses he has himself suffered; but also agreed that there are exceptions: these were variously explained on either the narrow or the broad ground mentioned in the *Linden Gardens* case. However, it was held that the exceptions apply only where the third party would otherwise be left without a remedy. On the facts of *Panatow*n, the contractors had been employed by Panatown to construct a building for the third party who owned the land. The contractors had executed a deed giving the landowners a direct remedy against the contractor for any failure on its part to exercise reasonable care and skill in the construction process.[134] The work was defective. It was held, by a majority, that because the third-party landowners had a direct remedy against the contractors, the employers could not recover substantial damages on the landowners' behalf.[135]

FURTHER READING

Borghetti, J-S, 'Breach of Contract and Liability to Third Parties in French Law: How to Break the Deadlock?' (2010) 18 ZEuP 279–303.

Borghetti, J-S, 'The Effects of Contracts and Third Parties' in J Cartwright and S Whittaker (eds), *The Code Napoléon Rewritten: French Contract Law after the 2016 Reforms* (Oxford: Hart Publishing, 2017) 227–53.

---

[129] s 4 of the Act provides that 'Section 1 does not affect any right of the promisee to enforce any term of the contract.'

[130] [1994] AC 85 (HL).

[131] [1995] 1 WLR 68 (CA) (see above, p 1265).

[132] (1998) 88 Building LR 67 (CA); [2000] UKHL 43, [2001] 1 AC 518.

[133] See *Chitty on Contracts*, 33rd ed by H Beale (gen ed) (London: Sweet & Maxwell/Thomson Reuters, 2018) paras 18-054 ff.

[134] Presumably the direct warranty was made by deed in part to avoid problems of consideration: see above, p 61. The reasons for this complex arrangement were said to be to reduce the incidence of VAT.

[135] For a further case in which the Supreme Court acknowledged the exceptions (which were described as examples of 'transferred loss'), but held that neither exception applied on the facts, see *Swynson Ltd v Lowick Rose LLP* [2017] UKSC 32, [2018] AC 313.

Ebers, M, Janssen, A and Meyer, O (eds), *European Perspectives on Producers' Liability: Direct Producers' Liability for Non-conformity and the Sellers' Right of Redress* (Munich: Sellier, 2009).

Jansen, CJH and van der Lely, AJ, 'Haftung für Auskünfte: ein Vergleich zwischen englischem, deutschem und niederländischem Recht' (1999) 7 ZEuP 229–45.

Kötz, H, *European Contract Law* (2nd edn, Oxford University Press, 2017) 319–35.

Markesinis, BS and Unberath, H, *The German Law of Torts: a Comparative Treatise* (4th edn, Oxford: Hart Publishing, 2002) 52–69.

Millner, MA, 'Ius Quaesitum Tertio: Comparison and Synthesis' (1967) 16 ICLQ 446–63.

Palmer, VV, 'Contracts in Favour of Third Persons in Europe: First Steps Toward Tomorrow's Harmonization' (2003) 11 ERPL 8–27.

du Perron, E, 'Contract and Third Parties' in AS Hartkamp et al (eds), *Towards a European Civil Code* (2nd edn, Nijmegen: Ars Aequi, 1998) 311–26.

Sutherland, P, 'Third-Party Contracts' in H MacQueen and R Zimmermann (eds), *European Contract Law: Scots and South African Perspectives* (Edinburgh University Press, 2006) 203–29.

Unberath, H, *Transferred Loss: Claiming Third Party Loss in Contract Law* (Oxford: Hart Publishing, 2003).

Vogenauer, S, 'Stipulation in Favour of a Third Party' in N Jansen and R Zimmermann (eds), *Commentaries on European Contract Laws* (Oxford University Press, 2018) 866–98.

Vogenauer, S, 'The Effects of Contracts on Third Parties: the Avant-projet de réforme in a Comparative Perspective' in J Cartwright, S Vogenauer and S Whittaker (eds), *Reforming the French Law of Obligations: Comparative Observations on the Avant-projet de réforme du droit des obligations et de la prescription (the 'Avant-projet Catala')* (Oxford: Hart Publishing, 2009) 235–68.

32.1 THE NOTION AND THE NATURE OF AGENCY

Principles of European Contract Law   32.1 (INT)

Article 3:201: Express, Implied, and Apparent Authority

(1) The principal's grant of authority to an agent to act in its name may be express or may be implied from the circumstances.

(2) The agent has authority to perform all acts necessary in the circumstances to achieve the purposes for which the authority was granted.

(3) A person is to be treated as having granted authority to an apparent agent if the person's statements or conduct induce the third party reasonably and in good faith to believe that the apparent agent has been granted authority for the act performed by it.

Article 3:202: Agent acting in Exercise of its Authority

Where an agent is acting within its authority as defined by Article 3:201, its acts bind the principal and the third party directly to each other. The agent itself is not bound to the third party.

Draft Common Frame of Reference   32.2 (INT)

Article II-6:101: Scope

(1) This Chapter applies to the external relationships created by acts of representation—that is to say, the relationships between:

    (a) the principal and the third party; and

    (b) the representative and the third party.

(2) It applies also to situations where a person purports to be a representative without actually being a representative.

(3) It does not apply to the internal relationship between the representative and the principal.

Article II-6:103: Authorisation

(1) The authority of a representative may be granted by the principal or by the law.

(2) The principal's authorisation may be express or implied.

(3) If a person causes a third party reasonably and in good faith to believe that the person has authorised a representative to perform certain acts, the person is treated as a principal who has so authorised the apparent representative.

Article II-6:105: When representative's act affects principal's legal position
When the representative acts:
(a) in the name of a principal or otherwise in such a way as to indicate to the third party an intention to affect the legal position of a principal; and
(b) within the scope of the representative's authority, the act affects the legal position of the principal in relation to the third party as if it had been done by the principal. It does not as such give rise to any legal relation between the representative and the third party.

The device of agency, or 'representation', as it is called in the Draft Common Frame of Reference (DCFR), is an unavoidable necessity in any developed economic system which depends on the division of labour for the production and distribution of goods and services. The most obvious example is the employee of a firm who has the power to enter into contracts that are binding on the firm. The firm may also confer such power on self-employed traders. Thus, a manufacturing company may delegate the sale of its products in a certain market to a 'commercial agent'. An export firm may ask a 'forwarding agent' to arrange for goods to be transported to a foreign destination. The entrepreneur who delegates the procurement of materials to a member of his staff, the heirs who commission an auctioneer to sell the inherited property, the landowner who has a 'factor' run the estate, the manufacturer whose distributive chain includes independent salesmen as well as staff of his own—all these people who, for one reason or another, cannot or will not act personally, expand their sphere of activity by engaging others to effect contracts with third parties 'for them', 'on their account', 'on their behalf', 'as their agents', 'in their interest' or 'in their name'.

In the common law, agency is defined as a relationship which arises when one person, called the principal, authorises another, called the agent, to act on his behalf, and the other agrees to do so. Its most important effect is that it enables the agent to affect the principal's legal position in respect of third parties, in particular by the making of contracts between the principal and third parties. A civil lawyer would regard this definition as too wide. What is needed in civil law systems is not only that the principal has conferred authority on the agent to act on his behalf; a contract made by the agent with a third party will bind the principal only if the agent acted 'in the name' of the principal and the third party therefore knows, or has reason to know, either from the agent or from the circumstances, that the contract was intended to become binding on the principal. If the agent acts 'in his own name', he alone acquires rights and liabilities under the contract with the third party even though he may have acted solely on the principal's business and account. Common lawyers, on the other hand, are perfectly willing to accept that if a duly authorised agent and a third party enter into a contract the third party acquires rights against both the agent and the principal even though the agency was 'undisclosed' at the time the contract was made. For these reasons, the term 'agency' is wider than the civil law term '*représentation*', '*rappresentanza*' or '*Stellvertretung*'.

Obligationenrecht   **32.3 (CH)**

Article 32: If somebody who is authorised to represent another enters into a contract in the other's name, it is the other, and not the representative, who acquires rights and duties under the contract.

BGB   **32.4 (DE)**

§164: Effect of a declaration made by the agent

(1) A declaration of intent which a person makes within the scope of his own power of agency in the name of a principal takes effect directly in favour of and against the principal. It is irrelevant whether the declaration is made explicitly in the name of the principal, or whether it may be gathered from the circumstances that it is to be made in his name.

(2) If the intent to act on behalf of another is not evident, the lack of intent on the part of the agent to act on his own behalf is not taken into consideration.

(3) The provisions of subsection (1) apply with the necessary modifications if a declaration of intent to be made to another is made to his agent.

Code civil   **32.5 (FR)**

Article 1154: Where a representative acts within his authority and in the name and on behalf of the person whom he represents, only the latter is bound to the undertaking so contracted.

Article 1388 of the Italian Civil Code is to similar effect.

The 1983 Geneva Convention on Agency in the International Sale of Goods[1] adopted the wider approach of the common law:

Geneva Convention on Agency in the International
Sale of Goods   **32.6 (INT)**

Article 1: (1) This Convention applies where one person, the agent, has authority or purports to have authority on behalf of another person, the principal, to conclude a contract of sale of goods with a third party.

...

(4) It applies irrespective of whether the agent acts in his own name or in that of the principal.

Note

The adoption of a broader notion of 'agency' does not require that the two different types of representation mentioned in Article 1(4) be treated alike. Indeed, different consequences are attached to them, depending on whether the third party did or did not know that the agent was acting as an agent, by Articles 12 and 13 of the Convention (discussed below). The distinction is drawn more clearly in the Principles of European Contract Law (PECL).

---

[1] UNIDROIT Convention on Agency in the International Sale of Goods (Geneva, 17 February 1983). The Convention needs to be ratified by five further States to enter into force. Articles 2.2.1–2.2.10 UNIDROIT PICC are largely modelled on the Convention.

Article 3:102: Categories of Representation

(1) Where an agent acts in the name of a principal, the rules on direct representation apply (Section 2). It is irrelevant whether the principal's identity is revealed at the time the agent acts or is to be revealed later.

(2) Where an intermediary acts on instructions and on behalf of, but not in the name of, a principal, or where the third party neither knows nor has reason to know that the intermediary acts as an agent, the rules on indirect representation apply (Section 3).

Most continental legal systems draw a sharp line between the authority of an agent and the contract linking him to the principal. They therefore distinguish between the *authorisation*, which they consider a purely unilateral act of the principal intended to confer on the agent the power to bind him directly, and the underlying *contractual relationship* between principal and agent, which produces rights and duties in their internal relationship. Once this approach is accepted, it becomes possible for the codes to draw a distinction between the general rules dealing, on a fairly high level of abstraction, with the authorisation of another and its legal consequences, and the rules on the various types of agency agreements. This system was first adopted by the German Civil Code and has been followed by the Swiss Law of Obligations (1911), the Swedish Contract Act (1915), the Greek Civil Code (1940), the Italian Civil Code (1942), the Portuguese Civil Code (1966) and the Dutch Civil Code (1992). The revised French Code civil also endorses this distinction as its Articles 1153 to 1161 provide for a general theory of representation which is dealt with independently[2] from the provisions governing the different ways through which the agent is given the authority to act on behalf of the principal.[3] These general provisions draw some inspiration from the rules on mandate but their scope of application is much wider and they take a generous approach. They create a general theory of representation in French law, much influenced by the PECL, the DCFR and the UNIDROIT Principles of International Commercial Contracts (UNIDROIT PICC).[4]

This chapter focuses exclusively on the external aspects of agency, such as the way in which the agent can affect the contractual relations between the principal and the third party, or whether there are remedies of the third party against the agent when the latter purports to bind the principal but fails to do so. Questions arising out of the relationship between principal and agent (the internal relationship) are only dealt with to the extent that they affect the external relationship.[5]

---

[2] See G Wicker, 'Le nouveau droit commun de la représentation dans le code civil' D 2016, 1942.

[3] The rules governing such aspects of the law of agency can notably be found in the section dedicated to the contract of mandate in the Code civil (Arts 1984 to 1990).

[4] F Ancel, B Fauvarque-Cosson and J Gest, *Aux sources de la réforme du droit des contrats* (Paris: Dalloz, 2017) no. 23-71.

[5] cf Art II-6:101(3) DCFR (see pp 1265–66 above) and Art 3:101(3) PECL. See also Council Directive 86/653/EEC of 18 December 1986 on the coordination of the laws of the Member States relating to self-employed commercial agents, [1986] OJ L382, p 17; MW Hesselink (ed), *Principles of European Law: Commercial Agency, Franchise and Distribution Contracts (PEL CAFDC)* (Munich: Sellier, 2006).

32.2 THE EFFECTS OF AGENCY

We have seen that legal systems differ in their definition of the notions of 'agency' and 'representation'. Some include cases where the agent did not 'act in the name of the principal' and some do not. Even those adopting the broader notion acknowledge that different rules are required for the legal effects carried out by the agent, depending on whether the third party knew or ought to have known that he was making a contract with someone other than the person he was negotiating with.

32.2.A DISCLOSED AGENCY

A disclosed principal is one of whose existence the third party is aware at the time of contracting. This will generally be the case where the agent entered into the contract 'as agent for X', 'for X', 'in the name of X', and also in situations where other circumstances existed from which the third party concluded, or had reason to conclude, that it was the agent's intention not to bind himself, but to bind another person as principal. The principal is a 'named' principal if the third party knows his identity. If the third party knows that the agent is contracting as an agent but is unaware of the principal's identity, there may still be a case of disclosed agency if the agent and the third party both know that the principal shall be identified at some later stage.

There may also be cases in which the third party knows that the agent is acting on behalf of another, but where it follows from the circumstances that the agent undertakes to bind himself only. This will be assumed if the agent has acted as a 'commission agent' (*commissionnaire, Kommissionär*). According to trade usage, custom or statute, a contract made by a commission agent will normally be held to be binding only on the agent, although the third party may not only know that the agent, as commission agent, acts on behalf of a principal, but may even be aware of the principal's identity. See, for example, Article 1731 of the Italian Civil Code, Article 425 of the Swiss Law of Obligations and the following provision from the German Commercial Code:

HGB	**32.8 (DE)**

§ 383: (1) A commission agent is a person who engages, for business purposes, in the sale or purchase in his own name of goods or securities for the account of another (the principal).

Suppose A, a shoe wholesaler, is buying shoes in large quantities from M, a manufacturer, and is reselling them to retail firms. In this case A bears the risk that the shoes become unsaleable or can be sold only at very low prices. If A wishes to shift this risk to M and M is willing to bear this risk, they may agree that A should operate on the basis of a 'commission contract'. Under a commission contract, A sells the shoes to retailers 'in his own name', and as a result the retailers will acquire contractual rights only against A (and will be insulated from contractual liabilities vis-à-vis M) even though they may be fully aware of M's identity and of A's role as M's agent. However, since A is dealing only 'on account' (*pour le compte, für Rechnung, per conto*) of M, the economic risk of his dealing in M's shoes will be borne by M, and A's reward will typically be only a percentage of what he is paid by the retailers.

Where a duly authorised agent has made a contract with a third party on behalf of a disclosed principal, a direct contractual relationship arises between principal and third party so that the principal can sue and be sued by the third party on such contract.

Geneva Convention on Agency in the International
Sale of Goods **32.9 (INT)**

Article 12: Where an agent acts on behalf of a principal within the scope of his authority and the third party knew or ought to have known that the agent was acting as an agent, the acts of the agent shall directly bind the principal and the third party to each other, unless it follows from the circumstances of the case, for example by a reference to a contract of commission, that the agent undertakes to bind himself only.

The revised French Code civil takes a similar position:

Code civil **32.10 (FR)**

Article 1154: Where a representative acts within his authority and in the name and on behalf of the person whom he represents, only the latter is bound to the undertaking so contracted.

Where a representative states that he is acting on behalf of another person but contracts in his own name, he alone is bound towards the other contracting party.

Further, Article 1156 of the revised Code civil provides that, in the case of a failure by the agent to disclose his status as an agent, the third party may still be contractually bound to the principal if he legitimately believed, at the time of the conclusion of the contract, that the agent was acting on behalf of the latter.[6]

These rules (see also Article 2.2.3 UNIDROIT PICC) are fairly clear in the abstract. However, the words used by contracting parties will not always facilitate the application of the rules. It may not be clear whether a person was contracting 'as agent' of another or whether it was intended by the parties that the contract should become binding only on the 'agent'. In other cases it may be clear that the person has been acting as agent for a principal, but there is doubt about who the principal is. Sometimes a person may contract both on his own behalf and on behalf of a principal. The following cases illustrate some of these difficulties, and the different approaches taken in the different systems studied.

Swiss Federal Court, 19 December 1934[7] **32.11 (CH)**

In the name of an unidentified group of banks

Where a party arranges finance for a borrower 'in the name of a group of banks' but those banks are not identified, that party should be treated as principal, so that the banks have no direct claim against the borrower.

---

[6] See below, p 1371.
[7] BGE 60 II 492.

Facts: Elektra Corp needed a substantial amount of money for an investment project. They approached the bankers Brupbacher & Co and obtained from them a loan of 5 million Swiss Francs under a contract dated 30 January 1929 which provided in its introductory passage that it was made between Elektra Corp, on the one hand, and 'Messrs CJ Brupbacher & Cie in Zurich, in the name of a group of banks, hereinafter called the "bank", on the other hand'. The same formula was used in a contract dated 4 June 1931 by which the loan was extended until 15 March 1933. In September 1930 Brupbacher became insolvent. An action was brought against Elektra Corp by 14 banks which, as members of a consortium formed by Brupbacher, had contributed shares ranging between 50,000 and 1.5 million Swiss Francs to be made available to Elektra Corp through Brupbacher. The defendant Elektra pleaded that, despite the wording of the contracts, its only creditor was Brupbacher, and that the plaintiffs had no cause of action.

Held: Brupbacher had been acting as principal, so the banks had no action against Elektra.

Judgment: 1. It is undisputed that Messrs Brupbacher & Cie concluded the two loan agreements of 30 January 1929 and 4 June 1931. The opening wording of those contracts merely stated that Brupbacher was acting 'in the name of a group of banks'. The defendant was not informed of the identity of the members of that group of banks, nor of the sums contributed by them. Indeed, it was not even certain, upon the conclusion of the first contract and, in part, on that of the second, who would be participating; on the contrary, it was only subsequently that the undertakings now claiming as the plaintiffs in this action, alternatively, their predecessors in title, committed themselves to the grant of the credit. Accordingly, they did not in any event, by virtue of the two contracts, become creditors of the defendant in accordance with the ordinary rules of agency, since it is normally a condition of direct agency (Articles 32 et seq of the Swiss Obligationenrecht), which alone is capable of having that effect, that the identity of the principal must, at the time when the contract is concluded, be objectively established and must, in addition, not be left unspecified in subjective terms, that is to say, vis-à-vis the other contracting party, or at least not intentionally.

However, the plaintiffs rely, in advancing their claims as alleged creditors, on the principle of 'acting on behalf of those whom it may concern'.

2. According to that principle, 'acting on behalf of those whom it may concern' takes place when, upon conclusion of the contract, an intermediary is involved on behalf of one of the parties and either the person for whom he is acting has not yet been specified in objective terms or, at least, his identity has not yet been revealed to the other contracting party. The most obvious example of this is where the intermediary buys something and 'reserves' to himself the right to identify the buyer. Since the intermediary makes it clear to the other contracting party that he is not contracting on his own behalf, such cases represent a particular type of direct agency. They differ from the form usually taken, in that the identity of the principal on whose behalf the transaction is entered into is for the time being left unspecified. Where the legal order permits this, the situation is such that the principal acquires direct rights and assumes direct obligations under the contract.

The plaintiffs rely on the opening wording of the contracts, which stated that Messrs Brupbacher & Cie were acting 'in the name of a group of banks'. According to normal legal parlance, that wording does indeed permit the conclusion to be drawn that direct agency was involved. However, that conclusion is not irrebuttable; it is open to the other party to adduce evidence to show that, in the particular case at issue, the formula in question bore a different meaning, and that the intention was that the rights and obligations arising under the contract should vest in the person of the alleged agent himself.

In that connection, the defendant ... correctly points out that the identity of the plaintiffs as contracting parties is not apparent from the ensuing wording of the contracts. In that further wording, the lender is specified as 'the Bank', without there being any clear indication from the explanation given in the opening wording whether that term was intended to constitute an abbreviated reference to Messrs Brupbacher & Cie or a reference to the group of banks. Moreover, no reference is made, in the context of the signature by Messrs Brupbacher & Cie, to its acting in any agency capacity. True, it may be argued that there was no need to repeat the reference to its involvement in the capacity of an agent, given that it had been definitively stated in the opening wording that the firm of Brupbacher & Cie was acting on behalf of the group of banks. However, had the contracting parties really considered that the group of banks was to stand directly, in legal terms, in the position of lender vis-à-vis the defendant, then it is clear, given the broad implications attaching to the question, that the position should have been expressed unambiguously, instead of merely being alluded to in a formula consisting of a few words in the opening wording …

The very nature of the transaction suggests that it was Messrs Brupbacher & Cie that was to be regarded as the creditor. In credit transactions, especially those involving millions, it is, from the outset, in the interests not only of the creditor but also, to a limited extent, of the debtor to know the identity of the other contracting party. The grant of the loan makes the debtor financially dependent on the creditor, with the result that the latter's identity cannot be a matter of indifference to him. One has only to consider in that regard that the debtor may subsequently run into problems over the making of payments and may have to ask for time to pay or for some other form of alleviation of his difficulties. For those reasons, it is hardly likely that an undertaking seeking such large amounts of credit would needlessly engage in a contract with unspecified third parties.

In addition, the plaintiffs claim that, even after the conclusion of the contracts, the defendant did not have the right to be informed of the composition of the consortium; and, in point of fact, the identity of its individual members did not come to light until the collapse of Messrs Brupbacher & Cie prompted them to emerge from their anonymity. As explained above, that in itself operates to deprive of all legal effect the plea that the case involved an agent 'acting on behalf of those whom it may concern'. Quite apart from this, however, it is apparent from the facts of this case that the parties cannot have had the intention alleged. It runs counter to the natural interpretation of the case, and to all normal business practice, to claim that, in the transaction of such a substantial deal, one party should remain, unidentified and unidentifiable, in the background and that the other party should renounce the right at any time to discover with whom it was dealing as the other party to the contract.

> *Note*
>
> Contrast the approach of the Swiss courts in this case with that of the English courts in *The Ariadne Irene* case:

House of Lords **32.12 (EN)**

Universal Steam Navigation Co Ltd v James McKelvie & Co (The Ariadne Irene)[8]

A party who signs 'as agent' is not personally liable even if elsewhere in the contract he is referred to as if he were the principal.

---

[8] [1923] AC 492.

Facts: A charterparty was expressed to be made between TH Seed & Co Ltd, as agents for the owners of a steamer, and 'James McKelvie & Co, Newcastle-on-Tyne, Charterers'. The charterparty contained numerous provisions imposing obligations on the 'Charterers', including an obligation to pay demurrage in the event of the steamer being detained beyond the stipulated time either at the port of loading or at the port of discharge. The charterparty was signed 'For and on behalf of James McKelvie & Co (as agents). JA McKelvie.' Liability for demurrage at the port of discharge having been incurred, the owner brought an action against the defendants. They pleaded that they had signed the charterparty merely 'as agents' for a third party and were therefore not personally liable.

Held: The defendants, having signed 'as agents', were not liable, notwithstanding that they were described as 'Charterers' in the body of the charterparty.

Judgment: Viscount Cave LC: If the respondents had signed the charterparty without qualification, they would of course have been personally liable to the shipowners; but by adding to their signature the words 'as agents' they indicated clearly that they were signing only as agents for others and had no intention of being personally bound as principals. I can imagine no other purpose for which these words could have been added; and unless they had that meaning, they appear to me to have no sense or meaning at all. ...

It is, as Bankes LJ said, to the interest of the commercial community that a signature 'as agent' should have a generally accepted meaning, and I agree with him that such a qualification of the signature should be taken as a deliberate expression of intention to exclude any personal liability on the part of the signatory.

Lord Shaw of Dunfermline: ... The first question is in what character Messrs McKelvie signed this document? I see no ground whatsoever for denying effect to the express word 'agents': it was undoubtedly in that character that the contract was signed: there is as little ground for cutting out the express character in which it was signed as for cutting out the signature itself.

The second question is, whether, although thus denominating themselves as 'agents,' Messrs McKelvie were yet signing a contract which by its terms made them principals therein. But its terms do not refer to either 'principals' or 'agents'; the body of the document can be applied to either category. As for the names of the parties, I hold that the names of McKelvie followed by 'Charterers' with nothing said of agency, is definitely stamped with agency by the express affirmation of the signature.

Lord Parmoor: ... My Lords, the question in this appeal is whether the respondents are personally liable, under the terms of a charter-party, for demurrage, in discharging the steamship Ariadne Irene. The defence of the respondents is that they signed the charterparty 'as agents', and did not incur thereunder any personal liability. The charterparty was signed as follows: 'For and on behalf of James McKelvie & Co (as agents).— JA McKelvie.' The words 'as agents' are, in my opinion, clearly words of qualification and not of description. They denote, in unambiguous language, that the respondents did not sign as principals, and did not intend to incur personal liability. The signature applies to the whole contract, and to every term in the contract. I think it would not be admissible to infer an implied term, or implied terms, in the contract inconsistent with the limitation of liability directly expressed in the qualification of the signature, since the effect of such an implication would be to contradict an express term of the contract. It is not impossible that by plain words in the body of the document, persons signing 'as agents', may expressly undertake some form of personal liability as principals, but I can find no trace of any intention of the respondents to incur any such liability in the charterparty, which is in question in the present appeal.

[Lord Sumner delivered a speech to the same effect. Lord Birkenhead concurred.]

Timber sold by non-owner

A person who makes a contract to sell timber 'as agent for the owner' is merely stating that he is acting on behalf of the person who instructed him and not on behalf of the true owner if that turns out to be someone else; therefore he is not liable for breach of warranty of authority on the basis that the true owner had not authorised the sale.

Facts: After R had bought a quantity of timber stored in a forest, he had authorised the defendant to sell the timber on his behalf. Thereupon the defendant had entered into a written contract with the plaintiff which was expressed to be made by the defendant 'as agent for the owners' of the timber. After paying the defendant the plaintiff tried to take possession of the timber, but was prevented from doing so by K, its real owner. The plaintiff brought an action (not against R, who had apparently become insolvent, but) against the defendant, arguing that the defendant had acted as agent (not for R, but) for the real owner and was therefore personally liable for breach of an implied warranty of authority.

Held: The appeal court dismissed the action; the BGH dismissed a further appeal.

Judgment: The appellate court has stated that when the defendant held himself out, on the conclusion of the contract, as acting 'as agent for the owner', without identifying the latter by name, he intended to act only on behalf of the person by whom he had in fact been given authority to act. According to that court, it is inconsistent with the realities of life to interpret his statement as meaning that he intended to act on behalf of the actual owner, regardless of who that person might be. On the contrary, the use of the word 'owner' in his contractual statement merely indicated he believed that the person whom he represented was the owner. On an objective assessment, the plaintiff must likewise have interpreted the defendant's statement as having that meaning. According to the appellate court, the plaintiff intended to conclude the contract not with someone who was completely unknown to him but with a person who, although not named, was nevertheless comprehensively specified, namely the person behind the defendant who had given the latter that authority to conclude the contract.

The criticisms levelled against those findings in the notice of appeal are without merit. The court below found that the defendant had acted on behalf of the person who had given him authority to sell the timber. It did not make any assumptions as to the identity of the person on whose behalf the defendant would have been acting had he known that K was in fact the owner of the timber; nor did it regard the defendant's intention, which was not revealed and which was never expressed in any way, as decisive. The reasons given by the court below for its finding that, on an objective assessment, the plaintiff would necessarily have likewise interpreted the defendant's declaration as meaning that the latter was acting on behalf of the person who actually gave him authority to act clearly show that that court chose the correct basis for its decision as to the nature of the intention declared to, and discernible by, the plaintiff, and as to the way in which the latter must, according to the principles of good faith, have construed that declaration. There exist no grounds in law for criticising the appellate court's conclusion, based on experience of life as it is lived, that an agent who declares that he is acting 'as agent for the owner' is not stating that he is contracting on behalf of a person unknown to him who may subsequently turn out to be the true owner of the goods sold, but is instead acting on behalf

---

[9] LM § 164 BGB no. 10, JZ 1957, 441.

of the person by whom he has been instructed to act and whose identity he has declined, for whatever reason, to specify, since he is assuming, like the other party to the contract, that the person who instructed him to act intended to sell something actually belonging to that person and not something which the latter had yet to acquire. In the light of the statements made, both parties should have regarded the defendant's principal as being the person who instructed the defendant to act on his behalf, and whom they assumed at the same time to be the owner of the goods. The question whether the plaintiff did in fact interpret the defendant's declaration in that way, or whether he may have regarded the defendant as being the agent of the true owner of the goods and intended to contract on that basis, is irrelevant, since it is only discernible conduct that counts. Nor can it be said on that basis that the present case concerns a hidden absence of consensus. According to the statements made by both parties, it was the person who had instructed the defendant to act who was the seller of the timber.

32.2.B UNDISCLOSED AGENCY

We now turn to cases in which the agent, by entering into a contract with a third party, has acted on behalf of a principal but without disclosing the existence of the agency relationship, so that the third party neither knew nor had reason to know that the agent was acting as an agent. The general rule in civil law systems is that in this case only the agent can sue and be sued on the contract and that the contract is for the principal a mere *res inter alios acta*.[10]

The common law adopts a different approach. Not only does it allow the undisclosed principal to sue the third party, but it also allows the third party, once the identity of the principal has been revealed to him, to bypass the agent and sue the principal directly. This is difficult to reconcile with the doctrine of privity, which says that a contract cannot confer rights or impose obligations arising under it on any person except the parties to it.[11] A good deal of academic discussion has been devoted to reconcile the doctrine of privity and the rules on undisclosed agency. But, in the words of Fridman:[12]

> all these varied, and imaginative theories do not completely explain this strange, peculiarly English doctrine. Perhaps the most satisfying attitude to adopt is that the idea of the undisclosed principal is an anomaly, introduced into and accepted by the common law for reasons of mercantile convenience.[13]

We shall first discuss cases in which the undisclosed principal is suing the third party. The paramount consideration is to avoid prejudice to the third party who honestly thought at the time of contracting that he was only dealing with the agent.

Given that there is no general 'doctrine of undisclosed agency' in civil law systems, the principal cannot generally proceed against the third party. However, if the principal

---

[10] Art 1156(1) of the revised French Code civil states that: 'an act made by a representative without authority or beyond his authority cannot be set up against the person whom he represents'. An exception to this rule is nevertheless provided by the aforementioned article (see above, p 1358 and below, p 1371).

[11] See above, pp 1261–62.

[12] GHL Fridman, *The Law of Agency* (7th edn, London: Butterworths, 1996) 258.

[13] On what these 'reasons of mercantile convenience' may be, see below, p 1366.

cannot obtain what he is owed by the agent he is sometimes allowed to intervene in a contract concluded on his behalf by an agent with a third party. If, for example, the agent is owed money by the third party under the contract and then becomes insolvent, the principal is given priority over the agent's general creditors in respect of his claim against the third party. This applies where goods have been sold on behalf of the principal by a 'commission agent'; see § 392(2) of the German Commercial Code (HGB) and § 61 of the Swedish Law on Commission Agents (1914). Other legal systems grant the same right to all undisclosed principals: see Article 401 of the Swiss Law of Obligations, Articles 1705(2) and 1721 of the Italian Civil Code and Article 6:421(1) of the New Dutch Civil Code. See further Article 2.2.4 UNIDROIT PICC, which broadly follows the Geneva Convention.

Geneva Convention on Agency in the International
Sale of Goods   **32.14 (INT)**

Article 13: (1) Where the agent acts on behalf of a principal within the scope of his authority, his acts shall bind only the agent and the third party if:
  (a) the third party neither knew nor ought to have known that the agent was acting as an agent, or
  (b) it follows from the circumstances of the case, for example by a reference to a contract of commission, that the agent undertakes to bind himself only.
  (2) Nevertheless:
  (a) where the agent, whether by reason of the third party's failure of performance or for any other reason, fails to fulfil or is not in a position to fulfil his obligations to the principal, the principal may exercise against the third party the rights acquired on the principal's behalf by the agent, subject to any defences which the third party may set up against the agent;
  (b) ...[14]

The following English case illustrates that, even though English law recognises undisclosed agency, there are constraints on the principal's ability to proceed against the third party:

King's Bench Division   **32.15 (EN)**

Said v Butt[15]

An undisclosed principal who knows that the third party would not have contracted with him directly cannot claim against the third party.

Facts: The plaintiff was minded to attend the first night of a play but the management of the theatre was ill-disposed towards him and would have refused to sell him a ticket, so he had the ticket purchased by a friend, Mr Pollock. This did him no good, since the defendant, the manager of the theatre, refused to allow the plaintiff to his seat. The plaintiff sued on the ground that he was entitled as undisclosed principal to demand admission on the basis of the contract concluded by Mr Pollock as his agent.

---

[14] See below, p 1367.
[15] [1920] 3 KB 497.

Held: The action was dismissed.

Judgment: McCardie J: ... A first night at the Palace Theatre is, as with other theatres, an event of great importance. The result of a first night may make or mar a play. If the play be good, then word of its success may be spread, not only by the critics, but by the members of the audience. The nature and social position and influence of the audience are of obvious importance. First nights have become to a large extent a species of private entertainment given by the theatrical proprietors and management to their friends and acquaintances, and to influential persons, whether critics or otherwise. The boxes, stalls and dress circle are regarded as parts of the theatre which are subject to special allocation by the management. Many tickets for those parts may be given away. The remaining tickets are usually sold by favour only. A first night, therefore, is a special event, with special characteristics. As the plaintiff himself stated in evidence, the management only disposes of first night tickets for the stalls and dress circle to those whom it selects. I may add that it is scarcely likely to choose those who are antagonistic to the management; or who have attacked the character of the theatre officials ...

In my opinion the defendant can rightly say, upon the special circumstances of this case, that no contract existed on 23 December 1919, upon which the plaintiff could have sued the Palace Theatre. The personal element was here strikingly present. The plaintiff knew that the Palace Theatre would not contract with him for the sale of a seat for 23 December. They had expressly refused to do so. He was well aware of their reasons. I hold that by the mere device of utilising the name and services of Mr Pollock, the plaintiff could not constitute himself a contractor with the Palace Theatre against their knowledge, and contrary to their express refusal. He is disabled from asserting that he was the undisclosed principal of Mr Pollock.

Geneva Convention on Agency in the International
Sale of Goods **32.16 (INT)**

Article 13: (6) The principal may not exercise against the third party the rights acquired on his behalf by the agent if it appears from the circumstances of the case that the third party, had he known the principal's identity, would not have entered into the contract.

In *Greer v Downs Supply Co*[16] the defendant made a purchase from an agent only because he had a time-barred claim against the agent which he hoped to be able to set off against the price; the undisclosed principal, on whose account the agent had contracted, was not allowed to sue. The third party can also defend on the ground that he has already performed to the agent, believing him to be the other party to the contract, and he can set off against the principal's claim any claim he had against the agent at the time the contract was formed (*Montagu v Forwood*[17]). It follows that the third party, if sued by an undisclosed principal, is protected much in the same way as a debtor who has a new creditor thrust on him without his consent by way of an assignment.[18]

While the common law and the civil law systems are not far apart in regard to the undisclosed principal's rights against the third party, the two systems diverge in relation

[16] [1927] 2 KB 28 (CA).
[17] [1893] 2 QB 350 (CA).
[18] See below, pp 1389–92.

to the third party's rights against the principal. Whilst the common law recognises the third party's right to sue the undisclosed principal, it is much harder for civil law systems to accept the view that the third party should be able to sue a principal of whom he was unaware when the contract was concluded. Take the case of an agent who bought goods on credit from a third party on behalf of an undisclosed principal: if the third party was unaware of the existence of a principal at the time of contracting, it is arguable that the third party, having failed to take the usual precaution of reserving title, should bear the risk of the agent's insolvency. Why should he be able to bypass the (insolvent) agent and sue the principal if his existence is revealed to him, perhaps by accident, at some later stage? The common lawyer would defend this result on the ground that the principal, by giving the agent authority to buy on his behalf, created the risk of his becoming insolvent and cannot complain if he is held liable to the third party for the consequences of his agent's activities:

Court of Appeal **32.17 (EN)**

Irvine v Watson[19]

An undisclosed principal is liable to the third party even though the principal has paid the agent, unless the third party has led the principal to believe that he had already settled with the agent.

Facts: The plaintiffs sold certain casks of oil, and on the face of the contract Conning appeared as the purchaser. Conning was acting for the defendants as principals. When the casks had been delivered to Conning the defendants paid the price to him. In the action brought against the defendants for payment of the price it was regarded by the court as self-evident that the plaintiffs had a right to sue them directly.

Held: The main issue was whether the defendants were discharged of their liability to the plaintiffs by having paid the agent. Bowen J had found in favour of the plaintiffs. The Court of Appeal affirmed his judgment.

Judgment: BRAMWELL LJ: The question is whether such payment discharged [the defendants] from their liability to the plaintiffs. I think it is impossible to say that it discharged them, unless they were misled by some conduct of the plaintiffs into the belief that [Conning] had already settled with the plaintiffs, and made such payment in consequence of such belief. But it is contended that the plaintiffs here did mislead the defendants into such belief, by parting with the possession of the oil to Conning without getting the money. The terms of the contract were 'cash on or before delivery', and it is said that the defendants had a right to suppose that the sellers would not deliver unless they received payment of the price at the time of delivery. I do not think, however, that that is a correct view of the case. The plaintiffs had a perfect right to part with the oil to the broker without insisting strictly upon their right to prepayment, and there is, in my opinion, nothing in the facts of the case to justify the defendants in believing that they would so insist. No doubt if there was an invariable custom in the trade to insist on prepayment where the terms of the contract entitled the seller to it, that might alter the matter; and in such cases non-insistence on prepayment might discharge the buyer if he paid the broker on the faith of the seller already having been paid. But that is not the case here; the evidence before Bowen J shows that there is no invariable custom to that effect.

---

[19] (1880) 5 QBD 414.

Apart from all authorities, then, I am of opinion that the defendants' contention is wrong, and upon looking at the authorities, I do not think that any of them are in direct conflict with that opinion. It is true that in *Thomson v Davenport* (1829) 9 B & C 78 both Lord Tenterden and Bayley J suggest in the widest terms that a seller is not entitled to sue the undisclosed principal on discovering him, if in the meantime the state of account between the principal and the agent has been altered to the prejudice of the principal. But it is impossible to construe the dicta of those learned judges in that case literally; it would operate most unjustly to the vendor if we did. I think the judges who uttered them did not intend a strictly literal interpretation to be put on their words. But whether they did or not, the opinion of Parke, B in *Heald v Kenworthy* (1855) 10 Exch 739 seems to me preferable; it is this, that 'If the conduct of the seller would make it unjust for him to call upon the buyer for the money, as for example, where the principal is induced by the conduct of the seller to pay his agent the money on the faith that the agent and seller have come to a settlement on the matter, or if any representation to that effect is made by the seller, either by words or conduct, the seller cannot afterwards throw off the mask and sue the principal'. That is in my judgment a much more accurate statement of the law.

[BRETT LJ and BAGGALLAY LJ delivered judgments to the same effect.]

The Geneva Agency Convention follows the common law approach. As seen above, Article 13(1) provides that, as a rule, the acts of an agent shall be binding on the agent and the third party only if the third party neither knew nor ought to have known that he was acting as an agent. However, according to Article 13(2)(b):

Geneva Convention on Agency in the International
Sale of Goods   **32.18 (INT)**

Article 13: (2)(b) where the agent fails to fulfil or is not in a position to fulfil his obligations to the third party, the third party may exercise against the principal the rights which the third party has against the agent, subject to any defences which the agent may set up against the third party and which the principal may set up against the agent.

BW   **32.19 (NL)**

Article 7:412: If a mandatary who has entered into a contract with a third person in his own name does not perform his obligations with respect to the mandator or goes bankrupt, the mandator can have those rights of the mandatary with respect to the third person, which are susceptible of transfer, transferred to him by a written declaration to both of them, except to the extent that these rights belong to the mandatary in his mutual relationship with the mandator.

Principles of European Contract Law   **32.20 (INT)**

Article 3:301: Intermediaries not acting in the name of a Principal
    (1) Where an intermediary acts:
        (a) on instructions and on behalf, but not in the name, of a principal, or
        (b) on instructions from a principal but the third party does not know and has no reason to know this,
        the intermediary and the third party are bound to each other.
    (2) The principal and the third party are bound to each other only under the conditions set out in Articles 3:302 to 3:304.

Article 3:302: Intermediary's Insolvency or Fundamental Non-performance to Principal

If the intermediary becomes insolvent, or if it commits a fundamental non-performance towards the principal, or if prior to the time for performance it is clear that there will be a fundamental non-performance:

(a) on the principal's demand, the intermediary shall communicate the name and address of the third party to the principal; and

(b) the principal may exercise against the third party the rights acquired on the principal's behalf by the intermediary, subject to any defences which the third party may set up against the intermediary.

Article 3:303: Intermediary's Insolvency or Fundamental Non-performance to Third Party

If the intermediary becomes insolvent, or if it commits a fundamental non-performance towards the third party, or if prior to the time for performance it is clear that there will be a fundamental non-performance:

(a) on the third party's demand, the intermediary shall communicate the name and address of the principal to the third party; and

(b) the third party may exercise against the principal the rights which the third party has against the intermediary, subject to any defences which the intermediary may set up against the third party and those which the principal may set up against the intermediary.

Article 3:304: Requirement of Notice

The rights under Articles 3:302 and 3:303 may be exercised only if notice of intention to exercise them is given to the intermediary and to the third party or principal, respectively. Upon receipt of the notice, the third party or the principal is no longer entitled to render performance to the intermediary.

32.3 AGENT ACTING WITH AUTHORITY AND ULTRA VIRES

32.3.A AUTHORITY

32.3.A.1 ACTUAL AUTHORITY

A principal will be bound to the third party only by acts which are within the agent's authority. Most obviously this applies to what the principal has expressly authorised the agent to do. However, a grant of authority may also be implied, either because (though it was not mentioned) it was a normal part of what the agent was expressly authorised to do (thus a lawyer retained to litigate a case has implied authority to accept an offer by the other side to settle the case out of court[20]) or if it is a normal duty of someone who is given the job that the agent has been appointed to do (thus a shop assistant may have authority to give information about the goods to customers as well as to sell them). It may also be implied from previous conduct between the parties, for example if a company executive who has no formal authority to enter certain types of transaction on behalf of the company has nonetheless done so on many occasions and the company board has

---

[20] *Waugh v HB Clifford* [1982] Ch 374 (CA).

always accepted what the executive has done without question.[21] But the principal may exclude authority which would normally be implied by indicating to the agent that he or she is not authorised to do the act in question. A contract made by the agent in excess of that authority will not affect the principal unless this is exceptionally provided for by statute[22] or the principal adopts what the agent has done in accordance with the doctrine of ratification.[23]

32.3.A.2 APPARENT AUTHORITY

Furthermore, a principal will be bound, despite the absence of a ratification, if, by words or conduct, he has allowed another person to appear to the outside world to be his agent and a third party, acting on the reasonable inference that the person is an agent, has entered into a contract with him. In this situation the principal cannot afterwards repudiate this 'apparent' or 'ostensible agency' if to do so would cause injury to the third party. See Articles 3:201(3) PECL and II-6:103(3) DCFR,[24] as well as:

BW

32.21 (NL)

Article 3:61(2): Where a juridical act has been performed in the name of another person, the other party who, on the basis of a declaration or conduct of that other person, has presumed and in the given circumstances could reasonably presume the existence of a sufficient authority, may not have invoked against him the inaccuracy of this presumption.

Geneva Convention on Agency in the International
Sale of Goods[25]

32.22 (INT)

Article 14: (1) Where an agent acts without authority or acts outside the scope of his authority, his acts do not bind the principal and the third party to each other.

(2) Nevertheless, where the conduct of the principal causes the third party reasonably and in good faith to believe that the agent has authority to act on behalf of the principal and that the agent is acting within the scope of that authority, the principal may not invoke against the third party the lack of authority of the agent.

Court of Appeal

32.23 (EN)

Freeman & Lockyer v Buckhurst Park Properties (Mangal) Ltd[26]

A director who has not been appointed as managing director of a company but who has been allowed by the board of directors to act as such has apparent authority to bind the company.

---

[21] eg *Hely-Hutchinson v Brayhead Ltd* [1968] 1 QB 549 (CA).
[22] See, eg, §§ 50, 54, 56 HGB.
[23] See below, pp 1372–74.
[24] See above, pp 1353–54.
[25] See also Art 2.2.5 UNIDROIT PICC.
[26] [1964] 2 QB 480.

Facts: The defendant company had bought a plot of land, intending to develop and resell it. Mr Kapoor was a director of the company but, not having been appointed managing director, had no actual authority to enter into contracts with third parties regarding the development of the land. Nevertheless, he instructed the plaintiffs to prepare an application for planning permission. The plaintiffs executed the work and filed an action against the defendant company claiming their fee. The defendant argued that Mr Kapoor had no authority to enter into the contract.

Held: It was held at first instance and by the Court of Appeal that Kapoor had authority to act.

Judgment: DIPLOCK LJ: It is necessary at the outset to distinguish between an 'actual' authority of an agent on the one hand, and an 'apparent' or 'ostensible' authority on the other. Actual authority and apparent authority are quite independent of one another. Generally they co-exist and coincide, but either may exist without the other and their respective scopes may be different. As I shall endeavour to show, it is upon the apparent authority of the agent that the contractor normally relies in the ordinary course of business when entering into contracts.

An 'actual' authority is a legal relationship between principal and agent created by a consensual agreement to which they alone are parties. Its scope is to be ascertained by applying ordinary principles of construction of contracts, including any proper implications from the express words used, the usages of the trade, or the course of business between the parties. To this agreement the contractor is a stranger; he may be totally ignorant of the existence of any authority on the part of the agent. Nevertheless, if the agent does enter into a contract pursuant to the 'actual' authority, it does create contractual rights and liabilities between the principal and the contractor.

An 'apparent' or 'ostensible' authority, on the other hand, is a legal relationship between the principal and the contractor created by a representation, made by the principal to the contractor, intended to be and in fact acted upon by the contractor, that the agent has authority to enter on behalf of the principal into a contract of a kind within the scope of the 'apparent' authority, so as to render the principal liable to perform any obligations imposed upon him by such contract. To the relationship so created the agent is a stranger. He need not be (although he generally is) aware of the existence of the representation but he must not purport to make the agreement as principal himself. The representation, when acted upon by the contractor by entering into a contract with the agent, operates as an estoppel, preventing the principal from asserting that he is not bound by the contract. It is irrelevant whether the agent had actual authority to enter into the contract …

The representation which creates 'apparent' authority may take a variety of forms of which the commonest is representation by conduct, that is, by permitting the agent to act in some way in the conduct of the principal's business with other persons. By so doing the principal represents to anyone who becomes aware that the agent is so acting that the agent has authority to enter on behalf of the principal into contracts with other persons of the kind which an agent so acting in the conduct of his principal's business has usually 'actual' authority to enter into.

[His Lordship then applied these rules to the case where the principal is not a natural person, but a corporation. In this case there were] four conditions which must be fulfilled to entitle a contractor to enforce against a company a contract entered into on behalf of the company by an agent who had no actual authority to do so. It must be shown:

(1) that a representation that the agent had authority to enter on behalf of the company into a contract of the kind sought to be enforced was made to the contractor;

(2) that such representation was made by a person or persons who had 'actual' authority to manage the business of the company either generally or in respect of those matters to which the contract relates;

(3) that he (the contractor) was induced by such representation to enter into the contract, that is, that he in fact relied upon it; and

(4) that under its memorandum or articles of association the company was not deprived of the capacity either to enter into a contract of the kind sought to be enforced or to delegate authority to enter into a contract of that kind to the agent ...

In the present case the findings of fact by the county court judge were sufficient to satisfy the four conditions. In particular the Court of Appeal could see no good ground for interfering with the judge's finding that Kapoor, although never appointed as managing director, had throughout been acting as such, and that this was well known to the board of the company. For these reasons it was held that Kapoor had 'apparent' authority to enter into contracts on behalf of the company for services in connection with the sale of the company's property, including the obtaining of development permission with respect to its use.

[PEARSON LJ and WILLMER LJ delivered judgments to the same effect.]

Note

The effect of corporate bodies, or 'organs', making a contract which is outside its powers has, since this case, been altered substantially by Article 9 of the First Company Law Directive.[27]

Code civil **32.24 (FR)**

Article 1156: An act made by a representative without authority or beyond his authority cannot be set up against the person whom he represents, unless the third party with whom he contracts legitimately believed that he had that person's authority, notably by reason of the latter's behaviour or statements.

Where a third party with whom a representative contracts was unaware that the act was concluded by the representative without authority or beyond his authority, the third party may invoke its nullity.

This approach towards apparent authority[28] applies equally to the context of an agent acting without authority and to the situation where his acts go beyond such authority. French law takes the position that, in both instances, the contract cannot be set up against the principal. Under French law a remedy is also given to the third party who may invoke the nullity of the contract. However, in both cases, it must be proven that the third party had no reason to legitimately believe that the agent had the authority to act or that he acted within the boundaries of that authority. In the case of an agent acting ultra vires, the principal may also invoke the nullity of the contract.

---

[27] First Council Directive 68/151/EEC of 9 March 1968 on co-ordination of safeguards which, for the protection of the interests of members and others, are required by Member States of companies within the meaning of the second paragraph of Article 58 of the Treaty, with a view to making such safeguards equivalent throughout the Community, [1968] OJ L65/8.

[28] Which is, to a large extent, the codification of the case law of the Cour de cassation; see Ass plén 13 December 1962, no. 57-11569, Bull AP no. 2.

Code civil **32.25 (FR)**

Article 1157:

   Where a representative abuses his authority to the detriment of the person whom he represents, the latter may invoke the nullity of any act concluded if the third party was aware of the abuse of authority or could not have been unaware of it.

The third party may nevertheless oppose such an action on the basis of the legitimate belief[29] that he held when he concluded the contract that the representative had the authority to enter into such contract on behalf of the principal.

   The revised French Code civil also provides for means to prevent an agent from acting beyond his authority. More precisely, it gives the possibility to a third party 'to request [in writing] the person represented to confirm to him within a time which he may fix and which must be reasonable, that the representative is empowered to conclude the act in question' (Article 1158).

32.3.B RATIFICATION

There is general agreement that a contract made by an unauthorised agent with a third party becomes binding on the principal if he ratifies it, ie affirms it either expressly or impliedly by conduct showing clearly that he approves and adopts what has been done on his behalf. Rules to this effect are laid down in most civil codes, although they differ in detail. See, for example, §§ 177, 178 BGB, Article 38 of the Swiss Law of Obligations, Article 1399 of the Italian Civil Code, Article 3:69 of the Dutch Civil Code and Article 1156 of the revised French Code civil.

Code civil **32.26 (FR)**

Article 1156: ...

   Neither an inability to set up an act against another person nor its nullity can be invoked once the person represented has ratified it.

Geneva Convention on Agency in the International
Sale of Goods[30] **32.27 (INT)**

Article 15: (1) An act by an agent who acts without authority or who acts outside the scope of his authority may be ratified by the principal. On ratification the act produces the same effects as if it had initially been carried out with authority.

   (2) Where, at the time of the agent's act, the third party neither knew nor ought to have known of the lack of authority, he shall not be liable to the principal if, at any time before ratification, he gives notice of his refusal to become bound by a ratification. Where the principal ratifies but does not do so within a reasonable time, the third party may refuse to be bound by the ratification if he promptly notifies the principal.

   (3) Where, however, the third party knew or ought to have known the lack of authority of the agent, the third party may not refuse to become bound by a ratification before the

---

[29] On the notion of a legitimate belief, see Cass civ (3) 3 June 2015, nos. 13-27143 and 14-12333.
[30] See also Art 2.2.9 UNIDROIT PICC.

expiration of any time agreed for ratification or, failing agreement, such reasonable time as the third party may specify.

(4) The third party may refuse to accept a partial ratification.

(5) Ratification shall take effect when notice of it reaches the third party or the ratification otherwise comes to his attention. Once effective, it may not be revoked.

(6) Ratification is effective notwithstanding that the act itself could not have been effectively carried out at the time of ratification. ...

(7) Where the act has been carried out on behalf of a corporation or other legal person before its creation, ratification is effective only if allowed by the law of the State governing its creation.

(8) Ratification is subject to no requirement as to form. It may be express or may be inferred from the conduct of the principal.

> *Note*
>
> Article 15(1) gives ratification retrospective effect: the situation is as if the agent had been authorised all along. See also *Bolton Partners v Lambert*[31] (the other party purported to repudiate the contract before the principal had ratified; it was held that if the principal ratified the repudiation was ineffective and the other party was bound).

| *Principles of European Contract Law* | **32.28 (INT)** |

Article 3:207: Ratification by Principal

(1) Where a person acting as an agent acts without authority or outside its authority, the principal may ratify the agent's acts.

(2) Upon ratification, the agent's acts are considered as having been authorised, without prejudice to the rights of other persons.

In civil law systems it follows from the wording of the code provisions that ratification by a principal is possible only where the agent's (unauthorised) statements were reasonably understood by the third party as being made in the name of a principal. Under the common law the principal can certainly ratify what was done by a person who indicated that he was acting as agent but had no authority; but what if the third party had no reason to assume that he was dealing with an agent? Can a principal, by way of a ratification, acquire rights and liabilities as a result of a contract made by an undisclosed agent acting outside his authority?

| *House of Lords* | **32.29 (EN)** |

Keighley, Maxstead & Co v Durant[32]

A person cannot ratify an act done by another who was not authorised to act as he did in advance and who did not disclose to the third party that he was acting as agent.

Facts: Roberts bought corn from the sellers at a price above that at which he had been instructed to buy by the appellants. He intended to buy for them, but did not disclose this fact to the sellers. The appellants later purported to ratify the contract, but then refused to accept delivery. The sellers sued them for damages.

---

[31] (1888) 41 ChD 295 (CA).
[32] [1901] AC 240.

Held: The Court of Appeal held for the sellers on the ground that the appellants' ratification was valid. The House of Lords allowed the appeal.

Judgment: LORD MACNAGHTEN: ... By a wholesome and convenient fiction, a person ratifying the act of another, who, without authority, has made a contract openly and avowedly on his behalf, is deemed to be, though in fact he was not, a party to the contract. Does the fiction cover the case of a person who makes no avowal at all, but assumes to act for himself and for no one else? ... Ought the doctrine of ratification to be extended to such a case? On principle I should say certainly not. It is, I think, a well-established principle in English law that civil obligations are not to be created by, or founded upon, undisclosed intentions. That is a very old principle ... and in my opinion it is not to be put aside or disregarded merely because it may be that, in a case like the present, no injustice might be done to the actual parties to the contract by giving effect to the undisclosed intentions of a would-be agent.

I think the appeal must be allowed.

LORD LINDLEY: ... It is not necessary to write a treatise on the doctrine of ratification in order to dispose of this case. Historically that doctrine is no doubt derived from the Roman law; but it has been extended and developed in this country conformably to our own legal principles and to meet our own commercial necessities; and it is to our own decisions rather than to the Digest and commentaries upon it that English Courts must look for guidance. It is well known that in matters of contract we pay far less attention judicially to unexpressed intentions than is paid to them in other countries which have followed the Roman law more closely than we have: see *Byrne v Van* Tienhoven (1880) 5 CPD 344 ...

It was strongly contended that there was no reason why the doctrine of ratification should not apply to undisclosed principals in general, and that no one could be injured by it if it were so applied. I am not convinced of this. But in this case there is no evidence in existence that, at the time when Roberts made his contract, he was in fact acting, as distinguished from intending to act, for the defendants as possible principals, and the decision appealed from, if affirmed, would introduce a very dangerous doctrine. It would enable one person to make a contract between two others by creating a principal and saying what his own undisclosed intentions were, and these could not be tested.

[Judgments to the same effect were delivered by the other Law Lords.]

32.3.C TERMINATION OF AUTHORITY

Principles of European Contract Law **32.30 (INT)**

Article 3:209: Duration of Authority
   (1) An agent's authority continues until the third party knows or ought to know that:
      (a) the agent's authority has been brought to an end by the principal, the agent, or both; or
      (b) the acts for which the authority had been granted have been completed, or the time for which it had been granted has expired; or
      (c) the agent has become insolvent or, where a natural person, has died or become incapacitated; or
      (d) the principal has become insolvent.
   (2) The third party is considered to know that the agent's authority has been brought to an end under paragraph (1)(a) above if this has been communicated or publicised

in the same manner in which the authority was originally communicated or publicised. (3) However, the agent remains authorised for a reasonable time to perform those acts which are necessary to protect the interests of the principal or its successors.

BGB   32.31 (DE)

§ 170: Period of effectiveness of the authority

If authority is granted by declaration to a third party, it remains in force in relation to this third party until he is notified by the principal of the expiry thereof.

Note

These provisions (see also Articles 17–20 of the Geneva Agency Convention and Article 2.2.10 UNIDROIT PICC) represent a general principle to which there are exceptions; for example, if the third party knows that an agent had been given authority for an indefinite period but does not know that the authority has in fact been terminated, the agent's acts on behalf of the principal will still bind the principal.[33] Thus, in *Waugh v HB Clifford*[34] a lawyer retained to litigate a case had implied authority to accept an offer by the other side to settle the case out of court. The lawyer had received an offer and had in fact contacted his client (the principal) to ask if he should accept. The client sent an instruction not to accept (thus revoking the implied authority) but the instruction never reached the lawyer, who accepted the offer. The other party knew nothing about the client's instruction not to accept. It was held that the lawyer had apparent authority to act and the client was bound by the settlement agreement.

32.3.D LIABILITY OF AGENT

Principles of European Contract Law   32.32 (INT)

Article 3:204: Agent acting without or outside its Authority

(1) Where a person acting as an agent acts without authority or outside the scope of its authority, its acts are not binding upon the principal and the third party.

(2) Failing ratification by the principal according to Article 3:207, the agent is liable to pay the third party such damages as will place the third party in the same position as if the agent had acted with authority. This does not apply if the third party knew or could not have been unaware of the agent's lack of authority.

The general principle of the common law is that everyone who professes to act as an agent on behalf of somebody else impliedly warrants that he has authority to make the contract which has been made unless the third party knows that he is lacking such authority. It follows that the self-styled agent will be liable to the third party even though he may have honestly believed in his authority.

---

[33] See H Kötz, *European Contract Law* (2nd edn, Oxford University Press, 2017) 305 n 64.
[34] [1982] Ch 374 (CA).

1375

Yonge v Toynbee[35]

An agent whose principal has become incapable by reason of insanity is liable on an implied warranty of authority, even though he had no reason to know of his lack of authority.

Facts: The defendant solicitor had been conducting litigation against the plaintiff on behalf of a client who became insane. After this had happened but before the solicitor had heard of it he took further steps in the lawsuit. The question was whether the plaintiff could recover from the solicitor the costs incurred by him in consequence of his having continued the litigation after his authority to do so had come to an end because of his client's incapacity.

Held: The plaintiff succeeded in recovering his costs from the solicitor.

Judgment: BUCKLEY LJ: ... I can see no distinction in principle between the case where the agent never had authority and the case where the agent originally had authority, but that authority has ceased without his knowledge or means of knowledge. In the latter case as much as in the former the proposition, I think, is true that without any mala fides he has at the moment of acting represented that he had an authority which in fact he had not. In my opinion he is then liable on an implied contract that he had authority, whether there was fraud or not. In *Collen v Wright* (1857) 8 E & B 647 Willes J in giving judgment of the Court uses the following language: 'I am of opinion that a person who induces another to contract with him, as the agent of a third party, by an unqualified assertion of his being authorised to act as such agent, is answerable to the person who so contracts for any damages which he may sustain by reason of the assertion of authority being untrue ... The fact that the professed agent honestly thinks that he has authority affects the moral character of his act; but his moral innocence, so far as the person whom he has induced to contract is concerned, in no way aids such person or alleviates the inconvenience and damage which he sustains. The obligation arising in such a case is well expressed by saying that a person professing to contract as agent for another, impliedly, if not expressly, undertakes to or promises the person who enters into such a contract, upon the faith of the professed agent being duly authorised, that the authority which he professes to have does in point of fact exist.' This language is equally applicable to each of the two classes of cases to which I have referred ... The question is not as to his honesty or bona fides. His liability arises from an implied undertaking or promise made by him that the authority which he professes to have does in point of fact exist. I can see no difference of principle between the case in which the authority never existed at all and the case in which the authority once existed and has ceased to exist ...

Note

Though an unauthorised agent's liability in English law is strict, an agent who acts without authority, and whose principal does not ratify what the agent has done, does not become liable 'in place of the principal'. The effect of the 'warranty of authority' is to entitle the third party to damages to put him into the position he would have been in if the agent had been authorised. In many cases this will enable the third party to

---

[35] [1910] KB 215.

recover his full loss from the agent. But if having rights against the principal would have been worthless because, for example, the principal is insolvent, the damages recoverable by the third party will be nil: see *Re National Coffee Place Co, ex p Panmure* (1883) 24 ChD 367, 371-72 (CA).

The same strict rule has been adopted by Article 3:70 of the Dutch Civil Code, Article 16 of the Geneva Agency Convention and Article 2.2.6 UNIDROIT PICC, and equally, the damages will be fixed so as to put the claimant into the position he would have been in had the agent had authority. In other jurisdictions the agent is treated more leniently. Under Italian law, he is only liable in the reliance measure. A reduction to the reliance interest is also possible under § 179(2) BGB, where it requires that the agent honestly believed in his authority. The same solution is adopted by Article 39 of the Swiss Law of Obligations; however, if the agent's belief in his authority was careless, judges may award higher damages if they think that it would be just and equitable to do so.[36]

FURTHER READING

Bonell, MJ, 'Agency' in AS Hartkamp et al (eds), *Towards a European Civil Code* (4th edn, Alphen aan den Rijn: Wolters Kluwer, 2011) 515–36.

Bonell, MJ, 'The 1983 Geneva Convention on Agency in the International Sale of Goods' (1984) 32 Am J Comp L 717–49.

Busch, D, *Indirect Representation in European Contract Law* (The Hague: Kluwer, 2005).

Busch, D and Macgregor, LJ, *The Unauthorised Agent: Perspectives from European and Comparative Law* (Cambridge University Press, 2009).

Festner, S, *Interessenkonflikte im deutschen und englischen Vertretungsrecht* (Tübingen: Mohr Siebeck, 2006).

Hesselink, MW (ed), *Principles of European Law: Commercial Agency, Franchise and Distribution Contracts* (PEL CAFDC) (Munich: Sellier, 2006).

Kleinschmidt, J, 'Stellvertretungsrecht in Deutschland und Frankreich' (2001) 9 ZEuP 697–736.

Kötz, H, *European Contract Law* (2nd edn, Oxford University Press, 2017) 293–318.

Mazeaud D, Schulze, R and Wicker, G, *La représentation en droit privé* (Paris: Société de législation comparée, vol 26, 2017).

Rademacher, L, 'Authority of Agents' in N Jansen and R Zimmermann (eds), *Commentaries on European Contract Laws* (Oxford University Press, 2018) 587–648.

[36] Although Art 1119-1(2) of the Avant projet de réforme du droit des obligations (one of the earlier versions of the 2016 reform) provided for the liability of the agent acting ultra vires, the revised French Code civil is silent on this issue. Some authors nevertheless suggest that an agent acting beyond his authority might still be liable for the damages caused to the principal even when the third party legitimately believed that the representative had the authority to conclude the said contract(s); see O Deshayes, T Genicon and YM Laithier, *Réforme du droit des contrats, du régime général et de la preuve des obligations, Commentaire article par article* (Paris: LexisNexis, 2016) 249.

33.1 INTRODUCTION

An assignment is a transaction whereby a right is transferred by its owner, called the assignor, to another person, called the assignee, as a result of which the assignee becomes entitled to sue the person liable, called the debtor. In most cases, an assignment will refer to the transfer of a money claim arising by way of contract, such as a seller's right to the purchase money, a contractor's right under a building contract to demand payment from his employer or an insured's right to be paid the agreed sum by the insurer. The rules on assignment are equally applicable to the transfer of other intangibles, such as patent rights and copyrights.

It is worth noting that under French law the notion of an assignment may refer to the assignment of a debt claim, a right arising from a contractual obligation or the very quality of party to the contract. The latter must be distinguished from the former as it consists in the transfer, by the assignor to the assignee, of his status as party to the contract. As a result, the assignor is substituted by the assignee in his entire contractual relationship. Accordingly, the French Code civil provides three different legal regimes for contractual assignments. Each legal regime is to be found in the sub-section of the Code civil which is devoted to it, forming either part of the section on plural obligations (assignment of debt claims and rights arising from obligations) or the section on the effects of contracts (assignment of contracts). These provisions were enacted through the 2016 reform. The law of assignment used to be solely governed by the provisions of Articles 1689 to 1701 of the French Code civil which can be found in the title on sales. Despite their limited scope, it is worth noting that the French courts developed a general theory of contractual assignment based on the interpretation of Article 1689 and former Article 1690 of the Code civil. The bulk of the novelties concerning the law of assignment introduced in 2016 can thus be understood, to a large extent, as a codification and clarification of that case law.

In each of the systems studied, special rules also apply to the assignment of contractual rights arising out of negotiable instruments, such as bills of exchange, promissory notes, cheques or other documents which have been held, either by statute or trade usage, to be negotiable. The essential feature of a negotiable instrument is that it represents the debt owed in physical form. If the holder of such an instrument endorses it, by writing his name on the back, and delivers it to another party, this party, upon taking the instrument in good faith and for value, obtains a good title despite any defect in the title of the transferor and any defences available to the debtor against his original creditor. Nor does it matter whether the debtor knew, or could have known, of the transfer of the instrument. In this respect, the position of the 'holder in due course' of a negotiable instrument is much stronger than if he had acquired the right by way of an ordinary assignment, since an assignee takes the right 'subject to equities', ie subject to any defects in the assignor's title and subject to certain defences which the debtor may have against the assignor.[1]

There is no assignment if the creditor simply requests his debtor to make payment to a third party. If the debtor pays the third party, he will be discharged not because the third party became his creditor by virtue of an assignment, but because the third party received payment as the creditor's agent and on his behalf (even though he may keep the money if that is what he and the creditor have agreed). Nor is there an assignment if the creditor and debtor have reached an agreement that a third party shall be entitled to demand performance from the debtor. In this case, the third party is a 'third party beneficiary', since his right arises directly from the agreement made between the creditor and the debtor, and not as a result of the transfer of the right by the creditor without the debtor's consent.[2]

An assignment may take place on the basis of different underlying agreements. It may occur because the assignor and the assignee are parties to a contract under which the assignor has assumed a duty, in consideration of the assignee's promise to pay a price, to transfer a right to the assignee as the buyer of that right. This seems to be the main situation the authors of the Code civil of 1804 had in mind when they drafted the provisions on assignment, since these provisions (Articles 1689 to 1701) form part of the title on sales. Today, the most common type of assignment is still the assignment of a claim to money, when the money claim is in effect sold for ready cash. However, it is clear that a right may also be assigned on the basis of a gift promise, in lieu of money owed or as security for a loan made by the assignee. One can also assign something by way of an outright gift with no prior promise. Even then there will be an agreement that the donee is to receive the assigned right without paying or owing anything in return. It is the very recognition of such a diversity that has led to the codification of a general theory of assignment in the French Code civil, through the enactment of the aforementioned provisions.[3]

Most assignments are made in the course of what is called 'receivables financing', ie the debt that is assigned is money that is originally owed to ('receivable' by) the assignor. Receivables financing may take one of two forms. One possibility is that the assignment is made by way of security, ie for the purpose of securing an obligation owed by the assignor to the assignee, for example, when a bank lending money to a customer accepts as security for repayment of the loan an assignment of the claims which the customer has against third parties. The other form of receivables financing is where the assignee takes an outright assignment by way of sale, and pays the assignee cash (or makes credit

---

[1] See below, pp 1405–13.

[2] See above, ch 31.

[3] See Rapport au Président de la République relative à l'ordonnance n°2016-131 du 10 février 2016 portant réforme du droit des contrats, du régime général et de la preuve des obligations, Section 4.

available to the assignor) immediately, later reimbursing itself by collecting the receivables. This is what happens in 'factoring', made when manufacturers or dealers whose customers have yet to settle their accounts need cash in hand now. They do not use their 'accounts receivable' as security but sell them outright to a factor for rather less than their nominal value, the difference representing the interest the factor forgoes on the cash advanced, the expense of collecting on the debts and sometimes the risk of non-payment.[4] Nowadays whole packages of claims are sold or transferred as security by a single transaction; credit institutions often take a bulk assignment of hundreds of claims at a time as security from those who borrow from them.

33.2 VALIDITY OF ASSIGNMENT

33.2.A AGREEMENT

The minimum requirement of a valid assignment is that there must be an agreement between the assignor and the assignee on the transfer of the right. In the continental legal systems many civil codes expressly provide that it is by virtue of a 'contract' between a creditor and another party that the creditor's claim may be transferred to that party.[5] English law does not see assignment as a 'contract'; accordingly there need not be any consideration[6] given or promised by the assignee.[7] However, in the words of Treitel, an assignment has no effect unless it is communicated to the assignee by the assignor or unless it is made in pursuance of a prior agreement between assignor and assignee.[8] If the assignee has become aware of the assignment, English law seems to allow him to repudiate the transfer.[9] If he does not do so, the assignment is valid. The same result would be reached on the continent, since it would normally be inferred from the circumstances that the assignee's silence constitutes an acceptance of the assignor's offer.

33.2.B FORMAL REQUIREMENTS

While an agreement between assignor and assignee is needed in each of the systems studied, it is highly controversial whether this agreement is sufficient to transfer the right

---

[4] Factoring may also be done on a 'recourse' basis under which the assignor either guarantees that the debt will be paid or agrees to repurchase any debt that is not paid.

[5] See Art 1321 of the French Civil Code concerning the assignment of rights arising from obligations; cf O Deshayes, T Genicon and YM Laithier, *Réforme du droit des contrats, du régime général et de la preuve des obligations, Commentaire article par article* (Paris: LexisNexis, 2016) 463: '[Article 1216] does not indicate the legal nature of the operation. However, it can only be considered as a contract, subject to the validity requirements outlined in Article 1128'.

[6] See above, ch 11.2.

[7] The debtor must pay the assignee if he is notified of the assignment. As between the assignor and assignee, no consideration is required if there has been a completed legal assignment. Where the agreement is one to transfer future debts, consideration is required. See *Treitel on the Law of Contract*, 14th edn by E Peel (London: Sweet & Maxwell, 2015) paras 15-025–15-036.

[8] ibid, para 15-019.

[9] ibid.

to the assignee so as to make him, as against the whole world, the new owner of the assigned claim.

The first point is that many systems do not require any particular form for an effective assignment. This is the position taken under German, Austrian and Swiss law, as well as under the proposals for a harmonisation of European contract law. Thus:

Principles of European Contract Law **33.1 (INT)**

Article 11:104: Form of assignment

An assignment need not be in writing and is not subject to any other requirement as to form. It may be proved by any means, including witnesses.

In contrast, in English law there cannot be what is termed a 'legal' or 'statutory assignment' giving the assignee the right to sue the debtor in the assignee's own name unless the assignment is in writing, signed by the assignor.[10] However, English law recognises what is termed an equitable assignment, which gives the assignee the right to sue if he joins the assignor in the action; and an equitable assignment need not be in any particular form.[11] Dutch law also requires a written document recording the transaction of the assignor and the assignee.[12]

33.2.C NOTICE TO AND CONSENT OF THE DEBTOR

The second point is whether the debtor must have been informed of the assignment or even have consented to it. There is considerable variation over whether there can be an effective assignment by an agreement or transfer as between the assignor and the assignee that is not known to the debtor. On these questions, German law has a particularly liberal position.

BGB **33.2 (DE)**

§ 398: Assignment

A claim or debt may, by agreement between the creditor and another, be transferred by the former to the latter (assignment). Upon the conclusion of such an agreement, the new creditor takes the place of the former creditor.

It follows that the assignment is fully effective without the debtor's consent and, indeed, even where the debtor knows nothing about it. Once the agreement referred to in § 398 BGB has been made, the right no longer forms part of the assignor's assets. It can no

---

[10] Law of Property Act 1925, s 136. There must also be notice in writing to the debtor, see below, p 1301.

[11] An equitable chose in action (such as the claim of a beneficiary under a trust, or of a legatee under a will, or interests in securities such as shares that are registered in the name of a broker or a bank but are held for the individual investor, who in English law is treated as the beneficial owner) may be assigned by way of a statutory or equitable assignment. According to s 53(1)(c) of the Law of Property Act 1925, an assignment of an equitable chose in action must be in writing. A debt is a legal interest and so the assignment of a debt will not be affected by s 53(1)(c).

[12] Arts 3:84 and 3:94(1) BW. There must also notification to the debtor, see below, p 1383.

longer be seized by the assignor's creditors, nor does it fall in the estate of a bank-rupt assignor, provided that the agreement referred to in § 398 BGB was made before the attachment order or the opening of the bankruptcy proceedings. If the assignor makes successive assignments of the same debt to two different assignees, the debt is acquired by the party to whom it was first assigned (*prior tempore potior iure*), while the second assignee takes nothing (*nemo dat quod non habet*). However, if the debtor pays the assignor, the payment will form part of the assignor's estate; the assignee will have merely a personal claim against the assignor. The claim may be of either a contractual or a restitutionary nature. This is for the protection of the debtor who has not been notified of the assignment and who pays the assignor.[13]

A different position is taken by the French Code civil and by most legal systems based on the French tradition. Under former Article 1689 Code civil, the agreement between assignor and assignee results in a transfer of the right only as between the par-ties. Article 1690 Code civil, which has not been amended by the 2016 reform, adds that, as against third parties, the assignment is to be treated as complete only when the assignor or assignee has notified the debtor of the assignment by making the appropriate communication through an official process-server (*signification*) or, alternatively, when the debtor has accepted the assignment by a notarial document (*acceptation faite par le débiteur dans un acte authentique*):

Code civil   33.3 (FR)

Article 1690: An assignee is vested with regard to third parties only by notice of the assignment served upon the debtor.

Nevertheless, the assignee may likewise be vested by acceptance of the assignment given by the debtor in an authentic act.

This rule was received, in one form or another, by most of the jurisdictions which have to some extent used the French Code civil as a model. In some cases, the assignment is valid as against third parties only if the debtor has been notified orally and in writing (eg the Netherlands: Articles 3:84 and 3:94(1) BW, together with Article 3:37 BW; notifica-tion is not required if the document recording the transaction between the assignor and the assignee has been registered: Article 3:94(3) BW) or if a 'secure date' of the assign-ment has been laid down in a public document evidencing the debtor's acknowledgement (eg in Italy: Articles 1264, 1265, 2704 Codice civile). Similarly, strict notice require-ments are applicable if a contractual right is to be pledged.

To some extent, the formalities prescribed by Article 1690 Cciv were mitigated by a number of legislative acts which excluded its application to the assignment of certain types of right.[14] The most important of these was the French Law of 2 January 1981 (Loi Dailly), which provided for the transfer on an *en masse* basis to banks and other credit institutions of contractual rights, either as outright sales (*cession*) or as collateral security (*nantissement*), by the simple delivery of a memorandum (*bordereau*) which

---

[13] See below, pp 1405–07.
[14] F Terré, P Simler and Y Lequette, *Les obligations* (11th edn, Paris: Dalloz, 2013) nos. 1283, 1297–1302.

identified the rights in prescribed form and was signed by the transferor. This statute was incorporated in the Code monétaire et financier in 2001.[15]

The courts have also mitigated the formalism of the aforementioned provisions of the Code civil by endorsing a generous approach when interpreting the scope of the obligation to signify the debtor. Thus it was held that the assignee's statement of claim against the debtor, if filed with the court, may amount to a *signification* within the meaning of Article 1690.

Cass com, 18 February 1969[16]   **33.4 (FR)**

Service of statement of claim

A statement of claim served on the debtor in an action by the assignor, if it gives sufficient detail to show that there has been an assignment, is sufficient to amount to a signification to the debtor perfecting the assignment.

Facts: The company Hercules assigned to another company, Epirotiki Lines, a debt owed to it by Rouquie. Epirotiki Lines did not give a formal notice to Rouquie but simply commenced a process to recover the debt from Rouquie.

Held: The service of a statement of claim was sufficient signification. Appeal dismissed.

Judgment: On the sole appeal ground:—Whereas the appellant contests the judgment of the lower court (Paris, 25 May 1966) on the ground that it accepted that the company Epirotiki Lines could bring an action against Rouquie pursuant to the assignment to Epirotiki of the debt owed by Rouquie to the company Hercules, the process served on the appellant having replaced notification of the assignment as provided for by Article 1690 Cciv, and according to the appellant, that was possible only if the process stated the date on which the assignment was effected and the price paid in consideration, which Rouquie formally contested without being in any way contradicted on that point by the judgment in issue.

— Whereas however, in order for the process to count as notification of the assignment of the debt, it is sufficient for it to provide, as notification, a copy of the assignment making the transfer unconditional; as in its notice and grounds of appeal, without pleading failure to mention the price paid for the assignment of the debt, Rouquie had maintained that the process contained no details of the essential provisions of that assignment; as the contested judgment rejects that plea, pointing out that the process stated that Hercules had assigned the debt owed to it to Epirotiki by private instrument of 31 March 1965 and that Rouquie challenged the locus standi of neither the assignor nor the assignee; as the cour d'appel therefore showed good reason for its decision.

— As the appeal ground is unfounded.

On those grounds: the Court dismisses the appeal against the judgment delivered by the cour d'appel, Paris, on 25 May 1966.

It followed that a statement amounts to a *signification* within the meaning of the provision, regardless of whether the statement contains a copy of the assignment agreement,

---

[15] See Arts L 313-23 to L 313-29-2 of the Code monétaire et financier.
[16] No. 66-13573, Bull civ IV no. 65.

in its entirety or in part.[17] The courts also endorsed the view that Article 1690 does not require the transfer price, that is to say the price paid by the assignee in consideration of the assignment, to be mentioned in the statement notifying the debtor.[18]

Similarly, the courts tended to be fairly generous in dispensing with the requirement of a formal notification or acceptance if enforcement of the assigned claim by the assignee could do no harm to any rights that may have accrued in the meantime to a third party. This was justified on the basis that the notification was only needed to make the assignment known to the third party.

Cass civ (1), 8 January 1955[19]   **33.5 (FR)**

Assignment of option to purchase

When an option to purchase land is assigned, the validity of the assignment is not affected by lack of a formal notification to the original grantor of the option if no third-party rights are affected by the enforcement of the option.

Facts: Landowners granted an option to purchase to Richepin, who assigned it to the Association Foncière et Immobilière, which assigned it to the claimants. The grantors were not formally notified before the claimants commenced proceedings.

Held: The last assignee could enforce the option.

Judgment: As to the first appeal ground:—Whereas it is apparent from the contested judgment that Jacques Richepin, the original promisee of a unilateral promise to sell made by Henri Bernard relating to property of approximately four hectares situated at Mougins, assigned the benefit thereof to the Association Foncière et Immobilière, which in turn assigned it to the Société de Golf de la Croix des Gardes;

— Whereas the appellant challenges the contested judgment on the grounds that while it declares that that assignment was duly made and may be relied on against Mr and Mrs Bernard, as the heirs of Henri Bernard, it does not find that the assignment was made in accordance with Article 1690 Cciv.

— Whereas however, while the right arising from a unilateral promise to sell is a personal right the assignment of which is governed by Article 1690 Cciv, and while service of notice of the assignment on the promisor or his acceptance of the assignment in a notarially recorded instrument is necessary, in principle, if the assignee is to be able to enforce against third parties the right which he has acquired, the fact nevertheless remains that failure to comply with those formalities does not mean that the assignee is estopped from requiring the promisor to perform his obligation, provided that that performance is not liable adversely to affect any right which has accrued since the debt was created, either to the person liable to pay the debt or perform the obligation assigned or to another person, a third party to the assignment.

— Whereas the contested judgment finds that the promise of sale signed by Henri Bernard in favour of Jacques Richepin had not lapsed at the time when Société de Golf de la Croix des Gardes claimed the rights under it; as furthermore, at no time did Mr and Mrs Bernard prove, offer to prove or even allege that they had received notification

---

[17] See C Ophèle, 'La cession de créance' in *Répertoire de droit civil* (Paris: Dalloz, avril 2008) no. 154.
[18] See Cass civ (1) 12 November 2015, no.14-23401, Bull 2016 no. 839, 1re Civ no. 419.
[19] Bull civ I no. 13.

from any other persons, transferees in particular, or creditors of intermediate promisees, of some right conflicting with that of the latest assignee.

— Whereas in the absence of any circumstance altering in favour of Henri Bernard, his heirs or third parties the legal situation arising from the original undertaking, no plea of inadmissibility based on failure to comply with the formalities of Article 1690 Cciv may be raised against Société de Golf de la Croix des Gardes in its action brought as the assignee of the right, this being outside the particular case contemplated by Article 2214 Cciv.

— As it follows that the first appeal ground is unfounded.

The same view has been taken in many other cases.[20] It applies only, however, if there is no third party who may have a better claim to the assigned right than the assignee. If, for example, the assignor makes successive assignments of the same claim to two different assignees, it is acquired not by the one to whom it was first assigned, but by the one who first complied with the formalities of Article 1690 Code civil. The same rule applies if the assigned claim has been attached by the assignor's creditors or is claimed by the assignor's trustee in bankruptcy.

The courts also interpreted ex-Article 1689 and Article 1690 (still in force) beyond their initial scope which used to be limited to the assignment of rights and debt claims arising from sales contracts. The courts thus recognised the existence of three types of assignment, that of the assignment of rights, of debt and of the assignor's status as a party to the contract which is to be assigned. In this process, the courts clarified the legal regimes of each legal operation, requiring the consent of the debtor for the assignment of debt[21] and for the assignment of the assignor's quality of party to a contract.[22] The same view was taken in other instances regardless of whether the contract was of a personal character (*intuit personae*)[23] (see below, 33.2.D.1) or not.[24]

The law of assignment has now been completely revised by the reform of 2016. These revisions can, to a large extent, be viewed as a codification of the case law outlined above.

Code civil **33.6 (FR)**

Article 1321: Assignment of rights is a contract by which the creditor (the assignor) transfers, whether or not for value, the whole or part of his rights against the assignment debtor to a third party (the assignee).

...

The consent of the debtor is not required unless the right was stipulated to be non-assignable.

Article 1324: Unless the debtor has already agreed to it, the assignment may be set up against him only if it has been notified to him or he has acknowledged it.

---

[20] See, eg, Cass civ (3) 26 February 1985, no. 83-17080, JCP 1986.II.20607, annotated by B Petit.

[21] See Cass com 2 June 1992, no. 90-18821, Bull IV no. 215; See Cass civ (1) 30 April 2009, no. 08-11093, Bull civ I no. 82, D 2009, 2400, annotated by L Andreu.

[22] See Cass com 6 May 1997, no. 94-16335, Bull IV no. 117; Cass com 6 May 1997, no. 95-10252, Bull IV no. 118.

[23] See Cass com 13 December 2005, no. 03-16878, Bull IV no. 255; Cass com 7 January 1992, no. 90-14831, Bull IV no. 3; Cass civ (1) 6 June 2000, no. 97-19347, Bull I no. 173; Cass com 3 June 2008, no. 06-18007, Bull IV no. 111.

[24] See Cass com 6 May 1997, no. 94-16335, Bull IV no. 117; Cass com 6 May 1997, no. 95-10252, Bull IV no. 118.

Article 1327: A debtor may assign his debt to another person with the agreement of the creditor. The assignment must be recorded in writing on pain of nullity.

Article 1327-1: If the creditor gave his agreement to the assignment in advance, or if he has not taken part in the assignment, he may find it set up against him, and may take advantage of it himself, only from the day when he was notified of it, or once he has acknowledged it.

In Belgium, mounting criticism of the formalism of Article 1690 of the Belgian Code civil (which corresponded to Article 1690 of the French Code civil) led to the replacement of this provision by a new text (enacted by Article 4 of the Law of 6 July 1994):[25]

Code civil (Belgium) **33.7 (BE)**

Article 1690 § 1: (1) By virtue of the conclusion of an agreement for the transfer or assignment of a debt, that transfer or assignment shall be effective against third parties other than the debtor whose debt has been transferred or assigned.

(2) The transfer or assignment shall not be effective against the debtor whose debt has been transferred or assigned until such time as notice thereof is given to the debtor or the transfer or assignment is acknowledged by him.

(3) Where the assignor has assigned the same rights to more than one assignee, preference shall be given to the assignee who is able in good faith to rely on the fact of having been the first to give the debtor notice of the transfer or assignment of the debt or of having been the first to receive acknowledgement thereof from the debtor.

(4) The transfer or assignment shall not be effective against a *bona fide* creditor of the assignor to whom the debtor has validly made payment in good faith and before he received notice of the transfer or assignment. ...

Article 1691: (1) A debtor who pays his debt in good faith before receiving notice of the transfer or assignment thereof or before acknowledging the same shall be discharged from liability.

(2) A *bona fide* debtor may rely, as against the assignee, on the consequences of any legal act executed in relation to the assignor before he received notice of the assignment or transfer or prior to his acknowledgement thereof.

English law at first sight seems to be the most restrictive, in that, for a legal assignment, statute requires both a document signed by the assignor and notice in writing to the debtor. However, in fact it is probably the most liberal regime of the three because, as mentioned earlier, it recognises the so-called 'equitable assignment', which requires neither a particular form nor notice to the debtor; and the effect of an equitable assignment is that the assignee obtains a proprietary right in the claim assigned. This means that, if the debtor is not notified of the assignment and so pays the assignor, the money paid is treated as the assignee's and (provided it remains traceable) it may be claimed by the assignee even if the assignor is insolvent.

---

[25] For a detailed discussion of the new provisions of the Belgian Civil Code, see P van Ommeslaghe, 'Le nouveau régime de la cession et de la dation en gage des créances' Journal des tribunaux 1995, 529. The introduction of new Art 1690 § 2 Belgian Civil Code, which was effected by Art 26 of the Law of 20 July 2006, is not relevant for our purposes.

Section 136: Legal assignment of things in action

(1) Any absolute assignment by writing under the hand of the assignor (not purporting to be by way of charge only) of any debt or other legal thing in action, of which express notice in writing has been given to the debtor, trustee or other person from whom the assignor would have been entitled to claim such debt or thing in action, is effectual in law (subject to equities having priority over the right of the assignee) to pass and transfer from the date of such notice—

(a) the legal right to such debt or thing in action;

(b) all legal and other remedies for the same; and

(c) the power to give a good discharge for the same without the concurrence of the assignor:

Provided that, if the debtor, trustee or other person liable in respect of such debt or thing in action has notice—

(a) that the assignment is disputed by the assignor or any person claiming under him; or

(b) of any other opposing or conflicting claims to such debt or thing in action; he may, if he thinks fit, either call upon the persons making the claim thereto to interplead concerning the same, or pay the debt or other thing in action into court under the provisions of the Trustee Act 1925.

...

Notes

(1) In English law a distinction is made between 'statutory assignments' and 'equitable assignments'. Before statute intervened, assignments were recognised only by the courts of equity, and the assignee could not sue without joining the assignor as a party to the action.

Under the Law of Property Act 1925, a 'legal' assignment is possible which enables the assignee to sue without joining the assignor. Section 136(1) of the Act provides that, for a statutory assignment to be effective, the assigned right must be a debt (such as a claim for the repayment of a loan, for the price of goods or for damages for breach of contract), notice must have been given in writing to the debtor, the assignment must be in writing, signed by the assignor, and the assignment must be 'absolute'. An assignment is not absolute if it is for only a part of the debt, if it is conditional (for instance, a debt is assigned as security for a loan until such time as the loan is repaid to the assignee) or if for some other reason the assignor retains an interest in the assigned right. These cases in which the assignment is not absolute are those in which it will normally be desirable to ensure that both the assignor and assignee are before the court, so the assignee cannot sue alone. Otherwise, as stated above, provided the formalities of section 136(1) of the Law of Property Act 1925 have been met, the assigned right will be acquired by the assignee so as to enable him to sue the debtor in his own name, and to sue alone, ie without joining the assignor as a party to the action. Adherence to the formalities also ensures that the assignor will seldom be able to dispute the existence of the assignment and will thus reduce litigation.

(2) If the requirements of an effective statutory assignment are not satisfied, be it because the debtor was not informed or because the assignment was oral or partial or not absolute, the transaction may still be a valid equitable assignment, with the result that the assignee may have to join the assignor in the action.

(3) Generally speaking, even an equitable assignment which has not been notified to the debtor will be effective as against the assignor's other creditors and his trustee in bankruptcy (or where the assignor is a company or its liquidator). Thus it gives the assignee the right to demand that payments falling due from the debtor are paid to the assignee. It also gives the assignee not just a personal right against the debtor but a proprietary claim to trace the proceeds (eg to pursue them into a bank account in which they may have been mixed with other money). This is obviously disadvantageous for other creditors; and this explains why in some cases an assignment of book debts (roughly speaking, these are trade receivables) may require registration in order to provide publicity.[26]

Principles of European Contract Law **33.9 (INT)**

Article 11:401: Priorities

...

(3) The assignee's interest in the assigned claim has priority over the interest of a creditor of the assignor who attaches that claim, whether by judicial process or otherwise, after the time the assignment has taken effect under Article 11:202.

(4) In the event of the assignor's bankruptcy, the assignee's interest in the assigned claim has priority over the interest of the assignor's insolvency administrator and creditors, subject to any rules of the law applicable to the bankruptcy relating to:

(a) publicity required as a condition of such priority;

(b) the ranking of claims; or

(c) the avoidance or ineffectiveness of transactions in the bankruptcy proceedings.

33.2.D FURTHER REQUIREMENTS

Some rights cannot be assigned.[27] Traditionally, the assignability of other rights was contested, though they have now been held to be assignable.

33.2.D.1 UNASSIGNABILITY OF RIGHTS TIED TO PERSONAL RELATIONSHIPS

A right cannot be assigned when it is 'of a strictly personal character' (Article 1260(1) of the Italian Civil Code) or when performance to an assignee would involve 'an alteration of its substance' (§ 399 BGB). Thus, like under French law, the right to the payment of

---

[26] A general assignment of book debts by an individual in trade or business requires registration as a Bill of Sale: Insolvency Act 1986, s 344. A charge created by a company over its book debts must be registered: Companies Act 2006, s 860(7)(f). However, outright sales of receivables by a company do not require registration.

[27] In addition, agreements providing for the transfer of a right are void, unenforceable or subject to being set aside where they have been entered into by a person lacking capacity, have been procured by undue influence, seek to defraud creditors, or are against public policy. These issues are not dealt with in this chapter.

salaries and pensions up to a certain amount, as well as entitlements to public benefits, are unassignable.[28] Nevertheless, French law does not take the position that all contracts of a personal character are unassignable. It appears that the courts have indeed concluded that the personal character of a right may preclude its assignability.[29] One of the early versions of the Ordonnance of February 2016 provided that the consent of the debtor is necessary and sufficient to overcome the unassignability of a right of a personal character.[30] Yet the revised Civil Code is silent on this issue.

Chancery Division **33.10 (EN)**

Griffith v Tower Publishing Co Ltd and Moncrieff[31]

A publishing contract may not be assigned by the publisher, even where the publisher is a company, because of the nature of the relationship between publisher and author.

Facts: The plaintiff was an author who had entered into three agreements with the defendant company for the publication of certain novels. The company became insolvent and Mr Moncrieff was appointed receiver. He informed the plaintiff of his intention to sell his books, together with all the company's rights under the above agreements, to another publishing firm. The plaintiff did not approve of this firm. He moved for an injunction to restrain the defendants from selling or assigning without his consent the company's rights under the above agreements.

Held: An injunction was granted to prevent the intended assignment.

Judgment: STIRLING J [after stating the facts and referring to the first agreement]: If the agreement in question had been entered into with an individual or a partnership firm, it is clear, upon the cases, that the contract would be of a personal nature, and that the benefit of it would not be assignable ... It is suggested that there is a difference between a company contractor and an individual contractor, and that though a contract entered into between an author and an individual publisher or a publishing firm consisting of individuals may not be assignable, yet a similar contract entered into between an author and a limited company is capable of assignment. I should hesitate long before accepting that view ... An author may have confidence in a limited company as well as in an individual publisher. A limited company may have a reputation for producing books in good style and attractive form, and an author selecting such a company as his publisher may do so in the reasonable expectation that the company, although its members and its officers may fluctuate, may nevertheless consider itself under an obligation to maintain its reputation. In the present case what attracted the plaintiff was that the company had published certain books in a form and style of which he approved. No doubt part of the inducement was also that the company had a very efficient manager. It was said that the company might have discharged him the next day without giving the plaintiff cause to complain. That observation is well founded. The company might have discharged its manager the next day, and appointed new officers at any time; but still the plaintiff might well act on the assumption that the Tower Company and those who directed its affairs would select a manager who would maintain the reputation of the company.

---

[28] § 400 BGB; Terré et al (n 14 above) no. 1278.
[29] Cass com 20 October 2015, no. 14-17896, Bull Joly 2016.II.11, annotated by H Barbier.
[30] Art 1322(4) of the avant-projet de la Chancellerie.
[31] [1897] 1 Ch 21.

It seems to me that it would be wrong to draw any such distinction as is suggested between an agreement entered into by an author with an individual publisher and a similar agreement between an author and a limited company; and agreements of the former kind being non-assignable, I hold that agreements of the latter description are also incapable of being assigned.

I think, therefore, that an injunction ought to be granted.

King's Bench Division **33.11 (EN)**

Peters v General Accident & Life Assurance Corp Ltd[32]

An insurance policy, as opposed to sums payable under a policy, cannot be assigned as the identity of the assured is material to the insurer.

Facts: The plaintiff had been injured in a road accident caused by Mr Pope's negligence while driving his car. Shortly before the accident Mr Pope had bought the car from Mr Coomber who had taken out liability insurance with the defendant insurance company under a policy which extended the cover to any person driving with the consent or permission of the insured. The car had been delivered to Mr Pope together with the policy. The plaintiff argued that there was an assignment of the policy and that he was therefore entitled to recover damages from the defendant company.

Held: The buyer was not entitled to the benefit of the policy.

Judgment: GODDARD J: ... The last point that was taken ... was that there was an assignment of the policy. I have already said why I do not think that there was an assignment in fact. I do not think that you can assign a policy of this nature at all. You can assign your right to receive money under it. If an accident has occurred, and you have a right to be indemnified by your insurers, or if your car has been destroyed, so that you have a right to be paid by your insurers, you can assign your right to anybody you choose, subject to the Road Traffic Act ... You cannot thrust a new assured upon a company against its will. If you do that, you must have a novation. You must have the release of the assured and the acceptance of a new assured. It is not a question of assigning a chose in action, such as a debt, a right to recover money. A little reflection, I think, will show what a serious state of affairs might otherwise exist. The proposal form in this case, as in every case of motor insurance, asks questions with regard to the previous driving history of the proposer. The company want to know whether he is a man whose record is such that they can take him, and, if so, at what premium. His driving history or his driving experience must, I think, be a material fact. The moral factor, as it has been called, enters into these matters very considerably, not only in motor insurance, but also in most classes of insurance of this description. For instance, take the case of a person who wishes to insure jewellery. There may be people whose character is such that no insurance company would insure their jewellery for a single moment. There may be people who have had such an unhappy record of fires or such an unhappy record of losses of jewellery that only the most charitable could believe that those were fortuitous happenings. An insurance company, in those circumstances, would probably be very shy—I mean, respectable insurance companies; there are some insurance companies which, I have no doubt, as long as they can get a premium, will take it, though whether they will pay out at the end is another matter. However, I am considering respectable and proper insurance companies, and the moral factor is a factor

---

[32] [1937] 4 All ER 628.

which is more common in an action, where the policy is disputed on the ground of non-disclosure, than to say: 'You have not disclosed a material fact here, namely, the accidents that you have had, or the fires that you have had, or the losses of jewellery that you have had.' I have no doubt therefore, that you cannot assign a motor policy in the way that it is suggested it was done here …

33.2.D.2 ASSIGNMENT OF FUTURE RIGHTS

There is general agreement that a right under an existing contract may be assigned even though the right is not yet due or is conditional on some event that has not yet occurred. If, for example, a building contractor secures a bank loan by assigning to the bank his claim under a construction contract which he has not yet (fully) performed, the assignment is valid even though the contractor's right to payment is conditioned on his own future performance of the contract.

A different problem arises where someone attempts to assign a right to payment under a contract he hopes to make with a third person in the future. Many courts had conceptual and practical difficulties in accepting such assignments as valid. The conceptual difficulty lies in the old rule that nobody is able to transfer property he does not yet own (*nemo dat quod non habet*). There is also the fear that by admitting the assignment of 'mere expectancies' the door to fraud might be opened or improvident assignors might be encouraged to sell or pledge all contract rights they might acquire at any time in the future. It is arguable that if there are clear policy reasons for disallowing the assignment of future claims such invalidity should be openly based on these reasons rather than on the view that the rights to be transferred are 'not yet in existence'. Moreover, there is a growing need of the business community to make use of future contract rights for the purpose of securing a present loan. English law has long recognised that it is possible to assign future debts. Technically, the agreement to assign is treated in equity as creating an assignment which takes effect as soon as the debt arises.

House of Lords   **33.12 (EN)**

Tailby v Official Receiver[33]

An assignment of book debts (broadly speaking, these are trade debts) is effective to transfer to the assignee even book debts which were not in existence at the time of the assignment, provided that when they come into existence they are sufficiently identifiable.

Facts: Izon assigned all his book debts to Tyrell; Tyrell's interest was later obtained by the appellant. Later Izon supplied goods to Wilson Brothers, who were notified by the appellant that they should pay him, which they did. Izon went bankrupt and his trustee in bankruptcy, the respondent, claimed that the appellant should repay this money.

Held: The Court of Appeal held that the assignment was ineffective because it was too vague. The House of Lords reversed this decision.

---

[33] (1888) 13 App Cas 523.

Judgment: Lord Watson: … My Lords, the circumstances which have given rise to this litigation may be very shortly stated.

Henry George Izon, who at that time carried on the business of a packing-case manufacturer in Birmingham, by mortgage dated the 13th of May 1879 assigned, for valuable consideration received, to the late John Tyrell, his stock-in-trade, and 'all the book debts due and owing or which may during the continuance of this security become due and owing to the said mortgagor.' In the months of October and November 1884 Izon supplied a firm of Wilson Brothers & Co, upon credit, with goods to the value of £10 7s 11d. The appellant, who had acquired Tyrell's interest in the debt, gave notice of the assignment to that firm, and required them to make payment of it to himself, which they accordingly did. Some time after the date of the notice Izon was adjudged bankrupt, and the respondent, who is trustee of his estate, now sues the appellant for repayment of the amount received by him from Wilson Brothers & Co.

It does not clearly appear whether the debt in question was incurred to the mortgagor in the business in which he was engaged in May 1879, or in some other trade. In the argument addressed to your Lordships it was rightly assumed that the assignment comprehends every future book debt becoming due to Izon, in any profession or trade which may be followed by him in any place and at any time during the continuance of the security constituted by the mortgage. The respondent admitted that the liability of Wilson Brothers & Co, whenever it emerged, was, and until satisfied by payment continued to be, a proper book debt, due and owing to the mortgagor. He maintained his right to it, in competition with the appellant, upon the single ground that the assignment of future book debts, in the mortgage of 1879, is ineffectual to carry any equitable interest to the assignee …

The rule of equity which applies to the assignment of future choses in action is, as I understand it, a very simple one. Choses in action do not come within the scope of the Bills of Sale Acts, and though not yet existing, may nevertheless be the subject of present assignment. As soon as they come into existence, assignees who have given valuable consideration will, if the new chose in action is in the disposal of their assignor, take precisely the same right and interest as if it had actually belonged to him, or had been within his disposition and control at the time when the assignment was made. There is but one condition which must be fulfilled in order to make the assignee's right attach to a future chose in action, which is, that, on its coming into existence, it shall answer the description in the assignment, or, in other words, that it shall be capable of being identified as the thing, or as one of the very things assigned. When there is no uncertainty as to its identification, the beneficial interest will immediately vest in the assignee. Mere difficulty in ascertaining all the things which are included in a general assignment, whether in esse or in posse, will not affect the assignee's right to those things which are capable of ascertainment or are identified. In the case of book debts, as in the case of choses in action generally, intimation of the assignee's right must be made to the debtor or obligee in order to make it complete. That is the only possession which he can attain, so long as the debt is unpaid, and is sufficient to take it out of the order and disposition of the assignor. In this case the appellant's right, if otherwise valid, was, in any question with the respondent, duly perfected by his notice to Wilson Brothers & Co before Izon became a bankrupt.

The learned judges of the Appeal Court were unanimously of opinion that the description of book debts in the assignment of Tyrell is 'too vague,' and it is upon that ground only that they have held the assignment to be invalid. The term which they have selected, in order to express what they conceived to be the radical defect of the assignment, is susceptible of at least two different meanings. It may either signify that the description is too wide and comprehensive, without implying that there will be any uncertainty as to the debts which it will include, if and when these come into existence, or it may signify that the language of the description is so obscure that it will be impossible, in the time to come, to determine with any degree of certainty to what particular debts it was intended to apply. In the latter sense the description of future book debts in the mortgage of 1879 does not incur the imputation of vagueness. No one has suggested that the expression 'book debt' is indefinite; and it is, in my opinion, very clear that every debt becoming due and owing to the mortgagor, which belongs to the class of book debts (a fact quite capable of ascertainment), is at once identified with the subject-matter of the assignment …

When the consideration has been given, and the debt has been clearly identified as one of those in respect of which it was given, a Court of Equity will enforce the covenant of the parties, and will not permit the assignor, or those in his right, to defeat the assignment upon the plea that it is too comprehensive.

Note

Lord Watson refers to the Bills of Sale Acts (Bills of Sale Acts 1878, 1890, 1891 and Bills of Sale (Amendment) Act 1882). This legislation requires any written agreement to sell goods which remain in the buyer's possession, or any written mortgage of goods, to be in a particular form and to be registered. As Lord Watson says, debts are not covered by this legislation. However, since the decision in *Tailby*, a statute has been enacted which requires a general assignment of book debts by an individual in trade or business to be registered as if it were a Bill of Sale, in order to warn other creditors that the debts have been assigned.[34]

The problem is of enormous practical significance in Germany since it is quite common for a buyer, having acquired on credit goods to be resold to third parties, to assign to the vendor his future claims against the buyers of those goods. So long as the goods are in the possession of the buyer, the vendor is protected by a reservation of title clause. Once the goods have been resold, the vendor's title is 'prolonged' into the contract rights to be acquired by the buyer against third parties upon the resale of the goods. The validity of such assignments used to be doubtful, partly because they were believed to be against public policy (§ 138 BGB), partly because they might be incompatible with the rule that there can be no effective transfer of property unless the asset to be transferred is 'determined' or at least 'determinable' at the time the transfer is made. All doubts were laid to rest when the Bundesgerichtshof decided that the assigned right need not be 'determinable' at the time of the assignment but only at the time when it comes into existence.

BGH, 25 October 1952[35] **33.13 (DE)**

The master plumber's debts

Where goods have been sold subject to a retention of title clause, with a provision that, if the goods are sold or otherwise disposed of, then the sums due from the persons to whom

---

[34] Insolvency Act 1986, s 344. This does not apply to assignment of debts by companies, see n 26 above.
[35] BGHZ 7, 365.

they were disposed of shall be assigned to the original supplier, with a provision for reassignment if the amount so received exceeds the sum due, the assignment is valid.

Facts: Between the end of May 1949 and January 1950, the defendant supplied goods having a total value of approximately DM 17,000 to S, a master plumber. Of the total purchase price, it received only approximately DM 1,700. The supplies were subject to the defendant's general terms and conditions of sale and delivery, clause 14 of which read as follows:

> Supplies shall be made by us solely on the basis of the reservation by us of title to and ownership of the goods supplied pending payment in full. Title to the goods shall not pass to the purchaser until such time as he has discharged all his liabilities and obligations arising from the supply of goods by us ... The purchaser shall be entitled to alienate the goods supplied in the ordinary course of business ... The alienation by the purchaser of the goods supplied by us—regardless of the state or condition thereof—shall operate with immediate effect as an assignment by him to us, pending the discharge in full of all debts due from him to us in respect of goods supplied by us, of claims vesting in him by virtue of [such] alienation against the person acquiring the goods in question, together with all ancillary rights relating thereto ... In the event that the value of the security provided to us exceeds, in the aggregate, the amount of our claims for goods supplied by more than 20 per cent, we shall be required, upon request by the purchaser, to re-assign to him our rights to that extent.

Under a contract with K, S had installed the materials bought from the defendant in K's house. Subsequently, S had assigned part of his outstanding claim against K to the claimant. Since K did not know which party had the better claim, he paid the money into court and left it to the parties to fight the matter out between themselves. The claimant claims an order requiring the defendant to consent to the payment, out of the sum paid into court, of the debts due to the claimant in priority to those due to the defendant. The claimant relies in support of his claim on the assignment of 8 December 1949, and asserts that the assignment of future claims provided for by clause 14 of the defendant's general terms and conditions of sale and delivery is ineffective and inoperative.

Held: The lower courts had found for the claimant on the ground that the assignment under clause 14 of the defendant's general terms of business was invalid. The BGH allowed the appeal and dismissed the action.

Judgment: ... The second sentence of § 398 BGB provides that, upon the conclusion of an assignment agreement, the new creditor takes the place of the former creditor. According to § 401 BGB, the ancillary and preferential rights specified in that provision are to pass, along with the claim assigned, to the new creditor. That provision is to be understood as meaning that the amount of an assigned claim must be adequately determined or determinable, since, if it is not, uncertainty will subsist as to the extent to which the claim remains vested in the old creditor and the extent to which it is vested in the new creditor. In the interests of legal certainty, however, it is necessary that the position should be clear in that regard. Thus, it is acknowledged in the relevant case law [citations omitted] and legal writings [citations omitted] that an assignment of future claims shall be valid in law only if the amount of the claim assigned is adequately determined or determinable.

The defendant bases its claim to entitlement to the moneys paid into court on the fact that the contracts concluded with S were subject to the its general terms and conditions of sale and delivery, and that these contained, in clause 14, a general assignment of future claims ...

The recent case law of the Reichsgericht has indeed attached excessively stringent requirements to the determinability of the scope of pre-assigned claims as provided for in standard-form legal documents. As stated above, it must be borne in mind that standard-form terms and conditions are to be construed without regard to the distinctive characteristics of individual cases. That follows from their very nature. Consequently, in the case of assignments of future claims under standard-form terms and conditions, it is necessary, first of all, to undertake an objective examination of the significance attaching to an assignment of future claims based on a standard-form document, leaving out of consideration the incidental aspects of the individual case in question. By means of the results thus obtained from the ascertainment of the meaning of the assignment clause, it is necessary then to proceed to examine whether the general assignment of future claims contained in the standard-form assignment clause, as construed from the interpretation of its standard characteristics, covers the claim at issue in the individual case. If it does, the next question will be whether that claim is adequately determined or determinable having regard to the results of the above-mentioned investigations. In the present case, the following results emerge from the test to be applied from those various standpoints: the nature of the defendant's business is such that it supplies goods to, in particular, plumbers and fitters who do not simply resell, according to sales contracts, the goods supplied to them by the defendant but conclude contracts for work and materials and use those goods in order to complete the works which they have contracted to carry out. The standard-form stipulations contained in clause 14 of the defendant's general terms and conditions of sale and delivery take those commercial circumstances into account. They provide for the possibility that the customer may process or adapt the goods subject to the retention of title clause, and that the customer may 'alienate them, in whatever state or condition they may be'. Thus, the possibility of alienation of the goods subject to the retention of title clause, even in a processed or adapted state, is covered by the clause at issue. It further follows from a logical interpretation of the contractual provision in question, having regard to the statement, set out above, of the principles of construction applying to standard-form legal documents, that the clause in issue also covers cases in which the customer has used the goods subject to the retention of title in carrying out contracts for work and materials (§ 651 BGB), has thereafter handed over the completed work to the person commissioning it, and has acquired, as against that person, a claim for remuneration under the contract. It further follows from this, however, that the phrase 'claims vesting in him by virtue of [such] alienation' contained in the clause must be understood as covering entitlement to the whole of the remuneration—in other words, the sum which, in the case of contracts for work and materials, is made up of the value of the goods, the business profit made and the reward for the labour itself. The fact that, contrary to the view taken by the appellate court, the defendant's standard-form terms and conditions of sale and delivery must be interpreted in that way is apparent, above all, from the final paragraph of clause 14. That paragraph provides that, in the event that the value of the security provided to the defendant exceeds, in the aggregate, the amount of its claims for goods supplied by more than 20 per cent, it is to be required, upon request by the purchaser, to re-assign to him its rights to that extent. That stipulation assumes that the assignment may cover not only the amount of the value of the goods subject to the retention of title but the entire remuneration which the purchaser of those goods is entitled to receive from the person who has commissioned the works pursuant to the contract for work and materials concluded with the latter. The appellate court, referring to the decision of the Reichsgericht reported at RGZ 155, 32, considered that such total assignment could not be regarded as feasible, especially having regard to the economic aspects involved. The doubts expressed by the appellate court might be justified, were it not for the existence of the final paragraph of clause 14. However, they are removed by the very fact of the stipulations contained in that final paragraph, which take into account the legitimate interests of both parties. If the provisions of the final paragraph of clause 14 are taken sufficiently into consideration, it becomes clear that the assignment of future claims does not excessively restrict the freedom of economic activity of the purchaser of the goods subject to the retention of title, and that the standard-form stipulations do not in themselves infringe § 138 BGB. This further has the result of removing the objection expressed by the Reichsgericht (RGZ 155, 32) that there could be an assignment the value of which was disproportionately high in relation to the value of the goods supplied. The following conclusions may be drawn from this objective interpretation of a standard-form document: the contract concluded between the defendant and S is legally valid, since the appellate court made no findings of fact concerning special circumstances which might have rendered it void under § 138 BGB. Furthermore, S assigned to the defendant in advance his claim against K for the whole of the fixed price agreed with the latter. That being so, the amount of the assigned claim is adequately determined, and there can thus be no doubt in that regard concerning the validity of the assignment in law.

Principles of European Contract Law   **33.14 (INT)**

Article 11:102: Contractual claims generally assignable
(1) ...
(2) A future claim under an existing or future contract may be assigned if at the time when it comes into existence, or at such other time as the parties agree, it can be identified as the claim to which the assignment relates.

The assignability of 'future' contract rights has also been recognised in France, both in the case law of the Cour de cassation,[36] in the Loi Dailly (now Article L 313-24 of the Code monétaire et financier[37]) and in the Code civil as reformed by the Ordonnance of February 2016 which inserted a new Article 1321 that provides for the assignment of future rights.[38]

Code civil   **33.15 (FR)**

Article 1321: Assignment of rights is a contract by which the creditor (the assignor) transfers, whether or not for value, the whole or part of his rights against the assignment debtor to a third party (the assignee).
It may concern one or more rights, present or future, ascertained or ascertainable. ...

Under Dutch law, it is possible to assign future claims (Articles 3:84 and 3:97 BW). However, since assignment normally requires notification to the debtor (Article 3:94(1) BW), the debtor must be known. In cases where notification is not required because the assignment has been registered (Article 3:94(3) BW), the future claim that is assigned must result from an already existing legal relationship.
In one English case, *Aluminium Industrie Vaassen BV v Romalpa Aluminium Ltd,*[39] it was held that, when goods were supplied under reservation of title and the seller

---

[36] Terré et al (n 14 above) no. 1278.

[37] The legal regime applicable to assignments undertaken on the basis of the Loi Dailly is distinct from the one provided by the Civil Code concerning the assignment of debt claims, rights or one's status as a party to a contract. Further, the latter does not have priority over the former. See Deshayes et al (n 5 above) 461.

[38] See also Cass civ (1) 20 March 2001, no. 99-14982, Bull I no. 76, D 2001, 3110, annotated by L Aynès.

[39] [1976] 1 WLR 676 (CA).

authorised the buyer to resell them on condition that he accounts for the proceeds of sale (a 'Romalpa clause'), the buyer held the proceeds in a fiduciary capacity for the seller, who was thus entitled to them in preference to the buyer's other creditors. Here the seller will be given an equitable right to 'trace' those proceeds and to recover them by a proprietary action. However, subsequent cases made it very difficult for the supplier to argue that the buyer holds the proceeds in a fiduciary capacity. There are two reasons. First, in the absence of the clearest indication to the contrary, the courts will assume that if the buyer receives the proceeds before he has to pay the seller he is free to use the proceeds for his own purposes. This is incompatible with him being a fiduciary. Secondly, if the entire proceeds belong to the seller, that means that the buyer will get nothing for his efforts in reselling the goods; and if the goods are resold for more than what the buyer paid for them (as will normally be the case), the seller would get a windfall if he were entitled to all the proceeds. Although, in principle, it is possible for the proceeds to belong to the supplier outright, the courts have been very reluctant to interpret the contract as giving the supplier entitlement to any more than the amount which it is owed by the buyer—and that would be a charge,[40] which will not be valid unless it is registered.[41] However, in the latest case[42] the majority reverted to the approach in the *Romalpa* case and held that the proceeds of re-sale should be held in trust for the first seller. Lord Justice Longmore delivered a strong dissenting judgment and the case has been subjected to powerful criticism.[43] In a later case of a 'retention of title clause' involving a different point the Supreme Court noted the criticisms but left the issue to be considered in a future case.[44]

33.2.D.3 ASSIGNMENTS CONTRARY TO NON-ASSIGNMENT CLAUSES

Principles of European Contract Law **33.16 (INT)**

Article 11:301: Contractual prohibition of assignment

(1) An assignment which is prohibited by or is otherwise not in conformity with the contract under which the assigned claim arises is not effective against the debtor unless:

(a) the debtor has consented to it; or

(b) the assignee neither knew nor ought to have known of the non-conformity; or

(c) the assignment is made under a contract for the assignment of future rights to payment of money.

(2) Nothing in the preceding paragraph affects the assignor's liability for the nonconformity.

Frequently, parties include in their contract a term prohibiting the creditor, without the written consent of the debtor, to assign to third parties rights arising under the contract.

---

[40] See, eg, *Pfeiffer Weinkellerei-Weineinkauf GmbH & Co v Arbuthnot Factors Ltd* [1988] 1 WLR 150 (QBD).

[41] Companies Act 2006, s 860.

[42] *Caterpillar (NI) Ltd (formerly FG Wilson (Engineering) Ltd) v John Holt & Co (Liverpool) Ltd* [2013] EWCA Civ 1232, [2014] 1 WLR 2365.

[43] L Gullifer, 'The interpretation of retention of title clauses: some difficulties' [2014] LMCLQ 564.

[44] *PST Energy 7 Shipping LLC v OW Bunker Malta Ltd (The Res Cogitans)* [2016] UKSC 23, [2016] AC 1034 at [57].

In the building industry, it is quite common for employers, particularly for the government, to include in their standard terms a 'non-assignment clause' and thereby to prevent the contractor from assigning his right to money under the building contract without the employer's consent.

Queen's Bench Division **33.17 (EN)**

Helstan Securities Ltd v Hertfordshire County Council[45]

A purported assignment of a claim under a contract which the contract states may not be assigned is ineffective.

Facts: Hertfordshire County Council (the county council) contracted with Renhold Road Surfacing Ltd (Renholds) for road-works to be carried out. There were a number of these agreements. They were all in the form of the Institution of Civil Engineers Conditions of Contract (known as the ICE Conditions of Contract 4th edn). Renholds got into very severe financial difficulties. They said that they were owed, in one way or another, £46,437 by the county council under the contracts and sold these debts to the plaintiffs. The plaintiffs gave notice of these assignments to the county council, who did not consent to the assignments. The plaintiffs as assignees of the debts sued the county council claiming that sum of £46,437.

Held: The purported assignment was without effect.

Judgment: CROOM-JOHNSON J: ... This case asks what is the effect, where there is a purported assignment of a chose in action, of a condition in the contract which forbids assignment without consent?

[He stated the facts as above and continued:]

The county council say that they are under no obligation to pay, for two reasons. The first is that each contract contained a condition prohibiting the assignment of the debts. It read as follows: '(3) The contractor [that is to say Renholds] shall not assign the contract or any part thereof or any benefit or interest therein or thereunder without the written consent of the employer [that is to say the county council].' Condition 4 of the contract forbids subletting the whole of the works and deals with subcontracting parts of the works ...

If the reported cases are not a sure guide, one is thrown back in this case on the agreement. There are certain kinds of choses in action which, for one reason or another, are not assignable and there is no reason why the parties to an agreement may not contract to give its subject-matter the quality of unassignability. In these circumstances, one has to look at the clause itself. The words 'benefit or interest therein or thereunder' do cover the debts which result from the performance of the contract. I cannot draw the distinction which the plaintiff's counsel asked me to draw, namely that there is a difference between a right to payment on an engineer's certificate and the resulting debt. If there is such a difference, both are caught by this clause. It is the contract which creates the entitlement to be paid, and that is a benefit or interest under the contract.

I find no ambiguity such as would lead me to consider the background against which the contract was made as an aid to interpretation. If I did, the background would not help the plaintiffs. The clause is obviously there to let the employer retain control of who does the work. Condition 4, which deals with subletting, has the same object. But closely associated with the right to control who does the work, is the right at the end of the day

---

[45] [1978] 3 All ER 262.

to balance claims for money due on the one had against counterclaims, for example, and for bad workmanship on the other. The plaintiffs say that such a counterclaim may be made against the assignees instead of against the assignors. But the debtors may only use it as a shield by way of set-off and cannot enforce it against the assignees if it is greater than the amount of the debt: *Young v Kitchin* (1878) 3 Ex D 127. And why should they have to make it against people whom they may not want to make it against, in circumstances not of their choosing, when they have contracted that they shall not?

Although arguments showing potential hardship cannot prevail over the construction of the clause, I should mention two which have been advanced. It is said by the plaintiffs that if the assignment is void, the debtor can take the benefit of the work done by the assignor and avoid paying the assignee. The defendants reply that the assignee must make proper enquiries before he buys a debt, and these enquiries may go to the likelihood of the debtor having the money with which to pay, or the prospect of a counterclaim which would extinguish the debt, or the existence of a prohibitory condition such as the present. On all of these things depends the price he is prepared to pay. There is no injustice in expecting the purchasers of debts to make these enquiries.

My decision ... is that condition 3 does in this case make the assignment invalid, and in those circumstances the defendants are entitled to judgment against the plaintiffs and this action fails.

The decision that the assignee had no right to sue the debtor in the assignee's own name was confirmed by the House of Lords in *Linden Gardens Trust Ltd v Lenesta Sludge Disposals Ltd.*[46]

Under § 399 BGB, Article 164(1) of the Swiss Law of Obligations and Article 3:83(2) BW, a claim is unassignable if an agreement between debtor and creditor so provides. The courts have treated no-assignment clauses as fully effective on the ground that the debtor has a legitimate interest to avoid the administrative expense of keeping track of one or more (partial) assignments and to protect himself against the risk of having to pay twice if he overlooks the receipt of a notice of assignment. A further reason is that, while the debtor can set up against the assignee all defences that have arisen before the receipt by him of a notice of assignment,[47] he may wish to set up 'new' defences as well and to avoid a fight with the assignee over the thorny question whether a defence is 'new' or 'old'.

Thus a non-assignment clause can prevent the assignee being able to claim against the debtor, and will preserve the rights the debtor acquires against the assignor after the date of notice. However, there is a separate question whether the prohibition prevents the assignment being effective as between the assignor and the assignee. The English courts have held that if the debt is assigned despite the clause, and the assignor receives the proceeds from the debtor, he holds them on trust for the assignee, so that they cannot be claimed by the assignor's other creditors.[48] There have even been suggestions that if the debtor fails to pay, though the assignee cannot sue the debtor in his own name, the

---

[46] [1994] AC 85, 108–09, per Lord Browne-Wilkinson.
[47] See below, pp 1405–13.
[48] See *Re Turcan* (1889) LR 40 Ch D 5 (CA); *Don King Productions Inc v Warren* [2000] Ch 291 (CA).

assignee may be able to force the assignor to sue the debtor and to pay the money to the assignee.[49]

It is clear that non-assignment clauses, if upheld as valid, can severely limit the creditor's ability to use his contract rights as security. An unassignable claim is not good security for a loan; indeed, it is arguable that the general recognition of non-assignment clauses has serious commercial implications, especially for small and medium-sized companies, which can, as a practical matter, finance their undertakings only by assigning book debts to financial institutions. In Germany such clauses are invalid if the right which the parties have purported to treat as unassignable arises from a commercial operation (as defined in §§ 343–345 HGB) or if the debtor is a government entity.

HGB   33.18 (DE)

§ 354a: (1) Where the assignment of a money claim is excluded by agreement with the debtor in accordance with § 399 BGB, and the transaction giving rise to that claim constitutes, for both parties, a commercial transaction, or the debtor is a legal person under public law …, the assignment shall nevertheless be valid. However, the debtor may, with the effect of discharging the debt, pay the sum due to the former creditor. Any agreement to the contrary shall be ineffective.

(2) …

The French Code civil says nothing on the validity of non-assignment clauses. It is nevertheless worth noting that Article 1321 of the revised French Code civil states that in the context of the assignment of a right, the consent of the debtor must, exceptionally, be obtained in the presence of a contractual clause precluding the establishment of such an assignment.[50] As a result, although the Code is silent on the validity of non-assignment clauses, it appears that it recognises their existence.[51] Further, it appears that French law takes the view that, in the context of the assignment of a right, the consent of the debtor is sufficient and necessary to overcome the aforementioned contractual prohibition. See also Article 1260(2) of the Italian Codice civile, which provides that a non-assignment clause does not prevent the assignee from acquiring a good title to the assigned right unless he had knowledge of the clause at the date of the assignment.

The trend towards the invalidity of non-assignment clauses has also manifested itself in the law of the US (see § 9-318(4) of the Uniform Commercial Code (UCC)) and in the UNIDROIT Convention on International Factoring. Article 6 of the Convention provides that the assignment of a contractual right by a supplier (assignor) to a factor (assignee) shall be effective 'notwithstanding any agreement between the supplier and the debtor prohibiting such assignment'.[52] In the UK, the government has taken the power to issue

---

[49] See *Barbados Trust Co Ltd v Bank of Zambia* [2007] EWCA Civ 148, [2007] 1 Lloyd's Rep 494. For a general discussion, see R Goode, 'Contractual prohibitions against assignment' [2009] LMCLQ 300.

[50] See Art 1321(3) Cciv: 'The consent of the debtor is not required unless the right was stipulated to be non-assignable'.

[51] See also Deshayes et al (n 5 above) 639.

[52] For details see, eg, R Goode, 'Conclusions of the Leasing and Factoring Conventions—II' [1988] Journal of Business Law 510; B Rebmann, 'Das UNIDROIT-Übereinkommen über das internationale Factoring (Ottawa 1988)' (1989) 53 RabelsZ 599.

regulations to render ineffective non-assignment clauses in contracts giving rise to trade receivables. It is expected that such regulations will be made in the course of the year 2018. They will probably cover the assignment of rights arising from many, if not all, types of contract if the assignee is a small or medium-sized enterprise (SME).[53]

33.3 PROTECTION OF THE DEBTOR

The law of assignment is dominated by the conflict between two interests. One of these is the interest of commerce in increasing the circulation of credit: money claims, like other items of wealth, should be capable of being transferred by mere agreement between assignor and assignee so that the transfer is effective against all third parties without any further requirement, especially without any need for any form of cooperation or agreement on the part of the debtor. Opposed to this is the interest of the debtor in not having his legal position adversely affected by the transfer of the claim against him.

The general principle recognised in all legal systems is that, while the assignee of a contract right succeeds to all the rights of the assignor, a debtor is not affected by the assignment unless he has notice thereof. If he pays his indebtedness to the assignor in ignorance of the assignment, he is relieved from all liability to the assignee.

In such a case the assignee will have to try to recover the money from the assignor.[54] The debtor may also set up against the claim of the assignee any defences, such as a release, a stay or a modification of the claim, acquired by way of an agreement made with the assignor prior to notice of the assignment.

French Law[55] also requires the debtor's consent to be obtained in order for the assignor to be discharged from his contractual duties[56] (the assignor is only discharged for the future). In the absence of such consent and in the context of a validly concluded assignment agreement, the assignor is liable jointly and severally to the performance of the contract (Articles 1216-1 and 1327-2 of the Code civil). These rules are not applicable in the context of the assignment of rights arising from obligations.

33.3.A DISCHARGE OF THE DEBTOR

The formulations used in different legal instruments vary to some extent. The debtor is not discharged by paying the assignor if he does so with 'knowledge of the assignment' (Article 11:303(4) PECL), after 'knowing' of the assignment (§ 407 BGB), after 'the assignee has been made known to him' (§ 1396 ABGB) or although he was not 'in good faith' in paying 'the previous creditor' (Article 167 of the Swiss Law of Obligations).

---

[53] Small Business, Employment and Enterprise Act 2015, s 1; cf reg 2 of the draft Business Contract Terms (Assignment of Receivables) Regulations 2018.

[54] The same applies under Dutch law. It follows from the rule that notification is required to assign validly (Arts 3:84 and 3:94(1) BW), and in the absence of notification, it is covered by Art 3:94(3) BW.

[55] See Art 1327-2 Cciv.

[56] The consent that must be provided by the debtor for the discharge of the assignor is distinct from the consent that underpins the validity of the assignment itself. See Deshayes et al (n 5 above) 468 and 662.

Similarly, Article L 313-28 of the Code monétaire et financier[57] provides that when the debtor has been notified of the assignment by the assignee bank he will not be discharged unless payment is made by him to the bank.[58]

French law takes the position that to be enforceable, the assignment of a contract as a whole or of debt claims must, in addition to having been agreed upon by the debtor, been notified to him when such consent was given in advance.[59] Further, although the debtor's consent is not required for the assignment of rights arising from contractual obligations, Article 1324 of the Code civil states that the assignment will not be enforceable as long as the debtor has not given its consent or, at least, been notified.

In English Law, the courts have, in applying the notice requirement, required the notification to record clearly and definitely the fact of the assignment and to indicate that payment must be made to the assignee.

Court of Appeal **33.19 (EN)**

James Talcott Ltd v John Lewis & Co Ltd and North American Dress Co Ltd[60]

A debtor who receives what was intended as a notice of assignment but which does not make it clear that the right to the debt has been transferred to the intended assignee cannot be made to pay a second time if he pays the assignor.

Facts: The second defendants, the North American Dress Co Ltd, agreed to sell certain goods to John Lewis & Co Ltd, the first defendants. They sent four instalments of goods to John Lewis and four invoices for payment. On each of the invoices there was a rubber stamp imposed in the following terms:

> To facilitate our accountancy and banking arrangements, it has been agreed that this invoice be transferred to and payment in London funds should be made to James Talcott, Ltd, 6–8 Sackville Street, London, W.1. Errors in this invoice must be notified to James Talcott, Ltd, immediately.

Subsequently, John Lewis paid the amount of the invoices to North American Dress by cheque and North American Dress received the money. Then the plaintiffs intervened, and made a claim on John Lewis that the debt represented by those invoices had been assigned to them, and that, therefore, they had a right to claim that John Lewis should pay the money to them a second time, basing their claim upon the ground that there had been an assignment of the debt to them, and that they had given notice thereof to John Lewis.

Held: The plaintiff's claim was dismissed at first instance. The Court of Appeal upheld this decision.

Judgment: MACKINNON LJ: This is a very short point, but, I think, not by any means an easy one. ... By correspondence between the solicitors for the plaintiffs and those for the first defendants, it was agreed that that question depended upon the construction of this clause which was stamped by the rubber stamp on the invoices. It was admitted by the solicitors for John Lewis & Co, Ltd, and it appears from a document with which I have been furnished—indeed, there is no doubt whatever—that the North American Dress Co, Ltd, had assigned those debts to the plaintiffs by a completely formal document.

---

[57] See above, p 1384 n 15.

[58] The same applies under Dutch law. It follows from the rule that notification is required to assign validly (Arts 3:84 and 3:94(1) BW), and in the absence of notification, it is covered by Art 3:94(3) BW.

[59] See Art 1327-2 Cciv.

[60] [1940] 3 All ER 592.

The whole question in this case is whether there was such sufficient notice to John Lewis & Co, Ltd, of that assignment, as created a legal obligation on John Lewis & Co, Ltd, to pay the plaintiffs, and to pay them only, so that, though they had paid the original debt, they must none the less pay the plaintiffs over again …

One may have a notice to a debtor from his creditor asking him to pay the money to a third party. The terms of it may be such as to indicate that it is to be paid to that third party because that third party has, by virtue of an assignment, become the person entitled to receive it. On the other hand, it may be a request to pay the debt to a third party, not because that third party has a right to it, but because, as a matter of convenience, the creditor desires that it shall be paid to that third party as his agent to receive it in respect of the right of the creditor still surviving to receive the debt himself. Plainness of meaning is necessary in order that the debtor who has received a notice to pay a third party shall be rendered liable to pay the money over again if he disregards the notice. The language is immaterial if the meaning is plain, but that plain meaning must be that the debt and the right to receive it have been transferred to the third party. It is not merely that I have made some arrangements by which I request another to pay this money to the third party as my agent. The question is whether this stamped clause put upon the invoices did amount to a plain intimation to the first defendants that the right to receive this money had been transferred to the plaintiffs.

First of all, it is not a notice sent by the plaintiffs at all. If it were sent direct by the plaintiffs to the first defendants, the mere fact that it emanated from them would go some little way to indicate that they were doing so pursuant to a right of theirs. I do not say that there is very much in that, but the fact that it is stamped on their own invoice by the North American Dress Co, Ltd, makes it a communication from them, and not a communication from John Lewis & Co, Ltd, to the plaintiffs … It would have been so simple for James Talcott Ltd, to give a correct notice, 'This debt has been assigned to us', or to insist that the North American Dress Co, Ltd should in clear terms give that intimation, that it is a matter of extreme wonder and speculation why this stamp should have been couched in this extremely vague and obscure language.

We have been told (I think that it appears from one of the letters) that the wording of this extraordinary sentence was actually settled by counsel. I can only conceive that it was couched in this obscure language to conceal the fact that the North American Dress Co, Ltd, were carrying on their business with borrowed money, and had assigned to the plaintiffs the money to which they themselves were entitled.

The words begin—and they are the first words to be read by anybody who did read them—'To facilitate our accountancy and banking arrangements …' The word 'our' suggests that it is still a debt due to the North American Dress Co, Ltd, and that it is only a matter of their internal business arrangements. It is true that the words go on 'it has been agreed', and it is suggested that that must mean an agreement between the North American Dress Co, Ltd, and the plaintiffs, though I do not know why it should. There is nothing to show that it has been agreed between those parties. There are the vague, uncertain words 'it has been agreed'. Then it goes on to say 'that this invoice be transferred to'. It is suggested that those words in themselves ought to be taken to mean that the debt due upon this invoice shall be assigned, but they do not say so. The invoice is transferred 'and payment in London funds should be made to James Talcott Ltd. … Errors in this invoice must be notified to James Talcott Ltd, immediately.'

As I have said, it is not enough to make the debtor liable to pay over again if he has creditors, if he has merely received a notice that he is to pay to some other party merely as agent for his creditor. He is not bound to pay over again unless he has received a sufficiently plain notice that the right to receive the money has been transferred to the third party, so that he will at his peril neglect that notice and neglect the right of the third party. I think that this notice stamped on the invoice was ambiguous. I think that it is equally consistent with being merely a request to pay to the plaintiffs, as agents of the creditor to receive the money, and it does not indicate sufficiently clearly that there has been an assignment of the debt to the plaintiffs so that they should become the real creditors of the first defendants, be the only persons entitled to be paid the money. That was the view taken by MacNaghten J, with the result that he dismissed the claim. I think that his decision was right, and that this appeal fails.

[Du Parcq LJ made a speech to the same effect. Goddard LJ dissented.]
Appeal dismissed.

33.3.B DEFENCES AVAILABLE TO THE DEBTOR

Principles of European Contract Law   **33.20 (INT)**

Article 11:307: Defences and rights of set-off
(1) The debtor may set up against the assignee all substantive and procedural defences to the assigned claim which the debtor could have used against the assignor.
(2) The debtor may also assert against the assignee all rights of set-off which would have been available against the assignor under Chapter 13 in respect of any claim against the assignor:
> (a) existing at the time when a notice of assignment, whether or not conforming to Article 11:303(1), reaches the debtor; or
> (b) closely connected with the assigned claim.

One type of defence is based on the debtor's contention that the assignment itself was invalid so that the assignee never became his true creditor. Assignment law requires the debtor to determine, at his own risk, the validity of assignment of claims against him. He will not get a good discharge if he pays the assignee and it later turns out that the assignment was a forgery, was procured by an assignee who lacked capacity to contract or, having been extorted by duress or fraud, was set aside by the assignor.

The problem of protecting the debtor can also arise when there is no doubt about the assignee's entitlement, but the question is what defences the debtor can raise against his claim for payment. Since the assignment can take place without the consent of the debtor, the invariable principle is that the assignment does not curtail the defences he can raise against the assignee. The common law's metaphor is that the assignee 'stands in the assignor's shoes' or that the assignee 'takes subject to equities'; in the civil law the rule is sometimes explained as being based on the principle that *nemo plus iuris transferre potest quam ipse habet*. Unlike the holder in due course of a negotiable instrument, the assignee of a non-negotiable claim has no greater rights against the debtor than the assignor.

It follows that the assignee is vulnerable to defences raised by the debtor on the ground that the assignor failed to perform the contract or that a condition limiting the debtor's duty to render the counter-performance occurred. This applies whether the events giving rise to the defence have occurred before or after the assignment or before or after the debtor has acquired notice thereof. Some code provisions seem to take a narrower view since defences available against the assignor are available against the assignee only 'if they were justified at the time of the assignment' (§ 404 BGB) or 'if they existed at the time when the debtor was notified of the assignment' (Article 169(1) of the Swiss Law of Obligations). However, it has been held in numerous cases that the debtor can invoke a breach committed by the assignor even though the facts giving rise to the breach did not occur until after the assignment and notice to the debtor.

These cases assert that the defence need not have fully materialised at the time of the assignment or of its notification; only a general basis for the defence must have existed at that time in the contractual relationship between the debtor and the assignor.

RG, 11 November 1913[61]   **33.21 (DE)**

Termination of building contract after date of assignment: Germany

If, after the assignment of money which should become payable under a contract, compensation becomes due to the debtor because of the assignor's failure to perform, the debtor may raise this as a defence against the assignee.

Facts: By a contract dated 23 October 1908, G, a building contractor, agreed to construct a new dwelling-house for the defendant. He accomplished part of the building works, but their completion was delayed. The defendant granted him a period of grace, until 5 April 1909, in which to resume the works, warning him that, in the event of failure by G to comply, the defendant would refuse to accept the services supplied and would claim damages for non-performance. Upon the failure by G to comply with the time-limit, the defendant ceased to employ him for the construction and had the building works carried out by another builder. Out of the amount due to him by way of remuneration for the partial work carried out to him, G had on 7 February 1909 assigned to the claimant, to whom he owed 4,441.10 marks for stones supplied for use in the construction, a claim in an equivalent sum, which the claimant proceeded to demand. The defendant was obliged to expend considerably more in order to have the construction completed than he would have had to pay to G under the contract with the latter. In opposition to the claim made against him, he sought compensation for that loss, which exceeded the remuneration due to G for the partial services performed by the latter.

Held: The Landgericht and the Oberlandesgericht dismissed the claimant's claim. The claimant's appeal on a point of law was likewise dismissed.

Judgment: According to the contract for work and services, the contractor was responsible for the performance of the building works in their entirety, and the customer was required, in consideration thereof, to pay the agreed remuneration. Even on the basis of a stipulation that instalments of the remuneration were to become payable to the contractor as the works proceeded, nevertheless, on a proper construction of the agreement, and having regard to the principle of good faith, it is clear from the particular nature of the synallagmatic contract concerned that the entitlement to partial remuneration was not definitively fixed, as to the existence and amount thereof, on an autonomous, independent basis; instead, it was dependent on the continuing existence of the legal relationship. For a contractor to demand, without any reduction, the remuneration corresponding to the completed part of the undivided whole of the work to be carried out by him, whilst at the same time being liable to pay his customer damages under the same contract on account of fault on his part, and particularly on account of delay, is contrary to the nature

---

[61] RGZ 83, 279.

of things, and is incompatible with the meaning of damages for non-performance of synallagmatic contracts pursuant to the second sentence of § 326(1) [now §§ 280(1) and (3), 281] BGB, as established by the case law of the Reichsgericht ... It is not permissible to determine the amount of the loss and then offset it against the remuneration for the work or against that part thereof which has become due. On the contrary, the contractor liable to pay damages has no further claim whatever arising out of the contract, not even for the partial remuneration which is due. The only significance of this remuneration is that of an invoiced sum which affects the amount of the claim for damages (citations omitted). If partial remuneration for work done is set against a claim for damages for non-performance arising out of the same contract for work and services, that amounts not to a set-off in accordance with § 387 of the BGB, but to a settlement of accounts, that is to say, the determination of the arithmetical result ...

The customer commissioning the works may argue, in opposition to the claim for part of the remuneration, that the change in the debt relationship, as described in the present case, occurred as a result of the delay on the part of the contractor. For the contractor to be able, by assigning his claim to partial remuneration for the work, to preclude the customer from raising any objection to that claim and to prevent the latter from thus recouping his losses by means of recourse to the partial remuneration due is not only contrary to the principle of good faith but also incompatible with § 404 BGB, according to which a debtor may raise, as against the new creditor, any objections and defences which were established against the former creditor at the time of the assignment. As at the date of the assignment in the present case (7 February 1909), the defendant's claim for damages was already established within the meaning of § 404 BGB, he had a legitimate objection or defence under § 326 [now §§ 280(1) and (3), 281] BGB, since it was based on the reciprocal debt relationship which existed at the time of the assignment, notwithstanding that the facts and matters as a result of which the legal basis of the objection or defence (inherent in the debt relationship) became effective did not occur until after the assignment (citations omitted). In the case of a synallagmatic contract in particular, the new creditor must accept that there may be raised against him all and any objections and defences which, like those asserted in the present case, do not emerge until a later stage in the legal relationship (citations omitted). The claim assigned passes, together with the preferential and ancillary rights attaching to it, but also with its weaknesses and defects, to the new creditor. Consequently, in this case too, the defendant is entitled to raise his claim for damages as against the claimant, with the effect described, since, in accordance with its legal basis, his defence lies in the debt relationship which already existed at the time of the assignment.

Cass com, 9 February 1993[62]　　　　　　　**33.22 (FR)**

Termination of building contract after date of assignment: France

If, after the assignment of money which should become payable under a contract, compensation becomes due to the debtor because of the assignor's failure to perform, the debtor may raise this as a defence against the assignee.

---

[62] No. 91-13601, Bull civ IV no. 51.

Facts: According to the contested judgment (Versailles, 4 January 1991), the Banque Populaire des Pyrénées-Orientales, de l'Aude et de l'Ariège ('the Bank') became, in the form provided for by the Law of 2 January 1981 (the Loi Dailly[63]), the assignee of a debt due from SCI (Société Immobilière pour le Commerce et l'Industrie, a company formed to let commercial and industrial premises) and notified that company of the assignment. When the debt fell due, the SCI claimed termination of the works contracts concluded with the assignor, since the latter had not completed the performance thereof.

Held: SCI need not pay the sum claimed by the bank. An appeal by the bank was dismissed.

Judgment: ...—Whereas the Bank challenges the contested judgment in that it allowed the objection pleaded against it to be relied upon, whereas, according to the appeal, Articles 1 and 4 of the Law of 2 January 1981 [now Articles L 313-23 and L 313-27 of the Code monétaire et financier] make it clear that a debtor may raise against an assignee only such objection as he could have raised against the assignor before the assignment; as having found that the termination of the works contract which gave rise to the assignment of debts of 2 May 1988 in favour of the Bank took place on 19 May 1988, that is to say, later than the assignment, from which it followed that the debtor's objection regarding the assignor's failure to perform its contractual obligations could not be pleaded against the assignee, the cour d'appel infringed those provisions by none the less relying on that fact in order to dismiss the Bank's application for payment.

   — Whereas however, since the debtor company had not consented to the assignment of the debt, the cour d'appel was fully entitled to hold that the objection relating to that non-performance could be relied upon against the assignee Bank, without there being any need to inquire whether the nonperformance of the contract on which the debt in issue was founded took place after notification of the assignment; as the appeal ground is accordingly unfounded.

   On those grounds, the appeal is dismissed.

Code civil   **33.23 (FR)**

Article 1324: The debtor may set up against the assignee defences inherent in the debt itself, such as nullity, the defence of non-performance, termination or the right to set off related debts. He may also set up defences which arose from the relations with the assignor before the assignment became enforceable against him, such as the grant of a deferral, the release of a debt, or the set-off of debts which are not related.

Article 1328: The substituted debtor, and the original debtor if he remains liable, may set up against the creditor defences inherent in the debt, such as nullity, the defence of non-performance, termination or the right to set off related debts. Each may also set up defences which are personal to him.

Similarly in English law, the assignee takes 'subject to equities'. This means that the debtor can always rely on any defence, or counter-claim that reduces the amount payable, if it arises under the original contract. In addition, the debtor may always rely on any other claim that is 'so closely connected with [the claimant's] demands that it would be manifestly unjust to allow him to enforce payment without taking into account the cross-claim.'[64] This is often referred to as 'equitable set-off'. Lastly, the debtor may set

---

[63] See above, p 1383.
[64] *Geldof Metaalconstructie NV v Simon Carves Ltd* [2010] EWCA Civ 667, [2010] 4 All ER 847, [2011] 1 Lloyd's Rep 517 at [43].

off against the assignee any other claim that it had against the assignor provided that the claim arose before the debtor had notice of the assignment.[65]

The rule under which a debtor may avail himself, as against the assignee, of all defences he could have raised against his original creditor renders the assignee's position somewhat precarious, and it comes as no surprise that assignees, dissatisfied with their vulnerability under this rule, have sought protection against the debtor's defences. One possibility is for the assignee to ask the debtor for an 'acknowledgement' of the debt, ie for a declaration by which the debtor confirms the existence of the assigned claim and states that he will raise no defences or counterclaims when payment is demanded. Since such waivers are as a rule made on forms provided by the assignee, ambiguities are interpreted *contra proferentem*. The courts are also inclined to consider defences as waived only to the extent to which the debtor at the time of the waiver knew, or ought to have known, of the facts giving rise to the defence.

BGH, 18 October 1972[66]   33.24 (DE)

Of tools assigned

Where a debtor has completed a form drafted by an assignee and confirmed that he has no claim against the assignor, any ambiguity in the form should be construed against the party who drafted it, ie the assignee.

Facts: On 20 January 1966 the defendant firm purchased tools from S GmbH. The purchase price was DM 97,850, and the tools were to be delivered over a period of time. S GmbH assigned its claim for payment to the claimant bank, which granted it credit. The defendant received a notice of assignment dated 29 June 1966; this was signed by S GmbH and was on a form used by the claimant. Attached to that form was a further form filled out by the claimant, which contained a clause stating that there existed no rights vested in any third party to the DM 80,000 residual debt or any counterclaims to that sum which the defendant itself might raise by way of set-off. The defendant signed the latter form, dated it 11 July 1966 and sent it, in accordance with an imprint on the form, to the claimant. In July 1967 S GmbH became bankrupt. By that time, it had provided the defendant with possession and ownership of only some of the tools sold. The claimant demanded from the defendant payment of a residual debt of DM 39,526.20 together with interest. The defendant refused to pay, on the ground that some of the tools had not yet been delivered and that it had already paid in excess of the sums due for those which had been delivered. The claimant argued that the defendant firm, by its 'confirmation' of 11 July 1966, had in any event lost any right to raise such a defence.

Held: The courts below found in favour of the claimant and ordered the defendant to pay the DM 39,526.20 claimed plus interest. This decision was reversed by the BGH.

Judgment: ... 2. (a) The court below regarded the defendant's statement of 20 January 1966 as a confirmatory acknowledgement of indebtedness, against which no objection can be raised.

According to that court, that acknowledgement must be interpreted as meaning that the defendant waived its right to assert, as against the claimant, the objection which it

---

[65] See *Bibby Factors Northwest Ltd v HFD Ltd* [2015] EWCA Civ 1908 at [30]-[33]. The last rule is said to be one reason why debtors sometimes insist on non-assignment clauses: the debtor is then entitled to ignore any notice of assignment and can continue to set off claims even if they only arise after notice has been, or would have been, given.

[66] NJW 1973, 39.

now raises, namely that the contract was not performed (§ 320 BGB). This Chamber, adjudicating in the dispute, is unable to concur with that interpretation.

(b) Where—as in the present case—a bank accepts from its customer, for the purposes of securing indebtedness, an assignment of a claim vested in the bank's customer against that customer's own customer, and obtains from the latter confirmation of the claim assigned, there arises a typical situation involving a juxtaposition of interests. On the one hand, the bank, in the interests of securing the credit given or to be given by it, attaches importance—in such a way that the debtor may be aware of it—to ensuring as far as possible that it is protected against any subsequent objections which the debtor may raise in relation to the claim assigned, by thus seeking to exclude such objections on the basis of the confirmation of the debt. On the other hand, as must ipso facto be manifestly apparent to the bank, it cannot as a general rule be in the interests of the debtor to waive his right to contest the claim assigned, since he has no reason to waive that right. Nor is he under any obligation vis-à-vis the creditor or the bank to declare, in response to the request made to him, that he confirms the debt claim. If he gives that confirmation, in accordance with normal commercial practice, the interpretation to be applied to it will depend on the way in which it should have been understood by the recipient of the declaration, that is to say, the bank. However, since the bank knows that it cannot necessarily reckon on a waiver by the debtor of his right to raise objections, it can only infer such a waiver from the debtor's declaration if and in so far as this is clearly and unambiguously expressed in that declaration, in such a way that it cannot be misunderstood by the debtor either. It is *a fortiori* necessary to apply that requirement where the debtor does not himself formulate the wording in which his declaration is couched but merely signs a declaration the wording of which has been prepared for him in advance by the bank. The consequences of any lack of clarity in the wording must be borne by the bank, which chose and filled out the form used. Where, however, the declaration contains an express waiver by the debtor of his right to raise any objection, such that, on a careful examination of its terms, it cannot be misconstrued by the debtor, then he must accept—subject to the possibility of contesting it on the ground of mistake, which does not arise in the present case—that his declaration is to be interpreted as a waiver of his right to raise objections, even where he was not conscious, when signing the declaration, that it would have that scope.

(c) In the form used in this case, the defendant confirmed on 11 July 1966 that it owed S GmbH a balance of DM 80,000 in respect of the supply of tools, and that there existed 'no rights vested in any third party to the DM 80,000 residual debt or any counterclaims to that sum which [the defendant itself] might raise by way of set-off'. Contrary to the view taken by the court below, the defendant had no reason necessarily to infer from the description of the sum in question as a 'residual debt'—which was the description applied to it by the claimant—that the claimant believed that S GmbH had already entirely performed its part of the contract or that the bank was relying on that belief. Where a bank agrees to take an assignment of debts owed to one of its customers and is unclear as to those debts, it must either obtain clarification from its customer, the assignor, or ask the debtor by whom the debts assigned are owed to explain the position in such a way as to clarify the point and remove any ambiguity … If it fails to do so, and instead contents itself with confirmation that the debt exists and that the debtor has no counterclaims which may be set off against that debt, then such a confirmation cannot be construed as a waiver by the debtor of his right under any circumstances to raise any such objections as he may be entitled to assert by reason of subsequent failure by the party with whom he has contracted properly to perform the contract (whether consisting of a total failure to provide consideration or of defective performance). In those circumstances, the confirmation of the debt dated 11 July 1966 cannot outweigh the objection by the defendant that the contract had (in part) not been performed. That objection was already 'established', within the meaning of § 404 BGB, at the time when the assignment took place (June 1966). It is sufficient for that purpose that, by that time, the sale and purchase contract from which the defendant derives its objections had already been concluded between it and S GmbH. Consequently, the defendant is entitled also to assert that objection against the claimant, as assignee.

Code monétaire et financier   **33.25 (FR)**

Article L 313-29: Upon demand by the person in whose favour the memorandum is provided, the debtor may undertake to make payment direct to that person; such undertaking shall be valid only if it is in writing and headed: 'Act of acceptance of the transfer, assignment or charge of a trade debt'. In such circumstances, the debtor may not raise against the credit establishment any objections founded on his personal relations with the signatory of the memorandum unless the credit establishment, in acquiring or taking over the benefit of the debt, knowingly acted to the detriment of the debtor.

Cass com, 3 December 1991[67]   **33.26 (FR)**

Acceptance of the debtor

If the debtor notifies the assignee that it accepts the debt, under Article 6 of the Loi Dailly [now Article L 313-29 of the Code monétaire et financier], he cannot then raise against the assignee any defence based on its relationship with the assignor.

Facts: According to the contested judgment (Douai, 23 November 1989), the company Cogny, a sub contractor of the company Santerne, executed successive assignments to three banks, in the form provided for by the Law of 2 January 1981 [the Loi Dailly], of the debt due to it from the latter company. The first of those assignees, Banque Hervet, obtained an acceptance of the arrangement from Santerne, but its right to receive payment of the amount of the debt was challenged both by that company and by the Banque du Bâtiment et des Travaux Publics, another assignee bank.

Held: The appeal court held that Santerne could not rely on the debtor's non-performance as against the Banque Hervet. The appeal was dismissed.

Judgment: On the sole appeal ground in the main appeal, taken in its two branches:— Whereas Santerne contests the judgment of the lower court on the ground that it ordered it to pay to Banque Hervet the total sum stated on the memorandum of transfer of the debt whereas by its appeal, it argues, first, that the assignment of a trade debt can only operate to transfer to the assignee a right to payment of the debt definitively found to be due and owing upon completion of the works, when they are accepted by the party commissioning them, and in accordance with their quantity and quality, and that such

---

[67] No. 89-21920, Bull civ IV no. 370.

assignment can only operate to require the debtor, even if he has accepted the assignment, to pay the debt thus determined upon the outcome of the works; as the appellant submits that, in deciding to the contrary, the contested judgment misapplied, and thus infringed, the second paragraph of Article 6 of the Law of 2 January 1981 [now Article L 313-29 of the Code monétaire and financier]; as on the other hand, it maintains that a debtor who has accepted an assignment may none the less raise against the assignee objections and defences which are based on his personal relations with the signatory of the memorandum but which had not yet come into existence as at the date of acceptance; as consequently, according to Santerne, it was entitled to raise, in opposition to Banque Hervet, the existence of bad workmanship affecting the works carried out by the assignor which did not become apparent until after the date of acceptance of the assignment, on which date those works had not yet even been carried out; as it asserts that the contested judgment thus infringed, the second paragraph of Article 6 of the Law of 2 January 1981.

— Whereas however, having found that Santerne had acknowledged its acceptance of an assignment of a debt in a fixed sum, which was not subject to the carrying out of the works, the cour d'appel correctly inferred from that finding, in accordance with the provisions of Article 6 of the Law of 2 January 1981, that that company was liable to pay the sum provided for on the due date, and that it could not raise against the assignee credit establishment any objections based on its personal relationship with the signatory of the memorandum; as it follows that none of the branches of the appeal ground is well founded ...

On those grounds, and without there being any need to rule on the second branch of the sole appeal ground advanced in the interlocutory appeal, the Court quashes and annuls the judgment delivered on 23 November 1989 by the Douai cour d'appel, restores the action and the parties to the position in which they found themselves prior to delivery of that judgment, and refers the case to the cour d'appel of Reims.

A seller planning to assign to his bank money claims arising under contracts of sale may include in his standard terms of business a waiver-of-defence clause under which the buyer agrees, in the event of an assignment, not to set up any defences against the assignee. Such clauses have been invalidated if the buyer is a consumer, ie a natural person who is acting for purposes which can be regarded as outside his trade or profession.

EU Consumer Credit Directive[68]   **33.27 (EU)**

Article 17: Assignment of rights

(1) In the event of assignment to a third party of the creditor's rights under a credit agreement or the agreement itself, the consumer shall be entitled to plead against the assignee any defence which was available to him against the original creditor, including set-off where the latter is permitted in the Member State concerned.

(2) The consumer shall be informed of the assignment referred to in paragraph 1 except where the original creditor, by agreement with the assignee, continues to service the credit vis-à-vis the consumer.

---

[68] Directive 2008/48/EC of the European Parliament and of the Council of 23 April 2008 on credit agreements for consumers and repealing Council Directive 87/102/EEC, [2008] OJ L133/6.

Note

According to Article 22(2) of the Directive, Member States 'shall ensure that consumers may not waive the rights conferred on them by the provisions of national law implementing or corresponding to this Directive'.

FURTHER READING

Jansen, N, 'Assignment of Claims' in N Jansen and R Zimmermann (eds), *Commentaries on European Contract Laws* (Oxford University Press, 2018) 1626–1727.
Kötz, H, *European Contract Law* (2nd edn, Oxford University Press, 2017) 337–55.
Salomons, AF, 'Deformalisation of Assignment Law and the Position of the Debtor in European Property Law' (2007) 15 ERPL 639–57.
Steffens, L, 'The new Rule on the Assignment of Rights in Rome I—The Solution to All our Proprietary Problems?: Determination of the Conflicts of Laws Rule in Respect of the Proprietary Aspects of Assignment' (2006) 14 ERPL 543–76.

INDEX

INTRODUCTORY NOTE

References such as '178–79' indicate (not necessarily continuous) discussion of a topic across a range of pages. Wherever possible in the case of topics with many references, these have either been divided into sub-topics or only the most significant discussions of the topic are listed. Because the entire work is about 'contract', the use of this term and certain others which occur constantly throughout the book as entry points has been minimized. Information will be found under the corresponding detailed topics.